Getting Started is as EASY as 1, 2, 3 . . . 4!

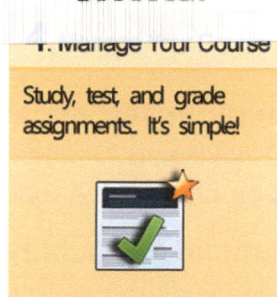

Provide Instruction and Practice 24/7

◆ Assign homework from your Cambridge Business Publishers textbook and have myBusinessCourse grade it for you automatically.

◆ With our eLectures, your students can revisit accounting topics as often as they like or until they master the topic.

◆ Guided Examples show students how to solve select problems.

◆ Make homework due before class to ensure students enter your classroom prepared.

◆ Additional practice and exam preparation materials are available to help students achieve better grades and content mastery.

STUDENT SELF-STUDY OPTION

Not all instructors choose to incorporate **myBusinessCourse** into their course. In such cases, students can access the Self-Study option for MBC. The Self-Study option provides most of the learning tools available in the Instructor-Led courses, including:

◆ eLectures
◆ Guided Examples
◆ Practice Quizzes

The Self-Study option does not include homework assignments from the textbook. Only the Instructor-Led option includes homework assignments.

Want to learn more about myBusinessCourse?

Contact your sales representative or visit **www.mybusinesscourse.com**.

STUDENTS: Find your access code on the myBusinessCourse insert on the following pages. If you have a used copy of this textbook, you can purchase access online at **www.mybusinesscourse.com**.

Cambridge Business Publishers
Series in Accounting

Computerized Accounting
- **QuickBooks Online**, by Williams
- **Computerized Accounting with QuickBooks® 2015**, by Williams

Financial Accounting
- **Financial Accounting for Undergraduates, 3e** by Wallace, Nelson, Christensen, and Ferris
- **Financial Accounting, 5e** by Dyckman, Hanlon, Magee, and Pfeiffer
- **Financial Accounting for MBAs, 7e** by Easton, Wild, Halsey, and McAnally
- **Financial Accounting for Executives & MBAs, 4e** by Simko, Ferris, and Wallace
- **Cases in Financial Reporting, 8e** by Drake, Engel, Hirst, and McAnally

Financial Accounting Using IFRS
- **Financial Accounting, 2e** by Wong, Dyckman, Hanlon, Magee, and Pfeiffer

Managerial Accounting
- **Managerial Accounting for Undergraduates, 1e** by Christensen, Hobson, and Wallace
- **Managerial Accounting, 8e** by Hartgraves & Morse
- **Cases in Managerial and Cost Accounting, 1e** by Allen, Brownlee, Haskins, and Lynch

Combined Financial & Managerial Accounting
- **Financial & Managerial Accounting for Decision Makers, 3e** by Dyckman, Hanlon, Magee, Pfeiffer, Hartgraves, and Morse
- **Financial & Managerial Accounting for MBAs, 5e** by Easton, Halsey, McAnally, Hartgraves, and Morse

Intermediate Accounting
- **Guide to Intermediate Accounting Research, 1e** by Collins
- **Cases in Financial Reporting, 8e** by Drake, Engel, Hirst, and McAnally

Cost Accounting
- **Cases in Managerial and Cost Accounting, 1e** by Allen, Brownlee, Haskins, and Lynch

Auditing
- **Alpine Cupcakes Audit Case** by Dee, Durtschi, and Mindak

Financial Statement Analysis & Valuation
- **Financial Statement Analysis & Valuation, 5e** by Easton, McAnally, Sommers, and Zhang
- **Corporate Valuation, 1e** by Holthausen & Zmijewski

Advanced Accounting
- **Advanced Accounting, 3e** by Hamlen, Huefner, and Largay
- **Advanced Accounting, 3e** by Halsey & Hopkins

Governmental and Not-For-Profit Accounting
- **Governmental and Not-for-Profit Accounting: An Active Learning Workbook** by Convery

FASB Codification and eIFRS
- **Skills for Accounting Research: Text & Cases, 3e** by Collins

Finance For Executives
- **Financial Management for Executives, 2e** by Prag & Wallace

my BusinessCourse

FREE WITH NEW COPIES OF THIS TEXTBOOK*

Start using **my BusinessCourse** Today: **www.mybusinesscourse.com**

my BusinessCourse is a web-based learning and assessment program intended to complement your textbook and faculty instruction.

Student Benefits

- **eLectures**: These videos review the key concepts of each Learning Objective in each chapter.
- **Guided examples**: These videos provide step-by-step solutions for select problems in each chapter.
- **Auto-graded assignments**: Provide students with immediate feedback on select assignments. (**with Instructor-Led course ONLY**).
- **Quiz and Exam preparation**: myBusinessCourse provides students with additional practice and exam preparation materials to help students achieve better grades and content mastery.

You can access **my BusinessCourse** 24/7 from any web-enabled device, including iPads, smartphones, laptops, and tablets.

Interactive content that runs on any device.

Built for PCs, iPads, Laptops, Tablets, Smartphones

Each access code is good for one use only. If the textbook is used for more than one course or term, students will have to purchase additional **my BusinessCourse** access codes. In addition, students who repeat a course for any reason will have to purchase a new access code. If you purchased a used book and the protective coating that covers the access code has been removed, your code may be invalid.

Access to **my BusinessCourse** is free ONLY with the purchase of a new textbook.

THIRD EDITION

Financial & Managerial Accounting for Decision Makers

THOMAS R. DYCKMAN
Cornell University

MICHELLE L. HANLON
Massachusetts Institute of Technology

ROBERT P. MAGEE
Northwestern University

GLENN M. PFEIFFER
Chapman University

AL L. HARTGRAVES
Emory University

WAYNE J. MORSE
Rochester Institute of Technology

Cambridge
BUSINESS PUBLISHERS

To my wife, Ann, and children, Daniel, James, Linda, and David;
and to Pete Dukes, a friend who is always there.
  —TRD

To my husband, Chris, and to our children, Clark and Josie.
  —MLH

To my wife, Peggy, and our family, Paul and Teisha, Michael and
Heather, and grandchildren Sage, Caillean, Rhiannon, Corin,
Connor, and Harrison.
  —RPM

To my wife, Kathie, and my daughter, Jaclyn.
  —GMP

To my wife Aline.
  —ALH

To my family and students.
  —WJM

Editor-in-Chief: George Werthman
Vice President, Brand Management: Marnee Fieldman
Managing Editor: Katie Jones-Aiello
Development Editor: Jocelyn Mousel
Product Developer: Jill Sternard
Digital Marketing Manager: Dana Vinyard
Compositor: T&D Graphics

Cambridge Business Publishers

Financial & Managerial Accounting for Decision Makers, Third Edition, by Thomas R. Dyckman, Michelle L. Hanlon, Robert P. Magee, Glenn M. Pfeiffer, Al L. Hartgraves, and Wayne J. Morse.

Student Edition ISBN: 978-1-61853-234-3

Bookstores & Faculty: To order this book, contact the company via email **customerservice@cambridgepub.com** or call 800-619-6473.

Students: To order this book, please visit the book's website and order directly online.

Printed in the United States of America.
10 9 8 7 6 5 4 3 2 1

About the Authors

Thomas R. Dyckman is Ann Whitney Olin Professor Emeritus of Accounting and Quantitative Analysis at Cornell University's Johnson Graduate School of Management. In addition to teaching accounting and quantitative analysis, he has taught in Cornell's Executive Development Program. He earned his doctorate degree from the University of Michigan. He is a former member of the Financial Accounting Standards Board Advisory Committee and the Financial Accounting Foundation, which oversees the FASB. He was president of the American Accounting Association in 1982 and received the association's *Outstanding Educator* Award for the year 1987. He also received the AICPA's *Notable Contributions to Accounting Literature Award* in 1966 and 1978.

Professor Dyckman has extensive industrial experience that includes work with the U.S. Navy and IBM. He has conducted seminars for Cornell Executive Development Program and Managing the Next Generation of Technology, as well as for Ocean Spray, Goodyear, Morgan Guaranty, GTE, Southern New England Telephone, and Goulds Pumps. Professor Dyckman was elected to The Accounting Hall of Fame in 2009.

Professor Dyckman has coauthored eleven books and written over 50 journal articles on topics from financial markets to the application of quantitative and behavioral theory to administrative decision making. He has been a member of the editorial boards of *The Accounting Review, The Journal of Finance and Quantitative Analysis, The Journal of Accounting and Economics, The Journal of Management Accounting Research,* and the *Journal of Accounting Education.*

Michelle L. Hanlon is the Howard W. Johnson Professor at the MIT Sloan School of Management. She earned her doctorate degree at the University of Washington. Prior to joining MIT, she was a faculty member at the University of Michigan. Professor Hanlon has taught financial accounting to undergraduates, MBA students, Executive MBA students, and Masters of Finance students. Professor Hanlon also teaches Taxes and Business Strategy to MBA students. She is the winner of the 2013 Jamieson Prize for Excellence in Teaching at MIT Sloan.

Professor Hanlon's research focuses primarily on the intersection of taxation and financial accounting. Her recent work examines the capital market effects of the accounting for income tax, the reputational effects of corporate tax avoidance, and the economic consequences of U.S. international tax policies for multinational corporations. She has published research studies in the *Journal of Accounting and Economics*, the *Journal of Accounting Research*, *The Accounting Review*, the *Review of Accounting Studies*, the *Journal of Finance*, the *Journal of Financial Economics*, the *Journal of Public Economics*, and others. She has won several awards for her research and has presented her work at numerous universities and conferences. Professor Hanlon has served on several editorial boards and currently serves as an editor at the *Journal of Accounting and Economics*.

Professor Hanlon is a co-author on another textbook, *Taxes and Business Strategy*. She has testified in front of the U.S. Senate Committee on Finance and the U.S. House of Representatives Committee on Ways and Means about the interaction of financial accounting and tax policy. She served as a U.S. delegate to the American-Swiss Young Leaders Conference in 2010 and worked as an Academic Fellow at the U.S. House Ways and Means Committee in 2015.

Robert P. Magee is Keith I. DeLashmutt Professor of Accounting Information and Management at the Kellogg School of Management at Northwestern University. He received his A.B., M.S. and Ph.D. from Cornell University. Prior to joining the Kellogg faculty in 1976, he was a faculty member at the University of Chicago's Graduate School of Business. For academic year 1980-81, he was a visiting faculty member at IMEDE (now IMD) in Lausanne, Switzerland.

Professor Magee's research focuses on the use of accounting information to facilitate decision-making and control within organizations. He has published articles in *The Accounting Review,* the *Journal of Accounting Research*, the *Journal of Accounting and Economics*, and a variety of other journals. He is the author of *Advanced Managerial Accounting* and co-author (with Thomas R. Dyckman and David H. Downes) of *Efficient Capital Markets and Accounting: A Critical Analysis*. The latter book received the Notable Contribution to the Accounting Literature Award from the AICPA in 1978. Professor Magee has served on the editorial boards of *The Accounting Review,* the *Journal of Accounting Research*, the *Journal of Accounting and Economics* and the *Journal of Accounting, Auditing and Finance*. From 1994–96, he served as Editor of *The Accounting Review*, the quarterly research journal of the American Accounting Association. He received the American Accounting Association's Outstanding Accounting Educator Award in 1999 and the Illinois CPA Society Outstanding Educator Award in 2000.

Professor Magee teaches financial accounting to MBA and Executive MBA students. He has received several teaching awards at the Kellogg School, including the Alumni Choice Outstanding Professor Award in 2003.

Glenn M. Pfeiffer is the Warren and Doris Uehlinger Professor of Business at the George L. Argyros School of Business and Economics at Chapman University. He received his M.S. and Ph.D. from Cornell University after he earned a bachelor's degree from Hope College. Prior to joining the faculty at the Argyros School, he held appointments at the University of Washington, Cornell University, the University of Chicago, the University of Arizona, and San Diego State University.

Professor Pfeiffer's research focuses on accounting and capital markets. He has investigated issues relating to lease accounting, LIFO inventory liquidation, earnings per share, management compensation, corporate reorganization, and technology investments. He has published articles in *The Accounting Review*, *Accounting Horizons*, the *Financial Analysts Journal*, the *International Journal of Accounting Information Systems*, the *Journal of High Technology Management Research*, the *Journal of Economics*, the *Journal of Accounting Education*, and several other academic journals. In addition, he has published numerous case studies in financial accounting and reporting.

Professor Pfeiffer teaches financial accounting and financial analysis to undergraduate, MBA, and Law students. He has also taught managerial accounting for MBAs. He has won several teaching awards at both the undergraduate and graduate levels.

Al L. Hartgraves is Professor Emeritus of Accounting at the Goizueta Business School at Emory University in Atlanta, Georgia. He has been a Guest Professor at Johannes Kepler University in Linz, Austria and at the Helsinki School of Economics and Business Administration and Aalto University in Finland. He is an honorary faculty member of the LIMAK Austrian Business School. He has also served as Senior Associate Dean, Acting Dean, and Director MBA Programs at Emory. His published scholarly and professional articles have appeared in *The Accounting Review, Accounting Horizons, Management Accounting, Journal of Accountancy, Journal of Accounting and Public Policy,* and many other journals. Students at Goizueta Business School selected him on six occasions to receive the Distinguished Educator Award. He is also the recipient of Emory University's highest teaching award, The Scholar/Teacher Award, and he was recognized as the Accounting Educator of the Year by the Georgia Society of CPAs. He has been recognized as an Outstanding Faculty Member in two editions of *The Business Week Guide to the Best Business Schools*. He is a Certified Public Accountant (inactive) and a Certified Management Accountant, having received the Certificate of Distinguished Performance on the CMA exam. He received his Ph.D. from Georgia State University, and in 2011 was granted an honorary doctorate by Johannes Kepler University.

Wayne J. Morse is Professor Emeritus at the Saunders College of Business at Rochester Institute of Technology. An author or co-author of more than fifty published papers, monographs, and textbooks, he was a founding member of the Management Accounting section of the American Accounting Association. His most notable writings are in the areas of learning curves, human resource accounting, and quality costs. He was a member of the IMA Committee on Research and an AICPA Board of Examiners subcommittee, and he has served on the editorial boards of *Advances in Accounting*, *Trends in Accounting Education*, *Issues in Accounting Education*, and *Management Accounting Research*. A Certified Public Accountant, he received his Ph.D. from Michigan State University. Prior to joining RIT, he was on the faculty of the University of Illinois, Duke University, the University of Tennessee, Clarkson University, and the University of Alabama-Huntsville.

Preface

Welcome to the third edition of *Financial & Managerial Accounting for Decision Makers,* and, to adopters of the first two editions, thank you for the great success those editions have enjoyed. We wrote this book to equip students with the accounting techniques and insights necessary to succeed in today's business environment. It reflects our combined experience in teaching accounting to college students at all levels. For anyone who pursues a career in business, the ability to read, analyze, and interpret accounting information is an essential skill. *Financial & Managerial Accounting for Decision Makers* is written for future business leaders who want to understand how accounting information is prepared and how the information is used by investors, creditors, financial analysts, and managers. Our goal is to provide the most engaging, relevant, and accessible textbook available.

TARGET AUDIENCE

Financial & Managerial Accounting for Decision Makers is intended for use in an introductory accounting course that combines financial and managerial accounting concepts, either the undergraduate or graduate level; one that balances the preparation of accounting information with its analysis and interpretation. This book accommodates mini-courses lasting only a few days as well as extended courses lasting a full semester.

This book is real-world oriented and focuses on the most salient aspects of accounting. It teaches students how to read, analyze, and interpret financial accounting data to make informed business decisions. To that end, it consistently incorporates **real company data**, both in the body of each chapter and throughout the assignment material.

REAL DATA INCORPORATED THROUGHOUT

Today's business students must be skilled in using real financial statements to make business decisions. We feel strongly that the more exposure students get to real financial statements, the more comfortable they become with the variety in financial statements that exists across companies and industries. Through their exposure to various financial statements, students will learn that, while financial statements do not all look the same, they can readily understand and interpret them to make business decisions. Furthermore, today's students must have the skills to go beyond basic financial statements to interpret and apply nonfinancial disclosures, such as footnotes and supplementary reports. We expose students to the analysis and interpretation of real company data and nonfinancial disclosures through the use of focus companies in each chapter, the generous incorporation of footnotes, financial analysis discussions in nearly every chapter, and an abundance of assignments that draw on real company data and disclosures.

Focus Companies for Each Chapter

Each chapter's content is explained through the accounting and reporting activities of real companies. Each chapter incorporates a "focus company" for special emphasis and demonstration. The enhanced instructional value of focus companies comes from the way they engage students in real analysis and interpretation. Focus companies were selected based on student appeal and the diversity of industries.

Footnotes and Management Disclosures

We incorporate footnote and other management disclosures, where appropriate, throughout the book. We explain the significance of the footnote and then demonstrate how to use the disclosed information to make managerial inferences and decisions. A representative sample follows.

Footnote Disclosures and Interpretations

In its balance sheets, Cisco reports Accounts receivables, net of allowance for doubtful accounts of $5,157 million at July 26, 2014, and $5,470 at July 27, 2013. In its MD&A (Management Discussion and Analysis), the company provides the following information.

Allowances for Receivables and Sales Returns
The allowances for receivables were as follows (in millions, except percentages):

	July 26, 2014	July 27, 2013
Allowance for doubtful accounts	$265	$228
Percentage of gross accounts receivable	4.9%	4.0%

The allowance for doubtful accounts is based on our assessment of the collectability of customer accounts. We regularly review the allowances to ensure their adequacy by considering internal factors such as historical experience, credit quality, age of the receivable balances as well as external factors such as economic conditions that may affect a customer's ability to pay. . . . We also consider the concentration of receivables outstanding with a particular customer in assessing the adequacy of our allowances . . .

Financial Analysis Discussions

Each financial accounting chapter includes a financial analysis discussion that introduces key ratios and applies them to the financial statements of the chapter's focus company. By weaving some analysis into each of these chapters, we try to instill in students a deeper appreciation for the significance of the accounting methods being discussed. One such analysis discussion follows.

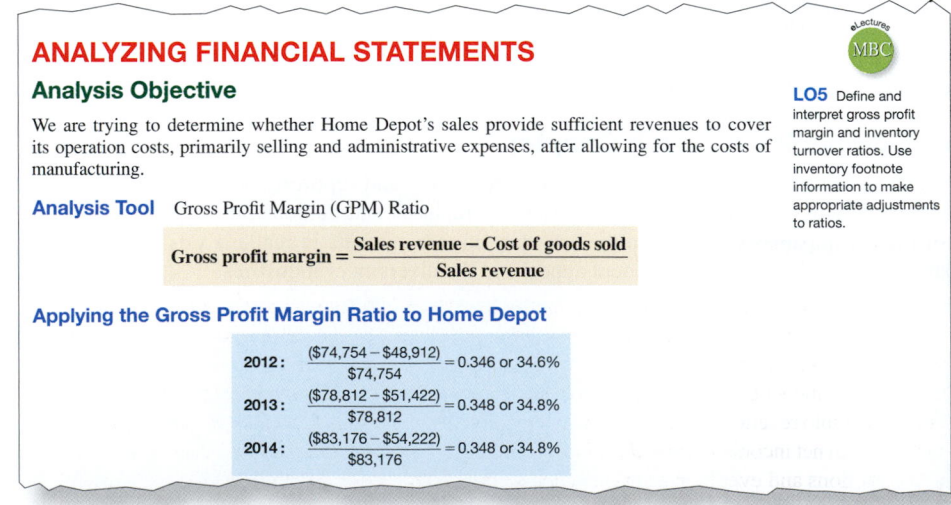

ANALYZING FINANCIAL STATEMENTS

Analysis Objective

We are trying to determine whether Home Depot's sales provide sufficient revenues to cover its operation costs, primarily selling and administrative expenses, after allowing for the costs of manufacturing.

Analysis Tool   Gross Profit Margin (GPM) Ratio

$$\text{Gross profit margin} = \frac{\text{Sales revenue} - \text{Cost of goods sold}}{\text{Sales revenue}}$$

Applying the Gross Profit Margin Ratio to Home Depot

2012: $\dfrac{(\$74,754 - \$48,912)}{\$74,754} = 0.346$ or 34.6%

2013: $\dfrac{(\$78,812 - \$51,422)}{\$78,812} = 0.348$ or 34.8%

2014: $\dfrac{(\$83,176 - \$54,222)}{\$83,176} = 0.348$ or 34.8%

LO5 Define and interpret gross profit margin and inventory turnover ratios. Use inventory footnote information to make appropriate adjustments to ratios.

Assignments that Draw on Real Data

It is essential for students to be able to apply what they have learned to real financial managerial decisions. Therefore, we have included an abundance of assignments in each chapter that draw on real data. A representative example follows.

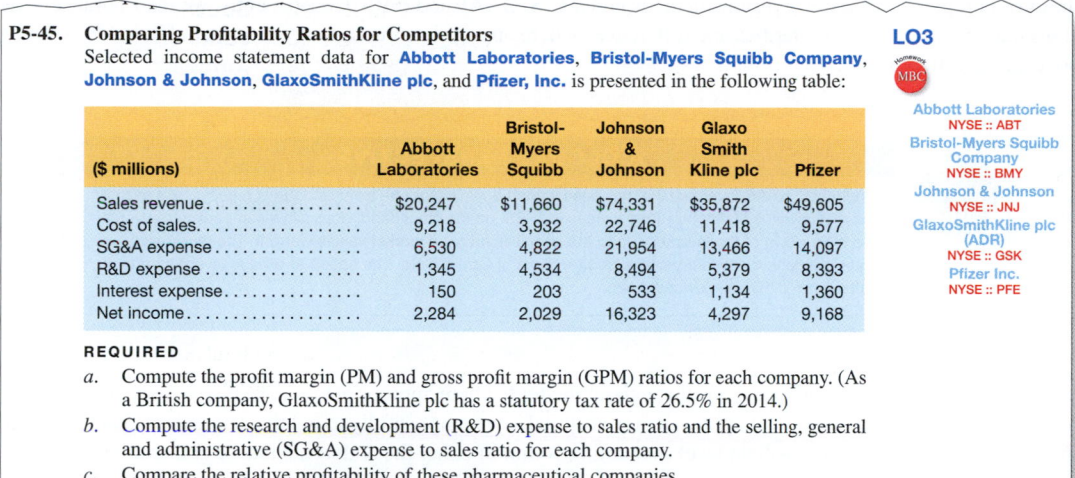

P5-45. Comparing Profitability Ratios for Competitors
Selected income statement data for **Abbott Laboratories**, **Bristol-Myers Squibb Company**, **Johnson & Johnson**, **GlaxoSmithKline plc**, and **Pfizer, Inc.** is presented in the following table:

LO3

Abbott Laboratories
NYSE :: ABT
Bristol-Myers Squibb
Company
NYSE :: BMY
Johnson & Johnson
NYSE :: JNJ
GlaxoSmithKline plc
(ADR)
NYSE :: GSK
Pfizer Inc.
NYSE :: PFE

($ millions)	Abbott Laboratories	Bristol-Myers Squibb	Johnson & Johnson	Glaxo Smith Kline plc	Pfizer
Sales revenue	$20,247	$11,660	$74,331	$35,872	$49,605
Cost of sales	9,218	3,932	22,746	11,418	9,577
SG&A expense	6,530	4,822	21,954	13,466	14,097
R&D expense	1,345	4,534	8,494	5,379	8,393
Interest expense	150	203	533	1,134	1,360
Net income	2,284	2,029	16,323	4,297	9,168

REQUIRED

a. Compute the profit margin (PM) and gross profit margin (GPM) ratios for each company. (As a British company, GlaxoSmithKline plc has a statutory tax rate of 26.5% in 2014.)

b. Compute the research and development (R&D) expense to sales ratio and the selling, general and administrative (SG&A) expense to sales ratio for each company.

c. Compare the relative profitability of these pharmaceutical companies.

BALANCED APPROACH

As instructors of introductory financial accounting, we recognize that the first financial accounting course serves the general business students as well as potential accounting majors. *Financial & Managerial Accounting for Decision Makers* embraces this reality. This book **balances reporting, analysis, interpretation**, and **decision making** with the more standard aspects of accounting such as **journal entries**, **T-accounts**, and the **preparation of financial statements**.

3-Step Process: Analyze, Journalize, Post

One technique we use throughout the financial accounting portion of the book to maintain a balanced approach is the incorporation of a 3-step process to analyze and record transactions. **Step 1** analyzes the impact of various transactions on the financial statements using the financial statement effects template. **Step 2** records the transaction using journal entries, and **Step 3** requires students to post the journal entries to T-accounts.

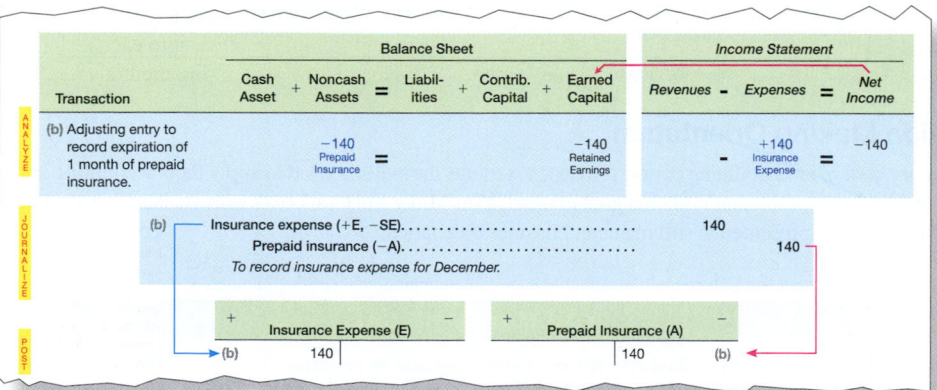

The template captures each transaction's effects on the four financial statements: the balance sheet, income statement, statement of stockholders' equity, and statement of cash flows. For the balance sheet, we differentiate between cash and noncash assets to identify the cash effects of transactions. Likewise, equity is separated into the contributed and earned capital components (the latter includes retained earnings as its major element). Finally, income statement effects are separated into revenues, expenses, and net income (the updating of retained earnings is denoted with an arrow line running from net income to earned capital). This template provides a convenient means to represent financial accounting transactions and events in a simple, concise manner for assessing their effects on financial statements.

INTERNATIONAL FINANCIAL REPORTING STANDARDS (IFRS)

The convergence of U.S. GAAP and International Financial Reporting Standards (IFRS) is in process. Our introductory students should be prepared for this eventuality with a basic understanding of the similarities and differences in the current reporting requirements and methods under U.S. GAAP and IFRS. Consequently, we incorporate discussions that examine these similarities and differences where appropriate throughout the book in Global Perspective boxes, as illustrated here:

A GLOBAL PERSPECTIVE

Under U.S. GAAP, inventory that has been written down cannot be revalued later at higher levels even if the market value of that inventory increases. IFRS, on the other hand, does allow companies to reverse the write-down of the inventory up to the acquisition cost if market values warrant. The revaluation results in a debit to Inventory and a credit to Cost of Goods Sold. The option to revalue inventory after a write-down differs across countries.

We also include exercises and problems throughout the text, where appropriate, to stimulate a discussion of international reporting differences. Our approach is conceptual—we purposefully avoid the detailed mechanics that are more appropriate for an intermediate level accounting course at either the undergraduate or graduate level. We feel strongly that our IFRS coverage exposes students to the similarities and differences without overwhelming them.

INNOVATIVE PEDAGOGY

Business Insights

Students appreciate and become more engaged when they can see the real world relevance of what they are learning in the classroom. We have included a generous number of current, real world examples throughout each chapter in Business Insight boxes. The following is a representative example:

BUSINESS INSIGHT

Alibaba's IPO   In September of 2014, **Alibaba Group** offered its shares to the general public for the first time. The first public sale of common stock by a corporation is called an initial public offering, or IPO for short. After the IPO, any offering of stock to the public is called a seasoned equity offering.

At the time, Alibaba's IPO was the largest in history, raising approximately $25 billion. The common stock had a par value of $0.000025, but was offered to the public for $68 per share. Within a couple of months after the stock opened for trade on the New York Stock Exchange, the price increased to almost $120 per share, but then began to fall. By the company's fiscal year end in March 2015, Alibaba's shares were trading for just over $83 per share, about 20% greater than their original offer price and almost 50 times their earnings per share.

Decision Making Orientation

One primary goal of an accounting course is to teach students the skills needed to apply their accounting knowledge to solving real business problems. With that goal in mind, **You Make the Call** boxes in each chapter encourage students to apply the material presented to solving actual business scenarios.

YOU MAKE THE CALL

You are the Division Manager   You are the division manager for a main operating division of your company. You are concerned that a declining PPE turnover is adversely affecting your division's profitability. What specific actions can you take to increase PPE turnover? [Answers on page 395]

Mid-Chapter and Chapter-End Reviews

Accounting can be challenging—especially for students lacking business experience or previous exposure to business courses. To reinforce concepts presented in each chapter and to ensure student comprehension, we include mid-chapter and chapter-end reviews that require students to recall and apply the accounting techniques and concepts described in each chapter.

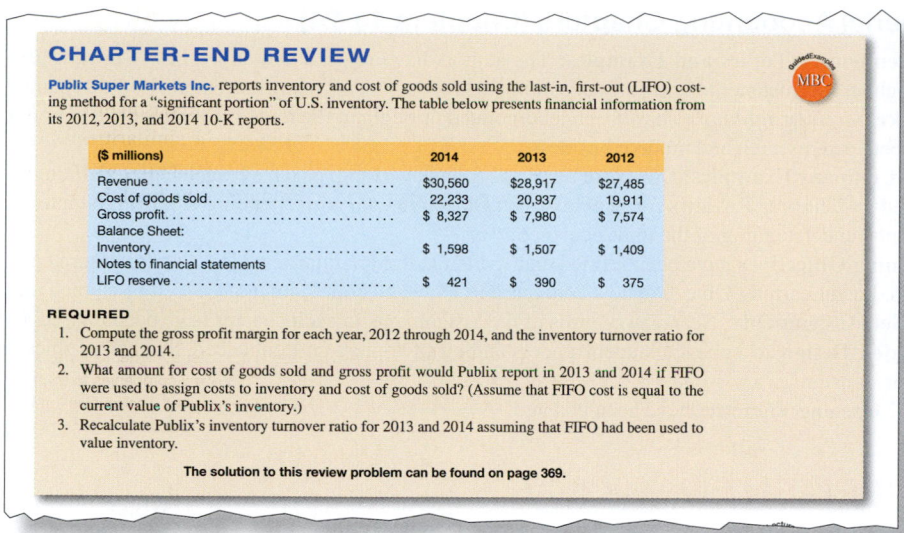

CHAPTER-END REVIEW

Publix Super Markets Inc. reports inventory and cost of goods sold using the last-in, first-out (LIFO) costing method for a "significant portion" of U.S. inventory. The table below presents financial information from its 2012, 2013, and 2014 10-K reports.

($ millions)	2014	2013	2012
Revenue	$30,560	$28,917	$27,485
Cost of goods sold	22,233	20,937	19,911
Gross profit	$ 8,327	$ 7,980	$ 7,574
Balance Sheet:			
Inventory	$ 1,598	$ 1,507	$ 1,409
Notes to financial statements			
LIFO reserve	$ 421	$ 390	$ 375

REQUIRED

1. Compute the gross profit margin for each year, 2012 through 2014, and the inventory turnover ratio for 2013 and 2014.
2. What amount for cost of goods sold and gross profit would Publix report in 2013 and 2014 if FIFO were used to assign costs to inventory and cost of goods sold? (Assume that FIFO cost is equal to the current value of Publix's inventory.)
3. Recalculate Publix's inventory turnover ratio for 2013 and 2014 assuming that FIFO had been used to value inventory.

The solution to this review problem can be found on page 369.

Research Insights for Business Students

Academic research plays an important role in the way business is conducted, accounting is performed, and students are taught. It is important for students to recognize how modern research and modern business practice interact. Therefore, we periodically incorporate relevant research to help students understand the important relation between research and modern business.

RESEARCH INSIGHT

Accounting Conservatism and Cost of Debt Research indicates that companies applying more conservative accounting methods incur a lower cost of debt. Research also suggests that while accounting conservatism can lead to lower-quality accounting income (because such income does not fully reflect economic reality), creditors are more confident in the numbers and view them as more credible. Evidence also implies that companies can lower the required return demanded by creditors (the risk premium) by issuing high-quality financial reports that include enhanced footnote disclosures and detailed supplemental reports.

NEW IN THE 3RD EDITION

- **New Co-author:** Michelle Hanlon, the Howard W. Johnson Professor and Professor of Accounting at the MIT Sloan School of Management, joined the 3rd edition. Michelle has won several awards for her research and is the winner of the 2013 Jamieson Prize for Excellence in Teaching at Sloan where she regularly teaches introductory financial accounting to MBAs. Hanlon recently testified in front of the U.S. Senate Committee on Finance and the U.S. House of Representatives Committee on Ways and Means regarding U.S. tax policy. She brings a wealth of knowledge and expertise to this best-selling author team.

- **myBusinessCourse:** myBusinessCourse (MBC) is a complete learning and assessment program that accompanies the textbook and contributes to student success in this course. MBC has been expanded to include nearly all the multiple choice questions, mini-exercises, and exercises from the 3rd edition. In addition, the Guided Examples and eLectures have been revised and improved.

Financial Accounting Chapters (1-12)

- **Updated Standards:** As appropriate, the text and assignments have been updated to reflect the latest standards. A brief discussion of the pending Revenue Recognition standard is included in Chapter 6 and the chapter-end appendix contains more detailed coverage of the new standard. The text and assignments have also been revised to reflect the change in accounting standards related to Extraordinary Items. Chapter 10 now includes a discussion of the new lease standard.

- In addition to the chapter specific changes, there have been several changes that span the entire book. Some of these global changes include: updated numbers for examples, illustrations, and assignments that use real data; updated footnotes and other nonfinancial disclosures; updated excerpts from the business and popular press; numerous assignments in each chapter have been revised or replaced with new assignments.

Managerial Accounting Chapters (Chapters 13-24)

- **Contemporary Topics and Examples:** The authors have revised and added new *Business Insight* boxes throughout each chapter to bring the accounting to life for students using current, real-world examples. Several new *Research Insight* boxes have been incorporated throughout the text to emphasize the important relationship between research and modern business.
- **Real Company Examples:** Dozens of new, real company examples have been integrated throughout the text.
- **Added In-Chapter Reviews** for each Learning Objective with corresponding Guided Example videos to test students' understanding of the topics covered.
- **Learning Objectives** have been refined and written at the granular level, in order to ensure coverage of all topics. Each Learning Objective now contains a Review and corresponding Guided Example video.
- **Revised Assignments:** Nearly two-thirds of the assignments in each chapter have been revised and updated.
- **Updated Design** to enhance student understanding of topics, and enhanced several graphics for student comprehension.
- All 12 Opening **Vignettes** have been updated.

SUPPLEMENT PACKAGE

Fundamentals of Financial Accounting Tutorial

This interactive tutorial is intended for use in programs that either require or would like to offer a pre-term tutorial that creates a baseline of accounting knowledge for students with little to no prior exposure to financial accounting. Initially developed as a pre-term tutorial for first year MBA students, this product can be used as a warm-up for any introductory level financial accounting course. It is designed as an asynchronous, interactive, self-paced experience for students.

Available Learning Modules (You Select)

1. Introducing Financial Accounting (approximate completion time 2 hours)
2. Constructing Financial Statements (approximate completion time 4 hours)
3. Adjusting Entries and Completing the Accounting Cycle (approximate completion time 4 hours)
4. Reporting and Analyzing Cash Flows (approximate completion time 3.5 hours)
5. Analyzing and Interpreting Financial Statements (approximate completion time 3.5 hours)

This is a separate, saleable item. Contact your sales representative to receive more information or email customerservice@cambridgepub.com.

For Instructors

Instructor CD-ROM: This convenient supplement provides the text's ancillary materials on a portable CD-ROM. All the faculty supplements that accompany the textbook are available, including PowerPoint, Solutions Manual, Test Bank, and Computerized Test Bank.

Solutions Manual: Created by the authors, the *Solutions Manual* contains complete solutions to all the assignment material in the text.

PowerPoint: The PowerPoint slides outline key elements of each chapter.

Test Bank: The Test Bank includes multiple-choice items, matching questions, short essay questions, and problems.

Website: All instructor materials are accessible via the book's Website (password protected) along with other useful links and marketing information. **www.cambridgepub.com**

myBusinessCourse: A web-based learning and assessment program intended to complement your textbook and classroom instruction. This easy-to-use course management system grades homework automatically and provides students with additional help when you are not available. In addition, detailed diagnostic tools assess class and individual performance. myBusinessCourse is ideal for online courses or traditional face-to-face courses for which you want to offer students more resources to succeed. Assignments with the MBC in the margin are available in myBusinessCourse. eLecture videos MBC are available for the chapter Learning Objectives, and Guided Examples MBC for the in-chapter Reviews are available for you to assign students.

For Students

Student Solutions Manual: Created by the authors, the student Solutions Manual contains solutions to the even numbered assignments in the textbook. This is a **restricted** item that is only available to students after their instructor has authorized its purchase.

Website: Practice quizzes and other useful links are available to students free of charge on the book's website.

eLectures: Each Learning Objective within a chapter includes an eLecture video available in myBusinessCourse (see below for more information).

Guided Examples: Guided Example videos are available for each in-chapter Review, also in myBusinessCourse (see below for more information).

myBusinessCourse: A web-based learning and assessment program intended to complement your textbook and faculty instruction. This easy-to-use program provides you with additional help when your instructor is not available. Guided Example videos are available for all in-chapter Reviews, and eLecture videos are available for each Learning Objective. With Instructor-Led MBC courses, assignments with the in the margin are also available and are automatically graded. Access is free with new copies of this textbook (look for page containing the access code towards the front of the book). If you buy a used copy of the book, you can purchase access at **www. mybusinesscourse.com**.

ACKNOWLEDGMENTS

This book has benefited greatly from the valuable feedback of focus group attendees, reviewers, students, and colleagues. We are extremely grateful to them for their help in making this project a success.

Ajay Adhikari, *American University*

Hank Adler, *Chapman University*

Kris Allee, *University of Wisconsin*

Bob Allen, *University of Utah*

Beverley Alleyne, *Belmont University*

Akinloye Akindayomi, *The University of Texas, Rio Grande Valley*

Elizabeth Arnold, *Citadel*

Frances Ayres, *University of Oklahoma*

Paul Bahnson, *Boise State University*

Jan Barton, *Emory University*

Progyan Basu, *University of Maryland*

James Benjamin, *Texas A&M University*

Anne Beyer, *Stanford University*

Robert Bowen, *University of San Diego*

Kimberly Brickler-Ulrich, *Lindenwood University*

Rada Brooks, *University of California, Berkeley*

Helen Brubeck, *San Jose State University*

Jacqueline Burke, *Hofstra University*

Richard J. Campbell, *University of Rio Grande*

Judson Caskey, *UCLA*

Sumantra Chakravarty, *California State University, Fullerton*

Paul Chaney, *Vanderbilt University*

Craig Chapman, *Northwestern University*

Sean Chen, *Furman University*

Hans Christensen, *University of Chicago*

Daniel Cohen, *University of Texas, Dallas*

John Core, *MIT*

Steve Crawford, *Rice University*

Somnath Das, *University of Illinois, Chicago*

Angela Davis, *University of Oregon*

Mark Dawkins, *University of Georgia*

David DeBoskey, *San Diego State University*

Mark DeFond, *University of Southern California*

Bruce Dehning, *Chapman University*

Bala G. Dharan, *Rice University*

Timothy Dimond, *Northern Illinois University*

Joe Dulin, *University of Oklahoma*

Reed Easton, *Seton Hall University*

Andrew Felo, *Nova Southeastern University*

Tom Fields, *Washington University*

Mark Finn, *Northwestern University*

Linda Flaming, *Monmouth University*

Elizabeth Foster, *College of William & Mary*

Micah Frankel, *California State University, East Bay*

George Geis, *University of California, Los Angeles*

Hubert Glover, *Drexel University*

Nancy Goble, *University of Southern California*

Rajul Gokarn, *Clark Atlanta University*

Jeff Gramlich, *University of Southern Maine*

Wayne Guay, *University of Pennsylvania*

Umit Gurun, *University of Texas, Dallas*

Rebecca Hann, *University of Maryland*

David Harvey, *University of Georgia*

Rayford Harwell, *California State University, East Bay*

Susan Hass, *Simmons College*

Joseph Hatch, *Lewis University*

Haihong He, *California State University, Los Angeles*

Kenneth Henry, *Florida International University*

Eric Hirst, *University of Texas, Austin*

Robert Hoskin, *University of Connecticut*

Marsha Huber, *Otterbein College*

Richard E. Hurley, *University of Connecticut*

Robert L. Hurt, *California State University, Pomona*

Marianne L. James, *California State University, LA*

Ross Jennings, *University of Texas*

Chris Jones, *George Washington University*

Jane Kennedy, *University of San Diego*

Suzanne Kiess, *Jackson College*

Irene Kim, *George Washington University*

Michael Kimbrough, *University of Maryland*

Kalin Kolev, *Yale University*

Gopal Krishnan, *George Mason University*

Benjamin Lansford, *Rice University*

James Ledwith, *San Diego State University*

Annette Leps, *Johns Hopkins University*

Alina Lerman, *Yale University*

Xu Li, *University of Texas, Dallas*

Thomas Lin, *University of Southern California*

Thomas J. Linsmeier, *University of Wisconsin*

Cathy Zishang Liu, *University of Houston, Downtown*

Jiangxia Liu, *Valparaiso University*

Frank Longo, *Centenary College*

Barbara Lougee, *University of San Diego*

Luann Lynch, *University of Virginia, Darden*

Bill Magrogan, *University of South Carolina*

Cathy Margolin, *Brandman University*

Maureen Mascha, *University of Wisconsin, Oshkosh*

Katie Maxwell, *University of Arizona*

Bruce McClain, *Cleveland State University*

Harvey McCown, *California State University, Bakersfield*

Jeff McMillan, *Clemson University*

John McCauley, *San Diego State University*

Marc McIntosh, *Augsburg College*

Greg Miller, *University of Michigan*

Jeffrey Miller, *University of Notre Dame*

Donald Minyard, *University of Alabama, Tuscaloosa*

Marilyn Misch, *Pepperdine University, Malibu*

Stephen Moehrle, *University of Missouri, Kansas City*

Matt Munson, *Chapman University*

Mark Myring, *Ball State University*

Sandeep Nabar, *Oklahoma State University*

James Naughton, *Northwestern University*

Karen Nelson, *Rice University*

Christopher Noe, *MIT*

Walter O'Connor, *Fordham University*

Jose Oaks, *University of Connecticut*

Shailendra Pandit, *University of Illinois, Chicago*

Simon Pearlman, *California State University, Long Beach*

Marietta Peytcheva, *Lehigh University*

Brandis Phillips, *North Carolina A&T State University*

Richard Price, *Utah State University*

S.E.C. Purvis, *University of Nevada, Reno*

Kathleen Rankin, *Chatham University*

Lynn Rees, *Texas A&M University*

Susan Riffe, *Southern Methodist University*

Leslie Robinson, *Dartmouth College*

Darren Roulstone, *Ohio State University*

Anwar Y. Salimi, *California State University, Pomona*

Haresh Sapra, *University of Chicago*

Robert Scharlach, *University of Southern California*

Nemit Shroff, *MIT*

Steve Sefcik, *University of Washington*

Timothy Shields, *Chapman University*

Andreas Simon, *California Polytechnic*

Robert Singer, *Lindenwood University*

Parveen Sinha, *Chapman University*

Kathleen Sobieralski, *University of Maryland*

Gregory Sommers, *Southern Methodist University*

David Smith, *University of Nebraska Lincoln*

Sri Sridharan, *Northwestern University*

Vic Stanton, *University of California, Berkeley*

Jack Stecher, *Carnegie Mellon University*

Doug Stevens, *Georgia State University*

Toby Stock, *Ohio University*

William Stout, *University of Louisville*

Shyam Sunder, *University of Arizona*

Robert J. Swieringa, *Cornell University*

Mary Tarling, *Aurora University*

Thomas Tallerico, *Dowling College*

Robin Tarpley, *George Washington University*

Nicole Thibodeau, *Willamette University*

Theresa Tiggeman *University of the Incarnate Word*

Rick Warne, *George Mason University*

Catherine Weber, *University of Houston*

Lourdes White, *University of Baltimore*

Donna Whitten, *Purdue University North Central*

Rahnl Wood, *Northwest Missouri State University*

Jia Wu, *University of Massachusetts, Dartmouth*

Jennifer Yin, *University of Texas, San Antonio*

Kimberly Zahller, *University of Colorado, Colorado Springs*

Stephen Zeff, *Rice University*

Yuping Zhao, *University of Houston*

We are grateful to Brian Cadman of the University of Utah for his contributions to this edition. We would also like to thank Lincoln Pinto of Concordia University, Chicago for his thorough accuracy checking. In addition, we are extremely grateful to George Werthman, Lorraine Gleeson, Jill Fischer, Katie Jones-Aiello, Beth Nodus, Jocelyn Mousel, Jill Sternard, Debbie McQuade, Terry McQuade, and the entire team at Cambridge Business Publishers for their encouragement, enthusiasm, and guidance.

Thomas   Michelle   Robert   Glenn   Al   Wayne

March 2017

Brief Contents

Contents

Chapter 5

Analyzing and Interpreting Financial Statements   218

Chapter 6

Reporting and Analyzing Revenues, Receivables, and Operating Income   270

Chapter 7

Reporting and Analyzing Inventory   326

Chapter 8

Reporting and Analyzing Long-Term Operating Assets   372

Chapter 9

Reporting and Analyzing Liabilities 412

Chapter 10

Reporting and Analyzing Leases, Pensions, and Income Taxes 460

Chapter 11

Reporting and Analyzing Stockholders' Equity 516

Chapter 12

Reporting and Analyzing Financial Investments 562

1

Introducing Financial Accounting

Learning Objectives *identify the key learning goals of the chapter.*

A **Focus Company** *introduces each chapter and illustrates the relevance of accounting in everyday business.*

LEARNING OBJECTIVES

1. Identify the users of accounting information and discuss the costs and benefits of disclosure. (p. 4)

2. Describe a company's business activities and explain how these activities are represented by the accounting equation. (p. 7)

3. Introduce the four key financial statements including the balance sheet, income statement, statement of stockholders' equity, and statement of cash flows. (p. 11)

4. Describe the institutions that regulate financial accounting and their role in establishing generally accepted accounting principles. (p. 17)

5. Compute two key ratios that are commonly used to assess profitability and risk—return on equity and the debt-to-equity ratio. (p. 21)

6. Appendix 1A: Explain the conceptual framework for financial reporting. (p. 25)

NIKE
www.Nike.com

Phil Knight majored in accounting and was a member of the track team at the University of Oregon. Today he is the chairman of the board of **Nike, Inc.**, the largest sports and fitness company in the world.

A few years after graduation, Knight teamed up with his former track coach, Bill Bowerman, to form a business called Blue Ribbon Sports to import, sell, and distribute running shoes from Japan. Blue Ribbon Sports, or BRS as it came to be known, was started on a shoestring—Knight and Bowerman each contributed $500 to start the business. A few years later, BRS introduced its own line of running shoes called Nike. It also unveiled a new logo, the now familiar Nike swoosh. Following the overwhelming success of the Nike shoe line, BRS officially changed its company name to Nike, Inc. Today, the company is worth more than $60 billion.

By 2014, Nike, Inc. products were marketed on six continents with total company sales of $28 billion and income of almost $2.7 billion. Nike owes much of its success to marketing prowess and innovative design and development of new products. The swoosh, along with advertising campaigns featuring taglines such as "just do it," have made the company and its products instantly recognizable to consumers all over the world. Endorsements by the most recognizable icons in sports, including Michael Jordan, Tiger Woods, Maria Sharapova, Tom Brady, LeBron James, and Mike Trout, add to Nike's brand recognition.

In recent years, Nike has expanded its product lines beyond the traditional offerings of athletic shoes, athletic apparel and sports equipment to include eyewear, watches such as the *Nike+ Sportwatch GPS*, and *Fuelband*, a wearable wristband which tracks energy output. In recent years, Nike further expanded its product offering by acquiring other companies such as Converse, an established athletic shoe company; Hurley International, a leading designer and distributor of surf, skate, and snowboarding apparel and footwear; and Umbro, specializing in soccer equipment, footwear, and apparel.

But as CEO Mark Parker recognizes, Nike needs to stay on its toes as newcomers **Under Armour** and **Quiksilver** challenge for customers. Nike also cannot ignore **Adidas**. As Nike's main competitor, it is more than two-thirds of Nike's size in terms of sales. Perhaps this situation, along with new product developments, explains Nike's major new marketing commitment that reached $2.3 billion in 2014 and continues to grow.

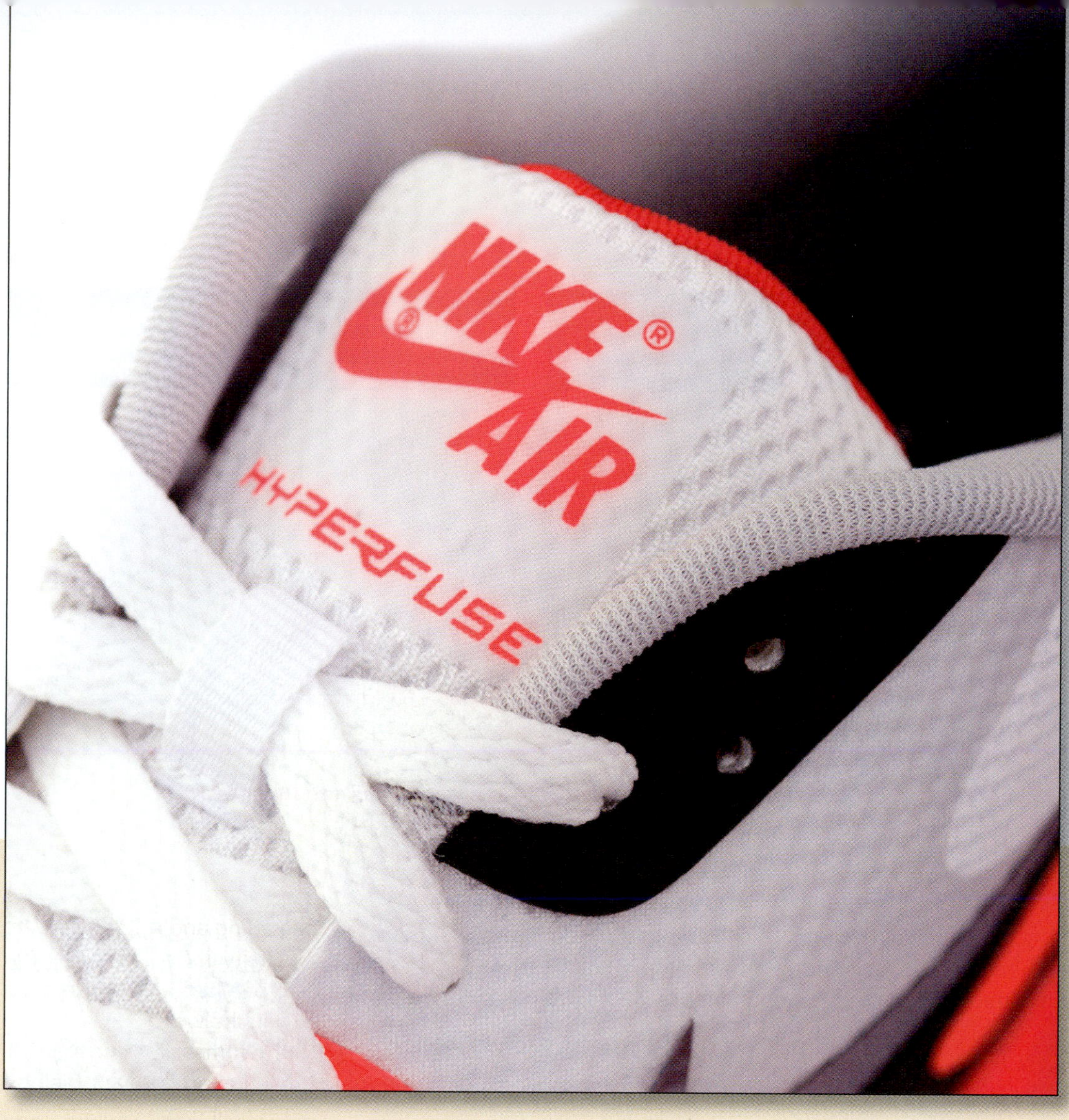

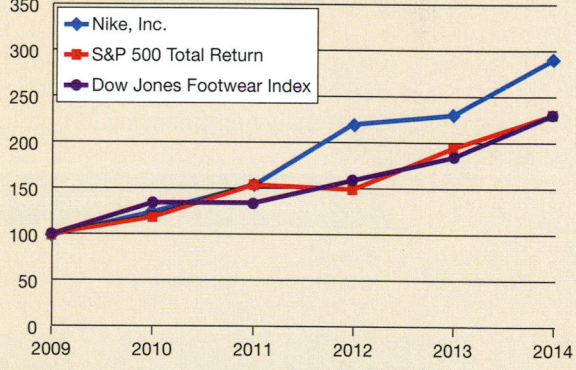

How does someone take a $1,000 investment and turn it into a company whose stock is worth more than $60 billion? Well, Nike's success is not an accident. Along the way, Nike management made countless decisions that ultimately led the company to where it is today. Each of these decisions involved identifying alternative courses of action and weighing their costs, benefits, and risks in light of the available information.

Accounting is the process of identifying, measuring, and communicating financial information to help people make *economic* decisions. People use accounting information to facilitate a wide variety of transactions, including assessing whether, and on what terms, they should invest in a firm, seek employment in a business, or continue purchasing its products. Accounting information is crucial to any successful business, and without it, most businesses would not even exist.

Comparison of 5-Year Cumulative Total Return for Nike, Inc., The S&P 500 Index, and The Dow Jones U.S. Footwear Index (Assumes an investment of $100 on May 31, 2009)

This book explains how to create and analyze financial statements, an important source of accounting information prepared by companies to communicate with a variety of users. We begin by introducing transactions between the firm and its investors, creditors, suppliers, employees, and customers. We continue by demonstrating how accounting principles are applied to these transactions to create the financial statements. Then, we "invert" the process and learn how to analyze the firm's financial statements to assess the firm's underlying economic performance. Our philosophy is simple—we believe it is crucial to have a deep understanding of financial accounting to become critical readers and users of financial statements. Financial statements tell a story—a business story. Our goal is to understand that story, and apply the knowledge gleaned from financial statements to make good business decisions.

Sources: Nike.com; Nike, Inc. 2014 10-K Report; *Business Week* (October 2007, August 2009); *Portland Business Journal* (October 2007); *Fortune* (February 2012).

CHAPTER ORGANIZATION

Chapter Organization *Charts visually depict the key topics and their sequence within the chapter.*

Introducing Financial Accounting

Demand for Accounting Information	Business Activities	Financial Statements	Financial Reporting Environment	Financial Statement Analysis
• Who Uses Financial Accounting Information? • Costs and Benefits of Disclosure	• Planning Activities • Investing Activities • Financing Activities • Operating Activities	• Balance Sheet • Income Statement • Statement of Stockholders' Equity • Statement of Cash Flows • Financial Statement Linkages	• Generally Accepted Accounting Principles • Regulation and Oversight • Role of the Auditor • A Global Perspective • Conceptual Framework (Appendix 1A)	• Profitability Analysis • Credit Risk Analysis

eLecture *icons identify topics for which there are instructional videos in* **myBusinessCourse** *(MBC). See the Preface for more information on MBC.*

eLectures
MBC

LO1 Identify the users of accounting information and discuss the costs and benefits of disclosure.

1

DEMAND FOR ACCOUNTING INFORMATION

Accounting can be defined as the process of recording, summarizing, and analyzing financial transactions. While accounting information attempts to satisfy the needs of a diverse set of users, the accounting information a company produces can be classified into two categories (see **Exhibit 1.1**):

- **Financial accounting**—designed primarily for decision makers outside of the company
- **Managerial accounting**—designed primarily for decision makers within the company

Financial accounting reports include information about company profitability and financial health. This information is useful to various economic actors who wish to engage in contracts with the firm, including investors, creditors, employees, customers, and governments. Managerial accounting information is not reported outside of the company because it includes proprietary information about the profitability of specific products, divisions, or customers. Company managers use managerial accounting reports to make decisions such as whether to drop or add products or divisions, or whether to continue serving different types of customers. This text focuses on understanding and analyzing financial accounting information.

EXHIBIT 1.1 | Information Needs of Decision Makers Who Use Financial and Managerial Accounting

	Decision Makers	Decisions	Information
Financial Accounting	• Investors and analysts • Creditors • Suppliers and customers	• Buy or sell stock? • Lend or not? • Purchase/sell goods or not?	• Sales and costs • Cash in and out • Assets and liabilities
Managerial Accounting	• Top management • Marketing teams • Production and operations	• Develop new strategy? • Launch a new product or not? • Manage operations	• Product sales and costs • Department performance reports • Budgets and quality reports

Who Uses Financial Accounting Information?

Demand for financial accounting information derives from numerous users including:

- Shareholders and potential shareholders
- Creditors and suppliers
- Managers and directors
- Financial analysts
- Other users

Shareholders and Potential Shareholders   Corporations are the dominant form of business organization for large companies around the world, and corporate shareholders are one important group of decision makers that have an interest in financial accounting information. A **corporation** is a form of business organization that is characterized by a large number of owners who are not involved in managing the day-to-day operations of the company.[1] A corporation exists as a legal entity that issues **shares of stock** to its owners in exchange for cash and, therefore, the owners of a corporation are referred to as *shareholders* or **stockholders**.

FYI Shareholders of a corporation are its owners; although managers can own stock in the corporation, most shareholders are not managers.

Because the shareholders are not involved in the day-to-day operations of the business, they rely on the information in financial statements to evaluate management performance and assess the company's financial condition.

In addition to corporations, sole proprietorships and partnerships are also common forms of business ownership. A **sole proprietorship** has a single owner who typically manages the daily operations. Small family-run businesses, such as corner grocery stores, are commonly organized as sole proprietorships. A **partnership** has two or more owners who are also usually involved in managing the business. Many professionals, such as lawyers and CPAs, organize their businesses as partnerships.

Most corporations begin as small, privately held businesses (sole proprietorships or partnerships). As their operations expand, however, they require additional capital to finance their growth. One of the principle advantages of a corporation over sole proprietorships and partnerships is the ability to raise large amounts of cash by issuing (selling) stock. For example, as Nike grew from a small business with only two owners into a larger company, it raised the funds needed for expansion by selling shares of Nike stock to new shareholders. In the United States, large corporations can raise funds by issuing stock on organized exchanges, such as the **New York Stock Exchange (NYSE)** or **NASDAQ** (which is an acronym for the National Association of Securities Dealers Automated Quotations system). Corporations with stock that is traded on public exchanges are known as *publicly traded corporations* or simply *public corporations*.

Financial statements and the accompanying footnotes provide information on the risk and return associated with owning shares of stock in the corporation, and they reveal how well management has performed. Financial statements also provide valuable insights into future performance by revealing management's plans for new products, new operating procedures, and new strategic directions for the company as well as for their implementation. Corporate management provides this information because the information reduces uncertainty about the company's future prospects which, in turn, increases the market price of its shares and helps the company raise the funds it needs to grow.

Creditors and Suppliers   Few businesses rely solely on shareholders for the cash needed to operate the company. Instead, most companies borrow from banks or other lenders known as **creditors**. Creditors are interested in the potential borrower's ability to repay. They use financial accounting information to help determine loan terms, loan amounts, interest rates, and collateral. In addition, creditors' loans often include contractual requirements based on information found in the financial statements.

FYI Financial statements are typically required when a business requests a bank loan.

---

[1] Most countries have business forms that are similar in structure to those of a U.S. corporation, though they are referred to by different names. For example, while firms that are incorporated in the United States have the extension, "Inc." appended to their names, similar firms in the United Kingdom are referred to as a Public Limited Company, which has the extension "PLC."

Suppliers use financial information to establish credit sales terms and to determine their long-term commitment to supply-chain relationships. Supplier companies often justify an expansion of *their* businesses based on the growth and financial health of their customers. Both creditors and suppliers rely on information in the financial statements to monitor and adjust their contracts and commitments with a company.

Managers and Directors

Financial statements can be thought of as a financial report card for management. A well-managed company earns a good return for its shareholders, and this is reflected in the financial statements. In most companies, management is compensated, at least in part, based on the financial performance of the company. That is, managers often receive cash bonuses, shares of stock, or other *incentive compensation* that is linked directly to the information in the financial statements.

Publicly traded corporations are required by law to have a **board of directors**. Directors are elected by the shareholders to represent shareholder interests and oversee management. The board hires executive management and regularly reviews company operations. Directors use financial accounting information to review the results of operations, evaluate future strategy, and assess management performance.

Both managers and directors use the published financial statements of *other companies* to perform comparative analyses and establish performance benchmarks. For example, managers in some companies are paid a bonus for financial performance that exceeds the industry average.

FYI The Sarbanes-Oxley Act requires issuers of securities to disclose whether they have a code of ethics for the senior officers.

BUSINESS INSIGHT

Recent court cases involving corporations such as **Enron**, **Tyco**, and **WorldCom** (now **MCI**) have found executives, including several CEOs, guilty of issuing fraudulent financial statements. These executives have received substantial fines and, in some cases, long jail sentences. These trials have resulted in widespread loss of reputation and credibility among corporate boards.

Financial Analysts

Many decision makers lack the time, resources, or expertise to efficiently and effectively analyze financial statements. Instead, they rely on professional financial analysts, such as credit rating agencies like **Moody's** investment services, portfolio managers, and security analysts. Financial analysts play an important role in the dissemination of financial information and often specialize in specific industries. Their analysis helps to identify and assess risk, forecast performance, establish prices for new issues of stock, and make buy-or-sell recommendations to investors.

Other Users of Financial Accounting Information

External decision makers include many users of accounting information in addition to those listed above. For example, *prospective employees* often examine the financial statements of an employer to learn about the company before interviewing for or accepting a new job.

Labor unions examine financial statements in order to assess the financial health of firms prior to negotiating labor contracts on behalf of the firms' employees. *Customers* use accounting information to assess the ability of a company to deliver products or services and to assess the company's long-term reliability.

Government agencies rely on accounting information to develop and enforce regulations, including public protection, price setting, import-export, taxation, and various other policies.[2] Timely and reliable information is crucial to effective regulatory policy. Moreover, accounting information is often used to assess penalties for companies that violate various regulations.

Costs and Benefits of Disclosure

The act of providing financial information to external users is called **disclosure**. As with every decision, the benefits of disclosure must be weighed against the costs of providing the information.

---

[2] A company's tax returns are distinctly different from its financial statements. Tax returns are prepared for tax authorities in order to comply with income tax rules. The financial statements are prepared to provide information to investors, creditors and other decision makers outside of the business.

One reason companies are motivated to disclose financial information to external decision makers is that it often lowers financing and operating costs. For example, when a company applies for a loan, the bank uses the company's financial statements to help determine the appropriate interest rate. Without adequate financial disclosures in its financial statements, the bank is likely to demand a higher interest rate or perhaps not make the loan at all. Thus, in this setting, a benefit of financial disclosure is that it reduces the company's cost of borrowing.

While there are benefits from disclosing financial information, there are also costs. Besides the obvious cost of hiring accountants and preparing the financial statements, financial disclosures can also result in costs being imposed by competitors. It is common practice for managers to scrutinize the financial statements of competitors to learn about successful products, new strategies, innovative technologies, and changing market conditions. Thus, disclosing too much information can place a company at a competitive disadvantage. Disclosure can also raise investors' expectations about a company's future profitability. If those expectations are not met, they may bring litigation against the managers.

There are also political costs that are potentially associated with accounting disclosure. Highly visible companies, such as defense contractors and oil companies, are often the target of scrutiny by the public and by government officials. When these companies report unusually large accounting profits, they are often the target of additional regulation or increased taxes.

Stock market regulators impose disclosure standards for publicly traded corporations, but the nature and extent of the required disclosures vary substantially across countries. Further, because the requirements only set the minimum level of disclosure, the quantity and quality of information provided by firms will vary. This variation in disclosure ultimately reflects differences among companies in the benefits and costs of disclosing information to the public.

You Make The Call requires you to assume various roles within a business and use your accounting knowledge to address an issue. Solutions are at the end of the chapter.

YOU MAKE THE CALL

You are a Product Manager   There is often friction between investors' needs for information and a company's desire to safeguard competitive advantages. Assume that you are the product manager for a key department at your company and you are asked for advice on the extent of information to disclose in the annual report on a potentially lucrative new product that your department has test marketed. What considerations affect the advice you provide and why? [Answer on page 29]

BUSINESS ACTIVITIES

Businesses produce accounting information to help develop strategies, attract financing, evaluate investment opportunities, manage operations, and measure performance. Before we can attempt to understand the information provided in financial statements, we must understand these business activities. That is, what does a business actually do? For example:

LO2 Describe a company's business activities and explain how these activities are represented by the accounting equation.

- Where does a company such as Nike find the resources to develop new products and open new retail stores?

- What new products should Nike bring to market?

- How much should Nike spend on product development? On advertising? On executive compensation?

- How does Nike's management determine if a product is a success?

Questions such as these define the activities of Nike and other companies.

Exhibit 1.2 illustrates the activities of a typical business. All businesses *plan* business activities, *finance* those activities, *invest* resources in those activities, and then engage in *operating* activities. Companies conduct all these activities while confronting a variety of *external forces,* including competition from other businesses, government regulation, economic conditions and market forces, and changing preferences of customers. The financial statements provide information that helps us understand and evaluate each of these activities.

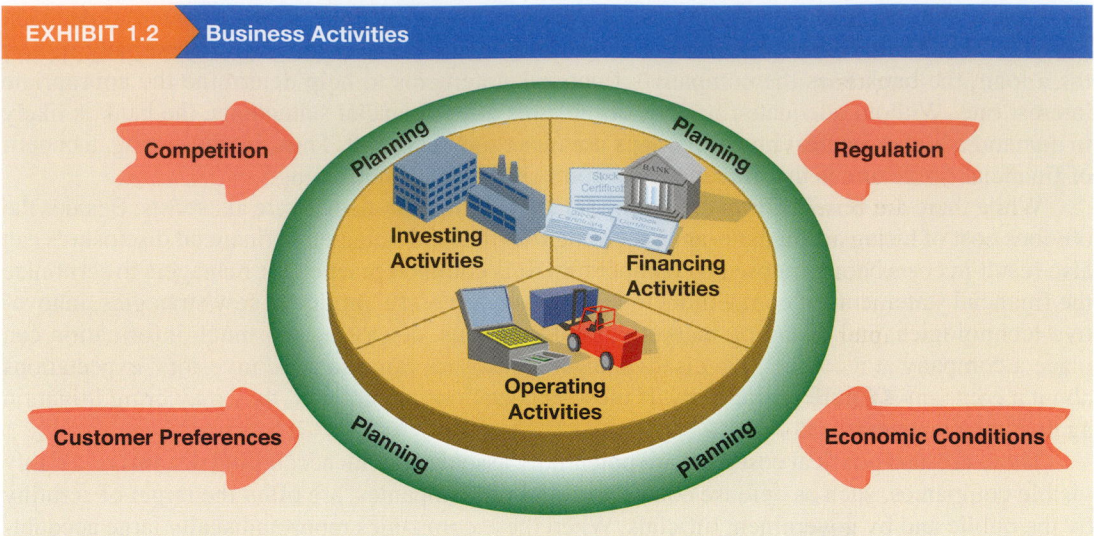

EXHIBIT 1.2 ▶ Business Activities

Planning Activities

A company's goals, and the strategies adopted to reach those goals, are the product of its **planning activities**. Nike, for example, states that its mission is "To bring inspiration and innovation to every athlete in the world" adding "If you have a body, you are an athlete." However, in its 2014 annual report to shareholders, Nike management suggests another goal that focuses on financial success and earning a return for the shareholders.

Excerpts from recent financial statements are used to illustrate and reinforce concepts.

> Our goal is to deliver value to our shareholders by building a profitable global portfolio of branded footwear, apparel, equipment, and accessories businesses.

As is the case with most businesses, Nike's primary goal is to create value for its owners, the shareholders. How the company plans to do so is the company's **strategy**.

A company's *strategic* (or *business*) *plan* describes how it plans to achieve its goals. The plan's success depends on an effective review of market conditions. Specifically, the company must assess both the demand for its products and services, and the supply of its inputs (both labor and capital). The plan must also include competitive analyses, opportunity assessments, and consideration of business threats. The strategic plan specifies both broad management designs that generate company value and tactics to achieve those designs.

Most information in a strategic plan is proprietary and guarded closely by management. However, outsiders can gain insight into planning activities through various channels, including newspapers, magazines, and company publications. Understanding a company's planning activities helps focus accounting analysis and place it in context.

Investing Activities

Key Terms are highlighted in bold, red font.

Investing activities consist of acquiring and disposing of the resources needed to produce and sell a company's products and services. These resources, called **assets**, provide future benefits to the company. Companies differ on the amount and mix of these resources. Some companies require buildings and equipment while others have abandoned "bricks and mortar" to conduct business through the Internet.

Some assets that a company invests in are used quickly. For instance, a retail clothing store hopes to sell its spring and summer merchandise before purchasing more inventory for the fall and winter. Other assets are acquired for long-term use. Buildings are typically used for several decades. The relative proportion of short-term and long-term investments depends on the type of business and the strategic plan that the company adopts. For example, Nike has relatively few long-term assets because it outsources most of the production of its products to other companies.

The graph in **Exhibit 1.3** compares the relative proportion of short-term and long-term assets held by Nike and seven other companies, several of which are featured in later chapters. Nike has adopted a business model that requires very little investment in long-term resources. A majority of its investments are short-term assets. In contrast, **Verizon**, **PepsiCo**, and **Procter & Gamble** all rely heavily on long-term investments. These companies hold relatively small proportions of short-term assets. This mix of long-term and short-term assets is described in more detail in Chapter 2.

Real Companies and Institutions are highlighted in bold, blue font.

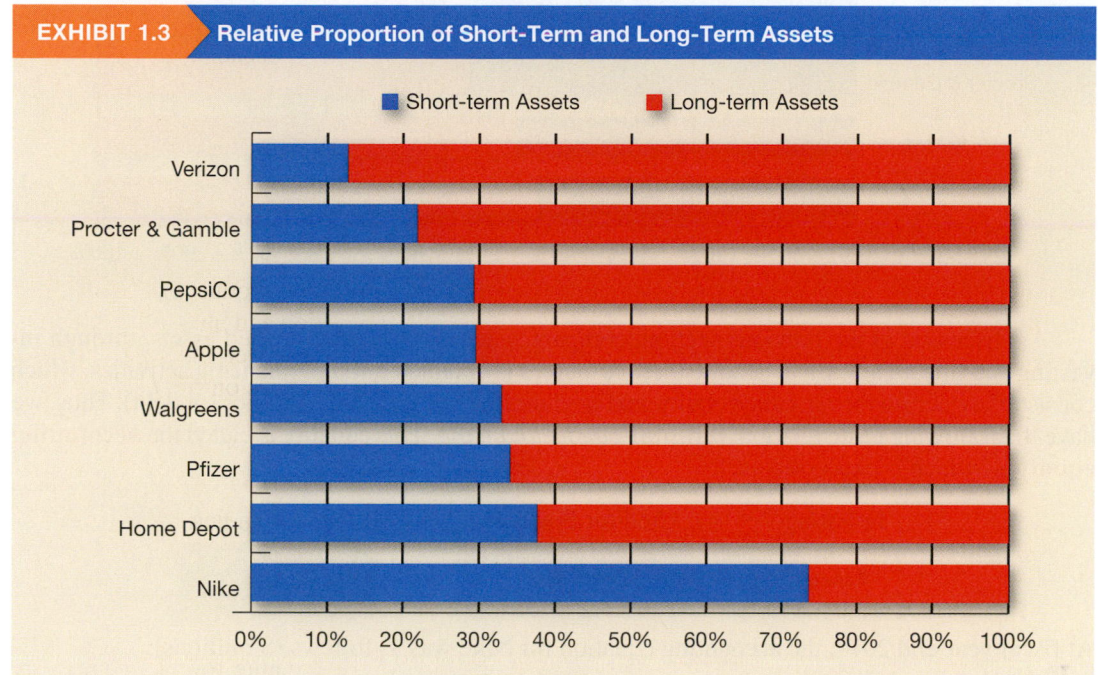

EXHIBIT 1.3   Relative Proportion of Short-Term and Long-Term Assets

Financing Activities

Investments in resources require funding, and **financing activities** refer to the methods companies use to fund those investments. *Financial management* is the planning of resource needs, including the proper mix of financing sources.

Companies obtain financing from two sources: equity (owner) financing and creditor (non-owner) financing. *Equity financing* refers to the funds contributed to the company by its owners along with any income retained by the company. One form of equity financing is the cash raised from the sale (or issuance) of stock by a corporation. *Creditor* (or debt) *financing* is funds contributed by nonowners, which create *liabilities*. **Liabilities** are obligations the company must repay in the future. One example of a liability is a bank loan. We draw a distinction between equity and creditor financing for an important reason: creditor financing imposes a legal obligation to repay, usually with interest, and failure to repay amounts borrowed can result in adverse legal consequences such as bankruptcy. In contrast, equity financing does not impose an obligation for repayment.

Exhibit 1.4 compares the relative proportion of creditor and equity financing for Nike and other companies. PepsiCo uses liabilities to finance 75% of its resources. In contrast, **Walgreen Co.** relies more heavily on its equity financing, receiving 45% of its financing from creditors. Nike has the lowest proportion of creditor financing in this sample of companies with just 42% of its assets financed by nonowners.

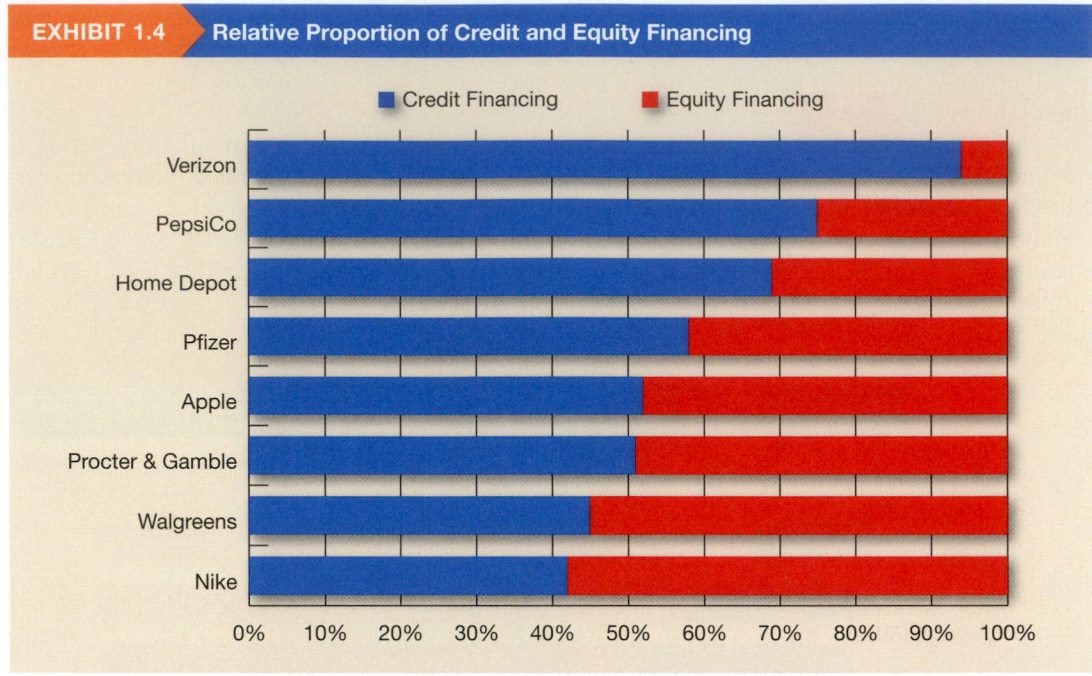

EXHIBIT 1.4   Relative Proportion of Credit and Equity Financing

Infographics are used to convey difficult concepts and procedures.

As discussed in the previous section, companies acquire resources, called assets, through investing activities. The cash to acquire these resources is obtained through financing activities, which consist of owner financing, called equity, and creditor financing, called liabilities (or debt). Thus, we have the following basic relation: *investing equals financing*. This equality is called the **accounting equation**, which is expressed as:

Investing   =   Creditor Financing   +   Owner Financing

| Assets | = | Liabilities | + | Equity |

At fiscal year-end 2014, the accounting equation for Nike was as follows ($ millions):

$$\$18{,}594 = \$7{,}770 + \$10{,}824$$

By definition, the accounting equation holds for all companies at all times. This relation is a very powerful tool for analyzing and understanding companies, and we will use it often throughout the text.

Operating Activities

Operating activities refer to the production, promotion, and selling of a company's products and services. These activities extend from a company's input markets, involving its suppliers, and to its output markets, involving its customers. Input markets generate *operating expenses* (or *costs*) such as inventory, salaries, materials, and logistics. Output markets generate *operating revenues* (or *sales*) from customers. Output markets also generate some operating expenses such as for marketing and distributing products and services to customers. When operating revenues exceed operating expenses, companies report *operating income*, also called *operating profit* or *operating earnings*. When operating expenses exceed operating revenues, companies report operating losses.

Revenue is the increase in equity resulting from the sale of goods and services to customers. The amount of revenue is determined *before* deducting expenses. An **expense** is the cost incurred to generate revenue, including the cost of the goods and services sold to customers as well as the cost of carrying out other business activities. **Income**, also called *net income*, equals revenues minus expenses, and is the net increase in equity from the company's operating activities.

| Income | = | Revenues | − | Expenses |

For fiscal year 2014, Nike reported revenues of almost $28 billion, yet its reported income was a fraction of that amount—just under $2.7 billion.

BUSINESS INSIGHT

Each year, *Fortune* magazine ranks the 500 largest corporations in the United States based on total revenues. For 2013, which is based on fiscal 2012 financial results, Nike ranked 126th on the *Fortune 500* list with revenues of just over $24 billion. The company also ranked 97th in profits, with net income of approximately $2.2 billion. For comparison, the largest corporation was **Wal-Mart Stores**, with revenues of $469.1 billion and $17 billion in net income. (Source: http://fortune.com/fortune500/2013/)

Nike's Net Income as a Fraction of Revenue

Expenses 91%

9% Net Income

FINANCIAL STATEMENTS

eLectures
MBC

LO3 Introduce the four key financial statements including the balance sheet, income statement, statement of stockholders' equity, and statement of cash flows.

Four financial statements are used to periodically report on a company's business activities. These statements are:

- **balance sheet**, which lists the company's investments and sources of financing using the accounting equation;
- **income statement**, which reports the results of operations;
- **statement of stockholders' equity**, which details changes in owner financing;
- **statement of cash flows**, which details the sources and uses of cash.

Exhibit 1.5 shows how these statements are linked across time. A balance sheet reports on a company's position at a point in time. The income statement, statement of stockholders' equity, and the statement of cash flows report on performance over a period of time. The three statements in the middle of **Exhibit 1.5** (period-of-time statements) link the balance sheet from the beginning of a period to the balance sheet at the end of a period.

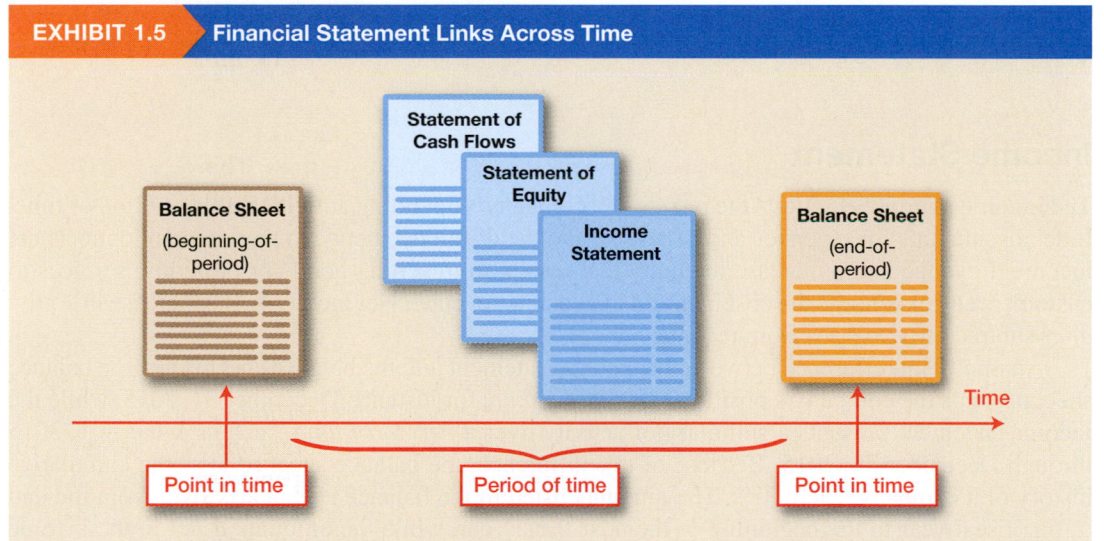

EXHIBIT 1.5 ▸ **Financial Statement Links Across Time**

A one-year, or annual, reporting period is common, which is called the *accounting*, or *fiscal year*. Semiannual, quarterly, and monthly reporting periods are also common. *Calendar-year* companies have a reporting period that begins on January 1 and ends on December 31. **Pfizer**, **Google**, and **Verizon** are examples of calendar-year companies. Some companies choose a fiscal year ending on a date other than December 31. Seasonal businesses, such as retail stores, often choose a fiscal year that ends when sales and inventories are at their lowest level. For example, **Home Depot**, the retail home improvement store chain, ends its fiscal year on the Sunday closest to February 1, after the busy holiday season. Nike has a May 31 fiscal year. The heading of each statement identifies the: (1) company name, (2) statement title, and (3) date or time period of the statement.

FYI The heading of each financial statement includes who, what, and when.

Balance Sheet

A **balance sheet** reports a company's financial position at a point in time. It summarizes the result of the company's investing and financing activities by listing amounts for assets, liabilities, and equity. The balance sheet is based on the accounting equation, also called the *balance sheet equation*: Assets = Liabilities + Equity.

Nike's balance sheet for fiscal year 2014, which ended May 31, 2014, is reproduced in a reduced format in **Exhibit 1.6** and reports that assets are $18,594 million, liabilities are $7,770 million, and equity is $10,824 million, where owner financing is the sum of contributed capital of $5,868 million, retained earnings of $4,871 million, and other equity of $85 million. Thus, the balance sheet equation holds true for Nike's balance sheet: assets equal liabilities plus equity.

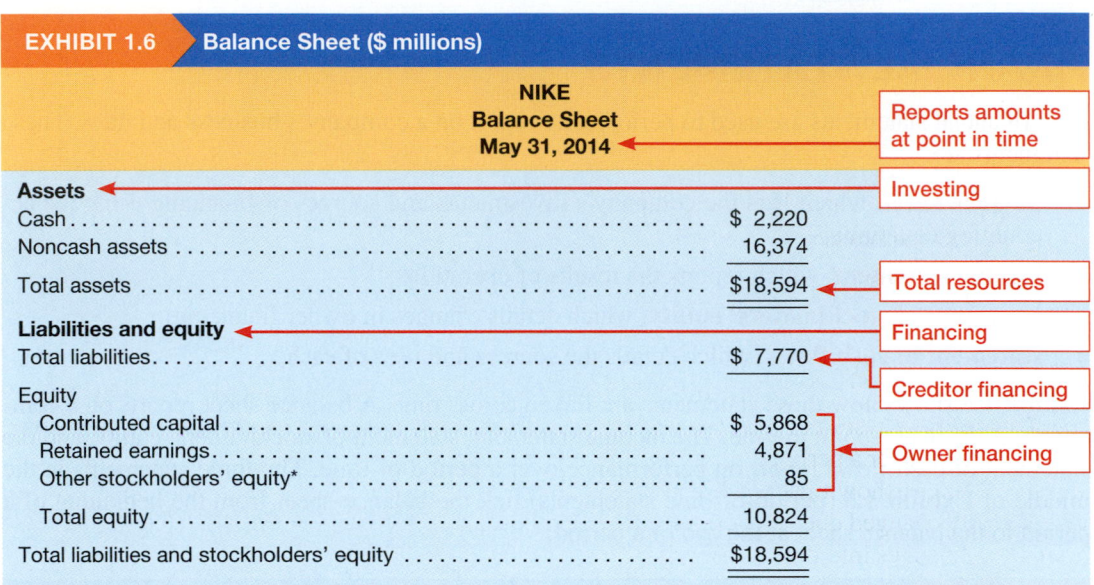

EXHIBIT 1.6   Balance Sheet ($ millions)

NIKE
Balance Sheet
May 31, 2014 — Reports amounts at point in time

Assets ←		Investing
Cash	$ 2,220	
Noncash assets	16,374	
Total assets	$18,594 ←	Total resources
Liabilities and equity ←		Financing
Total liabilities	$ 7,770 ←	Creditor financing
Equity		
Contributed capital	$ 5,868	
Retained earnings	4,871	Owner financing
Other stockholders' equity*	85	
Total equity	10,824	
Total liabilities and stockholders' equity	$18,594	

* Other stockholders' equity includes accumulated other comprehensive income. Other components of stockholders' equity are discussed in Chapter 11.

Income Statement

The **income statement** reports the results of a company's operating activities over a period of time. It details amounts for revenues and expenses, and the difference between these two amounts is net income. Revenue is the increase in equity that results from selling goods or providing services to customers and expense is the cost incurred to generate revenue. Net income is the increase in equity *after* subtracting expenses from revenues.

An important difference between the income statement and the balance sheet is that the balance sheet presents the company's position at a *point in time*, for instance December 31, 2015, while the income statement presents a summary of activity over a *period of time*, such as January 1, 2015 through December 31, 2015. Because of this difference, the balance sheet reflects the cumulative history of a company's activities. The amounts listed in the balance sheet carry over from the end of one fiscal year to the beginning of the next fiscal year, while the amounts listed in the income statement do not carry over from one year to the next.

Refer to Nike's income statement for the fiscal year ended May 31, 2014, shown in reduced format as **Exhibit 1.7**. It reports that revenues = $27,799 million, expenses = $25,106 million, and net income = $2,693 million. Thus, revenues minus expenses equals net income for Nike.

For manufacturing and merchandising companies, the **cost of goods sold** is an important expense that is typically disclosed separately in the income statement immediately following revenues. It is also common to report a subtotal for gross profit (also called gross margin), which is revenues less the cost of goods sold. The company's remaining expenses are then reported below gross profit. Nike's income statement is presented in this reduced format in **Exhibit 1.8**:

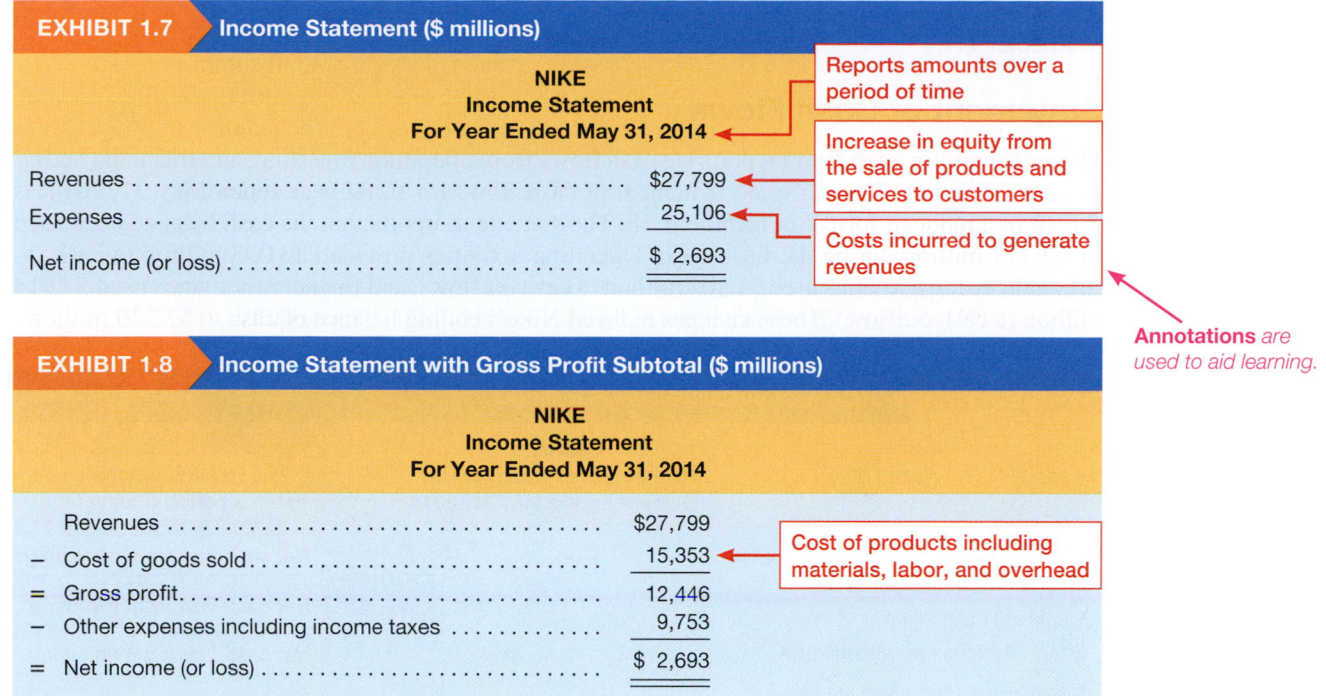

EXHIBIT 1.7 ▸ Income Statement ($ millions)

NIKE
Income Statement
For Year Ended May 31, 2014

Revenues	$27,799
Expenses	25,106
Net income (or loss)	$ 2,693

Reports amounts over a period of time

Increase in equity from the sale of products and services to customers

Costs incurred to generate revenues

Annotations are used to aid learning.

EXHIBIT 1.8 ▸ Income Statement with Gross Profit Subtotal ($ millions)

NIKE
Income Statement
For Year Ended May 31, 2014

	Revenues	$27,799
−	Cost of goods sold	15,353
=	Gross profit	12,446
−	Other expenses including income taxes	9,753
=	Net income (or loss)	$ 2,693

Cost of products including materials, labor, and overhead

Statement of Stockholders' Equity

The **statement of stockholders' equity**, or simply *statement of equity*, reports the changes in the equity accounts over a period of time. Nike's statement of stockholders' equity for fiscal year ended May 31, 2014, is shown in reduced format as **Exhibit 1.9**. During the year ended May 31, 2014, Nike's equity changed due to share issuance and income reinvestment. The exhibit details and classifies these changes into three categories:

- Contributed capital (includes common stock, and additional paid-in capital)
- Retained earnings (includes cumulative net income or loss, and deducts dividends)
- Other stockholders' equity

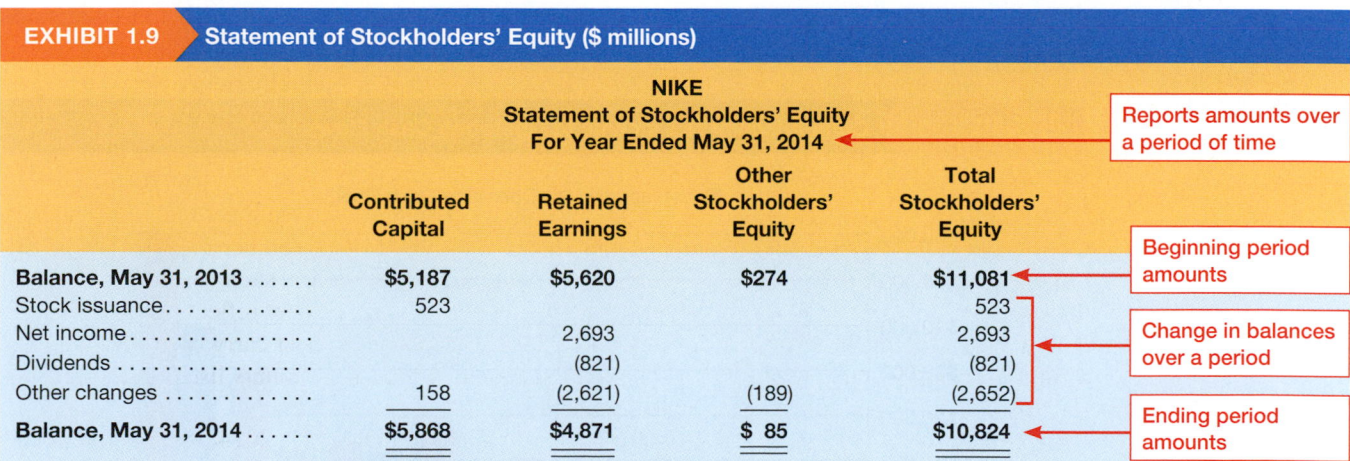

EXHIBIT 1.9 ▸ Statement of Stockholders' Equity ($ millions)

NIKE
Statement of Stockholders' Equity
For Year Ended May 31, 2014

	Contributed Capital	Retained Earnings	Other Stockholders' Equity	Total Stockholders' Equity
Balance, May 31, 2013	$5,187	$5,620	$274	$11,081
Stock issuance	523			523
Net income		2,693		2,693
Dividends		(821)		(821)
Other changes	158	(2,621)	(189)	(2,652)
Balance, May 31, 2014	$5,868	$4,871	$ 85	$10,824

Reports amounts over a period of time

Beginning period amounts

Change in balances over a period

Ending period amounts

Contributed capital represents the net amount received from issuing stock to shareholders (owners). **Retained earnings** (also called *earned capital*) represents the income the company has earned since its inception, minus the dividends it has paid out to shareholders. Thus, retained earnings equals the amount of income retained in the company. The change in retained earnings links consecutive balance sheets through the income statement. Nike's retained earnings decreased from $5,620 million at May 31, 2013 to $4,871 million at May 31, 2014. This decrease is explained by net income of $2,693 million, less dividends of $821 million and other reductions of $2,621 million. The category

FYI Dividends are reported in the statement of equity, and not in the income statement.

titled "other changes" refers to changes in equity that are not recorded in income and is discussed in Chapter 11.

Statement of Cash Flows

FYI Cash is critical to operations because it is necessary for purchasing resources and paying bills.

The **statement of cash flows** reports net cash flows from operating, investing, and financing activities over a period of time. Nike's statement of cash flows for fiscal year ended May 31, 2014, is shown in a reduced format in **Exhibit 1.10**. The statement reports that the cash balance decreased by $1,117 million during the fiscal year. Operating activities provided $3,003 million (a cash inflow), investing activities used $1,207 million (a cash outflow), and financing activities used $2,914 million (a cash outflow). These changes reduced Nike's ending balance of cash to $2,220 million.

EXHIBIT 1.10	Statement of Cash Flows ($ millions)

NIKE
Statement of Cash Flows
For Year Ended May 31, 2014 ← Reports amounts over a period of time

Operating cash flows	$3,003 ← Net cash flow from operating
Investing cash flows	(1,207) ← Net cash flow from investing
Financing cash flows	(2,914) ← Net cash flow from financing
Effect of exchange rate changes	1
Net increase (decrease) in cash	(1,117)
Cash, May 31, 2013	3,337 ←
Cash, May 31, 2014	$2,220 ← Cash amounts per balance sheet

FYI Common formatting for U.S. financial statements includes:
- Dollar sign next to first and last amount listed in a column
- Single underline before a subtraction or addition; double underline after a major total
- Assets listed in order of liquidity, which is nearness to cash
- Liabilities listed in order of due dates

Operating cash flow is the amount of cash generated from operating activities. This amount usually differs from net income due to differences between the time that revenues and expenses are recorded, and the time that the related cash receipts and disbursements occur. For example, a company may report revenues for goods sold to customers this period, but not collect the payment until next period. Consistent with most companies, Nike's operating cash flows of $3,003 million do not equal its net income of $2,693 million. **Exhibit 1.11** compares net income and operating cash flows for Nike and several other companies. The exhibit shows that there is large variation across companies in the amount of net income and operating cash flows.

Both cash flow and net income are important for making business decisions. They each capture different aspects of firm performance and together help financial statement users better understand and assess a company's past, present, and future business activities.

EXHIBIT 1.11	Comparison of Net Income to Operating Cash Flows

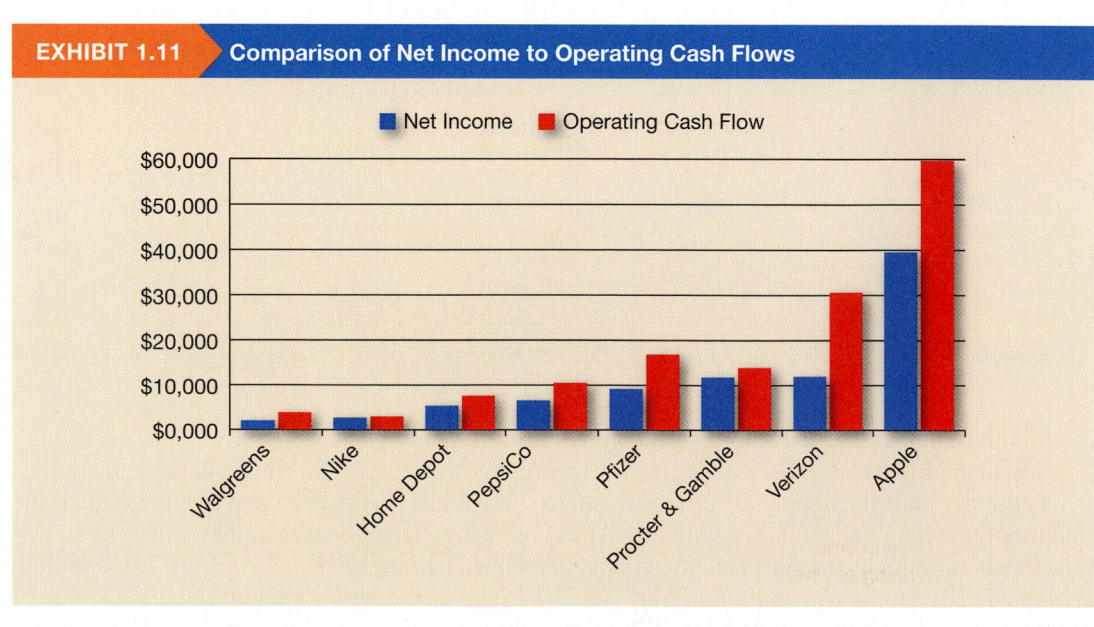

Financial Statement Linkages

A central feature of the accounting system is the linkage among the four primary statements, referred to as the *articulation* of the financial statements. Three of the key linkages are:

- The statement of cash flows links the beginning and ending cash in the balance sheet.
- The income statement links the beginning and ending retained earnings in the statement of stockholders' equity.
- The statement of stockholders' equity links the beginning and ending equity in the balance sheet.

Exhibit 1.12 demonstrates these links using Nike's financial statements from **Exhibits 1.6** through **1.10**. The left side of **Exhibit 1.12** presents Nike's beginning-year balance sheet for fiscal year 2014 (which is the same as the balance sheet for the end of fiscal year 2013) and the right side presents Nike's year-end balance sheet for fiscal year 2014. These balance sheets report Nike's investing and financing activities at the beginning and end of the fiscal year, two distinct points in time. The middle column of **Exhibit 1.12** presents the three financial statements

EXHIBIT 1.12   **Articulation of Nike Financial Statements ($ millions)**

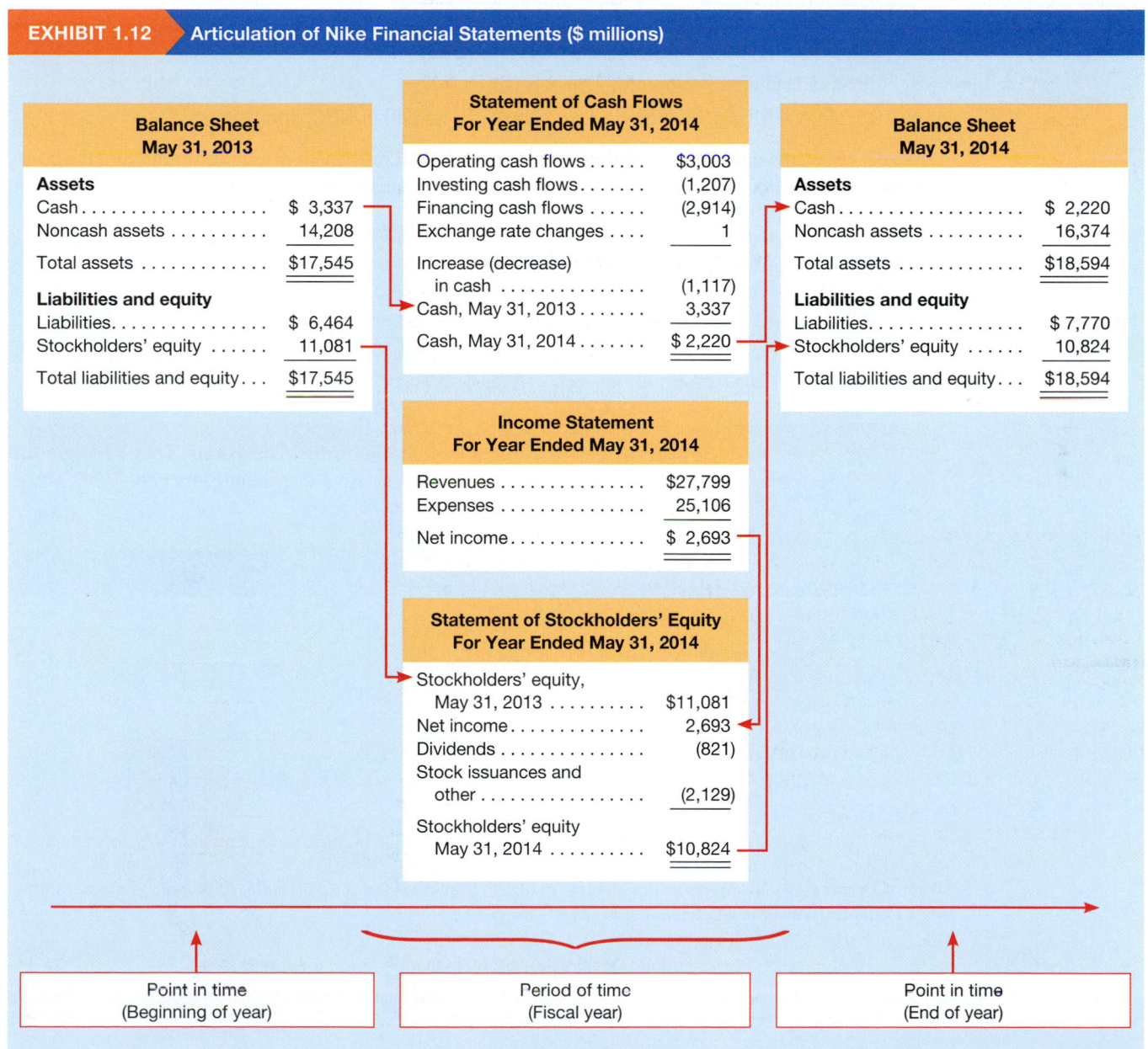

that report Nike's fiscal year 2014 business activities over time: the statement of cash flows, the income statement, and the statement of stockholders' equity. The three key linkages shown in **Exhibit 1.12** are:

- The statement of cash flows explains how operating, financing, and investing activities decreased the cash balance by $1,117 million, from the $3,337 million reported in the beginning-year balance sheet, to the $2,220 million reported in the year-end balance sheet.

- The net income of $2,693 million reported in the income statement is added to retained earnings in the statement of stockholders' equity.

- The statement of stockholders' equity explains how total equity of $11,081 million, reported in the beginning-year balance sheet, becomes total equity of $10,824 million, reported in the year-end balance sheet.

Information Beyond Financial Statements

FYI An analysis of a firm's activities requires extensive study of its footnotes and the MD&A.

Important information about a company is communicated to various decision makers through reports other than financial statements. These reports include the following:

- Management Discussion and Analysis (MD&A)
- Independent Auditor Report
- Financial statement footnotes
- Regulatory filings, including proxy statements and other SEC filings

We describe and explain the usefulness of these additional information sources throughout the book.

Review Problems are self-study tools that require the application of accounting. To aid learning, solutions are provided at the end of the chapter.

*Guided Example icons denote the availability of a demonstration video in **myBusinessCourse** (MBC)—see the Preface for more on MBC.*

MID-CHAPTER REVIEW

Based in Germany, **Adidas** is one of **Nike**'s primary competitors. It markets athletic shoes and apparel under the Adidas and Reebok brands. It also sells Solomon ski equipment as well as TaylorMade and Adams golf equipment. Adidas' financial statements are reported in Euros, the currency of the European Union. The following information is from the company's December 31, 2013, financial statements (€ millions):

	2013
Cash	€ 1,587
Cash flow from operations	634
Sales revenue	14,492
Stockholders' equity	5,481
Cost of goods sold	7,352
Cash flow used for financing	(439)
Total liabilities	6,118
Net other expenses	6,350
Noncash assets	10,012
Cash flow used for investing	(243)
Net income	790
Cash, beginning of year	1,670
Effect of exchange rates on cash	(35)

REQUIRED

a. Prepare Adidas' balance sheet at December 31, 2013, and its income statement and cash flow statement for the fiscal year ended December 31, 2013.

b. Compare Adidas' revenue, net income, and cash flow from operations to that of Nike (as reported in this chapter). Assume an exchange rate of €1.00 = $1.35.

The solution to this review problem can be found on pages 39–40.

FINANCIAL REPORTING ENVIRONMENT

Information presented in financial statements is of critical importance to external decision makers. Financial statements affect the prices paid for equity securities and interest rates attached to debt securities. To the extent that financial performance and condition are accurately communicated to business decision makers, debt and equity securities are more accurately priced. By extension, financial reporting plays a crucial role in efficient resource allocation within and across economies. Accounting information contributes to the efficient operation of securities markets, labor markets, commodity markets, and other markets.

To illustrate, imagine the consequences of a breakdown in the integrity of financial reporting. The Enron scandal provides a case in point. At the beginning of 2001, **Enron** was one of the more, if not the most, innovative and respected companies in the United States. With revenues of over $100 billion and total company value of over $60 billion, it was the fifth largest U.S. corporation based on market value. In October 2001, the company released its third quarter earnings report to the public. Although operating earnings were higher than in previous years, the income statement contained a $1 billion "special charge." Financial analysts began investigating the cause of this charge and discovered that it was linked to related-party transactions and questionable accounting practices. Once it became clear to the capital markets that Enron had not faithfully and accurately reported its financial condition and performance, people became unwilling to purchase its securities. The value of its debt and equity securities dropped precipitously and the company was unable to obtain the cash needed for operating activities. By the end of 2001, Enron was bankrupt!

The Enron case illustrates the importance of reliable financial reporting. Accountants recognize the importance of the information that they produce and, as a profession, they agree to follow a set of standards for the presentation of financial statements and the disclosure of related financial information. In the following paragraphs, we discuss these standards, or *principles*, as well as the institutional and regulatory environment in which accountants operate.

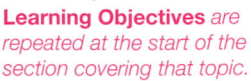

LO4 Describe the institutions that regulate financial accounting and their role in establishing generally accepted accounting principles.

Learning Objectives are repeated at the start of the section covering that topic.

Generally Accepted Accounting Principles

Decision makers who rely on audited financial statements expect that all companies follow similar procedures in preparing their statements. In response to these expectations, U.S. accountants have developed a set of standards and procedures called **generally accepted accounting principles (GAAP)**. GAAP is not a set of immutable laws. Instead, it is a set of standards and accepted practices, based on underlying principles, that are designed to guide the preparation of the financial statements. GAAP is subject to change as conditions warrant. As a result, specific rules are altered or new practices are formulated to fit changes in underlying economic circumstances or business transactions.

Some people mistakenly assume that financial accounting is an exact discipline—that is, companies select the proper standard to account for a transaction and then follow the rules. The reality is that GAAP allows companies considerable discretion in preparing financial statements. The choice of methods often yields financial statements that are markedly different from one company to another in terms of reported income, assets, liabilities, and equity amounts. In addition, financial statements depend on numerous estimates. Consequently, even though two companies may engage in the same transactions and choose the same accounting methods, their financial statements will differ because their managements have made different estimates about such things as the amount to be collected from customers who buy on credit, the length of time that buildings and equipment will be in use, and the future costs for product warranties.

Accounting standard setters walk a fine line regarding choice in accounting. On one hand, they are concerned that management discretion in preparing financial statements will lead to abuse by those seeking to influence the decisions of those who rely on the statements. On the other hand, they are concerned that companies are too diverse for a "one size fits all" financial accounting system. Ultimately, GAAP attempts to strike a balance by imposing constraints on the choice of accounting procedures, while allowing companies some flexibility within those constraints.

Regulation and Oversight

Following the U.S. stock market crash of 1929, the United States Congress passed the Securities Acts of 1933 and 1934. These acts were passed to require disclosure of financial and other information about securities being offered for public sale and to prohibit deceit, misrepresentations, and other fraud in the sale of securities. The 1934 Act created the **Securities and Exchange Commission (SEC)** and gave it broad powers to regulate the issuance and trading of securities. The act also provided that companies with more than $10 million in assets and whose securities are held by more than 500 owners must file annual and other periodic reports, including a complete set of financial statements.

While the SEC has ultimate authority over financial reporting by companies in the United States, it has ceded the task of setting accounting standards to a professional body, the **American Institute of Certified Public Accountants (AICPA)**. Over the years, this process has resulted in three standard-setting organizations.

Currently, accounting standards are established by the **Financial Accounting Standards Board (FASB)**. The FASB is a seven-member board that has the primary responsibility for setting financial accounting standards in the United States. It has published over 160 accounting statements governing the preparation of financial reports. These, along with numerous bulletins, interpretations, opinions, and earlier standards form the body of GAAP.

BUSINESS INSIGHT

Accounting can be complicated—but rule-makers are trying to make it a little simpler.
The Financial Accounting Standards Board, which sets accounting rules for U.S. companies, is expanding its effort to simplify some areas of accounting to make financial reporting a little less complex and reduce costs for companies and their accountants. The FASB has added five more projects it plans to tackle as part of that initiative, covering areas like how companies report their debt and when they record taxes on certain transactions.

The projects are low-hanging fruit—relatively narrow, straightforward changes in accounting that clearly would help reduce complexity and that the board expects to be able to make relatively quickly, without the years of work that often accompany major revisions in accounting rules.

"Complexity in accounting can be costly to both investors and companies," FASB Chairman Russ Golden said. The simplification initiative, which FASB began in June 2014, "is focused on identifying areas that we can address quickly and effectively, without compromising the quality of information provided to investors."

Besides setting standards for financial accounting, the FASB has developed a framework to form the basis for future discussion of proposed standards and serve as a guide to accountants for reporting information that is not governed by specific standards. A summary of this *Conceptual Framework* is presented in Appendix 1A at the end of this chapter.

In the wake of the Enron, Tyco, AOL, Global Crossing, Halliburton, Xerox, Adelphia, Bristol-Myers Squibb, and WorldCom scandals, concerns over the quality of corporate financial reporting led Congress to pass the **Sarbanes-Oxley Act** in 2002. The goal of this Act—sometimes referred to as SOX—was to increase the level of confidence that external users, particularly investors, have in the financial statements. To accomplish this objective, SOX imposed a number of requirements to strengthen audit committees and improve deficient **internal controls** by:

- increasing management's responsibility for accounting information,
- increasing the independence of the auditors,
- increasing the accountability of the board of directors,
- establishing adequate internal controls to prevent fraud.

SOX requires that the chief executive officer (CEO) and the chief financial officer (CFO) of a publicly traded corporation personally sign a statement attesting to the accuracy and completeness of financial statements. The prospect of severe penalties is designed to make these managers more vigilant in monitoring the financial accounting process. In addition, SOX established the **Public Company Accounting Oversight Board (PCAOB)** to approve auditing standards and monitor the quality of financial statements and audits.

SOX has had an impact on financial disclosures. A report by Glass, Lewis and Co. indicates that the number of publicly traded companies restating their financial reports increased to 1,295 in 2005, which is one restatement for every 12 reporting companies. That's triple the total in 2002 when SOX was passed.

The Sarbanes-Oxley Act is not without critics. Many small companies complain that the additional reporting and auditing requirements established in the act are prohibitively costly. In response to this criticism, the JOBS Act of 2012 relaxed the SOX reporting requirements for companies with less than one billion dollars in sales. Of even greater concern is the criticism that the penalties imposed on management for misstatements or errors are too severe. Some argue that managers have become less forthcoming in their disclosures and more conservative in choosing accounting methods and making accrual estimates to avoid the possibility of heavy fines or criminal charges.

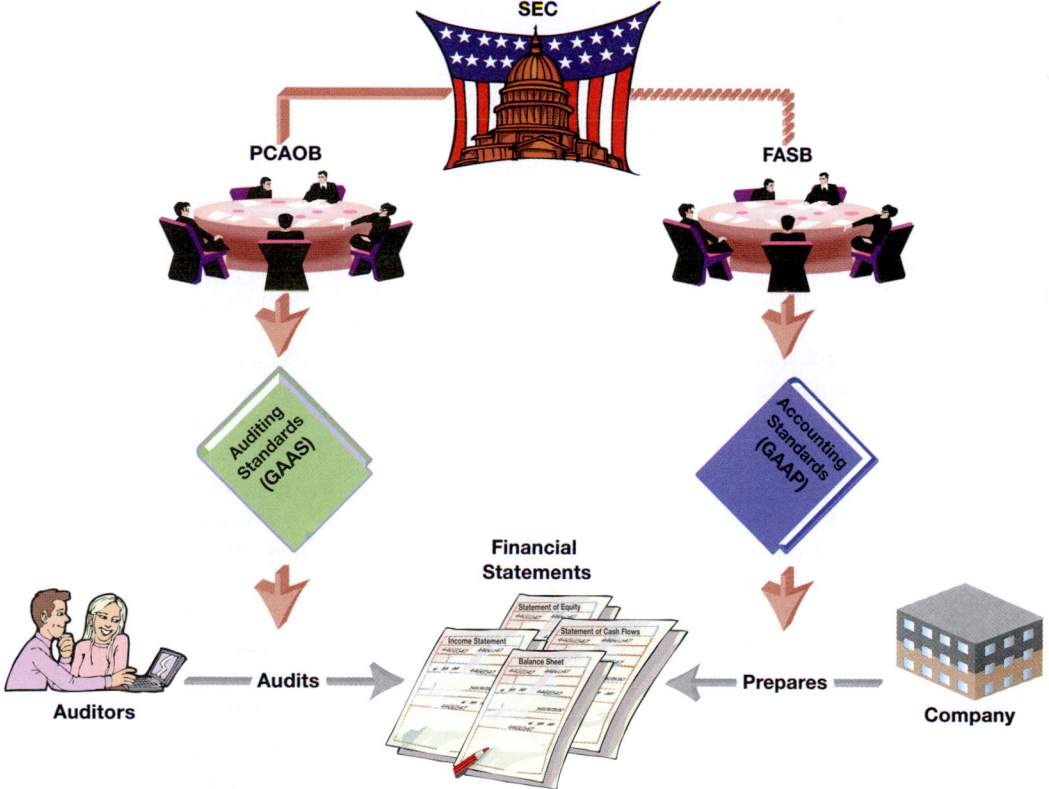

Role of the Auditor

What prevents a company from disclosing false or misleading information? For one thing, the financial statements are prepared by management, and management must take responsibility for what is disclosed. Management's reputation can be severely damaged by false disclosures when subsequent events unfold to refute the information. This situation can adversely affect the firm's ability to compete in capital, labor, and consumer markets. It can also lead to litigation and even criminal charges against management.

Even though management must personally attest to the accuracy and completeness of the financial statements, markets also demand assurances from independent parties. Therefore, the financial statements of publicly traded corporations must be **audited** by an *independent audit firm*. The auditors provide an opinion as to whether the statements *present fairly* and *in all material respects* a company's financial condition and the results of its operations.

The audit opinion is not a guarantee. Auditors only provide reasonable assurance that the financial statements are free of material misstatements. Even so, auditors provide a valuable service. Auditors effectively ensure that the information contained in the financial statements is reliable, thus increasing the confidence of outside decision makers in the information they use to make investment, credit, and other decisions. Therefore, creditors and shareholders of privately held corporations often demand that the financial statements be audited as well.

Public corporations are required to establish audit committees whose purpose is not to audit but, rather, to appoint the audit firm and assure that what is learned in the audit is disclosed to the firm's directors and shareholders.

YOU MAKE THE CALL

You are a Member of the Board of Directors   Until recently accounting firms were permitted to earn money for consulting activities performed for clients they audited. Do you see any reason why this might not be an acceptable practice? Do you see any advantage to your firm from allowing such activity? [Answer on page 29.]

A Global Perspective

Businesses increasingly operate in global markets. Consumers and businesses with access to the Internet can purchase products and services from anywhere in the world. Products produced in one country are often made with parts and materials imported from many different countries. Businesses outsource parts of operations to other countries to take advantage of better labor markets in those countries. Capital markets are global as well. Corporations whose securities trade on the New York Stock Exchange may also trade on exchanges in London, Toronto, Tokyo, or Hong Kong.

Because countries have a variety of laws and customs, accounting principles and practices vary considerably from one country to the next. Many companies based in countries other than the United States choose to present financial statements that conform to U.S. GAAP because they believe that doing so provides them better access to investors in the U.S. capital markets. Many other companies prepare financial statements following GAAP of the country in which they are based.

The globalization of capital markets, combined with the diversity of international accounting principles, has led to an effort to increase comparability of financial information across countries. The **International Accounting Standards Board (IASB)** oversees the development of accounting standards outside the United States. Over 100 countries, including those in the European Union, require the use of **International Financial Reporting Standards (IFRS)** developed by the IASB. The intention is to unify all public companies under one global set of reporting standards.

Early in the 2000s, the Financial Accounting Standards Board (FASB) and the IASB committed to developing the highest-quality standards useable for both domestic and cross-border financial reporting and to assure the standards would (a) be fully compatible as soon as practicable and (b) maintain that compatibility. In May 2011, the SEC proposed a transition method to incorporate IFRS into the U.S. reporting system but did not delineate a definitive time for implementation. A number of large international companies now issue IFRS-compliant financial statements, however without reconciling them with U.S. GAAP as previously required. Statements prepared under IFRS and U.S. GAAP are quite similar, yet important differences remain. For example, balance sheets prepared under IFRS often classify assets in reverse order of liquidity to those prepared under GAAP. Thus, intangible assets are listed first and cash last on the balance sheet. Both approaches require the same basic set of four financial statements, with explanatory footnotes. We shall examine some of the more important differences under a Global Perspective heading as they arise in future chapters. Websites maintained by the larger accounting firms as well as both the FASB and IASB provide considerable information.

Because it is international in its scope, the IASB has no legal authority to impose accounting standards on any country. However, by working with standard setters within countries, such as the FASB within the United States, the IASB is working to reduce diversity in financial reporting practice. Despite the push for comparability, not everyone is convinced that IFRS will improve the usefulness of accounting information. As one observer put it, "There is a real risk of a veneer of comparability that hides a lot of differences." A number of countries—over 30 at last count—have reserved the right to adopt exceptions to IFRS when they deem them to be appropriate. Perhaps this helps explain why the SEC on July 13, 2012, declined to recommend IFRS for adoption by the United States.

Global Perspectives *examine issues related to similarities and differences in accounting practices of the U.S. and other countries.*

A GLOBAL PERSPECTIVE

Prior to 2007, foreign-based companies wishing to sell securities in the United States were required to reconcile their financial statements to be consistent with U.S. GAAP. However, in June 2007, the SEC adopted a rule that allows foreign companies using international accounting standards to stop reconciling their financial statements to American rules. While this change made it easier for U.S. investors to purchase securities from around the world, a *New York Times* article referred to a "Tower of Babel in Accounting." The article raises concerns about the difficulty of comparing companies when their financial statements are based on diverse reporting standards. The situation is complicated by the fact that a number of developing countries have reserved the right to adopt exceptions to IFRS when deemed appropriate.

*Each chapter includes a section on **Analyzing Financial Statements** to emphasize the use of accounting information in making business decisions.*

ANALYZING FINANCIAL STATEMENTS

The financial statements provide insights into the financial health and performance of a company. However, the accounting data presented in these statements are difficult to interpret in raw form. For example, knowing that Nike's net income was $2,693 million in 2014 is, by itself, not very useful. Similarly, knowing the dollar amount of liabilities does not tell us whether or not Nike relies too heavily on creditor financing.

Financial analysts use a number of tools to help interpret the information found in the financial statements. They look at trends over time and compare one company to another. They calculate ratios using financial statement information to summarize the data in a form that is easier to interpret. Ratios also allow us to compare the performance and condition of different companies even if the companies being compared are dramatically different in size. Ratios also help analysts spot trends or changes in performance over time.

Throughout the book, we introduce ratios that are commonly used by financial analysts and other users who rely on the financial statements. Our goal is to develop an understanding of how to effectively use the information in the financial statements, as well as to demonstrate how these statements are prepared. In this chapter we introduce one important measure of **profitability** and one measure of financial **risk**.

LO5 Compute two key ratios that are commonly used to assess profitability and risk—return on equity and the debt-to-equity ratio.

5

Profitability Analysis

Profitability reveals whether or not a company is able to bring its product or service to the market in an efficient manner, and whether the market values that product or service. Companies that are consistently unprofitable are unlikely to succeed in the long run.

A key profitability metric for stockholders and other decision makers is company return on equity. This metric compares the level of net income with the amount of equity financing used to generate that income.

Analysis Objective

We are trying to determine Nike's ability to earn a return for its stockholders.

Analysis Tool Return on Equity

$$\text{Return on equity} = \frac{\text{Net income}}{\text{Average stockholders' equity}}$$

Applying the Return on Equity Ratio to Nike

$$\textbf{2012:} \quad \frac{\$2{,}211}{[(\$10{,}381 + \$9{,}843)/2]} = 0.219 \text{ or } 21.9\%$$

$$\textbf{2013:} \quad \frac{\$2{,}472}{[(\$11{,}081 + \$10{,}381)/2]} = 0.230 \text{ or } 23.0\%$$

$$\textbf{2014:} \quad \frac{\$2{,}693}{[(\$10{,}824 + \$11{,}081)/2]} = 0.246 \text{ or } 24.6\%$$

Guidance   Taken over time, ROE ratios that are over 10% and preferably increasing suggest the company is earning reasonable returns. For firms that are in more risky businesses, such as renewable power, even larger returns on equity would be appropriate, while firms in less risky endeavors, such as large food chains, would not be expected to generate as large returns.

Nike in Context

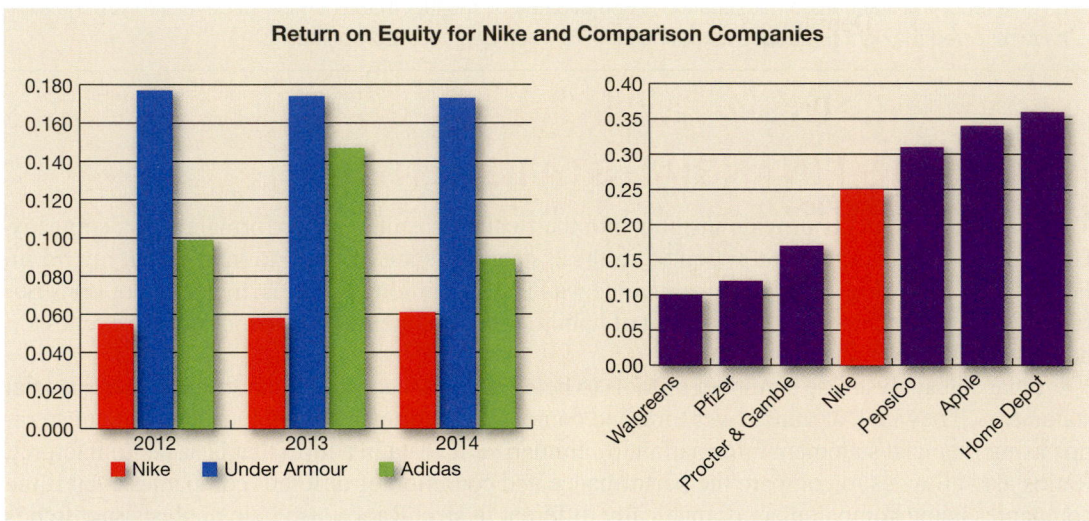

Takeaways   Over the time period covered by our calculations and by the graph, it is clear that Nike has done very well earning returns for its stockholders. Not only have returns been over 20% but the trend is one of increasing profitability. Whether Nike can continue to do so is less clear. Several new companies have entered the market and Nike will need to continue developing new products to preserve its market leadership.

Other Considerations   As with all ratios, care in their interpretation is essential. First, we need to be careful about comparing companies that operate in different product markets.

Second, firms with different customer or supplier demographics can also produce different conclusions. Furthermore, different management policies toward assets and liabilities have their own unique effect on ratios across firms. For example, the conversion of inventories to sales can be subject to slowdowns that affect companies differently, within the same industry.

Third, these measures can be altered by management decisions designed solely for cosmetic effects such as improving current earnings or an important ratio. Thus, delaying inventory orders or filling sales orders early can lead to increasing net income and ROE in current periods to the detriment of future periods.

Finally, differences in the fiscal year-end of companies can influence a comparison of ROE ratios. If one company's fiscal year ends in May and another company's fiscal year ends in December, economic conditions may change between May and December, creating differences in ROE that are not due to differences in the operations of the two companies. Among the companies compared above, fiscal year ends range from January 2014 (Home Depot) to December 2014 (Adidas and others).

Credit Risk Analysis

In addition to measuring profitability, analysts also frequently analyze the level of risk associated with investing in or lending to a given company. The riskier an investment is, the greater the return demanded by investors. For example, a low-risk borrower is likely to be able to borrow money at a lower interest rate than would a high-risk borrower. Similarly, there is a risk-return trade-off in equity returns. Investments in risky stocks are expected to earn higher returns than investments in low-risk stocks, and stocks are priced accordingly. The higher expected rate of return is compensation for accepting greater uncertainty in returns.

FYI Return cannot be evaluated without considering risk; the greater the risk of any decision, the greater the expected return.

Many factors contribute to the risk a company faces. One important factor is a company's *long-term solvency*. **Solvency** refers to the ability of a company to remain in business and avoid bankruptcy or financial distress. One such measure is the **debt-to-equity (D/E) ratio**.

Analysis Objective

We are interested in determining the ability of a company to make the necessary interest and principal payments on its debt.

Analysis Tool   Debt-to-Equity

$$\text{Debt-to-equity ratio} = \frac{\text{Total liabilities}}{\text{Total stockholders' equity}}$$

Applying the Debt-to-Equity Ratio to Nike

2012: $\dfrac{\$5,084}{\$10,381} = 0.49$

2013: $\dfrac{\$6,464}{\$11,081} = 0.58$

2014: $\dfrac{\$7,770}{\$10,824} = 0.72$

Guidance   Solvency is closely related to the extent a company relies on creditor financing. As the amount of creditor financing increases, the possibility of bankruptcy also increases. Short of bankruptcy, a company that has borrowed too much will occasionally find that the required interest payments are hurting the company's cash flow. The debt-to equity ratio is an important measure used by analysts and others to assess a company's ability to make the necessary interest and principal payments on its debt.

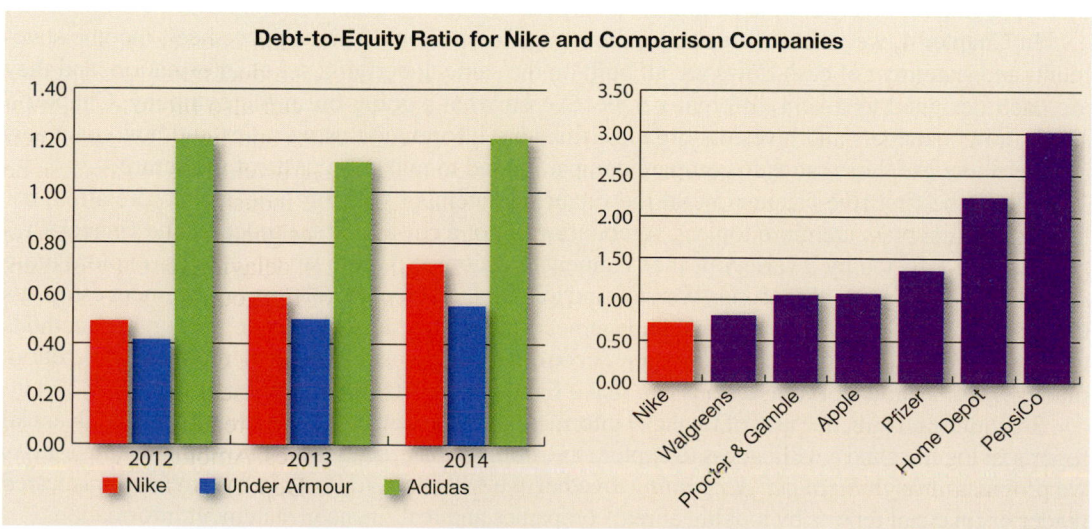

Debt-to-Equity Ratio for Nike and Comparison Companies

A debt-to equity ratio of one indicates that the company is using equal parts of debt and equity financing. Nike's borrowing has consistently been less than half its assets, resulting in a ratio substantially below one.

The appropriate D/E ratio level depends on the nature of the business and will differ appreciably as can be seen in the chart below. Typically, firms with large long-term commitments often reflected in fixed assets will find it appropriate to raise more capital through borrowing. The amount of debt relative to equity will also mirror the risk tolerance of the firm's management. If management believes it can earn a return above the debt interest cost, borrowing will increase the expected return to the owners.

Takeaways   Nike's D/E ratio has increased slightly over the three years presented. Nike's liabilities have been steadily increasing. Yet, stockholders' equity has not increased at the same pace, and in fact it declined in 2014. Nevertheless, Nike's D/E ratio remains low, which is reasonable given nearly all its production is carried out overseas.

Other Considerations   Comparisons with other companies in similar lines of business, such as Under Armour and Adidas, are always appropriate. New competitors, such as Quiksilver, could also prove insightful to examine in regards to strategic decisions. In Chapter 9, we will explore the accounting for liabilities in more depth. Balance sheets do not always recognize all obligations of a firm, and a careful reader will examine the footnotes to get a more complete picture of financial health in such comparisons. Nike might also consider increasing its debt level if profitable opportunities exist. The company has been, and remains, very successful, but new entrants are emerging indicating there is additional business to be had.

The graph shows that Nike had the lowest debt-to-equity ratio among this group of firms, followed closely by Walgreens. In contrast, PepsiCo had a debt-to-equity ratio of approximately 3.0. PepsiCo financed 75% of its assets with debt.

There are other measures of profitability and risk that will be introduced in later chapters. Collectively, these ratios, when placed in the context of the company's business activities, help to provide a clear picture of the *drivers* of a company's financial performance and the factors affecting its financial condition. Understanding these performance drivers and their impact on the financial health of a company is key to effectively using the information presented in the financial statements.

ORGANIZATION OF THE BOOK

In the pages that follow Chapter 1, we will explore the financial accounting model and how it reflects an organization's activities and events. Chapters 2 and 3 are focused on building the balance sheet and the income statement from transactions and a set of required adjustments. This process requires a structure for "bookkeeping" and also an understanding of the basic rules of the accounting language. When do we recognize revenue? When do we recognize an asset? We will look at these questions in a relatively simple setting.

In Chapter 4, we will construct the statement of cash flows. The balance sheet, income statement, and statement of cash flows are all built on the same underlying set of information, and they are each designed to give a different perspective on what's going on in the company. Chapter 5 shows how managers and investors organize financial information using ratios and how managers and investors use those ratios to compare companies and to make forecasts of the future.

While the first five chapters build the financial statement structure and its interpretation, the latter seven chapters are more topical. Accounting is not a cut-and-dried process, and financial reports can be affected by a variety of management decisions. So these seven chapters explore more sophisticated settings and analyses. We will find that financial reports rely on management estimates of future events, and that sometimes management has the freedom to choose accounting methods that affect income and assets. And, when accounting practices don't allow reporting discretion, management's choice of transactions can make financial reports look more favorable.

Becoming an effective user of financial information requires an understanding of how the financial reports fit together and a willingness to explore the footnote material to look for useful information. As we progress through *Financial Accounting* together, we will show you how to become a sophisticated reader of financial reports by looking at real companies and real financial statement information.

CHAPTER-END REVIEW

Adidas, a major competitor of Nike, markets athletic shoes and apparel under the Adidas and Reebok brands. It also sells Solomon ski equipment and TaylorMade golf equipment. The following information is from Adidas' 2013 financial statements (Adidas' financial statements are reported in Euros, the currency of the European Union):

(millions)	Adidas
Net income (loss) (2013)	€ 790
Stockholders' equity (2013 year-end)	5,481
Stockholders' equity (2012 year-end)	5,291
Total liabilities (2013 year-end)	6,118

REQUIRED

a. Calculate the 2013 return on equity (ROE) ratio for Adidas.
b. Calculate the 2013 debt-to-equity ratio for Adidas.
c. Compare the profitability and risk of Adidas to that of Nike.

The solution to this review problem can be found on page 40.

APPENDIX 1A: Conceptual Framework for Financial Reporting

LO6 Explain the conceptual framework for financial reporting.

6

The Financial Accounting Standards Board (FASB) has worked in conjunction with the International Accounting Standards Board (IASB) to develop a conceptual framework for financial reporting. The conceptual framework consists of a system of interrelated objectives that, if met, would help to identify desirable reporting standards. The FASB and the IASB expect that the two Boards will most directly benefit from the conceptual framework by using the framework as a common foundation in the development of future standards.

In this appendix, we focus on the objective for financial reporting as stated in the conceptual framework, as well as the characteristics of financial reporting that determine the degree of success in meeting that objective.

Objective of Financial Reporting

The objective of financial reporting is *to provide information that is useful to present and potential equity investors, as well as lenders and other creditors, in making decisions about providing resources to the entity.* The objective suggests that the information that is presented in financial statements is produced to 1) help the firm raise financing by providing information to equity investors and creditors about the financial health and performance of the firm, and 2) to provide ongoing information to those deciding whether to buy, sell, or hold equity and debt securities (including whether to settle loans and other types of credit). Information that is intended for investors and creditors may also be useful to other users of the financial statements.

This objective may be met by providing information for the assessment of the amount, timing, and uncertainty of future (net) cash flows to the firm, which enables investors and creditors to assess the amount, timing, and uncertainty of the cash flows which they will receive. The objective of financial reporting is not to provide a value of a firm, but to provide information for users' own assessments of value.

Qualitative Characteristics of Useful Financial Information

The conceptual framework identifies *relevance* and *faithful representation* as two fundamental qualitative characteristics of financial information that are necessary to fulfill the objective described in the previous section. As the conceptual framework states, "Neither a faithful representation of an irrelevant phenomenon, nor an unfaithful representation of a relevant phenomenon, helps users make good decisions." In addition, the conceptual framework identifies several enhancing qualitative characteristics that affect the usefulness of relevant and faithfully represented information. These qualitative characteristics and their relationship to the basic objective are depicted in **Exhibit 1A.1** and discussed below.

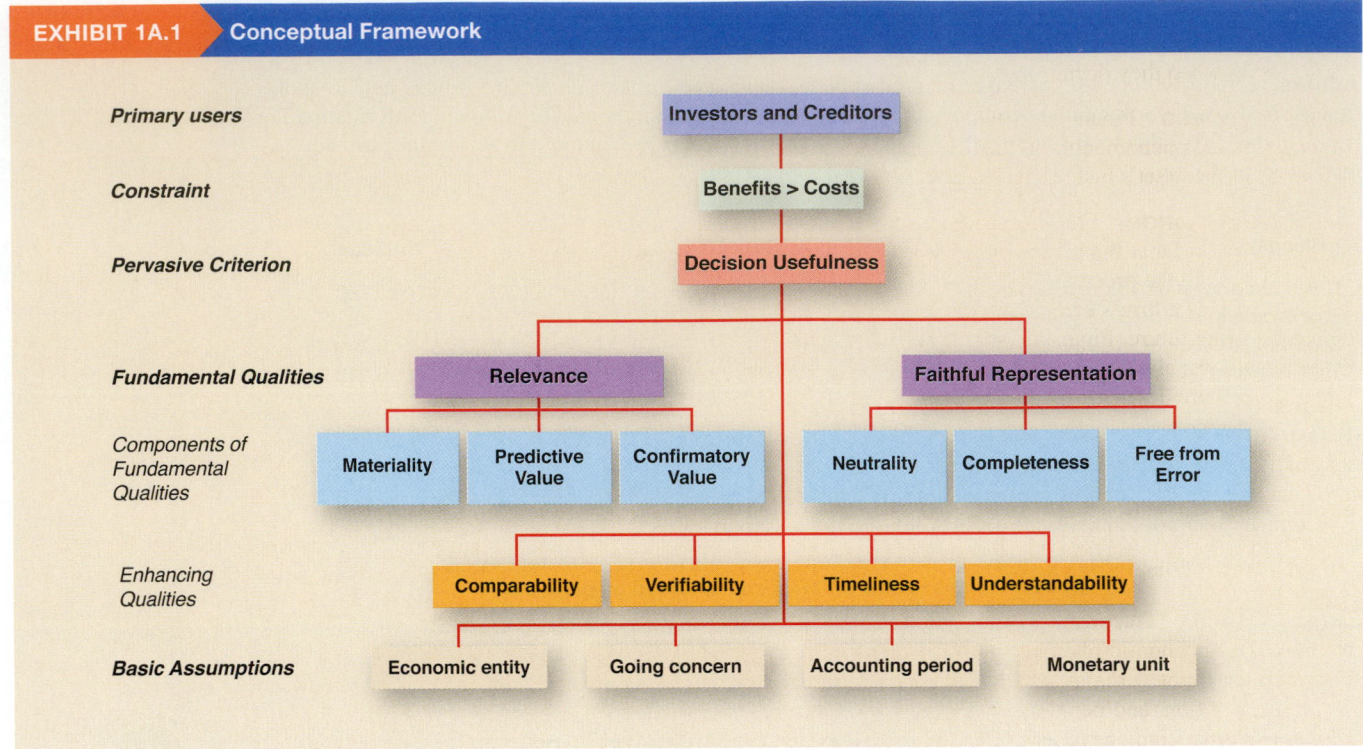

EXHIBIT 1A.1 ▸ Conceptual Framework

Relevance   To be relevant, accounting information must have the ability to make a difference in a decision. Such information may be useful in making predictions about future performance of a company or in providing confirmatory feedback to evaluate past events.

MATERIALITY   Materiality refers to whether a particular amount is large enough or important enough to affect the judgment of a reasonable decision maker. In practice, materiality is typically judged by the relative size of an item (e.g., relative to total assets, sales revenues, or net income).

PREDICTIVE VALUE   Financial information has predictive value if it can be used as an input in the decision processes employed by users to predict future outcomes. The information does not have to be a prediction or forecast itself, but if it can used by others in making predictions, it has predictive value.

CONFIRMATORY VALUE   Financial information has confirmatory value if it provides feedback about previous evaluations.

Faithful Representation   In addition to being relevant, financial information must report the economic events that it purports to report. Financial reports describe where an organization is at a point in time and how it arrived at that location from a previous one. To a traveler, a map would provide a faithful representation if the traveler can use the map to discern his or her actual location.

Information is a perfectly faithful representation if it is *complete*, *neutral*, and *free from error*. The objective stated in the conceptual framework does not expect to achieve such perfection, but the requirement of faithful representation for information provides a measuring stick for standard-setters when considering alternative reporting standards.

NEUTRALITY   While lack of bias is desirable in any reporting system, the effects of financial reports on management and investors create significant incentives to report outcomes and to choose disclosures that

RESEARCH INSIGHT

While neutrality is a desirable characteristic, the importance of financial reports in valuing companies, in lending terms and in management compensation creates significant incentives for managers to influence those reports. Accounting researchers have documented a wide variety of situations in which discretionary actions and/or estimates have been used to affect how financial reports may be perceived by users, usually to make the company look better or—on occasion—worse than it should. As we explore throughout the text, the accounting standards often provide the means for a careful reader to assess the neutrality of the reported numbers and to make adjustments where needed.

portray the firm in a favorable light. In choosing accounting standards, standard-setters aspire to reduce the ability of organizations to bias financial reports and to give financial statement users the ability to identify those biases when they occur.

COMPLETENESS   Financial information is complete if it enables the user to understand all the dimensions of an economic phenomenon. Achieving such completeness may require disclosure of additional numerical information (an asset's historical cost and its fair value) or descriptive information (ongoing litigation).

FREE FROM ERROR   Free from error means there are no errors or omissions in the description of the phenomenon and that the process used to produce the reported information has been selected and applied with no errors in the process. A common misconception about accounting is that it consists solely of a historical record of a firm's economic activities. It is such a record, but it is also dependent on management's forecasts of the future. Financial reports are very dependent on forecasts of the future, and forecasts of the future are almost always wrong (though we hope not by much). In this context, "free from error" means that any estimates are described clearly as such, with an explanation of the estimating process.

Enhancing Qualitative Characteristics

For financial information that is relevant to investors and faithfully represents an economic phenomenon, the conceptual framework describes several additional qualitative characteristics that – when present – enhance the usefulness of that information.

Comparability   Accounting information should enable users to identify similarities and differences between sets of economic phenomena. For instance, the financial statements of different companies should be presented in a way that allows users to make comparisons across companies concerning their activities, financial condition, and performance. In addition, the information supplied to decision makers should exhibit conformity from one reporting period to the next with unchanging policies and procedures. Companies can choose to change accounting methods, and sometimes they are required to do so by standard-setters. However, such changes make it difficult to evaluate financial performance over time. Accounting changes should be rare and supported as the better means of reporting the organization's financial condition and performance.

Verifiability   Verifiability means that consensus among independent observers could be reached that reported information is a faithful representation. An independent auditor should be able to examine the economic events and transactions underlying the financial statements and reach conclusions that are similar to those of management concerning how these events are measured and reported.

Timeliness   Financial reporting information must be available to decision makers before it loses its capacity to influence decisions.

Understandability   Modern organizations engage in a wide variety of transactions, and this complexity can make it difficult for a general user of the financial statements to assess the amount, timing, and uncertainty of the organization's future cash flows. The conceptual framework endeavors to take into consideration the reporting requirements for "users who have a reasonable knowledge of business and economic activities and who review and analyze the information diligently."

The Cost Constraint

Financial reporting requirements impose costs on companies. There are the costs of gathering, processing, and verifying the information, as well as the costs of publicly disclosing information to competitors. These costs are ultimately borne by the companies' investors and should be justified by the benefits of the information produced.

Additional Underlying Basic Assumptions

While not a part of the conceptual framework, four assumptions underlie the preparation of financial statements. Knowing these assumptions is helpful in understanding how the statements are prepared and in interpreting the information reported therein. These assumptions include:

Separate Economic Entity   For accounting purposes, the activities of a company are considered independent, distinct, and separate from the activities of its stockholders and from other companies.

Going Concern   Companies are assumed to have continuity in that they can be expected to continue in operation over time. This assumption is essential for valuing assets (future benefits) and liabilities (future obligations).

Accounting Period While continuity is assumed, company operations must be reported periodically, normally each fiscal year. Interim reporting periods, such as quarterly or monthly reports, allow companies to supplement the annual financial statements with more timely information.

Monetary Unit The unit of measure is the monetary unit of the country in which the firm's accounting reports are issued. The dollar is the monetary unit in the United States.

YOU MAKE THE CALL

You are the Bank Loan Officer **Hertz**, the rental car firm, has a fleet of relatively new automobiles that it rents to customers for usually short periods. Suppose that Hertz applied to your bank for a loan and offered their fleet of cars as collateral. Would you, as the loan officer, be satisfied with the value shown on Hertz's balance sheet as a measure of the fleet's value? If not, what value would you prefer and how might you estimate that value? [Answers on page 30.]

Summary offers key bullet point takeaways for each Learning Objective.

SUMMARY

LO1 **Identify the users of accounting information and discuss the costs and benefits of disclosure. (p. 4)**

- There are many diverse decision makers who use financial information.
- The benefits of disclosure of credible financial information must exceed the costs of providing the information.

LO2 **Describe a company's business activities and explain how these activities are represented by the accounting equation. (p. 7)**

- To effectively manage a company or infer whether it is well managed, we must understand its activities as well as the competitive and regulatory environment in which it operates.
- All corporations *plan* business activities, *finance* and *invest* in them, and then engage in *operations*.
- Financing is obtained partly from stockholders and partly from creditors, including suppliers and lenders.
- Investing activities involve the acquisition and disposition of the company's productive resources called assets.
- Operating activities include the production of goods or services that create operating revenues (sales) and expenses (costs). Operating profit (income) arises when operating revenues exceed operating expenses.

LO3 **Introduce the four key financial statements including the balance sheet, income statement, statement of stockholders' equity, and statement of cash flows. (p. 11)**

- The four basic financial statements used to periodically report the company's progress are the balance sheet, the income statement, the statement of stockholders' equity, and the statement of cash flows. These statements articulate with one another.
- The balance sheet reports the company's financial position *at a point* in time. It lists the company's asset, liability, and equity items, and it typically aggregates similar items.
- The income statement reports the firm's operating activities to determine income earned, and thereby the firm's performance *over a period* of time.
- The stockholders' equity statement reports the changes in the key equity accounts *over a period* of time.
- The statement of cash flows reports the cash flows into and out of the firm from its operating, investing, and financing sources *over a period* of time.

LO4 **Describe the institutions that regulate financial accounting and their role in establishing generally accepted accounting principles. (p. 17)**

- Generally Accepted Accounting Principles (GAAP) are established standards and accepted practices designed to guide the preparation of the financial statements.
- While the Securities and Exchange Commission (SEC) has ultimate authority over financial reporting by companies in the United States, it has ceded the task of setting accounting standards to the accounting profession.

- The Financial Accounting Standards Board (FASB) has the primary responsibility for setting financial accounting standards in the United States.
- The Sarbanes-Oxley Act established the Public Company Accounting Oversight Board (PCAOB) to approve auditing standards and monitor the quality of financial statements and audits.
- International Financial Reporting Standards (IFRS) are set by the International Accounting Standards Board (IASB).
- IFRS are an attempt to achieve a greater degree of commonality in financial reporting across different countries.

Compute two key ratios that are commonly used to assess profitability and risk—return on equity and the debt-to-equity ratio. (p. 21)   **LO5**

- **Return on equity (ROE)**—a measure of profitability that assesses the performance of the firm relative to the investment made by stockholders (equity financing)
- Return on equity (ROE) is an important profitability metric for stockholders.

$$ROE = \frac{\text{Net income}}{\text{Average stockholders' equity}}$$

- **Debt-to-equity ratio (D/E)**—a measure of long-term solvency that relates the amount of creditor financing to the amount of equity financing
- The debt-to-equity ratio is an important measure of long-term solvency, a determinant of overall company risk.

$$D/E = \frac{\text{Total liabilities}}{\text{Total stockholders' equity}}$$

Appendix 1A: Explain the conceptual framework for financial reporting. (p. 25)   **LO6**

- The conceptual framework includes, among other things, a statement of the *objectives* of financial reporting along with a discussion of the *qualitative characteristics* of accounting information that are important to users.

GUIDANCE ANSWERS . . . YOU MAKE THE CALL

You are a Product Manager   There are at least two considerations that must be balanced—namely, the disclosure requirements and your company's need to protect its competitive advantages. You must comply with all minimum required disclosures. The extent to which you offer additional disclosures depends on the sensitivity of the information; that is, how beneficial it is to your existing and potential competitors. Another consideration is how the information disclosed will impact your existing and potential investors. Disclosures such as this can be beneficial in that they convey the positive investments that are available to your company. Still, there are many stakeholders impacted by your decision and each must be given due consideration.

You are a Financial Analyst   This question has received a lot of discussion from both sides under the title "Economic Consequences." On one side are those who maintain that accounting rules should not only reflect a rule's economic consequences but should be designed to facilitate the attainment of a specific economic goal. One example is the case where the oil industry lobbied for an accounting rule that they and others believed would increase the incentive to explore and develop new oil deposits.

Those on the other side of the argument believe that accounting should try to provide data that is objective, reliable, and free from bias without considering the economic consequences of the decisions to be made. They believe that accounting rule makers have neither the insight nor the public mandate to attempt forecasts of the economic effects of financial reporting. Decisions that will affect the allocation of resources or that affect society's social structure should be made only by our elected representatives. While there are substantive points on both sides, we believe that it is the job of accounting rule makers to work toward the objective of financial reporting that reflects economic reality, subject to practical measurement limitations.

You are a Member of the Board of Directors   In order to perform a thorough audit, a company's auditors must gain an intimate knowledge of its operations, its internal controls, and its accounting system. Because of this familiarity, the accounting firm is in a position to provide insights and recommendations that another consulting firm might not be able to provide. However, the independence of the auditor is critical to the credibility of the audit and there is some concern that the desire to retain a profitable consulting engagement might lead the auditors to tailor their audit opinions to "satisfy the customer." Contrary to this concern, however, research finds that there is no evidence that auditors provide more optimistic audit reports for the companies they consult for. Rather, it appears that litigation and/or reputation concerns are reasonably effective in keeping auditors honest. Nevertheless, recent legislation in the United States now prohibits auditors from performing consulting services for their audit clients.

You are the Bank Loan Officer The value shown on Hertz's books will be the purchase price, though perhaps reduced for the time the fleet has been in use. However, the bank would want to know the current market value of the fleet, not its book value, and the bank would then adjust this market value. The current market value of a single car can be found in used-car market quotes. If the bank ultimately becomes the owner of the fleet, it will need to sell the cars, probably a few at a time through wholesalers. Therefore, the adjusted market value and the book value are likely to differ for several reasons, including:

1. Hertz would have been able to buy the fleet at a reduced value due to buying in large volume regularly (market value lower than used-car quotes).
2. Hertz is likely to have kept the cars in better condition than would the average buyer (market value higher than used-car quotes).
3. The bank would reduce the value by some percentage due to the costs associated with disposing of the fleet (including the wholesaler's discount) and the length of the bank loan (reduction to the value as otherwise determined).

KEY RATIOS

$$\text{Return on equity (ROE)} = \frac{\text{Net income}}{\text{Average stockholders' equity}} \qquad \text{Debt-to-equity (D/E)} = \frac{\text{Total liabilities}}{\text{Total stockholders' equity}}$$

← **Key Terms** *are listed for each chapter with references to page numbers within the chapter.*

KEY TERMS

Accounting (p. 4)

Accounting equation (p. 10)

American Institute of Certified Public Accountants (AICPA) (p. 18)

Assets (p. 8)

Audited (p. 20)

Balance sheet (p. 11, 12)

Board of directors (p. 6)

Conceptual framework (p. 25)

Corporation (p. 5)

Cost of goods sold (p. 12)

Creditors (p. 5)

Debt-to-equity (D/E) ratio (p. 23)

Disclosure (p. 6)

Economic consequences (p. 18)

Expense (p. 10)

Feedback value (p. 27)

Financial accounting (p. 4)

Financial Accounting Standards Board (FASB) (p. 18)

Financing activities (p. 9)

Generally accepted accounting principles (GAAP) (p. 17)

Income (p. 10)

Income statement (p. 11, 12)

Internal controls (p. 18)

International Accounting Standards Board (IASB) (p. 20)

International Financial Reporting Standards (IFRS) (p. 20)

Investing activities (p. 8)

Liabilities (p. 9)

Managerial accounting (p. 4)

Neutrality (p. 27)

Operating activities (p. 10)

Partnership (p. 5)

Planning activities (p. 8)

Predictive value (p. 27)

Profitability (p. 21)

Public Company Accounting Oversight Board (PCAOB) (p. 19)

Representational faithfulness (p. 27)

Retained earnings (p. 13)

Revenue (p. 10)

Risk (p. 21)

Sarbanes-Oxley Act (p. 18)

Securities and Exchange Commission (SEC) (p. 18)

Shares of stock (p. 5)

Sole proprietorship (p. 5)

Solvency (p. 23)

Statement of cash flows (p. 11, 14)

Statement of stockholders equity (p. 11, 13)

Stockholders (p. 5)

Strategy (p. 8)

Suppliers (p. 6)

Timeliness (p. 27)

Verifiability (p. 27)

Assignments with the ⊕ logo in the margin are available in **BusinessCourse**.
See the Preface of the book for details.

Multiple Choice questions with answers are provided for each chapter.

MULTIPLE CHOICE

1. Which of the following is a potential cost of the public disclosure of accounting information?
   a. Loss of competitive advantage caused by revealing information to competitors.
   b. Potential increased regulation and taxes due to reporting excessive profits in politically sensitive industries.
   c. Raising and then failing to meet the expectations of investors.
   d. All of the above are potential costs of disclosure.

2. Banks that lend money to corporations are considered
   a. creditors.
   b. stockholders.
   c. both *a* and *b* above.
   d. neither *a* nor *b* above.

3. Which of the following financial statements reports the financial condition of a company at a point in time?
   a. the balance sheet
   b. the income statement
   c. the statement of cash flows
   d. the statement of stockholders' equity

4. Which of the following is *not* one of the four basic financial reports?
   a. the balance sheet
   b. the income statement
   c. the statement of stockholders' equity
   d. the notes to the financial statements

5. Which of the following expressions is a correct statement of the accounting equation?
   a. Equity + Assets = Liability
   b. Assets − (Liabilities + Equity) = 0
   c. Liabilities − Equity = Assets
   d. Liabilities + Assets = Equity

Homework icons indicate which assignments are available in myBusinessCourse (MBC). This feature is only available when the instructor incorporates MBC in the course.

Superscript ᴬ denotes assignments based on Appendix 1A.

QUESTIONS

Q1-1. What are the three major business activities of a company that are motivated and shaped by planning activities? Explain each activity.

Q1-2. The accounting equation (Assets = Liabilities + Equity) is a fundamental business concept. Explain what this equation reveals about a company's sources and uses of funds and the claims on company resources.

Q1-3. Companies prepare four primary financial statements. What are those financial statements and what information is typically conveyed in each?

Q1-4. Does a balance sheet report on a period of time or at a point in time? Also, explain the information conveyed in that report. Does an income statement report on a period of time or at a point in time? Also, explain the information conveyed in that report.

Q1-5. Warren Buffett, CEO of Berkshire Hathaway, and known as the "Sage of Omaha" for his investment success, has stated that his firm is not interested in investing in a company whose business model he does not understand through reading its financial statements. Would you agree? Name several information items (3 or 4) reported in financial statements that corporate finance officers would find particularly relevant in considering whether to invest in a firm.

Q1-6. Does a statement of cash flows report on a period of time or at a point in time? Also, explain the information and activities conveyed in that report.

Q1-7. Explain what is meant by the articulation of financial statements.

Q1-8. The trade-off between risk and return is a fundamental business concept. Briefly describe both risk and return and their trade-off. Provide some examples that demonstrate investments of varying risk and the approximate returns that you might expect to earn on those investments.

Q1-9. Why might a company voluntarily disclose more information than is required by GAAP?

Q1-10. Financial statements are used by several interested stakeholders. Develop a listing of three or more potential external users of financial statements and their applications.

Q1-11. What ethical issues might managers face in dealing with confidential information?

Q1-12. Return on equity (ROE) is an important summary measure of financial performance. How is it computed? Describe what this metric reveals about company performance.

Q1-13. Business decision makers external to the company increasingly demand more financial information on business activities of companies. Discuss the reasons why companies have traditionally opposed the efforts of regulatory agencies like the SEC to require more disclosure.

Q1-14. What are generally accepted accounting principles and what organization presently establishes them?

Q1-15. What are International Financial Reporting Standards (IFRS)? Why are IFRS needed? What potential issues can you see with requiring all public companies to prepare financial statements using IFRS?

Q1-16. What is the primary function of the auditor? To what does the auditor attest in its opinion?

Q1-17.[A] What are the objectives of financial accounting? Which of the financial statements satisfies each of these objectives?

Q1-18.[A] What are the four qualitative characteristics of accounting information? Explain how each characteristic improves the quality of accounting disclosures.

MINI EXERCISES

LO2

WhiteWave Foods, Inc.
NYSE :: WWAV

M1-19. Financing and Investing Relations, and Financing Sources
Total assets of **WhiteWave Foods** equals $2,283.2 million and its equity is $961.4 million. What is the amount of its liabilities? Does WhiteWave Foods receive more financing from its owners or nonowners, and what percentage of financing is provided by its owners?

LO2

Coca-Cola Company
NYSE :: KO

M1-20. Financing and Investing Relations, and Financing Sources
Total assets of **The Coca-Cola Company** equals $90,055 million and its liabilities equal $56,615 million. What is the amount of its equity? Does Coke receive more financing from its owners or nonowners, and what percentage of financing is provided by its owners?

LO2

Hewlett-Packard
NYSE :: HPQ
General Mills
NYSE :: GIS
Harley-Davidson
NYSE :: HOG

M1-21. Applying the Accounting Equation and Computing Financing Proportions
Use the accounting equation to compute the missing financial amounts (a), (b), and (c). Which of these companies is more owner-financed? Which of these companies is more nonowner-financed?

($ millions)	Assets	=	Liabilities	+	Equity
Hewlett-Packard	$ 105,676		$ 78,020		$ (a)
General Mills	23,145.7		(b)		7,005.4
Harley-Davidson	(c)		6,395.5		3,009.5

LO3

Apple Inc.
NASDAQ :: AAPL

M1-22. Identifying Key Numbers from Financial Statements
Access the most recent 10-K for **Apple Inc.**, at the SEC's EDGAR database for financial reports (www.sec.gov). What are Apple's dollar amounts for assets, liabilities, and equity at September 27, 2014? Confirm that the accounting equation holds in this case. What percent of Apple's assets is financed from creditor financing sources?

LO3

Nike
NYSE :: NKE

M1-23. Verifying Articulation of Financial Statements
Access the 2014 10-K for **Nike** at the SEC's EDGAR database of financial reports (www.sec.gov). Using its consolidated statement of stockholders' equity, prepare a table similar to **Exhibit 1.9** showing the articulation of its retained (reinvested) earnings for the year ended May 31, 2013. Was Nike more or less profitable in 2014 compared to 2013?

LO3

M1-24. Identifying Financial Statement Line Items and Accounts
Several line items and account titles are listed below. For each, indicate in which of the following financial statement(s) you would likely find the item or account: income statement (IS), balance sheet (BS), statement of stockholders' equity (SE), or statement of cash flows (SCF).

a. Cash asset
b. Expenses
c. Noncash assets

d. Contributed capital
e. Cash outflow for land
f. Retained earnings

g. Cash inflow for stock issued
h. Cash outflow for dividends
i. Net income

M1-25. Ethical Issues and Accounting Choices

Assume that you are a technology services provider and you must decide whether to record revenue from the installation of computer software for one of your clients. Your contract calls for acceptance of the software by the client within six months of installation before payment is due. Although you have not yet received formal acceptance, you are confident that it is forthcoming. Failure to record these revenues will cause your company to miss Wall Street's earnings estimates. What stakeholders will be affected by your decision and how might they be affected?

LO1

LOs link assignments to the Learning Objectives of each chapter.

M1-26. Internal Controls and Their Importance

The Sarbanes-Oxley legislation requires companies to report on the effectiveness of their internal controls. What are internal controls and their purpose? Why do you think Congress felt it to be such an important area to monitor and report?

LO4

EXERCISES

E1-27. Applying the Accounting Equation and Assessing Financing Contributions

Determine the missing amount from each of the separate situations (a), (b), and (c) below. Which of these companies is more owner-financed? Which of these companies is more creditor-financed?

LO2

Motorola Solutions
NYSE :: MSI
Kraft Foods
NASDAQ :: KRFT
Merck & Co.
NYSE :: MRK

($ millions)	Assets	=	Liabilities	+	Equity
a. Motorola Solutions, Inc.	$ 11,851		$?		$3,689
b. Kraft Foods Group, Inc.	?		17,961		5,187
c. Merck & Co., Inc.	105,645		53,319		?

E1-28. Financial Information Users and Uses

Financial statements have a wide audience of interested stakeholders. Identify two or more financial statement users that are external to the company. Specify two questions for each user identified that could be addressed or aided by use of financial statements.

LO1

E1-29. Applying the Accounting Equation and Financial Statement Articulation

Answer the following questions. (*Hint:* Apply the accounting equation.)

LO2, 3

Intel
NASDAQ :: INTC
JetBlue Airways
NASDAQ :: JBLU

a. **Intel Corporation** had assets equal to $92,358 million and liabilities equal to $34,102 million for a recent year-end. What was the total equity for Intel's business at year-end?

b. At the beginning of a recent year, **JetBlue Airways Corporation**'s assets were $7,070 million and its equity was $1,888 million. During the year, assets increased $280 million and liabilities increased $34 million. What was its equity at the end of the year?

c. At the beginning of a recent year, **The Walt Disney Company**'s liabilities equaled $32,940 million. During the year, assets increased by $6,343 million, and year-end assets equaled $81,241 million. Liabilities increased $151 million during the year. What were its beginning and ending amounts for equity?

Walt Disney Company
NYSE :: DIS

E1-30. Financial Statement Relations to Compute Dividends

Colgate-Palmolive Company reports the following balances in its retained earnings.

LO3

Colgate-Palmolive
NYSE :: CL

($ millions)	2013	2012
Retained earnings	$17,952	$16,953

During 2013, Colgate-Palmolive reported net income of $2,410 million.

Ticker symbols are provided for companies so one can easily obtain additional information.

a. Assume that the only changes affecting retained earnings were net income and dividends. What amount of dividends did Colgate-Palmolive pay to its shareholders in 2013?

b. This dividend amount constituted what percent of its net income?

LO3

Colgate-Palmolive
NYSE :: CL

E1-31.   Calculating Gross Profit and Preparing an Income Statement

In 2013, **Colgate-Palmolive Company** reported sales revenue of $17,420 million and cost of goods sold of $7,219 million. Its net income was $2,410 million. Calculate gross profit and prepare an income statement using the format illustrated in **Exhibit 1.8**.

LO2, 5

Colgate-Palmolive
NYSE :: CL

E1-32.   Applying the Accounting Equation and Calculating Return on Equity and Debt-to-Equity Ratio

At the end of 2013, **Colgate-Palmolive Company** reported stockholders' equity of $2,536 million and total assets of $13,876 million. Its balance in stockholders' equity at the end of 2012 was $2,390 million. Net income in 2013 was $2,410 million.

a.   Calculate Colgate-Palmolive's return on equity ratio for 2013.

b.   Calculate its debt-to-equity ratio as of December 31, 2013. (*Hint:* Apply the accounting equation to determine total liabilities.)

LO2, 5

Daimler AG
OTC :: DDAIF

E1-33.   Applying the Accounting Equation and Computing Return on Equity and Debt-to-Equity Ratio

At the end of 2013, **Daimler AG**, reported stockholders' equity of €43,363 million and total assets of €168,518 million. Its stockholders' equity at the end of 2012 was €39,330 million. Net income in 2013 was €8,720 million.

a.   Calculate Daimler's return on equity ratio for 2013.

b.   Calculate Daimler's debt-to-equity ratio as of December 31, 2013.

LO1, 4

E1-34.   Accounting in Society

Financial accounting plays an important role in modern society and business.

a.   What role does financial accounting play in the allocation of society's financial resources?

b.   What are three aspects of the accounting environment that can create ethical pressure on management?

LO6

E1-35.ᴬ   Basic Assumptions, Principles, and Terminology in the Conceptual Framework

Match each item in the left column with the correct description in the right column.

_____ 1. Relevance
_____ 2. Verifiability
_____ 3. Going concern
_____ 4. Materiality
_____ 5. Measuring unit
_____ 6. Representational faithfulness
_____ 7. Accounting period
_____ 8. Consistency
_____ 9. Reliability
_____ 10. Economic entity

a.   Refers to whether or not a particular amount is large enough to affect a decision.

b.   The activities of a business are considered to be independent and distinct from those of its owners or from other companies.

c.   Whenever possible, information in concurrent periods should be presented without changes to policies and procedures

d.   Accounting information should be accurate and free of misstatement or bias.

e.   Information is useful if it has the ability to influence decisions.

f.   Consensus among measures assures that the information is free of error.

g.   Accounting information should reflect the underlying economic events that it purports to measure.

h.   The financial reports are presented in one consistent monetary unit, such as U.S. dollars.

i.   A business is expected to have continuity in that it is expected to continue to operate indefinitely.

j.   The life of a business can be divided into discrete accounting periods such as a year or quarter.

PROBLEMS

LO2, 5

Procter & Gamble
NYSE :: PG

P1-36.   Applying the Accounting Equation and Calculating Ratios

The following table contains financial statement information for **The Procter & Gamble Company** ($ millions):

Year	Assets	Liabilities	Equity	Net Income
2011...........	$138,354	$70,353	$?	$11,927
2012...........	?	68,209	64,035	10,904
2013...........	139,263	?	68,709	11,402

REQUIRED

a. Compute the missing amounts for assets, liabilities, and equity for each year.

b. Compute return on equity for 2012 and 2013. The median ROE for Fortune 500 companies is about 15%. How does P&G compare with this median?

c. Compute the debt-to-equity ratio for 2012 and 2013. The median debt-to-equity ratio for the Fortune 500 companies is 1.8. How does P&G compare to this median?

P1-37. Formulating Financial Statements from Raw Data

Following is selected financial information from **General Mills, Inc.**, for its fiscal year ended May 25, 2014 ($ millions):

LO2, 3

General Mills
NYSE :: GIS

Cash and cash equivalents	$ 867.3
Net cash from operations..	2,541.0
Sales..	17,909.6
Stockholders' equity	7,005.4
Cost of goods sold..	11,539.8
Net cash from financing	(1,824.1)
Total liabilities...	16,140.3
Other expenses, including income taxes...........................	4,508.5
Noncash assets	22,278.4
Net cash from investing	(561.8)
Net income...	1,861.3
Effect of exchange rate changes on cash	(29.2)
Cash, beginning year	741.4

REQUIRED

a. Prepare an income statement, balance sheet, and statement of cash flows for General Mills, Inc.

b. What portion of the financing is contributed by owners?

P1-38. Formulating Financial Statements from Raw Data

Following is selected financial information from **Abercrombie & Fitch** for its fiscal year ended February 1, 2014 ($ millions):

LO2, 3

Abercrombie & Fitch
NYSE :: ANF

Cash asset	$ 600.1
Cash flows from operations	175.5
Sales...	4,116.9
Stockholders' equity	1,729.5
Cost of goods sold..	1,541.5
Cash flows from financing	(40.8)
Total liabilities...	1,121.5
Other expenses, including income taxes...........................	2,520.8
Noncash assets	2,250.9
Cash flows from investing	(173.9)
Net income...	54.6
Effect of exchange rate changes on cash	(4.2)
Cash, beginning year	643.5

REQUIRED

a. Prepare an income statement, balance sheet, and statement of cash flows for Abercrombie & Fitch.

b. Determine the owner and creditor financing levels.

P1-39. Preparing Comparative Financial Statements from Raw Data

Following is selected financial information for **Tilly's, Inc.**

LO3

Tilly's, Inc.
NYSE :: TLYS

($ thousands)	Feb. 1, 2014	Feb. 2, 2013
Cash and cash equivalents	$ 25,412	$ 17,314
Cash flow from operations	43,794	41,730
Cost of goods sold	343,542	317,096
Total liabilities	91,484	88,085
Total assets	232,407	205,381
Cash flow from financing	1,834	22,819
Sales revenue	495,837	467,291
Cash flow from investing	(37,530)	(72,326)
Other expenses, including income taxes	134,158	126,302

REQUIRED

Prepare balance sheets, income statements and cash flow statements for the years ended February 1, 2014 and February 2, 2013.

LO3 **P1-40. Preparing Comparative Financial Statements from Raw Data**

Tesla Motors, Inc.
NASDAQ :: TSLA

Following is selected financial information for **Tesla Motors, Inc.**

($ thousands)	Dec. 31, 2013	Dec. 31, 2012
Cash and cash equivalents	$ 845,889	$ 201,890
Cash flow from operations	257,994	(266,081)
Cost of goods sold	1,557,234	383,189
Total liabilities	1,749,810	989,490
Total assets	2,416,930	1,114,190
Cash flow from financing	635,422	419,635
Sales revenue	2,013,496	413,256
Cash flow from investing	(249,417)	(206,930)
Other expenses, including income taxes	530,276	426,280

REQUIRED

Prepare balance sheets, income statements and cash flow statements for the years ended December 31, 2013 and 2012.

LO3 **P1-41. Formulating a Statement of Stockholders' Equity from Raw Data**

Crocker Corporation began calendar-year 2016 with stockholders' equity of $100,000, consisting of contributed capital of $70,000 and retained earnings of $30,000. During 2016, it issued additional stock for total cash proceeds of $30,000. It also reported $50,000 of net income, of which $25,000 was paid as a cash dividend to shareholders.

REQUIRED

Prepare the December 31, 2016 statement of stockholders' equity for Crocker Corporation.

LO3 **P1-42. Formulating a Statement of Stockholders' Equity from Raw Data**

DP Systems, Inc., reports the following selected information at December 31, 2016 ($ millions):

Contributed capital, December 31, 2015 and 2016	$ 550
Retained earnings, December 31, 2015	2,437
Cash dividends, 2016	281
Net income, 2016	859

REQUIRED

Use this information to prepare its statement of stockholders' equity for 2016.

LO3, 5 **P1-43. Analyzing and Interpreting Return on Equity**

Nokia Corp. manufactures, markets, and sells phones and other electronics. Stockholders' equity for Nokia are €6,660 million in 2013 and €9,239 million in 2012. In 2013, Nokia reported a loss of €739 million on sales of €12,709 million.

Nokia
NYSE :: NOK

REQUIRED

a. What is Nokia's return on equity for 2013?

b. Nokia's total assets were €25,191 million at the end of 2013. Compute its debt-to-equity ratio.

c. What are total expenses for Nokia in 2013?

P1-44. **Presenting an Income Statement and Computing Key Ratios**

LO3, 5

Best Buy Co., Inc., reported the following amounts in its February 1, 2014, and February 2, 2013, financial statements.

Best Buy
NYSE :: BBY

($ millions)	2014	2013
Sales revenue..	$42,410	$39,827
Cost of sales...	32,720	30,528
Net income (loss)	523	(420)
Total assets	14,013	16,787
Stockholders' equity	3,989	3,715

REQUIRED

a. Prepare an income statement for Best Buy for the year ended February 1, 2014, using the format illustrated in **Exhibit 1.8**.

b. Calculate Best Buy's return on equity for the year ended February 1, 2014.

c. Compute Best Buy's debt-to-equity ratio as of February 1, 2014.

P1-45. **Preparing Income Statements and Computing Key Ratios**

LO3, 5

Facebook, Inc. reported the following amounts in its 2012 and 2013 financial statements.

Facebook, Inc.
NASDAQ :: FB

($ millions)	Dec. 31, 2013	Dec. 31, 2012
Total assets	$17,895	$15,103
Total liabilities.....................................	2,425	3,348
Retained earnings	3,159	1,659
Revenue..	7,872	5,089
Operating expenses................................	5,068	4,551
Other expenses, including income taxes..................	1,304	485

REQUIRED

a. Prepare income statements for Facebook for 2013 and 2012. Use the format illustrated in **Exhibit 1.8**.

b. Compute Facebook's return on equity ratio for 2013 and 2012. Facebook's stockholders' equity at the end of 2011 was $4,899 million.

c. Compute Facebook's debt-to-equity ratio for 2013 and 2012.

d. What amount of dividends did Facebook pay to its shareholders in 2013?

CASES AND PROJECTS

C1-46. **Preparing Comparative Income Statements and Computing Key Ratios**

LO3, 5

Starbucks Corporation reported the following data in its 2013 and 2012 10-K reports.

Starbucks Corporation
NASDAQ :: SBUX

($ millions)	Sep. 29, 2013	Sep. 30, 2012
Total assets	$11,516.7	$ 8,219.2
Total liabilities.....................................	7,034.4	3,104.7
Sales revenue.......................................	14,892.2	13,299.5
Cost of goods sold..................................	6,382.3	5,813.3
Other expenses, including income taxes..................	8,501.1	6,101.5

REQUIRED

a. Prepare income statements for Starbucks for the years ended September 29, 2013 and September 30, 2012. Use the format illustrated in **Exhibit 1.8**.

b. Compute Starbucks' return on equity ratio for 2013 and 2012. Starbucks stockholders' equity at October 2, 2011 was $4,387.3 million.

c. Compute Starbucks' debt to equity ratio for 2013 and 2012.

d. Starbucks' net income and return on equity were considerably lower in 2013 than in 2012. In 2013, Starbucks reported a litigation charge of $2,784.1 million, which is included above in other expenses. What effect did this one-time charge have on the company's return on equity ratio? (*Hint:* Compute the ratio excluding the litigation charge from other expenses and compare to the ratio computed in *b.*)

e. Starbucks disclosed information about the pending litigation in the footnotes to its 2012 financial statements (before the case was settled). Discuss the costs and benefits of disclosing this information in its 2012 annual report.

LO2, 3, 5 **C1-47. Computing and Interpreting Key Ratios and Formulating an Income Statement**

The Gap
NYSE :: GPS
Nordstrom
NYSE :: JWN

Data from the financial statements of **The Gap, Inc.**, and **Nordstrom, Inc.**, are presented below.

($ millions)	The Gap	Nordstrom
Stockholders' equity, 2013	$ 3,062	$ 2,080
Stockholders' equity, 2012	2,894	1,913
Total assets, 2013	7,849	8,574
Total assets, 2012	7,470	8,089
Revenue, 2013	16,148	12,540
Cost of goods sold, 2013	9,855	7,737
Net income, 2013	1,280	734

REQUIRED

a. Compute the return on equity ratio for The Gap and Nordstrom for 2013. Which company earned the higher return for its shareholders?

b. Compute the debt-to-equity ratio for each company as of 2013. Which company relies more on creditor financing?

c. Prepare a 2013 income statement for each company using the format in **Exhibit 1.8**. For each firm, compute gross profit as a percentage of sales revenue.

d. Based on your answers to questions *a*, *b*, and *c*, compare these two retail companies. What might be the cause of any differences in the ratios that you computed?

LO5 **C1-48. Computing and Interpreting Key Ratios**

JetBlue Airways
NASDAQ :: JBLU
Southwest Airlines
NYSE :: LUV

Data from the financial statements of **JetBlue Airways** and **Southwest Airlines** are presented below.

($ millions)	JetBlue Airways	Southwest Airlines
Total liabilities, 2013	$5,216	$12,009
Total liabilities, 2012	5,182	11,604
Total assets, 2013	7,350	19,345
Total assets, 2012	7,070	18,596
Revenue, 2013	5,441	17,699
Net income, 2013	168	754

REQUIRED

a. Compute the return on equity ratio for JetBlue and Southwest for 2013. Which company earned the higher return for its shareholders?

b. Compute the debt-to-equity ratio for each company as of December 31, 2013. Which company relies more on creditor financing?

c. For each firm, compute net income as a percentage of revenue in 2013.

d. Based on your answers to questions *a*, *b*, and *c*, compare these two competitors. What might be the cause of any differences in the ratios that you computed?

LO1, 3, 5 **C1-49. Interpreting Financial Statement Information**

Paula Seale is negotiating the purchase of an extermination firm called Total Pest Control. Seale has been employed by a national pest control service and knows the technical side of the business. However, she knows little about accounting data and financial statements. The sole owner of the firm, Meg Krey, has provided Seale with income statements for the past three years, which show an average net income of $72,000 per year. The latest balance sheet shows total assets of $285,000 and liabilities of $45,000. Seale brings the following matters to your attention and requests advice.

1. Krey is asking $300,000 for the firm. She has told Seale that because the firm has been earning 30% on its investment, the price should be higher than the net assets on the balance sheet (net assets equals total assets minus total liabilities).

2. Seale has noticed no salary for Krey on the income statements, even though she worked half-time in the business. Krey explained that because she had other income, the firm only paid $18,000 in cash dividends to Krey (the sole shareholder). If she purchases the firm, Seale will hire a full-time manager for the firm at an annual salary of $36,000.

3. Krey's tax returns for the past 3 years report a lower net income for the firm than the amounts shown in the financial statements. Seale is skeptical about the accounting principles used in preparing the financial statements.

REQUIRED

a. How did Krey arrive at the 30% return figure in point 1? If Seale accepts Krey's average annual net income figure of $72,000, what would Seale's percentage return be, assuming that the net income remained at the same level and that the firm was purchased for $300,000?

b. Should the dividend to Krey affect the net income reported in the financial statements? What will Seale's percentage return be if she takes into consideration the $36,000 salary she plans to pay a full-time manager?

c. Could there be legitimate reasons for the difference between net income shown in the financial statements and net income reported on the tax returns, as mentioned in point 3? How might Seale obtain additional assurance about the propriety of the financial statements?

C1-50. Management, Auditing, and Ethical Behavior   **LO1, 4**

Jackie Hardy, CPA, has a brother, Ted, in the retail clothing business. Ted ran the business as its sole owner for 10 years. During this 10-year period, Jackie helped Ted with various accounting matters. For example, Jackie designed the accounting system for the company, prepared Ted's personal income tax returns (which included financial data about the clothing business), and recommended various cost control procedures. Ted paid Jackie for all these services. A year ago, Ted markedly expanded the business; Ted is president of the corporation and also chairs the corporation's board of directors. The board of directors has overall responsibility for corporate affairs. When the corporation was formed, Ted asked Jackie to serve on its board of directors. Jackie accepted. In addition, Jackie now prepares the corporation's income tax returns and continues to advise her brother on accounting matters.

Recently, the corporation applied for a large bank loan. The bank wants audited financial statements for the corporation before it will decide on the loan request. Ted asked Jackie to perform the audit. Jackie replied that she cannot do the audit because the code of ethics for CPAs requires that she be independent when providing audit services.

REQUIRED

a. Why is it important that a CPA be independent when providing audit services?

b. Which of Jackie's activities or relationships impair her independence?

SOLUTIONS TO REVIEW PROBLEMS

Mid-Chapter Review

SOLUTION

a.

ADIDAS Balance Sheet (€ millions) December 31, 2013			
Cash.................	€ 1,587	Total liabilities............................	€ 6,118
Noncash assets	10,012	Stockholders' equity	5,481
Total assets	€11,599	Total liabilities and stockholders' equity	€11,599

ADIDAS Income Statement (€ millions) For Year Ended December 31, 2013	
Sales revenue.	€14,492
Cost of goods sold.	7,352
Gross profit.	7,140
Other expenses	6,350
Net income (loss)	€ 790

ADIDAS Statement of Cash Flows (€ millions) For Year Ended December 31, 2013	
Cash flow from operations.	€ 634
Cash flow from investing	(243)
Cash flow from financing	(439)
Effect of exchange rates on cash.	(35)
Net increase (decrease) in cash.	(83)
Cash, beginning of year	1,670
Cash, end of year.	€ 1,587

b. Adidas reported revenues of €14,492 million (which is approximately equivalent to $19,564 million) compared to Nike's $27,799 million. Adidas reported net income of €790 million ($1,067 million) compared to Nike's $2,693 million. Adidas' operations produced cash flow of €634 million ($856 million) while Nike's cash flow from operations was $3,003 million. Hence, based on revenues, Nike is a larger company indicated by its substantially larger sales revenue. Its total assets of $18,594 million are also greater than Adidas' (€11,599 million or $15,659 million). Consistent with its larger size, Nike's operating cash flows and income are also larger than those of Adidas.

Chapter-End Review

SOLUTION

a. $$\text{ROE} = \frac{€790}{[(€5,481 + €5,291)/2]} = 0.147 \text{ or } 14.7\%$$

b. $$\text{Debt-to-equity} = \frac{€6,118}{€5,481} = 1.12$$

c. One additional benefit to using ratios to analyze financial information is that ratios can be computed for amounts denominated in any currency. Thus, we can compare Adidas and Nike without translating Euros into Dollars. Adidas' ROE of 14.7% is lower than Nike's of 24.6%. This means that Nike is more profitable in that it earned a higher return for its stockholders in 2014.

Adidas' debt-to-equity ratio is 1.12 compared to Nike's 0.72. This means that Adidas relies more on debt financing than does Nike. The higher debt-to-equity ratio indicates a higher level of risk associated with an investment in Adidas than with an investment in Nike.

Constructing Financial Statements

WALGREENS
www.walgreens.com

More than a hundred years have passed since Charles R. Walgreen, Sr. purchased his first pharmacy in 1901. In that time, the company that bears his name has grown remarkably. As of August 31, 2014, **Walgreen Co.** operated 8,309 locations in 50 states, the District of Columbia, Puerto Rico, and the U.S. Virgin Islands; it had 251,000 employees; and it filled 19% of the retail prescriptions in the United States.

Even with the company's recent success, Walgreens faces a number of challenges. The economic changes of the recent past have made consumers more cautious and cost-conscious. Pharmacy sales constitute two-thirds of Walgreens' sales, and almost all of those are paid for by a third party. The success of that business depends significantly on factors like the growth of generic pharmaceuticals, legislative changes such as the Affordable Care Act, and the relationships with Pharmacy Benefit Managers. Furthermore, Walgreens faces rising costs for pharmaceuticals and increasing competition from other drugstore chains like **CVS Health Corp.** and discount retailers like **Wal-Mart Stores, Inc.**

These factors, however, have not prevented Walgreens from reporting profits continuously for the last five years. Chief Executive Officer, Gregory D. Wasson, seems to have found a strategy for profitable growth by slowing the rate of new store openings and turning its focus to cost control and operating efficiencies.

Walgreens is poised to increase sales substantially and increase its geographic footprint with its recent decision to acquire **Alliance Boots GmbH**, an international health and beauty group. Subsequent to August 31, 2014, the merged companies have reorganized into Walgreens Boots Alliance, Inc.

As we discovered in Chapter 1, companies like Walgreens prepare financial statements annually. These financial statements allow investors and creditors to assess the impact of changing economic conditions on the company's financial health and performance.

This chapter will introduce and explain financial statements using Walgreens as its prime example. The chapter also introduces some key accounting procedures such as transaction analysis, journal entries, and posting. The general ledger, key accounting assumptions, and basic accounting definitions are also introduced.

Sources: "In the beginning…" Walgreens history on the corporate Web site; Walgreen Co. and Subsidiaries 2014 10-K annual report; *Fortune* magazine Web site.

CHAPTER ORGANIZATION

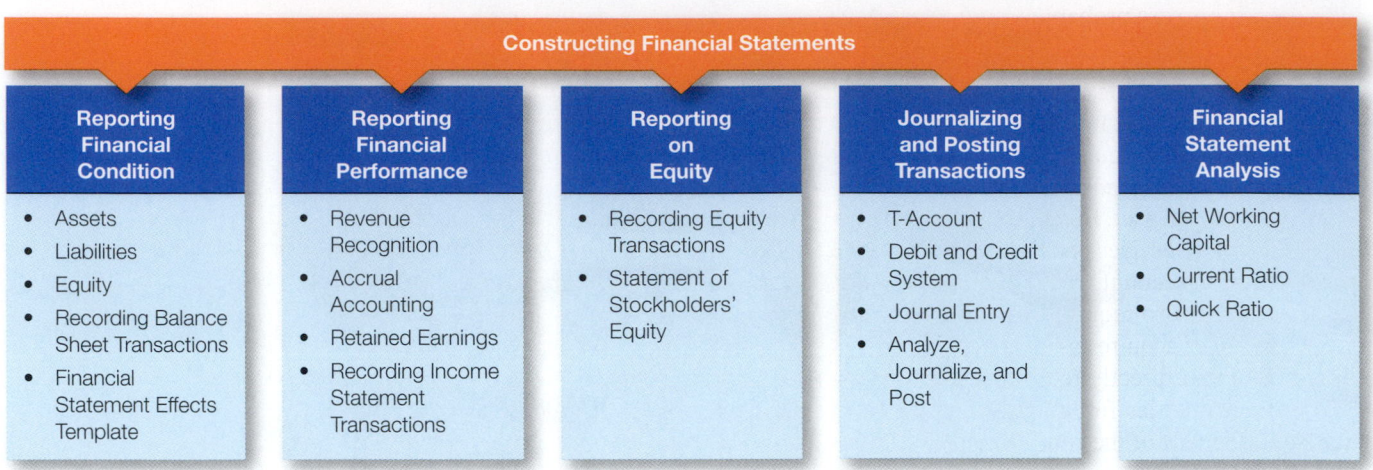

In Chapter 1, we introduced the four financial statements—the balance sheet, the income statement, the cash flow statement, and the statement of stockholders' equity. In this chapter and in Chapter 3, we turn our attention to how the balance sheet and income statement are prepared. The statement of cash flows is discussed in detail in Chapter 4, and the statement of stockholders' equity is discussed in detail in Chapter 11.

LO1 Describe and construct the balance sheet and understand how it can be used for analysis.

REPORTING FINANCIAL CONDITION

The balance sheet reports on a company's financial condition and is divided into three components: assets, liabilities, and stockholders' equity. It provides us with information about the resources available to management and the claims against those resources by creditors and shareholders. At the end of August 2014, Walgreens reports total assets of $37,182 million, total liabilities of $16,621 million, and equity of $20,561 million. Drawing on the **accounting equation**, Walgreens' balance sheet is summarized as follows ($ millions).

The balance sheet is prepared at a *point in time*. It is a snapshot of the financial condition of the company at that instant. For Walgreens, the above balance sheet amounts were reported at the close of business on August 31, 2014. Balance sheet accounts carry over from one period to the next; that is, the ending balance from one period becomes the beginning balance for the next period.

Walgreens' summarized 2014 and 2013 balance sheets are shown in **Exhibit 2.1**. These balance sheets report the assets and the liabilities and shareholders' equity amounts as of August 31, the company's fiscal year-end. Walgreens had $37,182 million in assets at the end of August 31, 2014, with the same amount reported in liabilities and shareholders' equity. Companies report their audited financial results on a yearly basis.[1] Many companies use the calendar year as their fiscal year. Other companies prefer to prepare their yearly report at a time when business activity is at a low level. Walgreens is an example of the latter reporting choice.

Assets

An **asset** is a resource owned or controlled by a company and expected to provide the company with future economic benefits. When a company incurs a cost to acquire future benefits, we say that cost is capitalized and an asset is recorded. An asset must possess two characteristics to be reported on the balance sheet:

---

[1] Companies also report quarterly financial statements, and these are reviewed by the independent accountant, but not audited.

1. It must be owned or controlled by the company.
2. It must possess probable future benefits that can be measured in monetary units.

The first requirement, that the asset must be owned or controlled by the company, implies that the company has legal title to the asset or has the unrestricted right to use the asset. This requirement presumes that the cost to acquire the asset has been incurred, either by paying cash, by trading other assets, or by assuming an obligation to make future payments.

The second requirement indicates that the company expects to receive some future benefit from ownership of the asset. Benefits can be the expected cash receipts from selling the asset or from selling products or services produced by the asset. Benefits can also refer to the receipt of other noncash assets, such as accounts receivable or the reduction of a liability (e.g., when assets are given up to settle debts). It also requires that a monetary value can be assigned to the asset.

Companies acquire assets to yield a return for their shareholders. Assets are expected to produce revenues, either directly (e.g., inventory that is sold) or indirectly (e.g., a manufacturing plant that produces inventories for sale). To create shareholder value, assets must yield resources that are in excess of the cost of the funds utilized to acquire the assets.

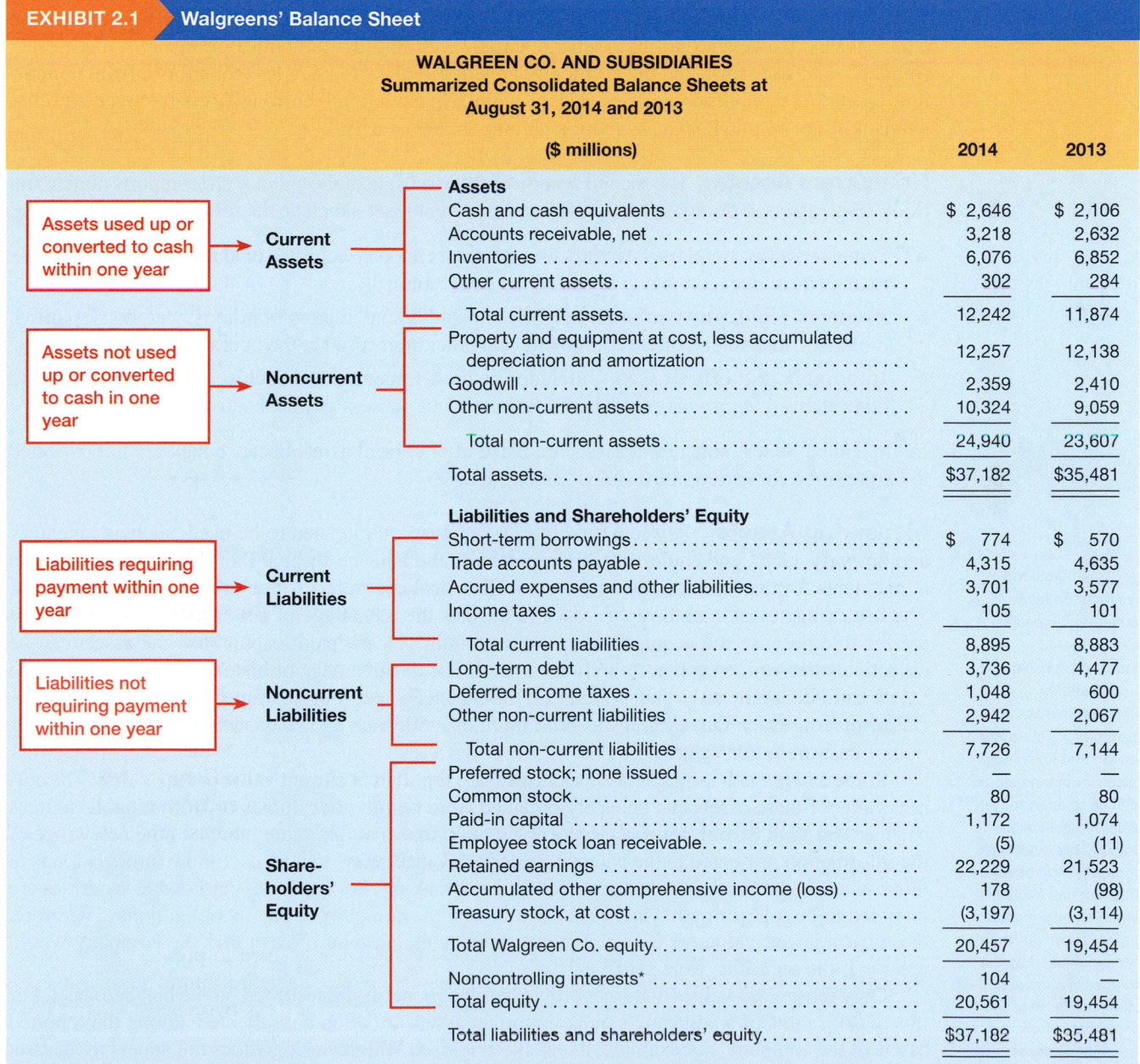

EXHIBIT 2.1 Walgreens' Balance Sheet

WALGREEN CO. AND SUBSIDIARIES
Summarized Consolidated Balance Sheets at
August 31, 2014 and 2013

($ millions)	2014	2013
Assets		
Cash and cash equivalents	$ 2,646	$ 2,106
Accounts receivable, net	3,218	2,632
Inventories	6,076	6,852
Other current assets	302	284
Total current assets	12,242	11,874
Property and equipment at cost, less accumulated depreciation and amortization	12,257	12,138
Goodwill	2,359	2,410
Other non-current assets	10,324	9,059
Total non-current assets	24,940	23,607
Total assets	$37,182	$35,481
Liabilities and Shareholders' Equity		
Short-term borrowings	$ 774	$ 570
Trade accounts payable	4,315	4,635
Accrued expenses and other liabilities	3,701	3,577
Income taxes	105	101
Total current liabilities	8,895	8,883
Long-term debt	3,736	4,477
Deferred income taxes	1,048	600
Other non-current liabilities	2,942	2,067
Total non-current liabilities	7,726	7,144
Preferred stock; none issued	—	—
Common stock	80	80
Paid-in capital	1,172	1,074
Employee stock loan receivable	(5)	(11)
Retained earnings	22,229	21,523
Accumulated other comprehensive income (loss)	178	(98)
Treasury stock, at cost	(3,197)	(3,114)
Total Walgreen Co. equity	20,457	19,454
Noncontrolling interests*	104	—
Total equity	20,561	19,454
Total liabilities and shareholders' equity	$37,182	$35,481

Labels on diagram:
- Assets used up or converted to cash within one year → Current Assets
- Assets not used up or converted to cash in one year → Noncurrent Assets
- Liabilities requiring payment within one year → Current Liabilities
- Liabilities not requiring payment within one year → Noncurrent Liabilities
- Shareholders' Equity

* Noncontrolling interests arise from the practice of consolidating subsidiaries that are controlled, but not wholly owned. Chapters 11 and 12 provide a brief introduction to this topic.

Current Assets   In the United States, the assets section of a balance sheet is presented in order of **liquidity**, which refers to the ease of converting noncash assets into cash. The most liquid assets are called **current assets**. Current assets are assets expected to be converted into cash or used in operations within the next year, or within the next operating cycle. Some typical examples of current assets include the following accounts, which are listed in order of their liquidity:

FYI Cash equivalents are short-term, highly liquid investments that mature in three months or less and can be easily converted to cash.

- **Cash** and **cash equivalents**—currency, bank deposits, certificates of deposit, and other cash equivalents;
- **Marketable securities**—short-term investments that can be quickly sold to raise cash;
- **Accounts receivable**—amounts due to the company from customers arising from the past sale of products or services on credit;
- **Inventory**—goods purchased or produced for sale to customers, and supplies used in operating activities;
- **Prepaid expenses**—costs paid in advance for rent, insurance, or other services.

The amount of current assets is an important component of liquidity (the ability to meet obligations when they come due). Companies require a degree of liquidity to effectively operate on a daily basis. However, current assets are expensive to hold—they must be insured, monitored, financed, and so forth—and they typically generate returns that are less than those from noncurrent assets. As a result, companies seek to maintain just enough current assets to cover liquidity needs, but not so much so as to reduce income unnecessarily.

Noncurrent Assets   The second section of the asset side of the balance sheet reports noncurrent (long-term) assets. **Noncurrent assets** (also non-current assets) include the following asset accounts:

- **Long-term financial investments**—investments in debt securities or shares of other firms that management does not intend to sell in the near future;
- **Property, plant, and equipment (PPE)**—includes land, factory buildings, warehouses, office buildings, machinery, office equipment, and other items used in the operations of the company;
- **Intangible and other assets**—includes patents, trademarks, franchise rights, goodwill, and other items that provide future benefits, but do not possess physical substance.

In the United States, noncurrent assets are listed after current assets because they are not expected to expire or be converted into cash within one year.

Measuring Assets   Physical (tangible) assets that are intended to be used, such as inventory and property, plant, and equipment, are reported on the balance sheet at their **historical cost** (with adjustments for depreciation in some cases). Historical cost refers to the original acquisition cost. The use of historical cost to report asset values has the advantage of **reliability**. Historical costs are reliable because the acquisition cost (the amount of cash paid to purchase the asset) can be objectively determined and accurately measured. The disadvantage of historical costs is that some assets can be significantly undervalued on the balance sheet. For example, the land in Anaheim, California, on which Disneyland was built more than 50 years ago, was purchased for a mere fraction of its current fair value.

FYI Excluded assets often relate to self-developed, knowledge-based assets, like organizational effectiveness and technology. This is one reason that knowledge-based industries are so difficult to analyze. Yet, excluded assets are presumably reflected in company market values. This fact can explain why the firm's market capitalization (its share price multiplied by the number of shares) is often greater than the book value shown on the balance sheet.

Some assets, such as marketable securities, are reported at current value or **fair value**. The current value of these assets can be easily obtained from online price quotes or from reliable sources such as **The Wall Street Journal**. Reporting certain assets at fair value increases the **relevance** of the information presented in the balance sheet. Relevance refers to how useful the information is to those who use the financial statements for decision making. For example, marketable securities are intended to be sold for cash when cash is needed by the company to pay its obligations. Therefore, the most relevant value for marketable securities is the amount of cash that the company would receive if the securities were sold.

Only those asset values that have probable future benefits are recorded on the balance sheet. For this reason, some of a company's most important assets are often not reflected among the reported assets of the company. For example, the well-recognized Walgreens logo does not appear as an asset on the company's balance sheet. The image of Mickey Mouse and that of the Aflac Duck are also absent from **The Walt Disney Company**'s and **Aflac Incorporated**'s balance sheets. Each of these items is referred to as an unrecognized intangible asset. These intangible assets and the Coke bottle silhouette, the Kleenex name, or a well-designed supply chain, are measured and reported on the balance sheet only when they are purchased from a third party (usually in a merger). As a result, *internally created* intangible assets, such as the Mickey Mouse image, are not reported on a balance sheet, even though many of these internally created intangible assets are of enormous value.

Liabilities and Equity

Liabilities and equity represent the sources of capital to the company that are used to finance the acquisition of assets. **Liabilities** represent the firm's obligations for borrowed funds from lenders or bond investors, as well as obligations to pay suppliers, employees, tax authorities, and other parties. These obligations can be interest-bearing or non-interest-bearing. **Equity** represents capital that has been invested by the shareholders, either directly via the purchase of stock (when issued by the company), or indirectly in the form of earnings that are reinvested in the business and not paid out as dividends (retained earnings). We discuss liabilities and equity in this section.

The liabilities and equity sections of Walgreens' balance sheets for 2014 and 2013 are reproduced in the lower section of **Exhibit 2.1**. Walgreens reports $16,621 million of total liabilities and $20,561 million of equity as of its 2014 fiscal year-end. The total of liabilities and equity equals $37,182—the same as the total assets—because the shareholders have the residual claim on the company.

A liability is a probable future economic sacrifice resulting from a current or past event. The economic sacrifice can be a future cash payment to a creditor, or it can be an obligation to deliver goods or services to a customer at a future date. A liability must be reported in the balance sheet when each of the following three conditions is met:

1. The future sacrifice is probable.
2. The amount of the obligation is known or can be reasonably estimated.
3. The transaction or event that caused the obligation has occurred.

When conditions 1 and 2 are satisfied, but the transaction that caused the obligation has not occurred, the obligation is called an **executory contract** and no liability is reported. An example of such an obligation is a purchase order. When a company signs an agreement to purchase materials from a supplier, it commits to making a future cash payment of a known amount. However, the obligation to pay for the materials is not considered a liability until the materials are delivered. Therefore, even though the company is contractually obligated to make the cash payment to the supplier, a liability is not recorded on the balance sheet. However, information about purchase commitments and other executory contracts is useful to investors and creditors, and the obligations, if material, should be disclosed in the footnotes to the financial statements. In its annual report, Walgreens reports open inventory purchase orders of $1,537 million at the end of fiscal year 2014.

Current Liabilities   Liabilities on the balance sheet are listed according to maturity. Obligations that are due within one year or within one operating cycle are called **current liabilities**. Some examples of common current liabilities include:

- **Accounts payable**—amounts owed to suppliers for goods and services purchased on credit. Walgreens uses another common name for this account—trade accounts payable.
- **Accrued liabilities**—obligations for expenses that have been recorded but not yet paid. Examples include accrued compensation payable (wages earned by employees but not yet paid), accrued interest payable (interest on debt that has not been paid), and accrued taxes (taxes due).
- **Short-term borrowings**—short-term debt payable to banks or other creditors.
- **Deferred (unearned) revenues**—an obligation created when the company accepts payment in advance for goods or services it will deliver in the future. Sometimes also called advances from customers or customer deposits.
- **Current maturities of long-term debt**—the current portion of long-term debt that is due to be paid within one year.

Noncurrent Liabilities

Noncurrent liabilities (also non-current liabilities) are obligations to be paid after one year. Examples of noncurrent liabilities include:

FYI Borrowings are often titled **Notes Payable**. When a company borrows money it normally signs a promissory note agreeing to pay the money back (including interest)—hence, the title notes payable.

- **Long-term debt**—amounts borrowed from creditors that are scheduled to be repaid more than one year in the future. Any portion of long-term debt that is due within one year is reclassified as a current liability called *current maturities of long-term debt*.
- **Other long-term liabilities**—various obligations, such as warranty and deferred compensation liabilities and long-term tax liabilities, that will be satisfied at least a year in the future. These items are discussed in later chapters.

Detailed information about a company's noncurrent liabilities, such as payment schedules, interest rates, and restrictive covenants, are provided in the footnotes to the financial statements.

BUSINESS INSIGHT

How Much Debt Is Reasonable? In August 2014, Walgreens reports total assets of $37,182 million, liabilities of $16,621 ($8,895 current + $7,726 non-current) million, and equity of $20,561 million. This means that Walgreens finances 45% of its assets with borrowed funds and 55% with shareholder investment. Liabilities represent claims for fixed amounts, while shareholders' equity represents a flexible claim (because shareholders have a residual claim). Companies must monitor their financing sources and amounts because borrowing too much increases risk, and investors must recognize that companies may have substantial obligations (like Walgreens' inventory purchase commitment) that do not appear on the balance sheet.

Stockholders' Equity

Equity reflects capital provided by the shareholders of the company. It is often referred to as a *residual interest*. That is, stockholders have a claim on any assets that are not needed to meet the company's obligations to creditors. The following are examples of items that are typically included in stockholders' equity:

Contributed Capital

- **Common stock**—the capital received from the primary owners of the company. Total common stock is divided into shares. One share of common stock represents the smallest fractional unit of ownership of a company.[2]
- **Additional paid-in capital**—amounts received from the common shareholders in addition to the par value or stated value of the common stock.
- **Treasury stock**—the amount paid for its own common stock that the company has reacquired, which reduces contributed capital.

Earned Capital

- **Retained earnings**—the accumulated earnings that have not been distributed to stockholders as dividends.
- **Accumulated other comprehensive income or loss**—accumulated changes in equity that are not reported in the income statement; discussed in Chapters 11 and 12.

The equity section of a balance sheet consists of two basic components: contributed capital and earned capital. **Contributed capital** is the net funding that a company has received from issuing and reacquiring its equity shares. That is, the funds received from issuing shares less any funds paid to repurchase such shares. In 2014, Walgreens' equity section reports $20,561 million in equity. Its contributed capital is a negative $1,950 million ($80 million in common stock plus $1,172 million in [additional] paid-in capital minus $5 million in an employee stock loan receivable and minus $3,197 million in treasury stock). The negative balance indicates that Walgreens has returned more

---

[2] Many companies' common shares have a par value, but that value has little economic significance. For instance, Walgreens' shares have a par value of $.078125 per share, while the market price of the stock is about $76 at the time of this writing. In most cases, the sum of common stock (at par) and additional paid-in capital represents the value of stockholders' contributions to the business in exchange for shares.

cash to its shareholders (by buying its own stock) than it has received in cash from its shareholder capital contributions.

Earned capital is the cumulative net income (and losses) retained by the company (not paid out to shareholders as dividends). Earned capital typically includes retained earnings and accumulated other comprehensive income or loss. Walgreens' earned capital is $22,407 million ($22,229 million in retained earnings plus $178 million in accumulated other comprehensive income). Other comprehensive income is discussed in Chapters 11 and 12.

RETAINED EARNINGS There is an important relation for retained earnings that reconciles its beginning and ending balances as follows:

> Beginning retained earnings
> + Net income (or − Net loss)
> − Dividends
> _____
> = Ending retained earnings

This relation is useful to remember, even though there are other items that sometimes impact retained earnings. We revisit this relation after our discussion of the income statement and show how it links the balance sheet and income statement.

> **FYI** **Equity** is a term used to describe owners' claims on the company. For corporations, the terms **shareholders' equity** and **stockholders' equity** are also used to describe owners' claims. We use all three terms interchangeably.

MID-CHAPTER REVIEW 1

Assume Schaefer's Pharmacy, Inc. has the following detailed accounts as part of its accounting system. Enter the letter of the balance sheet category A through E in the space next to the balance sheet items numbered 1 through 20. Enter an **X** in the space if the item is not reported on the balance sheet.

A. Current assets C. Current liabilities E. Equity
B. Noncurrent assets D. Noncurrent liabilities

_____ 1. Accounts receivable	_____ 11. Rent expense
_____ 2. Short-term notes payable	_____ 12. Cash
_____ 3. Land	_____ 13. Buildings
_____ 4. Retained earnings	_____ 14. Accounts payable
_____ 5. Intangible assets	_____ 15. Prepaid rent
_____ 6. Common stock	_____ 16. Borrowings (due in 25 years)
_____ 7. Repairs expense	_____ 17. Marketable securities
_____ 8. Equipment	_____ 18. Inventories
_____ 9. Treasury stock	_____ 19. Additional paid-in capital
_____ 10. Investments (noncurrent)	_____ 20. Unearned revenue

The solution to this review problem can be found on page 93.

Analyzing and Recording Transactions for the Balance Sheet

The balance sheet is the foundation of the accounting system. Every event, or transaction, that is recorded in the accounting system must be recorded so that the following accounting equation is maintained:

$$\text{Assets} = \text{Liabilities} + \text{Equity}$$

We use this fundamental relation throughout the book to help us assess the financial impact of transactions. This is our "step 1" when we encounter a transaction. Our "steps 2 and 3" are to journalize those financial impacts and then post them to individual accounts to emphasize the linkage from entries to accounts (steps 2 and 3 are explained later in this chapter).

> **LO2** Use the financial statement effects template (FSET) to analyze transactions.

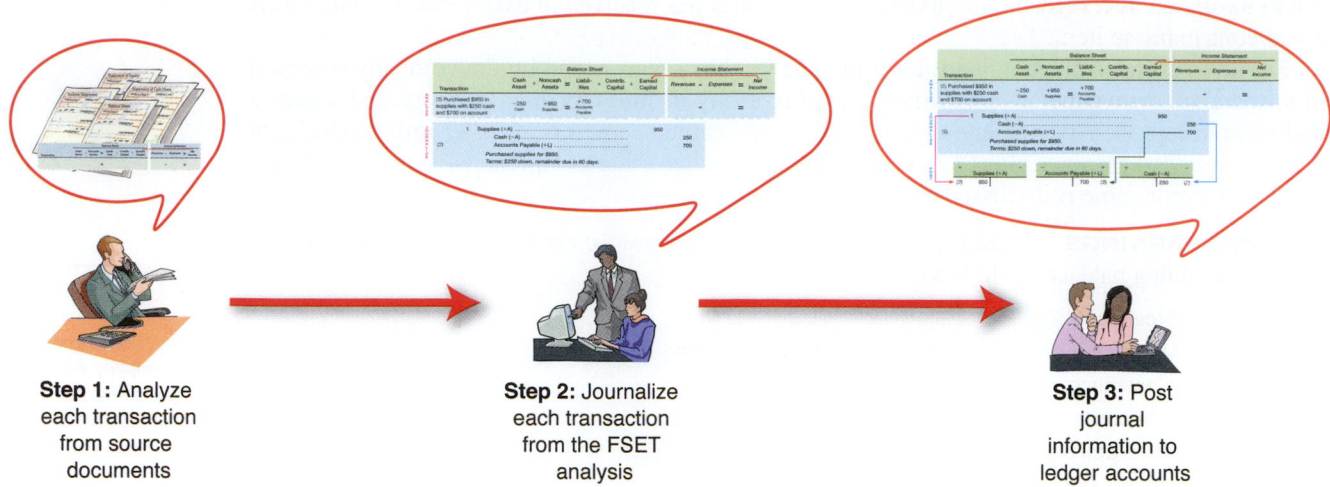

Step 1: Analyze each transaction from source documents

Step 2: Journalize each transaction from the FSET analysis

Step 3: Post journal information to ledger accounts

Financial Statement Effects Template   To analyze the financial impacts of transactions, we employ the following **financial statement effects template (FSET)**.

Transaction	Balance Sheet					Income Statement		
	Cash Asset	+ Noncash Assets	= Liabil- ities	+ Contrib. Capital	+ Earned Capital	Revenues	- Expenses	= Net Income
			=				-	=

The template accomplishes several things. First and foremost, it captures the transaction that must be recorded in the accounting system. That "recording" function is our focus for the next several pages. But accounting is not just recording financial data; it is also the reporting of information that is useful to financial statement readers. So, the template also depicts the effects of the transaction on the four financial statements: balance sheet, income statement, statement of stockholders' equity, and statement of cash flows. For the balance sheet, we differentiate between cash and noncash assets so as to identify the cash effects of transactions. Likewise, equity is separated into the contributed and earned capital components (the latter includes retained earnings as its major element). Finally, income statement effects are separated into revenues, expenses, and net income (the updating of retained earnings is denoted with an arrow line running from net income to earned capital). This template provides a convenient means to demonstrate the relationships among the four financial statements and of representing financial accounting transactions and events in a simple, concise manner for analyzing, journalizing, and posting.

The Account   An **account** is a mechanism for accumulating the effects of an organization's transactions and events. For instance, an account labeled "Merchandise Inventory" allows a retailer's accounting system to accumulate information about the receipts of inventory from suppliers and the delivery of inventory to customers.

Before a transaction is recorded, we first analyze the effect of the transaction on the accounting equation by asking the following questions:

● What accounts are affected by the transaction?

● What is the direction and magnitude of each effect?

To maintain the equality of the accounting equation, each transaction must affect (at least) two accounts. For example, a transaction might increase assets and increase equity by equal amounts. Another transaction might increase one asset and decrease another asset, while yet another might decrease an asset and decrease a liability. These *dual effects* are what constitute the **double-entry accounting system**.

The account is a record of increases and decreases for each important asset, liability, equity, revenue, or expense item. The **chart of accounts** is a listing of the titles (and identification codes) of all accounts for a company.[3] Account titles are commonly grouped into five categories: assets, liabilities, equity, revenues, and expenses. The accounts for Natural Beauty Supply, Inc. (introduced below), follow:

Assets	**Equity**
110 Cash	310 Common Stock
120 Accounts Receivable	320 Retained Earnings
130 Other Receivables	**Revenues and Income**
140 Inventory	410 Sales Revenue
150 Prepaid Insurance	420 Interest Revenue
160 Security Deposit	**Expenses**
170 Fixtures and Equipment	510 Cost of Goods Sold
175 Accumulated Depreciation—Fixtures and Equipment	520 Wages Expense
Liabilities	530 Rent Expense
210 Accounts Payable	540 Advertising Expense
220 Interest Payable	550 Depreciation Expense—Fixtures and Equipment
230 Wages Payable	560 Insurance Expense
240 Taxes Payable	570 Interest Expense
250 Unearned Revenue	580 Tax Expense
260 Notes Payable	

Each transaction entered in the template must maintain the equality of the accounting equation, and the accounts cited must correspond to those in its chart of accounts.

Transaction Analysis Using FSET

To illustrate the effect of transactions on the accounting equation and, correspondingly, the financial statements, we consider the business activities of Natural Beauty Supply, Inc. Natural Beauty Supply was established to operate as a retailer of organic beauty and health care products, though the owners hoped that they also would become a wholesale provider of such products to local salons. The company began business on November 1, 2015. The following transactions occurred on the first day of business:

(1) Nov. 1   Investors contributed $20,000 cash to launch Natural Beauty Supply, Inc. (NBS), in exchange for 10,000 shares of NBS stock.

(2) Nov. 1   NBS borrowed $5,000 cash from a family member of the company's founders by signing a note. The $5,000 must be paid back on November 30 with interest of $50.

(3) Nov. 1   NBS arranged to rent a storefront location and began to use the property. The landlord requires payment of $1,500 at the end of each month. NBS paid a $2,000 security deposit that will be returned at the end of the lease.

(4) Nov. 1   NBS purchased, on account (i.e., to be paid later), and received $17,000 of inventory consisting of natural soaps and beauty products.

Let's begin by analyzing the financial statement effects of the first transaction. At the beginning of its life, Natural Beauty Supply has accounts that show no balances, so the financial statements would be filled with zeroes. In the company's very first transaction, shareholders invested $20,000 cash in Natural Beauty Supply, and the company issued 10,000 shares of common stock, which increased equity (contributed capital). This transaction is reflected in the following financial statements effects template.

---

[3] Accounting systems at large organizations have much more detail in their account structures than we use here. The account structure's detail allows management to accumulate information by responsibility center or by product line or by customer.

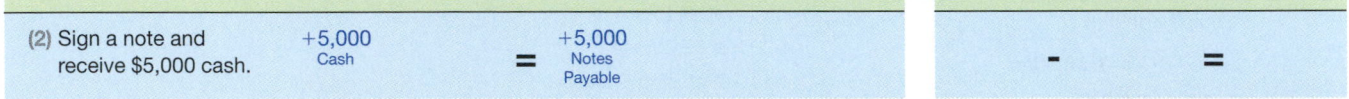

Transaction	Balance Sheet											Income Statement				
	Cash Asset	+	Noncash Assets	=	Liabil-ities	+	Contrib. Capital	+	Earned Capital			Revenues	-	Expenses	=	Net Income
(1) Issue stock for $20,000 cash.	+20,000 Cash			=			+20,000 Common Stock						-		=	

Assets (cash) and equity (common stock) increased by the same amount, and the accounting equation remains in balance (as it always must).

In the second transaction, Natural Beauty Supply borrowed cash by signing a note (loan agreement) with a family member. This transaction increased cash (an asset) and increased notes payable (a liability) by the same amount. The notes payable liability recognizes the obligation to repay the family member.

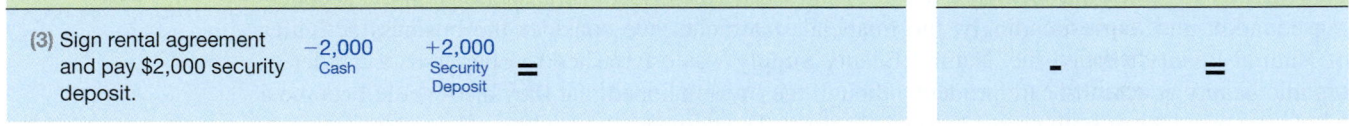

(2) Sign a note and receive $5,000 cash.	+5,000 Cash			=	+5,000 Notes Payable								-		=	

At this point, Natural Beauty Supply would not record anything for the interest that will eventually be paid. Interest expense occurs with the passage of time, and at the moment of borrowing on November 1, there is no interest obligation to be recognized.

Also on November 1, 2015, Natural Beauty Supply arranged for rental of a location and paid a security deposit which it expects to be returned at a future date. This transaction decreased cash (an asset) and increased security deposits (another asset). We'll assume that Natural Beauty Supply hopes to move to a more upscale location within a year, so the security deposit is considered a current asset.

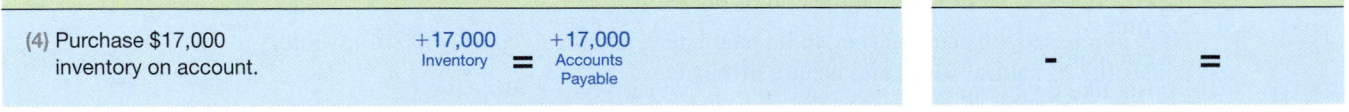

(3) Sign rental agreement and pay $2,000 security deposit.	−2,000 Cash		+2,000 Security Deposit	=									-		=	

Like the case of interest expense, Natural Beauty Supply would make no entry for rent expense on November 1, because the obligation to pay for the use of the location occurs with the passage of time.

Finally, Natural Beauty Supply purchased and received $17,000 of inventory on credit. This transaction increased inventory (an asset) by $17,000 and increased accounts payable (a liability) by $17,000, recognizing the obligation to the supplier. This transaction is recorded as follows:

(4) Purchase $17,000 inventory on account.			+17,000 Inventory	=	+17,000 Accounts Payable								-		=	

To summarize, the description of each transaction appears in the first column of the template. Then the financial statement effects of that transaction are recorded with a + or a − in the appropriate columns of the template. Under each number, the account title within that column of the balance sheet or income statement is entered. So far, Natural Beauty Supply's activities have not affected the revenue or expense accounts of the income statement.

After each transaction, the equality of the accounting equation is maintained. If we so choose, we can prepare a balance sheet at any time, reflecting the transactions up to that point in time. At the end of the day on November 1, 2015, Natural Beauty Supply's balance sheet appears as follows:

NATURAL BEAUTY SUPPLY, INC.
Balance Sheet
November 1, 2015

Assets		Liabilities and Equity	
Cash.................................	$23,000	Notes payable	$ 5,000
Inventory............................	17,000	Accounts payable.....................	17,000
Security deposit	2,000	Total current liabilities..................	22,000
Total current assets	42,000	**Equity**	
		Common stock.......................	20,000
Total assets..........................	$42,000	Total liabilities and equity..............	$42,000

MID-CHAPTER REVIEW 2

Assume that Schaefer's Pharmacy, Inc. enters into the following transactions. Record each of the following transactions in the financial statement effects template.

a. Issued common stock for $20,000 cash.
b. Purchased inventory costing $8,000 on credit.
c. Purchased equipment costing $10,000 for cash.
d. Paid suppliers $3,000 cash for part of the inventory purchased in *b.*

The solution to this review problem can be found on page 94.

REPORTING FINANCIAL PERFORMANCE

LO3 Describe and construct the income statement and discuss how it can be used to evaluate management performance.

3

While balance sheets provide useful information about the structure of a company's resources and the claims on those resources at a point in time, they provide little sense of recent movement or trajectory. The retained earnings balance represents the amount earned (but not paid out in dividends) over the entire life of the company. Looking at the difference between points in time doesn't give a clear picture about what happened between those points in time. For that perspective, we need the income statement to see whether our business activities generated more resources than they used. For instance, Walgreens' retained earnings increased by $706 million over fiscal year 2014, but that amount does not convey the volume of activity that occurred to accomplish it.

Walgreens' fiscal year summarized 2014 Statement of Earnings is shown in **Exhibit 2.2**. Walgreens reported net earnings of $2,031 million on revenues of $76,392 million, or about $0.027 of each revenue dollar ($2,031 million/$76,392 million). The remaining $0.973 of that revenue dollar relates to costs incurred to generate the revenues, such as the costs of products sold and equipment used, wages, advertising and promotion, interest and taxes. Interpretation of this $0.027 amount requires further analysis, as shown in Chapter 5, but we can compare it to previous amounts of $0.034 in fiscal year 2013, and $0.030 in fiscal year 2012.

To analyze an income statement, we need to understand some terminology. **Revenues** result in increases in **net assets** (assets minus liabilities) that are caused by the company's transferring goods or services to customers. **Expenses** result from decreases in net assets (assets minus liabilities) that are caused by the company's revenue-generating activities, including costs of products and services sold, operating costs like depreciation, wages and advertising, nonoperating costs like interest on debt and, finally, taxes on income. The difference between revenues and expenses is **net income** when revenues exceed expenses, or **net loss** when expenses exceed revenues. The connection to the balance sheet can be seen in that reporting net income means that revenues exceeded expenses, which in turn means that the company's business activities increased its net assets.

Operating expenses are the usual and customary costs that a company incurs to support its main business activities. These include cost of goods sold expense, selling expenses, depreciation expense, amortization expense, and research and development expense. Not all of these expenses are recognized in the period in which cash is disbursed. For example, depreciation expense is recognized in the time period during which the asset is used, not in the period when it was first acquired in exchange for cash. In contrast, other expenses, such as compensation expense, are recognized in

FYI The income statement is also called the statement of earnings or the statement of operations or the profit and loss statement. Walgreens uses all three terms (profit, income and earnings) in **Exhibit 2.2**.

FYI The terms revenues and sales are often used interchangeably.

EXHIBIT 2.2	Walgreens' Income Statement

WALGREEN CO. AND SUBSIDIARIES
Summarized Consolidated Statement of Earnings
Year ended August 31, 2014
($ millions)

Net sales.	$76,392
Cost of sales.	54,823
Gross profit.	21,569
Selling, general and administrative expenses	17,992
Equity earnings in Alliance Boots.	617
Operating income.	4,194
Interest (expense) income, net.	(156)
Other (expense) income.	(481)
Earnings before income tax provision	3,557
Income tax provision	1,526
Net earnings.	2,031
Net earnings attributable to non-controlling interests*	(99)
Net earnings attributable to Walgreen Co	$ 1,932

*Noncontrolling interests arise from the practice of consolidating subsidiaries that are controlled, but not wholly owned. Chapters 11 and 12 provide a brief introduction to this topic.

the period when the services are performed, which is often before cash is actually paid to employees. Walgreens' operating expenses in 2014 were $72,815 million ($54,823 million + $17,992 million).[4]

Nonoperating revenues and expenses relate to the company's financing and investing activities, and include interest revenue and interest expense. Business decision makers and analysts usually segregate operating and nonoperating activities as they offer different insights into company performance and condition. Walgreens' income statement reports net nonoperating expenses in 2014 of $637 million ($156 million + $481 million), followed by tax expense of $1,526 million.

It is helpful to distinguish income from continuing operations from nonrecurring items. Many readers of financial statements are interested in forecasting future company performance and focus their analysis on sources of operating income that are expected to *persist* into the future. Nonrecurring revenues and expenses are unlikely to arise in the future and are largely irrelevant to predictions of future performance. Consequently, many decision makers identify transactions and events that are unlikely to recur and separate them from operating income in the income statement. These nonrecurring items are described in greater detail in Chapter 6.

Accrual Accounting for Revenues and Expenses

LO4 Explain revenue recognition, accrual accounting, and their effects on retained earnings.

The income statement's ability to measure a company's periodic performance depends on the proper timing of revenues and expenses. Revenue should be recorded when the company has transferred goods or services to customers, in an amount that reflects how much the company expects to be entitled from the transfer—even if there is not an immediate increase in cash. This is called **revenue recognition**, a topic that receives more detailed attention in Chapter 6. Expenses are recognized when assets are diminished (or liabilities increased) as a result of earning revenue or supporting operations, even if there is no immediate decrease in cash. This is called **expense recognition**. **Accrual accounting** refers to this practice of recognizing revenues when earned through the company's operations and recognizing expenses as the assets used and obligations incurred in carrying out those operations.

An important consequence of accrual accounting for revenues and expenses is that the balance sheet depicts the resources of the company (in addition to cash) and the obligations which the company must fulfill in the future. Accrual accounting is required under U.S. GAAP and IFRS because it is considered to be the most useful information for making business decisions and evaluating business performance. (That is not to say that information on cash flows is not important—but it is conveyed by the statement of cash flows discussed in Chapter 4.)

---

[4] Walgreens also reports $617 million in Equity earnings in Alliance Boots, a company in which Walgreens invested. The operations of Alliance Boots are similar enough to Walgreens' operations that they include this as a component of operating income.

Walgreens' net sales in 2014 were $76,392 million. **Cost of goods sold** (cost of sales) is an expense item in the income statements of manufacturing and merchandising companies. It represents the cost of products that are delivered to customers during the period. The difference between revenues (at selling prices) and cost of goods sold (at purchase price or manufacturing cost) is called **gross profit**. Gross profit for merchandisers and manufacturers is an important number as it represents the remaining income available to cover all of the company's overhead and other expenses (selling, general and administrative expenses, research and development, interest, and so on). Walgreens' gross profit in 2014 is calculated as total net revenues less cost of sales, which equals $21,569 million ($76,392 million − $54,823 million).

The principles of revenue and expense recognition are crucial to income statement reporting. To illustrate, assume a company purchases inventories for $100,000 cash, which it sells later in that same period for $150,000 cash. The company would record $150,000 in revenue when the inventory is delivered to the customer, because at that point, the company has fulfilled its responsibilities in the exchange with the customer. Also assume that the company pays $20,000 cash for sales employee wages during the period. The income statement is designed to tell how effective the company was at generating more resources than it used, and it would appear as follows (ignoring income taxes for the moment):

Revenues	$150,000
Cost of goods sold.	100,000
Gross profit.	50,000
Wages expense	20,000
Net income (earnings) . .	$ 30,000

In this illustration, there is a correspondence between each of the revenues/expenses and a cash inflow/outflow within the accounting period. Net income was $30,000 and the increase in cash was $30,000.

However, that need not be the case under accrual accounting. Suppose that the company sells its product on **credit** (also referred to as *on account*) rather than for cash. Does the seller still report sales revenue? The answer is yes. Under GAAP, revenues are reported when a company has earned those sales at delivery. Earned means that the company has done everything required under the sales agreement—no material contingencies remain. The seller reports an accounts receivable asset on its balance sheet, and revenue can be recognized before cash collection.

Credit sales mean that companies can report substantial sales revenue and assets without receiving cash. When such receivables are ultimately collected, no further revenue is recorded because it was recorded earlier when the revenue recognition criteria were met. The collection of a receivable merely involves the decrease of one asset (accounts receivable) and the increase of another asset (cash), with no resulting increase in net assets.

Next, consider a different situation. Assume that the company sells gift cards to customers for $9,500. Should the $9,500 received in cash be recognized as revenue? No. Even though the gift cards were sold and cash was collected, there has been no transfer of goods or services to the customer. The revenue from gift cards is recognized when the product or service is provided. For example, revenue can be recognized when a customer purchases an item of merchandise using the gift card for payment. Hence, the $9,500 is then recorded as an increase in cash and an increase in *unearned revenue*, a liability, with no resulting increase in net assets.

The proper timing of revenue recognition suggests that the expenses incurred in earning that revenue be recognized in the same fiscal period. Thus, if merchandise inventory is purchased in one period and sold in another, the cost of the merchandise should be retained as an asset until the items are sold. It would not be proper to recognize expense when the inventory was purchased or the cash was paid. Accurate income determination requires the proper timing of revenue and expense recognition, and the exchange of cash is *not* the essential ingredient.

We have already seen that when a company incurs a cost to acquire a resource that produces benefits in the future (for example, merchandise inventory for future sale), it recognizes an asset. That asset represents costs that are waiting to be recognized as expenses in the future, when these assets are used to produce revenue or to support operations. When inventory is delivered to a customer, we recognize that the asset no longer belongs to the selling company. The inventory asset is decreased, and cost of goods sold is recognized as an expense.

FYI Purchase of inventories on credit or on account means that the buyer does not pay the seller at the time of purchase. The buyer reports a liability (accounts payable) on its balance sheet that is later removed when payment is made. The seller reports an asset (accounts receivable) on its balance sheet until it is removed when the buyer pays.

FYI Sales on credit will not always be collected. The potential for uncollectable accounts introduces additional risk to the firm.

FYI **Cash accounting** recognizes revenues only when received in cash and expenses only when paid in cash. This approach is not acceptable under GAAP.

The same principle applies when employees earn wages for work in one period, but are paid in the next period. Wages expense must be recognized when the liability (obligation) is *incurred*, regardless of when they are paid. If the company in the illustration doesn't pay its employees until the following reporting period, it recognizes a wages payable liability of $20,000 and, because this decreases net assets, it would recognize a wage expense of the same amount.

When wages are paid in the next reporting period, both cash and the wages payable liability are decreased. No expense is reported when the wages are paid, because the expense is recognized when the employees worked to generate sales in the prior period.

Accrual accounting principles are crucial for reporting the income statement revenues and expenses in the proper period, and these revenues and expenses provide a more complete view of the inflows and outflows of resources (including cash) for the firm. Was an outflow of cash supposed to produce benefits in the current period or in a future period? Was an inflow of cash the result of past operations or current operations? The accrual accounting model uses the balance sheet and income statement to answer such questions and to enable users of financial statements to make more timely assessments of the firm's economic performance.

However, accrual accounting's timeliness requires management to estimate future events in determining the amount of expenses incurred and revenue earned. The precise amount of cash to be received or disbursed may not be known until a later date. In the case of wages, the amount of the accrual is known with certainty. In other cases (e.g., incentive bonuses), it may not and thus require an estimate.

Retained Earnings

Net income for the period is added to the company's retained earnings, which, in turn, is part of stockholders' equity. The linkage between the income statement and the beginning- and end-of-period balance sheets, which we called articulation in Chapter 1, is achieved by tying net income to retained earnings because net income is, by definition, the *change* in retained earnings resulting from business activities during an accounting period. This link is highlighted by the red arrow at the top of the financial statement effects template (FSET).[5] There are typically other adjustments to retained earnings. The most common adjustment is for dividend payments to stockholders. **Exhibit 2.3** provides the annual adjustments to retained earnings for Walgreens.

EXHIBIT 2.3	Walgreens' Retained Earnings Reconciliation
WALGREEN CO. AND SUBSIDIARIES Year Ended August 31, 2014 ($ millions)	
Retained earnings, August 31, 2013	$21,523
Add: Net earnings attributable to Walgreen Co.	1,932
	23,455
Less: Cash dividends declared	1,226
Retained earnings, August 31, 2014	$22,229

Analyzing and Recording Transactions for the Income Statement

Earlier, we introduced the financial statement effects template as a tool to illustrate the effects of transactions on the balance sheet. In this section, we show how this template is used to analyze transactions that may affect the current period's income statement. To do so, we extend our illustration of Natural Beauty Supply (NBS) to reflect the following events in 2015:

(5) Nov. 2   NBS paid $670 to advertise in the local newspaper for November.

(6) Nov. 18   NBS paid $13,300 cash to its suppliers in partial payment for the earlier delivery of inventory.

---

[5] In the FSET, we show that each transaction that affects the income statement also impacts retained earnings. This approach is useful for *analyzing* the effect of the transaction on both the income statement and balance sheet. However, the impact of net income on retained earnings is *recorded* only once each accounting period, after all of the revenues and expenses have been recorded. This recording procedure is explained later in this chapter and in Chapter 3.

(7) Nov. —   During the month of November, NBS sold and delivered products to retail customers. The customers paid $7,000 cash for products that had cost NBS $4,000.

(8) Nov. —   During the month of November, sales and deliveries to wholesale customers totaled $2,400 for merchandise that had cost $1,700. Instead of paying cash, wholesale customers are required to pay for the merchandise within ten working days.

(9) Nov. —   NBS employed a salesperson who earned $1,400 for the month of November and was paid that amount in cash.

(10) Nov. 24   NBS received an order from a wholesale customer to deliver products in December. The agreed price of the products to be delivered is $700 and the cost is $450.

(11) Nov. 25   NBS introduced holiday gift certificates, which entitle the recipient to a one-hour consultation on the use of NBS's products. $300 of gift certificates were sold for cash, but none were redeemed before the end of November.

(12) Nov. 30   NBS received $1,450 in partial payment from customers billed in (8).

(13) Nov. 30   NBS repaid the loan and interest in (2).

(14) Nov. 30   NBS paid $1,680 for a twelve-month fire insurance policy. Coverage begins on December 1.

(15) Nov. 30   NBS paid $1,500 to the landlord for November rent.

In the fifth transaction, Natural Beauty Supply gave cash in return for advertising for the month of November. This payment does not create a benefit for future periods, so it does not create an asset. Nor does the payment discharge an existing obligation. Therefore, it decreases NBS's net assets (assets minus liabilities). The purpose of this decrease in net assets is to generate revenues for the company, so it is reported as an expense in the income statement.

We begin by entering the decrease in cash and an increase in expenses. (The minus sign in front of expenses insures that the accounting equation still holds.) Recording the expense allows the income statement to keep track of the flows of assets and liabilities that result from the company's operations.

Transaction	Balance Sheet							Income Statement		
	Cash Asset	+	Noncash Assets	=	Liabilities	+	Contrib. Capital	+	Earned Capital	
								Revenues − Expenses = Net Income		
(5) Pay $670 cash for November advertising.	−670 Cash			=					− +670 Advertising Expense =	

However, the FSET goes further than recording the accounting entry. It also depicts the effects of the expense on net income and of net income on retained earnings. So, the complete FSET description of transaction (5) is as follows. The FSET uses color to differentiate between the accounting entry (in blue) and the resulting effect on income and retained earnings (in black).

(5) Pay $670 cash for November advertising.	−670 Cash	=			−670 Retained Earnings		− +670 Advertising Expense =	−670

In the sixth transaction, Natural Beauty Supply made a partial payment of $13,300 in cash to the suppliers who delivered inventory on November 1. This transaction decreases cash by $13,300 and decreases the accounts payable liability by $13,300. The income statement is not affected by this payment. The cost of merchandise is reflected in the income statement when the merchandise is sold, not when it is paid for (as we will see shortly).

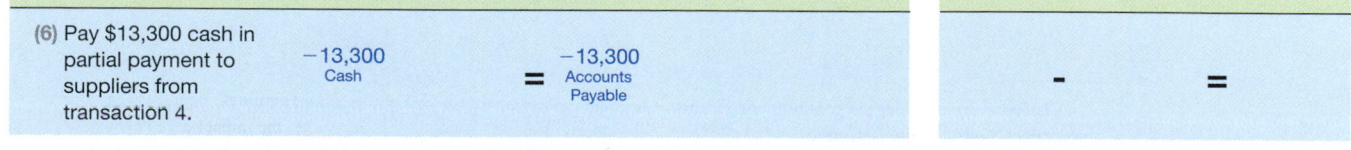

(6) Pay $13,300 cash in partial payment to suppliers from transaction 4.	−13,300 Cash	=	−13,300 Accounts Payable		− =

In transaction seven, Natural Beauty Supply sold and delivered products to customers who paid $7,000 in cash. NBS's transfer of products to customers results in the recognition of revenue in the income statement and an increase in net assets (cash) on the balance sheet. As in transaction 5, the FSET also depicts the impact of these sales on net income and on the retained earnings balance.

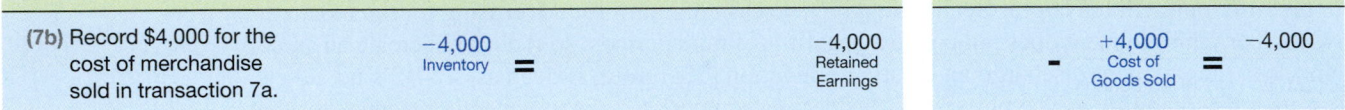

Transaction	Balance Sheet					Income Statement		
	Cash Asset +	Noncash Assets =	Liabil-ities +	Contrib. Capital +	Earned Capital	Revenues -	Expenses =	Net Income
(7a) Sell $7,000 of products for cash.	+7,000 Cash	=			+7,000 Retained Earnings	+7,000 Sales Revenue	-	+7,000 =

At the same time, NBS must recognize that these sales transactions involved an exchange, and cash was received while inventory costing $4,000 was delivered. Transaction (7b) recognizes that NBS no longer has this inventory and that this decrease in net assets produces an expense called cost of goods sold. In this way, the income statement portrays the increases in net assets (revenues) and the decreases in net assets (expenses like cost of goods sold and advertising) from the company's operating activities. (Again, the minus sign in front of all expenses insures that the accounting equation remains balanced.)

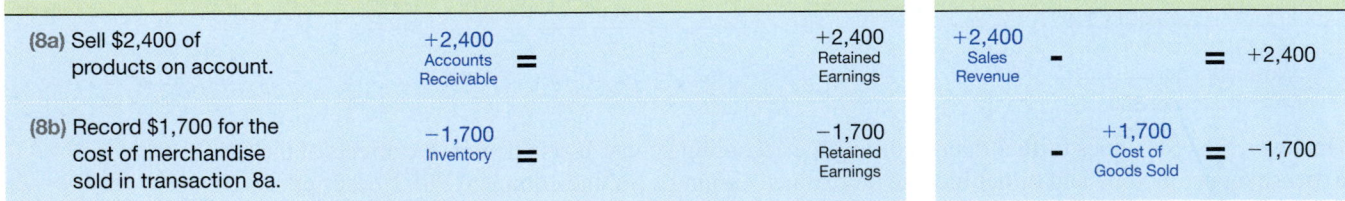

(7b) Record $4,000 for the cost of merchandise sold in transaction 7a.	−4,000 Inventory =				−4,000 Retained Earnings		+4,000 Cost of Goods Sold =	−4,000

The eighth transaction is very similar to the previous one, except that Natural Beauty Supply's customers will pay for the products ten days after they were delivered. Should NBS recognize revenue on these sales? The products have been delivered, so the revenue has been earned.[6] Therefore, NBS should recognize that it has a new asset—accounts receivable—equal to $2,400, and that it has earned revenue in the same amount. As above, NBS would also record cost of goods sold to recognize the cost of inventory delivered to the customers.

(8a) Sell $2,400 of products on account.	+2,400 Accounts Receivable =				+2,400 Retained Earnings	+2,400 Sales Revenue	-	= +2,400
(8b) Record $1,700 for the cost of merchandise sold in transaction 8a.	−1,700 Inventory =				−1,700 Retained Earnings		+1,700 Cost of Goods Sold =	−1,700

The ninth entry records wage expense. In this case, wages were paid in cash. Cash is decreased by $1,400, and this decrease in net assets results in a recognition of wages expense in the income statement (with resulting decreases in net income and retained earnings).

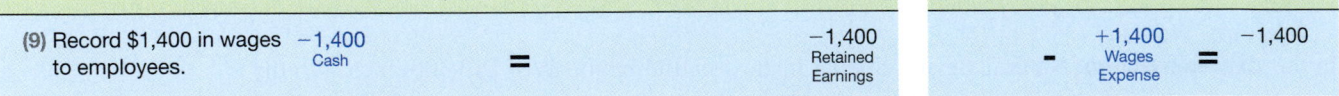

(9) Record $1,400 in wages to employees.	−1,400 Cash	=			−1,400 Retained Earnings		+1,400 Wages Expense =	−1,400

Transaction ten involves a customer order for products to be delivered in December. This transaction is an example of an *executory contract*, which does not require a journal entry (just like Walgreens' open purchase orders for inventory described earlier). NBS has not earned revenue, because it has not yet delivered the products.

---

[6] In Chapter 6, we consider the possibility that a customer might not pay the receivable. For the time being, we assume that the receivables' collectability is assured.

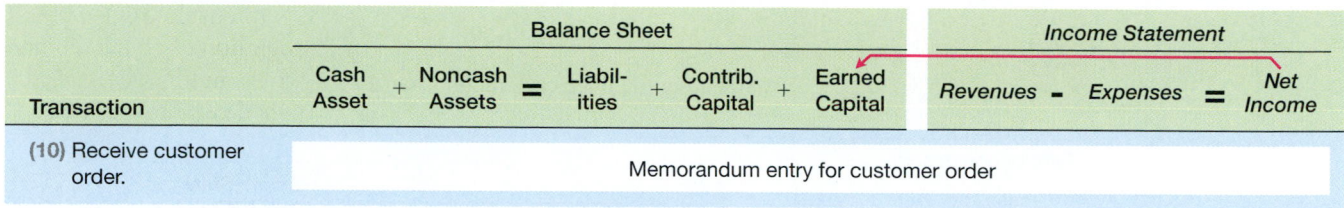

Transaction	Balance Sheet							Income Statement		
	Cash Asset	+	Noncash Assets	=	Liabil- ities	+	Contrib. Capital	+	Earned Capital	
									Revenues − Expenses = Net Income	
(10) Receive customer order.	Memorandum entry for customer order									

In transaction eleven, Natural Beauty Supply sold gift certificates for $300 cash, but none were redeemed. In this case, NBS has received cash, but revenue cannot be recognized because no goods or services have been transferred to the customers. Rather, NBS has accepted an obligation to provide services in the future when the gift certificates are redeemed. This obligation is recognized as a liability titled unearned revenue.

| (11) Sell gift certificates for $300 cash. | +300 Cash | | | = | +300 Unearned Revenue | | | | − = | |

In transaction twelve, NBS received $1,450 cash as partial payment from customers billed in transaction eight. Cash increases by $1,450 and accounts receivable decreases by $1,450. Recall that revenues are recorded when earned (transaction 8), not when cash is received.

| (12) Receive $1,450 cash as partial payment from customers billed in transaction 8. | +1,450 Cash | | −1,450 Accounts Receivable | = | | | | | − = | |

In transaction thirteen on November 30, Natural Beauty Supply paid back the family member who had loaned money to the business. The cash payment was the agreed-upon $5,050 ($5,000 principal and $50 interest). The repayment of the principal does not change the net assets of NBS; cash goes down by $5,000 and the note payable liability goes down an equal amount. However, the payment of $50 interest does cause the net assets to decrease, and this net asset decrease creates an interest expense in the income statement.

| (13) Pay interest of $50 and repay principal of $5,000. | −5,050 Cash | | | = | −5,000 Notes Payable | | | | −50 Retained Earnings | − +50 Interest Expense = −50 |

In the fourteenth transaction, NBS paid an annual insurance premium of $1,680 for coverage beginning December 1. NBS will receive the benefits of the insurance coverage in the future, so insurance expense will be recognized in those future periods. At this time, a noncash asset titled prepaid insurance is increased by $1,680, and cash is decreased by the same amount.

| (14) Pay $1,680 for one-year insurance policy. | −1,680 Cash | | +1,680 Prepaid Insurance | = | | | | | − = | |

In the last transaction of the month of November, Natural Beauty Supply paid $1,500 cash to the landlord for November's rent. This $1,500 reduction of net assets is balanced by rent expense in the income statement.

| (15) Pay $1,500 rent for November. | −1,500 Cash | | | = | | | | | −1,500 Retained Earnings | − +1,500 Rent Expense = −1,500 |

We can summarize the revenue and expense entries of these transactions to prepare an income statement for Natural Beauty Supply for the month ended November 30, 2015.

NATURAL BEAUTY SUPPLY, INC.
Income Statement
For Month Ended November 30, 2015

Sales revenue.	$ 9,400
Cost of goods sold.	5,700
Gross profit.	3,700
Wages expense	1,400
Rent expense	1,500
Advertising expense.	670
Operating income	130
Interest expense.	50
Net income.	$ 80

LO5 Illustrate equity transactions and the statement of stockholders' equity.

5

REPORTING ON EQUITY

Analyzing and Recording Equity Transactions

Earlier we recorded the effect of issuing common stock on the balance sheet of Natural Beauty Supply. To complete our illustration, we illustrate one final equity transaction—a dividend payment.

(16) Nov. 30   Natural Beauty Supply paid a $50 cash dividend to its shareholders.

To record the dividend payment, we decrease cash and decrease retained earnings.

	Balance Sheet						Income Statement		
Transaction	Cash Asset	+ Noncash Assets	= Liabil- ities	+ Contrib. Capital	+ Earned Capital		Revenues -	Expenses =	Net Income
(16) Pay $50 cash dividend to shareholders.	−50 Cash		=		−50 Retained Earnings		-		=

No revenue or income is recorded from a stock issuance. Similarly, no expense is recorded from a dividend. This is always the case. Companies cannot report revenues and expenses from capital transactions (transactions with stockholders relating to their investment in the company).

The FSET entries can be accumulated by account to determine the ending balances for assets, liabilities and equity. Natural Beauty Supply's balance sheet for November 30, 2015, appears in **Exhibit 2.4**. The balance in retained earnings is $30 (net income of $80 less the cash dividend of $50).

EXHIBIT 2.4	Natural Beauty Supply's Balance Sheet

NATURAL BEAUTY SUPPLY, INC.
Balance Sheet
November 30, 2015

Assets		Liabilities	
Cash.	$ 8,100	Accounts payable.	$ 3,700
Accounts receivable.	950	Unearned revenue	300
Inventory.	11,300	Total current liabilities.	4,000
Prepaid insurance.	1,680	Equity	
Security deposit	2,000	Common stock.	20,000
Total current assets	24,030	Retained earnings	30
		Total equity	20,030
Total assets.	$24,030	Total liabilities and equity	$24,030

Statement of Stockholders' Equity

The statement of stockholders' equity is a reconciliation of the beginning and ending balances of selected stockholders' equity accounts. The statement of stockholders' equity for Natural Beauty Supply for the month of November is in **Exhibit 2.5**.

EXHIBIT 2.5	Natural Beauty Supply's Statement of Stockholders' Equity

NATURAL BEAUTY SUPPLY, INC.
Statement of Stockholders' Equity
For Month Ended November 30, 2015

	Contributed Capital	Earned Capital	Total Equity
Balance, November 1, 2015.................	$ 0	$ 0	$ 0
Common stock issued	20,000	—	20,000
Net income.............................	—	80	80
Cash dividends.........................	—	(50)	(50)
Balance, November 30, 2015..............	$20,000	$30	$20,030

This statement highlights three main changes to Natural Beauty Supply's equity during November.

1. Natural Beauty raised $20,000 in equity capital during the month.
2. Natural Beauty Supply earned net income of $80. That is, its business activities increased the company's net assets by $80 during the month.
3. Natural Beauty Supply declared a $50 cash dividend.

At this point, we can make the important observation that the various financial statements are not the result of independent processes. That is, the process of constructing the income statement is intimately tied to the process of constructing the balance sheet. When we think about the fact that revenues reflect how much the company expects to receive from its delivery of goods to customers, while expenses measure the outflow of assets and increases in liabilities resulting from earning revenues and supporting operations, it should be apparent that an error on the income statement will, in all likelihood, lead to an error in the balance sheet. Understanding the connections among the various statements is a key step in becoming an effective reader of financial information.

YOU MAKE THE CALL

You are an Analyst   Walgreens reported a balance in retained earnings of $22,229 million at August 31, 2014. This amount compares to $21,523 million one year earlier at the end of 2013. In 2014, Walgreens reported net income of $1,932 million. Why did the company's retained earnings go up by less than reported net income? [Answer on page 74.]

MID-CHAPTER REVIEW 3

Part 1. Assume that Schaefer's Pharmacy, Inc.'s records show the following amounts at December 31, 2015. Use this information, as necessary, to prepare its 2015 income statement (ignore income taxes).

Cash........................	$ 3,000	Cash dividends.................	$ 1,000
Accounts receivable..............	12,000	Revenues	45,000
Office equipment	32,250	Cost of goods sold..............	20,000
Inventory......................	26,000	Rent expense..................	5,000
Land........................	10,000	Wages expense	8,000
Accounts payable................	7,500	Utilities expense................	2,000
Common stock.................	45,750	Other expenses	4,000

Part 2. Assume that Schaefer's Pharmacy, Inc. reports the following selected financial information for the year ended December 31, 2015.

Retained earnings, Dec. 31, 2015 . . .	$30,000	Dividends	$ 1,000
Net income	$ 6,000	Retained earnings, Dec. 31, 2014 . . .	$25,000

Prepare the 2015 calendar-year retained earnings reconciliation for this company.

Part 3. Use the listing of accounts and figures reported in part 1 along with the ending retained earnings from part 2 to prepare the December 31, 2015, balance sheet for Schaefer's Pharmacy, Inc.

The solution to this review problem can be found on pages 94–95.

LO6 Use journal entries and T-accounts to analyze and record transactions.

6

JOURNALIZING AND POSTING TRANSACTIONS

The financial statement effects template is a useful tool for illustrating the effects of a transaction on the balance sheet, income statement, statement of stockholders' equity, and statement of cash flows. However, when representing individual transactions or analyzing individual accounts, the accounting system records information in journal entries (step 2) that are collected in individual accounts. This section introduces the basics of that system. It also introduces the T-account as a useful tool for learning debits and credits and for representing accounts in the ledger (step 3).

T-Account

Accountants commonly use a graphic representation of an account called a **T-account**, so named because it looks like a large T. The typical form of a T-account is:

Account Title	
Debits	Credits
(Dr.)	(Cr.)
Always the left side	Always the right side

One side of the T-account is used to record increases to the account and the other side is used to record decreases.

> **FYI** Recall that an account is a record of increases and decreases in asset, liability, equity, revenue or expense items.

Accountants record individual transactions using the journal entry. A **journal entry** is an accounting entry in the financial records (journals) of a company. The journal entry is the *bookkeeping* aspect of accounting. Even if we never make a journal entry for a company, we still interact with accounting and finance professionals who do, and who will use this language. Further, journal entries and T-accounts can help in reconstructing transactions and interpreting their financial effects.

Debit and Credit System

> **FYI** Debit and credit are accounting terms meaning left and right, respectively.

Accountants describe increases and decreases in accounts using the terms **debit** and **credit**. The left side of each account is the debit side (abbreviated Dr.) and the right side of each account is the credit side (abbreviated Cr.). In some accounts, increases are recorded on the debit (left) side of the account and decreases are recorded on the credit (right) side of the account. In other accounts, just the opposite is true—increases are credits and decreases are debits. An easy way to remember what the words debit and credit reflect is to visualize a balance sheet in "T" account form with assets on the left and liabilities and equity on the right as follows:

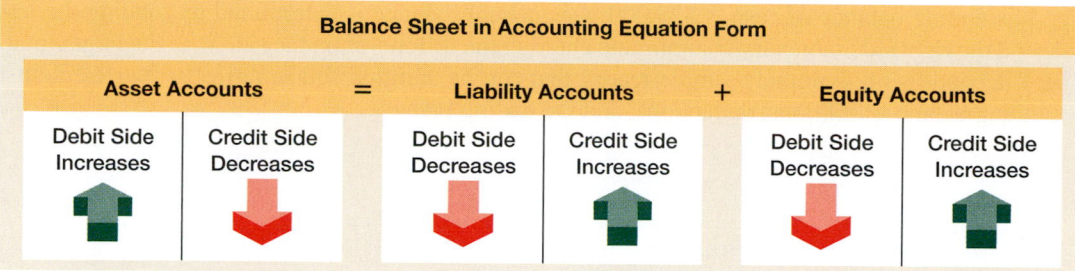

FYI In our everyday speech, the words "debit" and "credit" are often imbued with value connotations. For example, "To her credit, she took responsibility for the incident." But there are no value connotations within the accounting system. Every good event is recorded with both a debit and a credit, and the same is true for every bad event.

Thus, assets are assigned a *normal debit balance* because they are on the left side. Liabilities and equity are assigned a *normal credit balance* because they are on the right side. So, to reflect an increase in an asset, we debit the asset account. To reflect an increase in a liability or equity account we credit the account. Conversely, to reflect a decrease in an asset account, we credit it. To reflect a decrease in a liability or equity account we debit it. (There are exceptions to these normal balances; one case is accumulated depreciation, which is explained in Chapter 3.)

The balance sheet must always balance (assets = liabilities + equity). So too must total debits equal total credits in each journal entry. There can, however, be more than one debit and one credit in an entry. These so-called **compound entries** still adhere to the rule: *total debits equal total credits for each entry*. This important relation is extended below to show the *expanded accounting equation* in T-account form with the inclusion of debit (Dr.) and credit (Cr.) rules. Equity is expanded to reflect increases from stock issuances and revenues, and to reflect decreases from dividends and expenses.

FYI The rule that total debits equal total credits for each entry is known as double-entry accounting, or the duality of accounting.

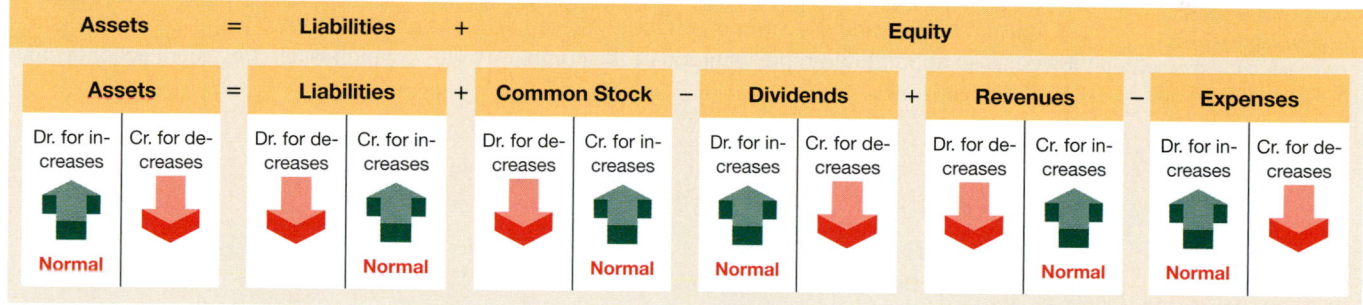

Income (revenues less expenses) feeds directly into retained earnings. Also, anything that increases equity is a credit and anything that decreases equity is a debit. So, to reflect an increase in revenues (which increases retained earnings and, therefore, equity), we credit the revenue account, and to reflect an increase in an expense account (which reduces retained earnings and, therefore, equity), we debit it.

To summarize, the following table reflects the use of the terms debit and credit to reflect increases and decreases to the usual balance sheet and the income statement relations.

FYI The **normal balance** of any account is on the side on which increases are recorded.

Accounting Relation		Debit	Credit
Balance sheet	Assets (A)	Increase	Decrease
	Liabilities (L)	Decrease	Increase
	Equity (SE)	Decrease	Increase
Income statement	Revenue (R)	Decrease	Increase
	Expense (E).	Increase	Decrease

T-Account with Debits and Credits

To illustrate use of debits and credits with a T-account, we use the Cash T-account for NBS transactions 1, 2, 3, and 4 (see page 51). There is a beginning balance of $0 on the left side (which is also the ending balance of the previous period). Increases in cash have been placed on the left side of the Cash T-account and the decreases have been placed on the right side. Transactions (1) and (2) increased the cash balance, while transaction (3) decreased it. Transaction (4) does not involve cash.

The ending balance of cash is $23,000. An account balance is determined by totaling the left side and the right side monetary columns and entering the difference on the side with the larger total. The T-account is an extremely simple record that can be summarized in terms of four elements: beginning balance, additions, deductions, and the ending balance.

+	Cash (A)	−
Beg. bal.	0	
(1)	20,000	2,000 (3)
(2)	5,000	
End. bal.	23,000	

Dates and other related data are usually omitted in T-accounts, but it is customary to *key* entries with a number or a letter to identify the similarly coded transaction. The number or letter is keyed to the journal entry (discussed next) that identifies the transaction involved. The type and number of accounts used by a business depend on the complexity of its operations and the degree of detail demanded by managers.

The Journal Entry

FYI We denote the transaction's effect on assets, liabilities, equity, revenues, and expenses in parentheses for each journal entry.

The journal entry records each transaction (step 2) by summarizing the debits and credits. To illustrate the use of journal entries and T-accounts (step 3), assume that Walgreens: (1) Paid employees $1,200 cash wages, recognizing that amount as an expense, and (2) Paid $9,500 cash to acquire equipment. The journal entries and T-accounts reflecting these two transactions follow. The T-accounts can be viewed as an abbreviated representation of the company *ledger,* which is a listing of all accounts and their dollar balances.

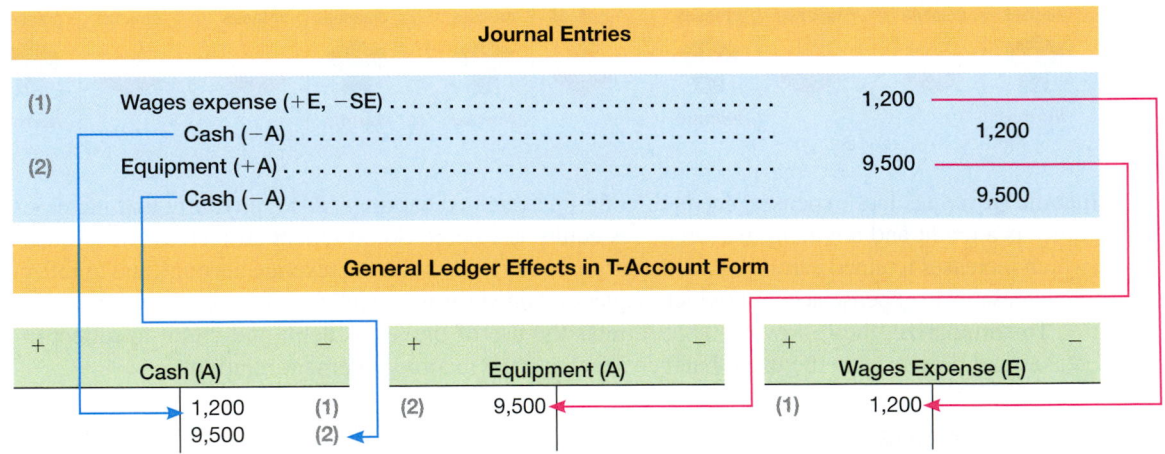

For journal entries, debits are recorded first followed by the credits. Credits are commonly indented. The dollar amounts are entered in both the debit (left) column and credit (right) column. In practice, recordkeepers also enter the date. An alternative presentation is to utilize the abbreviation *Dr* to denote debits and *Cr* to denote credits that precede the account title. We use the first approach in this book.

Analyze, Journalize, and Post

To illustrate the use of journal entries and T-accounts to record transactions, we return to Natural Beauty Supply and reexamine the same transactions recorded earlier in the financial statement effects template. The following layout illustrates our 3-step accounting process of analyzing, journalizing, and posting.

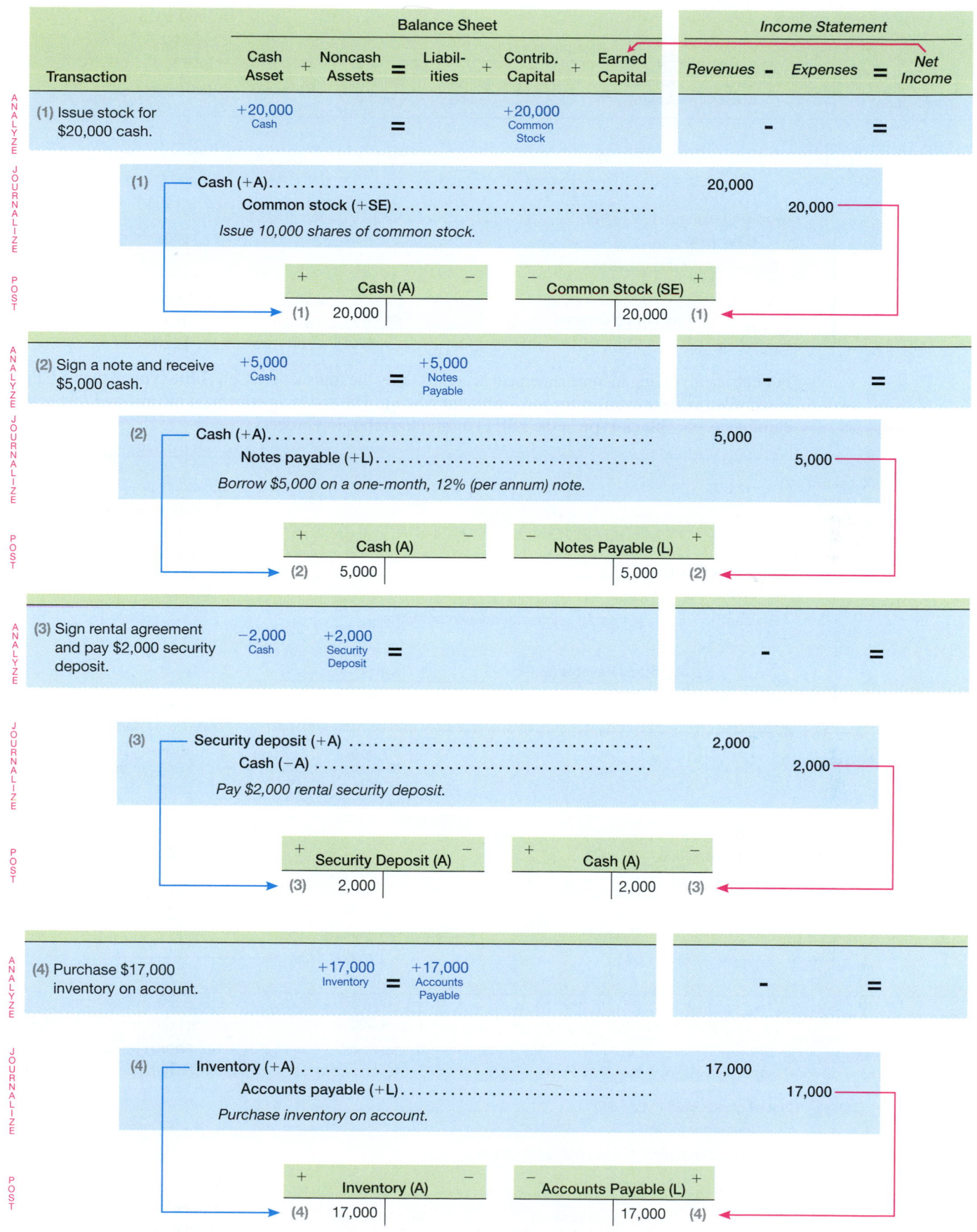

continued

continued from previous page

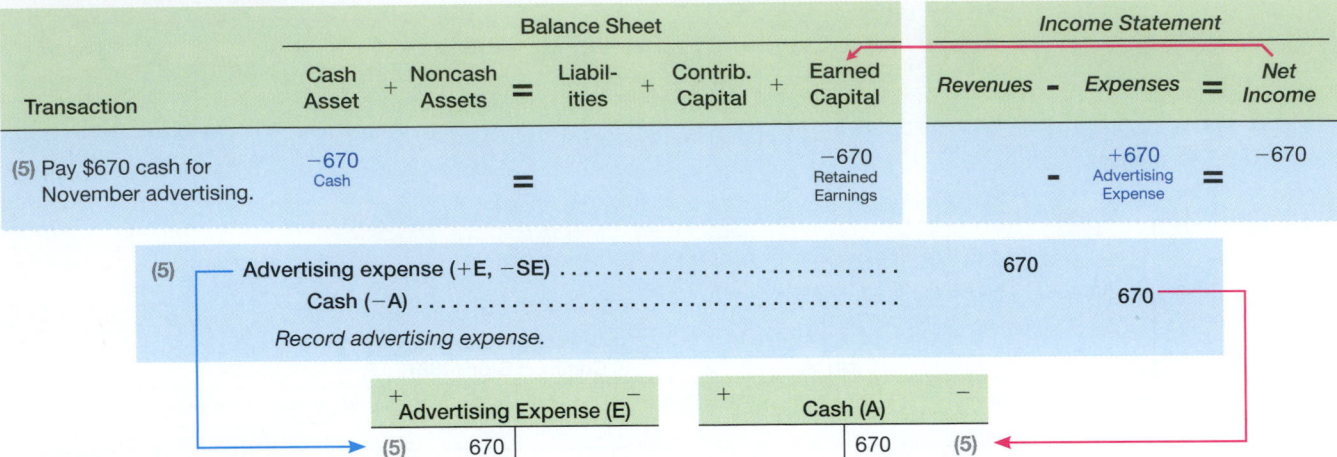

For entries involving income statement accounts, only the transaction itself (**blue type** in the FSET) is recorded in the journal entry and T-account posting. The resulting effects on income and retained earnings occur (**black type** in the FSET) during the reporting process.

(6) Pay $13,300 cash in partial payment to suppliers from transaction 4.

Transaction	Cash Asset	+	Noncash Assets	=	Liabilities	+	Contrib. Capital	+	Earned Capital		Revenues	–	Expenses	=	Net Income
(6)	−13,300 Cash			=	−13,300 Accounts Payable							–		=	

(6) ── Accounts payable (−L) 13,300
      Cash (−A) 13,300
      Pay cash to suppliers in partial payment for previous purchase.

− Accounts Payable (L) +	+ Cash (A) −
(6) 13,300	13,300 (6)

(7a) Sell $7,000 of products for cash.

Transaction	Cash Asset	+	Noncash Assets	=	Liabilities	+	Contrib. Capital	+	Earned Capital		Revenues	–	Expenses	=	Net Income
(7a)	+7,000 Cash			=					+7,000 Retained Earnings		+7,000 Sales Revenue	–		=	+7,000

(7a) ── Cash (+A)... 7,000
       Sales revenue (+R, +SE) 7,000
       Sell products for cash.

+ Cash (A) −	− Sales Revenue (R) +
(7a) 7,000	7,000 (7a)

(7b) Record $4,000 for the cost of merchandise sold in transaction 7a.

Transaction	Cash Asset	+	Noncash Assets	=	Liabilities	+	Contrib. Capital	+	Earned Capital		Revenues	–	Expenses	=	Net Income
(7b)			−4,000 Inventory	=					−4,000 Retained Earnings			–	+4,000 Cost of Goods Sold	=	−4,000

(7b) ── Cost of goods sold (+E, −SE) 4,000
       Inventory (−A)...................................... 4,000
       Record cost of merchandise sold as expense.

+ Cost of Goods Sold (E) −	+ Inventory (A) −
(7b) 4,000	4,000 (7b)

continued

continued from previous page

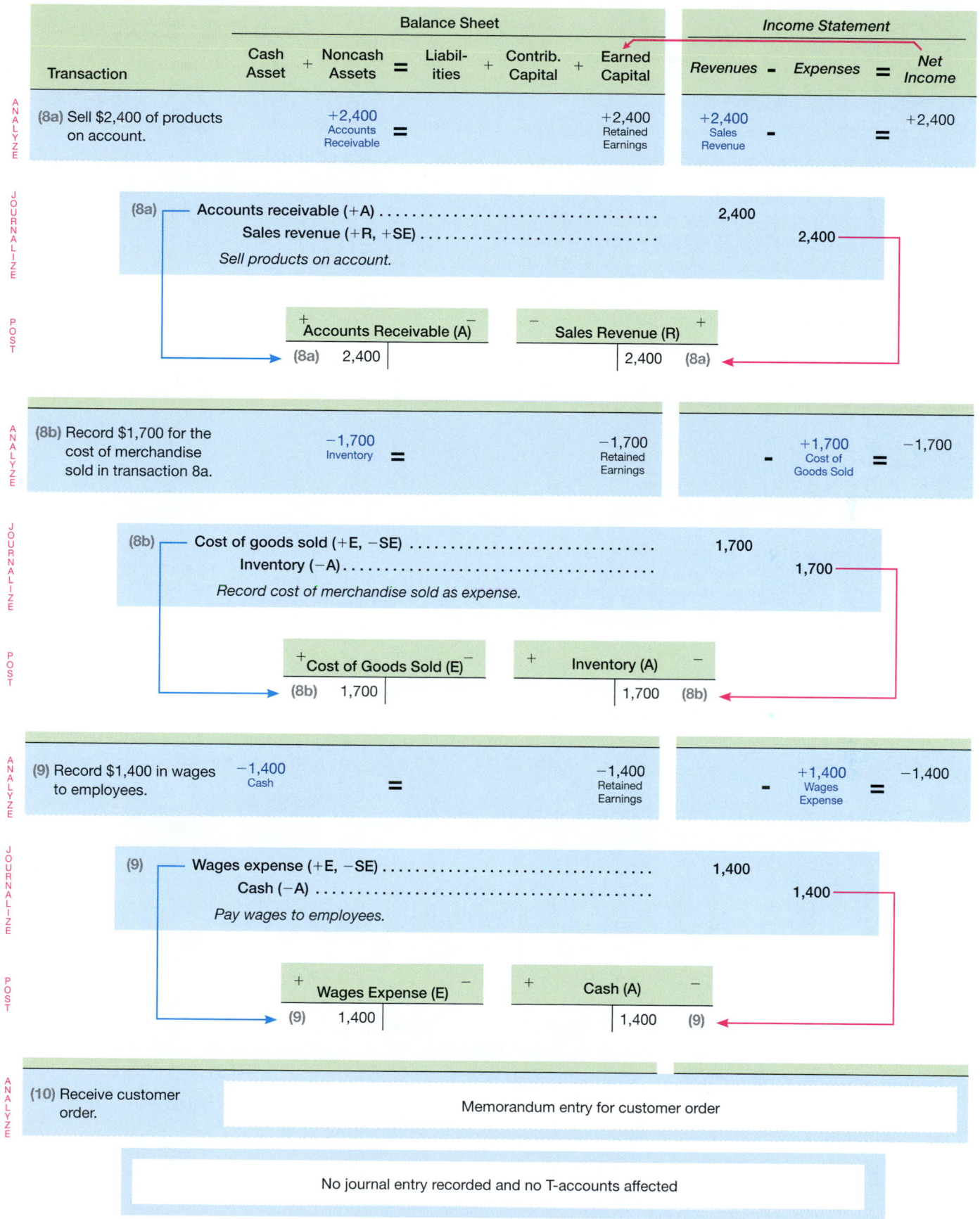

	Balance Sheet					Income Statement		
Transaction	Cash Asset	+ Noncash Assets	= Liabil- ities	+ Contrib. Capital	+ Earned Capital	Revenues	− Expenses	= Net Income
(8a) Sell $2,400 of products on account.		+2,400 Accounts Receivable =			+2,400 Retained Earnings	+2,400 Sales Revenue	−	= +2,400

(8a) Accounts receivable (+A) 2,400
      Sales revenue (+R, +SE)   2,400
    Sell products on account.

⁺ Accounts Receivable (A) [−]	[−] Sales Revenue (R) ⁺
(8a) 2,400	2,400 (8a)

	Balance Sheet					Income Statement		
(8b) Record $1,700 for the cost of merchandise sold in transaction 8a.		−1,700 Inventory =			−1,700 Retained Earnings		− +1,700 Cost of Goods Sold	= −1,700

(8b) Cost of goods sold (+E, −SE) 1,700
      Inventory (−A)   1,700
    Record cost of merchandise sold as expense.

⁺ Cost of Goods Sold (E) [−]	⁺ Inventory (A) [−]
(8b) 1,700	1,700 (8b)

	Balance Sheet					Income Statement		
(9) Record $1,400 in wages to employees.	−1,400 Cash		=		−1,400 Retained Earnings		− +1,400 Wages Expense	= −1,400

(9) Wages expense (+E, −SE) 1,400
      Cash (−A)   1,400
    Pay wages to employees.

⁺ Wages Expense (E) [−]	⁺ Cash (A) [−]
(9) 1,400	1,400 (9)

(10) Receive customer order.

Memorandum entry for customer order

No journal entry recorded and no T-accounts affected

continued

continued from previous page

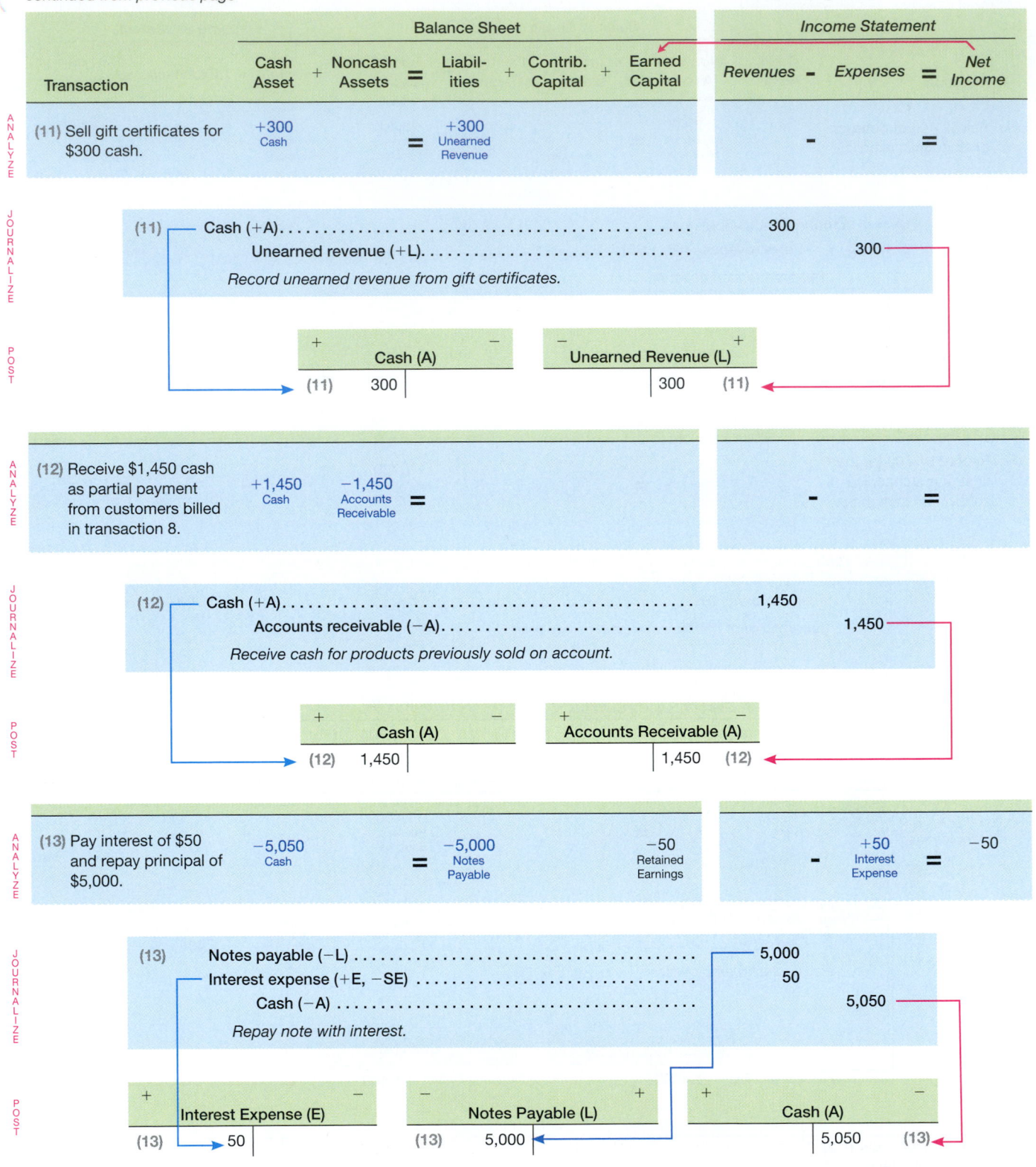

continued

continued from previous page

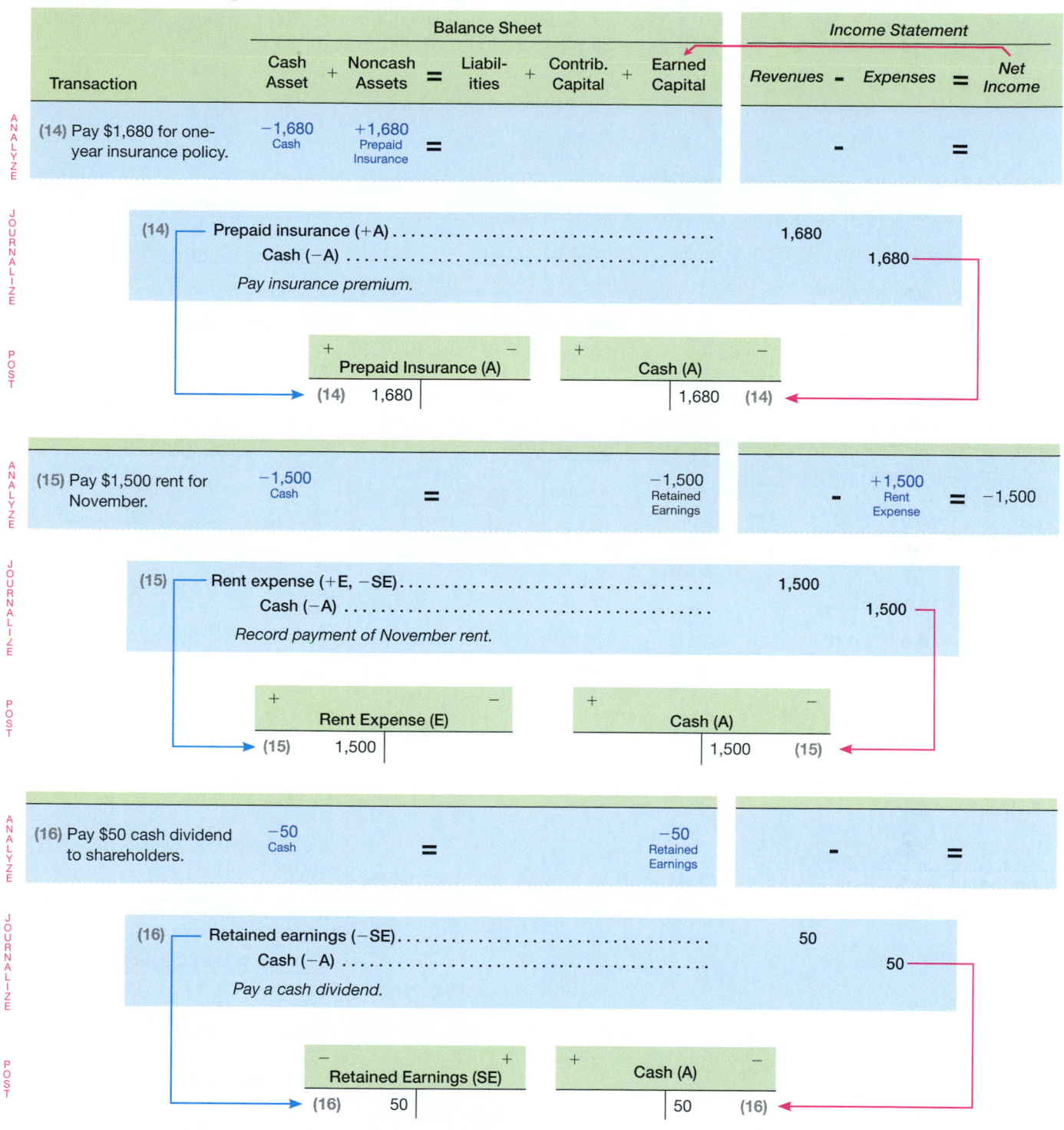

As shown above, each of the journal entries is posted to the appropriate T-accounts, which represent the general ledger. The complete general ledger reflecting each of these sixteen transactions follows, reflecting how the balance sheet and income statement are produced by the same underlying process. The dashed line around the six equity accounts indicates those that are reported in the income statement before becoming part of retained earnings. Each balance sheet T-account starts with an opening balance on November 1 (zero in this case), and the ending balances are the starting balances for December. Income statement T-accounts do not have an opening balance, for reasons we explore in Chapter 3.

As always, we see that: Assets = Liabilities + Equity. Specifically, $24,030 assets ($8,100 + $950 + $11,300 + $1,680 + $2,000) = $4,000 liabilities ($3,700 + $300) + $20,030 equity ($20,000 − $50 + $9,400 − $5,700 − $1,400 − $1,500 − $670 − $50).

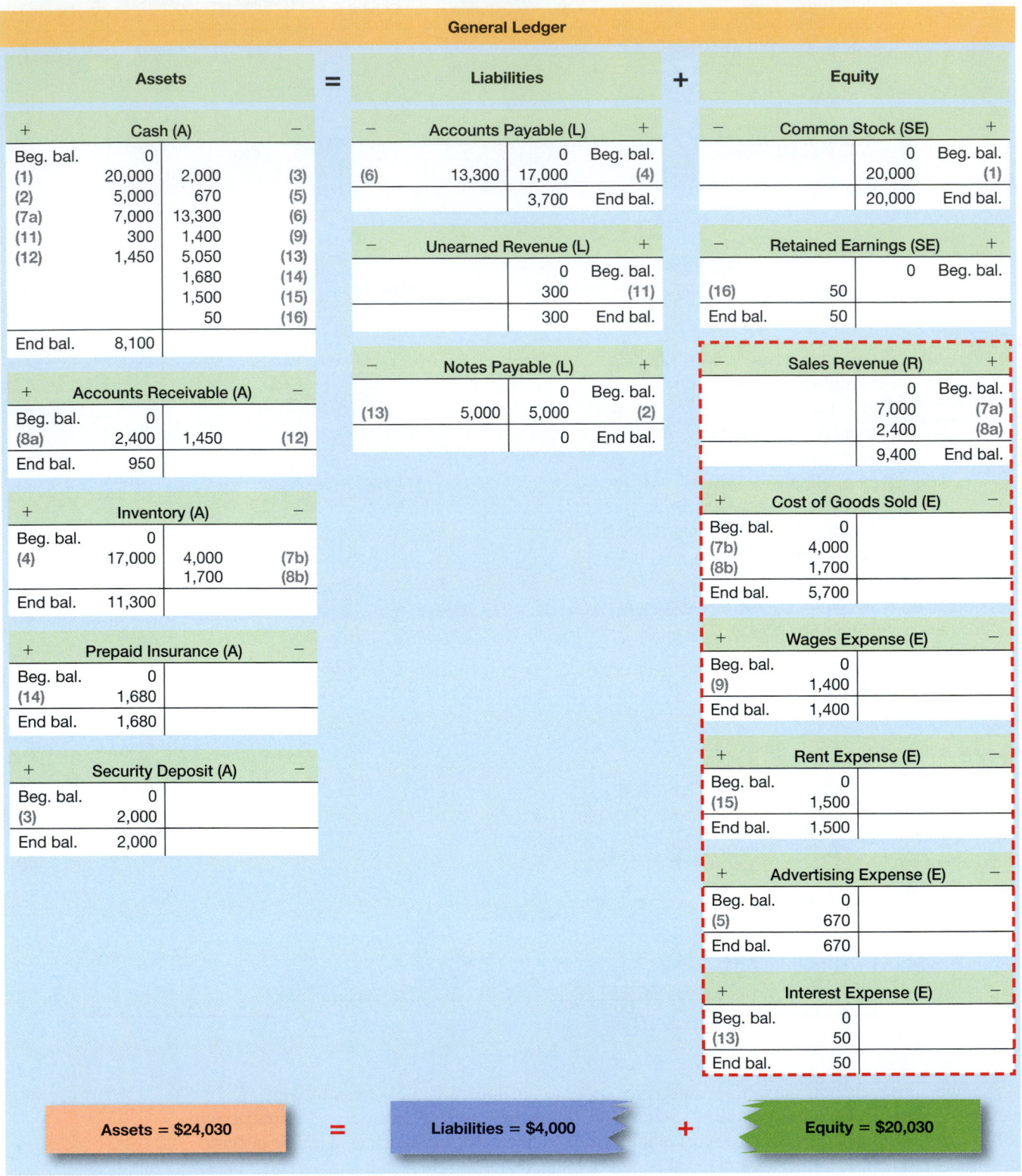

ANALYZING FINANCIAL STATEMENTS
Analysis Objective

We are trying to determine if Walgreens has sufficient funds to pay their short-term debts as they come due. To accomplish this task, we employ several measures of liquidity. We introduce three such measures below to assess liquidity.

LO7 Compute net working capital, the current ratio, and the quick ratio, and explain how they reflect liquidity.

7

Analysis Tool Net Working Capital

> **Net working capital = Current assets − Current liabilities**

Applying Net Working Capital to Walgreens

2012: $10,760 − $8,722 = $2,038
2013: $11,874 − $8,883 = $2,991
2014: $12,242 − $8,895 = $3,347

Guidance A company's net working capital is determined primarily by the time between paying for goods and employee services and the receipt of cash from sales for cash or on credit. This cycle is referred to as the firm's **cash operating cycle** (see **Exhibit 2.6**). The cash operating cycle can provide additional resources through trade credit financing. For example, inventory is typically bought on credit with terms that allow payment to be deferred for 30 to 90 days without penalty. The delay in payment allows the cash to be invested, thereby increasing the cash to be used in the following operating cycle. Of course, the reluctant supplier of the credit strives to reduce this payment delay, for example, through discounts for early payment.

A company's net working capital is a broad measure including all current assets even though some of them—inventories for one—require time to turn them into cash. Later in the book, we will discover that the accounting for some components of working capital, like inventory, needs to be adjusted with information found in the footnotes.

EXHIBIT 2.6 Operating Cycle

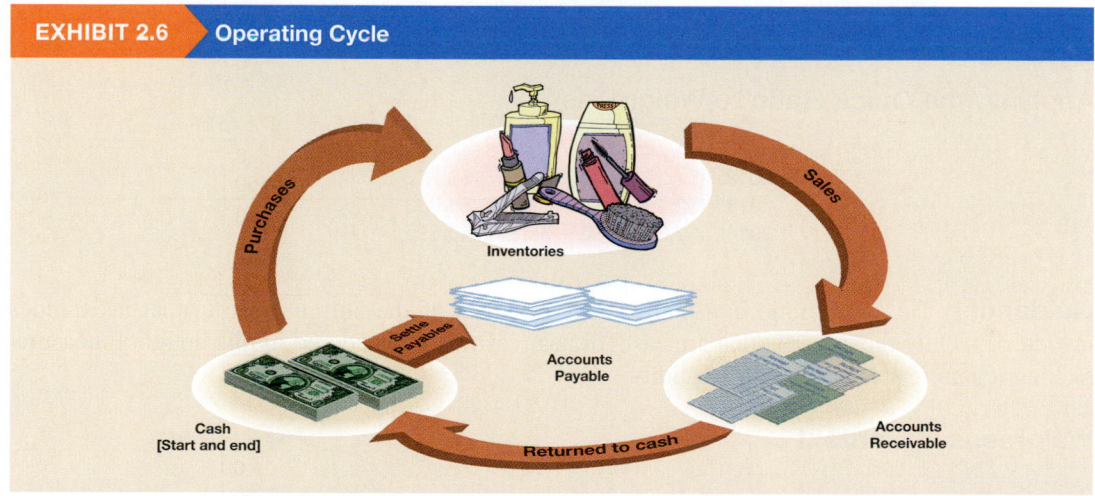

Analysis Tool Current Ratio

$$\text{Current ratio} = \frac{\text{Current assets}}{\text{Current liabilities}}$$

Applying the Current Ratio to Walgreens

2012: $10,760/$8,722 = 1.23
2013: $11,874/$8,883 = 1.34
2014: $12,242/$8,895 = 1.38

Guidance   The current ratio is just a different form of net working capital and as such simply provides a different viewpoint. Current ratios exceeding one indicate a positive net working capital. However, for firms that find difficulty in predicting sales and collections, a higher current ratio is desirable, as discussed in Chapter 5. Companies generally prefer a current ratio greater than one but less than two. The ratio allows us to discern whether the company is likely to have difficulty meeting its short-term obligations. The current ratio has additional value as a ratio because net working capital depends on the size of the company. This is useful when comparing companies as below.

Walgreens in Context

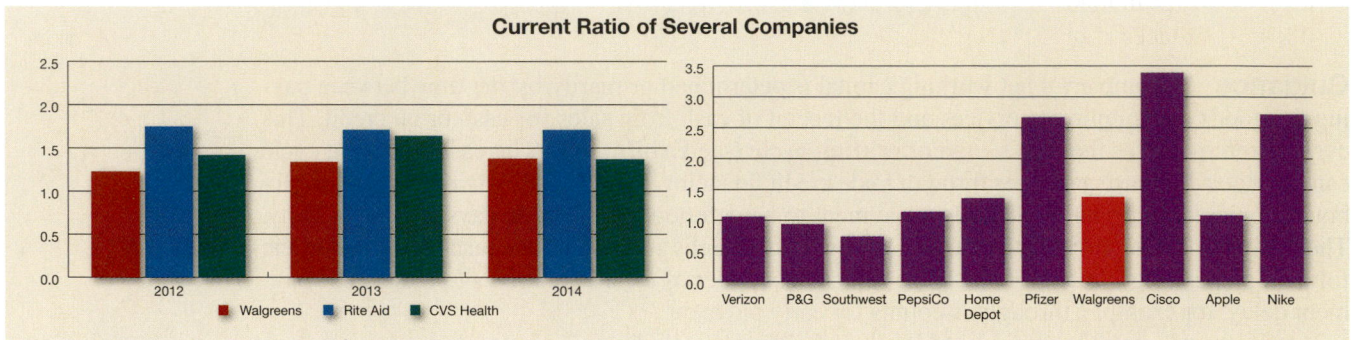

Analysis Tool   Quick Ratio

$$\text{Quick ratio} = \frac{\text{Cash} + \text{Short-term securities} + \text{Accounts receivable}}{\text{Current liabilities}}$$

Applying the Quick Ratio to Walgreens

2012: ($1,297 + $0 + $2,167)/$8,722 = 0.40
2013: ($2,106 + $0 + $2,632)/$8,883 = 0.53
2014: ($2,646 + $0 + $3,218)/$8,895 = 0.66

Guidance   The quick ratio is a more restrictive form of the current ratio in that it excludes inventories. Only those assets that are cash, or near cash, are considered in this liquidity measure, making it a more stringent test of liquidity.

Walgreens in Context

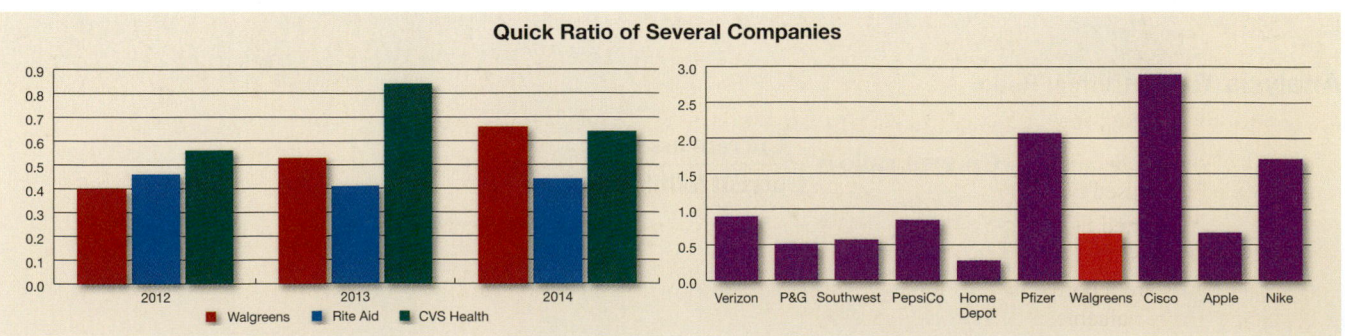

Takeaways   Over the three-year period covered by our calculations, we can conclude that Walgreens is in a strong position with respect to liquidity. Its net working capital, while declining slightly over the last several years has remained positive and is currently one-and-one-half times its liabilities. Our conclusions are bolstered by comparing Walgreens with two of its major competitors, CVS Health Corp. and **Rite Aid Corporation**. All three companies are quite similar on liquidity measures even though quite different in size. CVS is about 1.8 the size of Walgreens while Rite Aid is about one-third the size based on revenues.

Other Considerations   While the ratios above tell us about retail pharmacy chains, other companies with different operating cycles are likely to exhibit different values at optimal levels of activity. Thus grocery stores will have few current assets but consistent large operating cash inflows that ensure sufficient liquidity despite current ratios less than one. Additionally, companies that efficiently manage inventories, receivables and payables can also operate with current ratios below one. **Wal-Mart**, for example, uses its strong market power to extract extended credit terms from suppliers while simultaneously enforcing short payment periods on customers. In Chapter 10, we explore how many technology and pharmaceutical companies have adopted tax strategies that accumulate large amounts of assets that appear to be liquid, but which could be significantly reduced if brought back to the United States.

CHAPTER-END REVIEW

Assume that the following accounts appear in the ledger of M.E. Carter, a financial consultant to companies in the retail sector. Cash; Accounts Receivable; Office Equipment; Prepaid Subscriptions; Accounts Payable; Common Stock; Retained Earnings; Fees Earned; Salaries Expense; Rent Expense; and Utilities Expense. For each of the following 10 transactions: (a) analyze and enter each into the financial statement effects template, (b) prepare journal entries for each of the transactions, and (c) set up T-accounts for each of the ledger accounts and post the journal entries to those T-accounts—key all entries with the number identifying the transaction. Prepare the general ledger in T-account form, enter the financial effects of all transactions, and determine the ending balance for each account.

(1)   M.E. Carter started the firm by contributing $19,500 cash to the business in exchange for common stock.
(2)   The firm purchased $10,400 in office equipment on account.
(3)   Paid $700 cash for this period's office rent.
(4)   Paid $9,600 cash for subscriptions to online financial databases covering the next three periods.
(5)   Billed clients $11,300 for services rendered.
(6)   Made $6,000 cash payment on account for the equipment purchased in transaction 2.
(7)   Paid $2,800 cash for assistant's salary for this period.
(8)   Collected $9,400 cash from clients previously billed in transaction 5.
(9)   Received $180 invoice for this period's utilities; it is paid early in the next period.
(10) Paid $1,500 cash for dividends to shareholders.

The solution to this review problem can be found on pages 95–98.

SUMMARY

Describe and construct the balance sheet and understand how it can be used for analysis. (p. 44)   **LO1**

- Assets, which reflect investment activities, are reported (in order of their liquidity) as current assets (expected to be used typically within a year) and noncurrent (or plant) assets.
- Assets are reported at their historical cost and not at market values (with a few exceptions) and are restricted to those that can be reliably measured.
- Not all assets are reported on the balance sheet; a company's self-developed intellectual capital, often one of its more valuable assets, is one example.

- For an asset to be recorded, it must be owned or controlled by the company and carry future economic benefits.
- Liabilities and equity are the sources of company financing; ordered by maturity dates.

LO2 **Use the financial statement effects template (FSET) to analyze transactions. (p. 49)**

- The FSET captures the effects of transactions on the balance sheet, income statement, statement of stockholders' equity, and the statement of cash flows.
- Income statement effects are separated into revenues, expenses, and net income. The updating of retained earnings is denoted with an arrow line running from net income to earned capital.

LO3 **Describe and construct the income statement and discuss how it can be used to evaluate management performance. (p. 53)**

- The income statement presents the revenues, expenses, and net income recognized by the company during the accounting period.
- Net income (or loss) is the increase (decrease) in net assets that results from business activities.
- Net income is determined based on the use of accrual accounting.

LO4 **Explain revenue recognition, accrual accounting, and their effects on retained earnings. (p. 54)**

- Revenues must be recognized only when goods or services have been transferred to the customer.
- Expenses should be recognized as assets are used or liabilities incurred in order to earn revenues or carry out other operating activities.

LO5 **Illustrate equity transactions and the statement of stockholders' equity. (p. 60)**

- The statement of stockholders' equity reports transactions resulting in changes in equity accounts during the accounting period.
- Transactions between the company and its owners, such as dividend payments, are not reported in the income statement.

LO6 **Use journal entries and T-accounts to analyze and record transactions. (p. 62)**

- Transactions are recorded in the accounting system using journal entries.
- Journal entries are posted to a general ledger, represented by "T-accounts."
- Accountants use "debits" and "credits" to record transactions in the accounts.

LO7 **Compute net working capital, the current ratio, and the quick ratio, and explain how they reflect liquidity. (p. 71)**

- Net working capital: an indicator of a firm's ability to pay its short-term debts computed as the difference between current assets and current liabilities.
- Current ratio (CR): A measure of liquidity indicating the degree of coverage of current liabilities by current assets.
- Quick ratio (QR): A measure of the ability to cover current liabilities using only cash and cash equivalents (such as money market accounts), short-term securities, and accounts receivable.

GUIDANCE ANSWERS . . . YOU MAKE THE CALL

You are an Analyst In 2014, Walgreens paid cash dividends of $1,226 million. The net income and dividend payments account for the change in retained earnings ($22,229 million − $21,523 million = $1,932 million − $1,226 million). On occasion, companies pay dividends in excess of their earnings (or pay dividends even when earning losses), resulting in a decrease in retained earnings over the period.

KEY RATIOS

Net working capital = Current assets − Current liabilities

$$\text{Current ratio} = \frac{\text{Current assets}}{\text{Current liabilities}} \qquad \text{Quick ratio} = \frac{\text{Cash} + \text{Short-term securities} + \text{Accounts receivable}}{\text{Current liabilities}}$$

KEY TERMS

Account (p. 50)
Accounting equation (p. 44)
Accounts payable (p. 47)
Accounts receivable (p. 46)
Accrual accounting (p. 54)
Accrued liabilities (p. 47)
Accumulated other comprehensive income or loss (p. 48)
Additional paid-in capital (p. 48)
Asset (p. 44)
Cash (p. 46)
Cash accounting (p. 55)
Cash equivalents (p. 46)
Cash operating cycle (p. 71)
Chart of accounts (p. 51)
Common stock (p. 48)
Compound entries (p. 63)
Contributed capital (p. 48)
Cost of goods sold (p. 55)
Credit (p. 55, 62)
Current assets (p. 46)
Current liabilities (p. 47)
Current maturities of long-term debt (p. 47)

Debit (p. 62)
Deferred (unearned) revenues (p. 47)
Double-entry accounting system (p. 50)
Earned capital (p. 49)
Equity (p. 47, 49)
Executory contract (p. 47)
Expense recognition (p. 54)
Expenses (p. 53)
Fair value (p. 46)
Financial statement effects template (FSET) (p. 50)
Gross profit (p. 55)
Historical cost (p. 46)
Intangible and other assets (p. 46)
Inventory (p. 46)
Journal entry (p. 62)
Liabilities (p. 47)
Liquidity (p. 46)
Long-term debt (p. 48)
Long-term financial investments (p. 46)
Marketable securities (p. 46)
Net assets (p. 53)
Net income (p. 53)

Net loss (p. 53)
Noncurrent assets (p. 46)
Noncurrent liabilities (p. 48)
Nonoperating revenues and expenses (p. 54)
Normal balance (p. 63)
Notes payable (p. 48)
Operating expenses (p. 53)
Other long-term liabilities (p. 48)
Prepaid expenses (p. 46)
Property, plant, and equipment (PPE) (p. 46)
Relevance (p. 46)
Reliability (p. 46)
Retained earnings (p. 48)
Revenue recognition (p. 54)
Revenues (p. 53)
Shareholders' equity (p. 49)
Short-term borrowings (p. 47)
Stockholders' equity (p. 49)
T-account (p. 62)
Treasury stock (p. 48)

Assignments with the (MBC) logo in the margin are available in *my*BusinessCourse.
See the Preface of the book for details.

MULTIPLE CHOICE

1. Which of the following conditions must exist for an item to be recorded as an asset?
   a. Item is not owned or controlled by the company.
   b. Future benefits from the item cannot be reliably measured.
   c. Item must be a tangible asset.
   d. Item must be expected to yield future benefits.

2. Company assets that are excluded from the company financial statements
   a. are presumably reflected in the company's stock price.
   b. include all of the company's intangible assets.
   c. are known as intangible assets.
   d. include investments in other companies.

3. If an asset declines in value, which of the following must be true?
   a. A liability also declines.
   b. Equity also declines.
   c. Either a liability or equity also declines or another asset increases in value.
   d. Neither a nor b can occur.

4. Which of the following is true about accrual accounting?
   a. Accrual accounting requires that expenses always be recognized when cash is paid out.
   b. Accrual accounting is required under GAAP.
   c. Accrual accounting recognizes revenue only when cash is received.
   d. Recognition of a prepaid asset (e.g., prepaid rent) is not an example of accrual accounting.

5. Which of the following options accurately identifies the effects a cash sale of an iPhone has on Apple's accounts?
   a. Accounts receivable increases, sales revenue increases, cost of goods sold increases, and inventory decreases.
   b. Cash increases, sales revenue increases, cost of goods sold decreases, and inventory decreases.
   c. Accounts receivable increases, sales revenue increases, cost of goods sold decreases, and inventory decreases.
   d. Cash increases, sales revenue increases, cost of goods sold increases, and inventory decreases.

QUESTIONS

Q2-1. The balance sheet consists of assets, liabilities, and equity. Define each category and provide two examples of accounts reported within each category.

Q2-2. Two important concepts that guide income statement reporting are the revenue recognition principle and the expense recognition principle. Define and explain each of these two guiding principles.

Q2-3. GAAP is based on the concept of accrual accounting. Define and describe accrual accounting.

Q2-4. What is the statement of stockholders' equity? What information is conveyed in that statement?

Q2-5. What are the two essential characteristics of an asset?

Q2-6. What does the concept of liquidity refer to? Explain.

Q2-7. What does the term *current* denote when referring to assets?

Q2-8. Assets are recorded at historical costs even though current market values might, arguably, be more relevant to financial statement readers. Describe the reasoning behind historical cost usage.

Q2-9. Identify three intangible assets that are likely to be excluded from the balance sheet because they cannot be reliably measured.

Q2-10. How does the quick ratio differ from the current ratio?

Q2-11. What three conditions must be satisfied to require reporting of a liability on the balance sheet?

Q2-12. Define net working capital. Explain how increasing the amount of trade credit can reduce the net working capital for a company.

Q2-13. On December 31, 2015, Miller Company had $700,000 in total assets and owed $220,000 to creditors. If this corporation's common stock totaled $300,000, what amount of retained earnings is reported on its December 31, 2015, balance sheet?

MINI EXERCISES

LO1

M2-14. Determining Retained Earnings and Net Income Using the Balance Sheet

The following information is reported for Kinney Corporation at the end of 2015.

Accounts receivable	$ 23,000	Retained earnings	$?
Accounts payable	11,000	Supplies inventory	9,000
Cash	8,000	Equipment	138,000
Common stock	110,000		

a. Compute the amount of retained earnings at the end of 2015.
b. If the amount of retained earnings at the beginning of 2015 was $30,000, and $12,000 in cash dividends were declared and paid during 2015, what was its net income for 2015?

LO1

M2-15. Applying the Accounting Equation to the Balance Sheet

Determine the missing amount in each of the following separate company cases.

	Assets	Liabilities	Equity
a.	$200,000	$85,000	$?
b.	?	32,000	28,000
c.	93,000	?	52,000

M2-16. Applying the Accounting Equation to the Balance Sheet

LO1

Determine the missing amount in each of the following separate company cases.

	Assets	Liabilities	Equity
a.	$375,000	$105,000	$?
b.	?	43,000	11,000
c.	878,000	?	422,000

M2-17. Applying the Accounting Equation to Determine Unknown Values

LO1

Determine the following for each separate company case:

a. The stockholders' equity of Jensen Corporation, which has assets of $450,000 and liabilities of $326,000.

b. The liabilities of Sloan & Dechow, Inc., which has assets of $618,000 and stockholders' equity of $165,000.

c. The assets of Clem Corporation, which has liabilities of $400,000, common stock of $200,000, and retained earnings of $185,000.

M2-18. Analyzing Transaction Effects on Equity

LO2, 4, 5

Would each of the following transactions increase, decrease, or have no effect on equity?

a. Paid cash to acquire supplies.

b. Paid cash for dividends to shareholders.

c. Paid cash for salaries.

d. Purchased equipment for cash.

e. Shareholders invested cash in business in exchange for common stock.

f. Rendered service to customers on account.

g. Rendered service to customers for cash.

M2-19. Identifying and Classifying Financial Statement Items

LO1, 3, 4

For each of the following items, identify whether they would most likely be reported in the balance sheet (B) or income statement (I).

a. Machinery ____	e. Common stock ____	i. Taxes expense ____
b. Supplies expense ____	f. Factory buildings ____	j. Cost of goods sold ____
c. Prepaid advertising ____	g. Receivables ____	k. Long-term debt ____
d. Advertising expense ____	h. Taxes payable ____	l. Treasury stock ____

M2-20. Computing Net Income

LO3, 4

Healy Corporation recorded service revenues of $100,000 in 2015, of which $70,000 were for credit and $30,000 were for cash. Moreover, of the $70,000 credit sales for 2015, it collected $20,000 cash on those receivables before year-end 2015. The company also paid $60,000 cash for 2015 wages.

a. Compute the company's net income for 2015.

b. Suppose you discover that employees had earned an additional $10,000 in wages in 2015, but this amount had not been paid. Would 2015 net income change? If so, by how much?

M2-21. Classifying Items in Financial Statements

LO1, 3, 5

Next to each item, indicate whether it would most likely be reported on the balance sheet (B), the income statement (I), or the statement of stockholders' equity (SE).

a. Liabilities ____	d. Revenues ____	g. Assets ____
b. Net income ____	e. Stock issuance ____	h. Expenses ____
c. Cash ____	f. Dividends ____	i. Equity ____

M2-22. Classifying Items in Financial Statements

LO1, 3, 4, 5

For each of the following items, indicate whether it is most likely reported on the balance sheet (B), the income statement (I), or the statement of stockholders' equity (SE).

a.	Accounts receivable	_____	*e.*	Notes payable	_____
b.	Prepaid rent	_____	*f.*	Supplies expense	_____
c.	Net income	_____	*g.*	Land	_____
d.	Stockholders' equity	_____	*h.*	Supplies	_____

LO1, 3, 4, 5

M2-23. Classifying Items in Financial Statements

For each of the following items, indicate whether it is most likely reported on the balance sheet (B), the income statement (I), or the statement of stockholders' equity (SE).

a.	Cash (year-end balance)	_____	*e.*	Dividends	_____
b.	Advertising expense	_____	*f.*	Accounts payable	_____
c.	Common stock	_____	*g.*	Inventory	_____
d.	Printing fees earned	_____	*h.*	Equipment	_____

LO1, 5

L Brands, Inc.
NYSE :: LB

M2-24. Determining Company Performance and Retained Earnings Using the Accounting Equation

Use your knowledge of accounting relations to complete the following table for **L Brands, Inc.** (All amounts in $ millions.)

Fiscal year ending	February 2, 2013	February 1, 2014
Beginning retained earnings (deficit)	$ 24	$(672)
Net income (loss)	?	903
Dividends paid	(1,449)	?
Ending retained earnings (deficit).	$?	$(118)

LO1, 4

M2-25. Analyzing the Effect of Transactions on the Balance Sheet

Following the example in *a* below, indicate the effects of transactions *b* through *i* on assets, liabilities, and equity, including identifying the individual accounts affected.

a. Rendered legal services to clients for cash
    ANSWER: *Increase assets (Cash)*
            Increase equity (Service Revenues)
b. Purchased office supplies on account
c. Issued additional common stock in exchange for cash
d. Paid amount due on account for office supplies purchased in *b*
e. Borrowed cash (and signed a six-month note) from bank
f. Rendered legal services and billed clients
g. Paid cash to acquire a desk lamp for the office
h. Paid cash to cover interest on note payable to bank
i. Received invoice for this period's utilities

LO1, 4

M2-26. Analyzing the Effect of Transactions on the Balance Sheet

Following the example in *a* below, indicate the effects of transactions *b* through *i* on assets, liabilities, and equity, including identifying the individual accounts affected.

a. Paid cash to acquire a computer for use in office
    ANSWER: *Increase assets (Office Equipment)*
            Decrease assets (Cash)
b. Rendered services and billed client
c. Paid cash to cover rent for this period
d. Rendered services to client for cash
e. Received amount due from client in *b*
f. Purchased an office desk on account
g. Paid cash to cover this period's employee salaries
h. Paid cash to cover desk purchased in *f*
i. Declared and paid a cash dividend

M2-27. Constructing a Retained Earnings Reconciliation from Financial Data

Following is financial information from **Johnson & Johnson** for the year ended December 28, 2014. Prepare the 2014 fiscal-year retained earnings reconciliation for Johnson & Johnson ($ millions).

LO1, 5

Johnson & Johnson
NYSE :: JNJ

Retained earnings, Dec. 29, 2013	$89,493	Dividends	$7,768
Net earnings....................	16,323	Retained earnings, Dec. 28, 2014	?
Other retained earnings changes.....	$ (803)		

M2-28. Analyzing Transactions to Compute Net Income

Guay Corp., a start-up company, provided services that were acceptable to its customers and billed those customers for $350,000 in 2015. However, Guay collected only $280,000 cash in 2015, and the remaining $70,000 of 2015 revenues were collected in 2016. Guay employees earned $200,000 in 2015 wages that were not paid until the first week of 2016. How much net income does Guay report for 2015? For 2016 (assuming no new transactions)?

LO3, 4

M2-29. Analyzing Transactions Using the Financial Statement Effects Template

Report the effects for each of the following independent transactions using the financial statement effects template. If no entry should be made, answer "No entry."

LO1, 2

	Balance Sheet								Income Statement			
Transaction	Cash Asset	+	Noncash Assets	=	Liabil-ities	+	Contrib. Capital	+	Earned Capital	Revenues -	Expenses =	Net Income
a. Issue common stock for $20,000 cash.				=							-	=
b. Pay $2,000 rent in advance.				=							-	=
c. Purchase computer equipment for $7,000 cash.				=							-	=
d. Purchase and receive $13,000 of inventory on account (i.e., pay supplier later)				=							-	=
e. Pay supplier of inventory in part (d)				=							-	=

M2-30. Analyzing Transactions Using the Financial Statement Effects Template

Report the effects for each of the following independent transactions using the financial statement effects template. If no entry should be made, answer "No entry."

LO1, 2

	Balance Sheet								Income Statement			
Transaction	Cash Asset	+	Noncash Assets	=	Liabil-ities	+	Contrib. Capital	+	Earned Capital	Revenues -	Expenses =	Net Income
a. Borrow €19,000 from local bank.				=							-	=
b. Pay €3,000 insurance premium for coverage for following year.				=							-	=
c. Purchase vehicle for €32,000 cash.				=							-	=

continued

continued from previous page

Transaction	Balance Sheet					Income Statement		
	Cash Asset	+ Noncash Assets	= Liabil-ities	+ Contrib. Capital	+ Earned Capital	Revenues	- Expenses	= Net Income
d. Purchase and receive €2,500 of office supplies on account (i.e., pay supplier later).			=				-	=
e. Place order for €1,000 of additional supplies to be delivered next month.			=				-	=

LO1, 2, 3, 4 **M2-31. Analyzing Transactions Using the Financial Statement Effects Template**
Report the effects for each of the following independent transactions using the financial statement effects template. If no entry should be made, answer "No entry."

Transaction	Balance Sheet					Income Statement		
	Cash Asset	+ Noncash Assets	= Liabil-ities	+ Contrib. Capital	+ Earned Capital	Revenues	- Expenses	= Net Income
a. Receive merchandise inventory costing $9,000, purchased with cash.			=				-	=
b. Sell half of inventory in (a) for $7,500 on credit.			=				-	=
c. Place order for $5,000 of additional merchandise inventory to be delivered next month.			=				-	=
d. Pay employee $4,000 for compensation earned during the month.			=				-	=
e. Pay $7,000 rent for use of premises during the month.			=				-	=
f. Receive full payment from customer in part (b).			=				-	=

LO6 **M2-32. Journalizing Business Transactions**
 Refer to the transactions in M2-31. Prepare journal entries for each of the transactions (a) through (f).

LO6 **M2-33. Posting to T-Accounts**
 Refer to the transactions in M2-31. Set up T-accounts for each of the accounts referenced by the transactions and post the amounts for each transaction to those T-accounts.

EXERCISES

LO1, 7 **E2-34. Constructing Balance Sheets and Computing Working Capital**
 The following balance sheet data are reported for Beaver, Inc., at May 31, 2015.

Accounts receivable.............	$18,300	Accounts payable...............	$ 5,200
Notes payable	20,000	Cash...........................	12,200
Equipment	55,000	Common stock.................	42,500
Supplies	16,400	Retained earnings	?

Assume that on June 1, 2015, only the following two transactions occurred.

June 1   Purchased additional equipment costing $15,000, giving $2,000 cash and a $13,000 note payable.
         Declared and paid a $7,000 cash dividend.

a.   Prepare its balance sheet at May 31, 2015.
b.   Prepare its balance sheet at June 1, 2015.
c.   Calculate its net working capital at June 1, 2015. (Assume that Notes Payable are noncurrent.)

E2-35. Applying the Accounting Equation to Determine Missing Data   **LO1, 3, 5**

For each of the four separate situations *1* through *4* below, compute the unknown amounts referenced by the letters *a* through *d* shown.

	1	2	3	4
Beginning				
Assets	$28,000	$12,000	$28,000	$ (d)
Liabilities	18,600	5,000	19,000	9,000
Ending				
Assets	30,000	26,000	34,000	40,000
Liabilities	17,300	(b)	15,000	19,000
During Year				
Common Stock Issued	2,000	4,500	(c)	3,500
Revenues	(a)	28,000	18,000	24,000
Expenses	8,500	21,000	11,000	17,000
Cash Dividends Paid	5,000	1,500	1,000	6,500

E2-36. Preparing Balance Sheets, Computing Income, and Applying the Current and Quick Ratios   **LO1, 5, 7**

Balance sheet information for Lang Services at the end of 2014 and 2015 is:

	December 31, 2015	December 31, 2014
Accounts receivable	$22,800	$17,500
Notes payable	1,800	1,600
Cash	10,000	8,000
Equipment	32,000	27,000
Supplies	4,700	4,200
Accounts payable	25,000	25,000
Stockholders' equity	?	?

a.   Prepare its balance sheet for December 31 of each year.
b.   Lang Services raised $5,000 cash through issuing additional common stock early in 2015, and it declared and paid a $17,000 cash dividend in December 2015. Compute its net income or loss for 2015.
c.   Calculate the current ratio and quick ratio for 2015.
d.   Assume the industry average is 1.5 for the current ratio and 1.0 for the quick ratio. Comment on Lang's current and quick ratios relative to the industry.

E2-37. Constructing Balance Sheets and Determining Income   **LO1, 3, 5**

Following is balance sheet information for Lynch Services at the end of 2014 and 2015.

	December 31, 2015	December 31, 2014
Accounts payable	$ 6,000	$ 9,000
Cash	23,000	20,000
Accounts receivable	42,000	33,000
Land	40,000	40,000
Building	250,000	260,000
Equipment	43,000	45,000
Mortgage payable	90,000	100,000
Supplies	20,000	18,000
Common stock	220,000	220,000
Retained earnings	?	?

a. Prepare balance sheets at December 31 of each year.

b. The firm declared and paid a cash dividend of $10,000 in December 2015. Compute its net income for 2015.

LO1, 7 **E2-38.** **Constructing Balance Sheets and Applying the Current and Quick Ratios**

The following balance sheet data are reported for Brownlee Catering at September 30, 2015.

Accounts receivable..............	$17,000	Accounts payable.................	$24,000
Notes payable	12,000	Cash...........................	10,000
Equipment	34,000	Common stock..................	27,500
Supplies inventory	9,000	Retained earnings	?

Assume that on October 1, 2015, only the following two transactions occurred:

October 1 Purchased additional equipment costing $11,000, giving $3,000 cash and signing an $8,000 note payable.
Declared and paid a cash dividend of $3,000.

REQUIRED

a. Prepare Brownlee Catering's balance sheet at September 30, 2015.

b. Prepare the company's balance sheet at the close of business on October 1, 2015.

c. Calculate Brownlee's current and quick ratios on September 30 and October 1. (Assume that Notes Payable are noncurrent.)

d. The October 1, 2015 transactions have decreased Brownlee's current and quick ratios, reflecting a decline in liquidity. Identify two transactions that would increase the company's liquidity.

LO1, 3, 4 **E2-39.** **Constructing Financial Statements from Transaction Data**

Baiman Corporation commences operations at the beginning of January. It provides its services on credit and bills its customers $30,000 for January sales to be collected in February. Its employees also earn January wages of $12,000 that are not paid until the first of February. Complete the following statements for the month-end of January.

Income Statement		Balance Sheet	
Sales........................	$	Cash...........................	$ 8,000
Wages expense	_____	Accounts receivable..............	_____
Net income (loss)	$ _____	Total assets....................	$ _____
		Wages payable..................	$
		Common stock..................	8,000
		Retained earnings	_____
		Total liabilities and equity..........	$ _____

LO1, 3 **E2-40.** **Classifying Balance Sheet and Income Statement Accounts**

Following are selected accounts for **The Procter & Gamble Company** for June 30, 2014.

Procter & Gamble
NYSE :: PG

($ millions)	Amount	Classification
Net sales..	$83,062	
Income tax expense.............................	3,178	
Retained earnings	84,990	
Net earnings....................................	11,785	
Property, plant & equipment (net).................	22,304	
Selling, general & administrative expense	25,314	
Accounts receivable.............................	6,386	
Total liabilities..................................	74,290	
Stockholders' equity	69,976	
Net earnings from continuing operations...........	11,707	

a. Indicate the appropriate classification of each account as appearing in either its balance sheet (B) or its income statement (I).

b. Using the data, compute its amount for total assets.

E2-41.   Classifying Balance Sheet and Income Statement Accounts and Computing Current Ratio
Shoprite Holdings Ltd is an African food retailer listed on the Johannesburg Stock Exchange. The following accounts are selected from its annual report for the fiscal year ended June 30, 2014. The amounts below are in millions of South African Rand.

LO1, 3, 7

Shoprite Holdings Ltd
JSE :: SHP

(Rand millions)	Amount	Classification
Sales of merchandise..................................	R 102,204	
Depreciation and amortisation...........................	1,730	
Reserves (Retained earnings).........................	13,218	
Property, plant and equipment..........................	13,576	
Cost of goods and services	86,444	
Trade and other payables.............................	16,332	
Total equity and liabilities.............................	40,533	
Total equity..	17,283	
Salaries, wages and service benefits.....................	8,373	
Total non-current assets.............................	15,730	
Total non-current liabilities...........................	5,531	

a. Indicate the appropriate classification of each account as appearing in either its balance sheet (B) or its income statement (I). (Note: Shoprite presents a "Value-added Statement" in lieu of an income statement, but it provides the same information as an income statement.)

b. Using the data, compute Shoprite's total assets at June 30, 2014.

c. Calculate Shoprite's current ratio as of June 30, 2014.

E2-42.   Classifying Balance Sheet and Income Statement Accounts and Computing Quick Ratio
El Puerto de Liverpool (Liverpool) is a large retailer in Mexico. The following accounts are selected from its annual report for the fiscal year ended December 31, 2013. The amounts below are in thousands of Mexican pesos.

LO1, 3, 7

El Puerto de Liverpool
OTCMKTS :: ELPQF

(Pesos thousands)	Amount	Classification
Total revenue	$74,105,444	
Retained earnings	50,347,782	
Inventory..	11,421,969	
Administration expenses	19,397,781	
Total assets..	94,936,904	
Long-term loans from financial institutions	921,456	
Financing costs	1,088,892	
Total current assets	37,556,611	
Total stockholders' equity	54,827,332	
Prepaid expenses...................................	617,387	
Total non-current liabilities	14,483,101	

a. Indicate the appropriate classification of each account as appearing in either its balance sheet (B) or its income statement (I).

b. Determine Liverpool's total liabilities and current liabilities as of December 31, 2013.

c. Calculate Liverpool's quick ratio as of December 31, 2013. (Assume that Liverpool only has five types of current assets—cash, marketable securities, accounts receivable, inventory and prepaid expenses.)

E2-43.   Classifying Balance Sheet and Income Statement Accounts and Computing Debt-to-Equity
Following are selected accounts for **Kimberly-Clark Corporation** for 2014.

LO1, 3

Kimberly-Clark
NYSE :: KMB

($ millions)	Amount	Classification
Net sales...	$19,724	
Cost of goods sold.................................	13,041	
Retained earnings	8,470	
Net income.......................................	1,595	
Property, plant & equipment, net	7,359	
Marketing research and general expenses	3,709	
Accounts receivable, net	2,223	
Total liabilities....................................	14,527	
Total stockholders' equity	999	

a. Indicate the appropriate classification of each account as appearing in either its balance sheet (B) or its income statement (I).

b. Using the data, compute its amounts for total assets and for total expenses.

c. Compute Kimberly-Clark's debt-to-equity ratio. (Debt-to-equity was defined in Chapter 1.)

LO1, 2, 3, 4   **E2-44.   Analyzing Transactions Using the Financial Statement Effects Template**

Record the effect of each of the following independent transactions using the financial statements effects template provided. Confirm that Assets = Liabilities + Equity for each transaction.

	Balance Sheet						Income Statement		
Transaction	Cash Asset	+ Noncash Assets	= Liabil- ities	+ Contrib. Capital	+ Earned Capital		Revenues	- Expenses	= Net Income
(1) Receive €50,000 in exchange for common stock.			=					-	=
(2) Borrow €10,000 from bank.			=					-	=
(3) Purchase €2,000 of supplies inventory on credit.			=					-	=
(4) Receive €15,000 cash from customers for services provided.			=					-	=
(5) Pay €2,000 cash to supplier in transaction 3.			=					-	=
(6) Receive order for future services with €3,500 advance payment.			=					-	=
(7) Pay €5,000 cash dividend to shareholders.			=					-	=
(8) Pay employees €6,000 cash for compensation earned.			=					-	=
(9) Pay €500 cash for interest on loan in transaction 2.			=					-	=
Totals			=					-	=

LO6   **E2-45.   Recording Transactions Using Journal Entries and T-Accounts**

Use the information in Exercise 2-44 to complete the following.

a. Prepare journal entries for each of the transactions (1) through (9).

b. Set up T-accounts for each of the accounts used in part a and post the journal entries to those T-accounts. (The T-accounts will not have opening balances.)

LO1, 7   **E2-46.   Constructing Balance Sheets and Intrepreting Liquidity Measures**

The following balance sheet data are reported for Bettis Contractors at June 30, 2015.

Accounts payable	$ 8,900	Common stock	$100,000
Cash	14,700	Retained earnings	?
Supplies	30,500	Notes payable	30,000
Equipment	98,000	Accounts receivable	9,200
Land	25,000		

Assume that during the next two days only the following three transactions occurred:

July	1	Paid $5,000 cash toward the notes payable owed.
	2	Purchased equipment for $10,000, paying $2,000 cash and an $8,000 note payable for the remaining balance.
	2	Declared and paid a $5,500 cash dividend.

a. Prepare a balance sheet at June 30, 2015.
b. Prepare a balance sheet at July 2, 2015.
c. Calculate its current and quick ratios at June 30, 2015. (Notes Payable is a noncurrent liability.)
d. Assume the industry average is 3.0 for the current ratio and 2.0 for the quick ratio. Comment on Bettis's current and quick ratios relative to the industry.

E2-47. Analyzing Transactions Using the Financial Statement Effects Template   **LO1, 2, 3, 4**
Record the effect of each of the following independent transactions using the financial statement effects template provided. Confirm that Assets = Liabilities + Equity.

Transaction	Balance Sheet							Income Statement		
	Cash Asset	+	Noncash Assets	=	Liabil-ities	+	Contrib. Capital	+	Earned Capital	
									Revenues - Expenses = Net Income	
(1) Receive $20,000 cash in exchange for common stock.				=					-	=
(2) Purchase $2,000 of inventory on credit.				=					-	=
(3) Sell inventory for $3,000 on credit.				=					-	=
(4) Record $2,000 for cost of inventory sold in 3.				=					-	=
(5) Collect $3,000 cash from transaction 3.				=					-	=
(6) Acquire $5,000 of equipment by signing a note.				=					-	=
(7) Pay wages of $1,000 in cash.				=					-	=
(8) Pay $5,000 on a note payable that came due.				=					-	=
(9) Pay $2,000 cash dividend.				=					-	=
Totals				=					-	=

E2-48. Recording Transactions Using Journal Entries and T-Accounts   **LO6**
Use the information in Exercise 2-47 to complete the following.

a. Prepare journal entries for each of the transactions 1 through 9.
b. Set up T-accounts for each of the accounts used in part a and post the journal entries to those T-accounts. (The T-accounts will not have opening balances.)

PROBLEMS

LO1, 3   P2-49.   Comparing Operating Characteristics Across Industries

Comcast Corporation
NASDAQ :: CMCSA

Apple Inc.
NASDAQ :: AAPL

Nike, Inc.
NYSE :: NKE

Target Corporation
NYSE :: TGT

Harley-Davidson, Inc.
NYSE :: HOG

Review the following selected income statement and balance sheet data for fiscal years ending in 2014.

($ millions)	Sales	Cost of Sales	Gross Profit	Net Income	Assets	Liabilities	Equity
Comcast Corporation...	$ 68,775	$ 20,912	$47,863	$ 8,592	$159,339	$106,628	$ 52,711
Apple Inc.	182,795	112,258	70,537	39,510	231,839	120,292	111,547
Nike Inc.	27,799	15,353	12,446	2,693	18,594	7,770	10,824
Target Corporation	72,618	51,278	21,340	(1,636)	41,404	27,407	13,997
Harley-Davidson Inc. ...	6,229	3,707	2,522	845	9,528	6,619	2,909

REQUIRED

a. Compare and discuss how these companies finance their operations.

b. Which companies report the highest ratio of income to assets (net income/total assets)? Suggest a reason for this result.

c. Which companies have the highest estimated ROE? Is this result a surprise? Explain.

LO1, 3   P2-50.   Comparing Operating Characteristics Within an Industry

Hewlett-Packard Company
NYSE :: HPQ

Selected data from **Hewlett-Packard Company** at October 31, 2014, follow.

($ millions)	Sales	Cost of Sales	Gross Profit	Net Income	Assets	Liabilities	Equity
Hewlett-Packard.	$111,454	$84,839	$26,615	$5,013	$103,206	$76,475	$26,731

REQUIRED

Apple inc.
NASDAQ :: AAPL

a. Using the data for **Apple Inc.** in P2-49, compare and discuss the two companies on the basis of how they finance their operations.

b. Which company reports the higher ratio of income to assets (net income/total assets)? Suggest a reason for this result.

c. Which firm has the higher gross margin (gross profit as a percentage of sales)? What factors might account for the difference?

LO1, 3   P2-51.   Comparing Operating Characteristics Within an Industry

Verizon Communications Inc.
NYSE :: VZ

Review the following selected income statement and balance sheet data for **Verizon Communications Inc.** as of December 31, 2014.

($ millions)	Sales	Cost of Sales	Gross Profit	Net Income	Assets	Liabilities	Equity
Verizon Communications Inc. ...	$127,079	$49,931	$77,148	$9,625	$232,708	$220,410	$12,298

REQUIRED

Comcast Corporation
NASDAQ :: CMCSA

a. Using the data for **Comcast Corporation** in P2-49, compare and discuss how Verizon and Comcast finance their operations.

b. Which company reports the higher ratio of income to assets (net income/total assets)? Suggest a reason for this result.

c. Which company is likely better able to raise capital? Explain.

LO1, 7   P2-52.   Comparing Operating Structure Across Industries

Review the following selected income statement and balance sheet data from the fiscal years ending in 2014 and 2015.

($ millions)	Current Assets	Non-current Assets	Total Assets	Current Liab.	Non-current Liab.	Total Liab.	Equity
3M*	$11,765	$ 19,504	$ 31,269	$ 5,998	$12,162	$ 18,160	$ 13,109
Abercrombie & Fitch**	1,165	1,340	2,505	486	629	1,115	1,390
Apple†	68,531	163,308	231,839	63,448	56,844	120,292	111,547

*Manufacturer of consumer and business products

**Retailer of name-brand apparel at premium prices

†Computer company

3M Company
NYSE :: MMM
Abercrombie & Fitch Co.
NYSE :: ANF
Apple Inc.
NYSE :: AAPL

REQUIRED

a.   Compare and discuss how these companies finance their operations.

b.   Which company has the greatest net working capital? Which company has the highest current ratio? Do you have any concerns about any firm's net working capital position? Explain.

P2-53.   Preparing a Balance Sheet, Computing Net Income, and Understanding Equity Transactions

LO1, 5

At the beginning of 2015, Barth Company reported the following balance sheet.

Assets		Liabilities	
Cash	$ 4,800	Accounts payable	$12,000
Accounts receivable	14,700	**Equity**	
Equipment	10,000	Common stock	47,500
Land	50,000	Retained earnings	20,000
Total assets	$79,500	Total liabilities and equity	$79,500

REQUIRED

a.   At the end of 2015, Barth Company reported the following assets and liabilities: Cash, $8,800; Accounts Receivable, $18,400; Equipment, $9,000; Land, $50,000; and Accounts Payable, $7,500. Prepare a year-end balance sheet for Barth. (*Hint:* Report equity as a single total.)

b.   Assuming that Barth did not issue any common stock during the year but paid $12,000 cash in dividends, what was its net income or net loss for 2015?

c.   Assuming that Barth issued an additional $13,500 common stock early in the year but paid $21,000 cash in dividends before the end of the year, what was its net income or net loss for 2015?

P2-54.   Analyzing and Interpreting the Financial Performance of Competitors

Abercrombie & Fitch Co. and **Nordstrom, Inc.**, are major retailers that concentrate in the higher-end clothing lines. Following are selected data from their 2014 fiscal-year ended January 31, 2015, financial statements:

LO1, 3

Abercrombie & Fitch Co.
NYSE :: ANF
Nordstrom, Inc.
NYSE :: JWN

($ millions)	ANF	JWN
Total liabilities and equity	$2,505	$ 9,245
Net income	52	720
Net sales	3,744	13,506
Total liabilities	1,115	6,805

REQUIRED

a.   What is the total amount of assets invested in (1) ANF and (2) JWN? What are the total expenses for each company (1) in dollars and (2) as a percentage of sales?

b.   What is the return on equity (ROE) for (1) ANF and (2) JWN? ANF's total equity at the beginning of 2014 is $1,729 million and JWN's beginning 2014 equity is $2,080 million. (ROE was defined in Chapter 1.)

P2-55.   Analyzing Balance Sheet Numbers from Incomplete Data and Interpreting Liquidity Measures

LO1, 7

Kimberly-Clark Corp
NYSE :: KMB

Selected balance sheet amounts for **Kimberly-Clark Corp**, a consumer products company, for four recent years follow:

($ millions)	Current Assets	Non-current Assets	Total Assets	Current Liabilities	Non-current Liabilities	Total Liabilities	Equity
2011.........	$?	$13,090	$19,373	$5,397	$8,727	$14,124	$?
2012.........	6,589	13,284	?	?	8,797	?	4,985
2013.........	6,550	?	18,919	5,848	?	?	4,856
2014.........	?	9,967	15,526	6,226	?	14,797	?

REQUIRED

a. Compute the missing balance sheet amounts for each of the four years shown.
b. What types of accounts would you expect to be included in current assets? In noncurrent assets?
c. Calculate Kimberly-Clark's working capital and current ratio for 2011 and 2014.
d. Assume that the industry average is 2.0 for the current ratio. Comment on Kimberly-Clark's liquidity measures relative to the industry.

LO1, 7
Sears Holdings Corp.
NASDAQ :: SHLD

P2-56. Analyzing and Interpreting Balance Sheet Data and Interpreting Liquidity Measures
Selected balance sheet amounts for **Sears Holdings Corp.**, a retail company, for four recent fiscal years follow:

($ millions)	Current Assets	Non-current Assets	Total Assets	Current Liabilities	Non-current Liabilities	Total Liabilities	Equity
2011.........	$10,244	$11,137	$?	$9,212	$7,888	$17,100	$?
2012.........	?	10,075	19,340	?	8,171	16,585	?
2013.........	8,959	?	18,261	8,185	?	16,522	1,739
2014.........	5,863	7,346	?	6,076	?	14,160	?

REQUIRED

a. Compute the missing balance sheet amounts for each of the four years shown.
b. What asset category do you expect to constitute the majority of the company's current assets?
c. Calculate SHLD's current ratio for fiscal years 2011 and 2014.
d. Recent popular press articles have described SHLD's declining sales and deteriorating financial condition. What indications of financial deterioration do you see in the balance sheet numbers?

LO1, 2, 3, 4

P2-57. Analyzing Transactions Using the Financial Statement Effects Template and Preparing an Income Statement
On December 1, 2015, R. Lambert formed Lambert Services, which provides career and vocational counseling services to graduating college students. The following transactions took place during December, and company accounts include the following: Cash, Accounts Receivable, Land, Accounts Payable, Notes Payable, Common Stock, Retained Earnings, Counseling Services Revenue, Rent Expense, Advertising Expense, Interest Expense, Salary Expense, and Utilities Expense.

1. Raised $7,000 cash through common stock issuance.
2. Paid $750 cash for December rent on its furnished office space.
3. Received $500 invoice for December advertising expenses.
4. Borrowed $15,000 cash from bank and signed note payable for that amount.
5. Received $1,200 cash for counseling services rendered.
6. Billed clients $6,800 for counseling services rendered.
7. Paid $2,200 cash for secretary salary.
8. Paid $370 cash for December utilities.
9. Declared and paid a $900 cash dividend.
10. Purchased land for $13,000 cash to use for its own facilities.
11. Paid $100 cash to bank as December interest expense on note payable.

REQUIRED

a. Report the effects for each of the separate transactions 1 through 11 using the financial statement effects template. Total all columns and prove that (1) assets equal liabilities plus equity at December 31, and (2) revenues less expenses equal net income for December.
b. Prepare an income statement for the month of December.

P2-58.   Recording Transactions in Journal Entries and T-Accounts

Use the information in Problem 2-57 to complete the following requirements.

REQUIRED

a.   Prepare journal entries for each of the transactions 1 through 11.

b.   Set up T-accounts for each of the accounts used in part *a* and post the journal entries to those T-accounts.

P2-59.   Analyzing and Interpreting Balance Sheet Data and Interpreting Liquidity Measures

Selected balance sheet amounts for **Apple Inc.**, a retail company, for four recent fiscal years follow:

($ millions)	Current Assets	Non-current Assets	Total Assets	Current Liabilities	Non-current Liabilities	Total Liabilities	Stockholders' Equity
2011	$44,988	$?	$116,371	$?	$11,786	$ 39,756	$ 76,615
2012	57,653	118,411	?	38,542	?	57,854	118,210
2013	73,286	133,714	?	?	39,793	83,451	?
2014	?	163,308	231,839	63,448	?	120,292	111,547

REQUIRED

a.   Compute the missing balance sheet amounts for each of the four years shown.

b.   What asset category would you expect to constitute the majority of Apple's current assets? Of its long-term assets?

c.   Is the company conservatively financed; that is, is it financed by a greater proportion of equity than of debt?

d.   Calculate the current ratio for 2011 and 2014.

e.   Assume the industry average is 2.0 for the current ratio. Comment on Apple's current ratio relative to the industry.

P2-60.   Analyzing Balance Sheet Numbers from Incomplete Data and Interpreting Liquidity Measures

Selected balance sheet amounts for **Alibaba Group Holding Ltd**, a China-based online and mobile commerce company, for three recent fiscal years follow:

(millions of RMB)	Current Assets	Non-current Assets	Total Assets	Current Liabilities	Non-current Liabilities	Total Liabilities	Equity
2012	$27,899	$?	$?	$11,751	$?	$15,692	$31,518
2013	?	20,624	63,786	?	29,282	53,277	10,509
2014	?	43,716	111,549	37,384	34,426	?	?

REQUIRED

a.   Compute the missing balance sheet amounts for each of the three years shown.

b.   What asset category do you expect to constitute the majority of the company's current assets?

c.   Calculate Alibaba's current ratio for fiscal years 2012 and 2014.

d.   Calculate net working capital for 2012 and 2014.

P2-61.   Analyzing and Interpreting Income Statement Data

Selected income statement information for **Nike, Inc.**, a manufacturer of athletic footwear, for four recent fiscal years follows.

($ millions)	Revenues	Cost of Goods Sold	Gross Profit	Operating Expenses	Operating Income	Other Expenses	Net Income
2011	$20,117	$10,915	$?	$6,361	$2,841	$708	$?
2012	23,331	?	10,148	7,079	3,069	?	2,211
2013	?	14,279	11,034	7,796	3,238	766	?
2014	27,799	15,353	12,446	?	3,680	?	2,693

REQUIRED

a.   Compute the missing amounts for each of the four years shown.

b. Compute the gross profit margin (gross profit/sales) for each of the four years and comment on its level and any trends that are evident.

c. What would you expect to be the major cost categories constituting its operating expenses?

LO1, 2, 3, 4   P2-62.   Analyzing Transactions Using the Financial Statement Effects Template and Preparing an Income Statement

On June 1, 2015, a group of pilots in Melbourne, Australia, formed Outback Flights by issuing common stock for $50,000 cash. The group then leased several amphibious aircraft and docking facilities, equipping them to transport campers and hunters to outpost camps owned by various resorts in remote parts of Australia. The following transactions occurred during June 2015, and company accounts include the following: Cash, Accounts Receivable, Prepaid Insurance, Accounts Payable, Common Stock, Retained Earnings, Flight Services Revenue, Rent Expense, Entertainment Expense, Advertising Expense, Insurance Expense, Wages Expense, and Fuel Expense.

1. Issued common stock for $50,000 cash.
2. Paid $4,800 cash for June rent of aircraft, dockage, and dockside office.
3. Received $1,600 invoice for the cost of a reception to entertain resort owners in June.
4. Paid $900 cash for June advertising in various sport magazines.
5. Paid $1,800 cash for insurance premium for July.
6. Rendered flight services for various groups for $22,700 cash.
7. Billed client $2,900 for transporting personnel, and billed various firms for $13,000 in flight services.
8. Paid $1,500 cash to cover accounts payable.
9. Received $13,200 on account from clients in transaction 7.
10. Paid $16,000 cash to cover June wages.
11. Received $3,500 invoice for the cost of fuel used during June.
12. Declared and paid a $3,000 cash dividend.

REQUIRED

a. Report the effects for each of the separate transactions 1 through 12 using the financial statement effects template. Total all columns and prove that (1) assets equal liabilities plus equity at June 30, 2015, and (2) revenues less expenses equal net income for June.

b. Prepare an income statement for the month of June.

LO6   P2-63.   Recording Transactions in Journal Entries and T-Accounts

Use the information in Problem 2-62 to complete the following requirements.

REQUIRED

a. Prepare journal entries for each of the transactions 1 through 12.

b. Set up T-accounts for each of the accounts used in part *a* and post the journal entries to those T-accounts.

LO3   P2-64.   Analyzing and Interpreting Income Statement Numbers from Incomplete Data

Selected income statement information for **Starbucks Corporation**, a coffee-related restaurant chain, for four recent fiscal years follows.

Starbucks Corporation
NASDAQ :: SBUX

($ millions)	Revenues	Cost of Revenues	Gross Profit	Operating Expenses	Operating Income	Other Expenses	Net Income
2011	$?	$ 8,510	$3,190	$?	$1,729	$ 483	$?
2012	13,277	?	3,545	?	?	614	1,384
2013	14,867	10,668	?	4,400	(201)	?	9
2014	?	11,497	4,951	1,870	3,081	1,013	?

REQUIRED

a. Compute the missing amounts for each of the four years shown.

b. Compute the gross profit margin (gross profit/sales) for each of the four years and comment on its level and any trends that are evident.

c. What would you expect to be the major cost categories constituting its operating expenses?

LO3   P2-65.   Analyzing, Reconstructing, and Interpreting Income Statement Data

Siemens AG
OTCMKTS :: SIEGY

Selected income statement information for **Siemens AG**, a global technology company, for four fiscal years follows:

($ millions)	Revenues	Cost of Goods Sold	Gross Profit	Operating Expenses	Operating Income	Other Expense	Net Income
2011	€73,275	€51,046	€ ?	€ ?	€8,217	€ ?	€6,145
2012	?	55,470	21,925	15,210	6,715	2,565	?
2013	73,445	?	20,135	?	5,177	?	4,284
2014	71,920	51,165	?	14,038	?	1,344	5,373

REQUIRED

a.   Compute the missing amounts for each of the four years shown.

b.   Compute the gross profit margin (gross profit/sales) for each of the four years and comment on its level and any trends that are evident.

c.   What would we expect to be the major cost categories constituting Siemens' operating expenses?

P2-66.   Preparing the Income Statement, Statement of Stockholders' Equity, and the Balance Sheet   **LO1, 3, 5**
The records of Geyer, Inc., show the following information after all transactions are recorded for 2015.

Notes payable	$ 4,000	Supplies	$ 6,100
Service fees earned	67,600	Cash	14,800
Supplies expense..............	9,700	Advertising expense...........	1,700
Insurance expense.............	1,500	Salaries expense	30,000
Miscellaneous expense	200	Rent expense	7,500
Common stock (beg. year).......	4,000	Retained earnings (beg. year).....	6,200
Accounts payable.............	1,800		

Geyer, Inc., raised $1,400 cash through the issuance of additional common stock during this year and it declared and paid a $13,500 cash dividend near year-end.

REQUIRED

a.   Prepare its income statement for 2015.

b.   Prepare its statement of stockholders' equity for 2015.

c.   Prepare its balance sheet at December 31, 2015.

P2-67.   Analyzing Transactions Using the Financial Statement Effects Template and Preparing   **LO1, 2, 3, 4, 5**
Financial Statements

Schrand Aerobics, Inc., rents studio space (including a sound system) and specializes in offering aerobics classes. On January 1, 2015, its beginning account balances are as follows: Cash, $5,000; Accounts Receivable, $5,200; Equipment, $0; Notes Payable, $2,500; Accounts Payable, $1,000; Common Stock, $5,500; Retained Earnings, $1,200; Services Revenue, $0; Rent Expense, $0; Advertising Expense, $0; Wages Expense, $0; Utilities Expense, $0; Interest Expense, $0. The following transactions occurred during January.

1.   Paid $600 cash toward accounts payable.
2.   Paid $3,600 cash for January rent.
3.   Billed clients $11,500 for January classes.
4.   Received $500 invoice from supplier for T-shirts given to January class members as an advertising promotion.
5.   Collected $10,000 cash from clients previously billed for services rendered.
6.   Paid $2,400 cash for employee wages.
7.   Received $680 invoice for January utilities expense.
8.   Paid $20 cash to bank as January interest on notes payable.
9.   Declared and paid $900 cash dividend to stockholders.
10.   Paid $4,000 cash on January 31 to purchase sound equipment to replace the rental system.

REQUIRED

a.   Using the financial statement effects template, enter January 1 beginning amounts in the appropriate columns of the first row. (*Hint:* Beginning balances for columns can include amounts from more than one account.)

    b.   Report the effects for each of the separate transactions *1* through *10* in the financial statement effects template set up in part *a.* Total all columns and prove that (1) assets equal liabilities plus equity at January 31, and (2) revenues less expenses equal net income for January.

    c.   Prepare its income statement for January 2015.

    d.   Prepare its statement of stockholders' equity for January 2015.

    e.   Prepare its balance sheet at January 31, 2015.

LO6 **P2-68.** **Recording Transactions in Journal Entries and T-Accounts**

Use the information in Problem 2-67 to complete the following requirements.

REQUIRED

    a.   Prepare journal entries for each of the transactions 1 through 10.

    b.   Set up T-accounts, including beginning balances, for each of the accounts used in part *a.* Post the journal entries to those T-accounts.

LO1, 2, 3, 4, 5 **P2-69.** **Analyzing Transactions Using the Financial Statement Effects Template and Preparing Financial Statements**

Kross, Inc., provides appraisals and feasibility studies. On January 1, 2015, its beginning account balances are as follows: Cash, $6,700; Accounts Receivable, $14,800; Notes Payable, $2,500; Accounts Payable, $600; Retained Earnings, $12,400; and Common Stock, $6,000. The following transactions occurred during January, and company accounts include the following: Cash, Accounts Receivable, Vehicles, Accounts Payable, Notes Payable, Services Revenue, Rent Expense, Interest Expense, Salary Expense, Utilities Expense, Common Stock, and Retained Earnings.

    1. Paid $950 cash for January rent.

    2. Received $8,800 cash on customers' accounts.

    3. Paid $500 cash toward accounts payable.

    4. Received $1,600 cash for services performed for customers.

    5. Borrowed $5,000 cash from bank and signed note payable for that amount.

    6. Billed the city $6,200 for services performed, and billed other credit customers for $1,900 in services.

    7. Paid $4,000 cash for salary of assistant.

    8. Received $410 invoice for January utilities expense.

    9. Declared and paid a $6,000 cash dividend.

    10. Paid $9,800 cash to acquire a vehicle (on January 31) for business use.

    11. Paid $50 cash to bank for January interest on notes payable.

REQUIRED

    a.   Using the financial statement effects template, enter January 1 beginning amounts in the appropriate columns of the first row. (*Hint:* Beginning balances for columns can include amounts from more than one account.)

    b.   Report the effects for each of the separate transactions 1 through 11 in the financial statement effects template set up in part *a.* Total all columns and prove that (1) assets equal liabilities plus equity at January 31, and (2) revenues less expenses equal net income for January.

    c.   Prepare its income statement for January 2015.

    d.   Prepare its statement of stockholders' equity for January 2015.

    e.   Prepare its balance sheet at January 31, 2015.

LO6 **P2-70.** **Recording Transactions in Journal Entries and T-Accounts**

Use the information in Problem 2-69 to complete the following requirements.

REQUIRED

    a.   Prepare journal entries for each of the transactions 1 through 11.

    b.   Set up T-accounts, including beginning balances, for each of the accounts used in part *a.* Post the journal entries to those T-accounts.

CASES AND PROJECTS

LO1, 3, 4, 5 **C2-71.** **Constructing Financial Statements from Cash Data**

Sarah Penney operates the Wildlife Picture Gallery, selling original art and signed prints received on consignment (rather than purchased) from recognized wildlife artists throughout the country.

The firm receives a 30% commission on all art sold and remits 70% of the sales price to the artists. All art is sold on a strictly cash basis.

Sarah began the business on March 1, 2015. The business received a $10,000 loan from a relative of Sarah to help her get started; it took on a note payable agreeing to pay the loan back in one year. No interest is being charged on the loan, but the relative does want to receive a set of financial statements each month. On April 1, 2015, Sarah asks for your help in preparing the statements for the first month.

Sarah has carefully kept the firm's checking account up to date and provides you with the following complete listing of the cash receipts and cash disbursements for March 2015.

Cash Receipts	
Original investment by Sarah Penney.	$ 6,500
Loan from relative	10,000
Sales of art	95,000
Total cash receipts	111,500
Cash Disbursements	
Payments to artists for sales made	54,000
Payment of March rent for gallery space	900
Payment of March wages to staff.	4,900
Payment of airfare for personal vacation of Sarah (vacation will be in April)	500
Total cash disbursements.	60,300
Cash balance, March 31, 2015.	$ 51,200

Sarah also gives you the following documents she has received:

1. A $350 invoice for March utilities; payment is due by April 15, 2015.
2. A $1,700 invoice from Careful Express for the shipping of artwork sold in March; payment is due by April 10, 2015.
3. Sarah signed a one-year lease for the gallery space; as an incentive to sign the lease, the landlord reduced the first month's rent by 25%; the monthly rent starting in April is $1,200.

In your discussions with Sarah, she tells you that she has been so busy that she is behind in sending artists their share of the sales proceeds. She plans to catch up within the next week.

REQUIRED

From the above information, prepare the following financial statements for Wildlife Picture Gallery: (a) income statement for the month of March 2015; (b) statement of stockholders' equity for the month of March 2015; and (c) balance sheet as of March 31, 2015.

C2-72. Financial Records and Ethical Behavior   LO3

Andrea Frame and her supervisor are sent on an out-of-town assignment by their employer. At the supervisor's suggestion, they stay at the Spartan Inn (across the street from the Luxury Inn). After three days of work, they settle their lodging bills and leave. On the return trip, the supervisor gives Andrea what appears to be a copy of a receipt from the Luxury Inn for three nights of lodging. Actually, the supervisor indicates that he prepared the Luxury Inn receipt on his office computer and plans to complete his expense reimbursement request using the higher lodging costs from the Luxury Inn.

REQUIRED

What are the ethical considerations that Andrea faces when she prepares her expense reimbursement request?

SOLUTIONS TO REVIEW PROBLEMS

Mid-Chapter Review 1

SOLUTION

1. A	2. C	3. B	4. E	5. B	6. E	7. X	8. B	9. E	10. B
11. X	12. A	13. B	14. C	15. A	16. D	17. A	18. A	19. E	20. C

Mid-Chapter Review 2

SOLUTION

	Balance Sheet						Income Statement		
Transaction	Cash Asset	+ Noncash Assets	= Liabil- ities	+ Contrib. Capital	+ Earned Capital		Revenues	− Expenses	= Net Income
(a) Issue common stock for $20,000.	+20,000 Cash		=		+20,000 Common Stock			−	=
(b) Purchase $8,000 of inventory on credit.		+8,000 Inventory	= +8,000 Accounts Payable					−	=
(c) Purchase equipment for $10,000 cash.	−10,000 Cash	+10,000 Equipment	=					−	=
(d) Pay suppliers $3,000 cash.	−3,000 Cash		= −3,000 Accounts Payable					−	=
Totals	+7,000	+18,000	= +5,000		+20,000				

Assets = Liabilities + Equity

Mid-Chapter Review 3

SOLUTION TO PART 1

SCHAEFER'S PHARMACY, INC.
Income Statement
For Year Ended December 31, 2015

Revenues		$45,000
Expenses		
Cost of goods sold	$20,000	
Wages expense	8,000	
Rent expense	5,000	
Utilities expense	2,000	
Other expenses	4,000	
Total expenses		39,000
Net income		$ 6,000

SOLUTION TO PART 2

SCHAEFER'S PHARMACY, INC.
Retained Earnings Reconciliation
For Year Ended December 31, 2015

Retained earnings, Dec. 31, 2014	$25,000
Add: Net income	6,000
Less: Dividends	(1,000)
Retained earnings, Dec. 31, 2015	$30,000

SOLUTION TO PART 3

SCHAEFER'S PHARMACY, INC. Balance Sheet December 31, 2015			
Cash........................	$ 3,000	Accounts payable..............	$ 7,500
Accounts receivable.............	12,000		
Inventory......................	26,000		
Office equipment	32,250	Common stock.................	45,750
Land	10,000	Retained earnings	30,000
Total assets...................	$83,250	Total liabilities and equity	$83,250

Chapter-End Review

SOLUTION

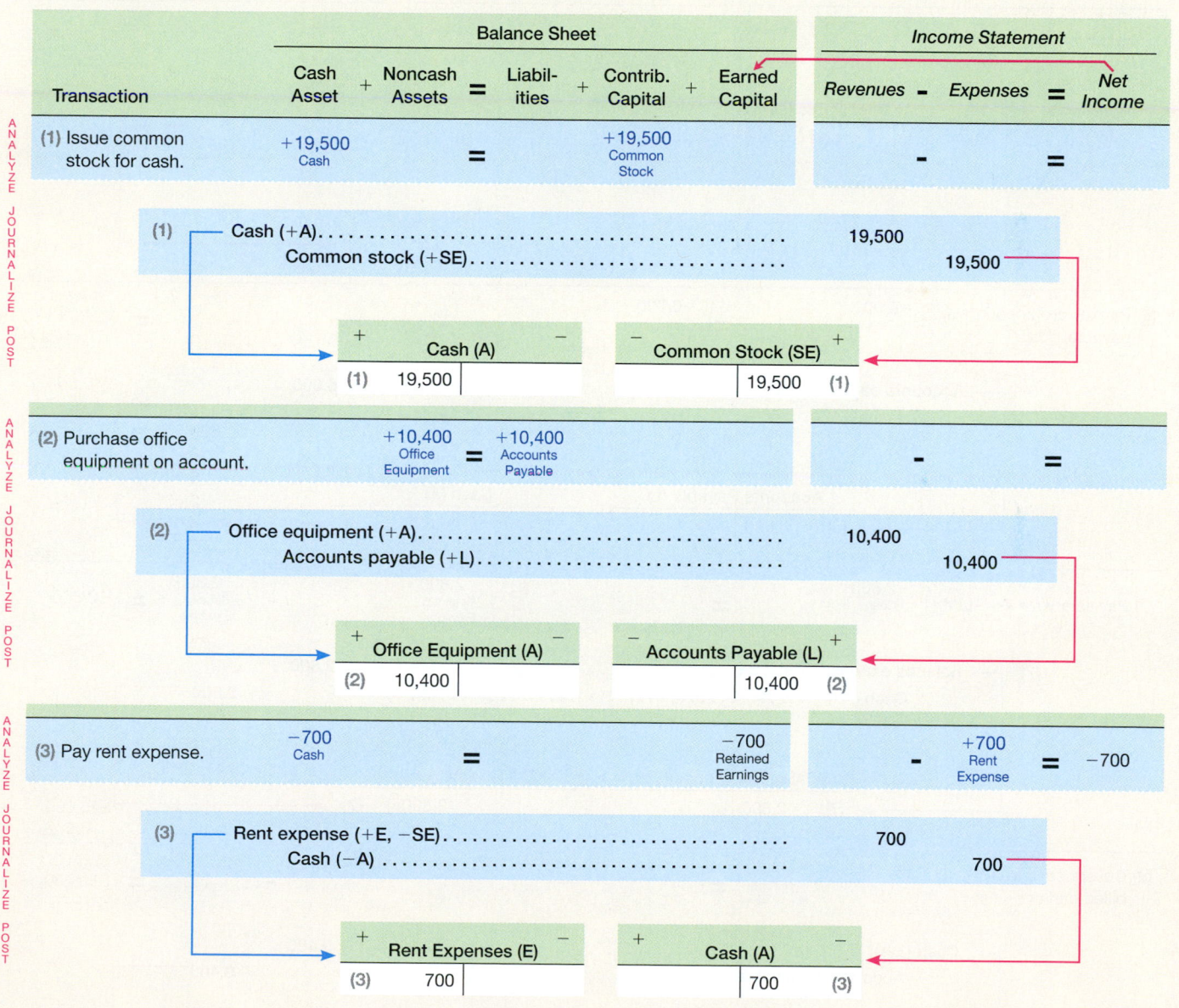

continued

continued from previous page

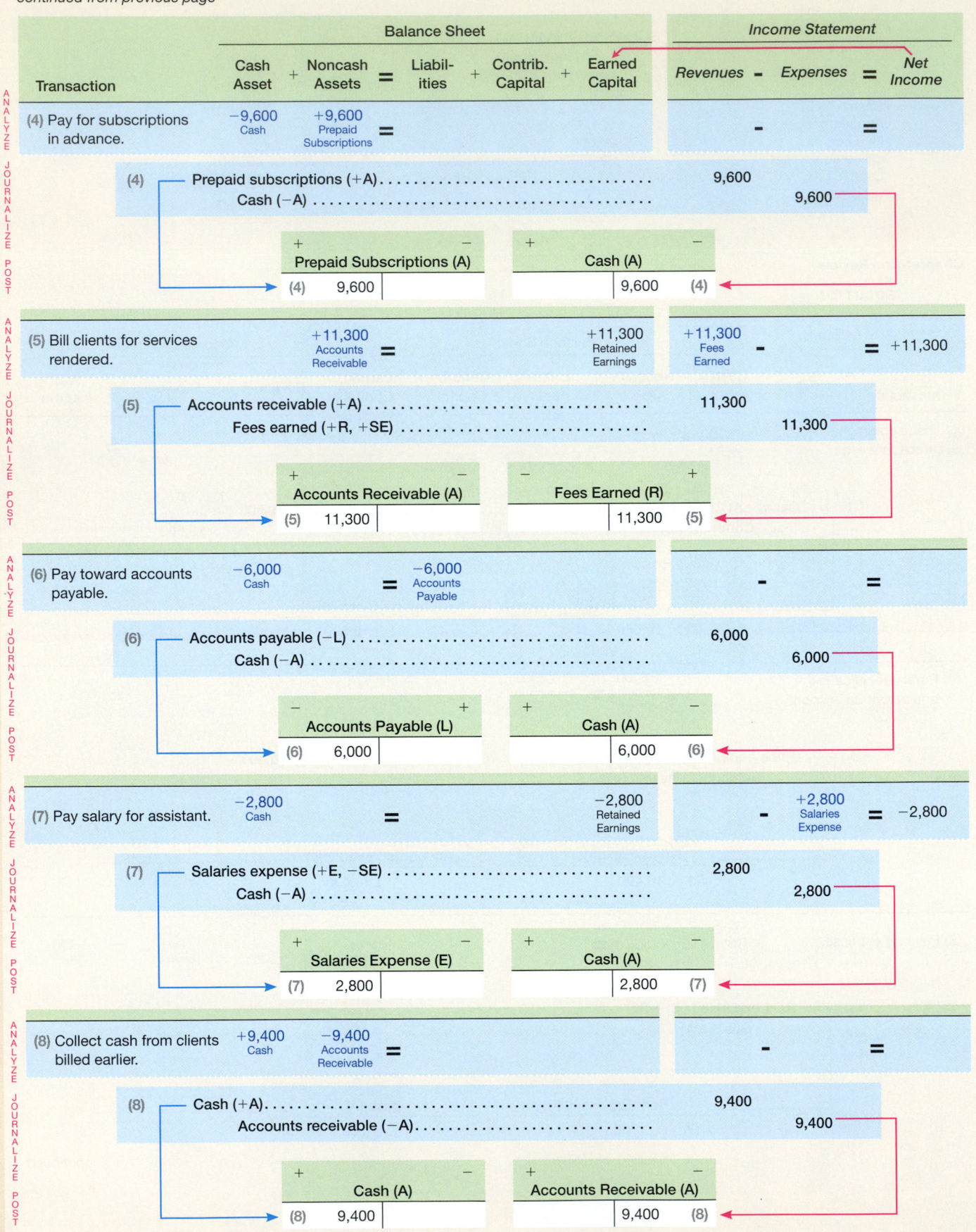

continued

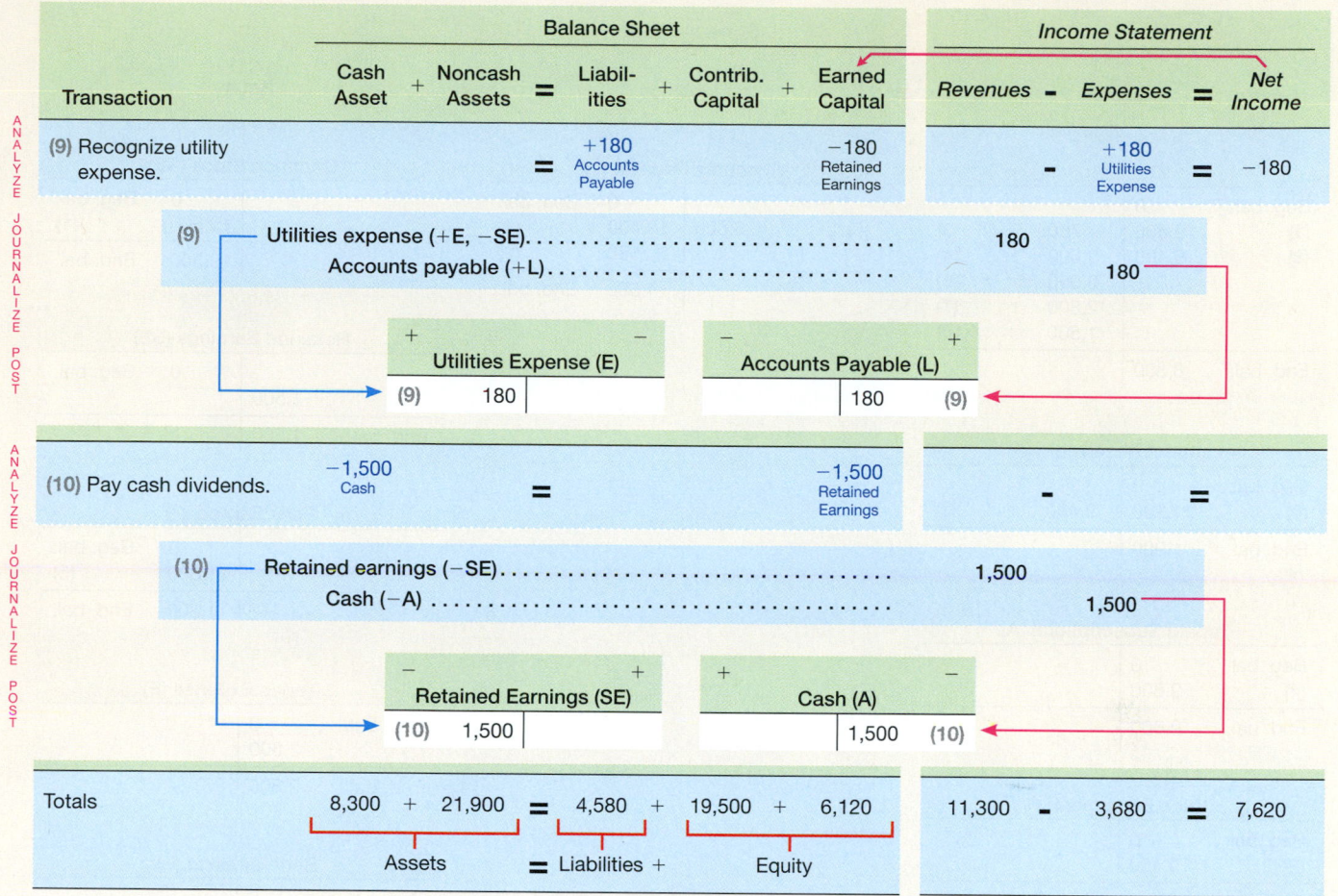

Transaction	Balance Sheet					Income Statement		
	Cash Asset +	Noncash Assets =	Liabil- ities +	Contrib. Capital +	Earned Capital	Revenues -	Expenses =	Net Income
(9) Recognize utility expense.		=	+180 Accounts Payable		−180 Retained Earnings	-	+180 Utilities Expense	= −180

(9) Utilities expense (+E, −SE)................................. 180
     Accounts payable (+L).............................. 180

+	−		−	+
Utilities Expense (E)			**Accounts Payable (L)**	
(9) 180			180 (9)	

Transaction	Balance Sheet					Income Statement		
(10) Pay cash dividends.	−1,500 Cash	=			−1,500 Retained Earnings	-		=

(10) Retained earnings (−SE)................................... 1,500
     Cash (−A) 1,500

−	+		+	−
Retained Earnings (SE)			**Cash (A)**	
(10) 1,500			1,500 (10)	

Totals	8,300 + 21,900	= 4,580 +	19,500 + 6,120	11,300 - 3,680 = 7,620
	Assets	= Liabilities +	Equity	

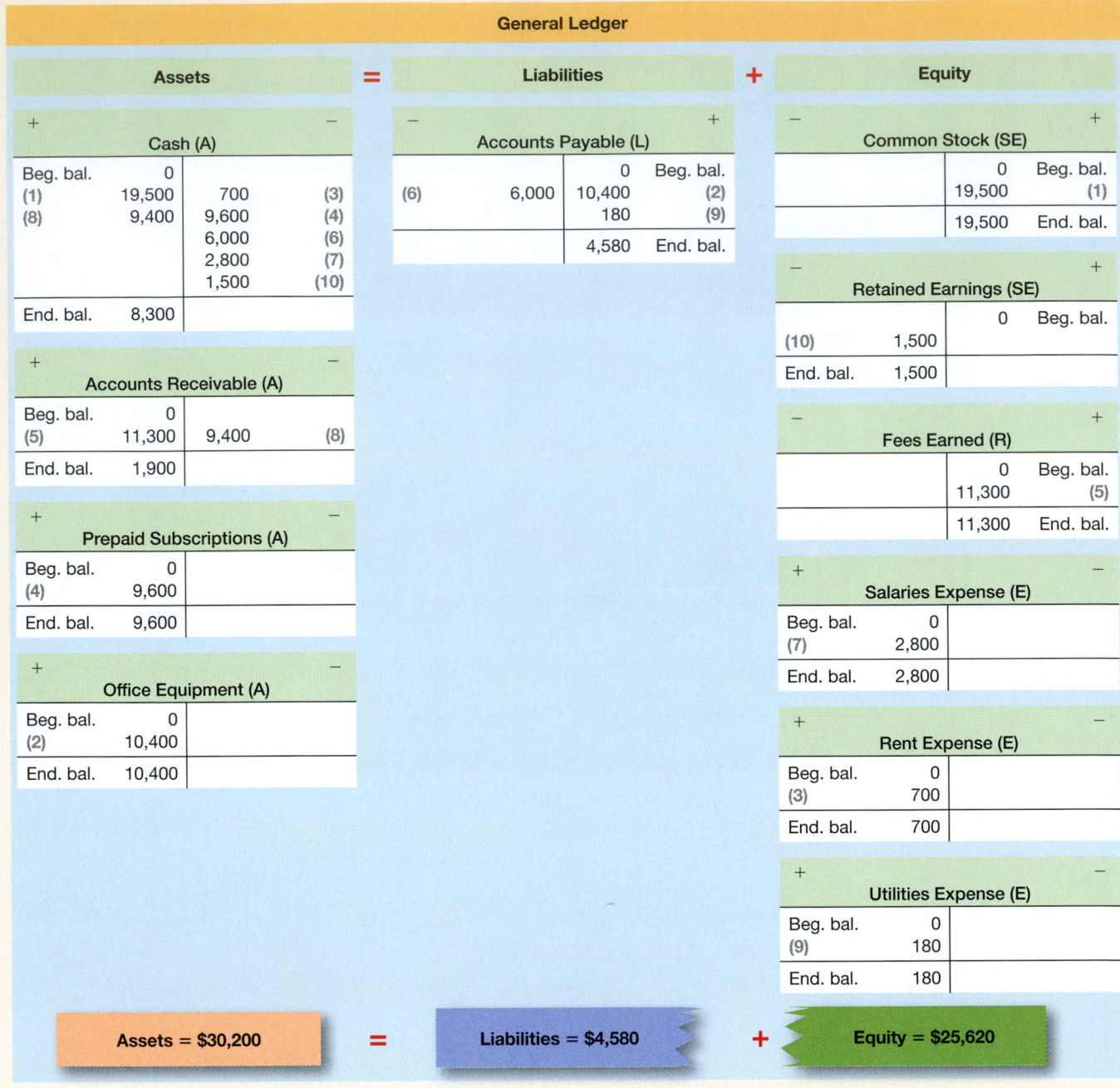

General Ledger

Assets = **Liabilities** + **Equity**

Cash (A)
+		−	
Beg. bal.	0	700	(3)
(1)	19,500	9,600	(4)
(8)	9,400	6,000	(6)
		2,800	(7)
		1,500	(10)
End. bal.	8,300		

Accounts Receivable (A)
+		−	
Beg. bal.	0	9,400	(8)
(5)	11,300		
End. bal.	1,900		

Prepaid Subscriptions (A)
+		−	
Beg. bal.	0		
(4)	9,600		
End. bal.	9,600		

Office Equipment (A)
+		−	
Beg. bal.	0		
(2)	10,400		
End. bal.	10,400		

Accounts Payable (L)
−		+	
(6)	6,000	0	Beg. bal.
		10,400	(2)
		180	(9)
		4,580	End. bal.

Common Stock (SE)
−		+	
		0	Beg. bal.
		19,500	(1)
		19,500	End. bal.

Retained Earnings (SE)
−		+	
		0	Beg. bal.
(10)	1,500		
End. bal.	1,500		

Fees Earned (R)
−		+	
		0	Beg. bal.
		11,300	(5)
		11,300	End. bal.

Salaries Expense (E)
+		−	
Beg. bal.	0		
(7)	2,800		
End. bal.	2,800		

Rent Expense (E)
+		−	
Beg. bal.	0		
(3)	700		
End. bal.	700		

Utilities Expense (E)
+		−	
Beg. bal.	0		
(9)	180		
End. bal.	180		

Assets = $30,200   =   Liabilities = $4,580   +   Equity = $25,620

3

Adjusting Accounts for Financial Statements

WALGREENS
www.walgreens.com

Walgreen Co.'s strategy for growth has three principal components. Within its network of more than 8,300 stores, it strives to create a "Well Experience" for customers, by store design and layout, by employee training and by digital applications. Their goal is to give the customer the "Three Ws"—What they want. Where they want it. When they want it. In fiscal year 2014, Walgreens reported an increase of 4.9% in same-store sales.

Pharmacy sales represent almost two-thirds of Walgreens' revenue, and the aging U.S. population will cause this to grow. In 2014, Walgreens completed multi-year agreements with major insurance companies, bringing greater stability to their pharmacy business. Finally, Walgreens made a significant international investment by purchasing 45% of the outstanding shares of **Alliance Boots GmbH**, plus an option to purchase the remaining 55% (which Walgreens exercised in late 2014). This acquisition creates the world's "leading pharmacy-led health and well-being enterprise," and provides the companies with a global platform for growth.

Because the financial statements should reflect the firm's underlying economic reality, Walgreens' management will need to "adjust" or "update" its financial statements to reflect the changes in its strategy and performance.

Accounting adjustments are a key part of creating the financial statements, and they are central to the difference between accrual and cash accounting. While cash accounting only records transactions that involve cash receipts and disbursements,

accrual accounting records revenues when they are earned (even if cash has not yet been received) and expenses as they are incurred (regardless of when the cash disbursement associated with that expense is made). The quality, or lack thereof, of the financial statements often hinges on the quality of those adjustments. Thus, understanding how and why accounting adjustments occur is fundamentally important to those who wish to analyze and interpret the financial statements.

This chapter describes the need for adjustments, how they are prepared, their financial statement effect, and the need for ethics and oversight in this process. We illustrate how financial statements are prepared from those adjusted accounts. Then, we end the chapter with the closing process for the financial statements. Such "closing of the books" enables firms to report their performance for the year and then "open the books" anew for the next period.

Sources: Walgreen Co. and Subsidiaries 2013 Annual Report and 2014 10-K.

CHAPTER ORGANIZATION

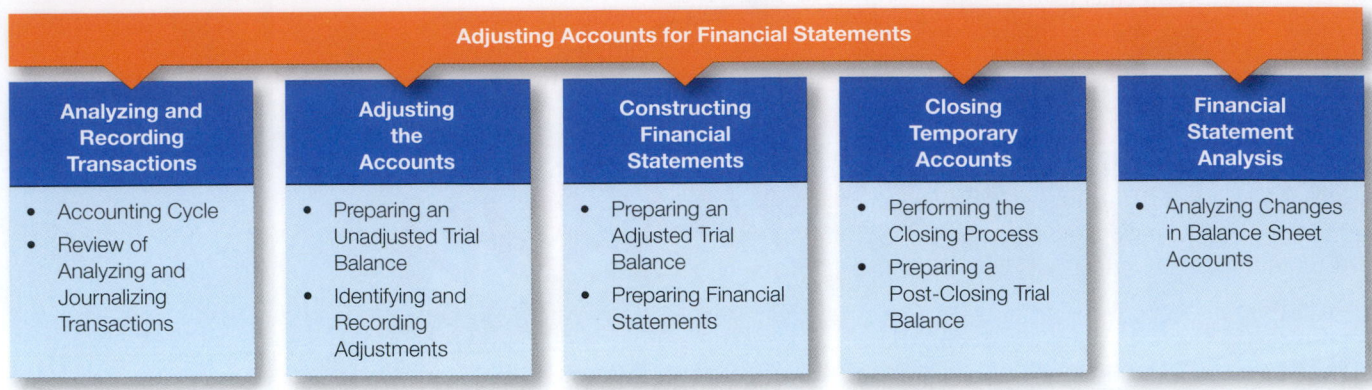

Adjusting Accounts for Financial Statements				
Analyzing and Recording Transactions	**Adjusting the Accounts**	**Constructing Financial Statements**	**Closing Temporary Accounts**	**Financial Statement Analysis**
• Accounting Cycle • Review of Analyzing and Journalizing Transactions	• Preparing an Unadjusted Trial Balance • Identifying and Recording Adjustments	• Preparing an Adjusted Trial Balance • Preparing Financial Statements	• Performing the Closing Process • Preparing a Post-Closing Trial Balance	• Analyzing Changes in Balance Sheet Accounts

The double-entry accounting system introduced in Chapter 2 provides us with a framework for the analysis of business activities, and we use that framework to record transactions and create financial reports. This chapter describes more fully the procedures companies use to account for the operations of a business during a specific time period. All companies, regardless of size or complexity, perform accounting steps, known as the *accounting cycle*, to accumulate and report their financial information. An important step in the accounting cycle is the *adjusting* process that occurs at the end of every reporting period. This chapter focuses on the accounting cycle with emphasis on the adjusting process.

eLectures
MBC

1

LO1 Identify the major steps in the accounting cycle.

ACCOUNTING CYCLE

Companies engage in business activities. These activities are analyzed for their financial impact, and the results from that analysis are entered into the accounting information system. When management and others want to know where the company stands financially, and what its recent performance tells about future prospects, the financial data often require adjustment prior to financial statements being prepared. At the end of this adjustment process, the company *closes the books*. This closing process prepares accounts for the next accounting period.

The process described constitutes the major steps in the **accounting cycle**—a sequence of activities to accumulate and report financial statements. The steps are: analyze, record, adjust, report, and close. **Exhibit 3.1** shows the sequence of major steps in the accounting cycle.

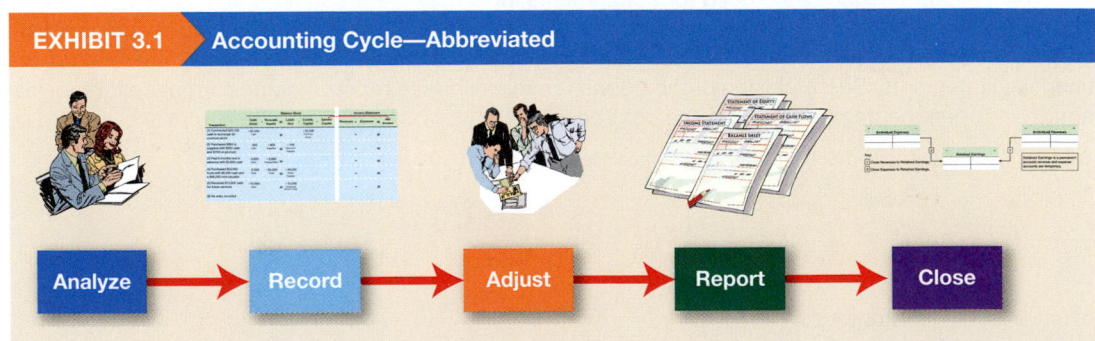

EXHIBIT 3.1   Accounting Cycle—Abbreviated

Analyze → Record → Adjust → Report → Close

The steps in the accounting cycle do not occur with equal frequency. That is, companies analyze and record daily transactions throughout the accounting period, but they adjust and report only when management requires financial statements, often monthly or quarterly, but at least annually. Closing occurs once during the accounting cycle, at the period-end.

The annual (one-year) accounting period adopted by a company is known as its **fiscal year**. Companies with fiscal year-ends on December 31 are said to be on a **calendar year**. About 60% of U.S. companies are on a calendar-year basis. Many companies prefer to have their accounting year coincide with their "natural" year; that is, the fiscal year ends when business is slow. For example,

L Brands, Inc., a specialty retailer, ends its fiscal year on the Saturday nearest January 31. **Starbucks Corporation** ends its fiscal year on the Sunday nearest to September 30. The **Manchester United Ltd.**, a professional soccer team, ends its fiscal year on June 30, during its off-season.

ANALYZING AND RECORDING TRANSACTIONS

The purpose of this section is to (1) review the analysis and recording of transactions as described in Chapter 2, and (2) to extend the Natural Beauty Supply example to illustrate the process of adjusting and closing accounts in the following sections. Natural Beauty Supply's fiscal year-end is December 31.

LO2 Review the process of journalizing and posting transactions.

Review of Accounting Procedures

The **chart of accounts** for Natural Beauty Supply is in **Exhibit 3.2**, and lists the titles and numbers of all accounts found in its general ledger. The account titles are grouped into the five major sections of the general ledger (assets, liabilities, equity, revenues, and expenses). We saw in Chapter 2 that the recording process involves analyzing, journalizing, and posting. The **general journal**, or *book of original entry*, is a tabular record where business activities are captured in debits and credits and recorded in chronological order before they are posted to the general ledger. The word *journalize* means to record a transaction in a **journal**. Each transaction entered in the journal must be stated in terms of equal dollar amounts of debits and credits—the double-entry system at work. The account titles cited must correspond to those in the general ledger (per the chart of accounts).

EXHIBIT 3.2	Chart of Accounts for Natural Beauty Supply

Assets	Equity
110 Cash	310 Common Stock
120 Accounts Receivable	320 Retained Earnings
130 Other Receivables	
140 Inventory	**Revenues and Income**
150 Prepaid Insurance	410 Sales Revenue
160 Security Deposit	420 Interest Income
170 Fixtures and Equipment	
175 Accumulated Depreciation—	**Expenses**
Fixtures and Equipment	510 Cost of Goods Sold
	520 Wages Expense
Liabilities	530 Rent Expense
210 Accounts Payable	540 Advertising Expense
220 Interest Payable	550 Depreciation Expense—
230 Wages Payable	Fixtures and Equipment
240 Taxes Payable	560 Insurance Expense
250 Unearned Revenue	570 Interest Expense
260 Notes Payable	580 Tax Expense

After transactions are journalized, the debits and credits in each journal entry are transferred to their related general ledger accounts. This transcribing process is called posting to the general ledger, or simply **posting**. Journalizing and posting occur simultaneously when recordkeeping is automated.

Review of Recording Transactions

In Chapter 2, we recorded the November activities of Natural Beauty Supply (NBS) and created the end-of-November financial statements. As NBS continues its activities into the next month, the end-of-November balance sheet provides the starting point for December. **Exhibit 3.3** provides a summary of Natural Beauty Supply's December 2015 transactions.

EXHIBIT 3.3		Transactions for Natural Beauty Supply for December 2015
Event	**Date**	**Description**
(17)	Dec. 1	NBS signed a three-year note to borrow $11,000 cash from a financial institution. NBS will pay interest on the first business day of every month (starting in January) at the rate of 12% per year or 1% per month. The $11,000 principal is due at the end of three years.
(18)	Dec. 1	NBS purchased and installed improved fixtures and equipment for $18,000 cash.
(19)	Dec. 10	NBS paid $700 to advertise in the local newspaper for December.
(20)	Dec. 20	NBS paid $3,300 cash to its suppliers in partial payment for the delivery of inventory in November.
(21)	Dec. —	During the month of December, NBS sold products costing $5,000 to retail customers for $8,500 cash.
(22)	Dec. —	During the month of December, sales to wholesale customers totaled $4,500 for merchandise that had cost $3,000. Instead of paying cash, wholesale customers are required to pay for the merchandise within ten business days.
(23)	Dec. —	$1,200 of gift certificates were sold during the month of December. Each gift certificate entitles the recipient to a one-hour consultation on the use of NBS' products.
(24)	Dec. —	NBS employed salespersons who were paid $1,625 in cash in December.
(25)	Dec. —	During the month of December, NBS received $3,200 in cash from wholesale customers for products that had been delivered earlier.
(26)	Dec. 28	NBS purchased and received $4,000 of inventory on account.
(27)	Dec. 31	NBS paid $1,500 to the landlord for December rent.
(28)	Dec. 31	NBS paid $50 cash dividend to its shareholders.

Most of these transactions are similar to those that we analyzed in Chapter 2. Each of the transactions involves an exchange of some kind. Suppliers provide inventory and employees provide labor services in exchange for cash or the promise of future cash payments. Customers receive products in exchange for cash or a promise to pay cash in the future. For each of these items, we analyze, journalize, and post as shown in Chapter 2.

NBS has the opportunity to secure long-term financing from a financial institution, and signs a note that must be paid back at the end of three years. Cash increases, and a noncurrent liability increases. Interest payments are made at the start of every month, beginning on January 2, 2016, but no entry is made for interest until time passes and an interest obligation is created.

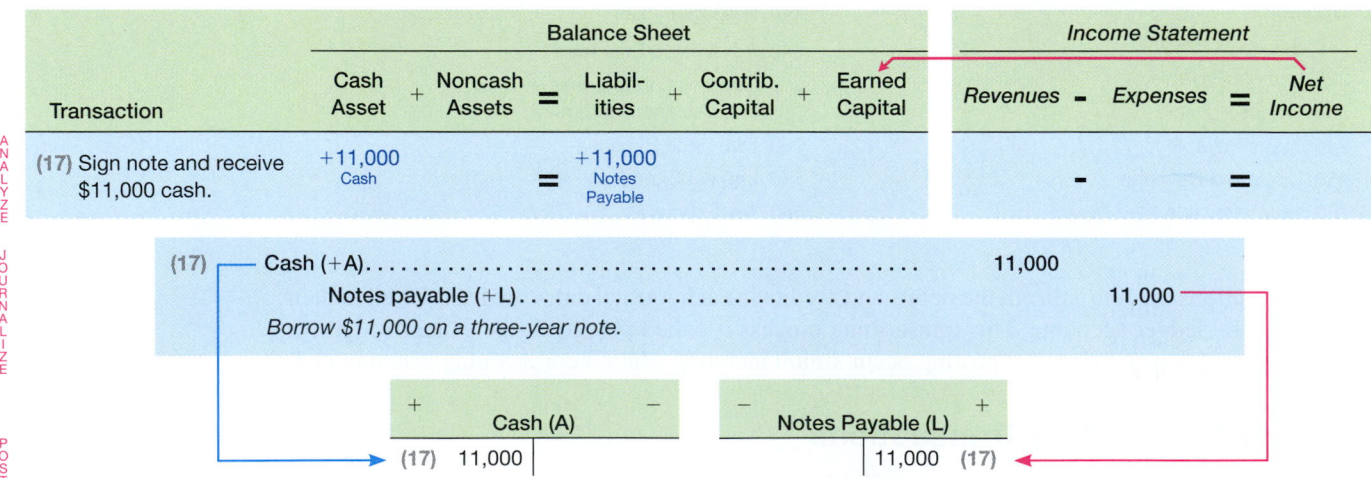

NBS pays $18,000 cash to purchase improved fixtures and equipment for its store location. One asset (cash) decreases, while a noncurrent asset (fixtures and equipment) is increased.

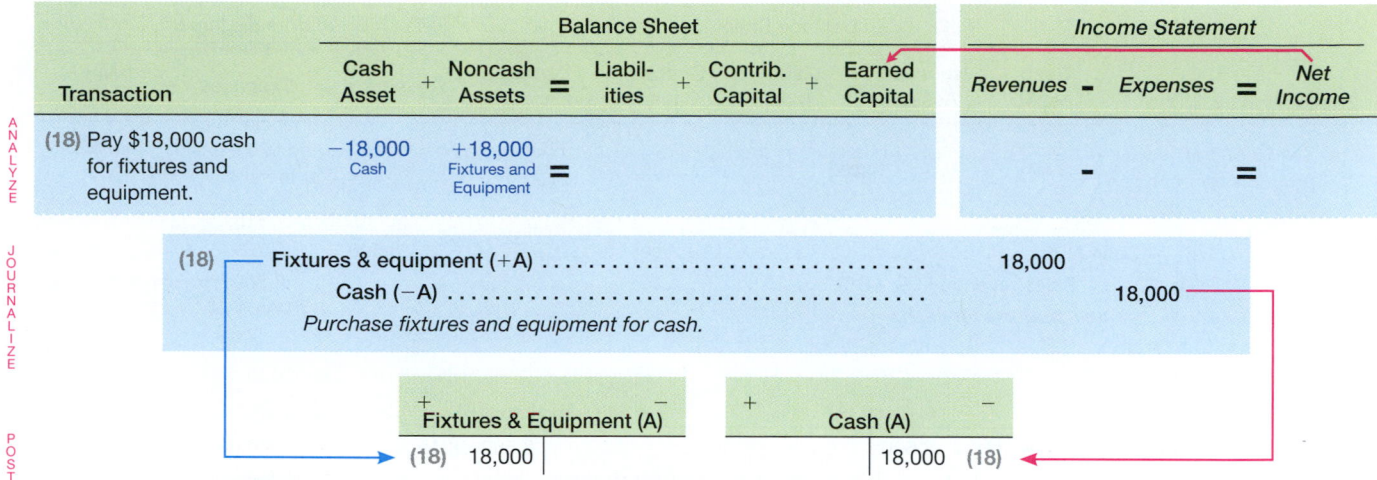

Transactions (19) and (20) are similar to ones that we saw in Chapter 2. The expenditure for advertising results in an expense that decreases net income and ultimately, retained earnings. The payment to suppliers fulfills (in part) an obligation that appeared in the November 30 balance sheet.

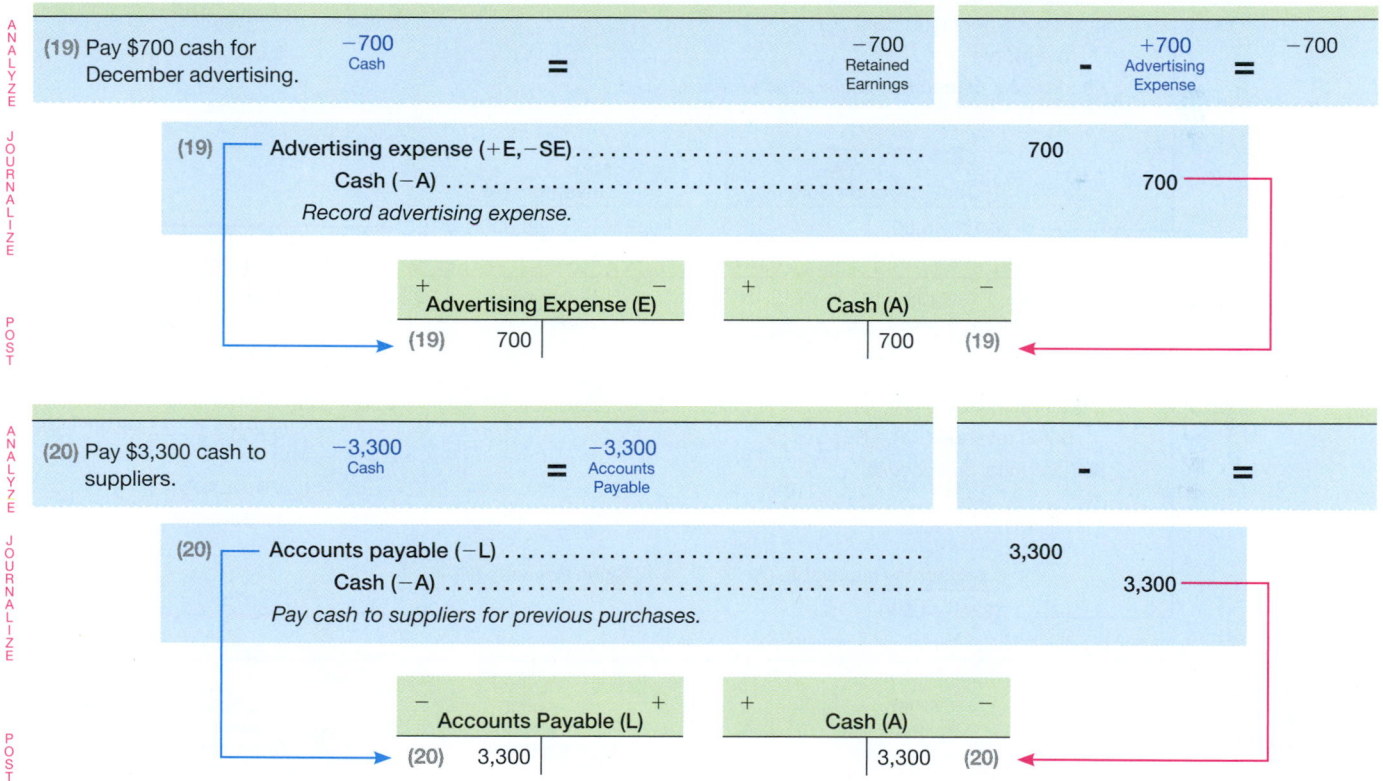

Sales to customers in (21), (22), and (23) are also similar to transactions in Chapter 2, and they are accounted for in similar fashion. Revenue is recognized when products are delivered to customers, rather than when cash is received. When cash is received after delivery, an accounts receivable asset is recognized; when cash is received before delivery, an unearned revenue liability is recognized. Cost of goods sold expense is recognized when the associated revenue is recognized.

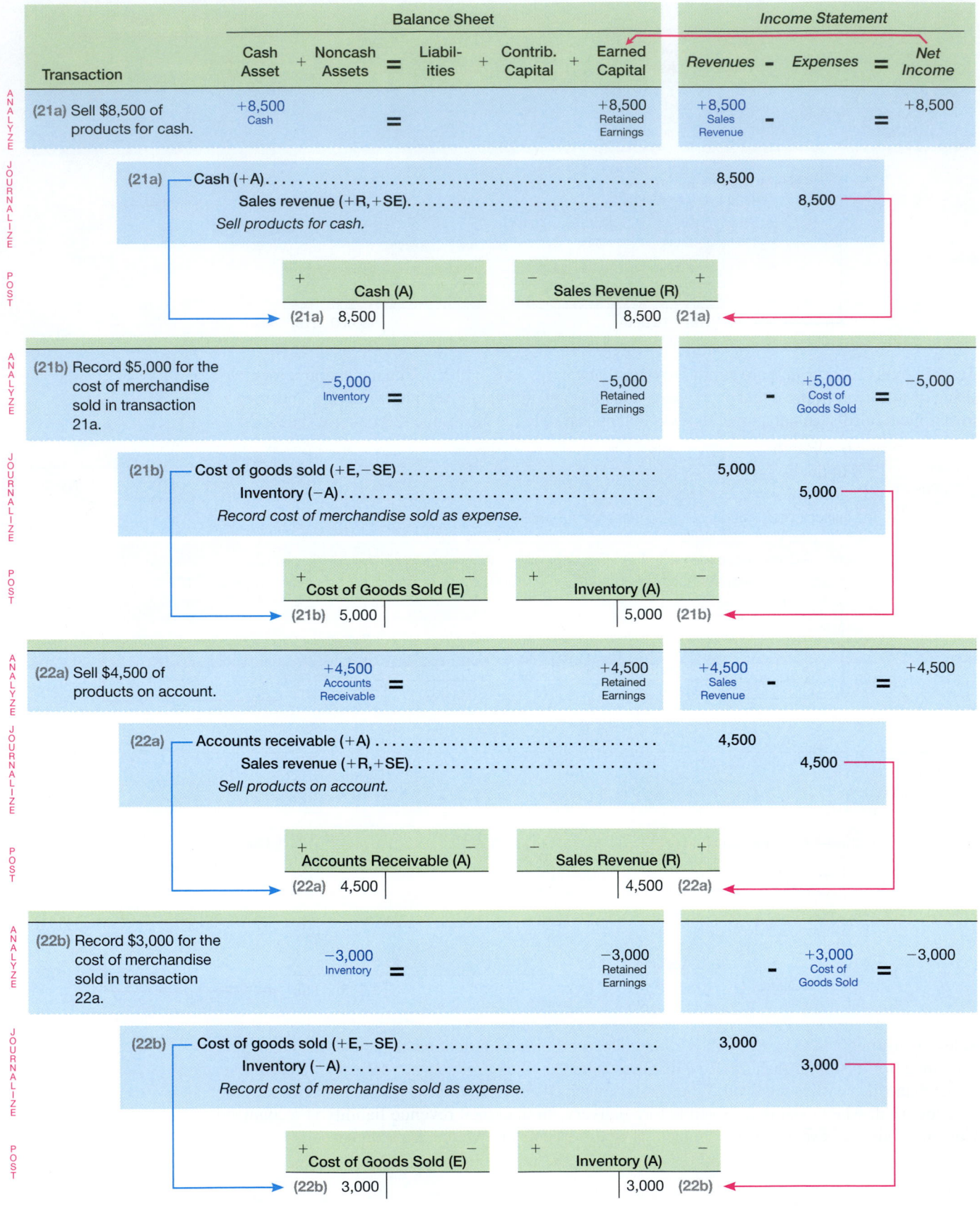

continued

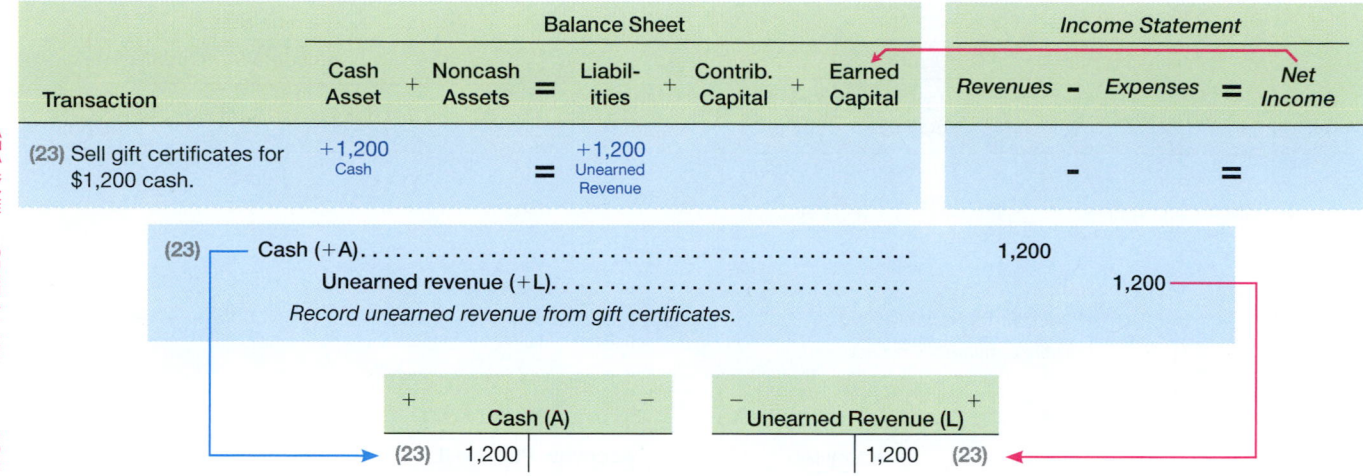

	Balance Sheet						Income Statement		
Transaction	Cash Asset	+ Noncash Assets	= Liabil- ities	+ Contrib. Capital	+ Earned Capital		Revenues	− Expenses	= Net Income
(23) Sell gift certificates for $1,200 cash.	+1,200 Cash		= +1,200 Unearned Revenue					−	=

(23)	Cash (+A)...	1,200	
	Unearned revenue (+L)..............................		1,200
	Record unearned revenue from gift certificates.		

+ Cash (A) −		− Unearned Revenue (L) +
(23) 1,200		1,200 (23)

The final five transactions in December also are similar to transactions that NBS had in November. Payment of wages to the employee is reflected in a wage expense. Cash received from wholesale (credit) customers does not cause revenue; rather the increase in cash is balanced by a decrease in accounts receivable. Purchase of inventory on account does not create an expense—the cost of the inventory is held in the inventory asset account until it is purchased by a customer. Payments to the landlord are balanced by a rent expense in the income statement. The cash dividend to shareholders decreases an asset (cash) and shareholders' equity (retained earnings), but does not affect the income statement.

	Balance Sheet						Income Statement		
Transaction	Cash Asset	+ Noncash Assets	= Liabil- ities	+ Contrib. Capital	+ Earned Capital		Revenues	− Expenses	= Net Income
(24) Record $1,625 in wages to employees.	−1,625 Cash		=		−1,625 Retained Earnings			− +1,625 Wages Expense	= −1,625

(24)	Wages expense (+E,−SE)...................................	1,625	
	Cash (−A)		1,625
	Pay wages to employees.		

+ Wages Expense (E) −		+ Cash (A) −
(24) 1,625		1,625 (24)

	Balance Sheet						Income Statement		
Transaction	Cash Asset	+ Noncash Assets	= Liabil- ities	+ Contrib. Capital	+ Earned Capital		Revenues	− Expenses	= Net Income
(25) Receive $3,200 cash from customers who purchased on credit.	+3,200 Cash	−3,200 Accounts Receivable	=					−	=

(25)	Cash (+A)...	3,200	
	Accounts receivable (−A)...........................		3,200
	Receive cash for products previously sold on account.		

+ Cash (A) −		+ Accounts Receivable (A) −
(25) 3,200		3,200 (25)

continued

continued from previous page

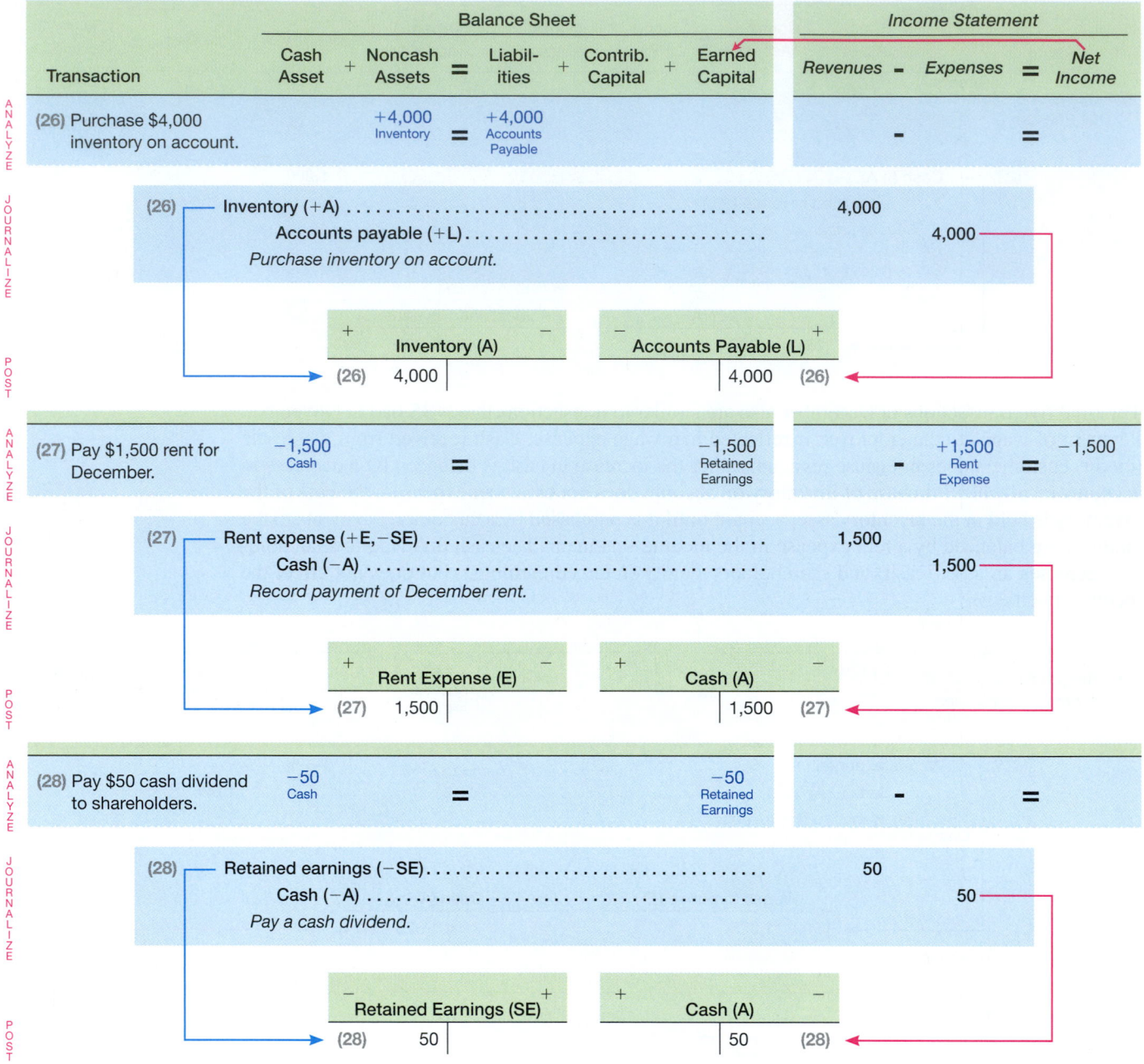

Exhibit 3.4 presents the general ledger accounts of Natural Beauty Supply in T-account form for December. Each balance sheet account has an opening balance equal to the end-of-November balance, and each income statement account starts with a zero balance so it records only the events of the current period. The December transactions (17–28) have been posted. We can trace each of the postings from the transactions above to these ledger accounts.

But the amounts in these accounts are not ready to be assembled into financial reports. There are revenues and expenses and changes in assets and liabilities that occur with the passage of time.[1] Accounting for these items is essential for us to determine how well a company has performed in an accounting period and to assess its financial standing.

---

[1] Natural Beauty Supply's November activities in Chapter 2 were carefully chosen so we could produce financial statements without adjusting entries. But, as **Exhibit 3.1** depicts, the adjusting process is an essential part of the accounting cycle.

EXHIBIT 3.4	General Ledger for Natural Beauty Supply before Adjustments

General Ledger

Assets		=	Liabilities		+	Equity	

Assets

+ Cash (A) −

Beg. bal.	8,100		
(17)	11,000	18,000	(18)
(21a)	8,500	700	(19)
(23)	1,200	3,300	(20)
(25)	3,200	1,625	(24)
		1,500	(27)
		50	(28)
Unadj. bal.	6,825		

+ Accounts Receivable (A) −

Beg. bal.	950		
(22a)	4,500	3,200	(25)
Unadj. bal.	2,250		

+ Inventory (A) −

Beg. bal.	11,300		
(26)	4,000	5,000	(21b)
		3,000	(22b)
Unadj. bal.	7,300		

+ Prepaid Insurance (A) −

Beg. bal.	1,680		
Unadj. bal.	1,680		

+ Security Deposit (A) −

Beg. bal.	2,000		
Unadj. bal.	2,000		

+ Fixtures and Equipment (A) −

Beg. bal.	0		
(18)	18,000		
Unadj. bal.	18,000		

Liabilities

− Accounts Payable (L) +

		3,700	Beg. bal.
(20)	3,300	4,000	(26)
		4,400	Unadj. bal.

− Unearned Revenue (L) +

		300	Beg. bal.
		1,200	(23)
		1,500	Unadj. bal.

− Notes Payable (L) +

		0	Beg. bal.
		11,000	(17)
		11,000	Unadj. bal.

Equity

− Common Stock (SE) +

		20,000	Beg. bal.
		20,000	Unadj. bal.

− Retained Earnings (SE) +

		30	Beg. bal.
(28)	50		
Unadj. bal.	20		

− Sales Revenue (R) +

		0	Beg. bal.
		8,500	(21a)
		4,500	(22a)
		13,000	Unadj. bal.

+ Cost of Goods Sold (E) −

Beg. bal.	0		
(21b)	5,000		
(22b)	3,000		
Unadj. bal.	8,000		

+ Wages Expense (E) −

Beg. bal.	0		
(24)	1,625		
Unadj. bal.	1,625		

+ Rent Expense (E) −

Beg. bal.	0		
(27)	1,500		
Unadj. bal.	1,500		

+ Advertising Expense (E) −

Beg. bal.	0		
(19)	700		
Unadj. bal.	700		

Assets = $38,055	=	Liabilities = $16,900	+	Equity = $21,155

ADJUSTING THE ACCOUNTS

It is important that accounts in financial statements be properly reported. For many accounts, the balances shown in the general ledger after all transactions are posted are not the proper balances for financial statements. So, when it is time to prepare financial statements, management must review account balances and make proper adjustments to these balances. The adjustments required are based on accrual accounting and generally accepted accounting principles. This section focuses on this adjustment process.

LO3 Describe the adjusting process and illustrate adjusting entries.

3

Preparing an Unadjusted Trial Balance

The T-accounts in **Exhibit 3.4** show balances for each account after recording all transactions. This set of balances is called an **unadjusted trial balance** because it shows account balances before any adjustments are made. The purpose of an unadjusted trial balance is to be sure the general ledger is in balance before management adjusts the accounts. Showing all general ledger account balances in one place also makes it easier to review accounts and determine which account balances require adjusting. Natural Beauty Supply's unadjusted trial balance at December 31 is shown in **Exhibit 3.5**.

EXHIBIT 3.5	Unadjusted Trial Balance		
NATURAL BEAUTY SUPPLY			
Unadjusted Trial Balance			
December 31, 2015			
		Debit	**Credit**
Cash		$ 6,825	
Accounts receivable		2,250	
Inventory		7,300	
Prepaid insurance		1,680	
Security deposit		2,000	
Fixtures & equipment		18,000	
Accounts payable			$ 4,400
Unearned revenue			1,500
Notes payable			11,000
Common stock			20,000
Retained earnings		20	
Sales revenue			13,000
Cost of goods sold		8,000	
Wages expense		1,625	
Rent expense		1,500	
Advertising expense		700	
Totals		$49,900	$49,900

Types of Adjustments

Accrual adjustments are caused by a variety of accounting practices. There are some revenues and expenses that arise with the passage of time, rather than in a transaction. There are asset and liability values that change over time or that require estimation based on recent events. All of these require adjustments before proper financial statements can be produced.

Adjusting entries have two common characteristics. First, they occur at the end of a reporting period, just before the construction of financial statements. Second, they (almost) never involve cash. Changes in cash require a transaction, and adjusting entries are not transactions.

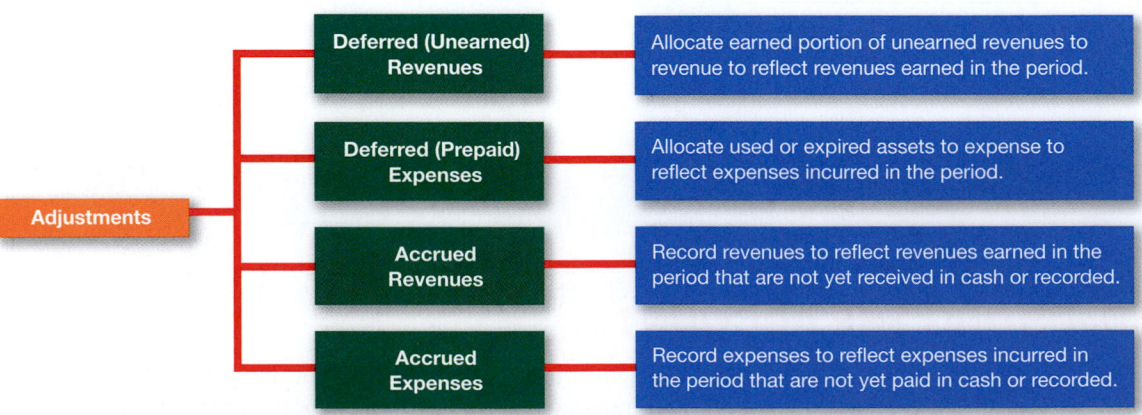

Through the course of this book, we will encounter quite a few required adjusting entries, but we will start with four general types of adjustments made at the end of an accounting period.

Journal entries made to reflect these adjustments are known as **adjusting entries**. Each adjusting entry usually affects a balance sheet account (an asset or liability account) and an income statement account (an expense or revenue account). The first two types of adjustments—allocating assets to expense and allocating unearned revenues to revenue—are often referred to as **deferrals**. The distinguishing characteristic of a deferral is that the adjustment deals with an amount previously recorded in a balance sheet account; the adjusting entry decreases the balance sheet account and increases an income statement account. The last two types of adjustments—accruing expenses and accruing revenues—are often referred to as **accruals**. The unique characteristic of an accrual is that the adjustment deals with an amount not previously recorded in any account; this type of adjusting entry increases both a balance sheet account and an income statement account. Both accruals and deferrals allow revenue to be recognized when it is earned and the expenses of the period to reflect asset decreases and liability increases from generating revenues or supporting that period's operations. Let's consider each of these adjustments in more detail.

Type 1: Deferred Revenue—Allocating Unearned Revenue to Revenue

Companies often receive fees for products or services before those products or services are rendered. Such transactions are recorded by debiting Cash and crediting a liability account for the **unearned revenue**—also referred to as **deferred revenue**. This account reflects the obligation for performing future services or delivering a product in the future. As services are performed or the product delivered, revenue is earned. At period-end, an adjusting entry records the revenue that was earned in the current accounting period and the liability amount that was reduced.

DEFERRED REVENUE   During November and December, Natural Beauty Supply sold gift certificates that entitled the recipient to a one-hour consultation with a salesperson on the use of natural and organic health and beauty products. When the gift certificates were purchased, NBS recognized an unearned revenue liability that reflected the obligation to provide these services. During the month of December, gift certificates totaling $900 were redeemed. On December 31, Natural Beauty Supply made the adjustment (a) in the following template, journal entry, and T-accounts to recognize the (partial) fulfillment of the obligation and to recognize the $900 of revenue to which it is now entitled. The $900 increase in sales revenue is reflected in net income and carried over to retained earnings.

> **FYI**   Chapter 2 explained that revenue recognition is key to determining net income under accrual accounting, which recognizes revenues when services are performed or when goods are sold and recognizes expenses in the period that they help to generate the recorded revenues.

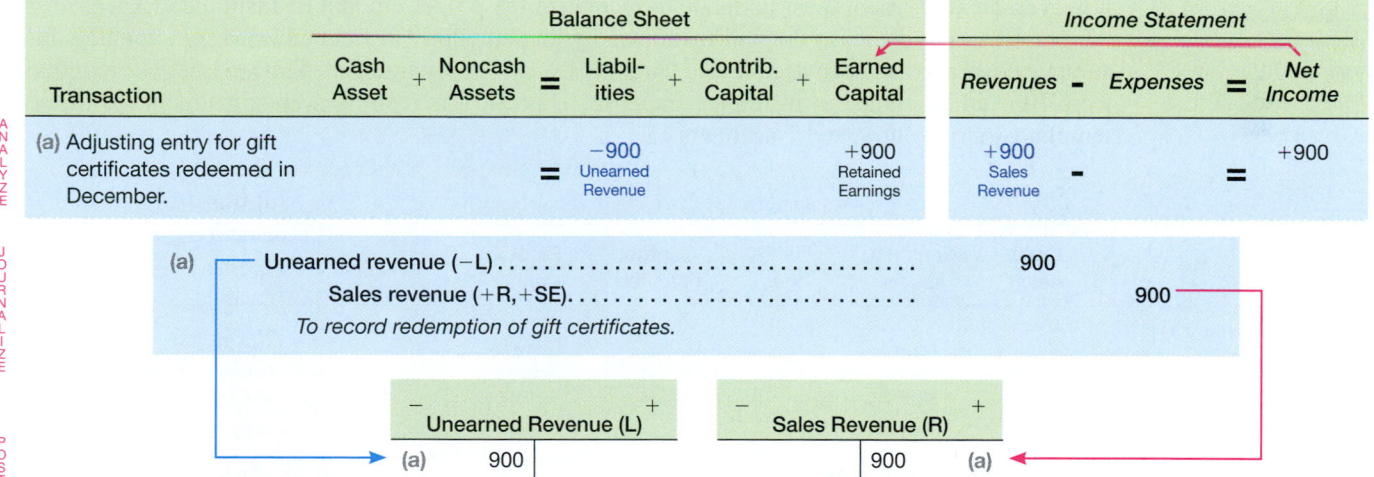

After this entry (a) is posted, the Unearned Revenue liability account has a balance of $600 for the remaining gift certificates outstanding, and the Sales Revenue account reflects the $900 earned in December.

In this case, the cost of the salesperson's time has already been recognized as an expense. If Natural Beauty Supply's gift certificates had been redeemable for products, then we would have recognized a Cost of Goods Sold expense for the items purchased with the redeemed certificates.

Other examples of revenues received in advance include gift cards, rental payments received in advance by real estate management companies, insurance premiums received in advance by insurance companies, subscription revenues received in advance by magazine and newspaper publishers, and membership fees received in advance by health clubs. In each case, a liability account is set up when the advance payment is received. Later, an adjusting entry is made to reflect the revenues earned from the services provided or products delivered during the period.

YOU MAKE THE CALL

You are the Chief Accountant   REI requires customers of its travel-vacation business to make an initial deposit equal to $400 when the trip is reserved and to make full payment two months before departure. REI's refunding policy is to return the entire deposit if the customer informs REI of the trip's cancellation three or more months in advance of the trip. REI will refund all but $400 of the deposit if the customer cancels between 60 and 90 days prior to the trip or 50% of the deposit if a customer cancels between 30 and 60 days prior to the trip. There is no refund if notification occurs within 30 days of the trip. REI's cancellation rate is very low. How should you account for deposits, and when should revenue be recorded? [Answers on page 128]

Type 2: Prepaid Expenses—Allocating Assets to Expenses   Many cash outlays benefit several accounting periods. Examples are purchases of buildings, equipment, and supplies; prepayments of rent and advertising; and payments of insurance premiums covering several periods. These outlays are added to (debited to) an asset account when the expenditure occurs. Then at the end of each accounting period, the estimated portion of the outlay that has expired in that period or has benefited that period, is transferred to an expense account.

We can usually see when adjustments of this type are needed by inspecting the unadjusted trial balance for costs that benefit several periods. Looking at the December 31 trial balance of Natural Beauty Supply (**Exhibit 3.5**), for example, adjustments are required to record the costs of prepaid insurance and the fixtures and equipment for the month of December.

PREPAID INSURANCE   On November 30, Natural Beauty Supply paid one year's insurance premium in advance and debited the $1,680 payment to Prepaid Insurance, an asset account. As each day passes and the insurance coverage is being used, insurance expense is being incurred, and the Prepaid Insurance asset is decreasing. It is not necessary to record insurance expense on a daily basis because financial statements are not prepared daily. At the end of an accounting period, however, an adjustment must be made to recognize the proper amount of Insurance Expense for the period and to decrease Prepaid Insurance by that amount. On December 31, one month's insurance coverage has been used up, so Natural Beauty Supply transfers $140 ($1,680/12 months) from Prepaid Insurance to Insurance Expense. This entry is identified as adjustment (b) in the template, journal entry, and T-accounts.

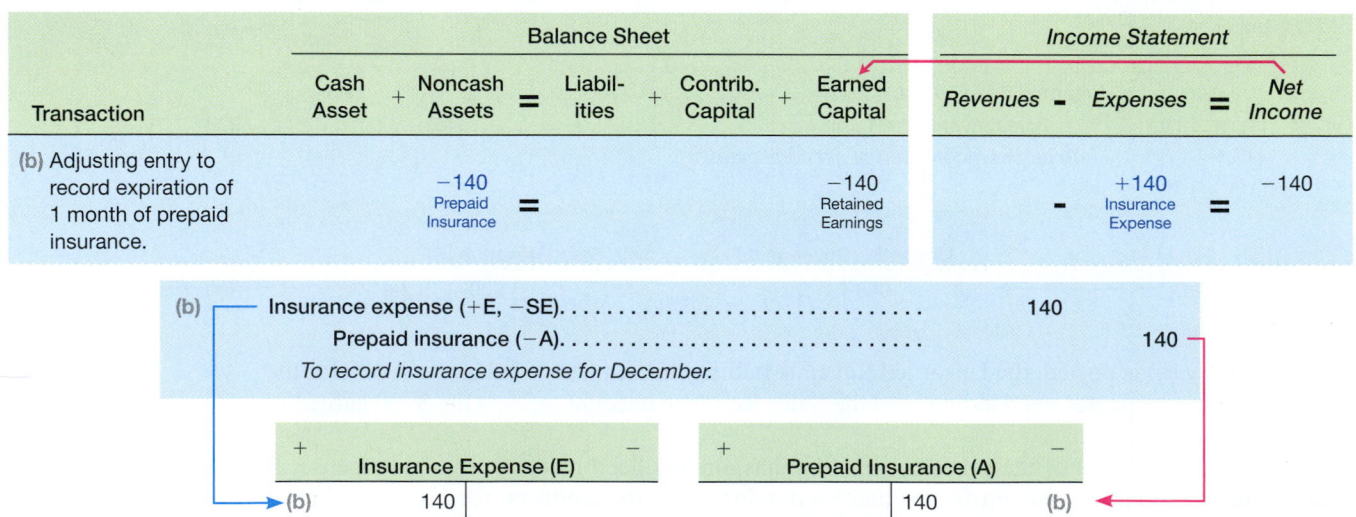

The posting of this adjusting entry creates the proper Insurance Expense of $140 for December in the Insurance Expense ledger account and reduces the Prepaid Insurance balance to the (eleven-month) amount that is prepaid as of December 31, which is $1,540.

Examples of other prepaid expenses for which similar adjustments are made include prepaid rent and prepaid advertising. When rent payments are made in advance, the amount is added to (debited to) a Prepaid Rent asset. At the end of an accounting period, an adjusting entry is made to record the portion of occupancy or usage that expired during the period. Rent Expense is debited (increased) and Prepaid Rent is credited (decreased). Similarly, when advertising services are purchased in advance, the payment is debited to Prepaid Advertising. At the end of an accounting period, an adjustment is needed to recognize the cost of any of the prepaid advertising used during the period. The adjusting entry debits (increases) Advertising Expense and credits (decreases) Prepaid Advertising.

DEPRECIATION   The process of allocating the costs of equipment, vehicles, and buildings to the periods benefiting from their use is called **depreciation**. Each accounting period in which such assets are used must reflect a portion of their cost as expense because these assets helped generate revenue or support operations for those periods. This periodic expense is known as *depreciation expense*. Periodic depreciation expense is an estimate. The procedure we use here estimates the annual amount of depreciation expense by dividing the asset cost by its estimated useful life. (We assume that the entire asset cost is depreciated—so-called zero salvage value; later in the book we consider salvage values other than zero.) This method is called **straight-line depreciation** and is used by the great majority of companies in their financial reports.

Expenses are recorded when business activities reduce net assets. But when we record depreciation expense, the asset amount is not reduced directly. Instead, the reduction is recorded in a **contra asset** account (labeled XA in the journal entries and T-accounts) called *Accumulated Depreciation*. **Contra accounts** are so named because they are used to record reductions in or offsets against a related account. The Accumulated Depreciation account normally has a credit balance and appears in the balance sheet as a deduction from the related asset amount. Use of the *contra asset* Accumulated Depreciation allows the original cost of the asset to be reported in the balance sheet, followed (and reduced) by the accumulated depreciation. Let's consider an example.

The fixtures and equipment purchased by Natural Beauty Supply for $18,000 are expected to last for four years. Straight-line depreciation recorded on the equipment is $4,500 per year ($18,000/4 years), or $375 per month ($18,000/48 months). At December 31, Natural Beauty Supply makes adjustment (c), as shown in the following template, journal entry, and T-accounts.

The introduction of contra assets requires a new column in the FSET for these accounts.[2] Increases in a contra asset decrease the net balance of the company's long-term assets. The new column is preceded by a minus sign to indicate that increases in contra assets create a decrease in the asset side of the accounting equation.

> **FYI**   Contra accounts are used to provide more information to users of financial statements. For example, Accumulated Depreciation is a contra asset reported in the balance sheet, which enables users to estimate asset age. For Natural Beauty Supply, the December 31 balance sheet reveals that its Fixtures and Equipment is nearly new as its accumulated depreciation is only $375, which is 1/48th of the $18,000 original cost.

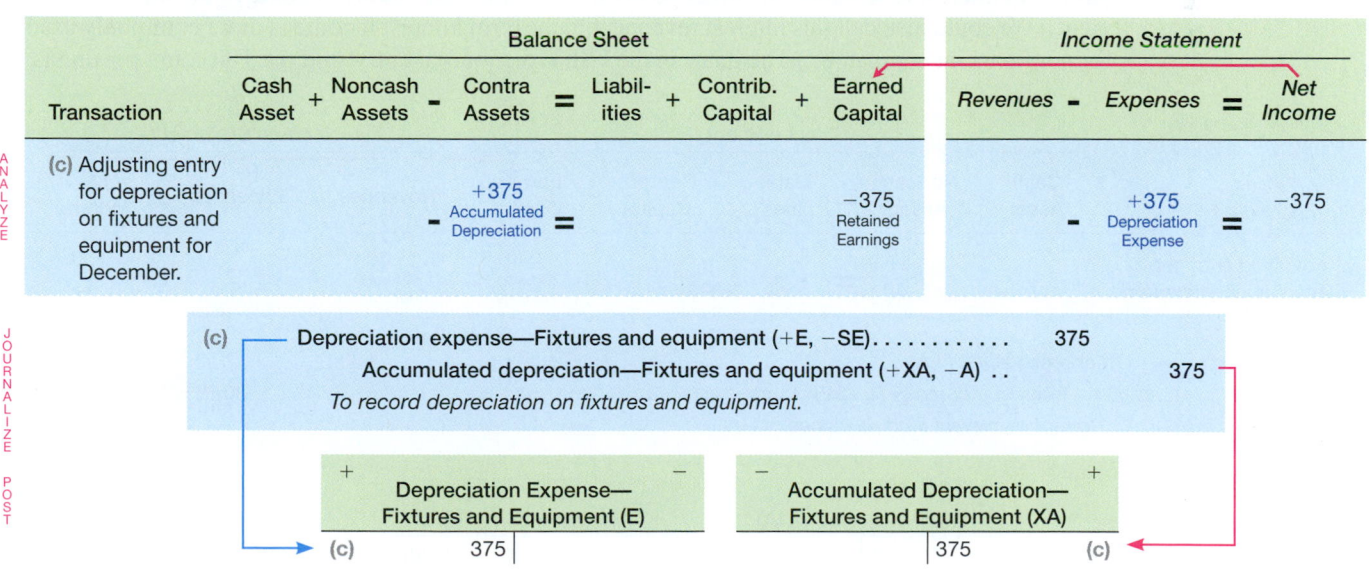

---

[2] Our practice is to include a separate FSET column where contra assets are required, but not to do so all the time. As we progress through the topics in this text, we will also see examples of contra liability accounts and contra equity accounts.

When this entry is posted, it properly reflects the cost of using this asset during December, and the $375 depreciation expense appears in the December income statement. On the balance sheet, the accumulated depreciation is an offset to the asset amount. The resulting balance (cost less accumulated depreciation), which is the asset's **book value**, represents the unexpired asset cost to be allocated as an expense in future periods. For example, the December 31, 2015, balance sheet reports the equipment with a book value of $17,625, as follows.

FYI An increase in the contra asset account Accumulated Depreciation reduces the book value of the asset.

Fixtures and equipment	$18,000
Less: Accumulated depreciation	375
Fixtures and equipment, net.	$17,625 (book value)

In each subsequent month, $375 is recognized as depreciation expense, and the Accumulated Depreciation contra asset is increased by the same amount (from $375 to $750 to $1,125 and so on). As a result, the book value of the fixtures and equipment is decreased by $375 each month. In Chapter 8, we will see the same principles applied to certain intangible assets.

Type 3: Accrued Revenues

Revenue should be recognized when the company has transferred goods or services to customers, and in an amount that reflects the amount to which the company expects to be entitled from the transfer. Yet, a company often provides services or earns income during a period that is neither paid for by clients or customers nor billed before the end of the period. Such values should be included in the firm's current period income statement, reflecting the company's fulfillment of its agreement with the customer. To properly account for such situations, end-of-period adjusting entries are made to reflect any revenues or income earned, but not yet billed or received. Such accumulated revenue is often called **accrued revenue** or **accrued income**.

ACCRUED SALES REVENUE/INCOME   At the end of December, Natural Beauty Supply learns that its bank has decided to provide interest on checking accounts for small businesses like NBS. Each month, NBS earns interest income based on the average balance in its checking account. The interest is paid into NBS's checking account on the fifth business day of the following month. Based on its average daily balance, NBS earned $30 in interest during December.

In this instance, Natural Beauty Supply does not receive the interest payment until January. Nevertheless, the company earned interest during the month of December. Therefore, it should recognize an interest receivable (or "other receivables") asset and interest income in the income statement. (We could also call this interest revenue, but the term interest income is more commonly used for nonfinancial companies.) The entry in the FSET, the journal entry, and the T-account posting is:

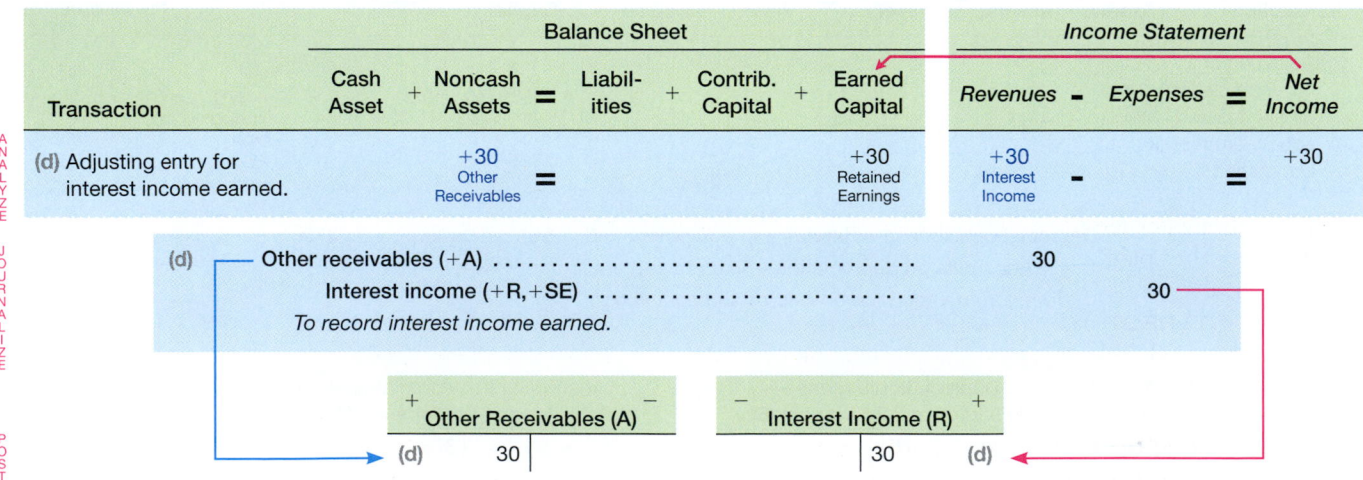

Revenue accruals also occur for landlords who receive rent payments after they are earned. In these cases, revenue has been earned over time as the customer receives and consumes the benefits of the services provided on a continuous basis. We look into these issues more closely in Chapter 6.

Type 4: Accrued Expenses

Companies often incur expenses before paying for them. Wages, interest, utilities, and taxes are examples of expenses that are incurred before cash payment is made. Usually the payments are made at regular intervals of time, such as weekly, monthly, quarterly, or annually. If the accounting period ends on a date that does not coincide with a scheduled cash payment date, an adjusting entry is required to reflect the expense incurred since the last cash payment. Such an expense is referred to as an **accrued expense**. Natural Beauty Supply has three such required adjustments for December 31; one for wages, one for interest and one for income tax.

ACCRUED WAGES Natural Beauty Supply employees are paid on a weekly basis. Recall that wages of $1,625 were paid during December in transaction 24. However, as of December 31, the company's employees have earned wages of $480 that will be paid in January. Wages expense of $480 must be recorded in the income statement for December because there is now an obligation to compensate employees, who helped generate revenues for December.

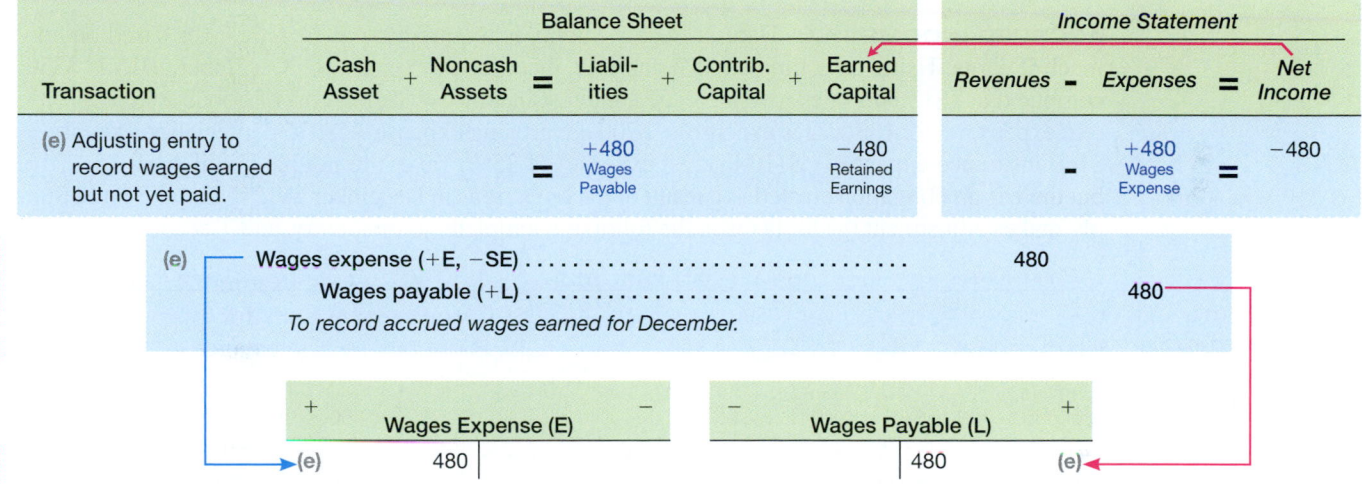

This adjustment enables the firm to reflect as December expense the cost of all wages *incurred* during the month rather than just the wages *paid*. In addition, the balance sheet shows the liability for unpaid wages at the end of the period.

When the employees are paid in January, the following entry is made.

Jan.	Wages payable (−L)	480	
	Cash (−A)		480

This entry eliminates the liability recorded in Wages Payable at the end of December and reduces Cash for the wages paid.

ACCRUED INTEREST On December 1, 2015, Natural Beauty Supply signed a three-year note payable for $11,000. This note has a 12% annual interest rate and requires monthly (interest-only) payments (1% per month), payable on the first business day of the following month. (The interest payment for the month of December is due on January 2.) The $11,000 principal on the note is due at the end of three years. An adjusting entry is required at December 31, 2015, to record interest expense for December and to recognize a liability. December's interest is $110 [$11,000 × (12%/12 months)], and at December 31, NBS makes adjustment (f) in the following template, journal entry, and T-accounts.

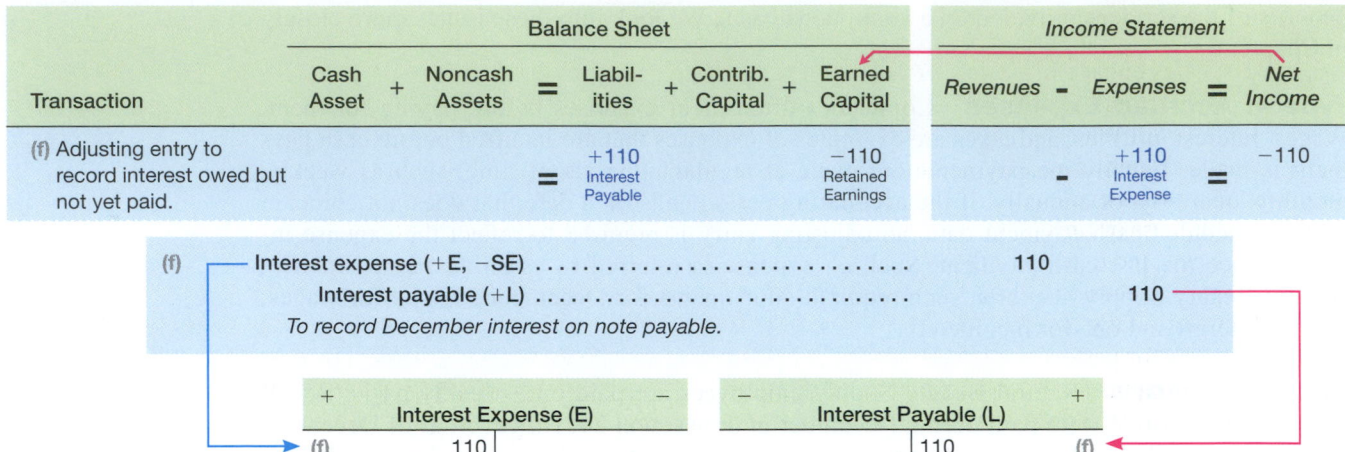

When these entries are posted to the general ledger, the accounts show the correct interest expense for December and the interest liability for one month's interest on the note that has accrued by December 31.

ACCRUED INCOME TAX   Natural Beauty Supply is required to pay income taxes based on how much it earns. Using an estimated 35% tax rate, income tax expense for December 2015 is $350, computed as ($13,900 sales revenue + $30 interest income − $8,000 cost of goods sold − $1,500 rent expense − $2,105 wages expense − $700 advertising expense − $375 depreciation expense − $140 insurance expense − $110 interest expense) × 35%. Taxes are not paid until April 15, 2016, but there is an obligation created as a result of the operations in December 2015. Natural Beauty Supply makes adjustment (g) for taxes in the following template, journal entry, and T-accounts.

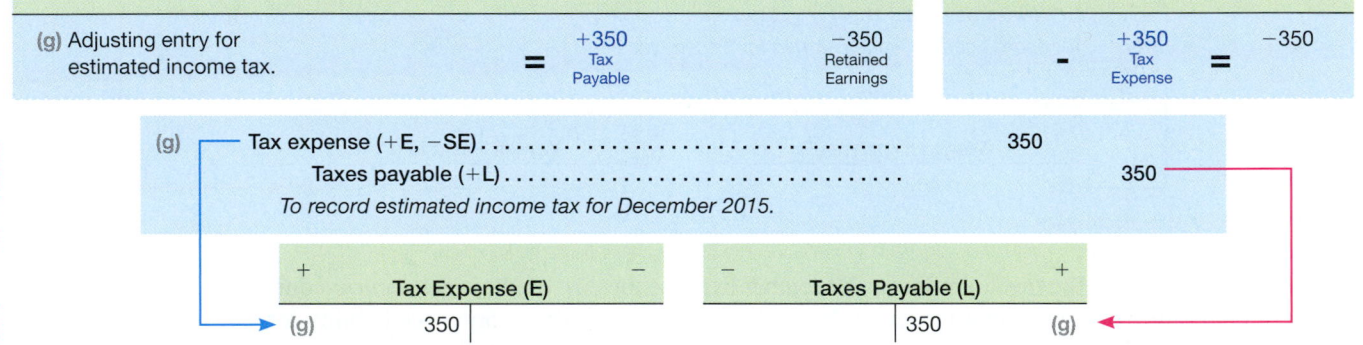

Exhibit 3.6 summarizes the four types of accounting adjustments, the usual journal entries required for each, and their financial impacts on the balance sheet and income statements.

EXHIBIT 3.6	Summary of Accounting Adjustments				
				Financial Effects if *Not* Adjusted	
Accounting Adjustment	Examples	Adjusting Entry		Balance Sheet	Income Statement
Deferrals: Unearned revenues	Delivery on advances from clients, gift cards, and subscribers	Dr. Liability Cr. Revenue		Liability overstated Equity understated	Revenue understated
Prepaid expenses	Expiration of prepaid rent, insurance, and advertising; depreciation of buildings and equipment	Dr. Expense Cr. Asset (or Contra asset)		Asset overstated Equity overstated	Expense understated
Accruals: Accrued revenues	Earned but not received service, sales, and interest revenues	Dr. Asset Cr. Revenue		Asset understated Equity understated	Revenue understated
Accrued expenses	Incurred but unpaid wages, interest, and tax expenses	Dr. Expense Cr. Liability		Liabilty understated Equity overstated	Expense understated

Ethics and Adjusting Entries

When companies engage in transactions, there is some evidence of the exchange. Cash increases or decreases; asset and liability levels change. Adjusting entries are much more dependent on estimation processes. What was the value of service provided to customers? What obligations have arisen in the past period without a transaction? What is their value? What is the expected useful life of our depreciable assets?

The usefulness of financial performance measures such as net income depends on these questions being answered to the best of management's ability. However, there often are pressures not to provide the most accurate information. For instance, an estimate might convey information about management's strategy that could be used by competitors. Or, the financial community may have set expectations for performance that management cannot meet by executing its current business plan. In these circumstances, managers are sometimes pressured to use the discretion inherent in the reporting process to meet analysts' expectations or to disguise a planned course of action.

The financial reporting environment described in Chapter 1 imposes significant controls on financial reporting, because that reporting process is important to the health of the economy. Managers who do not report accurately and completely are potentially subject to severe penalties. Moreover, adjusting entry estimates have a "self-correcting" character. Underestimating expenses today means greater expenses tomorrow; overestimating revenues today means lower revenues tomorrow.

MID-CHAPTER REVIEW

The following transactions relate to Lundholm Transport Company.

a. The Supplies and Parts balance on September 30, 2015, the company's accounting year-end, reveals $100,000 available. This amount reflects its beginning-year balance and all purchases for the year. A physical inventory indicates that much of this balance has been used in service operations, leaving supplies valued at $9,000 remaining at year-end September 30, 2015.

b. A $5,000 bill for September and October rent on the warehouse was received on September 29, but has not yet been paid or recorded.

c. A building holding its offices was purchased for $400,000 five years ago. The building's life was estimated at 8 years. Assume the entire asset cost is depreciated over its useful life. No depreciation has been recorded for this fiscal year.

d. An executive was hired on September 15 with a $120,000 annual salary. Payment and work are to start on October 15. No entry has yet been made to record this event.

e. A services contract is signed with the local university on September 1. Lundholm Transport Company received $1,200 cash on September 1 as a retainer for the months of September and October, but it has not yet been recorded. Lundholm Transport Company retains the money whether the university requires its services or not.

f. Employees are paid on the first day of the month following the month in which work is performed. Wages earned in September, but not yet paid or recorded as of September 30, amount to $25,000.

Lundholm Transport's ledger includes the following ledger accounts and unadjusted normal balances at September 30: Cash $80,000; Accounts Receivable $95,000; Supplies and Parts $100,000; Building $400,000; Accumulated Depreciation—Building $200,000; Land $257,500; Accounts Payable $20,000; Wages Payable $0; Unearned Revenue $0; Common Stock $80,000; Retained Earnings $380,000; Services Revenue $720,000; Rent Expense $27,500; Depreciation Expense $0; Wages Expense $440,000; Supplies and Parts Expense $0.

Required

1. For each of the six items described above, enter their effects in the financial statement effects template.
2. For each of the six items described above, enter their effects in journal entry form.
3. Set up T-accounts for all ledger accounts and enter the beginning unadjusted balance, the adjustments from part 2, and the adjusted ending balance.

The solution to this review problem can be found on pages 147–149.

4

LO4 Prepare financial statements from adjusted accounts.

CONSTRUCTING FINANCIAL STATEMENTS FROM ADJUSTED ACCOUNTS

This section explains the preparation of financial statements from the adjusted financial accounts.

Preparing an Adjusted Trial Balance

After adjustments are recorded and posted, the company prepares an adjusted trial balance. The **adjusted trial balance** lists all the general ledger account balances after adjustments. Much of the content for company financial statements is taken from an adjusted trial balance. **Exhibit 3.7** shows the general ledger accounts for Natural Beauty Supply after adjustments, in T-account form.

The adjusted trial balance at December 31 for Natural Beauty Supply is prepared from its general ledger accounts and is in the right-hand two columns of **Exhibit 3.8**. We show the unadjusted balances along with the adjustments to highlight the adjustment process.

Preparing Financial Statements

A company prepares its financial statements from the adjusted trial balance (and sometimes other supporting information). The set of financial statements consists of (and is prepared in the order of) the income statement, statement of stockholders' equity, balance sheet, and statement of cash flows. The following diagram summarizes this process.

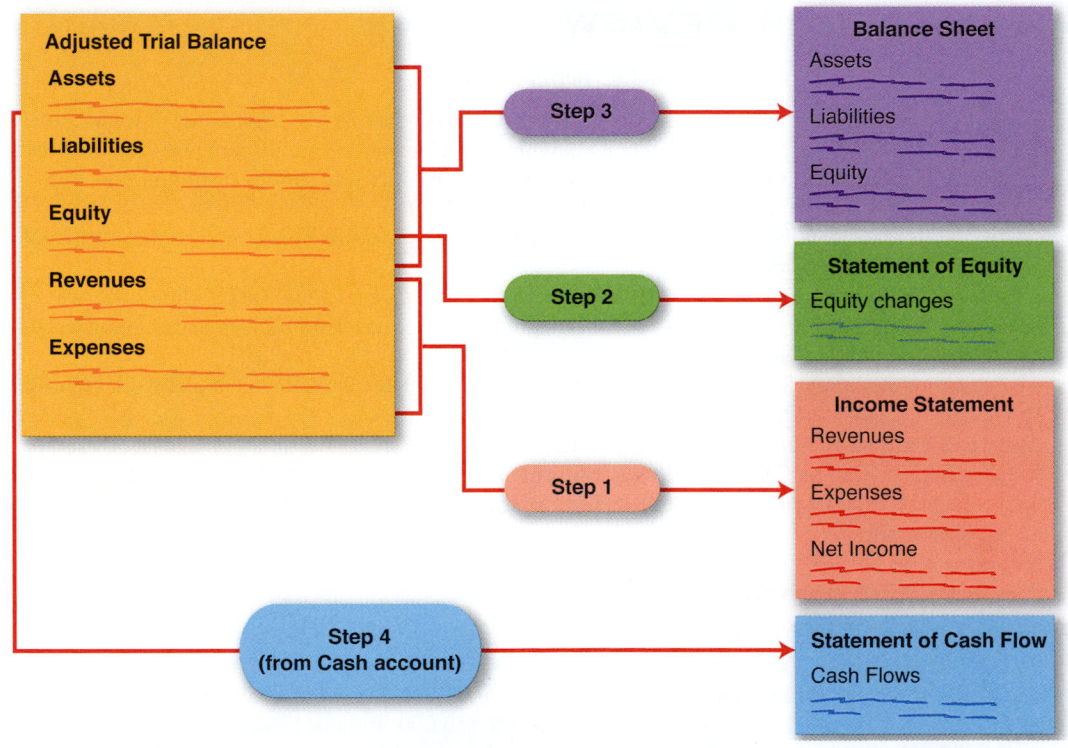

Income Statement   The income statement reports a company's revenues and expenses. Natural Beauty Supply's adjusted trial balance contains two revenue/income accounts and eight expense accounts. The revenues and expenses are reported in Natural Beauty Supply's income statement for December as shown in **Exhibit 3.9**. Its net income for December is $650.

EXHIBIT 3.7 General Ledger for Natural Beauty Supply after Adjustments

General Ledger

Assets	=	Liabilities	+	Equity

Assets

+	Cash (A)		−
Beg. bal.	8,100		
(17)	11,000	18,000	(18)
(21a)	8,500	700	(19)
(23)	1,200	3,300	(20)
(25)	3,200	1,625	(24)
		1,500	(27)
		50	(28)
Adj. bal.	6,825		

+	Accounts Receivable (A)		−
Beg. bal.			
950		3,200	(25)
(22a)	4,500		
Adj. bal.	2,250		

+	Other Receivables (A)		−
Beg. bal.	0		
(d)	30		
Adj. bal.	30		

+	Inventory (A)		−
Beg. bal.	11,300		
(26)	4,000	5,000	(21b)
		3,000	(22b)
Adj. bal.	7,300		

+	Prepaid Insurance (A)		−
Beg. bal.	1,680		
		140	(b)
Adj. bal.	1,540		

+	Security Deposit (A)		−
Beg. bal.	2,000		
Adj. bal.	2,000		

+	Fixtures and Equipment (A)		−
Beg. bal.	0		
(18)	18,000		
Adj. bal.	18,000		

−	Accumulated Depreciation— Fixtures and Equipment (XA)		+
		0	Beg. bal.
	375		(c)
		375	Adj. bal.

Liabilities

−	Accounts Payable (L)		+
		3,700	Beg. bal.
(20)	3,300	4,000	(26)
		4,400	Adj. bal.

−	Interest Payable (L)		+
		0	Beg. bal.
		110	(f)
		110	Adj. bal.

−	Wages Payable (L)		+
		0	Beg. bal.
		480	(e)
		480	Adj. bal.

−	Taxes Payable (L)		+
		0	Beg. bal.
		350	(g)
		350	Adj. bal.

−	Unearned Revenue (L)		+
		300	Beg. bal.
(a)	900	1,200	(23)
		600	Adj. bal.

−	Notes Payable (L)		+
		0	Beg. bal.
		11,000	(17)
		11,000	Adj. bal.

Equity

−	Common Stock (SE)		+
		20,000	Beg. bal.
		20,000	Adj. bal.

−	Retained Earnings (SE)		+
		30	Beg. bal.
(28)	50		
Adj. bal.	20		

−	Sales Revenue (R)		+
		0	Beg. bal.
		8,500	(21a)
		4,500	(22a)
		900	(a)
		13,900	Adj. bal.

−	Interest Income (R)		+
		0	Beg. bal.
		30	(d)
		30	Adj. bal.

+	Cost of Goods Sold (E)		−
Beg. bal.	0		
(21b)	5,000		
(22b)	3,000		
Adj. bal.	8,000		

+	Wages Expense (E)		−
Beg. bal.	0		
(24)	1,625		
(e)	480		
Adj. bal.	2,105		

+	Rent Expense (E)		−
Beg. bal.	0		
(27)	1,500		
Adj. bal.	1,500		

+	Advertising Expense (E)		−
Beg. bal.	0		
(19)	700		
Adj. bal.	700		

+	Depreciation Expense— Fixtures and Equipment (E)		−
Beg. bal.	0		
(c)	375		
Adj. bal.	375		

+	Insurance Expense (E)		−
Beg. bal.	0		
(b)	140		
Adj. bal.	140		

+	Interest Expense (E)		−
Beg. bal.	0		
(f)	110		
Adj. bal.	110		

+	Tax Expense (E)		−
Beg. bal.	0		
(g)	350		
Adj. bal.	350		

Assets = $37,570 = Liabilities = $16,940 + Equity = $20,630

EXHIBIT 3.8	Unadjusted and Adjusted Trial Balances

NATURAL BEAUTY SUPPLY, INC.
Trial Balance
December 31, 2015

	Unadjusted Trial Balance		Adjustments				Adjusted Trial Balance	
	Debit	Credit	Debit		Credit		Debit	Credit
Cash.	$ 6,825						$ 6,825	
Accounts receivable.	2,250						2,250	
Other receivables			(d)	$ 30			30	
Inventory.	7,300						7,300	
Prepaid insurance.	1,680				(b)	$ 140	1,540	
Security deposit	2,000						2,000	
Fixtures and equipment	18,000						18,000	
Accumulated depreciation					(c)	375		$ 375
Accounts payable.		$ 4,400						4,400
Interest payable					(f)	110		110
Wages payable.					(e)	480		480
Taxes payable.					(g)	350		350
Unearned revenue		1,500	(a)	900				600
Notes payable		11,000						11,000
Common stock.		20,000						20,000
Retained earnings	20						20	
Sales revenue.		13,000			(a)	900		13,900
Interest income.					(d)	30		30
Cost of goods sold.	8,000						8,000	
Wages expense	1,625		(e)	480			2,105	
Rent expense	1,500						1,500	
Advertising expense.	700						700	
Depreciation expense.			(c)	375			375	
Insurance expense.			(b)	140			140	
Interest expense.			(f)	110			110	
Tax expense			(g)	350			350	
Totals	$49,900	$49,900	$2,385		$2,385		$51,245	$51,245

EXHIBIT 3.9	Income Statement

NATURAL BEAUTY SUPPLY, INC.
Income Statement
For Month Ended December 31, 2015

Sales revenue.	$13,900
Cost of goods sold.	8,000
Gross profit	5,900
Wages expense	2,105
Rent expense	1,500
Advertising expense.	700
Depreciation expense.	375
Insurance expense	140
Operating income	1,080
Interest income.	30
Interest expense.	(110)
Income before tax expense	1,000
Tax expense	350
Net income.	$ 650

Statement of Stockholders' Equity   The statement of stockholders' equity reports the events causing the major equity components to change during the accounting period. **Exhibit 3.10** shows Natural Beauty Supply's statement of stockholders' equity for December. A review of its common stock account in the general ledger provides some of the information for this statement; namely, its balance at the beginning of the period and stock issuances during the period. The net income (or net loss) amount comes from the income statement. Dividends during the period are reflected in the retained earnings balance from the adjusted trial balance.

EXHIBIT 3.10 Statement of Stockholders' Equity

NATURAL BEAUTY SUPPLY, INC.
Statement of Stockholders' Equity
For Month Ended December 31, 2015

	Contributed Capital	Earned Capital	Total Equity
Balance, November 30, 2015..............	$20,000	$ 30	$20,030
Net income.....................	—	650	650
Common stock issued	—	—	—
Cash dividends.......................	—	(50)	(50)
Balances, December 31, 2015.............	$20,000	$630	$20,630

Balance Sheet The balance sheet reports a company's assets, liabilities, and equity. The assets and liabilities for Natural Beauty Supply's balance sheet at December 31, 2015, shown in **Exhibit 3.11**, come from the adjusted trial balance in **Exhibit 3.8**. The amounts reported for Common Stock and Retained Earnings in the balance sheet are taken from the statement of stockholders' equity for December (**Exhibit 3.10**).

FYI Financial statements are most commonly prepared for annual and quarterly accounting periods. A request for a bank loan is an example of a situation that can lead to financial statement preparation for a non-accounting period.

EXHIBIT 3.11 Balance Sheet

NATURAL BEAUTY SUPPLY, INC.
Balance Sheet
December 31, 2015

Assets			Liabilities		
Cash..........................		$ 6,825	Accounts payable...............		$ 4,400
Accounts receivable..............		2,250	Interest payable		110
Other receivables		30	Wages payable..................		480
Inventory......................		7,300	Taxes payable..................		350
Prepaid insurance................		1,540	Unearned revenue		600
Security deposit		2,000	Current liabilities..............		5,940
Current assets.................		19,945	Notes payable		11,000
Fixtures and equipment	$18,000		Total liabilities		16,940
Less: Accumulated depreciation	375		**Equity**		
Fixtures and equipment, net......		17,625	Common stock..................		20,000
			Retained earnings		630
Total assets		$37,570	Total liabilities and equity		$37,570

Statement of Cash Flows The statement of cash flows is formatted to report cash inflows and outflows by the three primary business activities:

- *Cash flows from operating activities* Cash flows from the company's transactions and events that relate to its primary operations.
- *Cash flows from investing activities* Cash flows from acquisitions and divestitures of investments and long-term assets.
- *Cash flows from financing activities* Cash flows from issuances of and payments toward equity, borrowings, and long-term liabilities.

The net cash flows from these three sections yield the change in cash for the period.

In analyzing the statement of cash flows, we should not necessarily conclude that the company is better off if cash increases and worse off if cash decreases. It is not the cash change that is most important, but the reasons for the change. For example, what are the sources of the cash inflows?

FYI The income statement, statement of stockholders' equity, and statement of cash flows report on periods of time. These statements illustrate the accounting period concept—the concept that useful statements can be prepared for arbitrary time periods within a company's life span. The purpose of adjusting entries is to obtain useful statements for specific time periods.

Are these sources mainly from operating activities? To what uses have cash inflows been put? Such questions (and their answers) are key to properly using the statement of cash flows. In Chapter 4, we examine the statement of cash flows more closely and answer these questions. The procedures for preparing a statement of cash flows are discussed in the next chapter. For completeness, we present Natural Beauty Supply's statement of cash flows for December in **Exhibit 3.12**.

EXHIBIT 3.12	Statement of Cash Flows

NATURAL BEAUTY SUPPLY, INC.
Statement of Cash Flows
For Month Ended December 31, 2015

Cash Flows from Operating Activities	
Cash received from customers	$12,900
Cash paid for inventory	(3,300)
Cash paid for wages	(1,625)
Cash paid for rent	(1,500)
Cash paid for advertising.	(700)
Net cash provided by operating activities	5,775
Cash Flows from Investing Activities	
Cash paid for fixtures and equipment	(18,000)
Net cash used for investing activities	(18,000)
Cash Flows from Financing Activities	
Cash received from loans	11,000
Cash paid for dividends.	(50)
Net cash provided by financing activities	10,950
Net change in cash.	(1,275)
Cash balance, November 30, 2015	8,100
Cash balance, December 31, 2015	$ 6,825

5 **LO5** Describe the process of closing temporary accounts.

CLOSING TEMPORARY ACCOUNTS

The chart of accounts contains two different types of accounts. Income statement accounts (revenues, expenses, etc.) are used to measure the net assets generated and used in a specific accounting period. As such, their end-of-period balances are reported in the income statement for that period. We use those balances to construct the statements of stockholders' equity and cash flows. But then these account balances have served their purpose, and we must get them ready to do the same thing for the following accounting period. Specifically, we must set their balances to zero so they can accumulate the revenues and expenses for that following period. For this reason, income statement accounts are called **temporary accounts**. Their end-of-period values do not carry over to the next reporting period.

In contrast, balance sheet account balances do carry over to the next reporting period. For example, the end-of-period balance in accounts receivable is the beginning-of-period balance for the next period. Therefore, balance sheet accounts are referred to as **permanent accounts**.

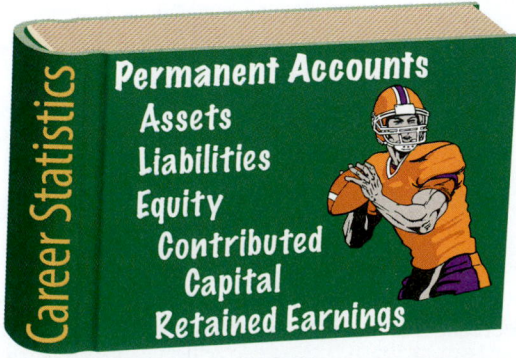
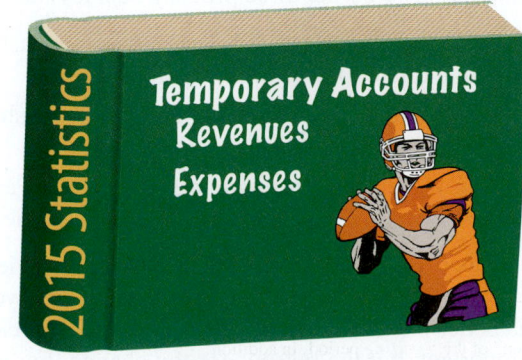

The **closing process** takes the end-of-period balances in the temporary accounts and moves them to a permanent account—the Retained Earnings account. A temporary account is *closed* when an entry is made that changes its balance to zero. The entry is equal in amount to the account's balance but is opposite to the balance as a debit or credit. An account that is closed is said to be closed *to* the account that receives the offsetting debit or credit. Thus, a closing entry simply transfers the balance of one account to another account. When closing entries bring temporary account balances to zero, the temporary accounts are then ready to accumulate data for the next accounting period.

Closing Process

The Retained Earnings account can be used to close the temporary revenue and expense accounts.[3] The entries to close temporary accounts are:

1. **Close revenue accounts**. Debit each revenue account for an amount equal to its balance, and credit Retained Earnings for the total of revenues.

2. **Close expense accounts**. Credit each expense account for an amount equal to its balance, and debit Retained Earnings for the total of expenses.

After these temporary accounts are closed, the difference equals the period's net income (if revenues exceed expenses) or net loss (if expenses exceed revenues) and that difference is now included in Retained Earnings. The closing process is graphically portrayed as follows.

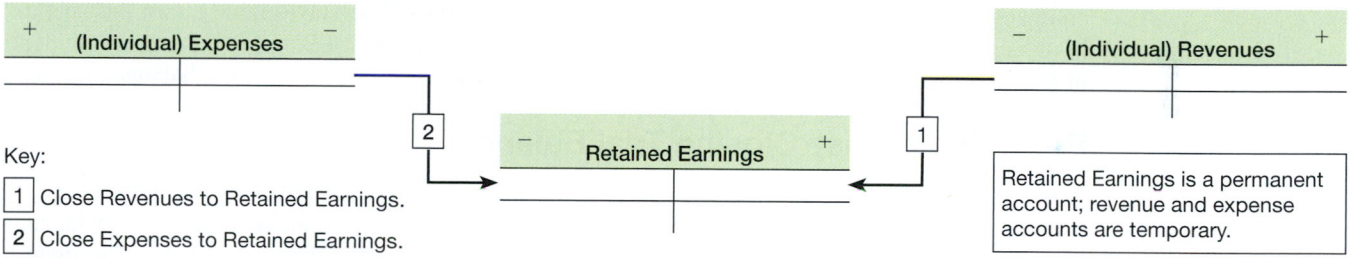

Closing Steps Illustrated

Exhibit 3.13 illustrates the entries for closing revenues and expenses for Natural Beauty Supply. The effects of these entries in T-accounts are shown after the journal entries. (We do not show the financial statement effects template for closing entries because the template automatically closes revenues and expenses to the Retained Earnings account as they occur—see earlier transactions for examples.)

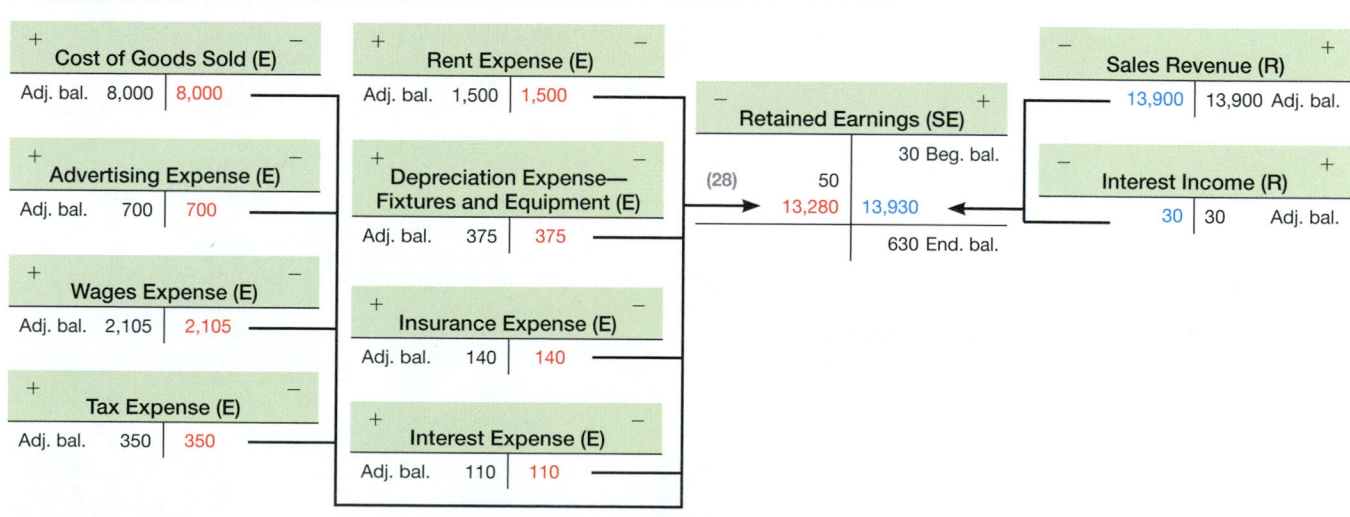

---

[3] *All* revenue and expense accounts are temporary accounts, so all revenue and expense accounts are closed to retained earnings at the end of the reporting period. In addition, companies often use a temporary account entitled Dividends Declared to record the amount of shareholder dividends declared during a reporting period. This account would accumulate a debit balance (because it reduces equity), and is closed to retained earnings at the end of the reporting period.

EXHIBIT 3.13		Closing Revenues and Expenses*		
1	Dec. 31	Sales revenue (−R)..	13,900	
		Interest income (−R).....................................	30	
		Retained earnings (+SE).........................		13,930
2	Dec. 31	Retained earnings (−SE)	13,280	
		Cost of goods sold (−E)		8,000
		Wages expense (−E)..............................		2,105
		Rent expense (−E).................................		1,500
		Advertising expense (−E)		700
		Depreciation expense (−E)		375
		Insurance expense (−E)...........................		140
		Interest expense (−E)		110
		Tax expense (−E).................................		350

* The two entries in this exhibit can be combined into a single entry where the credit (debit) to retained earnings would be net income (loss).

After these two steps, the net adjustment to the Retained Earnings account is a credit equal to the company's net income of $650, computed as $13,930 less $13,280. The Retained Earnings account in this case is increased by $650. We also recall that Natural Beauty Supply paid a cash dividend of $50 (transaction 28), which reduces retained earnings and results in the ending balance of $630.

Preparing a Post-Closing Trial Balance

After closing entries are recorded and posted to the general ledger, all temporary accounts have zero balances. At this point, a **post-closing trial balance** is prepared. A balancing of this trial balance is evidence that an equality of debits and credits has been maintained in the general ledger throughout the adjusting and closing process and that the general ledger is in balance to start the next accounting period. Only balance sheet accounts appear in a post-closing trial balance because all income statement accounts have balances of zero. The post-closing trial balance for Natural Beauty Supply is shown in **Exhibit 3.14**.

EXHIBIT 3.14	Post-Closing Trial Balance		
	NATURAL BEAUTY SUPPLY, INC. **Post-Closing Trial Balance** **December 31, 2015**		
		Debit	**Credit**
Cash...		$ 6,825	
Accounts receivable.......................................		2,250	
Other receivables		30	
Inventory..		7,300	
Prepaid insurance..		1,540	
Security deposit		2,000	
Fixtures and equipment		18,000	
Accumulated depreciation.................................			$ 375
Accounts payable..			4,400
Interest payable			110
Wages payable...			480
Taxes payable..			350
Unearned revenue			600
Notes payable			11,000
Common stock...			20,000
Retained earnings			630
Totals		$37,945	$37,945

Subsequent Events

There is usually a few weeks' delay between the end of the fiscal reporting period and the issuing of the financial reports for that period. What happens if a significant event occurs (e.g., a fire at a production facility, an acquisition, etc.) during that interim? Should the previous period's financial statements be changed to reflect the event?

If the event doesn't provide information about the company's condition on the balance sheet date, then the answer is no. So, neither the fire nor the acquisition would be reported in the previous period's financial statements. Such events should be disclosed in a footnote, if they are material.

SUMMARIZING THE ACCOUNTING CYCLE

The sequence of accounting procedures known as the accounting cycle occurs each fiscal year (period) and represents a systematic process for accumulating and reporting financial data of a company. **Exhibit 3.15** expands on **Exhibit 3.1** to include descriptions of the five major steps in the accounting cycle.

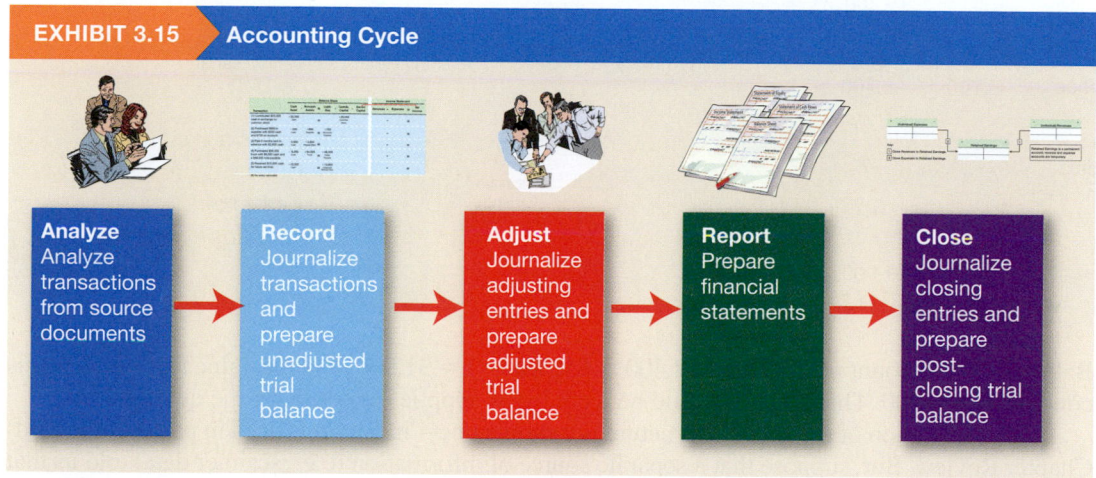

EXHIBIT 3.15 Accounting Cycle

| **Analyze** Analyze transactions from source documents | **Record** Journalize transactions and prepare unadjusted trial balance | **Adjust** Journalize adjusting entries and prepare adjusted trial balance | **Report** Prepare financial statements | **Close** Journalize closing entries and prepare post-closing trial balance |

FINANCIAL STATEMENT ANALYSIS

Using Information on Levels and Flows

A careful reader of financial statements must differentiate between those things that depict *levels* and those that depict *flows* or *changes*. The balance sheet portrays levels of resources and claims on those resources at a point in time, and the income statement portrays changes in those levels over a period of time. Knowing how the levels and flows relate to each other can be a very useful tool for analysis.

For instance, suppose that a service business has an inventory of office supplies. On July 1, an inventory count determined that the business has $2,400 of supplies inventory on hand. During the third calendar quarter, there were deliveries of office supplies with a cost of $5,700. And, at the end of the third quarter—on September 30—an inventory count finds $1,900 of supplies on hand. What amount of supplies expense should be recognized for the quarter?

Finding the answer to this question is easier if we recall the transactions that can affect the supplies inventory account, and that these transactions (changes) must lead from the beginning inventory level to the ending inventory level. At present, we know of two such transactions: the purchase of supplies inventory and the usage of supplies inventory.

LO6 Analyze changes in balance sheet accounts.

6

(a)	Supplies inventory (+A).	5,700	
	Cash (−A) or Accounts payable (+L).		5,700
	Purchase supplies inventory.		
(b)	Supplies expense (+E, −SE)	?	
	Supplies inventory (−A)		?
	Record expense for supplies used.		

The supplies inventory T-account must look like the following:

+	Supplies Inventory (A)		−
Beg. bal.	2,400		
(a)	5,700	?	(b)
End. bal.	1,900		

An FSET version of this analysis would look like the following, with the only noncash account being supplies inventory, and assuming that the inventory purchase was made with cash.

	Balance Sheet					Income Statement		
Transaction	Cash Asset	+ Supplies Inventory	= Liabil- ities	+ Contrib. Capital	+ Earned Capital	Revenues −	Expenses	= Net Income
Beginning balance	$2,400							
(a) Purchase office supplies	−5,700	+5,700						
(b) Office supplies taken for use in client service activities		−?			−? Retained Earnings		+? Supplies Expense	−?
Ending balance	$1,900							

Balancing the account requires that $2,400 + $5,700 − ? = $1,900$, and the value that satisfies this condition is $6,200. That amount would be recorded as supplies expense for the quarter.

This application of the account structure is a simple one—in fact, it is used in part *a* of the Mid-Chapter Review. But, suppose that a separate source of information (e.g., scanner data) told us that $5,900 in supplies had been taken from inventory for client service activities. When put into the FSET/T-account analysis above, this new fact would imply an additional $300 in supplies had been removed for reasons such as breakage, obsolescence, or pilferage.

As we progress through the topics in future chapters, we will find that accounting reports do not always provide the information that is most useful for assessment of a company's current performance or standing. In those cases, we can often use T-accounts and journal entries or the FSET to analyze levels and changes and to develop the numbers that do a better job of answering important questions.

CHAPTER-END REVIEW

Assume that Atwell Laboratories, Inc., operates with an accounting fiscal year ending June 30. The company's accounts are adjusted annually and closed on that date. Its unadjusted trial balance as of June 30, 2015, is as follows.

ATWELL LABORATORIES, INC. Unadjusted Trial Balance June 30, 2015	Debit	Credit
Cash.	$ 1,000	
Accounts receivable.	9,200	
Prepaid insurance.	6,000	
Supplies	31,300	
Equipment	270,000	
Accumulated depreciation—equipment.		$ 60,000
Accounts payable.		3,100
Unearned fees		4,000
Fees revenue		150,000
Wages expense	58,000	
Rent expense	22,000	
Common stock.		120,400
Retained earnings		60,000
Totals	$397,500	$397,500

Additional Information

1. Atwell acquired a two-year insurance policy on January 1, 2015. The policy covers fire and casualty; Atwell had no coverage prior to January 1, 2015.

2. An inventory of supplies was taken on June 30 and the amount available was $6,300.

3. All equipment was purchased on July 1, 2012, for $270,000. The equipment's life is estimated at 9 years. Assume the entire asset cost is depreciated over its useful life.

4. Atwell received a $4,000 cash payment on April 1, 2015, from Beave Clinic for diagnostic work to be provided uniformly over the next 4 months, beginning April 1, 2015. The amount was credited to Unearned Fees. The service was provided per the agreement.

5. Unpaid and unrecorded wages at June 30, 2015, were $600.

6. Atwell rents facilities for $2,000 per month. Atwell has not yet made or recorded the payment for June 2015.

In addition to the unadjusted accounts listed above, Atwell's ledger includes the following accounts, all with zero balances: Insurance Expense; Depreciation Expense; Supplies Expense; Wages Payable; and Rent Payable.

Required

1. Show the impact of the necessary adjusting entries using the FSET.

2. Show the impact of the necessary adjusting entries using journal entries.

3. Prepare T-accounts with the unadjusted balances as beginning balances and enter the adjusting entries from part 2. Prepare Atwell's June 30, 2015 adjusted trial balance by entering the adjusting journal entries into the T-accounts.

4. Prepare Atwell's closing journal entries and post them to the T-accounts (key the entries).

5. Prepare the company's June 30, 2015 balance sheet and its income statement and statement of stockholders equity for the year ended June 30, 2015.

The solution to this review problem can be found on pages 150–155.

SUMMARY

LO1   **Identify the major steps in the accounting cycle. (p. 102)**

- The major steps in the accounting cycle are
  a. Analyze   *b.* Record   *c.* Adjust   *d.* Report   *e.* Close

LO2   **Review the process of journalizing and posting transactions. (p. 103)**

- Transactions are initially recorded in a journal; the entries are in chronological order, and the journal shows the total effect of each transaction or adjustment.
- Posting is the transfer of information from a journal to the general ledger accounts.

LO3   **Describe the adjusting process and illustrate adjusting entries. (p. 109)**

- Adjusting entries achieve the proper recognition of revenues and the proper matching of expenses with those revenues; adjustments are summarized as follows.

Adjustment	Adjusting Entry
Adjusting prepaid (deferred) expenses............................	Increase expense
	Decrease asset
Adjusting unearned (deferred) revenues	Decrease liability
	Increase revenue
Accruing expenses..	Increase expense
	Increase liability
Accruing revenues	Increase asset
	Increase revenue

LO4   **Prepare financial statements from adjusted accounts. (p. 118)**

- An income statement, statement of stockholders' equity, balance sheet, and statement of cash flows are prepared from an adjusted trial balance and other information.

LO5   **Describe the process of closing temporary accounts. (p. 122)**

- *Closing the books* means closing (yielding zero balances) revenues and expenses—that is, all temporary accounts. Revenue and expense account balances are transferred (closed) to the Retained Earnings account.

LO6   **Analyze changes in balance sheet accounts. (p. 125)**

- The combination of balance sheet levels and income statement flows allows a financial statement reader to infer the effects of transactions and adjustments that are not disclosed directly.

GUIDANCE ANSWERS . . . YOU MAKE THE CALL

You are the Chief Accountant   Deposits represent a liability and should be included in REI's current liabilities at the time the cash or check is received. The account that would be used may have several names, including advances, trip deposits, and unearned revenues. Revenue should not be recognized until the trip has been completed. It is not unusual for events to occur that result in a refund of some portion or even all of the traveler's total payment. In the present case involving a low cancellation rate, waiting until the trip is over is not only conservative reporting, but is likely more efficient bookkeeping as well.

KEY TERMS

Accounting cycle (p. 102)
Accruals (p. 111)
Accrued expense (p. 115)
Accrued income (p. 114)
Accrued revenue (p. 114)
Adjusted trial balance (p. 118)
Adjusting entries (p. 111)
Book value (p. 114)
Calendar year (p. 102)
Chart of accounts (p. 103)

Close expense accounts (p. 123)
Close revenue accounts (p. 123)
Closing process (p. 123)
Contra accounts (p. 113)
Contra asset (p. 113)
Deferrals (p. 111)
Deferred revenue (p. 111)
Depreciation (p. 113)
Fiscal year (p. 102)
General journal (p. 103)

Journal (p. 103)
Permanent accounts (p. 122)
Post-closing trial balance (p. 124)
Posting (p. 103)
Straight-line depreciation (p. 113)
Temporary accounts (p. 122)
Unadjusted trial balance (p. 110)
Unearned revenue (p. 111)

Assignments with the 🔴 **logo in the margin are available in** *my*BusinessCourse.
See the Preface of the book for details.

MULTIPLE CHOICE

1. An end-of-period journal entry made to reflect accrual accounting is called

   a.　a posted journal entry.
   b.　an adjusting journal entry.
   c.　an erroneous journal entry.
   d.　a compound journal entry.

2. Posting refers to the process whereby journal entry information is transferred from
   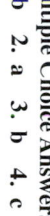
   a.　journal to general ledger accounts.
   b.　general ledger accounts to a journal.
   c.　source documents to a journal.
   d.　a journal to source documents.

3. Which of the following is an example of an adjusting entry?

   a.　Recording the purchase of supplies on account
   b.　Recording depreciation expense on a truck
   c.　Recording cash received from customers for services rendered
   d.　Recording the cash payment of wages to employees

4. A piece of equipment was placed in service on January 1, 2013. The cost of the equipment was
   $20,000, and it is expected to have no value at the end of its eight-year life. Using straight-line
   depreciation, what amounts will be seen for depreciation expense and accumulated depreciation for
   fiscal (and calendar) year 2015?

	Fiscal Year 2015 Depreciation Expense	Fiscal Year-End 2015 Accumulated Depreciation
a.	$2,500	$ 2,000
b.	–0–	$20,000
c.	$2,500	$ 7,500
d.	$7,500	$ 7,500

5. When a customer places an order, Custom Cakes requires a deposit equal to the full purchase price.
   However, Custom Cakes does not recognize revenue until the completed cake is delivered. During
   the month of November 2015, Custom Cakes received $24,000 in customer deposits. The balance
   in its unearned revenue liability was $4,000 at the beginning of November and $6,000 at the end of
   November. How much revenue did Custom Cakes recognize during the month of November?

   a.　$26,000
   b.　$24,000
   c.　$22,000
   d.　$4,000

QUESTIONS

Q3-1. What are the five major steps in the accounting cycle? List them in their proper order.

Q3-2. What does the term *fiscal year* mean?

Q3-3. What are three examples of source documents that underlie business transactions?

Q3-4. What is the nature and purpose of a general journal?

Q3-5. Explain the process of posting.

Q3-6. What is an adjusting journal entry?

Q3-7. What is a chart of accounts? Give an example of a coding system for identifying different types of accounts.

Q3-8. Why is the adjusting step of the accounting cycle necessary?

Q3-9. What four different types of adjustments are frequently necessary at the close of an accounting period? Give examples of each type.

Q3-10. On January 1, Prepaid Insurance was debited with the cost of a two-year premium, $1,872. What adjusting entry should be made on January 31 before financial statements are prepared for the month?

Q3-11. What is a contra account? What contra account is used in reporting the book value of a depreciable asset?

Q3-12. A building was acquired on January 1, 2011, at a cost of $4,000,000, and its depreciation is calculated using the straight-line method. At the end of 2015, the accumulated depreciation contra asset for the building is $800,000. What will be the balance in the building's accumulated depreciation contra asset at the end of 2022? What is the building's book value at that date?

Q3-13. The publisher of *International View*, a monthly magazine, received two-year subscriptions totaling $9,720 on January 1. (a) What entry should be made to record the receipt of the $9,720? (b) What entry should be made at the end of January before financial statements are prepared for the month?

Q3-14. Globe Travel Agency pays an employee $475 in wages each Friday for the five-day workweek ending on that day. The last Friday of January falls on January 27. What adjusting entry should be made on January 31, the fiscal year-end?

Q3-15. The Bayou Company earns interest amounting to $360 per month on its investments. The company receives the interest every six months, on December 31 and June 30. Monthly financial statements are prepared. What adjusting entry should be made on January 31?

Q3-16. Which groups of accounts are closed at the end of the accounting year?

Q3-17. What are the two major steps in the closing process?

Q3-18. What is the purpose of a post-closing trial balance? Which of the following accounts should *not* appear in the post-closing trial balance: Cash; Unearned Revenue; Prepaid Rent; Depreciation Expense; Utilities Payable; Supplies Expense; and Retained Earnings?

Q3-19. Dehning Corporation is an international manufacturer of films and industrial identification products. Included among its prepaid expenses is an account titled Prepaid Catalog Costs; in recent years, this account's size has ranged between $2,500,000 and $4,000,000. The company states that catalog costs are initially capitalized and then written off over the estimated useful lives of the publications (generally eight months). Identify and briefly discuss the accounting principles that support Dehning Corporation's handling of its catalog costs.

Q3-20. At the beginning of January, the first month of the accounting year, the supplies account had a debit balance of $825. During January, purchases of $260 worth of supplies were debited to the account. Although only $630 of supplies were still available at the end of January, the necessary adjusting entry was omitted. How will the omission affect (a) the income statement for January, and (b) the balance sheet prepared at January 31?

MINI EXERCISES

LO2

M3-21. Journalizing Transactions in Template, Journal Entry Form, and T-Accounts

Creative Designs, a firm providing art services for advertisers, began business on June 1, 2015. The following transactions occurred during the month of June.

June 1 Anne Clem invested $12,000 cash to begin the business in exchange for common stock.

      2 Paid $950 cash for June rent.

June 3 Purchased $6,400 of office equipment on account.

  6 Purchased $3,800 of art materials and other supplies; paid $1,800 cash with the remainder due within 30 days.

  11 Billed clients $4,700 for services rendered.

  17 Collected $3,250 cash from clients on their accounts.

  19 Paid $3,000 cash toward the account for office equipment suppliers (see June 3).

  25 Paid $900 cash for dividends.

  30 Paid $350 cash for June utilities.

  30 Paid $2,500 cash for June salaries.

REQUIRED

a. Record the above transactions for June using the financial statement effects template.

b. The following accounts in its general ledger are needed to record the transactions for June: Cash; Accounts Receivable; Supplies; Office Equipment; Accounts Payable; Common Stock; Retained Earnings; Service Fees Earned; Rent Expense; Utilities Expense; and Salaries Expense. Record the above transactions for June in journal entry form.

c. Set up T-accounts for each of the ledger accounts and post the entries to them (key the numbers in T-accounts by date).

M3-22. Journalizing Transactions in Template, Journal Entry Form, and T-Accounts

Minute Maid, a firm providing housecleaning services, began business on April 1, 2015. The following transactions occurred during the month of April.

April 1 A. Falcon invested $9,000 cash to begin the business in exchange for common stock.

  2 Paid $2,850 cash for six months' lease on van for the business.

  3 Borrowed $10,000 cash from bank and signed note payable agreeing to repay it in 1 year plus 10% interest.

  3 Purchased $5,500 of cleaning equipment; paid $2,500 cash with the remainder due within 30 days.

  4 Paid $4,300 cash for cleaning supplies.

  7 Paid $350 cash for advertisements to run in newspaper during April.

  21 Billed customers $3,500 for services performed.

  23 Paid $3,000 cash on account to cleaning equipment suppliers (see April 3).

  28 Collected $2,300 cash from customers on their accounts.

  29 Paid $1,000 cash for dividends.

  30 Paid $1,750 cash for April wages.

  30 Paid $995 cash to service station for gasoline used during April.

REQUIRED

a. Record the above transactions for April using the financial statement effects template.

b. The following accounts in its general ledger are needed to record the transactions for April: Cash; Accounts Receivable; Supplies; Prepaid Van Lease; Equipment; Accounts Payable; Notes Payable; Common Stock; Retained Earnings; Cleaning Fees Earned; Van Fuel Expense; Advertising Expense; and Wages Expense. Record the above transactions for April in journal entry form.

c. Set up T-accounts for each of the ledger accounts and post the entries to them (key the numbers in T-accounts by date).

M3-23. Journalizing Transactions and Adjusting Accounts

Deluxe Building Services offers custodial services on both a contract basis and an hourly basis. On January 1, 2015, Deluxe collected $20,100 in advance on a six-month contract for work to be performed evenly during the next six months. Assume that Deluxe closes its books and issues financial reports on a monthly basis.

a. Prepare the entry on January 1 to record the receipt of $20,100 cash for contract work (1) using the financial statements effect template and (2) in journal entry form.

b. Prepare the adjusting entry to be made on January 31, 2015, for the contract work done during January (1) using the financial statements effect template and (2) in journal entry form.

c. At January 31, a total of 30 hours of hourly rate custodial work was unbilled. The billing rate is $19 per hour. Prepare the adjusting entry needed on January 31, 2015, (1) using the financial statements effect template and (2) in journal entry form. (The firm uses the account Fees Receivable to reflect amounts due but not yet billed.)

LO3, 6

M3-24. Adjusting Accounts

Selected accounts of Ideal Properties, a real estate management firm, are shown below as of January 31, 2015, before any adjusting entries have been made.

Unadjusted Account Balances	Debits	Credits
Prepaid insurance.	$6,660	
Supplies inventory	1,930	
Office equipment	5,952	
Unearned rent revenue.		$ 5,250
Salaries expense	3,100	
Rent revenue		15,000

Monthly financial statements are prepared. Using the following information, record the adjusting entries necessary on January 31 (a) using the financial statements effect template and (b) in journal entry form.

1. Prepaid Insurance represents a three-year premium paid on January 1, 2015.
2. Supplies of $850 were still available on January 31.
3. Office equipment—purchased on January 1, 2015—is expected to last eight years.
4. On January 1, 2015, Ideal Properties collected six months' rent in advance from a tenant renting space for $875 per month.
5. Accrued employee salaries of $490 have not been recorded as of January 31.

LO2, 3, 6

El Puerto de Liverpool
OTCMKTS :: ELPQF

M3-25. Inferring Transactions from Financial Statements

El Puerto de Liverpool (Liverpool) is a large retailer in Mexico. The following accounts are selected from its annual report for the fiscal year ended December 31, 2013. For the fiscal year ended December 31, 2013, Liverpool purchased merchandise inventory costing 44,998,092 thousand Mexican pesos. Assume that all purchases were made on account. The following T-accounts reflect information contained in the company's 2013 and 2012 balance sheets (in thousands of Mexican pesos).

+ Inventories (A)	−		− Suppliers (Accounts Payable)	+
12/31/2012 Bal. 10,558,247				10,288,069 12/31/2012 Bal.
12/31/2013 Bal. 11,421,969				11,454,374 12/31/2013 Bal.

a. Prepare the entry, using the financial statement effects template and in journal entry form, to record Liverpool's purchases for the 2013 fiscal year.

b. What amount did Liverpool pay in cash to its suppliers for the fiscal year ended December 31, 2013? Explain. Assume that Suppliers (Accounts payable) is affected only by transactions related to inventory.

c. Prepare the entry, using the financial statement effects template and in journal entry form, to record cost of goods sold for the year ended December 31, 2013.

LO4

M3-26. Preparing a Statement of Stockholders' Equity

On December 31, 2014, the credit balances of the Common Stock and Retained Earnings accounts were $30,000 and $18,000, respectively, for Architect Services Company. Its stock issuances for 2015 totaled $6,000, and it paid $9,700 cash toward dividends in 2015. For the year ended December 31, 2015, the company had net income of $29,900. Prepare a 2015 statement of stockholders' equity for Architect Services.

LO5

M3-27. Applying Closing Procedures

Assume you are in the process of closing procedures for Echo Corporation. You have already closed all revenue and expense accounts to the Retained Earnings account. The total debits to Retained Earnings equal $308,800 and total credits to Retained Earnings equal $347,400. The Retained Earnings account had a credit balance of $99,000 at the start of this current year. What is the post-closing ending balance of Retained Earnings at the end of this current year?

LO5

M3-28. Preparing Closing Entries Using Journal Entries and T-Accounts

The adjusted trial balance at December 31, 2015, for Smith Company includes the following selected accounts.

Adjusted Account Balances	Debit	Credit
Commissions revenue		$84,900
Wages expense	$36,000	
Insurance expense.	1,900	
Utilities expense.	8,200	
Depreciation expense.	9,800	
Retained earnings		72,100

a. Prepare entries to close these accounts in journal entry form.

b. Set up T-accounts for each of these ledger accounts, enter the balances above, and post the closing entries to them. After these entries are posted, what is the post-closing balance of the Retained Earnings account?

M3-29. Inferring Transactions from Financial Statements   **LO2, 3, 6**

Amazon.com Inc. is one of the world's leading e-commerce companies, with almost $90 billion
in revenues for the fiscal year ended December 31, 2014. For the year ended December 31, 2014,
Amazon's cost of goods sold was $62,752 million. Assume that all purchases were made on ac-   **Amazon.com Inc.**
count. The following T-accounts reflect information contained in the company's 2014 and 2013   **NASDAQ :: AMZN**
balance sheets (in millions).

+	Inventories	−		−	Accounts Payable	+
12/31/2013 Bal.	$7,411				$15,133	12/31/2013 Bal.
12/31/2014 Bal.	$8,299				$16,459	12/31/2014 Bal.

a. Prepare the entry, using the financial statement effects template and in journal entry form, to record cost of goods sold for the year ended December 31, 2014.

b. Prepare the entry, using the financial statement effects template and in journal entry form, to record Amazon's inventory purchases for the year ended December 31, 2014. (Assume all purchases are made on account.)

c. What amount did Amazon pay in cash to its suppliers for the year ended December 31, 2014?

M3-30. Preparing Entries Across Two Periods   **LO2, 3, 5**

Hatcher Company closes its accounts on December 31 each year. On December 31, 2015, Hatcher
accrued $600 of interest income that was earned on an investment but not yet received or recorded
(the investment will pay interest of $900 cash on January 31, 2016). On January 31, 2016, the com-
pany received the $900 cash as interest on the investment. Prepare journal entries to:

a. Accrue the interest earned on December 31;

b. Close the Interest Income account on December 31 (the account has a year-end balance of $2,400 after adjustments); and

c. Record the cash receipt of interest on January 31, 2016.

EXERCISES

E3-31. Journalizing and Posting Closing Entries   **LO5**

The adjusted trial balance as of December 31, 2015, for Brooks Consulting Company contains the
following selected accounts.

Adjusted Account Balances	Debit	Credit
Service fees earned		€80,300
Rent expense	€20,800	
Salaries expense	45,700	
Supplies expense.	5,600	
Depreciation expense.	10,200	
Retained earnings		67,000

a. Prepare entries to close these accounts in journal entry form.

b. Set up T-accounts for each of the ledger accounts, enter the balances above, and post the closing entries to them. After these entries are posted, what is the post-closing balance of the Retained Earnings account?

LO3

Hartford Financial
Services Group
NYSE :: HIG

E3-32. **Preparing and Journalizing Adjusting Entries**
For each of the following separate situations, prepare the necessary adjustments (a) using the financial statement effects template, and (b) in journal entry form.

1.   Unrecorded depreciation on equipment is $610.
2.   On the date for preparing financial statements, an estimated utilities expense of $390 has been
     incurred, but no utility bill has yet been received or paid.
3.   On the first day of the current period, rent for four periods was paid and recorded as a $2,800
     debit to Prepaid Rent and a $2,800 credit to Cash.
4.   Nine months ago, the **Hartford Financial Services Group** sold a one-year policy to a
     customer and recorded the receipt of the premium by debiting Cash for $624 and crediting
     Unearned Premium Revenue for $624. No adjusting entries have been prepared during the
     nine-month period. Hartford's annual financial statements are now being prepared.
5.   At the end of the period, employee wages of $965 have been incurred but not yet paid or
     recorded.
6.   At the end of the period, $300 of interest income has been earned but not yet received or recorded.

LO2, 3, 5

E3-33. **Preparing Adjusting and Closing Entries Across Two Periods**
Norton Company closes its accounts on December 31 each year. The company works a five-day
work week and pays its employees every two weeks. On December 31, 2015, Norton accrued $4,700
of salaries payable. On January 7, 2016, the company paid salaries of $12,000 cash to employees.
Prepare journal entries to:

a.   Accrue the salaries payable on December 31;
b.   Close the Salaries Expense account on December 31 (the account has a year-end balance of
     $250,000 after adjustments); and
c.   Record the salary payment on January 7.

LO3, 6

E3-34. **Analyzing Accounts Using Adjusted Data**
Selected T-account balances for Fields Company are shown below as of January 31, 2016; adjusting entries have already been posted. The firm uses a calendar-year accounting period but prepares
monthly adjustments.

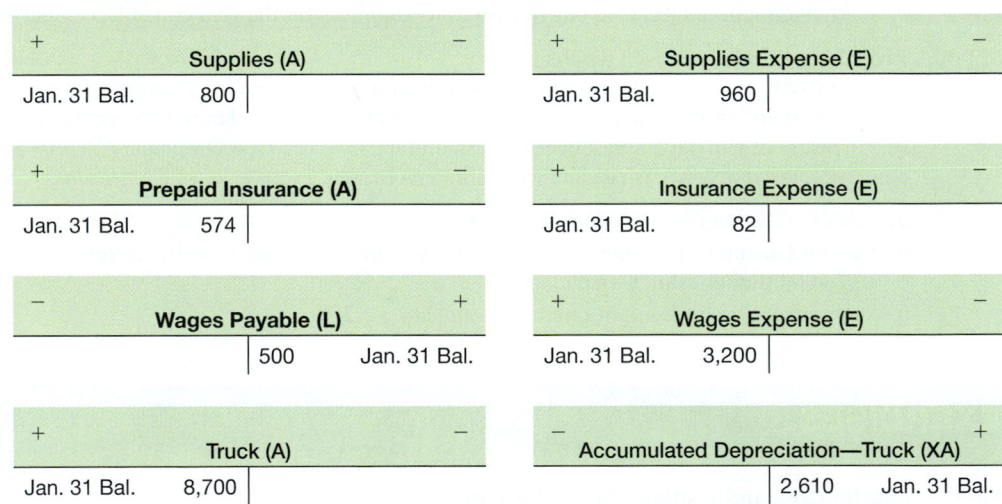

a.   If the amount in Supplies Expense represents the January 31 adjustment for the supplies used
     in January, and $620 worth of supplies were purchased during January, what was the January
     1 beginning balance of Supplies?
b.   The amount in the Insurance Expense account represents the adjustment made at January 31
     for January insurance expense. If the original insurance premium was for one year, what was
     the amount of the premium and on what date did the insurance policy start?
c.   If we assume that no beginning balance existed in wages payable or wages expense on January
     1, how much cash was paid as wages during January?
d.   If the truck has a useful life of five years, what is the monthly amount of depreciation expense
     and how many months has Fields owned the truck?

E3-35.   Preparing Adjusting Entries

LO2, 3, 6

Jake Thomas began Thomas Refinishing Service on July 1, 2015. Selected accounts are shown below as of July 31, before any adjusting entries have been made.

Unadjusted Account Balances	Debit	Credit
Prepaid rent	$5,700	
Prepaid advertising.	630	
Supplies inventory	3,000	
Unearned refinishing fees.		$ 600
Refinishing fees revenue		2,500

Using the following information, prepare the adjusting entries necessary on July 31 (a) using the financial statement effects template and (b) in journal entry form. (c) Set up T-accounts for each of the ledger accounts, enter the balances above, and post the adjusting entries to them.

1.   On July 1, the firm paid one year's advance rent of $5,700 in cash.
2.   On July 1, $630 cash was paid to the local newspaper for an advertisement to run daily for the months of July, August, and September.
3.   Supplies still available at July 31 total $1,100.
4.   At July 31, refinishing services of $800 have been performed but not yet recorded or billed to customers. The firm uses the account Fees Receivable to reflect amounts due but not yet billed.
5.   A customer paid $600 in advance for a refinishing project. At July 31, the project is one-half complete.

E3-36.   Inferring Transactions from Financial Statements

LO2, 3, 6

Abercrombie & Fitch Co.
NYSE :: ANF

Abercrombie & Fitch Co. (ANF) is a specialty retailer of casual apparel. The following information is taken from ANF's fiscal 10-K report for the fiscal year 2013, which ended February 1, 2014. (All amounts in $ thousands.)

Selected Balance Sheet Data	February 1, 2014	February 2, 2013
Inventory.	$530,192	$426,962
Accrued compensation	49,878	74,747

a.   ANF reported Cost of Goods Sold of $1,541,462 (thousand) for its fiscal year 2013. What was the cost that ANF incurred to acquire inventory for its fiscal year 2013?
b.   Assume that ANF reported Compensation Expense of $650,000 (thousand) for its fiscal year 2013. What amount of compensation was paid to its employees for fiscal year 2013?
c.   Where would you expect ANF to report its balance of Accrued Compensation?

E3-37.   Preparing Closing Procedures

LO5

The adjusted trial balance of Parker Corporation, prepared December 31, 2015, contains the following selected accounts.

Adjusted Account Balances	Debit	Credit
Service fees earned		$92,500
Interest income.		2,200
Salaries expense	$41,800	
Advertising expense.	4,300	
Depreciation expense.	8,700	
Income tax expense.	9,900	
Retained earnings		42,700

a.   Prepare entries to close these accounts in journal entry form.
b.   Set up T-accounts for each of the ledger accounts, enter the balances above, and post the closing entries to them. After these entries are posted, what is the post-closing balance of the Retained Earnings account?

E3-38.   Inferring Transactions from Financial Statements

LO2, 3, 6

Ethan Allen Interiors Inc.
NYSE :: ETH

Ethan Allen Interiors Inc., a leading manufacturer and retailer of home furnishings and accessories, sells products through an exclusive network of approximately 300 design centers. All of Ethan Allen's products are sold by special order. Customers generally place a deposit equal to 25%

to 50% of the purchase price when ordering. Orders take 4 to 12 weeks to be delivered. Selected fiscal-year information from the company's balance sheets is as follows ($ thousands):

Selected Balance Sheet Data	2014	2013
Inventories	$146,275	$137,256
Customer deposits..	59,684	59,098

a. In fiscal 2014, Ethan Allen reported total sales revenue of $746,659 (thousand). Assume that the company collected customer deposits equal to $200,000 (thousand) over the year. Prepare entries, using the financial statement effects template and in journal entry form, to record customer deposits and its sales revenue for fiscal year 2014.

b. Ethan Allen's cost of goods sold for 2014 was $340,163 (thousand). Prepare the adjusting entry, using the financial statement effects template and in journal entry form, that it made to record inventory acquisitions.

c. Where would you expect Ethan Allen to report its Customer Deposits?

LO4, 5 **E3-39. Preparing Financial Statements and Closing Procedures**

Solomon Corporation's adjusted trial balance for the year ending December 31, 2015, is:

SOLOMON CORPORATION Adjusted Trial Balance December 31, 2015	Debit	Credit
Cash	$ 4,000	
Accounts receivable...	6,500	
Equipment	78,000	
Accumulated depreciation		$ 14,000
Notes payable		10,000
Common stock...		43,000
Retained earnings		12,600
Service fees earned		71,000
Rent expense	18,000	
Salaries expense	37,100	
Depreciation expense...	7,000	
Totals	$150,600	$150,600

a. Prepare its income statement and statement of stockholders' equity for the current year, and its balance sheet for the current year-end. Cash dividends were $8,000 and there were no stock issuances or repurchases.

b. Prepare entries to close its temporary accounts in journal entry form.

c. Set up T-accounts for each of the ledger accounts, enter the balances above, and post the closing entries to them. After these entries are posted, what is the post-closing balance of the Retained Earnings account?

PROBLEMS

LO2, 3, 6   P3-40. Journalizing and Posting Transactions, and Preparing a Trial Balance and Adjustments

B. Lougee opened Lougee Roofing Service on April 1, 2015. Transactions for April are as follows:

Apr. 1 Lougee contributed $11,500 cash to the business in exchange for common stock.

1 Paid $2,880 cash for two-year premium toward liability insurance effective immediately.

2 Paid $6,100 cash for the purchase of a used truck.

2 Purchased $3,100 of ladders and other equipment; paid $1,000 cash, with the balance due in 30 days.

5 Purchased $1,200 of supplies on account.

5 Received an advance of $1,800 cash from a customer for roof repairs to be done during April and May.

12 Billed customers $5,500 for roofing services performed.

Apr 18 Collected $4,900 cash from customers on their accounts.

29 Paid $675 cash for truck fuel used in April.

30 Paid $100 cash for April newspaper advertising.

30 Paid $2,500 cash for assistants' wages.

30 Billed customers $4,000 for roofing services performed.

REQUIRED

a. Set up a general ledger in T-account form for the following accounts: Cash; Accounts Receivable; Supplies; Prepaid Insurance; Trucks; Accumulated Depreciation—Trucks; Equipment; Accumulated Depreciation—Equipment; Accounts Payable; Unearned Roofing Fees; Common Stock; Roofing Fees Earned; Fuel Expense; Advertising Expense; Wages Expense; Insurance Expense; Supplies Expense; Depreciation Expense—Trucks; and Depreciation Expense—Equipment.

b. Record these transactions for April (1) using the financial statement effects template and (2) in journal entry form. (3) Post these entries to their T-accounts (key numbers in T-accounts by date).

c. Prepare an unadjusted trial balance as of April 30, 2015.

d. Supplies still available on April 30 amount to $400; and depreciation for April was $125 on the truck and $35 on equipment; and one-fourth of the roofing fee received in advance was earned by April 30. Prepare entries to adjust the books for Insurance Expense, Supplies Expense, Depreciation Expense—Trucks, Depreciation Expense—Equipment, and Roofing Fees Earned (1) using the financial statement effects template and (2) in journal entry form. (3) Post adjusting entries to their T-accounts.

P3-41. Preparing an Unadjusted Trial Balance and Adjustments   **LO2, 3**

SnapShot Company, a commercial photography studio, has just completed its first full year of operations on December 31, 2015. General ledger account balances *before* year-end adjustments follow; no adjusting entries have been made to the accounts at any time during the year. Assume that all balances are normal.

Cash	$ 2,150	Accounts payable	$ 1,910
Accounts receivable	3,800	Unearned photography fees	2,600
Prepaid rent	12,600	Common stock	24,000
Prepaid insurance	2,970	Photography fees earned	34,480
Supplies	4,250	Wages expense	11,000
Equipment	22,800	Utilities expense	3,420

An analysis of the firm's records discloses the following.

1. Photography services of $925 have been rendered, but customers have not yet paid or been billed. The firm uses the account Fees Receivable to reflect amounts due but not yet billed.
2. Equipment, purchased January 1, 2015, has an estimated life of 10 years.
3. Utilities expense for December is estimated to be $400, but the bill will not arrive or be paid until January of next year.
4. The balance in Prepaid Rent represents the amount paid on January 1, 2015, for a 2-year lease on the studio.
5. In November, customers paid $2,600 cash in advance for photos to be taken for the holiday season. When received, these fees were credited to Unearned Photography Fees. By December 31, all of these fees are earned.
6. A 3-year insurance premium paid on January 1, 2015, was debited to Prepaid Insurance.
7. Supplies available at December 31 are $1,520.
8. At December 31, wages expense of $375 has been incurred but not paid or recorded.

REQUIRED

a. Prove that debits equal credits for SnapShot's unadjusted account balances by preparing its unadjusted trial balance at December 31, 2015.

b. Prepare its adjusting entries using the financial statement effects template.

c. Prepare its adjusting entries in journal entry form.

d. Set up T-accounts, enter the balances above, and post the adjusting entries to them.

P3-42. Preparing Adjusting Entries, Financial Statements, and Closing Entries   **LO2, 3, 4, 5, 6**

Murdock Carpet Cleaners ended its first month of operations on June 30, 2015. Monthly financial statements will be prepared. The unadjusted account balances are as follows.

MURDOCK CARPET CLEANERS Unadjusted Trial Balance June 30, 2015		
	Debit	Credit
Cash.	$ 1,180	
Accounts receivable.	450	
Prepaid rent	3,100	
Supplies	2,520	
Equipment	4,440	
Accounts payable.		$ 760
Common stock.		2,000
Retained earnings		5,300
Service fees earned		4,650
Wages expense	1,020	
	$12,710	$12,710

The following information is available.

1. The balance in Prepaid Rent was the amount paid on June 1 for the first four months' rent.
2. Supplies available at June 30 were $820.
3. Equipment, purchased June 1, has an estimated life of five years.
4. Unpaid and unrecorded employee wages at June 30 were $210.
5. Utility services used during June were estimated at $300. A bill is expected early in July.
6. Fees earned for services performed but not yet billed on June 30 were $380. The company uses the account Accounts Receivable to reflect amounts due but not yet billed.

REQUIRED

a. Prepare its adjusting entries at June 30, 2015 using the financial statement effects template.
b. Prepare its adjusting entries at June 30, 2015 in journal entry form.
c. Set up T-accounts, enter the balances above, and post the adjusting entries to them.
d. Prepare its income statement for June and its balance sheet at June 30, 2015.
e. Prepare entries to close its temporary accounts in journal entry form and post the closing entries to the T-accounts.

LO3   **P3-43.   Preparing Adjusting Entries**

The following information relates to the December 31 adjustments for Kwik Print Company. The firm's fiscal year ends on December 31.

1. Weekly employee salaries for a five-day week total $1,800, payable on Fridays. December 31 of the current year is a Tuesday.
2. Kwik Print has $20,000 of notes payable outstanding at December 31. Interest of $200 has accrued on these notes by December 31, but will not be paid until the notes mature next year.
3. During December, Kwik Print provided $900 of printing services to clients who will be billed on January 2. The firm uses the account Fees Receivable to reflect amounts due but not yet billed.
4. Starting December 1, all maintenance work on Kwik Print's equipment is handled by Richardson Repair Company under an agreement whereby Kwik Print pays a fixed monthly charge of $400. Kwik Print paid six months' service charge in advance on December 1, debiting Prepaid Maintenance for $2,400.
5. The firm paid $900 cash on December 15 for a series of radio commercials to run during December and January. One-third of the commercials have aired by December 31. The $900 payment was debited to Prepaid Advertising.
6. Starting December 16, Kwik Print rented 400 square feet of storage space from a neighboring business. The monthly rent of $0.80 per square foot is due in advance on the first of each month. Nothing was paid in December, however, because the neighbor agreed to add the rent for the one-half of December to the January 1 payment.
7. Kwik Print invested $5,000 cash in securities on December 1 and earned interest of $38 on these securities by December 31. No interest payment will be received until January, and the end-of-December market value of the securities remains at $5,000.
8. Annual depreciation on the firm's equipment is $2,175. No depreciation has been recorded during the year.

REQUIRED

Prepare its adjusting entries required at December 31:

a.   using the financial statement effects template, and

b.   in journal entry form.

P3-44.   Preparing Financial Statements and Closing Entries   LO4, 5

The following adjusted trial balance is for Trueman Consulting Inc. at December 31, 2015. The company had no stock issuances or repurchases during 2015.

	Debit	Credit
Cash.	$ 2,700	
Accounts receivable.	3,270	
Supplies	3,060	
Prepaid insurance.	1,500	
Equipment	6,400	
Accumulated depreciation—equipment.		$ 1,080
Accounts payable.		845
Long-term notes payable.		7,000
Common stock.		1,000
Retained earnings		3,305
Service fees earned		58,400
Rent expense	12,000	
Salaries expense	33,400	
Supplies expense.	4,700	
Insurance expense.	3,250	
Depreciation expense—equipment	720	
Interest expense.	630	
	$71,630	$71,630

REQUIRED

a.   Prepare its income statement and statement of stockholders' equity for 2015 and its balance sheet at December 31, 2015.

b.   Prepare entries to close its accounts in journal entry form.

P3-45.   Preparing Closing Entries   LO5

The following adjusted trial balance is for Wilson Company at December 31, 2015.

	Debit	Credit
Cash.	$ 8,500	
Accounts receivable.	8,000	
Prepaid insurance.	3,600	
Equipment	72,000	
Accumulated depreciation.		$ 12,000
Accounts payable.		600
Common stock.		25,000
Retained earnings		19,100
Service fees earned		97,200
Miscellaneous income		4,200
Salaries expense	42,800	
Rent expense	13,400	
Insurance expense.	1,800	
Depreciation expense.	8,000	
Income tax expense.	8,800	
Income tax payable		8,800
	$166,900	$166,900

REQUIRED

a.   Prepare closing entries in journal entry form.

b.   After the firm's closing entries are posted, what is the post-closing balance for the Retained Earnings account?

c.   Prepare its post-closing trial balance.

LO2, 3, 6 **P3-46.** **Preparing Entries Across Two Periods**

The following selected accounts appear in Shaw Company's unadjusted trial balance at December 31, 2015, the end of its fiscal year (all accounts have normal balances).

Prepaid advertising.	$ 1,200	Unearned service fees	$ 5,400
Wages expense	43,800	Service fees earned	87,000
Prepaid insurance.	3,420	Rental income	4,900

REQUIRED

a. Prepare its adjusting entries at December 31, 2015, (1) using the financial statement effects template, and (2) in journal entry form using the following additional information.
   1. Prepaid advertising at December 31 is $800.
   2. Unpaid and unrecorded wages earned by employees in December are $1,300.
   3. Prepaid insurance at December 31 is $2,280.
   4. Unearned service fees at December 31 are $3,000.
   5. Rent revenue of $1,000 owed by a tenant is not recorded at December 31.

b. Prepare entries on January 4, 2016, using the financial statement effects template and in journal entry form, to record (1) payment of $2,400 cash in wages, which includes the $1,300 accrued at December 31 and (2) cash receipt of the $1,000 rent revenue owed from the tenant.

LO2, 3, 6 **P3-47.** **Journalizing and Posting Transactions, and Preparing a Trial Balance and Adjustments**

Market-Probe, a market research firm, had the following transactions in June 2015, its first month of operations.

June 1 B. May invested $24,000 cash in the firm in exchange for common stock.
      1 The firm purchased the following: office equipment, $11,040; office supplies, $2,840. Terms are $4,400 cash with the remainder due in 60 days. (Make a compound entry requiring two credits.)
      2 Paid $875 cash for June rent owed to the landlord.
      2 Contracted for 3 months' advertising in a local newspaper at $310 per month and paid for the advertising in advance.
      2 Signed a 6-month contract with a customer to provide research consulting services at a rate of $3,200 per month. Received two months' fees in advance. Work on the contract started immediately.
      10 Billed various customers $5,800 for services rendered.
      12 Paid $3,600 cash for two weeks' salaries (5-day week) to employees.
      15 Paid $1,240 cash to employee for travel expenses to conference.
      18 Paid $520 cash to post office for bulk mailing of research questionnaire (postage expense).
      26 Paid $3,600 cash for two weeks' salaries to employees.
      28 Billed various customers $5,200 for services rendered.
      30 Collected $7,800 cash from customers on their accounts.
      30 Paid $1,500 cash for dividends.

REQUIRED

a. Set up a general ledger in T-account form for the following accounts: Cash; Accounts Receivable; Office Supplies; Prepaid Advertising; Office Equipment; Accumulated Depreciation—Office Equipment; Accounts Payable; Salaries Payable; Unearned Service Fees; Common Stock; Retained Earnings; Service Fees Earned; Salaries Expense; Advertising Expense; Supplies Expense; Rent Expense; Travel Expense; Depreciation Expense—Office Equipment; and Postage Expense.

b. Record these transactions (1) using the financial statement effects template, and (2) in journal entry form. (3) Post these entries to their T-accounts (key numbers in T-accounts by date).

c. Prepare an unadjusted trial balance at June 30, 2015.

d. Prepare adjusting entries (1) using the financial statement effects template and (2) in journal entry form, that reflect the following information at June 30, 2015:
   • Office supplies available, $1,530
   • Accrued employee salaries, $725
   • Estimated life of office equipment is 8 years

Adjusting entries must also be prepared for advertising and service fees per information in the June transactions. (3) Post all adjusting entries to their T-accounts.

P3-48.   Preparing an Unadjusted Trial Balance and Adjusting Entries   **LO3**

DeliverAll, a mailing service, has just completed its first full year of operations on December 31, 2015. Its general ledger account balances *before* year-end adjustments follow; no adjusting entries have been made to the accounts at any time during the year. Assume that all balances are normal.

Cash.	$ 2,300	Accounts payable.	$ 2,700
Accounts receivable.	5,120	Common stock.	9,530
Prepaid advertising.	1,680	Mailing fees earned	86,000
Supplies	6,270	Wages expense	38,800
Equipment	42,240	Rent expense	6,300
Notes payable	7,500	Utilities expense.	3,020

An analysis of the firm's records reveals the following.

1.   The balance in Prepaid Advertising represents the amount paid for newspaper advertising for one year. The agreement, which calls for the same amount of space and cost each month, covers the period from February 1, 2015, to January 31, 2016. DeliverAll did not advertise during its first month of operations.
2.   Equipment, purchased January 1, has an estimated life of eight years.
3.   Utilities expense does not include expense for December, estimated at $325. The bill will not arrive until January 2016.
4.   At year-end, employees have earned an additional $1,200 in wages that will not be paid or recorded until January.
5.   Supplies available at year-end amount to $1,520.
6.   At year-end, unpaid interest of $450 has accrued on the notes payable.
7.   The firm's lease calls for rent of $525 per month payable on the first of each month, plus an amount equal to 1/2% of annual mailing fees earned. The rental percentage is payable within 15 days after the end of the year.

REQUIRED

a.   Prove that debits equal credits for its unadjusted account balances by preparing its unadjusted trial balance at December 31, 2015.
b.   Prepare its adjusting entries: (1) using the financial statement effects template, and (2) in journal entry form.
c.   Set up T-accounts, enter the balances above, and post the adjusting entries to them.

P3-49.   Preparing Adjusting Entries   **LO3, 4, 5, 6**

Wheel Place Company began operations on March 1, 2016, to provide automotive wheel alignment and balancing services. On March 31, 2016, the unadjusted balances of the firm's accounts are as follows.

WHEEL PLACE COMPANY Unadjusted Trial Balance March 31, 2016		
	Debit	**Credit**
Cash.	$ 1,900	
Accounts receivable.	3,820	
Prepaid rent	4,770	
Supplies	3,700	
Equipment	36,180	
Accounts payable.		$ 2,510
Unearned service revenue		1,000
Common stock.		38,400
Service revenue		12,360
Wages expense	3,900	
Totals	$54,270	$54,270

The following information is available.

1.   The balance in Prepaid Rent was the amount paid on March 1 to cover the first 6 months' rent.
2.   Supplies available on March 31 amount to $1,720.
3.   Equipment has an estimated life of nine years and a zero salvage value.
4.   Unpaid and unrecorded wages at March 31 were $560.

5.   Utility services used during March were estimated at $390; a bill is expected early in April.
6.   The balance in Unearned Service Revenue was the amount received on March 1 from a car dealer to cover alignment and balancing services on cars sold by the dealer in March and April. The Wheel Place agreed to provide the services at a fixed fee of $500 each month.

REQUIRED

a.   Prepare its adjusting entries at March 31, 2016, (1) using the financial statement effects template, and (2) in journal entry form.
b.   Set up T-accounts, enter the balances above, and post the adjusting entries to them.
c.   Prepare its income statement for March and its balance sheet at March 31, 2016.
d.   Prepare entries to close its temporary accounts in journal entry form and post the closing entries to the T-accounts.

LO4, 5   P3-50.   Preparing Financial Statements and Closing Entries

Trails, Inc., publishes magazines for skiers and hikers. The company's adjusted trial balance for the year ending December 31, 2015 is:

TRAILS, INC. Adjusted Trial Balance December 31, 2015		
	Debit	**Credit**
Cash	$ 3,400	
Accounts receivable	8,600	
Supplies	4,200	
Prepaid insurance	930	
Office equipment	66,000	
Accumulated depreciation		$ 11,000
Accounts payable		2,100
Unearned subscription revenue		10,000
Salaries payable		3,500
Common stock		25,000
Retained earnings		23,220
Subscription revenue		168,300
Advertising revenue		49,700
Salaries expense	100,230	
Printing and mailing expense	85,600	
Rent expense	8,800	
Supplies expense	6,100	
Insurance expense	1,860	
Depreciation expense	5,500	
Income tax expense	1,600	
Totals	$292,820	$292,820

REQUIRED

a.   Prepare its income statement and statement of stockholders' equity for 2015, and its balance sheet at December 31, 2015. There were no cash dividends and no stock issuances or repurchases during the year.
b.   Prepare entries to close its accounts in journal entry form.

LO5   P3-51.   Preparing Closing Entries

The following adjusted trial balance is for Mayflower Moving Service at December 31, 2015.

MAYFLOWER MOVING SERVICE Adjusted Trial Balance December 31, 2015	Debit	Credit
Cash...	$ 3,800	
Accounts receivable.........................	5,250	
Supplies....................................	2,300	
Prepaid advertising.........................	3,000	
Trucks......................................	28,300	
Accumulated depreciation—trucks.............		$ 10,000
Equipment..................................	7,600	
Accumulated depreciation—equipment..........		2,100
Accounts payable...........................		1,200
Unearned service fees......................		2,700
Common stock..............................		5,000
Retained earnings..........................		15,550
Service fees earned........................		72,500
Wages expense.............................	29,800	
Rent expense..............................	10,200	
Insurance expense.........................	2,900	
Supplies expense..........................	5,100	
Advertising expense.......................	6,000	
Depreciation expense—trucks...............	4,000	
Depreciation expense—equipment............	800	
Totals.....................................	$109,050	$109,050

REQUIRED

a. Prepare closing entries in journal entry form.

b. After its closing entries are posted, what is the post-closing balance for the Retained Earnings account?

c. Prepare Mayflower's post-closing trial balance.

P3-52. **Preparing Entries Across Two Periods**   LO2, 3, 5, 6

The following selected accounts appear in Zimmerman Company's unadjusted trial balance at December 31, 2015, the end of its fiscal year (all accounts have normal balances).

Prepaid maintenance...........	$2,700	Commission fees earned.........	$84,000
Supplies.....................	8,400	Rent expense.................	10,800
Unearned commission fees.......	8,500		

Additional information is as follows.

1. On September 1, 2015, the company entered into a prepaid equipment maintenance contract. Zimmerman Company paid $2,700 to cover maintenance service for 6 months, beginning September 1, 2015. The $2,700 payment was debited to Prepaid Maintenance.
2. Supplies available on December 31 are $3,200.
3. Unearned commission fees at December 31 are $4,000.
4. Commission fees earned but not yet billed at December 31 are $2,800. (*Hint:* Debit Fees Receivable.)
5. Zimmerman Company's lease calls for rent of $900 per month payable on the first of each month, plus an annual amount equal to 1% of annual commissions earned. This additional rent is payable on January 10 of the following year. (*Hint:* Use the adjusted amount of commissions earned in computing the additional rent.)

REQUIRED

a. Prepare Zimmerman Company's adjusting entries at December 31, 2015 using the financial statement effects template.

b. Prepare entries on January 10, 2016, using the financial statement effects template to record (1) the billing of $4,600 in commissions earned (which includes the $2,800 of commissions earned but not billed at December 31) and (2) the cash payment of the additional rent owed for 2015. (*Hint for part (1)*: Zimmerman Company has two receivable accounts—Fees Receivable is used for amounts earned, but not yet billed, and Accounts Receivable for amounts that are earned and billed to the customer.)

c. Prepare the adjusting entries from part *a* and the transactions in part *b* in journal entry form.

LO2, 3, 4, 5, 6

P3-53. **Preparing Adjusting Entries, Financial Statements, and Closing Entries**

Fischer Card Shop is a small retail shop. Fischer's balance sheet at year-end 2014 is as follows. The following information details transactions and adjustments that occurred during 2015.

1. Sales total $145,850 in 2015; all sales were cash sales.
2. Inventory purchases total $76,200 in 2015; at December 31, 2015, inventory totals $14,500. Assume all purchases were made on account.
3. Accounts payable totals $4,100 at December 31, 2015.
4. Annual store rent of $24,000 was paid on March 1, 2015, covering the next 12 months. The balance in prepaid rent at December 31, 2014, was the balance remaining from the advance rent payment in 2014.
5. Wages are paid every other week on Friday; during 2015, Fischer paid $12,500 cash for wages. At December 31, 2015, Fischer owed employees unpaid and unrecorded wages of $350.
6. Depreciation on equipment totals $1,700 in 2015.

FISCHER CARD SHOP			
Balance Sheet			
December 31, 2014			
Cash........................	$ 8,500	Accounts payable.....................	$ 5,200
Inventories	12,000	Wages payable.......................	100
Prepaid rent	3,800	Total current liabilities.................	5,300
Total current assets	24,300	Total equity (includes retained earnings) ...	23,500
Equipment $7,500		Total liabilities and equity..............	$28,800
Less accumulated depreciation ... 3,000			
Equipment, net..............	4,500		
Total assets................	$28,800		

REQUIRED

a. Prepare any necessary transaction entries for 2015 and adjusting entries at December 31, 2015, using the financial statement effects template.

b. Prepare any necessary transaction entries for 2015 and adjusting entries at December 31, 2015, in journal entry form.

c. Set up T-accounts, enter the balances above, and post the transactions and adjusting entries to them.

d. Prepare its income statement for 2015, and its balance sheet at December 31, 2015.

e. Prepare entries to close its temporary accounts in journal entry form and post the closing entries to the T-accounts.

LO2, 3, 4, 5, 6

P3-54. **Applying the Entire Accounting Cycle**

Rhoades Tax Services began business on December 1, 2015. Its December transactions are as follows.

Dec. 1 Rhoades invested $20,000 in the business in exchange for common stock.
  2 Paid $1,200 cash for December rent to Bomba Realty.
  2 Purchased $1,080 of supplies on account.
  3 Purchased $9,500 of office equipment; paying $4,700 cash with the balance due in 30 days.
  8 Paid $1,080 cash on account for supplies purchased December 2.
  14 Paid $900 cash for assistant's wages for 2 weeks' work.
  20 Performed consulting services for $3,000 cash.
  28 Paid $900 cash for assistant's wages for 2 weeks' work.
  30 Billed clients $7,200 for December consulting services.
  31 Paid $1,800 cash for dividends.

Additional information:
1. Supplies available at December 31 are $710.
2. Accrued wages payable at December 31 are $270.
3. Depreciation for December is $120.
4. Rhoades has spent 30 hours on an involved tax fraud case during December. When completed in January, his work will be billed at $75 per hour. (The account Fees Receivable is used to reflect amounts earned but not yet billed.)

REQUIRED

a. Record these transactions and any necessary adjusting entries using the financial statement effects template.

b. Set up a general ledger in T-account form for the following accounts: Cash; Fees Receivable; Supplies; Office Equipment; Accumulated Depreciation—Office Equipment; Accounts Payable; Wages Payable; Common Stock; Retained Earnings; Consulting Revenue; Supplies Expense; Wages Expense; Rent Expense; and Depreciation Expense.

c. Record the above transactions in journal entry form and post these entries to their T-accounts (key numbers in T-accounts by date).

d. Prepare an unadjusted trial balance at December 31, 2015.

e. Journalize the adjusting entries at December 31 in journal entry form, drawing on the information above. Then post adjusting entries to their T-accounts and prepare an adjusted trial balance at December 31, 2015.

f. Prepare a December 2015 income statement and statement of stockholders' equity, and a December 31, 2015, balance sheet.

g. Record its closing entries in journal entry form. Post these entries to their T-accounts.

h. Prepare a post-closing trial balance at December 31, 2015.

CASES AND PROJECTS

C3-55. Preparing Adjusting Entries, Financial Statements, and Closing Entries   **LO2, 3, 4, 5, 6**

Seaside Surf Shop began operations on July 1, 2015, with an initial investment of $50,000. During the initial 3 months of operations, the following cash transactions were recorded in the firm's checking account.

Cash receipts		Cash payments	
Initial investment by owner........	$ 50,000	Rent	$ 24,000
Collected from customers	81,000	Fixtures and equipment	25,000
Borrowed from bank 7/1/2015.....	10,000	Merchandise inventory...........	62,000
Total cash receipts	$141,000	Salaries.....................	6,000
		Other expenses	13,000
		Total cash payments	$130,000

Additional information

1. Most sales were for cash, however, the store accepted a limited amount of credit sales; at September 30, 2015, customers owed the store $9,000.

2. Rent was paid on July 1 for six months.

3. Salaries of $3,000 per month are paid on the 1st of each month for salaries earned in the month prior.

4. Inventories are purchased for cash; at September 30, 2015, inventory worth $21,000 was available.

5. Fixtures and equipment were expected to last five years with zero salvage value.

6. The bank charges 12% annual interest (1% per month) on its bank loan.

REQUIRED

a. Prepare any necessary adjusting entries at September 30, 2015, (1) using the financial statement effects template, and (2) in journal entry form.

b. Set up T-accounts and post the adjusting entries to them.

c. Prepare its initial three-month income statement for 2015 and its balance sheet at September 30, 2015. (Ignore taxes.)

d. Analyze the statements from part c and assess the company's performance over its initial 3 months.

C3-56. Analyzing Transactions, Impacts on Financial Ratios, and Loan Covenants   **LO2, 3, 6**

Wyland Consulting, a firm started three years ago by Reyna Wyland, offers consulting services for material handling and plant layout. Its balance sheet at the close of 2015 is as follows.

WYLAND CONSULTING
Balance Sheet
December 31, 2015

Assets			Liabilities		
Cash......................		$ 3,400	Notes payable		$30,000
Accounts receivable..........		22,875	Accounts payable.....................		4,200
Supplies		13,200	Unearned consulting fees		11,300
Prepaid insurance............		4,500	Wages payable........................		400
Equipment	$68,500		Total liabilities......................		45,900
Less: accumulated			**Equity**		
depreciation	23,975	44,525	Common stock.......................		8,000
			Retained earnings		34,600
Total assets.................		$88,500	Total liabilities and equity..............		$88,500

Earlier in the year Wyland obtained a bank loan of $30,000 cash for the firm. One of the provisions of the loan is that the year-end debt-to-equity ratio (ratio of total liabilities to total equity) cannot exceed 1.0. Based on the above balance sheet, the ratio at the end of 2015 is 1.08. Wyland is concerned about being in violation of the loan agreement and requests assistance in reviewing the situation. Wyland believes that she might have overlooked some items at year-end. Discussions with Wyland reveal the following.

1. On January 1, 2015, the firm paid a $4,500 insurance premium for 2 years of coverage; the amount in Prepaid Insurance has not yet been adjusted.
2. Depreciation on the equipment should be 10% of cost per year; the company inadvertently recorded 15% for 2015.
3. Interest on the bank loan has been paid through the end of 2015.
4. The firm concluded a major consulting engagement in December, doing a plant layout analysis for a new factory. The $6,000 fee has not been billed or recorded in the accounts.
5. On December 1, 2015, the firm received an $11,300 advance payment from Croy Corporation for consulting services to be rendered over a 2-month period. This payment was credited to the Unearned Consulting Fees account. One-half of this fee was earned by December 31, 2015.
6. Supplies costing $4,800 were available on December 31; the company has made no entry in the accounts.

REQUIRED

a. What portion of the company is financed by debt versus equity (called the debt-to-equity ratio and defined in Chapter 1) at December 31, 2015?

b. Is the firm in violation of its loan agreement? Prepare computations to support the correct total liabilities and total equity figures at December 31, 2015.

LO2, 3   C3-57.   Ethics, Accounting Adjustments, and Auditors

It is the end of the accounting year for Juliet Javetz, controller of a medium-sized, publicly held corporation specializing in toxic waste cleanup. Within the corporation, only Javetz and the president know that the firm has been negotiating for several months to land a large contract for waste cleanup in Western Europe. The president has hired another firm with excellent contacts in Western Europe to help with negotiations. The outside firm will charge an hourly fee plus expenses, but has agreed not to submit a bill until the negotiations are in their final stages (expected to occur in another 3 to 4 months). Even if the contract falls through, the outside firm is entitled to receive payment for its services. Based upon her discussion with a member of the outside firm, Javetz knows that its charge for services provided to date will be $150,000. This is a material amount for the company.

Javetz knows that the president wants negotiations to remain as secret as possible so that competitors will not learn of the contract the company is pursuing in Europe. In fact, the president recently stated to her, "Now is not the time to reveal our actions in Western Europe to other staff members, our auditors, or the readers of our financial statements; securing this contract is crucial to our future growth." No entry has been made in the accounting records for the cost of contract negotiations. Javetz now faces an uncomfortable situation. The company's outside auditor has just asked her if she knows of any year-end adjustments that have not yet been recorded.

REQUIRED

a. What are the ethical considerations that Javetz faces in answering the auditor's question?

b. How should Javetz respond to the auditor's question?

C3-58. Inferring Adjusting Entries from Financial Statements   **LO2, 3, 4, 6**
Lady G's Fashions, a specialty retailer of women's apparel, markets its products through retail stores and catalogs. Selected information from its 2015 and 2014 balance sheets is as follows.

Selected Balance Sheet Data ($ thousands)	2014	2015
Prepaid catalog expenses (asset)	$3,894	$4,306
Advertising credits receivable	21	534
Customer deposits.	6,108	7,053

The following excerpts are from Lady G's Fashions accompanying footnotes:

*   Catalog costs in the direct segment are considered direct response advertising and as such are capitalized as incurred and amortized over the expected sales life of each catalog, which is generally a period not exceeding six months.

*   The Company periodically enters into arrangements with certain national magazine publishers whereby the Company includes magazine subscription cards in its catalog mailings in exchange for advertising credits or discounts on advertising.

REQUIRED

a. Assume that Lady G's Fashions spent $62,550 to design, print, and mail catalogs in 2015. Also assume that it received advertising credits of $849. Prepare the entry, using the financial statement effects template and in journal entry form, that Lady G's Fashions would have recorded when these costs were incurred.

b. Prepare the adjusting entry, using the financial statement effects template and in journal entry form, that would be necessary to record its amortization of prepaid catalog costs.

c. How do advertising credits expire? Prepare the adjusting entry, using both the financial statement effects template and in journal entry form, that Lady G's Fashions would record to reflect the change in advertising credits.

d. Assume that Lady G's Fashions sold gift certificates valued at $19,175 in 2015. Prepare the entry, using the financial statement effects template and in journal entry form, that Lady G's Fashions would make to record these sales. Next, prepare the entry, using the financial statement effects template and in journal entry form, that it makes to record merchandise sales to customers who pay with gift certificates.

SOLUTIONS TO REVIEW PROBLEMS

Mid-Chapter Review

SOLUTION TO PARTS 1 AND 2

a.

	Balance Sheet						Income Statement		
Transaction	Cash Asset	+ Noncash Assets	− Contra Assets	= Liabil- ities	+ Contrib. Capital	+ Earned Capital	Revenues	− Expenses	= Net Income
(a) Adjusting entry to record supplies and parts used.		−91,000 Supplies and Parts	− =			−91,000 Retained Earnings		+91,000 Supplies and Parts Expenses	− = −91,000

(a)	Supplies and parts expense (+E, −SE)	91,000	
	Supplies and parts (−A)		91,000

b.

Transaction	Balance Sheet						Income Statement		
	Cash Asset +	Noncash Assets −	Contra Assets =	Liabil- ities +	Contrib. Capital +	Earned Capital	Revenues −	Expenses =	Net Income
(b) Adjusting entry to record rent expense accrued but not yet paid.		−	=	+2,500 Accounts Payable		−2,500 Retained Earnings	−	+2,500 Rent Expense	= −2,500

(b)			
	Rent expense (+E, −SE)...............................	2,500	
	Accounts payable (+L)............................		2,500

The $2,500 expense for October is not recorded because it is not yet incurred as of September 30.

c.

Transaction	Balance Sheet						Income Statement		
(c) Adjusting entry to record depreciation on building.		−	+50,000 Accumulated Depreciation —Building =			−50,000 Retained Earnings	−	+50,000 Depreciation Expense	= −50,000

(c)			
	Depreciation expense (+E, −SE)	50,000	
	Accumulated depreciation—Building (+XA, −A)		50,000

d.   No entry required; the executive has not yet begun work and thus, no expense is incurred.

e.

Transaction	Balance Sheet						Income Statement		
(e) Adjusting entry to record cash advance, of which a part is earned.	+1,200 Cash	−	=	+600 Unearned Revenue		+600 Retained Earnings	+600 Services Revenue −		= +600

(e)			
	Cash (+A)...	1,200	
	Unearned revenue (+L).............................		600
	Services revenue (+R, +SE)		600

f.

Transaction	Balance Sheet						Income Statement		
(f) Adjusting entry to record wages earned but not yet paid.		−	=	+25,000 Wages Payable		−25,000 Retained Earnings	−	+25,000 Wages Expense	= −25,000

(f)			
	Wages expense (+E, −SE)	25,000	
	Wages payable (+L).................................		25,000

SOLUTION TO PART 3

General Ledger

Assets	=	Liabilities	+	Equity

Assets

+	Cash (A)	−
Unadj. bal. 80,000		
(e) **1,200**		
Adj. bal. 81,200		

+	Accounts Receivable (A)	−
Unadj. bal. 95,000		
Adj. bal. 95,000		

+	Supplies & Parts (A)	−
Unadj. bal. 100,000		
	91,000	(a)
Adj. bal. 9,000		

+	Building (A)	−
Unadj. bal. 400,000		
Adj. bal. 400,000		

−	Accumulated Depreciation—Building (XA)	+
	200,000 Unadj. bal.	
	50,000	(c)
	250,000 Adj. bal.	

+	Land (A)	−
Unadj. bal. 257,500		
Adj. bal. 257,500		

Liabilities

−	Accounts Payable (L)	+
	20,000 Unadj. bal.	
	2,500	(b)
	22,500 Adj. bal.	

−	Wages Payable (L)	+
	0 Unadj. bal.	
	25,000	(f)
	25,000 Adj. bal.	

−	Unearned Revenue (L)	+
	0 Unadj. bal.	
	600	(e)
	600 Adj. bal.	

Equity

−	Common Stock (SE)	+
	80,000 Unadj. bal.	
	80,000 Adj. bal.	

−	Retained Earnings (SE)	+
	380,000 Unadj. bal.	
	380,000 Adj. bal.	

−	Services Revenue (R)	+
	720,000 Unadj. bal.	
	600	(e)
	720,600 Adj. bal.	

+	Rent Expense (E)	−
Unadj. bal. 27,500		
(b) **2,500**		
Adj. bal. 30,000		

+	Depreciation Expense (E)	−
Unadj. bal. 0		
(c) **50,000**		
Adj. bal. 50,000		

+	Wages Expense (E)	−
Unadj. bal. 440,000		
(f) **25,000**		
Adj. bal. 465,000		

+	Supplies & Parts Expense (E)	−
Unadj. bal. 0		
(a) **91,000**		
Adj. bal. 91,000		

Assets = $592,700 = **Liabilities = $48,100** + **Equity = $544,600**

Transaction	Balance Sheet						Income Statement		
	Cash Asset +	Noncash Assets −	Contra Assets =	Liabil-ities +	Contrib. Capital +	Earned Capital	Revenues −	Expenses =	Net Income
(1) Adjustment to record insurance expense.	−1,500 Prepaid Insurance −	=				−1,500 Retained Earnings	−	+1,500 Insurance Expense =	−1,500

(1)	Insurance expense (+E, −SE)............................	1,500	
	Prepaid insurance (−A)................................		1,500
	Record insurance expired $6,000 × (6 months/24 months).		

Transaction	Balance Sheet						Income Statement		
(2) Adjustment to record supplies expense.	−25,000 Supplies −	=				−25,000 Retained Earnings	−	+25,000 Supplies Expense =	−25,000

(2)	Supplies expense (+E, −SE)	25,000	
	Supplies (−A)		25,000
	Record supplies used ($31,300 − $6,300).		

Transaction	Balance Sheet						Income Statement		
(3) Adjustment to record depreciation expense.	−	+30,000 Accumulated Depreciation —Equipment =			−30,000 Retained Earnings		−	+30,000 Depreciation Expense =	−30,000

(3)	Depreciation expense (+E, −SE)	30,000	
	Accumulated depreciation—Equipment (+XA, −A)		30,000
	Record depreciation [($270,000 − $0) ÷ 9 years].		

Transaction	Balance Sheet						Income Statement		
(4) Adjustment to record fees revenue.	−	=	−3,000 Unearned Fees	+3,000 Retained Earnings			+3,000 Fees Revenue −	=	+3,000

(4)	Unearned fees (−L).......................................	3,000	
	Fees revenue (+R, +SE).................................		3,000
	Record fees earned.		

Transaction	Balance Sheet						Income Statement		
(5) Adjustment to record wages expense.	−	=	+600 Wages Payable	−600 Retained Earnings			−	+600 Wages Expense =	−600

(5)	Wages expense (+E, −SE)	600	
	Wages payable (+L)		600
	Record employee wages incurred.		

	Balance Sheet							Income Statement		
Transaction	Cash Asset	+ Noncash Assets	− Contra Assets	= Liabil- ities	+ Contrib. Capital	+ Earned Capital		Revenues	− Expenses	= Net Income
(6) Adjustment to record rent expense.		−	=	+2,000 Rent Payable		−2,000 Retained Earnings			− +2,000 Rent Expense	= −2,000

(6)	Rent expense (+E, −SE).....................................	2,000	
	Rent payable (+L).....................................		2,000
	Record rent owed.		

SOLUTION TO PART 3

General Ledger

Assets	=	Liabilities	+	Equity

Assets

+ Cash (A) −

| Unadj. bal. | 1,000 | |
| Adj. bal. | 1,000 | |

+ Accounts Receivable (A) −

| Unadj. bal. | 9,200 | |
| Adj. bal. | 9,200 | |

+ Prepaid Insurance (A) −

Unadj. bal.	6,000		
		1,500	(1)
Adj. bal.	4,500		

+ Supplies (A) −

Unadj. bal.	31,300		
		25,000	(2)
Adj. bal.	6,300		

+ Equipment (A) −

| Unadj. bal. | 270,000 | |
| Adj. bal. | 270,000 | |

− Accumulated Depreciation— Equipment (XA) +

		60,000	Unadj. bal.
		30,000	(3)
		90,000	Adj. bal.

Liabilities

− Accounts Payable (L) +

| | | 3,100 | Unadj. bal. |
| | | 3,100 | Adj. bal. |

− Unearned Fees (L) +

		4,000	Unadj. bal.
(4)	3,000		
		1,000	Adj. bal.

− Wages Payable (L) +

		0	Unadj. bal.
		600	(5)
		600	Adj. bal.

− Rent Payable (L) +

		0	Unadj. bal.
		2,000	(6)
		2,000	Adj. bal.

Equity

− Common Stock (SE) +

| | | 120,400 | Unadj. bal. |
| | | 120,400 | Adj. bal. |

− Retained Earnings (SE) +

| | | 60,000 | Unadj. bal. |
| | | 60,000 | Adj. bal. |

− Fees Revenue (R) +

		150,000	Unadj. bal.
		3,000	(4)
		153,000	Adj. bal.

+ Insurance Expense (E) −

Unadj. bal.	0		
(1)	1,500		
Adj. bal.	1,500		

+ Supplies Expenses (E) −

Unadj. bal.	0		
(2)	25,000		
Adj. bal.	25,000		

+ Depreciation Expense (E) −

Unadj. bal.	0		
(3)	30,000		
Adj. bal.	30,000		

+ Rent Expense (E) −

Unadj. bal.	22,000		
(6)	2,000		
Adj. bal.	24,000		

+ Wages Expense (E) −

Unadj. bal.	58,000		
(5)	600		
Adj. bal.	58,600		

Assets = $201,000   =   **Liabilities = $6,700**   +   **Equity = $194,300**

ATWELL LABORATORIES, INC. Adjusted Trial Balance June 30, 2015	Debits	Credits
Cash.	$ 1,000	
Accounts receivable.	9,200	
Prepaid insurance.	4,500	
Supplies	6,300	
Equipment	270,000	
Accumulated depreciation—equipment.		$ 90,000
Accounts payable.		3,100
Rent payable		2,000
Wages payable.		600
Unearned fees		1,000
Fees revenue		153,000
Wages expense	58,600	
Rent expense.	24,000	
Insurance expense.	1,500	
Supplies expense.	25,000	
Depreciation expense.	30,000	
Common stock.		120,400
Retained earnings		60,000
Totals	$430,100	$430,100

SOLUTION TO PART 4

a.	Retained earnings (−SE).	139,100	
	Insurance expense (−E).		1,500
	Supplies expense (−E).		25,000
	Depreciation expense (−E)		30,000
	Rent expense (−E).		24,000
	Wages expense (−E)		58,600
b.	Fees revenue (−R).	153,000	
	Retained earnings (+SE)		153,000

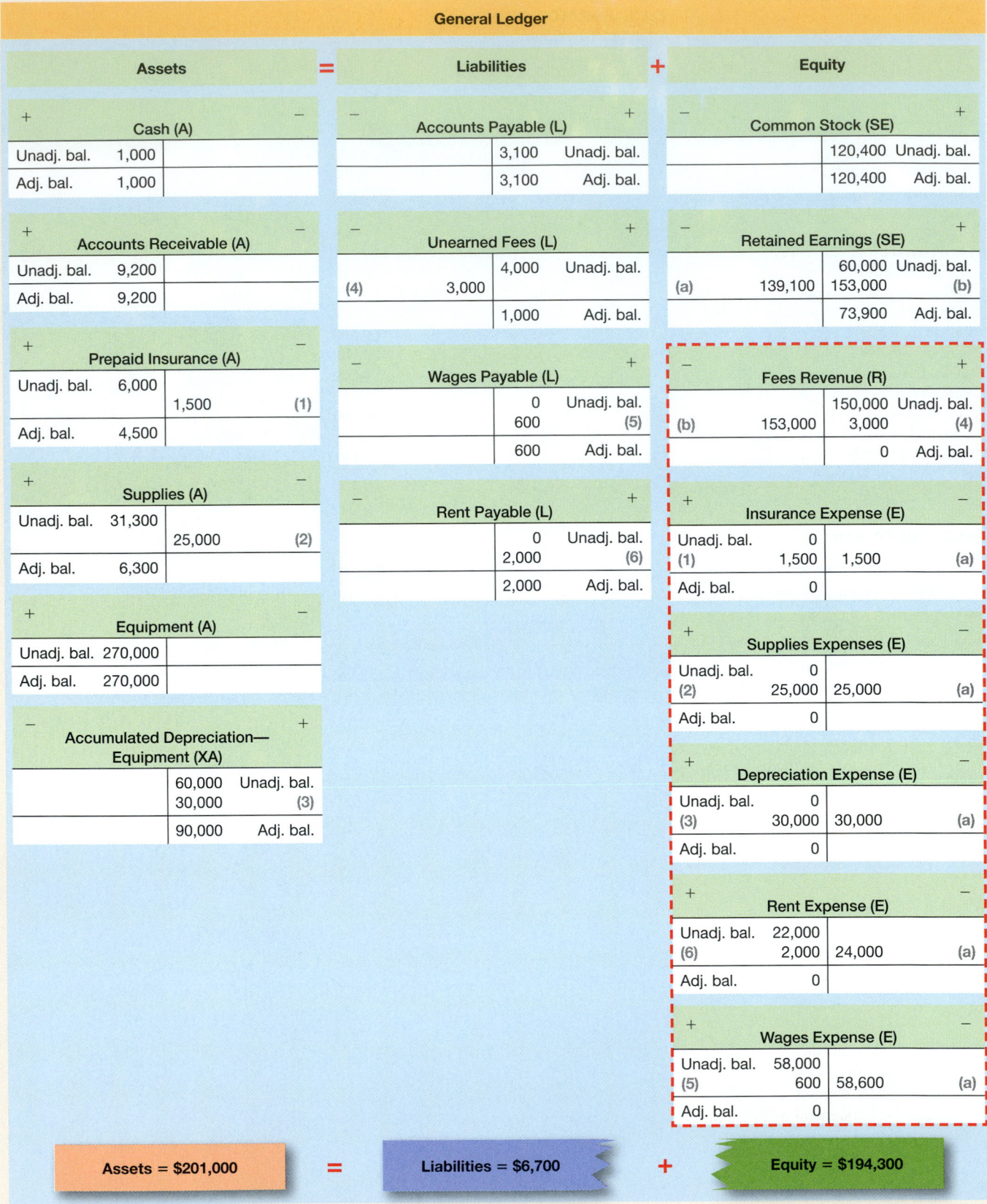

General Ledger

Assets	=	Liabilities	+	Equity

Cash (A)

+		−
Unadj. bal.	1,000	
Adj. bal.	1,000	

Accounts Receivable (A)

+		−
Unadj. bal.	9,200	
Adj. bal.	9,200	

Prepaid Insurance (A)

+		−	
Unadj. bal.	6,000		
		1,500	(1)
Adj. bal.	4,500		

Supplies (A)

+		−	
Unadj. bal.	31,300		
		25,000	(2)
Adj. bal.	6,300		

Equipment (A)

+		−
Unadj. bal.	270,000	
Adj. bal.	270,000	

Accumulated Depreciation— Equipment (XA)

−		+	
	60,000	Unadj. bal.	
	30,000		(3)
	90,000	Adj. bal.	

Accounts Payable (L)

−		+	
		3,100	Unadj. bal.
		3,100	Adj. bal.

Unearned Fees (L)

−		+	
		4,000	Unadj. bal.
(4)	3,000		
		1,000	Adj. bal.

Wages Payable (L)

−		+	
		0	Unadj. bal.
		600	(5)
		600	Adj. bal.

Rent Payable (L)

−		+	
		0	Unadj. bal.
		2,000	(6)
		2,000	Adj. bal.

Common Stock (SE)

−		+	
		120,400	Unadj. bal.
		120,400	Adj. bal.

Retained Earnings (SE)

−		+	
		60,000	Unadj. bal.
(a)	139,100	153,000	(b)
		73,900	Adj. bal.

Fees Revenue (R)

−		+	
		150,000	Unadj. bal.
(b)	153,000	3,000	(4)
		0	Adj. bal.

Insurance Expense (E)

+		−	
Unadj. bal.	0		
(1)	1,500	1,500	(a)
Adj. bal.	0		

Supplies Expenses (E)

+		−	
Unadj. bal.	0		
(2)	25,000	25,000	(a)
Adj. bal.	0		

Depreciation Expense (E)

+		−	
Unadj. bal.	0		
(3)	30,000	30,000	(a)
Adj. bal.	0		

Rent Expense (E)

+		−	
Unadj. bal.	22,000		
(6)	2,000	24,000	(a)
Adj. bal.	0		

Wages Expense (E)

+		−	
Unadj. bal.	58,000		
(5)	600	58,600	(a)
Adj. bal.	0		

Assets = $201,000 = **Liabilities = $6,700** + **Equity = $194,300**

SOLUTION TO PART 5

ATWELL LABORATORIES, INC.
Balance Sheet
June 30, 2015

Assets			Liabilities		
Cash..........................		$ 1,000	Accounts payable............		$ 3,100
Accounts receivable..............		9,200	Unearned fees		1,000
Prepaid insurance................		4,500	Wages payable..............		600
Supplies		6,300	Rent payable		2,000
Total current assets		21,000	Total current liabilities..........		6,700
Equipment, original cost...........	$270,000				
Less accumulated depreciation......	90,000	180,000	**Equity**		
			Common stock...............		120,400
			Retained earnings		73,900
Total assets.....................		$201,000	Totals liabilities and equity		$201,000

ATWELL LABORATORIES, INC.
Income Statement
For Year Ended June 30, 2015

Fees revenue		$153,000
Expenses		
Insurance expense	$ 1,500	
Supplies expense	25,000	
Depreciation expense...	30,000	
Rent expense...	24,000	
Wages expense	58,600	
Total expense...		139,100
Net income...		$ 13,900

ATWELL LABORATORIES, INC.
Statement of Stockholders' Equity
For Year Ended June 30, 2015

	Common Stock	Retained Earnings	Total
Balance at June 30, 2014.............	$120,400	$60,000	$180,400
Net Income........................	—	13,900	13,900
Balance at June 30, 2015.............	$120,400	$73,900	$194,300

Atwell's statement of stockholders' equity is much simpler than the usual statement because we have focused on the adjustment and closing process. In doing so, we did not consider additional activities in which corporations commonly engage, such as paying dividends, issuing stock, and repurchasing stock. (Requirements did not ask for a statement of cash flows. The next chapter is devoted to the statement of cash flows.)

4

Reporting and Analyzing Cash Flows

GOLDEN ENTERPRISES
www.goldenflake.com

In the southeastern United States, Golden Flake Snack Foods, Inc. is well-known for its tasty products. Founded in 1923 as Magic City Foods, it now operates as a wholly-owned subsidiary of **Golden Enterprises, Inc.** The company distributes potato chips, pork skins, tortilla chips, and many more products in fifteen states from Florida to Kentucky to Texas.

In 2014, sales at Golden Enterprises declined for the first time in five years from $137.3 million in fiscal 2013 to $135.9 million in fiscal 2014. Mark McCutcheon (Chairman and CEO) announced a restructuring of Golden Enterprises' operations in 2014, resulting in a $1 million charge against income in that fiscal year. As a consequence, net income declined for the fourth consecutive year to $921,829. The snack food market is highly competitive with large companies (Frito-Lay, Kraft Foods) competing with smaller firms like Golden Enterprises for market share. Small profit margins leave little leeway for increases in fuel or commodity costs, or significant shifts in consumer preferences. The graph below compares revenues for Golden Enterprises and three of its smaller competitors—**Snyder's-Lance** (LNCE: Snyder's of Hanover pretzels, Cape Cod potato chips), **J & J Snack Foods** (JJSF: Bavarian pretzels, ICEE beverages), and **Diamond Foods** (DMND: Diamond nuts, Pop Secret popcorn).

Golden Flake's headquarters and main production facilities are located in Birmingham, Alabama, and a second manufacturing plant is located in Florida. In addition to these properties, Golden Flake owns 20 warehouses and a fleet of delivery vehicles. The company's recent investments include improvements to its waste water treatment and a significant investment in an Enterprise Resource Planning (ERP) system that will improve the company's operating efficiency. Both of these investments should improve the company's margins in the future. Golden Flake spent almost $2.4 million in fiscal 2014 on additions to property, plant, and equipment. These costs are listed in Golden Flake's cash flow statement under *investing activities*.

In addition to making investments to improve operations, Golden Flake regularly returns about $1.5 million cash to its shareholders in the form of dividends or repurchases of its own stock (treasury shares). These cash outflows are reported in Golden Flake's statement of cash flows under *financing activities*.

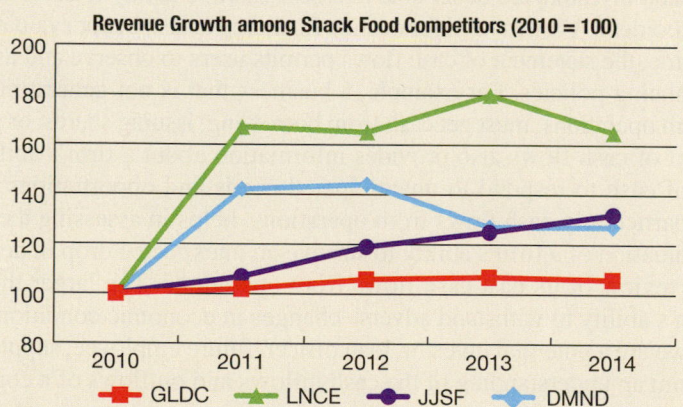

Revenue Growth among Snack Food Competitors (2010 = 100)

Legend: GLDC, LNCE, JJSF, DMND

How does a company with income of less than $1 million spend almost $4 million in investments and dividends? To accomplish its objectives, Golden Flake must generate positive cash flow from *operating activities*, and its operating activities produced cash flows of almost $3.3 million in the fiscal year ended May 30, 2014. The company's operations are the engine that produces cash that can be used to grow the business and to provide a return to shareholders.

As we will discover in this chapter, a business must make sure that its cash inflows are adequate to fund new investments, meet obligations to creditors as they come due, and pay dividends to shareholders. Even a profitable company can fail if it does not have a healthy cash flow. We will also discover why it is important to look at the cash flow statement along with the income statement and balance sheet when trying to assess the financial health of a company.

Sources: Golden Enterprises, Inc. Form 10-K 2010–2014; Golden Enterprises, Inc. Annual Report 2010–2014.

CHAPTER ORGANIZATION

Reporting and Analyzing Cash Flows			
Purpose of the Statement of Cash Flows	**Framework for the Statement of Cash Flows**	**Preparing the Statement of Cash Flows**	**Analysis of Cash Flows**
• What Do We Mean by Cash? • What Does a Statement of Cash Flows Look Like?	• Operating Activities • Investing Activities • Financing Activities • Usefulness of Classifications	• Cash Flows from Operating Activities • Cash Flows from Investing and Financing Activities • Additional Detail in the Statement of Cash Flows • Preparing the Statement of Cash Flows Using a Spreadsheet (Appendix 4A)	• Operating Cash Flow to Current Liabilities • Operating Cash Flow to Capital Expenditures • Free Cash Flow

LO1 Explain the purpose of the statement of cash flows and classify cash transactions by type of business activity: operating, investing or financing.

PURPOSE OF THE STATEMENT OF CASH FLOWS

In addition to the balance sheet and the income statement, corporations are required to report a statement of cash flows. The **statement of cash flows** tells us how a company generated cash (cash inflows) and how it used cash (cash outflows). The statement of cash flows complements the income statement and the balance sheet by providing information that neither the income statement nor the balance sheet can provide. For instance, slower collection of receivables doesn't affect income, but it does reduce the amount of cash coming into the company.

Understanding the statement of cash flows helps us understand trends in a firm's **liquidity** (ability to pay near-term liabilities and take advantage of investment opportunities), and it helps us assess a firm's **solvency** (ability to pay long-term liabilities). With information about how cash was generated or used, creditors and investors are better able to assess a firm's ability to settle its liabilities and pay dividends to shareholders. A firm's need for outside financing is also better evaluated when using cash flow data. Over time, the statement of cash flows permits users to observe and assess management's investing and financing policies. For example, a business that is not generating enough cash flow internally, i.e., from operations, must get cash from borrowing, issuing shares, or selling off its assets.

The statement of cash flows also provides information about a firm's ability to generate sufficient amounts of cash to respond to unanticipated needs and opportunities. Information about past cash flows, particularly cash flows from operations, helps in assessing a company's financial flexibility. An evaluation of a firm's ability to survive an unexpected drop in demand, for example, should include a review of its past cash flows from operations. The larger these cash flows, the greater is the firm's ability to withstand adverse changes in economic conditions.

So, whether we are a potential investor, loan officer, future employee, supplier, or customer, we greatly benefit from an understanding of the cash inflows and outflows of a company.

What Do We Mean by "CASH"?

The statement of cash flows explains the change in a firm's cash *and* cash equivalents. **Cash equivalents** are short-term, highly liquid investments that are (1) easily convertible into a known cash amount and (2) close enough to maturity that their market value is not sensitive to interest rate changes (generally, investments with remaining maturities of three months or less). Treasury bills, commercial paper (short-term notes issued by corporations), and money market funds are typical examples of cash equivalents.

When preparing a statement of cash flows, the cash and cash equivalents are added together and treated as a single sum. The addition is done because the purchase and sale of investments in cash equivalents are considered to be part of a firm's overall management of cash rather than a source or use of cash. As statement users evaluate and project cash flows, for example, it should not matter whether

FYI A cash equivalent is a short-term, highly liquid investment that is easily converted to cash and is close enough to maturity that its market value is not sensitive to interest rate changes.

the cash is readily available in a cash register or safe, deposited in a bank account, or invested in cash equivalents. Consequently, transfers back and forth between a firm's cash on hand, its bank accounts, and its investments in cash equivalents, are not treated as cash inflows and cash outflows in its statement of cash flows. When discussing the statement of cash flows, managers generally use the word *cash* rather than the phrase *cash and cash equivalents*. We will follow the same practice.

What Does a Statement of Cash Flows Look Like?

Exhibit 4.1 reproduces Golden Enterprises' cash flow statement for the fiscal year ended on May 30, 2014. During this fiscal year, Golden Enterprises generated $3,263,728 in cash from its operations. Investing activities used $2,332,162 in cash, and financing activities used another $528,047 of cash. Over the entire year, the company's cash balance increased by $757,111 and ended the year at $1,160,630 on May 30, 2014.

EXHIBIT 4.1	Golden Enterprises Cash Flow Statement

GOLDEN ENTERPRISES, INC. AND SUBSIDIARY
Consolidated Statement of Cash Flows
For the Fiscal Year Ended May 30, 2014

	2014
Cash Flows from Operating Activities	
Cash received from customers.	$135,015,577
Interest income.	1,956
Rental income.	29,783
Other operating cash payments/receipts	67,133
Cash paid to suppliers and employees for cost of goods sold	(68,774,050)
Cash paid for suppliers and employees for selling general and administrative	(62,094,737)
Income taxes	(645,342)
Interest expense	(336,592)
Net cash provided by operating activities.	3,263,728
Cash Flows from Investing Activities	
Purchase of property, plant and equipment	(2,380,287)
Proceeds from sale of property, plant and equipment	48,125
Net cash used in investing activities.	(2,332,162)
Cash Flows from Financing Activities	
Debt proceeds	35,726,909
Debt repayments	(35,316,537)
Change in checks outstanding in excess of bank balances*	528,162
Cash dividends paid	(1,466,581)
Net cash used in financing activities.	(528,047)
Net increase (decrease) in cash and cash equivalents	403,519
Cash and cash equivalents at beginning of year	757,111
Cash and cash equivalents at end of year	$1,160,630

* Golden Enterprises has an overdraft arrangement at one or more of its banks that allows it to write checks in excess of its balance. This negative balance creates a financial liability (essentially a loan) that must be settled according to its arrangement with the bank.

FRAMEWORK FOR THE STATEMENT OF CASH FLOWS

The statement of cash flows classifies cash receipts and payments into one of three categories: operating activities, investing activities, or financing activities. Classifying cash flows into these categories identifies the effects on cash of each of the major activities of a firm. The combined effects on cash of all three categories explain the net change in cash for the period. The period's net change in cash is then reconciled with the beginning and ending amounts of cash.

Operating Activities

A company's income statement mainly reflects the transactions and events that constitute its operating activities. The cash effects of these operating transactions and events determine the net cash flow from operating activities. The usual focus of a firm's **operating activities** is on selling goods or rendering services, but the activities are defined broadly enough to include any cash receipts or payments that are not classified as investing or financing activities. For example, Golden Enterprises reports cash received from customers and renters and borrowers. The company paid cash to suppliers and employees and tax authorities and to lenders for interest. The following are examples of cash inflows and outflows relating to operating activities.

Cash Inflows	**Cash Outflows**
1. Cash receipts from customers for sales made or services rendered (or in anticipation of future deliveries of goods or services).	1. Cash payments to employees or suppliers.
2. Cash receipts of interest and dividends.[1]	2. Cash payments to purchase inventories.
3. Other cash receipts that are not related to investing or financing activities, such as rentals, lawsuit settlements, and refunds received from suppliers.	3. Cash payments of interest to creditors.[1]
	4. Cash payments of taxes to government.
	5. Other cash payments that are not related to investing or financing activities, such as contributions to charity and lawsuit settlements.

Investing Activities

A firm's transactions involving (1) the acquisition and disposal of property, plant, and equipment (PPE) assets and intangible assets, (2) the purchase and sale of government securities and securities of other companies, including stocks, bonds, and other securities that are not classified as cash equivalents, and (3) the lending and subsequent collection of money constitute the basic components of its **investing activities**. The related cash receipts and payments appear in the investing activities section of the statement of cash flows and, if material in amount, inflows and outflows should be reported separately (not as a net amount). Examples of these cash flows follow:

Cash Inflows	**Cash Outflows**
1. Cash receipts from sales of property, plant, and equipment (PPE) assets and intangible assets.	1. Cash payments to purchase property, plant, and equipment (PPE) assets and intangible assets.
2. Cash receipts from sales of investments in government securities and securities of other companies (including divestitures).	2. Cash payments to purchase government securities and securities of other companies (including acquisitions).
3. Cash receipts from repayments of loans by borrowers.	3. Cash payments made to lend money to borrowers.

Financing Activities

A firm engages in **financing activities** when it receives cash from shareholders, returns cash to shareholders, borrows from creditors, and repays amounts borrowed. Cash flows related to these transactions are reported in the financing activities section of the statement of cash flows and again, inflows and outflows should be reported separately (not as a net amount) if material. For instance, Golden Enterprises reports proceeds from new debt and debt repayments separately, rather than as a net amount. Examples of these cash flows follow:

---

[1] Many financial statement readers believe that interest and dividends received should be considered cash inflows from investing activities and that interest payments should be considered cash outflows from financing activities. In fact, when the reporting standard was passed by the Financial Accounting Standards Board, three of the seven members dissented from the standard for this reason (among others). The majority based their decision on "the view that, in general, cash flows from operating activities should reflect the cash effects of transactions and other events that enter into the determination of net income." (Statement of Financial Accounting Standards No. 95, paragraph 88.)

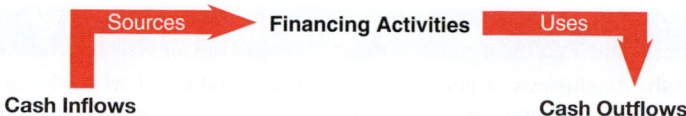

Cash Inflows	**Cash Outflows**
1. Cash receipts from issuances of common stock and preferred stock and from sales of treasury stock.	1. Cash payments to acquire treasury stock.
2. Cash receipts from issuances of bonds payable, mortgage notes payable, and other notes payable.	2. Cash payments of dividends.
	3. Cash payments to settle outstanding bonds payable, mortgage notes payable, and other notes payable.

Paying cash to settle such obligations as accounts payable, wages payable, interest payable, and income tax payable are operating activities, not financing activities because they are related to the daily operations of the company such as buying and selling inventory. Also, cash received as interest and dividends and cash paid as interest (not dividends) are classified as cash flows from operating activities. However, cash paid to shareholders as dividends is classified as cash flows from financing activities.

> **FYI** Treasury **stock** refers to the amount paid by a company to purchase its own common stock.

A GLOBAL PERSPECTIVE

Under U.S. accounting principles, payments for interest expense and receipts for interest and dividend income are considered part of cash from operations. International Financial Reporting Standards allow companies to report interest payments as part of either operating activities or financing activities and to report interest and dividend receipts as part of either operating activities or investing activities.

Usefulness of Classifications

The classification of cash flows into three categories of activities helps financial statement users interpret cash flow data. To illustrate, assume that Faultless, Inc., Peerless Co. and Dauntless Ltd. each reports a $100,000 cash increase during the current year. Information from their current-year statements of cash flows is summarized in **Exhibit 4.2**.

EXHIBIT 4.2 Summary Information for Three Competitors			
	Faultless	**Peerless**	**Dauntless**
Net cash provided by operating activities	$100,000	$ 0	$ 0
Cash flows from investing activities			
Sale of property, plant, and equipment	0	100,000	0
Cash flows from financing activities			
Issuance of notes payable	0	0	100,000
Net increase in cash.	$100,000	$100,000	$100,000

One of the keys to evaluating a company's worth is estimating its future cash flows based on the information available. Companies that can generate a stream of future cash flows are worth more than a company with a single cash flow. In **Exhibit 4.2**, each company's net cash increase was the same, but the source of the increase varied by company. This variation affects the analysis of the cash flow data, particularly for potential creditors who must evaluate the likelihood of obtaining repayment in the future for any funds loaned to the company. Based only on these cash flow data, a potential creditor would feel more comfortable lending money to Faultless than to either Peerless or Dauntless. This choice is because Faultless's cash increase came from its operating activities, and operations tend to be continuing. Both Peerless and Dauntless could only break even on their cash flows from operations. Also, Peerless's cash increase came from the sale of property, plant, and equipment (PPE) assets—a source of cash that is not likely to recur regularly. Dauntless's cash increase came entirely from borrowed funds. This means Dauntless faces additional cash burdens in the future when the interest and principal payments on the note payable become due.

MID-CHAPTER REVIEW 1

Assume **Golden Enterprises** executed the following transactions during 2015. Indicate whether the transaction creates a cash inflow (In) or outflow (Out). Next, determine how each item should be classified in the statement of cash flows: an operating activity (O), an investing activity (I), or a financing activity (F). For example: $50,000 cash received for the sale of snack foods. Answer: In/O

1. _____ $250,000 cash paid to purchase a warehouse
2. _____ $120,000 cash paid for interest on a loan
3. _____ $850,000 cash paid to employees as wages
4. _____ $20,000,000 cash raised through the issuance of stock
5. _____ $450,000 cash paid to the government for taxes
6. _____ $350,000 cash received as part of a settlement of a legal case
7. _____ $630,000 cash received from the sale of long-term securities
8. _____ $75,000 cash received from the sale of used office equipment
9. _____ $500,000 cash dividend paid to shareholders
10. _____ $90,000 cash received as interest earned on a government bond

The solution to this review problem can be found on page 214.

LO2 Construct the operating activities section of the statement of cash flows using the direct method.

PREPARING THE STATEMENT OF CASH FLOWS— OPERATING ACTIVITIES

In Chapter 3's **Exhibit 3.12**, we presented a statement of cash flows for Natural Beauty Supply (hereafter, NBS) for the month of December, 2015. This statement is reproduced in **Exhibit 4.3**. The statement details how NBS' cash balance decreases by $1,275 in December, from $8,100 to $6,825. The statement was prepared by examining all of the cash transactions that occurred during the month, and then grouping them according to the type of activity each represents—operating, investing, or financing. Transaction (17) was the loan, so that was a financing activity, transaction (18) was the purchase of fixtures and equipment, an investing activity, and so on. These cash transactions can be taken directly from the cash T-account, which is reproduced here:

+	Cash (A)		−
Beg. bal.	8,100		
(17)	11,000	18,000	(18)
(21)	8,500	700	(19)
(23)	1,200	3,300	(20)
(25)	3,200	1,625	(24)
		1,500	(27)
		50	(28)
End. bal.	6,825		

This approach to preparing the statement of cash flows is straightforward and doesn't require any additional bookkeeping steps, other than those introduced in Chapters 2 and 3.

EXHIBIT 4.3	NBS Statement of Cash Flows (Direct Method)

NATURAL BEAUTY SUPPLY, INC.
Statement of Cash Flows
For the Month Ended December 31, 2015

Cash Flows from Operating Activities		
Cash received from customers (entries 21, 23, 25)	$12,900	
Cash paid for inventory (entry 20)	(3,300)	
Cash paid for wages (entry 24)	(1,625)	
Cash paid for rent (entry 27)	(1,500)	
Cash paid for advertising (entry 19)	(700)	
Net cash provided by operating activities		$ 5,775
Cash Flows from Investing Activities		
Cash paid for fixtures and equipment (entry 18)	(18,000)	
Net cash used for investing activities		(18,000)
Cash Flows from Financing Activities		
Cash received from loans (entry 17)	11,000	
Cash paid for dividends (entry 28)	(50)	
Net cash provided by financing activities		10,950
Net change in cash		(1,275)
Cash balance, November 30, 2015		8,100
Cash balance, December 31, 2015		$ 6,825

However, for many companies, the number and variety of cash transactions that occur each period are so large that such an approach is often impractical. A company with revenues and assets and liabilities in the billions of dollars, like Walgreens for example, has thousands of cash transactions each day. It has accounts with several different banks in numerous locations, and regularly transfers cash from one account to another or back and forth between cash accounts and cash equivalents, as needed. For such a company, simply listing the cash transactions is not practical.

An alternative to this approach of compiling a list of cash flows is to reconcile the information in the income statement and balance sheet to prepare the cash flow statement. The statement of cash flows complements the balance sheet and the income statement. The balance sheet details the financial position of the company at a given point in time. Comparing two balance sheets prepared at the beginning and at the end of a period reveals changes that transpired during the accounting period. These changes are explained by the income statement and the statement of cash flows. Both the income statement and the cash flow statement summarize the events and transactions of the business during the accounting period, and as such, provide complementary descriptions of a company's activities. While the cash flow statement provides information that is not explicitly found in either of the other two statements, it must articulate with the balance sheet and income statement to present a complete picture of company activities.

One of the characteristics of the accounting system is that when an entry changes Net Income without a change in Cash, then it must change another account on the balance sheet. And, when an operating cash flow occurs without a change in Net Income, then there must be a change in some other balance sheet account. Therefore, we can start with information from the income statement and then use the balance sheet (and some additional information) to prepare the statement of cash flows. **Exhibit 4.4** presents the income statement and comparative balance sheets for NBS. We will use the data from these financial statements to prepare NBS' reconciliation of Net Income to Cash from Operating Activities.

Converting Revenues and Expenses to Cash Flows from Operating Activities

We know from Chapter 3 that net income consists of revenues and expenses. We also know that these are often not cash transactions. For example, sales on account will be considered revenue but are not cash inflows until collected. Depreciation is an expense, but is not a current-period cash outflow (the cash outflow presumably occurred when the underlying asset was acquired). We can compute cash flow from operating activities by making adjustments to the

EXHIBIT 4.4	NBS Income Statement and Comparative Balance Sheet

NATURAL BEAUTY SUPPLY Income Statement For the Month Ended December 31, 2015		
Sales revenue.............		$13,900
Cost of goods sold.........		8,000
Gross profit..............		5,900
Operating expenses:		
Rent	$1,500	
Wages..................	2,105	
Advertising	700	
Depreciation..............	375	
Insurance	140	
Total operating expenses....		4,820
Operating income.........		1,080
Interest income............		30
Interest expense...........		(110)
Income before taxes........		1,000
Income tax expense........		350
Net income...............		$ 650

NATURAL BEAUTY SUPPLY Comparative Balance Sheets	12/31/15	11/30/15
Assets:		
Cash....................	$ 6,825	$ 8,100
Interest receivable	30	
Accounts receivable........	2,250	950
Inventory.................	7,300	11,300
Prepaid insurance..........	1,540	1,680
Security deposit	2,000	2,000
Fixtures and equipment	18,000	
Accumulated depreciation ...	(375)	
Total assets..............	$37,570	$24,030
Liabilities:		
Accounts payable..........	$ 4,400	$ 3,700
Unearned revenue	600	300
Wages payable............	480	
Interest payable	110	
Income taxes payable	350	
Notes payable	11,000	
Stockholders' equity:		
Common stock............	20,000	20,000
Retained earnings	630	30
Total liabilities and equity....	$37,570	$24,030

revenues and expenses presented in the income statement. The adjustment amounts represent differences between revenues, expenses, gains, and losses recorded under accrual accounting and the related operating cash inflows and outflows. The adjustments are added to or subtracted from net income, depending on whether the related cash flow is more or less than the accrual amount.

Convert Sales Revenues to Cash Received from Customers

To illustrate this adjustment procedure for revenues and cash receipts from customers, consider the Chapter 3 transactions and adjusting entry that occurred for NBS in December 2015:

(21) Dec. During the month of December, NBS sold products costing $5,000 to retail customers for $8,500 cash.

(22) Dec. During the month of December, sales to wholesale customers totaled $4,500 for merchandise that had cost $3,000. Instead of paying cash, wholesale customers are required to pay for the merchandise within ten working days.

(23) Dec. $1,200 of gift certificates were sold during the month of December. Each gift certificate entitles the recipient to a one-hour consultation on the use of NBS' products.

(25) Dec. During the month of December, NBS received $3,200 in cash from wholesale customers for products that had been delivered earlier.

(a)   Dec. Gift certificates worth $900 were redeemed during the month.

We enter the revenue and cash receipts implications of each of these into the Financial Statement Effects Template (FSET) on the following page. Whenever there is a difference between the revenue recognized and the cash received, that difference affects an operating asset (accounts receivable) or an operating liability (unearned revenue). For instance, in transaction (22a), NBS recognizes credit sales revenue. That is, revenue increases, but cash does not, and the accounting equation is kept by increasing accounts receivable, an operating asset. When NBS received cash in advance of revenue recognition, as in transaction (23), the balancing entry is in unearned revenue, an operating liability. We will find that when an operating transaction affects cash or income—but not both—the operating assets and operating liabilities serve as a temporary buffer between the two.

The total of each of these columns is given in the last row, and because each individual entry is balanced, the totals are balanced.

| | Balance Sheet | | | | | Income Statement | | |
Transaction	Cash Asset +	Noncash Assets =	Liabilities +	Contrib. Capital +	Earned Capital	Revenues -	Expenses =	Net Income
(21a) Sell $8,500 of products for cash.	+8,500 Cash	=			+8,500 Retained Earnings	+8,500 Sales Revenue	-	= +8,500
(22a) Sell $4,500 of products on account.		+4,500 Accounts Receivable =			+4,500 Retained Earnings	+4,500 Sales Revenue	-	= +4,500
(23) Sell gift certificates for $1,200 cash.	+1,200 Cash	=	+1,200 Unearned Revenue				-	=
(25) Receive $3,200 cash from customers who purchased on credit.	+3,200 Cash	−3,200 Accounts Receivable =					-	=
(a) Adjusting entry for gift certificates redeemed in December.		=	−900 Unearned Revenue		+900 Retained Earnings	+900 Sales Revenue	-	= +900
Total changes	+12,900 Cash +	+1,300 Accounts Receivable =	+300 Unearned Revenue +	0 +	+13,900 Retained Earnings	+13,900 Sales Revenue	- 0	= +13,900

We can see that December's revenue was $13,900, and NBS collected $12,900 from customers during the month. Accounts receivable increased by $1,300 over the month, and unearned revenue increased by $300. The FSET maintains the accounting equation at every entry, so we know that the equality will hold for the totals in the last row.

$$\text{Cash flow (receipts)} + \text{Change in accounts receivable} = \text{Change in unearned revenue} + \text{Net income (Sales revenue)}$$

$$\$12,900 + \$1,300 = \$300 + \$13,900$$

And this relationship can be rewritten as the following:

$$\text{Cash flow} = \text{Net income} - \text{Change in accounts receivable} + \text{Change in unearned revenue}$$

$$\$12,900 = \$13,900 - \$1,300 + \$300$$

So, when we start with net income and then subtract the change in accounts receivable and add the change in unearned revenue, we convert the revenues in net income into the cash receipts from customers needed for cash from operations.

Convert Cost of Goods Sold to Cash Paid for Merchandise Purchased   As a second illustration, let's examine the December 2015 transactions involving NBS' inventory and its suppliers (**Exhibit 3.3** in Chapter 3).

(20) Dec. 20 NBS paid $3,300 cash to its suppliers in partial payment for the delivery of inventory in November.

(21) Dec.   During the month of December, NBS sold products costing $5,000 to retail customers for $8,500 cash.

(22) Dec.   During the month of December, sales to wholesale customers totaled $4,500 for merchandise that had cost $3,000. Instead of paying cash, wholesale customers are required to pay for the merchandise within ten working days.

(26) Dec. 28 NBS purchased and received $4,000 of inventory on account.

When a company like NBS purchases inventory for future sale, we know that the purchase will be followed by two events in the normal course of business. One event is that NBS will have to pay the supplier in cash according to the terms of the purchase, resulting in a cash outflow. The other event is the sale of that inventory to a customer of NBS, resulting in a cost of goods sold expense on the income statement. But these two events do not necessarily occur at the same point in time.

As we enter these events into the FSET, we see that the differences between cash payments for inventory and cost of goods sold expense are buffered by inventory, an operating asset, and accounts payable, an operating liability.

Transaction	Balance Sheet					Income Statement		
	Cash Asset	+ Noncash Assets	= Liabil- ities	+ Contrib. Capital	+ Earned Capital	Revenues –	Expenses =	Net Income
(20) Pay $3,300 cash to suppliers.	−3,300 Cash		= −3,300 Accounts Payable			–	=	
(21b) Record $5,000 for the cost of merchandise sold in transaction 21a.		−5,000 Inventory	=		−5,000 Retained Earnings	–	+5,000 Cost of Goods Sold	= −5,000
(22b) Record $3,000 for the cost of merchandise sold in transaction 22a.		−3,000 Inventory	=		−3,000 Retained Earnings	–	+3,000 Cost of Goods Sold	= −3,000
(26) Purchase $4,000 inventory on account.		+4,000 Inventory	= +4,000 Accounts Payable			–	=	
Total changes	−3,300 Cash	+ −4,000 Inventory	= +700 Accounts Payable	+ 0	+ −8,000 Retained Earnings	0 –	+8,000 Cost of Goods Sold	= −8,000

Again, the FSET keeps the accounting equation with every entry, so we know that the total changes in the last row must also conform to the accounting equation.

$$\underset{\text{(payments)}}{\text{Cash flow}} + \underset{\text{inventory}}{\text{Change in}} = \underset{\text{accounts payable}}{\text{Change in}} + \underset{\text{(COGS expense)}}{\text{Net income}}$$

$$-\$3,300 \ + \ -\$4,000 \ = \ \$700 \ + \ -\$8,000$$

And this relationship can be written as the following:

$$\underset{\text{flow}}{\text{Cash}} = \underset{\text{income}}{\text{Net}} - \underset{\text{inventory}}{\text{Change in}} + \underset{\text{accounts payable}}{\text{Change in}}$$

$$-\$3,300 = -\$8,000 - (-\$4,000) + \$700$$

The change in inventory is negative for NBS during December 2015, so when we subtract the change in inventory above, we must subtract a negative number, making a positive adjustment. (That is, $-(-\$4,000) = +\$4,000$.) And, when we subtract the change in inventory from net income and add the change in accounts payable to net income, we convert the (minus) cost of goods sold expense to the (minus) payments to suppliers we need for the cash from operations.

Stepping back to look at the big picture, we begin to see a pattern. The cash flow effect of an item is equal to its income statement effect, minus the change in any associated operating asset(s) plus the change in any associated operating liability(ies). That pattern can be confirmed as we look at the remaining necessary adjustments.

Convert Wages Expense to Cash Paid to Employees   To determine the adjustment needed for transactions involving employees, we look at the two entries from Chapter 3 related to the wages earned and paid during the month of December 2015.

(24) Record $1,625 in wages to employees.	−1,625 Cash		=		−1,625 Retained Earnings	–	+1,625 Wages Expense	= −1,625
(e) Adjusting entry to record wages earned but not yet paid.			= +480 Wages Payable		−480 Retained Earnings	–	+480 Wages Expense	= −480
Total changes	−1,625 Cash	+ 0	= +480 Wages Payable	+ 0	+ −2,105 Retained Earnings	0 –	+2,105 Wages Expense	= −2,105

Using the same approach as above, the FSET tells us the following about the totals:

$$\text{Cash flow (payments)} = \text{Change in wages payable} + \text{Net income (wage expense)},$$

which can be rewritten as

$$\text{Cash flow} = \text{Net income} + \text{Change in wages payable}$$
$$-\$1,625 = -\$2,105 + \$480$$

NBS recorded more wage expense than it paid to its employees, and that additional expense goes into an operating liability, wages payable. If wages payable had decreased over the period, it would imply that NBS had paid more to its employees than they had earned during the period (perhaps because they were owed compensation from a prior period).

Convert Rent Expense to Cash Paid for Rent and Advertising Expense to Cash Paid for Advertising

The December 2015 entries for rent and advertising are presented in the FSET below.

	Balance Sheet									Income Statement		
Transaction	Cash Asset	+	Noncash Assets	=	Liabil- ities	+	Contrib. Capital	+	Earned Capital	Revenues	- Expenses	= Net Income
(19) Pay $700 cash for December advertising.	−700 Cash			=					−700 Retained Earnings		− +700 Advertising Expense	= −700
(27) Pay $1,500 rent for December.	−1,500 Cash			=					−1,500 Retained Earnings		− +1,500 Rent Expense	= −1,500
Total changes	−2,200 Cash	+	0	=	0	+	0	+	−2,200 Retained Earnings	0	− +2,200 Advertising and Rent Expense	= −2,200

For these items, the amount paid is exactly equal to the amount recorded as expense, so no adjustment is necessary. The amounts included for advertising and rent in the determination of net income are exactly what we want in the cash from operations. If NBS had paid rent in advance or promised to pay later for its advertising, then operating assets and/or liabilities would have been created, and an adjustment would have been necessary (as we see in the case immediately following).

Other Adjustments

There are five more items in NBS' income statement that require adjustment to arrive at the amount of cash from operations for the month of December. Four of these items are insurance expense, interest income, interest expense and income tax expense. These items involved only adjusting entries during the month of December, so there were no cash flows involved, and we present the adjustments in an abbreviated fashion below.

	Balance Sheet									Income Statement		
(b) Adjusting entry to record expiration of 1 month of prepaid insurance.			−140 Prepaid insurance	=					−140 Retained Earnings		− +140 Insurance Expense	= −140
Total changes	0 Cash	+	−140 Prepaid Insurance	=	0	+	0	+	−140 Retained Earnings	0	− +140 Insurance Expense	= −140

$$\text{Cash flow} + \text{Change in prepaid insurance} = \text{Net income, or}$$
$$\text{Cash flow} = \text{Net income} - \text{Change in prepaid insurance, or}$$
$$\$0 \text{ (zero)} = -\$140 - (-\$140)$$

	Balance Sheet									Income Statement				
Transaction	Cash Asset	+	Noncash Assets	=	Liabil-ities	+	Contrib. Capital	+	Earned Capital	Revenues	-	Expenses	=	Net Income
(d) Adjusting entry for interest income earned.			+30 Other Receivables	=					+30 Retained Earnings	+30 Interest Income	-		=	+30
Total changes	0 Cash	+	+30 Other Receivables	=	0	+	0	+	+30 Retained Earnings	+30 Interest Income	-	0	=	+30

Cash flow + Change in other receivables = Net income, or

Cash flow = Net income − Change in other receivables, or

$$\$0 \text{ (zero)} = \$30 - \$30$$

Transaction	Cash Asset	+	Noncash Assets	=	Liabil-ities	+	Contrib. Capital	+	Earned Capital	Revenues	-	Expenses	=	Net Income
(f) Adjusting entry to record interest owed but not yet paid.				=	+110 Interest Payable				−110 Retained Earnings		-	+110 Interest Expense	=	−110
Total changes	0 Cash	+	0	=	+110 Interest Payable	+	0	+	−110 Retained Earnings	0	-	+110 Interest Expense	=	−110

Cash flow = Change in interest payable + Net income, or

Cash flow = Net income + Change in interest payable, or

$$\$0 \text{ (zero)} = -\$110 + \$110$$

Transaction	Cash Asset	+	Noncash Assets	=	Liabil-ities	+	Contrib. Capital	+	Earned Capital	Revenues	-	Expenses	=	Net Income
(g) Adjusting entry for estimated income tax.				=	+350 Tax Payable				−350 Retained Earnings		-	+350 Tax Expense	=	−350
Total changes	0 Cash	+	0	=	+350 Tax Payable	+	0	+	−350 Retained Earnings	0	-	+350 Tax Expense	=	−350

Cash flow = Change in tax payable + Net income, or

Cash flow = Net income + Change in tax payable, or

$$\$0 \text{ (zero)} = -\$350 + \$350$$

Each of the above four items involved only an adjusting entry (i.e., an entry at the end of the fiscal period). Adjusting entries rarely involve cash, so the adjustment simply cancels out the item in the income statement. We will see more examples in later chapters (e.g., write-downs of physical or intangible assets, restructuring charges, etc.).

Eliminate Depreciation Expense and Other Noncash Operating Expenses NBS recorded an adjusting entry for depreciation at the end of December 2015 for $375. That entry into the FSET was the following.

Transaction	Cash Asset	+	Noncash Assets	=	Liabil-ities	+	Contrib. Capital	+	Earned Capital	Revenues	-	Expenses	=	Net Income
(c) Adjusting entry for depreciation on fixtures and equipment for December.			+375 Accumulated Depreciation	=					−375 Retained Earnings		-	+375 Depreciation Expense	=	−375
Total changes	0	+	0	−	+375 Accumulated Depreciation	=	0	+	0	+	−375 Retained Earnings	0	-	+375 Depreciation Expense	=	−375

We can see that this entry reduced net income by $375, but it had no effect on cash. When we look at the total impact of this entry on the FSET (in the last row), its effect can be written in the following way.

$$\frac{\text{Cash}}{\text{flow}} - \frac{\text{Change in accumulated depreciation}}{\text{(for depreciation expense)}} = \frac{\text{Net}}{\text{income,}}$$

or

$$\text{Cash flow} = \text{Net income} + \text{Depreciation expense}$$
$$\$0 \text{ (zero)} = -\$375 + \$375$$

So, NBS' net income of $650 for December includes a depreciation expense of $375 that did not involve any cash outflow. When we add back depreciation expense (and similar items like amortization expense), we move the net income number one step closer to cash from operations.

Would increasing depreciation expense increase the cash flows from operations? That question is more complex than it initially appears. In Chapter 8, we will find that companies use different depreciation methods for tax reporting and financial reporting, and in Chapter 10 we will see how differences between tax and financial reporting are reconciled. Increasing the tax depreciation expense reduces taxable income and the amount of tax that has to be paid. Increasing depreciation expense in financial reports to shareholders has no effect on the amount of taxes paid and, therefore, no effect on the amount of cash generated.

A General Rule . . . with a Note of Caution   The relationships illustrated in the above examples suggest a general rule that we can use to prepare the cash flow statement:

> The difference between a revenue or an expense reported in the income statement and a related cash receipt or expenditure reported in the statement of cash flows will be reflected in the balance sheet as a change in one or more balance sheet accounts.

More specifically, all the above reconciliation adjustments for NBS can be summarized in a pattern:

$$\text{Net income} \pm \text{Adjustments} = \text{Cash from operations}$$

Or, more particularly

$$\frac{\text{Net}}{\text{income}} + \frac{\text{Depreciation}}{\text{expense}} - \frac{\text{Change in}}{\text{operating}\atop\text{assets}} + \frac{\text{Change in}}{\text{operating}\atop\text{liabilities}} = \frac{\text{Cash from}}{\text{operations}}$$

By "operating assets," we mean receivables, inventories, prepaid expenses and similar assets. "Operating liabilities" refers to accounts and wages payable, accrued expenses, unearned revenues, taxes payable, interest payable and similar items. Investing assets (like investment securities and property, plant, and equipment) and financing liabilities (like notes payable and long-term debt) would not be included in these adjustments.

Exhibit 4.5 summarizes the basic adjustments needed to convert the revenues, expenses, gains and losses presented in the income statement to cash receipts and payments presented in the statement of cash flows from operating activities. (The adjustments for non-operating gains and losses will be discussed shortly.)

We have now applied the adjustments to convert each accrual revenue and expense to the corresponding operating cash flow. We use these individual cash inflows and outflows to prepare the operating activities section of the statement of cash flows. The adjustments to convert revenues and expenses to operating cash flows are summarized in **Exhibit 4.6**, and this information can be used to produce NBS' cash from operating activities by using the information in the income statement and balance sheet.

Like all general rules, this one provides useful insights, but it also has limitations. As we learn more and more about business activities and the accounting for them, we find the need for refinements of this general rule. For instance, in Chapter 12, we will see that operating assets and liabilities can increase from acquisitions (an investing activity) as well as from operations. But for the time-being, the general rule is a useful way to approach the calculation of operating cash flow.

EXHIBIT 4.5 — Adjustments to Convert Income Statement Items to Cash Flows From Operating Activities

Net income	= Sales revenue	− Cost of goods sold	− Operating expenses	− Depreciation expense	+ Dividend and Interest income	− Interest expense	+ Gains − Losses	− Income tax expense
Adjustments:								
Add back depreciation expense				⊕ Depreciation expense				
Subtract (add) non-operating gains (losses)							⊖ Gains ⊕ Losses	
Subtract the change in operating assets (operating investments)	⊖ Change in accounts receivable	⊖ Change in inventory	⊖ Change in related prepaid expenses		⊖ Change in dividend and interest receivable			
Add the change in operating liabilities (operating financing)	⊕ Change in unearned revenue	⊕ Change in accounts payable	⊕ Change in related accrued liabilities			⊕ Change in interest payable		⊕ Change in income tax payable
Cash from operations	= Receipts from customers	− Payments for merchandise	− Payments for expenses	− 0	+ Receipts from dividends and interest	− Payments for interest	+ 0 − 0	− Payments for income tax

EXHIBIT 4.6 — Converting Revenues and Expenses to Cash Inflows and Outflows from Operating Activity (Natural Beauty Supply)

Net income	= Sales revenue	+ Interest income	− Cost of goods sold	− Wages expense	− Rent expense	− Advertising expense	− Insurance expense	− Interest expense	− Depreciation expense	− Income tax expense
$ 650	= $13,900	+ 30	− 8,000	− 2,105	− 1,500	− 700	− 140	− 110	− 375	− 350
Adjustments:										
Add back depreciation expense									⊕ 375 Depreciation expense	
Subtract the change in operating assets (operating investments)	⊖ 1,300 Change in accounts receivable	⊖ 30 Change in interest receivable	⊖ (−4,000)* Change in inventory				⊖ (−140)* Change in prepaid insurance			
Add the change in operating liabilities (operating financing)	⊕ 300 Change in unearned revenue		⊕ 700 Change in accounts payable	⊕ 480 Change in wages payable				⊕ 110 Change in interest payable		⊕ 350 Change in income tax payable
$5,775	= $12,900	+ 0	− 3,300	− 1,625	− 1,500	− 700	− 0	− 0	− 0	− 0
Cash from operations	= Receipts from customers	+ Receipts for interest	− Payments for merchandise	− Payments to employees	− Payments for rent	− Payments for advertising	− Payments for insurance	− Payments for interest	− 0	− Payments for income tax

* When the change in an operating asset is negative, subtracting that negative amount results in a positive adjustment.

MID-CHAPTER REVIEW 2

The income statement and comparative balance sheets for Mug Shots, Inc., (a photography studio) are presented below. Use the information in these financial statements and the frameworks in **Exhibits 4.5** and **4.6** to compute Mug Shots' cash flow from operating activities using the direct method.

MUG SHOTS, INC. Income Statement For Month Ended December 31, 2015		
Revenue		
Sales revenue......................		$31,000
Expenses		
Cost of goods sold	$16,700	
Wages expense	4,700	
Interest expense	300	
Advertising expense	1,800	
Rent expense....................	1,500	
Depreciation expense	700	
Total expenses..................		25,700
Income before taxes..............		5,300
Income tax expense.............		1,855
Net income.......................		$ 3,445

MUG SHOTS, INC. Comparative Balance Sheets	12/31/15	11/30/15
Assets		
Cash...........................	$10,700	$ 5,000
Accounts receivable.............	2,500	
Inventory	32,300	24,000
Prepaid rent	7,500	9,000
Equipment	30,000	18,000
Accumulated depreciation.........	(700)	
Total assets.....................	$82,300	$56,000
Liabilities		
Accounts payable	$25,000	$24,000
Interest payable.................	300	
Wages payable	2,200	
Income tax payable	1,855	
Unearned revenue	500	
Notes payable	30,000	12,000
Equity		
Common stock	20,000	20,000
Retained earnings	2,445	
Total liabilities and equity............	$82,300	$56,000

The solution to this review problem can be found on page 214.

Reconciling Net Income and Cash Flow from Operating Activities

LO3 Reconcile cash flows from operations to net income and use the indirect method to compute operating cash flows.

We now have two metrics to consider when examining the operations of a company over a period of time—net income and cash from operations. For December 2015, NBS reported net income of $650 and cash from operations of $5,775. For its fiscal year ended May 30, 2014, Golden Enterprises reported net income of $921,829 and cash from operations of $3,263,728. While both net income and cash from operations measure aspects of operations over the same time period, they can sometimes be very far apart, as seen in the following table.

	2013 ($ millions)	
	Net Income	Cash from Operations
Snyder's-Lance, Inc.......................................	$ 79	$ 141
Diamond Foods, Inc.	(165)	(102)
Verizon Communications, Inc.	23,547	38,818
Sprint Communications	(4,326)	2,999
Ford Motor Company......................................	7,155	10,444
Daimler AG..	10,139	3,285
Tesla Motors, Inc...	(74)	258
CarMax, Inc...	493	(613)
Starbucks Corp...	2,068	608
Keurig Green Mountain, Inc...............................	597	719
Delta Air Lines, Inc.	10,540	4,504
American Airlines Group, Inc..............................	(1,876)	1,279

It would be natural for a financial statement reader to want to understand the source(s) of the differences between net income and cash from operations. So, companies that present their statement of cash flows like Golden Enterprises must also present a reconciliation of net income to cash from operations. The reconciliation for Golden Enterprises' fiscal year ending May 30, 2014 is in **Exhibit 4.7**.

EXHIBIT 4.7	Golden Enterprises Income to Operating Cash Flows Reconciliation

GOLDEN ENTERPRISES, INC. AND SUBSIDIARY
CONSOLIDATED STATEMENT OF CASH FLOWS
For the Fiscal Year Ended May 30, 2014
RECONCILIATION OF NET INCOME TO NET CASH PROVIDED BY OPERATING ACTIVITIES

	2014
Net income.	$ 921,829
Adjustments to reconcile net income to net cash provided by operating activities:	
Depreciation.	3,778,563
Deferred income taxes	(298,467)
Gain on sale of property and equipment	(22,693)
Subtract:	
Change in receivables—net	(881,318)
Change in inventories	(703,826)
Change in prepaid expenses	276,876
Change in cash surrender value of insurance	93,408
Change in other assets—other.	434,287
Add:	
Change in accounts payable	(1,089,964)
Change in accrued expenses.	526,154
Change in salary continuation plan	(96,305)
Change in accrued income taxes.	325,184
Net cash provided by operating activities	$3,263,728

This reconciliation leads to exactly the same number that was presented in the operating section of **Exhibit 4.1**, but in a very different format. How is it produced? It is constructed using exactly the same adjustment process depicted in **Exhibits 4.5** and **4.6**.

Golden Enterprises' reconciliation contains a couple of entries that we did not see for Natural Beauty Supply. A company's income statement may contain gains and losses related to investing or financing activities. Examples include gains and losses from the sale of plant assets and gains and losses from the retirement of bonds payable. Golden Enterprises reported a $22,693 gain on sale of assets in its income statement. Because these gains and losses are not related to operating activities, **Exhibit 4.5** shows that we omit them as we convert income statement items to various cash flows from operating activities. The cash flows relating to these gains and losses are reported in the investing activities or financing activities sections of the statement of cash flows. NBS had no gains or losses in December, but Golden Enterprises made an adjustment for an investing activity gain in its reconciliation in **Exhibit 4.7**, and we will see an example of this type of adjustment in a later section.

Golden Enterprises also makes a $298,467 adjustment for deferred income taxes. Deferred income taxes occur when companies use different accounting methods for tax and financial reporting and are beyond our scope for the moment. It will be covered later in Chapter 10.

Cash Flow from Operating Activities Using the Indirect Method

Two alternative formats may be used to report the net cash flow from operating activities: the direct method and the indirect method. *Both methods report the same amount of net cash flow from operating activities.* Net cash flows from investing and financing activities are prepared in the same manner under both the indirect and direct methods; only the format for cash flows from operating activities differs.

For Natural Beauty Supply, we computed cash flow from operating activities using the direct method. The **direct method** presents the components of cash flow from operating activities as a list of gross cash receipts and gross cash payments. This format is illustrated in **Exhibit 4.3** and by Golden Enterprises' statement in **Exhibit 4.1**.

The direct method is logical and relatively easy to follow. In practice, however, nearly all statements of cash flows are presented using what is called the **indirect method**. Under this method, the reconciliation of net income to operating cash flow (e.g., **Exhibit 4.7**) is used for the presentation of cash flow from operations. The cash flow from operations section begins with net income and applies a series of adjustments to net income to convert it to net cash flow from operating activities. However, the adjustments to net income are not cash flows themselves, so the indirect method does not report any detail concerning individual operating cash inflows and outflows. In fact, there are no cash flows in the indirect method operating section of the cash flow statement, except the subtotal—cash flow from operations. The **Apple Inc.** statement of cash flows on page 206 is an example.

While accounting standard-setters prefer the direct method presentation, the AICPA's *Accounting Trends & Techniques 2011*, a survey of large U.S. companies, found that *more than 98% of companies preparing the statement of cash flows use the indirect method*, so the Golden Enterprises presentation is unusual. The indirect method is popular because (1) it is easier and less expensive to prepare than the direct method and (2) companies that use the direct method are required to present a supplemental disclosure showing the reconciliation of net income to cash from operations (thus, essentially requiring the company to report both methods for cash from operations). The same phenomenon occurs internationally. International standard-setters have stated a preference for the direct method, but the AICPA's *IFRS Accounting Trends & Techniques 2011*, a survey of large firms reporting under IFRS, found that only 23 (13.5%) used the direct method for cash from operations.

The procedure for presenting indirect method cash flows from operations uses the same approach that we applied above to convert income statement items to operating cash flows. In fact, the indirect method can be viewed as a "short-cut" calculation of the process shown in **Exhibit 4.5**. That is:

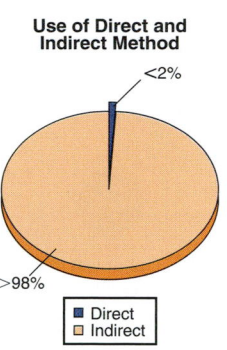

Use of Direct and Indirect Method

<2%
>98%
■ Direct
□ Indirect

> **Net income ± Adjustments = Cash flow from operating activities**

In **Exhibit 4.5**, revenue and expense components of the income statement are presented in the orange row that totals to net income. The yellow rows list the adjustments, and cash receipts and payments are listed in the green row at the bottom. The total of the green row is cash flow from operating activities. The indirect method skips the listing of individual revenues and expenses and starts with net income. After adjustments, we have total cash flow from operating activities, but not individual receipts and payments.

Cash flow from operating activities for NBS is presented using the indirect method in **Exhibit 4.8**. The calculation begins with the December net income of $650 and ends with cash flow from operating activities, $5,775. The total cash flow from operating activities is the same amount as was computed in **Exhibit 4.6** using the direct method. If we compare **Exhibit 4.6** and **Exhibit 4.8**, we see that the two exhibits are very similar. The only difference is that all of the revenues and expenses are listed in the orange row at the top of **Exhibit 4.6**, while **Exhibit 4.8** lists only the total—net income. Similarly, the green row at the bottom of **Exhibit 4.6** lists all of the cash inflows and outflows, while the bottom line of **Exhibit 4.8** lists only the net cash flow from operating activities. In both exhibits, the center rows list the adjustments.

FYI Managers can boost declining sales by lengthening credit periods or by lowering credit standards. The resulting increase in accounts receivable can cause net income to outpace operating cash flow. Consequently, many view a large receivables increase as a warning sign.

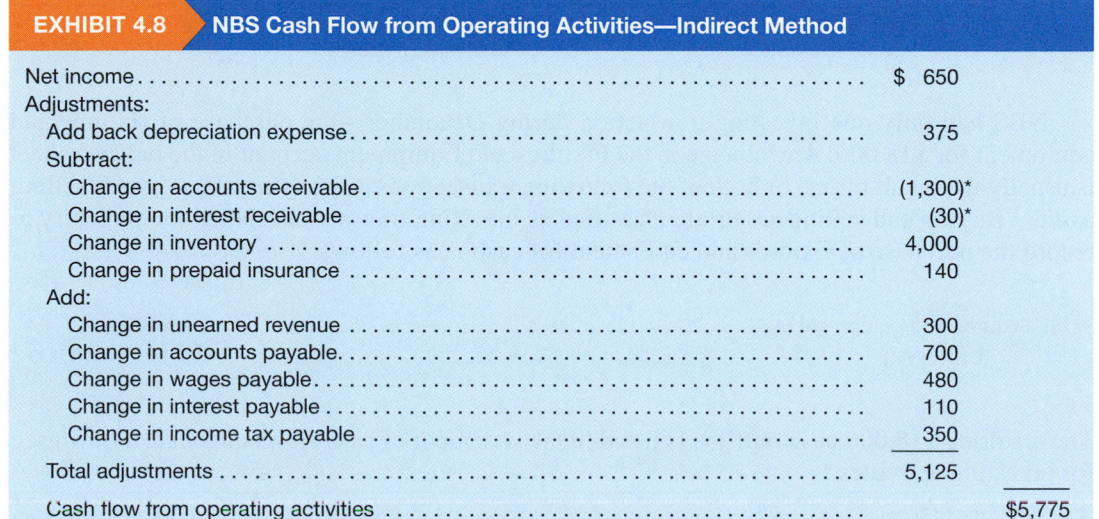

EXHIBIT 4.8	**NBS Cash Flow from Operating Activities—Indirect Method**
Net income...	$ 650
Adjustments:	
Add back depreciation expense.............................	375
Subtract:	
Change in accounts receivable...........................	(1,300)*
Change in interest receivable...........................	(30)*
Change in inventory....................................	4,000
Change in prepaid insurance............................	140
Add:	
Change in unearned revenue.............................	300
Change in accounts payable.............................	700
Change in wages payable...............................	480
Change in interest payable..............................	110
Change in income tax payable...........................	350
Total adjustments..	5,125
Cash flow from operating activities........................	$5,775

* When the change in an operating asset is negative, subtracting that negative amount results in a positive adjustment.

MID-CHAPTER REVIEW 3

Refer to the financial statements for Mug Shots, Inc. presented in Mid-Chapter Review 2. Compute cash flows from operating activities for Mug Shots, Inc. using the indirect method.

The solution to this review problem can be found on page 215.

LO4 Construct the investing and financing activities sections of the statement of cash flows.

PREPARING THE STATEMENT OF CASH FLOWS— INVESTING AND FINANCING ACTIVITIES

The remaining sections of the statement of cash flows focus on investing and financing activities. Investing activities are concerned with transactions affecting noncurrent (and some current) noncash assets. Financing activities are concerned with raising capital from owners and creditors. The presentation of the cash effects of investing and financing transactions is not affected by the method of presentation (direct or indirect) of cash flows from operating activities.

Accounting standard-setters (both in the United States and International) require that financing and investing items be presented in the statement of cash flows using gross amounts instead of net amounts. In **Exhibit 4.1**, Golden Enterprises reports that it spent $2,380,287 cash to acquire property, plant, and equipment in 2014, and it received $48,125 in cash from the sale of property, plant, and equipment. It would *not* be acceptable to show the net amount—an outflow of $2,332,162—as a single item unless one of the components is consistently immaterial.

Cash Flows from Investing Activities

Investing activities cause changes in noncash asset accounts. Usually the accounts affected (other than cash) are noncurrent operating asset accounts such as property, plant, and equipment assets and investing assets like marketable securities and long-term financial investments. Cash paid for acquisitions of other companies would be included as well. To determine the cash flows from investing activities, *we analyze changes in all noncash asset accounts not used in computing net cash flow from operating activities*. Our objective is to identify any investing cash flows related to these changes.

Purchases of noncash assets cause cash outflow. Conversely, a sale of a noncash asset results in cash inflow. This relationship is highlighted in the following decision guide:

Cash flows increase due to:	Cash flows decrease due to:
Sales of assets	Purchases of assets

NBS had only one investing transaction during December—the purchase of fixtures and equipment for $18,000. Any change in the Fixtures and Equipment account in the balance sheet is usually the result of one or both of the following transactions: (1) buying assets, or (2) selling assets.[2] Buying and selling assets are classified as investing transactions. NBS' journal entry to record the purchase of fixtures and equipment for cash is as follows:

| (18) Fixtures and equipment (+A) .... | 18,000 | |
| Cash (−A) .... | | 18,000 |

The resulting $18,000 cash outflow is listed in the statement of cash flows under cash flow used for investing activities.

---

[2] The Accumulated Depreciation—Fixtures and Equipment contra-asset account is affected by depreciation expense and selling assets.

Cash Flows from Financing Activities

Financing activities cause changes in financial liabilities and stockholders' equity accounts. Financial liabilities include current liability items like seasonal bank borrowing and the current portion of long-term debt due within the next year, plus noncurrent items like long-term debt issues and longer term borrowing from financial institutions. Cash receipts from the issuance of these liabilities and cash payments to settle outstanding principal balances are considered cash flows from financing activities. Stockholders' equity accounts include contributed capital (common stock, additional paid-in-capital and treasury stock) and retained earnings. Transactions with shareholders are always considered part of a company's financing activities. This relationship is highlighted in the following decision guide:

Cash flows increase due to:	Cash flows decrease due to:
Taking on a financial liability or issuing shares	Repaying principal on a financial liability or paying dividends to shareholders or making share repurchases

NBS had two financing transactions during December. It borrowed $11,000 on a three-year note, resulting in an increase in cash, and it paid $50 in cash dividends to shareholders. The journal entry to record the $11,000 note is illustrated as:

(17) Cash (+A).	11,000	
Notes payable (+L)		11,000

The resulting $11,000 cash inflow is listed in the statement of cash flows under cash flow from financing activities.

The journal entry to record dividends is illustrated as follows:

(28) Retained earnings (−SE).	50	
Cash (−A)		50

This dividend payment is a financing cash outflow and would be deducted from cash flow from financing activities.

When using the indirect method for the cash flow from operating activities, we should remember that there are some balance sheet accounts that will be affected by more than one type of activity. For instance, the balance in retained earnings will be affected by net income (which is going to appear in the operations section) and shareholder dividends (which will appear in the financing section).

The statement of cash flows lists cash flows from operating activities first (using either the direct or the indirect method), followed by cash flows from investing activities, then cash flows from financing activities. Once all three categories of cash flows have been listed, we total the three amounts to arrive at net cash flow for the period. The final step is to reconcile the cash balance from the beginning of the period to the ending balance. The completed statement of cash flows for NBS using the indirect method for operating cash flows is presented in **Exhibit 4.9**. We see from this statement that operating activities produced a cash inflow of $5,775, while investing activities resulted in a cash outflow of $18,000, and financing activities resulted in a cash inflow of $10,950. The sum of these three amounts ($5,775 − $18,000 + $10,950) equals the change in cash for December of −$1,275 ($6,825 − $8,100).

YOU MAKE THE CALL

You are the Chief Accountant   The February 24, 2012, *Wall Street Journal* reported that **Sears Holdings Corp.** "will unload more than 1,200 stores in an effort to raise up to $770 million of much-needed cash." How would the proceeds from the sales of Sears' stores be reflected in its cash flow statement? [Answer on page 189.]

EXHIBIT 4.9	NBS Statement of Cash Flows—Indirect Method

NATURAL BEAUTY SUPPLY
Statement of Cash Flows
For the Month Ended December 31, 2015

Operating activities:		
Net income		$ 650
Adjustments:		
Add back Depreciation expense		375
Subtract:		
Change in accounts receivable	(1,300)	
Change in interest receivable	(30)	
Change in inventory	4,000*	
Change in prepaid insurance	140*	
Add:		
Change in unearned revenue	300	
Change in accounts payable	700	
Change in wages payable	480	
Change in interest payable	110	
Change in income tax payable	350	
Total adjustments	5,125	
Cash flow from operating activities		$5,775
Investing activities:		
Purchase of fixtures and equipment	(18,000)	
Cash flow used for investing activities		(18,000)
Financing activities:		
Bank note	11,000	
Dividends paid	(50)	
Cash flow from financing activities		10,950
Net decrease in cash		(1,275)
Cash, November 30, 2015		8,100
Cash, December 31, 2015		$ 6,825

FYI   The net cash inflow or outflow for the period is the same amount as the increase or decrease in cash and cash equivalents for the period from the balance sheet.

* When the change in an operating asset is negative, subtracting that negative amount results in a positive adjustment.

MID-CHAPTER REVIEW 4

Refer to the financial statements for Mug Shots, Inc. in Mid-Chapter Review 2. Prepare a complete statement of cash flows for December using the indirect method for cash flows from operating activities. Follow the format used in **Exhibit 4.9**.

The solution to this review problem can be found on page 215.

ADDITIONAL DETAIL IN THE STATEMENT OF CASH FLOWS

There are two additional types of transactions that we must explore to understand the statement of cash flows. The first of these is the sale of investing assets like equipment or an investment security. The transaction itself isn't very complicated, but the use of the indirect method for operating cash flows makes it seem so. And, companies often engage in investing and financing activities that do not involve cash (e.g., acquiring another company through an exchange of stock). This section explores the accounting for these two types of transactions and their effect on the statement of cash flows.

Case Illustration   Natural Beauty Supply did not have any disposals of assets or repayments of debt in December 2015, so there is no adjustment to make in this case. However, let's consider the financial statements of One World Café, a coffee shop that is located next door to NBS. The income statement and comparative balance sheet for One World Café are presented in **Exhibit 4.10**. The cash flow statement is presented in **Exhibit 4.11**.

EXHIBIT 4.10	One World Café Income Statement and Comparative Balance Sheets

ONE WORLD CAFÉ, INC.
Income Statement
For Year Ended December 31, 2015

Revenue		
Sales revenue...............		$390,000
Expenses		
Cost of goods sold	$227,000	
Wages expense	82,000	
Advertising expense	9,800	
Depreciation expense	17,000	
Interest expense	200	
Loss on sale of plant assets ...	2,000	
Total expenses..............		338,000
Income before taxes..........		52,000
Income tax expense...........		17,000
Net income..................		$ 35,000

ONE WORLD CAFÉ, INC.
Comparative Balance Sheets
At December 31

	2015	2014
Assets		
Cash..........................	$ 8,000	$ 12,000
Accounts receivable...............	22,000	28,000
Inventory.......................	94,000	66,000
Prepaid advertising...............	12,000	9,000
Plant assets, at cost..............	208,000	170,000
Less accumulated depreciation.....	(72,000)	(61,000)
Total assets.....................	$272,000	$224,000
Liabilities		
Accounts payable................	$ 27,000	$ 14,000
Wages payable..................	6,000	2,500
Income tax payable	3,000	4,500
Notes payable	5,000	—
Equity		
Common stock..................	134,000	125,000
Retained earnings	97,000	78,000
Total liabilities and equity..........	$272,000	$224,000

EXHIBIT 4.11	Cash Flow Statement for One World Café

ONE WORLD CAFÉ, INC.
Statement of Cash Flows
For Year Ended December 31, 2015

Cash flows from operating activities		
Net income...	$35,000	
Add (deduct) items to convert net income to cash basis		
Add back depreciation	17,000	
Add back loss on sale of plant assets	2,000	
Subtract change in:		
Accounts receivable	6,000*	
Inventory	(28,000)	
Prepaid advertising..	(3,000)	
Add change in:		
Accounts payable	13,000	
Wages payable	3,500	
Income tax payable..	(1,500)	
Net cash provided by operating activities		$44,000
Cash flows from investing activities		
Purchase of plant assets..	(45,000)	
Proceeds from sale of plant assets	4,000	
Net cash used for investing activities.................................		(41,000)
Cash flows from financing activities		
Issuance of common stock	9,000	
Payment of dividends	(16,000)	
Net cash flows used for financing activities............................		(7,000)
Net cash decrease		(4,000)
Cash at beginning of year		12,000
Cash at end of year		$ 8,000

* When the change in an operating asset is negative, subtracting that negative amount results in a positive adjustment.

For One World Café, creation of the statement of cash flows requires information that cannot be discerned from the income statement and balance sheet. (After all, the statement of cash flows is *supposed* to provide additional information!) In particular, the following events occurred during the year.

- Plant assets were purchased for cash.
- Obsolete plant assets, with original cost of $12,000 and accumulated depreciation of $6,000, were sold for $4,000 cash, resulting in a $2,000 loss.
- Additional common stock was issued for cash.
- Cash dividends of $16,000 were declared and paid during the year.
- One World Café acquired $5,000 of plant assets by issuing notes payable.

Reviewing One World Café's comparative balance sheet, we see that plant assets at cost increased from $170,000 to $208,000, an increase of $38,000. In addition, the accumulated depreciation contra-asset increased by $11,000 from $61,000 to $72,000. However, these are *net* increases, and we need information on the individual components of the increases. Consequently, we need to determine the gross amounts to ensure the statement of cash flows we create properly presents the gross amounts in the investing activities section.

In addition to the changes in plant assets and accumulated depreciation, notes payable increased by $5,000 in 2015. The best way to fully understand what happened to cause the changes in balance sheet accounts during the year, and the impact of these changes on cash flows, is to "work backwards" to reconstruct the investing and financing transactions using journal entries and T-accounts, especially the plant assets and accumulated depreciation accounts.

Gains and Losses on Investing and Financing Activities

The focus of the income statement is on the revenues and expenses that are generated by a company's transactions with customers, suppliers, employees, and other operating activities. But the income statement also contains gains and losses that result from investing or financing transactions. Gains and losses from the sale of investments, property, plant, and equipment, or intangible assets result from investing activities, not operating activities. A gain or loss from the retirement of bonds payable is an example of a financing gain or loss. When these transactions occur, the income statement does not show a revenue and an expense, but rather shows only the net amount as a gain or loss.

The full cash flow effect from these types of events is reported in the investing or financing sections of the statement of cash flows. To illustrate, we record the sale of Old World Café's obsolete plant assets at a loss with the following journal entry:

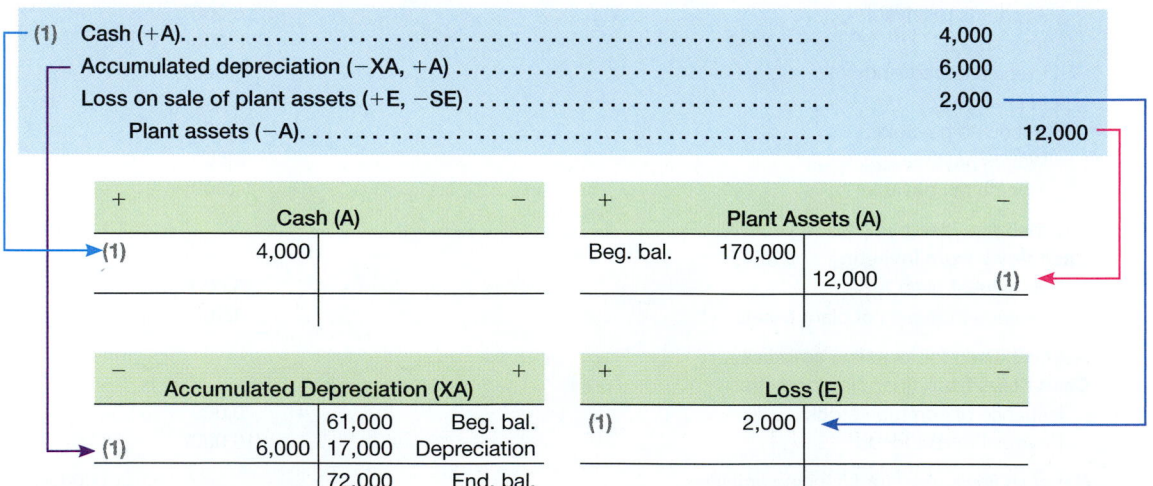

The $4,000 of cash received from this sale should be listed as a cash inflow under cash flows from investing activities, and it can be seen in **Exhibit 4.11**. The $4,000 cash flow is equal to the $6,000 net book value of the plant assets that were sold ($12,000 − $6,000) less the $2,000 loss on the sale.

If we were using the direct method to report the cash flows from operating activities, we wouldn't need to take any additional steps. But an indirect method operating cash flows starts with net income, and Old World Café's net income includes a $2,000 loss from this investing transaction (**Exhibit 4.10**). So, when we add back the investing loss to net income (or subtract an investing gain), we remove the effect of this investing transaction from the determination of cash flows from operating activities. It's one more step in the adjustments that are needed to reconcile net income to the cash flows from operating activities.

In Chapter 9, we will find that companies can experience financing gains (losses) from the early retirement of their debt. These gains and losses appear in the income statement, but they result from financing activities. In an indirect method statement of cash flows, the financing gains (losses) must be subtracted from (added to) net income to determine cash flows from operating activities.

We also see that the accumulated depreciation account started with a credit balance of $61,000, and the obsolete asset sale reduced this by $6,000 to $55,000. But the balance sheet in **Exhibit 4.10** tells us that the ending (credit) balance is $72,000. The difference is due to $17,000 depreciation expense for the year.

YOU MAKE THE CALL

You are the Securities Analyst   You are analyzing a company's statement of cash flows. The company has two items relating to its accounts receivable. First, the company finances the sale of its products to some customers with notes receivable; the increase to notes receivable is classified as an investing activity. Second, the company sells its accounts receivable to another company. As a result, the sale of receivables is reported as an asset sale, which reduces receivables and yields a gain or loss on sale. This action increases its operating cash flows. How should you interpret these items in the cash flow statement? [Answer on p. 189.]

Noncash Investing and Financing Activities

In addition to reporting how cash changed from one balance sheet to the next, cash flow reporting is intended to present summary information about a firm's investing and financing activities. Many of these activities affect cash and are therefore already included in the investing and financing sections of the statement of cash flows. Some significant investing and financing events, however, do not affect current cash flows. Examples of **noncash investing and financing activities** are the issuance of stocks, bonds, or leases in exchange for property, plant, and equipment (PPE) assets or intangible assets; the exchange of long-term assets for other long-term assets; and the conversion of long-term debt into common stock.

To illustrate the effect of noncash transactions on the preparation of the cash flow statement, consider One World Café's purchase of $5,000 of plant assets that was financed with notes payable. The journal entry to record the purchase is as follows:

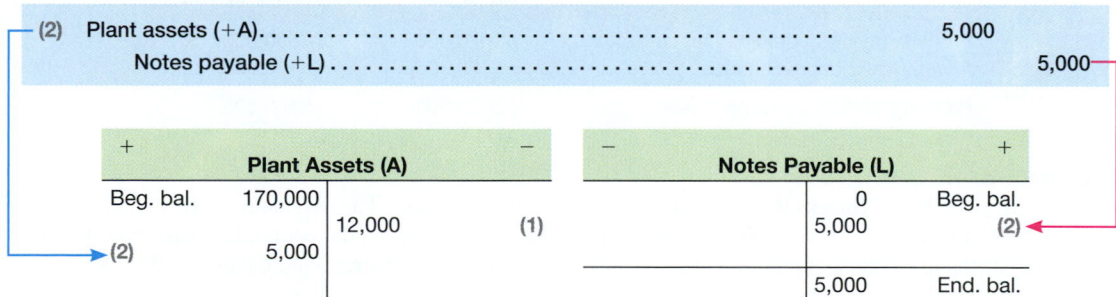

Because this purchase did not use any cash, it is not presented in the statement of cash flows. Only those capital expenditures that use cash are listed as cash flows from investing activities. That is, cash flows from investing activities should reflect the actual amount of cash spent to purchase plant assets or investment assets.

Noncash investing and financing transactions generally do affect *future* cash flows. Issuing notes payable to acquire equipment, for example, requires future cash payments for interest and principal on the notes, and should produce future operating cash flows from the equipment. Alternatively, converting bonds payable into common stock eliminates future cash payments related to the bonds, but may carry the expectation of future cash dividends. Knowledge of these types of events, therefore, is helpful to users of cash flow data who wish to assess a firm's future cash flows.

Information on noncash investing and financing transactions is disclosed in a schedule that is separate from the statement of cash flows. The separate schedule is reported either immediately below the statement of cash flows or among the notes to the financial statements.

Solving for Purchases of Plant Assets   The remaining entry affecting plant assets is the purchase of plant assets for cash. The amount of plant assets purchased can be determined by solving for the missing amount in the Plant Assets T-account:

+	Plant Assets (A)		−
Beg. bal.	170,000		
		12,000	(1)
(2)	5,000		
(3)	X		
End. bal.	208,000		

Balancing the account requires that we solve for the unknown amount:

$$\$170,000 + \$5,000 + X - \$12,000 \; = \; \$208,000$$
$$X \; = \; \$45,000$$

Thus, plant assets costing $45,000 were purchased for cash. This amount is listed as a cash outflow under cash flows for investing activities.

Examining the cash flow statement for One World Café in **Exhibit 4.11**, we see that two cash flows are listed under investing activities: (1) a $45,000 cash outflow for the purchase of plant assets, and (2) a $4,000 cash inflow from the sale of plant assets. The purchase of plant assets costing $5,000 by issuing notes payable is not listed; nor is the increase in notes payable listed under financing activities.

Appendix 4A at the end of this chapter introduces a spreadsheet approach that can be used to prepare the statement of cash flows. The appendix uses the One World Café financial statements as the illustration.

MID-CHAPTER REVIEW 5

The balance sheet of Jack's Snacks, Inc. reports the following amounts:

	End-of-year	Beginning-of-year
Property, plant & equipment at cost.	$670,000	$600,000
Accumulated depreciation	(150,000)	(140,000)
Property, plant & equipment, net	$520,000	$460,000

Additional information:
During the year, Jack's Snacks disposed of a used piece of equipment. The original cost of the equipment was $80,000 and, at the time of disposal, the accumulated depreciation on the equipment was $60,000. The purchaser of the used piece of equipment paid in cash, and Jack's Snacks reported a gain of $35,000 on the disposal.

All acquisitions of new property, plant, and equipment were paid for in cash.

Questions:
1. How much cash did Jack's Snacks receive from the used equipment disposal?
2. How much cash did Jack's Snacks spend to acquire new property, plant, and equipment during the year?
3. How much depreciation expense did Jack's Snacks record during the year?

The solution to this review problem can be found on pages 215–216.

The Effects of Foreign Currencies on the Cash Flow Statement

Multinational companies often engage in transactions that involve currencies other than U.S. dollars and may hold assets that were acquired with foreign currencies or liabilities that must be repaid in foreign currencies. Also, part of a company's cash balance may be held in a currency other than dollars. If the company prepares its financial statements in U.S. dollars, these foreign currency amounts must be converted, or *translated*, into dollars before preparing the financial statements. The process of translating transactions based in many currencies into one common currency for financial statement presentation is beyond the scope of an introductory text. However, foreign exchange rates fluctuate and these fluctuations can have an effect on the cash flow statement.

The statement of cash flows explains the change in the cash balance during the fiscal year, but part of this change may be due to changes in the dollar value of foreign currencies. This amount is typically small and it is not a cash flow, but it is included in the cash flow statement so that we can accurately reconcile the beginning balance in cash to the ending balance. The statement of cash flows for **Nike, Inc.** was summarized in Chapter 1 in **Exhibit 1.10** and is repeated here for illustration.

NIKE Statement of Cash Flows For the Year Ended May 31, 2014 ($ millions)	
Operating cash flows	$3,003
Investing cash flows	(1,207)
Financing cash flows	(2,914)
Effect of exchange rate changes	1
Net decrease in cash and cash equivalents	(1,117)
Cash and equivalents, beginning of year	3,337
Cash and equivalents, end of year	$2,220

Supplemental Disclosures

When the indirect method is used in the statement of cash flows, three separate supplemental disclosures are required: (1) two specific operating cash outflows—cash paid for interest and cash paid for income taxes, (2) a schedule or description of all noncash investing and financing transactions, and (3) the firm's policy for determining which highly liquid, short-term investments are treated as cash equivalents. If the direct method is used, a reconciliation of net income to cash flows from operating activities is also required. A firm's policy regarding cash equivalents is placed in the financial statement notes. The other disclosures are reported either in the notes or at the bottom of the statement of cash flows.

One World Café Case Illustration   One World Café incurred $200 of interest expense which was paid in cash. It also reported income tax expense of $17,000 and reported a decrease in income taxes payable of $1,500 ($4,500 − $3,000). Thus, One World Café paid $18,500 ($17,000 + $1,500) in income taxes during 2015. It also had the noncash investment in plant assets costing $5,000, which was financed with notes payable. One World Café would provide the following disclosure:

Supplemental cash flow information	
Cash payments for interest	$ 200
Cash payments for income taxes	18,500
Noncash transaction—investment in plant assets financed with notes payable	5,000

ANALYZING FINANCIAL STATEMENTS

Cash is a special resource for companies because of its flexibility. At short notice, it can be used to fulfill obligations and to take advantage of investment opportunities. When companies run short of cash, their suppliers may be reluctant to deliver and lenders may be able to take over control of decision making. In Chapter 2, we introduced the current ratio, which compares the level of current

LO5 Compute and interpret ratios that reflect a company's liquidity and solvency using information reported in the statement of cash flows.

5

assets to the level of current liabilities at a point in time. But the statement of cash flows gives us the opportunity to compare a company's ongoing cash generating activities to its obligations and to its investment opportunities.

Interpreting Indirect Method Cash from Operations

We want to interpret the cash flows from operations presented using the indirect method.

When companies use the indirect method to present their cash flows from operating activities, it is difficult to interpret the numbers presented to adjust net income to cash from operating activities. For instance, in **Exhibit 4.11**, One World Café reports $6,000 for the change in accounts receivable. Does that mean that the company received cash payments of $6,000 from its customers? It does not! Every item in the reconciliation has to be interpreted relative to the net income at the top. Net income includes revenue of $390,000, and the adjustment addition of $6,000 means that One World Café received payments of $390,000 + $6,000 = $396,000 from its customers.

The $3,500 adjustment for wages payable does not mean that One World Café received payments of $3,500 from its employees. Rather, the company paid its employees $3,500 less than it recognized as wage expense in determining net income. The adjustment for income tax payable was $(1,500), but that doesn't mean that One World Café's tax payments totaled $1,500 for the year. Rather, the $35,000 net income already reflects a charge for tax expense of $17,000, so the adjustment means that One World's payments for income tax totaled $17,000 + $1,500 = $18,500. Depreciation expense is added back not because it increases cash, but because it is an expense that doesn't require a cash outflow.

How should we interpret the changes in operating assets and liabilities? These assets and liabilities are a function of both the scale of the business and the practices of the business. If we're selling to 10% more customers this year, then we would expect an increase in receivables of about 10% over the previous year. If the increase is substantially more than that amount, then there must have been some other change as well. Perhaps increasing sales required that we give more favorable payment terms and customers are taking longer to pay. Such a development could cause an investor to question the "quality" of the company's earnings. If sales are constant and accounts payable are increasing, that may imply that the company is taking longer to pay its suppliers. That change would appear as a positive adjustment in the indirect method cash from operations, but it may indicate an unfavorable development for the company.

The indirect method may also alert us to gains and losses from non-operating transactions. These gains and losses are often in "other income" in the income statement, and therefore it's easy for a financial statement reader to miss them. The fact that gains must be subtracted and losses must be added back in the indirect cash from operations, gives them a prominence that they don't have in the income statement.

Analysis Objective

We are trying to gauge Golden Enterprises' generation of cash from its operating activities relative to its average short-term obligations found in the balance sheet.

Analysis Tool   Operating Cash Flow to Current Liabilities (OCFCL)

$$\text{Operating cash flow to current liabilities} = \frac{\text{Operating cash flow}}{\text{Average current liabilities}}$$

Applying the Operating Cash Flow to Current Liabilities Ratio to Golden Enterprises

2012: $\dfrac{\$5.747}{\$14.129} = 0.41 \text{ or } 41\%$

2013: $\dfrac{\$4.607}{\$14.044} = 0.33 \text{ or } 33\%$

2014: $\dfrac{\$3.264}{\$14.590} = 0.22 \text{ or } 22\%$

Guidance   Golden Enterprise's OCFCL is lower than the food industry average. Golden Enterprises' business is relatively low-margin, which means that it requires a large flow of resources to generate profits and cash from operations, and that large volume of activity results in high levels of current liabilities relative to the cash generated. The OCFCL ratio complements the current ratio and quick ratio introduced in Chapter 2. Golden Enterprises' current ratio is 1.32, also lower than average for the food industry, but its quick ratio of 0.95 is right at the industry average.

Golden Enterprises in Context

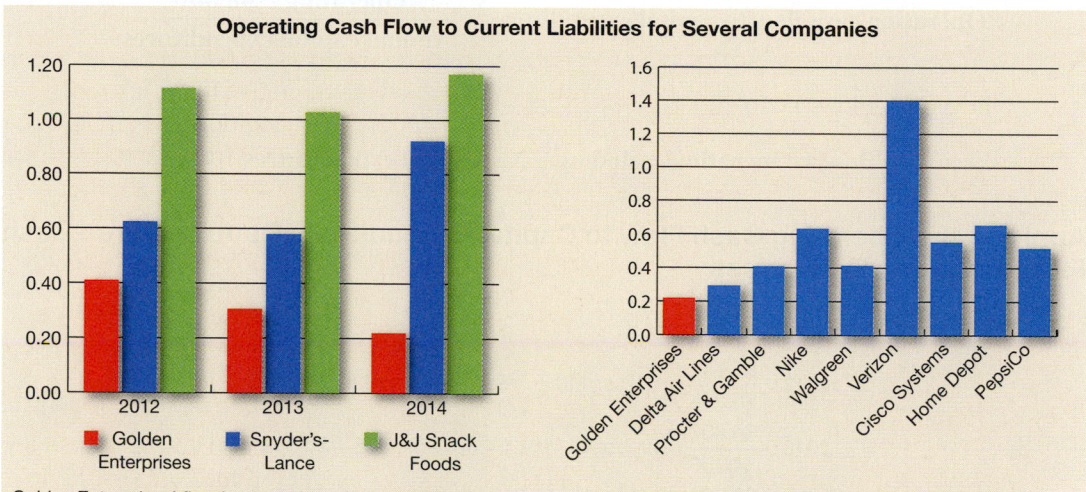

Golden Enterprises' fiscal year ends at the end of May each year. J&J Snack Foods' fiscal year ends at the end of September and Snyder's-Lance's year ends at the end of December. In the graph on the left, Golden Enterprises' end-of-May ratio is compared with J&J's end of September ratio and Snyder's-Lance's most recent December ratio.

Takeaways   Over the past three years, Golden Enterprises' OCFCL ratio is consistently lower than the two competitors that are included in the graph on the left. Snyder's-Lance's ratio is near the industry average for 2012 and 2013 but increases in 2014. J&J Snack Foods' ratio is well above the industry average all three years. There is also variation in the ratio from one year to the next. This is largely due to the fluctuation in operating cash flows. The comparison of focus companies' OCFCLs in the right-hand graph shows a range from 0.33 for Delta Air Lines to a high of over 1.40 for Verizon. Golden Enterprises is lower than any of these companies.

Other Considerations   There are some transactions that change both the numerator and the denominator, like using cash to pay current operating liabilities. Such a transaction would decrease both the numerator and the denominator, and these changes have an indeterminate effect on the ratio. Paying $100 to a creditor decreases operating cash flow and ending current liabilities by $100, with the average current liabilities decreasing by $50. If the OCFCL is below 2.0 prior to the transaction, it will be even lower after the transaction. If the OCFCL is greater than 2.0 prior to the transaction, it will be even higher after the transaction. Delaying a payment to the creditor would have the opposite effect.

It is also important to take a look at the components of current liabilities. Sometimes there is a large portion of long-term debt that comes due and increases current liabilities for one year. Or, in the case of Delta Air Lines, more than 25% of their current liabilities represent unearned revenue from customers who have purchased tickets in advance of travel (like the gift certificates at NBS). For this liability, Delta doesn't have to pay someone, they just need to keep flying.

Analysis Objective

We wish to determine Golden Enterprises' ability to fund the capital expenditures needed to maintain and grow its operations.

Does Golden Enterprises generate enough cash from its operations to make its capital investments? If it does not, then the company will have to finance those investments by selling other investments, by borrowing (resulting in future interest costs), by getting cash from shareholders or by reducing cash balances. If it generates more cash than needed for capital expenditures, then the additional cash can be used to grow the business (e.g., by acquisition) or to distribute cash to investors. Two measures may be used in making this assessment. The first of these measures, operating cash flow to capital expenditures, is a ratio that facilitates comparisons with other companies. The second, free cash flow,[3] is a monetary amount that reflects the funds available for investing in new ventures, buying back stock, paying down debt, or returning funds to stockholders in the form of dividends. The concept is also used in mergers and acquisitions to indicate cash that would be available to the acquirer for investment.

Analysis Tools   Operating Cash Flow to Capital Expenditures (OCFCX)

$$\text{Operating cash flow to capital expenditures} = \frac{\text{Operating cash flow}}{\text{Annual capital expenditures}}$$

Free Cash Flow (FCF)

$$\text{Free cash flow} = \text{Operating cash flow} - \text{Net capital expenditures}$$

Applying the Operating Cash Flow to Capital Expenditures Ratio and Free Cash Flow to Golden Enterprises

	OCFCX	FCF
2012:	$\frac{\$5.747}{\$5.214} = 1.10$ or 110%	$\$5.747 - \$4.992 = \$0.755$
2013:	$\frac{\$4.607}{\$4.150} = 1.11$ or 111%	$\$4.607 - \$4.075 = \$0.532$
2014:	$\frac{\$3.264}{\$2.380} = 1.37$ or 137%	$\$3.264 - \$2.332 = \$0.932$

Guidance   Operating cash flows to capital expenditures ratios that exceed 1.0 (or free cash flows that are positive) mean that the company can make its capital investments without obtaining additional financing or reducing its cash balances. The excess cash could be used to reduce borrowing, or it could be returned to shareholders. In both 2012 and 2013, Golden Enterprises' cash from operations exceeded its capital expenditures, though not by a large margin. The ratio increased in 2014 despite a drop in operating cash flows. In 2013, the company completed a major investment in an enterprise resource planning system and capital expenditures subsequently declined.

Golden Enterprises in Context

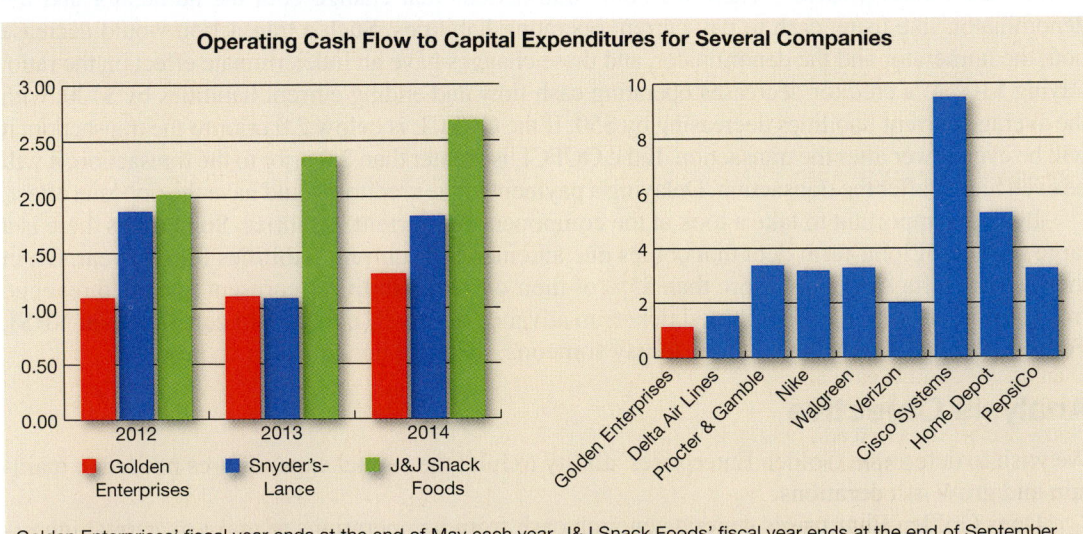

Operating Cash Flow to Capital Expenditures for Several Companies

Golden Enterprises' fiscal year ends at the end of May each year. J&J Snack Foods' fiscal year ends at the end of September and Snyder's-Lance's year ends at the end of December. In the graph on the left, Golden Enterprises' end-of-May ratio is compared with J&J's end of September ratio and Snyder's-Lance's most recent December ratio.

---

[3] Free cash flow can be defined in several ways, but it always includes a measure of the cash resources generated by the company's current operations minus a measure of the cash required to sustain those operations. One of the simpler, more common definitions is presented here.

Takeaways   OCFCX increased over the last three years for Golden Enterprises, but its OCFCX is substantially lower than either of the two comparison companies from the same industry. Snyder's-Lance and J&J Snack Foods have used the additional cash flow to acquire other businesses, pay dividends and repay long-term debt. We can see that all of the focus companies have OCFCX well above the levels of Golden Enterprises. These companies can use the cash in excess of capital expenditures to make acquisitions or to return cash to shareholders in the form of dividends or common stock repurchases.

Other Considerations   Measurement of cash flows is regarded as more objective than measures of income and less dependent on management judgments and estimates. But it may be subject to "lumpy" behavior from management's decisions, particularly for a smaller company. Capital expenditures may differ significantly from year to year if management takes on large, but infrequent, projects. A series of high values of OCFCX followed by a low value might mean deterioration in cash generating performance, but it might also mean that management has been accumulating cash in anticipation of a major project.

RESEARCH INSIGHT

Is the Cash Flow Statement Useful?   Some analysts rely on cash flow forecasts to value common stock. Research shows that both net income and operating cash flows are correlated with stock prices, but that stock prices are more highly correlated with net income than with cash flows. So, do we need both statements? Evidence suggests that by using *both* net income and cash flow information, we can improve our forecasts of *future* cash flows. Also, net income and cash flow together are more highly correlated with stock prices than either net income or cash flow alone. This result suggests that, for purposes of stock valuation, information from the cash flow statement complements information from the income statement.

CHAPTER-END REVIEW

Refer to One World Café's statement of cash flows and comparative balance sheets from **Exhibits 4.10** and **4.11** to complete the following.

Required

1. Calculate the operating cash flow to current liabilities (OCFCL) ratio for One World Café and interpret your findings. Assume that the notes payable are due within the year and are a current liability.
2. Calculate One World Café's operating cash flow to capital expenditures (OCFCX) ratio. What observations can you make about your findings?
3. Calculate the free cash flow (FCF) for One World Café.

The solution to this review problem can be found on page 216.

APPENDIX 4A: A Spreadsheet Approach to Preparing the Statement of Cash Flows

LO6 Use a spreadsheet to construct the statement of cash flows.

6

Preparing the statement of cash flows is aided by the use of a spreadsheet. The procedure is somewhat mechanical and is quite easy once someone has mastered the material in the chapter. We illustrate this procedure using the data for One World Café presented in the chapter in **Exhibit 4.10**. By following the steps presented below, we are able to readily prepare One World Café's cash flow statement for 2015.

To set up the spreadsheet, we list all of the accounts in the balance sheet in the first column of the spreadsheet. We list depreciable assets net of accumulated depreciation. In column C, we list the most recent balance sheet (the ending balances) followed by the earlier balance sheet (beginning balances) in column D. There is no need to list totals such as total assets or total current liabilities. See **Exhibit 4A.1**. We will build the statement of cash flows in columns F, G and H.

Step 1: Classify the balance sheet accounts.   For each of the accounts (other than cash), classify them in column B as Operating (O), Investing (I) or Financing (F) according to where the effect of changes in that account will appear in the statement of cash flows. There are two accounts that have a

EXHIBIT 4A.1	Cash Flow Spreadsheet for One World Café

	A	B	C	D	E	F	G	H	I	J
1		O, I or F?	2015	2014	Change	Effect of change on cash flow			No effect on cash	Total F,G,H,I
2						Operating	Investing	Financing		
3	**Assets**									
4	Cash..........................		8,000	12,000	(4,000)					
5										
6	Accounts receivable............	O	22,000	28,000	(6,000)	6,000				6,000
7	Inventory.....................	O	94,000	66,000	28,000	(28,000)				(28,000)
8	Prepaid advertising............	O	12,000	9,000	3,000	(3,000)				(3,000)
9	Plant assets, net..............	O,I	136,000	109,000	27,000					
10	Depreciation expense........					17,000				
11	Plant assets purchased						(45,000)		(5,000)	(27,000)
12	Plant assets sold............					2,000	4,000			
13										
14	**Liabilities**									
15	Accounts payable.............	O	27,000	14,000	13,000	13,000				13,000
16	Wages payable...............	O	6,000	2,500	3,500	3,500				3,500
17	Income tax payable	O	3,000	4,500	(1,500)	(1,500)				(1,500)
18	Notes payable	F	5,000	—	5,000					
19	New borrowing								5,000	5,000
20	Borrowing repayments........									
21										
22	**Shareholders' Equity**									
23	Common stock...............	F	134,000	125,000	9,000					
24	New issue of common stock ...							9,000		9,000
25	Repurchase of common stock ..									
26	Retained earnings	O,F	97,000	78,000	19,000					
27	Net income					35,000				19,000
28	Dividends							(16,000)		
29										
30	**Totals........................**					44,000	(41,000)	(7,000)	—	(4,000)

double classification. Changes in the plant assets, net account can be caused by depreciation expense (which will appear in the indirect method cash from operations) and by investing activities, so we label it as (O, I). Changes in the retained earnings account are caused by net income (which appears in the indirect method cash from operations) and dividends, so we label it as (O, F).

For those rows labeled I or F, insert two rows below: one for increases in the account and one for decreases in the account because we must report increases and decreases separately. For plant assets, net, insert three rows below: one for depreciation expense, one for plant asset acquisitions and one for plant asset sales. For retained earnings, insert two rows below: one for net income and one for dividends.

Step 2: Compute the changes in the balance sheet accounts.
Subtract the beginning balances in each account from the ending balances and record these in column E. We highlight the change in the cash balance, because this is the amount that we are trying to explain. At this point it is useful to verify that the change in cash is equal to the changes in liabilities plus the changes in stockholders' equity minus the changes in noncash assets:

$$\Delta \text{ Cash} = \Delta \text{ Liabilities} + \Delta \text{ Stockholders' Equity} - \Delta \text{ Noncash Assets}$$

In effect, we're going to use changes on the right-hand side of this equation to explain the changes in cash on the left-hand side.

Step 3: Handle the accounts that have single classifications.
For those accounts that are operating-only assets (accounts receivable, inventory, prepaid expenses, etc.), we enter in column F the *negative* of the value in column E. The $28,000 increase in inventories in column E results in $(28,000) for the operating cash flows in column F. Changes in assets have the opposite effect on cash. Increases in assets have a negative effect on cash, while decreases in assets lead to positive adjustments to cash.

For those accounts that are operating only liabilities (accounts payable, wages payable, taxes payables, etc.), we enter in column F the value in column E. The $13,000 increase in accounts payable produces a $13,000 entry in column F.

For those accounts that are financing only (notes payable, common stock), we enter in column H the cash effect(s) of the change in column E. For example, we must be aware that the common stock account could have changed due to both issuing stock for cash and repurchasing stock for cash. For One World Café, there was only a $9,000 inflow due to a new stock issue in column H. (We will deal with the notes payable changes in the next step.)

One World Café has no assets that are investing only, but for such accounts (marketable securities, investments, etc.), we would again make entries for increases and decreases separately. And, since these are assets, the change in the balance sheet has the opposite sign of the entry in the cash flow columns. For instance, if One World Café had invested $10,000 in a financial security, its investments asset would increase, and we would put an entry of $(10,000) in column G.

Step 4: Enter the effect of investing/financing transactions that do not involve cash.
We know from the information provided about One World Café that it arranged the purchase of $5,000 of plant assets by signing a note payable for the same amount. This transaction affected an investing asset and a financing liability at the same time, and we put the effects into column I. $5,000 is put in the new borrowing row (19), and $(5,000) is put in the plant assets purchased row (11). This transaction will not appear in the cash flow statement in columns F, G and H, but it does explain some of the changes in the company's assets and liabilities.

Step 5: Analyze the change in retained earnings.
Some accounts require special attention because the change in the account balance involves two types of cash flow effects. For example, the change in retained earnings is actually two changes—net income, which is related to operations, and dividends, which is a financing cash outflow.

One World Café's retained earnings increased by $19,000. It reported net income of $35,000, which is listed as an operating item (because we're using the indirect method), and paid dividends of $16,000, a cash outflow listed under financing activities. For clarity, it is helpful to list each of these changes on a separate line. Thus, we have inserted two lines into the spreadsheet immediately below retained earnings—the first for net income and the second for dividends. The $35,000 inflow and the $16,000 outflow net to $19,000.

Step 6: Analyze the change in plant assets.
A change in depreciable assets is actually the result of both operating and investing items. The change in plant assets can be explained by looking at the individual transactions that caused the change. As was the case with retained earnings, it is helpful to list each of these transactions in a separate row in the spreadsheet. Thus, we have inserted three rows into the spreadsheet immediately below the change in plant assets. First, we recall that One World Café reported depreciation expense of $17,000, which reduced its plant assets, net. This is listed in the first row under plant assets as a positive adjustment to cash flow from operations because cash flow effects on the asset side have the opposite sign.

In the next row, we list purchases of plant assets. One World Café purchased plant assets for $45,000 in cash, which is listed under investing as a cash outflow in column F. There was also the $5,000 purchase of plant assets that was financed with notes payable. This transaction did not affect cash so it's in column I.

In the third row below plant assets, we list the sale of plant assets. One World Café sold plant assets for $4,000 cash, recognizing a loss of $2,000. The loss is listed in the operations column (as a positive adjustment to operating cash flow) and the proceeds from the sale are listed under investing as a cash inflow in column F.

When all of the balance sheet changes have been analyzed, the change for each account should add up to the sum of the effect on operating, investing, and financing cash flows, plus the amount in the "no effect" column. That is, for each change listed in the spreadsheet in column E, we can add columns F, G, H and I to get the change in the balance sheet account in column J. For retained earnings: $35,000 − $16,000 = $19,000. For assets, the total will be the *negative* of the change. Adding up entries for plant assets: $17,000 − $45,000 − $5,000 + $2,000 + $4,000 = −$27,000, which is minus the amount in column E, row 9.

Step 7: Total the columns.
We add up the effects listed in columns F, G, H and I to get the cash flow subtotals. One World Café had cash flow from operations of $44,000, investing cash flows of −$41,000 and financing cash flows of −$7,000. The total for the "no effect" column (column I) should be $0, because the entries in this column had no effect on cash flow. Finally, we add up these totals to make sure that the cash flow effects equal the change in cash: $44,000 − $41,000 − $7,000 − $0 = −$4,000. If the totals do not add up to the change in cash, then there must be an error in analyzing one or more of the balance sheet changes. For example, if we had forgotten to subtract dividends, then the cash flow effects in columns F, G and H would not add up to the change in retained earnings listed in column E. Likewise, if we had mistakenly omitted the sale of plant assets, then the change in plant assets would not add up correctly. Totaling the columns and rows is a check to verify that our analysis is complete and correct.

Step 8: Prepare the cash flow statement.
Starting with operating cash flows (column F), we list each of the items in the statement of cash flows. We start with net income, and then add depreciation and the loss on the sale of plant assets, then we list the remaining adjustments, starting with the change in accounts receivable and working down the column. Next, we do the same for the items listed in the investing (column G) and financing (column H) sections of the cash flow statement. The resulting statement is identical to the statement presented in **Exhibit 4.11**.

APPENDIX 4A REVIEW

The comparative balance sheets and income statement for Rocky Road Bicycles, Inc., are as follows.

ROCKY ROAD BICYCLES, INC. Comparative Balance Sheets		
At December 31	2015	2014
Assets		
Cash	$ 106,000	$ 96,000
Accounts receivable	156,000	224,000
Inventory	752,000	528,000
Prepaid rent	68,000	72,000
Plant assets	1,692,000	1,360,000
Less accumulated depreciation	(562,000)	(488,000)
Total assets	$2,212,000	$1,792,000
Liabilities		
Accounts payable	$ 216,000	$ 112,000
Wages payable	18,000	20,000
Income tax payable	44,000	36,000
Equity		
Common stock	1,142,000	1,000,000
Retained earnings	792,000	624,000
Total liabilities and equity	$2,212,000	$1,792,000

Additional Information:

- Rocky Road reported net income of $326,000 in 2015.
- Depreciation expense was $122,000 in 2015.
- Rocky Road sold plant assets during 2015. The plant assets originally cost $88,000, with accumulated depreciation of $48,000, and were sold for a gain of $16,000.
- Rocky Road declared and paid a $158,000 cash dividend in 2015.

REQUIRED

Use a spreadsheet to create a statement of cash flows for Rocky Road Bicycles, Inc.

The solution to this review problem can be found on page 217.

SUMMARY

LO1   **Explain the purpose of the statement of cash flows and classify cash transactions by type of business activity: operating, investing or financing. (p. 158)**

- The statement of cash flows summarizes information about the flow of cash into and out of the business.
- Operating cash flow includes any cash transactions related to selling goods or rendering services, as well as interest payments and receipts, tax payments and any transaction not specifically classified as investing or financing.
- Investing cash flow includes acquiring and disposing of plant assets, buying and selling securities, including securities of other companies, and lending and subsequently collecting funds from a borrower.
- Financing cash flow includes all cash received or paid to shareholders, including stock issued or repurchased and dividends paid. In addition, it includes amounts borrowed and repaid to creditors.

LO2   **Construct the operating activities section of the statement of cash flows using the direct method. (p. 162)**

- The direct method presents net cash flow from operating activities by showing the major categories of operating cash receipts and payments.
- The operating cash receipts and payments are usually determined by converting the accrual revenues and expenses to corresponding cash amounts.

Reconcile cash flows from operations to net income and use the indirect method to compute operating cash flows. (p. 171)

LO3

- Because operating cash flow differs from net income, a reconciliation of these two amounts helps financial statement users understand the sources of this difference.
- The indirect method reconciles net income and operating cash flows by making adjustments for noncash revenues and expenses and changes in balance sheet accounts related to operations.

Construct the investing and financing activities sections of the statement of cash flows. (p. 174)

LO4

- Cash investment outlays are captured in the investing section along with any cash receipts from asset disposals. Because cash receipts include any gain on sale (or reflect any loss), the gain (loss) must be subtracted from (added to) net income in the operating section to avoid double-counting.
- Cash obtained from the issuance of securities or borrowings, and any repayments of debt, are disclosed in the financing section. Cash dividends are also included in this section. Interest payments are included in the operating section of the statement.
- Some events, for example assets donated to the firm, provide resources to the business that are important but which do not involve cash outlays. These events are disclosed separately, along with the statement of cash flows, as supplementary disclosures or in the notes.

Compute and interpret ratios that reflect a company's liquidity and solvency using information reported in the statement of cash flows. (p. 181)

LO5

- Interpreting indirect method cash from operations requires reference to those items that comprise net income. Each adjustment is intended to modify an income statement item to bring it to cash from operations.
- Two ratios of importance that are based on cash flows include:
  - Operating cash flow to current liabilities—a measure of the adequacy of current operations to cover current liability payments.
  - Operating cash flow to capital expenditures—a reflection of a company's ability to replace or expand its activities based on the level of current operations.
- Free cash flow is defined as: Cash flow from operations − Net capital expenditures.
- Free cash flow is a measure of a company's ability to apply its resources to new endeavors.

Appendix 4A: Use a spreadsheet to construct the statement of cash flows. (p. 185)

LO6

- A spreadsheet helps to prepare the statement of cash flows by classifying the effect of each change in the balance sheet as operating, investing, financing, or not affecting cash.
- The spreadsheet approach relies on the key relationship:

$$\text{Cash} = \text{Liabilities} + \text{Stockholders' equity} - \text{Noncash assets}$$

GUIDANCE ANSWERS . . . YOU MAKE THE CALL

You are the Chief Accountant   The transaction's effect will appear in the investing section of the cash flow statement in the amount of a positive $770 million.

You are the Securities Analyst   Many companies, but not all, treat customers' notes receivable as an investing activity. In 2005, the SEC became concerned with this practice and issued letters to a number of companies objecting to this accounting classification. "Presenting cash receipts from receivables generated by the sale of inventory as investing activities in the company's consolidated statements of cash flows is not in accordance with GAAP," wrote the chief accountant for the SEC's division of corporation finance, in her letter to the companies ("Little Campus Lab Shakes Big Firms—Georgia Tech Crew's Report Spurs Change in Accounting for Operating Cash Flow," March 1, 2005, *The Wall Street Journal*). The SEC's position is that these notes receivable are an operating activity and analysts are certainly justified in treating them likewise. Concerning the sale of receivables, the transaction can be treated as a sale with a consequent reduction in receivables and a gain or loss on the sale recorded in the income statement. Many analysts treat this as a financing activity and argue that the cash inflow should not be regarded as an increase in operating cash flows. Bottom line: many argue that operating cash flows do not increase as a result of these two transactions and analysts should adjust the statement of cash flows to properly classify the financing of notes receivable as an operating activity and the sale of receivables as a financing activity.

KEY RATIOS

$$\text{Operating cash flow to current liabilities} = \frac{\text{Operating cash flow}}{\text{Average current liabilities}}$$

$$\text{Operating cash flow to capital expenditures} = \frac{\text{Operating cash flow}}{\text{Annual capital expenditures}}$$

$$\text{Free cash flow} = \text{Operating cash flow} - \text{Net capital expenditures}$$

KEY TERMS

Cash equivalents (p. 158)
Direct method (p. 172)
Financing activities (p. 160)
Indirect method (p. 172)

Investing activities (p. 160)
Liquidity (p. 158)
Noncash investing and financing activities (p. 179)

Operating activities (p. 160)
Solvency (p. 158)
Statement of cash flows (p. 158)
Treasury stock (p. 161)

Assignments with the ⊙ logo in the margin are available in **BusinessCourse**.
See the Preface of the book for details.

MULTIPLE CHOICE

1. Which of the following is not disclosed in a statement of cash flows?
   a. A transfer of cash to a cash equivalent investment
   b. The amount of cash at year-end
   c. Cash outflows from investing activities during the period
   d. Cash inflows from financing activities during the period

2. Which of the following events appears in the cash flows from investing activities section of the statement of cash flows?
   a. Cash received from customers
   b. Cash received from issuance of common stock
   c. Cash purchase of equipment
   d. Cash payment of dividends

3. Which of the following events appears in the cash flows from financing activities section of the statement of cash flows?
   a. Cash purchase of equipment
   b. Cash purchase of bonds issued by another company
   c. Cash received as repayment for funds loaned
   d. Cash purchase of treasury stock

4. Tyler Company has a net income of $49,000 and the following related items:

Depreciation expense.	$ 5,000
Accounts receivable increase.	2,000
Inventory decrease.	10,000
Accounts payable decrease.	4,000

   Using the indirect method, what is Tyler's net cash flow from operations?
   a. $42,000
   b. $46,000
   c. $58,000
   d. $38,000

5. Refer to information in Mid-Chapter Review 2. Assume that notes payable are not due within the coming year and are classified as a noncurrent liability. The operating cash flow to current liabilities ratio for Mug Shots, Inc. in December is

   a. 6.4%.

   b. 2.9%.

   c. 2.6%.

   d. impossible to determine from the data provided.

Superscript ^A denotes assignments based on Appendix 4A.

QUESTIONS

Q4-1. What is the definition of *cash equivalents*? Give three examples of cash equivalents.

Q4-2. Why are cash equivalents included with cash in a statement of cash flows?

Q4-3. What are the three major types of activities classified on a statement of cash flows? Give an example of a cash inflow and a cash outflow in each classification.

Q4-4. In which of the three activity categories of a statement of cash flows would each of the following items appear? Indicate for each item whether it represents a cash inflow or a cash outflow:

   a. Cash purchase of equipment.

   b. Cash collection on loans.

   c. Cash dividends paid.

   d. Cash dividends received.

   e. Cash proceeds from issuing stock.

   f. Cash receipts from customers.

   g. Cash interest paid.

   h. Cash interest received.

Q4-5. Traverse Company acquired a $3,000,000 building by issuing $3,000,000 worth of bonds payable. In terms of cash flow reporting, what type of transaction is this? What special disclosure requirements apply to a transaction of this type?

Q4-6. Why are noncash investing and financing transactions disclosed as supplemental information to a statement of cash flows?

Q4-7. Why is a statement of cash flows a useful financial statement?

Q4-8. What is the difference between the direct method and the indirect method of presenting net cash flow from operating activities?

Q4-9. In determining net cash flow from operating activities using the indirect method, why must we add depreciation back to net income? Give an example of another item that is added back to net income under the indirect method.

Q4-10. Vista Company sold for $98,000 cash land originally costing $70,000. The company recorded a gain on the sale of $28,000. How is this event reported in a statement of cash flows using the indirect method?

Q4-11. A firm uses the indirect method. Using the following information, what is its net cash flow from operating activities?

Net income.	$88,000
Accounts receivable decrease	13,000
Inventory increase	9,000
Accounts payable decrease.	3,500
Income tax payable increase	1,500
Depreciation expense.	6,000

Q4-12. What separate disclosures are required for a company that reports a statement of cash flows using the indirect method?

Q4-13. If a business had a net loss for the year, under what circumstances would the statement of cash flows show a positive net cash flow from operating activities?

Q4-14. A firm is converting its accrual revenues to corresponding cash amounts using the direct method. Sales on the income statement are $925,000. Beginning and ending accounts receivable on the balance sheet are $58,000 and $44,000, respectively. What is the amount of cash received from customers?

Q4-15. A firm reports $86,000 wages expense in its income statement. If beginning and ending wages payable are $3,900 and $2,800, respectively, what is the amount of cash paid to employees?

Q4-16. A firm reports $43,000 advertising expense in its income statement. If beginning and ending prepaid advertising are $6,000 and $7,600, respectively, what is the amount of cash paid for advertising?

Q4-17. Rusk Company sold equipment for $5,100 cash that had cost $35,000 and had $29,000 of accumulated depreciation. How is this event reported in a statement of cash flows using the direct method?

Q4-18. What separate disclosures are required for a company that reports a statement of cash flows using the direct method?

Q4-19. How is the operating cash flow to current liabilities ratio calculated? Explain its use.

Q4-20. How is the operating cash flow to capital expenditures ratio calculated? Explain its use.

MINI EXERCISES

LO1, 3

Target
NYSE :: TGT

M4-21. **Identifying the Impact of Account Changes on Cash Flow from Operating Activities (Indirect Method)**

The following account information was presented as adjustments to net income in a recent statement of cash flows for **Target Corporation**. Determine whether each item would be a positive adjustment or a negative adjustment to net income in determining cash from operations. ($ millions).

a. Operating activities increased accounts payable by $625.
b. Operating activities increased inventories by $885.
c. Operating activities decreased other noncurrent liabilities by $50.
d. Depreciation and amortization expense was $2,223.
e. Operating activities decreased other noncurrent assets by $19.

LO1

M4-22. **Classifying Cash Flows**

For each of the items below, indicate whether the cash flow relates to an operating activity, an investing activity, or a financing activity.

a. Cash receipts from customers for services rendered.
b. Sale of long-term investments for cash.
c. Acquisition of plant assets for cash.
d. Payment of income taxes.
e. Bonds payable issued for cash.
f. Payment of cash dividends declared in previous year.
g. Purchase of short-term investments (not cash equivalents) for cash.

LO1, 3

Dole Food Company, Inc.
NYSE :: DOLE

M4-23. **Classifying Cash Flow Statement Components**

The following table presents selected items from a recent cash flow statement of **Dole Food Company, Inc.** For each item, determine whether the amount would be disclosed in the cash flow statement under operating activities, investing activities, or financing activities. (Dole uses the indirect method of reporting cash flows from operating activities.)

DOLE FOOD COMPANY, INC.
Selected Items from its Cash Flow Statement
1   Long-term debt repayments
2   Change in receivables
3   Depreciation and amortization
4   Change in accrued liabilities
5   Dividends paid
6   Change in income taxes payable
7   Cash received from sales of assets and businesses
8   Net income
9   Change in accounts payable
10 Short-term debt borrowings
11 Capital expenditures

LO1, 4

M4-24. **Classifying Cash Flows**

For each of the items below, indicate whether it is (1) a cash flow from an operating activity, (2) a cash flow from an investing activity, (3) a cash flow from a financing activity, (4) a noncash investing and financing activity, or (5) none of the above.

a.   Paid cash to retire bonds payable at a loss.
b.   Received cash as settlement of a lawsuit.
c.   Acquired a patent in exchange for common stock.
d.   Received advance payments from customers on orders for custom-made goods.
e.   Gave large cash contribution to local university.
f.   Invested cash in 60-day commercial paper (a cash equivalent).

M4-25. Reconciling Net Income and Cash Flow from Operations Using FSET
For fiscal year 2015, Beyer GMBH had the following summary information available concerning its operating activities. The company had no investing or financing activities this year.

LO2, 3

1. Sales of merchandise to customers on credit	€507,400
2. Sales of merchandise to customers for cash	91,500
3. Cost of merchandise sold on credit	320,100
4. Cost of merchandise sold for cash	63,400
5. Purchases of merchandise from suppliers on credit	351,600
6. Purchases of merchandise from suppliers for cash	47,700
7. Collections from customers on accounts receivable	483,400
8. Cash payments to suppliers on accounts payable	340,200
9. Operating expenses (all paid in cash)	172,300

REQUIRED
a.   Enter the items above into the Financial Statement Effects Template. Under noncash assets, use two separate columns for accounts receivable and inventories. Calculate the totals for each column.
b.   What was the company's net income for the year? What was the cash flow from operating activities? (Use the direct method.)
c.   Indicate the direction and amounts by which each of the following accounts changed during the year.
    1.   Accounts receivable
    2.   Merchandise inventory
    3.   Accounts payable
d.   Using your results above, prepare the operating activities section of the statement of cash flows using the indirect format.

M4-26. Calculating Net Cash Flow from Operating Activities (Indirect Method)
The following information was obtained from Galena Company's comparative balance sheets. Assume that Galena Company's 2016 income statement showed depreciation expense of $8,000, a gain on sale of investments of $9,000, and net income of $45,000. Calculate the net cash flow from operating activities using the indirect method.

LO3

	Dec. 31, 2016	Dec. 31, 2015
Cash	$ 19,000	$ 9,000
Accounts receivable	44,000	35,000
Inventory	55,000	49,000
Prepaid rent	6,000	8,000
Long-term investments	21,000	34,000
Plant assets	150,000	106,000
Accumulated depreciation	40,000	32,000
Accounts payable	24,000	20,000
Income tax payable	4,000	6,000
Common stock	121,000	92,000
Retained earnings	106,000	91,000

M4-27. Reconciling Net Income and Cash Flow from Operations Using FSET
For fiscal year 2016, Riffe Enterprises had the following summary information available concerning its operating activities. The company had no investing or financing activities this year.

LO2, 3

1.	Sales of services to customers on credit	$769,200
2.	Sales of services to customers for cash	46,200
3.	Employee compensation earned	526,700
4.	Cash payment in advance to landlord for offices.	149,100
5.	Cash paid to employees for compensation	521,600
6.	Rental expense for offices used over the year.	117,900
7.	Collections from customers on accounts receivable.	724,100
8.	Operating expenses (all paid in cash)	122,800
9.	Depreciation expense.	23,000

REQUIRED

a. Enter the items above into the Financial Statement Effects Template. Under noncash assets, use three separate columns for accounts receivable and prepaid rent and the accumulated depreciation contra-asset. Calculate the totals for each column.

b. What was the company's net income for the year? What was the cash flow from operating activities? (Use the direct method.)

c. Indicate the direction and amounts by which each of the following accounts changed during the year.

    1. Accounts receivable

    2. Prepaid rent

    3. Accumulated depreciation

    4. Wages payable

d. Using your results above, prepare the operating activities section of the statement of cash flows using the indirect format.

LO3   **M4-28.** **Calculating Net Cash Flow from Operating Activities (Indirect Method)**

Weber Company had a $21,000 net loss from operations for 2016. Depreciation expense for 2016 was $8,600 and a 2016 cash dividend of $6,000 was declared and paid. Balances of the current asset and current liability accounts at the beginning and end of 2016 follow. Did Weber Company's 2016 operating activities provide or use cash? Use the indirect method to determine your answer.

	Ending	Beginning
Cash	$ 3,500	$ 7,000
Accounts receivable.	16,000	25,000
Inventory.	50,000	53,000
Prepaid expenses.	6,000	9,000
Accounts payable.	12,000	8,000
Accrued liabilities	5,000	7,600

LO1   **M4-29.** **Classifying Cash Flow Statement Components and Determining Their Effects**

The following table presents selected items from a recent cash flow statement of **Nordstrom, Inc.**

Nordstrom, Inc.
NYSE :: JWN

a. For each item, determine whether the amount would be disclosed in the cash flow statement under operating activities, investing activities, or financing activities. (Nordstrom uses the indirect method of reporting.)

b. For each item, determine whether it will appear as a positive or negative in determining the net increase in cash and cash equivalents.

NORDSTROM, INC.
Consolidated Statement of Cash Flows—Selected Items

1. Increase in accounts receivable
2. Capital expenditures
3. Proceeds from long-term borrowings
4. Increase in deferred income tax net liability
5. Principal payments on long-term borrowings
6. Increase in merchandise inventories
7. Decrease in prepaid expenses and other assets
8. Proceeds from issuances under stock compensation plans
9. Increase in accounts payable
10. Net earnings
11. Payments for repurchase of common stock
12. Increase in accrued salaries, wages and related benefits
13. Cash dividends paid
14. Depreciation and amortization expenses

M4-30. Calculating Operating Cash Flows (Direct Method)

Calculate the cash flow for each of the following cases.

LO2

a. Cash paid for rent:

Rent expense	$60,000
Prepaid rent, beginning year	10,000
Prepaid rent, end of year	8,000

b. Cash received as interest:

Interest income.	$16,000
Interest receivable, beginning year.	3,000
Interest receivable, end of year	3,700

c. Cash paid for merchandise purchased:

Cost of goods sold.	$98,000
Inventory, beginning year	19,000
Inventory, end of year.	22,000
Accounts payable, beginning year.	11,000
Accounts payable, end of year.	7,000

M4-31. Calculating Operating Cash Flows (Direct Method)

Chakravarthy Company's current year income statement reports the following:

LO2

Sales.	$825,000
Cost of goods sold.	550,000
Gross profit.	$275,000

Chakravarthy's comparative balance sheets show the following (accounts payable relate to merchandise purchases):

	End of Year	Beginning of Year
Accounts receivable.	$ 71,000	$60,000
Inventory.	109,000	96,000
Accounts payable.	31,000	37,000

Compute Chakravarthy's current-year cash received from customers and cash paid for merchandise purchased.

EXERCISES

LO5   **E4-32.   Comparing Firms Using Ratio Analysis**

Consider the following 2013 data for several pharmaceutical firms ($ millions):

	Average current liabilities	Cash from operations	Expenditures on PPE	Proceeds from the sale of PPE
Merck & Co., Inc.	$18,108	$11,654	$1,548	$ 0
Pfizer Inc.	26,276	17,765	1,206	0
Abbott Laboratories	11,394	3,324	1,145	0
Johnson & Johnson	24,969	17,414	3,595	458

Merck & Co.
NYSE :: MRK
Pfizer Inc.
NYSE :: PFE
Abbott Laboratories
NYSE :: ABT
Johnson & Johnson
NYSE :: JNJ

a.   Compute the operating cash flow to current liabilities (OCFCL) ratio for each firm.
b.   Compute the free cash flow for each firm.
c.   Comment on the results of your computations.

LO5   **E4-33.   Comparing Firms Using Ratio Analysis**

Consider the following data for several firms from 2013 ($ millions):

	Average current liabilities	Cash from operations	Expenditures on PPE	Proceeds from the sale of PPE
Wal-Mart Stores, Inc.	$70,582	$23,257	$13,115	$ 727
The Coca-Cola Company	27,816	10,542	2,550	111
Exxon Mobil Corporation	67,932	44,914	33,669	2,707

Wal-Mart
NYSE :: WMT
The Coca-Cola
Company
NYSE :: KO
Exxon Mobil Corp.
NYSE :: XOM

a.   Compute the operating cash flow to current liabilities (OCFCL) ratio for each firm.
b.   Compute the free cash flow for each firm.
c.   Comment on the results of your computations.

LO2   **E4-34.   Preparing a Statement of Cash Flows (Direct Method)**

Use the following information about the 2016 cash flows of Mason Corporation to prepare a statement of cash flows under the direct method. Refer to **Exhibit 4.3** for the appropriate format.

Cash balance, end of 2016	$ 12,000
Cash paid to employees and suppliers	148,000
Cash received from sale of land	40,000
Cash paid to acquire treasury stock	10,000
Cash balance, beginning of 2016	16,000
Cash received as interest	6,000
Cash paid as income taxes	11,000
Cash paid to purchase equipment	89,000
Cash received from customers	194,000
Cash received from issuing bonds payable	30,000
Cash paid as dividends	16,000

LO3, 5   **E4-35.   Calculating Net Cash Flow from Operating Activities (Indirect Method)**

Lincoln Company owns no plant assets and reported the following income statement for the current year:

Sales		$750,000
Cost of goods sold	$470,000	
Wages expense	110,000	
Rent expense	42,000	
Insurance expense	15,000	637,000
Net income		$113,000

Additional balance sheet information about the company follows:

	End of Year	Beginning of Year
Accounts receivable.	$54,000	$49,000
Inventory.	60,000	66,000
Prepaid insurance.	8,000	7,000
Accounts payable.	22,000	18,000
Wages payable.	9,000	11,000

Use the information to

a. calculate the net cash flow from operating activities under the indirect method.

b. compute its operating cash flow to current liabilities (OCFCL) ratio. (Assume current liabilities consist of accounts payable and wages payable.)

E4-36. Accounting Sleuth: Reconstructing Entries

Meubles Fischer SA had the following balances for its property, plant, and equipment accounts (in thousands of euros):

LO4

	September 30, 2015	September 30, 2016
Property, plant, and equipment at cost	€1,000	€1,200
Accumulated depreciation	(350)	(390)
Property, plant, and equipment, net.	€ 650	€ 810

During fiscal year 2016, Meubles Fischer acquired €100 thousand in property by signing a mortgage, plus another €300 thousand in equipment for cash. The company also received €100 thousand in cash from the sale of used equipment, and its income statement reveals a €20 thousand gain from this transaction.

a. What was the original cost of the used equipment that Meubles Fischer SA sold during fiscal year 2016?

b. How much depreciation had been accumulated on the used equipment at the time it was sold?

c. How much depreciation expense did Meubles Fischer SA recognize in its fiscal year 2016 income statement?

E4-37. Accounting Sleuth: Reconstructing Entries

Kasznik Ltd. had the following balances for its property, plant, and equipment accounts (in millions of pounds):

LO4

	December 31, 2015	December 31, 2016
Property, plant, and equipment at cost	£175	£183
Accumulated depreciation	(78)	(83)
Property, plant, and equipment, net.	£ 97	£100

During 2016, Kasznik Ltd. paid £28 million in cash to acquire property and equipment, and this amount represents all the acquisitions of property, plant, and equipment for the period. The company's income statement reveals depreciation expense of £17 million and a £5 million loss from the disposal of used equipment.

a. What was the original cost of the used equipment that Kasznik Ltd. sold during 2016?

b. How much depreciation had been accumulated on the used equipment at the time it was sold?

c. How much cash did Kasznik Ltd. receive from its disposal of used equipment?

E4-38. Reconciling Changes in Balance Sheet Accounts

The following table presents selected items from the 2014 and 2013 balance sheets and 2014 income statement of **Walgreen Company**.

LO2, 4

Walgreen Company
NYSE :: WAG

WALGREEN CO. AND SUBSIDIARIES ($ millions)					
Selected Balance Sheet Data			Selected Income Statement Data		
	2014	2013			2014
Inventories	$ 6,076	$ 6,852	Cost of merchandise sold		$54,823
Property and equipment, less			Depreciation expense.		1,316
accumulated depreciation	12,257	12,138			
Trade accounts payable.	4,315	4,635	Net earnings.		2,031
Retained earnings	22,229	21,523			

a. Compute the cash paid for merchandise inventories in 2014. Assume that trade accounts payable is only for merchandise purchases.

b. Compute the net cost of property acquired in 2014.

c. Compute the cash dividends paid in 2014.

LO4 **E4-39. Analyzing Investing and Financing Cash Flows**

During 2016, Paxon Corporation's long-term investments account (at cost) increased $15,000, which was the net result of purchasing stocks costing $80,000 and selling stocks costing $65,000 at a $6,000 loss. Also, its bonds payable account decreased $10,000, the net result of issuing $130,000 of bonds and retiring bonds with a book value of $140,000 at a $9,000 gain. What items and amounts appear in the (a) cash flows from investing activities and (b) cash flows from financing activities sections of its 2016 statement of cash flows?

LO4 **E4-40. Reconciling Changes in Balance Sheet Accounts**

The following table presents selected items from the 2014 and 2013 balance sheets and 2014 income statement of **Golden Enterprises, Inc.**

Golden Enterprises, Inc.
NASDAQ :: GLDC

GOLDEN ENTERPRISES, INC.					
Selected Balance Sheet Data			Selected Income Statement Data		
	2014	2013			2014
Property and equipment, cost	$95,174,198	$93,022,443	Depreciation expense.		$3,778,563
Accumulated depreciation	69,502,854	65,927,389	Gain on sale of property		
			and equipment		22,693
Retained earnings	18,728,462	19,273,214	Net income.		921,829

Golden Enterprises reported expenditures for property and equipment of $2,380,287 in 2014.

a. What was the original cost of the property and equipment that Golden Enterprises sold during 2014? What was the accumulated depreciation on that property and equipment at the time of sale?

b. Compute the cash proceeds from the sale of property and equipment in 2014.

c. Prepare the journal entry to describe the sale of property and equipment.

d. Determine the cash dividends paid in 2014.

LO2 **E4-41. Calculating Operating Cash Flows (Direct Method)**

Calculate the cash flow for each of the following cases.

a. Cash paid for advertising:

Advertising expense.	$62,000
Prepaid advertising, beginning of year.	11,000
Prepaid advertising, end of year.	15,000

b. Cash paid for income taxes:

Income tax expense.	$29,000
Income tax payable, beginning of year	7,100
Income tax payable, end of year	4,900

c. Cash paid for merchandise purchased:

Cost of goods sold.	$180,000
Inventory, beginning of year	30,000
Inventory, end of year.	25,000
Accounts payable, beginning of year.	10,000
Accounts payable, end of year.	12,000

E4-42. **Preparing a Statement of Cash Flows (Indirect Method)**   **LO3, 4**

The following financial statements were issued by Hoskins Corporation for the fiscal year ended December 31, 2016. All amounts are in millions of U.S. dollars.

Balance Sheets	December 31, 2015		December 31, 2016	
Assets				
Cash.		$ 300		$ 550
Accounts receivable.		600		1,500
Inventory.		400		500
Prepaid expenses.		400		150
Current assets.		1,700		2,700
Property, plant, and equipment at cost	6,200		6,100	
Less accumulated depreciation	(2,100)		(1,750)	
Property, plant, and equipment, net.		4,100		4,350
Total assets.		$5,800		$7,050
Liabilities and Shareholders' Equity				
Accounts payable.		$ 400		$ 800
Income tax payable		200		100
Short-term debt		1,200		2,700
Current liabilities.		1,800		3,600
Long-term debt		1,000		0
Total liabilities		2,800		3,600
Contributed capital.		800		800
Retained earnings		2,200		2,650
Total shareholders' equity.		3,000		3,450
Total liabilities and shareholders' equity.		$5,800		$7,050

Income Statement	Fiscal year 2016
Sales revenues	$6,500
Cost of goods sold.	3,400
Gross profit.	3,100
Selling, general and administrative expenses	1,450
Depreciation expense.	350
Operating income	1,300
Interest expense.	350
Income before income tax expense	950
Income tax expense.	250
Net income	$ 700

Additional information:

1. During fiscal year 2016, Hoskins Corporation acquired new equipment for $1,200 in cash. In addition, the company disposed of used equipment that had original cost of $1,300 and accumulated depreciation of $700, receiving $600 in cash from the buyer.

2. During fiscal year 2016, Hoskins Corporation arranged short-term bank financing and borrowed $1,500, using a portion of the cash to repay all of its outstanding long-term debt.

3. During fiscal year 2016, Hoskins Corporation engaged in no transactions involving its common stock, though it did declare and pay in cash a common stock dividend of $250.

REQUIRED

Prepare a statement of cash flows (all three sections) for Hoskins Corporation's fiscal year 2016, using the indirect method for the cash from operations section.

LO2, 5
E4-43. **Analyzing Operating Cash Flows (Direct Method)**
Refer to the information in Exercise 4-35. Calculate the net cash flow from operating activities using the direct method. Show a related cash flow for each revenue and expense. Also, compute its operating cash flow to current liabilities (OCFCL) ratio. (Assume current liabilities consist of accounts payable and wages payable.)

LO2, 3
E4-44. **Interpreting Cash Flow from Operating Activities**
Carter Company's income statement and cash flow from operating activities (indirect method) are provided as follows ($ thousands):

Income statement		Cash flow from operating activities	
Revenue	$400	Net income	$35
Cost of goods sold	215	Plus depreciation expense	70
Gross profit	185		
Operating expenses	110	Operating asset adjustments	
		Less increase in accounts receivable	(25)
Operating income	75	Less increase in inventories	(50)
Interest expense	25	Less increase in prepaid rent	(5)
		Plus increase in accounts payable	65
Income before taxes	50	Plus increase in income tax payable	5
Income tax expense	15		
Net income	$ 35	Cash flow from operating activities	$95

a. For each of the four statements below, determine whether the statement is true or false.
b. If the statement is false, provide the (underlined) dollar amount that would make it true.
   1. Carter collected $375 from customers in the current period.
   2. Carter paid $0 interest in the current period.
   3. Carter paid $20 in income taxes in the current period.
   4. If Carter increased the depreciation expense by $50, it would increase its cash from operations by $50.

PROBLEMS

LO3 **P4-45.** **Reconciling and Computing Operating Cash Flows from Net Income**
Petroni Company reports the following selected results for its calendar year 2016.

Net income	$135,000
Depreciation expense	25,000
Gain on sale of assets	5,000
Accounts receivable increase	10,000
Accounts payable increase	6,000
Prepaid expenses decrease	3,000
Wages payable decrease	4,000

REQUIRED

Prepare the operating section only of Petroni Company's statement of cash flows for 2016 under the indirect method of reporting.

P4-46. **Preparing a Statement of Cash Flows (Indirect Method)**   **LO3, 4**
Wolff Company's income statement and comparative balance sheets follow.

WOLFF COMPANY
Income Statement
For Year Ended December 31, 2016

Sales.		$635,000
Cost of goods sold.	$430,000	
Wages expense	86,000	
Insurance expense.	8,000	
Depreciation expense.	17,000	
Interest expense.	9,000	
Income tax expense.	29,000	579,000
Net income.		$ 56,000

WOLFF COMPANY
Balance Sheets

	Dec. 31, 2016	Dec. 31, 2015
Assets		
Cash.	$ 11,000	$ 5,000
Accounts receivable.	41,000	32,000
Inventory.	90,000	60,000
Prepaid insurance.	5,000	7,000
Plant assets	250,000	195,000
Accumulated depreciation	(68,000)	(51,000)
Total assets.	$329,000	$248,000
Liabilities and Stockholders' Equity		
Accounts payable.	$ 7,000	$ 10,000
Wages payable.	9,000	6,000
Income tax payable	7,000	8,000
Bonds payable	130,000	75,000
Common stock.	90,000	90,000
Retained earnings	86,000	59,000
Total liabilities and equity	$329,000	$248,000

Cash dividends of $29,000 were declared and paid during 2016. Also in 2016, plant assets were purchased for cash, and bonds payable were issued for cash. Bond interest is paid semiannually on June 30 and December 31. Accounts payable relate to merchandise purchases.

REQUIRED

a. Compute the change in cash that occurred during 2016.
b. Prepare a 2016 statement of cash flows using the indirect method.
c. Compute and interpret Wolff's
  (1) operating cash flow to current liabilities ratio, and
  (2) operating cash flow to capital expenditures ratio.

P4-47. **Computing Cash Flow from Operating Activities (Direct Method)**   **LO2**
Refer to the income statement and comparative balance sheets for Wolff Company presented in P4-46.

REQUIRED

a. Compute Wolff Company's cash flow from operating activities using the direct method. Use the format illustrated in **Exhibit 4.5** in the chapter.
b. What can we learn from the direct method that may not be readily apparent when reviewing a cash flow statement prepared using the indirect method?

LO3, 4   P4-48.   Preparing a Statement of Cash Flows (Indirect Method)

Arctic Company's income statement and comparative balance sheets follow.

ARCTIC COMPANY Income Statement For Year Ended December 31, 2016		
Sales.		$728,000
Cost of goods sold.	$534,000	
Wages expense	190,000	
Advertising expense.	31,000	
Depreciation expense.	22,000	
Interest expense.	18,000	
Gain on sale of land	(25,000)	770,000
Net loss		$ (42,000)

ARCTIC COMPANY Balance Sheets	Dec. 31, 2016	Dec. 31, 2015
Assets		
Cash.	$ 49,000	$ 28,000
Accounts receivable.	42,000	50,000
Inventory.	107,000	113,000
Prepaid advertising.	10,000	13,000
Plant assets	360,000	222,000
Accumulated depreciation	(78,000)	(56,000)
Total assets.	$490,000	$370,000
Liabilities and Stockholders' Equity		
Accounts payable.	$ 17,000	$ 31,000
Interest payable	6,000	—
Bonds payable	200,000	—
Common stock.	245,000	245,000
Retained earnings	52,000	94,000
Treasury stock	(30,000)	—
Total liabilities and equity	$490,000	$370,000

During 2016, Arctic sold land for $70,000 cash that had originally cost $45,000. Arctic also purchased equipment for cash, acquired treasury stock for cash, and issued bonds payable for cash in 2016. Accounts payable relate to merchandise purchases.

REQUIRED

a.   Compute the change in cash that occurred during 2016.

b.   Prepare a 2016 statement of cash flows using the indirect method.

c.   Compute and interpret Arctic's

   (1) operating cash flow to current liabilities ratio, and

   (2) operating cash flow to capital expenditures ratio.

LO2   P4-49.   Computing Cash Flow from Operating Activities (Direct Method)

Refer to the income statement and comparative balance sheets for Arctic Company presented in P4-48.

REQUIRED

a.   Compute Arctic Company's cash flow from operating activities using the direct method. Use the format illustrated in **Exhibit 4.5** in the chapter.

b.   What can we learn from the direct method that may not be readily apparent when reviewing a cash flow statement prepared using the indirect method?

P4-50. **Preparing a Statement of Cash Flows (Indirect Method)**   **LO3, 4, 5**

Dair Company's income statement and comparative balance sheets follow.

DAIR COMPANY Income Statement For Year Ended December 31, 2016		
Sales..		$700,000
Cost of goods sold..	$440,000	
Wages and other operating expenses	95,000	
Depreciation expense......................................	22,000	
Amortization expense......................................	7,000	
Interest expense..	10,000	
Income tax expense..	36,000	
Loss on bond retirement	5,000	615,000
Net income..		$ 85,000

DAIR COMPANY Balance Sheets	Dec. 31, 2016	Dec. 31, 2015
Assets		
Cash..	$ 27,000	$ 18,000
Accounts receivable.......................................	53,000	48,000
Inventory...	103,000	109,000
Prepaid expenses..	12,000	10,000
Plant assets	360,000	336,000
Accumulated depreciation..................................	(87,000)	(84,000)
Intangible assets	43,000	50,000
Total assets..	$511,000	$487,000
Liabilities and Shareholders' Equity		
Accounts payable..	$ 32,000	$ 26,000
Interest payable	4,000	7,000
Income tax payable	6,000	8,000
Bonds payable...	60,000	120,000
Common stock..	252,000	228,000
Retained earnings	157,000	98,000
Total liabilities and equity.............................	$511,000	$487,000

During 2016, the company sold for $17,000 cash old equipment that had cost $36,000 and had $19,000 accumulated depreciation. Also in 2016, new equipment worth $60,000 was acquired in exchange for $60,000 of bonds payable, and bonds payable of $120,000 were retired for cash at a loss. A $26,000 cash dividend was declared and paid in 2016. Any stock issuances were for cash.

REQUIRED

a. Compute the change in cash that occurred in 2016.

b. Prepare a 2016 statement of cash flows using the indirect method.

c. Prepare separate schedules showing

  (1) cash paid for interest and for income taxes and

  (2) noncash investing and financing transactions.

d. Compute its

  (1) operating cash flow to current liabilities ratio,

  (2) operating cash flow to capital expenditures ratio, and

  (3) free cash flow.

LO2, 3, 4   **P4-51.**   **Interpreting the Statement of Cash Flows**
CVS Health Corp.   Following is the statement of cash flows of **CVS Health Corp.**
NYSE :: CVS

CVS HEALTH CORP. Consolidated Statement of Cash Flows Year Ended December 31, 2013 ($ millions)	
Cash flows from operating activities:	
Cash receipts from customers	$114,993
Cash paid for inventory and prescriptions dispensed by retail network pharmacies	(91,178)
Cash paid to other suppliers and employees	(14,295)
Interest received	8
Interest paid	(534)
Income taxes paid	(3,211)
Net cash provided by operating activities	5,783
Cash flows from investing activities:	
Purchases of property and equipment	(1,984)
Proceeds from sale-leaseback transactions	600
Proceeds from sale of property and equipment and other assets	54
Acquisitions (net of cash acquired) and other investments	(415)
Purchase of available-for-sale investments	(226)
Maturity of available-for-sale investments	136
Net cash used in investing activities	(1,835)
Cash flows from financing activities:	
Increase (decrease) in short-term debt	(690)
Proceeds from issuance of long-term debt	3,964
Dividends paid	(1,097)
Proceeds from exercise of stock options	500
Excess tax benefits from stock-based compensation	62
Repurchase of common stock	(3,976)
Net cash used in financing activities	(1,237)
Effect of exchange rate changes on cash and cash equivalents	3
Net increase (decrease) in cash and cash equivalents	2,714
Cash and cash equivalents at the beginning of the year	1,375
Cash and cash equivalents at the end of the year	$ 4,089
Reconciliation of net income to net cash provided by operating activities:	
Net income	$ 4,592
Adjustments to reconcile net income to net cash provided by operating activities:	
Depreciation and amortization	1,870
Stock-based compensation	141
Deferred income taxes and other noncash items	(86)
Change in operating assets and liabilities, net of effects from acquisitions:	
Accounts receivable, net	(2,210)
Inventories	12
Other current assets	105
Other assets	(135)
Accounts payable and claims and discounts payable	1,024
Accrued expenses	471
Other long-term liabilities	(1)
Net cash provided by operating activities	$ 5,783

REQUIRED

a. Does CVS use the direct method or the indirect method to present its statement of cash flows? Explain.

b. Based on the information presented in its statement of cash flows, what amount of revenues should CVS report in its income statement?

c.   CVS reported retained earnings of $24,998 million at the end of 2012. What amount of re-
     tained earnings did the company report in its 2013 balance sheet?
d.   Why is "stock-based compensation" listed under "adjustments to reconcile net income to net
     cash provided by operating activities"?
e.   Why does CVS list the "effect of exchange rate changes on cash and cash equivalents" in its
     statement of cash flows? What does this amount represent?
f.   Using three bullet points, explain what CVS did with the $5.8 billion in cash that was provided
     by operating activities in 2013.

P4-52.   **Preparing a Statement of Cash Flows (Indirect Method)**   **LO3, 4, 5**
Rainbow Company's income statement and comparative balance sheets follow.

RAINBOW COMPANY Income Statement For Year Ended December 31, 2016		
Sales.		$750,000
Dividend income.		15,000
Total revenue		765,000
Cost of goods sold.	$440,000	
Wages and other operating expenses	130,000	
Depreciation expense.	39,000	
Patent amortization expense	7,000	
Interest expense.	13,000	
Income tax expense.	44,000	
Loss on sale of equipment.	5,000	
Gain on sale of investments.	(3,000)	675,000
Net income.		$ 90,000

RAINBOW COMPANY Balance Sheets		
	Dec. 31, 2016	Dec. 31, 2015
Assets		
Cash and cash equivalents	$ 19,000	$ 25,000
Accounts receivable.	40,000	30,000
Inventory.	103,000	77,000
Prepaid expenses.	10,000	6,000
Long-term investments	—	57,000
Land.	190,000	100,000
Buildings.	445,000	350,000
Accumulated depreciation—buildings.	(91,000)	(75,000)
Equipment	179,000	225,000
Accumulated depreciation—equipment.	(42,000)	(46,000)
Patents.	50,000	32,000
Total assets.	$903,000	$781,000
Liabilities and Stockholders' Equity		
Accounts payable.	$ 20,000	$ 16,000
Interest payable	6,000	5,000
Income tax payable	8,000	10,000
Bonds payable	155,000	125,000
Preferred stock ($100 par value)	100,000	75,000
Common stock ($5 par value)	379,000	364,000
Paid-in capital in excess of par value—common.	133,000	124,000
Retained earnings	102,000	62,000
Total liabilities and equity.	$903,000	$781,000

During 2016, the following transactions and events occurred:

1.   Sold long-term investments costing $57,000 for $60,000 cash.
2.   Purchased land for cash.
3.   Capitalized an expenditure made to improve the building.

4. Sold equipment for $14,000 cash that originally cost $46,000 and had $27,000 accumulated depreciation.
5. Issued bonds payable at face value for cash.
6. Acquired a patent with a fair value of $25,000 by issuing 250 shares of preferred stock at par value.
7. Declared and paid a $50,000 cash dividend.
8. Issued 3,000 shares of common stock for cash at $8 per share.
9. Recorded depreciation of $16,000 on buildings and $23,000 on equipment.

REQUIRED

a. Compute the change in cash and cash equivalents that occurred during 2016.
b. Prepare a 2016 statement of cash flows using the indirect method.
c. Prepare separate schedules showing (1) cash paid for interest and for income taxes and (2) noncash investing and financing transactions.
d. Compute its (1) operating cash flow to current liabilities ratio, (2) operating cash flow to capital expenditures ratio, and (3) free cash flow.

LO2, 3, 4   P4-53.   Preparing a Statement of Cash Flows (Direct Method)
Refer to the data for Rainbow Company in Problem 4-52.

REQUIRED

a. Compute the change in cash that occurred in 2016.
b. Prepare a 2016 statement of cash flows using the direct method. Use one cash outflow for "cash paid for wages and other operating expenses." Accounts payable relate to inventory purchases only.
c. Prepare separate schedules showing (1) a reconciliation of net income to net cash flow from operating activities and (2) noncash investing and financing transactions.

LO3, 4   P4-54.   Interpreting Cash Flow Information

Apple Inc.
NASDAQ :: AAPL

The 2014 cash flow statement for **Apple Inc.** is presented below (all $ amounts in millions):

APPLE INC.
Consolidated Statement of Cash Flows
Year Ended September 27, 2014

Cash and cash equivalents, beginning of the year	$ 14,259
Operating activities	
Net income	39,510
Adjustments to reconcile net income to cash generated by operating activities:	
Depreciation, and amortization	7,946
Share-based compensation expense	2,863
Deferred income tax expense	2,347
Changes in operating assets and liabilities:	
Accounts receivable, net	(4,232)
Inventories	(76)
Vendor non-trade receivables	(2,220)
Other current and non-current assets	167
Accounts payable	5,938
Deferred revenue	1,460
Other current and non-current liabilities	6,010
Cash generated by operating activities	59,713
Investing activities	
Purchases of marketable securities	(217,128)
Proceeds from maturities of marketable securities	18,810
Proceeds from sales of marketable securities	189,301
Payments made in connection with business acquisitions, net of cash acquired	(3,765)
Payments for acquisition of property, plant and equipment	(9,571)
Payments made for acquisitions of intangible assets	(242)
Other	16
Cash used in investing activities	(22,579)

continued

Financing activities

Proceeds from issuance of common stock	730
Excess tax benefits from equity awards.	739
Taxes paid related to net share settlement of equity awards	(1,158)
Dividends and dividend equivalents paid.	(11,126)
Repurchase of common stock	(45,000)
Proceeds from issuance of long-term debt, net.	11,960
Proceeds from issuance of commercial paper, net	6,306
Cash used in financing activities.	(37,549)
Increase (decrease) in cash and cash equivalents.	(415)
Cash and cash equivalents, end of the year	$13,844

Supplemental cash flow disclosure:

Cash paid for income taxes, net	$10,026
Cash paid for interest.	$ 339

REQUIRED

a. Did Apple's accounts receivable go up or down in 2014? Explain. Apple reported net sales of $182,795 million in its fiscal 2014 income statement. What amount of cash did Apple collect from customers during the year? (Ignore the Vendor non-trade receivables account, which relates to Apple's suppliers.)

b. Apple's cost of goods sold was $112,258 million in 2014. Assuming that accounts payable applies only to the purchase of inventory, what amount did Apple pay to purchase inventory in 2014?

c. At September 27, 2014, Apple reported a balance of $20.6 billion in property, plant, and equipment, net of accumulated depreciation, and its footnotes revealed that depreciation expense for fiscal 2014 was $6.9 billion. What was the balance in property, plant, and equipment, net of accumulated depreciation at the end of fiscal 2013?

d. Apple lists stock based compensation as a positive amount—$2,863 million—under cash flow from operating activities. Why is this amount listed here? Explain how this amount increases cash flow from operating activities.

P4-55.^A Preparing the Statement of Cash Flows Using a Spreadsheet

The table below provides the balance sheets for **Golden Enterprises, Inc.** for the fiscal years ended May 30, 2014 and May 31, 2013.

LO5, 6
Golden Enterprises, Inc.
NASDAQ :: GLDC

	Year Ended	
Consolidated Balance Sheets	**May 30, 2014**	**May 31, 2013**
Assets		
Cash and cash equivalents	$ 1,160,630	$ 757,111
Receivables, net.	11,341,024	10,459,706
Inventories	5,659,639	4,955,813
Prepaid expenses.	1,277,861	1,554,737
Deferred income taxes	559,672	596,267
Total current assets.	19,998,826	18,323,634
Property, plant and equipment at cost.	95,174,198	93,022,443
Accumulated depreciation	(69,502,854)	(65,927,389)
Property, plant and equipment, net	25,671,344	27,095,054
Cash surrender of life insurance.	602,353	695,761
Other.	1,207,743	1,642,030
Total assets	$47,480,266	$47,756,479

continued

continued from previous page

	May 30, 2014	May 31, 2013
Liabilities & stockholders' equity		
Checks outstanding in excess of bank balances.................	$ 1,971,076	$ 1,442,915
Accounts payable.......................................	3,719,102	4,809,066
Accrued income taxes	378,659	53,475
Current portion of long-term debt	369,979	392,850
Line of credit outstanding...............................	2,528,511	1,725,289
Other accrued expenses	5,953,171	5,427,017
Salary continuation plan................................	212,970	196,649
Total current liabilities.................................	15,133,468	14,047,261
Note payable to bank, non-current	4,944,233	5,314,213
Salary continuation plan................................	920,184	1,032,810
Deferred income taxes..................................	2,969,389	3,304,451
Total liabilities.......................................	23,967,274	23,698,735
Common stock at par..................................	9,219,195	9,219,195
Additional paid-in capital...............................	6,497,954	6,497,954
Retained earnings	18,728,462	19,273,214
Treasury shares, at cost................................	(10,932,619)	(10,932,619)
Total stockholders' equity.............................	23,512,992	24,057,744
Total liabilities and stockholders' equity	$47,480,266	$47,756,479

Additional information:

1. Net income for the year ended May 30, 2014 was $921,829.
2. Depreciation expense for the year ended May 30, 2014 was $3,778,563.
3. Accounts for the life insurance asset and salary continuation liabilities are operating.
4. Checks outstanding in excess of bank balances should be treated as a financing liability.
5. During the year ended May 30, 2014, Golden Enterprises sold used property, plant, and equipment, receiving $48,125 in cash and recognizing a gain of $22,693.
6. For the year ended May 30, 2014, debt proceeds (encompassing the liabilities for current portion of long-term debt, line of credit outstanding and note payable to bank, non-current) were $35,726,909 and debt repayments were $35,316,538.

REQUIRED

a. Set up a spreadsheet to analyze the changes in Golden Enterprises' comparative balance sheets. Use the format illustrated in **Exhibit 4A.1**.

b. Prepare a statement of cash flows (including operations, investing and financing) for Golden Enterprises for the year ended May 30, 2014 using the indirect method for the operating section.

c. Using information in the statement of cash flows prepared in part *b*, compute (1) the operating cash flow to current liabilities ratio and (2) the operating cash flow to capital expenditures ratio.

LO3, 4, 5
Groupon, Inc.
NASDAQ :: GRPN

P4-56. **Interpreting the Statement of Cash Flows**

Groupon, Inc. provides an electronic marketplace to connect local merchants to consumers. Merchants offer discounts which customers purchase through Groupon, and Groupon makes payments (keeping approximately 40%) to the merchants over the next few weeks. Its growth prior to the company's initial public offering in November 2011 can only be described as meteoric. The company's revenues grew from $5 thousand in 2008 to $312,941 thousand in 2010 to $1,118,266 thousand in the first nine months of 2011. The sales growth did not translate into profitability, and Groupon reported net losses of $1,542 thousand in 2008, $413,386 thousand in 2010 and $238,083 thousand in the first nine months of 2011. However, the company generated positive cash flow from operating activity as can be seen in the accompanying nine-month statement of cash flows issued just prior to its initial public offering (Page F-52 of Form S-1/A filed with the Securities and Exchange Commission on November 1, 2011). While Groupon's net loss was $238,083 thousand for the period, its cash from operating activities was $129,511.

REQUIRED

a. Groupon uses the indirect method to present its cash from operating activities. The largest single positive adjustment is $314,872 for Accrued Merchant Payable. Explain the causes of this adjustment and its magnitude. Is this adjustment likely to recur in future periods? Explain.

b. How much of Groupon's investing cash flows are being spent on property and equipment? Calculate the company's operating cash flow to capital expenditures ratio.

c. What are the significant items in the financing cash flows section? Groupon raised $509,692 thousand through the issuing of shares. What did the company do with most of those funds?

GROUPON, INC. CONDENSED CONSOLIDATED STATEMENTS OF CASH FLOWS (UNAUDITED)		
	Nine Months Ended September 30,	
(in thousands)	2010	2011
Operating activities		
Net loss	$(77,783)	$(238,083)
Adjustments to reconcile net loss to net cash provided by operating activities:		
Depreciation and amortization	6,908	22,754
Stock-based compensation	8,739	60,922
Deferred income taxes	(4,615)	602
Excess tax benefit on stock-based compensation	—	(11,323)
Losses in equity interests	—	19,974
Non cash interest expense	106	—
Acquisition-related	37,844	(4,793)
Gain on return of common stock	—	(4,916)
Change in assets and liabilities, net of acquisitions:		
Accounts receivable	(16,071)	(69,690)
Prepaid expenses and other current assets	1,916	(41,023)
Accounts payable	12,178	(21,924)
Accrued merchant payable	47,518	314,872
Accrued expenses and other current liabilities	23,690	108,963
Due to related parties	682	361
Other	(6,146)	(7,185)
Net cash provided by operating activities	34,966	129,511
Investing activities		
Purchases of property and equipment	(6,092)	(29,825)
Acquisitions of businesses, net of acquired cash	6,495	(12,553)
Purchases of intangible assets	(707)	(15,072)
Changes in restricted cash	200	(8,141)
Purchases of investments in subsidiaries	—	(34,887)
Purchases of equity investments	—	(20,189)
Net cash used in investing activities	(104)	(120,667)
Financing activities		
Issuance of shares, net of issuance costs	134,932	509,692
Excess tax benefit on stock-based compensation	—	11,323
Loans from related parties	5,035	—
Repayments of loans to related parties	—	(14,358)
Repurchase of common stock	(119,891)	(353,550)
Proceeds from exercise of stock options	68	2,269
Proceeds from sale of common stock	—	137
Redemption of preferred stock	—	(35,221)
Net cash provided by financing activities	20,144	120,292
Effect of exchange rate changes on cash and cash equivalents	1,316	(4,034)
Net increase in cash and cash equivalents	56,322	125,102
Cash and cash equivalents, beginning of period	12,313	118,833
Cash and cash equivalents, end of period	$ 68,635	$ 243,935

CASES AND PROJECTS

LO3, 4   **C4-57.** **Analyzing a Projected Statement of Cash Flows and Loan Covenants**

The President and CFO of Lambert Co. will be meeting with their bankers next week to discuss the short-term financing needs of the company for the next six months. Lambert's controller has provided a projected income statement for the next six-month period, and a current balance sheet along with a projected balance sheet for the end of that six-month period. These statements are presented below ($ millions).

LAMBERT CO.
Projected Six-Month Income Statement

Revenues	$400
Cost of goods sold	200
Gross profit	200
Selling and administrative expense	50
Depreciation expense	120
Income before income taxes	30
Income taxes	12
Net income	$ 18

LAMBERT CO.
Current and Projected Six-Month Balance Sheets

	Current	6-month projected
Cash	$ 50	$???
Accounts receivable	180	220
Inventory	200	180
Total current assets	430	???
Property, plant & equipment, cost	400	500
Less accumulated depreciation	(150)	(220)
Property, plant & equipment, net	250	280
Total assets	$680	???
Accounts payable	$150	$180
Income taxes payable	20	10
Short-term borrowing	50	???
Long-term debt	200	180
Total liabilities	420	???
Common stock at par	100	125
Retained earnings	160	148
Total liabilities and shareholders' equity	$680	???

Additional Information (already reflected in the projected income statement and balance sheet):

- Lambert's current long-term debt includes $100 that is due within the next six months. During the next six months, the company plans to take advantage of lower interest rates by issuing new long-term debt that will provide $80 in cash proceeds.
- During the next six months, the company plans to dispose of equipment with an original cost of $125 and accumulated depreciation of $50. An appraisal by an equipment broker indicates that Lambert should be able to get $75 in cash for the equipment. In addition, Lambert plans to acquire new equipment at a cost of $225.
- A small issue of common stock for cash ($25) and a cash dividend to shareholders ($30) are planned in the next six months.
- Lambert's outstanding long-term debt imposes a restrictive loan covenant on the company that requires Lambert to maintain a debt-to-equity ratio below 1.75.

REQUIRED

The CFO says, "I would like a clear estimate of the amount of short-term borrowing that we will need six months from now. I want you to prepare a forecasted statement of cash flows that we can take to the meeting next week."

Prepare the required statement of cash flows, using the indirect method to compute cash flow from operating activities. The forecasted statement should include the needed amount of short-term borrowing and should be consistent with the projected balance sheet and income statement, as well as the loan covenant restriction.

C4-58. Reconstructing Journal Entries and T-Accounts from Completed Financial Statements **LO1, 3, 4**

Lundholm Company's comparative balance sheets, income statement, and statement of cash flows for July are presented below:

LUNDHOLM COMPANY
Comparative Balance Sheets

	July 1	July 31
Cash	$ 600	$ 1,184
Accounts receivable	6,500	6,800
Inventory	2,400	1,800
Prepaid rent	—	400
Current assets	9,500	10,184
Fixtures and equipment at cost	1,900	2,620
Accumulated depreciation	(800)	(880)
Plant and equipment, net	1,100	1,740
Total assets	$10,600	$11,924
Accounts payable	$ 3,000	$ 3,100
Salaries and wages payable	100	70
Taxes payable	—	374
Bank loan payable	1,600	—
Current liabilities	4,700	3,544
Long-term loan	—	2,000
Common stock	4,600	4,600
Retained earnings	1,300	1,780
Total liabilities and shareholders' equity	$10,600	$11,924

LUNDHOLM COMPANY
Income Statement
Month Ended July 31

Revenue		$3,800
Operating expenses:		
Cost of goods sold	$1,800	
Salaries and wages	700	
Rent	200	
Depreciation	150	
Total operating expenses		2,850
Operating income		950
Interest expense		16
Income before taxes		934
Income taxes		374
Net income		$ 560

LUNDHOLM COMPANY
Statement of Cash Flows
Month Ended July 31

Operating activities:

Net income	$ 560
Adjustments:	
Depreciation	150
Increase in accounts receivable	(300)
Decrease in inventory	600
Increase in prepaid rent	(400)
Increase in accounts payable	100
Decrease in salaries and wages payable	(30)
Increase in taxes payable	374
Total adjustments	494
Cash flow from operating activities	1,054
Investing activities:	
Proceeds from disposal of fixtures and equipment	10
Purchases of fixtures and equipment	(800)
Cash flow used for investing activities	(790)
Financing activities:	
Loan repayment	(1,600)
Proceeds from new loan	2,000
Dividends paid to shareholders	(80)
Cash flow from financing activities	320
Net increase in cash	584
Cash balance, July 1	600
Cash balance, July 31	$1,184

REQUIRED

a. Set up T-accounts and enter beginning and ending balances for each account in Lundholm Company's balance sheet.

b. Provide a set of *summary journal entries* for July that would produce the financial statements presented above. For simplicity, you may assume that all of Lundholm Company's sales are made on account and that all of its purchases are made on account. One such entry is provided as an example.

(1)	Accounts receivable (+A)	3,800	
	Sales revenue (+R, +SE)		3,800

c. Post the journal entries from part b to T-accounts and verify ending balances.

C4-59. **Interpreting the Statement of Cash Flows**

The statement of cash flows for **Daimler AG** follows:

LO1, 2, 3, 4, 5
Daimler AG
ETR :: DAI

DAIMLER AG Consolidated Statement of Cash Flows Year Ended December 31, 2013 (€ millions)	
Profit before income taxes	€10,139
Depreciation and amortization	4,368
Other non-cash expense and income	(3,345)
(Gains)/losses on disposals of assets	193
Change in operating assets and liabilities	
Inventories	(592)
Trade receivables	(695)
Trade payables	610
Receivables from financial services	(5,334)
Vehicles on operating leases	(2,990)
Other operating assets and liabilities	2,240
Income taxes paid	(1,309)
Cash provided by/used for operating activities	3,285
Additions to property, plant and equipment	(4,975)
Additions to intangible assets	(1,932)
Proceeds from disposals of property, plant and equipment and intangible assets	180
Investments in share property	(969)
Proceeds from disposals of share property	2,414
Acquisition of marketable debt securities	(6,566)
Proceeds from sales of marketable debt securities	4,991
Other	28
Cash used for investing activities	(6,829)
Change in short-term financing liabilities	845
Additions to long-term financing liabilities	37,602
Repayment of long-term financing liabilities	(31,987)
Dividend paid to shareholders of Daimler AG	(2,349)
Dividends paid to non-controlling interests	(269)
Proceeds from issuance of share capital	101
Acquisition of treasury shares	(24)
Acquisition of non-controlling interests in subsidiaries	(73)
Proceeds from disposals of interests in subsidiaries without loss of control	9
Cash provided by/used for financing activities	3,855
Effect of foreign exchange rate changes on cash and cash equivalents	(254)
Net increase/decrease in cash and cash equivalents	57
Cash and cash equivalents at the beginning of the period	10,996
Cash and cash equivalents at the end of the period	€11,053

REQUIRED

a. Daimler begins its cash flow statement with net income of €10,139 million, then adds €4,368 million for depreciation and amortization. Why is Daimler adding depreciation and amortization to net income in this computation?

b. Why does Daimler add €193 million of losses on disposals of assets in its indirect method cash flows from operating activities? If these losses are all created by disposals of property, plant, and equipment and intangible assets, what was the book value of the assets Daimler disposed of during fiscal year 2013?

c. Daimler shows a negative €592 million for inventories in the statement of cash flows. Does this mean that Daimler paid €592 million for inventories in 2013? Explain.

d. Compute Daimler's free cash flow for 2013. How did the company finance its investing activities?

e. Daimler reports a cash flow from operating activities of only €3,285 million, despite reporting net income of €10,139 million. What principal activities account for this difference? Does this raise concerns about the health of Daimler AG?

f. Why does Daimler list the "effect of foreign exchange rate changes on cash and cash equivalents" in its statement of cash flows? What does this amount represent?

SOLUTIONS TO REVIEW PROBLEMS

Mid-Chapter Review 1

SOLUTION

1. Out/I; 2. Out/O; 3. Out/O; 4. In/F; 5. Out/O; 6. In/O; 7. In/I; 8. In/I; 9. Out/F; 10. In/O

Mid-Chapter Review 2

SOLUTION

MUG SHOTS, INC.
Computation of Cash Flow from Operating Activities
For Month Ended December 31, 2015

Net income $3,445	= Sales revenue $31,000	− Cost of goods sold 16,700	− Wage expenses 4,700	− Interest expense 300	− Advertising expense 1,800	− Rent expense 1,500	− Depreciation expense 700	− Income tax expense 1,855
Adjustments:								
Add back depreciation expense							⊕ 700 Depreciation expense	
Subtract (add) non-operating gains (losses)								
Subtract the change in operating assets (operating investments)	⊖ 2,500 Change in accounts receivable	⊖ 8,300 Change in inventory				⊖ (−1,500) Change in prepaid rent		
Add the change in operating liabilities (operating financing)	⊕ 500 Change in unearned revenue	⊕ 1,000 Change in accounts payable	⊕ 2,200 Change in wages payable	⊕ 300 Change in interest payable				⊕ 1,855 Change in income tax payable
$700 Cash from operations	= $29,000 = Receipts from customers	− 24,000 − Payments for merchandise	− 2,500 − Payments for wages	− 0 − Payments for interest	− 1,800 − Payments for advertising	− 0 − Payments for rent	− 0 −	− 0 − Payments for income tax

Mid-Chapter Review 3

SOLUTION

MUG SHOTS, INC. Cash Flow from Operating Activities—Indirect Method		
Net income..		$3,445
Adjustments:		
Add back depreciation expense...........................	$ 700	
Subtract changes in:		
Accounts receivable	(2,500)	
Inventory	(8,300)	
Prepaid rent..	1,500	
Add changes in:		
Unearned revenue....................................	500	
Accounts payable	1,000	
Wages payable	2,200	
Interest payable.....................................	300	
Income tax payable...................................	1,855	
Total adjustments		(2,745)
Cash flow from operating activities		$700

Mid-Chapter Review 4

SOLUTION

MUG SHOTS, INC. Statement of Cash Flows For Month Ended December 31, 2015		
Cash flow from operating activities		
Net income..	$ 3,445	
Add back depreciation	700	
Subtract changes in:		
Accounts receivable	(2,500)	
Inventory	(8,300)	
Prepaid rent......................................	1,500	
Add changes in:		
Accounts payable	1,000	
Unearned revenue.................................	500	
Income tax payable................................	1,855	
Wages payable	2,200	
Interest payable...................................	300	
Net cash provided by operating activities		$700
Cash flow from investing activities		
Purchase of equipment...............................	(12,000)	
Net cash used by investing activities....................		(12,000)
Cash flow from financing activities		
Bank loan	18,000	
Payment of dividend.................................	(1,000)	
Net cash provided by financing activities.................		17,000
		5,700
Cash, beginning of period		5,000
Cash, end of period		$10,700

Mid-Chapter Review 5

SOLUTION

There are three entries that affected the balance sheet accounts of Property, Plant, and Equipment at cost and Accumulated Depreciation. We know some of the amounts involved, but not all. Let P be the proceeds on the sale of used equipment, let A be the cash spent to acquire new property, plant, and equipment, and let D be the year's depreciation expense. Here are the entries:

1. Disposal:

DR Cash (+A)	P	
DR Accumulated depreciation (−XA, +A)	60,000	
CR Property, plant, and equipment at cost (−A)		80,000
CR Gain on equipment disposal (+R, +SE)		35,000

The value of P must be $55,000, because Jack's Snacks reported a gain of $35,000 on selling an asset with book value of $20,000 (= $80,000 − $60,000).

2. Acquisition:

DR Property, plant, and equipment at cost (+A)	A	
CR Cash (−A)		A

We can determine the cost of acquired assets by looking at the T-account for Property, Plant, and Equipment at Cost.

+	Property, Plant, and Equipment at Cost		−
Beg. bal.	600,000		
Purchases	A	80,000	Disposal
End. bal.	670,000		

The value of A, i.e., the amount spent on acquiring PPE, must have been $150,000.

3. Depreciation expense:

DR Depreciation expense (+E, −SE)	D	
CR Accumulated depreciation (+XA, −A)		D

We can determine the depreciation expense by looking at the T-account for the Accumulated Depreciation contra-asset.

+	Accumulated Depreciation		−
		140,000	Beg. bal.
Disposal	60,000	D	Deprec. Exp.
		150,000	End. bal.

The depreciation expense for the year, D, must have been $70,000, because the contra-asset increased by $10,000 even though the disposal decreased it by $60,000.

Chapter-End Review

SOLUTION

1. We assume that One World Café's notes payable are classified as current liabilities. If so, current liabilities are $41,000 ($27,000+$6,000+$3,000+$5,000) in 2015 and $21,000 ($14,000+$2,500+$4,500) in 2014.
    $44,000 / [($41,000 + $21,000)/2] = 1.42
    One World Café is generating cash flows from operations in excess of its current liabilities. Assuming that this continues, it should have no difficulty meeting its obligations.
2. $44,000 / $45,000 = 0.98
    One World Café spent a little more on plant capacity than it generated through operations. However, for a small business, capital expenditures are often irregular. Thus, this ratio is not alarmingly low.
3. $44,000 − ($45,000 − $4,000) = $3,000.

Appendix 4A Review

SOLUTION

Cash Flow Spreadsheet for Rocky Road Bicycles, Inc.

	A	B	C	D	E	F	G	H	I	J
						Effect of change on cash flow			**No effect**	**Total**
		O, I, or F?	**2015**	**2014**	**Change**	**Operating**	**Investing**	**Financing**	**on cash**	**F, G, H, I**
3	**Assets**									
4	Cash..........................		106,000	96,000	10,000					
5										
6	Accounts receivable.............	O	156,000	224,000	(68,000)	68,000				68,000
7	Inventory......................	O	752,000	528,000	224,000	(224,000)				(224,000)
8	Prepaid rent	O	68,000	72,000	(4,000)	4,000				4,000
9	Plant assets, net................	O, I	1,130,000	872,000	258,000					
10	Depreciation expense..........					122,000				
10	Plant assets purchased						(420,000)			(258,000)
12	Plant assets sold...............						(16,000)	56,000		
13										
14	**Liabilities**									
15	Accounts payable...............	O	216,000	112,000	104,000	104,000				104,000
16	Wages payable.................	O	18,000	20,000	(2,000)	(2,000)				(2,000)
17	Income tax payable	O	44,000	36,000	8,000	8,000				8,000
18	Notes payable	F								
19	New borrowing									
20	Borrowing repayments									—
21										
22	**Shareholders' Equity**									
23	Common stock.................	F	1,142,000	1,000,000	142,000					
24	New issue of common stock							142,000		142,000
25	Repurchase of common stock ...									
26	Retained earnings	O, F	792,000	624,000	168,000					
27	Net income...................					326,000				168,000
28	Dividends							(158,000)		
29										
30	Totals					390,000	(364,000)	(16,000)	—	10,000

$390,000 − $364,000 − $16,000 = $10,000.

ROCKY ROAD BICYCLES, INC.
Statement of Cash Flows
For Year Ended December 31, 2015

Cash flows from operating activities		
Net income..		$326,000
Add (deduct) items to convert net income to cash basis		
Depreciation		122,000
Gain on sale of plant assets		(16,000)
Accounts receivable...........................		68,000
Inventory.....................................		(224,000)
Prepaid rent		4,000
Accounts payable.............................		104,000
Wages payable...............................		(2,000)
Income tax payable		8,000
Net cash provided by operating activities		$390,000
Cash flows from investing activities		
Purchase of plant assets	(420,000)	
Proceeds from sale of plant assets	56,000	
Net cash used for investing activities...............		(364,000)
Cash flows from financing activities		
Issuance of common stock......................	142,000	
Payment of dividends..........................	(158,000)	
Net cash used for financing activities		(16,000)
Net cash increase...............................		10,000
Cash at beginning of year		96,000
Cash at end of year		$106,000

5

Analyzing and Interpreting Financial Statements

PEPSICO
www.pepsico.com

In recent years, **PepsiCo** CEO Indra K. Nooyi faced increasing pressure from shareholders. Its flagship soft drink—Pepsi-Cola—was unseated as the second best-selling brand in the U.S. by Diet Coke in 2010, and revenue at its principal beverage unit has increased only marginally. The company's North American snack foods unit has experienced solid growth, accounting for 22% of PepsiCo's revenue and 36% of its operating profit in 2014. This disparity in performance has activist shareholders calling for a split-up of the company. Ms. Nooyi maintains that PepsiCo will do better keeping all its business units and has taken several steps to improve performance.

PepsiCo was created by the merger of Pepsi-Cola and the Frito-Lay Company in 1965. Since then, the company has grown through selective acquisitions and creative marketing of its products to become the largest food and beverage company in the United States. By 2014, its sales topped $66.6 billion, and the company ranked 44th in the Fortune 500 ranking of the largest companies based on revenues. Yet, between 2008 and 2014, PepsiCo's stock price has performed below the level of the S&P 500 index, and below that of its chief competitor, Coca-Cola, as well.

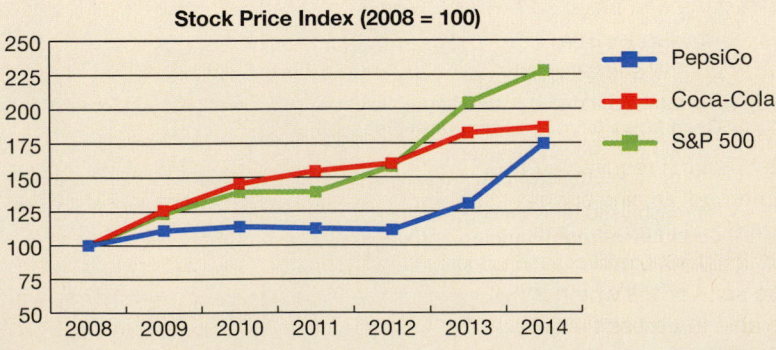

As is the case in most companies, PepsiCo's management employs a number of financial measures to assess the performance and financial condition of its operating units. These measures include ratios related to profitability and asset

utilization as well as return on investment. Investors, creditors and financial analysts use similar measures to evaluate company performance, assess credit risk, and estimate share value.

This chapter focuses on the analysis of information reported in the financial statements. We discuss a variety of measures that provide insights into a company's performance to answer questions such as: Is it managed efficiently and profitably? Does it use assets efficiently? Is the performance achieved with an optimal amount of debt? We pay especially close attention to measures of return. In Chapter 1, we introduced one such return metric, namely return on equity (ROE). In this chapter, we review ROE and add another return metric—return on assets (ROA).

ROE and ROA differ by the use of debt financing, or financial leverage. Companies can increase ROE by borrowing money and using these funds to finance investment in operating assets. However, debt financing can increase company risk and, if not used judiciously, can have a detrimental effect on ROE and even lead to financial distress. In the latter part of this chapter, we examine metrics that measure liquidity and solvency that allow us to assess that risk.

PepsiCo tackled its sluggish beverage sales by launching a major "rebranding" program for all of its beverage product lines, including Pepsi, Gatorade, Tropicana, SoBe Lifewater, Sierra Mist, and others. Rebranding requires creating new product logos, new packaging, new slogans and, most importantly, new advertising campaigns. PepsiCo's most recent efforts include reducing headcount by almost 9,000, modifying products to make them more appealing to health-conscious consumers, and investing an additional $600 million in marketing to maintain its brand equity and ability to charge premium prices. It is too soon to tell whether these efforts will produce the growth that investors desire. Ultimately, we will be able to assess the success of this initiative by looking at specific measures of PepsiCo's performance. In doing so, we seek the answer to the root question: Can the company achieve a high return on investment and, if so, is that return sustainable?

Sources: PepsiCo annual report 2014; *New York Times*, April 26, 2012; *Wall Street Journal*, May 15, 2012, July 25, 2012. *The New Yorker*, May 16, 2011, *USA Today*, April 24, 2015

CHAPTER ORGANIZATION

Analyzing and Interpreting Financial Statements			
Common-Size Statements	**Return on Investment**	**Liquidity and Solvency**	**Appendices**
• Vertical Analysis • Horizontal Analysis	• Return on Equity • Return on Assets • Return on Financial Leverage • Disaggregating ROA into Profit Margin and Asset Turnover	• Short-term Liquidity: Current Ratio and Quick Ratio • Long-term Solvency: Debt-to-Equity and Times Interest Earned • Limitations of Ratio Analysis	• Analyzing Core Operating Activities • Pro Forma Financial Statements

INTRODUCTION

Companies prepare financial statements to be used. These statements are used by investors who rely on financial statement information to assess investment risk, forecast income and dividends, and estimate value. They are used by creditors to assess credit risk and monitor outstanding loans for compliance with debt covenants. And, as the PepsiCo example illustrates, they are used by management to evaluate the performance of operating units. **Financial statement analysis** identifies relationships between numbers within the financial statements and trends in these relationships from one period to the next. The goal is to help users such as investors, creditors, and managers interpret the information presented in the financial statements.

Financial statement analysis is all about making comparisons. Accounting information is difficult to interpret when the numbers are viewed in isolation. For example, a company that reports net income of $7 million may have had a good year or a bad year. However, if we know that total sales were $100 million, assets total $90 million, and that the previous year's net income was $6 million, we have a better idea about how well the company performed. If we go a step further and compare these numbers to those of a competing company or to an industry average, we begin to make an assessment about the relative quality of management, the prospects for future growth, overall company risk, and the potential to earn sustainable returns.

Assessing the Business Environment

Financial statement analysis cannot be undertaken in a vacuum. A meaningful interpretation of financial information requires an understanding of the business, its operations, and the environment in which it operates. That is, before we begin crunching the numbers, we must consider the broader business context in which the company operates. This approach requires starting with the Management's Discussion and Analysis section of the financial reports and asking questions about the company and its business environment, including:

- *Life cycle*—At what stage in its life is this company? Is it a start-up, experiencing the growing pains that often result from rapid growth? Is it a mature company, reaping the benefits of its competitive advantages? Is it in decline?

- *Outputs*—What products does it sell? Are its products new, established, or dated? Do its products have substitutes? Are its products protected by patents? How complicated are its products to produce?

- *Customers*—Who are its customers? How often do customers purchase the company's products? What demographic trends are likely to have an effect on future sales?

- *Competition*—Who are the company's competitors? How is it positioned in the market relative to its competition? Is it easy for new competitors to enter the market for its products? Are its products differentiated from competitors' products? Does it have any cost advantages over its competitors?

- *Inputs*—Who are the company's suppliers? Are there multiple supply sources? Does the company depend on one (or a few) key supply sources creating the potential for high input costs?

- *Labor*—Who are the company's managers? How effective are they? Is the company unionized? Does it depend on a skilled or educated workforce?

- *Technology*—What technology does the company employ to produce its products? Does the company outsource production? What transport systems does the company rely on to deliver its products?

- *Capital*—To what extent does the company rely on public markets to raise needed capital? Has it recently gone public? Does it have expansion plans that require large sums of cash to carry out? Is it planning to acquire another company? Is it in danger of defaulting on its debt?

- *Political*—How does the company interact with the communities, states, and countries in which it operates? What government regulations affect the company's operations? Are any proposed regulations likely to have a significant impact on the company?

These are just a few of the questions that we should ask before we begin analyzing a company's financial statements. Ultimately, the answers will help us place our numerical analysis in the proper context, so that we can effectively interpret the accounting numbers.

In this chapter, we introduce the tools that are used to analyze and interpret financial statements. These tools include common-size financial statements that are used in vertical and horizontal analysis and ratios that measure return on investment and help to assess liquidity and solvency.

VERTICAL AND HORIZONTAL ANALYSIS

LO1 Prepare and analyze common-size financial statements.

1

Companies come in all sizes, a fact that presents difficulties when making comparisons between firms and over time. **Vertical analysis** is a method that attempts to overcome this obstacle by restating financial statement information in ratio (or percentage) form. Specifically, it is common to express components of the income statement as a percent of net sales, and balance sheet items as a percent of total assets. This restatement is often referred to as **common-size financial statements** and it facilitates comparisons across companies of different sizes as well as comparisons of accounts within a set of financial statements.

Exhibit 5.1 presents PepsiCo's summarized comparative balance sheets for 2014 and 2013. Next to the comparative balance sheets are common-size balance sheets for the same two years. Vertical analysis helps us interpret the composition of the balance sheet. For example, as of the end of 2014, 29.3% of PepsiCo's assets were current assets and 24.5% were property, plant, and equipment. Intangible assets made up a greater share of the company's total assets. In addition, 75.1% of PepsiCo's total assets were financed with liabilities—up from 68.5% in 2013 (and 56.2% in 2009). Long-term debt obligations were 33.8% of total assets in 2014, but as recent as 2009, long-term liabilities were 18.6% of total assets. This significant change in liabilities is largely due to the acquisition of Pepsi Bottling Group, Inc. (PBG) and PepsiAmericas, Inc. (PAS) in February 2010. Financial statement analysts should be aware of changes in a company's organization that produce significant changes in financial statement relationships. It is not uncommon for companies to use lower-cost debt financing to finance expansion, especially if management believes that low stock prices prevent them from issuing common stock. However, increasing debt levels are a concern if profits and cash flows are not growing fast enough to cover the rising interest and principal payments.

In **Exhibit 5.2**, we present PepsiCo's summarized comparative income statements for 2014 and 2013, along with common-size income statements for the same years. Vertical analysis reveals that cost of sales is 46.3% of net revenue, down from 47.0% in 2013, while the increased percentage for selling, general and administrative expenses left operating profit slightly lower as a percentage of revenue compared to the year before. An increase in selling, general and administrative expenses could be due to higher marketing and advertising costs, supply chain or distribution problems, or increased management costs. PepsiCo's management noted that the increased cost of international operations was a significant contributor to the lower operating profit as a percentage of sales in 2014. While further analysis would be necessary to determine the exact causes of any fluctuation, common size financial statements highlight important changes and help to reveal the factors that may contribute to these changes.

EXHIBIT 5.1 | PepsiCo Comparative Balance Sheets

PEPSICO, INC.
Balance Sheets and Common-Size Balance Sheets
December 27, 2014 and December 28, 2013

	As reported ($ millions)		As a percentage of Total Assets	
	2014	2013	2014	2013
Assets				
Current assets				
Cash and cash equivalents	$ 6,134	$ 9,375	8.7%	12.1%
Short-term investments	2,592	303	3.7	0.4
Accounts and notes receivable, net	6,651	6,954	9.4	9.0
Inventories	3,143	3,409	4.5	4.4
Prepaid expenses and other current assets	2,143	2,162	3.0	2.8
Total current assets	20,663	22,203	29.3	28.7
Property, plant, and equipment, net	17,244	18,575	24.5	24.0
Amortizable intangible assets, net	1,449	1,638	2.1	2.1
Goodwill	14,965	16,613	21.2	21.4
Other nonamortizable intangible assets	12,639	14,401	17.9	18.6
Investments in noncontrolled affiliates	2,689	2,623	3.8	3.4
Other assets	860	1,425	1.2	1.8
Total assets	$70,509	$77,478	100.0%	100.0%
Liabilities and equity				
Current liabilities				
Short-term obligations	$ 5,076	$ 5,306	7.2%	6.8%
Accounts payable and other current liabilities	13,016	12,533	18.5	16.2
Total current liabilities	18,092	17,839	25.7	23.0
Long-term debt obligations	23,821	24,333	33.8	31.4
Other liabilities	5,744	4,931	8.1	6.4
Deferrred income taxes	5,304	5,986	7.5	7.7
Total liabilities	52,961	53,089	75.1	68.5
Total equity	17,548	24,389	24.9	31.5
Total liabilities and equity	$70,509	$77,478	100.0%	100.0%

EXHIBIT 5.2 | PepsiCo Comparative Income Statements

PEPSICO, INC.
Income Statements and Common-Size Income Statements
Fiscal years ended December 27, 2014 and December 28, 2013

	As reported ($ millions)		As a percentage of Net Revenue	
	2014	2013	2014	2013
Net revenue	$66,683	$66,415	100.0%	100.0%
Cost of sales	30,884	31,243	46.3	47.0
Gross profit	35,799	35,172	53.7	53.0
Selling, general and administrative expenses	26,126	25,357	39.2	38.2
Amortization of intangible assets	92	110	0.1	0.2
Operating profit	9,581	9,705	14.4	14.6
Interest expense	(909)	(911)	(1.4)	(1.4)
Interest income and other	85	97	0.1	0.1
Income before income taxes	8,757	8,891	13.1	13.4
Provision for income taxes	2,199	2,104	3.3	3.2
Net income	$ 6,558	$ 6,787	9.8%	10.2%

Horizontal analysis examines changes in financial data across time. Comparing data across two or more consecutive periods is helpful in analyzing company performance and in predicting future performance. **Exhibit 5.3** presents a horizontal analysis of a few selected items from PepsiCo's income statement—revenue, operating income, and net income. The dollar amounts reported in each year from 2010 through 2014 are shown for each item along with a percentage change for each item. The amount of the change for a given year is computed by subtracting the amount for the prior year from the amount for the current year. The change is then divided by the reported amount for the prior year to get the percentage change. For example, PepsiCo's percentage change in net revenue was 0.4% in 2014, computed as follows:

$$0.4\% = \frac{\$66{,}683 \text{ million} - \$66{,}415 \text{ million}}{\$66{,}415 \text{ million}}$$

Exhibit 5.3 highlights some important changes in PepsiCo's income statement. The table shows that, since 2011 both revenue and net income have increased by a very small amount and operating profit has actually decreased. In 2014, revenues increased by only 0.4% and net income decreased by 3.4%. The decline in net income is largely due to the increase in operating expenses as well as higher income taxes.

EXHIBIT 5.3	Horizontal Analysis of Selected Income Statement Items				
PEPSICO, INC. **Revenue, Operating Income and Net Income** **($ millions and percent changes)**					
	2014	**2013**	**2012**	**2011**	**2010**
Revenue	$66,683	$66,415	$65,492	$66,504	$57,838
	0.4%	1.4%	−1.5%	15.0%	
Operating profit	$ 9,581	$ 9,705	$ 9,112	$ 9,633	$ 8,332
	−1.3%	6.5%	−5.4%	15.6%	
Net income	$ 6,558	$ 6,787	$ 6,214	$ 6,462	$ 6,338
	−3.4%	9.2%	−3.8%	2.0%	

Horizontal analysis is useful in identifying unusual changes that might not be obvious when looking at the reported numbers alone. At the same time, it is important to look at both the percentage change and the reported dollar amount. If a reported amount is close to $0 in one year, the percentage change will likely be very large the following year, even if the amount reported in that year is small. Similarly, if reported earnings is negative one year and positive the next, the percentage change will be negative even though the earnings increased. Horizontal analysis that is based on a denominator that is negative or zero is not meaningful.

MID-CHAPTER REVIEW 1

Following are summarized 2014 and 2013 income statements and balance sheets for **The Coca-Cola Company**.

Required

Prepare common-size income statements and balance sheets for Coca-Cola. Comment on any noteworthy relationships that you observe.

THE COCA-COLA COMPANY AND SUBSIDIARIES
Consolidated Statements of Income
($ millions)

Year ended December 31	2014	2013
Net operating revenues	$45,998	$46,854
Cost of goods sold	17,889	18,421
Gross profit	28,109	28,433
Selling, general and administrative expenses	17,218	17,310
Other operating charges	1,183	895
Operating income	9,708	10,228
Interest income	594	534
Interest expense	(483)	(463)
Other income (loss)—net	(494)	1,178
Income before income taxes	9,325	11,477
Income taxes	2,201	2,851
Consolidated net income	$ 7,124	$ 8,626

THE COCA-COLA COMPANY AND SUBSIDIARIES
Consolidated Balance Sheets
($ millions)

December 31,	2014	2013
ASSETS		
Cash and cash equivalents	$ 8,958	$10,414
Short-term investments and marketable securities	12,717	9,854
Trade accounts receivable	4,466	4,873
Inventories	3,100	3,277
Prepaid expenses and other assets	3,745	2,886
Total current assets	32,986	31,304
Equity method investments	9,947	10,393
Other investments	3,678	1,119
Property, plant, and equipment, net	14,633	14,967
Goodwill and other intangible assets	26,372	27,611
Other assets	4,407	4,661
Total assets	$92,023	$90,055
LIABILITIES AND EQUITY		
Accounts payable and accrued expenses	$ 9,234	$ 9,577
Loans and notes payable	19,188	16,901
Current maturities of long-term debt	3,552	1,024
Accrued income taxes	400	309
Total current liabilities	32,374	27,811
Long-term debt	19,063	19,154
Other liabilities	4,389	3,498
Deferred income taxes	5,636	6,152
Total liabilities	61,462	56,615
Total equity	30,561	33,440
Total liabilities and equity	$92,023	$90,055

The solution to this review problem can be found on page 265.

LO2 Compute and interpret measures of return on investment, including return on equity (ROE), return on assets (ROA), and return on financial leverage (ROFL).

RETURN ON INVESTMENT

Common-size financial statements and percentage changes are useful, but there is a limit to what we can learn from this type of analysis. While vertical and horizontal analysis focuses on relationships within a particular financial statement, either the income statement or the balance sheet, many of the questions that we might ask about a company can be answered only by comparing amounts between statements. For example, return on investment measures are ratios that divide some measure of performance—typically reported in the income statement—by the average amount of investment as reported in the balance sheet.

In this section, we discuss three important return metrics—return on equity (ROE), return on assets (ROA), and return on financial leverage (ROFL). We also examine return on investment in detail by disaggregating ROA into performance drivers that capture profitability and efficiency.

Return on Equity (ROE)

Return on equity (ROE) is the primary summary measure of company performance and is defined as:

$$\text{ROE} = \frac{\text{Net income}}{\text{Average stockholders' equity}}$$

ROE relates net income to the average investment by shareholders as measured by total stockholders' equity from the balance sheet. The net income number in the numerator measures the performance of the firm for a specific period (typically a fiscal year). Therefore, in order to accurately capture the return for that period, we use the average level of stockholders' equity for the same period as the denominator. The average is computed by adding the beginning and ending stockholders' equity balances and then dividing by two.

PepsiCo's ROE was 31.3% in 2014. This return is computed as $6,558 million/[($17,548 million + $24,389 million)/2]. PepsiCo's ROE has been consistently high over the past 5 years, ranging from a low of 28.7% in 2012 to a high of 32.6% in 2010.

ROE is widely used by analysts, investors, and managers as a key overall measure of company performance. Billionaire investor Warren Buffett highlights ROE as part of his acquisition criteria: "businesses earning good returns on equity while employing little or no debt." Companies can use debt to increase their return on equity, but too much debt increases risk as the failure to make required debt payments is likely to yield many legal consequences, including bankruptcy. This is one reason why many analysts focus on returns generated by assets used in operations, rather than on returns produced by increasing the amount of debt financing. Next, we discuss each of these sources of return in more detail.

> **FYI** Whenever we compare an income statement amount with a balance sheet amount, the balance sheet amount should be the *average* balance for the period (beginning balance plus ending balance divided by 2) rather than the year-end balance.

Return on Assets (ROA)

ROE measures the return on the investment made by the firm's stockholders. In contrast, **return on assets (ROA)** measures the return earned on each dollar that the firm invests in assets. By focusing on the asset side of the balance sheet, ROA captures the returns generated by the firm's operating and investing activities, without regard for how those activities are financed. ROA is defined as:

$$\text{Return on assets (ROA)} = \frac{\text{Earnings without interest expense (EWI)}}{\text{Average total assets}}$$

Average total assets is computed in much the same way that we calculated average stockholders' equity for ROE. We add the beginning and ending balances in total assets and then divide by two. The numerator in this ratio, **earnings without interest expense (EWI)**, is defined to be:

$$\text{Earnings without interest expense (EWI)} =$$
$$\text{Net income} + [\text{Interest expense} \times (1 - \text{Statutory tax rate})]$$

EWI measures the income generated by the firm before taking into account any of its financing costs. Interest costs should be excluded from the ROA calculation so that return is measured without the effect of debt financing. Because interest expense is subtracted when net income is calculated, it must be added back to net income when we compute EWI. However, interest expense is tax deductible and, as such, it reduces the firm's tax obligation. That is, interest expense produces a tax *savings* for the firm. This tax savings is equal to the interest expense times the statutory tax rate. In order to eliminate the full effect of interest cost on EWI, we must add back the interest expense *net* of the resulting tax savings. To accomplish this, we multiply the interest expense by (1 − the statutory tax rate). This amount is then added to net income to get EWI. Thus, we can compute ROA as follows:

$$\text{Return on assets (ROA)} = \frac{\text{Net income} + [\text{Interest expense} \times (1 - \text{Statutory tax rate})]}{(\text{Beginning total assets} + \text{Ending total assets}) / 2}$$

ROA is an important measure of how well a company's management has utilized assets to earn a profit. If ROA is high, the firm can pay its interest costs to creditors and still have sufficient resources left over to distribute to stockholders as a dividend or to reinvest in the firm.

PepsiCo's ROA was 9.7% in 2014. PepsiCo's return is computed as follows: [1]

$$\text{ROA} = \frac{\$6{,}558 \text{ million} + [\$909 \text{ million} \times (1 - 35\%)]}{(\$77{,}478 \text{ million} + \$70{,}509 \text{ million}) / 2} = 9.7\%$$

PepsiCo's return on assets has fluctuated over the past 5 years from a high of 12.8% in 2010 to a low of 9.2% in 2012.

Return on Financial Leverage (ROFL)

The principal difference between ROE and ROA is the effect that liabilities (including debt financing) have on the return measure. ROA is calculated so that it is independent of financing costs, whereas ROE is computed net of the cost of debt financing. **Financial leverage** refers to the effect that liabilities (including debt financing) have on ROE. A firm's management can increase the return to shareholders (ROE) by effectively using financial leverage. On the other hand, too much financial leverage can be risky. To help gauge the effect that financial leverage has on a firm, the **return on financial leverage (ROFL)** is defined as:

$$\text{ROFL} = \text{ROE} - \text{ROA}$$

This return metric captures the amount of ROE that can be attributed to financial leverage. In the case of PepsiCo, the ROFL is 21.6% (31.3% − 9.7%). Over the past 5 years, financial leverage has had a significant impact on PepsiCo's performance. The impact of financial leverage on PepsiCo's ROE is illustrated in **Exhibit 5.4**. The height of each bar in the graph reflects PepsiCo's ROE for that year. Each bar is split into two components—ROA for the same year (the lower portion of each bar) and ROFL (the upper portion of each bar).

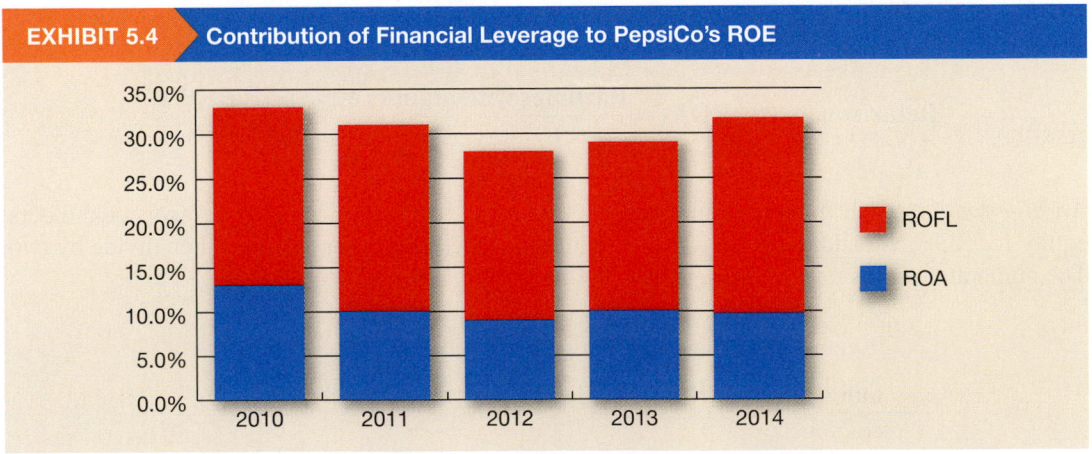

EXHIBIT 5.4   Contribution of Financial Leverage to PepsiCo's ROE

---

[1] The statutory federal tax rate for corporations is 35% (per U.S. tax code). In addition, many states tax corporate income, and those state taxes are deductible for federal tax purposes. Consequently, the net state tax rate is the statutory state tax rate less the federal tax benefit. Most companies provide both the federal tax rate and the state tax rate (net of the federal tax deduction) as percentages in the income tax footnote. If this information is available, the statutory tax rate is the sum of the two percentages. However, state tax rates (net of the federal tax deduction) vary from one company to the next and are typically small. Therefore, for purposes of illustration, we ignore state income taxes and use the federal statutory tax rate of 35% in these ratio calculations.

In **Exhibit 5.5**, we compare the ROE, ROA and ROFL of PepsiCo to that of several other companies featured in this text. As in **Exhibit 5.4**, the height of each bar represents the company's ROE for 2014. The lower portion of each bar is the company's ROA and the upper portion reflects the contribution of financial leverage (ROFL). The graph suggests that, with the possible exception of Verizon and Delta Air Lines, PepsiCo's ROE is influenced to a greater extent by financial leverage than the other companies.

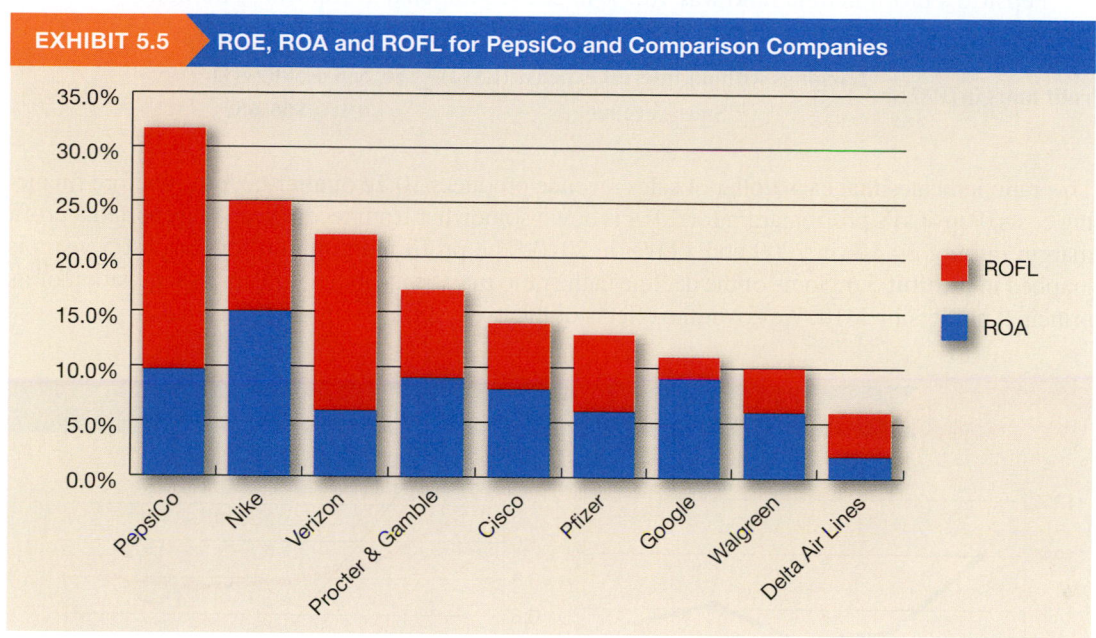

EXHIBIT 5.5 ROE, ROA and ROFL for PepsiCo and Comparison Companies

Later in this chapter, we examine the effects of financial leverage more closely and discuss several ratios that measure liquidity and solvency. These ratios help us to evaluate the risk associated with using financial leverage.

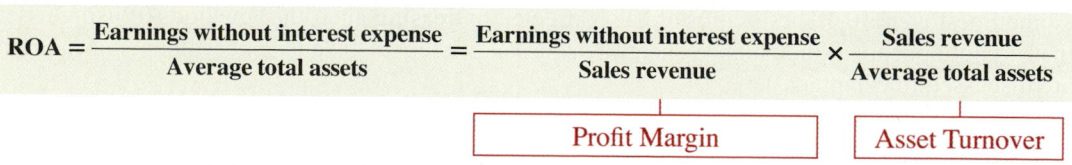

MID-CHAPTER REVIEW 2

Required

Refer to the financial statements for the **Coca-Cola Company** presented in Mid-Chapter Review 1 earlier in this chapter. Calculate Coca-Cola's ROE, ROA and ROFL for 2014.

The solution to this review problem can be found on page 266.

Disaggregating ROA

LO3 Disaggregate ROA into profitability (profit margin) and efficiency (asset turnover) components.

We can gain further insights into return on investment by disaggregating ROA into performance drivers that capture profitability and efficiency. ROA can be restated as the product of two ratios—profit margin and asset turnover—by simultaneously multiplying and dividing ROA by sales revenue:

$$\text{ROA} = \frac{\text{Earnings without interest expense}}{\text{Average total assets}} = \underbrace{\frac{\text{Earnings without interest expense}}{\text{Sales revenue}}}_{\text{Profit Margin}} \times \underbrace{\frac{\text{Sales revenue}}{\text{Average total assets}}}_{\text{Asset Turnover}}$$

The first ratio on the right-hand side of the above relationship is the **profit margin (PM)**. This ratio measures the profit, without interest expense, that is generated from each dollar of sales revenue. All other things being equal, a higher profit margin is preferable. Profit margin is affected by the level of gross profit that the company earns on its sales (sales revenue minus cost of goods sold), which depends on product prices and the cost of manufacturing or purchasing its product. It is also affected by operating expenses that are required to support sales of products or services. These include wages and salaries, marketing, research and development, as well as depreciation and other **capacity costs**. Finally, profit margin is affected by the level of competition, which affects product pricing, and by the company's operating strategy, which affects operating costs, especially discretionary costs such as advertising and research and development.

PepsiCo's profit margin ratio was 10.7% in 2014, computed as follows ($ millions):

$$\text{Profit margin (PM)} = \frac{\text{Earnings without interest expense (EWI)}}{\text{Sales revenue}} = \frac{\$6{,}558 + \$909 \times (1 - 35\%)}{\$66{,}683} = 10.7\%$$

This ratio indicates that each dollar of sales revenue produces 10.7¢ of after-tax profit before financing costs. PepsiCo's profit margin for 2014 is down somewhat from recent years. It reported a profit margin ratio of 14.4% in 2009 and 12.0% in 2010. The profit margin ratio for the past 5 years is graphed in **Exhibit 5.6**. Some of the decline in the ratio may be attributed to Pepsi's acquisition of its principal bottlers in 2010. We cover the effects of this type of transaction in Chapter 12.

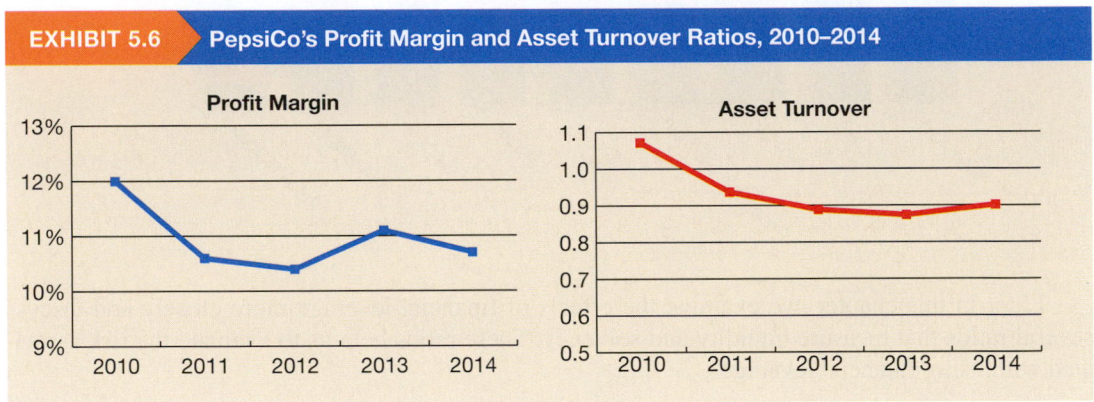

EXHIBIT 5.6 PepsiCo's Profit Margin and Asset Turnover Ratios, 2010–2014

The **asset turnover (AT)** ratio reveals insights into a company's productivity and efficiency. This metric measures the level of sales generated by each dollar that a company invests in assets. A high asset turnover ratio suggests that assets are being used efficiently so, all other things being equal, a high asset turnover ratio is preferable. The ratio is affected by inventory management practices, credit policies, and most of all, the technology employed to produce a company's products or deliver its services.

The asset turnover ratio can be improved by increasing the level of sales for a given level of assets, or by efficiently managing assets. For many companies, efficiently managing working capital—primarily inventories and receivables—is the easiest way to limit investment in assets and increase turnover. On the other hand, it is usually more difficult to increase asset turnover by managing investment in long-term assets. Capital intensive companies, such as those in the telecommunications or energy production industries, tend to have lower asset turnover ratios (often less than 1.0) because the production technology employed by these firms requires a large investment in property, plant, and equipment. Retail companies, on the other hand, tend to have a relatively small investment in plant assets. As a result, they tend to have higher asset turnover ratios (sometimes over 3.0). These ratios are also affected by leasing and other methods of using assets that do not appear on the balance sheet. Leasing and other off-balance-sheet financing methods are discussed in Chapter 10.

PepsiCo's asset turnover ratio is computed as follows ($ millions):

$$\text{Asset turnover (AT)} = \frac{\text{Sales revenue}}{\text{Average total assets}} = \frac{\$66{,}683}{(\$77{,}478 + \$70{,}509) / 2} = 0.901$$

The ratio indicates that each dollar of assets generates 90.1¢ in sales revenue each year. Over the past five years, PepsiCo's asset turnover has ranged from 0.87 in 2013 to 1.07 in 2010 as illustrated by the graphic in **Exhibit 5.6**.

YOU MAKE THE CALL

You are the Entrepreneur   You are analyzing the performance of your start-up company. Your analysis of ROA reveals the following (industry benchmarks in parentheses): ROA is 16% (10%), PM is 18% (17%), and AT is 0.89 (0.59). What interpretations do you draw that are useful for managing your company? [Answer, page 250.]

Trade-Off Between Profit Margin and Asset Turnover

ROA is the product of profit margin and asset turnover. By decomposing ROA in this way, we can identify the source of PepsiCo's decline in ROA between 2010 and 2014:

	ROA	=	Profit Margin	×	Asset Turnover
2010:	12.8%	=	11.97%	×	1.071
2014:	9.7%	=	10.72%	×	0.901

Between 2010 and 2014, PepsiCo's profit margin declined from 11.97% to 10.72% while, at the same time, asset turnover declined from 1.071 to 0.901. These changes are due in part to PepsiCo's acquisition of its principal bottlers, which contributed to a substantial increase in the company's reported assets (from $40 billion at the end of 2009 to $68 billion at the end of 2010). The usual cause of a decline in asset turnover is a decline in sales revenue, but PepsiCo's revenues increased substantially since 2010. As we saw earlier in the chapter when we examined PepsiCo's common-size income statement, a major cause of the profit margin decline was the increase in operating costs as a percentage of sales revenue. Because sales revenue appears to be increasing substantially, it is likely that management's best opportunity to increase ROA in the future would be to focus its efforts on increasing profitability.

Basic economics tells us that any successful business must earn an acceptable return on investment if it wants to attract capital from investors and survive. Yet, there are an infinite number of combinations of asset turnover and profit margin that will yield a given ROA. The trade-off between profit margin and asset turnover is heavily influenced by a company's business model. A company can attempt to increase its ROA by targeting higher profit margins, or by increasing its asset turnover. To an extent, this trade-off is the result of strategic decisions made by management. However, to a greater extent, the relative mix of margin and turnover is dictated by the industry in which the company operates. As mentioned earlier, one determinant of a company's profit margin is its competitive environment, while asset turnover is heavily influenced by the production technology employed. For this reason, companies in the same industry tend to exhibit similar combinations of margin and turnover while comparisons between industries can exhibit much greater variation. That is, within a given industry, differences in the mix of profit margin and asset turnover often reflect the specific strategy employed by each individual firm, while variations between industries are caused by differences in the competitive environment and production technology of each industry.

This trade-off is illustrated in **Exhibit 5.7**. The solid curved line represents the average ROA for all companies over the period from 2012 through 2014. Each point along that curve represents a combination of asset turnover and profit margin that yields the average ROA. Industries that are plotted near the upper left side of the graph are those that achieve their ROA targets by maintaining a high asset turnover. These industries are often characterized by intense competition and low profit margins. On the other hand, industries in the lower right-hand portion of the graph have lower asset turnover ratios because they typically employ capital-intensive production technologies. At the same time, the competitive environment within these industries allows companies to achieve higher profit margins to offset the lower turnover ratios.

EXHIBIT 5.7 ▶ **Profit Margin and Turnover Across Industries**

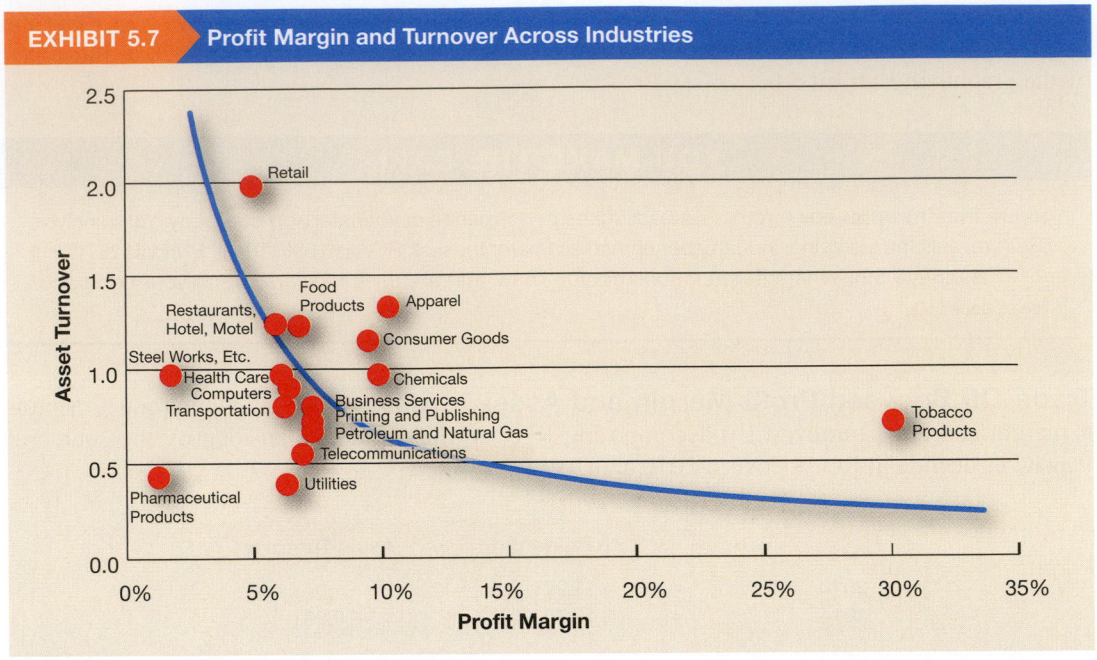

The DuPont Model Disaggregation of return on equity (ROE) into three components—profitability, turnover, and financial leverage—was initially introduced by the **E.I. DuPont de Nemours and Company** to aid its managers in performance evaluation. DuPont realized that management's focus on profit alone was insufficient because profit can be increased simply by adding investments in low-yielding, but safe, assets. Further, DuPont wanted managers to think like investors and to manage their portfolio of activities using investment principles that allocate scarce investment capital to competing projects based on a goal of maximizing return on investment.

The basic DuPont model disaggregates ROE as the product of three ratios as follows:

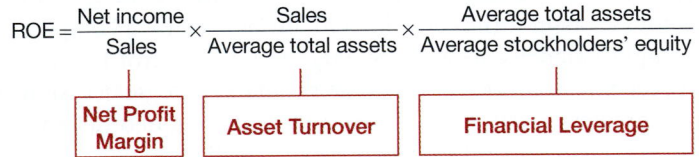

$$ROE = \frac{\text{Net income}}{\text{Sales}} \times \frac{\text{Sales}}{\text{Average total assets}} \times \frac{\text{Average total assets}}{\text{Average stockholders' equity}}$$

| **Net Profit Margin** | **Asset Turnover** | **Financial Leverage** |

An important limitation of the DuPont model is that net profit margin is measured using net income in the numerator rather than earnings without interest expense (EWI). This means that this measure of profitability is affected by financial leverage—as financial leverage increases, interest expense increases and the net profit margin decreases. As a consequence, the model fails to adequately separate the effects of operating profitability on ROE from the effects of financial leverage. Despite this limitation, the DuPont model is widely used as a simple, straightforward way to disaggregate ROE.

Further Disaggregation of Profit Margin and Asset Turnover

While disaggregation of ROA into profit margin and asset turnover yields useful insights into the factors driving company performance, analysts, investors, creditors, and managers often disaggregate these measures even further. The purpose of this analysis is to be more precise about the specific determinants of profitability and efficiency.

To disaggregate profit margin (PM), we examine gross profit on products sold and individual expense accounts that contribute to the total cost of operations. The key ratios include the gross profit margin and expense-to-sales ratios. **Gross profit margin (GPM)** is defined as:

$$\text{Gross profit margin (GPM)} = \frac{\text{Sales revenue} - \text{Cost of goods sold}}{\text{Sales revenue}}$$

PepsiCo's GPM is 53.7% ([$66,683 million − $30,884 million]/$66,683 million). That is, just over half (53.7%) of every sales dollar is gross profit while slightly less than half (46.3%) goes to cover the cost of products sold.

Gross profit margin measures the percentage of each sales dollar that is left over after product costs are subtracted. It is easily determined by looking at the common-size income statement. This ratio is discussed in more detail in Chapter 7.

An **expense-to-sales (ETS)** ratio measures the percentage of each sales dollar that goes to cover a specific expense item and is computed by dividing the expense by sales revenue. Expense items that might be examined with ETS ratios include selling, general and administrative (SG&A) expenses, advertising expense, or research and development (R&D) expense, among others. Which specific ETS ratio is appropriate depends on the company being analyzed. For instance, advertising expense is an important expense item for a consumer products company, such as PepsiCo, while R&D expense is important for an R&D intensive pharmaceutical company, such as **Pfizer**. Analysts study trends in ETS ratios over time in an effort to uncover clues that might explain changes in profit margin and make predictions about future profitability.

PepsiCo's SG&A ETS ratio is computed by dividing selling, general and administrative expenses by net revenue. The resulting ETS ratio is 39.2% ($26,126 million/$66,683 million). This ratio indicates that 39.2¢ of every sales dollar goes to pay marketing and administrative costs. This ETS ratio is relatively high because this expense item includes PepsiCo's advertising expenditures.

To disaggregate asset turnover (AT), we examine individual asset accounts and compare them to sales or cost of goods sold. We focus on three specific turnover ratios—accounts receivable turnover (ART), inventory turnover (INVT), and property, plant, and equipment turnover (PPET).

Accounts receivable turnover (ART) is defined as follows:

$$\text{Accounts receivable turnover (ART)} = \frac{\text{Sales revenue}}{\text{Average accounts receivable}}$$

ART measures how many times receivables have been turned (collected) during the period. More turns indicate that accounts receivable are being collected more quickly, while low turnover often indicates difficulty with a company's credit policies. PepsiCo's ART is 9.8 times ($66,683 million/[{$6,954 million + $6,651 million}/2]). ART is discussed in Chapter 6.

Inventory turnover (INVT) is defined as:

$$\text{Inventory turnover (INVT)} = \frac{\text{Cost of goods sold}}{\text{Average inventory}}$$

INVT measures the number of times during a period that total inventory is turned (sold). A high INVT indicates that inventory is managed efficiently. Retail companies, such as **Wal-Mart** and **Home Depot** focus a great deal of management attention on maintaining a high INVT ratio. PepsiCo's INVT is 9.4 times ($30,884 million/[{$3,409 million + $3,143 million}/2]). This ratio is discussed further in Chapter 7.

Property, plant, and equipment turnover (PPET) measures the sales revenue produced for each dollar of investment in PP&E. It is computed as the ratio of sales to average PP&E assets:

$$\text{Property, plant, and equipment turnover (PPET)} = \frac{\text{Sales revenue}}{\text{Average PP \& E}}$$

PPET provides insights into asset utilization and how efficiently a company operates given its production technology. PepsiCo's PPET is 3.7 times ($66,683 million/[{$18,575 million + $17,244 million}/2]). This ratio is revisited in Chapter 8.

In the next section, we examine ratios that focus on liquidity and solvency. These ratios help us evaluate the risk associated with debt financing and weigh the costs and benefits of financial leverage. **Exhibit 5.8** presents a schematic summary of the disaggregation of ROE. It identifies the two primary components of ROE—ROA and ROFL—and highlights the disaggregation of ROA into profit margin and asset turnover, along with the drivers of these ratios. In addition, the link between ROFL and liquidity and solvency analysis is highlighted.

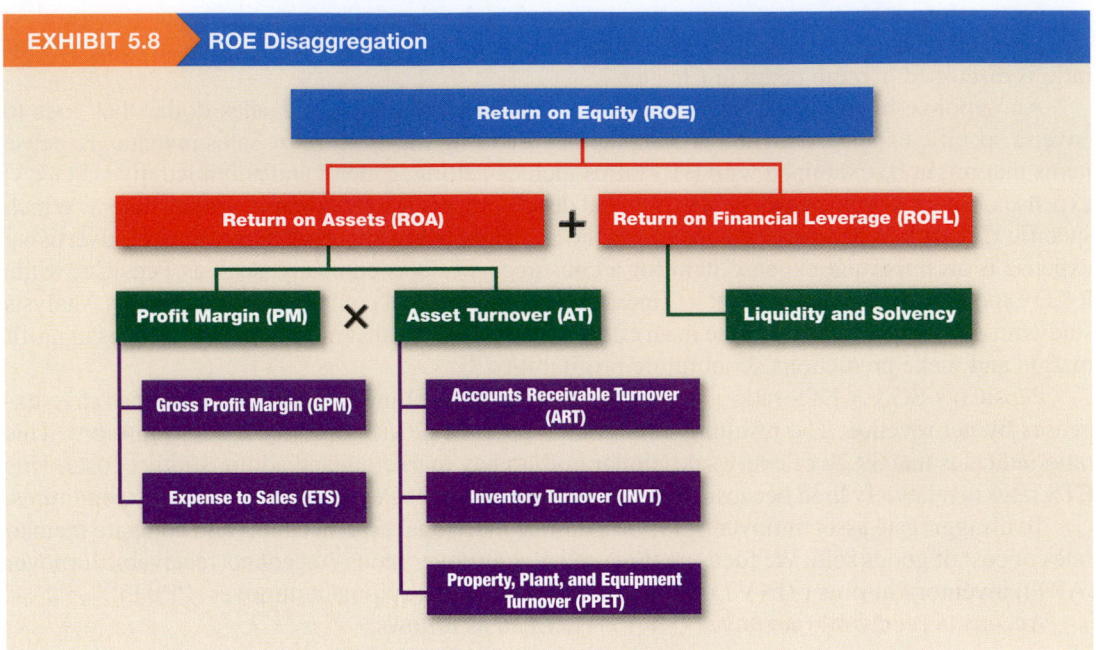

EXHIBIT 5.8 ROE Disaggregation

MID-CHAPTER REVIEW 3

Required

Refer to the financial statements for the **Coca-Cola Company** presented in Mid-Chapter Review 1 earlier in this chapter.

1. Calculate Coca-Cola's profit margin (PM) and asset turnover (AT) ratios for 2014.
2. Show that ROA = PM × AT using Coca-Cola's financial data.
3. Calculate Coca-Cola's gross profit margin (GPM), accounts receivable turnover (ART), inventory turnover (INVT), and property, plant, and equipment turnover (PPET) ratios for 2014.
4. Evaluate Coca-Cola's ratios in comparison to those of PepsiCo.

The solution to this review problem can be found on page 266.

LO4 Compute and interpret measures of liquidity and solvency.

LIQUIDITY AND SOLVENCY

Companies can use debt to increase financial leverage and boost ROE. The increase in ROE due to the use of debt is called *return on financial leverage (ROFL)*. The primary advantage of debt financing is that it is typically less costly than equity financing; the cost of debt financing is currently a little over 2%, while equity financing averages about 8%.[2]

---

[2] Equity financing is more costly than debt because, in the event that the firm fails, creditors collect their investment first, while stockholders collect the residual. Stockholders, therefore, demand a greater return on investment to compensate for assuming greater risk.

Exhibit 5.9 illustrates a comparison between two companies—one (Company A) is financed with 100% equity and the other (Company B) is financed with 50% debt and 50% equity. Both companies have $1,000 in (average) assets and EWI of $100, producing an ROA of 10% ($100/$1,000). Because Company A does not use debt financing, average equity equals average total assets. Also, it reports no interest expense in its income statement so net income equals EWI. Therefore, for Company A, ROE = ROA, and its ROFL = 0%.

EXHIBIT 5.9	The Effect of Debt Financing on ROE (ROA > interest rate)		
		Company A	Company B
Assets (average)		$1,000	$1,000
EWI		100	100
ROA (EWI/Assets)		10%	10%
Equity (average)		$1,000	$ 500
Debt		0	500
Interest expense (4% of debt)		0	20
Net income (EWI − interest)		100	80
ROE (Net income/equity)		10%	16%
ROFL (ROE − ROA)		0%	6%

In contrast, Company B has $500 of equity financing and $500 of debt financing. It reports interest expense of $20 ($500 × 4%) leaving net income of $80 ($100 − $20). Company B's ROE is 16% ($80/$500), which means that its ROFL is 6% (16% − 10%). Company B has made effective use of debt financing to increase its ROE. As long as a company's ROA is greater than its cost of debt, its ROFL will be positive.[3]

We might further ask: If a higher ROE is desirable, why don't companies use as much debt financing as possible? The answer is that there are risks associated with debt financing. As the amount of debt in a company's balance sheet increases, so does the burden of interest costs on income and debt payments on cash flows. In the best of times, financial leverage increases returns to stockholders (ROE). In contrast, when earnings are depressed, financial leverage has the effect of making a bad year even worse. In the worst case, too much debt can lead to financial distress and even bankruptcy.

To illustrate how debt financing can reduce shareholder returns, **Exhibit 5.10** compares Company A and Company B in a year when reported profits are lower than in the previous example. Both companies have $1,000 in (average) assets and both report EWI of $30, producing an ROA of 3% ($30/$1,000). Company A does not use debt financing, so its ROE = 3%, and its ROFL = 0%. Because Company B has $500 of equity and $500 of debt, it reports interest expense of $20 ($500 × 4%) leaving net income of $10 ($30 − $20). Company B's ROE is 2% ($10/$500), which means that its ROFL is −1% (2% − 3%). That is, for Company B, the use of financial leverage has a negative effect on ROE. As this example illustrates, whenever ROA is less than the interest rate on the debt, debt financing reduces the return to shareholders.

EXHIBIT 5.10	The Effect of Debt Financing on ROE (ROA < interest rate)		
		Company A	Company B
Assets (average)		$1,000	$1,000
EWI		30	30
ROA (EWI/Assets)		3%	3%
Equity (average)		$1,000	$ 500
Debt		0	500
Interest expense (4% of debt)		0	20
Net income (EWI − interest)		30	10
ROE (Net income/equity)		3%	2%
ROFL (ROE − ROA)		0%	−1%

---

[3] The interest cost on debt is tax deductible. Therefore, the relevant cost of debt to use to compare to ROA is the after-tax interest rate.

As a general rule, shareholders benefit from increased use of debt financing provided that the assets financed with the debt earn a return that exceeds the cost of the debt. However, increasing levels of debt result in successively higher interest rates charged by creditors. At some point, the cost of debt exceeds the return on assets that a company can expect from the debt financing. Thereafter, further debt financing does not make economic sense. The market, in essence, places a limit on the amount that a company can borrow.

In addition, creditors usually require a company to execute a loan agreement that places various restrictions on its operating activities. These restrictions, called **covenants**, help safeguard debtholders in the face of increased risk. This occurs because debtholders do not have a voice on the board of directors like stockholders do. These debt covenants impose a "cost" on the company beyond that of the interest rate, and these covenants are more stringent as a company increases its reliance on debt financing.

The median ratio of total liabilities to stockholders' equity, which measures the relative use of debt versus equity in a company's capital structure, is just over 1.0 for all publicly traded companies. This means that the typical company relies more on debt financing than on equity. However, the relative use of debt varies considerably across industries as illustrated in **Exhibit 5.11**.

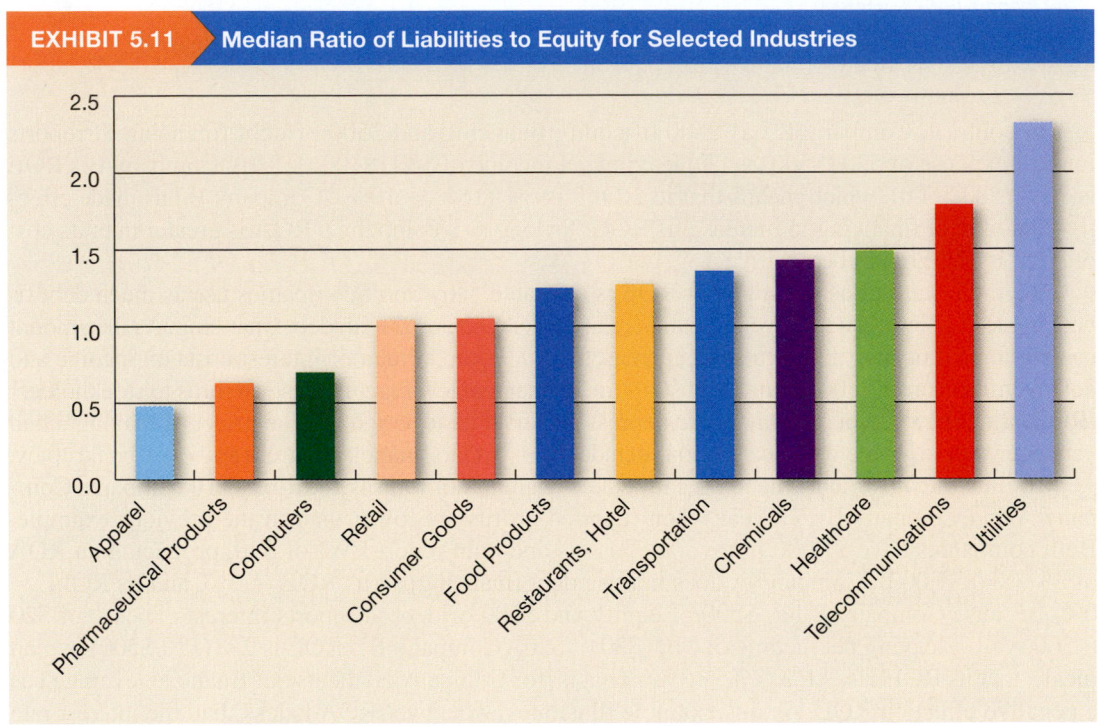

EXHIBIT 5.11 Median Ratio of Liabilities to Equity for Selected Industries

Companies in the utilities industry have relatively high proportions of debt. Because the utilities industry is regulated, profits and cash flows are relatively certain and stable and, as a result, utility companies can support a higher debt level. The healthcare and telecommunications industries also utilize a relatively high proportion of debt. These industries are not regulated, but their heavy investments in property, plant, and equipment require significant long-term debt. At the lower end of debt financing are pharmaceuticals and apparel companies. Historically, these industries have been characterized by relatively uncertain profits and cash flows. In addition, success in these industries depends heavily on intellectual property and human resources devoted to research and product development. These "assets" do not appear on the balance sheet and cannot be used as collateral when borrowing funds. Consequently, they use less debt in their capital structures.

To summarize, companies can effectively use debt to increase ROE. Although it reduces financing costs, debt increases **default risk**: the risk that the company will be unable to repay debt when it comes due. Because of this risk, analysts carefully examine a company's financial statements to determine if it is using debt financing effectively and judiciously.

The core of our analysis relating to debt is the examination of a company's ability to generate cash to *service* its debt (that is, to make required debt payments of both interest and principal).

Analysts, investors, and creditors are primarily concerned about whether the company has sufficient cash available or, alternatively, whether it is able to generate the required cash in the future to cover its debt obligations. The analysis of available cash is called **liquidity analysis**. The analysis of the company's ability to generate sufficient cash in the future is called **solvency analysis** (so named because a bankrupt company is said to be "insolvent").

Liquidity Analysis

Liquidity refers to cash availability: how much cash a company has, and how much it can raise on short notice. The most common ratios used to assess the degree of liquidity are the current ratio and the quick ratio, which were first introduced in Chapter 2, as well as the operating cash flow to current liabilities ratio, which was introduced in Chapter 4. Each of these ratios links required near-term payments to cash available in the near term.

Current Ratio   *Current assets* are those assets that a company expects to convert into cash within the next operating cycle, which is typically a year. *Current liabilities* are those liabilities that come due within the next year. An excess of current assets over current liabilities (Current assets − Current liabilities), is known as *net working capital* or simply **working capital**. Positive working capital implies more expected cash inflows than cash outflows in the short run. The **current ratio** expresses working capital as a ratio and is computed as follows:

$$\text{Current ratio (CR)} = \frac{\text{Current assets}}{\text{Current liabilities}}$$

A current ratio greater than 1.0 implies positive working capital. Both working capital and the current ratio consider existing balance sheet data only and ignore cash inflows from future sales or other sources. The current ratio is more commonly used than working capital because ratios allow comparisons across companies of different sizes. Generally, companies prefer a higher current ratio; however, an excessively high current ratio indicates inefficient asset use. Furthermore, a current ratio less than 1.0 is not always problematic for at least two reasons:

1. A cash-and-carry company (like a grocery store) can have little or no receivables (and a low current ratio), but consistently large operating cash inflows ensure the company will be sufficiently liquid. A company can efficiently manage its working capital by minimizing receivables and inventories and maximizing payables. **The Kroger Company** and **Wal-Mart**, for example, use their buying power to exact extended credit terms from suppliers. Consequently, because both companies are essentially cash-and-carry companies, their current ratios are less than 1.0 and both are sufficiently liquid.

2. A service company will typically report little or no inventories among its current assets. In addition, some service companies do not report significant accounts receivable. If short-term borrowings and accrued expenses exceed cash and temporary investments, a current ratio of less than 1.0 would result. **United Continental Holdings, Inc.** is an example of such a firm.

The aim of current-ratio analysis is to discern if a company is having, or is likely to have, difficulty meeting its short-term obligations. If a company cannot cover its short-term debts with cash provided by operations, it may need to liquidate current assets to meet its obligations. **PepsiCo**'s current ratio was 1.14 ($20,663 million / $18,092 million) at December 31, 2014. At the end of 2013, its current ratio was 1.24 ($22,203 million / $17,839 million).

Quick Ratio   The **quick ratio** is a variant of the current ratio. It focuses on quick assets, which are those assets likely to be converted to cash within a relatively short period of time, usually less than 90 days. Specifically, quick assets include cash, marketable securities, and accounts receivable; they exclude inventories and prepaid assets. The quick ratio is defined as follows:

$$\text{Quick ratio (QR)} = \frac{\text{Cash} + \text{Short-term securities} + \text{Accounts receivable}}{\text{Current liabilities}}$$

The quick ratio reflects on a company's ability to meet its current liabilities without liquidating inventories that could require markdowns. It is a more stringent test of liquidity than the current ratio and may provide more insight into company liquidity in some cases.

In 2014, PepsiCo's quick ratio was 0.85 ([$6,134 million + $2,592 million + $6,651 million]/$18,092 million), which was down from 0.93 in 2013 ([$9,375 million + $303 million + $6,954 million]/$17,839 million). While it is not uncommon for a company to report a quick ratio less than 1.0, PepsiCo's quick ratio has declined along with its current ratio.

Operating Cash Flow to Current Liabilities

The **operating cash flow to current liabilities (OCFCL)** ratio was introduced in Chapter 4 and is defined as follows:

$$\text{Operating cash flow to current liabilities (OCFCL)} = \frac{\text{Cash flow from operations}}{\text{Average current liabilities}}$$

Cash flow from operations is taken directly from the statement of cash flows. It represents the net amount of cash derived from operating activities during the year. Ultimately the ability of a company to pay its debts is determined by whether its operations can generate enough cash to cover debt payments. Thus, a higher OCFCL ratio is generally preferred by analysts.

PepsiCo reported an OCFCL ratio of 0.58 in 2014 ($10,506 million / [($17,839 million + $18,092 million)/2]). Its 2013 OCFCL ratio was 0.55 ($9,688 million / [($17,089 million + $17,839 million)/2]). PepsiCo's OCFCL ratio has increased slightly over the past two years after a few years of decline. The increase in the OCFCL ratio, combined with the decline in the CR and QR suggests that PepsiCo's sources of liquidity should be examined further. Improvement in the ratio of cash flows to short-term obligations is generally a good sign, but this improvement appears to be the result of reducing the level of inventories and receivables from 2013 to 2014. In Chapter 4 we saw that reductions in inventory and receivables *increased* operating cash flows. As a consequence, the improvement may not be sustainable and continued improvement is certainly limited. **Exhibit 5.12** provides a plot of all three liquidity ratios over the past 5 years.

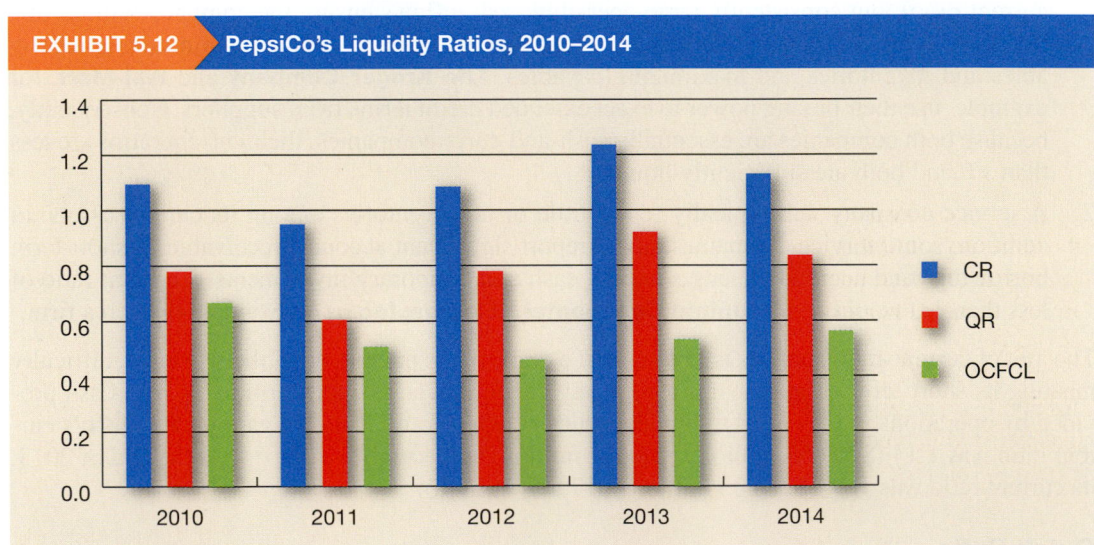

EXHIBIT 5.12 PepsiCo's Liquidity Ratios, 2010–2014

Solvency Analysis

Solvency refers to a company's ability to meet its debt obligations, including both periodic interest payments and the repayment of the principal amount borrowed. Solvency is crucial because an insolvent company is a failed company. There are two general approaches to measuring solvency. The first approach uses balance sheet data and assesses the proportion of capital raised from creditors. The second approach uses income statement data and assesses the profit generated relative to debt payment obligations. We discuss each approach in turn.

Debt-to-Equity   The **debt-to-equity ratio**, which was introduced in Chapter 1, is a useful tool for the first type of solvency analysis. It is defined as follows:

$$\textbf{Debt-to-equity ratio} = \frac{\textbf{Total liabilities}}{\textbf{Total stockholders' equity}}$$

This ratio conveys how reliant a company is on creditor financing (which are fixed claims) compared with equity financing (which are flexible or residual claims). A higher ratio indicates less solvency, and more risk. PepsiCo's debt-to-equity ratio is 3.02 for 2014 ($52,961 million/$17,548 million). In 2013, its ratio was 2.18 ($53,089 million/$24,389 million). Between 2010 and 2013, PepsiCo's debt-to-equity ratio remained below 2.5 (see graph). The dramatic increase in 2014 was caused by a significant decrease in stockholders' equity from 2013 to 2014, and not by an increase in total liabilities. The decrease in stockholders' equity was due to negative foreign currency translation adjustments in 2014. Such adjustments are often beyond the ability of management to control. Nevertheless, the increase in the debt-to-equity ratio can have an impact on PepsiCo's ability to borrow at favorable interest rates. PepsiCo's debt-to-equity ratio is well above the average of approximately 1.2 for other companies in the food industry.

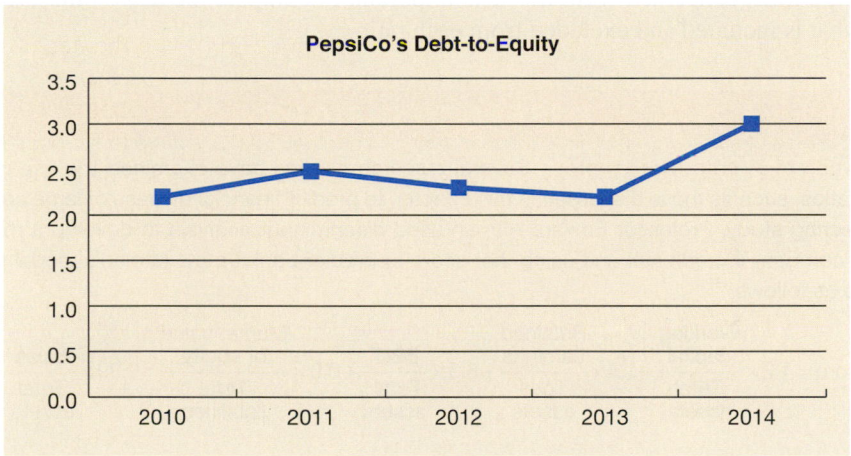

In practice, analysts use a variety of solvency measures that are similar to the debt-to-equity ratio. One variant of this ratio considers a company's *long-term* debt divided by equity. This approach assumes that current liabilities are repaid from current assets (so-called self-liquidating). Thus, it assumes that creditors and stockholders need only focus on the relative proportion of long-term capital.

Times Interest Earned   The second type of solvency analysis compares profits to liabilities. This approach assesses how much operating profit is available to cover debt obligations. A common measure for this type of solvency analysis is the **times interest earned (TIE)** ratio (see Chapter 9) defined as follows:

$$\textbf{Times interest earned} = \frac{\textbf{Earnings before interest expense and taxes}}{\textbf{Interest expense}}$$

The times interest earned ratio reflects the operating income available to pay interest expense. The underlying assumption is that only interest needs to be paid because the principal will be refinanced. This ratio is sometimes abbreviated as EBIT/I. The numerator is similar to earnings without interest (EWI), but it is *pretax* instead of after tax.

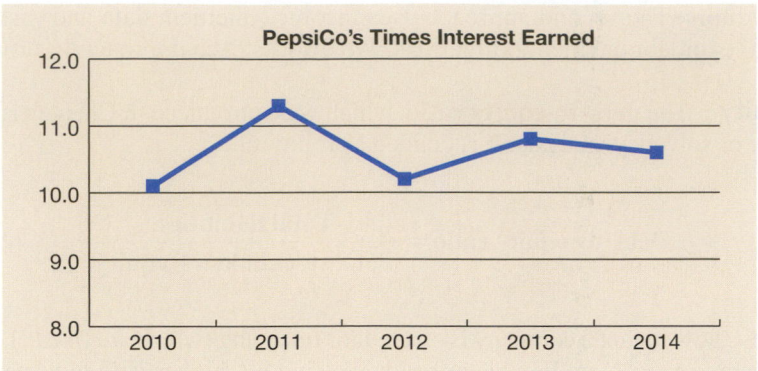

Management wants this ratio to be sufficiently high so that there is little risk of default. PepsiCo's TIE ratio was 10.63 times in 2014 ([$8,757 million + $909 million]/$909 million), which is only slightly down from 10.76 times in 2013 ([$8,891 million + $911 million]/$911 million). Over the 5-year period between 2010 and 2014, PepsiCo's TIE ratio has ranged from a low of 10.12 in 2010 to a high of 11.32 in 2011. The current level of this ratio suggests that PepsiCo is more than capable of earning income that is sufficient to cover its financing costs.

There are many variations of solvency and liquidity analysis and the ratios used. The basic idea is to construct measures that reflect a company's credit risk exposure. There is not one "best" financial leverage ratio. Instead, as financial statement users, we want to use measures that capture the risk we are most concerned with. It is also important to compute the ratios ourselves to ensure we know what is included and excluded from each ratio.

RESEARCH INSIGHT

Using Ratios to Predict Bankruptcy Several research studies have examined the use of various financial ratios, such as those discussed in this chapter, to predict financial distress of large companies. In a pioneering study, Professor Edward Altman used discriminant analysis to develop a method for scoring a company's credit risk and using that score to predict bankruptcy. Altman's model produced a **Z-score** as follows:

$$\text{Z-score} = 1.2 \times \frac{\text{Working capital}}{\text{Total assets}} + 1.4 \times \frac{\text{Retained earnings}}{\text{Total assets}} + 3.3 \times \frac{\text{EBIT}}{\text{Total assets}} + 0.6 \times \frac{\text{Market value of equity}}{\text{Total liabilities}} + 0.99 \times \frac{\text{Sales}}{\text{Total assets}}$$

The first variable is a measure of liquidity. The second and third variables measure long-term and short-term profitability. The fourth variable captures a company's financial leverage and the last variable is asset turnover. A Z-score greater than 3.0 indicates a healthy company, while a Z-score below 1.8 suggests a high potential for near-term bankruptcy. The model was 95% accurate at predicting bankruptcy one year in advance and 72% accurate two years in advance. Today, credit scoring models like Altman's Z-score are used by nearly all financial institutions and many other businesses to evaluate credit risk. (Altman, E., "Financial Ratios, Discriminant Analysis and the Prediction of Corporate Bankruptcy," *Journal of Finance*, September, 1968.)

Limitations of Ratio Analysis

The quality of financial statement analysis depends on the quality of financial information. We ought not blindly analyze numbers; doing so can lead to faulty conclusions and suboptimal decisions. Instead, we need to acknowledge that current accounting rules (GAAP) have limitations, and be fully aware of the company's environment, its competitive pressures, and any structural and strategic changes. **Exhibit 5.13** shows how ratios can differ significantly across industries, so comparisons to companies with similar customers, technologies and competitive pressures will be most meaningful. Even within industries, there may be differences in strategy that create big differences in ratio values. There can be other factors that limit the usefulness of financial accounting information for ratio analysis.

EXHIBIT 5.13	Industry Ratios: Medians of Companies with Market Capitalization > $500 Million (2012-2014)													
	ROE	ROA	ROFL	PM	GPM	AT	ART	INVT	PPET	DE	TIE	CR	QR	OCFCL
Apparel..............	16.3%	9.5%	5.4%	10.3%	50.5%	1.34	9.79	3.20	7.87	0.48	32.36	2.84	1.54	0.75
Business Services	9.9%	5.0%	3.7%	7.3%	64.7%	0.81	5.64	28.30	10.52	0.83	9.22	1.80	1.62	0.48
Chemicals...........	18.1%	8.1%	8.6%	9.9%	32.7%	0.98	6.53	5.17	3.13	1.43	8.95	2.18	1.24	0.54
Computers	9.8%	5.4%	4.0%	6.4%	52.5%	0.91	5.52	7.16	11.00	0.70	12.44	2.07	1.71	0.45
Consumer Goods......	13.9%	8.3%	6.7%	9.5%	47.8%	1.16	7.19	5.44	6.67	1.05	14.37	1.70	1.11	0.43
Food Products	13.3%	7.0%	5.9%	6.8%	32.4%	1.24	12.26	6.29	4.80	1.25	7.48	1.82	0.88	0.52
Healthcare	11.7%	5.9%	5.3%	6.1%	21.9%	0.98	7.39	44.73	4.74	1.49	4.39	1.52	1.16	0.60
Petroleum...........	8.5%	5.3%	2.9%	7.3%	45.4%	0.68	6.83	15.94	0.44	1.13	3.87	1.26	0.84	1.10
Pharmaceutical........	-3.1%	-3.1%	-1.1%	1.3%	62.6%	0.44	5.85	2.39	4.48	0.63	3.50	4.14	3.50	0.11
Printing & Publishing ...	12.5%	5.7%	7.1%	7.3%	55.5%	0.73	6.58	19.82	7.62	1.52	5.45	1.32	0.91	0.43
Restaurants, Hotel	14.5%	6.4%	6.7%	5.9%	26.0%	1.25	30.37	55.46	2.37	1.27	6.12	1.02	0.66	0.78
Retail	14.6%	7.5%	6.0%	5.0%	34.0%	1.99	46.25	5.40	6.77	1.04	9.75	1.70	0.63	0.51
Steel...............	5.6%	3.4%	1.4%	1.8%	17.5%	0.98	7.68	5.26	2.84	1.19	3.44	2.34	1.22	0.42
Telecommunications....	12.1%	6.1%	5.2%	6.9%	51.2%	0.56	7.13	25.51	1.65	1.79	3.38	1.14	0.91	0.69
Tobacco	13.1%	14.2%	9.0%	30.1%	52.7%	0.72	40.01	3.34	7.84	2.15	9.36	1.02	0.49	0.49
Transportation	11.1%	5.5%	4.6%	6.2%	30.0%	0.81	10.24	32.27	1.00	1.36	4.22	1.33	1.09	0.69
Utilities	9.6%	4.1%	5.4%	6.3%	28.9%	0.40	7.47	13.55	0.46	2.32	3.12	0.93	0.59	0.66
Overall	11.0%	5.7%	5.3%	7.1%	34.6%	0.87	7.19	5.48	4.77	1.25	7.35	1.81	1.19	0.48

GAAP Limitations   Several limitations in GAAP can distort financial ratios. Limitations include:

1. **Measurability**. Financial statements reflect what can be reliably measured. This results in nonrecognition of certain assets, often internally developed assets, the very assets that are most likely to confer a competitive advantage and create value. Examples are brand name, a superior management team, employee skills, and a reliable supply chain.

2. **Non-capitalized costs**. Related to the concept of measurability is the expensing of costs relating to "assets" that cannot be identified with enough precision to warrant capitalization. Examples are brand equity costs from advertising and other promotional activities, and research and development costs relating to future products.

3. **Historical costs**. Assets and liabilities are usually recorded at original acquisition or issuance costs. Subsequent increases in value are not recorded until realized, and declines in value are recognized only if deemed permanent.

Thus, GAAP balance sheets omit important and valuable assets. Our analysis of ROE, including that of liquidity and solvency, must consider that assets can be underreported and that ratios can be distorted. We discuss many of these limitations in more detail in later chapters.

Company Changes   Many companies regularly undertake mergers, acquire new companies, and divest subsidiaries. Such major operational changes can impair the comparability of company ratios across time. Companies also change strategies, such as product pricing, R&D, and financing. We must understand the effects of such changes on ratios and exercise caution when we compare ratios from one period to the next. Companies also behave differently at different points in their life cycles. For instance, growth companies possess a different profile than do mature companies. Seasonal effects also markedly impact analysis of financial statements at different times of the year. Thus, we must consider life cycle and cyclicality when we compare ratios across companies and over time.

Conglomerate Effects   Few companies are pure-play; instead, most companies operate in several businesses or industries. Most publicly traded companies consist of a parent company and multiple subsidiaries, often pursuing different lines of business. PepsiCo reports financial information for six separate business segments. Most heavy equipment manufacturers, for example, have finance subsidiaries (**Ford Credit Corporation** and **Cat Financial** are subsidiaries of **Ford** and **Caterpillar** respectively). Financial statements of such conglomerates are consolidated and include the financial statements of the parent and its subsidiaries. Consequently, such consolidated statements are challenging to analyze. Typically, analysts break the financials apart into their component businesses and separately analyze each component. Fortunately, companies must report financial information (albeit limited) for major business segments in their 10-Ks.

Means to an End Ratios reduce, to a single number, the myriad complexities of a company's operations. No one number can accurately capture the qualitative aspect of a company. Ratios cannot hope to capture the innumerable transactions and events that occur each day between a company and various parties. Ratios cannot meaningfully convey a company's marketing and management philosophies, its human resource activities, its financing activities, its strategic initiatives, and its product management. In our analysis we must learn to look through the numbers and ratios to better understand the operational factors that drive financial results. Successful analysis seeks to gain insight into what a company is really about and what the future portends. Our overriding purpose in analysis is to understand the past and present to better predict the future. Computing and examining ratios is just one step in that process.

CHAPTER-END REVIEW

Refer to the income statements and balance sheets for the **Coca-Cola Company** presented in Mid-Chapter Review 1 earlier in this chapter.

Required
Compute the following liquidity and solvency ratios for Coca-Cola and interpret your results in comparison to those of PepsiCo.

1. Current ratio
2. Quick ratio
3. Debt-to-equity ratio
4. Times interest earned

The solution to this review problem can be found on pages 266-267.

5

LO5 Measure and analyze the effect of operating activities on ROE.

APPENDIX 5A: Analyzing and Interpreting Core Operating Activities

In Chapter 4, we analyzed cash flows by grouping them into three categories—operating, investing, and financing. Similarly, the income statement and balance sheet can be formatted to distinguish between operating and nonoperating (investing and financing) activities. In this appendix, we consider the effect of operating activities on the return on investment. The distinction between returns earned from operating activities and those generated by nonoperating activities is important. Operations provide the primary value drivers for stockholders. It is for this reason that many analysts argue that operating activities must be executed successfully if a company expects to remain profitable in the long run.

Operating activities refer to the core transactions and events of a company. They consist of those activities required to deliver a company's products and services to its customers. A company is engaged in operating activities when it conducts research and development, establishes supply chains, assembles administrative support, produces and markets its products, and follows up with after-sale customer service. Although nonoperating activities, namely investing and financing activities, are important and must be managed well, they are not the primary value drivers for investors and creditors.

Operating returns are measured by the **return on net operating assets (RNOA)**. This return metric is defined as follows:

$$\text{RNOA} = \frac{\text{Net operating profit after taxes (NOPAT)}}{\text{Average net operating assets (NOA)}}$$

In order to calculate this ratio, we must first classify the income statement and balance sheet accounts into operating and nonoperating components so that we can assess each separately. First, we will consider operating components of the income statement and the calculation of NOPAT. Then, we consider operating and nonoperating components of the balance sheet and the calculation of NOA.

Reporting Operating Activities in the Income Statement The income statement reports operating activities through accounts such as sales revenue, cost of goods sold, selling, general and administrative (SG&A) expenses, depreciation, rent, insurance, wages, advertising, and R&D expenses. These activities create the most long-lasting effects on profitability and cash flows. Nonoperating items in the income statement include interest expense on borrowed funds and interest and dividend income on investments as well as gains and losses on those investments.

A commonly used measure of operating income is **net operating profit after taxes (NOPAT)**. NOPAT is calculated as:

$$\text{NOPAT} = \text{Net income} - [(\text{Nonoperating revenues} - \text{Nonoperating expenses}) \times (1 - \text{Marginal tax rate})]$$

NOPAT is an important measure of profitability. It is similar to net income except that NOPAT focuses exclusively on after-tax *operating* performance.

Computation of NOPAT requires that we separate nonoperating revenues and expenses from operating sources of income. Companies often report income from operations as a subtotal (before income taxes) within the income statement. These numbers should be interpreted with caution. Currently, there are no requirements within GAAP that specify which revenue and expense items should be included in operating income.[4] As a consequence, some nonoperating items may be included (as part of SG&A expense, for example). PepsiCo has investments in affiliated companies that distribute its snack foods in certain parts of the world. PepsiCo's income from these investments is included in its SG&A expense in the income statement, but the amount is not disclosed. While this income might appear to be nonoperating, most analysts would argue that this amount should be included in the calculation of NOPAT for PepsiCo, because these distribution operations are part of the core operating activities of the business.

The tax rate used to compute NOPAT is the **marginal tax rate**. This rate is the effective tax rate on nonoperating revenues and expenses. As we have done throughout this chapter, we use the federal statutory tax rate of 35% to approximate the marginal tax rate.[5] PepsiCo's NOPAT can be computed using this tax rate:

$$\text{NOPAT} = \$6{,}558 \text{ million} - [(\$85 \text{ million} - \$909 \text{ million}) \times (1 - 0.35)] = \$7{,}093.6 \text{ million}$$

PepsiCo's NOPAT is greater than its net income of $6,558 million in 2014. The difference between net income and NOPAT is the interest expense on its debt and interest income on its investments.

Reporting Operating Activities in the Balance Sheet The balance sheet also reflects both operating and nonoperating activities. The asset side of the balance sheet reports resources devoted to operating activities in accounts such as cash, receivables, inventories, property, plant, and equipment, and intangible assets. Among liabilities, accounts payable, accrued expenses, and some long-term liabilities such as deferred compensation and pension benefits arise out of operating activities. In addition, accrued and deferred income taxes are generally considered operating liabilities.

Investments in securities of other companies are usually considered nonoperating. The exception is that some equity-type investments are related to operations. PepsiCo's investment in its snack foods distributors is an example of this type of investment. Equity investments are discussed further in Chapter 12. Among a company's liabilities, short-term and long-term debt accounts are classified as nonoperating. These include accounts such as notes payable, interest payable, current maturities of long-term debt, capital leases, and long-term debt.

PepsiCo reports short-term investments of $2,592 million in 2014 ($303 million in 2013), which are nonoperating. It also reports long-term investments in non-controlled affiliates of $2,689 in 2014 ($2,623 in 2013). These long-term investments are the aforementioned equity investments in companies distributing PepsiCo's snack foods, and most analysts would consider them to be part of operations. PepsiCo's footnotes show that its noncurrent Other assets account includes nonoperating assets of $447 million in 2014 ($419 million in 2013). Its nonoperating liabilities include short-term debt obligations of $5,076 million in 2014 ($5,306 million in 2013) and long-term debt obligations of $23,821 million in 2014 ($24,333 million in 2013).

By subtracting total operating liabilities from total operating assets, we get **net operating assets (NOA)**.[6] PepsiCo's NOA for 2014 and 2013 is calculated as follows ($ millions):

---

[4] The FASB recently released a preliminary draft of a proposal for presenting financial statements in a new format. Among other things, the objective is to better distinguish operating and nonoperating activities.

[5] As we argued earlier in this chapter, the federal statutory tax rate is a reasonable approximation of the marginal tax rate in many instances, including our analysis of PepsiCo. However, some nonoperating sources of revenue and expense are not taxed at this 35% rate. For example, most dividend income received from investments in the stock of other corporations is excluded from taxable income. A detailed analysis of marginal tax rates is beyond the scope of this text. Nevertheless, a thorough analysis of operating return would normally include a close examination of a company's income taxes.

[6] Total operating assets can be computed by subtracting nonoperating assets from total assets. Similarly, we can determine operating liabilities either by adding up the operating items or by subtracting the nonoperating items from total liabilities.

	2014	2013
Operating assets	$70,509 − $2,592 − $447 = $67,470	$77,478 − $303 − $419 = $76,756
Operating liabilities...	$52,961 − $5,076 − $23,821 = $24,064	$53,089 − $5,306 − $24,333 = $23,450
NOA	$43,406	$53,306

Given NOPAT and NOA we can compute PepsiCo's RNOA as follows:

$$\text{RNOA} = \frac{\text{NOPAT}}{\text{Average NOA}} = \frac{\$7,093.6 \text{ million}}{(\$53,306 \text{ million} + \$43,406 \text{ million}) / 2} = 14.7\%$$

PepsiCo's ROE is 31.3% in 2014. Its RNOA is 14.7%, which represents less than half of the total return earned by stockholders.

Disaggregating RNOA

We gain further insights into operating returns by disaggregating RNOA into operating profit margin and asset turnover. RNOA can be presented as the product of net operating profit margin (NOPM) and net operating asset turnover (NOAT). We define **net operating profit margin (NOPM)** as the amount of operating profit produced as a percentage of each sales dollar. NOPM is similar to the profit margin (PM) ratio defined in the chapter, except that it excludes all nonoperating revenues and expenses from the calculation. PepsiCo's NOPM was 10.64% in 2014, computed as:

$$\text{NOPM} = \frac{\text{NOPAT}}{\text{Sales revenue}} = \frac{\$7,093.6 \text{ million}}{\$66,683 \text{ million}} = 10.64\%$$

The ratio indicates that each dollar of sales revenue generated 10.6¢ of after-tax operating profit. PepsiCo's NOPAT is very close to PepsiCo's EWI because the primary nonoperating item in the company's income statement is interest expense. Thus its NOPM is almost identical to its profit margin of 10.7%.

Net operating asset turnover (NOAT) is defined as the ratio of sales revenue to average net operating assets (NOA). NOAT captures the amount of sales revenue generated by each dollar of net investment in operating assets. PepsiCo's NOAT is 1.38 times, computed as:

$$\text{NOAT} = \frac{\text{Sales revenue}}{\text{Average NOA}} = \frac{\$66,683 \text{ million}}{(\$53,306 \text{ million} + \$43,406 \text{ million}) / 2} = 1.38$$

This ratio suggests that each dollar of investment in net operating assets generates $1.38 of sales revenue. This ratio is considerably higher than PepsiCo's asset turnover (AT) ratio of 0.901. This difference is caused by the difference between net operating assets (NOA) and total assets. NOAT is computed using average NOA in the denominator rather than average total assets. Thus, nonoperating assets are excluded, and operating assets are presented net of operating liabilities. The resulting denominator is, therefore, considerably smaller.

PepsiCo's RNOA is 14.7%. This return can be disaggregated into the product of NOPM and NOAT as follows:

$$\text{RNOA} = \text{NOPM} \times \text{NOAT}$$
$$14.7\% = 10.64\% \times 1.38$$

APPENDIX 5A REVIEW

Refer to the financial statements of the Coca-Cola Company presented in Mid-Chapter Review 1. Calculate Coca-Cola's return on net operating assets (RNOA) and then disaggregate RNOA into net operating profit margin (NOPM) and net operating asset turnover (NOAT).

The solution to this review problem can be found on page 267.

LO6 Prepare *pro forma* financial statements.

APPENDIX 5B: Pro Forma Financial Statements

The ability to forecast future financial activities is an important aspect of many business decisions. We might, for example, wish to estimate the value of a company's common stock before purchasing its shares. Or, we might want to evaluate the creditworthiness of a prospective borrower. We might also be interested in comparing the financial impact of alternative business strategies or tactics. For each of these decision contexts, a forecast of future earnings and cash flows would be relevant to such an evaluation.

Pro forma financial statements are hypothetical statements prepared to reflect specific assumptions about the company and its transactions. The most common type of pro forma statements are those prepared for future periods based on assumptions about the future activities of a business.[7] By varying the assumptions, pro forma statements allow us to ask "what if" questions about the future activities of the company, the answers to which provide the necessary inputs underlying most business decisions.

In this appendix, we present a common, yet simple method for preparing pro forma financial statements. This method proceeds in seven steps:

1. Forecast sales revenue.
2. Forecast operating expenses, such as cost of goods sold and SG&A expenses.
3. Forecast operating assets and liabilities, including accounts receivable, inventory, property, plant, and equipment, accounts payable, and prepaid and accrued expenses.
4. Forecast nonoperating assets, liabilities, contributed capital, revenues and expenses.
5. Forecast net income, dividends and retained earnings.
6. Forecast the amount of cash required to balance the balance sheet.
7. Prepare a pro forma cash flow statement based on the pro forma income statement and balance sheet.

Step 1. Forecast Sales Revenue

The sales forecast is the crucial first step in the preparation of pro forma financial statements, because many of the accounts in the pro forma income statement and balance sheet depend on their relation to the sales forecast. The general method for forecasting sales is to assume a revenue growth rate and apply that rate to the current sales revenue amount:

$$\text{Forecasted revenues} = \text{Current revenues} \times (1 + \text{Revenue growth rate})$$

A good starting point for estimating the revenue growth rate is the historical rate of sales growth. This is obtained by using data from the horizontal analysis discussed earlier in the chapter. For example, over the past four years, PepsiCo has experienced an average sales growth rate of 3.6%. Once we have this historical rate as a starting point, we can then adjust the growth rate up or down based on other relevant information. For example, we might attempt to answer the following questions:

- How will future sales be affected by economic conditions? What will happen in the economy in the coming year? Do we expect economic growth or a recession? How will economic growth vary in various markets, such as the United States, Europe, Asia, and Latin America?

- What changes are expected from the company? Are there any new strategic initiatives planned? Is the company planning to open new stores, launch new products, new advertising campaigns, or new pricing tactics? Do we expect any acquisitions of other businesses?

- What changes in the competitive environment do we expect? Are new competitors entering the market? How will existing competitors respond to changes in the company's strategy? How will substitute products affect sales?

To answer each of the above questions, we rely on a variety of information sources, not the least of which is the management's discussion and analysis (MD&A) section of the company's 10-K report. We can also use publicly available information from competitors, suppliers, customers, industry organizations and government agencies to provide some insight into trends that can have an effect on future revenues. Our objective is to be able to adjust the historical growth rate up or down to reflect the insights we gain from reviewing this additional information. Using the historical growth rate of 3.6%, we forecast the 2015 revenue to be $69,084 million ($66,683 million × 1.036).

Step 2. Forecast Operating Expenses

Given our forecast of sales revenue, we then turn to forecasting operating expenses. We rely on the common-size income statement as a starting point to identify the relationship between operating expense items and sales revenue. That is, we use the expense-to-sales (ETS) ratio for each operating expense item to compute the forecasted expense:

$$\text{Forecasted operating expense} = \text{Forecasted revenues} \times \text{ETS ratio}$$

---

[7] The term "pro forma financial statements" is a term that is also used to describe *current* period financial statements prepared under alternative assumptions. For example, management might use the term pro forma earnings when referring to earnings computed after excluding a major revenue or expense item, such as restructuring charges or income from discontinued operations. The term can also be used to describe financial statements prepared under a different set of accounting principles.

While historical ETS ratios provide a good place to start, we may want to adjust these ratios up or down based on observed trends or any additional information that we might have. For example, when we examined PepsiCo's common-size income statements, we learned that cost of goods sold decreased to 46.3% of sales in 2014, up from 47.0% in 2013. Will this trend continue into 2015? Or, alternatively, do we anticipate that this expense item will revert to historical levels in relation to sales? Has the company taken any steps to alter the trend in this ETS ratio? As was the case with the sales forecast, there are numerous sources of information that are potentially useful for making adjustments to the historical relationships.

For the purpose of illustration, we assume that the ETS ratios for all operating expense items remain the same in 2015 as they were in 2014. For example, we forecast PepsiCo's 2015 SG&A expense to be $27,081 million ($69,084 million × 39.2%).

Step 3. Forecast Operating Assets and Liabilities

The sales forecast can also be used to forecast operating assets and liabilities. The relationship between operating assets and revenues is based on asset turnover analysis. For example, when we compute accounts receivable turnover (ART), sales revenue is divided by average accounts receivable. When forecasting accounts receivable, we assume a relationship between sales revenue and year-end accounts receivable:

$$\text{Forecasted accounts receivable} = \frac{\text{Forecasted sales revenue} \times \text{Reported accounts receivable}}{\text{Reported sales revenue}}$$

PepsiCo reports accounts and notes receivable of $6,651 million in 2014, which is 9.97% of the reported sales revenue of $66,683 million. The forecasted accounts receivable for 2015 is, therefore, $6,888 million ($69,084 million × 9.97%).

The same procedure can be used to forecast other operating assets, such as inventories, prepaid expenses and property, plant, and equipment, as well as operating liabilities such as accounts payable and accrued expenses.

Step 4. Forecast Nonoperating Assets, Liabilities, Revenues and Expenses

While operating expenses, assets, and liabilities tend to be related to sales revenue, this is typically not the case for nonoperating items. Instead, nonoperating revenues, such as interest and dividend income, tend to be related to investments, while nonoperating expense, namely interest expense, is related to debt financing. As a starting point, we forecast each of these items by assuming no change from the current amounts. For example, PepsiCo reported long-term debt of $23,821 million in 2014 along with short-term obligations of $2,592 million. We forecast the same level of debt financing in 2015. Likewise, interest expense should remain the same at $909 million.

There may be information in the notes or in the MD&A section of the 10-K report to suggest other assumptions. For example, the notes typically reveal the amount of long-term debt that will come due in each of the next five years. This information can be used to adjust the balance in short-term obligations, because current maturities of long-term debt would be included under this item. Nevertheless, an assumption of no change is a good place to start.

Step 5. Forecast Net Income, Dividends, and Retained Earnings

Once we have forecasts of sales revenue (from step 1), operating expenses (step 2), and nonoperating revenues and expenses (step 4), we can calculate pretax earnings, income tax expense, and net income. Income tax expense is forecasted by multiplying pretax income by the effective tax rate:

$$\text{Forecasted income tax expense} = \text{Forecasted pretax income} \times \text{Effective tax rate}$$

The **effective tax rate** is the average tax rate applied to pretax earnings, and is computed by dividing reported income tax expense by reported pretax earnings. PepsiCo's effective tax rate was 25.1% in 2014 ($2,199 million/$8,757 million). Although this rate can be adjusted up or down based on additional information, we apply the 2014 effective tax rate to compute 2015 forecasted income taxes. This assumption results in forecasted income taxes of $2,284 million ($9,098 million × 25.1%) and forecasted net income of $6,814 million ($9,098 million − $2,284 million). PepsiCo's 2015 pro forma income statement is presented in **Exhibit 5B.1** alongside its 2014 reported income statement.

Our forecast of dividends relies on the **dividend payout ratio**, defined as dividend payments divided by net income.

$$\text{Forecasted dividends} = \text{Forecasted net income} \times \text{Dividend payout ratio}$$

PepsiCo paid cash dividends of $3,730 million in 2014, which is 56.9% of its net income of $6,558 million. Using this dividend payout ratio, we forecast 2015 dividends to be $3,877 million ($6,814 million × 56.9%).

Next, we can forecast retained earnings using the forecasts of net income and dividends:

$$\text{Forecasted retained earnings} = \text{Beginning retained earnings} + \text{Forecasted net income} - \text{Forecasted dividends}$$

Throughout this chapter, we have presented PepsiCo's stockholders' equity as a single amount, without separating retained earnings from contributed capital. Contributed capital increases when common stock is issued, and decreases when common stock is repurchased. PepsiCo has repurchased shares every year for the past five years and every indication is that they will continue to repurchase shares in 2015. Stock repurchases, net of common stock issued, have averaged 40% of net income over the past five years. If we assume that this rate will continue in 2015, we can estimate stock repurchases totaling $2,726 million ($6,814 million × 40%). Thus, total stockholders' equity in 2015 will equal $17,759 computed as follows:

$$\text{Forecasted stockholders' equity} = \text{Beginning stockholders' equity} + \text{Forecasted net income} - \text{Forecasted dividends} - \text{Forecasted stock repurchases}$$

$$\$17,759 \text{ million} = \$17,548 \text{ million} + \$6,814 \text{ million} - \$3,877 \text{ million} - \$2,726 \text{ million}$$

EXHIBIT 5B.1	PepsiCo Pro Forma Income Statement

PEPSICO, INC.
2014 Income Statement and 2015 Pro Forma Income Statement

($ millions)	Pro forma 2015	As reported 2014
Net revenue ($66,683 × 1.036)	$69,084	$66,683
Cost of sales ($69,084 × 46.3%).	31,986	30,884
Selling, general and administrative expenses ($69,084 × 39.2%).	27,081	26,126
Amortization of intangible assets ($69,084 × 0.14%)	95	92
Operating profit	9,922	9,581
Interest expense (no change).	(909)	(909)
Interest income and other (no change).	85	85
Income before income taxes	9,098	8,757
Provision for income taxes (25.1% × pretax income)	2,284	2,199
Net income.	$ 6,814	$ 6,558

Step 6. Forecast Cash

If the forecasts of all other components of the balance sheet are in place, we can then forecast the cash balance. This forecast is simply a "plug" amount that makes the balance sheet balance:

$$\text{Forecasted cash} = \text{Forecasted liabilities} + \text{Forecasted stockholders' equity} - \text{Forecasted noncash assets}$$

It is possible that the resulting forecast of cash will be negative or unreasonably small or large. If this occurs, we then revisit steps 4 and 5. If the cash forecast is negative or too low, we adjust our forecast of short-term debt and interest expense to reflect increased borrowing to cover cash needs. If the cash forecast is too large, we can assume that excess cash is invested in marketable securities and increase the amount of interest income. In either case, we then modify our forecast of income taxes, net income, dividends and retained earnings, before recalculating the cash forecast.

PepsiCo's 2015 pro forma balance sheet is presented in **Exhibit 5B.2**, alongside the company's 2014 actual balance sheet. The cash balance is forecasted to decrease slightly, from $6,134 million in 2014 to $6,081 million in 2015.

Step 7. Prepare the Pro Forma Cash Flow Statement

Once we have a pro forma income statement and balance sheet, we can prepare a pro forma cash flow statement using the methods illustrated in Chapter 4. To do so, we need a forecast of depreciation expense (if that

EXHIBIT 5B.2	PepsiCo Pro Forma Balance Sheet		

PEPSICO, INC.
2014 Balance Sheet and 2015 Pro Forma Balance Sheet

($ millions)	Pro forma 2015	As reported 2014
Assets		
Cash and cash equivalents (plug to balance).............................	$ 6,081	$ 6,134
Short-term investment (no change)...	2,592	2,592
Accounts and notes receivable, net ($69,084 × 9.97%)...................	6,888	6,651
Inventories ($69,084 × 4.71%)...	3,254	3,143
Prepaid expenses and other current assets ($69,084 × 3.21%)..............	2,218	2,143
Total current assets..	21,033	20,663
Property, plant, and equipment, net ($69,084 × 25.86%)....................	17,865	17,244
Amortizable intangible assets, net ($69,084 × 2.17%).....................	1,499	1,449
Goodwill (no change)..	14,965	14,965
Other nonamortizable intangible assets (no change)........................	12,639	12,639
Investments in noncontrolled affiliates (no change).......................	2,689	2,689
Other assets ($69,084 × 1.29%)..	891	860
Total assets...	$71,581	$ 70,509
Liabilities and shareholders' equity		
Short-term obligations (no change)..	$ 5,076	$ 5,076
Accounts payable and other current liabilities ($69,084 × 19.52%)........	13,485	13,016
Total current liabilities...	18,561	18,092
Long-term debt obligations (no change)....................................	23,821	23,821
Other liabilities ($69,084 × 8.61%).......................................	5,948	5,744
Deferred income taxes ($69,084 × 7.95%)...................................	5,492	5,304
Total liabilities..	53,822	52,961
Total equity ($17,548 + $6,814 − $3,877 − $2,726)........................	17,759	17,548
Total liabilities and equity...	$71,581	$70,509

item is not explicitly listed as an operating expense in the income statement). The procedure for forecasting depreciation expense is the same as was used for other operating expenses—we simply use the depreciation ETS ratio.

PepsiCo reported depreciation and amortization expense of $2,625 million in 2014, which was 3.94% of sales revenue. Using this ETS ratio, we can forecast depreciation expense of $2,722 million in 2015 ($69,084 million × 3.94%). Using this forecast, along with other items forecasted earlier, we can prepare the pro forma cash flow statement, which is presented in **Exhibit 5B.3**.

Additional Considerations

Pro forma financial statements are based on a set of assumptions about the future. Any decisions that are based on pro forma statements are only as good as the quality of these assumptions. Therefore it is important that we appreciate the effect that each assumption has on the forecasted amounts. To this end, it is often helpful to use **sensitivity analysis** to examine the effect of alternative assumptions on the pro forma statements. For example, we might prepare three different pro forma income statements, one using our "most-likely" assumption for the sales forecast, and one each for the "best-case" and "worst-case" scenarios. In some situations, a change in the sales forecast can have a dramatic effect on net income and cash flows. Sensitivity analysis helps to identify these effects before a decision is made so that costly mistakes can be avoided.

It is also important to remember that these statements are predictions about the future and, as such, are bound to be wrong. That is, we expect that there will be **forecast errors**—differences between the forecasted and the actual amounts. The goal of a good forecast is accuracy, which means that we want the forecast errors to be as small as possible. Generating pro forma statements using a computer is relatively easy and the efficiency and precision of spreadsheet software can provide a false sense of confidence in the numbers. Spreadsheets routinely calculate forecasted amounts to the "nth" decimal place whether or not such precision is justified. However, an amount forecasted to the nearest penny may not be useful if the forecast is off by millions of dollars. It is better to be imprecisely accurate than to be precisely inaccurate.

EXHIBIT 5B.3	PepsiCo Pro Forma Cash Flow Statement

PEPSICO, INC.
2015 Pro Forma Cash Flow Statement

($ millions)	Pro forma 2015
Operations:	
Net income.	$6,814
Adjustments:	
Depreciation and amortization ($69,084 × 3.94%)	2,722
Minus change in accounts and notes receivable	(237)
Minus change in inventories	(111)
Minus change in prepaid expenses and other current assets	(75)
Minus change in other assets.	(31)
Plus change in accounts payable and other current liabilities	469
Plus change in other liabilities	204
Plus change in income taxes payable and deferred income taxes	188
Cash flow from operations	9,943
Investing activities:	
Investment in property, plant, and equipment, net and amortizable intangible assets	(3,393)
Cash used for investing activities.	(3,393)
Financing activities:	
Cash dividends paid	(3,877)
Share repurchases, net	(2,726)
Cash used for financing activities.	(6,603)
Net decrease in cash (10,785 − 4,534 − 3,423)	(53)
Cash and cash equivalents, 2014	6,134
Cash and cash equivalents, 2015	$6,081

APPENDIX 5B REVIEW

Refer to the income statements and balance sheets of the Coca-Cola Company presented in Mid-Chapter Review 1.

Required

Make the following assumptions:

- 2015 sales revenue is $50,000 million.
- Operating expenses increase in 2015 in proportion to sales revenue.
- Operating assets and liabilities increase based on their 2014 relation to sales revenue. Classify "Goodwill and other intangible assets," "Other assets," and "Other liabilities" as operating.
- Assume that nonoperating revenues, expenses, assets and liabilities do not change from 2014 to 2015.
- Dividend payout is 60% of net income.
- Assume 20% income tax rate.

Prepare a pro forma income statement and balance sheet for 2015.

The solution to this review problem can be found on pages 267–268.

SUMMARY

Prepare and analyze common-size financial statements. (p. 221)   **LO1**

- Vertical analysis restates items in the income statement as a percentage of sales revenue and items in the balance sheet as a percentage of total assets.
- Horizontal analysis examines the percentage change from one year to the next for specific items in the income statement and balance sheet.

LO2   **Compute and interpret measures of return on investment, including return on equity (ROE), return on assets (ROA), and return on financial leverage (ROFL). (p. 224)**

- ROE is the primary measure of company performance. It captures the return earned by shareholder investment in the firm.
- ROA measures the return earned on the firm's investment in assets. It is not affected by the way those assets are financed.
- ROFL is the difference between ROE and ROA and measures the effect that financial leverage has on ROE.

LO3   **Disaggregate ROA into profitability (profit margin) and efficiency (asset turnover) components. (p. 227)**

- ROA can be disaggregated as the product of profit margin (PM) and asset turnover (AT).
- PM can be analyzed further by examining the gross profit margin and expense-to-sales ratios.
- AT can be analyzed further by examining accounts receivable turnover (ART), inventory turnover (INVT), and property, plant, and equipment turnover (PPET).
- The trade-off between PM and AT is determined by the company's strategy and its competitive environment.

LO4   **Compute and interpret measures of liquidity and solvency. (p. 232)**

- The current ratio (CR) and quick ratio (QR) measure short-term liquidity by comparing liquid assets to short-term obligations.
- The debt-to-equity ratio (D/E) and times interest earned ratio (TIE) measure long-term solvency by comparing sources of financing and the level of earnings to the cost of debt (interest).

LO5   **Appendix 5A: Measure and analyze the effect of operating activities on ROE. (p. 240)**

- Net operating profit after taxes (NOPAT) measures the portion of income that results from a business' core operating activities.
- Return on net operating assets (RNOA), defined as NOPAT/average net operating assets, measures the return on a company's net investment in operating assets.

LO6   **Appendix 5B: Prepare *pro forma* financial statements. (p. 242)**

- *Pro forma* financial statements are statements prepared for future periods based on assumptions about the future activities of the business.
- *Pro forma* statements can be used to evaluate the effects of alternative actions or assumptions on the financial statements.

KEY RATIOS

RETURN MEASURES

$$\text{Return on equity (ROE)} = \frac{\text{Net income}}{\text{Average stockholders' equity}}$$

$$\text{Earnings without interest expense (EWI)} = \text{Net income} + [\text{Interest expense} \times (1 - \text{Statutory tax rate})]$$

$$\text{Return on assets (ROA)} = \frac{\text{Earnings without interest expense (EWI)}}{\text{Average total assets}}$$

$$\text{Return on financial leverage (ROFL)} = \text{ROE} - \text{ROA}$$

PROFITABILITY RATIOS

$$\text{Profit margin (PM)} = \frac{\text{Earnings without interest expense (EWI)}}{\text{Sales revenue}}$$

$$\text{Gross profit margin (GPM)} = \frac{\text{Sales revenue} - \text{Cost of goods sold}}{\text{Sales revenue}}$$

$$\text{Expense-to-sales (ETS)} = \frac{\text{Individual expense items}}{\text{Sales revenue}}$$

TURNOVER RATIOS

$$\text{Asset turnover (AT)} = \frac{\text{Sales revenue}}{\text{Average total assets}}$$

$$\text{Accounts receivable turnover (ART)} = \frac{\text{Sales revenue}}{\text{Average accounts receivable}}$$

$$\text{Inventory turnover (INVT)} = \frac{\text{Cost of goods sold}}{\text{Average inventory}}$$

$$\text{Property, plant, and equipment turnover (PPET)} = \frac{\text{Sales revenue}}{\text{Average PP \& E}}$$

LIQUIDITY RATIOS

$$\text{Current ratio (CR)} = \frac{\text{Current assets}}{\text{Current liabilities}}$$

$$\text{Quick ratio (QR)} = \frac{\text{Cash + Short-term securities + Accounts receivable}}{\text{Current liabilities}}$$

$$\text{Operating cash flow to current liabilities (OCFCL)} = \frac{\text{Operating cash flow}}{\text{Average current liabilities}}$$

SOLVENCY RATIOS

$$\text{Times interest earned (TIE)} = \frac{\text{Earnings before interest expense and taxes (EBIT)}}{\text{Interest expense}}$$

$$\text{Debt-to-equity (DE)} = \frac{\text{Total liabilities}}{\text{Total stockholders' equity}}$$

KEY TERMS

Accounts receivable turnover (ART) (p. 231)

Asset turnover (AT) (p. 228)

Capacity costs (p. 228)

Common-size financial statements (p. 221)

Covenants (p. 234)

Current ratio (p. 235)

Debt-to-equity ratio (p. 237)

Default risk (p. 234)

Dividend payout ratio (p. 244)

Earnings without interest expense (EWI) (p. 225)

Effective tax rate (p. 244)

Expense-to-sales (ETS) (p. 231)

Financial leverage (p. 226)

Financial statement analysis (p. 220)

Forecast error (p. 246)

Gross profit margin (GPM) (p. 230)

Horizontal analysis (p. 223)

Inventory turnover (INVT) (p. 231)

Liquidity (p. 235)

Liquidity analysis (p. 235)

Marginal tax rate (p. 241)

Net operating assets (NOA) (p. 241)

Net operating asset turnover (NOAT) (p. 242)

Net operating profit after taxes (NOPAT) (p. 241)

Net operating profit margin (NOPM) (p. 242)

Operating cash flow to current liabilities (OCFCL) (p. 236)

Profit margin (PM) (p. 227)

Pro forma financial statements (p. 243)

Property, plant, and equipment turnover (PPET) (p. 231)

Quick ratio (p. 235)

Return on assets (ROA) (p. 225)

Return on equity (ROE) (p. 225)

Return on financial leverage (ROFL) (p. 226)

Return on net operating assets (RNOA) (p. 240)

Sensitivity analysis (p. 246)

Solvency (p. 236)

Solvency analysis (p. 235)

Times interest earned (TIE) (p. 237)

Vertical analysis (p. 221)

Working capital (p. 235)

Assignments with the logo in the margin are available in BusinessCourse.
See the Preface of the book for details.

MULTIPLE CHOICE

1. Which of the following ratios would not be affected by an increase in cost of goods sold?
   a. ROA
   b. INVT
   c. Quick ratio
   d. PM

2. A company has the following values: PM = 0.07; EWI = $1,885; Average total assets = $37,400. AT equals
   a. 0.05
   b. 0.72
   c. 0.36
   d. AT is not determinable because its sales are not reported.

3. A company's current ratio is 2 and its quick ratio is 1. What can be said about the sum of the company's cash + marketable securities + accounts receivable?
   a. The sum exceeds the current liabilities.
   b. The sum is equal to the sum of the current liabilities.
   c. The sum is equal to 1/2 of the total current liabilities.
   d. None of the above is correct.

4. A company's interest expense is $500,000 and its net income is $14 million. If the company's effective tax rate is 30%, what is the company's times interest earned (TIE) ratio?
   a. 90
   b. 41
   c. 32
   d. 16

5. If a company's ROFL is negative, which of the following is *not* true?
   a. ROA > ROE
   b. The DE ratio is negative.
   c. ROA < net interest rate
   d. The company likely has a low TIE ratio.

GUIDANCE ANSWERS . . . YOU MAKE THE CALL

You are the Entrepreneur   Your company is performing substantially better than its competitors. Namely, your ROA of 16% is markedly superior to competitors' ROA of 10%. However, ROA disaggregation shows that this is mainly attributed to your AT of 0.89 versus competitors' AT of 0.59. Your PM of 18% is essentially identical to competitors' PM of 17%. Accordingly, you will want to maintain your AT as further improvements are probably difficult to achieve. Importantly, you are likely to achieve the greatest benefit with efforts at improving your PM of 18%, which is only marginally better than the industry norm of 17%.

Superscript [A(B)] denotes assignments based on Appendix 5A (5B).

QUESTIONS

Q5-1.   Explain in general terms the concept of return on investment. Why is this concept important in the analysis of financial performance?

Q5-2.   (a) Explain how an increase in financial leverage can increase a company's ROE. (b) Given the potentially positive relation between financial leverage and ROE, why don't we see companies with 100% financial leverage (entirely nonowner financed)?

Q5-3.   Gross profit margin [(Sales revenue − Cost of goods sold)/Sales revenue] is an important determinant of profit margin. Identify two factors that can cause gross profit margin to decline. Is a reduction in the gross profit margin always bad news? Explain.

Q5-4.   Explain how a reduction in operating expenses as a percentage of sales can produce a short-term gain at the cost of long-term performance.

Q5-5.   Describe the concept of asset turnover. What does the concept mean and why is it so important to understanding and interpreting financial performance?

Q5-6.   Explain what it means when a company's ROE exceeds its ROA.

Q5-7.   What are common-size financial statements? What role do they play in financial statement analysis?

Q5-8.   How does a firm go about increasing its AT ratio? What strategies are likely to be most effective?

Q5-9.[A]   What is meant by the term "net" in net operating assets (NOA)?

Q5-10.   Why is it important to disaggregate ROA into profit margin (PM) and asset turnover (AT)?

Q5-11.   What insights do we gain from the graphical relation between profit margin and asset turnover?

Q5-12.   Explain the concept of liquidity and why it is crucial to company survival.

Q5-13.   Identify at least two factors that limit the usefulness of ratio analysis.

MINI EXERCISES

M5-14.   Return on Investment, DuPont Analysis and Financial Leverage
The following table presents selected 2016 financial information for Sunder Company.

LO2

SUNDER COMPANY Selected 2016 Financial Data	
Balance Sheet:	
Average total assets.	$1,000,000
Average total liabilities	500,000
Average stockholders' equity.	500,000
Income statement:	
Sales revenue.	$1,000,000
Earnings before interest (net of tax)	20,000
Interest expense (net of tax).	15,000
Net income.	5,000

a.   Compute Sunder's ROE, ROA and ROFL for 2016.

b.   Use the DuPont analysis described in the Business Insight on page 230 to disaggregate ROE.

c.   How did the use of financial leverage affect Sunder's ROE in 2016? Explain.

M5-15.   Common-Size Balance Sheets
Following is the balance sheet for **Target Corporation**. Prepare Target's common-size balance sheets as of January 31, 2015 and February 1, 2014.

LO1

Target Corporation
NYSE :: TGT

($ millions)	January 31, 2015	February 1, 2014
Assets		
Cash and cash equivalents	$ 2,210	$ 670
Inventory.	8,790	8,278
Other current assets.	3,087	2,625
Total current assets.	14,087	11,573
Property and equipment, net	25,958	26,412
Other noncurrent assets.	1,359	6,568
Total assets.	$41,404	$44,553
Liabilities and shareholders' investment		
Accounts payable.	$ 7,759	$ 7,335
Accrued and other current liabilities.	3,886	4,299
Current portion of long-term debt and notes payable	91	1,143
Total current liabilities	11,736	12,777
Long-term debt	12,705	11,429
Deferred income taxes.	1,321	1,349
Other noncurrent liabilities	1,645	2,767
Total shareholders' investment.	13,997	16,231
Total liabilities and shareholders' investment.	$41,404	$44,553

LO1

Target Corporation
NYSE :: TGT

M5-16.   Common-Size Income Statements

Following is the income statement for **Target Corporation**. Prepare Target's common-size income statement for the fiscal year ended January 31, 2015.

($ millions)	Fiscal year ended January 31, 2015
Sales revenue.	$72,618
Cost of sales.	51,278
Selling, general and administrative expenses	14,676
Depreciation and amortization.	2,129
Earnings from continuing operations before interest and income taxes	4,535
Net interest expense	882
Earnings from continuing operations before income taxes	3,653
Provision for income taxes.	1,204
Net earnings from continuing operations.	2,449
Discontinued operations, net of tax.	(4,085)
Net earnings (loss)	$ (1,636)

LO2, 3

Target Corporation
NYSE :: TGT

M5-17.   Compute ROA, Profit Margin, and Asset Turnover

Refer to the financial information for **Target Corporation**, presented in M5-15 and M5-16.

a.   Compute its return on assets (ROA) for the fiscal year ending January 31, 2015. Compute two ROA measures, one using net earnings from continuing operations and one using net earnings.

b.   Disaggregate ROA into profit margin (PM) and asset turnover (AT). Confirm that ROA = PM × AT.

LO4

Target Corporation
NYSE :: TGT

M5-18.   Analysis and Interpretation of Liquidity and Solvency

Refer to the financial information of **Target Corporation** in M5-15 and M5-16 to answer the following.

a.   Compute Target's current ratio and quick ratio for January 2015 and February 2014. Comment on any observed trends.

b.   Compute Target's times interest earned for the year ended January 31, 2015, and its debt-to-equity ratios for January 2015 and February 2014. Comment on any trends observed.

c.   Summarize your findings in a conclusion about the company's liquidity and solvency. Do you have any concerns about Target's ability to meet its debt obligations?

LO1

3M Company
NYSE :: MMM

M5-19.   Common-Size Balance Sheets

Following is the balance sheet for **3M Company**. Prepare common-size balance sheets for 2014 and 2013.

3M COMPANY AND SUBSIDIARIES		
December 31 ($ millions, except per share amount)	2014	2013
Assets		
Cash, cash equivalents and marketable securities	$ 2,523	$ 3,337
Accounts receivable.	4,238	4,253
Total inventories.	3,706	3,864
Other current assets.	1,298	1,279
Total current assets	11,765	12,733
Investments.	930	1,575
Property, plant, and equipment—net.	8,489	8,652
Goodwill.	7,050	7,345
Intangible assets—net.	1,435	1,688
Other assets.	1,600	1,557
Total assets.	$31,269	$33,550

continued

continued from previous page

	2014	2013
Liabilities and Stockholders' Equity		
Short-term borrowings and current portion of long-term debt	$ 106	$ 1,683
Accounts payable	1,807	1,799
Accrued payroll	732	708
Accrued income taxes	435	417
Other current liabilities	2,918	2,891
Total current liabilities	5,998	7,498
Long-term debt	6,731	4,326
Other liabilities	5,398	3,778
Total liabilities	18,127	15,602
Stockholders' equity—net	13,142	17,948
Total liabilities and stockholders' equity	$31,269	$33,550

M5-20. Common-Size Income Statements

Following is the income statement for **3M Company**. Prepare common-size income statements for 2014 and 2013.

3M COMPANY AND SUBSIDIARIES		
Year ended December 31 ($ millions)	**2014**	**2013**
Net sales	$31,821	$30,871
Operating expenses		
Cost of sales	16,447	16,106
Selling, general and administrative expenses	6,469	6,384
Research, development and related expenses	1,770	1,715
Operating income	7,135	6,666
Interest expense and income		
Interest expense	142	145
Interest income	(33)	(41)
Net interest	109	104
Income before income taxes and minority interest	7,026	6,562
Provision for income taxes	2,028	1,841
Net income	$ 4,998	$ 4,721

M5-21. Compute ROA, Profit Margin, and Asset Turnover

Refer to the balance sheet and income statement information for **3M Company**, presented in M5-19 and M5-20.

a. Compute 3M's 2014 return on assets (ROA).

b. Disaggregate ROA into profit margin (PM) and asset turnover (AT). Confirm that ROA = PM × AT.

M5-22. Compute ROA, Profit Margin and Asset Turnover for Competitors

Selected balance sheet and income statement information from **Urban Outfitters, Inc.** and **TJX Companies**, clothing retailers in the high-end and value-priced segments, respectively, follows.

Company ($ millions)	2014 Sales	2014 Earnings Without Interest Expense (EWI)	2014 Total Assets	2013 Total Assets
Urban Outfitters	$ 3,323	$ 232.4	$ 1,889	$ 2,221
TJX Companies	29,078	2,241.0	11,128	10,201

a. Compute the 2014 return on assets (ROA) for both companies.

b. Disaggregate ROA into profit margin (PM) and asset turnover (AT) for each company. Confirm that ROA = PM × AT.

c. Discuss differences observed with respect to PM and AT and interpret these differences in light of each company's business model.

LO4

Verizon
Communications, Inc.
NYSE :: VZ

M5-23.   Compute and Interpret Liquidity and Solvency Ratios

Selected balance sheet and income statement information from **Verizon Communications, Inc.**, follows.

($ millions)	2014	2013
Current assets	$ 29,623	$ 70,994
Current liabilities	28,064	27,050
Total liabilities	219,032	178,682
Equity	13,676	95,416
Earnings before interest and taxes	20,185	31,944
Interest expense	4,915	2,667
Net cash flow from operating activities	30,631	38,818

a.   Compute the current ratio for each year and discuss any change in liquidity. How does Verizon's current ratio compare to the median for the telecommunications industry in **Exhibit 5.13**? What additional information about the numbers used to calculate this ratio might be useful in helping us assess liquidity? Explain.

b.   Compute times interest earned, the debt-to-equity, and the operating cash flow to current liabilities ratios for each year and discuss any trends for each. (In 2012, current liabilities totaled $26,956 million.) Compare Verizon's ratios to those that are typical for its industry (refer to **Exhibit 5.13**). Do you have any concerns about the extent of Verizon's financial leverage and the company's ability to meet interest obligations? Explain.

c.   Verizon's capital expenditures are expected to remain high as it seeks to respond to competitive pressures to upgrade the quality of its communication infrastructure. Assess Verizon's liquidity and solvency in light of this strategic direction.

LO2, 3

The Procter & Gamble
Company
NYSE :: PG

CVS Health Corporation
NYSE :: CVS

Valero Energy
Coporation
NYSE :: VLO

M5-24.   Computing Turnover Ratios for Companies in Different Industries

Selected data from recent financial statements of **The Procter & Gamble Company**, **CVS Health Corporation**, and **Valero Energy Corporation** are presented below:

($ millions)	Procter & Gamble	CVS Health	Valero Energy
Sales	$ 83,062	$139,367	$130,844
Cost of sales	42,460	114,000	118,141
Average receivables	6,447	9,208	7,315
Average inventories	6,834	11,488	6,191
Average PP&E	21,985	8,729	34,933
Average total assets	141,765	72,889	46,405

a.   Compute the asset turnover (AT) ratio for each company.

b.   Compute the accounts receivable turnover (ART), inventory turnover (INVT), and PP&E turnover (PPET) for each company.

c.   Discuss any differences across these three companies in the turnover ratios computed in a and b.

EXERCISES

LO2, 3

McDonald's Corporation
NYSE :: MCD

Yum! Brands, Inc.
NYSE :: YUM

E5-25.   Compute and Interpret ROA, Profit Margin, and Asset Turnover of Competitors

Selected balance sheet and income statement information for **McDonald's Corporation** and **Yum! Brands, Inc.**, follows.

($ millions)	Sales Revenue	Interest Expense	Net Income	Average Total Assets
McDonald's	$27,441	$571	$4,758	$35,454
Yum! Brands	13,279	130	1,021	8,520

a.   Compute the return on assets (ROA) for each company.

b.   Disaggregate ROA into profit margin (PM) and asset turnover (AT) for each company.

c.   Discuss any differences in these ratios for each company. Your interpretation should reflect the distinct business strategies of each company.

E5-26. **Compute ROA, ROE and ROFL and Interpret the Effects of Leverage**

LO2

Basic income statement and balance sheet information is given below for six different cases. For each case, the assets are financed with a mix of non-interest-bearing liabilities, 10% interest-bearing liability and stockholders' equity. In all cases, the income tax rate is 40%.

Case	A	B	C	D	E	F
Average assets	1,000	1,000	1,000	1,000	1,000	1,000
Non-interest-bearing liabilities	0	0	0	0	200	200
Interest-bearing liabilities	0	250	500	500	0	300
Average shareholders' equity	1,000	750	500	500	800	500
Earnings before interest and taxes (EBIT)	120	120	120	80	100	80

a. For each case, calculate the return on equity (ROE), return on assets (ROA) and return on financial leverage (ROFL).

b. Consider cases A, B and C. How does increasing leverage affect the three ratios? Why does the ROE grow from case A to case C?

c. Consider cases C and D. When does leverage work in favor of shareholders? Does that hold for case E?

d. Case F has two types of liabilities. How does ROA compare to the rate on interest-bearing liabilities? Does leverage work in favor of the shareholders? Why?

E5-27. **Compute, Disaggregate, and Interpret Competitors' Rates of Return**

LO2, 3

Selected balance sheet and income statement information for the drug retailers **CVS Health Corporation** and **Walgreen Co.** follows.

CVS Health Corporation
NYSE :: CVS
Walgreen Co.
NYSE :: WAG

($ millions)	CVS Health	Walgreen
Sales revenue—2014	$139,367	$76,392
Interest expense—2014	600	156
Net income—2014	4,644	2,031
Total assets—2014	74,252	37,182
Total assets—2013	71,526	35,481
Stockholders' equity—2014	37,963	20,561
Stockholders' equity—2013	37,938	19,454

a. Compute the 2014 return on assets (ROA) for each company.

b. Disaggregate ROA into profit margin (PM) and asset turnover (AT) for each company.

c. Compute the 2014 return on equity (ROE) and return on financial leverage (ROFL) for each company.

d. Discuss any differences in these ratios for each company. Identify the factor(s) that drives the differences in ROA observed from your analyses in parts *a* through *c*.

E5-28. **Compute, Disaggregate, and Interpret ROE**

LO2, 3

Selected fiscal year balance sheet and income statement information for the computer chip maker, **Intel Corporation**, follows ($ millions).

Intel Corporation
NASDAQ :: INTC

Balance sheet information ($ millions)	2014	2013	2012
Total assets	$91,956	$92,358	$84,351
Total shareholders' equity	55,865	58,256	51,203

Income statement information ($ millions)	2014	2013	2012
Sales revenue	$55,870	$52,708	$53,341
Interest expense	192	244	90
Net income	11,704	9,620	11,005

a. Calculate Intel's return on equity (ROE) for fiscal years 2014 and 2013.

b. Calculate Intel's return on assets (ROA) and return on financial leverage (ROFL) for each year. Is financial leverage working to the advantage of Intel's shareholders?

c. Use the DuPont formulation in the Business Insight on page 230 to analyze the variations in Intel's ROE over this period. How does this analysis differ from your answers to *a* and *b* above?

LO2, 3 **E5-29. Return on Investment, Financial Leverage, and DuPont Analysis**

The following tables provide information from the recent annual reports of HD Rinker, AG.

Balance sheets (€ millions)	2016	2015	2014	2013
Total assets..........................	€6,108	€6,451	€7,173	€6,972
Total liabilities.......................	5,970	4,974	4,989	5,097
Total shareholders' equity	138	1,477	2,184	1,875

Income statements (€ millions) 52 weeks ended	2016	2015	2014
Sales revenue......................................	€10,364	€9,613	€8,632
Earnings before interest and income taxes	1,473	1,459	887
Interest expense....................................	246	208	237
Earnings before income taxes	1,227	1,251	650
Income tax expense.................................	377	446	202
Net earnings......................................	€ 850	€ 805	€ 448

  a. Calculate HD Rinker's return on equity (ROE) for fiscal years 2016, 2015, and 2014.

  b. Calculate HD Rinker's return on assets (ROA) and return on financial leverage (ROFL) for each year. Is financial leverage working to the advantage of HD Rinker's shareholders?

  c. Use the DuPont formulation in the Business Insight on page 230 to analyze the variations in HD Rinker's ROE over this period. How does this analysis differ from your answers to *a* and *b* above?

LO2, 3 **E5-30. Compute, Disaggregate and Interpret ROE and ROA**

Staples, Inc.
NASDAQ :: SPLS

Selected balance sheet and income statement information from **Staples, Inc.**, follows ($ millions).

Sales	Interest Expense	Net Income	Total Assets		Stockholders' Equity	
2014	2014	2014	2014	2013	2014	2013
$22,492	$49	$135	$10,314	$11,175	$5,313	$6,141

  a. Compute the 2014 return on equity (ROE), return on assets (ROA), and return on financial leverage (ROFL).

  b. Disaggregate ROA into profit margin (PM) and asset turnover (AT).

  c. What inferences do we draw from PM compared to AT? How do these ratios compare to industry medians?

LO2, 3 **E5-31. Compute, Disaggregate and Interpret ROE and ROA**

Intuit Inc.
NASDAQ :: INTU

Selected balance sheet and income statement information from the software company, **Intuit Inc.**, follows ($ millions).

Sales	Interest Expense	Net Income	Total Assets		Stockholders' Equity	
2014	2014	2014	2014	2013	2014	2013
$4,506	$31	$907	$5,201	$5,486	$3,078	$3,531

  a. Compute the 2014 return on equity (ROE), return on assets (ROA), and return on financial leverage (ROFL).

  b. Disaggregate the ROA from part *a* into profit margin (PM) and asset turnover (AT).

  c. What can we learn by comparing PM to AT? What explanation can we offer for the relation between ROE and ROA observed and for Intuit's use of financial leverage?

LO4 **E5-32. Compute and Interpret Liquidity and Solvency Ratios**

Comcast Corporation
NASDAQ :: CMCSA

Selected balance sheet and income statement information from **Comcast Corporation** for 2012 through 2014 follows ($ millions).

	Total Current Assets	Total Current Liabilities	Pretax Income	Interest Expense	Total Assets	Stockholders' Equity
2012	$19,991	$16,714	$11,609	$2,521	$164,971	$49,796
2013	14,075	18,912	11,115	2,574	158,813	51,058
2014	13,531	17,410	12,465	2,617	159,339	53,068

a. Compute the current ratio for each year and discuss any trend in liquidity. Do you believe the company is sufficiently liquid? Explain. What additional information about the accounting numbers comprising this ratio might be useful in helping you assess liquidity? Explain.

b. Compute times interest earned and the debt-to-equity ratio for each year and discuss any trends for each.

c. How do Comcast's ratios compare to the industry medians for the telecommunications industry in **Exhibit 5.13**?

d. What is your overall assessment of the company's liquidity and solvency from the analyses above? Explain.

E5-33. Compute and Interpret Liquidity and Solvency Ratios

Selected balance sheet and income statement information from **Siemens, AG**, for 2012 through 2014 follows (€ millions).

LO4

Siemens AG
NYSE :: SI

	Total Current Assets	Total Current Liabilities	Cash Flow from Operations	Pretax Income	Interest Expense	Total Liabilities	Stockholders' Equity
2012	€52,128	€42,627	€6,923	€6,636	€760	€77,396	€30,855
2013	46,937	37,868	7,186	5,813	784	73,825	28,111
2014	48,076	36,598	7,230	7,427	764	73,925	30,954

a. Compute the current ratio for each year and discuss any trend in liquidity. Also compute the operating cash flow to current liabilities (OCFCL) ratio for each year. (In 2011, current liabilities totaled €43,560 million.) Do you believe the company is sufficiently liquid? Explain. What additional information about the accounting numbers comprising this ratio might be useful in helping you assess liquidity? Explain.

b. Compute times interest earned and the debt-to-equity ratio for each year and discuss any trends for each.

c. What is your overall assessment of the company's liquidity and solvency from the analyses in a and b? Explain.

E5-34. Compute, Disaggregate and Interpret ROE and ROA

Income statements for **The Gap, Inc.**, follow, along with selected balance sheet information ($ millions).

LO2, 3

The Gap, Inc.
NYSE :: GPS

THE GAP, INC. Consolidated Statement of Earnings		
Fiscal year ended	**Jan. 31, 2015**	**Feb. 1, 2014**
Net sales.	$16,435	$16,148
Cost of goods sold and occupancy expenses.	10,146	9,855
Gross profit.	6,289	6,293
Operating expenses.	4,206	4,144
Operating income.	2,083	2,149
Interest expense.	75	61
Interest income.	(5)	(5)
Income before income taxes	2,013	2,093
Income taxes	751	813
Net earnings.	$1,262	$1,280

THE GAP, INC. Selected Balance Sheet Data		
	Jan. 31, 2015	**Feb. 1, 2014**
Merchandise inventories	$1,889	$1,928
Total assets.	7,690	7,849
Total stockholders' equity	2,983	3,062

a. Compute the return on equity (ROE), return on assets (ROA), and return on financial leverage (ROFL) for the fiscal year ended January 31, 2015.

b. Disaggregate ROA into profit margin (PM) and asset turnover (AT).

c. Compute the gross profit margin (GPM) and inventory turnover (INVT) ratios for the fiscal year ended January 31, 2015.

d. Assess the Gap's performance. What are the most important drivers of the Gap's success?

LO1, 6   **E5-35.**[B] **Common-Size and Pro Forma Income Statements**

The Gap, Inc.
NYSE :: GPS

Refer to the income statements for **The Gap, Inc.**, presented in E5-34.

a. Prepare common-size income statements for fiscal years 2014 (ending January 31, 2015) and 2013 (ending February 1, 2014).

b. Prepare a pro forma income statement for the fiscal year 2015 (ending January 30, 2016), based on the following assumptions:

- Net sales total $15,000 million.
- Cost of goods sold and occupancy expenses are 64% of sales.
- Operating expenses total 26% of sales.
- Interest income and interest expense are unchanged from the 2014 amounts.
- The Gap's effective tax rate is 39%.

c. Given the Gap's business strategy, what are the factors that ultimately determine the accuracy of the pro forma statement prepared in *b*?

PROBLEMS

LO2, 3   **P5-36.**   **Analysis and Interpretation of Return on Investment for Competitors**

Nike, Inc.
NYSE :: NKE

Adidas Group, AG
OTC :: ADDDF

Balance sheets and income statements for **Nike, Inc.**, and **Adidas Group** follow. Refer to these financial statements to answer the requirements.

	NIKE, INC. Balance Sheets ($ millions) May 31,		ADIDAS GROUP, AG Balance Sheets (€ millions) December 31,	
	2014	2013	2014	2013
Assets				
Cash and cash equivalents	$ 2,220	$ 3,337	€ 1,683	€ 1,587
Short-term investments	2,922	2,628	403	224
Accounts receivable	3,434	3,117	1,946	1,809
Inventories	3,947	3,484	2,526	2,634
Other current assets	1,173	1,064	789	603
Total current assets	13,696	13,630	7,347	6,857
Property, plant, and equipment	2,834	2,452	1,454	1,238
Intangible assets and goodwill	413	420	2,763	2,787
Long-term investments	—	—	171	150
Other noncurrent assets	1,651	1,043	682	567
Total assets	$18,594	$17,545	€12,417	€11,599
Liabilities and shareholders' equity				
Short-term debt	$ 174	$ 155	€ 288	€ 681
Accounts payable	1,930	1,669	1,652	1,825
Accrued expenses	2,491	2,036	1,249	1,147
Income taxes payable	432	84	294	240
Other current liabilities	—	18	894	839
Total current liabilities	5,027	3,962	4,378	4,732
Long-term debt	1,199	1,210	1,584	653
Other noncurrent liabilities	1,544	1,292	837	733
Total liabilities	7,770	6,464	6,799	6,118
Shareholders' equity	10,824	11,081	5,618	5,481
Total liabilities and shareholders' equity	$18,594	$17,545	€12,417	€11,599

	NIKE, INC. Income Sheets ($ millions) Year ended May 31,		ADIDAS GROUP, AG Income Sheets (€ millions) Year ended December 31,	
	2014	**2013**	**2014**	**2013**
Net sales.	$27,799	$25,313	€14,534	€14,203
Cost of sales.	15,353	14,279	7,610	7,202
Gross profit.	12,446	11,034	6,924	7,001
Operating expenses, net	8,766	7,796	6,041	5,820
Operating profit	3,680	3,238	883	1,181
Interest and other income (expense)	(83)	38	19	26
Interest expense.	53	20	67	94
Income before income taxes	3,544	3,256	835	1,113
Income taxes	851	805	271	340
Income from continuing operations	2,693	2,451	564	773
Gain (loss) from discontinued operations.	—	21	(68)	17
Net income.	$ 2,693	$ 2,472	€ 496	€ 790

REQUIRED

a. Compute return on equity (ROE), return on assets (ROA), and return on financial leverage (ROFL) for Nike and Adidas in 2014. The corporate tax rate in Germany, where Adidas is headquartered, is about 30%.

b. Disaggregate the ROA's computed into profit margin (PM) and asset turnover (AT) components. Which of these factors drives ROA for each company?

c. Compute the gross profit margin (GPM) and operating expense-to-sales ratios for each company. How do these companies' profitability measures compare?

d. Compute the accounts receivable turnover (ART), inventory turnover (INVT), and property, plant, and equipment turnover (PPET) for each company. How do these companies' turnover measures compare?

e. Nike's fiscal year ends on May 31, 2014, while Adidas's fiscal year ends on December 31, 2014 (a difference of seven months). How does this difference affect your analysis of ROE and ROA for these two companies?

f. Nike's financial statements are prepared in accordance with U.S. GAAP, while Adidas, a German company, follows IFRS rules. How does this difference in financial reporting standards affect your comparison of these companies' financial statements?

P5-37. Analysis and Interpretation of Liquidity and Solvency for Competitors

Refer to the financial statements of **Nike** and **Adidas** presented in P5-36.

REQUIRED

a. Compute each company's current ratio and quick ratio for each year. Comment on any changes that you observe.

b. Compute each company's times interest earned ratio and debt-to-equity ratio for each year. Comment on any observed changes.

c. Compare these two companies on the basis of liquidity and solvency. Do you have any concerns about either company's ability to meet its debt obligations?

P5-38. Analysis and Interpretation of Return on Investment for Competitors

Balance sheets and income statements for **The Home Depot, Inc.**, and **Lowe's Companies, Inc.**, follow. Refer to these financial statements to answer the requirements.

LO4
Nike, Inc.
NYSE :: NKE
Adidas Group, AG
OTC :: ADDDF

LO2, 3
The Home Depot, Inc.
NYSE :: HD
Lowe's Companies, Inc.
NYSE :: LOW

($ millions)	HOME DEPOT, INC. Balance Sheets		LOWE'S COMPANIES Balance Sheets	
	2014	2013	2014	2013
Assets				
Cash and cash equivalents	$ 1,723	$ 1,929	$ 466	$ 391
Short-term investments	—	—	125	185
Receivables, net	1,484	1,398		
Merchandise inventories	11,079	11,057	8,911	9,127
Other current assets	1,016	895	578	593
Total current assets	15,302	15,279	10,080	10,296
Property and equipment, net	22,720	23,348	20,034	20,834
Goodwill	1,353	1,289	—	—
Long-term investments	—	—	354	279
Other assets	571	602	1,359	1,323
Total assets	$39,946	$40,518	$31,827	$32,732
Liabilities and shareholders' equity				
Short-term debt and current maturities of long-term debt	$ 328	$ 33	$ 552	$ 435
Accounts payable	5,807	5,797	5,124	5,008
Accrued compensation and related expenses	1,391	1,428	773	785
Deferred revenue	1,468	1,337	979	892
Income taxes payable	35	12	—	—
Other current liabilities	2,240	2,142	1,920	1,756
Total current liabilities	11,269	10,749	9,348	8,876
Long-term debt, excluding current maturities	16,869	14,691	10,815	10,086
Deferred income taxes	642	514	97	291
Other long-term liabilities	1,844	2,042	1,599	1,626
Total liabilities	30,624	27,996	21,859	20,879
Total stockholders' equity	9,322	12,522	9,968	11,853
Total liabilities and shareholders' equity	$39,946	$40,518	$31,827	$32,732

($ millions)	HOME DEPOT, INC. Income Statements		LOWE'S COMPANIES Income Statements	
	2014	2013	2014	2013
Net sales	$83,176	$78,812	$56,223	$53,417
Cost of sales	54,222	51,422	36,665	34,941
Gross profit	28,954	27,390	19,558	18,476
Selling, general and administrative	16,834	16,597	13,281	12,865
Depreciation and amortization	1,651	1,627	1,485	1,462
Operating income	10,469	9,166	4,792	4,149
Investment and other income	337	12	6	4
Interest expense	830	711	522	480
Earnings before income taxes	9,976	8,467	4,276	3,673
Provision for income taxes	3,631	3,082	1,578	1,387
Net earnings	$ 6,345	$ 5,385	$ 2,698	$ 2,286

REQUIRED

a. Compute return on equity (ROE), return on assets (ROA), and return on financial leverage (ROFL) for each company in 2014.

b. Disaggregate the ROA's computed into profit margin (PM) and asset turnover (AT) components. Which of these factors drives ROA for each company?

c. Compute the gross profit margin (GPM) and operating expense-to-sales ratios for each company. How do these companies' profitability measures compare?

    d. Compute the accounts receivable turnover (ART), inventory turnover (INVT), and property, plant, and equipment turnover (PPET) for each company. How do these companies' turnover measures compare?

    e. Compare and evaluate these competitors' performance in 2014.

P5-39. Analysis and Interpretation of Liquidity and Solvency for Competitors

Refer to the financial statements of **Home Depot** and **Lowe's** presented in P5-38.

LO4
Home Depot, Inc.
NYSE :: HD
Lowe's Companies, Inc.
NYSE :: LOW

REQUIRED

    a. Compute each company's current ratio and quick ratio for each year. Comment on any changes that you observe.

    b. Compute each company's times interest earned ratio and debt-to-equity ratio for each year. Comment on any observed changes.

    c. Compare these two companies on the basis of liquidity and solvency. Do you have any concerns about either company's ability to meet its debt obligations?

P5-40.ᴬ Analysis of the Effect of Operations on ROE

Refer to the financial statements of **Home Depot** and **Lowe's** presented in P5-38.

LO5
Home Depot, Inc.
NYSE :: HD
Lowe's Companies, Inc.
NYSE :: LOW

REQUIRED

    a. Compute each company's net operating profit after taxes (NOPAT) for 2014 and net operating assets (NOA) for 2014 and 2013. Classify other assets and other liabilities (both current and noncurrent) as operating assets and liabilities in the balance sheet.

    b. Compute each company's return on net operating assets (RNOA) for 2014.

    c. Compute the 2014 net operating profit margin (NOPM) and net operating asset turnover (NOAT) for each company.

    d. Compare operating returns for these two companies. How does RNOA compare to ROA? What insights are gained by focusing on operating returns?

P5-41. Analysis and Interpretation of Profitability

Balance sheets and income statements for **United Parcel Service, Inc., (UPS)** follow. Refer to these financial statements to answer the following requirements.

LO2, 3
United Parcel Service, Inc.
NYSE :: UPS

UNITED PARCEL SERVICE, INC. Income Statement			
Years Ended December 31 ($ millions)	**2014**	**2013**	**2012**
Revenue...	$58,232	$55,438	$54,127
Compensation and benefits	32,045	28,557	33,102
Other operating expenses	21,219	19,847	19,682
Operating profit	4,968	7,034	1,343
Investment income....................................	22	20	24
Interest expense......................................	353	380	393
Income before income taxes	4,637	6,674	974
Income tax expense...................................	1,605	2,302	167
Net income...	$ 3,032	$ 4,372	$ 807

UNITED PARCEL SERVICE, INC. Balance Sheet			
December 31 ($ millions)	2014	2013	2012
Assets			
Cash and cash equivalents	$ 2,291	$ 4,665	$ 7,327
Marketable securities	992	580	597
Accounts receivable, net	6,661	6,502	6,111
Deferred income tax assets	590	684	583
Other current assets	1,274	956	973
Total current assets	11,808	13,387	15,591
Property, plant & equipment, net	18,281	17,961	17,894
Goodwill and other intangible assets, net	3,031	2,965	2,776
Noncurrent investments and restricted cash	489	444	307
Other noncurrent assets	1,862	1,455	2,295
Total assets	$35,471	$36,212	$38,863
Liabilities and shareowners' equity			
Current maturities of long-term debt and commercial paper	$ 923	$ 48	$ 1,781
Accounts payable	2,754	2,478	2,278
Accrued wages and withholdings	2,373	2,325	1,927
Self-insurance reserves, current portion	656	719	763
Other current liabilities	1,933	1,561	1,641
Total current liabilities	8,639	7,131	8,390
Long-term debt	9,864	10,824	11,089
Pension and postretirement benefit obligations	11,452	7,051	11,068
Deferred income tax liabilities	83	1,244	48
Self-insurance reserves	1,916	2,059	1,980
Other noncurrent liabilities	1,359	1,415	1,555
Total liabilities	33,313	29,724	34,130
Total shareowners' equity	2,158	6,488	4,733
Total liabilities and shareowners' equity	$35,471	$36,212	$38,863

REQUIRED

a. Compute ROA and disaggregate it into profit margin (PM) and asset turnover (AT) for 2014 and 2013. Comment on the drivers of the ROA.

b. Compute any expense to sales (ETS) ratios that you think might help explain UPS's profitability.

c. Compute return on equity (ROE) for 2014 and 2013.

d. Comment on the difference between ROE and ROA. What does this relation suggest about UPS's use of debt?

LO4
United Parcel Service
NYSE :: UPS

P5-42. **Analysis and Interpretation of Liquidity and Solvency**

Refer to the financial information of **United Parcel Service** in P5-41 to answer the following requirements.

REQUIRED

a. Compute its current ratio and quick ratio for 2014 and 2013. Comment on any observed trends.

b. Compute its times interest earned and its debt-to-equity ratios for 2014 and 2013. Comment on any trends observed.

c. Summarize your findings in a conclusion about the company's liquidity and solvency. Do you have any concerns about its ability to meet its debt obligations?

LO5
United Parcel Service
NYSE :: UPS

P5-43.[A] **Computing and Analyzing Operating Returns**

Refer to the financial statements of **United Parcel Service** in P5-41 to answer the following requirements.

REQUIRED

a. Compute net operating profit after taxes (NOPAT) for 2014 and net operating assets (NOA) for 2013 and 2014.

b. Compute the return on net operating assets (RNOA) for 2014. What percentage of UPS's ROE is generated by operations?

c. Decompose RNOA by computing net operating profit margin (NOPM) and net operating asset turnover (NOAT) for 2014.

d. What can be inferred about UPS from these ratios?

P5-44.[B] **Preparing Pro Forma Financial Statements**

Refer to the financial statements of **United Parcel Service** in P5-41 to answer the following requirements. The following assumptions should be useful:

- UPS's sales forecast for 2015 is $60,000 million.
- Operating expenses and operating profits increase in proportion to sales.
- Investment income and interest expense are unchanged in 2015.
- Income taxes are 35% of pretax earnings.
- Marketable securities and noncurrent investments are unchanged in 2015; all other assets (except cash) increase in proportion to sales.
- Long-term debt and current maturities of long-term debt are unchanged in 2015; all other liabilities increase in proportion to sales.
- Dividends are 50% of net income. Income and dividends are the only changes to stockholders' equity in 2015.

REQUIRED

a. Prepare a pro forma income statement for 2015.

b. Prepare a pro forma balance sheet for 2015.

LO6

United Parcel Service
NYSE :: UPS

P5-45. **Comparing Profitability Ratios for Competitors**

Selected income statement data for **Abbott Laboratories**, **Bristol-Myers Squibb Company**, **Johnson & Johnson**, **GlaxoSmithKline plc**, and **Pfizer, Inc.** is presented in the following table:

LO3

Abbott Laboratories
NYSE :: ABT
Bristol-Myers Squibb
Company
NYSE :: BMY
Johnson & Johnson
NYSE :: JNJ
GlaxoSmithKline plc
(ADR)
NYSE :: GSK
Pfizer Inc.
NYSE :: PFE

($ millions)	Abbott Laboratories	Bristol-Myers Squibb	Johnson & Johnson	Glaxo Smith Kline plc	Pfizer
Sales revenue	$20,247	$11,660	$74,331	$35,872	$49,605
Cost of sales	9,218	3,932	22,746	11,418	9,577
SG&A expense	6,530	4,822	21,954	13,466	14,097
R&D expense	1,345	4,534	8,494	5,379	8,393
Interest expense	150	203	533	1,134	1,360
Net income	2,284	2,029	16,323	4,297	9,168

REQUIRED

a. Compute the profit margin (PM) and gross profit margin (GPM) ratios for each company. (As a British company, GlaxoSmithKline plc has a statutory tax rate of 26.5% in 2014.)

b. Compute the research and development (R&D) expense to sales ratio and the selling, general and administrative (SG&A) expense to sales ratio for each company.

c. Compare the relative profitability of these pharmaceutical companies.

P5-46. **Comparing Profitability and Turnover Ratios for Retail Companies**

Selected financial statement data for **Best Buy Co., Inc.**, **The Kroger Co.**, **Nordstrom, Inc.**, **Staples, Inc.**, and **Walgreen Co.** is presented in the following table:

LO3

Best Buy Co., Inc.
NYSE :: BBY
The Kroger Co.
NYSE :: KR
Nordstrom, Inc.
NYSE :: JWN
Staples, Inc.
NASDAQ :: SPLS
Walgreen Co.
NYSE :: WAG

($ millions)	Best Buy	Kroger	Nordstrom	Staples	Walgreen
Sales revenue	$40,339	$108,465	$13,506	$22,492	$76,392
Cost of sales	31,292	85,512	8,406	16,691	54,823
Interest expense	90	488	138	49	156
Net income	1,233	1,728	720	135	1,932
Average receivables	1,294	1,191	2,489	1,883	2,925
Average inventories	5,275	5,670	1,632	2,236	6,464
Average PP&E	2,447	17,403	3,145	1,788	12,198
Average total assets	14,635	29,919	8,910	10,744	36,332

REQUIRED

a. Compute return on assets (ROA) profit margin (PM) and asset turnover (AT) for each company. Discuss the relative importance of PM and AT for each company.

b. Compute accounts receivable turnover (ART), inventory turnover (INVT) and property, plant, and equipment turnover (PPET) for each company. Discuss any difference that you observe.

c. Compute the gross profit margin (GPM) for each company. How does the GPM differ across companies? Does this difference seem to correlate with differences in ART or INVT? Explain.

CASES AND PROJECTS

LO3 **C5-47.** **Management Application: Gross Profit and Strategic Management**

One way to increase overall profitability is to increase gross profit. This can be accomplished by raising prices and/or by reducing manufacturing costs.

REQUIRED

a. Will raising prices and/or reducing manufacturing costs unambiguously increase gross profit? Explain.

b. What strategy might you develop as a manager to (i) yield a price increase for your product, or (ii) reduce product manufacturing cost?

LO3 **C5-48.** **Management Application: Asset Turnover and Strategic Management**

Increasing net operating asset turnover requires some combination of increasing sales and/or decreasing net operating assets. For the latter, many companies consider ways to reduce their investment in working capital (current assets less current liabilities). This can be accomplished by reducing the level of accounts receivable and inventories, or by increasing the level of accounts payable.

REQUIRED

a. Develop a list of suggested actions to achieve all three of these objectives as manager.

b. Examine the implications of each. That is, describe the marketing implications of reducing receivables and inventories, and the supplier implications of delaying payment. How can a company achieve working capital reduction without negatively impacting its performance?

LO2, 3, 4 **C5-49.** **Ethics and Governance: Earnings Management**

Companies are aware that analysts focus on profitability in evaluating financial performance. Managers have historically utilized a number of methods to improve reported profitability that are cosmetic in nature and do not affect "real" operating performance. These are typically subsumed under the general heading of "earnings management." Justification for such actions typically includes the following arguments:

- Increasing stock price by managing earnings benefits shareholders; thus, no one is hurt by these actions.

- Earnings management is a temporary fix; such actions will be curtailed once "real" profitability improves, as managers expect.

REQUIRED

a. Identify the affected parties in any scheme to manage profits to prop up stock price.

b. Do the ends (of earnings management) justify the means? Explain.

c. To what extent are the objectives of managers different from those of shareholders?

d. What governance structure can you envision that might prohibit earnings management?

SOLUTIONS TO REVIEW PROBLEMS

Mid-Chapter Review 1

SOLUTION

THE COCA-COLA COMPANY AND SUBSIDIARIES
Consolidated Statements of Income
($ millions)

Year ended December 31	2014	2013
Net operating revenues	100.0%	100.0%
Cost of goods sold	38.9%	39.3%
Gross profit	61.1%	60.7%
Selling, general and administrative expenses	37.4%	36.9%
Other operating charges	2.6%	1.9%
Operating income	21.1%	21.8%
Interest income	1.3%	1.1%
Interest expense	−1.1%	−1.0%
Other income (loss)—net	−1.1%	2.5%
Income before income taxes	20.3%	24.5%
Income taxes	4.8%	6.1%
Net income	15.5%	18.4%

THE COCA-COLA COMPANY AND SUBSIDIARIES
Common Size Balance Sheets

December 31,	2014	2013
Assets		
Cash and cash equivalents	9.7%	11.6%
Short-term investments and marketable securities	13.8%	10.9%
Trade accounts receivable	4.9%	5.4%
Inventories	3.4%	3.6%
Prepaid expenses and other current assets	4.1%	3.2%
Total current assets	35.8%	34.8%
Investments	14.8%	12.8%
Property, plant, and equipment, net	15.9%	16.6%
Goodwill and other intangible assets	28.7%	30.7%
Other assets	4.8%	5.2%
Total assets	100.0%	100.0%
Liabilities and Stockholders' Equity		
Accounts payable and accrued expenses	10.0%	10.6%
Loans and notes payable	20.9%	18.8%
Current maturities of long-term debt	3.9%	1.1%
Accrued income taxes	0.4%	0.3%
Total current liabilities	35.2%	30.9%
Long-term debt	20.7%	21.3%
Other liabilities	4.8%	3.9%
Deferred income taxes	6.1%	6.8%
Total liabilities	66.8%	62.9%
Total equity	33.2%	37.1%
Total liabilities and equity	100.0%	100.0%

Mid-Chapter Review 2

SOLUTION ($ MILLIONS)

$$ROE = \frac{\$7,124}{(\$33,440 + \$30,561)/2} = 22.26\%$$

$$ROA = \frac{\$7,124 + \$483 \times (1 - 0.35)}{(\$90,055 + \$92,023)/2} = 8.17\%$$

$$ROFL = 22.26\% - 8.12\% = 14.14\%$$

Mid-Chapter Review 3

SOLUTION ($ MILLIONS)

$$PM = \frac{\$7,124 + \$483 \times (1 - 0.35)}{\$45,998} = 16.17\%$$

$$AT = \frac{\$45,998}{(\$90,055 + \$92,023)/2} = 0.505 \text{ times}$$

$$16.17\% \times 0.505 = 8.17\%$$

$$GPM = \frac{\$45,998 - \$17,889}{\$45,998} = 61.11\%$$

$$ART = \frac{\$45,998}{(\$4,873 + \$4,466)/2} = 9.85 \text{ times}$$

$$INVT = \frac{\$17,889}{(\$3,277 + \$3,100)/2} = 5.61 \text{ times}$$

$$PPET = \frac{\$45,998}{(\$14,967 + \$14,633)/2} = 3.11 \text{ times}$$

PepsiCo and Coca-Cola have similar business models, and both companies achieve high returns on the capital invested by their shareholders. PepsiCo has a higher ROE, while the difference in ROA is much smaller (9.7% vs. 8.2%). Most of the difference in ROE is due to the fact that PepsiCo has a higher ROFL, caused by its higher use of liabilities as a source of financing. Coca-Cola has higher PM and GPM, while PepsiCo achieves a higher turnover of total assets. Closer analysis of turnover ratios reveals that ART is similar, implying that they employ similar credit policies. PepsiCo's inventory turns over significantly more quickly than Coca-Cola's inventory, perhaps reflecting differences in their product mix (e.g., PepsiCo's snack foods). This difference plays a significant role in PepsiCo's superior asset turnover.

Chapter-End Review

SOLUTION ($ MILLIONS)

$$\text{Current ratio} = \frac{\$32,986}{\$32,374} = 1.02$$

$$\text{Quick ratio} = \frac{\$8,958 + \$12,717 + \$4,466}{\$32,374} = 0.81$$

$$\text{Debt-to-equity ratio} = \frac{\$61,462}{\$30,561} = 2.01$$

$$\text{Times interest earned} = \frac{\$9,325 + \$483}{\$483} = 20.31$$

PepsiCo is slightly more liquid than Coca-Cola as indicated by a higher current ratio (1.14 vs. 1.02) and a higher quick ratio (0.85 vs. 0.81). In addition, PepsiCo has a much higher debt-to-equity ratio than Coke (3.02 vs. 2.01) suggesting that PepsiCo is relying more on debt financing. This is consistent with the higher ROFL ratio computed in Mid-Chapter Review 2. Nevertheless, neither company has significant issues related to solvency. Both report reasonably high times-interest-earned ratios (10.6 for PepsiCo and 20.3 for Coca-Cola).

Appendix 5A Review

SOLUTION ($ MILLIONS)

Operating assets:
2014: $92,023 - $3,678 - $12,717 = $75,628$
2013: $90,055 - $1,119 - $9,854 = $79,082$

Operating liabilities:
2014: $61,462 - $19,063 - $3,552 - $19,188 = $19,659$
2013: $56,615 - $19,154 - $1,024 - $16,901 = $19,536$

Net operating assets (NOA):
2014: $75,628 - $19,659 = $55,969$
2013: $79,082 - $19,536 = $59,546$

$$NOPAT = \$7,124 - [(\$594 - \$483 - \$494) \times (1 - 0.35)] = \$7,373.0$$

$$RNOA = \frac{\$7,373}{(\$55,969 + \$59,546)/2} = 12.8\%$$

$$NOPM = \frac{\$7,373}{\$45,998} = 16.0\%$$

$$NOAT = \frac{\$45,998}{(\$55,969 + \$59,546)/2} = 0.80$$

Appendix 5B Review

SOLUTION ($ MILLIONS)

THE COCA-COLA COMPANY AND SUBSIDIARIES Pro Forma Statements of Income ($ millions)	
Year ended December 31	**2015**
Net operating revenues	$50,000 (8.7% growth)
Cost of goods sold ($50,000 × 38.9%)	19,450
Gross profit	30,550
Selling, general and administrative expenses ($50,000 × 37.4%)	18,700
Other operating charges ($50,000 × 2.6%)	1,300
Operating income	10,550
Interest income	594
Interest expense	(483)
Other income (loss)—net	(494)
Income before income taxes	10,167
Income taxes ($10,170 × 20.0%)	2,033
Net income	$ 8,134

THE COCA-COLA COMPANY AND SUBSIDIARIES
Pro Forma Balance Sheet
($ millions)

December 31,	2015
Assets	
Cash and cash equivalents	$ 8,987
Marketable securities	12,717
Trade accounts receivable ($4,466 × 1.087)	4,855
Inventories ($3,100 × 1.087)	3,370
Prepaid expenses and other current assets ($3,745 × 1.087)	4,071
Total current assets	34,000
Investments	13,625
Property, plant, and equipment, net ($14,633 × 1.087)	15,906
Goodwill and other intangible assets ($26,372 × 1.087)	28,666
Other assets ($4,407 × 1.087)	4,790
Total assets	$96,987
Liabilities and Shareowners' Equity	
Accounts payable and accrued expenses ($9,234 × 1.087)	$10,037
Loans and notes payable	19,188
Current maturities of long-term debt	3,552
Accrued income taxes ($400 × 1.087)	435
Total current liabilities	33,212
Long-term debt	19,063
Other liabilities ($4,389 × 1.087)	4,771
Deferred income taxes ($5,636 × 1.087)	6,126
Total liabilities	63,172
Shareowners' equity ($30,561 + $8,134 − $4,880)	33,815
Total liabilities and shareowners' equity	$96,987

6

Reporting and Analyzing Revenues, Receivables, and Operating Income

CISCO SYSTEMS
www.cisco.com

Cisco Systems, Inc., manufactures and sells networking and communication products for transporting data, voice, and video. It is the worldwide leader in networking for the Internet.

Its engineers have been prominent in the development of Internet Protocol (IP)-based networking technologies in the core areas of routing and switching, along with advancing technologies in areas such as IP telephony, wireless LAN, storage networking, and home networking. Its products are seemingly everywhere:

- Cisco routers and switches are a crucial component of all networks.

- Cisco wireless network and IP telephony products allow people to communicate freely and reduce the cost of long distance communications.

- Cisco wireless technology allows employees to connect to corporate networks over a virtual private network (VPN), and it has medical applications such as telerobotics that aid in surgery. Commercial applications include wireless displays on shopping carts, targeted advertisements, and quick checkout.

- Enterprise collaboration including enterprise content management, enterprise voice, and enterprise social networks is an area of recent growth for Cisco.

- Virtual classrooms, powered by Cisco's switching technology and web collaboration software, are part of the distance learning revolution.

- Cisco video kiosks serve customers, constituents, and students in the healthcare, transportation, retail, banking, and education sectors of the economy.

- Cisco offers the Unified Data Center platform designed to automate IT resulting in increased efficiency, more agile business responsiveness, and simplified IT operations.

After a decade of rapid annual growth, Cisco ran smack into the tech decline in 2001. The company reported a $1 billion loss after taking a massive $1.2 billion restructuring charge. The restructuring led to inventory write-downs and the severance of 6,000 employees and seemed to undermine Cisco's claims of cutting-edge e-efficiency. In 2011, Cisco announced a second restructuring costing $1.1 billion, mostly for early retirement and severance costs. Effectively, in less than a decade, Cisco spent over $3 billion to restructure its business from the ground up.

Cisco's then-CEO, John Chambers, commented to *BusinessWeek*, "success in the 1990s was often based on how fast you could get to market and how fast you could blow a product through your distribution [channels]. Our market changed dramatically in terms of what customers expected; we needed to have engineering and manufacturing and professional services and [sales] and customer support working together in a way that wasn't required before."

Profitability is the primary measure by which financial statement users gauge a company's success in efficiently offering products and services that receive a favorable response from customers. In this chapter, we focus on how companies report operating income. Operating income is determined by decisions about how and when to recognize revenues and expenses. In addition, the income statement also includes *nonrecurring* (or *transitory*) *items*, such as restructuring charges. Transitory items are often important events reflecting very large dollar amounts and are distinguished by the fact that they are unlikely to recur in subsequent years. Understanding how such nonrecurring items are reported is crucial to interpreting a company's profitability.

Cisco's performance cannot be measured by profits alone. In order to control costs and improve operating profits, Cisco has to effectively manage operating assets. For example, accounts receivable is an important operating asset at Cisco because all of its sales are on account. By extending credit to customers on favorable credit terms, Cisco stimulates sales. However, extending credit exposes the company to collectibility risk—the risk that some customers will not pay the amounts owed. In addition, accounts receivable do not earn interest, and involve administrative costs associated with billing and collection. Hence, management of receivables is critical to financial success. This chapter describes the reporting of receivables. The reporting of other operating assets is covered in subsequent chapters.

Cisco has named its new CEO who will succeed John Chambers in July of 2015. The company has done well over time but faces continual challenges in the fast-changing technology industry.

Sources: *Cisco Systems, Inc.,* 10-K Reports; www.Cisco.com; *The Wall Street Journal,* February 7, 2005; *BusinessWeek,* November/December 2003; *USA Today,* August 7, 2007; *Wall Street Journal*, June 2, 2009; *The Economist*, April 15, 2010; *The Wall Street Journal* May 4, 2015.

CHAPTER ORGANIZATION

Reporting and Analyzing Revenues, Receivables, and Operating Income			
Reporting Operating Income	**Reporting Receivables**	**Analyzing Financial Statements**	**Further Considerations**
• Revenue Recognition • Accounting for Transactions with Future Deliverables • Accounting for Long-term Projects	• Allowance for Uncollectible Accounts • Footnote Disclosures and Interpretations	• Net Operating Profit After Taxes • Return on Net Operating Assets • Net Operating Profit Margin • Accounts Receivable Turnover • Average Collection Period	• Earnings Management • Reporting Nonrecurring Items (Appendix A) • New Standards for Revenue Recognition (Appendix B)

REPORTING OPERATING INCOME

The income statement is the primary source of information about recent company performance. This information is used to predict future performance for investment purposes and to assess the credit-worthiness of a company. The income statement is also used to evaluate the quality of management.

This section describes the information reported in the income statement and its analysis implications. The central questions that the income statement attempts to answer are:

- How profitable has the company been recently?
- How did it achieve that profitability?
- Will the current profitability level persist?

To answer these three profitability questions, it is not enough to focus on a company's net income. Rather, we must use the various classifications within the income statement to see how profits were achieved and what the future prospects look like. **Exhibit 6.1** provides a schematic of the primary income statement classifications.

EXHIBIT 6.1   Income Statement Classifications

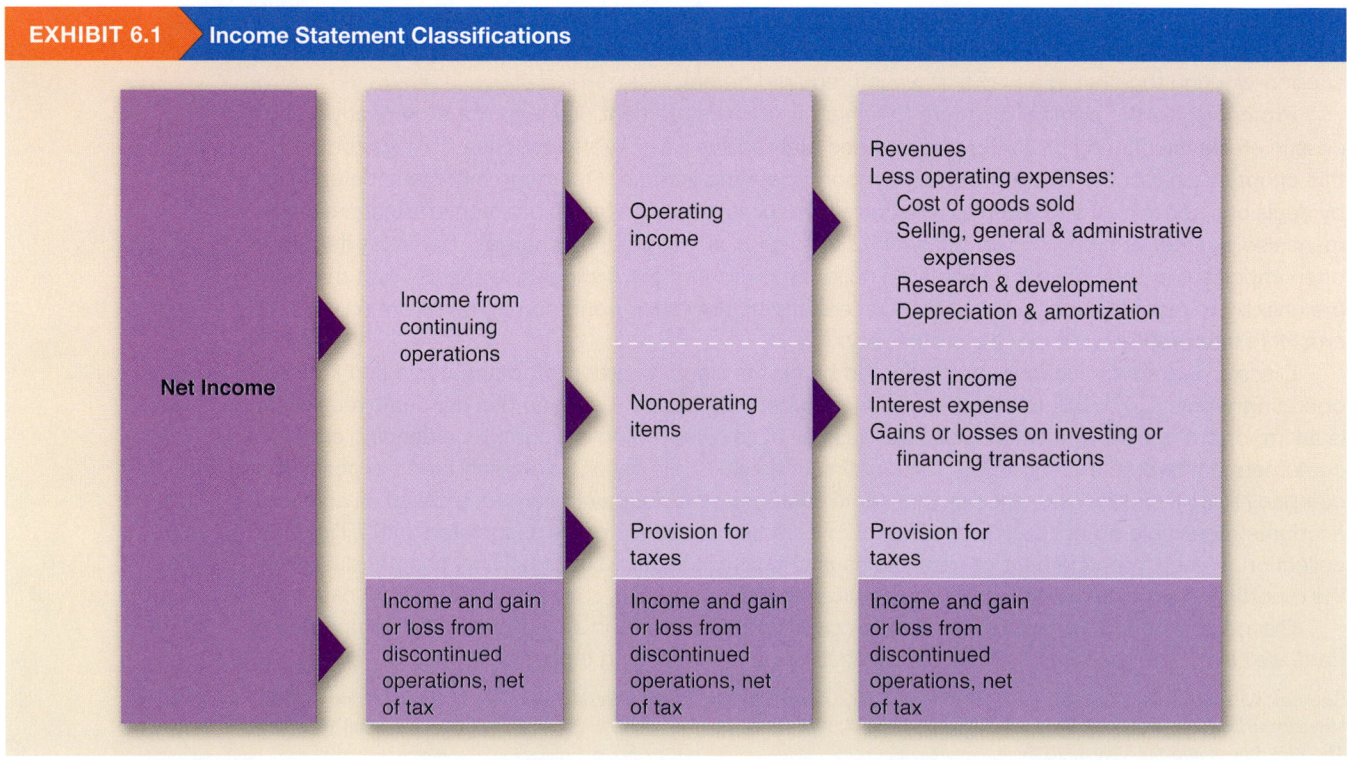

Operating activities refer to the primary transactions and events of a company. These include the purchase of goods from suppliers, the conversion of materials into finished products, the promotion and distribution of goods, the sale of goods and services to customers, and post-sale customer support. Operating activities are reported in the income statement under items such as sales, cost of goods sold, and selling, general, and administrative expenses. They represent a company's primary activities, which must be executed successfully for a company to remain consistently profitable.

Nonoperating activities relate to the financial (borrowing) and securities investment activities of a company. These activities are typically reported in the income statement under items such as interest income and expenses, dividend revenues, and gains and losses on sales of securities. Distinguishing income components by operating versus nonoperating is an important part of effective financial statement analysis because operating activities drive company performance. It is of interest, for example, to know whether company profitability results from operating activities, or whether poorly performing operating activities are being masked by income from nonoperating activities.

All the line items in income from continuing operations are presented before taxes, with the final line item being provision for income taxes, or tax expense. The accounting for income taxes is discussed more fully in Chapter 10.

If the company has income or loss items that qualify as discontinued operations, these will be presented after income from continuing operations. Discontinued operations are reported net of income tax expense or benefit. The appendix at the end of this chapter provides a detailed description of nonrecurring items. Finally, many large corporations report something called net income attributable to **noncontrolling interests**. Such an amount arises when a company consolidates a subsidiary that it controls, but for which it holds less than 100% ownership. This topic is covered in later chapters.

Exhibit 6.2 presents the 2014, 2013, and 2012 income statements (also called statements of operations) for Cisco Systems. Cisco has no discontinued operations during this time period, so

FYI When analyzing a company's income statement, it is important to distinguish operating activities from nonoperating activities and recurring activities from nonrecurring activities.

EXHIBIT 6.2	Distinguishing Operating and Nonoperating Sources of Income		

CISCO SYSTEMS, INC.
Consolidated Statements of Operations
($ millions)

Year ended	July 26, 2014	July 27, 2013	July 28, 2012
Net sales:			
Product...	$36,172	$38,029	$36,326
Service	10,970	10,578	9,735
Total net sales..................................	47,142	48,607	46,061
Cost of sales:			
Product...	15,641	15,541	14,505
Service	3,732	3,626	3,347
Total cost of sales..............................	19,373	19,167	17,852
Gross Margin	27,769	29,440	28,209
Operating expenses:			
Research and development	6,294	5,942	5,488
Sales and marketing.............................	9,503	9,538	9,647
General and administrative.......................	1,934	2,264	2,322
Amortization of purchased intangible assets	275	395	383
Restructuring and other charges	418	105	304
Total operating expenses........................	18,424	18,244	18,144
Operating income...................................	9,345	11,196	10,065
Interest income....................................	691	654	650
Interest expense...................................	(564)	(583)	(596)
Other income, net..................................	243	(40)	40
Interest and other income, net	370	31	94
Income before provision for income taxes................	9,715	11,227	10,159
Provision for income taxes...........................	1,862	1,244	2,118
Net Income.....................................	$ 7,853	$ 9,983	$ 8,041

income from continuing operations is the same as net income. Like many companies, Cisco presents operating income as a subtotal in its income statement. Cisco's operating income is computed by subtracting its total operating expenses (including cost of sales, research and development, sales and marketing, general and administrative, amortization, and restructuring charges) from total sales revenues. Nonoperating income and expenses, such as interest income and expense, and other income and expense, are added to or deducted from the subtotal for operating income.

At this time, GAAP does not have specific rules for classifying revenue and expense items as either operating or nonoperating, so management must use judgment in reporting and financial statement users must be careful to examine each revenue and expense item to determine if it is appropriately listed as part of operating income. Specifically, sales, cost of goods sold, and most selling, general, and administrative expenses are categorized as operating activities. Alternatively, investment-related income from dividends and interest is nonoperating, as is interest expense. Gains and losses on debt retirements and sales of investments are also nonoperating.[1]

While we think of Cisco as a networking and communications company, it has more than $45 billion (43% of its assets) invested in financial instruments (mostly government and government-backed securities) at 2014 fiscal year-end. And these assets provided $691 million in interest income for 2014. So, making predictions about Cisco's profitability for 2015 would be improved by separating the results of its product and service operations from those of its investing activities. In addition, operating income is the normal focus of business unit managers in a company—financing activities and investments in financial instruments and tax administration are usually determined at the central corporate level.

Revenue Recognition

LO1 Describe and apply the criteria for determining when revenue is recognized.

Revenue is one of the most important metrics of a company's operating success. The objective of almost all operating activities is to obtain a favorable response from customers, and revenue is a primary indicator of how customers view the company's product and service offerings. Companies can improve profits by reducing costs, but the effects of those improvements are limited unless revenues are increasing. Accordingly, growth in revenue is carefully monitored by management and by investors, as exemplified by the attention given to "same-store sales growth" in the retail industry.

---

[1] To further complicate matters, the classification of some items in the income statement as nonoperating is not consistent with their classification in the cash flow statement. Specifically, interest and dividend income and interest expense are classified as operating in the cash flow statement and nonoperating in most income statements. Of course, the distinction between operating and nonoperating items depends on the company's business. For Cisco Systems, interest income and expense would be classified as nonoperating, but for a financial institution (e.g., a bank), those same items would be considered part of their operations. Purchases and sales of production equipment would be considered nonoperating for Cisco, but operating for a company in the business of buying and selling used equipment.

Revenue recognition refers to the timing and amount of revenue reported by the company. The decision of when to recognize revenue depends on certain criteria. Determining whether the criteria for revenue recognition are met is often subjective and requires judgment. Therefore, financial statement readers should pay careful attention to companies' revenue recognition, particularly when companies face market pressures to meet income targets. Indeed, many SEC enforcement actions against companies for inaccurate, and sometimes fraudulent financial reporting are for improper (usually premature) revenue recognition.

GAAP dictates two **revenue recognition criteria** that must be met for revenue to be recognized (and reported) on the income statement. Revenue must be (1) **realized or realizable**, and (2) **earned**. *Realized or realizable* means that the company's net assets increase. That is, it receives an asset or satisfies a liability as a result of a transaction or event. *Earned* means that the seller has executed its duties under the terms of the sales agreement and that the title has passed to the buyer.

Many companies recognize revenues when the product or service is delivered to the customer. For these companies, delivery occurs at the same time, or shortly after, the sale takes place. Revenue recognition complications arise if there is uncertainty about collectibility or when the sale is contingent on product performance, product approval, or similar contingencies. In some industries, it is standard practice to allow customers to return the product within a specified period of time. When the customer retains a **right of return**, it is sometimes inappropriate to recognize revenue at the time of delivery. For many companies, returns are either immaterial in amount or relatively easy to predict based on history of a large number of similar transactions. For these companies, revenue can be recognized when the product is delivered to the customer. The expected returns are estimated and deducted from revenue when reporting the sale in the income statement. However, if the amount of returns is difficult to estimate, revenues should not be recognized until the return period expires.

BUSINESS INSIGHT

Product Returns at Pfizer   Following is an excerpt from **Pfizer Inc.**'s accounting policies as reported in its annual report.

> We record revenues from product sales when the goods are shipped and title passes to the customer. At the time of sale, we also record estimates for a variety of sales deductions, such as sales rebates, discounts and incentives, and product returns. When we cannot reasonably estimate the amount of future product returns, we record revenues when the risk of product return and/or additional sales deductions have been substantially eliminated.

Pfizer's policy regarding product returns is consistent with GAAP in that expected returns are estimated and deducted from sales at the time that the sale is recorded. If returns cannot be estimated, the sales revenue is deferred until the company is relatively certain that the product will not be returned.

The term "delivery" does not refer only to transportation to the customer's location, but also the transfer of title and the risks and rewards of ownership. In a **consignment** sale, a *consignor* delivers product to a *consignee*, but retains ownership until the consignee sells the product to the ultimate customer. As long as ownership remains with the consignor, a sale has not taken place. Only when the consignee sells the product should the consignor record the sales revenue.

Revenue Recognition Subsequent to Customer Purchase   There are many businesses in which customers purchase a product or a service prior to its delivery. For instance, a customer may pay for a year's subscription to a periodical. The publisher receives the cash at the start of the subscription, but it earns revenue when it delivers the periodical to the subscriber. Or, a homeowner may pay for the upcoming year's casualty insurance, but the insurance company can only recognize revenue as it provides insurance coverage.

LO2 Illustrate revenue and expense recognition when the transaction involves future deliverables and/or multiple elements.

In settings where a company's customers pay for the product or service prior to its delivery, the company must recognize a liability (usually called **unearned revenue** or **deferred revenue**)[2] at the time of the customer's payment. Then this liability is reduced, and revenue recognized, as the product or service is delivered.

Suppose that on January 1, a subscriber pays $36 for an annual subscription to a monthly magazine. At the time of payment, the publisher would make the following entry:

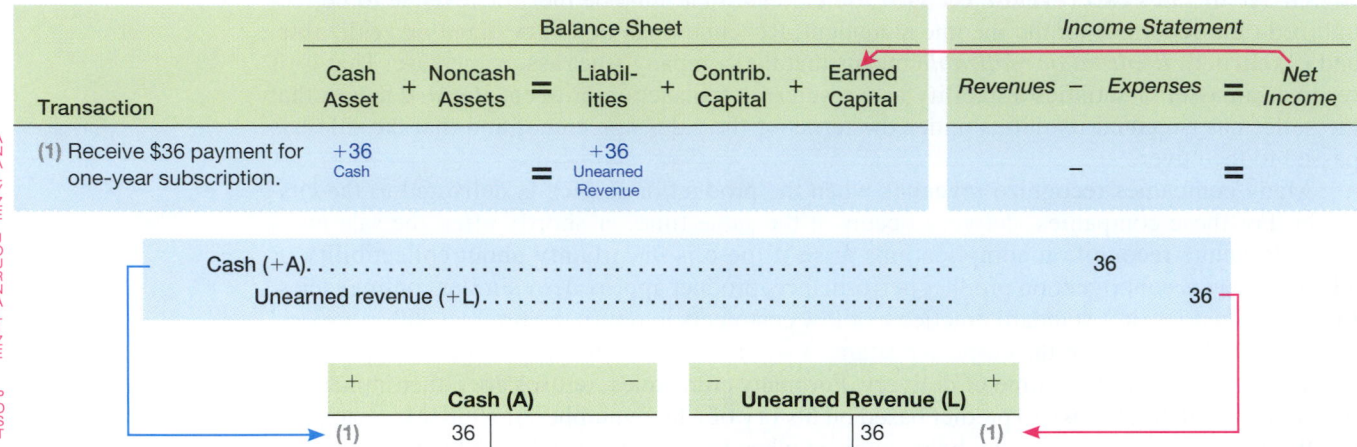

The unearned revenue liability represents the publisher's obligation—not to make a payment, but to provide the promised publication. Most liabilities reflect obligations to make a future payment, but unearned revenue is one of a handful of *deferred performance liabilities* that represent an obligation for future performance.

On March 31, at the end of its first quarter, the publisher would recognize that three magazines had been delivered to the subscriber, and the publisher has earned three times the monthly revenue of $3, or $9. The entry to recognize this revenue is the following.

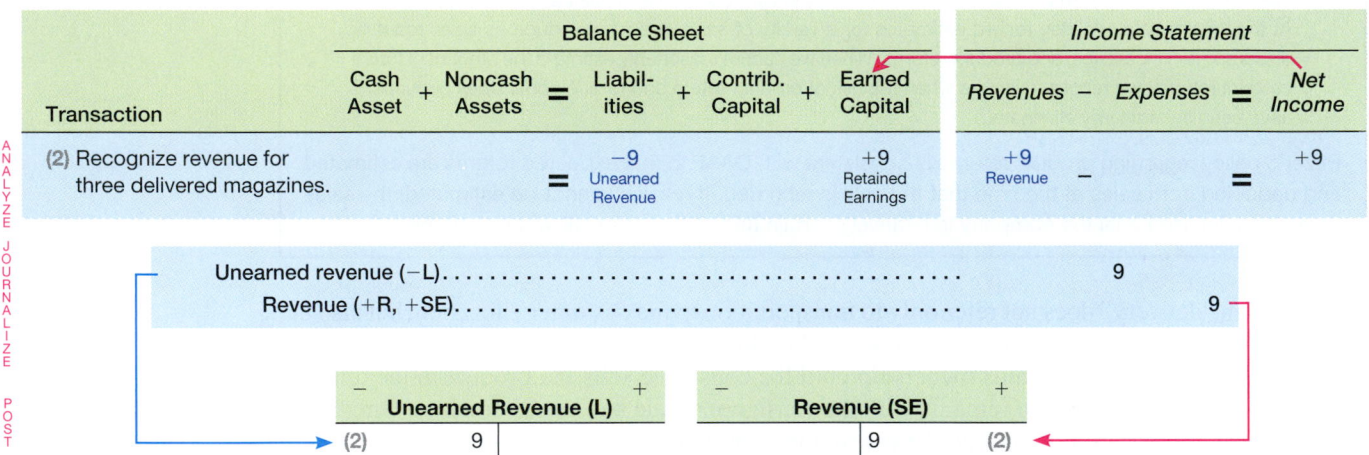

The same entries would be made until the subscription expired. In the March 31 balance sheet, the publisher would have a deferred revenue liability of $27, reflecting the remaining obligation for nine months of subscription delivery. And, the quarter's indirect method operating cash flows would include $9 in revenue (in net income) and the $27 increase in unearned revenue liability which, in total, reflect the $36 received from the customer.

---

[2] The term used for unearned revenue may be particular to the company's business. For instance, **Delta Air Lines** shows an Air Traffic Liability of $4,296 million at the end of 2014 which represents customers' purchases of tickets in advance of their flights. **The Allstate Corporation** uses the term *Unearned Premiums*. The new revenue recognition accounting standard uses the general term *contract liability*.

Unearned revenue is seen in a growing number of financial statements as companies increase their promises of future deliveries of products and service due to the changing nature of products and services in the economy and also in an effort to build a continuing relationship with their customers. From the point of view of a financial analyst, one implication of revenue deferral is that the change in revenue from one period to the next is not equal to the change in customer purchases over the same period. In the case of our publisher with one-year subscriptions, quarterly revenue is actually a composite of subscriber purchases over the current quarter plus the last three quarters and, therefore, not an ideal indicator of how current customers are responding to the publisher's offerings. Both the revenue and unearned revenue accounts need to be analyzed to obtain a complete picture.

A revenue recognition complication arises when two or more products or services are sold under the same sales agreement for one lump-sum price. These bundled sales are called **multiple element arrangements** and are commonplace in the software industry, where developers sell software, training, maintenance, and customer support in one transaction. In these circumstances, GAAP requires that the sales price be allocated among the various elements of the sale in proportion to their fair value. Revenue allocated to the elements that have not been delivered (such as maintenance and customer support) must be deferred and recognized as the service is rendered in future periods.

BUSINESS INSIGHT

Cisco's Revenue Recognition Following is an excerpt from Cisco Systems' policies on revenue recognition as reported in footnotes to its recent annual report.

> The Company recognizes revenue when persuasive evidence of an arrangement exists, delivery has occurred, the fee is fixed or determinable, and collectibility is reasonably assured. In instances where final acceptance of the product, system, or solution is specified by the customer, revenue is deferred until all acceptance criteria have been met. For hosting arrangements, the Company recognizes subscription revenue ratably over the subscription period, while usage revenue is recognized based on utilization. Software subscription revenue is deferred and recognized ratably over the subscription term upon delivery of the first product and commencement of the term. Technical support services revenue is deferred and recognized ratably over the period during which the services are to be performed, which is typically from one to three years.
>
> . . . The Company enters into revenue arrangements that may consist of multiple deliverables of its product and service offerings due to the needs of its customers. For example, a customer may purchase routing products along with a contract for technical support services. This arrangement would consist of multiple elements, with the products delivered in one reporting period and the technical support services delivered across multiple reporting periods . . .

Cisco goes on to discuss how it then allocates revenue among the various components of a multiple element contract using either vendor-specific objective evidence of price, third-party evidence of a selling price, or estimated selling prices. Cisco also states that it determines its price on which to allocate revenue based on the normal pricing practices for the specific product or service if that product or service is sold separately.

Cisco's criteria and methods of revenue recognition reflect current accounting standards and SEC guidance. In its recent 10-K, Cisco describes the new accounting standard and states that they are currently evaluating the impact of this accounting standard update on its financial reporting.

To illustrate revenue recognition for a multiple element arrangement (or bundled sale), assume that Software Innovations, Inc., develops marketing software designed to track customer questions and comments on the Internet and through social media. The software license sells for $125,000 and includes user training for up to 12 individuals and customer support for three years. Software Innovations estimates that the software, if licensed without training or customer support, would sell for $120,000. In addition, it estimates that the value of the user training services, if sold separately, would be $18,000 and the customer support would sell for $12,000. Software Innovations would allocate the $125,000 sales price as illustrated in **Exhibit 6.3**.

EXHIBIT 6.3	Allocation of the Sales Price in a Multiple Element Arrangement				
Element		Estimated value	Percent of total value	Bundle sales price	Sales price allocated to each element
Software license		$120,000	80%	× $125,000 =	$100,000
Training		18,000	12	× 125,000 =	15,000
Customer support		12,000	8	× 125,000 =	10,000
Total		$150,000	100%		$125,000

The sale would be recorded as revenue for the portion that was allocated to software and as deferred (or unearned) revenue for that portion that was allocated to training and customer support:

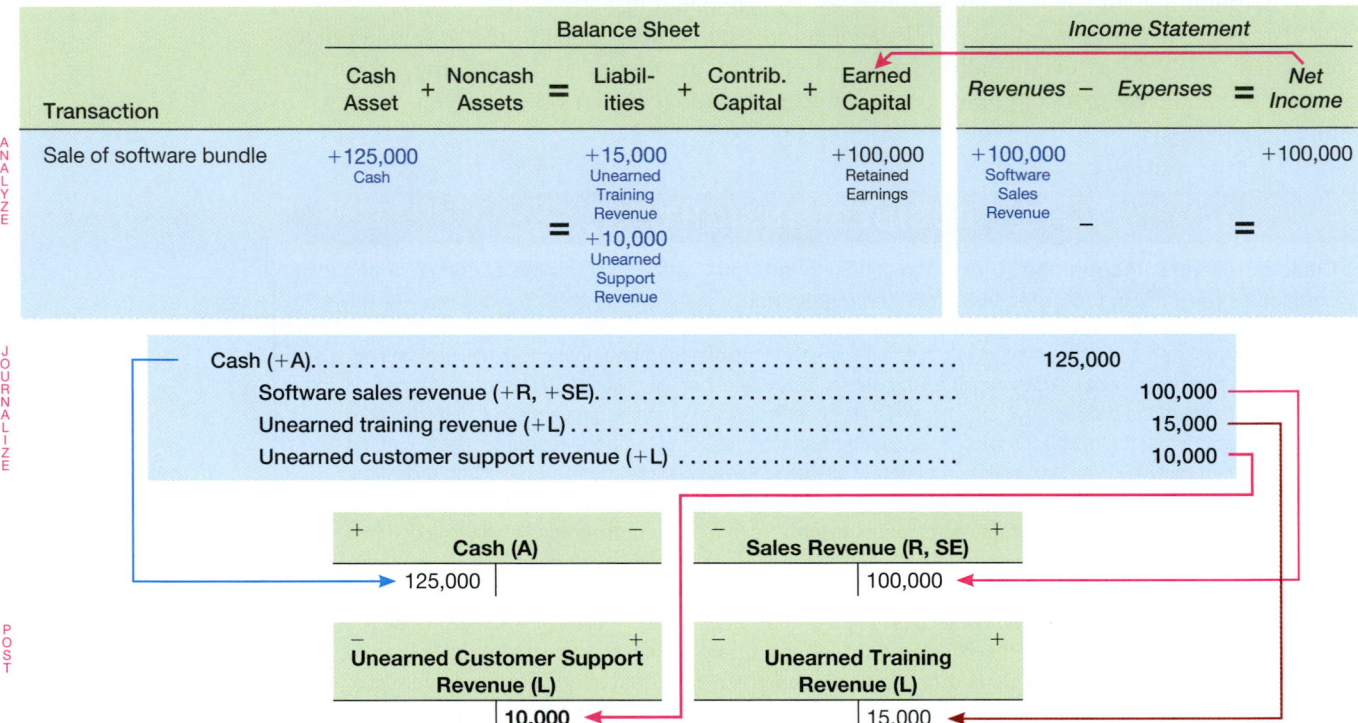

The unearned training revenue would be recognized as training services are provided. Software Innovations might recognize 1/12 of the $15,000, or $1,250 for each individual trained. The unearned customer support revenue would be recognized over time ($10,000/3 = $3,333 each year).

MID-CHAPTER REVIEW 1

When **Microsoft Corporation** sells software, it recognizes part of the revenue at the time of customer purchase and defers the rest because it will deliver support and upgrades in the future. For instance, in its 2014 annual report, it states

> Revenue recognition for multiple-element arrangements requires judgment to determine if multiple elements exist, whether elements can be accounted for as separate units of accounting, and if so, the fair value for each of the elements. Where elements are delivered over different periods of time, and when allowed under U.S. GAAP, revenue is allocated to the respective elements based on their relative selling prices at the inception of the arrangement, and revenue is recognized as each element is delivered. . . . Technology guarantee programs are accounted for as multiple-element arrangements as customers receive free or significantly discounted rights to use upcoming new versions of a software product if they license existing versions of the product during the eligibility period. Revenue is allocated between the existing product and the new product, and revenue allocated to the new

product is deferred until that version is delivered . . . Software updates that will be provided free of charge are evaluated on a case-by-case basis to determine whether they meet the definition of an upgrade and create a multiple-element arrangement, which may require revenue to be deferred and recognized when the upgrade is delivered, or if it is determined that implied post-contract customer support ("PCS") is being provided, the arrangement is accounted for as a multiple-element arrangement and all revenue from the arrangement is deferred and recognized over the implied PCS term. If updates are determined to not meet the definition of an upgrade, revenue is generally recognized as products are shipped or made available.

In its income statement, Microsoft reports revenues for the past three years.

(in millions)	2014	2013	2012
Revenue	$86,833	$77,849	$73,723

In its indirect-method operating cash flows, Microsoft makes many adjustments to its net income in arriving at cash from operations. Two of the adjustments are the following:

(in millions)	2014	2013	2012
Deferral of unearned revenue.	$44,325	$44,253	$36,104
Recognition of unearned revenue	(41,739)	(41,921)	(33,347)

"Deferral of unearned revenue" provides the amount of customer purchases made during a year that were not recognized as revenue at the time of customer purchase. That is the amount that was put into the unearned revenue liability during the year. "Recognition of unearned revenue" refers to the amounts of revenue recognized during the year that derived from customer purchases made in earlier periods. This amount was taken out of the unearned revenue liability during the year and recognized as revenue on the income statement.

Required

1. Calculate the revenue growth rates for fiscal years 2013 and 2014.
2. From the information on revenues and on changes in the unearned revenue liability, determine the amount of customer purchases for fiscal years 2012, 2013, and 2014.
3. Calculate the growth rates in customer purchases for fiscal years 2013 and 2014. Why do these differ from those calculated in part 1?

The solution to this review problem can be found on page 321.

Revenue Recognition for Long-term Projects

Challenges arise in determining revenue recognition for companies with long-term production processes (spanning more than one reporting period) such as consulting firms, construction companies, and defense contractors. For these companies, revenue is often recognized using the **percentage-of-completion method**, which recognizes revenue based on the costs incurred under the contract relative to its total expected costs.[3] In addition to determining when to recognize revenues to properly measure and report a company's performance, we must also decide when to recognize expenses. The idea of **expense recognition** was introduced in Chapter 2. Expenses are recognized when assets are diminished (or liabilities increased) as a result of earning revenue or supporting operations, even if there is no immediate decrease in cash. The following illustration demonstrates the appropriate recognition of revenues and expenses using the percentage-of-completion method.

LO3 Illustrate revenue and expense recognition for long-term projects.

3

PERCENTAGE-OF-COMPLETION METHOD   To illustrate the percentage-of-completion method, assume that Built-Rite Construction signs a $10 million contract to construct a building. The company estimates $7.5 million in construction costs, yielding an expected gross profit of $2.5 million. Further assume that Built-Rite incurs $4.5 million in construction costs during the first year of construction, and the remaining $3 million in costs during the second year. The amount of revenue and gross profit that Built-Rite would report each year is illustrated in **Exhibit 6.4**.

---

[3] In some circumstances, a company may use some other indicator of progress, like employee time or the achievement of customer-specified milestones.

EXHIBIT 6.4 ▶ **Revenue Recognition Using the Percentage-of-Completion Method**

Year	Percentage completed	Revenue recognized	Expense recognized	Gross profit
1.............	$4,500,000/$7,500,000 = 60%	$10,000,000 × 60% = $ 6,000,000	$4,500,000	$1,500,000
2.............	$3,000,000/$7,500,000 = 40%	$10,000,000 × 40% = 4,000,000	3,000,000	1,000,000
Totals..........	100%	$10,000,000	$7,500,000	$2,500,000

Using the percentage-of-completion method, Built-Rite would report $1.5 million in gross profit from this project in the first year and $1.0 million in the second year. The timing of revenue and gross profit coincides with the amount of work completed.

The percentage-of-completion method of revenue recognition requires an estimate of total costs. This estimate is made at the beginning of the contract and is typically the one used to initially bid the contract. However, estimates are inherently prone to estimation error. If total construction costs are underestimated, the percentage of completion is overestimated (the denominator is too low) and too much revenue and gross profit are recognized in the early years of the project. The estimation process used in this method has the potential for inaccurate or, even, improper revenue recognition. Estimates of costs to complete projects are also difficult to verify for auditors. This uncertainty adds additional risk to financial statement analysis.

To justify use of the percentage-of-completion method, a company must have a contract with the customer that specifies a fixed or determinable price. In addition, project costs must be reasonably estimable. When a long-term project fails to meet these criteria, all revenue should be deferred until the contract is complete. This approach is known as the **completed contract method**. **Exhibit 6.5** provides a comparison of the gross profit calculations using each of these two accounting methods for the Built-Rite Construction contract described earlier.

EXHIBIT 6.5 ▶ **Comparison of the Percentage-of-Completion and Completed Contract Methods**

	Percentage-of-Completion Method		Completed Contract Method	
	Year 1	Year 2	Year 1	Year 2
Revenues......	$6,000,000	$4,000,000	$0	$10,000,000
Expenses......	4,500,000	3,000,000	0	7,500,000
Gross profit.....	$1,500,000	$1,000,000	$0	$ 2,500,000

The total revenue and gross profit are the same under either revenue recognition method. Likewise, there is no difference in the costs incurred to construct the building. The only difference between the percentage-of-completion method and the completed contract method is *when* the revenue and gross profit are reported in the income statement.

It is very likely that Built-Rite would have received some cash payments from the customer during the construction period. However, neither the percentage-of-completion method nor the completed contract method is affected by the schedule of cash payments from the customer. It would not make sense for Built-Rite to enter into this contract unless it had a high degree of confidence in the customer's ability and willingness to pay.

A GLOBAL PERSPECTIVE

Currently, International Financial Reporting Standards do not allow the completed contract method to be used for long-term contracts when percentage-of-completion is not appropriate. Instead, companies are required to use the **cost-recovery method**, in which revenues are recognized in an amount equal to the cost incurred (and expensed) in each period. The pattern of profit recognition is the same as (or very similar to) completed contract, but the revenues and expenses occur differently. IFRS will adopt the new converged revenue recognition standard as described briefly in the Business Insight Box on page 274 and in more detail in Appendix 6B and will recognize revenue either over time or at a point in time similar to the new standard in GAAP.

MID-CHAPTER REVIEW 2

Following is a footnote from a recent annual report of Adler Corporation.

Note 2: Revenue Recognition
Revenue from long-term government contracts is recognized using the percentage-of-completion method of accounting. Production costs are capitalized by project and are expensed based on the ratio of current period costs to estimated total contract costs. Revenue from contracts with private organizations is recognized using the completed contract method.

Required

1. Speculate as to possible reasons why Adler Corporation uses different revenue recognition policies for long-term government contracts and for contracts with private organizations.

2. Assume that Adler signed a contract in 2016 for a long-term project at a contract price of $40,000,000. The project is estimated to take three years to complete and cost $30,000,000. The cost incurred in 2016 was $12,000,000, and projected costs in 2017 and 2018 are $13,500,000 and $4,500,000 respectively. Compute gross profit for each year assuming that the contract is reported using the

   a. percentage-of-completion method
   b. completed contract method

3. Assume that Adler Corporation overestimated the cost of the contract in question 2, such that the actual cost incurred in 2018 was $1,500,000 instead of $4,500,000. What effect would this overestimate have on income in each year?

The solution to this review problem can be found on page 321.

REPORTING ACCOUNTS RECEIVABLE

Receivables are usually a major part of operating working capital. They must be carefully managed as they represent a substantial asset for most companies. GAAP requires companies to report receivables at the amount they expect to collect, necessitating an estimation of uncollectible accounts. These estimates determine the amount of receivables reported on the balance sheet as well as revenues and expenses reported on the income statement. Accordingly, it is important that companies accurately assess uncollectible accounts and report them. It is also necessary that readers of financial reports understand management's accounting choices and the effects of those choices on reported balance sheets and income statements.

When companies sell to other companies, they usually do not expect cash upon delivery as is common with retail customers. Instead, they offer credit terms, and the resulting sales are called **credit sales** or *sales on account*.

Companies establish credit policies (to determine which customers receive credit) by weighing the expected losses from uncollectible accounts against the expected profits generated by offering credit. Sellers know that some buyers will be unable to pay their accounts when they become due. Buyers, for example, can suffer business downturns that are beyond their control and which limit their cash available to meet liabilities. They must, then, make choices concerning which of their liabilities to pay. Liabilities to the IRS, to banks, and to bondholders are usually paid, as those creditors have enforcement powers and can quickly seize assets and disrupt operations, leading to bankruptcy and eventual liquidation. Buyers also try to cover their payroll, as they cannot exist without employees. Then, if there is cash remaining, these customers will pay suppliers to ensure a continued flow of goods.

When a customer faces financial difficulties, suppliers are often the last creditors to receive payment and are often not paid in full. Consequently, there is risk in the collectibility of accounts receivable. This *collectibility risk* is crucial to analysis of accounts receivable.

Accounts receivable are reported on the balance sheet of the seller at **net realizable value**, which is the net amount that the seller expects to collect. Cisco reports $5,157 million of accounts receivable in the current asset section of its 2014 balance sheet. Its receivables are reported net of allowances for doubtful accounts of $265 million. This means that the total amount owed to Cisco

FYI The phrase *trade receivables* refers to accounts receivable from customers.

FYI Receivables are claims held against customers and others for money, goods, or services.

by customers is $5,422 million ($5,157 million + $265 million), but the company *estimates* that $265 million of these receivables will be uncollectible. Thus, only the net amount that Cisco expects to collect is reported on the balance sheet.

We might ask why Cisco would sell to companies from whom they do not expect to collect the amounts owed. The answer is they would not *if* they knew beforehand who those companies were. That is, Cisco probably cannot identify those companies that constitute the $265 million in uncollectible accounts as of its statement date. Yet, Cisco knows from past experience that a certain portion of its receivables will prove uncollectible. GAAP requires a company to estimate the dollar amount of uncollectible accounts each time it issues its financial statements (even if it cannot identify specific accounts that are uncollectible), and to report its accounts receivable at the resulting *net realizable value* (total receivables less an **allowance for uncollectible accounts**).

Determining the Allowance for Uncollectible Accounts

The amount of expected uncollectible accounts is usually estimated based on an **aging analysis**. When aging the accounts, an analysis of receivables is performed as of the balance sheet date. Specifically, each customer's account balance is categorized by the number of days or months that the related invoices are outstanding. Based on prior experience, assessment of current economic conditions, or on other available statistics, uncollectible (bad debt) percentages are applied to each of these categorized amounts, with larger percentages applied to older accounts. The result of this analysis is a dollar amount for the allowance for uncollectible accounts (also called allowance for doubtful accounts) at the balance sheet date.

To illustrate, **Exhibit 6.6** shows an aging analysis for a seller that began operations this year and is owed $100,000 of accounts receivable at year-end. Those accounts listed as current consist of those outstanding that are still within their original credit period. Accounts listed as 1–60 days past due are those 1 to 60 days past their due date. This classification would include an account that is 45 days outstanding for a net 30-day invoice. This same logic applies to all aged categories.

EXHIBIT 6.6	Aging of Accounts Receivable		
Age of Accounts Receivable	**Receivable Balance**	**Estimated Percent Uncollectible**	**Accounts Estimated Uncollectible**
Current	$ 50,000	2%	$1,000
1–60 days past due	30,000	3	900
61–90 days past due	15,000	4	600
Over 90 days past due	5,000	8	400
Total	$100,000		$2,900

The calculation illustrated in **Exhibit 6.6** also reflects the seller's experience with uncollectible accounts, which manifests itself in the uncollectible percentages for each aged category. For example, on average, 3% of buyers' accounts that are 1–60 days past due prove uncollectible for this seller. Hence, it estimates a potential loss of $900 for those $30,000 in receivables for that aged category.

Another means of estimating uncollectible accounts is to use the **percentage of sales**. To illustrate, if our seller reports sales of $100,000 and estimates the uncollectible accounts at 3% of sales, estimated uncollectible accounts would be $3,000. The percentage of sales approach focuses on the amount of potentially uncollectible accounts among current-period sales, whereas the aging analysis is based on the current balance in accounts receivable. Thus, these two methods nearly always result in different estimates of uncollectible accounts. While the percentage of sales method is arguably simpler, an aging analysis generally provides more accurate estimates.

Reporting the Allowance for Uncollectible Accounts

How does the accounting system record this estimate? The amount that appears in the balance sheet as accounts receivable represents a collection of individual accounts—one or more receivables for each customer. Because we need to keep track of exactly how much each customer owes us, we cannot simply subtract estimated uncollectibles from accounts receivable.

In Chapter 3, we introduced contra-asset accounts to record accumulated depreciation. A contra-asset account is directly associated with an asset account, but serves to offset the balance of the asset account. To record the estimated uncollectible accounts without disturbing the balance in accounts receivable, we use another contra-asset—the allowance for uncollectible accounts.

To illustrate, we use the data from **Exhibit 6.6**. The summary journal entry to reflect credit sales follows.

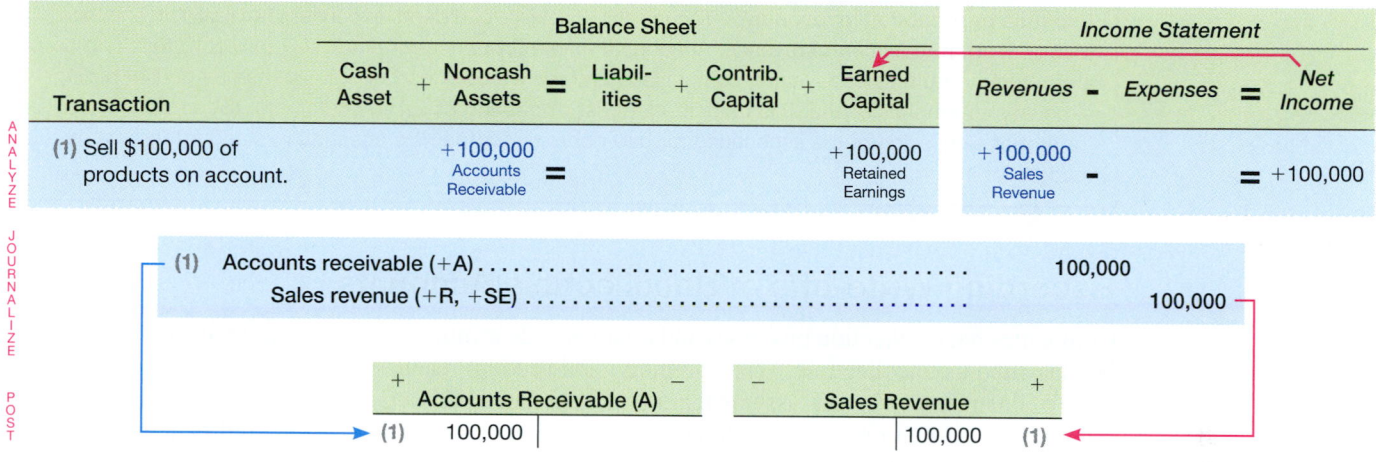

For an adjusting entry at year-end, uncollectible accounts are estimated and recorded as follows as **bad debts expense** (also called *provision for uncollectible accounts*). The allowance for uncollectible accounts is a contra-asset account. It offsets (reduces) accounts receivable.

> **FYI** The term *provision* is sometimes used as a substitute for expense; often when the reported expense is an estimate.

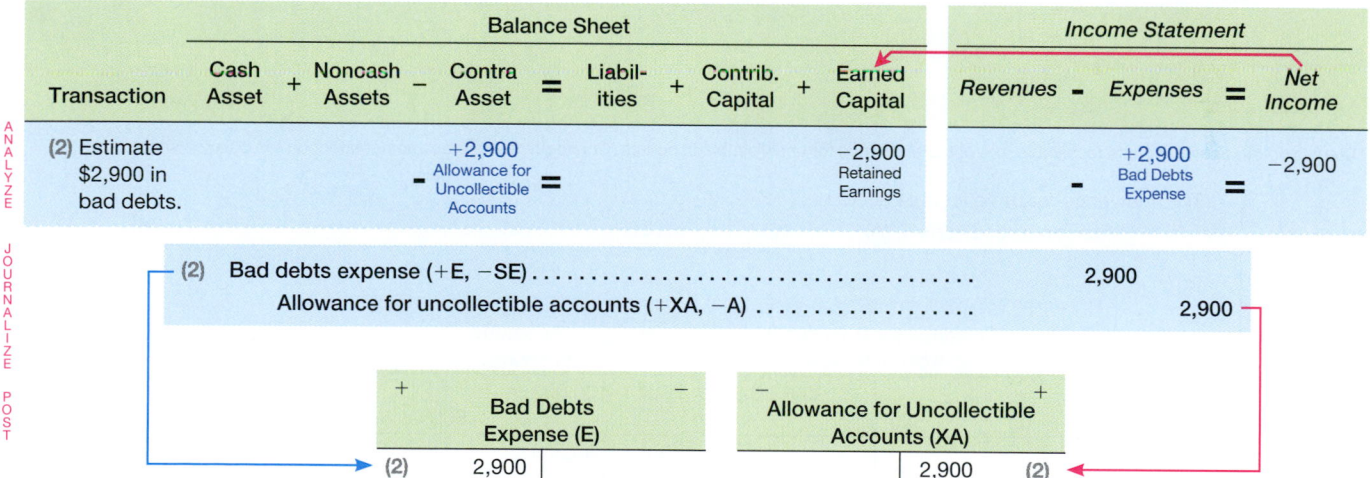

This accounting treatment serves three purposes. First, the balance in accounts receivable is reported in the balance sheet net of estimated uncollectible accounts as follows:

> Accounts receivable, net of $2,900 in allowances. $97,100

The $97,100 is the net realizable value of the accounts receivable. Second, the original value of accounts receivable is preserved. The individual accounts that add up to the $100,000 in accounts receivable have not been altered. Third, bad debts expense of $2,900, which is part of the cost of offering credit to customers, is matched against the $100,000 sales generated on credit and reported in the income statement. Bad debts expense is usually included in SG&A expenses.

The allowance for uncollectible accounts is increased by bad debts expense (estimated provision for uncollectibles) and decreased when an account is written off. Because the allowance for uncollectible accounts is a contra-asset account, credit entries increase its balance. The greater the balance in the contra-asset account, the more the corresponding asset account is offset.

BUSINESS INSIGHT

Expense or reduction in revenue?   Technically speaking, bad debts expense is not really an expense. It is, instead, a reduction of revenue. Although it is correct under current GAAP to record this item as a subtraction from sales revenue, companies commonly record bad debts expense as part of selling expenses to emphasize that this amount is a cost of offering credit to customers. (See Appendix 6B for a brief discussion of the accounting for bad debts under the new accounting standard for revenue recognition.)

Recording Write-offs of Uncollectible Accounts

Companies have collection processes and policies to determine when an overdue receivable should be classified as uncollectible. When an individual account reaches that classification, it is written off. To illustrate a write-off, assume that in the next period (Year 2), the company described above receives notice that one of its customers, owing $500 at the time, has declared bankruptcy. The seller's attorneys believe that the legal costs necessary to collect the amount would exceed the $500 owed. The seller could then decide to write off the account with the following entry.

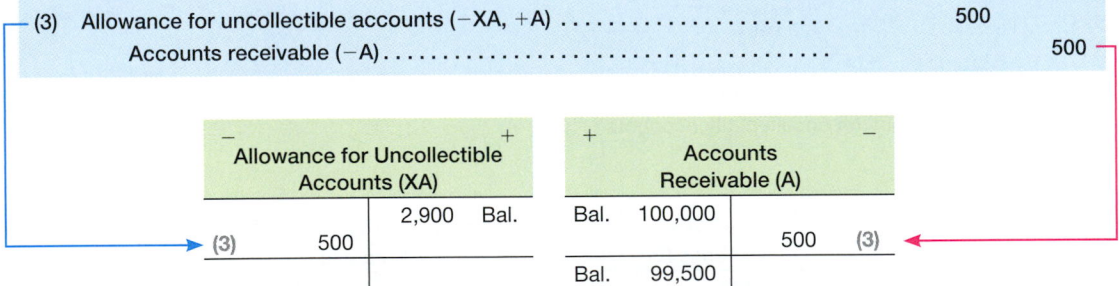

*There is no effect on accounts receivable, net of the allowance for uncollectible accounts. Consequently, there is no *net* effect on the balance sheet.

Exhibit 6.7 summarizes the effects of this write-off on the individual accounts.

EXHIBIT 6.7	Effects of an Accounts Receivable Write-Off		
	Before Write-Off	**Effects of Write-Off**	**After Write-Off**
Accounts receivable..............................	$100,000	$ (500)	$99,500
Less: Allowance for uncollectible accounts...........	2,900	500	2,400
Accounts receivable, net of allowance..............	$ 97,100		$97,100

The net amount of accounts receivable that is reported in the balance sheet after the write-off is the same amount that was reported before the write-off. This is always the case. The individual account receivable was reduced and the contra-asset was reduced by the same amount. Also, no entry was made to the income statement. The expense was estimated and recorded in the period when the credit sales were recorded.[4]

To complete the illustration, assume that management's aging of accounts at the end of Year 2 shows that the ending balance in the allowance account should be $3,000, so another $600 should be added to the allowance account at the end of Year 2. This $600 amount would reflect sales made in Year 2, as well as the seller's experience with collections during Year 2. The entry to record the Year 2 provision follows.

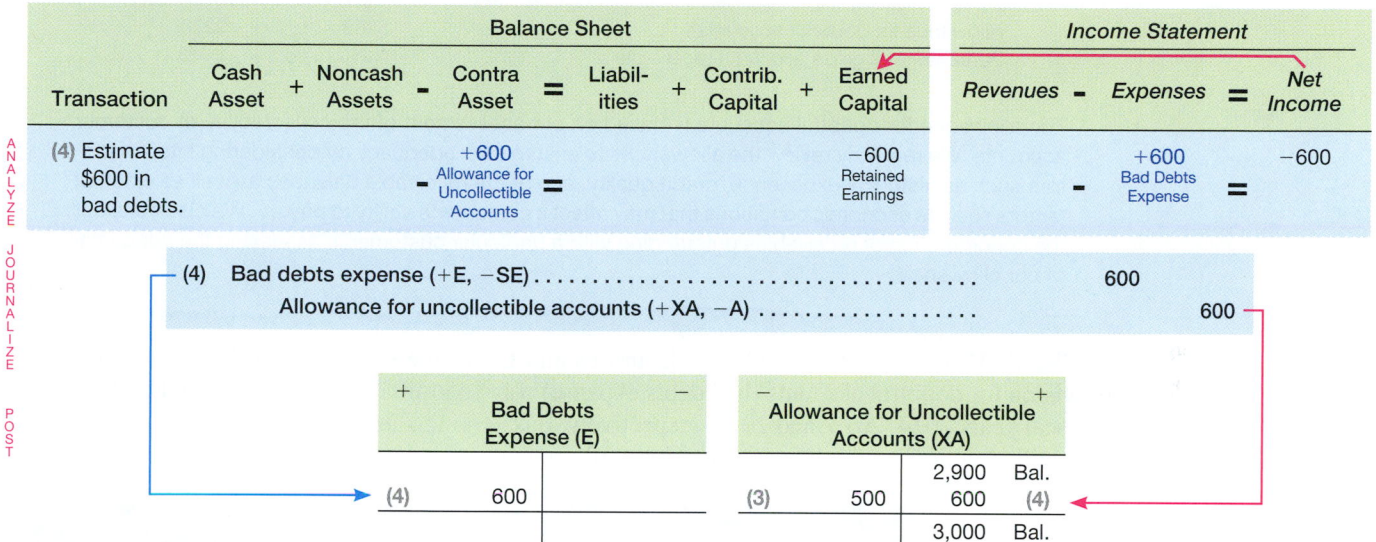

This entry is the same (albeit with a different dollar amount) as the entry made to record the estimate in Year 1. A reconciliation of allowance for uncollectible accounts for the two years follows.

	Year 1	Year 2
Allowance for uncollectible accounts, beginning balance	$ 0	$2,900
Add: provision for uncollectible accounts (bad debts expense estimate)	2,900	600
Subtract: write-offs of uncollectible accounts receivable	0	(500)
Allowance for uncollectible accounts, ending balance	$2,900	$3,000

To summarize, the *main balance sheet and income statement effects occur when the provision is made to the allowance for uncollectible accounts*. Accounts receivable (net) is reduced, and that reduction is reflected in the income statement as bad debts expense (usually part of selling, general, and administrative expenses). The net income reduction yields a corresponding equity reduction (via reduced retained earnings). Importantly, the main financial statement effects are at the point of *estimation*, not upon the event of *write-off*. In this way, the net accounts receivable reflects the most up-to-date judgments about future customer payments, and bad debts expense matches the current period's sales and incorporates any changes in management's assessment of the likelihood that customers will pay.

[4] Suppose a previously written off account is unexpectedly paid. If that occurs, the write-off entry (3) is reversed (reinstating the receivable and increasing the allowance), and the payment of this reinstated receivable is accounted for in the usual fashion.

Footnote Disclosures and Interpretations

In its balance sheets, Cisco reports Accounts receivables, net of allowance for doubtful accounts of $5,157 million at July 26, 2014, and $5,470 at July 27, 2013. In its MD&A (Management Discussion and Analysis), the company provides the following information.

Allowances for Receivables and Sales Returns

The allowances for receivables were as follows (in millions, except percentages):

	July 26, 2014	July 27, 2013
Allowance for doubtful accounts	$265	$228
Percentage of gross accounts receivable	4.9%	4.0%

The allowance for doubtful accounts is based on our assessment of the collectability of customer accounts. We regularly review the allowances to ensure their adequacy by considering internal factors such as historical experience, credit quality, age of the receivable balances as well as external factors such as economic conditions that may affect a customer's ability to pay. . . . We also consider the concentration of receivables outstanding with a particular customer in assessing the adequacy of our allowances . . .

In Cisco's 10-K report filed with the Securities and Exchange Commission, it discloses that its provision for doubtful accounts (bad debts expense) was $65 million, $33 million, and $19 million in fiscal years 2014, 2013, and 2012, respectively. Based on this information, we could construct a reconciliation of Cisco's allowance for doubtful accounts as presented in **Exhibit 6.8**.

EXHIBIT 6.8	Reconciliation of Cisco's Allowance for Doubtful Accounts

Allowance for Doubtful Accounts ($ millions)	
Balance at July 27, 2013	$228
Provision for doubtful accounts	65
Write-offs	(28)
Balance at July 26, 2014	$265

The footnotes may also disclose whether or not a company has *pledged* its accounts receivable as collateral for a short-term loan. If this is the case, a short-term loan is presented in the liabilities section of the balance sheet and a footnote explains the arrangement. As an alternative to borrowing, a company may *factor* (or sell) its accounts receivable to a bank or other financial institution. If the receivables have been factored, the bank or other financial institution accepts all responsibility for collection. Consequently, the receivables do not appear on the balance sheet of the selling company because they have been sold.

The reconciliation of Cisco's allowance account provides insight into the level of its annual provision (bad debts expense) relative to its write-offs. In 2014, Cisco wrote off $28 million in uncollectible accounts while recording a provision for doubtful accounts (bad debts expense) of $65 million. Because the provision exceeded the write-offs, the total allowance increased from $228 million in 2013 to $265 million in 2014.

Cisco's bad debts expense (or provision) has been volatile in recent years. It reported a provision for bad debts of $19 million in 2012 and $7 million in 2011. The changes in bad debts expense, both in absolute amount and as a percentage of sales revenue, could be caused by a number of factors. For example, the creditworthiness of Cisco's customers may have changed. These changes can be caused by changing economic conditions or changes in Cisco's credit policies (including collection efforts).

The magnitude of Cisco's uncollectible accounts relative to the company's overall size and profitability makes it an unlikely place for earnings management. But companies in other industries (banking, publishing, retail) often have receivables that require substantial adjustments for expected returns or uncollectible accounts. For instance, the publisher **John Wiley & Sons, Inc.**, reports accounts receivable of $149.7 million in its April 30, 2014, balance sheet, but this amount is net of an allowance for doubtful accounts of $7.9 million and an allowance for sales returns of $41.1 million. So, Wiley only expects to collect about 75% of the amounts it has billed customers. For such companies, modest changes in expectations of returns or collections can have a material effect on reported income.

Experience tells us that many companies have used the allowance for uncollectible accounts to shift income from one period into another. For instance, a company may overestimate its allowance in some years. Such an overestimation may have been unintentional, or it may have been an intentional attempt to manage earnings by building up a reserve (during good years) that can be drawn down in subsequent periods in order to increase reported income. Such a reserve is sometimes called a **cookie jar reserve**. Alternatively, a company may underestimate its provision in some years. This underestimation may be unintentional, or it may be an attempt to boost earnings to achieve some desired target. Looking at the patterns in the reconciliation of the allowance for uncollectible accounts may provide some indicators of this behavior.[5]

The MD&A section of a company's 10-K report often provides insights into changes in company policies, customers, or economic conditions to help explain changes in the allowance account. Further, the amount and timing of the uncollectible provision is largely controlled by management. Although external auditors assess the reasonableness of the allowance for uncollectible accounts, auditors do not possess the inside knowledge of management and are, therefore, at an information disadvantage, particularly if a dispute arises.

Some insight can be gained by comparing Cisco's allowance to those of its competitors. **Exhibit 6.9** illustrates that Cisco's allowance as a percentage of total receivables is significantly above that of its competitors, **F5 Networks, Inc.**, **Hewlett-Packard Company**, and **Juniper Networks, Inc.** This result suggests that Cisco is either more liberal in its credit policies or more conservative in its estimate of uncollectible accounts. In addition, Cisco increased the allowance as a percentage of receivables over this period, while none of its competitors did.

EXHIBIT 6.9	Allowance for Doubtful Accounts as a Percentage of Gross Receivables

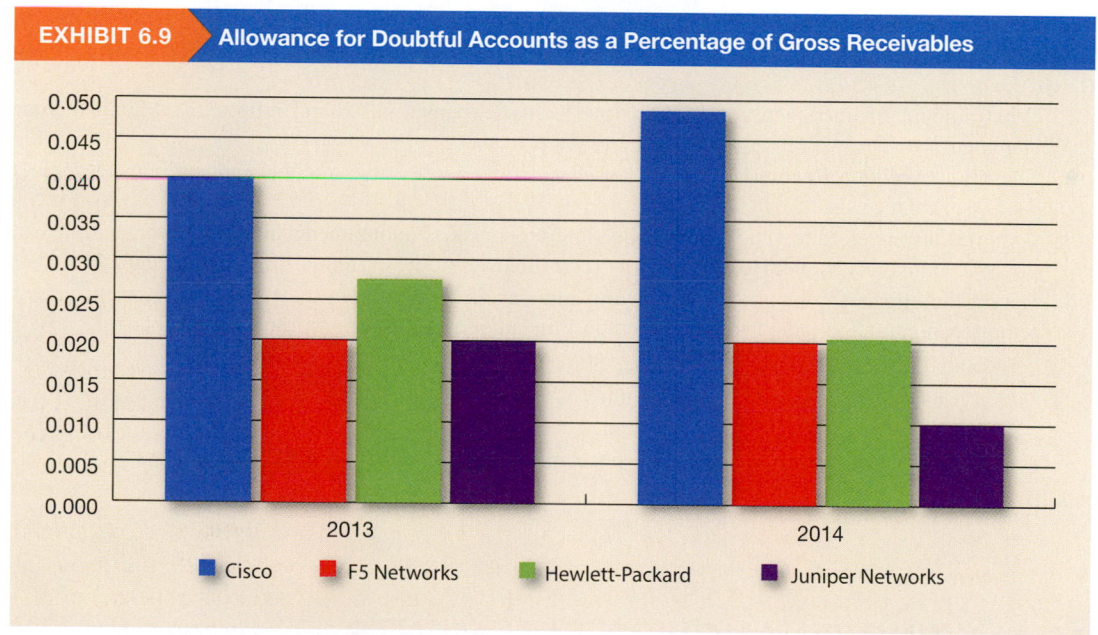

These companies do not have identical fiscal year-ends. Cisco's fiscal year ends in late July, F5 Networks on September 30, Hewlett-Packard on October 31, and Juniper Networks on December 31. The comparisons in this exhibit (and in those following) are based on the most recent financial statements for each company available prior to Cisco's statements.

Ultimately, a company makes two representations when reporting accounts receivable (net) in the current asset section of its balance sheet:

[5] See McNichols, Maureen and G. Peter Wilson, "Evidence of Earnings Management from the Provision for Bad Debts," *Journal of Accounting Research*, Supplement 1988.

1. It expects to collect the asset amount reported on the balance sheet (remember, accounts receivable are reported net of allowance for uncollectible accounts).

2. It expects to collect the asset amount within the next year (implied from its classification as a current asset).

From an analysis viewpoint, we scrutinize the adequacy of a company's provision for its uncollectible accounts. If the provision is inadequate, the cash ultimately collected will be less than what the company is reporting as net receivables.

The financial statement effects of uncollectible accounts are at the point of estimation, not at the time of a write-off. Nevertheless, it is important to remember that management sets the size of the allowance, albeit with auditor assurances.

MID-CHAPTER REVIEW 3

At December 31, 2016, Engel Company had a balance of $770,000 in its Accounts Receivable account and an unused balance of $7,000 in its Allowance for Uncollectible Accounts. The company then analyzed and aged its accounts receivable as follows:

Current	$468,000
1–60 days past due	244,000
61–180 days past due	38,000
Over 180 days past due	20,000
Total accounts receivable	$770,000

In the past, the company experienced losses as follows: 1% of current balances, 5% of balances 1–60 days past due, 15% of balances 61–180 days past due, and 40% of balances over 180 days past due. The company bases its provision for credit losses on the aging analysis.

Required

1. What amount of uncollectible accounts (bad debts) expense will Engel report in its 2016 income statement?

2. Show how Accounts Receivable and the Allowance for Uncollectible Accounts appear in its December 31, 2016, balance sheet.

3. Assume that Engel's allowance for uncollectible accounts has maintained a historical average of 2% of gross accounts receivable. How do you interpret the level of the current allowance percentage?

4. Report the effects for each of the following summary transactions in the financial statement effects template, prepare journal entries, and then post the amounts to the appropriate T-accounts.

    a. Bad debts expense estimated at $23,580.

    b. Write off $5,000 in customer accounts.

The solution to this review problem can be found on pages 322–323.

LO5 Calculate return on net operating assets, net operating profit after taxes, net operating profit margin, accounts receivable turnover, and average collection period.

ANALYZING FINANCIAL STATEMENTS

We began this chapter with a discussion of operating income and revenues and proceeded to examine receivables. We now introduce ratios that will aid in our analysis of income, revenue, and receivables. The first ratio is a measure of performance that relates the firm's operating achievements to the resources available. The next ratio, net operating profit margin, relates operating profit to sales. The last two ratios, accounts receivable turnover ratio and the average collection period, aid in the analysis of receivables. Before we discuss these ratios, we examine a commonly-used measure of operating profit first introduced in Chapter 5, net operating profit after taxes (NOPAT).

Net Operating Profit After Taxes (NOPAT)

Net operating profit after taxes (NOPAT) is a widely used measure of operating profitability. NOPAT is calculated as follows:

$$\text{NOPAT} = \text{Net income} - [(\text{Nonoperating revenues} - \text{Nonoperating expenses}) \times (1 - \text{Statutory tax rate})]$$

As described in Appendix A of Chapter 5, we assume that the applicable statutory tax rate on nonoperating revenues and expenses is equal to the federal statutory tax rate of 35%. To illustrate the calculation of NOPAT, refer to Cisco's income statement presented in **Exhibit 6.2**. Cisco reported net income of $7,853 million in 2014. It also reported net interest and other income of $370 million. Therefore, Cisco's NOPAT for 2014 is $7,613 million [$7,853 million − ($370 million × (1 − 0.35))]. In 2013, Cisco's NOPAT was $9,963 million [$9,983 million − ($31 million × (1 − 0.35))].

NOPAT is an important measure of profitability. It is similar to net income except that NOPAT focuses exclusively on after-tax operating performance, while net income measures the overall performance of the company and includes both operating and nonoperating components. NOPAT is used as a performance measure by management and analysts alike and it is also used in a number of ratios, such as the net operating profit margin.

Next, we examine two ratios that allow us to compare operating profitability across firms.

Analysis Objective

We want to gauge the profitability of a company's operations.

Analysis Tool   Return on net operating assets (RNOA).

$$\text{Return on net operating assets (RNOA)} = \frac{\text{NOPAT}}{\text{Average net operating assets}}$$

Applying the Ratio to Cisco Systems

$$\textbf{2013:}\ \text{RNOA} = \frac{\$9,963}{\$30,683} = 0.325 \text{ or } 32.5\%$$

$$\textbf{2014:}\ \text{RNOA} = \frac{\$7,613}{\$32,438} = 0.235 \text{ or } 23.5\%$$

Cisco's average total assets for fiscal 2014 total $103,162.5 million ([$105,134 million + $101,191 million]/2), but $44,016.5 of this amount represents average investments in marketable securities. So, average operating assets are $59,146 million. Cisco also reports average operating liabilities of $26,708 million. Subtracting this amount from average operating assets gives average net operating assets of $32,438 million.

BUSINESS INSIGHT

What constitutes "cash" and when is cash operating and when is it nonoperating?   To compute RNOA in this book we make a simplifying assumption and consider marketable securities and other investments as nonoperating assets, but we consider cash to be an operating asset. This is a matter of judgment for the financial statement user when doing financial statement analysis. The categorization of investment securities as cash or as investments varies across firms. Some companies, such as Hewlett-Packard classify a significant amount of investments as cash equivalents, and thus include the amount in the cash balance on the balance sheet. Other companies include investments in a separate line item on the balance sheet (either in current, long-term assets, or some in each).

Guidance   **Return on net operating assets (RNOA)** is conceptually similar to return on assets (ROA) except that it excludes all nonoperating components of income and investment from the calculation. The resulting ratio is a measure of how well the company is performing relative to its core objective. A company can use investments in securities and financial leverage to report a satisfactory level of profit and return overall, even when its primary operating activities are not performing well. RNOA can reveal weaknesses in a company's operating strategy that are not readily apparent from overall measures such as return on equity and return on assets.

A variation on RNOA is the **return on capital employed**. This ratio examines the return on net operating assets *before* income taxes and is often used to measure performance of business units and division managers within a large organization. Operating managers generally do not have responsibility for income taxes or financing activities. (These functions are typically the responsibility of central management.) Consequently, return on capital employed excludes income taxes and focuses exclusively on the resources made available to the unit manager.

Cisco does not provide enough information to calculate return on capital employed for individual business units, but we can do so for the company as a whole. From **Exhibit 6.2**, we see that pretax operating income is $9,345 million. Average net operating assets, adjusted for income tax assets and liabilities, total $31,701 million.[6] Thus, Cisco's return on capital employed is 29% (=$9,345 million/$31,701 million).

Cisco Systems in Context

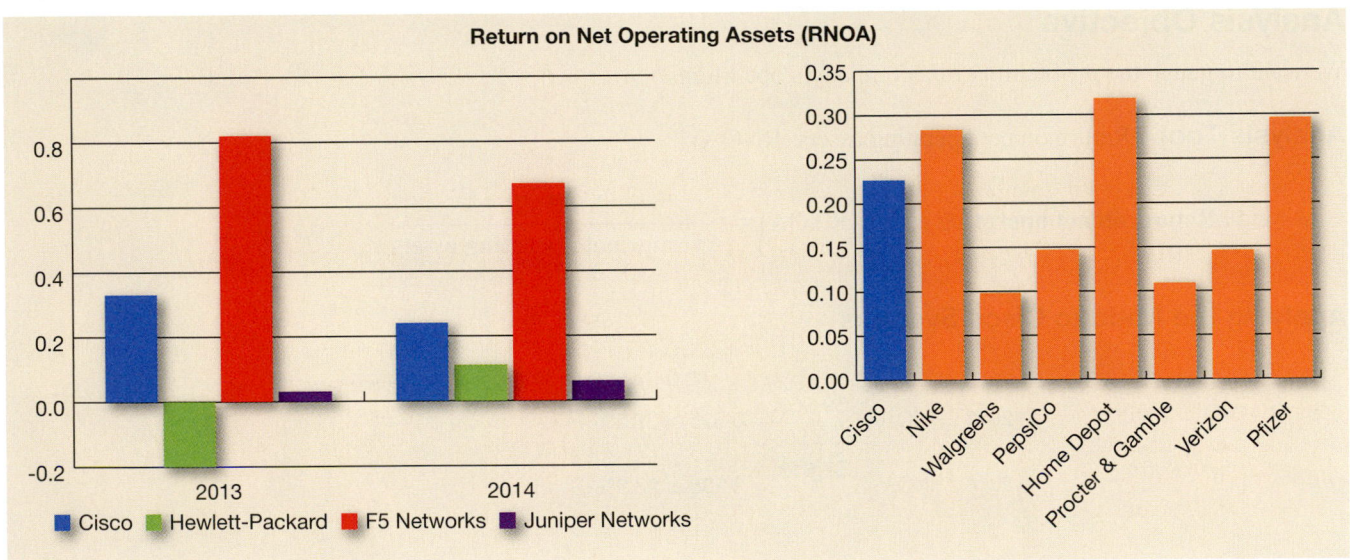

Analysis Tool   Net operating profit margin (NOPM)

$$\text{Net operating profit margin (NOPM)} = \frac{\text{NOPAT}}{\text{Sales revenue}}$$

Applying the Ratio to Cisco Systems

$$\textbf{2013: } \text{NOPM} = \frac{\$9,963}{\$48,607} = 0.205 \text{ or } 20.5\%$$

$$\textbf{2014: } \text{NOPM} = \frac{\$7,613}{\$47,142} = 0.161 \text{ or } 16.1\%$$

---

[6] Because we use operating profit before taxes, accrued income taxes payable and deferred income taxes (assets and liabilities) should be excluded when computing net operating assets for this ratio. Cisco reported average deferred tax assets of $2,712 million and income taxes payable of $1,975 million. Thus, the average net operating assets used to calculate return on capital employed equals $32,438 million − ($2,712 million − $1,975 million) = $31,701 million.

Guidance   Profit margins are commonly used to compare a company to its competitors and to evaluate the performance of business segments. **Net operating profit margin (NOPM)** is a useful summary measure that focuses on the overall operating profitability of the company relative to its sales revenue.

Cisco Systems in Context

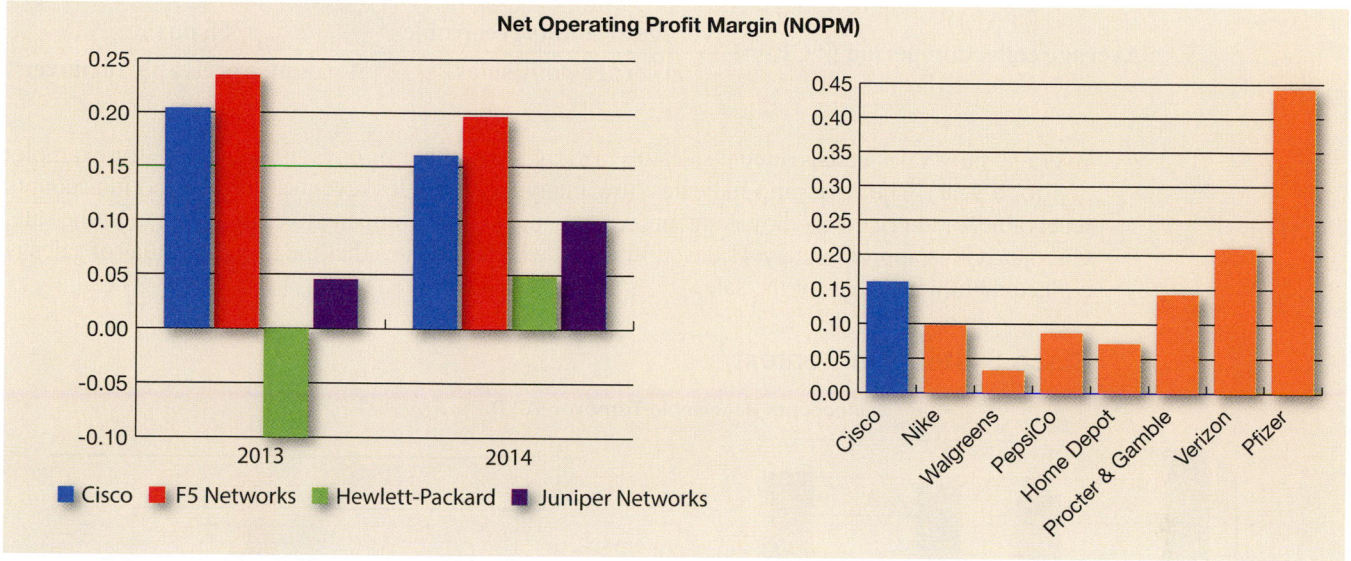

Takeaways   Cisco's return on net operating assets and net operating profit margin are both within the range of the other companies we examine in this text. Retail businesses, such as **Walgreen Co.** and **Home Depot**, tend to have lower operating profit margins than companies in other industries. This does not necessarily translate into lower operating returns. Retail companies rely more heavily on turnover of operating assets to produce returns, relative to other industries.

Cisco's return on net operating assets is higher than two of its primary competitors, Hewlett-Packard and Juniper Networks, but has decreased slightly from 2013 to 2014. Only F5 Networks reported a higher return on net operating assets and operating profit margin than Cisco Systems. In sum, Cisco's operating performance appears to be relatively strong and it does not appear that the company relies too heavily on nonoperating sources of income to generate its returns. However, the decline in returns and margins from 2013 to 2014 may be cause for further investigation.

Analysis Objective

We want to evaluate a company's management of its receivables.

Analysis Tool   Accounts receivable turnover (ART) and average collection period (ACP)

$$\text{Accounts receivable turnover (ART)} = \frac{\text{Sales revenue}}{\text{Average accounts receivable}}$$

Applying the Accounts Receivable Turnover Ratio to Cisco Systems

$$\textbf{2013:} \ \text{ART} = \frac{\$48,607}{(\$5,470 + \$4,369)/2} = 9.9 \text{ times}$$

$$\textbf{2014:} \ \text{ART} = \frac{\$47,142}{(\$5,157 + \$5,470)/2} = 8.9 \text{ times}$$

Guidance **Accounts receivable turnover** measures the number of times each year that accounts receivable is converted into cash. A high turnover ratio suggests that receivables are well managed and that sales revenue quickly leads to cash collected from customers.

A companion measure to accounts receivable turnover is the **average collection period**, also called *days sales outstanding* which is defined as:

$$\text{Average collection period (ACP)} = \frac{\text{Average accounts receivable}}{\text{Average daily sales}} = \frac{\text{365 days}}{\text{Accounts receivable turnover}}$$

Average daily sales equals annual sales divided by the number of days in the period (for example, 365 for a year). The ACP ratio indicates how many days of sales revenue are invested in accounts receivable, or alternatively, how long, on average, it takes the company to collect cash after the sale. Cisco's ACP is approximately 41 days (365/8.9), which indicates that the average dollar of sales is collected within 41 days of the sale.

Cisco Systems in Context

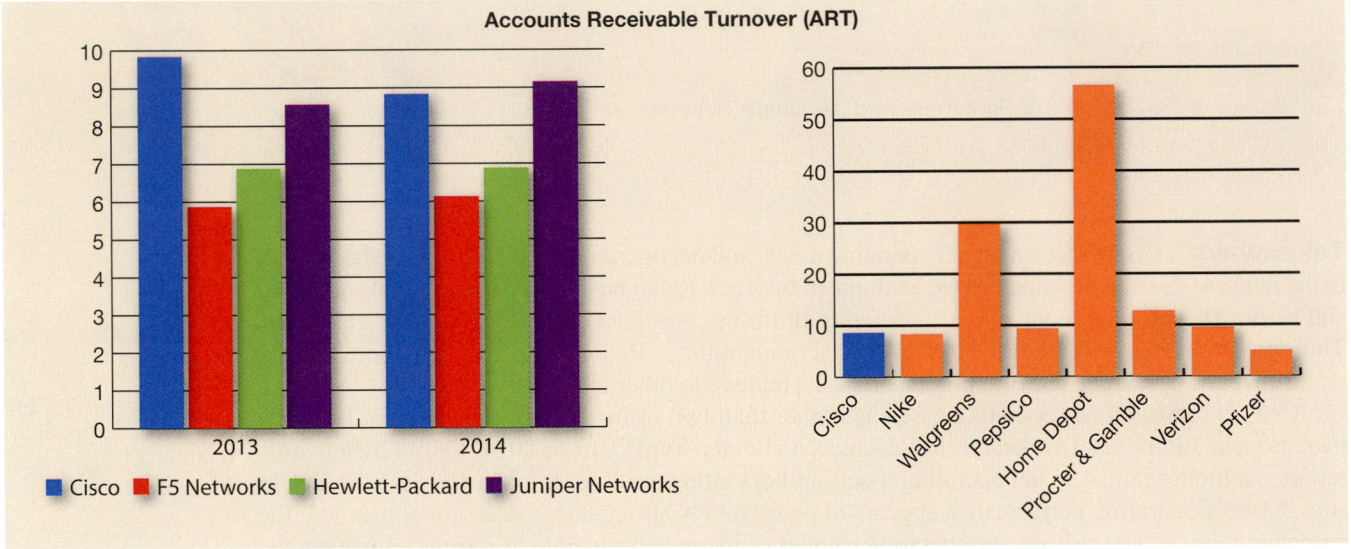

Takeaways The accounts receivable turnover and the average collection period yield valuable insights on at least two dimensions:

1. *Receivables quality.* A change in receivables turnover (and collection period) provides insight into accounts receivable quality. If turnover slows (collection period lengthens), the reason could be deterioration in collectibility of receivables. However, before reaching this conclusion, consider at least three alternative explanations:

   a. A seller can extend its credit terms. If the seller is attempting to enter new markets or take market share from competitors, it may extend credit terms to attract buyers.

   b. A seller can take on longer-paying customers. For example, facing increased competition, many computer and automobile companies began leasing their products, thus reducing the cash outlay for customers and stimulating sales. The change in mix away from cash sales and toward leasing had the effect of reducing receivables turnover and increasing the collection period.

c. The seller can increase the allowance provision. Receivables turnover is often computed using net receivables (after the allowance for uncollectible accounts). Overestimating the provision reduces net receivables and increases turnover.

2. *Asset utilization*. Asset turnover is an important measure of financial performance, both by managers for internal performance goals, as well as by the market in evaluating companies. High performing companies must be both efficient (controlling margins and operating expenses) and productive (getting the most out of their asset base). An increase in receivables ties up cash as the receivables must be financed, and slower-turning receivables carry increased risk of loss. One of the first "low-hanging fruits" that companies pursue in efforts to improve asset utilization is efficiency in receivables collection.

Other Considerations Accounts receivable are sometimes used by companies to obtain financing. This is done in one of two ways: (1) the company can use accounts receivable as collateral for a short-term loan in a transaction called *securitization*, or (2) the company can sell its receivables, which is referred to as *factoring*. A thorough discussion of these transactions is beyond the scope of this text. Nonetheless, if a firm uses securitization or factoring of receivables to obtain short-term financing, the amount of accounts receivable listed on the balance sheet is altered which, in turn, affects the ART ratio.

YOU MAKE THE CALL

You are the Receivables Manager You are analyzing your receivables turnover report for the period, and you are concerned that the average collection period is lengthening, causing a drop in cash flow from operations. What specific actions can you take to reduce the average collection period?
[Answers on page 301]

EARNINGS MANAGEMENT

Management choices about transactions, accounting principles, estimates, disclosure, and presentation of income components are an inevitable part of financial reporting. Earnings management occurs when management uses this discretion to mask the underlying economic performance of a company.

LO6 Discuss earnings management and explain how it affects analysis and interpretation of financial statements.

There are many motives for earnings management, but these motives generally fall into one of two categories:

1. A desire to mislead some financial statement users about the financial performance of the company to gain economic advantage, or

2. A desire to influence legal contracts that use reported accounting numbers to specify contractual obligations and outcomes.[7]

Most earnings management practices relate to aggressive revenue or expense recognition practices. However, financial statement presentation can also be a concern. Below, we identify several examples of potentially misleading reporting.

FYI Earnings management involves earnings quality and management ethics. For the latter, management must consider both legal and personal ethical standards of conduct.

- *Overly optimistic (or overly pessimistic) estimates.* The use of estimates in accrual accounting is extensive. For instance, revenue recognition based on percentage of completion requires estimates of future construction costs. Depreciation expense depends on estimates of useful life, and bad debts expense depends on estimates of future customer payments. Although changes in estimates may be warranted by changes in business conditions, they can have a significant effect on reported net income and, thereby, may provide opportunities for managers to report income that is better (or worse) than it should be.

---

[7] See Healy, Paul M., and James M. Wahlen, "A Review of Earnings Management Literature and Its Implications for Standard Setting," *Accounting Horizons*, December 1999.

- *Channel stuffing.*   **Channel stuffing** arises when a company uses its market power over customers or distributors to induce them to purchase more goods than necessary to meet their normal needs. Or, the seller may offer significant price reductions to encourage buyers to stock up on its products. Channel stuffing usually occurs immediately before the end of an accounting period and boosts the seller's revenue for that period (while increasing the buyer's inventory). The practice is not illegal and revenue may be recorded, as long as the transactions meet the necessary criteria for a sale.

- *Strategic timing and disclosure of transactions and nonrecurring gains and losses.*   Management has some discretion over the timing of transactions that can affect financial statements. If management has an asset (e.g., a tract of land) with book value less than market value, it can choose when to sell the asset to recognize a gain and maintain steady improvements in net income. This practice is known as **income smoothing**. In some cases, these smoothing effects are reported in combination with other items, making it more difficult to separate recurring amounts from nonrecurring amounts. Or, a company could take a **big bath** by recording a nonrecurring loss in a period of already depressed income. Concentrating bad news in a single period reduces the amount of bad news recognized in other periods. Given adequate disclosure, the astute reader of the financial statements will separate nonrecurring income items from persistent operating income, making these income management tactics transparent.

> **FYI** An arm's-length transaction is any transaction between two unrelated parties.

- *Mischaracterizing transactions as arm's-length.*   Transfers of inventories or other assets to related entities typically are not recorded until later **arm's-length** sales occur. Sometimes sales are disguised as being sold to unrelated entities to inflate income when (1) the buyer is a related party to the seller, or (2) financing is provided or guaranteed by the seller, or (3) the buyer is a special-purpose entity that fails to meet independence requirements. This financial reporting practice is not consistent with GAAP and may be fraudulent.

BUSINESS INSIGHT

Sell-through Accounting at Cisco   Following is an excerpt from Cisco System's revenue recognition policies from its annual report.

> Distributors hold inventory and typically sell to systems integrators, service providers, and other resellers. We refer to sales through distributors as our two-tier system of sales to the end customer. Revenue from distributors is recognized based on a sell-through method using information provided by them.

> The "sell-through" method is essentially the same as the accounting for consignment arrangements. By not recognizing revenue until its distributors and retail partners sell its products to the final customer, Cisco greatly reduces the likelihood of any channel stuffing behavior.

The consequence of earnings management is that the usefulness of the information presented in the income statement is compromised. **Quality of earnings** is a term that analysts often use to describe the extent to which reported income reflects the underlying economic performance of a company. Financial statement users must be careful to examine the quality of a company's earnings before using that information to evaluate performance or value its securities.[8]

YOU MAKE THE CALL

You are the Controller   While evaluating the performance of your sales staff, you notice that one of the salespeople consistently meets his quarterly sales quotas but never surpasses his goals by very much. You also discover that his customers often return an unusually large amount of product at the beginning of each quarter. What might be happening here? How would you investigate for potential abuse? [Answer on page 301]

---

[8] See Dechow, Patricia, Weili Ge, and Catherine Schrand, "Understanding Earnings Quality: A Review of the Proxies, their Determinants, and their Consequences," *Journal of Accounting and Economics*, December, 2010.

CHAPTER-END REVIEW

The following data were taken from the 2014 10-K reports of **Comcast Corporation** and **Time Warner, Inc.**:

($ millions)	Comcast	Time Warner
Sales revenue	$68,775	$27,359
Net income	8,592	3,827
Nonoperating revenues	296	0
Nonoperating expenses	2,832	1,296
Accounts receivable, net (end-of-year)	6,321	7,720
Accounts receivable, net (beginning-of-year)	6,376	7,305
Operating assets (end-of-year)	155,602	60,933
Operating assets (beginning-of-year)	151,470	65,990
Operating liabilities (end-of-year)	56,971	16,289
Operating liabilities (beginning-of-year)	58,951	17,284

REQUIRED

1. Compute the following for each company:
   a. Net operating profit after taxes (NOPAT). Assume a 35% statutory tax rate.
   b. Return on net operating assets (RNOA).
   c. Net operating profit margin (NOPM).
   d. Accounts receivable turnover (ART).
   e. Average collection period (ACP).
2. Compare these two companies based on the ratios computed in (1). What inferences can you make about these competitors?

The solution to this review problem can be found on page 323.

APPENDIX 6A: Reporting Nonrecurring Items

In addition to categorizing income statement elements as either operating or nonoperating, it is also useful to separate **recurring** sources of income from those sources that are **nonrecurring**. Isolating nonrecurring earnings is useful for two reasons. First, to evaluate company performance or management quality, it is helpful to make comparisons of current performance with prior years and with other companies facing similar economic circumstances. It is easier to make these comparisons if we focus on recurring income components. Nonrecurring income components are likely to be specific to one company and one accounting period, making them irrelevant for comparative purposes. Second, estimation of company value involves forecasts of income and cash

LO7 Describe and illustrate the reporting for nonrecurring items.

7

flows. Such forecasts are better when we can identify any nonrecurring effects in income and cash flows and then eliminate them from projections. Recurring earnings and cash flows are more **persistent** and, therefore, more useful in estimating company value.

Accounting standards attempt to distinguish some nonrecurring income components. Two of the most common nonrecurring items are:

FYI Previously, a third category, extraordinary items, existed that reported gains or losses from unusual and infrequent items. FASB has eliminated this third category effective for fiscal years beginning after December 15, 2015. The category was eliminated in an effort toward simplification. See Accounting Standards Update 2015-01.

- **Discontinued operations**—income related to business units that the company has discontinued and sold or plans to sell.
- **Restructuring charges**—expenses and losses related to significant reorganization of a company's operations.

Discontinued Operations

Discontinued operations refer to separately identifiable components of the company that management sells or intends to sell. Recent guidance for discontinued operations (ASU 2014-08) provides that only disposals representing a strategic shift in operations should be reported as discontinued operations. Examples include a disposal of a major geographical segment, a major line of business, or a major equity investment. The new guidance was issued because of concerns that too many disposals of small asset groups were being classified as discontinued operations.

The income or loss of the discontinued operations (net of tax), and the after-tax gain or loss on sale of the unit, are reported in the income statement below income from continuing operations. The segregation of discontinued operations means that its revenues and expenses are *not* reported with revenues and expenses from continuing operations.

To illustrate, assume that Chapman Company's income statement results were the following.

	Continuing Operations	Discontinued Operations	Total
Revenues	$10,000	$3,000	$13,000
Expenses	7,000	2,000	9,000
Pretax income	3,000	1,000	4,000
Tax expense (40%).	1,200	400	1,600
Net income.	$ 1,800	$ 600	$ 2,400

The reported income statement would then appear with the separate disclosure for discontinued operations (shown in bold, separately net of any related taxes) as follows.

Revenues	$10,000
Expenses	7,000
Pretax income	3,000
Tax expense (40%).	1,200
Income from continuing operations	1,800
Income from discontinued operations, net of income taxes	**600**
Net income.	$ 2,400

FYI Income, gains, and losses from discontinued operations are reported separately from other items to alert readers to their transitory nature.

Revenues and expenses reflect the continuing operations only, and the (persistent) income from continuing operations is reported after deducting the related tax expense. Results from the (transitory) discontinued operations are collapsed into one line item and reported separately net of any related taxes. The same is true for any gain or loss from sale of the discontinued operation's net assets. The net income figure is unchanged by this presentation, but our ability to evaluate and interpret income information is greatly improved.

Exit or Disposal Costs

Exit or disposal costs include but are not limited to **restructuring costs**. Exit and disposal costs typically include activities such as consolidating production facilities, reorganizing sales operations, outsourcing product lines, or discontinuing product lines within a business unit or that do not represent a strategic shift in operations. These costs should be separately disclosed if material, but if not material are not required to be shown as a separate line item on the income statement. Often these costs, such as restructuring costs, are material in nature and are shown as a separate line item or are detailed in the notes to the financial statements. These costs are considered transitory because many companies do not engage in restructuring activities every year. As such, these costs should be classified to a transitory category for analysis purposes even though the costs are included in income from continuing operations. Restructuring costs include, but are not limited to, the following types of costs:

1. Employee severance costs
2. Costs to consolidate and close facilities, including asset write-downs

The first of these, **employee severance costs**, represent accrued (estimated) costs for termination of employees as part of a restructuring program. The second part of restructuring costs consists of **asset write-downs**, also called *write-offs* or *charge-offs*. Restructuring activities usually involve closure or relocation of manufacturing or administrative facilities. This process can require the write-down of long-term assets (such as plant assets), and the write-down of inventories that are no longer salable at current carrying costs.

Cisco reported restructuring charges of $418 million in its fiscal 2014 income statement and $105 million (net) in its 2013 income statement. These charges were discussed in the footnotes.

In August 2013, the Company announced a workforce reduction plan that would impact up to 4,000 employees, or 5% of the Company's global workforce. In connection with this restructuring action, the Company incurred charges of $418 million during fiscal 2014. The Company has completed the Fiscal 2014 restructuring and does not expect any remaining charges related to this action. The Fiscal 2011 Plans consist primarily of the realignment and restructuring of the Company's business announced in July 2011 and of certain consumer product lines as announced during April 2011. . . . The following table summarizes the activities related to the restructuring and other charges pursuant to the Company's Fiscal 2014 Plan and the Fiscal 2011 Plans related to the realignment and restructuring of the Company's business (in millions):

	Fiscal 2011 Plans	Employee Severance	Other	Total
Balance as of July 27, 2013	$28	$ 0	$ 0	$ 28
Gross charges in fiscal 2014		366	52	418
Cash payments	(22)	(326)	(4)	(352)
Non-cash items	(3)		(22)	(25)
Balance as of July 26, 2014	$ 3	$ 40	$26	$ 69

Most of Cisco's restructuring costs were in the form of severance pay to employees and payments to retirement programs as compensation to employees who elect to take early retirement. As of the end of fiscal 2014, Cisco had $69 million in restructuring charges that had been accrued but not yet paid.

RESEARCH INSIGHT

Restructuring Costs and Managerial Incentives   Research has investigated the circumstances and effects of restructuring costs. Some research finds that stock prices increase upon announcement of a restructuring as if the market appreciates the company's candor. Research also finds that many companies that reduce income through restructuring costs later reverse those costs, resulting in a substantial income boost for the period of reversal. These reversals often occur when their absence would have yielded an earnings decline. Whether or not the market responds favorably to trimming the fat or simply disregards such transitory items as uninformative, managers have incentives to exclude such income-decreasing items from operating income. These incentives are contractually-based, extending from debt covenants and restrictions to managerial bonuses.

YOU MAKE THE CALL

You are the Financial Analyst   You are analyzing the financial statements of a company that has reported a large restructuring cost, involving both employee severance and asset write-downs, in its income statement. How do you interpret and treat this cost in your analysis of its current and future period profitability? [Answer on page 301]

APPENDIX 6A REVIEW

On April 30, 2016, Singh Corporation decided to close its operations in Fiji. During the first four months of the year (January through April) these operations had reported a loss of $120,000. Singh paid its employees $12,000 in severance pay. The assets of this operation were sold at a loss of $18,000. The tax rate in Fiji is 30%.

REQUIRED

a. If this closure is recorded as discontinued operations, how should it be presented in Singh's income statement?

b. If this closure is classified as a restructuring charge, how would it be presented in Singh's income statement?

c. What would determine whether this event should be reported as discontinued operations or a restructuring charge?

The solution to this review problem can be found on page 324.

LO8 Describe the new standard for revenue recognition and discuss its potential effects.

APPENDIX 6B: New Standards for Revenue Recognition

The FASB and the IASB issued new, converged accounting standards for revenue recognition in May of 2014.[9] The new standard is intended to develop a common revenue standard between U.S. GAAP and IFRS and to consolidate the guidance and rules for revenue recognition into one standard as opposed to the patchwork of standards and sources of guidance that had developed over time for various transactions and industries. In addition, the new standard aims to eliminate inconsistencies that exist across industries and transactions. The new standard is more principles based and will require management to exercise more judgment; however, it broadly employs many of the same overriding concepts to revenue recognition as the current standards. The standard setters intend for the new standards to improve comparability and disclosure for financial statement users.

In August 2015, FASB and IASB deferred the effective dates of the new standards by one year from the originally stated effective dates. The new effective dates are as follows. Public business entities, certain not-for-profit entities, and certain employee benefit plans are required to apply the guidance in Update 2014-09 to annual reporting periods beginning after December 15, 2017, including interim reporting periods within that reporting period. Thus, for calendar year-end companies, the required effective date is January 1, 2018.[10] All other entities, including private business entities, are required to apply the guidance in Update 2014-09 to annual reporting periods beginning after December 15, 2018, and interim reporting periods within annual reporting periods beginning after December 15, 2019.[11] Thus, the required effective dates are more than two years away at the time of the writing of this text. As a result, we do not have examples of companies applying the new standard and we cannot show any disclosures under the new standard. In this appendix, we discuss the overriding principles of the new standard and conjecture about potential implications of the new standard based on industry reports and company disclosures available at this time.

The new standard's core principle is that an entity should recognize revenue to depict the transfer of goods or services to customers in an amount that reflects the consideration to which the entity expects to be entitled in the exchange for those goods and services. FASB outlines the following five steps in the revenue recognition process:

Step 1.   Identify the contract with a customer
Step 2.   Identify the performance obligations in the contract
Step 3.   Determine the transaction price
Step 4.   Allocate the transaction price
Step 5.   Recognize revenue when or as the entity satisfies a performance obligation

Collectibility of payment (broadly similar to the idea of realized or realizable discussed as part of the current accounting standards for revenue recognition) continues to be an important issue for revenue recognition. Under

---

[9] FASB issued Accounting Standards Update (ASU) 2014-09 and the IASB issued International Financial Reporting Standards 15, both entitled *Revenue from Contracts with Customers*. ASU 2014-09 creates Topic 606, *Revenue from Contracts with Customers*, in codified GAAP, which supersedes the revenue recognition requirements in Topic 605, *Revenue Recognition*, including most industry-specific revenue recognition guidance.

[10] Early adoption is permitted, but only as of annual reporting periods beginning after December 15, 2016, including interim reporting periods within that reporting period.

[11] Early adoption is also permitted for these entities, but only as early as annual reporting periods beginning after December 15, 2016, including interim reporting periods within that reporting period (or within annual reporting periods beginning one year after the annual reporting period in which the entity first applies the guidance in Update 2014-09).

the new standard, collectibility should be assessed in determining whether a contract exists (i.e., whether the entity has passed Step 1 of the 5-step revenue recognition process listed above).

In general, the new revenue recognition standard does not conceptually change the accounting for bad debts from the current rules. However, the new standard will require more judgment on the part of management in determining whether the expectation of partial payment on a sales contract is 1) evidence that the contract lacks collectibility in which case revenue cannot be recorded, 2) due to a price concession in which case revenue should be recorded but at the expected lower amount, or 3) a bad debt, in which case sales should be recognized in full but with bad debt provision recorded. The additional required judgment about collectibility could lead to uncertainty and potentially significant changes to revenue recognition for some entities. As firms apply the standard in future years, we will be able to observe and discuss more fully the consequences of these changes.

Long-Term Contracts

With respect to the accounting for long-term contracts, the new revenue recognition standard does not use the terms percentage-of-completion method, cost-recovery method, or completed contract method. All contracts fall under the 5-step process outlined above and revenue is recognized as performance obligations are satisfied, that is, when control of the good or service transfers to the customer. This can occur either at a point in time or over time. For most long-term contracts, revenue will be recognized over time. Under the new standard, measuring progress toward completion is done using either what is called the input method or the output method. It is likely that for many long-term contracts, such as construction contracts, most performance obligations will be measured over time using the input method. This method of revenue recognition is consistent with the percentage-of-completion method that is often applied under the current standard. Thus, the general overriding principles for revenue recognition are similar between the old and new standards for long-term contracts.

Disclosure

Significant changes in disclosure are required in the new standard. Companies will need to provide both qualitative and quantitative disclosure about contracts with customers including revenues recognized, disaggregation of revenues, contract balances, and performance obligations (including transaction prices allocated to remaining performance obligations). Additional disclosures will also be required about judgments and changes in judgments such as determining the timing of satisfaction of performance obligations (over time or at a point in time) and determining the transaction price and amounts allocated to performance obligations.

Potential Effects of Accounting Standards Update 2014-09 (Topic 606)

The effects of the new accounting standard for revenue recognition are not entirely clear at the time of this writing. The new standard calls for enhanced disclosure and additional documentation of internal controls over revenue recognition. In addition, while the overall spirit of the new standard is similar to current GAAP, it is likely the new standard will affect the reporting of revenues to some extent for many companies, especially those with multiple element contracts requiring revenue to be deferred and recognized across multiple periods. Some examples of potential and expected impacts are as follows.

- In **Microsoft**'s most recent annual report they state that they "*anticipate this standard will have a material impact on our consolidated financial statements and we are currently evaluating its impact.*"
- **Electronic Arts, Inc.** (see P6-47) states in its most recent annual report that "*. . . We recognize all of the revenue from bundled sales (i.e., online-enabled games that include updates on a when-and-if-available basis or a matchmaking service) on a deferred basis over an estimated offering period . . . We believe the current proposal by the FASB would require us to materially change the way we account for revenue by requiring us to recognize more revenue upon delivery of the primary product than we currently do under current accounting standards.*"
- A recent *Wall Street Journal* article (January 26, 2015) reports that **Ford Motor Co.** and **General Motors Co.** say that the new rules might force them to account separately for each car sold rather than allowing a grouping into comparable transactions.
- Airline companies may also be affected. It is likely that airlines will have to change the way they account for loyalty programs (e.g., frequent flier programs). For example, it appears likely that loyalty points will be treated as a revenue element and some portion of the transaction price will have to be allocated to the loyalty element based on the estimated standalone selling price of each performance obligation (Source: E&Y Technical Line, "The New Revenue Recognition Standard—Airlines").
- In a similar example as the airlines, companies that provide promotions or "free" goods may have to allocate revenues differently than they do currently. For example, when a wireless carrier sells a service contract and gives a free or discounted phone to the customer, it is likely that under the new standard

more revenue will likely be allocated to the sale of the phone, reducing margins on the service contracts. Even a simple retailer that offers a promotion such as buy three and get one free, will have to allocate revenue across the four products under the new standard.

- A panel of experts suggested that companies should be aware of changes to footnote disclosure requirements and should not regard those as an insignificant event. Lynne Triplett, a partner at Grant Thornton, said her greatest concern, "*is that companies aren't going to be prepared for the disclosures aspect.*" (Source: Bloomberg BNA conference entitled, "Inside Revenue Recognition: A Deep Dive into Assessment & Implementation Under the New Revenue Recognition Standard" held on September 17, 2015, reported on in Bloomberg BNA on September 22, 2015).

At a high level, the new standard applies many of the same broad principles of revenue recognition as the current standard. However, there will likely be significant changes for many companies in terms of the timing of recognition, the allocation of revenue to transactions, and the disclosures about the revenue recognition process. These changes could have far reaching implications. For example, revenue recognition changes could affect operational decisions and outcomes such as the use of coupons, compensation in the form of sales commissions, and many others. As companies start to apply the standard, the standard setters may issue additional guidance or clarifications. In future editions of this text, we will incorporate examples from company disclosures as the new standard is applied and will discuss any future updates and guidance from the standard setters.

SUMMARY

LO1   **Describe and apply the criteria for determining when revenue is recognized. (p. 274)**

- Revenue is recognized when it is earned and realized (or realizable).

LO2   **Illustrate revenue and expense recognition when the transaction involves future deliverables and/or multiple elements. (p. 275)**

- When customers pay prior to the delivery of all elements of the product (or service) package, an unearned revenue liability must be recognized.
- When a company recognizes an unearned revenue liability, its reported revenue for a period does not coincide with the purchases made by customers in that period.

LO3   **Illustrate revenue and expense recognition for long-term projects. (p. 279)**

- Long-term contracts are recorded using the percentage-of-completion method when a signed contract exists with a fixed or determinable price, collection is reasonably assured, and the cost of completing the contract can be estimated.
- The completed contract method is used when the conditions for using percentage-of-completion are not met.

LO4   **Estimate and account for uncollectible accounts receivable. (p. 282)**

- Uncollectible accounts are usually estimated by aging the accounts receivable.
- Estimated uncollectible accounts are recorded as a contra-asset called allowance for uncollectible accounts.
- Write-offs of uncollectible accounts are deducted from accounts receivable and from the allowance account.

LO5   **Calculate return on net operating assets, net operating profit after taxes, net operating profit margin, accounts receivable turnover, and average collection period. (p. 288)**

- Net operating profit after taxes (NOPAT) and the net operating profit margin (NOPM) are measures of the profitability of operating activities.
- Return on net operating assets measures after-tax operating performance relative to available net operating assets; similarly, return on capital employed is a pretax measure that is used to evaluate business unit performance.
- Accounts receivable turnover (ART) and average collection period (ACP) measure the ability of the company to convert receivables into cash through collection.

LO6   **Discuss earnings management and explain how it affects analysis and interpretation of financial statements. (p. 293)**

- Earnings management occurs when management uses its discretion to mask the underlying economic performance of a company.
- The consequence of earnings management is that the usefulness of the information presented in the income statement is compromised.

Appendix 6A: Describe and illustrate the reporting for nonrecurring items. (p. 295)   LO7

- Income or loss from discontinued operations is a transitory (nonrecurring) item that is reported net of income taxes after earnings from continuing operations.
- Restructuring charges include asset write-downs and employee severance costs. Even though these charges are typically reported among earnings from continuing operations, they are classified as transitory for analysis purposes.

Appendix 6B: Describe the new standard for revenue recognition and discuss its potential effects. (p. 298)   LO8

- New standards for revenue recognition were issued to create a common revenue standard between IFRS and U.S. GAAP and to consolidate various rules and industry guidance into one standard.
- The effective date for calendar year companies that are publicly traded is January 1, 2018 and is January 1, 2019 for calendar year companies that are privately held
- The new revenue standard is, at a high level, conceptually similar to the current standard. However, the timing of revenue recognition will likely change for many companies, especially those with multiple element sales contracts. The new standard also requires much more disclosure about a company's revenue recognition process.

GUIDANCE ANSWERS . . . YOU MAKE THE CALL

You are the Receivables Manager   First, you must realize that the extension of credit is an important tool in the marketing of your products, often as important as advertising and promotion. Given that receivables are necessary, there are some methods we can use to speed their collection. (1) We can better screen the customers to whom we extend credit. (2) We can negotiate advance or progress payments from customers. (3) We can use bank letters of credit or other automatic drafting prcedures so that billings need not be sent. (4) We can make sure products are sent as ordered to reduce disputes. (5) We can improve administration of past due accounts to provide for more timely notices of delinquencies and better collection procedures.

You are the Controller   The salesperson may be channel stuffing or recording sales without a confirmed sales order. The unusual amount of returns suggests that sales revenues are most likely being recognized prematurely. To investigate, you could examine specific sales orders from customers who returned goods early in the following quarter, or contact customers directly. Most companies delay bonuses until after an appropriate return period expires and only credit the sales staff with net sales.

You are the Financial Analyst   There are two usual components to a restructuring charge: asset write-downs (such as inventories, property, plant, and goodwill) and severance costs. Write-downs occur when the cash flow generating ability of an asset declines, thus reducing its current market value below its book value reported on the balance sheet. Arguably, this decline in cash flow generating ability did not occur solely in the current year and, most likely, has developed over several periods. Delays in loss recognition, such as write-downs of assets, are not uncommon. Thus, prior period income is arguably not as high as reported, and the current period loss is not as great as is reported. Turning to severance costs, their recognition can be viewed as an investment decision by the company that is expected to increase future cash flows (through decreased wages). If this cost accrual is capitalized on the balance sheet, current period income is increased and future period income would bear the amortization of this "asset" to match against future cash flow benefits from severance. This implies that current period income is not as low as reported; however, this adjustment is not GAAP as such severance costs cannot be capitalized. Yet, we can make such an adjustment in our analysis.

KEY RATIOS

Net operating profit after taxes (NOPAT)

$$NOPAT = Net\ income - [(Nonoperating\ revenues - Nonoperating\ expenses) \times (1 - Statutory\ tax\ rate)]$$

Return on net operating assets (RNOA)

$$RNOA = \frac{NOPAT}{Average\ net\ operating\ assets}$$

Net operating profit margin (NOPM)

$$NOPM = \frac{Net\ operating\ profit\ after\ taxes\ (NOPAT)}{Sales\ revenue}$$

Accounts receivable turnover (ART)

$$ART = \frac{Sales\ revenue}{Average\ accounts\ receivable}$$

Average collection period (ACP)

$$ACP = \frac{Average\ accounts\ receivable}{Average\ daily\ sales} = \frac{365}{Accounts\ receivable\ turnover\ (ART)}$$

$$Return\ on\ capital\ employed = \frac{Income\ from\ operations\ before\ taxes}{Average\ net\ operating\ assets}$$

KEY TERMS

Accounts receivable turnover (p. 292)

Aging analysis (p. 282)

Allowance for uncollectible accounts (p. 282)

Arm's-length (p. 294)

Asset write-downs (p. 297)

Average collection period (p. 292)

Bad debts expense (p. 283)

Big bath (p. 294)

Channel stuffing (p. 294)

Completed contract method (p. 280)

Consignment (p. 275)

Cookie jar reserve (p. 287)

Cost-recovery method (p. 280)

Credit sales (p. 281)

Deferred revenue (p. 276)

Discontinued operations (p. 296)

Earned (p. 275)

Employee severance costs (p. 297)

Expense recognition (p. 279)

Income smoothing (p. 294)

Multiple element arrangements (p. 277)

Net operating profit after taxes (NOPAT) (p. 289)

Net operating profit margin (NOPM) (p. 291)

Net realizable value (p. 281)

Noncontrolling interest (p. 273)

Non-GAAP (p. 295)

Nonrecurring (p. 295)

Notes payable (p. 282)

Notes receivable (p. 282)

Percentage-of-completion method (p. 279)

Percentage of sales (p. 282)

Persistent (p. 296)

Pro forma income (p. 295)

Quality of earnings (p. 294)

Realized or realizable (p. 275)

Recurring (p. 295)

Restructuring charges (p. 296)

Restructuring costs (p. 296)

Return on capital employed (p. 290)

Return on net operating assets (RNOA) (p. 290)

Revenue recognition (p. 275)

Revenue recognition criteria (p. 275)

Right of return (p. 275)

Unearned revenue (p. 276)

Assignments with the **MBC** logo in the margin are available in **myBusinessCourse**.
See the Preface of the book for details.

MULTIPLE CHOICE

1. Which of the following best describes the condition(s) that must be present for the recognition of revenue?
   a. Revenue must be earned and collected.
   b. There are no uncertainties in measurement of income.
   c. Revenue must be earned and realizable.
   d. Expenses must be measurable and directly associated with the revenues.

2. When multiple products or services are bundled and sold for one price, the revenue should be
   a. Recognized when the bundle of products is sold
   b. Allocated among the different elements and recognized as each element is delivered to the customer
   c. Deferred until all elements of the bundle are delivered to the customer.
   d. Recognized when the customer pays cash for the products or services.

3. The percentage-of-completion method is preferable to the completed contract method and should be used unless:
   a. There is a lack of dependable estimates or inherent hazards cause forecasts to be doubtful.
   b. Completion rates are certain.
   c. Profits are low.
   d. Projects are more than five years to completion.

4. When management selectively excludes some revenues, expenses, gains, and losses from earnings calculated using generally accepted accounting principles, it is an example of
   a. income smoothing.
   b. big bath accounting.
   c. cookie jar accounting.
   d. pro forma earnings.

5. If bad debts expense is determined by estimating uncollectible accounts receivable, the entry to record the write-off of a specific uncollectible account would decrease
   a. allowance for uncollectible accounts.
   b. net income.

  c.   net book value of accounts receivable.
  d.   bad debts expense.

6. If management intentionally underestimates bad debts expense, then net income is
  a.   overstated and assets are understated.
  b.   understated and assets are overstated.
  c.   understated and asset are understated.
  d.   overstated and assets are overstated.

Superscript ^A denotes assignments based on Appendix 6A.

QUESTIONS

Q6-1.   What are the criteria that guide firms in recognition of revenue? What does each of the criteria mean? How are the criteria met for a company like **Abercrombie & Fitch Co.,** a clothing retailer? How are the criteria met for a construction company that builds offices under long-term contracts with developers?

Q6-2.   Why are discontinued operations reported separately from continuing operations in the income statement?

Q6-3.   Identify the two typical categories of restructuring costs and their effects on the balance sheet and the income statement.

Q6-4.   Explain the concept of a *big bath* and why restructuring costs are often identified with this event.

Q6-5.   Why might companies want to manage earnings? Describe some of the tactics that some companies use to manage earnings.

Q6-6.   What is the concept of *pro forma income* and why has this income measure been criticized?

Q6-7.   Why does GAAP allow management to make estimates of amounts that are included in financial statements? Does this improve the usefulness of financial statements? Explain.

Q6-8.   How might earnings forecasts that are published by financial analysts encourage companies to manage earnings?

Q6-9.   Explain how management can shift income from one period into another by its estimation of uncollectible accounts.

Q6-10.   During an examination of Wallace Company's financial statements, you notice that the allowance for uncollectible accounts has decreased as a percentage of accounts receivable. What are the possible explanations for this change?

Q6-11.   Under what circumstances would it be correct to say that a company would be better off with more uncollectible accounts?

Q6-12.   Estimating the bad debts expense by aging accounts receivable generally results in smaller errors than the percentage of credit sales approach. Can you explain why?

MINI EXERCISES

M6-13.   Computing Percentage-of-Completion Revenues
Bartov Corporation agreed to build a warehouse for $2,500,000. Expected (and actual) costs for the warehouse follow: 2016, $400,000; 2017, $1,000,000; and 2018, $500,000. The company completed the warehouse in 2018. Compute revenues, expenses, and income for each year 2016 through 2018 using the percentage-of-completion method.

LO3

M6-14.   Assessing Revenue Recognition of Companies
Identify and explain when each of the following companies should recognize revenue.

  a.   **The GAP Inc.:** The GAP is a retailer of clothing items for all ages.
  b.   **Merck & Company Inc.:** Merck engages in the development, manufacturing, and marketing of pharmaceutical products. It sells its drugs to retailers like **CVS Caremark Corporation** and **Walgreen Co.**
  c.   **Deere & Company**: Deere manufactures heavy equipment. It sells equipment to a network of independent distributors, who in turn sell the equipment to customers. Deere provides financing and insurance services both to distributors and customers.

LO1

d. **Bank of America Corporation**: Bank of America is a banking institution. It lends money to individuals and corporations and invests excess funds in marketable securities.

e. **Johnson Controls Inc.**: Johnson Controls manufactures products for the U.S. Government under long-term contracts.

f. **Syngenta AG**: Syngenta is a Swiss global agribusiness operating in crop protection, seeds, lawn and garden. Its products are consumed mainly by growers of diverse size and often sold through distributers. Some product return rates can be reliably estimated and some cannot be estimated.

LO1

M6-15. Estimating Revenue Recognition with Right of Return

The Unlimited Company offers an unconditional return policy for its retail clothing business. It normally expects 2% of sales at retail selling prices to be returned at some point prior to the expiration of the return period, and returned items cannot be resold. Assuming that it records total sales of $5 million for the current period, how much net revenue would it report for this period?

LO3

M6-16. Using Percentage-of-Completion and Completed Contract Methods

Halsey Building Company signed a contract to build an office building for $40,000,000. The scheduled construction costs follow.

Year	Cost
2016	$ 9,000,000
2017	15,000,000
2018	6,000,000
Total	$30,000,000

The building is completed in 2018.

For each year, compute the revenue, expense, and gross profit reported for this construction project using each of the following methods.

a. Percentage-of-completion method
b. Completed contract method

LO1, 2

M6-17. Explaining Revenue Recognition and Bundled Sales

A.J. Smith Electronics is a retail consumer electronics company that also sells extended warranty contracts for many of the products that it carries. The extended warranty provides coverage for three years beyond expiration of the manufacturer's warranty. In 2016, A.J. Smith sold extended warranties amounting to $1,700,000. The warranty coverage for all of these begins in 2017 and runs through 2019. The total expected cost of providing warranty services on these contracts is $500,000.

a. How should A.J. Smith recognize revenue on the extended warranty contracts?
b. Estimate the revenue, expense, and gross profit reported from these contracts in the year(s) that the revenue is recognized.
c. In 2017, as a special promotion, A.J. Smith sold a digital camera (retail price $300), a digital photograph printer (retail price $125), and an extended warranty contract for each (total retail price $75) as a package for a special price of $399. The extended warranty covers the period from 2018 through 2020. The company sold 200 of these camera–printer packages. Compute the revenue that A.J. Smith should recognize in each year from 2017 through 2020.

LO4

M6-18. Reporting Uncollectible Accounts and Accounts Receivables

Mohan Company estimates its uncollectible accounts by aging its accounts receivable and applying percentages to various aged categories of accounts. Mohan computes a total of $2,100 in estimated losses as of December 31, 2016. Its Accounts Receivable has a balance of $98,000, and its allowance for Uncollectible Accounts has an unused balance of $500 before adjustment at December 31, 2016.

a. What is the amount of bad debts expense that Mohan will report in 2016?
b. Determine the net amount of accounts receivable reported in current assets at December 31, 2016.
c. Set up T-accounts for both Bad Debt Expense and for Allowance for Uncollectible Accounts. Enter any beginning balances and effects from the information above (including your results from parts *a* and *b*). Explain the numbers for each of your T-accounts.

M6-19. **Explaining the Allowance Method for Accounts Receivable**

LO4

At a recent board of directors meeting of Ascot, Inc., one of the directors expressed concern over the allowance for uncollectible accounts appearing in the company's balance sheet. "I don't understand this account," he said. "Why don't we just show accounts receivable at the amount owed to us and get rid of that allowance?" Respond to that director's question. Include in your response (a) an explanation of why the company has an allowance account, (b) what the balance sheet presentation of accounts receivable is intended to show, and (c) how the concept of expense recognition relates to the analysis and presentation of accounts receivable.

M6-20. **Analyzing the Allowance for Uncollectible Accounts**

LO4, 5

Following is the current asset section from the **Ralph Lauren Corporation** balance sheet:

Ralph Lauren Corporation
NYSE :: RL

At March 29, 30 ($ millions)	2014	2013
Cash and cash equivalents	$ 797	$ 974
Short-term investments	488	325
Accounts receivable, net of allowances of $270 in 2014 and $245 in 2013 ...	588	458
Inventories	1,020	896
Income tax receivable	62	29
Deferred tax assets	150	120
Prepaid expenses and other current assets.	224	161
Total current assets	$3,329	$2,963

a.   Compute the gross amount of accounts receivable for both 2014 and 2013. Compute the percentage of the allowance for uncollectible accounts relative to the gross amount of accounts receivable for each of these years.

b.   How do you interpret the change in the percentage of the allowance for uncollectible accounts relative to total accounts receivable computed in part *a*?

c.   Ralph Lauren reported net sales of $7,284 million in 2014. Compute its accounts receivable turnover and average collection period.

M6-21. **Analyzing Accounts Receivable Changes**

LO4

The comparative balance sheets of Sloan Company reveal that accounts receivable (before deducting allowances) increased by $15,000 in 2016. During the same time period, the allowance for uncollectible accounts increased by $2,100. If sales revenue was $120,000 in 2016 and bad debts expense was 2% of sales, how much cash was collected from customers during the year?

M6-22. **Evaluating Accounts Receivable Turnover for Competitors**

LO5

The **Procter & Gamble Company** and **Colgate-Palmolive Company** report the following sales and accounts receivable balances ($ millions):

The Procter & Gamble Company
NYSE :: PG

Colgate-Palmolive Company
NYSE :: CL

	Procter & Gamble			Colgate-Palmolive		
Fiscal year	Sales	Accounts Receivable	Fiscal year	Sales	Accounts Receivable	
June 30, 2014...	$83,062	$6,386	December 31, 2013 ..	$17,420	$1,636	
June 30, 2013...	82,581	6,508	December 31, 2012 ..	17,085	1,668	

a.   Compute accounts receivable turnover and average collection period for both companies.

b.   Identify and discuss a potential explanation for the difference between these competitors' accounts receivable turnover.

M6-23. **Analyzing Accounts Receivable Changes**

LO4

In 2016, Grant Corporation recorded credit sales of $3,200,000 and bad debts expense of $42,000. Write-offs of uncollectible accounts totaled $39,000 and one account, worth $12,000, that had been written off in an earlier year was collected in 2016.

a.   Prepare journal entries to record each of these transactions.

b.   If net accounts receivable increased by $220,000, how much cash was collected from credit customers during the year? Prepare a journal entry to record cash collections.

c.   Set up T-accounts and post each of the transactions in parts *a* and *b* to them.

d. Record each of the above transactions in the financial statement effects template to show the effect of these entries on the balance sheet and income statement.

LO2 **M6-24. Analyzing Unearned Revenue Changes**

Finn Publishing Corp. produces a monthly publication aimed at competitive swimmers, with articles profiling current stars of the sport, advice from coaches, and advertising by swimwear companies, training organizations and others. The magazine is distributed through newsstands and bookstores, and by mail to subscribers. The most common subscription is for twelve months. When Finn Publishing receives payment of an annual subscription, it records an Unearned Revenue liability that is reduced by 1/12th each month as publications are provided.

The table below provides four years of revenues from the income statement and unearned revenue from the balance sheet. (All amounts in $ thousands.)

Fiscal year	Revenue	Unearned revenue liability (end of year)
2015	$48,000	$20,000
2016	55,000	24,000
2017	62,000	26,000
2018	62,000	25,000

a. Calculate the growth in revenue from 2015 to 2016, 2016 to 2017, and from 2017 to 2018.
b. Calculate the amount of customer purchases in 2016, 2017, and 2018. Customer purchases are defined as sales made at newsstands and bookstores, plus the amount paid for new or renewal subscriptions. Again, calculate the growth rates from 2016 to 2017 and from 2017 to 2018.
c. Explain the differences in growth rates between parts *a* and *b* above.

LO2 **M6-25. Applying Revenue Recognition Criteria**

Commtech, Inc., designs and sells cellular phones. The company creates the technical specifications and the software for its products, though it outsources the production of the phones to an overseas contract manufacturer. Commtech has arrangements to sell its phones to the major wireless communications companies who, in turn, sell the phones to end customers packaged with calling plans.

The product life cycle for a phone model is about six months, and Commtech recognizes revenue at the time of delivery to the wireless communications company. The product team for the CD924 model has met to consider a possible modification to the phone. The software team has developed an improved global positioning application for a new phone model, and this application works in the CD924. It could be uploaded to existing phones through the wireless networks.

Marketing's analysis of focus groups and customer feedback is that further sales of the CD924 would be enhanced significantly if the new application were made available. The software engineers have demonstrated that the new GPS application can be successfully sent wirelessly to the CD924.

However, the finance manager points out that Commtech's financial statements have been based on the assumption that the company's phones do not involve "multiple deliverables," like upgrades. All revenue is recognized at the point of sale to the wireless communications companies. Like many communications hardware companies, Commtech has been under pressure to demonstrate its financial performance. Offering an upgrade to the CD924's navigation capabilities would probably be viewed as a significant deliverable in terms of customer value, and the finance manager says that "the accounting won't let us do it."

How should the product team proceed?

LO6 **M6-26. Earnings Management and the Allowance for Doubtful Accounts**

Verdi Co. builds and sells PC computers to customers. The company sells most of its products for immediate payment but also extends credit to some customers. The industry is competitive and in the most recent year many competitors showed declines in revenue. However, Verdi Co. showed stable revenues. It is later revealed that Verdi Co. made sales and extended credit to customers previously deemed to have credit scores too low for the company to extend credit. The company did not disclose this practice in its financial statements or elsewhere.

a. Explain how this practice would have enabled Verdi Co. to show stable sales.
b. How should Verdi Co. have accounted for these additional sales and related receivables in its financial statements?

c.   How would the actions by Verdi Co. in the current period affect financial statements in future periods if the customers cannot pay for the computers they purchased on credit?

EXERCISES

E6-27.   Assessing Revenue Recognition Timing

Discuss and justify when each of the following businesses should recognize revenues:

a.   A clothing retailer like **Limited Brands, Inc.**

b.   A contractor like **The Boeing Company** that performs work under long-term government contracts.

c.   An operator of grocery stores like **SUPERVALU, INC.**

d.   A producer of television shows, such as **MTV** that syndicates its content to television stations.

e.   A residential real estate developer who constructs only speculative houses and later sells these houses to buyers.

f.   A banking institution like **Wells Fargo & Company** that lends money for home mortgages.

g.   A manufacturer like **Harley-Davidson, Inc.**

h.   A publisher of magazines such as **Time-Warner Inc.**

LO1, 2
Limited Brands, Inc.
NYSE :: LTD
Boeing Company
NYSE :: BA
Supervalu, Inc.
NYSE :: SVU
Wells Fargo & Company
NYSE :: WFC
Harley-Davidson, Inc.
NYSE :: HOG
Time-Warner Inc.
NYSE :: TWX

E6-28.   Assessing Revenue Recognition Timing and Income Measurement

Discuss and justify when each of the following businesses should recognize revenue and identify any income measurement issues that are likely to arise.

a.   **RealMoney.Com**, a division of **TheStreet.Com** provides investment advice to customers for an up-front fee. It provides these customers with password-protected access to its website where customers can download certain investment reports. Real Money has an obligation to provide updates on its website.

b.   **Oracle Corporation** develops general ledger and other business application software that it sells to its customers. The customer pays an up-front fee to gain the right to use the software and a monthly fee for support services.

c.   **Intuit Inc.** develops tax preparation software that it sells to its customers for a flat fee. No further payment is required and the software cannot be returned, only exchanged if defective.

d.   A developer of computer games sells its software with a 10-day right of return period during which the software can be returned for a full refund. After the 10-day period has expired, the software cannot be returned.

LO1, 2

Oracle Corporation
NASDAQ :: ORCL

Intuit Inc.
NASDAQ :: INTU

E6-29.   Constructing and Assessing Income Statements Using Percentage of Completion

Assume that **General Electric Company** agreed in February 2016 to construct an electricity generating facility for **Eversource Energy**, a utility serving the Boston area. The contract price of $500 million is to be paid as follows: $200 million at the time of signing; $100 million on December 31, 2016; and $200 million at completion in May 2017. General Electric incurred the following costs in constructing the power plant: $100 million in 2016, and $300 million in 2017.

a.   Compute the amount of General Electric's revenue, expense, and income for both 2016 and 2017 under the percentage-of-completion revenue recognition method.

b.   Compute the amount of GE's revenue, expense, and income for both 2016 and 2017 using the completed contract method.

c.   Discuss whether you believe that the percentage-of-completion method or the completed contract method provides a good measure of GE's performance under the contract.

LO3

General Electric Company
NYSE :: GE
Eversource Energy
NYSE :: ES

E6-30.   Constructing and Assessing Income Statements Using Percentage of Completion

On March 15, 2017, Frankel Construction is contracted to build a shopping center at a contract price of $120 million. The schedule of expected (equals actual) cash collections and contract costs follows:

LO3

Year	Cash Collections	Cost Incurred
2017	$ 30 million	$15 million
2018	50 million	40 million
2019	40 million	30 million
Total	$120 million	$85 million

a. Calculate the amount of revenue, expense, and income for each of the three years 2017 through 2019 using (1) the percentage-of-completion method, and (2) the completed contract method. Which method more closely follows the cash flows produced by this project?

b. Discuss which method you believe provides the better measure of the construction company's performance under this contract.

LO2   **E6-31.   Accounting for Multiple-Element Arrangements**

Amazon.com, Inc. provides the following description of its revenue recognition policies in its 2014 10-K report:

Amazon.com
NASDAQ :: AMZN

We recognize revenue from product sales or services rendered when the following four criteria are met: persuasive evidence of an arrangement exists, delivery has occurred or service has been rendered, the selling price is fixed or determinable, and collectability is reasonably assured. Revenue arrangements with multiple deliverables are divided into separate units and revenue is allocated using estimated selling prices if we do not have vendor-specific objective evidence or third-party evidence of the selling prices of the deliverables. We allocate the arrangement price to each of the elements based on the relative selling prices of each element. Estimated selling prices are management's best estimates of the prices that we would charge our customers if we were to sell the standalone elements separately and include considerations of customer demand, prices charged by us and others for similar deliverables, and the price if largely based on the cost of producing the product or service. Sales of our digital devices, including Kindle e-readers, Fire tablets, Fire TVs, Echo, and Fire phones, are considered arrangements with multiple deliverables, consisting of the device, undelivered software upgrades and/or undelivered non-software services such as cloud storage and free trial memberships to other services. The revenue allocated to the device, which is the substantial portion of the total sale price, and related costs are generally recognized upon delivery. Revenue related to undelivered software upgrades and/or undelivered non-software services is deferred and recognized generally on a straight-line basis over the estimated period the software upgrades and non-software services are expected to be provided for each of these devices. Sales of Amazon Prime memberships are also considered arrangements with multiple deliverables, including shipping benefits, Prime Instant Video, Prime Music, Prime Photo, and access to the Kindle Owners' Lending Library. The revenue related to the deliverables is amortized over the life of the membership based on the estimated delivery of services. Amazon Prime membership fees are allocated between product sales and service sales. Costs to deliver Amazon Prime benefits are recognized as cost of sales as incurred.

a. What is an "arrangement with multiple deliverables?" How are revenues recognized in such arrangements?

b. Assume that Amazon sells a Kindle with 3G wireless access and a commitment for future software upgrades for $190. Also assume that the device, if sold alone, would sell for $170 and that management estimates the selling price of the 3G access and software upgrades would be $30 if they were to be sold separately. What amount of revenue would Amazon recognize in the year of the sale? How would the remaining revenues be recognized?

c. Record the transaction described in part *b* using the financial statement effects template and in journal entry form.

LO5   **E6-32.   Computing NOPAT, NOPM and RNOA**

Selected information from the financial statements of **GoPro, Inc.** is provided below:

GoPro, Inc.
NASDAQ :: GPRO

($ thousands)	2014	2013
Revenue	$1,394,205	$985,737
Operating income.	187,035	98,703
Net interest expense and other nonoperating expense.	6,060	7,374
Net income.	128,088	60,578
Operating assets	815,364	439,671
Operating liabilities.	276,487	254,227

a. Compute GoPro's net operating profit after taxes (NOPAT) for 2014 and 2013.

b. Compute GoPro's net operating profit margin (NOPM) for each year.

c. Compute GoPro's return on net operating assets (RNOA) for 2014.

LO1, 6   **E6-33.   Applying Revenue Recognition Criteria**

Simpyl Technologies, Inc., manufactures electronic equipment used to facilitate control of production processes and tracking of assets using RFID and other technologies. Since its initial public offering in 1996, the company has shown consistent growth in revenue and earnings, and the stock price has reflected that impressive performance.

Operating in a very competitive environment, Simpyl Technologies provides significant bonus incentives to its sales representatives. These representatives sell the company's products directly to end customers, to value-added resellers, and to distributers.

Consider the four situations below. In each case, determine whether Simpyl Technologies can recognize revenue at this time. Describe the reasons for your judgment.

a. When selling directly to the end customer, Simpyl Technologies requires a sales contract with authorized signatures from the customer company. At the end of Simpyl's fiscal year, sales representative A asks to book revenue from a customer. The customer's purchasing manager has confirmed the intention to complete the purchase, but the contract has only one of the two required signatures. The second person is traveling and will return to the office in a few days (but after the end of Simpyl's fiscal year). The inventory to fulfill the order is sitting in Simpyl's warehouse. Can Simpyl recognize revenue at this time?

b. Sales representative B has an approved contract to deliver units that must be customized to meet the customer's specifications. Just prior to the end of the fiscal year, the uncustomized units are shipped to an intermediate staging area where they will be reconfigured to meet the customer's requirements. Can Simpyl recognize revenue on the basic, uncustomized units at this time?

c. Sales representative C has finalized an order from a value-added reseller who regularly purchases significant volumes of Simpyl's products. The products have been delivered to the customer at the beginning of the fiscal year, and Simpyl Technologies has no further responsibilities for the items. However, the sales representative (with the regional sales manager) is still conducting negotiations with the value-added reseller as to the volume discounts that will be offered for the current year. Can Simpyl recognize revenue on the items delivered to the customer?

d. Sales representative D has finalized an order from a distributor, and the items have been delivered. However, an examination of the distributor's financial condition shows that it does not have the resources to pay Simpyl for the items it has purchased. It needs to sell those items, so the resulting proceeds can be used to pay Simpyl. Can Simpyl recognize revenue on the items delivered to the distributor?

E6-34. **Reporting Uncollectible Accounts and Accounts Receivable**   **LO4**
LaFond Company analyzes its accounts receivable at December 31, 2016, and arrives at the aged categories below along with the percentages that are estimated as uncollectible.

Age Group	Accounts Receivable	Estimated Loss %
Current (not past due)	$250,000	0.5%
1–30 days past due	90,000	1
31–60 days past due	20,000	2
61–120 days past due	11,000	5
121–180 days past due	6,000	10
Over 180 days past due.....................	4,000	25
Total accounts receivable	$381,000	

At the beginning of the fourth quarter of 2016, there was a credit balance of $4,350 in the Allowance for Uncollectible Accounts. During the fourth quarter, LaFond Company wrote off $3,830 in receivables as uncollectible.

a. What amount of bad debts expense will LaFond report for 2016?

b. What is the balance of accounts receivable that it reports on its December 31, 2016, balance sheet?

c. Set up T-accounts for both Bad Debts Expense and for the Allowance for Uncollectible Accounts. Enter any unadjusted balances along with the dollar effects of the information described (including your results from parts a and b). Explain the numbers in each of the T-accounts.

E6-35. **Analysis of Accounts Receivable and Allowance for Doubtful Accounts**   **LO4, 5**
Steelcase, Inc. reported the following amounts in its 2014 and 2013 10-K reports (years ended February 28, 2014 and February 22, 2013).

Steelcase, Inc.
NYSE :: SCS

($ millions)	2014	2013
From the income statement:		
Net sales.....	$2,989	$2,869
From the balance sheet:		
Accounts receivable, net	306.8	287.3
Customer deposits.....	16.0	13.5
From the disclosure on allowance for doubtful accounts:		
Balance at beginning of period.....	14.5	19.6
Additions (reductions) charged to income	2.8	3.1
Adjustments or deductions.....	(4.3)	(8.2)
Balance at end of period	13.0	14.5

a. Prepare the journal entry to record accounts receivable written off as uncollectible in 2014. Also prepare the entry to record the provision for doubtful accounts (bad debts expense) for 2014. What effect did these entries have on Steelcase's income for that year?

b. Calculate Steelcase's gross receivables for the years given, and then determine the allowance for doubtful accounts as a percentage of the gross receivables.

c. Calculate Steelcase's accounts receivable turnover for 2014. (Use Accounts receivable, net for the calculation.)

d. How much cash did Steelcase receive from customers in 2014?

LO4 **E6-36.** **Analyzing and Reporting Receivable Transactions and Uncollectible Accounts (Using Percentage-of-Sales Method)**

At the beginning of 2017, Penman Company had the following (normal) account balances in its financial records:

Accounts receivable.....	$122,000
Allowance for uncollectible accounts.....	7,900

During 2017, its credit sales were $1,173,000 and collections on credit sales were $1,150,000. The following additional transactions occurred during the year:

Feb. 17   Wrote off Nissim's account, $3,600.
May 28   Wrote off White's account, $2,400.
Dec. 15   Wrote off Ohlson's account, $900.
Dec. 31   Recorded the provision for uncollectible accounts at 0.8% of credit sales for the year. (*Hint*: The allowance account is increased by 0.8% of credit sales regardless of any prior write-offs.)

Compute and show how accounts receivable and the allowance for uncollectible accounts are reported in its December 31, 2017, balance sheet.

LO4 **E6-37.** **Estimating Bad Debts Expense and Reporting of Receivables**

At December 31, 2016, Sunil Company had a balance of $375,000 in its accounts receivable and an unused balance of $4,200 in its allowance for uncollectible accounts. The company then aged its accounts as follows:

Current.....	$304,000
0–60 days past due	44,000
61–180 days past due	18,000
Over 180 days past due.....	9,000
Total accounts receivable	$375,000

The company has experienced losses as follows: 1% of current balances, 5% of balances 0–60 days past due, 15% of balances 61–180 days past due, and 40% of balances over 180 days past due. The company continues to base its provision for credit losses on this aging analysis and percentages.

a. What amount of bad debts expense does Sunil report on its 2016 income statement?

b. Show how accounts receivable and the allowance for uncollectible accounts are reported in its December 31, 2016, balance sheet.

c. Set up T-accounts for both Bad Debts Expense and for the Allowance for Uncollectible Accounts. Enter any unadjusted balances along with the dollar effects of the information described (including your results from parts *a* and *b*). Explain the numbers in each of the T-accounts.

E6-38. **Estimating Uncollectible Accounts and Reporting Receivables over Multiple Periods**   **LO4**
Barth Company, which has been in business for three years, makes all of its sales on credit and does not offer cash discounts. Its credit sales, customer collections, and write-offs of uncollectible accounts for its first three years follow:

Year	Sales	Collections	Accounts Written Off
2015	$751,000	$733,000	$5,300
2016	876,000	864,000	5,800
2017	972,000	938,000	6,500

a. Barth uses the allowance method of recognizing credit losses that provides for such losses at the rate of 1% of sales. (This means the allowance account is increased by 1% of credit sales regardless of any write-offs and unused balances.) What amounts for accounts receivable and the allowance for uncollectible accounts are reported on its balance sheet at the end of 2017? What total amount of bad debts expense appears on its income statement for each of the three years?

b. Comment on the appropriateness of the 1% rate used to provide for bad debts based on your results in part *a*. (*Hint*: T-accounts can help with this analysis.)

E6-39.[A] **Evaluating Business Segment Information**   **LO5, 7**
Hewlett-Packard Company reports that its "organizational structure is based on a number of factors that management uses to evaluate, view and run its business operations." In its disclosures of segment information, there are seven segments—Personal Systems, Printing, Enterprise Group, Enterprise Services, Software, HP Financial Services, and Corporate Investments. The company provides the following information about these business segments:

Hewlett-Packard
NYSE :: HPQ

($ millions)	2014	2013
Total net revenue:		
Personal systems	$34,303	$32,179
Printing	22,979	23,896
Enterprise group	27,814	28,081
Enterprise services	22,398	24,061
Software	3,933	4,021
HP financial services	3,498	3,629
Corporate investments	302	24
Earnings from operations:		
Personal systems	$ 1,270	$ 980
Printing	4,185	3,933
Enterprise group	4,008	4,259
Enterprise services	803	679
Software	872	868
HP financial services	389	399
Corporate investments	(199)	(316)
Total assets:		
Personal systems	$12,104	$11,690
Printing	10,063	11,088
Enterprise group	27,236	29,759
Enterprise services	13,472	16,217
Software	11,575	11,940
HP financial services	13,529	12,746
Corporate investments	34	105

a. Calculate the 2014 return on capital employed for each segment. (Base the calculation on total assets instead of net operating assets in the denominator—HP does not disclose operating liabilities by segment.)

b. Which segments are more profitable? Which are growing more quickly?

c.   In 2014, HP reported restructuring charges of $1,619 million. Assume these charges are mostly attributable to the Enterprise Services segment. How should restructuring charges be reported in the income statement? How do these charges affect your interpretation of the return on capital employed by the Enterprise Services segment?

LO1, 2   **E6-40.**   **Analyzing Unearned Revenue Liabilities**

The Lyric Opera of Chicago was founded in 1954 and is widely regarded as one of the world's greatest opera companies. Each year, The Lyric has an eight-opera season that extends from September to March, and its loyal subscribers (numbering more than 30,000) eagerly reserve their seats for coming performances. In fact, many subscribers purchase their tickets for the upcoming year before the close of The Lyric's fiscal year. For these ticket purchases, The Lyric recognizes a liability entitled Deferred Ticket and Other Revenue and defined in its footnotes as "Deferred ticket revenue relates to ticket sales for the following opera season."

Information about The Lyric Opera's ticket revenue and deferred ticket revenue liability is given below ($ thousands). Assume that the "Other" portion of deferred revenue is negligible.

Fiscal year ended	Ticket Sales (Revenue)	Deferred Ticket and Other Revenue (Year-end Liability)
2014	$28,878	$13,750
2013	26,671	14,525
2012	25,030	12,638
2011	23,775	12,711

a.   What revenue recognition principle(s) drive The Lyric's deferral of advance ticket purchases?

b.   Recreate the summary journal entries to recognize ticket sales revenue for The Lyric's fiscal year 2014 and advance sales for the fiscal year 2015 season.

c.   The Lyric Opera's season changes every year, with a mixture of classical and contemporary operas. At the end of each fiscal year, management of The Lyric can observe the revenue generated by the season just concluded and also its subscribers' enthusiasm for the upcoming season. How might that information be used in managing the organization?

LO2   **E6-41.**   **Accounting for Membership Fees and Rewards Program**

Costco Wholesale
NASDAQ :: COST

Costco Wholesale Corporation provides the following description of its revenue recognition policies for membership fees and rewards in its 10-K report dated August 31, 2014:

Membership fee revenue represents annual membership fees paid by substantially all of the Company's members. The Company accounts for membership fee revenue, net of estimated refunds, on a deferred basis, whereby revenue is recognized ratably over the one-year membership period. The Company's Executive Members qualify for a 2% reward (beginning November, 1, 2011 the reward increased from a maximum of $500 to $750 per year on qualified purchases), which can be redeemed at Costco warehouses. The Company accounts for this reward as a reduction in sales. The sales reduction and corresponding liability are computed after giving effect to the estimated impact of non-redemptions based on historical data. The net reduction in sales was $1,051, $970, and $900 in 2014, 2013, and 2012, respectively.

The following data were extracted from Costco's 2014 income statement and balance sheet:

($ millions)	2014	2013
Revenue		
Net sales	$110,212	$102,870
Membership fees	2,428	2,286
Total revenue	112,640	105,156
Current Liabilities		
Accounts payable	$ 8,491	$ 7,872
Accrued salaries and benefits	2,231	2,037
Accrued member rewards	773	710
Accrued sales and other taxes	442	382
Deferred membership fees	1,254	1,167
Other current liabilities	1,221	1,089
Total current liabilities	$14,412	$13,257

a. Explain Costco's accounting for membership fees and rewards programs.
b. Prepare journal entries to record (1) membership fees collected in cash in fiscal 2014 and (2) membership fee revenue recognized in 2014.
c. Prepare journal entries to record (1) member rewards earned by "executive members" in fiscal 2014 and (2) rewards redeemed during the year.

PROBLEMS

P6-42. Identifying Operating and Nonrecurring Income Components

Following is the **The Dow Chemical Company** income statement.

LO5, 7

MBC

The Dow Chemical Company
NYSE :: DOW

($ millions) For Year Ended December 31	2014	2013
Net sales.	$58,167	$57,080
Cost of sales.	47,464	47,594
Research and development expenses	1,647	1,747
Selling, general, and administrative expenses	3,106	3,024
Amortization of intangibles	436	461
Goodwill and other intangible asset impairment losses	50	—
Restructuring charges (credits)	(3)	(22)
Asbestos-related charge	78	—
Equity in earnings of nonconsolidated affiliates	835	1,034
Sundry income (expense)—net.	(27)	2,554
Interest income	51	41
Interest expense and amortization of debt discount	983	1,101
Income before income taxes	5,265	6,804
Provision for income taxes	1,426	1,988
Net income	$ 3,839	$ 4,816

REQUIRED
a. Identify the components in its statement that you would consider operating.
b. Identify those components that you would consider nonrecurring.
c. Compute net operating profit after taxes (NOPAT) and net operating profit margin (NOPM) for each year.

P6-43. Percentage-of-Completion and Completed Contract Methods

Philbrick Company signed a three-year contract to provide sales training to the employees of Elliot Company. The contract price is $1,200 per employee and the estimated number of employees to be trained is 400. The expected number to be trained in each year and the expected training costs follow.

LO3

MBC

	Number of employees	Training costs incurred
2016	125	$ 60,000
2017	200	75,000
2018	75	40,000
Total	400	$175,000

REQUIRED
a. For each year, compute the revenue, expense, and gross profit reported assuming revenue is recognized using the following method.
   1. Percentage-of-completion method, where percentage-of-completion is determined by the number of employees trained.
   2. Percentage-of-completion method, where percentage-of-completion is determined by the costs incurred.
   3. Completed contract method.
b. Which method do you believe is most appropriate in this situation? Explain.

LO6 **P6-44.** **Incentives for Earnings Management**

Harris Corporation pays senior management an annual bonus from a bonus pool. The size of the bonus pool is determined as follows.

Reported net income	Bonus pool
Less than or equal to $10 million	$0
Greater than $10 million, but less than or equal to $20 million.	10% of income in excess of $10 million
Greater than $20 million.	$1 million

REQUIRED

a. Assume that senior management expects current earnings to be $21 million and next year's earnings to be $18 million. What incentive does management of Harris Corporation have for managing earnings?

b. Assume that senior management expects current earnings to be $17 million and next year's earnings to be $24 million. What incentive does management of Harris Corporation have for managing earnings?

c. Assume that senior management expects current earnings to be $9.5 million and next year's earnings to be $12 million. What incentive does management of Harris Corporation have for managing earnings?

d. How might the bonus plan be structured to minimize the incentives for earnings management?

LO4 **P6-45.** **Interpreting Accounts Receivable and Uncollectible Accounts**

Nordstrom, Inc.
NYSE :: JWN

Nordstrom, Inc. provided the following information concerning its accounts receivable in note 3 of its 10-K report dated February 1, 2014 (fiscal year 2013):

NOTE 3: ACCOUNTS RECEIVABLE

The components of accounts receivable are as follows:

	2013	2012
Total credit card receivables	$2,184	$2,142
Allowance for credit losses	(80)	(85)
Credit card receivables, net	2,104	2,057
Other accounts receivable	73	72
Accounts receivable, net	**$2,177**	**$2,129**

Activity in the allowance for credit losses for the past two fiscal years is as follows:

Fiscal year	2013	2012
Allowance at beginning of year	$85	$115
Bad debt provision.	52	42
Write-offs	(80)	(97)
Recoveries	23	25
Allowance at end of year	**$80**	**$ 85**

Credit Quality

The primary indicators of the credit quality of our credit card receivables are aging and delinquency, particularly the levels of account balances delinquent 30 days or more as these are the accounts most likely to be written off. The following table illustrates the aging and delinquency status of our credit card receivables:

	February 1, 2014		February 2, 2013	
	Balance	% of Total	Balance	% of Total
Current	$2,046	93.7%	$2,018	94.2%
1–29 days delinquent	99	4.5%	84	3.9%
30+ days delinquent:				
30–59 days delinquent	16	0.7%	15	0.7%
60–89 days delinquent	9	0.4%	10	0.5%
90 days or more delinquent	14	0.7%	15	0.7%
Total 30+ days delinquent.	39	1.8%	40	1.9%
Total credit card receivables.	$2,184	100.0%	$2,142	100.0%

REQUIRED

a. What amount did Nordstrom report as accounts receivable, net in its February 1, 2014 balance sheet?

b. Prepare journal entries to record the provision for bad debts, write-offs of uncollectible accounts, and recoveries in fiscal 2014. Post these entries to T-accounts. How should Nordstrom record recoveries?

c. Compute the ratio of allowance for credit losses to total credit card receivables for fiscal 2012 and 2013. Speculate as to what might be the cause of any change that you observe.

d. Nordstrom reported net sales of $12,166 million in fiscal 2013. Compute its accounts receivable turnover and average collection period for that year.

P6-46.   Accounting for Product Returns

In its income statement for fiscal year 2013, **The Gap, Inc.**, reported net sales of $16,148 million and cost of goods sold and occupancy expenses of $9,855 million, resulting in a gross profit of $6,293 million. In its footnotes, The Gap reports that "Allowances for estimated returns are recorded based on estimated gross profit using our historical return patterns."

When The Gap accounts for estimated sales returns, it reduces sales revenue by the returns' expected sales price, reduces cost of goods sold by the returns' expected cost and recognizes a sales return allowance as a liability equal to the returns' expected gross profit.

A sales returns allowance of $26 million was reported among The Gap's liabilities at the end of fiscal year 2013, and the footnotes report that $896 million in allowance for returns was added to this liability during fiscal year 2013. Actual returns were reported at $897 million and subtracted from the liability.

REQUIRED

a. What was the balance in The Gap's sales returns allowance liability at the beginning of fiscal year 2013?

b. Suppose The Gap sells 100 units of an item for $50 each, and its gross profit on each unit is $20. Further, suppose The Gap expects that 10 of the units will be returned. What entries will be made to record the sale of 100 units (for cash) and the expected returns? What entry is made when ten customers subsequently return the items and receive a cash refund? Assume that the units are undamaged and can be sold to other customers.

c. Assume that the gross profit margin (gross profit divided by sales revenue) for returned items is the same as that for those that are not returned. Reconstruct the entry The Gap made to account for expected product returns in 2013. What were the 2013 gross sales for The Gap? What percentage of its sales does The Gap expect to be returned?

d. Suppose The Gap entered a new market in which it did not have the ability to predict product returns. How should it deal with the prospect of returns when it sells products to customers?

P6-47.   Analyzing Unearned Revenue Changes

Electronic Arts Inc. (EA) is a developer, marketer, publisher and distributor of video game software and content to be played on a variety of platforms. There is an increasing demand for the ability to play these games in an online environment, and EA has developed this capability in many of its products. In addition, EA maintains servers (or arranges for servers) for the online activities of its customers. When customers purchase online subscriptions, revenue is recognized ratably over the subscription period.

LO4

The GAP, Inc.
NYSE :: GPS

LO2

MBC

Electronic Arts Inc.
NASDAQ :: EA

EA treats a significant portion of its software sales as "multiple-element arrangements" and—through fiscal 2007—deferred a portion of customer purchases based on the estimated value of the online services offered. Beginning in fiscal 2008, it was not possible to estimate the separate value of the software and the online services, so EA began to defer all such revenue over a six-month period. Starting July 1, 2013, based on an analysis by the company, revenue continues to be recognized over six months for games distributed online, but for physical games purchased at retailers revenue will be recognized over a nine-month period. EA's 2014 10-K states that U.S. GAAP requires the company to account for the consumer's right to receive unspecified updates or their matchmaking service for no additional fee as a "bundled" sale, or multiple-element arrangement.

Information from Electronic Arts' financial statements is given below. Prior to fiscal year 2006, no revenue was deferred. All amounts are in $ millions.

Fiscal year ending March 31	Net revenue	Deferred net revenue (liability)
2005	$3,129	$ 0
2006	2,951	9
2007	3,091	32
2008	3,665	387
2009	4,212	261
2010	3,654	766
2011	3,589	1,005
2012	4,143	1,048
2013	3,797	1,044
2014	3,575	1,490

REQUIRED

a. Calculate the growth rates in net revenue over the years in the table.

b. What are the purchases by customers in each of these years? What are the growth rates? Why do you think they differ from the growth rates in net revenue?

c. Would you predict a growth in 2015 revenue equal to that in 2014? Why?

CASES AND PROJECTS

LO1, 2

Groupon, Inc.
NASDAQ :: GRPN

C6-48. **Revenue Recognition and Refunds**

Groupon, Inc. is an internet-based marketing company which sells coupons (called "Groupons") for products and services offered by other merchants (merchant partners). Groupon offers a "daily deal" to subscribers. The daily deal provides significant savings on a variety of products and services provided that a minimum number of customers purchase the Groupon for each deal offered. This feature guarantees a sufficient volume of customers to ensure that the deal is profitable to the merchant partner.

When Groupon sells a coupon, it collects the proceeds from the customer (gross billings) and then remits a payment to the merchant partner. These payments are typically paid out over a 60-day period. Groupon's revenue recognition policy is described in its 10-K as follows:

Revenue Recognition

The Company recognizes revenue from Groupons when the following criteria are met: persuasive evidence of an arrangement exists; delivery has occurred; the selling price is fixed or determinable; and collectability is reasonably assured. These criteria are met when the number of customers who purchase the daily deal exceeds the predetermined threshold, the Groupon has been electronically delivered to the purchaser and a listing of Groupons sold has been made available to the merchant. At that time, the Company's obligations to the merchant, for which it is serving as an agent, are substantially complete. The Company's remaining obligations, which are limited to remitting payment to the merchant and continuing to make available on the Company's website the listing of Groupons previously provided to the merchant, are inconsequential or perfunctory. The Company records the net amount it retains from the sale of Groupons after paying an agreed upon percentage of the purchase price to the featured merchant excluding any applicable taxes. Revenue is recorded on a net basis because the Company is acting as an agent of the merchant in the transaction.

Groupon reported gross billings of $3,985.5 million in 2011, up from $745.3 million in 2010. Its net revenues were $1,610.4 million in 2011 and $312.9 million in 2010. Groupon also reported that it changed its method of revenue recognition during 2011:

The Company restated the Condensed Consolidated Statements of Operations for the three months ended March 31, 2011, included in the Form S-1 filed with the SEC on June 2, 2011, to correct for an error in its presentation of revenue. Most significantly, the Company restated its reporting of revenues from Groupons to be net of the amounts related to merchant fees. Historically, the Company reported the gross amounts billed to its subscribers as revenue. The Condensed Consolidated Statement of Operations for the three months ended March 31, 2011, was restated to show the net amount the Company retains after paying the merchant fees. The effect of the correction resulted in a reduction of previously reported revenues and corresponding reductions in cost of revenue in those periods. The change in presentation had no effect on pre-tax loss, net loss or any per share amounts for the period.

Groupon's refund policy is also described in its 2012 10-K report:

Our Groupon Promise states that we will provide our customers with a refund of the purchase price of a Groupon if they believe that we have let them down. . . . Our standard agreements with our merchant partners generally limit the time period during which we may seek reimbursement for customer refunds or claims. Our customers may make claims for refunds with respect to which we are unable to seek reimbursement from our merchant partners.

   At the time revenue is recorded, we record an allowance for estimated customer refunds. We accrue costs associated with refunds in accrued expenses on the consolidated balance sheets. The cost of refunds where the amount payable to the merchant is recoverable is recorded in the consolidated statements of operations as a reduction to revenue. The cost of refunds when there is no amount recoverable from the merchant are presented as a cost of revenue.

   To determine the amount of our refund reserve, we track refund patterns of prior deals, use that data to build a model and apply that model to current deals. Further analysis of our refund activity into 2012 indicated deviations from modeled refund behavior for deals featured in late 2011, particularly due to a shift in our fourth quarter deal mix and higher price point offers. Accordingly, we updated our refund model to reflect changes in the deal mix and price point of our deals over time and we believe this updated model will enable us to more accurately track and anticipate refund behavior.

REQUIRED

a. Assume that Groupon offers a daily deal that costs $200 per Groupon. It sells 600 of the Groupons and agrees to remit 50% of the gross revenue to the merchant within 60 days. Using journal entries, illustrate how Groupon would record the sale of this Groupon deal.

b. In the first quarter of 2011, Groupon changed its revenue recognition policy. How did this change affect its income statement?

c. Refer to the facts presented in part *a* above. Assume that Groupon expects that 10% of the Groupon customers will demand a refund within the first 60 days. How does Groupon record this estimate of returns? How are actual refunds recorded?

d. Now assume that an additional 5% of Groupon's customers demand refunds after the first 60 days. How are these refunds handled?

e. Given the uncertainty surrounding refunds, what alternative accounting approaches might Groupon consider for handling refunds?

C6-49. **Interpreting Revenue Recognition Policies and Earnings Management**   **LO1, 2, 6**
A *Wall Street Journal* article dated October 31, 2007, reported that an internal investigation at **Dell Inc.** had uncovered evidence of earnings management. The article states: **Dell Inc.**
NASDAQ :: DELL

An internal investigation found that senior executives and other employees manipulated the company's financial statements to give the appearance of hitting quarterly performance goals.

   One of the biggest problems uncovered in the investigation was the way Dell recognized revenue on software products it sells. Dell, a large reseller of other companies' software products, said it historically recognized revenue from software licenses at the time that the products were sold. . . . Based on its internal review, it should have deferred more revenue from software sales.

   Another issue was product warranties. In some cases, Dell said it improperly recognized revenue associated with [extended] warranties over a shorter period of time than the duration of the contract.

The income statements from Dell's 2007 10-K report are presented below, along with the footnote outlining Dell's revenue recognition policies:

	Fiscal Year Ended		
	February 2, 2007	**February 3, 2006 As Restated**	**January 28, 2005 As Restated**
Net revenue	$57,420	$55,788	$49,121
Cost of net revenue	47,904	45,897	40,103
Gross margin	9,516	9,891	9,018
Operating expenses:			
Selling, general, and administrative	5,948	5,051	4,352
Research, development, and engineering ..	498	458	460
Total operating expenses...............	6,446	5,509	4,812
Operating income....................	3,070	4,382	4,206
Investment and other income, net	275	226	197
Income before income taxes	3,345	4,608	4,403
Income tax provision	762	1,006	1,385
Net income.........................	$ 2,583	$ 3,602	$ 3,018

Revenue Recognition Net revenue includes sales of hardware, software and peripherals, and services (including extended service contracts and professional services). These products and services are sold either separately or as part of a multiple-element arrangement. Dell allocates revenue from multiple-element arrangements to the elements based on the relative fair value of each element, which is generally based on the relative sales price of each element when sold separately. The allocation of fair value for a multiple-element arrangement involving software is based on vendor specific objective evidence ("VSOE"), or in the absence of VSOE for delivered elements, the residual method. Under the residual method, Dell allocates revenue to software licenses at the inception of the license term when VSOE for all undelivered elements, such as Post Contract Customer Support ("PCS"), exists and all other revenue recognition criteria have been satisfied. In the absence of VSOE for undelivered elements, revenue is deferred and subsequently recognized over the term of the arrangement. For sales of extended warranties with a separate contract price, Dell defers revenue equal to the separately stated price. Revenue associated with undelivered elements is deferred and recorded when delivery occurs. Product revenue is recognized, net of an allowance for estimated returns, when both title and risk of loss transfer to the customer, provided that no significant obligations remain. Revenue from extended warranty and service contracts, for which Dell is obligated to perform, is recorded as deferred revenue and subsequently recognized over the term of the contract or when the service is completed. Revenue from sales of third-party extended warranty and service contracts or software PCS, for which Dell is not obligated to perform, and for which Dell does not meet the criteria for gross revenue recognition under EITF 99-19 is recognized on a net basis. All other revenue is recognized on a gross basis.

REQUIRED

a. Explain how Dell accounts for sales of other companies' software products. What are the potential risks of abuse of these accounting policies as a means to manage earnings?

b. Explain how Dell accounts for sales of extended warranty contracts. How did Dell employees manipulate these policies to manage earnings?

c. Discuss the incentives that exist to manage earnings to "give the appearance of hitting quarterly performance goals." How can a company such as Dell prevent earnings management in circumstances such as this?

LO2, 4, 5
John Wiley and Sons, Inc.
NYSE :: JW

C6-50. Accounting for Doubtful Accounts and Returns

John Wiley and Sons, Inc. publishes books, periodicals, software and other digital content. Its April 30, 2012 balance sheet reported the following amounts for accounts receivable ($ thousands):

April 30,	2012	2011
Accounts receivable...	$171,561	$168,310

Wiley's income statement provided the following detail of operating income ($ thousands):

Year ended April 30	2012	2011
Revenue	$1,782,742	$1,742,551
Cost of sales.	543,396	539,043
Operating and administrative expenses.	922,177	910,847
Additional provision for doubtful accounts	—	9,290
Amortization of intangibles.	36,750	35,223
Operating income.	280,419	248,148

Wiley normally charges operating and administrative expenses for estimated doubtful accounts. However, in fiscal 2011, the company recorded an additional charge to reflect estimated losses from the **Borders Group, Inc.** bankruptcy. This was explained in note 9 of its financial statements:

Note 9—Additional Provision for Doubtful Trade Account

In fiscal year 2011, the Company recorded a pre-tax bad debt provision of $9.3 million, or $6.0 million after-tax ($0.10 per diluted share), related to the Company's customer, Borders Group, Inc. ("Borders"). The net charge was reflected in the Additional Provision for Doubtful Trade Account line item in the Consolidated Statements of Income and represented the difference between the Company's outstanding receivable with Borders, net of existing reserves and recoveries. There were no additional charges or bad debt expense with respect to this customer. On February 16, 2011, Borders filed a petition for reorganization relief under Chapter 11 of the U.S. Bankruptcy code.

Wiley provided the following supplemental information concerning doubtful accounts and returns in its footnotes ($ thousands):

	Balance at Beginning of Period	Charged to Costs and Expenses	Deductions from Reserve	Balance at End of Period
Year ended April 30, 2012				
Allowance for sales returns	$48,909	$82,901	$ 96,037	$35,773
Allowance for doubtful accounts	19,642	2,111	14,903	6,850
Year ended April 30, 2011				
Allowance for sales returns	55,311	96,841	103,243	48,909
Allowance for doubtful accounts	6,859	13,989	1,206	19,642

Net sales return reserves are reflected in the following accounts of the Consolidated Statements of Financial Position—increase (decrease):

April 30,	2012	2011
Accounts receivable.	$(48,612)	$(65,664)
Inventory.	7,246	9,485
Accounts and royalties payable.	(5,593)	(7,270)
Decrease in net assets.	$(35,773)	$(48,909)

REQUIRED

a. Prepare journal entries (and post to the related T-accounts) to record bad debts expense and accounts receivable write-offs for 2011 and 2012.

b. Compute the allowance for doubtful accounts as a percentage of accounts receivable. How does the "additional provision for doubtful accounts" affect your analysis of Wiley's accounts receivable?

c. Wiley has also established an allowance for returns. How do returns differ from doubtful accounts? Under what circumstances might this difference affect the accounting for returns?

d. Assume that Wiley accepted returns totaling $130 million in 2012 and that the inventory returned had a cost of $20 million. Moreover, assume that the returned merchandise was returned to inventory and can be resold. Prepare a journal entry to record estimated returns for 2012.

e. Calculate the accounts receivable turnover ratio and average collection period for 2012 using net accounts receivable.

LO7

DreamWorks
AnimationSKG, Inc.
NASDAQ :: DWA

C6-51.[A] **Interpreting Restructuring Charges**

The following is from the most recent 10-K of **DreamWorks Animation SKG, Inc.** for the year ended December 31, 2014.

> In January 2015, we announced our 2015 Restructuring Plan involving the Company's core feature animation business intended to maximize our creative talent and resources, reduce costs and improve profitability. As a result, we recorded charges totaling approximately $210.1 million for the year ended December 31, 2014, including approximately $43.4 million relating to employee termination costs. . .
>
> As of December 31, 2014, we employed approximately 2,700 people, many of whom were covered by employment agreements, which generally include non-disclosure agreements. In connection with the 2015 Restructuring Plan, we anticipate reducing our workforce by approximately 500 employees. . .
>
> In connection with the 2015 Restructuring Plan, the Company has made changes in its senior leadership team and has also made changes based on its reevaluation of its feature film slate. The Company expects that the 2015 Restructuring Plan activities will result in charges related to employee-related costs resulting from headcount reductions, . . . costs were incurred during the three months ended December 31, 2014 . . . The Company expects that the remaining costs will be primarily incurred during the year ending December 31, 2015 and will result in total cash payments of approximately $76.0 million, primarily related to severance, benefits and contractual obligations. This excludes cash payments associated with anticipated excess labor costs as further described below. The actions associated with the restructuring plan are expected to be substantially completed during 2015.
>
> The following tables summarizes the costs that we incurred during the year ended December 31, 2014, as well as the remaining costs we expect to incur in order to execute upon our 2015 Restructuring Plan:

	Year Ended December 31, 2014	Future Periods
Employee termination costs..............................	$ 43.4	$12.3
Relocation and other employee-related costs..............	—	7.1
Lease obligations and related charges	—	6.7
Accelerated depreciation charges	—	19.3
Film and other inventory write-offs........................	155.5	—
Other contractual obligations.............................	11.2	—
Additional labor and other excess costs	—	38.3
Total restructuring and related charges....................	$210.1	$83.7

Employee Termination Costs. Employee termination costs consist of severance and benefits (including stock-based compensation) which are accounted for based on the type of employment arrangement between the Company and the employee. Certain of these arrangements include obligations that are accounted for as non-retirement postemployment benefits. We also employ individuals under employment contracts. Charges related to non-retirement postemployment benefits and amounts due under employment contracts for employees who will no longer provide services are accrued when probable and estimable. Severance and benefits related to all other employees are accounted for in accordance with accounting guidance on costs associated with exit or disposal activities. Thus, such costs are recorded in the period in which the terms of the restructuring plan have been established, management with the appropriate authority commits to the plan and communication to employees has occurred.

Relocation and Other Employee-Related Costs. Relocation and other employee-related costs primarily consist of expected costs to relocate employees from our Northern California facility to our Southern California facility. Such costs are expensed as incurred and will be primarily incurred during the year ending December 31, 2015.

REQUIRED

a. Describe where on the income statement the above described restructuring charges are included.

b. Describe how an analyst of the company should treat the costs when doing financial statement analysis.

c. What incentives might management have to either overstate or understate the above described restructuring charges? Describe how future financial statements would be affected if the costs were overstated or understated when these charges were recorded in 2014.

SOLUTIONS TO REVIEW PROBLEMS

Mid-Chapter Review 1

SOLUTION

(All dollar amounts are in millions.)

1.

	2014	2013
Revenue growth rates	($86,833 − $77,849)/$77,849 = 11.5%	($77,849 − $73,723)/$73,723 = 5.6%

2. To determine the customer purchases during the year, we start with the revenue, then add the "Deferral of unearned revenue," then subtract the "Recognition of unearned revenue."

	2014	2013	2012
Revenue	$86,833	$77,849	$73,723
Plus "Deferral of unearned revenue"	44,325	44,253	36,104
Less "Recognition of unearned revenue".	41,739	41,921	33,347
Purchases made by customers	$89,419	$80,181	$76,480

3.

	2014	2013
Purchase growth rates	($89,419 − $80,181)/$80,181 = 11.5%	($80,181 − $76,480)/$76,480 = 4.8%

When a customer makes a purchase, Microsoft defers a substantial portion of the amount received and recognizes that portion over future periods. Therefore, revenue reported on the income statement is a combination of customer purchases in the current period, plus customer purchases in previous periods (up to three years ago). This has the effect of smoothing Microsoft's revenues over time.

Mid-Chapter Review 2

SOLUTION

1. The terms of the contract are likely different for government contracts and contracts with private organizations. To justify the use of the percentage-of-completion method, there must be a contract that specifies a fixed or determinable price. The contracts for private organizations might have more ambiguity as far as the pricing is concerned. Alternatively, Adler most likely has experience that would indicate that government contracts are less likely to be cancelled.

2. The percentage completed in each year is 40% in 2016 ($12,000,000/$30,000,000), 45% in 2017 ($13,500,000/$30,000,000), and 15% in 2018 ($4,500,000/$30,000,000).

   a. Percentage-of-completion method

	2016	2017	2018
Percentage completed.	40%	45%	15%
Contract revenue	$16,000,000	$18,000,000	$ 6,000,000
(Percentage completed × $40,000,000)			
Contract expense.	12,000,000	13,500,000	4,500,000
Gross profit.	$ 4,000,000	$ 4,500,000	$ 1,500,000

   b. Completed contract method

	2016	2017	2018
Contract revenue	$ 0	$ 0	$40,000,000
Contract expense.	0	0	30,000,000
Gross profit.	$ 0	$ 0	$10,000,000

3. Income would be understated in 2016 and 2017, but the difference would be made up in 2018 with higher than expected earnings. The gross profit in 2018 would be $6,000,000 − $1,500,000 = $4,500,000.

Mid-Chapter Review 3

SOLUTION

1.   As of December 31, 2016,

Current....................	$468,000 × 1%	=	$ 4,680
1–60 days past due	244,000 × 5%	=	12,200
61–180 days past due	38,000 × 15%	=	5,700
Over 180 days past due......	20,000 × 40%	=	8,000
Amount required...........			$30,580
Unused allowance balance ...			7,000
Provision.................			$23,580 2016 bad debts expense

2.   Current assets section of balance sheet.

Accounts receivable, net of $30,580 in allowances..................	$739,420

3.   Engel Company has markedly increased the percentage of the allowance for uncollect-
     ible accounts to gross accounts receivable—from the historical 2% to the current 4%
     ($30,580/$770,000). There are at least two possible interpretations:

   a.   The quality of Engel Company's receivables has declined. Possible causes include the
          following: (1) sales can stagnate and the company can feel compelled to sell to lower-
          quality accounts to maintain sales volume; (2) it may have introduced new products for
          which average credit losses are higher; and (3) its administration of accounts receivable
          can become lax.

   b.   The company has intentionally increased its allowance account above the level needed
          for expected future losses so as to reduce current period income and "bank" that income
          for future periods (income shifting).

4.   Transaction effects shown in the financial statement effects template.

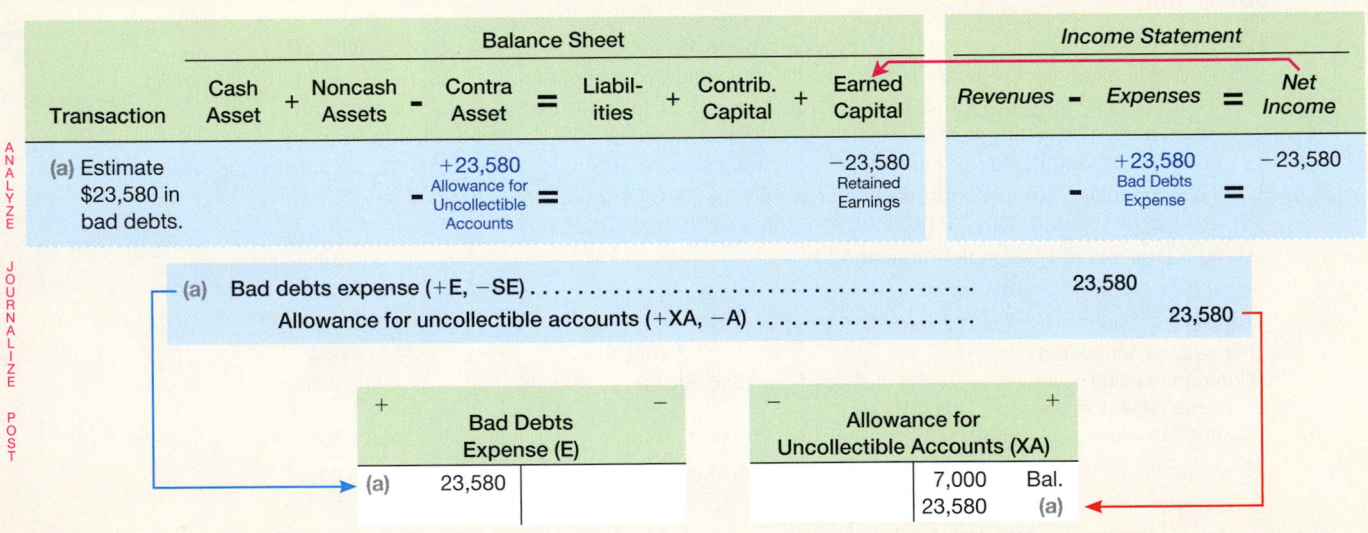

	Balance Sheet								Income Statement		
Transaction	Cash Asset	+ Noncash Assets	− Contra Asset	= Liabil- ities	+ Contrib. Capital	+ Earned Capital			Revenues −	Expenses	= Net Income
(a) Estimate $23,580 in bad debts.			+23,580 − Allowance for Uncollectible Accounts =			−23,580 Retained Earnings				− +23,580 Bad Debts Expense =	−23,580

(a) Bad debts expense (+E, −SE)....................................... 23,580
         Allowance for uncollectible accounts (+XA, −A)   23,580

+ Bad Debts Expense (E)	−	− Allowance for Uncollectible Accounts (XA)	+
(a) 23,580			7,000 Bal.
			23,580 (a)

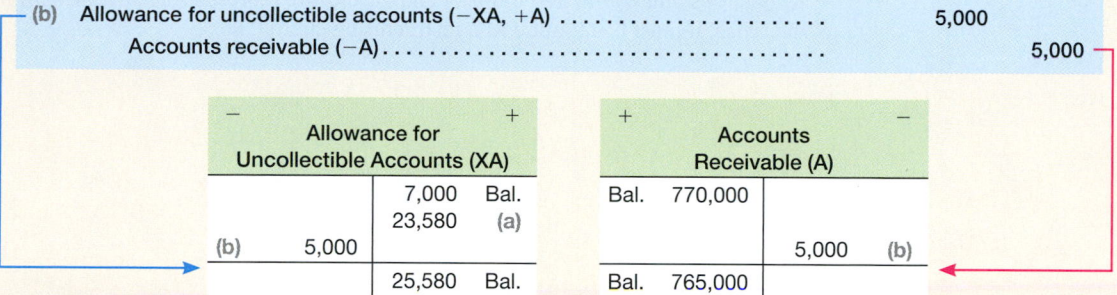

			Balance Sheet						Income Statement		
Transaction	Cash Asset	+	Noncash Assets	−	Contra Asset	=	Liabil-ities	+	Contrib. Capital	+	Earned Capital
(b) Write off $5,000 in accounts receivable.*			−5,000 Accounts Receivable	−	−5,000 Allowance for Uncollectible Accounts	=					

	Income Statement		
Revenues	−	Expenses	= Net Income
-			=

* There is no effect on net accounts receivable.

(b)	Allowance for uncollectible accounts (−XA, +A)	5,000	
	Accounts receivable (−A)		5,000

−	Allowance for Uncollectible Accounts (XA)	+
	7,000	Bal.
	23,580	(a)
(b) 5,000		
	25,580	Bal.

+	Accounts Receivable (A)	−
Bal. 770,000		
	5,000	(b)
Bal. 765,000		

Chapter-End Review

SOLUTION

1.

($ millions)	Comcast	Time Warner
NOPAT	$8,592 − [($296 − $2,832) × (1 − 0.35)] = $10,240.4	$3,827 − [($0 − $1,296) × (1 − 0.35)] = $4,669.4
Average net operating assets	[($155,602 − $56,971) + ($151,470 − $58,951)]/2 = $95,575	[($60,933 - $16,289) + ($65,990 − $17,284)]/2 = $46,675
Return on net operating assets	$10,240.4/$95,575 = 0.107	$4,669.4/$46,675 = 0.100
Net operating profit margin	$10,240.4/$68,775 = 0.149	$4,669.4/$27,359 = 0.171
Accounts receivable turnover...........	$68,775/[($6,321 + $6,376)/2] = 10.8	$27,359/[($7,720 + $7,305)/2] = 3.64
Average collection period	= 365/10.8 = 33.8 days	= 365/3.64 = 100.3 days

2. These two companies are similar in their performance ratios. Comcast reports a 10.7% return on net operating assets and a 14.9% net operating profit margin while Time Warner reports a 10.0% RNOA and a 17.1% NOPM. Thus, these companies generate nearly identical returns on their assets, but Time Warner appears to control costs better per dollar of revenue as shown in their higher margins.

   However, there is a significant difference between these two competitors when it comes to accounts receivable. Time Warner turns its receivables 3.64 times per year, for an average collection period (ACP) of 100.3 days. Comcast, on the other hand, has an accounts receivable turnover of 10.8 times and an ACP of 33.8 days. Thus, Comcast collects receivables nearly three times faster than Time Warner.

Appendix 6A Review

SOLUTION

a. A loss from discontinued operations of $105,000 would be reported below income from continuing operations. The loss is net of tax and is calculated as follows:
$105,000 = ($120,000 + $12,000 + $18,000) \times (1 - 30\%)$.

b. A restructuring charge of $30,000 ($12,000 + $18,000) would be reported as part of operating income. The loss is before taxes. The tax effect of the restructuring charge would be included in the provision for income taxes (income tax expense).

c. Singh could report this loss as discontinued operations only if the closure represented a separate business unit within the company and the closure represents a strategic shift in operations. Otherwise, it must be reported as a restructuring charge.

7

Reporting and Analyzing Inventory

LEARNING OBJECTIVES

1. Interpret disclosures of information concerning operating expenses, including manufacturing and retail inventory costs. (p. 328)

2. Account for inventory and cost of goods sold using different costing methods. (p. 332)

3. Apply the lower of cost or market rule to value inventory. (p. 337)

4. Evaluate how inventory costing affects management decisions and outsiders' interpretations of financial statements. (p. 341)

5. Define and interpret gross profit margin and inventory turnover ratios. Use inventory footnote information to make appropriate adjustments to ratios. (p. 345)

6. Appendix 7A: Analyze LIFO liquidations and the impact they have on the financial statements. (p. 351)

HOME DEPOT
www.HomeDepot.com

The Home Depot, Inc. is the world's largest home improvement retailer and the second largest specialty retailer in the United States. At February 1, 2015, the company operated 2,269 retail stores worldwide, and reported sales of $83 billion. This performance represents a fifth year of increasing revenues.

Management of The Home Depot has focused in recent years on "improving the performance of our existing stores,"[1] with less emphasis on expansion. Indeed, their stated strategic framework consists of three key initiatives—1) customer service, 2) product authority, and 3) disciplined capital allocation, productivity, and efficiency. The Home Depot's net operating profit margin (net operating profit divided by sales revenue) has increased significantly between 2011 and 2014, reflecting a combination of management's attention to costs and an improving economy. The company has performed very well in recent years.

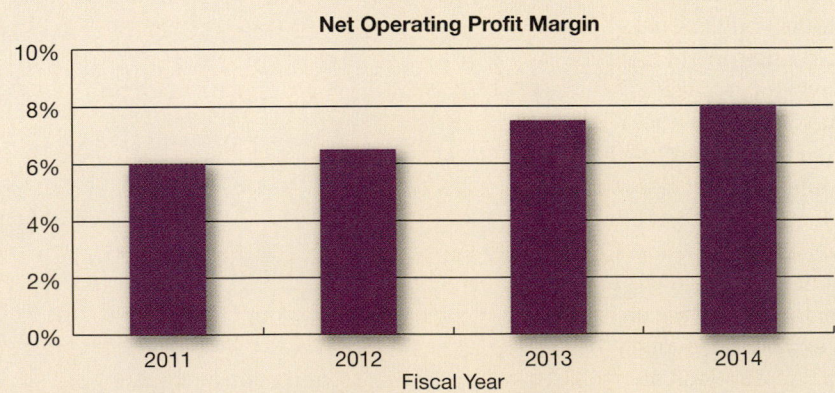

Net Operating Profit Margin

---

[1] Home Depot CEO Frank Blake in an interview with Rachel Tobin Blake published in *The Atlantic Journal-Constitution*, February 1, 2009.

A key element of Home Depot's operating strategy is inventory management. Inventory represents one of the largest assets on Home Depot's balance sheet. A typical Home Depot store carries 30,000 to 40,000 products during the year, ranging from garden supplies to hardware and lumber to household appliances. These stores are stocked through a sophisticated logistics program designed to ensure product availability for customers and low supply chain costs. The fiscal 2014 annual report states that the company "continued to focus on optimizing our supply chain network and improving our inventory, transportation and distribution productivity." As of February 1, 2015, the company operated 34 bulk distribution centers, 21 stocking distribution centers, 10 specialty distribution centers, and 19 Rapid Deployment Centers (RDCs) where merchandise from manufacturers is received and prepared for immediate delivery to stores. The company also utilizes its retail stores as a network of locations for customers who shop online.

In this chapter, we examine the reporting of inventory and cost of goods sold. For most retail and manufacturing businesses, cost of goods sold and the related inventory management costs represent the largest source of expenses in the income statement. Carrying large stocks of inventory is costly for any business. The more that a business can minimize the amount of resources tied up in merchandise or materials, while still meeting customer demand, the more profitable it will be. Moreover, excessive inventory balances can indicate poor inventory management, obsolete products, and weakening sales. We explore accounting methods designed to measure inventory costs and determine cost of goods sold. We also look at measures that help us assess the effectiveness of inventory management practices for companies such as The Home Depot.

Sources: *Fortune*, May 2012; The Home Depot, Inc. 2010-2014 10-K reports; The Home Depot does not end its fiscal year on December 31, but rather on the Sunday closest to January 31. So, "Fiscal Year 2014" actually ended on February 1, 2015. One interesting aspect of this practice is that most of The Home Depot's fiscal years have 52 weeks, but periodically a fiscal year will have 53 weeks. (Fiscal Year 2012 was the most recent year of this event.)

CHAPTER ORGANIZATION

Reporting and Analyzing Inventory			
Reporting Operating Expenses	**Inventory Costing Methods**	**Financial Statement Effects and Disclosure**	**Analyzing Financial Statements**
• Expense Recognition • Recording and Reporting Inventory Costs • Manufacturing Inventory	• FIFO • LIFO • Average Cost • Lower of Cost or Market	• Footnote Disclosures • Income Statement Effects • Balance Sheet Effects • Cash Flow Effects	• Gross Profit Analysis • Inventory Turnover • LIFO Liquidation (Appendix 7A)

LO1 Interpret disclosures of information concerning operating expenses, including manufacturing and retail inventory costs.

REPORTING OPERATING EXPENSES

In Chapter 6, we introduced the concept of operating income and discussed issues surrounding revenue recognition and how best to measure and report a company's performance. But the amount of revenue from customers must be interpreted relative to the resources that were required to achieve it. Operating expenses include the costs of acquiring the products (and services) that customers purchase, plus the costs of selling efforts, administrative functions, and any other activities that support the operations of the company. Careful examination of these costs allows financial statement users to judge management's performance, to identify emerging problems, and to make predictions of future performance. For instance, we may address the following questions.

- Are the company's costs of providing products increasing or decreasing?
- Is the company able to maintain its margins in the face of changes in costs or competition?
- Does management's ability to judge customer tastes and preferences allow it to avoid overstocks of unpopular inventory and the resulting price discounts that reduce margins?

In this chapter, we begin our examination of operating expenses by studying inventory and cost of goods sold. The reporting of inventory and cost of goods sold is important for three reasons. First, cost of goods sold is often the largest single expense in a company's income statement, and inventory may be one of the largest assets in the balance sheet. Consequently, information about inventory and cost of goods sold is critical for interpreting the financial statements. Second, in order to effectively manage operations and resources, management needs accurate and timely information about inventory quantities and costs. Finally, alternative methods of accounting for inventory and cost of goods sold can distort interpretations of margins and turnovers unless the information in the financial statement footnotes is used.

Expense Recognition Principles

In addition to determining when to recognize revenues to properly measure and report a company's performance, we must also determine when to recognize expenses. In general, expenses are recognized when assets are diminished (or liabilities increased) as a result of earning revenue or supporting operations, even if there is no immediate decrease in cash. Expense recognition can be generally divided into the following three approaches.

- **Direct association.** Any cost that can be *directly* associated with a specific source of revenue should be recognized as an expense at the same time that the related revenue is recognized. For a merchandising company (a retailer or a wholesaler), an example of direct association is recognizing cost of goods sold and sales revenue when the product is delivered to the customer. The cost of acquiring the inventory is recorded in the inventory asset account where it remains until the item is sold. At that point, the inventory cost is removed from the inventory asset and transferred to expenses. The future costs of any obligations arising from current revenues should also be estimated and recognized as liabilities and matched as expenses against those revenues. An example of such an expense is expected warranty costs, a topic covered in Chapter 9.

  For a manufacturing company, the accounting system distinguishes between *product costs* and *period costs*. Product costs are incurred to benefit the company's manufacturing activities and include raw materials, production workers and supervisors, depreciation on equipment and facilities, utilities, and so on. Even though some of these costs cannot be directly associated with a unit of production, the accounting system accumulates product costs and assigns them to inventory assets until the unit is sold. All costs not classified as product costs are considered period costs.

● **Immediate recognition**.   Many period costs are necessary for generating revenues and income but cannot be directly associated with specific revenues. Some costs can be associated with all of the revenues of an accounting period, but not with any specific sales transaction that occurred during that period. Examples include most administrative and marketing costs. These costs are recognized as expenses in the period when the costs are incurred. Other expense items, such as research and development (R&D) expense, are recognized immediately because of U.S. GAAP requirements.

● **Systematic allocation**.   Costs that benefit more than one accounting period and cannot be associated with specific revenues or assigned to a specific period must be allocated across all of the periods benefited. The most common example is depreciation expense. When an asset is purchased, it is capitalized (recorded in an asset account). The asset cost is then converted into an expense over the duration of its useful life according to a depreciation formula or schedule established by management. Depreciation of long-term assets is discussed in Chapter 8.

Inventory and cost of goods sold expense are important for product companies—manufacturers, wholesalers, and retailers. But before turning to an examination of these accounts at The Home Depot, we should recognize that cost of sales expense is also a critical performance component for many service companies, particularly those who engage in projects for their clients and customers. For fiscal 2014, the consulting firm **Accenture PLC** reports revenues of $31.9 billion and cost of services of $22.2 billion; the professional staffing company **Kelly Services, Inc.** reported net service revenues of $5.6 billion and direct costs of services of $4.7 billion; and **Google Inc.** reported revenue of $66 billion and cost of sales of $25.7 billion. While these companies report no inventory, the relationship of revenues to costs of revenues remains important.

Reporting Inventory Costs in the Financial Statements

To help frame our discussion of inventory, **Exhibits 7.1** and **7.2** present information from the current asset section of the balance sheet and the continuing operations section of the income statement for The Home Depot. We highlight merchandise inventories in the balance sheet as well as cost of goods sold in the income statement.

When inventory is purchased or produced, it is capitalized and carried on the balance sheet as an asset until it is sold, at which time its cost is transferred from the balance sheet to the income statement as an expense (cost of goods sold). Cost of goods sold (COGS) is then subtracted from sales revenue to yield **gross profit**:

$$\text{Gross profit} = \text{Sales revenue} - \text{Cost of goods sold}$$

The manner in which inventory costs are transferred from the balance sheet to the income statement affects both the level of inventories reported on the balance sheet and the amount of gross profit (and net income) reported on the income statement.

EXHIBIT 7.1	Balance Sheets (Current Assets Only)	
THE HOME DEPOT, INC. **Consolidated Balance Sheets**		
($ millions)	**February 1, 2015**	**February 2, 2014**
Assets		
Current assets:		
Cash and cash equivalents	$ 1,723	$ 1,929
Receivables, net.	1,484	1,398
Merchandise inventories	11,079	11,057
Other current assets.	1,016	895
Total current assets	$15,302	$15,279

EXHIBIT 7.2	Income Statement (Continuing Operations Only)

THE HOME DEPOT, INC.
Consolidated Statement of Earnings

($ millions)	Fiscal year 2014
Net sales.	$83,176
Cost of sales.	**54,222**
Gross profit.	28,954
Total operating expenses	18,485
Operating income.	10,469
Interest and other, net	493
Earnings from continuing operations before provision for income taxes.	9,976
Provision for income taxes.	3,631
Earnings from continuing operations	$ 6,345

Recording Inventory Costs in the Financial Statements

To illustrate the inventory purchasing and selling cycle, assume that a start-up company purchases 800 units of merchandise inventory at a cost of $4 cash per unit. We account for this transaction as follows:

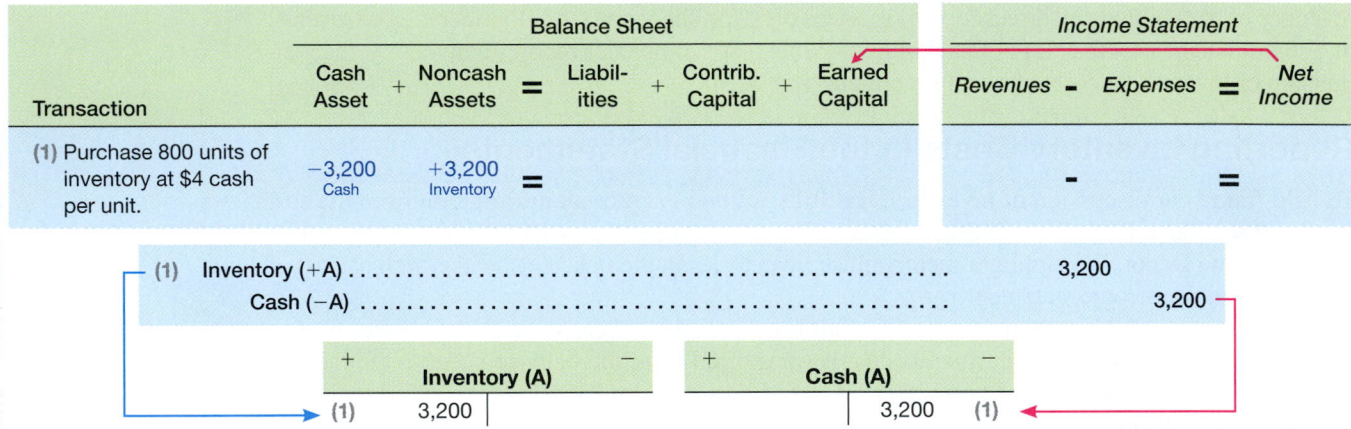

Next, assume this company sells 500 of those units for $7 cash per unit. The two following entries are required to record (a) the sales revenue and (b) the expense for the cost of the inventory sold.

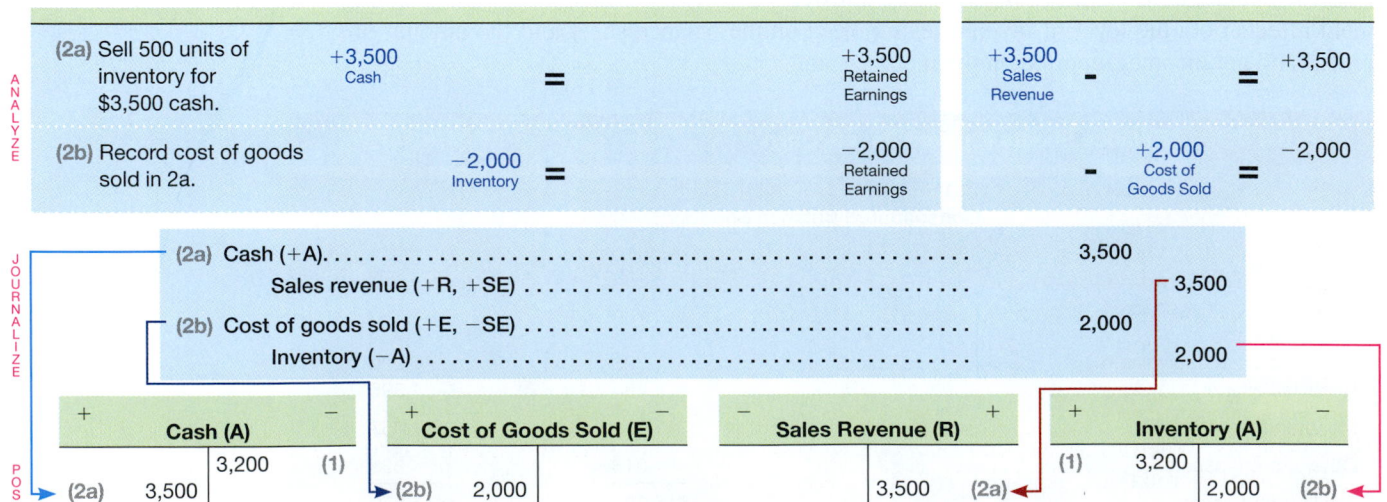

The gross profit from this sale is $1,500 ($3,500 − $2,000). Also, $1,200 worth of merchandise remains in inventory (300 units × $4 per unit).

Inventory and the Cost of Acquisition

In general, a company should recognize all inventories to which it holds legal title, and that inventory should be recognized at the cost of acquiring the inventory. On occasion, that means that the company will recognize items in inventory that are not on its premises. For instance, if a company purchases inventory from a supplier on an "FOB shipping point" basis, meaning that the purchasing company receives title to the goods as soon as they are shipped by the supplier, the purchasing company should recognize the inventory as soon as it receives notice that the goods have been shipped. A similar situation occurs when a company ships its own products to a customer, but has not yet fulfilled the requirements for recognizing revenue on the shipment. In this case, the cost of the products remains in the selling company's inventory account until revenue (and cost of goods sold) can be recognized.

It is also possible for a company to have physical possession of inventory items, but not to have legal title. **Target Corporation**, for example, reports the following in a recent 10-K.

> We routinely enter into arrangements with certain vendors whereby we do not purchase or pay for merchandise until the merchandise is ultimately sold to a guest. Activity under this program is included in sales and cost of sales in the Consolidated Statements of Operations, but the merchandise received under the program is not included in inventory in our Consolidated Statements of Financial Position because of the virtually simultaneous purchase and sale of this inventory.

Inventory is reported in the balance sheet at its cost, including any cost to acquire, transport, and prepare goods for sale. In some cases, determining the cost of inventory requires accounting for various incentives that suppliers offer to purchase more or to pay promptly. If a company qualifies for a supplier's volume discount or rebate, it should immediately recognize the effective reduction in the cost of inventory and cost of goods sold. Or, if the company purchases inventory on credit, suppliers often grant **cash discounts** to buyers if payment is made within a specified time period. Cash discounts are usually established as part of the credit terms and stated as a percentage of the purchase price. For example, credit terms of 1/10, n/30 (one-ten, net-thirty) indicate that a 1% cash discount is allowed if the payment is made within 10 days. If the cash discount is not taken, the full purchase price is due in 30 days. Cash discounts are discussed in greater detail in Chapter 9.

Inventory Reporting by Manufacturing Firms

Retail and wholesale businesses purchase merchandise for resale to customers. In contrast, a manufacturing firm produces the goods it sells. Its inventory reporting is designed to reflect this difference in the nature of its operations.

Manufacturing firms typically report three categories of inventory account:

- **Raw materials inventory**—the cost of parts and materials purchased from suppliers for use in the production process. When raw materials are used in the production process, the cost of the materials used is transferred from raw materials inventory into the work-in-process inventory account.

- **Work-in-process inventory**—the cost of the inventory of partially completed goods. Work-in-process (abbreviated WIP) includes the materials used in the production of the product as well as labor cost and overhead cost. (Methods by which labor and overhead costs are assigned to products in the WIP account is a *managerial accounting* topic.) When the production process is completed, the cost of goods produced is transferred from WIP into the finished goods inventory account.

- **Finished goods inventory**—the cost of the stock of completed product ready for delivery to customers. When finished goods are sold, cost of goods sold is debited and finished goods inventory is credited, much the same as in a retail business.

FYI The term **FOB** ("free on board") **shipping point** means that title passes to the purchaser as soon as it is shipped by the seller. **FOB destination** means that the seller retains title until the item arrives at the purchaser's location.

FYI Only one inventory account appears in the financial statements of a merchandiser. A manufacturer normally has three inventory accounts: Raw Materials, Work-in-Process, and Finished Goods.

EXHIBIT 7.3	Components of Inventory for Cisco Systems, Inc.	
		July 26, 2014
Inventories ($ millions):		
Raw materials..		$ 77
Work in process..		5
Finished goods		
Distributor inventory and deferred cost of sales...............		595
Manufactured finished goods..................................		606
Total finished goods..		1,201
Service-related spares...		273
Demonstration systems...		35
Total..		$1,591

A complete illustration of the accounting process for a manufacturing business is beyond the scope of this text. However, it is useful to understand how these inventory accounts are presented in the financial statements of manufacturing firms. In some cases, each of the three categories of inventory is presented in the balance sheet. Usually, however, the balance sheet only presents the combined total of the three accounts, leaving the detail to be presented in the footnotes. **Cisco Systems** reported inventory of $1,591 million in its balance sheet dated July 26, 2014. **Exhibit 7.3** details the components of Cisco's inventory balance as presented in its 10-K report. It shows that finished goods inventory represented the largest portion of the total inventory balance and that almost half of these finished goods are held by Cisco's distributors. (Cisco's "sell-through" revenue recognition was described in Chapter 6.) Cisco reports two additional categories of inventory—spare parts and systems used in product demonstrations. **Exhibit 7.3** is representative of the footnote disclosure provided by many manufacturing companies.

BUSINESS INSIGHT

If a manufacturing company has an unexpected buildup of inventory, the interpretation depends on the type of inventory. A larger-than-normal buildup of finished goods would imply that the company was having difficulty getting customers to purchase its products. However, if the buildup is in work-in-process inventory, it might imply a problem with manufacturing processes, particularly if accompanied by a decrease in finished goods inventory.

MBC
eLectures

LO2 Account for inventory and cost of goods sold using different costing methods.

2

INVENTORY COSTING METHODS

The computation of cost of goods sold is important and is shown in **Exhibit 7.4**.

EXHIBIT 7.4	Cost of Goods Sold Computation
	Beginning inventory value (prior period ending balance sheet)
+	Cost of inventory purchases and/or production
	Cost of goods available for sale
−	Ending inventory value (current period balance sheet)
	Cost of goods sold (current income statement)

The cost of inventory available at the beginning of a period is a carryover from the ending inventory balance of the prior period. The costs of current period purchases of inventory (or costs of newly manufactured inventories) are added to the costs of beginning inventory on the balance sheet, yielding the total cost of goods (inventory) available for sale. Then, the total cost of goods available either ends up in cost of goods sold for the period (reported on the income statement) or is carried forward as inventory to start the next period (reported on the ending balance sheet). This cost flow is schematically shown in **Exhibit 7.5**.

Understanding the flow of inventory costs is important. If the beginning inventory plus all inventory purchased or manufactured during the period is sold, then COGS is equal to the cost of the goods available for sale. However, when inventory remains at the end of a period, companies must identify the cost of those inventories that have been sold and the cost of those inventories that remain.

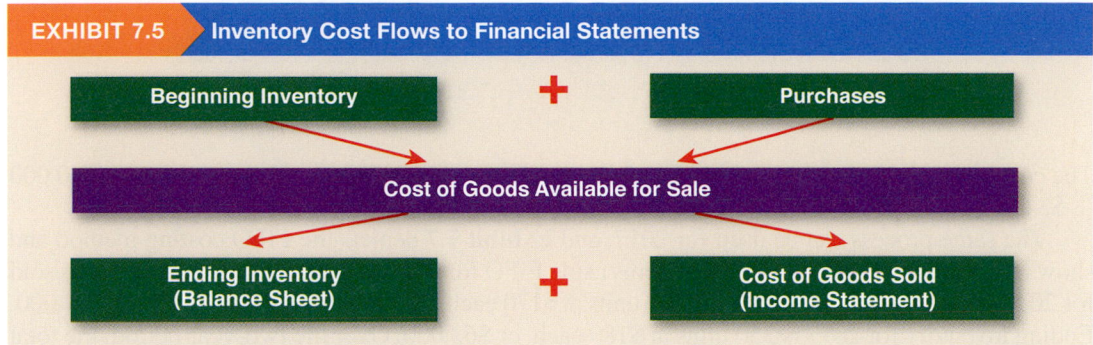

EXHIBIT 7.5 | **Inventory Cost Flows to Financial Statements**

Most companies will organize the physical flow of their inventories to keep the cost of inventory management low, while minimizing the likelihood of spoilage or obsolescence. However, the accounting for inventory and cost of goods sold does not have to follow the physical flow of the units of inventory, so companies may report using a **cost flow assumption** that does not conform to the actual movement of product through the firm. (For instance, many grocery chains use last-in, first-out to account for inventory costs, but that doesn't mean that they put the newest produce out to sell while keeping the older produce back in the storeroom.)

Illustration   To illustrate the possible cost flow assumptions that companies can adopt, assume that **Exhibit 7.6** reflects the inventory records of Butler Company.

EXHIBIT 7.6 | **Summary Inventory Records for Butler Company**

		Number of Units	Cost per Unit	Total Cost	Number of Units	Price per Unit	Total Revenue
January 1, 2016	Beginning inventory	500	$100	$ 50,000			
2016	Inventory purchased.	200	170	34,000			
	Inventory sold.				450	$250	$112,500
2017	Inventory purchased.	600	180	108,000			
	Inventory sold.				500	255	127,500

Butler Company began the period with inventory consisting of 500 units it purchased at a total cost of $50,000 ($100 each). During the two-year period, the company purchased an additional 200 units costing $34,000 and 600 units costing $108,000. The total cost of goods available for sale for this two-year period equals $192,000.

Tracking the number of units available for sale each year and in inventory at the end of each year is simple. However, the changing cost per unit makes it more complicated to determine the cost of goods sold and the ending inventory. The relationships depicted in **Exhibit 7.5** can hold in multiple ways, depending on the cost flow assumption chosen. Three inventory costing methods are acceptable under U.S. GAAP (though only two are permitted under IFRS, as we discuss later).[2]

First-In, First-Out (FIFO)

The **first-in, first-out (FIFO)** inventory costing method transfers costs from inventory in the order that they were initially recorded. That is, FIFO assumes that the first costs recorded in inventory (first-in) are the first costs transferred from inventory (first-out) to cost of goods sold. Conversely, the costs of the last units purchased are the costs that remain in inventory at year-end. Applying FIFO to the data in **Exhibit 7.6** means that the costs relating to the 450 units sold

> **FYI** First-in, first-out (FIFO) assumes that goods are used in the order in which they are purchased; the inventory remaining represents the most recent purchases.

---

[2] Of the firms in the Standard and Poor's 500 Index as of December 31, 2013, 17.2% have a LIFO reserve reported on Compustat (database of annual reports). A few additional firms may be on LIFO but have a zero reserve. (An example is Hollyfrontier Corporation. It reported a zero LIFO reserve in 2014 caused by the large decline in oil prices during 2014.)

are all taken from its *beginning* inventory, which consists of 500 units. The company's 2016 cost of goods sold and gross profit, using FIFO, is computed as follows:

Sales..	$112,500
COGS (450 @ $100 each)...........................	45,000
Gross profit.....................................	$ 67,500

The cost remaining in inventory and reported on its 2016 year-end balance sheet is $39,000 ($50,000 + $34,000 − $45,000; also computed 50 × $100 + 200 × $170).

The same process can be used for 2017, and **Exhibit 7.7** depicts the FIFO costing method and shows the resulting financial statement items using FIFO for 2016 and 2017. FIFO cost of goods sold for 2017 is 50 units at $100 each plus 200 units at $170 each plus 250 units at $180 each, or $84,000. Ending inventory for 2017 is 350 units at $180 each, or $63,000. Over the two-year period, the total cost of goods available for sale of $192,000 is either recognized as cost of goods sold ($45,000 + $84,000 = $129,000) or remains in ending inventory ($63,000).

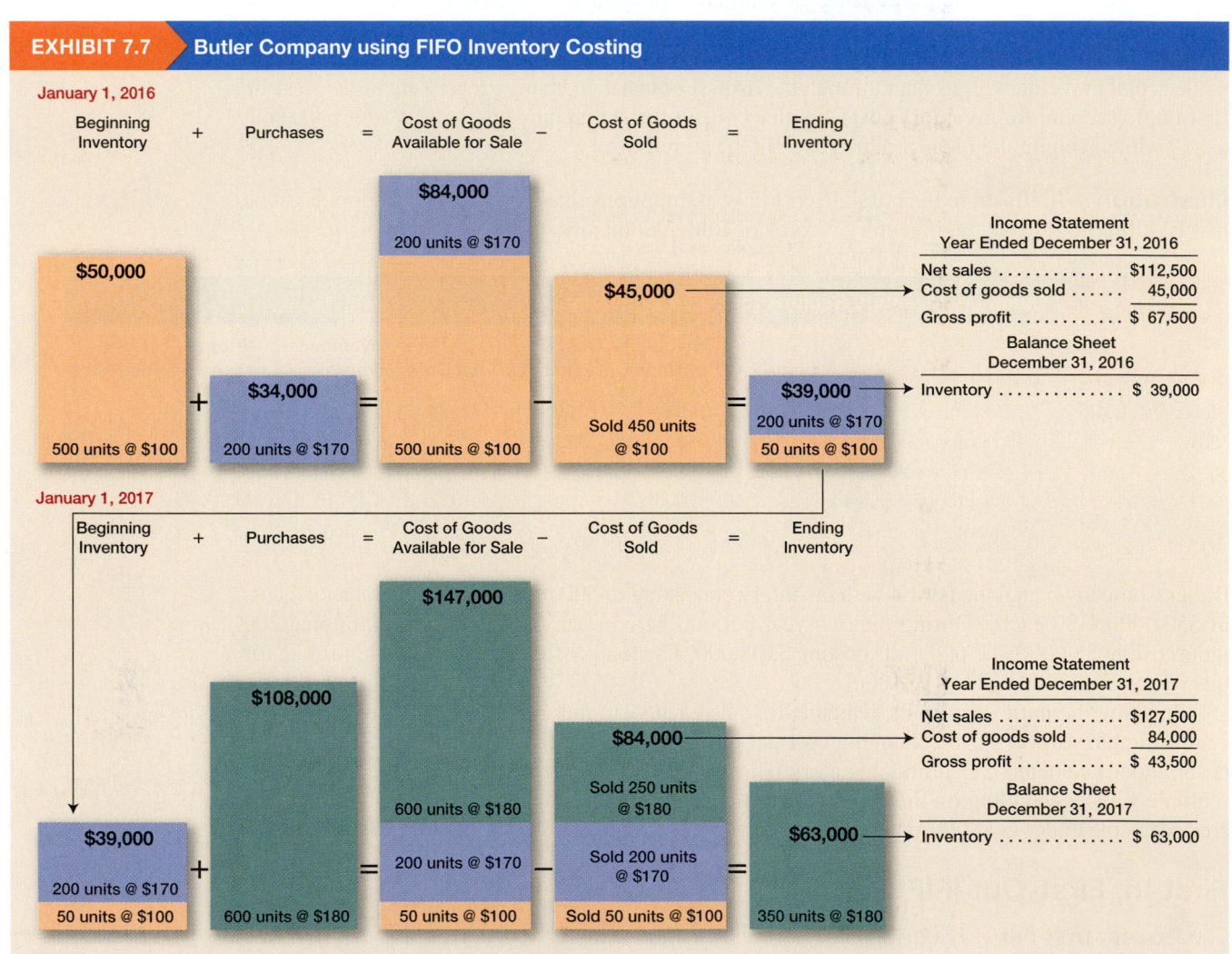

EXHIBIT 7.7   Butler Company using FIFO Inventory Costing

Last-In, First-Out (LIFO)

FYI Last-in, first-out (LIFO) matches the cost of the last goods purchased against revenue.

The **last-in, first-out (LIFO)** inventory costing method transfers to cost of goods sold the most recent costs that were recorded in inventory. That is, we assume that the most recent costs recorded in inventory (last-in) are the first costs transferred from inventory (first-out). Conversely, the costs of the first units purchased are the costs that remain in inventory at year-end. Butler Company's 2016 cost of goods sold and gross profit, using LIFO, are computed as follows:

Sales.	$112,500
COGS: (200 @ $170 each = $34,000)	
(250 @ $100 each = $25,000).	59,000
Gross profit.	$ 53,500

The cost remaining in inventory and reported on its 2016 balance sheet is $25,000 ($50,000 +
$34,000 − $59,000; also computed 250 × $100).

The same process can be used for 2017, and **Exhibit 7.8** depicts the LIFO costing method and
shows the resulting financial statement values using LIFO for both years. LIFO cost of goods sold for
2017 is 500 units at $180 each, or $90,000. Ending inventory is 250 units at $100 each plus 100 units
at $180 each, or $43,000. Again, the two-year total cost of goods available for sale of $192,000 is either
recognized as cost of goods sold ($59,000 + $90,000 = $149,000) or remains in inventory ($43,000).

EXHIBIT 7.8   **Butler Company using LIFO Inventory Costing**

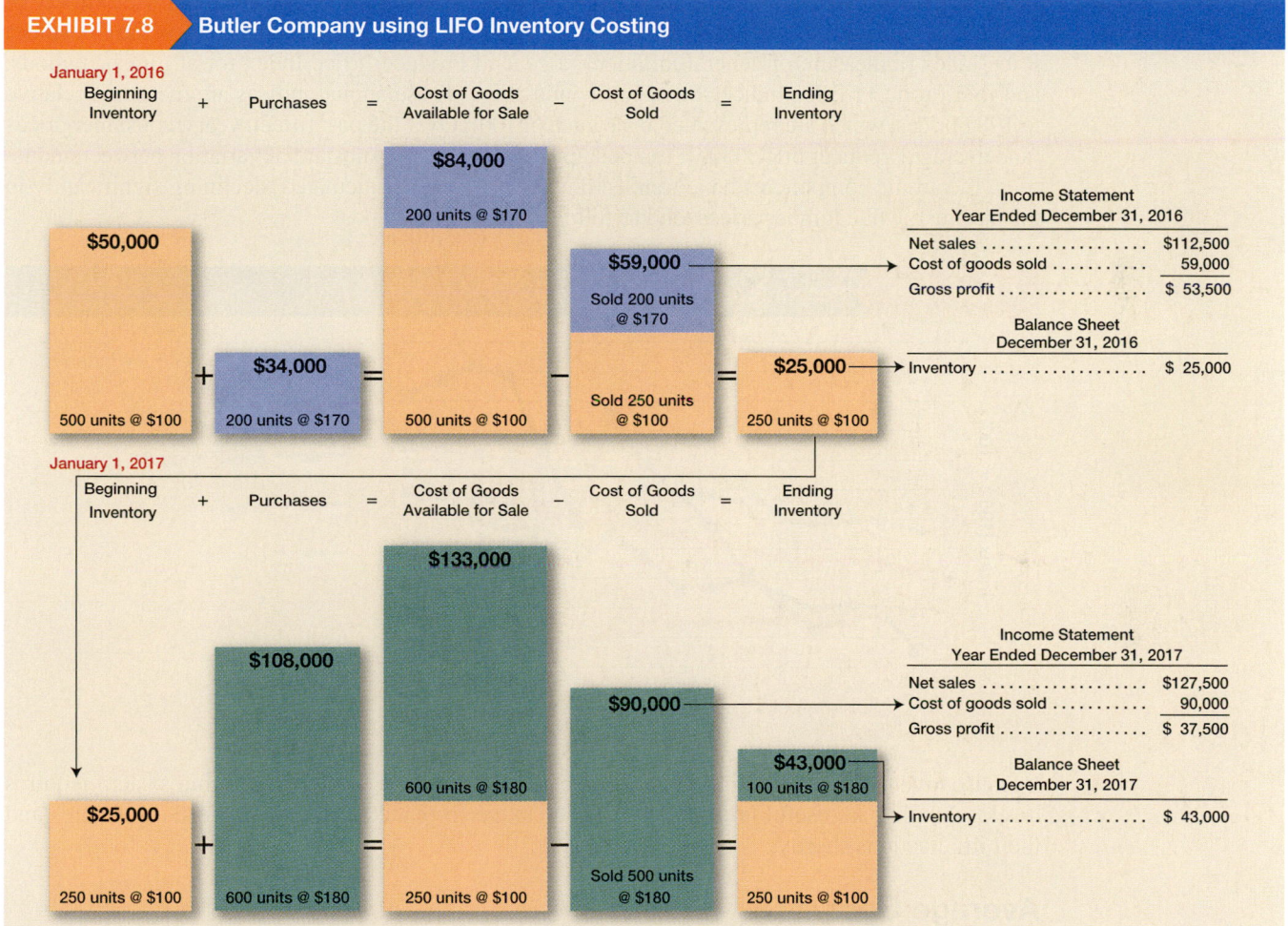

The exhibit shows that **LIFO layers** of inventories added in each year are kept separately. So,
the ending inventory in 2017 consists of a pre-2016 layer of 250 units at $100 each plus a 2017
layer of 100 units at $180 each. When unit sales exceed purchases (as we discuss in the appen-
dix), the first costs carried to cost of goods sold are those purchased in the current year, followed
by the most recent layer of LIFO inventory and working down to the oldest layers. So, the 2016
beginning inventory value of $100 per unit remains in LIFO inventory as long as there are 250
units remaining at the end of the year. One aspect of this flow assumption is that reported LIFO
inventory values can be significantly lower than the current cost of acquiring the same inventory.

LIFO inventory costing is always applied on a periodic, annual basis. This means that Butler's
cost of goods sold and ending inventory for 2017 do not depend on the timing of the sales and purchases within the year. Inventory levels might be drawn down below 250 units *during* the year, but

the 250 unit LIFO layer at $100 each remains in ending inventory as long as inventory is built up to 250 units by the *end* of the year.

Inventory Costing and Price Changes

There are several important aspects of inventory costing that are illustrated by the Butler Company example. First, both LIFO and FIFO are historical cost methods, though they allocate the costs of inventory differently. All costs are accounted for, but in different ways.

Second, the differences between LIFO and FIFO arise when the costs of inventory change over time. In general, LIFO puts more recent costs into cost of goods sold expense, so LIFO cost of goods sold is higher than FIFO cost of goods sold (and gross profit correspondingly lower) when the costs of inventory are rising over time. This phenomenon can be seen in years 2016 and 2017 for Butler Company. If the costs of inventory are falling, then FIFO cost of goods sold exceeds LIFO cost of goods sold.

One place where we can observe the cost trends of acquiring inventory is in the U.S. Bureau of Labor Statistics' Producer Price Indices. These indices track the costs of producing a wide variety of products in the United States. **Exhibit 7.9** shows the recent trends (and fluctuations) in the Consumer Price Index (a measure of general inflation), a general Producer Price Index for all finished goods, and four Producer Price Indices for specific industries. (These annual indices are measured relative to 1982 prices, which are represented by a value of 100.) Over the past fifteen years, consumer prices (and average producer prices) have trended upward, but there is substantial variation between industries. Electronic components have trended down, gasoline has fluctuated, declining significantly in the last year, while lumber prices tend to follow construction trends.

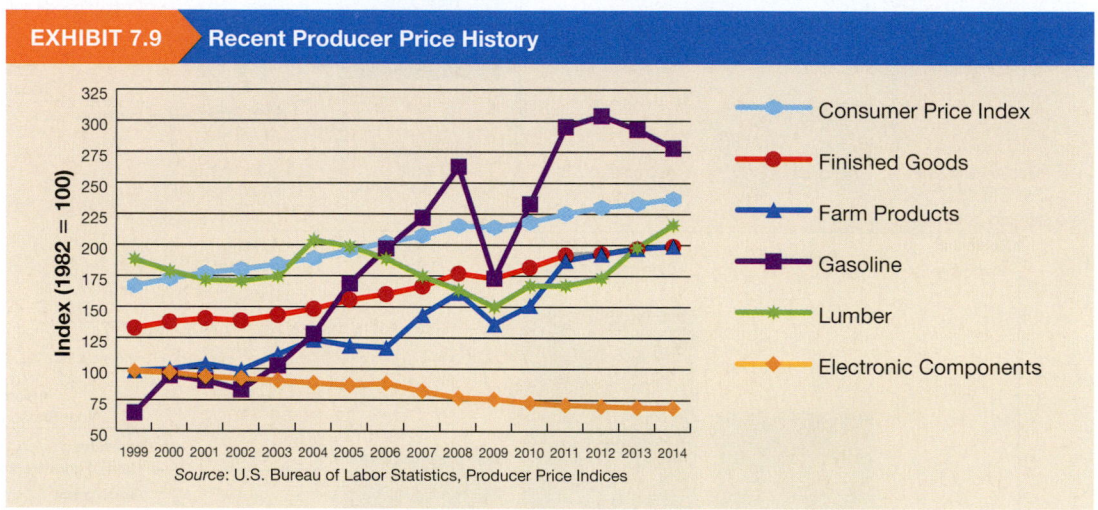

EXHIBIT 7.9 ▶ **Recent Producer Price History**

Source: U.S. Bureau of Labor Statistics, Producer Price Indices

Because inventories are so important for many companies, the financial reporting system requires disclosures that are useful in interpreting financial performance. We turn to those disclosures and their implications shortly.

Average Cost (AC)

FYI Average cost values inventory on the basis of the average cost of all similar goods available during the period.

The **average cost (AC)** method computes the 2016 cost of goods sold as an average of the cost to purchase all of the inventories that were available for sale during the period as follows:

Sales..	$112,500
COGS (450 @ $120 [{$50,000 + $34,000}/700 units] each)	54,000
Gross profit...................................	$ 58,500

The average cost of $120 per unit is determined from the total cost of goods available for sale divided by the number of units available for sale ($84,000/700 units). The cost remaining in inventory and reported on its 2016 balance sheet is $30,000 ($84,000 − $54,000; also computed 250 × $120).

When average cost is applied to the future years, the beginning inventory balance's average cost is again averaged with the inventory acquisitions made during the year. This new average is used to assign costs to that year's ending inventory and cost of goods sold. For the Butler Company, the average cost is $120 for 2016 and $162.35 (rounded) for 2017. The average cost for 2017 is the opening inventory balance plus the period's purchases ($30,000 + $108,000) divided by the total number of units available for sale (250 + 600). So, 2017 cost of goods sold is 500 units at $162.35 each, and ending inventory is 350 units at that same average cost. **Exhibit 7.10** depicts the average cost method and shows the resulting financial statement values using average cost for both years.

EXHIBIT 7.10	Butler Company using Average Cost Inventory Costing

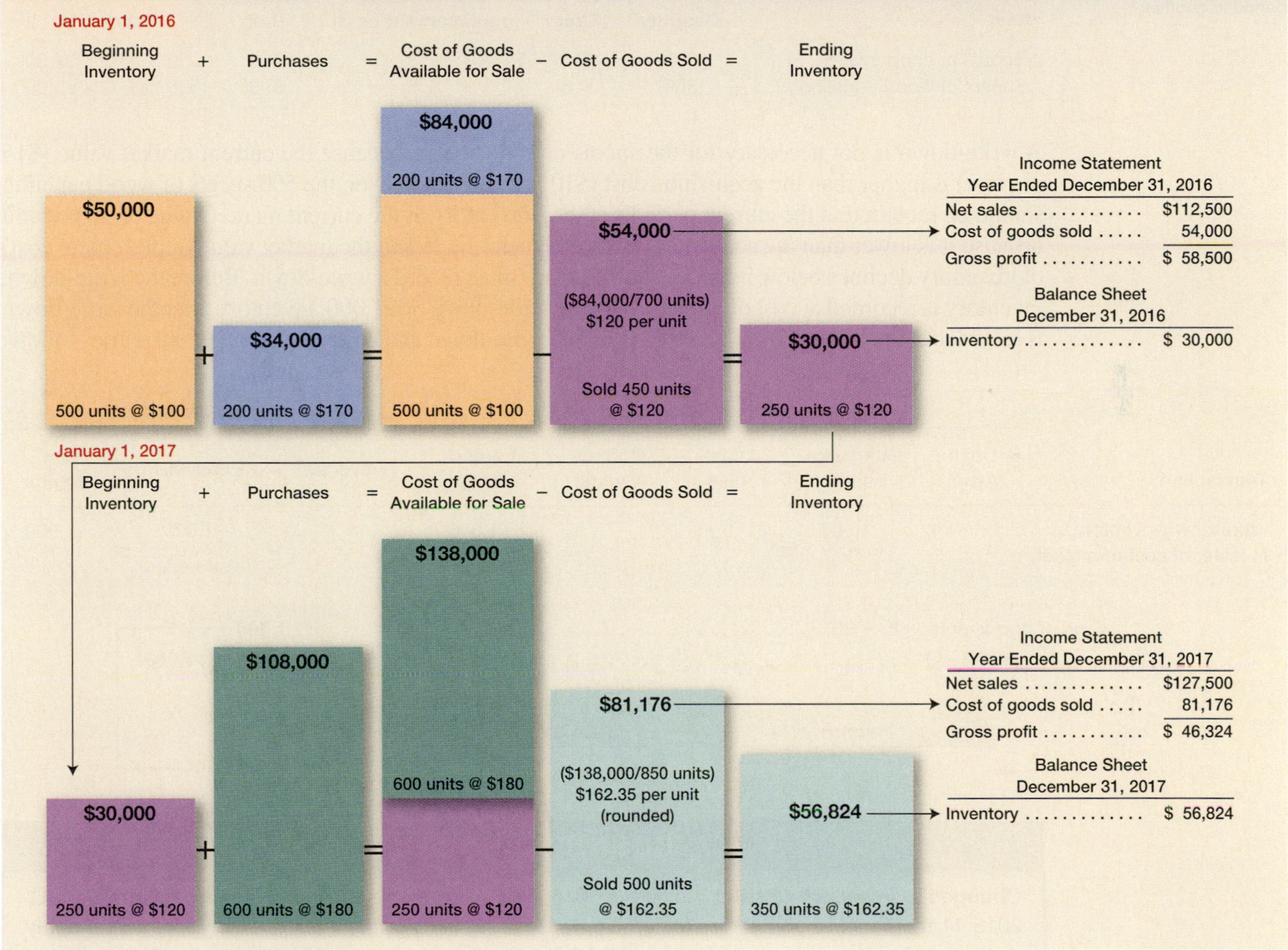

January 1, 2016

Beginning Inventory + Purchases = Cost of Goods Available for Sale − Cost of Goods Sold = Ending Inventory

$84,000
200 units @ $170

$50,000
500 units @ $100

$34,000
200 units @ $170

$84,000
500 units @ $100

$54,000
($84,000/700 units)
$120 per unit
Sold 450 units @ $120

$30,000
250 units @ $120

Income Statement
Year Ended December 31, 2016
Net sales $112,500
Cost of goods sold 54,000
Gross profit . . . . $ 58,500

Balance Sheet
December 31, 2016
Inventory . . . . $ 30,000

January 1, 2017

Beginning Inventory + Purchases = Cost of Goods Available for Sale − Cost of Goods Sold = Ending Inventory

$138,000

$108,000

$30,000
250 units @ $120

$108,000
600 units @ $180

$138,000
250 units @ $120

$81,176
($138,000/850 units)
$162.35 per unit
(rounded)
Sold 500 units @ $162.35

$56,824
350 units @ $162.35

Income Statement
Year Ended December 31, 2017
Net sales $127,500
Cost of goods sold 81,176
Gross profit . . . . $ 46,324

Balance Sheet
December 31, 2017
Inventory . . . . $ 56,824

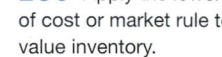

Lower of Cost or Market

Companies are required to write down the carrying amount of inventories on the balance sheet, *if* the reported cost (using FIFO, for example) exceeds the market value. This process is called reporting inventories at the **lower of cost or market (LCM)**. Should the market value be less than reported cost, the inventories must be written down from cost to market value, resulting in the following financial statement effects.

LO3 Apply the lower of cost or market rule to value inventory.

3

- Inventory book value is written down to current market value, reducing total assets.
- Inventory write-down is reflected as an expense (part of cost of goods sold) on the income statement, reducing current period gross profit, income, and equity.

The most common occurrence of inventory write-downs is in connection with restructuring activities. These write-downs are either included in cost of goods sold or on a separate line in the income statement.

FYI If inventory declines in value below its original cost, for whatever reason, the inventory is written down to reflect this loss.

The write-down of inventories can potentially shift income from one period to another. If, for example, inventories were written down below current replacement cost (too conservative), future gross profit would be increased as lower future costs would be reflected in cost of goods sold. GAAP anticipates this possibility by requiring that inventories not be written down below a floor that is equal to net realizable value less a normal markup. Although this does allow some discretion (and the ability to manage income), the net realizable value and markup values must be confirmed by the company's auditors.[3]

> **FYI** Standards require the consistent application of costing methods from one period to another.

Illustration   To illustrate the lower of cost or market rule, assume Home Depot has the following items in its current period ending inventory:

Item	Quantity	Cost per Unit	Market Value (replacement cost)	LCM per Unit	Total LCM
Spools of copper wire	250	$10	$15	$10	250 × $10 = $2,500
Sheets of wood paneling	500	$ 8	$ 6	$ 6	500 × $ 6 = $3,000

A write-down is not necessary for the spools of copper wire because the current market value ($15 per unit) is higher than the acquisition cost ($10 per unit). However, the 500 sheets of wood paneling should be recorded in the current period's ending inventory at the current market value of $6 per unit because it is lower than the acquisition cost of $8 per unit. When the market value (replacement cost) of inventory declines below its acquisition cost, we must record a write-down. Before the write-down, inventory is recorded at cost of $6,500. With the write-down of $1,000, inventory after the write-down is recorded at LCM of $5,500. The effects of this write-down and corresponding journal entries follow:

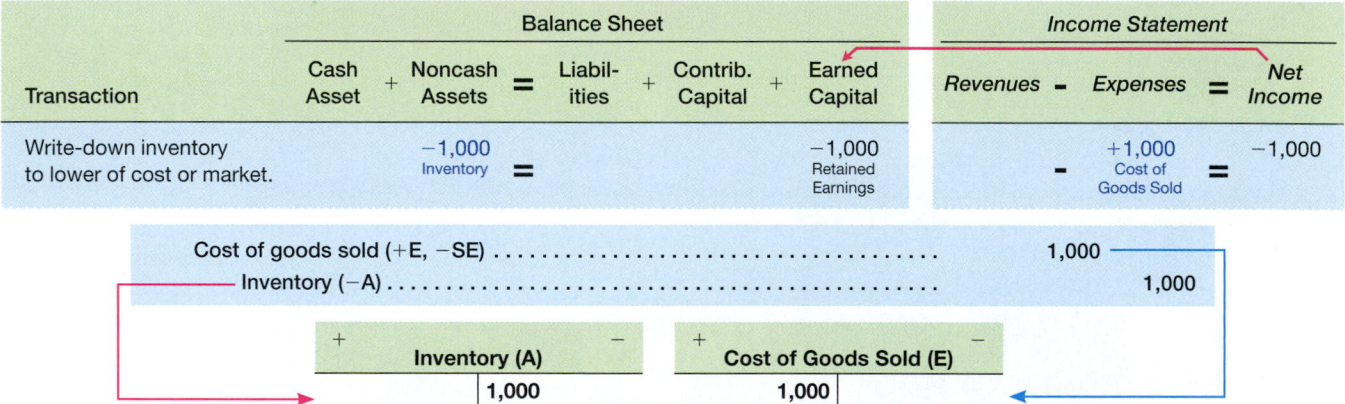

BUSINESS INSIGHT

Changes to Inventory Costing   In July of 2015, FASB issued an Accounting Standards Update (ASU) 2015-11 that requires companies (other than those using LIFO or the retail inventory method) to apply the lower of cost or net realizable value (LCNRV) rather than the lower of cost or market. Net realizable value (NRV) is the estimated selling price less costs to complete the sale. This ASU essentially provides a narrower definition of "market" and aligns U.S. GAAP more closely with IFRS. The new rules are effective for fiscal years beginning after December 15, 2016.

A GLOBAL PERSPECTIVE

Under U.S. GAAP, inventory that has been written down cannot be revalued later at higher levels even if the market value of that inventory increases. IFRS, on the other hand, does allow companies to reverse the write-down of the inventory up to the acquisition cost if market values warrant. The revaluation results in a debit to Inventory and a credit to Cost of Goods Sold. The option to revalue inventory after a write-down differs across countries.

---

[3] Recall Cisco's inventory write-down discussed in the opening pages of Chapter 6.

MID-CHAPTER REVIEW

PART 1

At the beginning of the current period, Hutton Company holds 1,000 units of its only product with a per-unit cost of $18. A summary of purchases during the current period follows:

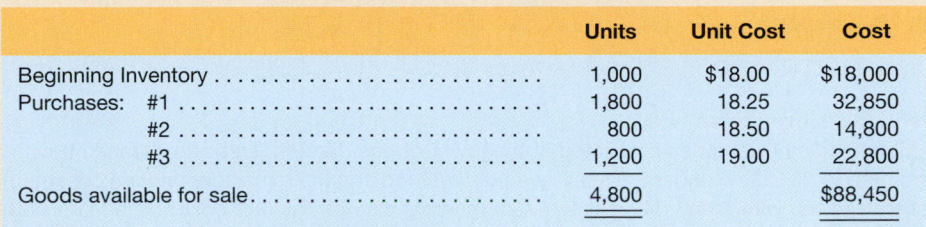

	Units	Unit Cost	Cost
Beginning Inventory	1,000	$18.00	$18,000
Purchases: #1	1,800	18.25	32,850
#2	800	18.50	14,800
#3	1,200	19.00	22,800
Goods available for sale.	4,800		$88,450

During the current period, Hutton sells 2,800 units.

Required

1. Assume that Hutton uses the first-in, first-out (FIFO) method. Compute the cost of goods sold for the current period and the ending inventory balance.
2. Assume that Hutton uses the last-in, first-out (LIFO) method. Compute the cost of goods sold for the current period and the ending inventory balance.
3. Assume that Hutton uses the average cost (AC) method. Compute the cost of goods sold for the current period and the ending inventory balance.
4. As manager, which one of these three inventory costing methods would you choose:
   a. To reflect what is probably the physical flow of goods? Explain.
   b. To minimize income taxes for the period? Explain.
5. Assume that Hutton utilizes the LIFO method and instead of purchasing lot #3, the company allows its inventory level to decline and delays purchasing lot #3 until the next period. Compute cost of goods sold under this scenario and discuss the effect of end-of-year purchases under LIFO.
6. Record the effects of each of the following summary transactions *a* and *b* in the financial statement effects template, prepare journal entries, set up T-accounts for each of the accounts used, and post the journal entries to those T-accounts.
   a. Purchased inventory for $70,450 cash.
   b. Sold $50,850 of inventory for $85,000 cash.

PART 2

Venner Company had the following inventory at December 31, 2017.

	Quantity	Unit Price Cost	Market
Fans			
Model X1	300	$18	$19
Model X2	250	22	24
Model X3	400	29	26
Heaters			
Model B7	500	24	28
Model B8	290	35	32
Model B9	100	41	38

Required

1. Determine ending inventory by applying the lower of cost or market rule to
   a. Each item of inventory.
   b. Each major category of inventory.
   c. Total inventory.
2. Which of the LCM procedures from requirement 1 results in the lowest net income for 2017? Explain.

The solution to this review problem can be found on pages 367–369.

FINANCIAL STATEMENT EFFECTS AND DISCLOSURE

FYI Standards require financial statement disclosure of (1) the composition of the inventory (in the balance sheet or a separate schedule in the notes), (2) significant or unusual inventory financing arrangements, and (3) inventory costing methods employed (which can differ for different types of inventory).

The notes to the financial statements describe, at least in general terms, the inventory accounting method used by a company. To illustrate, The Home Depot reports $11,079 million in merchandise inventory on its February 1, 2015, balance sheet as a current asset. The following note was taken from that 10-K report:

Merchandise Inventories

Our Merchandise Inventories are stated at the lower of cost (first-in, first-out) or market, with approximately 74% valued under the retail inventory method and the remainder under a cost method. Retailers like us, with many different types of merchandise at low unit cost and a large number of transactions, frequently use the retail inventory method. Under the retail inventory method, Merchandise Inventories are stated at cost, which is determined by applying a cost-to-retail ratio to the ending retail value of inventories. As our inventory retail value is adjusted regularly to reflect market conditions, our inventory valued under the retail method approximates the lower of cost or market. We evaluate our inventory valued under a cost method at the end of each quarter to ensure that it is carried at the lower of cost or market. The valuation allowance for Merchandise Inventories valued under a cost method was not material to our Consolidated Financial Statements as of the end of fiscal 2014 or 2013.

Independent physical inventory counts or cycle counts are taken on a regular basis in each store and distribution center to ensure that amounts reflected in the accompanying Consolidated Financial Statements for Merchandise Inventories are properly stated. During the period between physical inventory counts in our stores, we accrue for estimated losses related to shrink on a store-by-store basis. Shrink (or in the case of excess inventory, "swell") is the difference between the recorded amount of inventory and the physical inventory. Shrink may occur due to theft, loss, inaccurate records for the receipt of inventory or deterioration of goods, among other things. We estimate shrink as a percent of Net Sales using the average shrink results from the previous two physical inventories. The estimates are evaluated quarterly and adjusted based on recent shrink results and current trends in the business. Actual shrink results did not vary materially from estimated amounts for fiscal 2014, 2013 or 2012.

This note includes several items that would be of interest to financial statement users:

1. The Home Depot uses the FIFO method to determine the cost of its inventory suggesting several methods are likely to be in use.

2. Inventory is reported at the lower of cost or market value, and the amount of write-down (the valuation allowance) was not material at the financial statement date.

3. The company periodically takes a physical count of inventory to identify "shrink." Shrink refers to the loss of inventory due to theft, breakage or damage, spoilage (for perishable goods), or other losses, as well as inaccurate records.

When businesses adjust inventory balances for shrink, the loss is debited to cost of goods sold. Hence, cost of goods sold expense on the income statement includes the actual cost of products sold during the period plus the loss due to shrink as well as losses resulting from lower of cost or market adjustments and discounts lost.

Another illustration of inventory disclosure is taken from the notes of **Kaiser Aluminum Corporation**. Kaiser reports an inventory of $214.7 million on its December 31, 2014, balance sheet. The following note was taken from its 2014 10-K report ($ millions):

Inventories. Inventories are stated at the lower of cost or market value. Finished products, work-in-process and raw material inventories are stated on the last-in, first-out ("LIFO") basis. The excesses of current cost over the stated LIFO value of inventory at December 31, 2014 and December 31, 2013 were $37.6 and $0.4, respectively. Other inventories, principally operating supplies and repair and maintenance parts, are stated at average cost. Inventory costs consist of material, labor and manufacturing overhead, including depreciation.

There are several interesting items disclosed in Kaiser's note:

1. Kaiser uses LIFO to report the cost of its raw materials, work in process, and finished goods inventory, but uses average cost for supplies and other. Neither U.S. GAAP nor tax authorities such as the IRS require the use of a single inventory costing method. That is, companies are allowed to, and frequently do, use different inventory costing methods for different categories of inventory. In addition, multinational companies may use one costing method in the United States and a different method for foreign inventory stocks.

2. Although Kaiser reports inventory costs at the lower of cost or market, the market value of its inventory (indicated by its current or FIFO cost) is significantly higher than its cost based on LIFO accounting. In fact, the note reports that current cost exceeded the $214.7 million LIFO cost by $37.6 million. That means that the replacement cost of its inventory was $252.3 million ($214.7 + $37.6). Companies using LIFO are required to report the difference between the LIFO cost and current value—determined either as market value or replacement cost or as the FIFO cost. The difference between the ending inventory's FIFO cost (or current cost) and its LIFO cost is called the **LIFO reserve**.

Why do companies disclose such details on inventory, and why is so much attention paid to inventory in financial statement analysis? First, the magnitude of a company's investment in inventory is often large—impacting both balance sheets and income statements. Second, risks of inventory losses are often high, as they are tied to technical obsolescence and consumer tastes. Third, it can provide insight into future performance—both good and bad. Fourth, high inventory levels result in substantial costs for the company, such as:

*   Financing costs to purchase inventories (when not purchased on credit)
*   Storage costs of inventories (such as warehousing and related facilities)
*   Handling costs of inventories (including wages)
*   Insurance costs of inventories

Consequently, companies seek to keep inventories at levels that balance these costs against the cost of insufficient inventory (stock-out and resulting lost sales and delays in production, as machines and employees sit idle awaiting inventories to process).

Next, we turn our focus on the effects of the different inventory costing assumptions on the financial statements.

Financial Statement Effects of Inventory Costing

LO4 Evaluate how inventory costing affects management decisions and outsiders' interpretations of financial statements.

The three inventory costing methods described a few pages earlier yield differing levels of gross profit for our illustrative example, as shown in **Exhibit 7.11**.

We emphasize that, even though the various methods produce different financial statements, the underlying events are the same. That is, different accounting methods can make similar situations seem more different than they really are.

LIFO Reserve   **Exhibit 7.11** demonstrates one of the income statement/balance sheet links that proves useful in analyzing financial statements. In the beginning inventory for 2016, LIFO and FIFO start from the same point—500 units at $100 each. But during 2016, FIFO would record cost of goods sold that is $14,000 less than LIFO ($45,000 versus $59,000). During 2016, LIFO put $14,000 more into cost of goods sold than FIFO did, but that also means that LIFO put $14,000 less into ending inventory. We can see that the LIFO reserve has grown from zero to $14,000, the same amount. This relationship continues in 2017: the LIFO reserve increased by $6,000 (from $14,000 to $20,000), and the LIFO cost of goods sold was $6,000 greater than the FIFO cost of goods sold ($90,000 versus $84,000). The LIFO reserve equals the ending inventory's FIFO cost less LIFO cost, but it is also the *cumulative* difference between LIFO and FIFO cost of goods sold. The *change* in the LIFO reserve is the difference between LIFO and FIFO cost of goods sold for the current period.

So, if Butler Company chose to report using LIFO, we could estimate what the company's FIFO cost of goods sold would have been by seeing how the LIFO reserve changed.

FYI If ending inventory is misstated, then (1) the inventory, retained earnings, working capital, and current ratio in the balance sheet are misstated, and (2) the cost of goods sold and net income in the income statement are misstated.

> **FIFO cost of goods sold = LIFO cost of goods sold − Change in the LIFO reserve**

EXHIBIT 7.11	Financial Statement Effects of Inventory Costing Methods for Butler Company			
		FIFO	LIFO	Average Cost
January 1, 2016	**Balance Sheet**			
	Beginning inventory	$ 50,000	$ 50,000	$ 50,000
	LIFO Reserve	—	—	—
Year Ended 2016	**Income Statement**			
	Revenue	$112,500	$112,500	$112,500
	Cost of goods sold:			
	Beginning inventory	50,000	50,000	50,000
	Add: Purchases	34,000	34,000	34,000
	Goods available for sale	84,000	84,000	84,000
	Subtract: Ending inventory	39,000	25,000	30,000
	Cost of goods sold	45,000	59,000	54,000
	Gross profit	67,500	53,500	58,500
	Selling, general and administrative expenses (assumed number)	10,000	10,000	10,000
	Income before income taxes	57,500	43,500	48,500
	Income tax expense (35%)	20,125	15,225	16,975
	Net income	$ 37,375	$ 28,275	$ 31,525
December 31, 2016	**Balance Sheet**			
	Ending inventory	$ 39,000	$ 25,000	$ 30,000
	LIFO Reserve	—	$ 14,000	—
Year Ended 2017	**Income Statement**			
	Revenue	$127,500	$127,500	$127,500
	Cost of goods sold:			
	Beginning inventory	39,000	25,000	30,000
	Add: Purchases	108,000	108,000	108,000
	Goods available for sale	147,000	133,000	138,000
	Subtract: Ending inventory	63,000	43,000	56,824
	Cost of goods sold	84,000	90,000	81,176
	Gross profit	43,500	37,500	46,324
	Selling, general and administrative expenses (assumed number)	10,000	10,000	10,000
	Income before income taxes	33,500	27,500	36,324
	Income tax expense (35%)	11,725	9,625	12,713
	Net income	$ 21,775	$ 17,875	$ 23,611
December 31, 2017	**Balance Sheet**			
	Ending inventory	63,000	43,000	56,824
	LIFO Reserve	—	20,000	—

That relationship proves useful if we want to compare Butler Company's gross profit to that of another company using FIFO. Changes in the LIFO reserve also give a rough indication of how a company's inventory costs changed over the period. If costs increase, the LIFO reserve increases; if costs decrease, the LIFO reserve decreases.

Income Statement Effects   The income differences between inventory accounting methods are a function of two factors. First is the speed and direction of inventory cost changes. For Butler Company, inventory costs have increased from $100 per unit to $180 per unit in a two-year period. If costs increased more slowly, the difference between LIFO and FIFO would decrease. And, if costs decreased, the differences would reverse: FIFO cost of goods sold would be greater than LIFO cost of goods sold.

The second factor determining the differences is the length of time inventory is held by the company. If Butler Company were able to operate with zero inventory (or at least begin and end the reporting period with zero inventory), the three inventory accounting methods would yield exactly the same cost of goods sold. On the other hand, if inventory must be held for a long period, the differences would increase.

Effects of Changing Costs

When the cost of a company's products is changing, management usually makes corresponding changes in the prices it charges for those products. If costs are declining, competitive pressures are likely to push down the prices customers are willing to pay. If costs are increasing, the company will try to increase prices to recover at least some of the greater cost. When costs fluctuate (for example, for a commodity), management may act to cause its prices to fluctuate in an effort to maintain its target profit margin.[4]

If costs and prices are rising, then FIFO reports a higher gross margin, because the costs of older, lower-cost inventory are being matched against current selling prices. For tax purposes, the company would prefer to use LIFO because it would decrease gross profit and decrease taxable income. If Butler Company were subject to a 35% income tax rate, the use of LIFO rather than FIFO reduces taxes by $4,900 in 2016 ($20,125 − $15,225 in **Exhibit 7.11**, or 35% of the $14,000 difference in 2016 cost of goods sold) and by $2,100 in 2017 ($11,725 − $9,625 in **Exhibit 7.11**, or 35% of the $6,000 difference in 2017 cost of goods sold). In total over the two years, using LIFO (rather than FIFO) would reduce Butler's tax bill by $7,000 (which equals 35% of the $20,000 LIFO reserve at the end of 2017).

In the United States, LIFO is a popular tax method for accounting for inventories that have an upward trend in costs. But, the Internal Revenue Service has imposed a LIFO conformity requirement. If Butler Company is using LIFO for tax reporting, it must use LIFO for reporting to its shareholders. For inventories with a decreasing trend in costs, FIFO reduces the amount of taxes paid. FIFO is allowed by the Internal Revenue Service, but there is no corresponding conformity requirement for firms that use FIFO.

> **FYI** When a company adopts LIFO in its tax filings, the company is required to use LIFO for reporting to its shareholders (in its 10-K). This requirement is known as the LIFO conformity rule.

Balance Sheet Effects

The ending inventory using LIFO for our illustration is less than that reported using FIFO. In prolonged periods of rising costs, using LIFO yields ending inventories that are markedly lower than FIFO. As a result, balance sheets using LIFO do not accurately represent the cost that a company would incur to replace its current investment in inventories.

Kaiser, for example, reported that the current value of its inventory was $37.6 million higher than the LIFO cost at the end of 2014. That is, the amount presented in its balance sheet was understated (relative to current value) by more than $37 million. For purposes of analysis, the value of the LIFO reserve can be viewed as an **unrealized holding gain**—a gain resulting from holding inventory as prices are rising. That is, there is a holding gain due to rising inventory costs that has not been recorded in the financial statements. This gain is not recognized until the inventory is sold. In its December 31, 2014, balance sheet, Kaiser reported current assets of $825.2 million and current liabilities of $426.4 million, for a current ratio of $825.2 ÷ $426.4, or about 1.94. However, Kaiser's inventory is not reported at an up-to-date amount, while the accounts payable would reflect the current prices owed to suppliers. Therefore, an improved measure of the current ratio would be [$825.2 + $37.6] ÷ $426.4, or about 2.02.

In contrast, by assigning the most recently purchased inventory items to ending inventory, FIFO costing tends to approximate current value in the balance sheet. Hence, companies using FIFO tend not to have large unrealized inventory holding gains. However, if prices fall, companies using FIFO are more likely to adjust inventory values to the lower of cost or market.

> **FYI** Some companies highlight this in their disclosures. For example, another company that uses LIFO, Chevron Corporation, mentions the current ratio effect in the notes to their statements saying "The current ratio was adversely affected by the fact that Chevron's inventories are valued on a last-in, first-out basis."

Cash Flow Effects

The increased gross profit using FIFO results in higher pretax income and, consequently, higher taxes payable (assuming FIFO is also used for tax reporting). Conversely, the use of LIFO in an inflationary environment results in a lower tax liability.

Use of LIFO has reduced the dollar amount of Kaiser inventories by $37.6 million, resulting in a cumulative increase in cost of goods sold and a cumulative decrease in gross profit and pretax profit of that same amount.[5] The decrease in cumulative pretax profits has lowered Kaiser's tax bill over the life of the company by roughly $13.2 million ($37.6 million × 35% assumed corpo-

---

[4] LIFO has a reporting advantage when inventory costs fluctuate, in that it matches current period costs against current period revenues. For a company that holds one quarter's worth of inventory, FIFO matches the costs from three months ago against current period revenues. Such a "mismatch" might make it difficult for management to convey its success in maintaining its current profit margin.

[5] Cost of Goods Sold = Beginning Inventories + Purchases − Ending Inventories. Thus, as ending inventories decrease, cost of goods sold increases.

rate tax rate), which has increased Kaiser's cumulative operating cash flow by that same amount. The increased cash flow from tax savings is often cited as a compelling reason for management to adopt LIFO.

Adjusting the Balance Sheet to FIFO   For analysis purposes, we can use the LIFO reserve to adjust the balance sheet and income statement to achieve comparability between companies that utilize different inventory costing methods. For example, if we wanted to compare Kaiser with another company using FIFO, we add the LIFO reserve to its LIFO inventory. As explained above, this $37.6 million increase in 2014 inventories increases its cumulative pretax profits by $37.6 million and taxes by $13.2 million. Thus, the balance sheet adjustments involve increasing inventories by $37.6 million, tax liabilities by $13.2 million, and retained earnings by the remaining after-tax amount of $24.4 million (computed as $37.6 million − $13.2 million).

A GLOBAL PERSPECTIVE

One of the important differences in inventory accounting between U.S. GAAP and IFRS is that the latter does not allow the use of last-in, first-out (LIFO) accounting. Only FIFO and Average Cost are allowed for companies reporting under IFRS.

An analyst comparing a U.S. GAAP company to an IFRS company would need to keep an eye on these inventory differences and, when necessary, do the conversions described in the preceding paragraphs. While FIFO firms are not required to disclose what they would have looked like under LIFO, LIFO firms must disclose enough information to do a rough approximation of what they would have looked like under FIFO—making for an improved comparison with an IFRS company.

The fact that IFRS does not allow LIFO—combined with the U.S. Internal Revenue Service's conformity requirement—creates a dilemma if the United States were to adopt IFRS. For instance, if Kaiser were to have adopted IFRS for fiscal year 2014, reporting FIFO inventory and cost of goods sold in subsequent financial reports, the IRS would consider that Kaiser had given up its LIFO election and would require payment of the $13.2 million in taxes that had been deferred by the use of LIFO. This concern often appears in companies' comment letters to the Securities and Exchange Commission on the proposed move to IFRS in the United States.

It is also worth noting that when comparing companies in the same industry, accounting choices can differ. For example, GM and Ford use LIFO while Honda, a Japanese firm, uses FIFO.

Adjusting the Income Statement to FIFO   To adjust the income statement from LIFO to FIFO, we use the *change* in the LIFO reserve. For Kaiser, the LIFO reserve changed from $0.4 million in 2013 to $37.6 million in 2014, an increase of $37.2 million. To adjust the income statement to FIFO, we subtract $37.2 from the cost of goods sold (reported using LIFO) and add the same amount to gross profit and pretax income. To estimate net income, we need to adjust for income taxes. Assuming a corporate tax rate of 35%, the use of LIFO provides Kaiser with tax savings of $13 million ($37.2 million × 0.35). Thus, 2014 net income using FIFO would be higher by $24.2 million ($37.2 million − $13 million).

RESEARCH INSIGHT

LIFO and Stock Prices   The value-relevance of inventory disclosures depends at least partly on whether investors rely more on the income statement or the balance sheet to assess future cash flows. Under LIFO, cost of goods sold reflects current costs, whereas FIFO ending inventory reflects current costs. This implies that LIFO enhances the usefulness of the income statement to the detriment of the balance sheet. This trade-off partly motivates the required LIFO reserve disclosure (the adjustment necessary to restate LIFO ending inventory and cost of good sold to FIFO).

Research suggests that LIFO-based income statements better reflect stock prices than do pro forma FIFO income statements that are constructed using the LIFO reserve. Research also shows a negative relation between stock prices and LIFO reserve—meaning that higher magnitudes of LIFO reserve are associated with lower stock prices. This is consistent with the LIFO reserve being viewed as an inflation indicator (for either current or future inventory costs) detrimental to company value.

ANALYZING FINANCIAL STATEMENTS

Analysis Objective

LO5 Define and interpret gross profit margin and inventory turnover ratios. Use inventory footnote information to make appropriate adjustments to ratios.

We are trying to determine whether Home Depot's sales provide sufficient revenues to cover its operation costs, primarily selling and administrative expenses, after allowing for the costs of manufacturing.

Analysis Tool   Gross Profit Margin (GPM) Ratio

$$\text{Gross profit margin} = \frac{\text{Sales revenue} - \text{Cost of goods sold}}{\text{Sales revenue}}$$

Applying the Gross Profit Margin Ratio to Home Depot

2012: $\dfrac{(\$74{,}754 - \$48{,}912)}{\$74{,}754} = 0.346$ or 34.6%

2013: $\dfrac{(\$78{,}812 - \$51{,}422)}{\$78{,}812} = 0.348$ or 34.8%

2014: $\dfrac{(\$83{,}176 - \$54{,}222)}{\$83{,}176} = 0.348$ or 34.8%

Guidance   The gross profit margin is commonly used instead of the dollar amount of gross profit as it allows for comparisons across companies and over time. A decline in GPM is usually cause for concern because it indicates that the company has less ability to pass on to customers increased costs in its products. Because companies try to charge the highest price the market will bear, a decline in GPM is often the result of market forces beyond the company's control. Some possible reasons for a GPM decline are:

- Product line is stale. Perhaps it is out of fashion and the company must resort to markdowns to reduce overstocked inventories. Or, perhaps the product lines have lost their technological edge, yielding reduced demand.

- A change in product mix resulting from a change in buyers' behavior (more generic brands, more necessities, fewer big-ticket items).

- New competitors enter the market. Perhaps substitute products or new technologies are now available from competitors, yielding increased pressure to reduce selling prices.

- General decline in economic activity. Perhaps an economic downturn reduces product demand. The weak housing market during the latter half of the decade likely affected the gross profits of home improvement companies.

- Inventory is overstocked. Perhaps the company overproduced goods and finds itself in an overstock position. This can require reduced selling prices to move inventory.

Takeaways   The Home Depot's sales revenue has increased from fiscal year 2012 to fiscal year 2014. The company was successful in maintaining its gross profit margin. However, to properly evaluate gross profit margin, it is useful to make comparisons with other companies in the same industry. **Exhibit 7.12** graphically compares The Home Depot's gross profit margin with that of its largest (but smaller) competitor, **Lowe's Companies, Inc.**

As the bar graph illustrates, The Home Depot and Lowe's have reported nearly identical, and very stable, gross profit margins in the last three years. In addition, in 2014 The Home Depot's sales revenue increased by 5.5%, while Lowe's revenues increased by 5.3%.

To gain further insights, **Exhibit 7.13** compares the gross profit margin of The Home Depot with that of several other retailers: **Target Corporation**, a national chain of retail variety stores; **Staples, Inc.**, a retail office supply store; and **Whole Foods Market Inc.**, a retail specialty grocery store chain. The graph illustrates that the highest gross profit margin belongs to Whole Foods, the specialty grocery store, while the lowest was that of Staples. Also, while the percentages fluctuate

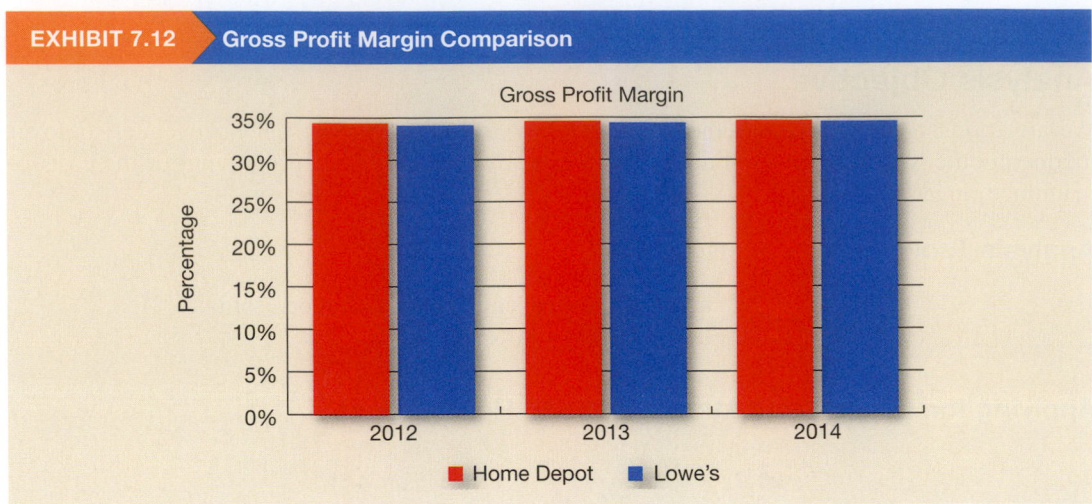

EXHIBIT 7.12 | **Gross Profit Margin Comparison**

slightly from year to year, the *relative* level of gross profit percentage remains the same over time, reflecting the fact that the industry or type of business is a major determinant of gross profit margin.

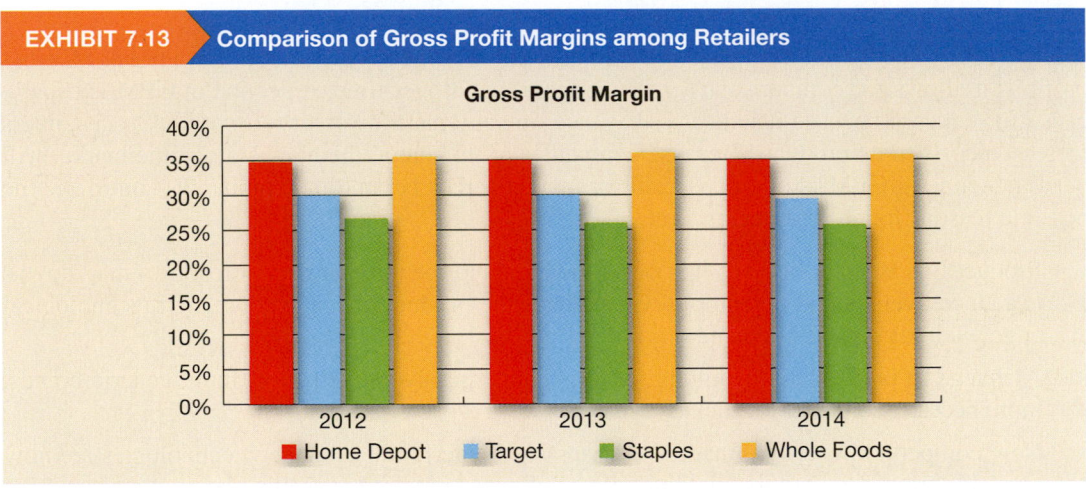

EXHIBIT 7.13 | **Comparison of Gross Profit Margins among Retailers**

Because of competitive pressures, companies rarely have the opportunity to affect gross margin with price increases. (Of course, an astute choice of product offerings is likely to reduce pricing discounts and improve the gross profit margin.) Most improvements in gross margin that we witness are the result of better management of supply chains, production processes, or distribution networks. Similarly, a decline in gross profit margin suggests problems or inefficiencies in these processes. Companies that succeed typically do so because of better performance on basic business processes. This is one of The Home Depot's primary objectives.

Comparison of gross profit margins across selected focus companies:

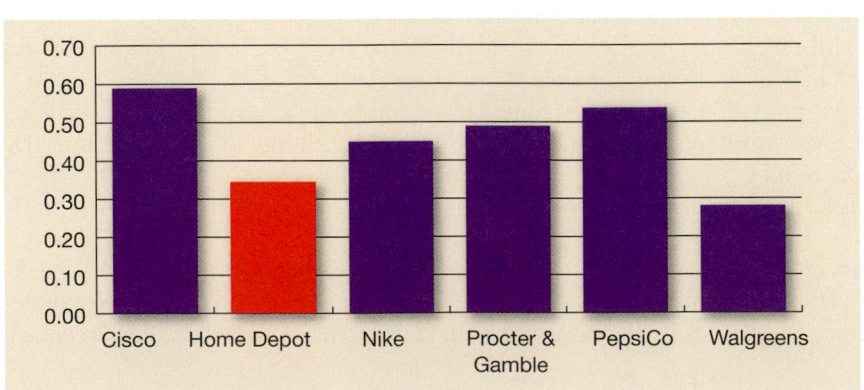

Analysis Objective

We wish to determine how quickly inventory passes through the production process and results in sales.

Analysis Tool   Inventory Turnover (INVT) Ratio

$$\text{Inventory turnover} = \frac{\text{Cost of goods sold}}{\text{Average inventory}}$$

Applying Inventory Turnover Ratio to Home Depot

2012: $48,912/[($10,710 + $10,325)/2] = 4.7 Times per year
2013: $51,422/[($11,057 + $10,710)/2] = 4.7 Times per year
2014: $54,222/[($11,079 + $11,057)/2] = 4.9 Times per year

Home Depot in Context

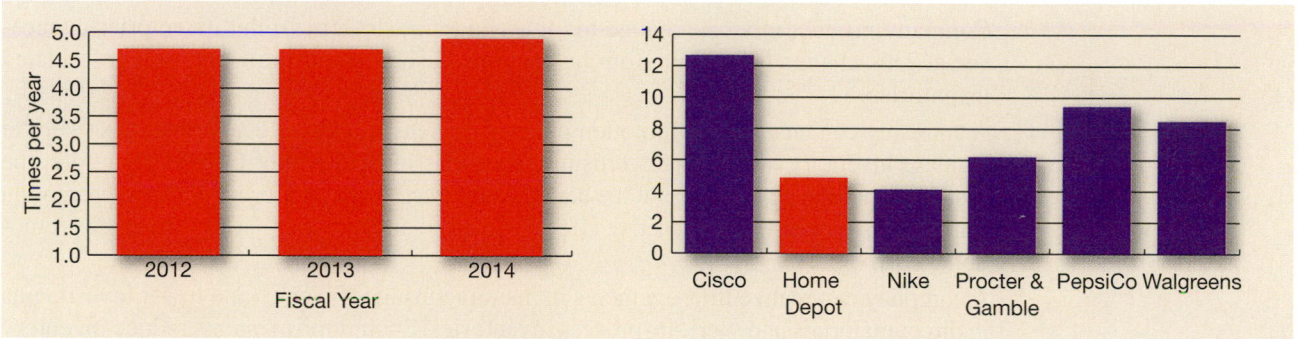

Cost of goods sold is in the numerator because inventory is reported at cost. The denominator is the average of beginning inventory and ending inventory to recognize growth (or decline) in the company's investment in inventory over the period. Inventory turnover indicates how many times inventory turns (is sold) during a period. More turns indicate that inventory is being sold more quickly.

Analysis Tool   Average inventory days outstanding (AIDO), also called *days inventory outstanding*:

$$\text{Average inventory days outstanding} = \frac{\text{Average inventory}}{\text{Average daily cost of goods sold}}$$

Applying Average Inventory Days Outstanding Ratio to Home Depot

2012:   [($10,710 + $10,325)/2]/[$48,912/365] = 78 Days
2013:   [($11,057 + $10,710)/2]/[$51,422/365] = 77 Days
2014:   [($11,079 + $11,057)/2]/[$54,222/365] = 75 Days

Home Depot in Context

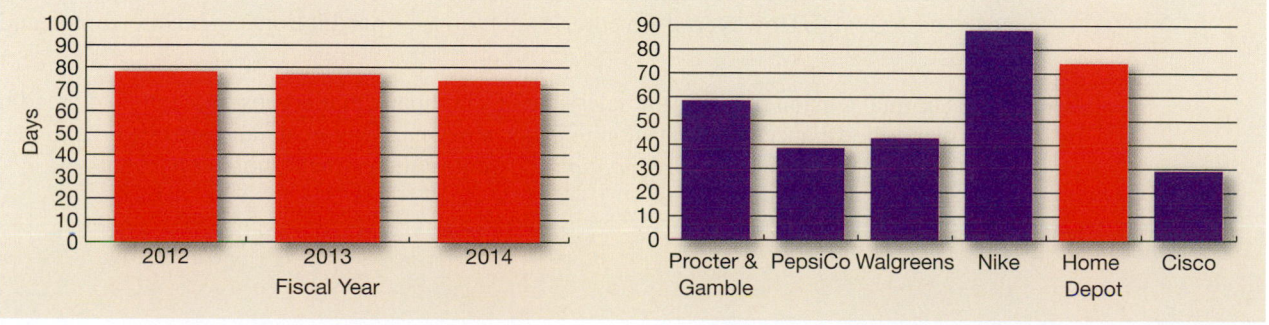

The average daily cost of goods sold equals cost of goods sold divided by the number of days in the period (for our example, 365 for a year).

Average inventory days outstanding indicates how long, on average, inventories are on the shelves or in production before being sold. For example, if a retailer's annual cost of goods sold is $1,200 and average inventories are $300, inventories are turning four times and are on the shelves 91.25 days [$300/($1,200/365)] on average. This performance might be an acceptable turnover for the retail fashion industry where it needs to sell out its inventories each retail selling season, but it would not be acceptable for the grocery industry.

Guidance   Analysis of inventory turnover is important for at least two reasons:

1. *Inventory quality.* Inventory turnover can be compared with those of prior periods and competitors. Higher turnover is viewed favorably, implying that products are salable, preferably without undue discounting of selling prices, or that production processes are functioning smoothly. Conversely, lower turnover implies that inventory is on the shelves for a longer period of time, perhaps from excessive purchases or production, missed fashion trends or technological advances, increased competition, and so forth. Our conclusions about higher or lower turnover must consider alternative explanations including:

    a. Company product mix can change to higher-margin, slower-turning inventories or vice-versa. This change can occur from business acquisitions and the resulting consolidated inventories.

    b. A company can change its promotion policies. Increased, effective advertising is likely to increase inventory turnover. Advertising expense is in SG&A, not COGS. Therefore, the cost is in operating expenses, but the benefit is in gross profit and turnover. If the promotion campaign is successful, the positive effects in margin and turnover should offset the promotion cost in SG&A.

    c. A company can realize improvements in manufacturing efficiency and lower investments in direct materials and work-in-process inventories. Such improvements reduce inventory and, consequently, increase inventory turnover. Although positive, such improvements do not yield any information about the desirability of a company's product line.

2. *Asset utilization.* Companies strive to optimize their inventory investment. Carrying too much inventory is expensive, and too little inventory risks stock-outs and lost sales (current and future). There are operational changes that companies can make to reduce inventory including:

    a. Improved manufacturing processes can eliminate bottlenecks and the consequent build-up of work-in-process inventories.

    b. Just-in-time (JIT) deliveries from suppliers that provide raw materials to the production line when needed can reduce the level of raw materials required.

    c. Demand-pull production, in which raw materials are released into the production process when final goods are demanded by customers instead of producing for estimated demand, can reduce inventory levels. **Dell Inc.** was founded on a business model that produced for actual, rather than estimated, demand; many of its computers are manufactured after the customer order is received.

Reducing inventories reduces inventory carrying costs, thus improving profitability and increasing cash flow (asset reduction is reflected as a cash inflow adjustment in the statement of cash flows). However, if inventories get too low, production can be interrupted and sales lost.

There is normal tension between the sales side of a company that argues for depth and breadth of inventory and the finance side that monitors inventory carrying costs and seeks to maximize cash flow. Companies, therefore, seek to *optimize* inventory investment, not *minimize* it.

Takeaways   **Exhibit 7.14** compares inventory turnover for The Home Depot with that of its chief rival, Lowe's. Both Home Depot's and Lowe's inventory turnover and AIDO improved over the period 2012–2014. Lowe's inventory turnover decreased, but increases in inventories probably helped it to maintain revenues and gross profit in the changing economic climate.

EXHIBIT 7.14	**Inventory Turnover Comparison**

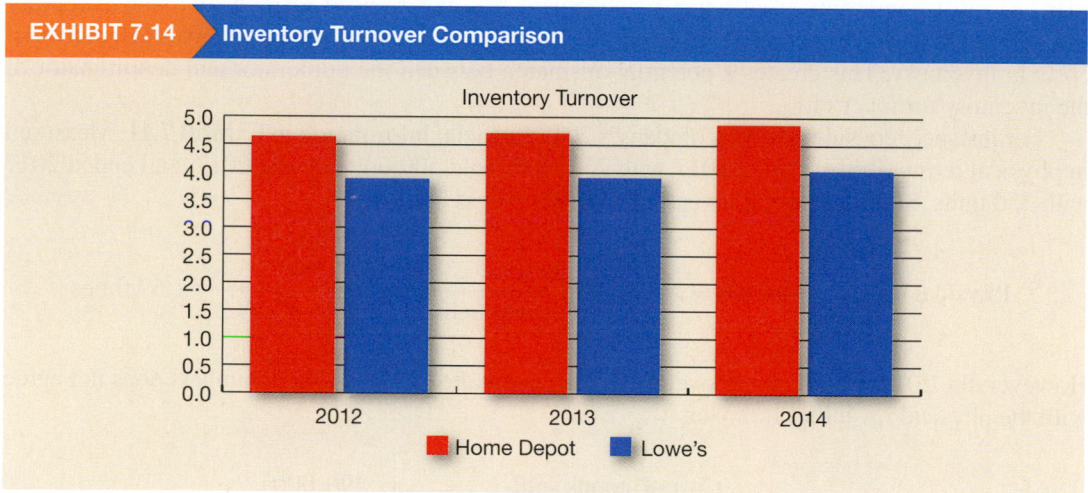

It is also instructive to compare the home improvement retail industry, represented by The Home Depot, with other retailers as illustrated in **Exhibit 7.15**.

EXHIBIT 7.15	**Inventory Turnover for Various Retail Companies**

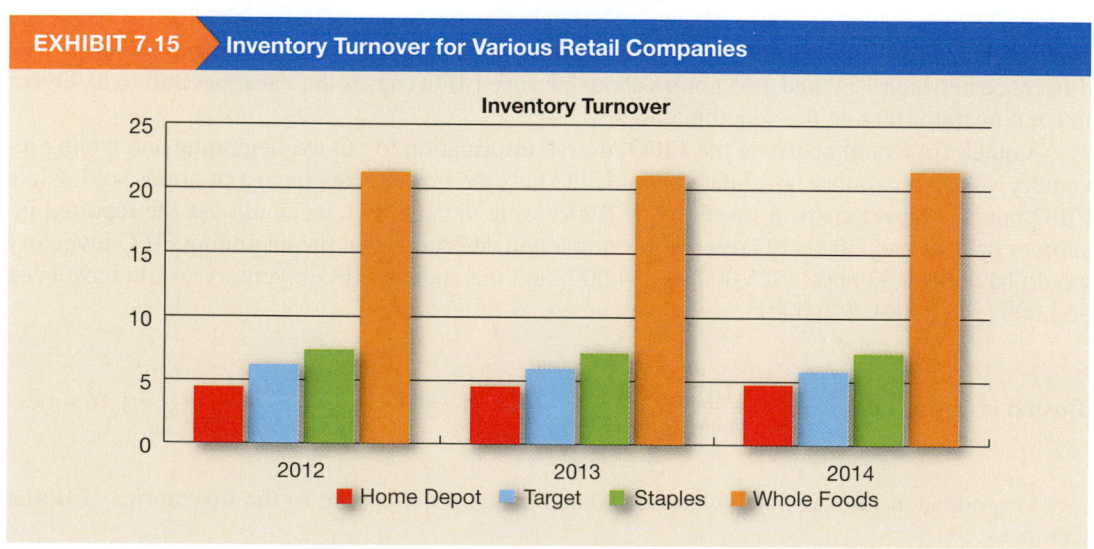

---

[6] "More Accounting Deficiencies Linked to Inventory," *Wall Street Journal* August 26, 2014.

[7] See Feng, Mei, Chan Li, Sarah E. McVay, and Hollis Skaife, "Does Ineffective Internal Control over Financial Reporting affect a Firm's Operations? Evidence from Firms' Inventory Management." The Accounting Review, March 2015.

In the retail grocery industry, high inventory turnover is a necessity given that a significant portion of a grocer's inventory is perishable. Whole Foods' high turnover is typical of what we might expect from retail grocers. The Home Depot's turnover is lower than any of the comparison companies. Target's turnover is lower than that of Staples, the consumer office products retailer, despite the fact that part of Target's sales is food related. The small portion of food product sales as a percentage of total sales explains why Target's turnover is not comparable to that of Whole Foods.

Adjusting Turnover Ratios For a company using the last-in, first-out (LIFO) inventory method, it is advisable to make an adjustment before calculating the inventory turnover ratio. LIFO is most commonly used when management has experienced a trend of rising inventory costs. As a result, LIFO puts higher (newer) costs into cost of goods sold and leaves lower (older) costs in inventory. This creates a potential mismatch between the numerator and denominator of the inventory turnover ratio.

For instance, consider Butler Company's 2017 financial information in **Exhibit 7.11**. Measured in physical terms, Butler started 2017 with 250 units, sold 500 units during 2017, and ended 2017 with 350 units. So, the physical inventory turnover would be

$$\text{Physical inventory turnover} = \frac{\text{Units sold}}{\text{Average units held}} = \frac{500}{(250+350)/2} = 1.67 \text{ times}$$

However, the 2017 inventory turnover calculated using the LIFO reported numbers does not agree with the physical inventory turnover.

$$\text{LIFO inventory turnover} = \frac{\text{Cost of goods sold}}{\text{Average inventory}} = \frac{\$90,000}{(\$25,000+\$43,000)/2} = 2.65 \text{ times}$$

Why is the LIFO inventory turnover higher? The distortion occurs because the LIFO cost of goods sold is 500 units valued at $180 each, while the beginning inventory is 250 units valued at $100 each and the ending inventory is 250 units valued at $100 each plus 100 units valued at $180 each. The difference between 1.67 and 2.65 comes about because LIFO causes the value per unit to be higher in the numerator than in the denominator.

A quick fix would be to use the LIFO reserve information to put the beginning and ending inventory values on a more up-to-date basis. LIFO puts the newer costs in cost of goods sold, while FIFO puts the newer costs in inventory. If Butler were using LIFO, we could use the reported inventory balances and the LIFO reserve information to determine that the beginning FIFO inventory would have been $39,000 ($25,000 + $14,000) and the ending FIFO inventory would have been $63,000 ($43,000 + $20,000).

$$\text{Adjusted inventory turnover} = \frac{\text{LIFO cost of good sold}}{\text{Average FIFO inventory}} = \frac{\$90,000}{(\$39,000+\$63,000)/2} = 1.76 \text{ times}$$

This adjusted ratio is much closer to what's actually happening to the inventories at Butler Company.

The magnitude of this adjustment can be significant. For instance, **Chevron Corporation** in its 2014 annual report states that its 2014 expense for "Purchased crude oil and products" was $119,671 million. Chevron's balance sheet totals for inventories were $6,380 million at the end of 2013 and $6,505 million at the end of 2014, for an average of $6,442.5 million. These numbers would give an inventory turnover ratio of $119,671 million ÷ $6,442.5 million, or 18.6 times, implying that inventory is held less than 20 days on average.

However, we know that the LIFO inventory balances are out of date. Chevron's LIFO reserve disclosure says that the replacement cost of inventories was higher than the reported amounts by $9,150 million at the end of 2013 and $8,135 million at the end of 2014, making the replacement cost of inventories equal to $15,530 million at the end of 2013 and $14,640 million at the end of 2014. The adjusted inventory turnover ratio would be $119,671/[($15,530 + $14,640)/2] = 7.9, implying that inventory is held about 46 days.

Following a similar line of analysis, it would be possible to construct a FIFO inventory turnover for Chevron, which could be useful in making comparisons to another company that uses IFRS in its financial reports.

CHAPTER-END REVIEW

Publix Super Markets Inc. reports inventory and cost of goods sold using the last-in, first-out (LIFO) costing method for a "significant portion" of U.S. inventory. The table below presents financial information from its 2012, 2013, and 2014 10-K reports.

($ millions)	2014	2013	2012
Revenue	$30,560	$28,917	$27,485
Cost of goods sold	22,233	20,937	19,911
Gross profit	$ 8,327	$ 7,980	$ 7,574
Balance Sheet:			
Inventory	$ 1,598	$ 1,507	$ 1,409
Notes to financial statements			
LIFO reserve	$ 421	$ 390	$ 375

REQUIRED

1. Compute the gross profit margin for each year, 2012 through 2014, and the inventory turnover ratio for 2013 and 2014.

2. What amount for cost of goods sold and gross profit would Publix report in 2013 and 2014 if FIFO were used to assign costs to inventory and cost of goods sold? (Assume that FIFO cost is equal to the current value of Publix's inventory.)

3. Recalculate Publix's inventory turnover ratio for 2013 and 2014 assuming that FIFO had been used to value inventory.

The solution to this review problem can be found on page 369.

APPENDIX 7A: LIFO Liquidation

When companies use LIFO inventory costing, the most recent costs of purchasing inventory are transferred to cost of goods sold, while older costs remain in ending inventory. Each time inventory is purchased at a different price, a new *layer* (also called a **LIFO layer**) is added to the inventory balance. As long as a year's purchases equal or exceed the quantity sold, older cost layers remain in inventory—sometimes for several years. On the other hand, when the quantity sold exceeds the quantity purchased, inventory costs from these older cost layers are transferred to cost of goods sold. This situation is called **LIFO liquidation**. Because these older costs are usually much lower than current replacement costs, LIFO liquidation normally yields a boost to current gross profit as these older costs are matched against current revenues.

To illustrate the effects of LIFO liquidation, we return to the example of Butler Company in **Exhibit 7.6** and add an additional year. At the end of 2017, Butler has 350 units in inventory, 250 at $100 each and 100 at $180 each. Suppose that during 2018, the company purchases 500 units at $190 and sells 650 units. At the end of 2018, Butler will have only 200 units remaining in inventory and, under LIFO, those units will be assigned a cost of $100 each. The determination of cost of goods sold and ending inventory for 2018 can be seen in **Exhibit 7A.1**.

LO6 Analyze LIFO liquidations and the impact they have on the financial statements.

EXHIBIT 7A.1	Calculation of 2018 LIFO Inventory and Cost of Goods Sold	
Beginning Inventory	250 units at $100 each plus 100 units at $180 each	$ 43,000
Purchases.	500 units at $190 each	95,000
Cost of goods available for sale.		138,000
Ending inventory.	200 units at $100 each	20,000
Cost of goods sold.	500 units at $190 each plus 100 units at $180 each plus 50 units at $100 each	$118,000

Exhibit 7A.2 portrays graphically that the inventory reduction in 2018 eliminated the LIFO layer added in 2017 and reduced the original LIFO layer from the start of 2016.

EXHIBIT 7A.2	Butler Company LIFO Inventory Flows

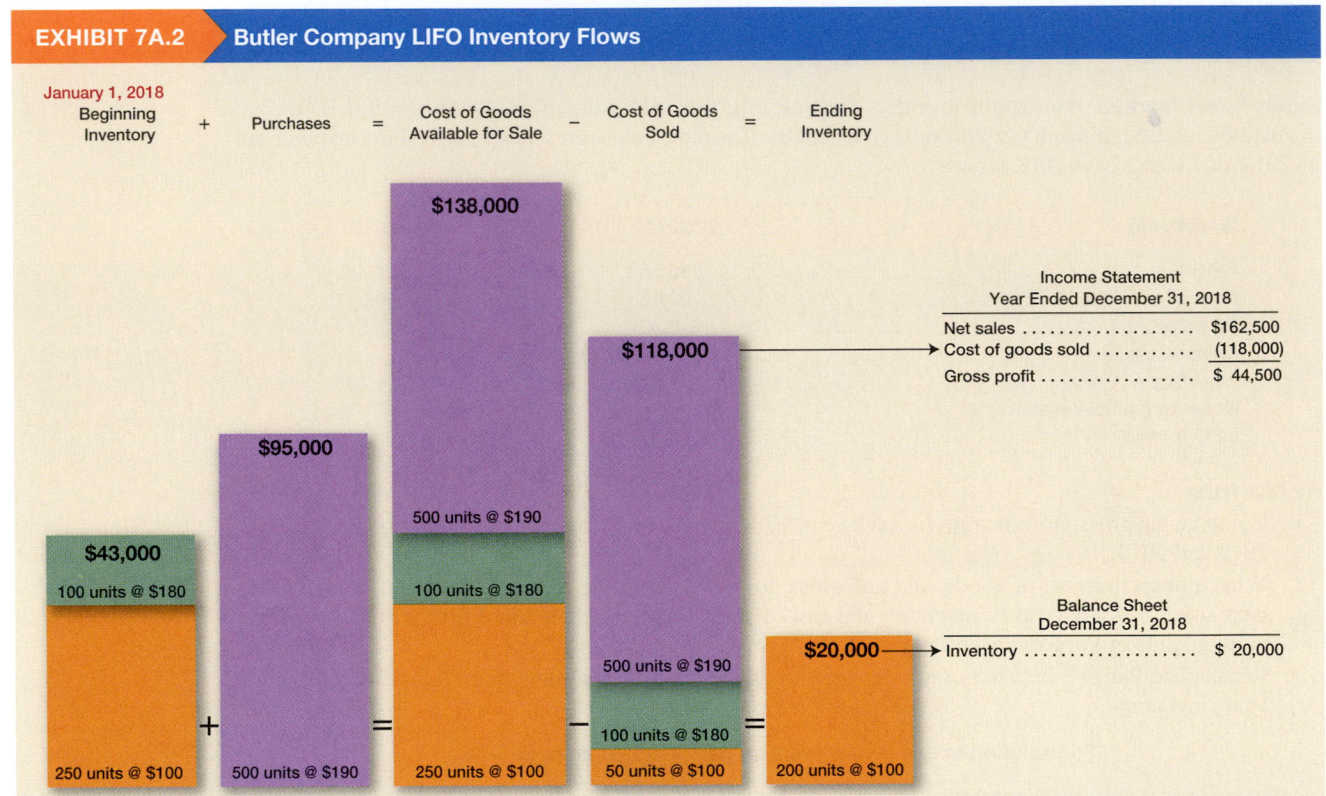

What would have happened if Butler had purchased 650 units at $190 in 2018? The ending inventory would have been identical to the beginning inventory. And, the cost of goods sold would have been $123,500 (650 units at $190 each), higher than the $118,000 cost of goods sold in **Exhibit 7A.1**. This difference can be attributed to the differences between the current unit cost of inventory ($190) and the old unit costs ($180 and $100) that had been in inventory but are now in cost of goods sold.

Thus, Butler's cost of goods sold has been *reduced* by $5,500 due to the LIFO liquidation, and its gross profit and income before tax have been *increased* by the same amount. If Butler's tax rate were 35%, the net income would be increased by $3,575. This **LIFO liquidation gain** must be disclosed in the company's footnotes.

The effect of LIFO liquidation is evident in the following footnote information from Notes A and G to **Alcoa Inc.**'s 2014 annual report.

Notes A and G: Inventories
Inventory Valuation. Inventories are carried at the lower of cost or market, with cost for a substantial portion of U.S. and Canadian inventories determined under the last-in, first-out (LIFO) method. The cost of other inventories is principally determined under the average-cost method.

Note G: (dollars in millions) At December 31, 2014 and 2013, the total amount of inventories valued on a LIFO basis was $1,514 and $1,169, respectively. If valued on an average-cost basis, total inventories would have been $767 and $691 higher at December 31, 2014 and 2013, respectively. During 2013 and 2012, reductions in LIFO inventory quantities caused partial liquidations of the lower cost LIFO inventory base. These liquidations resulted in the recognition of income of $26 ($17 after-tax) in 2013 and $1 ($1 after-tax) in 2012.

Alcoa reports that reductions in inventory quantities led to the sale (at current selling prices) of products that carried costs from prior years that were less than current costs. As a result of these inventory reductions, pretax income increased by $26 million in 2013 and by $1 million in 2012.

Analysis Implications

LIFO liquidation boosts gross profit when older, lower costs are matched against revenues based on current sales prices. This increase in gross profit is transitory. Once an old LIFO layer is liquidated, it can only be replaced at current prices. The transitory boost in gross profit temporarily distorts the gross profit margin (GPM) ratio.

It is important that we ask why the LIFO liquidation happened. Involuntary LIFO liquidations result from circumstances beyond the company's control, such as disruptions in supply due to a natural disaster. Voluntary LIFO liquidations are the result of a management decision to reduce inventory levels. While this result is sometimes the result of efforts to lower costs and improve efficiency, it can also be the consequence of earnings management.

If a voluntary LIFO liquidation is the result of earnings management, we should remember that the extra gross profit that is reported is taxable. These tax consequences provide an incentive for companies to *avoid* LIFO liquidations by maintaining ending inventories at levels equal to or greater than beginning inventory quantities. Maintaining these inventory levels can be inefficient, leading to higher inventory holding costs. However, in the short run, the tax savings can be greater than the costs.

On one hand, management could liquidate LIFO inventories to report higher earnings. On the other hand, management may hold too much inventory to avoid paying extra taxes. A careful evaluation of future cash flows usually identifies the preferred course of action.

APPENDIX 7A REVIEW

Dickhaut Corporation imports and sells a product that is produced in the Dominican Republic. In the summer of 2016, a hurricane disrupted production and affected Dickhaut's supply of this product. Dickhaut uses LIFO to determine the cost of its inventory and cost of goods sold. On January 1, 2016, Dickhaut's inventory of this product consisted of the following:

Year Purchased	Quantity (units)	Cost Per Unit	Total Cost
2014	2,000	$20	$ 40,000
2015	3,000	30	90,000
Total	5,000		$130,000

Through mid-December, purchases were limited to 7,000 units, because the cost had increased to $70 per unit. Dickhaut sold 11,500 units during 2016 at a price of $65 per unit, which significantly depleted its inventory. However, the cost was expected to drop to $55 per unit by early January 2017.

Required

a. Assume that Dickhaut makes no further purchases during 2016. Compute its gross profit for 2016.
b. Assume that Dickhaut purchases 4,500 units for $70 per unit before the end of December 2016, so that it maintains its balance of inventory at 5,000 units. Compute its gross profit for 2016.
c. How should Dickhaut disclose the LIFO liquidation if it chooses not to make a year-end purchase?
d. If Dickhaut's corporate tax rate is 35%, should it make a year-end purchase? If so, how many units should the company purchase before December 31, 2016? Assume that the management of Dickhaut believes it is efficient (in the long run) to carry 5,000 units in inventory.

The solution to this review problem can be found on page 370.

SUMMARY

Interpret disclosures of information concerning operating expenses, including manufacturing and retail inventory costs. (p. 328)   **LO1**

● Inventory is reported in the balance sheet at its cost, including any cost to acquire, transport and prepare goods for sale.

- Manufacturing inventory consists of raw materials, work in process and finished goods. The cost of manufacturing inventory includes the cost of materials and labor used to produce goods, as well as overhead cost.

LO2 **Account for inventory and cost of goods sold using different costing methods. (p. 332)**

- FIFO places the cost of the most recent purchases in ending inventory and older costs in the cost of goods sold.
- LIFO places the cost of the most recent purchases in cost of goods sold and older costs in inventory.
- The average cost method computes an average unit cost, which is used to value inventories *and* cost of goods sold.

LO3 **Apply the lower of cost or market rule to value inventory. (p. 337)**

- If the market value of inventory falls below its cost, the inventory is written down to market value, thereby reducing total assets.
- The loss is added to cost of goods sold and reported in the income statement (unless it is large enough to warrant separate disclosure).

LO4 **Evaluate how inventory costing affects management decisions and outsiders' interpretations of financial statements. (p. 341)**

- When inventory costs are rising, LIFO costing reports higher cost of goods sold and lower income than either FIFO or average costing.
- If LIFO is used for tax reporting, it must be used for financial reporting.
- Companies that use LIFO have an incentive to hold inventories to avoid LIFO *liquidation* and the resulting higher income taxes.
- LIFO distorts the inventory turnover ratio because inventories are often severely undervalued (relative to current cost of goods sold). Management can boost earnings by liquidating these undervalued inventories.
- International Financial Reporting Standards (IFRS) allows FIFO and average costing methods. LIFO is not permitted.

LO5 **Define and interpret gross profit margin and inventory turnover ratios. Use inventory footnote information to make appropriate adjustments to ratios. (p. 345)**

- Gross profit margin (GPM)—a measure of profitability that focuses on the amount of revenue in excess of cost of goods sold as a percentage of revenue
- Gross profit margin is defined as Gross profit/Sales revenue.
- Inventory turnover (INVT)—a measure of the frequency at which the average balance in inventory is sold each year
- Inventory turnover is defined as Cost of goods sold/Average inventory.
- These ratios provide insight into how efficiently the company is managing inventory.
- Footnote disclosures enable a financial statement reader to determine the up-to-date costs of LIFO inventories, to estimate what cost of goods sold would have been under FIFO, and to compute an inventory turnover ratio that is not subject to the distortions noted above in LO4.

LO6 **Appendix 7A: Analyze LIFO liquidations and the impact they have on the financial statements. (p. 351)**

- LIFO liquidation is the result of selling and not replenishing inventory stocks purchased in previous accounting periods.
- When inventory costs are increasing, LIFO liquidation results in higher net income as the unrealized holding gains from LIFO are realized.

GUIDANCE ANSWERS . . . YOU MAKE THE CALL

You are the Plant Manager   Companies need inventories to avoid lost sales opportunities; however, there are several ways to minimize inventory needs. (1) We can reduce product costs by improving product design to eliminate costly features not valued by customers. (2) We can use more cost-efficient suppliers, possibly including production in lower wage-rate parts of the world. (3) We can reduce raw material inventories with just-in-time delivery from suppliers. (4) We can eliminate bottlenecks in the production process that increase work-in-process inventories. (5) We can manufacture for orders rather than for estimates of demand to reduce finished goods inventories. (6) We can improve warehousing and distribution to reduce duplicate inventories. (7) We can monitor product sales and adjust product mix as demand changes to reduce finished goods inventories.

KEY RATIOS

Gross profit (GP)

$$GP = \text{Sales revenue} - \text{Cost of goods sold}$$

Gross profit margin (GPM)

$$\text{Gross profit margin} = \frac{\text{Sales revenue} - \text{Cost of goods sold}}{\text{Sales revenue}}$$

Inventory turnover (INVT)

$$INVT = \frac{\text{Cost of goods sold}}{\text{Average inventory}}$$

Average inventory days outstanding (AIDO)

$$AIDO = \frac{\text{Average inventory}}{\text{Average daily cost of goods sold}}$$

KEY TERMS

Average cost (AC) (p. 336)
Cash discounts (p. 331)
Cost flow assumption (p. 333)
Direct association (p. 328)
Finished goods
  inventory (p. 331)
First-in, first-out (FIFO) (p. 333)
FOB destination (p. 331)

FOB shipping point (p. 331)
Gross profit (p. 329)
Immediate recognition (p. 329)
Last-in, first-out (LIFO) (p. 334)
LIFO layer (p. 351)
LIFO layers (p. 335)
LIFO liquidation (p. 351)
LIFO liquidation gain (p. 352)

LIFO reserve (p. 341)
Lower of cost or market
  (LCM) (p. 337)
Raw materials inventory (p. 331)
Systematic allocation (p. 329)
Unrealized holding gain (p. 343)
Work-in-process
  inventory (p. 331)

Assignments with the 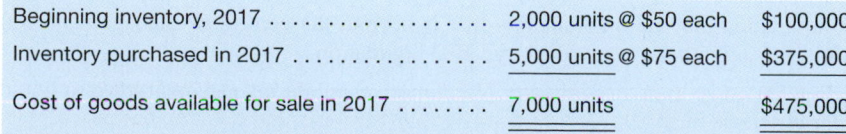 **logo in the margin are available in BusinessCourse.**
See the Preface of the book for details.

MULTIPLE CHOICE

1. Which of the following is not normally reported as part of total manufacturing inventory cost?
   a. work-in-process
   b. finished goods
   c. property, plant, and equipment
   d. raw materials

2. When the current year's ending inventory amount is overstated, then the
   a. current year's cost of goods sold is overstated.
   b. current year's total assets are understated.
   c. current year's net income is overstated.
   d. next year's income is overstated.

3. In a period of rising prices, the inventory cost allocation method that tends to result in the lowest reported net income is
   a. LIFO.
   b. FIFO.
   c. average cost.
   d. specific identification.

4. Assume that Beyer Corporation has the following initial balance and subsequent purchase of inventory:

Beginning inventory, 2017	2,000 units @ $50 each	$100,000
Inventory purchased in 2017	5,000 units @ $75 each	$375,000
Cost of goods available for sale in 2017	7,000 units	$475,000

During 2017, Beyer Corporation sold 6,000 units. Which of the following is not true?
a. FIFO cost of goods sold would be $400,000.
b. FIFO ending inventory would be $75,000.
c. LIFO cost of goods sold would be $425,000.
d. LIFO ending inventory would be $75,000.

5. Sletten Industries uses the last-in, first-out (LIFO) method of accounting for the inventories of its single product. For fiscal year 2017, the company reported sales revenue of $200 million and cost of goods sold of $135 million. The following table was reported in the financial statement footnotes.

($ millions)	January 1, 2017	December 31, 2017
Inventory value at LIFO	$25	$28
LIFO Reserve	14	22
Inventory value at FIFO	$39	$50

If Sletten Industries had used FIFO to account for its inventory, its 2017 gross profit would be
a. $87 million.
b. $73 million.
c. $57 million.
d. $65 million.

Superscript ^A denotes assignments based on Appendix 7A.

QUESTIONS

Q7-1. Under what circumstances is it justified to include transportation costs in the value of the inventory purchased?

Q7-2. Why do relatively stable inventory costs reduce the importance of management's choice of an inventory costing method?

Q7-3. What is one explanation for increased gross profit during periods of rising inventory costs when FIFO is used?

Q7-4. If inventory costs are rising, which inventory costing method—first-in, first-out; last-in, first-out; or average cost—yields the (a) lowest ending inventory? (b) lowest net income? (c) largest ending inventory? (d) largest net income? (e) greatest cash flow assuming that method is used for tax purposes?

Q7-5. Even though it does not reflect their physical flow of goods, why might companies adopt last-in, first-out inventory costing in periods when costs are consistently rising?

Kaiser Aluminum
Corporation
NASDAQ :: KALU

Q7-6. In a recent annual report, **Kaiser Aluminum Corporation** made the following statement in reference to its inventories: "The Company recorded pretax charges of approximately $19.4 million because of a reduction in the carrying values of its inventories caused principally by prevailing lower prices for alumina, primary aluminum, and fabricated products." What basic accounting principle caused Kaiser Aluminum to record this $19.4 million pretax charge? Briefly describe the rationale for this principle.

Q7-7. Under what conditions would each of the inventory costing methods discussed in the chapter produce the same results?

Q7-8. What is inventory "shrink?" How does a company determine the amount of inventory shrink that may have occurred?

Q7-9. What is a LIFO reserve? How is the LIFO reserve related to unrealized holding gains?

Q7-10. Analysts claim that it is more difficult to forecast net income for a company that uses LIFO. Why might this be true?

Q7-11.^A LIFO liquidation may be involuntary—that is beyond the control of management. Suggest two situations that might lead to involuntary LIFO liquidation.

Q7-12.^A LIFO liquidation is often discretionary. What motives might management have to liquidate LIFO inventory?

MINI EXERCISES

M7-13. Recording an Inventory Purchase   **LO1**

Shields Company has purchased inventories incurring the following costs: (a) the invoice amount of $500, (b) shipping charges of $30, (c) interest of $10 on the $500 borrowed to finance the purchase, and (d) $5 for the cost of moving the inventory to the company's warehouse.

REQUIRED

Determine the cost to be assigned to the inventory and record the purchase using "T" accounts.

M7-14. Recording Inventory Costs   **LO1**

Schrand Inc., a merchandiser, is requesting help in determining what costs ought to be considered as costs when incurred or treated as inventory costs, which are expensed as COGS. The costs include: sales persons wages, utilities such as heat and light in the store, the floor supervisor's salary, the cost of merchandise to be sold, costs of packaging and shipping to buyers.

REQUIRED

Determine the items above that should be included in inventory.

M7-15. Determining Cost of Goods Sold for a Manufacturing Company   **LO1**

Ybarra Products began operations in 2017. During its first year, the company purchased raw materials costing $84,000 and used $63,000 of those materials in the production of its products. The company's manufacturing operations also incurred labor costs of $58,000 and overhead costs of $28,000. At year end 2017, Ybarra had $19,000 of partially completed product in work-in-process inventory and $35,000 in finished goods inventory. What was Ybarra Company's cost of goods sold in 2017?

M7-16. Calculating Gross Profit Margin   **LO5**

Johnson & Johnson reported the following revenue and cost of goods sold information in its 10-K report for 2014, 2013, and 2012.

Johnson & Johnson
NYSE :: JNJ

($ millions)	2014	2013	2012
Sales to customers.	$74,331	$71,312	$67,224
Cost of products sold.	22,746	22,342	21,658

Compute Johnson & Johnson's gross profit margin for each year.

M7-17. Calculating Effect of Inventory Errors   **LO1**

For each of the following scenarios, determine the effect of the error on income in the current period and in the subsequent period. To answer these questions, rely on the inventory equation:

$$\textbf{Beginning inventory} + \textbf{Purchases} - \textbf{Cost of goods sold} = \textbf{Ending inventory}$$

a.   Porter Company received a shipment of merchandise costing $32,000 near the end of the fiscal year. The shipment was mistakenly recorded at a cost of $23,000.

b.   Chiu, Inc., purchased merchandise costing $16,000. When the shipment was received, it was determined that the merchandise was damaged in shipment. The goods were returned to the supplier, but the accounting department was not notified and the invoice was paid.

c.   After taking a physical count of its inventory, Murray Corporation determined that it had "shrink" of $12,500, and the books were adjusted accordingly. However, inventory costing $5,000 was never counted.

M7-18. Calculating LIFO, FIFO, Income and Cash Flows   **LO2, 4**

An acquaintance has proposed the following business plan to you. A local company requires a consistent quantity of a commodity and is looking for a reliable supplier. You could become that reliable supplier.

The cost of the commodity is expected to rise steadily over the foreseeable future, but the company is willing to pay more than the price that is current at the time. All you would need to do is make an investment, purchase the inventory and then deliver inventory to the company over the following year. One complication is that the commodity is available for purchase only seasonally, so at the end of every year you would need to purchase the supply for the following year. The customer pays promptly on delivery.

An initial cash investment of $62,000 would be used to purchase $50,000 of inventory in December 2016. The remaining cash would be held for liquidity needs. In the following year, you would deliver this inventory to the customer. Inventory costs are expected to increase by $10,000 per year, and the customer agrees to pay $15,000 more than the current cost of inventory. So, during 2017, you would deliver inventory that originally cost $50,000, receive payment of $75,000 and pay $60,000 to purchase inventory for the current year. This pattern would continue in future years, but with annually increasing costs of inventory and corresponding increases in the price charged the customer.

If you accept this proposal, your objective would be to receive $9,000 in dividends (about a 15% return on the $62,000 investment) at the end of each year. Assume your business would have an income tax rate of 40%.

a. Construct a projected balance sheet as of the end of December 2016.

b. Construct financial forecasts of income statements, cash flows (direct method) and balance sheets for the next three years (through 2019). Assume that your business would operate in a tax jurisdiction that requires the use of FIFO for inventory. Would this opportunity meet your financial objective?

c. Suppose that your business would operate in a tax jurisdiction that allowed the use of LIFO for inventory. Would this opportunity meet your financial objective? Why?

LO2 **M7-19. Computing Cost of Goods Sold and Ending Inventory Under FIFO, LIFO, and Average Cost**

Assume that Gode Company reports the following initial balance and subsequent purchase of inventory:

Beginning inventory, 2017	1,000 units @ $100 each	$100,000
Inventory purchased in 2017	2,000 units @ $150 each	300,000
Cost of goods available for sale in 2017	3,000 units	$400,000

Assume that 1,700 units are sold during 2017. Compute the cost of goods sold for 2017 and the balance reported as ending inventory on its 2017 balance sheet under the following inventory costing methods:

a. FIFO

b. LIFO

c. Average Cost

LO2 **M7-20. Inferring Purchases Using Cost of Goods Sold and Inventory Balances**

Geiger Corporation, a retail company, reported inventories of $1,320,000 in 2016 and $1,460,000 in 2017. The 2017 income statement reported cost of goods sold of $6,980,000.

a. Compute the amount of inventory purchased during 2017.

b. Prepare journal entries to record (1) purchases, and (2) cost of goods sold.

c. Post the journal entries in part b to their respective T-accounts.

d. Record each of the transactions in part b in the financial statement effects template to show the effect of these entries on the balance sheet and income statement.

LO2 **M7-21. Computing Cost of Goods Sold and Ending Inventory**

Bartov Corporation reports the following beginning inventory and purchases for 2017:

Beginning inventory, 2017	400 units @ $10 each	$ 4,000
Inventory purchased in 2017	700 units @ $12 each	8,400
Cost of goods available for sale in 2017	1,100 units	$12,400

Bartov sells 600 of these units in 2017. Compute its cost of goods sold for 2017 and the ending inventory reported on its 2017 balance sheet under each of the following inventory costing methods:

a. FIFO

b. LIFO

c. Average cost

M7-22.   Computing and Evaluating Inventory Turnover

LO5

Wal-Mart Stores, Inc.
NYSE :: WMT

Target Corporation
NYSE :: TGT

Wal-Mart Stores, Inc., and **Target Corporation** reported the following in their financial reports:

($ billions) Fiscal Year	Wal-Mart			Target		
	Sales	COGS	Inventory	Sales	COGS	Inventory
2014	$476	$358	$44.9	$72.6	$51.3	$8.79
2013	469	352	43.8	71.3	50.0	8.28
2012	447	335	40.7	72.0	50.6	7.90

a.   Compute the 2014 and 2013 inventory turnovers for each of these two retailers.

b.   Discuss any changes that are evident in inventory turnover across years and companies from part *a*.

c.   Describe ways in which a retailer can improve its inventory turnover. Are there ways to increase inventory turnover that are not beneficial to the company's long-term interests?

M7-23.   Inferring Purchases Using Cost of Goods Sold and Inventory Balances

LO2

MBC

Penno Company reported ending inventories of $23,560,000 in 2017 and $25,790,000 in 2016. Cost of goods sold totaled $142,790,000 in 2017.

a.   Prepare the journal entry to record cost of goods sold.

b.   Set up a T-account for inventory and post the cost of goods sold entry from part *a* to this account.

c.   Using the T-account from *b*, determine the amount of inventory that was purchased in 2017. Prepare a journal entry to record those purchases.

d.   Using the financial statement effects template, show the effects of the entries in parts *a* and *c* on the balance sheet and income statement.

M7-24.   Determining Lower of Cost or Market

LO3

MBC

The following data refer to Froning Company's ending inventory.

Item Code	Quantity	Unit Cost	Unit Market
LXC.	60	$45	$48
KWT	210	38	34
MOR.	300	22	20
NES	100	27	32

Determine the ending inventory amount by applying the lower of cost or market rule to (*a*) each item of inventory and (*b*) the total inventory.

EXERCISES

E7-25.   Analyzing Inventory and Margin in a Seasonal Business

LO5

MBC

West Marine, Inc.
NASDAQ :: WMAR

West Marine, Inc., opened its first boating supply store in 1975. Since that time, the company has grown to be one of the largest boating supply companies in the world, with fiscal year 2014 revenues in excess of $675 million. The accompanying table provides financial information for two recent years. West Marine's fiscal year is closely aligned with the calendar year. All amounts are in millions.

Time Period	Net Revenues	Cost of Goods Sold	Ending Inventory
Fiscal year 2012	—	—	$189
First quarter 2013	$114	$ 89	238
Second quarter 2013	237	149	237
Third quarter 2013	193	136	217
Fourth quarter 2013	119	98	203
Fiscal year 2013	**663**	**472**	**203**
First quarter 2014	113	88	245
Second quarter 2014	236	154	244
Third quarter 2014	197	138	215
Fourth quarter 2014	130	103	214
Fiscal year 2014	**676**	**483**	**214**

  a. Using the fiscal year (annual) information for 2013 and 2014, calculate the gross profit margin and the inventory turnover ratio.

  b. West Marine is in a seasonal business, in which the sales total for the second and third quarters is substantially higher than the sales total for the first and fourth quarters. Calculate the company's gross profit margin by quarter. What do you learn from the seasonal pattern in the gross profit margin?

  c. What is the seasonal pattern in inventory balances? What effect does West Marine's choice of fiscal year-end have on the inventory turnover ratio calculated in *a*?

  d. Recalculate West Marine's inventory turnover ratios for 2013 and 2014 using a weighted average of the company's inventory investment over the year.

LO2, 4 **E7-26.** **Applying and Analyzing Inventory Costing Methods**

At the beginning of the current period, Chen carried 1,000 units of its product with a unit cost of $20. A summary of purchases during the current period follows:

	Units	Unit Cost	Cost
Beginning Inventory	1,000	$20	$20,000
Purchases: #1	1,800	22	39,600
#2	800	26	20,800
#3	1,200	29	34,800

During the current period, Chen sold 2,800 units.

  a. Assume that Chen uses the first-in, first-out method. Compute its cost of goods sold for the current period and the ending inventory balance.

  b. Assume that Chen uses the last-in, first-out method. Compute its cost of goods sold for the current period and the ending inventory balance.

  c. Assume that Chen uses the average cost method. Compute its cost of goods sold for the current period and the ending inventory balance.

  d. Which of these three inventory costing methods would you choose to:

   1. Reflect what is probably the physical flow of goods? Explain.

   2. Minimize income taxes for the period? Explain.

   3. Report the largest amount of income for the period? Explain.

LO2 **E7-27.** **Computing Cost of Sales and Ending Inventory**

Stocken Company has the following financial records for the current period:

	Units	Unit Cost
Beginning inventory	100	$46
Purchases: #1	650	42
#2	550	38
#3	200	36

Ending inventory at the end of this period is 350 units. Compute the ending inventory and the cost of goods sold for the current period using (*a*) first-in, first-out, (*b*) average cost, and (*c*) last-in, first-out.

LO3 **E7-28.** **Determining Lower of Cost or Market**

Crane Company had the following inventory at December 31, 2017.

		Unit Price	
	Quantity	Cost	Market
Desks			
Model 9001	70	$190	$210
Model 9002	45	280	268
Model 9003	20	350	360
Cabinets			
Model 7001	120	60	64
Model 7002	80	95	88
Model 7003	50	130	126

a. Determine the ending inventory amount by applying the lower of cost or market rule to
1. Each item of inventory.
2. Each major category of inventory.
3. Total inventory.

b. Which of the LCM procedures from requirement *a* results in the lowest net income for 2017? Explain.

E7-29. Analyzing Inventory Footnote Disclosure

General Motors Corporation reported the following information in its 10-K report:

LO2, 4

General Motors
NYSE :: GM

Inventories at December 31 ($ millions)	2008	2007
Productive material, work in process, and supplies.	$ 4,849	$ 6,267
Finished product, service parts, etc.	9,426	10,095
Total inventories at FIFO.	14,275	16,362
Less LIFO allowance	(1,233)	(1,423)
Total automotive and other inventories, less allowances.	$13,042	$14,939

The company reports its inventory using the LIFO costing method during 2007 and 2008.

a. At what dollar amount are inventories reported on its 2008 balance sheet?

b. At what dollar amount would inventories have been reported in 2008 if FIFO inventory costing had been used?

c. What cumulative effect has the use of LIFO had, as of year-end 2008, on GM's pretax income, compared to the pretax income that would have been reported using the FIFO costing method?

d. Assuming a 35% income tax rate, what is the cumulative effect on GM's tax liability as of year-end 2008?

e. In July 2009, GM changed its inventory accounting to FIFO costs. Why do you suppose GM made that choice?

E7-30. Analyzing of Inventory and Footnote Disclosure

The inventory footnote from **Deere & Company**'s 2013 10-K follows ($ millions).

LO2, 4

Deere & Company
NYSE :: DE

15. INVENTORIES

Most inventories owned by Deere & Company and its US equipment subsidiaries are valued at cost, on the "last-in, first-out" (LIFO) basis. Remaining inventories are generally valued at the lower of cost, on the "first-in, first-out" (FIFO) basis, or market. The value of gross inventories on the LIFO basis represented 63 percent and 61 percent of worldwide gross inventories at FIFO value on October 31, 2013 and 2012, respectively. If all inventories had been valued on a FIFO basis, estimated inventories by major classification at October 31 in millions of dollars would have been as follows:

	2013	2012
Raw materials and supplies.	$1,954	$1,874
Work-in-process.	753	652
Finished goods and parts.	3,757	4,065
Total FIFO value	6,464	6,591
Less adjustment to LIFO value.	(1,529)	(1,421)
Inventories	$4,935	$5,170

We note that not all of Deere's inventories are reported using the same inventory costing method (companies can use different inventory costing methods for different inventory pools).

a. At what dollar amount are Deere's inventories reported on its 2013 balance sheet?

b. At what dollar amount would inventories have been reported on Deere's 2013 balance sheet had it used FIFO inventory costing?

c. What *cumulative* effect has the use of LIFO inventory costing had, as of year-end 2013, on its pretax income compared with the pretax income it would have reported had it used FIFO inventory costing? Explain.

d. Assuming a 35% income tax rate, by what *cumulative* dollar amount has Deere's tax liability been affected by use of LIFO inventory costing as of year-end 2013? Has the use of LIFO inventory costing increased or decreased its cumulative tax liability?

e.   What effect has the use of LIFO inventory costing had on Deere's pretax income and tax liability for 2013 (assume a 35% income tax rate)?

f.   Deere's 2014 annual report has similar disclosures but also states: "The pretax favorable income effect from the liquidation of LIFO inventory during 2014 was approximately $13 million." Explain what happened in 2014 with respect to Deere's inventory and why there was a favorable income effect.

LO2, 4, 5

Whole Foods
NASDAQ :: WFMI

E7-31.   Analyzing Inventories Using LIFO Inventory Footnote

The footnote below is from the 2014 10-K report of **Whole Foods Market, Inc.**, a Texas-based retail grocery chain.

Inventories

The Company values inventories at the lower of cost or market. Cost was determined using the dollar value retail last-in, first-out ("LIFO") method for approximately 93.5% and 92.8% of inventories in fiscal years 2014 and 2013, respectively. Under the LIFO method, the cost assigned to items sold is based on the cost of the most recent items purchased. As a result, the costs of the first items purchased remain in inventory and are used to value ending inventory. The excess of estimated current costs over LIFO carrying value, or LIFO reserve, was approximately $48 million and $32 million at September 28, 2014 and September 29, 2013, respectively. Costs for remaining inventories are determined by the first-in, first-out method. Cost before the LIFO adjustment is principally determined using the item cost method, which is calculated by counting each item in inventory, assigning costs to each of these items based on the actual purchase cost (net of vendor allowances) of each item and recording the actual cost of items sold.

Whole Foods operates the world's largest chain of natural and organic food stores. In 2014, Whole Foods reported sales revenue of $14,194 million and cost of goods sold of $9,150 million. The following information was extracted from the company's 2014 and 2013 balance sheets:

($ millions)	2014	2013
Merchandise inventories	$441	$414

a.   Calculate the amount of inventories purchased by Whole Foods in 2014.

b.   What amount of gross profit would Whole Foods have reported if the FIFO method had been used to value all inventories?

c.   Calculate the gross profit margin (GPM) as reported and assuming that the FIFO method had been used to value all inventories.

LO5

Tiffany & Co.
NYSE :: TIF

Zale Corporation
NYSE :: ZLC

Blue Nile, Inc.
NASDAQ :: NILE

E7-32.   Calculating Gross Profit Margin and Inventory Turnover

The following table presents sales revenue, cost of goods sold, and inventory amounts for three retailers of fine jewelry, **Tiffany & Co.**, **Zale Corporation**, and **Blue Nile, Inc.** (an Internet retailer).

($ millions)	2013	2012
Tiffany & Co.		
Revenues................................	$4,031	$3,794
Cost of goods sold	1,691	1,631
Inventory	2,327	2,234
Zale Corporation		
Revenues................................	$1,888	$1,867
Cost of goods sold	904	906
Inventory	768	742
Blue Nile, Inc.		
Revenues................................	$ 450	$ 400
Cost of goods sold	366	325
Inventory	35	33

a.   Compute the gross profit margin (GPM) for each of these companies for 2013 and 2012.

b.   Compute the inventory turnover ratio and the average inventory days outstanding for 2013 for each company.

c.   What factors might determine the differences among these three companies' ratios?

d.   Zale reports that as of July 31, 2013 its LIFO reserve totaled $63 million while at July 31, 2012 it totaled $58.3 million. Using a 35% tax rate, how much money did Zale save in fiscal 2013 using LIFO and how much has Zale saved since it began using LIFO to value its inventories?

P7-33. Analyzing Inventory and Its Footnote Disclosure

LO2, 4, 5
Caterpillar, Inc.
NYSE :: CAT
Komatsu Ltd. (ADR)
OTC :: KMTUY

Caterpillar Inc. and **Komatsu Ltd.** are international manufacturers of industrial and construction equipment. Caterpillar's headquarters is in the United States, while Komatsu's headquarters is in Japan. The following information comes from their recent financial statements.

Caterpillar—fiscal year ending December 31, 2013 ($ millions)

Cost of goods sold	$40,727
Beginning inventory	15,547
Ending inventory	12,625

Komatsu—fiscal year ending March 31, 2014 (¥ millions)

Cost of goods sold	¥1,393,048
Beginning inventory	633,647
Ending inventory	625,077

In its footnotes, Caterpillar also provides the following information (assume no LIFO liquidation):

Inventories

Inventories are stated at the lower of cost or market. Cost is principally determined using the last-in, first-out (LIFO) method. The value of inventories on the LIFO basis represented about 60 percent of total inventories at December 31, 2013 and 2012, and about 65 percent at December 31, 2011. If the FIFO (first-in, first-out) method had been in use, inventories would have been $2,504 million, $2,750 million and $2,422 million higher than reported at December 31, 2013, 2012 and 2011, respectively.

REQUIRED

a. Calculate the inventory turnover ratios for Caterpillar and Komatsu using the information reported in their financial statements. Describe some operational reasons that companies might have differing inventory turnover ratios, even if they are in the same industry.

b. Did the cost of Caterpillar's acquiring (i.e., producing) products go up or down in 2013?

c. Assuming a 35% income tax rate, by what cumulative dollar amount has Caterpillar's tax liability been affected by use of LIFO inventory costing as of fiscal year-end 2013? Has the use of LIFO inventory costing increased or decreased its cumulative tax liability?

d. What effect has the use of LIFO inventory costing had on Caterpillar's pretax income and tax liability for fiscal year 2013? (Assume a 35% tax rate.)

e. In its footnotes, Komatsu reports that it "determines cost of work in process and finished products using the specific identification method based on actual costs accumulated under a job-order cost system. The cost of finished parts is determined principally using the first-in, first-out method." What effect does this footnote have on your interpretation in question *a* above? Use the information available to make a more appropriate comparison of the two companies' inventory turnover.

P7-34. Analyzing Inventory Disclosure Comparing LIFO and FIFO

LO2, 4, 5

Kroger
NYSE :: KR

The current asset section of the 2014 and 2013 fiscal year end balance sheets of **The Kroger Co.** are presented in the accompanying table:

($ millions)	January 31, 2015	February 1, 2014
Current assets		
Cash and temporary cash investments	$ 268	$ 401
Deposits in-transit	988	958
Receivables	1,266	1,116
FIFO inventory	6,933	6,801
LIFO credit	(1,245)	(1,150)
Prepaid and other current assets	701	704
Total current assets	$8,911	$8,830

In addition, Kroger provides the following footnote describing its inventory accounting policy (assume the following is their complete disclosure):

Inventories are stated at the lower of cost (principally on a LIFO basis) or market. In total, approximately 95% of inventories in 2014 and 2013 were valued using the LIFO method. Cost for the balance of the inventories, including substantially all fuel inventories, was determined using the FIFO method. Replacement cost was higher than the carrying amount by $1,245 million at January 31, 2015 and $1,150 million at February 1, 2014. We follow the Link-Chain, Dollar-Value LIFO method for purposes of calculating our LIFO charge or credit.

REQUIRED

a. At what dollar amount does Kroger report its inventory in its January 31, 2015, balance sheet?
b. What is the cumulative effect (through January 31, 2015) of the use of LIFO on Kroger's pretax earnings?
c. Assuming a 35% tax rate, what is the cumulative (through January 31, 2015) tax effect of the use of LIFO to determine inventory costs?
d. Kroger reported net earnings of $1,728 million in its fiscal year 2014 income statement. Assuming a 35% tax rate, what amount of net earnings would Kroger report if the company used the FIFO inventory costing method?
e. Kroger reported merchandise costs (cost of goods sold) of $85,512 million in fiscal year 2014. Compute its inventory turnover for the year.
f. How would the inventory turnover ratio differ if the FIFO costing method had been used?

LO5

P7-35. Calculating Gross Profit and Inventory Turnover

Samsung Electronics Co. Ltd.
KRX: 005930

Hewlett-Packard and Company
NYSE :: HPQ

Apple Inc.
NASDAQ :: AAPL

The following table presents sales revenue, cost of goods sold, and inventory amounts for three computer/electronics companies, **Samsung Electronics Co.**, **Hewlett-Packard Company**, and **Apple Inc.**

($ millions)	Fiscal year ending		
Samsung Electronics Co. Ltd. (S. Korean won)	Dec. 31, 2014	Dec. 31, 2013	Dec. 31, 2012
Revenues	206,205,987	228,692,667	201,103,613
Cost of goods sold	128,278,800	137,696,309	126,651,931
Inventory	17,317,504	19,134,868	17,747,413
Hewlett-Packard Company (US dollar)	Oct. 31, 2014	Oct. 31, 2013	Oct. 31, 2012
Revenues (products only)	73,726	72,398	77,887
Cost of goods sold	56,469	55,632	59,468
Inventory	6,415	6,046	6,317
Apple Inc. (US dollar)	Sep. 27, 2014	Sep. 28, 2013	Sep. 29, 2012
Revenues	182,795	170,910	156,508
Cost of goods sold	112,258	106,606	87,846
Inventory	2,111	1,764	791

REQUIRED

a. Compute the gross profit margin (GPM) for each of these companies for all three fiscal years.
b. Compute the inventory turnover ratio and the average inventory days outstanding for each company for the last two fiscal years. (All three firms use FIFO inventory costing.)
c. What factors might determine the differences among these three companies' ratios?

LO2, 4, 6

Seneca Foods Corporation
NASDAQ :: SENEA

P7-36.ᴬ Analyzing and Interpreting Inventories and Its Related Ratios and Disclosures

The current asset section from **Seneca Foods Corporation**, a low-cost producer and distributor of quality fruits and vegetables, March 31, 2014 annual report follows:

($ thousands)	March 31, 2014	March 31, 2013
Current Assets		
Cash and cash equivalents	$ 13,839	$ 14,104
Accounts receivable, net	76,964	78,240
Inventories	451,250	479,730
Deferred income taxes	8,412	9,400
Other current assets	33,594	25,299
Total current assets	$584,059	$606,773

Seneca reports the following related to its gross profit:

($ thousands)	Years Ended	
	2014	2013
Net sales.	$1,340,208	$1,276,297
Cost of sales.	1,249,245	1,134,985
Gross profit.	$ 90,963	$ 141,312

Seneca further reports the following footnote:

11. Inventories

Effective December 30, 2007 (beginning of 4th quarter of Fiscal Year 2008), the Company changed its inventory valuation method from the lower of cost, determined under the FIFO method, or market to the lower of cost, determined under the LIFO method, or market. In the high inflation environment that the Company was experiencing, the Company believed that the LIFO inventory method was preferable over the FIFO method because it better compares the cost of current production to current revenue. The effect of LIFO was to reduce net earnings by $13.2 million in 2014, increase net earnings by $2.7 million in 2013 and reduce net earnings by $30.8 million in 2012, compared to what would have been reported using the FIFO inventory method. The reduction in earnings per share was $1.19 ($1.19 diluted) in 2014, increase in earnings per share was $0.24 ($0.24 diluted) in 2013, and the reduction in earnings per share was $2.53 ($2.52 diluted) in 2012. During 2014 and 2012, certain inventory quantities accounted for on the LIFO method were reduced, resulting in the liquidation of certain quantities carried at costs prevailing in prior years. The impact on net earnings of these liquidations was an increase of $4.8 million and $2.9 million during 2014 and 2012, respectively. The excess of FIFO cost of inventory over the LIFO cost of inventory was $153 million in 2014 and $133 million in 2013.

In prior financial statements, Seneca has stated that it "manages the Company for cash, not reported earnings" and that the "decision to switch to LIFO has turned out to be a very prudent one of the last five years."

a.   Compute the ratio of inventories to total current assets for both 2014 and 2013. Is the change observed for the ratio a positive development for a company such as Seneca? Explain.

b.   Compute inventory turnover for both 2014 and 2013 (2012 ending inventories were $432,433). Interpret and explain the change in inventory turnover as positive or negative for the company.

c.   What inventory costing method does Seneca use? What effect has the use of this method (relative to FIFO or LIFO) had on its reported income for 2014? Was the result an increase or decrease? Explain.

d.   Seneca claims that it manages its company for cash flow. Does its inventory reporting help the Company to do so? How much in taxes has Seneca saved, assuming a 35% tax rate, by the inventory approach it adopted?

CASES AND PROJECTS

C7-37.[A] **Analyzing Effects of LIFO on Inventory Turnover Ratios**

The current assets of **Exxon Mobil Corporation** follow:

LO2, 4, 5, 6

MBC

Exxon Mobil Corp.
NYSE :: XOM
BP, p.l.c.
NYSE :: BP

($ millions)	2014	2013
Current assets		
Cash and cash equivalents	$ 4,658	$ 4,913
Notes and accounts receivable, less estimated doubtful amounts	28,009	33,152
Inventories:		
Crude oil, products and merchandise	12,384	12,117
Materials and supplies.	4,294	4,018
Other current assets.	3,565	5,108
Total current assets	$52,910	$59,308

In addition, the following note was provided in its 2014 10-K report:

Inventories. Crude oil, products and merchandise inventories are carried at the lower of current market value or cost (generally determined under the last-in, first-out method—LIFO). Inventory costs include expenditures and other charges (including depreciation) directly and indirectly incurred in bringing the inventory to its existing condition and location. Selling expenses and general and administrative expenses are reported as period costs and excluded from inventory cost. Inventories of materials and supplies are valued at cost or less.

In 2014, 2013 and 2012, net income included gains of $187 million, $282 million and $328 million, respectively, attributable to the combined effects of LIFO inventory accumulations and drawdowns. The aggregate replacement cost of inventories was estimated to exceed their LIFO carrying values by $10.6 billion and $21.2 billion at December 31, 2014, and 2013, respectively.

REQUIRED

a. Exxon Mobil reported pretax earnings of $51,630 million in 2014. What amount of pretax earnings would have been reported by the company if inventory had been reported using the FIFO costing method?

b. Exxon Mobil reported cost of goods sold of $225,972 million in 2014. Compute its inventory turnover ratio for 2014 using total inventories.

c. **BP, p.l.c.** (BP) reports its financial information using IFRS. For fiscal year 2014, BP reported cost of goods sold of $281,907 million, beginning inventory of $29,231 million and ending inventory of $18,373 million. Compute BP's inventory turnover ratio for fiscal year 2014.

d. Compare your answers in parts b and c. BP can't use LIFO to report under IFRS, so revise your calculations in such a way as to find out which company has faster inventory turnover.

e. What is meant by the statement that "2014 net income included gains of $187 million attributable to the combined effects of LIFO inventory accumulations and draw-downs"?

LO2, 4 **C7-38. Analyzing Effects of Change from LIFO to FIFO Inventory Costing**

Virco Manufacturing Corp.
NASDAQ :: VIRC

Virco Manufacturing Corp. provided the following note in its annual report for the year ended January 31, 2011:

On January 31, 2011, the Company elected to change its costing method for the material component of raw materials, work in process, and finished goods inventory to the lower of cost or market using the first-in first-out ("FIFO") method, from the lower of cost or market using the last-in first out ("LIFO") method. The labor and overhead components of inventory have historically been valued on a FIFO basis. The Company believes that the FIFO method for the material component of inventory is preferable as it conforms the inventory costing methods for all components of inventory into a single costing method and better reflects current acquisition costs of those inventories on our consolidated balance sheets. Additionally, presentation of inventory at FIFO aligns the financial reporting with the Company's borrowing base under its line of credit (see Note 3 for further discussion of the line of credit). Further, this change will promote greater comparability with companies that have adopted International Financial Reporting Standards, which does not recognize LIFO as an acceptable accounting method. In accordance with FASB ASC Topic 250, "Accounting Changes and Error Corrections," all prior periods presented have been adjusted to apply the new accounting method retrospectively. In addition, as an indirect effect of the change in our inventory costing method from LIFO to FIFO, the Company recorded additional inventory lower of cost or market expenses and changes in deferred tax assets and income tax expense. The retroactive effect of the change in our inventory costing method…increased the February 1, 2008, opening retained earnings balance by $4.1 million, and increased our inventory and retained earnings balances by $8.5 million and $5.4 million as of January 31, 2009, by $6.9 million and $4.3 million as of January 31, 2010, and by $7.6 million and $4.7 million as of January 31, 2011, respectively.

REQUIRED

a. What do the stated changes in inventory in each year represent (e.g., the $7.6 million in 2011)? Equity? What is the difference between the two?

b. What were Virco's stated reasons for the change to FIFO?

c. In the Annual Report for the year ended January 2010, Virco states the following: "Inventories are stated at the lower of cost or market. Cost is determined using the last-in, first-out ("LIFO") method of valuation for the material content of inventories and the first-in, first-out ("FIFO") method for labor and overhead. The Company uses LIFO as it results in a better matching of costs and revenues." What are some possible motivations behind why Virco changed to the FIFO method of accounting beyond those listed by management?

SOLUTIONS TO REVIEW PROBLEMS

Mid-Chapter Review Part 1

SOLUTION

Preliminary computation: Units in ending inventory = 4,800 available − 2,800 sold = 2,000

1. First-in, first-out (FIFO)

Cost of goods sold computation:	Units		Cost		Total
	1,000	@	$18.00	=	$18,000
	1,800	@	$18.25	=	32,850
	2,800				$50,850

Cost of goods available for sale. $88,450
Less: Cost of goods sold 50,850
Ending inventory ($22,800 + $14,800). $37,600

2. Last-in, first-out (LIFO)

Cost of goods sold computation:	Units		Cost		Total
	1,200	@	$19.00	=	$22,800
	800	@	$18.50	=	14,800
	800	@	$18.25	=	14,600
	2,800				$52,200

Cost of goods available for sale. $88,450
Less: Cost of goods sold 52,200
Ending inventory [$18,000 + (1,000 × $18.25)]. $36,250

3. Average cost (AC)

Average unit cost	= $88,450/4,800	= $18.427
Cost of goods sold	= 2,800 × $18.427	= $51,596
Ending inventory	= 2,000 × $18.427	= $36,854

4. *a.* FIFO in most circumstances reflects physical flow. For example, FIFO would apply to the physical flow of perishables and to situations where the earlier items acquired are moved out first because of risk of deterioration or obsolescence.

   b. LIFO results in the lowest ending inventory amount during periods of rising costs, which in turn yields the lowest net income and the lowest income taxes.

5. Last-in, first-out with LIFO liquidation

Cost of goods sold computation:	Units		Cost		Total
	800	@	$18.50	=	$14,800
	1,800	@	$18.25	=	32,850
	200	@	$18.00	=	3,600
	2,800				$51,250

Cost of goods available for sale. $65,650
Less: Cost of goods sold 51,250
Ending inventory (800 × $18). $14,400

The company's LIFO gross profit has increased by $950 ($52,200 − $51,250). This increase is from LIFO liquidation, which is the reduction of inventory quantities that results in matching older (lower) cost layers against current selling prices. The company has, in effect, dipped into lower-cost layers to boost current period profit—all from a simple delay of inventory purchases.

6. Transaction effects shown in the financial statement effects template, journal entries, and T-accounts.

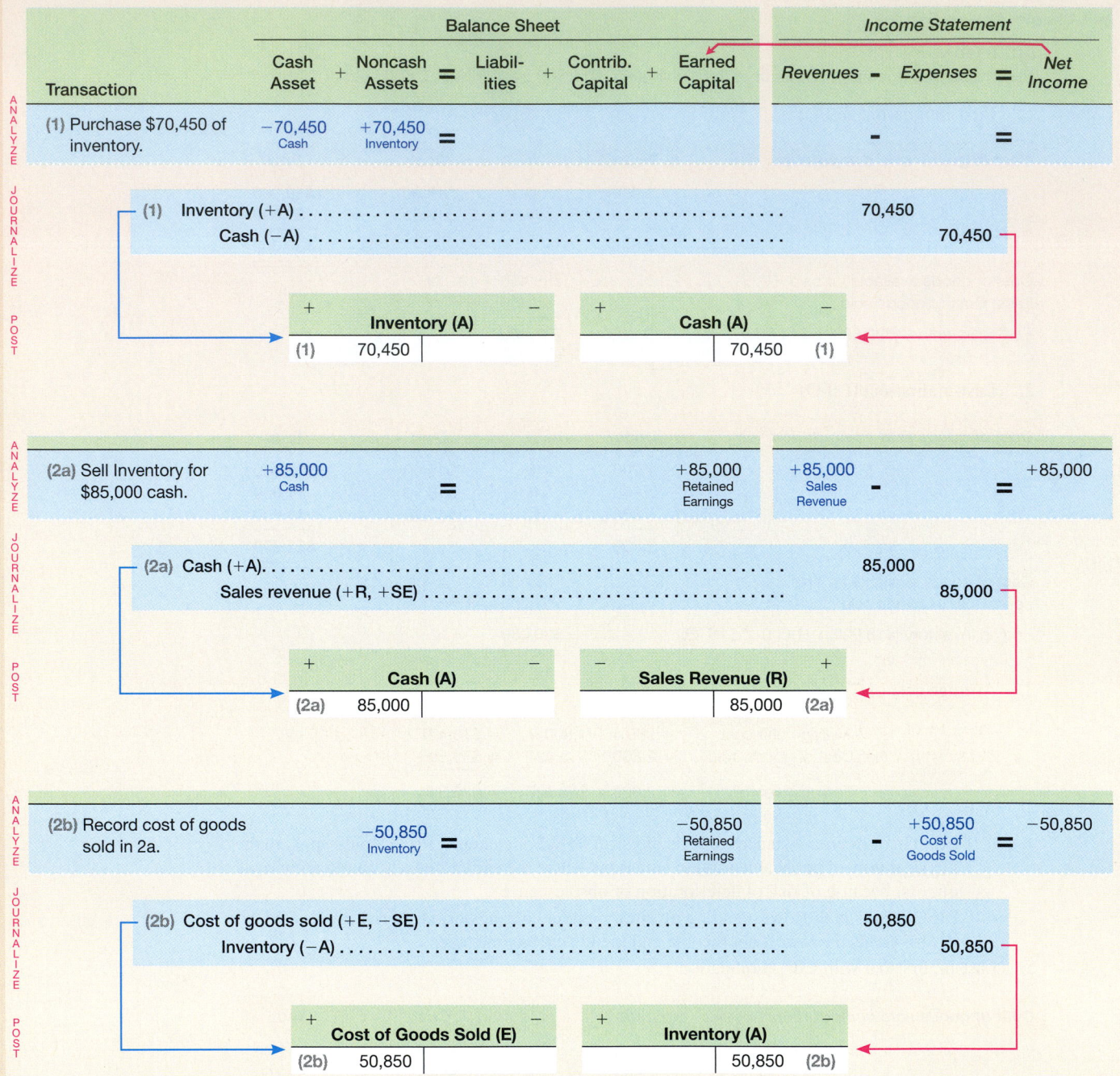

Mid-Chapter Review Part 2

SOLUTION

1.

Item	Quantity	Cost	Market	Inventory Amounts Cost	Inventory Amounts Market	LCM (by Item)
Fans						
Model X1	300	$18	$19	$ 5,400	$ 5,700	$ 5,400
Model X2	250	22	24	5,500	6,000	5,500
Model X3	400	29	26	11,600	10,400	10,400
Totals				$22,500	$22,100	$21,300
Heaters						
Model B7	500	24	28	$12,000	$14,000	$12,000
Model B8	290	35	32	10,150	9,280	9,280
Model B9	100	41	38	4,100	3,800	3,800
Totals				26,250	27,080	25,080
Totals				$48,750	$49,180	$46,380

 a. As shown in this schedule, applying the lower of cost or market rule to each item of the inventory results in an ending inventory amount of $46,380.

 b. Applying the lower of cost or market rule to each major category of the inventory results in an ending inventory amount of $48,350, calculated as follows:

Fans	$22,100
Heaters.	26,250
	$48,350

 c. As shown in this schedule, applying the lower of cost or market rule to the total inventory results in an ending inventory amount of $48,750.

2. The LCM procedure that results in the lowest ending inventory amount also results in the lowest net income for the year (the lower the ending inventory amount, the higher the cost of goods sold). Applying the lower of cost or market rule to each item of the inventory results in the lowest net income for the year.

Chapter-End Review

SOLUTION

1. The gross profit margin is calculated as follows:

Gross profit margin:
2012:	$7,574/$27,485 =	0.276 (or 27.6%)
2013:	$7,980/$28,917 =	0.276 (or 27.6%)
2014:	$8,327/$30,560 =	0.272 (or 27.2%)

Inventory turnover:
2013:	$20,937/[($1,507 + $1,409)/2] =	14.4 times
2014:	$22,233/[($1,598 + $1,507)/2] =	14.3 times

2. Cost of goods sold and gross profit must be adjusted by the change in the LIFO reserve to convert to FIFO.

Cost of goods sold
2013:	$20,937 − ($390 − $375) = $20,922
2014:	$22,233 − ($421 − $390) = $22,202

Gross profit
2013:	$7,980 + ($390 − $375) = $ 7,995
2014:	$8,327 + ($421 − $390) = $ 8,358

 The use of LIFO resulted in a higher cost of goods sold and a lower gross profit for both years.

3.   Restated inventory turnover calculations:

2013:	$20,922/[($1,897 + $1,784)/2] =	11.4 times
2014:	$22,202/[($2,019 + $1,897)/2] =	11.3 times

Because inventory values are higher and cost of goods sold is lower under FIFO, the inventory turnover ratio is slightly lower when FIFO numbers are used.

Appendix 7A Review

SOLUTION

a.

Sales revenue	
(11,500 × $65).	$747,500
Cost of goods sold	
(7,000 × $70) + (3,000 × $30) + (1,500 × $20)	610,000
Gross profit.	$137,500

b.

Sales revenue	
(11,500 × $65).	$747,500
Cost of goods sold	
(11,500 × $70).	805,000
Gross profit.	$ (57,500)

c.   Dickhaut should report in its footnotes that gross profit was increased by $195,000 [$137,500 − $(57,500)] due to LIFO liquidation. It's worth noting that Dickhaut could report any gross profit between $(57,500) and $137,500 by adjusting its end-of-year purchases.

d.   The replenishment decision should depend on the cash flows from each alternative over the planning period (until the point where inventory could be replenished next year at $55). The following table looks at three alternatives—no year-end purchase, a year-end purchase of 4,500 units, and a year-end purchase of 1,500 units. The second alternative would retain all the LIFO layers that were in the beginning inventory, while the third alternative would retain only the 2014 layer at $20 per unit. For this last alternative, cost of goods sold would be $685,000 (8,500 units at $70 each plus 3,000 units at $30 each).

As the table shows, the second alternative is preferred to the first, but the third alternative is preferred over the other two. (Of course, this analysis is based on the assumption that 5,000 units will be held in inventory for the entire planning horizon. If Dickhaut anticipates future inventory reductions, e.g., due to product changes, end-of-year purchases would only defer the payment of taxes and their relative advantage would decrease.)

	No purchase		Purchase 4,500 units		Purchase 1,500 units	
	Income	Cash Flows	Income	Cash Flows	Income	Cash Flows
Revenue	$747,500	$747,500	$747,500	$747,500	$747,500	$747,500
COGS.	610,000		805,000		685,000	
Gross profit.	137,500		(57,500)		62,500	
Tax (35%)	(48,125)	(48,125)	20,125	20,125	(21,875)	(21,875)
Year-end purchases				(315,000)		(105,000)
2017 purchases		(247,500)				(165,000)
Total cash flows		$451,875		$452,625		$455,625

Reporting and Analyzing Long-Term Operating Assets

LEARNING OBJECTIVES

1. Describe and distinguish between tangible and intangible assets. (p. 374)

2. Determine which costs to capitalize and report as assets and which costs to expense. (p. 375)

3. Apply different depreciation methods to allocate the cost of assets over time. (p. 377)

4. Determine the effects of asset sales and impairments on financial statements. (p. 381)

5. Describe the accounting and reporting for intangible assets. (p. 388)

6. Analyze the effects of tangible and intangible assets on key performance measures. (p. 393)

PROCTER & GAMBLE
www.pg.com

The Procter & Gamble Company (P&G) has successfully reinvented itself . . . again. Founded in 1837 by William Procter and James Gamble, P&G is the largest consumer products company in the world today. P&G markets its products in more than 180 countries and its annual sales now are in excess of $83 billion, which far exceeds competitors such as Colgate-Palmolive Company and Kimberly-Clark Corporation. P&G has focused on its higher-margin products such as those in beauty care. P&G's advertising budget is 11% of sales, which is slightly larger than Colgate's and more than twice as large as Kimberly-Clark's.

P&G's financial performance has been impressive. Its return on equity (ROE) in 2014 was 17%. Although more financially leveraged than the average publicly traded company, there is little need for concern because P&G generates almost $14 billion in operating cash flow, which is more than sufficient to cover its $700 million in interest payments. P&G also paid almost $7 billion in dividends and repurchased more than $6 billion of its own shares in 2014. (Stock repurchases are covered more fully in Chapter 11.)

P&G has made divesting underperforming brands a strategic goal. For example, P&G recently sold off its pet care business to Mars, Inc. and Spectrum Brands Holdings, Inc. In addition, P&G agreed to divest its Duracell batteries business to Berkshire Hathaway, Inc. and has entered into deals to exit Vicks VapoStream, Camay and Zest bar soap brands, and several skin care and fragrance brands.

P&G's remaining product stable consists of numerous well-recognized household brands. Surveys in the business press show that the company is widely admired. A partial listing follows by business segment, including some "Billion Dollar Brands" in each segment:

- **Baby and Family Care**—Bounty, Charmin, Pampers
- **Beauty**— CoverGirl, Head & Shoulders, Olay, Pantene, Wella
- **Fabric and Home Care**—Ace, Febreze, Cascade, Cheer, Dawn, Downy, Gain, Tide
- **Grooming**—Braun, Gillette, Mach3
- **Health Care**—Always, Crest, Oral-B

However, substantial risks exist. In the fiscal 2014 annual report, management states that "Our business model relies on continued growth and success of existing brands and products, as well as the creation of new products. The markets and industry segments in which we offer our products are highly competitive. . . Achieving our business results depends, in part, on the successful development, introduction, and marketing of new products and improvements to our equipment and manufacturing processes." External risks also exist. For example, in recent years commodity costs have risen rapidly and significantly, and cautious consumers have made it difficult for P&G to increase prices and maintain margins. In the last year, the strength of the dollar also hurt P&G. Around 60% of the company's business is generated outside North America. Lower consumption in several countries due to pricing actions taken to offset the effects of currency changes negatively affected sales.

In this chapter, we explore the reporting and analysis of long-term operating assets. In order to maintain growth in sales, income, and cash flows, capital-intensive companies like P&G must be diligent in managing long-term operating assets. As is the case with P&G, many companies have made large investments in innovation and brand value. These investments are not always reflected adequately in the balance sheet. Management's choices and GAAP rules concerning the reporting of long-term operating assets can have a marked impact on the analysis and interpretation of financial statements.

Sources: *Procter & Gamble* 2014 Annual Report and 10-K.

CHAPTER ORGANIZATION

Reporting and Analyzing Long-Term Operating Assets		
Property, Plant, and Equipment	**Analyzing Financial Statements**	**Intangible Assets**
• Determining Costs to Capitalize • Depreciation Methods • Changes in Accounting Estimates • Asset Sales and Impairments • Footnote Disclosures	• PPE Turnover • Percent Depreciated Ratio • Cash Flow Effects	• Research and Development Costs • Patents, Trademarks, and Franchises • Amortization and Impairment • Goodwill • Footnote Disclosures • Analysis Implications

LO1 Describe and distinguish between tangible and intangible assets.

INTRODUCTION

Investments in long-term operating assets often represent the largest component of a company's balance sheet. Effectively managing long-term operating assets is crucial, because these investments affect company performance for several years and are frequently irreversible. To evaluate how well a company is managing operating assets, we need to understand how they are measured and reported.

This chapter describes the accounting, reporting, and analysis of long-term operating assets including tangible and intangible assets. **Tangible assets** are assets that have physical substance. They are frequently included in the balance sheet as *property, plant, and equipment*, and include land, buildings, machinery, fixtures, and equipment. **Intangible assets**, such as trademarks and patents, do not have physical substance, but provide the owner with specific rights and privileges.

Long-term operating assets have two common characteristics. First, unlike inventory, these assets are not acquired for resale. Instead, they are necessary to produce and deliver the products and services that generate revenues for the company. Second, these assets help produce revenues for multiple accounting periods. Consequently, accountants focus considerable attention on how they are reported in the balance sheet and how these costs are transferred over time to the income statement as expenses.

To illustrate the size and importance of long-term operating assets, the asset section (only) of P&G's balance sheet is reproduced in **Exhibit 8.1**. We can see as of June 30, 2014, the end of P&G's fiscal year, P&G's net investment in property, plant, and equipment totaled approximately $22.3 billion and its intangible assets represent an $84.5 billion investment. Together, these two categories of assets make up almost three-fourths of P&G's total assets.

This chapter is divided into two main sections. The first section focuses on accounting for tangible property, plant, and equipment and the related depreciation expense that is reported each period in the income statement. The second section examines the measurement and reporting of intangible assets.

PROPERTY, PLANT, AND EQUIPMENT (PPE)

For many companies, the largest category of operating assets is its long-term property, plant, and equipment (PPE) assets. The size and duration of this asset category raises several important questions, including:

- Which costs should be **capitalized** on the balance sheet as assets? Which should be expensed?
- How should capitalized costs be allocated to the accounting periods that benefited from the asset?
- How should asset sales or significant changes in assets' fair values be reported?

This section explains the accounting, reporting, and analysis of PPE assets and related items.

EXHIBIT 8.1	Procter & Gamble Balance Sheet (assets only)		
		June 30	
($ millions)		2014	2013
Assets			
Current assets			
Cash and cash equivalents		$ 8,558	$ 5,947
Available-for-sale investment securities		2,128	—
Accounts receivable		6,386	6,508
Inventories			
Materials and supplies		1,742	1,704
Work in process		684	722
Finished goods		4,333	4,483
Total inventories		6,759	6,909
Deferred income taxes		1,092	948
Prepaid expenses and other current assets		3,845	3,678
Assets held for sale		2,849	—
Total current assets		31,617	23,990
Property, plant, and equipment			
Buildings		8,022	7,829
Machinery and equipment		32,398	31,070
Land		893	878
Construction in progress		3,114	3,235
		44,427	43,012
Accumulated depreciation		(22,123)	(21,346)
Net property, plant, and equipment		22,304	21,666
Goodwill and other intangible assets			
Goodwill		53,704	55,188
Trademarks and other intangible assets, net		30,843	31,572
Net goodwill and other intangible assets		84,547	86,760
Other noncurrent assets		5,798	6,847
Total assets		$ 144,266	$ 139,263

Determining Costs to Capitalize

LO2 Determine which costs to capitalize and report as assets and which costs to expense.

When a company acquires an asset, it must first decide which portion of the cost should be included among the expenses of the current period and which costs should be capitalized as part of the asset and reported in the balance sheet. Outlays to acquire PPE are called **capital expenditures**. Expenditures that are recorded as an asset must possess each of the following two characteristics:

1. The asset is owned or controlled by the company.

2. The asset is expected to provide future benefits.

All normal costs incurred to acquire an asset and prepare it for its intended use should be capitalized and reported in the balance sheet. These costs would include the purchase price of the asset plus any of the following: installation costs, taxes, shipping costs, legal fees, and setup or calibration costs. If owning an asset carries legal obligations at the end of the asset's life (for example, to remove the asset or to perform environmental remediation), the current cost of those obligations should be included in the asset's cost and recognized as a liability at the time the asset is acquired. This cost will be included in the subsequent depreciation of the asset.

Determining the specific costs that should be capitalized requires judgment. There are two important considerations to address when deciding which costs to capitalize. First, companies can only capitalize costs that are *directly linked* to future benefits. Incidental costs or costs that would be incurred regardless of whether the asset is purchased should not be capitalized. Second, the costs capitalized as an asset can be no greater than the expected future benefits to be derived from use of the asset. This requirement means that if a company reports a $200 asset, we can reasonably expect that it will derive at least $200 in expected future cash inflows from the use and ultimate disposition of the asset.

Sometimes, companies construct assets for their own use rather than purchasing a similar asset from another company. In this case, all of the costs incurred to construct the asset—including materials, labor, and a reasonable amount of overhead—should be included in the cost that is capitalized. In addition, in many cases, a portion of the interest expense incurred during the construction period should also be capitalized as part of the asset's cost. This interest is called **capitalized interest**. Capitalizing some of a company's interest cost as part of the cost of a self-constructed asset reduces interest expense in the current period and increases depreciation expense in future periods when the asset is placed in service.

Once an asset is placed in service, additional costs are often incurred to maintain and improve the asset. Routine repairs and maintenance costs are necessary to realize the full potential benefits of ownership of the asset and should be treated as expenses of the period in which the maintenance is performed. However, if the cost can be considered an *improvement or betterment* of the asset, the cost should be capitalized. An improvement or betterment is an outlay that either enhances the usefulness of the asset or extends the asset's useful life beyond the original expectation.

YOU MAKE THE CALL

You are the Company Accountant Your company has just purchased a plot of land as a building site for an office building. After the purchase, you discover that the building site was once the site of an oil well. Before construction can commence, your company must spend $40,000 to properly cap the oil well and prepare the site to meet current environmental standards. How should you account for the $40,000 cleanup cost? [Answers on page 395]

Depreciation

> **FYI** Depreciation is a systematic allocation of asset cost over the useful life—not a measure of the change in fair value.

Once an asset has been recorded in the balance sheet, the cost must be transferred over time from the balance sheet to the income statement and reported as an expense. The nature of long-term operating assets is that they benefit more than one period. As a consequence, it is impossible to match a specific portion of the cost *directly* to the revenues of a particular period. Accounting principles require that this expense be recognized as equitably as possible over the asset's useful economic life. Therefore, we rely on a *systematic allocation* to assign a portion of the asset's cost to each period benefited. This systematic allocation of cost is called **depreciation**.

The concept of systematic allocation of an asset's cost is important. When depreciation expense is recorded, the reported value of the asset (also called the *book value* or *carrying value*) is reduced. Naturally, it is tempting to infer that the fair value of the asset is lower as a result. However, this reported value does not reflect the fair value of the asset. The fair value of the asset may decline by more or less than the amount of depreciation expense, and can even increase in some periods. Depreciation expense should only be interpreted as an assignment of costs to an accounting period and not a measure of the decline in fair value of the asset.

The amount of cost that is allocated to a given period is recorded as depreciation expense in the income statement with a balancing entry in **accumulated depreciation** in the balance sheet. Accumulated depreciation is a contra-asset account (denoted "XA" in the journal entry). Like all contra-asset accounts, it offsets the balance in the corresponding asset account. To illustrate, assume that Dehning Company purchases a heavy-duty delivery truck for $100,000 and decides to record $18,000 of depreciation expense in the first year of operation. The following entries would be recorded with a cash outflow reflected in the investing section of the statement of cash flows.

The asset would be presented in the balance sheet at period-end at its net book value.

Truck, at cost	$100,000	
Less accumulated depreciation	18,000	
Truck, net	$ 82,000	(Book Value)

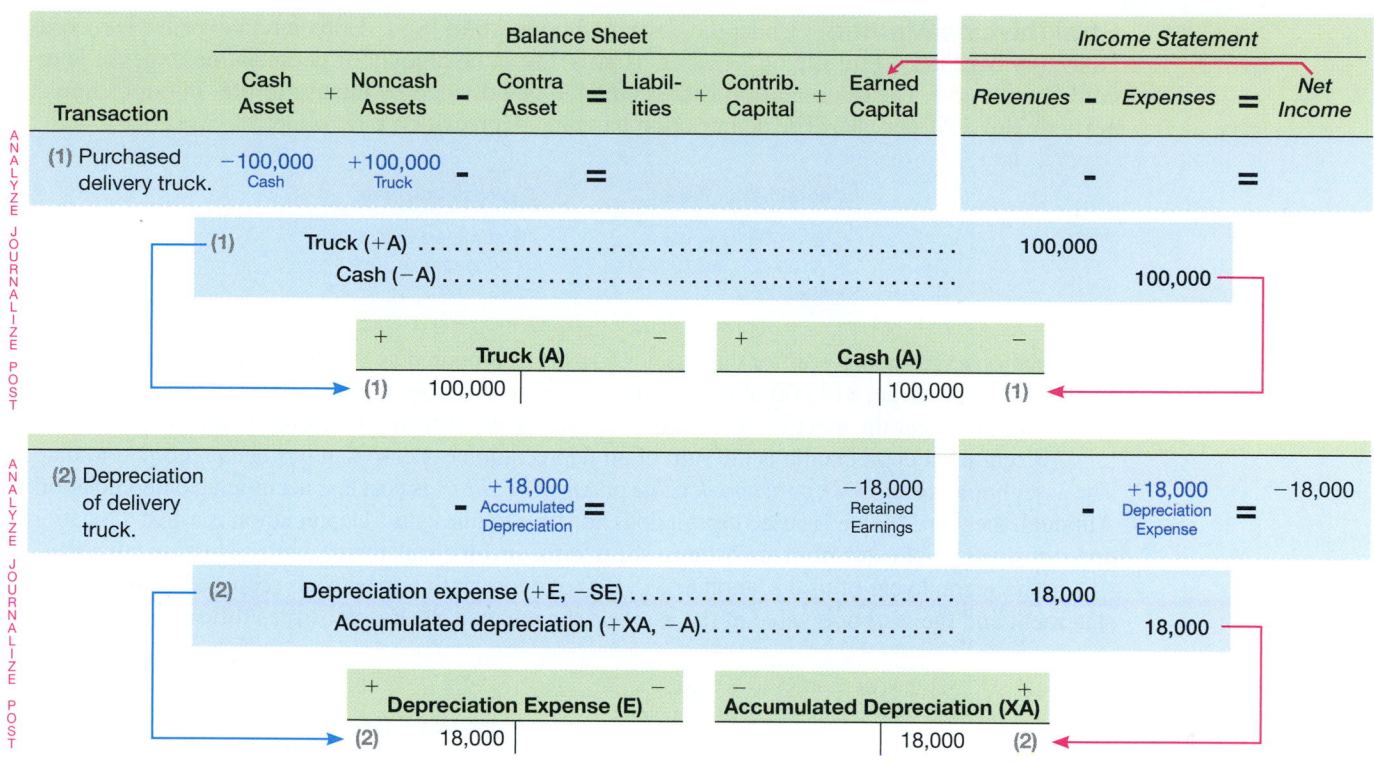

By presenting the information using a contra-asset account, the original acquisition cost of the asset is preserved in the asset account. The net book value of the asset reflects the acquisition cost less the balance in the accumulated depreciation account. The balance in the accumulated depreciation account is the sum of the depreciation expense that has been recorded to date. In **Exhibit 8.1**, Procter & Gamble reports that the original cost of its property, plant, and equipment is $44,427 million and the depreciation accumulated as of June 30, 2014 is $22,123 million. The result is a net book value of $22,304 million.

Depreciation Methods

Two estimates are required to compute the amount of depreciation expense to record each period.

LO3 Apply different depreciation methods to allocate the cost of assets over time.

1. **Useful life**. The useful life is the period of time over which the asset is expected to provide economic benefits to the company. The useful life is not the same as the physical life of the asset. An asset may or may not provide economic benefits to the company for its entire physical life. This useful life should not exceed the period of time that the company intends to use the asset. For example, if a company has a policy of replacing automobiles every two years, the useful life should be set at no longer than two years, even if the automobiles physically last three years or more.

2. **Residual (or salvage) value**. The residual value is the expected realizable value of the asset at the end of its useful life. This value may be the disposal or scrap value, or it may be an estimated resale value for a used asset.

These factors must be estimated when the asset is acquired. The **depreciation base**, also called the *nonrecoverable cost*, is the portion of the cost that is depreciated. The depreciation base is the capitalized cost of the asset less the estimated residual value. This amount is allocated over the useful life of the asset according to the *depreciation method* that the company has selected.

To illustrate alternative depreciation methods, we return to the example presented earlier. Assume that Dehning Company purchases a delivery truck for $100,000. The company expects the truck to last five years and estimates a residual value of $10,000. The depreciation base is $90,000 ($100,000 − $10,000). We illustrate the three most common depreciation methods:

1. Straight-line method
2. Double-declining-balance method
3. Units-of-production method

Straight-Line Method   Under the **straight-line method (SL)**, depreciation expense is recorded evenly over the useful life of the asset. That is, the same amount of depreciation expense is recorded each year. The **depreciation rate** is equal to one divided by the useful life. In our example, 1/5 = 0.2 or 20% per year. The depreciation base and depreciation rate follow.

Depreciation Base	Depreciation Rate
Cost − Salvage value = $100,000 − $10,000 = $90,000	1/Estimated useful life = 1/5 years = 20%

Depreciation expense per year for this asset is $18,000, computed as $90,000 × 20%. For the asset's first full year of usage, $18,000 of depreciation expense is reported in the income statement. At the end of that first year the asset is reported on the balance sheet as shown earlier in the chapter.

Accumulated depreciation is the sum of all depreciation expense that has been recorded to date. The asset **book value (BV)**, or *net book value* or *carrying value*, is cost less accumulated depreciation. Although the word "value" is used here, it does not refer to fair value. Depreciation is a cost allocation concept (transfer of costs from the balance sheet to the income statement), not a valuation concept.

In the second year of usage, another $18,000 of depreciation expense is recorded in the income statement and the net book value of the asset on the balance sheet is shown as follows:

Truck, at cost	$100,000
Less accumulated depreciation	36,000
Truck, net	$ 64,000

Accumulated depreciation now includes the sum of the first and second years' depreciation ($36,000), and the net book value of the asset is now reduced to $64,000. After the fifth year, a total of $90,000 of accumulated depreciation will be recorded, yielding a net book value for the truck of $10,000, its estimated salvage value.

Double-Declining-Balance Method   GAAP allows companies to use **accelerated depreciation** methods. Accelerated depreciation methods record more depreciation expense in the early years of an asset's useful life and less expense in the later years. The total depreciation expense recorded *over the entire useful life* of the asset is the same as with straight-line depreciation. The only difference is in the amount of depreciation recorded for *any given year*.

The **double-declining-balance (DDB) method** is an accelerated depreciation method that computes the depreciation rate as twice the straight-line rate. This double rate is then multiplied by the net book value of the asset, which declines each period as accumulated depreciation increases. For Dehning Company, the depreciation base and the depreciation rate are computed as follows:

Depreciation Base	Depreciation Rate
Net Book Value = Cost − Accumulated Depreciation	2 × SL rate = 2 × 20% = 40%

FYI When calculating DDB depreciation, the depreciation rate is multiplied by the book value; residual value is not subtracted from book value.

The depreciation expense for the first year of usage for this asset is $40,000, computed as $100,000 × 40%. At the end of the first full year, $40,000 of depreciation expense is reported on the income statement (compared with $18,000 under the SL method), and the asset is reported on the balance sheet as follows:

Truck, at cost	$100,000
Less accumulated depreciation	40,000
Truck, net	$ 60,000

In the second year, $24,000 ($60,000 × 40%) of depreciation expense is reported in the income statement and the net book value of the asset on the balance sheet is shown as follows:

Truck, at cost	$100,000
Less accumulated depreciation	64,000
Truck, net	$ 36,000

The double-declining-balance method continues to record depreciation expense in this manner until the salvage amount is reached, at which point the depreciation process is discontinued. This leaves a net book value equal to the salvage value as with the straight-line method. The DDB depreciation schedule for the life of this asset is illustrated in **Exhibit 8.2**.

EXHIBIT 8.2 ▸ **Double-Declining-Balance Depreciation Schedule**

Year	Book Value at Beginning of Year	Depreciation Expense	Book Value at End of Year
1.	$100,000	100,000 × 40% = $40,000	$60,000
2.	60,000	60,000 × 40% = 24,000	36,000
3.	36,000	36,000 × 40% = 14,400	21,600
4.	21,600	21,600 × 40% = 8,640	12,960
5.	12,960	12,960 − 10,000 = 2,960*	10,000

*The depreciation expense in the fifth year is not calculated as 40% × $12,960 because the resulting depreciation would reduce the net book value below the $10,000 residual value. Instead, the residual value ($10,000) is subtracted from the remaining book value ($12,960), resulting in depreciation expense of $2,960.

Exhibit 8.3 compares the depreciation expense and net book value for both the SL and DDB methods. During the first two years, the DDB method yields higher depreciation expense in comparison with the SL method. Beginning in the third year, this pattern reverses and the SL method produces higher depreciation expense. Over the asset's life, the same $90,000 in total depreciation expense is recorded, leaving a residual value of $10,000 on the balance sheet under both methods.

EXHIBIT 8.3 ▸ **Comparison of Straight-Line and Double-Declining-Balance Depreciation**

	Straight-Line		Double-Declining-Balance	
Year	Depreciation Expense	Book Value at End of Year	Depreciation Expense	Book Value at End of Year
1.	$18,000	$82,000	$40,000	$60,000
2.	18,000	64,000	24,000	36,000
3.	18,000	46,000	14,400	21,600
4.	18,000	28,000	8,640	12,960
5.	18,000	10,000	2,960	10,000
	$90,000		$90,000	

> All depreciation methods yield the same salvage value

> Total depreciation over asset life is identical for all methods

Units-of-Production Method

Under the **units-of-production method**, the useful life of the asset is defined in terms of the number of units of service provided by the asset. For instance, this could be the number of units produced, the number of hours that a machine is operated, or, as with Dehning Company's delivery truck, the number of miles driven. To illustrate, assume that Dehning Company estimates that the delivery truck will provide 150,000 miles of service before it is sold for its residual value of $10,000. The depreciation rate is expressed in terms of a cost per mile driven, computed as follows:

$$\frac{\$100,000 - \$10,000}{150,000 \text{ miles}} = \$0.60 \text{ per mile}$$

If the delivery truck is driven 35,000 miles in year 1, the depreciation expense for that year would be $21,000 (35,000 × $0.60). This method produces an amount of depreciation that varies from year to year as the use of the asset varies.

The units-of-production method is used by companies with natural resources such as oil reserves, mineral deposits, or timberlands. These assets are often referred to as **wasting assets**, because the asset is consumed as it is used. The acquisition cost of a natural resource, plus any costs incurred to prepare the asset for its intended use, should be capitalized and reported among PPE assets in the balance sheet.

When the natural resource is used or extracted, inventory is created. The cost of the resource is transferred from the long-term asset account into inventory and, once the inventory is sold, to the income statement as cost of goods sold. The process of transferring costs from the resource account into inventory is called **depletion**.

Depletion is very much like depreciation of tangible operating assets, except that the amount of depletion recorded each period should reflect the amount of the resource that was actually extracted or used up during that period. As a result, depletion is usually calculated using the units-of-production method. The depletion rate is calculated as follows:

$$\text{Depletion rate per unit consumed} = \frac{\text{Acquisition cost} - \text{Residual value}}{\text{Estimated quantity of resource available}}$$

The calculation requires an estimate of the quantity of the resource available, which usually requires the assistance of experts, such as geologists or engineers, who are trained to make these determinations.

Depreciation for Tax Purposes   Most companies use the straight-line method for financial reporting purposes and an accelerated depreciation method for tax returns.[1] Governments allow accelerated depreciation, in part, to provide incentives for taxpayers to invest. As a result of the differing depreciation methods used for financial accounting and tax purposes, lower depreciation expense (and higher income) is reported for financial accounting purposes early in the life of an asset relative to tax purposes. Even though this difference reverses in later years, companies prefer to defer the tax payments so that the cash savings can be invested to produce earnings. Further, even with the reversal in the later years of an asset's life, if total depreciable assets are growing at a fast enough rate, the additional first-year depreciation on newly acquired assets more than offsets the lower depreciation expense on older assets, yielding a continuing deferral of taxable income and taxes paid. There are other differences between financial reporting and tax reporting that create issues in determining a company's tax expense. In Chapter 10, we explore these differences further and examine deferred tax liabilities and deferred tax assets.

Changes in Accounting Estimates

The estimates required in the depreciation process are made when the asset is acquired. When necessary, companies can, and do, change these estimates during the useful lives of assets. When either the useful life or residual value estimates change, the change is applied prospectively. That is, companies use the new estimates from the date of the change going forward and do not restate the financial statements of prior periods.

To illustrate, assume that, after three years of straight-line depreciation, Dehning Company decided to extend the useful life of its truck from 5 years to 6 years. From **Exhibit 8.3**, the book value of the delivery truck at the end of the third year is $46,000. The change in estimated useful life would not require a formal accounting entry. Instead, depreciation expense would be recalculated for the remaining three years of the truck's useful life:

$$\frac{\$46,000 - \$10,000}{3 \text{ years}} = \$12,000 \text{ per year}$$

Thus, beginning in year four, depreciation expense of $12,000 (instead of $18,000) would be recorded each year.

---

[1] The IRS mandates the use of MACRS (Modified Accelerated Cost Recovery System) for tax purposes. This method fixes the useful life for various classes of assets, assumes no salvage value, and generally produces depreciation amounts consistent with the double-rate, double-declining-balance method. When a declining balance method is used with zero salvage, the depreciation schedule must switch after the midpoint of the asset's life to straight-line depreciation of the remaining balance over the remaining life.

Asset Sales and Impairments

This section discusses gains and losses from asset sales and computation and disclosure of asset impairments.

Gains and Losses on Asset Sales The gain or loss on the sale (disposition) of a long-term asset is computed as follows:

LO4 Determine the effects of asset sales and impairments on financial statements.

> **Gain or loss on asset sale = Proceeds from sale − Book value of asset sold**

The book (carrying) value of an asset is its acquisition cost less accumulated depreciation. When an asset is sold, its acquisition cost and related accumulated depreciation are removed from the balance sheet and any gain or loss is reported in income from continuing operations. To illustrate such a transaction, assume that Dehning Company decided to sell the delivery truck after four years of straight-line depreciation. From **Exhibit 8.3**, we know that the book value of the truck is $28,000 ($100,000 − $72,000). If the truck is sold for $30,000, the entry to record the sale follows.

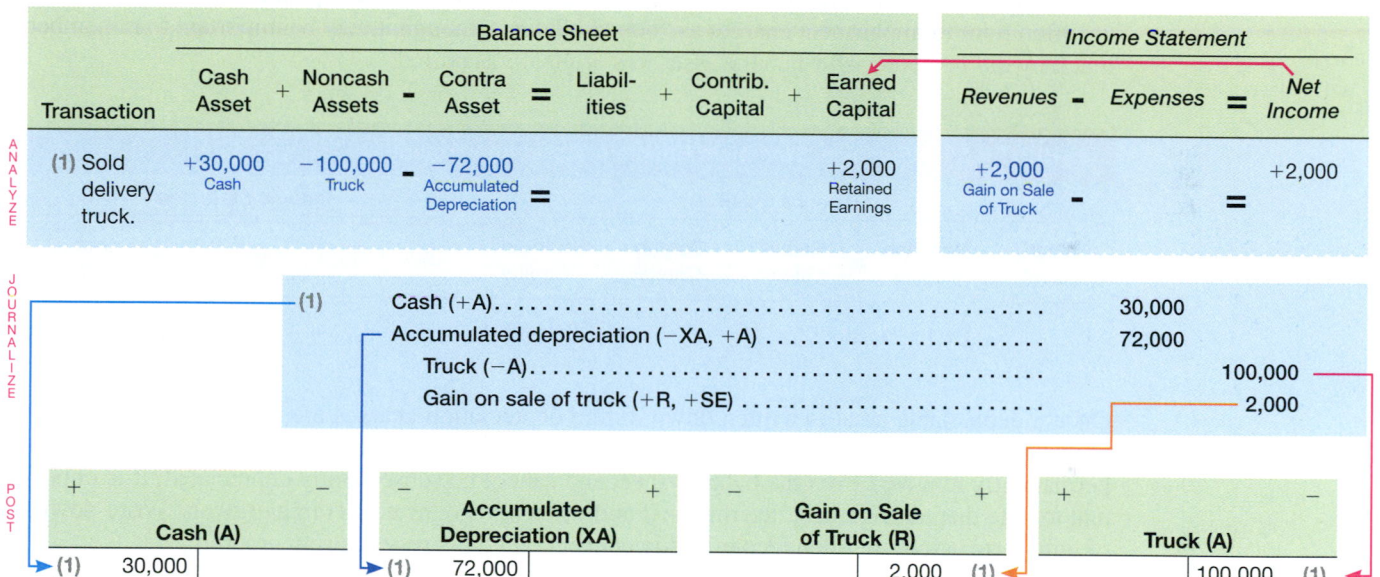

Gains and losses on asset sales can be large, and analysts must be aware of these nonrecurring operating income components. Further, if the gains are deemed immaterial, companies often include such gains and losses in general line items of the income statement—often as a component of selling, general and administrative expenses. As described in Chapter 4, the $30,000 increase in cash is an investing cash inflow in the statement of cash flows, and the $2,000 gain would be subtracted from net income in an indirect-method statement of cash flows from operating activities.

Asset Impairments Property, plant, and equipment assets are reported at their net book values (original cost less accumulated depreciation). This is the case even if fair values of these assets increase subsequent to acquisition. As a result, there can be unrecognized gains hidden in the balance sheet.

However, if fair values of PPE assets subsequently decrease—and it can be determined that the asset value is permanently impaired—then companies must recognize losses on those assets. **Impairment** of PPE assets is determined by comparing the sum of *expected* future (undiscounted) cash flows from the asset with its net book value. If these expected cash flows are greater than net book value, no impairment is deemed to exist. However, if the sum of expected cash flows is less than net book value, the asset is deemed impaired and it is written down to its current fair value (generally, the discounted present value of those expected cash flows). **Exhibit 8.4** depicts this impairment analysis.

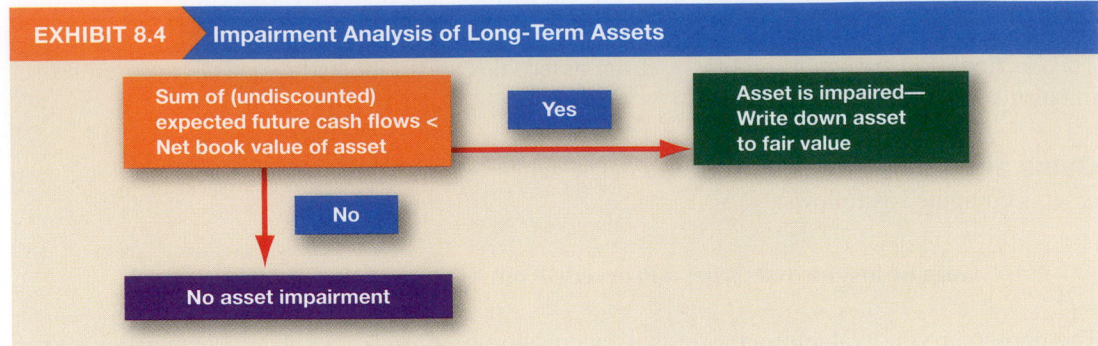

EXHIBIT 8.4   Impairment Analysis of Long-Term Assets

When a company records an impairment charge, assets are reduced by the amount of the write-down and the loss is recognized in the income statement, which reduces current period income. These effects are illustrated in **Exhibit 8.5**. Impairment charges are often included as part of **restructuring costs** along with future costs of workforce reductions. The entry in **Exhibit 8.5** reduces net income, but does not affect current cash flows, so the impairment charges would be added back to net income when reporting an indirect-method cash flows from operating activities. Managers often refer to impairment charges as "noncash" items, though it may be important to remember that they did involve cash when the asset was originally acquired.

EXHIBIT 8.5   Financial Statement Effects of Asset Impairment

Balance Sheet					Income Statement		
Cash Asset	+ Noncash Assets	= Liabilities	+ Contrib. Capital	+ Earned Capital	Revenues -	Expenses	= Net Income
Decrease =				Decrease	-	Increase	= Decrease

Once a depreciable asset is written down, future depreciation charges are reduced by the amount of the write-down. This result occurs because that portion of the asset's cost that is written down is permanently removed from the balance sheet and cannot be subsequently depreciated. It is important to note that management determines if and when to recognize asset impairments. Write-downs of long-term assets are often recognized in connection with a restructuring program.

Analysis of asset write-downs presents two potential challenges:

1. *Insufficient write-down.* Assets sometimes are impaired to a larger degree than is recognized. This situation can arise if management is overly optimistic about future prospects or is reluctant to recognize the full loss in income. Underestimation of an impairment causes current income to be overstated and income in future years to be lower relative to income that would have been reported had the impairment been correctly recorded.

2. *Aggressive write-down.* This *big bath* scenario can arise if income is currently and severely depressed by recognizing a larger impairment charge than the actual costs. Management's view is that the market will not penalize the firm for an extra write-off, and that doing so purges the balance sheet of costs that would otherwise reduce future years' income. This leads to income being overstated for several years after the write-down.

Neither of these cases is condoned under GAAP. Yet, because management is estimating future cash flows for the impairment test and such estimates are difficult to verify, it has some degree of latitude over the timing and amount of the write-off and can use that discretion to manage reported income.

Footnote Disclosure

Procter & Gamble provides the following information in footnote 1 of its 2014 Annual Report to describe its accounting for PPE assets.

Property, plant, and equipment

Property, plant, and equipment is recorded at cost reduced by accumulated depreciation. Depreciation expense is recognized over the assets' estimated useful lives using the straight-line method.

Machinery and equipment includes office furniture and fixtures (15-year life), computer equipment and capitalized software (3- to 5-year lives) and manufacturing equipment (3- to 20-year lives). Buildings are depreciated over an estimated useful life of 40 years. Estimated useful lives are periodically reviewed and, where appropriate, changes are made prospectively. Where certain events or changes in operating conditions occur, asset lives may be adjusted and an impairment assessment may be performed on the recoverability of the carrying amounts.

The note details P&G's depreciation method (straight-line) and the estimated useful lives of various classes of PPE assets. Later in the notes, the company reports "asset-related costs" included in its restructuring charges of $179 million for the year ended June 30, 2014. The company describes these costs as follows:

Asset-related costs

Asset-related costs consist of both asset write-downs and accelerated depreciation. Asset write-downs relate to the establishment of a new fair value basis for assets held-for-sale or disposal. These assets were written down to the lower of their current carrying basis or amounts expected to be realized upon disposal, less minor disposal costs. Charges for accelerated depreciation relate to long-lived assets that will be taken out of service prior to the end of their normal service period. These assets related primarily to manufacturing consolidations and technology standardization. The asset-related charges will not have a significant impact on future depreciation charges.

Based on other disclosures in the statements, most of the assets held for sale noted above are related to the goodwill and other intangible assets of Pet Care, a business Procter & Gamble is in the process of selling.

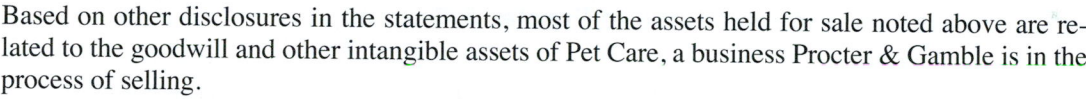

A GLOBAL PERSPECTIVE

International Financial Reporting Standards (IFRS) are very similar to U.S. GAAP in the recognition of asset values when acquired and in the depreciation methods allowed. However, IFRS requires that companies recognize depreciation separately on the significant components of an asset. So, a U.S. company that acquires a building might recognize a single asset and depreciate it over the expected useful life of the building. An IFRS company would be required to recognize a bundle of assets like the structure, the roof, the elevators, the HVAC system, etc. Each of these components would be depreciated separately over its expected useful life, generally producing a more accelerated depreciation expense.

One implication of this difference is that subsequent expenditures might be dealt with differently. The U.S. company that replaces the HVAC system after its expected fifteen-year life would classify the expenditure as a maintenance expense. But the IFRS company would have fully depreciated the original HVAC system, and the new system would be treated as a capital expenditure, creating a new asset.

International Financial Reporting Standards for changes in long-term operating asset values have significant differences from U.S. GAAP. IFRS allows companies to report their property, plant, and equipment on a revalued basis. That is, companies may choose to conduct regular appraisals of their property, plant, and equipment and to adjust their balance sheet amounts to those appraised values. Depreciation expense is also adjusted for changes in values. While this option is allowed under IFRS, it appears that the vast majority of companies use historical cost to account for property, plant, and equipment. (IFRS also has provisions for companies operating in hyperinflationary environments.)

For IFRS companies using historical cost, impairment is a single-step process in which an asset's book value is compared to the larger of its value in use (present value of future cash flows) and its net selling price (fair value less cost to sell). If the book value is higher, an impairment is reported. Unlike U.S. GAAP, if an impairment is subsequently recovered, an IFRS company may increase the asset's value to what it would have been without the prior impairment.

ANALYZING FINANCIAL STATEMENTS

Most companies produce their financial performance with their long-term operating assets like property, plant, and equipment and with their intellectual property. Effective use of these assets represents one of the key components of success for companies. In addition, these assets are acquired with the anticipation that they will provide benefits for an extended period of time. They are often expensive relative to their annual benefit, and most of these assets require replenishment on an ongoing basis.

Analysis Objective

We are trying to gauge the effectiveness of Procter & Gamble's use of its physical productive assets.

Analysis Tool   PPE Turnover (PPET)

$$\text{Turnover (PPET)} = \frac{\text{Sales revenue}}{\text{Average PPE, net}}$$

Applying the PPE Turnover Ratio to Procter & Gamble

$$2012: \frac{\$83,680}{\$20,835} = 4.02$$

$$2013: \frac{\$84,167}{\$21,021.5} = 4.00$$

$$2014: \frac{\$83,062}{\$21,985} = 3.78$$

Guidance   Property, plant, and equipment turnovers vary greatly by industry and are affected by companies' manufacturing strategies, so it is difficult to give specific guidance. In general, a higher ratio is preferred, as it is one significant component of the company's return on assets.

Procter & Gamble in Context

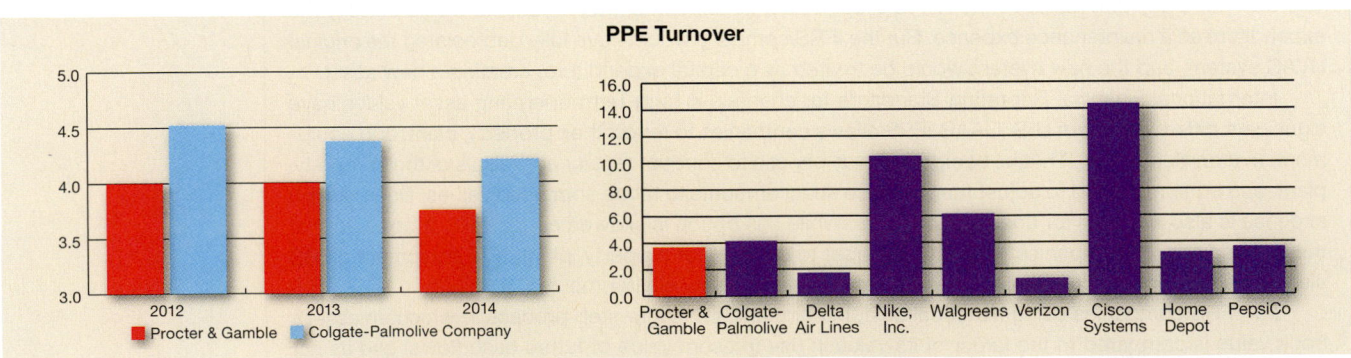

These companies do not have identical fiscal year-ends. Procter & Gamble's year end is June 30, 2014. For the other companies we used financial statements ending as follows: Colgate-Palmolive, Delta, Verizon Communications, and PepsiCo—all December 2014; Nike—May 2014; Walgreens—August 2014; Cisco—July 2014; Home Depot—February 2014.

---

[2] See Christensen, Hans B., and Valeri V. Nikolaev, "Does fair value accounting for non-financial assets pass the market test?" *Review of Accounting Studies*, September 2013.

Takeaways   P&G's fiscal 2014 and 2013 PPET decreased from the value in 2012. Companies prefer that PPET be higher rather than lower, because it implies a lower level of capital investment is required to achieve a given level of sales revenue. P&G's PPET is lower than Colgate-Palmolive, though it is higher than some others in its industry. We can also see that PPET differs considerably by industry—capital-intensive businesses with long-lived assets like Delta Air Lines and Verizon Communications have a low ratio.

Other Considerations   Besides effectiveness of asset usage, PPET depends on a number of factors that affect the denominator and that should be taken into account in interpreting the numbers. First, it reflects the company's manufacturing strategy; a company that outsources its production will have a very high PPET, like Nike. Or, a company that has assets that are more fully depreciated will also report a high PPET. In Chapter 12, we discuss how ratios mixing income statement and balance sheet information can be affected by acquisitions of other companies. Finally, we find in Chapter 10 that there are (at the time of this writing) ways for a company to acquire the use of productive resources that do not appear among its assets (e.g., operating leases), increasing the ratio.

Analysis Objective

We are trying to gauge the age of P&G's long-term tangible operating assets relative to their expected useful lives.

Analysis Tool   Percent Depreciated

$$\text{Percent depreciated} = \frac{\text{Accumulated depreciation}}{\text{Cost of depreciable assets}}$$

Applying the Percent Depreciated Ratio to Procter & Gamble   Accumulated depreciation can be seen in the balance sheet or footnotes. The original cost of depreciable assets can be found in the same places. (See **Exhibit 8.1** for P&G's presentation.) Two types of property, plant, and equipment are not depreciated. Land is one type, and the other is construction in progress. Land is not depreciated because it has an indefinite life, and construction in progress is not depreciated until the constructed asset is placed in service. For P&G, the $44,427 million original cost of property, plant, and equipment includes $893 million for land and $3,114 for construction in progress, which must be removed from the denominator.

$$2012: \quad \frac{\$19,856}{(\$40,233 - \$2,687)} = 54.2\%$$

$$2013: \quad \frac{\$21,346}{(\$43,012 - \$878 - \$3,235)} = 54.9\%$$

$$2014: \quad \frac{\$22,123}{(\$44,427 - \$893 - \$3,114)} = 54.7\%$$

Guidance   Percent depreciated depends on a company's age and on the occurrence of disruptive technological shifts in products and production methods. A new company will have a lower ratio, as will a company that has just made substantial investments in new productive facilities. A high ratio could mean that a company's productive resources are nearing the end of their useful lives and that substantial investments will be required in the near future.[3]

---

[3] Some companies do not provide complete disclosure for this computation. For example, Cisco Systems combines land and buildings in one line item and thus, an external reader of the statements cannot subtract the book value of land from the denominator to compute the percent depreciated accurately.

Procter & Gamble in Context

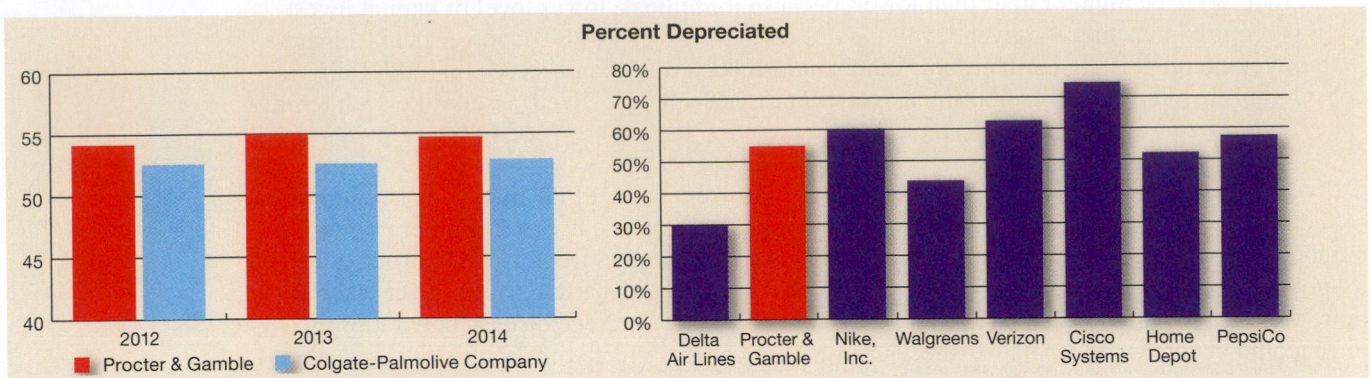

Takeaways   Both Procter & Gamble and Colgate-Palmolive are mature companies experiencing long-term steady growth. They acquire assets on a continuing basis and, as a result, they have some assets that are brand-new and others that are reaching the end of their productive lives. The net result is that the percent depreciated ratio is approximately 50% to 55% for both companies.

Other Considerations   Companies' percent depreciated ratio may differ because they are using different depreciation methods (straight-line or accelerated) or because they have chosen different useful lives for their assets. For instance, one airline depreciates its aircraft over twenty-five years to zero salvage value, while another depreciates its aircraft over fifteen years to ten percent salvage. A percent depreciated ratio of 50% for the first company would mean its average aircraft is 12.5 years old, while the same 50% ratio would imply aircraft that was 8.3 years old for the second company. As a result, it is always advisable to check companies' footnotes to make sure that the ratios are interpreted correctly.

BUSINESS INSIGHT

Federal authorities arrested **WorldCom, Inc.**'s CEO, Bernie Ebbers, and chief financial officer, Scott Sullivan, in August 2002 for allegedly conspiring to alter the telecommunications giant's financial statements to meet analyst expectations. They were accused of *cooking the books* so the company would not show a loss for 2001 and subsequent quarters.

Specifically, WorldCom incurred large costs in anticipation of an increase in Internet-related business that did not materialize. The executives shifted these costs to the balance sheet and recorded them as PPE, thereby inflating current profitability. By capitalizing these costs (moving them from the income statement to the balance sheet), WorldCom was able to disguise these costs as an asset to be allocated as future costs. Contrary to WorldCom's usual practices and prevailing accounting principles, no support existed for capitalization.

Although the WorldCom case also involved alleged fraud, an astute analyst would have suspected something was amiss from analysis of WorldCom's property, plant, and equipment turnover (Sales/Average property, plant, and equipment) as shown below. The decline in turnover reveals that its assets constituted an ever-increasing percent of total sales during 1995 to 2002, by quarter. This finding does not, in itself, imply fraud. It does, however, raise serious questions that should have been answered by WorldCom executives in meetings with analysts.

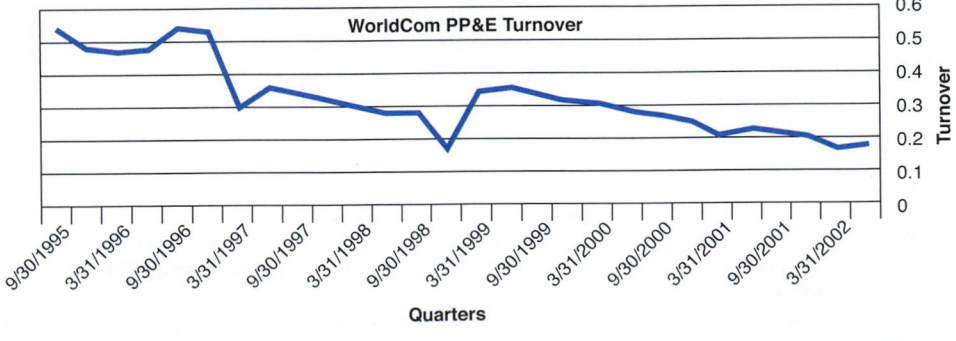

Cash Flow Effects

When cash is involved in the acquisition of plant or equipment, the cash amount is reported as a use of cash in the investment section of the statement of cash flows as discussed in Chapter 4. Any cash received from asset sales is reported as a source of cash. The investing section of Procter & Gamble's 2014 annual report is shown below.

($ millions)	2014	2013	2012
Investing activities			
Capital expenditures	$(3,848)	$(4,008)	$(3,964)
Proceeds from asset sales	570	584	2,893
Acquisitions, net of cash acquired	(24)	(1,145)	(134)
Purchase of available-for-sale investment securities	(568)	(1,605)	—
Proceeds from sales of available-for-sale investment securities	24	—	—
Change in investments	(261)	(121)	112
Total investing activities	$(4,107)	$(6,295)	$(1,093)

In 2014, P&G paid cash of $3,848 million to acquire plant assets and received cash of $570 million on the disposal of plant and equipment. Losses (gains) on these disposal transactions would be added (subtracted) as adjustments in the operating section. Acquisitions of other companies was small in terms of cash outlays in 2014 but in the year ended June 2013 constituted 18% of P&G's net investing activities.

For the Dehning Company delivery truck sale described earlier in this chapter, the investing section of the cash flow statement would show $30,000 of cash proceeds. The gain on the sale would be subtracted from net income in the operating section. No receivable was involved in the sale.

YOU MAKE THE CALL

You are the Division Manager   You are the division manager for a main operating division of your company. You are concerned that a declining PPE turnover is adversely affecting your division's profitability. What specific actions can you take to increase PPE turnover? [Answers on page 395]

MID-CHAPTER REVIEW

On January 2, Lev Company purchases equipment for use in fabrication of a part for one of its key products. The equipment costs $95,000, and its estimated useful life is five years, after which it is expected to be sold for $10,000.

REQUIRED

1. Compute depreciation expense for each year of the equipment's useful life for each of the following depreciation methods:
   a. Straight-line
   b. Double-declining-balance
2. Assume that Lev Company uses the straight-line depreciation method. Show the effects of these entries on the balance sheet and the income statement using the financial statement effects template. Prepare journal entries to record the initial purchase of the equipment on January 2 and the year-end depreciation adjustment on December 31, and post the journal entries to T-accounts.
3. Show how the equipment is reported on Lev's balance sheet at the end of the third year assuming straight-line depreciation.
4. Assume that this is the only depreciable asset the company owns and that it uses straight-line depreciation. Using the depreciation expense computed in 1a and the balance sheet presentation from 3, estimate the percent depreciated for this asset at the end of the third year.

The solution to this review problem can be found on pages 409–410.

LO5 Describe the accounting and reporting for intangible assets.

INTANGIBLE ASSETS

Intangible assets are assets that lack physical substance but provide future benefits to the owner in the form of specific property rights or legal rights. For many companies, these assets have become an important source of competitive advantage and company value.

For financial accounting purposes, intangible assets are classified as either *separately transferable or not separately transferable*. *Separately transferable* intangible assets generally fall into one of two categories. The first category is assets that are the product of contractual or other legal rights. These intangibles include patents, trademarks, copyrights, franchises, license agreements, broadcast rights, mineral rights, and noncompetition agreements. The second category of separately transferable intangible assets includes benefits that are not contractually or legally defined, but can be separated from the company and sold, transferred, or exchanged. Examples include customer lists, unpatented technology, formulas, processes, and databases. There are also intangible assets that are not separately transferable, primarily goodwill. Procter & Gamble reports its intangible assets on its 2014 balance sheet in just two categories ($ in millions): Goodwill $53,704; Trademarks and Other Intangible Assets $30,843. The majority of these assets resulted from the acquisition of **The Gillette Company**.

The issues involved in reporting intangible assets are conceptually similar to those of accounting for property, plant, and equipment. We must first decide which costs to capitalize and then we need to determine how and when those costs will be transferred to the income statement. However, intangible assets often pose a particularly difficult problem for accountants. This problem arises because the benefits provided by these assets are often uncertain and difficult to quantify. In addition, the useful life of an intangible asset is often impossible to estimate with confidence.

As was the case with property, plant, and equipment, intangible assets are either purchased from another individual or company or internally developed. Like PPE assets, the cost of purchased intangible assets is capitalized. Unlike PPE assets, though, we generally do not capitalize the cost of internally developed intangible assets. Research and development (R&D) costs, and the patents and technologies that are created as a result of R&D, serve as useful examples.

Research and Development Costs

R&D activities are a major expenditure for most companies, especially for those in technology and pharmaceutical industries where R&D expenses can exceed 10% of revenues. These expenses include employment costs for R&D personnel, R&D-related contract services, and R&D plant asset costs.

Companies invest millions of dollars in R&D because they expect that the future benefits resulting from these activities will eventually exceed the costs. Successful R&D activities create new products that can be sold and new technologies that can be utilized to create and sustain a competitive advantage. Unfortunately, only a fraction of R&D projects reach commercial production, and it is difficult to predict which projects will be successful. Moreover, it is often difficult to predict when the benefits will be realized, even if the project is successful.

Because of the uncertainty surrounding the benefits of R&D, accounting for R&D activities follows a uniform method—*immediate recognition as an expense*. This approach applies to all R&D costs incurred prior to the start of commercial production, including the salaries and wages of personnel engaged in R&D activities, the cost of materials and supplies, and the equipment and facilities used in the project. Should any of the R&D activities prove successful, the benefits should result in higher net income in future periods. Costs incurred internally to develop new software products do not satisfy the capitalization requirement of providing expected future profits until the technological feasibility of the product is established. Therefore, until the feasibility requirement can be met, these costs are expensed.

If equipment and facilities are purchased for a specific R&D project, and have no other use, their cost is expensed immediately even though their useful life would typically extend beyond the current period. The expensing of R&D equipment and facilities is in stark contrast to the capitalization-and-depreciation of non-R&D plant assets. The expensing of R&D plant assets is mandated unless those assets have alternative future uses (in other R&D projects or otherwise). For example, a general research facility housing multi-use lab equipment should be capitalized and depreciated like any other depreciable asset. However, project-directed research buildings and equipment with no alternate uses must be expensed.

Patents

Successful research and development activity often leads a company to obtain a **patent** for its discoveries. A patent is an exclusive right to produce a product or use a technology. Patents are granted to protect the inventor of the new product or technology by preventing other companies from copying the innovation. The fair value of a patent depends on the commercial success of the product or technology. For example, a patent on the formula for a new drug to treat diabetes could be worth billions of dollars.

If a patent is purchased from the inventor, the purchase price is capitalized and reported in the balance sheet as an intangible asset. On the other hand, if the patent is developed internally, only the legal costs and registration fees are capitalized. The R&D cost to develop the new product or technology is expensed as incurred. This accounting illustrates the marked difference between purchased and internally created intangible assets.

Copyrights

A copyright is an exclusive right granted by the government to an individual author, composer, play writer, or similar individual for the life of the creator plus 70 years. Corporations can also obtain a copyright for varying periods set by law. Copyrights, like patents, can be acquired. The acquisition cost would be capitalized and amortized over the expected remaining economic life.

Trademarks

A **trademark** is a registered name, logo, package design, image, jingle, or slogan that is associated with a product. Many trademarks are easily recognizable, such as the **Nike** "swoosh," the shape of a **Coca-Cola** bottle, **McDonald's** golden arches, and the musical tones played in computer advertisements featuring **Intel** computer chips. Companies spend millions of dollars developing and

---

[4] See Bushee, Brian, "The Influence of Institutional Investors on Myopic R&D Investment Behavior." *Accounting Review*, 1998; Graham, John R., Cam Harvey and Shiva Rajgopal, "The Economic Implications of Corporate Financial Reporting." *Journal of Accounting and Economics*, 2005; and Sloan, Richard and P. Dechow. "Executive Incentives and the Horizon Problem: An Empirical Investigation," *Journal of Accounting and Economics*, 1991, for examples of research on this topic.

[5] See Koh, P.S., and D. M. Reeb. "Missing R&D". *Journal of Accounting and Economics*, Forthcoming.

protecting trademarks and their value is enhanced by advertising programs that increase their recognition. If a trademark is purchased from another company, the purchase price is capitalized. However, the cost of internally developed trademarks is expensed as incurred. Likewise, all advertising costs are expensed immediately, even if the value of a trademark is enhanced by the advertisement. For these reasons, many trademarks are not presented in the balance sheet.

BUSINESS INSIGHT

Trademarks and Patents at P&G Procter & Gamble has acquired many of the products it currently markets to consumers. Others were developed internally. The following paragraph from the Management Discussion and Analysis section of P&G's 2014 annual report emphasizes the importance of these intangible assets to the company.

> *Ability to Achieve Business Plans.* We are a consumer products company and rely on continued demand for our brands and products. To achieve business goals, we must develop and sell products that appeal to consumers and retail trade customers. Our continued success is dependent on innovation with respect to both products and operations and on the continued positive reputations of our brands. This means we must be able to obtain and maintain patents and trademarks and respond to technological advances and patents granted to competition. Our success is also dependent on effective sales, advertising and marketing programs in a more fast-paced and rapidly changing environment.

Franchise Rights

A **franchise** is a contractual agreement that gives a company the right to operate a particular business in an area for a particular period of time. For example, a franchise may give the owner the right to operate a number of fast-food restaurants in a particular geographic region for twenty years. *Operating rights* and *licenses* are similar to franchise rights, except that they are typically granted by government agencies. Most franchise rights are purchased and, as a result, the purchase price should be capitalized and presented as an intangible asset in the balance sheet.

Amortization and Impairment of Identifiable Intangible Assets

When intangible assets are acquired and capitalized, a determination must be made as to whether the asset has a **definite life**. Examples of intangible assets with definite lives include patents and franchise rights. An intangible asset with a definite life must be *amortized* over the expected useful life of the asset. **Amortization** is the systematic allocation of the cost of an intangible asset to the periods benefited, similar to depreciation of tangible assets.

Amortization expense is generally recorded using the straight-line method. The expense is included in the income statement as a component of operating income, and is often included among selling, general and administrative expenses. The cost of the intangible asset is presented in the balance sheet net of accumulated amortization.

Amortization To illustrate, assume that Landsman Company spent $100,000 in early 2016 to purchase a patent. The entry to record the capitalization of this cost follows.

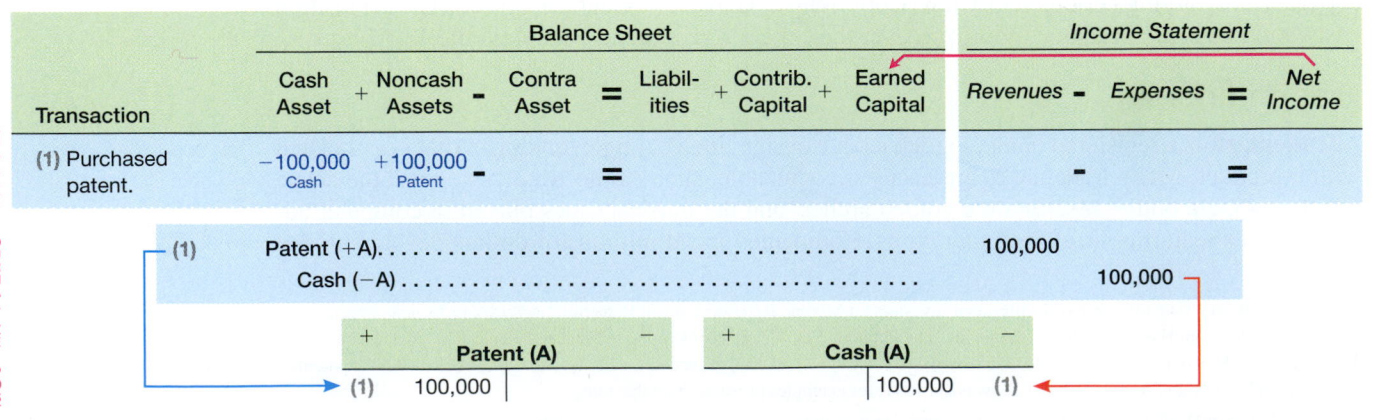

Although the patent had a remaining legal life of 12 years, Landsman estimated that the useful life of the patent was 5 years. Thus the intangible asset has a definite life. The entry to record the annual amortization expense at the end of 2016 follows.

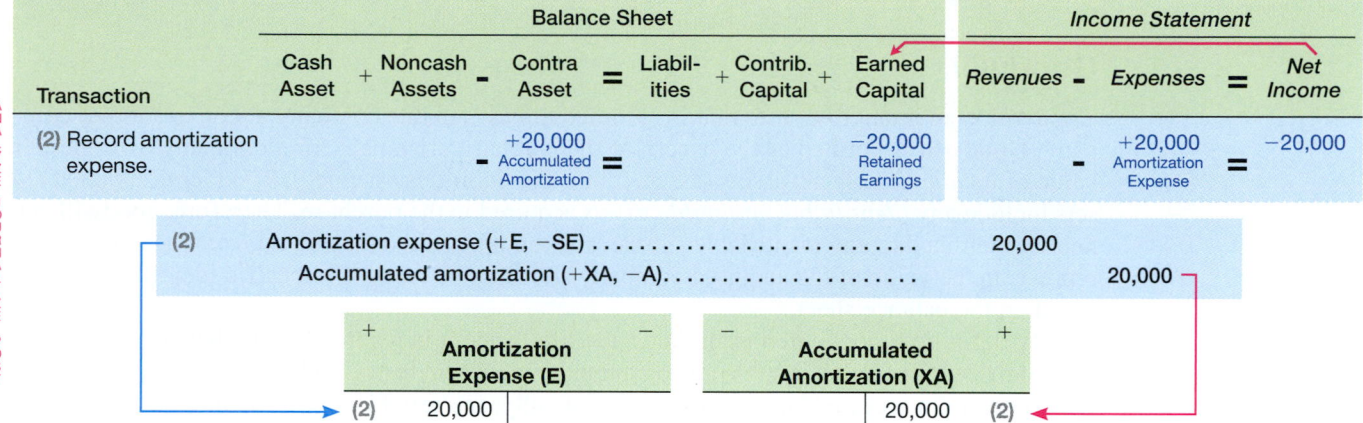

Impairment

Impairment   Some transferable intangible assets, such as some trademarks, have indefinite lives. For these assets, the expected useful life extends far enough into the future that it is impossible for management to estimate a useful life. An intangible asset with an indefinite life should not be amortized until the useful life of the asset can be specified. That is, no expense is recorded until management can reasonably estimate the useful life of the asset.

Although intangible assets with indefinite lives are not subject to amortization, they must be tested annually to determine if their value has been impaired. The impairment test for intangibles is slightly different from the impairment test used to evaluate PPE assets. The intangible asset is impaired if the book value of the asset exceeds its fair value and the write-down is equal to the difference between the book value and the fair value.

To illustrate, assume that Norell Company purchased a trademark in 2014 for $240,000 and determined that the intangible asset had an indefinite life. The entry to record the purchase of the trademark follows.

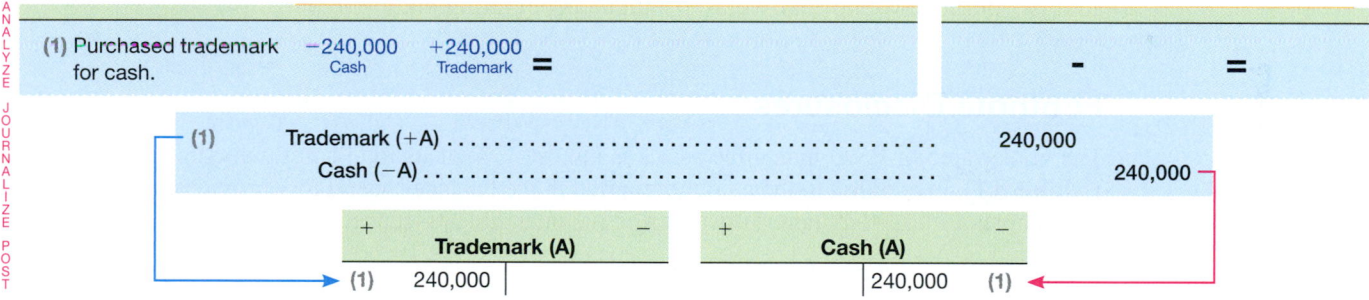

In 2017, changes in regulations caused Norell to conclude that the value of the trademark had been impaired. They estimated the current fair value was $100,000, resulting in a loss of $140,000 ($240,000 – $100,000). The entry to record the impairment of the trademark would be as follows.

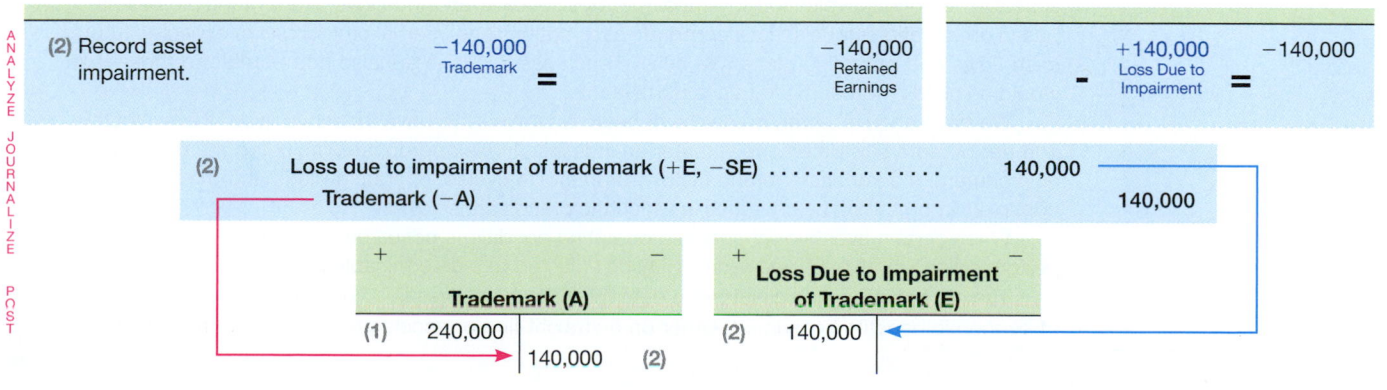

If the value of the trademark subsequently decreases further, additional impairment losses would be recorded. However, increases in the fair value of the asset would not be recorded. Furthermore, if, at any time, Norell determined that the trademark had a definite life, the company would begin amortizing the remaining value over the remaining estimated life.

Goodwill

Goodwill is an intangible asset that is recorded only when one company acquires another company. **Goodwill** is defined as the excess of the purchase price paid for a company over the fair value of its *identifiable* net assets (assets minus the liabilities assumed). The identifiable net assets include any *identifiable intangible assets* acquired in the purchase. Therefore, goodwill can neither be linked to any identifiable source, nor can it be sold or separated from the company. It represents the value of the acquired company above and beyond the specific identifiable assets listed on the balance sheet.

By definition, goodwill has an indefinite life. Once it is recorded in the balance sheet, it is not amortized. Instead, it is subject to an annual impairment test. Goodwill is impaired when the fair value of the acquired business (more specifically, any testable reporting unit) is less than the recorded book value. If this occurs, goodwill is written down to an imputed value. The goodwill write-down (also called a goodwill write-off) results in the immediate transfer of some or all of a company's goodwill book value from the balance sheet to the income statement as an expense. The book value of goodwill is immediately reduced and a corresponding expense is reported in the income statement. Like the impairment write-down of tangible assets, the write-down of goodwill is a discretionary expense whose amount and timing are largely determined by management (with auditor acceptance).

It is commonplace to see goodwill impairment write-downs related to unsuccessful acquisitions, particularly those from the acquisition boom of the late 1990s and the recent recession of 2008–2009. Goodwill write-downs usually represent material amounts. For example, **Time Warner Inc.** wrote off $54 billion of goodwill in the second quarter of 2002, which arose from the $106 billion merger of AOL and Time-Warner. This write-off exceeded the *total revenues* of 483 of the Fortune 500 companies (*Fortune*, 2002). Goodwill write-downs are usually nonrecurring, but are typically reported by companies in income from continuing operations. For analysis purpose we normally classify them as operating and nonrecurring.

Footnote Disclosures

The book value of P&G intangible assets is almost 60% of its total asset value in 2014 (refer to **Exhibit 8.1**). In addition to the amount reported in the balance sheet, P&G provides the following in footnotes 1 and 2 that more fully describes its intangible asset accounting.

Note 1: Summary of Significant Accounting Policies—
Goodwill and Other Intangible Assets

Goodwill and indefinite-lived intangible assets are not amortized, but are evaluated for impairment annually or more often if indicators of a potential impairment are present. Our annual impairment testing of goodwill is performed separately from our impairment testing of indefinite-lived intangible assets. The annual evaluation for impairment of goodwill and indefinite-lived intangible assets is based on valuation models that incorporate assumptions and internal projections of expected future cash flows and operating plans. We believe such assumptions are also comparable to those that would be used by other marketplace participants.

We have acquired brands that have been determined to have indefinite lives. We evaluate a number of factors to determine whether an indefinite life is appropriate, including the competitive environment, market share, brand history, product life cycles, operating plans and the macroeconomic environment of the countries in which the brands are sold.

When certain events or changes in operating conditions occur, an impairment assessment is performed and indefinite-lived assets may be adjusted to a determinable life.

The cost of intangible assets with determinable useful lives is amortized to reflect the pattern of economic benefits consumed, either on a straight-line or accelerated basis over the estimated

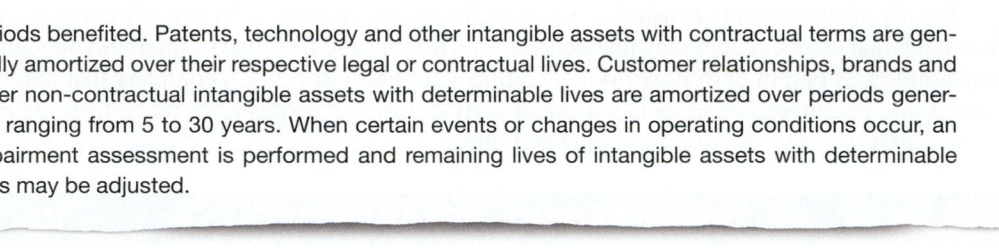

periods benefited. Patents, technology and other intangible assets with contractual terms are generally amortized over their respective legal or contractual lives. Customer relationships, brands and other non-contractual intangible assets with determinable lives are amortized over periods generally ranging from 5 to 30 years. When certain events or changes in operating conditions occur, an impairment assessment is performed and remaining lives of intangible assets with determinable lives may be adjusted.

Procter & Gamble's largest intangible is goodwill ($53.7 billion). The acquisition of Gillette in 2006 resulted in the recognition of $35.3 billion of goodwill, some of which remains as part of goodwill currently on the balance sheet. P&G paid $53.4 billion for Gillette upon acquisition in 2006, and at the time allocated $29.7 billion to other intangibles.

Note 2: Goodwill and Intangible Assets

Identifiable intangible assets were comprised of:

	2014		2013	
	Gross Carrying Amount	Accumulated Depreciation	Gross Carrying Amount	Accumulated Depreciation
Intangible assets with determinable lives				
Brands	$ 4,154	$(2,205)	$ 4,251	$(2,020)
Patents and technology	2,850	(2,082)	2,976	(2,032)
Customer relationships	2,002	(763)	2,118	(703)
Other.	355	(164)	348	(168)
Total	9,361	(5,214)	9,693	(4,923)
Brands with indefinite lives. . . .	26,696	—	26,802	—
Total	$36,057	$(5,214)	$36,495	$(4,923)

There are two observations that we can make from the above disclosures. First, P&G has purchased a significant amount of intangible assets by acquiring other companies. We can infer this from the large amount of goodwill assets reported in the balance sheet ($53.7 billion). Second, most of P&G's identifiable intangible assets are trademarks and most have indefinite lives. Hence, we might expect that the amount of amortization expense in any given year would be small, as indicated by the total in the above table. However, goodwill impairment write-offs could be substantial in any given year.

Analysis Implications

Because internally generated intangible assets are not capitalized, an important component of a company's assets is potentially hidden from users of the financial statements. Moreover, differential treatment of purchased and internally created assets makes it difficult to compare companies. If one company generates its patents and trademarks internally, while another company purchases these intangibles, their balance sheets can differ dramatically, even if the two companies are otherwise very similar.

LO6 Analyze the effects of tangible and intangible assets on key performance measures.

These hidden intangible assets can distort our analysis of the financial statements. For example, when a company expenses R&D costs, especially R&D equipment and facilities that can potentially benefit more than one period, both the income statement and balance sheet are distorted. Net income, assets, and stockholders' equity are all understated.

The income statement effects may be small if a company regularly purchases R&D assets and the amount of purchases is relatively constant from year to year. Specifically, after the average useful life is reached, say in 5 to 10 years, the expensing of current-year purchases will be approximately the same as the depreciation that would have been reported had the assets been capitalized. Thus, the income statement effect is mitigated. However, the recorded assets and equity are still understated. This accounting produces an upward bias in asset turnover ratios and ROE.

Finally, the statement of cash flows is also affected by the manner in which a company acquires its intellectual assets. A company that generates its patents and trademarks internally recognizes the expenditures as part of cash flow from operating activities. However, a company that purchases its patents and trademarks from an independent party or through acquisitions recognizes the expenditures as part of cash flow from investing activities.

A GLOBAL PERSPECTIVE

Under International Financial Reporting Standards, development costs can be capitalized as intangible assets when specific criteria are met. For instance, the company must be able to demonstrate that it has the ability and the intention to complete the development process and to produce an intangible asset that will generate future benefits through use or sale.

Here is an example from GlaxoSmithKline plc's footnotes:

Research and development

Research and development expenditure is charged to the income statement in the period in which it is incurred. Development expenditure is capitalised when the criteria for recognising an asset are met, usually when a regulatory filing has been made in a major market and approval is considered highly probable. Property, plant, and equipment used for research and development is capitalised and depreciated in accordance with the Group's policy.

Under IFRS, similar to under U.S. GAAP, goodwill must be periodically evaluated for impairment. The overall concepts are very similar between IFRS and GAAP but the details differ. For example, under IFRS companies are required to compare the recoverable amount (defined as the higher of the fair value or value-in-use) of a cash-generating unit to the carrying value of that unit to determine an impairment loss. Just as under U.S. GAAP, once impaired, goodwill cannot be revalued upward. Although, note that this is different from the treatment of PPE under IFRS, as discussed earlier in the chapter.

CHAPTER-END REVIEW

In 2016, Bowen Company's R&D department developed a new production process that significantly reduced the time and cost required to manufacture its product. R&D costs were $120,000. The process was patented on July 1, 2016. Legal costs and fees to acquire the patent totalled $12,500. Bowen estimated the useful life of the patent at 10 years.

On July 1, 2018, Bowen sold the nonexclusive right to use the new process to Kennedy Company for $90,000. Because Bowen retained the patent, the agreement allows Kennedy to use, but not sell, the new technology for a period of 5 years. Both Bowen Company and Kennedy Company have December 31 fiscal years.

On July 1, 2020, another competitor obtained a patent on a new process that made Bowen's patent obsolete.

Required

1. How should Bowen Company account for the R&D costs and legal costs incurred to obtain the patent? Show the effects of these entries using the financial statement effects template, prepare the appropriate journal entries necessary to account for the costs incurred in 2016, and post the entries to T-accounts.

2. What amount of amortization expense would Bowen record each year? Show the effects of these transactions using the financial statement effects template, prepare a journal entry to record amortization expense on December 31, 2016, and post the entries to T-accounts.

3. How would Kennedy Company record the acquisition of the rights to use the new technology? Show the effects of this transaction using the financial statement effects template, prepare a journal entry to record the purchase of the technology rights, and post the entry to T-accounts.

4. What effect would the new patent registered by the other competitor have on Bowen Company? On Kennedy Company? Show the effects of this transaction using the financial statement effects template, prepare a journal entry to record the impairment loss for Kennedy Company, and post the entry to T-accounts.

The solution to this review problem can be found on pages 410–411.

SUMMARY

Describe and distinguish between tangible and intangible assets. (p. 374)   **LO1**

- Tangible assets, including land, buildings, machinery, and equipment are assets with physical substance and are usually classified as property, plant, and equipment.
- Intangible assets are long-term assets lacking in physical substance, such as patents, trademarks, franchise rights and goodwill.

Determine which costs to capitalize and report as assets and which costs to expense. (p. 375)   **LO2**

- All costs incurred to acquire an asset and prepare it for its intended use should be capitalized and reported in the balance sheet.
- The cost of self-constructed assets should include all costs incurred during construction, including the interest cost of financing the construction.

Apply different depreciation methods to allocate the cost of assets over time. (p. 377)   **LO3**

- Depreciation methods generally fall into three categories:
  (1) Straight-line depreciation
  (2) Accelerated depreciation, such as the double-declining-balance method
  (3) Units-of-production method

Determine the effects of asset sales and impairments on financial statements. (p. 381)   **LO4**

- The sale of a long-term asset will result in a gain or loss if the proceeds from the sale are greater than or less than the book value of the asset.
- If the expected benefits (undiscounted cash flows) derived from an asset fall below its book value, the asset is impaired and should be written down to fair value.

Describe the accounting and reporting for intangible assets. (p. 388)   **LO5**

- For the most part, internally generated intangible assets are not recognized in the balance sheet.
- Intangible assets purchased from other companies are capitalized and presented separately in the balance sheet.
- Intangible assets with definite lives are amortized using the straight-line method.
- Intangible assets with indefinite lives are not amortized.

Analyze the effects of tangible and intangible assets on key performance measures. (p. 393)   **LO6**

- PPE turnover and long-term asset turnover ratios provide insights into the capital intensity of a company and how efficiently the company is utilizing these investments.
- The ratio of accumulated depreciation divided by the cost of depreciable assets measures the percent depreciated.

GUIDANCE ANSWERS . . . YOU MAKE THE CALL

You are the Company Accountant   Any cost that is necessary in order to bring an asset into service should be capitalized as a part of the cost of the asset. In this case, your company cannot build an office building on this property until the oil well is properly capped. Therefore, the $40,000 cost of capping the oil well should be capitalized as part of the cost of the land.

You are the Division Manager   To increase PPE turnover one must either increase sales or reduce PPE assets. The first step is to identify unproductive or inefficiently utilized assets. Unnecessary assets can be sold, and some processes can be outsourced. Also, by reducing down time, effective maintenance practices will increase asset productivity.

KEY RATIOS

$$\text{PPE Turnover (PPET)} = \frac{\text{Sales revenue}}{\text{Average PP \& E, net}} \qquad \text{Percent depreciated} = \frac{\text{Accumulated depreciation}}{\text{Cost of depreciable asset}}$$

KEY TERMS

Accelerated depreciation (p. 378)
Accumulated depreciation (p. 376)
Amortization (p. 390)
Book value (BV) (p. 378)
Capital expenditures (p. 375)
Capitalized (p. 374)
Capitalized interest (p. 376)
Definite life (p. 390)
Depletion (p. 380)

Depreciation (p. 376)
Depreciation base (p. 377)
Depreciation rate (p. 378)
Double-declining-balance (DDB) method (p. 378)
Franchise (p. 390)
Goodwill (p. 392)
Impairment (p. 381)
Intangible assets (p. 374)
Patent (p. 389)

Residual (or salvage) value (p. 377)
Restructuring costs (p. 382)
Straight-line method (p. 378)
Straight-line method (SL) (p. 378)
Tangible assets (p. 374)
Trademark (p. 389)
Units-of-production method (p. 379)
Useful life (p. 377)
Wasting assets (p. 380)

Assignments with the 🔴 logo in the margin are available in 𝓶𝔂BusinessCourse.
See the Preface of the book for details.

MULTIPLE CHOICE

1. Burgstahler Corporation bought a lot to construct a new corporate office building. An older building on the lot was razed immediately so that the office building could be constructed. The cost of razing the older building should be
   a. recorded as part of the cost of the land.
   b. written off as a loss in the year of purchase.
   c. written off as an extraordinary item in the year of purchase.
   d. recorded as part of the cost of the new building.

2. The purpose of recording periodic depreciation of long-term PPE assets is to
   a. report declining asset values on the balance sheet.
   b. allocate asset costs over the periods benefited by use of the assets.
   c. account for costs to reflect the change in general price levels.
   d. set aside funds to replace assets when their economic usefulness expires.

3. When the estimate of an asset's useful life is changed,
   a. depreciation expense for all past periods must be recalculated.
   b. there is no change in the amount of depreciation expense recorded for future years.
   c. only depreciation expense for current and future years is affected.
   d. only depreciation expense in the current year is affected.

4. If the sale of a depreciable asset results in a loss, the proceeds from the sale were
   a. less than current fair value.
   b. greater than cost.
   c. greater than book value.
   d. less than book value.

5. Which of the following principles best describes the current method of accounting for research and development costs?
   a. Revenue recognition method
   b. Systematic and rational allocation
   c. Immediate recognition as an expense
   d. Income tax minimization

6. Goodwill should be recorded in the balance sheet as an intangible asset only when
   a. it is sold to another company.
   b. it is acquired through the purchase of another business.
   c. a company reports above-normal earnings for five or more consecutive years.
   d. it can be established that a definite benefit or advantage has resulted from some item such as an excellent reputation for service.

QUESTIONS

Q8-1. How should companies account for costs, such as maintenance or improvements, which are incurred after an asset is acquired?

Q8-2. What is the effect of capitalized interest on the income statement in the period that an asset is constructed? What is the effect in future periods?

Q8-3. Why is the recognition of depreciation expense necessary for proper expense recognition?

Q8-4. Why do companies use accelerated depreciation for income tax purposes, when the total depreciation taken over the asset's useful life is identical to straight-line depreciation?

Q8-5. How should a company treat a change in an asset's estimated useful life or residual value? Which period(s)—past, present, or future—is affected by this change?

Q8-6. What factors determine the gain or loss from the sale of a long-term operating asset?

Q8-7. When is a PPE asset considered to be impaired? How is the impairment loss determined?

Q8-8. What is the proper accounting treatment for research and development costs? Why are R&D costs not capitalized under GAAP?

Q8-9. Why are some intangible assets amortized while others are not? What is meant by an intangible asset with an "indefinite life"?

Q8-10. Under what circumstances should a company report goodwill in its balance sheet? What is the effect of goodwill on the income statement?

MINI EXERCISES

M8-11. Determining Whether to Capitalize or Expense   **LO2**

For each of the following items, indicate whether the cost should be capitalized or expensed immediately:

a. Paid $1,200 for routine maintenance of machinery

b. Paid $5,400 to rent equipment for two years

c. Paid $2,000 to equip the production line with new instruments that measure quality

d. Paid $20,000 to repair the roof on the building

e. Paid $1,600 to refurbish a machine, thereby extending its useful life

f. Purchased a patent for $5,000

M8-12. Computing Depreciation Under Straight-Line and Double-Declining-Balance   **LO3**

A delivery van costing $18,000 is expected to have a $1,500 salvage value at the end of its useful life of 5 years. Assume that the truck was purchased on January 1, 2016. Compute the depreciation expense for 2017 (its second year) under each of the following depreciation methods:

a. Straight-line

b. Double-declining-balance

M8-13. Computing Depreciation Under Alternative Methods   **LO3**

Equipment costing $130,000 is expected to have a residual value of $10,000 at the end of its six-year useful life. The equipment is metered so that the number of units processed is counted. The equipment is designed to process 1,000,000 units in its lifetime. In 2016 and 2017, the equipment processed 180,000 units and 140,000 units respectively. Calculate the depreciation expense for 2016 and 2017 using each of the following methods:

a. Straight-line

b. Double-declining-balance

c. Units of production

M8-14. Recording the Sale of PPE Assets   **LO4**

As part of a renovation of its showroom, O'Keefe Auto Dealership sold furniture and fixtures that were eight years old for $3,500 in cash. The assets had been purchased for $40,000 and had been depreciated using the straight-line method with no residual value and a useful life of ten years.

a. Prepare a journal entry to record this transaction.

b. Show how the sale of the furniture and fixtures affects the balance sheet and income statement using the financial statement effects template.

LO4

M8-15.   Recording the Sale of PPE Assets

Gaver Company sold machinery that had originally cost $75,000 for $25,000 in cash. The machinery was three years old and had been depreciated using the double-declining-balance method assuming a five-year useful life and a residual value of $5,000.

a.   Prepare a journal entry to record this sale.

b.   Using the financial statement effects template, show how the sale of the machinery affects the balance sheet and income statement.

LO3

M8-16.   Computing Depreciation Under Straight-Line and Double-Declining-Balance for Partial Years

A machine costing $145,800 is purchased on May 1, 2016. The machine is expected to be obsolete after three years (36 months) and, thereafter, no longer useful to the company. The estimated salvage value is $5,400. Compute depreciation expense for both 2016 and 2017 under each of the following depreciation methods:

a.   Straight-line

b.   Double-declining-balance

LO1, 2, 5

Siemens AG
NYSE :: SI

M8-17.   Accounting for Research and Development Under IFRS

The following information on **Siemens AG**'s treatment of research and development is extracted from its 2014 financial statements. Siemens AG is an integrated technology company with activities in the fields of industry, energy and healthcare. The company is incorporated under the laws of Germany and reports using International Financial Reporting Standards (IFRS).

Research and development costs—Costs of research activities undertaken with the prospect of gaining new scientific or technical knowledge and understanding are expensed as incurred.

Costs for development activities, whereby research findings are applied to a plan or design for the production of new or substantially improved products and processes, are capitalized if (1) development costs can be measured reliably, the product or process is (2) technically and (3) commercially feasible, (4) future economic benefits are probable and (5) Siemens intends, and (6) has sufficient resources, to complete development and to use or sell the asset. The costs capitalized include the cost of materials, direct labour and other directly attributable expenditure that serves to prepare the asset for use. Such capitalized costs are included in line item Other intangible assets as software and other internally generated intangible assets. Other development costs are expensed as incurred. Capitalized development costs are stated at cost less accumulated amortization and impairment losses with an amortization period of generally three to five years.

a.   How does the reporting under IFRS differ from reporting under U.S. GAAP for research and development?

b.   At year-end September 30, 2014 Siemens had a gross carrying amount of Other Intangible Assets of 10.8 billion Euros and accumulated amortization and impairment related to those assets of 6.3 billion Euros. Should the amounts capitalized be tested annually for impairment?

LO3

M8-18.   Computing Double-Declining-Balance Depreciation

DeFond Company purchased equipment for $50,000. For each of the following sets of assumptions, prepare a depreciation schedule (all years) for this equipment assuming that DeFond uses the double-declining-balance depreciation method.

Useful life	Residual value
a. Four years	$8,000
b. Five years	$3,000
c. Ten years	$1,000

LO3

M8-19.   Computing and Recording Depletion Expense

The Nelson Oil Company estimated that the oil reserve that it acquired in 2016 would produce 4 million barrels of oil. The company extracted 300,000 barrels the first year, 500,000 barrels in 2017, and 600,000 barrels in 2018. Nelson paid $32,000,000 for the oil reserve.

a.   Compute the depletion expense for each year—2016, 2017, and 2018.

b.   Prepare the journal entries to record (i) the acquisition of the oil reserve, and (ii) the depletion for 2016.

c.   Open T-accounts and post the entries from part b in the accounts.

LO6

Texas Instruments
Incorporated
NYSE :: TXN

Intel Corporation
NASDAQ :: INTC

M8-20.   Computing and Comparing PPE Turnover for Two Companies

Texas Instruments Incorporated and **Intel Corporation** report the following information:

($ millions)	Texas Instruments		Intel Corp	
	Sales	PPE, net	Sales	PPE, net
2014	$13,045	$2,840	$55,870	$33,238
2013	12,205	3,399	52,708	31,428

a. Compute the 2014 PPE turnover for both companies. Comment on any difference you observe.
b. Discuss ways in which high-tech manufacturing companies like these can increase their PPE turnover.

M8-21. Assessing Research and Development Expenses

LO5, 6

Abbott Laboratories reports the following income statement (in partial form):

Abbott Laboratories
NYSE :: ABT

Year Ended December 31 ($ millions)	2014
Net sales.	$20,247
Cost of products sold.	9,218
Amortization of intangible assets	555
Research and development*	1,345
Selling, general and administrative	6,530
Total operating cost and expenses	17,648
Operating earnings.	$ 2,599

* including acquired in-process and collaborations R&D

a. Compute the percent of net sales that Abbott Laboratories spends on research and development (R&D). How would you assess the appropriateness of its R&D expense level?
b. Using the financial statement effects template, describe how the accounting for R&D expenditures affects Abbot Laboratories' balance sheet and income statement.

EXERCISES

E8-22. Recording Asset Acquisition, Depreciation, and Disposal

LO2, 3, 4

On January 2, 2016, Verdi Company acquired a machine for $85,000. In addition to the purchase price, Verdi spent $2,000 for shipping and installation, and $2,500 to calibrate the machine prior to use. The company estimates that the machine has a useful life of five years and residual value of $7,000.

a. Prepare journal entries to record the acquisition costs.
b. Calculate the annual depreciation expense using straight-line depreciation and prepare a journal entry to record depreciation expense for 2016.
c. On December 31, 2019, Verdi sold the machine to another company for $12,000. Prepare the necessary journal entry to record the sale.

E8-23. Computing Straight-Line and Double-Declining-Balance Depreciation

LO3

On January 2, Haskins Company purchases a laser cutting machine for use in fabrication of a part for one of its key products. The machine cost $80,000, and its estimated useful life is five years, after which the expected salvage value is $5,000. Compute depreciation expense for each year of the machine's useful life under each of the following depreciation methods:

a. Straight-line
b. Double-declining-balance

E8-24. Computing Depreciation, Asset Book Value, and Gain or Loss on Asset Sale

LO3, 4

Sloan Company uses its own executive charter plane that originally cost $800,000. It has recorded straight-line depreciation on the plane for six full years, with an $80,000 expected salvage value at the end of its estimated 10-year useful life. Sloan disposes of the plane at the end of the sixth year.

a. At the disposal date, what is the (1) accumulated depreciation and (2) net book value of the plane?
b. Prepare a journal entry to record the disposal of the plane assuming that the sales price is
1. Cash equal to the book value of the plane.
2. $195,000 cash.
3. $600,000 cash.

LO3

E8-25.   Computing Straight-Line and Double-Declining-Balance Depreciation

On January 2, 2016, Dechow Company purchases a machine to help manufacture a part for one of its key products. The machine cost $218,700 and is estimated to have a useful life of six years, with an expected salvage value of $23,400.

Compute each year's depreciation expense for 2016 and 2017 for each of the following depreciation methods.

a.   Straight-line
b.   Double-declining-balance

LO3, 4

E8-26.   Computing Depreciation, Asset Book Value, and Gain or Loss on Asset Sale

Palepu Company owns and operates a delivery van that originally cost $27,200. Straight-line depreciation on the van has been recorded for three years, with a $2,000 expected salvage value at the end of its estimated six-year useful life. Depreciation was last recorded at the end of the third year, at which time Palepu disposes of this van.

a.   Compute the net book value of the van on the sale date.
b.   Compute the gain or loss on sale of the van if its sales price is for:
  1.   Cash equal to book value of van.
  2. $15,000 cash.
  3. $12,000 cash.

LO3

E8-27.   Computing Depreciation and Accounting for a Change of Estimate

Lambert Company acquired machinery costing $110,000 on January 2, 2016. At that time, Lambert estimated that the useful life of the equipment was 6 years and that the residual value would be $15,000 at the end of its useful life. Compute depreciation expense for this asset for 2016, 2017, and 2018 using the

a.   straight-line method.
b.   double-declining-balance method.
c.   Assume that on January 2, 2018, Lambert revised its estimate of the useful life to 7 years and changed its estimate of the residual value to $10,000. What effect would this have on depreciation expense in 2018 for each of the above depreciation methods?

LO3

E8-28.   Computing Depreciation and Accounting for a Change of Estimate

In January 2016, Rankine Company paid $8,500,000 for land and a building. An appraisal estimated that the land had a fair value of $2,500,000 and the building was worth $6,000,000. Rankine estimated that the useful life of the building was 30 years, with no residual value.

a.   Calculate annual depreciation expense using the straight-line method.
b.   Calculate depreciation for 2016 and 2017 using the double-declining-balance method.
c.   Assume that in 2018, Rankine changed its estimate of the useful life of the building to 25 years. If the company is using the double-declining-balance method of depreciation, what amount of depreciation expense would Rankine record in 2018?

LO6

E8-29.   Estimating the Percent Depreciated

The property and equipment footnote from the **Deere & Company** balance sheet follows ($ millions):

PROPERTY AND DEPRECIATION

A summary of property and equipment at October 31, 2014, in millions of dollars follows:

	2014
Land	$ 124
Buildings and building equipment	3,108
Machinery and equipment	5,089
Dies, patterns, tools, etc.	1,552
All other	926
Construction in progress	530
Total at cost	11,329
Less accumulated depreciation	5,751
Property and equipment—net	$ 5,578

During 2014, the company reported $696 million of depreciation expense.

Estimate the percent depreciated of Deere's depreciable assets. How do you interpret this figure?

E8-30. Computing and Evaluating Receivables, Inventory, and PPE Turnovers

3M Company reports the following financial statement amounts in its 10-K report:

($ millions)	Sales	Cost of Sales	Receivables	Inventories	PPE, net
2014	$31,821	$16,447	$4,238	$3,706	$8,489
2013	30,871	16,106	4,253	3,864	8,652
2012	29,904	15,685	4,061	3,837	8,378

a. Compute the receivables, inventory, and PPE turnover ratios for both 2014 and 2013. (Receivables turnover and inventory turnover are discussed in Chapters 6 and 7, respectively.)

b. What changes are evident in the turnover rates of 3M for these years? Discuss ways in which a company such as 3M can improve its turnover within each of these three areas.

E8-31. Identifying and Accounting for Intangible Assets

On the first day of 2016, Holthausen Company acquired the assets of Leftwich Company including several intangible assets. These include a patent on Leftwich's primary product, a device called a plentiscope. Leftwich carried the patent on its books for $1,500, but Holthausen believes that the fair value is $200,000. The patent expires in seven years, but competitors can be expected to develop competing patents within three years. Holthausen believes that, with expected technological improvements, the product is marketable for at least 20 years.

The registration of the trademark for the Leftwich name is scheduled to expire in 15 years. However, the Leftwich brand name, which Holthausen believes is worth $500,000, could be applied to related products for many years beyond that.

As part of the acquisition, Leftwich's principal researcher left the company. As part of the acquisition, he signed a five-year noncompetition agreement that prevents him from developing competing products. Holthausen paid the scientist $300,000 to sign the agreement.

a. What amount should be capitalized for each of the identifiable intangible assets?

b. What amount of amortization expense should Holthausen record in 2016 for each asset?

E8-32. Computing and Recording Depletion Expense

In 2016, Eldenburg Mining Company purchased land for $7,200,000 that had a natural resource reserve estimated to be 500,000 tons. Development and road construction costs on the land were $420,000, and a building was constructed at a cost of $50,000. When the natural resources are completely extracted, the land has an estimated residual value of $1,200,000. In addition, the cost to restore the property to comply with environmental regulations is estimated to be $800,000. Production in 2016 and 2017 was 60,000 tons and 85,000 tons, respectively.

a. Compute the depletion charge for 2016 and 2017. (You should include depreciation on the building, if any, as part of the depletion charge.)

b. Prepare a journal entry to record each year's depletion expense as determined in part a.

E8-33. Computing and Interpreting Percent Depreciated and PPE Turnover

The following footnote is from Note 4 to the 2011 10-K of **Adams Golf, Inc.**, a Texas-based manufacturer of golf equipment ($ thousands):

Property and Equipment, net		
Property and equipment consist of the following at December 31	2011	2010
Equipment	$ 2,691	$ 2,629
Computers and software	8,011	7,854
Furniture and fixtures	1,117	993
Leaseholds improvements	447	328
Accumulated depreciation and amortization	(11,320)	(10,925)
	$ 946	$ 879

a. Calculate the percent depreciated ratio for each year.

b. Sales revenue totaled $96,504 in 2011 (all values are in $ thousands). Calculate the PPE turnover ratio (PPET).

c. Comment on these ratios. Do you notice anything unusual?

LO5

Callaway Golf Co.
NYSE :: ELY

Apple, Inc.
NASDAQ :: AAPL

Samsung Electronics
Co., Ltd
KS :: 005930

Intel Corporation
NASDAQ :: INTC

Microsoft Corporation
NASDAQ :: MSFT

Baxter International, Inc.
NYSE :: BAX

Pfizer, Inc.
NYSE :: PFE

Merck & Co., Inc
NYSE :: MRK

Monsanto Co.
NYSE :: MON

Syngenta AG
NYSE :: SYT

Deere & Co.
NYSE :: DE

E8-34. **Evaluating R&D Expenditures of Companies**

R&D intensity is measured by the ratio of research and development expense to sales revenue. The following table compares the R&D intensity for various companies.

Company	R&D Intensity
Callaway Golf Co.	3.53%
Samsung Electronics Co., Ltd (Korea)	6.46%
Apple, Inc.	3.30%
Intel Corporation	20.65%
Microsoft Corporation	13.11%
Baxter International, Inc.	8.52%
Pfizer, Inc.	16.90%
Merck & Co., Inc.	17.00%
Monsanto Co.	10.88%
Syngenta AG (Switzerland)	9.45%
Deere & Company	4.03%

a. Comment on the differences among these companies. To what extent are the differences related to industry affiliation?

b. What other factors (besides industry affiliation) might determine a company's R&D intensity?

LO4

E8-35. **Computing and Assessing Plant Asset Impairment**

Zeibart Company purchases equipment for $225,000 on July 1, 2012, with an estimated useful life of 10 years and expected salvage value of $25,000. Straight-line depreciation is used. On July 1, 2016, economic factors cause the fair value of the equipment to decline to $90,000. On this date, Zeibart examines the equipment for impairment and estimates $125,000 in future cash inflows related to use of this equipment.

a. Is the equipment impaired at July 1, 2016? Explain.

b. If the equipment is impaired on July 1, 2016, compute the impairment loss and prepare a journal entry to record the loss.

c. What amount of depreciation expense would Zeibart record for the 12 months from July 1, 2016 through June 30, 2017? Prepare a journal entry to record this depreciation expense. (*Hint:* Assume no change in salvage value.)

d. Using the financial statement effects template, show how the entries in parts b and c affect Zeibart Company's balance sheet and income statement.

PROBLEMS

LO4

Golden Enterprises, Inc.
NASDAQ :: GLDC

P8-36. **Computing and Recording Gain or Loss on Asset Sale**

The following information was provided in the 2014 10-K report of **Golden Enterprises, Inc.**

Note 10: Land, Buildings and Equipment

	May 30, 2014	May 31, 2013
Property, plant, and equipment, Gross, Total	$95,174,198	$93,022,443
Less: Accumulated depreciation	69,502,854	65,927,389
Property, plant, and equipment, Net, Total	$25,671,344	$27,095,054

The company's statement of cash flows, including the reconciliation of net income to cash from operations, provided the following information for the year ended May 30, 2014:

- Depreciation expense was $3,778,563.
- Purchases of property, plant, and equipment were $2,380,287.
- Proceeds from the sale of property, plant, and equipment were $48,125.

REQUIRED

Using this information, prepare a journal entry to record the sale of property, plant, and equipment.

LO5

Agilent Technologies,
Inc.
NYSE :: A

Hewlett-Packard
Company
NYSE :: HPQ

P8-37. **Analyzing and Assessing Research and Development Expenses**

Agilent Technologies, Inc., the high-tech spin-off from **Hewlett-Packard Company**, reports the following operating profit for 2014 in its 10-K ($ millions):

Net revenue	
Products.	$5,686
Services and other.	1,295
Total net revenue.	6,981
Costs and expenses	
Cost of products	2,673
Cost of services and other.	715
Total costs.	3,388
Research and development.	719
Selling, general and administrative	2,043
Total costs and expenses	6,150
Income from operations.	$ 831

REQUIRED

a. What percentage of its total net revenue is Agilent spending on research and development?

b. How are its balance sheet and income statement affected by the accounting for R&D costs?

c. In 2003, Agilent's spending on R&D was $1,051 million—17.4% of its total net revenue. What are some possible ways that the company might have reduced its R&D intensity from 2003 to 2014? What are some of the possible implications for the company?

P8-38. **Analyzing PPE Accounts and Recording PPE Transactions, Including Discontinued Operations**

LO4

Target Corporation
NYSE :: TGT

The 2014 and 2013 income statements and balance sheets (asset section only) for **Target Corporation** follow, along with its footnote describing Target's accounting for property and equipment. Target's cash flow statement for fiscal 2014 reported capital expenditures of $1,786 million and disposal proceeds for property and equipment of $95 million. No gain or loss was reported on property and equipment disposals. In addition, Target acquired property and equipment through non-cash acquisitions not reported on the statement of cash flows. *(Note some numbers were added to make the disclosure complete.)*

Consolidated Statements of Operations			
($ millions)	2014	2013	2012
Sales.	$72,618	$71,279	$71,960
Credit card revenues	—	—	1,341
Total revenues	72,618	71,279	73,301
Cost of sales.	51,278	50,039	50,568
Selling, general and administrative expenses	14,676	14,465	14,643
Credit card expenses	—	—	467
Depreciation and amortization.	2,129	1,996	2,044
Gain on receivables transaction.	—	(391)	(161)
Earnings from continuing operations before interest expense and income taxes.	4,535	5,170	5,740
Net interest expense	882	1,049	684
Earnings from continuing operations before income taxes	3,653	4,121	5,056
Provision for income taxes.	1,204	1,427	1,741
Net earnings from continuing operations.	2,449	2,694	3,315
Discontinued operations, net of tax.	(4,085)	(723)	(316)
Net (loss)/earnings	$ (1,636)	$ 1,971	$ 2,999

Consolidated Statements of Financial Position (Asset Section Only)		
($ millions)	January 31, 2015	February 1, 2014
Assets		
Cash and cash equivalents, including short-term investments of $1,520 and $3	$ 2,210	$ 670
Inventory	8,790	8,278
Assets of discontinued operations	1,333	793
Other current assets	1,754	1,832
Total current assets	14,087	11,573
Property and equipment		
Land	6,127	6,143
Buildings and improvements	26,614	25,984
Fixtures and equipment	5,346	5,199
Computer hardware and software	2,553	2,395
Construction-in-progress	424	757
Accumulated depreciation	(15,106)	(14,066)
Property and equipment, net	25,958	26,412
Noncurrent assets of discontinued operations	442	5,461
Other noncurrent assets	917	1,107
Total assets	$41,404	$44,553

12. Property and Equipment

Property and equipment is depreciated using the straight-line method over estimated useful lives or lease terms if shorter. We amortize leasehold improvements purchased after the beginning of the initial lease term over the shorter of the assets' useful lives or a term that includes the original lease term, plus any renewals that are reasonably assured at the date the leasehold improvements are acquired. Depreciation expense for 2014, 2013 and 2012 was $2,108 million, $1,975 million and $2,027 million, respectively. For income tax purposes, accelerated depreciation methods are generally used. Repair and maintenance costs are expensed as incurred **and were $715 million in 2014, $643 million in 2013, and $650 in 2012.** Facility pre-opening costs, including supplies and payroll, are expensed as incurred.

Estimated Useful Lives	Life (in years)
Buildings and improvements	8-39
Fixtures and equipment	2-15
Computer hardware and software	2-7

Long-lived assets are reviewed for impairment when events or changes in circumstances, such as a decision to relocate or close a store or make significant software changes, indicate that the asset's carrying value may not be recoverable. For asset groups classified as held for sale, the carrying value is compared to the fair value less cost to sell. We estimate fair value by obtaining market appraisals, valuations from third party brokers or other valuation techniques.

Impairments ($ millions)	2014	2013	2012
Impairments included in segment SG&A	$108	$58	$37
Unallocated impairments	16	19	—
Total impairments	$124	$77	$37

REQUIRED

a. Prepare journal entries to record the following for 2014:
   i. Depreciation expense
   ii. Capital expenditures
   iii. Disposal of property, plant, and equipment
   iv. Repair and maintenance costs
   v. Impairments and write-downs (Assume that impairments and write-downs reduce the property and equipment account, rather than increasing accumulated depreciation.)
b. Estimate the amount of property and equipment that was acquired through non-cash transactions.

P8-39. **Reporting PPE Transactions and Asset Impairment**

Note B from the fiscal 2010 10-K report of **Williams-Sonoma, Inc.**, (January 30, 2011) follows. Its cash flow statement reported that the company made capital expenditures of $61,906,000 during fiscal 2010, impaired assets of $5,453,000 and recorded depreciation expense of $144,630,000. In addition, the company reported a gain on the disposal of property and equipment of $1,139,000.

Note B: Property and Equipment
Property and equipment consists of the following:

($ thousands)	Jan. 30, 2011	Jan. 31, 2010
Leasehold improvements..................................	$ 809,239	$ 831,757
Fixtures and equipment..................................	572,155	576,488
Capitalized software.....................................	292,424	267,724
Land and buildings......................................	126,061	135,692
Corporate systems projects in progress	56,602	65,989
Construction in progress	1,568	14,905
Corporate aircraft (held for sale).........................	0	10,029
Total	1,858,049	1,902,584
Accumulated depreciation and amortization	(1,127,493)	(1,073,557)
Property and equipment—net	$ 730,556	$ 829,027

We review the carrying value of all long-lived assets for impairment, primarily at a store level, whenever events or changes in circumstances indicate that the carrying value of an asset may not be recoverable. We review for impairment all stores for which current or projected cash flows from operations are not sufficient to recover the carrying value of the assets. Impairment results when the carrying value of the assets exceeds the estimated undiscounted future cash flows over the remaining life of the lease. Our estimate of undiscounted future cash flows over the store lease term (generally 5 to 22 years) is based upon our experience, historical operations of the stores and estimates of future store profitability and economic conditions. The future estimates of store profitability and economic conditions require estimating such factors as sales growth, gross margin, employment rates, lease escalations, inflation on operating expenses and the overall economics of the retail industry, and are therefore subject to variability and difficult to predict. If a long-lived asset is found to be impaired, the amount recognized for impairment is equal to the difference between the net carrying value and the asset's fair value.

REQUIRED
Prepare journal entries to record the following for fiscal 2010:

a. Depreciation expense
b. Capital expenditures
c. Impairment of property and equipment (Assume that impairments and write-downs reduce the property and equipment account, rather than increasing accumulated depreciation.)
d. Disposal of property and equipment

CASES AND PROJECTS

C8-40. **Interpreting and Reporting Property, Plant, and Equipment (PPE) Expenditures**

General Mills, Inc. is a global consumer foods company. The firm manufactures and sells a wide range of branded products and is a major supplier to the foodservice and baking industries. The company's core product areas are ready-to-eat cereal, super-premium ice cream, convenient meal solutions, and healthy snacking. The following data are taken from the company's 2014 annual report. From the balance sheet:

($ millions)	May 25, 2014	May 26, 2013
Land, buildings, and equipment:		
Land	$ 106.9	$ 101.2
Buildings	2,228.4	2,168.3
Buildings under capital lease	0.3	0.3
Equipment	5,979.7	5,731.1
Equipment under capital lease	9.0	9.0
Capitalized software	468.0	427.9
Construction in progress	600.8	495.1
Total land, buildings, and equipment	9,393.1	8,932.9
Less accumulated depreciation	(5,451.2)	(5,054.8)
Total	$3,941.9	$3,878.1

From the income statement ($ millions):

	2014	2013
Net sales	$17,909.6	$ 17,774.1

REQUIRED

a.   Compute the PPE turnover for 2014. Assuming an average PPE turnover of 4.0 for the company's closest competitors, does General Mills appear to be capital intensive?

b.   Calculate the percentage depreciated of General Mills' depreciable assets at the end of fiscal year 2014. What implications might the result suggest for the company's future cash flows?

c.   General Mills reports depreciation expense of approximately $585 million in 2014. Estimate the average useful life of its depreciable assets by dividing average depreciable assets by depreciation expense.

d.   During 2014, General Mills purchased $664 million of land, buildings and equipment for cash. Create the necessary journal entries to reflect the asset purchases and the year's depreciation charge.

LO6   **C8-41.**   **Managing Operating Assets to Improve Performance. A Management Application**
Return on a company's net operating assets is commonly used to evaluate financial performance. One way to increase performance is to focus on operating assets.

REQUIRED
Indicate how this might be done in relation to the following asset categories. Indicate also any potential problems a given action might create.

a.   Receivables

b.   Inventories

c.   Property, plant, and equipment

d.   Intangibles

LO4, 5, 6   **C8-42.**   **Determining the Effects of Capitalizing Versus Expensing Software Development Costs**
Take-Two Interactive Software, Inc.
NASDAQ ::TTWO

The following excerpts are taken from the March 31, 2014 annual report of **Take-Two Interactive Software, Inc.**, a maker and distributor of video games. All amounts are in thousands of U.S dollars.

Income Statement Information:	2014	2013
Net sales	$2,350,568	$1,214,483
Cost of goods sold	1,414,327	715,837
Operating expenses	520,985	493,407
Income (loss) from operations	$ 415,256	$ 5,239

Information from the Management Discussion, Balance Sheet and Note 8:

Software Development Costs and Licenses
Capitalized software development costs include direct costs incurred for internally developed titles and payments made to third-party software developers under development agreements. We capitalize internal software development costs (including stock-based compensation, specifically identifiable employee payroll expense and incentive compensation costs related to the completion and release of titles), third-party production and other content costs, subsequent to establishing technological feasibility of a software title.

Technological feasibility of a product includes the completion of both technical design documentation and game design documentation. Significant management judgments and estimates are utilized in the assessment of when technological feasibility is established. For products where proven technology exists, this may occur early in the development cycle. Technological feasibility is evaluated on a product by product basis. Amortization of capitalized software development costs and licenses commences when a product is released and is recorded on a title-by-title basis in cost of goods sold. For capitalized software development costs, amortization is calculated using (1) the proportion of current year revenues to the total revenues expected to be recorded over the life of the title or (2) the straight-line method over the remaining estimated useful life of the title, whichever is greater. For capitalized licenses, amortization is calculated as a ratio of (1) current period revenues to the total revenues expected to be recorded over the remaining life of the title or (2) the contractual royalty rate based on actual net product sales as defined in the licensing agreement, whichever is greater. …We evaluate the future recoverability of capitalized software development costs and licenses on a quarterly basis. Recoverability is primarily assessed based on the actual title's performance. For products that are scheduled to be released in the future, recoverability is evaluated based on the expected performance of the specific products to which the cost or license relates. We utilize a number of criteria in evaluating expected product performance, including: historical performance of comparable products developed with comparable technology; market performance of comparable titles; orders for the product prior to its release; general market conditions; and, past performance of the franchise. When management determines that the value of the title is unlikely to be recovered by product sales, capitalized costs are charged to cost of goods sold in the period in which such determination is made.

Capitalized Software Development Costs and Licenses	2014	2013
Beginning balance	$294,196	$315,979
Additions	197,046	208,965
Amortization and write-downs	(265,533)	(230,748)
Ending balance.	$225,709	$294,196

Assume an income tax rate of 35% where necessary.

REQUIRED

a. You wish to compare the performance of Take-Two with one of its competitors, **Electronic Arts, Inc.** However, Electronic Arts does not capitalize any significant amounts of its software development costs. Estimate Take-Two's 2014 Income from operations if it did not capitalize any software development costs. *Briefly* explain your adjustment(s).

b. Is there any indication that Take-Two might have changed its software amortization estimates from 2013 to 2014? Explain *briefly*.

C8-43.   Analyzing Impairment Charges

In the last quarter of 2014, **DreamWorks Animation SKG Inc.** recorded a loss. Part of this loss was due to impairment charges. In their annual report the company stated:

LO4

DreamWorks Animation SKG Inc.

NASDAQ :: DWA

We are required to amortize capitalized production costs over the expected revenue streams as we recognize revenue from the associated films or other projects. The amount of production costs that will be amortized each quarter depends on, among other things, how much future revenue we expect to receive from each project. Unamortized production costs are evaluated for impairment each reporting period on a project-by-project basis. If estimated remaining revenue is not sufficient to recover the unamortized production costs, the unamortized production costs will be written down to fair value. In any given quarter, if we lower our previous forecast with respect to total anticipated revenue from any individual feature film or other project, we may be required to accelerate amortization or record impairment charges with respect to the unamortized costs, even if we have previously recorded impairment charges for such film or other project. For instance, in the quarter ended December 31, 2013, we incurred a write-down of $13.5 million for our film *Turbo* and in the year ended December 31, 2014, we incurred write-downs of $66.5 million for our film *Mr. Peabody and Sherman* and $30.3 million for our film *The Penguins of Madagascar*. Such impairment charges adversely impacted our business, operating results and financial condition.

REQUIRED

a. DreamWorks reported an $86.2 million pre-tax loss for the year 2014. What would pre-tax income or loss have been without the above described impairment charges?

b. DreamWorks is in the film production/media industry. From the paragraph above, describe how companies in this industry account for their film production costs – when incurred and over time.

c. Show the journal entry for 2014 to record the impairment charges related to *Mr. Peabody and Sherman* and *The Penguins of Madagascar*.

LO4, 5, 6
**Vodafone Public Limited
Company**
NASDAQ :: VOD

C8-44.   Goodwill Impairment Under IFRS

Vodafone Group Public Limited Company's (UK) Annual Report reports the following information (year ended March 31, 2014):

	2014 £m
Revenue	**$38,346**
Cost of sales	(27,942)
Gross profit	**10,404**
Selling and distribution expenses	(3,033)
Administrative expenses	(4,245)
Share of results of equity accounted associates and joint ventures	278
Impairment losses	(6,600)
Other income and expense	(717)
Operating (loss)/profit	**(3,913)**
Non-operating income and expense	(149)
Investment income	346
Financing costs	(1,554)
(Loss)/profit before taxation	(5,270)
Income tax credit/(expense)	16,582
Profit/(loss) for the financial year from continuing operations	11,312
Profit for the financial year from discontinued operations	48,108
Profit for the financial year	**$59,420**

The company also provides the following disclosures in the notes to their financial statements:

Impairment reviews

IFRS requires management to perform impairment tests annually for indefinite lived assets and, for finite lived assets, if events or changes in circumstances indicate that their carrying amounts may not be recoverable. Impairment testing requires management to judge whether the carrying value of assets can be supported by the net present value of future cash flows that they generate. Calculating the net present value of the future cash flows requires assumptions to be made in respect of highly uncertain matters . . .

Accounting Policies—Goodwill

Goodwill is not subject to amortisation but is tested for impairment annually or whenever there is an indication that the asset may be impaired. For the purpose of impairment testing, assets are grouped at the lowest levels for which there are separately identifiable cash flows, known as cash-generating units. If the recoverable amount of the cash-generating unit is less than the carrying amount of the unit, the impairment loss is allocated first to reduce the carrying amount of any goodwill allocated to the unit and then to other assets of the unit pro-rata on the basis of the carrying amount of each asset in the unit. Impairment losses recognised for goodwill are not reversible in subsequent periods. The recoverable amount is the higher of fair value less costs to sell and value in use. In assessing value in use, the estimated future cash flows are discounted to their present value using a pre-tax discount rate that reflects current market assessments of the time value of money and the risks specific to the asset for which the estimates of future cash flows have not been adjusted.

Assets
Goodwill and other intangible assets

Our total intangible assets increased to £46.7 billion from £44.1 billion. The increase primarily arose as a result of £11.5 billion additions as a result of the Group's acquisitions . . . partially offset by £6.6 billion of goodwill impairments, reductions of £2.6 billion as a result of unfavourable movements in foreign exchange rates and £3.5 billion of amortisation.

REQUIRED

a.   Briefly describe the general goodwill impairment rules that Vodafone used relative to those that would apply under U.S. GAAP. Are they very different?

b.   How would you treat the goodwill impairment if you were a financial analyst evaluating the company? How did the charge affect pre-tax income for Vodafone?

c.   How does such an impairment charge affect the cash flows of the company?

SOLUTIONS TO REVIEW PROBLEMS

Mid-Chapter Review

SOLUTION

1a. Straight-line Depreciation expense = ($95,000 − $10,000)/5 years = $17,000 per year

1b. Double-declining-balance (twice straight-line rate = 2 × (1/5) = 40%

Year	Book Value × Rate	Depreciation Expense
1	$95,000 × 0.40 =	$38,000
2	($95,000 − $38,000) × 0.40 =	22,800
3	($95,000 − $60,800) × 0.40 =	13,680
4	($95,000 − $74,480) × 0.40 =	8,208
5	($95,000 − $82,688) × 0.40 =	2,312*

*The formula value of $4,925 is not reported because it would depreciate the asset below residual value. Only the $2,312 needed to reach residual value is depreciated.

2.

3.

Equipment, cost	$95,000
Less accumulated depreciation	51,000
Equipment, net	$44,000

Equipment is reported on Lev's balance sheet at its net book value of $44,000.

4. The percent depreciated is computed as: Accumulated Depreciation/Depreciable Asset Cost = $51,000/$95,000 − 53.7%. The equipment is more than one half depreciated at the end of the third year. Again, the lack of knowledge of salvage value has resulted in an underestimate of the percent depreciated. Still, this estimate is useful in that we know that the company's asset

is over one-half depreciated and is likely to require replacement in about 2 years (less than one-half of its useful life of 5 years). This replacement will become a cash outflow or financing need when it arises and should be considered in our projections of future cash flows.

Chapter-End Review

SOLUTION

1. Bowen Company would expense the $120,000 in R&D costs in 2016. The $12,500 in legal fees to obtain the patent would be capitalized. As a result, the book value of the patent would be $12,500 on July 1, 2016. The entries to record these costs would be:

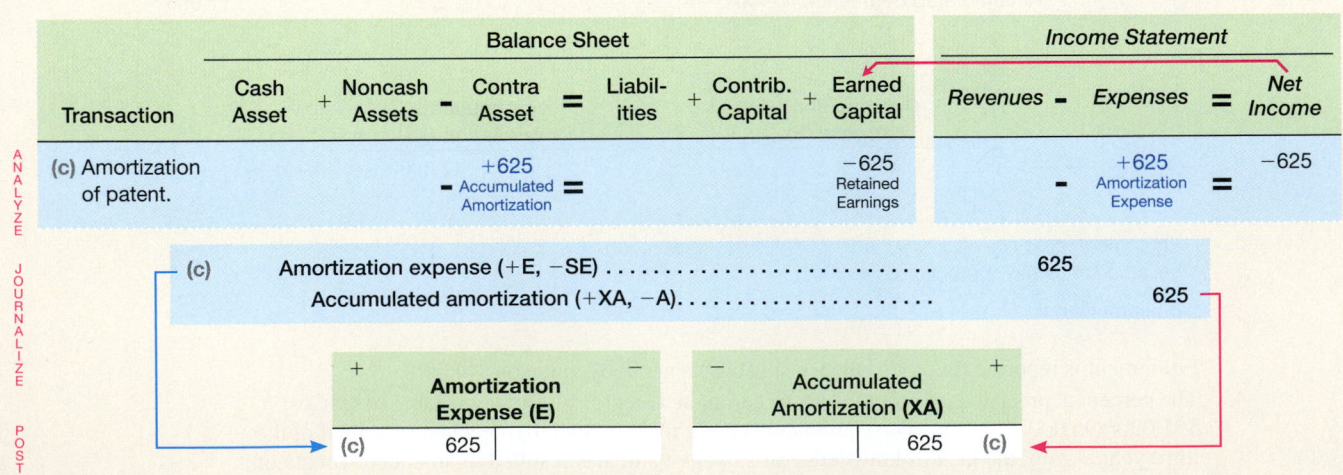

Transaction	Balance Sheet						Income Statement		
	Cash Asset	+ Noncash Assets	− Contra Asset	= Liabil- ities	+ Contrib. Capital	+ Earned Capital	Revenues −	Expenses	= Net Income
(a) Record R&D costs as R&D expense.	−120,000 Cash	−	=			−120,000 Retained Earnings	−	+120,000 R&D Expense	= −120,000

```
(a)  R&D expense (+E, −SE) ...................................   120,000
         Cash (−A) ..........................................             120,000
```

+ Research & Development Expense (E) −		+ Cash (A) −
(a) 120,000		120,000 (a)

Transaction	Balance Sheet						Income Statement		
(b) Record acquisition of patent.	−12,500 Cash	+12,500 Patent	−	=			−		=

```
(b)  Patent (+A) ............................................   12,500
         Cash (−A) ..........................................             12,500
```

+ Patent (A) −		+ Cash (A) −
(b) 12,500		120,000 (a)
		12,500 (b)

2. Each year, beginning on July 1, 2016, Bowen would record amortization expense of $1,250 ($12,500/10). For 2016, six months of amortization expense, or $625, would be recorded ($1,250/2). The journal entry would be:

Transaction	Balance Sheet						Income Statement		
	Cash Asset	+ Noncash Assets	− Contra Asset	= Liabil- ities	+ Contrib. Capital	+ Earned Capital	Revenues −	Expenses	= Net Income
(c) Amortization of patent.			+625 − Accumulated Amortization	=		−625 Retained Earnings	−	+625 Amortization Expense	= −625

```
(c)  Amortization expense (+E, −SE) ............................   625
         Accumulated amortization (+XA, −A) ...................             625
```

+ Amortization Expense (E) −		− Accumulated Amortization (XA) +
(c) 625		625 (c)

3. Because Kennedy purchased the right to use the technology, the purchase price can be capitalized as an intangible asset and amortized over the five-year length of the agreement. Kennedy would record amortization expense of $18,000 ($90,000/5) each year, beginning July 1, 2018. (Bowen would recognize the $90,000 as revenue.) The journal entry that Kennedy Company would need to record the acquisition of the technology rights would be as follows:

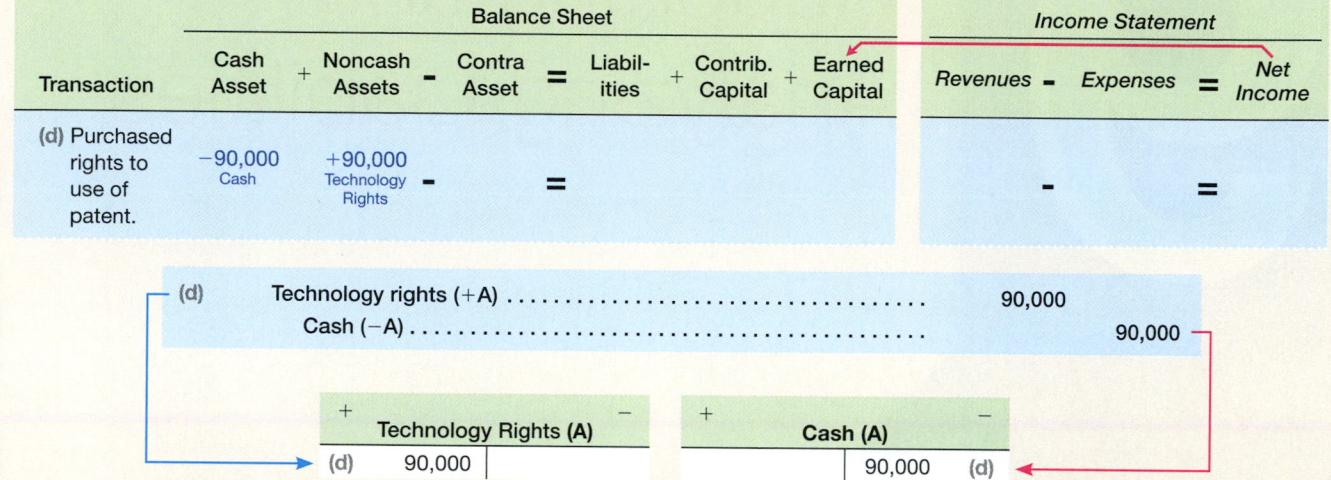

4. Given that the patent is obsolete, both Bowen Company and Kennedy Company would record impairment losses. Bowen would write off the unamortized balance in the patent account, resulting in a loss of $7,500 [$12,500 − ($1,250 × 4)]. Kennedy Company would write off the remaining value of the technology agreement, recording an impairment loss of $54,000 [$90,000 − ($18,000 × 2)]. Kennedy's journal entry would be:

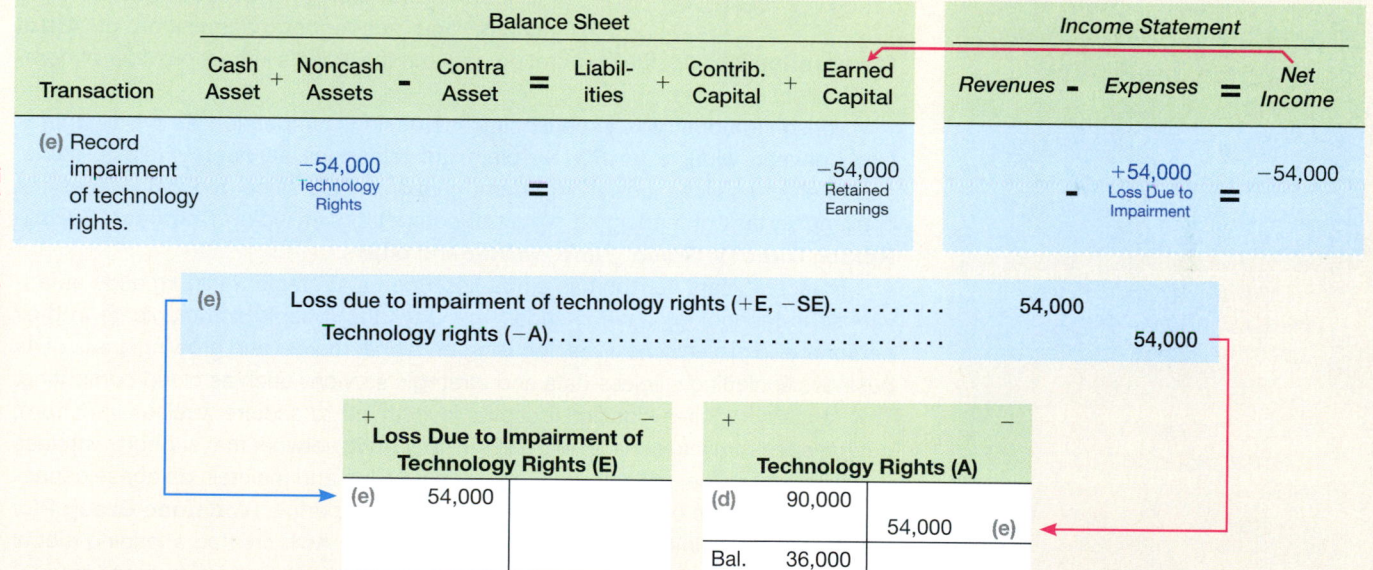

9

Reporting and Analyzing Liabilities

VERIZON
www.verizon.com

In 2000, **Bell Atlantic Corporation** merged with **GTE** to form **Verizon Communications**. After its 2006 acquisition of **MCI Communications Corp.** and subsequent acquisition of **Alltel Corporation** in 2008, the corporation became the world's largest provider of communications services.

Verizon's industry is experiencing increasing competition as product lines blur between wireline (or POTS—plain old telephone service), wireless, cable, and Internet services. Lowell McAdam, Verizon's CEO since mid-2011, faces the challenging task of fending off a host of competitors including **Comcast**, **Sprint-Nextel**, **DirecTV Group**, **Time Warner** and others.

In recent years Verizon has embarked upon a strategic transformation as advances in technology have changed the ways that people communicate in their personal and professional lives, focusing on higher margin and growing areas of its business, including wireless data and strategic services such as cloud computing. This strategy requires significant capital investment to acquire wireless spectrum, put the spectrum into service, expand the fiber optic network that supports wireless and wireline service, maintain networks and develop and maintain database capacity. In 2014, Verizon bought out the 45% interest of a partner (**Vodafone Group Plc**) in its wireless business, and its 2015 acquisition of **AOL** created a leading global media technology company. This investment program requires a significant amount of cash at a time when the company is faced with more than $110.5 billion in debt and $33.3 billion in employee benefit obligations. Fortunately, Verizon's operating cash flow remains strong at $30.6 billion in 2014.

Previous chapters focused on the reporting of operating assets, including receivables, inventories, property, plant, and equipment, and intangible assets, along with the related expenses. We now turn our attention to the other side of the balance sheet. Chapter 9 examines how we value liabilities and how debt financing along with the subsequent payment of interest and principal affect the financial statements. We also discuss the required disclosures that enable us to effectively analyze a company's ability to make its liability payments as they mature. Chapter 10 focuses on the reporting for three specific types of liabilities, and Chapter 11 examines the reporting of stockholders' equity.

As Verizon faces increased competition from other telecom companies, cable, and Internet providers, it must continue to innovate in order to maintain its position as the industry leader. This objective will require large investments in technology and infrastructure, only part of which will come from its operating cash flow. To be successful, McAdam will need to manage Verizon's increased debt burden and efficiently allocate cash resources between strategic investments and debt payments.

Sources: *The Wall Street Journal* 5/2011; *Verizon* 2014 10-K.

CHAPTER ORGANIZATION

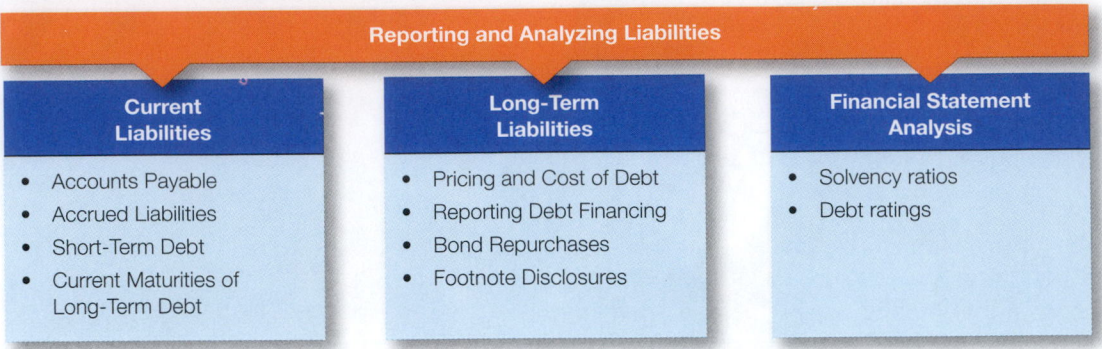

INTRODUCTION

Just as asset disclosures provide us with information on where a company invests its funds, the disclosures concerning liabilities and equity inform us as to how those assets are financed. To be successful, a company must not only invest funds wisely, but must also be astute in the manner in which it finances those investments.

Companies hope to finance their assets at the lowest possible cost. The cost of financing assets with liabilities is the interest charged by the lender. While many liabilities bear explicit interest rates, many other liabilities (such as accounts payable and accrued liabilities) are non-interest-bearing. This fact does not mean that these liabilities are cost-free. For example, while a supplier may appear to offer interest-free credit terms, the cost of that credit is implicitly included in the price it charges for the goods or services it sells.

Verizon's liabilities and equity, as taken from its 2014 10-K report, are presented in **Exhibit 9.1**. Just as assets are classified as either current or noncurrent, so are liabilities presented in the balance sheet as either current or noncurrent.

Current liabilities, as the name implies, are short-term in nature, generally requiring payment within the coming year. As a result, they are not a suitable source of funding for long-term assets that generate cash flows over several years. Instead, companies often finance long-term assets with long-term liabilities that require payments over several years, so that the cash outflows required by the financing source match the cash inflows produced by the assets to which they relate.

EXHIBIT 9.1	Verizon Communications' Liabilities and Equity		
At December 31 ($ millions)		**2014**	**2013**
Current liabilities..			
Debt maturing within one year........................		$ 2,735	$ 3,933
Accounts payable and accrued liabilities............		16,680	16,453
Other..		8,649	6,664
Total current liabilities................................		28,064	27,050
Long-term debt		110,536	89,658
Employee benefit obligations...........................		33,280	27,682
Deferred income taxes..................................		41,578	28,639
Other liabilities		5,574	5,653
Total liabilities..		219,032	178,682
Total equity...		13,676	95,416
Total liabilities and equity............................		$232,708	$274,098

When a company acquires assets, and finances them with liabilities, its **financial leverage** increases. Because the magnitude of required liability payments increases with the level of liability financing, those larger payments increase the chance of default should a downturn in business occur. Increasing levels of liabilities make the company riskier to creditors who, consequently, demand a higher return on the financing they provide to the company. The assessment of default risk is part of liquidity and solvency analysis.

This chapter, along with Chapter 10, focuses on liabilities that are reported on the balance sheet and the corresponding interest costs reported in the income statement. All such liabilities represent probable, nondiscretionary, future obligations that are the result of events that have already occurred. Chapter 10 also addresses *off-balance sheet financing*, which encompasses future obligations that are reported in the notes, but not on the face of the balance sheet. An understanding of both on-balance-sheet and off-balance-sheet financing is central to evaluating a company's financial condition and assessing its risk of default.

CURRENT LIABILITIES

Liabilities are separated on the balance sheet into current and noncurrent (long-term). We first focus our attention on current liabilities, which are obligations that must be met (paid) within one year. Most current liabilities such as those related to utilities, wages, insurance, rent, and taxes, generate a corresponding impact on operating expenses.

Verizon reports three categories of current liabilities: (1) debt maturing within one year, which includes short-term borrowings as well as long-term obligations that are scheduled for payment in the upcoming year, (2) accounts payable and accrued liabilities, and (3) other current liabilities, which consist mainly of customer deposits, dividends declared but not yet paid, and miscellaneous short-term obligations too small to list separately.

It is helpful to separate current liabilities into operating and nonoperating components. These two components primarily consist of:

1. Current operating liabilities

   - **Accounts payable** Obligations to others for amounts owed on purchases of goods and services. These are usually non-interest-bearing.

   - **Accrued liabilities** Obligations for expenses incurred that have not been paid as of the end of the current period. These include, for example, accruals for employee wages earned but yet unpaid, accruals for taxes (usually quarterly) on payroll and current-period profits, and accruals for other liabilities such as rent, utilities, interest, and insurance. Accruals are made to properly reflect the liabilities owed as of the statement date and the expenses incurred in the period. Each one is journalized by a debit to an expense account and a credit to a related liability.

   - **Deferred performance liabilities** Obligations that will be satisfied, not by paying cash, but instead, by providing products or services to customers. Examples of deferred performance liabilities include customer deposits, unearned gift card revenues for retail companies, and liabilities for frequent flier programs offered by airlines.

2. Current nonoperating liabilities

   - **Short-term interest-bearing debt** Short-term bank borrowings and notes expected to mature in whole or in part during the upcoming year.

   - **Current maturities of long-term debt** Long-term borrowings that are scheduled to mature in whole or in part during the upcoming year.

The remainder of this section describes current liabilities.

Accounts Payable

LO1 Identify and account for current operating liabilities.

Accounts payable, which are part of current operating liabilities, arise from the purchase of goods and services from others on credit. Verizon reports $16,680 million in accounts payable and accrued liabilities as of December 31, 2014. Its accounts payable represent $5,598 million, or 34%, of this total amount.

Accounts payable are a non-interest-bearing source of financing. Increased payables reduce the amount of net working capital, because these payables are deducted from current assets in the computation of net working capital. Also, increased payables improves operating cash flow (because inventories were purchased without using cash). An increase in accounts payable also increases profitability because it causes a reduction in the level of interest-bearing debt that is required to finance operating assets. ROE increases when companies make use of this low-cost financing source.

However, management must be careful to avoid excessive "**leaning on the trade**" because short-term income and cash flow gains can result in long-term costs such as damaged supply channels.[1]

When a company purchases goods or services on credit, suppliers often grant **cash discounts** to buyers if payment is made within a specified time period. Cash discounts are usually established as part of the credit terms and stated as a percentage of the purchase price. For example, credit terms of 1/10, n/30 (one-ten, net-thirty) indicate that a 1% cash discount is allowed if the payment is made within 10 days. If the cash discount is not taken, the full purchase price is due in 30 days.

Net-of-Discount Method To illustrate a cash discount, assume that a company purchases 1,000 units of merchandise at \$4 per unit on terms of 1/10, n/30. The total purchase price is 1,000 × \$4 = \$4,000. However, if payment is made within 10 days, the net purchase price would then be \$3,960 (\$4,000 − \$40). While this difference seems like a small amount, consider the cost of not taking the discount. If the discount is missed, the buyer is afforded an extra 20 days to pay for the merchandise, for which it pays a penalty of \$40, or \$2 per day. Two dollars per day is the equivalent of \$730 dollars per year which, in turn, is equivalent to paying interest at an annual rate of 18.4% (\$730/\$3,960).[2]

When cash discounts are offered, the inventory purchase should be recorded at its cost using the **net-of-discount method**. When the net-of-discount method is used, inventory is capitalized at the net cost, assuming that the discount will be taken by the buyer. Continuing with our example, the following entry would be recorded by the buyer at the time of purchase:

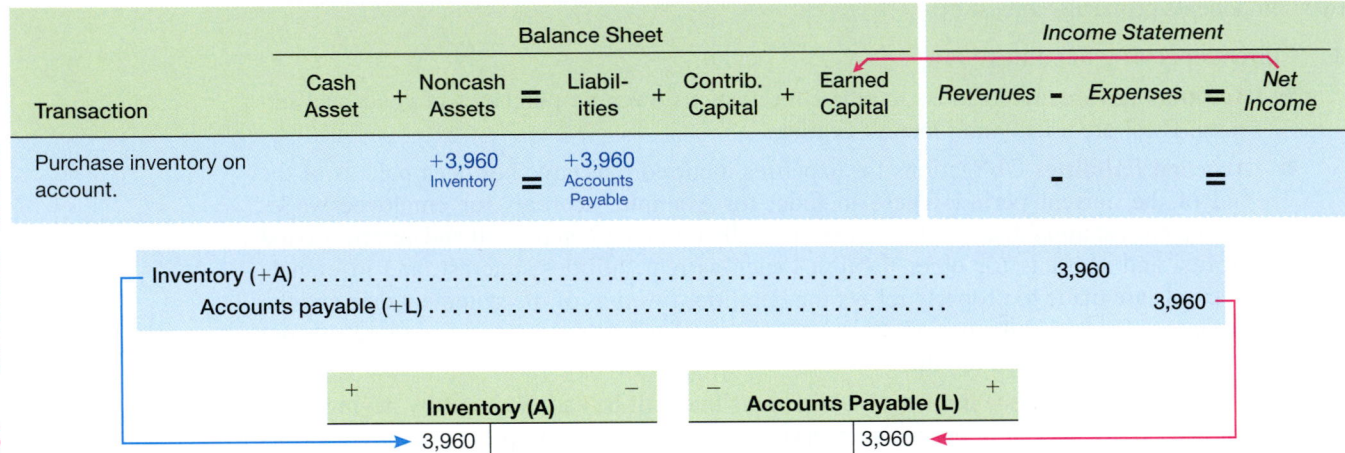

When payment is made within the 10-day discount period, accounts payable is debited and cash is credited:

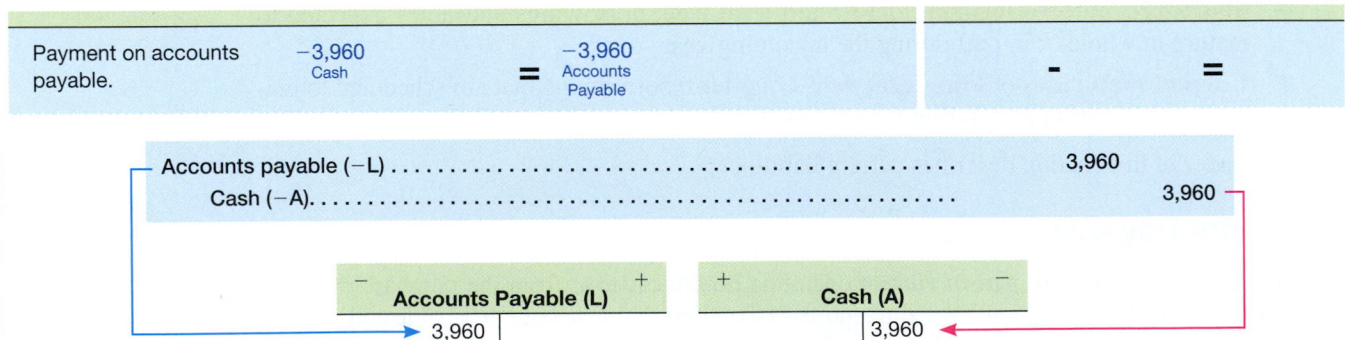

However, when a discount is missed, the lost discount must be recorded. For example, if full payment is made after the 10-day discount period, the payment is recorded as follows:

---

[1] One must be careful, because excessive delays in the payment of payables can result in suppliers charging a higher price for their goods or, ultimately, refusing to sell to certain buyers. This situation is a hidden "financing" cost that, even though it is not interest, is a real cost.

[2] Compound interest methods (introduced in Appendix A) would arrive at a slightly higher annual rate of interest, about 19.6%.

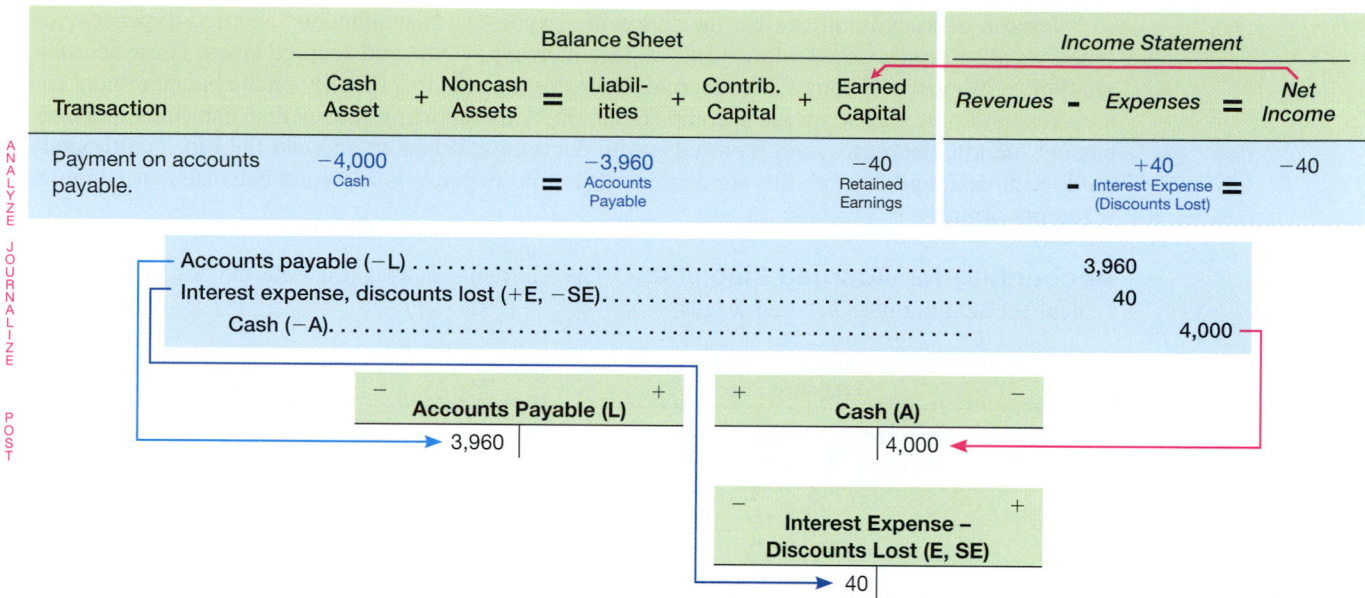

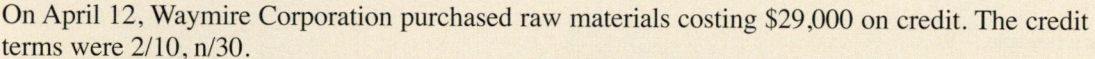

The missed discount is an expense in the period when the discount is lost. This serves two purposes. First, discounts lost are not capitalized as part of inventory and are not added to cost of goods sold. Instead, the lost discounts are treated like a finance charge and recorded as an expense of the period when the discount is missed. Second, the net-of-discount method highlights late payments by explicitly keeping a record of lost discounts. Given the high cost of missed cash discounts, most businesses would likely want to minimize the amount of discounts lost. Thus, keeping a record of discounts lost is useful when it comes to managing cash and accounts payable.

MID-CHAPTER REVIEW 1

On April 12, Waymire Corporation purchased raw materials costing $29,000 on credit. The credit terms were 2/10, n/30.

a. If Waymire paid for the materials on April 19, how much would it pay?
b. Compute the cost of a lost discount as an annual percentage interest rate.

The solution to this review problem can be found on page 456.

Accrued Liabilities

Accrued liabilities are identified at the end of an accounting period to reflect liabilities and expenses that have been incurred during the period but are not yet paid.[3] **Verizon** reports details of its $16,680 million accounts payable and accrued liabilities, including its $5,598 accounts payable, in footnote 16 to its 2014 10-K report:

December 31 ($ millions)	2014	2013
Accounts payable.	$ 5,598	$ 4,954
Accrued expenses	4,016	3,954
Accrued vacation pay, salaries and wages	4,131	4,790
Interest payable	1,478	1,199
Taxes payable.	1,457	1,556
Total	$16,680	$16,453

---

[3] Accruals can also be made for recognition of revenue and a corresponding receivable. An example of this situation would be revenue recognition on a long-term contract that has reached a particular milestone, or for interest earned but not received on an investment in bonds that is still outstanding at period-end.

Verizon accrues liabilities for the following expenses: miscellaneous accrued expenses, accrued vacation pay, accrued salaries and wages, interest payable, and accrued taxes. These accruals are typical of most companies. The accruals are recognized with a liability on the balance sheet and a corresponding expense on the income statement. This reporting means that liabilities increase, current income decreases, and reported equity decreases. When an accrued liability is ultimately paid, both cash and the liability are decreased (but no expense is recorded because it was recognized previously).

Accounting for Accrued Liabilities   The following entries illustrate the accounting for a typical accrued liability, accrued wages:

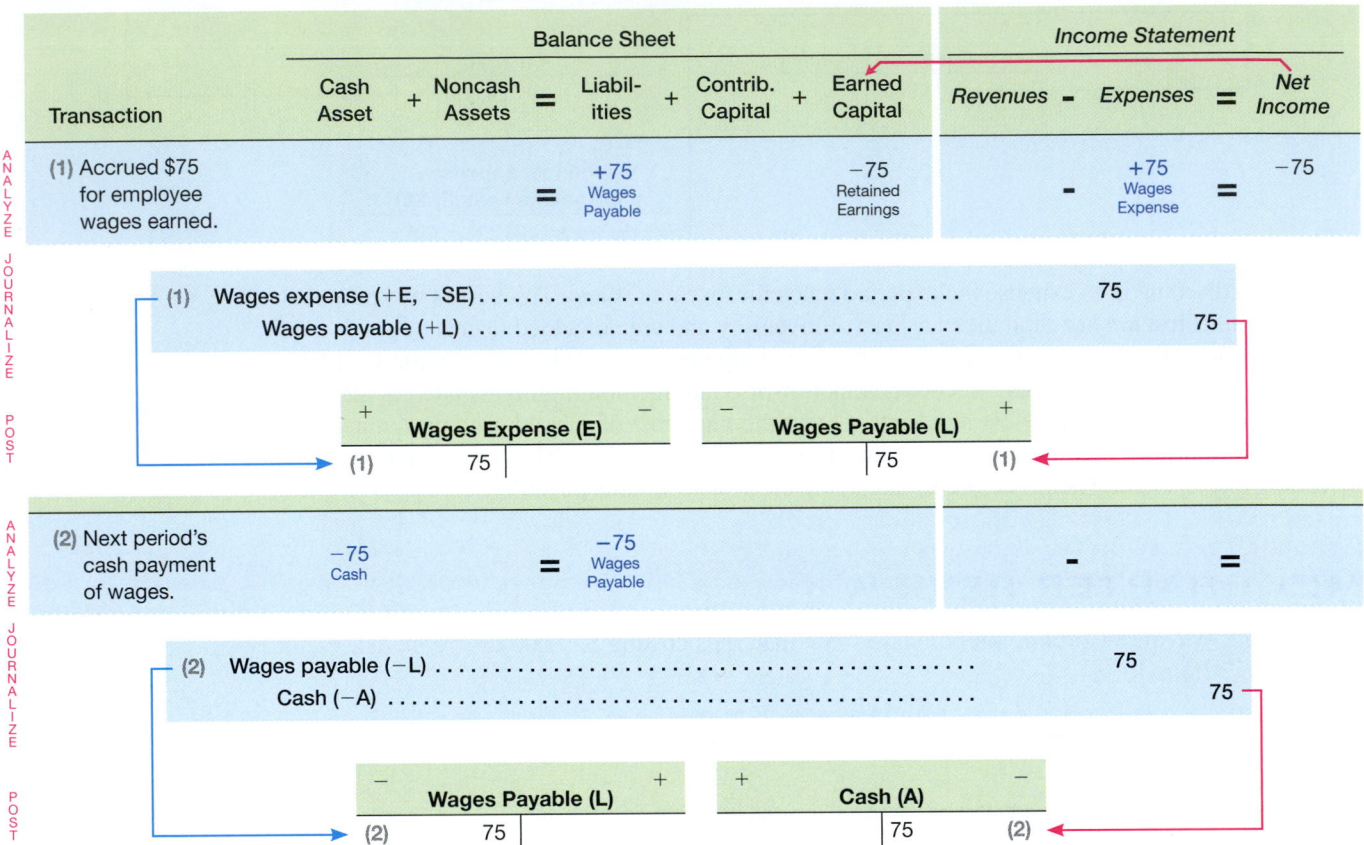

The following financial statement effects result from this accrual of employee wages:

- Employees have worked during a period and have not yet been paid. The effect of this accrual is to increase wages payable on the balance sheet and to recognize wages expense on the income statement. Failure to recognize this liability and associated expense would understate liabilities on the balance sheet and overstate income.

- Employees are paid in the following period, resulting in a cash decrease and a reduction in wages payable. This payment does not result in expense because the expense was recognized in the prior period when incurred.

Contingent Liabilities   The accrued wages illustration relates to events that are fairly certain. We know, for example, when wages are incurred but not paid. Other examples of such accruals are rental costs, insurance premiums due but not yet paid, and taxes owed.

Some accrued liabilities, however, are less certain than others. Consider a company facing a lawsuit. Should it record the possible liability and related expense? The answer depends on the likelihood of occurrence and the ability to estimate the obligation. Specifically, if the obligation is *probable* **and** the amount *estimable,* then a company will recognize this obligation, called a **contingent liability**, with a corresponding charge to income. If an obligation is only *reasonably possible,* regardless of the company's ability to estimate the amount, the contingent liability is not reported on the balance sheet and is merely disclosed in the footnotes. All other contingent liabilities that are less than reasonably possible are not accrued—disclosure in a note is permitted but not required.

A GLOBAL PERSPECTIVE

Reporting Contingent Liabilities U.S. GAAP and IFRS are similar with respect to reporting accrued liabilities. The one exception is contingencies. IFRS uses the term *provisions* to refer to contingent liabilities that are accrued and reported on the balance sheet while an obligation that is disclosed in the notes is labeled *contingent liability*. Both GAAP and IFRS require accrual of the "best estimate" of the liability. However, if the best estimate of the future payments required to settle the obligation is a range of values, IFRS requires that the midpoint of the range be used as the estimated value of the contingent liability or provision. In the same situation, U.S. GAAP requires that the low end of the range be used, with disclosure of the maximum.

Warranties

The new revenue recognition standard discussed in Chapter 6 has implications for the accounting for warranty obligations. When a company delivers a product with a warranty, is the warranty simply assurance that the product will function as intended, or should it be considered a separate performance obligation? If it is considered a separate performance obligation, then the company would allocate the purchase price between the product and the warranty and recognize an unearned revenue liability at the time of purchase, as shown in Chapter 6.[4] However, if the warranty is not a separate performance obligation (e.g., it cannot be purchased separately from the product and is intended as assurance that the product will perform as expected), a liability accrual for the warranty obligation must be made at the time of purchase.

The expected cost of the warranty commitment usually is reasonably estimated at the time of sale based on past experience. GAAP requires manufacturers to record the expected cost of warranties as a liability, and to record the related expected warranty expense in the income statement to match against the sales revenue reported for that period.

To illustrate, the effects of an accrual of a $1,000 warranty liability are:

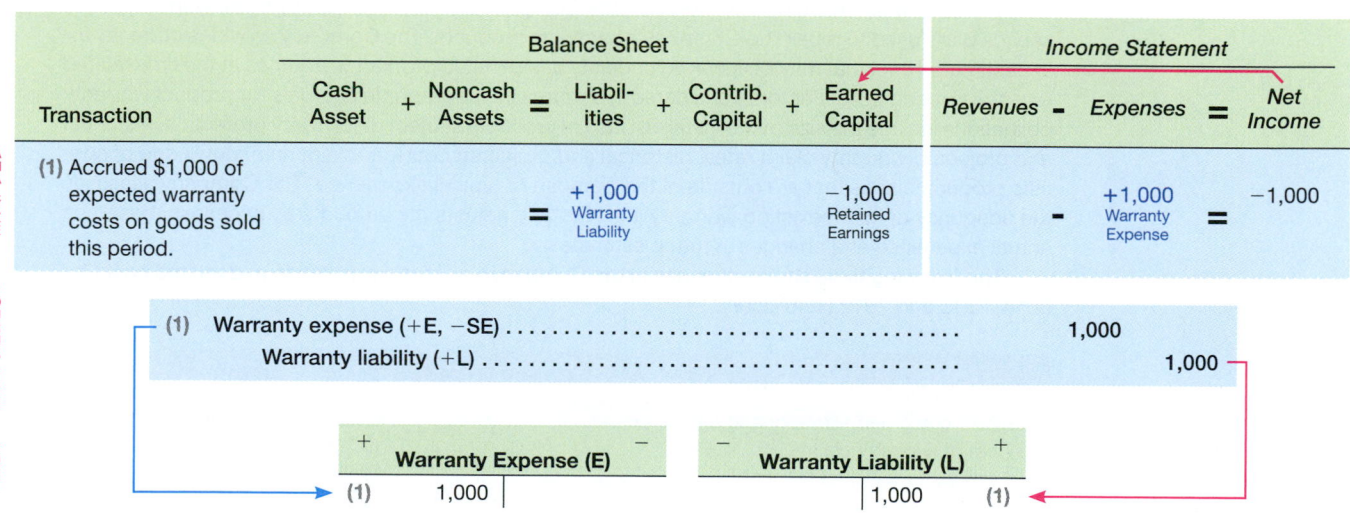

---

[4] Under current GAAP, deferral of revenue is required for extended warranties that are purchased separately from the product.

	Balance Sheet						Income Statement		
Transaction	Cash Asset	+ Noncash Assets	= Liabil-ities	+ Contrib. Capital	+ Earned Capital		Revenues −	Expenses =	Net Income
(2) Next period's costs (sent $950 in replacement products) to cover failures under warranty.		−950 Inventory	= −950 Warranty Liability				−	=	

(2)	Warranty liability (−L)	950	
	Inventory (−A)		950

− Warranty Liability (L) +		+ Inventory (A) −	
(2)	950	950	(2)

Reporting of warranty liabilities has the same effect on financial statements as does the accrual of wages expense in the previous section. That is, a liability is recorded on the balance sheet and an expense is reported in the income statement, reducing income by the warranty accrual. When the defective product is later replaced (or repaired), the liability is reduced together with the cost of the inventory (or other assets) spent to satisfy the claim. (Only a portion of the products estimated to fail does so in the current period; we expect other product failures in future periods. Using methods similar to the aging of accounts in Chapter 6, management monitors this estimate and adjusts it if failure is higher or lower than expected.) As in the accrual of wages, the expense is reported when it is incurred and the liability is estimated at that time, not when payments are made.

Apple Inc. reports $4,159 million of warranty liability in its 2014 balance sheet. The footnotes reveal the following additional information:

Accrued Warranty and Indemnification   The Company offers a basic limited parts and labor warranty on its hardware products. The basic warranty period for hardware products is typically one year from the date of purchase by the end-user. The Company also offers a 90-day basic warranty for its service parts used to repair the Company's hardware products. The Company provides currently for the estimated cost that may be incurred under its basic limited product warranties at the time related revenue is recognized. Factors considered in determining appropriate accruals for product warranty obligations include the size of the installed base of products subject to warranty protection, historical and projected warranty claim rates, historical and projected cost-per-claim and knowledge of specific product failures that are outside of the Company's typical experience. The Company assesses the adequacy of its preexisting warranty liabilities and adjusts the amounts as necessary based on actual experience and changes in future estimates.

The following table shows changes in the Company's accrued warranties and related costs for 2014, 2013 and 2012 (in millions):

	2014	2013	2012
Beginning accrued warranty and related costs	$2,967	$1,638	$1,240
Cost of warranty claims	(3,760)	(3,703)	(1,786)
Accruals for product warranty	4,952	5,032	2,184
Ending accrued warranty and related costs.	$4,159	$2,967	$1,638

In 2014, Apple incurred $3,760 million in cost to replace or repair defective products during the year, reducing the liability by this amount. This cost can be in the form of cash paid to customers or to employees as wages, and in the form of parts used for repairs. The company accrued an additional $4,952 million in new warranty liabilities in 2014. It is important to realize that only the increase in the liability resulting from additional accruals affects the income statement, reducing income through the additional warranty expense. Warranty payments reduce the warranty liability but have no impact on the income statement.

U.S. GAAP requires that the warranty liability reflect the estimated amount of cost that the company expects to incur as a result of warranty claims. This amount is often difficult to estimate and is prone to error. There is also the possibility that a company might intentionally underestimate its warranty liability to report higher current income, or overestimate it so as to depress current income and create an additional liability on the balance sheet that can be used to absorb future warranty costs without the need to record additional expense. Doing so would shift income from the current period to one or more future periods. Warranty liabilities should be compared with sales levels. Any deviations from the historical relation of the warranty liability to sales may indicate a change in product quality or, alternatively, it may reveal earnings management.

All accrued liabilities result in a liability on the balance sheet and an expense on the income statement. Management has some latitude in determining the amount and timing for accruals. This latitude can lead to misreporting of income and liabilities (unintentional or otherwise). For example, if accruals are underestimated, then liabilities are underestimated, income is overestimated, and retained earnings are overestimated. In subsequent periods when an understated accrued liability is reversed (it is recognized in the account), reported income is lower than it should be; this is because prior period income was higher than it should have been. (The reverse holds for overestimated accruals.) The over- and under-reporting of accruals, therefore, results in the shifting of income from one period into another.

Experience tells us that some accrued liabilities are more prone to misstatement than others. Estimated accruals that are linked with restructuring programs, including severance accruals and accruals for asset write-downs, are often overstated, as are estimated environmental liabilities. Companies sometimes overestimate these "one-time" accruals, resulting in early recognition of expenses (as "nonrecurring items") and a corresponding reduction in current period income. This choice, in turn, boosts income in future years when management decides that the accrual can be reversed because it was initially too large. This may suggest that management is conservative and wants to avoid understating liabilities. It can also reflect a desire by management to show earnings growth in the future by shifting current income to future periods. Accrued liabilities set up to smooth income over future periods are called "**cookie jar reserves**." The terms "clearing the decks" and "taking a big bath" have also been applied to such accounting practices.

YOU MAKE THE CALL

You are the Analyst   Dow Chemical Company reported accrued environmental liabilities in excess of $706 million in its 2014 balance sheet. What conditions needed to be met before these liabilities could be reported? The company also indicated in a footnote that actual environmental liabilities could be twice this amount. How does this uncertainty potentially affect Dow's balance sheet?   [Answers on page 443]

MID-CHAPTER REVIEW 2

MBC GuidedExamples

The **Toro Company** reported warranty liabilities of $72,177,000 in its October 31, 2013 balance sheet. On its October 31, 2014 balance sheet, it reported a liability of $71,080,000. It recognized $37,471,000 in net warranty expenses during fiscal year 2014, ending October 31, 2014. What amount of cost did Toro incur to cover warranty claims in 2014? How would the fulfillment of these claims be recorded?

The solution to this review problem can be found on pages 456–457.

LO2 Describe and account for current nonoperating (financial) liabilities.

Current Nonoperating (Financial) Liabilities

Current nonoperating (financial) liabilities include short-term bank loans, the accrual of interest on those loans, and the current maturities of long-term debt. Companies generally try to structure their financing so that debt service requirements (payments) of those financing obligations coincide with the cash inflows from the assets financed. This strategy means that current assets are usually financed with current liabilities, and that long-term assets are financed with long-term liability (and equity) sources.

The use of short-term financing is particularly important for companies that have seasonal sales. To illustrate, a seasonal company's investment in current assets tends to fluctuate during the year as depicted in the graphic below:

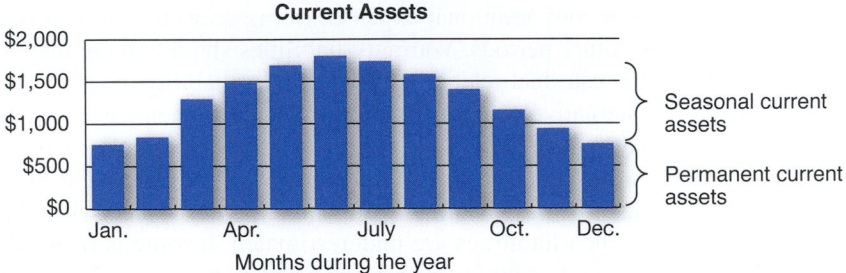

This particular company does most of its selling in the summer months. More inventory is purchased and manufactured in the early spring than at any other time of the year. Sales of the company's manufactured goods are also greater during the summer months, giving rise to accounts receivable that are higher than normal during the summer and fall. The peak working capital level is reached at the height of the selling season and is lowest when the business slows in the off-season. There is a permanent level of working capital required for this business (about $750), and a seasonal component (maximum of about $1,000). Businesses differ in their working capital requirements, but many have permanent and seasonal components.

If a company's working capital needs fluctuate from one season to the next, then the financing needs of the company are also seasonal. Some assets can be financed with short-term operating liabilities. For example, seasonal increases in inventory balances are typically financed with increased levels of accounts payable. However, operating liabilities are unlikely to meet all of the financing needs of a company. Additional financing is provided by short-term interest-bearing debt.

This section focuses on short-term nonoperating liabilities. These include short-term debt and interest as well as current maturities of long-term liabilities.

Short-Term Interest-Bearing Debt

Seasonal swings in working capital are often financed with a bank line of credit (short-term debt). In this case the bank provides a commitment to lend up to a given level with the understanding that the amounts borrowed are repaid in full sometime during the year. An interest-bearing note is evidence of such borrowing.

When these short-term funds are borrowed, the cash received is reported on the balance sheet together with an increase in liabilities (notes payable). The note is reported as a current liability because the expectation is that it will be paid within a year. This borrowing transaction has no effect on income or equity, but there will be a financing cash inflow on the statement of cash flows. The borrower incurs (and the lender earns) interest on the note as time passes. U.S. GAAP requires the borrower to accrue the interest liability and the related interest expense each time financial statements are issued.

To illustrate, assume that Verizon borrows $1,000 cash from 1st Bank on January 1. The note bears interest at a 12% annual (3% quarterly) rate, and the interest is payable on the first of each subsequent quarter (April 1, July 1, October 1, January 1). Assuming that Verizon issues calendar-quarter financial statements, this borrowing results in the following financial statement effects for the period January 1 through April 1:

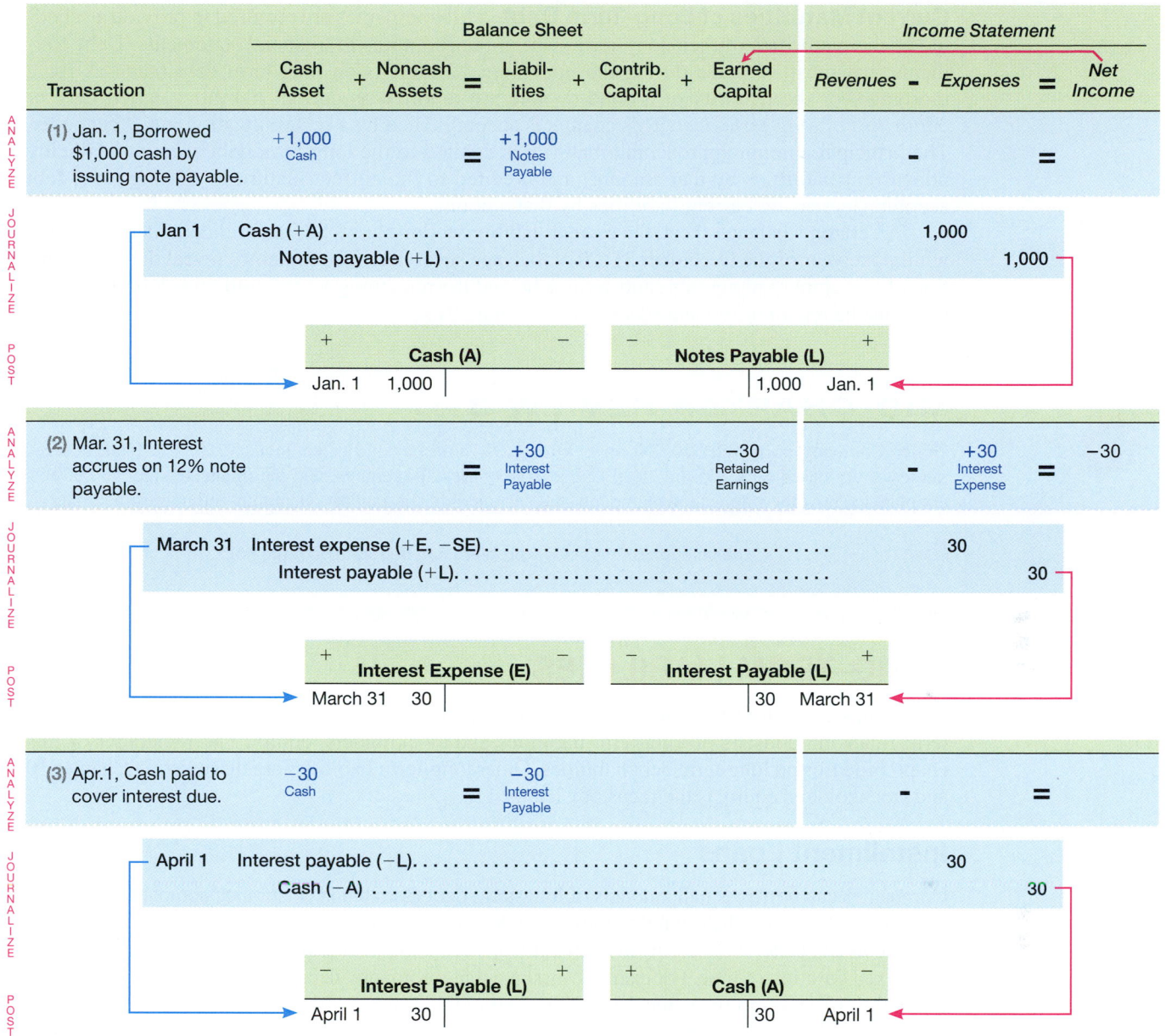

The January 1 borrowing is reflected by an increase in cash and in notes payable. On March 31, this company issues its quarterly financial statements. Although interest is not paid until April 1, the company has incurred three months' interest obligation as of March 31. Failure to recognize this liability and the expense incurred would not fairly present the financial condition of the company. Accordingly, the quarterly accrued interest is computed as follows:

Interest Expense = Principal × Annual Rate × Portion of Year Outstanding

$$\$30 = \$1{,}000 \times 12\% \times 3/12$$

The subsequent interest payment on April 1 is reflected in the financial statements as a reduction of cash and a reduction of the interest payable liability accrued on March 31. There is no expense reported on April 1, because it was recorded the previous day (March 31) when the financial statements were prepared, however the payment of interest would be an operating cash outflow in the statement of cash flows for the quarter beginning April 1. (For fixed-maturity borrowings specified in days, such as a 90-day note, we use a 365-day year for interest accrual computations, see Mid-Chapter Review 3.)

Current Maturities of Long-Term Debt   All companies are required to provide a schedule of the maturities of their long-term debt in the footnotes to financial statements. Debt payments that must be made during the upcoming 12 months on long-term debt (such as for a mortgage) or the maturity of a bond or note are reported as current liabilities called *current maturities of long-term debt*. This change is accomplished by a reclassification in the accounts. The principal amount approaching maturity is debited to the long-term debt account (reducing noncurrent liabilities by that amount) and credited to the current maturities of long-term debt account (increasing current liabilities by that amount).

In Verizon's balance sheet, the current liability section shows $2,735 million in debt maturing within one year of the December 31, 2014, balance sheet date. The footnotes reveal that $338 million of this amount represents short-term debt, and the remaining $2,397 million is long-term debt that must be repaid or refinanced sometime during 2015.

MID-CHAPTER REVIEW 3

Gigler Company borrowed $10,000 on a 90-day, 6% note payable dated January 15. The bank accrues interest daily based on a 365-day year. Use journal entries, T-accounts, and the financial statement effects template to show the implications (amounts and accounts) of the January 31 month-end interest accrual.

The solution to this review problem can be found on page 457.

LONG-TERM LIABILITIES

Companies generally try to fund long-term investments in assets with long-term financing. Long-term financing consists of long-term liabilities and stockholders' equity. The remainder of this chapter focuses on long-term debt liabilities. Other long-term liabilities are discussed in Chapter 10 and stockholders' equity is the focus of Chapter 11.

Installment Loans

Companies can borrow small amounts of long-term debt from banks, insurance companies, or other financial institutions. These liabilities are often designed as installment loans and may be secured by specific assets called **collateral**. Installment loans are loans that require a fixed periodic payment for a fixed duration of time. For example, assume that a company decides to finance an office building with a 15-year mortgage requiring 180 equal monthly payments (180 payments = 15 years × 12 months). The fixed payment on an installment loan includes a portion of the principal (i.e., the amount borrowed) plus any interest that has accrued on the loan.

To illustrate the accounting for installment loans, assume that Shevlin Company borrowed $40,000 from 1st Bank on July 1, 2015. The terms of the loan require that Shevlin repay the loan in 12 equal quarterly payments over a three-year period and require 8% interest per year. The quarterly payment is $3,782 and can be calculated using the Table A3 (page 639) present value factor for 12 periods (3 years × 4 quarters) and 2% interest (8% per year ÷ 4 quarters) as follows:

$$\text{Present Value} = \text{Payment} \times \text{Present Value Factor}$$

$$\frac{\text{Present Value}}{\text{Present Value Factor}} = \text{Payment}$$

$$\frac{\$40,000}{10.57534} = \$3,782$$

Using a financial calculator, we can compute the payment by letting N be the number of quarters and setting I/Yr equal to the interest rate per quarter. The payment can then be calculated as follows: N = 12; I/Yr = 2; PV = 40,000; FV = 0:

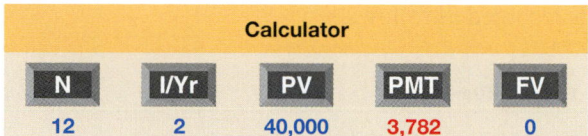

When Shevlin Company agrees to the loan terms, it receives the loan amount, $40,000 in cash, and incurs a $40,000 liability (installment loan payable). The loan is recorded on July 1 as follows:

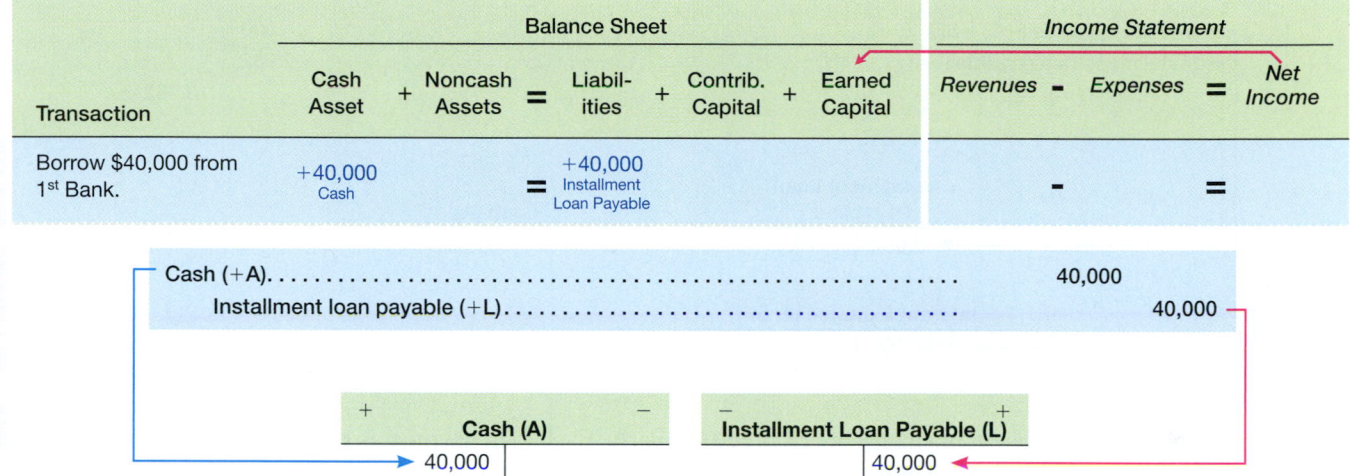

On October 1, 2015, the first payment of $3,782 is due. The payment includes both interest for the three months from July 1 through September 30, and some portion of the original loan amount (the **principal**). The division of the payment between interest and principal is best illustrated using a **loan amortization table**, like the one in **Exhibit 9.2**. (Pages 624–634 in Appendix A demonstrate the use of Excel to calculate the required payment and the amortization table.)

Each payment includes interest and principal. The first loan payment, due on October 1, 2015, is summarized in the second row of the table. Column [B] is the quarterly loan payment. Column [C] is the interest expense, computed by multiplying column [A] by the interest rate (2 percent per quarter). Column [D] is the principal portion of the payment, which is the cash payment (column [B]) less the interest (column [C]). The remaining balance on the loan is in column [E], which is equal to the beginning balance in column [A] less the principal payment from column [D]. The loan balance decreases with each payment until the loan is paid off on July 1, 2018.

EXHIBIT 9.2	Loan Amortization Table				
Date	**[A]** **Beginning** **Balance**	**[B]** **Cash** **Payment**	**[C]** **([A] × interest %)** **Interest**	**[D]** **([B] – [C])** **Principal**	**[E]** **([A] – [D])** **Balance**
07/01/15.............					40,000
10/01/15.............	40,000	3,782	800	2,982	37,018
01/01/16.............	37,018	3,782	740	3,042	33,976
04/01/16.............	33,976	3,782	679	3,103	30,873
07/01/16.............	30,873	3,782	617	3,165	27,708
10/01/16.............	27,708	3,782	554	3,228	24,480
01/01/17.............	24,480	3,782	489	3,293	21,187
04/01/17.............	21,187	3,782	423	3,359	17,828
07/01/17.............	17,828	3,782	356	3,426	14,402
10/01/17.............	14,402	3,782	288	3,494	10,908
01/01/18.............	10,908	3,782	218	3,564	7,344
04/01/18.............	7,344	3,782	146	3,636	3,708
07/01/18.............	3,708	3,782	74	3,708	0

The first payment is recorded as follows:

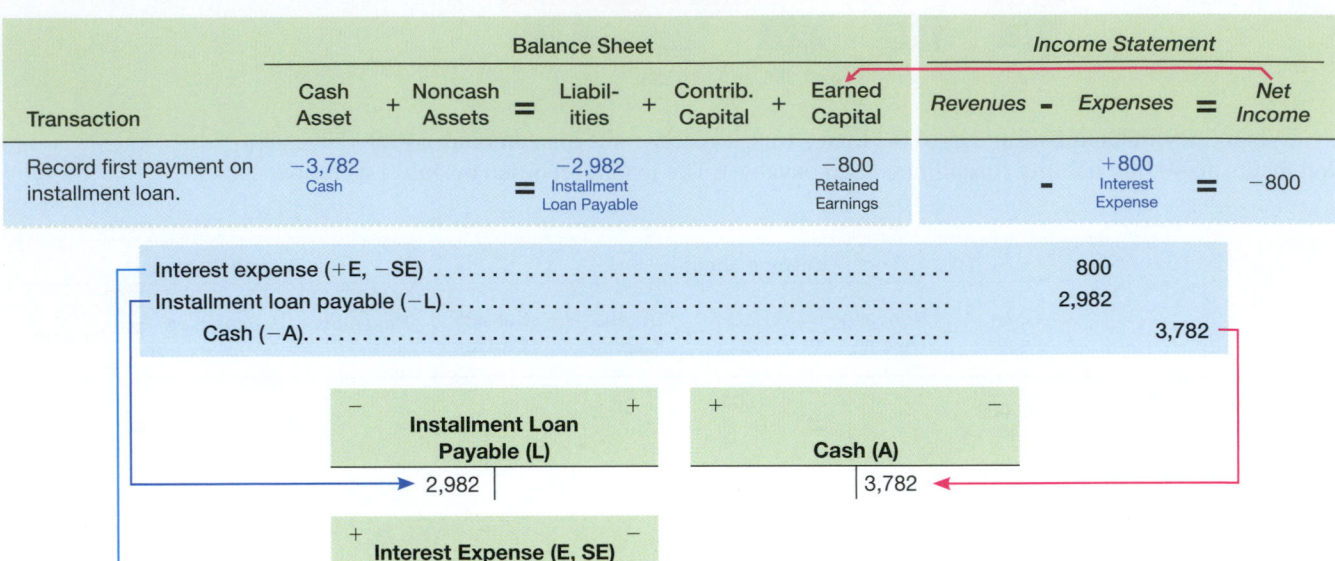

	Balance Sheet					Income Statement		
Transaction	Cash Asset	+ Noncash Assets	= Liabil- ities	+ Contrib. Capital	+ Earned Capital	Revenues −	Expenses =	Net Income
Record first payment on installment loan.	−3,782 Cash		= −2,982 Installment Loan Payable		−800 Retained Earnings	−	+800 Interest Expense	= −800

Interest expense (+E, −SE)	800	
Installment loan payable (−L).	2,982	
Cash (−A).		3,782

− Installment Loan Payable (L) +	+ Cash (A) −
2,982	3,782

+   Interest Expense (E, SE) −
800

ANALYZE   JOURNALIZE   POST

Subsequent payments are recorded similarly. Each loan payment is the same amount, quarter after quarter. And each period's interest expense is equal to the beginning loan balance times the periodic interest rate. Any difference between the payment and the interest expense affects the loan balance. In **Exhibit 9.2**, each payment contains some portion of interest expense and some portion of principal repayment, and the amounts change over time. As principal is repaid, the loan balance decreases, reducing the subsequent periods' interest expense and increasing the subsequent periods' principal repayment.

Bonds

Sometimes the amount or duration of financing required by a company is greater than the amount that a bank or insurance company can provide. Companies can borrow larger amounts of money by issuing bonds (or notes) in the capital markets. Bonds and notes are debt securities issued by companies and traded in the bond markets. When a company issues bonds, it is borrowing money. The investors who buy the bonds are lending money to the issuing company. That is, the bondholders are the company's creditors. Because the bond markets provide companies with access to large amounts of capital, bonds represent a very common, cost-effective source of long-term debt financing.

Bonds and notes are structured like any other borrowing. The borrower receives cash and agrees to pay it back with interest. Generally, the entire **face amount** (principal) of the bond or note is repaid at maturity and interest payments are made (usually semiannually) in the interim.

Companies wishing to raise funds in the bond market normally work with an underwriter (e.g., **Goldman Sachs**) to set the terms of the bond issue. The underwriter sells individual bonds (usually in $1,000 denominations) from this general bond issue to its retail clients, corporations and professional portfolio managers (e.g., **The Vanguard Group**), and it receives a fee for underwriting the bond issue.

Once issued, the bonds can be traded in the secondary market between investors just like stocks. Market prices of bonds fluctuate daily despite the fact that the company's obligation for payment of principal and interest remains fixed throughout the life of the bond. This occurs because of fluctuations in the general level of interest rates and changes in the financial condition of the borrowing company.

The following sections analyze and interpret the reporting for bonds. We first examine the mechanics of bond pricing. In a subsequent section, we address the accounting for and reporting of bonds.

Pricing of Bonds

Two different interest rates are crucial for understanding how a bond is priced.

LO3 Explain and illustrate the pricing of long-term nonoperating liabilities.

3

- **Coupon (contract** or **stated) rate** The coupon rate of interest is stated in the bond contract. It is used to compute the dollar amount of (semiannual) interest payments that are paid to bondholders during the life of the bond issue.

- **Market (yield) rate** The market rate is the interest rate that investors expect to earn on the investment for this debt security. This rate is used to price the bond issue.

The coupon (contract) rate is used to compute interest payments and the market (yield) rate is used to price the bond. The coupon rate and the market rate are nearly always different. The coupon rate is fixed prior to issuance of the bond and remains so throughout its life (unless the interest rate "floats" with market rates). Market rates of interest, on the other hand, fluctuate continually with the supply and demand for bonds in the marketplace, general macroeconomic conditions, and the financial condition of borrowers.

The bond price equals the **present value** of the expected cash flows to the bondholder. Specifically, bondholders normally expect to receive two different cash flows:

1. **Periodic interest payments** (usually semiannual) during the bond's life. These cash flows are typically in the form of equal payments at periodic intervals, called an **annuity**.

2. **Single payment** of the face (principal) amount of the bond at maturity.

The bond price equals the present value of the periodic interest payments plus the present value of the principal payment at maturity. We next illustrate the issuance of bonds at three different prices: at par, at a discount, and at a premium.

Bonds Issued at Par When a bond is issued at par, its coupon rate is identical to the market rate. Under this condition, a $1,000 bond sells for $1,000 in the market. To illustrate bond pricing, assume that investors wish to value a bond issue with a face amount of $100,000, a 6% annual coupon rate with interest payable semiannually (3% semiannual rate), and a maturity of 4 years.[5] Investors purchasing this issue receive the following cash flows:

	Number of Payments	Dollars per Payment	Total Cash Flows
Semiannual interest payments	4 years × 2 = 8	$100,000 × 3% = $ 3,000	$ 24,000
Principal payment at maturity.	1	$100,000	100,000
			$124,000

Specifically, the bond agreement dictates that the borrower makes 8 semiannual payments of $3,000 each, computed as $100,000 × (6%/2), plus the $100,000 face amount at maturity, for a total of $124,000 in cash flows. Each $1,000 bond in this bond issue provides the bondholder with an annuity of 8 payments of $30 and a principal payment of $1,000 at maturity. For an individual bond, the cash flows total $1,240 (= $30 × 8 + $1,000).

When pricing bonds, the number of periods used for computing the present value is the number of interest (coupon) payments required by the bond. In this case, there are 8 semiannual interest payments required, so we use 8, six-month periods to value the bond. The market interest rate (yield) is 6% per year, which is 3% per six-month period.

The bond price is the present value of the interest annuity plus the present value of the principal payment. Assuming that investors desire a 6% annual market rate (yield), the bond sells for exactly $100,000, which is computed as follows:

---

[5] Semiannual interest payments are typical for bonds. With semiannual interest payments, the issuer pays bondholders two interest payments per year. The semiannual interest rate is the annual rate divided by two.

	Payment	Present Value Factor[a]	Present Value
Interest	$ 3,000	7.01969[b]	$ 21,059
Principal	$100,000	0.78941[c]	78,941
			$100,000

[a] Mechanics of using tables to compute present values are explained in Appendix A at the end of the text. Present value factors are taken from tables provided in Appendix A.

[b] Present value of ordinary annuity for 8 periods discounted at 3% per period.

[c] Present value of single payment in 8 periods hence discounted at 3% per period.

Because the bond contract pays investors a 6% annual rate when investors demand a 6% market rate, investors purchase these bonds at the **par (face) value** of $1,000 per bond, or $100,000 in total.[6] Using a financial calculator, we can compute the bond value as follows: N = 8; I/Yr = 3; PMT = 3,000; FV = 100,000:

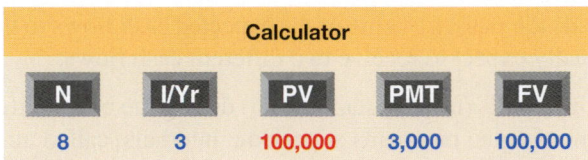

Bonds Issued at a Discount As a second illustration, assume that market conditions are such that investors demand an 8% annual yield (4% semiannual) for the 6% coupon bond, while all other details remain the same. The bond now sells for $93,267, computed as follows:

	Payment	Present Value Factor	Present Value
Interest	$ 3,000	6.73274[a]	$20,198
Principal	$100,000	0.73069[b]	73,069
			$93,267

[a] Present value of ordinary annuity for 8 periods discounted at 4% per period.

[b] Present value of single payment in 8 periods hence discounted at 4% per period.

Using a financial calculator, the bond is priced as follows: N = 8; I/Yr = 4; PMT = 3,000; FV = 100,000:

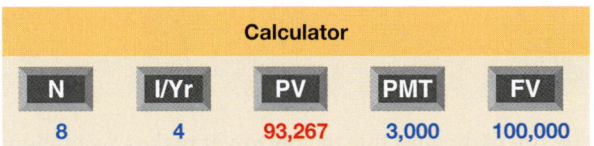

The market price of the bond issue is, therefore, $93,267. The price of each bond in the bond issue is $932.67 (= $93,267/100).

Because the bond carries a coupon rate *lower* than that which investors demand, the bond is less desirable and sells at a **discount**. In general, bonds sell at a discount whenever the coupon rate is less than the market rate.[7]

Bonds Issued at a Premium As a third illustration, assume that investors in the bond market demand a 4% annual yield (2% semiannual) for the 6% coupon bonds, while all other details remain the same. The bond issue now sells for $107,325, computed as follows:

---

[6] If we purchase a bond after the semiannual interest date, we must pay accrued interest in addition to the purchase price. This interest is returned to us in the regular interest payment. (This procedure makes the bookkeeping easier for the issuer/underwriter.)

[7] Bond prices are often stated in percent form. For example, a bond sold at par is said to be sold at 100 (that is, 100% of its face value, par). The bond sold at $932.67 is said to be sold at 93.267 (93.267% of par, computed as $932.67/$1,000).

	Payment	Present Value Factor	Present Value
Interest	$ 3,000	7.32548[a]	$ 21,976
Principal	$100,000	0.85349[b]	85,349
			$107,325

[a] Present value of ordinary annuity for 8 periods discounted at 2% per period.

[b] Present value of single payment in 8 periods hence discounted at 2% per period.

Using a financial calculator, the bond is priced as follows: N = 8; I/Yr = 2; PMT = 3,000; FV = 100,000:

Calculator				
N	**I/Yr**	**PV**	**PMT**	**FV**
8	2	107,325	3,000	100,000

The market price of the bond issue is, therefore, $107,325. The price of each bond in the bond issue is $1,073.25 (= $107,325/100).

Because the bond carries a coupon rate higher than that which investors demand, the bond is more desirable and sells at a **premium**. In general, bonds sell at a premium whenever the coupon rate is greater than the market rate. **Exhibit 9.3** summarizes this relation for bond pricing.

EXHIBIT 9.3	Coupon Rate, Market Rate, and Bond Pricing
Coupon rate > market rate →	Bond sells at a **premium** (above face amount)
Coupon rate = market rate →	Bond sells at **par** (at face amount)
Coupon rate < market rate →	Bond sells at a **discount** (below face amount)

Effective Cost of Debt

When a bond sells for par, the cost to the issuing company is the cash interest paid. In our first illustration where the bond is issued at par, the *effective cost* of the bond is the 6% interest paid by the issuer.

When a bond sells at a discount, the issuer's effective cost consists of two parts: (1) the cash interest paid and (2) the discount incurred. The discount, which is the difference between par and the lower issue price, is a cost that must eventually be reflected in the issuer's income statement as an expense. This fact means that the effective cost of a discount bond is greater than if the bond had sold at par. A discount is a cost and, like any other cost, must eventually be transferred from the balance sheet to the income statement as an expense. In the previous section's discount example, the economic substance is that the bond issuer has not borrowed $100,000 at 6%, but rather $93,267 at 8%.

When a bond sells at a premium, the issuer's effective cost consists of (1) the cash interest paid and (2) a cost reduction due to the premium received. The premium is a benefit that must eventually find its way from the balance sheet to the income statement as a *reduction* of interest expense. As a result of the premium, the effective cost of a premium bond is less than if the bond had sold at par. Effectively, the bond issuer has borrowed $107,325 at 4% in the premium example above.

Bonds are priced to yield the return (market rate) demanded by investors in the bond market, which results in the effective interest rate of a bond *always* equaling the yield (market) rate, regardless of the coupon (stated) rate of the bond. Bond prices are set by the market so as to always yield the rate required by investors based on the terms and qualities of the bond. Companies cannot influence the effective cost of debt by raising or lowering the coupon rate. We discuss the factors affecting the market yield later in the chapter.

The effective cost of debt is ultimately reflected in the amount reported in the issuer's income statement as interest expense. This amount can be, and usually is, different from the cash interest paid. The two are the same only for a bond issued at par. The next section discusses how management reports bonds on the balance sheet and interest expense on the income statement.

Reporting of Bond Financing

LO4 Analyze and account for financial statement effects of long-term nonoperating liabilities.

This section identifies and describes the financial statement effects of bond transactions.

Bonds Issued at Par When a bond sells at par, the issuing company receives the cash proceeds and accepts an obligation to make payments per the bond contract. Specifically, cash is increased and a liability (bonds payable) is increased by the same amount. Using the facts from our earlier illustration, the issuance of bonds at par has the following financial statement effects (there is no revenue or expense at the date the bond is issued):

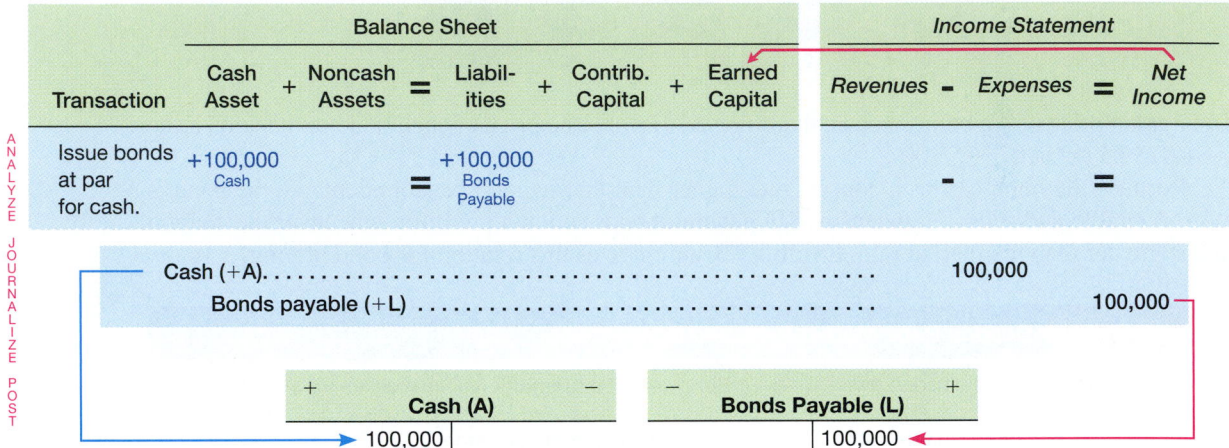

Bonds Issued at a Discount For the discount bond case, cash is increased by the proceeds from the sale of the bonds, and the liability increases by the same amount. However, the net liability consisting of the two components shown below (including a bond discount contra liability) is reported on the balance sheet.

FYI "Bonds Payable, Net" is a common title reflecting the face value of the bond less the unamortized discount.

Bonds payable, face.	$100,000
Less bond discount	(6,733)
Bonds payable, net	$ 93,267

Using the facts above from our bond discount illustration, the financial statement effects follow:

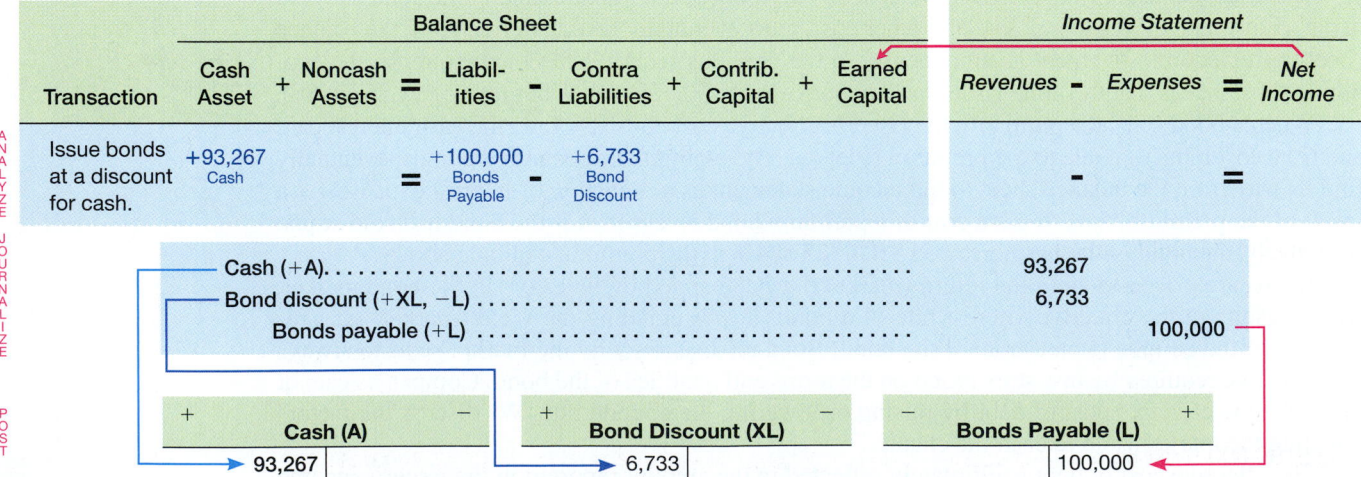

Bonds are reported on the balance sheet net of any discount (or plus any premium). When the bond matures, however, the company is obligated to repay $100,000. Accordingly, at maturity, the bond liability must read $100,000, the amount that is owed. Therefore, between the bond issuance and its maturity, the discount must decline to zero. This reduction of the discount over the life of the bond is called **amortization**. This amortization causes the effective interest expense to be greater than the periodic cash interest payments based on the coupon rate.

BUSINESS INSIGHT

Zeros and Strips   Zero coupon bonds and notes, called *zeros*, do not carry an explicit coupon rate. However, the pricing of these bonds and notes is done in the same manner as those with coupon rates—the exception is the absence of an interest annuity. This omission means that the price is the present value of just the principal payment at maturity; hence the bond is sold at a *deep discount*. For example, consider a 4-year, $100,000 zero coupon bond, priced to yield a market rate of 6%. The only payment would be the return of principal 4 years away. We already know that the present value of this single payment is $78,941. This "zero" would initially sell for $78,941 resulting in a substantial discount of $21,059.

Another interesting variation on traditional bonds is a *strip*, which is short for **S**eparately **TR**aded *I*nterest and *P*rincipal. Initially, a strip is priced and sold just like an ordinary bond. Subsequently, the two payment components—the periodic coupon payments and the *balloon* payment of principal which is due when the bond matures—are sold separately. A 4-year, $100,000 bond priced at $100,000 to yield 6% would be separated into two securities: 1) a zero, selling for $78,941, representing the present value of this single payment, and, 2) another security, priced at $21,059, representing the present value of the coupon payments.

Bonds Issued at a Premium

When a bond is sold at a premium, the cash proceeds and net bond liability are recorded at the amount of the proceeds received (not the face amount of the bond). Again, using the facts above from our premium bond illustration, the financial statement effects are:

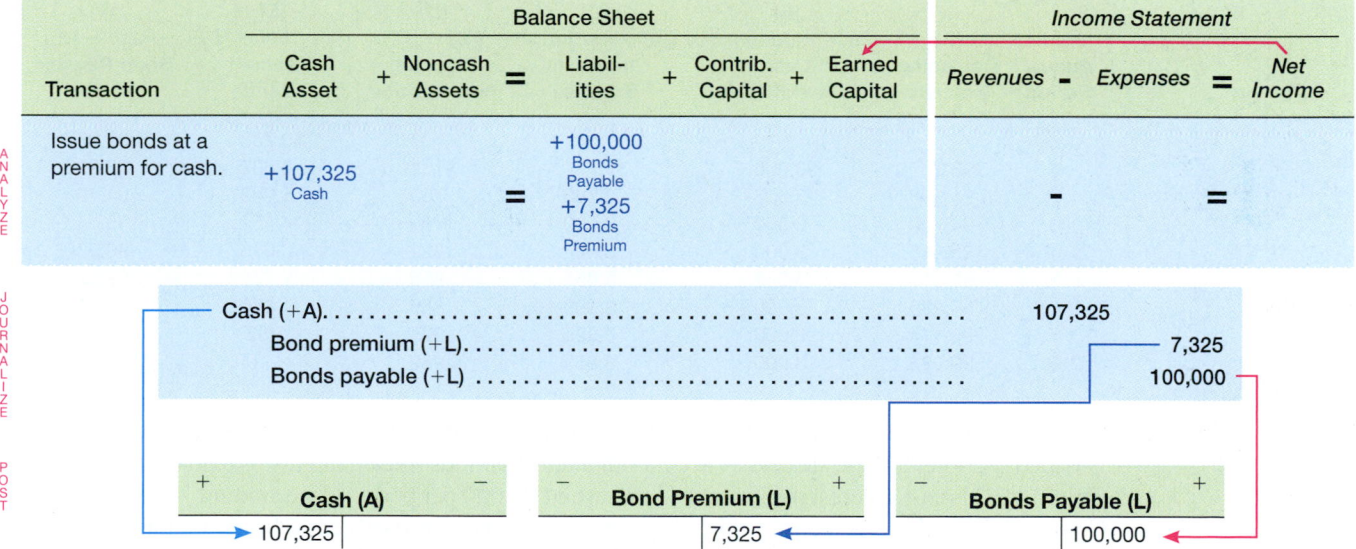

The net bond liability amount reported on the balance sheet, again, consists of two parts:

Bonds payable, face.	$100,000
Add bond premium	7,325
Bonds payable, net	$107,325

The $100,000 must be repaid at maturity, and the premium is amortized to zero over the life of the bond. The premium represents a *benefit*, which yields a *reduction* in interest expense on the income statement.

Effects of Discount and Premium Amortization

The amount of interest expense that is reported on the income statement always equals the loan balance at the beginning of the period (bonds payable, net of discount or premium) times the market interest rate at the time of issue. For bonds issued at par, interest expense equals the cash interest payment. However, for bonds issued at a discount or premium, interest expense reported on the income statement equals interest paid adjusted for the amortization of the discount or premium:

	Cash interest paid				Cash interest paid
+	Amortization of discount	or	−		Amortization of premium
	Interest expense				Interest expense

Specifically, periodic amortization of a discount is added to the cash interest paid to get interest expense for a discount bond. Amortization of the discount reflects the additional cost the issuer incurs from issuance of the bonds at a discount and its recognition, via amortization, as an increase to interest expense. For a premium bond, the premium is a benefit the issuer receives at issuance. Amortization of the premium reduces interest expense over the debt term. Consequently, interest expense on the income statement represents the *effective cost* of debt (the *nominal cost* of debt is the cash interest paid). This is true whether the bonds are issued at par, at a discount, or at a premium.

Companies amortize discounts and premiums using the effective interest method. To illustrate, recall the assumptions of the discount bond above—face amount of $100,000, a 6% annual coupon rate payable semiannually (3% semiannual rate), a maturity of 4 years, and a market (yield) rate of 8% annual (4% semiannual). These facts resulted in a bond issue price of $932.67 per bond or $93,267 for the entire bond issue. **Exhibit 9.4** illustrates a bond discount amortization table for this bond.

| **EXHIBIT 9.4** | **Bond Discount Amortization Table** |

Semi-Annual Period	[A] Beginning Balance	[B] (Face × coupon%) Cash Interest Paid	[C] ([A] × market%) Interest Expense	[D] ([C] − [B]) Discount Amortization	[E] (Prior bal − [D]) Discount Balance	[F] (Face − [E]) Bond Payable Net
0					$6,733	$ 93,267
1	$93,267	$3,000	$3,731	$731	6,002	93,998
2	93,998	3,000	3,760	760	5,242	94,758
3	94,758	3,000	3,790	790	4,452	95,548
4	95,548	3,000	3,822	822	3,630	96,370
5	96,370	3,000	3,855	855	2,775	97,225
6	97,225	3,000	3,889	889	1,886	98,114
7	98,114	3,000	3,925	925	962	99,038
8	99,038	3,000	3,962	962	0	100,000

The interest period is denoted in the left-most column. Period 0 is the point in time at which the bond is issued. Periods 1–8 are successive six-month interest periods (recall, interest is paid semiannually). Column [B] is cash interest paid, which is a constant $3,000 per period (face amount × coupon rate). Column [C] is interest expense, which is reported in the income statement. This column is computed as the carrying amount of the bond at the beginning of the period (column [A]) multiplied by the 4% semiannual yield rate used to compute the bond issue price. Column [D] is discount amortization, which is the difference between interest expense and cash interest paid. Column [E] is the discount balance, which is the previous balance of the discount less the discount amortization in column [D]. Column [F] is the net bond payable, which is the $100,000 face amount less the unamortized discount from column [E]. Column [A] is the value from the previous period's column [F].

The amortization process continues until period 8, at which time the discount balance is $0 and the net bond payable is $100,000 (the maturity value). An amortization table reveals the financial statement effects of the bond for its duration. Specifically, we see the cash effects in column [B], the income statement effects in column [C], and the balance sheet effects in columns [D], [E], and [F].

To record the interest payment at the end of period 1, we use the values in row 1 of the amortization table. The resulting entry is recorded as follows:

	Balance Sheet							Income Statement		
Transaction	Cash Asset	+ Noncash Assets	= Liabil-ities	− Contra Liabilities	+ Contrib. Capital	+ Earned Capital		Revenues −	Expenses =	Net Income
Record interest payment and interest expense on bond.	−3,000 Cash		=	− −731 Bond Discount		−3,731 Retained Earnings		−	+3,731 Interest Expense	= −3,731

Interest expense (+E, −SE)	3,731	
Cash (−A)		3,000
Bond discount (−XL, +L)		731

+ Interest Expense (E) −	+ Cash (A) −	+ Bond Discount (XL) −
3,731	3,000	731

To illustrate amortization of a premium bond, we use the assumptions of the premium bond above—$100,000 face value, a 6% annual coupon rate payable semiannually (3% semiannual rate), a maturity of 4 years, and a 4% annual market (yield) rate (2% semiannual). These parameters resulted in a bond issue price of $1,073.25 per bond or $107,325 for the entire bond issue. **Exhibit 9.5** shows the bond premium amortization table for this bond.

EXHIBIT 9.5	Bond Premium Amortization Table					
Semi-Annual Period	**[A]** Beginning Balance	**[B]** (Face × coupon%) Cash Interest Paid	**[C]** ([A] × market%) Interest Expense	**[D]** ([B] − [C]) Premium Amortization	**[E]** (Prior bal − [D]) Premium Balance	**[F]** (Face + [E]) Bond Payable Net
0					$7,325	$107,325
1	$107,325	$3,000	$2,147	$853	6,472	106,472
2	106,472	3,000	2,129	871	5,601	105,601
3	105,601	3,000	2,112	888	4,713	104,713
4	104,713	3,000	2,094	906	3,807	103,807
5	103,807	3,000	2,076	924	2,883	102,883
6	102,883	3,000	2,058	942	1,941	101,941
7	101,941	3,000	2,039	961	980	100,980
8	100,980	3,000	2,020	980	0	100,000

Interest expense is computed using the same process that we used for discount bonds. The difference is that the yield rate is 4% (2% semiannual) in the premium case. Cash interest paid follows from the bond contract (face amount × coupon rate), and the other columns' computations reflect the premium amortization. After period 8, the premium is fully amortized (equals zero) and the net bond payable balance is $100,000, the amount owed at maturity. The book value of bonds issued at a discount starts below the face value and, over time, increases. The book value of bonds issued at a premium starts above the bonds' face value and, over time, decreases. At maturity, the book value of both types of bonds equals the face value that must be paid to the bondholders. Again, an amortization table reveals the financial statement effects of the bond—the cash effects in column [B], the income statement effects in column [C], and the balance sheet effects in columns [D], [E], and [F].

To record the interest payment at the end of period 1, we, again, use the values in row 1 of the amortization table. The resulting entry is recorded as follows:

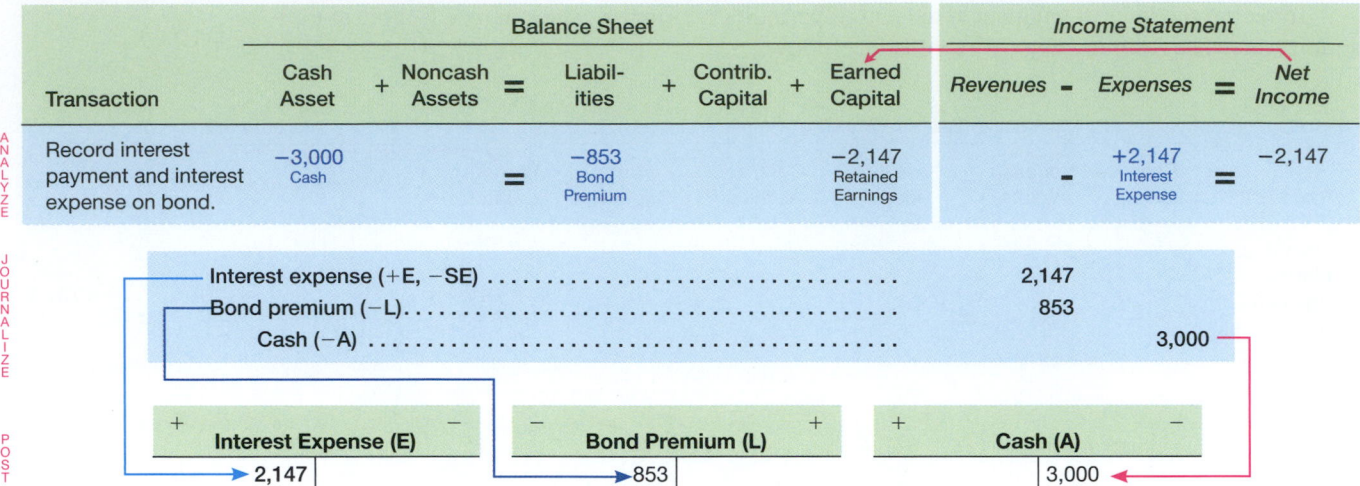

The Fair Value Option

Thus far, we have described the reporting of liabilities at *historical cost*. This means that all financial statement relationships are established on the date that the liability is created and do not subsequently change. For example, the interest rate used to value a bond is the market rate of interest on the date that the bond is issued and the reported value of the bond is the face value plus the unamortized premium or minus the unamortized discount. Yet, once issued, bonds can be traded in secondary markets. Market interest rates fluctuate and, as a consequence, the market value of a bond is likely to change after the bond is issued.

As an alternative to historical cost, a company may elect to report some or all of its financial liabilities at *fair value*. Moreover, a company may choose to report some of its liabilities at historical cost and others at fair value. It must make this choice at the inception of the liability (e.g., at the time that a bond is issued) and cannot subsequently switch between fair value and historical cost for that liability. If a company elects to report a liability at fair value in its balance sheet, then any changes in fair value are reported as a gain or loss in its income statement. If a liability is to be reported at historical cost, then its fair value is disclosed in the notes.

To illustrate how we report a liability at fair value, we refer to our example of a 4-year, 6% bond issued at a discount to yield 8%. The issue price of this bond is $93,267 and we assume that the bond is issued on June 30, 2015. Six months later, on December 31, the issuing company pays the first of eight coupon payments of $3,000. From **Exhibit 9.4**, we know that after this coupon payment, the bond payable, net of the discount, is equal to $93,998. Now assume that the market value of the bond has increased to $96,943. (This price increase is consistent with a market interest rate that has decreased to 7%.) The bond would now be reported on the balance sheet at a value of $96,943:

Bonds payable	$100,000
Less, unamortized discount	6,002
Bond payable, net (historical cost)	$ 93,998
Plus, fair value adjustment	2,945
Bond payable, net (fair value)	$ 96,943

The increase in the bond's fair value must be added to an account that adjusts the bond payable liability. The balancing entry is included as a loss in the income statement, and ends up in retained earnings. The fair value adjustment would be recorded as follows:

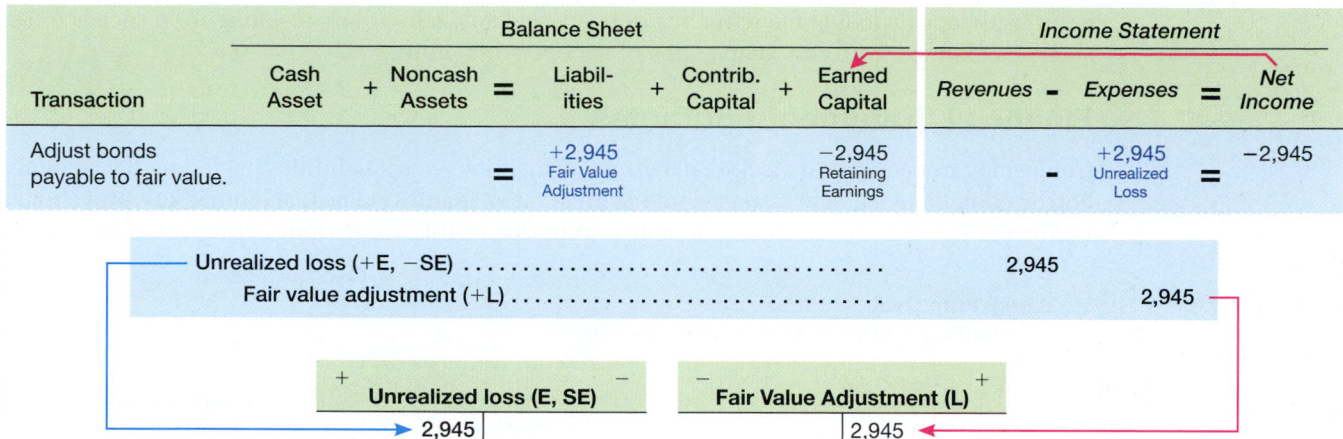

The fair value computation does not affect the calculation of interest expense or the amortization of the bond discount in this or any subsequent period. The unrealized loss does have an effect on the income statement. For this illustration, the total effect on income for 2015 is $6,676, which is computed as:

Coupon payment, July 1—December 31.......	$3,000
Amortization of the bond discount...........	731
Interest expense.........................	$3,731
Unrealized loss..........................	2,945
Total effect (decrease) on earnings...........	$6,676

If the fair value of this bond decreases (e.g., because interest rates increase), the fair value adjustment account would be debited and an unrealized gain would be credited and reported in the income statement. We discuss the fair value option further in Chapter 12.[8]

Effects of Bond Repurchase

Companies can and sometimes do repurchase (also called *redeem*) their bonds prior to maturity. The bond indenture (contract agreement) often includes a **call provision** giving the company the right to repurchase its bond by paying a small premium above face value. Alternatively, the company can repurchase bonds in the open market. When a company uses historical cost to account for its bonds, a bond repurchase usually results in a gain or loss, and is computed as follows:

Gain or loss on bond repurchase = Book value of the bond − Repurchase payment

The *book (carrying) value of the bond* is the net amount reported on the balance sheet. If the issuer pays more to retire the bonds than the amount carried on its balance sheet, a loss is reported on its income statement, usually called *loss on bond retirement*. The issuer reports a *gain on bond retirement* if the repurchase price is less than the book value of the bond.

GAAP dictates that any gains or losses on bond repurchases be reported as part of ordinary income unless they meet the criteria for treatment as part of discontinued operations. Relatively few debt retirements meet these criteria and, hence, most gains and losses on bond repurchases are reported as part of income from continuing operations.

The question arises as to how gains and losses on the redemption of bonds should affect our analysis of a company's profitability. Because bonds and notes payable represent nonoperating

---

[8] At the time of this textbook writing, the FASB is considering a change in the fair value accounting for companies' own debt. When a company's credit standing deteriorates under current fair value accounting, the fair value of its debt decreases and produces a gain on the company's income statement. Likewise, when a company's credit standing improves, the company reports a loss from the increased fair value of its debt. Many investors find these effects counter-intuitive. It is projected that the FASB will require these gains and losses to be reported in Other Comprehensive Income (discussed in Chapter 12) and have no effect on Net Income until the company's debt is redeemed.

items, activities including the refunding of bonds and any gain or loss resulting from such activity should be omitted from our computation of net operating profit.

Financial Statement Footnotes

Companies are required to disclose details about their long-term liabilities, including the amounts borrowed under each debt issuance, the interest rates, maturity dates, and other key provisions. Following is Verizon's disclosure in note 8 to its 2014 10-K for its long-term debt ($ millions):

Long-Term Debt

Outstanding long-term obligations are as follows:

At December 31	Interest Rates %	Maturities	(dollars in millions)	
			2014	2013
Verizon Communications—notes payable and other...........................	0.30—3.85	2015—2042	$ 27,617	$20,416
	4.15—5.50	2018—2054	40,701	20,226
	5.85—6.90	2018—2054	24,341	31,965
	7.35—8.95	2018—2039	2,264	5,023
	Floating	2015—2025	14,600	5,500
Verizon Wireless—notes payable and other....	8.75—8.88	2015—2018	676	3,931
Verizon—Alltel assumed notes..............	6.80—7.88	2029—2032	686	1,300
Telephone subsidiaries—debentures.........	5.13—6.86	2027—2033	1,075	1,075
	7.38—7.88	2022—2032	1,099	1,099
	8.00—8.75	2019—2031	880	880
Other subsidiaries—debentures and other	6.84—8.75	2018—2028	1,432	1,700
Capital lease obligations (average rate of 4.0% and 8.1% in 2014 and 2013, respectively)			516	293
Unamortized discount, net of premium			(2,954)	(264)
Total long-term debt, including current maturities			112,933	93,144
Less long-term debt maturing within one year..........................			2,397	3,486
Total long-term debt...			$110,536	$89,658

Verizon reports a book value for long-term debt of $112,933 million at year-end 2014. Of this amount, $2,397 million matures in the next year, hence its classification as a current liability (current maturities of long-term debt) and the remainder matures after 2015. Verizon also reports $2,954 million in unamortized discount (net of unamortized premium) on this debt.

In addition to amounts, rates, and due dates on its long-term debt, Verizon also reports aggregate maturities for the 5 years subsequent to its balance sheet date:

Maturities of Long-Term Debt

Maturities of long-term debt outstanding at December 31, 2014, are as follows ($ millions):

2015	$ 2,397
2016	6,114
2017	3,911
2018	6,529
2019	6,088
Thereafter...............................	87,894

This reporting reveals that Verizon is required to make principal payments of $25,039 million between 2015 and 2019, and $87,894 million thereafter. Such maturities are important as a company must meet its required payments, negotiate a rescheduling of the indebtedness, or refinance the debt to avoid default. The latter (default) usually has severe consequences as debt holders have legal remedies available to them, which can result in bankruptcy of the company.

Verizon's disclosure on the fair value of its total debt follows:

> The fair value of our debt is determined using various methods, including quoted prices for identical terms and maturities . . . as well as quoted prices for similar terms and maturities in inactive markets and future cash flows discounted at current rates. . . The fair value of our short-term and long-term debt, excluding capital leases, was as follows ($ millions):
>
> | At December 31, | 2014 | | 2013 | |
> | --- | --- | --- | --- | --- |
> | | Carrying Amount | Fair Value | Carrying Amount | Fair Value |
> | Short-term and long-term debt, excluding capital leases . . . . | $112,755 | $126,549 | $93,298 | $103,527 |

As of December 31, 2014, indebtedness with a book value of $112,755 million had a fair value of $126,549 million, resulting in an unrecognized liability (and loss if the debt is redeemed) of $13,794 million (due mainly to a decline in interest rates subsequent to bond issuance). The justification for not recognizing unrealized gains and losses on the balance sheet and income statement is that such amounts can reverse with future fluctuations in interest rates. Further, because only the face amount of debt is repaid at maturity, unrealized gains and losses that arise during intervening years are not necessarily relevant. (This same logic is used to justify the nonrecognition of gains and losses on held-to-maturity investments in debt securities, a topic covered in Chapter 12.) At this time, Verizon, like most U.S. companies, has elected to report liabilities at historical cost in the financial statements and disclose fair values in the footnotes.

Interest and the Statement of Cash Flows

GAAP requires that interest payments (and receipts) be included in cash flows from operating activities. For companies using the indirect method for operating cash flows, net income already includes interest expense. Because interest expense does not equal interest payments, the reconciliation of net income to cash flows from operating activities should include an adjustment for any amortization of bond discounts or premiums.

However, interest income and interest expense are typically related to nonoperating assets (investments in securities) and nonoperating liabilities (interest-bearing bonds and notes), respectively. As such, they should be omitted from all computations of net operating profit (as in Appendix A to Chapter 5) and also separated from other cash flows when analyzing a company's operations, even though it sometimes requires some digging in the financial statements to determine their magnitudes.

ANALYZING FINANCIAL STATEMENTS

A major concern of managers and analysts is the solvency of the corporation. In this chapter we revisit two ratios discussed in previous chapters, both of which are designed to measure a firm's solvency. The first ratio is the debt-to-equity ratio (D/E), first introduced in Chapter 1. It measures the extent to which a company relies on debt financing, also known as financial leverage. The second ratio is times-interest-earned (TIE), which measures the ability of current operations to cover interest costs.

LO5 Explain how solvency ratios and debt ratings are determined and how they impact the cost of debt.

Analysis Objective

We want to gauge the ability of a company to satisfy its long-term debt obligations and remain solvent.

Analysis Tool   Debt-to-Equity Ratio

$$\text{Debt-to-equity ratio (D/E)} = \frac{\text{Total liabilities}}{\text{Total stockholders' equity}}$$

Applying the Ratio to Verizon

$$2012: \quad \frac{\$139{,}689}{\$85{,}533} = 1.63 \text{ or } 163\%$$

$$2013: \quad \frac{\$178{,}682}{\$95{,}416} = 1.87 \text{ or } 187\%$$

$$2014: \quad \frac{\$219{,}032}{\$13{,}676} = 16.02 \text{ or } 1602\%$$

Guidance   A debt-to-equity ratio equal to 1.0 implies that the company is relying on debt and equity financing in equal amounts. As a company's reliance on debt increases and the company's long-term solvency becomes more of a concern, this ratio increases. A debt-to-equity ratio of about 1.5 is about average, though **Exhibit 5.13** (in Chapter 5) shows that the ratio varies by industry.

Verizon in Context

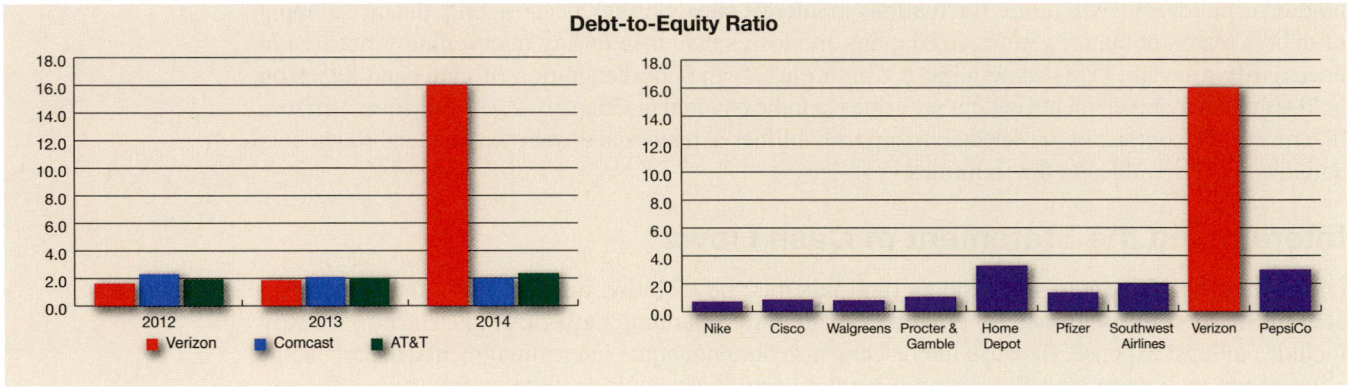

Analysis Tool   Times Interest Earned

$$\text{Times interest earned (TIE)} = \frac{\textbf{Earnings before interest and taxes}}{\textbf{Interest expense}}$$

Applying the Ratio to Verizon

$$2012: \quad \frac{\$12{,}468}{\$2{,}571} = 4.85 \text{ times}$$

$$2013: \quad \frac{\$31{,}944}{\$2{,}667} = 11.98 \text{ times}$$

$$2014: \quad \frac{\$20{,}185}{\$4{,}915} = 4.11 \text{ times}$$

Guidance   When a company relies on debt financing, it assumes the burden of paying the interest on the debt. The times interest earned ratio measures the burden of interest costs by comparing earnings before interest and taxes (EBIT) to annual interest expense. A high TIE ratio indicates that a company is able to meet its interest costs without adversely affecting profitability.

Verizon in Context

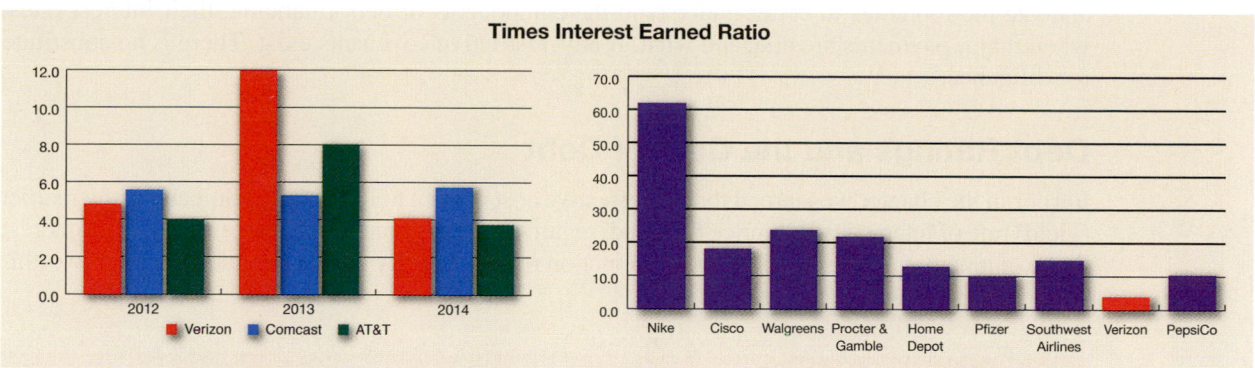

Times Interest Earned Ratio

Takeaways   Before 2014, Verizon's debt-to-equity ratio was lower than either Comcast or AT&T, two of its competitors. In 2014, Verizon engaged in a transaction to buy out the 45% equity interest of its wireless partner (Vodafone Group Plc) that had the effect of reducing its cash and reducing its shareholders equity by a substantial amount. Verizon's debt-to-equity ratio has been higher than most of the companies we have looked at in this text, and in 2014, it is substantially higher. Its times interest earned ratio is lower than many companies, though it remains higher than its competitor, AT&T. The size of this ratio is driven by two factors—the amount of debt financing, which in turn determines interest expense, as well as profitability. We should also take into account that Verizon's depreciation and amortization expense is almost as large as its earnings before interest and taxes. Therefore, its cash from operating activities may be able to support a higher debt load.

In sum, Verizon appears to be a company with a very high level of financial leverage, as indicated by a debt-to-equity ratio that is much higher than average and a lower than average times interest earned ratio. However, we must also recognize that financial reports do not recognize the values of many company resources, particularly opportunities for future growth. At the time of this writing, the total market value of Verizon's common stock is more than $193.7 billion, while the book value of shareholders' equity at the end of 2014 was $13.7 billion.

Other Considerations   In Chapter 5 we learned that debt financing is a double-edged sword. When used effectively, financial leverage increases return on equity because debt financing is generally less costly than equity financing. However, debt carries with it the risk of **default**, which is the risk that the company will be unable to pay its obligations when they come due (insolvency). To provide some protection against default risk, creditors usually require a company to execute a loan agreement that places restrictions on the company's activities. These restrictions, called covenants, impose indirect costs on a firm beyond the explicit cost of interest, and these indirect costs tend to increase as a company increases its reliance on debt financing. When a company's solvency ratios are close to the limits specified by its covenants, management is more likely to pass up profitable investment opportunities or engage in counterproductive earnings management activities to avoid violating these restrictions.

Walgreen Co. has two lines of credit totaling $1.35 billion as of the end of its 2014 fiscal year. In its footnotes, Walgreens reports:

> The Company's ability to access these facilities is subject to compliance with the terms and conditions of the credit facilities, including financial covenants. The covenants require the Company to maintain certain financial ratios related to minimum net worth and priority debt, along with limitations on the sale of assets and purchases of investments. At August 31, 2014, the Company was in compliance with all such covenants.

There are several variations on the ratios that we have discussed here and there is no single ratio that can be described as the best measure of company solvency. As with all ratios, solvency measures can be distorted by uncertain, inappropriate or inaccurate data. It is always helpful to analyze the footnotes to better understand the components of debt financing, their interest rates, when major payments are due, and what, if any, restrictive covenants exist. There is no substitute for diligence.

Debt Ratings and the Cost of Debt

Earlier in the chapter we learned that the effective cost of debt to the issuing company is the market (yield) rate of interest used to price the bond, regardless of the bond coupon rate. The rate of interest that a company must pay on its debt is a function of the maturity of that debt and the creditworthiness of the issuing company.

RESEARCH INSIGHT

Accounting Conservatism and Cost of Debt   Research indicates that companies applying more conservative accounting methods incur a lower cost of debt. Research also suggests that while accounting conservatism can lead to lower-quality accounting income (because such income does not fully reflect economic reality), creditors are more confident in the numbers and view them as more credible. Evidence also implies that companies can lower the required return demanded by creditors (the risk premium) by issuing high-quality financial reports that include enhanced footnote disclosures and detailed supplemental reports.

A company's debt rating, also referred to as credit quality and creditworthiness, is related to default risk. Companies seeking to obtain bond financing from the capital markets, normally first seek a rating on their proposed debt issuance from one of several rating agencies such as **Standard & Poor's**, **Moody's Investors Service**, or **Fitch**. The aim of rating agencies is to rate debt so that its default risk is more accurately determined and priced by the market. Such debt issuances carry debt ratings from one or more of the three large rating agencies as shown in **Exhibit 9.6**. This exhibit includes the general description attached to the debt for each rating class—for example, AAA is assigned to debt of prime maximum safety (maximum creditworthiness). Bonds with credit ratings below investment grade (below Baa or BBB) are referred to as "high yield" bonds or, more pejoratively, "junk bonds," which may not be purchased by many professionally managed portfolios.

EXHIBIT 9.6	Corporate Debt Ratings and Descriptions		
Moody's	**S&P**	**Fitch**	**Description**
Aaa	AAA	AAA	Prime Maximum Safety
Aa	AA	AA	High Grade, High Quality
A	A	A	Upper-Medium Grade
Baa	BBB	BBB	Lower-Medium Grade
Ba	BB	BB	Non-Investment Grade
B	B	B	Speculative
Caa	CCC	CCC	Substantial Risk
Ca	CC	CC	Extremely Speculative
C	C	C	Exceptionally High Risk
	D		Default

Verizon bonds are rated A− according to Fitch, and BBB+ according to S&P, as of 2015.[9] It is this rating that, in conjunction with the maturity of its bonds, establishes the market interest rate and consequent selling price. There are a number of considerations that affect the rating of a bond. **Standard & Poor's** lists the following factors among its credit rating criteria:

> **Business Risk**
>   Industry characteristics
>   Competitive position (e.g., marketing, technology, efficiency, regulation)
>   Management
> **Financial Risk**
>   Financial characteristics
>   Financial policy
>   Profitability
>   Capital structure
>   Cash flow protection
>   Financial flexibility

Rating agencies use a number of accounting ratios to help establish creditworthiness, including measures of liquidity, solvency and profitability. These ratios are variants of the ratios we describe in Chapter 5 and in this chapter, especially those used to assess solvency.

There are other relevant factors in setting debt ratings, including the following:

- **Collateral**   Companies can provide security for debt in the form of mortgages on assets. To the extent debt is secured, the debt holder is in a preferred position vis-à-vis other creditors.

- **Covenants**   Debt agreements (indentures) can contain restrictions on the issuing company to protect debt holders. Examples are restrictions on excessive dividend payment, on other company acquisitions, on further borrowing, and on maintaining minimum levels for key liquidity and solvency ratios. These covenants provide debt holders some means of control over the issuer's operations because, unlike equity investors, they do not have voting rights.

- **Options**   Debt obligations involve contracts between the borrowing company and debt holders. Options are sometimes written into debt contracts. Examples are options to convert debt into stock (so that debt holders have a stake in value creation) and options allowing the issuing company to repurchase its debt before maturity (usually at a premium).

CHAPTER-END REVIEW

On January 1, 2016, Givoly Company issues $300,000 of 15-year, 10% bonds payable for $351,876, yielding an effective interest rate of 8%. Interest is payable semiannually on June 30 and December 31. (1) Show computations to confirm the issue price of $351,876, and (2) provide Givoly's journal entries, T-accounts, and complete financial statement effects template for (a) bond issuance, (b) semiannual interest payment and premium amortization on June 30, 2016, and (c) semiannual interest payment and premium amortization on December 31, 2016.

The solution to this review problem can be found on pages 457-458.

[9] Standard & Poor's reports that ratings "may be modified by the addition of a plus (+) or minus (-) sign to show relative standing within the major rating categories."

SUMMARY

LO1   Identify and account for current operating liabilities. (p. 415)

- Current liabilities are short-term and generally non-interest-bearing; accordingly, firms try to maximize the financing of their assets using these sources of funds.

- ROE increases when firms make use of accounts payable increases to finance operating assets; a firm must avoid excessive "leaning on the trade" for short-term gains that can damage long-term supplier relationships.

- When cash discounts are offered by creditors, companies use the net of discount method to report accounts payable information.

- Accrued liabilities reflect amounts that have been recognized as expenses in the current (or a prior) period, but not yet paid.

- While all accruals result in a liability on the balance sheet and an expense on the income statement, management has latitude in determining (in some cases, estimating) their amount and timing; this discretion offers the opportunity for managing earnings.

LO2   Describe and account for current nonoperating (financial) liabilities. (p. 422)

- Management will generally try to assure that the debt service on financial (nonoperating) liabilities coincides with the cash flows from the assets financed.

- When large amounts of financing are required for, say, plant and equipment, firms find that bonds, notes, and other forms of long-term financing provide a cost-efficient means of raising capital.

LO3   Explain and illustrate the pricing of long-term nonoperating liabilities. (p. 427)

- The coupon rate indicated on a bond contract determines the periodic interest payment. The required return on any bond called the market (yield or effective) rate is determined by market conditions and rarely equals the coupon (contract) rate. The market rate is used to price the bond and determines the effective cost of the debt to the issuer.

- If the market rate is below the coupon rate, the bond will sell at a premium to its face value, assuring that the owner of the bond earns only the market rate of interest. If the market rate exceeds the coupon rate, the bond will sell at a discount so that the bond is issued at less than its face value.

LO4   Analyze and account for financial statement effects of long-term nonoperating liabilities. (p. 430)

- A discount for a bond selling below its face value represents additional interest expense over time to the issuer because the issuer received less than face value upon issuance, but must pay the holder the face value at the bond's maturity; this discount represents additional interest beyond the coupon payment to the holder. The premium on a bond selling above its face value lowers the interest cost to the issuer.

- Companies may choose to report liabilities at fair value; if the fair value option is elected, changes in fair value are reported as gains and losses in the income statement.[10]

- Gains and losses on bonds repurchased must be reported in operating income, unless they are part of discontinued operations. Such transactions do not represent operating activities, and gains/losses should be removed when determining cash from operations with the indirect method.

LO5   Explain how solvency ratios and debt ratings are determined and how they impact the cost of debt. (p. 437)

- Two debt-related ratios that are particularly useful in evaluating a company's solvency include the debt-to-equity ratio and the times interest earned ratio.

- The market rate of interest to a firm reflects the creditworthiness of the particular issuer. Credit agencies play an important role in this process by issuing debt ratings.

- Borrowing is typically secured by collateral that places the lender in a superior position to other creditors and covenants that put restrictions on the borrower's activities; bonds can also contain options including those for conversion or repurchase.

---

[10] A projected change in accounting standards may result in these gains and losses being reported in other comprehensive income—described in Chapter 12—until the debt is retired.

GUIDANCE ANSWERS . . . YOU MAKE THE CALL

You are the Analyst   Accrued liabilities must be probable and estimable before they can be reported in the balance sheet. If Dow's environmental costs turn out to be higher than management estimates, it may be understating its liabilities (and overstating equity). As an analyst, if you suspect that Dow's estimate is too low, you should add an additional estimated liability to the company's balance sheet.

You are the Vice President of Finance   The types of restructurings you might consider are those yielding a strengthening of the financial ratios typically used to assess liquidity and solvency by the rating agencies. Such restructurings include inventory reduction to generate cash, the reallocation of cash outflows from investing activities (PPE or intangible assets) to debt reduction, and reducing the cash outflows for repurchases of the company's stock (treasury stock). These actions increase liquidity or reduce financial leverage and, thus, should yield an improved debt rating. An improved debt rating gives the company access to more debt holders, as the current debt rating is below investment grade and is not a suitable investment for many professionally managed portfolios. An improved debt rating also yields a lower interest rate on debt. Offsetting these benefits are costs such as the following: (1) potential loss of sales from inventory stock-outs; (2) potential future cash flow reductions and loss of market power from reduced investing in PPE and intangibles; and (3) possible reductions in share price if shareholders were expecting more cash to be returned in the form of dividends and stock buybacks. All cost and benefits must be assessed before you pursue any restructurings.

KEY RATIOS

$$\text{Debt-to-equity (D/E)} = \frac{\text{Total liabilities}}{\text{Total stockholders' equity}} \qquad \text{Times interest earned (TIE)} = \frac{\text{Earnings before interest and taxes}}{\text{Interest}}$$

KEY TERMS

Accounts payable (p. 415)
Accrued liabilities (p. 415)
Amortization (p. 431)
Annuity (p. 427)
Call provision (p. 435)
Cash discounts (p. 416)
Collateral (p. 424, 441)
Contingent liability (p. 419)
Cookie jar reserves (p. 421)
Coupon (contract or stated) rate (p. 427)

Covenants (p. 441)
Current maturities of long-term
  debt (p. 415)
Default (p. 439)
Deferred performance liabilities (p. 415)
Discount (p. 428)
Face amount (p. 426)
Financial leverage (p. 414)
Leaning on the trade (p. 416)
Loan amortization table (p. 425)

Market (yield) rate (p. 427)
Net-of-discount method (p. 416)
Options (p. 441)
Par (face) value (p. 428)
Periodic interest payments (p. 427)
Premium (p. 429)
Present value (p. 427)
Principal (p. 425)
Short-term interest-bearing debt (p. 415)
Single payment (p. 427)

Assignments with the logo in the margin are available in *my* BusinessCourse.
See the Preface of the book for details.

MULTIPLE CHOICE

1. Which of the following statements is correct? A decrease in accrued wages liability:
   a.   decreases cash flows from operations.
   b.   decreases working capital.
   c.   increases net income.
   d.   increases net nonoperating (financial) assets.

Multiple Choice Answers
1. a 2. b 3. b
4. c 5. a, b, and d

2. On April 1, 2015, a firm borrows $12,000 at an annual interest rate of 10% with payments required semiannually on September 30 and March 31. How much interest payable and how much interest expense should appear on the firm's annual report at the end of the firm's fiscal year, December 31, 2015?
    a. $900 payable and $300 expense.
    b. $300 payable and $900 expense.
    c. $600 payable and $600 expense.
    d. $900 payable and $600 expense.

3. A firm issues $30,000,000 of 10-year bonds and receives $29.5 million in cash. Which of the following statements is correct?
    a. The bonds do not have a coupon rate because they are zeros.
    b. The market rate exceeds the coupon rate.
    c. The contract rate exceeds the market rate.
    d. The bonds were issued at par.

4. A firm issues $5 million of 10-year, 6% notes with interest paid semiannually. At issuance the firm received $5,817,565 cash reflecting a 4% yield. What is the amount of premium written off against interest expense in the first year the notes are outstanding?
    a. $48,318
    b. $24,527
    c. $67,971
    d. $33,649

5. On May 1, 2016, Wild, Inc. makes an early repayment of long-term debt due to mature on June 1, 2018. Which of the following ratios for the year 2016 is (are) decreased by this repayment?
    a. Current Ratio
    b. Quick Ratio
    c. Times Interest Earned
    d. Debt-to-Equity

QUESTIONS

Q9-1. What does the term *current liabilities* mean? What assets are usually used to settle current liabilities?

Q9-2. What is the justification for using the net-of-discount method to record inventory purchases when cash discounts are offered?

Q9-3. What is an accrual? How do accruals impact the balance sheet and the income statement?

Q9-4. What is the difference between a bond coupon rate and its market interest rate (yield)?

Q9-5. How does issuing a bond at a premium or discount affect the bond's *effective* interest rate vis-à-vis the coupon (stated) rate?

Q9-6. Why do companies report a gain or loss on the repurchase of their bonds (assuming the repurchase price is different from bond book value)?

Q9-7. How do debt ratings affect the cost of borrowing for a company?

Q9-8. How would you interpret a company's reported gain or loss on the repurchase of its bonds?

Q9-9. What do the following terms mean? (a) bonds payable, (b) call provision, (c) face value, (d) coupon, (e) bond discount, (f) bond premium, and (g) amortization of bond premium or discount.

Q9-10. What are the advantages and disadvantages of issuing bonds rather than common stock?

Q9-11. A $3,000,000 issue of 10-year, 9% bonds was sold at 98 plus accrued interest three months after the bonds were dated. What net amount of cash is received?

Q9-12. How does issuing bonds at a premium or discount "adjust the contract rate to the applicable market rate of interest"?

Q9-13. Regardless of whether premium or discount is involved, what generalization can be made about the change in the book value of bonds payable during the period in which they are outstanding?

Q9-14. If the effective interest amortization method is used for bonds payable, how does the periodic interest expense change over the life of the bonds when they are issued (a) at a discount and (b) at a premium?

Q9-15. How should premium and discount on bonds payable be presented in the balance sheet?

Q9-16. On April 30, 2016, one year before maturity, Weber Company retired $200,000 of 9% bonds payable at 101. The book value of the bonds on April 30 was $197,600. Bond interest was last paid on April 30, 2016. What is the gain or loss on the retirement of the bonds?

Q9-17. Brownlee Company borrowed money by issuing a 20-year mortgage note payable. The note will be repaid in equal monthly installments. The interest expense component of each payment decreases with each payment. Why?

MINI EXERCISES

M9-18. Recording Cash Discounts

On November 15, 2015, Shields Company purchased inventory costing $6,200 on credit. The credit terms were 2/10, n/30.

LO1

a. Assume that Shields Company paid the invoice on November 23, 2015. Prepare journal entries to record the purchase of this inventory and the cash payment to the supplier using the net-of-discount method.

b. Set up the necessary T-accounts and post the journal entries from question *a* to the accounts.

c. Compute the cost of a lost discount as an annual percentage rate.

M9-19. Recording Cash Discounts

Schrand Corporation purchases materials from a supplier that offers credit terms of 2/15, n/60. It purchased $12,500 of merchandise inventory from that supplier on January 20, 2016.

LO1

a. Assume that Schrand Corporation paid the invoice on February 15, 2016. Prepare journal entries to record the purchase of this inventory and the cash payment to the supplier using the net-of-discount method.

b. Set up the necessary T-accounts and post the journal entries from question *a* to the accounts.

c. Compute the cost of a lost discount as an annual percentage rate.

M9-20. Analyzing and Computing Financial Statement Effects of Loan Interest

Huddart Company gave a creditor a 90-day, 8% note payable for $7,200 on December 16.

LO2

a. Prepare the journal entry to record the year-end December 31st accounting adjustment Huddart must make.

b. Post the journal entries from part *a* to their respective T-accounts.

c. Record the transaction from part *a* in the financial statement effects template.

	Balance Sheet					Income Statement		
Transaction	Cash Asset	+ Noncash Assets	= Liabil- ities	+ Contrib. Capital	+ Earned Capital	Revenues −	Expenses =	Net Income

M9-21. Analyzing and Determining the Amount of a Liability

For each of the following situations, indicate the liability amount, if any, which is reported on the balance sheet of Hirst, Inc., at December 31, 2015.

LO1, 2

a. Hirst owes $110,000 at year-end 2015 for its inventory purchases.

b. Hirst agreed to purchase a $28,000 drill press in January 2016.

c. During November and December of 2015, Hirst sold products to a firm with a 90-day warranty against product failure. Estimated 2016 costs of honoring this warranty are $2,200.

d. Hirst provides a profit-sharing bonus for its executives equal to 5% of its reported pretax annual income. The estimated pretax income for 2015 is $600,000. Bonuses are not paid until January of the following year.

M9-22. Interpreting Relations Between Bond Price, Coupon, Yield, and Rating

In early February 2015, **Microsoft Corporation** issued a series of corporate bonds with maturities ranging from 5 years to 40 years. The bond issue was rated AAA by Standard & Poor's and Aaa by Moody's. Two of the bond offerings are described below.

LO3, 5

Microsoft Corporation
NASDAQ :: MSFT

Amount: $2.25 billion; Maturity: February 12, 2025; Coupon: 2.7%; Price: 99.37; Yield: 2.772%.

Amount: $2.25 billion; Maturity: February 12, 2055; Coupon: 4.0%; Price: 98.76; Yield: 4.063%.

a. Discuss the relation between the coupon rate, issuance price, and yield for the 2025 issue.

b. Compare the yields on the two bond issues. Why are the yields different when the bond ratings are the same?

LO4

M9-23. Determining Gain or Loss on Bond Redemption

On January 1, 2016, two years before maturity, Easton Company retires $400,000 of its 8.5% bonds payable at the current market price of 102 (102% of the bond face amount, or $400,000 × 1.02 = $408,000). The bond book value on January 1, 2016 is $397,000 reflecting an unamortized discount of $3,000. Bond interest is presently fully paid and recorded up to the date of retirement. What is the gain or loss on retirement of these bonds?

LO4

Pfizer, Inc.
NYSE :: PFE

M9-24. Interpreting Bond Footnote

In its 2014 balance sheet, **Pfizer, Inc.** reports a value of $3,011 million as current portion of long-term debt. In addition, Pfizer reports the following maturity schedule for its remaining $31,481 million in long-term debt outstanding:

($ millions)	2016	2017	2018	2019	After 2019
Maturities	$3,990	$3,963	$2,339	$4,771	$16,418

a. Why does the table not include 2015? How much long-term debt is due in 2015?
b. What implications does the payment schedule have for your evaluation of Pfizer's liquidity and solvency?

LO1

M9-25. Classifying Debt Accounts into the Balance Sheet or Income Statement

Indicate the proper financial statement classification (balance sheet or income statement) for each of the following accounts:

a. Gain on Bond Retirement
b. Discount on Bonds Payable
c. Mortgage Notes Payable
d. Bonds Payable

e. Bond Interest Expense
f. Bond Interest Payable (due next period)
g. Premium on Bonds Payable
h. Loss on Bond Retirement

LO4

Cencosud SA
NYSE :: CNCO

M9-26. Interpreting Bond Footnote Disclosures

Cencosud SA is a leading Latin American retailer, with approximately US$3.34 billion in short- and long-term debt outstanding as of December 31, 2013. In its 20-F filing with the Securities and Exchange Commission, Cencosud reports the following:

Our loan agreements and outstanding bonds contain a number of covenants requiring us to comply with certain financial ratios and other tests. The most restrictive financial covenants under these loan agreements and bonds require us to maintain:

- a ratio of consolidated Net Financial Debt to consolidated net worth not exceeding 1.2 to 1;
- a ratio of consolidated Net Financial Debt to EBITDA (as defined in the relevant credit agreements) for the most recent four consecutive fiscal quarters for such period of less than 5.25 to 1;
- unencumbered assets in an amount equal to at least 120% of the outstanding principal amount of total liabilities;
- minimum consolidated assets of at least UF 50.5 million[11]; and
- minimum consolidated net worth of at least UF 28.0 million.

As of the date of this annual report, we are in compliance with all of our loan and debt instruments.

a. Why do creditors impose restrictive covenants on borrowers?
b. How might restrictive covenants such as these affect management decisions?
c. What implications do these restrictions have on an analysis of the company and its solvency?

LO4

M9-27. Analyzing Financial Statement Effects of Bond Redemption

Holthausen Corporation issued $400,000 of 11%, 20-year bonds at 108 on January 1, 2010. Interest is payable semiannually on June 30 and December 31. Through January 1, 2016, Holthausen amortized $4,191 of the bond premium. On January 1, 2016, Holthausen retires the bonds at 103.

a. Prepare journal entries to record the issue and retirement of these bonds.
b. Post the journal entries from part *a* to their respective T-accounts.
c. Record each of the transactions from part *a* in the financial statement effects template.

---

[11] "UF" refers to *Unidades de Fomento*. The UF is an inflation-indexed Chilean monetary unit with a value in Chilean pesos that is adjusted daily to reflect changes in the official Consumer Price Index ("CPI").

M9-28. Analyzing Financial Statement Effects of Bond Redemption

Dechow, Inc., issued $250,000 of 8%, 15-year bonds at 96 on July 1, 2009. Interest is payable semiannually on December 31 and June 30. Through June 30, 2016, Dechow amortized $3,186 of the bond discount. On July 1, 2016, Dechow retired the bonds at 101.

a. Prepare journal entries to record the issue and retirement of these bonds. (Assume the June interest expense has already been recorded.)

b. Post the journal entries from part *a* to their respective T-accounts.

c. Record each of the transactions from part *a* in the financial statement effects template.

M9-29. Analyzing and Computing Accrued Interest on Notes

Compute any interest accrued for each of the following notes payable owed by Penman, Inc., as of December 31, 2015 (use a 365-day year):

Lender	Issuance Date	Principal	Interest Rate (%)	Term
Nissim...................	11/21/15	$18,000	10%	120 days
Klein	12/13/15	14,000	9	90 days
Bildersee................	12/19/15	16,000	12	60 days

M9-30. Debt Ratings and Capital Structure **LO5**

General Mills, Inc. reports the following information in the Management Discussion & Analysis section of its 2014 10-K report:

General Mills, Inc.
NYSE :: GIS

Cash Flows from Financing Activities ($ millions)	2014
Change in notes payable	$ 572.9
Issuance of long-term debt	1,673.0
Payment of long-term debt	(1,444.8)
Proceeds from common stock issued on exercised options, including tax benefit.	177.4
Purchases of common stock for treasury	(1,745.3)
Dividends paid	(983.3)
Dividends to noncontrolling interests and other, net	(74.0)
Net cash used by financing activities.	$(1,824.1)

a. General Mills reported net income of $1,861.3 million in 2014. What effect did these financing cash flows have on General Mills solvency measures in 2014? Explain.

b. Would the changes in financing tend to lower or increase the firm's debt rating? (Currently General Mills long-term debt is rated at upper medium grade.)

M9-31. Computing Bond Issue Price

Bushman, Inc., issues $500,000 of 9% bonds that pay interest semiannually and mature in 10 years. Compute the bond issue price assuming that the bonds' market rate is:

a. 8% per year compounded semiannually.

b. 10% per year compounded semiannually.

M9-32. Computing Issue Price for Zero-Coupon Bonds

Baiman, Inc., issues $500,000 of zero-coupon bonds that mature in 10 years. Compute the bond issue price assuming that the bonds' market rate is:

a. 8% per year compounded semiannually.

b. 10% per year compounded semiannually.

c. If prior to the debt issue at 10%, the firm had total assets of $3 million and total equity of $1 million, what would be the effect of the new borrowing on the financial leverage of the firm?

M9-33. Financial Statement Effects of Accounts Payable Transactions

Petroni Company engages in the following sequence of transactions every month:

1. Purchases $300 of inventory on credit.
2. Sells $300 of inventory for $420 on credit.
3. Pays other operating expenses of $110 in cash.
4. Collects $420 in cash from customers.
5. Pays supplier of inventory $300.

a. Create a monthly income statement and statement of operating cash flow (direct method) for four consecutive months.

b. The CFO is disappointed with the cash flows from the business. They do not provide the support for investment and growth that she wants. She proposes delaying supplier payments by a month. That is, each month's inventory purchase will be paid for in the following month. How would this change the monthly income statements and operating cash flows in part *a*? Would it provide the steady flow of cash that the CFO is looking for? Why?

LO3, 4

M9-34. **Computing Bond Issue Price and Preparing an Amortization Table in Excel**
On December 31, 2015, Kaplan, Inc., issues $500,000 of 9% bonds that pay interest semiannually and mature in 10 years (December 31, 2025).

a. Using the Excel PV worksheet function, compute the issue price assuming that the bonds' market rate is 8% per year compounded semiannually. (Refer to Appendix A for illustration.)

b. Prepare an amortization table in Excel to demonstrate the amortization of the book (carrying) value to the $500,000 maturity value at the end of the 20th semiannual period. (Refer to Appendix A for illustration.)

LO4

M9-35. **Classifying Bond-Related Accounts**
Indicate the proper financial statement classification for each of the following accounts:

> Gain on Bond Retirement (material amount)
> Discount on Bonds Payable
> Mortgage Notes Payable
> Bonds Payable
> Bond Interest Expense
> Bond Interest Payable
> Premium on Bonds Payable

LO3, 4

M9-36. **Recording and Assessing the Effects of Installment Loans**
On December 31, 2015, Thomas, Inc., borrowed $700,000 on a 12%, 15-year mortgage note payable. The note is to be repaid in equal semiannual installments of $50,854 (payable on June 30 and December 31).

a. Prepare journal entries to record (1) the issuance of the mortgage note payable, (2) the payment of the first installment on June 30, 2016, and (3) the payment of the second installment on December 31, 2016. Round amounts to the nearest dollar.

b. Post the journal entries from part *a* to their respective T-accounts.

c. Record each of the transactions from part *a* in the financial statement effects template.

LO3

M9-37. **Determining Bond Prices**
Lunar, Inc., plans to issue $900,000 of 10% bonds that will pay interest semiannually and mature in 5 years. Assume that the effective interest rate is 12% per year compounded semiannually. Compute the selling price of the bonds. Use Tables 2 and 3 in Appendix A near the end of the book.

EXERCISES

LO1

E9-38. **Analyzing and Computing Accrued Warranty Liability and Expense**
Waymire Company sells a motor that carries a 60-day unconditional warranty against product failure. Waymire estimates that between the sale and lapse of the product warranty, 2% of the 69,000 units sold this period will require repair at an average cost of $50 per unit. The warranty liability for this product had a beginning-of-period balance of $30,000, and $27,000 has already been spent on warranty repairs and replacements during the period.

a. How much warranty expense must Waymire report in its income statement and what amount of warranty liability must it report on its balance sheet for this year?

b. What analysis issues do we need to consider with respect to the amount of reported warranty liability?

c. What solvency ratios are increased if warranty liabilities rise?

E9-39. **Analyzing Contingencies and Assessing Liabilities**

LO1
MBC

The following independent situations represent various types of liabilities. Analyze each situation and indicate which of the following is the proper accounting treatment for each company: (1) record in accounts, (2) disclose in a financial statement footnote, or (3) neither record nor disclose.

 a. A stockholder has filed a lawsuit against Clinch Corporation. Clinch's attorneys have reviewed the facts of the case. Their review revealed that similar lawsuits have never resulted in a cash award and it is highly unlikely that this lawsuit will either.

 b. Foster Company signed a 60-day, 10% note when it purchased (and received) items from another company.

 c. The Department of Environment Protection notifies Shevlin Company that a state where it has a plant is filing a lawsuit for groundwater pollution against Shevlin and another company that has a plant adjacent to Shevlin's plant. Test results have not identified the exact source of the pollution. Shevlin's manufacturing process often produces by-products that can pollute groundwater.

 d. Sloan Company manufactured and sold products to a retailer that sold the products to consumers. The Sloan Company warranty offers replacement of the product if it is found to be defective within 90 days of the sale to the consumer. Historically, 1.2% of the products are returned for replacement.

E9-40. **Analyzing and Computing Accrued Wages Liability and Expense**

LO1

Demski Company pays its employees on the 1st and 15th of each month. It is March 31 and Demski is preparing financial statements for this quarter. Its employees have earned $25,000 since the 15th of this month and have not yet been paid. How will Demski's balance sheet and income statement change to reflect the accrual of wages that must be made at March 31? What balance sheet and income statement accounts would be incorrectly reported if Demski failed to make this accrual (for each account indicate whether it would be overstated or understated)?

E9-41. **Analyzing and Reporting Financial Statement Effects of Bond Transactions**

LO3, 4
MBC

On January 1, 2016, Hutton Corp. issued $300,000 of 15-year, 11% bonds payable for $377,814, yielding an effective interest rate of 8%. Interest is payable semiannually on June 30 and December 31.

 a. Show computations to confirm the issue price of $377,814.

 b. Prepare journal entries to record the bond issuance, semiannual interest payment and premium amortization on June 30, 2016, and semiannual interest payment and premium amortization on December 31, 2016. Use the effective interest rate method.

 c. Post the journal entries from part *b* to their respective T-accounts.

 d. Record each of the transactions from part *b* in the financial statement effects template.

E9-42. **Computing the Bond Issue Price**

LO3
MBC

D'Souza, Inc., issues $900,000 of 11% bonds that pay interest semiannually and mature in seven years. Assume that the market interest (yield) rate is 12% per year compounded semiannually. Compute the bond issue price.

E9-43. **Interpreting Warranty Liability Disclosures**

LO1
MBC

The following disclosures were provided by **Siemens AG** in its 2014 annual report:

Siemens AG
OTCMKTS :: SIEGY

Product-related expenses

Provisions for estimated costs related to product warranties are recorded in line item Cost of sales at the time the related sale is recognized, and are established on an individual basis, except for the standard product business. The estimates reflect historic experience of warranty costs, as well as information regarding product failure experienced during construction, installation or testing of products. In the case of new products, expert opinions and industry data are also taken into consideration in estimating product warranty provisions.

Note 23 Provisions

(in millions of €)	Provision for Warranties Year ended September 30	
	2014	**2013**
Beginning balance	€3,350	€3,405
Additions	1,776	1,544
Usage	(771)	(828)
Reversals	(657)	(683)
Translation differences and other	23	(88)
Ending balance	€3,721	€3,350

a. The Provision that Siemens reports is an estimated warranty liability. What would constitute "additions" to the provision? Prepare a journal entry to record this addition.

b. What constitutes "usage" of the provision? Besides the provision, what other accounts are likely to be affected by usage? Prepare a journal entry to record usage of €771 million.

c. "Reversals" are corrections of previous estimates of warranty obligations. Why would it be useful to report reversals separately from additions?

d. Siemens reported sales revenue of €71,920 million in 2014 and €73,445 in 2013. Calculate the ratio of warranty expense to sales for each year.

LO4 **E9-44. Reporting Financial Statement Effects of Bond Transactions**

Lundholm, Inc., which reports financial statements each December 31, is authorized to issue $500,000 of 9%, 15-year bonds dated May 1, 2015, with interest payments on October 31 and April 30. Assume the bonds are issued at par on May 1, 2015.

a. Prepare journal entries to record the bond issuance, payment of the first semiannual period's interest, and retirement of $300,000 of the bonds at 101 on November 1, 2016.

b. Post the journal entries from part *a* to their respective T-accounts.

c. Record each of the transactions from part *a* in the financial statement effects template.

LO3, 4 **E9-45. Reporting Financial Statement Effects of Bond Transactions**

On January 1, 2016, McKeown, Inc., issued $250,000 of 8%, 9-year bonds for $220,776, yielding a market (yield) rate of 10%. Semiannual interest is payable on June 30 and December 31 of each year.

a. Show computations to confirm the bond issue price.

b. Prepare journal entries to record the bond issuance, semiannual interest payment and discount amortization on June 30, 2016, and semiannual interest payment and discount amortization on December 31, 2016. Use the effective interest rate.

c. Post the journal entries from part *b* to their respective T-accounts.

d. Record each of the transactions from part *b* in the financial statement effects template.

LO3, 4 **E9-46. Reporting Financial Statement Effects of Bond Transactions**

On January 1, 2016, Shields, Inc., issued $800,000 of 9%, 20-year bonds for $879,172, yielding a market (yield) rate of 8%. Semiannual interest is payable on June 30 and December 31 of each year.

a. Show computations to confirm the bond issue price.

b. Prepare journal entries to record the bond issuance, semiannual interest payment and premium amortization on June 30, 2016, and semiannual interest payment and premium amortization on December 31, 2016. Use the effective interest rate method.

c. Post the journal entries from part *b* to their respective T-accounts.

d. Record each of the transactions from part *b* in the financial statement effects template.

LO3, 4 **E9-47. Analyzing Bond Pricing, Interest Rates, and Financial Statement Effect of a Bond Issue**

Deere & Company
NYSE :: DE

Following is a price quote for $200 million of 6.55% coupon bonds issued by **Deere & Company** that mature in October 2028:

Ratings/Industry	Issue/Call Information	Coupon/Maturity	Price/YTM
A2/A	**Deere & Company**	6.550	123.962
Industrial	Non Callable, NYBE, DE. . . .	10-01-2028	4.178

This quote indicates that, on this day, Deere's bonds have a market price of 123.962 (123.962% of face value), resulting in a yield of 4.178%.

a. Assuming that these bonds were originally issued at or close to par value, what does the above market price reveal about the direction that interest rates have changed since Deere issued its bonds? (Assume that Deere's debt rating has remained the same.)

b. Does the change in interest rates since the issuance of these bonds affect the amount of interest expense that Deere is reporting in its income statement? Explain.

c. If Deere were to repurchase its bonds at the above market price of 123.962, how would the repurchase affect its current income? Assume that the bonds were issued at face value (100).

d. Assuming that the bonds remain outstanding until their maturity, at what market price will the bonds sell on their due date of October 1, 2028?

E9-48. **Analyzing and Reporting Financial Statement Effects of Bond Transactions**

LO3, 4

On January 1, 2016, Trueman Corp. issued $600,000 of 20-year, 11% bonds for $554,860, yielding a market (yield) rate of 12%. Interest is payable semiannually on June 30 and December 31.

   a.   Confirm the bond issue price.
   b.   Prepare journal entries to record the bond issuance, semiannual interest payment and discount amortization on June 30, 2016, and semiannual interest payment and discount amortization on December 31, 2016. Use the effective interest rate method.
   c.   Post the journal entries from part *b* to their respective T-accounts.
   d.   Trueman elected to report these bonds in its financial statements at fair value. On December 31, 2016, these bonds were listed in the bond market at a price of 101 (or 101% of par value). What entry is required to adjust the reported value of these bonds to fair value?
   e.   Prepare a table summarizing the effect of these bonds on earnings for 2016.

E9-49. **Reporting and Interpreting Bond Disclosures**

LO2, 4

The adjusted trial balance for the Hass Corporation at the end of 2015 contains the following accounts:

$ 25,000	Bond Interest Payable
600,000	9% Bonds Payable due 2017
500,000	10% Bonds Payable due 2016
19,000	Discount on 9% Bonds Payable
2,000	Premium on 8% Bonds Payable
170,500	Zero-Coupon Bonds Payable due 2018
100,000	8% Bonds Payable due 2020

Prepare the long-term liabilities section of the balance sheet. Indicate the proper balance sheet classification for accounts listed above that do not belong in the long-term liabilities section.

E9-50. **Recording and Assessing the Effects of Installment Loans**

LO3, 4

On December 31, 2015, Dehning, Inc., borrowed $500,000 on an 8%, 10-year mortgage note payable. The note is to be repaid in equal quarterly installments of $18,278 (beginning March 31, 2016).

   a.   Prepare journal entries to reflect (1) the issuance of the mortgage note payable, (2) the payment of the first installment on March 31, 2016, and (3) the payment of the second installment on June 30, 2016. Round amounts to the nearest dollar.
   b.   Post the journal entries from part *a* to their respective T-accounts.
   c.   Record each of the transactions from part *a* in the financial statement effects template.

PROBLEMS

P9-51. **Interpreting Warranty Liability Disclosures**

LO1

Hewlett-Packard
NYSE :: HPQ
Cisco Systems, Inc.
NASDAQ :: CSCO

The following information was extracted from the 2014 10-K reports of **Hewlett-Packard Company** and **Cisco Systems, Inc.**

	Hewlett-Packard		Cisco Systems, Inc.	
($ millions)	2014	2013	2014	2013
Revenue from product sales	$73,726	$72,398	$36,172	$38,029
Warranty expense.........................	1,840	2,007	704	649
Accrued warranty liability.................	1,956	2,031	446	402

REQUIRED

   a.   Compute the amount of warranty costs incurred in 2014 for each company. (That is, what amount was spent for warranty repairs and settlements in 2014?)
   b.   Compare these two companies on the basis of the ratio of warranty expense to sales. What factors might explain any difference that you observe?

P9-52. **Recording and Assessing the Effects of Bond Financing (with Accrued Interest)**

LO3, 4

Eskew, Inc., which closes its books on December 31, is authorized to issue $500,000 of 9%, 15-year bonds dated May 1, 2015, with interest payments on November 1 and May 1.

REQUIRED

Assuming that the bonds were sold at 100 plus accrued interest on October 1, 2015, prepare the necessary journal entries for items *a.–f.* below.

a. The bond issuance.

b. Payment of the first semiannual period's interest on November 1, 2015.

c. Accrual of bond interest expense at December 31, 2015.

d. The adjustment to fair value on December 31, 2015 assuming that Eskew, Inc. elected to use the fair value option. On that date, the bond traded at a price of 99 (99% of par value) in the bond market.

e. Payment of the semiannual interest on May 1, 2016. (The firm does not make reversing entries.)

f. Retirement of $300,000 of the bonds at 101 on May 1, 2020 (immediately after the interest payment on that date). Assume that the fair value adjustment account for the entire issue has a debit balance of $15,000 as of that date. *Hint:* Sixty percent of the outstanding bonds were retired in this transaction.

g. Suppose fair value adjustments of bond values were not posted to net income, but rather to other comprehensive income. How would Eskew, Inc.'s December 31, 2015 financial statements change?

LO3, 4

CVS Health Corp.
NYSE :: CVS

P9-53. **Interpreting Debt Footnotes on Interest Rates and Expense**

CVS Health Corp. discloses the following footnote in its 10-K relating to its debt:

BORROWING AND CREDIT AGREEMENTS

Following is a summary of the Company's borrowings as reported in note 5 to the firm's 10-K.

In millions	2014	2013
Commercial paper	$ 685	$ —
4.875% senior notes due 2014	—	550
3.25% senior notes due 2015	550	550
6.125% senior notes due 2016	421	421
1.2% senior notes due 2016	750	750
5.75% senior notes due 2017	1,080	1,310
2.25% senior notes due 2018	1,250	1,250
6.6% senior notes due 2019	394	394
2.25% senior notes due 2019	850	—
4.75% senior notes due 2020	450	450
4.125% senior notes due 2021	550	550
2.75% senior notes due 2022	1,250	1,250
4.0% senior notes due 2023	1,250	1,250
3.375% senior notes due 2024	650	—
6.25% senior notes due 2027	453	1,000
6.125% senior notes due 2039	734	1,500
5.75% senior notes due 2041	493	950
5.3% senior notes due 2043	750	750
Capital lease obligations	391	390
Other	4	87
	12,955	13,402
Less:		
Short-term debt (commercial paper)	(685)	—
Current portion of long-term debt	(575)	(561)
Long-term debt	$11,695	$12,841

CVS also discloses that its interest expense was $615 million in 2014, after deducting capitalized interest of $19 million. It paid interest of $647 million.

REQUIRED

a. What was the average interest rate on CVS debt in 2014?

b. Does your computation in part *a* seem reasonable given the disclosure relating to specific bond issues? Explain.

c. Why can the amount of interest paid be different from the amount of interest expense recorded in the income statement?

P9-54. **Recording and Assessing the Effects of Bond Financing (with Accrued Interest)**   **LO3, 4**
Petroni, Inc., which closes its books on December 31, is authorized to issue $800,000 of 9%, 20-year bonds dated March 1, 2016, with interest payments on September 1 and March 1.

REQUIRED
Assuming that the bonds were sold at 100 plus accrued interest on July 1, 2016, prepare the necessary journal entries, post the journal entries to their respective T-accounts, and record each transaction in the financial statement effects template.

- *a.* The bond issuance.
- *b.* Payment of the semiannual interest on September 1, 2016.
- *c.* Accrual of bond interest expense at December 31, 2016.
- *d.* Payment of the semiannual interest on March 1, 2017. (The firm does not make reversing entries.)
- *e.* Retirement of $200,000 of the bonds at 101 on March 1, 2017 (immediately after the interest payment on that date).

P9-55. **Preparing an Amortization Schedule and Recording the Effects of Bonds**   **LO3, 4**
On December 31, 2015, Kasznik, Inc., issued $720,000 of 11%, 10-year bonds for $678,708, yielding an effective interest rate of 12%. Semiannual interest is payable on June 30 and December 31 each year. The firm uses the effective interest method to amortize the discount.

REQUIRED
- *a.* Prepare an amortization schedule showing the necessary information for the first two interest periods. Round amounts to the nearest dollar.
- *b.* Prepare the journal entries for (1) the bond issuance on December 31, 2015, (2) to record bond interest expense and discount amortization at June 30, 2016, and (3) to record bond interest expense and discount amortization at December 31, 2016.
- *c.* Post the journal entries from part *b* to their respective T-accounts.
- *d.* Record each of the transactions from part *b* in the financial statement effects template.

P9-56. **Preparing an Amortization Schedule and Recording the Effects of Bonds**   **LO3, 4**
On April 30, 2016, Cheng, Inc., issued $250,000 of 6%, 15-year bonds for $206,770, yielding an effective interest rate of 8%. Semiannual interest is payable on October 31 and April 30 each year. The firm uses the effective interest method to amortize the discount.

REQUIRED
- *a.* Prepare an amortization schedule showing the necessary information for the first two interest periods. Round amounts to the nearest dollar.
- *b.* Prepare the journal entries (1) for the bond issuance on April 30, 2016, (2) to record the bond interest payment and discount amortization at October 31, 2016, (3) the adjusting entry to record bond interest expense and discount amortization at December 31, 2016, the close of the firm's accounting year, and (4) to record the bond interest payment and discount amortization at April 30, 2017.
- *c.* Post the journal entries from part *b* to their respective T-accounts.
- *d.* Record each of the transactions from part *b* in the financial statement effects template.

P9-57. **Recording and Assessing the Effects of Installment Loans: Semiannual Installments**   **LO3, 4**
On December 31, 2015, Wasley Corporation borrowed $500,000 on a 10%, 10-year mortgage note payable. The note is to be repaid with equal semiannual installments, beginning June 30, 2016.

REQUIRED
- *a.* Compute the amount of the semiannual installment payment. Use the appropriate table (in Appendix A near the end of the book) or a financial calculator, and round amount to the nearest dollar.
- *b.* Prepare the journal entry (1) to record Wasley's borrowing of funds on December 31, 2015, (2) to record Wasley's installment payment on June 30, 2016, and (3) to record Wasley's installment payment on December 31, 2016. (Round amounts to the nearest dollar.)
- *c.* Post the journal entries from part *b* to their respective T-accounts.
- *d.* Record each of the transactions from part *b* in the financial statement effects template.

P9-58. **Recording and Assessing the Effects of Installment Loans: Quarterly Installments**   **LO3, 4**
On December 31, 2015, Watts Corporation borrowed $950,000 on an 8%, 5-year mortgage note payable. The note is to be repaid with equal quarterly installments, beginning March 31, 2016.

REQUIRED

a. Compute the amount of the quarterly installment payment. Use the appropriate table (in Appendix A near the end of the book) or a financial calculator, and round amount to the nearest dollar.

b. Prepare the journal entries (1) to record the borrowing of funds by Watts Corporation on December 31, 2015, (2) to record the installment payment by Watts Corporation on March 31, 2016, and (3) to record the installment payment by Watts Corporation on June 30, 2016.

c. Post the journal entries from part *b* to their respective T-accounts.

d. Record each of the transactions from part *b* in the financial statement effects template.

LO1

BP, PLC
NYSE :: BP

P9-59.   Contingent Liabilities

BP operates off-shore oil drilling platforms including rigs in the Gulf of Mexico. In April 2010, explosions and a fire on the Deepwater Horizon rig led to the death of 11 crew members and a 200-million-gallon oil spill in the Gulf of Mexico. BP's 2010 annual report included the following description of its contingent liabilities (provision) related to this accident:

In estimating the amount of the provision, BP has determined a range of possible outcomes for Individual and Business Claims, and State and Local Claims.... BP has concluded that a reasonable range of possible outcomes for the amount of the provision at December 31, 2010, is $6 billion to $13 billion. BP believes that the provision recorded at December 31, 2010, of $9.2 billion represents a reliable best estimate from within this range of possible outcomes.

REQUIRED

a. BP prepares its financial statements in accordance with IFRS. How did BP report the $9.2 billion estimate in its 2010 financial statements?

b. How would the accounting for this provision differ if BP prepared its financial statements in accordance with U.S. GAAP?

CASES AND PROJECTS

LO3, 4, 5

Comcast
NASDAQ :: CMCSA

C9-60.   Interpreting Debt Disclosures

Comcast Corporation's 2014 income statement and partial balance sheet (liabilities and equity, only) are presented below. In addition, footnote 10 pertaining to Comcast's long-term debt obligations is provided. All $ amounts are presented in millions.

Summarized Consolidated Statement of Income		
Year ended December 31 (in millions)	2014	2013
Revenue	$68,775	$64,657
Costs and expenses:		
Programming and production........................	20,912	19,670
Other operating and administrative	19,862	18,584
Advertising, marketing and promotion	5,078	4,969
Depreciation and amortization	8,019	7,871
	53,871	51,094
Operating income..................................	14,904	13,563
Other income (expense)		
Interest expense.................................	(2,617)	(2,574)
Other..	178	126
	(2,439)	(2,448)
Income before income taxes	12,465	11,115
Income tax expense...............................	(3,873)	(3,980)
Net income......................................	$ 8,592	$ 7,135

Summarized Consolidated Balance Sheet (Liabilities and Equity only) December 31 (in millions)	2014	2013
Current liabilities:		
Accounts payable and accrued expenses related to trade creditors....	$ 5,638	$ 5,528
Accrued participations and residuals...............................	1,347	1,239
Deferred revenue	915	898
Accrued expenses and other current liabilities.....................	5,293	7,967
Current portion of long-term debt	4,217	3,280
Total current liabilities..	17,410	18,912
Long-term debt, less current portion...............................	44,017	44,567
Deferred income taxes...	32,959	31,935
Other noncurrent liabilities..	11,885	12,341
Total liabilities..	106,271	107,755
Total equity...	53,068	51,058
Total liabilities and equity...	$159,339	$158,813

Note 10: Long-term Debt

Long-term Debt Outstanding December 31 (in millions)	Weighted-Average Interest Rate as of December 31, 2014	2014	2013
Commercial paper	0.373%	$ 845	$ 1,350
Revolving bank credit facilities.....................	—%	—	1,250
Senior notes with maturities of 5 years or less	4.642%	15,334	15,080
Senior notes with maturities between 5 and 10 years ...	4.822%	10,527	11,533
Senior notes with maturities greater than 10 years[a]	5.737%	20,937	18,010
Other, including capital lease obligations.............	—%	591	624
Total debt	4.95%[b]	48,234	47,847
Less: Current portion		4,217	3,280
Long-term debt		$44,017	$44,567

[a] The December 31, 2014 and 2013 amounts include £625 million of 5.50% notes due 2029 translated at $974 million and $1 billion, respectively, using the exchange rates at these dates.

[b] Includes the effects of our derivative financial instruments.

As of December 31, 2014 and 2013, our debt had an estimated fair value of $55.3 billion and $51.8 billion, respectively. The estimated fair value of our publicly traded debt is primarily based on Level 1 inputs that use the quoted market values for the debt. The estimated fair value of debt for which there are no quoted market prices is based on Level 2 inputs that use interest rates available to us for debt with similar terms and remaining maturities. See Note 20 for additional information on our cross-guarantee structure.

Debt Maturities (in millions)	Weighted-Average Interest Rate as of December 31, 2014	
2015	4.990%	$ 4,217
2016	4.158%	3,530
2017	6.973%	2,558
2018	4.124%	4,117
2019	3.159%	2,205
Thereafter...	5.425%	31,607

REQUIRED

a. Comcast provided cash flow information revealing that the company paid interest equal to $2,389 million in 2014. Explain why this amount is different from the amount of interest expense reported in its 2014 income statement.

b. Comcast reports its debt using historical cost. What would be the impact on the financial statements if the company elected to report all of its debt at fair value? Be specific.

c.   The financial ratios specified in Comcast's loan agreements include the solvency measures described in this chapter. Calculate Comcast's debt-to-equity ratio and times-interest-earned for 2014. Explain why creditors might include these ratios in the restrictive covenants of loan agreements.

d.   Violation of debt covenants can be a serious event that can impose substantial costs on a company. What actions might management take to avoid violating debt covenants if the company's ratios are near the covenant limits?

LO3, 4, 5   C9-61.   Assessing Debt Financing, Company Interests, and Managerial Ethics

Foster Corporation is in the third quarter of the current year, and projections are that net income will be down about $600,000 from the previous year. Foster's return on assets is also projected to decline from its usual 15% to approximately 13%. If earnings do decline, this year will be the second consecutive year of decline. Foster's president is quite concerned about these projections (and his job) and has called a meeting of the firm's officers for next week to consider ways to "turn things around—and fast."

Margot Barth, treasurer of Foster Corporation, has received a memorandum from her assistant, Lorie McNichols. Barth had asked McNichols if she had any suggestions as to how Foster might improve its earnings performance for the current year. McNichols' memo reads as follows:

> As you know, we have $3,000,000 of 4%, 20-year bonds payable outstanding. We issued these bonds 10 years ago at face value, so they have 10 years left to maturity. When they mature, we would probably replace them with other bonds. The economy is expecting a period of greater inflation, and interest rates have increased to about 8%. My proposal is to replace these bonds right now. More specifically, I propose:
>
> 1.   Immediately issue $3,000,000 of 20-year, 8% bonds payable. These bonds will be issued at face value.
> 2.   Use the proceeds from the new bonds to buy back and retire our outstanding 4% bonds. Because of the current high rates of interest, these bonds are trading in the market at about $2,200,000.
> 3.   The benefits to Foster are that (a) the retirement of the old bonds will generate an $800,000 gain for the income statement and (b) there will be an extra $800,000 of cash available for other uses.

Barth is intrigued by the possibility of generating an $800,000 gain for the income statement. However, she is not sure this proposal is in the best long-run interests of the firm and its stockholders.

REQUIRED

a.   How is the $800,000 gain calculated from the retirement of the old bonds? Where would this gain be reported in Foster's income statement?

b.   Why might this proposal not be in the best long-run interests of the firm and its stockholders?

c.   What possible ethical conflict is present in this proposal?

SOLUTIONS TO REVIEW PROBLEMS

Mid-Chapter Review 1

SOLUTION

a.   The discount would be $580 ($29,000 × 0.02). Thus, Waymire would pay $28,420 ($29,000 − $580).

b.   The cost of the lost discount is $29 per day ($580/20) or $10,585 per year (simple interest). The implicit financing cost of the lost discount is 37.24% ($10,585/$28,420).

Mid-Chapter Review 2

SOLUTION

Toro Company incurred $38,568 thousand in warranty claims in 2014 ($000):

$$\$72,177 + \$37,471 - \text{warranty claims} = \$71,080. \text{ Warranty claims} = \$38,568.$$

This cost would be recorded as follows:

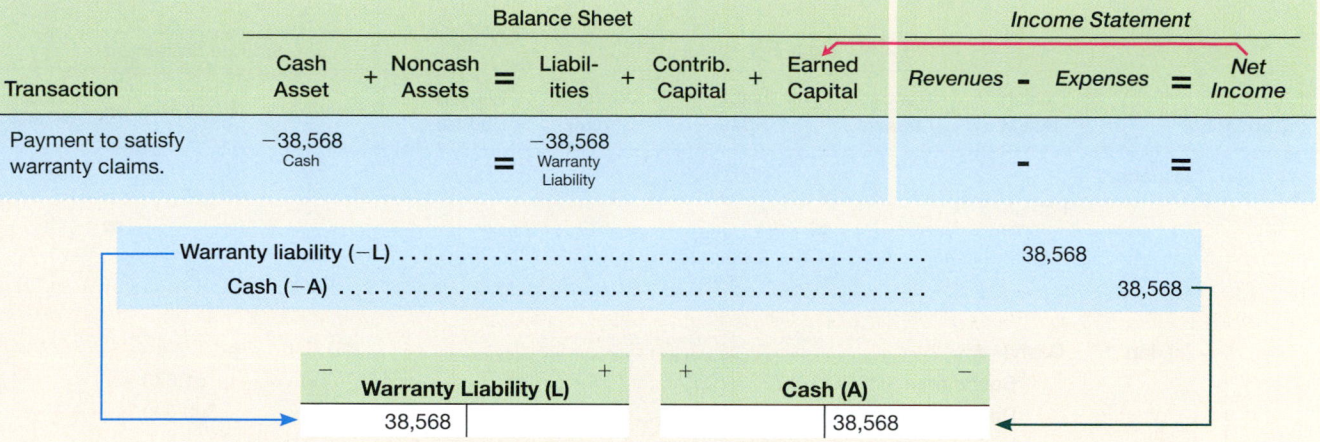

	Balance Sheet						Income Statement			
Transaction	Cash Asset	+ Noncash Assets	= Liabil- ities	+ Contrib. Capital	+ Earned Capital		Revenues	- Expenses	= Net Income
Payment to satisfy warranty claims.	−38,568 Cash		= −38,568 Warranty Liability				-		=

Warranty liability (−L)		38,568	
Cash (−A)			38,568

− Warranty Liability (L) +	+ Cash (A) −
38,568		38,568

The credit entry to cash assumes that cash was paid to satisfy the warranty claims. Toro could also have credited wages payable, or parts inventory as needed.

Mid-Chapter Review 3

SOLUTION

The related journal entry to recognize the accrual of interest is:

	Balance Sheet						Income Statement			
Transaction	Cash Asset	+ Noncash Assets	= Liabil- ities	+ Contrib. Capital	+ Earned Capital		Revenues	- Expenses	= Net Income
Accrued $26 of interest as of January 31*.			= +26 Interest Payable		−26 Retained Earnings		-	+26 Interest Expense	= −26

Interest expense (+E, −SE)		26	
Interest payable (+L)...			26

+ Interest Expense (E) −	− Interest Payable (L) +
26		26

*Accrued interest for a 16-day period at January 31 = $10,000 × 0.06 × 16/365 = $26.

Chapter-End Review

SOLUTION

1. Issue price for $300,000, 15-year, 10% semiannual bonds discounted at 8%:

Present value of principal payment ($300,000 × 0.30832)	$ 92,496
Present value of semiannual interest payments ($15,000 × 17.29203).....	259,380
Issue price of bonds...	$351,876

2.

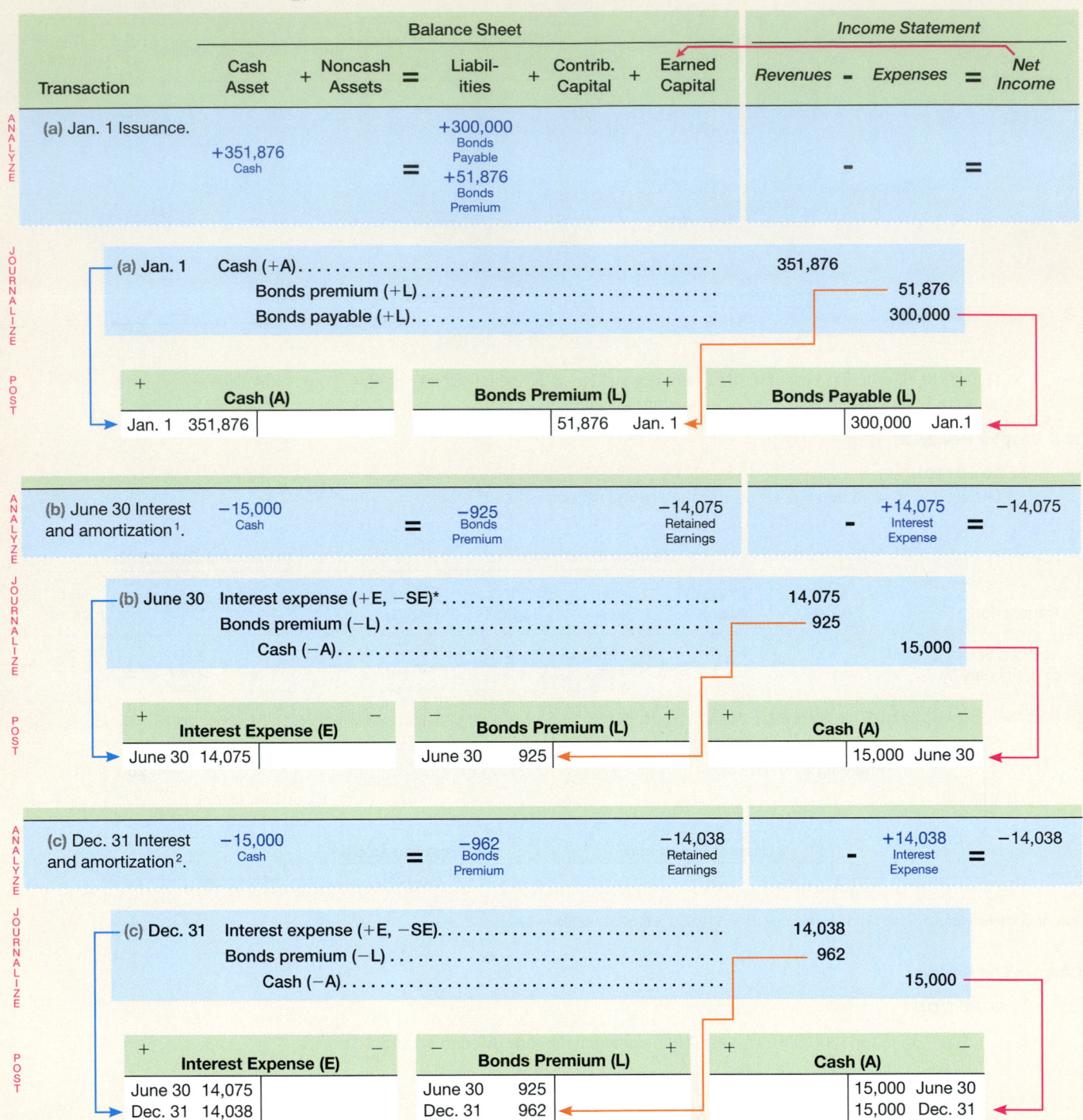

[1] $300,000 \times 0.10 \times 6/12 = \$15,000$ cash payment; $0.04 \times \$351,876 = \$14,075$ interest expense; the difference is the bond premium amortization, a reduction of the net bond carrying amount.

[2] $0.04 \times (\$351,876 - \$925) = \$14,038$ interest expense. The difference between this amount and the $15,000 cash payment is the premium amortization, a reduction of the net bond carrying amount.

10

Reporting and Analyzing Leases, Pensions, and Income Taxes

LEARNING OBJECTIVES

1. Define off-balance-sheet financing and explain its effects on financial analysis. (p. 462)

2. Account for leases using the operating lease method and the capital lease method. (p. 463)

3. Convert off-balance-sheet operating leases to the capital lease method. (p. 469)

4. Explain and interpret the reporting for pension plans. (p. 475)

5. Analyze and interpret pension footnote disclosures. (p. 478)

6. Describe and interpret accounting for income taxes. (p. 484)

DELTA AIR LINES
www.delta.com

Delta Air Lines confronts competing demands for its available cash flow as a result of a heavy debt load that includes borrowed money, aircraft leases, and pension and other postemployment obligations. The magnitude of obligations arising from aircraft leases often surprises those outside the industry. Many airlines do not own all the planes that they fly. The airlines often lease a significant portion of their planes from commercial leasing companies rather than own the planes themselves.

In many cases, neither the leased planes (the assets) nor the lease obligations (the liabilities) would be on Delta's balance sheet. That omission can alter investors' perceptions of the capital investment Delta needs to operate its business as well as the level of debt it carries. Methods that companies apply to avoid reporting potential liabilities (and related expenses), are commonly referred to as *off-balance-sheet financing*.

We describe an analytical procedure that provides an alternative view of the company's investing and financing activities. The analytical adjustment increases the liability on Delta's balance sheet. We estimate that Delta has lease payment obligations not recorded on the balance sheet of nearly $9 billion in 2014, which is

a significant amount when compared to the company's reported noncurrent liabilities of $28 billion. This chapter discusses the accounting for leases, explains the analytical adjustment, and illustrates how to apply the adjustment.

Pensions and deferred income taxes are major liabilities or assets reported in many firm's financial statements, including Delta Air Lines. In this chapter, we will explore the reporting of leases, pensions, and income taxes, along with the various assumptions that underlie the reported figures. We also examine the impact that these items have on reported earnings and cash flows, and how they affect the company's financial position and performance. Understanding this information is essential if we are to assess the future potential of Delta Air Lines and other companies.

Sources: Delta Air Lines 2014 Annual Report

CHAPTER ORGANIZATION

Reporting and Analyzing Leases, Pensions, and Income Taxes		
Leases	**Pensions**	**Income Taxes**
• Lessee Reporting of Leases • Footnote Disclosures • Capitalization of Operating Leases • Analyzing Financial Statements	• Reporting of Defined Benefit Pension Plans • Footnote Disclosures • Other Postretirement Benefits	• Reporting Tax Expense • Footnote Disclosures • Book-Tax Differences • Computation and Analysis

LO1 Define off-balance-sheet financing and explain its effects on financial analysis.

1

INTRODUCTION

Investors, creditors, and other users of financial statements assess the composition of a company's balance sheet and its relation to the income statement. Chapter 6 introduced the concept of earnings quality to refer to the extent to which reported income reflects the underlying economic performance of a company. Similarly, the quality of the balance sheet refers to the extent to which the assets and liabilities of a company are reported in a manner that accurately reflects its economic resources and obligations. For example, in previous chapters, we highlighted the reporting of LIFO inventories and noncapitalized intangible assets to illustrate how some assets can be undervalued or even excluded from the balance sheet. This chapter focuses on the reporting of liabilities that can often only be found in the notes to the financial statements.

Financial managers are keenly aware of the importance that financial markets place on the quality of balance sheets. This importance creates pressure on companies to *window dress* their financial statements in order to report their financial condition and performance in the best possible light. One means of improving the perceived financial condition of the company is by keeping debt off the

---

BUSINESS INSIGHT

Nike's Off-Balance-Sheet Obligations Lebron James, Maria Sharapova, and Tom Brady are just some of the marquee athletes who endorse **Nike, Inc.** products. These athletes sign long-term, multimillion dollar contracts to use and promote Nike shoes, apparel, and accessories. These long-term endorsement contracts are just one of Nike's off-balance-sheet obligations. Consider the following note from Nike's 10-K report.

Contractual Obligations
Our significant long-term contractual obligations as of May 31, 2014, and significant endorsement contracts entered into through the date of this report are as follows ($ millions):

	Cash Payments Due During the Year Ended May 31,						
Description of Commitment	**2015**	**2016**	**2017**	**2018**	**2019**	**Thereafter**	**Total**
Operating leases	$ 427	$ 399	$ 366	$311	$251	$1,050	$ 2,804
Capital leases	36	35	1	1	1	—	74
Long-term debt	46	145	79	56	37	1,488	1,851
Endorsement contracts	991	787	672	524	349	1,381	4,704
Product purchase obligations	3,688	—	—	—	—	—	3,688
Other	309	108	78	7	3	12	517
Total	$5,497	$1,474	$1,196	$899	$641	$3,931	$13,638

Of these obligations disclosed, only its long-term debt is included in the balance sheet. If the other obligations were presented in the balance sheet at their present values (ignoring any related off-balance-sheet assets that might also need to be capitalized), Nike's debt-to-equity ratio would increase in 2014 by 135% from 0.72 to 1.69.

balance sheet. **Off-balance-sheet financing** refers to financial obligations of a company that are not reported as liabilities in the balance sheet.

Off-balance-sheet financing reduces the amount of debt reported on the balance sheet, thereby lowering the company's financial leverage ratios. Additionally, many off-balance-sheet financing techniques (e.g., operating leases and contract manufacturing) remove assets from the balance sheet, along with the liabilities, without reducing revenues or markedly affecting net income. Such techniques cause operation ratios, such as return on assets (ROA), to appear stronger than they are.

This chapter focuses on three common financial obligations that companies report in their financial statements—leases, pensions, and income taxes. The liability section of Delta Air Lines' balance sheet is presented in **Exhibit 10.1**. The amounts reported on Delta's balance sheet related to leases and pensions are highlighted. Delta reports a deferred asset related to income taxes for 2013 and 2014; we discuss what this means later in the chapter.

FYI Off-balance-sheet financing usually requires off-balance-sheet assets—this means the off-balance-sheet remains balanced!

EXHIBIT 10.1	Delta Air Lines Balance Sheet (Liabilities Only)		
($ millions)		2014	2013
Current Liabilities:			
Current maturities of long-term debt and capital leases		$1,216	$1,547
Air traffic liability		4,296	4,122
Accounts payable		2,622	2,300
Accrued salaries and related benefits		2,266	1,926
Hedge derivatives liability		2,772	146
Frequent flyer deferred revenue		1,580	1,861
Other accrued liabilities		2,127	2,250
Total current liabilities		16,879	14,152
Noncurrent Liabilities:			
Long-term debt and capital leases		8,561	9,795
Pension, postretirement and related benefits		15,138	12,392
Frequent flyer deferred revenue		2,602	2,559
Other noncurrent liabilities		2,128	1,711
Total noncurrent liabilities		28,429	26,457
Total liabilities		$45,308	$40,609

In addition to the obligations presented in its balance sheet, Delta reports most of its leases in its footnotes and not on its balance sheet. Whether they are reported in the footnotes or on the balance sheet, management enjoys considerable discretion in determining the value of these obligations and how they are presented. Understanding the information in these disclosures enables us to analyze the impact of these obligations on the financial condition of the company.

LEASES

A lease is a contract between the owner of an asset (the **lessor**) and the party desiring to use that asset (the **lessee**). Because this is a private contract between two willing parties, it is governed only by applicable commercial law, and can include whatever provisions are negotiated between the parties. The lessor and lessee can be any legal form of organization, including private individuals, corporations, partnerships, and joint ventures.

Leases generally contain the following terms:

- The lessor allows the lessee the unrestricted right to use the asset during the lease term.
- The lessee agrees to make periodic payments to the lessor and to maintain the asset.
- The legal title to the asset remains with the lessor. At the end of the lease, either the lessor takes physical possession of the asset, or the lessee purchases the asset from the lessor at a price specified in the lease contract.

LO2 Account for leases using the operating lease method and the capital lease method.

2

From the lessor's standpoint, lease payments are set at an amount that yields an acceptable return on investment, commensurate with the credit standing of the lessee. The lessor, thus, obtains a quality investment, and the lessee gains use of the asset.

From the lessee's perspective, the lease serves as a financing vehicle, similar to an intermediate-term secured bank loan. However, there are several advantages to leasing over bank financing:

- Leases often require less equity investment than bank financing. That is, banks often only lend a portion of the asset's cost and require the borrower to make up the difference from its available cash.

- Leases often require payments to be made at the beginning of the period (e.g., the first of the month). However, because leases are contracts between two parties, their terms can be structured in any way to meet their respective needs. For example, a lease can allow variable payments to match seasonal cash inflows of the lessee, or have graduated payments for companies in their start-up phase.

- If the lessee requires the use of the asset for only a part of its useful life, leasing avoids the need to sell a used asset.

- Because the lessor retains ownership of the asset, leases provide the lessor with tax benefits such as accelerated depreciation deductions. This fact can lead to lower payments for lessees.

- According to current U.S. GAAP, if the lease is properly structured, neither the leased asset nor the lease liability is reported on the lessee's balance sheet. Accordingly, leasing can be a form of off-balance-sheet financing.

FYI New standards are forthcoming that will put almost all leases on the balance sheet. We discuss this new treatment below.

Lessee Reporting of Leases

GAAP identifies two different approaches for the reporting of leases by the lessee:

- **Capital lease method**. This method requires that both the leased asset and the lease liability be reported on the balance sheet. The leased asset is depreciated like any other long-term asset. The lease liability is amortized like debt, where lease payments are separated into interest expense and principal repayment.

- **Operating lease method**. Under this method, neither the leased asset nor the lease liability is on the balance sheet. Lease payments are recorded as rent expense by the lessee when paid.

To illustrate the two approaches to lease accounting, assume that Richardson Electronics agrees to lease retail store space in a shopping center. The lease is a 5-year lease with annual payments of $10,000 due at each year-end. (Most leases require payments at the beginning of each period; we use year-end payments here for simplification.) Using a 7% interest rate, the present value of the five annual lease payments equals $41,002, computed as $10,000 × 4.10020 (Appendix A, Table A.3). This amount is used for valuing the lease under the capital lease method.

Using a calculator, the present value of the annual lease payments is computed as follows:[1]

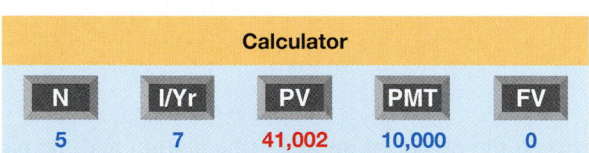

Calculator				
N	**I/Yr**	**PV**	**PMT**	**FV**
5	7	41,002	10,000	0

Operating Leases   When the operating lease method is used, leased assets and lease liabilities are not recorded in the balance sheet. No accounting entry is recorded when the lease

---

[1] The result produced by the financial calculator is actually −41,002. The present value will always have the opposite sign from the payment. So, if the payment is positive, the present value will be negative. **Appendix A** illustrates the use of a financial calculator to compute present values. In this calculation, it is important to set the payments per year (period) to 1 and make sure that the payments are set to occur at the end of each period.

agreement is signed. At each year-end, Richardson would record the rent payment as rent expense as follows.

Rent expense (+E, −SE)..	10,000	
Cash (−A)		10,000

Because no asset or liability is reported, the only time an operating lease affects the balance sheet is if rent is prepaid (resulting in prepaid rent in current assets) or if unpaid rent is accrued (resulting in accrued rent payable, a current liability). The income statement reports the lease payment as rent expense. The existence and key details of the lease agreement are disclosed in a footnote.

Capital Leases   When the capital lease method is applied, the lessee records an asset and a liability at the time that the lease agreement is signed. Both the asset and the liability are valued using the present value of the lease payments. The entry that would be recorded when Richardson Electronics signs its lease is:

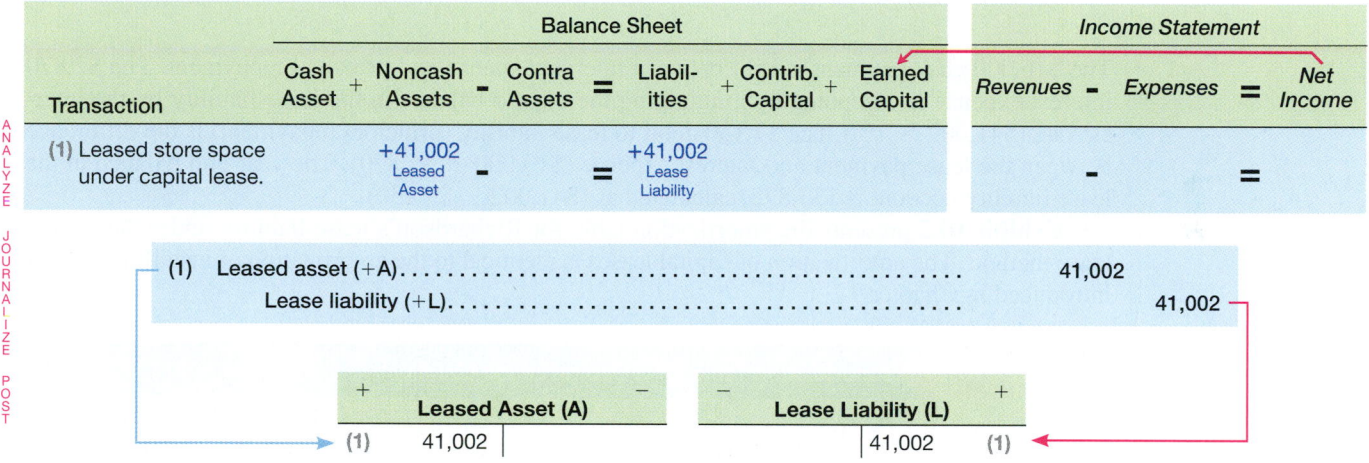

The asset is reported among long-term (PPE) assets in the balance sheet and the liability is reported in long-term debt.

At the end of the first year, two entries are required, one to account for the asset and the other to account for the lease payment. Like other long-term assets, the leased asset must be depreciated. The entry to depreciate Richardson's leased asset (assuming straight-line depreciation, a useful life of 5 years, and zero residual value [$41,002/5 = $8,200]) is:

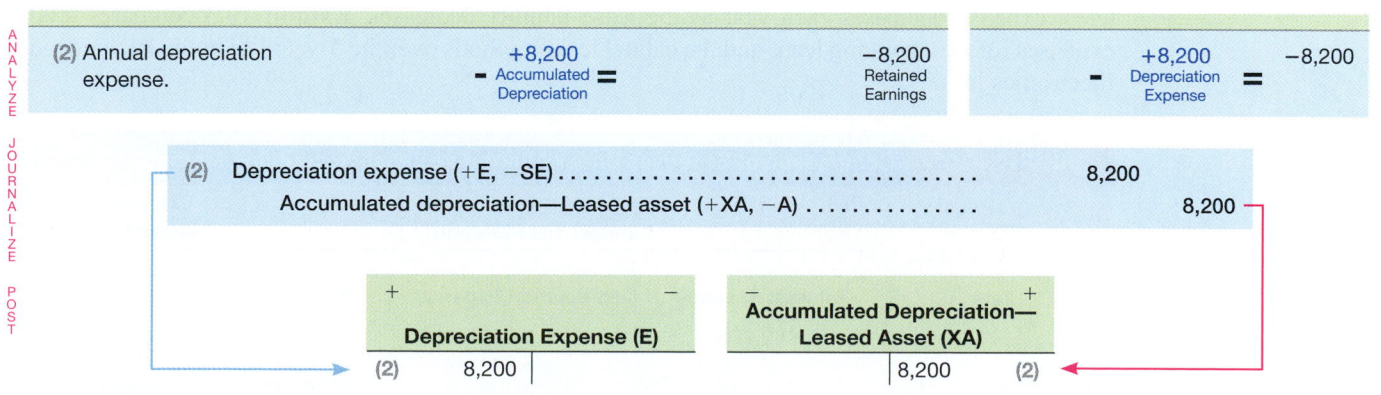

The financial statement effects and related entry to record the annual lease payment are:

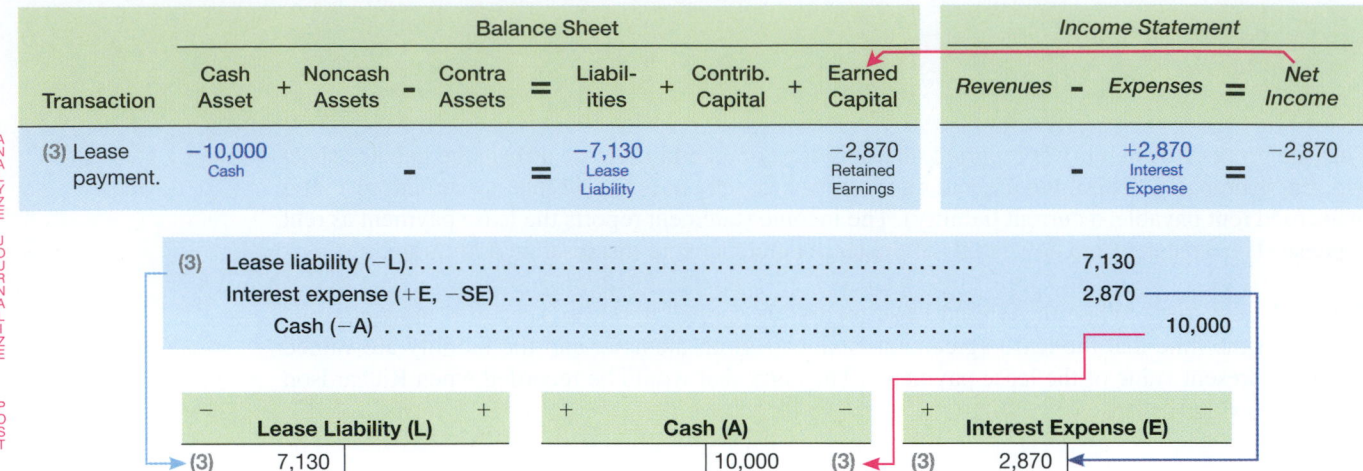

The $10,000 cash payment is split between interest expense and principal repayment. The $2,870 interest expense is computed by multiplying the unpaid balance in the lease liability by the interest rate ($41,002 × 7%). The $7,130 debit to lease liability (principal repayment) is the difference between the lease payment and interest expense ($10,000 − $2,870). The year-end balance in the lease liability account is $33,872, calculated as ($41,002 − $7,130).

Exhibit 10.2 presents the amortization table for Richardson's lease liability under the capital lease method. The amortization of capital leases is identical to the amortization of installment loans introduced in Chapter 9.

EXHIBIT 10.2	Amortization Table for a Capital Lease Liability				
A	**B**	**C**	**D**	**E**	**F**
Year	**Beginning-year Lease Liability**	**Interest Expense (B × 7%)**	**Payment**	**Principal Repayment (D − C)**	**Ending-year Lease Liability (B − E)**
1........	$41,002	$2,870	$10,000	$7,130	$33,872
2........	33,872	2,371	10,000	7,629	26,243
3........	26,243	1,837	10,000	8,163	18,080
4........	18,080	1,266	10,000	8,734	9,346
5........	9,346	654	10,000	9,346	0

Comparing Operating Lease and Capital Lease Methods In **Exhibit 10.2**, the interest expense decreases each year as the lease liability decreases. **Exhibit 10.3** compares total expenses for the operating lease and the capital lease methods over the 5-year life of the Richardson Electronics lease.

EXHIBIT 10.3	Comparison of Expenses Under Alternative Lease Accounting Methods			
		Capital Lease Method		Operating Lease Method
Year	**Interest Expense**	**Depreciation Expense**	**Total Expense**	**Rent Expense**
1................	$2,870	$ 8,200	$11,070	$10,000
2................	2,371	8,200	10,571	10,000
3................	1,837	8,200	10,037	10,000
4................	1,266	8,201	9,467	10,000
5................	654	8,201	8,855	10,000
Total	$8,998	$41,002	$50,000	$50,000

Exhibit 10.3 shows how the capital lease method reports a higher total expense (depreciation plus interest) in the early years of the lease and a lower total expense in the later years. Total expense over the 5-year life of the lease is the same under both methods and is equal to the total of the lease payments ($50,000).

The effects of these two accounting methods on the lessee's financial statements are summarized in **Exhibit 10.4**.

EXHIBIT 10.4	Financial Statement Effects of Lease Methods for the Lessee			
Lease Type	**Assets**	**Liabilities**	**Expenses**	**Cash Flows**
Capital	Leased asset reported	Lease liability reported	Depreciation and interest expense	Interest is operating cash flow; principal is financing
Operating	Leased asset not reported	Lease liability not reported	Rent expense	Payment is operating cash flow

U.S. GAAP defines four criteria to determine the classification of a lease as capital or operating. FASB considers meeting one or more of these criteria as an indication that the benefits and risks of ownership are effectively transferred to the lessee. The lessee *must* capitalize the lease *if one or more* of these criteria are met:

1. The lease automatically transfers ownership of the leased asset to the lessee at the lease-end.

2. The lease agreement allows the lessee to purchase the asset at a discounted price (say $1) at the lease-end; this is called a bargain purchase option.

3. The lease term is at least 75% of the economic useful life of the asset.

4. The present value of the lease payments is at least 90% of the asset's fair value.

BUSINESS INSIGHT

The Financial Accounting Standards Board has been working on new standards for leases for several years. Much of this time was spent on a convergence project with the International Accounting Standards Board on the topic. The Boards could not come to agreement on the treatment of leases in the income statement, and thus differences will remain between GAAP and IFRS with regard to leases.

U.S. GAAP will change significantly, however. The proposed change to the lease standard will require that all leases be recorded by the lessee as an asset and a liability, except very short-term rental agreements (less than twelve months). Recognizing that a lease represents the right to use an asset for a specified period of time, the proposed standard refers to the leased asset as a right-of-use asset to be capitalized on a company's balance sheet. Thus, once the new standard is effective, both an asset and a liability will be recorded and the concept of operating leases being off-balance-sheet will no longer apply (unless the lease is short term in duration). The income statement, however, will continue to reflect different treatment between the two types of leases—operating and capital (or finance). The finance type leases (capital leases) will require a recording of interest expense and depreciation, consistent with how current capital leases are accounted for under existing leases guidance. The operating type leases will be expensed on a straight-line basis (rather than high interest costs early in the term of the lease), which is consistent with how current operating leases are accounted for under the exisiting guidance for leases. The FASB does not have a defined effective date for the new standards at the current time.

A GLOBAL PERSPECTIVE

IFRS accounting for leases will also change significantly. The International Accounting Standards Board has proposed a single lease model for IFRS. All leases will be recorded in the same manner on the balance sheet and on the income statement in a manner similar to the capital lease method under U.S. GAAP. In contrast, as described in the Business Insight box above, U.S. GAAP retained a dual model because the income statement treatment varies between the types of leases. In addition to the short-term lease exception that is proposed under U.S. GAAP, there will also be an exception under IFRS if the lease is for a small asset defined in terms of asset value.

Accounting for leases using the operating lease method offers several reporting benefits to the lessee:

- The leased asset is not reported on the balance sheet. This reporting means that asset turnover ratios are higher because reported operating assets are lower and revenues are unaffected.

- The lease liability is not reported on the balance sheet. This means that common balance sheet measures of leverage (such as liabilities divided by equity) are improved. Consequently, many managers believe the company would then command a better debt rating and a lower interest rate on borrowed funds.

- For the early years of the lease term, rent expense reported for an operating lease is less than the sum of depreciation and interest expense reported for a capital lease. This reporting means that net income is higher in those early years with an operating lease. (However, the corporation's net *operating* profit after taxes is *lower* for an operating lease because rent expense is an operating expense whereas only depreciation expense [not interest expense] is considered an operating expense for a capital lease.)

The benefits of using the operating method to account for leases are quite clear to managers, leading them to avoid lease capitalization if possible. Furthermore, the lease accounting standard is structured around rigid requirements relating to capitalization. Whenever accounting standards are rigidly defined, clever managers that are so inclined can structure lease contracts to meet the letter of the standard to achieve a desired accounting result even though the essence of the transaction would suggest a different accounting treatment.

Footnote Disclosures of Leases

Disclosures of expected payments for leases are required under both operating and capital lease methods. Delta Air Lines provides a typical disclosure from its 2014 annual report:

Note 9: Lease Obligations

We lease aircraft, airport terminals, maintenance facilities, ticket offices and other property and equipment from third parties. Rental expense for operating leases, which is recorded on a straight-line basis over the life of the lease term, totaled $1.2 billion for the year ended December 31, 2014 and $1.1 billion for the years ended December 31, 2013 and 2012. Amounts due under capital leases are recorded as liabilities, while assets acquired under capital leases are recorded as property and equipment. Amortization of assets recorded under capital leases is included in depreciation and amortization expense.

The following tables summarize, as of December 31, 2014, our minimum rental commitments under capital leases and noncancelable operating leases (including certain aircraft flown by Contract Carriers) with initial or remaining terms in excess of one year:

Year Ending December 31 ($ millions)	Operating Leases	Capital Leases
2015	$ 1,707	$ 157
2016	1,493	139
2017	1,323	97
2018	1,120	51
2019	929	33
Thereafter	6,169	42
Total minimum lease payments	$12,741	519
Less: amount representing interest		(121)
Present value of future minimum lease payments		398
Less: current obligations under capital leases		(107)
Long-term capital lease obligations		$ 291

Delta Air Lines' footnote disclosure reports minimum contractual lease payment obligations for each of the next five years (2015 through 2019) and the total lease payment obligations that come due in 2020 and beyond. This presentation is similar to disclosures of future maturities for long-term debt. The company also must provide separate disclosures for operating leases and capital leases (Delta has both operating and capital leases outstanding).

The purpose of this lease disclosure is to provide information concerning current and future payment obligations. These contractual obligations are similar to debt payments. While the obligations under capital leases are reported in long-term debt, the operating lease obligations are not reported in the balance sheet. However, the operating lease obligations must be considered in our evaluation of the company's financial condition.

Capital Leases and the Cash Flow Statement

A capital lease results in an increase to long-term operating assets and an increase in long-term liabilities. However, in many cases, there is no effect on cash flows at the inception of the lease—see entry (1) on page 463. As a consequence, the initial inception of the lease should be reported as a material noncash transaction and not presented in the cash flow statement under either investing or financing cash flows. Subsequently, the depreciation of the leased asset is added (in an indirect method cash flow statement) to cash flow from operations (an expense that does not require a cash outlay) and the principal portion of the lease payment is treated as debt repayment under cash flows from financing activities.

YOU MAKE THE CALL

You are the Division President   You are the president of an operating division. Your CFO recommends operating lease treatment for asset acquisitions to reduce reported assets and liabilities on your balance sheet. To achieve this classification, you must negotiate leases with terms that you feel are not advantageous to your company. What is your response? [Answer on page 493]

Capitalization of Operating Leases

LO3 Convert off-balance-sheet operating leases to the capital lease method.

When a company uses the operating lease method to report its leases, it can have significant resources that are not recognized as assets and significant obligations that are not recognized as liabilities on its balance sheet. As a result, there are distortions in many important measures of financial condition and performance.

- Return on assets (ROA) and asset turnover ratios are overstated due to nonreporting of leased assets.

- Financial leverage ratios are understated by the nonreporting of lease liabilities.

- Net operating profit margin (NOPM) is understated. Although, over the life of the lease, rent expense under operating leases equals depreciation plus interest expense under capital leases, only depreciation expense is included in net operating profit after tax (NOPAT)—interest is a nonoperating expense.

- While cash payments are the same whether the lease is classified as operating or capital, cash flow from operations is higher for capital leases because part of the lease payment (the principal) is treated as a financing cash outflow.

When operating leases are not capitalized, the balance sheet neither reflects all of the assets that are used in the business, nor the nonoperating obligations for which the company is liable. Such noncapitalization of leases makes ROE appear to be of higher quality. This result is, of course, an important reason why managers want to exclude leases from the balance sheet.

Despite structuring leases to achieve off-balance-sheet financing, required lease disclosures allow us to capitalize operating leases for analysis purposes. This capitalization process involves four steps (these are the same steps that the company would follow to record the asset and liability on the balance sheet if the leases had been classified as capital leases):

1. Estimate the discount rate.
2. Estimate the future payments required under operating leases.
3. Compute the present value of future operating lease payments.
4. Adjust the financial statements to include the present value from Step 3 as both a leased asset and a lease liability.

Step 1. There are at least two approaches to determine the appropriate discount rate for our analysis: (1) If the company discloses capital leases, we can impute (infer) an implicit rate of return: a rate that yields the present value computed by the company given the future capital lease payments (see the Business Insight box later in this section for an illustration). (2) Use the rate that corresponds to the company's credit rating or the rate from any recent borrowings involving intermediate-term secured obligations. Companies typically disclose these details in their long-term debt footnote. To illustrate the capitalization of operating leases, we use the Delta Air Lines lease footnote (page 466). For this illustration, we assume a discount rate of 7%, which is approximately equal to the average rate of interest on Delta's debt.

BUSINESS INSIGHT

Imputed Discount Rate Computation for Leases When companies report both operating and capital leases, the average rate used to discount capital leases can be imputed (inferred) from disclosures in the leasing footnote. **Southwest Airlines** presents the following table in the footnotes to its 2014 10-K report:

($ millions)	Capital Leases	Operating Leases, Net
2015	$ 33	$ 684
2016	42	636
2017	45	592
2018	44	496
2019	43	430
Thereafter	202	2,317
Total minimum lease payments	409	$5,155
Less amount representing interest	75	
Present value of minimum lease payments	334	
Less current portion	23	
Long-term portion	$311	

The note reports that the total of the minimum lease payments under capital leases is $409 million and the present value of those payments is $334 million. Using Excel, we estimate the discount rate that Southwest used for its capital lease computations with the IRR function (=**IRR(values)**) as shown in the following spreadsheet. The entries in cells B2 through G2 are taken from Southwest's reported schedule of lease maturities, and those in cells H2 through L2 assume a continuation of the $43 million in capital lease payments in 2020 until the $202 million of estimated payments after 2019 is accounted for. The spreadsheet method yields an estimate of 4% for the discount rate that Southwest implicitly used for capitalization of its capital leases in its 2014 balance sheet.

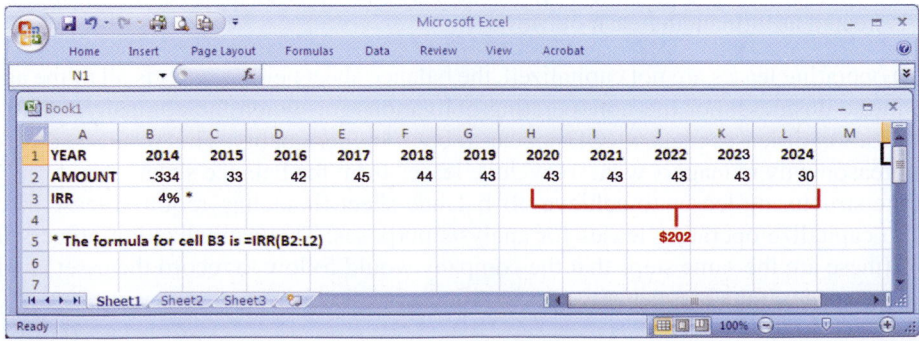

Step 2. The future payments required under operating leases are detailed in Delta's footnotes. The leases footnote typically provides the required cash payment for each of the next five years and then an amount representing total payments for all years after that. In Delta's 2014 10-K report, it reported cash payments for operating leases due each year from 2015 through 2019. In addition, it reports that scheduled lease payments after 2019 total $6,169 million.

One limitation of the footnote disclosure is that the information about the lease payments occurring after the next five years (in 2020 and later) is presented as a lump sum instead of specific payment amounts for each year. Unless we have detailed information about operating leases beyond that which is presented in the footnotes, we are limited to making an assumption about these cash payments. One approach is to assume that the lease payment that we know is due in 2019 ($929 million) is repeated in 2020 and each subsequent year until the total amount of lease payments is reached. This usually requires that we assume a smaller, residual lease payment in the last year to reach the total payments exactly. Using this assumption, Delta's operating lease payments would be $929 million each year from 2020 through 2025, and $595 million in 2026.[2]

Step 3. Once we have a discount rate from Step 1 and a series of cash flows from Step 2, we are ready to compute the present value of the cash flows. Because the lease payments vary from year to year, we cannot compute the present value as an ordinary annuity. One approach is to compute the present value of each payment and then total the present values. This approach is presented in **Exhibit 10.5** using present value factors from **Table A.2** in Appendix A.

EXHIBIT 10.5	Present Value of Delta Air Lines, Inc. Operating Lease Payments ($ millions)		
Year	Operating Lease Payment	Present Value Factor (Table A.2, 7%)	Present Value (Payment × PV Factor)
1 2015	$ 1,707	0.93458	$1,595
2 2016	1,493	0.87344	1,304
3 2017	1,323	0.81630	1,080
4 2018	1,120	0.76290	854
5 2019	929	0.71299	662
6 2020	929	0.66634	619
7 2021	929	0.62275	579
8 2022	929	0.58201	541
9 2023	929	0.54393	505
10 2024	929	0.50835	472
11 2025	929	0.47509	441
12 2026	595	0.44401	264
	$12,741		$8,918*

* Rounded total rather than the sum of the rounded present values.

As an alternative to using the present value tables from Appendix A, we can use the NPV function in Excel to compute the present value.[3] This approach is illustrated in the spreadsheet below:

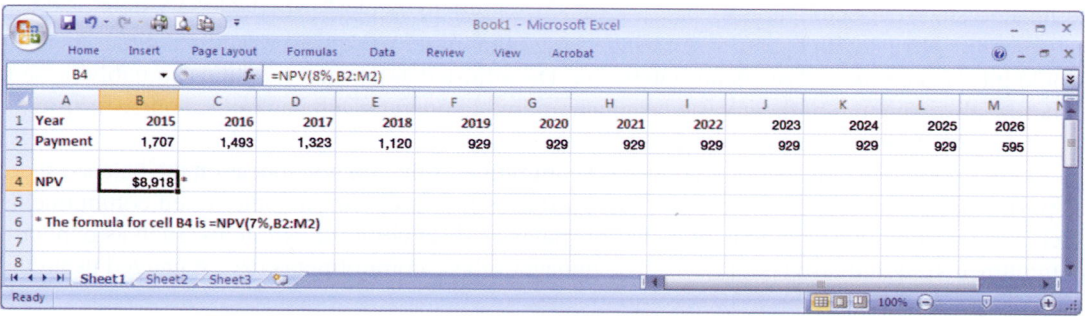

---

[2] There are other reasonable assumptions that we could make that would be consistent with the facts presented in the footnotes. As outsiders analyzing the financial statements, we are limited to estimating the present value of a company's operating leases and to do that, some assumptions are unavoidable.

[3] The NPV function is also available on most financial calculators.

Step 4. Once we've computed the present value of the operating lease payments, we can use the computed amount to adjust the balance sheet and income statement as we illustrate in **Exhibit 10.6**.

EXHIBIT 10.6	Analytical Adjustments from Capitalization of Delta Air Lines' Operating Leases			
($ millions)	Reported	Adjustments	Adjusted	Percent Increase
Assets..............................	$54,121	$8,918	$63,039	16.5%
Liabilities..........................	45,308	8,918	54,226	19.7%
Equity.............................	8,813		8,813	—

By adding the present value of the operating lease payments to both the assets and the liabilities in the balance sheet, we are, in effect, treating these leases as capital leases. If this is the first year of the leases, the initial entry the company would use to record the leases if they were capital leases (and the entry we will use to adjust the balance sheet to be "as if" the leases are capital leases) would be as shown in the following financial statement effects template.[4]

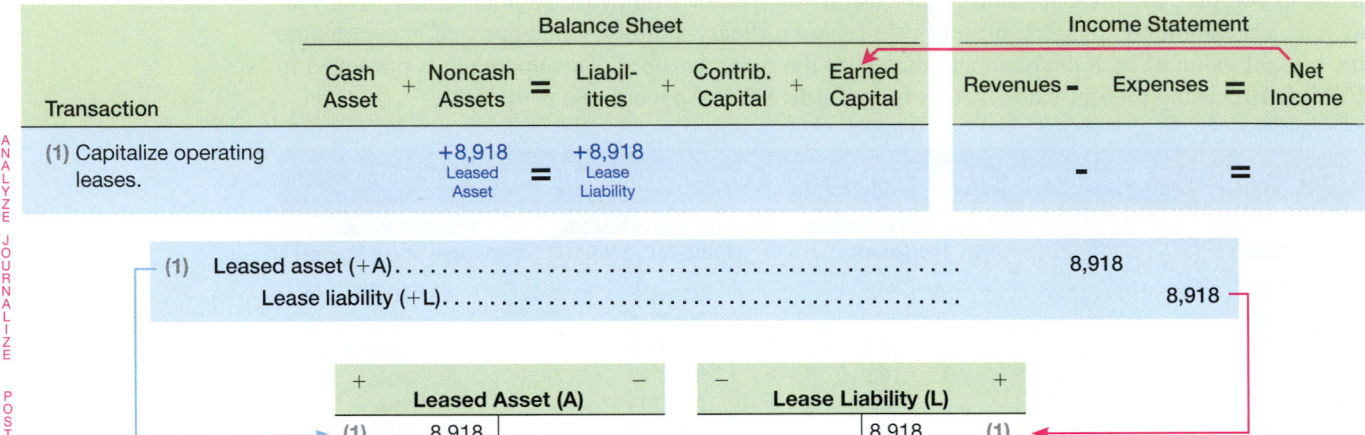

Operating Leases and Financial Ratios

An asset acquired under an operating lease will not appear in the company balance sheet and the related liability will not appear among the liabilities. The omission also affects the income statement, although to a lesser extent. Depreciation is understated but the rent expense offsets the understatement. However, as we have seen, it is possible to estimate the capitalized value of the assets and the size of the associated obligation, which can then be considered in an analysis of the firm using the ratios we have previously introduced.

The capitalization of operating leases has a marked impact on Delta's balance sheet. For the airline and retailing industries, in particular, leased assets (airplanes and real estate) comprise a large portion of net operating assets and these leases are usually classified as operating.

Using the year-end data presented in **Exhibit 10.6** and given revenues of $40,362 million, asset turnover (using year-end figures) decreases from 0.75 ($40,362/$54,121) to 0.64 ($40,362/$63,039). In general for firms with operating leases, leverage (liabilities to equity) would be higher than we would infer from reported financial statements. The adjusted assets and liabilities arguably present a more realistic picture of the invested capital required to operate Delta as well as other firms with significant operating lease commitments.

It is important to consider operating lease commitments that do not appear on the balance sheet as payments that must be satisfied with cash, just as is the case with the other fixed commitments such as interest on outstanding debt. Other off-balance-sheet commitment items, such as purchase commitments, should also be included. The impact of these commitments can be gauged using the ratio of operating cash flow to fixed commitments.

---

[4] For simplicity, we assume the initial year of the lease. Realistically, the leases will be at various stages in their terms. Thus, to consider what the financial statements would look like if the leases were capital, we need to think about how the asset and liability change over time. Generally, depreciation of the asset will be straight-line. On the liability side, early in lease life, most of the lease payments will be interest, not principal. As a result, the balance of the asset will decline faster than the balance of the liability. Thus, we would have to adjust the asset and liability by different amounts. See pages 463-464 and Mid-Chapter Review 1 for examples.

ANALYZING FINANCIAL STATEMENTS

Analysis Objective

We want to assess the effect of financial obligations, including off-balance-sheet commitments, on financial solvency and liquidity.

Analysis Tool   Fixed Commitments Ratio

$$\text{Fixed commitments ratio} = \frac{\text{Operating cash flow before fixed commitments}}{\text{Fixed commitments}}$$

Applying the Fixed Commitments Ratio to Delta Air Lines   Some fixed commitments, such as operating lease payments and purchase commitments, are cash outflows that are classified as operating activities in the cash flow statement. Others (for example, payments due on long-term debt) are classified as financing cash flows and some can be classified as investing (for example, commitments to purchase plant assets). Delta reports total fixed commitments of $8,504 million in its 10-K report. Of these, $1,219 million is for non-interest payments on long-term debt and capital leases (financing) and $1,480 million is for aircraft purchase commitments (investing). Subtracting these amounts leaves the amount of fixed commitments that are part of operating cash flows ($8,504 million − $1,219 million − $1,480 million = $5,805 million). To compute the **fixed commitments ratio**, we start with operating cash flows, add back the fixed commitments that are classified as operating and then divide by the total amount of fixed commitments.[5]

$$\textbf{2012:} \quad 1.00 = \frac{\$2,467 + \$6,317}{\$8,793}$$

$$\textbf{2013:} \quad 1.14 = \frac{\$4,504 + \$5,649}{\$8,890}$$

$$\textbf{2014:} \quad 1.26 = \frac{\$4,947 + \$5,805}{\$8,504}$$

Guidance   A fixed commitments ratio less than 1.0 indicates that a company is generating insufficient cash flows from operations to meet its contractual obligations. Some commitments may be met by selling assets, or by raising additional financing. For example, when long-term debt comes due, it can be refinanced with new debt if the company is otherwise in sound financial health.

Delta Air Lines in Context

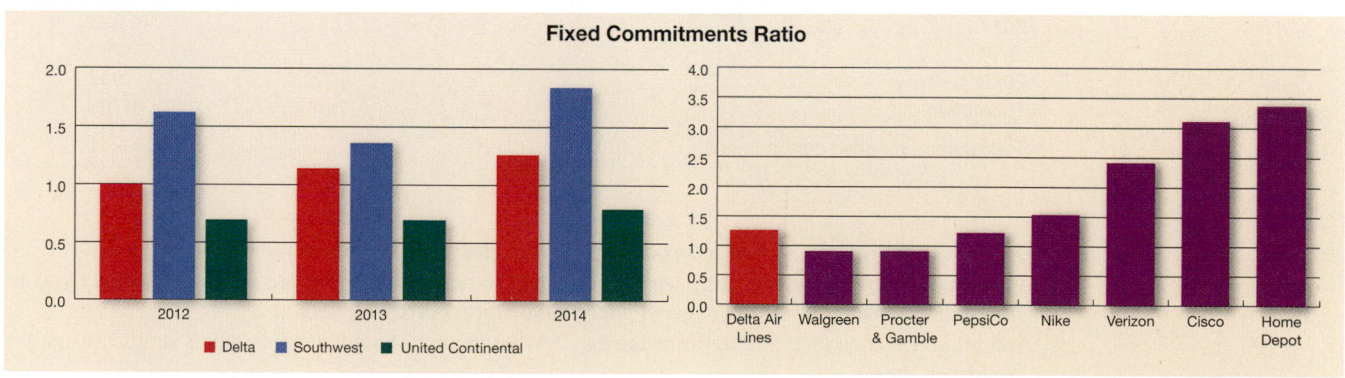

[5] Companies often disclose future fixed commitments by year. For ease of computation in our examples, we use cash flows from 2014 and fixed commitments for 2015 to compute the 2014 ratio. Thus, we are making an implicit assumption that the fixed commitments for the next year are similar to those for the current year.

Takeaways   There is a range of values across firms within an industry and across industries. In our set of companies above for 2014, the ratio ranges from 0.80 for United Continental to 3.37 for Home Depot. Historically, airlines have had relatively low ratios due to large amounts of operating leases, pension commitments, and other obligations. Southwest has always been an exception and now that Delta has improved its performance and cash flows, their ratio is near the middle of the companies we display above. The key takeaway is that off-balance-sheet obligations can have a significant impact on our analysis and understanding of a company's solvency and liquidity.

Other Considerations   The fixed commitments ratio is but one measure of financial solvency and liquidity. It should be used in conjunction with other ratios, such as the debt-to-equity ratio and the current ratio in an effort to gauge the ability of the firm to meet its financial obligations.

MID-CHAPTER REVIEW 1

PART A

Assume that **The Gap Inc.** leased a vacant retail space with the intention of opening another store. The lease calls for annual lease payments of $32,000, due at the end of each of the next ten years. Assume the appropriate discount rate is 7%.

1. If the lease is treated as a capital lease, what journal entry(ies) would Gap make to record the initial signing of the lease agreement?
2. How would Gap record depreciation expense and the first lease payment at the end of the first year of the lease?
3. If this lease is accounted for as an operating lease, what entry(ies) would be necessary during the first year?

PART B

Following is the leasing footnote disclosure from note 12 in **The Gap Inc.**'s 2014 10-K report.

> We lease most of our store premises and some of our corporate facilities and distribution centers. These operating leases expire at various dates through 2030. Most store leases are for a five-year base period and include options that allow us to extend the lease term beyond the initial base period, subject to terms agreed upon at lease inception. Some leases also include early termination options, which can be exercised under specific conditions. The aggregate minimum non-cancelable annual lease payments under leases in effect on January 31, 2015, are:

Fiscal Year	(in millions)
2015	$1,136
2016	1,096
2017	920
2018	760
2019	638
Thereafter	1,701
Total minimum lease commitment	$6,251

1. Does Gap classify these leases as operating or capital leases? How do you know?
2. Assuming its leases are operating leases, compute the adjustments that are necessary for analysis of Gap's balance sheet. (Use Gap's recent intermediate term borrowing rate of 5%.)
3. Assuming the same facts as determined in part 2, what income statement adjustments should an analyst consider, if any?

The solution to this review problem can be found on pages 513-514.

PENSIONS

Companies frequently offer retirement or pension plans as a benefit for their employees. There are two general types of pension plans:

LO4 Explain and interpret the reporting for pension plans.

1. **Defined contribution plan**. This type of plan is one in which the employer, employee, or both make contributions on a regular basis. Individual accounts are set up for participants. Future benefits are not guaranteed but instead fluctuate on the basis of investment earnings. Following retirement, the employee makes periodic withdrawals from that account. The amount that can be withdrawn is determined by how much is contributed to the plan and the rate of return earned on the investment. A tax-advantaged 401(k) account is a typical example. Under a 401(k) plan, the employee makes contributions that are exempt from federal taxes until they are withdrawn after retirement.

2. **Defined benefit plan**. This type of plan is one in which benefits are defined (promised). Defined benefit plans require the company to make periodic payments to a third party, which then makes payments to an employee after retirement. Retirement benefits are usually based on years of service and the employee's salary, not on the amount invested or the rate of return. It is possible for companies to set aside insufficient funds to cover these obligations (federal law does set minimum funding requirements). As a result, defined benefit plans can be overfunded or underfunded. All pension investments are retained by the third party until paid to the employee. In the event of bankruptcy, employees have the standing of a general creditor, but usually have additional protection from the Pension Benefit Guaranty Corporation (PBGC), an independent agency of the U.S. government funded by premiums paid from the participating companies.

For a defined contribution plan, the company contribution is recorded as an expense in the income statement when the cash is paid or the liability accrued. A defined benefit plan is more complex. Although the company contributes cash or securities to the pension investment account, the pension obligation is not satisfied until the employee receives pension benefits, which may be many years into the future. This section focuses on how a defined benefit plan is reported in the financial statements, and how we assess company performance and financial condition when such a plan exists.

Balance Sheet Effects of Defined Benefit Pension Plans

Pension plan assets are primarily investments in stocks and bonds (mostly of other companies, but it is not uncommon for companies to invest pension funds in their own stock). Pension liabilities (called the **projected benefit obligation** or **PBO**) are the company's obligations to pay current and former employees. The difference between the fair value of the pension plan assets and the projected benefit obligation is called the **funded status** of the pension plan. If the PBO exceeds the pension plan assets, the pension is **underfunded**. Conversely, if pension plan assets exceed the PBO, the pension plan is **overfunded**. Under current U.S. GAAP, companies are required to record only the funded status on their balance sheets (that is, the *net* amount, not the pension plan assets and PBO separately), either as an asset if the plan is overfunded, or as a liability if it is underfunded.

Pension plan assets consist of stocks and bonds whose value changes each period in three ways. First, the value of the investments increases or decreases as a result of interest, dividends, and gains or losses on the stocks and bonds held. Second, the pension plan assets increase when the company contributes additional cash or stock to the investment account. Third, the pension plan assets decrease by the amount of benefits paid to retirees during the period. These three changes in the pension plan assets are articulated below.

Pension Plan Assets
Pension plan assets, beginning balance
+ Actual returns on investments (interest, dividends, gains and losses)
+ Company contributions to pension plan
− Benefits paid to retirees
= Pension plan assets, ending balance

The pension liability, or PBO (projected benefit obligation), is computed as the present value of the expected future benefit payments to employees. The future payments depend on the number of years the employee is expected to work (years of service) and the employee's salary level at retirement. Consequently, companies must estimate future wage increases, as well as the number of employees expected to reach retirement age (or the vesting requirement) with the company. In addition, in order to compute the present value of benefit payments, the company has to estimate how long the plan participants are likely to receive pension benefits following retirement (that is, how long the employee—and often surviving spouse—will live). Once the future retiree pool is determined and the expected future payments under the plan are estimated, the expected payments are then discounted to arrive at the present value of the pension obligation. This is the PBO. A reconciliation of the PBO from beginning balance to year-end balance follows.

Projected Benefit Obligation
Projected benefit obligation, beginning balance
+   Service cost
+   Interest cost
+/− Actuarial losses (gains)
−   Benefits paid to retirees
=   Projected benefit obligation, ending balance

As this reconciliation shows, the balance in the PBO changes during the period for four reasons.

- First, as employees continue to work for the company, their pension benefits increase. The annual **service cost** represents the additional (future) pension benefits earned by employees during the current year.

- Second, **interest cost** accrues on the outstanding pension liability, just as it would with any other long-term liability (see the accounting for bond liabilities in Chapter 9). Because there are no scheduled interest payments on the PBO, the interest cost accrues each year, that is, interest is added to the existing liability.

- Third, the PBO can increase (or decrease) due to **actuarial losses (and gains)**, which arise when companies make changes in their pension plans or make *changes in actuarial assumptions* (including assumptions that are used to estimate the PBO, such as the rate of wage inflation, termination and mortality rates, and the discount rate used to compute the present value of future obligations). For example, if a company increases the discount rate used to compute the present value of future pension plan payments from, say, 8% to 9%, the present value of future benefit payments declines (just like bond prices) and the company records a gain. Conversely, if the discount rate is reduced to 7%, the present value of the PBO increases and a loss is recorded. Other assumptions used to estimate the pension liability (such as the expected wage inflation rate or the expected life span of current and former employees) can create similar actuarial losses or gains.

- Fourth, pension benefit payments to retirees reduce the PBO (that portion of the liability is now paid).

Finally, the net pension liability (or asset) that is reported in a company's balance sheet, then, is computed as follows:

Net Pension Asset (or Liability)
Pension plan assets (at fair value)
− Projected benefit obligation (PBO)
Funded status

If the funded status is positive (assets exceed liabilities), the overfunded pension plan is reported on the balance sheet as an asset, typically called prepaid pension cost. If the funded status is negative (liabilities exceed assets), it is reported as a liability.[6] During the early 2000s, long-term interest

---

[6] Companies that have a defined benefit plan typically maintain many pension plans. Some are overfunded and others are underfunded. Current U.S. GAAP requires companies to group all of the overfunded and underfunded plans together, and to present a net asset for the overfunded plans and a net liability for the underfunded plans.

rates declined drastically and many companies lowered their discount rate for computing the present value of future pension payments. Lower discount rates meant higher PBO values. This period also witnessed two bear markets—the "dot com crash" in 2000–2001 and the financial crisis of 2008–2010—and pension plan assets declined in value. The combined effect of the increase in PBO and the decrease in asset values caused many pension funds to become severely underfunded. They have not fully recovered. Of the 1,500 largest U.S companies reporting pension plans (pension plan data available on the Compustat database) in 2014, 81% reported pension plans that were underfunded. Delta Air Lines reported an underfunded pension obligation of $12.5 billion in 2014. This amount was equal to 23 percent of its total assets. Many companies with a defined benefit plan report that their plans are underfunded. The underfunded liability as a percent of total assets for Delta and several other companies is reported in the graphic below.[7]

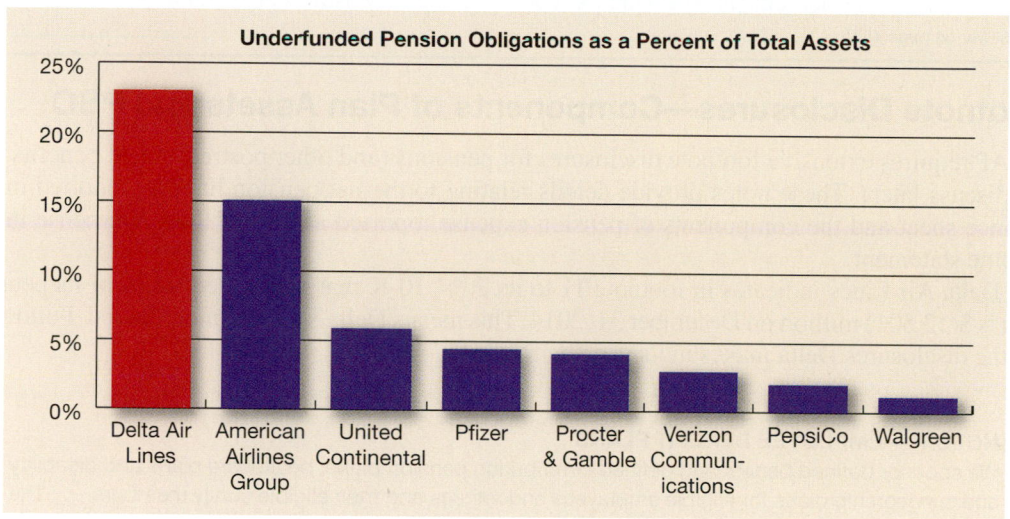

Income Statement Effects of Defined Benefit Pension Plans

In a defined benefit plan, pension expense is not determined by the company's contribution to the pension fund. Instead, net pension expense is computed as follows.

Net Pension Expense
Service cost
+ Interest cost
− *Expected* return on pension plan assets
± Amortization of deferred amounts
Net pension expense

The net pension expense is rarely reported separately on the income statement. Instead, it is included with other forms of compensation expense in selling, general and administrative (SG&A) expenses. However, pension expense is disclosed separately in footnotes.

The net pension expense has four components. The previous section about the PBO described the first two components: service costs and interest costs. The third component of pension expense relates to the return on pension plan assets, which *reduces* total pension expense. To compute this component, companies use the long-term *expected* rate of return on the pension plan assets, rather than the *actual* return, and multiply that expected rate by the balance in the pension plan assets account. Use of the expected return rather than actual return is an important distinction. Company CEOs and CFOs dislike income variability because they believe that stockholders react negatively to it, so company executives intensely (and successfully) lobbied the FASB to use the more stable expected long-term investment return, rather than the actual return, in computing pension expense. Thus, the pension plan assets' expected return is subtracted to compute net pension expense.

Any difference between the expected and the actual return is accumulated, together with other deferred amounts, off-balance-sheet and reported in the footnotes. Other deferred amounts include

---

[7] Southwest Airlines does not offer a defined benefit plan, but does offer a defined contribution plan.

changes in PBO resulting from changes in estimates used to compute the PBO and from amendments to the pension plans made by the company. However, if the deferred amounts exceed certain limits, the excess is recognized on-balance-sheet with a corresponding amount recognized as amortization in the income statement.[8] This amortization is the fourth component of pension expense and can be either a positive or negative amount depending on the sign of the difference between expected and actual return on plan assets.

YOU MAKE THE CALL

You are a Consultant to the FASB The Board has asked your input on whether the assets in the pension fund should be netted against Pension Benefit Obligation (PBO) or whether the pension asset and the pension obligation should be reported separately. How would you advise the Board?
[Answer on page 493]

LO5 Analyze and interpret pension footnote disclosures.

Footnote Disclosures—Components of Plan Assets and PBO

GAAP requires extensive footnote disclosures for pensions (and other postretirement benefits that we discuss later). These notes provide details relating to the net pension liability reported in the balance sheet and the components of pension expense reported as part of SG&A expense in the income statement.

Delta Air Lines indicates in footnote 11 to its 2014 10-K that the funded status of its pension plan is $(12,501) million on December 31, 2014. This means Delta's plan is underfunded. Following are the disclosures Delta makes in its pension footnote.

NOTE 11—EMPLOYEE BENEFIT PLANS

We sponsor defined benefit and defined contribution pension plans, healthcare plans and disability and survivorship plans for eligible employees and retirees and their eligible family members. . . . The defined benefit plans are closed to new entrants and frozen for future benefit accruals. The Pension Protection Act of 2006 allows commercial airlines to elect alternative funding rules . . . under which the unfunded liability for a frozen defined benefit plan may be amortized over a 17-year period. . . . We estimate that the funding requirements under these plans will total at least $950 million in 2015.

Benefit Obligations, Fair Value of Plan Assets and Funded Status ($ millions):	2014	2013
Benefit obligation at beginning of period	$19,060	$21,489
Service cost	—	—
Interest cost	928	861
Actuarial loss (gain)	2,923	(2,212)
Benefits paid, including lump sums and annuities	(1,055)	(1,078)
Participant contributions	—	—
Benefit obligation at end of period	$21,856	$19,060
Fair value of plan assets at beginning of period	$8,937	$8,196
Actual gain on plan assets	556	905
Employer contributions	917	914
Participant contributions	—	—
Benefits paid, including lump sums and annuities	(1,055)	(1,078)
Fair value of plan assets at end of period	$9,355	$8,937
Funded status at end of period	$(12,501)	$(10,123)

---

[8] To avoid amortization, the deferred amounts must be less than 10% of the PBO or pension investments, whichever is less. The excess, if any, is amortized until no further excess remains. When the excess is eliminated (by investment returns or company contributions, for example), the amortization ceases.

Delta's PBO began 2014 with a balance of $19,060 million. It increased by the accrual of $928 million in interest cost. During the year, Delta also realized an actuarial loss of $2,923 million, which increased the pension liability. The PBO decreased as a result of $1,055 million in benefits paid to retirees, leaving a balance of $21,856 million at year-end.

Pension plan assets began the year with a fair value of $8,937 million, which increased by $556 million from investment returns (gains) and increased by $917 million from company contributions. The company drew down its investments to make pension payments of $1,055 million to retirees, leaving the pension plan assets with a year-end balance of $9,355 million. The funded status of Delta's pension plan at year-end is $(12,501) million ($21,856 million − $9,355 million). The negative balance indicates that its pension plan is underfunded. The PBO and pension plan assets accounts cannot be separated into operating and nonoperating components; thus, most analysts treat the entire funded status as an operating item (either asset or liability).

Footnote Disclosures—Components of Pension Expense

Delta Air Lines incurred $784 million of pension expense in 2014. This is not broken out separately in its income statement. Instead, it is included in SG&A expense. Details of this expense are found in its pension footnote. Delta reported $551 million in pension cost related to defined contribution plans. In addition, Delta reported its expense related to its defined benefit plans as follows ($ millions):

	2014	2013
Service cost	$ —	$ —
Interest cost	928	861
Expected return on assets	(829)	(734)
Recognized net actuarial loss	134	221
Net periodic cost for defined benefit plans	$233	$354

Most analysts consider the service cost portion of pension expense to be an operating expense, similar to salaries and other benefits. However, the interest cost component is generally viewed as a financing cost. Similarly, the expected return on plan assets is not considered operating. Because Delta's defined benefit pension plan is closed and further accrual of benefits is frozen, it reported no service cost in 2014 and the entire $233 million of defined benefit pension cost would be treated as nonoperating for analysis purposes. The costs related to the defined contribution plan are considered operating expenses.

RESEARCH INSIGHT

Valuation of Pension Footnote Disclosures   The FASB requires footnote disclosure of the major components of pension cost presumably because it is useful for investors. Pension-related research has examined whether investors assign different valuation multiples to the components of pension cost when assessing company market value. Research finds that the market does, indeed, attach different interpretation to pension components, reflecting differences in information about recurring vs. nonrecurring expenses.

Interest cost is the product of the PBO and the discount rate. This discount rate is set by the company. The expected dollar return on pension assets is the product of the pension plan asset balance and the expected long-run rate of return on the investment portfolio. This rate is also set by the company. Further, the PBO is affected by the expected rate of wage inflation, termination and mortality rates, all of which are estimated by the company.

U.S. GAAP requires disclosure of several rates used by the company in its estimation of PBO and the related pension expense. Delta Air Lines discloses the following table in its pension footnote:

	2014	2013
Weighted-average assumptions used to determine net periodic benefit cost for the years ended December 31		
Discount rate	4.99%	4.10%
Expected long-term rate of return on plan assets	8.94	8.94

During 2014, Delta increased its assumed discount rate, which is used to compute the present value of the PBO and determine interest cost component of pension expense. The expected rate of return on plan assets remained constant.

Changes in these assumptions have the following general effects on pension expense and, thus, profitability. This table summarizes the effects of increases in the various rates. Decreases have the exact opposite effects of increases.

Estimate change	Probable effect on pension expense	Reason for effect
Discount rate increase	Increases	While the higher discount rate reduces the PBO, the lower PBO is multiplied by a higher interest rate. The rate effect is generally larger than the discount effect, resulting in increased pension expense.
Investment return increase .	Decreases	The dollar amount of expected return on plan assets is the product of the plan assets balance and the expected long-term rate of return. Increasing the return increases the expected return on plan assets, thus reducing pension expense.
Wage inflation increase	Increases	The expected rate of wage inflation affects future wage levels that determine expected pension payments. An increase, thus, increases PBO, which increases both the service and interest cost components of pension expense.

In the case of Delta Air Lines, for example, a higher discount rate increased interest cost in 2014 relative to 2013. However, Delta recorded a higher expected return on plan assets (the expected rate was constant but the base must have changed) and a lower amount of recognized net actuarial loss in 2014 compared to 2013. Thus, the net cost in 2014 is lower. It is often the case that companies reduce the expected investment returns with a lag, but increase them without a lag, to favorably impact profitability. We must be aware of the impact of these changes in assumptions in our evaluation of company profitability.

BUSINESS INSIGHT

Pension Buyout at GM   **General Motors'** pension obligation was at one time the largest of any company in the world. In 2011, its defined benefit plans were underfunded by $25.4 billion. Because pension fund assets are invested in securities, the underfunded balance can increase if the stock market falls. Analysts argued that the size, risk, and long duration of these obligations depressed GM's credit rating and its stock price.

In an effort to remove some of the projected obligations from its balance sheet, GM offered to buy out the pensions of 42,000 retirees in 2012. The pensions of an additional 76,000 retirees were transferred to **Prudential Financial** who will make the annuity payments to the retirees. Although the buyout required an immediate cash payment, the move removed approximately $26 billion of pension obligations from GM's 2012 balance sheet, thus improving solvency ratios. In addition, the reduced obligation means that future income statements will reflect lower pension expense due to reduced interest costs. GM's 2014 financial statement shows that the defined benefit pension plans are still underfunded by $24.1 billion. The related pension expense included in the income statement for 2014 was $151 million, considerably less than the pension expense in 2012 of $2.9 billion.

Footnote Disclosures and Future Cash Flows

The net periodic pension cost (expense) of $233 million is considerably less than the $917 million in cash that Delta contributed to its defined benefit plans. In addition, Delta paid $551 million into its defined contribution plans. Thus, its total pension expense for 2014 was $784 million ($233 million + $551 million) and its cash contributions totaled $1,468 million ($917 million + $551 million).

BUSINESS INSIGHT

How Pensions Confound Income Analysis   Overfunded pension plans and boom markets can inflate income. Specifically, when the stock market is booming, pension investments realize large gains that flow to income (via reduced pension expense). Although pension plan assets do not belong to shareholders (as they are the legal entitlement of current and future retirees), the gains and losses from those plan assets are reported in income. The following graph plots the funded status of **General Electric Company**'s pension plan together with pension expense (revenue) that GE reported from 2000 to 2014.

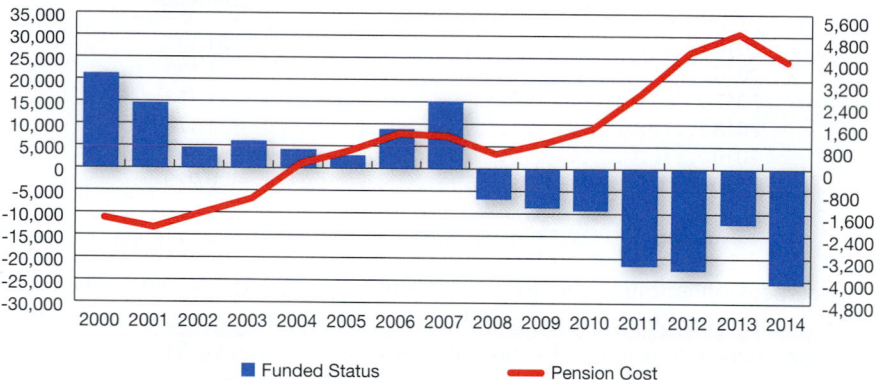

GE's funded status was consistently positive (indicating an overfunded plan) until 2008. The degree of overfunding peaked in 1999 at the height of the stock market, and began to decline during the bear market of the early 2000s. GE reported pension *revenue* (not expense) during this period. In 2001, GE's reported pension *revenue* was $2,095 million (10.6% of its pretax income). Because of the plan's overfunded status, the expected return and amortization of deferred gains components of pension expense amounted to $5,288 million, far in excess of the service and interest costs of $3,193 million. Since 2004, GE has recorded pension expense (rather than revenue) as the pension plan's overfunding and expected long-term rates of return declined, and in 2008 the funded status turned negative. In 2014, GE reported an unfunded liability of $25.7 billion and a pension expense of $4.0 billion.

Companies use their pension plan assets to pay pension benefits to retirees. When markets are booming, as was true during the 1990s, pension plan assets can grow rapidly. However, when markets reverse, as in the bear market of the early 2000s and in 2008–2009, the value of pension plan assets can decline. The company's annual pension plan contribution is an investment decision influenced, in part, by market conditions and minimum required contributions specified by law.[9] Companies' cash contributions come from borrowed funds or operating cash flows.

RESEARCH INSIGHT

Why Do Companies Offer Pensions?   Research examines why companies choose to offer pension benefits. It finds that deferred compensation plans and pensions help align the long-term interests of owners and employees. Research also examines the composition of pension investments. It finds that a large portion of pension fund assets are invested in fixed-income securities, which are of lower risk than other investment securities. This implies that pension assets are less risky than nonpension assets. However, in severe economic downturns, some corporations curtail their pension plan contributions in order to protect cash flow.

Delta Air Lines paid $1,055 million in pension benefits to retirees in 2014, yet it contributed only $917 million to pension assets that year. The remaining amount was paid out of available funds in the investment account. Cash contributions to the pension plan assets are the relevant amounts for an analysis of projected cash flows. Benefits paid in relation to the pension liability balance

---

[9] The Pension Protection Act of 2006 tightens funding requirements so employers make greater cash contributions to pension funds, closes loopholes that allow companies with underfunded plans to skip cash pension payments, prohibits employers and union leaders from promising extra benefits if pension plans are markedly underfunded, and strengthens disclosure rules to give workers and retirees more information about the status of their pension plan.

can provide a clue about the need for *future* cash contributions. Companies are required to disclose the expected benefit payments for five years after the statement date and the remaining obligations thereafter. Following is Delta's benefit disclosure statement:

The following table summarizes the benefit payments that are scheduled to be paid in the years ending December 31 ($ millions):

	Pension Benefits
2015	$1,124
2016	1,133
2017	1,153
2018	1,173
2019	1,191
2020–2024	6,229

Delta's unfunded pension amount grew by over $2 billion from 2013 to 2014. The company was, however, able to contribute $917 million and the plan assets had an actual return of $556 million. Thus, the company was able to cover its current year cash outflows of $1,055 million from these sources, which has not always been the case for Delta. The reason for the growth in the net unfunded balance in its pension plan is from increases in the pension liability. In general for pension plans, and as is true at Delta, life expectancies are getting longer but retirement ages are not increasing. Thus, pension payments are expected to be paid for a longer period of time, increasing the liability. In addition, market rates of interest are low requiring discount rates used to value the liabilities to be (somewhat) low, which makes the liability higher.

One application of the pension footnote is to assess the likelihood that the company will be required to increase its cash contributions to the pension plan. This estimate is made by examining the funded status of the pension plan and the projected payments to retirees. For severely underfunded plans, the projected payments to retirees will not be covered by existing pension assets and current negative investment returns. When this occurs, the company will need to divert operating cash flow from other prospective projects to cover its pension plan. Alternatively, if operating cash flows will not be sufficient, it will likely need to borrow to fund those payments. This decision can be especially troublesome as the debt service payments include interest, thus, effectively increasing the cost of the pension contribution.

Other Post-Employment Benefits

In addition to pension benefits, many companies provide health care and insurance benefits to retired employees. These benefits are referred to as **other post-employment benefits (OPEB)**. These benefits present reporting challenges similar to pension accounting. However, companies most often provide these benefits on a "pay-as-you-go" basis and it is rare for companies to make contributions in advance for OPEB. As a result, this liability, known as the **accumulated post-employment benefit obligation (APBO)**, is largely, if not totally, unfunded. GAAP requires that the unfunded APBO liability, net of any unrecognized amounts, be reported in the balance sheet and the annual service costs and interest costs be accrued as expenses each year. This requirement is controversial for two reasons. First, future health care costs are especially difficult to estimate, so the value of the resulting APBO (the present value of the future benefits) is fraught with error. Second, these benefits are provided at the discretion of the employer and can be altered or terminated at any time. Consequently, employers argue that without a legal obligation to pay these benefits, the liability should not be reported in the balance sheet.

Other post-employment benefits can produce large liabilities. For example, Delta Air Lines reports an underfunded health care obligation of $2,505 million and a related expense of $101 million in 2014. Our analysis of cash flows related to pension obligations can be extended to other post-employment benefit obligations. For example, in addition to its pension payments, Delta also discloses that it is obligated to make health care payments to retirees totaling $2,633 million over the next 10 years. Our analysis of projected cash flows must consider this potential cash outflow.

RESEARCH INSIGHT

Valuation of Nonpension Post-Employment Benefits   The FASB requires employers to accrue the costs of all nonpension post-employment benefits; known as *accumulated post-employment benefit obligation* (APBO). These benefits consist primarily of health care and insurance. This requirement is controversial due to concerns about the reliability of the liability estimate. Research finds that the APBO (alone) is associated with company value. However, when other pension-related variables are included in the research, the APBO liability is no longer useful in explaining company value. Research concludes that the pension-related variables do a better job at conveying value-relevant information than the APBO number alone, which implies that the APBO number is less reliable.

A GLOBAL PERSPECTIVE

Pension Fund Status   IFRS and U.S. GAAP require companies to report the funded status of their defined benefit pension plans on the balance sheet. IFRS, however, calculates pension expense differently. First, unlike U.S. GAAP, IFRS requires that the expected return on pension assets must be the same rate as the discount rate used to value the PBO. In addition, IFRS recognizes the cost of plan amendments in the income statement immediately, rather than amortizing those costs over the service life of employees. There are still other differences that make direct comparison across IFRS and U.S. GAAP firms difficult.

MID-CHAPTER REVIEW 2

The following pension data is taken from footnote 8 of **United Continental Holdings, Inc.**, 10-K report.

($ millions)	2014
Change in Benefit Obligation	
Projected benefit obligation at beginning of year	$4,000
Service cost	98
Interest cost	201
Actuarial (gains) losses	807
Gross benefits paid and settlements	(281)
Other	(22)
Projected benefit obligation at end of year	$4,803
Change in Plan Assets	
Fair value of plan assets at beginning of year	$2,397
Actual gains (losses) on plan assets	151
Employer contributions	307
Gross benefits paid and settlements	(281)
Other	(12)
Fair value of plan assets at end of year	$2,562
Funded status of the plans	$(2,241)

Following is United Continental's footnote for its pension cost as reported in its income statement.

Components of Net Periodic Benefit Cost	Defined Benefit Pension 2014
Service cost	$ 98
Interest cost	201
Expected return on plan assets	(180)
Amortization and other	13
Net periodic benefit cost	$132

Required

1. In general, what factors impact a company's pension benefit obligation during a period?
2. In general, what factors impact a company's pension plan investments during a period?
3. What amount is reported on the balance sheet relating to the United Continental pension plan?
4. How does the expected return on plan assets affect pension cost?
5. How does United Continental's expected return on plan assets compare with its actual return (in $s) for 2014?
6. How much net pension cost is reflected in United Continental's 2014 income statement?
7. Assess United Continental's ability to meet payment obligations to retirees.

The solution to this review problem can be found on pages 514-515.

LO6 Describe and interpret accounting for income taxes.

ACCOUNTING FOR INCOME TAXES

Companies maintain two sets of books, one for reporting to their shareholders and creditors and one to report to tax authorities. This is not unethical or illegal. In fact, it is often required. Companies with publicly traded securities compute and report financial accounting income under the rules (e.g., GAAP or IFRS) provided by the financial accounting standards setters (e.g., FASB in the United States). As we have discussed, this income computation is done on the accrual basis, and it is meant to provide information about firm performance to outside stakeholders, such as investors and creditors.[10] Companies must also compute taxable income and report the amount on their tax return(s) filed with the tax authorities in the jurisdictions in which they are required to file (e.g., the Internal Revenue Service and state tax authorities in the United States). Taxable income is determined under the rules promulgated by the government of the taxing jurisdiction (e.g., the Internal Revenue Code in the United States). Tax authorities have different objectives from financial accounting standard setters. The tax rules are set in order to raise money to fund government activities, to encourage or discourage certain behaviors, and (hopefully) based on some sense of fairness and equity. In contrast, financial accounting income is meant to provide information about firm performance to investors, creditors, and other stakeholders so that these parties can make informed decisions about investments and loans. The rules and objectives are very different for the two income measures, and as a result, the two resulting income numbers for a company can be very different.

Our objective here is to learn how to determine a corporation's income tax expense that is reported on the income statement for financial accounting purposes. Financial accounting uses accrual accounting, thus, income tax expense is determined using accrual accounting just like all other expenses. As a result, income tax expense on the income statement is not the cash taxes paid for the reporting period. Instead, it is the accrual-based expense measure, meaning it is the total income tax expense related to the financial accounting income reported in the period regardless of whether those income taxes are paid in the current period or in the future. Furthermore, because it is accrual-based, there will be resulting assets and liabilities that need to be accounted for on the balance sheet. These include what are called deferred tax liabilities and deferred tax assets.

Book-Tax Differences

There are two general types of differences between taxable income and financial accounting income, also known as book-tax differences—permanent differences and temporary differences.

A permanent difference is an item of income or expense that is accounted for differently for book and tax purposes in the current year and never reverses in a future year. A simple example of a permanent difference is interest income on municipal bonds. Municipal bond interest income is included in financial accounting income. However, municipal bond interest is tax exempt at the federal level, meaning it is not included in taxable income. Thus, if a company has municipal bond interest income, its financial accounting income will be higher than its taxable income by the amount of municipal bond interest. This difference will not reverse in the future

---

[10] All companies have to report to tax authorities but many privately held companies do not have to comply with GAAP.

because the municipal bond interest is never included in taxable income. The accounting for income tax with respect to a permanent difference is straightforward; no deferred tax assets or liabilities are created. Income tax expense is lower (in this case) in the current year as a result of the taxes saved by investing in municipal bonds.

A temporary difference is an item of income or expense that is different between book and taxable income in the current year, but will reverse in a future year such that the same amount is included in taxable income and book income over time. Temporary differences are:

1. created by using accrual accounting for book and cash accounting for tax, and/or
2. created by using different rules for determining the accrual amount for book than for tax.

A common example of a temporary difference is depreciation. For financial accounting purposes companies often use straight-line depreciation as discussed in Chapter 8. For U.S. tax purposes, however, companies use an accelerated method of depreciation (the Modified Accelerated Cost Recovery System (MACRS)). Thus, early in an asset's life, tax depreciation will be greater than book depreciation. However, over the life of the asset the same amount of depreciation will be recorded for book and tax (assuming zero salvage value). This is a temporary difference because tax depreciation is higher earlier on but will be equal to or less than book depreciation in later years in the asset's life. In other words, the book-tax difference will reverse. The computation of the income tax expense is more difficult in this case. We need to account for the taxes due on taxable income (the cash taxes) *and* an accrual of taxes that are known to be due in a future period when the depreciation difference reverses. In other words, our total income tax expense is the tax expense related to financial accounting income for the period regardless of whether the taxes are actually paid this year. The accrual for the portion not yet paid creates a **deferred tax liability**—the book-tax difference in this period will lead to higher taxable income relative to book income in the future. This higher relative taxable income means higher cash taxes to be paid in the future—that is, a liability.

FYI   We use the term book income to refer to income before income taxes, as reported in financial statements. Taxable income refers to income reported in the income tax return.

Example   Assume Clark Corporation is in its first year of business. It purchases a piece of equipment that costs $200,000 with a useful life of 4 years and no net salvage value. The firm uses straight-line depreciation for financial reporting purposes and accelerated depreciation under MACRS for tax purposes (we will use double declining balance depreciation as an approximation for our example). Comparing the depreciation schedules reveals the following information:

FYI   Income tax expense is also titled **provision for income tax**.

Year	Tax Reporting DDB Depreciation	Financial Reporting Straight-Line Depreciation	Tax vs. Book Difference	Cumulative Tax-Book Difference
1	$100,000	$50,000	$50,000	$50,000
2	50,000	50,000	0	50,000
3	25,000	50,000	(25,000)	25,000
4	25,000	50,000	(25,000)	0

Assume the corporate statutory tax rate is 40%, we expect the tax rate to stay at 40% for the entire 4 years, and that depreciation is the only book-tax difference for the Clark Corporation. The deferred tax liability at the end of each year is the cumulative book-tax difference times the tax rate. The tax rate to be used is the tax rate expected to be in effect when the book-tax difference reverses. The deferred tax expense each period is the current year book-tax difference (which is the change in the cumulative book-tax difference) times the tax rate. The deferred tax liability at the end of each year and the deferred tax expense for each year for Clark Corporation would be:

Year	Cumulative Tax-Book Difference	Tax Rate	Deferred Tax Liability, End of Year	Deferred Tax Expense
1	$50,000	40%	$20,000	$20,000
2	50,000	40%	20,000	0
3	25,000	40%	10,000	(10,000)
4	0	40%	0	(10,000)

Now assume for illustration that financial accounting earnings each year before depreciation and taxes are $125,000 and there are no other book-tax differences. The yearly calculation of financial reporting and taxable income along with the income tax expense is as follows:

	Tax			
Year	1	2	3	4
Earnings before depreciation	$125,000	$125,000	$125,000	$125,000
Depreciation deduction	(100,000)	(50,000)	(25,000)	(25,000)
Taxable income	25,000	75,000	100,000	100,000
Tax due on the tax return (@ 40%)	10,000	30,000	40,000	40,000

	Financial Reporting			
Year	1	2	3	4
Earnings before depreciation	$125,000	$125,000	$125,000	$125,000
Depreciation expense.	(50,000)	(50,000)	(50,000)	(50,000)
Earnings before tax	75,000	75,000	75,000	75,000
Tax expense	30,000	30,000	30,000	30,000

The entry to record income tax expense in Year 1 follows using the financial statement effects template and journal entry form:

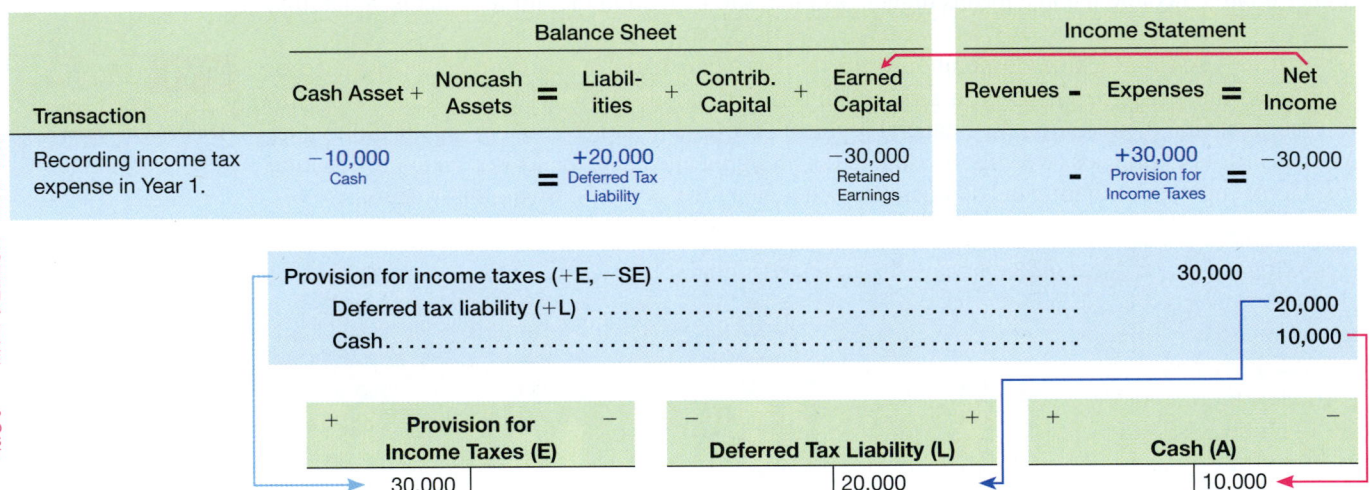

In Year 4, Clark Corporation records its income tax expense. The entry is recorded as follows:

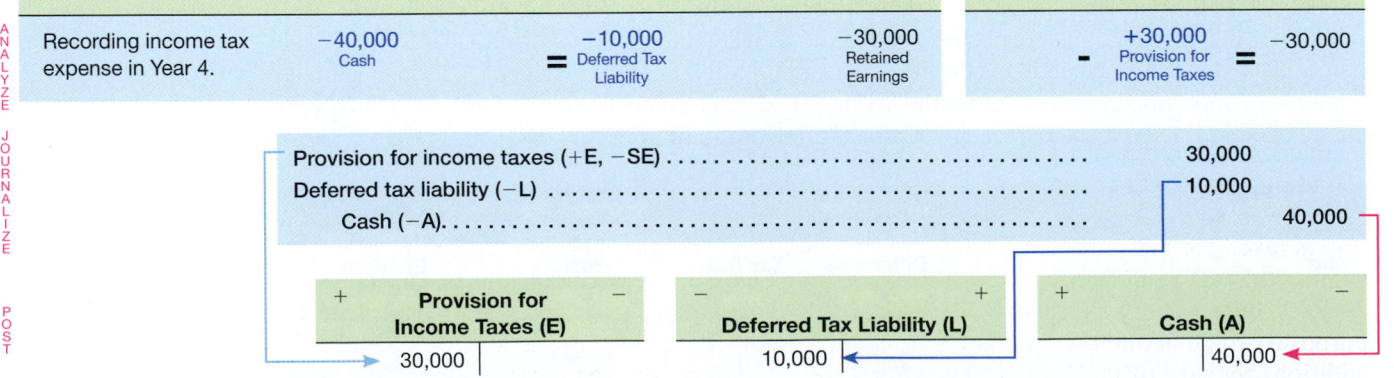

The analysis highlights several facts:

1. Over the 4 years, tax payments to the IRS total $120,000 = $10,000 + $30,000 + $40,000 + $40,000. Total tax expense on the books for the 4 years also equals $120,000 = 4 × $30,000.

2. The timing of the tax payments differs from the tax expense recognized on the books.

3. The deferred tax liability created in the first year because the tax code allows a larger deduction for depreciation, is reduced to zero in the 4th year when the useful life of the asset is over and the timing of the depreciation deductions reverse.

4. The cash flow takes place consistent with the tax code. The accounting expense amount is an accrual-basis measure.

5. In year 1, the corporation's provision for income tax consists of current income tax expense of $10,000 and deferred income tax expense of $20,000 for the total income tax expense of $30,000. In year 4, the corporation has current income tax expense of $40,000 and deferred income tax expense of $(10,000) for a total income tax expense of $30,000. The total income tax expense is shown on the income statement and the more detailed breakout into current and deferred expense is disclosed in the notes to the financial statements.

Depreciation generally will lead to a deferred tax liability because tax depreciation is usually faster than book depreciation. There are also transactions that generate the necessity to record a **deferred tax asset**. For example, bad debts, warranty expense, and many other accrued expenses usually require an associated deferred tax asset to be recorded. For financial accounting purposes, bad debt expense and warranty expense are expensed using management estimates before the receivable actually goes bad and before the warranty costs are actually paid. Again, this is because financial accounting is done on the accrual method and expenses that are associated with the revenue recorded generally are estimated and accrued before they are paid in cash. This is the conservative nature of financial reporting. For tax purposes, these expenses cannot be estimated but instead are deductible generally only when paid. This difference in timing between tax reporting and financial accounting leads to temporary differences where the tax deduction is later in time than the financial accounting expense (opposite of what we just illustrated for depreciation). Because in this case a tax deduction will occur in the future due to a transaction or event in the current period, the company has a deferred tax asset (future benefit) that needs to be recorded.

Temporary book-tax differences also occur with items of revenue. Take for example, unearned revenue we described in Chapter 6. If a company receives cash in advance of being able to recognize revenue, the company will record unearned revenue (a liability) until the revenue is earned and can be recognized. For tax purposes, however, the cash received is generally recorded as income in the period it is received. Thus, there is a book-tax difference. In this case, the revenue is recorded for tax in an earlier period than for financial accounting, meaning that in some future year(s) taxable income will be less than financial accounting income when the revenue is recognized according to the GAAP rules. That means the company has a deferred tax asset to record in the year the cash is received because in a future period taxable income will be lower than book income because of the unearned revenue recorded in the current year.

As a brief example, let's say that the corporation Josie's Jewelry, Inc. makes sales of $100,000 in the current period and estimates and records a bad debt expense of $5,000. This is an expense for financial reporting purposes but there is no deduction allowed for tax purposes in the current period. The tax deduction is not allowed until the receivable actually goes bad (i.e., is deemed to be uncollectible). Using a tax rate of 40%, Josie's Jewelry would report an increase in a deferred tax asset in the current period of $2,000 ($5,000 × 40%) and a corresponding deferred tax benefit (i.e., a negative deferred tax expense) on the income statement. When the receivable is deemed uncollectible and written off in a future period and the deduction is taken for tax purposes, the corporation will reverse the deferred tax asset to zero (assuming the full $5,000 is the amount that eventually is deducted for tax purposes) and record a $2,000 deferred tax expense. Notice that in this future period, the deduction is taken for tax purposes so the actual tax paid is lower and thus, current tax expense is lower by $2,000. In addition, because of the deferred tax asset reversal, deferred tax expense is increased. Thus, the net effect on income in the future period is zero. This is correct because the tax benefit was accrued in the first period when the revenue was earned, bad debt expense was recorded, and deferred tax asset was established.[11]

BUSINESS INSIGHT

The United States has a worldwide tax system, meaning the United States taxes multinational corporations incorporated in the United States on their worldwide earnings. Operating earnings earned by a subsidiary in a foreign jurisdiction, however, are not taxed in the United States when earned, but are taxed in the United States when repatriated to the U.S. parent company as a dividend (tax credits for foreign income taxes paid are allowed to mitigate double taxation). Because the United States has a high corporate statutory tax rate, many U.S. corporations do not repatriate earnings from their foreign subsidiaries in order to avoid (defer) the U.S. tax on those earnings. As of the time of this writing, most estimates are that there is in excess of $2 trillion of unremitted earnings in foreign subsidiaries of U.S. multinational corporations (the estimates of how much of this is in cash versus reinvested in property, plant, and equipment vary).

How do companies account for the current and future taxes on these unremitted foreign earnings? The earnings of the foreign subsidiaries are included in financial accounting income in the same manner as earnings from domestic subsidiaries. But, as just described, the operating earnings of the foreign subsidiaries are not included in taxable income until repatriated to the United States. Thus, a temporary book-tax difference exists. This temporary book-tax difference creates a deferred tax liability (because future taxable income will be greater than future financial accounting income when the earnings are repatriated) in the amount of unremitted earnings times the U.S. tax rate (less foreign tax credits). However, the accounting standards allow for an exception to normal deferred tax accounting if management expects to leave the earnings in the foreign subsidiaries and not return the earnings to the U.S. parent. In such a case the foreign earnings are called indefinitely reinvested (also known as permanently reinvested) and the corporation does not have to accrue the expected U.S. income taxes but can instead treat the book-tax difference related to unremitted foreign earnings as a permanent difference. As a result, the company's effective tax rate can be significantly reduced, and accounting earnings increased.

An example of a company with a substantial amount of offshore earnings and cash is Apple, Inc. In its 2014 10-K, Apple provides very good disclosure about its income tax expense and the effect of U.S. taxation of its foreign earnings. Apple reports that the company has $69.7 billion of unremitted foreign earnings on which it has not accrued any U.S. income tax expense. The company reports that it estimates that the U.S. income tax associated with those earnings would be $23.3 billion. Thus, Apple has not recorded $23.3 billion in income tax expense over the life of the company that it otherwise would have had to record if the exception to deferred tax accounting did not exist. This has increased earnings by $23.3 billion over the life of the company. In 2014, the company's effective tax rate is 26% (not the statutory federal rate of 35%) almost entirely because of foreign earnings in lower taxed jurisdictions on which Apple does not accrue U.S. income taxes. The United States is currently contemplating corporate tax reform, particularly with respect to how the United States taxes the foreign earnings of U.S. corporations. Whether any legislation will pass remains to be seen, but if successful there could be significant financial statement effects.

Net Operating Losses   Another book-tax difference is a net operating loss carryover. For tax purposes, corporations can carryover operating losses to future years.[12] Financial accounting does not have such a rule; if a corporation has a loss for financial reporting, the loss is recorded and the corporation starts the next year with a clean slate and measures income for that next year only. Thus, the net operating loss carryover is a temporary book-tax difference. Because the loss carryover represents future deductions for tax purposes, the company has and must record an increase to deferred tax assets and a deferred tax benefit (i.e., negative deferred tax expense) in the

---

[11] When a company has both deferred tax assets and deferred tax liabilities, the assets and liabilities are first separated into current and long-term amounts. The current deferred tax assets and current deferred tax liabilities are then reported net in the balance sheet under current assets or current liabilities, whichever is greater. Long-term amounts are treated similarly. It is not uncommon, therefore to see a company report deferred tax assets under current assets in the balance sheet, while reporting deferred tax liabilities under long-term liabilities. The FASB in 2015 issued a proposed Accounting Standard Update to change this accounting, however, such that all deferred tax assets and liabilities would be reported as long-term.

[12] Under current rules, corporations can carry net operating losses back two years for tax purposes and forward for 20 years. In essence, allowing loss carryovers for tax purposes approximates an averaging of income over time so companies with volatile income are not required to pay high taxes in years with high income and then get no relief in years with losses. We ignore the carryback in our discussion for simplicity (and because it does not create a deferred tax asset).

amount of the loss carryover times the tax rate (the tax rate expected to be in effect when the loss carryover will be used to offset taxes). Thus, even though the corporation is not getting the cash benefits of the deduction yet, the accounting rules require the company to accrue the benefit to the current period.

Valuation Allowance   After a corporation computes its income tax expense and records its deferred tax assets and liabilities, the corporation has yet another step to complete. The corporation must evaluate the realizability of the deferred tax assets. This means that management must estimate whether the company will have sufficient future taxable income to offset the future deductions represented by the deferred tax assets. If management does not think the company will have enough future taxable income to be able to use all the deferred tax assets (i.e., future deductions), then a reserve (i.e., a contra-asset) must be established against the deferred tax assets. Thus, the deferred tax assets on the balance sheet will not be overstated. As an analogy, recall that when a company has accounts receivables it must evaluate the collectability of those receivables and establish an allowance for doubtful accounts to ensure the accounts receivable asset is not overstated. In addition, inventory is valued at lower of cost or market (or soon to be lower of cost or net realizable value) so that inventory is not overstated on the balance sheet. Again, this is the conservative nature of the financial accounting rules. Similarly, if a corporation has deferred tax assets (i.e., future tax deductions) that management does not expect to be able to use to offset future taxable income, then the company must record a **valuation allowance**. When the contra-asset is recorded, deferred tax expense is increased which decreases accounting income (and if a valuation allowance is reduced, deferred tax expense is reduced, increasing income). A more detailed discussion is beyond the scope of this text, but net operating losses and associated valuation allowances have been an important part of many companies', including Delta's, accounting for income taxes as we will see below.

RESEARCH INSIGHT

Recent research has examined how important the exception to deferred tax accounting is to managers when making "real" decisions such as whether to operate outside the United States and whether to repatriate cash to the United States. While the importance of cash tax savings is well known, the evidence in the studies suggests that lowering income tax expense for financial accounting purposes is statistically just as important as saving the cash taxes.[13] This suggests that the numbers reported as financial accounting income are extremely important to managers.

Income Tax Disclosures

Delta Air Lines reported income before income taxes of $1,072 million in 2014. Delta reported an income tax expense of $413 million in 2014. In 2013, Delta reported income before income taxes of $2,527 million and income tax benefit (the opposite of an income tax expense) of $8,013 million.

To fully understand how income tax expense (or benefit) is determined, we refer to the footnotes. Note 13 to Delta's 2014 10-K report contains the table shown in **Exhibit 10.7**.

EXHIBIT 10.7	Delta Air Lines Income Tax Expense		
Year ended December 31 ($ millions)		**2014**	**2013**
Current income tax (provision) benefit		$ 1	$ 22
Deferred tax (provision) benefit net of valuation allowance		(414)	7,991
Income tax (provision) benefit		$(413)	$8,013

The income tax expense or benefit reported in the income statement consists of two primary components:

---

[13] See John Graham, Michelle Hanlon, Terry Shevlin, "Real Effects of Accounting Rules: Evidence from Multinational Firms' Investment Location and Repatriation Decisions," *Journal of Accounting Research*, March 2011.

Current tax expense—this can be thought of for our purposes as the amount that has been paid or is payable to tax authorities in the current period (it also usually contains the income effects of some tax accruals that are beyond the scope of this text).

Deferred tax expense—this is the effect on tax expense due to changes in deferred tax liabilities and assets. It is the result of temporary differences between the reported income statement and the tax return.

Based on the table shown in **Exhibit 10.7**, Delta reported a tax benefit of $1 million for current taxes. This tax benefit potentially suggests that Delta reported a loss on its tax return in 2014 and potentially expects tax refunds of $1 million. It also reported a net deferred tax expense of $414 million.

Companies must also disclose the components of deferred tax assets and liabilities. The components of Delta's deferred tax assets and liabilities are presented in **Exhibit 10.8**.

EXHIBIT 10.8	**Components of Delta Air Lines' Deferred Income Taxes**		
December 31 ($ millions)		**2014**	**2013**
Deferred tax assets:			
Net operating loss carryforwards		$ 4,782	$ 6,024
Pension, postretirement and other benefits		6,033	4,982
Fuel derivatives MTM adjustments		777	0
AMT credit carryforwards		357	378
Deferred revenue		1,824	1,965
Other		659	698
Valuation allowance		(46)	(177)
Total deferred tax assets, net of valuation allowance		$14,386	$13,870
Deferred tax liabilities:			
Depreciation		$ 4,663	$ 4,799
Intangible assets		1,684	1,704
Other		444	639
Total deferred tax liabilities		$ 6,791	$ 7,142
Deferred tax assets, net		$ 7,595	$ 6,728

Delta's deferred tax assets were greater than its deferred tax liabilities in both 2014 and 2013. Notice that Delta has a large deferred tax liability for depreciation. We would expect this for a capital intensive company like an airline (assuming not all planes are leased via operating leases). Notice also that Delta has a large deferred tax asset for pensions and other postretirement benefits. As we discussed earlier in the chapter, Delta has a large unfunded pension liability. The company has to record the liability and a pension expense for financial accounting on the accrual basis but does not get a tax deduction until funds are contributed to the plan. Thus, larger expenses have been recorded for book relative to the deductions taken for tax. In the future, this will reverse (assuming Delta eventually funds its pension) and the deductions for tax will be greater than the expenses for book. Finally, note that Delta's other large deferred tax asset is for net operating loss carryforwards. In prior years, as recent as 2011 and 2012, Delta established a large valuation allowance against its deferred tax assets indicating that management did not think the company would have enough future taxable income to be able to offset the net operating loss carryovers. However, starting in 2012 and to a large degree in 2013, Delta decreased the valuation allowance (by $8 billion in 2013) indicating that management thinks that taxable income will be high enough in the future to use all the tax loss carryforwards. In the 2014 10-K, management states that "During 2014 we continued our trend of sustained profitability, recording pre-tax profit of $1.1 billion for the year. After considering all available positive and negative evidence, we released additional valuation allowance related to net operating losses . . . " As Delta reduces the valuation allowance, more of the deferred tax assets related to the net operating loss carryovers are recognized on the balance sheet. Analysts sometimes consider management's assessment and changes in valuation allowances an indicator of future prospects for the company. In addition, one has to consider large increases to net income from changes in the valuation allowance (like Delta had in 2013) and understand that such large changes will not happen every year; the income from the valuation allowance release is nonrecurring.

Companies also report in the footnotes a reconciliation of differences between the statutory U.S. tax rate (currently 35%) and the tax expense reported in the income statement. The **effective tax rate** is determined by dividing the provision for income taxes (tax expense) by the income before income taxes. Delta's effective tax rate for 2014 was 38.5% ($413 million/$1,072 million). Effective tax rates can vary considerably from one company to another due to permanent differences, tax credits, and other factors. A comparison of the effective tax rate for several companies is presented in **Exhibit 10.9**. The exhibit also splits the tax expense into current and deferred amounts. For example, the highest effective tax rates were reported by **Walgreen**, **Delta**, **Southwest Airlines**, and **Chevron Corporation**. Each of their effective tax rates are greater than the U.S. statutory rate of 35%. However, most of Chevron's and Walgreen's taxes are current while the airlines' taxes are largely deferred. On the other extreme, **Cisco**, **Procter & Gamble**, and **Verizon** reported effective tax rates around 20%.

EXHIBIT 10.9	Comparison of Effective Tax Rates

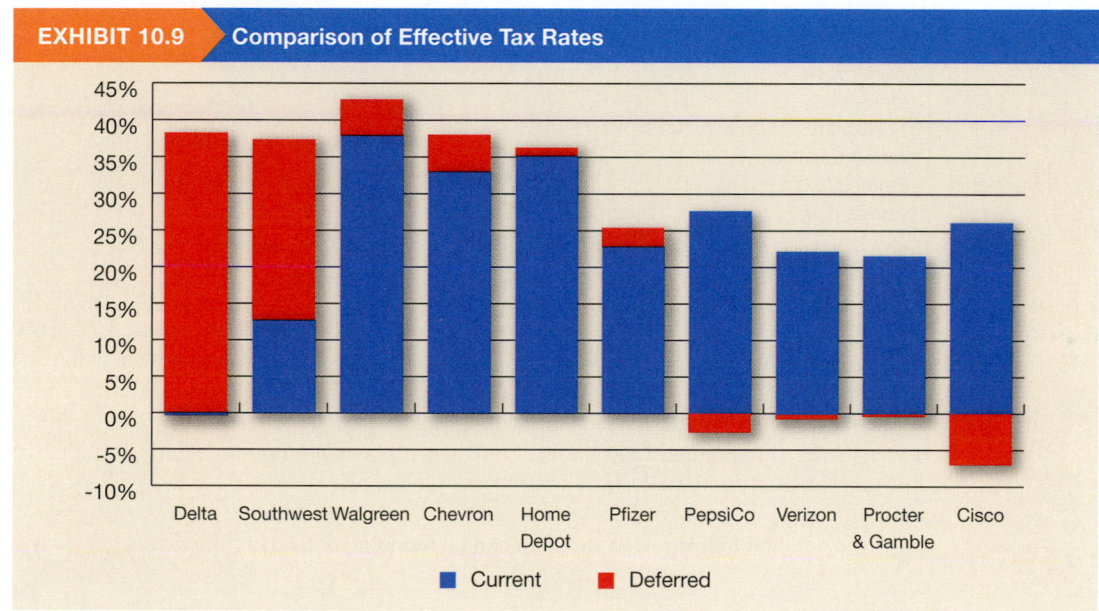

Deferred Taxes in the Cash Flow Statement

Income taxes, including deferred income taxes, are reported in the operating section of the cash flow statement. When the cash flow statement is prepared using the direct method, deferred income taxes are excluded from taxes paid in cash. When the indirect (or reconciliation) method is used, the deferred portion of the income tax expense must be added back to net income as an expense not requiring the use of cash. The amount of income taxes paid in cash is then reported at the bottom of the cash flow statement or in the footnotes.

Computation and Analysis of Taxes

An analysis of deferred taxes can yield useful insights. An increase in deferred tax liabilities indicates that a company is reporting higher profits in its income statement than in its tax return. The difference between reported corporate profits and taxable income increased substantially in the late 1990s, just prior to the stock market decline.

Although an increase in deferred tax liabilities can be the result of legitimate differences between financial reporting standards and tax rules, we must be aware of the possibility that such differences can also be caused by tax avoidance or by earnings management, improper revenue recognition, or other questionable accounting practices. More advanced courses cover the accounting for income taxes in more depth.

CHAPTER-END REVIEW

The following footnote is from the 2016 annual report of Adler Corporation.

Note 9: Income Taxes
The provision for income taxes includes the following

($ thousands)	2016
Current provision	
Domestic	$1,342
Foreign.	146
Deferred provision (credit)	
Domestic	960
Foreign.	(58)
Total	$2,390

Required

1. (a) What is the amount of income tax expense reported on its income statement? (b) How much of its income tax expense is payable in cash? (c) Assuming that its deferred tax liability increased, identify an example that could account for such a change.
2. Prepare the entry, using both the financial statement effects template and in journal entry form, to record its income tax expense for 2016. Post journal entries to the appropriate T-accounts.

The solution to this review problem can be found on page 515.

SUMMARY

LO1   Define off-balance-sheet financing and explain its effects on financial analysis. (p. 462)

- Off-balance-sheet financing refers to financial obligations of the company that are not recognized as liabilities in the balance sheet. Recognizing these obligations often requires recognizing off-balance-sheet assets.

- Off-balance-sheet financing improves financial leverage ratios and its corresponding unrecognized assets improve performance measures.

LO2   Account for leases using the operating lease method and the capital lease method. (p. 463)

- Operating lease payments are treated as ordinary rent expense. No asset or liability is recorded.

- A capital lease records an asset and a liability equal to the present value of the minimum lease payments. The income statement reports interest expense on the liability and depreciation on the asset.

LO3   Convert off-balance-sheet operating leases to the capital lease method. (p. 469)

- Compute the present value of future cash payments required under operating leases. These cash obligations are disclosed in footnotes.

- Add a leased asset and a lease liability to the balance sheet equal to the present value of the future cash payments.

---

[14] See the following studies: 1) Phillips, John, Mort Pincus, and Sonja Rego, "Earnings Management: New Evidence Based on Deferred Tax Expense." *The Accounting Review*, 1999, 2) Lev, Baruch and Doron Nissim, "Taxable Income, Future Earnings, and Equity Values," *The Accounting Review*, October 2004, and 3) Hanlon, Michelle, "The Persistence and Pricing of Earnings, Accruals, and Cash Flows When Firms Have Large Book-Tax Differences," *The Accounting Review*, January 2005.

Explain and interpret the reporting for pension plans. (p. 475)   **LO4**

- Pension and other postretirement obligations represent one of the largest obligations for most companies.
- The projected benefit obligation is the present value of the estimated future benefits that a company expects to pay retired employees.
- The net liability that a company reports on the balance sheet is the projected benefit obligation offset by the plan assets.

Analyze and interpret pension footnote disclosures. (p. 478)   **LO5**

- Pension footnotes provide detailed information about changes in pension obligations, changes in plan assets, and the determinants of pension expense.
- Pension footnotes provide information allowing us to interpret pension expenses and cash flows.

Describe and interpret accounting for income taxes. (p. 484)   **LO6**

- While income tax expense is reported below income from operations, it is an operating expense. The initial item in an indirect cash flow statement is net income, which reflects the deduction of the tax expense.
- Income tax expense is determined as the sum of the tax computed as due to the government and the net change in deferred taxes.
- Deferred taxes occur because of differences between U.S. GAAP reporting and the tax due based on the rules of the tax authority. The former are based on accrual accounting while the latter are often based on a cash-based accounting system.

GUIDANCE ANSWERS . . . YOU MAKE THE CALL

You are the Division President   You must take care in accepting lease terms that are not advantageous to your company merely to achieve off-balance-sheet financing. Long-term shareholder value is created by managing your operation well, including negotiating leases with acceptable terms. Lease footnote disclosures also provide sufficient information for skilled analysts to undo the operating lease treatment. This means that you can end up with effective capitalization of a lease with lease terms that are not in the best interests of your company and with few benefits from off-balance-sheet financing. There is also the potential for lost credibility with stakeholders.

You are a Consultant to the FASB   This issue is one of the questions confronting the FASB. Normally accountants do not favor offsetting liabilities against the related assets as is currently the reporting practice required under GAAP. However, because the pension fund is a separate legal entity, there is a problem with reporting the pension plan assets among the firm's assets. A company does not have unilateral control over a pension trust. It can put assets into the trust but can not easily get them out of the trust. For this reason, the pension assets do not meet the criteria we normally require for recognition. While we do not know how the FASB will resolve this matter, we suspect the reporting of the net asset or liability will continue to be required.

KEY RATIOS

$$\text{Fixed commitments ratio} = \frac{\text{Operating cash flow before fixed commitments}}{\text{Fixed commitments}}$$

$$\text{Effective tax rate} = \frac{\text{Provision for income taxes (expense)}}{\text{Income before income taxes}}$$

KEY TERMS

Accumulated post-employment benefit obligation (APBO) (p. 482)

Actuarial losses and gains (p. 476)

Capital lease method (p. 464)

Deferred tax asset (p. 487)

Deferred tax liability (p. 485)

Defined benefit plan (p. 475)

Defined contribution plan (p. 475)

Effective tax rate (p. 491)

Fixed commitments ratio (p. 473)

Funded status (p. 475)

Interest cost (p. 476)

Lessee (p. 463)

Lessor (p. 463)

Off-balance-sheet
  financing (p. 463)
Operating lease method (p. 464)
Other post-employment benefits
  (OPEB) (p. 482)

Overfunded (p. 475)
Pension plan assets (p. 475)
Projected benefit obligation
  (PBO) (p. 475)

Provision for income
  tax (p. 485)
Service cost (p. 476)
Underfunded (p. 475)
Valuation allowance (p. 489)

Assignments with the 🔴 logo in the margin are available in my**BusinessCourse**.
See the Preface of the book for details.

MULTIPLE CHOICE

Multiple Choice Answers
1. a   2. d   3. d   4. b   5. d   6. c

1. U.S. GAAP requires that certain leases be accounted for as *capital leases*. The reason for this treatment is that this type of lease
  a. conveys the benefits and risks of ownership of the asset.
  b. is an example of form over substance.
  c. provides the use of the leased asset to the lessee for a limited period of time.
  d. is an example of off-balance-sheet financing.

2. For a lease that is accounted for as an operating lease by the lessee, the monthly rental payments should be
  a. allocated between interest expense and depreciation expense.
  b. allocated between a reduction in the liability for leased assets and interest expense.
  c. recorded as a reduction in the liability for leased assets.
  d. recorded as rent expense.

3. The balance sheet liability for a capital lease would be reduced each period by the
  a. lease payment.
  b. lease payment plus the amortization of the related asset.
  c. lease payment less the amortization of the related asset.
  d. lease payment less the periodic interest expense.

4. Which of the following statements characterizes defined benefit pension plans?
  a. The employer's obligation is satisfied by making the necessary periodic contribution.
  b. Retirement benefits are based on the plan's benefit formula.
  c. Retirement benefits depend on how well pension fund assets have been managed.
  d. Contributions are made in equal amounts by employer and employees.

5. When the value of pension plan assets is greater than the projected benefit obligation,
  a. the difference is added to pension expense.
  b. the difference is reported as deferred pension cost.
  c. the difference is reported as a contra equity adjustment.
  d. the pension plan is overfunded.

6. Which of the following is *not* a component of net pension expense?
  a. Interest cost
  b. Expected return on plan assets
  c. Benefits paid to retirees
  d. Amortization of actuarial gains or losses

QUESTIONS

Q10-1. What are the financial reporting differences between an operating lease and a capital lease? Explain.

Q10-2. Are footnote disclosures sufficient to overcome nonrecognition on the balance sheet of assets and related liabilities for operating leases? Explain.

Q10-3. Is the expense of a lease over its entire life the same whether or not it is capitalized? Explain.

Q10-4. What are the economic and accounting differences between a defined contribution plan and a defined benefit plan?

Q10-5. Under what circumstances will a company report a net pension asset? A net pension liability?

Q10-6. What are the components of pension expense that is reported in the income statement?

Q10-7. What effect does the use of expected returns on pension investments and the deferral of unexpected gains and losses on those investments have on income?

Q10-8. How is the initial valuation determined for the asset and the liability with a capital lease?

Q10-9. Over what time period should the cost of providing retirement benefits to employees be expensed?

Q10-10. What is the conceptual reason why income tax expense on the income statement is not equal to cash taxes paid?

Q10-11. Under what circumstances would a tax payment be made that also requires the recording of a deferred tax asset or liability?

MINI EXERCISES

M10-12. Accounting for Leases

LO2

On January 3, 2017, Hanna Corporation signed a lease on a machine for its manufacturing operation. The lease requires Hanna to make six annual lease payments of $12,000 with the first payment due December 31, 2017. Hanna could have financed the machine by borrowing the purchase price at an interest rate of 7%.

   a.   Prepare the journal entries that Hanna Corporation would make on January 3 and December 31, 2017, to record this lease assuming

       i.   the lease is reported as an operating lease.

       ii.   the lease is reported as a capital lease.

   b.   Assuming that the lease is treated as a capital lease, post the journal entries of part *a* to the appropriate T-accounts.

   c.   Show how the entries posted in part *b* would affect the financial statements using the financial statement effects template.

M10-13. Accounting for Leases

LO2

On July 1, 2017, Shroff Company leased a warehouse building under a 10-year lease agreement. The lease requires quarterly lease payments of $4,500. The first lease payment is due on September 30, 2017. The lease was reported as a capital lease using an 8% annual interest rate.

   a.   Prepare the journal entry to record the initial signing of the lease on July 1, 2017.

   b.   Prepare the journal entries that would be necessary on September 30 and December 31, 2017.

   c.   Post the entries from parts *a* and *b* in their appropriate T-accounts.

   d.   Prepare a financial statement effects template to show the effects of the entries from parts *a* and *b* on the balance sheet and income statement.

   e.   Redo parts *a* and *b* assuming that the lease is reported as an operating lease. Is the expense recognized in 2017 under the operating lease method higher or lower than under the capital lease method? Explain.

M10-14. Accounting for Operating and Capital Leases

LO2, 3

On January 1, 2017, Weber, Inc., entered into two lease contracts. The first lease contract was a six-year lease for computer equipment with $15,000 annual lease payments due at the end of each year. Weber took possession of the equipment on January 1, 2017. The second lease contract was a six-month lease, beginning January 1, 2017, for warehouse storage space with $1,000 monthly lease payments due the first of each month. Weber made the first month's payment on January 1, 2017. The present value of the lease payments under the first contract is $74,520. The present value of the lease payments under the second contract is $5,853.

REQUIRED

   a.   Assume that the first lease contract is a capital lease. Prepare the appropriate journal entry for this lease on January 1, 2017.

   b.   Assume the second lease contract is an operating lease. Prepare the proper journal entry for this lease on January 1, 2017.

M10-15. Analyzing and Interpreting Leasing Footnote Disclosures

LO2

YUM! Brands
NYSE :: YUM

YUM! Brands, Inc., reports the following information related to non-cancelable leases in Note 11 of its 2014 10-K.

At December 27, 2014, we operated nearly 8,700 restaurants, leasing the underlying land and/or building in approximately 7,775 of those restaurants with the vast majority of our commitments expiring within 20 years from the inception of the lease. In addition, the Company leases or subleases approximately 875 units to franchises principally in the United States, UK, China, and Mexico. We also lease office space for headquarters and support functions, as well as certain office and restaurant equipment. We do not consider any of these individual leases material to our operations. Most leases require us to pay related executory costs, which include property taxes, maintenance, and insurance.

a. Yum has both capital and operating leases. In general, what effects does each of these lease types have on Yum's balance sheet and its income statement?
b. What types of adjustments might you consider to Yum's balance sheet for analysis purposes?

LO3

YUM! Brands
NYSE :: YUM

M10-16. Analyzing and Capitalizing Operating Lease Payments Disclosed in Footnotes

YUM! Brands, Inc. discloses the following in Note 11 to its 2014 10-K report relating to its lease commitments:

(In millions)	Capital Leases	Operating Leases
2015	$ 20	$ 709
2016	21	661
2017	20	609
2018	20	555
2019	20	501
Thereafter	181	2,444
Total minimum lease payments	$282	$5,479

At December 27, 2014, the present value of minimum payments under capital leases was $175 million.

Operating leases are not reflected on-balance-sheet. In our analysis of a company, we often desire to capitalize these operating leases, that is, add the present value of these lease payments to both the reported assets and liabilities.

a. What is the implied interest rate in the capital leases?
b. Compute the present value of Yum!'s operating lease payments assuming a discount rate equal to the rate computed in part a.
c. What effect does capitalization of Yum!'s operating leases have on its total liabilities (it reported total liabilities of $6,732 million for 2014)?

LO4

M10-17. Accounting for Pension Benefits

Bartov Corporation has a defined contribution pension plan for its employees. Each year, Bartov contributes to the plan an amount equal to 4% of the employee payroll for the year. Bartov's 2016 payroll was $400,000. Bartov also provides a life insurance benefit that pays a $50,000 death benefit to the beneficiaries of retired employees. At the end of 2016, Bartov estimates that its liability under the life insurance program is $625,000. Bartov has assets with a fair value of $175,000 in a trust fund that are available to meet the death benefit payments.

REQUIRED

a. Prepare the journal entry at December 31, 2016, to record Bartov's 2016 defined contribution to a pension trustee who will manage the pension funds for the firm's employees.
b. What amount of liability for death benefit payments must Bartov report in its December 31, 2016, balance sheet? Explain.

LO4, 5

Exxon Mobil Corporation
NYSE :: XOM

M10-18. Analyzing and Interpreting Pension Disclosures—Expenses and Returns

Exxon Mobil Corporation discloses the following information in footnote 17 in its 10-K report:

(In millions)	2014
Service cost	$1,267
Interest cost	1,945
Expected return on plan assets	(1,992)
Amortization of actuarial loss (gain)	1,037
Net pension enhancement and curtailment/settlement cost	276
Amortization of prior service cost...	128
Net periodic pension benefit cost	$2,661

a. How much pension expense does Exxon Mobil Corporation report in its 2014 income statement?

b. What effect does its "expected return on plan assets" have on its reported pension expense? Explain.

c. Explain use of the word *expected* as it relates to results of pension plan investments.

M10-19. Analyzing and Interpreting Pension Disclosures—Expenses and Returns

YUM! Brands, Inc., discloses the following pension footnote in its 10-K report:

(In millions)	Pension Benefits	
	2014	**2013**
Service cost	$17	$21
Interest cost	54	54
Amortization of prior service cost	1	2
Expected return on plan assets	(56)	(59)
Amortization of net loss	17	48
Net periodic benefit cost	$33	$66

LO4, 5
YUM! Brands
NYSE :: YUM

a. How much pension expense does Yum report in its 2014 income statement?

b. What effect does its "expected return on plan assets" have on its reported pension expense? Explain.

c. Explain use of the word *expected* as it relates to results of pension plan investments.

M10-20. Analyzing and Interpreting Retirement Benefit Footnote

Abercrombie & Fitch Co. discloses the following footnote relating to its retirement plans in its 2014 10-K report:

LO4, 5
Abercrombie & Fitch
NYSE :: ANF

15. RETIREMENT BENEFITS   The Company maintains the Abercombie & Fitch Co. Savings & Retirement Plan, a qualified plan. All U.S. associates are eligible to participate in this plan if they are at least 21 years of age and have completed a year of employment with 1,000 or more hours of service. In addition, the Company maintains the Abercrombie & Fitch Nonqualified Savings and Supplemental Retirement Plan. . . Participation in these plans is based on service and compensation. The Company's contributions are based on a percentage of associates' eligible annual compensation. The cost of the Company's contributions to these plans was $13.8 million, $18.3 million, and $21.1 million in fiscal 2014, 2013, and 2012, respectively.

a. Does Abercrombie have a defined contribution or defined benefit pension plan? Explain.

b. How does Abercrombie account for its contributions to its retirement plan?

c. How is Abercrombie's obligation to its retirement plan reported on its balance sheet?

M10-21. Analyzing and Interpreting Footnote on Contract Manufacturers

Nike, Inc. reports the following information relating to its manufacturing activities in the footnotes to its 2014 10-K report:

LO1
Nike
NYSE :: NKE

MANUFACTURING   Virtually all of our footwear is manufactured outside of the United States by independent contract manufacturers who often operate multiple factories. In fiscal 2014, contract factories in Vietnam, China, and Indonesia manufactured approximately 43%, 28%, and 25% of total NIKE Brand footwear, respectively. We also have manufacturing agreements with independent factories in Argentina, Brazil, India, and Mexico to manufacture footwear for sale primarily within those countries. In fiscal 2014, five footwear contract manufacturers each accounted for greater than 10% of fiscal 2014 footwear production, and in aggregate accounted for approximately 67% of NIKE Brand footwear production in fiscal 2014.

a. What effect does the use of contract manufacturers have on Nike's balance sheet?

b. Nike executes purchase contracts with its contract manufacturers to purchase their output. How are executory contracts reported under GAAP? Does your answer suggest a possible motivation for the use of contract manufacturing?

M10-22. Computing and Reporting Deferred Income Taxes

Fisk, Inc., purchased $600,000 of construction equipment on January 1, 2014. The equipment is being depreciated on a straight-line basis over six years with no expected salvage value. MACRS depreciation is being used on the firm's tax returns. At December 31, 2016, the equipment's book value is $300,000 and its tax basis is $173,000 (this is Fisk's only temporary difference). Over the next three years, straight-line depreciation will exceed MACRS depreciation by $31,000 in 2017, $31,000 in 2018, and $65,000 in 2019. Assume that the income tax rate in effect for all years is 40%.

LO6
Homework
MBC

a.   What amount of deferred tax liability should appear in Fisk's December 31, 2016, balance sheet?
b.   What amount of deferred tax liability should appear in Fisk's December 31, 2017, balance sheet?
c.   What amount of deferred tax liability should appear in Fisk's December 31, 2018, balance sheet?
d.   Where should the deferred tax liability accounts be classified in Fisk's 2016, 2017, and 2018
     year-end balance sheets?

EXERCISES

LO2, 3

Target
NYSE :: TGT

E10-23.   Analyzing and Interpreting Leasing Footnote

The 2014 10-K report of **Target Corporation** provides the following footnote ($ thousands).

21. Leases   We lease certain retail locations, warehouses, distribution centers, office space, land, equipment, and software. Assets held under capital lease are included in property and equipment. Operating lease rentals are expensed on a straight-line basis over the life of the lease. . . . we determine the lease term by assuming the exercise of those renewal options that are reasonably assured. The exercise of lease renewal options is at our sole discretion. The lease term is used to determine whether a lease is capital or operating and is used to calculate straight-line rent expense. Additionally, the depreciable life of leased assets and leasehold improvements is limited by the expected lease term.

Rent expense is included in SG&A. Some of our lease agreements include rental payments based on a percentage of retail sales over contractual levels . . . Certain leases require us to pay real estate taxes, insurance, maintenance, and other operating expenses associated with the leased premises. These expenses are classified in SG&A consistent with similar costs for owned locations.

Most long-term leases include one or more options to renew, with renewal terms that can extend the lease term from one to more than fifty years. Certain leases also include options to purchase the leased property.

Future Minimum Lease Payments (millions)	Operating Leases	Capital Leases
2015	$ 186	$ 123
2016	178	94
2017	170	58
2018	165	55
2019	154	54
After 2019.	2,974	1,019
Total future minimum lease payments	$3,827	1,403
Less: Interest		614
Present value of future minimum capital lease payments		$ 789

a.   Compute the present value of Target's operating leases. Assume a 5% discount rate.
b.   If the operating leases are classified as capital leases, indicate how the amount in part *a* would be reported in Target's balance sheet using the financial statement effects template.
c.   Would recognition of the operating leases affect the current ratio? Explain.
d.   Prepare journal entries to record the capitalization of Target's operating leases at the end of fiscal 2014. Enter them in the appropriate T-accounts.
e.   Do these leases represent a substantial fixed commitment to Target given Target's operating cash flow of $4,439 million in 2014?

LO4, 5

Target
NYSE :: TGT

E10-24.   Analyzing and Interpreting Pension Plan Benefit Footnote

Target Corporation provides the following footnote relating to its retirement plans in its 2014 10-K report:

Defined Contribution Plans   Team members who meet eligibility requirements can participate in a defined contribution 401(k) plan by investing up to 80 percent of their compensation, as limited by statute or regulation. Generally, we match 100 percent of each team member's contribution up to 5 percent of total compensation. Company match contributions are made to funds designated by the participant. Benefits expense related to these matching contributions was $220 million, $229 million, and $218 million in 2014, 2013, and 2012, respectively.

a. Does Target have a defined contribution or defined benefit pension plan? Explain.

b. How would Target account for its contributions to its retirement plan?

c. How is Target's obligation to its retirement plan reported on its balance sheet?

d. Do you see any problems for employees in Target's plan?

E10-25. Analyzing and Interpreting Leasing Footnote

LO2, 3

The Home Depot
NYSE :: HD

The Home Depot, Inc. included the following footnote in its fiscal 2014 10-K report:

The approximate future minimum lease payments under capital and all other leases at February 1, 2015 were as follows (amounts in millions):

Fiscal year	Capital Leases	Operating Leases
2015	$ 113	$ 893
2016	111	817
2017	108	737
2018	101	638
2019	97	561
Thereafter	880	4,059
Total minimum lease payments	1,410	$7,705
Less imputed interest	726	
Present value of minimum lease payments	684	
Amount included in current liabilities	36	
Long-term lease obligations excluding current installments	$ 648	

The assets under capital leases recorded in Property and Equipment, net of amortization, totaled $557 million and $374 million at February 1, 2015 and February 2, 2014, respectively.

The Home Depot reported stockholders' equity of $9,322 million and total assets of $39,946 million in its fiscal 2014 balance sheet.

a. What was the total amount of capital lease obligations reported in The Home Depot's fiscal 2014 balance sheet? Why is this amount not equal to the $557 million that it reported for assets under capital leases on that date?

b. Using a 4% discount rate, compute the present value of Home Depot's scheduled operating lease payments.

c. Estimate the effect that capitalizing operating leases would have on The Home Depot's debt-to-equity ratio.

E10-26. Analyzing and Interpreting Footnote on Both Operating and Capital Leases

LO2, 3

Verizon
NYSE :: VZ

Verizon Communications Inc. provides the following footnote relating to its leasing activities in its 10-K report.

The aggregate minimum rental commitments under noncancelable leases for the periods shown at December 31, 2014, are:

Years (dollars in millions)	Capital Leases	Operating Leases
2015	$181	$ 2,499
2016	137	2,245
2017	113	1,960
2018	68	1,660
2019	39	1,369
Thereafter	60	4,670
Total minimum rental commitments	598	$14,403
Less interest and executory costs	82	
Present value of minimum lease payments	516	
Less current installments	158	
Long-term obligation at December 31, 2014	$358	

    a. Assuming that this is the only available information relating to its leasing activities, what amount does Verizon report on its balance sheet for its lease obligations? Does this amount represent its total obligation to lessors? How do you know?

    b. What effect has its lease classification as capital or operating had on Verizon's balance sheet? Over the life of its leases, what effect does this lease classification have on its net income?

    c. Based on the information provided by Verizon in this footnote, what amount of interest expense will it report on capital leases in 2015? (Hint: prepare a journal entry to record the 2015 lease payment.)

    d. Estimate the present value of Verizon's operating leases using a 5% discount rate. What would be the effect on Verizon's balance sheet if these leases were reported as capital leases?

LO2, 3

Walgreen Co.
NASDAQ :: WAG

E10-27. Analyzing, Interpreting, and Capitalizing Operating Leases

Walgreen Co. provided the following information in footnote 3 of its 2014 10-K report ($ millions):

Future minimum rental payments under operating leases with remaining noncancelable terms in excess of one year are as follows:

(in millions)	Operating
2015	$ 2,569
2016	2,533
2017	2,493
2018	2,407
2019	2,295
Thereafter	22,168
Total	$34,465

    a. Assuming a 5% discount rate, what adjustments to Walgreen's balance sheet would be necessary to convert these operating leases into capital leases?

    b. If the leases were reported as capital leases instead of operating leases, what would be the effect on Walgreen's 2015 income statement (assuming no other changes)?

LO2, 3

Nike
NYSE :: NKE

E10-28. Analyzing, Interpreting, and Capitalizing Operating Leases

Nike, Inc. reports the following data concerning leases in its 2014 10-K.

Note 14—Commitments and Contingencies
The Company leases space for certain of its offices, warehouses and retail stores under leases expiring from 1 to 20 years after May 31, 2014. . . . Amounts of minimum future annual rental commitments under noncancelable operating leases in each of the five years ending May 31, 2015 through 2019 are $427 million, $399 million, $366 million, $311 million, $251 million, respectively, and $1,050 million in later years.

    a. What adjustment(s) might you consider to Nike's balance sheet given this information and assuming that Nike's discount rate is 4%? Explain.

    b. Show how the amount computed in part *a* would be reported in the balance sheet using the financial statement effects template.

    c. Prepare journal entries to record the capitalization of these operating leases at the end of fiscal 2014. What journal entries would be required to record lease payments and lease related expenses in 2015 if these leases were accounted for as capital leases? Assume straight-line depreciation and a ten-year life.

    d. Post the journal entries from part *c* to the appropriate T-accounts.

LO4, 5

YUM! Brands
NYSE :: YUM

E10-29. Analyzing and Interpreting Pension Footnote—Funded and Reported Amounts

YUM! Brands, Inc., reports the following pension footnote in Note 13 of its 10-K report.

December 27 (in millions)	Pension Benefits 2014
Change in benefit obligation	
Projected benefit obligation at beginning of year	$1,025
Service cost	17
Interest cost	54
Curtailments	(2)
Plan amendments	1
Special termination benefits	3
Benefits paid	(65)
Settlements	(17)
Actuarial (gain) loss	290
Administrative expenses	(5)
Projected benefit obligation at end of year	$1,301
Change in plan assets	
Fair value of plan assets at beginning of year	$ 933
Actual return on plan assets	124
Employer contributions	21
Benefits paid	(65)
Settlements	(17)
Administrative expenses	(5)
Fair value of plan assets at end of year	$ 991
Funded status—end of year	$ (310)

a. Describe what is meant by *service cost* and *interest cost*.
b. What is the source of funds to make payments to retirees?
c. Show the computation of the 2014 funded status for Yum.
d. What net pension amount is reported on its 2014 balance sheet?

E10-30. Analyzing and Interpreting Pension Footnote—Funded and Reported Amounts   **LO4, 5**
    Verizon Communications Inc. reports the following pension data in Note 12 to its 2014 10-K report.
         Verizon
         NYSE :: VZ

At December 31 ($ millions)	Pension 2014
Change in Benefit Obligations	
Beginning of year	$23,032
Service cost	327
Interest cost	1,035
Plan amendments	(89)
Actuarial loss (gain), net	2,977
Benefits paid and settlements	(1,973)
Curtailment and termination benefits	11
End of year	25,320
Change in Plan Assets	
Beginning of year	17,111
Actual return on plan assets	1,778
Company contributions	1,632
Benefits paid and settlements	(1,973)
End of year	18,548
Funded Status	
End of year	$ (6,772)

a. Describe what is meant by *service cost* and *interest cost*.
b. What is the source of funds to make payments to retirees?
c. Show the computation of Verizon's 2014 funded status.
d. What net pension amount is reported on its 2014 balance sheet?

LO6 **E10-31. Computing and Reporting Deferred Income Taxes**

Early in January 2016, Oler, Inc., purchased equipment costing $16,000. The equipment had a 2-year useful life and was depreciated in the amount of $8,000 in 2016 and 2017. Oler deducted the entire $16,000 on its tax return in 2016. This difference was the only one between its tax return and its financial statements. Oler's income before depreciation expense and income taxes was $236,000 in 2016 and $245,000 in 2017. The tax rate in each year was 40%.

REQUIRED

a. What amount of deferred tax liability should Oler report in 2016 and 2017?
b. Prepare the journal entries to record income taxes for 2016 and 2017.
c. Repeat requirement *b* if the tax rate in 2016 was only 35%.

LO6 **E10-32. Calculating and Reporting Deferred Income Taxes**

Bens' Corporation paid $12,000 on December 31, 2016, for equipment with a three-year useful life. The equipment will be depreciated in the amount of $4,000 each year. Bens' took the entire $12,000 as an expense in its tax return in 2016. Assume this is the only timing difference between the firm's books and its tax return. Bens' tax rate is 40%.

REQUIRED

a. What amount of deferred tax liability should appear in Bens' 12/31/2016 balance sheet?
b. Where in the balance sheet should the deferred tax liability appear?
c. What amount of deferred tax liability should appear in Bens' 12/31/2017 balance sheet?

LO6 **E10-33. Recording Income Tax Expense**

Nike, Inc., reports the following tax information in Note 9 to its 2014 financial report.
Income before income taxes is as follows:

Nike
NYSE :: NKE

Year Ended May 31 (In millions)	2014	2013	2012
Income before income taxes:			
United States	$3,066	$1,231	$ 799
Foreign	478	2,025	2,212
	$3,544	$3,256	$3,011

The provision for income taxes is as follows:

Year Ended May 31 (In millions)	2014	2013	2012
Current:			
United States			
Federal	$371	$432	$286
State	93	69	51
Foreign	398	398	488
	862	899	825
Deferred:			
United States			
Federal	8	0	(47)
State	(3)	(4)	5
Foreign	(16)	(90)	(29)
	(11)	(94)	(71)
	$851	$805	$754

a. Record Nike's provision for income taxes for 2014 using the financial statement effects template.
b. Record Nike's provision for income taxes for 2014 using journal entries.
c. Explain how the provision for income taxes affects Nike's financial statements.
d. Calculate and compare Nike's effective tax rate for 2014, 2013 and 2012.

LO6 **E10-34. Recording Income Tax Expense**

The Boeing Company reports the following tax information in Note 4 to its 2014 financial report.

Boeing
NYSE :: BA

Year ended December 31,	2014	2013	2012
Current tax expense			
U.S. federal.	$ 676	$ (82)	$ 657
Non-U.S..	91	76	52
U.S. state	69	11	19
	836	5	728
Deferred tax expense			
U.S. federal.	828	1,531	1,209
Non-U.S..	34	41	(13)
U.S. state	(7)	69	83
	855	1,641	1,279
Total income tax expense.	$1,691	$1,646	$2,007

a.   Record Boeing's provision for income taxes for 2014 using the financial statement effects template.

b.   Record Boeing's provision for income taxes for 2014 using journal entries.

c.   Explain how the provision for income affects Boeing's financial statements.

PROBLEMS

P10-35. Analyzing, Interpreting, and Capitalizing Operating Leases

Staples, Inc., reports the following footnote relating to its capital and operating leases in its fiscal 2014 10-K report ($ thousands).

LO2, 3

Staples, Inc.
NASDAQ :: SPLS

Future minimum lease commitments due for retail distribution, fulfillment, and support facilities (including restructured facilities and lease commitments for 11 retail stores not yet opened at January 31, 2015) and equipment leases under noncancellable operating leases are as follows (in thousands):

Fiscal Year	Total
2015	$ 703,905
2016	599,304
2017	479,441
2018	348,146
2019	254,085
Thereafter	545,640
	$2,930,521

Rent expense was approximately $767.5 million, $801.4 million, and $838.9 million for 2014, 2013, and 2012, respectively.

a.   What dollar adjustment(s) might you consider to Staples' balance sheet given this information and assuming that Staples intermediate-term borrowing rate is 5%? Explain. (Staples reported total liabilities of $5 billion for 2014.) Round the average life to the nearest year.

b.   Show how the amount computed in part a would be reported in the balance sheet using the financial statement effects template.

c.   Prepare journal entries to record the capitalization of these operating leases at the end of fiscal 2014. What journal entries would be required to record lease payments and lease related expenses in 2015 if these leases were accounted for as capital leases? Assume leased assets are depreciated over a 9-year life using the straight-line method.

d.   Post the journal entries from part c to the appropriate T-accounts.

P10-36. Capitalizing Operating Leases

The 2014 10-K report of **CVS Health Corporation** included the following footnote.

LO2, 3

CVS Health Corporation
NYSE :: CVS

Leases

The Company leases most of its retail and mail order locations, ten of its distribution centers and certain corporate offices under noncancelable operating leases, typically with initial terms of 15 to 25 years and with options that permit renewals for additional periods. The Company also leases certain equipment and other assets under noncancelable operating leases, typically with initial terms of 3 to 10 years. Minimum rent is expensed on a straight-line basis over the term of the lease. In addition to minimum rental payments, certain leases require additional payments based on sales volume, as well as reimbursement for real estate taxes, common area maintenance and insurance, which are expensed when incurred.

The following table is a summary of the Company's net rental expense for operating leases for the years ended December 31:

(in millions)	2014	2013	2012
Minimum rentals.....................................	$2,320	$2,210	$2,165

The following table is a summary of the future minimum lease payments under capital and operating leases as of December 31, 2014:

(in millions)	Capital Leases	Operating Leases
2015	$ 47	$ 2,279
2016	47	2,220
2017	47	2,121
2018	48	2,007
2019	48	1,861
Thereafter	573	16,794
Total future lease payments	810	$27,282
Less: imputed interest	(419)	
Present value of capital lease obligations	$391	

The Company finances a portion of its store development program through sale-leaseback transactions. The properties are generally sold at net book value, which generally approximates fair value, and the resulting leases generally qualify and are accounted for as operating leases. The operating leases that resulted from these transactions are included in the above table. The Company does not have any retained or contingent interests in the stores and does not provide any guarantees, other than a guarantee of lease payments, in connection with the sale-leaseback transactions. Proceeds from sale-leaseback transactions totaled $515 million in 2014, $600 million in 2013 and $529 million in 2012.

REQUIRED

a. Prepare the journal entry to record CVS's rent expense under operating leases on December 31, 2014. Assume that this expense was paid in cash and none of this expense was prepaid or accrued in other years.

b. Assume that CVS reclassified its operating leases as capital leases and that the appropriate discount rate is 4%. What amount would CVS report as a lease liability in its December 31, 2014 balance sheet?

c. If these leases are treated as capital leases instead of operating leases, what would be the effect on CVS's 2014 income statement? Its 2015 income statement? The assets are depreciated on a straight-line basis over 10 years.

d. Show the results of capitalization using the financial statement effects template.

e. If these leases had been treated as capital leases instead of operating leases, what would be the effect on CVS's 2014 statement of cash flows?

f. Briefly, describe the effects of CVS's sale-leaseback transaction on the company's balance sheet.

LO2, 3

Best Buy
NYSE :: BBY

P10-37. Analyzing, Interpreting, and Capitalizing Leasing Disclosures

The **Best Buy Co., Inc.,** 10-K report has the following footnote (8) related to its leasing activities.

The future minimum lease payments under our capital, financing, and operating leases by fiscal year (not including contingent rentals) at January 31, 2015, were as follows ($ millions):

Fiscal Year	Capital Leases	Financing Leases	Operating Leases
2016	$22	$24	$ 873
2017	11	18	771
2018	7	14	641
2019	4	9	499
2020	2	6	365
Thereafter	15	9	727
Subtotal	61	80	$3,876
Less: imputed interest	(9)	(11)	
Present value	$52	$69	

REQUIRED

a. What does Best Buy report on its balance sheet in regard to its leases?

b. What is the general effect that capitalization of Best Buy's operating leases would have on its balance sheet? Over the life of the lease, what effect does this classification have on its net income?

c. Using a 7% discount rate, estimate the assets and liabilities that it fails to report as a result of its off-balance-sheet lease financing.

d. Using the financial statement effects template, show how capitalizing these operating leases would affect the balance sheet and income statement. Assume straight-line depreciation over a 10-year life.

e. Prepare journal entries to record the capitalization of these operating leases at January 31, 2015. What journal entries would be required to record the operating lease and lease related expenses in the year ended January, 2016 if these leases were accounted for as capital leases?

f. Post the journal entries from part *e* to the appropriate T-accounts.

g. What impact would capitalization of the company's operating leases have on analyzing Best Buy? What ratios might be affected?

P10-38. Analyzing and Interpreting Pension Disclosures   **LO4, 5**

Hoopes Corporation's December 31, 2015, 10-K report has the following disclosures related to its retirement plans.

The following table provides a reconciliation of the changes in the pension and postretirement healthcare plans' benefit obligations and fair value of assets over the two-year period ended December 31, 2015, and a statement of the funded status as of December 31, 2015 and 2014 (in millions):

(in millions)	Pension Plans	
	2015	2014
Changes in Projected Benefit Obligation ("PBO")		
PBO at beginning of year.	$14,484	$11,050
Service cost	521	417
Interest cost	900	823
Actuarial (gain) loss.	1,875	2,607
Benefits paid.	(468)	(391)
Other.	60	(22)
PBO at end of year.	$17,372	$14,484
Change in Plan Assets		
Fair value of plan assets at beginning of year	$13,295	$10,812
Actual return on plan assets.	2,425	1,994
Company contributions	557	900
Benefits paid.	(468)	(391)
Other.	32	(20)
Fair value of plan assets at end of year	$15,841	$13,295

Net periodic benefit cost for the three years ended December 31 were as follows (in millions):

(in millions)	Pension Plans		
	2015	2014	2013
Service cost	$ 521	$417	$ 499
Interest cost	900	823	798
Expected return on plan assets	(1,062)	(955)	(1,059)
Recognized actuarial (gains) losses and other.	184	23	(61)
Net periodic benefit cost	$ 543	$308	$ 177

Weighted-average actuarial assumptions for our primary U.S. pension plans, which represent substantially all of our PBO, are as follows:

(in millions)	Pension Plans		
	2015	2014	2013
Discount rate used to determine benefit obligation.	5.76%	6.37%	7.68%
Rate of increase in future compensation levels used to determine benefit obligation.	4.58	4.63	4.42
Expected long-term rate of return on assets	8.00	8.00	8.50

REQUIRED

a. How much pension expense (revenue) does Hoopes report in its 2015 income statement?

b. Hoopes reports a $1,062 million expected return on plan assets as an offset to 2015 pension expense. Approximately, how is this amount computed? What is the actual gain or loss realized on its 2015 plan assets? What is the purpose of using this estimated amount instead of the actual gain or loss?

c. What factors affected its 2015 pension liability? What factors affected its 2015 plan assets?

d. What does the term *funded status* mean? What is the funded status of the 2015 Hoopes retirement plans? What amount of asset or liability does Hoopes report on its 2015 balance sheet relating to its retirement plans?

e. Hoopes decreased its discount rate from 6.37% to 5.76% in 2015. What effect(s) does this have on its balance sheet and its income statement?

f. Hoopes changed its estimate of expected annual wage increases used to determine its defined benefit obligation in 2015. What effect(s) does this change have on its financial statements? In general, how does such a change affect income?

LO4, 5
Johnson and Johnson
NYSE :: JNJ

P10-39. Analyzing and Interpreting Pension Footnote—Funded and Reported Amounts

Johnson and Johnson reports the following pension footnote as part of its 2014 10-K report.

(in millions)	Pension Benefits 2014
Change in Benefit Obligation	
Projected benefit obligation—beginning of year	$21,488
Service cost	882
Interest cost	1,018
Plan participant contributions	59
Amendments	(60)
Actuarial (gains) losses.	5,395
Divestitures and acquisitions	(121)
Curtailments, settlements and restructuring	(53)
Benefits paid from plan	(813)
Effect of exchange rates.	(906)
Projected benefit obligation—end of year	$26,889

continued

continued from previous page

(in millions)	2014
Change in Plan Assets	
Plan assets at fair value—beginning of year	$20,901
Actual return on plan assets.	2,078
Company contributions	1,176
Plan participant contributions	59
Settlements	(40)
Divestitures and acquisitions	(109)
Benefits paid from plan assets.	(813)
Effect of exchange rates.	(677)
Plan assets at fair value—end of year	$22,575
Funded status—end of year.	$ (4,314)

a. Describe what is meant by *service cost* and *interest cost*.

b. What is the actual return on pension investments in 2014?

c. Provide an example under which an "actuarial loss," such as the $5,395 million loss that Johnson and Johnson reports in 2014, might arise.

d. What is the source of funds to make payments to retirees?

e. How much cash did Johnson and Johnson contribute to its pension plans in 2014?

f. How much cash did the company pay to retirees in 2014?

g. Show the computation of its 2014 funded status.

h. What net pension amount is reported on its 2014 balance sheet?

P10-40. **Interpreting the Income Tax Expense Footnote**

LO6

General Electric Company reports the following tax information in its 2014 financial report.

General Electric
NYSE :: GE

($ millions)	2014	2013	2012
Earnings before provision for income taxes.	$17,229	$16,151	$17,381
Provision for income taxes:			
Current tax expense.	2,958	3,971	3,686
Deferred tax expense (benefit)	(1,186)	(3,295)	(1,152)
Total provision (benefit) for income taxes.	$ 1,772	$ 676	$ 2,534

REQUIRED

a. What amount of tax expense is reported in GE's 2014 income statement? In 2013? In 2012? How much of each year's income tax expense is current tax expense and how much is deferred tax expense?

b. Compute GE's effective tax rate for each year.

c. Assume that GE's deferred tax benefit in 2014 is due to a decrease in deferred tax liabilities. Provide an example that would be consistent with this situation.

d. Assume that GE's deferred tax benefit in 2014 is due to an increase in a deferred tax asset. Explain how temporary differences would create a deferred tax asset. What would cause this asset to increase in value?

P10-41. **Calculating and Reporting Income Tax Expense**

LO6

Lynch Company began operations in 2016. The company reported $24,000 of depreciation expense on its income statement in 2016 and $26,000 in 2017. On its tax returns, Lynch deducted $32,000 for depreciation in 2016 and $37,000 in 2017. The 2017 tax return shows a tax obligation (liability) of $19,200 based on a 40% tax rate.

REQUIRED

a. Determine the temporary difference between the book value of depreciable assets and the tax basis of these assets at the end of 2016 and 2017.

b. Calculate the deferred tax liability for each year.

c. Calculate the income tax expense for 2017.

d. Prepare a journal entry to record income tax expense and post the entry to the appropriate T-accounts for 2017.

LO6   P10-42. Calculating and Reporting Income Tax Expense

Carter Inc. began operations in 2016. The company reported $130,000 of depreciation expense on its 2016 income statement and $128,000 in 2017. Carter Inc. deducted $140,000 for depreciation on its tax return in 2016 and $122,000 in 2017. The company reports a tax obligation of $45,150 for 2017 based on a tax rate of 35%.

REQUIRED

a.   Determine the temporary difference between the book value of depreciable assets and the tax basis of these assets at the end of 2016 and 2017.
b.   Calculate the deferred tax liability at the end of each year.
c.   Calculate the income tax expense for 2017.
d.   Prepare a journal entry to record income tax for 2017 and post the entry to the appropriate T-accounts.

LO6   P10-43. Computing and Reporting Deferred Income Taxes

Robinson Inc. paid $12,000 on December 31, 2016, for equipment with a two-year useful life. The equipment was depreciated for book purposes at $6,000 in 2017 and 2018. Robinson deducted the entire amount on its 2016 tax return. Assume this was the firm's only depreciable asset and that the firm's tax rate was 35% for 2016 and 2017 and 40% for 2018. The tax rate increase is not known until 2018. Assume, further, that Robinson's income before depreciation and taxes was $320,000 in 2016, $400,000 in 2017, and $420,000 in 2018.

REQUIRED

a.   Calculate the book value of the asset on 12/31 for 2016, 2017, and 2018.
b.   Calculate the tax basis of the asset on 12/31 for 2016, 2017, and 2018.
c.   What deferred tax liability should be reported for 2016, 2017, and 2018?
d.   Prepare journal entries to record income taxes for 2016, 2017, and 2018.

CASES AND PROJECTS

LO4, 5   C10-44. Analyzing and Interpreting Pension Disclosures

Dow Chemical
NYSE :: DOW

The Dow Chemical Company provides the following footnote disclosures in its 10-K report relating to its pension plans.

(in millions)	Defined Benefit Pension Plans	
	2014	**2013**
Service cost	$ 411	$ 471
Interest cost	1,096	1,012
Expected return on plan assets	(1,322)	(1,248)
Amortization of prior service cost	22	25
Amortization of unrecognized loss (gain)	500	788
Curtailment/settlement/other	(2)	5
Net periodic cost	$ 705	$ 1,053
Change in projected benefit obligation		
Benefit obligation at beginning of year.	$25,027	$26,840
Service cost	411	471
Interest cost	1,096	1,012
Plan participants' contributions	21	17
Amendments	(500)	0
Actuarial changes in assumptions and experience	4,096	(2,029)
Acquisition/divestiture/other activity	(1)	0
Benefits paid	(1,316)	(1,322)
Currency impact.	(779)	123
Termination benefits/curtailment cost	(76)	(85)
Benefit obligation at end of year	$27,979	$25,027

continued

continued from previous page

	2014	2013
Fair value of plan assets at beginning of year	$18,827	$17,725
Actual return on plan assets.	1,961	1,548
Currency impact.	(593)	85
Employer contributions	815	865
Plan participants' contributions	21	17
Acquisition/divestiture/other activity	(86)	(91)
Benefits paid	(1,316)	(1,322)
Fair value of plan assets at end of year	$19,629	$18,827

	Benefit Obligations at December 31	
Weighted Average Assumptions for All Pension Plans	**2014**	**2013**
Discount rate	3.60%	4.54%
Rate of increase in future compensation levels	4.13%	4.15%
Expected long-term rate of return on plan assets	—	—

REQUIRED

a. How much pension expense (revenue) does Dow Chemical report in its 2014 income statement?

b. Dow reports a $1,322 million expected return on plan assets as an offset to 2014 pension expense. Estimate the rate of return Dow expected to earn on its plan assets in 2014.

c. What factors affected its 2014 pension liability? What factors affected its 2014 plan assets?

d. What does the term *funded status* mean? What is the funded status of the 2014 Dow retirement plans at the end of 2014? What amount of asset or liability should Dow report on its 2014 balance sheet relating to its retirement plans?

e. Dow changed its discount rate from 4.54% to 3.60% in 2014. What effect(s) does this change have on its balance sheet and its income statement?

f. Suppose Dow increased its estimate of expected returns on plan assets in 2015. What effect(s) would this increase have on its income statement? Explain.

g. Dow provides us with its weighted-average discount rate. The company operates with manufacturing facilities in over 201 sites in 35 countries. Would you expect that the discount rate differed in the United States from the average rate outside the United States? Explain. What would you expect for future compensation levels?

C10-45. **Interpreting Capital and Operating Leases**

JetBlue Airways Corporation reports the following leasing information in its 2014 10-K.

LO1, 2, 3
JetBlue Airways Corporation
NASDAQ: JBLU

Excerpt from Note 2—Long-term Debt, Short-term Borrowings and Capital Lease Obligations

As of December 31, 2014, four capital leased Airbus A320 aircraft and two capital leased Airbus A321 aircraft were included in property and equipment at a cost of $253 million with accumulated amortization of $40 million. As of December 31, 2013, four capital leased Airbus A320 aircraft were included in property and equipment at a cost of $152 million with accumulated amortization of $33 million. The future minimum lease payments under these noncancelable leases are $23 million in 2015, $23 million in 2016, $23 million in 2017, $23 million in 2018, $23 million in 2019 and $98 million in the years thereafter. Included in the future minimum lease payments is $43 million representing interest, resulting in a present value of capital leases of $170 million with a current portion of $15 million and a long-term portion of $155 million.

Note 3—Operating Leases

We lease aircraft, all of our facilities at the airports we serve, office space and other equipment. These leases have varying terms and conditions, with some having early termination clauses which we determine to be the lease expiration date. The length of the lease depends upon the type of asset being leased, with the latest lease expiring in 2035. Total rental expense for all operating leases was $298 million in 2014, $295 million in 2013 and $284 million in 2012. As of December 31, 2014, 60 of the 203 aircraft in our fleet were leased under operating leases, with lease expiration dates ranging from 2016 to 2026. . . . Our aircraft lease agreements contain termination provisions which include standard maintenance and return conditions. Our policy is to record these lease return conditions when they are probable and the costs can be estimated.

Future minimum lease payments under noncancelable operating leases, including those described above, with initial or remaining terms in excess of one year at December 31, 2014, are as follows (in millions):

	Aircraft	Other	Total
2015	$150	$ 85	$ 235
2016	90	80	170
2017	75	65	140
2018	75	60	135
2019	58	57	115
Thereafter	213	487	700
Total minimum operating lease payments	$661	$834	$1,495

In the past we have entered into sale-leaseback arrangements with a third party lender for 45 of our operating aircraft. The sale-leasebacks occurred simultaneously with the delivery of the related aircraft to us from their manufacturers. Each sale-leaseback transaction was structured with a separate trust set up by the third party lender, the assets of which consist of the one aircraft initially transferred to it following the sale by us and the subsequent lease arrangement with us. Because of their limited capitalization and the potential need for additional financial support, these trusts are VIEs as defined in the *Consolidations* topic of the Codification and must be considered for consolidation in our financial statements. Our assessment of each trust considers both quantitative and qualitative factors, including whether we have the power to direct the activities and to what extent we participate in the sharing of benefits and losses of the trusts. JetBlue does not retain any equity interests in any of these trusts and our obligations to them are limited to the fixed rental payments we are required to make to them. These were approximately $585 million as of December 31, 2014 and are reflected in the future minimum lease payments in the table above. Our only interest in these entities is the purchase options to acquire the aircraft as specified above. Since there are no other arrangements, either implicit or explicit, between us and the individual trusts that would result in our absorbing additional variability from the trusts, we concluded we are not the primary beneficiary of these trusts. We account for these leases as operating leases, following the appropriate lease guidance as required by the *Leases* topic in the Codification.

REQUIRED

a. What entry did JetBlue make to record rent payments on operating leases in 2014? What entry will be required in 2015?

b. What is the total liability for leases that JetBlue reports in its 2014 balance sheet? How much of this liability is current? Noncurrent? Is this (total liability) amount representative of its obligations? Explain.

c. JetBlue reported that it operated four aircraft under capital leases at the end of 2013. Assume that all these leases were still in effect at the end of 2014. Prepare journal entries to record (i) new capital lease agreements signed during 2014, and (ii) depreciation of leased assets in 2014. Post your entries to T-accounts.

d. Based on the information above, prepare the entry that JetBlue would make in 2015 to record lease payments on capital leases. Record your entry in the financial statement effects template and in journal entry form. Post your entry to T-accounts.

e. Using a 4% discount rate, estimate the asset and liability that JetBlue would report if it capitalized all of its operating leases. JetBlue reports long-term debt of $1,968 million in its 2014 balance sheet. Would this amount be affected substantially if operating leases were capitalized?

f. Based on your calculations in part *e*, what journal entry would be necessary to record lease payments in 2015 if all of JetBlue's operating leases are capitalized at the end of 2014?

LO6   **C10-46. Interpreting Income Tax Footnotes**

The following information is taken from **Williams-Sonoma, Inc.**'s 10-K ($ thousands).

Note D: Income Taxes

The components of earnings before income taxes, by tax jurisdiction, are as follows:

	Fiscal Year Ended		
(in thousands)	Feb. 1, 2015 (52 Weeks)	Feb. 2, 2014 (52 Weeks)	Feb. 3, 2013 (53 Weeks)
United States	$482,739	$448,764	$401,542
Foreign	19,464	3,918	8,414
Total earnings before income taxes	$502,203	$452,682	$409,956

The provision for income taxes consists of the following:

(in thousands)	Fiscal Year Ended		
	Feb. 1, 2015 (52 Weeks)	Feb. 2, 2014 (52 Weeks)	Feb. 3, 2013 (53 Weeks)
Current			
Federal	$157,227	$173,686	$136,742
State	31,959	25,748	22,072
Foreign	4,411	2,690	3,441
Total current	193,597	202,124	162,255
Deferred			
Federal	2,719	(26,324)	(7,827)
State	(2,547)	(1,277)	(1,202)
Foreign	(420)	(743)	(0)
Total deferred	(248)	(28,344)	(9,029)
Total provision	$193,349	$173,780	$153,226

We have historically elected not to provide for U.S. income taxes with respect to the undistributed earnings of our foreign subsidiaries as we intended to utilize those earnings in our foreign operations for an indefinite period of time. As of February 1, 2015 the accumulated undistributed earnings of all foreign subsidiaries were approximately $43,300,000 and are sufficient to support our anticipated future cash needs for our foreign operations. We currently intend to utilize those undistributed earnings for an indefinite period of time and will only repatriate such earnings when it is tax effective to do so. It is currently not practical to estimate the tax liability that might be payable if these foreign earnings were to be repatriated.

Significant components of our deferred tax accounts are as follows:

(in thousands)	Feb. 1, 2015	Feb. 2, 2014
Current:		
Compensation	$ 15,968	$ 14,378
Merchandise inventories	30,328	27,337
Accrued liabilities	28,866	26,461
Customer deposits	60,989	58,479
Prepaid catalog expenses	(12,753)	(12,576)
Other	7,220	7,407
Total current	130,618	121,486
Non-current:		
Depreciation	(9,888)	(4,216)
Deferred rent	18,925	17,500
Deferred lease incentives	(37,098)	(33,065)
Stock-based compensation	19,857	28,948
Executive deferral plan	5,437	5,699
Uncertainties	7,061	4,378
Valuation allowance	(1,568)	(1,048)
Other	1,539	(4,372)
Total non-current	4,265	13,824
Total deferred tax assets, net	$134,883	$135,310

REQUIRED

a. What amount of income tax expense did Williams-Sonoma report for the year ended February 1, 2015?

b. Calculate Williams-Sonoma's effective tax rate for each year reported. In addition, calculate the rate of U.S. federal taxes on U.S. income in the fiscal year ended February 1, 2015.

    c.   Williams-Sonoma reported income taxes payable of $32,488 thousand in its February 1, 2015 balance sheet, and $49,365 thousand at February 2, 2014. What amount of income taxes did it pay in cash during the fiscal year ended February 1, 2015?[15]

    d.   Prepare a journal entry to record income tax expense for the fiscal year ended February 1, 2015.

    e.   The company reported a net book value of property, plant, and equipment of $883,012 thousand on February 1, 2015. Given a tax rate of 35%, what is an estimate of the tax basis of these assets on that date?

    f.   The company reported prepaid catalog expense of $33,942 thousand as a current asset in its February 1, 2015, balance sheet. The company provided the following explanation of this asset in footnote A to its 10-K:

> *Advertising and Prepaid Catalog Expenses*
> Advertising expenses consist of media and production costs related to catalog mailings, e-commerce advertising and other direct marketing activities. All advertising costs are expensed as incurred, or upon the release of the initial advertisement, with the exception of prepaid catalog expenses. Prepaid catalog expenses consist primarily of third party incremental direct costs, including creative design, paper, printing, postage and mailing costs for all of our direct response catalogs. Such costs are capitalized as prepaid catalog expenses and are amortized over their expected period of future benefit. . . . Each catalog is generally fully amortized over a six to nine month period, with the majority of the amortization occurring within the first four to five months.

         Explain how this expense results in a temporary difference between tax and financial reporting. Did the item create a current or long-term deferred tax asset or a liability and in what amount?

    g.   How much in unremitted foreign earnings on which no U.S. tax has been accrued (i.e., indefinitely reinvested earnings) does the company have in its foreign subsidiaries? If the company were required to estimate and record an accrual for the amount of U.S. tax on those earnings, how would accounting earnings be affected?

    h.   Williams-Sonoma has a valuation allowance listed in its schedule of deferred tax assets and liabilities. Briefly and in general explain what a valuation allowance is and how it affects deferred taxes and reported income.

LO6

C10-47. Interpreting Income Tax Disclosures

     Google Inc. reported the following in note 14 to its 2014 10-K report:

Note 14. Income Taxes
Income from continuing operations before income taxes included income from domestic operations of $6,447 million, $7,044 million, and $7,936 million for the years ended December 31, 2012, 2013, and 2014, and income from foreign operations of $8,021 million, $8,855 million, and $9,323 million for the years ended December 31, 2012, 2013, and 2014.

     The provision for income taxes consists of the following (in millions):

	Year Ended December 31,		
	2012	**2013**	**2014**
Current:			
Federal	$2,484	$2,217	$2,424
State	169	117	140
Foreign	312	711	774
Total	2,965	3,045	3,338
Deferred:			
Federal	(109)	(421)	29
State	5	0	7
Foreign	55	(72)	(43)
Total	(49)	(493)	(7)
Provision for income taxes	$2,916	$2,552	$3,331

---

[15] For this problem, assume a simple case. The complicating factors that would change the answer are beyond the scope of this text. For those readers aware of these complicating factors, assume there are no acquisitions of other companies during the year and that Williams-Sonoma has no unrecognized tax benefits.

We have not provided U.S. income taxes and foreign withholding taxes on the undistributed earnings of foreign subsidiaries as of December 31, 2014 because we intend to permanently reinvest such earnings outside the U.S. If these foreign earnings were to be repatriated in the future, the related U.S. tax liability may be reduced by any foreign income taxes previously paid on these earnings. As of December 31, 2014, the cumulative amount of earnings upon which U.S. income taxes have not been provided is approximately $47.4 billion. Determination of the amount of unrecognized deferred tax liability related to these earnings is not practicable.

REQUIRED

a. Compute Google's effective tax rate for each year presented. Also, compute Google's domestic tax rate (federal plus state) and its tax rate on income from foreign operations.

b. Explain what is meant by the disclosure in the final paragraph of the footnote regarding the "undistributed earnings of foreign subsidiaries."

c. Estimate the amount of taxes that Google might owe if all of the undistributed earnings were repatriated to the United States. Why is it "not practicable" to determine an amount of deferred income taxes on these undistributed earnings?

SOLUTIONS TO REVIEW PROBLEMS

Mid-Chapter Review 1

SOLUTION TO PART A

1. The present value of the lease payments is $224,755, computed as $32,000 × 7.02358.

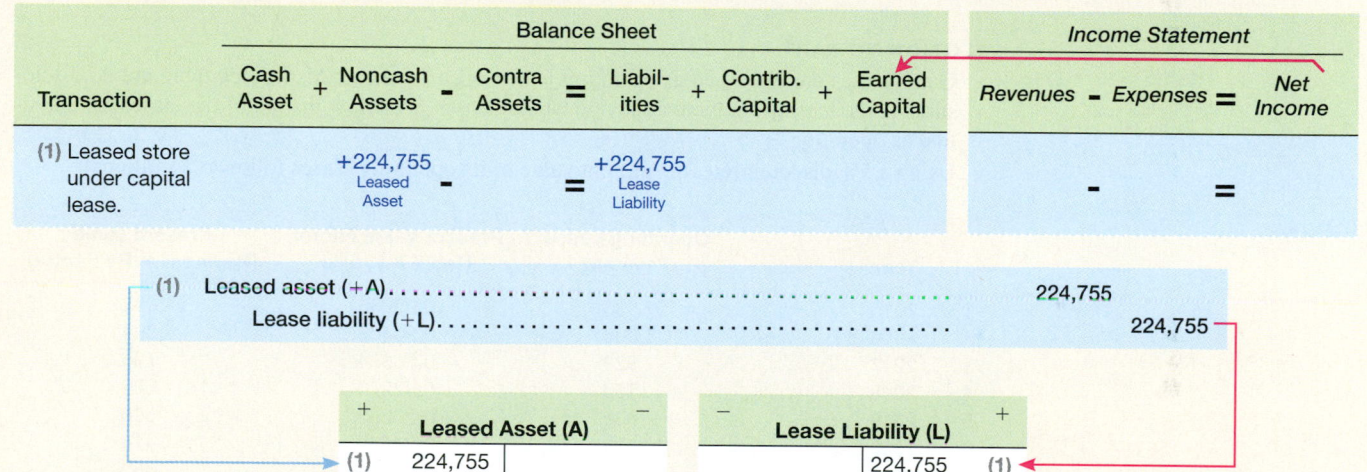

2. At the first year-end, Gap would record depreciation expense of $22,476 ($224,755/10) and interest expense of $15,733 ($224,755 × .07).

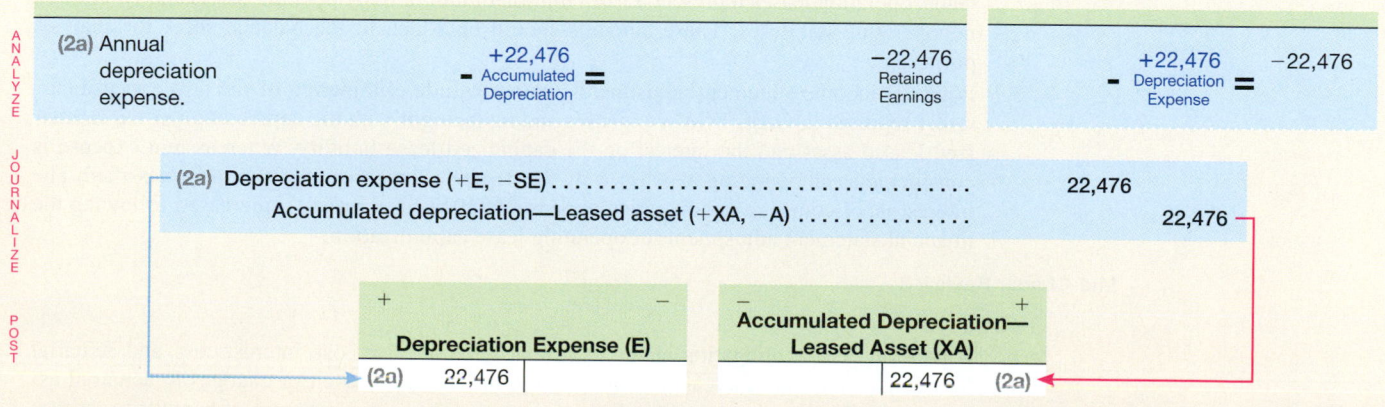

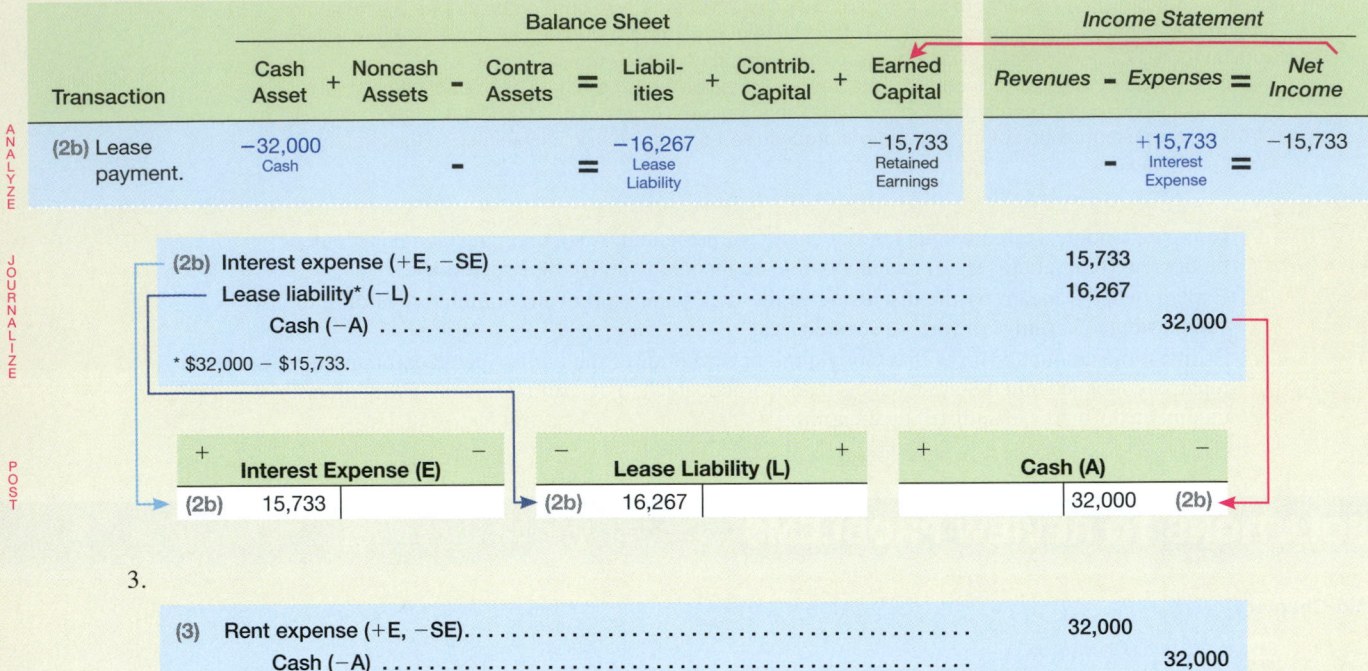

	Balance Sheet						Income Statement		
Transaction	Cash Asset	+ Noncash Assets	− Contra Assets	= Liabil- ities	+ Contrib. Capital	+ Earned Capital	Revenues	− Expenses	= Net Income
(2b) Lease payment.	−32,000 Cash		−	= −16,267 Lease Liability		−15,733 Retained Earnings		− +15,733 Interest Expense	= −15,733

(2b) Interest expense (+E, −SE) 15,733
    Lease liability* (−L) 16,267
        Cash (−A) 32,000
* $32,000 − $15,733.

+ Interest Expense (E) −		− Lease Liability (L) +		+ Cash (A) −	
(2b) 15,733		(2b) 16,267			32,000 (2b)

3.

(3) Rent expense (+E, −SE).. 32,000
    Cash (−A) 32,000

SOLUTION TO PART B

1. Gap's leases are classified as operating leases—see footnote. Also, since there are no disclosures in the leasing footnote related to capital leases, we know that all of the leases are classified as operating.

2. Using a 5% discount rate, the present value of its operating leases follows ($ millions):

Year		Operating Lease Payment	Present Value Factor (Table A.2, 5%)	Present Value (Payment × PV Factor)
1	2015	$1,136	0.95238	$1,082
2	2016	1,096	0.90703	994
3	2017	920	0.86384	795
4	2018	760	0.82270	625
5	2019	638	0.78353	500
6	2020	638	0.74622	476
7	2021	638	0.71068	453
8	2022	425	0.67684	288
Total		$6,251		$5,213

Gap's operating leases represent $5,213 million of unreported operating assets and unreported nonoperating liabilities. These amounts should be added to the balance sheet for analysis purposes.

3. Potential income statement adjustments would include elimination of the rent expense currently reported in Gap's SG&A expenses and replacing it with the depreciation of the capitalized leased asset and the interest on the capitalized lease liability. Whereas rent expense is considered as an operating expense, only the depreciation expense is similarly classified. The interest is, of course, a nonoperating expense. NOPAT, as a result, is increased following the financial statement adjustment for operating lease capitalization.

Mid-Chaper Review 2

SOLUTION

1. A pension benefit obligation increases primarily by service cost, interest cost, and actuarial losses. The latter are increases in the pension liability as a result of changes in actuarial assumptions. The pension benefit obligation is decreased by the payment of benefits to retirees and by actuarial gains.

2. Pension investments increase through positive investment returns for the period and by cash contributions made by the company. Investments decrease by payments made to retirees and investment losses.

3. United Continental's funded status is $(2,241) million ($4,803 million PBO − $2,562 million pension assets) as of 2014. The negative amount indicates that the plan is underfunded. Therefore, this amount is reported as a liability on the company's balance sheet.

4. Expected return on plan assets acts as an offset to service cost and interest cost in computing the net pension cost. As the expected return increases (decreases), net pension cost decreases (increases).

5. United Continental's expected return of $180 million exceeded its actual return of $151 million in 2014.

6. United Continental reports net pension expense of $132 million in 2014.

7. United Continental's funded status is negative, indicating an underfunded plan. The company contributed $307 million to the pension plan in 2014. It is likely that the company will need to increase its future funding levels to cover the plan's requirements. This action is likely to have negative consequences for its ability to fund other operating needs, and could damage its competitive position in the future.

Chapter-End Review

SOLUTION

1. *a.* $2,390.
   b. $1,488 = $1,342 + $146 is currently payable or has already been paid in 2016.
   c. The most obvious example would be depreciation allowed in 2016 by the tax code exceeded that calculated by the straight-line method.

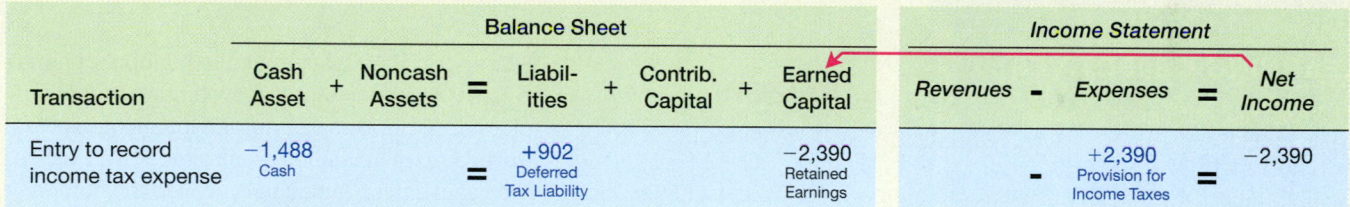

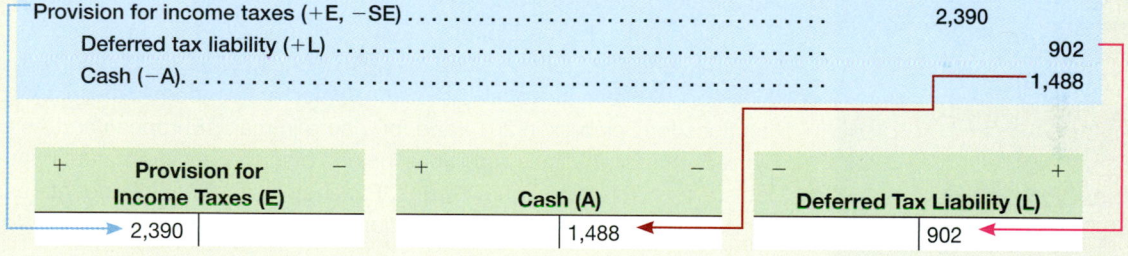

11

Reporting and Analyzing Stockholders' Equity

LEARNING OBJECTIVES

1. Describe business financing through stock issuances. (p. 518)

2. Explain and account for the issuance and repurchase of stock. (p. 521)

3. Describe how operations increase the equity of a business. (p. 525)

4. Explain and account for dividends and stock splits. (p. 525)

5. Define and illustrate comprehensive income. (p. 530)

6. Describe and illustrate the basic and diluted earnings per share computations. (p. 533)

7. Appendix 11A: Analyze the accounting for convertible securities, stock rights, and stock options. (p. 535)

PFIZER
www.pfizer.com

Pfizer Inc. is a research-based, global pharmaceutical company that discovers, develops, manufactures, and markets prescription medicines. Pfizer's 2014 revenues were almost $50 billion, down from almost $55 billion just two years earlier. Although Lyrica led the company with 10% of sales, Enbrel, Celebrex, Lipitor, and Viagra also contributed substantially to Pfizer's bottom line.

Unfortunately, the Lipitor patent expired in 2011 and many of Pfizer's other pharmaceutical patents are due to expire in the near future, causing Pfizer's projections of 2015 revenue to fall by 8%. Of immediate concern is the loss of patent protections for Celebrex in 2014 and for Viagra in major European and Asian markets. Pfizer's primary business activities include discovering and marketing new, patentable drugs. To discover new drugs, Pfizer spends sizeable amounts each year on research and development: $6.7 billion in 2013 and $8.4 billion in 2014.

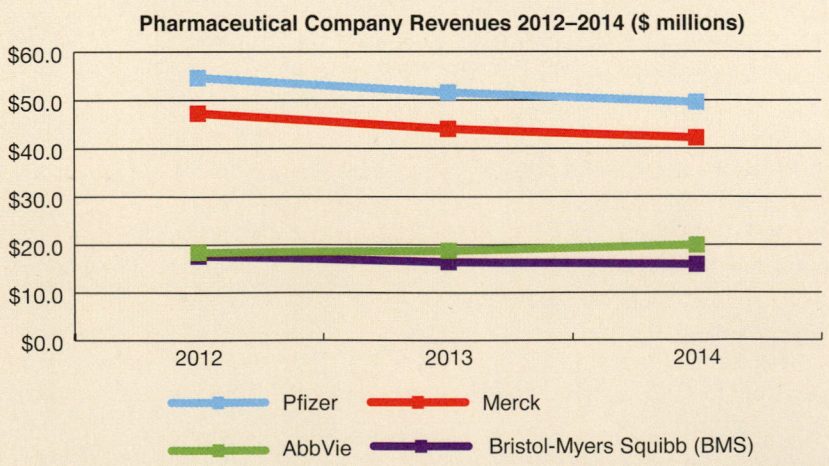

Pharmaceutical Company Revenues 2012–2014 ($ millions)

Pfizer faces increased competition from its major rivals, **Merck & Co., Inc.**, **AbbVie Inc.**, and **Bristol-Myers Squibb**, and also from generic manufacturers. In addition,

Pfizer reports that the "Patient Protection and Affordable Care Act" of 2010 cost the company almost $1 billion in 2014 and will continue to affect the company in future years.

One critical component of Pfizer's recent strategy has been to spread its high overhead costs across a broader sales base and to rationalize its production and sales activities. In 2000, Pfizer merged with **Warner-Lambert Company**, and in 2003 it acquired **Pharmacia**. The merger with Warner-Lambert and acquisition of Pharmacia made Pfizer the largest pharmaceutical company in the world. Since 2003, Pfizer has continued to acquire other companies, including **Esperion Therapeutics, Inc.** (2004), **Vicuron Pharmaceuticals, Inc.** (2005), **BioRexis Pharmaceuticals Corporation** (2007), **Coley Pharmaceutical Group** (2008), **Wyeth** (2009), and **King Pharmaceuticals, Inc.** in 2011. In 2014, Pfizer made an unsuccessful $119 billion bid to acquire **AstraZeneca plc**, which has $26 billion in revenues. Pfizer divested its animal health business in 2013 and its nutrition business in 2012 to focus more on its core businesses.

Pfizer must balance the capital needs of its acquisition strategy and its heavy commitment to research and development with the expectations of shareholders. From 2012 through 2014, the company reports $51 billion of net cash flow from operating activities, but it also paid $49 billion in cash to shareholders in the form of dividends and share repurchases. Other transactions involving shareholders' equity included share-based compensation for employees and conversions of one form of shareholders' equity to another.

This chapter describes the reporting and analysis of equity transactions, including sales and repurchases of stock, dividends, comprehensive income, and convertible securities.

Sources: *The Wall Street Journal* (January 27, 2009; May 21, 2009; April 21, 2015), *New York Times* (January 27, 2009; May 27, 2014), *Business Week* (April and June, 2009), *Fortune* (August, 2009), and Pfizer 2014 10-K Report.

CHAPTER ORGANIZATION

Reporting and Analyzing Stockholders' Equity			
Contributed Capital	**Earned Capital**	**Earnings per Share**	**Further Considerations (Appendix 11A)**
• Classes of Stock • Accounting for Stock	• Cash Dividends • Stock Dividends and Splits • Comprehensive Income	• Basic EPS • Diluted EPS	• Convertible Securities • Stock Rights • Stock Options

eLectures
MBC

1

LO1 Describe business financing through stock issuances.

INTRODUCTION

A company finances its assets from one of three sources: either it borrows funds from creditors, it obtains funds from shareholders or it reinvests excess cash flow from operations. On average, companies obtain about 60% of their external financing from borrowed sources and the remaining 40% from shareholder investment. This chapter describes the issues relating to stockholders' equity, including the accounting for stock transactions (issues and repurchases of stock, and dividends), the accounting for stock options, and the computation of earnings per share. Finally, we discuss the accounting for convertible securities, an increasingly prevalent financing vehicle.

When a company issues stock to the investing public, it records the receipt of cash (or other assets) and an increase in contributed capital, a part of stockholders' equity, representing investment in the company by shareholders. The increases in cash and equity equal the issue price of the stock on the issue date multiplied by the number of shares sold.

Contributed capital is accounted for at *historical cost*. Consequently, fluctuations in the market price of the issuer's stock subsequent to the initial public offering do not directly affect the financial statements of the issuing company. These fluctuations are the result of transactions between outside parties not involving the issuer. When and if stock is repurchased and subsequently resold, the issuer's contributed capital decreases (increases) by the current purchase (sales) price of the shares.

There is an important difference between accounting for stockholders' equity and accounting for transactions involving assets and liabilities: *there is never any gain or loss reported on the purchase and sale of stock or the payment of dividends*. Instead, these "gains and losses" are reflected as increases and decreases in the contributed capital component of the issuing company's stockholders' equity.

This chapter focuses on the two broad categories of shareholder investment: contributed capital and earned capital. **Exhibit 11.1** provides an illustration of this breakdown using Pfizer's stockholders' equity as of December 31, 2014.

> **FYI** Corporations never record gains or losses resulting from transactions between the company and its owners.

EXHIBIT 11.1   Stockholders' Equity from Pfizer's Balance Sheet

	Shareholders' Equity (millions except preferred stock issued and per common share data)	Dec. 31, 2014
Contributed capital	Preferred stock, no par value, at stated value; 27 shares authorized; issued: 2014—717	$ 29
	Common stock, $0.05 par value; 12,000 shares authorized; issued: 2014—9,110.	455
	Additional paid-in capital	78,977
	Treasury stock, shares at cost: 2014—2,819.	(73,021)
Earned capital	Retained earnings	72,176
	Accumulated other comprehensive income (loss)	(7,316)
	Total Pfizer Inc. shareholders' equity	71,301
	Equity attributable to noncontrolling interests	321
	Total equity.	$71,622

Pfizer, like other companies, has two broad categories of stockholders' equity:

1. **Contributed capital**   This section reports the proceeds received by the issuing company from original stock issuances. Contributed capital often includes common stock, preferred stock, and additional paid-in capital. Netted against these capital accounts is treasury stock, the amounts

paid to repurchase shares of the issuer's stock from its investors less the proceeds from the resale of such shares. Collectively, these accounts are generically referred to as contributed capital (or *paid-in capital*).

2. **Earned capital**   This section consists of (a) retained earnings (or accumulated deficit, if negative), which represent the cumulative income and losses of the company less any dividends to shareholders, and (b) accumulated other comprehensive income (AOCI), which includes changes to equity that are not included in income and are, therefore, not reflected in retained earnings. For Pfizer, AOCI includes foreign currency translation adjustments, changes in market values of derivatives, unrecognized gains and losses on available-for-sale securities, and pension adjustments.

Before turning to a discussion of contributed capital and earned capital, we note one other item in **Exhibit 11.1**—Equity attributable to **noncontrolling interests**. This amount results from the practice of consolidating subsidiaries that are controlled, but not wholly owned, and it represents neither capital contributed to Pfizer nor capital earned by Pfizer's shareholders. Chapter 12 provides a brief introduction to this topic.

CONTRIBUTED CAPITAL

We begin our discussion with contributed capital. Contributed capital represents the cumulative cash inflow that the company has received from the sale of various classes of stock, less the net cash that it has paid out to repurchase its stock from the market.

Pfizer's contributed capital consists of preferred and common stock, additional paid-in capital, less costs of treasury stock (repurchased shares).

Classes of Stock

There are two general classes of stock: preferred and common. The difference between the two lies in the respective legal rights conferred upon each class.

Common Stock   Shares of **common stock** represent the primary ownership unit in a corporation. Common stockholders have voting rights which allow them to participate in the governance of the corporation. The total number of common shares is usually presented on the face of the balance sheet. There are three numbers of shares to be aware of:

- The number of **shares authorized** represents the upper limit on the number of shares that the corporation can issue. This number is established in the *articles of incorporation* and can only be increased by an affirmative shareholder vote.

- The number of **shares issued** is the actual number of shares that have been sold to stockholders by the corporation.

- The number of **shares outstanding** is the number of issued shares less the number of shares repurchased as treasury stock.

Pfizer's common stock is described as follows in its 2014 balance sheet (shares in millions):

Common stock, $0.05 par value; 12,000 shares authorized; issued: 2014—9,110

The Pfizer common stock has the following important characteristics:

- Pfizer common stock has a par value of $0.05 per share. The **par value** is an arbitrary amount set by company organizers at the time of formation. Generally, par value has no substance from a financial reporting or statement analysis perspective (there are some legal implications, which are usually minor). Its main impact is in specifying the allocation of proceeds from stock issuances between the two contributed capital accounts on the balance sheet: common stock and additional paid-in capital.

- Pfizer has authorized the issuance of 12,000 million shares. As of December 31, 2014, 9,110 million shares are issued yielding a total par value of $455 million = $0.05 \times 9,110 million shares. When shares are first issued, the number of shares outstanding equals those issued. Any shares subsequently repurchased as treasury stock are subtracted from issued shares to derive outstanding shares.

Some corporations issue multiple classes of stock, with differential voting rights. For instance, **Google Inc.** has Class A common stock with one vote per share, Class B common stock with ten votes per share, and Class C capital stock with no voting rights at all. All shares participate equally in dividends, but this structure has allowed the original management team to raise capital while retaining voting control over the corporation.

Preferred Stock **Preferred stock** generally has some preference, or priority, with respect to common stock but does not have voting rights. Two typical preferences are:

1. **Dividend preference** Preferred shareholders receive dividends on their shares before common shareholders do. If dividends are not paid in a given year, those dividends are normally forgone. However, some preferred stock contracts include a *cumulative provision* stipulating that any forgone dividends must first be paid to preferred shareholders, together with the current year's dividends, before any dividends are paid to common shareholders.

2. **Liquidation preference** If a company fails, its assets are sold (liquidated) and the proceeds are paid to the creditors and shareholders, in that order. Shareholders, therefore, have a greater risk of loss than do creditors. Among shareholders, the preferred shareholders receive payment in full before any proceeds are paid to common shareholders. This liquidation preference makes preferred shares less risky than common shares. Any liquidation payment to preferred shares is normally at its par value, although it is sometimes specified in excess of par, called a **liquidating value**.

The preferred stock of Pfizer is described in Note 12 to its 2014 10-K:

The Series A convertible perpetual preferred stock is held by an Employee Stock Ownership Plan "Preferred ESOP" Trust and provides dividends at the rate of 6.25%, which are accumulated and paid quarterly. The per-share stated value is $40,300 and the preferred stock ranks senior to our common stock as to dividends and liquidation rights. Each share is convertible, at the holder's option, into 2,574.87 shares of our common stock with equal voting rights. The conversion option is indexed to our common stock and requires share settlement, and therefore, is reported at the fair value at the date of issuance. We may redeem the preferred stock at any time or upon termination of the Preferred ESOP, at our option, in cash, in shares of common stock or a combination of both at a price of $40,300 per share.

Following are several important features of the Pfizer preferred stock:

- There are 27 million preferred shares authorized, of which 717 shares are issued as of December 31, 2014. The articles of incorporation set the number of shares authorized for issuance. Once that limit is reached, shareholders must approve any increase in authorized shares.

- Pfizer preferred stock has a preference with respect to dividends and liquidation; meaning that preferred shareholders are paid before common shareholders.

- Pfizer preferred stock pays a dividend of 6.25% of its par (stated) value of $40,300. This feature means that each preferred share is entitled to annual dividends of $2,518.75 ($40,300 × 6.25%), payable quarterly.

- Pfizer preferred stock is convertible into common stock at the option of the holder and at a predetermined exchange rate. A preferred share is convertible, at the holder's option, into 2,574.87 common shares.

- Pfizer can redeem (repurchase) its preferred stock at any time in cash, common stock, or both.

Pfizer's cumulative preferred shares carry a dividend yield of 6.25%. This dividend yield compares favorably with the $1.04 per share (3.47% yield on a $30 average share price) paid to its common shareholders. Generally, preferred stock can be an attractive investment for shareholders seeking higher dividend yields, especially when tax laws wholly or partially exempt such dividends from taxation.

There are three additional features sometimes seen in preferred stock agreements:

1. **Call feature** The call feature provides the issuer with the right, but not the obligation, to repurchase the preferred shares at a specified price. This price can vary according to a specified time. A decline in the market rate of interest is one event that can lead to the firm exercising

the call provision. While of value to the issuer of the preferred stock, the call provision makes the issue less attractive to potential investors. The result is a lower offering price per share.

2. **Conversion feature**   The yield on preferred stock, especially when coupled with a cumulative feature, is similar to the interest rate on a bond or note. Further limited protection is offered because preferred shareholders receive the par value at liquidation like debtholders receive face value. The fixed yield and liquidation value for the preferred stock limit the upside potential return of preferred shareholders. This constraint can be overcome by inclusion of a *conversion feature* that allows preferred stockholders to convert their shares into common shares at their option at a predetermined conversion ratio. Some preferred contracts give the company an option to force conversion.

   The conversion feature causes the shares to be more attractive to potential investors because the preferred stockholders now have the opportunity to share in the fruits of a successful company with the common stockholders. Indeed, the market price of preferred stock tends to reflect the added value of the conversion feature.

3. **Participation feature**   Preferred shares sometimes carry a *participation feature* that allows preferred shareholders to share ratably with common stockholders in dividends. The dividend preference over common shares can be a benefit when dividend payments are meager, but a fixed dividend yield limits upside potential if the company performs exceptionally well. This limitation can be overcome with a participation feature.

A GLOBAL PERSPECTIVE

Under IFRS, convertible debt securities are termed compound financial instruments because the conversion feature has a value even if it is not legally detachable for sale. IFRS (but not GAAP) splits the convertible bonds' value into the separate debt and equity values for reporting purposes.

Accounting for Stock Transactions

We cover the accounting for stock transactions in this section, including the accounting for stock issuances and for stock repurchases.

LO2 Explain and account for the issuance and repurchase of stock.

2

Stock Issuance   Stock issuances, whether common or preferred, yield an increase in both assets and stockholders' equity. Companies use stock issuances to obtain cash and other assets for use in their business.

   Stock issuances increase assets (cash) by the number of shares sold multiplied by the issuance price of the stock on the issue date. Equity increases by the same amount, which is reflected in contributed capital accounts. Specifically, assuming the issuance of common stock, the common stock account increases by the number of shares sold multiplied by its par value and the additional paid-in capital account is increased for the remainder of the purchase price.[1]

BUSINESS INSIGHT

Alibaba's IPO   In September of 2014, **Alibaba Group** offered its shares to the general public for the first time. The first public sale of common stock by a corporation is called an initial public offering, or IPO for short. After the IPO, any offering of stock to the public is called a seasoned equity offering.

   At the time, Alibaba's IPO was the largest in history, raising approximately $25 billion. The common stock had a par value of $0.000025, but was offered to the public for $68 per share. Within a couple of months after the stock opened for trade on the New York Stock Exchange, the price increased to almost $120 per share, but then began to fall. By the company's fiscal year end in March 2015, Alibaba's shares were trading for just over $83 per share, about 20% greater than their original offer price and almost 50 times their earnings per share.

---

[1] Companies who offer their shares for sale to the general public are called *public corporations*. In a *private company*, ownership is limited to a smaller number of investors and the stock is not available to the general public. The distinction between public and private corporations should not be confused with media references to the public sector and the private sector. The *public sector* refers to government entities. Virtually all business entities, including public corporations, are considered part of the *private sector*.

To illustrate, assume that Davis Company issues 10,000 shares of $1 par value common stock at a market price of $43 cash per share. The financial statement effects and entries for this stock issuance follow.

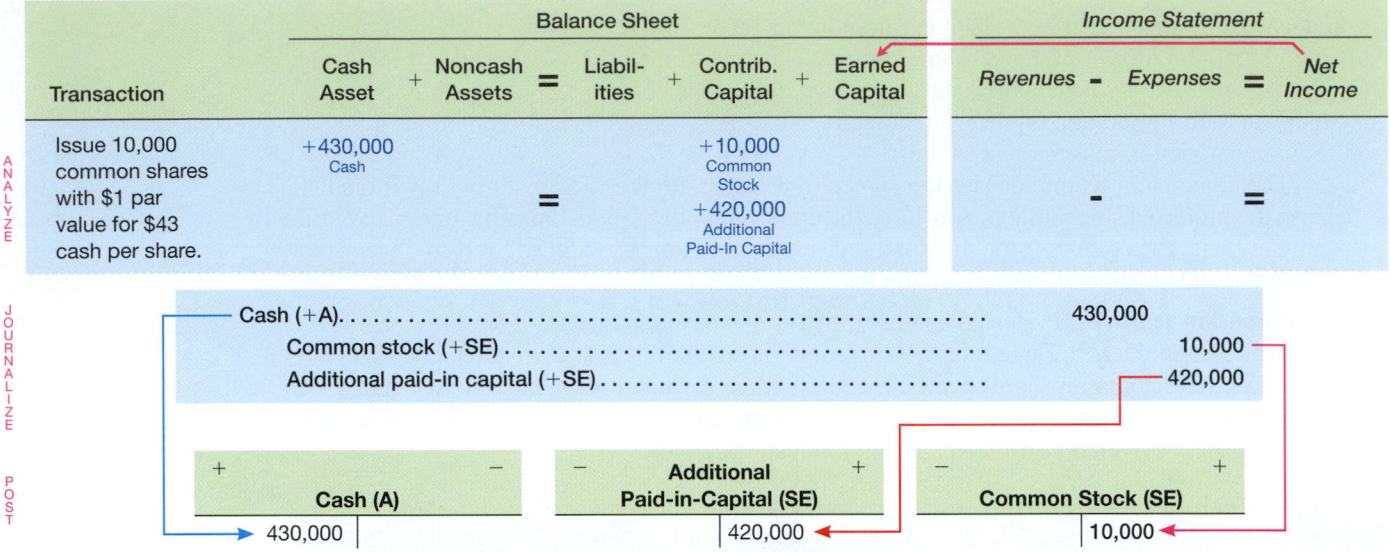

Specifically, the following financial statement effects of the stock issuance are:

1. Cash increases by $430,000 (10,000 shares × $43 per share) and is reported as a cash inflow from financing activities on the statement of cash flows.

2. Common stock increases by the $10,000 par value of shares sold (10,000 shares × $1 par value).[2]

3. Additional paid-in capital increases by the $420,000 difference between the issue price and par value ($430,000 − $10,000).

Once shares are issued, they are freely traded in the market among investors. The proceeds of those sales and any gains and losses on those sales do not affect the issuing company and are not recorded in its accounting records. Further, fluctuations in the issuing company's stock price subsequent to issuance do not directly affect its financial statements. Hence, the equity section of the balance sheet cannot be used to determine the current market value of the company. The market value (or market capitalization) is given by the product of the number of common shares outstanding times the current per-share price of the stock.

Pfizer's outstanding common shares, repeated from **Exhibit 11.1** are (in millions):

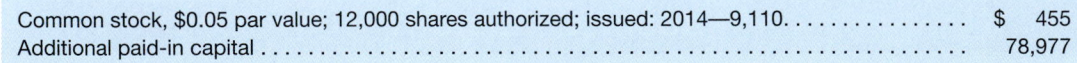

Common stock, $0.05 par value; 12,000 shares authorized; issued: 2014—9,110.	$ 455
Additional paid-in capital	78,977

Pfizer's common stock, in the amount of $455 million, equals the number of shares issued multiplied by the common stock's par value: 9,110 million × $0.05 = $455 million.[3] The balance of the proceeds from stock issuances ($78,977 million) is included in the additional paid-in capital account. Total proceeds from stock issuances are $79,432 million, or $8.72 per share ($79,432 million/9,110 million shares).

FYI Stock issuance affects the balance sheet, the statement of cash flows and the statement of stockholders' equity. There is never any revenue or gain from stock issuance reported in the income statement.

---

[2] Common stock can also be issued as "no par" or as "no par with a stated value." For no par stock, the common stock account is increased by the entire proceeds of the sale and no amount is assigned to additional paid-in capital. For no par stock with a stated value, the stated value is treated just like par value; that is, common stock is increased by the number of shares multiplied by the stated value, and the remainder is assigned to the additional paid-in capital account.

[3] The number of shares issued and the par value of those shares are both rounded to the nearest million.

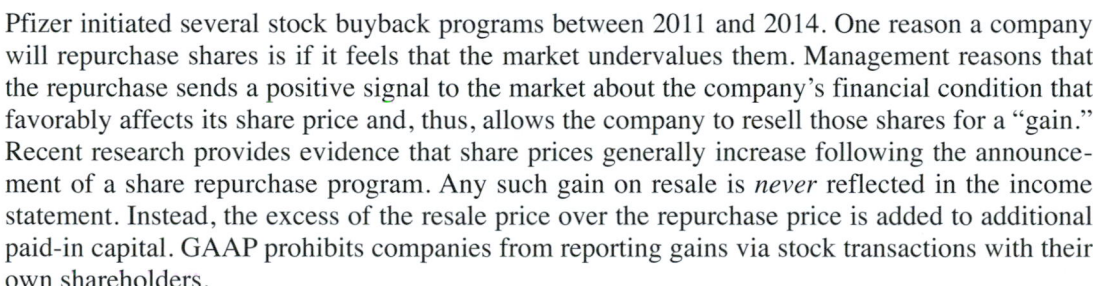

Stock Repurchase   Pfizer provides the following description of its stock repurchase program in notes to its 10-K report.

Our December 2011 $10 billion share-purchase plan was exhausted in the first quarter of 2013. Our November 2012 $10 billion share-purchase plan was exhausted in the fourth quarter of 2013. On June 27, 2013, we announced that the Board of Directors had authorized an additional $10 billion share-purchase plan, and share purchases commenced thereunder in October 2013. On October 23, 2014, we announced that the Board of Directors had authorized an additional $11 billion share-purchase plan . . . After giving effect to share purchases through year-end 2014, our remaining share-purchase authorization was approximately $11.5 billion at December 31, 2014.

Pfizer initiated several stock buyback programs between 2011 and 2014. One reason a company will repurchase shares is if it feels that the market undervalues them. Management reasons that the repurchase sends a positive signal to the market about the company's financial condition that favorably affects its share price and, thus, allows the company to resell those shares for a "gain." Recent research provides evidence that share prices generally increase following the announcement of a share repurchase program. Any such gain on resale is *never* reflected in the income statement. Instead, the excess of the resale price over the repurchase price is added to additional paid-in capital. GAAP prohibits companies from reporting gains via stock transactions with their own shareholders.

Another reason shares are repurchased is to offset the dilutive effects of an employee stock option program. When an employee exercises stock options, the number of shares outstanding increases. These additional shares reduce earnings per share and are, therefore, viewed as *dilutive*. In response, many companies repurchase an equivalent number of shares in a desire to keep outstanding shares constant. Corporations also buy back their own shares in order to concentrate ownership to avoid an unwelcome takeover action. Repurchased shares do not participate in dividends or in shareholder votes.

A GLOBAL PERSPECTIVE

The accounting for share repurchases under IFRS is similar to GAAP. IFRS allows the repurchase also to be recorded as a decrease to the common equity, additional paid-in capital, and retained earnings or some combination.

A stock repurchase has the opposite financial statement effects from a stock issuance. That is, cash is reduced by the price of the shares repurchased (number of shares repurchased multiplied by the purchase price per share) and stockholders' equity is reduced by the same amount. The reduction in equity is achieved by increasing a contra equity account called **treasury stock**. *A contra equity account is a negative equity account with a debit balance,* which reduces stockholders' equity. Thus, when a contra equity account increases, total equity decreases.

Any subsequent reissuance of treasury stock does not yield a gain or loss. Instead, the difference between the proceeds received and the repurchase price of the treasury stock is reflected as an increase or decease to additional paid-in capital.

To illustrate, assume that 3,000 common shares of Davis Company stock previously issued for $43 are later repurchased for $40. The financial statement effects and entries for this stock repurchase follow.

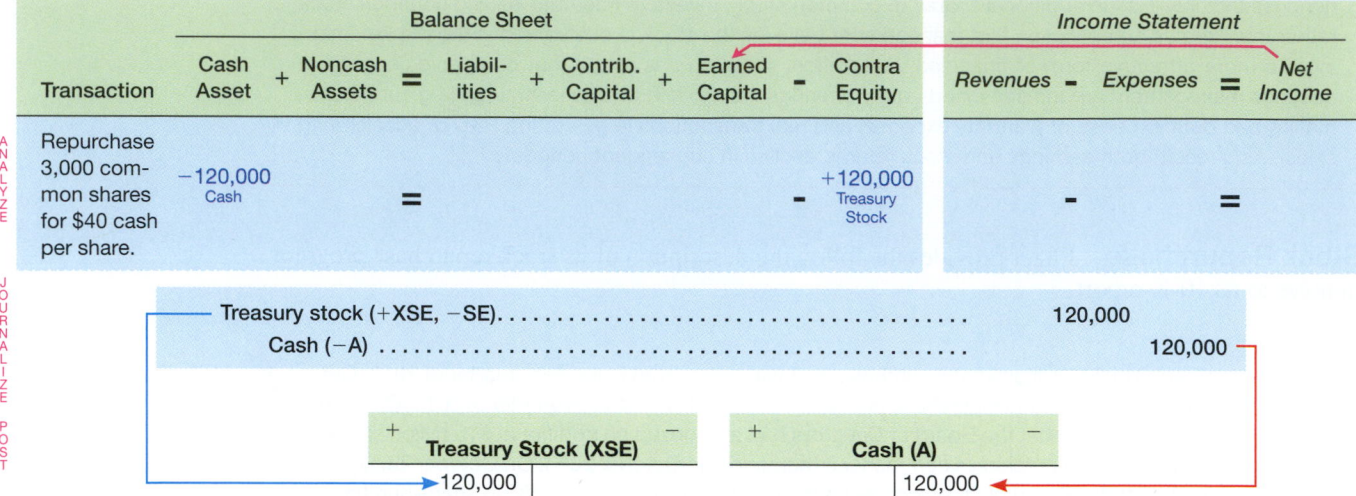

Assets (cash) and equity both decrease. Treasury stock (a contra equity account) increases by $120,000, which reduces stockholders' equity by that same amount.

Assume that these 3,000 shares are then subsequently resold for $42 cash per share. The financial statement effects and entries for this treasury stock sale follow.

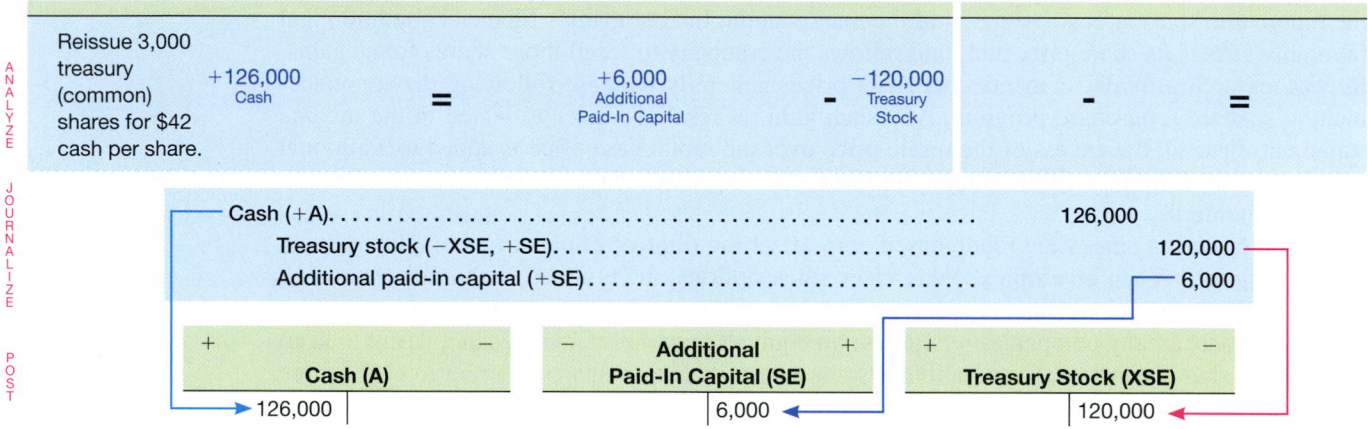

Cash assets increase by $126,000 (3,000 shares × $42 per share), the treasury stock account is reduced by the $120,000 cost of the treasury shares issued, and the $6,000 excess (3,000 shares × $2 per share) is reported as an increase in additional paid-in capital.[4] Again, there is no effect on the income statement—companies are prohibited from reporting gains and losses from repurchases and reissuances of their own stock.

The treasury stock section of Pfizer's 2014 balance sheet is reproduced below.

At December 31 (millions)	2014
Treasury stock, shares at cost: 2014—2,819..............................	$(73,021)

Pfizer has repurchased a cumulative total of 2,819 million shares of its common stock for $73,021 million, an average repurchase price of $25.90 per share. This compares with total contributed

---

[4] If the reissue price is below the repurchase price, then additional paid-in capital is reduced until it reaches a zero balance, after which retained earnings is reduced.

capital of $79,461 million ($29 million + $455 million + $78,977 million). Although some of Pfizer's treasury purchases were to offset increases in shares outstanding due to the exercise of stock options, it appears that most of these purchases are motivated by a perceived low stock price by Pfizer management. When there have been several repurchases and sales of treasury stock, a question arises as to which shares were sold. Typically the solution is to assume a flow such as the first shares repurchased are the first ones assumed to be sold (first-in, first-out).

YOU MAKE THE CALL

You are the Chief Financial Officer You believe that your company's stock price is lower than its real value. You are considering various alternatives to increase that price, including the repurchase of company stock in the market. What are some considerations relating to this decision? [Answer on page 540]

MID-CHAPTER REVIEW 1

Plesko Corporation reported the following transactions relating to its stock accounts in 2015.

Jan.   15   Issued 10,000 shares of $5 par value common stock at $17 cash per share.

Mar.   31   Purchased 2,000 shares of its own common stock at $15 cash per share.

June   25   Reissued 1,000 shares of its treasury stock at $20 cash per share.

Show the financial impact of each transaction using the financial statement effects template, provide the appropriate journal entry for each transaction, and post the journal entries to the related T-accounts.

The solution to this review problem can be found on page 558.

EARNED CAPITAL

We now turn our attention to the earned capital portion of stockholders' equity. Earned capital represents the cumulative profit that has been retained by the company. Recall that earned capital is increased by income earned and decreased by any losses incurred. Earned capital is also decreased by dividends paid to shareholders. Not all dividends are paid in the form of cash, however. In fact, companies can pay dividends in many forms, including property (such as land, for example) or additional shares of stock. We cover both cash and stock dividends in this section. Earned capital also includes the positive or negative effects of accumulated other comprehensive income (AOCI). The earned capital of Pfizer is highlighted in the following graphic:

LO3 Describe how operations increase the equity of a business.

Shareholders' Equity (millions, except preferred shares issued and par value)	Dec. 31, 2014
Preferred stock, no par value, at stated value; 27 shares authorized; issued: 2014—717	$ 29
Common stock, $0.05 par value; 12,000 shares authorized; issued: 2014—9,110	455
Additional paid-in capital	78,977
Treasury stock, shares at cost: 2014—2,819	(73,021)
Retained earnings	72,176
Accumulated other comprehensive income (loss)	(7,316)
Total Pfizer Inc. shareholders' equity	71,301
Equity attributable to noncontrolling interests	321
Total equity	$71,622

Cash Dividends

Many companies, but not all, pay dividends. Their reasons for dividend payments are varied. Most dividends are paid in cash on a quarterly basis. The following is a description of Pfizer's dividend policy from its 2014 10-K.

LO4 Explain and account for dividends and stock splits.

Dividends on Common Stock

We paid dividends on our common stock of $6.6 billion in 2014, $6.6 billion in 2013 and $6.5 billion in 2012. In December 2014, our Board of Directors declared a first-quarter 2015 dividend of $0.28 per share, payable on March 3, 2015, to shareholders of record at the close of business on February 6, 2015. The first-quarter 2015 cash dividend will be our 305th consecutive quarterly dividend.

Our current and projected dividends provide a return to shareholders while maintaining sufficient capital to invest in growing our businesses and to seek to increase shareholder value. Our dividends are not restricted by debt covenants. While the dividend level remains a decision of Pfizer's Board of Directors and will continue to be evaluated in the context of future business performance, we currently believe that we can support future annual dividend increases, barring significant unforeseen events.

Outsiders closely monitor dividend payments. It is generally perceived that the level of dividend payments is related to the expected long-term core income. Accordingly, dividend increases are usually accompanied by stock price increases, and companies rarely reduce their dividends unless absolutely necessary. Dividend reductions are, therefore, met with substantial stock-price declines.

Financial Effects of Cash Dividends   Cash dividends reduce both cash and retained earnings by the amount of the cash dividends paid. To illustrate, Pfizer paid $6.6 billion in 2014 cash dividends on its common and preferred shares. The financial statement effects of this cash dividend payment are reflected as a reduction in assets (cash) and a reduction in retained earnings as follows.

($ billions)	Balance Sheet					Income Statement		
Transaction	Cash Asset	+ Noncash Assets	= Liabil- ities	+ Contrib. Capital	+ Earned Capital	Revenues −	Expenses =	Net Income
Paid $6.6 billion cash dividends on common and preferred shares.	−6.6 Cash	=			−6.6 Retained Earnings	−	=	

Retained earnings (−SE).. 6.6

    Cash (−A) 6.6

−	Retained Earnings (SE)	+		+	Cash (A)	−
	6.6				6.6	

Dividend payments have no effect on profitability. They are a direct reduction to retained earnings and bypass the income statement.

BUSINESS INSIGHT

While many technology companies appear to have ample financial resources to pay dividends, the tax strategies described in Chapter 10 make it costly to use those resources. For instance, **Apple Inc.** reported end-of-fiscal year 2014 cash and financial investments of $155 billion, 67% of the company's total assets. However, $137 billion of this amount was held by Apple's foreign subsidiaries and had not yet been subject to U.S. taxation. If Apple repatriated some portion of these resources to pay dividends to its shareholders, it would have to pay approximately one-third of the amount to U.S. tax authorities. As a result, Apple borrowed a total of $35 billion in fiscal years 2013 and 2014, at least in part to return cash to shareholders in the form of dividends and repurchases of common stock.

Preferred stock dividends have priority over those for common shares, including unpaid prior years' preferred dividends (dividends in arrears) when preferred stock is cumulative. To illustrate, assume that Hanna Company has 15,000 shares of $50 par value, 8% preferred stock outstanding and 50,000 shares of $5 par value common stock outstanding. During its first three years in business, assume that Hanna declares $20,000 dividends in the first year, $260,000 of dividends in the second year, and $60,000 of dividends in the third year. If the preferred stock is cumulative, the total amount of dividends paid to each class of stock in each of the three years would be:

	Preferred Stock	Common Stock
Year 1		
Current-year dividend ($15,000 × $50 × 8%;	$20,000	
but only $20,000 is paid, leaving $40,000 in arrears)......		
Balance to common.................................		$ 0
Year 2		
Arrearage from Year 1 [($15,000 × $50 × 8%) − $20,000]....	40,000	
Current-year dividend ($15,000 × $50 × 8%).............	60,000	
Balance to common [$260,000 − ($40,000 + $60,000)].....		160,000
Year 3		
Current-year dividend ($15,000 × $50 × 8%).............	60,000	
Balance to common.................................		0

MID-CHAPTER REVIEW 2

Finn Corporation has outstanding 10,000 shares of $100 par value, 5% preferred stock and 50,000 shares of $5 par value common stock. During its first three years in business, Finn declared no dividends in the first year, $300,000 of cash dividends in the second year, and $80,000 of cash dividends in the third year.

a. If the preferred stock is cumulative, determine the total amount of dividends paid to each class of stock for each of the three years.
b. If the preferred stock is not cumulative, determine the total amount of dividends paid to each class of stock for each of the three years.

The solution to this review problem can be found on page 559.

Stock Dividends and Splits

Dividends need not be paid in cash. Many companies pay **stock dividends**, that is dividends in the form of additional shares of stock. Companies can also distribute additional shares to their stockholders with a stock split. We cover both of these distributions in this section.

Stock Dividends   When dividends are paid in the form of the company's stock, retained earnings are reduced and contributed capital is increased. However, the amount by which retained earnings are reduced depends on the proportion of the outstanding shares distributed to the total outstanding shares on the issue date. **Exhibit 11.2** illustrates two possibilities depending on whether a stock dividend is classified as either a small stock dividend or a large stock dividend. When the additional number of shares issued as a stock dividend is so great that it is likely to have a negative impact on the market price per share of the stock, the dividend must be treated as a large stock dividend. Dividends of less than 20%–25% of the outstanding shares are considered to be small stock dividends, while dividends of more than 20%–25% are classified as large stock dividends.

EXHIBIT 11.2	Analysis of Stock Dividend Effects	
Percentage of Outstanding Shares Distributed	**Retained Earnings**	**Contributed Capital**
Less than 20%–25% *(small stock dividend)*	Reduce by **market value** of shares distributed	Common stock increased by par value of shares distributed; additional paid-in capital increased for the balance
More than 20%–25% *(large stock dividend)*	Reduce by **par value** of shares distributed	Common stock increased by par value of shares distributed

For *small stock dividends,* retained earnings are reduced by the *market* value of the shares distributed (dividend shares × market price per share) and contributed capital is increased by the same amount. For the contributed capital increase, the common stock is increased by the par value of the shares distributed and the remainder [dividend shares × (market value per share − par value per share)] increases additional paid-in capital. For *large stock dividends,* retained earnings are reduced by the *par* value of the shares distributed (dividend shares × par value per share), and common stock is increased by the same amount (no change to additional paid-in capital).

To illustrate the financial statement effects of dividends, assume that a company has 1 million shares of $5 par common stock outstanding. It then declares a small stock dividend of 15% of the outstanding shares (1,000,000 shares × 15% = 150,000 shares) when the market price of the stock is $30 per share. This small stock dividend has the following financial statement effects:

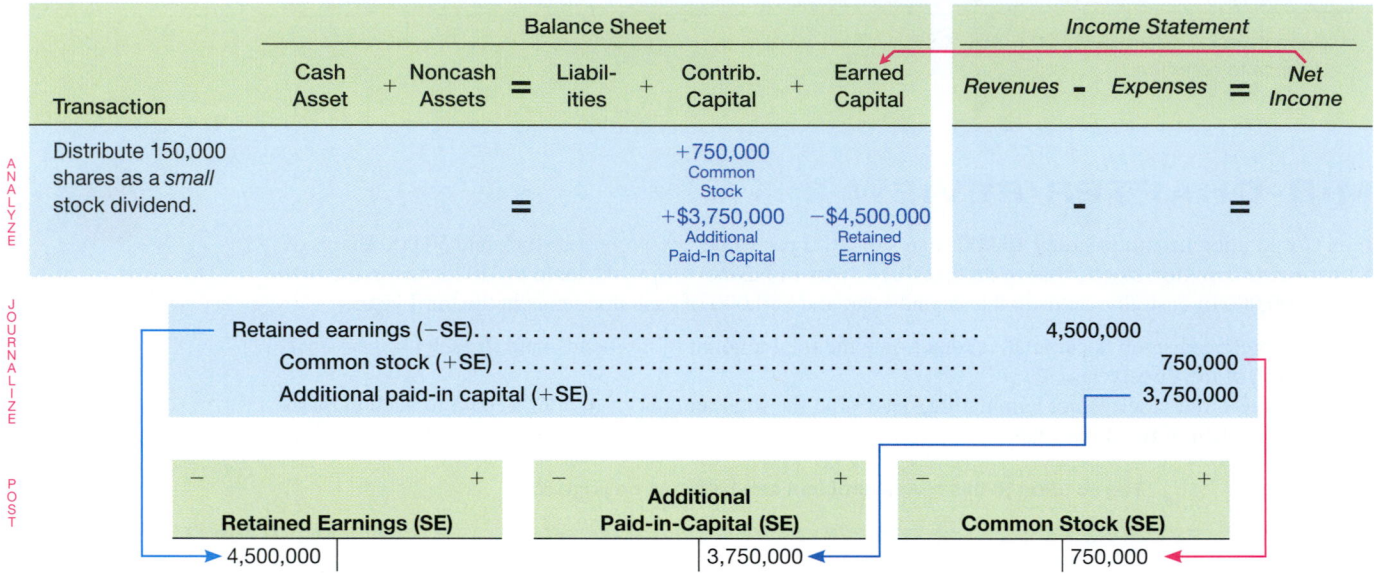

Retained earnings are reduced by $4,500,000, which equals the market value of the small stock dividend (150,000 shares × $30 market price per share). The increase in contributed capital is treated as follows: common stock is increased by the par value of $750,000 (150,000 shares × $5 par value), and the remainder of $3,750,000 increases additional paid-in capital. Similar to cash dividend payments, the stock dividends, whether large or small, never impact income. But unlike cash dividends, stock dividends do not affect the cash flows from financing activities.

Next, assume instead that a company declares a large stock dividend of 70% of the 1 million outstanding common ($5 par) shares when the market price of the stock is $30 per share. This large stock dividend has the following financial statement effects and related entries:

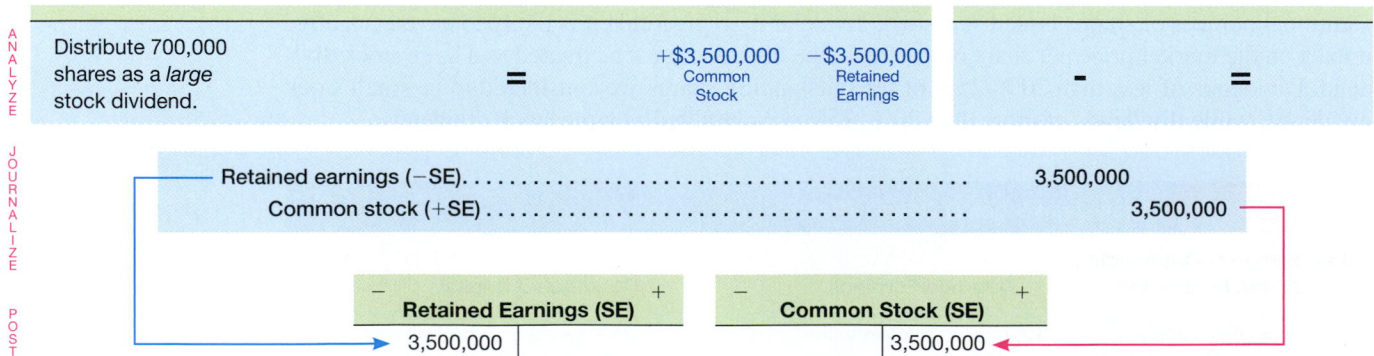

Retained earnings are reduced by $3,500,000, which equals the par value of the large stock dividend (700,000 shares × $5 par value per share). Common stock is increased by the par value of $3,500,000. There is no effect on additional paid-in capital because the dividend is reported at par value.

For both large and small stock dividends, companies are required to show comparable shares outstanding for all prior periods for which earnings per share (EPS) is reported in the statements. The reasoning is that a stock dividend has no effect on the ownership percentage of each common stockholder. As such, to show a dilution in reported EPS would erroneously suggest a decline in profitability when it is simply due to an increase in shares outstanding.

Stock Splits   A **stock split** is a proportionate distribution of shares and, as such, is similar in substance to a stock dividend. A typical stock split is 2-for-1, which means that the company distributes one additional share for each share owned by a shareholder. Following the distribution, each investor owns twice as many shares, yet their percentage ownership in the company is unchanged.

A stock split is not a monetary transaction and, as such, there are no financial statement effects. However, companies must disclose the new number of shares outstanding for all periods presented in the financial statements. Further, many states require that the par value of shares be proportionately adjusted as well (for example, halved for a 2-for-1 split).[5]

Stock Transactions and the Cash Flows Statement

The issuance of common stock, the acquisition of treasury stock, and cash (but not stock) dividends affect the financing section of the cash flow statement as follows:

Transaction	Effect on Cash Flow from Financing Activities
Issuance of Common Stock.	Increase
Acquisition of Treasury Stock.	Decrease
Sale of Treasury Stock	Increase
Cash Dividends Paid	Decrease

Stock splits and stock dividends do not influence the cash flows statement and are often used when cash is short but the continuation of a dividend is considered necessary.

MID-CHAPTER REVIEW 3

The stockholders' equity of Zhang Corporation at December 31, 2014, follows.

5% preferred stock, $100 par value, 10,000 shares authorized; 4,000 shares issued and outstanding	$ 400,000
Common stock, $5 par value, 200,000 shares authorized; 50,000 shares issued and outstanding	250,000
Paid-in capital in excess of par value—Preferred stock	40,000
Paid-in capital in excess of par value—Common stock	300,000
Retained earnings	656,000
Total stockholders' equity	$1,646,000

The following transactions occurred during 2015. Show the financial impact of each transaction using the financial statement effects template, provide the appropriate journal entry for each transaction, and post the journal entries to the related T-accounts.

Apr. 1   Declared and issued a 100% stock dividend on all outstanding shares of common stock when the market value of the stock was $11 per share.

Dec. 7   Declared and issued a 3% stock dividend on all outstanding shares of common stock when the market value of the stock was $7 per share.

Dec. 31   Declared and paid a cash dividend of $1.20 per share on all outstanding common shares.

The solution to this review problem can be found on pages 559–560.

[5] If state law requires that par value not be reduced for a stock split, this event should be described as a *stock split effected in the form of a dividend*.

LO5 Define and illustrate comprehensive income.

Comprehensive Income

Comprehensive income is a more inclusive notion of company performance than net income. It includes all recognized changes in equity that occur during a period except those resulting from contributions by and distributions to owners.

Specifically, comprehensive income includes net income *plus* additional gains and losses not included in the income statement. These additional gains and losses are called *other comprehensive income* and include, for example, foreign currency adjustments, unrealized gains or losses on available-for-sale securities and derivatives, and adjustments to pension and other benefit plans. Comprehensive income includes the effects on a company of some economic events that are often outside of management's control. Accordingly, some observers assert that net income is a measure of management's performance, while comprehensive income is a measure of company performance.

Comprehensive income can be reported by firms in one of two ways. The first reporting method is to present a statement of comprehensive income that combines net income and other comprehensive income in one statement. Such a statement begins much like any income statement, with revenues, cost of goods sold, operating expenses and so forth. However, in the statement of comprehensive income, net income is a subtotal, followed by the gains and losses that are classified as other comprehensive income. The second reporting approach presents other comprehensive income in a separate statement immediately following the income statement. Pfizer follows the second reporting approach. Its statement of comprehensive income is presented in **Exhibit 11.3**.

EXHIBIT 11.3	Pfizer's 2014 Abridged Consolidated Statement of Comprehensive Income ($ millions)	
Net income.		$9,168
Other comprehensive income:		
Foreign currency translation adjustments, net	(2,054)	
Unrealized holding gains on derivative financial instruments, net	501	
Unrealized holding gains/(losses) on available-for-sale securities, net	(418)	
Benefit plans: actuarial gains/(losses), net	(3,690)	
Benefit plans: prior service credit and other, net	672	
Tax benefit/(provision) on other comprehensive income/(loss).	946	
Total other comprehensive income/(loss).		(4,042)
Comprehensive income before allocation to noncontrolling interests.		$5,126
Less: Comprehensive income attributable to noncontrolling interests		36
Comprehensive income attributable to Pfizer Inc.		$5,090

Unlike net income, other comprehensive income is not closed to retained earnings at the end of each accounting period. Instead, other comprehensive income is closed to a separate earned capital account called **accumulated other comprehensive income** (abbreviated AOCI).

In its 2014 balance sheet, Pfizer reports accumulated other comprehensive income of $(7,316), compared to $(3,271) in 2013. The $4,045 decrease from 2013 to 2014 is (almost) equal to the $(4,042) other comprehensive income for 2014 that Pfizer reported in its statement of comprehensive income (**Exhibit 11.3**). (The $3 million "slippage" is due to noncontrolling interests' share of other comprehensive income items.)

A GLOBAL PERSPECTIVE

As with U.S. GAAP, companies reporting under IFRS have a choice of presenting a single statement including components of profit and loss and other comprehensive income or presenting two statements—one for profit and loss (the income statement) and one that begins with profit or loss and then provides other comprehensive income components.

Summary of Stockholders' Equity

A summary of transactions that affect stockholders' equity is included in the statement of stockholders' equity. This statement reports a reconciliation of the beginning and ending balances of important stockholders' equity accounts. Pfizer's statement of stockholders' equity is shown in **Exhibit 11.4**. Pfizer's statement of shareholders' equity reveals the following key transactions for 2014:

- Total comprehensive income increased shareholders' equity by $5,090 million (net income of $9,135 million less other comprehensive loss of $4,045 million).

- Dividends to preferred and common shareholders decreased stockholders' equity by $6,692 million ($2 million + $6,690 million).

- Employee share-based compensation increased equity by $1,597 million.

- Common stock repurchases decreased equity by $5,000 million.

- Conversion of preferred stock into common stock and redemptions decreased the preferred stock account, for a net decrease in stockholders' equity of $8 million.

EXHIBIT 11.4	**Pfizer's Stockholders' Equity (December 31, 2014)**											
	Preferred Stock		**Common Stock**			**Treasury Stock**			**Accum.**			
(Millions, Except Preferred Shares)	Shares	Stated Value	Shares	Par Value	Additional Paid-In Capital	Shares	Cost	Retained Earnings	Other Comp. Loss	Share-holders' Equity	Non-controlling Interests	Total Equity
Balance December 31, 2013	829	$33	9,051	$453	$77,283	(2,652)	$(67,923)	$69,732	$(3,271)	$76,307	$313	$76,620
Net income								9,135		9,135	32	9,168
Other comprehensive income/ (loss), net of tax									(4,045)	(4,045)	3	(4,042)
Cash dividends declared:												
Common stock								(6,690)		(6,690)		(6,690)
Preferred stock								(2)		(2)		(2)
Noncontrolling interests											(6)	(6)
Share-based payment transactions			59	3	1,693	(2)	(100)			1,597		1,597
Purchases of common stock						(165)	(5,000)			(5,000)		(5,000)
Preferred stock conversions and redemptions	(112)	(4)			(4)	—	1			(8)		(8)
Other	—	—	—	(1)	5	—	—	—	—	5	(22)	(17)
Balance December 31, 2014	717	$29	9,110	$455	$78,977	(2,819)	$(73,021)	$72,176	$(7,316)	$71,301	$321	$71,622

ANALYZING FINANCIAL STATEMENTS

Analysis Objective

We want to measure the return on investment by common shareholders.

Before getting to the specifics of the performance ratio, we must address a complexity introduced when a company (like Pfizer) has a subsidiary that is not 100% owned. Suppose Company A owns 85% of the common stock of Company B. The remaining 15% of B's shareholders are called a "non-controlling interest." Company A would be required to incorporate the assets, liabilities, revenues and expenses of Company B in its reports. As a result, Company A's reported net income would include all the income from both A and B. But then there is an adjustment in which 15% of B's income is subtracted (as "net income attributable to noncontrolling interests"), and the resulting number is "net income attributable to common shareholders." We use this information to develop the following measure of profit that can be attributed to common shareholders of the reporting company.

> **Net income available for common shareholders =**
> **Net income − Net income attributable to noncontrolling interests − Preferred dividends**

A similar adjustment is required on the balance sheet, where total equity consists of "equity attributable to noncontrolling interests" plus "common shareholders' equity" (as can be seen in **Exhibit 11.4**).

Analysis Tool   Return on Common Equity (ROCE)

> $$\text{Return on Common Equity (ROCE)} = \frac{\text{Net income available for common shareholders}}{\text{Average common shareholders' equity}}$$

Applying the Ratio to Pfizer

$$2013 \text{ ROCE} = \frac{\$22{,}072 - \$69 - \$2}{[(\$76{,}620 - \$313 - \$33) + (\$81{,}678 - \$418 - \$39)]/2} = 0.279, \text{ or } 27.9\%$$

$$2014 \text{ ROCE} = \frac{\$9{,}168 - \$32 - \$2}{[(\$71{,}622 - \$321 - \$29) + (\$76{,}620 - \$313 - \$33)]/2} = 0.124, \text{ or } 12.4\%$$

Guidance   ROCE is similar to ROE except that when we compute ROCE, we remove the effect of noncontrolling interests and preferred stock from both the numerator and denominator.

Pfizer in Context

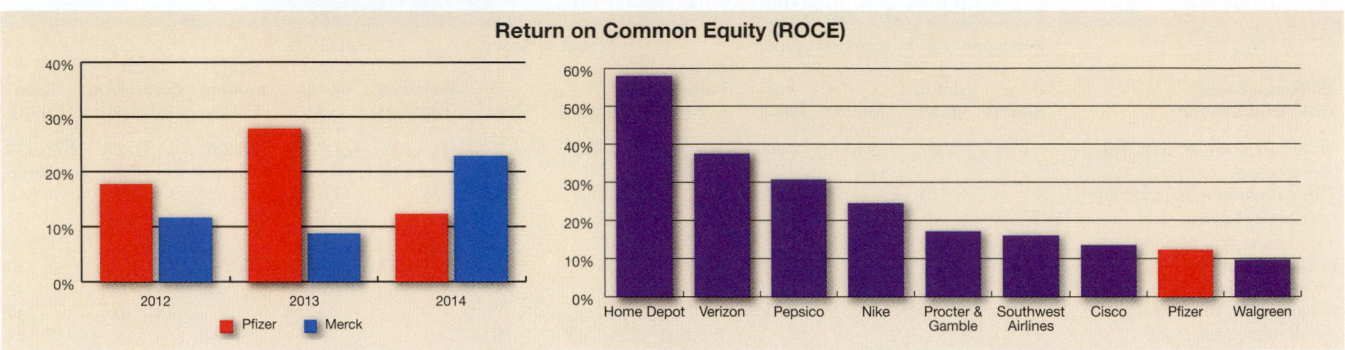

Return on Common Equity (ROCE)

Takeaways   Neither Pfizer's nor Merck's ROCE has been stable for the past few years. The large values in 2013 for Pfizer and in 2014 for Merck reflect unusual gains from the sale of discontinued businesses. Such items are not likely to recur on a regular basis. Relative to other focus companies in this text, Pfizer's ROCE is low. It is about the same as that of Cisco and higher than Walgreens.

Many companies have little or no preferred stock or noncontrolling interests. So the difference between return on common equity (ROCE) and return on equity (ROE) will be immaterial for these firms. When preferred stock is present, ROCE is a more accurate measure of return to common shareholders.

Other Considerations   In Chapter 5, we learned that ROE can be decomposed into two components: return on assets and return on financial leverage. Differences between firms may reflect a difference in performance, or a difference in the reliance on debt financing. A similar division can be done with ROCE with the caveat that ROCE essentially treats preferred stock as debt rather than equity.

One final point: the financial press sometimes refers to a measure called **book value per share**. This amount is the net book value of the company that is available to common shareholders, defined as: stockholders' equity less preferred stock less equity attributable to noncontrolling interest divided by the number of common shares outstanding (issued common shares less treasury shares). Pfizer's 2014 book value per share is computed as: ($71,622 million − $29 million − $321 million)/ (9,110 million shares − 2,819 million shares) = $11.33 book value per common share.

MID-CHAPTER REVIEW 4

The stockholders' equity of Sloan Corporation at December 31, 2014, follows.

Common stock, $5 par value, 400,000 shares authorized; 160,000 shares issued and outstanding...	$800,000
Paid-in capital in excess of par value..	920,000
Retained earnings	513,000

During 2015, the following transactions occurred:

June 28   Declared and issued a 10% common stock dividend when the market value is $11 per share.
Dec. 5   Declared and paid a cash dividend of $1.25 per share.
Dec. 31   Updated retained earnings for net income of $412,000.

Compute the year-ending balance of retained earnings for 2015.

The solution to this review problem can be found on page 560.

EARNINGS PER SHARE

The income statement reports at least one, and potentially two, earnings per share (EPS) numbers: basic and diluted. The difference between the two measures is illustrated as follows:

LO6 Describe and illustrate the basic and diluted earnings per share computations.

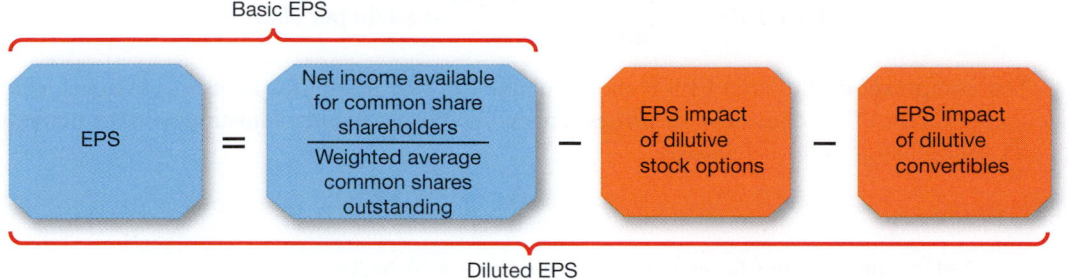

All public companies are required to report basic EPS. If the company has a complex capital structure, it is also required to report diluted EPS. A company is said to have a **complex capital structure** if it has certain *dilutive securities* outstanding. **Dilutive securities** are securities that can be converted into shares of common stock and would therefore reduce (or dilute) the earnings per share upon conversion. The three primary types of dilutive securities are:

- Stock options
- Convertible debt
- Convertible preferred stock

The Appendix at the end of this chapter details the accounting for these securities. A company with none of these dilutive securities outstanding is said to have a **simple capital structure**.

Basic EPS (BEPS) is computed as earnings available for common shareholders (net income less net income attributable to noncontrolling interests and preferred dividends) divided by the weighted average number of common shares outstanding for the year. (The number of shares is "weighted" by the amount of time each share was outstanding during the year.) The subtraction of net income attributable to noncontrolling interests and preferred stock dividends yields the income per common share available for dividend payments to common shareholders. The preferred dividends are subtracted because this portion of net income does not accrue to the common stockholders.

Computation of **Diluted EPS (DEPS)** reflects the added shares that would have been issued if all "in the money" stock options and other convertible securities had been exercised at the beginning of the year. When DEPS is calculated, the corporation needs to consider the maximum potential reduction (dilution) of its BEPS that could occur if the conversion of these securities took place. To do so means that any of these securities that do not reduce BEPS upon conversion are not to be considered converted. The result must be a figure that is lower than BEPS. The actual calculation can be quite complex. This does not detract from the importance of the DEPS value. The diluted earnings per share figure is favored by analysts as a better indicator of performance compared to basic earnings per share. Because reported DEPS never exceeds reported BEPS, the calculation is considered conservative.

Computation and Analysis of EPS

The computation of basic EPS is relatively straightforward, particularly when the firm neither issues nor buys any of its shares during the year. The formula is:

$$\text{Basic EPS (BEPS)} = \frac{\text{Net income available for common shareholders}}{\text{Weighted average number of common shares outstanding}}$$

To illustrate this calculation, assume that United Bridge Corporation reported net income of $200,000 in 2015 and paid $24,000 in preferred dividends. At the beginning of the year, the company had 44,000 shares of common stock outstanding. On June 30 (exactly the midpoint of the year) United Bridge purchased 8,000 shares of stock as treasury stock. Thus, the number of shares outstanding for the first six months of 2015 was 44,000 and, for the second half of the year, the company had 36,000 shares outstanding. The weighted average number of shares outstanding was, therefore, 40,000 [(44,000 + 36,000)/2]. Basic EPS would be calculated as follows:

$$\text{Basic EPS} = \frac{\$200,000 - \$24,000}{40,000 \text{ shares}} = \$4.40 \text{ per share}$$

The computation of diluted EPS is more complex in that it requires adjusting the basic EPS calculation for the effect of dilutive securities. This will typically require adjusting both the numerator and denominator of the calculation.

Diluted earnings per share (DEPS) =

$$\frac{\text{Net income available for common shareholders} + \text{Add-backs}}{\text{Weighted average number of common shares} + \text{Shares of convertible securities and stock options assumed to be converted}}$$

To illustrate, assume that United Bridge Corporation's preferred stock is convertible into 8,000 shares of common stock. To calculate diluted EPS, we must assume that the convertible preferred shares were converted at the beginning of the year. If this had occurred, two things would have been different for United Bridge. First, the weighted average number of shares outstanding would be higher by 8,000 shares. Second, the company would not have paid preferred dividends of $24,000. The resulting calculation would be:

$$\text{Diluted EPS} = \frac{\$200,000}{48,000 \text{ shares}} = \$4.17 \text{ per share}$$

A full description of the procedures for calculating diluted EPS is beyond the scope of this text. However, as the calculation above illustrates, diluted EPS adjusts basic EPS for the effect of dilutive securities. Reported DEPS must be no larger than BEPS to reflect its conservative message.

Pfizer reports both basic and diluted EPS. The table below, drawn from Pfizer's 2014 consolidated income statement, presents its basic and diluted EPS figures.

Year Ended December 31	2014	2013
Earnings per common share—basic		
Income from continuing operations attributable to Pfizer Inc. common shareholders.....	$1.43	$1.67
Discontinued operations—net of tax...	0.01	1.56
Net income attributable to Pfizer Inc. common shareholders.......................	$1.44	$3.23
Earnings per common share—diluted		
Income from continuing operations attributable to Pfizer Inc. common shareholders.....	$1.41	$1.65
Discontinued operations—net of tax...	0.01	1.54
Net income attributable to Pfizer Inc. common shareholders.......................	$1.42	$3.19
Weighted average shares—basic (millions).....................................	6.346	6,813
Weighted average shares—diluted (millions)...................................	6,424	6,895

Several observations should be made regarding Pfizer's EPS disclosures:

1. Pfizer reports basic EPS of $1.44 in 2014 and $3.23 in 2013. Diluted EPS is $0.02 lower and $0.04 lower in 2014 and 2013, respectively. The difference between basic and diluted EPS is caused by the effect of dilutive securities. Specifically, Pfizer has outstanding stock options and convertible preferred stock. Most publicly traded companies have at least one type of dilutive security outstanding. However, the dilutive effect of these securities on Pfizer's EPS is negligible.

2. The income statement further separates these EPS figures into EPS from continuing operations and EPS from discontinued operations. In 2014, discontinued operations increased Pfizer's EPS by $0.01 per share, but the effects of discontinued operations were much larger in 2013. GAAP requires separate reporting of the effects of nonrecurring items on EPS, including discontinued operations (see Chapter 6).

3. Pfizer used weighted average shares outstanding of 6,346 million shares to calculate basic EPS. This number is not the same as the number of shares outstanding in its December 31, 2014 balance sheet. Nor is it the simple average of the beginning and ending numbers of shares outstanding. The precise number of shares used in the EPS calculations requires knowing exactly when common stock and treasury stock transactions occurred during the year so that the weighted average number of shares outstanding can be calculated. Such detailed information is seldom available in a company's 10-K report.

EPS figures are sometimes used as a method of comparing operating results for companies of different sizes under the assumption that the number of shares outstanding is proportional to the income level (that is, a company twice the size of another will report double the income and will have double the common shares outstanding, leaving EPS approximately equal for the two companies). This assumption is erroneous. Management controls the number of common shares outstanding. Different companies also have different philosophies regarding share issuance and repurchase. For example, consider that most companies report annual EPS of less than $5, while **Berkshire Hathaway Inc.** reported EPS of $12,092 for 2014! The large amount occurs because Berkshire Hathaway has so few common shares outstanding, not necessarily because it has stellar profits.

Most analysts prefer to concentrate their attention on diluted EPS versus basic EPS as the more important measure, but the value of the EPS number is influenced by a number of factors including the number of common shares outstanding. For this reason, comparisons are more useful over time than across firms, but a careful reader should differentiate between EPS growth that comes from increases in the numerator and EPS growth that comes from decreases in the denominator. For these reasons, EPS may be of limited use in evaluating a firm's operational performance.

BUSINESS INSIGHT

From 2012 to 2014, **International Business Machines Corp.**'s Basic EPS from continuing operations increased by 5.4%. However, the company's income from continuing operations fell by 7.3% over the same period. The reason for these differing directions is IBM's repurchases of its own stock. The weighted-average number of basic common shares outstanding fell by 12.1% from 2012 to 2014.

CHAPTER-END REVIEW

Petroni Corporation reported net income of $1,750 million in 2015. The weighted average number of common shares outstanding during 2015 was 760 million shares. Petroni paid $40 million in dividends on preferred stock, which was convertible into 10 million shares of common stock.

1. Calculate Petroni's basic earnings per share for 2015.
2. Calculate Petroni's diluted earnings per share for 2015.
3. What EPS numbers should Petroni report on its 2015 income statement?

The solution to this review problem can be found on page 561.

APPENDIX 11A: Dilutive Securities: Further Considerations

Convertible Securities

LO7 Analyze the accounting for convertible securities, stock rights, and stock options.

Convertible securities are debt and equity securities that provide the holder with an option to convert those securities into other securities. Convertible debentures, for example, are debt securities that give the holder the option to convert the debt into common stock at a predetermined conversion price. Preferred stock can also contain a conversion privilege.

To illustrate, assume 5,000 shares of preferred stock were issued at a stated value of $100 per share, with each share convertible into 12 shares of $5 par value common stock. The appropriate journal entry would be:

Cash (+A)..	500,000	
Preferred stock (stated value) (+SE)............................		500,000

Now assume that 2,000 shares are converted to (2,000 × 12) = 24,000 shares of common stock. The appropriate journal entry is:

Preferred stock (stated value) (−SE) 200,000	
Common stock (par $5) (+SE)	10,000
Additional paid-in capital (+SE)....................................	190,000

Conversion privileges offer an additional benefit to the holder of a security. That is, debtholders and preferred stockholders carry senior positions as claimants in bankruptcy, and carry a fixed-interest or dividend yield. With a conversion privilege, they can enjoy the residual benefits of common shareholders should the company perform well.

A conversion option is valuable and yields a higher price for the securities than they would otherwise command. However, conversion privileges impose a cost on common shareholders. That is, the higher market price received for convertible securities is offset by the cost imposed on the subordinate (common) securities. Conversion of these securities into common shares dilutes the ownership percentage of existing holders of the firm's common stock.

Accounting for the issuance of a convertible security is straightforward: the conversion option is *not* valued on the balance sheet unless it is detachable from the security (and, thus, separately saleable). Instead, the convertible preferred stock or convertible debt is recorded just like preferred stock or debt that does not have a conversion feature.

When securities are converted, the book value of the converted security is removed from the balance sheet and a corresponding increase is made to contributed capital. To illustrate the most commonly used method, assume that a company has convertible bonds with a face value of $1,000 and an unamortized premium of $100. Its holders convert them into 20 shares of $10 par value common stock. The financial statement effects and related entries of this conversion would be:

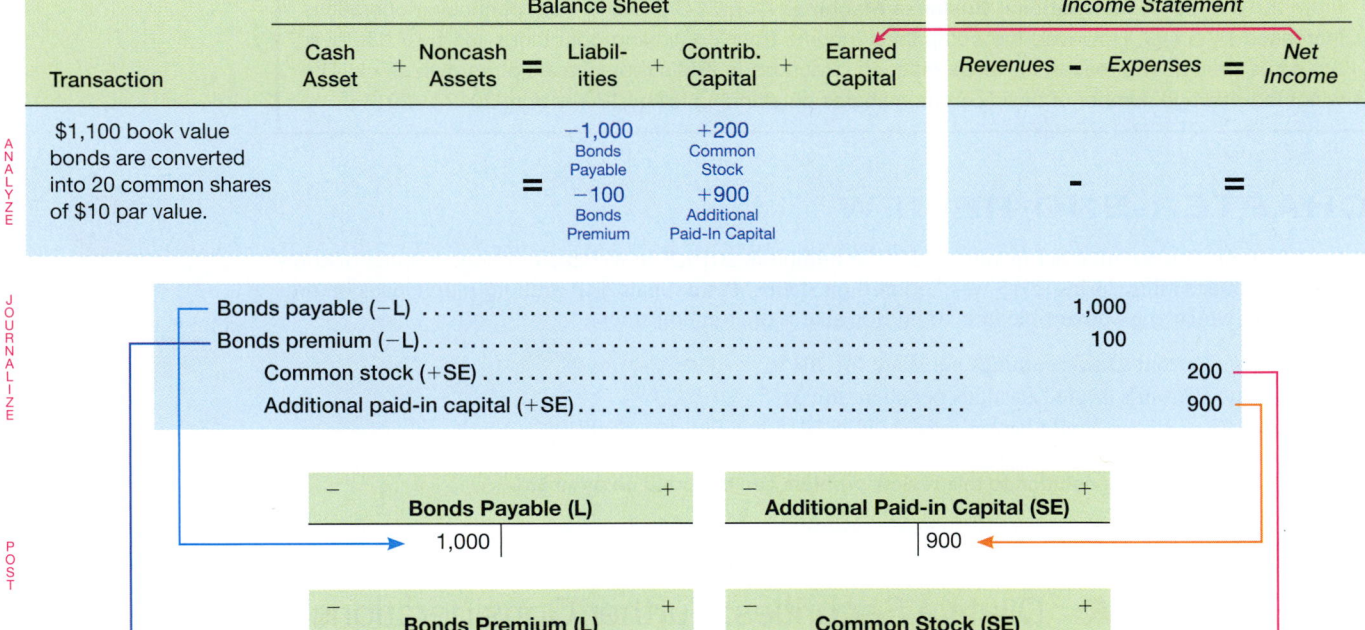

The key financial statement effects of this transaction are:

- The bond's face value ($1,000) and unamortized premium ($100) of the bonds are removed from the balance sheet.
- Common stock increases by the par value of the shares issued (20 shares × $10 par = $200) and additional paid-in capital increases for the balance ($900).
- There is no effect on income from this conversion unless an interest accrual is required.

One final note: the potentially dilutive effect of convertible securities is taken into account in the computation of diluted earnings per share (DEPS). Specifically, the diluted EPS computation assumes conversion at the beginning of the year (or when the security is issued if during the year). The earnings available to common shares in the numerator are increased by any forgone after-tax interest expense or preferred dividends, and the additional shares to be issued in the conversion increase the shares outstanding in the denominator.

Stock Rights

Corporations often issue **stock rights** that give the holder an option to acquire a specified number of shares of capital stock under prescribed conditions and within a stated period. The evidence of stock rights is a certificate called a **stock warrant**. Stock rights are issued for several reasons that include the following:

- To compensate outside parties (such as underwriters, promoters, board members, and other professionals) for services provided to the company;
- As a preemptive right that gives existing stockholders the first chance to buy additional shares when the corporation decides to raise additional equity capital through share issuances;
- To compensate officers and other employees of the corporation (rights in this form are referred to as **stock options**);
- To enhance the marketability of other securities issued by the company (an example is issuing rights to purchase common stock with convertible bonds).

Stock rights or warrants specify the:

- Number of rights represented by the warrant
- Option price per share (which can be zero)
- Number of rights needed to obtain a share of the stock
- Expiration date of the rights
- Instructions for the exercise of rights

Accounting for stock rights is complex. The goals of this discussion are to understand the essence of (1) stock rights issued to current stockholders and (2) stock options issued to employees and others.

Stock rights issued to current stockholders have three important dates: (1) Announcement date of the rights offering; (2) Issuance date of the rights; and (3) Expiration date of the rights. Between the announcement date and the issuance date, the price of the stock will reflect the value of the rights. After the issuance date, the shares and the rights trade separately. Shareholders can exercise their rights, sell their stock, or allow the rights to lapse.

To illustrate, assume on December 10, 2014, a company announces the issue of rights to purchase one additional share of its $5 par value common stock for every 10 shares currently held on January 1, 2015. The exercise price per share is $20 and the rights expire September 1, 2015. Assume further that 7,000 of the rights are exercised.

- No recognition is required at the announcement date and at the issuance date.
- The first entry is made when the first stock right is exercised. We give only the summary entry that would be appropriate after September 1, 2015.

Sept 1: To record the issuance of 7,000 shares of common stock on exercise of stock rights:
The financial statement effects and related entries would be (amounts in millions):

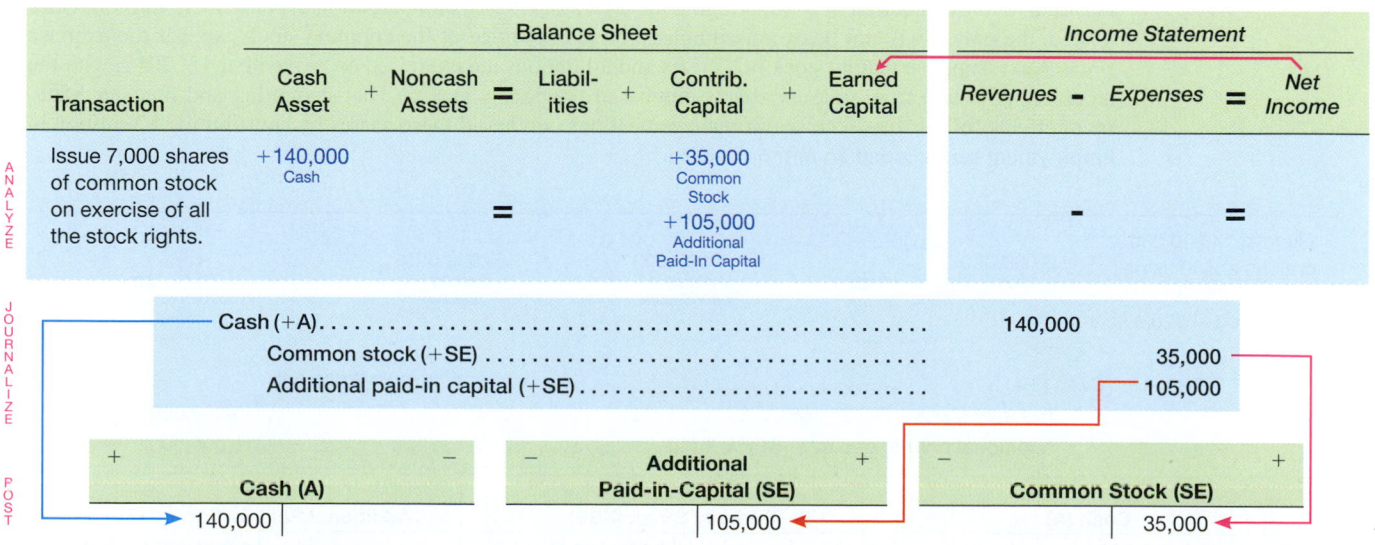

Stock Options

Accounting for stock options has been a contentious issue for a number of years. Accounting standard setters, on the one hand, argue that the options to purchase a corporation's stock at a discount (or even without a discount) are valuable. They point to the willingness of senior management and others to accept stock options instead of cash in payment for services rendered as evidence of their value. Thus, the FASB concluded that the fair value of each stock option award must be recognized as an expense on the firm's income statement.

However, senior managements of start-up firms typically argue that it is necessary in the face of cash shortages to compensate those providing service at least partly using stock options. If these option grants are treated as an expense, it will cause their firms to appear less profitable, thereby stifling investment and business growth. Those arguing against recognizing an expense also point to the difficulties in obtaining precise values for these options.

These difficulties are real, but methods of valuing options do exist that provide reasonable estimates of option values. The FASB decided that such awards are expenses and the expense must be reported at the fair value of the option grant. For example, in Note 13 to its 2014 10-K report, Pfizer reports the fair value of stock option grants to be $196.2 million (44.6 million options granted × $4.40 per option).

Stock option grants normally require a vesting period. The **vesting period** is a period of time during which the employee is not allowed to exercise the stock option. For example, a stock option may expire in 5 years and vest over a period of 3 years. Such an option would be exercisable in the fourth or fifth year of its life. Rather than recognizing the entire option value as compensation expense at the time that the option grant is awarded, GAAP requires that the fair value of the option be recorded ratably over the vesting period.

To illustrate stock option accounting, suppose that on January 1, 2015, a company grants options to purchase 200,000 shares to senior management as part of its performance bonus plan. The options are granted with an exercise price of $30 (the current price), and can be exercised after vesting in 2 years. The firm uses an accepted valuation method (not discussed here) to obtain a fair value of $10 per option. The accounting and financial statement effects and related entries for 2015 would be:

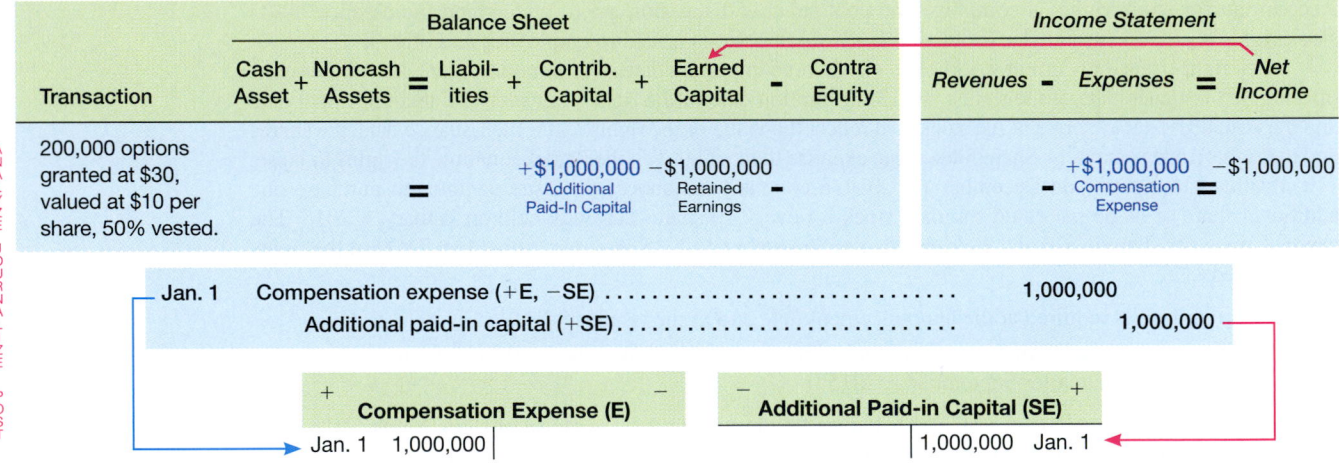

A similar entry is required in 2016, bringing the total stock-based compensation expense to $2 million. Once vested, the option will not be exercised unless the market price of the common stock exceeds the exercise price. Next, suppose that its stock price rises and all options are exercised on November 15, 2017, with the stock being issued from treasury shares purchased previously at $25. The accounting and financial statement effects follow. In effect, senior management has purchased these shares by contributing $2 million in employment services and $6 million in cash.

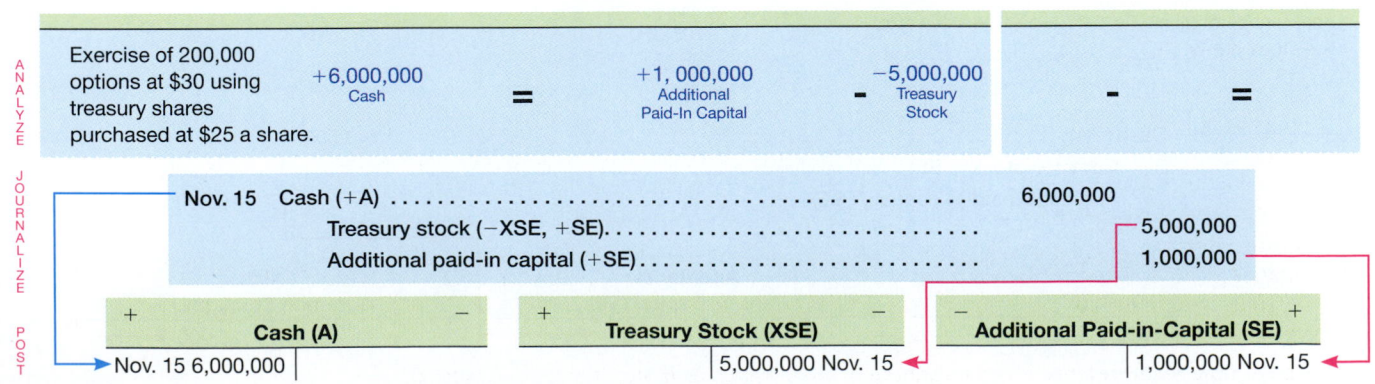

APPENDIX 11A REVIEW

Kallapur, Inc. has issued convertible debentures: each $1,000 bond is convertible into 200 shares of $1 par common stock. Assume that the bonds were sold at a discount, and that each bond has a current unamortized discount equal to $150.

REQUIRED

1. Using the financial statement effects template, illustrate the effects of the conversion of one of its bonds.
2. Prepare journal entries for the transaction assuming conversion of one bond.
3. Post the journal entries to the related T-accounts.

The solution to this review problem can be found on page 561.

SUMMARY

Describe business financing through stock issuances. (p. 518)   **LO1**

- Contributed capital represents the cumulative cash (or other asset) inflow that the company has received from the sale of various classes of stock, preferred and common.

- Preferred stock receives preference in terms of dividends before common and, if cumulative, receives all dividends not paid in the past before common dividends can be paid. Preferred stock can also be designated as convertible into common stock at the holder's option and at a predetermined conversion ratio. Voting privileges reside only with the common stock.

Explain and account for the issuance and repurchase of stock. (p. 521)   **LO2**

- Common stock is often repurchased by the firm for use in stock award programs or to signal management confidence in the company or simply to return cash to shareholders. Repurchased stock is either cancelled or held for reissue. The repurchase is debited to a contra equity account titled treasury stock.

Describe how operations increase the equity of a business. (p. 525)   **LO3**

- Earned capital includes retained earnings, which represents the cumulative profit that has been retained by the company. Earned capital is increased by income earned and decreased by losses and dividends declared by the firm. Earned capital also includes the effects of items included in other comprehensive income.

Explain and account for dividends and stock splits. (p. 525)   **LO4**

- Dividends in the form of stock decrease retained earnings and increase contributed capital by an equivalent amount.

- A stock split is a proportionate distribution similar in substance to a stock dividend. The new number of shares outstanding must be disclosed. Otherwise, no further accounting is required unless the state of incorporation requires that the par value be proportionally adjusted.

Define and illustrate comprehensive income. (p. 530)   **LO5**

- Comprehensive income includes several additional items not recognized in net income including: adjustments for changes in foreign exchange rates, unrealized changes in available-for-sale securities, and pension liability adjustments. The concept is designed to highlight impacts on net assets that are beyond management's control.

Describe and illustrate the basic and diluted earnings per share computations. (p. 533)   **LO6**

- Earnings per share is a closely watched number reported for all publicly traded firms. Basic EPS is computed as the ratio of net income (less preferred dividends and noncontrolling interests) to the weighted average number of outstanding shares for the period. The value of this performance metric is subject to all the difficulties in measuring net income including the fact that net income can increase due to an acquisition or divestiture that can have no impact on the number of outstanding shares.

- Most analysts are more interested in what is termed diluted earnings per share. This conservative calculation, which, if reported, never exceeds basic EPS, reflects the maximum reduction in basic EPS possible assuming conversion of the convertible securities.

- Stock options that are "in the money" are always dilutive.

- Convertible securities that would be antidilutive are treated as if they were not converted.

LO7 **Appendix 11A: Analyze the accounting for convertible securities, stock rights, and stock options. (p. 535)**

- Convertible securities are debt and equity instruments, including stock rights, that allow these securities to be exchanged for other securities, typically common stock. The convertible feature adds value to the security to which it is attached.

- Stock options, one form of stock right, allow the holders to exchange them at a specified (strike) price for common stock. This right is valuable and should create an expense when granted to an employee or other individual. Expense recognition is appropriate, using the value obtained by applying an options-pricing model, even though the calculation is not precise. The option will not be exercised unless the market price of the common stock exceeds the strike price.

- Convertible preferred stock and convertible debt securities need to be considered in the calculation of DEPS to the extent conversion reduces reported BEPS.

GUIDANCE ANSWERS . . . YOU MAKE THE CALL

You are the Chief Financial Officer Several points must be considered. (1) Treasury shares are likely to prop up earnings per share (EPS). While the numerator (earnings) is likely dampened by the use of cash for the stock repurchase, EPS is likely to increase because of the reduced shares in the denominator. (2) If the shares are sufficiently undervalued (in management's opinion), the stock repurchase and subsequent resale can provide a better return than some alternative investments. (3) Stock repurchases send a strong signal to the market that management feels its stock is undervalued. This is more credible than merely making that argument with analysts. On the other hand, company cash is diverted from other investments. This is bothersome if such investments are mutually exclusive either now or in the future.

KEY RATIOS

Net income available for common shareholders =
Net income − Net income attributable to noncontrolling interests − Preferred dividends

$$\text{Return on Common Equity (ROCE)} = \frac{\text{Net income available for common shareholders}}{\text{Average common shareholders' equity}}$$

$$\text{Basic earnings per share (BEPS)} = \frac{\text{Net income available for common shareholders}}{\text{Weighted average number of common shares outstanding}}$$

Diluted earnings per share (DEPS) =

$$\frac{\text{Net income available for common shareholders} + \text{Add-backs}}{\text{Weighted average number of common shares} + \text{Shares of convertible securities and stock options assumed to be converted}}$$

KEY TERMS

Accumulated other comprehensive income (p. 530)
Basic EPS (p. 533)
Book value per share (p. 532)
Call feature (p. 520)
Common stock (p. 519)

Complex capital structure (p. 533)
Comprehensive income (p. 530)
Contributed capital (p. 518)
Conversion feature (p. 521)
Convertible securities (p. 535)
Diluted EPS (p. 533)
Dilutive securities (p. 533)

Dividend preference (p. 520)
Earned capital (p. 519)
Liquidating value (p. 520)
Liquidation preference (p. 520)
Noncontrolling interest (p. 519)
Participation feature (p. 521)
Par value (p. 519)

Assignments with the **logo in the margin are available in** BusinessCourse**.**
See the Preface of the book for details.

MULTIPLE CHOICE

1. Suppose Pfizer issues 100,000 shares of its common stock, $0.05 par value, to obtain a warehouse and the accompanying land when the price of the stock is $22.00. Which one of the following statements is not true?
    a. The newly acquired assets will increase total assets by $2.2 million.
    b. Retained earnings are unaffected.
    c. The common stock account increases by $5,000.
    d. Total shareholders' equity increases by $2,195,000.

2. Assume Pfizer resells 10,000 shares of its stock that were purchased when the market price of the stock was $25. If the shares are resold for $22, which one of the following statements holds?
    a. Additional paid-in capital decreases by $30,000.
    b. The treasury stock account increases by $30,000.
    c. Additional paid-in capital increases by $30,000.
    d. The treasury stock account decreases by $30,000.

3. Suppose Pfizer declares a 200,000 common stock dividend (par $0.05) when the market value of a share is $20.00. Which one of the following statements is true?
    a. The common stock account increases by $10,000.
    b. Additional paid-in capital decreases by $3.99 million.
    c. Retained earnings increases by $4 million.
    d. Additional paid-in capital increases by $4 million.

4. Which of the following statements is true?
    a. When a *large stock dividend* is paid, retained earnings are reduced by the market value of the shares distributed.
    b. Neither stock dividends nor stock splits affect basic earnings per share calculations.
    c. A three-for-one stock split increases the total outstanding shares by 300%.
    d. A stock split has no financial statement effects because it is not a monetary transaction.

5. Which of the following statements is not true in relation to diluted EPS (DEPS)?
    a. Stock options that are in the money will always cause DEPS to be less than basic EPS.
    b. Convertible bonds, if dilutive, will cause changes in both the numerator and the denominator of DEPS.
    c. Stock analysts tend to concentrate their attention on DEPS instead of basic EPS.
    d. A company's only equity contract that can lead to dilution is stock options.

Multiple Choice Answers
1. d 2. a 3. a 4. d 5. d

QUESTIONS

Q11-1. Define *par value stock*. What is the significance of a stock's par value from an accounting and analysis perspective?

Q11-2. What are the basic differences between preferred stock and common stock? What are the typical features of preferred stock?

Q11-3. What features make preferred stock similar to debt? Similar to common stock?

Q11-4. What is meant by dividend arrearage on preferred stock? If dividends are two years in arrears on $500,000 of 6% preferred stock, and dividends are declared at the end of this year, what amount of total dividends must preferred shareholders receive before any distributions are made to common shareholders?

Q11-5. Distinguish between authorized stock and issued stock. Why might the number of shares issued be more than the number of shares outstanding?

Q11-6. Describe the difference between contributed capital and earned capital. Specifically, how can earned capital be considered as an investment by the company's shareholders?

Q11-7. How does the account "additional paid-in capital" (APIC) arise? What inferences, if any, can you draw from the amount of APIC as reported on the balance sheet relative to the common stock amount in relation to the financial condition of the company?

Q11-8. Define *stock split*. What are the major reasons for a stock split?

Q11-9. Define *treasury stock*. Why might a corporation acquire treasury stock? How is treasury stock reported in the balance sheet?

Q11-10. If a corporation purchases 600 shares of its own common stock at $10 per share and resells them at $14 per share, where would the $2,400 increase in capital be reported in the financial statements? Why is no gain reported?

Q11-11. A corporation has total stockholders' equity of $4,628,000 and one class of $2 par value common stock. The corporation has 500,000 shares authorized; 300,000 shares issued; 260,000 shares outstanding; and 40,000 shares as treasury stock. What is its book value per share?

Q11-12. What is a stock dividend? How does a common stock dividend distributed to common shareholders affect their respective ownership interests?

Q11-13. What is the difference between the accounting for a small stock dividend and the accounting for a large stock dividend?

Q11-14. Employee stock options have a potentially dilutive effect on earnings per share (EPS) that is recognized in the diluted EPS computation. What can companies do to offset these dilutive effects and how might this action affect the balance sheet?

Q11-15. What information is reported in a statement of stockholders' equity?

Q11-16. What items are typically reported under the stockholders' equity category of other comprehensive income (OCI)?

Q11-17. What is a stock option vesting period? How does the vesting period affect the recognition of compensation expense for stock options?

Q11-18. Describe the accounting for a convertible bond. Would this accounting ever result in the recognition of a gain in the income statement?

MINI EXERCISES

LO1

M11-19. Analyzing and Identifying Financial Statement Effects of Stock Issuances

On June 1, Beatty Corp. issues (*a*) 8,000 shares of $50 par value preferred stock at $68 cash per share and it issues (*b*) 12,000 shares of $1 par value common stock at $10 cash per share.

a. Do these transactions increase contributed capital or earned capital?

b. What is the effect of these transactions on Beatty Corp.'s income statement?

c. What are the differences between the preferred stock and the common stock issued by Beatty Corp.?

LO2

M11-20. Analyzing and Identifying Financial Statement Effects of Stock Issuances

On September 1, Magliolo, Inc., (*a*) issues 18,000 shares of $10 par value preferred stock at $48 cash per share and (*b*) issues 120,000 shares of $2 par value common stock at $37 cash per share.

a. Using the financial statement effects template, illustrate the effects of these two issuances.

b. Prepare the journal entries for the two issuances.

c. Post the journal entries from *b* to the related T-accounts.

LO2

M11-21. Distinguishing between Common Stock and Additional Paid-in Capital

Following is the stockholders' equity section from the **Cisco Systems, Inc.,** balance sheet (in millions, except par value).

Shareholders' equity	July 26, 2014
Preferred stock, no par value: 5 shares authorized; none issued and outstanding	$ —
Common stock and additional paid-in capital, $0.001 par value: 20,000 shares authorized; 5,107 shares issued and outstanding	41,884
Retained earnings	14,093
Accumulated other comprehensive income.	677
Total Cisco shareholders' equity	56,654
Noncontrolling interests	7
Total equity.	$56,661

For the $41,884 million reported as "common stock and additional paid-in capital," what portion is common stock and what portion is additional paid-in capital? Explain.

M11-22. Identifying and Analyzing Financial Statement Effects of Stock Issuance and Repurchase   **LO2**

On January 1, 2016, Bartov Company issues 5,000 shares of $100 par value preferred stock at $250 cash per share. On March 1, the company repurchases 5,000 shares of previously issued $1 par value common stock at $83 cash per share.

    a.   Using the financial statement effects template, illustrate the effects of these two transactions.
    b.   Prepare the journal entries for the two transactions.
    c.   Post the journal entries from *b* to the related T-accounts.

M11-23. Assessing the Financial Statement Effects of a Stock Split   **LO4**

In its second quarter 2015 10-Q, **Starbucks Corporation** included the following information:

Starbucks Corporation
NASDAQ :: SBUX

> On April 9, 2015, we effected a two-for-one stock split of our $0.001 par value common stock for shareholders of record as of March 30, 2015. All share and per-share data in our consolidated financial statements and notes has been retroactively adjusted to reflect this stock split.

Starbucks effected this stock split as a large stock dividend. What changes has Starbucks made to its balance sheet as a result of this action?

M11-24. Computing Basic and Diluted Earnings per Share   **LO2, 6**

Zeller Corporation began 2015 with 120,000 shares of common stock and 16,000 shares of convertible preferred stock outstanding. On March 1 an additional 10,000 shares of common stock were issued. On August 1, another 16,000 shares of common stock were issued. On November 1, 6,000 shares of common stock were acquired for the treasury. The preferred stock has a $2 per-share dividend rate, and each share may be converted into one share of common stock. Zeller Corporation's 2015 net income is $501,000.

    a.   Compute basic earnings per share for 2015.
    b.   Compute diluted earnings per share for 2015.
    c.   If the preferred stock were not convertible, Zeller Corporation would have a simple capital structure. How would this change Zeller's earnings per share presentation?

M11-25. Assessing Common Stock and Treasury Stock Balances   **LO2, 6**

Following is the stockholders' equity section from the **Toyota Motor Corporation**'s balance sheet for the 2015 fiscal year, which ended on March 31, 2015.

Toyota Motor
Corporation (ADR)
NYSE :: TM

Toyota Motor Corporation Shareholders' Equity (Millions of Yen)	March 31, 2015
Common stock, no par value: authorized 10,000,000,000 shares, issued 3,417,997,492 shares at March 31, 2015.	¥ 397,050
Additional paid-in capital	547,054
Retained earnings	15,591,947
Accumulated other comprehensive income (loss)	1,477,545
Treasury stock, at cost: 271,183,861 shares at March 31, 2015	(1,225,465)
Total Toyota Motor Corporation shareholders' equity	¥16,788,131

    a.   Toyota has repurchased 271,183,861 shares that comprise its March 31, 2015 treasury stock account. Compute the number of outstanding shares as of March 31, 2015.
    b.   Assume that all of this treasury stock had been acquired in one purchase on July 1, 2014. What would have been the effect on the denominator of the basic EPS calculation?

LO4   **M11-26. Identifying and Analyzing Financial Statement Effects of Cash Dividends**

Freid Corp. has outstanding 6,000 shares of $50 par value, 6% preferred stock, and 40,000 shares of $1 par value common stock. The company has $328,000 of retained earnings. At year-end, the company declares and pays the regular $3 per share cash dividend on preferred stock and a $2.20 per share cash dividend on common stock.

a. Using the financial statement effects template, illustrate the effects of these two dividend payments.
b. Prepare the journal entries for the two dividend payments.
c. Post the journal entries from b to the related T-accounts.

LO4   **M11-27. Analyzing and Identifying Financial Statement Effects of Stock Dividends**

Dutta Corp. has outstanding 70,000 shares of $5 par value common stock. At year-end, the company declares and issues a 4% common stock dividend when the market price of the stock is $21 per share.

a. Using the financial statement effects template, illustrate the effects of this dividend declaration and payment.
b. Prepare the journal entries for the stock dividend declaration and payment.
c. Post the journal entries from b to the related T-accounts.

LO4   **M11-28. Analyzing, Identifying, and Explaining the Effects of a Stock Split**

On September 1, Weiss Company has 250,000 shares of $15 par value ($165 market value) common stock that are issued and outstanding. Its balance sheet on that date shows the following account balances relating to the common stock.

Common stock.	$3,750,000
Paid-in capital in excess of par value.	2,250,000

On September 2, Weiss splits its stock 3-for-2 and reduces the par value to $10 per share.

a. How many shares of common stock are issued and outstanding immediately after the stock split?
b. What is the dollar balance of the common stock account immediately after the stock split?
c. What is the likely reason that Weiss Company split its stock?

LO4   **M11-29. Distributing Cash Dividends to Preferred and Common Shareholders**

Dechow Company has outstanding 20,000 shares of $50 par value, 6% cumulative preferred stock, and 80,000 shares of $10 par value common stock. The company declares and pays cash dividends amounting to $160,000.

a. If no arrearage on the preferred stock exists, how much in total dividends, and in dividends per share, is paid to each class of stock?
b. If one year's dividend arrearage on the preferred stock exists, how much in total dividends, and in dividends per share, is paid to each class of stock?

LO3, 4   **M11-30. Analyzing and Preparing a Retained Earnings Reconciliation**

Use the following data to prepare the 2015 retained earnings reconciliation for Bamber Company.

Total retained earnings, December 31, 2014	$347,000
Stock dividends declared and paid in 2015.	28,000
Cash dividends declared and paid in 2015	35,000
Net income for 2015.	94,000

LO4   **M11-31. Accounting for Large Stock Dividend and Stock Split**

Watts Corporation has 40,000 shares of $10 par value common stock outstanding and retained earnings of $820,000. The company declares a 100% stock dividend. The market price at the declaration is $17 per share.

a. Prepare the general journal entry for the stock dividend.
b. Assume that the company splits its stock two shares for one share and reduces the par value from $10 to $5 rather than declaring a 100% stock dividend. How does the accounting for the stock split differ from the accounting for the 100% stock dividend?

M11-32. Computing Basic and Diluted Earnings per Share

During 2015, Park Corporation had 50,000 shares of $10 par value common stock and 10,000 shares of 8%, $50 par value convertible preferred stock outstanding. Each share of preferred stock may be converted into three shares of common stock. Park Corporation's 2015 net income was $440,000.

a. Compute the basic earnings per share for 2015.
b. Compute the diluted earnings per share for 2015.

LO6

M11-33. Computing Earnings per Share

Kingery Corporation began the calendar (and fiscal) year with a simple structure consisting of 38,000 shares of common stock outstanding. On May 1, 10,000 additional shares were issued, and another 1,000 shares were issued on September 1. The company had a net income for the year of $234,000.

a. Compute the earnings per share of common stock.
b. Assume that the company also had 6,000 shares of 6%, $50 par value cumulative preferred stock outstanding throughout the year. Compute the basic earnings per share of common stock.

LO6

M11-34. Defining and Computing Earnings per Share

Siemens AG reports the following basic and diluted earnings per share in its 2014 annual report.

LO6

Siemens AG (ADR)
OTCMKTS :: SIEGY

(shares in thousands; earnings per share in €)	Year Ended September 30, 2014	2013
Income from continuing operations attributable to shareholders of Siemens AG ...	€ 5,267	€ 4,059
Weighted average shares outstanding—basic............................	843,449	843,819
Effect of dilutive share-based payment	8,485	8,433
Weighted average shares outstanding—diluted	€851,934	€852,252
Basic earnings per share (from continuing operations)	€ 6.24	€ 4.81
Diluted earnings per share (from continuing operations).....................	€ 6.18	€ 4.76

a. Describe the accounting definitions for basic and diluted earnings per share.
b. Identify the Siemens numbers that make up both EPS computations.
c. What calculation limits the reported value of diluted EPS?

M11-35. Analyzing Stock Option Expense for Income

Merck & Co., Inc., reported net income attributable to Merck & Co., Inc. of $11,920 million for the 2014 fiscal year. Its 2014 10-K report contained the following information regarding its stock options.

LO7

Merck & Co.
NYSE :: MRK

Employee stock options are granted to purchase shares of Company stock at the fair market value at the time of grant. These awards generally vest one-third each year over a three-year period, with a contractual term of 7-10 years . . . The weighted average exercise price of options granted in 2014 was $58.14 per option . . . The weighted average fair value of options granted in 2014 was $6.79 per option.

a. Merck granted 4,872,000 options to employees in 2014. Using a journal entry, show how the stock option grants would be recorded in 2014. (Assume all grants took place on January 1, 2014.)
b. How does the granting of stock options affect EPS?
c. Merck employees exercised 39,293,000 options in 2014, paying a total of $1,560 million in cash to the company. Using a summary journal entry, show how these option exercises would be recorded in 2014.
d. How does the exercise of stock options affect EPS?

M11-36. Examining the Effect of Stock Transactions

Year 1: Noreen Company issues 10,000 shares of its no-par common stock for $30/share in cash.
Year 2: Noreen Company buys 1,000 shares of its no-par common stock for $28/share in cash.
Year 3: Noreen Company declares but has not yet paid a dividend on its no-par common stock of $2 per share. The company's basic earnings per share were $10 in the third year.

LO2, 4, 6

Indicate the effect (increase, decrease, no effect) of each of these stock decisions for each year on the items listed.

Year	Total Assets	Total Liabilities	Total Stockholders' Equity	EPS	Operating Income
1					
2					
3					

LO1, 2, 3, 6

M11-37. Reporting Stockholders' Equity

Bonner Company began business this year and immediately sold 600,000 common shares for $18,000,000 cash and paid $1,000,000 in common dividends. At midyear, the firm bought back some of its own shares. The company reports the following additional information at year-end:

Net income	$5,000,000
Common stock, at par	$6,000,000
Retained earnings beginning of year	$ 0
Common shares authorized:	1,000,000
Common shares outstanding at year's end:	550,000

a. What was the average sales price of a common share when issued?

b. What is the par value of the common?

c. How much is in the Additional paid-in capital account at the end of the year?

d. Determine the retained earnings amount at the end of the year.

e. How many shares of stock are in the treasury at the end of the year?

f. Compute BEPS.

LO6

JetBlue
NASDAQ :: JBLU

M11-38. Analyzing Earnings Per Share Effects of Convertible Securities

JetBlue Airways Corporation reports the following data in its 2014 10-K. The data relate to the corporation's computation of its earnings per share calculations. (Dollar and share data are in millions.)

Numerator:	**2014**
Net income	$401
Effect of dilutive securities:	
Interest on convertible debt, net of income taxes and profit sharing	7
Net income applicable to common stockholders after assumed conversions for diluted earnings per share	$408
Denominator:	
Weighted average shares outstanding for basic earnings per share	294.7
Effect of dilutive securities:	
Employee stock options and restricted stock units	2.4
Convertible debt	46.2
Adjusted weighted average shares outstanding and assumed conversions for diluted earnings per share	343.3

REQUIRED

a. What is the objective behind the calculation of diluted EPS?

b. Calculate JetBlue's basic EPS.

c. Calculate JetBlue's diluted EPS.

d. JetBlue excluded 6.9 million stock options from the computation of diluted EPS. Under what circumstances would this be appropriate?

E11-39. **Identifying and Analyzing Financial Statement Effects of Stock Transactions**   **LO2**
Lipe Company reports the following transactions relating to its stock accounts.

Feb. 20   Issued 10,000 shares of $1 par value common stock at $25 cash per share.
Feb. 21   Issued 15,000 shares of $100 par value, 8% preferred stock at $275 cash per share.
Jun. 30   Purchased 2,000 shares of its own common stock at $15 cash per share.
Sep. 25   Sold 1,000 shares of the treasury stock at $21 cash per share.

   a.   Using the financial statement effects template, illustrate the effects of these transactions.
   b.   Prepare the journal entries for these transactions.
   c.   Post the journal entries from *b* to the related T-accounts.

E11-40. **Analyzing and Identifying Financial Statement Effects of Stock Transactions**   **LO2**
McNichols Corp. reports the following transactions relating to its stock accounts.

Jan. 15   Issued 25,000 shares of $5 par value common stock at $17 cash per share.
Jan. 20   Issued 6,000 shares of $50 par value, 8% preferred stock at $78 cash per share.
Mar. 31   Purchased 3,000 shares of its own common stock at $20 cash per share.
June 25   Sold 2,000 shares of the treasury stock at $26 cash per share.
July 15   Sold the remaining 1,000 shares of treasury stock at $19 cash per share.

   a.   Using the financial statement effects template, illustrate the effects of these transactions.
   b.   Prepare the journal entries for these transactions.
   c.   Post the journal entries from *b* to the related T-accounts.

E11-41. **Analyzing and Computing Average Issue Price and Treasury Stock Cost**   **LO1, 2, 6**
Following is the stockholders' equity section from the **The Coca-Cola Company** 2014 balance
sheet. (All amounts in millions except par value.)

The Coca-Cola
Company
NYSE :: KO

The Coca-Cola Company Shareowners' Equity	December 31, 2014
Common stock—$0.25 par value; authorized—11,200 shares; issued—7,040 shares....	$ 1,760
Capital surplus	13,154
Reinvested earnings.	63,408
Accumulated other comprehensive income (loss)	(5,777)
Treasury stock, at cost—2,674 shares.	(42,225)
Equity attributable to shareowners of The Coca-Cola Company	$30,320

   a.   Compute the number of shares outstanding.
   b.   At what average price were the Coca-Cola shares issued?
   c.   At what average cost were the Coca-Cola treasury stock shares purchased?
   d.   How should treasury stock be treated in calculating EPS?

E11-42. **Analyzing and Distributing Cash Dividends to Preferred and Common Stocks**   **LO4**
Moser Company began business on March 1, 2015. At that time, it issued 20,000 shares of $60
par value, 7% cumulative preferred stock and 100,000 shares of $5 par value common stock.
Through the end of 2017, there has been no change in the number of preferred and common shares
outstanding.

   a.   Assume that Moser declared and paid cash dividends of $0 in 2015, $183,000 in 2016, and
$200,000 in 2017. Compute the total cash dividends and the dividends per share paid to each
class of stock in 2015, 2016, and 2017.
   b.   Assume that Moser declared and paid cash dividends of $0 in 2015, $84,000 in 2016, and
$150,000 in 2017. Compute the total cash dividends and the dividends per share paid to each
class of stock in 2015, 2016, and 2017.

E11-43. **Computing Basic and Diluted Earnings per Share**   **LO6**
Nichols Corporation began the year 2015 with 25,000 shares of common stock and 5,000 shares
of convertible preferred stock outstanding. On May 1, an additional 9,000 shares of common
stock were issued. On July 1, 6,000 shares of common stock were acquired for the treasury. On
September 1, the 6,000 treasury shares of common stock were reissued. The preferred stock has

a $4 per-share dividend rate, and each share may be converted into two shares of common stock. Nichols Corporation's 2015 net income is $230,000.

    a. Compute earnings per share for 2015.

    b. Compute diluted earnings per share for 2015.

    c. If the preferred stock were not convertible, Nichols Corporation would have a simple capital structure. How would this change Nichols's earnings per share presentation?

LO4, 6

E11-44. Analyzing and Distributing Cash Dividends to Preferred and Common Stocks

Potter Company has outstanding 15,000 shares of $50 par value, 8% preferred stock and 50,000 shares of $5 par value common stock. During its first three years in business, it declared and paid no cash dividends in the first year, $280,000 in the second year, and $60,000 in the third year.

    a. If the preferred stock is cumulative, determine the total amount of cash dividends paid to each class of stock in each of the three years.

    b. If the preferred stock is noncumulative, determine the total amount of cash dividends paid to each class of stock in each of the three years.

    c. How should each type of preferred dividends be treated in calculating EPS?

LO1, 2

Chipotle Mexican Grill
NYSE :: CMG

E11-45. Analyzing and Computing Issue Price, Treasury Stock Cost, and Shares Outstanding

The following is the stockholders' equity section from **Chipotle Mexican Grill, Inc.**'s balance sheet (in thousands, except per share data).

Shareholders' Equity	December 31, 2014
Preferred stock, $0.01 par value, 600,000 shares authorized, no shares issued as of December 31, 2014	$ —
Common stock, $0.01 par value, 230,000 shares authorized, and 35,394 shares issued as of December 31, 2014	354
Additional paid-in capital	1,038,932
Treasury stock, at cost, 4,367 common shares at December 31, 2014	(748,759)
Accumulated other comprehensive income	(429)
Retained earnings	1,722,271
Total shareholders' equity	$2,012,369

    a. Show the computation to derive the $354 thousand for common stock.

    b. At what average price has Chipotle issued its common stock?

    c. How many shares of Chipotle common stock are outstanding as of December 31, 2014?

    d. At what average cost has Chipotle repurchased its treasury stock as of December 31, 2014?

    e. Give three reasons why a company such as Chipotle would want to repurchase almost $750 million of its common stock.

LO4

E11-46. Analyzing and Distributing Cash Dividends to Preferred and Common Stocks

Skinner Company began business on June 30, 2015. At that time, it issued 18,000 shares of $50 par value, 6% cumulative preferred stock and 90,000 shares of $10 par value common stock. Through the end of 2017, there has been no change in the number of preferred and common shares outstanding.

    a. Assume that Skinner declared and paid cash dividends of $63,000 in 2015, $0 in 2016, and $378,000 in 2017. Compute the total cash dividends and the dividends per share paid to each class of stock in 2015, 2016, and 2017.

    b. Assume that Skinner declared and paid cash dividends of $0 in 2015, $108,000 in 2016, and $189,000 in 2017. Compute the total cash dividends and the dividends per share paid to each class of stock in 2015, 2016, and 2017.

LO4

E11-47. Analyzing and Identifying Financial Statement Effects of Dividends

Chaney Company has outstanding 25,000 shares of $10 par value common stock. It also has $405,000 of retained earnings. Near the current year-end, the company declares and pays a cash dividend of $1.90 per share and declares and issues a 4% stock dividend. The market price of the stock at the declaration date is $35 per share.

    a. Using the financial statement effects template, illustrate the effects of these two separate dividends.

    b. Prepare the journal entries for these two separate dividend transactions.

    c. Post the journal entries from *b* to the related T-accounts.

E11-48. Identifying and Analyzing Financial Statement Effects of Dividends
The stockholders' equity of Palepu Company at December 31, 2015, appears below.

LO3, 4

Common stock, $10 par value, 200,000 shares authorized;	
80,000 shares issued and outstanding	$800,000
Paid-in capital in excess of par value.	480,000
Retained earnings	305,000

During 2016, the following transactions occurred:

May 12   Declared and issued a 7% stock dividend; the common stock market value was $18 per share.

Dec. 31   Declared and paid a cash dividend of 75 cents per share.

a.   Using the financial statement effects template, illustrate the effects of these transactions.
b.   Prepare the journal entries for these transactions.
c.   Post the journal entries from b to the related T-accounts.
d.   Prepare a retained earnings reconciliation for 2016 assuming that the company reports 2016 net income of $283,000.

E11-49. Analyzing and Identifying Financial Statement Effects of Dividends
The stockholders' equity of Kinney Company at December 31, 2015, is shown below:

LO3, 4

5% preferred stock, $100 par value, 10,000 shares authorized;	
4,000 shares issued and outstanding	$ 400,000
Common stock, $5 par value, 200,000 shares authorized;	
50,000 shares issued and outstanding	250,000
Paid-in capital in excess of par value—preferred stock.	40,000
Paid-in capital in excess of par value—common stock.	300,000
Retained earnings	656,000
Total stockholders' equity	$1,646,000

The following transactions, among others, occurred during 2016.

Apr. 1   Declared and issued a 100% stock dividend on all outstanding shares of common stock. The market value of the stock was $11 per share.

Dec. 7   Declared and issued a 3% stock dividend on all outstanding shares of common stock. The market value of the stock was $14 per share.

Dec. 20   Declared and paid (1) the annual cash dividend on the preferred stock and (2) a cash dividend of 80 cents per common share.

a.   Using the financial statement effects template, illustrate the effects of these transactions.
b.   Prepare the journal entries for these transactions.
c.   Post the journal entries from b to the related T-accounts.
d.   Prepare a 2016 retained earnings reconciliation assuming that the company reports 2016 net income of $253,000.

E11-50. Analyzing, Identifying, and Explaining the Effects of a Stock Split
On March 1 of the current year, Xie Company has 400,000 shares of $20 par value common stock that are issued and outstanding. Its balance sheet shows the following account balances relating to common stock.

LO4, 6

Common stock.	$8,000,000
Paid-in capital in excess of par value.	3,400,000

On March 2, Xie Company splits its common stock 2-for-1 and reduces the par value to $10 per share.

a.   How many shares of common stock are issued and outstanding immediately after the stock split?
b.   What is the dollar balance in its common stock account immediately after the stock split?
c.   What is the dollar balance in its paid-in capital in excess of par value account immediately after the stock split?
d.   What is the effect of a stock split on the calculation of EPS?

LO3, 4

Intuit Inc.
NASDAQ :: INTU

E11-51. Analyzing and Computing Dividends and Effect of Options Exercises

Following is the stockholders' equity section of the **Intuit Inc.** balance sheet (dollars in millions, except par value; shares in thousands). Changes in the company's outstanding shares are due to (1) treasury share purchases by the company and (2) issues of treasury shares for employee stock options.

Stockholders' Equity ($ millions)	July 31, 2014	July 31, 2013
Preferred stock, $0.01 par value		
Authorized—1,345 shares total; 145 shares designated Series A;		
250 shares designated Series B Junior Participating		
Issued and outstanding—none.	$ —	$ —
Common stock, $0.01 par value		
Authorized—750,000 shares		
Outstanding—284,950 shares at July 31, 2014 and 299,503 shares at		
July 31, 2013.	3	3
Additional paid-in capital	3,558	3,198
Treasury stock, at cost.	(6,430)	(4,952)
Accumulated other comprehensive income (loss)	(2)	20
Retained earnings	5,949	5,262
Total stockholders' equity	**$3,078**	**$3,531**

    a. In the fiscal year ended July 31, 2014, Intuit reported net income of $907 million. How much did Intuit pay in dividends to its common shareholders?

    b. In the fiscal year ended January 31, 2014, Intuit repurchased 22,467 thousand of its common shares. How many shares were issued to employees under stock option plans?

    c. Intuit's issuance of shares for stock option plans increased the Additional paid-in capital balance by $74 million. Was the (average) option exercise price greater or less than the (average) amount Intuit paid to acquire the treasury shares that were reissued?

LO2

Merck & Co.
NYSE :: MRK

E11-52. Analyzing and Computing Issue Price, Treasury Stock Cost, and Shares Outstanding

Following is the stockholders' equity section of the **Merck & Co., Inc.**, balance sheet.

Merck & Co., Inc. Stockholders' Equity ($ millions)	Dec. 31, 2014	Dec. 31, 2013
Common stock, $0.50 par value		
Authorized—6,500,000,000 shares		
Issued—3,577,103,522 shares in 2014 and 2013.	$ 1,788	$ 1,788
Other paid-in capital	40,423	40,508
Retained earnings	46,021	39,257
Accumulated other comprehensive loss	(4,323)	(2,197)
	83,909	79,356
Less treasury stock, at cost:		
738,963,326 shares in 2014 and 649,576,808 shares in 2013 . . .	35,262	29,591
Total Merck & Co., Inc. stockholders' equity	$48,647	$49,765

    a. Explain the derivation of the $1,788 million in the common stock account.

    b. Using December 31, 2014 balances, at what average issue price were the Merck common shares issued?

    c. At what average cost was the Merck treasury stock as of December 31, 2014?

    d. How many common shares are outstanding as of December 31, 2014?

LO7

McKesson Corporation
NYSE :: MCK

E11-53. Assessing Effects of Employee Stock Options for Income and EPS

The following data is taken from the March 31, 2015, income statement of **McKesson Corporation** (millions, except for per share amounts). McKesson has neither preferred stock nor convertible securities outstanding.

Earnings (Loss) Per Common Share Attributable to McKesson Corporation	
Diluted	
Continuing operations	$ 7.54
Discontinued operations...	(1.27)
Total...	$ 6.27
Basic	
Continuing operations	$ 7.66
Discontinued operations...	(1.29)
Total...	$ 6.37
Weighted average common shares	
Diluted	235
Basic	232

a.   Estimate McKesson's loss from discontinued operations in the year ended March 31, 2015. Is the amount you calculated before or after tax?

b.   Estimate McKesson's net earnings from continuing operations for fiscal year 2015.

c.   McKesson reports diluted earnings per share of $6.27 in 2015. What might have caused the dilution?

E11-54. Interpreting Information in the Statement of Shareholders' Equity   **LO2, 4**
The 2014 statement of stockholders' equity for **Walt Disney Co.** is presented below. (Disney includes both par value and additional paid-in capital under the heading "Common Stock." Noncontrolling interests have been excluded for simplicity. All amounts in millions.)

Walt Disney Co.
NYSE :: DIS

				Equity Attributable to Disney		
	Shares	**Common Stock**	**Retained Earnings**	**Accumulated Other Comprehensive Income (Loss)**	**Treasury Stock**	**Total Disney Equity**
Balance at September 28, 2013....	1,773	$33,440	$47,758	$(1,187)	$(34,582)	$45,429
Comprehensive income	—	—	7,501	(781)	—	6,720
Equity compensation activity	18	844	—	—	—	844
Common stock repurchases	(84)	—	—	—	(6,527)	(6,527)
Dividends	—	17	(1,525)	—	—	(1,508)
Contributions	—	—	—	—	—	—
Distributions and other...........	—	—	—	—	—	—
Balance at September 27, 2014....	1,707	$34,301	$53,734	$(1,968)	$(41,109)	$44,958

REQUIRED

a.   Did Disney issue any additional common shares in fiscal year 2014 (ending on September 27, 2014)?

b.   What was Disney's total comprehensive income in 2014?

c.   Show how Disney recorded the purchase of treasury shares in 2014 using the financial statement effects template. Prepare the journal entry and post to the related T-accounts.

d.   According to its statement of cash flows, Disney paid common dividends of $1,508 million in fiscal year 2014. What might be a possible explanation for the fact that dividends reduced retained earnings by $1,525 million?

PROBLEMS

LO2, 3, 6 **P11-55.** **Analyzing and Identifying Financial Statement Effects of Stock Transactions**
The stockholders' equity section of Gupta Company at December 31, 2014, follows.

8% preferred stock, $25 par value, 50,000 shares authorized;	
6,800 shares issued and outstanding	$170,000
Common stock, $10 par value, 200,000 shares authorized;	
50,000 shares issued and outstanding	500,000
Paid-in capital in excess of par value—preferred stock.	68,000
Paid-in capital in excess of par value—common stock.	200,000
Retained earnings	270,000

During 2015, the following transactions occurred:

Jan. 10   Issued 28,000 shares of common stock for $17 cash per share.
Jan. 23   Purchased 8,000 shares of common stock for the treasury at $19 cash per share.
Mar. 14   Sold one-half of the treasury shares acquired January 23 for $21 cash per share.
July 15   Issued 3,200 shares of preferred stock for $128,000 cash.
Nov. 15   Sold 1,000 of the treasury shares acquired January 23 for $24 cash per share.

REQUIRED
a.   Using the financial statement effects template, illustrate the effects of each transaction.
b.   Prepare the journal entries for these transactions.
c.   Post the journal entries from *b* to the related T-accounts.
d.   Indicate the impact of each transaction on the calculation of basic EPS.
e.   Prepare the December 31, 2015, stockholders' equity section of the balance sheet assuming the company reports 2015 net income of $59,000.

LO2, 3, 4, 5, 6 **P11-56.** **Analyzing and Identifying Financial Statement Effects of Stock Transactions**
The stockholders' equity of Sougiannis Company at December 31, 2014, follows.

7% Preferred stock, $100 par value, 20,000 shares authorized;	$ 500,000
5,000 shares issued and outstanding	
Common stock, $15 par value, 100,000 shares authorized;	600,000
40,000 shares issued and outstanding	
Paid-in capital in excess of par value—preferred stock.	24,000
Paid-in capital in excess of par value—common stock.	360,000
Retained earnings	325,000
Total stockholders' equity	$1,809,000

The following transactions, among others, occurred during 2015.

Jan. 12   Announced a 3-for-1 common stock split, reducing the par value of the common stock to $5 per share. The authorized shares were increased to 300,000 shares.
Sept. 1   Acquired 10,000 shares of common stock for the treasury at $10 cash per share.
Oct. 12   Sold 1,500 treasury shares acquired September 1 at $12 cash per share.
Nov. 21   Issued 5,000 shares of common stock at $11 cash per share.
Dec. 28   Sold 1,200 treasury shares acquired September 1 at $9 cash per share.

REQUIRED
a.   Using the financial statement effects template, illustrate the effects of each transaction.
b.   Prepare the journal entries for these transactions.
c.   Post the journal entries from *b* to the related T-accounts.
d.   Indicate the impact of each transaction on the calculation of basic EPS.
e.   Prepare the December 31, 2015, stockholders' equity section of the balance sheet assuming that the company reports 2015 net income of $83,000.
f.   Compute return on common equity for 2015.

P11-57. Identifying and Analyzing Financial Statement Effects of Stock Transactions   **LO2, 3, 6**

The stockholders' equity of Verrecchia Company at December 31, 2014, follows.

Common stock, $5 par value, 350,000 shares authorized;	
150,000 shares issued and outstanding	$750,000
Paid-in capital in excess of par value.......................................	600,000
Retained earnings	346,000

During 2015, the following transactions occurred.

Jan. 5   Issued 10,000 shares of common stock for $12 cash per share.

Jan. 18   Purchased 4,000 shares of common stock for the treasury at $14 cash per share.

Mar. 12   Sold one-fourth of the treasury shares acquired January 18 for $17 cash per share.

July 17   Sold 500 shares of the remaining treasury stock for $13 cash per share.

Oct. 1   Issued 5,000 shares of 8%, $25 par value preferred stock for $35 cash per share. This is the first issuance of preferred shares from 50,000 authorized shares.

REQUIRED

a.   Using the financial statement effects template, illustrate the effects of each transaction.

b.   Prepare the journal entries for these transactions.

c.   Post the journal entries from b to the related T-accounts.

d.   Prepare the December 31, 2015, stockholders' equity section of the balance sheet assuming that the company reports net income of $72,500 for the year.

e.   How will each transaction affect the calculation of basic EPS?

P11-58. Identifying and Analyzing Financial Statement Effects of Stock Transactions   **LO2, 4**

Following is the stockholders' equity of Dennis Corporation at December 31, 2014.

8% preferred stock, $50 par value, 10,000 shares authorized;	
7,000 shares issued and outstanding	$ 350,000
Common stock, $20 par value, 50,000 shares authorized;	
25,000 shares issued and outstanding	500,000
Paid-in capital in excess of par value—preferred stock......................	70,000
Paid-in capital in excess of par value—common stock.....................	385,000
Retained earnings	238,000
Total stockholders' equity	$1,543,000

The following transactions, among others, occurred during 2015.

Jan. 15   Issued 1,000 shares of preferred stock for $62 cash per share.

Jan. 20   Issued 4,000 shares of common stock at $36 cash per share.

May 18   Announced a 2-for-1 common stock split, reducing the par value of the common stock to $10 per share. The authorization was increased to 100,000 shares.

June 1   Issued 2,000 shares of common stock for $60,000 cash.

Sept. 1   Purchased 2,500 shares of common stock for the treasury at $18 cash per share.

Oct. 12   Sold 900 treasury shares at $21 cash per share.

Dec. 22   Issued 500 shares of preferred stock for $59 cash per share.

REQUIRED

a.   Using the financial statement effects template, illustrate the effects of each transaction.

b.   Prepare the journal entries for these transactions.

c.   Post the journal entries from b to the related T-accounts.

P11-59. Analyzing and Interpreting Stockholders' Equity and EPS   **LO1, 2, 5, 7**

Following is the stockholders' equity section of the balance sheet for **The Procter & Gamble Company** along with selected earnings and dividend data. For simplicity, balances for noncontrolling interests have been left out of income and shareholders' equity information.

Procter & Gamble
NYSE :: PG

($ millions except per share amounts)	2014	2013
Net earnings attributable to Procter & Gamble shareholders	$11,643	$11,312
Common dividends	6,658	6,275
Preferred dividends	253	244
Basic net earnings per common share.	$ 4.19	$ 4.04
Diluted net earnings per common share	$ 4.01	$ 3.86
Shareholders' equity:		
Convertible class A preferred stock, stated value $1 per share.	$ 1,111	$ 1,137
Common stock, stated value $1 per share	4,009	4,009
Additional paid-in capital	63,911	63,538
Treasury stock, at cost (shares held: 2014—1,298.4, 2013—1,266.9).	(75,805)	(71,966)
Retained earnings	84,990	80,197
Accumulated other comprehensive income/(loss)	(7,662)	(7,499)
Other.	(1,340)	(1,352)
Shareholders' equity attributable to Procter & Gamble shareholders	$69,214	$68,064

a. Compute the number of shares outstanding at the end of each fiscal year. Estimate the average number of shares outstanding during 2014. How do these two computations compare?

b. Calculate the average cost per share of the shares held as treasury stock at the end of each fiscal year.

c. In 2014, preferred shareholders elected to convert 3.2 million shares of preferred stock ($26 million book value) into common stock. Rather than issue new shares, the company granted to the preferred shareholders 3.2 million common shares held in treasury stock with a total cost of $22 million. Prepare a journal entry to illustrate how this transaction would have been recorded.

d. P&G has no convertible debt outstanding. What could explain the reported diluted EPS?

e. Calculate P&G's return on common equity (ROCE) for fiscal 2014.

LO5, 7

Google Inc.
NASDAQ :: GOOG

P11-60. Analyzing and Interpreting Equity Accounts and Comprehensive Income

The 2012 and 2013 statements of stockholders' equity for **Google Inc.** are presented below along with portions on Note 12 relating to stockholders' equity.

GOOGLE INC.
Consolidated Statements of Stockholders' Equity
(In millions, except for share amounts which are reflected in thousands)

($ millions)	Class A and Class B Common Stock and Additional Paid-in Capital		Accumulated Other Comprehensive Income	Retained Earnings	Total Stock- holders' Equity
	Shares	Amount			
Balance at Dec. 31, 2011.	324,895	$20,264	$276	$37,605	$58,145
Common stock issued	5,084	736	0	0	736
Stock-based compensation expense		2,692	0	0	2,692
Stock-based compensation tax benefits		166	0	0	166
Tax withholding related to vesting of restricted stock units		(1,023)	0	0	(1,023)
Net income.		0	0	10,737	10,737
Other comprehensive income		0	262	0	262
Balance at Dec. 31, 2012.	329,979	22,835	538	48,342	71,715
Common stock issued	5,853	1,174	0	0	1,174
Stock-based compensation expense		3,343	0	0	3,343
Stock-based compensation tax benefits		449	0	0	449
Tax withholding related to vesting of restricted stock units		(1,879)	0	0	(1,879)
Net income.		0	0	12,920	12,920
Other comprehensive income		0	(413)	0	(413)
Balance at Dec. 31, 2013.	335,832	$25,922	$125	$61,262	$87,309

Note 12: Stockholders' Equity

Class A and Class B Common Stock

Our board of directors has authorized two classes of common stock, Class A and Class B. At December 31, 2013, there were 9,000,000,000 and 3,000,000,000 shares authorized and there were 279,325,564 and 56,506,728 shares outstanding of Class A and Class B common stock, $0.001 par value. The rights of the holders of Class A and Class B common stock are identical, except with respect to voting. Each share of Class A common stock is entitled to one vote per share. Each share of Class B common stock is entitled to 10 votes per share. Shares of Class B common stock may be converted at any time at the option of the stockholder and automatically convert upon sale or transfer to Class A common stock. We refer to Class A and Class B common stock as common stock throughout the notes to these financial statements, unless otherwise noted.

Stock Plans

We maintain the 1998 Stock Plan, the 2000 Stock Plan, the 2003 Stock Plan, the 2003 Stock Plan (No. 2), the 2003 Stock Plan (No. 3), the 2004 Stock Plan, the 2012 Stock Plan, and plans assumed through acquisitions, all of which are collectively referred to as the "Stock Plans." Under our Stock Plans, incentive and non-qualified stock options or rights to purchase common stock may be granted to eligible participants. Options are generally granted for a term of 10 years. Under the Stock Plans, we have also issued RSUs. An RSU award is an agreement to issue shares of our stock at the time the award vests. Except for options granted pursuant to our stock option exchange program completed in March 2009 (the Exchange), options granted and RSUs issued to participants under the Stock Plans generally vest over four years contingent upon employment or service with us on the vesting date.

We estimated the fair value of each option award on the date of grant using the BSM option pricing model. Our assumptions about stock-price volatility have been based exclusively on the implied volatilities of publicly traded options to buy our stock with contractual terms closest to the expected life of options granted to our employees. We estimate the expected term based upon the historical exercise behavior of our employees. The risk-free interest rate for periods within the contractual life of the award is based on the U.S. Treasury yield curve in effect at the time of grant.

The following table summarizes the activities for our options for the year ended December 31, 2013:

	Number of Shares	Weighted-Average Exercise Price	Aggregate Intrinsic Value ($ millions)
Balance at December 31, 2012	8,551,395	$405.98	
Granted	1,571	$723.25	
Exercised	(3,299,276)	$355.56	
Forfeited/canceled	(220,827)	$595.92	
Balance at December 31, 2013	5,032,863	$431.00	$3,470

The aggregate intrinsic value is calculated as the difference between the exercise price of the underlying awards and the closing stock price of $1,120.71 of our Class A common stock on December 31, 2013. The weighted-average estimated fair value of options granted during 2013 was $214.39 per share.

REQUIRED

a. What is the difference between Google's Class A common stock and its Class B common stock? Why do they have two different classes of common stock? In fiscal year 2014, Google created shares of Class C capital stock, which participate in any common dividends, but have no voting rights. What might be the purpose of the Class C stock?

b. Google granted 1,571 stock options in 2013. Compute the aggregate fair value of the options that Google granted to employees in 2013.

c. Prepare a journal entry to record the 2013 option grants. Assuming a four-year vesting period, what impact did these grants have on Google's earnings before income taxes in 2013?

d. Google refers to the fair value of options granted as well as the *intrinsic* value of the options. Calculate the aggregate intrinsic value of options granted in 2013. Why is this amount different from the fair value of those options?

e. Google reported net income of $12,920 million in 2013 and basic EPS of $38.82 per share. Estimate the weighted average number of shares used to calculate basic EPS.

f. If all outstanding stock options were exercised in 2013, what would be the impact on Google's basic EPS?

g. Google reported diluted EPS of $38.13 in 2013. Why is this amount different from the answer that you gave in f?

CASES AND PROJECTS

LO7

C11-61. Interpreting Disclosure on Convertible Preferred Securities

Northrop Grumman Corporation reports the following in footnote 4 to its 2008 10-K related to its convertible preferred stock.

Conversion of Preferred Stock – On February 20, 2008, the company's board of directors approved the redemption of the 3.5 million shares of mandatorily redeemable convertible preferred stock on April 4, 2008. Prior to the redemption date, substantially all of the preferred shares were converted into common stock at the election of shareholders. All remaining unconverted preferred shares were redeemed by the company on the redemption date. As a result of the conversion and redemption, the company issued approximately 6.4 million shares of common stock.

REQUIRED

a. What do you believe is meant by the terms "mandatorily redeemable" prior to the words "preferred stock"?

b. Northrop's balance sheet at December 31, 2007, shows preferred stock of $350 million and $0 million on December 31, 2008. Northrop originally sold the preferred shares at par. What was the preferred par value per share?

c. The fair market value of a preferred share, as reported by Northrop on December 31, 2008, was $146. What could account for the substantial increase in the value per share?

d. How should preferred stock be treated in an analysis of a company?

e. Discuss the general effects of the April 4th conversion on Northrop Grumman's balance sheet.

LO1, 2

C11-62. Identifying Corporate Takeover, Stock Ownership, and Managerial Ethics

Ron King, chairperson of the board of directors and chief executive officer of Image, Inc., is pondering a recommendation to make to the firm's board of directors in response to actions taken by Jack Hatcher. Hatcher recently informed King and other board members that he (Hatcher) had purchased 15% of the voting stock of Image at $12 per share and is considering an attempt to take control of the company. His effort to take control would include offering $16 per share to stockholders to induce them to sell shares to him. Hatcher also indicated that he would abandon his takeover plans if the company would buy back his stock at a price 50% over its current market price of $13 per share.

King views the proposed takeover by Hatcher as a hostile maneuver. Hatcher has a reputation of identifying companies that are undervalued (that is, their underlying net assets are worth more than the price of the outstanding stock), buying enough stock to take control of such a company, replacing top management, and, on occasion, breaking up the company (that is, selling off the various divisions to the highest bidder). The process has proven profitable to Hatcher and his financial backers. Stockholders of the companies taken over also benefited because Hatcher paid them attractive prices to buy their stock.

King recognizes that Image is currently undervalued by the stock market but believes that eventually the company will significantly improve its financial performance to the long-run benefit of its stockholders.

REQUIRED

What are the ethical issues that King should consider in arriving at a recommendation to make to the board of directors regarding Hatcher's offer to be "bought out" of his takeover plans?

LO1, 2, 3

C11-63. Understanding Shareholders' Meeting, Managerial Communications, and Financial Interpretations

The stockholders' equity section of Pillar Corporation's comparative balance sheet at the end of 2014 and 2015 is presented below. It is part of the financial data just reviewed at a stockholders' meeting.

	December 31, 2015	December 31, 2014
Common stock, $10 par value, 600,000 shares authorized; issued at December 31, 2015, 275,000 shares; 2014, 250,000 shares	$ 2,750,000	$2,500,000
Paid-in capital in excess of par	4,575,000	4,125,000
Retained earnings (see Note)	2,960,000	2,825,000
Total stockholders' equity	$10,285,000	$9,450,000

Note: Availability of retained earnings for cash dividends is restricted by $2,000,000 due to a planned plant expansion.

The following items were also disclosed at the stockholders' meeting: net income for 2015 was $1,220,000; a 10% stock dividend was issued December 14, 2015; when the stock dividend was declared, the market value was $28 per share; the market value per share at December 31, 2015, was $26; management plans to borrow $500,000 to help finance a new plant addition, which is expected to cost a total of $2,300,000; and the customary $1.54 per share cash dividend had been revised to $1.40 when declared and issued the last week of December 2015. As part of its investor relations program, during the stockholders' meeting management asked stockholders to write any questions they might have concerning the firm's operations or finances. As assistant controller, you are given the stockholders' questions.

REQUIRED

Prepare brief but reasonably complete answers to the following questions:

a. What did Pillar do with the cash proceeds from the stock dividend issued in December?

b. What was my book value per share at the end of 2014 and 2015?

c. I owned 7,500 shares of Pillar in 2014 and have not sold any shares. How much more or less of the corporation do I own at December 31, 2015 and what happened to the market value of my interest in the company?

d. I heard someone say that stock dividends don't give me anything I didn't already have. Why did you issue one? Are you trying to fool us?

e. Instead of a stock dividend, why didn't you declare a cash dividend and let us buy the new shares that were issued?

f. Why are you cutting back on the dividends I receive?

g. If you have $2,000,000 put aside in retained earnings for the new plant addition, which will cost $2,300,000, why are you borrowing $500,000 instead of just the $300,000 needed?

C11-64. Assessing Stock Buybacks, Corporate Accountability, and Managerial Ethics   **LO2, 3, 6**

Liz Plummer, vice president and general counsel, chairs the Executive Compensation Committee for Sunlight Corporation. Four and one-half years ago, the compensation committee designed a performance bonus plan for top management that was approved by the board of directors. The plan provides an attractive bonus for top management if the firm's earnings per share grows each year over a five-year period. The plan is now in its fifth year; for the past four years, earnings per share has grown each year. Last year, earnings per share was $1.95 (net income was $7,800,000 and the weighted average common shares outstanding was 4,000,000). Sunlight Corporation has no preferred stock and has had 4,000,000 common shares outstanding for several years. Plummer has recently seen an estimate that Sunlight's net income this year will decrease about 5% from last year because of a slight recession in the economy.

Plummer is disturbed by an item on the agenda for the board of directors meeting on June 20 and an accompanying note from Rob Lundy. Lundy is vice president and chief financial officer for Sunlight. Lundy is proposing to the board that Sunlight buy back 600,000 shares of its own common stock on July 1. Lundy's explanation is that the firm's stock is undervalued now and that Sunlight has excess cash available. When the stock subsequently recovers in value, Lundy notes, Sunlight will reissue the shares and generate a nice increase in contributed capital.

Lundy's note to Plummer merely states, "Look forward to your support of my proposal at the board meeting."

REQUIRED

Why is Plummer disturbed by Lundy's proposal and note? What possible ethical problem does Plummer face when Lundy's proposal is up for a vote at the board meeting?

SOLUTIONS TO REVIEW PROBLEMS

Mid-Chapter Review 1

SOLUTION

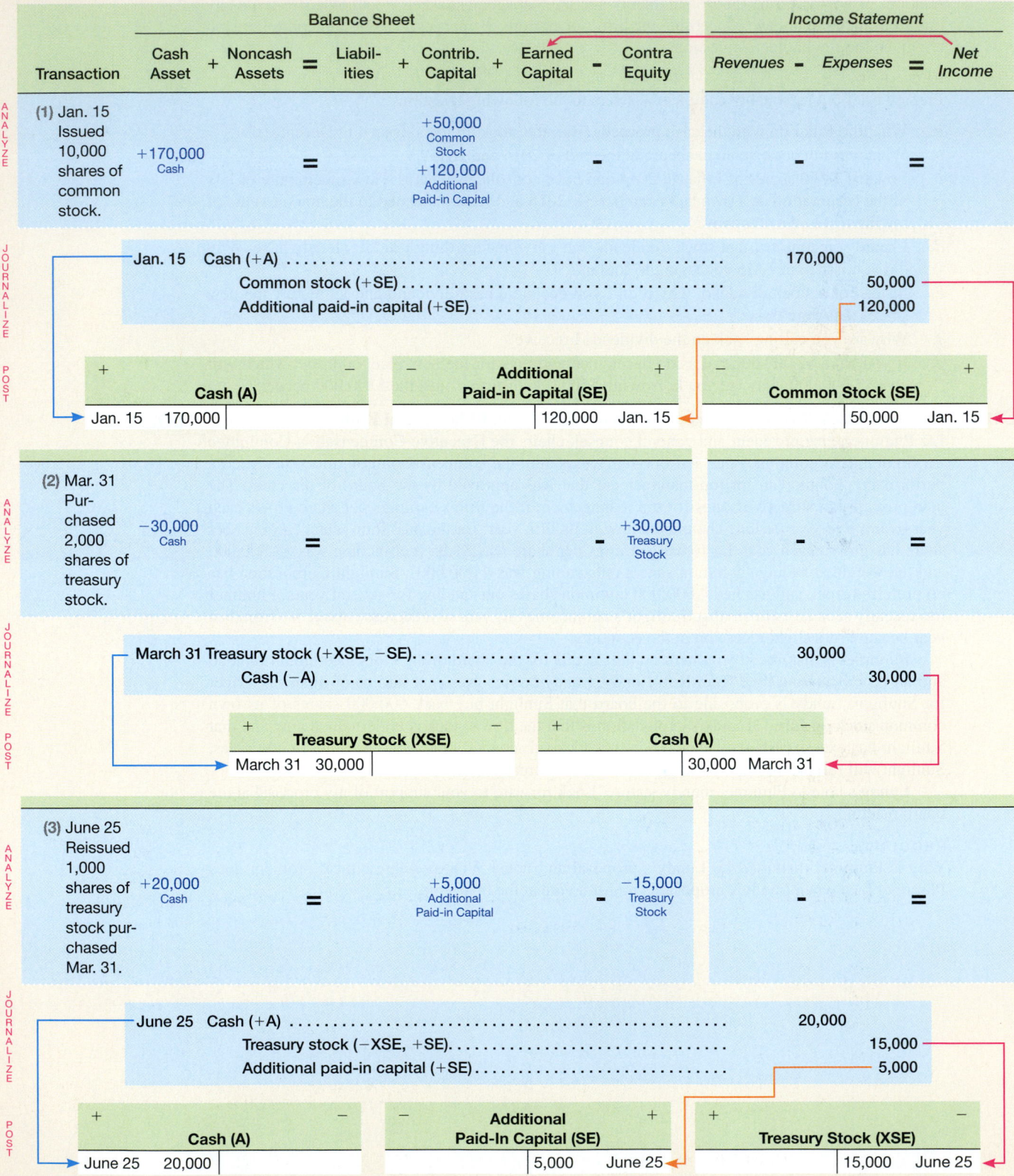

Mid-Chapter Review 2

SOLUTION

a.

	Preferred Stock	Common Stock
Year 1	$ 0	$ 0
Year 2		
Arrearage from Year 1 ($1,000,000 × 5%)	50,000	
Current-year dividend ($1,000,000 × 5%)	50,000	
Balance to common		200,000
Year 3		
Current-year dividend ($1,000,000 × 5%)	50,000	
Balance to common		30,000

b.

	Preferred Stock	Common Stock
Year 1	$ 0	$ 0
Year 2		
Current-year dividend ($1,000,000 × 5%)	50,000	
Balance to common		250,000
Year 3		
Current-year dividend ($1,000,000 × 5%)	50,000	
Balance to common		30,000

Mid-Chapter Review 3

SOLUTION

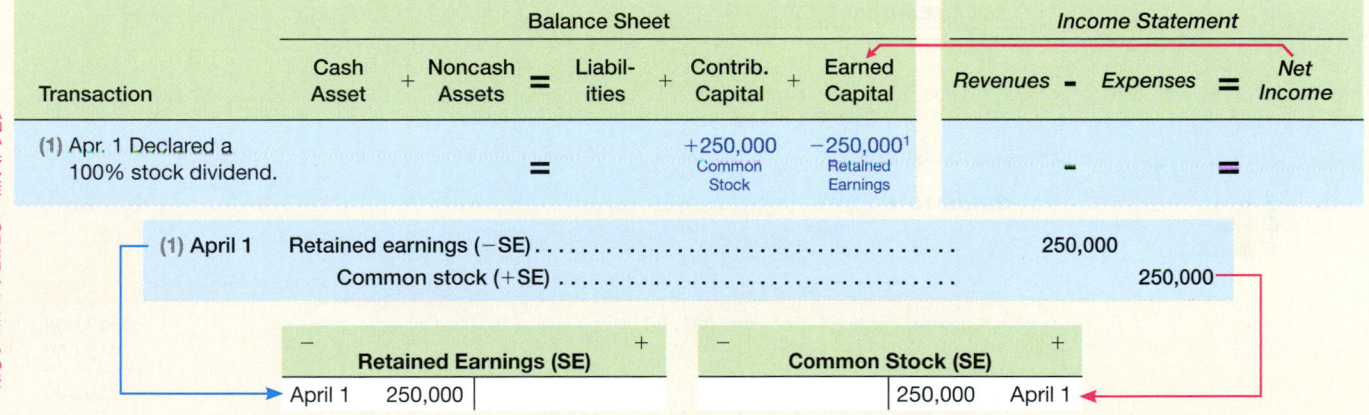

1 This large stock dividend reduces retained earnings at the par value of shares distributed (50,000 shares × 100% × $5 par value = $250,000). Contributed capital (common stock) increases by the same amount.

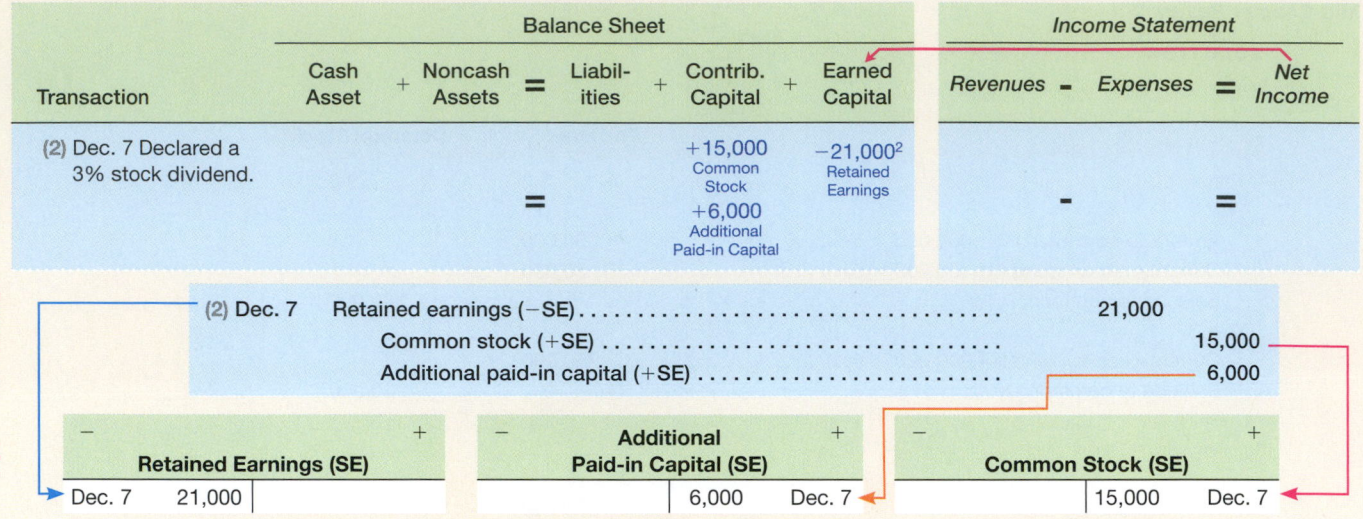

2 This small stock dividend reduces retained earnings at the market value of shares distributed (3% × 100,000 shares × $7 per share = $21,000). Contributed capital increases by the same amount ($15,000 to common stock and $6,000 to paid-in capital).

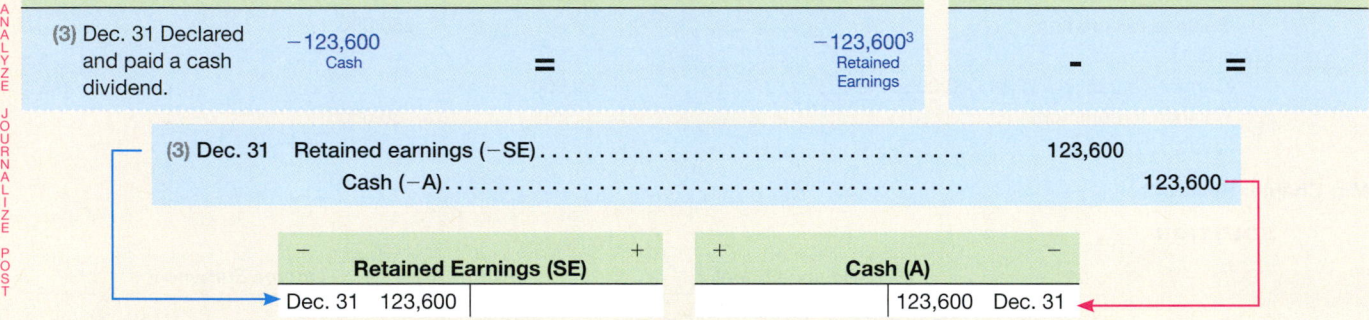

3 At the time of the cash dividend, there are 103,000 shares outstanding. The cash paid is, therefore, 103,000 shares × $1.20 per share = $123,600.

Mid-Chapter Review 4

SOLUTION

Retained Earnings Reconciliation For Year Ended December 31, 2015		
Retained earnings, December 31, 2014.		$513,000
Add: Net income.		412,000
		925,000
Less: Cash dividends declared $1.25 × [160,000 + (0.10 × 160,000)] .	$220,000	
Stock dividends declared $11 × (160,000 × 0.10)	176,000	396,000
Retained earnings, December 31, 2015.		$529,000

Chapter-End Review

SOLUTION

1. Basic EPS would be calculated as follows (millions, except per share amount):

$$\text{Basic EPS} = \frac{\$1{,}750 - \$40}{760 \text{ shares}} = \$2.25 \text{ per share}$$

2. Diluted EPS is calculated as follows (millions, except per share amounts):

$$\text{Diluted EPS} = \frac{\$1{,}750}{770 \text{ shares}} = \$2.27 \text{ per share}$$

3. Petroni would only report basic EPS on its income statement. Diluted EPS, as calculated in requirement 2, is actually higher than basic EPS because the convertible preferred stock is anti-dilutive. GAAP requires that reported diluted EPS must be lower than basic EPS. Consequently, Petroni would not report the diluted EPS number.

Apendix 11A Review

SOLUTION

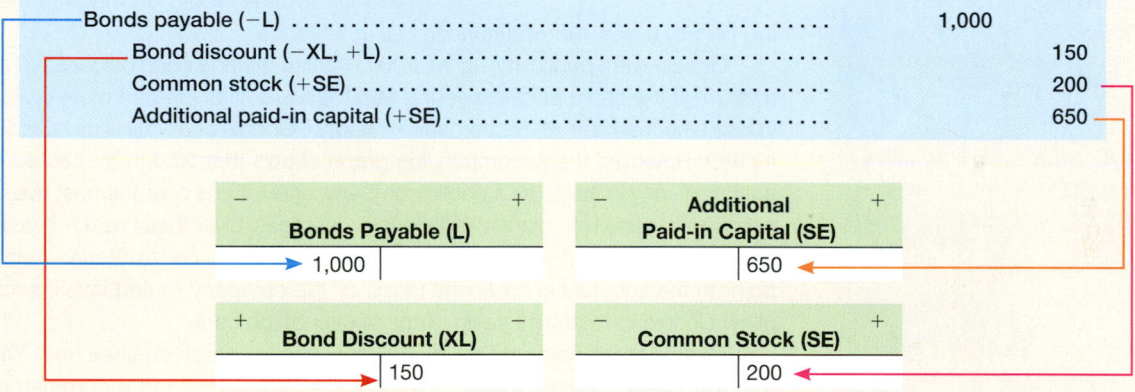

	Balance Sheet									Income Statement			
Transaction	Cash Asset	+	Noncash Assets	=	Liabil-ities	−	Contra Liabilities	+	Contrib. Capital	+	Earned Capital		Revenues − Expenses = Net Income
Conversion of an $850 book-value bond into 200 common shares of $1 par value.				=	−1,000 Bonds Payable	−	−150 Bond Discount		+200 Common Stock +650 Additional Paid-In Capital				− ▮ =

Bonds payable (−L)	1,000	
Bond discount (−XL, +L)		150
Common stock (+SE)		200
Additional paid-in capital (+SE)		650

− Bonds Payable (L) +	− Additional Paid-in Capital (SE) +
1,000	650

+ Bond Discount (XL) −	− Common Stock (SE) +
150	200

12

Reporting and Analyzing Financial Investments

LEARNING OBJECTIVES

1. Explain and interpret the three levels of investor influence over an investee—passive, significant, and controlling. (p. 564)

2. Describe the term "fair value" and the fair value hierarchy. (p. 566)

3. Describe and analyze accounting for passive investments. (p. 567)

4. Explain and analyze accounting for investments with significant influence. (p. 575)

5. Describe and analyze accounting for investments with control. (p. 579)

6. Appendix 12A: Illustrate and analyze accounting mechanics for equity method investments. (p. 589)

7. Appendix 12B: Apply consolidation accounting mechanics. (p. 590)

8. Appendix 12C: Discuss the reporting of derivative securities. (p. 591)

GOOGLE
www.google.com

When Sergey Brin and Larry Page, Stanford computer science students, started **Google Inc.**, in September, 1998, they were probably unaware that their fortune would be made in the advertising field that now generates nearly all its revenue.

Google went public in August, 2004, with an offering price below $100 a share. By mid-2012, the share price exceeded $630! Google "has created more investor wealth in less time than any other company in history." Google currently is up over 500% since its IPO. However, the accompanying graph shows that Google's spectacular returns occurred early in its life as a public company, and returns over the past five years have been more in line with market and industry averages. Over these past five years, Google has met investor expectations (which are high), but has not exceeded them. Analysts point to the substantial challenge faced by the company to find investments that will allow Google to match its past returns of over 50 percent.

Google faces competition in general purpose search engines from **Yahoo, Inc.** and **Microsoft Corporation**, in vertical search engines and e-commerce websites from **Kayak.com**, **Monster Worldwide, Inc.**, **Amazon.com, Inc.** and others, in social networks from **Facebook, Inc.** and **Twitter, Inc.** The company also competes fiercely with **Apple Inc.** in the mobile applications market. In addition, the company faces legal challenges from competitors and anti-trust investigations in the United States and other countries. Google faces substantial competition as it attempts to build its presence in the second largest Internet market, China.

Google addresses these growth challenges in several ways. More than one-third of Google's employees engage in research and development to advance the company's provision of cutting-edge products and services to its users. In addition, Google acquires companies with technology that the company can leverage. Most of these acquisitions are small, but Google acquired **YouTube, Inc.** in 2006 for $1.19 billion, **DoubleClick, Inc.** in 2008 for $3.19 billion, **Motorola Mobility Holdings, Inc.** in 2012 for $12.4 billion and **Nest Labs, Inc.** in 2014 for $2.7 billion. In addition to these investments for operating growth, Google's 2014 balance sheet shows that approximately 50% of its reported assets are cash and securities.

As we discuss in this chapter, the accounting method used to report investments depends on the investor company's purpose in making the investment and on the

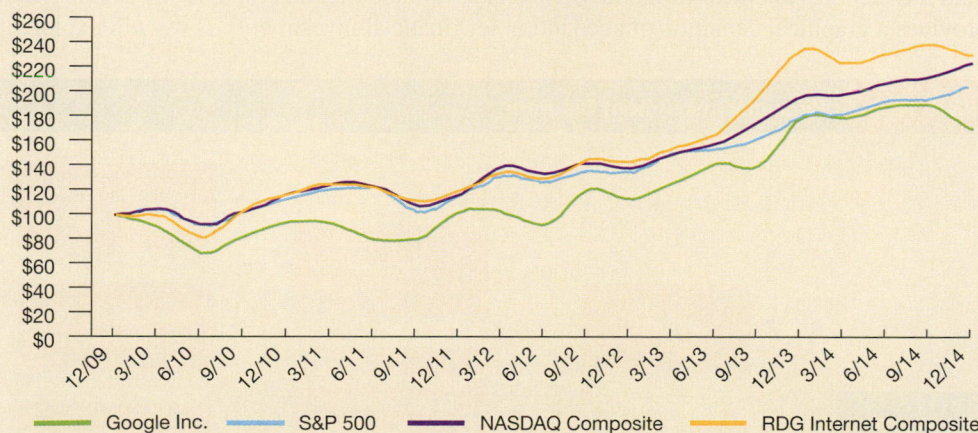

COMPARISON OF 5 YEAR CUMULATIVE TOTAL RETURN*
Among Google Inc., the S&P 500 Index, the
NASDAQ Composite Index, and the RDG Internet Composite Index

Legend:
— Google Inc.　— S&P 500　— NASDAQ Composite　— RDG Internet Composite

*$100 invested on 12/31/09 in stock or index, including reinvestment of dividends. Fiscal year ending December 31.

degree of influence or control that the investor company can exert over the investee company (the company whose securities are being purchased). One consequence of these accounting methods is that small changes in the amount invested can produce significant changes in the investor's financial statements. (Note: In August, 2015, Google formed a holding company called Alphabet, Inc., the largest subsidiary of which is Google.)

Sources: Google 2014 10-K report, *Wall Street Journal*, Aug. 10, 2015.

CHAPTER ORGANIZATION

Reporting and Analyzing Financial Investments			
Passive Investments	**Investments with Significant Influence**	**Investments with Control**	**Further Considerations**
• Trading Securities • Available-for-Sale Securities • Held-to-Maturity Securities	• Accounting and Reporting • Equity Method and Effects on Ratios	• Accounting and Reporting • Acquired Assets and Liabilities • Accounting for Goodwill • Noncontrolling Interest	• Equity Method Mechanics (Appendix 12A) • Consolidation Accounting Mechanics (Appendix 12B) • Reporting Derivative Securities (Appendix 12C)

LO1 Explain and interpret the three levels of investor influence over an investee— passive, significant, and controlling.

1

INTRODUCTION

Most companies invest in government securities or the securities of other companies. These investments often have the following strategic goals:

- **Short-term investment of excess cash.** Companies often generate excess cash for investment either during slow times of the year (after receivables are collected and before seasonal production begins) or for liquidity needs (such as to counter strategic moves by competitors or to quickly respond to acquisition opportunities).[1]

- **Alliances for strategic purposes.** Companies often acquire an equity interest in other companies for strategic purposes, such as gaining access to their research and development activities, to supply or distribution markets, or to their production and marketing expertise.

- **Market penetration or expansion.** Acquisitions of controlling interests in other companies can achieve vertical or horizontal integration in existing markets or can be avenues to penetrate new and growing markets.

Investments in government securities and in the securities of other companies are usually referred to as **financial investments**. Firms make these investments for different purposes, so accounting for the investments can follow one of five different methods, each of which affects the balance sheet and the income statement differently. To help assimilate the materials in this chapter, **Exhibit 12.1** provides a graphical depiction of accounting for financial investments as we will explore it.

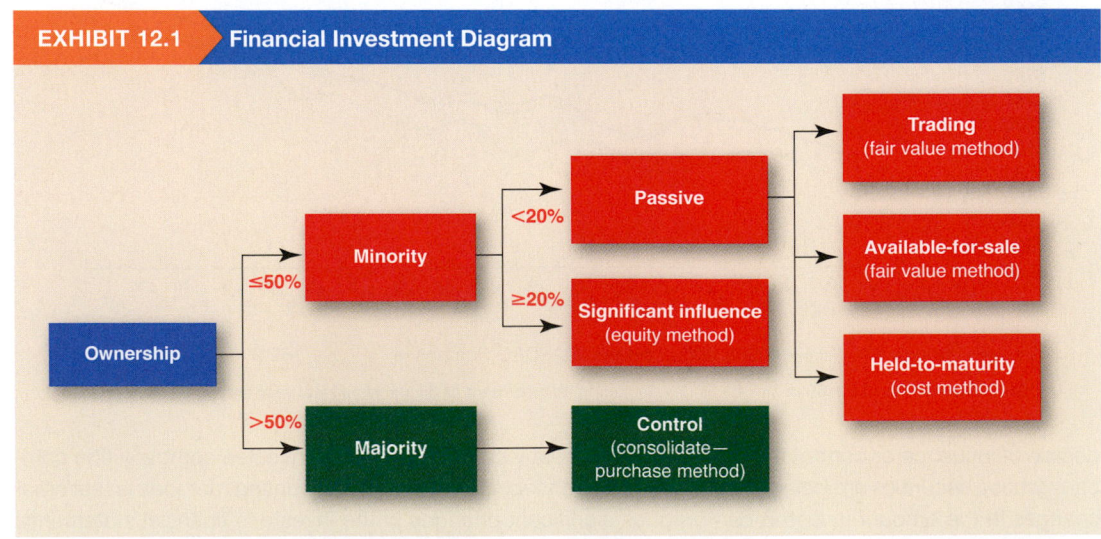

EXHIBIT 12.1 ▶ Financial Investment Diagram

---

[1] Many U.S. firms operate subsidiaries in foreign countries with lower tax rates. The income earned by those subsidiaries is subject to U.S. income tax only when the income is repatriated in the form of dividends. The desire to delay those tax payments results in a cash build-up in the subsidiaries.

The degree of influence or control that the investor company (purchaser) can exert over the investee organization (the company or government whose securities are being purchased) determines the accounting method. U.S. GAAP identifies three levels of influence/control:

1. **Passive influence**. In this case, the purchasing company is merely an investor and cannot exert influence over the investee organization. The purchaser's goal for this investment is to realize dividends and capital gains. Generally, passive investor status is presumed if the investor company owns less than 20% of the outstanding voting stock of the investee. Investments in debt securities, such as bonds or notes of other organizations, are also classified as passive investments.

2. **Significant influence**. An investor company can sometimes exert significant influence over, but not control, the activities of an investee company. This level of influence can result from the percentage of voting stock owned. It also can result from legal agreements, such as a license to use technology, a formula, or a trade secret like production know-how. It also can occur when the investor company is the sole supplier or customer of the investee. Generally, significant influence is presumed if the investor company owns 20% to 50% of the voting stock of the investee.

3. **Controlling influence**. When a company has control over another, it has the ability to elect a majority of the board of directors and, as a result, the ability to determine its strategic direction and hiring of executive management. Control is generally presumed if the investor company owns more than 50% of the outstanding voting stock of the investee company. Control can sometimes occur at less than 50% stock ownership by virtue of legal agreements, technology licensing, or other contractual means.

Once the level of influence/control is determined, the appropriate accounting method is applied as outlined in **Exhibit 12.2**.

EXHIBIT 12.2		Investment Type, Accounting Treatment, and Financial Statement Effects		
	Accounting	**Balance Sheet Effects**	**Income Statement Effects**	**Cash Flow Effects**
Passive	Trading	Investment balance reported as end-of-period fair value	Dividend payments from investee are included in income Capital gain/loss recognized in the period in which it occurs	Purchase/sale of investee yields investing cash flows Dividend payments received from investee are operating cash inflows
	Available-for-Sale	Investment balance reported as end-of-period fair value	Dividend payments from investee are included in income Capital gain/loss recognized when investment sold; interim gain/loss reported as AOCI*	Purchase/sale of investee yields investing cash flows Dividend payments received from investee are operating cash inflows
	Held-to-Maturity	Investment balance reported at acquisition cost	Dividend payments from investee are included in income Capital gain/loss recognized when investment sold	Purchase/sale of investee yields investing cash flows Dividend payments received from investee are operating cash inflows
Significant Influence	Equity Method	Investment balance reflects purchase price and subsequent changes in proportion owned of investee's equity	Investor reports income equal to percent owned of investee income Sale of investee yields gains/losses	Purchase/sale of investee yields investing cash flows Dividend payments received from investee are operating cash inflows
Control	Consolidation	Balance sheets of investor and investee are presented as if one entity	Income statements of investor and investee are presented as if one entity Sale of investee yields gains/losses	Purchase/sale of investee yields investing cash flows Cash flows of investor and investee are presented as if one entity

*AOCI is defined on page 528 and discussed further in the following pages.

There are two basic reporting issues with investments: (1) how investment income should be recognized and (2) at what amount (cost or fair value) the investment should be reported on the balance sheet. We next discuss both of these issues under each of the three investment types.

2

LO2 Describe the term "fair value" and the fair value hierarchy.

FAIR VALUE: AN INTRODUCTION

The term **fair value** is finding increasing use in the language of accounting, but it is particularly prevalent in the accounting for financial investments. When an investor purchases a security for $100, the relevance of that acquisition cost fades rather quickly. If the investor considers selling the security a year later, the original $100 cost is much less meaningful than the current price for the security in the markets. Or, if we were to look at the balance sheet of a company, it would be useful to know how much its investments are worth today, rather than what was paid for them at various points in the past.

When accounting requires the use of fair value, U.S. GAAP defines fair value as the amount that an independent buyer would be willing to pay for an asset (or the amount that would need to be paid to discharge a liability) in an orderly transaction. For an asset that is actively traded on financial markets, fair value is the amount that we would receive by selling that asset at the balance sheet date. But fair value is also used when there is no active market for the asset. When Google accounts for its acquisition of Motorola, it must report the fair value of the patent portfolio that it obtained in that transaction. In such cases, fair value is not "mark-to-market," but rather "mark-to-model." For instance, fair value might be determined by a discounted cash flow analysis as in Chapter 9. U.S. GAAP allows various methods to be used in determining the "most representative" fair value at the appropriate date.

While fair values are often deemed to be more relevant than historical cost, they are also viewed as more subjective—particularly when fair value is determined by reference to a model rather than a liquid market. For this reason, U.S. GAAP requires that firms disclose the methods used to determine fair value for their assets using a **fair value hierarchy**.

Level 1: Values based on quoted prices in active markets for identical assets/liabilities. An example would be a common share of a company traded on an active exchange. For instance, Google's class A common stock closed at a price of $530.66 per share on December 31, 2014. That price would be used to determine the fair value of another company's investment in Google stock.

Level 2: Values based on observable inputs other than Level 1 (e.g., quoted prices for similar assets/liabilities or interest rates or yield curves). An example would be a bond that is infrequently traded, but that is similar to bonds that are actively traded. Moody's rates Google bonds at Aa2. Other bonds with that rating would likely have a similar yield, which could be used to compute the present value of the bond payments to estimate the fair value of a bond investment.

Level 3: Values based on inputs observable only to the reporting entity (e.g., management estimates or assumptions). An example would be an operating asset that is judged to be impaired.

Google's use of fair value to report its investments is presented in the coming pages. The purpose of the classification is to provide an assessment of the subjectivity that underlies the numbers in the balance sheet (and sometimes, the income statement), with Level 1 being the most reliable and Level 3 being the most subjective.

In addition, companies have a **fair value option** that provides them with the *option* of using fair value to measure the value of most financial assets and liabilities. This option extends the use of fair value to a wide range of financial assets and liabilities, including accounts and notes receivable, accounts and notes payable, and bonds payable. This standard is optional, however, and thus far its application has been limited mostly to financial institutions such as banks and insurance companies.[2]

---

[2] Other assets that *must* be reported at fair value include (1) derivative securities, such as options, futures and forward contracts, that are purchased to hedge price, interest rate, or foreign exchange rate fluctuations, (2) long-term assets that are impaired, and (3) inventories that have been written down to fair value based on the lower-of-cost-or-market rule. In addition, U.S. GAAP provides companies with the *option* of using fair value to measure the value of most financial assets and liabilities.

PASSIVE INVESTMENTS

LO3 Describe and analyze accounting for passive investments.

The term "passive" refers to the investor's role in trying to influence the operations of the investee organization. So, short-term investments of excess cash are typically passive investments, usually in liquid securities. In addition, investors seeking trading profits from short-term capital gains would be considered passive investors, even though their trading style may be active. Passive investments can involve either equity or debt securities. Debt securities have no ownership interest, so they are always passive. Equity investments are passive when the ownership level is not sufficient to influence or control the investee. Passive investments can be broadly grouped into two categories: those reported at cost and those reported at fair value. Furthermore, there are two methods for reporting investments at fair value. These alternative treatments are discussed below.

Acquisition and Sale

When an investment is acquired, regardless of the amount of shares purchased or the percentage of outstanding shares acquired, the investment is initially recorded on the balance sheet at its fair value, that is, its price on the date of purchase. This accounting is the same as that for the acquisition of other assets such as inventories or plant assets. Subsequent to acquisition, investments are carried on the balance sheet as current or long-term assets, depending on management's expectations about their ultimate holding period (the assets are reported as current assets if management expects to dispose of them within one year).

When investments are sold, any recognized gain or loss on sale usually is equal to the difference between the proceeds received and the book (carrying) value of the investment on the balance sheet. However, there is one passive investment method where that is not true.

To illustrate the simplest acquisition and sale of a passive investment, assume that Pownall Company purchases an investment in King Company consisting of 1,000 shares for $20 cash per share (the acquisition price includes transaction costs such as brokerage fees). Later in the same reporting period, Pownall sells 400 of the 1,000 shares for $30 cash per share. The financial statement effects of these transactions and their related entries for Pownall follow:

	Balance Sheet								Income Statement			
Transaction	Cash Asset	+	Noncash Assets	=	Liabilities	+	Contrib. Capital	+	Earned Capital	Revenues −	Expenses =	Net Income
(1) Purchase 1,000 common shares for $20 cash per share.	−20,000 Cash		+20,000 Investments	=							-	=

(1) Investment in King Company (+A).. 20,000
          Cash (−A)   20,000

	+ Investment in King Company (A)	−		+ Cash (A)	−
(1)	20,000				20,000	(1)

	Balance Sheet								Income Statement			
(2) Sell 400 common shares for $30 cash per share.	+12,000 Cash		−8,000 Investments	=					+4,000 Retained Earnings	+4,000 Gain on Sale −	=	+4,000

(2) Cash (+A)... 12,000
          Investment in King Company (−A)...............................   8,000
          Gain on sale of investment (+R, +SE)..........................   4,000

	+ Cash (A)	−		− Gain on Sale (R)	+		+ Investment in King Company (A)	−
(2)	12,000	20,000	(1)		4,000	(2)	(1) 20,000	8,000	(2)

The gain or loss on sale is reported as a component of *other income,* which is commonly commingled with interest and dividend revenue in the income statement.

On the statement of cash flows, the $20,000 purchase (transaction 1) would be an investing cash outflow, and the $12,000 proceeds (transaction 2) would be an investing cash inflow. If Pownall Company presents its cash flows from operating activities using the indirect method, we would see a subtraction of the $4,000 gain on sale among the adjustments from net income to cash from operations.

Accounting for the purchase and sale of investments is similar to any other asset. Further, there is no difference in accounting for purchases and sales across the different types of passive investments when those purchases and sales occur in the same reporting period.

However, as Pownall Company reaches the end of its fiscal reporting period (a quarter- or year-end), we can see that there are different ways in which we might determine the balance sheet value of the 600 shares of King Company that Pownall Company still owns. And, that balance sheet value will be the asset's book value going forward, affecting gains and losses now and when the shares are ultimately sold.

Investments Marked to Fair Value

The following two classifications of marketable securities require the investment to be reported on the balance sheet at current fair value:

1. **Trading (T) securities**. These are investments in securities that management intends to actively buy and sell for trading profits as market prices fluctuate.
2. **Available-for-sale (AFS) securities**. These are investments in securities that management intends to hold for capital gains and dividend revenue; although it may sell them if the price is right or if the organization needs cash.

Investments in both equity and debt securities qualify for these classifications. Management's assignment of securities between these two classifications depends on the degree of turnover (transaction volume) it expects in the investment portfolio, which reflects its intent to actively trade the securities or not. Available-for-sale portfolios exhibit less turnover than do trading portfolios. Once that classification is established, reporting for a portfolio follows procedures detailed in **Exhibit 12.3**.

FYI GAAP permits companies to have multiple portfolios, each with a different classification. Management can change portfolio classification provided it adheres to strict disclosure and reporting requirements if its expectations of turnover change.

EXHIBIT 12.3	**Accounting Treatment for Trading and Available-for-Sale Investments**		
Investment Classification	**Reporting of Fair Value Changes**	**Reporting Gains and Losses on Sale**	**Reporting Dividends Received**
Trading (T)	Balance sheet values are updated to reflect fair value changes; unrealized gains and losses are reported as investment income; affects equity via retained earnings	Gain or loss on sale equals proceeds minus the most recent book (fair) value	Reported as investment income in income statement
Available-for-Sale (AFS)	Balance sheet values are updated to reflect fair value changes; unrealized gains and losses bypass the income statement and are reported directly in accumulated other comprehensive income (AOCI), a component of equity; these changes are reported in the statement of shareholders' equity	Gain or loss on sale equals proceeds minus the original acquisition cost of the investment; any unrealized gains or losses in accumulated other comprehensive income must be eliminated	Reported as investment income in income statement

Both trading (T) and available-for-sale (AFS) investments are reported at fair values on the statement date. Whether the change in fair value affects current income depends on the investment classification: available-for-sale securities have no immediate income effect; trading securities have an income effect. The impact on equity is similar for both classifications, with the only difference being whether the change is reflected in retained earnings or in accumulated other comprehensive income (AOCI) in equity. Dividends and any gains or losses on security sales are reported in the investment income section of the income statement for both classifications.[3]

FYI When trading securities are marked-to-fair value, the unrealized gain is recorded as income and reported in the income statement. For available-for-sale investments, unrealized gains are reported as other comprehensive income.

Fair Value Adjustments   To illustrate the accounting for changes in fair value subsequent to purchase (and before sale), assume that Pownall's investment in King Co. (600 remaining shares purchased for $20 per share) could be sold for $25 per share at year-end. The investment must be marked to fair value in an adjusting entry to reflect the $3,000 unrealized gain ($5 per share increase for 600 shares).

If the investment is classified as trading securities (T) the entry would be:

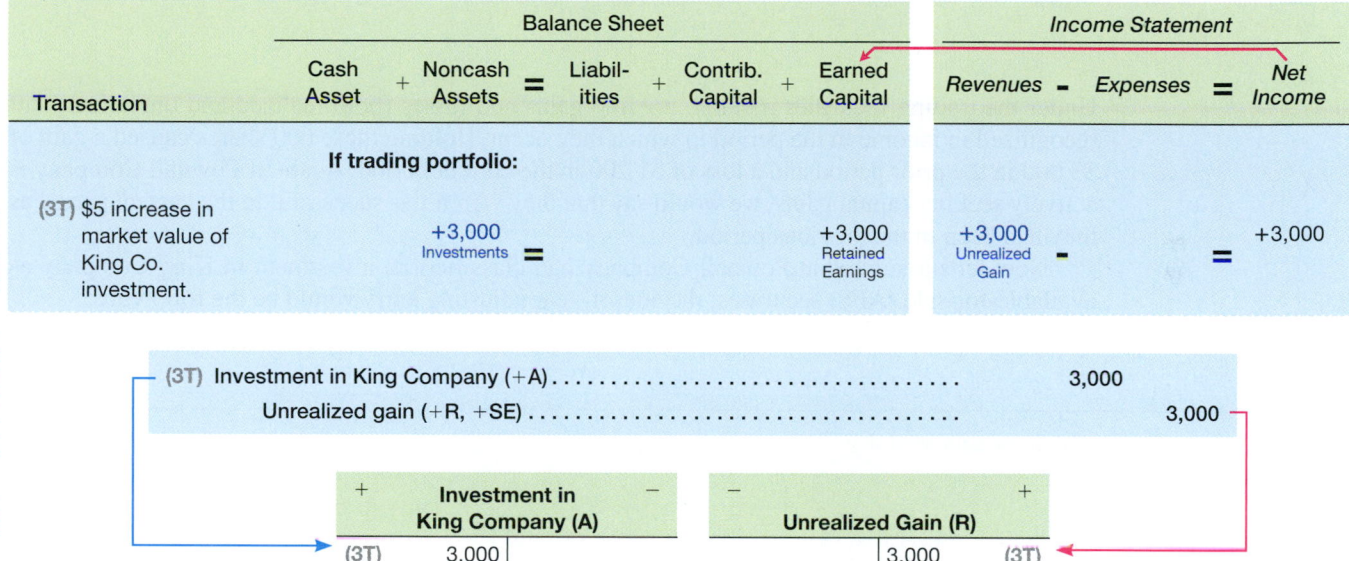

The investment account is increased by $3,000, making the end-of-year book value of Pownall's investment equal to $15,000, its fair value. Total investment income reported on Pownall's income statement would be $7,000, consisting of $4,000 in realized holding gains and $3,000 in unrealized holding gains. If Pownall is actively trading to achieve capital gains, then this approach seems like the correct way to "keep score."

This entry to adjust the balance sheet to reflect the fair value of the securities is an adjusting entry. It would need to be made at the end of every fiscal period as financial reports are being prepared.

What happens when the securities are subsequently sold? Assume that Pownall Company sells its 600 shares of King Company for $23 per share shortly after the end of the last reporting period. Pownall receives $13,800 in cash, and it no longer owns the shares of King Company. When the trading method is used, the accounting for the sale of shares is relatively simple:

---

[3] At the time of this textbook writing, the FASB is considering a change in the fair value accounting for investments in equity securities. The proposal would force companies to report changes in fair value for all securities on the income statement as unrealized gains or losses. Unrealized gains and losses on available-for-sale securities would no longer be recorded in AOCI. This change, if implemented, would effectively eliminate the distinction between trading securities and available-for-sale securities.

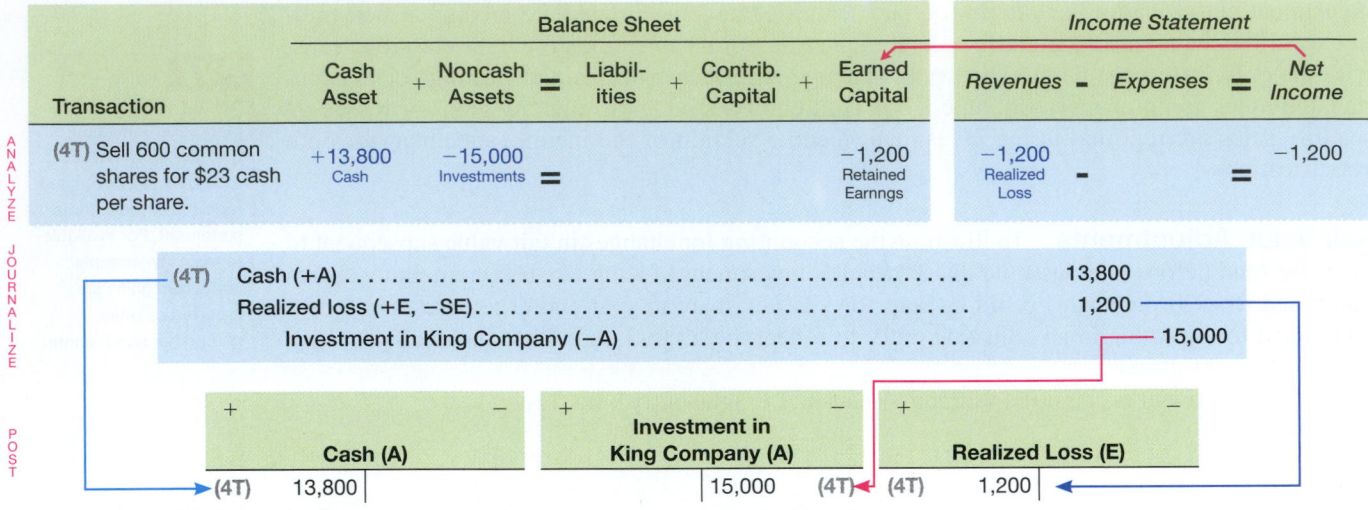

Under the trading securities method, holding gains and losses (both realized and unrealized) are recognized in income in the period in which they occur. Holding these 600 shares caused a gain of $3,000 in the prior period and a loss of $1,200 in the current period. Again, if Pownall Company is actively seeking capital gains, we would say that they weren't as successful in the current period as they had been in the previous period.

Now let's assume that Pownall Company had classified its investment in King Company as available-for-sale (AFS) securities; the end-of-year adjusting entry would be the following:

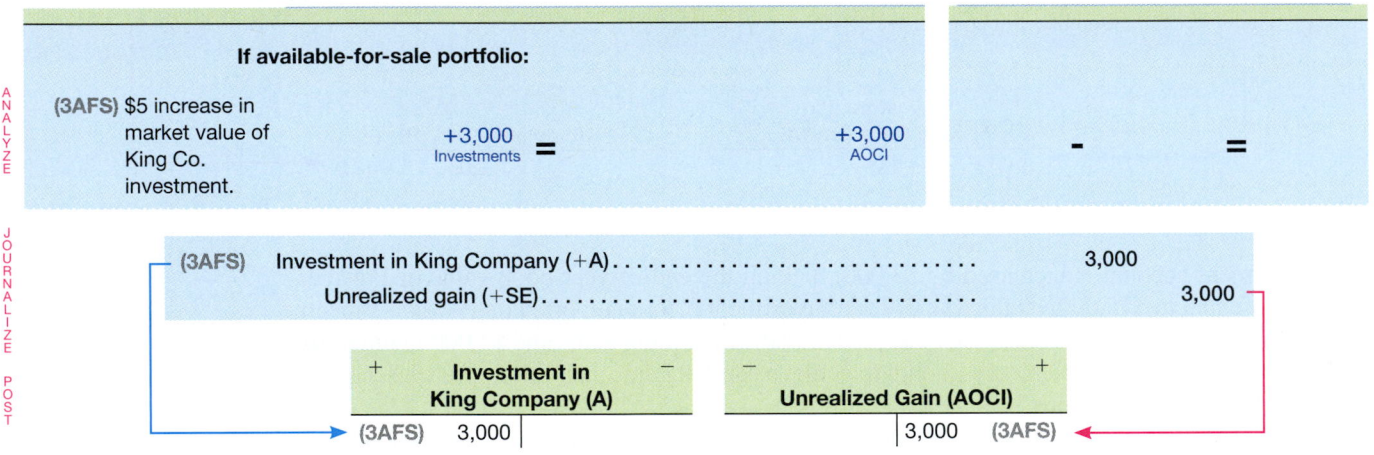

As under the trading method, the investment account is increased by $3,000 to reflect the increase in fair value of the shares owned. However, when accounted for as an AFS security, the unrealized gain (or loss) is recorded as an increase in accumulated other comprehensive income (AOCI), a separate component of shareholders' equity. Therefore, the increase in the investment does not result in an immediate income statement effect. Under AFS, Pownall Company's investment income for this period would reflect only the $4,000 realized gain from the sale of 400 shares. The $3,000 unrealized gain is reflected in stockholders' equity, but not reported on the income statement. In a sense, the balance sheet has been updated to reflect the current values, but the income statement has been left out of the picture for the time being.

When Pownall Company sells the 600 shares for $13,800 in the subsequent period, the entry under AFS would be the following:

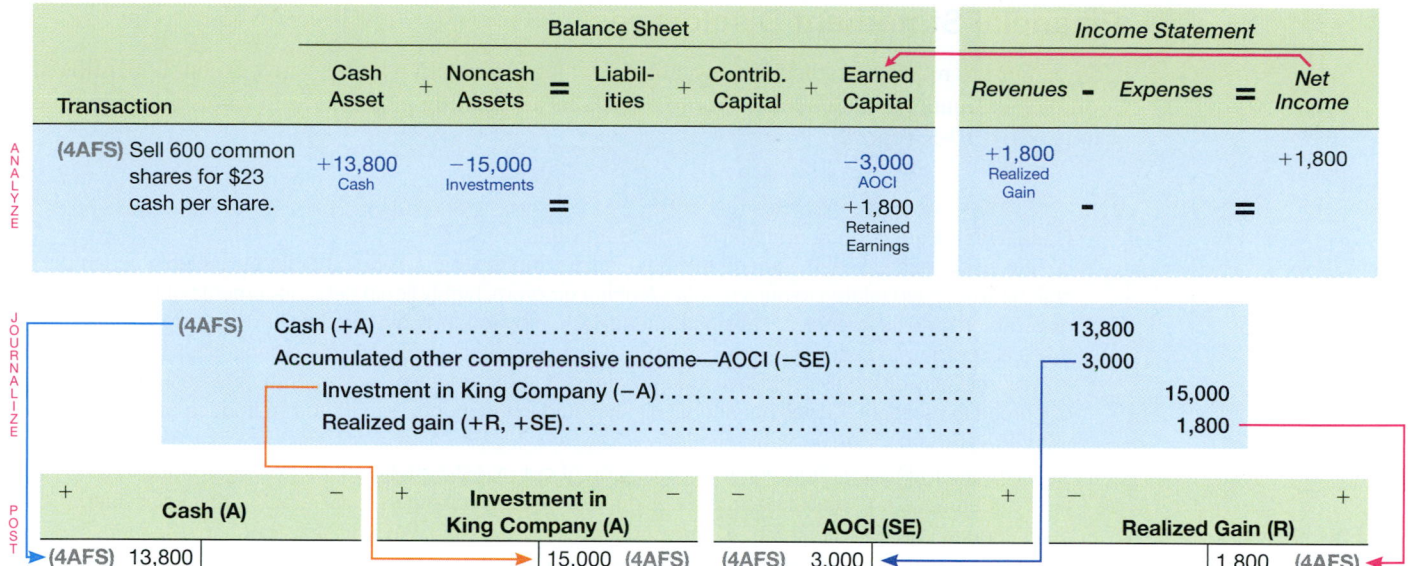

Under AFS, the realized gain (loss) goes into income when the security is sold, and the amount is determined by comparing the amount received when the shares are sold ($23 per share) to the amount paid for the shares when originally purchased ($20 per share). When the investment is sold, the entry must delete the investment (which was valued at $25 per share at the end of last period) *and* the unrealized holding gain ($5 per share) that was put into accumulated other comprehensive income when those shares were revalued. Both the Investment in King Company account and the AOCI for King Company have zero balances after this transaction.

The principal difference between trading and available-for-sale accounting is in the income statement. Under the trading security method, Pownall Company records income of $7,000 ($4,000 as a realized gain + $3,000 as an unrealized gain) in the first period and a loss of $1,200 in the second period. Under available-for-sale, Pownall Company records income of $4,000 in the first period and income of $1,800 in the second period. The total income from the investment in King Company is the same, but the timing is different. These differences are summarized in the following table:

	Income reported in income statement from investment in 1,000 shares at a cost of $20 per share	
	Trading	Available-for-sale
Period 1:		
Sell 400 shares at $30 per share	$4,000	$4,000
Adjust remaining 600 shares to fair value of $25 per share	3,000	—
Total period 1 income.	$7,000	$4,000
Period 2:		
Sell 600 shares at $23 per share	($1,200)	$1,800
Total period 2 income (loss)	($1,200)	$1,800
Total income – period 1 plus period 2	$5,800	$5,800

Because of the difference in the way unrealized gains and losses are reported, the classification of investments as either trading or available-for-sale will have an effect on key ratios that might be used to evaluate the performance of a company. Ratios that use net income in the calculation are affected. Return on equity (ROE), return on assets (ROA) and profit margin (PM) are among the ratios affected. Return on net operating assets (RNOA), which is discussed in Appendix A at the end of Chapter 5, would not be affected by this classification because passive investments would be considered nonoperating assets and excluded from the calculation of net operating assets and the gains and losses would be excluded from net operating profit after taxes (NOPAT).

Financial Statement Disclosures

Companies are required to disclose cost and fair value information on their investment portfolios in footnotes to financial statements. **Google** reports its accounting policies for its investments in note 1 to its 2014 10-K report:

Cash, Cash Equivalents, and Marketable Securities

We invest our excess cash primarily in time deposits, money market and other funds, including cash collateral received related to our securities lending program, highly liquid debt instruments of the U.S. government and its agencies, debt instruments issued by foreign governments and municipalities in the U.S., corporate securities, mortgage-backed securities, and asset-backed securities.

We classify all highly liquid investments with stated maturities of three months or less from date of purchase as cash equivalents and all highly liquid investments with stated maturities of greater than three months as marketable securities.

We determine the appropriate classification of our investments in marketable securities at the time of purchase and reevaluate such designation at each balance sheet date. We have classified and accounted for our marketable securities as available-for-sale. We may or may not hold securities with stated maturities greater than 12 months until maturity. After consideration of our risk versus reward objectives, as well as our liquidity requirements, we may sell these securities prior to their stated maturities. As we view these securities as available to support current operations, we classify securities with maturities beyond 12 months as current assets under the caption marketable securities in the accompanying Consolidated Balance Sheets. We carry these securities at fair value, and report the unrealized gains and losses, net of taxes, as a component of stockholders' equity, except for unrealized losses determined to be other-than-temporary, which we record within interest and other income, net. We determine any realized gains or losses on the sale of marketable securities on a specific identification method, and we record such gains and losses as a component of interest and other income, net.

This footnote reveals that Google reports investments with maturities of three months or less as cash equivalents. These investments are most likely treated as trading securities and any changes in their fair value would result in a gain or loss that would be reported in the income statement. Because of the short maturity of these investments, the gains and losses due to changes in fair value are generally very small. Those investments with longer maturities are reported as marketable securities and classified as available-for-sale. Consistent with this accounting treatment, Google notes that its marketable securities are carried in the balance sheet at fair value and it reports the "unrealized gains and losses, net of taxes, as a component of stockholders' equity." The cash, cash equivalents, and marketable securities are presented under current assets in the balance sheet:

December 31 ($ millions)	2014
Cash and cash equivalents	$18,347
Marketable securities	46,048
Total cash, cash equivalents, and marketable securities	64,395

In note 2 to its 10-K, Google provides further information about the composition of its investment portfolio:

Cash, Cash Equivalents, and Marketable Securities

The following tables summarize our cash, cash equivalents and marketable securities by significant investment categories (in millions):

	As of December 31, 2014					
	Adjusted Cost	Gross Unrealized Gains	Gross Unrealized Losses	Fair Value	Cash and Cash Equivalents	Marketable Securities
Cash.....................	$ 9,863	$ 0	$ 0	$ 9,863	$ 9,863	$ 0
Level 1:						
Money market and other funds	2,532	0	0	2,532	2,532	0
U.S. government notes	15,320	37	(4)	15,353	1,128	14,225
Marketable equity securities ..	988	428	(64)	1,352	0	1,352
	18,840	465	(68)	19,237	3,660	15,577
Level 2:						
Time deposits..............	2,409	0	0	2,409	2,309	100
Money market and other funds	1,762	0	0	1,762	1,762	0
Fixed-income bond funds	385	0	(38)	347	0	347
U.S. government agencies....	2,327	8	(1)	2,334	750	1,584
Foreign government bonds ...	1,828	22	(10)	1,840	0	1,840
Municipal securities	3,370	33	(6)	3,397	3	3,394
Corporate debt securities.....	11,499	114	(122)	11,491	0	11,491
Agency residential mortgage-backed securities	8,196	109	(42)	8,263	0	8,263
Asset-backed securities......	3,456	1	(5)	3,452	0	3,452
	35,232	287	(224)	35,295	4,824	30,471
Total	$63,935	$752	$(292)	$64,395	$18,347	$46,048

A large portion of Google's investment in marketable securities is in government debt securities, including U.S. government debt, foreign government bonds, and municipal securities. The various types of securities are divided into two groups, labeled "Level 1" and "Level 2." These labels refer to the method used to determine the fair value of each investment. The fair values of the investments listed as Level 1 are determined by looking at quoted prices in active markets. For most of Google's marketable securities, fair value is determined by a "mark-to-model" approach where the model uses information from publicly available sources (Level 2). None of Google's investments are listed as Level 3.

For each type of investment, Google reports its cost, its fair value, and the gross unrealized gains and losses; the latter equaling the difference between the cost and fair value. Google reports the cost of its cash and investments at $63,935 million and its fair value at $64,395 million. The fair value total is then divided into cash and cash equivalents of $18,347 million and marketable securities of $46,048 million.

The note reports gross unrealized gains of $752 million and gross unrealized losses of $292 million. These gains and losses can be almost entirely attributed to the portfolio of marketable securities, which are classified as available-for-sale investments. The net gain of $460 million ($752 million − $292 million) is reported net of tax in accumulated other comprehensive income (AOCI), which is included in the stockholders' equity section of the balance sheet.

Potential for Earnings Management

The difference between available-for-sale investments and trading securities—as far as the way changes in fair value are reported—creates the potential for earnings management. For example, if management wishes to report higher net income, investments that have increased in value could be classified as trading securities while investments that have declined in value could be classified as available-for-sale securities. This classification would mean that the unrealized gains on the trading securities would be reported on the income statement, while the unrealized losses on available-for-sale securities would bypass the income statement and be subtracted from AOCI. In addition, management is free to reclassify investments if it sees fit to do so.

Because of the potential for earnings management, the FASB requires that investments be measured at fair value at the time that a security is reclassified from one category to another. If trading securities are reclassified as available-for-sale securities, for example, any unrealized gain or loss must be recognized as income at the time of the reclassification. This prevents management from moving investments between categories to hide a loss in AOCI.

Nevertheless, available-for-sale securities offer the opportunity for earnings management, because management can decide when to recognize the unrealized gain (or loss) in the income statement. When investments are classified as available-for-sale securities, any unrealized gain or loss is recorded directly in stockholders' equity as AOCI until one of two things happens: (1) management decides to sell the securities, or (2) management decides to reclassify the investment as trading securities. In either case, the unrealized gain or loss is immediately recognized in the income statement and thus transferred from AOCI to retained earnings.

Google's footnote allows us to observe how a firm might use its investments in marketable securities to manage its net income for the year. Suppose, for example, that Google wanted to increase net income for the 2014 reporting year. Google reports gross unrealized gains of $752 million on its marketable securities. Because these securities are classified as available-for-sale, these gains have not been reported previously in Google's income statement. So, if Google decided to reclassify these available-for-sale securities as trading securities, it could immediately recognize the $752 million unrealized gain and report it on its 2014 income statement.

Instead of reclassifying the investments, Google could sell the securities and recognize the gain. (The unrealized gain would now be realized.) In fact, Google could sell the investment to record the gain and then immediately buy back similar securities at the same price (or very near to it). The company would incur some transaction costs, but it would be able to increase its income without changing its portfolio or reclassifying its investments.

One way to determine whether a company is selling and buying available-for-sale securities to manage earnings is to examine the cash flow statement. Under the heading of investing activities, companies are required to report cash flows from buying and selling investments separately. During 2014, Google reported that cash proceeds from the sale or maturity of marketable securities totaled $51,315 million, while cash spent to buy marketable securities totaled $56,310 million. These two cash flow numbers were, by far, the largest cash flows reported in Google's cash flow statement. Of course, we cannot automatically conclude that these transactions were the result of earnings management. Realized gains and losses on available-for-sale investments should be disclosed in a company's footnotes, and Google's footnotes report realized gains of $238 million and realized losses of $85 million for 2014. In addition, we could look at the adjustments to net income in the indirect method cash from operations to identify gains and losses from investing activities.

Investments Reported at Cost

Investments for which fair value cannot be determined must be accounted for using the cost method. Under the **cost method**, the investment is continually reported at its historical cost, and any cash dividends and interest received are recognized in current income. Gains or losses on investments carried at cost are only recorded when an investment is sold and the resulting gain or loss is realized.

Debt securities that management intends to hold to maturity are also reported using the cost method. These debt securities are classified as **held-to-maturity (HTM)**. **Exhibit 12.4** summarizes the reporting of these securities.

EXHIBIT 12.4	Accounting Treatment for Held-to-Maturity Investments	
Investment Classification	**Reporting of Fair Value Changes**	**Reporting Interest Received and Gains and Losses on Sale**
Held-to-Maturity (HTM)	Fair value changes are not reported in either the balance sheet or income statement	Reported as other income in income statement

Fluctuations in fair value are not reflected on either the balance sheet or the income statement. The presumption is that these investments are held to maturity, at which time they are settled at their face value. Fluctuations in fair value, as a result, are less relevant for this investment classification. Any interest received, and gains and losses on the sale of these investments, are recorded in current income.

MID-CHAPTER REVIEW 1

PART 1: AVAILABLE-FOR-SALE SECURITIES

Show the effects (amount and account) of the following four transactions involving investments in marketable securities classified as available-for-sale in the financial statement effects template, prepare the journal entries, and post the journal entries to the appropriate T-accounts.

1. Purchased 1,000 shares of Pincus common stock for $15 cash per share.
2. Received cash dividend of $2 per share on Pincus common stock.
3. Year-end market price of Pincus common stock is $18 per share.
4. Sold all 1,000 shares of Pincus common stock for $19,000 cash.

PART 2: TRADING SECURITIES

Using the same transaction information 1 through 4 from part 1, enter the effects (amount and account) relating to these transactions in the financial statement effects template, prepare the journal entries and post the journal entries to the related T-accounts assuming that the investments are classified as trading securities.

The solution to this review problem can be found on pages 613–615.

INVESTMENTS WITH SIGNIFICANT INFLUENCE

LO4 Explain and analyze accounting for investments with significant influence.

4

Many companies make investments in other companies that yield them significant influence over those other companies. These intercorporate investments are usually made for strategic reasons including:

- **Prelude to acquisition.** Significant ownership can allow the investor company to gain a seat on the board of directors from which it can learn much about the investee company, its products, and its industry.

- **Strategic alliance.** One example of a strategic alliance is an investment in a company that provides inputs for the investor's production process. This relationship is closer than the usual supplier-buyer relationship, often because the investor company provides trade secrets or technical know-how of its production process.

- **Pursuit of research and development.** Many research activities in the pharmaceutical, software, and oil and gas industries are conducted jointly. The common motivation is to reduce risk or the amount of capital invested by the investor. The investor company's equity investment often carries an option to purchase additional shares or the entire company, which it can exercise if the research activities are fruitful.

A crucial feature in each of these investments is that the investor company has ownership sufficient to exert *significant influence* over the investee company. GAAP requires that such investments be accounted for using the *equity method*.

Significant influence is the ability of the investor to affect the financing or operating policies of the investee. Ownership levels of 20% to 50% of the outstanding common stock of the investee presume significant influence. Significant influence can also exist when ownership is less than 20%. Evidence of such influence can be that the investor company is able to gain a seat on the board of directors of the investee by virtue of its equity investment, or the investor controls technical know-how or patents that are used by the investee, or the investor is able to exert significant influence by virtue of legal contracts between it and the investee. There is growing pressure for determining significant influence by the facts and circumstances of the investment instead of the strict ownership percentage rule reflected in current corporate reporting.

Accounting for Investments with Significant Influence

Investments with significant influence must be accounted for using the **equity method**. The equity method of accounting for investments reports the investment on the balance sheet at an amount equal to the proportion of the investee's equity owned by the investor; hence the name equity method. (This accounting assumes acquisition at book value. Acquisition at an amount greater than book value is covered in Appendix 12A.) Contrary to passive investments that are reported at fair value, equity method investments increase (decrease) with increases (decreases) in the equity of the investee.

Equity method accounting is summarized as follows:

● Investments are initially recorded at their purchase cost.

● Dividends received are treated as a recovery of the investment and, thus, reduce the investment balance (unlike passive investments, dividends are *not* reported as income).

● The investor reports income equal to its proportionate share of the reported income of the investee; the investment account is increased by that income or decreased by its share of any loss.

● The investment is *not* reported at fair value as is the case with most passive investments.

To illustrate the accounting for investments using the equity method, consider the following scenario: Assume that Google acquires a 30% interest in Mitel Networks, a company seeking to develop a new technology in a strategic alliance with Google. At acquisition, Mitel reports $1,000 of stockholders' equity, and Google purchases its 30% stake for $300. At the first year-end, Mitel reports profits of $100 and pays $20 in cash dividends to its shareholders ($6 to Google). Following are the financial statement effects for Google (the investor company) for this investment using the equity method:

	Balance Sheet						Income Statement		
Transaction	Cash Asset	+ Noncash Assets	= Liabil-ities	+ Contrib. Capital	+ Earned Capital		Revenues −	Expenses =	Net Income
(1) Purchased 30% investment in Mitel for $300 cash.	−300 Cash	+300 Investment in Mitel	=				−	=	
(2) Mitel reports $100 income.		+30 Investment in Mitel	=		+30 Retained Earnings		+30 Investment Income −	=	+30
(3) Mitel pays $20 cash dividends, $6 to Google.	+6 Cash	−6 Investment in Mitel	=				−	=	
Ending balance of Google's investment account.		324							

The related journal entries and T-accounts are:

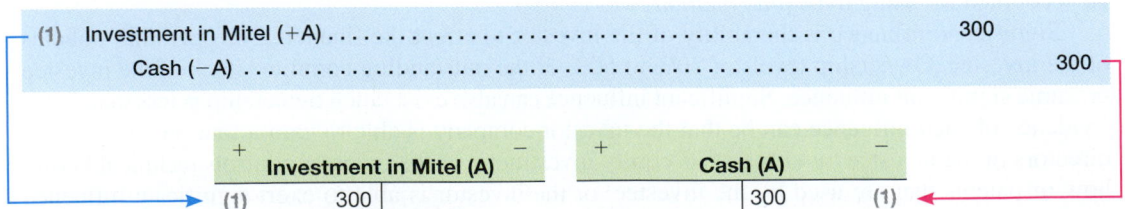

(1) Investment in Mitel (+A)		300	
Cash (−A)			300

+ Investment in Mitel (A) −			+ Cash (A) −	
(1) 300			300	(1)

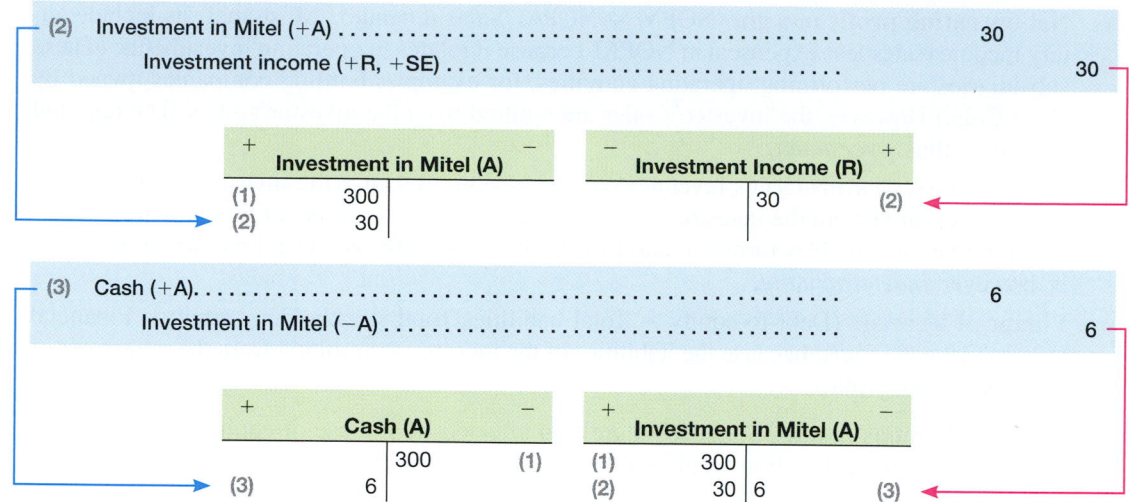

The investment is initially reported on Google's balance sheet at its purchase price of $300, representing a 30% interest in Mitel's equity of $1,000. During the year, Mitel's equity increases to $1,080 ($1,000 plus $100 income and less $20 dividends). Likewise, Google's investment increases by $30 to reflect its 30% share of Mitel's $100 income and decreases by $6 from Mitel's $20 of dividends (30% × $20). After these transactions, Google's investment in Mitel is reported on Google's balance sheet at 30% of $1,080, or $324. Appendix 12A covers the case in which Google might have paid a premium over 30% of the fair value of Mitel's net assets.

On the statement of cash flows, the original investment in Mitel would be seen as a $300 investing cash outflow. The $6 dividend received would be an operating cash inflow. However, the indirect method presentation would start with net income, which includes $30 in income from Mitel. Therefore, a negative $24 adjustment would be necessary (entitled something like "excess of equity income over dividends received") to arrive at the correct operating cash inflow.

Two final points about equity method accounting: First, just as the equity of a company is different from its fair value, so is the balance of the equity investment account different from its fair value. Indeed, there can be a substantial difference between the book value of an investment and its fair value. Second, if the investee company reports income, the investor company also reports income. Recognition of equity income by the investor, however, does not mean that it has received that income in cash. Cash is only received if the investee's directors declare a dividend payment.

FYI Investee dividend-paying ability can be (a) restricted by regulatory agencies or foreign governments, (b) prohibited under debt agreements for highly leveraged borrowers, and/or (c) influenced by directors that the investor does not control.

RESEARCH INSIGHT

Equity Income and Stock Prices   The equity method of accounting for investments does not recognize any dividends received from the investee or any fair value changes for the investee in the investor's income until the investment is sold. However, research has found a positive relation between investors' and investees' stock prices at the time of investees' earnings and dividend announcements. This relation suggests that the fair value includes information regarding investees' earnings and dividends when assessing the stock prices of investor companies. This finding implies the market looks beyond the book value of the investment account in determining stock prices of investor companies. The finding also reflects the fact that the earnings from the operations of subsidiaries are considered earnings of the parent corporation.

Equity Method Accounting and Effects on Ratios

Under equity method accounting, only the net equity owned is reported on the balance sheet (not the assets and liabilities to which the investment relates), and only the net equity in earnings is reported in the income statement (not the investee's sales and expenses). Both the balance sheet and income statements are, therefore, markedly affected. Further, because the gross assets and liabilities are left off the balance sheet, and because the sales and expenses are omitted from the income statement, several financial ratios are also affected. Some important examples are highlighted:

- **Net operating profit margin** (NOPM = NOPAT/Sales revenue). Most analysts include equity income (sales less expenses) in NOPAT because it relates to operating investments. (These subsidiaries are performing operating activities, for example, bottling companies owned by Coca-Cola.) However, the investee's sales are omitted from the investor's sales. The reported NOPM is, thus, *overstated*.

- **Asset turnover ratios** (Sales revenue/Average assets). Because the investee's sales and its assets are omitted from the investor's financial statements, asset turnover ratios such as inventory turnover, receivables turnover, and PPE turnover are affected. The direction of the effect is, however, *indeterminable*.

- **Financial leverage** (Debt-to-equity = Total liabilities/Total stockholders' equity). Financial leverage is *understated* because the liabilities of the investee are omitted from the numerator of the debt-to-equity ratio.

Profitability ratios like ROE and ROA are also affected by the use of equity method investments, though the exact direction would require a careful analysis of the noncontrolling interests described on page 585. Analysts frequently adjust reported financial statements for equity investments before conducting their analysis. One approach to adjusting the reported financial statements would be to consolidate the equity method investee with the investor company.

Financial Statement Disclosures

Coca-Cola Company reports its interest in three of its international affiliates using the equity method. It reported the following amounts in its 2014 and 2013 financial statements:

Coca-Cola—Financial Statement Effects of Equity Investments		
($ millions)	2014	2013
Balance sheet:		
Equity method investments	$9,947	$10,393
Income statement:		
Equity income—net	$ 769	$ 602
Cash flow statement:		
Equity income, net of dividends	$ 371	$ 201

Coca-Cola's equity method investment of $9,947 million represents 10.8% of its total assets of $92,023 million. Its equity income of $769 million is (coincidentally) 10.8% of its consolidated net income of $7,124 million. Pertinent portions of note 6 from Coca-Cola's 2014 10-K report are presented below:

The Company's equity method investments include our ownership interests in Coca-Cola FEMSA, Coca-Cola Hellenic and Coca-Cola Amatil. As of December 31, 2014, we owned 28 percent, 23 percent and 29 percent, respectively, of these companies' outstanding shares. As of December 31, 2014, our investment in our equity method investees in the aggregate exceeded our proportionate share of the net assets of these equity method investees by $1,671 million. This difference is not amortized.

A summary of financial information for our equity method investees in the aggregate is as follows (in millions):

Year ended December 31,	2014
Net operating revenues	$52,627
Cost of goods sold	31,810
Gross profit	20,817
Operating income	4,489
Consolidated net income	$ 2,440
Less: Net income attributable to noncontrolling interests	74
Net income attributable to common shareowners	$ 2,366
Equity income (loss)—net	$ 769

December 31,	2014
Current assets	$16,184
Noncurrent assets	40,080
Total assets	$56,264
Current liabilities	12,477
Noncurrent liabilities	16,657
Total liabilities	$29,134
Equity attributable to shareowners of investees	26,363
Equity attributable to noncontrolling interests	767
Total equity	27,130
Company equity investment	$ 9,947

YOU MAKE THE CALL

You are the Chief Financial Officer   A substantial percentage of your company's sales are made through a key downstream producer, who combines your product with other materials to make the product that is ultimately purchased by consumers. In the last two years, this downstream producer has been branching out into other products that limit the capacity that can be devoted to your product. As a result, the growth prospects for your company have been diminished. What potential courses of action can you consider? Explain. (Answer on page 536.)

MID-CHAPTER REVIEW 2

Show the effects (amount and account) relating to the following four transactions involving investments in marketable securities accounted for using the equity method in the financial statement effects template, prepare the journal entries, and post the journal entries to the related T-accounts.

1. Purchased 5,000 shares of Hribar common stock at $10 cash per share. These shares reflect 30% ownership of Hribar.
2. Received a $2 per share cash dividend on Hribar common stock.
3. Made an adjustment to reflect $100,000 income reported by Hribar.
4. Sold all 5,000 shares of Hribar common stock for $90,000.

The solution to this review problem can be found on pages 615–616.

INVESTMENTS WITH CONTROL

LO5 Describe and analyze accounting for investments with control.

5

If the investor company owns enough of the voting stock of the investee company such that it can exercise control over the investee, it must report **consolidated financial statements**. For example, in footnote 1 to its 2014 10-K describing its accounting policies, Google reports:

Basis of Consolidation   The Consolidated Financial Statements include the accounts of Google and our subsidiaries. All intercompany balances and transactions have been eliminated.

This statement means that Google's financial statements are an aggregation of those of the parent company and all its subsidiary companies to create the financial statements of the total economic entity. This process involves adding up the separate financial statements, while being careful to remove the effect of transactions between the separate entities.

Accounting for Investments with Control

Accounting for business combinations (acquisitions) involves one additional step to equity method accounting. Under the equity method, the investment balance represents the proportion of the investee's equity owned by the investor, and the investor company income statement includes its proportionate share of the investee's income. Consolidation accounting (1) replaces the investment balance with the investee's assets and liabilities to which it relates, and (2) replaces the equity income reported by the investor with the investee's sales and expenses to which it relates. Specifically, the consolidated balance sheet includes the gross assets and liabilities of the investee company, and the income statement includes the gross sales and expenses of the investee.

To illustrate, consider the following scenario. Penman Company acquires all of the common stock of Nissim Company by exchanging $3,000 cash for all of Nissim's common stock. In this case, the $3,000 purchase price is equal to the book value of Nissim's stockholders' equity (contributed capital of $2,000 and retained earnings of $1,000), and we assume that the fair values of Nissim's assets and liabilities are the same as their book values. On Penman's balance sheet, the investment in Nissim Co. appears as a financial investment (GAAP only requires consolidation for financial statements issued to the public, not for the internal financial records of the separate companies). Penman records an initial balance in the investment account of $3,000, which equals the purchase price. The balance sheets for Penman and Nissim immediately after the acquisition, together with the required consolidating adjustments (or eliminations), and the consolidated balance sheet that the two companies report are shown in **Exhibit 12.5**.

EXHIBIT 12.5	Mechanics of Consolidation Accounting (Purchased at Book Value, where Book Values = Fair Values)			
	Penman Company	Nissim Company	Consolidating Adjustments*	Consolidated
Current assets	$ 5,000	$1,000		$ 6,000
Investment in Nissim	3,000	0	$(3,000)	0
PPE, net	10,000	4,000		14,000
Total assets.	$18,000	$5,000		$20,000
Liabilities.	$ 5,000	$2,000		$ 7,000
Contributed capital.	10,000	2,000	(2,000)	10,000
Retained earnings	3,000	1,000	(1,000)	3,000
Total liabilities and equity	$18,000	$5,000		$20,000

*The accounting equation remains in balance with these adjustments.

Penman controls the activities of Nissim, so GAAP requires consolidation of the two balance sheets. That is, Penman must report a balance sheet as if the two companies were one economic entity. For the most part, this process involves adding together the companies' resources and obligations. However, if one company has a claim on the other (e.g., a receivable) and the other company has an obligation to the first (e.g., a payable), the consolidation process must eliminate both the claim and the obligation. In the case of Penman Company and Nissim Company, the consolidated balances for current assets, PPE, and liabilities are the sum of those accounts on each balance sheet. Penman's asset investment in Nissim represents a claim on Nissim Company, and Nissim's stockholders' equity accounts represent an obligation that is held by Penman, and this intercompany claim/obligation must be eliminated to complete the consolidation. This elimination is accomplished by removing the financial investment of $3,000, and removing Nissim's equity to which that investment relates.

The consolidated balance sheet is shown in the far right column of **Exhibit 12.5**. It shows total assets of $20,000, total liabilities of $7,000, and stockholders' equity of $13,000. Consolidated equity equals that of the parent company—this is always the case when the parent owns 100% of the subsidiary's shares.

Comparing the left and right columns of **Exhibit 12.5** demonstrates the difference between the equity method and consolidation. In the left column, it appears that Penman spent $3,000 to acquire a financial asset. However, in the right column, it appears that Penman spent $3,000 to acquire a "bundle" of assets and liabilities consisting of $1,000 in cash plus $4,000 in PPE minus $2,000 in liabilities. The purchase of the financial asset was the means by which this bundle was acquired. The net value of this bundle is $3,000, so the net assets don't change. But the financial statement reader gets more information about what was acquired.

Penman Company's statement of cash flows would show an investing cash outflow for the acquisition of Nissim Company. However, the outflow is shown net of the cash received in the acquisition, which was $1,000. Therefore, the investing section would have a line item showing something like "Cash paid for acquisitions, net of cash acquired" with an outflow of $2,000.

In addition, the changes in Penman's operating assets and liabilities on this year's balance sheet from last year's balance sheet will no longer match the adjustments for operating assets and liabilities on the indirect method statement of cash flows from operations. For instance, the change in Penman's receivables will be changes due to its own operations (including Nissim after the acquisition) plus any receivables acquired in the Nissim acquisition.

The illustration above assumes that the purchase price of the acquisition equals book value and the fair values of the acquired company's assets and liabilities are equal to their book values. What changes, if any, occur when the purchase price and book value are different? To explore this case, consider an acquisition where purchase price exceeds book value (the typical scenario). This situation might arise, for example, if an investor company believes it is acquiring something of value that is not reported on the investee's balance sheet—such as tangible assets whose fair values have risen above book value, or unrecorded intangible assets like patents or corporate synergies. If an acquisition is made at a price in excess of book value, all net assets acquired (both tangible and intangible) must be recognized on the consolidated balance sheet.

To illustrate an acquisition where purchase price exceeds book value, assume that Penman Company acquires 100% of Nissim Company for $4,000 instead of the $3,000 purchase price we used in the previous illustration. Also assume that in determining its purchase price, Penman feels that the additional $1,000 ($4,000 vs. $3,000) is justified because (1) Nissim's PPE is worth $300 more than its book value, and (2) Penman expects to realize $700 in additional value from corporate synergies.

The $4,000 investment account reflects two components: the book value acquired of $3,000 (as before) and an additional $1,000 of newly acquired assets. The post-acquisition balance sheets of the two companies, together with the consolidating adjustments and the consolidated balance sheet, are shown in **Exhibit 12.6**.

EXHIBIT 12.6 | Mechanics of Consolidation Accounting (Purchased above Book Value)

	Penman Company	Nissim Company	Consolidating Adjustments	Consolidated
Current assets	$ 4,000	$1,000		$ 5,000
Investment in Nissim	4,000	0	$(4,000)	0
PPE, net	10,000	4,000	300	14,300
Goodwill			700	700
Total assets	$18,000	$5,000		$20,000
Liabilities	$ 5,000	$2,000		$ 7,000
Contributed capital	10,000	2,000	(2,000)	10,000
Retained earnings	3,000	1,000	(1,000)	3,000
Total liabilities and equity	$18,000	$5,000		$20,000

The consolidated balances for current assets, PPE, and liabilities are the sum of those accounts on each company's balance sheet. The investment account, however, includes newly acquired assets that must be reported on the consolidated balance sheet. The consolidation process in this case has two steps. First, the $3,000 equity of Nissim Company is eliminated against the investment account as before. Then, the remaining $1,000 of the investment account is eliminated through the adjustments for newly acquired assets on the consolidated balance sheet ($300 of

PPE and $700 of goodwill not reported on Nissim's balance sheet). Thus, the consolidated balance sheet reflects the book value of Penman and the *fair value* (book value plus the excess of Nissim's fair value over book value) for Nissim Company at the acquisition date.

Reporting of Acquired Assets and Liabilities

Acquisitions are often made at a purchase price in excess of the book value of the investee company's equity. The excess purchase price must be allocated to all of the assets and liabilities acquired, including those that do not currently appear on the balance sheet of the investee. This allocation can be done in three steps:

Step 1: Adjust the book value of all tangible assets acquired and all liabilities assumed to fair value. This adjustment addresses the issue of misvalued assets and liabilities on the investee firm's balance sheet.

Step 2: Assign a fair value to any identifiable intangible assets. Recall from Chapter 8 that intangible assets are only reported on the balance sheet if they are purchased; internally created intangible assets are not capitalized. This step allows the acquiring firm to assign a value to the investee's intangible assets, even if those assets are not reported on the investee firm's balance sheet.

Step 3: Assign the residual amount to goodwill. Goodwill is the excess of the acquisition price over the fair value of identifiable net assets acquired. That is, whatever value cannot be assigned to identifiable tangible and intangible assets is considered goodwill.[4]

The acquiring company is required to disclose relevant information about the allocation of the purchase price in its footnotes.

For example, consider Google's reported allocation of its total $2.6 billion purchase price in February 2014 for Nest Labs, Inc. as reported in Note 5 to its 2014 10-K report:

Note 5. Acquisitions

In February 2014, we completed the acquisition of Nest Labs, Inc. (Nest), a company whose mission is to reinvent devices in the home such as thermostats and smoke alarms. Prior to this transaction, we had an approximately 12% ownership interest in Nest. The acquisition is expected to enhance Google's suite of products and services and allow Nest to continue to innovate upon devices in the home, making them more useful, intuitive, and thoughtful, and to reach more users in more countries.

Of the total $2.6 billion purchase price and the fair value of our previously held equity interest of $152 million, $51 million was cash acquired, $430 million was attributed to intangible assets, $2.3 billion was attributed to goodwill, and $84 million was attributed to net liabilities assumed. The goodwill of $2.3 billion is primarily attributable to synergies expected to arise after the acquisition. Goodwill is not expected to be deductible for tax purposes. . . .

For all acquisitions completed during the year ended December 31, 2014, patents and developed technology have a weighted-average useful life of 5.1 years, customer relationships have a weighted-average useful life of 4.5 years, and trade names and other have a weighted-average useful life of 6.9 years.

Of the total acquisition price of $2.7 billion, Google assigned $2.3 billion to goodwill. The remaining (approximately) $400 million includes $51 million in cash plus $430 million in intangible assets, less $84 million in liabilities. The $430 million in intangible assets and the $84 million in liabilities were recorded at fair value at the time of the acquisition.

Google reports its aggregated goodwill separately on its balance sheet, but combines its other intangible assets in its balance sheet under the title "Intangible assets, net." Goodwill can only be recognized as an asset in an acquisition and only then in the amount by which the purchase price exceeds the fair value of the net assets acquired, including all identifiable intangible assets.

---

[4] What happens if goodwill is negative? Such a "bargain purchase" is uncommon, because it implies that the "whole" of the acquired company is worth less than the sum of its parts. Therefore, when an acquirer believes that it has made a bargain purchase, it must carefully check its valuation of all the components of the goodwill calculation. If that review confirms that the acquirer has made a bargain purchase, then it recognizes a gain in its income from continuing operations.

For the acquisitions it made in 2014, Google estimates customer relationships have a weighted average useful life of 4.5 years. Patents and developed technology have a weighted average useful life of 5.1 years. Tradenames and other intangibles have a weighted average useful life of 6.9 years. The majority of these assets are not deductible for tax purposes. These estimated lives determine the annual amortization expense associated with these assets on the firm's financial books. Goodwill is not amortized under GAAP although it is subject to impairment write-down. The effect of this accounting treatment is to relieve the income statement of the annual amortization expense. The SEC is sufficiently concerned with the impact on the income statement that it scrutinizes acquisition accounting for excessive goodwill capitalization.

Reporting of Goodwill   GAAP requires companies to test goodwill annually for impairment just like any other asset. The impairment test is a two-step process:

1.   The fair value of the investee company (the reporting unit) is compared with the book value of the investor's investment account.[5]

2.   If the fair value is less than the investment balance, the investment is deemed impaired. The company must then estimate the goodwill value as if the subsidiary were acquired for its current fair value, and the imputed balance for goodwill becomes the amount at which it is recorded. If this imputed amount is less than its book value, goodwill must be written down, resulting in an impairment loss that is reported in the consolidated income statement.

To illustrate the impairment computation, assume that an investment, currently reported at $1 million on the investor's balance sheet, has a current fair value of $900,000. The consolidated balance sheet reports net assets (absent goodwill) at $700,000 and goodwill at $300,000. Analysis reveals that the current fair value of the net assets of the investee company (absent goodwill) is $700,000. This analysis indicates goodwill is impaired by $100,000, which is computed as follows.

Fair value of investee company	$ 900,000
Fair value of net assets (absent goodwill)	(700,000)
Implied goodwill	200,000
Current goodwill balance	(300,000)
Impairment loss	$(100,000)

The financial statement effects and related journal entry and T-accounts are:

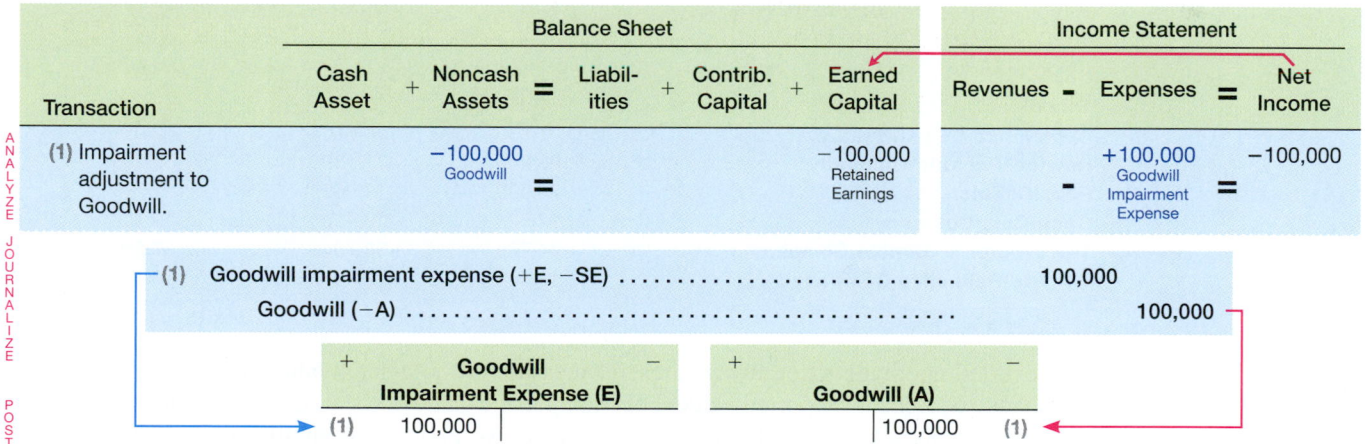

This analysis of investee company implies that goodwill must be written down by $100,000. The impairment loss is reported as a separate line item in the consolidated income statement. The related footnote disclosure describes the reasons for the write-down.

   Yahoo! Inc. reports the following goodwill impairment in excerpts from note 5 of its 2014 10-K:

---

[5] The fair value of the investee company can be determined using market comparables or another valuation method (such as the discounted cash flow model, residual operating income model, or P/E multiples).

The changes in the carrying amount of goodwill for the year ended December 31, 2014 were as follows (in thousands):

	Americas	EMEA	Asia Pacific	Total
Net balance as of December 31, 2013......	$3,802,334	$546,856	$330,458	$4,679,648
Acquisitions and other..................	533,894	110,203	(607)	643,490
Goodwill impairment charge		(79,135)	(9,279)	(88,414)
Foreign currency translation adjustments ...	(2,271)	(46,109)	(22,690)	(71,070)
Net balance as of December 31, 2014......	$4,333,957	$531,815	$297,882	$5,163,654

In 2014, as a result of the annual goodwill impairment test, the Company concluded that the carrying value of the Middle East reporting unit, included in the EMEA reportable segment, and the carrying value of the India & Southeast Asia reporting unit included in the Asia Pacific reportable segment both exceeded their respective fair values. As required by the second step of the impairment test, the Company performed an allocation of the fair value to all the assets and liabilities of the reporting unit, including identifiable intangible assets, based on their estimated fair values, to determine the implied fair value of goodwill. Accordingly, the Company recorded a goodwill impairment charge related to the Middle East and India & Southeast Asia reporting units of $79 million and $9 million, respectively, during the quarter ended December 31, 2014 for the difference between the carrying value of the goodwill in the reporting unit and its implied fair value with no goodwill remaining in either reporting unit. The impairment resulted from a decline in business conditions in the Middle East and India & Southeast Asia during the latter half of 2014.

At the end of 2014, Yahoo had a goodwill balance of $5,164 million. The goodwill balance represented 8.3% of its total assets and 13.3% of its stockholders' equity. The $88.4 million impairment charge in 2014 was 61.9% of its operating income. Yahoo's disclosures hint at the complexity of the process that a company follows to determine goodwill impairment charges.

Reported goodwill across companies differs widely in total and as a percentage of company assets as the following fiscal 2014 figures indicate ($ millions).

Company	Total Assets	Reported Goodwill	Goodwill Percentage
Google, Inc.	$131,133	$15,599	11.9%
Yahoo! Inc.	61,960	5,164	8.3%
Apple, Inc.	231,839	4,616	2.0%
Hewlett-Packard Company	103,206	31,139	30.2%
PepsiCo, Inc.	70,509	14,965	21.2%
Coca-Cola Company......................	92,023	12,100	13.1%
The Procter & Gamble Company	144,266	53,704	37.2%
Colgate-Palmolive Company..............	13,459	2,307	17.1%

Reported goodwill is not always a useful measure of the asset's value, particularly when the actual value exceeds the reported value. For example, the value of the Coca-Cola brand name alone exceeds the reported total asset value of the firm, yet its reported goodwill is only 13.1% of total assets.

BUSINESS INSIGHT

In competitive bidding situations, the winning bidder is likely to be the one who most overvalued the item, a phenomenon known as the "winner's curse." Therefore, acquisition goodwill is viewed with some skepticism by financial analysts. Does the goodwill represent synergies like future cost savings or business opportunities that are available only to the combined companies? Or, does it represent an overpayment?

A *Wall Street Journal* article described multi-billion dollar goodwill impairment charges by Hewlett-Packard, Microsoft and Boston Scientific and ascribes these charges to acquisitions that did not "pan out." The article identified more companies whose goodwill assets exceeded their total market value.

When companies record a goodwill impairment charge, they often emphasize that the impairment was a "non-cash charge," implying that it is therefore less important. That statement is true as far as the current period is concerned, but acquisitions involve cash or some other item of value. In Hewlett-Packard's case, its $8 billion goodwill impairment in the third quarter of 2012 was primarily related to its acquisition of EDS, which required a cash outflow of more than $13 billion when the deal closed in 2008 and resulted in about $10.4 billion in goodwill. Goodwill impairment requires no *current* cash outflows, but it does reflect on the wisdom of *past* cash outflows.

Source: Scott Thurm, "Buyers Beware: The Goodwill Games," *Wall Street Journal*, August 14, 2012.

Noncontrolling Interest

Noncontrolling interest represents the equity of shareholders who own a minority of the shares of one or more of the subsidiaries in a consolidated entity. When a company acquires a controlling interest in a company, it must consolidate the subsidiary when preparing its financial statements by reporting all of the subsidiary's assets and liabilities in the consolidated balance sheet and all of the subsidiary's revenues and expenses in the consolidated income statement. This is true even when the controlling parent company acquires less than 100% of the subsidiary. When less than 100% of the subsidiary's shares are acquired, there are two groups of shareholders: the parent company's shareholders and the noncontrolling shareholders who own a minority of the subsidiary's shares. These noncontrolling shareholders have a claim on the net assets and the earnings of the subsidiary company.

To illustrate the reporting of noncontrolling interest, assume that Penman Company acquires 80% of Nissim Company for $2,400 (80% of $3,000). Because Penman must consolidate 100% of the assets and liabilities of Nissim, Penman's equity must increase to maintain the accounting equation. A new equity account titled noncontrolling interests is added to Penman's stockholders' equity. The consolidation worksheet is presented in **Exhibit 12.7**.

EXHIBIT 12.7 **Mechanics of Consolidation Accounting (Less than 100% of Subsidiary Shares Purchased at Book Value)**

	Penman Company	Nissim Company	Consolidating Adjustments	Consolidated
Current assets	$ 5,600	$1,000		$ 6,600
Investment in Nissim	2,400	0	$(2,400)	0
PPE, net	10,000	4,000		14,000
Total assets	$18,000	$5,000		$20,600
Liabilities	$ 5,000	$2,000		$ 7,000
Contributed capital	10,000	2,000	(2,000)	10,000
Retained earnings	3,000	1,000	(1,000)	3,000
Penman shareholders' equity	13,000			13,000
Noncontrolling interests			600	600
Total equity	13,000			13,600
Total liabilities and equity	$18,000	$5,000		$20,600

The contributed capital of the consolidated entity (common stock, additional paid-in capital, treasury stock, etc.) refers to the parent company's shareholders' equity (in this example, Penman Company). The net assets owned by the noncontrolling shareholders are represented in one account, labeled noncontrolling interests. Each period, the noncontrolling interests equity account is increased by the noncontrolling shareholders' share of the subsidiary's net income, and decreased by any dividends paid to those shareholders.

The consolidated income statement lists total consolidated revenues and expenses and consolidated net income. After net income is computed, the portion of net income that is attributed to noncontrolling interests is subtracted. If the noncontrolling shareholders own 20% of the subsidiary's shares, then 20% of the earnings of the subsidiary are subtracted from the consolidated entity's income statement. (This is not 20% of the consolidated company's earnings, only 20% of the subsidiary's earnings.)

The stockholders' equity section of Yahoo!'s 2014 balance sheet is shown as an illustration of the presentation of noncontrolling interests in the balance sheet:

Yahoo! Inc. Consolidated Balance Sheet (Stockholders' equity section only)	
($ thousands)	December 31, 2014
Preferred stock, $0.001 par value	—
Common stock, $0.001 par value	$ 945
Additional paid-in capital	8,496,683
Treasury stock, at cost	(712,455)
Retained earnings	8,937,036
Accumulated other comprehensive income	22,019,628
Total Yahoo! Inc. stockholders' equity	38,741,837
Noncontrolling interests	43,755
Total equity	$38,785,592

Total Yahoo! Inc. stockholders' equity is listed at $38,741.8 million. This is the equity claim of those investors who own shares in Yahoo!. Next, the $43.8 million of noncontrolling interests is listed. This amount represents the share of Yahoo! subsidiaries' net assets that is owned by minority shareholders. The final line lists the total equity, which is the sum of Yahoo!'s stockholders' equity and the noncontrolling interests. Yahoo!'s income statement presents noncontrolling interests as follows:

Yahoo! Inc. Consolidated Income Statement (excerpts)	
($ thousands)	Year ended December 31, 2014
Income before income taxes and earnings in equity interests	$10,512,381
Provision for income taxes	(4,038,102)
Earnings in equity interests, net of tax	1,057,863
Net income	7,532,142
Net income attributable to noncontrolling interests	(10,411)
Net income attributable to Yahoo! Inc.	$ 7,521,731

Yahoo! presents its earnings in equity method investments after the provision for income taxes so these earnings are presented net of income taxes. Yahoo! then presents net income of $7,532.1 million. This is income for the consolidated entity, including the share of income for Yahoo!'s shareholders as well as that portion that is for the noncontrolling interests. Next, the income attributable to noncontrolling interests ($10.4 million) is subtracted, leaving net income attributable to Yahoo!'s shareholders ($7,521.7 million).

A GLOBAL PERSPECTIVE

U.S. GAAP and IFRS are very similar in their treatment of the accounting for investments as covered in this chapter. IFRS defines the term fair value in the same way and requires disclosure of fair values according to their determination as Level 1, Level 2 or Level 3. Passive investments are classified as being for trading purposes or as being held-to-maturity, with all other passive investments accounted as available-for-sale.

GAAP uses the term "equity" or "affiliate" to describe an investment involving significant influence (usually between 20% and 50%). IFRS uses the term "associate" to describe such an investment, with the same 20% threshold. The investment balance is equal to the investor's cost plus the proportionate share of changes in the investee's net assets since the date of investment. If the investor's cost exceeds the proportionate book value, the excess is attributed to individual assets (including goodwill) and liabilities and subsequent earnings will include the appropriate amortizations of those value adjustments.

The process of accounting for an acquisition and issuing subsequent consolidated financial statements is very similar to that described in the previous section.

Under International Financial Reporting Standards (IFRS), trading, available-for-sale, and held-to-maturity portfolios are accounted for similarly to GAAP.

Limitations of Consolidation Reporting Consolidation of financial statements is meant to present a financial picture of the entire set of companies under control of the parent. Because investors typically purchase stock in the parent company and not in the subsidiaries, the view is more relevant than would be one of the parent company's own balance sheet with subsidiaries reported as equity investments. Still, we must be aware of certain limitations that the consolidation process entails:

1. Consolidated income does not imply that cash is received by the parent company and is available for subsidiaries. The parent can only receive cash via dividend payments, and dividend payments may trigger tax obligations. It is readily possible, therefore, for an individual subsidiary to experience cash flow problems even though the consolidated group has strong cash flows. Likewise, debts of a subsidiary are not obligations of the consolidated group. Thus, even if the consolidated balance sheet is strong, creditors of a failing subsidiary are often unable to sue the parent or other subsidiaries to recoup losses.

2. Consolidated balance sheets and income statements are a mix of the subsidiaries, often from different industries. Comparisons across companies, even if in similar industries, are often complicated by the different mix of subsidiary companies. Companies are required to report some financial results for their business segments. For instance, **General Electric** reports revenues, operating profits and assets for each of its six operating segments—Energy Infrastructure, Aviation, Healthcare, Transportation, Home & Business Solutions, and GE Capital.

3. Segment disclosures on individual subsidiaries are affected by intercorporate transfer-pricing policies that can artificially inflate the profitability of one segment at the expense of another. Companies also have considerable discretion in the allocation of corporate overhead to subsidiaries, which can markedly affect segment and subsidiary profitability.

FINANCIAL STATEMENT ANALYSIS

This section introduces no new ratios, but the topics covered in Chapter 12 do have implications for ratios covered in other chapters. For instance, gains and losses on available-for-sale securities are not recognized in income until those securities are sold. Therefore, management can increase net income by selling securities on which it has gains or decrease net income by selling securities on which it has losses. As a result, management may have a means to smooth the variations in income over time, using gains and losses from previous periods that have nothing to do with current performance. As careful financial statement users, we can read the footnotes to find the realized gains and losses included in income for the period.

Financial ratio comparisons are also affected by the percentage ownership of affiliated companies. For instance, suppose Naughton Group has 50% ownership in the company that distributes its products. Chapman Enterprises, a competitor of Naughton, owns 55% of the shares of the company that distributes its products. While the difference between 50% and 55% ownership probably has little economic significance, the accounting reports for Naughton and Chapman will look very different. Naughton's income statement will report only its own revenues and expenses, while Chapman's income statement will report its own revenues and expenses *and* the revenues and expenses of the distribution company (less any intercompany adjustments). Naughton's balance sheet will report its own assets, including its 50% equity in the distributor, while Chapman's balance sheet will report its own assets *plus* the assets of the distribution company. Financial statement readers should interpret comparisons of ratios like PPE Turnover in light of these effects.

A similar "quantum" change in accounting occurs at 20% ownership. There may appear to be little economic difference between owning 19% of a company's shares and owning 20% of those shares. But there is a significant difference in the accounting for those two alternatives, and this difference sometimes affects the choice between a 19% investment and a 20% investment. If the investee is a start-up earning losses, a 20% investment would require the investor to recognize 20% of those losses in its own income. A 19% investment would not recognize any share of the losses.

Finally, acquisitions disrupt the usual relationships between income statement and balance sheet items. When one company acquires another, the acquirer consolidates the acquired company as of the date that the deal closes. At that point, it includes the acquired company's assets and liabilities on the consolidated balance sheet, and it begins to report the acquired company's revenues and expenses from that time forward. So, if Hoskin Corp. acquires 100% of Lynch, Inc. on December 31, 2016, how will the inventory turnover ratio be affected? The 2016 cost of goods sold for Hoskin will reflect a year of Hoskin's COGS plus one day of Lynch's COGS. The beginning-of-year inventory will be 100% of Hoskin's inventory at that time, but the end-of-year inventory will be 100% of Hoskin's inventory *plus* 100% of Lynch's inventory. The inventory turnover ratio is likely to decrease significantly, but that decrease is due to the acquisition, not necessarily a decline in Hoskin's performance. A careful reader of the financial statements should try to separate out the effects of the acquisition from the ongoing performance of the company.

CHAPTER-END REVIEW

On January 1 of the current year, Bradshaw Company purchased all of the common shares of Dukes Company for $600,000 cash—this is $200,000 in excess of Dukes's book value of its equity. The balance sheets of the two firms immediately after the acquisition follow:

	Bradshaw (Parent)	Dukes (Subsidiary)	Consolidating Adjustments	Consolidated
Current assets	$1,000,000	$100,000		
Investment in Dukes.	600,000	—		
PPE, net	3,000,000	400,000		
Goodwill	—	—		_____
Total assets.	$4,600,000	$500,000		
Liabilities.	$1,000,000	$100,000		
Contributed capital.	2,000,000	200,000		
Retained earnings	1,600,000	200,000		_____
Total liabilities and equity	$4,600,000	$500,000		

During purchase negotiations, Dukes's PPE was appraised at $500,000, and all of Dukes's remaining assets and liabilities were appraised at values approximating their book values. Also, Bradshaw concluded that payment of an additional $100,000 was warranted because of anticipated corporate synergies. Show the impact of the transaction in the financial statement effects template, prepare the appropriate journal entry, post the journal entry to the related T-accounts, and prepare the consolidated balance sheet at acquisition.

The solution to this review problem can be found on page 617.

APPENDIX 12A: Equity Method Mechanics

The appendix provides a comprehensive example of accounting for an equity method investment. Assume that Petroni Company acquires a 30% interest in the outstanding voting shares of Wahlen Company on January 1, 2016, for $234,000 in cash. On that date, Wahlen's book value of equity is $560,000. Petroni agrees to pay $234,000 for a company with a book value of equity equivalent to $168,000 ($560,000 × 30%) because it feels that (1) Wahlen's balance sheet is undervalued by $140,000 (Petroni estimates PPE is undervalued by $50,000 and that Wahlen has unrecorded patents valued at $90,000) and (2) the investment is expected to yield intangible benefits valued at $24,000. (The $140,000 by which the balance sheet is undervalued translates into an investment equivalent of $42,000 [$140,000 × 30%]. This, plus the intangible benefits valued at $24,000, comprises the $66,000 difference between the purchase price [$234,000] and the book value equivalent [$168,000].)

The effect of the investment on Petroni's books is to reduce cash by $234,000 and to report the investment in Wahlen for $234,000. The investment is reported at its fair value at acquisition, just like all other asset acquisitions, and it is reported as a noncurrent asset because the expected holding period of equity method investments is in excess of one year. Subsequent to this purchase there are three main aspects of equity method accounting:

1. Dividends received from the investee are treated as a return *of* the investment rather than a return *on* the investment (investor company records an increase in cash received and a decrease in the investment account).

2. When the investee company reports net income for a period, the investor company reports its proportionate ownership of that income. This amount is usually reported in the investment income section of its income statement. Thus, both income and the investment account increase from equity method income. If the investee company reports a net *loss* for the period, income of the investor company is reduced as well as its investment account by its proportionate share.

3. The investment balance is not marked-to-fair value (market) as with passive investments. Instead, it is recorded at its historical cost and is increased (decreased) by the investor company's proportionate share of investee income (loss) and decreased by any cash dividends received. Unrecognized gains (losses) can, therefore, occur if the fair value of the investment differs from this adjusted cost. (If a decline in value is deemed "other than temporary," then the investment would be written down.)

To illustrate these mechanics, let's return to our illustration and assume that subsequent to acquisition, Wahlen reports net income of $50,000 and pays $10,000 cash dividends. Petroni would reflect these events in the FSET as follows:

Transaction	Balance Sheet									Income Statement				
	Cash Asset	+	Noncash Assets	=	Liabil- ities	+	Contrib. Capital	+	Earned Capital		Revenues	-	Expenses	=	Net Income
(1) Purchase 30% of Wahlen Co. stock.	−234,000 Cash		+234,000 Investment in Wahlen	=								-		=	
(2) Recognize 30% of Wahlen net income.			+15,000 Investment in Wahlen						+15,000 Retained Earnings		+15,000 Investment Income				+15,000
(3) Receive 30% of Wahlen dividends.	+3,000 Cash		−3,000 Investment in Wahlen												

After these entries, the investment balance is $246,000. Petroni has an investing cash outflow of $234,000 and an operating cash inflow of $3,000. Retained earnings increase by $15,000 from recognizing the 30% share of Wahlen's net income.

However, Petroni must also account for the differential values that accounted for the purchase premium. If Wahlen's PPE is undervalued by $50,000 and has an expected remaining life of twenty years, Petroni must depreciate $750 (= 30%*$50,000/20 years) in value for each of the next twenty years. And, if the unrecorded patents have an expected useful life of nine years, Petroni must amortize $3,000 (= 30%*$90,000/9 years) of the investment's value for each of the coming nine years. These amortizations are deducted from the investment income recognized by Petroni. The entries are the following:

Transaction	Balance Sheet									Income Statement				
(4) Depreciate additional PPE value.			−750 Investment in Wahlen	=					−750 Retained Earnings		−750 Investment Income	-		=	−750
(5) Amortize additional patent assets.			−3,000 Investment in Wahlen						−3,000 Retained Earnings		−3,000 Investment Income				−3,000

A part of the premium paid by Petroni is attributed to items that have definite lives (PPE and patents), and we must account for those amounts in judging the investment's performance. In this case, Petroni records income of $11,250 on its $234,000 investment − $15,000 for its share of Wahlen's income, minus the $3,750 amortization of the premium paid for PPE and patents. The Investment in Wahlen asset has a value of $242,250 ($234,000 + 15,000 − 3,000 − 750 − 3,000) after all entries.

The amount attributed to goodwill is tested for impairment annually, but it is not subject to periodic amortization.

LO7 Apply consolidation accounting mechanics.

7

APPENDIX 12B: Consolidation Accounting Mechanics

This appendix is a continuation of the example we introduced in Appendix 12A, extended to the consolidation of a parent company and one wholly owned subsidiary. Assume that Petroni Company acquires 100% (rather than 30% as in Appendix 12A) of the outstanding voting shares of Wahlen Company on January 1, 2016. To obtain these shares, Petroni pays $420,000 cash and issues 20,000 shares of its $10 par value common stock. On this date, Petroni's stock has a fair value of $18 per share, and Wahlen's book value of equity is $560,000. Petroni is willing to pay $780,000 ($420,000 plus 20,000 shares at $18 per share) for this company with a book value of equity of $560,000 because it believes Wahlen's balance sheet is understated by $140,000 (its PPE is undervalued by $50,000 and it has unrecorded patents valued at $90,000). The remaining $80,000 of the purchase price excess over book value is ascribed to corporate synergies and other unidentifiable intangible assets (goodwill). Thus, the purchase price consists of the following three components:

Investment ($780,000)	Book value of Wahlen ($560,000)
	Excess fair value over book ($140,000)
	Goodwill ($80,000)

The investment in Wahlen appears as a financial asset on Petroni's books. This means that at acquisition, Petroni's assets increase by $360,000 (cash decreases by $420,000 and the investments account increases by $780,000) and its equity (contributed capital) increases by the same amount.

The balance sheets of Petroni and Wahlen at acquisition follow, including the adjustments that occur in the consolidation process and the ultimate consolidated balance sheet.

Accounts	Petroni Company	Wahlen Company	Consolidation Adjustments*		Consolidated Balance Sheet
			Entry S	Entry A	
Cash.......................	$ 168,000	$ 80,000			$ 248,000
Receivables, net...............	320,000	180,000			500,000
Inventory...................	440,000	260,000			700,000
Investment in Wahlen...........	780,000	0	$(560,000)	$(220,000)	0
Land......................	200,000	120,000			320,000
PPE, net...................	1,040,000	320,000		50,000	1,410,000
Patents....................	0	0		90,000	90,000
Goodwill...................	0	0		80,000	80,000
Totals	$2,948,000	$960,000			$3,348,000
Accounts payable..............	$ 320,000	$ 60,000			$ 380,000
Long-term liabilities	760,000	340,000			1,100,000
Contributed capital............	1,148,000	80,000	(80,000)		1,148,000
Retained earnings	720,000	480,000	(480,000)		720,000
Totals	$2,948,000	$960,000			$3,348,000

*Entry S refers to elimination of subsidiary stockholders' equity, and Entry A refers to adjustment of assets and liabilities acquired.

The initial balance of the investment account at acquisition ($780,000) reflects the $700,000 fair value of Wahlen's net tangible assets and patents ($560,000 book value + $140,000 undervaluation of assets) plus the goodwill ($80,000) acquired. Goodwill is the excess of the purchase price over the fair value of the net assets acquired. It does not appear on Petroni's balance sheet as an explicit asset at this point. It is, however, included in the investment balance and will emerge as a separate asset during consolidation.

The process of completing the initial consolidated balance sheet involves eliminating Petroni's investment account and replacing it with the assets and liabilities of Wahlen Company to which it relates. Recall the investment account consists of three items: the book value of Wahlen ($560,000), the excess of net asset fair value over book value ($140,000), and goodwill ($80,000). The consolidation process eliminates each item as follows:

Entry S: Elimination of Wahlen's book value of equity: Investment account is reduced by the $560,000 book value of Wahlen, and each of the components of Wahlen's equity ($80,000 common stock and $480,000 retained earnings) are eliminated.

Entry A: Elimination of the excess of purchase price over book value: Investment account is reduced by $220,000 to zero. The remaining adjustments increase assets (A) by the additional purchase price paid. PPE is written up by $50,000, and a $90,000 patent asset and an $80,000 goodwill asset are reported.

Stepping back from the consolidation process, we can see its effects by comparing the Petroni Company (parent) balance sheet to the consolidated balance sheet. The Petroni Company balance sheet shows a financial asset valued at $780,000. Consolidation gives us a different perspective. Rather than viewing this as a financial investment, consolidation views the financial investment as the *means* by which Petroni Company acquired a bundle of assets and liabilities. That is, the financial asset of $780,000 has been replaced by Cash ($80,000), Receivables ($180,000), Inventory ($260,000), Land ($120,000), PPE – net ($370,000), Patent ($90,000), Goodwill ($80,000), Payables ($60,000) and Long-term liabilities ($340,000). This bundle has a net value equal to the $780,000, but it provides much more detail about the transaction in which Petroni engaged.

The one part of the balance sheet that is not changed by the consolidation is the shareholders' equity section. The consolidated shareholders' equity accounts are the same as the parent company shareholders' equity accounts when the parent owns 100% of the subsidiary.

Consolidation is similar in successive periods. To the extent that the excess purchase price has been assigned to depreciable assets, or identifiable intangible assets that are amortized over their useful lives, the new assets recognized initially are depreciated. If the PPE value adjustment has an estimated life of 20 years, then the consolidated income statement would include depreciation of 1/20 of this $50,000 each year. Amortization of the $90,000 patent would also appear in the consolidated income statement. Finally, because goodwill is not amortized under GAAP, it remains at its carrying amount of $80,000 on the consolidated balance sheet unless and until it is impaired and written down.

APPENDIX 12C: Accounting for Investments in Derivatives

LO8 Discuss the reporting of derivative securities.

Derivatives refer to financial instruments that are utilized by companies to reduce various kinds of risks. Some examples follow:

- A company expects to purchase raw materials for its production process and wants to reduce the risk that the purchase price increases prior to the purchase.

- A company has an accounts receivable on its books that is payable in a foreign currency and wants to reduce the risk that exchange rates move unfavorably prior to collection.

- A company borrows funds on a floating rate of interest (such as linked to the prime rate) and wants to convert the loan to a fixed rate of interest.

Companies are commonly exposed to these and many similar types of risk. Although companies are generally willing to assume the normal market risks that are inherent in their business, many of these financial-type risks can add variability to income and are uncontrollable. Fortunately, commodities, currencies, and interest rates are all traded on various markets and, further, securities have been developed to manage all of these risks. These securities fall under the label of derivatives. They include forward contracts, futures contracts, option contracts, and swap agreements.

Companies use derivatives to manage many of these financial risks. The reduction of risk comes at a price: the fee that another party (called the counterparty) is charging to assume that risk. Most counterparties are financial institutions, and managing financial risk is their business and a source of their profits. Although derivatives can be used effectively to manage financial risk, they can also be used for speculation with potentially disastrous results. It is for this reason that regulators passed standards regarding their disclosure in financial statements.

Reporting of Derivatives   Derivatives work by offsetting the gain or loss for the asset or liability to which they relate. Derivatives thus shelter the company from such fluctuations. For example, if a hedged receivable denominated in a foreign currency declines in value (due to a strengthening of the $US), the derivative security will increase in value by an offsetting amount, at least in theory. As a result, net equity remains unaffected and no gain or loss arises, nor is a loss reported in income.[6]

Although accounting for derivatives is complex, it essentially boils down to this: the derivative contract, and the asset or liability to which it relates, are both reported on the balance sheet at fair value. The asset and liability are offsetting *if* the hedge is effective and, thus, net equity is unaffected. Likewise, the related gains and losses are largely offsetting, leaving income unaffected. Income is impacted only to the extent that the hedging activities are ineffective or result from speculative activities. It is this latter activity, in particular, that regulators were concerned about in formulating accounting standards for derivatives.

Disclosure of Derivatives   Companies are required to disclose both qualitative and quantitative information about derivatives in notes to their financial statements and elsewhere (usually in Management's Discussion and Analysis section). The aim of these disclosures is to inform outsiders about potential risks underlying derivative securities.

Following is **Southwest Airlines Co.**'s disclosures from note 1 to its 2014 10-K report relating to its use of derivatives.

Financial Derivative Instruments

The Company accounts for financial derivative instruments at fair value and applies hedge accounting rules where appropriate. The Company utilizes various derivative instruments, including crude oil, unleaded gasoline, and heating oil-based derivatives, to attempt to reduce the risk of its exposure to jet fuel price increases. These instruments consist primarily of purchased call options, collar structures, call spreads, put spreads, and fixed-price swap agreements, and upon proper qualification are accounted for as cash-flow hedges. The Company also has interest rate swap agreements to convert a portion of its fixed-rate debt to floating rates and has swap agreements that convert certain floating-rate debt to a fixed-rate. These interest rate hedges are appropriately designated as either fair value hedges or as cash flow hedges.

Since the majority of the Company's financial derivative instruments are not traded on a market exchange, the Company estimates their fair values. Depending on the type of instrument, the values are determined by the use of present value methods or option value models with assumptions about commodity prices based on those observed in underlying markets. Also, since there is not a reliable forward market for jet fuel, the Company must estimate the future prices of jet fuel in order to measure the effectiveness of the hedging instruments in offsetting changes to those prices. Forward jet fuel prices are estimated through utilization of a statistical-based regression equation with data from market forward prices of like commodities. This equation is then adjusted for certain items, such as transportation costs, that are stated in the Company's fuel purchasing contracts with its vendors.

For the effective portion of settled fuel hedges, the Company records the associated gains or losses as a component of Fuel and oil expense in the Consolidated Statement of Income. For amounts representing ineffectiveness, as defined, or changes in fair value of derivative instruments for which hedge accounting is not applied, the Company records any gains or losses as a component of Other (gains) losses, net, in the Consolidated Statement of Income. Amounts that are paid or received in connection with the purchase or sale of financial derivative instruments (i.e., premium costs of option contracts) are classified as a component of Other (gains) losses, net, in the Consolidated Statement of Income in the period in which the instrument settles or expires. All cash flows associated with purchasing and selling derivatives are classified as operating cash flows in the Consolidated Statement of Cash Flows, within Changes in certain assets and liabilities.

Southwest Airlines' derivative use is mainly to hedge against fuel cost. Those hedges act to place a ceiling on fuel cost. For 2014, these instruments covered 34% of the company's fuel requirements.

From a reporting standpoint, unrealized gains and losses on these option contracts are accumulated in the Accumulated Other Comprehensive Income (AOCI) portion of its stockholders' equity until the fuel is purchased. Once that fuel is purchased, those unrealized gains and losses are removed from AOCI and the gain (loss) on the option is used to offset the loss (gain) on fuel. While the effect of fuel hedging on Southwest Airlines' profitability was minor in 2014, it has had a much bigger impact in previous years.

Although the fair value of derivatives and their related assets or liabilities can be substantial, the net effect on earnings and stockholders' equity is usually minor because companies are mainly using them as

---

[6] Unrealized gains and losses on derivatives classified as effective *cash flow hedges* (such as those relating to planned purchases of commodities) are accumulated in other comprehensive income (OCI) and are not recognized in current income until the transaction is complete (such as when both the purchase and sale of inventory occurs). Unrealized gains and losses on derivatives classified as *fair value hedges* (such as those relating to interest rate hedges and swaps, and the hedging of asset values such as relating to securities) as well as the changes in value of the hedged asset (liability) are recorded in current income.

hedges and not as speculative securities. The accounting standards for derivative instruments were enacted in response to a concern that speculative activities were not adequately disclosed. Subsequent to its passage, the financial effects have often appeared modest (with occasional exceptions such as **JP Morgan Chase**'s "London Whale"). Either these companies were not speculating to the extent expected, or they have since reduced their level of speculation in response to increased scrutiny from better disclosures.

SUMMARY

Explain and interpret the three levels of investor influence over an investee–passive, significant, and controlling. (p. 564)   **LO1**

- Ownership of 20% or less in another corporation is treated as a passive investment by the investor.
- Significant influence is assumed to be available to the investor corporation if it owns more than 20% but not over 50% of the outstanding voting stock of the investee corporation.
- Control is generally presumed if the investing firm owns more than 50% of the outstanding voting stock of the investee corporation.

Describe the term "fair value" and the fair value hierarchy. (p. 566)   **LO2**

- Fair value is the amount that an independent buyer would be willing to pay for an asset (or the amount that would need to be paid to discharge a liability) in an orderly transaction.
- Fair value can be determined by reference to a market price when available, but it may also be determined by other methods (discounted cash flow analysis, pricing of comparable assets, etc.). GAAP defines three levels of fair value determination:
  - Level 1: Values based on quoted prices in active markets for identical assets/liabilities
  - Level 2: Values based on observable inputs other than Level 1 (e.g., quoted prices for similar assets/liabilities or interest rates or yield curves)
  - Level 3: Values based on inputs observable only to the reporting entity (e.g., management estimates or assumptions.)
- GAAP requires that companies disclose their fair value determinations in the footnotes of their financial statements.

Describe and analyze accounting for passive investments. (p. 567)   **LO3**

- Ownership of 20% or less in another corporation is treated as a passive investment by the investor. Investing for returns is the objective rather than influencing another corporation's decisions. The investment is reported as a long-term asset only if the intention is to retain the asset for longer than a year. Passive investments are segregated into two types, called trading securities or securities available-for-sale.
- Trading securities are securities that will be converted into cash in a very short period of time. Any trading securities held at the end of an accounting period are marked to their fair value. The value change is recognized as an unrealized gain (or loss) in the income statement.
- Available-for-sale securities are held for long-term capital gains or dividends. Any securities held at the end of an accounting period are also marked to their fair value. However, the value change bypasses the income statement to become part of retained earnings called other comprehensive income.
- Gains and losses realized on sale, and dividends on passive investments are reported as other income in the income statement.
- Debt securities that management intends to hold to maturity are carried at cost unless their value is considered impaired in which case the security is written down. Otherwise changes in fair value are not recognized on the balance sheet or the income statement.

Explain and analyze accounting for investments with significant influence. (p. 575)   **LO4**

- Significant influence is assumed to be available to the investor corporation if it owns more than 20% but not over 50% of the outstanding voting stock of the investee corporation. Typically, the investment is initially recorded as a long-term asset at the purchase price.
- In the case of significant influence, the equity method of reporting is followed.
- Under the equity method, the investor recognizes its proportionate share of the investee's net income as income and an increase in the investment account. Any dividends received by the investor are treated as a recovery of the investment and reduce the investment balance.

LO5   Describe and analyze accounting for investments with control. (p. 579)

- If a corporation is considered to have control of another corporation, the financial statements of both firms are consolidated and reported as though they were a single entity.
- Control means that the investor has the ability to affect the strategic direction of the investee. Control is generally presumed if the investing firm owns more than 50% of the outstanding voting stock of the investee corporation.
- At the time of the acquisition, acquired assets and liabilities are restated at fair value in the consolidated balance sheet.
- If the purchase price exceeds the fair value of acquired assets, the remainder is labeled "goodwill." Goodwill is not amortized, but tested for impairment annually.

LO6   Appendix 12A: Illustrate and analyze accounting mechanics for equity method investments. (p. 589)

- Under the equity method of accounting, neither the investee's assets nor its liabilities are reported on the investor's balance sheet. Only the proportionate investment is reported. Further, only the investor's net equity is reported in income; and the investee's sales and expenses are omitted.
- The result is that revenues and expenses, but not NOPAT, are understated; NOPM (NOPAT/Sales) is overstated; and net operating assets (NOA) are understated. Also, financial leverage is understated. ROE remains unaffected.

LO7   Appendix 12B: Apply consolidation accounting mechanics. (p. 590)

- Identifiable intangible assets (such as patents, trademarks, customer lists) often result from the acquisition of one corporation by another. This is a situation in which the acquirer will have control and consolidation accounting is required.
- Intangibles are valued at the purchase date and then amortized over their economic life. Any remaining purchase price not allocated to tangible or identifiable intangible assets is treated as goodwill.
- Goodwill is not amortized but is written down when and if considered impaired. The write-down is an expense of the period.
- Reports of consolidated corporations are often difficult to understand because they commingle the assets, liabilities, revenues, expenses, and cash flows of several businesses that can be very different. General Electric and its subsidiary provide an example.

LO8   Appendix 12C: Discuss the reporting of derivative securities. (p. 591)

- Derivatives refer to financial instruments that are utilized by companies to reduce various kinds of risks.
- Derivatives work by offsetting the gain or loss for the asset or liability to which they relate.
- The accounting for derivatives boils down to this: the derivative contract and the asset or liability to which it relates are both reported on the balance sheet at fair value. The asset and liability are offsetting if the hedge is effective. Likewise, the related gains and losses are largely offsetting, leaving income unaffected.

GUIDANCE ANSWERS . . . YOU MAKE THE CALL

You are the Chief Financial Officer   When a key component of a company's distribution process begins to turn its attention to other products, it can have a detrimental effect of the prospects for future growth. For instance, the soft-drink companies depend heavily on their bottling companies to get the product to the consumer. In these circumstances, companies may purchase enough shares in the distribution company to exert significant influence (or even control) over the key distributor.

KEY TERMS

Asset turnover ratios (p. 578)

Available-for-sale (AFS) securities (p. 568)

Consolidated financial statements (p. 579)

Controlling influence (p. 565)

Cost method (p. 574)

Derivatives (p. 591)

Equity method (p. 576)

Fair value (p. 566)

Fair value hierarchy (p. 566)

Fair value option (p. 566)

Financial investments (p. 564)

Financial leverage (p. 578)

Held-to-maturity (HTM) (p. 574)

Net operating profit margin (p. 578)

Passive influence (p. 565)

Significant influence (p. 565)

Trading (T) securities (p. 568)

Assignments with the Ⓜ logo in the margin are available in BusinessCourse.
See the Preface of the book for details.

MULTIPLE CHOICE

1. Corporation A owns 50% of corporation B. This is a case where:
   a. Corporation A controls corporation B.
   b. Corporation A does not control corporation B.
   c. Corporation A has significant influence on corporation B.
   d. Corporation A does not have a significant influence on corporation B.
   e. Both *a* and *c* are correct.

2. In accounting for available-for-sale securities, the:
   a. Securities are reported at their fair value, along with their fair value adjustment from cost.
   b. Securities are reported at cost.
   c. Increases in fair value are reported in income.
   d. Increases in fair value are not reported in income.
   e. Both *a* and *d* are correct.

3. Which of the following statements is true of investments accounted for under the equity method?
   a. Investor reports its percentage share of the investee's income in its operating income.
   b. Investor reports dividends received from the investee in its operating income.
   c. Investment is reported at its fair value.
   d. Investment is reported at cost plus any dividends received from the investee.
   e. Investment is reported at fair value less any dividends received from the investee.

4. Which of the following statements is true about goodwill?
   a. Current reporting standards require that goodwill be amortized over its economic life.
   b. Goodwill is written down when the fair value of the investee implies a goodwill value below the investor's goodwill account.
   c. Goodwill can be recognized only when the acquisition price does not exceed the value of the tangible and identifiable intangible assets acquired.
   d. The recording of goodwill can be based on the acquisition of assets such as patents and trademarks.
   e. Goodwill equals retained earnings.

Multiple Choice Answers
1. c   2. e   3. a   4. b

Superscript $^{A\,(B,\,C)}$ denotes assignments based on Appendix 12A (12B, 12C).

QUESTIONS

Q12-1. What measure (fair value or amortized cost) is used for the balance sheet to report (a) trading securities, (b) available-for-sale securities, and (c) held-to-maturity securities?

Q12-2. What is an unrealized holding gain (loss)? Explain.

Q12-3. Where are unrealized holding gains and losses related to trading securities reported in the financial statements? Where are unrealized holding gains and losses related to available-for-sale securities reported in the financial statements?

Q12-4. What does *significant influence* imply regarding financial investments? Describe the accounting procedures used for such investments.

Q12-5. On January 1 of the current year, Yetman Company purchases 40% of the common stock of Livnat Company for $250,000 cash. During the year, Livnat reports $80,000 of net income and pays $60,000 in cash dividends. At year-end, what amount should appear in Yetman's balance sheet for its investment in Livnat?

Q12-6. What accounting method is used when a stock investment represents more than 50% of the investee company's voting stock? Explain.

Q12-7. What is the underlying objective of consolidated financial statements?

Q12-8. Finn Company purchases all of the common stock of Murray Company for $750,000 when Murray Company has $300,000 of common stock and $450,000 of retained earnings. If a consolidated balance sheet is prepared immediately after the acquisition, what amounts are eliminated in preparing it? Explain.

Q12-9.[B] Bradshaw Company owns 100% of Dee Company. At year-end, Dee owes Bradshaw $75,000. If a consolidated balance sheet is prepared at year-end, how is the $75,000 handled? Explain.

Q12-10. What are some limitations of consolidated financial statements?

MINI EXERCISES

LO1

M12-11. Classifying Investments as Passive, Significant or Controlling

For each of the situations below, determine if the investment should be reported as a passive investment (P), an investment reflecting significant influence (SI), or a controlling interest (C).

a. _____ Griffin Company purchased 25% of the common stock of Wright, Inc. Griffin is one of several suppliers that Wright, Inc. relies on to supply subcomponents.

b. _____ Dye Corporation purchased 20% of the 2016 $40 million bond issue offered by Glover Company.

c. _____ Zhao, Inc. purchased 2,000 shares of Google, Inc. common stock, paying $1.1 million.

d. _____ Watts Corporation purchased 65% of the common stock of Zimmerman, Inc. common stock for cash. Watts and Zimmerman had been engaged in several strategic alliances prior to the purchase.

e. _____ Shevlin, Inc. purchased 15% of Bowen Company's common stock. Shevlin is Bowen Company's largest customer, buying more than 60% of its output.

LO3

Cisco Systems, Inc.
NASDAQ :: CSCO

M12-12. Interpreting Disclosures of Available-for-Sale Securities

Use the following year-end footnote information from **Cisco Systems, Inc.**'s 10-K report to answer parts *a* and *b*.

($ millions)	2014
Cost of available-for-sale investments securities.........................	$44,619
Gross unrealized gains...	759
Gross unrealized losses..	(30)
Fair value of available-for-sale investments securities....................	$45,348

a. At what amount is its available-for-sale investments reported on Cisco's 2014 balance sheet? Explain.

b. How is its net unrealized gain of $729 million ($759 million − $30 million) reported by Cisco in its financial statements?

LO3

M12-13. Accounting for Available-for-Sale and Trading Securities

Assume that Wasley Company purchases 6,000 common shares of Pincus Company for $12 cash per share. During the year, Wasley receives a cash dividend of $1.10 per common share from Pincus, and the year-end market price of Pincus common stock is $13 per share. How much income does Wasley report relating to this investment for the year if it accounts for the investment as:

a. Available-for-sale investment?

b. Trading investment?

LO2

Cisco Systems, Inc.
NASDAQ :: CSCO

M12-14. Analyzing Disclosures of Investment Securities

On its July 26, 2014 balance sheet, **Cisco Systems, Inc.** reports available-for-sale investments with a value of $45,348 million. As available-for-sale securities, these investments are reported at their fair value, and Cisco provides the following information in its footnotes.

	July 26, 2014 Fair Value Measurements			
	Level 1	Level 2	Level 3	Total Balance
Available-for-sale investments:				
U.S. government securities	$ —	$31,734	$ —	$31,734
U.S. government agency securities	—	1,063	—	1,063
Non-U.S. government and agency securities	—	861	—	861
Corporate debt securities.	—	9,159	—	9,159
Mortgage-backed securities	—	579	—	579
Publicly traded equity securities	$1,952	—	—	$ 1,952

  a. Explain the differences between the three columns labeled Level 1, Level 2 and Level 3.
  b. Are all of these investments "marked-to-fair value"? If not, which ones are not marked-to-fair value? Which investment values do you regard as most subjective? Least subjective?
  c. If Cisco needed to raise cash to take advantage of an investment opportunity, which of these investments do you regard as most liquid (i.e., most easily turned into cash)? Least liquid?

M12-15. Analyzing and Interpreting Equity Method Investments   **LO4**

Stober Company purchases an investment in Lang Company at a purchase price of $1 million cash, representing 30% of the book value of Lang. During the year, Lang reports net income of $100,000 and pays cash dividends of $40,000. At the end of the year, the fair value of Stober's investment is $1.2 million.

  a. At what amount is the investment reported on Stober's balance sheet at year-end?
  b. What amount of income from investments does Stober report? Explain.
  c. Stober's $200,000 unrealized gain in investment fair value (choose one and explain):
      (1) Is not reflected on either its income statement or balance sheet.
      (2) Is reported in its current income.
      (3) Is reported on its balance sheet only.
      (4) Is reported in its other comprehensive income.
  d. Prepare journal entries to record the transactions and events above.
  e. Post the journal entries from d to their respective T-accounts.
  f. Record each of the transactions from d in the financial statement effects template.

M12-16. Calculating Income for Equity Method Investments   **LO4**

Kross Company purchases an equity investment in Penno Company at a purchase price of $5 million, representing 40% of the book value of Penno. During the current year, Penno reports net income of $600,000 and pays cash dividends of $200,000. At the end of the year, the market value of Kross's investment is $5.3 million. What amount of income does Kross report relating to this investment in Penno for the year? Explain.

M12-17. Computing Consolidating Adjustments and Noncontrolling Interest   **LO5**

Philipich Company purchases 80% of Hirst Company's common stock for $600,000 cash when Hirst Company has $300,000 of common stock and $450,000 of retained earnings. If a consolidated balance sheet is prepared immediately after the acquisition, what amounts are eliminated when preparing that statement? What amount of noncontrolling interest appears in the consolidated balance sheet?

M12-18. Computing Consolidated Net Income   **LO5**

Benartzi Company purchased a 90% interest in Liang Company on January 1 of the current year. Benartzi Company had $600,000 net income for the current year *before* recognizing its share of Liang Company's net income. If Liang Company had net income of $150,000 for the year, what is the consolidated net income for the year?

M12-19. Effect of Investing on Ratios   **LO4, 5**

DeFond Company wishes to secure a reliable supply of a key component for its production processes, and its management is considering two alternative investments. Verduzco Company produces exactly the supply that DeFond needs, so DeFond could use cash to purchase 100% of the common stock of Verduzco. Lin Company produces twice as much of the component that DeFond needs, but DeFond could form a joint venture with another company where each would purchase 50% of Lin Company's common stock and each take 50% of Lin Company's output.

The table that follows gives the balance sheet information for all three companies prior to any investment by DeFond. For the questions below, assume that DeFond would be able to purchase shares at the investee companies' book values and that the investee companies' assets and liabilities have fair values equal to their book values.

	DeFond Company	Verduzco Company	Lin Company
Cash...	$ 800	$ 100	$ 200
Investment	—	—	—
Noncash assets	2,000	900	1,800
Liabilities...................................	2,200	700	1,400
Shareholders' Equity	600	300	600

a. Suppose that DeFond purchases 100% of Verduzco's common stock for $300. Produce the consolidated balance sheet for DeFond immediately after the acquisition.

b. Suppose that DeFond purchases 50% of Lin's common stock for $300. Produce the balance sheet for DeFond immediately after the investment (using the equity method).

c. From a business perspective, either of these investments will accomplish the objective of obtaining a reliable supply of components. How will the financial ratios differ between the two alternatives?

LO3

M12-20. Reporting of and Analyzing Financial Effects of Trading (Debt) Securities

Hartgraves Company had the following transactions and adjustments related to a bond investment that is a trading security.

2015

Oct. 1   Purchased $500,000 face value of Skyline, Inc.'s 7% bonds at 97 plus a brokerage commission of $1,000. The bonds pay interest on September 30 and March 31 and mature in 20 years. Hartgraves Company expects to sell the bonds in the near future.

Dec. 31   Made the adjusting entry to record interest earned on investment in the Skyline bonds.

     31   Made the adjusting entry to record the current fair value of the Skyline bonds. At December 31, 2015, the fair value of the Skyline bonds was $490,000.

2016

Mar. 31   Received the semiannual interest payment on investment in the Skyline bonds.

Apr. 1   Sold the Skyline bond investment for $492,300 cash.

a. Prepare journal entries to record these transactions.

b. Post the journal entries from *a* to their respective T-accounts.

c. Record each of the transactions in the financial statement effects template.

LO3

M12-21. Reporting of and Analyzing Financial Effects of Trading (Equity) Securities

Blouin Company had the following transactions and adjustment related to a stock investment that is a trading security.

2015

Nov. 15   Purchased 10,000 shares of Lane, Inc.'s common stock at $17 per share plus a brokerage commission of $1,200. Blouin expects to sell the stock in the near future.

Dec. 22   Received a cash dividend of $1.00 per share of common stock from Lane.

     31   Made the adjusting entry to reflect year-end fair value of the stock investment in Lane. The year-end fair value of the Lane common stock is $15.50 per share.

2016

Jan. 20   Sold all 10,000 shares of the Lane common stock for $150,000.

a. Prepare journal entries to record these transactions.

b. Post the journal entries from *a* to their respective T-accounts.

c. Record each of the transactions in the financial statement effects template.

LO3

M12-22. Reporting of and Analyzing Financial Effects of Available-for-Sale (Equity) Securities

Refer to the data for Blouin Company in Mini Exercise 12-21. Assume that when the shares were purchased, management did not intend to sell the stock in the near future. Record the transactions and adjustments for Blouin Company as an available-for-sale security.

M12-23. Computing Stockholders' Equity in Consolidation

LO5

On January 1 of the current year, Halen Company purchased all of the common shares of Jolson Company for $575,000 cash. On this date, the stockholders' equity of Halen Company consisted of $600,000 in common stock and $310,000 in retained earnings. Jolson Company had $350,000 in common stock and $225,000 in retained earnings. What amount of total stockholders' equity appears on the consolidated balance sheet?

EXERCISES

E12-24. Assessing Financial Statement Effects of Trading and Available-for-Sale Securities

LO1, 3

Four transactions involving investments in marketable securities classified as trading follow.

    (1) Purchased 6,000 common shares of Liu, Inc., for $12 cash per share.
    (2) Received a cash dividend of $1.10 per common share from Liu.
    (3) Year-end market price of Liu common stock is $11.25 per share.
    (4) Sold all 6,000 common shares of Liu for $66,900.

  a. Prepare journal entries to record the four transactions.
  b. Post the journal entries from *a* to their respective T-accounts.
  c. Record each of the transactions from *a* in the financial statement effects template.
  d. Using the same transaction information as above and assuming the investments in marketable securities are classified as available-for-sale, (i) prepare journal entries to record the transactions, (ii) post the journal entries to their respective T-accounts, and (iii) record each of the transactions in the financial statement effects template.

E12-25. Assessing Financial Statement Effects of Trading and Available-for-Sale Securities

LO1, 3

For the following transactions involving investments in marketable securities, assume that:

  a. Investments are classified as trading.
    (1) Ohlson Co. purchases 5,000 common shares of Freeman Co. at $16 cash per share.
    (2) Ohlson Co. receives a cash dividend of $1.25 per common share from Freeman.
    (3) Year-end market price of Freeman common stock is $17.50 per share.
    (4) Ohlson Co. sells all 5,000 common shares of Freeman for $86,400 cash.
    (i) prepare journal entries to record the four transactions, (ii) post the journal entries to their respective T-accounts, and (iii) record each of the transactions in the financial statement effects template.
  b. Investments are classified as available-for-sale (for same four transactions from *a*).
    (i) prepare journal entries to record the transactions, (ii) post the journal entries to their respective T-accounts, and (iii) record each of the transactions in the financial statement effects template.

E12-26. Interpreting Footnotes on Security Investments

LO1, 3, 4

SunTrust Banks, Inc.
NYSE :: STI
The Coca-Cola Company
NYSE :: KO

SunTrust Banks, Inc. is a bank holding company based in Atlanta, Georgia. Founded in 1891 as the Commercial Travelers' Savings Bank, the organization underwrote **The Coca-Cola Company**'s initial public offering in 1919, receiving Coca-Cola stock in lieu of underwriting fees. Over the ensuing 91 years, the SunTrust organization has maintained a close relationship with Coca-Cola. Robert Woodruff, Coca-Cola's president from 1923 to 1954, was the son of long-time SunTrust president, Ernest Woodruff. The original copy of the famous Coca-Cola formula is stored in a safe deposit box at one of SunTrust's Atlanta branches.

The financial crisis of 2007-2009 put pressure on most large American financial institutions, including SunTrust. Although the company did not suffer the spectacular drops in asset values that made headlines at other banks, its exposure to property markets and securities connected to these markets caused the bank's regulatory capital to decline.

The following information is taken from Note 5 of SunTrust's 2006 annual report:

Note 5: Securities Available for Sale
Securities available for sale at December 31 were as follows:

($ thousands)	2006			
	Amortized Cost	Unrealized Gains	Unrealized Losses	Fair Value
U.S. Treasury and other U.S. government agencies and corporations...............	$ 1,607,999	$ 8,602	$ 16,144	$ 1,600,457
States and political subdivisions	1,032,247	13,515	4,639	1,041,123
Asset-backed securities.....................	1,128,032	1,891	17,584	1,112,339
Mortgage-backed securities	17,337,311	37,365	243,762	17,130,914
Corporate bonds	468,855	1,477	7,521	462,811
Common stock of The Coca-Cola Company....	110	2,324,716	—	2,324,826
Other securities	1,423,799	5,446	—	1,429,245
Total securities available for sale	$22,998,353	$2,393,012	$289,650	$25,101,715

a.   On December 31, 2006, SunTrust owned 48.183 million shares of Coca-Cola stock. What was the amortized cost of this investment? (This is the value imputed to the underwriting services provided in 1919 plus the historical value of any dividends reinvested in Coca-Cola stock over the ensuing 87 years.) What was the fair value of SunTrust's investment in Coca-Cola on December 31, 2006?

b.   What is the maximum amount by which SunTrust Banks, Inc. could have increased its retained earnings by sales of Coca-Cola stock on December 31, 2006? Assume a 35% tax rate would be applied to gains from disposal of available-for-sale securities. Also, assume that taxes would be paid in cash immediately, i.e., on December 31.

c.   Beginning in 2007, the pressures of the financial crisis caused SunTrust to use its investment in Coca-Cola to boost its required capital. SunTrust sold 4.605 million shares of Coca-Cola's stock in 2007 for a price of $51 per share. Assume that the sale took place early in the year. Provide a journal entry for this transaction (ignore taxes).

LO1, 3

E12-27. Reporting of and Analyzing Financial Effects of Trading (Debt) Securities
Barclay, Inc., had the following transactions and adjustments related to a bond investment that is classified as a trading security.

2015

Nov. 1   Purchased $300,000 face value of Joos, Inc.'s 9% bonds at 102 plus a brokerage commission of $900. The bonds pay interest on October 31 and April 30 and mature in 15 years. Barclay expects to sell the bonds in the near future.

Dec. 31   Made the adjusting entry to record interest earned on investment in the Joos bonds.

     31   Made the adjusting entry to record the current fair value of the Joos bonds. At December 31, 2015, the fair value of the Joos bonds was $301,500.

2016

Apr. 30   Received the semiannual interest payment on investment in the Joos bonds.

May 1   Sold the Joos bond investment for $300,900 cash.

a.   Prepare journal entries to record these transactions.

b.   Post the journal entries from a to their respective T-accounts.

c.   Record each of the transactions in the financial statement effects template.

LO5

E12-28. Reporting of Stockholders' Equity in Consolidation
Baylor Company purchased 75% of the common stock of Reed Company for $600,000 in cash when the stockholders' equity of Reed Company consisted of $500,000 in common stock and $300,000 in retained earnings. On the acquisition date, the stockholders' equity of Baylor Company consisted of $900,000 in common stock and $440,000 in retained earnings. Prepare the stockholders' equity section in the consolidated balance sheet as of the acquisition date.

LO3

E12-29. Interpreting Footnote Disclosures for Investments
CNA Financial Corporation provides the following information from its 2014 10-K report:

Valuation of investments: The Company classifies its fixed maturity securities and its equity securities as either available-for-sale or trading, and as such, they are carried at fair value. Changes in fair value of trading securities are reported within Net investment income on the Consolidated Statements of Operations. Changes in fair value related to available-for-sale securities are reported as a component of Other comprehensive income. The cost of fixed maturity securities classified as available-for-sale is adjusted for amortization of premiums and accretion of discounts to maturity, which are included in Net investment income on the Consolidated Statements of Operations. Losses may be recognized within Net realized investment gains (losses) on the Consolidated Statements of Operations when a decline in value is determined by the Company to be other-than-temporary.

Summary of Fixed Maturity and Equity Securities

December 31, 2014 ($ millions)	Cost or Amortized Cost	Gross Unrealized Gains	Gross Unrealized Losses	Estimated Fair Value
Fixed maturity securities available-for-sale:				
Corporate and other bonds	$17,210	$1,721	$61	$18,870
States, municipalities and political subdivisions	11,285	1,463	8	12,740
Asset-backed				
Residential mortgage-backed....................	5,028	218	13	5,233
Commercial mortgage-backed..................	2,056	93	5	2,144
Other asset-backed	1,234	11	10	1,235
Total asset-backed	8,318	322	28	8,612
U.S. Treasury and obligations of government-sponsored enterprises	26	5	—	31
Foreign government	438	16	—	454
Redeemable preferred stock	39	3	—	42
Total fixed maturity securities available-for-sale	37,316	3,530	97	40,749
Total fixed maturity securities trading.	19	—	—	19
Equity securities available-for-sale:				
Common stock................................	38	9	—	47
Preferred stock..............................	172	5	2	175
Total equity securities available-for-sale	210	14	2	222
Total	$37,545	$3,544	$99	$40,990

   a. At what amount is its investment portfolio reflected on its balance sheet? In your answer identify its fair value, cost, and any unrealized gains and losses.

   b. How are its unrealized gains and/or losses reflected in CNA's balance sheet and income statement?

   c. How are any impairment losses and the gains and losses realized from the sale of securities reflected in CNA's balance sheet and income statement?

E12-30. Assessing Financial Statement Effects of Equity Method Securities

The following transactions involve investments in marketable securities and are accounted for using the equity method.

   (1) Purchased 12,000 common shares of Barth Co. at $9 cash per share; the shares represent 30% ownership in Barth.

   (2) Received a cash dividend of $1.25 per common share from Barth.

   (3) Recorded income from Barth stock investment when Barth's net income is $80,000.

   (4) Sold all 12,000 common shares of Barth for $120,500.

   a. Prepare journal entries to record these four transactions.

   b. Post the journal entries from *a* to their respective T-accounts.

   c. Record each of the transactions in the financial statement effects template.

E12-31. Assessing Financial Statement Effects of Equity Method Securities

The following transactions involve investments in marketable securities and are accounted for using the equity method.

   (1) Healy Co. purchases 15,000 common shares of Palepu Co. at $8 cash per share; the shares represent 25% ownership of Palepu.

   (2) Healy receives a cash dividend of $0.80 per common share from Palepu.

   (3) Palepu reports annual net income of $120,000.

   (4) Healy sells all 15,000 common shares of Palepu for $140,000 cash.

    a.   Prepare journal entries to record these four transactions.

    b.   Post the journal entries from *a* to their respective T-accounts.

    c.   Record each of the transactions in the financial statement effects template.

LO1, 3, 4

E12-32. Assessing Financial Statement Effects of Passive and Equity Method Investments

On January 1, 2016, Ball Corporation purchased, as a stock investment, 10,000 shares of Leftwich Company common stock for $15 cash per share. On December 31, 2016, Leftwich announced net income of $80,000 for the year and paid a cash dividend of $1.10 per share. At December 31, 2016, the market value of Leftwich's stock was $19 per share.

    a.   Assume that the stock acquired by Ball represents 15% of Leftwich's voting stock and that Ball classifies it as available-for-sale. For the following transactions, (1) prepare journal entries, (2) post those journal entries to their respective T-accounts, and (3) record each of the transactions in the financial statement effects template.

        (1)   Ball purchased 10,000 common shares of Leftwich at $15 cash per share; the shares represent a 15% ownership in Leftwich.

        (2)   Leftwich reported annual net income of $80,000.

        (3)   Received a cash dividend of $1.10 per common share from Leftwich.

        (4)   Year-end market price of Leftwich common stock is $19 per share.

    b.   Assume that the stock acquired by Ball represents 30% of Leftwich's voting stock and that Ball accounts for this investment using the equity method since it is able to exert significant influence. For the same four transactions as above, (1) prepare journal entries, (2) post those journal entries to their respective T-accounts, and (3) record each of the transactions in the financial statement effects template.

LO1, 3

E12-33. Reporting Passive Investments

The following was disclosed in Note 10 to the September 30, 2014 annual report of **Siemens AG**:

Available-for-sale financial assets

The following tables summarize the current portion of the Company's investment in available-for-sale financial assets:

(€ millions)	September 30, 2014			
	Cost	Fair Value	Unrealized Gain	Unrealized Loss
Equity instruments	€ 1	€ 1	€—	€—
Debt instruments	693	702	9	—
Fund shares	194	222	28	—
	€888	€925	€37	€—

(€ millions)	September 30, 2013			
	Cost	Fair Value	Unrealized Gain	Unrealized Loss
Equity instruments	€ 6	€ 8	€ 2	€—
Debt instruments	379	382	3	—
Fund shares	195	211	16	(1)
	€580	€601	€21	€(1)

Noncurrent available-for-sale financial assets, which are included in line item Other financial assets are measured at fair value, if reliably measurable. They primarily consist of equity instruments, including shares in AtoS and in OSRAM. As of September 30, 2014 and 2013 non-current available-for-sale financial assets measured at cost amount to €192 million and €167 million, respectively; noncurrent available-for-sale financial assets measured at fair value amount to €1,611 million and €1,394 million, respectively.

    a.   What was the total amount that was reported for available-for-sale securities in Siemens' 2014 balance sheet? Where are the unrealized gains and losses reported?

    b.   In fiscal 2014, Siemens purchased short-term (current) available-for-sale securities costing €613 million and sold short-term (current) available-for-sale securities for €317 in cash. What amount of gain or loss was realized on the sale of these securities? Where was this gain or loss reported?

c. What amount of gain or loss would Siemens report in its 2014 income statement if the current portion of available-for-sale securities were classified as trading securities?

E12-34. Allocation of Acquisition Purchase Price
On January 26, 2015, Medtronic completed the acquisition of Covidien plc in a cash and stock transaction valued at approximately $50 billion. In connection with the transaction, Medtronic, Inc., a Minnesota corporation (Medtronic, Inc.), and Covidien were combined under and became subsidiaries of **Medtronic plc**, a public limited company organized under the laws of Ireland. Medtronic plc reported the allocation of the $50 billion purchase price to various assets and liabilities acquired in its April 2015 10-K as presented below ($ billions):

LO5
Medtronic, PLC
NYSE :: MDT

Current assets	$ 6.5
Property, plant and equipment	2.4
Intangible assets	26.3
Goodwill	?
Other assets	0.7
Current liabilities	3.3
Long-term liabilities, net	12.2

a. How are the values in the above table determined?
b. How much goodwill would Medtronic recognize from this acquisition? How will that goodwill be treated in subsequent periods?
c. Do you think Medtronic's shareholders would prefer to see an allocation that gives a lot of value to separately-identifiable assets or an allocation where most of the acquistion price goes to goodwill? Why?

E12-35. Reporting of and Analyzing Financial Effects of Trading (Equity) Securities
Guay Company had the following transactions and adjustment related to a stock investment classified as a trading security.

LO1, 3

2015

Nov. 15 Purchased 5,000 shares of Core, Inc.'s common stock at $16 per share plus a brokerage commission of $900. Guay Company expects to sell the stock in the near future.
Dec. 22 Received a cash dividend of $1.25 per share of common stock from Core.
31 Made the adjusting entry to reflect year-end fair value of the stock investment in Core. The year-end market price of the Core common stock is $17.50 per share.

2016
Jan. 20 Sold all 5,000 shares of the Core common stock for $86,400.

a. Prepare journal entries to record these transactions.
b. Post the journal entries from *a* to their respective T-accounts.
c. Record each of the transactions in the financial statement effects template.

E12-36. Reporting of and Analyzing Financial Effects of Available-for-Sale (Equity) Securities
Refer to the data for Guay Company in Exercise 12-35. Assume that when the shares were purchased, management did not intend to sell the stock in the near future. Record the transactions and adjustments for Guay Company under this assumption.

LO1, 3

E12-37. Reporting and Interpreting Stock Investment Performance
Kasznik Company began operations in 2016 and, by year-end (December 31), had made six stock investments. Year-end information on these stock investments follows.

LO1, 3, 4

Company	Cost or Equity Basis (as appropriate)	Year-End Fair Value	Investment Classification
Barth, Inc.	$ 68,000	$ 65,300	Trading
Foster, Inc.	162,500	160,000	Trading
McNichols, Inc.	197,000	192,000	Available-for-sale
Patell, Inc.	157,000	154,700	Available-for-sale
Ertimur, Inc.	100,000	102,400	Equity method
Soliman, Inc.	136,000	133,200	Equity method

a. At what total amount are the trading stock investments reported at in the December 31, 2016, balance sheet?

b. At what total amount are the available-for-sale stock investments reported at in the December 31, 2016, balance sheet?

c. At what total amount are the equity method stock investments reported at in the December 31, 2016, balance sheet?

d. What total amount of unrealized holding gains or unrealized holding losses related to stock investments appears in the 2016 income statement?

e. What total amount of unrealized holding gains or unrealized holding losses related to stock investments appears in the stockholders' equity section of the December 31, 2016, balance sheet?

f. What total amount of fair value adjustment to stock investments appears in the December 31, 2016, balance sheet? Which category of stock investments does the fair value adjustment relate to? Does the fair value adjustment increase or decrease the financial statement presentation of these stock investments?

LO1, 4

Merck & Co., Inc.
NYSE :: MRK

E12-38. Analyzing Equity Method Investment Footnotes

Merck & Co., Inc. reports a December 31, 2013 balance of $1.6 billion in "Investments in affiliates accounted for using the equity method" ("Investments in affiliates"). Provide the entries for the following events for fiscal year 2014:

a. Merck's share of income from its affiliates was $257 million.

b. Merck received dividends and distributions from its affiliates of $185 million during fiscal year 2014.

c. During fiscal year 2014, Merck divested its $1.4 billion investment in AstraZeneca LP, recognizing a gain of $650 million.

d. After these events, what should be the balance in Merck's investments in affiliates account at December 31, 2014? The actual balance was $337 million. What might explain any differences between these two values?

LO7

E12-39.ᴮ Constructing the Consolidated Balance Sheet at Acquisition

On January 1 of the current year, Healy Company purchased all of the common shares of Miller Company for $500,000 cash. Balance sheets of the two firms at acquisition follow.

	Healy Company	Miller Company	Consolidating Adjustments	Consolidated
Current assets	$1,700,000	$120,000		
Investment in Miller	500,000	—		
Plant assets, net.	3,000,000	410,000		
Goodwill	—	—		
Total assets.	$5,200,000	$530,000		_____
Liabilities.	$ 700,000	$ 90,000		
Contributed capital.	3,500,000	400,000		
Retained earnings	1,000,000	40,000		
Total liabilities and equity	$5,200,000	$530,000		_____

During purchase negotiations, Miller's plant assets were appraised at $425,000; and, all of its remaining assets and liabilities were appraised at values approximating their book values. Healy also concluded that an additional $45,000 (in goodwill) demanded by Miller's shareholders was warranted because Miller's earning power was better than the industry average. (1) Prepare the consolidating adjustments, (2) Prepare the consolidated balance sheet at acquisition, (3) Prepare journal entries to record the transactions, (4) Post the journal entries to their respective T-accounts, and (5) Record each of the transactions in the financial statement effects template.

LO7

E12-40.ᴮ Constructing the Consolidated Balance Sheet at Acquisition

Rayburn Company purchased all of Kanodia Company's common stock for cash on January 1, at which time the separate balance sheets of the two corporations appeared as follows:

	Rayburn Company	Kanodia Company	Consolidating Adjustments	Consolidated
Investment in Kanodia	$ 600,000	—		
Other assets	2,300,000	$700,000		
Goodwill	—	—		
Total assets.	$2,900,000	$700,000		
Liabilities.	$ 900,000	$160,000		
Contributed capital.	1,400,000	300,000		
Retained earnings	600,000	240,000		
Total liabilities and equity	$2,900,000	$700,000		

During purchase negotiations, Rayburn determined that the appraised value of Kanodia's other assets was $720,000; and, all of its remaining assets and liabilities were appraised at values approximating their book values. The remaining $40,000 of the purchase price was ascribed to goodwill. (1) Prepare the consolidating adjustments, (2) Prepare the consolidated balance sheet at acquisition, (3) Prepare journal entries to record the transactions, (4) Post the journal entries to their respective T-accounts, and (5) Record each of the transactions in the financial statement effects template.

E12-41. Assessing Goodwill Impairment

On January 1, 2016, Engel Company purchases 100% of Ball Company for $16.8 million. At the time of acquisition, Ball's stockholders' equity is reported at $16.2 million. Engel ascribes the excess of $600,000 to goodwill. Assume that the fair value of Ball declines to $12.5 million and that the fair value of Ball's tangible net assets is estimated at $12.3 million as of December 31, 2016.

LO5

a. Provide computations to determine if the goodwill has become impaired and, if so, the amount of the impairment.

b. What impact does the impairment of goodwill have on Engel's financial statements?

E12-42.B Constructing the Consolidated Balance Sheet at Acquisition

Easton Company acquires 100 percent of the outstanding voting shares of Harris Company on January 1, 2016. To obtain these shares, Easton pays $210,000 in cash and issues 5,000 of its $10 par value common stock. On this date, Easton's stock has a fair value of $36 per share, and Harris's book value of stockholders' equity is $280,000. Easton is willing to pay $390,000 for a company with a book value for equity of $280,000 because it believes that (1) Harris buildings are undervalued by $40,000, and (2) Harris has an unrecorded patent that Easton values at $30,000. Easton considers the remaining balance sheet items to be fairly valued (no book-to-fair value difference). The remaining $40,000 of the purchase price excess over book value is ascribed to corporate synergies and other general unidentifiable intangible assets (goodwill). The January 1, 2016, balance sheets at the acquisition date follow:

LO5, 7

	Easton Company	Harris Company	Consolidating Adjustments	Consolidated
Cash	$ 84,000	$ 40,000		
Receivables	160,000	90,000		
Inventory.	220,000	130,000		
Investment in Harris	390,000	—		
Land	100,000	60,000		
Buildings, net	400,000	110,000		
Equipment, net	120,000	50,000		
Total assets.	$1,474,000	$480,000		
Accounts payable.	$ 160,000	$ 30,000		
Long-term liabilities	380,000	170,000		
Common stock.	500,000	40,000		
Additional paid-in capital	74,000	—		
Retained earnings	360,000	240,000		
Total liabilities & equity	$1,474,000	$480,000		

a. Show the breakdown of the investment into the book value acquired, the excess of fair value over book value, and the portion of the investment representing goodwill.

b.   Prepare the consolidating adjustments and the consolidated balance sheet. Identify the adjustments by whether they relate to the elimination of stockholders' equity [S] or the excess of
purchase price over book value [A].

c.   How will the excess of the purchase price over book value acquired be treated in years subsequent to the acquisition?

LO6   **E12-43.^A Accounting for Equity Method Investments**

Refer to the Easton Company acquisition described in E12-42. Instead of a 100% acquisition, assume that Easton purchased 40% of the outstanding shares of Harris Company on January 1, 2016,
for $156,000 in cash. Also assume that the undervalued buildings have an estimated remaining
useful life of 20 years and the unrecorded patent has a useful life of 5 years.

During 2016, Harris reported net income of $80,000 and paid cash dividends to shareholders
totaling $40,000.

a.   Prepare journal entries to record Easton Company's equity in the earnings of Harris Company,
including any amortization of the excess of fair value over book value of assets acquired.

b.   What is the value of the investment in Harris Company reported on Easton Company's balance sheet as of December 31, 2016?

LO8   **E12-44.^C Reporting and Analyzing Derivatives**

Hewlett-Packard
Company
NYSE :: HPQ

Hewlett-Packard Company reports the following information on its cash-flow hedges (derivatives) in comprehensive income (net income plus other comprehensive income) in its 2014 10-K
report:

($ millions)	Total
Net earnings.	$5,013
Net unrealized gain on available-for-sale securities.	6
Net unrealized gain on cash flow hedges	488
Net unrealized components of defined benefit pension plans.	(2,446)
Net cumulative translation adjustment.	(85)
Provision for income taxes.	(66)
Comprehensive income	$2,910

a.   Identify and describe the usual applications for derivatives.

b.   How are derivatives and their related assets (and/or liabilities) reported on the balance sheet?

c.   By what amount has the unrealized gain or loss on the HP derivatives affected its current income? What are the analysis implications?

PROBLEMS

LO1, 2, 3   **P12-45.   Analyzing and Interpreting Available-for-Sale Securities Disclosures**

Metlife Inc.
NYSE :: MET

Following is a portion of the investments footnote 8 from **MetLife Inc.**'s 2014 10-K report.
Investment earnings are a crucial component of the financial performance of insurance companies
such as MetLife, and investments comprise a large part of its assets. MetLife accounts for its bond
investments as available-for-sale securities.

Fixed Maturity Securities Available-for-Sale

The following tables present the fixed maturity securities AFS by sector.

	December 31, 2014				
(in millions)	Cost or Amortized Cost	Gross Unrealized			Estimated Fair Value
		Gains	Temporary Losses	OTTI Losses	
Fixed Maturity Securities:					
U.S. corporate	$ 96,235	$10,343	$ 624	$ —	$105,954
Foreign corporate.........................	57,695	4,651	664	7	61,675
U.S. Treasury and agency	54,654	6,892	30	—	61,516
Foreign government.......................	47,327	5,500	161	—	52,666
RMBS...................................	38,064	2,102	214	106	39,846
State and political subdivision	12,922	2,291	26	—	15,187
CMBS..................................	13,762	615	46	(1)	14,332
ABS	14,121	240	112	—	14,249
Total fixed maturity securities..............	$334,780	$32,634	$1,877	$112	$365,425

	December 31, 2013				
(in millions)	Cost or Amortized Cost	Gross Unrealized			Estimated Fair Value
		Gains	Temporary Losses	OTTI Losses	
Fixed Maturity Securities:					
U.S. corporate	$100,203	$ 7,495	$1,229	$ —	$106,469
Foreign corporate.........................	59,778	3,939	565	—	63,152
U.S. Treasury and agency	43,928	2,251	1,056	—	45,123
Foreign government.......................	50,717	4,107	387	—	54,437
RMBS...................................	34,167	1,584	490	206	35,055
State and political subdivision	13,233	903	306	—	13,830
CMBS..................................	16,115	605	170	—	16,550
ABS	15,458	296	171	12	15,571
Total fixed maturity securities..............	$333,599	$21,180	$4,374	$218	$350,187

REQUIRED

a. At what amount does MetLife report its bond investments on its balance sheets for 2014 and 2013?

b. What are its net unrealized gains (losses) for 2014 and 2013? By what amount did these unrealized gains (losses) affect its reported income?

c. What is the difference between *realized* and *unrealized* gains and losses? Are realized gains and losses treated differently in the income statement than unrealized gains and losses? MetLife's 2014 pre-tax income was $8,804 million. What is the maximum amount MetLife could have increased pre-tax income by selling available-for-sale securities on the last day of 2014?

d. Many analysts compute a *mark-to-market investment return* as follows: Net investment income + Realized gains and losses + Change in unrealized gains and losses. Do you think that this metric provides insights into the performance of MetLife's investment portfolio beyond that which is included in GAAP income statements? Explain.

P12-46.[B] **Preparing the Consolidated Balance Sheet**   **LO5, 7**

On January 1, 2016, Gem Company purchased for $392,000 cash a 70% stock interest in Alpine, Inc., which then had common stock of $420,000 and retained earnings of $140,000. Balance sheets of the two companies immediately after the acquisition were as follows:

	Gem	Alpine
Current assets	$258,000	$160,000
Stock investment—Controlling (Alpine)	392,000	—
Plant and equipment (net)	265,000	460,000
Total assets...	$915,000	$620,000

continued

continued from previous page

	Gem	Alpine
Liabilities.	$ 50,000	$ 60,000
Common stock.	700,000	420,000
Retained earnings	165,000	140,000
Total liabilities and stockholders' equity.	$915,000	$620,000

At the time of Gem's investment, the fair values of Alpine's assets and liabilities were equal to their book values.

REQUIRED
Prepare the consolidated balance sheet on the acquisition date; include a column for consolidating adjustments (see **Exhibit 12.7** for guidance).

LO1, 2, 3, 4, 5 **P12-47. Analyzing and Reporting Debt Investment Performance**
Columbia Company began operations in 2016 and by year-end (December 31) had made six bond investments. Year-end information on these bond investments follows.

Company	Face Value	Cost or Amortized Cost	Year-End Fair Value	Classification
Ling, Inc..	$100,000	$102,400	$105,300	Trading
Wren, Inc..	$250,000	$262,500	$270,000	Trading
Olanamic, Inc.	$200,000	$197,000	$199,000	Available for sale
Fossil, Inc.	$150,000	$154,000	$160,000	Available for sale
Meander, Inc.	$100,000	$101,200	$102,400	Held to maturity
Resin, Inc..	$140,000	$136,000	$137,000	Held to maturity

REQUIRED

a. At what total amount will the trading bond investments be reported in the December 31, 2016, balance sheet?

b. At what total amount will the available-for-sale bond investments be reported in the December 31, 2016, balance sheet?

c. At what total amount will the held-to-maturity bond investments be reported in the December 31, 2016, balance sheet?

d. What total amount of unrealized holding gains or unrealized holding losses related to bond investments will appear in the 2016 income statement?

e. What total amount of unrealized holding gains or unrealized holding losses related to bond investments will appear in the stockholders' equity section of the December 31, 2016, balance sheet?

f. What total amount of fair value adjustment to bond investments will appear in the December 31, 2016, balance sheet? Which category of bond investments does the fair value adjustment relate to? Does the fair value adjustment increase or decrease the financial statement presentation of these bond investments?

LO1, 4, 5, 6, 7 **P12-48.**[A, B] **Analyzing and Interpreting Disclosures on Consolidations**
Caterpillar Inc.
NYSE :: CAT
Caterpillar Inc. consists of two business units: the manufacturing company (parent corporation) and a wholly owned finance subsidiary. These two units are consolidated in Caterpillar's 2014 10-K report. Following is a supplemental disclosure that Caterpillar includes in its 10-K report that shows the separate balance sheets of the parent and its subsidiary, as well as consolidating adjustments and the consolidated balance sheet presented to shareholders. This supplemental disclosure is not mandated under GAAP, but is voluntarily reported by Caterpillar as useful information for investors and creditors.

| | | Supplemental Consolidating Data | | |
	Consolidated	Machinery, Energy & Transportation	Financial Products	Consolidating Adjustments
Assets				
Current assets				
Cash and short-term investments	$ 7,341	$ 6,317	$ 1,024	$ —
Receivables—trade and other	7,737	4,215	300	3,222
Receivables—finance.	9,027	—	13,458	(4,431)
Deferred and refundable income taxes.	1,739	1,644	95	—
Prepaid expenses and other current assets.	818	399	432	(13)
Inventories	12,205	12,205	—	—
Total current assets	38,867	24,780	15,309	(1,222)
Property, plant and equipment—net	16,577	12,392	4,185	—
Long-term receivables—trade and other.	1,364	154	268	942
Long-term receivables—finance	14,644	—	15,618	(974)
Investments in unconsolidated affiliated companies	257	257	—	—
Investments in Financial Products subsidiaries	—	4,488	—	(4,488)
Noncurrent deferred and refundable income taxes	1,404	1,980	98	(674)
Intangible assets	3,076	3,069	7	—
Goodwill	6,694	6,677	17	—
Other assets.	1,798	391	1,407	—
Total assets.	$84,681	$54,188	$36,909	$(6,416)
Liabilities				
Current liabilities				
Short-term borrowings	$ 4,708	$ 9	$ 5,807	$(1,108)
Accounts payable.	6,515	6,436	180	(101)
Accrued expenses	3,548	3,273	288	(13)
Accrued wages, salaries and employee benefits	2,438	2,396	42	—
Customer advances	1,697	1,697	—	—
Dividends payable	424	424	—	—
Other current liabilities	1,754	1,361	402	(9)
Long-term debt due within one year	6,793	510	6,283	—
Total current liabilities.	27,877	16,106	13,002	(1,231)
Long-term debt due after one year	27,784	9,525	18,291	(32)
Liability for postemployment benefits	8,963	8,963	—	—
Other liabilities	3,231	2,768	1,128	(665)
Total liabilities.	67,855	37,362	32,421	(1,928)
Stockholders' equity				
Common stock.	5,016	5,016	911	(911)
Treasury stock.	(15,726)	(15,726)	—	—
Profit employed in the business	33,887	33,887	3,756	(3,756)
Accumulated other comprehensive income (loss)	(6,431)	(6,431)	(311)	311
Noncontrolling interests	80	80	132	(132)
Total stockholders' equity	16,826	16,826	4,488	(4,488)
Total liabilities and stockholders' equity	$84,681	$54,188	$36,909	$(6,416)

REQUIRED

a. Does each individual company (unit) maintain its own financial statements? Explain. Why does GAAP require consolidation instead of providing the financial statements of individual companies (units)?

b. What is the balance of Investments in Financial Products Subsidiaries as of December 31, 2014, on the parent's balance sheet (Machinery, Energy & Transportation)? What is the equity balance of the financial products subsidiary to which this relates as of December 31, 2014? Do you see a relation? Will this relation always exist?

c. Refer to your answer for *a*. How does the equity method of accounting for the investment in the subsidiary company obscure the actual financial condition of the parent company that is revealed in the consolidated financial statements?

d. Refer to the Consolidating Adjustments column reported—it is used to prepare the consolidated balance sheet. Generally, what do these adjustments accomplish?

e. Compare the consolidated balance of stockholders' equity with the stockholders' equity of the parent company (Machinery, Energy & Transportation). Will the relation that is evident always hold? Explain.

f. Recall that the parent company uses the equity method of accounting for its investment in the subsidiary, and that this account is eliminated in the consolidation process. What is the relation between consolidated net income and the net income of the parent company? Explain.

g. What do you believe is the implication for the consolidated balance sheet if the fair value of the Financial Products subsidiary is greater than the book value of its stockholders' equity?

CASES AND PROJECTS

LO1, 3, 4

Yahoo! Inc.
NASDAQ :: YHOO
Alibaba Group
NYSE :: BABA

C12-49. Effect of Investment Accounting on Performance Ratios

Since 2005, **Yahoo! Inc.** has held a significant investment in **Alibaba Group**. In September, 2014, Alibaba Group closed its initial public offering (IPO) of American Depository Shares (shares). Yahoo! sold 140 million shares in the IPO realizing a pretax gain of $10.3 billion. Following completion of the IPO, Yahoo! retained 383.6 million shares of Alibaba Group representing approximately 15% of the outstanding shares. Note 2 to Yahoo!'s 2014 10-K report details its remaining investment in Alibaba.

($ thousands)	Cost Basis	Fair Value
Alibaba Group equity securities	$ 2,713,484	$39,867,789

Yahoo! reported the following (abridged) income statements in its 2014 10-K report ($ thousands):

Year Ended December 31,	2014	2013
Revenue	$4,618,133	$4,680,380
Operating expenses	4,475,191	4,090,454
Income from operations	142,942	589,926
Other income, net	10,369,439	43,357
Income before income taxes and earnings in equity interests	10,512,381	633,283
Provision for income taxes	(4,038,102)	(153,392)
Earnings in equity interests, net of tax	1,057,863	896,675
Net income	$7,532,142	$1,376,566

The following is from Yahoo!'s balance sheets as presented in its 2014 and 2013 10-K reports ($ thousands):

As of December 31,	2014	2013	2012
Total assets	$61,960,344	$16,804,959	$17,103,253
Net operating assets (operating assets – operating liabilities)	$11,416,323	$11,144,097	$10,961,873

REQUIRED

a. At the end of 2013, Yahoo! owned 24% of the shares in Alibaba Group and reported its investment as an equity method investment. Describe the impact of the Alibaba Group IPO on Yahoo!'s financial statements. What method does Yahoo! appear to be using to report its investment in Alibaba in 2014?

b. Compute Yahoo!'s return on assets (ROA) for 2014 and 2013.

c. Compute Yahoo!'s 2014 and 2013 net operating profit after taxes (NOPAT) and its return on net operating assets (RNOA = NOPAT ÷ average net operating assets; refer to Appendix A at the end of Chapter 5 for further discussion). How does this ratio compare to the ROA ratios computed in b?

d. Yahoo! is using the available-for-sale accounting method to report its investment in Alibaba Group at the end of 2014. What amount is reported in Yahoo!'s 2014 balance sheet for this investment? What is reported in Yahoo!'s income statement related to this investment?

e. What would be the effect on Yahoo!'s ROA and RNOA ratios if it had classified its investment in Alibaba Group as trading securities?

f. If, in 2014, Yahoo! continued to use the equity method to report its investment in Alibaba, what would be the impact on Yahoo!'s ROA and RNOA? (Do not attempt to calculate ROA or RNOA under the equity method.)

C12-50. Analyzing Financial Statement Effects of Passive and Equity Investments   **LO1, 3, 4**

On January 2, 2016, Magee, Inc., purchased, as a stock investment, 20,000 shares of Dye, Inc.'s common stock for $21 per share, including commissions and taxes. On December 31, 2016, Dye announced a net income of $280,000 for the year and declared a dividend of 80 cents per share, payable January 15, 2017, to stockholders of record on January 5, 2017. At December 31, 2016, the market value of Dye's stock was $18 per share. Magee received its dividend on January 18, 2017.

REQUIRED

a. Assume that the stock acquired by Magee represents 10% of Dye's voting stock and is classified in the trading category. Prepare all journal entries appropriate for this investment, beginning with the purchase on January 2, 2016, and ending with the receipt of the dividend on January 18, 2017. (Magee recognizes dividend income when received.)

b. Post the journal entries from part a to their respective T-accounts.

c. Record each of the transactions from part a in the financial statement effects template.

d. Assume that the stock acquired by Magee represents 40% of Dye's voting stock. Prepare all journal entries appropriate for this investment, beginning with the purchase on January 2, 2016, and ending with the receipt of the dividend on January 18, 2017.

e. Post the journal entries from part d to their respective T-accounts.

f. Record each of the transactions from part d in the financial statement effects template.

C12-51. Assessing Management Interpretation of Consolidated Financial Statements   **LO1, 2, 3, 4, 5**

Demski, Inc., manufactures heating and cooling systems. It has a 75% interest in Asare Company, which manufactures thermostats, switches, and other controls for heating and cooling products. It also has a 100% interest in Demski Finance Company, created by the parent company to finance sales of its products to contractors and other consumers. The parent company's only other investment is a 25% interest in the common stock of Knechel, Inc., which produces certain circuits used by Demski, Inc. A condensed consolidated balance sheet of the entity for the current year follows.

DEMSKI, INC., AND SUBSIDIARIES Consolidated Balance Sheet December 31, 2016		
Assets		
Current assets		$19,300,000
Stock investment—Influential (Knechel)		2,600,000
Other assets		71,400,000
Excess of cost over equity acquired in net assets of Asare Company		1,700,000
Total assets		$95,000,000
Liabilities and shareholders' equity		
Current liabilities		$10,300,000
Long-term liabilities		14,200,000
Shareholders' equity		
Common stock	$50,000,000	
Retained earnings	16,700,000	
Demski, Inc. shareholders' equity	66,700,000	
Noncontrolling interests	3,800,000	
Total shareholders' equity		70,500,000
Total liabilities and shareholders' equity		$95,000,000

This balance sheet, along with other financial statements, was furnished to shareholders before their annual meeting, and all shareholders were invited to submit questions to be answered at the meeting. As chief financial officer of Demski, you have been appointed to respond to the questions at the meeting.

REQUIRED

Answer the following shareholder questions.

a.   What is meant by *consolidated* financial statements?

b.   Why is the investment in Knechel shown on the consolidated balance sheet, but the investments in Asare and Demski Finance are omitted?

c.   Explain the meaning of the asset Excess of Cost over Equity Acquired in Net Assets of Asare Company.

d.   What is meant by *noncontrolling interest* and to what company is this account related?

LO1, 2, 3, 4   **C12-52.   Understanding Intercorporate Investments, Accounting Practices, and Managerial Ethics**
Doug Stevens, controller of Nexgen, Inc., has asked his assistant, Gayle Sayres, for suggestions as to how the company can improve its financial performance for the year. The company is in the last quarter of the year and projections to the end of the year show the company will have a net loss of about $400,000.

"My suggestion," said Sayres, "is that we sell 1,000 of the 200,000 common shares of Heflin Company that we own. The 200,000 shares gives us a 20% ownership of Heflin, and we have been using the equity method to account for this investment. We have owned this stock a long time and the current market value of the 200,000 shares is about $750,000 above our book value for the stock."

"That sale will only generate a gain of about $3,750," replied Stevens.

"The rest of the story," continued Sayres, "is that once we sell the 1,000 shares, we will own less than 20% of Heflin. We can then reclassify the remaining 199,000 shares from the influential category to the trading category. Once in the trading category, we value the stocks at their current fair value, include the rest of the $750,000 gain in this year's income statement, and finish the year with a healthy net income."

"But," responded Stevens, "we aren't going to sell all the Heflin stock; 1,000 shares maybe, but certainly not any more. We own that stock because they are a long-term supplier of ours. Indeed, we even have representation on their board of directors. The 199,000 shares do not belong in the trading category."

Sayres rolled her eyes and continued, "The classification of an investment as trading or not depends on management's intent. This year-end we claim it was our intent to sell the stock. Next year we change our minds and take the stock out of the trading category. Generally accepted accounting principles can't legislate management intent, nor can our outside auditors read our minds. Besides, why shouldn't we take advantage of the flexibility in GAAP to avoid reporting a net loss for this year?"

REQUIRED

a.   Should generally accepted accounting principles permit management's intent to influence accounting classifications and measurements?

b.   Is it ethical for Doug Stevens to implement the recommendation of Gayle Sayres?

SOLUTIONS TO REVIEW PROBLEMS

Mid-Chapter Review 1

SOLUTION TO PART 1

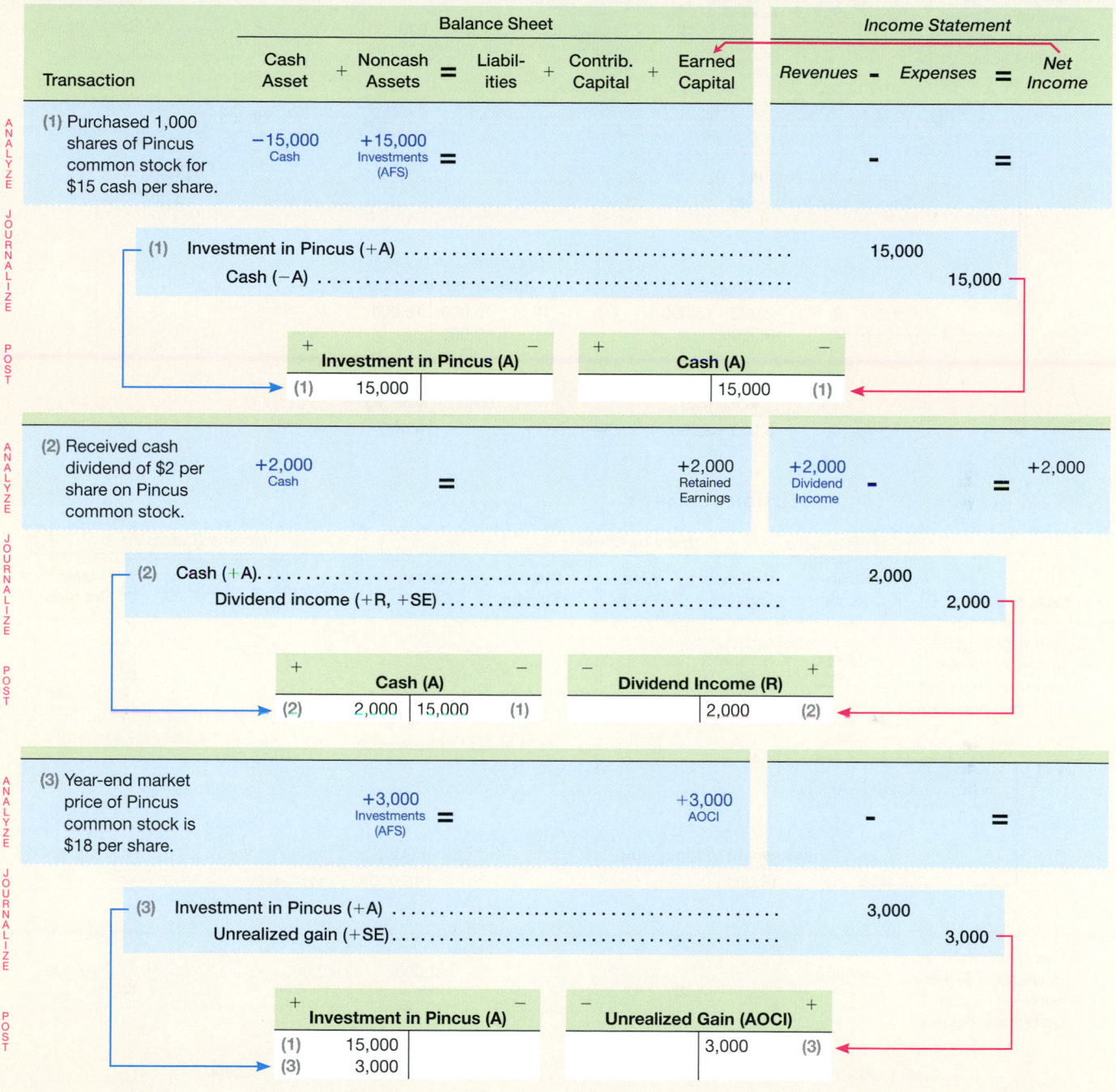

continued

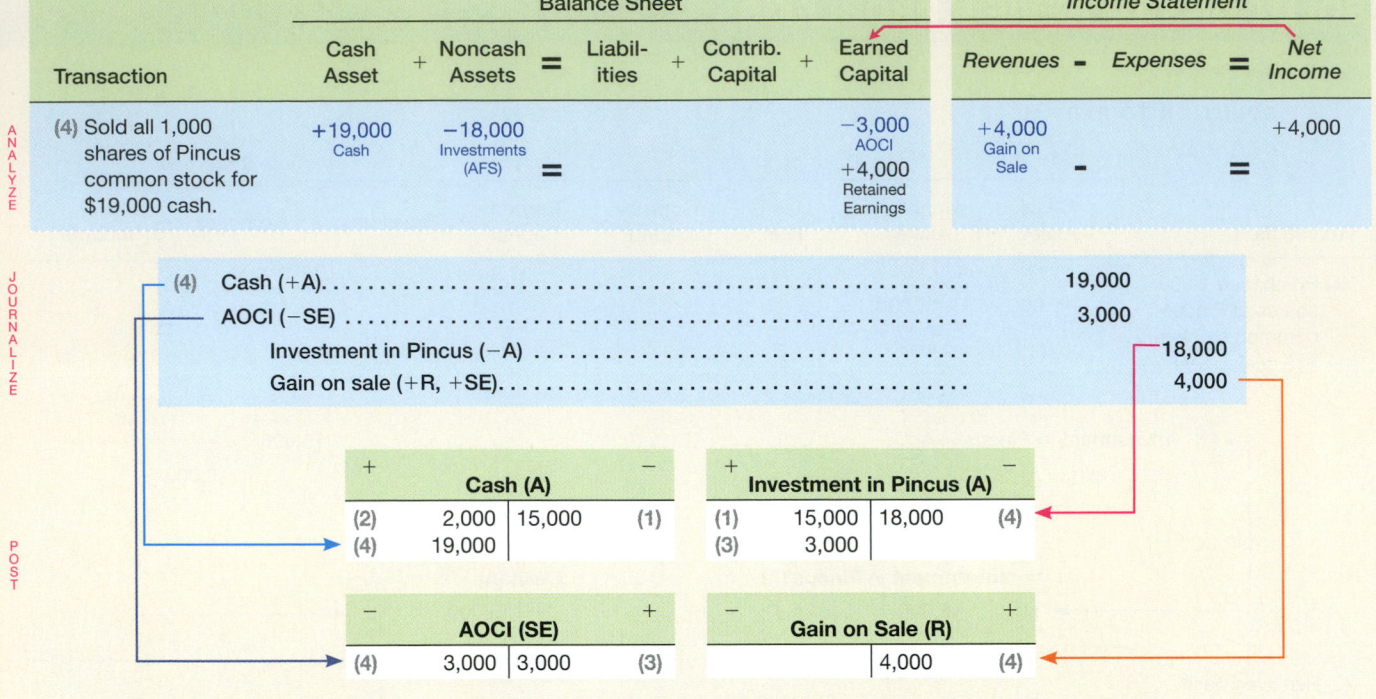

	Balance Sheet					Income Statement		
Transaction	Cash Asset	+ Noncash Assets	= Liabil- ities	+ Contrib. Capital	+ Earned Capital	Revenues	- Expenses	= Net Income
(4) Sold all 1,000 shares of Pincus common stock for $19,000 cash.	+19,000 Cash	−18,000 Investments (AFS) =			−3,000 AOCI +4,000 Retained Earnings	+4,000 Gain on Sale	-	= +4,000

(4) Cash (+A)... 19,000
    AOCI (−SE)... 3,000
        Investment in Pincus (−A)................................. 18,000
        Gain on sale (+R, +SE)................................... 4,000

+	Cash (A)	−
(2)	2,000	15,000 (1)
(4)	19,000	

+	Investment in Pincus (A)	−
(1)	15,000	18,000 (4)
(3)	3,000	

−	AOCI (SE)	+
(4)	3,000	3,000 (3)

−	Gain on Sale (R)	+
		4,000 (4)

SOLUTION TO PART 2

	Balance Sheet					Income Statement		
Transaction	Cash Asset	+ Noncash Assets	= Liabil- ities	+ Contrib. Capital	+ Earned Capital	Revenues	- Expenses	= Net Income
(1) Purchased 1,000 shares of Pincus common stock for $15 cash per share.	−15,000 Cash	+15,000 Investments (Trading) =					-	=

(1) Investment in Pincus (+A)..................................... 15,000
        Cash (−A)... 15,000

+	Investment in Pincus (A)	−
(1)	15,000	

+	Cash (A)	−
		15,000 (1)

	Balance Sheet					Income Statement		
(2) Received cash dividend of $2 per share on Pincus common stock.	+2,000 Cash		=		+2,000 Retained Earnings	+2,000 Dividend Income	-	= +2,000

(2) Cash (+A).. 2,000
        Dividend income (+R, +SE).................................. 2,000

+	Cash (A)	−
(2)	2,000	15,000 (1)

−	Dividend Income (R)	+
		2,000 (2)

continued

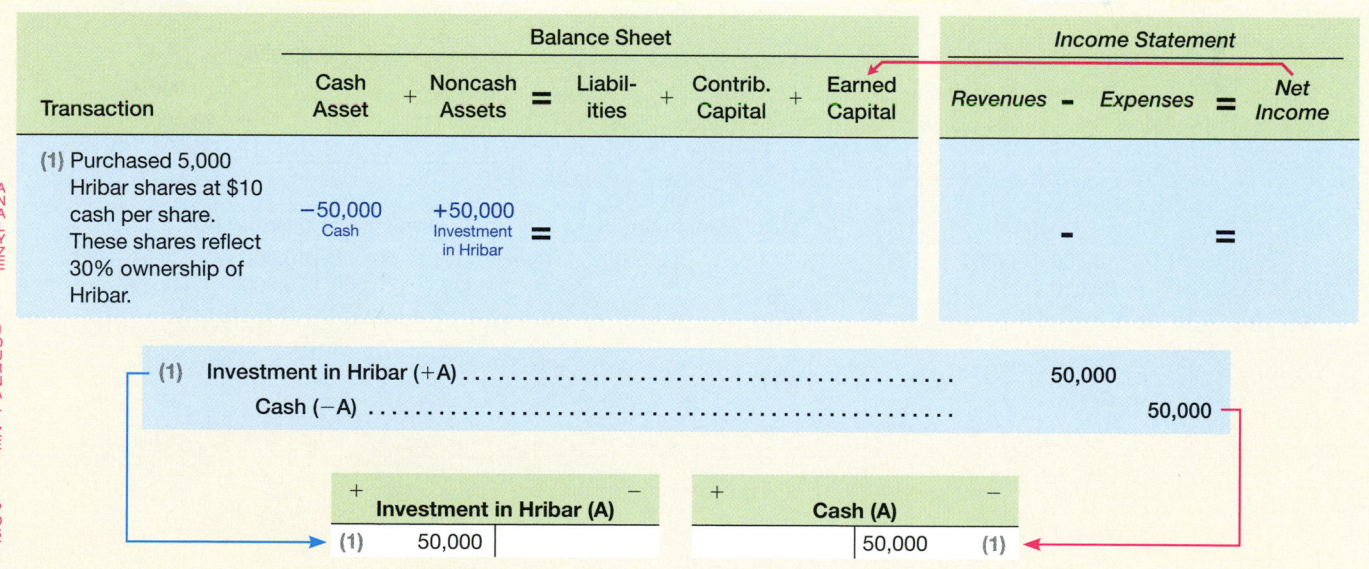

	Balance Sheet					Income Statement		
Transaction	Cash Asset	+ Noncash Assets	= Liabil- ities	+ Contrib. Capital	+ Earned Capital	Revenues	− Expenses	= Net Income
(3) Year-end market price of Pincus common stock is $18 per share.		+3,000 Investments (Trading) =			+3,000 Retained Earnings	+3,000 Unrealized Gain	−	= +3,000

(3) Investment in Pincus (+A) 3,000
   Unrealized gain (+R, +SE) 3,000

+ Investment in Pincus (A) −		− Unrealized Gain (R) +	
(1) 15,000			3,000 (3)
(3) 3,000			

	Balance Sheet					Income Statement		
Transaction	Cash Asset	+ Noncash Assets	= Liabil- ities	+ Contrib. Capital	+ Earned Capital	Revenues	− Expenses	= Net Income
(4) Sold all 1,000 shares of Pincus common stock for $19,000 cash.	+19,000 Cash	−18,000 Investments (Trading) =			+1,000 Retained Earnings	+1,000 Gain on Sale	−	= +1,000

(4) Cash (+A)... 19,000
   Investment in Pincus (−A) 18,000
   Gain on sale (+R, +SE)...................................... 1,000

+ Cash (A) −		− Gain on Sale (R) +		+ Investment in Pincus (A) −	
(2) 2,000	15,000 (1)		1,000 (4)	(1) 15,000	18,000 (4)
(4) 19,000				(3) 3,000	

Mid-Chapter Review 2

SOLUTION

	Balance Sheet					Income Statement		
Transaction	Cash Asset	+ Noncash Assets	= Liabil- ities	+ Contrib. Capital	+ Earned Capital	Revenues	− Expenses	= Net Income
(1) Purchased 5,000 Hribar shares at $10 cash per share. These shares reflect 30% ownership of Hribar.	−50,000 Cash	+50,000 Investment in Hribar =					−	=

(1) Investment in Hribar (+A).. 50,000
   Cash (−A) 50,000

+ Investment in Hribar (A) −		+ Cash (A) −	
(1) 50,000			50,000 (1)

continued

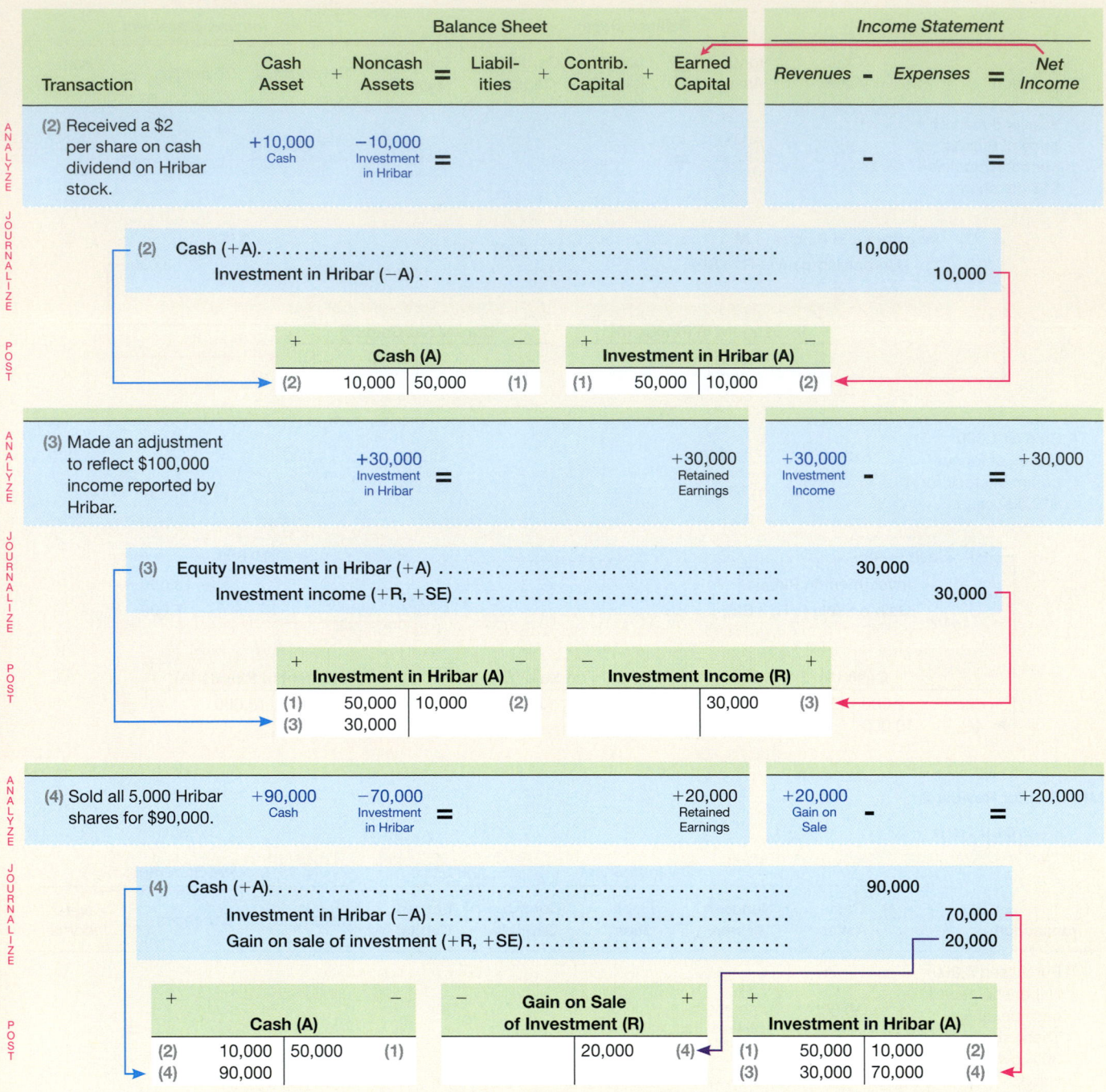

Chapter-End Review

SOLUTION

	Balance Sheet							Income Statement		
Transaction	Cash Asset	+	Noncash Assets	=	Liabil- ities	+	Contrib. Capital	+	Earned Capital	Revenues − Expenses = Net Income
(1) Consolidation adjustment for Bradshaw.			+100,000 PPE, net +100,000 Goodwill −600,000 Investment in Dukes	=			−200,000 Dukes Common Stock		−200,000 Dukes Retained Earnings	− =

ANALYZE

JOURNALIZE

(1)	PPE, net (+A)..	100,000	
	Goodwill (+A)	100,000	
	Dukes common stock (−SE)...................................	200,000	
	Dukes retained earnings (−SE)................................	200,000	
	Investment in Dukes (−A)...................................		600,000

POST

+ PPE (A) −		+ Goodwill (A) −		− Dukes Common Stock (SE) +
(1) 100,000		(1) 100,000		(1) 200,000

− Dukes Retained Earnings (SE) +		+ Investment in Dukes (A) −
(1) 200,000		600,000 (1)

	Bradshaw (Parent)	Dukes (Subsidiary)	Consolidating Adjustments	Consolidated
Current assets	$1,000,000	$100,000		$1,100,000
Investment in Dukes.........	600,000	—	$(600,000)	
PPE, net	3,000,000	400,000	100,000	3,500,000
Goodwill	—	—	100,000	100,000
Total assets...............	$4,600,000	$500,000		$4,700,000
Liabilities.................	$1,000,000	$100,000		$1,100,000
Contributed capital..........	2,000,000	200,000	(200,000)	2,000,000
Retained earnings	1,600,000	200,000	(200,000)	1,600,000
Total liabilities and equity.....	$4,600,000	$500,000		$4,700,000

Notes: The $600,000 investment account is eliminated together with the $400,000 book value of Dukes's equity to which it mainly relates. The remaining $200,000 consists of the additional $100,000 in PPE assets and the $100,000 in goodwill from expected corporate synergies. Following these adjustments, the balance sheet items are summed to yield the consolidated balance sheet.

Managerial Accounting: Tools for Decision Making

MODCLOTH
www.modcloth.com

Shopping for women's apparel has traditionally been a collaborative experience. Women shop with their mothers, daughters, sisters, and friends and rely on their advice in determining what styles best suit them. Yet Internet commerce has transformed what was once a social outing into an impersonal and solitary activity. One company, **ModCloth**, is putting the social aspect back into e-retailing.

ModCloth is headquartered in San Francisco and sells vintage and or vintage-inspired apparel, accessories, and décor. It was founded in 2002 by husband-and-wife team Eric Koger and Susan Gregg Koger, while they were in college at Carnegie Mellon University. ModCloth has been named "America's Fastest-Growing Retailer" by **Inc.** magazine (which also ranked the company number two for the fastest-growing private company). ModCloth's sales exceeded $160 million in 2015, and the company is working to expand its international operations. The company's physical capacity is rapidly expanding both in property and staff to support planned growth. Three hundred and fifty employees now work in San Francisco, Los Angeles, and Pittsburgh.

The information provided by the managerial accounting system is critical to thriving, young companies as they build upon their corporate vision. Startup companies must search for capital while honing their strategy and making calculated decisions regarding their position in the competitive landscape. For example, ModCloth set out to target women in the technologically savvy millennial generation (18 to 34 years old). Understanding customers' demographics facilitates the company's planning activities. ModCloth's planners know that millennials are not content to be passive consumers, and they've plotted the company's growth strategy to provide increased customer participation in the shopping experience.

Not only do ModCloth's managers use managerial accounting information to plan their long-run and day-to-day operations, they evaluate the feedback produced by the system to control their operations. For example, the company has found that its mobile applications (for smartphones and tablets) result in, on average, more frequent visits per customer and higher purchase amounts per visit than the company's traditional website application. ModCloth managers also utilize customer comments to identify segments of their key demographic that are currently underserved. Throughout this book, we will learn how managerial accounting provides useful information for making informed business decisions.

Sources: Kim Bhasin, "ModCloth Plans Huge Expansion Under New CEO," *Bloomberg.Com*, August 31, 2015; Sandra Guy, "ModCloth Hires a Chief Technology Officer," *Internetretailer.Com*, May 24, 2016; Douglas MacMillan, "At ModCloth, Vintage Fashion Goes Mobile," *Bloomberg Businessweek*, August 8, 2013; Meghan Casserly, "ModCloth Hits $100 Million in Revenue, Gives Social All the Credit," *Forbes*, July 23, 2013; and Bridget Brennan, "The Retailer Winning the Battle for Millennial Women," *Forbes*, November 16, 2012.

CHAPTER ORGANIZATION

Managerial Accounting: Tools for Decision Making				
Uses of Accounting Information	**Organizations: Missions, Goals, and Strategies**	**Changing Environment of Business**	**Ethics in Managerial Accounting**	**Cost Drivers**
• Financial Accounting • Managerial Accounting • Strategic Cost Management	• Strategic Position Analysis • Managerial Accounting and Goal Attainment • Planning, Organizing, and Controlling	• Global Competition and Its Key Dimensions • Big Data and Analysis • Enterprise Risk Management (ERM)	• Codes of Ethics • Corporate Governance • Sustainability Accounting and Corporate Social Responsibility	• Structural Cost Drivers • Organizational Cost Drivers • Activity Cost Drivers

Managers of organizations such as **ModCloth** are required to make strategic decisions every day in order to remain competitive in the marketplace. These decisions might involve answering questions such as: What is our target market? How do we create awareness within our target market? What products should we offer and at what price? How many employees should we hire? How much should we pay our employees? Which suppliers should we use to fulfill our orders? And, how much money should we invest in capital resources? In order to make these decisions, and to achieve their organizations' goals, managers must have an understanding of, and access to, timely and reliable information.

Managerial accounting is defined as the activities carried out to provide managers and other employees with financial reporting information and control to assist management in the formulation and implementation of an organization's strategy. We begin our exploration of managerial accounting by discussing the differences between managerial and financial accounting and by investigating how competitive strategy affects the way organizations use managerial accounting information. Next, we explore how the emergence of global competition and changes in technology have increased the need to understand managerial accounting concepts. We also examine the interrelationships among measurement, management, and ethics. Finally, we provide an overview of factors that influence costs in an organization and how these factors have changed in recent years.

LO1 Contrast the different uses of financial and managerial accounting information.

USES OF ACCOUNTING INFORMATION

Accounting information attempts to satisfy the needs of a variety of individuals and agencies that make decisions about and for organizations. These decision makers can be classified by their relation to a business as either external users or internal users. **Financial accounting** is designed primarily for decision makers outside of the company, whereas managerial accounting is designed primarily for decision makers within the company.

Financial Accounting

Financial accounting is an information-processing system that generates general-purpose reports of financial operations (income statement and statement of cash flows) and financial position (balance sheet) for an organization. Although financial accounting is used by decision makers inside and outside the firm, financial accounting typically emphasizes external users, such as security investors, analysts, and lenders. Adding to this external orientation are external financial reporting requirements determined by law and generally accepted accounting principles.

Financial accounting is also concerned with keeping records of the organization's assets, obligations, and the collection and payment of cash. An organization cannot survive without converting sales into cash, paying for purchases, meeting payroll, and keeping track of its assets.

Managers often use income statements and balance sheets as a starting point in evaluating and planning the firm's overall activities. Managers learn a great deal by performing a comparative analysis of their firm and competing firms. Corporate goals are often stated using financial accounting numbers such as net income, or ratios such as return on investment and earnings per common share. However, internal decision makers often find the information provided in financial statements of limited value in managing day-to-day operating activities. They often complain that financial accounting information is too aggregated, prepared too late, based on irrelevant past costs, and not action oriented. For example, the costs of all items produced and sold or all services rendered are summarized in a single line in most financial statements, making it impossible to determine the costs of individual products or services. Financial accounting procedures, acceptable for costing inventories as a whole, often produce misleading information when applied to individual products. Even when they are accurately determined, the costs of individual products or services are rarely detailed enough in overall financial statements to provide the information needed for decisions concerning the factors that influence costs. Financial accounting reports, seldom prepared more than once a month, are not timely enough for use in the management of day-to-day activities that cause excess costs. Finally, financial accounting reports, to a great extent, are based on historical costs rather than on current or future costs. Managers are more interested in future costs than in historical costs such as last year's depreciation. While financial accounting information is useful in making some management decisions, its primary emphasis is not on internal decision making.

Managerial Accounting

As emphasized in our ModCloth example, managers are constantly faced with the need to understand and control costs, make important product decisions, coordinate resources, and guide and motivate employees. Managerial accounting provides an information framework to organize, evaluate, and report proprietary data in light of an organization's goals. This information is directed to managers and other employees within the organization. Managerial accounting reports can be designed to meet the information needs of internal decision makers. Top management may need only summary information prepared once a month for each business unit. An engineer responsible for hourly production scheduling may need continuously updated and detailed information concerning the cost of alternative ways of producing a product.

Because of the intensity of competition and the shorter life cycles of new products and services, managerial accounting is crucial to an organization's success. All managers must understand the financial implications of their decisions. While accountants are available to assist in obtaining and evaluating relevant information, individual managers are responsible for requesting information, analyzing it, and making the final decisions.

BUSINESS INSIGHT

Strategic Thinking Requires a Company to Think Inside the Consumer's Sphere   Emerging markets represent significant opportunities, but companies must check their preconceptions at the door when formulating their strategies. For example, a company building a mobile network in Africa will be dealing with customers who may have never had a landline telephone. Cost structures based on landline companies are outdated because building a mobile network is far cheaper than extending telephone wire to each business and home. The desktop and laptop computer market may skip Africa entirely as consumers leap to smartphones for their computing needs. And traditional brick-and-mortar banks need to rethink their functionality in a region where customers are doing the majority of their banking on their phones.

In Kenya, 40 percent of the population lives on less than $2 per day, but more and more Kenyans are purchasing low-cost smartphones. Safaricom, East Africa's telecom market leader, and the Commercial Bank of Africa have partnered in a service that allows mobile phone users to apply for and receive loans through their phones. This partnership is serving a population that is new to the entire concept of banking. The next project on Safaricom's horizon is to use cell phone technology to access and pay for health care. Managerial accounting helps guide companies like Safaricom through the myriad of growth opportunities available to them, while providing information about their costs of delivering a product or service and making a determination of what price to charge consumers for those products and services.

Sources: Eric Ombok, "Safaricom, Commercial Bank Africa Start Mobile Loan Service," *Bloomberg Businessweek*, November 27, 2012; and Tim Worstall, "Africa Might Just Skip the Entire PC Revolution," *Forbes*, August 17, 2011.

Managerial accounting information exists to serve the needs of management. Hence, it is subject to a cost-benefit analysis and should be developed only if the perceived benefits exceed the costs of development and use. Also, while financial measures are often used in managerial accounting, they are not used to the exclusion of other measures. Money is simply a convenient way of expressing events in a form suitable to summary analysis. When this is not possible or appropriate, nonfinancial measures are used. Time, for example, is often an important element of quality or service. Hence, many performance measures focus on time, for example:

- Internet vendors such as **ModCloth** and **Amazon.com** track delivery time.
- Fire departments and police departments measure the response time to emergency calls.
- Airlines, such as **Delta Airlines** as well as the Federal Aviation Administration monitor the number of on-time departures and arrivals.

About IMA® (Institute of Management Accountants)   No external standards (such as requirements of the Securities and Exchange Commission) are imposed on information provided to internal users. However the IMA®—the association of accountants and financial professionals in business—acts as a guide for defining the role and best practices of managerial accounting. Globally, IMA supports the profession through research, the CMA® (Certified Management Accountant) program, continuing education, networking, and advocacy of the highest ethical business practices. In 2016, the IMA developed a Management Accounting Competency Framework. The framework emphasizes the need for management accountants to partner in planning and decision making, to create performance management systems, and to provide expertise in financial reporting and control.[1]

The IMA's CMA program focuses specifically on the competencies required by organizations and CFOs to protect investors and drive business value. The CMA tests professional competency in financial planning and analysis, risk management and internal controls, strategic costing, decision support, performance management, corporate finance, ethics, and more. CMA-certified professionals work within organizations of all sizes, industries, and types, including manufacturing and services, public and private enterprises, not-for-profit organizations, academic institutions, government entities, and multinational corporations. To become certified, a qualified professional must be a member of IMA, pass a two-part exam, stay current through continuing education, and abide by IMA's *Statement of Ethical Professional Practice*. According to a 2016 IMA salary survey, professionals who have completed the CMA program earn 31 percent more in the United States than noncertified professionals. For more information about IMA, please visit www.imanet.org.

The significant differences between financial and managerial accounting are summarized in **Exhibit 13.1**.

EXHIBIT 13.1	Differences Between Financial and Managerial Accounting
Financial Accounting	**Managerial Accounting**
Information for internal *and* external users	Information for internal users
General-purpose financial statements	Special-purpose information and reports
Statements are highly aggregated	Information is aggregated or detailed, depending on need
Relatively long reporting periods	Reporting periods are long or short, depending on need
Report on past decisions	Oriented toward current and future decisions
Follows generally accepted accounting principles	Not constrained by generally accepted accounting principles
Must conform to external standards	No external standards
Emphasizes objective data	Encourages subjective data, if relevant

---

[1] http://www.imanet.org/tools-and-resources/competency-framework

MID-CHAPTER REVIEW 1

The previous discussion has focused on understanding the difference between financial and managerial accounting and the broader context of managerial accounting within a company.

REQUIRED
Identify the statements and phrases from the following list that are primarily relevant to managerial accounting, as opposed to financial accounting:

1. Preparing periodic financial statements
2. A company's strategic position
3. Calculates earnings per share for stockholders
4. Summarizes information about past events
5. Is not based on generally accepted accounting principles
6. Must conform to external standards
7. Helping managers make decisions is its primary purpose
8. Encourages use of selective data, if relevant
9. Is tailored to the needs of the company and its managers
10. Receives guidance from the IMA as to its role in helping an organization achieve its goals.

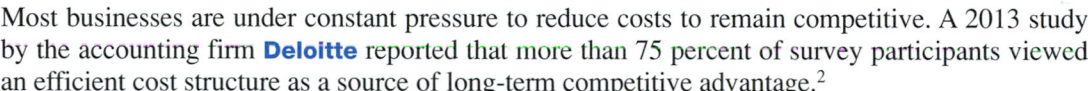

The solution to this review problem can be found on page 645.

Strategic Cost Management

LO2 Describe the three themes of strategic cost management and illustrate how strategic cost management can be used to create a long-term competitive advantage.

Most businesses are under constant pressure to reduce costs to remain competitive. A 2013 study by the accounting firm **Deloitte** reported that more than 75 percent of survey participants viewed an efficient cost structure as a source of long-term competitive advantage.[2]

During recent years, the rapid introduction of improved and new products and services has shortened the market lives of products and services. Some products, such as personal computers, can be obsolete within two or three years after introduction. At the same time, the increased use of complex automated equipment makes it difficult to change production procedures after production begins. Combining short product life cycles with automated production results in an environment where most costs are determined by decisions made before production begins (decisions concerning product design and production procedures).

In response to these trends, a strategic approach to managerial accounting, referred to as *strategic cost management* has emerged. Strategic cost management is a blending of three themes:

1. **Strategic position analysis**—an examination of an organization's basic way of competing to sell products or services.

2. **Cost driver analysis**—the study of factors that cause or influence costs.

3. **Value chain analysis**—the study of value-producing activities, stretching from basic raw materials to the final consumer of a product or service.[3]

We define **strategic cost management** as making decisions concerning specific cost drivers within the context of an organization's business strategy, internal value chain, and position in a larger value chain stretching from the development and use of resources to final consumers. Strategic position analysis is considered in this chapter as part of an organization's strategy. Cost driver analysis is also introduced in this chapter and examined further in Chapter 14. Value chain analysis is discussed in Chapter 20.

---

[2] "Cutting Costs to Drive Growth: Trends Among the Fortune 1000," Deloitte's Third Biennial Cost Survey: Cost-Improvement Practices and Trends in the Fortune 1000, 2013.

[3] John K. Shank, "Strategic Cost Management: New Wine, or Just New Bottles?" *Journal of Management Accounting Research*, Fall 1989, p. 50.

MID-CHAPTER REVIEW 2

Discuss the three themes that are blended to form the idea of strategic cost management. Do some research online in newspapers and identify a business that seems to demonstrate the use of each of the strategies.

The solution to this review problem can be found on pages 645–646.

LO3 Examine how an organization's mission, goals, and strategies affect managerial accounting.

MISSIONS, GOALS, AND STRATEGIES

An Organization's Mission and Goals

An organization's **mission** is the basic purpose toward which its activities are directed. **ModCloth's** current mission is to "inspire personal style and help our community and customers feel like the best version of themselves."[4] **TED** is a nonprofit devoted to spreading ideas, usually in the form of short, powerful talks (18 minutes or less). TED's mission statement is simply two words: "Spread ideas."[5] Organizations vary widely in their missions. One benefit of a mission statement is to help focus all the activities of an organization. For instance, the former chairman and CEO of Coca-Cola stated that the mission of **The Coca-Cola Company** is "to create value over time for the owners of our business." He went on to say:

> Our society is based on democratic capitalism. In such a society, people create specific institutions to help meet specific needs. Governments are created to help meet social needs. . . Businesses such as ours are created to meet economic needs. The common thread between these institutions is that they can flourish only when they stay focused on the specific need they were created to fulfill. When institutions try to broaden their scope beyond their natural realms, when for example they try to become all things to all people, they fail.[6]

The CEO of Coca-Cola believed that Coca-Cola best contributes to society and helps government and other organizations fulfill their missions by staying focused on shareholder value. He believed focusing on economics keeps a company financially healthy, and a healthy company fulfills its responsibilities. Conversely, a bankrupt company is incapable of paying taxes, employing people, serving customers, supporting charitable institutions, or making other contributions to society. Coca-Cola's current mission statement, "To refresh the world. To inspire moments of optimism and happiness. And to create value and make a difference," still emphasizes the creation of shareholder value.

We frequently distinguish between organizations on the basis of profit motive. **For-profit organizations** have profit as a primary objective, whereas **not-for-profit organizations** do not have profit as a primary objective. Clearly, the Coca-Cola Company is a for-profit organization, whereas **TED** and **United Way** are not-for-profit organizations. (The term *nonprofit* is frequently used to refer to what we have identified as not-for-profit organizations.) Regardless of whether a profit motive exists, organizations must use resources wisely. Every dollar **United Way** spends for administrative salaries is a dollar that cannot be used to support charitable activities. Not-for-profit organizations, including governments, can go bankrupt if they are unable to meet their financial obligations. All organizations, for-profit and not-for-profit, should use managerial accounting concepts to ensure that resources are used wisely.

A **goal** is a definable, measurable objective. Based on the organization's mission, management sets a number of goals. For-profit organizations have some measure of profitability or shareholder value as one of their stated or implicit goals. The mission of a paper mill located in a small town is to provide quality paper products in order to earn a profit for its owners. The paper mill's goals might include earning an annual profit equal to 10 percent of average total

---

[4] Modcloth.com
[5] https://www.ted.com/about/our-organization
[6] Roberto Goizueta, "Why Shareholder Value?" *CEO Series Issue No. 13,* February 1997, Center for the Study of American Business, Washington University in St. Louis, p. 2.

assets, maintaining annual dividends of $2 per share of common stock, developing a customer reputation for above-average quality and service, providing steady employment for area residents, and meeting or exceeding environmental standards.

A clear statement of mission and well-defined goals provides an organization with an identity and unifying purpose, thereby ensuring that all employees are heading in the same direction. Having developed a mission and a set of goals, employees are more apt to make decisions that move the organization toward its defined purpose.

A **strategy** is a course of action that will assist in achieving one or more goals. Much of this text will focus on the financial aspects of selecting strategies to achieve goals. For example, if an organization's goal is to improve product quality, possible strategies for achieving this goal include investing in new equipment, implementing additional quality inspections, prescreening suppliers, reducing batch size, redesigning products, training employees, and rearranging the shop floor. Managerial accounting information will assist in determining which of the many alternative strategies for achieving the goal of quality improvement are cost effective. The distinction between mission, goals, and strategies is illustrated in **Exhibit 13.2**.

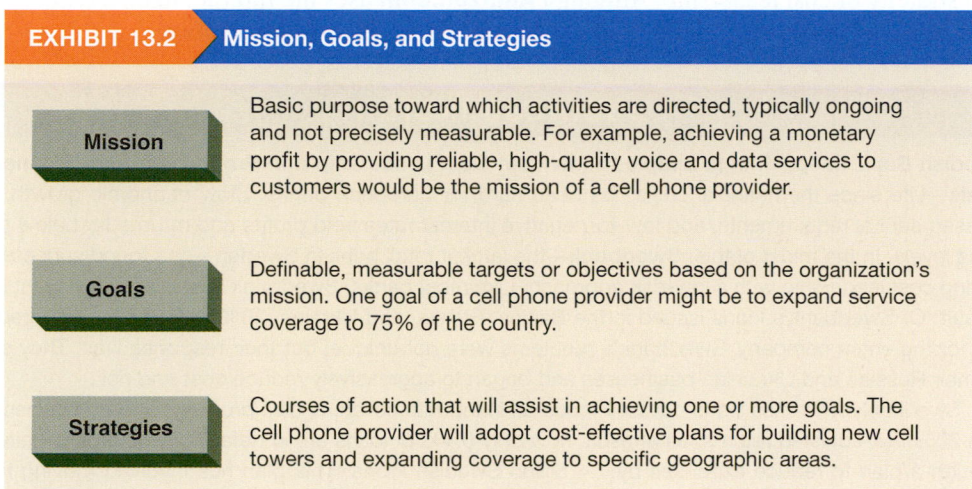

Strategic Position Analysis

In competitive environments, managers must make a fundamental decision concerning their organization's goal for positioning itself in comparison to competitors. This goal is referred to as the organization's **strategic position**. Much of the organization's strategy depends on this strategic positioning goal. Michael Porter, a highly regarded expert on business strategy, has identified three possible strategic positions that lead to business success.[7]

1. Cost leadership
2. Product or service differentiation
3. Market niche

According to Porter, cost leadership

requires aggressive construction of efficient-scale facilities, vigorous pursuit of cost reductions from experience, tight cost and overhead control, avoidance of marginal customer accounts, and cost minimization in areas like R&D [research and development], service, sales force, advertising, and so on. A great deal of managerial attention to cost control is necessary to achieve these aims. Low cost relative to competitors becomes the theme running through the entire strategy, though quality, service, and other areas cannot be ignored.[8]

[7] Michael E. Porter, *Competitive Strategy* (New York: The Free Press, 1980), p. 35.
[8] Porter, p. 35.

Achieving cost leadership allows an organization to achieve higher profits selling at the same price as competitors or by allowing the firm to aggressively compete on the basis of price while remaining profitable. One of the first companies to successfully use a cost leadership strategy was **Carnegie Steel Company**.

> Carnegie's operating strategy was to push his own direct costs below his competitors so that he could charge prices that would always ensure enough demand to keep his plants running at full capacity. This strategy prompted him to require frequent information showing his direct costs in relation to those of his competitors. Possessing that information and secure in the knowledge that his costs were the lowest in the industry, Carnegie then mercilessly cut prices during economic recessions. While competing firms went under, he still made profits. In periods of prosperity, when customers' demands exceeded the industry's capacity to produce, Carnegie joined others in raising prices.[9]

Southwest Airlines and **Costco** are current examples of successful businesses competing with a strategy of cost leadership. Although **Amazon.com** uses the Internet to differentiate itself from traditional booksellers, its primary strategic position is cost leadership.

BUSINESS INSIGHT

Swedish Bank Keeps Things Simple to Maintain Cost Leadership and Profitability Post-Financial-Crisis   Life since the financial crisis has been hard for European banks. Slow economic growth, increased capital requirements, and low-to-negative interest rates hold profits and returns far below pre-crisis levels. In the midst of this, **Swedbank**—the largest retail bank in Sweden—has found success by pairing cost leadership with a low-risk approach. Like most banks, Swedbank had assets that went into default. Of Swedbank's loans issued in the Baltics, Russia, and Ukraine, 20% defaulted, compared to 3% for the entire company. Swedbank's problems were not unique, but their response was. They sold off their Russian and Ukrainian businesses and began to aggressively reduce cost and risk.

Swedbank still writes loans but they focus on loans with collateral (i.e., property) and on businesses with 20% risk-adjusted returns; as a result, now only 0.4% of loans are in default. Swedbank is halfway through a plan to reduce expenses by 1.4 billion Swedish krona. This plan has involved moving their headquarters out of the expensive center of Stockholm to a nearby suburb, shifting some workforce to the Baltic states (where cost of living is lower), and renegotiating service contracts such as telecommunications. These decreases in costs have put the bank in a strong position; Swedbank has nearly two times the risk-weighted capital and two times the profitability of the average EU bank. This success is driven by a cost-to-income ratio of 43% (16 percentage points above the average for the EU). Managerial accounting tools can help companies analyze and establish their strategic position in their markets.

Source: "Bank to Basics," *The Economist*, May 21, 2016.

Conversely, while an organization might compete primarily on the basis of price, management must take care to ensure their product or service remains attuned to changing customer needs and preferences. In the early twentieth century, **General Motors** employed a differentiation strategy, focusing on the rapid introduction of technological change in new automobile designs to overcome the market dominance of the Model T produced by **Ford Motor Company**. While successfully following a cost leadership strategy for years, Ford made the mistake of excluding other considerations such as vehicle performance and customer desires for different colors. ModCloth follows a product differentiation strategy by using community collaboration to drive product design and selection that results in a unique array of merchandise compared to its competitors.

---

[9] H. Thomas Johnson and Robert S. Kaplan, *Relevance Lost: The Rise and Fall of Management Accounting* (Boston: Harvard Business School Press, 1987), pp. 33–34.

The third possible strategic position according to Porter, focuses on a specific market niche such as a buyer group, segment of the product line, or geographic market and

rests on the premise that the firm is thus able to serve its narrow strategic target more effectively or efficiently than competitors who are competing more broadly. As a result, the firm achieves either differentiation from better meeting the needs of the particular target, or lower costs in serving the target, or both. Even though the focus strategy does not achieve low costs or differentiation for the market as a whole, it does achieve one or both of these positions vis-à-vis its narrow market target.[10]

BUSINESS INSIGHT

Managerial Accounting Is Key to Adapting Proven Business Models to New Markets   Nollywood, the Nigerian movie industry, is a busy place. Without a studio system, independent filmmakers produce and distribute a thousand films each year on budgets of about $20,000. **Iroko**, an African-based Internet streaming company, has been applying a subscription-for-streaming business model similar to that of **Hulu** and **Netflix** to the Nollywood catalogue since 2011. The service is off to a promising start with an estimated 65,000 subscribers and two successful rounds of investor funding. However, the telecommunication infrastructure of the Nigerian market makes penetration into that market difficult. Iroko reports that only 11% of their subscribers are actually in Nigeria.

Most computing in Nigeria is mobile, which presents a challenge for Iroko. It is the cost of mobile data, and not the 500-naira ($2.50) monthly subscription, that prevents Nigerian customers from streaming. Iroko is in the process of implementing three modifications to its business model that address the use of mobile data for streaming. Because downloading requires less data than streaming, Iroko allows customers to download low-quality versions of the movie for offline viewing. To minimize download times and storage demands, the company produces shows with shorter episodes. Finally, Iroko is negotiating deals with local telecommunication firms to lower the cost of data while customers are streaming. Managerial accounting helps companies like Iroko understand the cost of delivering their service, and the costs of adapting their business model to access new markets. Accurate cost data and forecasts will be central to Iroko's negotiations with telecommunication providers.

Source: Alexis Okeowo, "The Netflix of Africa Doesn't Need Hollywood to Win," *Bloomberg Businessweek*, February 22, 2016.

Iroko, highlighted in the Business Insight box above, is following a market niche strategy. It identified behaviors of its target market, and using management accounting information, is adapting its model to better fit its market's needs.

Managerial Accounting and Goal Attainment

A major purpose of managerial accounting is to support the achievement of goals. Hence, determining an organization's strategic position goal has implications for the operation of an organization's managerial accounting system.

Careful budgeting and cost control with frequent and detailed performance reports are critical with a goal of cost leadership. When the product is difficult to distinguish from that of competitors', price is the primary basis of competition. Under these circumstances, everyone in the organization should continuously apply managerial accounting concepts to achieve and maintain cost leadership. The managerial accounting system should constantly compare actual costs with budgeted costs and signal the existence of significant differences. A simplified version of a *performance report* for costs during a budget period is as follows:

Budgeted (planned) Costs	Actual Costs	Deviation from Budget	Percent Deviation
$560,000	$595,000	$35,000 unfavorable	6.25%

---

[10] Porter, pp. 38–39.

Frequent and detailed comparisons of actual and budgeted costs are less important when a differentiation strategy is followed. This is especially true when products have short life cycles or production is highly automated. In these situations, most costs are determined before production begins and there is little opportunity to undertake cost reduction activities thereafter.

With short product lives or automated manufacturing, exceptional care must go into the initial design of a product or service and the determination of how it will be produced or delivered. Here, detailed cost information assists in design and scheduling decisions. A simplified version of the predicted costs of producing one batch of a specialty product is as follows:

Engineering and scheduling (12 hours @ $70).	$ 840
Materials (detail omitted)	3,500
Equipment setup (2.5 hours @ $100).	250
Machine operation (9.5 hours @ $90).	855
Materials movement.	150
Packing and shipping.	675
Total	$6,270

When a differentiation strategy is followed, it often pays to work closely with customers to find ways to enhance the perceived value of a product or service. This leads to an analysis of costs from the customer's viewpoint. The customer may not want a costly feature. Alternatively, the customer may be willing to pay more for an additional feature that will reduce subsequent operating costs.

Planning, Organizing, and Controlling

The process of selecting goals and strategies to achieve these goals is often referred to as **planning**. The implementation of plans requires the development of subgoals and the assignment of responsibility to achieve subgoals to specific individuals or groups within an organization. This process of making the organization into a well-ordered whole is called **organizing**. In organizing, the authority to take action to implement plans is delegated to other managers and employees.

Developing an **organization chart** illustrating the formal relationships that exist between the elements of an organization is an important part of organizing. An organization chart for Crown Department Stores is illustrated in **Exhibit 13.3**. The blocks represent organizational units, and the lines represent relationships between the units. Authority flows down through the organization. Top management delegates authority to use resources for limited purposes to subordinate managers who, in turn, delegate to their subordinates more limited authority for accomplishing more structured tasks. Responsibility flows up through the organization. People at the bottom are responsible for specific tasks, but the president is responsible for the operation of the entire organization.

A distinction is often made between line and staff departments. *Line departments* engage in activities that create and distribute goods and services to customers. *Staff departments* exist to facilitate the activities of line departments. In **Exhibit 13.3**, we see that Crown Department Stores has two levels of staff organizations—corporate and store. The corporate staff departments are Purchasing, Advertising, Operations, Treasurer, and Controller. Staff departments at the store level are Personnel, Accounting, and Maintenance. All other units are line departments. A change in plans can necessitate a change in the organization. For example, Crown's plan to discontinue the sale of hardware and add an art department during the coming year will necessitate an organizational change.

Controlling is the process of ensuring that results agree with plans. A brief example of a performance report for costs was presented previously on page 627. In the process of controlling operations, actual performance is compared with plans.

With a cost leadership strategy and long-lived products, if actual results deviate significantly from plans, an attempt is made to bring operations into line with plans, or the plans are adjusted. The original plan is adjusted if it is deemed no longer appropriate because of changed circumstances.

With a differentiation strategy and short-lived products, design and scheduling personnel will consider previous errors in predicting costs as they plan new products and services. Hence, the process of controlling feeds forward into the process of planning to form a continuous cycle coordinated through the management accounting system. This cycle is illustrated in **Exhibit 13.4**.

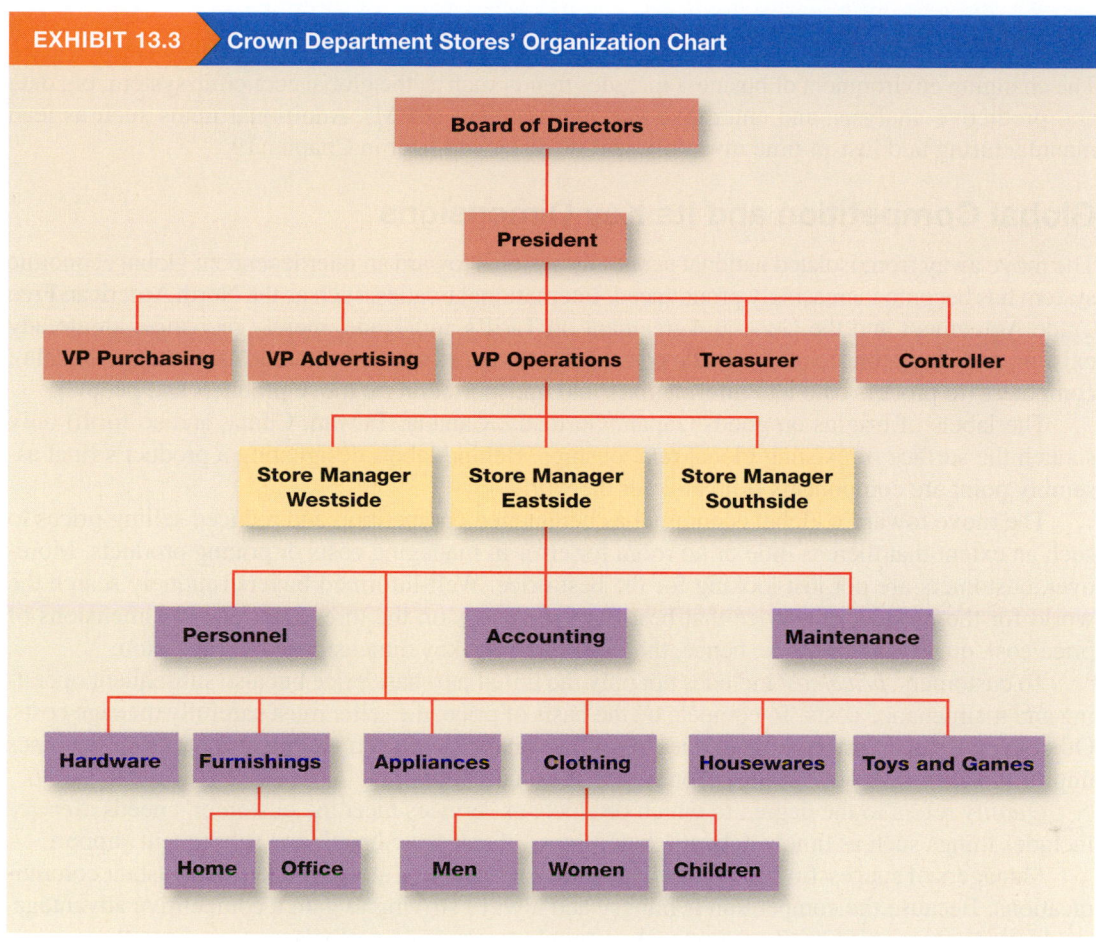

EXHIBIT 13.3 ▸ **Crown Department Stores' Organization Chart**

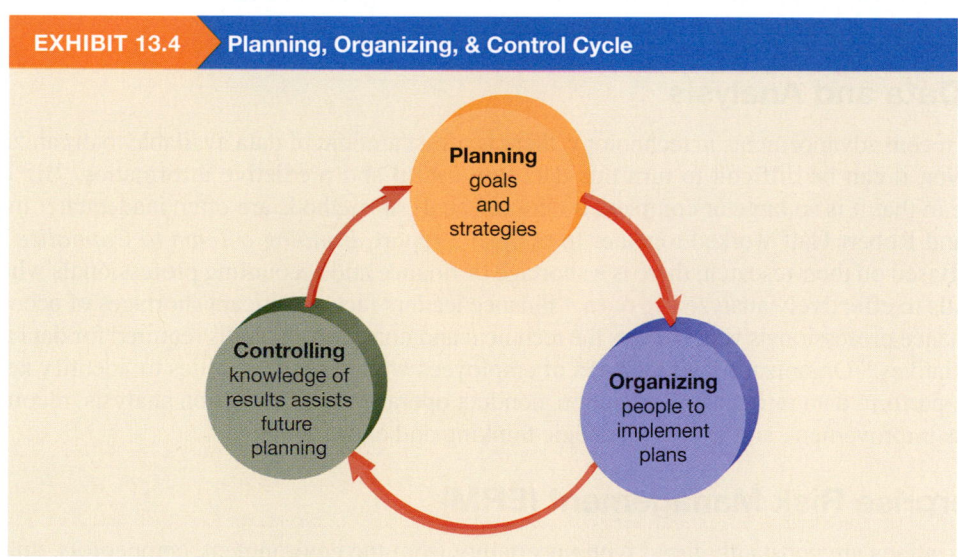

EXHIBIT 13.4 ▸ **Planning, Organizing, & Control Cycle**

MID-CHAPTER REVIEW 3

A major purpose of managerial accounting is to support the achievement of goals. Discuss a few ways that managerial accountants can help support the achievement of goals, specifically those of cost leadership and differentiation.

The solution to this review problem can be found on page 646.

LO4 Analyze how trends in the business environment impact the role of management accounting.

4

CHANGING ENVIRONMENT OF BUSINESS

The changing environment of business includes trends such as the global economic system, big data and predictive analysis, and enterprise risk management (ERM). Additional items such as lean manufacturing and just-in-time inventory will be discussed later in Chapter 19.

Global Competition and Its Key Dimensions

The move away from isolated national economic systems toward an interdependent global economic system has become increasingly pronounced. International treaties, such as the North American Free Trade Agreement and the General Agreement on Tariffs and Trade, merely recognize an already existing and inevitable condition made possible by advances in telecommunications (to move data), computers (to process data into information), and transportation (to move products and people).

The labels of origins on goods (Japan, Germany, Canada, Taiwan, China, and so forth) only scratch the surface of existing global relationships. Behind labels designating a product's final assembly point are components from all over the world.

The move toward a global economy has heightened competition and reduced selling prices to such an extent that there is little or no room for error in managing costs or pricing products. Moreover, customers are not just looking for the best price. Well-informed buyers routinely search the world for the product or service that best fits their needs on the three interrelated dimensions of price/cost, quality, and service; hence, these are the three key dimensions of competition.

To customers, *price/cost* includes not only the initial purchase price but also subsequent operating and maintenance costs. To compete on the basis of price, the seller must carefully manage costs. Otherwise, reduced prices might squeeze product margins to such an extent that a sale becomes unprofitable. Hence, price competition implies cost competition.

Quality refers to the degree to which products or services meet the customer's needs. *Service* includes things such as timely delivery, helpfulness of sales personnel, and subsequent support.

Managers of successful companies know they compete in a global market with instant communications. Because the competition is hungry and always striving to gain a competitive advantage, world-class companies must continuously struggle to improve performance on these three interrelated dimensions: price/cost, quality, and service. Throughout this text, we examine how firms successfully compete on these three dimensions.

Big Data and Analysis

Given recent advancements in technology, there is a vast amount of data available to organizations. However, it can be difficult to turn this data into useful and predictive information. Big data is unique in that it is so large or complex, traditional analysis methods are often inadequate. In 2016, IMA and Robert Half worked together to publish a report, *Building a Team to Capitalize in Big Data*. Based on their research, there is a shortage of finance and accounting professionals who have the skills to effectively analyze **big data**. "Finance leaders face significant shortages of accounting and finance professionals who possess the technical and nontechnical skills required for data analytics initiatives." Organizations are in need of employees who have the abilities to: identify key data trends, perform data mining and extraction, conduct operational and decision analysis, recommend process improvement, and conduct strategic thinking and execution.

Enterprise Risk Management (ERM)

Organizations are constantly faced with uncertainty from the environment, competitors, and other factors that could result in significant risk or loss. The Committee of Sponsoring Organizations (COSO) defines **enterprise risk management (ERM)** as "a process, effected by an entity's board of directors, management and other personnel, applied in strategy setting and across the enterprise, designed to identify potential events that may affect the entity, and manage risk to be within its risk appetite, to provide reasonable assurance regarding the achievement of entity objectives."[11] By better understanding the types and potential costs of these risks, management accountants can help their

---

[11] *Enterprise Risk Management—Integrated Framework: Executive Summary (PDF)*. Committee of Sponsoring Organizations of the Treadway Commission. *September 2004. Retrieved 2008-09-16.*

organizations devise strategies to better predict and minimize their exposures to risk. In Chapter 21 we will discuss how an organization's budgeting model is used to evaluate the financial impact of a risk and to determine, from a financial perspective, the best response to risk.

MID-CHAPTER REVIEW 4

Big data analysis and ERM are of growing interest to leaders of organizations. Discuss briefly how the influence of each might affect the role of management accountants.

The solution to this review problem can be found on page 646.

ETHICS IN MANAGERIAL ACCOUNTING

Ethics deals with the moral quality, fitness, or propriety of a course of action that can injure or benefit people. Ethics goes beyond legality, which refers to what is permitted under the law, to consider the moral quality of an action. Because situations involving ethics are not guided by well-defined rules, they are often subjective.

LO5 Assess the nature of the ethical dilemmas managers and accountants confront.

Although some actions are clearly ethical (working a full day in exchange for a full day's pay) and others are clearly unethical (pumping contaminants into an underground aquifer used as a source of drinking water), managers are often faced with situations that do not fall clearly into either category such as the following:

- Accelerating or decelerating shipments at the end of the quarter to meet current earnings forecasts.
- Keeping inventory that is unlikely to be used so as to avoid recording a loss.
- Purchasing supplies from a relative or friend rather than seeking bids.
- Basing a budget on an overly optimistic sales forecast.
- Assigning some costs of Contract A to Contract B to avoid an unfavorable performance report on Contract A.

Many ethical dilemmas involve actions that are perceived to have desirable short-run consequences and highly probable undesirable long-run consequences. The ethical action is to face an undesirable situation now to avoid a worse situation later, yet the decision maker prefers to believe that things will work out in the long run, be overly concerned with the consequences of not doing well in the short run, or simply not care about the future because the problem will then belong to someone else. In a situation that is clearly unethical, the future consequences are known to be avoidable and undesirable. In situations involving questionable ethics, there is some hope that things will work out:

- Next year's sales will more than make up for the accelerated shipments.
- The obsolete inventory can be used in a new nostalgia line of products.
- The relative or friend may charge more but provides excellent service.
- A desire to have more confidence in the sales staff.
- Making up for the cost shift by working extra hard and more efficiently with the remaining work on Contract B.

When forced to think about the situation, most employees want to act in an ethical manner. The problem faced by personnel involved in measurement and reporting is that while they may question the propriety of a proposed action, and the arguments may be plausible, they want to be team players, and their careers can be affected by "whistle-blowing." Of course, careers are also affected when individuals are identified as being involved in unethical behavior. The careers of people who fail to point out unethical behavior are also affected, especially if they have a responsibility for measurement and reporting.

Major ethical dilemmas often evolve from a series of small compromises, none of which appears serious enough to warrant taking a stand on ethical grounds. **WorldCom** is such a case, in which managers deferred expenses inappropriately over several periods to meet profit forecasts, expecting to recognize them at a later time when sales improved. Unfortunately, these small compromises establish a pattern of behavior that is increasingly difficult to reverse. The key to avoiding these situations is recognizing the early warning signs of situations that involve questionable ethical behavior and taking whatever action is appropriate.

Codes of Ethics

Codes of ethics are often developed by professional organizations to increase members' awareness of the importance of ethical behavior and to provide a reference point for resisting pressures to engage in actions of questionable ethics. These professional organizations include the American Bar Association, the American Institute of Certified Public Accountants, the American Medical Association, and the Institute of Management Accountants (IMA).

Many corporations have established codes of ethics. Hershey's has a 44 page published document "Code of Ethical Business Conduct." One of the important goals of corporate codes of ethics is to provide employees with a common foundation for addressing ethical issues. These codes provide a summary of a company's policies that define ethical standards of employee conduct and they often include broad philosophical statements about behavior. Hershey's code states, "Every day provides new opportunities to do the right thing. Let this Code and your good judgment be your guide."[12]

BUSINESS INSIGHT

Violations of Ethical Standards for Management Accountants at Toshiba   **Toshiba** is a 140-year-old company that started making telegraph equipment in 1875 and has since expanded into a diverse line of products. In 2015, Toshiba had over 200,000 employees worldwide and ranked as 356 in the list of the world's largest public companies.

At the end of 2015, Japanese regulators fined Toshiba Corporation with a record fine of ¥7.37 billion ($60 million). This fine was in response to accounting violations between 2008 and 2014 that inflated profits by $1.2 billion to meet unrealistic profit targets. Toshiba's accountants, under pressure from executives, delayed the recognition of losses.

The Institute of Management Accountants (IMA) has developed four standards of ethical conduct for management accountants and financial managers.

1. Competence: Perform their professional duties in accordance with relevant laws, regulations, and technical standards.
2. Confidentiality: Refrain from disclosing confidential information acquired in the course of their work except when authorized, unless legally obligated to do so.
3. Integrity: Refrain from engaging in or supporting any activity that would discredit the profession.
4. Credibility: Communicate information fairly and objectively.

Toshiba and its auditors violated all or part of each of these standards.

Sources: Pavel Alpeyev and Takashi Amano, "Toshiba Said to Face Biggest Fine by Japan's Financial Regulator," *Bloomberg Technology*, December 6, 2015.

Pavel Alpeyev and Takashi Amano, "Toshiba to Restate at Least 152 Billion Yen of Past Profits," *Bloomberg Technology*, July 20, 2015.

"Standards of Ethical Conduct for Management Accountants," *Accountingverse*, accessed 19 July, 2016.

Corporate Governance

Corporate governance refers to the system of policies, processes, laws, and regulations that affect the way a company is directed and controlled. At the highest level, the system of corporate governance for a company is the responsibility of the board of directors, but it affects all stakeholders, including employees, creditors, customers, vendors, and the community at large. The large number of corporate failures of the last decade brought the topic of corporate governance to the forefront.

The collapse of **Enron**, along with its independent auditor, **Arthur Andersen**, prompted the U.S. Congress to pass the Sarbanes-Oxley Act of 2002 (or SOX), which was intended to address

---

[12] https://www.thehersheycompany.com/content/dam/corporate-us/documents/investors/business-code-of-conduct.pdf

weaknesses affecting U.S. capital markets. Although SOX deals primarily with issues pertaining to the relationship between publicly traded companies and the capital markets, some of its requirements have become a standard for corporate responsibility and governance affecting both public and private companies, as well as not-for-profit organizations.

SOX consists of 66 sections, including such topics as external auditing standards, auditor conflicts of interest, codes of ethics for financial officers, review of internal controls, and criminal penalties for fraud. Probably the most important provisions of SOX, from a managerial accounting standpoint, are those related to internal control systems. **Internal control systems** generally are made up of the policies and procedures that exist to ensure that company objectives are achieved with regard to (a) effectiveness and efficiency of operations, (b) reliability of financial reporting, and (c) compliance with laws and regulations.

SOX imposes the requirement that CEOs and CFOs annually review and assess the effectiveness of their company's internal controls over financial reporting, and issue a report of their assessment. Although many CEOs and CFOs have argued that the cost of SOX compliance is unjustified by the benefits to investors, the following Research Insight provides evidence that SOX is improving the quality of financial reporting. Even though SOX limits the internal control review to aspects of the system related to financial reporting, in practice there is very little that takes place in any organization that does not impact the financial statements. Therefore, if SOX is resulting in improvements in data that goes into financial reports, it is likely that data supporting managerial accounting is also enhanced by a more reliable internal control system.

Many of the models and processes that we discuss in this text have either a direct or indirect impact on a company's financial statements; hence, they are likely subject to the SOX internal control review. An overlap often exists between the systems that produce the data for the external financial statements and those that produce data for internal decision making. For example, cost data produced by the product costing system is often used for both financial reporting and managerial decision making purposes. A more detailed discussion of SOX and internal control systems can typically be found in financial accounting and auditing textbooks.

RESEARCH INSIGHT

SOX Gives Important Internal Control Information to Financial Markets   An important question that accounting researchers ask about any disclosure is whether the disclosure is useful to the financial markets. A team of researchers from Shanghai and Hong Kong have shown that information provided by SOX about internal controls directly influences the pricing of Credit Default Swaps (CDS), a transaction that allows lenders to hedge the risk of their loans. CDS provide the firm's owners with insurance if the firm goes bankrupt, so the connection between information about internal control and the price of this type of insurance suggests that SOX is releasing important information about the way the firm is run.

The impact of good internal control on annual debt interest expense is meaningful. Firms with good controls book, on average, $35.7 million less in annual debt interest expense than firms with material weaknesses in their internal controls. This study shows that the relationship between CDS pricing and internal control holds, not only for the material weakness disclosures, but also as internal controls deteriorate over time, leading up to the material weakness. To the extent that the firm is concerned about the cost of debt, SOX-mandated disclosures provide pressure for good internal controls. This may improve the information that is provided to management accounting systems.

Source: Dragon Yongjun Tang, Feng Tian, and Hong Yan, "Internal Control Quality and Credit Default Swap Spreads," *Accounting Horizons*, September 2015, Vol. 29, No. 3, pp. 603-629.

Sustainability Accounting and Corporate Social Responsibility

Sustainability accounting and corporate social responsibility are increasingly important to managers. "Since the 1960s environmentalists have been concerned with the impact of economic growth and the increasingly rapid use of the world's resources. In recent years, these concerns have increased because of the impact of greenhouse gases, caused by the burning of fossil fuels, on global warming."[13] John Elkington introduced the concept of the Triple Bottom Line (TBL), which in-

---

[13] *The Evolution of Accountability Sustainability Reporting for Accountants*, IMA 2014.

corporates traditional financial performance and accountability to shareholders, as well as broader accountability through both environmental and social impacts.[14]

These concepts entail balancing the objective of profitability with the objective of giving proper attention to issues such as environmental sustainability and energy conservation, and avoiding actions that would lower the quality of life in the communities in which a company operates and sells its products or services. In earlier generations it would have meant giving a day's wage for a day's labor, not hiring underage children, or not dumping untreated waste into the local river.

Managerial accounting includes a variety of models that help managers determine the cost of a particular activity or product, or the benefits and costs of various decision alternatives. Although such models in their current state of development may not take into account all external social costs, accountants are more aware today than in the past of the need to consider such costs. For example, when calculating the cost of building a new capital asset that is going to last for 25 years, it is necessary to include in that calculation the present value of the cost of the ultimate disposal of the asset, including any environmental cleanup.

Being a socially responsible company does not mean abandoning the profit motive or the goal of providing an attractive return to investors. It means that while pursuing these essential objectives, a for-profit company attempts to measure the total benefits and costs of its actions and accepts the responsibility for those actions. Also, being a good competitor should not be confused with social responsibility. For example, many companies offer certain fringe benefits, such as on-site child-care, because it attracts better employees, not because they feel they have a social responsibility to provide such services. Obviously, the line between being a good competitor and being socially responsible is sometimes blurred.

RESEARCH INSIGHT

Environmental Disclosures—Silence Is Not Golden Various regulatory sources have been calling for increased disclosure regarding a firm's effect on the environment, including a report on the firm's carbon emissions. Shareholder activists have also driven increased reporting of climate-change risks to their investee firms. In 2004, only 14 percent of shareholder resolutions involved environmental initiatives, but that number had grown to 27 percent by 2009, according to a report by **EY**. The authors of a recent study note that firms with a reputation for environmental responsibility enjoy higher revenues, lower compliance costs, more motivated employees, and positive perceptions among customers and suppliers.

EY analyzed carbon emissions data from 2006 to 2008 for S&P 500 firms and found that for each additional thousand metric tons of carbon emissions produced by the firm, the firm's value (as measured by market value of equity) decreases by $212,000. The difference in value between the first and third quartiles of carbon emission levels correlates to a 1.4-billion-dollar difference in firm value. However, silence is not golden. The authors state that although all firms are penalized for their carbon emissions, those firms that do not disclose the information to the public are penalized to a larger extent by the stock market.

Source: Ella Mae Matsumura, Rachna Prakash, and Sandra Vera-Munoz, "Firm-Value Effects of Carbon Emissions and Carbon Disclosures," *The Accounting Review*, forthcoming.

MID-CHAPTER REVIEW 5

How can managerial accounting help support corporate social responsibility?

The solution to this review problem can be found on page 646.

---

[14] John Elkington, founder of "SustainAbility," 1987.

COST DRIVERS

The foundation for the managerial accounting concepts covered in this text, is the ability to identify and measure the activities of an organization. In this chapter, we introduce the idea of business activities and what drives the costs related to those activities.

An **activity** is a unit of work. To serve a customer at a restaurant such as **Fleming's Prime Steakhouse**, a server might perform the following units of work:

- Seat customer and offer menu
- Take customer order
- Send order to kitchen
- Bring food to customer
- Serve and replenish beverages
- Determine and bring bill to customer
- Accept and process payment
- Clear and reset table

Each of these is an activity, and the performance of each activity consumes resources that cost money. To manage activities and their costs, it is necessary to understand how costs respond to **cost drivers**, which are the factors that cause or influence costs.

The most basic cost driver is customer demand. Without customer demand for products or services, the organization cannot exist. To serve customers, managers and employees make a variety of decisions and take numerous actions. These decisions and actions, undertaken to satisfy customer demand, drive costs. While these cost drivers may be classified in a variety of ways, we believe that dividing them into the three categories of structural, organizational, and activity cost drivers, as summarized in **Exhibit 13.5**, provides a useful foundation for the study of managerial accounting.

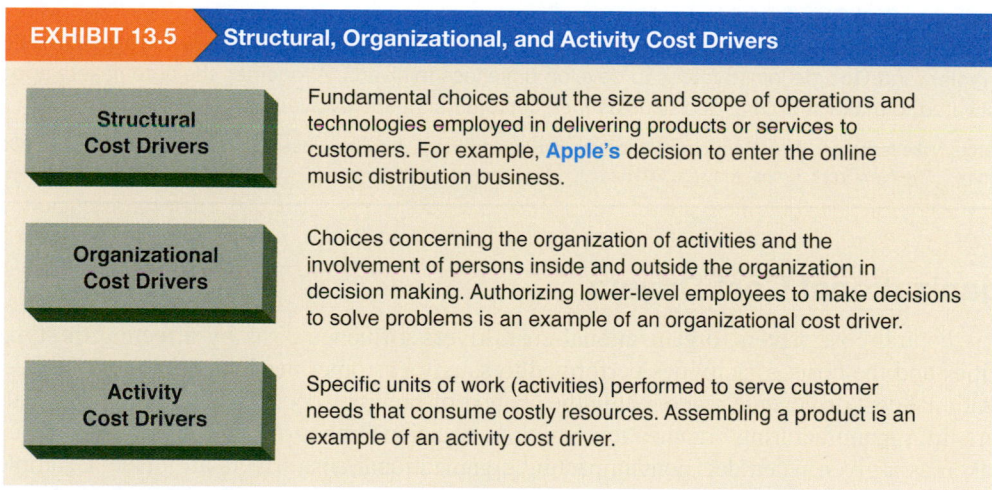

EXHIBIT 13.5   Structural, Organizational, and Activity Cost Drivers

Structural Cost Drivers	Fundamental choices about the size and scope of operations and technologies employed in delivering products or services to customers. For example, **Apple's** decision to enter the online music distribution business.
Organizational Cost Drivers	Choices concerning the organization of activities and the involvement of persons inside and outside the organization in decision making. Authorizing lower-level employees to make decisions to solve problems is an example of an organizational cost driver.
Activity Cost Drivers	Specific units of work (activities) performed to serve customer needs that consume costly resources. Assembling a product is an example of an activity cost driver.

Structural Cost Drivers

The types of activities and the costs of activities performed to satisfy customer needs are influenced by an organization's size, its location, the scope of its operations, and the technologies used. Decisions affecting structural cost drivers are made infrequently, and once made, the organization is committed to a course of action that will be difficult to change. For a chain of retail stores such as **Target**, possible structural cost drivers include:

- *Determining the size of stores*. This affects the variety of merchandise that can be carried and operating costs.
- *Determining the type of construction*. While a lean warehouse type of construction is less expensive, it is not an appropriate setting for selling high-fashion clothing.

- *Determining the location of stores.* Locating in a shopping mall can cost more and subject the store to mall regulations but provides for more customer traffic and shared advertising.
- *Determining types of technology to employ in stores.* A computerized system for maintaining all inventory and sales data requires a large initial investment and fixed annual operating costs while providing more current information. However, the computerized inventory and sales systems can be less expensive at high sales volumes than a less costly system relying more on clerks taking physical inventory.

An important structural cost driver for many companies is the decision to redefine their company's product offering. The following Business Insight illustrates how the auto industry is rethinking what "product" they bring to market. Traditionally their product was manufacturing cars. Now they are thinking broader in terms of transportation. This has led to investments in ride hailing apps, the creation of their own driver services, and driverless car technology.

BUSINESS INSIGHT

Auto Industry Begins Structural Shift to Match Changing Car Culture A company's long-term viability depends on its ability to change with its customers. Structural cost decisions made decades ago can make it tough for large, mature firms to adapt. This problem is easy to see in the American auto industry. American automakers paid the price for producing oversized, overpowered cars during the fuel price spikes in the early 2000s.

As apps like **Lyft**, **Uber**, and **Gett** and ride-sharing programs like **Zipcar** change the way people get around, automakers are making moves to keep up. In many cities, owning or even knowing how to drive a car is becoming less of a necessity. While industry analysts don't see a decrease in auto sales due to these changes, automakers have been actively investing in ride-hailing apps. **Toyota** has invested an undisclosed amount in Uber, the leader in app-based driver services. **Volkswagen** has invested $300 million in Gett, Uber's largest European competitor. **General Motors**, not to be left behind, has invested $500 million in Lyft. **BMW** and **Mercedes-Benz** are also testing the waters with their own driver services. Tech companies are also interested in this shift in the way transportation works, as Apple has invested $1 billion in **Didi Chuxing**, a rival of Uber's in China.

Driverless car technology is a particularly dramatic shift in this marketplace, but in May 2016 **Fiat**, **Chrysler**, and **Google** joined forces to develop driverless minivans. Altogether, the automakers appear motivated to make structural decisions as their customers' needs evolve.

Source: Mike Isaac and Neal Boudette, "Automakers Befriend Start-Ups Like Uber, Girding Against a Changing Car Culture," *The New York Times*, May 24, 2016.

Organizational Cost Drivers

Like structural cost drivers, organizational cost drivers influence costs by affecting the types of activities and the costs of activities performed to satisfy customer needs. Decisions that affect organizational cost drivers are made within the context of previous decisions affecting structural cost drivers. In a manufacturing organization, previous decisions about plant, equipment, and location are taken as a given when decisions impacting organizational cost drivers are made. Examples of organizational cost drivers at a manufacturing organization such as **Harley-Davidson** include making decisions regarding:

- *Working closely with a limited number of suppliers.* This can help achieve proper materials in the proper quantities at the optimal time. Developing linkages with suppliers can also result in suppliers' initiatives that improve the profitability of both organizations.
- *Providing employees with cost information and authorizing them to make decisions.* This helps improve decision speed and reduce costs while making employees more customer oriented. Production employees may, for example, offer product design suggestions that reduce manufacturing costs or reduce defects.
- *Reorganizing the existing equipment in the plant so that sequential operations are closer.* This more efficient layout reduces the cost of moving inventory between workstations.

- *Designing components of a product so they can fit together only in the correct manner.* This can reduce defects as well as assembly time and cost.

- *Manufacturing a low-volume product on low-speed, general-purpose equipment rather than high-speed, special-purpose equipment.* Assuming the special-purpose equipment is more difficult and costly to set up for a new job, this decision can increase operating time and operating cost while reducing setup time and setup cost.

The following Business Insight illustrates how an innovative software startup managed a key organizational cost driver to keep down costs and achieve profitability.

BUSINESS INSIGHT

Software Company Increases Sales at a Lower Cost without Sales Department   **Atlassian**, a company without salespeople, sold $320 million of business software last year. The company, known for its flagship project management product JIRA, is valued at $5 billion and is competing with industry giants such as **Oracle**, **IBM**, and **HP**. While unconventional, the benefit to Atlassian's approach shows up in its 19% revenue-to-sales/marketing cost ratio, where Atlassian beats its peers by 30% or more.

The decision to develop the business without a sales department was an organic one. Launched while the founders Scott Farquhar and Mike Cannon-Brooks were in school, at first they simply lacked the time and resources for a formal sales department. Effort was focused on developing and delivering the product, not on selling it. Now customers are guided through the purchase process online, and requests for a sales rep visit are politely declined. As the company has matured, they have learned that this strategy has increased sales at a low cost.

As young firms develop, management accountants can help decision makers think carefully about the future organizational costs associated with structural decisions like those Cannon-Brooks and Farquhar faced as students.

Source: Dina Bass, "This $5 Billion Software Company Has No Sales Staff," *Bloomberg Businessweek*, May 19, 2016.

Activity Cost Drivers

Activity cost drivers are specific units of work (activities) performed to serve customer needs that consume costly resources. Several examples of activities in a restaurant were mentioned previously. The customer may be outside the organization, such as a client of an advertising firm, or inside the organization, such as an accounting office that receives maintenance services. Because the performance of activities consumes resources and resources cost money, the performance of activities drives costs.

The basic decisions concerning which available activities will be used to respond to customer requests precede the actual performance of activities. At the activity level, execution of previous plans and following prescribed activities are important. All of the examples of structural and organizational cost drivers involved making decisions. In the following list of activity cost drivers for a manufacturing organization, note the absence of the decision-oriented words.

- Placing a purchase order for raw materials
- Inspecting incoming raw materials
- Moving items being manufactured between workstations
- Setting up a machine to work on a product
- Spending machine time working on a product
- Spending labor time working on a product
- Hiring and training a new employee
- Packing an order for shipment
- Processing a sales order
- Shipping a product

In managing costs, management makes choices concerning structural and organizational cost drivers. These decisions affect the types of activities required to satisfy customer needs. Because different types of activities have different costs, management's decisions concerning structural and organizational cost drivers ultimately affect activity costs and profitability. Good decision making at the level of structural and organizational cost drivers requires an understanding of the linkages among the types of cost drivers and the costs of different activities.

YOU MAKE THE CALL

You are the CEO   How can you use information about structural, organizational, and activity cost drivers to help you in implementing the organization's strategy? [Answer, p. 638]

CHAPTER-END REVIEW

Classify each of the following as a structural, organizational, or activity cost driver.

a. Meals served to airplane passengers aboard **Delta Airlines**.
b. **GM**'s decision to manufacture the Volt, an all-electric automobile.
c. **Zenith**'s decision to sell its computer operations and focus on the core television business.
d. Number of tax returns filed electronically by **H&R Block**.
e. Number of passenger cars in an **Amtrak** train.
f. **Coors**' decision to expand its market area east from the Rocky Mountains.
g. **Boeing**'s decision to invite airlines to assist in designing the model 777 airplane.
h. **Daimler Benz**'s decision to use cross-disciplinary teams to design a new automobile.
i. **St. Jude Hospital**'s decision to establish review committees on the appropriateness and effectiveness of medical procedures for improving patient care.
j. **Harley-Davidson**'s efforts to restructure production procedures to reduce inventories and machine setup times.

The solution to this review problem can be found on page 646.

GUIDANCE ANSWERS . . . YOU MAKE THE CALL

You are the CEO   It is important that an organization's cost structure be aligned with its strategy. If your goal is to be a cost leader (such as Wal-Mart or Costco), you will want to make sure that the structural cost drivers, such as the type of buildings acquired and the displays used, are consistent with this strategy. As the CEO of Wal-Mart you would not permit many of the costs that would be incurred in an organization such as Tiffany or Nordstrom.

KEY TERMS

activity, 635
activity cost drivers, 637
big data, 630
controlling, 628
corporate governance, 632
cost driver analysis, 623
cost drivers, 635
enterprise risk management (ERM), 630

ethics, 631
financial accounting, 620
for-profit organizations, 624
goal, 624
internal control systems, 633
managerial accounting, 620
mission, 624
not-for-profit organizations, 624
organization chart, 628

organizing, 628
planning, 628
strategic cost management, 623
strategic position, 625
strategic position analysis, 623
strategy, 625
sustainability accounting, 633
value chain analysis, 623

Assignments with the ⬤ logo in the margin are available in my BusinessCourse.
See the Preface of the book for details.

MULTIPLE CHOICE

1. Which of the following is not a characteristic of Managerial Accounting?
   a. No external standards
   b. Reports primarily on past decisions
   c. Provides information for internal users
   d. Information is more detailed

2. Controlling is the process of:
   a. Selecting goals and adopting strategies for achieving them
   b. Delegating authority to others to take action to implement plans
   c. Organizing employees into line and staff functions
   d. Ensuring that results agree with plans

3. Which of the following is not likely to be regarded as an action that has ethical implications in today's business environment?
   a. Purchasing supplies from a relative or friend rather than seeking bids
   b. Using different depreciation methods for calculating depreciation expense for the financial statements and the income tax return
   c. Failing to recognize obsolete inventory to avoid missing a profit forecast
   d. Shifting costs for one contract to another to make the profits of the contracts line up with initial forecasts

4. Which of the following is not a cost driver?
   a. The gender of the wait staff at a restaurant
   b. The number of customers in a restaurant
   c. The size of a restaurant
   d. The policy of empowering a server to make the decision to give a customer a free dessert because of the delay in delivering the main entrée

5. Which of the following is not one of the three basic types of cost drivers discussed in the text?
   a. Activity cost drivers
   b. Organizational cost drivers
   c. Direct cost drivers
   d. Structural cost drivers

Multiple Choice Answers
1. b 2. d 3. b 4. a 5. c

QUESTIONS

Q13-1. Contrast financial and managerial accounting on the basis of user orientation, purpose of information, level of aggregation, length of time period, orientation toward past or future, conformance to external standards, and emphasis on objective data.

Q13-2. What three themes are a part of strategic cost management?

Q13-3. Distinguish between a mission and a goal.

Q13-4. Describe the three strategic positions that Porter views as leading to business success.

Q13-5. Distinguish between how managerial accounting would support the strategy of cost leadership and the strategy of product differentiation.

Q13-6. Why are the phases of planning, organizing, and controlling referred to as a *continuous cycle*?

Q13-7. Identify three advances that have fostered the move away from isolated national economic systems toward an interdependent global economy.

Q13-8. What are the three interrelated dimensions of today's competition?

Q13-9. How can top management establish an ethical tone in an organization?

Q13-10. Describe how pressures to have desirable short-run outcomes can lead to ethical dilemmas.

Q13-11. Differentiate among structural, organizational, and activity cost drivers.

MINI EXERCISES

LO1, 2, 3, 5, 6   **M13-12. Management Accounting Terminology**

Match the following terms with the best descriptions. Each description is used only once.

TERMS

1. Ethics
2. Mission
3. Controlling
4. Goal
5. Cost drivers
6. Quality
7. Balance sheet
8. Income statement
9. Strategic cost management
10. Financial accounting
11. Activity cost driver
12. Structural cost driver
13. Managerial accounting
14. Resources
15. Product differentiation

DESCRIPTION

a. Making decisions concerning specific cost drivers
b. Factors that influence costs
c. Reports a company's financial position
d. Accounting for external users
e. Increase year 2017 sales by 10 percent over year 2016 sales
f. Shows the results of operations for a period of time
g. Packing an order for shipment
h. Deciding to limit market focus to a region rather than the entire nation
i. The degree to which a new e-book reader meets a buyer's expectations
j. Used internally to make decisions
k. Consumed by activities
l. The propriety of taking some action
m. Reduces customer price sensitivity
n. Basic purpose toward which activities are directed
o. Comparing the budget with the actual results

M13-13. Financial and Managerial Accounting

Indicate whether each phrase is more descriptive of financial accounting or managerial accounting.

a. May be subjective
b. Often used to state corporate goals
c. Typically prepared quarterly or annually
d. May measure time or customer satisfaction
e. Future oriented
f. Has a greater emphasis on cost-benefit analysis
g. Keeps records of assets and liabilities
h. Highly aggregated statements
i. Must conform to external standards
j. Special-purpose reports
k. Decision-making tool
l. Income statement, balance sheet, and statement of cash flows

LO1   **M13-14. Institute of Managerial Accountants**

What is the role of managerial accounting according to the IMA, and how does the IMA try to influence the best practices of managerial accountants?

LO3   **M13-15. Missions, Goals, and Strategies**

Identify each of the following as a mission, goal, or strategy.

a. Budget time for study, sleep, and relaxation
b. Provide shelter for the homeless
c. Provide an above-average return to investors
d. Protect the public
e. Locate fire stations so that the average response time is less than five minutes

f. Overlap police patrols so that there are always police cars on major thoroughfares

g. Achieve a 12 percent market share

h. Lower prices and costs

i. Select the most scenic route to drive between Las Vegas and Denver

j. Graduate from college

M13-16. Line and Staff Organization

LO3

Presented are the names of several departments often found in a merchandising organization such as **Target**.

Target
NYSE :: TGT

a. Maintenance   *d.* Payroll

b. Home Furnishings   *e.* Human Resources

c. Store Manager   *f.* Advertising

REQUIRED

Identify each as a line or a staff department.

M13-17. Line and Staff Organization

LO3

Presented are the names of several departments often found in a manufacturing organization such as **KraftHeinz**.

KraftHeinz
NASDAQ :: KHC

a. Manager, Plant 2   *d.* Controller

b. Design Engineering   *e.* Property Accounting

c. President   *f.* Sales Manager, District 1

REQUIRED

Identify each as a line or a staff department.

M13-18. Changing Business Environment

LO4

Identify some trends that should be considered when developing the role and processes of an organization's managerial accounting strategy.

M13-19. Classifying Cost Drivers

LO6

Classify each of the following as structural, organizational, or activity cost drivers.

Apple Inc.
NASDAQ :: AAPL

a. **Apple Inc.** reorganizes production facilities from a layout in which all similar types of machines are grouped together to a layout in which a set of machines is designated for the production of a particular product and that set of machines is grouped together.

b. A cable television company decides to start offering telephone service.

c. **IBM** decides to stop making personal computers.

IBM
NYSE :: IBM

d. **Canon** decides to start making high-volume photocopy equipment to compete head-to-head with Xerox.

Canon
NYSE :: (CAJ)

e. The number of meals a cafeteria serves.

f. The number of miles a taxi is driven.

g. A company eliminates the position of supervisor and has each work group elect a team leader.

h. **Tesla** empowers employees to halt production if a quality problem is identified.

Tesla Motors Inc.
NASDAQ :: TSLA

i. The number of tons of grain a ship loads.

j. Northbrook Mall decides to build space for 80 additional stores.

M13-20. Classifying Cost Drivers

LO6

Henderson Construction managers provide design and construction management services for various commercial construction projects. Senior managers are trying to apply cost driver concepts to their firm to better understand Henderson's costs.

REQUIRED

Classify each of the following actions or decisions as structural, organizational, or activity cost drivers.

a. The decision to be a regional leader in computer-assisted design services.

b. The decision to allow staff architects to follow a specific project through to completion.

c. The daily process of inspecting the progress on various construction projects.

d. The process of conducting extensive client interviews to assess the exact needs for Henderson services.

e. The decision to expand the market area by establishing an office in another state.

f. The decision to use only Henderson staff rather than relying on subcontractors.

g. The process of receiving approval from government authorities along with appropriate permits for each project.

h. The decision to organize the workforce into project teams.

i. The decision to build a new headquarters facility with areas for design and administration as well as storage and maintenance of construction equipment.

j. The process of grading building sites and preparing forms for foundations.

EXERCISES

LO1

KraftHeinz
NASDAQ :: KHC

E13-21. Financial and Managerial Accounting

Assume Katie Milling has just been promoted to product manager at **KraftHeinz**. Although she is an accomplished sales representative and well versed in market research, her accounting background is limited to reviewing her paycheck, balancing her checkbook, filing income tax returns, and reviewing the company's annual income statement and balance sheet. She commented that while the financial statements are no doubt useful to investors, she just doesn't see how accounting can help her be a good product manager.

REQUIRED

Based on her remarks, it is apparent that Katie's view of accounting is limited to financial accounting. Explain some of the important differences between financial and managerial accounting and suggest some ways managerial accounting can help Katie be a better product manager.

LO3

E13-22. Developing an Organization Chart

Develop an organization chart for a three-outlet bakery chain with a central baking operation and deliveries every few hours. Assume the business is incorporated and that the president has a single staff assistant. Also assume that the delivery truck driver reports to the bakery manager.

LO3

Stanford University
Good Samaritan Hospital
Walgreen Boots Alliance
NASDAQ :: WBA
Starwood Hotels and Resorts
NYSE :: HOT
United Parcel Service
NYSE :: UPS

E13-23. Identifying Monetary and Nonmonetary Performance Measures

Identify possible monetary and nonmonetary performance measures for each of the following situations. One nonmonetary measure should relate to quality, and one should relate to time.

a. **Stanford University** wishes to evaluate the success of last year's graduating class.

b. **Good Samaritan Hospital** wishes to evaluate the performance of its emergency room.

c. **Walgreen Boots Alliance** wishes to evaluate the performance of its online order–filling operations.

d. **Starwood Hotels** wishes to evaluate the performance of registration activities at one of its hotels.

e. **United Parcel Service** wishes to evaluate the success of its operations in Knoxville.

LO3

EarthLink
NASDAQ :: ELNK
Comcast
NASDAQ :: CMCSA
ASUSTEK Computer Inc.
NASDAQ :: ASUUY
Target Corporation
NYSE :: TGT
Emory University

E13-24. Identifying Monetary and Nonmonetary Performance Measures

Identify possible monetary and nonmonetary performance measures for each of the following situations. One nonmonetary measure should relate to quality, and one should relate to time.

a. **EarthLink**'s evaluation of the performance of its Internet service in Chicago.

b. **Comcast Cable**'s evaluation of the performance of new customer cable installations in Springfield.

c. **ASUS**'s evaluation of the performance of its logistical arrangements for delivering computers to its U.S. customers.

d. **Target**'s evaluation of the performance of its Web site.

e. **Emory University**'s evaluation of the success of its freshman admissions activities.

LO3

Toyota
NYSE :: TM
General Motors
NYSE :: GM

E13-25. Identifying Information Needs of Different Managers

Matt Parker operates a number of auto dealerships for **Toyota** and **General Motors**. Identify possible monetary and nonmonetary performance measures for each of the following situations. One nonmonetary measure should relate to quality, and one should relate to time.

a. An individual sales associate.

b. The sales manager of a single dealership.

c. The general manager of a particular dealership.

d. The corporate chief financial officer.

e. The president of the corporation.

E13-26. **Activities and Cost Drivers**

For each of the following activities, select the most appropriate cost driver. Each cost driver may be used only once.

Activity		Cost Driver
1. Pay vendors	a.	Number of different raw material items
2. Receive material deliveries	b.	Number of classes offered
3. Inspect raw materials	c.	Number of machine hours
4. Plan for purchases of raw materials	d.	Number of employees
5. Packaging	e.	Number of maintenance hours
6. Supervision	f.	Number of units of raw materials received
7. Employee training	g.	Number of new customers
8. Operating machines	h.	Number of deliveries
9. Machine maintenance	i.	Number of checks issued
10. Opening accounts at a bank	j.	Number of customer orders

CASES AND PROJECTS

C13-27. **Goals and Strategies**   LO3

a. What is your instructor's goal for students in this course? What strategies has he or she developed to achieve this goal?

b. What is your goal in this course? What strategies will help you achieve this goal?

c. What is your goal for this semester or term? What strategies will help you achieve this goal?

d. What is your next career goal? What strategies will help you achieve this goal?

C13-28. **Product Differentiation**   LO3

You are the owner of Lobster's Unlimited. You have no trouble catching lobsters, but you have difficulty in selling all that you catch. The problem is that all lobsters from all vendors look the same. You do catch high-quality lobsters, but you need to be able to tell your customers that your lobsters are better than those sold by other vendors.

REQUIRED

a. What are some possible ways of distinguishing your lobsters from those of other vendors?

b. Explain the possible results of this differentiation.

C13-29. **Ethics and Short-Term Borrowing**   LO5

Rory, an administrative assistant, is in charge of petty cash for a local law firm. Normally, about $300 is kept in the petty cash box. When Rory is short on cash and needs some for lunch or to pay her babysitter, she sometimes takes a few dollars from the box. Because she is in charge of the box, nobody knows that she takes the money, and she always replaces it within a few days.

REQUIRED

a. Is Rory's behavior ethical?

b. Assume that Rory has recently had major problems meeting her bills. She also is in charge of purchasing supplies for the office from petty cash. Last week when she needed $50 for the babysitter, she falsified a voucher for the amount of $50. Is this behavior ethical?

C13-30. **Ethics and Travel Reimbursement**   LO5

Jake takes many business trips throughout the year. All of his expenses are paid by his company. Last week he traveled to Rio De Janeiro, Brazil, and stayed there on business for five days. He is allowed a maximum of $50 per day for food and $150 per day for lodging. To his surprise, the food and accommodations in Brazil were much less than he expected. Being upset about traveling last week and having to sacrifice tickets he'd purchased to a Cubs baseball game, he decided to inflate his expenses a bit. He increased his lodging expense from $80 per day to $100 per day and his food purchased from $30 per day to $40 per day. Therefore, for the five-day trip, he overstated his expenses by $150 total. After all, the allowance was higher than the amount he spent.

REQUIRED ·

Assume that the company would never find out that he had actually spent less. Are Jake's actions ethical? Are they acceptable?

LO5   **C13-31.   Ethical Issues with Supplier-Buyer Partnerships**

Tom Wopat was excited to learn of his appointment as Circuit Electronics Corporation's sales representative to Household Appliance Inc. For the past four years, Circuit Electronics has supplied all of the electric switches used in Household's washers and dryers. As Circuit Electronics' sales representative, Tom's job involves the following tasks.

1. Working with Household engineers to design electric switches that can be manufactured to meet Household's cost and quality requirements.
2. Assisting Household in resolving any problems related to electric switches.
3. Monitoring the inventory levels of electric switches at Household and placing orders for additional switches when appropriate.

This appointment will require Tom to move to Stutgart, Germany, for two years. Although Tom has mixed feelings about the move, he is familiar with the success of the program in improving Circuit Electronics' financial performance. He is also very much aware of the fact that the two previous sales representatives received promotions at the end of their appointments.

As Tom toured the Household factory in Stutgart with his predecessor, Catherine Bach, his excitement turned to concern. It became apparent that Circuit Electronics had not been supplying Household with the best available switches at the lowest possible costs. Although the switches were adequate, they were more likely to wear out after five or six years of use than would switches currently on the market (and being used by Household's competitors). Furthermore, taking into account the current number of switches in transit by ship from North America to Europe, it also appeared that the inventory level of electric switches would soon be more than enough to satisfy Household's needs for the next four months.

REQUIRED
If you were Tom, what would you do?

LO5   **C13-32.   Expected Values of Questionable Decisions**

Exxon Mobil
NYSE :: XOM

The members of the jury had to make a decision in a lawsuit brought by the State of Alabama against **Exxon Mobil**. The suit revolved around natural-gas wells that Exxon drilled in state-owned waters. After signing several leases obligating Exxon to share revenues with Alabama, company officials started questioning the terms of the agreement that prohibited deducting several types of processing costs before paying the state royalties.

Royal Dutch/Shell
NYSE :: RDS-B

During the course of the trial, a memo by an in-house attorney of Exxon Mobil came to light. The memo noted that **Royal Dutch/Shell**, which had signed a similar lease, interpreted it "in the same manner as the state." The memo then presented arguments the company might use to claim the deduction, estimated the probability of the arguments being successful (less than 50 percent), and proceeded to consider whether Exxon should obey the law using a cost-benefit analysis. According to the memo, "If we adopt anything beyond a 'safe' approach, we should anticipate a quick audit and subsequent litigation." The memo also observed that "our exposure is 12 percent interest on underpayments calculated from the due date, and the cost of litigation." Deducting the questionable costs did, indeed, result in an audit and a lawsuit. Source: *Business Week.*[15]

REQUIRED
If you were a member of the jury, what would you do? Why?

LO6   **C13-33.   Management Decisions Affecting Cost Drivers**

An avid bicycle rider, you have decided to use an inheritance to start a new business to sell and repair bicycles. Two college friends have already accepted offers to work for you.

REQUIRED
a.   What is the mission of your new business?
b.   Suggest a strategic positioning goal you might strive for to compete with area hardware and discount stores that sell bicycles.
c.   Identify two items that might be long-range goals.
d.   Identify two items that might be goals for the coming year.
e.   Mention two decisions that will be structural cost drivers.
f.   Mention two decisions that will be organizational cost drivers.
g.   Identify two activity cost drivers.

---

[15] Mike France, "When Big Oil Gets Too Slick," *Business Week,* April 9, 2001, p. 70.

C13-34. **Success Factors and Performance Measurement**   **LO3**

Three years ago, Vincent Chow completed his college degree. The economy was in a depressed state at the time, and Vincent managed to get an offer of only $25,000 per year as a bookkeeper. In addition to its relatively low pay, this job had limited advancement potential. Since Vincent was an enterprising and ambitious young man, he instead started a business of his own. He was convinced that because of changing lifestyles, a drive-through coffee establishment would be profitable. He was able to obtain backing from his parents to open such an establishment close to the industrial park area in town. Vincent named his business The Cappuccino Express and decided to sell only two types of coffee: cappuccino and decaffeinated.

As Vincent had expected, The Cappuccino Express was very well received. Within three years, Vincent had added another outlet north of town. He left the day-to-day management of each site to a manager and turned his attention toward overseeing the entire enterprise. He also hired an assistant to do the record keeping and other selected chores.[16]

REQUIRED

a. Develop an organization chart for The Cappuccino Express.

b. What factors can be expected to have a major impact on the success of The Cappuccino Express?

c. What major tasks must Vincent undertake in managing The Cappuccino Express?

d. What are the major costs of operating The Cappuccino Express?

e. Vincent would like to monitor the performance of each site manager. What measure(s) of performance should he use?

f. If you suggested more than one measure, which of these should Vincent select if he could use only one?

g. Suppose that last year, the original site had yielded total revenues of $146,000, total costs of $122,000, and hence, a profit of $24,000. Vincent had judged this profit performance to be satisfactory. For the coming year, Vincent expects that due to factors such as increased name recognition and demographic changes, the total revenues will increase by 20 percent to $175,200. What amount of profit should he expect from the site? Discuss the issues involved in developing an estimate of profit.

SOLUTIONS TO REVIEW PROBLEMS

Mid-Chapter Review 1

SOLUTION

2, 5, 7, 8, 9, and 10

Mid-Chapter Review 2

SOLUTION

Below are the three themes involved in strategic position analysis and a possible example of each.

1. **Strategic position analysis is an examination of an organization's basic way of competing to sell products or services.** This might be relevant for a company like Uber. Uber originally started as a luxury brand, using high-end "black" cars. Their position was "everyone's private driver." As the first to market this concept, they have been very successful and have caused a number of changes in the industry. Uber's strategic positioning is very different from Lyft's, which according to their CMO, is more environmental. Lyft wants to focus on having fewer cars on the road and filling empty seats.[17]

2. **Cost driver analysis is the study of factors that cause or influence costs.** IKEA is a Swedish furniture retailer that changed the industry with its low-cost leadership. They offer inexpensive but stylish furniture and keep prices low by controlling their costs. They offer a basic level of service and do not assemble or deliver furniture. They also produce their products in low-wage countries.[18]

---

[16] Based on Chee W. Chow, "Instructional Case: Vincent's Cappuccino Express—A Teaching Case to Help Students Master Basic Cost Terms and Concepts Through Interactive Learning," *Issues in Accounting Education,* Spring 1995, pp. 173–190.

[17] Dean Millson, "Uber vs Lyft – Brand positioning, customer expectation and internal culture," Brand & Strategy, February 18, 2016. http://brandingandstrategyblog.com/brand-strategy/uber-vs-lyft-brands-effect-customer-expectation-internal-culture/

[18] http://smallbusiness.chron.com

3. **Value chain analysis is the study of value-producing activities, stretching from basic raw materials to the final consumer of a product or service.** Starbucks is a well-known example of value chain analysis. They focus on selecting the highest quality beans, operate in 65 countries, and have few if any intermediaries involved in the selling of their products; they have a high level of customer service with a related commitment to human resources management.[19]

Mid-Chapter Review 3

SOLUTION

When an organization's goal is cost leadership, managerial accountants can partner with management to develop budgets and to prepare frequent and detailed performance reports against those budgets. This allows managers and employees to analyze areas in which the company's activities cost more than expected and to work together to find ways to further reduce those costs. When an organization's goal is differentiation, managerial accountants can partner with customers, marketing, and sales to help identify ways to increase the perceived value of the products or services. This might be done through an analysis of costs from a customer's point of view, enabling the organization to better understand what features the customer is willing to pay for.

Mid-Chapter Review 4

SOLUTION

Big Data and Analysis—Given recent advancements in technology, there is a vast amount of data available to organizations. However, it can be difficult to turn this data into useful and predictive information. Organizations are in need of employees who have the abilities to: identify key data trends, perform data mining and extraction, conduct operational and decision analysis, recommend process improvement, and conduct strategic thinking and execution.

ERM—Organizations are constantly faced with uncertainty from the environment, competitors, and other factors that could result in significant risk or loss. By better understanding the types and potential costs of these risks, management accountants can help their organizations devise strategies to better predict and minimize exposure to risk.

Mid-Chapter Review 5

SOLUTION

Managerial accounting includes a variety of models that help managers determine the cost of a particular activity or product or the benefits and costs of various decision alternatives. Although such models in their current state of development may not take into account all external social costs, accountants are more aware today than in the past of the need to consider such costs. Being a socially responsible company does not mean abandoning the profit motive or the goal of providing an attractive return to investors. It means that while pursuing these essential objectives, a for-profit company attempts to measure the total benefits and costs of its actions and accepts the responsibility for those actions.

Chapter-End Review

SOLUTION

a. Activity cost driver
b. Structural cost driver
c. Structural cost driver
d. Activity cost driver
e. Activity cost driver
f. Structural cost driver
g. Organizational cost driver
h. Organizational cost driver
i. Organizational cost driver
j. Organizational cost driver

---

[19] Prableen Bajpai, "Starbucks As An Example of the Value Chain Model," *Investopedia*, October 31, 2014.

14

Cost Behavior, Activity Analysis, and Cost Estimation

SQUARE, INC.
www.squareup.com

The creator of **Twitter**, Jack Dorsey, founded **Square, Inc.** in 2009 to address a void in payment processing services for small, portable businesses. Square makes a postage stamp-sized plastic card reader that attaches to smartphones, which gives businesses such as food trucks, kiosk boutiques, taxi drivers, and the like the ability to accept credit card payments. Square also has an online payment app, and in 2016, Square introduced Virtual Terminal, which enables sellers to accept payments from their computers through the Square Dashboard.

The San Francisco–based company has been so successful that it now processes over $40 billion in transactions each year. Square provides the card readers, the Dashboard App, and the Virtual Terminal to businesses free of charge but collects a per transaction fee to compensate for its services.

In recent years, Square has expanded beyond payment processing to offer a broad range of services, including marketing, analytics, and payroll. With Square's hand in so many business lines coupled with the company's phenomenal growth, it's difficult for outsiders and insiders, including Square's management team, to predict future costs. This is an important task because the company's growth plans require either internally generated profit or external financing to continue on its trajectory.

The cost of making the card readers is directly related to the number of new businesses adopting the technology. In other words, the hardware cost is driven by the number of new merchants in any given period. But the number of new adoptions is difficult to estimate in advance. The costs associated with processing payments are even more difficult to predict. Consider that the company remits most of the payments received from customers' credit card companies to the merchant, minus Square's fee. However, what is Square's cost of processing each payment? Does the cost of processing a payment differ based on volume or seasonality?

In order to predict processing costs, we must be able to predict merchant sales volume or number of transactions. If the processing costs vary proportionately with this activity, the processing costs are referred to as variable costs. And what about the costs that do not vary with the number or type of transactions processed? Many of Square's employees are salaried engineers and software developers. These costs are likely to be unrelated to the number of card readers issued or payments processed. We call costs that do not vary with activity fixed costs. As we'll see throughout the chapter, many costs are neither variable nor fixed, but a mixture of the two. Mixed costs present a challenge to a company in estimating future costs.

Square needs the ability to accurately predict its future costs if it is to maintain the financial flexibility necessary to go up against its competitors. This requires a thorough understanding of cost behavior, activity analysis, and cost estimation, which are the topics of this chapter.

Source: www.SquareUp.com; Michal Lev-Ram, "Jack Dorsey: The Pride of St. Louis," *Fortune*, September 19, 2013; Greg Bensinger, "Square Takes on PayPal Online," *Wall Street Journal*, June 26, 2013, p. B5; Tomio Geron, "Square Launches Stand, A New Point of Sale Device," *Forbes*, May 14, 2013; Danielle Kucera, "Square Introduces Hardware to Convert iPads into Cash Registers," *Bloomberg Businessweek*, May 14, 2013; Danielle Kucera, "Square Debuts Mobile Gift Cards in Challenge to PayPal," *Bloomberg Businessweek*, December 10, 2012; and Amir Efrati and Annie Gasparro, "Starbucks Invests in Square," *Wall Street Journal*, August 8, 2012, p. B8.

CHAPTER ORGANIZATION

Cost Behavior, Activity Analysis, and Cost Estimation			
Cost Behavior Analysis	**Cost Estimation**	**Additional Issues in Cost Estimation**	**Alternative Cost Driver Classifications**
• Four Basic Cost Behavior Patterns • Factors Affecting Cost Behavior Patterns • Total Cost Function for an Organization or Segment • Relevant Range • Additional Cost Behavior Patterns • Committed and Discretionary Fixed Costs	• High-Low Cost Estimation • Scatter Diagrams • Least-Squares Regression	• Changes in Technology and Prices • Matching Activity and Costs • Identifying Activity Cost Drivers	• Manufacturing Cost Hierarchy • Customer Cost Hierarchy

eLectures
MBC

LO1 Identify basic patterns of how costs respond to changes in activity cost drivers.

1

COST BEHAVIOR ANALYSIS

This chapter introduces **cost behavior**, which refers to the relationship between a given cost item and the quantity of its related cost driver. Cost behavior, therefore, explains how the total amount for various costs responds to changes in activity volume. Understanding cost behavior is essential for estimating future costs. In this chapter we examine several typical cost behavior patterns and methods for developing cost equations that are useful for predicting future costs.

Four Basic Cost Behavior Patterns

Although there are an unlimited number of ways that costs can respond to changes in cost drivers, as a starting point it is useful to classify cost behavior into four categories: **variable costs**, **fixed costs**, **mixed costs**, and **step costs**. Graphs of each are presented in **Exhibit 14.1**. Observe that total cost (the dependent variable) is measured on the vertical axis, and total activity (the independent variable) is measured on the horizontal axis. Consider pizza franchise **Papa Murphy's Pizza**. Papa Murphy's specializes in "take and bake," meaning they are made to order and cooked in the customer's oven at home. Customers can pick from signature pies like Chicken Artichoke and Spicy Fennel Sausage, or they can create their own and choose the type of dough, sauce, and toppings. Papa Murphy's scores top marks for customer satisfaction and expects to see significant growth over the next few years. To manage its growth, the company must understand the behavior underlying its cost structure.

1. **Variable costs** change in total in direct proportion to changes in activity. Their total amount increases as activity increases, equaling zero dollars when activity is zero and increasing at a constant amount per unit of activity. The higher the variable cost per unit of activity, the steeper the slope of the line representing total cost. With the number of pizzas served as the activity cost driver for Papa Murphy's restaurants, the cost of cheese is an example of a variable cost.

2. **Fixed costs** do not change in response to a change in activity volume. Hence, a line representing total fixed costs is flat with a slope (incline) of zero. With the number of Papa Murphy's pizzas sold as the activity cost driver, annual depreciation, property taxes, and property insurance are examples of fixed costs. While fixed costs may respond to structural and organizational cost drivers over time, they do not respond to short-run changes in activity cost drivers.

3. **Mixed costs** (sometimes called **semivariable costs**) contain a fixed and a variable cost element. Total mixed costs are positive (like fixed costs) when activity is zero, and they increase in a linear fashion (like total variable costs) as activity increases. With the number of pizzas sold as the cost driver, the cost of electric power is an example of a mixed cost. Some electricity is required to provide basic lighting (fixed cost), while an increasing amount of electricity is required to prepare food as the number of pizzas served increases (variable cost).

EXHIBIT 14.1   **Cost Behavior Patterns**

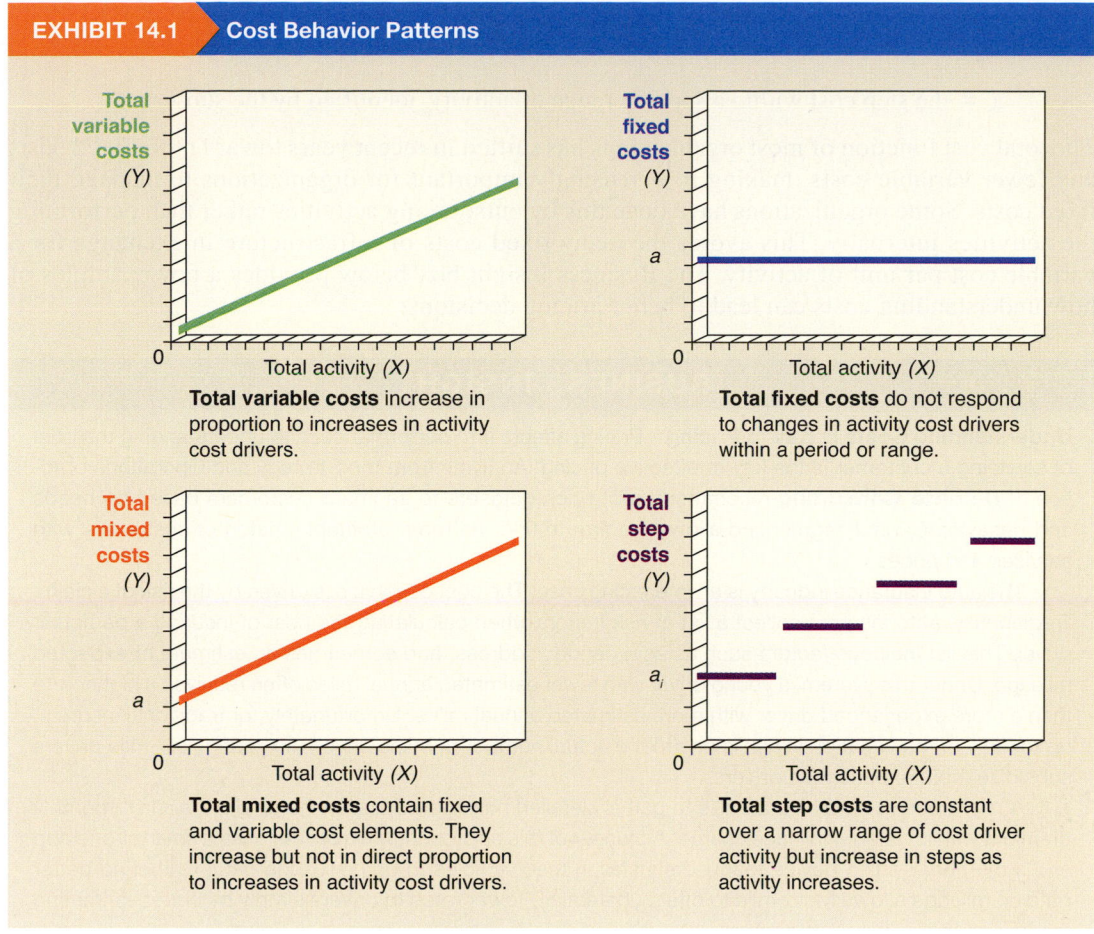

Total variable costs increase in proportion to increases in activity cost drivers.

Total fixed costs do not respond to changes in activity cost drivers within a period or range.

Total mixed costs contain fixed and variable cost elements. They increase but not in direct proportion to increases in activity cost drivers.

Total step costs are constant over a narrow range of cost driver activity but increase in steps as activity increases.

4. **Step costs** are constant within a narrow range of activity but shift to a higher level when activity exceeds the range. Total step costs increase in a steplike fashion as activity increases. With the number of pizzas served as the cost driver, employee wages is an example of a step cost. Up to a certain number of pizzas, only a small staff needs to be on duty. Beyond that number, additional employees are needed for quality service and so forth.

The relationship between total cost (Y axis) and total activity (X axis) for the four cost behavior patterns is mathematically expressed as follows:

$$\text{Variable cost: } Y = bX$$

where
   b = the variable cost per unit, sometimes referred to as the slope of the cost function.

$$\text{Fixed cost: } Y = a$$

where
   a = total fixed costs. The slope of the fixed cost function is zero because fixed costs do not change with activity.

$$\text{Mixed cost: } Y = a + bX$$

where
   a = total fixed cost element
   b = variable cost element per unit of activity.

$$\text{Step cost: } Y = a_i$$

where

a_i = the step cost within a specific range of activity, identified by the subscript i.

The total cost function of most organizations has shifted in recent years toward more fixed costs and fewer variable costs, making it increasingly important for organizations to manage their fixed costs. Some organizations have done this by outsourcing activities rather than performing the activities internally. This avoids the many fixed costs of infrastructure in exchange for a variable cost per unit of activity. The Business Insight box below provides a few examples of how understanding costs can lead to better pricing decisions.

BUSINESS INSIGHT

Understanding Costs Is Key to Pricing   Pricing affects firm performance, and understanding the cost of servicing a customer is the key to effective pricing. Analysts from the Strategy and Operations practice of **Deloitte Consulting** recommend using rich datasets to segment customers based on needs and behavior. Careful segmenting allows the firm to find the most profitable match of customers with services and prices.

The auto insurance industry is an interesting case. The cost of service is driven by the risk of a claim. Traditionally, auto insurers collect a list of risk factors when calculating the cost of insuring a particular driver. This list includes factors such as age, gender, address, and sometimes an estimate of expected mileage. Under this system, a young driver with fewer estimated annual miles often receives a higher rate than a more experienced driver with more estimated annual miles. Unfortunately for traditional insurers, up to 70% of the variation in risk is due to the actual number of miles driven; so young, low-mile drivers subsidize more experienced drivers.

A new trend in auto insurance is to gather detailed mileage data and charge drivers a low monthly premium with a variable mileage charge. A pioneer of this approach, **Metromile**, uses a smartphone app and a thumbnail-sized device that users install in their vehicles to gather usage data. Gathering better data on mileage allows Metromile to offer substantially lower rates to drivers simply by better estimating the cost of insuring each customer.

Sources: Quentin Hardy, "Technology Transforms How Insurers Calculate Risk," *The New York Times*, April 6, 2016. John Hagel, John Brown, Maggie Wooll, and Andrew de Maar, "Align Price With Use," *Deloitte University Press*, February 12, 2016. Julie Meehan, Chuck Davenport, and Shruti R. Kahlon, "The Price of Pricing Effectiveness: Is the View Worth the Climb?" *Deloitte University Press*, July 1, 2012.

Factors Affecting Cost Behavior Patterns

The four cost behavior patterns presented are based on the fundamental assumption that a unit of final output is the primary cost driver. The implications of this assumption are examined later in this chapter.

Another important assumption is that the time period is too short to incorporate changes in strategic cost drivers such as the scale of operations. Although this assumption is useful for short-range planning, for the purpose of developing plans for extended time periods, it is more appropriate to consider possible variations in one or more strategic cost drivers. When this is done, many costs otherwise classified as fixed are better classified as variable.

Even the cost of depreciable assets can be viewed as variable if the time period is long enough. Assuming that the number of pizzas served is the cost driver, for a single month the depreciation on all Papa Murphy's restaurants in the world is a fixed cost. Over several years, if sales are strong, a strategic decision will be made to open additional restaurants; if sales are weak, strategic decisions will likely be made to close some restaurants. Hence, over a multiple-year period, the number of restaurants varies with sales volume, making depreciation appear as a variable cost with sales revenue as the cost driver.

Fixed costs are easily identified. They are the same at each activity level. Variable and mixed costs can be determined by dividing total costs by monthly sales at two activity levels. The quotients of variable costs will be the same at both levels. The quotients of mixed costs will be lower at the higher activity level. This is because the fixed costs are spread over a larger number of units.

MID-CHAPTER REVIEW 1

Assume a local **Subway** reported the following results for April and May:

	April	May
Sandwiches sold	2,100	2,700
Cost of food sold	$1,575	$2,025
Wages and salaries	1,525	1,675
Rent on building	1,500	1,500
Depreciation on equipment	200	200
Utilities	710	770
Supplies	225	255
Miscellaneous	113	131
Total	$5,848	$6,556

REQUIRED

Identify each cost as being fixed, variable, or mixed.

The solution to this review problem can be found on page 682.

Total Cost Function for an Organization or Segment

LO2 Determine a linear total cost estimating equation.

To obtain a general understanding of an organization, to compare the cost structures of different organizations, or to perform preliminary planning activities, managers are often interested in how total costs respond to a single measure of overall activity such as units sold or sales revenue. This overview can be useful, but presenting all costs as a function of a single cost driver is seldom accurate enough to support decisions concerning products, services, or activities. Doing so implies that all of an organization's costs can be manipulated by changing a single cost driver. This is seldom true.

In developing a total cost function, the independent variable usually represents some measure of the goods or services provided customers, such as total student credit hours in a university, total sales revenue in a store, total guest-days in a hotel, or total units manufactured in a factory. The resulting cost function is illustrated in **Exhibit 14.2**.

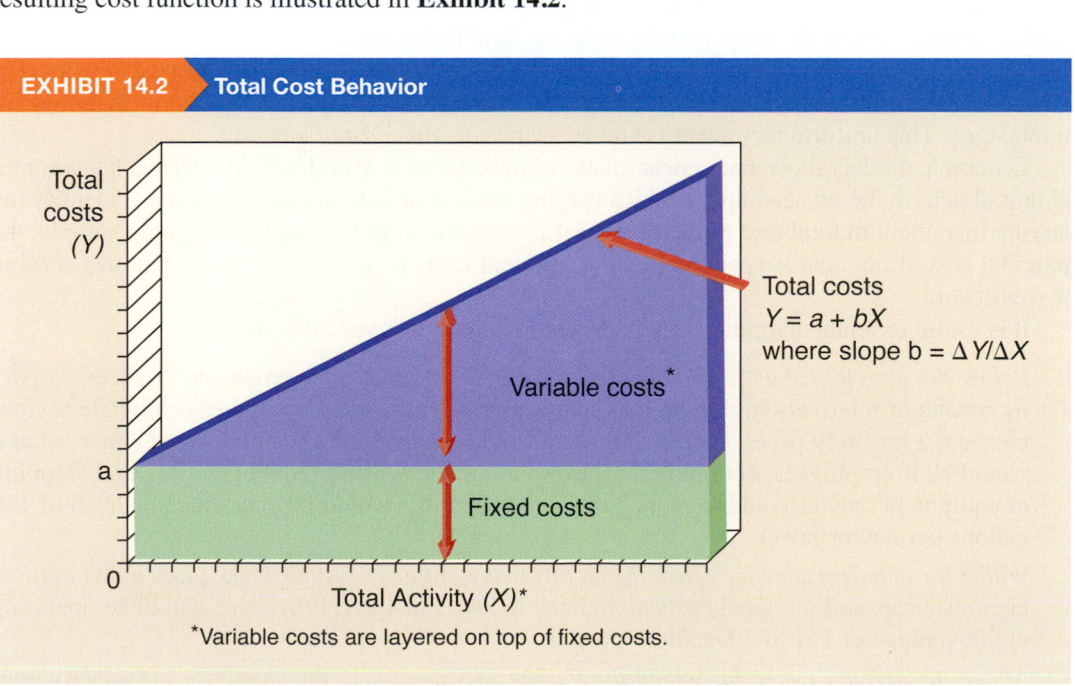

EXHIBIT 14.2   Total Cost Behavior

The equation for total costs is:

$$Y = a + bX$$

where

> Y = total costs
> a = vertical axis intercept (an approximation of fixed costs)
> b = slope (an approximation of variable costs per unit of X)
> X = value of independent variable

In situations where the variable, fixed, and mixed costs, and the related cost functions, can be determined, a total cost equation can be useful in predicting future costs for various activity levels. For example, assume that **Coco Froyo** frozen yogurt shop's only fixed cost is the depreciation on its frozen yogurt making machines. Coco Froyo's monthly depreciation is $1,200. Also assume that the variable cost per frozen yogurt served is $3.25. Therefore, the total cost equation for Coco Froyo is:

$$Y = \$1,200 + \$3.25 \text{ (number of yogurts served)}$$

If the shop expects to serve 1,600 frozen yogurts in July, they can then estimate their total July costs to be:

$$\$6,400 = \$1,200 + \$3.25\ (1,600)$$

Relevant Range

Generally, a total cost equation is useful for predicting costs in only a limited range of activity. The **relevant range** of a total cost equation is that portion of the range associated with the fixed cost of the current or expected capacity. In our Coco Froyo example, they are able to produce a maximum of 50 gallons of frozen yogurt per day with a single machine. If it has four machines in operation, and if it can readily adjust its fixed capacity cost by increasing or decreasing the number of machines, the relevant range of activity for the shop's current total cost equation is 151 to 200 gallons. In the future, if the shop expects to operate at more than 200 gallons per day, the current total cost equation would not predict total cost accurately, because fixed costs would have to be increased for additional machines. Conversely, if it expects to operate at 150 gallons or fewer, it may reduce the number of machines in the shop, thereby reducing total fixed costs.

The use of straight lines in accounting models of cost behavior assumes a linear relationship between cost and activity with each additional unit of activity accompanied by a uniform increment in total cost. This uniform increment is known as the *variable cost of one unit.*

Economic models show a nonlinear relationship between cost and activity with each incremental unit of activity being accompanied by a varying increment in total cost. Economists identify the varying increment in total cost as the **marginal cost** *of one unit.* For our Coco Froyo example, the marginal cost of one unit is specifically the additional costs incurred with each additional serving of yogurt sold.

It is useful to relate marginal costs to the following three levels of activity:

1. *Below the activity range for which the facility was designed,* the existence of excess capacity results in relatively high marginal costs. Having extra time, employees complete assignments at a leisurely pace, increasing the time and the cost to produce each unit above what it would be if employees were more pressed to complete work. Frequent starting and stopping of equipment may also add to costs. For Coco Froyo this would be operating at a level of 150 gallons per day or fewer.

2. *Within the activity range for which the facility was designed,* activities take place under optimal circumstances and marginal costs are relatively low. For Coco Froyo this would be operating within a range of 151 to 200 gallons per day.

3. *Above the activity range for which the facility was designed,* the existence of capacity constraints again results in relatively high marginal costs. Near capacity, employees may be paid

overtime wages, less-experienced employees may be used, regular equipment may operate less efficiently, and old equipment with high energy requirements may be placed in service. For Coco Froyo this would be operating at a level of more than 200 gallons per day.

Based on marginal cost concepts, the economists' short-run total cost function is illustrated in the first graph in **Exhibit 14.3**. To clarify the concept, we use the capacity information for Coco Froyo. The vertical axis intercept represents capacity costs. In this simple example, our only capacity, or fixed cost, is depreciation. Corresponding to the high marginal costs at low levels of activity, the initial slope is quite steep. In the normal activity range, where marginal costs are relatively low, the slope becomes less steep. Then, corresponding to high marginal costs above the normal activity range, the slope of the economists' total cost function increases again.

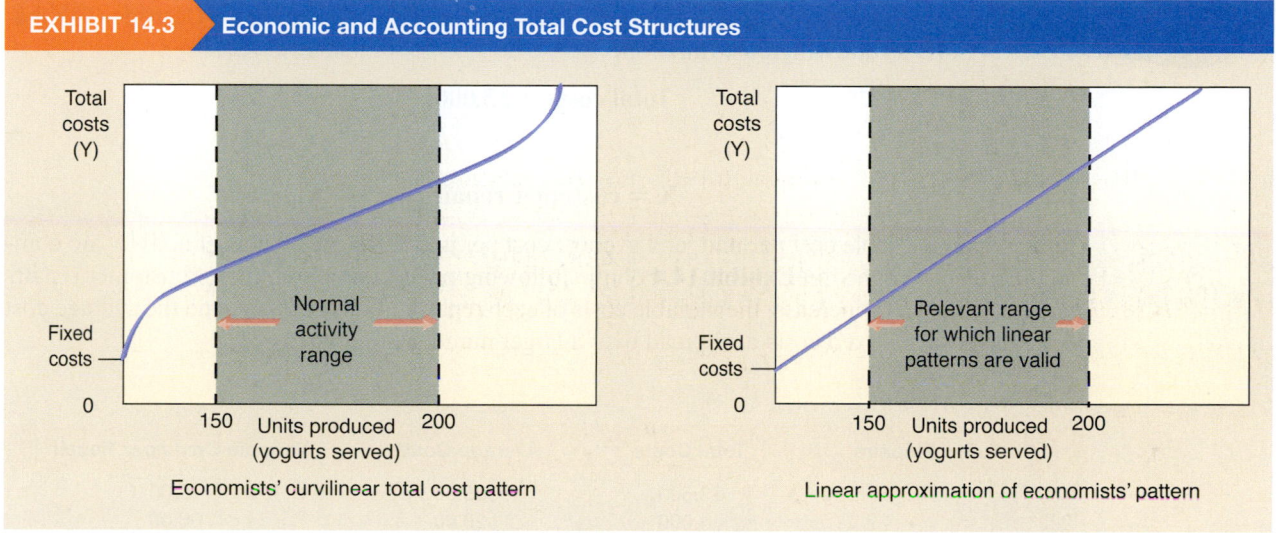

| EXHIBIT 14.3 | Economic and Accounting Total Cost Structures |

Economists' curvilinear total cost pattern

Linear approximation of economists' pattern

If the economists' total cost curve is valid, how can we reasonably approximate it with a straight line? The answer to this question is in the notion of a *relevant range*. A linear pattern may be a poor approximation of the economists' curvilinear pattern over the entire range of possible activity, but a linear pattern as illustrated in the right-hand graph in **Exhibit 14.3** is often sufficiently accurate within the range of probable operations. The range of activity within which a linear cost function is valid is called the *relevant range*. Linear estimates of cost behavior are valid only within the relevant range. Extreme care must be exercised when making comments about cost behavior outside the relevant range.

Additional Cost Behavior Patterns

Although we have considered the most frequently used cost behavior patterns, remember that there are numerous ways that costs can respond to changes in activity. Avoid the temptation to automatically assume that the cost in question conforms to one of the patterns discussed in this chapter. As illustrated by the preceding Business Insight box, it is important to think through each situation and then select a behavior pattern that seems logical and fits the known facts.

Particular care needs to be taken with the vertical axis. So far, all graphs have placed *total* costs on the vertical axis. Miscommunication is likely if one party is thinking in terms of *total* costs while the other is thinking in terms of *variable* or *average* costs. **FIXthat4U** is a smartphone and tablet repair store. FIXthat4U's monthly fixed costs include rent and depreciation on tools and furniture. Its variable costs include direct labor and any materials used up in the repair such as new screens. Consider FIXthat4U's following cost function:

$$\text{Total costs} = \$3,000 + \$5X$$

where

$$X = \text{customer repairs}$$

The total, variable cost per unit, and average cost per unit at various levels of activity are computed here and graphed in **Exhibit 14.4** on the following page. As the number of customer repairs increases, total costs increase, the variable costs of each repair remain constant, and the average cost decreases because fixed costs are spread over a larger number of repairs.

Customer Repairs	Total Costs	Average Cost*	Variable Costs per Repair
100	$3,500	$35.00	$5.00
200	4,000	20.00	5.00
300	4,500	15.00	5.00
400	5,000	12.50	5.00
500	5,500	11.00	5.00

* Total costs/customer repairs

To predict total costs for the coming period, FIXthat4U's management will use the first graph in **Exhibit 14.4**. To determine the minimum price required to avoid a loss on each additional repair, management is interested in the variable costs per customer repair, yet if a manager inquired as to the cost of each customer repair, a financial accountant would probably provide average cost information, as illustrated in the third graph in **Exhibit 14.4**. The specific average cost would likely be a function of the number of customer repairs during the most recent accounting period.

Errors can occur if last period's average costs, perhaps based on a volume of 500 repairs, were used to predict total costs for a future period when the anticipated volume was some other amount, say 300 repairs. Using average costs, based on the 500 repairs, the predicted total costs of 300 repairs are $3,300 ($11 × 300). In fact, using the proper total cost function, a more accurate prediction of total costs is $4,500 [$3,000 + ($5 × 300)]. The prediction error could cause a number of problems. If management budgeted $3,300 to pay bills and the bills actually totaled $4,500, the company might have to curtail activities or borrow under unfavorable terms to avoid running out of cash.

EXHIBIT 14.4	Total Costs, Variable Costs, and Average Costs

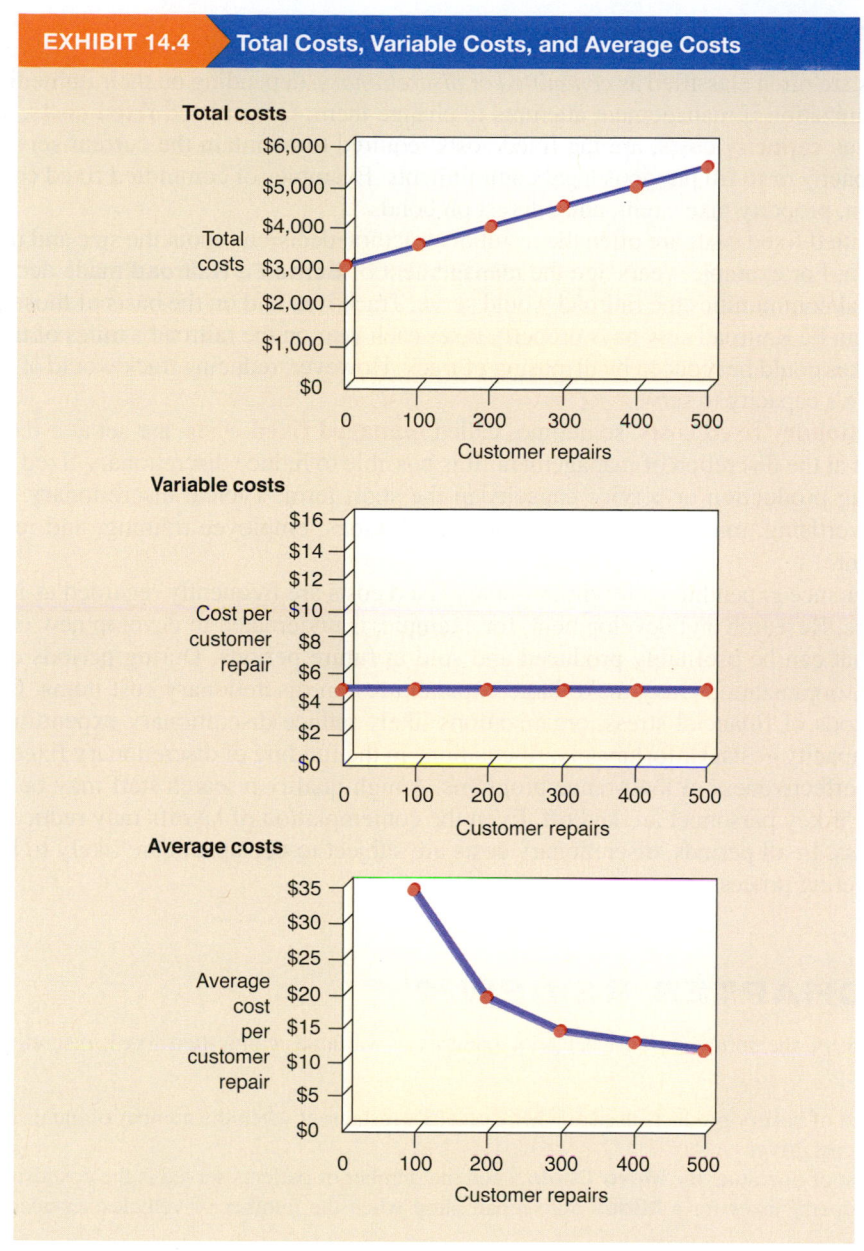

RESEARCH INSIGHT

Managers Use Procurement to Control Risk   In a recent study of cost data from California Hospitals, researchers analyzed the way that firms adjust committed costs in response to external risk. The study shows that managers seek to mitigate the effects of both demand uncertainty and financial risk through procurement decisions. The study considers three procurement choices that affect committed costs:

1. Deliver new services through outsourcing or onsite.
2. Rent or purchase new equipment.
3. Structure labor costs to be more flexible versus fixed.

The researchers found that hospitals facing greater uncertainty limited committed costs, for example, limiting capital expenditures on equipment. This study highlights that managers can make cost-structure decisions that protect their organizations from the risk of demand uncertainty.

Source: Martin Holzhacker, Ranjani Krishnan, and Matthias D. Mahlendorf, "Unraveling the Black Box of Cost Behavior: An Empirical Investigation of Risk Drivers, Managerial Resource Procurement, and Cost Elasticity," *The Accounting Review* 90, no. 6 (2015): 2305-2335.

Committed and Discretionary Fixed Costs

Fixed costs are often classified as *committed* or *discretionary,* depending on their immediate impact on the organization if management attempts to change them. **Committed fixed costs**, sometimes referred to as **capacity costs**, are the fixed costs required to maintain the current service or production capacity or to fill previous legal commitments. Examples of committed fixed costs include depreciation, property taxes, rent, and interest on bonds.

Committed fixed costs are often the result of structural decisions about the size and nature of an organization. For example, years ago the management of **Santa Fe Railroad** made decisions concerning what communities the railroad would serve. Track was laid on the basis of those decisions, and the Santa Fe Railroad now pays property taxes each year on the railroad's miles of track. These property taxes could be reduced by disposing of track. However, reducing track would also diminish the Santa Fe's capacity to serve.

Discretionary fixed costs, sometimes called **managed fixed costs**, are set at a fixed amount each period at the discretion of management. It is possible to reduce discretionary fixed costs without reducing production or service capacity in the short term. Typical discretionary fixed costs include advertising, maintenance, charitable contributions, employee training, and research and development.

Maintenance expenditures for discretionary fixed costs are frequently regarded as investments in the future. Research and development, for example, is undertaken to develop new or improved products that can be profitably produced and sold in future periods. During periods of financial well-being, organizations may make large expenditures on discretionary cost items. Conversely, during periods of financial stress, organizations likely reduce discretionary expenditures before reducing capacity costs. Unfortunately, fluctuations in the funding of discretionary fixed costs may reduce the effectiveness of long-range programs. A high-quality research staff may be difficult to reassemble if key personnel are laid off. Even the contemplation of layoffs may reduce the staff's effectiveness. In all periods, discretionary costs are subject to debate and are likely to be changed in the budgeting process.

MID-CHAPTER REVIEW 2

Identify each of the following cost behavior patterns as variable, committed fixed, discretionary fixed, mixed, or step.

a. Total cost of bakery products used at a **McDonald's** restaurant when the number of meals served is the activity cost driver.

b. Total cost of operating the **Mayo Clinic** when the number of patients served is the cost driver.

c. Total property taxes for a **Midas** auto repair shop when the number of vehicles serviced is the cost driver.

d. Total cost of motherboards used by **Apple** when the number of computers manufactured and shipped is the cost driver.

e. Total cost of secretarial services at **Indiana University** with each secretary handling the needs of ten faculty members and where part-time secretarial help is not available. The number of faculty is the cost driver.

f. Total advertising costs for **International Business Machines** (IBM).

g. Automobile rental costs incurred by **Alamo** in Orlando, Florida, when there is no mileage charge. The cost driver is the number of miles driven.

h. Automobile rental cost incurred by **Hertz** in Dallas, Texas, which has a base charge plus a mileage charge. The cost driver is the number of miles driven.

i. Salaries paid to personnel while conducting on-campus employment interviews for **Champion International**. Number of on-campus interviews is the cost driver.

j. The cost of contributions to educational institutions by **Microsoft Corporation**.

The solution to this review problem can be found on page 682.

COST ESTIMATION

Cost estimation, the determination of the relationship between activity and cost, is an important part of cost management. In this section, we develop equations for the relationship between total costs and total activity.

LO3 Calculate and compare three different approaches to cost estimation.

To properly estimate the relationship between activity and cost, we must be familiar with basic cost behavior patterns and cost estimating techniques. Costs known to have a variable or a fixed pattern are readily estimated by interviews or by analyzing available records. Sales commission per sales dollar, a variable cost, might be determined to be 15 percent of sales. In a similar manner, annual property taxes might be determined by consulting tax documents.

Mixed (semivariable) costs, which contain fixed and variable cost elements, are more difficult to estimate. According to a basic rule of algebra, two equations are needed to determine two unknowns. Following this rule, at least two observations are needed to determine the variable and fixed elements of a mixed cost.

High-Low Cost Estimation

The most straightforward approach to determining the variable and fixed elements of mixed costs is to use the **high-low method of cost estimation**. This method utilizes data from two time periods, a *representative* high-activity period and a *representative* low-activity period, to estimate fixed and variable costs. Assuming identical fixed costs in both periods, any difference in total costs between these two periods is due entirely to variable costs. The variable costs per unit are found by dividing the difference in total costs by the difference in total activity:

$$\text{Variable costs per unit} = \frac{\text{Difference in total costs}}{\text{Difference in activity}}$$

Once variable costs are determined, fixed costs, which are identical in both periods, are computed by subtracting the total variable costs of either the high or the low activity period from the corresponding total costs.

$$\text{Fixed costs} = \text{Total costs} - \text{Variable costs}$$

Assume a retailer such as **Pottery Barn** wants to develop a monthly cost function for its packaging department and that the number of shipments is believed to be the primary cost driver. The following observations are available for the first four months of 2017.

		Number of Shipments	Packaging Costs
(Low-activity period)	January	6,000	$17,000
	February	9,000	26,000
(High-activity period)	March	12,000	32,000
	April	10,000	20,000

Equations for total costs for the packaging department in January and March (the periods of lowest and highest activity) follow:

January: $17,000 = a + b (6,000 shipments)
March: $32,000 = a + b (12,000 shipments)

where

a = fixed costs per month
b = variable costs per shipment

Solving for the estimated variable costs per shipment:

$$b = \frac{\text{Difference in total costs}}{\text{Difference in activity}}$$

$$b = \frac{\$32,000 - \$17,000}{12,000 - 6,000}$$

$$= \$2.50$$

Next, the estimated monthly fixed costs are determined by subtracting variable costs from total costs of *either* the January or March equation:

$$a = \text{Total costs} - \text{Variable costs}$$

January: $a = \$17,000 - (\$2.50 \text{ per shipment} \times 6,000 \text{ shipments})$

$$= \$2,000$$

or

March: $a = \$32,000 - (\$2.50 \text{ per shipment} \times 12,000 \text{ shipments})$

$$= \$2,000$$

The cost estimating equation for total packaging department costs is

$$Y = \$2,000 + \$2.50X$$

where

$$X = \text{number of shipments}$$

$$Y = \text{total costs for the packaging department}$$

The concepts underlying the high-low method of cost estimation are illustrated in **Exhibit 14.5**.

Cost prediction, the forecasting of future costs, is a common purpose of cost estimation. Previously developed estimates of cost behavior are often the starting point in predicting future costs. Continuing the Pottery Barn example, if 5,000 shipments are budgeted for June 2017, the predicted June 2017 packaging department costs are $14,500 [$2,000 + ($2.50 per shipment × 5,000 shipments)].

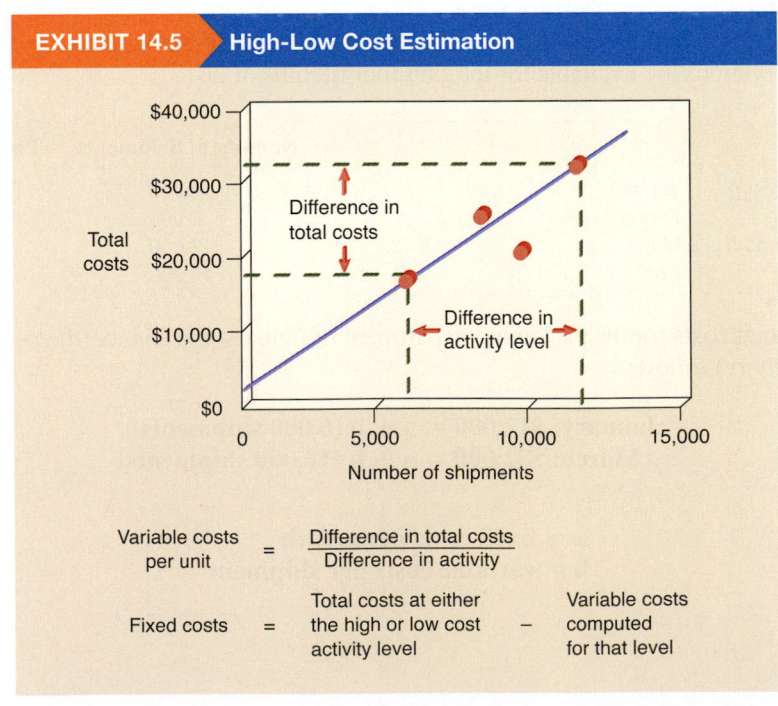

EXHIBIT 14.5   High-Low Cost Estimation

Scatter Diagrams

A **scatter diagram** is a graph of past activity and cost data, with individual observations represented by dots. Plotting historical cost data on a scatter diagram is a useful approach to cost estimation, especially when used in conjunction with other cost-estimating techniques. As illustrated in **Exhibit 14.6**, a scatter diagram helps in selecting high and low activity levels representative of normal operating conditions. The periods of highest or lowest activity may not be representative because of the cost of overtime, the use of less efficient equipment, strikes, and so forth. If the goal is to develop an equation to predict costs under normal operating conditions, then the equation should be based on observations of normal operating conditions. A scatter diagram is also useful in determining whether costs can be reasonably approximated by a straight line.

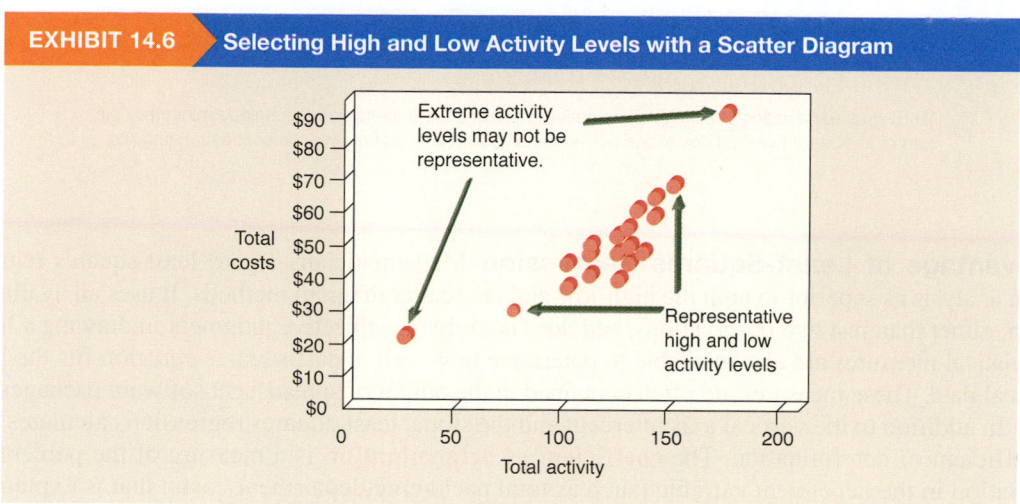

EXHIBIT 14.6   Selecting High and Low Activity Levels with a Scatter Diagram

Scatter diagrams are sometimes used alone as a basis of cost estimation. This requires the use of professional judgment to draw a representative straight line through the plot of historical data. Typically, the analyst tries to ensure that an equal number of observations are on either side of the line while minimizing the total vertical differences between the line and actual cost observations at each value of the independent variable. Once a line is drawn, cost estimates at any representative volume are made by studying the line. Alternatively, an equation for the line may be developed by applying the high-low method to any two points on the line.

Least-Squares Regression

Least-squares regression analysis uses a mathematical technique to fit a cost-estimating equation to the observed data. The technique mathematically accomplishes what the analyst does visually with a scatter diagram. The least-squares technique creates an equation that minimizes the sum of the vertical squared differences between the estimated and the actual costs at each observation. Each of these differences is an estimating error. Using the packaging department example, the least-squares criterion is illustrated in **Exhibit 14.7**. Estimated values of total monthly packaging costs are represented by the straight line, and the actual values of total monthly packaging costs are represented by the dots. For each dot, such as the one at a volume of 10,000 shipments, the line is fit to minimize the vertical squared differences.

Values of a and b can be manually calculated using a set of equations developed by mathematicians or by using spreadsheet software packages such as **Microsoft** Excel®. Many calculators also have built-in functions to compute these coefficients. The least-squares equation for monthly packaging costs is:

$$Y = \$3{,}400 + \$2.20X$$

Using the least-squares equation, the predicted June 2017 packaging department costs with 5,000 budgeted shipments are $14,400 [$3,400 + ($2.20 per shipment × 5,000 shipments)]. Recall that the high-low method predicted June 2017 costs of $14,500. Although this difference is small, we should consider which prediction is more reliable.

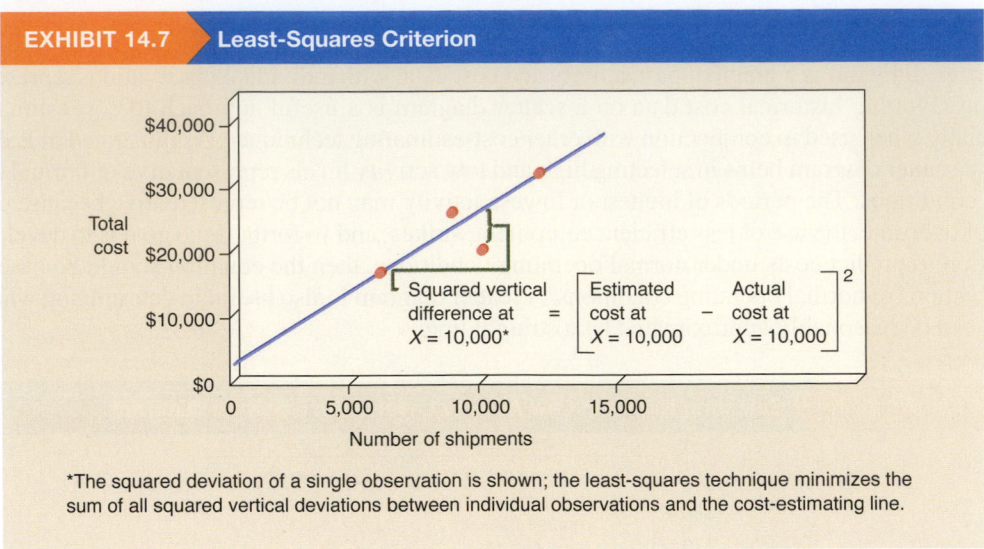

| EXHIBIT 14.7 | Least-Squares Criterion |

*The squared deviation of a single observation is shown; the least-squares technique minimizes the sum of all squared vertical deviations between individual observations and the cost-estimating line.

Advantage of Least-Squares Regression Mathematicians regard least-squares regression analysis as superior to both the high-low and the scatter diagram methods. It uses all available data, rather than just two observations, and does not rely on subjective judgment in drawing a line. Statistical measures are also available to determine how well a least-squares equation fits the historical data. These measures are often contained in the output of spreadsheet software packages.

In addition to the vertical axis intercept and the slope, least-squares regression calculates the coefficient of determination. The **coefficient of determination** is a measure of the percent of variation in the dependent variable (such as total packaging department costs) that is explained by variations in the independent variable (such as total shipments). Statisticians often refer to the coefficient of determination as R-squared and represent it as R^2.

The coefficient of determination can have values between zero and one, with values close to zero suggesting that the equation is not very useful and values close to one indicating that the equation explains most of the variation in the dependent variable. When choosing between two cost-estimating equations, the one with the higher coefficient of determination is generally preferred. The coefficient of determination for the packaging department cost estimation equation, determined using least-squares regression analysis, is 0.68. This means that 68 percent of the variation in packaging department costs is explained by the number of shipments.

Managers, Not Models, Are Responsible Although computers make least-squares regression easy to use, the generated output should not automatically be accepted as correct. Statistics and other mathematical techniques are tools to help managers make decisions. Managers, not mathematical models, are responsible for decisions. Judgment should always be exercised when considering the validity of the least-squares approach, the solution, and the data. If the objective is to predict future costs under normal operating conditions, observations reflecting abnormal operating conditions should be deleted. Also examine the cost behavior pattern to determine whether it is linear. Scatter diagrams assist in both of these judgments. Finally, the results should make sense. When the relationships between total cost and several activity drivers are examined, it is possible to have a high R-squared purely by chance. Even though the relationship has a high R-squared, if it "doesn't make sense" there is probably something wrong.

Simple and Multiple Regression Least-squares regression analysis is identified as "simple regression analysis" when there is only one independent variable and as "multiple regression analysis" when there are two or more independent variables. The general form for simple regression analysis is:

$$Y = a + bX$$

The general form for multiple regression analysis is:

$$Y = a + \Sigma b_i X_i$$

In this case, the subscript i is a general representation of each independent variable. When there are several independent variables, i is set equal to 1 for the first, 2 for the second, and so forth. The total variable costs of each independent variable is computed as $b_i X_i$, with b_i representing the variable cost per unit of independent variable X_i. The Greek symbol sigma, Σ, indicates that the costs of all independent variables are summed in determining total variable costs.

As an illustration, assume that **Staples**' costs are expressed as a function of the unit sales of its two products: executive desks and task desks. Assume fixed costs are $18,000 per month and the variable costs are $250 per executive desk and $120 per task desk. The mathematical representation of monthly costs with two variables is:

$$Y = a + b_1 X_1 + b_2 X_2$$

where

$$a = \$18,000$$
$$b_1 = \$250 \text{ per executive desk}$$
$$b_2 = \$120 \text{ per task desk}$$
$$X_1 = \text{unit sales of executive desks}$$
$$X_2 = \text{unit sales of task desks}$$

During a month if 105 executive desks and 200 task desks are sold, Staples' estimated total costs are:

$$Y = \$18,000 + \$250(105) + \$120(200)$$
$$= \$68,250$$

In addition to estimating costs, multiple regression analysis can be used to determine the effect of individual product features on the market value of a product or service. The following Research Insight reports on insurance companies that use lifestyle and health behaviors to predict future health issues using a model similar to multiple regression analysis. These predictions are used to motivate changes in behavior that will ultimately improve employee health and reduce costs.

RESEARCH INSIGHT

Employers and Insurers Partner to Reduce Health Care Costs   Improving employee health reduces sick leave and insurance premiums. Insurance companies are partnering with large employers such as **J.P. Morgan Chase** and **WalMart** to use data to reduce health care costs and to help employees improve their health. Some of these opportunities are as simple as using an app to provide information about in-network providers for employees. **Cigna** and **J.P. Morgan Chase** have shifted 2% of claims into network by making a smartphone app with provider information available to employees.

Other solutions use lifestyle and health data to identify at-risk employees and implement lifestyle changes and treatments that reduce the need for expensive procedures and sick leave. **Castlight Healthcare Inc.** uses health data, which the employer is not permitted to see directly, to identify employees who are prediabetic or suffering from back pain. These two conditions have high health care costs, so Castlight sends personalized messages and recommendations for lifestyle changes. Research suggests that 30% of patients considering spinal surgery who get a second opinion elect not to have the surgery. Because spinal surgery is an invasive and costly procedure with a long recovery, Castlight sends personalized recommendations for second opinions to employees who have met with specialists. Another firm, **HealthMine Inc.**, analyzes health records to identify prediabetic employees and provide targeted recommendations for diet and exercise changes.

While issues of privacy around health data are complex, employers and insurers are finding ways to use data to improve employee health and reduce costs.

Source: Rachel Silverman, "Bosses Tap Outside Firms to Predict Which Workers Might Get Sick," *The Wall Street Journal*, February 17, 2016.

MID-CHAPTER REVIEW 3

Assume a local **Subway** reported the following results for April and May:

	April	May
Sandwiches sold	2,100	2,700
Cost of food sold	$1,575	$2,025
Wages and salaries	1,525	1,675
Rent on building	1,500	1,500
Depreciation on equipment	200	200
Utilities	710	770
Supplies	225	255
Miscellaneous	113	131
Total	$5,848	$6,556

REQUIRED

a. Using the high-low method, create an equation for each of the following costs in April: cost of food, wages and salaries, rent on building, and total monthly costs.
b. Predict total costs for monthly volumes of 1,000 and 2,000 sandwiches.
c. Predict the average cost per unit at monthly volumes of 1,000 and 2,000 sandwiches. Explain why the average costs differ at these two volumes.

The solution to this review problem can be found on pages 682–683.

LO4 Identify and discuss problems encountered in cost estimation.

4

ADDITIONAL ISSUES IN COST ESTIMATION

We have mentioned several items to be wary of when developing cost estimating equations:

- Data that are not based on normal operating conditions.
- Nonlinear relationships between total costs and activity.
- Obtaining a high R-squared purely by chance.

Additional items of concern include:

- Changes in technology or prices.
- Matching activity and cost within each observation.
- Identifying activity cost drivers.

Changes in Technology and Prices

Changes in technology and prices make cost estimation and prediction difficult. When telecommunications companies changed from using landlines to voice over internet protocol (VOIP) to place long-distance telephone calls, cost estimates based on the use of fiber optic cables were of little or no value in predicting future costs. Care must be taken to make sure that data used in developing cost estimates are based on the existing technology. When this is not possible, professional judgment is required to make appropriate adjustments.

Only data reflecting a single price level should be used in cost estimation and prediction. If prices have remained stable in the past but then uniformly increase by 20 percent, cost-estimating equations based on data from previous periods will not accurately predict future costs. In this case, all that is required is a 20 percent increase in the prediction. Unfortunately, adjustments for price changes are seldom this simple. The prices of various cost elements are likely to change at different rates and at different times. Furthermore, there are probably several different price levels included in the past data used to develop cost-estimating equations. If data from different price levels are used, an attempt should be made to restate them to a single price level.

Matching Activity and Costs

The development of accurate cost-estimating equations requires the matching of the activity to related costs within each observation. This accuracy is often difficult to achieve because of the time lag between an activity and the recording of the cost of resources consumed by the activity. Current activities usually consume electricity, but the electric bill won't be received and recorded until next month. Driving an automobile requires routine maintenance for items such as lubrication and oil, but the auto can be driven several weeks or even months before the maintenance is required. Consequently, daily, weekly, and perhaps even monthly observations of miles driven and maintenance costs are unlikely to match the costs of oil and lubrication with the cost-driving activity, miles driven.

In general, the shorter the time period, the higher the probability of error in matching costs and activity. The cost analyst must carefully review the database to verify that activity and cost are matched within each observation. If matching problems are found, it may be possible to adjust the data (perhaps by moving the cost of electricity from one observation to another). Under other circumstances, it may be necessary to use longer periods to match costs and activity.

Identifying Activity Cost Drivers

Identifying the appropriate activity cost driver for a particular cost requires judgment and professional experience. In general, the cost driver should have a logical, causal relationship with costs. In many cases, the identity of the most appropriate activity cost driver, such as miles driven for the cost of automobile gasoline, is apparent. In other situations, where different activity cost drivers might be used, scatter diagrams and statistical measures, such as the coefficient of determination, are helpful in selecting the activity cost driver that best explains past variations in cost. When scatter diagrams are used, the analyst can study the dispersion of observations around the cost-estimating line. In general, a small dispersion is preferred. If regression analysis is used, the analyst considers the coefficient of determination. In general, a higher coefficient of determination is preferred. The relationship between the activity cost driver and the cost must seem logical, and the activity data must be available.

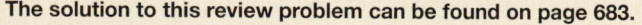

MID-CHAPTER REVIEW 4

Identify some common activity drivers that might be used to state a volume of activity in a manufacturing operation. What general criterion might be used in choosing a driver?

The solution to this review problem can be found on page 683.

ALTERNATIVE COST DRIVER CLASSIFICATIONS

So far we have examined cost behavior and cost estimation using only a unit-level approach, which assumes changes in costs are best explained by changes in the number of units of product or service provided customers. This approach may have worked for **Carnegie Steel Company**, but it is inappropriate for multidimensional organizations, such as **Square**. The unit-level approach becomes increasingly inaccurate for analyzing cost behavior when organizations experience the following types of changes:

LO5 Describe and develop alternative classifications for activity cost drivers.

5

- From face-to-face customer interactions to web-based interface,
- From stand-alone products to products with multiple layers of customer interface, such as Square's hardware versus the processing of payments executed by Square for its customers, and

● From internet-based operations to mobile platforms, thus engaging a more geographically diverse set of customers.

Exhibit 14.8 illustrates the composition of total manufacturing costs for the past century, illustrating changes in the percentage of manufacturing costs for three major cost categories.

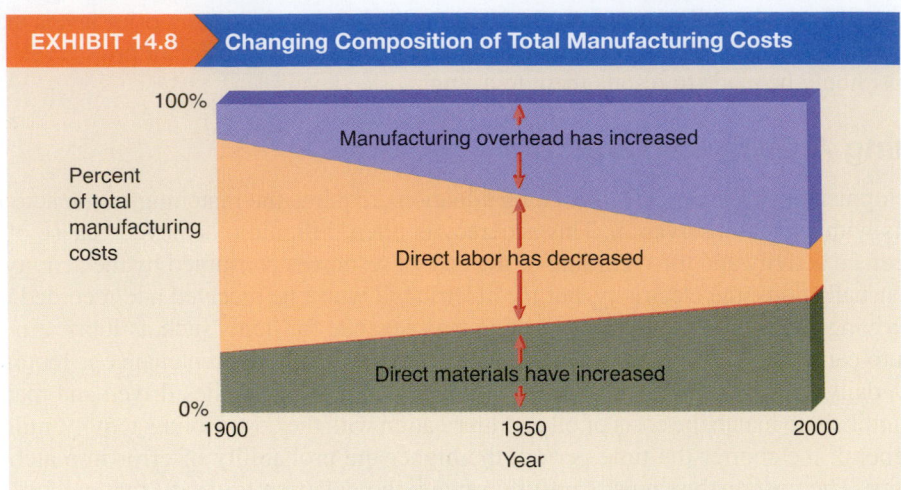

1. **Direct materials**, the cost of primary raw materials converted into finished goods, have increased slightly as organizations purchase components they formerly fabricated. The word "direct" is used to indicate costs that are easily or directly traced to a finished product or service.

2. **Direct labor**, the wages earned by production employees for the time they spend converting raw materials into finished products, has decreased significantly as employees spend less time physically working on products and more time supporting automated production activities.

3. **Manufacturing overhead**, which includes all manufacturing costs other than direct materials and direct labor, has increased significantly due to automation, product diversity, and product complexity.

Changes in the composition of manufacturing costs have implications for the behavior of total costs and the responsiveness of costs to changes in cost drivers. Because direct materials and direct labor vary directly with the number of units, they are easy to measure. In the past, when manufacturing overhead was relatively small, it was possible to assume units of product or service was the primary cost driver. This is no longer true. Units of final product is no longer an adequate explanation of changes in manufacturing overhead for many organizations.

The past tendency to ignore overhead, while focusing on direct materials and direct labor, led one researcher to describe overhead-causing activities as "the hidden factory."[1] To better understand the hidden factory, several researchers have developed frameworks for categorizing cost-driving activities. The crucial feature of these frameworks is the inclusion of nonunit cost drivers. Depending on the characteristics of a particular organization, as well as management's information needs, there are an almost unlimited number of cost driver classification schemes. We consider two frequently applied cost driver classification schemes: one based on a manufacturing cost hierarchy and a second based on a customer cost hierarchy. We also illustrate variations of each.

Manufacturing Cost Hierarchy

The most well-known framework, developed by Cooper[2] and Cooper and Kaplan[3] for manufacturing situations, classifies activities into the following four categories.

---

[1] Jeffrey G. Miller and Thomas E. Vollmann, "The Hidden Factory," *Harvard Business Review,* September-October 1985, pp. 142–150.

[2] Robin Cooper, "Cost Classification in Unit-Based and Activity-Based Manufacturing Cost Systems," *The Journal of Cost Management,* Fall 1990, pp. 4–14.

[3] Robin Cooper and Robert S. Kaplan, "Profit Priorities from Activity-Based Costing," *Harvard Business Review,* May-June 1991, pp. 130–135.

1. A **unit-level activity** is performed *for each unit* of product produced. **Christofle** is a French manufacturer of high-end silver flatware. In the production of forks, the stamping of each fork into the prescribed shape is an example of a unit-level cost driver.

2. A **batch-level activity** is performed *for each batch* of product produced. At Christofle, a batch is a number of identical units (such as a fork of a specific design) produced at the same time. Batch-level activities include setting up the machines to stamp each fork in an identical manner, moving the entire batch between workstations (i.e., molding, stamping, and finishing), and inspecting the first unit in the batch to verify that the machines are set up correctly.

3. A **product-level activity** is performed *to support* the production of *each different type of product*. At Christofle, product-level activities for a specific pattern of fork include initially designing the fork, producing and maintaining the mold for the fork, and determining manufacturing operations for the fork.

4. A **facility-level activity** is performed *to maintain* general manufacturing capabilities. At Christofle, facility-level activities include plant management, building maintenance, property taxes, and electricity required to sustain the building.

Several additional examples of the costs driven by activities at each level are presented in **Exhibit 14.9**.

EXHIBIT 14.9	Hierarchy of Activity Costs	
Activity Level	**Reason for Activity**	**Examples of Activity Cost**
1. Unit level	Performed for each unit of product produced or sold	• Cost of raw materials • Cost of inserting a component • Utilities cost of operating equipment • Some costs of packaging • Sales commissions
2. Batch level	Performed for each batch of product produced or sold	• Cost of processing sales order • Cost of issuing and tracking work order • Cost of equipment setup • Cost of moving batch between workstations • Cost of inspection (assuming same number of units inspected in each batch)
3. Product level	Performed to support each different product that can be produced	• Cost of product development • Cost of product marketing such as advertising • Cost of specialized equipment • Cost of maintaining specialized equipment
4. Facility level	Performed to maintain general manufacturing capabilities	• Cost of maintaining general facilities such as buildings and grounds • Cost of nonspecialized equipment • Cost of maintaining nonspecialized equipment • Cost of real property taxes • Cost of general advertising • Cost of general administration such as the plant manager's salary

When using a cost hierarchy for analyzing and estimating costs, total costs are broken down into the different cost levels in the hierarchy, and a separate cost driver is determined for each level of cost. For example, using the above hierarchy, the costs that are related to the number of units produced (such as direct materials or direct labor) may have direct labor hours or machines hours as the cost driver; whereas, batch costs may be driven by the number of setups of production machines or the number of times materials are moved from one machine to another. Other costs may be driven by the number of different products produced. Facility-level costs are generally regarded as fixed costs and do not vary unless capacity is increased or decreased.

Customer Cost Hierarchy

The manufacturing hierarchy presented is but one of many possible ways of classifying activities and their costs. Classification schemes should be designed to fit the organization and meet user needs. A merchandising organization or the sales division of a manufacturing organization might use the following hierarchy.

1. **Unit-level activity**: performed for each unit sold.
2. **Order-level activity**: performed for each sales order.
3. **Customer-level activity**: performed to obtain or maintain each customer.
4. **Facility-level activity**: performed to maintain the general manufacturing function.

This classification scheme assists in answering questions concerning the cost of individual orders or individual customers.

If an organization sells to distinct market segments (for profit, not for profit, and government), the cost hierarchy can be modified as follows:

1. Unit-level activity
2. Order-level activity
3. Customer-level activity
4. **Market-segment-level activity**: performed to obtain or maintain operations in a segment.
5. Facility-level activity

The market-segment-level activities and their related costs differ with each market segment. This classification scheme assists in answering questions concerning the profitability of each segment.

Finally, an organization that completes unique projects for different market segments (such as buildings for **IBM** and the **U.S. Department of Defense**) can use the following hierarchy to determine the profitability of each segment:

1. **Project-level activity:** performed to support the completion of each project.
2. Market-segment-level activity
3. Facility-level activity

The possibilities are endless. The important point is that both the cost hierarchy and the costs included in the hierarchy be tailored to meet the specific circumstances of an organization and the interests of management.

CHAPTER-END REVIEW

Customer Cost Hierarchy Consider the pizza chain **Blaze Pizza**. They custom build and cook each pizza to order. Items 1–6 represent cost activities a particular store might incur.

1. Pepperoni on the pizza
2. Wood to fuel the fire used to cook the pizzas
3. Insurance on the building
4. The labor hours worked by the employee building and cooking each pizza
5. The sales calls made to local organizations to promote the pizzas for catering special events
6. The number of pizza orders received

REQUIRED

Classify each cost activity above, in the most appropriate level of the proposed customer cost hierarchy. Each cost activity may be used more than once.

_____ *a.* Unit-level—performed for each unit sold
_____ *b.* Order-level—performed for each sales level
_____ *c.* Customer-level—performed to obtain or maintain each customer
_____ *d.* Store(facility)-level—performed to maintain the general store functions

The solution to this review problem can be found on page 683.

GUIDANCE ANSWERS . . . YOU MAKE THE CALL

You are the Purchasing Manager   One of the quickest methods for gaining a general understanding of the relationship between a given cost and its cost driver is to graph the relationship using data from several recent periods. As purchasing manager you could probably quickly obtain information about the amount of the total purchasing department costs and number of purchase orders processed for each of the most recent eight or ten periods. By graphing these data with costs on the vertical axis and number of purchase orders on the horizontal axis, you should be able to visually determine if there is an obvious behavioral pattern (variable, fixed, or mixed). Since costs have been declining as volume has increased, this would suggest that there are some fixed costs, and that they have been declining on a per unit basis as they are spread over an increasing number of purchase orders. Using two representative data points in the scatter diagram, you can plot a cost curve on the graph, and then use the data for those two points to calculate the estimated fixed and variable costs using the high-low cost estimation method. Using these cost estimates, you can predict the total cost for next period. This method may not give you a precise estimate of the cost, but coupled with your subjective estimate of cost based on your experience as manager of the department, it should give you more confidence than merely making a best guess. Hopefully, you will have an opportunity before presenting your budget for the next period to conduct additional analyses using more advanced methods.

KEY RATIOS

Variable costs: $Y = bX$

Where b = the variable cost per unit, sometimes referred to as the slope of the cost function.

Fixed costs: $Y = a$

Where a = total fixed costs. The slope of the fixed cost function is zero because fixed costs do not change with activity.

Mixed costs: $Y = a + bX$

Where a = total fixed cost element and b = variable cost element per unit of activity.

Step cost: $Y = a_i$

Where a_i = the step cost within a specific range of activity, identified by the subscript i.

Total costs: $Y = a + bX$

Where Y = total costs, a = vertical axis intercept (an approximation of fixed costs), b = slope (an approximation of variable costs per unit of X) and X = value of independent variable.

$$\text{Variable costs per unit} = \frac{\text{Difference in total costs}}{\text{Difference in activity}}$$

Fixed costs = Total costs − Variable costs

General form for simple regression analysis: $Y = a + bX$

Where a = total fixed cost element and b = the variable cost per unit of independent variable X.

General form for multiple regression analysis is: $Y = a + \sum b_i X_i$

Where the subscript i is a general representation of each independent variable. When there are several independent variables, i is set equal to 1 for the first, 2 for the second, and so forth. The total variable costs of each independent variable is computed as $b_i X_i$, with b_i representing the variable cost per unit of independent variable X_i. The Greek symbol sigma, $\sum$, indicates that the costs of all independent variables are summed in determining total variable costs.

KEY TERMS

batch-level activity, 667

capacity costs, 658

coefficient of determination, 662

committed fixed costs, 658

cost behavior, 650

cost estimation, 659

cost prediction, 660

customer-level activity, 668

direct labor, 666

direct materials, 666

discretionary fixed costs, 658

facility-level activity, 667, 668

fixed costs, 650

high-low method of cost
    estimation, 659

least-squares regression analysis,
    661

managed fixed costs, 658

manufacturing overhead, 666

marginal cost, 654

market-segment-level activity,
    668

mixed costs, 650

order-level activity, 668

product-level activity, 667

project-level activity, 668

relevant range, 654

scatter diagram, 661

semivariable costs, 650

step costs, 650

unit-level activity, 667, 668

variable costs, 650

Assignments with the (MBC) logo in the margin are available in *my*BusinessCourse.
See the Preface of the book for details.

MULTIPLE CHOICE

1. A graph of the total cost of ingredients used in **Papa Murphy's** pizzas most closely resembles this total cost behavior pattern:
   a. Variable cost
   b. Fixed cost
   c. Mixed cost
   d. Step cost

2. Increasing the length of the time period included in each observation of activity and cost will assist in overcoming this possible problem in cost estimation:
   a. Data not based on normal operations
   b. Nonlinear relationship between total costs and activity
   c. Changes in technology or prices
   d. Failure to match activity and costs within each observation

3. At a sales volume of 50 units the average cost is $410 per unit and the variable cost is $10 per unit. Assuming a linear cost behavior pattern, if sales double to 100 units the average cost will be:
   a. $10
   b. $200
   c. $205
   d. $210

4. Employees of Chelsea, a financial consulting firm, often travel to client sites for project meetings. The firm's business manager is attempting to better understand the costs associated with the employees' company cars. Below is data for the first four months of the year related to miles incurred and costs associated with the cars, including leases, insurance, maintenance, and gas. Use the high-low method to calculate the fixed costs associated with the company cars.

	Mileage	Costs
Jan.	450	$29,300
Feb.	325	$22,550
Mar.	418	$27,572
Apr.	380	$25,520

   a. $0.54
   b. $3,215
   c. $5,000
   d. $4,500

5. Which of the following situations would cause concern when an analyst is developing a cost-estimating equation?

   a. A relatively linear relationship exists between total costs and activity.
   b. The data is based on normal operating conditions.
   c. The industry incurs significant changes in technology.
   d. The cost driver has a logical, causal relationship with costs.

6. Arch manufactures a product with the following manufacturing cost hierarchy for its only current product:

	Cost
Unit.	$20/unit
Batch	$500/batch
Product.	$10,000/year
Facility	$50,000/year

   Next year Arch plans to manufacture 50,000 units of product in batches of 500 units. Arch's predicted manufacturing costs for next year are:

   a. $1,560,000
   b. $1,500,000
   c. $1,110,000
   d. $660,000

7. West sells specialized products produced by electronics companies to 100 engineering firms. West sells these products at a price based on West's purchase price. West's customer cost hierarchy is as follows:

	Cost
Unit.	80 percent of selling price
Batch	$200 per sales order
Customer	$1,000 per customer per year
Facility	$120,000 per year

   Next year West plans to sell $4,000,000 of product to the 100 engineering firms they serve. They anticipate that each firm will place an average of 4 orders. West's predicted customer costs for next year are:

   a. $80,000
   b. $300,000
   c. $3,200,000
   d. $3,500,000

QUESTIONS

Q14-1. Briefly describe variable, fixed, mixed, and step costs and indicate how the total cost function of each changes as activity increases within a time period.

Q14-2. Why is presenting all costs of an organization as a function of a single independent variable, although useful in obtaining a general understanding of cost behavior, often not accurate enough to make specific decisions concerning products, services, or activities?

Q14-3. Explain the term "relevant range" and why it is important in estimating total costs.

Q14-4. How are variable and fixed costs determined using the high-low method of cost estimation?

Q14-5. Distinguish between cost estimation and cost prediction.

Q14-6. Why is a scatter diagram helpful when used in conjunction with other methods of cost estimation?

Q14-7. Identify two advantages of least-squares regression analysis as a cost estimation technique.

Q14-8. Why is it important to match activity and costs within a single observation? When is this matching problem most likely to exist?

Q14-9. During the past century, how have direct materials, direct labor, and manufacturing overhead changed as a portion of total manufacturing costs? What is the implication of the change in manufacturing overhead for cost estimation?

Q14-10. Distinguish between the unit-, batch-, product-, and facility-level activities of a manufacturing organization.

MINI EXERCISES

LO1

M14-11. Classifying Cost Behavior
Classify the total costs of each of the following as variable, fixed, mixed, or step. Sales volume is the cost driver.

  a. Salary of the department manager
  b. Memory chips in a computer assembly plant
  c. Real estate taxes
  d. Salaries of quality inspectors when each inspector can evaluate a maximum of 1,000 units per day
  e. Wages paid to production employees for the time spent working on products
  f. Electric power in a factory
  g. Raw materials used in production
  h. Automobiles rented on the basis of a fixed charge per day plus an additional charge per mile driven
  i. Sales commissions
  j. Depreciation on office equipment

LO1

M14-12. Classifying Cost Behavior
Classify the total costs of each of the following as variable, fixed, mixed, or step.

  a. Straight-line depreciation on a building
  b. Maintenance costs at a hospital
  c. Rent on a photocopy machine charged as a fixed amount per month plus an additional charge per copy
  d. Cost of goods sold in a bookstore
  e. Salaries paid to temporary instructors in a college as the number of course sessions varies
  f. Lumber used by a house construction company
  g. The costs of operating a research department
  h. The cost of hiring a dance band for three hours
  i. Laser printer paper for a department printer
  j. Electric power in a restaurant

LO1, 2, 3

M14-13. Classifying Cost Behavior
For each of the following situations, select the most appropriate cost behavior pattern (as shown in the illustrations following this problem) where the lines represent the cost behavior pattern, the vertical axis represents costs, the horizontal axis represents total volume, and the dots represent actual costs. Each pattern may be used more than once.

  a. Variable costs per unit
  b. Total fixed costs
  c. Total mixed costs
  d. Average fixed costs per unit
  e. Total current manufacturing costs
  f. Average variable costs
  g. Total costs when employees are paid $15 per hour for the first 40 hours worked each week and $20 for each additional hour
  h. Total costs when employees are paid $15 per hour and guaranteed a minimum weekly wage of $300
  i. Total costs per day when a consultant is paid $200 per hour with a maximum daily fee of $1,000

j.   Total variable costs

k.   Total costs for salaries of social workers where each social worker can handle a maximum of 25 cases

l.   A water bill where a flat fee of $800 is charged for the first 100,000 gallons and additional water costs $0.005 per gallon

m.   Total variable costs properly used to estimate step costs

n.   Total materials costs

o.   Rent on exhibit space at a convention

GRAPHS FOR MINI EXERCISE 14-13

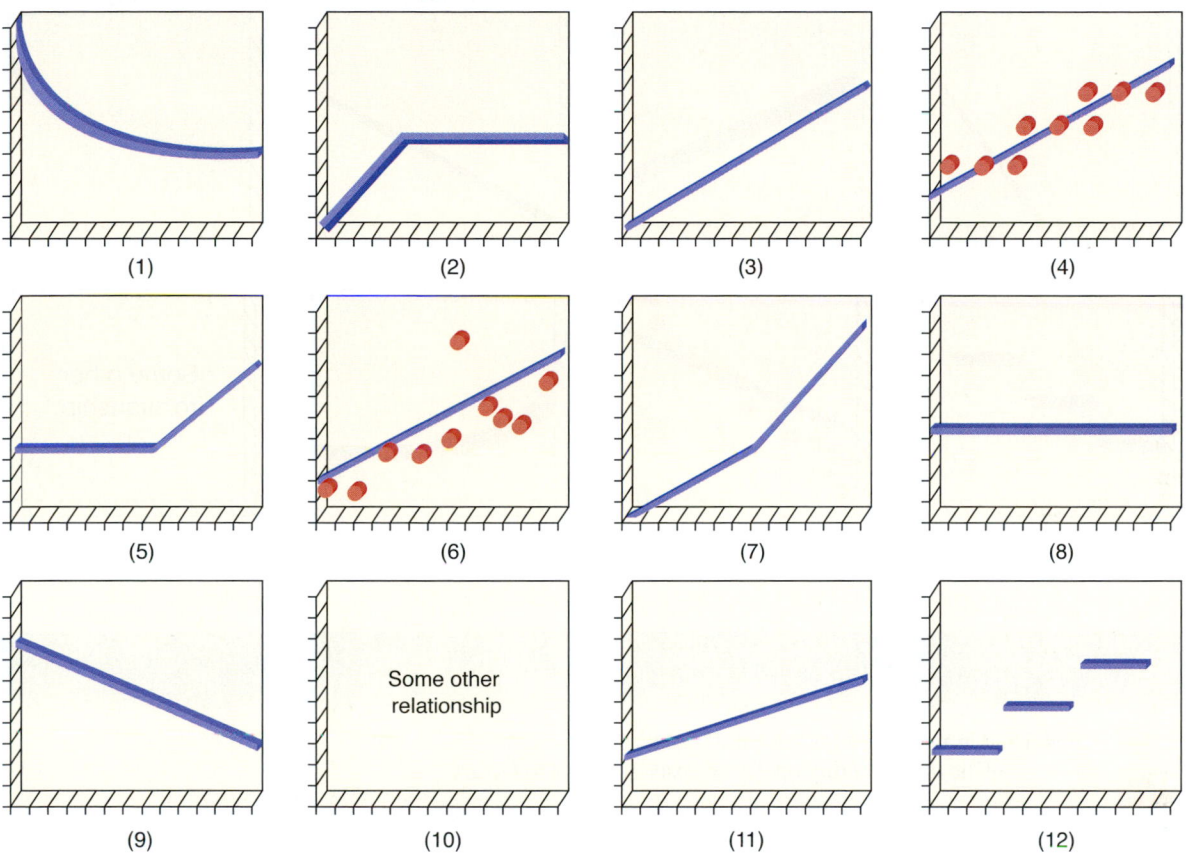

M14-14. Classifying Cost Behavior

LO1, 2, 3

For each of the graphs displayed following this problem, select the most appropriate cost behavior pattern where the lines represent the cost behavior pattern, the vertical axis represents total costs, the horizontal axis represents total volume, and the dots represent actual costs. Each pattern may be used more than once.

a.   A cellular telephone bill when a flat fee is charged for the first 500 minutes of use per month and additional use costs $0.25 per minute

b.   Total selling and administrative costs

c.   Total labor costs when employees are paid per unit produced

d.   Total overtime premium paid production employees

e.   Average total cost per unit

f.   Salaries of supervisors when each one can supervise a maximum of 10 employees

g.   Total idle time costs when employees are paid for a minimum 40-hour week

h.   Materials costs per unit

i.   Total sales commissions

j.   Electric power consumption in a restaurant

k.   Total costs when high volumes of production require the use of overtime and obsolete equipment

l.   A good linear approximation of actual costs

m.   A linear cost estimation valid only within the relevant range

GRAPHS FOR MINI EXERCISE 14-14

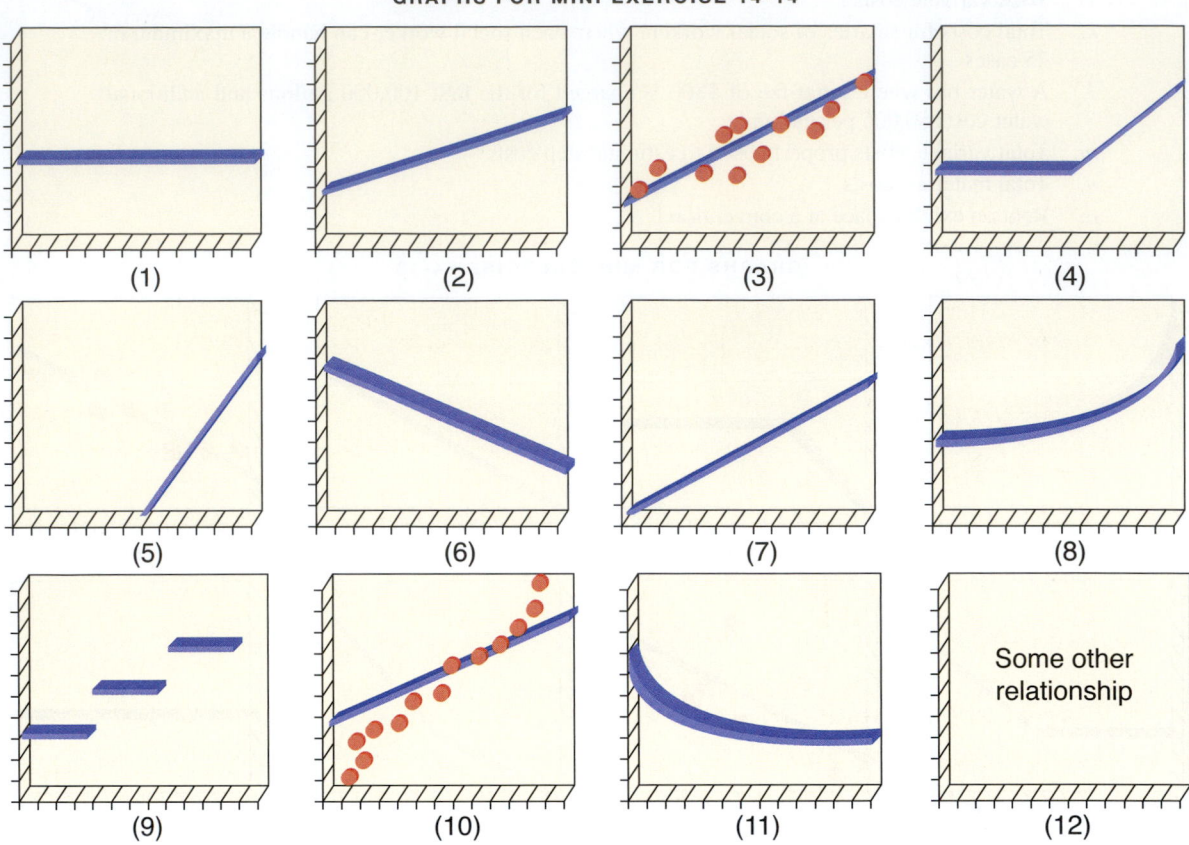

(1)   (2)   (3)   (4)

(5)   (6)   (7)   (8)

(9)   (10)   (11)   (12)

Some other relationship

EXERCISES

LO2   **E14-15. Computing Average Unit Costs**

MBC

The total monthly operating costs of Salads to Go are:

$$\$10,000 + \$0.30X$$

where

$$X = \text{Number of salads}$$

REQUIRED

a.   Determine the average cost per salad at each of the following monthly volumes: 100; 1,000; 5,000; and 10,000.

b.   Determine the monthly volume at which the average cost per serving is $0.70.

LO2   **E14-16. Automatic versus Manual Processing**

MBC

Image Solutions operates a printing service for customers with digital cameras. The current service, which requires employees to download photos from customer cameras, has monthly operating costs of $7,000 plus $0.3 per photo printed. Management is evaluating the desirability of acquiring a machine that will allow customers to download and make prints without employee assistance. If the machine is acquired, the monthly fixed costs will increase to $13,000 and the variable costs of printing a photo will decline to $0.05 per photo.

REQUIRED

a.   Determine the total costs of printing 20,000 and 50,000 photos per month:

    1.   With the current employee-assisted process.

    2.   With the proposed customer self-service process.

b.   Determine the monthly volume at which the proposed process becomes preferable to the current process.

E14-17. **Automatic versus Manual Processing**

LO2

Red Star Copy Service processes 2,100,000 photocopies per month at its service center. Approximately 50 percent of the photocopies require collating. Collating is currently performed by high school and college students who are paid $9 per hour. Each student collates an average of 5,000 copies per hour. Management is contemplating the lease of an automatic collating machine that has a monthly capacity of 6,000,000 photocopies, with lease and operating costs totaling $1,550, plus $0.05 per 1,000 units collated.

REQUIRED

a.   Determine the total costs of collating 500,000 and 1,700,000 per month:
   1. With student help.
   2. With the collating machine.
b.   Determine the monthly volume at which the automatic process becomes preferable to the manual process.

E14-18. **High-Low Cost Estimation**

LO3

YRC Worldwide
NASDAQ :: YRCW

Assume the local **YRC Worldwide** delivery service hub has the following information available about fleet miles and operating costs:

Year	Miles	Operating Costs
2017	556,000	$175,600
2018	684,000	214,000

REQUIRED

Use the high-low method to develop a cost-estimating equation for total annual operating costs.

E14-19. **Scatter Diagrams and High-Low Cost Estimation**

LO2, 3

Pearle Vision
NYSE :: LUX

Assume the local **Pearle Vision** has the following information on the number of sales orders received and order-processing costs.

Month	Sales Orders	Order-Processing Costs
1	3,000	$ 82,700
2	1,500	50,375
3	4,400	120,700
4	2,800	81,900
5	2,300	69,775
6	1,200	43,100
7	2,000	62,500

REQUIRED

a.   Use information from the high- and low-volume months to develop a cost-estimating equation for monthly order-processing costs.
b.   Plot the data on a scatter diagram. Using the information from representative high- and low-volume months, develop a cost-estimating equation for monthly production costs.
c.   What factors might have caused the difference in the equations developed for requirements (*a*) and (*b*)?

E14-20. **Scatter Diagrams and High-Low Cost Estimation**

LO2, 3

Coles County

From April 1 through October 31, **Coles County Highway Department** hires temporary employees to mow and clean the right-of-way along county roads. The County Road Commissioner has asked you to help her in determining the variable labor cost of mowing and cleaning a mile of road. The following information is available regarding current-year operations:

Month	Miles Mowed and Cleaned	Labor Costs
April	350	$ 9,600
May.	300	8,800
June	400	10,400
July.	250	8,000
August	375	10,000
September	200	7,200
October	100	6,200

REQUIRED

a. Use the information from the high- and low-volume months to develop a cost-estimating equation for monthly labor costs.

b. Plot the data on a scatter diagram. Using the information from representative high- and low-volume months, use the high-low method to develop a cost-estimating equation for monthly labor costs.

c. What factors might have caused the difference in the equations developed for requirements (*a*) and (*b*)?

d. Adjust the equation developed in requirement (*b*) to incorporate the effect of an anticipated 8 percent increase in wages.

LO2, 3

Potbelly's
NASDAQ :: PBPB

E14-21. Cost Behavior Analysis in a Restaurant: High-Low Cost Estimation

Assume a **Potbelly's** restaurant has the following information available regarding costs at representative levels of monthly sales:

	Monthly sales in units		
	5,000	8,000	10,000
Cost of food sold	$10,000	$16,000	$20,000
Wages and fringe benefits	4,200	4,320	4,400
Fees paid delivery help.	1,100	1,760	2,200
Rent on building	1,100	1,100	1,100
Depreciation on equipment	900	900	900
Utilities	800	920	1,000
Supplies (soap, floor wax, etc.)	250	340	400
Administrative costs.	1,700	1,700	1,700
Total	$20,050	$27,040	$31,700

REQUIRED

a. Identify each cost as being variable, fixed, or mixed.

b. Use the high-low method to develop a schedule identifying the amount of each cost that is mixed or variable per unit. Total the amounts under each category to develop an equation for total monthly costs.

c. Predict total costs for a monthly sales volume of 9,800 units.

LO2, 3

E14-22. Developing an Equation from Average Costs

Paradise Pup is a high-end dog hotel located in New York. Assume that in March, when dog-days occupancy was at an annual low of 500 days, the average cost per dog-day was $26. In July, when dog-days were at a capacity level of 4,500, the average cost per dog-day was $10.

REQUIRED

a. Develop an equation for monthly operating costs.

b. Determine the average cost per dog-day at an annual volume of 28,000 dog-days.

LO2, 3

E14-23. Selecting an Independent Variable: Scatter Diagrams

Eclipse Co. produces backpacks that are designed specifically for business executives and managers. The backpacks are sold to department stores throughout the northeast region. Presented is information on production costs and inventory changes for five recent months:

	January	February	March	April	May
Finished goods inventory in units:					
Beginning	30,000	40,000	50,000	30,000	60,000
Manufactured	60,000	90,000	80,000	90,000	100,000
Available	90,000	130,000	130,000	120,000	160,000
Sold	(50,000)	(80,000)	(100,000)	(60,000)	(120,000)
Ending	40,000	50,000	30,000	60,000	40,000
Manufacturing costs	$300,000	$500,000	$450,000	$450,000	$550,000

REQUIRED

a. With the aid of scatter diagrams, determine whether units sold or units manufactured is a better predictor of manufacturing costs.

b. Prepare an explanation for your answer to requirement (a).

c. Which independent variable, units sold or units manufactured, should be a better predictor of selling costs? Why?

E14-24. Selecting a Basis for Predicting Shipping Expenses (Requires Computer Spreadsheet*)   **LO2, 3**
Boom Company assembles and sells portable speaker systems throughout the midwest. In an effort to improve the planning and control of shipping expenses, management is trying to determine which of three variables—units shipped, weight shipped, or sales value of units shipped—has the closest relationship with shipping expenses. The following information is available:

Month	Units Shipped	Weight Shipped (lbs.)	Sales Value of Units Shipped	Shipping Expenses
May	6,000	9,300	$200,000	$ 8,960
June	10,000	12,000	220,000	12,320
July	8,000	12,150	160,000	10,400
August	14,000	15,000	228,000	16,640
September	12,000	10,500	280,000	13,760
October	9,000	12,000	320,000	13,120

REQUIRED

a. With the aid of a spreadsheet program, determine whether units shipped, weight shipped, or sales value of units shipped has the closest relationship with shipping expenses.

b. Using the independent variable that appears to have the closest relationship to shipping expenses, develop a cost-estimating equation for total monthly shipping expenses.

c. Use the equation developed in requirement (b) to predict total shipping expenses in a month when 5,000 units, weighing 7,000 lbs., with a total sales value of $114,000 are shipped.

PROBLEMS

P14-25. High-Low and Scatter Diagrams with Implications for Regression   **LO2, 3**
Signature Cookies produces and sells gourmet cookies at each of its restaurants. Presented is monthly cost and sales information for one of Signature's restaurants.

Month	Sales (Dozens)	Total Costs
January	3,750	$14,400
February	3,000	13,200
March	2,000	10,200
April	750	9,600
May	2,500	10,800
June	2,750	11,700

* This assignment requires the use of a computer spreadsheet such as Excel® to solve. This assignment assumes previous knowledge of computer spreadsheets.

REQUIRED

a. Using the high-low method, develop a cost-estimating equation for total monthly costs.

b. 1. Plot the equation developed in requirement (a).

2. Using the same graph, develop a scatter diagram of all observations for the bagel shop. Select representative high and low values and draw a second cost-estimating equation.

c. Which is a better predictor of future costs? Why?

d. If you decided to develop a cost-estimating equation using least-squares regression analysis, should you include all the observations? Why or why not?

e. Mention two reasons that the least-squares regression is superior to the high-low and scatter diagram methods of cost estimation.

LO5 **P14-26. Multiple Cost Drivers**

Lettuce Serve manufactures a variety of specialty salad dressings. Production runs are both high-volume and low-volume activities, depending on customer orders. Presented is Lettuce Serve's 2017 general manufacturing costs (manufacturing overhead) and each cost's related activity cost driver.

Level	Total Cost	Units of Cost Driver
Unit....................................	$500,000	10,000 machine hours
Batch	50,000	500 customer orders
Product.................................	100,000	25 products

Their cranberry vinaigrette dressing required 3,000 machine hours to fill 10 customer orders for a total of 8,000 units.

REQUIRED

a. Assuming all manufacturing overhead is estimated and predicted on the basis of machine hours, determine the predicted total overhead costs to produce the 8,000 units of cranberry vinaigrette.

b. Assuming manufacturing overhead is estimated and predicted using separate rates for machine hours, customer orders, and products (a multiple-level cost hierarchy), determine the predicted total overhead costs to produce the 8,000 units of cranberry vinaigrette.

c. Calculate the error in predicting manufacturing overhead using machine hours versus using multiple cost drivers. Indicate whether the use of only machine hours results in overpredicting or underpredicting the costs to produce 8,000 units of cranberry vinaigrette.

d. Determine the error in the prediction of cranberry vinaigrette batch-level costs resulting from the use of only machine hours. Indicate whether the use of only machine hours results in over-predicting or underpredicting the batch-level costs of cranberry vinaigrette.

e. Determine the error in the prediction of cranberry vinaigrette product-level costs resulting from the use of only machine hours. Indicate whether the use of only machine hours results in overpredicting or underpredicting the product-level costs of cranberry vinaigrette.

LO5 **P14-27. Unit- and Batch-Level Cost Drivers**

KC, a fast-food restaurant, serves fried chicken, fried fish, and french fries. The managers have estimated the costs of a batch of fried chicken for KC's all-you-can-eat Friday Fried Fiesta. Each batch must be 50 pieces. The chicken is precut by the chain headquarters and sent to the stores in 10-piece bags. Each bag costs $4. Preparing a batch of 50 pieces of chicken with KC's special coating takes one employee two hours. The current wage rate is $9 per hour. Another cost driver is the cost of putting fresh oil into the fryers. New oil, costing $6.50, is used for each batch.

REQUIRED

a. Determine the cost of preparing one batch of 50 pieces.

b. If management projects that it will sell 150 pieces of fried chicken, determine the total batch and unit costs.

c. If management estimates the sales to be 350 pieces, determine the total costs.

d. How much will the batch costs increase if the government raises the minimum wage to $10 per hour?

e. If management decided to increase the number of pieces in a batch to 100, determine the cost of preparing 350 pieces. Assume that the batch would take twice as long to prepare, and management wants to replace the oil after 100 pieces are cooked.

P14-28. Optimal Batch Size

LO5

This is a continuation of parts *c* and *e* of P14-27.

REQUIRED

Should management increase the batch size to 100? Why or why not?

CASES AND PROJECTS

C14-29. Significance of High R-Squared

LO3

Drew Conner had always been suspicious of "newfangled mathematical stuff," and the most recent suggestion of his new assistant merely confirmed his belief that schools are putting a lot of useless junk in students' heads. It seems that after an extensive analysis of historical data, the assistant suggested that the number of pounds of scrap was the best basis for predicting manufacturing overhead. In response to Mr. Conner's rage, the slightly intimidated assistant indicated that of the 35 equations he tried, pounds of scrap had the highest coefficient of determination with manufacturing overhead.

REQUIRED

Comment on Conner's reaction. Is it justified? Is it likely that the number of pounds of scrap is a good basis for predicting manufacturing overhead? Is it a feasible basis for predicting manufacturing overhead?

C14-30. Estimating Machine Repair Costs

LO3

In an attempt to determine the best basis for predicting machine repair costs, the production supervisor accumulated daily information on these costs and production over a one-month period. Applying simple regression analysis to the data, she obtained the following estimating equation:

$$Y = \$800 - \$2.60X$$

where

$$Y = \text{total daily machine repair costs}$$
$$X = \text{daily production in units}$$

Because of the negative relationship between repair costs and production, she was somewhat skeptical of the results, even though the R-squared was a respectable 0.765.

REQUIRED

a. What is the most likely explanation of the negative variable costs?

b. Suggest an alternative procedure for estimating machine repair costs that might prove more useful.

C14-31. Ethical Problem Uncovered by Cost Estimation

LO4

Sounders Management Company owns and provides management services for several shopping centers. After five years with the company, James Heller was recently promoted to the position of manager of **Brunswick**, an 18-store mall on the outskirts of a downtown area. When he accepted the assignment, James was told that he would hold the position for only a couple of years because Brunswick would likely be torn down to make way for a new sports stadium. James was also told that if he did well in this assignment, he would be in line for heading one of the company's new 200-store operations that were currently in the planning stage.

While reviewing Brunswick's financial records for the past few years, James observed that last year's oil consumption was up by 8 percent, even though the number of heating degree days was down by 4 percent. Somewhat curious, James uncovered the following information:

Brunswick
NYSE :: BC

- Brunswick is heated by forced-air oil heat. The furnace is five years old and has been well maintained.
- Fuel oil is kept in four 5,000-gallon underground oil tanks. The oil tanks were installed 25 years ago.
- Replacing the tanks would cost $80,000. If pollution was found, cleanup costs could go as high as $2,000,000, depending on how much oil had leaked into the ground and how far it had spread.
- Replacing the tanks would add more congestion to Brunswick's parking situation.

REQUIRED

What should James do? Explain.

LO5   **C14-32. Activity Cost Drivers and Cost Estimation**

Market Street Soup Company produces ten varieties of soup in large vats, several thousand gallons at a time. The soup is distributed to several categories of customers. Some soup is packaged in large containers and sold to college and university food services. Some is packaged in half-gallon or small containers and sold through wholesale distributors to grocery stores. Finally, some is packaged in a variety of individual servings and sold directly to the public from trucks owned and operated by Market Street Soup Company. Management has always assumed that costs fluctuated with the volume of soup, and cost-estimating equations have been based on the following cost function:

$$\textbf{Estimated costs} = \textbf{Fixed costs} + \textbf{Variable costs per gallon} \times \textbf{Production in gallons}$$

Lately, however, this equation has not been a very accurate predictor of total costs. At the same time, management has noticed that the volumes and varieties of soup sold through the three distinct distribution channels have fluctuated from month to month.

REQUIRED

a.   What *relevant* major assumption is inherent in the cost-estimating equation currently used by Market Street Soup Company?

b.   Why might Market Street Soup Company wish to develop a cost-estimating equation that recognizes the hierarchy of activity costs? Explain.

c.   Develop the general form of a more accurate cost-estimating equation for Market Street Soup Company. Clearly label and explain all elements of the equation, and provide specific examples of costs for each element.

LO3   **C14-33. Multiple Regression Analysis for a Special Decision (Requires Computer Spreadsheet[*])**

For billing purposes, Galaxy Health Clinic classifies its services into one of four major procedures, X1 through X4. A local business has proposed that Galaxy provide health services to its employees and their families at the following set rates per procedure:

X1	$ 45
X2	90
X3	60
X4	105

Because these rates are significantly below the current rates charged for these services, management has asked for detailed cost information on each procedure. The following information is available for the most recent 12 months.

Month	Total Cost	Number of Procedures			
		X1	X2	X3	X4
1..............	$11,500	15	50	103	38
2..............	12,500	19	60	90	45
3..............	13,500	25	40	70	75
4..............	9,500	10	45	60	50
5..............	10,000	34	25	80	40
6..............	13,500	45	38	105	53
7..............	12,750	10	55	95	55
8..............	10,750	8	60	88	40
9..............	13,000	30	43	62	70
10..............	11,000	10	45	50	70
11..............	11,400	10	35	75	65
12..............	13,250	36	30	100	60

REQUIRED

a.   Use multiple regression analysis to determine the unit cost of each procedure. How much variation in monthly cost is explained by your cost-estimating equation?

b.   Evaluate the rates proposed by the local business. Assuming Galaxy has excess capacity and no employees of the local business currently patronize the clinic, what are your recommendations regarding the proposal?

---

[*] This assignment requires the use of a computer spreadsheet such as Excel® to solve. This assignment assumes previous knowledge of computer spreadsheets.

c. Evaluate the rates proposed by the local business. Assuming Galaxy is operating at capacity and would have to turn current customers away if it agrees to provide health services to the local business, what are your recommendations regarding the proposal?

C14-34. Cost Estimation, Interpretation, and Analysis (Requires Computer Spreadsheet*) **LO3**

Brady Table Company produces two styles of modern dining room and kitchen tables. Presented is monthly information on production volume and manufacturing costs:

	Total Manufacturing Costs	Total Tables Produced	Dining Room Tables Produced	Kitchen Tables Produced
June 2017.	$ 69,975	375	75	300
July.	76,332	308	158	150
August	90,945	428	158	270
September	59,615	315	60	255
October	63,180	263	113	150
November.	78,863	315	165	150
December.	79,527	368	135	233
January 2018	70,988	375	75	300
February	70,853	330	105	225
March	66,713	270	120	150
April	146,700	473	270	203
May.	89,900	420	158	263
June	78,065	383	113	270
July.	83,070	353	165	188
August	69,335	293	128	165
September	90,653	390	180	210
October	80,562	375	135	240
November.	86,400	405	150	255
December.	56,475	248	90	158

REQUIRED

a. Use the high-low method to develop a cost-estimating equation for total manufacturing costs. Interpret the meaning of the "fixed" costs and comment on the results.

b. Use the chart feature of a spreadsheet to develop a scatter graph of total manufacturing costs and total units produced. Use the graph to identify any unusual observations.

c. Excluding any unusual observations, use the high-low method to develop a cost-estimating equation for total manufacturing costs. Comment on the results, comparing them with the results in requirement (a).

d. Use simple regression analysis to develop a cost-estimating equation for total manufacturing costs. What advantages does simple regression analysis have in comparison with the high-low method of cost estimation? Why must analysts carefully evaluate the data used in simple regression analysis?

e. A customer has offered to purchase 50 dining room tables for $220 per table. Management has asked your advice regarding the desirability of accepting the offer. What advice do you have for management? Additional analysis is required.

C14-35. Simple and Multiple Regression (Requires Computer Spreadsheet*) **LO3**

Dan Mullen is employed by a mail-order distributor and reconditions used desktop computers, broadband routers, and laser printers. Dan is paid $12 per hour, plus an extra $6 per hour for work in excess of 40 hours per week. The distributor just announced plans to outsource all reconditioning work. Because the distributor is pleased with the quality of Dan's work, he has been asked to enter into a long-term contract to recondition used desktop computers at a rate of $40 per computer, plus all parts. The distributor also offered to provide all necessary equipment at a rate of $200 per month. Dan has been informed that he should plan on reconditioning as many computers as he can handle, up to a maximum of 20 per week.

Dan has room in his basement to set up a work area, but he is unsure of the economics of accepting the contract, as opposed to working for a local Radio Stuff store at $11 per hour. Data related to the time spent and the number of units of each type of electronic equipment Dan has reconditioned in recent weeks is as follows:

*This assignment requires the use of a computer spreadsheet such as Excel® to solve. This assignment assumes previous knowledge of computer spreadsheets.

Week	Laser Printers	Broadband Routers	Desktop Computers	Total Units	Total Hours
1.................	4	5	5	14	40
2.................	0	7	6	13	42
3.................	4	3	7	14	40
4.................	0	2	12	14	46
5.................	11	6	4	21	48
6.................	5	8	3	16	44
7.................	5	8	3	16	44
8.................	5	6	5	16	43
9.................	2	6	10	18	53
10................	8	4	6	18	46
Total.............				160	446

REQUIRED

Assuming he wants to work an average of 40 hours per week, what should Dan do?

SOLUTIONS TO REVIEW PROBLEMS

Mid-Chapter Review 1

SOLUTION

Fixed costs are easily identified. They are the same at each activity level. Variable and mixed costs are determined by dividing the total costs for an item at two activity levels by the corresponding units of activity. The quotients of the variable cost items will be identical at both activity levels. The quotients of the mixed costs will differ, being lower at the higher activity level because the fixed costs are being spread over a larger number of units.

Cost	April	May	Behavior
Cost of food sold	$1,575/2,100 = 0.750	$2,025/2,700 = 0.750	Variable
Wages and salaries	$1,525/2,100 = 0.726	$1,675/2,700 = 0.620	Mixed
Rent on building	NA	NA	Fixed
Depreciation on equipment	NA	NA	Fixed
Utilities	$710/2,100 = 0.338	$770/2,700 = 0.285	Mixed
Supplies	$225/2,100 = 0.107	$255/2,700 = 0.094	Mixed
Miscellaneous................	$113/2,100 = 0.054	$131/2,700 = 0.049	Mixed

Mid-Chapter Review 2

SOLUTION

a. Variable cost
b. Mixed cost
c. Committed fixed cost
d. Variable cost
e. Step cost
f. Discretionary fixed cost
g. Fixed cost (Without knowing the purpose of renting the car, the cost cannot be classified as committed or discretionary.)
h. Mixed cost
i. Step cost
j. Discretionary fixed cost

Mid-Chapter Review 3

SOLUTION

a. The cost of food sold was classified as a variable cost. Hence, the cost of food may be determined by dividing the total cost of food sold at either observation by the corresponding number of sandwiches.

$$b = \frac{\$1{,}575 \text{ total variable costs}}{2{,}100 \text{ units}}$$

$$= \$0.75X$$

Wages and salaries were previously classified as a mixed cost. Hence, the cost of wages and salaries is determined using the high-low method.

(variable cost)

$$b = \frac{\$1{,}675 - \$1{,}525}{2{,}700 - 2{,}100}$$

$$= 0.25X$$

(fixed cost)

$$a = \$1{,}525 \text{ total cost} - (\$0.25 \times 2{,}100) \text{ variable cost}$$

$$= \$1{,}000$$

Rent on building was classified as a fixed cost.

$$a = \$1{,}500$$

Total monthly costs most likely follow a mixed cost behavior pattern. Hence, they can be determined using the high-low method.

$$b = \frac{\$6{,}556 - \$5{,}848}{2{,}700 - 2{,}100}$$

$$= \$1.18X$$

$$a = \$5{,}848 - (\$1.18 \times 2{,}100)$$

$$= \$3{,}370$$

$$\text{Total costs} = \$3{,}370 + \$1.18X$$

where

$$X = \text{unit sales}$$

b. and *c*.

Volume	Total Costs	Average Cost per Sandwich
1,000.	$3,370 + ($1.18 × 1,000) = $4,550	$\dfrac{\$4{,}550}{\$1{,}000} = \$4.550$
2,000.	$3,370 + ($1.18 × 2,000) = $5,730	$\dfrac{\$5{,}730}{\$2{,}000} = \$2.865$

The average costs differ at 1,000 and 2,000 units because the fixed costs are being spread over a different number of units. The larger the number of units, the smaller the average fixed cost per unit.

Mid-Chapter Review 4

SOLUTION

Some common activity drivers for stating volume of activity in a manufacturing operation might include direct labor hours, machine hours, units of material produced, and units of finished product. The selection of the most appropriate basis requires judgment and professional experience. The relationship between the activity cost driver and the cost must seem logical and the activity data must be available.

Chapter-End Review

SOLUTION

1. *a*; Unit-level
2. *b*; Store-level
3. *c*; Store-level
4. *d*; Unit-level
5. *e*; Customer-level
6. *f*; Order-level

15

Cost-Volume-Profit Analysis and Planning

RAZOR USA, LLC
www.razor.com

Based in Cerritos, California, **Razor USA, LLC** designs and manufactures an array of rideable devices ranging from kick scooters to self-balancing hoverboards. Razor, as it is commonly known, was founded in 2000 and has experienced tremendous growth. Razor's first product, the model A kick scooter, sold over 5 million units within six months of its introduction and won the 2000 Toy of The Year award. By 2010, Razor had sold over 35 million scooters. Razor built on its kick scooter success and expanded its product line to include electric scooters, a modern version of the Scream Machine ™, go-karts, electric motor bikes, and self-balancing hoverboards.

Razor is redefining the "ride on" category of toys and is well positioned for continued success, but how much should it charge for its products? How many units does Razor need to sell to breakeven? How many units does it need to sell to reach its target profit? These are questions that managers within Razor must answer.

Profitability analysis involves examining the relations between revenues, costs, and profits. Performing profitability analysis requires an understanding of selling prices and the behavior of activity cost drivers. Profitability analysis is widely used to make better decisions regarding existing or proposed products or services. Typically, it is performed before decisions are finalized in the operating budget for a future period.

If Razor is to accomplish its goals, it must generate profits, meaning that its revenues must exceed its costs. Razor's manufacturing processes consume energy and raw materials. The price of these inputs changes over time. By decomposing Razor's costs into its variable and fixed components, the company can perform profitability analyses to determine where to direct its future efforts. In fact, Razor can utilize the tools presented in this chapter to determine how much revenue it has to generate to achieve a desired profit.

This chapter introduces basic approaches to profitability analysis and planning. We consider single product, multiple-product, and service organizations; income taxes; sales mix; and the effects of cost structure on the relation between profit potential and the risk of loss.

Source: Parija Kavilanz, "Next for Razor after massive recall: Hovertrax 2.0," *CNN Money*, July 7, 2106; Matt Malmlund, "Are Hoverboards Safe to Ride Yet? The Razor Hovertrax 2.0 Is," Heavy.Com, December 13, 2016; Bloomberg.com 2017; and Razor.com 2017.

CHAPTER ORGANIZATION

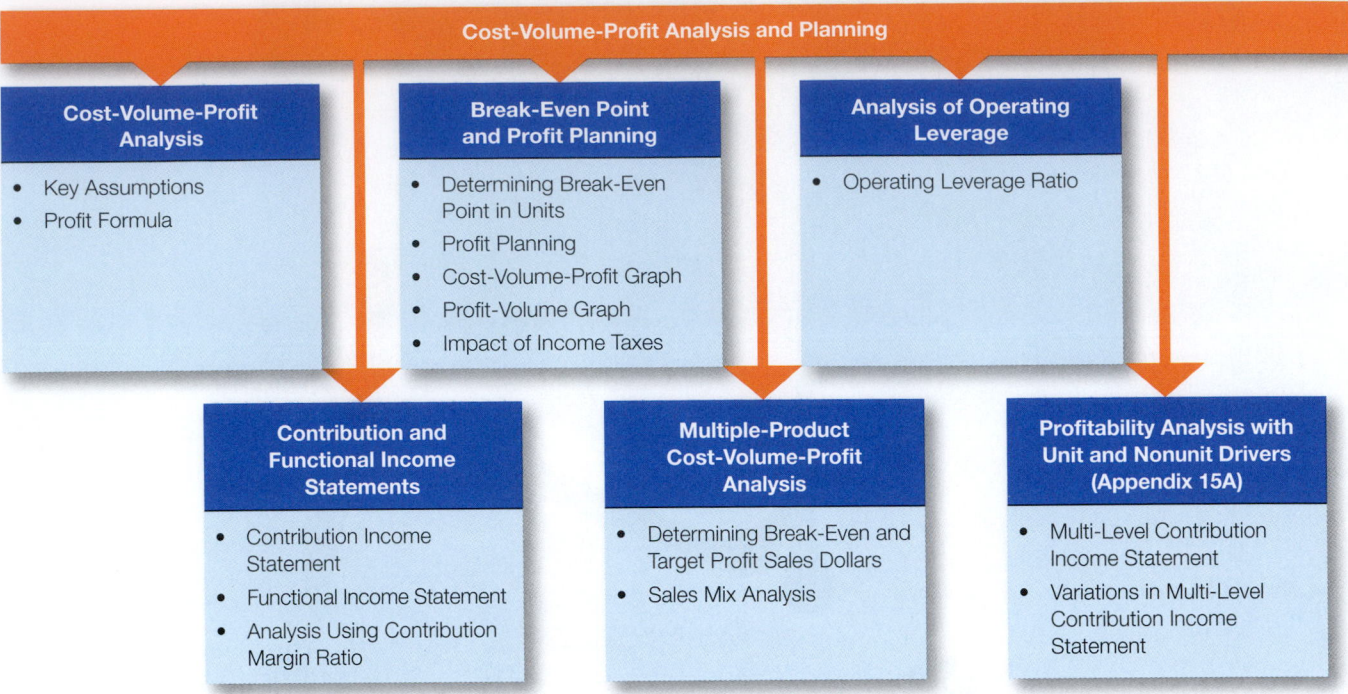

What fee should we charge for a subscription to our services? How many units do we need to sell to break even? How many units do we need to sell to reach our target profit?

Profitability analysis involves examining the relationships among revenues, costs, and profits. Performing profitability analysis requires an understanding of selling prices and the behavior of activity cost drivers. Profitability analysis is widely used to make better decisions regarding existing or proposed products or services. Typically, it is performed before decisions are finalized in the operating budget for a future period.

This chapter introduces basic approaches to profitability analysis and planning. We consider single-product, multiple-product, and service organizations; income taxes; sales mix; and the effects of cost structure on the relation between profit potential and the risk of loss.

COST-VOLUME-PROFIT ANALYSIS

LO1 Describe the uses and limitations of traditional cost-volume-profit analysis.

Cost-volume-profit (CVP) analysis is a technique used to examine the relationships among the total volume of an independent variable, total costs, total revenues, and profits for a time period (typically a quarter or year). With CVP analysis, volume refers to a single activity cost driver, such as unit sales, that is assumed to correlate with changes in revenues, costs, and profits.

Cost-volume-profit analysis is useful in the early stages of planning because it provides an easily understood framework for discussing planning issues and organizing relevant data. CVP analysis is widely used by for-profit as well as not-for-profit organizations. It is equally applicable to service, merchandising, and manufacturing firms.

In for-profit organizations, CVP analysis is used to answer such questions as these: How many photocopies must the local **Staples** store produce to earn a profit of $80,000? At what dollar sales volume will **Whole Foods**' total revenues and total costs be equal? What profit will **Target** earn at an annual sales volume of $75 billion? What will happen to the profit of **Panera Bread** if there is a 20 percent increase in the cost of food and a 10 percent increase in the selling price of meals? The Research Insight box on the following page indicates how the role of managerial accounting is expanding. With greater availability of data, managers can efficiently perform more analyses to help guide CVP decisions.

In not-for-profit organizations, CVP analysis is used to establish service levels, plan fund-raising activities, and determine funding requirements. How many meals can the downtown **Salvation**

Army serve with an annual budget of $600,000? How many tickets must be sold for the benefit concert to raise $20,000? Given the current cost structure, current tuition rates, and projected enrollments, how much money must **DePaul University** raise from other sources?

Key Assumptions

CVP analysis is subject to a number of assumptions. Although these assumptions do not negate the usefulness of CVP models, especially for a single product or service, they do suggest the need for further analysis before plans are finalized. Among the more important assumptions are:

1. *All costs are classified as fixed or variable.* This assumption is most reasonable when analyzing the profitability of a specific event (such as a concert) or the profitability of an organization that produces a single product or service on a continuous basis.

2. *The total cost function is linear within the relevant range.* This assumption is often valid within a relevant range of normal operations, but over the entire range of possible activity, changes in efficiency are likely to result in a nonlinear cost function.

3. *The total revenue function is linear within the relevant range.* Unit selling prices are assumed constant over the range of possible volumes. This implies a purely competitive market for final products or services. In some economic models in which demand responds to price changes, the revenue function is nonlinear. In these situations, the linear approximation is accurate only within a limited range of activity.

4. *The analysis is for a single product, or the sales mix of multiple products is constant.* The **sales mix** refers to the relative portion of unit or dollar sales derived from each product or service. If products have different selling prices and costs, changes in the mix affect CVP model results.

5. *There is only one cost driver: unit or sales dollar volume.* In a complex organization it is seldom possible to represent the multitude of factors that drive cost with a single cost driver.

RESEARCH INSIGHT

Data-Driven Planning Central to Management Accounting   The role of management accounting is expanding to include planning driven by data science. This work is often called financial planning and analysis (FP&A) and is used widely enough that a professional accrediting program has been launched by the **Association for Financial Professionals (AFP)**.

The central function of the FP&A group within a company is to inform decisions with data. **GoDaddy Inc.** called on its FP&A group to help guide the domain-name seller's international expansion. The team developed purpose-built growth metrics to help executives allocate marketing dollars across the 40 countries where GoDaddy does business. By finding the correct metric to drive resource decisions, GoDaddy was able to increase the share of sales from foreign markets to 26% of total sales. Its CFO claims that the FP&A group's contribution tripled foreign growth.

At **Dunkin Brands Group Inc.**, the FP&A group has influence in every department, helping managers and employees across the organization find ways to improve processes and practices. Dunkin's 36-member FP&A team took on the key job of mining loyalty data to find ways to get customers back into the store throughout the day and increasing the amount that the customers spent. This effort led to a 2.2% growth in same-store sales over nine months.

While Dunkin is deeply committed to FP&A (its CFO was the VP of FP&A), other firms are adopting this approach more slowly. The consulting firm CEB notes that 61% of FP&A directors do not feel that top managers take their contributions seriously. As this perception changes, accountants trained in management accounting principles will have the chance to influence companies with their analyses.

Source: Alix Stuart, "Metrics Sell Doughnuts and More," *Wall Street Journal*, December 21, 2015.

When applied to a single product (such as pounds of potato chips), service (such as the number of pages printed), or event (such as the number of tickets sold to a banquet), it is reasonable to assume the single independent variable is the cost driver. The total costs associated with the single product, service, or event during a specific time period are often determined by this single activity cost driver.

Although cost-volume-profit analysis is often used to understand the overall operations of an organization or business segment, accuracy decreases as the scope of operations being analyzed increases.

Profit Formula

The profit associated with a product, service, or event is equal to the difference between total revenues and total costs as follows:

$$\pi = R - Y$$

where

$$\pi = \text{Profit}$$
$$R = \text{Total revenues}$$
$$Y = \text{Total costs}$$

The revenues are a function of the unit sales volume and the unit selling price, while total costs for a time period are a function of the fixed costs per period and the unit variable costs as follows:

$$R = pX$$
$$Y = a + bX$$

where

$$p = \text{Unit selling price}$$
$$a = \text{Fixed costs}$$
$$b = \text{Unit variable costs}$$
$$X = \text{Unit sales}$$

The equation for profit can then be expanded to include the above details of the total revenue and total cost equations as follows:

$$\pi = pX - (a + bX)$$

Using information on the selling price, fixed costs per period, and variable costs per unit, this formula is used to predict profit at any specified activity level.

To illustrate, assume that **Razor's** only product is a standard kick scooter that it manufactures and sells to merchandisers at $60 per completed scooter. Applying inventory minimization techniques, Razor does not maintain inventories of raw materials or finished goods. Instead, newly purchased raw materials are delivered directly to the factory, and finished goods are loaded directly onto trucks for shipment. Razor's variable and fixed costs follow.

1. **Direct materials** refer to the cost of the primary raw materials converted into finished goods. Because the consumption of raw materials increases as the quantity of goods produced increases, *direct materials represents a variable cost*. Razor's raw materials consist primarily

of nuts and bolts, rubber wheels, bearings, steel frames, and packaging materials. Razor also treats the costs of purchasing, receiving, and inspecting these materials as part of the cost of direct materials. Assume that all together, these costs are $20 per completed scooter.

2. **Direct labor** refers to wages earned by production employees for the time they spend working on the conversion of raw materials into finished goods. Based on Razor's manufacturing procedures, *direct labor represents a variable cost.* Further assume these costs are $10 per completed scooter.

3. **Variable manufacturing overhead** includes all other variable costs associated with converting raw materials into finished goods. Assume Razor's variable manufacturing overhead costs include the costs of lubricants for cutting and packaging machines, electricity to operate these machines, and the cost to move materials between receiving and shipping. These costs are $3 per completed scooter.

4. **Variable selling and administrative costs** include all variable costs other than those directly associated with converting raw materials into finished goods. Assume at Razor, these costs include sales commissions and transportation of finished goods to merchandisers. These costs are $5 per completed scooter.

5. **Fixed manufacturing overhead** includes all fixed costs associated with converting raw materials into finished goods. Suppose Razor's fixed manufacturing costs include the depreciation, property taxes, and insurance on buildings and machines used for manufacturing, the salaries of manufacturing supervisors, and the fixed portion of electricity used to light the factory. Further assume these costs are $35,000 per month.

6. **Fixed selling and administrative costs** include all fixed costs other than those directly associated with converting raw materials into finished goods. These costs include the salaries of Razor's divisional manager and many other staff personnel such as accounting and marketing. Also included are depreciation, property taxes, insurance on facilities used for administrative purposes, and any related utilities costs. Assume these costs are $15,000 per month.

Razor's hypothetical variable and fixed costs are summarized here.

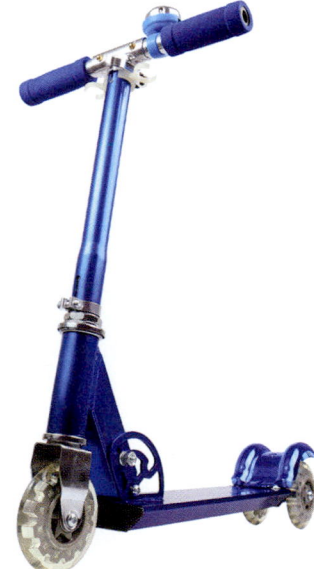

Variable Costs per Scooter			Fixed Costs per Month	
Manufacturing			Manufacturing overhead	$35,000
Direct materials	$20		Selling and administrative	15,000
Direct labor	10		Total	$50,000
Manufacturing overhead	3	$33		
Selling and administrative		5		
Total		$38		

The cost estimation techniques discussed in Chapter 14 can be used to determine many detailed costs. Least-squares regression, for example, might be used to determine the variable and monthly fixed amount of electricity used in manufacturing. Assume Razor manufactures and sells a single product on a continuous basis with all sales to merchandisers under standing contracts. Therefore, it is reasonable to assume that in the short run, Razor's total monthly costs respond to a single cost driver, scooters sold. Combining all this information, Razor's profit equation is assumed to be:

$$\text{Profit} = \$60X - (\$50,000 + \$38X)$$

where

$$X = \text{scooters sold}$$

Using this equation, Razor's profit at a volume of 5,400 units is $68,800, computed as ($60 × 5,400) − [$50,000 + ($38 × 5,400)].

MID-CHAPTER REVIEW 1

Benchmark Paper Company's only product is high-quality photocopy paper that it manufactures and sells to wholesale distributors at $14 per carton. Applying inventory minimization techniques, Benchmark does not maintain inventories of raw materials or finished goods. Newly purchased raw materials are delivered

Continued

Continued from previous page

directly to the factory, and finished goods are loaded directly onto trucks for shipment. Benchmark's variable and fixed costs follow:

Variable Costs per Carton			Fixed Costs per Month	
Manufacturing			Manufacturing overhead...........	$ 2,000
Direct materials	$1.25		Selling and administrative.........	8,000
Direct labor.................	0.50		Total	$10,000
Manufacturing overhead	2.50	$4.25		
Selling and administrative.......		1.00		
Total		$5.25		

REQUIRED
a. Determine Benchmark's profit equation.
b. Using your equation, calculate Benchmark's profit at a volume of 6,200 cartons.

The solution to this review problem can be found on page 721.

eLectures
MBC

LO2 Prepare and contrast contribution and functional income statements.

2

CONTRIBUTION AND FUNCTIONAL INCOME STATEMENTS

Contribution Income Statement

To provide more detailed information on anticipated or actual financial results at a particular sales volume, a contribution income statement is often prepared. Razor's hypothetical contribution income statement for a volume of 5,400 units is in **Exhibit 15.1**. In a **contribution income statement**, costs are classified according to behavior as variable or fixed, and the **contribution margin** (the difference between total revenues and total variable costs) that goes toward covering fixed costs and providing a profit is emphasized.

EXHIBIT 15.1	Contribution Income Statement

RAZOR COMPANY
Contribution Income Statement
For a Monthly Volume of 5,400 Scooters

Sales (5,400 × $60)		$324,000
Less variable costs		
Direct materials (5,400 × $20)	$108,000	
Direct labor (5,400 × $10)...	54,000	
Manufacturing overhead (5,400 × $3)	16,200	
Selling and administrative (5,400 × $5)	27,000	(205,200)
Contribution margin		118,800
Less fixed costs		
Manufacturing overhead...	35,000	
Selling and administrative...	15,000	(50,000)
Profit...		$ 68,800

Functional Income Statement

Contrast the contribution income statement in **Exhibit 15.1** with Razor's hypothetical income statement in **Exhibit 15.2**. This statement is called a **functional income statement** because costs are classified according to function (rather than behavior), such as manufacturing, selling, and administrative. This is the type of income statement typically included in corporate annual reports.

A problem with a functional income statement is the difficulty of relating it to the profit formula in which costs are classified according to behavior rather than function. The relationship between sales volume, costs, and profits is not readily apparent in a functional income statement. Consequently, we emphasize contribution income statements because they provide better information to internal decision makers.

EXHIBIT 15.2	Functional Income Statement

RAZOR COMPANY
Functional Income Statement
For a Monthly Volume of 5,400 Cartons

Sales (5,400 × $60)		$324,000
Less cost of goods sold		
Direct materials (5,400 × $20)	$108,000	
Direct labor (5,400 × $10)	54,000	
Variable manufacturing overhead (5,400 × $3)	16,200	
Fixed manufacturing overhead	35,000	(213,200)
Gross margin		110,800
Less other expenses		
Variable selling and administrative (5,400 × $5)	27,000	
Fixed selling and administrative	15,000	(42,000)
Profit		$ 68,800

Analysis Using Contribution Margin Ratio

While the contribution income statement (shown in **Exhibit 15.1**) presents information on total sales revenue, total variable costs, and so forth, it is sometimes useful to present information on a per-unit or portion of sales basis.

	Total	Per Unit	Ratio to Sales
Sales (5,400 units)	$324,000	$60	1.0000
Variable costs	(205,200)	38	0.6333*
Contribution margin	118,800	$22	0.3667
Fixed costs	(50,000)		
Profit	$ 68,800		

* Rounded

The per-unit information assists in short-range planning. The **unit contribution margin** is the difference between the unit selling price and the unit variable costs. It is the amount, $22 in this case, that each unit contributes toward covering fixed costs and earning a profit.

The contribution margin is widely used in **sensitivity analysis** (the study of the responsiveness of a model to changes in one or more of its independent variables). Razor's income statement is an economic model of the firm, and the unit contribution margin indicates how sensitive Razor's income model is to changes in unit sales. If, for example, sales increase by 100 scooters per month, the increase in profit is readily determined by multiplying the 100-scooter increase in sales by the $22 unit contribution margin as follows:

100 (scooter sales increase) × $22 (unit contribution margin) = $2,200 (profit increase)

There is no increase in fixed costs, so the new profit level becomes $71,000 ($68,800 + $2,200) per month.

When expressed as a ratio to sales, the sales margin is identified as the **contribution margin ratio**. It is the portion of each dollar of sales revenue contributed toward covering fixed costs and earning a profit. In the abbreviated income statement above, the portion of each dollar of sales revenue contributed toward covering fixed costs and earning a profit is $0.3667 ($118,800 ÷ $324,000).

This is Razor's assumed contribution margin ratio. If sales revenue increases by $6,000 per month, the increase in profits is computed as follows:

$6,000 (sales increase) × 0.3667 (contribution margin ratio) = $2,200 (profit increase)

The contribution margin ratio is especially useful in situations involving several products or when unit sales information is not available.

MID-CHAPTER REVIEW 2

Assume **Solo Cup Company** produces 16-ounce beverage containers. Further assume Solo sells the cups for $40 per box of 50 containers. Variable and fixed costs follow:

Variable Costs per Box			Fixed Costs per Month	
Manufacturing			Manufacturing overhead	$15,000
Direct materials	$15		Selling and administrative	10,000
Direct labor	3		Total	$25,000
Manufacturing overhead	10	$28		
Selling and administrative		2		
Total		$30		

Suppose in September 2017, Solo produced and sold 3,000 boxes of beverage containers.

REQUIRED
a. Prepare a contribution income statement for September 2017.
b. Determine Solo's unit contribution margin and contribution margin ratio.

The solution to this review problem can be found on page 722.

LO3 Apply cost-volume-profit analysis to find a break-even point and for preliminary profit planning.

BREAK-EVEN POINT AND PROFIT PLANNING

The **break-even point** occurs at the unit or dollar sales volume when total revenues equal total costs. The break-even point is of great interest to management. Until break-even sales are reached, the product, service, event, or business segment of interest operates at a loss. Beyond this point, increasing levels of profits are achieved. Also, management often wants to know the **margin of safety**, the amount by which actual or planned sales exceed the break-even point. Other questions of interest include the probability of exceeding the break-even sales volume and the effect of some proposed change on the break-even point.

Determining Break-Even Point in Units

In determining the break-even point, the equation for total revenues is set equal to the equation for total costs and then solved for the break-even unit sales volume. Using the general equations for total revenues and total costs, the following results are obtained. Setting total revenues equal to total costs:

$$\text{Total revenues} = \text{Total costs}$$
$$pX = a + bX$$

Solving for the break-even unit sales volume:

$$pX - bX = a$$
$$(p - b)X = a$$
$$X = a/(p - b)$$

In words:

$$\text{Break-even unit sales volume} = \frac{\text{Fixed costs}}{\text{Selling price per unit} - \text{Variable costs per unit}}$$

Because the denominator is the unit contribution margin, the break-even point is also computed by dividing fixed costs by the unit contribution margin:

$$\text{Break-even unit sales volume} = \frac{\text{Fixed costs}}{\text{Unit contribution margin}}$$

With an assumed $22 unit contribution margin and fixed costs of $50,000 per month, Razor's break-even point is 2,273[*] units per month ($50,000 ÷ $22). Stated another way, at a $22 per-unit contribution margin, 2,273 units of sales are required to cover $50,000 of fixed costs. With a break-even point of 2,273 units, the monthly margin of safety for a sales volume of 5,400 units is 3,127 units (5,400 expected unit sales − 2,273 break-even unit sales). The expected profit at a sales volume of 5,400 units is $68,794 (3,127 unit margin of safety × $22 unit contribution margin). (The difference between the calculated $68,794 and the profit of $68,800 in **Exhibits 15.1** and **15.2** is due to rounding.)

[*] Rounded UP to the nearest whole unit

The break-even point concept is applicable to a wide variety of business and personal planning situations. The following Research Insight box illustrates how a personal financial planner might use break-even point concepts to assist a client making a retirement decision.

RESEARCH INSIGHT

Determining the Cash Break-Even Point for Delaying Retirement Social Security retirement benefits are a function of years worked, contributions to the Social Security System, and the age at which the recipient files for Social Security retirement benefits. Currently, persons retiring at age 67 are entitled to "full" retirement benefits, while those retiring at age 62 are eligible for only 70 percent of "full" benefits. A person contemplating retirement at age 62 might ask: (1) how large is the reduction in benefits and (2) what is the break-even age at which the benefits from delaying retirement until age 67 equals the cumulative benefits from retiring at age 62?

An individual with the analytic skills obtained from a managerial accounting course can readily determine the answers to these questions after consulting the Social Security web site www.ssa.gov. Others might consult a personal financial planner.

(1) Assume the individual's full Social Security retirement benefits at age 67 are $2,265 per month. If that person started receiving benefits at age 62 their monthly benefits are reduced by 30 percent or $679.50 ($2,265 × 0.30) to $1,585.50.

(2) With retirement at age 62, the early retiree would receive total benefits of $95,130 ($1,585.50 × 12 months × 5 years) by age 67, the normal "full" age. Treating this as a fixed amount to be recovered by the subsequent incremental monthly benefits of $679.50 from delaying the receipt of monthly benefits to age 67, the break-even age is computed as follows:

Months beyond age 67 = $95,130/$679.50 = 140 months or 11.67 years.
Hence, the break-even age is 78.67 years (67 + 11.67).

The analysis suggests that life expectancy is an important consideration in deciding when to start taking Social Security benefits.

Note that this analysis does not consider any return on the $95,130 that might be earned by investing the benefits received during early retirement. Such returns would increase the break-even age. Nor does it consider the lost wages that could have been earned between age 62 and age 67.

Source: www.ssa.gov

Profit Planning

Establishing profit objectives is an important part of planning in for-profit organizations. Profit objectives are stated in many ways. They can be set as a percentage of last year's profits, as a percentage of total assets at the start of the current year, or as a percentage of owners' equity. They might be based on a profit trend, or they might be expressed as a percentage of sales. The economic outlook for the firm's products as well as anticipated changes in products, costs, and technology are also considered in establishing profit objectives.

Before incorporating profit plans into a detailed budget, it is useful to obtain some preliminary information on the feasibility of those plans. Cost-volume-profit analysis is one way of doing this. By manipulating cost-volume-profit relationships, management can determine the sales volume corresponding to a desired profit. Management might then evaluate the feasibility of this sales volume. If the profit plans are feasible, a complete budget might be developed for this activity level. The required sales volume might be infeasible because of market conditions or because the required volume exceeds production or service capacity, in which case management must lower its profit objective or consider other ways of achieving it. Alternatively, the required sales volume might be less than management believes the firm is capable of selling, in which case management might raise its profit objective.

Assume that Razor's management desires to know the unit sales volume required to achieve a monthly profit of $75,000. Using the profit formula, the required unit sales volume is determined by setting profits equal to $75,000 and solving for **X**, the unit sales volume.

$$\textbf{Profit} = \textbf{Total revenues} - \textbf{Total costs}$$
$$\$75{,}000 = \$60X - (\$50{,}000 + \$38X)$$

Solving for **X**

$$\$60X - \$38X = \$50{,}000 + \$75{,}000$$
$$X = (\$50{,}000 + \$75{,}000) \div \$22$$
$$= 5{,}682 \text{ units (rounded UP to the nearest whole unit)}$$

The total contribution must cover the desired profit as well as the fixed costs. Hence, the target sales volume required to achieve a desired profit is computed as the fixed costs plus the desired profit, all divided by the unit contribution margin.

$$\textbf{Target unit sales volume} = \frac{\textbf{Fixed costs} + \textbf{Desired profit}}{\textbf{Unit contribution margin}}$$

The Business Insight box below considers CVP analysis for **Costco**, a large wholesale club whose strategic position for consumer goods focuses on cost leadership.

BUSINESS INSIGHT

Cost, Volume, What Profit? **Costco** customers are loyal. Its competitors have lost customers to Internet retailers, but Costco's sales have grown by nearly 40 percent over the past several years. Costco's customers are happy, its employees are happy, and its management is happy. The company's workers are paid on average $20.89 per hour, which is nearly 65 percent higher than the average **Wal-Mart** worker. Nearly 90 percent of its employees have company-sponsored health insurance, whereas slightly over half of Wal-Mart workers do. Employees rarely leave the company—its turnover rate is only 5 percent.

But once Costco accounts for its real estate costs and wages for its employees, its merchandise barely breaks even. The company passes along its cost savings from buying its merchandise in bulk to the consumer, which ensures the company will have plenty of volume in its CVP analysis. But how has the company been in business for three decades without turning a profit on its merchandise? The company's profit is earned from its annual membership dues. Each member pays $55 per year, but clearly Costco's customers believe this is a good bargain. Ninety percent of members renew their membership year over year. By selling their products to the customer at their break-even points, Costco will always make its necessary profit. Now that's a business model.

Source: Brad Stone, "Costco CEO Craig Jelinek Leads the Cheapest, Happiest Company in the World," *Bloomberg Businessweek*, June 6, 2013.

Cost-Volume-Profit Graph

A **cost-volume-profit graph** illustrates the relationships among activity volume, total revenues, total costs, and profits. Its usefulness comes from highlighting the break-even point and depicting revenue, cost, and profit relationships over a range of activity. This representation allows management to view the relative amount of important variables at any graphed volume. Razor's hypothetical monthly CVP graph is in **Exhibit 15.3**. Total revenues and total costs are measured on the vertical axis, with unit sales measured on the horizontal axis. Separate lines are drawn for total variable costs, total costs, and total revenues. The vertical distance between the total revenue and the total cost lines depicts the amount of profit or loss at a given volume. Losses occur when total revenues are less than total costs; profits occur when total revenues exceed total costs.

The total contribution margin is shown by the difference between the total revenue and the total variable cost lines. Observe that as unit sales increase, the contribution margin first goes to cover the fixed costs. Beyond the break-even point, any additional contribution margin provides a profit.

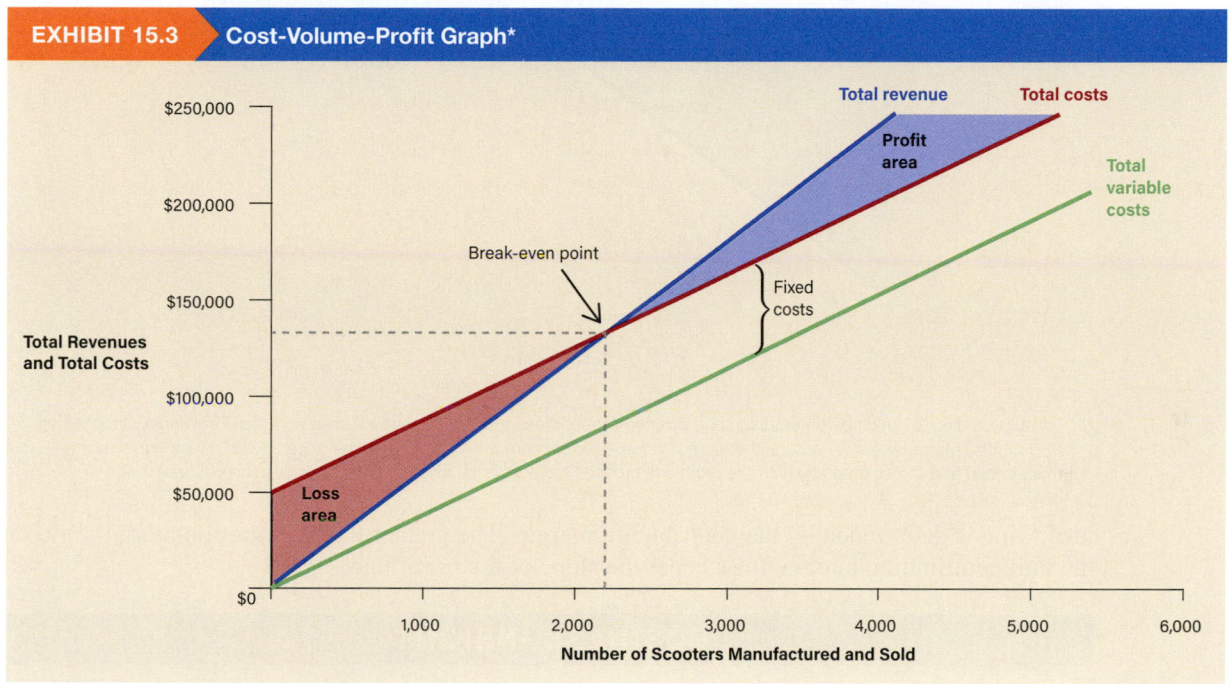

EXHIBIT 15.3	Cost-Volume-Profit Graph*

* The three lines are developed as follows:

1. **Total variable costs** line is drawn between the origin and total variable costs at an arbitrary sales volume. At 3,000 units, total variable costs are $114,000 (3,000 × $38).

2. **Total revenues** line is drawn through the origin and a point representing total revenues at some arbitrary sales volume. At 3,000 units, Razor's hypothetical total revenues are $180,000 (3,000 × $60).

3. **Total costs** line is computed by layering fixed costs, $50,000 in this case, on top of total variable costs. This gives a vertical axis intercept of $50,000 and total costs of $164,000 at 3,000 units.

Profit-Volume Graph

In cost-volume-profit graphs, profits are represented by the difference between total revenues and total costs. When management is primarily interested in the impact of changes in sales volume on profits and less interested in the related revenues and costs, a **profit-volume graph** is sometimes used. A profit-volume graph illustrates the relationship between volume and profits; it does not show revenues and costs. Profits are read directly from a profit-volume graph, rather than being computed as the difference between total revenues and total costs. Profit-volume graphs are developed by plotting either unit sales or total revenues on the horizontal axis.

The Business Insight box on the following page discusses that GlaxoSmithKline expects a future reduction in its process costs. This would lead to a reduction in its required sales to breakeven.

Razor's assumed monthly profit-volume graph is presented in **Exhibit 15.4**. Profit or loss is measured on the vertical axis, and volume (total revenues) is measured on the horizontal axis, which intersects the vertical axis at zero profit. A single line, representing total profit, is drawn intersecting the vertical axis at zero sales volume with a loss equal to the fixed costs. The profit line crosses the horizontal axis at the break-even sales volume. The profit or loss at any volume is depicted by the vertical difference between the profit line and the horizontal axis. The slope of the

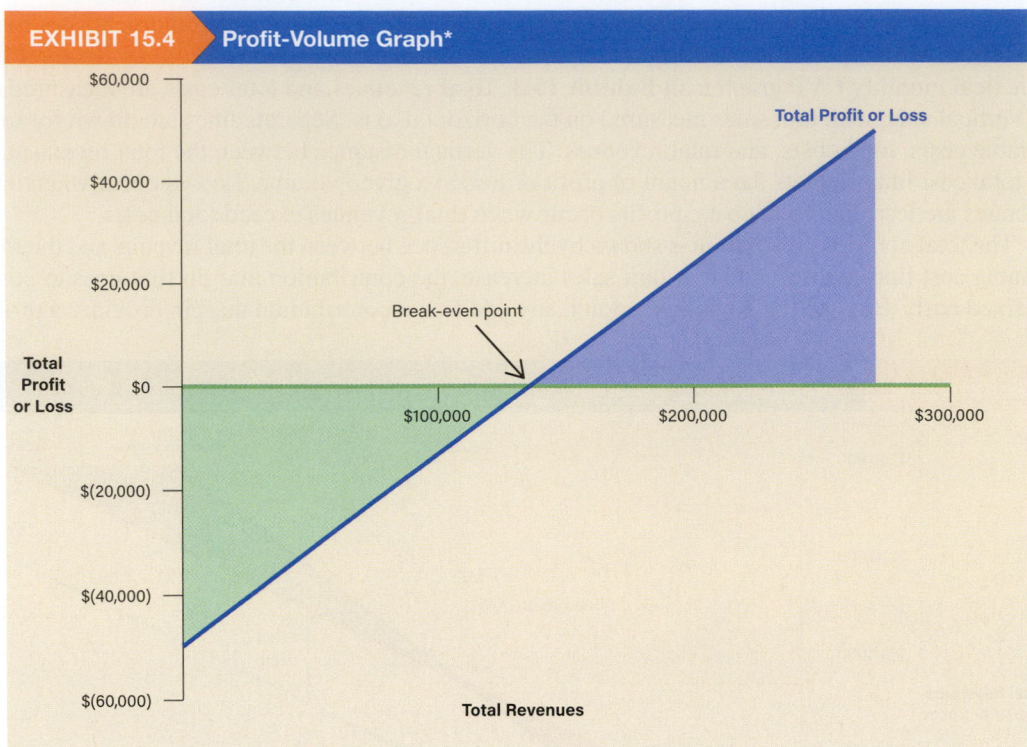

EXHIBIT 15.4 | Profit-Volume Graph*

* The profit line is drawn by determining and plotting profit or loss at two different volumes and then drawing a straight line through the plotted values. Perhaps the easiest values to select are the loss at a volume of zero (with a loss equal to the fixed costs) and the volume at which the profit line crosses the horizontal axis (this is the break-even volume).

profit line is determined by the contribution margin. The greater the contribution margin ratio or the unit contribution margin, the steeper the slope of the profit line.

BUSINESS INSIGHT

Drugmaker Looks to Bioelectronics to Change Cost Structure   At **GlaxoSmithKline's** (GSK) bioelectronics unit, treatments are not pills or serums delivering doses of chemicals to the entire body but rice-sized devices attached to nerve bundles. The innovation here is treating illness as a programming problem rather than as a chemical problem. The nervous system can be viewed as a communication system carrying messages about the body's operations. To the extent that problematic messages can be edited, many health problems can be solved by implanting and programming these devices. In addition to finding new solutions to old pathologies, GSK hopes to eventually change the cost structure of drug companies. GSK has started a venture capital effort worth $50 million that funds 100 independent researchers and 30 employees.

Development costs are exploding for conventional molecular drug therapies. The average drug takes 10 years and $2.6 billion to bring to market. GSK is betting that basic engineering innovations in bioelectronics will allow new therapies to be tested and implemented more quickly and at lower cost. This could potentially change some therapies into software problems rather than manufacturing problems, eliminating many of the process costs involved in manufacturing drugs under the current model. These investments remain risky, but GSK is hoping that its investment in this technology changes the cost structure of the drug business.

Source: Matthew Campbell, "Only One Big Drugmaker Is Working on a Nanobot Cure," *Bloomberg Businessweek*, June 9, 2016.

Impact of Income Taxes

Income taxes are imposed on individuals and for-profit organizations by government agencies. The amount of an individual's or organization's income tax is determined by laws that specify the calculation of taxable income (the income subject to tax) and the calculation of the amount of tax on taxable income. Income taxes are computed as a percentage of taxable income, with increases in taxable income usually subject to progressively higher tax rates. The laws governing the computation of taxable income differ in many ways from the accounting principles that guide the computation of accounting income. Consequently, taxable income and accounting income are seldom the same.

In the early stages of profit planning, income taxes are sometimes incorporated in CVP models by assuming that taxable income and accounting income are identical and that the tax rate is constant. Although these assumptions are seldom true, they are useful for assisting management in developing an early prediction of the sales volume required to earn a desired after-tax profit. Once management has developed a general plan, this early prediction should be refined with the advice of tax experts.

Assuming taxes are imposed at a constant rate per dollar of before-tax profit, income taxes are computed as before-tax profit multiplied by the tax rate. After-tax profit is equal to before-tax profit minus income taxes.

$$\textbf{After-tax profit} = \textbf{Before-tax profit} - (\textbf{Before-tax profit} \times \textbf{Tax rate})$$

After-tax profit can also be expressed as before-tax profit times 1 minus the tax rate.

$$\textbf{After-tax profit} = \textbf{Before-tax profit} \times (1 - \textbf{Tax rate})$$

This formula can be rearranged to isolate before-tax profit as follows:

$$\textbf{Before-tax profit} = \frac{\textbf{After-tax profit}}{(1 - \textbf{Tax rate})}$$

Since all costs and revenues in the profit formula are expressed on a before-tax basis, the most straightforward way of determining the unit sales volume required to earn a desired after-tax profit is to:

1. Determine the required before-tax profit.
2. Substitute the required before-tax profit into the profit formula.
3. Solve for the required unit sales volume.

To illustrate, assume that Razor is subject to a 40 percent tax rate and that management desires to earn an after-tax profit of $75,000 for November 2017. The required before-tax profit is $125,000 [$75,000 ÷ (1 − 0.40)], and the unit sales volume required to earn this profit is 7,955 units [($50,000 + $125,000) ÷ $22]. Rounded to the nearest whole unit.

Income taxes increase the sales volume required to earn a desired after-tax profit. A 40 percent tax rate increased the sales volume required for Razor to earn an after-tax profit of $75,000 from 5,682 to 7,955 units. These amounts are verified in **Exhibit 15.5**.

Another way to remember the computation of before-tax profit is shown on the right side of **Exhibit 15.5**. The before-tax profit represents 100 percent of the pie, with 40 percent going to income taxes and 60 percent remaining after taxes. Working back from the remaining 60 percent ($75,000), we can determine the 100 percent (before-tax profit) by dividing after-tax profit by 0.60.

EXHIBIT 15.5	Contribution Income Statement with Income Taxes

RAZOR COMPANY
Contribution Income Statement
Planned for the Month of November 2017

Sales (7,955 × $60)		$477,300	
Less variable costs			
Direct materials (7,955 × $20)	$159,100		
Direct labor (7,955 × $10)	79,550		
Manufacturing overhead (7,955 × $3)	23,865		
Selling and administrative (7,955 × $5)	39,775	(302,290)	
Contribution margin		175,010	
Less fixed costs			
Manufacturing overhead	35,000		
Selling and administrative	15,000	50,000	
Before-tax profit		125,000*	100%
Income taxes ($125,000 × 0.40)		(50,000)	(40)%
After-tax profit		$ 75,000	60%

*Calculated total is $125,010. Difference is due to rounding.

MID-CHAPTER REVIEW 3

Assume **Solo Cup Company** produces 16-ounce beverage containers. Further assume Solo sells the cups for $40 per box of 50 containers. Variable and fixed costs follow:

Variable Costs per Box			Fixed Costs per Month	
Manufacturing			Manufacturing overhead...........	$15,000
Direct materials	$15		Selling and administrative.........	10,000
Direct labor....................	3		Total	$25,000
Manufacturing overhead........	10	$28		
Selling and administrative........		2		
Total		$30		

Suppose in September 2017, Solo produced and sold 3,000 boxes of beverage containers.

REQUIRED
a. Prepare a cost-volume-profit graph with unit sales as the independent variable. Label the revenue line, total costs line, fixed costs line, loss area, profit area, and break-even point. The recommended scale for the horizontal axis is 0 to 5,000 units, and the recommended scale for the vertical axis is $0 to $200,000.
b. Determine Solo's monthly break-even point in units.
c. Determine the monthly dollar sales required for a monthly profit of $5,000 (ignoring taxes).
d. Assuming Solo is subject to a 40 percent income tax, determine the monthly unit sales required to produce a monthly after-tax profit of $4,500.

The solution to this review problem can be found on pages 722–723.

LO4 Analyze the profitability and sales mix of a multiple-product firm.

MULTIPLE-PRODUCT COST-VOLUME-PROFIT ANALYSIS
Determining Break-Even and Target Profit Sales Dollars

Unit cost information is not always available or appropriate when analyzing cost-volume-profit relationships of multiple-product firms. Assuming the sales mix is constant, the contribution margin ratio (the portion of each sales dollar contributed toward covering fixed costs and earning a profit) can be used to determine the break-even dollar sales volume or the dollar sales volume required to achieve a desired profit. Treating a dollar of sales revenue as a unit, the break-even point in dollars is computed as fixed costs divided by the contribution margin ratio (the number of cents from each dollar of revenue contributed to covering fixed costs and providing a profit).

$$\text{Dollar break-even point} = \frac{\text{Fixed costs}}{\text{Contribution margin ratio}}$$

If unit selling price and cost information were not available, Razor's dollar break-even point could be computed as $136,351 ($50,000 ÷ 0.3667). Rounded to the nearest whole unit.

Corresponding computations can be made to find the dollar sales volume required to achieve a desired profit as follows.

$$\text{Target dollar sales volume} = \frac{\text{Fixed costs} + \text{Desired profit}}{\text{Contribution margin ratio}}$$

To achieve a desired profit of $82,000, Razor needs sales of $359,967 [($50,000 + $82,000) ÷ 0.3667]. Rounded to the nearest whole unit.

These relationships can be graphed by placing sales dollars, rather than unit sales, on the horizontal axis. The slope of the variable and total cost lines, identified as the **variable cost ratio**, presents variable costs as a portion of sales revenue. It indicates the number of cents from each sales dollar required to pay variable costs. The Business Insight box below demonstrates how CVP information can be developed from the published financial statements of a multiple-product firm.

BUSINESS INSIGHT

Using CVP for Financial Analysis and Prediction **Apple Inc.** manufactures consumer electronics including the iPhone, Mac computers, and other devices. We can use historical data to predict future costs through the cost-volume-profit method. We used data from the condensed 2013 and 2014 income statements (in millions) to predict 2015 costs:

	For the Year Ending	
	September 31, 2014	September 31, 2013
Sales	$182,795	$170,910
Cost of sales and operating expenses	(130,292)	(121,911)
Operating profit	$ 52,503	$ 48,999

We can use the high-low method to understand Apple's cost-volume-profit relationships and forecast profits based on expected sales. The first step is to calculate variable costs as a percentage of sales:

$$\text{Variable cost ratio} = \frac{\$130,292 - \$121,911}{\$182,795 - \$170,910} = 0.7052$$

Next, use this ratio to estimate Apple's fixed costs by subtracting variable costs from total costs for either period. Based on 2014 revenues and variable costs, we can calculate fixed costs as:

Annual fixed costs = $130,292 − ($182,795 × 0.7052) = $1,385 million

Our estimate of Apple's cost function is:

Total annual costs = $1,385 million + (0.7052 × Sales)

Apple's break-even sales can be calculated using fixed cost and contribution margin (1 minus the variable cost ratio).

Break-even point = $1,385 million/(1 − 0.7052) = $4,698 million

In 2015 sales were $233,715 million and operating income was $71,230 million. Based on the CVP relationships developed above and 2015 sales, the predicted level of operating income is:

Predicted operating income = $233,715 − [($233,715 × 0.7052) + $1,385] = $67,514

The error in this estimate suggests that Apple's cost structure has changed somewhat over the past three years.

Sales Mix Analysis

Sales mix refers to the relative portion of unit or dollar sales that are derived from each product. One of the limiting assumptions of the basic cost-volume-profit model is that the analysis is for a single product or the sales mix is constant. When the sales mix is constant, managers of multiple-product organizations can use the average unit contribution margin, or the average contribution margin ratio, to determine the break-even point or the sales volume required for a desired profit. Often, however, management is interested in the effect of a change in the sales mix rather than a change in the sales volume at a constant mix. In this situation, it is necessary to determine either the average unit contribution margin or the average contribution margin ratio for each alternative mix.

Unit Sales Analysis   Assume the **Hallmark Cards** sells two kinds of greeting cards, regular and deluxe. At a 1:1 (one-to-one) unit sales mix in which Hallmark sells one box of regular cards for every box of deluxe cards, assume the following revenue and cost information is available:

	Regular Box	Deluxe Box	Average Box*
Unit selling price..................................	$4	$12	$8
Unit variable costs	(3)	(3)	(3)
Unit contribution margin.........................	$1	$ 9	$5
Fixed costs per month			$15,000

* At a 1:1 sales mix, the average unit contribution margin is $5[{($1 × 1 unit) + ($9 × 1 unit)} ÷ 2 units].

At a 1:1 mix, Hallmark's assumed monthly break-even sales volume is 3,000 units ($15,000 ÷ $5), consisting of 1,500 boxes of regular cards and 1,500 boxes of deluxe cards. The top line in **Exhibit 15.6** represents the current sales mix. Suppose management wants to know the break-even sales volume if the unit sales mix became 3:1; that is, on average, a sale of 4 units contains 3 regular units and 1 deluxe unit. With no changes in the selling prices or variable costs of individual products, the average contribution margin becomes $3[{($1 × 3 units) + ($9 × 1 unit)} ÷ 4 units], and the revised break-even sales volume is 5,000 units ($15,000 ÷ $3). The revised break-even sales volume includes 3,750 boxes of regular cards [5,000 × $\frac{3}{4}$] and 1,250 boxes of deluxe cards [5,000 × $\frac{1}{4}$].

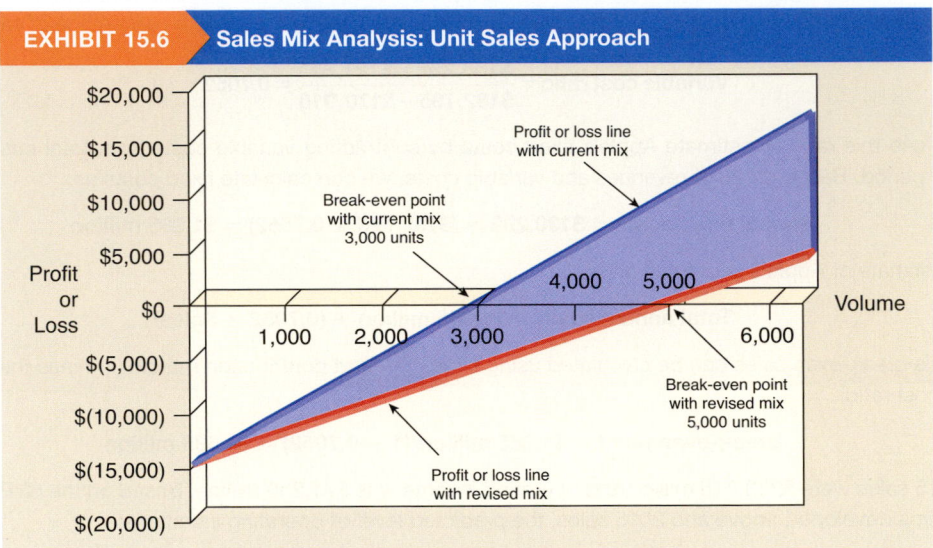

EXHIBIT 15.6   Sales Mix Analysis: Unit Sales Approach

The bottom line in **Exhibit 15.6** represents the revised sales mix. Because a greater portion of the revised mix consists of lower contribution margin regular cards, the shift in the mix increases the break-even point.

Sales Dollar Analysis   The preceding analysis focused on units and the unit contribution margin. An alternative approach focuses on sales dollars and the contribution margin ratio. Following this approach, the sales mix is expressed in terms of sales dollars.

Assume Hallmark's current sales dollars are 25 percent from regular cards and 75 percent from deluxe cards. The following display indicates the contribution margin ratios at the current sales mix and monthly volume of 5,400 units.

	Regular	Deluxe	Total
Unit sales	2,700	2,700	
Selling price	$4.00	$12.00	
Sales...	$10,800	$32,400	$43,200
Variable costs......................................	8,100	8,100	16,200
Contribution margin	$ 2,700	$24,300	$27,000
Contribution margin ratio	0.25	0.75	0.625

If monthly fixed costs are $15,000, Hallmark's current break-even sales revenue is $24,000 ($15,000 ÷ 0.625), consisting of $6,000 from regular cards ($24,000 × 0.25) and $18,000 from deluxe cards ($24,000 × 0.75). The top line in **Exhibit 15.7** illustrates the current sales mix.

Now suppose management wants to know the break-even sales volume if the dollar sales mix became 70 percent regular and 30 percent deluxe. With no changes in the selling prices or variable costs of individual products, the total contribution margin ratio becomes 0.40 [(0.25 × 0.70) + (0.75 × 0.30)], and the revised break-even sales volume is $37,500 ($15,000 ÷ 0.40). The revised break-even sales volume includes $26,250 from regular cards ($37,500 × 0.70) and $11,250 from deluxe cards (37,500 × 0.30).

The bottom line in **Exhibit 15.7** represents the revised sales mix. Because a greater portion of the revised mix consists of lower contribution ratio regular cards, the shift in the mix increases the break-even point.

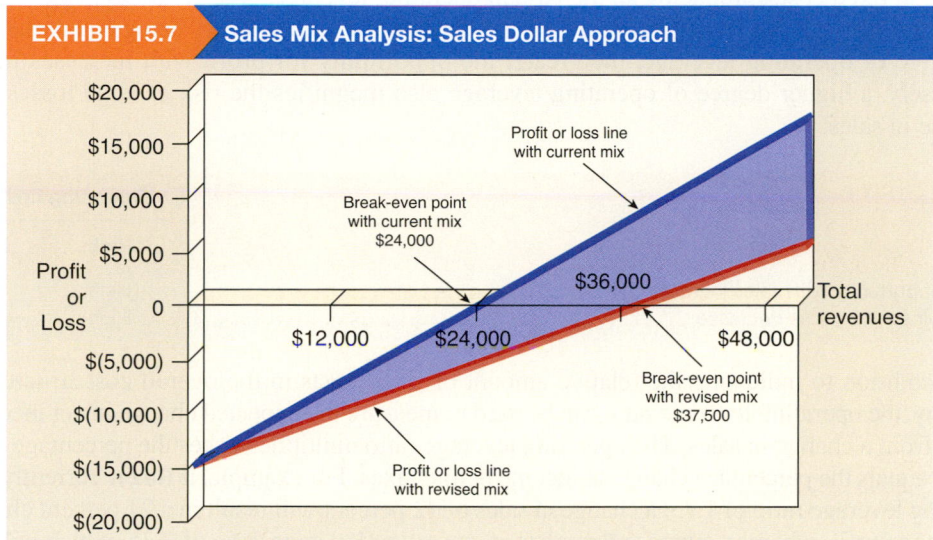

EXHIBIT 15.7   Sales Mix Analysis: Sales Dollar Approach

Sales mix analysis is important in multiple-product or service organizations. Management is just as concerned with the mix of products as with the total unit or dollar sales volume. A shift in the sales mix can have a significant impact on the bottom line. Profits may decline, even when sales increase, if the mix shifts toward products or services with lower unit margins. Conversely, profits may increase, even when sales decline, if the mix shifts toward products or services with higher unit margins. Other things being equal, managers of for-profit organizations strive to increase sales of high-margin products or services.

MID-CHAPTER REVIEW 4

Suppose the Coffee Bean has a new shop in a Cambridge village shopping center that sells high-end teas and coffees. Further, suppose it has added smoothie drinks to its product line. Below are the assumed sales and cost data for the company:

	Coffee	Tea	Smoothie
Sales price per (12 oz.) serving.	$1.35	$1.25	$1.95
Variable cost per serving.	0.60	0.45	0.75
Fixed costs per month $8,000			

Suppose the company sells each month an average of 6,000 servings of coffee, 3,750 servings of tea, and 2,250 servings of smoothies.

REQUIRED

a. Calculate the current before-tax profit, contribution margin ratio, and sales mix based on sales dollars.
b. Using a sales dollar analysis, calculate the monthly break-even point assuming the sales mix does not change.

The solution to this review problem can be found on page 723.

LO5 Apply operating leverage ratio to assess opportunities for profit and the risks of loss.

ANALYSIS OF OPERATING LEVERAGE

Operating leverage refers to the extent that an organization's costs are fixed. The **operating leverage ratio** is computed as the contribution margin divided by before-tax profit as follows.

$$\text{Operating leverage ratio} = \frac{\text{Contribution margin}}{\text{Before-tax profits}}$$

The rationale underlying this computation is that as fixed costs are substituted for variable costs, the contribution margin as a percentage of income before taxes increases. Hence, a high degree of operating leverage signals the existence of a high portion of fixed costs. As noted in Chapter 13, the shift from labor-based to automated activities has resulted in a decrease in variable costs and an increase in fixed costs, producing an increase in operating leverage.

Operating leverage is a measure of risk and opportunity. Other things being equal, the higher the degree of operating leverage, the greater the opportunity for profit with increases in sales. Conversely, a higher degree of operating leverage also magnifies the risk of large losses with a decrease in sales.

	Operating Leverage	
	High	**Low**
Profit opportunity with sales increase	High	Low
Risk of loss with sales decrease	High	Low

In addition to indicating the relative amount of fixed costs in the overall cost structure of a company, the operating leverage ratio can be used to measure the expected change in net income resulting from a change in sales. The operating leverage ratio multiplied times the percentage change in sales equals the percentage change in income before taxes. For example, if **Razor** currently has an operating leverage ratio of 1.73, a change in sales of 12 percent will result in a 21 percent change in before-tax profit; whereas, suppose **Envy** has an operating leverage ratio of 2.35, which will result in an increase in before-tax profit of 28%.

	Current		Projected	
	Razor	**Envy**	**Razor**	**Envy**
Unit selling price.........................	$ 60	$ 60	$ 60	$ 60
Unit variable costs	(38)	(30)	(38)	(30)
Unit contribution margin..................	$ 22	$ 30	$ 22	$ 30
Unit sales	× 5,400	× 5,400	× 6,048	× 6,048
Contribution margin	$118,800	$162,000	$133,056	$181,440
Fixed costs.............................	(50,000)	(93,200)	(50,000)	(93,200)
Before-tax profit........................	$ 68,800	$ 68,800	$ 83,056	$ 88,240
Contribution margin	$118,800	$162,000		
Before-tax profit........................	÷ 68,800	÷ 68,800		
Operating leverage ratio.................	1.73*	2.35*		
Percent increase in sales			12%	12%
Percent increase in income before taxes.....			21%*	28%*

* Rounded

Although both companies have identical before-tax profits at a sales volume of 5,400 units, assume Envy has a higher degree of operating leverage and its profits vary more with changes in sales volume.

If sales are projected to increase by 12 percent, from 5,400 to 6,048 units, the percentage of increase in each firm's profits is computed as the percent change in sales multiplied by the degree of operating leverage.

	Razor	Envy
Increase in sales.	12%	12%
Degree of operating leverage.	× 1.73	× 2.35
Increase in profits.	21%*	28%*

* Rounded

As noted in the following Business Insight box, operating leverage is an important consideration when changes in demand, and consequently sales, occur.

Management is interested in measures of operating leverage to determine how sensitive profits are to changes in sales. Risk-averse managers strive to maintain a lower operating leverage, even if this results in some loss of profits. One way to reduce operating leverage is to use more direct labor and less automated equipment. Another way is to contract outside organizations to perform tasks that could be done internally. While operating leverage is a useful analytic tool, long-run success comes from keeping the overall level of costs down, while providing customers with the products or services they want at competitive prices.

BUSINESS INSIGHT

Mining Companies Fight for Financial Flexibility When Prices Fall   While larger mining companies like **BHP Billiton** and **Rio Tinto** have the flexibility to maintain output when ore prices fall, smaller miners like the **Australian Fortescue Metals Group** struggle to deal with low prices. Cost cutting can only help so much when debt is nearly four times earnings. This makes Fortescue's profit exceptionally sensitive to sale price and volume; hence, China's slowdown in economic growth has corresponded to a 90% drop in profit for the company. As a result, Fortescue and other mid-sized mining firms are rushing to restructure their debt.

In response to the same pressures, other mining companies, like **AngloAmerican**, are selling assets to reduce operational leverage. In contrast, **South32**, a recent BHP Billiton spin-off, is less sensitive to demand fluctuations because its net debt is less than a quarter of pretax earnings. South32's more nimble financial structure makes it much easier for the company to deal with fluctuations in price and demand. Financial flexibility is an important consideration in industries such as mining, where fixed costs are high and demand is sensitive to macroeconomic fluctuations.

Source: "Miners: In Search of Flexibility," *Financial Times*, August 25, 2015, London edition, 14.

YOU MAKE THE CALL

You are the Division Manager   As manager of a division responsible for both production and sales of products and, hence, division profits, you are looking for ways to leverage the profits of your division to a higher level. You are considering changing your cost structure to include more fixed costs and less variable costs by automating some of the production activities currently performed by people. What are some of the considerations that you should keep in mind as you ponder this decision? [Answer, p. 707]

CHAPTER-END REVIEW

Suppose the Coffee Bean has a new shop in a Cambridge village shopping center that sells high-end teas and coffees. Further, suppose it has added smoothie drinks to its product line. Below are the assumed sales and cost data for the company:

	Coffee	Tea	Smoothie
Sales price per (12 oz.) serving.	$1.35	$1.25	$1.95
Variable cost per serving.	0.60	0.45	0.75
Fixed costs per month $8,000			

Suppose the company sells each month an average of 6,000 servings of coffee, 3,750 servings of tea, and 2,250 servings of smoothies.

Continued

Continued from previous page

REQUIRED
Calculate Coffee Bean's operating leverage ratio. If sales increase by 20 percent, by how much will before-tax income be expected to change? If sales decrease by 20 percent, by how much will before-tax income be expected to change?

The solution to this review problem can be found on page 724.

LO6 Perform profitability analysis with unit and nonunit cost drivers.

6

APPENDIX 15A: Profitability Analysis with Unit and Nonunit Cost Drivers

A major limitation of cost-volume-profit analysis and the related contribution income statement is the exclusive use of unit-level activity cost drivers. Even when multiple products are considered, the CVP approach either restates volume in terms of an average unit or in terms of a dollar of sales volume. Additionally, CVP analysis does not consider other categories of cost drivers.

We now expand profitability analysis to incorporate nonunit cost drivers. While the addition of multiple levels of cost drivers makes it difficult to develop graphical relationships (illustrating the impact of cost driver changes on revenues, costs, and profits), it is possible to modify the traditional contribution income statement to incorporate a hierarchy of cost drivers. The expanded framework is not only more accurate, but it encourages management to ask important questions concerning costs and profitability.

Multi-Level Contribution Income Statement

To illustrate the use of profitability analysis with unit and nonunit cost drivers, assume **Anthropologie**, a multiple-product merchandising organization, has the following cost hierarchy:

Unit-level activities	
Cost of goods sold	$0.80 per sales dollar
Order-level activities	
Cost of processing order	$20 per order
Customer-level activities	
Mail, phone, sales visits, recordkeeping, etc.	$200 per customer per year
Facility-level costs	
Depreciation, manager salaries, insurance, etc.	$120,000 per year

Assume that Anthropologie is subject to a 40 percent income tax rate and has the following plans for the year 2017:

Sales	$3,000,000
Number of sales orders	3,200
Number of customers	**400**

While Anthropologie's plans could be summarized in a functional income statement, we have previously considered the limitations of such statements for management. Contribution income statements are preferred because they correspond to the cost classification scheme used in CVP analysis. In this case, Anthropologie's cost structure (unit level, order level, customer level, and facility level) does not correspond to the classification scheme used in traditional contribution income statements (variable and fixed). The problem occurs because traditional contribution income statements consider only unit-level cost drivers. When a larger set of unit and nonunit cost drivers is used for cost analysis, an expanded contribution income statement should be used for profitability analysis.

A hypothetical multi-level contribution income statement for Anthropologie is presented in **Exhibit 15A.1**. Costs are separated using a cost hierarchy and there are several contribution margins, one for each level of costs that responds to a short-run change in activity. Suppose that in the case of Anthropologie, the contribution margins are at the unit level, order level, and customer level. Because the facility-level costs do not vary with short-run variations in activity, the final customer-level contribution goes to cover facility-level costs and to provide for a profit. If a company had a different activity cost hierarchy, it would use a different set of contribution margins.

EXHIBIT 15A.1 **Multi-Level Contribution Income Statement with Taxes**

ANTHROPOLOGIE
Multi-Level Contribution Income Statement
For Year 2017

Sales.	$3,000,000
Less unit-level costs	
Cost of goods sold ($3,000,000 × 0.80)	(2,400,000)
Unit-level contribution margin	600,000
Less order-level costs	
Cost of processing order (3,200 orders × $20)	(64,000)
Order-level contribution margin	536,000
Less customer-level costs	
Mail, phone, sales visits, recordkeeping, etc. (400 customers × $200).	(80,000)
Customer-level contribution margin.	456,000
Less facility-level costs	
Depreciation, manager salaries, insurance, etc..	(120,000)
Before-tax profit.	336,000
Income taxes ($336,000 × 0.40)	(134,400)
After-tax profit	$ 201,600

A number of additional questions of interest to management can be formulated and answered using the multi-level hierarchy. Consider the following examples:

- Holding the number of sales orders and customers constant, what is the break-even dollar sales volume? The answer is found by treating all other costs as fixed and dividing the total nonunit-level costs by the contribution margin ratio. Here the contribution margin ratio indicates how many cents of each sales dollar is available for profits and costs above the unit level.

$$\text{Unit-Level Break-Even Point In Dollars With No Changes In Other Costs} = \frac{\text{Current Order-Level Costs} + \text{Current Customer-Level Costs} + \text{Facility-Level Costs}}{\text{Contribution Margin Ratio}}$$

$$= (\$64{,}000 + \$80{,}000 + \$120{,}000) \div (1 - 0.80)$$
$$= \$1{,}320{,}000$$

- What order size is required to break even on an individual order? Answering this question might help management to evaluate the desirability of establishing a minimum order size. To break even, each order must have a unit-level contribution equal to the order-level costs. Any additional contribution is used to cover customer- and facility-level costs and provide for a profit.

$$\text{Break-even order size} = \$20 \div (1 - 0.80)$$
$$= \$100$$

- What sales volume is required to break even on an average customer? Answering this question might help management to evaluate the desirability of retaining certain customers. Based on the preceding information, an average customer places 8 orders per year (3,200 orders ÷ 400 customers). With costs of $20 per order and $200 per customer, the sales to an average customer must generate an annual contribution of $360 [($20 × 8) + $200]. Hence, the break-even level for an average customer is $1,800 [$360 ÷ (1 − 0.80)]. Management might consider discontinuing relations with customers with annual purchases of less than this amount. Alternatively, they might inquire as to whether such customers could be served in a less costly manner.

The concepts of multi-level break-even analysis and profitability analysis are finding increasing use as companies such as **FedEx**, **Best Buy**, and **Bank of America** strive to identify profitable and unprofitable customers. At FedEx, customers are sometimes rated as "the good, the bad, and the ugly." FedEx strives to retain the "good" profitable customers, turn the "bad" into profitable customers, and ignore the "ugly" who seem unlikely to become profitable.

Variations in Multi-Level Contribution Income Statement

Classification schemes should be designed to fit the organization and user needs. In Chapter 14, when analyzing the costs of a manufacturing company, we used a manufacturing cost hierarchy. While formatting issues can seem mundane and routine, format is important because the way information is presented encourages certain types of questions while discouraging others. Hence, management accountants must inquire as to user needs before developing management accounting reports, just as users of management accounting information should be knowledgeable enough to request appropriate information and know whether the information they are receiving is the information they need. With computers to reduce computational drudgery and to provide a wealth of available data, the most important issues involve identifying the important questions and presenting information to address those questions.

In the case of Anthropologie, we used a customer cost hierarchy with information presented in a single column. A multiple-column format is also useful for presenting and analyzing information. Assume that Anthropologie's managment believes that the differences between the in-store and internet-based markets are such that these markets could be better served with separate marketing activities. They would have two market segments, one for the in-store customers and one for internet-based customers, giving the following cost hierarchy:

1. Unit-level activities
2. Order-level activities
3. Customer-level activities
4. Market segment activities
5. Facility-level activities

One possible way of presenting Anthropologie's 2017 hypothetical multi-level income statement with two market segments is shown in **Exhibit 15A.2**. The details underlying the development of this statement are not presented. In developing the statement, we assume the mix of units sold, their cost structure, and the costs of processing an order are unchanged. Finally, we present new market segment costs and assume that the addition of the segments allows for some reduction in previous facility-level costs.

The information in the total column is all that is required for a multi-level contribution income statement. The information in the two detailed columns for the government and private segments can, however, prove useful in analyzing the profitability of each. Observe that the facility-level costs, incurred for the benefit of both segments, are not assigned to specific segments. Depending on the nature of the goods sold, it may be possible to further analyze the profitability of each product (or type of product) sold in each market segment. The profitability analysis of business segments is more closely examined in Chapter 23.

EXHIBIT 15A.2	Multi-Level Contribution Income Statement with Segments and Taxes		

ANTHROPOLOGIE
Multi-Level Contribution Income Statement
For Year 2017

	In-Store Segment	Internet Segment	Total
Sales.	$1,500,000	$2,000,000	$3,500,000
Less unit-level costs			
Cost of goods sold (0.80)	(1,200,000)	(1,600,000)	(2,800,000)
Unit-level contribution margin	300,000	400,000	700,000
Less order-level costs			
Cost of processing order			
(1,000 × $20; 3,000 × $20)	(20,000)	(60,000)	(80,000)
Order-level contribution margin	280,000	340,000	620,000
Less customer-level costs			
Mail, phone, sales visits, recordkeeping, etc.			
(150 × $200, 300 × $200)	(30,000)	(60,000)	(90,000)
Customer-level contribution margin.	250,000	280,000	530,000
Less market segment-level costs.	(80,000)	(20,000)	(100,000)
Market segment-level contribution.	$ 170,000	$ 260,000	430,000
Less facility-level costs			
Depreciation, manager salaries, insurance, etc.			(90,000)
Before-tax profit			340,000
Income taxes ($340,000 × 0.40)			(136,000)
After-tax profit			$ 204,000

APPENDIX 15A REVIEW

7-Eleven operates a number of convenience stores worldwide. Assume that an analysis of operating costs, customer sales, and customer patronage reveals the following:

Fixed costs per store	$80,000/year
Variable cost ratio	0.80
Average sale per customer visit	$17.00
Average customer visits per week	1.50
Customers as portion of city population	0.05

REQUIRED
Determine the city population required for a single 7-Eleven to earn an annual profit of $40,000.

The solution to this review problem can be found on page 724.

GUIDANCE ANSWERS . . . YOU MAKE THE CALL

You are the Division Manager Fixed costs represent a two-edged sword. When a company is growing its sales, fixed costs cause profits to grow faster than sales; however, if a company should experience declining sales, the rate of reduction in profits is greater than the rate of reduction in sales. When sales decline, variable costs decline proportionately, while fixed costs continue. For this reason, when a company faces serious declines that are expected to continue, one of the first steps its top management should consider is reducing capacity in order to reduce fixed costs. The automobile companies in the U.S. have been employing this technique in recent years to try to offset the effect of sales lost to importers.

KEY RATIOS

Profit = Revenues − Total costs

Revenues = Unit selling price × Unit sales volume

Total costs = Fixed costs + (Unit variable costs × Unit sales)

Profit: $\pi = pX 2 (a + bX)$
Where p = unit selling price, X = unit sales, a = fixed costs, b = unit variable costs.

$$\text{Break-even unit sales volume} = \frac{\text{Fixed costs}}{\text{Selling price per unit} - \text{Variable costs per unit}}$$

$$\text{Break-even unit sales volume} = \frac{\text{Fixed costs}}{\text{Unit contribution margin}}$$

$$\text{Target unit sales volume} = \frac{\text{Fixed costs} + \text{Desired profit}}{\text{Unit contribution margin}}$$

After-tax profit = Before-tax profit × (1 − Tax rate)

$$\text{Dollar break-even point} = \frac{\text{Fixed costs}}{\text{Contribution margin ratio}}$$

$$\text{Target dollar sales volume} = \frac{\text{Fixed costs} + \text{Desired profit}}{\text{Contribution margin ratio}}$$

$$\text{Operating leverage ratio} = \frac{\text{Contribution margin}}{\text{Before-tax profits}}$$

KEY TERMS

break-even point, 692

contribution income statement, 690

contribution margin, 690

contribution margin ratio, 691

cost-volume-profit (CVP) analysis, 686

cost-volume-profit graph, 694

direct labor, 689

direct materials, 688

fixed manufacturing overhead, 689

fixed selling and administrative costs, 689

functional income statement, 690

margin of safety, 692

operating leverage, 702

operating leverage ratio, 702

profitability analysis, 686

profit-volume graph, 695

sales mix, 687, 699

sensitivity analysis, 691

unit contribution margin, 691

variable cost ratio, 698

variable manufacturing overhead, 689

variable selling and administrative costs, 689

Assignments with the 🔴 **logo in the margin are available in** BusinessCourse.
See the Preface of the book for details.

MULTIPLE CHOICE

1. With fixed costs of $20,000/month and variable costs of $3/unit, Ace reported a monthly profit of $5,000 at a volume of 12,500 units. The unit selling price was:
   a. $1.60
   b. $3.00
   c. $4.60
   d. $5.00

2. Presented is information from Wayne's contribution income statement:

Sales..		$70,000
Less variable costs:		
Manufacturing	$20,000	
Selling and administrative	10,000	(30,000)
Contribution margin		40,000
Less fixed costs:		
Manufacturing	15,000	
Selling and administrative	8,000	(23,000)
Profit..		$17,000

With a functional income statement Wayne would have reported a gross margin of:
   a. $35,000
   b. $40,000
   c. $47,000
   d. $50,000

3. Based on the information in question 2, if Wayne had a $5,000 increase in sales, profits would increase by:
   a. $5,000
   b. $3,570
   c. $2,857
   d. $2,500

4. Penn Company produces a product sold for $40 per unit. Variable and fixed cost information is presented below:

Variable costs per unit		Fixed costs per month	
Manufacturing	$ 8	Manufacturing	$29,000
Selling and administrative	2	Selling and administrative	16,000
Total	$10	Total	$45,000

The sales volume required for a monthly profit of $36,000 is:
a.   900 units
b.   2,050 units
c.   2,700 units
d.   3,600 units

5.   Based on the information in question 4, with an income tax rate of 40 percent the sales volume required for a monthly after-tax profit of $36,000 is:
a.   2,000 units
b.   3,500 units
c.   3,700 units
d.   4,500 units

6.   The Pitch sells 1 select style soccer ball for every 3 classic style balls. The select and classic style balls, respectively, sell for $40 and $20 and have unit variable costs of $20 and $10. Assuming a constant sales mix and total fixed costs for the company of $120,000, the break-even unit sales volume is:
a.   7,200
b.   384,000
c.   9,600
d.   9,023

7.   Each of the following is true *except*:
a.   Operating leverage is a measure of a firm's fixed costs.
b.   Operating leverage is a measure of risk and opportunity.
c.   The lower the degree of operating leverage, the greater the opportunity for profit with increases in sales.
d.   Operating leverage can be used to measure the expected change in net income resulting from a change in sales.

QUESTIONS

Q15-1.   What is cost-volume-profit analysis and when is it particularly useful?
Q15-2.   Identify the important assumptions that underlie cost-volume-profit analysis.
Q15-3.   When is it most reasonable to use a single independent variable in cost-volume-profit analysis?
Q15-4.   Distinguish between a contribution and a functional income statement.
Q15-5.   What is the unit contribution margin? How is it used in computing the unit break-even point?
Q15-6.   What is the contribution margin ratio and when is it most useful?
Q15-7.   How is the break-even equation modified to take into account the sales required to earn a desired profit?
Q15-8.   How does a profit-volume graph differ from a cost-volume-profit graph? When is a profit-volume graph most likely to be used?
Q15-9.   What impact do income taxes have on the sales volume required to earn a desired after-tax profit?
Q15-10. How are profit opportunities and the risk of losses affected by operating leverage?

MINI EXERCISES

M15-11. Profitability Analysis

LO3

Assume Strands, a local hair salon, provides cuts, perms, and hairstyling services. Annual fixed costs are $150,000, and variable costs are 40 percent of sales revenue. Last year's revenues totaled $300,000.

REQUIRED
a.   Determine its break-even point in sales dollars.
b.   Determine last year's margin of safety in sales dollars.
c.   Determine the sales dollar required for an annual profit of $80,000.

LO3 **M15-12. Cost-Volume-Profit Graph: Identification and Sensitivity Analysis**

A typical cost-volume-profit graph is presented below.

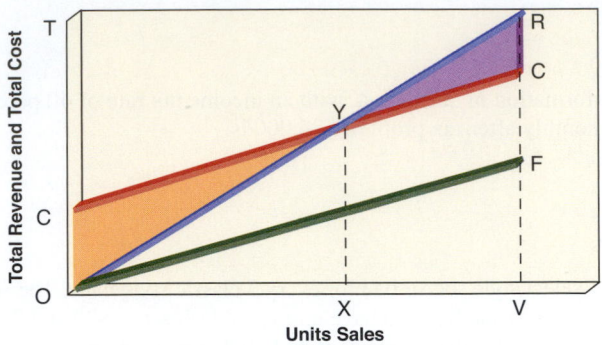

REQUIRED

a. Identify each of the following:
1. Line OF
2. Line OR
3. Line CC
4. The difference between lines OF and OV at any given number of unit sales
5. The difference between lines CC and OF at any given number of unit sales
6. The difference between lines CC and OV at any given number of unit sales
7. The difference between lines OR and OF at any given number of unit sales
8. Point X
9. Area CYO
10. Area RCY

b. Indicate the effect of each of the following independent events on lines CC, OR, and the break-even point:
1. A decrease in fixed costs
2. An increase in unit selling price
3. An increase in the variable costs per unit
4. An increase in fixed costs and a decrease in the unit selling price
5. A decrease in fixed costs and a decrease in the unit variable costs

LO3 **M15-13. Profit-Volume Graph: Identification and Sensitivity Analysis**

A typical profit-volume graph follows.

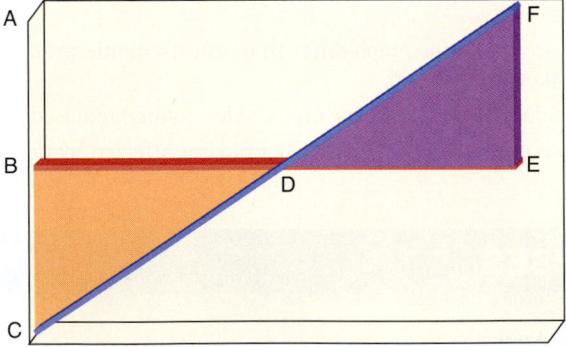

REQUIRED

a. Identify each of the following:
1. Area BDC
2. Area DEF
3. Point D
4. Line AC
5. Line BC
6. Line EF

b. Indicate the effect of each of the following on line CF and the break-even point:
1. An increase in the unit selling price
2. An increase in the variable costs per unit
3. A decrease in fixed costs
4. An increase in fixed costs and a decrease in the unit selling price
5. A decrease in fixed costs and an increase in the variable costs per unit

M15-14. Preparing Cost-Volume-Profit and Profit-Volume Graphs

LO3
Connie's Pizza

Assume a **Connie's Pizza** shop has the following monthly revenue and cost functions:

Total revenues = $10.00X

Total costs = $17,000 + $4.00X

REQUIRED

a. Prepare a graph (similar to that in **Exhibit 15.3**) illustrating Connie's cost-volume-profit relationships. The vertical axis should range from $0 to $72,000, in increments of $12,000. The horizontal axis should range from 0 units to 6,000 units, in increments of 2,000 units.
b. Prepare a graph (similar to that in **Exhibit 15.4**) illustrating Connie's profit-volume relationships. The horizontal axis should range from 0 units to 6,000 units, in increments of 2,000 units.
c. When is it most appropriate to use a profit-volume graph?

M15-15. Preparing Cost-Volume-Profit and Profit-Volume Graphs

LO3

Tacos Locos is a taco concession business operating at five soccer parks. It sells large carnitas tacos for $6.00 each. Variable costs are $4.50 per taco, and fixed operating costs are $750,000 per year.

REQUIRED

a. Determine the annual break-even point in tacos.
b. Prepare a cost-volume-profit graph for the company. Use a format that emphasizes the contribution margin. The vertical axis should vary between $0 and $5,000,000 in increments of $1,000,000. The horizontal axis should vary between 0 tacos and 1,000,000 tacos, in increments of 250,000 tacos. Label the graph in thousands.
c. Prepare a profit-volume graph for the company. The vertical axis should vary between $(750,000) and $750,000 in increments of $150,000. The horizontal axis should vary as described in requirement (b). Label the graph in thousands.
d. Evaluate the profit-volume graph. In what ways is it superior and in what ways is it inferior to the traditional cost-volume-profit graph?

M15-16. Multiple Product Break-Even Analysis

LO4
MBC
Reebok
NYSE :: RBK
Bauer
ETR: B5A
Titan

Slapshot company sells three styles of youth hockey sticks: **Reebok**, **Bauer** and **Titan**. Presented is information for Slapshot's three products.

	Reebok	Bauer	Titan
Unit selling price.	$150	$200	$80
Unit variable costs	115	132	40
Unit contribution margin.	$ 35	$ 68	$40

With monthly fixed costs of $250,000, the company sells two Reebok sticks for each Bauer, and three Bauer for each Titan.

REQUIRED

Determine the number of Reebok sticks sold at the monthly break-even point.

EXERCISES

LO2, 3

E15-17. Contribution Income Statement and Cost-Volume-Profit Graph

Kopi Company produces dog cages that are sold for $40 per unit. The company produced and sold 6,000 dog cages during July 2017. There were no beginning or ending inventories. Variable and fixed costs follow.

Variable Costs per Unit			Fixed Costs per Month	
Manufacturing:			Manufacturing overhead	$40,000
Direct materials.	$10		Selling and administrative	20,000
Direct labor	2			
Manufacturing overhead.	5	$17	Total	$60,000
Selling and administrative		5		
Total		$22		

REQUIRED

a.   Prepare a contribution income statement for July.

b.   Prepare a cost-volume-profit graph. Label the horizontal axis in units with a maximum value of 10,000. Label the vertical axis in dollars with a maximum value of $400,000. Draw a vertical line on the graph for the current (6,000) unit sales level, and label total variable costs, total fixed costs, and total profits at 6,000 units.

LO3, 4

E15-18. Contribution Margin Concepts

The following information is taken from the 2017 records of Hendrix's Guitar Center.

	Fixed	Variable	Total
Sales.			$750,000
Costs			
Goods sold		$337,500	
Labor.	$160,000	60,000	
Supplies	2,000	5,000	
Utilities	12,000	13,000	
Rent	24,000	—	
Advertising	6,000	24,500	
Miscellaneous.	6,000	10,000	
Total costs.	$210,000	$450,000	(660,000)
Net income.			$ 90,000

REQUIRED

a.   Determine the annual break-even dollar sales volume.

b.   Determine the current margin of safety in dollars.

c.   Prepare a cost-volume-profit graph for the guitar shop. Label both axes in dollars with maximum values of $1,000,000. Draw a vertical line on the graph for the current ($750,000) sales level, and label total variable costs, total fixed costs, and total profits at $750,000 sales.

d.   What is the annual break-even dollar sales volume if management makes a decision that increases fixed costs by $35,000?

LO3, 4

E15-19. Multiple Product Planning with Taxes

In the year 2017, Pyramid Consulting had the following contribution income statement:

PYRAMID CONSULTING		
Contribution Income Statement		
For the Year 2017		
Sales revenue...		$1,300,000
Variable costs		
Cost of services	$420,000	
Selling and administrative...........................	200,000	(620,000)
Contribution margin		680,000
Fixed costs—selling and administrative		(285,000)
Before-tax profit.......................................		395,000
Income taxes (36%)		(142,200)
After-tax profit		$ 252,800

REQUIRED

a. Determine the annual break-even point in sales revenue.

b. Determine the annual margin of safety in sales revenue.

c. What is the break-even point in sales revenue if management makes a decision that increases fixed costs by $57,000?

d. With the current cost structure, including fixed costs of $285,000, what dollar sales revenue is required to provide an after-tax net income of $200,000?

e. Prepare an abbreviated contribution income statement to verify that the solution to requirement (d) will provide the desired after-tax income.

E15-20. Not-for-Profit Applications

LO3

Determine the solution to each of the following independent cases:

a. Collings College has annual fixed operating costs of $12,500,000 and variable operating costs of $1,000 per student. Tuition is $8,000 per student for the coming academic year, with a projected enrollment of 1,500 students. Expected revenues from endowments and federal and state grants total $250,000. Determine the amount the college must obtain from other sources.

b. The Collings College Student Association is planning a fall concert. Expected costs (renting a hall, hiring a band, etc.) are $30,000. Assuming 3,000 people attend the concert, determine the break-even price per ticket. How much will the association lose if this price is charged and only 2,700 tickets are sold?

c. City Hospital has a contract with the city to provide indigent health care on an outpatient basis for $25 per visit. The patient will pay $5 of this amount, with the city paying the balance ($20). Determine the amount the city will pay if the hospital has 10,000 patient visits.

d. A civic organization is engaged in a fund-raising program. On Civic Sunday, it will sell newspapers at $1.25 each. The organization will pay $0.75 for each newspaper. Costs of the necessary permits, signs, and so forth are $500. Determine the amount the organization will raise if it sells 5,000 newspapers.

e. Christmas for the Needy is a civic organization that provides Christmas presents to disadvantaged children. The annual costs of this activity are $5,000, plus $10 per present. Determine the number of presents the organization can provide with $20,000.

E15-21. Alternative Production Procedures and Operating Leverage

LO3, 5

Newell Brands
NYSE :: NWL

Assume Sharpie, a brand of **Newell Brands**, is planning to introduce a new executive pen that can be manufactured using either a capital-intensive method or a labor-intensive method. The predicted manufacturing costs for each method are as follows:

	Capital Intensive	Labor Intensive
Direct materials per unit.....................................	$ 5.00	$ 6.00
Direct labor per unit	$ 5.00	$10.00
Variable manufacturing overhead per unit	$ 4.00	$ 2.00
Fixed manufacturing overhead per year.......................	$2,440,000	$700,000

Sharpie's market research department has recommended an introductory unit sales price of $40. The incremental selling costs are predicted to be $500,000 per year, plus $2 per unit sold.

REQUIRED

a. Determine the annual break-even point in units if Sharpie uses the:
    1. Capital-intensive manufacturing method.
    2. Labor-intensive manufacturing method.
b. Determine the annual unit volume at which Sharpie is indifferent between the two manufacturing methods.
c. Management wants to know more about the effect of each alternative on operating leverage.
    1. Explain operating leverage and the relationship between operating leverage and the volatility of earnings.
    2. Compute operating leverage for each alternative at a volume of 250,000 units.
    3. Which alternative has the higher operating leverage? Why?

LO3, 5   **E15-22. Contribution Income Statement and Operating Leverage**

Stateline Berry Farm harvests early-season blueberries for shipment throughout Michigan and Illinois in July. The blueberry farm is maintained by a permanent staff of 10 employees and seasonal workers who pick and pack the blueberries. The blueberries are sold in crates containing 100 individually packaged one-quart containers. Affixed to each one-quart container is the distinctive Stateline Berry Farm logo inviting buyers to "Enjoy the berry best blueberries in the world!" The selling price is $90 per crate, variable costs are $80 per crate, and fixed costs are $280,000 per year. In the year 2017, Stateline Berry Farm sold 50,000 crates.

REQUIRED

a. Prepare a contribution income statement for the year ended December 31, 2017.
b. Determine the company's 2017 operating leverage.
c. Calculate the percentage change in profits if sales decrease by 10 percent.
d. Management is considering the purchase of several berry-picking machines. This will increase annual fixed costs to $375,000 and reduce variable costs to $77.50 per crate. Calculate the effect of this acquisition on operating leverage and explain any change.

LO4   **E15-23. Multiple Product Break-Even Analysis**

Joe's Tax Service prepares tax returns for low- to middle-income taxpayers. Its service operates January 2 through April 15 at a counter in a local grocery store. All jobs are classified into one of three categories: standard, multiform, and complex. Following is information for last year. Also, last year, the fixed cost of rent, utilities, and so forth were $50,000.

	Standard	Multiform	Complex
Billing rate.	$50	$125	$250
Average variable costs.	(30)	(75)	(150)
Average contribution margin	$20	$ 50	$100
Number of returns prepared.	1,750	500	250

REQUIRED

a. Determine Joe's break-even dollar sales volume.
b. Determine Joe's margin of safety in sales dollars.
c. Prepare a profit-volume graph for Joe's Tax Service.

LO3   **E15-24. Cost-Volume-Profit Relations: Missing Data**

Following are data from 4 separate companies.

	Case A	Case B	Case C	Case D
Unit sales	1,200	800	?	?
Sales revenue.	$20,000	?	?	$80,000
Variable cost per unit	$ 10	$ 1	$ 12	?
Contribution margin	?	$800	?	?
Fixed costs.	$ 7,000	?	$82,000	?
Net income.	?	$450	?	?
Unit contribution margin.	?	?	?	$ 15
Break-even point (units)	?	?	4,000	2,000
Margin of safety (units).	?	?	300	1,000

REQUIRED
Supply the missing data in each independent case.

E15-25. Cost-Volume-Profit Relations: Missing Data

Following are data from 4 separate companies.

	Case 1	Case 2	Case 3	Case 4
Sales revenue.........................	$120,000	$100,000	?	?
Contribution margin	$ 60,000	?	$20,000	?
Fixed costs.........................	$ 40,000	?	?	?
Net income.........................	?	$ 5,000	$12,000	?
Variable cost ratio....................	?	0.50	?	0.22
Contribution margin ratio	?	?	0.40	?
Break-even point (dollars)	?	?	?	$25,000
Margin of safety (dollars)	?	?	?	$20,000

REQUIRED
Supply the missing data in each independent case.

E15-26. Customer-Level Planning

Circle K

Circle K operates a number of convenience stores worldwide. Assume that an analysis of operating costs, customer sales, and customer patronage reveals the following:

Fixed costs per store	$80,000.00/year
Variable cost ratio..	0.80
Average sale per customer visit	$15.00
Average customer visits per week	1.75
Customers as portion of city population	0.04

REQUIRED
Determine the city population required for a single Circle K to earn an annual profit of $40,000.

E15-27. Multiple-Level Break-Even Analysis

Kucera Associates provides marketing services for a number of small manufacturing firms. Kucera receives a commission of 10 percent of sales. Operating costs are as follows:

Unit-level costs.......................................	$0.04 per sales dollar
Sales-level costs	$300 per sales order
Customer-level costs	$900 per customer per year
Facility-level costs	$60,000 per year

REQUIRED
a.   Determine the minimum order size in sales dollars for Kucera to break even on an order.
b.   Assuming an average customer places four orders per year, determine the minimum annual sales required to break even on a customer.
c.   What is the average order size in (b)?
d.   Assuming Kucera currently serves 100 customers, with each placing an average of four orders per year, determine the minimum annual sales required to break even.
e.   What is the average order size in (d)?
f.   Explain the differences in the answers to (a), (c), and (e).

PROBLEMS

P15-28. Profit Planning with Taxes

LO3

Rebounder Company produces a rebounding net that can be used for soccer, baseball and lacrosse. The net sells for $40 per unit. Last year, the company manufactured and sold 20,000 nets to obtain an after-tax profit of $54,000. Variable and fixed costs follow.

Variable Costs per Unit		Fixed Costs per Year	
Manufacturing	$18	Manufacturing	$ 80,000
Selling and administrative	9	Selling and administrative	30,000
Total	$27	Total	$110,000

REQUIRED

a. Determine the tax rate the company paid last year.

b. What unit sales volume is required to provide an after-tax profit of $100,000?

c. If the company reduces the unit variable cost by $3 and increases fixed manufacturing costs by $22,000, what unit sales volume is required to provide an after-tax profit of $100,000?

d. What assumptions are made about taxable income and tax rates in requirements (a) through (c)?

LO2, 3   P15-29. Contribution Income Statement, Cost-Volume-Profit Graph, and Taxes

New York Tours (NYT) provides daily sightseeing tours that include transportation, admission to selected attractions, and lunch. Ticket prices are $85 each. During June 2017, NYT provided 3,000 tours.

Variable Costs per Customer		Fixed Costs per Month	
Admission fees.	$30	Operations	$25,000
Lunch	17	Selling and administration	15,000
Overhead	10		
Selling and administrative	8		
Total	$65	Total	$40,000

NYT is subject to an income tax rate of 40 percent.

REQUIRED

a. Prepare a contribution income statement for June.

b. Determine NYT's monthly break-even point in units.

c. Determine NYT's margin of safety for June 2017.

d. Determine the unit sales required for a monthly after-tax profit of $15,000.

e. Prepare a cost-volume-profit graph. Label the horizontal axis in units with a maximum value of 4,000. Label the vertical in dollars with a maximum value of $300,000. Draw a vertical line on the graph for the current (3,000) unit level and label total variable costs, total fixed costs, and total before-tax profits at 3,000 units.

LO3, 4   P15-30. High-Low Cost Estimation and Profit Planning

Comparative 2017 and 2018 income statements for Bismark Products Inc. follow:

BISMARK PRODUCTS INC. Comparative Income Statements For Years Ending December 31, 2017 and 2018		
	2017	**2018**
Unit sales	6,000	11,000
Sales revenue.	$78,000	$143,000
Expenses	(70,000)	(85,000)
Profit (loss)	$ 8,000	$ 58,000

REQUIRED

a. Determine the break-even point in units.

b. Determine the unit sales volume required to earn a profit of $12,000.

LO3, 4   P15-31. CVP Analysis and Special Decisions

Smoothie Citrus Company buys a variety of citrus fruit from growers and then processes the fruit into a product line of fresh fruit, juices, and fruit flavorings. The most recent year's sales revenue was $4,400,000. Variable costs were 60 percent of sales and fixed costs totaled $1,400,000.

Smoothie is evaluating two alternatives designed to enhance profitability.

- One staff member has proposed that Smoothie purchase more automated processing equipment. This strategy would increase fixed costs by $300,000 but decrease variable costs to 54 percent of sales.
- Another staff member has suggested that Smoothie rely more on outsourcing for fruit processing. This would reduce fixed costs by $300,000 but increase variable costs to 65 percent of sales.

REQUIRED

a. What is the current break-even point in sales dollars?

b. Assuming an income tax rate of 34 percent, what dollar sales volume is currently required to obtain an after-tax profit of $500,000?

c. In the absence of income taxes, at what sales volume will both alternatives (automation and outsourcing) provide the same profit?

d. Briefly describe one strength and one weakness of both the automation and the outsourcing alternatives.

P15-32. Break-Even Analysis in a Not-for-Profit Organization   **LO3**

Melford Hospital operates a general hospital but rents space to separately owned entities rendering specialized services such as pediatrics and psychiatry. Melford charges each separate entity for patients' services (meals and laundry) and for administrative services (billings and collections). Space and bed rentals are fixed charges for the year, based on bed capacity rented to each entity. Melford charged the following costs to Pediatrics for the year ended June 30, 2017:

	Patient Services (Variable)	Bed Capacity (Fixed)
Dietary	$ 600,000	
Janitorial		$ 70,000
Laundry	300,000	
Laboratory	450,000	
Pharmacy	350,000	
Repairs and maintenance		30,000
General and administrative		1,300,000
Rent		1,500,000
Billings and collections	300,000	
Total	$2,000,000	$2,900,000

In addition to these charges from Melford Hospital, Pediatrics incurred the following personnel costs:

	Annual Salaries*
Supervising nurses	$100,000
Nurses	200,000
Assistants	180,000
Total	$480,000

* These salaries are fixed within the ranges of annual patient-days considered in this problem.

During the year ended June 30, 2017, Pediatrics charged each patient $300 per day, had a capacity of 60 beds, and had revenues of $6,000,000 for 365 days. Pediatrics operated at 100 percent capacity on 90 days during this period. It is estimated that during these 90 days, the demand exceeded 80 beds. Melford has 20 additional beds available for rent for the year ending June 30, 2018. This additional rental would proportionately increase Pediatrics' annual fixed charges based on bed capacity.

REQUIRED

a. Calculate the minimum number of patient-days required for Pediatrics to break even for the year ending June 30, 2018, if the additional beds are not rented. Patient demand is unknown, but assume that revenue per patient-day, cost per patient-day, cost per bed, and salary rates for the year ending June 30, 2018, remain the same as for the year ended June 30, 2017.

b. Assume Pediatrics rents the extra 20-bed capacity from Melford. Determine the net increase or decrease in earnings by preparing a schedule of increases in revenues and costs for the year ending June 30, 2018. Assume that patient demand, revenue per patient-day, cost per patient-day, cost per bed, and salary rates remain the same as for the year ended June 30, 2017.

(CPA adapted)

LO3   P15-33. CVP Analysis of Alternative Products

Pegasus Shoe Company plans to expand its manufacturing capacity to allow up to 20,000 pairs of a new product each year. Because only one product can be produced, management is deciding between the production of the Roadrunner for backpacking and the Trail Runner for exercising. A marketing analysis indicates Pegasus could sell between 8,000 and 14,000 pairs of either product. The accounting department has developed the following price and cost information:

	Product	
	Roadrunner	**Trail Runner**
Selling price per pair.	$ 90	$ 75
Variable costs per pair	60	50
Product costs.	$130,000	$50,000

Facility costs for expansion, regardless of product, are $150,000. Pegasus is subject to a 40 percent income tax rate.

REQUIRED

a. Determine the number of pairs of Roadrunner shoes Pegasus must sell to obtain an after-tax profit of $30,000.

b. Determine the number of pairs of each product Pegasus must sell to obtain identical before-tax profit.

c. For the solution to requirement *b*, calculate Pegasus' after-tax profit or loss.

d. Which product should Pegasus produce if both products were guaranteed to sell at least 13,000 pairs? Verify your solution with calculations.

e. How much would the variable costs per pair of the product *not* selected in requirement *d* have to fall before both products provide the same profit at sales of 13,000 pairs? Verify your solution with calculations.

LO3, 4   P15-34. CVP Analysis Using Published Financial Statements

Condensed data in millions of dollars from **Apple**'s 2014 and 2015 income statements follow:

	2015	**2014**
Revenues	$233,715	$182,795
Total cost of revenues and operating expenses.	(162,485)	(130,292)
Operating income.	$ 71,230	$ 52,503

REQUIRED

a. Develop a cost-estimation equation for Apple's annual cost of revenues and operating expenses.

b. Determine Apple's annual break-even point.

c. Predict operating profit for 2016, assuming 2016 sales of $284,000 million.

d. Identify the assumptions required to use the equations and amounts computed above.

LO6   P15-35. Multiple-Product Profitability Analysis, Multiple-Level Profitability Analysis

College Avenue Bookstore sells new college textbooks at the publishers' suggested retail prices. It then pays the publishers an amount equal to 75 percent of the suggested retail price. The store's other variable costs average 5 percent of sales revenue and annual fixed costs amount to $360,000.

REQUIRED

a. Determine the bookstore's annual break-even point in sales dollars.

b. Assuming an average textbook has a suggested retail price of $120, determine the bookstore's annual break-even point in units.

c. College Avenue Bookstore is planning to add used book sales to its operations. A typical used book costs the store 25 percent of the suggested retail price of a new book. The bookstore plans to sell used books for 75 percent of the suggested retail price of a new book. Assuming unit sales are unchanged, describe the effect on bookstore profitability of shifting sales toward more used and fewer new textbooks.

d. College Publishing produces and sells new textbooks to college and university bookstores. Typical project-level costs total $325,000 for a new textbook. Production and distribution costs amount to 20 percent of the net amount the publisher receives from the bookstores. Textbook authors are paid a royalty of 15 percent of the net amount received from the bookstores. Determine the dollar sales volume required for College Publishing to break even on a new textbook. This is the amount the bookstore pays the publisher, not the bookstore's sales revenue.

e. For a project with predicted sales of 8,000 new books at $120 each, determine:
   1. The bookstores' contribution.
   2. The publisher's contribution.
   3. The author's royalties.

P15-36. Multiple-Product Profitability Analysis

LO3, 4

SKYZ Company produces two models of basketball hoops, Ausom Garage Mount and Delux Ground Mount. Presented is sales information for the year 2017.

	Ausom	Delux	Total
Units manufactured and sold.	1,000	1,500	2,500
Sales revenue.	$300,000	$700,000	$1,000,000
Variable costs.	(200,000)	(420,000)	(620,000)
Contribution margin	$100,000	$280,000	380,000
Fixed costs.			(252,510)
Before-tax profit			127,490
Income taxes (40 percent)			(50,996)
After-tax profit			$ 76,494

REQUIRED

a. Determine the current break-even point in sales dollars.

b. With the current product mix and break-even point, determine the average unit contribution margin and unit sales.

c. Sales representatives believe that the total sales will increase to 3,000 units, with the sales mix likely shifting to 80 percent Ausom Garage Mount and 20 percent Delux Ground Mount over the next few years. Evaluate the desirability of this projection.

P15-37. Multiple-Product Break-Even Analysis

LO3, 4

Currently, Corner Lunch Counter sells only Super Burgers for $2.50 each. During a typical month, the Counter reports a profit of $9,000 with sales of $50,000 and fixed costs of $21,000. Management is considering the introduction of a new Super Chicken Sandwich that will sell for $3.50 and have variable costs of $2.30. The addition of the Super Chicken Sandwich will require hiring additional personnel and renting additional equipment. These actions will increase monthly fixed costs by $7,760.

In the short run, management predicts that Super Chicken sales will average 10,000 sandwiches per month. However, almost all short-run sales of Super Chickens will come from regular customers who switch from Super Burgers to Super Chickens. Consequently, management predicts monthly sales of Super Burgers will decline by 10,000 units to $25,000. In the long run, management predicts that Super Chicken sales will increase to 15,000 sandwiches per month and that Super Burger sales will increase to 30,000 burgers per month.

REQUIRED

a. Determine each of the following:
   1. The current monthly break-even point in sales dollars.
   2. The short-run monthly profit and break-even point in sales dollars subsequent to the introduction of Super Chickens.
   3. The long-run monthly profit and break-even point in sales dollars subsequent to the introduction of Super Chickens.

b. Based on your analysis, what are your recommendations?

LO6 **P15-38. Multi-Level Profitability Analysis**

AccuMeter manufactures and sells its only product (Z1) in lot sizes of 500 units. Because of this approach, lot (batch)-level costs are regarded as variable for CVP analysis. Presented is sales and cost information for the year 2017:

Sales revenue (50,000 units at $45).	$2,250,000
Direct materials (50,000 units at $12).	600,000
Processing (50,000 units at $18)	900,000
Setup (100 lots at $2,000)	200,000
Batch movement (100 lots at $400).	40,000
Order filling (100 lots at $200)	20,000
Fixed manufacturing overhead.	800,000
Fixed selling and administrative.	300,000

REQUIRED

a. Prepare a traditional contribution income statement in good form.

b. Prepare a multi-level contribution income statement in good form. (*Hint:* First determine the appropriate cost hierarchy.)

c. What is the current contribution per lot (batch) of 500 units?

d. Management is contemplating introducing a limited number of specialty products. One product would sell for $65 per unit and have direct materials costs of $17 per unit. All other costs and all production and sales procedures will remain unchanged. What lot (batch) size is required for a contribution of $700 per lot?

CASES AND PROJECTS

LO1 **C15-39. Ethics and Pressure to Improve Profit Plans**

Art Conroy is the assistant controller of New City Muffler, Inc., a subsidiary of New City Automotive, which manufactures tailpipes, mufflers, and catalytic converters at several plants throughout North America. Because of pressure for lower selling prices, New City Muffler has had disappointing financial performance in recent years. Indeed, Conroy is aware of rumblings from corporate headquarters threatening to close the plant.

One of Conroy's responsibilities is to present the plant's financial plans for the coming year to the corporate officers and board of directors. In preparing for the presentation, Conroy was intrigued to note that the focal point of the budget presentation was a profit-volume graph projecting an increase in profits and a reduction in the break-even point.

Curious as to how the improvement would be accomplished, Conroy ultimately spoke with Paula Mitchell, the plant manager. Mitchell indicated that a planned increase in productivity would reduce variable costs and increase the contribution margin ratio.

When asked how the productivity increase would be accomplished, Mitchell made a vague reference to increasing the speed of the assembly line. Conroy commented that speeding up the assembly line could lead to labor problems because the speed of the line was set by union contract. Mitchell responded that she was afraid that if the speedup were opened to negotiation, the union would make a big "stink" that could result in the plant being closed. She indicated that the speedup was the "only way to save the plant, our jobs, and the jobs of all plant employees." Besides, she did not believe employees would notice a 2 or 3 percent increase in speed. Mitchell concluded the meeting observing, "You need to emphasize the results we will accomplish next year, not the details of how we will accomplish those results. Top management does not want to be bored with details. If we accomplish what we propose in the budget, we will be in for a big bonus."

REQUIRED

What advice do you have for Art Conroy?

LO1, 3, 5 **C15-40. CVP Analysis with Changing Cost Structure**

Homestead Telephone was formed in the 1940s to bring telephone services to remote areas of the U.S. Midwest. The early equipment was quite primitive by today's standards. All calls were handled manually by operators, and all customers were on party lines. By the 1970s, however, all customers were on private lines, and mechanical switching devices handled routine local and long distance calls. Operators remained available for directory assistance, credit card calls, and emergencies. In the 1990s

Homestead Telephone added local Internet connections as an optional service to its regular customers. It also established an optional cellular service, identified as the Home Ranger.

REQUIRED

a. Using a unit-level analysis, develop a graph with two lines, representing Homestead Telephone's cost structure (1) in the 1940s and (2) in the late 1990s. Be sure to label the axes and lines.

b. With sales revenue as the independent variable, what is the likely impact of the changed cost structure on Homestead Telephone's (1) contribution margin percent and (2) break-even point?

c. Discuss how the change in cost structure affected Homestead's operating leverage and how this affects profitability under rising or falling sales scenarios.

C15-41. Cost Estimation and CVP Analysis   **LO2, 3, 4**
Presented are the 2017 and 2018 functional income statements of Regional Distribution Inc.:

REGIONAL DISTRIBUTION INC. Functional Income Statements For Years Ending December 31, 2017 and 2018				
	2017		**2018**	
Sales.		$2,760,000		$2,500,000
Expenses				
Cost of goods sold	$2,070,000		$1,875,000	
Shipping	107,700		100,000	
Sales order processing.	26,250		25,000	
Customer relations	60,000		50,000	
Depreciation	40,000		40,000	
Administrative.	125,000	(2,428,950)	125,000	(2,215,000)
Before-tax profit		331,050		285,000
Income taxes (40%)		(132,420)		(114,000)
After-tax profit		$ 198,630		$ 171,000

REQUIRED

a. Determine Regional Distribution's break-even point in sales dollars.

b. What dollar sales volume is required to earn an after-tax profit of $480,000?

c. Assuming budgeted 2017 sales of $6,000,000, prepare a 2017 contribution income statement.

d. Discuss the reliability of the calculations in requirements a-c, including the limitations of the CVP model and how they affect the reliability of the model.

SOLUTIONS TO REVIEW PROBLEMS

Mid-Chapter Review 1

SOLUTION

a. Profit = $14X − ($10,000 + 5.25X)

b. At a volume of 6,200 cartons, Benchmark's profit is $44,250.
   Computed as ($14 × 6,200) − [$10,000 + ($5.25 × 6,200)]
   $86,800 − $42,550 = $44,250

Mid-Chapter Review 2

SOLUTION

a.

SOLO CUP COMPANY Contribution Income Statement For the Month of September 2017		
Sales (3,000 × $40)		$120,000
Less variable costs		
Direct materials (3,000 × $15)	$45,000	
Direct labor (3,000 × $3).	9,000	
Manufacturing overhead (3,000 × $10)	30,000	
Selling and administrative (3,000 × $2)	6,000	(90,000)
Contribution margin		30,000
Less fixed costs		
Manufacturing overhead.	15,000	
Selling and administrative.	10,000	(25,000)
Profit.		$ 5,000

b.

Selling price	$40 per unit
Variable costs	(30) per unit
Contribution margin	$10 per unit

$$\text{Contribution margin ratio} = \frac{\text{Unit contribution margin}}{\text{Unit selling price}}$$

$$= \$10 \div \$40$$

$$= 0.25$$

Mid-Chapter Review 3

SOLUTION

a.

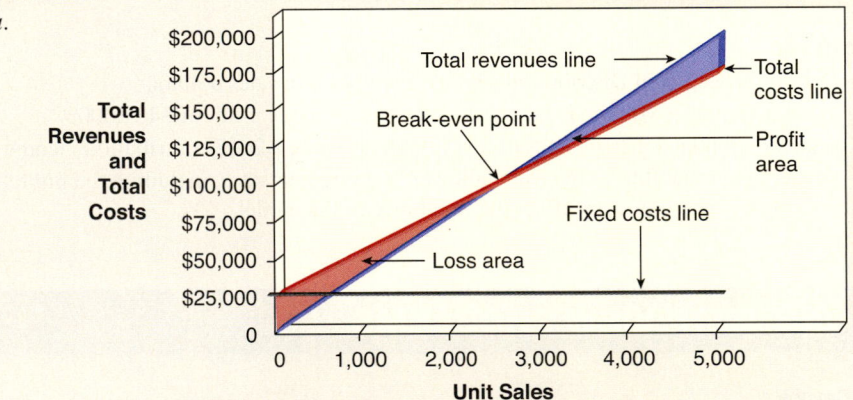

b.

$$\text{Break-even point} = \frac{\text{Fixed costs}}{\text{Unit contribution margin}}$$

$$= \$25,000 \div \$10$$

$$= 2,500 \text{ units}$$

c.

$$\text{Required dollar sales} = \frac{\text{Fixed costs} + \text{Desired profit}}{\text{Contribution margin ratio}}$$

$$= (\$25,000 + \$5,000) \div 0.25$$

$$= \$120,000$$

d.
$$\text{Required unit sales} = \frac{\text{Fixed costs} + \text{Desired before-tax profit}}{\text{Unit contribution margin}}$$

$$\text{Desired before-tax profit} = \$4,500 \div (1 - 0.40) = \$7,500$$

$$\text{Required unit sales} = (\$25,000 + \$7,500) \div \$10$$

$$= 3,250 \text{ units}$$

Mid-Chapter Review 4

SOLUTION

a.

	Coffee	Tea	Smoothies	Total
Monthly unit sales	6,000	3,750	2,250	
Selling price	$1.35	$1.25	$1.95	
Sales	$8,100.00	$4,687.50	$4,387.50	$17,175.00
Variable costs	3,600.00	1,687.50	1,687.50	6,975.00
Contribution margin	$4,500.00	$3,000.00	$2,700.00	10,200.00
Fixed costs				8,000.00
Before-tax profit				$ 2,200.00
Contribution margin (CM) ratio	0.5556	0.6400	0.6154	0.5939
Current sales mix (based on sales dollars)	47.16%	27.29%	25.55%	

b. **Break-even = Fixed costs/Total contribution margin ratio**

      = $8,000/0.5939

      = $13,470

Proof:		Sales		C/M Ratio
Coffee:	$13,470 × 47.16% =	$ 6,352.45	× 0.5556 =	$3,529.42
Tea:	$13,470 × 27.29% =	3,675.96	× 0.6400 =	2,352.62*
Smoothies:	$13,470 × 25.55% =	3,441.59	× 0.6154 =	2,117.96*
		$13,470.00		
Total contribution margin				8,000.00
Fixed costs				8,000.00
Before-tax profit				–0–

* Amounts adjusted to correct for minor rounding error.

Chapter-End Review

SOLUTION

The Coffee Bean has an operating leverage of 4.636, calculated as a contribution margin of $10,200 divided by before-tax profit of $2,200. Therefore, if sales dollars increase by 20% to $20,610, before-tax profit should increase by 4.636 times 20%, or 92.72%, to $4,240. Because of the leverage caused by fixed costs, a 20% increase in sales results in a 92.72% increase in before-tax profit. Conversely, a 20% decrease in sales would result in a 92.72% decrease in before-tax profits to $160.

Proof:	20% Sales Increase	20% Sales Decrease
Sales......................................	$20,610	$13,740
CM %......................................	× 0.5939	× 0.5939
Total CM...................................	12,240	8,160
Fixed costs................................	8,000	8,000
Before-tax profit...........................	$ 4,240	$ 160

Current before-tax profit of $2,200 × (1 + 0.9272) = $4,240
Current before-tax profit of $2,200 × (1 − 0.9272) = $160

Appendix 15A Review

SOLUTION

Weekly contribution per average customer:

$17 sales per visit × (1 − 0.80) contribution ratio × 1.50 visits = $5.10

Annual contribution per customer = $5.10 × 52 weeks = $265.20

Customers required for desired profit = ($80,000 + $40,000)/$265.20 = 453

(rounded up to the next whole number)

Required population = 453 customers/0.05 customers in population = 9,060

16

Relevant Costs and Benefits for Decision Making

UBER

www.uber.com

Every day companies, both large and small, are faced with making critical decisions that can drastically alter their likelihood of success. Some of these decisions are long term in nature, such as where a company should invest in property, plant, and equipment. Others are short-run decisions, such as whether or not to sell product or service to a new customer at a price that is below the normal market price.

San Francisco startup company **Uber** got its start from pondering a common dilemma: how to get home from the club late at night. CEO Travis Kalanick explains that he and friend joked, ". . . let's go buy 10 **Mercedes** S-Classes, let's go hire 20 drivers, let's get parking garages and let's make it so we could push a button and an S-Class would roll up, for only us, in the city of San Francisco, where you cannot get a ride." Shortly thereafter, an iPhone application called Uber was launched in 2010. Uber has now expanded to 551 cities in 81 countries.

Uber's intent was to act as a broker by matching riders to available drivers with a summons via smartphones. But the company first had to decide whether it should purchase cars and pay for insurance, storage, and other associated costs or whether to contract with existing drivers, either limousine companies or individual drivers. In the end, Uber decided to contract with partners (limo companies or individuals) who had their own vehicles. These partners take responsibility for licensing, vehicle cost and maintenance, gas, auto insurance, and storage. In return, Uber trains the drivers on the software platform and pays them 80 percent of the fare.

By acting as a broker instead of owning its own vehicles, Uber was able to minimize its fixed costs. This "operating leverage" results in a greater benefit from increases in customers, because the fixed costs don't need to increase to handle the higher capacity. However, the company's capacity is limited by how many drivers it has on contract. This limited resource can be maximized by minimizing the downtime of its drivers. Uber invested in engineers to build algorithms to manage its supply of drivers and demand of riders. The efficient management of this limited resource benefits both drivers (who are more likely to be engaged in fare-generating activity) and riders, who can use the software's tracking feature to see their car's progress toward the predetermined pickup destination.

Uber has successfully changed the way people think about transportation. It is expected to achieve greater than $5.5 billion in net revenue in 2016. However it also spent approximately $1.55 for every $1.00 of revenue it earned, with total losses for the year expected to amass approximately $3 billion.

As Uber emphasizes growth over pofits, the company is betting that investing in areas such as mapping technology, food delivery, and autonomous vehicles will reduce the real cost of transportation.

In this chapter, we will learn how to incorporate the relevant revenues and costs to simplify decision making, even when operating in a complex, changing environment.

Source: Eric Newcomer, "Uber's Loss Exceeds $800 Million in Third Quarter on $1.7 Billion in Net Revenues," *Bloomberg Technology*, December 19, 2016; Jessi Hempel, "Hey, Taxi Company, You Talkin' to Me?" *Fortune*, September 23, 2013; Joshua Brustein, "From Google, Uber Gets Money and Political Muscle," *Bloomberg Businessweek*, August 26, 2013; Josh Linkner, "Uber's Borrowed Creativity," *Forbes*, August 19, 2013; and Andy Kessler, "The Transportation Trustbuster," *Wall Street Journal*, January 26, 2013, p. A13.

CHAPTER ORGANIZATION

Relevant Costs and Benefits for Decision Making			
Identifying Relevant Costs	**Differential Analysis of Relevant Costs**	**Applying Differential Analysis**	**Use of Limited Resources**
• Relevance of Future Revenues • Relevance of Outlay Costs • Irrelevance of Sunk Costs • Sunk Costs Can Cause Ethical Dilemmas • Relevance of Disposal and Salvage Values • Relevance of Opportunity Costs	• Differential Cost Analysis	• Multiple Changes in Profit Plans • Special Orders • Outsourcing Decisions • Sell or Process Further	• Single Constraint • Multiple Constraints • Theory of Constraints • Limitations of Decision Analysis Models

The purpose of this chapter is to examine approaches to identifying and analyzing revenue and cost information for specific decisions, such as the decision to outsource. Our emphasis is on identifying **relevant costs** (future costs that differ among competing decision alternatives) and distinguishing relevant costs from **irrelevant costs** that do not differ among competing decision alternatives. We consider a number of frequently encountered decisions: to make multiple changes in profit plans, to accept or reject a special order, to acquire a component or service internally or externally, to sell a product or process it further, and how to best use limited capacity. These decision situations are not exhaustive; they only illustrate relevant cost concepts. Once we understand these concepts, we can apply them to a variety of decision scenarios.

Although our focus in this chapter is on profit maximization, decisions should not be based solely on this criterion, especially maximizing profit in the short run. Managers must consider the implications decision alternatives have on long-run profit, as well as legal, ethical, social, and other nonquantitative factors. These factors can lead management to select a course of action other than that selected by financial information alone.

LO1 Distinguish between relevant and irrelevant revenues and costs.

IDENTIFYING RELEVANT COSTS

For a specific decision, the key to relevent cost analysis is first to identify the relevant costs (and revenues) and then to organize them in a manner that clearly indicates how they differ under each alternative. Consider the following equipment replacement decision.

Beats by Dr. Dre (Beats), a subsidiary of **Apple Inc.,** produces headphones and supplies high-quality components and equalizer software to HP for its line of personal computers. Assume that one of its components used in wireless headsets is forecasted to sell 10,000 units during the coming year at a price of $20 per unit. Further assume that each of Beats' components is manufactured with separate machines in a shared plant.

The machine used in the manufacture of headset components is two years old and has a remaining useful life of four years. Its purchase price was $90,000 (new), and it has an estimated salvage value of zero dollars at the end of its useful life. Its current book value (original cost less accumulated depreciation) is $60,000, but it could be sold today for only $35,000.

Headset Component Costs:	
Direct materials...	$3.00 per unit
Conversion	5.00 per unit
Selling and distribution..	1.00 per unit
Inspection and adjustment...	$500 per batch
	(1,000 units)
Depreciation on machines	$15,000 per year
Machine maintenance..	$200 per month
Advertising	$5,000 per year

continued

Common Costs:	
Administrative salaries	$65,000 per year
Building operations.	23,000 per year
Building rent	24,000 per year

Management is evaluating the desirability of replacing the machine with a new machine. The new machine costs $80,000, has a useful life of four years, and a predicted salvage value of zero dollars at the end of its useful life. Although the new machine has the same production capacity as the old machine, its predicted operating costs are lower because it consumes less electricity. Further, because of a computer control system, the new machine allows production of twice as many units between inspections and adjustments, and the cost of inspections and adjustments is lower. The new machine requires only annual, rather than monthly, overhauls. Hence, machine maintenance costs are lower. Costs for the new machine are predicted as follows:

Conversion costs	$4.00 per unit
Inspection and adjustment.	$ 300 per batch (2,000 units)
Machine maintenance	$ 200 per year

All other costs and all revenues remain unchanged.

The decision alternatives are to keep the old machine or to replace it with a new machine. An analysis of how costs and revenues differ under each alternative assists management in making the best choice. The first objective of this chapter is to study the distinction between relevant and irrelevant items. After evaluating the relevance of each item, we develop an analysis of relevant costs.

Relevance of Future Revenues

Revenues, which are inflows of resources from the sale of goods and services, are relevant to a decision only if they differ between alternatives. In this example, revenues are not relevant because they are identical under each alternative. They would be relevant if the new machine had greater capacity or if management intended to change the selling price should it acquire the new machine. (The $35,000 disposal value of the old machine is an inflow. However, *revenues* refer to resources from the sale of goods and services to customers in the normal course of business. We include the sale of the old machine under disposal and salvage values.)

The hypothetical keep-or-replace decision facing Beats' management might be called a **cost reduction proposal** because it is based on the assumption that the organization is committed to an activity and that management desires to minimize the cost of activities. Here, the two alternatives are either to continue operating with the old machine or to replace it with a new machine.

Although this approach is appropriate for many activities, managers should remember that they have another alternative—discontinue operations. To simplify the analysis, managers normally do not consider the alternative to discontinue when operations appear to be profitable. However, if there is any doubt about an operation's profitability, this alternative should be considered. Because revenues change if an operation is discontinued, revenues are relevant whenever this alternative is considered.

Relevance of Outlay Costs

Outlay costs are costs that require future expenditures of cash or other resources. Outlay costs that differ under the decision alternatives are relevant; outlay costs that do not differ are irrelevant. Assume Beats' relevant and irrelevant outlay costs for the equipment replacement decision follow.

Relevant Outlay Costs	Irrelevant Outlay Costs
Conversion Costs	Direct Materials
Inspection and Adjustment Costs	Selling and Distributon
Cost of New Machine	Advertising
Machine Maintenance	Common Outlay Costs

Irrelevance of Sunk Costs

Sunk costs result from past decisions that cannot be changed. Suppose we purchased a car for $30,000 five years ago. Today we must decide whether to purchase another car or have major maintenance performed on our current car. In making this decision, the purchase price of our current car is a sunk cost.

Although the relevance of outlay costs is determined by the decision scenario, sunk costs are never relevant. The cost of the old machine is a sunk cost, not a future cost. This cost and the related depreciation result from the past decision to acquire the old machine. Even though all the outlay costs discussed earlier would be relevant to a decision to continue or discontinue operations, the sunk cost of the old machine is not relevant even to this decision.

If management elects to keep the old machine, its book value will be depreciated over its remaining useful life of four years. However, if management elects to replace the old machine, its book value is written off when it is replaced. Even if management elects to discontinue operations, the book value of the old machine must be written off.

Sunk Costs Can Cause Ethical Dilemmas

Although the book value of the old machine has no economic significance, the accounting treatment of past costs may make it psychologically difficult for managers to regard them as irrelevant. If management replaces the old machine, a $25,000 accounting loss is recorded in the year of replacement:

Book value	$60,000
Disposal value	(35,000)
Loss on disposal	$25,000

The possibility of recording an accounting loss can create an ethical dilemma for managers. Although an action may be desirable from the long-run viewpoint of the organization, in the short run, choosing the action may result in an accounting loss. Fearing the loss will lead superiors to question her judgment, a manager might prefer to use the old machine (with lower total profits over the four-year period) as opposed to replacing it and being forced to record a loss on disposal. Although this action may avoid raising troublesome questions in the near term, the cumulative effect of many decisions of this nature is harmful to the organization's long-run economic health.

From an economic viewpoint, the analysis should focus on future costs and revenues that differ. The decision should not be influenced by sunk costs. Although there is no easy solution to this behavioral and ethical problem, managers and management accountants should be aware of its potential impact.

YOU MAKE THE CALL

You are the Vice President of Manufacturing   You recently made the decision to purchase a very expensive machine for your manufacturing plant that used technology that was well established over several years. The purchase of this machine was a major decision supported by the chief financial officer, based solely on your recommendation. Shortly after making the purchase, you were attending a trade convention where you learned of new technology that is now available that essentially renders obsolete the machine you recently purchased. You feel that it may be best for the company to acquire the new technology since most of your competitors will be using it soon; however, you feel that this cannot be done now that you have recently purchased the new machine. What should you do? [Answer, p. 747]

Relevance of Disposal and Salvage Values

Beats' assumed revenues (inflows of resources from operations) from the sale of headset components were discussed earlier. The sale of fixed assets is also a source of resources. Because the sale of fixed assets is a nonoperating item, cash inflows obtained from these sales are discussed separately.

The disposal value of the old machine is a relevant cash inflow. It is obtained only if the replacement alternative is selected. Any salvage value available at the end of the useful life of either machine is also relevant. A loss on disposal can have a favorable tax impact if the loss can be offset against taxable gains or taxable income. To simplify the analysis, we ignore any tax implications at this point. The tax effects related to capital asset transactions are discussed in Chapter 24.

Relevance of Opportunity Costs

When making a decision between alternative courses of action, accepting one alternative results in rejecting the other alternative(s). Any benefit foregone as a result of rejecting one opportunity in favor of another opportunity is described as an **opportunity cost** of the accepted alternative. For example, if you are employed at a salary of $40,000 per year and you have the opportunity to continue to work or the opportunity to go back to school full-time for two years to earn a graduate degree, the cost of getting the degree includes not only all the outlay costs for tuition, books, and so forth, it also includes the salary foregone (or opportunity cost) of $40,000 per year. So, if your tuition and other outlay costs are going to be $25,000 per year for two years, the cost of earning the degree will be $50,000 of outlay costs and $80,000 of opportunity costs, for a total cost of earning the degree of $130,000. Opportunity costs are always relevant in making decisions among competing alternatives.

The following is a summary of all the relevant and irrelevant costs discussed in this section.

Relevant Costs		Irrelevant Costs	
Future costs that differ among competing alternatives		Future costs that do not differ among competing alternatives	
Opportunity Costs	**Relevant Outlay Costs**	**Irrelevant Outlay Costs**	**Sunk Costs**
Net benefits foregone of rejected alternatives	Future costs requiring future expenditures that differ	Future costs requiring future expenditures that do not differ	Historical costs resulting from past decisions

RESEARCH INSIGHT

Why Don't Managers Always Ignore Sunk Costs?   For decades, business school students have learned that sunk costs are irrelevant to decision making; however, managers still find these costs difficult to ignore. Researchers have shown that, far from ignoring sunk costs, many managers increase commitment to a project as sunk costs increase. Recent experimental research from a team at the University of Melbourne in Australia sheds more light on the precise motivations of managers who choose not to ignore sunk costs. The researchers found that the managers' personal motivations interact with the context of the specific project and the related sunk costs. Their study found that individuals who are focused on promotion become increasingly fixated on completion as the end of the project nears. While other managers are able to ignore fixed costs more consistently throughout the project life cycle, those who are focused on promotion are most likely to continue to invest in a project that should be abandoned when the project is close to completion. As managerial accountants advise executive teams, this type of bias should be kept in mind.

Source: Adam P. Barsky, and Michael J. Zyphur, "Disentangling sunk-costs and completion proximity: The role of regulatory focus," *Journal of Experimental Social Psychology* 65 (2016): 105-108.

MID-CHAPTER REVIEW 1

TaylorMade-Adidas Golf Company, a subsidiary of Adidas, manufactures golf clubs using "adjustable weight technology" or AWT. Suppose a European machine company has proposed to sell TaylorMade a new highly automated machine that would reduce significantly the labor cost of producing its golf clubs. The cost of the machine is $1,000,000, and would have an expected life of 5 years, at the end of which it would have a residual value of $100,000. It has an estimated operating cost of $10,000 per month. The direct labor cost savings per club from using the machine is estimated to be $5 per club. In addition, one monthly salaried manufacturing manager, whose salary is $6,000 per month would no longer be needed. Assume the Vice President of Manufacturing earns $10,000 per month. Also, the new machine would free up about 5,000 square feet of space from the displaced workers. Assume TaylorMade's building is held under a 10-year lease that has eight years remaining. The current lease cost is $1 per square foot per month. TaylorMade may be able to use the space for other purposes, and it has received an offer to rent it to a nearby related company for $3,500 per month.

REQUIRED
Identify all of the costs described above as either "relevant" or "irrelevant" to the decision to acquire the new machine.

The solution to this review problem can be found on page 763.

LO2 Analyze relevant costs and indicate how they differ under alternative decision scenarios.

DIFFERENTIAL ANALYSIS OF RELEVANT COSTS

Differential cost analysis is an approach to the analysis of relevant costs that focuses on the costs that differ under alternative actions. A differential analysis of relevant costs for Beats' equipment replacement decision is in **Exhibit 16.1**. Replacement provides a net advantage of $17,800 over the life of both machines versus keeping the old machine.

EXHIBIT 16.1	Differential Analysis for Beats' Equipment Replacement

	Four-Year Totals		
	Replace with New Machine	Keep Old Machine	Difference (effect of replacement on income)
Conversion:			
Old machine (10,000 units × $5 × 4 years)		$200,000	
New machine (10,000 units × $4 × 4 years)	$160,000		($40,000)
Inspection and adjustment:			
Old machine (10* setups × $500 × 4 years)		20,000	
New machine (5** setups × $300 × 4 years)	6,000		(14,000)
Machine maintenance:			
Old machine ($200 per month × 12 months × 4 years). . .		9,600	
New machine ($200 per year × 4 years)	800		(8,800)
Disposal of old machine.	(35,000)		(35,000)
Cost of new machine	80,000		80,000
Totals	$211,800	$229,600	($17,800)
Advantage of replacement		$17,800	

* Old machine: 10,000 units ÷ 1,000 units per batch
** New machine: 10,000 units ÷ 2,000 units per batch

An alternative analysis to that presented in **Exhibit 16.1** is to present all revenues and costs (relevant and irrelevant) for each alternative in separate columns, such that the bottom line of the analysis is the total profit or loss for each alternative. This method is preferred if the goal is to determine the total profitability of each alternative. If the goal is to determine which of the two alternatives is most profitable, then a differential analysis is preferred.

Assuming the organization is committed to providing a particular product or service, a differential analysis of relevant costs (as shown in **Exhibit 16.1**) is preferred to a complete analysis of all costs and revenues for a number of reasons:

- A differential analysis focuses on only those items that differ, providing a clearer picture of the impact of the decision. Management is less apt to be confused by this analysis than by one that combines relevant and irrelevant items.

- A differential analysis contains fewer items, making it easier and quicker to prepare.

- A differential analysis can help to simplify complex situations (such as those encountered by multiple-product or multiple-plant firms), when it is difficult to develop complete firmwide statements to analyze all decision alternatives.

Before preparing a differential analysis, it is always desirable to reassess the organization's commitment to a product or service. This helps avoid "throwing good money after bad." If Beats currently had large annual losses, acquiring the new machine would merely reduce total losses over the next four years by $17,800. In this case, discontinuing operations (a third alternative) should also be considered.

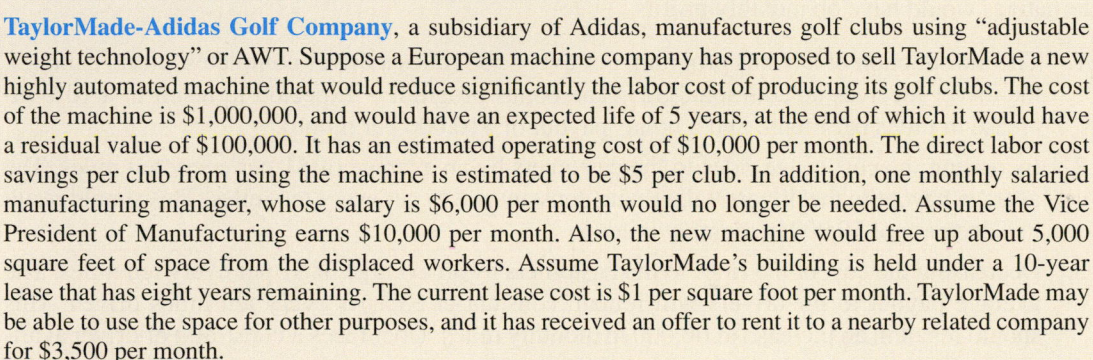

MID-CHAPTER REVIEW 2

TaylorMade-Adidas Golf Company, a subsidiary of Adidas, manufactures golf clubs using "adjustable weight technology" or AWT. Suppose a European machine company has proposed to sell TaylorMade a new highly automated machine that would reduce significantly the labor cost of producing its golf clubs. The cost of the machine is $1,000,000, and would have an expected life of 5 years, at the end of which it would have a residual value of $100,000. It has an estimated operating cost of $10,000 per month. The direct labor cost savings per club from using the machine is estimated to be $5 per club. In addition, one monthly salaried manufacturing manager, whose salary is $6,000 per month would no longer be needed. Assume the Vice President of Manufacturing earns $10,000 per month. Also, the new machine would free up about 5,000 square feet of space from the displaced workers. Assume TaylorMade's building is held under a 10-year lease that has eight years remaining. The current lease cost is $1 per square foot per month. TaylorMade may be able to use the space for other purposes, and it has received an offer to rent it to a nearby related company for $3,500 per month.

REQUIRED

a. Assuming the new machine would be used to produce an average of 5,000 clubs per month, prepare a differential analysis of the relevant costs of buying the machine and using it for the next five years, versus continuing to use hand labor.

b. In addition to the quantitative analysis in requirement b., what qualitative considerations are important for making the right decision?

The solution to this review problem can be found on page 764.

APPLYING DIFFERENTIAL ANALYSIS

Differential analysis is used to provide information for a variety of planning and decision-making situations. This section illustrates some of the more frequently encountered applications of differential analysis. To focus on differential analysis concepts, we will continue with the **Uber** discussion introduced in the opening vignette of this chapter. For the purposes of our example, we assume a simplified financial model, which consists of variable costs based on number of miles driven and costs that are fixed in the short run. As Uber is primarily a technology company, other than driver fees, its costs are generally related to the processing, storage, and communication of information. Also, for this example, we assume that the entire amount of the customer fees collected by the drivers is categorized as revenue for Uber and the fees paid out to the drivers are categorized as variable driver fees.

LO3 Apply differential analysis to evaluate changes in profit plans.

3

Multiple Changes in Profit Plans

Assume Uber collects an average of $45 for every ten miles of customer rides. Variable costs per every ten miles and fixed costs per month are as follows:

Variable Costs*		Fixed Costs per Month	
Driver fees	$35.00	Platform and cloud based data storage...	$ 40,000
Platform and cloud-based data storage ...	1.50	Mapping technology.................	75,000
Mapping technology..................	2.00	Advertising	5,000
Customer service....................	0.50	Total	$120,000
Total	$39.00		

*Per every ten miles

Assume the contribution margin per every ten miles driven is $6 ($45 customer collection less $39 variable costs). Uber's hypothetical contribution income statement for April 2017 is presented in **Exhibit 16.2**. Assume the April operations are typical and monthly miles driven average 300,000 miles, with monthly profits averaging $60,000.

Management wants to know the effect that each of the following three mutually exclusive alternatives would have on monthly profits.

1. The introduction of a bonus program. For every 500 miles a driver completes within a month, the driver receives an additional $25. The bonus program is expected to result in a 10% increase in miles per month and a bonus payout of $10,000 per month.

2. Increasing the cost of the rides to the customers by an average of $1 per every ten miles. The average payout to the drivers will remain constant at $35 per every ten miles. This should result in a decrease of 50,000 in monthly miles.

3. Decreasing the cost of the rides to the customers by an average of $1 per every ten miles. The average payout to the drivers will remain constant at $35 per every ten miles driven. This should result in an increase of 60,000 in monthly miles. Uber faces a constraint of driver availability. To encourage its drivers to work more, Uber is offering to pay an extra $1 for every ten miles, after a driver completes 1,200 miles within a one-week period. Assume that 30,000 miles will be paid out at the higher rate.

It is possible to develop contribution income statements for each alternative and then determine the profit impact of the proposed change by comparing the new income with the current income. A more direct approach is to use differential analysis and focus on only those items that differ under each alternative.

Alternative 1	
Profit increase from increased miles (3,000* × $6)...................................	$18,000
Profit decrease from bonus	(10,000)
Increase in monthly profit...	$ 8,000

*(300,000 × 10%) divided by 10

Alternative 2	
Profit decrease from reduced miles (5,000* × $6)	$(30,000)
Profit increase from increased price**...	25,000
Decrease in monthly profit	$ (5,000)

*50,000 divided by 10
**[(300,000 current miles − 50,000 lost miles) divided by 10] × $1

Alternative 3
Profit increase from increase in miles (6,000* × $6)..	$36,000
Profit decrease from reduced selling price (36,000** × $1).............................	(36,000)
Profit decrease from increased driver fees (3,000*** × $1).............................	($3,000)
Decrease in monthly profit...	($3,000)

*60,000 divided by 10

**(300,000 current miles + 60,000 increased miles) divided by 10

***30,000 divided by 10

Alternatives 2 and 3 are undesirable because they would each result in a decrease in monthly profit. Because Alternative 1 results in an increase in monthly profit, it is preferred to both Alternatives 2 and 3.

MID-CHAPTER REVIEW 3

Epson produces color cartridges for inkjet printers. Suppose cartridges are sold to mail-order distributors for $4.80 each and that manufacturing and other costs are as follows:

Variable Costs per Unit		Fixed Costs per Month	
Direct materials.....................	$2.00	Factory overhead	$15,000
Direct labor	0.20	Selling and administrative............	5,000
Factory overhead	0.25	Total	$20,000
Distribution	0.05		
Total	$2.50		

The variable distribution costs are for transportation to mail-order distributors. Also assume the current monthly production and sales volume is 15,000 and monthly capacity is 20,000 units.

REQUIRED
Determine the effect of the following independent situations on monthly profits.

a.   A $1.50 increase in the unit selling price should result in an 1,800 unit decrease in monthly sales.

b.   A $1.80 decrease in the unit selling price should result in a 6,000 unit increase in monthly sales. However, because of capacity constraints, the last 1,000 units would be produced during overtime, when the direct labor costs increase by 50 percent.

The solution to this review problem can be found on page 764.

Special Orders

Assume that a not-for-profit is hosting a fundraising dinner, and it would like to offer its attendees Uber rides home from the event at a reduced rate of $40 for every ten miles. The total expected miles related to the fundraiser are 3,000. Uber drivers will not be called to the site via the online app as the drivers will be ready and waiting at the event when it is over. Therefore, the mapping technology fees can be reduced to $1.50 per every ten miles. Also assume that the driver fees will remain constant at $35 per every ten miles. Uber has sufficient driver capacity to handle the event without reducing its rides to other customers. Uber's management wants to know the profit impact of accepting the offer. The following analysis focuses on those costs and revenues that will differ if the offer is accepted.

LO4 Apply differential analysis to evaluate whether to accept a special order.

4

Increase in revenues (300* × $40)		$12,000
Increase in costs		
Driver fees (300* × $35)	$10,500	
Platform and cloud-based data storage (300* × $1.50)	450	
Mapping technology (300* × $1.50)	450	
Customer service (300* × $0.50)	150	11,550
Increase in profits		$ 450

*3,000 divided by 10

Accepting the offer will result in a profit increase of $450. Although this is not a significant increase, management might consider this to be a great marketing opportunity and a chance to convert the attendees into future customers.

If management were unaware of relevant cost concepts, they might be tempted to compare the special event price of $40 to the average cost per every ten miles as developed from the accounting reports. Based on Uber's hypothetical April contribution income statement in **Exhibit 16.2**, the average cost per every ten miles was $43, calculated as follows.

Total variable costs	$1,170,000
Total fixed costs	120,000
Total costs	1,290,000
Total miles divided by 10 (300,000/10)	30,000
Average cost per every 10 miles	$ 43

Comparing the special event price of $40 per ten miles to the average cost of $43, management might conclude the event would result in a loss of $3 per ten miles.

It is apparent that the $43 figure encompasses variable costs of $39 per ten miles (including irrelevant variable mapping technology costs of $0.50 per ten miles) and irrelevant fixed costs of $120,000 spread over 3,000 miles. But remember, management may not have detailed cost information. To obtain appropriate information for decision-making purposes, management must ask its accounting staff for the specific information needed. Different configurations of cost information are provided for different purposes. In the absence of special instructions, the accounting staff might not supply relevant cost information.

EXHIBIT 16.2	Contribution Income Statement	

UBER
Contribution Income Statement
For the Month of April 2017

Revenue (30,000* × $45.00)		$1,350,000
Less variable costs		
Driver fees (30,000* × $35.00)	$1,050,000	
Platform and cloud-based data storage (30,000* × $1.50)	45,000	
Mapping technology (30,000* × $2.00)	60,000	
Customer service (30,000* × $0.50)	15,000	(1,170,000)
Contribution margin		180,000
Less fixed costs		
Platform and cloud-based data storage	40,000	
Mapping technology	75,000	
Advertising	5,000	(120,000)
Profit		$ 60,000

*300,000 divided by 10

Importance of Time Span and Opportunity Costs The special event is a one-time contract for 3,000 miles that will use current excess driver capacity. Because no special setups or technology are required to manage the event, it is appropriate to consider only variable costs in computing the event's profitability.

But what if the not-for-profit wanted Uber to sign a multiyear contract to provide 3,000 miles per month at $40 per every ten miles? Under these circumstances, management would be well advised to reject the contract because there is a high probability that cost increases would make the order unprofitable in later years. At the very least, management should insist that a cost escalation clause be added to the agreement, specifying that the customer price would increase to cover any cost increases and detailing the cost computation.

Of more concern is the variable nature of all long-run costs. Given adequate time, management must replace fixed assets and may have to adjust the amount and quality of its equipment and technology. Accordingly, *in the long run, all costs (including costs classified as fixed in a given period) are relevant*. To remain in business in the long run, Uber must replace equipment, pay taxes, pay administrative salaries, and so forth. Consequently, management should consider *all costs,* fixed and variable, in evaluating a long-term contract.

Full costs include all costs, regardless of their behavior pattern or activity level. The average full cost per unit is sometimes used to approximate long-run variable costs. If accepting a long-term contract increases the monthly miles to 303,000, the average full cost per every ten miles will be $42.97.

Driver fees	$35.00
Platform and cloud-based data storage	1.50
Mapping technology.	2.00
Customer service support	0.50
Platform and cloud-based data storage (40,000/30,300*)	1.32**
Mapping technology (75,000/30,300*)	2.48**
Advertising (5,000/30,300*)	0.17**
Average full cost per every 10 miles.	$42.97**

*303,000 divided by 10
**Rounded

In this case, the estimated long-run variable costs are $42.97 per every ten miles. Many managers would say this is the minimum acceptable selling price, especially if the order extends over a long period of time.

Because Uber has excess productive driver capacity, no opportunity cost is associated with accepting the not-for-profit's one-time offer. There is no alternative use of the driving time related to the event, in the short run, so there is no opportunity cost.

But what if Uber was operating at driver capacity? In that case, accepting the special offer would require reducing regular miles. Assume hiring new drivers is not a possibility in the short run and there are safety concerns with having the current drivers driving too many miles. With an alternative use of the drivers' time, an opportunity cost is associated with using the drivers to drive for the fundraising event.

Every ten miles driven at the event could otherwise generate a $6 contribution from regular customers. Accepting the special event would cause Uber to incur an opportunity cost of $1,800 for the contribution margin lost from foregoing rides to regular customers.

Lost fees to regular customers (3,000 miles/10)	300
Regular contribution margin per ten miles	× $6
Opportunity cost of accepting special event	$1,800

Because this opportunity cost exceeds the $450 contribution derived from the special event, management might reject the special event. Accepting the event will reduce profits by $1,350 ($450 contribution − $1,800 opportunity cost). As discussed previously, there are also qualitative considerations. Even though there is a loss expected from accepting the special event, management might consider this a great marketing opportunity to reach out to new customers and decide that it is worthwhile to accept the order.

Qualitative Considerations Although an analysis of cost and revenue information may indicate that a special order is profitable in the short run, management might still reject the order because of qualitative considerations. Any concerns regarding the order's impact on regular customers might lead management to reject the order even if there is excess capacity. If the order involves a special low price, regular customers might demand a similar price reduction and threaten to take their business elsewhere. Alternatively, management might accept the special order while operating at capacity if they believed there were long-term benefits associated with penetrating a new market. Legal factors must also be considered if the special order is from a buyer who competes with regular customers.

MID-CHAPTER REVIEW 4

Epson produces color cartridges for inkjet printers. Suppose cartridges are sold to mail-order distributors for $4.80 each and that manufacturing and other costs are as follows:

Variable Costs per Unit		Fixed Costs per Month	
Direct materials	$2.00	Factory overhead	$15,000
Direct labor	0.20	Selling and administrative	5,000
Factory overhead	0.25	Total	$20,000
Distribution	0.05		
Total	$2.50		

The variable distribution costs are for transportation to mail-order distributors. Also assume the current monthly production and sales volume is 15,000 and monthly capacity is 20,000 units.

REQUIRED
Determine the effect of the following independent situations on monthly profits.

a. A Russian distributor has proposed to place a special, one-time order for 4,000 units next month at a reduced price of $4.00 per unit. The distributor would pay all transportation costs. There would be additional fixed selling and administrative costs of $500.00.

b. An Austrian distributor has proposed to place a special, one-time order for 8,000 units at a special price of $4.00 per unit. The distributor would pay all transportation costs. There would be additional fixed selling and administrative costs of $500.00. Assume overtime production is not possible.

The solution to this review problem can be found on page 765.

LO5 Apply differential analysis to evaluate outsourcing decisions.

5

Outsourcing Decisions (Make or Buy)

One of the most common applications of relevant cost analysis involves the make-or-buy decision. Virtually any service, product, or component that can be produced or manufactured internally can also be acquired from an external source. The procurement of services, products or components from an external source is called **outsourcing**. For example, the management of the bookstore at your college or university is likely outsourced to **Barnes and Noble** or **Follett**, and the dining facilities may be outsourced to **Compass Group North America** or **Aramark Corporation**. Similarly, **HP** and more recently, **Samsung**, actually manufacture very few of the components of their computers. Instead the manufacture of components is outsourced to other firms such as **Intel** for computer chips and **Seagate** for storage devices. Virtually all computer manufacturers, with the exception of **Apple**, outsource their operating systems to **Microsoft**.

Any time you call a customer support call center, the representative reached is likely to be working in a different country. A growing number of companies even outsource employees from employee leasing companies. In the past 25 years, outsourcing of goods and services has expanded exponentially with the emergence of well-trained, low-cost labor forces in China and India and other parts of the world.

As the above discussion reveals, the decision to outsource rather than to produce a service or product internally involves a vast array of qualitative issues. The quantitative issues surrounding the outsourcing (or make-or-buy) decision are often less challenging. To illustrate, we continue the Uber example. Suppose a technology firm, DataTech, offers Uber a one-year contract to manage all of Uber's data storage service at a cost of $15,000 per month. Uber is now faced with the decision to continue to supply the data storage service internally or outsource the technology to DataTech. An analysis of the decision reveals that if Uber accepts the offer, it will be able to reduce the following:

- Variable platform and data storage costs by $0.20 per ten miles.
- Fixed platform and data storage costs by $5,000.

BUSINESS INSIGHT

When Being Liked Is Worth the Money   **Comcast** wants to be loved. After years of being enthusiastically anchored to the bottom of customer satisfaction surveys, Comcast is changing strategies. Finally faced with competition from on-demand services such as Netflix, Hulu, and Amazon, Comcast has decided that it is time to court its customers. This initiative has two parts. First, the company has begun to improve customer service by redesigning physical locations to feel more welcoming and Apple-like. Second, it has developed a new app to help customers plan around service visits, tracking the technician's estimated time of arrival to make the visit convenient for customers.

The second part of this effort also takes a page from the Apple playbook: make Internet, TV, and home-security devices that people can connect with. Fraser Stirling, head of hardware development at Comcast, says, "we are genuinely trying to create an emotional experience, whether that's love, or whatever, like you have with your phone. We want people to be able to put something from Comcast in their study or their living room and people can look at it and go 'Oof, what is that? It's amazing.'"

Differential analysis helps a company like Comcast weigh the increased costs associated with customer satisfaction and hardware design against the forecasted loss of customers to on-demand entertainment. This sort of analysis helps companies deal with the changing realities of their markets. For years Comcast had significant market power and, thus, sought to deliver cable at the lowest possible cost; now facing competition, the company finds it profitable to invest in the customer's experience. Ultimately, it may be the answer to managerial accounting questions that drive increased satisfaction.

Source: Felix Gillette, "Can a Company You Hate Make a Cable Box You Love?" *Bloomberg Businessweek*, June 23, 2016.

A differential analysis of Uber's decision to supply storage service internally or to outsource it is presented in **Exhibit 16.3**. Continuing to provide the service internally has a net advantage of $4,000.

EXHIBIT 16.3	Differential Analysis of Outsourcing Decision		
	Cost to do Internally	**Cost to Outsource**	**Difference (income effect of outsourcing)**
Cost to outsource data storage		$15,000	$(15,000)
Cost to do internally			
Variable costs related to data storage ($0.20 × 30,000*). . .	$ 6,000		6,000
Fixed costs related to data storage	5,000		5,000
Total	$11,000	$15,000	$ (4,000)
Advantage of providing service internally		$4,000	

*300,000 miles divided by 10

But what if the data storage capacity created by outsourcing to DataTech can be used to provide storage services to another company for $7,000 per month? In this case, the storage capacity has an alternative use, and the net cash flow from this alternative use is an opportunity cost of providing the service internally. Treating the revenue Uber will not receive if it continues to source data storage internally as an opportunity cost, the analysis in **Exhibit 16.4** indicates that outsourcing now has a net advantage of $3,000.

EXHIBIT 16.4	Differential Analysis of of Outsourcing Decision with Opportunity Cost		
	Cost to do Internally	Cost to Outsource	Difference (income effect of outsourcing)
Cost to outsource data storage		$15,000	$(15,000)
Cost to do internally			
Variable costs related to data storage ($0.20 × 30,000*). . .	$ 6,000		6,000
Fixed costs related to data storage	5,000		5,000
Opportunity cost of lost subscription revenue	7,000		7,000
Total	$18,000	$15,000	$ 3,000
Advantage of providing service internally		$3,000	

*300,000 miles divided by 10

Although outsourcing has become widely accepted across virtually all industries, the results of outsourcing are not uniformly positive. Some companies that made a strong commitment to extensive outsourcing have discovered that there are many problems that can occur when they shift key processes and functions to other companies. It is usually easier to make major changes and to correct problems related to in-house functions and processes than for those outsourced to other companies, especially if they are located offshore. The following Business Insight discusses the outsourcing experience of Boeing.

BUSINESS INSIGHT

Boeing Rethinks Outsourcing **Boeing** made headlines in 2007 when aggressive outsourcing led to unanticipated delays in the launch of their new flagship aircraft, the 787 Dreamliner. At the time, the company believed that the radically outsourced production process would eventually be "more efficient and profitable than existing construction methods." However, under pressure from customers the airline has moved more and more production back in-house. In fact, upon ordering the 777x, Emirates Airline publicly asked Boeing not to outsource production of the planes to avoid the delays faced by Dreamliner customers.

Boeing's enthusiasm for outsourcing the Dreamliner and other planes was quickly tempered as language barriers, further outsourcing by contractors, and poor communication across the production process led to issues of quality and schedule delays. Now even more production is being moved back in-house, as Boeing reconsiders the costs and benefits of outsourcing parts of its complex design, production, and manufacturing processes.

Sources: Jon Ostrower, "Boing Insources Jumbo Work," *The Wall Street Journal*, September 17, 2015; David Kesmodel and Daniel Michaels, "For Boeing, It's Been a Long, Strange Trip," *The Wall Street Journal*, September 23, 2011; and Lynn Lunsford "Boeing Scrambles to Repair Problems With New Plane," *The Wall Street Journal*, December 7, 2007.

Even if outsourcing appears financially advantageous in the short run, management should not decide to outsource before considering a variety of qualitative risk factors. Is the outside supplier interested in developing a long-term relationship or merely attempting to use some temporarily idle capacity? If so, what will happen at the end of the contract period? What impact would a decision to outsource have on the morale of a company's employees? Will it have to rehire laid-off employees after the contract expires? Will the outside supplier meet delivery schedules? Does the supplied part meet quality standards? Will it continue to meet them? Organizations often manufacture products or provide services they can obtain elsewhere in order to control quality, to have an assured supply source, to avoid dealing with a potential competitor, or to maintain a core competency. Some of these issues are discussed in the Business Insight that follows.

The qualitative risk factors discussed above are often magnified when a company goes global, either as an outsourcing buyer or provider. Global outsourcing is often motivated by the desire to get projects completed "on time" and "within budget." In the following Research Insight, PricewaterhouseCoopers views outsourcing as a way to focus resources on operations that truly differentiate the firm.

BUSINESS INSIGHT

Outsourcing Changes Cost Structure, Brings New Risks   Firms are finding that flexibility from outsourcing can come with significant costs, largely in holding the supplier to quality standards. Bert Ahill, who advises firms on outsourcing, feels that companies regularly forget the risks that they are exposing themselves to when outsourcing. Often firms forget to account for economic, political, and weather hazards that affect their international suppliers. Firms should take care to build redundancy into outsourced supply chains to control disruptions that could come from these sources.

Some firms are finding that the costs of monitoring outsourced contractors outweigh the benefits of outsourcing. **Boston Scientific**, a maker of medical devices, has been manufacturing its own batteries for 10 years. While companies like **Boeing** were making radical moves in the opposite direction, Boston Scientific found it more cost-effective to keep battery production in-house, as the quality and longevity of a battery implanted in a patient is of paramount importance. In addition to quality and stability, other supply chain issues arise with outsourcing. **Taylor Guitars** uses exotic woods in its products, and when concerns arose about the sustainability of its suppliers' practices it chose to purchase a Cameroonian mill to improve sourcing. The organic soap maker **Dr. Bronner's** ran into similar issues with its palm oil supply, so it formed a company to manage sustainable sourcing of palm oil in Ghana.

Careful analysis of the costs and benefits of both outsourcing and vertical integration should be undertaken on an ongoing basis to make sure that the company chooses the correct supply chain.

Sources: Alexis Bateman, "Guest Voices: New Supplier Strategies Revive Important Corporate Questions," *The Wall Street Journal*, March 7, 2016 and Ben DiPietro, "When Manufacturing Means Building Supply-Chain Resilience," *The Wall Street Journal*, October 21, 2015.

RESEARCH INSIGHT

Role of Outsourcing in Operations   PricewaterhouseCoopers's latest Global Operations Survey offers a new, narrower view of the role of outsourcing in operations. Rather than recommending outsourcing as a way to change the firm's cost structure, PwC views outsourcing as a way to focus on operations that truly differentiate the firm. The PwC study divides a company's capabilities into four groups:

1. Differentiating capabilities,
2. Competitive necessities,
3. Basic capabilities, and
4. Other activities.

PwC recommends focusing resources on those activities where being best-in-category offers greatest returns (item 1). Investments in attention, staff, and capital should center on these differentiating operations. PwC recommends aggressive cost management and efficiency in activities that are required for participation in the market sector, where excellence in these areas offers no advantage, but is required for participation in a market (item 2). For example, consumers expect all banks to have excellent security; thus, banks should find ways to meet the excellent security standards with the greatest efficiency. PwC recommends outsourcing basic capabilities (item 3). As there is no return for excelling in these areas, they are the areas in which cost minimization is the best strategy. Most firms outsource facilities maintenance and other operations that are unrelated to success in their sector but are required to function. All other activities that do not fit into the first three groups and deviate from the core business should be eliminated if possible (item 4).

Source: "2015 Global Operations Survey: Reimagining Operations," *PricewaterhouseCoopers*, 2015, p. 17. Link: http://operationssurvey.pwc.com/PwC-2015-Global-Operations-Survey.pdf

MID-CHAPTER REVIEW 5

Epson produces color cartridges for inkjet printers. Suppose cartridges are sold to mail-order distributors for $4.80 each and that manufacturing and other costs are as follows:

Variable Costs per Unit		Fixed Costs per Month	
Direct materials	$2.00	Factory overhead	$15,000
Direct labor	0.20	Selling and administrative.	5,000
Factory overhead	0.25	Total	$20,000
Distribution	0.05		
Total	$2.50		

The variable distribution costs are for transportation to mail-order distributors. Also assume the current monthly production and sales volume is 15,000 and monthly capacity is 20,000 units.

REQUIRED
Determine the effect of the following situation on monthly profits.

A Mexican manufacturer has offered a one-year contract to supply ink for the cartridges at a cost of $1.00 per unit. If Epson accepts the offer, it will be able to reduce variable manufacturing costs by 40 percent and rent some of its factory space to another company for $1,000.00 per month.

The solution to this review problem can be found on page 765.

LO6 Apply differential analysis to evaluate whether to sell or further process a product.

Sell or Process Further

When a product is salable at various stages of completion, management must determine the product's most advantageous selling point. As each stage is completed, management must determine whether to sell the product then or to process it further. For example, petroleum companies have to determine how much crude oil to refine as diesel fuel and how much to process further as gasoline. We consider two types of sell or process further decisions: (1) for a single product and (2) for joint products.

Single Product Decisions Assume that **Scandinavian Furniture Inc.** manufactures modular wood furniture from precut and shaped wood. Although all units are salable before they are sanded and painted, Scandinavian Furniture Inc. sands and paints all units before they are sold. Management wishes to know if this is the optimal selling point.

A complete listing of unit costs and revenues for the alternative selling points for a low-end storage cabinet follows:

	Per Cabinet		
	Sell after Assembly	Sell after Painting	Difference (income effect of painting)
Selling price	$40	$75	$35
Assembly costs	(25)	(25)	
Sanding and painting costs		(12)	(12)
Contribution margin	$15	$38	$23
Advantage of painting		$23	

The sanding and painting operation has an additional contribution of $23 per unit. The storage cabinets should be sold after they are painted.

The assembly costs are the same under both alternatives. This illustrates that *all costs incurred prior to the decision point are irrelevant*. Given the existence of an assembled chair, the decision alternatives are to sell it now or to process it further. A differential analysis for the decision to sell or process further should include only revenues and the incremental costs of further processing as follows.

Increase in revenues		
Sell after painting	$75	
Sell after assembly	(40)	$35
Additional costs of sanding and painting		(12)
Advantage of sanding and painting		$23

The identical solution is obtained if the selling price without further processing is treated as an opportunity cost as follows.

Revenues after painting		$75
Additional costs of sanding and painting	$12	
Opportunity cost of not selling after assembly	40	(52)
Advantage of sanding and painting		$23

By processing a chair further, Scandinavian Furniture has foregone the opportunity to receive $40 from its sale. Since the chair is already assembled, and the cost of assembly is an irrelevant sunk cost, this $40 is the net cash inflow from the most desirable alternative; it is the opportunity cost of painting.

Joint Product Decisions Two or more products simultaneously produced by a single process from a common set of inputs are called **joint products**. Joint products are often found in basic industries that process natural raw materials such as dairy, chemical, meat, petroleum, and wood products. In the petroleum industry, crude oil is refined into fuel oil, gasoline, kerosene, diesel, lubricating oil, and other products.

The point in the process where the joint products become separately identifiable is called the **split-off point**. Materials and conversion costs incurred prior to the split-off point are called **joint costs**. For external reporting purposes, a number of techniques are used to allocate joint costs among joint products. We do not discuss these techniques here (interested students should consult a cost accounting textbook), except to note that none of the methods provide information useful for determining what to do with a joint product once it is produced. Because joint costs are incurred prior to the decision point, they are sunk costs. Consequently, *joint costs are irrelevant to a decision to sell a joint product or to process it further*. The only relevant factors are the alternative costs and revenues subsequent to the split-off point.

BUSINESS INSIGHT

Product Mix Decisions in Consumer Electronics The changing consumer electronics landscape is driving changes in product mix at companies like **Apple** and **Microsoft**. Microsoft, long a software company, is aggressively shifting its product mix to include smartphones, laptops, and a smart watch. This shift to hardware alongside software is a product mix similar to Apple's. There is a notable exception—desktop computers. Apple will need to rethink its commitment to the desktop computer to keep pace with customers' changing preferences for devices.

Apple's Mac line is estimated to be the most profitable product in its class, and this year Apple reported its highest ever revenue from its desktop computer business. At the same time, Mac revenue is at its lowest ebb as a share of Apple's total revenue. This suggests that while Apple is clearly successful in the PC space, changes will be required in the future. The product mix decisions that Apple and Microsoft are making rely on the decision relevance framework introduced in this chapter.

Sources: Shira Ovide, "Microsoft Pushes Deeper Into Hardware," *The Wall Street Journal*, October 6, 2015 and Christopher Mims, "Why Apple Should Kill Off the Mac," *The Wall Street Journal*, June 14, 2015.

MID-CHAPTER REVIEW 6

Epson produces color cartridges for inkjet printers. Suppose cartridges are sold to mail-order distributors for $4.80 each and that manufacturing and other costs are as follows:

Variable Costs per Unit		Fixed Costs per Month	
Direct materials	$2.00	Factory overhead	$15,000
Direct labor	0.20	Selling and administrative	5,000
Factory overhead	0.25	Total	$20,000
Distribution	0.05		
Total	$2.50		

The variable distribution costs are for transportation to mail-order distributors. Also assume the current monthly production and sales volume is 15,000 and monthly capacity is 20,000 units.

REQUIRED
Determine the effect of the following situation on monthly profits.

The cartridges are currently unpackaged; that is, they are sold in bulk. Individual packaging would increase costs by $0.10 per unit. However, the units could then be sold for $5.05.

The solution to this review problem can be found on page 765.

USE OF LIMITED RESOURCES

LO7 Allocate limited resources for purposes of maximizing short-run profit.

All of us have experienced time as a limiting or constraining resource. With two exams the day after tomorrow and a paper due next week, our problem is how to allocate limited study time. The solution depends on our objectives, our current status (grades, knowledge, skill levels, and so forth), and available time. Given this information, we devise a work plan to best meet our objectives.

Managers must also decide how to best use limited resources to accomplish organizational goals. A supermarket may lose sales because limited shelf space prevents stocking all available brands of soft drinks. A manufacturer may lose sales because limited machine hours or labor hours prevent filling all orders. Managers of for-profit organizations will likely find the problems of capacity constraints less troublesome than the problems of excess capacity; nonetheless, these problems are real. Ultimately, the problem often boils down to a product-mix decision, in which we must decide the mix of products or services we are going to offer our customers with the limited resources available to us.

If the limited resource is not a core business activity, it may be appropriate to outsource additional units of the limited resource externally. For example, many organizations have a small legal staff to handle routine activities; if the internal staff becomes fully committed, the organization seeks outside legal counsel.

The long-run solution to the problem of limited resources to perform core activities may be to expand capacity. However, this is usually not feasible in the short run. Economic models suggest that another solution is to reduce demand by increasing the price. Again, this may not be desirable. A hotel, for example, may want to maintain competitive prices. A manufacturer might want to maintain a long-run price to retain customer goodwill to avoid attracting competitors, or to prevent accusations of "price gouging."

Single Constraint

The allocation of limited resources should be made only after a careful consideration of many qualitative factors. The following rule provides a useful starting point in making short-run decisions of how to best use limited resources: *To achieve short-run profit maximization, a for-profit organization should allocate limited resources in a manner that maximizes the contribution per unit of the limited resource.* The application of this rule is illustrated in the following example.

Assume **Snap Fitness** offers three different personal training packages (A, B, and C) to its customers. These packages vary from a personalized nutrition and exercise training to a one-time consultation. Suppose a limitation of 120 labor hours per week prevents Snap from meeting the demand for its services. Information for the three service packages is as follows:

	A	B	C
Unit selling price...	$100	$80	$50
Unit variable costs	(60)	(35)	(25)
Unit contribution margin......................................	$ 40	$45	$25
Hours per unit..	4	3	1

Package A has the highest selling price and Package B has the highest unit contribution margin. Package C is shown below to have the highest contribution per hour.

	A	B	C
Unit contribution margin.......................................	$40	$45	$25
Hours per unit..	÷ 4	÷ 3	÷ 1
Contribution per hour..	$10	$15	$25

Following the rule of maximizing the contribution per unit of a single constraining factor (labor hours), Snap should use its limited labor hours to sell Package C. As shown in the following analysis, any other plan would result in lower profits:

	A Highest Selling Price per Unit	B Highest Contribution per Unit	C Highest Contribution per Constraining Factor
Hours available....................	120	120	120
Hours per unit.....................	÷ 4	÷ 3	÷ 1
Weekly production in units..........	30	40	120
Unit contribution margin............	× $40	× $45	× $25
Total weekly contribution margin	$1,200	$1,800	$3,000

Despite this analysis, management may decide on a product mix that includes some units of A or B or both to satisfy the requests of some "good" customers or to offer a full product line. However, such decisions sacrifice short-run profits.

Multiple Constraints

Continuing our illustration, assume a second constraint; that is, the maximum weekly demand for C is only 90 units, although the company is capable of producing 120 units of C each week. In this case, the limited labor resource should first be used to satisfy the demand for Package C, with any remaining capacity going to produce Package B, which has the next highest contribution per unit of constraining factor. This allocation provides a total weekly contribution of $2,700 as follows.

Available hours..	120
Required for C (90 units × 1 hour)................................	(90)
Hours available for B	30
Labor hours per unit...	÷ 3
Production of B in units	10
Unit contribution margin of B......................................	× $45
Contribution from B	$ 450
Contribution from C ($25 per unit × 90 units)	2,250
Total weekly contribution margin	$2,700

When an organization has alternative uses for several limited resources, such as limited labor hours and limited space, the optimal use of those resources cannot be determined using the rule for short-run profit maximization. In these situations, techniques such as linear programming can be used to assist in determining the optimal mix of products or services.

Theory of Constraints

The **theory of constraints** states that every process has a bottleneck (constraining resource) and that production cannot take place faster than it is processed through that bottleneck. The goal of the theory of constraints is to maximize **throughput** (defined as sales revenue minus direct materials costs) in a constrained environment.[1] The theory has several implications for management.

- Management should identify the bottleneck. This is often difficult when several different products are produced in a facility containing many different production activities. One approach is to walk around and observe where inventory is building up in front of workstations. The bottleneck will likely have the largest piles of work that have been waiting for the longest time.

- Management should schedule production to maximize the efficient use of the bottleneck resource. Efficiently using the bottleneck resource might necessitate inspecting all units before they reach the bottleneck rather than after the units are completed. The bottleneck resource is too valuable to waste on units that may already be defective.

- Management should schedule production to avoid a buildup of inventory. Reducing inventory lowers the cost of inventory investments and the cost of carrying inventory. It also assists in improving quality by making it easier to identify quality problems that might otherwise be hidden in large piles of inventory. Reducing inventory will require a change in the attitude of managers who like to see machines and people constantly working. To avoid a buildup of inventory in front of the bottleneck, it may be necessary for people and equipment to remain idle until the bottleneck resource calls for additional input.

- Management should work to eliminate the bottleneck, perhaps by increasing the capacity of the bottleneck resource, redesigning products so they can be produced with less use of the bottleneck resource, rescheduling production procedures to substitute nonbottleneck resources, or outsourcing work performed by bottleneck resources.

The theory of constraints has implications for management accounting performance reports. Keeping people and equipment working on production full-time is often a goal of management. To support this goal, management accounting performance reports have traditionally highlighted underutilization as an unfavorable variance (see Chapter 22). This has encouraged managers to have people and equipment producing inventory, even if the inventory is not needed or cannot be further processed because of bottlenecks. The theory of constraints suggests that it is better to have nonbottleneck resources idle than it is to have them fully utilized. To support the theory of constraints, performance reports should:

- Measure the utilization of bottleneck resources
- Measure factory throughput
- Not encourage the full utilization of nonbottleneck resources
- Discourage the buildup of excess inventory

While the theory of constraints is *similar* to our general rule for how to best use limited resources, it emphasizes throughput (selling price minus direct materials) rather than contribution (selling price minus variable costs) in allocating the limited resource. The exclusion of direct labor and variable manufacturing overhead yields larger unit margins, and it may affect resource allocations based on throughput rankings. The result will likely be a reduction in profits from those that could be achieved using our general rule for how to allocate limited resources. Although the theory of constraints has not been widely embraced by companies, many of its users are enthusiastic about its benefits.

---

[1] *The Goal,* by Eliyah M. Goldratt and Jeff Cox, presents the concepts underlying the theory of constraints in the form of a novel.

Limitations of Decision Analysis Models

Analytical models, such as the relevant cost analysis model and applications presented in this chapter, are very useful in organizing information for purposes of determining the economics of a decision. However, it is important always to keep in mind that models do not make decisions—managers make decisions. The results of analytical models are an essential and necessary starting point in many decisions, but often there are other factors that weigh heavily on a decision that may cause the manager to go against the most economical alternative. There may be human resource, marketing, cultural, logistical, technological, or other factors that outweigh the analytics of a decision situation. It is in these situations where managers demonstrate leadership, problem-solving, and executive skill and potential, or the lack thereof.

CHAPTER-END REVIEW

Assume that **Innovative Components Inc.** produces only three different types of injection-molded knobs. They produce the Pointer Knob which is used for on/off devices, the Instrument Knob which is used for precision adjustment, and the Star Knob which is used for snowblowers and lawnmowers. The factory machine capacity is the company's constraining resource. It operates at 90% capacity and management wants to devote the unused capacity to one of the products. The following data represents their current operations:

	Pointer Knob	Instrument Knob	Star Knob
Per-case data:			
Sales price	$20	$22	$6
Variable cost.	8	16	2
Contribution margin	$12	$ 6	$4
Fixed costs*	6	2	1
Net income.	$ 6	$ 4	$3

*Allocated on basis of machine hours at $1 per hour.

REQUIRED

Which product should management produce with its extra capacity?

The solution to this review problem can be found on page 766.

GUIDANCE ANSWERS . . . YOU MAKE THE CALL

You are the Vice President of Manufacturing   This is a decision that has both economic and ethical dimensions. Economically, the cost of the old machine is a sunk cost, since the expenditure to acquire it has already been made. If it can be sold to another company to recover part of the initial cost, that amount would be relevant to the decision regarding the new technology. However, you should ignore the cost of the recently purchased machine and consider only the outlay costs that will differ between keeping the recently purchased machine and purchasing the new technology, plus any opportunity costs that may be involved with disposing of the existing machine and acquiring the new machine. From an ethical standpoint, managers are often hesitant to recommend an action that reflects poorly on their past decisions. The temptation is to try to justify the past decision. If you have evaluated all of the relevant costs and have considered all of the qualitative issues associated with upgrading the machine, these should be the basis for making your recommendation, not what it will do to your reputation with your superiors.

KEY TERMS

cost reduction proposal, 729

differential cost analysis, 732

full costs, 737

irrelevant costs, 728

joint costs, 743

joint products, 743

opportunity cost, 731

outlay costs, 729

outsourcing, 738

relevant costs, 728

revenues, 729

split-off point, 743

sunk costs, 730

theory of constraints, 746

throughput, 746

Assignments with the Ⓜ️ logo in the margin are available in *my*BusinessCourse.
See the Preface of the book for details.

MULTIPLE CHOICE

Multiple Choice Answers
1. a   2. c   3. d   4. a   5. a

1. Jabo Inc. is considering a new bifro-spectra machine for its production plant to replace an old machine that originally cost $12,000 and has $9,000 of accumulated depreciation. The new machine can be purchased at a cash cost of $18,000, but the distributor of the new machine has offered to take the old machine in as a trade-in, thereby reducing the cost of the new machine to $16,000. Based only on this information, calculate the total relevant cost of acquiring the new machine.

    a. $16,000, or the net cash paid to the distributor
    b. $18,000, or the gross cost of the new machine
    c. $19,000, or the net cash paid plus the book value ($3,000) of the old machine
    d. $17,000, or the gross cost of the new machine minus the $1,000 loss on disposing of the old machine

2. Bruno Company is a Rhode Island company that sells a branded product regionally to retail customers in New England. It normally sells its product for $30 per unit; however, it has received a one-time offer from a private-brand company on the West Coast to buy 1,000 units at $19 per unit. Even though the company has excess capacity to produce the units, the President of the company immediately rejected the offer; however, the chief accountant stated that it might be a profitable opportunity for the company, even though $19 is below its unit cost of $21, calculated as follows:

Direct materials	$ 9.00
Direct labor.	5.00
Variable overhead.	4.00
Depreciation and other fixed overhead	3.00
Total unit cost.	$21.00

    Also, the special order will save $1 per unit in packaging costs since the product will be bulk packaged instead of being individually packaged. Calculate the amount of profit or loss per unit if Bruno accepts the special order.

    a. $2 loss
    b. $1 loss
    c. $2 profit
    d. $1 profit

3. Sitro, LTD had been making a component for one of its products, but is now considering outsourcing the component to a Chinese company, which has offered to sell an unlimited quantity of components for $6 per unit. If Sitro outsources, it could shut down a whole department and rent the building for $2,000 per month. The cost of making the component is $5 per unit, which includes $1.50 of fixed costs, of which only $1.00 per unit can be avoided if the department is shut down. Sitro currently produces about 1,000 units per month. What is the cost advantage or disadvantage of per unit of outsourcing the component?

    a. $1.00 disadvantage
    b. $1.50 disadvantage
    c. $1.00 advantage
    d. $0.50 advantage

4. Mitrex Company makes a semi-finished machine component for the heavy equipment industry that has a unit contribution margin of $250 to Mitrex. A major customer has been purchasing 100 units per month from Mitrex for many years, but has indicated that it would prefer to purchase them already machined to its specifications. It has offered to pay an additional $50 per unit for the finished units. To meet those specifications, Mitrex would have to rent additional equipment at a cost of $2,000 per month and incur labor and other direct costs of $15 per unit. Calculate the per-unit advantage or disadvantage of further processing.

    a. $15 advantage
    b. $35 advantage
    c. $50 advantage
    d. $15 disadvantage

5. Giko, LTD makes three products (Abba, Babba, and Cabba), all of which use a very rare ingredient called Mecogen. Giko can purchase only 500 ounces of Mecogen per month from its East Asian source. Below are data for the three products:

	Abba	Babba	Cabba
Unit selling price...................................	$80	$65	$100
Unit variable costs	45	40	60
Unit contribution margin...........................	35	25	40
Mecogen (ounces per unit).........................	10	15	20

How should Giko allocate the 500 ounces of Mecogen assuming it can sell unlimited quantities of all three produces?

    a. All 500 ounces should be allocated to Abba
    b. All 500 ounces should be allocated to Babba
    c. All 500 ounces should be allocated to Cabba
    d. None of the above

QUESTIONS

Q16-1. Distinguish between relevant and irrelevant costs.

Q16-2. In evaluating a cost reduction proposal, what three alternatives are available to management?

Q16-3. When are outlay costs relevant and when are they irrelevant?

Q16-4. Relate the manufacturing cost hierarchy discussed in Chapter 14 to the concept of relevant costs. Under what conditions would product-level costs be relevant?

Q16-5. Why is a differential analysis of relevant items preferred to a detailed listing of all costs and revenues associated with each alternative?

Q16-6. When are opportunity costs relevant to the evaluation of a special order?

Q16-7. Identify some important qualitative considerations in evaluating a decision to make or buy a part.

Q16-8. In a decision to sell or to process further, of what relevance are costs incurred prior to the decision point? Explain your answer.

Q16-9. How should limited resources be used to achieve short-run profit maximization?

Q16-10. What should performance reports do in support of the theory of constraints?

LO1

M16-11. Relevant Cost Terms: Matching

SoundBite produces three different versions of portable digital music players, the Deluxe, Sport and Zip. SoundBite is evaluating a proposal that will result in doubling the production of Sport and discontinuing the production of Zip. The facilities currently used to produce Zip will be devoted to the production of Sport. Furthermore, additional machinery will be acquired to produce Sport. The production of Deluxe will not be affected. All products have a positive contribution margin.

REQUIRED

Presented below are a number of phrases related to the proposal followed by a list of cost terms. For each phrase, select the most appropriate cost term. Each term is used only once.

PHRASES

1. Cost of equipment to produce Zip
2. Increased variable costs of Sport
3. Property taxes on the new machinery
4. Revenues from the sale of Deluxe
5. Increased revenue from the sale of Sport
6. Contribution margin of Zip
7. Variable costs of Deluxe
8. Company president's salary

COST TERMS

a. Opportunity cost
b. Sunk cost
c. Irrelevant variable outlay cost
d. Irrelevant fixed outlay cost
e. Relevant variable outlay cost
f. Relevant fixed outlay cost
g. Relevant revenues
h. Irrelevant revenues

LO1

M16-12. Relevant Cost Terms: Matching

Studio produces and sells 4,000 specialty handbags per month and has the capacity to produce 5,000 units per month. Studio is evaluating a one-time, special order for 2,000 units from a Bloomingdales. Accepting the order will increase variable manufacturing costs and certain fixed selling and administrative costs. It will also require the company to forego the sale of 1,000 units to regular customers.

REQUIRED

Presented below are a number of statements related to the proposal followed by a list of cost terms. For each statement, select the most appropriate cost term. Each term is used only once.

STATEMENTS

1. Increased revenues from special order
2. Lost contribution margin from foregone sales to regular customers
3. Revenues from 4,000 units sold to regular customers
4. Variable cost of 4,000 units sold to regular customers
5. Increase in fixed selling and administrative expenses
6. Cost of existing equipment used to produce special order
7. Salary paid to current supervisor who oversees manufacture of special order
8. Increased variable costs of special order

COST TERMS

a. Irrelevant variable outlay cost
b. Irrelevant fixed outlay cost
c. Sunk cost
d. Relevant variable outlay cost
e. Relevant fixed outlay cost
f. Opportunity cost
g. Relevant revenues
h. Irrelevant revenues

M16-13. Identifying Relevant Costs and Revenues

The Village of Bomont operates a power plant on a river that flows through town. The village uses some of this generated electricity to operate a water treatment plant and sells the excess electricity to a local utility. The city council is evaluating two alternative proposals:

- *Proposal A* calls for replacing the generators used in the plant with more efficient generators that will produce more electricity and have lower operating costs. The salvage value of the old generators is higher than their removal cost.
- *Proposal B* calls for raising the level of the dam to retain more water for generating power and increasing the force of water flowing through the dam. This will significantly increase the amount of electricity generated by the plant. Operating costs will not be affected.

REQUIRED

Presented are a number of cost and revenue items. Indicate in the appropriate columns whether each item is relevant or irrelevant to proposals A and B.

	Proposal A	Proposal B
1. Cost of new furniture for the city manager's office	_____	_____
2. Cost of old generators	_____	_____
3. Cost of new generators	_____	_____
4. Operating cost of old generators	_____	_____
5. Operating cost of new generators	_____	_____
6. The police chief's salary	_____	_____
7. Depreciation on old generators	_____	_____
8. Salvage value of old generators	_____	_____
9. Removal cost of old generators	_____	_____
10. Cost of raising dam	_____	_____
11. Maintenance costs of water plant	_____	_____
12. Revenues from sale of electricity	_____	_____

M16-14. Classifying Relevant and Irrelevant Items

The law firm of Hannan, Taylor, and Masteller has been asked to represent a local client. All legal proceedings will be held out of town in Boston.

REQUIRED

The law firm's accountant has asked you to help determine the incremental cost of accepting this client. Classify each of the following items on the basis of their relationship to this engagement. Items may have multiple classifications.

	Relevant costs		Irrelevant costs	
	Opportunity	Outlay	Outlay	Sunk
1. The case will require three attorneys to stay four nights in a Boston hotel. The predicted hotel bill is $2,400.	_____	_____	_____	_____
2. Hannan, Taylor, and Masteller's professional staff is paid $2,000 per day for out-of-town assignments.	_____	_____	_____	_____
3. Last year, depreciation on Hannan, Taylor, and Masteller's office was $25,000.	_____	_____	_____	_____
4. Round-trip transportation to Boston is expected to cost $250 per person.	_____	_____	_____	_____
5. The firm has recently accepted an engagement that will require partners to spend two weeks in Chicago. The predicted out-of-pocket costs of this trip are $8,500.	_____	_____	_____	_____
6. The firm has a maintenance contract on its computer equipment that will cost $2,200 next year.	_____	_____	_____	_____
7. If the firm accepts the client and sends attorneys to Boston, it will have to decline a conflicting engagement in Miami that would have provided a net cash inflow of $15,000.	_____	_____	_____	_____

continued

continued from previous page

| | Relevant costs | | Irrelevant costs | |
	Opportunity	Outlay	Outlay	Sunk
8. The firm's variable overhead is $80 per client hour.	_____	_____	_____	_____
9. The firm pays $250 per year for Mr. Masteller's subscription to a law journal.	_____	_____	_____	_____
10. Last year the firm paid $3,500 to increase the insulation in its building.	_____	_____	_____	_____

LO1, 2

M16-15. Relevant Costs for Equipment Replacement Decision

Dr. Heller paid $50,000 for X-ray equipment four years ago. The equipment was expected to have a useful life of 10 years from the date of acquisition with annual operating costs of $32,000. Technological advances have made the machine purchased four years ago obsolete with a zero salvage value. An improved X-ray device incorporating the new technology is available at an initial cost of $55,000 and annual operating costs of $21,000. The new machine is expected to last only six years before it, too, is obsolete. Asked to analyze the financial aspects of replacing the obsolete but still functional machine, Dr. Heller's accountant prepared the following analysis. After looking over these numbers, the company's manager rejected the proposal.

Six-year savings [($32,000 − $21,000) × 6]	$ 66,000
Cost of new machine	(55,000)
Undepreciated cost of old machine	(30,000)
Advantage (disadvantage) of replacement	$(19,000)

REQUIRED

Perform an analysis of relevant costs to determine whether the manager made the correct decision.

LO1, 2, 4

M16-16. Special Order

Soni LTD produces wall mounts for flat panel television sets. The forecasted income statement for 2017 is as follows:

SONI, LTD Budgeted Income Statement For the Year 2017	
Sales ($44 per unit)	$4,400,000
Cost of good sold ($36 per unit)	(3,600,000)
Gross profit	800,000
Selling expenses ($3 per unit)	(300,000)
Net income	$ 500,000

ADDITIONAL INFORMATION

(1) Of the production costs and selling expenses, $800,000 and $100,000, respectively, are fixed. (2) Soni LTD received a special order from a hospital supply company offering to buy 12,500 wall mounts for $30. If it accepts the order, there will be no additional selling expenses, and there is currently sufficient excess capacity to fill the order. The company's sales manager argues for rejecting the order because "we are not in the business of paying $36 to make a product to sell for $30."

REQUIRED

Do you think the company should accept the special order? Should the decision be based only on the profitability of the sale, or are there other issues that Soni should consider? Explain.

LO1, 2, 6

M16-17. Sell or Process Further

Bear Lake Boat Company manufactures sailboat hulls at a cost of $5,200 per unit. The hulls are sold to boat-yards for $6,000. The company is evaluating the desirability of adding masts, sails, and rigging to the hulls prior to sale at an additional cost of $1,500. The completed sailboats could then be sold for $7,000 each.

REQUIRED

Determine whether the company should sell sailboat hulls or process them further into complete sailboats. Assume sales volume will not be affected.

EXERCISES

E16-18. Special Order

LO1, 2, 4

Great Oaks Farm grows organic vegetables and sells them to local restaurants after processing. The farm's leading product is Salad-in-a-Bag, which is a mixture of organic green salad ingredients prepared and ready to serve. The company sells a large bag to restaurants for $25. It calculates the variable cost per bag at $19 (including $1 for local delivery), and the average total cost per bag is $22. Because the vegetables are perishable and Great Oaks Farm is experiencing a large crop, the farm has extra capacity. A representative of a restaurant association in another city has offered to buy fresh salad stock from the company to augment its regular supply during an upcoming international festival. The restaurant association wants to buy 2,500 bags during the next month for $21 per bag. Delivery to restaurants in the other city will cost the company $0.75 per bag. It can meet most of the order with excess capacity but would sacrifice 400 bags of regular sales to fill this special order. Please assist Great Oaks Farm's management by answering the following questions.

REQUIRED

a. Using differential analysis, what is the impact on profits of accepting this special order?

b. What nonquantitative issues should management consider before making a final decision?

c. How would the analysis change if the special order were for 2,500 bags per month for the next five years?

E16-19. Special Order

LO1, 2, 4

Nature's Garden, a new restaurant situated on a busy highway in Pomona, California, specializes in a chef's salad selling for $7. Daily fixed costs are $1,200, and variable costs are $4 per meal. With a capacity of 800 meals per day, the restaurant serves an average of 750 meals each day.

REQUIRED

a. Determine the current average cost per meal.

b. A busload of 30 Girl Scouts stops on its way home from the San Bernardino National Forest. The leader offers to bring them in if the scouts can all be served a meal for a total of $150. The owner refuses, saying he would lose $0.60 per meal if he accepted this offer. How do you think the owner arrived at the $0.60 figure? Comment on the owner's reasoning.

c. A local businessman on a break overhears the conversation with the leader and offers the owner a one-year contract to feed 300 of the businessman's employees one meal each day at a special price of $4.50 per meal. Should the restaurant owner accept this offer? Why or why not?

E16-20. Special Order: High-Low Cost Estimation

LO1, 2, 4

ABS Inc. produces air bag systems that it sells to North American automobile manufacturers. Although the company has a capacity of 150,000 units per year, it is currently producing at an annual rate of 90,000 units. ABS Inc. has received an order from a Japanese manufacturer to purchase 30,000 units at $8.75 each. Budgeted costs for 90,000 and 120,000 units are as follows:

	90,000 Units	120,000 Units
Manufacturing costs		
Direct materials	$ 225,000	$ 300,000
Direct labor	157,500	210,000
Factory overhead	607,500	630,000
Total	990,000	1,140,000
Selling and administrative	382,500	390,000
Total	$1,372,500	$1,530,000
Costs per unit		
Manufacturing	$11.00	$ 9.50
Selling and administrative	4.25	3.25
Total	$15.25	$12.75

Sales to North American manufacturers are priced at $20 per unit, but the sales manager believes the company should aggressively seek the Japanese business even if it results in a loss of $4.00 per unit. She believes obtaining this order would open up several new markets for the company's product. The general manager commented that the company cannot tighten its belt to absorb the $120,000 loss ($4.00 × 30,000) it would incur if the order is accepted.

REQUIRED

a. Determine the financial implications of accepting the order. (*Hint:* Use the high-low method to determine variable costs per unit.)

b. How would your analysis differ if the company were operating at capacity? Determine the advantage or disadvantage of accepting the order under full-capacity circumstances.

MBC

Hewlett-Packard
NYSE: HPQ
Sanmina Corp.
NASDAQ: SANM

E16-21. Outsourcing (Make-or-Buy) Decision

Assume a division of **Hewlett-Packard** currently makes 10,000 circuit boards per year used in producing diagnostic electronic instruments at a cost of $36 per board, consisting of variable costs per unit of $24 and fixed costs per unit of $12. Further assume **Sanmina Corporation** offers to sell Hewlett-Packard the 10,000 circuit boards for $36 each. If Hewlett-Packard accepts this offer, the facilities currently used to make the boards could be rented to one of Hewlett-Packard's suppliers for $30,000 per year. In addition, $5 per unit of the fixed overhead applied to the circuit boards would be totally eliminated.

REQUIRED

Should HP outsource this component from Sanmina Corporation? Support your answer with relevant cost calculations.

E16-22. Outsourcing (Make-or-Buy) Decision

Mountain Air Limited manufactures a line of room air purifiers. Management is currently evaluating the possible production of an air purifier for automobiles. Based on an annual volume of 10,000 units, the predicted cost per unit of an auto air purifier follows.

Direct materials	$ 9.00
Direct labor.	1.40
Factory overhead	10.00
Total	$20.40

These cost predictions include $80,000 in fixed factory overhead averaged over 10,000 units.

The completed air purifier units include a battery-operated electric motor, which Mountain Air assembles with parts purchased from an outside vendor for $2.00 per motor. Mini Motor Company has offered to supply an assembled battery-operated motor at a cost of $5.50 per unit, with a minimum annual order of 5,000 units. If Mountain Air accepts this offer, it will be able to reduce the variable labor and variable overhead costs of the auto air purifier by 50 percent.

REQUIRED

a. Determine whether Mountain Air should continue to make the electric motor or outsource it from Mini Motor Company. (Hint: analyze the relevant costs of making the "motors," not the entire air purifier.)

b. If it could otherwise rent the motor-assembly space for $25,000 per year, should it make or outsource this component?

c. What additional factors should it consider in deciding whether to make or outsource the electric motors?

E16-23. Make or Buy

Priya Rahavy, M.D., is a general practitioner whose offices are located in the Lake Forest Professional Building. In the past, Dr. Rahavy has operated her practice with a nurse, a receptionist/secretary, and a part-time bookkeeper. Dr. Rahavy, like many small-town physicians, has billed her patients and their insurance companies from her own office. The part-time bookkeeper, who works 15 hours per week, is employed exclusively for this purpose.

North Avenue Physician's Service Center has offered to take over all of Dr. Rahavy's billings and collections for an annual fee of $24,000. If Dr. Rahavy accepts this offer, she will no longer need the bookkeeper. The bookkeeper's wages and fringe benefits amount to $20 per hour, and the bookkeeper works 50 weeks per year. With all the billings and collections done elsewhere, Dr. Rahavy will have three additional hours available per week to see patients. She sees an average of four patients per hour at an average fee of $30 per visit. Dr. Rahavy's practice is expanding, and new patients often have to wait several weeks for an appointment. She has resisted expanding her office hours or working more than 50 weeks per year. Finally, if Dr. Rahavy signs on with the center, she will no longer need to rent a records storage facility for $200 per month.

REQUIRED

Conduct a relevant cost analysis to determine if it is profitable to outsource the bookkeeping.

E16-24. Sell or Process Further

LO1, 2, 6

Port Allen Chemical Company processes raw material D into joint products E and F. Raw material D costs $12 per liter. It costs $100 to convert 100 liters of D into 60 liters of E and 40 liters of F. Product F can be sold immediately for $12 per liter or processed further into Product G at an additional cost of $10 per liter. Product G can then be sold for $26 per liter.

REQUIRED

Determine whether Product F should be sold or processed further into Product G.

E16-25. Limited Resources

LO7

Fender Musical Instruments Corp.
NASDAQ :: FNDR

Assume **Fender** produces only three guitars: the Stratocaster, Dreadnought and Telecaster. A limitation of 720 labor hours per week prevents Fender from meeting the sales demand for these products. Product information is as follows:

	Stratocaster	Dreadnought	Telecaster
Unit selling price.	$960	$600	$1,260
Unit variable costs	(600)	(300)	(1,080)
Unit contribution margin.	$360	$300	$ 180
Labor hours per unit.	36	24	36

REQUIRED

a. Determine the weekly contribution from each product when total labor hours are allocated to the product with the highest
1. Unit selling price.
2. Unit contribution margin.
3. Contribution per labor hour.
(*Hint:* Each situation is independent of the others.)

b. What generalization can be made regarding the allocation of limited resources to achieve short-run profit maximization?

c. Determine the opportunity cost the company will incur if management requires the weekly production of 20 Telecasters.

d. Give reasons why a company may not allocate resources in the most economical way in some situations.

E16-26. Limited Resources

LO7

Maria Pajet, a regional sales representative for UniTec Systems Inc. has been working about 80 hours per week calling on a total of 123 regular customers each month. Because of family and health considerations, she has decided to reduce her hours to a maximum of 160 per month. Unfortunately, this cutback will require Maria to turn away some of her regular customers or, at least, serve them less frequently than once a month. Maria has developed the following information to assist her in determining how to best allocate time:

	Customer Classification		
	Large Business	Small Business	Individual
Number of customers.	8	35	80
Average monthly sales per customer.	$2,500	$1,500	$600
Commission percentage	5%	8%	10%
Hours per customer per monthly visit	5.0	3.0	2.5

REQUIRED

a. Develop a monthly plan that indicates the number of customers Maria should call on in each classification to maximize her monthly sales commissions.

b. Determine the monthly commissions Maria will earn if she implements this plan.

c. Give one or two reasons why Maria might decide not to follow the conclusions of the above analysis entirely.

PROBLEMS

LO1, 2, 3   **P16-27. Multiple Changes in Profit Plans**

In an attempt to improve profit performance, Anderson Company's management is considering a number of alternative actions. An October 2017 contribution income statement for Anderson Company follows.

ANDERSON COMPANY Contribution Income Statement For Month of October 2017		
Sales (10,000 units × $40)..		$400,000
Less variable costs		
Direct materials (10,000 units × $5).............................	$ 50,000	
Direct labor (10,000 units × $14)...............................	140,000	
Variable factory overhead (10,000 units × $6)....................	60,000	
Selling and administrative (10,000 units × $5)...................	50,000	(300,000)
Contribution margin (10,000 units × $10)........................		100,000
Less fixed costs		
Factory overhead..	50,000	
Selling and administrative..................................	60,000	(110,000)
Net income (loss)..		$ (10,000)

REQUIRED

Determine the effect of each of the following independent situations on monthly profit.

a. Purchasing automated assembly equipment, which should reduce direct labor costs by $5 per unit and increase variable overhead costs by $2 per unit and fixed factory overhead by $22,000 per month.

b. Reducing the selling price by $5 per unit. This should increase the monthly sales by 5,000 units. At this higher volume, additional equipment and salaried personnel would be required. This will increase fixed factory overhead by $2,800 per month and fixed selling and administrative costs by $2,500 per month.

c. Buying rather than manufacturing a component of Anderson's final product. This will increase direct materials costs by $12 per unit. However, direct labor will decline $4 per unit, variable factory overhead will decline $1 per unit, and fixed factory overhead will decline $15,000 per month.

d. Increasing the unit selling price by $4 per unit. This action should result in a 1,000-unit decrease in monthly sales.

e. Combining alternatives (a) and (d).

LO1, 2, 3   **P16-28. Multiple Changes in Profit Plans: Multiple Products**

Information on Guadalupe Ltd.'s three products follows:

	A	B	C
Unit sales per month	900	1,400	900
Selling price per unit..	$10.00	$15.00	$8.00
Variable costs per unit	(10.40)	(12.00)	(4.00)
Unit contribution margin.....................................	$ (0.40)	$ 3.00	$4.00

REQUIRED

Determine the effect each of the following situations would have on monthly profits. Each situation should be evaluated independently of all others.

a. Product A is discontinued.

b. Product A is discontinued, and the subsequent loss of customers causes sales of Product B to decline by 100 units.

c. The selling price of A is increased to $11.00 with a sales decrease of 150 units.

d. The price of Product B is increased to $16.00 with a resulting sales decrease of 200 units. However, some of these customers shift to Product A; sales of Product A increase by 140 units.

e. Product A is discontinued, and the plant in which A was produced is used to produce D, a new product. Product D has a unit contribution margin of $0.60. Monthly sales of Product D are predicted to be 600 units.

f. The selling price of Product C is increased to $9.0, and the selling price of Product B is decreased to $14.00. Sales of C decline by 200 units, while sales of B increase by 300 units.

P16-29. Relevant Costs and Differential Analysis

LO1, 2

Cornerstone Bank paid $120,000 for a check-sorting machine in January 2013. The machine had an estimated life of 10 years and annual operating costs of $110,000, excluding depreciation. Although management is pleased with the machine, recent technological advances have made it obsolete. Consequently, as of January 2017, the machine has a book value of $72,000, a remaining operating life of 6 years, and a salvage value of $0.

The manager of operations is evaluating a proposal to acquire a new optical scanning and sorting machine. The new machine would cost $168,000 and reduce annual operating costs to $70,000, excluding depreciation. Because of expected technological improvements, the manager believes the new machine will have an economic life of 6 years and no salvage value at the end of that life. Prior to signing the papers authorizing the acquisition of the new machine, the president of the bank prepared the following analysis:

Six-year savings [($110,000 − $70,000) × 6 years]	$240,000
Cost of new machine	(168,000)
Loss on disposal of old machine	(72,000)
Advantage (disadvantage) of replacement	$ 0

After looking at these numbers, the manager rejected the proposal and commented that he was "tired of looking at marginal projects. This bank is in business to make a profit, not to break even. If you want to break even, go work for the government."

REQUIRED

a. Evaluate the president's analysis.
b. Prepare a differential analysis of six-year totals for the old and the new machines.
c. Speculate on some limitations of the model or other issues that might be a factor in making a final decision.

P16-30. Special Order

LO1, 2, 4

Cruise Company produces a variety of electric scooters. Management follows a pricing policy of manufacturing cost plus 60 percent. In response to a request from Pulse Cycles, LLC, the following price has been developed for an order of 300 scooters (the smallest scooter Cruise produces):

Manufacturing costs	
Direct materials	$24,000
Direct labor	30,000
Factory overhead	36,000
Total	90,000
Markup (60%)	54,000
Selling price	$144,000

Pulse Cycles rejected this price and offered to purchase the 300 scooters at a price of $120,000. The following additional information is available:

- Cruise has sufficient excess capacity to produce the scooters.
- Factory overhead is applied on the basis of direct labor dollars.
- Budgeted factory overhead is $800,000 for the current year. Of this amount, $200,000 is fixed. Of the $36,000 of factory overhead assigned to the Pulse Cycles order, only $27,000 is driven by the special order; $9,000 is a fixed cost.
- Selling and administrative expenses are budgeted as follows:

Fixed	$180,000 per year
Variable	$40 per unit manufactured and sold

REQUIRED

a. The president of Cruise wants to know if he should allow Pulse Cycles to have the scooters for $120,000. Determine the effect on profits of accepting Pulse Cycles' offer.

b. Briefly explain why certain costs should be omitted from the analysis in requirement (a).

c. Assume Cruise is operating at capacity and could sell the 300 scooters at its regular markup.
   1. Determine the opportunity cost of accepting Pulse Cycles' offer.
   2. Determine the effect on profits of accepting Pulse Cycles' offer.

d. What other factors should Cruise consider before deciding to accept the special order?

LO1, 2, 4   **P16-31. Special Order**

Every Halloween, Peterson's Ice Cream Shop offers a trick-or-treat package of 25 coupons for $8. The coupons are redeemable by children 12 years or under, for a single-scoop cone, with a limit of one coupon per child per visit. Coupon sales average 500 books per year. The printing costs are $100. A single-scoop cone of Peterson's ice cream normally sells for $1.20. The variable costs of a single-scoop cone are $0.80.

REQUIRED

a. Determine the loss if all coupons are redeemed without any other effect on sales.

b. Assume all coupons will not be redeemed. With regular sales unaffected, determine the coupon redemption rate at which Peterson's will break even on the offer.

c. Assuming regular sales are not affected and one additional single-scoop cone is sold at the regular price each time a coupon is redeemed, determine the coupon redemption rate at which Peterson's will break even on the offer.

d. Determine the profit or loss incurred on the offer if the coupon redemption rate is 60 percent and:
   1. One-fourth of the redeemed coupons have no effect on sales.
   2. One-fourth of the redeemed coupons result in additional sales of two single-scoop cones.
   3. One-fourth of the redeemed coupons result in additional sales of three single-scoop cones.
   4. One-fourth of the redeemed coupons come out of regular sales of single-scoop cones.

LO1, 2, 3, 4, 5   **P16-32. Applications of Differential Analysis**

Nantucket Optics Company manufactures high-end sunglasses that it sells to mail-order distributors for $60. Manufacturing and other costs follow:

Variable Costs per Unit		Fixed Costs per Month	
Direct materials	$13	Factory overhead	$20,000
Direct labor.	12	Selling and administrative	10,000
Factory overhead	2	Total	$30,000
Distribution.	3		
Total	$30		

The variable distribution costs are for transportation to mail-order distributors. The current monthly production and sales volume is 5,000 units. Monthly capacity is 6,000 units.

REQUIRED

Determine the effect of each of the following independent situations on monthly profits.

a. A $2.00 increase in the unit selling price should result in a 1,200-unit decrease in monthly sales.

b. A 10% decrease in the unit selling price should result in a 2,000-unit increase in monthly sales. However, because of capacity constraints, the last 1,000 units would be produced during overtime with the direct labor costs increasing by 60 percent.

c. A British distributor has proposed to place a special, one-time order for 1,000 units at a reduced price of $55 per unit. The distributor would pay all transportation costs. There would be additional fixed selling and administrative costs of $1,000.

d. A Swiss distributor has proposed to place a special, one-time order for 2,500 units at a special price of $55 per unit. The distributor would pay all transportation costs. There would be additional fixed selling and administrative costs of $1,500. Assume overtime production is not possible.

    e.   Nantucket Optics provides a designer case for each pair of sunglasses that it manufactures. A Chinese manufacturer has offered a one-year contract to supply the cases at a cost of $4 per unit. If Nantucket Optics accepts the offer, it will be able to reduce variable manufacturing costs by 10%, reduce fixed costs by $1,500, and rent out some freed-up space for $2,000 per month.

    f.   The glasses also come with four different color inserts that allow the user to change the appearance of the glasses to match her or his clothing. Making the glasses in only one color without the color inserts would reduce the cost by $5, and Nantucket Optics believes the selling price would have to decrease to $55.

P16-33. Applications of Differential Analysis   **LO1, 2, 3, 4, 5**

Adventure Expeditions offers guided back-country hiking/camping trips in British Columbia. Adventure provides a guide and all necessary food and equipment at a fee of $50 per person per day. Adventure currently provides an average of 600 guide-days per month in June, July, August, and September. Based on available equipment and staff, maximum capacity is 800 guide-days per month. Monthly variable and fixed operating costs (valued in Canadian dollars) are as follows:

Variable Costs per Guide-Day		Fixed Costs per Month	
Food............................	$ 5	Equipment rental	$ 5,000
Guide salary	25	Administration	5,000
Supplies	2	Advertising	2,000
Insurance	8	Total	$12,000
Total	$40		

REQUIRED

Determine the effect of each of the following situations on monthly profits. Each situation is to be evaluated independently of all others.

    a.   A $12 increase in the daily fee should result in a 150-unit decrease in monthly sales.

    b.   A $7 decrease in the daily fee should result in a 300-unit increase in monthly sales. However, because of capacity constraints, the last 100 guide-days would be provided by subcontracting to another firm at a cost of $46 per guide-day.

    c.   A French tour agency has proposed to place a special, one-time order for 75 guide-days at a reduced fee of $45 per guide-day. The agency would pay all insurance costs. There would be additional fixed administrative costs of $200.

    d.   An Italian tour agency has proposed to place a special, one-time order for 300 guide-days next month at a special fee of $40 per guide-day. The agency would pay all insurance costs. There would be additional fixed administrative costs of $200. Assume additional capacity beyond 800 guide-days is not available.

    e.   An Alberta outdoor supply company has offered to supply all necessary food and camping equipment at $7.50 per guide-day. This eliminates the current food costs and reduces the monthly equipment rental costs to $1,800.

    f.   Clients currently must carry a backpack and assist in camp activities such as cooking. Adventure is considering the addition of mules to carry all food and equipment and the hiring of college students to perform camp activities such as cooking. This will increase variable costs by $12 per guide-day and fixed costs by $1,000 per month. However, 600 full-service guide-days per month could now be sold at $75 each.

P16-34. Continue or Discontinue   **LO1, 2**

Westview Eye Clinic primarily performs three medical procedures: cataract removal, corneal implants, and laser keratotomy. At the end of the first quarter of this year, Dr. Rajan, president of Westview, expressed grave concern about the cataract sector because it had reported a loss of $100,000. He rationalized that "since the cataract market is losing $100,000, and the overall practice is making $330,000, if we eliminate the cataract market, our total profits will increase to $430,000."

REQUIRED

    a.   Is the president's analysis correct?

    b.   Will total profits increase if the cataract section is dropped?

    c.   Is it possible total profits will decline?

CASES AND PROJECTS

LO1, 2, 3   **C16-35. Assessing the Impact of an Incentive Plan[2]**

OVERVIEW

Ladbrecks is a major department store with fifty retail outlets. The company's stores compete with outlets run by companies such as Nordstrom, Macys, Bloomingdales, and Saks Fifth Avenue. During the early nineties the company decided that providing excellent customer service was the key ingredient for success in the retail industry. Therefore, during the mid 1990s the company implemented an incentive plan for its sales associates in twenty of its stores. Your job is to assess the financial impact of the plan and to provide a recommendation to management to continue or discontinue the plan based on your findings.

INCENTIVES IN RETAIL

The past decade has evidenced a concerted effort by many firms to empower and motivate employees to improve performance. A recent *New York Times* article reported that more and more firms are offering bonus plans to hourly workers. An Ernst and Young survey of the retail industry indicates that virtually all department stores currently offer incentive programs such as straight commissions, base salary plus commission, and quota bonus programs. Although these programs can add to payroll costs, the survey respondents indicated that they believe these plans have contributed to major improvements in customer service.

COMPANY'S BACKGROUND

Ladbrecks was founded by members of the Ladbreck family in the 1880s. The first store opened under the name Ladbreck Dry Goods. Growth was fueled through acquisitions as the industry consolidated during the 1960s. Over this hundred-year period, sales associates were paid a fixed hourly wage. Raises were based on seniority. Sales associates were expected to be neat and courteous to customers. The advent of specialty stores and the stated intention of an upscale west coast retailer to begin opening stores in the Midwest concerned Ladbreck's management. Building on its history of excellence in customer service, the company initiated its performance-based incentive plan to support its stated firm-wide strategy of "customer emphasis" with "employee empowerment." Management expected it to result in further enhancement of customer service and, consequently, in an increase in sales generated at its stores.

INCENTIVE PLAN

The plan was implemented in stores sequentially as company managers intended to examine and evaluate the plan's impact on sales and profitability. Initially, the firm selected one store from a group of similar stores in the same general area to begin the implementation. By the end of 1994, ten stores had implemented the plan. In 1995, ten more stores implemented the plan, bringing the total to 20 out of a total of 50.

   The performance-based incentive plan is best described as a bonus program. At the time of the plan's implementation, sales associates received little in the form of annual merit increases, and promotions were rare. The bonus payment became the only significant reward for high performance. Each week sales associates are paid a base hourly rate times hours worked. In addition, under the plan sales associates could increase their compensation by receiving a bonus at the end of each quarter. The contract provides sales-force personnel with a cash bonus only if the actual quarterly sales generated by the employee exceed a quarterly sales goal. Individualized pre-specified sales goals were established for each employee based only on the individual's base hourly rate, hours worked and a multiplier (multiplier = 1/bonus rate). The bonus is computed as a fixed percentage of the excess sales (actual sales minus a pre-specified sales goal) by the employee in a quarter (see Exhibit 1).

$$\text{Employee's Bonus} = 0.08 \times \text{(Employee's actual sales for quarter} - \text{employee's targeted sales for quarter)}$$

$$\text{Where employee's targeted sales for quarter} = \text{Employee's hourly wage} \times \text{Hours worked in quarter} \times 12.5$$

---

[2] Written to illustrate the use of relevant costs and revenues for decision making. This example is based on an actual company's experience with implementing an incentive plan. The company name and the financial numbers and key ratios have been altered.

Senior managers regarded the incentive plan as a major change for the firm and its sales force. Management expected that the new incentive scheme would motivate many changes in employee behavior that would enhance customer service. Sales associates were now expected to build a client base to generate repeat sales. Actions consistent with this approach include developing and updating customer address lists (including details of their needs and preferences), writing thank you notes and contacting customers about upcoming sales and new merchandise that matched their preferences.

CONSULTANT'S TASK

Management decided to call you in to provide an independent assessment. While the company thought that sales had increased with the plan's implementation, the human resource department did not know exactly how to quantify the plan's impact on sales and expenses. It suspected that employee salaries, cost of goods sold, and inventory carrying costs, as well as sales, may have changed due to the plan's implementation. You, therefore, requested information on these financial variables.

Sales Analysis: Because each of the twenty stores implemented the plan at different dates, and store sales fluctuated greatly with the seasons and the economy, you could not simply plot store sales. Instead, for each of the twenty stores, you picked another Ladbreck store as a control and computed for 48 months the following series of monthly sales:[3]

$$\text{Percent Change in Sales} = \frac{[(\text{Plan Store Sales in Month t} \div \text{Plan Store Sales in Month t-24}) -}{(\text{Control Store Sales in Month t} \div \text{Control Store Sales in Month t-24})] \times 100}$$

The plan's implementation was denoted as month 25, so you had 24 months prior to the plan and 24 months after the plan. Averages were then taken for the twenty stores. If the control procedure worked then you expected that the first 24 months of the series would fluctuate around zero. The actual results are reported in Figure 1 page 763. Month 25 is denoted as the rollout month, the month the incentive plan began.

Expense Analysis: You then plotted wage expense/sales, cost of goods sold/sales, and inventory turnover for the twenty stores for the 24 months preceding the plan and the first 24 months after plan implementation. After pulling out seasonal effects these monthly series are presented in Figures 2, 3 and 4. If the plan has no impact on these expenses then you would expect no dramatic change in the series around month 25.

Figure 2   plots (wage expense in month t/sales in month t)
Figure 3   plots (cost of goods sold in month t/sales in month t)
Figure 4   plots "annual" turnover computed as (12 × cost of goods sold in month t/inventory at beginning of month t)

For example, if monthly cost of sales is $100 and the annual inventory turnover ratio is 4, it suggests a monthly turnover of 0.333 with the firm holding an average inventory of $300 throughout the year. (Note that a monthly inventory turnover of .333 implies an annual turnover of 4 (from 12 × 0.333).)

Financial Report for Store: A typical annual income statement for a pre-plan Ladbreck store before fixed charges, taxes and incidentals looks as follows.

	Total	Percent
Sales...	10,000,000	100
Cost of goods sold..	6,300,000	63
Gross profit...	3,700,000	37
Employee salaries	800,000	8
Profit before fixed charges..............................	2,900,000	29

A store also has substantial charges for rent, management salaries, insurance, etc. but they are fixed with respect to the incentive plan.

---

[3] For instance, assume sales for plan store were $2,200 this January and $2,000 two Januarys ago. Also assume that sales in the control store were $4,400 this January and $4,000 two Januarys ago. Percent change = 2,200/2,000 − 4,400/4,000 = 0.

REQUIRED

a. Suppose the goal of the firm is to now provide superior customer service by having the sales consultant identify and sell to the specific needs of the customer. What does this goal suggest about a change in managerial accounting and control systems?

b. Provide an estimate of the impact of the incentive plan on sales.

c. Did the sales impact occur all at once, or did it occur gradually?

d. What is the impact of the incentive plan on wage expense as a percent of sales?

e. What is the impact of the incentive plan on cost of good sold as a percent of sales?

f. What is the impact of incentive plan on inventory turnover (turnover = cost of goods sold ÷ inventory)? [If sales go up then stores are selling more goods; therefore, more goods need to be on the floor or those goods on floor need to turn over faster.]

g. What is the additional dollar amount of inventory that must be held?

h. Using the information on sales and expenses for a typical store, provide an analysis of the additional store profit contributed by the plan. Assume that it costs 12% a year to carry the added inventory.

i. Look at Exhibit 1, which provides a partial listing of employee pay for one small department within a store. Which "type" of employee is receiving the bonus?

j. Should the company keep the plan? Explain your estimate of the financial impact of the plan and also incorporate any nonfinancial information you feel is relevant in justifying your decision.

EXHIBIT 1	Wages by subset of employees in Ladbreck's fashion department						
Name	**Years of Service**	**Hourly Wage Rate**	**Hours Worked in Quarter**	**Regular Pay**	**Actual Sales for Quarter**	**Bonus**	**Total Pay Quarter**
BOB MARLEY	2	4.00	400	1,600	25,000	400	2,000
JIMI HENDRIX	16	7.50	440	3,300	41,000	0	3,300
MILLIE SMALL	24	9.99	440	4,396	40,000	0	4,396
AL GREEN	11	6.00	400	2,400	36,000	480	2,880
BOB DYLAN	4	5.00	400	2,000	30,000	400	2,400
JANIS JOPLIN	10	6.00	400	2,400	30,000	0	2,400
WILSON PICKETT	16	7.50	440	3,300	50,000	700	4,000
BRUCE SPRINGSTEEN	23	9.99	440	4,396	30,000	0	4,396
MICHIGAN & SMILEY	13	7.00	400	2,800	38,000	240	3,040
RICHIE FURAY	22	9.90	400	3,960	30,000	0	3,960
JOHN LENNON	5	5.00	400	2,000	34,000	720	2,720
JULIO IGLESIAS.	4	5.00	480	2,400	46,000	1,280	3,680
TOMMY PETTY	11	6.00	400	2,400	36,000	480	2,880
JOAN BAEZ	21	9.90	400	3,960	40,000	0	3,960
BB KING.	8	6.00	400	2,400	38,000	640	3,040
GLADYS KNIGHT.	14	8.00	480	3,840	46,000	0	3,840
NEIL YOUNG	15	8.00	480	3,840	36,000	0	3,840
BO DIDDLEY	4	5.00	400	2,000	30,000	400	2,400

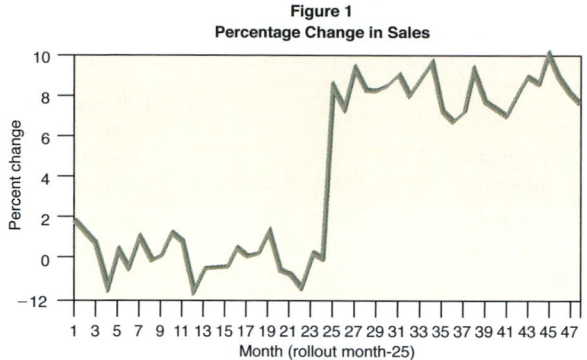

Figure 1
Percentage Change in Sales

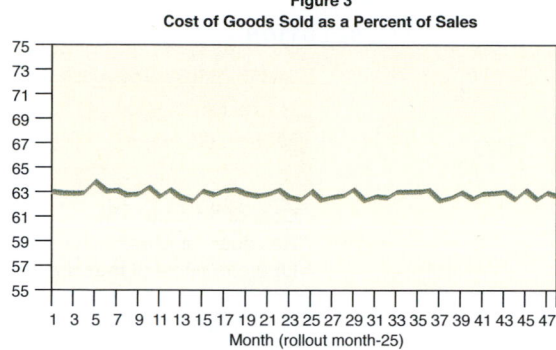

Figure 3
Cost of Goods Sold as a Percent of Sales

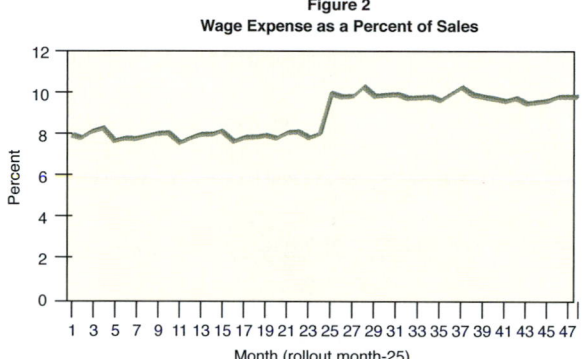

Figure 2
Wage Expense as a Percent of Sales

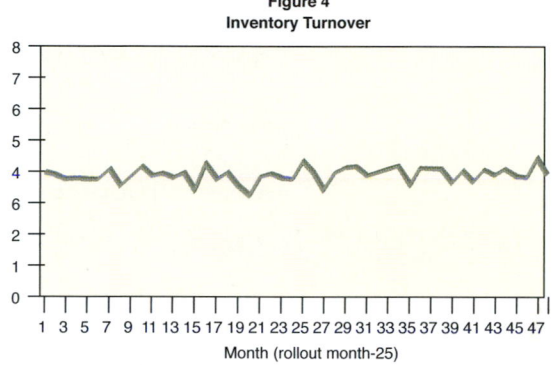

Figure 4
Inventory Turnover

SOLUTIONS TO REVIEW PROBLEMS

Mid-Chapter Review 1

SOLUTION

Relevant costs	Irrelevant costs
Cost of machine	Building lease cost
Residual value of machine	Vice president's salary
Operating cost of machine	
Direct labor savings	
Cost of manager	
Opportunity cost of renting released space	

Mid-Chapter Review 2

SOLUTION

a.

	Purchase Machine	Use Labor	Difference (in total cost of purchasing machine)
Cost of new machine	$1,000,000		$1,000,000
Residual value of machine	(100,000)		(100,000)
Operating cost of machine ($10,000 × 60 months).	600,000		600,000
Cost of direct laborers (5,000 clubs × $5 × 60 months) . . .		$1,500,000	(1,500,000)
Cost of one manager ($6,000 × 60 months).		360,000	(360,000)
Rental value of freed up space ($3,500 × 60 months)		210,000	(210,000)
Total costs	$1,500,000	$2,070,000	$ (570,000)
Advantage of purchasing machine. . .		$570,000	

b. Even though the new machine would save estimated costs of $570,000 over the next five years, there are several qualitative questions that should be answered, including the following:

- Will the new machine provide the same quality product as the current workers?
- How important is it to have a cost structure that includes variable labor costs versus more fixed machine costs? If a business decline should occur, variable costs are often easier to eliminate than fixed costs.
- What is the expected effect on worker morale and community image of eliminating a significant number of jobs in the plant?
- How important is it for the sales staff to be able to promote the product as primarily hand-made, versus machine made?

Mid-Chapter Review 3

SOLUTION

Unit selling price.	$4.80
Unit variable costs	(2.50)
Unit contribution margin.	$2.30

a.

Profit decrease from reduced sales given no changes in prices or costs (1,800 units × $2.30)	$ (4,140)
Profit increase from increase in selling price [(15,000 units − 1,800 units) × $1.50]	19,800
Increase in monthly profit.	$15,660

b.

Profit increase from increased sales given no changes in prices or costs (6,000 units × $2.30)	$13,800
Profit decrease from reduced selling price of all units [(15,000 units + 6,000 units) × $1.80]	(37,800)
Profit decrease from increased direct labor costs for the last 1,000 units [1,000 units × ($0.20 × 0.50)].	(100)
Decrease in monthly profit	$(24,100)

Mid-Chapter Review 4

SOLUTION

a.

Increase in revenues (4,000 units × $4.00)		$16,000
Increase in costs		
Direct materials (4,000 units × $2.00)	$8,000	
Direct labor (4,000 units × $0.20).	800	
Factory overhead (4,000 units × $0.25)	1,000	
Selling and administrative.	500	(10,300)
Increase in profits		$ 5,700

b.

Increase in revenues (8,000 units × $4.00)		$32,000
Increase in costs		
Direct materials (8,000 units × $2.00)	$16,000	
Direct labor (8,000 units × $0.20).	1,600	
Factory overhead (8,000 units × $0.25)	2,000	
Selling and administrative.	500	
Opportunity cost of lost regular sales		
[(15,000 units + 8,000 units − 20,000 unit capacity) × $2.30]. . . .	6,900	(27,000)
Increase in profits		$ 5,000

Mid-Chapter Review 5

SOLUTION

	Cost to Make	Cost to Buy	Difference (income effect of buying)
Cost to buy (15,000 units × $1.00)		$15,000	$(15,000)
Cost to make			
Direct materials			
(15,000 units × $2.00 × 0.40).	$12,000		12,000
Direct labor			
(15,000 units × $0.20 × 0.40).	1,200		1,200
Factory overhead			
(15,000 units × $0.25 × 0.40).	1,500		1,500
Opportunity cost.	1,000		1,000
Totals.	$15,700	$15,000	$ 700
Advantage of buying		$700	

Mid-Chapter Review 6

SOLUTION

Increase in revenues		
Package individually (15,000 units × $5.05)	$75,750	
Sell in bulk (15,000 units × $4.80)	(72,000)	$3,750
Additional packaging costs (15,000 units × $0.10)		(1,500)
Advantage of individual packaging		$2,250

Chapter-End Review

SOLUTION

Intuition suggests that the extra capacity should be devoted either to produce the Instrument Knob, which has the highest sales price, or the Pointer Knob, which has the highest per-unit contribution margin and net income. However, an analysis of the contribution margin of each product per unit of constraining factor reveals that the Star Knob should receive the extra capacity.

Note that fixed costs are allocated among products on the basis of machine hours—the constraining resource in our example. Furthermore, the unit allocations of fixed costs indicate that the Pointer Knob requires three times as many machine hours as the Instrument Knob and six times as many as the Star Knob. The contribution per unit of machine capacity for each product is as follows:

	Pointer Knob	Instrument Knob	Star Knob
Contribution margin per case.....................	$12	$6	$4
Divided by units machine capacity required	6	2	1
Contribution margin per unit of machine capacity (the constraining resource).....................	$ 2	$3	$4

Use of the remaining capacity generates a greater contribution margin if devoted to the Star Knob.

17

Product Costing: Job and Process Operations

SAMSUNG

www.samsung.com

Merchandising firms such as **ModCloth** have one type of inventory—the goods purchased from suppliers that will be resold to customers. However, the inventory of a manufacturing firm such as South Korea's **Samsung Electronics** is more complicated. Let's consider Samsung's smartphones. First, there are several components used in the manufacturing process of a smartphone, including external cases, batteries, SIM cards, circuit boards, motherboards, speaker assemblies, cameras, flash memory, controller chips, and numerous other elements. Of these components, some are purchased from outside vendors, whereas others are made internally by Samsung. In fact, one of Samsung's competitive advantages is that it makes everything from chips to screens in its own factories, thereby controlling the processing time and technological know-how that goes into its smartphones. This allows the company to bring its products to market more quickly than its competitors, especially because its competitors often buy their components from Samsung. Clearly, Samsung will satisfy its own demand for the components before selling its output to its competitors.

Given that Samsung makes many of its smartphone components internally, the company will have something called raw materials inventory. These are materials that will be transformed during the manufacturing process to become smartphone components. Examples of Samsung's raw materials include steel, glass, chemicals, wood, papers, metals, and polycarbonates. However, Samsung purchases some components from external vendors, for example, chips for the American version of its smartphones come from the San Diego–based company **Qualcomm**. These components are also considered raw materials inventory until they are requisitioned into the manufacturing process.

Samsung's smartphone manufacturing complex, called Gumi, is located 150 miles south of Seoul and employs more than 10,000 people. Within the factory, employees assemble smartphones at a three-sided workbench that has all the needed tools and raw materials within arm's reach. Once the raw materials are requisitioned into this part of the facility and direct labor and overhead are added to the raw materials to manufacture the smartphones, these costs are accumulated in another type of inventory called work-in-process inventory. When the smartphones are completed, they are transferred into a third type of inventory called finished goods, where they will await sale to a customer. This means that for manufacturing companies, the line item "inventory" on the balance sheet may be the sum of three types of inventory: raw materials inventory, work in process inventory, and finished goods inventory.

This chapter will illustrate how the costs of products and services flow through these inventory accounts and how we allocate costs to individual products or services based on those products' or services' consumption of the resources. Sometimes, this allocation is straightforward; for example, we can track the amount of raw materials or direct labor hours that go into a product or service. Other times, however, this allocation is more complicated.

Source: Tim Worstall, "Why Samsung Beats Apple or Perhaps Vice Versa," *Forbes*, September 9, 2013; and Sam Grobart, "How Samsung Became the World's No. 1 Smartphone Maker," *Bloomberg Businessweek*, March 28, 2013.

CHAPTER ORGANIZATION

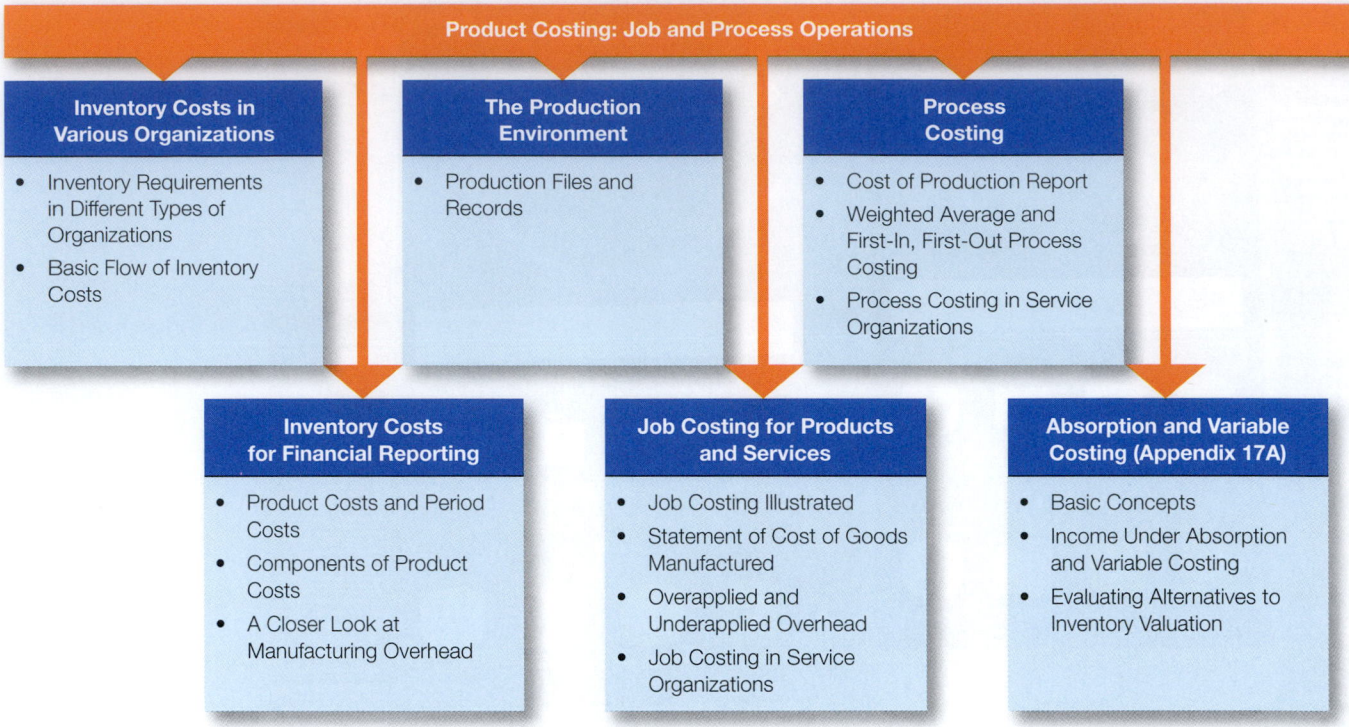

This chapter provides an overview of product costing systems and a framework for understanding costs in a production environment. It also examines aspects of the production environment that can affect product costing systems and discusses costing issues related to the production of physical products versus the production of services.

LO1 Describe inventory requirements and measurement issues for service, merchandising, and manufacturing organizations.

INVENTORY COSTS IN VARIOUS ORGANIZATIONS

Organizations can be classified as service, merchandising, or manufacturing. **Service organizations**, such as **SportClips** hair salons, **Shriners Hospitals for Children**, **The Cheesecake Factory** restaurants, and **Delta Air Lines**, perform services for others. **Merchandising organizations**, such as **Wal-Mart**, **Urban Outfitters**, and **Best Buy**, buy and sell goods. **Manufacturing organizations**, such as **Garmin Ltd.**, **The Boston Beer Company**, and **Hershey**, process raw materials into finished products for sale to others.

Service organizations typically have a low percentage of their assets invested in inventory, which usually consists only of the supplies needed to facilitate their operations. In contrast, merchandising organizations usually have a high percentage of their assets invested in inventory. Their largest inventory investment is merchandise purchased for resale, but they also have supplies inventories.

Manufacturing organizations, like merchandisers, have a high percentage of their assets invested in inventories. However, rather than just one major inventory category, manufacturing organizations typically have three: raw materials, work-in-process, and finished goods. **Raw materials inventories** contain the physical ingredients and components that will be converted by machines and/or human labor into a finished product. **Work-in-process inventories** are the partially completed goods that are in the process of being converted into a finished product. **Finished goods inventories** are the completely manufactured products held for sale to customers. As of December 26, 2015, The Boston Beer Company reported the following inventories:

Raw materials..	$42.1 million
Work-in-process..	8.9 million
Finished goods...	8.3 million
Total	$59.3 million

Manufacturing organizations also have supplies inventories used to facilitate production and selling and administrative activities. **Exhibit 17.1** illustrates the flow of inventory costs in service, merchandising, and manufacturing organizations. In all three types of organizations, the financial accounting system initially records costs of inventories as assets; when they are eventually consumed or sold, inventory costs are recorded as expenses.

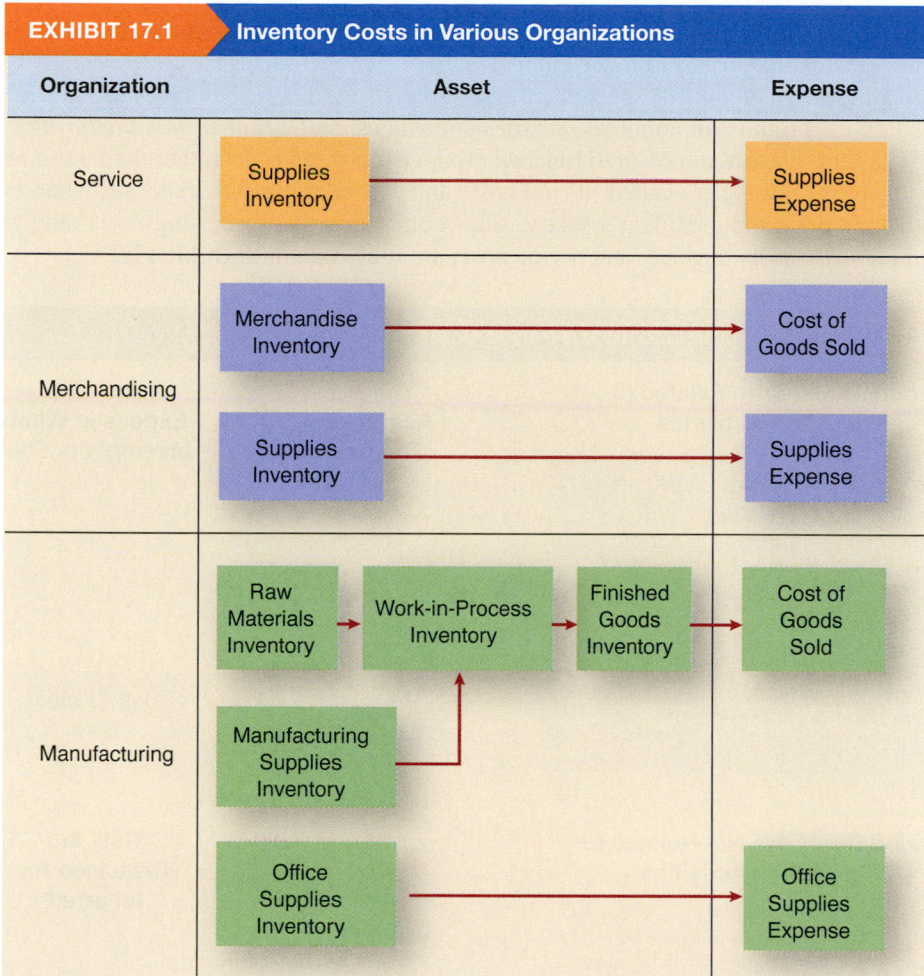

EXHIBIT 17.1	Inventory Costs in Various Organizations	
Organization	**Asset**	**Expense**

Most formal inventory costing systems are designed to provide information for general purpose financial statements. Before the balance sheet and income statement are prepared, the cost of ending inventory and the cost of inventory sold or used during the period must be determined.

MID-CHAPTER REVIEW 1

Below is a list of asset accounts a company might maintain in its accounting records.

1. Office supplies inventory.
2. Merchandise inventory.
3. Finished goods inventory.
4. Manufacturing supplies inventory.

REQUIRED

For each of the above accounts, identify which type of organization; service, merchandising, or manufacturing, is most likely to maintain the account in its records. You may list more than one organization type if it is relevant. Discuss where each of the above asset accounts would be presented in the organization's financial statements. As each of the above asset accounts is eventually consumed or sold, identify how it would be presented in the organization's financial statements.

The solution to this review problem can be found on page 816.

LO2 Explain the framework of inventory costing for financial reporting.

INVENTORY COSTS FOR FINANCIAL REPORTING

In financial reporting for manufacturing organizations, an important distinction is made between the cost of *producing* products and the cost of all other activities such as selling and administration.

Product Costs and Period Costs

For financial reporting, all costs incurred in the *manufacturing* of products are called **product costs**; these costs are carried in the accounts as an asset (inventory) until the product is sold, at which time they are recognized as an expense (cost of goods sold). Product costs include the costs of raw materials, production employee salaries and wages, and all other *manufacturing* costs incurred to transform raw materials into finished products. Expired costs (other than those related to manufacturing inventory) are called **period costs** and are recognized as expenses when incurred. Period costs include the president's salary, sales commissions, advertising costs, and all other *nonmanufacturing* costs. Product and period costs are illustrated in **Exhibit 17.2**.

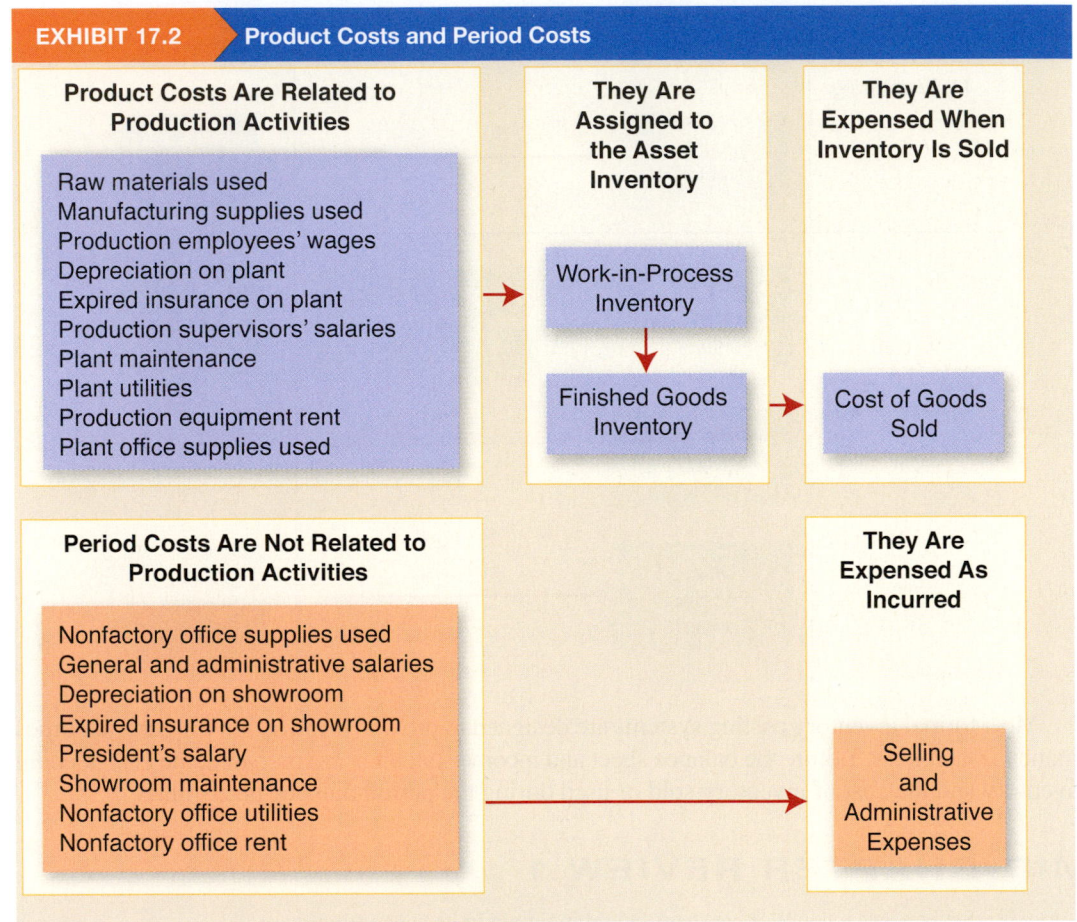

EXHIBIT 17.2   Product Costs and Period Costs

Costs such as research and development, marketing, distribution, and customer service are important for strategic analyses; however, since these costs are not incurred in the production process, they are not product costs for *financial reporting purposes*. For *internal managerial purposes*, accountants and managers often use the term *product costing* to embrace all costs incurred in connection with a product or service throughout the value chain.

To summarize, in the *product cost* versus *period cost* framework of *financial reporting*, costs are classified based on whether or not they are related to the production process. If they are related to the production process, they are product costs; otherwise, they are period costs. In this framework, costs that seem very similar may be treated quite differently. For example, note in **Exhibit 17.2** that the expired cost of insurance on the *plant* is a *product cost,* but the expired cost of insurance on the *showroom* is a *period cost.* The reason is that the plant is used in production, but the showroom is not. This method of accounting for inventory that assigns all production costs to inventory is sometimes referred to as the **absorption cost** (or **full absorption cost**) method because all production costs are said to be fully absorbed into the cost of the product.

Three Components of Product Costs

The manufacture of even a simple product, such as a small wooden table, requires three basic ingredients: materials (wood), labor (the skill of a worker) and production facilities (a building to work in, a saw, and other tools). Corresponding to these three basic ingredients of any product are three basic categories of product costs: direct materials, direct labor, and manufacturing overhead.

Direct materials are the costs of the primary raw materials converted into finished goods. Examples of primary raw materials include iron ore to a steel mill, coiled aluminum to a manufacturer of aluminum siding, cow's milk to a dairy, logs to a sawmill, and lumber to a builder. The finished product of one firm may be the raw materials of another firm down the value chain. For example, rolled steel is a finished product of **U.S. Steel**, but it is the raw material of the **Whirlpool Corporation** for the manufacture of washers and dryers. **Direct labor** consists of wages earned by *production employees for the time they actually spend working on a product,* and **manufacturing overhead** includes all manufacturing costs other than direct materials and direct labor. (Manufacturing overhead is also called *factory overhead, burden, manufacturing burden,* and just *overhead.* Merchandising organizations occasionally refer to administrative costs as *overhead.*) **Conversion cost** consists of the combined costs of direct labor and manufacturing overhead incurred to convert raw materials into finished goods.

Examples of manufacturing overhead are manufacturing supplies, depreciation on manufacturing buildings and equipment, and the costs of plant taxes, insurance, maintenance, security, and utilities. Also included are production supervisors' salaries and all other manufacturing-related labor costs for employees who do not work directly on the product (such as maintenance, security, and janitorial personnel).

Just as raw materials, labor, and production facilities are combined to produce a finished product, direct materials costs, direct labor costs, and manufacturing overhead costs are accumulated to obtain the total cost of goods produced. **Exhibit 17.3** illustrates that these product costs are accumulated in the general ledger in Work-in-Process Inventory (or just Work-in-Process) as production takes place and then are transferred to Finished Goods Inventory when production is completed. Product costs are finally assigned to Cost of Goods Sold when the finished goods are sold. (Account titles are capitalized to make it easier to determine when reference is being made to a physical item, such as

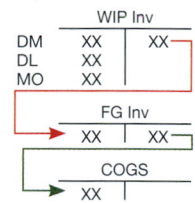

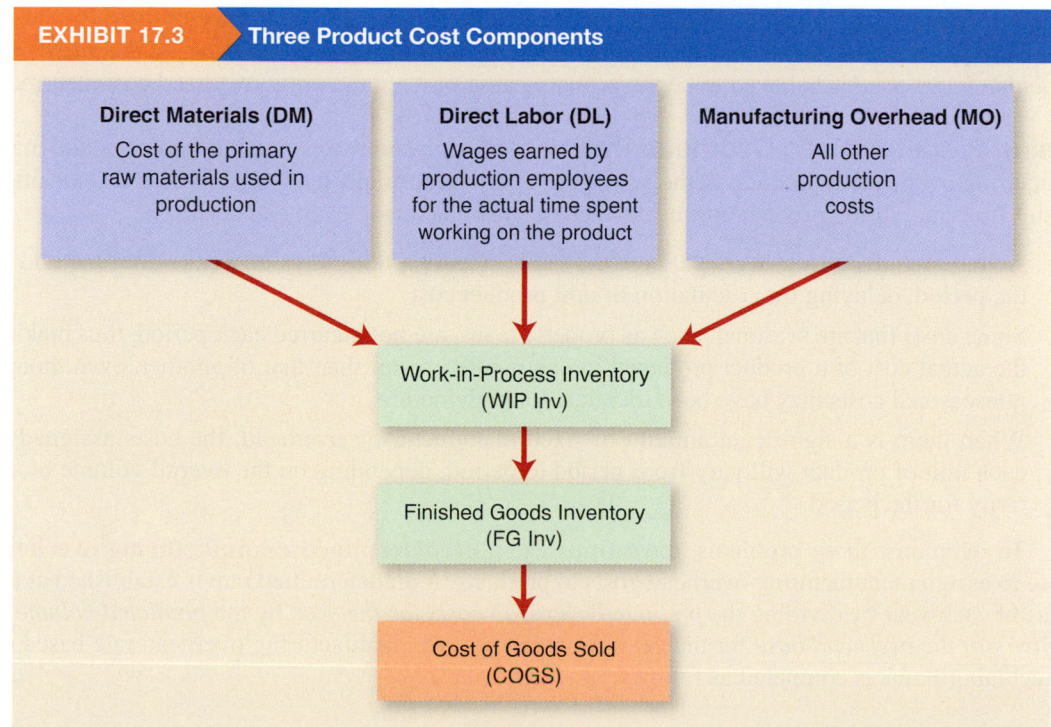

EXHIBIT 17.3 ▶ **Three Product Cost Components**

work-in-process inventory, or to the account, Work-in-Process Inventory, in which costs assigned to the work-in-process inventory are accumulated.)

A Closer Look at Manufacturing Overhead

The biggest challenge in measuring the cost of a product is determining the amount of overhead incurred to produce it. Direct materials cost is driven by the number of raw materials units used; hence, its cost is simply the number of units of raw materials used multiplied by the related cost per unit. Direct labor cost is driven by the number of directly traceable labor hours worked on the product; so its cost is the number of direct labor hours used times the appropriate rate per hour. But what about manufacturing overhead? Manufacturing overhead often consists of dozens of different cost elements, potentially with many different cost drivers. Electricity cost is based on kilowatt-hours and water cost on gallons used; depreciation is usually measured in years of service and insurance in premium dollars per thousand dollars of coverage; and supervisors' salaries are a fixed amount per month.

Historically, accountants have believed that, even when possible, it is not cost effective to try to separately measure the cost incurred for each manufacturing overhead item to produce a unit of finished product. Instead of identifying separate cost drivers for each individual cost component in manufacturing overhead, all overhead costs for a department or plant are frequently placed in a cost pool and a single unit-level cost driver is used to assign (or apply) overhead to products.

If a company produced only one product, it would be simple to assign (or apply) overhead to the units produced because it would merely involve dividing total manufacturing overhead cost incurred by the number of units produced to get a cost per unit. For example, if total manufacturing overhead costs were $100,000 for a period when 20,000 units of product were produced, the overhead cost assigned to each unit would be $5.

Selecting a Basis (or Cost Driver) for Assigning Overhead
When multiple products are manufactured in the same facilities, using a simple average of manufacturing overhead cost per unit seldom provides a good estimate of the overhead costs incurred to produce each product. Units requiring extensive manufacturing activity will have too little cost assigned to them, while others requiring only a small amount of manufacturing effort will absorb too much cost. In these cases, units of production is not an appropriate cost driver for manufacturing overhead.

To solve this allocation problem, an overhead application base (or cost driver) other than number of units produced is used. The overhead application base selected is typically a unit-level activity that is common to all products and has a causal relationship with the incurrence of overhead costs. For example, *machine hours* may be used to assign manufacturing overhead costs if the *number of machine hours used* is believed to be the primary cause of manufacturing overhead cost incurred.

Using Predetermined Overhead Rates
Although some organizations assign actual manufacturing overhead to products at the end of each period (normally a month), three problems often result from measuring product cost using "actual" manufacturing overhead costs:

1. Actual manufacturing overhead cost may not be known until days or weeks after the end of the period, delaying the calculation of unit product cost.

2. Some costs that are seasonal, such as property taxes, are not incurred each period, thus making the actual cost of a product produced in one month greater than that of another, even though nonseasonal costs may have been identical for both months.

3. When there is a significant amount of fixed manufacturing overhead, the costs assigned to each unit of product will vary from period to period, depending on the overall volume of activity for the period.

To overcome these problems, most firms use a **predetermined manufacturing overhead rate** to assign manufacturing overhead costs to products. A predetermined rate is established at the start of each year by dividing the *predicted overhead costs for the year* by the *predicted volume of activity in the overhead base* for the year. A predetermined manufacturing overhead rate based on direct labor hours is computed as follows:

$$\begin{array}{l} \text{Predetermined manufacturing} \\ \text{overhead rate per direct labor hour} \end{array} = \frac{\begin{array}{c}\text{Predicted total manufacturing} \\ \text{overhead cost for the year}\end{array}}{\begin{array}{c}\text{Predicted total direct labor} \\ \text{hours for the year}\end{array}}$$

If management believes machine hours is the major driver of manufacturing overhead, the denominator should be predicted machine hours.

Using a predetermined manufacturing overhead rate based on direct labor hours, we compute the assignment of overhead to Work-in-Process Inventory as follows:

$$\begin{array}{l} \text{Manufacturing} \\ \text{overhead applied to} \\ \text{Work-in-Process Inventory} \end{array} = \begin{array}{l} \text{Actual} \\ \text{direct labor} \\ \text{hours} \end{array} \times \begin{array}{l} \text{Predetermined manufacturing} \\ \text{overhead rate per direct} \\ \text{labor hour} \end{array}$$

To illustrate, assume that late in 2017, one of **Garmin**'s plants predicted a 2018 activity level of 25,000 direct labor hours with manufacturing overhead totaling $187,500. Using this information, its 2018 predetermined overhead rate per direct labor hour was computed as follows:

$$\begin{array}{l} \text{Predetermined} \\ \text{overhead rate} \end{array} = \frac{\$187{,}500}{25{,}000 \text{ direct labor hours}}$$

$$= \$7.50 \text{ per direct labor hour}$$

If 2,000 direct labor hours were used in September 2018, the applied overhead for September would be $15,000, as shown here:

$$2{,}000 \times \$7.50 = \$15{,}000$$

When a predetermined rate is used, monthly variations between actual and applied manufacturing overhead are expected because of the seasonality in costs and the variations in monthly activity. Hence, in some months overhead will be "overapplied" as applied overhead exceeds actual overhead; in other months overhead will be "underapplied" as actual overhead exceeds applied overhead. If the beginning-of-the-year estimates are accurate for annual overhead costs and annual activity, monthly over- and underapplied amounts during the year should offset each other by the end of the year. Later in this chapter, we consider accounting for any over- or underapplied manufacturing overhead balance that may exist at the end of the year.

Changing Cost Structures Affect the Basis of Overhead Application   By using a single overhead rate, we assume that overhead costs are primarily caused by a single cost driver. Historically, a single plantwide overhead application rate based on direct labor hours was widely used when direct labor was the predominant cost factor in production, and manufacturing overhead costs were driven by the utilization of direct labor.

Changes in manufacturing processes have produced major shifts in the composition of conversion costs, resulting in significantly less direct labor and significantly more manufacturing overhead. An example of this shift is the automobile industry where firms such as **Ford** and **Toyota** have spent billions of dollars on robotics and other technologies, thereby reducing direct labor in the production process. In many cases, direct labor hours are no longer an appropriate basis for assigning manufacturing costs to products. In others, these changes mean there is no longer a single cost driver that is appropriate for assigning manufacturing overhead to products.

Although some companies continue to use a single manufacturing overhead rate because it is convenient, many companies no longer use this approach. Instead, they have adopted multiple overhead rates based on either major departments or activities within the organization. One method for using multiple overhead rates is activity-based costing, discussed in Chapter 18.

MID-CHAPTER REVIEW 2

Assume that the following predictions were made for 2018 for one of the plants of **Milliken & Company**:

Total manufacturing overhead for the year.	$40,000,000
Total machine hours for the year	3,200,000

Actual results for February 2018 were as follows:

Manufacturing overhead	$4,410,000
Machine hours	410,000

REQUIRED
a. Determine the 2018 predetermined overhead rate per machine hour.
b. Using the predetermined overhead rate per machine hour, determine the manufacturing overhead applied to Work-in-Process during February.
c. As of February 1, actual overhead was underapplied by $400,000. Determine the cumulative amount of any overapplied or underapplied overhead at the end of February.

The solution to this review problem can be found on page 816.

LO3 Describe the production environment as it relates to product costing systems.

THE PRODUCTION ENVIRONMENT

Production personnel need to know the specific products to produce on specific machines on a daily or even hourly basis. The detailed scheduling of products on machines is performed by production scheduling personnel. Exactly how production is scheduled depends on whether process manufacturing or job production is used and whether production is in response to a specific customer sales order or for the company's inventory in anticipation of future sales.

In **process manufacturing**, production of identical units is on a *continuous* basis; a production facility may be devoted exclusively to one product or to a set of closely related products. Companies where you would likely find a process manufacturing environment include **Exxon Mobil** and **Procter & Gamble**. Process manufacturing is discussed later in this chapter.

In **job production**, also called **job order production**, products are manufactured in single units or in batches of identical units. Of course, the products included in different jobs may vary considerably. Examples of single-unit jobs are found at **Schumacher Homes**, a builder of custom-designed homes; **Bechtel Corporation**, the largest commercial construction company in the U.S., and **Cray Inc.** which manufactures supercomputers. Examples of multiple-unit jobs are found at **True Religion Brand Jeans**, a clothing manufacturer, and **Herman Miller**, a large producer of office chairs including the ergonomic Aeron model.

In a job production environment, when a customer's order is received, the marketing department forwards the order to production scheduling, where employees determine when and how the product is to be produced. Important scheduling considerations include the overall workload, raw materials availability, specific equipment or labor requirements, and the delivery date(s) of the finished product.

Important staff groups involved in production planning and control include engineering, scheduling, and accounting. Engineering is primarily concerned with determining how a product should be produced. Based on an engineering analysis and cost data, engineering personnel develop manufacturing specifications for each product. These manufacturing specifications are often summarized in two important documents: a bill of materials and an operations list. Each product's **bill of materials** specifies the kinds and quantities of raw materials required for one unit of product. The **operations list** (sometimes called an **activities list**) specifies the manufacturing operations and related times required for one unit or batch of product. The operations list should also include information on any machine setup time, movements between work areas, and other scheduled activities, such as quality inspections.

Scheduling personnel prepare a production order for each job. The **production order** contains a job's unique identification number and specifies such details as the quantity to be produced, raw materials requirements, manufacturing operations and other activities to be performed, and perhaps even the time when each manufacturing operation should be performed. In preparing a production order, scheduling personnel use the product's bill of materials and operations list to determine the materials, operations, and manufacturing times required for the job.

A **job cost sheet** is a document used to accumulate the costs for a specific job. The job cost sheet serves as the basic record for recording actual progress on the job. As production takes place, the materials, labor, and machine resources utilized are recorded on the job cost sheet along with the related costs. When a job is completed, the final cost of the job is determined by totalling the costs on the job cost sheet.

Production Files and Records

Certain files in the cost system (typically in a computer database) provide the necessary detail for amounts maintained in total in the general ledger. For example, the raw materials inventory file contains separate records for each type of raw materials, indicating increases, decreases, and the available balance for both units and costs. Every time there is a change in the Raw Materials Inventory general ledger account, there must be an equal change in one or more individual inventory records. Therefore, at any given time, the total of the balances in the raw materials inventory file for all raw materials inventory items should equal the balance in the Raw Materials Inventory general ledger account. Because of this relationship between the raw materials inventory file and Raw Materials Inventory in the general ledger, Raw Materials Inventory is called a *control account* and the raw materials file of detailed records is called a *subsidiary ledger*. Other general ledger accounts related to the product cost system that have subsidiary files are Work-in-Process, Finished Goods Inventory, and Cost of Goods Sold.

Other records required to operate a job cost system include production orders, job cost sheets, materials requisition forms, and work tickets. Production orders and job cost sheets were previously discussed. The production order serves as authorization for production supervisors to obtain materials from the storeroom and to issue work orders to production employees, and the job cost sheet accumulates the cost of the job.

A **materials requisition form** indicates the type and quantity of each raw material issued to the factory. This form is used to record the transfer of responsibility for materials and to record materials changes on raw materials and job cost sheet records. The materials requisition form has a place to record the job number; the job cost sheet has a place to record the requisition number. If a question arises regarding the issuance of materials, the requisition number and job number provide a trail for tracing the destination and the source of the materials. The materials requisition form also identifies the materials warehouse employee who issued the materials and the production employee who received them.

A **work ticket** is used to record the time a job spends in a specific manufacturing operation. Each manufacturing operation performed on a job is documented by a work ticket. The completed work tickets for a job should correspond to the operations specified on the job production order. Time information on the work tickets is used by production scheduling or expediting personnel to determine whether the job is on schedule, and to assign costs to the job.

A production operation can involve a single employee, a group of employees, a machine, or even heating, cooling, or aging processes. When the operation involves a single employee, the rate recorded on the work ticket is simply the employee's wage rate. When it involves a group of employees, the rate is composed of the wage rates of all employees in the group. When the work involves a machine operation, the rate includes a charge for machine time, as well as the time of any machine operators. Other operations, such as heating, cooling, or aging, will also have a rate for each unit of time.

MID-CHAPTER REVIEW 3

Which term below (a–f) is best associated with the following statements?

a. Process costing
b. Job order costing
c. Production order
d. Job cost sheet
e. Materials requisition
f. Work ticket

___1. Authorization to production supervisors to obtain materials and issue work orders.
___2. The accounting system most likely used to capture the costs of the production of rolls of paper that are sold as finished goods to print newspaper companies.
___3. Accumulates the costs of the job.
___4. The accounting system used to capture the costs of the production of custom-built boats.
___5. Records the time a job spends in a specific manufacturing operation.
___6. Transfers responsibility for materials.

The solution to this review problem can be found on page 816.

LO4 Explain the operation of a job costing system.

JOB COSTING FOR PRODUCTS AND SERVICES

Exhibit 17.4 shows how inventory costs in a manufacturing organization flow in a logical pattern through the financial accounting system. Pay particular attention to the major inventory accounts (Raw Materials, Work-in-Process, and Finished Goods Inventory), Manufacturing Overhead, and the flow of costs through the inventory accounts. Each of the numbered items, representing a cost flow affecting an inventory account or Manufacturing Overhead, is explained here:

1. The costs of purchased raw materials and manufacturing supplies are recorded in Raw Materials and Manufacturing Supplies, respectively. An increase in Accounts Payable typically offsets these increases.

2. As primary raw materials are requisitioned to the factory, direct materials costs are transferred from Raw Materials to Work-in-Process.

3. Direct labor costs are assigned to Work-in-Process on the basis of the time devoted to processing raw materials. Indirect labor costs associated with production employees are initially assigned to Manufacturing Overhead.

4–6.   Other production related costs are also assigned to Manufacturing Overhead. Other Payables represents the incurrence of a variety of costs such as repairs and maintenance, utilities, and property taxes.

7. Costs assigned to Manufacturing Overhead are periodically reassigned (applied) to Work-in-Process, preferably with the use of a predetermined overhead rate such as direct labor hours, machine hours, or some other cost assignment base.

8. When products are completed, their accumulated product costs are totaled on a job cost sheet and transferred from Work-in-Process to Finished Goods Inventory.

9. When the completed products are sold, their costs are transferred from Finished Goods Inventory to Cost of Goods Sold.

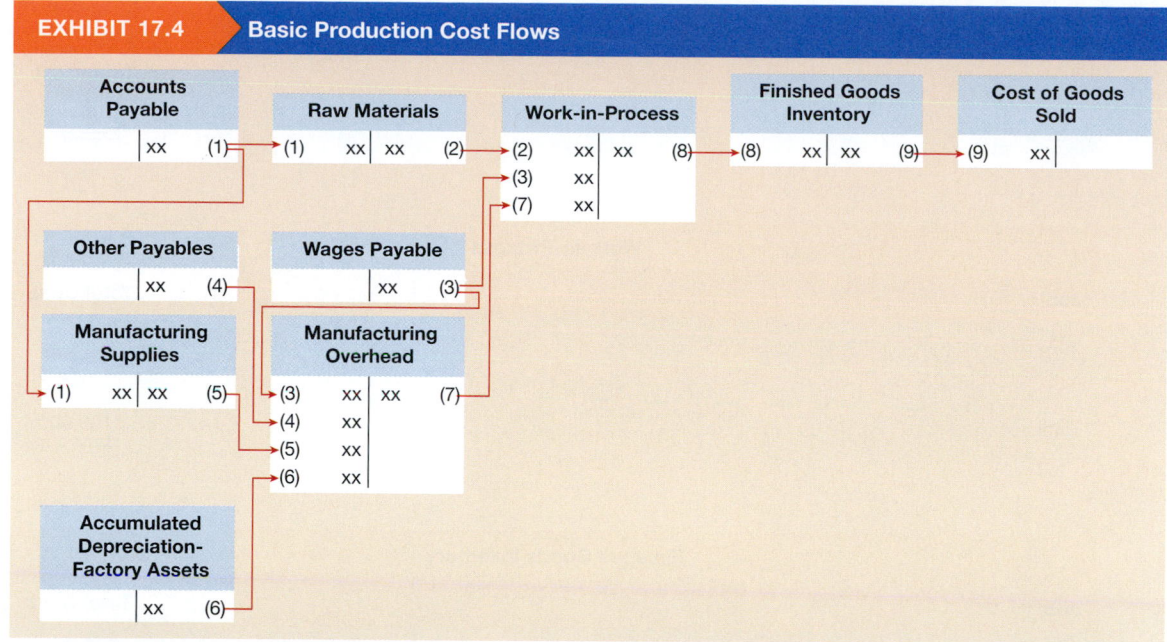

EXHIBIT 17.4   Basic Production Cost Flows

Job Costing Illustrated

Even though data are almost always processed with computerized systems, data processing procedures are best illustrated within the context of a paper-based manual system. Consider the **Burberry** custom scarves featured in the Business Insight box. Because variations in styles cause differences in costs, detailed records are kept concerning the costs assigned to specific jobs. Suppose raw materials consist of outer fabric, liner fabric, and thread.

Assume total inventory on August 1, 2017, included Raw Materials, $71,000; Work-in-Process, $109,900; and Finished Goods, $75,000. In addition there were manufacturing supplies of $1,600, consisting of various items such as thread, needles, sheers, and machine lubricant. The August 1 balance in Manufacturing Overhead was $0.

Raw Materials			
Description	**Quantity**	**Unit Cost**	**Total Cost**
Outer fabric	3,000 square yards	$20	$60,000
Liner	2,000 square yards	3	6,000
Thread	1,000 units	5	5,000
Total			$71,000

Manufacturing Supplies

Item	Total Cost
Various	$1,600

Work-in-Process

Job	Total Cost
425	$ 58,600
426	51,300
Total	$109,900

Finished Goods Inventory

Job	Total Cost
424	$75,000

To illustrate manufacturing cost flows in a job cost system, "T" accounts are presented in the margin for the cost system transactions for Burberry, for August 2017. Each cost assignment is supported by documented information that is recorded in subsidiary cost system records. The hypothetical manufacturing cost transactions for Burberry for August 2017 are discussed here. The numbered jobs combine scarf orders that share the same outer and liner fabric choices.

1. Raw materials and manufacturing supplies are purchased on account. The vendor's invoice totals $31,000, including $1,000 of manufacturing supplies and $30,000 of raw materials. The cost of the raw materials must be assigned to specific raw materials inventory records:

RM Inv	
BB	71,000
(1)	30,000

Mfg. Supplies	
BB	1,600
(1)	1,000

Accounts Payable	
	31,000 (1)

Outer fabric	850 square yards × $20 =	$17,000
Liner	2,000 square yards × $3 =	6,000
Thread	1,400 units × $5 =	7,000
Total		$30,000

2. Materials needed to complete Jobs 425 and 426 are requisitioned. Two new jobs, 427 and 428, were also started and direct materials were requisitioned for them. A total of $54,300 of raw materials was requisitioned:

WIP Inv	
BB	109,900
(2)	54,300

RM Inv	
BB	71,000	54,300 (2)
(1)	30,000	

	Job 425	Job 426	Job 427	Job 428	Total
Outer fabric					
975 sq. yds. × $20			$19,500		$19,500
955 sq. yds. × $20				$19,100	19,100
Liner					
500 sq. yds. × $3			1,500		1,500
1,100 sq. yds. × $3				3,300	3,300
Thread					
960 units × $5	$4,800				4,800
720 units × $5		$3,600			3,600
500 × $5			2,500		2,500
Total	$4,800	$3,600	$23,500	$22,400	$54,300

3. Assume the August payroll liability was $41,650, including $34,450 for direct labor and $7,200 for indirect labor. Direct labor was assigned to the jobs as follows:

	Job 425	Job 426	Job 427	Job 428	Total
Labor hours	600	900	1,000	945	
Labor rate	× $10	× $10	× $10	× $10	
Total	$6,000	$9,000	$10,000	$9,450	$34,450

Note: The $7,200 of indirect labor costs is assigned to products as part of applied overhead.

4–6. In addition to indirect labor, suppose Burberry incurred the following manufacturing overhead costs:

Manufacturing Supplies	$ 950
Accumulated Depreciation—Factory Assets	2,400
Miscellaneous (Other Payables)	3,230

7. Assume manufacturing overhead is applied to jobs using a predetermined rate of $4 per direct labor hour. Assignments to individual jobs are as follows:

	Job 425	Job 426	Job 427	Job 428	Total
Labor hours	600	900	1,000	945	
Overhead rate per labor hour	× $4	× $4	× $4	× $4	
Total	$2,400	$3,600	$4,000	$3,780	$13,780

8. Jobs 425, 426, and 427 are completed with the following costs:

	Job 425	Job 426	Job 427	Total
Beginning balance	$58,600	$51,300	$ 0	$109,900
Current costs:				
Direct materials (entry 2)	4,800	3,600	23,500	31,900
Direct labor (entry 3)	6,000	9,000	10,000	25,000
Applied overhead (entry 7)	2,400	3,600	4,000	10,000
Total	$71,800	$67,500	$37,500	$176,800

Additional analysis for the completed jobs indicates the following:

	Job 425	Job 426	Job 427
Total cost of job	$71,800	$67,500	$37,500
Units in job	÷ 1,200	÷ 900	÷ 500
Unit cost	$ 59.83	$ 75.00	$ 75.00

9. Jobs 424, 425, and 426 are delivered to customers for a sales price of $400,000. Determining the costs transferred from Finished Goods Inventory to Cost of Goods Sold requires summing the total cost of jobs sold.

Job 424	$ 75,000
Job 425	71,800
Job 426	67,500
Total	$214,300

WIP Inv
BB 109,900
(2) 54,300
(3) 34,450

MO
BB –0–
(3) 7,200

Wages Payable
41,650 (3)

MO
BB –0–
(3) 7,200
(4) 950
(5) 2,400
(6) 3,230

Mfg Supplies
BB 1,600 | 950 (4)
(1) 1,000

Accum. Depr
2,400 (5)

Other Payables
3,230 (6)

WIP Inv
BB 109,900
(2) 54,300
(3) 34,450
(7) 13,780

MO
BB –0– | 13,780 (7)
(3) 7,200
(4) 950
(5) 2,400
(6) 3,230

FG Inv
BB 75,000
(8) 176,800

WIP Inv
BB 109,900 | 176,800 (8)
(2) 54,300
(3) 34,450
(7) 13,780

COGS
(9) 214,300

FG Inv
BB 75,000 | 214,300 (9)
(8) 176,800

At this point we can determine the gross profit on the completed jobs:

Sales.	$400,000
Cost of goods sold.	(214,300)
Gross profit.	$185,700

If inventory were produced in anticipation of future sales rather than in response to specific customer orders, it is likely that not all units in a job would be sold at the same time. In this case, the unit cost information is used to determine the amount transferred from Finished Goods Inventory to Cost of Goods Sold.

Exhibit 17.5 shows the cost system records supporting the ending balances in the major inventory accounts and Cost of Goods Sold. Note the importance of the job cost sheets for determining cost transfers affecting Work-in-Process and Finished Goods Inventory. The job cost sheets are also used in determining the ending balances of these accounts.

EXHIBIT 17.5   General Ledger Accounts and Subsidiary Records for Inventory Categories and Cost of Goods Sold

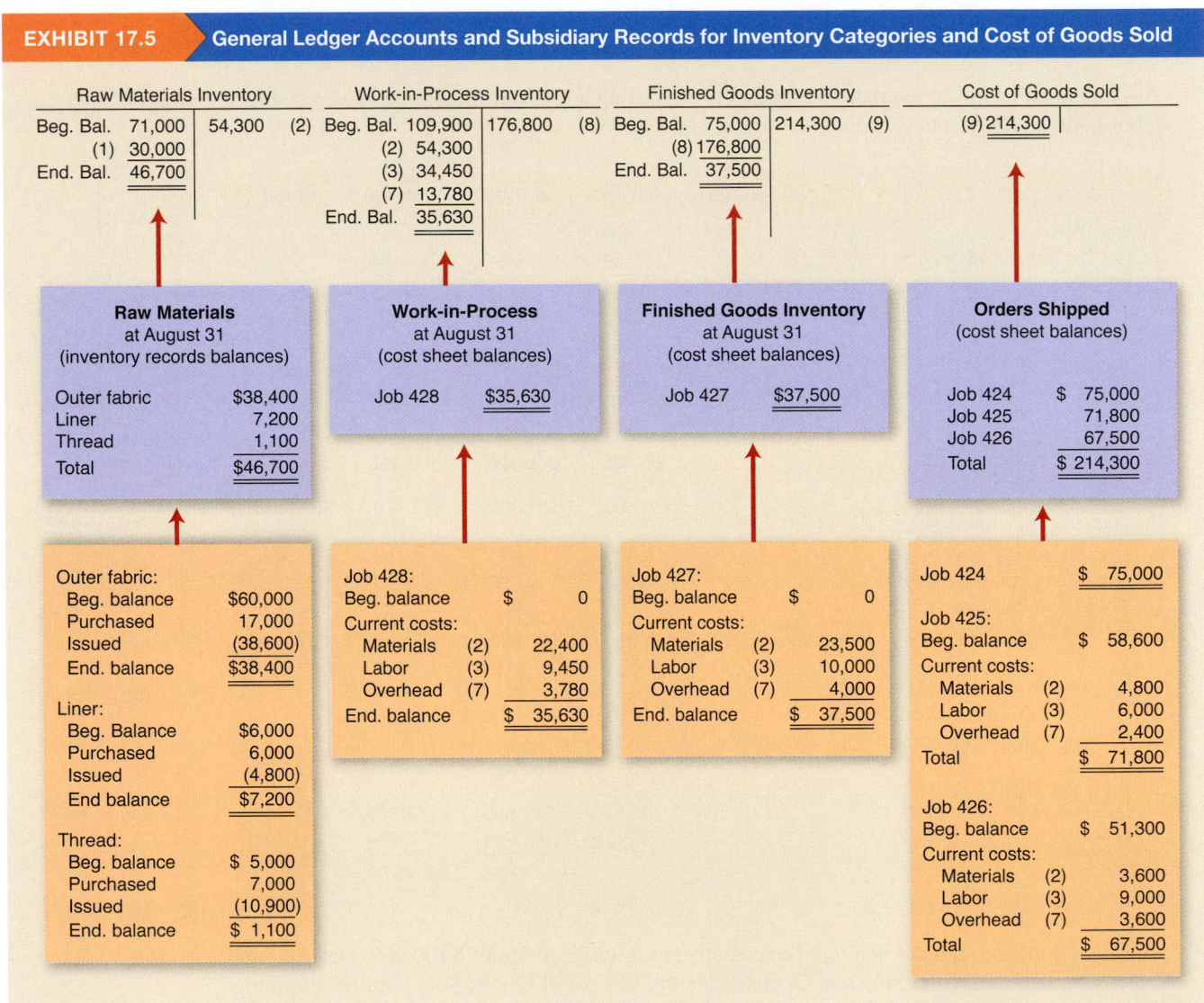

Burberry's product costing system is adequate for determining the cost for each job for purposes of valuing ending inventories and cost of goods sold in its external financial statements. The costing system recognizes the differences in materials costs by carefully tracking each type of material as a separate cost pool. Assuming all direct labor employees are paid the same rate, it is necessary to maintain only one labor cost pool. Although there are three distinct operations in making scarves (cutting, sewing, and finishing), the various styles of scarves likely require the same proportionate times on each operation. Hence, even with only one plantwide manufacturing overhead cost pool applied on the basis of direct labor hours, individual product costs are reasonably accurate.

Although Burberry's assumed costing system may be adequate for inventory costing for financial statement purposes, the data it routinely generates will not provide management with information for many management decisions. To evaluate product or customer profitability, management needs additional information concerning marketing, distributing, selling, and customer service costs, which are not included in the product cost system. The following Business Insight illustrates the importance of distribution costs in decision making at **Coca-Cola**.

Furthermore, the cost system does not provide information for decisions concerning individual operations, such as cutting. To answer questions regarding how best to perform operations, Burberry's accountants should perform a special cost study to obtain relevant activity-cost information.

BUSINESS INSIGHT

Coca-Cola Sheds Shipping and Production to Focus on Sales and Marketing For a global brand like **Coca-Cola**, distribution costs can become quite large and can distract the company from its core business. Coca-Cola has announced that it is overhauling its U.S. supply chain by selling both production and distribution portions of the business to partner companies. Coca-Cola will focus on selling and marketing drink concentrate to production partners and bottlers.

This trend seems to be meaningful enough for logistics and distribution businesses to take note. **FedEx** and **UPS** have both announced acquisitions of logistics firms that offer supply chain tasks traditionally done in-house, such as processing returns and other distribution. In fact, **Coyote Logistics**, which UPS purchased in 2015, arranges shipping for 12,000 firms including beverage giant **Heineken**.

Sources: Mike Esterl, "Coke Plans to Sell Nine U.S. Production Plants," *The Wall Street Journal*, September 24, 2015; Laura Stevens, "FedEx Pays $1.4 Billion for GENCO," *The Wall Street Journal*, March 19, 2015; and Laura Stevens, "UPS Agrees to Buy Coyote Logistics for $1.8 Billion," *The Wall Street Journal*, July 31, 2015.

Statement of Cost of Goods Manufactured

The income statement for a merchandising organization normally includes a calculation of cost of goods sold as follows:

Sales.		$X,XXX
Less cost of goods sold		
Beginning inventory	$X,XXX	
Plus purchases	X,XXX	
Goods available for sale	X,XXX	
Less ending inventory	(X,XXX)	
Cost of goods sold		(X,XXX)
Gross profit.		X,XXX
Less selling and administrative expenses		(X,XXX)
Net income.		$X,XXX

Manufacturing organizations modify only one line of this income statement format, changing purchases to cost of goods manufactured. Since a manufacturer acquires finished goods from the factory, its cost of goods manufactured is the total cost transferred from Work-in-Process to Finished Goods Inventory during the period.

For internal reporting purposes, most companies prepare a separate **statement of cost of goods manufactured**, which summarizes the cost of goods completed and transferred into Finished Goods Inventory during the period. A hypothetical statement of cost of goods manufactured and an income statement for Burberry, are presented in **Exhibit 17.6** for August 2017.

EXHIBIT 17.6	Statement of Cost of Goods Manufactured and Income Statement

BURBERRY
Statement of Cost of Goods Manufactured
For Month Ending August 31, 2017

Current manufacturing costs			
Cost of materials placed in production			
Raw materials, 8/1/17	$ 71,000		
Purchases	30,000		
Total available	101,000		
Raw materials, 8/31/17	(46,700)	$ 54,300	
Direct labor		34,450	
Manufacturing overhead.		13,780	$102,530
Work-in-process, 8/1/17.			109,900
Total costs in process.			212,430
Work-in-process, 8/31/17.			(35,630)
Cost of goods manufactured			$176,800

BURBERRY
Income Statement
For Month Ending August 31, 2017

Sales.			$400,000
Cost of goods sold			
Finished goods inventory, 8/1/17		$ 75,000	
Cost of goods manufactured		176,800	
Total goods available for sale		251,800	
Finished goods inventory, 8/31/17		(37,500)	214,300
Gross profit.			185,700
Selling and administrative expenses*.			(90,000)
Net income.			$ 95,700

* Selling and administrative expenses for Burberry are assumed to be $90,000.

Overapplied and Underapplied Overhead

In the Burberry example, assume that the predetermined manufacturing overhead rate of $4 per direct labor hour was based on predicted manufacturing overhead for the year of $100,000 and predicted direct labor hours of 25,000. Assume further that it was determined that the company actually incurred $100,000 in manufacturing overhead during the year and that actual direct labor hours for the year were 25,000, resulting in applied overhead of $100,000 (25,000 hours × $4). The activity in Manufacturing Overhead is summarized as follows:

Manufacturing Overhead	
Beginning balance	$ 0
Actual overhead	100,000
Total	100,000
Applied overhead	(100,000)
Ending balance.	$ 0

With identical amounts of actual and applied overhead, the ending balance in Manufacturing Overhead is zero. However, if either the actual overhead cost or the actual level of the production activity base differed from its predicted value, there would be a balance in Manufacturing Overhead representing overapplied or underapplied overhead.

Assume, for example, that the prediction of 25,000 direct labor hours was correct but that actual overhead cost was $105,000. In this case, Manufacturing Overhead shows a $5,000 positive balance, representing underapplied manufacturing overhead:

Manufacturing Overhead	
Beginning balance	$ 0
Actual overhead	105,000
Total	105,000
Applied overhead	(100,000)
Ending balance.	$ 5,000*

* Underapplied; actual exceeds applied.

If actual manufacturing overhead were only $98,000, Manufacturing Overhead would be overapplied and show a $2,000 negative balance.

If the *prediction* of total manufacturing overhead cost is not accurate, there will be an underapplied or overapplied balance in Manufacturing Overhead at the end of the year. A similar result occurs when the *predicted* activity level used in computing the predetermined rate differs from the actual activity level. It is not uncommon for such differences to occur. Predictions are exactly that—predictions.

Month-to-month balances in Manufacturing Overhead are usually allowed to accumulate during the year. In the absence of evidence to the contrary, it is assumed that such differences result from seasonal variations in production or costs or both. However, any year-end balance in Manufacturing Overhead must be eliminated.

Theoretically, the disposition of any year-end balance in Manufacturing Overhead should be accomplished in a manner that adjusts every account to what its balance would have been if an actual, rather than a predetermined, overhead rate had been used. This involves adjusting the ending balances in Work-in-Process, Finished Goods Inventory, and Cost of Goods Sold. Procedures to do this are examined in cost accounting textbooks.

In most situations, the simple procedure of treating the remaining overhead as an adjustment to Cost of Goods Sold is adequate. Unless there are large ending balances in inventories and a large year-end balance in Manufacturing Overhead, this simple procedure produces acceptable results. Underapplied overhead indicates that the assigned costs are less than the actual costs, understating Cost of Goods Sold. Hence, disposing of an underapplied balance in Manufacturing Overhead increases the balance in Cost of Goods Sold.

Manufacturing Overhead		
Beginning balance	$ 0	
Actual overhead	105,000	
Total	105,000	
Applied overhead	(100,000)	
Ending balance.	$ 5,000*	← Increase Cost of Goods Sold

* Underapplied; actual exceeds applied.

Conversely, overapplied overhead indicates that the assigned costs are more than the actual costs, overstating Cost of Goods Sold. Hence, disposing of an overapplied balance in Manufacturing Overhead decreases Cost of Goods Sold.

Job Costing in Service Organizations

Service costing, the assignment of costs to services performed, uses job costing concepts to determine the cost of filling customer service orders in organizations such as automobile repair shops, charter airlines, CPA firms, hospitals, and law firms. Many of these organizations bill clients on the basis of resources consumed. Consequently, they maintain detailed records for billing purposes. On the invoice sent to the client, the organization itemizes any materials consumed on the job at a selling price per unit, the labor hours worked on the job at a billing rate per hour, and the time special facilities were used at a billing rate per unit of time. Employees with different capabilities and experience often have different billing rates. In a CPA firm, for example, a partner or a senior manager has a higher billing rate than a staff accountant.

The prices and rates must be high enough to cover costs not assigned to specific jobs and to provide for a profit. To evaluate the contribution to common costs and profit from a job, a comparison must be made between the price charged the customer and the actual cost of the job. This is easily done when the actual cost of resources itemized on the customer's invoice is presented on a job cost sheet. A CPA firm, for example, should accumulate the actual hardware and software costs of an accounting system installed for a client, along with the actual wages earned by employees while working on the job and any related travel costs. Comparing the total of these costs with the price charged, the client indicates the total contribution of the job to common costs and profit.

Although service organizations may identify costs with individual jobs for management accounting purposes, there is considerable variation in the way job cost information is presented in financial statements. Some organizations report the cost of jobs completed in their income statements using an account such as Cost of Services Provided. They use procedures similar to those outlined in **Exhibit 17.6**; the only major change involves replacing Cost of Goods Sold with Cost of Services Provided.

BUSINESS INSIGHT

The Versatility of Job Costing—A Perfect Fit for Designers   Brand design firms provide an incredible host of design and branding services to clients. **Sandstrom Partners** has run focus groups in Oregon to help the state understand how best to name and market the Oregon Health Insurance Exchange. **Hornall Anderson**, another global brand design firm based in Seattle, helped **La Brea Bakery** redesign its iconic packaging because customers assumed that the bread was made by the grocery store rather than a premium baker, and helped **Quaker** put a small window on its granola box so that shoppers can see what they are getting. The agency **Design by Structure Ltd.** has advised private equity firms **Dunedin LLP**, **Gresham Private Equity**, and **RJD Partners**, as they rebrand to focus on impressing the management teams of the firms they plan to purchase.

This multitude of services with a focus on individuality illustrates the value of job costing in service organizations. By tracking the resources to jobs, these firms have the flexibility to accurately adapt the costing system to the structure of the work being done for the client.

Sources: Becky Pritchard, "Investors Struggle to Find the Differences Between Firms," *The Wall Street Journal*, May 16, 2016; Sarah Nassauer, "See-Through Food Packaging Boosts Sales," *The Wall Street Journal*, August 13, 2014; Sarah Nassauer, "The Marketing Decoder: La Brea Bakery," March 26, 2014; and Louise Radnofsky, "States' Puzzle: What to Call Health Insurance Exchanges," *The Wall Street Journal*, August 7, 2012.

More often, however, service organizations do not formally establish detailed procedures to trace the flow of service costs. Instead, service job costs are left in their original cost categories such as materials expense, salaries and wages expense, travel expense, and so forth. Because all service costs are typically regarded as expenses rather than product costs, either procedure is acceptable for financial reporting. Regardless of the formal treatment of service costs in financial accounting records and statements, the managers of a well-run service organization need information regarding job cost and contribution. The previous Business Insight considers the importance of accurate cost estimation by service firms that focus on providing unique and customized service to each client.

All preceding examples of service costing involve situations in which the order is filled in response to a specific customer request. Job order costing can also be used to determine the cost of making services available even when the names of specific customers are not known in advance and the service is being provided on a speculative basis. A regularly scheduled airline flight, for example, could be regarded as a job. Management is interested in knowing the cost of the job in order to determine its profitability. This is but another example of the versatility of job order costing.

YOU MAKE THE CALL

You are the Chief Financial Officer   You have asked the accounting staff to provide you with cost information on each of the products manufactured by your company so you can conduct profitability analysis on each product. Accounting provided you with the costs that are used in the company's external financial statements. What additional information are you going to need before you can conduct a complete profitability analysis? [Answer p. 798]

MID-CHAPTER REVIEW 4

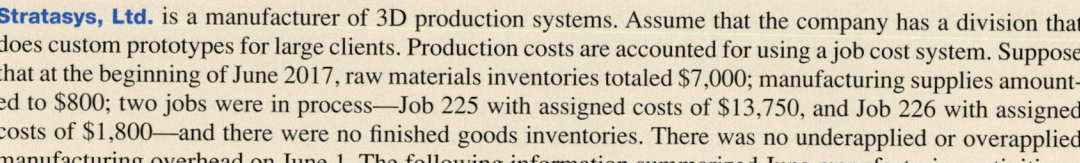

Stratasys, Ltd. is a manufacturer of 3D production systems. Assume that the company has a division that does custom prototypes for large clients. Production costs are accounted for using a job cost system. Suppose that at the beginning of June 2017, raw materials inventories totaled $7,000; manufacturing supplies amounted to $800; two jobs were in process—Job 225 with assigned costs of $13,750, and Job 226 with assigned costs of $1,800—and there were no finished goods inventories. There was no underapplied or overapplied manufacturing overhead on June 1. The following information summarized June manufacturing activities:

- Purchased raw materials costing $40,000 on account.
- Purchased manufacturing supplies costing $9,000 on account.
- Requisitioned materials needed to complete Job 226. Started two new jobs, 227 and 228, and requisitioned direct materials for them as follows:

Job 226	$ 2,600
Job 227	18,000
Job 228	14,400
Total	$35,000

- Incurred June salaries and wages as follows:

Job 225 (500 hours × $10 per hour)	$ 5,000
Job 226 (1,500 hours × $10 per hour)........................	15,000
Job 227 (2,050 hours × $10 per hour)........................	20,500
Job 228 (800 hours × $10 per hour)	8,000
Total direct labor...	48,500
Indirect labor	5,000
Total	$53,500

- Used manufacturing supplies costing $5,500.
- Recognized depreciation on factory fixed assets of $5,000.
- Incurred miscellaneous manufacturing overhead cost of $10,750 on account.
- Applied manufacturing overhead at the rate of $5 per direct labor hour.
- Completed Jobs 225, 226, and 227.
- Delivered Jobs 225 and 226 to customers.

REQUIRED

a. Prepare "T" accounts showing the flow of costs through the Work-in-Process, Finished Goods, and Cost of Goods Sold accounts.

b. Show the job cost details to support the June 30, 2017, balances in Work-in-Process, Finished Goods and Cost of Goods Sold.

c. Prepare a statement of cost of goods manufactured for June 2017.

The solution to this review problem can be found on pages 817–818.

PROCESS COSTING

LO5 Explain the operation of a process costing system.

5

A job costing system works well when products are made one at a time (building houses) or in batches of identical items (making blue jeans). However, if products are produced in a continuous manufacturing environment, where production does not have a distinct beginning and ending (refining fossil fuels such as gasoline or diesel), companies usually use a process costing system.

In job costing, the unit cost is the total cost of the "job" divided by the units produced in the job. Costs are accumulated for each job on a job cost sheet, and those costs remain in Work-in-Process until the job is completed, regardless of how long the job is in progress. A multiple-unit job is not considered completed until all units in the job are finished. The cost is not determined until the job is completed, which will not necessarily coincide with the end of an accounting period. Large jobs (such as construction projects) and jobs started near the end of the period frequently overlap two or more accounting periods.

In process costing, the cost of a single unit is equal to the total product costs assigned to a "process" or "department" during the accounting period (frequently a month) divided by the number of units produced. Since goods in the beginning and ending work-in-process inventory are only partially processed during the period, it is necessary to determine the total production for the period in terms of the equivalent number of completed units. For example, if 300 units were started and completed through 40 percent of the process during the period, then the equivalent of 120 fully completed units (300 units $\times$ 0.40) were produced. The average cost per unit is computed as total product costs divided by the number of equivalent units produced.

A good example of a process costing environment involving continuous production is the soft drink bottling process. At **Coca-Cola**'s bottling facility in Atlanta, more than 2,000 twelve-ounce cans of Coca-Cola are produced per minute in a continuous process. The process adds the ingredients (concentrate syrup, water, sweetener, and the carbonation agent) at various points in the process and blends the ingredients in the can. At the end of the process, the cans are automatically wrapped in either 6-pack or 12-pack sizes.

In a job cost system, job cost sheets are used to collect cost information for each and every job. In a process costing system, cost accumulation requires fewer records because each department's production is treated as the only job worked on during the period. In a department that has just one manufacturing process, process costing is particularly straightforward because the Work-in-Process account is, in effect, the departmental cost record. If a department has more than one manufacturing process, separate records should be maintained for each process.

BUSINESS INSIGHT

3D Printing Builds Customization into the Production Process   Breakthroughs in technology are making customization available to the masses with customization built in as part of the production process. In the past, bespoke suit makers and automakers often had a lot in common. There was a time when automakers like **Bugatti**, **Duesenberg**, and **Roller** would build custom automobiles as personalized as any suit from Savile Row, a renowned street in London with custom-tailored suit offerings. The customer paid a lot of money and the producer made the product substantially to order. Skilled craftsmen were tasked with producing the customizations one job at a time. Cost management in the presence of dramatic customization was only possible through job costing.

3D printing and other new technology has made customization less costly, and brings changes to cost management. The custom knit wear manufacturer **Unmade** uses proprietary software and programmable knitting machines to produce unique sweaters and scarves for clients. While each garment is unique, the variation in cost due to customization is largely captured by conventional drivers like direct materials (yarn), direct labor (programming), and machine hours. In addition, this business model saves costs by allowing Unmade to hold very little inventory while still delivering to the customer within 10 days. Similar changes have come to auto manufacturing. **Daihatsu Copen**, a Toyota subsidiary, uses 3D printing to allow customers to customize portions of their cars. **Local Motors**, an Arizona automaker, is more aggressive in its use of 3D printing. The LM3D Roadster, expected to be available for retail purchase in 2017, is 75% printed, and Local Motors envisions local micro-factories developing cars with the customer rather than dealerships.

Sources: Michael Pooler, "Makers Follow the Techies to Create a 'Nurture' Space of Their Own," *Financial Times*, December 17, 2015 and "Print My Ride," *The Economist*, June 23, 2016.

Cost of Production Report

To illustrate process costing procedures, consider **Intel**, which manufactures memory chips for microcomputers using sophisticated machinery. Assume each finished unit requires one unit of raw materials added at the beginning of the manufacturing process. Hypothetical production and cost data for the month of July 2017 for Intel is as follows:

July Production Data	
Units in process, beginning of period (75% converted)	4,000
Units started	36,000
Completed and transferred to finished goods	35,000
Units in process, end of period (20% converted)	5,000

July Cost Data		
Beginning work-in-process		
Materials costs		$ 16,000
Conversion costs		9,000
Total		$ 25,000
Current manufacturing costs		
Direct materials (36,000 × $4)		$144,000
Conversion costs		
Direct labor	$62,200	
Manufacturing overhead applied	46,700	108,900
Total		$252,900

Developing a cost of production report is a useful way of organizing and accounting for costs in a process costing environment. A **cost of production report**, which summarizes unit and cost data for each department or process for each period, consists of the following sections:

- Summary of units in process
- Equivalent units
- Total cost to be accounted for and cost per equivalent unit
- Accounting for total costs

The cost of production report for Intel is shown in **Exhibit 17.7**, and its four sections are discussed next.

EXHIBIT 17.7	Cost of Production Report for Process Costing

INTEL
Cost of Production Report
For the Month Ending July 31, 2017

Summary of units in process

Beginning	4,000
Units started	36,000
In process	40,000
Completed	(35,000)
Ending	5,000

Equivalent units in process	Materials	Conversion
Units completed	35,000	35,000
Plus equivalent units in ending inventory	5,000	1,000*
Equivalent units in process.	40,000	36,000

Total cost to be accounted for and cost per equivalent unit in process	Materials	Conversion	Total
Beginning work-in-process	$ 16,000	$ 9,000	$ 25,000
Current cost	144,000	108,900**	252,900
Total cost in process	$160,000	$117,900	$277,900
Equivalent units in process.	÷ 40,000	÷ 36,000	
Cost per equivalent unit in process	$ 4.00	$ 3.275	$ 7.275
Accounting for total costs			
Transferred out (35,000 × $7.275)			$254,625
Ending work-in-process			
Materials (5,000 × $4.00)		$20,000	
Conversion (1,000 × $3.275)		3,275	23,275
Total cost accounted for.			$277,900

* 5,000 units, 20% converted

** Includes direct labor of $62,200 and applied manufacturing overhead of $46,700

Summary of Units in Process

This section of the cost of production report provides a summary of all units in the department during the period—both from an input and an output perspective—regardless of their stage of completion. From an input perspective, total units in process during the period consisted of the following:

- Units in process at the beginning of the period, **plus**
- Units started during the period.

From an output perspective, these units in process during the period were either

- Completed and transferred out of the department, **or**
- Still on hand at the end of the period.

In the summary of units in process, all units are treated as the same, regardless of the amount of processing that took place on them during the period. The objective here is to account for all discrete units of product in process at any time during the period. In the summary of units in process in **Exhibit 17.7**, suppose 40,000 individual units were in process, including 4,000 partially completed units in the beginning inventory and 36,000 new units started during the month. During the period, 35,000 units were completed, and the remaining 5,000 were still in process at the end of the month.

Equivalent Units in Process

This section of the report translates the number of units in process during the period into equivalent completed units of production. The term **equivalent completed units** refers to the number of completed units that is equal, in terms of production effort, to a given number of partially completed units. For example, 80 units for which 50 percent of the expected total processing cost has been incurred is the equivalent of 40 completed units (80 × 0.50).

Frequently, direct materials costs are incurred largely, if not entirely, at the beginning of the process, whereas direct labor and manufacturing overhead costs are added throughout the production process. If direct labor and manufacturing costs are added to the process simultaneously, it is common to treat them jointly as conversion costs. Assume Intel adds all materials at the beginning of the process; all conversion costs are added evenly throughout the process. Therefore, separate computations are made for equivalent units of materials and equivalent units of conversion. Although the department worked on 40,000 units during the period, the total number of equivalent units in process with respect to conversion costs was only 36,000 units, consisting of 35,000 finished units plus 1,000 equivalent units in ending inventory (5,000 units 20 percent converted). Because all materials are added at the start of the process, 40,000 equivalent units (35,000 finished and 5,000 in process) were in process with respect to materials costs.

Total Cost to Be Accounted for and Cost per Equivalent Unit in Process

This section of the report summarizes total costs in Work-in-Process during the period and calculates the cost per equivalent unit for materials, conversion, and in total. Total cost consists of the beginning Work-in-Process balance (if any) plus current costs incurred. For our Intel example, the total cost to be accounted for during July was $277,900, consisting of $25,000 in Work-in-Process at the beginning of the period plus current costs of $252,900 incurred in July. **Exhibit 17.7** shows these amounts broken down between materials costs and conversion costs.

To compute cost per equivalent unit, divide total cost in process by the equivalent units in process. This is done separately for materials cost and conversion cost. The total cost per equivalent unit is the sum of the unit costs for materials and conversion. Because the number of equivalent units in process was different for materials and conversion, it is not possible to get the total cost per unit by dividing total costs of $277,900 by some equivalent unit amount.

Accounting for Total Costs

This section shows the disposition of the total costs in process during the period divided between units completed (and sent to finished goods) and units still in process at the end of the period. As noted in the previous section, total cost in process is $277,900 and each equivalent unit in process has $4.00 of materials cost and $3.275 of conversion costs for a total of $7.275.

The first step in assigning total costs is to calculate the cost of units transferred out by multiplying the units completed during the period by the total cost per unit (35,000 units × $7.275). This assigns $254,625 of the total cost to units transferred out, leaving $23,275 ($277,900 − $254,625) to be assigned to ending Work-in-Process. To verify that $23,275 is the correct amount of cost remaining in ending Work-in-Process, the materials and conversion costs in ending Work-in-Process are calculated separately. Recall that the 5,000 units in process at the end of the period are 100 percent completed with materials costs, but only 20 percent completed with conversion costs. Therefore, in ending Work-in-Process, the materials cost component is $20,000 (5,000 $\times$ 1.00 $\times$ $4.00), the conversion cost component is $3,275 (5,000 $\times$ 0.20 $\times$ $3.275), and the total cost of ending Work-in-Process is $23,275 ($20,000 + $3,275).

The cost of production report summarizes manufacturing costs assigned to Work-in-Process during the period and provides information for determining the transfer of costs from Work-in-Process to Finished Goods Inventory. The supporting documents are similar to those previously illustrated for job costing, except that the single cost of production report replaces all the job cost sheets that flow through a department or process. The flow of costs through Work-in-Process is as follows:

Work-in-Process		
Beginning balance		$ 25,000
Current manufacturing costs		
Direct materials.	$144,000	
Direct labor	62,200	
Applied overhead	46,700	252,900
Total		277,900
Cost of goods manufactured		(254,625)
Ending balance.		$ 23,275

The reduction in Work-in-Process for the units completed during the period is determined in the cost of production report (see **Exhibit 17.7**). This amount is transferred to Finished Goods Inventory. The $23,275 ending balance in Work-in-Process is also determined in the cost of production report as the amount assigned to units in ending Work-in-Process.

Weighted Average and First-In, First-Out Process Costing

Because the costs of materials, labor, and overhead are constantly changing, unit costs are seldom exactly the same from period to period. Hence, if a unit is manufactured partially in one period and partially in the following period, its actual cost is seldom equal to the unit cost of units produced in either period.

In the cost of production report in **Exhibit 17.7**, we made no attempt to account separately for the completed units that came from beginning inventory and those that were started during the current period. The method illustrated in **Exhibit 17.7** is called the **weighted average method**, and it simply spreads the combined beginning inventory cost and current manufacturing costs (for materials, labor, and overhead) over the units completed and those in ending inventory on an average basis. For example, the total cost in process for conversion ($117,900) included both beginning inventory cost and current costs; the 36,000 equivalent units in process for conversion included both units from beginning inventory and units started during the current period. Hence, the average cost per unit of $3.275 (or $117,900 ÷ 36,000) is a weighted average cost of the partially completed units in beginning inventory (prior period costs) and units started during the current period. It is not a precise cost per unit for the current period's production activity but an average cost that includes the cost of partially completed units in beginning inventory carried over from the previous period.

An alternative, more precise process costing method is the **first-in, first-out (FIFO) method**. It accounts for unit costs of beginning inventory units separately from those started during the current period. Under this method, the first costs incurred each period are assumed to have been used to complete the unfinished units carried over from the previous period. Hence, the cost of the beginning inventory is partially based on the prior period's unit costs and partially based on the current period's unit costs.

If unit costs are changing from period to period and beginning inventories are large in relation to total production for the period, the FIFO method is more accurate. However, with the current trend toward smaller inventories, the additional effort and cost of the FIFO method may not be justified. Detailed coverage of the FIFO method is included in cost accounting textbooks. Unless stated otherwise, weighted average process costing is used in chapter assignments.

Process Costing in Service Organizations

There are many applications of process costing for service organizations. Process costing in service organizations is similar to that in manufacturing organizations, the primary purpose being to assign costs to cost objects. Generally, the use of process costing techniques for service organizations is easier than for manufacturing organizations because the raw materials element is not necessary. The applications for the labor and overhead costs are similar, if not identical, to those of a manufacturing firm.

Process costing for services is similar to job costing for batches in that an average cost for similar or identical services is determined. There are important differences, though, between batch and process costing. In a batch environment, a discrete group of services is identified, but in a process environment, services are performed on a continuous basis. Batch costing accumulates the cost for a specific group of services as the batch moves through the various activities that make up the service. Process service costing measures the average cost of identical or similar services performed each period (each month) in a department. An example of batch service costing is determining the cost of registering a student at your college during the fall term registration period; an example of process service costing is determining the cost each month of processing a check by a bank. If continuously performed services involved multiple processes, the total cost of the service would be the sum of the costs for each process.

After it is determined that process costing would be appropriate for a service activity, the actual decision to use it is generally contingent on two important factors about the items being evaluated. First, is average cost per unit acceptable as an input item to the decision process? For some activities, the answer is obvious. For instance, tracking the actual cost of processing each check through a bank would probably not be as useful as determining the average cost of processing checks for a given period; therefore, average cost is acceptable. For other activities, the answer is more difficult to determine. Should the decision model include average cost per patient-day or actual cost per individual patient?

The second issue relates to the benefits versus the costs of the resulting information. Normally, it is easier to track and record the cost of an activity or process than it is to track and record the cost of each individual item in the activity. Often actual cost tracking is impossible for practical reasons (the actual cost of processing a check through a banking system, for example). Although process costing will not work in every situation, it has many applications in service organizations. As illustrated in this text, there are many possibilities for applying either job or process costing to activities in service organizations.

CHAPTER-END REVIEW

SanDisk manufactures USB flash drives that are used in computing. Since there is little product differentiation between SanDisk's products, assume it uses a process costing system to determine inventory costs. Production and manufacturing cost data for 2017 are as follows:

Production Data (units)	
Units in process, beginning of period (60% converted).	3,000,000
Units started.	27,000,000
Completed and transferred to finished goods	25,000,000
Units in process, end of period (30% converted).	5,000,000

Manufacturing Costs	
Work-in-Process, beginning of period (materials, $468,000; conversion, $252,000)	$ 720,000
Current manufacturing costs:	
Raw materials transferred to processing	6,132,000
Direct labor for the period.	1,550,000
Overhead applied for the period.	3,498,000

REQUIRED

Prepare a cost of production report for SanDisk for 2017.

The solution to this review problem can be found on page 819.

APPENDIX 17A: Absorption and Variable Costing

LO6 Evaluate the differences between absorption and variable costing income.

Product costing for inventory valuation is the link between financial and managerial accounting. Product costing systems determine the cost-based valuation of the manufactured inventories used in making key financial accounting measurements (cost of goods sold and income on the income statement as well as inventory and total assets on the balance sheet). They also provide vital information to managers for setting prices, controlling costs, and evaluating management performance. The influence of financial accounting on product costing systems is apparent in the design of traditional job order and process costing systems. These systems reflect the requirement of financial accounting (i.e., generally accepted accounting principles) that all manufacturing costs be included in inventory valuations for external financial reporting purposes. In these systems, all other costs incurred, such as selling, general, and administrative costs, are treated as expenses of the period.

Basic Concepts

A debate exists over how to treat fixed manufacturing overhead costs in the valuation of inventory. The debate centers around whether fixed costs such as depreciation on manufacturing equipment should be considered an *inventoriable product cost* and treated as an asset cost until the inventory is sold, or as a *period cost* and recorded immediately as an operating expense. **Absorption costing** (also called **full costing**) treats fixed manufacturing overhead as a product cost, whereas **variable costing** (also called **direct costing**) treats it as a period cost. Therefore, fixed manufacturing overhead is recorded initially as an asset (inventory) under absorption costing but as an operating expense under variable costing.

> **Fixed manufacturing costs:**
>
> **Absorption costing** treats **fixed manufacturing costs** as **product costs**.
>
> **Variable costing** treats **fixed manufacturing costs** as **period costs**.

Since fixed product costs are eventually recorded as expenses under both variable and absorption costing by the time the inventory is sold, why does it matter whether fixed overhead is treated as a product cost or a period cost? It matters because the way it is treated affects the measurement of income for a particular period and the valuation assigned to inventory on the balance sheet at the end of the period. Because absorption costing presents fixed manufacturing overhead as a cost per unit rather than a total cost per period, management's perceptions of cost behavior, and decisions based on perceptions of cost behavior, may also be affected.

Inventory Valuations   To illustrate the difference in inventory valuations between absorption and variable costing, assume the following cost data for a single component of a **Trek** bicycle at a monthly volume of 4,000 units:

Direct materials	$ 5	per unit
Direct labor	2	per unit
Variable manufacturing overhead	3	per unit
Total variable cost	$ 10	per unit
Fixed manufacturing overhead	$8,000	per month

To determine the unit cost of inventory using absorption costing, an average fixed overhead cost per unit is calculated by dividing the monthly fixed manufacturing overhead by the monthly volume. Even though fixed manufacturing overhead is not a variable cost, under absorption costing it is applied to inventory on a per-unit basis, the same as variable costs. At a monthly volume of 4,000 units, Trek's total component inventory cost per unit, is $10 under variable costing, and $12 under absorption costing.

The $2 difference in total unit cost is attributed to the treatment of fixed overhead of $8,000 divided by 4,000 units. The difference in the total component inventory valuation on the balance sheet between absorption and variable costing is the number of units in ending inventory times $2. So if 1,000 units are on hand at the end of the month, they are valued at $12,000 if absorption costing is used but at only $10,000 with variable costing.

Income Under Absorption and Variable Costing

The income statement formats used for variable and absorption costing are not the same. One benefit of variable costing is that it separates costs into variable and fixed costs, making it possible to present the income statement in a contribution format. As illustrated in Chapter 15, in a contribution income statement, variable costs are subtracted from revenues to compute contribution margin; fixed costs are then subtracted from contribution margin to calculate profit, also called net income or earnings.

When absorption costing is used, the income statement is usually formatted using the functional format, which classifies costs based on cost function, such as manufacturing, selling, or administrative. The functional income statement, used for financial reporting, subtracts manufacturing costs (represented by cost of goods sold) from revenues to calculate gross profit; selling and administrative costs are then subtracted from gross profit to calculate profit or income.

The contribution format provides information for determining the contribution margin ratio, which is calculated as total contribution margin divided by total sales. It also provides the total amount of fixed costs. These are the primary items of data needed to determine the break-even point and to conduct other cost-volume-profit analysis (see Chapter 15).

Not only is the income statement format different for absorption and variable costing methods, but also as illustrated in the following hypothetical examples for Trek, the amount of income reported on the income statement might not be the same because of the difference in the treatment of fixed manufacturing overhead. The following additional information is assumed for the Trek component examples:

Selling price	$ 30	per unit
Variable selling and administrative expenses.	$ 3	per unit
Fixed selling and administrative expenses.	$10,000	per month

Production Equals Sales

Assume Trek has no component inventory on June 1, 2017. Production and sales for the third quarter of 2017 are:

Month	Production	Sales
June	3,200 units	3,200 units
July	4,000 units	3,500 units
August	4,000 units	4,500 units
Third quarter	11,200 units	11,200 units

Production and sales both total 11,200 units for the third quarter. A summary of unit production, sales, and inventory levels is presented in **Exhibit 17A.1**. Using previously presented cost and a selling price of $30 per unit, monthly contribution (variable costing) and functional (absorption costing) income statements are presented in **Exhibit 17A.1** parts B and C. An analysis of fixed manufacturing overhead with absorption costing is presented in part D.

In June, with 3,200 units produced and sold all $8,000 of fixed manufacturing overhead is deducted as a period cost under variable costing and expensed as part of the cost of goods sold under absorption costing. No costs were assigned to ending inventory under either method.

Production Exceeds Sales

July production of 4,000 units exceeded sales of 3,500 units by 500 units. The ending inventory under variable costing consisted of only the variable cost of production, $5,000 (500 × $10). The entire $8,000 of fixed manufacturing overhead is deducted as a period cost.

Under absorption costing, in addition to the variable cost of production, a portion of the fixed manufacturing overhead is assigned to the ending inventory. As shown in the July column of **Exhibit 17A.1**, part D, absorption costing assigns $1,000 of the month's fixed manufacturing overhead to the July ending inventory and $7,000 to the cost of goods sold. Consequently, under absorption costing the July ending inventory is $1,000 higher, the July expenses are $1,000 lower, and the July net income is $1,000 higher than under variable costing.

EXHIBIT 17A.1	Contribution (Variable Costing) and Functional (Absorption Costing) Income Statements with Variations in Production and Sales

	June (Production equals sales)	July (Production exceeds sales)	August (Sales exceed production)
A. Trek's Component: Summary of Unit Inventory Changes			
Beginning inventory	0	0	500
Production	3,200	4,000	4,000
Total available	3,200	4,000	4,500
Sales	(3,200)	(3,500)	(4,500)
Ending inventory	0	500	0
B. Contribution (Variable Costing) Income Statements			
Sales ($30/unit)	$96,000	$105,000	$135,000
Less variable expenses:			
Cost of goods sold ($10/unit)	$32,000	$ 35,000	$ 45,000
Selling & admin. ($3/unit)	9,600	10,500	13,500
Total	(41,600)	(45,500)	(58,500)
Contribution margin	54,400	59,500	76,500
Less fixed expenses			
Manufacturing overhead	8,000	8,000	8,000
Selling & admin.	10,000	10,000	10,000
Total	(18,000)	(18,000)	(18,000)
Net income	$36,400	$ 41,500	$ 58,500
C. Functional (Absorption Costing) Income Statements			
Sales ($30/unit)	$96,000	$105,000	$135,000
Cost of goods sold (Part D.)	(40,000)	(42,000)	(54,000)
Gross profit	56,000	63,000	81,000
Selling & admin. expenses			
Variable ($3/unit)	9,600	10,500	13,500
Fixed	10,000	10,000	10,000
Total	(19,600)	(20,500)	(23,500)
Net income	$36,400	$ 42,500	$ 57,500
D. Analysis of Fixed Manufacturing Overhead under Absorption Costing			
Fixed manufacturing overhead	$ 8,000	$ 8,000	$ 8,000
Units produced	÷ 3,200	÷ 4,000	÷ 4,000
Absorption fixed cost per unit*	$ 2.50	$ 2.00	$ 2.00
Units in ending inventory	× 0	× 500	× 0
Fixed costs in ending inv.	$ 0	$ 1,000	$ 0
Fixed cost of goods sold:			
From beginning inventory	$ 0	$ 0	$ 1,000
June (3,200 units × $2.50)	8,000		
July (3,500 units × $2.00)		7,000	
August (4,000 × $2.00)			8,000
Total fixed	8,000	7,000	9,000
Variable cost of goods sold	32,000	35,000	45,000
Absorption cost of goods sold	$40,000	$ 42,000	$ 54,000

* To simplify the illustration, the example does not use a predetermined overhead rate. If a predetermined overhead rate were used, an increase or decrease in the balance of Manufacturing Overhead is treated as an adjustment to ending inventory.

Sales Exceed Production

In August just the opposite of July's situation occurred: sales of 4,500 units exceeded production of 4,000 units by 500 units. The additional units came from the July production. Under variable costing all current manufacturing costs are expensed either as the variable cost of goods sold or as part of the fixed expense. Additionally, the August variable cost of goods sold includes variable costs assigned the July ending inventory.

Under absorption costing all current manufacturing costs are expensed as part of the cost of goods sold. Additionally, the cost of goods sold includes the variable and fixed costs assigned the July ending inventory. The inclusion of the July fixed costs caused absorption costing net income to be $1,000 lower than the corresponding variable costing amount.

The above relationships between absorption and variable costing are summarized in **Exhibit 17A.2**.

EXHIBIT 17A.2	Comparative Effects of Absorption and Variable Costing		
Relationship between period production and sales	**Effect on inventory costs**	**Effect on operating income**	**Explanation**
Production = Sales	No change in inventory costs.	Absorption costing income = Variable costing income	All current fixed manufacturing costs are expensed under both absorption and variable costing.
Production > Sales	Absorption costing ending inventory increases more than variable costing inventory.	Absorption costing income > Variable costing income	Under absorption costing some current fixed manufacturing costs are assigned to ending inventory. Under variable costing all current fixed manufacturing costs are expensed.
Sales > Production	Absorption costing ending inventory declines more than variable costing inventory.	Absorption costing income < Variable costing income	Under absorption costing fixed manufacturing costs previously assigned to ending inventory are expensed along with current fixed manufacturing costs. Under variable costing only current fixed manufacturing costs are expensed.

Exhibits 17A.1 and **17A.2** reveal several important relationships between absorption costing net income and variable costing net income, as well as the way net income responds to changes in sales and production under both methods.

For each period, the income differences between absorption and variable costing can be explained by analyzing the change in inventoried fixed manufacturing overhead under absorption costing net income. In general, the following relationship exists:

Variable costing net income	+	**Increase (or minus decrease) in inventoried fixed manufacturing overhead**	=	**Absorption costing net income**

Using Trek's July information, the equation is as follows:

$$\$41,500 + (500 \times \$2.00) = \$42,500$$

For any given time period, regardless of length, if total units produced equals total units sold, net income is the same for absorption costing and variable costing, all other things being equal. Under absorption costing, all fixed manufacturing overhead is released as a product cost through cost of goods sold when inventory is sold. Under variable costing, all fixed manufacturing overhead is reported as a period cost and expensed in the period incurred. Consequently, over the life of a product, the income differences within periods are offset since they occur only because of the timing of the release of fixed manufacturing overhead to the income statement.

Evaluating Alternatives to Inventory Valuation

The issue in the variable costing debate is whether or not fixed manufacturing costs add value to products. Proponents of variable costing argue that these costs do not add value to a product. They believe that fixed costs are incurred to provide the capacity to produce during a given period, and these costs expire with the passage of time regardless of whether the related capacity was used. Variable manufacturing costs, on the other hand, are incurred only if production takes place. Consequently, these costs are properly assignable to the units produced.

Proponents of variable costing also argue that inventories have value only to the extent that they avoid the necessity of incurring costs in the future. Having inventory available for sale avoids the necessity of incurring some future variable costs, but the availability of finished goods inventory does not avoid the incurrence of future fixed manufacturing costs. Proponents conclude that inventories should be valued at their variable manufacturing cost, and fixed manufacturing costs should be expensed as incurred.

Opponents of variable costing argue that fixed manufacturing costs are incurred for only one purpose, namely, to manufacture the product. Because they are incurred to manufacture the product, they should be assigned to the product. It is also argued that in the long run all costs are variable. Consequently, by omitting fixed costs, variable costing understates long-run variable costs and misleads decision makers into underestimating true production costs.

On a pragmatic level, the central arguments for variable costing center around the fact that use of variable costing facilitates the development of contribution income statements and cost-volume-profit analysis. With costs accumulated on an absorption costing basis, contribution income statements are difficult to develop, and cost-volume-profit analysis becomes very complicated unless production and sales are equal.

Proponents of activity-based costing typically do not favor variable costing because ABC is based on the assumption that, in the long run, all costs are variable and that fixed costs should be assigned to products or services to represent long-run variable costs. Hence, inventory valuation using an ABC approach will tend to be closer to absorption costing values than variable costing values.

As inventory levels have remained steady in recent years (see the following Research Insight), the significance of the debate over absorption versus variable costing has quieted. If a company has no inventories, all its costs are deducted as expenses (either as operating expenses or cost of goods sold expense) during the current period whether it uses absorption or variable costing. Hence, from an income determination standpoint, it does not matter in such cases whether fixed costs are considered a product or period cost.

RESEARCH INSIGHT

Inventory Levels Are Holding Steady   Using data from 2012 financial statements from 1,000 public companies, research has found that overall U.S. inventory levels have remained flat since 2005 when compared to sales. There was a temporary spike in the inventory-to-sales ratio immediately after the recession of 2008 when companies were temporarily left with excess inventory in the face of decreased demand. The construction equipment, food manufacturing, and contract manufacturing sectors decreased their inventory holdings over the past year, whereas the spirits, electric utilities, and retail wireless services sectors saw an increase in their inventories over the same period.

Total Business Inventories/Sales Ratios: 2004 to 2013
(Data adjusted for seasonal, holiday and trading—day differences but not for price changes)

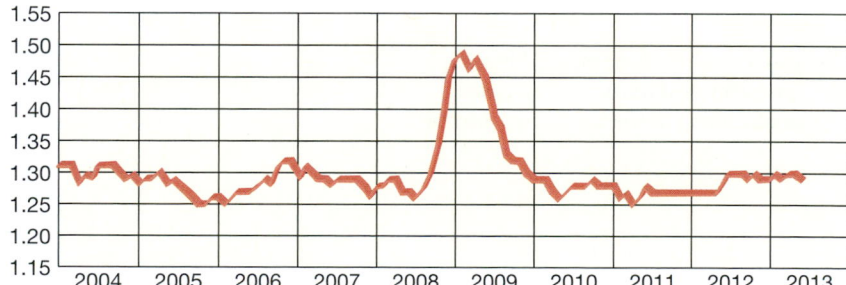

Source: Dan Gilmore, "Supply Chain News: Inventory Performance 2013," *Supply Chain Digest*, July 26, 2013.

APPENDIX 17A REVIEW

Boxtel Inc. has a highly automated assembly line that uses very little direct labor. Therefore, direct labor is part of variable overhead. For October, assume that it incurred the following unit costs:

Direct materials	$250
Variable overhead...	220
Fixed overhead...	80

The 100 units of beginning inventory for October had an absorption costing value of $45,000 and a variable costing value of $38,000. For October, assume that Boxtel Inc. produced 500 units and sold 540 units.

REQUIRED

a. Compute Boxtel's October amount of ending inventory under both absorption and variable costing if the FIFO inventory method was used.

b. Compute Boxtel's October Cost of Goods Sold using both the variable and absorption costing methods.

The solution to this review problem can be found on pages 819–820.

GUIDANCE ANSWERS . . . YOU MAKE THE CALL

You are the Chief Financial Officer   Inventory costs that are provided for financial statement purposes for external stockholders and lenders are required by generally accepted accounting principles to include only the manufacturing costs of the product for direct materials, direct labor, and manufacturing overhead. To conduct a complete profitability analysis, the CFO will need to gather data for all other costs that relate to the marketing, sales, and distribution of each product, as well as any costs related to providing service to customers who buy the products.

KEY RATIOS

$$\text{Predetermined manufacturing overhead rate per direct labor hour} = \frac{\text{Predicted total manufacturing overhead cost for the year}}{\text{Predicted total direct labor hours for the year}}$$

$$\text{Manufacturing overhead applied to Work-in-Process Inventory} = \text{Actual direct labor hours} \times \text{Predetermined manufacturing overhead rate per direct labor hour}$$

$$\text{Variable costing net income} + \text{Increase (or minus decrease) in inventoried fixed manufacturing overhead} = \text{Absorption costing net income}$$

KEY TERMS

absorption cost, 773	full absorption cost, 773	process manufacturing, 776
absorption costing, 793	full costing, 793	product costs, 772
activities list, 776	job cost sheet, 777	production order, 777
bill of materials, 776	job order production, 776	raw materials inventories, 770
conversion cost, 773	job production, 776	service costing, 785
cost of production report, 789	manufacturing organizations, 770	service organizations, 770
direct costing, 793	manufacturing overhead, 773	statement of cost of goods
direct labor, 773	materials requisition form, 777	manufactured, 783
direct materials, 773	merchandising organizations, 770	variable costing, 793
equivalent completed units, 790	operations list, 776	weighted average method, 791
finished goods inventories, 770	period costs, 772	work-in-process inventories, 770
first-in, first-out (FIFO)	predetermined manufacturing	work ticket, 777
method, 791	overhead rate, 774	

Assignments with the (MBC) **logo in the margin are available in** BusinessCourse.
See the Preface of the book for details.

MULTIPLE CHOICE

1. Which of the following statements best represents manufacturing organizations?

    a.   A manufacturing organization always uses process costing.
    b.   A manufacturing organization typically has a low percentage of its assets invested in inventory.
    c.   A manufacturing organization typically has three major inventory categories.
    d.   A manufacturing organization is the only type of organization that has a cost of goods sold account reported on the income statement.

2. Kay Company's formula for annual manufacturing overhead is:

    $Y = \$120,000 + \$10X$, where x is direct labor dollars

    The predicted activity for 2017 is 50,000 direct labor hours and the actual activity for January of 2017 was 4,000 direct labor hours. Using a predetermined overhead rate the applied January overhead is:

    a. $40,000
    b. $49,600
    c. $160,000
    d. $169,600

3. Which of the following statements best represents job order costing?

    a.   Job order costing works best when there is production of identical units on a continuous basis.
    b.   Job order costing works best for companies like Kraft Heinz and SanDisk.
    c.   In job order costing, scheduling personnel prepare a production order for each job.
    d.   In job order costing, a process cost sheet is used to accumulate the costs for each job.

4. Presented is selected information from Took's April income statement and statement of cost of goods manufactured:

Cost of goods sold.	$230,000
Cost of goods manufactured	$210,000
Finished goods inventory, April 30	$ 40,000

    Took's finished goods inventory on April 1 was:

    a. $20,000
    b. $40,000
    c. $60,000
    d. $80,000

5. Presented is selected information from Fred's January statement of cost of goods manufactured.

Predetermined overhead rate........................	80 percent of direct labor dollars
Direct materials	$ 60,000
Cost of goods manufactured	$150,000

Fred's January direct labor was:

   a. $40,000
   b. $50,000
   c. $75,000
   d. $90,000

6. The beginning inventory consisted of 10,000 units, 30 percent complete and the ending inventory consisted of 8,000 units, 40 percent complete. There were 22,000 units started during the period. Determine the equivalent units of conversion in process.

   a.   17,800
   b.   20,800
   c.   25,200
   d.   27,200

7. Presented is selected information from Micro Systems cost of production report:

Cost per equivalent unit in process	$ 20
Units completed..	30,000
Total costs in process..	$664,000
Equivalent units of materials in ending inventory.....................	4,000
Cost per equivalent unit of materials	$ 12

The ending inventory of work-in-process is complete as to materials. The cost of conversion in the ending inventory is:

   a. $16,000
   b. $32,000
   c. $48,000
   d. $64,000

8. Chandler Company sells its product for $100 per unit. Variable manufacturing costs per unit are $40, and fixed manufacturing costs at the normal operating level of 12,000 units are $240,000. Variable expenses are $16 per unit sold. Fixed administration expenses total $104,000. Chandler had no beginning inventory in 2017. During 2017, the company produced 12,000 units and sold 9,000. What would the net income be for Chandler Company in 2017 using both variable costing and absorption costing?

   a.   Variable costing $60,000; absorption costing $60,000
   b.   Variable costing $112,000; absorption costing $52,000
   c.   Variable costing $112,000; absorption costing $125,000
   d.   Variable costing $52,000; absorption costing $112,000

QUESTIONS

Q17-1. Distinguish among service, merchandising, and manufacturing organizations on the basis of the importance and complexity of inventory cost measurement.

Q17-2. Distinguish between product costing and service costing.

Q17-3. When is depreciation a product cost? When is depreciation a period cost?

Q17-4. What are the three major product cost elements?

Q17-5. How are predetermined overhead rates developed? Why are they widely used?

Q17-6. Briefly distinguish between process manufacturing and job order production. Provide examples of products typically produced under each system.

Q17-7. Briefly describe the role of engineering personnel and production scheduling personnel in the production planning process.

Q17-8.   Identify the primary records involved in the operation of a job cost system.

Q17-9.   Describe the flow of costs through the accounting system of a labor-intensive manufacturing organization.

Q17-10.   Identify two reasons that a service organization should maintain detailed job cost information.

Q17-11.   What are the four major elements of a cost of production report?

Q17-12.   What are equivalent completed units?

Q17-13.   Under what conditions will equivalent units in process be different for materials and conversion costs?

MINI EXERCISES

M17-14. Classification of Product and Period Costs

Classify the following costs incurred by a manufacturer of golf clubs as product costs or period costs. Also classify the product costs as direct materials or conversion costs.

LO2

    a.   Depreciation on computer in president's office
    b.   Salaries of legal staff
    c.   Graphite shafts
    d.   Plant security department
    e.   Electricity for the corporate office
    f.   Rubber grips
    g.   Golf club heads
    h.   Wages paid assembly line maintenance workers
    i.   Salary of corporate controller
    j.   Subsidy of plant cafeteria
    k.   Wages paid assembly line production workers
    l.   National sales meeting in Orlando
    m.   Overtime premium paid assembly line workers
    n.   Advertising on national television
    o.   Depreciation on assembly line

M17-15. Developing and Using a Predetermined Overhead Rate

Assume that the following predictions were made for 2018 for one of the plants of **Milliken & Company**:

LO2

Milliken & Company

Total manufacturing overhead for the year.	$20,000,000
Total machine hours for the year	1,600,000

Actual results for February 2018 were as follows:

Manufacturing overhead	$2,205,000
Machine hours	205,000

REQUIRED

    a.   Determine the 2018 predetermined overhead rate per machine hour.
    b.   Using the predetermined overhead rate per machine hour, determine the manufacturing overhead applied to Work-in-Process during February.
    c.   As of February 1, actual overhead was underapplied by $400,000. Determine the cumulative amount of any overapplied or underapplied overhead at the end of February.

M17-16. Job Order Costing and Process Costing Applications

For each of the following manufacturing situations, indicate whether job order or process costing is more appropriate and why.

LO4, 5

    a.   Manufacturer of chocolate candy bars
    b.   Manufacturer of carbonated beverages
    c.   Manufacturer of high-quality men's suits
    d.   Manufacturer of subway cars
    e.   Book printing

LO4, 5   **M17-17. Job Order Costing and Process Costing Applications**

For each of the following situations, indicate whether job order or process costing is more appropriate and why.

a. Building contractor for residential dwellings
b. Manufacturer of nylon yarn that sells to fabric-making textile companies
c. Evening gown manufacturer that makes gowns in several different fabrics, colors, styles, and sizes
d. Hosiery mill that manufactures a one-size-fits-all product
e. Vehicle battery manufacturer that has just received an order for 400,000 identical batteries to be delivered as completed over the next 12 months

LO5   **M17-18. Process Costing**

Clarke Manufacturing Company makes a single product that is produced on a continuous basis in one department. All materials are added at the beginning of production. The total cost per equivalent unit in process in March was $6.00, consisting of $4.80 for materials and $1.40 for conversion. During the month, 9,000 units of product were transferred to finished goods inventory; on March 31, 3,500 units were in process, 10 percent converted. The company uses weighted average costing.

REQUIRED

a. Determine the cost of goods transferred to finished goods inventory.
b. Determine the cost of the ending work-in-process inventory.
c. What was the total cost of the beginning work-in-process inventory plus the current manufacturing costs?

LO6   **M17-19. Absorption and Variable Costing; Inventory Valuation**

Bondware Inc. has a highly automated assembly line that uses very little direct labor. Therefore, direct labor is part of variable overhead. For March, assume that it incurred the following unit costs:

Direct materials	$500
Variable overhead.	440
Fixed overhead.	160

The 100 units of beginning inventory for March had an absorption costing value of $90,000 and a variable costing value of $76,000. For March, assume that Bondware Inc. produced 500 units and sold 540 units.

REQUIRED

Compute Bondware's March amount of ending inventory under both absorption and variable costing if the FIFO inventory method was used.

LO6   **M17-20. Absorption and Variable Costing; Cost of Goods Sold**

Use data from Mini Exercise 17-19.

REQUIRED

Compute Bondware's March Cost of Goods Sold using both the variable and absorption costing methods.

EXERCISES

E17-21. Analyzing Activity in Inventory Accounts

LO2, 4

Selected data concerning operations of Ridgeview Manufacturing Company for the past fiscal year follow:

Raw materials used	$300,000
Total manufacturing costs charged to production during the year (includes raw materials, direct labor, and manufacturing overhead applied at a rate of 60 percent of direct labor costs)	681,000
Cost of goods available for sale.	826,000
Selling and general expenses.	30,000

	Inventories	
	Beginning	Ending
Raw materials.	$70,000	$ 80,000
Work-in-process.	85,000	30,000
Finished goods.	90,000	110,000

REQUIRED

Determine each of the following:

a. Cost of raw materials purchased
b. Direct labor costs charged to production
c. Cost of goods manufactured
d. Cost of goods sold

E17-22. Statement of Cost of Goods Manufactured and Income Statement

LO4

Information from the records of the Bridgeview Manufacturing Company for August 2017 follows:

Sales.	$315,000
Selling and administrative expenses	127,500
Purchases of raw materials	45,000
Direct labor.	30,000
Manufacturing overhead	55,500

	Inventories	
	August 1	August 31
Raw materials.	$ 8,000	$ 5,000
Work-in-process.	14,000	11,000
Finished goods.	15,000	19,000

REQUIRED

Prepare a statement of cost of goods manufactured and an income statement for August 2017.

E17-23. Statement of Cost of Goods Manufactured from Percent Relationships

LO4

Information about Blue Line Products Company for the year ending December 31, 2017, follows:

- Sales equal $475,000.
- Direct materials used total $68,000.
- Manufacturing overhead is 150 percent of direct labor dollars.
- The beginning inventory of finished goods is 20 percent of the cost of goods sold.
- The ending inventory of finished goods is twice the beginning inventory.
- The gross profit is 20 percent of sales.
- There is no beginning or ending work-in-process.

REQUIRED

Prepare a statement of cost of goods manufactured for 2017. (*Hint:* Prepare an analysis of changes in Finished Goods Inventory.)

LO2, 4   **E17-24. Account Activity and Relationships**

	Case A	Case B	Case C	Case D
Sales.	$85,000	(b)	$110,000	(b)
Direct materials	15,000	21,000	(f)	21,000
Direct labor.	5,000	(c)	20,000	(c)
Total direct costs	(a)	32,000	(e)	30,000
Conversion cost	(b)	26,000	(g)	(g)
Manufacturing overhead	8,000	(d)	10,000	(f)
Current manufacturing costs	(c)	(e)	95,000	79,000
Work in process, beginning	7,000	10,000	(d)	21,000
Work in process, ending.	5,000	(f)	21,000	(e)
Cost of goods manufactured	(d)	32,000	(c)	82,000
Finished goods inventory, beginning	9,000	8,000	7,000	12,000
Finished goods inventory, ending.	6,000	(g)	8,000	(d)
Cost of goods sold.	(e)	35,000	(b)	80,000
Gross profit.	(f)	(a)	18,000	15,000
Selling and administrative expenses	20,000	15,000	(a)	(a)
Net income.	(g)	22,000	12,000	6,000

REQUIRED

Each case is independent. Solve for missing data in alphabetical order. (*Hint:* Refer to Exhibit 17.6, p. 784 and the WIP table, p. 791.)

LO2   **E17-25. Developing and Using a Predetermined Overhead Rate: High-Low Cost Estimation**

For years, Mattoon Components Company has used an actual plantwide overhead rate and based its prices on cost plus a markup of 30 percent. Recently the marketing manager, Holly Adams, and the production manager, Sue Walsh, confronted the controller with a common problem. The marketing manager expressed a concern that Mattoon's prices seem to vary widely throughout the year. According to Adams, "It seems irrational to charge higher prices when business is bad and lower prices when business is good. While we get a lot of business during high-volume months because we charge less than our competitors, it is a waste of time to even call on customers during low-volume months because we are raising prices while our competitors are lowering them." Walsh also believed that it was "folly to be so pushed that we have to pay overtime in some months and then lay employees off in others." She commented, "While there are natural variations in customer demand, the accounting system seems to amplify this variation."

REQUIRED

a.   Evaluate the arguments presented by Adams and Walsh. What suggestions do you have for improving the accounting and pricing procedures?

b.   Assume that the Mattoon Components Company had the following total manufacturing overhead costs and direct labor hours in 2016 and 2017:

	2016	2017
Total manufacturing overhead	$210,000	$248,000
Direct labor hours.	20,000	28,000

Use the high-low method (see Chapter 14) to develop a cost estimating equation for total manufacturing overhead.

c.   Develop a predetermined rate for 2018, assuming 25,000 direct labor hours are budgeted for 2018.

d.   Assume that the actual level of activity in 2018 was 30,000 direct labor hours and that the total 2018 manufacturing overhead was $250,000. Determine the underapplied or overapplied manufacturing overhead at the end of 2018.

e.   Describe two ways of handling any underapplied or overapplied manufacturing overhead at the end of the year.

E17-26. Manufacturing Cost Flows with Machine Hours Allocation

LO4

On April 1, Telecom Manufacturing Company's beginning balances in manufacturing accounts and finished goods inventory were as follows:

Raw Materials	$16,000
Manufacturing Supplies	1,500
Work-in-Process	6,500
Manufacturing Overhead	0
Finished Goods	30,000

During April, Telecom Manufacturing completed the following manufacturing transactions:

1. Purchased raw materials costing $47,000 and manufacturing supplies costing $3,000 on account.
2. Requisitioned raw materials costing $45,000 to the factory.
3. Incurred direct labor costs of $27,000 and indirect labor costs of $4,800.
4. Used manufacturing supplies costing $2,500.
5. Recorded manufacturing depreciation of $15,000.
6. Miscellaneous payables for manufacturing overhead totaled $3,600.
7. Applied manufacturing overhead, based on 2,250 machine hours, at a predetermined rate of $10 per machine hour.
8. Completed jobs costing $90,000.
9. Finished goods costing $100,000 were sold.

REQUIRED

a. Prepare "T" accounts showing the flow of costs through all manufacturing accounts, Finished Goods Inventory, and Cost of Goods Sold.

b. Calculate the balances at the end of April for Work-in-Process Inventory and Finished Goods Inventory.

E17-27. Service Cost Flows

LO4

Vente Marketing, Ltd., produces television advertisements for businesses that are marketing products in the western provinces of Canada. To achieve cost control, Vente Marketing uses a job cost system similar to that found in a manufacturing organization. It uses some different account titles:

Account	Replaces
Videos-in-Process	Work-in-Process
Video Supplies Inventory	Manufacturing Supplies Inventory
Cost of Videos Completed	Cost of Goods Sold
Accumulated Depreciation, Studio Assets	Accumulated Depreciation, Factory Assets
Studio Overhead	Manufacturing Overhead

Vente Marketing does not maintain Raw Materials or Finished Goods Inventory accounts. Materials, such as props needed for videos, are purchased as needed from outside sources and charged directly to Videos-in-Process and the appropriate job. Videos are delivered directly to clients upon completion. The April 1, balances were as follows:

Video Supplies	$1,300	
Videos-in-Process	2,000	
Studio Overhead	250	underapplied

During April, Vente Marketing completed the following production transactions:

1. Purchased video supplies costing $1,675 on account.
2. Purchased materials for specific jobs costing $27,000 on account.
3. Incurred direct labor costs of $65,000 and indirect labor costs of $3,100.
4. Used production supplies costing $850.
5. Recorded studio depreciation of $3,500.
6. Incurred miscellaneous payables for studio overhead of $1,800.
7. Applied studio overhead at a predetermined rate of $18 per studio hour, with 520 studio hours.
8. Completed jobs costing $100,000 and delivered them directly to clients.

REQUIRED

a.   Prepare "T" accounts showing the flow of costs through all service accounts and Cost of Videos Completed.

b.   Calculate the cost incurred as of the end of April for the incomplete jobs still in process.

LO5   **E17-28.   Cost of Production Report: No Beginning Inventories**

Atlanta Paper Company produces newsprint paper through a special recycling process using scrap paper products. Production and cost data for October 2017, the first month of operations for the company's new Brunswick plant, follow:

Units of product started in process during October	80,000 tons
Units completed and transferred to finished goods.	75,000 tons
Machine hours operated	7,000
Direct materials costs incurred.	$486,000
Direct labor costs incurred.	$190,800

Raw materials are added at the beginning of the process for each unit of product produced, and labor and manufacturing overhead are added evenly throughout the manufacturing process. Manufacturing overhead is applied to Work-in-Process at the rate of $24 per machine hour. Units in process at the end of the period were 60 percent converted.

REQUIRED

Prepare a cost of production report for Atlanta Paper Company for October.

LO5   **E17-29.   Cost of Production Report: No Beginning Inventories**

Howell Paving Company manufactures asphalt paving materials for highway construction through a one-step process in which all materials are added at the beginning of the process. During April 2017, the company accumulated the following data in its process costing system:

Production data	
Work-in-process, 10/1/17.	0 tons
Raw materials transferred to processing	25,000 tons
Work-in-process, 10/31/17 (75% converted).	5,000 tons
Cost data	
Raw materials transferred to processing	$650,000
Conversion costs	
Direct labor cost incurred	$47,500
Manufacturing overhead applied	?

Manufacturing overhead is applied at the rate of $6 per equivalent unit (ton) processed.

REQUIRED

Prepare a cost of production report for April.

LO6   **E17-30.   Absorption and Variable Costing Comparisons: Production Equals Sales**

The J.M. Smucker Company
NYSE :: SJM

Assume that **Smuckers** manufactures and sells 30,000 cases of peanut butter each quarter. The following data are available for the third quarter of 2017.

Total fixed manufacturing overhead.	$90,000
Fixed selling and administrative expenses.	20,000
Sales price per case.	32
Direct materials per case	15
Direct labor per case	6
Variable manufacturing overhead per case	3

REQUIRED

a.   Compute the cost per case under both absorption costing and variable costing.

b.   Compute net income under both absorption costing and variable costing.

c.   Reconcile any differences in income. Explain.

LO6   **E17-31.   Absorption and Variable Costing Income Statements: Production Exceeds Sales**

Glenview Company sells its product at a unit price of $13.00. Unit manufacturing costs are direct materials, $2.50; direct labor, $3.00; and variable manufacturing overhead, $1.50. Total fixed manufacturing costs are $50,000 per year. Selling and administrative expenses are $1.00 per unit variable and $20,000 per year fixed. Though 50,000 units were produced during 2017, only 44,000 units were sold. There was no beginning inventory.

REQUIRED

a. Prepare a functional income statement using absorption costing.

b. Prepare a contribution income statement using variable costing.

E17-32. Absorption and Variable Costing Comparisons: Sales Exceed Production   **LO6**

Wright Development purchases, develops, and sells commercial building sites. As the sites are sold, they are cleared at an average cost of $3,000 per site. Storm drains and driveways are also installed at an average cost of $5,500 per site. Selling costs are 10 percent of sales price. Administrative costs are $425,000 per year. During 2016, the company bought 1,000 acres of land for $5,000,000 and divided it into 200 sites of equal size. The average selling price per site was $90,000 during 2016 when 50 sites were sold. During 2017, the company purchased and developed another 1,000 acres, divided into 200 sites. The purchase price was again $5,000,000. Sales totaled 300 sites in 2017 at an average price of $90,000.

REQUIRED

a. Prepare 2016 and 2017 functional income statements using absorption costing.

b. Prepare 2016 and 2017 contribution income statements using variable costing.

PROBLEMS

P17-33. Cost of Goods Manufactured and Income Statement   **LO4**

Following is information from the records of the Savoy Company for July 2017.

Purchases	
Raw materials	$ 90,000
Manufacturing supplies	3,500
Office supplies	1,200
Sales.	445,800
Administrative salaries	12,000
Direct labor	117,500
Production employees' fringe benefits*	4,000
Sales commissions.	55,000
Production supervisors' salaries	7,200
Plant depreciation	14,000
Office depreciation	22,000
Plant maintenance	10,000
Plant utilities	35,000
Office utilities	8,000
Office maintenance	2,000
Production equipment rent.	6,000
Office equipment rent.	1,300

* Classified as manufacturing overhead

Inventories	July 1	July 31
Raw materials.	$18,000	$27,000
Manufacturing supplies	2,500	4,000
Office supplies	1,600	2,000
Work-in-process.	52,000	41,000
Finished goods.	36,000	28,100

REQUIRED

Prepare a statement of cost of goods manufactured and an income statement. Actual overhead costs are assigned to products.

P17-34. Cost of Goods Manufactured and Income Statement with Predetermined Overhead and Labor Cost Classifications

Assume information pertaining to **Performance Sports Group Ltd.** for April 2017 follows.

Sales.	$250,000
Purchases	
Raw materials.	40,000
Manufacturing supplies	800
Office supplies	500
Salaries (including fringe benefits)	
Administrative.	6,000
Production supervisors.	3,600
Sales.	15,000
Depreciation	
Plant and machinery.	8,000
Office and office equipment	4,000
Utilities	
Plant.	5,250
Office	890

Inventories	April 1	April 30
Raw materials.	$8,000	$ 9,000
Manufacturing supplies	2,000	2,300
Office supplies	1,900	1,600
Work-in-process.	4,000	4,500
Finished goods.	9,000	10,200

Additional information follows:
- Manufacturing overhead is applied to products at 85 percent of direct labor dollars.
- Employee base wages are $12 per hour.
- Employee fringe benefits amount to 40 percent of the base wage rate. They are classified as manufacturing overhead.
- During April, production employees worked 5,600 hours, including 4,800 regular hours and 200 overtime hours spent working on products. There were 600 indirect labor hours.
- Employees are paid a 50 percent overtime premium. Any overtime premium is treated as manufacturing overhead.

REQUIRED

a. Prepare a statement of cost of goods manufactured and an income statement for April.
b. Determine underapplied or overapplied overhead for April.
c. Recompute direct labor and actual manufacturing overhead assuming employee fringe benefits for direct labor hours are classified as direct labor.

P17-35. Actual and Predetermined Overhead Rates

Raceway Engines, which builds high performance auto engines for race cars, started operations on January 1, 2017. During the month, the following events occurred:
- Materials costing $7,000 were purchased on account.
- Direct materials costing $5,000 were placed in process.
- A total of 390 direct labor hours was charged to individual jobs at a rate of $15 per hour.
- Overhead costs for the month of January were as follows:

Depreciation on building and equipment.	$ 800
Indirect labor	1,500
Utilities	600
Property taxes on building.	450
Insurance on building.	550

- On January 31, only one job (A06) was in process with materials costs of $550, direct labor charges of $400 for 30 direct labor hours, and applied overhead.

- The building and equipment were purchased before operations began and the insurance was prepaid. All other costs will be paid during the following month.

Note: Predetermined overhead rates are used throughout the chapter. An alternative is to accumulate actual overhead costs for the period in Manufacturing Overhead, and apply actual costs at the close of the period to all jobs in process during the period.

REQUIRED

a. Assuming Raceway Engines assigned actual monthly overhead costs to jobs on the basis of actual monthly direct labor hours, prepare an analysis of Work-in-Process for the month of January.

b. Assuming Raceway Engines uses a predetermined overhead rate of $10.50 per direct labor hour, prepare an analysis of Work-in-Process for the month of January. Describe the appropriate treatment of any overapplied or underapplied overhead for the month of January.

c. Review the overhead items and classify each as fixed or variable in relation to direct labor hours. Next, predict the actual overhead rates for months when 200 and 1,500 direct labor hours are used. Assuming jobs similar to A06 were in process at the end of each month, determine the costs assigned to these jobs. (*Hint:* Determine a variable overhead rate.)

d. Why do you suppose predetermined overhead rates are preferred to actual overhead rates?

P17-36. Job Costing with Predetermined Overhead Rate

LO2, 4
Kubota Corporation
OTCMKTS :: KUBTY

Kubota Corporation manufactures equipment in batches for inventory stock. Assume that Kubota's production costs are accounted for using a job cost system. At the beginning of April raw materials inventories totaled $8,500,000, manufacturing supplies amounted to $1,200,000 and finished goods inventories totaled $6,000,000. Two jobs were in process: Job 522 with assigned costs of $5,750,000 and Job 523 with assigned costs of $2,600,000. The following information summarizes April manufacturing activities:

- Purchased raw materials costing $25,000,000 on account.
- Purchased manufacturing supplies costing $3,000,000 on account.
- Requisitioned materials needed to complete Job 523. Started two new jobs, 524 and 525, and requisitioned direct materials for them.

Direct materials	
Job 523.	$ 3,000,000
Job 524.	12,900,000
Job 525.	9,600,000
Total	$25,500,000

- Recorded April salaries and wages as follows:

Direct labor	
Job 522 (300,000 hours × $20 per hour)	$ 6,000,000
Job 523 (800,000 hours × $20 per hour)	16,000,000
Job 524 (1,200,000 hours × $20 per hour)	24,000,000
Job 525 (1,000,000 hours × $20 per hour)	20,000,000
Total direct labor.	66,000,000
Indirect labor	6,400,000
Total	$72,400,000

- Used manufacturing supplies costing $2,250,000.
- Recognized depreciation on factory fixed assets of $4,000,000.
- Incurred miscellaneous manufacturing overhead costs of $5,500,000 on account.
- Applied manufacturing overhead at the rate of $6 per direct labor hour.
- Completed Jobs 522, 523, and 524.

REQUIRED

Prepare a complete analysis of all activity in Work-in-Process. Be sure to show the beginning and ending balances, all increases and decreases, and label each item. Provide support information on decreases with job cost sheets.

LO2, 4   **P17-37.   Job Costing with Predetermined Overhead Rate**

SnoBlo Company manufactures a variety of gasoline-powered snow blowers for discount hardware and department stores. SnoBlo uses a job cost system and treats each customer's order as a separate job. The primary snow blower components (motors, chassis, and wheels) are purchased from three different suppliers under long-term contracts that call for the direct delivery of raw materials to the production floor as needed. When a customer's order is received, a raw materials purchase order is electronically placed with suppliers. The purchase order specifies the scheduled date that production is to begin as the delivery date for motors and chassis; the scheduled date production is to be completed is specified as the delivery date for the wheels. As a consequence, there are no raw materials inventories; raw materials are charged directly to Work-in-Process upon receipt. Upon completion, goods are shipped directly to customers rather than transferred to finished goods inventory. At the beginning of July SnoBlo had the following work-in-process inventories:

Job 365	$23,000
Job 366	15,400
Job 367	16,000
Job 368	8,500
Total	$62,900

During July, the following activities took place:
- Started Jobs 369, 370, and 371.
- Ordered and received the following raw materials for specified jobs:

Job	Motors	Chassis	Wheels	Total
366	$ 0	$ 0	$ 800	$ 800
367	0	0	1,200	1,200
368	0	0	1,600	1,600
369	14,000	5,000	1,000	20,000
370	9,000	3,500	900	13,400
371	8,500	3,800	0	12,300
Total	$31,500	$12,300	$5,500	$49,300

- Incurred July manufacturing payroll:

Direct labor	
Job 365	$ 500
Job 366	3,300
Job 367	3,400
Job 368	4,160
Job 369	1,300
Job 370	2,620
Job 371	1,500
Total	16,780
Indirect labor	3,436
Total	$20,216

- Incurred additional manufacturing overhead costs for July:

Manufacturing supplies purchased on account and used	$ 2,800
Depreciation on factory fixed assets	6,000
Miscellaneous payables	5,100
Total	$13,900

- Applied manufacturing overhead using a predetermined rate based on predicted annual overhead of $190,000 and predicted annual direct labor of $200,000.
- Completed and shipped Jobs 365 through 370.

REQUIRED

Prepare a complete analysis of all activity in Work-in-Process. Be sure to show the beginning and ending balances, all increases and decreases, and label each item. Provide support information on decreases with job cost sheets.

P17-38. Weighted Average Process Costing   **LO5**

Minot Processing Company manufactures one product on a continuous basis in two departments, Processing and Finishing. All materials are added at the beginning of work on the product in the Processing Department. During November 2017, the following events occurred in the Processing Department:

Units started.	17,000 units
Units completed and transferred to Finishing Department	14,500 units

Costs assigned to processing	
Raw materials (one unit of raw materials for each unit of product started)	$296,200
Manufacturing supplies used	18,000
Direct labor costs incurred	103,000
Supervisors' salaries.	12,000
Other production labor costs	14,000
Depreciation on equipment	6,000
Other production costs.	18,000

Additional information follows:

*   Minot uses weighted average costing and applies manufacturing overhead to Work-in-Process at the rate of 100 percent of direct labor cost.
*   Ending inventory in the Processing Department consists of 4,500 units that are one-third converted.
*   Beginning inventory contained 2,000 units, one-half converted, with a cost of $27,300 ($17,300 for materials and $10,000 for conversion).

REQUIRED

a. Prepare a cost of production report for the Processing Department for November.
b. Prepare an analysis of all changes in Work-in-Process.

P17-39. Weighted Average Process Costing   **LO5**

Assume that **JIF**, which is part of **The J.M. Smucker Company**, processes its only product, 12-ounce jars of peanut butter, in a single process and uses weighted average process costing to account for inventory costs. All materials are added at the beginning of production. Assume the following inventory, production, and cost data are provided for September 2017:

JIF
The J.M. Smucker
Company
NYSE :: SJM

Production data	
Beginning inventory (25% converted).	300,000 units
Units started	650,000 units
Ending inventory (50% converted)	250,000 units

Manufacturing costs	
Beginning inventory in process:	
Materials cost	$238,700
Conversion cost	88,000
Raw materials cost added at beginning of process	739,800
Direct labor cost incurred	461,150
Manufacturing overhead applied	333,600

REQUIRED

a. Prepare a cost of production report for September.
b. Prepare a statement of cost of goods manufactured for September.

P17-40. Weighted Average Process Costing with Error Correction   **LO5**

Capital Manufacturing Company began operations on December 1. On December 31 a new accounting intern was assigned the task of calculating and costing ending inventories.

The intern estimated that the ending work-in-process inventory was 40 percent complete as to both materials and conversion, resulting in 4,000 equivalent units of materials and conversion. The ending work-in-process was then valued at $80,000, including $40,000 for materials and $40,000 for conversion. A subsequent review of the intern's work revealed that although the materials portion of the ending inventory was correctly estimated to be 40 percent complete, the units in ending inventory, on average, were only 20 percent complete as to conversion.

REQUIRED

a. Determine the number of units in the ending inventory.
b. How many equivalent units of conversion were in the ending inventory?
c. What cost per unit did the intern calculate for conversion?
d. Assuming 9,000 units were completed during the month of December, determine the correct cost per equivalent unit. (*Hint:* Find the total conversion costs in process.)
e. Determine the corrected cost of the ending inventory.
f. By how much was the cost of goods manufactured misstated as a result of the intern's error? Indicate whether the cost of goods manufactured was overstated or understated.

LO6   P17-41. Absorption and Variable Costing Comparisons

Fartlek Shoe Company is concerned with changing to the variable costing method of inventory valuation for making internal decisions. Functional income statements using absorption costing for January and February follow.

FARTLEK SHOE COMPANY Functional (Absorption Costing) Income Statements For January and February 2017		
	January	**February**
Sales (8,000 units)	$160,000	$160,000
Cost of goods sold.	(104,000)	(116,000)
Gross profit.	56,000	44,000
Selling and administrative expenses	(30,000)	(30,000)
Net income	$ 26,000	$ 14,000

Production data follow.

Production units.	12,000	8,000
Variable costs per unit	$ 10	$ 10
Fixed overhead costs.	$36,000	$36,000

The preceding selling and administrative expenses include variable costs of $1 per unit sold.

REQUIRED

a. Compute the absorption cost per unit manufactured in January and February.
b. Explain why the net income for January was higher than the net income for February when the same number of units was sold in each month.
c. Prepare contribution income statements for both months using variable costing.
d. Reconcile the absorption costing and variable costing net income figures for each month. (Start with variable costing net income.)

LO6   P17-42. Absorption and Variable Costing Comparisons

Red Arrow Blueberries manufactures blueberry jam. Because of bad weather, its blueberry crop was small. The following data have been gathered for the summer quarter of 2017:

Beginning inventory (cases)	0
Cases produced.	9,000
Cases sold	8,700
Sales price per case.	$60
Direct materials per case	$8
Direct labor per case	$9
Variable manufacturing overhead per case	$3
Total fixed manufacturing overhead.	$300,000
Variable selling and administrative cost per case	$2
Fixed selling and administrative cost.	$48,000

REQUIRED

a. Prepare a functional income statement for the quarter using absorption costing.
b. Prepare a contribution income statement for the quarter using variable costing.
c. What is the value of ending inventory under absorption costing?
d. What is the value of ending inventory under variable costing?
e. Reconcile the difference in ending inventory under absorption costing and variable costing.

P17-43. Variable and Absorption Costing with High-Low Cost Estimation and CVP Analysis Including Taxes   **LO6**

Presented are the Charger Company's functional income statements for January and February of 2017.

CHARGER COMPANY
Functional (Absorption Costing) Income Statements
For the Months of January and February 2017

	January	February
Production and sales	40,000	50,000
Sales Revenue	$1,000,000	$1,250,000
Cost of goods manufactured and sold	(525,000)	(625,000)
Gross profit	475,000	625,000
General and administrative expenses	(235,000)	(235,000)
Net income before taxes	240,000	390,000
Income taxes at 0.35	(84,000)	(136,500)
Net income after taxes	$ 156,000	$ 253,500

REQUIRED

a. Using the high-low method (see Chapter 14), develop a cost estimating equation for total monthly manufacturing costs.
b. Determine Charger Company's monthly break-even point.
c. Determine the unit sales required to earn a monthly after-tax income of $175,000.
d. Prepare a January 2017 contribution income statement using variable costing.
e. If the January 2017 net income amounts differ using absorption and variable costing, explain why. If they are identical, explain why.

CASES AND PROJECTS

C17-44. Cost Data for Financial Reporting and Special Order Decisions   **LO2, 4**

Harman Greeting Card Company produces a full range of greeting cards sold through pharmacies and department stores. Each card is designed by independent artists. A production master is then prepared for each design. The production master has an indefinite life. Product designs for popular cards are deemed to be valuable assets. If a card sells well, many batches of the design will be manufactured over a period of years. Hence, Harman Greeting maintains an inventory of production masters so that cards may be periodically reissued. Cards are produced in batches that may vary by increments of 1,000 units. An average batch consists of 10,000 cards. Producing a batch requires placing the production master on the printing press, setting the press for the appropriate paper size, and making other adjustments for colors and so forth. Following are facility-, product-, batch-, and unit-level cost information:

Walgreens Boots Alliance
NASDAQ :: WBA

Product design and production master per new card	$ 2,000.00
Batch setup (typically per 10,000 cards)	200.00
Materials per 1,000 cards	100.00
Conversion per 1,000 cards	80.00
Shipping	
Per batch	25.00
Per card	0.02
Selling and administrative	
Companywide	200,000.00
Per product design marketed	500.00

Information from previous year:

Product designs and masters prepared for new cards	90
Product designs marketed	120
Batches manufactured	500
Cards manufactured and sold	5,000,000

REQUIRED

You may need to review materials in Chapter 16 to complete the requirements.

a. Describe how you would determine the cost of goods sold and the value of any ending inventory for financial reporting purposes. (No computations are required.)

b. You have just received an inquiry from Walgreens department stores to develop and manufacture 20 special designs for sale exclusively in Walgreens stores. The cards would be sold for $1.50 each, and Walgreens would pay Harman Greeting $0.35 per card. The initial order is for 20,000 cards of each design. If the cards sell well, Walgreens plans to place additional orders for these and other designs. Because of the preestablished sales relationship, no marketing costs would be associated with the cards sold to Walgreens. How would you evaluate the desirability of the Walgreens proposal?

c. Explain any differences between the costs considered in your answer to requirement (a) and the costs considered in your answer to requirement (b).

LO2, 4   C17-45. Continue or Discontinue: Plantwide Overhead with Labor- and Machine-Intensive Operations

When Dart Products started operation five years ago, its only product was a radar detector known as the Bear Detector. The production system was simple, with Bear Detectors manually assembled from purchased components. With no ending work-in-process inventories, unit costs were calculated once a month by dividing current manufacturing costs by units produced.

Last year, Dart Products began to manufacture a second product, code-named the Lion Tamer. The production of Lion Tamers involves both machine-intensive fabrication and manual assembly. The introduction of the second product necessitated a change in the firm's simple accounting system. Dart Products now separately assigns direct material and direct labor costs to each product using information contained on materials requisitions and work tickets. Manufacturing overhead is accumulated in a single cost pool and assigned on the basis of direct labor hours, which is common to both products. Following are last year's financial results by product:

	Bear Detector		Lion Tamer	
Sales				
Units		5,000		2,000
Dollars		$ 500,000		$ 300,000
Cost of goods sold				
Direct materials	$110,000		$65,000	
Direct labor	150,000		45,000	
Applied overhead	270,000		81,000	
Total		(530,000)		(191,000)
Gross profit		$ (30,000)		$ 109,000

Management is concerned about the mixed nature of last year's financial performance. It appears that the Lion Tamer is a roaring success. The only competition, the Nittney Company, has been selling a competing product for considerably more than Dart's Lion Tamer; this company is in financial difficulty and is likely to file for bankruptcy. The management of Dart Products attributes the Lion Tamer's success to excellent production management. Management is concerned, however, about the future of the Bear Detector and is likely to discontinue that product unless its profitability can be improved. You have been asked to help with this decision and have obtained the following information:

- The labor rate is $15 per hour.
- Dart has two separate production operations, fabrication and assembly. Bear Detectors undergo only assembly operations and require 2.5 assembly hours per unit. Lion Tamers undergo both fabrication and assembly and require 1.5 fabrication hour and 0.5 assembly hour per unit.
- The annual Fabricating Department overhead cost function is:

$$\$200{,}000 + \$5 \text{ (labor hours)}$$

- The annual Assembly Department overhead cost function is:

$$\$20{,}000 + \$11 \text{ (labor hours)}$$

REQUIRED

You may need to review materials in Chapters 15 and 16 to complete this case. Evaluate the profitability of Dart's two products and make any recommendations you believe appropriate.

C17-46. **Absorption Costing and Performance Evaluation**   **LO6**

On July 2, 2017 Maddon Financial acquired 90 percent of the outstanding stock of Kluber Industries in exchange for 2,000 shares of its own stock. Maddon Financial has a reputation as a "high flier" company that commands a high price-to-earnings ratio because its management team works wonders in improving the performance of ailing companies.

At the time of the acquisition, Kluber was producing and selling at an annual rate of 100,000 units per year. This is in line with the firm's average annual activity. Fifty thousand units were produced and sold during the first half of 2017.

Immediately after the acquisition Maddon Financial installed its own management team and increased production to practical capacity. One-hundred thousand units were produced during the second half of 2017.

At the end of the year, the new management declared another dramatic turnaround and a $100,000 cash dividend when the following set of income statements were issued:

KLUBER INDUSTRIES Income Statement For the first and second half-years of 2017			
	First	**Second**	**Total**
Sales.	$1,400,000	$1,400,000	$2,800,000
Cost of goods sold*	(1,200,000)	(700,000)	(1,900,000)
Gross profit.	200,000	700,000	900,000
Selling and administrative expenses	(200,000)	(400,000)	(600,000)
Net income.	$ 0	$ 300,000	$ 300,000

* Absorption costing with any under-absorbed or over-absorbed overhead written off as an adjustment to cost of goods sold. Kluber applies manufacturing overhead using a predetermined overhead rate based on predicted annual fixed overhead of $1,000,000 and annual production of 100,000 units.

REQUIRED

As the only representative of the minority interest on the board of directors, evaluate the performance of the new management team.

SOLUTIONS TO REVIEW PROBLEMS

Mid-Chapter Review 1

SOLUTION

1. **Office supplies inventory**

   Each of the three types of organizations might include an office supplies inventory account on its balance sheet. Office supplies will typically be classified on the balance sheet as "other current asset." A manufacturing organization is most likely to have a supplies inventory account including the term "office" in order to distinguish it from manufacturing supplies. As the office supplies are consumed, they will move to the income statement and be classified as supply expense.

2. **Merchandise inventory**

   Merchandise inventory is an inventory account in the current asset section of the balance sheet of a merchandising company. As the inventory is sold, it moves to the income statement and is reported as a cost of goods sold expense.

3. **Finished goods inventory**

   Finished goods inventory is an inventory account in the current asset section of the balance sheet of a manufacturing company. As the inventory is sold, it moves to the income statement and is reported as a cost of goods sold expense.

4. **Work in process inventory**

   Work in process inventory is an inventory account in the current asset section of the balance sheet of a manufacturing company. As the work in process inventory is completed, it moves on to the finished goods inventory account in the current asset section of the balance sheet. Then, as discussed above, as the finished goods inventory is sold, it moves to the income statement and is reported as a cost of goods sold expense.

Mid-Chapter Review 2

SOLUTION

a. Predetermined overhead rate per machine hour = $40,000,000/3,200,000 = $12.50

b. Applied overhead = $12.50 × 410,000 = $5,125,000

c. February overhead:

Actual..	$4,410,000
Applied...	(5,125,000)
Overapplied for February...	(715,000)
Underapplied overhead, February 1................................	400,000
Overapplied overhead, end of February	$ (315,000)

Mid-Chapter Review 3

SOLUTION

1. *c.* Production order
2. *a.* Process costing
3. *d.* Job cost sheet
4. *b.* Job order costing
5. *f.* ork ticket
6. *e.* Materials requisition

Mid-Chapter Review 4

SOLUTION

a.

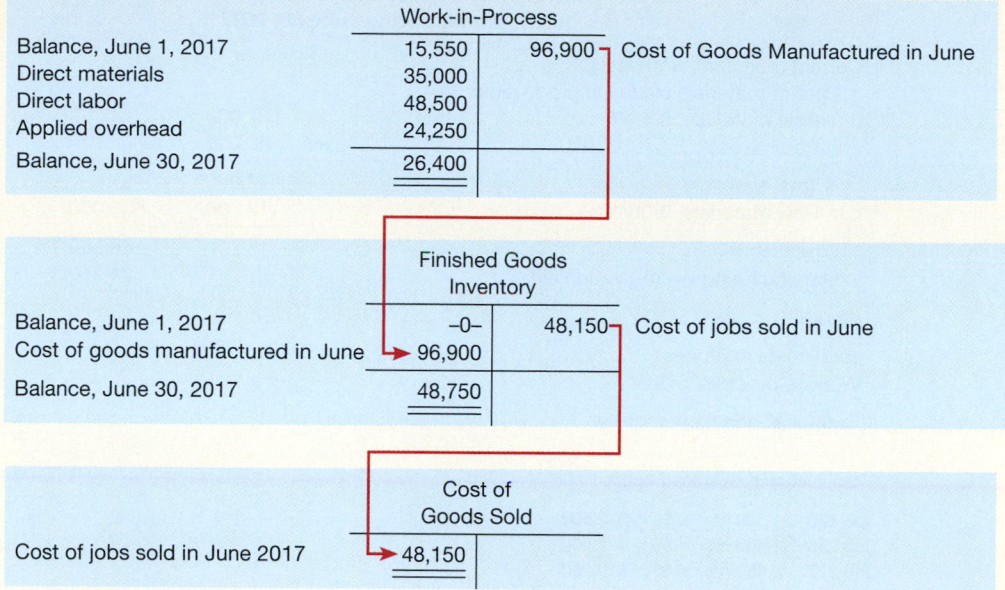

b.   Job in Work-in-Process at June 30, 2017:

	Job 228
Direct materials	$14,400
Direct labor.	8,000
Applied overhead (800 × $5)	4,000
Total	$26,400

Job in Finished Goods at June 30, 2017:

	Job 227
Direct materials	$18,000
Direct labor.	20,500
Applied overhead (2,050 × $5)	10,250
Total	$48,750

Jobs sold in June 2017:

	Job 225	Job 226	Total
Costs assigned from prior period.	$13,750	$ 1,800	$15,550
June Costs: Direct materials	–0–	2,600	2,600
Direct labor	5,000	15,000	20,000
Applied overhead (500 & 1,500 × $5).	2,500	7,500	10,000
Total	$21,250	$26,900	$48,150

c. Statement of cost of goods manufactured for June 2017.

STRATASYS LTD. Statement of Cost of Goods Manufactured For Month Ending June 30, 2017			
Current manufacturing costs			
Cost of materials placed in production			
Raw materials, 6/1/17	$ 7,000 ^		
Purchases	40,000 ^		
Total available	47,000		
Raw materials, 6/30/17	(12,000)	$35,000 ^	
Direct labor		48,500	
Manufacturing overhead applied		24,250 *	$107,750
Work-in-process, 6/1/17			15,550 **
Total costs in process			123,300
Work-in-process, 6/30/17			(26,400) ***
Cost of goods manufactured			$ 96,900

*Manufacturing Overhead Applied

Job 225:   500 hrs. × $5 = $ 2,500
Job 226: 1,500 hrs. × $5 = $ 7,500
Job 227: 2,050 hrs. × $5 = $10,250
Job 228:   800 hrs. × $5 = $ 4,000
                             $24,250

**Work-in-process, 6/1/17

Job 225: $13,750^
Job 226: $ 1,800^
         $15,550

***Work-in-process, 6/30/17 (see part *b.*)
^ Given

Chapter-End Review

SOLUTION

SANDISK Cost of Production Report For the Year 2017			
Summary of units in process			
Beginning	3,000,000		
Units started	27,000,000		
In process	30,000,000		
Completed	(25,000,000)		
Ending	5,000,000		

Equivalent units in process	**Materials**	**Conversion**	
Units completed	25,000,000	25,000,000	
Plus equivalent units in ending inventory	5,000,000	1,500,000	
Equivalent units in process	30,000,000	26,500,000	

Total costs to be accounted for and cost per equivalent unit in process	**Materials**	**Conversion**	**Total**
Work-in-Process, beginning	$ 468,000	$ 252,000	$ 720,000
Current cost	6,132,000	5,048,000	11,180,000
Total cost in process	$ 6,600,000	$ 5,300,000	$11,900,000
Equivalent units in process	÷ 30,000,000	÷26,500,000	
Cost per equivalent unit in process	$0.22	$0.20	$0.42
Accounting for total costs:			
Transferred out (25,000,000 × $0.42)			$10,500,000
Work-in-Process, ending:			
Materials (5,000,000 × $0.22)		$ 1,100,000	
Conversion (1,500,000 × $0.20)		300,000	1,400,000
Total cost accounted for			$11,900,000

Appendix 17A Review

SOLUTION

a.

Ending inventory = 100 BI + 500 PROD − 540 SOLD = 60	
Absorption costing	
Direct materials ($250 × 60)	$15,000
Variable overhead ($220 × 60)	13,200
Fixed overhead ($80 × 60)	4,800
Total	$33,000
Variable costing	
Direct materials ($250 × 60)	$15,000
Variable overhead ($220 × 60)	13,200
Total	$28,200

b.

Absorption Costing		
Beginning inventory		$ 45,000
Production		
Direct materials (500 × $250)	$125,000	
Variable overhead (500 × $220)	110,000	
Fixed overhead (500 × $80)	40,000	275,000
Goods available for sale		320,000
Less ending inventory ($275,000/500 × 60)		33,000
Cost of goods sold		$287,000

Variable Costing		
Beginning inventory		$ 38,000
Production		
Direct materials (500 × $250)	$125,000	
Variable overhead (500 × $220)	110,000	235,000
Goods available for sale		273,000
Less ending inventory ($235,000/500 × 60)		28,200
Cost of goods sold		$244,800

18

Activity-Based Costing, Customer Profitability, and Activity-Based Management

UNILEVER
www.unilever.com

We learned in the last chapter that indirect product costs need to be allocated to units of products or services based on a cost driver—a measure of activity that causes that cost to increase. However, the choice of one activity driver over another may result in widely differing costs for the same unit. In this chapter, we will address which driver is the correct driver; in many instances, product costing will be improved if we incorporate multiple drivers into the computation, choosing the drivers based on the activities undertaken to produce the good or service.

Consider the Anglo-Dutch company **Unilever**, which makes consumer food and drink, personal care, and home care products. The company's well-known brands include Lipton, Ben & Jerry's, Dove Beauty Products, Vaseline, and Pond's. The company is in the midst of two overarching strategic shifts: increasing market share in emerging markets and sustainability. Unilever is moving into new markets such as Central Africa and Myanmar where there is increased demand for grooming products. Although Unilever has been in Indonesia for nearly a century, changing demographics require that the company rethink its packaging and distribution strategies. Women in Indonesia cannot afford the $10 price of Pond's Skin Cream. By repackaging into single-serve containers and selling through street vendors, the product line has experienced tremendous growth in sales throughout the region.

Unilever's sustainability plan spans its sourcing of raw materials to its production facilities to the communities it serves. Unilever is the world's biggest consumer of palm oil, which is used in many of its products, including Dove soap, Magnum ice cream, and Vaseline lotion. Traditionally, rain forests in Indonesia and Malaysia have made way for palm plantations, which has destroyed wildlife habitats. Unilever built a $100 million palm-oil processing plant in an attempt to slow the rate of deforestation. Unilever's factories have greatly diminished waste generated by production processes by recycling the waste products into new products. The company is also investing its profits into community health and hygiene projects such as sanitation and safe drinking water campaigns.

These investments are made possible by streamlining operations and reducing manufacturing and distribution inefficiencies. Specifically, by analyzing the activities undertaken in producing and delivering its products to consumers, the company has been able to better determine the cost of each activity in its value chain, thereby eliminating waste and redundancies from costly activities. As a result, engineering has adopted "cookie-cutter" templates for factories, product designs, and supplier specifications to reduce inconsistencies in product quality across geographic regions. The company's 22 geographic segments were reorganized down to 6 markets, vastly reducing duplicative activities and allowing Unilever to better determine where to re-allocate its resources and effort. Distribution systems have been pushed down to mobile platforms, which allows for more efficient and effective servicing of remote and emerging markets. Even the financial reporting system and marketing efforts have been streamlined.

When we break down our costs by activity and then allocate those costs based on the set of activities a product or service consumes, we provide the basis by which a company such as Unilever can make broad strategic and operational changes to its business. This chapter will demonstrate how to develop and implement costing systems based on activity consumption, which will lead to better decision making regarding product, geographic, and customer selection.

Source: Unilever 2012 Annual Report; Paul Sonne and Simon Zekaria, "Unilever Tallies Hefty Sales Gain," *Wall Street Journal*, January 24, 2013, p. B6; Matthew Boyle, "In Emerging Markets, Unilever Finds a Passport to Profit," *Bloomberg Businessweek*, January 3, 2013; and Paul Sonne, "Unilever Takes Palm Oil in Hand," *Wall Street Journal*, April 12, 2012, p. B3.

CHAPTER ORGANIZATION

Activity-Based Costing, Customer Profitability, and Activity-Based Management

Activity-Based Costing (ABC)	Traditional Product Costing and ABC Compared	Implementation of ABC	ABC and Customer Profitability Analysis	Activity-Based Management
• Changing Cost Environment • ABC Concepts • ABC Product Costing Model	• Applying Overhead with Plantwide Rate • Applying Overhead with Department Rates • Applying Overhead with ABC	• Limitations of ABC • Comparing Traditional and ABC Models • Implementation Issues	• Customer Profitability Profile • ABC Customer Profitability Analysis	• The Difference Between ABC and Activity-Based Management

ACTIVITY-BASED COSTING (ABC)

What are appropriate prices for our products and services? What are the current activities that contribute to our firm's costs? Does each of our activities add value for our customers? Which customers contribute the most to our profitability and which customers are unprofitable?

In a competitive business environment, it is imperative that a firm understand its costs in order to make good business decisions. It has become increasingly difficult to appropriately link overhead (indirect) costs to the products and services they support. In this chapter we will discuss some of the reasons behind the growing complexity of appropriately costing products and services and how activity-based costing can provide better information for decision making.

Changing Cost Environment

LO1 Explain the changes in the modern production environment that have affected cost structures.

As technology has advanced and competition has intensified over the last century, there has been a fundamental shift in manufacturing organizations from labor-intensive to automated assembly techniques. These changes have influenced the activities performed to meet customer needs and, consequently, the costs of producing goods and services.

At the beginning of the twentieth century, products had long life cycles, production procedures were relatively straightforward, production was labor based, and only a limited number of related products were produced in a single plant. It was said of the Model T Ford that "you could have any color you wanted, as long as it was black." The largest cost elements of most manufactured goods were the cost of raw materials and the wages paid to production employees. Manufacturing overhead was a relatively small portion of the overall cost of manufacturing products.

The twentieth century saw an accelerating shift from traditional labor-based activities to production procedures requiring large investments in automated equipment. In the past, production employees used equipment to assist them in performing their jobs. Now employees spend considerable time scheduling, setting up, maintaining, and moving materials to and from, equipment. They spend relatively little time on actual production. The equipment does the work, and the employees keep it running efficiently. Increased complexity of production procedures and an increase in the variety of products produced in a single facility have also caused a shift toward more support personnel and fewer production employees. The result is a significant increase in manufacturing overhead as a percentage of total product cost. This change in the typical production cost structure over the past century is illustrated in **Exhibit 18.1**.

In the "low-tech," labor-intensive manufacturing environment, factors related to direct labor were often the primary drivers of manufacturing overhead costs; however, in today's "high-tech" automated environment there are many other factors that drive manufacturing overhead costs, and the specific set of cost drivers differs from organization to organization.

The previous chapter on product costing illustrated a simplified traditional system for allocating manufacturing overhead to products using a single, volume-based cost driver, such as direct labor hours. The following section introduces activity-based costing, which recognizes the multiple activities that drive manufacturing overhead costs in today's production environment.

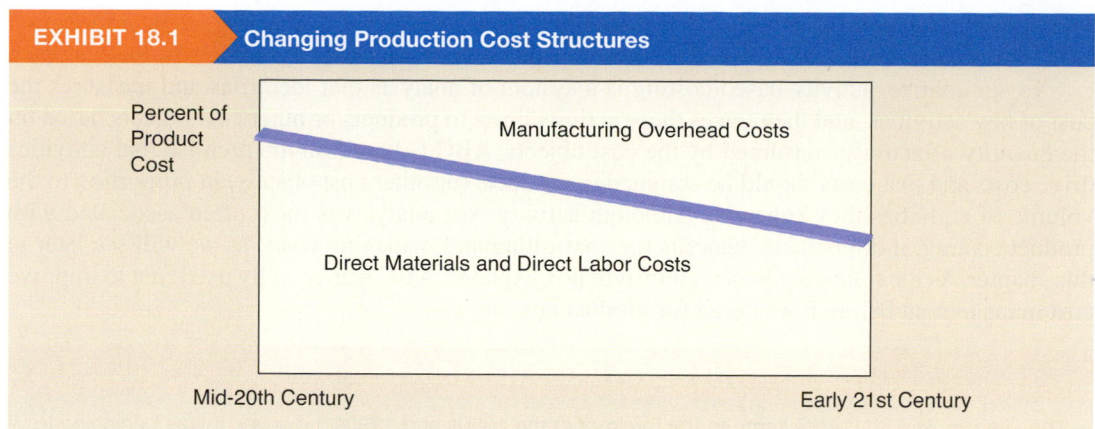

EXHIBIT 18.1   Changing Production Cost Structures

MID-CHAPTER REVIEW 1

In a competitive business environment, it is imperative that a firm understand its costs in order to make good business decisions. These decision might include: What are appropriate prices? What current activities contribute to a firm's costs? Which customers contribute the most to profitability?

REQUIRED
Discuss some of the factors in the U.S. economy that make it increasingly difficult to accurately assign costs to products and services.

The solution to this review problem can be found on page 859.

Activity-Based Costing Concepts

The manufacturing overhead cost pool has been referred to as a "blob" of common costs. The constant growth of costs classified as overhead has forced us to search for increasingly detailed methods to analyze these costs. If overhead costs are low in comparison with other costs and if factories produce few products in large production runs, the use of an overhead rate based on direct labor hours or machine hours may be adequate. However, as the amount of overhead costs continues to grow, as manufacturing facilities produce a wider variety of products, and as competition intensifies, the inadequacies of a single overhead rate based on a single cost driver such as direct labor hours become evident.

Fortunately, advances in information technology and the declining costs of computerized information systems have facilitated the development and maintenance of increasingly detailed databases. The increased complexity of the production environment, coupled with faster and cheaper computing technology, gave rise to the emergence and development of activity-based costing during the 1980s and 1990s.

Activity-based costing involves determining the cost of activities and tracing their costs to cost objects on the basis of the cost object's utilization of units of activity.

The concepts underlying ABC can be summarized in the following two statements and illustrations:

LO2 Outline the concept of activity-based costing and how it is applied.

1. Activities performed to fill customer needs consume resources that cost money.

2. The cost of resources consumed by activities should be assigned to cost objects on the basis of the units of activity consumed by the cost object.

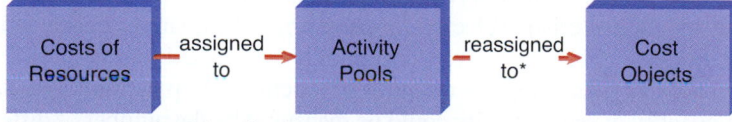

*Based on units of activity utilized by the cost object.

The cost object is typically a product or service provided to a customer. Depending on the information needs of decision makers, as we will discuss later in this chapter, the cost object might be the customer.

To summarize, activity-based costing is a system of analysis that identifies and measures the cost of key activities, and then traces these activity costs to products or other cost objects based on the quantity of activity consumed by the cost objects. ABC is based on the premise that activities drive costs and that costs should be assigned to products (or other cost objects) in proportion to the volume of activities they consume. Although activity cost analysis is most often associated with product costing, it offers many benefits for controlling and managing costs, as we will see later in this chapter. As the following Research Insight box explains, ABC was actually used first to improve cost management before it was used for product costing.

RESEARCH INSIGHT

The History of ABC   ABC came to the forefront in the 1980s and 1990s; however, it was beginning to evolve as early as the 1960s when General Electric's (GE) finance and accounting staff attempted to improve the usefulness of accounting information in controlling ever-increasing indirect costs. The GE staff noted that indirect costs were often the result of "upstream" decisions, such as engineering design and change orders, which were made long before the costs were actually incurred. Frequently, the engineering department was not informed of the consequences their actions had on the other parts of the organization.

The second phase of the development of ABC was accomplished by business consultants, professors, and manufacturing companies during the 1970s and early 1980s. By generating more accurate cost and profitability measures for the various products offered by companies, these consultants and professors hoped to improve product cost information used in pricing and product mix decisions. ABC has since been extended to assess customer profitability.

In the late 1980s and 1990s, ABC was being promoted by many of the leading consulting firms, and it almost became a fad, much as TQM and JIT had become before it. Consequently, many companies that jumped on the ABC bandwagon early in its life, later determined that it was not for them. Most of the companies that abandoned ABC, probably adopted it initially for the wrong reasons.

Knowledge of the historical development of activity-based costing is important in order to clearly understand what ABC analysis was intended to accomplish, as well as what it was not intended to accomplish.

Source: Latshaw, Craig A. Cortese-Danile, Teresa M., "Activity-based costing: usage and pitfalls," *Review of Business*, Winter, 2002.

ABC Product Costing Model

Traditional costing considers the cost of a product to be its direct costs for materials and labor plus some allocated portion of factory overhead, using overhead rates typically based on direct labor or machine hours. Activity-based costing is based on the notion that companies incur costs because of the activities they conduct in pursuit of their goals and objectives. For example, various activities take place to produce a particular product, such as setting up, maintaining, or monitoring the machines to make the product, physically moving raw materials and work in process, and so forth. Each of these activities has a cost; therefore, the total cost of producing a product using ABC is the sum of the direct materials and direct labor costs of that product, plus the cost of other activities conducted to produce that product.

The general two-stage ABC product cost model is illustrated in **Exhibit 18.2**. The first stage includes the assignment of manufacturing overhead resource costs, such as indirect labor, depreciation, and utilities, to activity cost pools for the key activities identified. Typical activity cost pools in a manufacturing environment include pools for machine setup, material movement, and engineering. The second stage assigns those activity cost pools to products.

Notice in **Exhibit 18.2** that direct product costs, such as direct materials and direct labor, are directly assigned to products and are excluded from the activity cost pools. Only indirect product costs (manufacturing overhead) are assigned to products via activity cost pools.

Probably the most critical step in ABC is identifying cost drivers. The activity cost driver for a particular cost (or cost pool) is the characteristic selected for measuring the quantity of the activity for a particular period of time. For example, if an activity cost pool is established for machine setup, it is necessary to select some basis for measuring the quantity of machine setup activity associated with the costs in the pool. The quantity of setup activity could be measured by the number of different

EXHIBIT 18.2	Two-Stage Activity-Based Costing Model

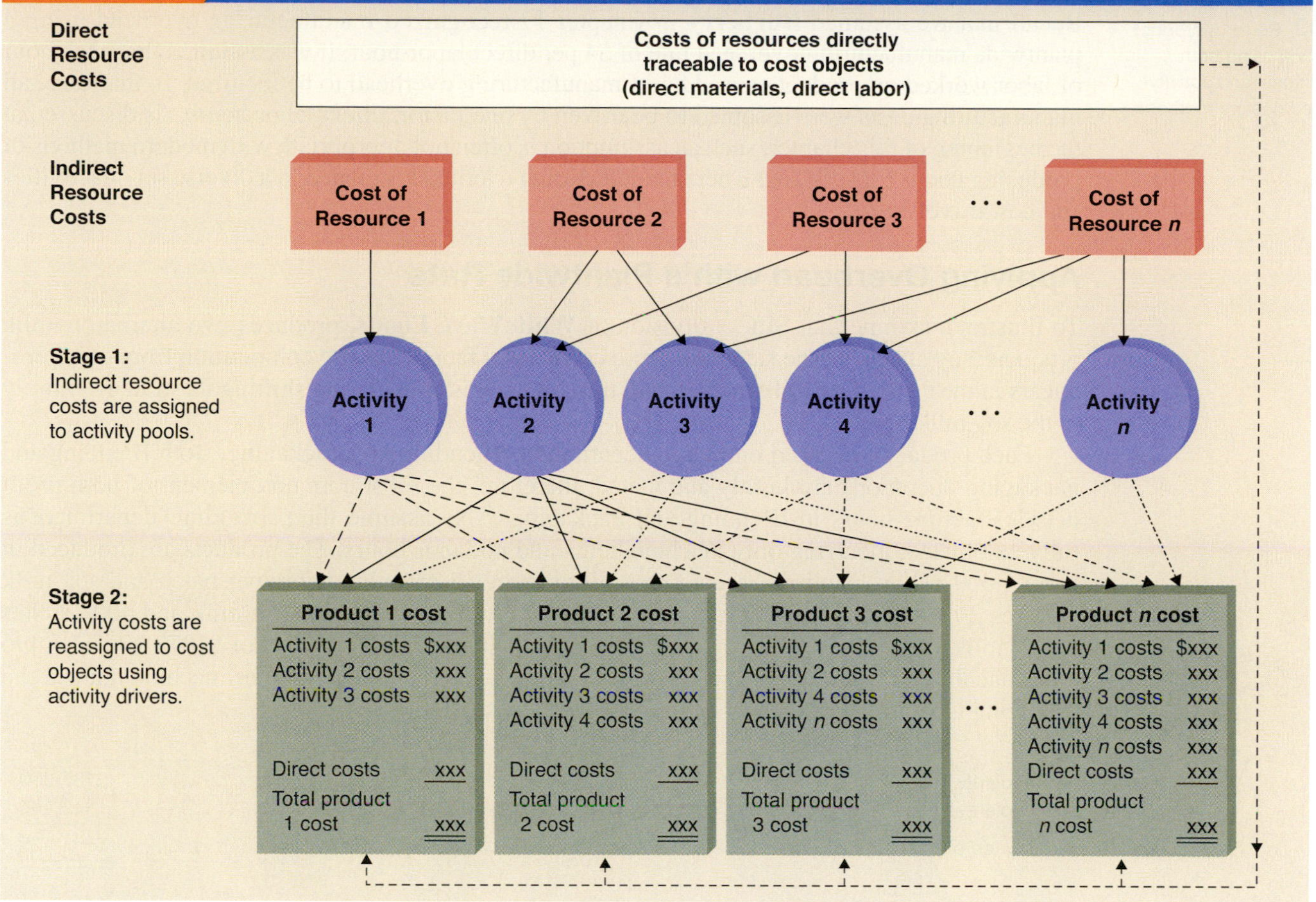

Direct Resource Costs

Costs of resources directly
traceable to cost objects
(direct materials, direct labor)

Indirect Resource Costs

Cost of Resource 1   Cost of Resource 2   Cost of Resource 3   . . .   Cost of Resource n

Stage 1:
Indirect resource costs are assigned to activity pools.

Activity 1   Activity 2   Activity 3   Activity 4   . . .   Activity n

Stage 2:
Activity costs are reassigned to cost objects using activity drivers.

Product 1 cost		**Product 2 cost**		**Product 3 cost**		**Product n cost**	
Activity 1 costs	$xxx	Activity 1 costs	$xxx	Activity 1 costs	$xxx	Activity 1 costs	$xxx
Activity 2 costs	xxx	Activity 2 costs	xxx	Activity 2 costs	xxx	Activity 2 costs	xxx
Activity 3 costs	xxx	Activity 3 costs	xxx	Activity 4 costs	xxx	Activity 3 costs	xxx
		Activity 4 costs	xxx	Activity n costs	xxx	Activity 4 costs	xxx
						Activity n costs	xxx
Direct costs	xxx	Direct costs	xxx	Direct costs	xxx	Direct costs	xxx
Total product 1 cost	xxx	Total product 2 cost	xxx	Total product 3 cost	xxx	Total product n cost	xxx

times machines are set up to produce a different product, the amount of time used in completing machine setups, the number of staff working on setups, or some other measure. It is critical that the activity measure used has a logical causal relationship to the costs in the pool and that the quantity of the activity is highly correlated with the amount of cost in the pool. Statistical methods, such as regression analysis and correlation analysis, can be very useful in selecting activity cost drivers.

Once the total cost in the activity pool and the activity cost driver have been determined, the cost per unit of activity is calculated as the total cost divided by the total amount of activity. For example, if total costs assigned to the setup activity pool in July were $100,000 and 200 setups were completed in July, the cost per setup for the month would be $500. If during July machines were set up 10 times to make product JX2, the total setup cost that would be assigned to product JX2 would be $5,000 ($500 × 10).

MID-CHAPTER REVIEW 2

Mobile Health Screening (MHS) offers onsite general health screening services for a flat rate of $35 per screening. MHS typically provides its services to businesses that offer fitness and health programs as a benefit to their employees. A representative of MHS arrives at a business early in the morning and sets up a room with the necessary equipment and supplies. MHS sees participating employees throughout the day and screens for basic health measures such as blood pressure, weight, blood screening, and health behaviors. MHS sends samples to an outside lab for testing. MHS then compiles the results of all the tests and provides employees access to their individual results via a logon identification and password on the website.

REQUIRED

Identify likely activities and related cost drivers that MHS might engage in throughout the processes of providing the health screening services.

The solution to this review problem can be found on page 859.

LO3 Perform product costing using both traditional and activity-based costing methods.

TRADITIONAL PRODUCT COSTING AND ABC COMPARED

Recall that we assumed **Burberry** in Chapter 17 recognized manufacturing overhead using a plantwide manufacturing overhead rate of $4 per direct labor hour. It was assumed that each hour of labor worked on product caused $4 of manufacturing overhead to be incurred. In that case, all manufacturing costs were assumed to be driven by one factor, direct labor hours. As discussed at the beginning of this chapter, such an assumption is often not appropriate with modern methods of producing goods (or services) where manufacturing overhead is related to a diverse set of activities and cost drivers.

Applying Overhead with a Plantwide Rate

To illustrate, assume that **Silk**, a division of **WhiteWave Foods**, produces two alternative milk products, soy and rice. The rice milk product has been facing intense competition from other producers in the alternative milk market, and the company is considering shifting its strategy entirely to the soy milk product.

Each product is worked on in two departments, Blending and Packaging. Both Blending and Packaging operations are highly automated; therefore, the most common element of both products is machine hours in Blending and Packaging. Also assume the packaging department is fully automated, incurring only machine hours and no labor hours. The products are produced in large 1,000-gallon batches. Assume rice milk requires 3 machine hours per batch and soy milk requires 2 machine hours per batch. Suppose for July, 232 batches of rice milk and 400 batches of soy milk were produced, with total plantwide manufacturing overhead of $187,000 and 1,496 total machine hours. The plantwide overhead rate is calculated as $125 per machine hour in the following tabulation.

Total plantwide manufacturing overhead	$187,000
Total plantwide machine hours.	÷ 1,496
Plantwide overhead rate per machine hour	$ 125

Assigning $125 to each machine hour used is the simplest method of assigning manufacturing overhead to the products and, as the tabulation below shows, results in a total cost per batch of $610 for rice milk and $400 for soy milk after adding the direct materials and direct labor costs.

A plantwide overhead allocation method is often used in situations where companies produce only one product in a plant, or where multiple products are very similar in regard to the use of activities, such as machine or labor hours, that drive most of the overhead costs. If multiple products are produced that consume varying levels of activities in multiple production departments, departmental overhead allocation rates will produce a more accurate allocation of overhead costs to the various products.

	Unit Costs	
	Rice Milk	**Soy Milk**
Direct materials	$125	$120
Direct labor.	110	30
Manufacturing overhead		
Rice milk: 3 machine hours × $125	375	
Soy milk: 2 machine hours × $125.		250
Total unit cost.	$610	$400

Applying Overhead with Department Rates

For Silk to establish separate overhead allocation rates for each of the two production departments, it is necessary first to assign the $187,000 of total overhead costs for the plant to the two production departments, some of which is directly assignable to the departments. For example, the departmental supervisors' salaries could be directly assignable to the departments. Other manufacturing overhead costs, such as support costs for maintenance, payroll, and so forth, are allocated to the production departments. Assume that after these allocations, the total costs assigned to the departments were $59,100 for Blending and $127,900 for Packaging.

The next step in the product costing process is to assign the departmental costs to the products. For this example, assume that the manufacturing process in the Blending Department is labor intensive, while the process in the Packaging Department is fully automated. Manufacturing overhead is applied to products as follows:

Department	Manufacturing Overhead Application Base
Blending	Direct labor hours
Packaging	Machine hours

During the month of July, 500 direct labor hours were worked in Blending. Packaging used 800 machine hours. Assume rice milk requires a total of 3 machine hours per batch with 1 of those hours incurred in Packaging. Soy milk requires a total of 2 machine hours per batch with 1.42 of those hours incurred in Packaging. The department manufacturing overhead rates based on actual costs for July, and the total product costs using departmental overhead rates, are calculated in the following tables:

Department manufacturing overhead rates for July	Blending	Packaging
Total department manufacturing overhead (direct department costs plus allocated costs)...	$59,100	$127,900
Quantity of overhead application base		
Direct labor hours....	÷ 500	
Machine hours		÷ 800
Department manufacturing overhead rates....	$118.20	$159.875
	Per direct labor hour	Per machine hour

	Unit Costs per Batch	
Total costs per unit for July using department rates	Rice Milk	Soy Milk
Direct materials	$125	$120
Direct labor.....	110	30
Manufacturing overhead		
Blending: 1 labor hr. × $118.20	118	
0.67 labor hrs. × $118.20		79
Packaging: 1 machine hr. × $159.875.....	160	
1.42 machine hrs. × $159.875		227
Total costs....	$513	$456

Allocating factory overhead costs based on department rates (rather than on a plantwide rate of $125 per machine hour) causes a shift in costs from rice to soy milk because rice milk's overhead activity is incurred evenly in both Blending and Packaging (1.00 hour each) while soy milk incurs more of its overhead activity in Packaging (1.42 hours versus 0.67 hour).

The per-unit costs with multiple allocations are substantially different from the per-unit costs when using plantwide rates and, in fact, show the cost of rice milk to be slightly below a competitor's bid of $525 that was offered to one of soy milk's customers. Assume that based on the plantwide rate, the cost of $610 for rice milk was higher than the competitor's price.

By creating separate manufacturing overhead cost allocation pools, allocation bases, and overhead application rates for Blending and Packaging, it is possible to recognize overhead cost differences in various products based on differences in Blending Department labor hours used and Packaging Department machine hours used for each product. In most multiproduct manufacturing environments, this approach represents a cost system improvement over using a single, plantwide overhead rate, and it reduces the likelihood of cost cross-subsidization, which occurs when one product is assigned too much cost as a result of another being assigned too little cost. While department overhead rates may improve product costing results for many organizations, and in fact may be satisfactory, this method does not attempt to reflect the actual activities used in producing the different product.

Applying Overhead with Activity-Based Costing

An even more precise method of measuring the cost of products than plantwide or departmental rates is the activity-based costing method. As stated earlier, activity-based costing involves determining the cost of activities associated with a particular cost object. ABC for product costing identifies and measures the cost of activities used to produce the various products and sums the cost of those activities to determine the cost of the products. The following Business Insight compares three key benefits regarding the accuracy of cost systems for ABC users and non-ABC users.

For WhiteWave's Silk division, assume Blending and Packaging have overhead costs of $59,100 and $127,900, respectively. The overhead rates for each department were determined in the last section as $118.20 and $159.875, respectively, per relevant hour of use. The easiest way to assign these costs to products is by using one base and one rate for all products going through a given process (e.g., blending). However, different products typically use different amounts of resources from a given process and using the same base and overhead rate for all may distort the cost for some or all products.

Overhead costs in the Blending and Packaging departments consisted of two types of costs: direct department costs and allocated costs from other support departments. Direct department overhead costs are costs that are incurred directly by the department such as indirect labor, indirect materials, depreciation on equipment, supervisory wages, and so forth. Allocated support costs are costs allocated from other departments (specifically, engineering, support services, and building and grounds) that provide services to both Blending and Packaging. WhiteWave's accountants determined that the *direct* department overhead costs in Blending were driven primarily by labor hours, whereas *direct* department overhead costs in Packaging were driven primarily by machine hours. It was also determined that each component of engineering, support services, and building and grounds represents a separate activity cost pool, and that these costs support both the Blending and Packaging Departments. Therefore, these costs should be assigned to the products based on specific cost drivers rather than a single department cost driver.

The following is a detailed analysis of overhead cost data for July's operations:

Overhead Activity	Total Activity Cost	Activity Cost Driver	Quantity of Activity	Unit Activity Rates
Direct departmental overhead costs				
Blending	$ 25,000	Labor hours	500	$ 50.00
Packaging.	105,000	Machine hours	800	$131.25
Common overhead costs				
Support Services				
Receiving.	14,000	Purchase orders	100	140.00
Inventory control	13,000	Units produced.	632	20.57
Engineering Resources				
Production setup.	12,000	Production runs	20	600.00
Engineering and testing	8,000	Machine hours	1,496	5.35
Building and Grounds				
Maintenance, machines	4,000	Machine hours	1,496	2.67
Depreciation, machines.	6,000	Units produced.	632	9.49
Total	$187,000			

BUSINESS INSIGHT

Key Benefits of Using ABC   A 2009 study of 348 manufacturing and service companies worldwide indicated that activity-based costing continues to provide strategic and operational benefits. Although the study showed that there has been a decline in ABC users since the 1990s, when it was first widely adopted, the following graphics from the study report support the conclusion that users of ABC have a higher level of confidence than non-ABC users that their cost system provides more accurate cost measurements.

Comparisons of ABC to Non-ABC Users on Three Key Benefits

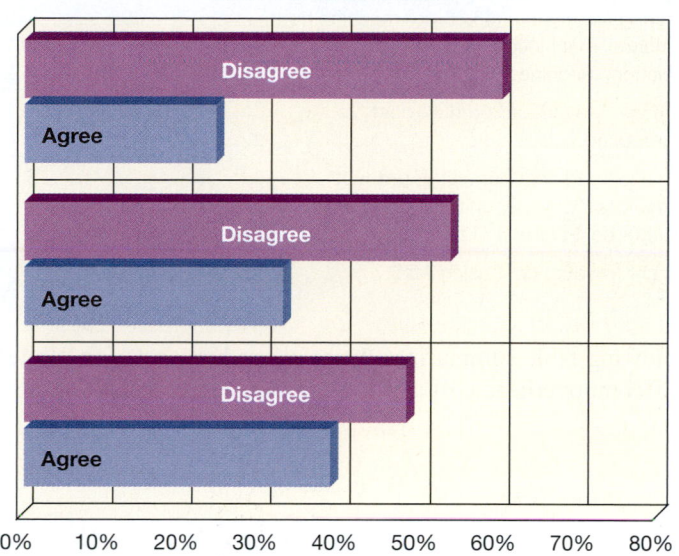

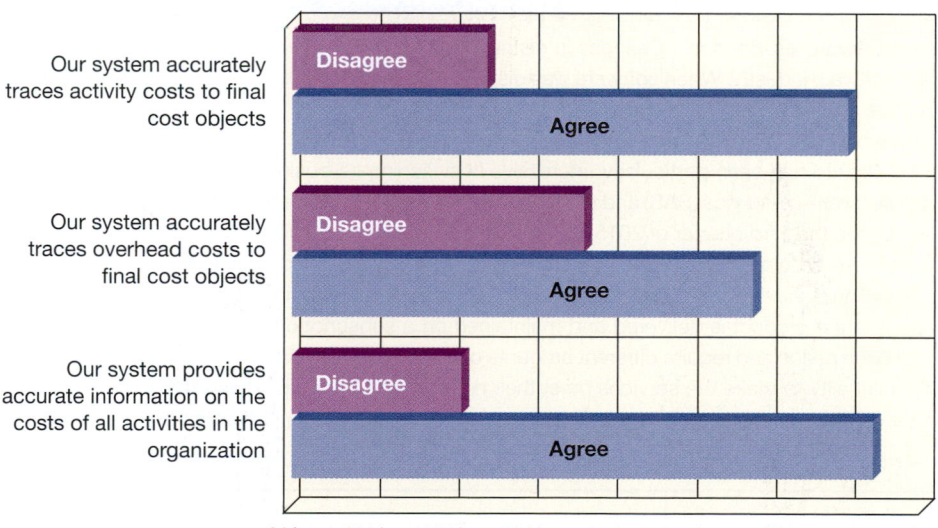

Source: William O. Stratton, Denis Desroches, Raef Lawson, and Toby Hatch, "Activity-Based Costing: Is It Still Relevant?" *Management Accounting Quarterly*, Spring 2009, Vol. 10, No. 3, pp. 31-40.

Suppose the amounts of activity attributed to rice and soy milk and the factory overhead cost per unit based on ABC costs are as follows:

Activity (cost per unit of driver activity)	Rice Milk Quantity of Activity	Rice Milk Cost of Activity	Soy Milk Quantity of Activity	Soy Milk Cost of Activity
Blending ($50.00 per labor hour)	232	$11,600	268	$ 13,400
Packaging ($131.25 per machine hour)	232	30,450	568	74,550
Receiving ($140.00 per order)	40	5,600	60	8,400
Inventory control ($20.57 per unit produced).	232	4,772	400	8,228
Production setup ($600.00 per run)	5	3,000	15	9,000
Engineering and testing ($5.35 per machine hour).	696	3,724	800	4,280
Maintenance, machines ($2.67 per machine hour)	696	1,858	800	2,136
Depreciation, machines ($9.49 per unit produced)	232	2,202*	400	3,796
Total factory overhead product cost.		$63,206		$123,790
Units produced.		÷ 232		÷ 400
Factory overhead cost per unit of product*		$ 272		$ 309
Direct materials cost per unit of product		125		120
Direct labor cost per unit of product		110		30
Total unit product cost using ABC		$ 507		$ 459

The following table summarizes the total product costs for WhiteWave's two products using the three different overhead cost assignment methods:

	Rice Milk	Soy Milk
Plantwide overhead rate.	$610	$400
Departmental overhead rates.	513	456
ABC	507	459

BUSINESS INSIGHT

ABC and Software-as-Service Changes in distribution have altered the business model and cost structure of the software industry. When software was distributed on physical discs, both the business model and cost structure of the software industry were rather traditional, dominated by direct labor and shipping costs. With the rise of the Internet and cloud-based computing, the software industry's business model is changing rapidly. **Oracle** has been particularly aggressive in switching its business from traditional software-as-product to software-as-service (SAS) and platform-as-service with revenue from these sectors climbing 30% to $372 million in the third quarter of 2015. This year its cloud business will generate $1 billion in revenue.

All three business sections highlight the importance of activity-based costing for an SAS business like Oracle. Providing SAS requires both production of the software product and ongoing hardware and networking support as the product is delivered and maintained on a subscription basis. Each customer will have different service needs and require different amounts of various services from storage to support, as well as added functionality to make the services meet their needs on an ongoing basis. ABC is particularly useful in this type of business where units sold offer a very incomplete picture of the costs of serving the client.

Source: Mamta Badkar and Eric Platt, "Oracle Tops the S&P 500 Leaderboard," *Financial Times*, March 20, 2015.

ABC product costing reveals a different cost picture. Using either a plantwide overhead rate or departmental rates, the rice milk product is bearing more than its share of total overhead costs. Using either of these methods could lead the company into a potentially poor strategy of abandoning the rice milk market. With an actual per-batch cost of $507, rather than $513 or $610, the company clearly has more latitude to compete on price with other companies in this market and remain profitable. Inaccurate costing can affect management's assessment of product profitability and its decisions regarding which products to continue to produce and which products to discontinue. Flawed product costing information can cause management mistakenly to decide to keep products that are losing money, while deciding to discontinue products that are profitable. Using a plantwide or departmental overhead allocation method could have led WhiteWave's management to shift its emphasis from the rice milk to the soy milk market, a decision that could have been a poor decision for the company.

ABC often reveals product cross-subsidization problems. This is when ABC produces costs for some products that are higher, and costs for other products that are lower, than costs produced by traditional costing methods. This is referred to as cross-subsidization.

YOU MAKE THE CALL

You are the Controller   You have heard about companies that have adopted ABC and experienced significant differences in product costs compared with previous cost calculations using traditional costing methods. Consequently, you were surprised when your newly implemented ABC system provided product costs that were almost identical to those from the old costing system. You are, therefore, thinking about abandoning the ABC system, since it is quite costly to maintain. Should you abandon your ABC system? [Answer, p. 841]

MID-CHAPTER REVIEW 3

Assume that one of **Illinois Tool Works Inc's (ITW)** divisions has the following predicted indirect costs and cost drivers for 2017 for the given activity cost pools:

	Fabrication Department	Finishing Department	Cost Driver
Maintenance.	$ 20,000	$10,000	Machine hours
Materials handling	30,000	15,000	Material moves
Machine setups	70,000	5,000	Machine setups
Inspections	—	25,000	Inspection hours
	$120,000	$55,000	

The following activity predictions were also made for the year:

	Fabrication Department	Finishing Department
Machine hours	10,000	5,000
Materials moves	3,000	1,500
Machine setups	700	50
Inspection hours	—	1,000

It is assumed that the cost per unit of activity for a given activity does not vary between departments.

Suppose ITW's divisional manager is trying to evaluate the company's product mix strategy regarding two of its five product models, Cobra Latch and GrimLoc. The company has been using a plantwide overhead rate based on machine hours but is considering switching to either department rates or activity-based rates. The production manager has provided the following data for the production of a batch of 100 units for each of these models:

	Cobra Latch	GrimLoc
Direct materials cost.	$12,000	$18,000
Direct labor cost.	$ 5,000	$ 4,000
Machine hours (Fabrication).	500	700
Machine hours (Finishing).	200	100
Materials moves.	30	50
Machine setups	5	9
Inspection hours.	30	60

continued

continued from previous page

REQUIRED

a. Determine the cost of one unit each of Cobra Latch and GrimLoc, assuming a plantwide overhead rate is used based on total machine hours.

b. Determine the cost of one unit of Cobra Latch and GrimLoc, assuming department overhead rates are used. Overhead is assigned based on machine hours in both departments.

c. Determine the cost of one unit of Cobra Latch and GrimLoc, assuming activity-based overhead rates are used for maintenance, materials handling, machine setup, and inspection activities.

The solution to this review problem can be found on pages 859–860.

LO4 Compare activity-based costing to traditional methods. Assess implementation issues involved in activity-based costing systems.

IMPLEMENTATION OF ABC

Limitations of ABC Illustration

Several limitations of WhiteWave's Silk division illustration should be mentioned. For the sake of simplicity, the example was limited to manufacturing cost considerations. A complete analysis would also require considerations of nonmanufacturing costs, such as marketing, distribution, and customer service, before a final determination of product profitability could be made. Finally, in calculating the activity cost per unit of activity, it is necessary to decide how to measure the total quantity of activity. For example, for the Silk division, the receiving cost per purchase order was calculated as $140.00 based on the actual quantity of 100 purchase orders for the period. Alternatively, the receiving cost could have been calculated based on **practical capacity**, which is the maximum possible volume of activity, while allowing for normal downtime for repairs and maintenance. If the plant has a practical capacity to prepare 140 purchase orders per period, the cost per purchase order based on the practical capacity is $100 per purchase order, or $14,000 ÷ 140. Using this overhead rate in costing product, only $10,000 would have been assigned to the two products, which required only 100 purchase orders, and the remaining $4,000 for the 40 purchase orders of excess (or idle) capacity not used would be written off as an operating expense of the period as underapplied overhead. Practical capacity is generally regarded as better than actual capacity for calculating activity costs because it does not hide the cost of idle capacity within product costs, and it gives a truer cost of the activities used to produce the product.

Comparing Traditional and Activity-Based Costing

Procedurally, ABC is not a new method for assigning costs to cost objects. Traditional costing systems have used a two-stage allocation model (similar to the ABC model) to assign costs to cost pools (such as departments) and subsequently assign those cost pools to products using an allocation base. In most traditional costing systems, overhead is assigned to one or more cost pools based on departments and functional characteristics (such as labor-related, machine-related, and space-related costs) and then reassigned to products using a general allocation base such as direct labor hours or machine hours. ABC is different in that it divides the overall manufacturing processes into activities. ABC accumulates costs in cost pools for the major activities and then assigns the costs of these activities to products or other cost objects that benefit from these activities. *Conceptually*, ABC is different because of the way it views the operations of the company; *procedurally*, it uses a methodology that has been around for a long time.

The challenge in using ABC is specifying the model; that is, determining how many activity pools should be established for a given cost measurement purpose, which costs should be assigned to each activity pool, and the appropriate activity driver for each pool. Specifying the model also includes determining the resource cost drivers for assigning indirect resource costs to the various activity cost pools.

When evaluating whether to implement an ABC model, management must weigh the value of more accurate information against the administrative efforts of producing it. This can be complicated by the fact that it is often more difficult to measure the benefits of a process than it is to measure tangible costs. Further, once a company makes the decision to implement an ABC system, it also needs to assess the level of accuracy it wants the system to provide. In his article,

"Implementing Activity-Based Costing," Gary Cokins emphasizes that the "quest for perfection is expensive," and that a reasonable level of accuracy might be sufficient.[1]

BUSINESS INSIGHT

Batch Size Matters   Two trends are pushing American businesses to **Maker's Row**, a matchmaker for firms and factories in the United States. The rise of crowdfunding platforms like **Kickstarter** and **IndieGogo** has produced a large and growing number of small firms with a product and the cash required to produce it. Since these firms do not have the scale or resources to consider overseas production, they need local factories. At the same time, global manufacturing is shifting homeward. Large firms are trading lower labor costs and weaker regulatory environments at foreign plants for better supervision, more control, and lower shipping costs at U.S. plants. The crowdfunding and the "re-shoring" trends are both driving demand for domestic production, and Maker's Row is helping to match firms with factories that fit their needs.

According to Maker's Row cofounder Tanya Menendez, part of the problem with finding a factory is that the factory operators consider much of what they do to be a trade secret. Simple Internet searches yield little information of value, and even larger companies have difficulty finding the best option for their production. Maker's Row is a kind of online dating site for these manufacturers, allowing them to share information with potential clients and partners without making too much information public. By delivering information about factories to firms, Maker's Row helps firms make better production decisions about potential products.

Source: T.J. McCue, "80,000 Businesses Receive Manufacturing Help from Maker's Row," *Forbes*, September 3, 2015.

ABC Implementation Issues

The distortion in product costs for WhiteWave's Silk division from using traditional cost systems based on plantwide or departmental rates, while hypothetical, is not uncommon. Studies have shown that distortions of this type occur regularly in traditional systems in which a significant variation exists in the volume and complexity of products and services produced.[2] Traditional systems tend to overcost high-volume, low-complexity products, and they tend to undercost low-volume, high-complexity products. These studies indicate that the typical amount of overcosting is up to 200 percent for high-volume products with low complexity and that the typical undercosting can be more than 1,000 percent for low-volume, highly complex products. In companies with a large number of different products, traditional costing can show that most products are profitable. After changing to ABC, however, these companies might find that 10 to 15 percent of the products are profitable while the remainder are unprofitable. Adopting ABC often leads to increased profits merely by changing the product mix to minimize the number of unprofitable products.

Most companies initially do not abandon their traditional cost system and move to a system that uses ABC for management and financial reporting purposes because financial statements must withstand the scrutiny of auditors and tax authorities. This scrutiny typically implies more demands on the cost accounting system for consistency, objectivity, and uniformity than required when the system is used only for management purposes. In addition, ABC systems must be built facility by facility rather than being embedded in a software program that can be used by all facilities within the company.[3] Often companies maintain traditional costing for external reporting purposes and ABC for pricing and other internal decision-making purposes.

Once an ABC system has been developed for a production facility, including an activities list (sometimes called an activities dictionary), identification of activity cost drivers, and calculation of cost per unit of driver activity, the activity costs of a current or proposed product can be readily determined. In ABC, as illustrated for WhiteWave, manufacturing a product is viewed simply as the combination of activities selected to make it; therefore, the activity cost of a product or service is the sum of the costs of those activities. This approach to viewing a product enables management to evaluate the importance of each of the activities consumed in making a product. Possibly some activities can be eliminated or a lower cost activity substituted for a more costly one without reducing the quality or performance of the product. In the 1980s, the **Coca-Cola Company** used ABC to determine that it was less costly—and thus, more profitable—to deliver soft drink concentrate to some

---

[1] Gary Cokins, *Implementing Activity-Based Costing* (Institute of Management Accountants, 2014).

[2] Gary Cokins, Alan Stratton, and Jack Helbling, *An ABC Manager's Primer* (Montvale, NJ: Institute of Management Accountants, 1993).

[3] Robert S. Kaplan and Robin Cooper, *Cost and Effect* (Boston: Harvard Business School Press, 1998), p. 105.

fountain drink retailers (such as fast-food restaurants) in nonreturnable, disposable containers rather than in returnable stainless steel containers, which had been standard in the industry for many years.

Although an ABC system may be complex, it merely mirrors the complexity of an organization's design, manufacturing, and distribution systems. If a firm's products are diverse and its production and distribution procedures complex, the ABC system will also be complex; however, if its products are homogeneous and its production environment relatively simple, its ABC system should also be relatively simple. Even in highly complex manufacturing environments, ABC systems usually have no more than 10 to 20 cost pools. Many ABC experts in practice have observed that creating a large number of activity cost pools for a given costing application normally does not significantly improve cost accuracy above that of a smaller number of cost pools. As with any information system design, the costs of developing and maintaining the system must not exceed its benefits; hence, although adding more activity cost pools may result in some small amount of increased accuracy, it may be so small as not to be cost effective.

In addition to using ABC for product costing purposes, other important uses for ABC have also been found. One of the most useful applications for ABC discussed in the next section is in evaluating customer costs and distribution channel costs. Other applications include costing administrative functions such as processing accounts receivable or accounts payable; costing the process of hiring and training employees; and costing such menial tasks as processing a letter or copying a document. Any process, function, or activity performed in an organization, whether it is related to production, marketing and sales, finance and accounting, human resources, or even research and development, is a candidate for ABC analysis. In short, almost any cost object that has more than an insignificant amount of indirect costs can be more effectively measured using ABC.

RESEARCH INSIGHT

A Time-Based Refinement of ABC for Health Care   ABC's complexity is both a strength and a weakness. To successfully implement ABC, an organization must be able to model and measure its production process in great detail. In industries such as health care this is all but impossible. Kaplan and his colleagues introduced a refinement to ABC in 2004 and tested its application to health care in 2011 with the help of several hospitals. Time-Driven Activity-Based Costing (TDABC) makes the patient and the diagnoses the unit of analysis. Rather than defining complex sets of activities and their rates, TDABC uses historical data to estimate two relationships—the cost of each resource used in treatment and the amount of time the patient spends with each resource.

These estimated relationships allow hospitals and other organizations to implement ABC without completely characterizing their activities. It also allows hospitals to determine which resources are particularly costly and focus on those resources for cost control. Thus, the benefits of ABC can be realized without the implementation issues discussed in this chapter. TDABC integrates easily with existing resource planning processes. The **Mayo Clinic** is a successful example of the benefits of TDABC implementation. It treats the TDABC process like it would any other improvement in medical care—as a scientific inquiry. It assembles a project team from every level of the organization and the group uses Kaplan's principles to estimate time/resource cost relationships. These relationships lead to experiments for improvement where they test the changes suggested in the TDABC process. Their findings are then shared with the whole organization.

Sources: Derek Haas, Richard Helmers, March Rucci, Meredith Brady, and Robert Kaplan, "The Mayo Clinic Model for Running a Value-Improvement Program," *Harvard Business Review*, October 22, 2015; Robert Kaplan and Michael Porter, "The Big Idea: How to Solve the Cost Crisis in Health Care," *Harvard Business Review*, September 2011; Alex Santana and Paulo Afonso, "Analysis of Studies on Time-Driven Activity Based Costing," *International Journal of Management Science & Technology Information* 15; 133-157 (2015).

MID-CHAPTER REVIEW 4

Assume that one of **Illinois Tool Works Inc's (ITW)** divisions has the following predicted indirect costs and Refer to Review 18-3 on page 833 and review your unit cost calculations in parts *a.*, *b.*, and *c.*

REQUIRED
Based on your calculations, compare and contrast the unit costs of the Cobra Latch and GrimLoc using the plantwide, department, and activity-based rates to assign manufacturing overhead.

The solution to this review problem can be found on page 861.

ABC AND CUSTOMER PROFITABILITY ANALYSIS

LO5 Analyze customer profitability using activity-based costing.

One of the most beneficial applications of activity-based costing is in the analysis of the profitability of customers. Companies that have a large number of diverse customers also usually have widely varied profits from serving those customers. Many companies never attempt to calculate the profit earned from individual customers. They merely assume that if they are selling products above their costs, and that overall the company is earning a profit, then each of the customers must be profitable. Unfortunately, the cost incurred to sell goods and services, and to provide service, to individual customers is not usually proportionate with the gross profits generated by those sales. Customers with high sales volume are not necessarily the most profitable. Profitability of individual customers depends on whether the gross profits from sales to those customers exceed the customer-specific costs of serving those customers. Some customers are simply more costly than others, and some may even be unprofitable, and the unprofitable customers are eating away at the total profits of the company. In an ideal world, only profitable customers would be retained, and unprofitable customers would be either converted to a profitable status or they would be dropped as customers.

Customer Profitability Profile

If a company knows the amount of profits (or losses) generated by each of its customers, a **customer profitability profile** can be prepared similar to the one illustrated in **Exhibit 18.3**.

This hypothetical company has 350 customers and has current total profits of $5 million, but only 200 of its customers are profitable. Cumulative profits reach $7.5 million when the 200th customer is added to the graph, but the 201st through the 350th customers cause cumulative profits to decline to $5 million because they are unprofitable. Once a company has profitability data on each of its customers (or categories of customers), only then can it proceed to try to convert them to profitability, or seek to terminate the relationship with those customers. Just as we saw that ABC provided a model for producing more accurate product cost data, ABC is also a valuable tool for generating customer profitability data.

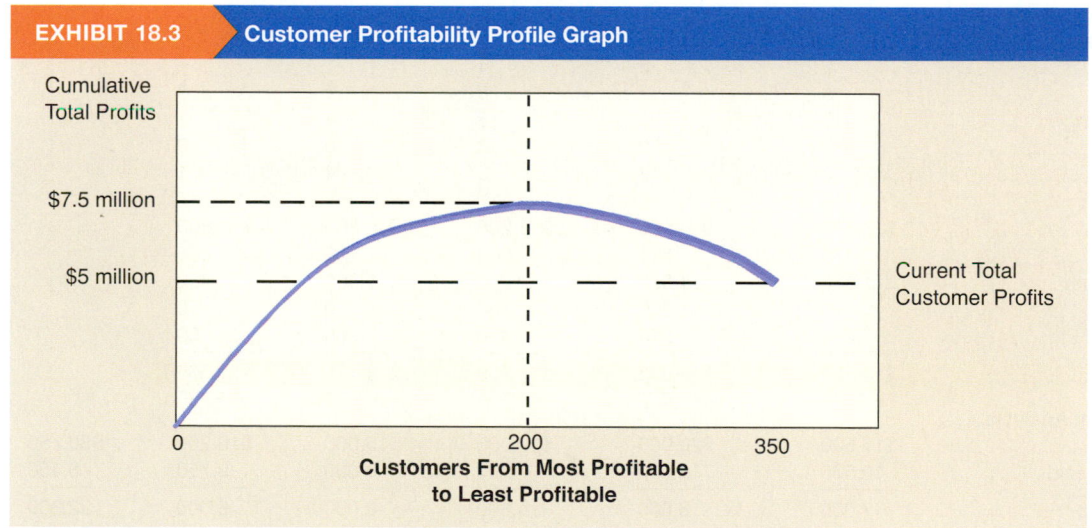

EXHIBIT 18.3   Customer Profitability Profile Graph

ABC Customer Profitability Analysis Illustrated

Pure Water Company is a "green" company located in the Midwest that manufactures and sells all-natural compounds for purifying water distributed through large public water systems. The CEO and founder of Pure Water, personally developed the compounds using natural materials obtained from remote regions of the world. He knows that he has a product that is far superior to the traditional processes based on synthetic chemicals that have been used for generations to purify water. After five years in business, Pure Water has built a solid and growing customer base, but it has to invest significant time and expense servicing customers, especially those who have recently embraced its approach to water purification. Some customers require a lot of "hand-holding" with frequent visits and telephone calls, and they tend to purchase frequently in small amounts, often requiring repackaging. Other customers require little attention and support, and many of them purchase in large amounts once a year.

Although the company is making money, there is concern that profits could be higher if sales and other customer-related costs could be decreased. Pure Water's accountant has decided to conduct a customer profitability analysis using activity-based costing. As a first step, she determined that there were five primary activities related to serving customers: visits of customers by sales representatives, remote contacts (phone, email, fax), processing and shipping of customer orders, repackaging, and billing and collection. After extensive analysis, including numerous interviews and statistical analyses of activity and cost data, the accountant determined the following cost drivers and cost per unit of activity for the five customer-related activities:

Activity	Activity Cost Driver	Cost per Unit of Driver Activity
Visits to customers.....................................	Visits	$800
Remote contacts	Number of contacts	75
Processing & shipping	Customer orders	450
Repackaging	Number of requests	250
Billing & collection	Invoices	90

After collecting activity driver data on each of these activities for its major customers, the accounting group prepared the customer activity cost and profitability analysis presented in **Exhibit 18.4** for its five largest customers (in terms of sales dollars) in the order of greatest to least profit for the most recent year.

EXHIBIT 18.4	Pure Water Company					
Customer Activity Cost and Profitability Analysis						
	Seattle Water District	Manhattan Water Authority	Great Lakes Utility	Gulf Coast Utilities	Consolidated Water, Inc.	Total
Customer Activity Cost Analysis:						
Activity Cost Driver Data						
Visits to customers	3	5	4	1	1	
Remote contacts	5	7	8	2	3	
Processing & shipping	3	3	5	4	1	
Repackaging..................	0	2	3	0	0	
Billing & collection.............	3	3	5	4	1	
Customer Activity Cost						
Visits to customers	$ 2,400	$ 4,000	$ 3,200	$ 800	$ 800	
Remote contacts	375	525	600	150	225	
Processing & shipping	1,350	1,350	2,250	1,800	450	
Repackaging..................	0	500	750	0	0	
Billing & collection.............	270	270	450	360	90	
Total Activity Cost.............	$ 4,395	$ 6,645	$ 7,250	$ 3,110	$ 1,565	
Customer Profitability Analysis:						
Customer sales................	$17,500	$20,000	$12,000	$15,000	$16,250	$80,750
Less cost of goods sold	10,500	12,000	7,200	9,000	9,750	48,450
Gross profit on sales............	7,000	8,000	4,800	6,000	6,500	32,300
Less activity costs	4,395	6,645	7,250	3,110	1,565	22,965
Customer profitability	$ 2,605	$ 1,355	$ (2,450)	$2,890	$4,935	$ 9,335
Customer profitability ratio*	14.9%	6.8%	(20.4%)	19.3%	30.4%	11.6%

* Customer profitability ÷ Sales

Since Pure Water is selling only one product to all of its customers, and has the same pricing policy for all customers, there is a constant 40% gross profit ratio across all customers, and the combined net profitability of these customers is 11.6% of sales. However, all customers are not equally profitable. The high level of support required by Manhattan and Great Lakes resulted in a net customer loss from sales to Great Lakes and only a 6.8% customer profitability ratio for Manhattan.

Armed with the information in the customer activity cost and profitability analysis, Pure Water can take proactive steps to increase its overall profitability ratio. An obvious option would be to try to terminate its relationship with Great Lakes since the company is clearly losing money on that customer. If Great Lakes were terminated as a customer, and assuming that all of the activity costs associated with Great Lakes could be avoided by the termination, Pure Water's total sales would drop to $68,750 (or $80,750 minus $12,000), but its total profit would increase to $11,785 (or $9,335 plus $2,450), resulting in a profitability ratio on the remaining four customers of 17.1%.

A more proactive approach would be to work with Great Lakes and Manhattan that have high support requirements, such as repackaging, frequent visits, and phone contacts to try to lower the level of high-cost support activities without reducing sales to those customers. This could result in maintaining the current level of gross profit, but generating a significantly higher level of total net customer profitability.

Two caveats should be considered when using activity cost data to manage customer profitability. First, there may be justifiable reasons (such as having a new customer that requires a high level of early-stage support, trying to penetrate a new geographic market, or existing relationships with other more profitable customers) for keeping customers that have lower profitability, or even customers that are not profitable. If so, these customers should be managed intensely to attempt to reduce the activities devoted to their support. Another caveat is that eliminating a customer may not immediately translate into an immediate reduction of activity costs. Some activity costs may not have a variable cost behavior pattern, and eliminating customers may merely create excess capacity in the short term. Of course, as stated previously, activity-based costing views virtually all costs as variable in the longer term. As the following Business Insight illustrates, despite these limitations, customer profitability analysis can provide valuable information to help keep an organization focused on its most profitable customers. In the case of **General Growth Properties**, understanding its customer profitability profile allowed it to adjust its leasing strategy to meet the changing needs of the retail industry.

BUSINESS INSIGHT

Activity-Based Costing Helps Malls Adapt   Department stores, once the center of the American mall experience, are on the decline, and mall owners are taking back their space. **General Growth Properties Inc.**, a large mall property owner, reports that between 2005 and 2015, sales at mall specialty stores have grown 33% while sales at department stores have fallen 10%. In response, mall owners are asking department stores to move out. General Growth and the **Simon Property Group**, another large mall property owner, have turned over more than 100 department stores at malls they own.

When the department store drew customers, mall owners leased space to them at a discount. Rent for a department store like **Nordstrom's** or **Saks Fifth Avenue** was as low as $2 per square foot. Now, rents for new anchor stores like **Dick's Sporting Goods** and **H&M** are often closer to $15 per square foot. The big question facing mall owners is the type of store that will replace the department store. Will it be a large retailer like Dick's, or will the space be split among many smaller stores that can pay rents as high as $100 per square foot? The investment in remodeling has paid off for malls. When **Sears** left the Cool Springs Galleria in Franklin, Tennessee, owner **CBL & Associates Inc.** remodeled the space to house H&M, **The Cheesecake Factory**, and **American Girl**. This change has led to a 15% rise in annual sales at the mall. ABC can help mall owners analyze the costs and benefits of shifting their lessee mix away from department stores and toward smaller specialty retailers.

Source: Suzanne Kapner, "Mall Owners Push Out Department Stores," *Wall Street Journal*, July 10, 2016.

MID-CHAPTER REVIEW 5

Suppose SAP is a systems design and implementation firm that serves five different types of customers. Assume SAP's design and installation projects are fairly standardized and routine; hence, the pricing is also standardized for all customers. While the company is profitable overall, the CFO thinks the net margins should be higher. She is concerned that customer support costs are eating up some of the margin and has decided to do a customer profitability analysis based on the five different types of customers to see if some of the customer groups may actually be less profitable than others. The following data for the most recent period have been collected to support the analysis.

Support Activity		Driver	Cost per Driver Unit
A.	Minor systems maintenance	Hours on jobs	$160
B.	Visits to customer	Number of visits	$300
C.	Communication	Number of calls	$ 50

Customer Group	Activity A	Activity B	Activity C	Profit Before Support Costs
1	69	25	128	$80,000
2	141	42	205	85,000
3	74	19	99	83,000
4	61	28	106	90,000
5	136	39	189	78,000

REQUIRED

a. Calculate the customer profitability for each customer group taking into account the support activity required for each customer group.

b. Comment on the usefulness of this type of analysis. What reasonable actions might the company take as a result of this analysis?

The solution to this review problem can be found on page 861.

LO6   xplain the
difference between
activity-based costing
and activity-based
management.

6

ACTIVITY-BASED MANAGEMENT

The Difference Between ABC and Activity-Based Management

Activity-based costing has been highly touted as a technique for improving the measurement of the cost and profitability of products, customers, and other cost objects. In the early development of ABC, it was discovered that a by-product of accurately measuring the cost using ABC is that management invariably gains a much better understanding of the processes and activities that are used to create cost objects, such as products. Although ABC could be justified on the basis of its value as a tool in helping produce more accurate cost measurements for various cost objects, its greatest potential value may be in its by-products. The access to ABC data enables managers to engage in **activity-based management (ABM)**, defined as the identification and selection of activities to maximize the value of the activities while minimizing their cost from the perspective of the final consumer. In other words, ABM is concerned with how to efficiently and effectively manage activities and processes to provide value to the final consumer.

Defining processes and identifying key activities helps management better understand the business and to evaluate whether activities being performed add value to the customer. ABM focuses managerial attention on what is most important among the activities performed to create value for customers.

A helpful analogy in understanding what ABC can do for a company is to compare a company's operations with a large retail store, such as a **Home Depot** store. In a Home Depot store there is a clearly marked price on each of the tens of thousands of individual items that customers may decide to purchase. Similarly, every activity that takes place in any organization has a cost that can be determined and that management can use to make a judgment about the activity's value. In an ideal world, a manager could walk through the business and evaluate the cost of every activity being performed—maybe thousands of different activities—and then decide which ones are worth the cost and which ones are not adding value. Since generating ABC data has a cost, management must decide which ABC data are likely to be useful and cost beneficial. Our discussion here is only an introduction to activity-based costing and some of its applications. As the following Research Insight points out, over the past quarter of a century, ABC has matured well beyond merely accurately measuring cost of products and customers. More advanced topics such as those shown in the graphic are covered in advanced managerial accounting (or cost accounting) courses.

RESEARCH INSIGHT

The Maturing of Activity-Based Costing One of the leading thinkers and authors on the topic of activity-based costing over the past 25 years has been Peter B. B. Turney. He recently traced the evolution of ABC within the context of a product life cycle showing how ABC functionality has expanded since it was first introduced in the 1980s. As this graphic shows, ABC is now in its fourth generation, where it has become "an integral part of business performance management solutions, including profitability management, performance measurement, financial management, sustainability, and human capital management." In its current state of development, a single ABC model can support a number of needs, including historical cost measurement, resource planning, performance measurement, and other analyses.

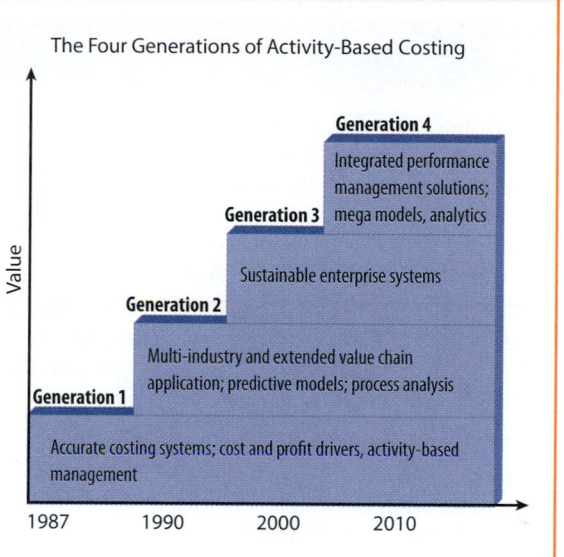

The Four Generations of Activity-Based Costing

Source: Peter B. B. Turney, "Activity-Based Costing: An Emerging Foundation for Performance Management," *Cost Management*, July/August 2010, pp. 33-42.

CHAPTER-END REVIEW

Although ABC could be justified on the basis of its value as a tool in helping produce more accurate cost measurements for various cost objects, its greatest potential value may be in its by-products.

REQUIRED

Discuss the relationship between activity-based management and activity-based costing.

The solution to this review problem can be found on page 861.

GUIDANCE ANSWERS . . . YOU MAKE THE CALL

You are the Controller It probably is not the right decision to abandon the ABC system because there are many benefits to using ABC other than just calculating product costs. Indeed, in cases where companies produce multiple products that are fairly homogeneous in terms of the use of resources, ABC may not produce more accurate costs than traditional methods; however, there are many uses of ABC information beyond just calculating the cost of products. Having detailed information about activities and their costs can significantly improve the management of those activities. Identifying key activities and measuring their costs often causes companies to seek more efficient processes, possibly considering outsourcing activities that are currently performed internally, or even looking for ways to eliminate activities altogether. Activity cost information can also be used to identify best practices within an organization, or to benchmark internal activity costs with other organizations.

KEY TERMS

activity-based costing (ABC), 825

activity-based management (ABM), 840

practical capacity, 834

customer profitability profile, 837

Assignments with the ⬤ logo in the margin are available in *my* BusinessCourse.
See the Preface of the book for details.

MULTIPLE CHOICE

1. Assume that Arco, Inc. has three activity pools which have the following costs: Machine Setups, $30,000; Material Moves, $45,000; and Machine Operations, $28,000. The activity cost drivers (and driver quantity) for the three pools are, respectively, number of setups (200), number of material moves (450), and number of machine hours (350). Product XJ3 used the following quantity of activity drivers to produce 100 units of final product: 25 setups, 40 material moves, and 75 machine hours. The total ABC cost and unit ABC cost assigned to Product XJ3 is:

   a. $103,000 total ABC cost and $1,030 unit ABC cost
   b. $103,000 total ABC cost and $103 unit ABC cost
   c. $13,750 total ABC cost and $137.50 unit ABC cost
   d. $3,300 total ABC cost and $330 unit ABC cost

2. Marko Company produces two products, Xeon and Zeon in a small manufacturing plant which had total manufacturing overhead of $45,000 in January and used 600 direct labor hours. The factory has two departments, Preparation, which incurred $25,000 of manufacturing overhead, and Processing which incurred $20,000 of manufacturing overhead. Preparation used 400 hours of direct labor and Processing used 160 machine hours. During January, 300 direct labor hours were used in making 100 units of Xeon, and 300 were used in making 100 units of Zeon. If Marko uses a plantwide rate based on direct labor hours to assign manufacturing costs to products, the total manufacturing overhead assigned to each unit of Xeon and Zeon in January were:

   a. $22,500 for Xeon and $22,500 for Zeon
   b. $225 for Xeon and $225 for Zeon
   c. $25,000 for Xeon and $20,000 for Zeon
   d. $107.14 for Xeon, and $42.86 for Zeon

3. Refer to the previous question. Assume that instead of using a plantwide overhead rate, Marko used departmental rates based on direct labor hours for the Preparation Department and machine hours for the Processing Department. The departmental overhead rates for the Preparation and Processing Departments were:

   a. $75 per direct labor hour for both Preparation and Processing
   b. $62.50 per direct labor hour for Preparation, and $125 per machine hour for Processing
   c. $125 per direct labor hour for Preparation, and $62.50 per machine hour for Processing
   d. $80.35 per direct labor hour for Preparation, and $80.35 per machine hour for Processing

4. Refer to the previous questions regarding Marko Company. Assume that Xeon used 175 direct labor hours and Zeon used 225 direct labor hours in the Preparation Department. Also, assume that Xeon used 100 machine hours and Zeon used 60 machine hours in the Processing Department. The overhead costs assigned to each unit of Xeon and Zeon were:

   a. $253.50 for Xeon and $196.50 for Zeon
   b. $62.50 for Xeon and $125 for Zeon
   c. $215.63 for Zeon and $215.63 for Xeon
   d. $234.38 for Xeon and $215.63 for Zeon

5. Refer to the previous questions regarding Marko Company. Assume that Marko used an ABC product costing system and that its total manufacturing overhead costs of $45,000 were assigned to the following ABC cost pools:

Material inspections & preparation ($20,000)...............	$20 per pound of raw materials
Material moves ($5,000).....................................	$50 per move
Machine setups ($6,000)	$300 per setup
Machine operations ($14,000)	$87.50 per machine hour

Xeon and Zeon used the following quantities of the four activity drivers:

	Xeon	Zeon
Pounds of raw materials...	500	500
Material moves..	60	40
Setups	12	8
Machine hours	100	60

The overhead costs assigned to each unit of Xeon and Zeon were:
a. $253.50 for Xeon and $196.50 for Zeon
b. $62.50 for Xeon and $125 for Zeon
c. $215.63 for Xeon and $234.63 for Zeon
d. $234.38 for Xeon and $215.63 for Zeon

QUESTIONS

Q18-1. Summarize the concepts underlying activity-based costing in two sentences.

Q18-2. What steps are required to implement the two-stage activity-based costing model?

Q18-3. Define activity cost pool, activity cost driver, and cost per unit of activity.

Q18-4. Name two possible activity cost drivers for each of the following activities: maintenance, materials movement, machine setup, inspection, materials purchases, and customer service.

Q18-5. What is the premise of activity-based costing for product costing purposes?

Q18-6. In what ways does ABC product costing differ from traditional product cost methods?

Q18-7. Explain why ABC often reveals existing product cost cross-subsidization problems.

Q18-8. How can ABC be used to improve customer profitability analysis?

Q18-9. Explain activity-based management and how it differs from activity-based costing.

MINI EXERCISES

M18-10. Activities and Cost Drivers

LO2

For each of the following activities, select the most appropriate cost driver. Each cost driver may be used only once.

Activity	Cost Driver
1. Pay vendors	*a.* Number of different kinds of raw materials
2. Evaluate vendors	*b.* Number of classes offered
3. Inspect raw materials	*c.* Number of tables
4. Plan for purchases of raw materials	*d.* Number of employees
5. Packaging	*e.* Number of operating hours
6. Supervision	*f.* Number of units of raw materials received
7. Employee training	*g.* Number of moves
8. Clean tables	*h.* Number of vendors
9. Machine maintenance	*i.* Number of checks issued
10. Move in-process product from one work	*j.* Number of customer orders station to the next

LO2   **M18-11. Developing a List of Activities for Baggage Handling at an Airport**

As part of a continuous improvement program, you have been asked to determine the activities involved in the baggage-handling process of a major airline at one of the airline's hubs. Prior to conducting observations and interviews, you decide that a list of possible activities would help you to better observe key activities and ask meaningful questions.

REQUIRED

For incoming aircraft only, develop a sequential list of baggage-handling activities. Your list should contain between 8 and 10 activities.

LO2   **M18-12. Stage 1 ABC at a College: Assigning Costs to Activities**

An accounting professor at Middleton University devotes 60 percent of her time to teaching, 30 percent of her time to research and writing, and 10 percent of her time to service activities such as committee work and student advising. The professor teaches two semesters per year. During each semester, she teaches one section of an introductory financial accounting course (with a maximum enrollment of 40 students) and one section of a graduate financial accounting course (with a maximum enrollment of 25 students). Including course preparation, classroom instruction, and appointments with students, each course requires an equal amount of time. The accounting professor is paid $120,000 per year.

REQUIRED

Determine the activity cost of instruction per student in both the introductory and the graduate financial accounting courses.

LO2   **M18-13. Stage 1 ABC for a Machine Shop: Assigning Costs to Activities**

As the chief engineer of a small fabrication shop, Christine Ford refers to herself as a "jack-of-all-trades." When an order for a new product comes in, Christine must do the following:

1. Design the product to meet customer requirements.
2. Prepare a bill of materials (a list of materials required to produce the product).
3. Prepare an operations list (a sequential list of the steps involved in manufacturing the product).

Each time the foundry manufactures a batch of the product, Christine must perform these activities:

1. Schedule the job.
2. Supervise the setup of machines that will work on the job.
3. Inspect the first unit produced to verify that it meets specifications.

Christine supervises the production employees who perform the actual work on individual units of product. She is also responsible for employee training, ensuring that production facilities are in proper operating condition, and attending professional meetings. Christine's estimates (in percent) of time spent on each of these activities last year are as follows:

Designing product	12%
Preparing bills of materials	7
Preparing operations lists	10
Scheduling jobs	16
Supervising setups	8
Inspecting first units	6
Supervising production	22
Training employees	13
Maintaining facility	4
Attending professional meetings	2
	100%

REQUIRED

Assuming Christine Ford's salary is $85,000 per year, determine the dollar amount of her salary assigned to unit-, batch-, product-, and facility-level activities. (You may need to review Chapter 14 before answering this question.)

M18-14. Stage 2 ABC for a Wholesale Company

Information is presented for the activity costs of Brighton Wholesale Company:

Activity	Cost per Unit of Activity Driver
Customer relations............................	$80.00 per customer per month
Selling.......................................	0.07 per sales dollar
Accounting...................................	5.00 per order
Warehousing..................................	0.50 per unit shipped
Packing......................................	0.25 per unit shipped
Shipping.....................................	0.30 per pound shipped

The following information pertains to Brighton Wholesale Company's activities in Colorado for the month of June 2017:

Number of orders..	320
Sales revenue...	$197,100
Cost of goods sold..	$103,680
Number of customers...	40
Units shipped..	5,400
Pounds shipped...	81,000

REQUIRED

Determine the profitability of sales in Colorado for June 2017.

M18-15. Stage 2 ABC for Manufacturing: Reassigning Costs to Cost Objects

Woodland Corporation has developed the following activity cost information for its manufacturing activities:

Activity	Activity Cost
Machine setup..	$70.00 per batch
Movement..	12.00 per batch move
	0.12 per pound
Drilling..	5.00 per hole
Welding..	3.00 per inch
Shaping..	20.00 per hour
Assembly..	16.00 per hour
Inspection..	1.50 per unit

Filling an order for a batch of 100 fireplace inserts (each insert weighing 50 pounds) required the following:

- Three batch moves
- Two sets of inspections
- Drilling six holes in each unit
- Completing 90 inches of welds on each unit
- Thirty minutes of shaping for each unit
- One hour of assembly per unit

REQUIRED

Determine the activity cost of converting the raw materials into 100 fireplace inserts.

M18-16. Two-Stage ABC for Manufacturing

Bismark Inc., a large manufacturer of heavy equipment components, has determined the following activity cost pools and cost driver levels for the year:

Activity Cost Pool	Activity Cost	Activity Cost Driver
Machine setup................................	$600,000	15,000 setup hours
Material handling.............................	90,000	3,000 tons of materials
Machine operation............................	420,000	12,000 machine hours

The following data are for the production of single batches of two products, Camshafts and Swing Drives during the month of August:

	Camshafts	Swing Drives
Units produced..	1,500	900
Machine hours	4	5
Direct labor hours......................................	300	500
Direct labor cost..	$7,000	$12,000
Direct materials cost.	$40,000	$30,000
Tons of materials	10	7
Setup hours	5	8

REQUIRED

Determine the unit costs of Camshafts and Swing Drives using ABC.

LO2 **M18-17. Two-Stage ABC for Manufacturing**

Sherwin-Williams
NYSE :: SHW

Assume Sherwin-Williams Company, a large paint manufacturer, has determined the following activity cost pools and cost driver levels for the latest period:

Activity Cost Pool	Activity Cost	Activity Cost Driver
Machine setup	$990,000	3,000 setup hours
Material handling	840,000	6,000 material moves
Machine operation	200,000	25,000 machine hours

The following data are for the production of single batches of two products, Mirlite and Subdue:

	Mirlite	Subdue
Gallons produced..	30,000	20,000
Direct labor hours.......................................	300	150
Machine hours	650	200
Direct labor cost...	$12,300	$9,500
Direct materials cost.	$240,000	$110,000
Setup hours	12	10
Material moves...	40	25

REQUIRED

Determine the batch and unit costs per gallon of Mirlite and Subdue using ABC.

LO5 **M18-18. Customer Profitability Analysis**

Elite Services, Inc. provides residential painting services for three home building companies, Brookside, Edgewater, and Hillrose, and it uses a job costing system for determining the costs for completing each job. The job cost system does not capture any cost incurred by Elite for return touchups and refinishes after the homeowner occupies the home. Elite paints each house on a square footage contract price, which includes painting as well as all refinishes and touchups required after the homes are occupied. Each year, the company generates about one-third of its total revenues and gross profits from each of the three builders. The Elite owner has observed that the builders, however, require substantially different levels of support following the completion of jobs. The following data have been gathered:

Support Activity	Driver	Cost per Driver Unit
Major refinishes	Hours on jobs	$ 80
Touchups	Number of visits	$130
Communication	Number of calls	$ 25

Builder	Major Refinishes	Touchups	Communication
Brookside...........................	130	250	610
Edgewater	70	210	365
Hillrose	79	215	350

REQUIRED

Assuming that each of the three customers produces gross profits of $125,000, calculate the profitability from each builder after taking into account the support activity required for each builder.

E18-19. Two-Stage ABC for Manufacturing

LO2

Thornton Company has determined its activity cost pools and cost drivers to be the following:

Cost pools	
Setup	$ 45,000
Material handling	9,600
Machine operation	180,000
Packing	54,000
Total indirect manufacturing costs	$288,600
Cost drivers	
Setups	500
Material moves	600
Machine hours	18,000
Packing orders	1,200

One product made by Merlot, metal casements, used the following activities during the period to produce 500 units:

Setups	40
Material moves	100
Machine hours	2,100
Packing orders	180

REQUIRED

a.   Calculate the cost per unit of activity for each activity cost pool for Thornton Company.

b.   Calculate the manufacturing overhead cost per metal casement manufactured during the period.

E18-20. Calculating Manufacturing Overhead Rates

LO3, 4

Windsor Company, accumulated the following data for 2017:

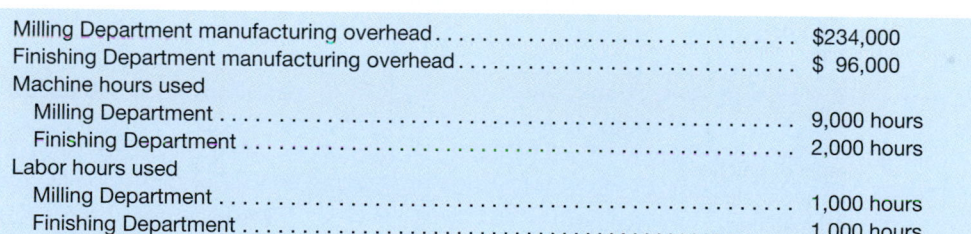

Milling Department manufacturing overhead	$234,000
Finishing Department manufacturing overhead	$ 96,000
Machine hours used	
Milling Department	9,000 hours
Finishing Department	2,000 hours
Labor hours used	
Milling Department	1,000 hours
Finishing Department	1,000 hours

REQUIRED

a.   Calculate the plantwide manufacturing overhead rate using machine hours as the allocation base.

b.   Calculate the plantwide manufacturing overhead rate using direct labor hours as the allocation base.

c.   Calculate department overhead rates using machine hours in Milling and direct labor hours in Finishing as the allocation bases.

d.   Calculate department overhead rates using direct labor hours in Milling and machine hours in Finishing as the allocation bases.

e.   Which of these allocation systems seems to be the most appropriate? Explain.

LO2, 3, 4

E18-21. Calculating Activity-Based Costing Overhead Rates

Assume that manufacturing overhead for Windsor Company in the previous exercise consisted of the following activities and costs:

Setup (1,000 setup hours)	$ 92,000
Production scheduling (300 batches).	24,000
Production engineering (70 change orders)	70,000
Supervision (2,200 direct labor hours)	66,000
Machine maintenance (13,000 machine hours)	78,000
Total activity costs	$330,000

The following additional data were provided for Job 845:

Direct materials costs. $6,000
Direct labor cost (5 Milling direct labor hours; 25 Finishing direct labor hours) $1,000
Setup hours . . . . .5 hours
Production scheduling . . . . .1 batch
Machine hours used (15 Milling machine hours;
5 Finishing machine hours). . . . . .20 hours
Production engineering . . . . .2 change orders

REQUIRED

a. Calculate the cost per unit of activity driver for each activity cost category.

b. Calculate the cost of Job 845 using ABC to assign the overhead costs.

c. Calculate the cost of Job 845 using the plantwide overhead rate based on machine hours calculated in the previous exercise.

d. Calculate the cost of Job 845 using a machine hour departmental overhead rate for the Milling Department and a direct labor hour overhead rate for the Finishing Department (see E18-20).

LO2, 3, 4

E18-22. Activity-Based Costing and Conventional Costs Compared

Hickory Grill Company manufactures two types of cooking grills: the Gas Cooker and the Charcoal Smoker. The Cooker is a premium product sold in upscale outdoor shops; the Smoker is sold in major discount stores. Following is information pertaining to the manufacturing costs for the current month.

	Gas Cooker	Charcoal Smoker
Units.	2,000	8,000
Number of batches.	50	20
Number of batch moves.	90	50
Direct materials	$70,000	$130,000
Direct labor.	$44,000	$56,000

Manufacturing overhead follows:

Activity	Cost	Cost Driver
Materials acquisition and inspection	$ 68,000	Amount of direct materials cost
Materials movement.	19,600	Number of batch moves
Scheduling	43,400	Number of batches
	$131,000	

REQUIRED

a. Determine the total and per-unit costs of manufacturing the Gas Cooker and Charcoal Smoker for the month, assuming all manufacturing overhead is assigned on the basis of direct labor dollars.

b. Determine the total and per-unit costs of manufacturing the Gas Cooker and Charcoal Smoker for the month, assuming manufacturing overhead is assigned using activity-based costing.

E18-23. **Activity-Based Costing Versus Conventional Costing**   **LO1, 3, 4**
Refer to the previous exercise in E18-22 for Hickory Grill.

REQUIRED

a. Comment on the differences between the solutions to requirements (a) and (b). Which is more accurate? What errors might managers make if all manufacturing overhead costs are assigned on the basis of direct labor dollars?

b. Hickory Grill's manufacturing process has become increasingly automated over the past few years. Discuss how this will likely impact its ability to accurately measure product costs.

c. Comment on the adequacy of the preceding data to meet management's needs.

E18-24. **Traditional Product Costing versus Activity-Based Costing**   **LO2, 3, 4**
Assume that **Panasonic Company** has determined its estimated total manufacturing overhead cost for one of its plants to be $318,200, consisting of the following activity cost pools for the current month:

Panasonic Company
OTCMKTS :: PCRFY

Activity Centers	Activity Costs	Cost Drivers	Activity Level
Assembly setups	$ 66,000	Setup hours	2,000
Materials handling	32,400	Number of moves.	600
Assembly	180,000	Assembly hours	18,000
Maintenance.	39,800	Maintenance hours.	1,990
Total	$318,200		

Total direct labor hours used during the month were 14,800. Panasonic produces many different electronic products, including the following two products produced during the current month:

	Model X301	Model Z205
Units produced.	1,500	1,500
Direct materials costs.	$22,000	$22,000
Direct labor costs	$17,000	$17,000
Direct labor hours.	700	700
Setup hours	60	120
Materials moves	30	60
Assembly hours	900	900
Maintenance hours.	20	80

REQUIRED

a. Calculate the total per-unit cost of each model using direct labor hours to assign manufacturing overhead to products.

b. Calculate the total per-unit cost of each model using activity-based costing to assign manufacturing overhead to products.

c. Comment on the accuracy of the two methods for determining product costs.

d. Discuss some of the strategic implications of your answers to the previous requirements.

E18-25. **Traditional Product Costing versus Activity-Based Costing**   **LO2, 3, 4**
Ridgeland Inc. makes backpacks for large sporting goods chains that are sold under the customers' store brand names. The Accounting Department has identified the following overhead costs and cost drivers for next year:

Overhead Item	Expected Costs	Cost Driver	Maximum Quantity
Setup costs	$489,600	Number of setups.	7,200
Ordering costs	130,000	Number of orders	65,000
Maintenance.	920,000	Number of machine hours	80,000
Power	88,000	Number of kilowatt hours.	440,000

Total predicted direct labor hours for next year is 42,500. The following data are for two recently completed jobs:

	Job 201	Job 202
Cost of direct materials	$10,500	$12,000
Cost of direct labor	$18,600	$62,300
Number of units completed	900	750
Number of direct labor hours	220	270
Number of setups	15	19
Number of orders	21	42
Number of machine hours	450	360
Number of kilowatt hours	200	300

REQUIRED

a. Determine the unit cost for each job using a traditional plantwide overhead rate based on direct labor hours.

b. Determine the unit cost for each job using ABC. (Round answers to two decimal places.)

c. As the manager of Ridgeland, is there additional information that you would want to help you evaluate the pricing and profitability of Jobs 201 and 202?

d. Assuming the company has been using the method required in part *a,* how should management react to the findings in part *b?*

LO5, 6   **E18-26. Customer Profitability Analysis**

Leahy Inc. has 10 customers that account for all of its $4,200,000 of net income. Its activity-based costing system is able to assign all costs, except for $650,000 of general administrative costs, to key activities incurred in connection with serving its customers. A customer profitability analysis based on activity costing produced the following customer profits and losses:

Customer	#1	$ 306,000
	#2	624,000
	#3	(257,000)
	#4	909,000
	#5	950,000
	#6	872,000
	#7	598,000
	#8	322,000
	#9	(105,000)
	#10	631,000
Total		$4,850,000

REQUIRED

Prepare a customer profitability profile like the one in Exhibit 18.3.

LO5   **E18-27. Customer Profitability Analysis**

Refer to the previous exercise E18-26 for Leahy Inc.

REQUIRED

a. If Leahy were to notify customers 3 and 9 that it will no longer be able to provide them services in the future, will that increase company profits by $362,000? Why or why not?

b. What is the primary benefit of preparing a customer profitability analysis?

PROBLEMS

P18-28. Two-Stage ABC for Manufacturing with ABC Variances LO2, 3, 4

Meade Manufacturing has developed the following activity cost pool information for its 2017 manufacturing activities:

	Budgeted Activity Cost	Activity Cost Driver at Practical Capacity
Purchasing and materials handling	$1,920,000	800,000 kilograms
Setup	880,000	1,600 setups
Machine operations	768,000	12,000 hours
First unit inspection	60,000	1,200 batches
Packaging.	423,900	471,000 units

Actual 2017 production information is as follows:

	Standard Product A	Standard Product B	Specialty Products
Units.	100,000	80,000	60,000
Batches	80	60	500
Setups*.	200	140	800
Machine operations (hours)	5,000	2,000	3,000
Kilograms of raw materials.	500,000	400,000	300,000
Direct materials costs.	$1,000,000	$700,000	$960,000

* Some products require setups on two or more machines.

REQUIRED

a. Determine the unit cost of each product for Meade Manufacturing.

b. Explain why the unit cost of the specialty products is so much higher than the unit cost of Standard Product A or Standard Product B.

P18-29. ABC—A Service Application LO2, 3, 4

Grand Haven is a senior living community that offers a full range of services including independent living, assisted living, and skilled nursing care. The assisted living division provides residential space, meals, and medical services (MS) to its residents. The current costing system adds the cost of all of these services (space, meals, and MS) and divides by total resident days to get a cost per resident day for each month. Recognizing that MS tends to vary significantly among the residents, Grand Haven's accountant recommended that an ABC system be designed to calculate more accurately the cost of MS provided to residents. She decided that residents should be classified into four categories (A, B, C, D) based on the level of services received, with group A representing the lowest level of service and D representing the highest level of service. Two cost drivers being considered for measuring MS costs are number of assistance calls and number of assistant contacts. A contact is registered each time an assistance professional provides medical services or aid to a resident. The accountant has gathered the following data for the most recent annual period:

Resident Classification	Annual Resident Days	Annual Assistance Hours	Number of Assistance Contacts
A	7,700	12,000	52,000
B	5,600	20,000	48,000
C	3,300	24,000	48,000
D	1,900	30,000	48,000
	18,500	86,000	196,000

Other data:

Total cost of medical services for the period	$2,479,400
Total cost of meals and residential space.	$1,276,500

REQUIRED

(round all calculations to two decimal places)

a. Determine the ABC cost of a resident day for each category of residents using assistance hours as the cost driver.

b. Determine the ABC cost of a resident day for each category of residents using assistance contacts as the cost driver.

c. Which cost driver do you think provides the more accurate measure of the cost per day for a Grand Haven resident?

LO2, 3, 4   P18-30. ABC Costing for a Service Organization

New Liberty Mortgage Company is a full-service residential mortgage company in the Chicago area that operates in a very competitive market. The CEO, David Ross, is concerned about operating costs associated with processing mortgage applications and has decided to install an ABC costing system to help him get a handle on costs. Although labor hours seem to be the primary driver of the cost of processing a new mortgage, the labor cost for the different activities involved in processing new loans varies widely. The Accounting Department has provided the following data for the company's five major cost pools for 2017:

Activity Cost Pools		Activity Drivers	
Taking customer applications.......	$ 364,900	Time—assistant managers.........	17,800 hours
Conducting credit investigations	350,000	Time—credit managers	12,500 hours
Underwriting....................	787,500	Time—Underwriting Department	15,000 hours
Preparing loan packages	585,000	Time—Processing Department	22,500 hours
Closing loans	1,485,000	Time—Legal Department..........	18,000 hours
	$3,572,400		85,800 hours

During 2017, the company processed and issued 9,000 new mortgages, two of which are summarized here with regard to activities used to process the mortgages:

	Loan 7023	Loan 8955
Application processing hours..................................	2.00	3.00
Credit investigating hours.....................................	2.50	2.50
Underwriting hours...	1.50	1.50
Processing hours	3.00	3.50
Legal hours...	1.50	2.50
Total hours	10.50	13.00

REQUIRED

a. Determine the cost per unit of activity for each activity cost pool.

b. Determine the cost of processing loans 7023 and 8955.

c. Determine the cost of preparing loans 7023 and 8955 assuming that an average cost per hour for all activities is used.

d. Compare and discuss your answers to requirements (*b*) and (*c*).

LO2, 3, 4, 6   P18-31. Activity-Based Costing in a Service Organization

Banctronics Inc. has ten automatic teller machines (ATMs) spread throughout the city maintained by the ATM Department. You have been assigned the task of determining the cost of operating each machine. Management will use the information you develop, along with other information pertaining to the volume and type of transactions at each machine, to evaluate the desirability of continuing to operate each machine and/or changing security arrangements for a particular machine.

The ATM Department consists of a total of six employees: a supervisor, a head cashier, two associate cashiers, and two maintenance personnel. The associate cashiers make between two and four daily trips to each machine to collect and replenish cash and to replenish supplies, deposit tickets, and so forth. Each machine contains a small computer that automatically summarizes and reports transactions to the head cashier. The head cashier reconciles the activities of the two associate cashiers to the computerized reports. The supervisor, who does not handle cash, reviews the reconciliation. When an automatic teller's computer, a customer, or a cashier reports a problem, the two maintenance employees and one cashier are dispatched immediately. The cashier removes all cash and transaction records, and the maintenance employees repair the machine.

Maintenance employees spend all of their time on maintenance-related activities. The associate cashiers spend approximately 50 percent of their time on maintenance-related activities and 50 percent on daily trips. The head cashier's time is divided, with 75 percent directly related to daily trips to each machine and 25 percent related to supervising cashiers on maintenance calls. The supervisor devotes 20 percent of the time to daily trips to each machine and 80 percent to the equal supervision of each employee. Cost information for a recent month follows:

Salaries	
Supervisor.	$ 5,500
Head cashier.	4,000
Other ($2,100 each)	8,400
Lease and operating costs	
Cashiers' service vehicle	1,600
Maintenance service vehicle.	1,500
Office rent and utilities	4,000
Machine lease, space rent, and utilities ($1,700 each).	17,000
Total	$42,000

Related monthly activity information for this month follows:

Machine	Routine Trips	Maintenance Hours
1	20	5
2	60	17
3	40	15
4	40	30
5	80	15
6	20	10
7	70	25
8	100	5
9	30	20
10	40	18
Total	500	160

Additional information follows:

- The office is centrally located with about equal travel time to each machine.
- Maintenance hours include travel time.
- The cashiers' service vehicle is used exclusively for routine visits.
- The office space is divided equally between the supervisor and the head cashier.

REQUIRED

a. Determine the monthly operating costs of machines 7 and 8 when cost assignments are based on the number of machines.

b. Determine the activity cost of a routine trip and a maintenance hour for the month given. Round answers to the nearest cent.

c. Determine the operating costs assigned and reassigned to machines 7 and 8 when activity-based costing is used.

d. How can ABC cost information be used by Banctronics Inc. to improve the overall management of monthly operating costs?

P18-32. Product Costing: Plantwide Overhead versus Activity-Based Costing LO3, 4

Sterling Industries produces machine parts as a contract provider for a large manufacturing company. Sterling produces two particular parts, shafts and gears. The competition is keen among contract producers, and Sterling's top management realizes how vulnerable its market is to cost-cutting competitors. Hence, having a very accurate understanding of costs is important to Sterling's survival.

Sterling's president, Sheila Hudson, has observed that the company's current cost to produce shafts is $21.41, and the current cost to produce gears is $12.73. She indicated to the controller that she suspects some problems with the cost system because Sterling is suddenly experiencing extraordinary competition on shafts, but it seems to have a virtual corner on the gears market. She is even considering dropping the shaft line and converting the company to a one-product manufacturer of gears. She asked the controller, George Coleman, to conduct a thorough cost study and to consider whether changes in the cost system are necessary. The controller collected the following data about the company's costs and various manufacturing activities for the most recent month:

	Shafts	Gears
Production units.	47,000	16,000
Selling price	$31.95	$23.50
Overhead per unit (based on direct labor hours)	$12.34	$6.25
Materials and direct labor cost per unit	$9.07	$6.48
Number of production runs	15	25
Number of purchasing and receiving orders processed	50	110
Number of machine hours	12,750	6,000
Number of direct labor hours.	29,000	5,000
Number of engineering hours.	5,000	5,000
Number of material moves.	40	30

The controller was able to summarize the company's total manufacturing overhead into the following pools:

Setup costs	$ 40,000
Machine costs	180,000
Purchasing and receiving costs	200,000
Engineering costs.	190,000
Materials handling costs	70,000
Total	$680,000

REQUIRED

a. Calculate Sterling's current plantwide overhead rate based on direct labor hours.

b. Verify Sterling's calculation of overhead cost per unit of $12.34 for shafts and $6.25 for gears.

c. Calculate the manufacturing overhead cost per unit for shafts and gears using activity-based costing, assuming each of the five cost pools represents a separate activity pool. Use the most appropriate activity driver for assigning activity costs to the two products.

d. Comment on Sterling's current cost system and the reason the company is facing fierce competition for shafts but little competition for gears.

LO2, 5, 6 **P18-33. Customer Profitability Analysis**

Remington Aeronautics LTD is a British aeronautics subcontract company that designs and manufactures electronic control systems for commercial airlines. The vast majority of all commercial aircraft are manufactured by Boeing in the U.S. and Airbus in Europe; however, there is a relatively small group of companies that manufacture narrow-body commercial jets. Assume for this exercise that Remington does contract work for the two major manufacturers plus three companies in the second tier.

Because competition is intense in the industry, Remington has always operated on a fairly thin 20% gross profit margin; hence, it is crucial that it manage non-manufacturing overhead costs effectively in order to achieve an acceptable net profit margin. With declining profit margins in recent years, Remington Aeronautics' CEO, John Remington, has become concerned that the cost of obtaining contracts and maintaining relations with its five major customers may be getting out of hand. You have been hired to conduct a customer profitability analysis.

Remington Aeronautics' non-manufacturing overhead consists of $2.5 million of general and administrative (G&A) expense, (including, among other expenses, the CEO's salary and bonus and the cost of operating the company's corporate jet) and selling and customer support expenses of $3 million (including 5% sales commissions and $1,050,000 of additional costs).

The accounting staff determined that the $1,050,000 of additional selling and customer support expenses related to the following four activity cost pools:

Activity	Activity Cost Driver	Cost per Unit of Activity
1. Sales visits	Number of visit days	$1,400
2. Product adjustments	Number of adjustments	1,200
3. Phone and email contacts	Number of calls/contacts	200
4. Promotion and entertainment events	Number of events	1,600

Financial and activity data on the five customers follows (Sales and Gross Profit data in millions):

Customer	Sales	Gross Profit	Quantity of Sales and Support Activity			
			Activity 1	Activity 2	Activity 3	Activity 4
A.	$17	$3.4	106	23	220	82
B.	12	2.4	130	36	354	66
C.	3	0.6	52	10	180	74
D.	4	0.8	34	6	138	18
E.	3	0.6	16	5	104	10
	$39	$7.8	338	80	996	250

In addition to the above, the sales staff used the corporate jet at a cost of $800 per hour for trips to customers as follows:

Customer A	24 hours
Customer B	36 hours
Customer C	5 hours
Customer D	0 hours
Customer E.	6 hours

The total cost of operating the airplane is included in general and administrative expense; none is included in selling and customer support costs.

REQUIRED

a. Prepare a customer profitability analysis for Remington Aeronautics that shows the gross profits less all expenses that can reasonably be assigned to the five customers.

b. Now assuming that the remaining general and administrative costs are assigned to the five customers based on relative sales dollars, calculate net profit for each customer.

c. Discuss the merits of the analysis in part a. versus part b.

CASES AND PROJECTS

C18-34. Designing an ABC System for a Country Club

LO2, 5, 6

The Reserve Club is a traditional private golf and country club that has three different categories of memberships: golf, tennis & swimming, and social. Golf members have access to all amenities and programs in the Club, Tennis & Swimming members have access to all amenities and programs except use of the golf course, and Social members have access to only the social activities of the club, excluding golf, tennis, and swimming. All members have clubhouse privileges, including use of the bar and restaurant, which is operated by an outside contractor. During the past year, the average membership in each category, along with the number of club visits during the year, was

	Members	Visits
Golf.	250	9,360
Tennis & Swimming	55	1,500
Social	125	2,160

Some members of the Club have been complaining that heavy users of the Club are not bearing their share of the costs through their membership fees. Dess Rosmond, General Manager of the Reserve Club, agrees that monthly fees paid by the various member groups should be based on the annual average amount of cost-related activities provided by the Club for the three groups, and he intends to set fees on that basis for the coming year. The annual direct costs of operating the golf course, tennis courts, and swimming pool have been calculated by the Club's controller as follows:

Golf course.	$1,000,000
Swimming pool.	50,000
Tennis courts	25,000

The operation of the bar and restaurant and all related costs, including depreciation on the bar and restaurant facilities, are excluded from this analysis. In addition to the above costs, the Club incurs general overhead costs in the following amounts for the most recent (and typical) year:

General Ledger Overhead Accounts	Amounts
Indirect labor for the Club management staff (the general manager, assistant general manager, membership manager, and club controller)	$300,000
Utilities (other than those directly related to golf, swimming and tennis).	24,000
Website maintenance.	2,000
Postage	5,000
Computers and information systems maintenance	7,500
Clubhouse maintenance & depreciation	30,000
Liability insurance.	4,000
Security contract	12,000
	$384,500

Dess believes that the best way to assign most of the overhead costs to the three membership categories is with an activity-based system that recognizes four key activities that occur regularly in the club:

- Recruiting and providing orientation for new members
- Maintaining the membership roster and communicating with members
- Planning, scheduling and managing Club events
- Maintaining the financial records and reporting for the Club

REQUIRED

a. Identify and explain which overhead costs can reasonably be assigned to one or more of the four key activities, and suggest a basis for making the assignment.

b. Identify a cost driver for each activity cost pool that would seem to be suitable for assigning the activity cost pool to the three membership categories.

c. Suggest a method for assigning any overhead costs to the three membership categories that cannot reasonably be assigned to activity pools.

d. Comment on the suitability of ABC to this cost assignment situation.

LO2, 4, 6   C18-35. Product Costing: Department versus Activity-Based Costing for Overhead

Advertising Technologies, Inc. (ATI) specializes in providing both published and online advertising services for the business marketplace. The company monitors its costs based on the cost per column inch of published space printed in print advertising media and based on the cost per minute of telephone advertising time delivered on "The AD Line," a computer-based, online advertising service. ATI has one new competitor, Tel-a-Ad, in its local teleadvertising market; and with increased competition, ATI has seen a decline in sales of online advertising in recent years. ATI's president, Robert Beard, believes that predatory pricing by Tel-a-Ad has caused the problem. The following is a recent conversation between Robert and Jane Minnear, director of marketing for ATI.

Jane: I just received a call from one of our major customers concerning our advertising rates on "The AD Line" who said that a sales rep from another firm (it had to be Tel-a-Ad) had offered the same service at $1 per minute, which is $1.50 per minute less than our price.

Robert: It's costing about $1.27 per minute to produce that product. I don't see how they can afford to sell it so cheaply. I'm not convinced that we should meet the price. Perhaps the better strategy is to emphasize producing and selling more published ads, which we're more experienced with and where our margins are high and we have virtually no competition.

Jane: You may be right. Based on a recent survey of our customers, I think we can raise the price significantly for published advertising and still not lose business.

Robert: That sounds promising; however, before we make a major recommitment to publishing, let's explore other possible explanations. I want to know how our costs compare with our competitors. Maybe we could be more efficient and find a way to earn a good return on teleadvertising.

After this meeting, Robert and Jane requested an investigation of production costs and comparative efficiency of producing published versus online advertising services. The controller, Tim Gentry, indicated that ATI's efficiency was comparable to that of its competitors and prepared the following cost data:

	Published Advertising	Online Advertising
Estimated number of production units..........................	200,000	10,000,000
Selling price	$200	$2.50
Direct product costs.......................................	$21,000,000	$5,000,000
Overhead allocation*	$10,175,000	$8,325,000
Overhead per unit...	$49	$0.77
Direct costs per unit......................................	$105	$0.50
Number of customers......................................	180,000	25,000
Number of salesperson days...............................	28,500	3,500
Number of art and design hours	35,000	5,000
Number of creative services subcontract hours	100,000	25,000
Number of customer service calls	72,000	8,000

* Based on direct labor costs

Upon examining the data, Robert decided that he wanted to know more about the overhead costs since they were such a high proportion of total production costs. He was provided the following list of overhead costs and told that they were currently being assigned to products in proportion to direct labor costs.

Selling costs...	$8,000,000
Visual and audio design costs	3,000,000
Creative services costs	5,500,000
Customer service costs	2,000,000

REQUIRED

Using the data provided by the controller, prepare analyses to help Robert and Jane in making their decisions. (*Hint:* Prepare cost calculations for both product lines using ABC to see whether there is any significant difference in their unit costs.) Should ATI switch from the fast-growing, online advertising market back into the well-established published advertising market? Does the charge of predatory pricing seem valid? Why are customers likely to be willing to pay a higher price to get published services? Do traditional costing and activity-based costing lead to the same conclusions?

C18-36.   Unit-Level and Multiple-Level Cost Assignments with Decision Implications   LO2, 3, 4, 6

CarryAll Company[4] produces briefcases from leather, fabric, and synthetic materials in a single production department. The basic product is a standard briefcase made from leather and lined with fabric. CarryAll has a good reputation in the market because the standard briefcase is a high-quality item that has been produced for many years.

Last year, the company decided to expand its product line and produce specialty briefcases for special orders. These briefcases differ from the standard in that they vary in size, contain both leather and synthetic materials, and are imprinted with the buyer's logo (the standard briefcase is simply imprinted with the CarryAll name in small letters). The decision to use some synthetic materials in the briefcase was made to hold down the materials cost. To reduce the labor costs per unit, most of the cutting and stitching on the specialty briefcases is done by automated machines, which are used to a much lesser degree in the production of the standard briefcases. Because of these changes in the design and production of the specialty briefcases, CarryAll management believed that they would cost less to produce than the standard briefcases. However, because they are specialty items, they were priced slightly higher; standards are priced at $30 and specialty briefcases at $32.

---

[4] The CarryAll Company case, prepared by Professors Harold Roth and Imogene Posey, was originally published in the *Management Accounting Campus Report.*

After reviewing last month's results of operations, CarryAll's president became concerned about the profitability of the two product lines because the standard briefcase showed a loss while the specialty briefcase showed a greater profit margin than expected. The president is wondering whether the company should drop the standard briefcase and focus entirely on specialty items. Units and cost data for last month's operations as reported to the president are as follows:

	Standard	Specialty
Units produced.	10,000	2,500
Direct materials		
Leather (1 sq. yd. × $15.00; ½ sq. yd. × $15.00)	$15.00	$ 7.50
Fabric (1 sq. yd. × $5.00; 1 sq. yd. × $5.00)	5.00	5.00
Synthetic.		5.00
Total materials.	20.00	17.50
Direct labor (½ hr. × $12.00, ¼ hr. × $12.00)	6.00	3.00
Manufacturing overhead (½ hr. × $8.98; ¼ hr. × $8.98)	4.49	2.25
Cost per unit.	$30.49	$22.75

Factory overhead is applied on the basis of direct labor hours. The rate of $8.98 per direct labor hour was calculated by dividing the total overhead ($50,500) by the direct labor hours (5,625). As shown in the table, the cost of a standard briefcase is $0.49 higher than its $30 sales price; the specialty briefcase has a cost of only $22.75, for a gross profit per unit of $9.25. The problem with these costs is that they do not accurately reflect the activities involved in manufacturing each product. Determining the costs using ABC should provide better product costing data to help gauge the actual profitability of each product line.

The manufacturing overhead costs must be analyzed to determine the activities driving the costs. Assume that the following costs and cost drivers have been identified:

- The Purchasing Department's cost is $6,000. The major activity driving these costs is the number of purchase orders processed. During the month, the Purchasing Department prepared the following number of purchase orders for the materials indicated:

Leather	20
Fabric	30
Synthetic material.	50

- The cost of receiving and inspecting materials is $7,500. These costs are driven by the number of deliveries. During the month, the following number of deliveries were made:

Leather	30
Fabric	40
Synthetic material.	80

- Production line setup cost is $10,000. Setup activities involve changing the machines to produce the different types of briefcases. Each setup for production of the standard briefcases requires one hour; each setup for specialty briefcases requires two hours. Standard briefcases are produced in batches of 200, and specialty briefcases are produced in batches of 25. During the last month, there were 50 setups for the standard item and 100 setups for the specialty item.
- The cost of inspecting finished goods is $8,000. All briefcases are inspected to ensure that quality standards are met. However, the final inspection of standard briefcases takes very little time because the employees identify and correct quality problems as they do the hand cutting and stitching. A survey of the personnel responsible for inspecting the final products showed that 150 hours were spent on standard briefcases and 250 hours on specialty briefcases during the month.
- Equipment-related costs are $6,000. Equipment-related costs include repairs, depreciation, and utilities. Management has determined that a logical basis for assigning these costs to products is machine hours. A standard briefcase requires 1/2 hour of machine time, and a specialty briefcase requires two hours. Thus, during the last month, 5,000 hours of machine time relate to the standard line and 5,000 hours relate to the specialty line.
- Plant-related costs are $13,000. These costs include property taxes, insurance, administration, and others. For the purpose of determining average unit costs, they are to be assigned to products using machine hours.

REQUIRED

a. Using activity-based costing concepts, what overhead costs should be assigned to the two products?

b. What is the unit cost of each product using activity-based costing concepts?

c. Reevaluate the president's concern about the profitability of the two product lines.

d. Discuss the merits of activity-based management as it relates to CarryAll's ABC cost system.

SOLUTIONS TO REVIEW PROBLEMS

Mid-Chapter Review 1

SOLUTION

Indirect expenses are displacing direct expenses. This may be attributed to the advancement of technology and equipment. It may also be largely related to an increase in the number of different types of products and services that companies offer. As companies move away from one simple product, the need for more indirect costs such as equipment design, changeover, and even the movement of products can increase. As the pool of indirect expenses becomes a more significant part of product costs, it is increasingly difficult yet important to come up with methods to reasonably assign indirect costs to products.

Mid-Chapter Review 2

SOLUTION

Answers may vary but likely activities and related drivers might include:

- Reception and admission of participating employees/number of participating employees
- Consultations with physician/number of minutes of consultation services
- Administration of tests/number of tests
- Processing and distributing test results/number of participating employees
- Room set up/number of participating employees
- External lab processing/number of tests
- Technology support for website/number of participating employees

Mid-Chapter Review 3

SOLUTION

a. **Plantwide overhead rate= Total manufacturing overhead ÷ Total machine hours**
$$= (\$120{,}000 + \$55{,}000) \div (10{,}000 + 5{,}000)$$
$$= \$175{,}000 \div 15{,}000$$
$$= \$11.67 \text{ per machine hour}$$

	Cobra Latch	GrimLoc
Product costs per unit		
Direct materials....................................	$12,000	$18,000
Direct labor..	5,000	4,000
Manufacturing overhead		
700 machine hours × $11.67......................	8,169	
800 machine hours × $11.67......................		9,336
Total cost per batch..............................	$25,169	$31,336
Number of units per batch........................	÷ 100	÷ 100
Cost per unit......................................	$251.69	$313.36

b. **Departmental overhead rates = Total departmental overhead ÷ Dept. allocation base**
$$\text{Fabrication} = \$120{,}000 \div 10{,}000 \text{ machine hours}$$
$$= \$12 \text{ per machine hour}$$
$$\text{Finishing} = \$55{,}000 \div 5{,}000 \text{ machine hours}$$
$$= \$11 \text{ per machine hour}$$

	Cobra Latch	GrimLoc
Product costs per unit		
Direct materials.	$12,000	$18,000
Direct labor	5,000	4,000
Manufacturing overhead		
Fabrication Department		
500 machine hours × $12.	6,000	
700 machine hours × $12.		8,400
Finishing Department		
200 machine hours × $11.	2,200	
100 machine hours × $11.		1,100
Total cost per batch	$25,200	$31,500
Number of units per batch	÷ 100	÷ 100
Cost per unit.	$252.00	$315.00

c.

Activity-based overhead rates = Activity cost pool ÷ Activity cost driver

$$\text{Maintenance} = \$30,000 \div 15,000 \text{ machine hours}$$
$$= \$2 \text{ per machine hour}$$
$$\text{Materials handling} = \$45,000 \div 4,500 \text{ materials moves}$$
$$= \$10 \text{ per materials move}$$
$$\text{Machine setups} = \$75,000 \div 750 \text{ setups}$$
$$= \$100 \text{ per machine setup}$$
$$\text{Inspections} = \$25,000 \div 1,000 \text{ inspection hours}$$
$$= \$25 \text{ per inspection hour}$$

	Cobra Latch	GrimLoc
Product costs per unit		
Direct materials.	$12,000	$18,000
Direct labor	5,000	4,000
Manufacturing overhead		
Maintenance activity		
700 machine hours × $2.	1,400	
800 machine hours × $2.		1,600
Materials handling activity		
30 materials moves × $10.	300	
50 materials moves × $10.		500
Machine setups activity		
5 machine setups × $100.	500	
9 machine setups × $100.		900
Inspections activity		
30 inspection hours × $25	750	
60 inspection hours × $25		1,500
Total cost per batch	$19,950	$26,500
Number of units per batch	÷ 100	÷ 100
Cost per unit.	$199.50	$265.00

Mid-Chapter Review 4

SOLUTION

Following is a summary of product costs for Cobra Latch and GrimLoc assigning overhead costs based on a plantwide rate, department rates, and activity-based rates:

	Cobra Latch	GrimLoc
Plantwide rate.	$251.69	$313.36
Department rates	$252.00	$315.00
Activity rates.	$199.50	$265.00

Changing from a plantwide rate to department rates had little effect on unit costs because the department rates per machine hour are close to the plantwide rate per machine hour. Based on machine hours, both departments have similar cost structures.

When using activity rates, however, the cost of these two products drops dramatically because they use only a small portion (less than 2 percent) of the activities of setup (14 of 750) and materials moves (80 of 4,500). Neither a plantwide rate nor department rates recognize this fact, resulting in a large amount of cost cross-subsidization of other products by Cobra Latch and GrimLoc for these costs. Although this problem did not include cost analysis of the other three products, it shows that they are less profitable and that Cobra Latch and GrimLoc are much more profitable than management previously thought.

Mid-Chapter Review 5

SOLUTION

a.   Activity A—Minor systems maintenance
Activity B—Visits to customers
Activity C—Communications via phone

Activity	1	2	3	4	5
A (@ $160)	$11,040	$22,560	$11,840	$ 9,760	$21,760
B (@ $300)	7,500	12,600	5,700	8,400	11,700
C (@ $50)	6,400	10,250	4,950	5,300	9,450
Total support costs.	$24,940	$45,410	$22,490	$23,460	$42,910
Profit before support Costs	80,000	85,000	83,000	90,000	78,000
Customer profits.	$55,060	$39,590	$60,510	$66,540	$35,090
Ratio of support costs to profit before support costs:. . . .	31%	53%	27%	26%	55%

b.   This analysis is beneficial to SAP because it shows that Groups 2 and 5 are outliers among the five customer groups in terms of support services required. Groups 2 and 5 are significantly larger consumers of activities for all three of the support activities. Note also that Group 4 customers are relatively light users of minor systems maintenance, and Group 3 are relatively light users of phone communications. Calculating the ratio of total support costs to profit before support costs provides additional insight into the relative profitability of the customer groups. All five customer groups are profitable; however, this analysis provides useful information for improving profits by working with Groups 2 and 5 to control support activities and related costs and attempt to bring their support costs in line with the other customer groups.

Chapter-End Review

SOLUTION

Activity-based costing requires a company to understand, identify, and measure the activities it engages in in order to deliver its products or services. Activity-based management is the process of assessing those activities to make sure they align with companies' goals and objectives. It allows for a review of activities to identify which ones ultimately add value for its customers and can change or remove those activities that do not add value. It may also wish to make changes to activities that add value, to further a company's initiative. For example, **Safety-Kleen** is a subsidiary of **Clean Harbor**. Safety-Kleen states, "We are committed to continually examining our own operations to identify areas where we can reduce energy consumption, as well as determine innovative ways to drive enhancements across our entire network."[5] A firm is not in a position to do this effectively and profitably if it does not have a grasp of the costs and values of each of its activities.

---

[5] http://www.safety-kleen.com/about-us/sustainability

Additional Topics in Product Costing

WHOLE FOODS
www.wholefoodsmarket.com

Whole Foods is trying to shed its nickname "Whole Paycheck." The Austin, Texas, grocery company specializes in quality food offered in upscale locations with a focus on excellent customer service. However, the recent economic crisis along with intensified competition from companies like **Fresh Market** and **Sprouts Farmers Markets** has Whole Foods rethinking its premium-brand pricing strategy. Even large-scale grocers such as **Kroger Company** are encroaching on what was once Whole Foods' private domain by offering premium meats, cheeses, and health foods.

Because the bulk of Whole Foods' inventory is organic or certified on other dimensions (i.e., gluten- or allergen-free, kosher, etc.), the cost of its inventory is higher than that of mass-market grocers. Yet increased competition necessitates that the company uses accurate cost accounting methods and finds innovative ways to contain its operating costs. One way the company is doing this is by building new stores that are smaller in size and located in lower-rent locations like Detroit and New Orleans. But inside the store, Whole Foods must be careful not to cut costs in a way that curtails its competitive advantage. The company successfully utilizes a decentralized supply chain structure that highlights the geographic diversity of a store's local markets. To that point, the company employs "foragers" to seek out high-quality local products for the Whole Foods located within that region.

Moreover, a grocery operation has numerous support departments—areas that are necessary to the operation of the store, but not directly attributable to any one product or group of products. Examples of support departments include human resources, accounting, and custodial services. Whole Foods must develop a system of service cost allocation that will minimize distortions in profitability across grocery departments. The company must also operate as efficiently as possible; however, that efficiency shouldn't come at the expense of the quality that has become Whole Foods' bedrock. In fact, in the grocery industry, quality should arise from maintaining a clean, safe, and efficient work environment and by adhering to rigorous standards, the very same actions that should simultaneously improve efficiency.

The last, but perhaps most important factor for the company is its inventory management. Holding inventory is costly due to storage and insurance costs; and in the case of a grocer, perishable inventory is prone to spoilage and waste. Indeed, inventory turnover should be much more frequent for produce, meats, and bakery items than for vitamins and supplements. One common method in preventing spoilage is to discount certain goods that are getting close to their expiration date. By doing so, the company is betting that the lost revenue on the discounted goods will draw the customer in for repeat business, as opposed to a "one-shot" shopping experience. The deep discounts have helped the company better manage its inventory of products with short shelf lives. This chapter discusses how companies such as Whole Foods assign the cost of their internal service departments to their products, and how they can benefit from adopting a lean operations philosophy in managing their inventory levels.

Source: Julie Jargon, "The Battle for the Organic Shopper," *Wall Street Journal*, August 22, 2013, pp. B1–B2; Clair Suddath, "Whole Foods Local Forager Elly Truesdell Is a Grocery Tastemaker," *Bloomberg Businessweek*, May 2, 2013; Annie Gasparo, "Whole Foods Lifts Outlook as Sales Rise," *Wall Street Journal*, February 9, 2012, p. B4; and Katie Agin, "Lean Manufacturing 2.0," *Whole Foods Magazine*, January 2010.

CHAPTER ORGANIZATION

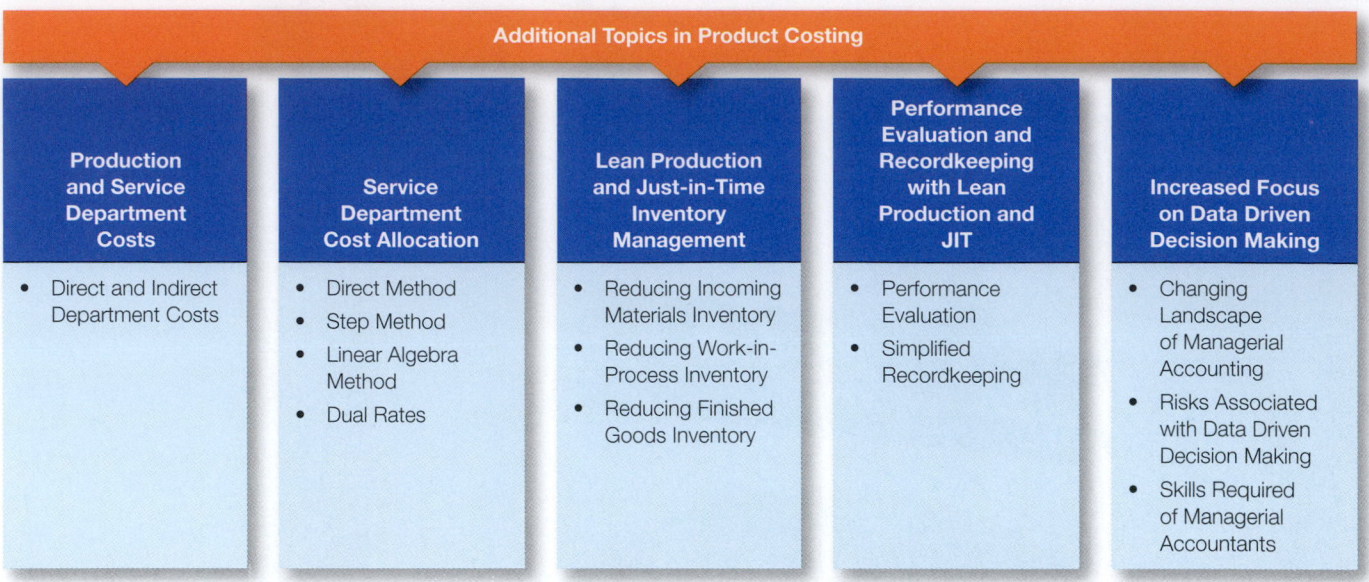

Additional Topics in Product Costing				
Production and Service Department Costs	**Service Department Cost Allocation**	**Lean Production and Just-in-Time Inventory Management**	**Performance Evaluation and Recordkeeping with Lean Production and JIT**	**Increased Focus on Data Driven Decision Making**
• Direct and Indirect Department Costs	• Direct Method • Step Method • Linear Algebra Method • Dual Rates	• Reducing Incoming Materials Inventory • Reducing Work-in-Process Inventory • Reducing Finished Goods Inventory	• Performance Evaluation • Simplified Recordkeeping	• Changing Landscape of Managerial Accounting • Risks Associated with Data Driven Decision Making • Skills Required of Managerial Accountants

1

LO1 Differentiate between production and service department costs and direct and indirect department costs.

PRODUCTION AND SERVICE DEPARTMENT COSTS

In Chapter 17, we discussed two basic methods (job order costing and process costing) for accumulating, measuring and recording the costs of producing goods. In Chapter 18, we discussed both traditional and activity-based methods for assigning indirect costs to products. We now look in more detail at another aspect of assigning indirect costs.

In addition to *production* departments that actually perform work on a product, many companies have production *support* departments, such as payroll, human resources, information technology, security, and facilities, that provide support services for all of the production departments, and sometimes even for each other. These departments are typically called **service departments**. The cost of producing products, therefore, includes the costs incurred within production departments, as well as the cost of services received from service departments.

A **direct department cost** is a cost assigned directly to a department (production or service) when it is incurred. For a production department, direct department costs include both *direct* product costs (direct materials and direct labor) as well as *indirect* product costs (such as indirect labor and indirect materials) incurred directly in the department. An **indirect department cost** is a cost assigned to a department as a result of an indirect allocation, or reassignment, from another department, such as a service department.

The product costing system must include a policy for assigning to products the cost of services received from service departments. For companies that use a plantwide overhead rate, the costs of all service departments are added to the indirect product costs incurred within all of the producing departments to get total plantwide manufacturing overhead, which is then assigned to products using a single overhead rate based on a common factor such as direct labor hours. For companies that use departmental overhead rates, service department costs are allocated to the production departments that utilize their services, and the allocated service department costs are added to the indirect costs incurred within the department to arrive at total departmental overhead and allocation rates. Also, as illustrated in Chapter 18, service department costs may also be assigned to products using activity-based costing. As discussed in the following Business Insight, service department cost allocation can impact the amount of revenue received for some organizations.

MID-CHAPTER REVIEW 1

Most companies have production support departments, such as payroll, human resources, and information technology that provide support services for multiple production departments. To create meaningful product and service cost information, the costs associated with support departments must be allocated to the ultimate products or services in a meaningful way.

REQUIRED
Discuss how a company using each of the product costing systems—plantwide overhead rate, department overhead rate, and activity-based costing—would handle the allocation of support department costs.

The solution to this review problem can be found on page 890.

SERVICE DEPARTMENT COST ALLOCATION

LO2 Describe the allocation of service department costs under the direct, step, and linear algebra methods.

As discussed above, service departments (maintenance, administration, information technology, security, etc.) provide a wide range of support functions, primarily for one or more production departments. These departments, which are considered essential elements in the overall manufacturing process, do not work directly on the "product" but provide auxiliary support to the producing departments. In addition to providing support for the various producing departments, some service departments also provide services to *other service departments*. For example, the payroll and personnel departments typically provide services to all departments (producing and service), and engineering may provide services to only the producing departments. Services provided by one service department to other service departments are called **interdepartment services**.

To illustrate service department cost allocations, suppose the **Dasani** Division of **The Coca-Cola Company**, has two producing departments, three service departments, and two products. The service departments and their respective service functions and cost allocation bases are as follows:

Department	Service Functions	Allocation Base
Support Services	Receiving and inventory control	Total amount of department capital investment
Engineering Resources	Production setup and engineering and testing	Number of employees
Building and Grounds	Machinery maintenance and depreciation	Amount of square footage occupied

Difficulty in choosing an allocation base for service department costs is not uncommon. For example, Dasani may have readily determined the appropriate allocation bases for the Engineering Resources and the Building and Grounds Departments but may have found the choice for Support Services to be less clear. Perhaps after conducting correlation studies, the most equitable base for allocating Support Services costs to other departments was determined to be total capital investment in the departments because they included expensive computer-tracking equipment, both manual and automated forklifts, and other material-moving equipment.

Assume direct department costs and allocation base information used to illustrate Dasani's July service department cost allocations are summarized as follows:

	Direct Department Costs	Number of Employees		Amount of Square Footage Occupied		Total Amount of Department Capital Investment	
Service departments							
Support Services	$ 27,000	15	15%	4,000	8%	—	—
Engineering Resources. . . .	20,000	—	—	2,000	4	$ 45,000	8%
Building and Grounds.	10,000	5	5	—	—	50,000	9
Producing departments							
Mixing.	40,000*	24	24	11,000	22	180,000	33
Bottling	90,000*	56	56	33,000	66	270,000	50
	$187,000	100	100%	50,000	100%	$545,000	100%

*Direct department overhead

The preceding information omitted the amount of capital investment in the Support Services Department, the number of employees in the Engineering Resources Department, and the amount of square footage used by the Building and Grounds Department. These data were omitted because a department normally does not allocate costs to itself; it allocates costs only to the departments it serves.

The three methods commonly used for service department cost allocations—direct, step, and linear algebra—are discussed in this section. Each of these methods eventually results in all service department costs being assigned to the production departments. Once this is done, Dasani can then use either department overhead rates or activity-based costing to further assign the indirect costs that are accumulated in the producing departments to the actual products. If Dasani were to use a plantwide overhead rate to allocate indirect costs, the service department costs would not be allocated to the producing departments; they would merely be added to the one plantwide indirect cost pool and allocated directly to the product using one plantwide overhead rate.

Direct Method

The **direct method** allocates all service department costs based only on the amount of services provided to the producing departments. **Exhibit 19.1** shows the flow of costs using the direct method. All arrows depicting the cost flows extend directly from service departments to producing departments; under the direct method there are no cost allocations between the service departments.

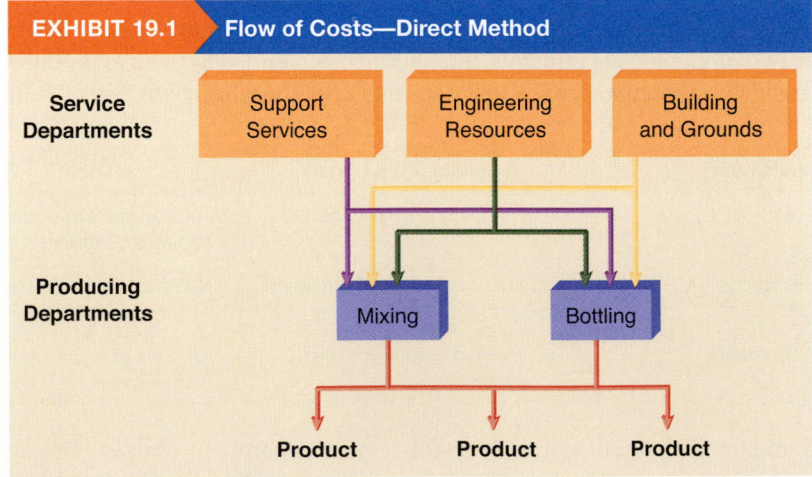

EXHIBIT 19.1   Flow of Costs—Direct Method

Exhibit 19.2 shows the service department cost allocations for the direct method. Notice the allocation base used to allocate Engineering Resources costs; only the employees in the producing departments are considered in computing the allocation percentages—24 in Mixing and 56 in Bottling, for a total of 80 employees in the allocation base. Thirty percent (24 ÷ 80) of the producing department employees work in Mixing; therefore, 30 percent of Engineering Resources costs are allocated to Mixing. Applying the same reasoning, 70 percent of Engineering Resources costs are allocated to Bottling. Similar logic is followed in computing the cost allocations for Building and Grounds and Support Services.

EXHIBIT 19.2	**Service Department Cost Allocations—Direct Method**		
	Total	**Mixing**	**Bottling**
Support Services Department			
Allocation base (capital investment)	$450,000	$180,000	$270,000
Percent of total base.	100%	40%	60%
Cost allocations	$ 27,000	$ 10,800	$ 16,200
Engineering Resources Department			
Allocation base (number of employees)	80	24	56
Percent of total base.	100%	30%	70%
Cost allocations	$ 20,000	$ 6,000	$ 14,000
Building and Grounds Department			
Allocation base (square footage occupied)	44,000	11,000	33,000
Percent of total base.	100%	25%	75%
Cost allocations	$ 10,000	$ 2,500	$ 7,500

Cost Allocation Summary

	Support Services	**Engineering Resources**	**Building and Grounds**	**Mixing**	**Bottling**	**Total**
Department cost before allocations	$27,000	$20,000	$10,000	$40,000	$ 90,000	$187,000
Cost allocations						
Support Services.	(27,000)			10,800	16,200	—
Engineering Resources		(20,000)		6,000	14,000	—
Building and Grounds			(10,000)	2,500	7,500	—
Department costs after allocations.	$ 0	$ 0	$ 0	$59,300	$127,700	$187,000

The cost allocation summary at the bottom of **Exhibit 19.2** shows that all service department costs have been allocated, decreasing the service department costs to zero and increasing the producing department overhead balances by the amounts of the respective allocations. Also, total costs are not affected by the allocations; the total of $187,000 was merely redistributed so that all costs are reassigned to the producing departments. Total department overhead costs of the producing departments after allocation of service costs are $59,300 for Mixing and $127,700 for Bottling.

The advantage of the direct method of allocating service department costs is that it is easy and convenient to use. Its primary disadvantage is that it does not recognize the costs for interdepartment services provided by one service department to another. Instead, any costs incurred to provide services to other service departments are passed directly to the producing departments. The step method improves on the allocation procedure by redirecting some of the costs to other service departments before they are finally allocated to the production departments.

Step Method

The **step method** gives partial recognition of interdepartmental services by using a methodology that allocates the service department costs *sequentially* both to the remaining service departments and the producing departments. Any indirect costs allocated to a service department in this process are added to that service department's direct costs to determine the total costs to allocate to the remaining departments. Through this procedure, all service department costs are assigned to the production departments and ultimately to the products.

To illustrate a problem that can result from using the direct method, assume that Prestige Company has two service departments, S1 and S2, and two producing departments, P1 and P2, that provide services as follows:

Provider of Services	Receiver of Services			
	S1	S2	P1	P2
S1...	0%	0%	70%	30%
S2...	50%	0%	25%	25%

If the direct method is used to allocate service department costs to the producing departments, S2 total costs will be allocated equally to the producing departments because they use the same amount of S2 services (25 percent each). Is this an equitable allocation of S2 costs? S2 actually provides half of its services to the other service department (S1), which, in turn, provides the majority of its services to P1. Assume that S2 has total direct department costs of $100,000. If the direct method is used to allocate service department costs, the entire $100,000 will be divided equally between the two producing departments, each being allocated $50,000, with no allocation to S1.

	S1	S2	P1	P2
Direct allocation of S2 to P1 and P2	$0	$(100,000)	$50,000	$50,000

Consider the following alternative allocation of the $100,000 of S2 costs that takes into account interdepartment services. First, 25 percent, or $25,000, is allocated to each of the producing departments, and 50 percent, or $50,000, is allocated to S1. Next, the $50,000 allocated to S1 from S2 is reallocated to the producing departments in proportion to the amount of services provided to them by S1: 70 percent and 30 percent, respectively. In this scenario, the $100,000 of S2 costs is ultimately allocated $60,000 to P1 and $40,000 to P2 as follows:

	S1	S2	P1	P2
Step 1:				
Allocate S2 costs to S1, P1, and P2............	$50,000	$(100,000)	$25,000	$25,000
Step 2:				
Reallocate S1 costs to P1 and P2	(50,000)	0	35,000	15,000
Total allocation of S2 costs via step method	$ 0	$ 0	$60,000	$40,000

This calculation shows only the ultimate allocation of S2 costs. Of course, any S1 direct department costs would also have to be allocated to P1 and P2 on a 70:30 basis. If interdepartmental services are ignored, P1 is allocated only $50,000 of S2 costs; by considering interdepartmental services, P1 is allocated $60,000. Certainly, a more accurate measure of both the direct and indirect services received by P1 from S2 is $60,000, not $50,000.

As long as all producing departments use approximately the same percentage of services of each service department, the direct method provides a reasonably accurate cost assignment. In this example, the percentages of services used by the producing departments were quite different: 70 percent and 30 percent for S1, and 50 percent and 50 percent for S2. In such situations, the direct method can result in significantly different allocations.

The step method is illustrated graphically in **Exhibit 19.3** for Dasani. Notice the sequence of the allocations: Engineering Resources, Support Services, and Building and Grounds.

When using the step method, the sequence of allocation is typically based on the relative percentage of services provided to other service departments, with the largest provider of interdepartmental services allocated first and the smallest provider of interdepartmental services allocated last. For Dasani, Engineering Resources is allocated first because, of the three service departments, it provides the largest percentage (20 percent) of its services to other service departments: 15 percent to Support Services and 5 percent to Building and Grounds (see previous cost allocation data). Building and Grounds is allocated last because it provides the least amount (12 percent) of its services to other service departments: 8 percent to Support Services and 4 percent to Engineering Resources. The service department cost allocations for Dasani using the step method are shown in **Exhibit 19.4**.

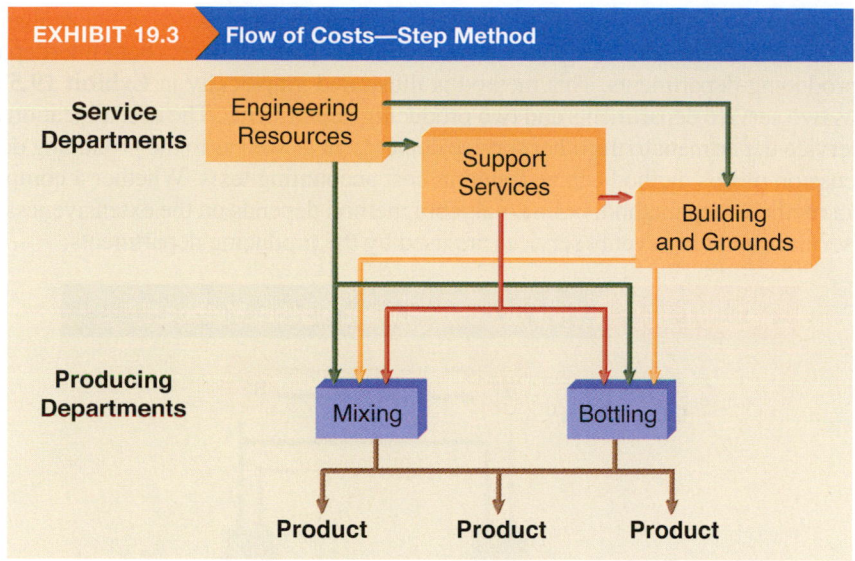

EXHIBIT 19.3   **Flow of Costs—Step Method**

EXHIBIT 19.4   **Service Department Cost Allocations—Step Method**

	Total	Support Services	Building and Grounds	Mixing	Bottling
Engineering Resources Department					
Allocation base (number of employees)	100	15	5	24	56
Percent of total base.	100%	15%	5%	24%	56%
Cost allocations	$20,000	$3,000	$1,000	$4,800	$11,200
Support Services Department					
Allocation base (capital investment)	$500,000		$50,000	$180,000	$270,000
Percent of total base.	100%		10%	36%	54%
Cost allocations	$30,000		$3,000	$10,800	$16,200
Building and Grounds Department					
Allocation base (square footage occupied)	44,000			11,000	33,000
Percent of total base.	100%			25%	75%
Cost allocations	$14,000			$3,500	$10,500

Cost Allocation Summary

	Engineering Resources	Support Services	Building and Grounds	Mixing	Bottling	Total
Department costs before allocations	$ 20,000	$ 27,000	$ 10,000	$40,000	$ 90,000	$187,000
Cost allocations						
Engineering Resources.	(20,000)	3,000	1,000	4,800	11,200	—
Support Services.		(30,000)	3,000	10,800	16,200	—
Building and Grounds			(14,000)	3,500	10,500	—
Department costs after allocations.	$ 0	$ 0	$ 0	$59,100	$127,900	$187,000

Linear Algebra (Reciprocal) Method

The disadvantage of the step method is that it provides only partial recognition of interdepartmental services. For Dasani, the step method recognizes Engineering Resources services provided to the other two service departments; however, no services received by Engineering Resources from the other two departments are recognized. Similarly, services from Support Services to Building and Grounds are recognized, but not the reverse. To achieve the most mathematically accurate service department cost allocation, there should be full recognition of services between service departments as well as between service and producing departments. This requires using the linear algebra method, sometimes called the *reciprocal method*. The **linear algebra (reciprocal) method** uses a series of linear algebraic equations, which are solved simultaneously, to allocate service department costs both interdepartmentally and to the producing departments. This method is illustrated graphically in **Exhibit 19.5** for a company that has two service departments and two producing departments. The cost allocation arrows run from each service department to the other service department as well as to the producing departments. Further discussion of this method can be found in cost accounting texts. Whether a company should use the direct method, step method, or linear algebra method depends on the extensiveness of interdepartmental services and how evenly services are used by the producing departments.

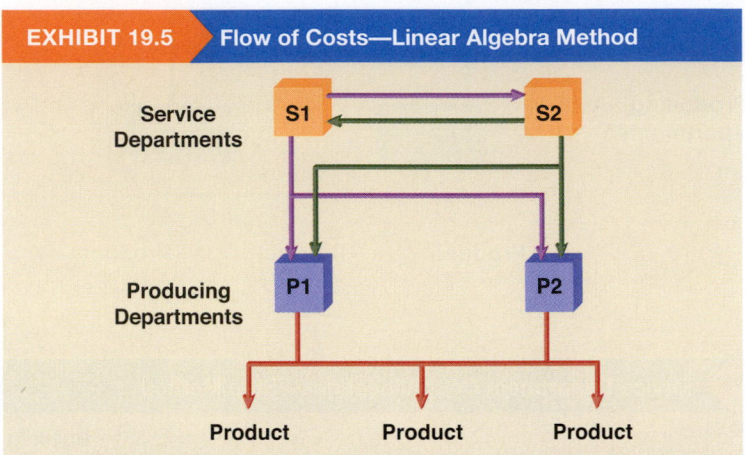

EXHIBIT 19.5 Flow of Costs—Linear Algebra Method

YOU MAKE THE CALL

You are the Controller As the person responsible for the product costing system, you are trying to decide which method is best to use in allocating service department costs to the producing departments and to the products. Some of the service departments provide services only to producing departments; whereas, others provide services to both producing and service departments. You would like to use the method that provides reliable cost measurements, but without creating more costs than the benefits derived. Which method do you recommend? [Answer, p. 879]

Dual Rates

When allocating service department costs, it can be useful to provide separate allocations for fixed costs and variable costs. This will result in cost allocations that more accurately reflect the factors that drive costs. The capacity provided most often drives fixed costs, whereas some type of actual activity usually drives variable costs. Dual rates involve establishing separate bases for allocating fixed and variable costs. Dual rates may be used for one or all service departments, depending on the size and nature of the costs in each service department. They may also be used in conjunction with the direct, step, or linear algebra methods.

It is important to remember the relationship between capacity and cost when selecting the allocation method. Total variable costs change as activity changes. Fixed costs, however, are the same whether the activity is at or below capacity. Fixed costs should usually be allocated based on the relative capacity provided the benefiting department, while variable costs should be allocated on the basis of actual usage. The allocation methods and bases also may be different for variable and fixed costs.

Fixed costs based on capacity provided eliminates the possibility that the amount of the cost allocation to one department is affected by the level of services utilized by other departments. When fixed service department costs are allocated based on the capacity provided to the user department, managers of the user departments are charged for that capacity whether they use it or not, and their use of services has no effect on the amount of costs allocated to other departments. A benefit of this allocation system is that it reduces the temptation for managers to avoid or delay services to minimize fixed cost allocations to their departments. Dual rates are examined in more detail in most cost accounting texts.

MID-CHAPTER REVIEW 2

Suppose a **Buckle** retail store is organized into four departments: Women's Apparel, Men's Apparel, Administrative Services, and Facilities Services. The first two departments are the primary producing departments; the last two departments provide services to the producing departments as well as to each other. Top management has decided that, for internal reporting purposes, the cost of service department operations should be allocated to the producing departments. Administrative Services costs are allocated on the basis of the number of employees, and Facilities Services costs are allocated based on the amount of square footage of floor space occupied. Hypothetical data pertaining to the cost allocations for February 2017 are as follows:

Department	Direct Department Cost	Number of Employees	Square Footage Occupied
Women's Apparel	$ 60,000	15	15,000
Men's Apparel	50,000	9	7,500
Administrative Services	18,000	3	2,500
Facilities Services	12,000	2	1,000
Total	$140,000	29	26,000

REQUIRED

a. Determine the amount of service department costs to be allocated to the producing departments under both the *direct method* and the *step method* of service department cost allocation.
b. Discuss the *linear algebra method* of service department cost allocation, explaining circumstances when it should be considered over the direct and step methods.
c. Should Buckle consider using the linear algebra method?

The solution to this review problem can be found on pages 891–892.

LEAN PRODUCTION AND JUST-IN-TIME INVENTORY MANAGEMENT

LO3 Understand lean production and just-in-time inventory management.

3

Previously, our discussions about inventories have centered around how to measure the cost of products. A related issue is how to manage the production process and physical inventory levels. Cost accounting textbooks, as well as operations management textbooks, usually discuss models that have been used for decades to determine the economic order quantities for products, given the particular level of inventory a company wants to maintain. Although these models are still relevant in many situations, managing the production process and inventory levels has changed dramatically for companies that have adopted a value chain approach to management. No longer do most managers consider only their company's strategies, goals, and objectives in deciding the characteristics and quantities of inventory that should be acquired or produced and maintained.

A value chain approach to inventory management requires that managers consider their suppliers' and customers' strategies, goals, and objectives as well if they hope to compete successfully in a global marketplace. Computer technology has affected the way inventories are manufactured and handled (using robotics, fully computerized manufacturing and product handling systems, bar code identification systems, etc.), and it is changing the way companies relate to other parties in the value chain. It has spawned worldwide use of alternative inventory production and management techniques and processes including just-in-time (JIT) inventory management and lean production methods.

Just-in-time (JIT) inventory management is a comprehensive inventory management philosophy that emerged in the 1970s that stresses policies, procedures, and attitudes by managers and other workers that result in the efficient production of high-quality goods while maintaining the minimum level of inventories. JIT is often described simply as an inventory model that maintains only the level of inventories required to meet current production and sales requirements, but it is, in reality, much more than that. The key elements of the JIT philosophy, which has come to be known as the "lean production" philosophy, include increased coordination throughout the value chain, reduced inventory, reduced production times, increased product quality, and increased employee involvement and empowerment.

In sum, the concept of a JIT/lean approach is that in a manufacturing environment, the customers pull the production through the system with customer orders. Instead of the business making the decisions of what and when to produce, the customer does. JIT/lean production is a system aimed at reducing or eliminating waste, increasing cost efficiency, and securing a competitive advantage. Accordingly, it emphasizes a nimble production process with small lot sizes, short setup and changeover times, effective and efficient quality controls, a minimum number of bottlenecks and backups, and maximum efficiency of people.

Reducing Incoming Materials Inventory

The JIT/lean approach to reducing incoming materials includes these elements:

1. Developing long-term relationships with a limited number of vendors.
2. Selecting vendors on the basis of service and material quality, as well as price.
3. Establishing procedures for key employees to order materials for current needs directly from approved vendors.
4. Accepting vendor deliveries directly to the shop floor, and only as needed.

When fully implemented, these steps minimize or eliminate many materials inventories. Sufficient materials would be on hand to meet only immediate needs, and the materials inventories in the manufacturing setting are located on the shop floor.

To achieve this reduction, it is apparent that vendors and buyers must work as a team and that key employees must be involved in decision making. The goal of the JIT approach to purchasing is not to shift materials carrying costs to vendors. A close, long-term working relationship between purchasers and vendors should be beneficial to both. Purchasers' scheduling information is provided to vendors so that vendors also can reduce inventories and minimize costs. Vendors are therefore able to manufacture small batches frequently, rather than manufacturing large batches infrequently. Further, vendors are more confident of future sales.

BUSINESS INSIGHT

Costs of Mismanaged Inventories   Fast fashion requires attentive inventory management. Updating product lines several times a year and moving inventory from factory to shelf quickly are essential. Clothing companies have struggled to keep this pace using overseas production. The troubled clothing manufacturer **American Apparel**, with its LA-based production and design, should have been well positioned to lead the fast-fashion revolution as other manufacturers struggled to "re-shore" production. The brand should have been able to produce new styles quickly. However, lawsuits and mismanagement led to supply chain issues.

Supply chain issues led to an excess stock of clothes. In an industry where products are outdated in mere months, it is almost impossible to sell through these stocks. At American Apparel, unsold inventory resulted in styles staying on the shelf for up to four years. Shoppers turned away from stores when they came looking for new trends and found the same designs as the previous year. For a fast-fashion brand to work, the time from design to release of clothing items in stores needs to be minimized. Low sales made the inventory problems even worse. Together, these issues contributed to the end of the founder's tenure as CEO, and to the company's eventual bankruptcy.

Sources: "American Apparel: Ticking Clock," *Financial Times*, June 13, 2015, London edition: 20.
Sujeet Indap, "A Plan to Move from Chaotic to Iconic," *Financial Times*, July 10, 2015, London edition: 16.

Reducing Work-in-Process Inventory

Reducing the total time required to complete a process, or the **cycle time**, is the key to reducing work-in-process inventories and is central to a lean production approach. In a manufacturing organization, cycle time is composed of the time needed for setup, processing, movement, waiting, and inspection. **Setup time** is the time required to prepare equipment to produce a specific product, or to change from producing one product to another product. **Processing time** is the time spent working on units. **Movement time** is the time units spend moving between work or inspection stations. **Waiting time** is the time units spend in temporary storage waiting to be processed, moved, or inspected. **Inspection time** is the amount of time it takes units to be inspected. Of the five elements of cycle time, only processing time adds value to the product. Efforts to reduce cycle time are appropriate for both continuous and batch production.

Devising means of reducing setup times will directly reduce the cycle time for batch production and thus reduce setup costs. Setup times can also be reduced by shifting from batch to continuous production whenever practical. Rearranging the shop floor to eliminate unnecessary movements of materials can help reduce movement time for both continuous and batch production.

Many companies have created **quality circles**, which are groups of employees involved in production who have the authority, within certain parameters, to address and resolve quality problems as they occur, without seeking management approval. Giving employees more authority and responsibility for quality, including the right to stop production whenever quality problems are noted, can reduce the need for separate inspection time.

Waiting time can be reduced by moving from a materials push to a materials pull approach to production. Under a traditional **materials push system,** employees work to reduce the pile of inventory building up at their workstations. Workers at each station remove materials from an in-process storage area, complete their operation, and place the output in another in-process storage area. Hence, they *push* the work to the next workstation. The emphasis is on production efficiency at each station. In a push system, one of the functions of work-in-process inventory is to help make workstations independent of each other. Inventories are large enough to allow for variations in processing speeds, for discarding defective units without interrupting production, and for machine downtime.

Under a **materials pull system** (often called a **Kanban system**), employees at each station work to provide inventory for the next workstation only as needed. (*Kanban*, the Japanese word for *card*, is a system created in Japan that originally used cards to indicate that a department needed additional components.) The building of excess inventories is strictly prohibited. When the number of units in inventory reaches a specified limit, work at the station stops until workers at a subsequent station pull a unit from the in-process storage area. Hence, the *pull* of inventory by a subsequent station authorizes production to continue.

A pull, or Kanban, system's low inventory levels require a team effort. To avoid idle time, processing speeds must be balanced and equipment must be kept in good repair. Quality problems are identified immediately, and the low inventory levels require immediate correction of quality problems. To make a pull system work, management must accept the notion that it is better to have employees idle than to have them building excess inventory. A pull system also requires careful planning by management and active participation in decision making by employees. A lean production process involves minimizing cycle time, eliminating waste, producing inventory only as needed, and ensuring the highest level of quality and efficiency. To achieve these results on a continuing basis, there is a strong emphasis on continuous improvement programs (see Chapter 20).

BUSINESS INSIGHT

Inventory Management and Supply Chain Risk   Toyota's just-in-time inventory system is central to the company's global manufacturing success; however, this system also creates vulnerabilities. **Toyota** keeps as little inventory on site as possible—it holds only several hours' worth of parts, working with suppliers to maintain a steady supply of parts for production. This lowers cost and increases quality control, as defects are noticed immediately. However, Toyota is vulnerable to events affecting its suppliers.

In 1997, a fire at a supplier halted Toyota's production for five days. A 2007 earthquake left the Toyota plants unscathed but still stopped production due to damage at the site of their supplier of piston rings. The massive 2011 earthquake affected 660 of Toyota's suppliers. Since 2011 Toyota has aggressively sought to manage this risk. While some earthquake risk is inherent in manufacturing in Japan, Toyota has worked with suppliers to diversify geographically. These measures should reduce the supply chain effects of future disasters.

Source: Yoko Kubota, "Japan Earthquakes Rattle Toyota's Vulnerable Supply Chain," *Wall Street Journal*, April 19, 2016.
Link: http://www.wsj.com/articles/japan-earthquakes-rattle-toyotas-supply-chain-1460986805

Reducing Finished Goods Inventory

Finished goods inventory can be reduced by reducing cycle time and by better predicting customer demand for finished units. Lowering cycle times reduces the need for speculative inventories. If finished goods can be replenished quickly, the need diminishes for large inventory levels to satisfy customer needs and to provide for unanticipated fluctuations in customer orders. Anticipating customers' demand for goods can be improved by adopting a value chain approach to inventory management by which the manufacturer or supplier is working as a partner with its customers to meet their inventory needs. This frequently involves having online computer access to customers' inventory levels on a real-time basis and being able to synchronize changes in production with changes in customers' inventory levels as they occur.

Sharing this type of information obviously requires an enormous amount of mutual trust between a manufacturer or supplier and its customers, but it is becoming increasingly common among world-class organizations. An example of this type of vendor-customer relationship is the relationship between **Procter & Gamble**, one of the world's largest consumer products companies, and its largest customer, **Wal-Mart**. By having access to Wal-Mart's computer inventory system, Procter & Gamble is better able to determine and fill Wal-Mart's specific needs for products, such as disposable diapers.

MID-CHAPTER REVIEW 3

1. An element of lean production and just-in-time inventory management.
2. An element of a traditional inventory model that focuses on a partial level of inventory that a company wants to maintain.
3. Cycle time.

REQUIRED

For each of the statements *a–f* below, identify which of the concepts listed in above is the most relevant. You can use each concept more than once.

_____ *a.* Nimble production process with small lot sizes and short setup and changeover times.
_____ *b.* Material push system.
_____ *c.* Key to managing work-in-process inventories and central to a lean production approach.
_____ *d.* Selecting venders on the basis of service and material quality, as well as price.
_____ *e.* Accepting vendor deliveries directly to the shop floor, and only as needed.
_____ *f.* Employees at each station work to provide inventory for the next workstation only as needed (Kanban system).

The solution to this review problem can be found on page 892.

LO4 Explain how lean production and just-in-time affect performance evaluation and recordkeeping.

PERFORMANCE EVALUATION AND RECORDKEEPING WITH LEAN PRODUCTION AND JIT

Movement toward a JIT/lean production philosophy requires changes in performance evaluation procedures and offers opportunities for significant reductions in recordkeeping costs. These changes are discussed in this section.

Performance Evaluation

JIT regards inventory as something to be eliminated. Hence, in a manufacturing organization, inventories are kept as small as possible. Under the JIT ideal, inventories do not exist because vendors deliver raw materials in small batches directly to the shop floor. JIT also strives to minimize, or eliminate, work-in-process inventory by minimizing the non-processing elements of cycle time and by having processing times as short as possible.

Dysfunctional Effects of Traditional Performance Measures A potential conflict exists between the goals of JIT and lean production and those of traditional performance measures applied at the level of the department or cost center. Although lean production emphasizes overall efficiency, many traditional performance measures emphasize local (departmental) cost savings and local (departmental) efficiency. Consider the following traditional performance measures for a purchasing agent and a departmental production supervisor:

- To achieve quantity discounts and favorable prices, a purchasing agent might order excess inventory, thereby increasing subsequent storage, obsolescence, and handling costs.

- To obtain a low price, a purchasing agent might order from a supplier whose goods have not been certified as meeting quality specifications, thereby causing subsequent inspection, rework, and spoilage costs, and perhaps, dissatisfied customers further down the value chain.

- To avoid having idle employees and equipment, a supervisor might refuse to halt production to determine the cause of a quality problem, thereby increasing inspection, rework, and spoilage costs.

- To obtain low fixed costs per unit under absorption costing, a supervisor might produce in excess of current needs (preferably in long production runs), thereby causing subsequent increases in storage, obsolescence, and handling costs.

Performance Measures Under Lean Production and JIT In accordance with the goal of eliminating inventory and reducing cycle time to processing time, JIT supportive performance measures emphasize inventory turnover, cycle time, and **cycle efficiency** (the ratio of value-added to non-value-added manufacturing activities).

When applied to a specific item of raw materials or finished goods, **inventory turnover** is computed as the annual demand in units divided by the average inventory in units:

$$\text{Inventory turnover} = \frac{\textbf{Annual demand in units}}{\textbf{Average inventory in units}}$$

Progress toward the goal of reducing inventory is measured by comparing successive inventory turnover ratios. Generally, the higher the inventory turnover, the better.

When measured with inventory dollars instead of inventory units, inventory turnover can be used as a measure of the organization's overall success in reducing inventory, or in increasing sales in relation to inventories. This financial measure can be derived directly from a firm's financial statements.

$$\text{Inventory turnover} = \frac{\textbf{Cost of goods sold}}{\textbf{Average inventory (in dollars)}}$$

Another ratio often used to monitor the effectiveness of inventory levels in retail organizations, such as **Whole Foods** or **Macy's**, is gross margin return on inventory investment (GMROI), calculated as follows:

$$\text{GMROI} = \frac{\textbf{Gross margin (in dollars)}}{\textbf{Average inventory (in dollars)}}$$

Cycle time is a measure of the total time required to produce one unit of a product:

$$\frac{\textbf{Cycle}}{\textbf{time}} = \frac{\textbf{Setup}}{\textbf{time}} + \frac{\textbf{Processing}}{\textbf{time}} + \frac{\textbf{Movement}}{\textbf{time}} + \frac{\textbf{Waiting}}{\textbf{time}} + \frac{\textbf{Inspection}}{\textbf{time}}$$

Under ideal circumstances, cycle time would consist of only processing time, and processing time would be as low as possible. Only processing time adds value to the product; hence, the time required for all other activities should be driven toward zero. The use of flexible manufacturing systems, properly sequencing jobs, and properly placing tools will minimize setup time. If the shop floor is optimally arranged, workers pass products directly from one workstation to the next. If production is optimally scheduled, inventory will not wait in temporary storage between workstations. If raw materials are of high quality and products are manufactured so that they always conform to specifications, separate inspection activities are not needed.

Cycle efficiency is computed as the ratio of processing time to total cycle time:

$$\text{Cycle efficiency} = \frac{\text{Processing time}}{\text{Cycle time}}$$

The highest cycle efficiency possible is always sought. If all non-value-added activities are eliminated, this ratio equals one.

Simplified Recordkeeping

Lean production and JIT enable significant reductions in the number of accounting transactions required for purchasing and production activities. This results in cost savings for bookkeeping activities and in shifting accounting resources from detailed bookkeeping to the development of more useful activity cost data.

Purchasing In a traditional accounting system, every purchase results in the preparation of several documents. Additional documents are prepared for the issuance of raw materials to the factory. JIT, on the other hand, attempts to minimize inventory levels and stresses long-term relationships with a limited number of vendors who have demonstrated their ability to provide quality raw materials on a timely basis, as well as at a competitive price. Under a JIT inventory system, a company often has standing purchase orders for specified materials from specified vendors at specified prices. Production personnel are authorized to requisition materials directly from authorized vendors, who deliver limited quantities of materials as needed directly to the shop floor. Production personnel verify receipt of the raw materials. Periodically, each vendor sends an invoice for several shipments, which the company acknowledges and pays.

Product Costing Another advantage of a lean production system is that it reduces the amount of detailed bookkeeping required for financial accounting purposes. If ending inventories are nonexistent, or so small that the costs assigned to them are insignificant in comparison with the costs assigned to Cost of Goods Sold, it makes little sense to track product costs through several inventory accounts. Instead of using a traditional product cost accounting system (as illustrated in Chapter 17), firms that have implemented JIT often use what is sometimes referred to as a backflush approach to accounting for product costs.

Under **backflush costing**, all costs of direct materials, direct labor, and manufacturing overhead are assigned as incurred to Cost of Goods Sold. If there are no inventories on hand at the end of the period, no additional steps are required. However, if there are inventories on hand at year-end, costs are backed out of Cost of Goods Sold and assigned to the appropriate inventory accounts. For a complete discussion of backflush costing, refer to a cost accounting text.

Also under a JIT inventory approach, many of the distinctions and arguments regarding absorption versus variable costing are moot (see Appendix 17A). If the quantity of inventory is insignificant, it matters little whether inventory cost includes only variable manufacturing costs or both variable and fixed manufacturing costs. Whether absorption or variable costing is used, the total cost assigned to inventory on the balance sheet will be small, and there is little difference in the amount of profit reported on the income statement.

As we discussed in previous chapters, traditional product costing systems go to great lengths to calculate the materials, labor, and manufacturing overhead cost per unit for each unit produced. Overhead is typically assigned to inventory using a predetermined overhead rate based on an assumed volume-based driver such as direct labor hours or machine hours. If actual production is less than budgeted production, there will be underapplied overhead, which is usually written off as an expense of the period. To avoid this expense, managers are often motivated to overproduce product in order to ensure that all overhead is allocated to product. Also, by budgeting a large amount of produced units, fixed overhead cost is spread over more units, resulting in a lower cost per unit. Such overproduction is equivalent to a cardinal sin in a lean production company.

As we will see in Chapter 22, many companies also adopt standard cost systems where they account for product cost components on both an actual and budgeted cost basis, with variances between actual cost and standard (or allowed) costs reported on the internal performance reports as increased expenses if they are unfavorable and as a reduction of expenses if they are favorable. In such cases, managers are motivated to maximize favorable variances and minimize or eliminate unfavorable variances. Such systems of reporting often lead managers to actions that are contrary to the lean production philosophy.

MID-CHAPTER REVIEW 4

Assume **Titleist** is trying to decide which automated production line to use to produce its new Pro VI golf balls. Suppose the two best systems under consideration have the following estimated performance characteristics, based on minutes per 1,000 balls produced:

	System A	System B
Setup time	25	10
Movement time from start to finish	10	14
Waiting time	3	16
Inspection time	5	7
Processing time	40	30
Total time in minutes	83	77

REQUIRED

a. Determine the cycle time per batch for each system.
b. Determine the cycle efficiency for each system.
c. Which system do you recommend and why?
d. Assuming Titleist is a "lean" manufacturer, what improvements in the selected system is it likely to pursue?

The solution to this review problem can be found on page 892.

INCREASED FOCUS ON DATA-DRIVEN DECISION MAKING

LO5 Evaulate ways in which the increasing availability of data might change the responsibilities of managerial accountants.

Increased access to data is changing the landscape of managerial accounting. Business leaders should be able to increasingly rely on data to answer difficult questions. Which products or services are most profitable? What are the best prices to charge for our services? Which manufacturing process is the most efficient? When business leaders can rely on data to answer these types of questions, they can then focus efforts on understanding which questions to ask. What is our business's core competency? What is our organization's strategic position (as discussed in Chapter 13)? Which products or services should we offer, or in which markets should we compete?

In order to rely on data, it must be accurate and timely. Costing models such as ABC, step, and linear algebra can help provide more accurate information on product costs. However, the accuracy of this data relies on management choosing relevant activity cost pools and cost drivers, and reasonable additional assumptions. Further, employees throughout the organization must understand and support the costing model. The concept of GIGO (garbage in, garbage out) refers to the idea that incorrect information going into a system results in incorrect data coming out. The system does not magically fix the information.[1]

Even when analysts have reliable and timely data, there are risks associated with data-driven decision making. A common issue is the misunderstanding of correlation versus causation. The

---
[1] Rod Koch, "Big Data or Big Empathy," *Strategic Finance*, December 1, 2015.

idea behind big data analytics is to uncover hidden patterns and correlation among activities, and then to use this information to make decisions and to predict outcomes.[2] Often, just because there is a high correlation between two events, it does not mean that one caused the other. Using this information to then extrapolate further outcomes will be inaccurate. An example often referenced to demonstrate this issue is the windmill. The faster the windmill rotates, the more wind can be observed. Can we conclude that windmills cause wind? As ice cream sales increase, the rate of drowning increases. Does ice cream consumption cause drowning? These examples make it fairly obvious that one event does not cause the other, even though they are correlated. However, as managers are inundated with data, it may not always be so easy to understand the distinction between correlation and causation, resulting in poor decision making.

As the environment changes in terms of the availability of managerial accounting information, so too do the skills required of managerial accountants. **Exhibit 19.6** summarizes the research conducted by the IMA to better understand the talent gap between the skills business leaders perceive as important factors of success and the skills their finance teams possess.[3] Finance professionals seem to be reasonably prepared with the more traditional skills such as financial analysis; budgeting, planning, and forecasting; and operations analysis. However, a more significant talent gap exists related to data skills such as technological acumen; identifying key data trends; data mining and extraction; and statistical modeling and data analysis skills. The study also emphasizes that softer skills are also increasingly sought. Business leaders expect finance teams to be capable of using data to improve business performance through skills such as process improvement, strategic thinking and execution, adaptability to change, and communications.

EXHIBIT 19.6	Technical Skills Gap	Important to Success	Possessed by Your Team	Talent Gap
Financial analysis		87%	69%	18%
Budgeting, planning, and forecasting		85%	63%	22%
Operational analysis		82%	54%	28%
Cost management		81%	61%	20%
Technological acumen		77%	50%	27%
Identifying key data trends		75%	46%	29%
Data mining and extraction		71%	43%	28%
Statistical modeling and data analysis		62%	35%	27%
Enterprise resource planning (ERP) systems		61%	40%	21%
Customer lifetime value (CLV)		55%	32%	23%

CHAPTER-END REVIEW

Increased access to data can help business leaders make better and more timely decisions. This can also allow them to focus more of their efforts toward more strategic analysis and thinking. Even though there are many benefits to the increasing availability of data, there are also risks and concerns.

REQUIRED
Discuss some accompanying risks and concerns of growing access to big data.

The solution to this review problem can be found on page 893.

---

[2] http://www.sas.com/en_us/insights/analytics/big-data-analytics.html

[3] Kip Krumweide, "Building a Team to Capitalize on the Promise of Big Data," *IMA*, January 2016.

GUIDANCE ANSWERS . . . YOU MAKE THE CALL

You are the Controller   Designing any information processing system is a matter of weighing benefits with the costs of designing and operating the system. The same is true for a cost allocation system. Also, you have to decide how the cost information will be used. If it is used only for external financial reporting purposes, a high degree of precision may not be necessary. However, if it is used to determine the most profitable product mix, it may be crucial to have the most precise cost information. For the service departments that provide only services to producing departments and that receive no services from other service departments, a direct allocation method might be adequate. For departments that provide and/or receive interdepartmental services, you should consider using either a step or linear algebra approach to assigning costs. Whether you use a direct, step or linear algebra approach, you will have to decide whether to assign the costs using a single volume-based cost driver (such as square footage or number of employees) or using multiple cost drivers that reflect the actual activities performed. In most cases, the ABC approach (discussed in Chapter 18) will give a higher level of precision, but at considerably greater cost.

KEY RATIOS

$$\text{Inventory turnover} = \frac{\text{Annual demand in units}}{\text{Average inventory in units}}$$

$$\text{Inventory turnover} = \frac{\text{Cost of goods sold}}{\text{Average inventory (in dollars)}}$$

$$\text{Gross margin return on inventory investment} = \frac{\text{Gross margin (in dollars)}}{\text{Average inventory (in dollars)}}$$

$$\frac{\text{Cycle}}{\text{time}} = \frac{\text{Setup}}{\text{time}} + \frac{\text{Processing}}{\text{time}} + \frac{\text{Movement}}{\text{time}} + \frac{\text{Waiting}}{\text{time}} + \frac{\text{Inspection}}{\text{time}}$$

$$\text{Cycle efficiency} = \frac{\text{Processing time}}{\text{Cycle time}}$$

KEY TERMS

backflush costing, 876
cycle efficiency, 875
cycle time, 872
direct department cost, 864
direct method, 866
indirect department cost, 864
inspection time, 873
interdepartment services, 865

inventory turnover, 875
just-in-time (JIT) inventory management, 871
Kanban system, 873
linear algebra (reciprocal) method, 870
materials pull system, 873
materials push system, 873

movement time, 873
processing time, 873
quality circles, 873
service departments, 864
setup time, 873
step method, 867
waiting time, 873

Assignments with the ⓂⒷⒸ logo in the margin are available in *my*BusinessCourse.
See the Preface of the book for details.

MULTIPLE CHOICE

Multiple Choice Answers
1. d 2. a 3. c 4. c 5. d 6. d 7. c

1. Which of the following statements regarding production and service department costs is incorrect?
   a. For a production department, direct department costs include both direct and indirect product costs.
   b. An indirect department cost is a cost assigned to a department as a result of a reassignment from another service department.
   c. Companies that use departmental overhead rates likely allocate service department costs to production departments.
   d. Companies that use activity-based costing likely do not allocate service department costs to production departments.

2. The following budgeted information pertains to Trawbing Company:

	Service Departments		Producing Departments	
	Human Resources	Facilities	Mixing	Molding
Direct department costs..............	$75,000	$50,000	$520,000	$860,000
Direct labor hours...................	6,000	4,000	20,000	36,000
Square footage.....................	2,000	3,000	24,000	36,000
# of employees....................	3	2	18	12

   The direct department costs for Mixing and Molding represent the direct department overhead costs of those departments, not including any direct material or direct labor. Human Resource Department costs are assigned to other departments based on the number of employees, and Facilities Department costs are assigned to other departments based on square footage occupied. If the direct method is used to allocate service department costs to the producing departments, the total budgeted overhead for the Molding Department after service department costs are allocated is
   a. $920,000.00
   b. $585,000.00
   c. $584,062.50
   d. $920,937.50

3. Refer to the previous question. If the step method is used to allocate service departments to the producing departments, the total budgeted overhead for the Mixing Department after service department costs are allocated is (round all calculations to two decimal places)
   a. $920,000.00
   b. $585,000.00
   c. $584,062.50
   d. $920,937.50

4. Refer to question 2 above. Assume that the Molding Department uses a predetermined overhead rate for assigning overhead costs to products based on budgeted total overhead after service department costs are allocated using the direct allocation method. The predetermined overhead rate for the Molding Department is (round all calculations to two decimal places)
   a. $26.88 per direct labor hour
   b. $23.89 per direct labor hour
   c. $25.56 per direct labor hour
   d. $29.25 per direct labor hour

5. The key elements of JIT/lean production include which of the following?
   a. Increased coordination throughout the value chain
   b. Reduced inventories and production times
   c. Increased product quality and employee empowerment
   d. All of the above are elements of JIT/lean production

6. Topaz Company sold and produced 40,000 units of product at a cost of $1,200,000 for a sales price of $60 per unit during the most recent year. Throughout the year its average inventory was 4,000 units with an average cost of $120,000. Based on this information, which of the following cannot be determined about Topaz's inventory management performance?
   a. Topaz's inventory turnover in units was 10 times.
   b. Topaz's gross margin return on average inventory investment was 1,000%.
   c. Topaz's inventory turnover in dollars was 10 times.
   d. Topaz's production cycle efficiency was 100%.

7. Which of the following is not a characteristic of a business environment with increasing availability of data?
   a. There is potential risk of misinterpretation between correlation and causation.
   b. It is increasingly important that data be accurate and timely.
   c. There is decreasing reliance on the softer skills such as strategic analysis and communication.
   d. The largest technical skills talent gaps occur in areas of identifying key data trends and data mining and extraction.

QUESTIONS

Q19-1. Distinguish between the following sets of terms:
   a. Direct product costs and indirect product costs.
   b. Direct department costs and indirect department costs.

Q19-2. Define the terms direct cost and indirect cost.

Q19-3. Differentiate between cost assignment and cost allocation.

Q19-4. Explain how a cost item can be both a direct cost and an indirect cost.

Q19-5. What is the primary advantage of separately allocating fixed and variable indirect costs?

Q19-6. Define interdepartmental services.

Q19-7. To what extent are interdepartmental services recognized under the direct, step, and linear algebra methods of service department cost allocation?

Q19-8. Is it feasible to assign interdepartmental services to production departments using ABC?

Q19-9. Explain the concept of just-in-time inventory management.

Q19-10. What are the major elements of lean production?

Q19-11. What is the relationship between JIT and the lean production concept?

Q19-12. Explain how computer technology has affected the way companies approach JIT inventory management and lean production methods.

Q19-13. What elements of the JIT approach contribute to reducing materials inventories?

Q19-14. Define and identify the elements of cycle time. Which of these elements adds value to the product?

Q19-15. Explain briefly how JIT/lean production benefits organizations that take a value-chain approach to management.

Q19-16. Explain how traditional performance evaluation systems using standard costs conflict with the lean production concept.

MINI EXERCISES

M19-17. Allocating Service Department Costs: Allocation Basis Alternatives

Weld-Rite Fabricators has two producing departments, P1 and P2, and one service department, S1. Estimated direct overhead costs per month are as follows:

P1	$300,000
P2	500,000
S1	182,000

LO2

Other data follow:

	P1	P2
Number of employees	150	50
Production capacity (units)...................................	100,000	60,000
Space occupied (square feet)................................	5,000	15,000
Five-year average percent of S1's service output used............	65%	35%

REQUIRED

a. For each of the following allocation bases, determine the total estimated overhead cost for P1 and P2 after allocating S1 cost to the producing departments.

1. Number of employees
2. Production capacity in units
3. Space occupied
4. Five-year average percentage of S1 services used
5. Estimated direct overhead costs. (Round your answer to the nearest dollar.)

b. For each of the five allocation bases, explain the circumstances (including examples) under which each allocation base might be most appropriately used to allocate service department cost in a manufacturing plant such as Weld-Rite Fabricators. Also, discuss the advantages and disadvantages that might result from using each of the allocation bases.

LO2 **M19-18. Indirect Cost Allocation: Direct Method**

Charlie Manufacturing Company has two production departments, Melting and Molding. Direct general plant management and plant security costs benefit both production departments. Charlie allocates general plant management costs on the basis of the number of production employees and plant security costs on the basis of space occupied by the production departments. In November, the following overhead costs were recorded:

Melting Department direct overhead	$350,000
Molding Department direct overhead................................	600,000
General plant management	180,000
Plant security	70,000

Other pertinent data follow:

	Melting	Molding
Number of employees	50	90
Space occupied (square feet)...............................	20,000	80,000
Machine hours	10,000	2,000
Direct labor hours..	4,000	20,000

REQUIRED

a. Prepare a schedule allocating general plant management costs and plant security costs to the Melting and Molding Departments.

b. Determine the total departmental overhead costs for the Melting and Molding Departments.

c. Assuming the Melting Department uses machine hours and the Molding Department uses direct labor hours to apply overhead to production, calculate the overhead rate for each production department.

LO2 **M19-19. Interdepartment Services: Direct Method**

Wilhelm Manufacturing Company has five operating departments, two of which are producing departments (P1 and P2) and three of which are service departments (S1, S2, and S3). All costs of the service departments are allocated to the producing departments. The following table shows the distribution of services from the service departments.

		Services Provided to			
Services provided from	**S1**	**S2**	**S3**	**P1**	**P2**
S1..	—	5%	25%	50%	20%
S2..	10%	—	5	45	40
S3..	15	5	—	20	60

The direct operating costs of the service departments are as follows:

S1...	$ 98,000
S2...	187,000
S3...	36,000

REQUIRED
Using the direct method, prepare a schedule allocating the service department costs to the producing departments.

M19-20. Inventory Ratio Calculations

Anka Inc. provided the following data for 2016 and 2017:

Inventory	
December 31, 2015	$ 404,800
December 31, 2016	571,200
December 31, 2017	365,000
Cost of goods sold	
2016	$1,284,000
2017	1,448,000
Gross margin	
2016	$ 680,000
2017	820,000

REQUIRED
(round all calculations to two decimal places)
a.   Calculate the inventory turnover ratio for 2016 and 2017.
b.   Calculate the gross margin return on inventory investment for 2016 and 2017.

M19-21. Inventory Ratio Calculations

Sanchez LTD. provided the following data for 2016 and 2017:

Inventory	
December 31, 2015	$ 352,000
December 31, 2016	555,000
December 31, 2017	388,000
Cost of goods sold	
2016	$1,172,000
2017	1,258,000
Gross margin	
2016	$ 512,000
2017	574,000

REQUIRED
(round all calculations to two decimal places)
a.   Calculate the inventory turnover ratio for 2016 and 2017.
b.   Calculate the gross margin return on inventory investment for 2016 and 2017.

EXERCISES

E19-22. Interdepartment Services: Step Method

Refer to the data in Mini Exercise M19-19. Using the step method, prepare a schedule for Wilhelm Manufacturing Company allocating the service department costs to the producing departments. (Round calculations to the nearest dollar.)

E19-23. Interdepartment Services: Step Method

Jane Cooper's Department Stores allocates the costs of the Personnel and Payroll departments to three retail sales departments, Housewares, Clothing, and Furniture. In addition to providing services to the operating departments, Personnel and Payroll provide services to each other. Cooper's allocates Personnel Department costs on the basis of the number of employees and

Payroll Department costs on the basis of gross payroll. Cost and allocation information for June is as follows:

	Personnel	Payroll	Housewares	Clothing	Furniture
Direct department cost........	$15,600	$6,400	$24,400	$40,000	$33,500
Number of employees	15	12	24	32	12
Gross payroll	$12,000	$6,600	$21,200	$26,100	$16,200

REQUIRED

a. Determine the percentage of total Personnel Department services that was provided to the Payroll Department.

b. Determine the percentage of total Payroll Department services that was provided to the Personnel Department.

c. Prepare a schedule showing Personnel Department and Payroll Department cost allocations to the operating departments, assuming Cooper's uses the step method. (Round calculations to the nearest dollar.)

LO3, 4 E19-24. **Product Costing in a JIT/Lean Environment**

Johanna Computer manufactures laptop computers under its own brand, but acquires all the components from outside vendors. No computers are assembled until the order is received online from customers, so there is no finished goods inventory. When an order is received, the bill of materials required to fill the order is prepared automatically and sent electronically to the various vendors. All components are received from vendors within three days and the completed order is shipped to the customer immediately when completed, usually on the same day the components are received from vendors. The number of units in process at the end of any day is negligible.

The following data are provided for the most recent month of operations:

Actual components costs incurred	$1,850,000
Actual conversion costs incurred..	$ 406,000
Units in process, beginning of month	0
Units started in process during the month.................................	5,500
Units in process, end of month	0

REQUIRED

a. Assuming Johanna uses traditional cost accounting procedures:
   1. How much cost was charged to Work-in-Process during the month?
   2. How much cost was charged to cost of goods sold during the month?

b. Assuming Johanna is a lean production company and uses backflush costing method:
   1. How much cost was charged to Work-in-Process during the month?
   2. How much cost was charged to cost of goods sold during the month?

LO4 E19-25. **Inventory Management Metrics**

Costco
NASDAQ :: COST
Target
NYSE :: TGT

Large retailers like **Costco** and **Target** typically use gross margin ratio (gross margin ÷ sales), inventory turnover (sometimes referred to as inventory turns), and gross margin return on investment (GMROI) to evaluate how well inventory has been managed. The goal is to maximize profits while minimizing the investment in inventory. Below are data for four scenarios, a base scenario (A) followed by three modifications (B, C, & D) to the base scenario.

	Scenario A	Scenario B	Scenario C	Scenario D
Sales..........................	$30,000	$60,000	$36,000	$30,000
Cost of goods sold..............	18,000	30,000	15,000	15,000
Gross profit.....................	$12,000	$30,000	$21,000	$15,000
Average inventory................	$ 9,000	$ 9,000	$ 9,000	$ 7,500

REQUIRED

For each scenario calculate the gross margin percent, the inventory turnover, and GMROI.

E19-26. Evaluating Inventory Management Metrics LO4
Refer to E19-25.

REQUIRED

a. For Scenarios B through D, explain what change occurred relative to Scenario A to cause GMROI to change. For example, was the change in GMROI caused by a change in inventory turns, a change in gross margin percent, or by reducing inventory levels?

b. What general conclusions can be made from the calculations and observations regarding the factors that influence GMROI?

E19-27. Technical Skills Gap LO5
Katie Dempsey works as a recruiter, placing accounting and finance professionals. Katie's current project is to fill an open managerial accounting position at PepsiCo. Identify the technical skills that Katie will be looking for in the applicant's resume and application materials that will likely lead to success in the position. Do you think these skills will be difficult to find in candidates? If so, what are some ways PepsiCo might be able to develop these skills in-house?

PROBLEMS

P19-28. Selecting Cost Allocation Bases and Direct Method Allocations LO2
Seattle Company has three producing departments (P1, P2, and P3) for which direct department costs are accumulated. In January, the following indirect costs of operation were incurred.

Plant manager's salary and office expense	$30,600
Plant security	4,800
Plant nurse's salary and office expense	6,600
Plant depreciation	8,000
Machine maintenance	10,800
Plant cafeteria cost subsidy	7,200
	$68,000

The following additional data have been collected for the three producing departments:

	P1	P2	P3
Number of employees	10	15	5
Space occupied (square feet)	2,000	5,000	3,000
Direct labor hours	1,600	4,000	750
Machine hours	4,800	8,000	3,200
Number of nurse office visits	30	35	10

REQUIRED

a. Group the indirect cost items into cost pools based on the nature of the costs and their common basis for allocation. Identify the most appropriate allocation basis for each cost pool and determine the total January costs in the pool. (*Hint:* A cost pool may consist of one or more cost items.)

b. Allocate the cost pools directly to the three producing departments using the allocation bases selected in requirement (*a*).

c. How much indirect cost would be allocated to each producing department if Seattle Company were using a plantwide rate based on direct labor hours? Based on machine hours?

d. Comment on the benefits of allocating costs in pools compared with using a plantwide rate.

P19-29. Evaluating Allocation Bases and Direct Method Allocations LO2
Brahtz Company has two service departments, Maintenance and Information Technology (IT), that serve two producing departments, Mixing and Packaging. The following data have been collected for these departments for the current year:

	IT	Maintenance	Mixing	Packaging
Direct department costs..............	$368,000	$284,000	$930,000	$590,000
Number of employees			50	30
Number of ethernet connections			90	70
Number of maintenance hours used.....			800	600
Number of maintenance orders			180	170

REQUIRED

a. Using the direct method, allocate the service department costs under the following indepen-dent assumptions:
1. IT costs are allocated based on the number of employees, and Maintenance costs are al-located based on the number of maintenance hours used.
2. IT costs are allocated based on the number of ethernet connections served, and Mainte-nance costs are allocated based on the number of maintenance orders.

b. Comment on the reasonableness of the bases used in the calculations in requirement (a). What considerations should determine which bases to use for allocating IT and Maintenance costs?

LO2   **P19-30. Cost Reimbursement and Step Allocation Method**

Hope Clinic is a not-for-profit outpatient facility that provides medical services to both fee-paying patients and low-income government-supported patients. Reimbursement from the government is based on total actual costs of services provided, including both direct costs of patient services and indirect operating costs. Patient services are provided through two producing departments, Medical Services and Ancillary Services (includes X-ray, therapy, etc.). In addition to the direct costs of these departments, the clinic incurs indirect costs in two service departments, Administration and Facilities. Administration costs are allocated first based on the number of full-time employees, and Facilities costs are then allocated based on space occupied. Costs and related data for the current month are as follows:

	Administration	Facilities	Medical Services	Ancillary Services
Direct costs	$72,000	$24,000	$257,600	$79,200
Number of employees	5	4	13	7
Amount of space occupied (square feet)....	1,500	750	8,000	2,000
Number of patient visits.................	—	—	4,000	1,500

REQUIRED

a. Using the step method, prepare a schedule allocating the common service department costs to the producing departments.

b. Determine the amount to be reimbursed from the government for each low-income patient visit.

LO2   **P19-31. Budgeted Service Department Cost Allocation: Pricing a New Product**

Fit & Active Company is adding a new diet food concentrate called Body Fit & Healthy to its line of bodybuilding and exercise products. A plant is being built for manufacturing the new prod-uct. Management has decided to price the new product based on a 100 percent markup on total manufacturing costs. A direct cost budget for the new plant projects that direct department costs of $6,500,000 will be incurred in producing an expected normal output of 700,000 pounds of fin-ished product. In addition, indirect costs for Administration and Technical Support will be shared by Body Fit & Healthy with the two exercise products divisions, Commercial Products and Retail Products. Budgeted annual data to be used in making the allocations are summarized here.

	Administration	Technical Support	Commercial Products	Retail Products	Body Fit & Healthy
Number of employees	5	5	50	30	20
Amount of technical support time (hours)	500	—	1,500	1,250	750

Direct costs are budgeted at $410,000 for the Administration Department and $560,000 for the Technical Support Department.

REQUIRED

a. Using the step method, determine the total direct and indirect costs of Body Fit & Healthy.

b. Determine the selling price per pound of Body Fit & Healthy. (Round calculations to the nearest cent.)

P19-32. Allocation and Responsibility Accounting **LO2**

Assume that **Timberland Company** uses a responsibility accounting system for evaluating its managers, and that abbreviated performance reports for the company's three divisions for the month of March are as follows (amounts in thousands).

Timberland
Company
NYSE :: TBL

	Total	East	Central	West
Income	$412,000	$146,000	$160,000	$106,000
Less allocated costs:				
Information Technology	(210,000)	(70,000)	(70,000)	(70,000)
Personnel	(150,000)	(56,250)	(56,250)	(37,500)
Division income	$ 52,000	$ 19,750	$ 33,750	$ (1,500)

The West Division manager is very disturbed over his performance report and recent rumors that his division may be closed because of its failure to report a profit in recent periods. He believes that the reported profit figures do not fairly present operating results because his division is being unfairly burdened with service department costs. He is particularly concerned over the amount of Information Technology costs charged to his division. He believes that it is inequitable for his division to be charged with one-third of the total cost when it is using only 20 percent of the services. He believes that the Personnel Department's use of the Information Technology Department should also be considered in the cost allocations. Cost allocations were based on the following distributions of service provided:

		Services Receiver			
Services Provider	**Personnel**	**Computer Services**	**East**	**Central**	**West**
Information Technology	40%	—	20%	20%	20%
Personnel	—	20%	30	30	20

REQUIRED

a. What method is the company using to allocate Personnel and Information Technology costs?

b. Recompute the cost allocations using the step method. (Round calculations to the nearest dollar.)

c. Revise the performance reports to reflect the cost allocations computed in requirement (b).

d. Comment on the complaint of the West Division's manager.

P19-33. Allocating Service Department Costs: Direct and Step Methods; Department and Plantwide Overhead Rates **LO2**

Assume that Pennington Group, a manufacturer of fine casual outdoor furniture, allocates Human Resources Department costs to the producing departments (Cutting and Welding) based on number of employees; Facilities Department costs are allocated based on the amount of square footage occupied. Direct department costs, labor hours, and square footage data for the four departments for October are as follows:

	Human Resources	Facilities	Cutting	Welding
Direct department overhead costs.	$100,000	$300,000	$1,800,000	$740,000
Number of employees	5	15	40	60
Number of direct labor hours	—	—	8,000	10,000
Amount of square footage	10,000	3,000	150,000	50,000

Assume that two jobs, A1 and A2, were completed during October and that each job had direct materials costs of $2,400. Job A1 used 80 direct labor hours in the Cutting Department and 20 direct labor hours in the Welding Department. Job A2 used 20 direct labor hours in the Cutting Department and 80 direct labor hours in the Welding Department. The direct labor rate is $80 in both departments.

REQUIRED

a. Find the cost of each job using a plantwide rate based on direct labor hours.

b. Find the cost of each job using department rates with *direct* service department cost allocation.

c. Find the cost of each job using department rates with *step* service department cost allocation.

d. Explain the differences in the costs computed in requirements (*a*)–(*c*) for each job. Which costing method is best for product pricing and profitability analysis?

LO4 **P19-34. JIT/Lean Production and Product Costing**

Presented is information pertaining to the standard or budgeted unit cost of a product manufactured in a JIT/Lean Production environment at CNN Systems Inc.:

Direct materials	$40
Conversion	30
Total	$70

All materials are added at the start of the production process. All raw materials purchases and conversion costs are directly assigned to Cost of Goods Sold. At the end of the period, costs are backed out and assigned to Raw Materials in Process (only for materials still in the plant) and Finished Goods Inventory (for materials and conversion costs for completed units). Costs assigned to inventories are based on the standard or budgeted cost multiplied by the number of units in inventory. Conversion costs are assigned to inventories only for fully converted units. Since inventory levels tend to be small in this JIT environment, partially completed units are assigned no conversion costs. CNN Systems had no beginning inventories on August 1, 2017. During the month, it incurred the following manufacturing-related costs:

Purchase of raw materials on account	$700,000
Factory wages	260,000
Factory supervision salaries	60,000
Utilities bill for month	34,000
Factory supplies purchased	30,000
Depreciation	19,000

The end-of-month inventory included raw materials in process of 750 units and finished goods of 500 units. One hundred units of raw materials were zero percent converted; the other 650 units averaged 60 percent converted.

REQUIRED

a. Calculate the total cost charged to Cost of Goods Sold during August.

b. Calculate the balances in Raw Materials in Process, Finished Goods Inventory, and Cost of Goods Sold at the end of August.

c. Assuming that August is a typical month, is it likely that using the company's shortcut backflush accounting procedures will produce misleading financial statements? Explain.

LO4 **P19-35. Just-in-Time Performance Evaluation**

To control operations, Sirius Company makes extensive and exclusive use of financial performance reports for each department. Although all departments have been reporting favorable cost variances in most periods, management is perplexed by the firm's low overall return on investment. You have been asked to look into the matter. Believing the purchasing department is typical of the company's operations, you obtained the following information concerning the purchases of parts for a product it started producing in 2012:

Year	Purchase Price Variance	Quantity Used (units)	Average Inventory (units)
2012	$ 3,000 F	20,000	4,000
2013	21,000 F	30,000	6,000
2014	24,000 F	35,000	7,750
2015	40,000 U	25,000	5,000
2016	16,000 F	36,000	7,200
2017	19,000 F	29,000	5,800

REQUIRED

a. Compute the inventory turnover for each year. What conclusions can be drawn from a yearly comparison of the purchase price variance and the inventory turnover?

b. Identify problems likely to be caused by evaluating purchasing only on the basis of the purchase price variance.

c. Offer whatever recommendations you believe appropriate.

P19-36. Dual Allocation Approach and Charging for Services　　　　　　　　　　　　　**LO2**

The Maintenance Department of Management Just Like Home Suites Hotel has fixed costs of $1,000,000 a year. It also incurs $60 in out-of-pocket expenses for every hour of work. During the year the Rooms Department used 30,000 maintenance hours. The Food and Beverage (F&B) Department used 10,000 maintenance hours. When the Maintenance Department was established the Rooms and F&B departments estimated they would need 30,000 and 20,000 maintenance hours, respectively. It turns out F&B cut back on maintenance hours used to insure it would meet its budget.

REQUIRED

a. Calculate the amount of Maintenance Department costs to allocate to Rooms and F&B based entirely on actual usage.

b. Calculate the amount of Maintenance Department costs to allocate to Rooms and F&B using a dual allocation approach where fixed cost is allocated based on estimated capacity needed and variable cost is allocated based on actual usage.

c. Which of the two methods applied in parts a. and b. is more fair to the two departments?

d. Assume that the Maintenance Department allocates costs to the producing departments using a user charge. What amount would you suggest for the user charge? Is it a good idea to use a user charge for allocating costs?

CASES AND PROJECTS

C19-37. Materials Push and Materials Pull Systems　　　　　　　　　　　　　　　　　**LO3, 4**

Data Storage Inc. produces three models of external storage devices for personal computers. Each model is produced on a separate assembly line. Production consists of several operations in separate work centers. Because of a high demand for Data's products, management is most interested in high-production volume and operating efficiency. Each work center is evaluated on the basis of its operating efficiency. To avoid idle time caused by defective units, variations in machine times, and machine breakdowns, significant inventories are maintained between each workstation.

At a recent administrative committee meeting, the director of research announced that the firm's engineers have made a dramatic breakthrough in designing a low-cost, read/write optical storage device. Data Storage's president is very enthusiastic, and the vice president of marketing wishes to add an assembly line for optical storage devices as soon as possible. The equipment necessary to manufacture the new product can be purchased and installed in less than 60 days. Unfortunately, all available plant space is currently devoted to the production of conventional storage devices, and expansion is not possible at the current plant location. It appears that adding the new product will require dropping a current product, relocating the entire operation, or manufacturing the optical storage devices at a separate location.

The vice president of marketing is opposed to dropping a current product. The vice president of finance is opposed to relocating the entire operation because of financing requirements and the associated financial risks. The vice president of production is opposed to splitting up production activities because of the loss of control and the added costs for various types of overhead.

REQUIRED

Explain how switching to a materials pull (Kanban) system can help solve Data Storage's space problems while improving quality and cycle time. Describe how a materials pull system works and the changes required in management attitude toward inventory and efficiency to make it work.

C19-38. Product Costing Using Activity-Based Costing and Just-in-Time: A Value Chain Approach　**LO3, 4**

Wearwell Carpet Company is a small residential carpet manufacturer started by Don Stegall, a longtime engineer and manager in the carpet industry. Stegall began Wearwell in the early 1990s after learning about ABC, JIT, total quality management, and several other manufacturing concepts being used successfully in Japan and other parts of the world. Although it was a small company, he believed that with his many years of experience and by applying these advanced techniques, Wearwell could very quickly become a world-class competitor.

Stegall buys dyed carpet yarns for Wearwell from three different major yarn manufacturers with which he has done business for many years. He chose these companies because of their reputation for producing high-quality products and their state-of-the art research and development departments. He has arranged for two carpet manufacturing companies to produce (tuft) all of his carpets on a contractual basis. Both companies have their own brands, but they also do contract work for other companies. For each manufacturer, Stegall had to agree to use the full output of one manufacturing production line at least one day per month. Each production line was dedicated to producing only one style of carpet, but each manufacturer had production lines capable of running each type of carpet that Wearwell sold.

Stegall signed a contract with a large transport company (CTC), which specializes in carpet-related shipping, to pick up and deliver yarn from the yarn plants to the tufting mills. This company will then deliver the finished product from the tufting mills to Wearwell's ten customers, which are carpet retailers in the ten largest residential building markets in the country. These retailers pay the shipping charges to have the carpets delivered to them. Wearwell maintains a small sales staff (which also doubles as a customer service staff) to deal with the retailers and occasionally with the end customers on quality problems that arise.

Wearwell started selling only one line of carpet, a medium-grade plush, but as new carpet styles were developed, it added two additional lines, a medium-grade berber carpet and a medium-grade textured carpet. Three colors are offered in each carpet style. By selling only medium grades with limited color choices, Stegall felt that he would reach a very large segment of the carpet market without having to deal with a large number of different products. As textured (trackless) carpets have become more popular, sales of plush have diminished substantially.

REQUIRED

a. Describe the value chain for Wearwell Carpet Company, and identify the parties who compose this value chain.

b. Identify and discuss the cost categories that would be included in the cost of the product for financial reporting purposes.

c. Identify and discuss the cost categories that would be included in the cost of the product for pricing and other management purposes.

d. Discuss some of the challenges that Stegall will have trying to apply JIT to regulate the levels of control at Wearwell. Suggest changes that might be necessary to make JIT work.

e. Does Wearwell seem to be an appropriate setting for implementing ABC? If so, what are likely to be the most important activities and related cost drivers?

SOLUTIONS TO REVIEW PROBLEMS

Mid-Chapter Review 1

SOLUTION

Plantwide overhead rate—The costs of all service departments are added to the indirect product costs incurred within all the producing departments to get total plantwide manufacturing overhead, which is then assigned to products using a single overhead rate based on a common factor such as direct labor hours.

Department overhead rate—Service department costs are allocated to the production departments that use their services, and the allocated service department costs are added to the indirect costs incurred within the department to arrive at total department overhead and allocation rates.

Activity-based costing—Service department costs are assigned to activity cost pools; then the activity cost pools are assigned to the product based on an activity driver allocation rate.

Mid-Chapter Review 2

SOLUTION
Service Department Cost Allocation
a.   Direct Method

	Total	Women's	Men's
Administrative Services Department			
Allocation base (number of employees)	24	15	9
Percent of total base.	100%	62.5%	37.5%
Cost allocation	$18,000	$11,250	$6,750
Facilities Services Department			
Allocation base (square footage)	22,500	15,000	7,500
Percent of total base.	100%	66.7%	33.3%
Cost allocation	$12,000	$ 8,000	$4,000

Cost Allocation Summary

	Administrative	Facilities	Women's	Men's	Total
Departmental costs					
before allocation	$18,000	$12,000	$60,000	$50,000	$140,000
Cost allocations					
Administrative	(18,000)	—	11,250	6,750	0
Facilities	—	(12,000)	8,000	4,000	0
Departmental costs					
after allocation	$ 0	$ 0	$79,250	$60,750	$140,000

Step Method

Allocation Sequence

	Administrative	Facilities
Allocation base.	Number of employees	Amount of square footage
Total base for other service and		
producing departments (a)	26	25,000
Total base for other service departments (b)	2	2,500
Percent of total services provided to other		
service departments (b ÷ a).	7.7%	10.0%
Order of allocation	Second	First

Step Allocations

	Total	Administrative	Women's	Men's
Facilities Services Department				
Allocation base (square footage)	25,000	2,500	15,000	7,500
Percent of total base.	100%	10%	60%	30%
Cost allocation	$12,000	$1,200	$ 7,200	$3,600
Administrative Services Department				
Allocation base (number of				
employees)	24	—	15	9
Percent of total base.	100%	—	62.5%	37.5%
Cost allocation ($18,000 + $1,200)	$19,200	—	$12,000	$7,200

Cost Allocation Summary					
	Facilities	**Administrative**	**Women's**	**Men's**	**Total**
Departmental costs before allocation	$12,000	$18,000	$60,000	$50,000	$140,000
Cost allocations					
Facilities	(12,000)	1,200	7,200	3,600	0
Administrative	—	(19,200)	12,000	7,200	0
Departmental costs after allocations	$ 0	$ 0	$79,200	$60,800	$140,000

b. Another service department cost allocation method is the *linear algebra method*. This method simultaneously allocates service department costs both to other service departments and to the producing departments. It has an advantage over the *step method* in that it fully recognizes interdepartmental services.

c. If **Buckle** wants the most precise allocation of service department costs to the producing departments, considering both direct services and indirect services, it must use the linear algebra method of service department allocation. As indicated in the Allocation Sequence section of the step method in (*a*), Facilities provides 10 percent of its services to Administrative, and Administrative provides 7.7 percent of its services to Facilities. The step method recognized the Facilities services provided to Administrative, but it did not recognize the Administrative services provided to Facilities.

In this case, the producing departments are using approximately the same proportion of services from each of the service departments (60.0 percent to 62.5 percent for the Women's Department and 30.0 percent to 37.5 percent for the Men's Department). Hence, using a more precise measure of cost allocation is not likely to produce significantly different results, especially since the interdepartmental services are so close (7.7 percent versus 10.0 percent). Just as the step method allocation results were quite close to the direct method results, the linear method results would likely be quite close to both the direct and step method results. Use of the linear algebra method is not recommended in this case. On the basis of simplicity and convenience, the direct method is probably the best method for Buckle to use.

Mid-Chapter Review 3

SOLUTION

 1 *a.* Nimble production process with small lot sizes and short setup and changeover times.
 2 *b.* Material push system.
 3 *c.* Key to managing work-in-process inventories and central to a lean production approach.
 1 *d.* Selecting venders on the basis of service and material quality, as well as price.
 1 *e.* Accepting vendor deliveries directly to the shop floor, and only as needed.
 1 *f.* Employees at each station work to provide inventory for the next workstation only as needed (Kanban system).

Mid-Chapter Review 4

SOLUTION

a. Cycle time is the total time required to produce one batch, including both value-added and non-value-added activities: System A = 83; System B = 77

b. The cycle efficiency is the percent of total time used in value-added activities. In this case, only the processing time is adding value to the product. Cycle efficiency: System A = 40/83 = 0.48; System B = 30/77 = 0.39

c. In selecting between A and B, the system with the higher efficiency would not likely be chosen because it has the longer total cycle time. Assuming both systems produce products of equal quality and characteristics, B is appealing because it requires one-fourth less processing time than A and offers greater opportunity for continuous improvement.

d. In a lean environment, management and all employees involved will be seeking ways to reduce the cycle time while maintaining a high-quality product. For B, the most likely opportunity for significant reduction is to reduce the large amount of movement and waiting time. If these components of total cycle time can be reduced, B becomes even more attractive.

SOLUTION

Students will have a variety of answers. Here are a few possible responses.

1. The data must be timely and reliable. Incorrect or misleading data can result in bad information and lead to incorrect and poor decisions.

2. Softer skills such as communication, strategic thinking, and execution are also of growing importance as organizations focus more on the need to communicate and execute business strategies.

3. Analysts must be careful when drawing conclusions based on data. Often, events may seem to be linked when there may be no causal relationship driving the correlation. The cause may be inverted as in the windmill example. The machine does not cause the wind, but the wind causes the windmill to move. Or there may be additional factors to consider as in the ice cream/drowning relationship. The missing link here is that higher temperatures likely lead to more swimming and therefore, more drowning, and higher temperatures also lead to more ice cream consumption.

20

Pricing and Other Product Management Decisions

ROKU

www.roku.com

The key to a startup company's success is to have a unique product or service that customers are willing to pay for, to be able to identify what price they will pay for it, and to produce the good or service within the price constraint such that the company can generate a profit. A tall order, especially when the startup company is sailing in relatively uncharted waters. Such is the case for **Roku**, the California startup that has become one of the most popular streaming video device makers alongside **Apple**'s Apple TV, **Alphabet**'s Google Chromecast, and **Amazon**'s Fire TV. If a company's value chain is the set of activities that a customer is willing to pay for, then Roku is the proverbial and literal "black box" that sits on top of the TV and allows customers to enhance their home entertainment systems.

Roku, Apple TV, Google Chromecast, and Amazon's Fire TV all offer video-streaming services such as Netflix, Hulu Plus, and HBO Now, photo services such as Flickr, and streamed sporting events from the NBA, MLB, and NHL. Ordinarily, a company would like to set its price above the cost to produce its good or service plus some desired profit. We refer to this as cost-based pricing. Yet when a company is engaged in intense competition, it may not be able to capture a price that is any higher than an entrenched rival's price. In other words, the market price is established by the more powerful rival(s). The Apple TV sells for $149 while Google Chromecast is priced at $35. Streaming video consumers have a range of options from inexpensive products of lower quality and fewer features to more costly products of higher quality and extensive features. Given the dominant market share of Apple TV and Google Chromecast, their prices define the market. Accordingly, Roku prices its units between $29.99 and $129.99. We refer to this as "target costing," or setting a price at what the market is willing to pay and producing within those revenue constraints.

Given the fledgling industry's vast uncertainty, we must assume that product life-cycle stages will be abbreviated either from competition or regulation. To maximize its sales and profits in the short run, a company like Roku must compete on the functionality, quality, and continuous improvement of its product. The managerial tools discussed throughout this chapter are increasingly important for managers involved in the development, production, and marketing of products and services that compete in contested environments. A company that truly understands the value chain of its production and delivery systems will remain nimble and flexible in the face of a changing regulatory and competitive landscape.

Source: AP News, "Roku Raises $60M from Hearst, News Corp, Others," *Bloomberg Businessweek*, May 29, 2013; Kyle Stock, "Roku Sales Hit 5 Million Units, Thanks to Amazon, Netflix," *Bloomberg Businessweek*, April 11, 2013; Larry Magid, "Roku Reaches Milestone as Networks Consider Dropping Free Broadcast," *Forbes*, April 10, 2013; Larry Magid, "Review of Roku 3: Could It Kill Cable and Satellite TV?' *Forbes*, April 1, 2013; Walter Mossberg, "Roku 3: Easier Streaming and Remote Headphones," *Wall Street Journal*, March 6, 2013, pp. D1–D3; and Robert Hof, "Could TiVo and Roku Beat Apple to TV Nirvana?" *Forbes*, February 27, 2013.

CHAPTER ORGANIZATION

Pricing and Other Product Management Decisions

Understanding the Value Chain	The Pricing Decision	Target Costing	Other Costing Techniques
• Usefulness of a Value Chain Perspective • Value-Added and Value Chain Perspectives	• Economic Approaches to Pricing • Cost-Based Approaches to Pricing	• Target Costing and Cost Management • Target Costing and Design • Target Costing and Product Life Cycles	• Continuous Improvement Costing • Benchmarking

Strategic cost management techniques, such as target costing and continuous improvement costing, represent important concepts for product management professionals involved in the development, manufacture, and marketing of products and services. Virtually all such techniques are grounded in the notion of managing the value chain. This chapter examines pricing, the interrelation between price and cost, and the role of benchmarking in meeting customer needs at the lowest possible price.

We begin with a discussion of the value chain, followed by an overview of the pricing model economists use to explain price equilibrium. Given the limitations of this long-run equilibrium model for determining price of a product or service, we consider the widely used cost-plus approach to identifying initial prices. We then examine how intense competition (such as that for the green car market) has inverted the cost-plus pricing model into one that starts with an acceptable market price and subtracts a desired profit to determine a target cost. We also consider life cycle costs from the perspectives of both the seller, who increasingly plans for all costs before production begins, and the buyer, who regards subsequent operating, maintenance, repair, and disposal costs as important as price. Finally, we consider how benchmarking can assist in improving competitiveness and profitability.

LO1 Explain the importance of the value chain in managing products and describe the key components of an organization's internal and external value chain.

UNDERSTANDING THE VALUE CHAIN

The **value chain** for a product or service is the set of value-producing activities that stretches from basic raw materials to the final consumer. Each product or service has a distinct value chain, and all entities along the value chain depend on the final customer's perception of the value and cost of a product or service. It is the final customer who ultimately pays all costs and provides all profits to all organizations along the entire value chain. Consequently, the goal of every organization is to maximize the value, while minimizing the cost, of a product or service to final customers.

The value chain provides a viewpoint that encompasses all activities performed to deliver products and services to final customers. Depending on the needs of management, value chains are developed at varying levels of detail. Analyzing a value chain from the perspective of the final consumer requires working backward from the end product or service to the basic raw materials entering into the product or service. Analyzing a value chain from the viewpoint of an organization that is in the middle of a value chain requires working forward (downstream) to the final consumer and backward (upstream) to the source of raw materials. The paper industry provides a convenient context for illustrating the value chain concept.

Exhibit 20.1 presents the value chain for the paperboard cartons used to package beverages, such as **Coca-Cola**, **Pepsi**, or **Evían** products. The value chain is presented at three levels, with each successive level containing additional details. The first level depicts the various business entities in the value chain:

- Timber producers grow the pulp wood (usually pine) used as the basic input into paper products. Some large paper companies, such as **Boise Cascade** and **Georgia Pacific**, harvest much of their pulp wood from timberlands that they manage. Other companies, including **International Paper**, which is a leading producer of paperboard, do not manage their own timberlands, but purchase pulp for their mills on the open market through pulp intermediaries.

- Pulp mills produce the kraft (unbleached) paper used to produce the paperboard. Some of the smaller paperboard manufacturers purchase the kraft paper product from pulp mills; **Graphic**

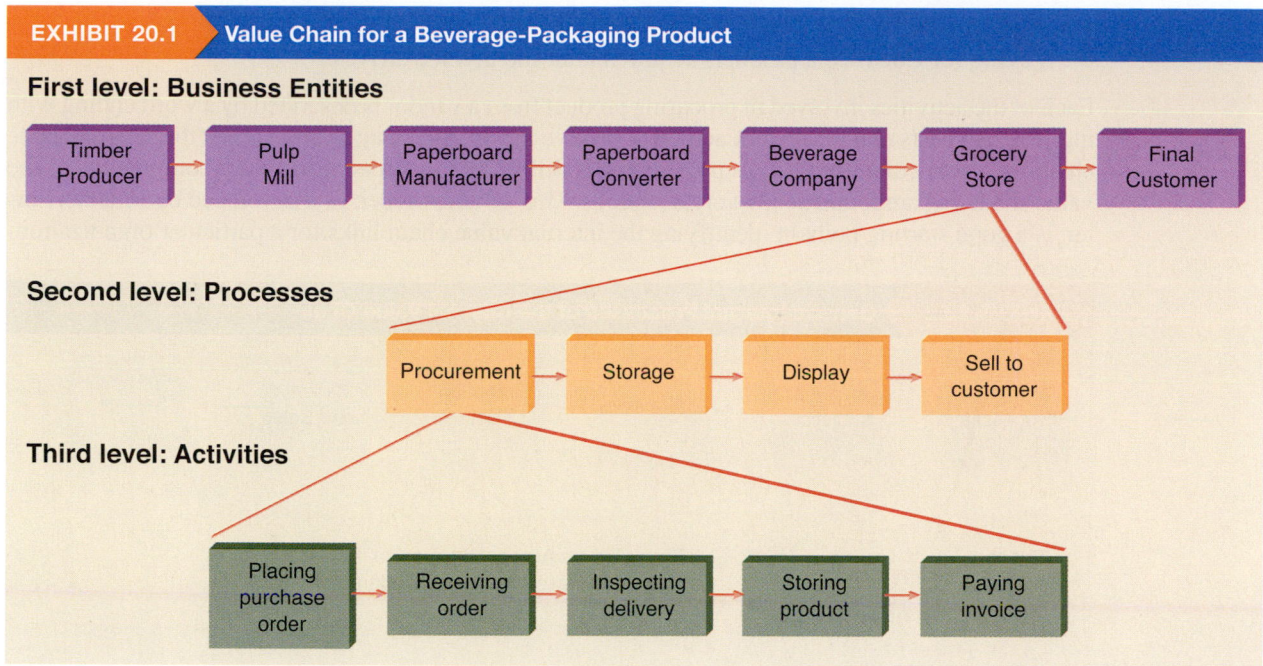

EXHIBIT 20.1   Value Chain for a Beverage-Packaging Product

First level: Business Entities

Timber Producer → Pulp Mill → Paperboard Manufacturer → Paperboard Converter → Beverage Company → Grocery Store → Final Customer

Second level: Processes

Procurement → Storage → Display → Sell to customer

Third level: Activities

Placing purchase order → Receiving order → Inspecting delivery → Storing product → Paying invoice

Packaging, however, owns its own paper mills that produce paper for its paperboard production facilities.

- Paperboard manufacturers perform a laminating process of coating paperboard material used to produce beverage packages. The paperboard consists of two layers of paper product plus three layers of coating that gives the top surface a high gloss finish that is water resistant and suitable for multicolor printing.

- The paperboard converter uses manufactured paperboard to print and produce the completed beverage packaging product, such as the cartons used to package the Diet **Coca-Cola** 12-pack.

- Beverage distributors, such as **Coca-Cola Enterprises** and **Anheuser-Busch**, purchase the completed paperboard packages from Graphic Packaging to package their many different brands in various package sizes and shapes.

- Grocery and convenience stores, such as **Publix** and **7-Eleven**, display and sell beverages packaged in the paperboard containers.

- The final customer purchases beverages packaged in paperboard packages and uses the packages to carry the beverages and to store them until consumed. The packages not only perform a transport and storage function but also serve as an advertising medium for the beverage company. The beverage company's advertising on the paperboard packages is intended to entice customers to purchase the beverage company's product and to help create a sense of satisfaction for the customer.

To better understand how business entities within the chain add value and incur costs, management might further refine the value chain into **processes**, collections of related activities intended to achieve a common purpose. The second level in **Exhibit 20.1** represents major processes concerning the procurement and sale of Coca-Cola products by a grocery store. To simplify our illustration, we show only the processes for the grocery store related to the purchase and sale of Coca-Cola products packaged in paperboard packages. These processes include procuring Coca-Cola products from the bottling company, storing and displaying the product, and selling the product to the final consumer.

An **activity** is a unit of work. In the third level of **Exhibit 20.1**, the grocery store process to procure Coca-Cola products is further broken up into the following activities:

- Placing a purchase order for Coca-Cola products packaged in paperboard packages.

- Receiving delivery of the Coca-Cola products in paperboard packages.

- Inspecting the delivery to make sure it corresponds with the purchase order and to verify that the products are in good condition.

- Storing Coca-Cola products in paperboard packages until needed for display.
- Paying for Coca-Cola products acquired after the invoice arrives.

Each of the activities involved in procuring product from a vendor is described by a word ending with ing. This suggests that most work activities involve action. One way to think about the internal value chain for a particular company is provided in **Exhibit 20.2** in terms of the basic components of the value chain that are found in most organizations. This generic model, first developed by Michael Porter, is a good starting point in identifying the internal value chain links for a particular organization.

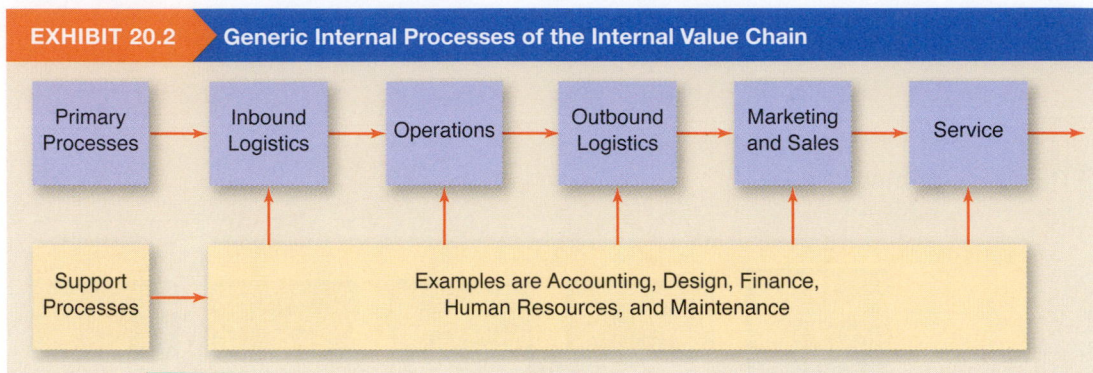

EXHIBIT 20.2 Generic Internal Processes of the Internal Value Chain

Usefulness of a Value Chain Perspective

The goal of maximizing final customer value while minimizing final customer cost leads organizations to examine internal and external links in the value chain rather than the departments, processes, or activities independently. From a value chain perspective, it is total cost across the entire value chain, not the cost of individual businesses, departments, processes, or activities that is most important.

Value Chain Perspective Fosters Supplier–Buyer Partnerships In the past, relationships between suppliers and buyers were often adversarial. Contact between suppliers and buyers was solely through the selling and purchasing departments. Suppliers attempted merely to meet purchasing contract specifications at the lowest possible cost. Buyers encouraged competition among suppliers with the primary—and often single—goal of obtaining the lowest purchase price.

As discussed in Chapter 19 with JIT and lean production, exploiting cost reduction and value-enhancing opportunities in the value chain has led many buyers and suppliers to view each other as partners rather than as adversaries. Buyers have reduced the number of suppliers they deal with, often developing long-term partnerships with a single supplier. Once they establish mutual trust, both proceed to share detailed information on internal operations and help each other solve problems. Partners work closely to examine mutual opportunities by studying their common value chain. Supplier engineers might determine that a minor relaxation in buyer specifications would significantly reduce supplier manufacturing costs with only minor increases in subsequent buyer processing costs. Working together, they determine how best to modify processes to reduce overall costs and share increased profits.

Companies such as **Hewlett-Packard** and **Boeing** involve suppliers in design, development, and manufacturing decisions. **Motorola** has even developed a survey asking suppliers to assess Motorola as a buyer. Among other questions, the survey asks sellers to evaluate Motorola's performance in helping suppliers to identify major cost drivers and to increase their profitability. These questions represent the concerns of a partner rather than those of an adversary. Michael Dell, at **Dell Computers**, stated that "rather than closely guarding our information databases, which took us years to develop, we used Internet browsers to essentially give that information to our customers and suppliers—bringing them into our business."[1] The following Business Insight box describes how **General Motors** is strengthening its relationships with its suppliers, in the hopes of working together to develop cost cutting strategies.

---

[1] *Direct from Dell*, Michael Dell with Catherine Fredman, Harper Collins Publishers, 1999. Also, see http://money.cnn.com/magazines/fortune/fortune500/2007/full_list/index.html

BUSINESS INSIGHT

Cost Control: For Starters, Your Suppliers Don't Need to Hate You   **General Motors** is seeking to improve historically poor supplier relationships. The company's purchasing chief, Steve Kiefer, says that the company is now negotiating parts contracts that span two vehicle generations—up to a decade. North America's largest automaker hopes that this will give them access to both lower costs and advanced technology. Strengthening relationships with suppliers and then partnering on cost cutting is a new approach for GM. In the past, GM's suppliers saw the automaker's planning and cost-cutting processes as heavy handed, which made suppliers unwilling to give GM access to new technologies. Kiefer hopes that long-term commitments to suppliers will lead to more attention and productive partnerships for the company.

Source: Jeff Bennett, "GM Seeks Longer-Term Supplier Contracts in Bid to Cut Costs," *Wall Street Journal*, April 15, 2015.

On a smaller scale, the grocery store in **Exhibit 20.1** should examine its external links. It may be willing to pay more for **Coca-Cola** products if the distributors cooperate to help reduce costs such as the following:

- Making more frequent deliveries in small lots would reduce storage costs.
- Being responsible for maintaining and changing the product displays would relieve store workers of these tasks.
- Streamlining ordering and payment procedures would reduce bookkeeping costs.

If partnership arrangements with upstream suppliers enable the grocery store to reduce its total costs, the store can enhance or maintain its competitive position by reducing prices charged to its consumers. Remember that competitors are also striving to reduce costs and enhance their competitive position. Hence, failing to strive for improvements will likely result in reduced sales and profits.

Value Chain Perspective Fosters Focus on Core Competencies

Using value chain concepts, relationships with suppliers often begin to represent an extended family, allowing companies to focus on core competencies; this capability provides a distinct competitive advantage. In addition, a new breed of contract manufacturers, such as **Sanmina-SCI** has emerged in recent years. Sanmina-SCI promotes itself as an end-to-end solution. It partners with customers across a variety of industries to design and make complex optical, electronic, and mechanical products. This allows Sanmina-SCI's customers to focus on marketing and product development while Sanmina-SCI focuses on efficient, low-cost manufacturing.

Interestingly, because their facilities are available to all innovators with the necessary financing, the emergence of contract manufacturers may speed innovation. **Toyota** attributes much of its rapid growth and profitability to virtual integration with suppliers. **Virtual integration** is the use of information technology and partnership concepts to allow two or more entities along a value chain to act as if they were a single economic entity.

BUSINESS INSIGHT

***Keiretsu*: Focus on Core Competencies**   The Japanese concept of *keiretsu* has attractive features for the auto industry. Traditionally, Japanese automakers would keep their business within a tight group of suppliers who were part owners of the automaker. These close-knit relationships have benefits for just-in-time inventory and allow firms to focus on their core competencies. On the other hand, *keiretsu* can stifle competition, creativity, and responsibility.

Honda has been plagued by a slow response to serious malfunctions by its airbag supplier **Takata Corp.**, widely thought to be symptomatic of the industry's overly insular nature. To deal with these shortcomings, automakers across Japan have begun to modify or abandon *keiretsu*. **Nissan Motor Co.** slashed costs in the 1990's by dismantling their *keiretsu* network, while Honda has been slowly introducing international suppliers to its supply chain. Toyota has been modifying its longstanding relationships, contracting with one break-system supplier. When the best supplier is not available in its network, Toyota looks elsewhere, even overseas. *Keiretsu* networks can help firms focus, but firms should be careful that this focus does not lead to other problems.

Source: Yoko Kubota and Eric Pfanner, "Toyota Shakes Up a Japanese Tradition," *Wall Street Journal*, October 28, 2015.

Value-Added and Value Chain Perspectives

The value chain perspective is often contrasted with a value-added perspective. Under a value-added perspective, decision makers consider only the cost of resources to their organization and the selling price of products or services to their immediate customers. Using a value-added perspective, the goal is to maximize the value added (the difference between the selling price and costs) by the organization. To do this, the value-added perspective focuses primarily on internal activities and costs. Under a value chain perspective, the goal is to maximize value and minimize cost to final customers, often by developing linkages or partnerships with suppliers and customers.

Although initial efforts to enhance competitiveness might start with a value-added perspective, it is important to expand to a value chain perspective. World-class competitors utilize both a value-added and a value chain perspective. These firms always keep the final customer in mind and recognize that the profitability of each entity in the value chain depends on the overall value and cost of the products and services delivered to final customers.

The value-added perspective is the foundation of the make or buy (outsourcing) decision considered in Chapter 16. The key differences between the partnering decisions considered here and the make or buy decision in Chapter 16 concern time frame, perspective, and attitude. The make or buy decision is a stand-alone decision, often in the short run, that does not view vendors and customers as partners. In contrast, characteristics of the value chain perspective are as follows:

- Comprehensive.
- Focused on the final customers.
- Strategic.
- Basis for partnerships between vendors and customers.

Enhancing or maintaining a competitive position requires an understanding of the entire system used to develop and deliver value to final customers, including interactions among organizations along the value chain. All organizations in the value chain are in business together and should work together as partners rather than as adversaries.

MID-CHAPTER REVIEW 1

Peruse **Starbucks**' corporate website at https://www.starbucks.com. Think about the different processes that Starbucks likely conducts as a part of its business model.

REQUIRED
Using Michael Porter's generic model presented in **Exhibit 20.2**, identify probable elements of each of the primary processes in Starbucks's value chain (i.e., inbound logistics, operations, outbound logistics, marketing and sales, and service).

The solution to this review problem can be found on page 922.

LO2 Distinguish between economic and cost-based approaches to pricing.

THE PRICING DECISION

Pricing products and services is one of the most important and complex decisions facing management. Pricing decisions directly affect the salability of individual products or services, as well as the profitability, and even the survival, of the organization. Many economists have spent their entire careers examining the foundations of pricing. To respond to the needs of pricing hundreds or thousands of individual items, managers have developed pricing guidelines that are typically based on costs. More recently, global competition has turned cost-based approaches upside down. Managers of world-class organizations increasingly start with a price that customers are willing to pay and then determine allowable costs.

Economic Approaches to Pricing

In economic models, the firm has a profit-maximizing goal and known cost and revenue functions. Typically, increases in sales quantity require reductions in selling prices, causing **marginal revenue** (the varying increment in total revenue derived from the sale of an additional unit) to decline as sales increase. Increases in production cause an increase in **marginal cost** (the varying increment in total cost required to produce and sell an additional unit of product). In economic models, profits are maximized at the sales volume at which marginal revenues equal marginal costs. Firms continue to produce as long as the marginal revenue derived from the sale of each additional unit exceeds the marginal cost of producing that unit.

Economic models provide a useful framework for considering pricing decisions. The ideal price is the one that will lead customers to purchase all units a firm can provide up to the point at which the last unit has a marginal cost exactly equal to its marginal revenue.

Despite their conceptual merit, economic models are seldom used for day-to-day pricing decisions. Perfect information and an indefinite time period are required to achieve equilibrium prices at which marginal revenues equal marginal costs. In the short run, most for-profit organizations attempt to achieve a target profit rather than a maximum profit. One reason for this is an inability to determine the single set of actions that will lead to profit maximization. Furthermore, managers are more apt to strive to satisfy a number of goals (such as profits for investors, job security for themselves and their employees, and being a "good" corporate citizen) than to strive for the maximization of a single profit goal. In any case, to maximize profits, a company's management would have to know the cost and revenue functions of every product the firm sells. For most firms, this information cannot be developed at a reasonable cost.

Cost-Based Approaches to Pricing

Although cost is not the only consideration in pricing, it has traditionally been the most important for several reasons.

- *Cost data are available.* When hundreds or thousands of different prices must be set in a short time, cost could be the only feasible basis for product pricing.

- *Cost-based prices are defensible.* Managers threatened by legal action or public scrutiny feel secure using cost-based prices. They can argue that prices are set in a manner that provides a "fair" profit.

- *Revenues must exceed costs if the firm is to remain in business.* In the long run, the selling price must exceed the full cost of each unit.

Cost-based pricing is illustrated in **Exhibit 20.3**. The process begins with market research to determine customer wants. If the product requires components to be designed and produced by vendors,

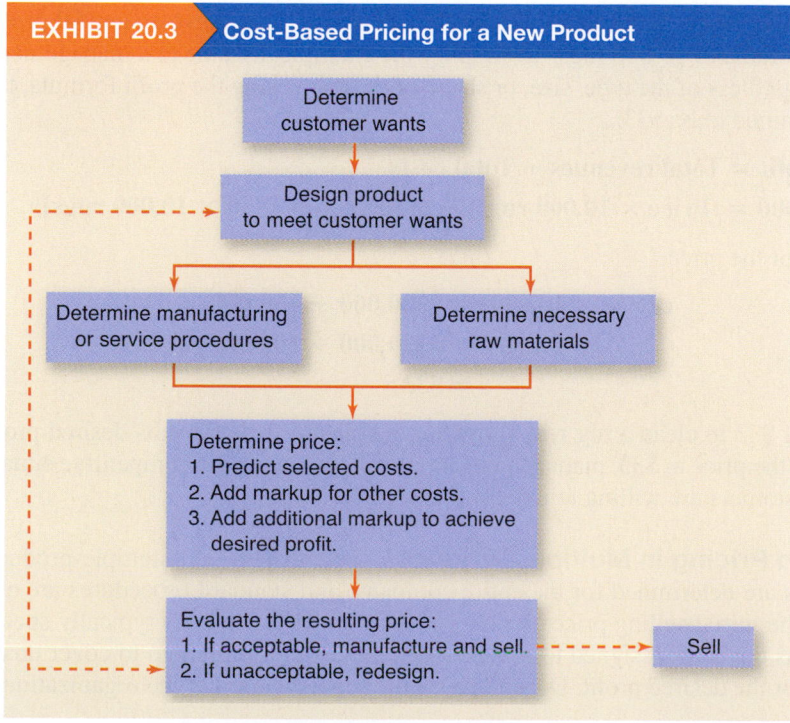

EXHIBIT 20.3   **Cost-Based Pricing for a New Product**

Determine customer wants

Design product to meet customer wants

Determine manufacturing or service procedures

Determine necessary raw materials

Determine price:
1. Predict selected costs.
2. Add markup for other costs.
3. Add additional markup to achieve desired profit.

Evaluate the resulting price:
1. If acceptable, manufacture and sell.
2. If unacceptable, redesign.

Sell

the process of obtaining prices can be time consuming. When some costs, such as those fixed costs at the facility level, are not assigned to specific products, a markup is added to cover these costs. An additional markup is added to achieve a desired profit. The selling price is then set as the sum of the assigned costs, the markup to cover unassigned costs, and the markup to achieve the desired profit.

The proposed selling price should be evaluated with regard to competitive information and what customers are willing to pay. If the price is acceptable, the product or service is produced. If the price is too high, the product might be redesigned, manufacturing procedures might be changed, and different types of materials might be considered until either an acceptable price is achieved or it is determined that the product cannot be produced at an acceptable price. On the other hand, as the Business Insight below shows, the price can sometimes be a major driver of a company's growth.

BUSINESS INSIGHT

For a Better Price, Make a Better Product   While traditional media companies and advertising firms are struggling to adapt to the Internet age, **Vice Media** has cracked the code. Vice has found a way to connect with millennial viewers, born between 1980 and 2000. Vice Media's unique foothold in the millennial market allows the company to change the way ads are delivered and allows Vice to name its price.

Vice's partnership with **A&E**, called Viceland, airs on the A&E network but is not a part of traditional ad buys. Companies must pay a premium to access the Vice audience. For example, instead of a traditional spot on a website or before a BuzzFeed or YouTube video, Vice charges between $83,000 and $413,000 per episode to sponsor any one of its 70 original video series. Vice's advertising is often integrated into its content in a way that differs dramatically from traditional commercial-break or sidebar ads. Vice programs are marketed as being "produced with" the sponsor rather than simply showing an ad. By accessing a new group of consumers in new ways, Vice has changed the price the market will bear for its ads.

Sources: Mike Shields, "Vice, BuzzFeed Tread on Madison Avenue's Turf," *Wall Street Journal*, June 22, 2016.
Aaron Taube, "How Vice Media Will Make $500 Million This Year," *Business Insider*, June 21, 2014.
Jason Lynch, "Viceland Is Shaking Up TV Advertising by Running More Native Ads That Look Editorial," *ADWEEK*, March 1, 2016.
Jane Martinson, "The Virtues of Vice: How Punk Magazine Was Transformed into Media Giant," *The Guardian*, January 1, 2015.

Cost-Based Pricing in Single-Product Companies

Implementing cost-based pricing in a single-product company is straightforward if everything is known but the selling price. In this case, all known data are entered into the profit formula, which is then solved for the variable price. Assume that a **ServiceMaster** location's annual fixed facility-level costs are $200,000 and the unit cost of cleaning a rug is $10. Suppose management desires to achieve an annual profit of $30,000 at an annual volume of 10,000 rugs. To simplify the example, assume that management charges the same price regardless of the type, size, or shape of the rug. Using the profit formula, the cost-based price is determined to be $33:

$$\textbf{Profit} = \textbf{Total revenues} - \textbf{Total costs}$$

$$\$30{,}000 = (\textbf{Price} \times \textbf{10,000 rugs}) - (\$200{,}000 + [\$10 \times \textbf{10,000 rugs}])$$

Solving for the price:

$$(\textbf{Price} \times \textbf{10,000}) = \$300{,}000 + \$30{,}000$$

$$\textbf{Price} = \$330{,}000 \div \textbf{10,000}$$

$$= \$33$$

A price of $33 to clean a rug will allow ServiceMaster to achieve its desired profit. However, before setting the price at $33, management should also evaluate the competitive situation and consider what customers are willing to pay for this service.

Cost-Based Pricing in Multiple-Product Companies

In multiple-product companies, desired profits are determined for the entire company, and standard procedures are established for determining the initial selling price of each product. These procedures typically specify the initial selling price as the costs assigned to products or services plus a markup to cover unassigned costs and provide for the desired profit. Depending on the sophistication of the organization's accounting system, possible cost bases in a manufacturing organization include markups based on a combination of cost behavior and function. The possible cost bases include:

- Direct materials costs.
- Variable manufacturing costs.
- Total variable costs (manufacturing, selling, and administrative).
- Full manufacturing costs.

Regardless of the cost base, the general approach to developing a markup is to recognize that the markup must be large enough to provide for costs not included in the base plus the desired profit.

$$\textbf{Markup on cost base} = \frac{\textbf{Costs not included in the base} + \textbf{Desired profit}}{\textbf{Costs included in the base}}$$

First we illustrate a pricing decision with variable costs as the cost base; full manufacturing costs is the cost base in the second illustration.

1. When the markup is based on variable costs, it must be large enough to cover all fixed costs and the desired profit. Assume that the predicted annual variable and fixed costs for one of **Roku**'s divisions are are as follows:

Variable		Fixed	
Manufacturing	$600,000	Manufacturing	$300,000
Selling and administrative	200,000	Selling and administrative	100,000
Total	$800,000	Total	$400,000

Furthermore, assume that Roku's division has total assets of $1,250,000; management believes that an annual return of 16 percent on total assets is appropriate in Roku's industry. A 16 percent return translates into a desired annual profit of $200,000 ($1,250,000 3 0.16). Assuming all cost predictions are correct, obtaining a profit of $200,000 requires a 75 percent markup on variable costs:

$$\textbf{Markup on variable costs } = \frac{\$400,000 + \$200,000}{\$800,000}$$

$$= \textbf{0.75}$$

If the predicted variable costs for Product A1 are $12 per unit, the initial selling price for Product A1 is $21:

$$\textbf{Initial selling price } = \$12 + (\$12 \times 0.75)$$

$$= \$21$$

2. When the markup is based on full manufacturing costs, it must be large enough to cover selling and administrative expenses and to provide for the desired profit. Again, it is necessary to determine the desired profit and predict all costs for the pricing period. The initial prices of individual products are then determined as their unit manufacturing costs plus the markup. For Roku's, the markup on manufacturing costs would be 55.6 percent:

$$\textbf{Markup on manufacturing costs } = \frac{\$300,000 + \$200,000}{\$900,000}$$

$$= \textbf{0.556}$$

If the predicted manufacturing costs for Product B1 are $10, the initial selling price for Product B1 is $15.56:

$$\text{Initial selling price} = \$10 + (\$10 \times 0.556)$$
$$= \$15.56$$

Cost-Based Pricing for Special Orders   Many organizations use cost-based pricing to bid on unique projects. If the project requires dedicated assets, the acquisition of new fixed assets, or an investment in employee training, the desired profit on the special order or project should allow for an adequate return on the dedicated assets or additional investment.

Critique of Cost-Based Pricing   Cost-based pricing has four major drawbacks:

1. Cost-based pricing requires accurate cost assignments. If costs are not accurately assigned, some products could be priced too high, losing market share to competitors; other products could be priced too low, gaining market share but being less profitable than anticipated.

2. The higher the portion of unassigned costs, the greater is the likelihood of over- or under-pricing individual products.

3. Cost-based pricing assumes that goods or services are relatively scarce and, generally, customers who want a product or service are willing to pay the price.

4. In a competitive environment, cost-based approaches increase the time and cost of bringing new products to market.

Cost-based pricing became the dominant approach to pricing during an era when products were relatively long-lived and there was relatively little competition. Also, these systems tend to focus on organizational units such as departments, plants, or divisions and not on activities or cost drivers. While easy to implement, reflecting the need to recover costs and earn a return on investment, and easily justified, cost-based prices might not be competitive. Competition puts intense downward pressure on prices and removes slack from pricing formulas. There is little margin for error in pricing. In a highly competitive market, small variations in pricing make significant differences in success.

MID-CHAPTER REVIEW 2

Assume that **Prince**, a tennis equipment manufacturer, has the following 2017 contribution income statement:

PRINCE Contribution Income Statement For Year Ended December 31, 2017		
Sales (100,000 units at $12 per unit)		$1,200,000
Less variable costs		
Manufacturing.	$300,000	
Selling and administrative.	150,000	(450,000)
Contribution margin		750,000
Less fixed costs		
Manufacturing.	400,000	
Selling and administrative.	200,000	(600,000)
Net income.		$ 150,000

Assume Prince has total assets of $2,000,000, and management desires an annual return of 10 percent on total assets.

continued

REQUIRED

a. Determine the dollar amount by which Prince exceeded or fell short of the desired annual rate of return in 2017.

b. Given the current sales volume and cost structure, determine the unit selling price required to achieve an annual profit of $250,000.

c. Assume that management wants to state the selling price as a percentage of variable manufacturing costs. Given your answer to requirement (b) and the current sales volume and cost structure, determine the selling price as a percentage of variable manufacturing costs.

d. Restate your answer to requirement (c), dividing into two separate markup percentages:

  1. The markup on variable manufacturing costs required to cover unassigned costs.

  2. The additional markup on variable manufacturing costs required to achieve an annual profit of $250,000.

The solution to this review problem can be found on pages 922–923.

TARGET COSTING

LO3 Explain target costing and discuss its acceptance in highly competitive industries.

Economists argue that cost-based prices are not realistic, because in the real world prices are determined by the confluence of supply and demand. However, when a new product is introduced into the market for which there is no previously existing supply or demand, there has to be a starting point. As discussed above, cost has often been the baseline for determining initial selling prices. All too often, however, companies introduce new products into the market based on what the designers and engineers "think" the market wants (or based on inadequate market research), only to find out later that either the market does not want the product, or it is not willing to buy the new product at a price sufficient to cover its cost plus an acceptable profit to the producer. This often leads to costly redesign, or in many cases, complete abandonment of the product, typically resulting in substantial financial losses.

Toyota, which has pioneered many innovations in manufacturing systems, turned the notion of cost-based pricing around and came up with the idea of price-based costing, referred to as target costing. Toyota determined that before a new product is introduced into the market, it must be able to be produced at a cost that will make it profitable when sold at a price acceptable to customers. The acceptable selling price to the marketplace determines the acceptable cost of producing the product.

Target Costing Is Proactive for Cost Management

Target costing starts with determining what customers are willing to pay for a product or service and then subtracts a desired profit on sales to determine the allowable, or target, cost of the product or service. This target cost is then communicated to a cross-functional team of employees representing such diverse areas as marketing, product design, manufacturing, and management accounting. Reflecting value chain concepts and the notion of partnerships up and down the value chain, suppliers of raw materials and components are often included in the teams. The target costing team is assigned the task of designing a product that meets customer price, function, and quality requirements while providing a desired profit. Its job is not completed until the target cost is met, or a determination is made that the product or service cannot be profitably introduced under the current circumstances. See **Exhibit 20.4** for an overview of target costing.

Although a formula can be used to determine a markup on cost, it is not possible to develop a formula indicating how to achieve a target cost. Hence, target costing is not a technique. It is more a philosophy or an approach to pricing and cost management. It takes a proactive approach to cost management, reflecting the belief that costs are best managed by decisions made during product development. This contrasts with the more passive cost-plus belief that costs result from design, procurement, and manufacture. Like the value chain, target costing helps orient employees toward the final customer and reinforces the notion that all departments within the organization and all organizations along the value chain must work together. Target costing also empowers employees who will be assigned the responsibility for carrying out activities necessary to deliver a product or service with the authority to determine what activities will be selected. Like process mapping, it helps employees to better understand their role in serving the customer. The following Research Insight discusses how target costing can improve margins for companies engaged in global sourcing.

RESEARCH INSIGHT

Target Costing and Global Sourcing   Creating and meeting cost targets in an age of global supply and distribution is fundamentally an information technology problem. Researchers with the **Deloitte Consulting LLP Supply Chain Strategy Practice** point to **Toyota's** response to the 2011 tsunami as an example of evolution toward modern supply chain management. Toyota's supply system now anticipates the impact of catastrophes on each part used in production. Parts are now designed to allow flexibility in sourcing. This focus is a shift from the optimization and cost minimization of the past. Toyota has adjusted its cost targets to build flexibility and durability into the supply chain, which requires data collection and analysis capabilities that are new for many organizations.

To meet these needs, **Nordstrom Inc.** has purchased a minority stake in the supply-chain software firm **DS Co.,** a move specifically intended to help the retail giant manage inventories among its department stores, online business, and suppliers. This allows the company to maintain its traditional storefront business while also shipping directly from its suppliers to its online customers.

Information technology helps firms meet cost targets and manage inventories in a global marketplace.

Sources: Kelly Marchese and Bill Lam, "Anticipatory Supply Chains," Deloitte University Press, March 31, 2014.
Loretta Chao, "Nordstrom Buys Stake in Software Firm," *Wall Street Journal*, July 8, 2016.

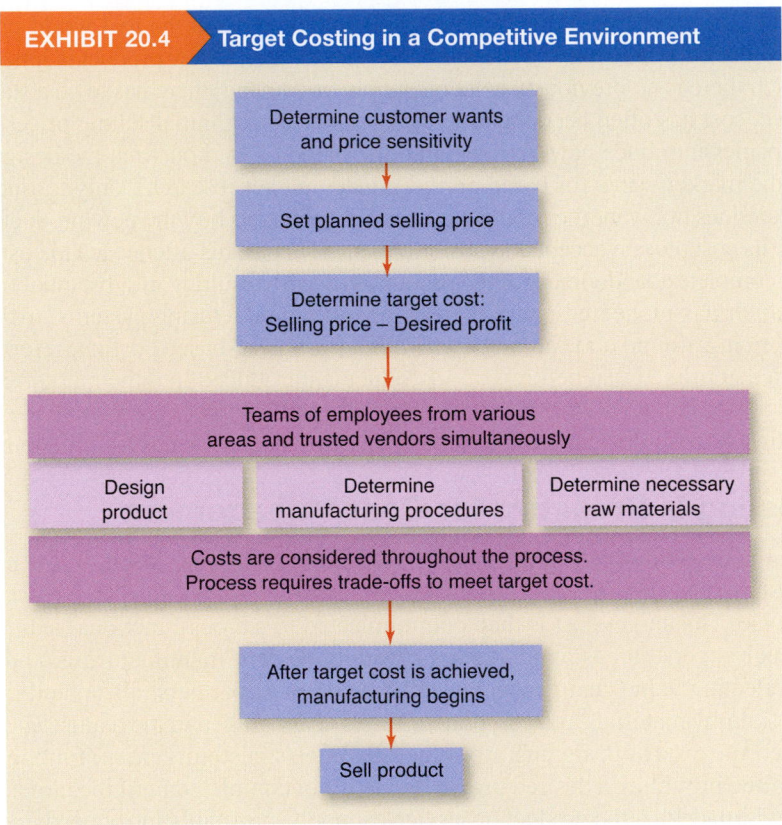

EXHIBIT 20.4   Target Costing in a Competitive Environment

Target Costing Encourages Design for Production

In the absence of a target costing approach, design engineers are apt to focus on incorporating leading-edge technology and the maximum number of features in a product. Target costing keeps the customer's function, quality, and price requirements in the forefront at all times. If customers do not want leading-edge technology (which could be expensive and untested) and several product features, they will resist paying for them. Focusing on achieving a target cost keeps design engineers tuned in to the final customer.

Left on their own, design engineers might believe that their job ends when they design a product that meets the customer's functional requirements. The tendency is to simply pass on the design to manufacturing and let manufacturing determine how best to produce the product. Further down the line, if the product needs servicing, it becomes the service department's responsibility to determine how best to service the product. A target costing approach forces design engineers to explicitly consider the costs of manufacturing and servicing a product while it is being designed. This is known as **design for manufacture**.

Minor changes in design that do not affect the product's functioning can often produce dramatic savings in manufacturing and servicing costs. Examples of design for manufacture include the following:

- Using molded plastic parts to avoid assembling several small parts.
- Designing two parts that must be fit together so that joining them in the correct manner is obvious to assembly workers.
- Placing an access panel in the side of an appliance so service personnel can make repairs quickly.
- Using standard-size parts to reduce inventory requirements, to reduce the possibility of assembly personnel inserting the incorrect part, and to simplify the job of service personnel.
- Ensuring that tolerance requirements for parts that must fit together can be met with available equipment.
- Using manufacturing procedures that are common to other products.

The successful implementation of target costing requires employees from all involved disciplines to be familiar with costing concepts and the notions of value-added and non-value-added activities. When considering the manufacturing process, team members should minimize non-value-added activities such as movement, storage, inspection, and setup. They should also select the lowest-cost value-added activities that do the job properly.

Target Costing Reduces Time to Introduce Products

By designing a product to meet a target cost (rather than evaluating the marketability of a product at a cost-plus price and having to recycle the design through several departments), target costing reduces the time required to introduce new products. Involving vendors in target costing design teams makes the vendors aware of the necessity of meeting a target cost. This facilitates the concurrent engineering of components to be produced outside the organization and reduces the time required to obtain components.

Target Costing Requires Cost Information

Implementing target costing requires detailed information on the cost of alternative activities. This information allows decision makers to select design and manufacturing alternatives that best meet function and price requirements. Tables that contain detailed databases of cost information for various manufacturing variables are occasionally used in designing products and selecting processes to meet target costs.

Target Costing Requires Coordination

Limitations of target costing are employee and supplier attitudes and the many meetings required to coordinate product design and to select manufacturing processes. All people involved must have a basic understanding of the overall processes required to bring a product to market and an appreciation of the cost consequences of alternative actions. They must also respect, cooperate, and communicate with other team members and be willing to engage in a negotiation process involving trade-offs. Finally, they must understand that although the total time required to bring a new product to market can be reduced, the countless coordinating meetings could be quite intrusive on the individuals' otherwise orderly schedules. See **Exhibit 20.5** for an evaluation of target costing.

This aspect of the process is even more difficult when suppliers must be brought in as part of the coordination process. This concept is frequently referred to as **chained target costing** because the supply chain's support is critical for the product to be both competitively priced and delivered to the final customer in a timely manner. When multiple suppliers are required, the organization must obtain everyone's support or the process will probably not be successful due to gaps in the reliability of delivery, quality, and cost control. Each organization and unit must understand that if the product is not brought to market within the defined constraints, all will lose. They must make firm commitments for the project undertaken and to have faith that each participant will carry out whatever part of the supply chain it has promised to fulfill. Coordination across the supply chain is vital in the overall process of continuous improvement as discussed later in this chapter.

EXHIBIT 20.5	Pros and Cons of Target Costing

Pros

- Takes proactive approach to cost management.
- Orients organization toward customer.
- Breaks down barriers between departments.
- Enhances employee awareness and empowerment.
- Fosters partnerships with suppliers.
- Minimizes non-value-added activities.
- Encourages selection of lowest-cost value-added activities.
- Reduces time to market.

Cons

- To be effective, requires the development of detailed cost data.
- Requires willingness to cooperate.
- Requires many meetings for coordination.

Target Costing is Key for Products with Short Life Cycles

From a traditional marketing perspective, products with a relatively long life go through four distinct stages during their life cycle:

1. *Start-up.* Sales are low when a product is first introduced. Traditionally, initial selling prices are set high, and customers tend to be relatively affluent trendsetters.

2. *Growth.* Sales increase as the product gains acceptance. Traditionally, prices have remained high during this stage because of customer loyalty and the absence of competitive products.

3. *Maturity.* Sales level off as the product matures. Because of increased competition, pressure on prices is increasing; some price reductions could be necessary.

4. *Decline.* Sales decline as the product becomes obsolete. Significant price cuts could be required to sell remaining inventories.

Target costing is more important for products with a relatively short market life cycle. Products with a long life cycle present many opportunities to continuously improve design and manufacturing procedures that are not available when a product has a short life cycle. Hence, extra care must go into the initial planning for short-lived products. This is especially true when short product life cycles are combined with increased worldwide competition. It is important to introduce a product first and at a price that ensures rapid market penetration.

BUSINESS INSIGHT

Pricing Must Consider Customers' Purchasing Power   Exchange rates add a wrinkle for pricing and target costing. The Japanese central bank is allowing the yen to slowly strengthen over the course of 2016. The exchange rate is expected to move from 120 yen to the dollar in early 2016 to an expected average of 105 yen to the dollar for the year. This affects profits, pricing, and costs for both foreign and domestic firms. **Ford** executives have complained that the weak yen gave **Toyota** a $10 billion advantage, and Toyota has announced that its recent financial performance has been artificially inflated by the weak yen. Weak currencies favor exports of domestic production as producing in yen and selling in dollars is a way for manufacturers to buy low and sell high. At the same time, foreign firms in the Japanese market are forced to either lower their prices or see sales drop, as the exchange rate makes imports more expensive. The Japanese experience highlights how foreign currency exchange rates are important considerations in setting price targets.

Sources: Sean Mclain and Yoko Kubota, "Toyota Warns Stronger Yen Will Drive Profits Down," *Wall Street Journal*, May 11, 2016. Keith Naughton, "Ford CFO Says Toyota Gains $10 Billion Advantage on Weak Yen," *Japan Times*, February 2, 2015.

Target Costing Helps Manage Life Cycle Costs

An awareness of the impact of today's actions on tomorrow's costs underlies the notion of **life cycle costs**, which include all costs associated with a product or service ranging from those incurred with the initial conception through design, pre-production, production, and after-production support.

The lower line in **Exhibit 20.6** illustrates the cumulative expenditure of funds over the life of a product. For low-technology products with relatively long product lives, decisions committing the organization to spend money are made at approximately the same time the money is spent. However, for high-technology products with relatively short product lives, most of the critical decisions affecting cost, such as product design and the selection of manufacturing procedures, are made before production begins. The top line in **Exhibit 20.6** represents decisions committing the organization to expenditures for a product. It has been estimated that as much as 70 percent of the cost of the typical automobile, and 95 percent of the cost of high-technology products, is committed during the design stage.

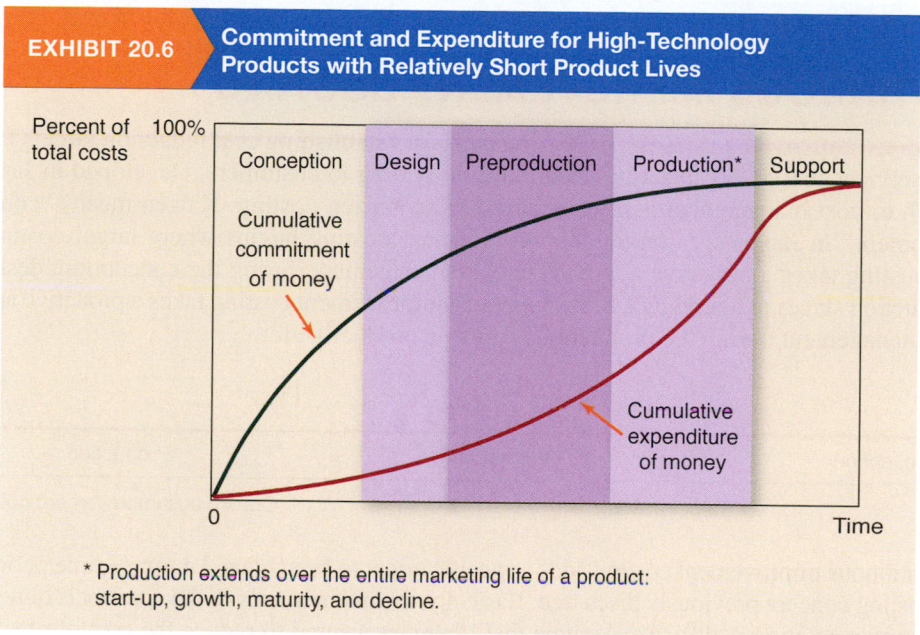

EXHIBIT 20.6   **Commitment and Expenditure for High-Technology Products with Relatively Short Product Lives**

Percent of total costs

100%

Conception   Design   Preproduction   Production*   Support

Cumulative commitment of money

Cumulative expenditure of money

0

Time

* Production extends over the entire marketing life of a product: start-up, growth, maturity, and decline.

Reflecting significant changes in vehicle production since the time of Henry Ford and the Model T, **General Motors** estimates that 70 percent of the cost of manufacturing truck transmissions is determined during design. Others estimate that up to 95 percent of the total costs associated with high-technology products are committed before the first unit is produced.

Life cycle cost concepts have also been usefully applied to low-technology issues, such as repair versus replace decisions. The New York State Throughway Authority uses life cycle concepts to determine the point at which it is more expensive to repair than to replace bridges.

YOU MAKE THE CALL

You are the Vice President of Product Development   As head of new product development for your electronics company, you are concerned that so many of the ideas for new products coming from your research and development group are not succeeding in the market. Many recent attempts to take new products to market have failed, not because of technological deficiencies in the products, but because the market would not support the high prices for new products that were necessary to produce a satisfactory profit. What should you do to try to reverse this trend of new product failures? [Answer, p. 913]

MID-CHAPTER REVIEW 3

Chrysler has been conducting early-stage research on hydrogen powered automobiles and is nearing the point where product development will soon begin. In order to determine the feasibility of the product, assume Chrysler has conducted marketing research that indicates that the price target for the product must be no more than $35,000 if it is to appeal to a large enough market segment to sell a minimum of 150,000 automobiles in the first year of production. The CFO has indicated that the new product must meet a 15% minimum profit margin requirement.

REQUIRED
a. Calculate the target cost per unit to produce the hydrogen powered automobile.
b. How would Chrysler go about determining whether the target cost can be achieved?
c. What should Chrysler do if the estimated cost to produce the product exceeds the target cost?

The solution to this review problem can be found on page 923.

LO4 Illustrate the relation between target costing and continuous improvement costing.

4

CONTINUOUS IMPROVEMENT COSTING

Continuous improvement (Kaizen) costing calls for establishing cost reduction targets for products or services that an organization is currently providing to customers. Developed in Japan, this approach to cost management is often referred to as Kaizen costing. Kaizen means "continuous improvement" in Japanese. Continuous improvement costing begins where target costing ends. Target costing takes a proactive approach to cost management during the conception, design, and preproduction stages of a product's life; continuous improvement costing takes a proactive approach to cost management during the production stage of a product's life:

Time

Conception	Design	Preproduction	Production
	Target costing		Continuous improvement costing

Continuous improvement costing adds a specific target to be achieved during a time period to the target costing concept previously discussed. Basically, the mathematics of the concept is quite simple, but its implementation is difficult. Assume that **Walmart** wanted to reduce the cost of merchandise handling in each of its stores, and management set a target reduction of 2 percent a year. If a given store had current annual merchandise handling costs of $100,000 and expected an increase the next year due to 10 percent growth, the budget for the next year would be $107,800 [($100,000 3 1.10) 3 0.98]. The budget for next year based on growth is $110,000 less the continuous improvement factor of 0.02.

Like target costing, Kaizen costing should be viewed as a serious attempt to make processes more efficient, while maintaining or improving quality, thereby making the company more competitive and profitable. In Kaizen costing, cost reductions can be achieved both internally and externally through continuous redesign and improved internal processes, and by working with vendors to improve their designs and processes. Kaizen is a team effort involving everyone who has an influence on costs. Kaizen is typically found in companies that have adopted a lean production philosophy. The following Business Insight discusses **Daisin**'s use of Kaizen to compete with Japanese suppliers for Toyota's business.

Successful companies use continuous improvement costing to avoid complacency. Competitors are constantly striving to win market share through better quality or lower prices. **Hewlett-Packard** studied **Epson** to determine its strengths and weaknesses. To fend off competition, prices and costs must be continuously reduced. To maintain its competitive position, Hewlett-Packard has reduced the list price of the basic inkjet printer from nearly $400 when first introduced to less than $50 today. This could not have been done without continuous reductions in costs.

The "Toyota Way" describes **Toyota's** method to set Kaizen cost reduction targets for each cost element, including purchased parts per car, direct materials per car, labor hours per car, and office utilities. Performance reports developed at the end of each month compare targeted and actual cost reductions. If actual cost reductions are more than the targeted cost reductions, the results are favorable; if the actual cost reductions are less than the targeted cost reductions, the results are unfavorable.

Because cost reduction targets are set before it is known how they will be achieved, continuous improvement costing can be stressful to employees. A critical element in motivating employee co-operation and teamwork in aggressive cost management techniques, such as target and continuous improvement costing, is to avoid using performance reports to place blame for failure. The proper response to an unfavorable performance report must be an offer of assistance to correct the failure.

BUSINESS INSIGHT

Thai Manufacturer Uses *Kaizen* to Compete   Thai auto component manufacturer **Daisin** uses the Japanese concept of *kaizen*, or continual improvement, to compete with Japanese suppliers for Toyota's business. The firm was founded as a joint venture with Japanese brake parts maker **Nissin Kogyo**. Since the firm became independent in 2000, it has focused on developing production efficiency and quality control skills to rival other Toyota suppliers. To differentiate itself from other suppliers, the company has developed design capabilities. This allows Toyota to delegate important design steps to Daisin and to look to the supplier for design improvements. Daisin's efforts to differentiate fit with its effort to apply continuous improvement to costing. The firm's factory is designed to optimize use of time and space. The company produces jigs and molds in-house so that it can improve production of these expensive and time-consuming tools. At the same time, bringing these tooling steps in-house makes its design focus possible. Daisin's application of kaizen has helped it carve out a place in Toyota's highly competitive supply chain.

Source: Kohei Fujimura and Natsuko Katsuki, "Thai Car Parts Makers Muscle into Supply Chains, Venture Abroad," *Nikkei Asian Review*, December 31, 2015.

MID-CHAPTER REVIEW 4

Patel Company does contract manufacturing of compact video cameras. At its Pacific plant, cost control has become a concern of management. The actual costs per unit for the years 2016 and 2017 were as follows:

	2016	2017
Direct materials		
Plastic case.	$ 4.50	$ 4.40
Lens set	17.00	17.20
Electrical component set	6.60	5.70
Film track	11.00	10.00
Direct labor.	32.00 (1.6 hours)	30.00 (1.5 hours)
Indirect manufacturing costs		
Variable.	7.50	7.10
Fixed.	3.00 (100,000 unit base)	2.85 (120,000 unit base)

The company manufactures all of the camera components except the lens sets, which it purchases from several vendors. The company has used target costing in the past but has not been able to meet the very competitive global pricing. Beginning in 2017, the company implemented a continuous improvement program that requires cost reduction targets.

REQUIRED

If continuous improvement (Kaizen) costing sets a first-year target of a 5 percent reduction of the 2016 base, how successful was the company in meeting 2017 per unit cost reduction targets? Support your answer with appropriate computations.

The solution to this review problem can be found on page 923.

LO5 Explain how benchmarking enhances quality management, continuous improvement, and process reengineering.

5

BENCHMARKING

When **Hewlett-Packard** studies **Epson** to identify Epson's strengths and weaknesses, each company is engaging in benchmarking, a practice that has been around for centuries. In recent years, however, as globalization and increased competitiveness have forced businesses to more aggressively compete on the bases of cost, quality, and service, benchmarking has become more formalized and open. No longer regarded as spying, **benchmarking** is now a systematic approach to identifying the best practices to help an organization take action to improve performance.

The formalization of benchmarking is largely attributed to a book written in the 1980s by Robert Camp of **Xerox**. Since then, many managers have come to believe that benchmarking is a requirement for success. Although benchmarking can focus on anything of interest, it typically deals with target costs for a product, service, or operation, customer satisfaction, quality, inventory levels, inventory turnover, cycle time, and productivity. Benchmarking initially focused on studying competitors, but benchmarking efforts have changed dramatically in recent years to include competitors, as well as companies in very different industries. For example, an electronics company like **Samsung** may benchmark its order fulfillment processes against **Amazon**, or a grocery company like the **Kroger Company** may benchmark its inventory management processes against an apparel company like **Gap**.

In considering how to go about benchmarking, an organization must be careful because it must consider nonfinancial limitations. No single numerical measurement can completely describe the performance of a complex device such as a microprocessor or a television camera, but benchmarks can be useful tools for comparing different products, components, and systems. The only totally accurate way to measure the performance of a given product is to test it against other products while performing the exact same activity. The following Business Insight box describes how **Intel Corporation** makes benchmarks available with some information on how to use them.

BUSINESS INSIGHT

Intel Benchmarks Performance   **Intel Corporation** divides its benchmarks into two types, component and system. Component benchmarks measure the performance of specific parts of a computer system, such as a microprocessor or hard disk drive. System benchmarks typically measure the performance of the entire computer system. The performance obtained will almost certainly vary from benchmark performance for a number of reasons. First, individual components must usually be tested in a complete computer system, and it is not always possible to eliminate the considerable effects that differences in system design and configuration have on benchmark results. For instance, vendors sell systems with a wide variety of disk capabilities and speeds, system memory, and video and graphics capabilities, all of which influence how the system components perform in actual use. Differences in software, including operating systems and compilers, also affect component and system performance. Finally, benchmark tests are typically written to be exemplary for only a certain type of computer application, which might or might not be similar to what is being compared.

A benchmark is, at most, only one type of information that an organization might use during the purchasing or manufacturing process. To get a true picture of the performance of a component or system being considered, the organization should consult industry sources, publicly available research reports, and even government publications of related information.

Source: As described on the Intel website at: http://www.intel.com/content/www/us/en/benchmarks/resources-benchmark-limitations.html

---

Benchmarking provides measurements that are useful in setting goals. It can lead to dramatic innovations, and it can help overcome resistance to change. When presented with a major cost reduction target, employees often believe they are being asked to do the impossible. Benchmarking can be a psychological tool that helps overcome resistance to change by showing how others have already met the target.

Although each organization has its own approach to benchmarking, the following six steps are typical:

1. Decide what to benchmark.
2. Plan the benchmark project.

3. Understand your own performance.
4. Study others.
5. Learn from the data.
6. Take action.

In recent years, professional organizations, such as the Institute of Management Accountants, have set up clearinghouses for benchmark information or have performed benchmarking studies of interest to members as have certain corporations such as **Intel**.

CHAPTER-END REVIEW

Visit the website iSixSigma.com. **iSixSigma** provides information on the Lean Six Sigma process and training and tools for Six Sigma certifications. The website dedicates a page to understanding the purpose and use of benchmarking.

REQUIRED

Visit: https://www.isixsigma.com/methodology/benchmarking/understanding-purpose-and-use-benchmarking/. Identify a few differences between benchmarking and traditional customer research.

The solution to this review problem can be found on page 924.

GUIDANCE ANSWERS . . . YOU MAKE THE CALL

You are the Vice President of Product Development   You should consider adopting target costing methods for new product development. Great product research ideas are successful only when they translate into products that can be produced and sold for an acceptable profit. Creating and producing new products before determining what the customer wants and is willing to pay often leads to failure. Target costing methods reverse this process by applying value chain concepts to bring customers and suppliers along the value chain together to produce a product only if it has features and a selling price that are acceptable to potential customers, and if its production costs allow the seller to make an acceptable profit.

KEY RATIOS

$$\text{Markup on cost base} = \frac{\text{Costs not included in the base} + \text{Desired profit}}{\text{Costs included in the base}}$$

KEY TERMS

activity, 897
benchmarking, 912
chained target costing, 907
continuous improvement
  (Kaizen) costing, 910

design for manufacture, 907
life cycle costs, 909
marginal cost, 901
marginal revenue, 900

processes, 897
target costing, 905
value chain, 896
virtual integration, 899

Assignments with the ⓜ logo in the margin are available in my BusinessCourse.
See the Preface of the book for details.

MULTIPLE CHOICE

1. In a value chain analysis:
   a.   The links of the chain are the various entities beginning with the producers of raw materials and ending with the final customer
   b.   Processes are collections of related activities intended to achieve a common purpose, such as procurement or production
   c.   Activities are the units of work that take place within the various processes, such as moving products from one workstation to another
   d.   All of the above

2. In a cost-based pricing model, the markup percentage is determined by an equation that:
   a.   Has the cost base in the denominator and any remaining costs plus the desired profit in the numerator
   b.   Has variable costs plus fixed costs in the denominator and total profit in the numerator
   c.   Always has only variable costs in the numerator
   d.   Always has desired profit as part of the denominator

3. Brown manufacturing makes profits with varying pricing structures, but it wants to determine the minimum markup percentage for all products based on manufacturing costs that will ensure that it does not fall below break-even point. It has estimated the following costs for the coming year for its planned production of all products.

Variable manufacturing costs.	$600,000
Fixed manufacturing costs.	200,000
Selling expenses	100,000
Administrative expenses	150,000

   The markup percentage required for Brown Company to break even is:
   a.   320%
   b.   31.25%
   c.   75%
   d.   Cannot be determined unless desired profit is known

4. Electronics Inc. is considering producing a new MP3 player that will offer several new features, including wireless earphones and wireless download of music and videos from any computer to the device. After much market research, it has determined that the appropriate target price for the new product is $90. To achieve its normal minimum profit margin of 20 percent, Electronics must be able to produce the product at a maximum total cost of:
   a. $108
   b. $70
   c. $72
   d. $18

5. Orange Inc. produces electronic devices such as computers and cell phones. It has recently introduced a digital reader, called the e-pad, but realizes that to compete effectively in the future, it must be able to lower the cost of production and the selling price. The current cost per unit for producing the e-pad is $138, and Orange is estimating inflation on e-pad components and supplies purchased externally to be 1.5 percent in the coming year. In the most recent period, these items had a cost of $74. Despite these cost increases, Orange has adopted a Kaizen cost improvement model that targets a 5 percent cost decrease. Orange's Kaizen cost target (rounded to two decimal places) for the e-pad is:
   a. $131.11
   b. $132.15
   c. $133.07
   d. $130.05

6. Typical characteristics of benchmarking include each of the following except:
   a.   Planning the benchmarking project
   b.   Understanding your own performance
   c.   Focusing on performance measures
   d.   Studying others

QUESTIONS

Q20-1. What are the relationships among an organization's value chain, processes, and activities?

Q20-2. What should be the goal of every organization along the value chain?

Q20-3. Distinguish between the value-added perspective and the value chain perspective.

Q20-4. Why are economic models seldom used for day-to-day pricing decisions?

Q20-5. Identify three reasons that cost-based approaches to pricing have traditionally been important.

Q20-6. Identify four drawbacks to cost-based pricing.

Q20-7. How does target costing differ from cost-based pricing?

Q20-8. Why is cost-based pricing more a technique, and target costing is more a philosophy? Which approach takes a more proactive approach to cost management?

Q20-9. Distinguish between the marketing life cycles of products incorporating advanced technology (such as household electronic equipment) and those using more traditional technology (such as household paper products). Why would life cycle costing be more important to a manufacturer of household electronic equipment than to a manufacturer of household paper products?

Q20-10. What is the relationship between target costing and continuous improvement (Kaizen) costing?

Q20-11. Distinguish between the seller's and the buyer's perspective of life cycle costs.

Q20-12. What advantage is derived from benchmarking against firms other than competitors?

MINI EXERCISES

M20-13. Developing a Value Chain from the Perspective of the Final Customer   LO1
Prepare a value chain for bottled orange juice that was purchased for personal consumption at an on-campus cafeteria.

M20-14. Developing a Value Chain: Upstream and Downstream Entities   LO1
Prepare a value chain for a firm that produces gasoline fuel. Clearly identify upstream and downstream entities in the value chain.

M20-15. Classifying Activities Using the Generic Internal Value Chain: Aluminum Cable Manufacturer   LO1
Using the generic internal value chain shown in **Exhibit 20.2**, classify each of the following activities of an aluminum cable manufacturer as inbound logistics, operations, outbound logistics, marketing and sales, service, or support.

   a.   Advertising in a construction magazine

   b.   Inspecting incoming aluminum ingots

   c.   Placing bar codes on coils of finished products

   d.   Borrowing money to finance a buildup of inventory

   e.   Hiring new employees

   f.   Heating aluminum ingots

   g.   Drawing wire from aluminum ingots

   h.   Coiling wire

   i.   Visiting a customer to determine the cause of cable breakage

   j.   Filing tax returns

M20-16. Classifying Activities Using the Generic Internal Value Chain: Cable TV Company   LO1
Using the generic internal value chain shown in **Exhibit 20.2**, classify each of the following activities of a cable television company as inbound logistics, operations, outbound logistics, marketing and sales, service, or support.

   a.   Installing coaxial cable in the apartment of a new customer

   b.   Repairing coaxial cable after a windstorm

   c.   Mailing brochures to prospective customers

   d.   Discussing a rate increase with members of a regulatory agency

   e.   Selling shares of stock in the company

   f.   Monitoring the quality of reception at the company's satellite downlink

   g.   Preparing financial statements

   h.   Visiting a customer to determine the cause of poor-quality television reception

i.   Traveling to a conference to learn about technological changes affecting the industry
j.   Replacing old routers with updated technology

LO2

Sue Bee Honey

M20-17. Product Pricing: Single Product

Sue Bee Honey is one of the largest processors of its product for the retail market. Assume that one of its plants has annual fixed costs totalling $12,000,000, of which $4,500,000 is for administrative and selling efforts. Sales are anticipated to be 800,000 cases a year. Variable costs for processing are $30 per case, and variable selling expenses are 25 percent of selling price. There are no variable administrative expenses.

REQUIRED

If the company desires a profit of $7,500,000, what is the selling price per case?

LO2

M20-18. Product Pricing: Single Product

Assume that you plan to open a soft ice cream franchise in a resort community during the summer months. Fixed operating costs for the three-month period are projected to be $9,080. Variable costs per serving include the cost of the ice cream and cone, $0.75, and a franchise fee payable to Austrian Ice, AG, $0.23. A market analysis prepared by Austrian Ice indicates that summer sales in the resort community should total 24,000 units.

REQUIRED

Determine the price you should charge for each ice cream cone to achieve a $25,000 profit for the three-month period.

LO3

M20-19. Target Pricing

A few years ago, Hotel Klingerhoffer, a large hotel chain, announced that because occupancy rates had declined during the previous quarter, it was raising room rates to cover the cost of its increase in vacant rooms. Although not referring to accounting or economics, several business journalists during the week following the announcement questioned the basis for the rate increases. One stated that "Hotel Klingerhoffer increases rates of vacant rooms."

REQUIRED

a.   Did the journalist mean that vacant rooms would be more expensive? Explain.
b.   Do you think Hotel Klingerhoffer's action to raise room rates was based on economics, accounting, or both?

LO5

M20-20. Benchmarking

Your company is developing a new product for the computer printer industry. You have talked to several material vendors about being able to supply quality components for the new product. The product designers are satisfied with the company's ability to make the product in the current facilities. Numerous potential customers also have been surveyed, and most have indicated a willingness to buy the product if the price is competitive.

REQUIRED

What are some means of benchmarking the development and production of your new product?

EXERCISES

LO2

E20-21. Product Pricing: Single Product

Presented is the 2017 contribution income statement of Grafton Products.

GRAFTON PRODUCTS Contribution Income Statement For Year Ended December 31, 2017		
Sales (13,000 units)		$2,925,000
Less variable costs		
Cost of goods sold	$780,000	
Selling and administrative	208,000	(988,000)
Contribution margin		1,937,000
Less fixed costs		
Manufacturing overhead	780,000	
Selling and administrative	315,000	(1,095,000)
Net income		$ 842,000

During the coming year, Grafton expects an increase in variable manufacturing costs of $12 per unit and in fixed manufacturing costs of $39,000.

REQUIRED

a. If sales for 2018 remain at 13,000 units, what price should Grafton charge to obtain the same profit as last year?

b. Management believes that sales can be increased to 16,000 units if the selling price is lowered to $200. Is this action desirable?

c. After considering the expected increases in costs, what sales volume is needed to earn a profit of $254,800 with a unit selling price of $200?

E20-22.   Cost-Based Pricing and Markups with Variable Costs

LO2

Computer Consultants provides computerized inventory consulting. The office and computer expenses are $800,000 annually and are not assigned to specific jobs. The consulting hours available for the year total 20,000, and the average consulting hour has $25 of variable costs.

REQUIRED

a. If the company desires a profit of $150,000, what should it charge per hour?

b. What is the markup on variable costs if the desired profit is $200,000?

c. If the desired profit is $75,000, what is the markup on variable costs to cover (1) unassigned costs and (2) desired profit?

E20-23.   Computing Markups

LO2

The predicted 2017 costs for Mighty Motors are as follows:

Manufacturing Costs		Selling and Administrative Costs	
Variable....................	$200,000	Variable....................	$600,000
Fixed........................	400,000	Fixed........................	300,000

Average total assets for 2017 are predicted to be $7,000,000.

REQUIRED

a. If management desires a 12 percent rate of return on total assets, what are the markup percentages based on total variable costs and based on total manufacturing costs?

b. If the company desires a 10 percent rate of return on total assets, what is the markup percentage on total manufacturing costs for (1) unassigned costs and (2) desired profit?

E20-24.   Product Pricing: Two Products

LO2

Disks for You manufactures two products, CDs and DVDs, both on the same assembly lines and packaged 10 disks per pack. The predicted sales are 400,000 packs of CDs and 500,000 packs of DVDs. The predicted costs for the year 2017 are as follows:

	Variable Costs	Fixed Costs
Materials...	$300,000	$600,000
Other..	350,000	900,000

Each product uses 50 percent of the materials costs. Based on manufacturing time, 40 percent of the other costs are assigned to the CDs, and 60 percent of the other costs are assigned to the DVDs. The management of Disks for You desires an annual profit of $200,000.

REQUIRED

a. What price should Disks for You charge for each disk pack if management believes the DVDs sell for 20 percent more than the CDs?

b. What is the total profit per product using the selling prices determined in part *a*?

E20-25.   Product Pricing: Two Products

LO2

Refer to the previous exercise, E20-24. Based on your calculations of the selling price and profit for CDs and DVDs, how should Disks for You evaluate the status of these two products? Should either CDs or DVDs be discontinued? What additional information does the management of Disks for You need in order to make an appropriate judgment on the future status of these two products?

E20-26.   Target Costing

LO3

Portland Equipment Company wants to develop a new log-splitting machine for rural homeowners. Market research has determined that the company could sell 6,000 log-splitting machines per year at a retail price of $850 each. An independent catalog company would handle sales for an annual fee of $6,000 plus $59 per unit sold. The cost of the raw materials required to produce the log-splitting machines amounts to $95 per unit.

REQUIRED

If company management desires a return equal to 10 percent of the final selling price, what is the target unit cost?

PROBLEMS

LO2

Macquarium Inc.

P20-27. Product Pricing: Two Products

Macquarium Inc. provides computer-related services to its clients. Its two primary services are are Web page design (WPD), and Internet consulting services (ICS). Assume that Macquarium's management expects to earn a 20 percent annual return on the assets invested. Macquarium has invested $9 million since its opening. The annual costs for the coming year are expected to be as follows:

	Variable Costs	Fixed Costs
Consulting support..................................	$600,000	$1,500,000
Sales and administration	180,000	900,000

The two services expend about equal costs per hour, and the predicted hours for the coming year are 40,000 for WPD and 20,000 for ICS.

REQUIRED

a.   If markup is based on variable costs, how much revenue must each service generate to provide the profit expected by corporate headquarters? What is the anticipated revenue per hour for each service?

b.   If the markup is based on total costs, how much revenue must each service generate to provide the expected profit?

c.   Explain why answers in requirements (a) and (b) are either the same or different.

d.   Comment on the advantages and disadvantages of using a cost-based pricing model.

LO3

Redback Networks Inc.

NASDAQ :: RBAK

P20-28. Target Costing

Redback Networks Inc., a subsidiary of Ericsson, provides networking services and related systems for 75 percent of the world's largest telephone companies. Assume that it is developing a new networking system for smaller, private telephone companies. To attract small companies, Redback must keep the price low without giving up too many of the features of larger networking systems. A marketing research study conducted on the company's behalf found that the price range must be $75,000 to $95,000. Management has determined a target price to be $85,000. The company's minimum profit percentage of sales is normally 25 percent, but the company is willing to reduce it to 18 percent to get the new product on the market. The fixed costs for the first year are anticipated to be $9,000,000. If sales reach 500 installed networks, the company needs to know how much it can spend on variable costs, which are primarily related to installation.

REQUIRED

a.   What is the amount of total cost allowed if the 18 percent profit target is allowed and the sales target is met? Show the amount for fixed and for variable costs.

b.   What is the amount of total costs allowed if the 25 percent normal profit target is desired at the 500 sales target? Show the amount for fixed and for variable costs.

c.   Discuss the advantages of using a target costing model versus using cost-based pricing.

LO4

P20-29. Continuous Improvement (Kaizen) Costing

Samira Company does contract manufacturing of compact video cameras. At its Pacific plant, cost control has become a concern of management. The actual costs per unit for the years 2016 and 2017 were as follows:

	2016		2017	
Direct materials				
Plastic case.	$ 7.50		$ 7.40	
Lens set	19.00		19.20	
Electrical component set	6.60		5.70	
Film track	11.00		9.50	
Direct labor.	32.00	(1.6 hours)	28.00	(1.5 hours)
Indirect manufacturing costs				
Variable.	7.50		7.10	
Fixed.	3.00	(100,000 unit base)	2.85	(120,000 unit base)

The company manufactures all of the camera components except the lens sets, which it purchases from several vendors. The company has used target costing in the past but has not been able to meet the very competitive global pricing. Beginning in 2017, the company implemented a continuous improvement program that requires cost reduction targets.

REQUIRED

a.   If continuous improvement (Kaizen) costing sets a first-year target of a 10 percent reduction of the 2016 base, how successful was the company in meeting 2017 per unit cost reduction targets? Support your answer with appropriate computations.

b.   Evaluate and discuss Samira's use of Kaizen costing.

P20-30.   Continuous Improvement (Kaizen) Costing

Assume that GE Capital, a division of **General Electric**, has been displeased with the costs of servicing its consumer loans. Assume that it has decided to implement a Kaizen-based cost improvement program. For 2017, GE Capital incurred the following costs ($ millions):

LO4

General Electric
NYSE :: GE

Loan processing.	$10,850
Customer relations.	2,100
Printing, mailing, and postage	490

For the next two years, GE Capital expects an increase in consumer loans of 6 percent annually with related increases in costs.

REQUIRED

a.   If the company has a continuous improvement goal of 3 percent each year, develop a budget for the next two years for the consumer loan department.

b.   Identify some possible ways that GE Capital can achieve the Kaizen costing goal.

c.   Discuss the potential benefits and limitations of GE's Kaizen costing model.

P20-31.   Price Setting: Multiple Products

Tech Com's predicted 2017 variable and fixed costs are as follows:

LO2

	Variable Costs	Fixed Costs
Manufacturing	$480,000	$315,900
Selling and administrative	216,000	60,500
Total	$696,000	$376,400

Tech Com is a small company producing a wide variety of computer interface devices. Per-unit manufacturing cost information about one of these products, a high-capacity flash drive, is as follows:

Direct materials	$10
Direct labor.	9
Manufacturing overhead	
Variable.	7
Fixed.	9
Total manufacturing costs	$35

Variable selling and administrative costs for the flash drive is $6 per unit. Management has set a 2017 target profit of $250,000 on the sale of the flash drive.

REQUIRED

a. Determine the markup percentage on variable costs required to earn the desired profit.
b. Use variable cost markup to determine a suggested selling price for the flash drive.
c. For the flash drive, break the markup on variable costs into separate parts for fixed costs and profit. Explain the significance of each part.
d. Determine the markup percentage on manufacturing costs required to earn the desired profit.
e. Use the manufacturing costs markup to determine a suggested selling price for the flash drive.
f. Evaluate the variable and the manufacturing cost approaches to determine the markup percentage.

LO2   P20-32.   Price Setting: Multiple Products

Pipestem Golf produces a wide variety of golfing equipment. In the past, product managers set prices using their professional judgment. Samuel Snead, the new controller, believes this practice has led to the significant underpricing of some products (with lost profits) and the significant overpricing of other products (with lost sales volume). You have been asked to assist Snead in developing a corporate approach to pricing. The output of your work should be a cost-based formula that can be used to develop initial selling prices for each product. Although product managers are allowed to adjust these prices to meet competition and to take advantage of market opportunities, they must explain such deviations in writing. The following 2017 cost information from the accounting records is available:

	Manufacturing Costs	Selling and Administrative Costs
Variable.....................	$412,500	$125,000
Fixed.......................	150,000	250,000

In 2017, Pipestem Golf reported earnings of $175,000. However, the controller believes that proper pricing should produce earnings of at least $225,000 on the same sales mix and unit volume. Accordingly, you are to use the preceding cost information and a target profit of $225,000 in developing a cost-based pricing formula. Selling and administrative expenses are not currently associated with individual products. However, you have obtained the following unit production cost information for the TW Irons:

Variable manufacturing costs...	$175
Fixed manufacturing costs...	75
Total	$250

REQUIRED

a. Determine the standard markup percentage for each of the following cost bases. Round answers to two decimal places.
  1. Full costs, including fixed and variable manufacturing costs, and fixed and variable selling and administrative costs.
  2. Manufacturing costs plus variable selling and administrative costs.
  3. Manufacturing costs.
  4. Variable costs.
  5. Variable manufacturing costs.
b. Explain why the markup percentages become progressively larger from requirement (a), parts (1) through (5).
c. Determine the initial price of a set of TW Irons using the manufacturing cost markup and the variable manufacturing cost markup.
d. Do you believe the controller's approach to product pricing is reasonable? Why or why not?

CASES AND PROJECTS

C20-33. Telephone Pole Rental Rates   **LO2, 3**

Most utility poles carry electric and telephone lines. In areas served by cable television, they also carry television cables. However, cable television companies rarely own any utility poles. Instead, they pay utility companies a rental fee for the use of each pole on a yearly basis. The determination of the rental fee is a source of frequent disagreement between the pole owners and the cable television companies. In one situation, pole owners were arguing for a $10 annual rental fee per pole; this was the standard rate the electric and telephone companies charged each other for the use of poles.

"We object to that," stated the representative of the cable television company. "With two users, the $10 fee represents a rental fee for one-half the pole. This fee is too high because we only use about six inches of each 40-foot pole."

"You are forgetting federal safety regulations," responded a representative of the electric company. "They specify certain distances between different types of lines on a utility pole. Television cables must be a minimum of 40 inches below power lines and 12 inches above telephone lines. If your cable is added to the pole, the total capacity is reduced because this space cannot be used for anything else. Besides, we have an investment in the poles; you don't. We should be entitled to a fair return on this investment. Furthermore, speaking of fair, your company should pay the same rental fee that the telephone company pays us and we pay them. We do not intend to change this fee."

In response, the cable television company representative made two points. First, any fee represents incremental income to the pole owners because the cable company would pay all costs of moving existing lines. Second, because the electric and telephone companies both strive to own the same number of poles in a service area, their pole rental fees cancel themselves. Hence, the fee they charge each other is not relevant.

REQUIRED

Evaluate the arguments presented by the cable television and electric company representatives. What factors should be considered in determining a pole rental fee?

C20-34. Target Costing   **LO3**

The president of Houston Electronics was pleased with the company's newest product, the HE Versatile CVD. The product is portable and can be attached to a computer to play or record computer programs or sound, attached to an amplifier to play or record music, or attached to a television to play or record TV programs. It can even be attached to a camcorder to record videos directly on compact disks rather than on tape. It also can be used with a headset to play or record sound. The proud president announced that this unique and innovative product would be an important factor in reestablishing the North American consumer electronics industry.

Based on development costs and predictions of sales volume, manufacturing costs, and distribution costs, the cost-based price of the HE Versatile CVD was determined to be $425. Following a market-skimming strategy, management set the initial selling price at $525. The marketing plan was to reduce the selling price by $50 during each of the first two years of the product's life to obtain the highest contribution possible from each market segment.

The initial sales of the HE Versatile CVD were strong, and Houston Electronics found itself adding second and third production shifts. Although these shifts were expensive, at a selling price of $525, the product had ample contribution margin to remain highly profitable. The president was talking with the company's major investors about the desirability of obtaining financing for a major plant expansion when the bad news arrived. A foreign company had announced that it would shortly introduce a similar product that would incorporate new design features and sell for only $350. The president was shocked. "Why," she remarked, "it costs us $375 to put a complete unit in the hands of customers."

REQUIRED

How could the foreign competitor profitably sell a similar product for less than the manufacturing costs to Houston Electronics? What advice do you have for the president concerning the HE Versatile CVD? What advice would you have to help the company avoid similar problems in the future?

SOLUTIONS TO REVIEW PROBLEMS

Mid-Chapter Review 1

SOLUTION

Student answers will vary; possible responses include:

Inbound Logistics:
    Company-appointed buyers
    Unroasted coffee beans are brought in from growers in farming communities in key coffee growing regions
    Starbucks roasting facilitates, storage sites, and regional distribution centers
Operations:
    Direct stores operated by company
    Licensed stores
    Stores add to customer value by offering free Wi-Fi and phone charging stations
Outbound Logistics:
    Customers buy from company-operated and licensed stores
    Online sales for limited products are available
    Limited selection of products can be purchased in leading supermarket chains
Marketing and Sales:
    Traditionally Starbucks has relied on customer loyalty through customer service and high quality.
    As competition increases, it is increasing its budget for promotions, advertising, and public relations activities.
Service:
    Strives for customer loyalty through customer service and quality products. Its mission statement is, "To inspire and nurture the human spirit—one person, one cup and one neighborhood at a time."[2]

Mid-Chapter Review 2

SOLUTION

a.

Desired annual profit ($2,000,000 × 0.10)		$200,000
Actual profit		(150,000)
Amount actual profit fell short of achieving the desired return		$ 50,000

b.

Predicted costs		
Variable	$450,000	
Fixed	600,000	$1,050,000
Desired profit		250,000
Required revenue		$1,300,000
Unit sales		÷ 100,000
Required unit selling price		$ 13

c.

Variable manufacturing costs per unit ($300,000/100,000 unit)	= $3
Selling price as a percent of variable manufacturing costs	= $13/3
	= 433⅓%
Markup as a percent of variable manufacturing costs ($10/$3)	= 333⅓%

---

[2] http://investor.starbucks.com/

d. Detail of markup on variable manufacturing costs:

1. Unassigned costs

Variable selling and administrative.	$150,000	
Fixed costs.	600,000	$750,000
Variable manufacturing costs.		÷300,000
Markup on variable manufacturing costs to cover unassigned costs . .		250%

2. | | |
|---|---|
| Desired profit . . . . | $250,000 |
| Variable manufacturing costs. . . . . | ÷300,000 |
| Additional markup on variable manufacturing costs to achieve desired profit ($250,000) . . . . | 83⅓% |

Mid-Chapter Review 3

SOLUTION

a.

Total revenue (150,000 × $35,000)	$5,250,000,000
Required profit margin (15%).	−787,500,000
Total cost	$4,462,500,000
Number of units	÷ 150,000
Target cost per unit.	$ 29,750

b. A new product such as an automobile is an extremely complex product with hundreds, if not thousands, of different components, involving many different vendors. Once Chrysler has determined what product features potential customers want, its engineers must determine how best to provide those features, working with vendors and potential vendors. The idea is to determine how best to provide the final product that the customers want at a cost that will provide a reasonable profit to Chrysler and its vendors.

c. Teams of engineers, accountants, designers, etc. from Chrysler and its vendors should work together to try to achieve the target cost. If initial cost estimates are too high, they should explore every possibility, including redesign of the product, using components from existing products, developing new production systems, etc. to meet the target cost. If it is finally determined that the target cannot be reached, then management has to decide if it is willing to go forward with the product with a lower than desired initial profit margin. In some cases, managers will proceed with the idea that additional cost savings will be found (using Kaizen costing methods) after the product is in production.

Mid-Chapter Review 4

SOLUTION

Item	2016 Base	× 95%	2017 Target	2017 Actual	Variance
Direct materials:					
Plastic case.	$ 4.50	0.95	$ 4.275	$ 4.40	$0.125 U
Lens set	17.00	0.95	16.15	17.20	1.05 U
Electrical set	6.60	0.95	6.27	5.70	0.57 F
Film track	11.00	0.95	10.45	10.00	0.45 F
Direct labor.	32.00	0.95	30.40	30.00	0.40 F
Indirect mfg:					
Variable costs	7.50	0.95	7.125	7.10	0.025 F
Fixed costs	3.00	0.95	2.85*	2.85	0.00*

*If 120,000 were used to adjust the 2017 base, the target would be $2.375 [(100,000 × $3 × 0.95)/120,000], providing for a variance of $0.475 U ($2.375 − $2.85).

The company made progress during the year 2017 with favorable variances for all components except cases and lens sets. The unfavorable lens items may require more consideration since they are vendor purchased. Maybe new vendors can be found, or current vendor contracts may be renegotiated.

The fixed manufacturing costs also need attention. The total fixed costs increased from $300,000 (100,000 × $3) to $342,000 (120,000 × $2.85). If they are fixed, why did they increase? Did increased production or other factors cause the increase? If it was volume driven, maybe some of the costs are not fixed.

SOLUTION

Student responses will vary. According to iSixSigma.com, neither approach is superior to the other. Which approach to use will depend on an organization's available time and resources. A few of the differences identified by iSixSigma.com include:

Differences Between Benchmarking and Competitor Research	
Benchmarking	**Competitor Research**
Focuses on best practices	Focuses on performance measures
Strives for continuous improvement	Bandage or quick fix
Partnering to share information	Considered corporate spying by some
Needed to maintain a competitive edge	Simply a "nice to have"
Adapting based on customer needs after examination of the best	Attempting to mirror another company/process

Source: https://www.isixsigma.com/methodology/benchmarking/understanding-purpose-and-use-benchmarking/

21

Operational Budgeting and Profit Planning

LEARNING OBJECTIVES

1. Discuss the importance of budgets. (p. 928)

2. Describe basic approaches to budgeting. (p. 929)

3. Explain the relations among elements of a master budget and develop a basic budget. (p. 932)

4. Explain and develop a basic manufacturing cost budget. (p. 941)

5. Analyze the relationship between budget development and manager behavior. (p. 946)

PINTEREST

www.pinterest.com

Every experienced executive knows that budgeting is the lifeblood of a business enterprise. It is the mechanism by which we plan the entity's operations for the upcoming year, or even decade. It's the way we quantitatively communicate those plans and coordinate the employees' efforts throughout the organization. The budget is unambiguous and unassailable; you either make your numbers or you don't, which makes the budget a valuable feedback loop by which to evaluate past operations. More importantly, preparing a budget alerts management ahead of time to the risks faced by the entity in the coming periods, whether those risks are a shortage of cash, too few or too many employees, or idle versus excess capacity.

Each period, businesses prepare what is called a "master budget." The master budget covers every aspect of the financial (and often nonfinancial) operations. The first step in the master budget is to budget or forecast sales revenue. But how do you prepare a budget for a company that, until recently, generated zero revenue while experiencing explosive growth? Pinterest has, at last count, 150 million users worldwide each month and has been valued at $11 billion. Pinterest was founded in 2010 but didn't even have a revenue model until 2014. The company works with businesses to understand how Pinterest traffic can generate sales revenue for those businesses by advertising on Pinterest. The advertising fees paid by those companies reached an estimated $100 million in 2015.

The way Pinterest generates traffic on its site is by allowing members to use the site as a virtual scrapbook, "pinning" places that they'd eventually like to travel to, recipes that they'd eventually like to prepare, and items that they'd eventually like to buy. Pinterest introduced corporate memberships that allow companies to use their corporate name on their pinboards, which offer its Pinterest followers a sneak peak of the company's upcoming product lineup before the items hit the store shelves. More recently, Pinterest launched Promoted Videos for showing Pinners how their ideas will work for others. The benefit to potential advertisers is clear cut.

From a budgeting perspective, the company may need to prepare its sales budget using several what-if scenarios to help it determine the proper pricing for its advertisements. In the meantime, Pinterest will need to develop expense budgets for everything from labor to selling to general and administrative expenses. At the time of this writing, the company had grown to over 500 employees, including new hires from Facebook, Google, and Amazon. It has a sprawling 58,000 square-foot office space in San Francisco, and it has invested in major information technology systems to extend its applications.

Clearly, Pinterest is an evolving, dynamic company, but it will have to pay close attention to its budgeting to manage its cash flow and capital investments. More importantly, if it wants to continue to raise funds from external sources, those investors and creditors will want to analyze the company's forecasted financial statements to estimate the expected rate of return on their investment in Pinterest. The budgeting techniques discussed in this chapter will aid the manager in planning and managing the organization's revenues, costs, and other quantitative variables in the face of constantly changing business conditions.

Source: Robert Hof, "Pinterest: Here Come the Ads (But They'll Be Tasteful)," *Forbes*, September 19, 2013; Lydia Dishman, "J. Crew's Smart Pinterest Play: Move Beyond Inspiration to Make a Sale," *Forbes*, August 20 2013; Kyle Stock, "Nordstrom Racks Now Powered by Pinterest," Bloomberg Businessweek, July 2, 2013; Jessi Hempel, "CEO Outlines the Future of Pinterest," *Fortune*, May 30, 2013; Eric Spitznagel, "Dude! The Battle to Become the Male Pinterest!" *Bloomberg Businessweek*, April 10, 2013; and Pui-Wing Tam and Spencer Ante, "As Pinterest Grows, Startup Seeks $2.5 Billion Valuation," *Wall Street Journal*, February 6, 2013, pp. B1–B2.

CHAPTER ORGANIZATION

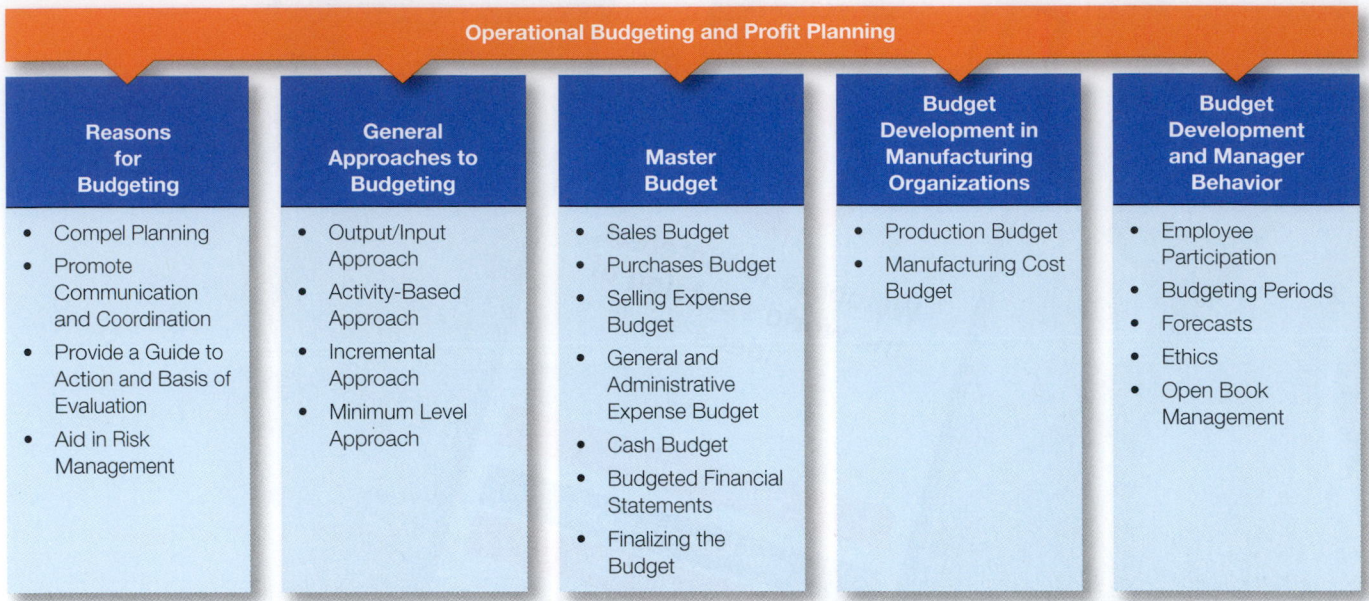

A **budget** is a formal plan of action expressed in monetary terms. The purpose of this chapter is to examine the concepts, relationships, and procedures used in budgeting. Our emphasis is on **operating budgets**, which concern the development of detailed plans to guide operations throughout the budget period. We consider the reasons that organizations budget and alternative approaches to budget development. We also examine budget assembly and consider issues related to manager behavior and the budgeting process.

LO1 Discuss the importance of budgets.

REASONS FOR BUDGETING

Operating managers frequently regard budgeting as a time-consuming task that diverts attention from current problems. Indeed, the development of an effective budget is a difficult job. It is also a necessary one. Organizations that do not plan are likely to wander aimlessly and ultimately succumb to the swirl of current events. The formal development of a budget helps to ensure both success and survival. As discussed below, budgeting compels planning; it improves communications and coordination among organizational elements; it provides a guide to action; and it provides a basis of performance evaluation. Budget models are also used to analyze and prepare for various business risks.

Compel Planning

Formal budgeting procedures require people to think about the future. Without the discipline of formal planning procedures, busy operating managers would not find time to plan. Immediate needs would consume all available time. Formal budgeting procedures, with specified deadlines, force managers to plan for the future by making the completion of the budget another immediate need. Budgeting moves an organization from an informal "reactive" style to a formal "proactive" style of management. As a result, management and other employees spend less time solving unanticipated problems and more time on positive measures and preventative actions.

Promote Communication and Coordination

When operating responsibilities are divided, it is difficult to synchronize activities. Production must know what marketing intends to sell. Purchasing and personnel must know the factory's material and labor requirements. The treasurer must plan to ensure the availability of the cash to support receivables, inventories, and capital expenditures. Budgeting forces the managers of these diverse functions to communicate their plans and coordinate their activities. It helps ensure that plans are feasible (Can purchasing obtain adequate inventories to support projected sales?) and that they are synchronized (Will inventory be available in advance of an advertising campaign?). The final version of the budget emerges after an extensive (often lengthy) process of communication and coordination.

Provide a Guide to Action and Basis of Evaluation

Once the budget has been finalized, the various operating managers know what is expected of them, and they can set about doing it. If employees do not have a guide to action, their efforts could be wasted on unproductive or even counterproductive activities.

After employees accept the budget as a guide to action, they can be held responsible for their portion of the budget. When results do not agree with plans, managers attempt to determine the cause of the divergence. This information is then used to adjust operations or to modify plans. More generally, budgeting is an important part of **management by exception**, whereby management directs attention only to those activities not proceeding according to plan. Without the budget, management might spend an inordinate amount of time seeking explanation of past activities and not enough time planning future activities.

Aid in Risk Management

The models used for budgeting are also used in managing risk. **Risk** is the danger that things will not go according to plan. Although some risk results from anticipated events having a positive impact, such as an increase in sales volume or selling prices, risk is more typically associated with events that have a negative impact, like a work stoppage at a key supplier, a fire, or hackers shutting down a retail website for an extended period of time.

Risk management (also called enterprise risk management) is the process of identifying, evaluating, and planning possible responses to risks that could impede an organization from achieving its plans. It also involves monitoring the sources of risk. An organization's budget model can be used to evaluate the financial impact of a risk and to determine, from a financial perspective, the best response to a risk. The Research Insight on the following page summarizes a proposed approach to risk management. The performance evaluation procedures considered in Chapter 22, if completed on a timely basis, assist in monitoring risk.

MID-CHAPTER REVIEW 1

Mark Fisher was recently hired as an intern at Mobile Innovations, a small manufacturer and seller of conveyer systems, which are used by other businesses in their manufacturing processes. After recently finishing a course in management accounting, Mark asks his manager if he can see a copy of the current year's operating budget. His manager replies that as a small business, they are too busy focusing on day-to-day operations to take the time to create a budget.

REQUIRED
Discuss some ways that an operating budget might benefit Mobile Innovations.

The solution to this review problem can be found on page 964.

GENERAL APPROACHES TO BUDGETING

Before an organization can develop operating budgets, management must decide which approaches to budget planning will be used for the various revenue and expenditure activities and organizational units. Widely used planning approaches to budgeting include the output/input, activity-based, incremental, and minimum level approaches.

LO2 Describe basic approaches to budgeting.

2

Output/Input Approach

The **output/input approach** budgets physical inputs and costs as a function of planned unit-level activities. This approach is often used for service, merchandising, manufacturing, and distribution activities that have defined relationships between effort and accomplishment. If each unit produced requires 2 pounds of direct materials that cost $5 each, and the planned production volume is 25 units, the budgeted inputs and costs for direct materials are 50 pounds (25 units × 2 pounds per unit) and $250 (50 pounds × $5 per pound).

The budgeted inputs are a function of the planned outputs. The output/input approach starts with the planned outputs and works backward to budget the inputs. It is difficult to use this approach for costs that do not respond to changes in unit-level cost drivers.

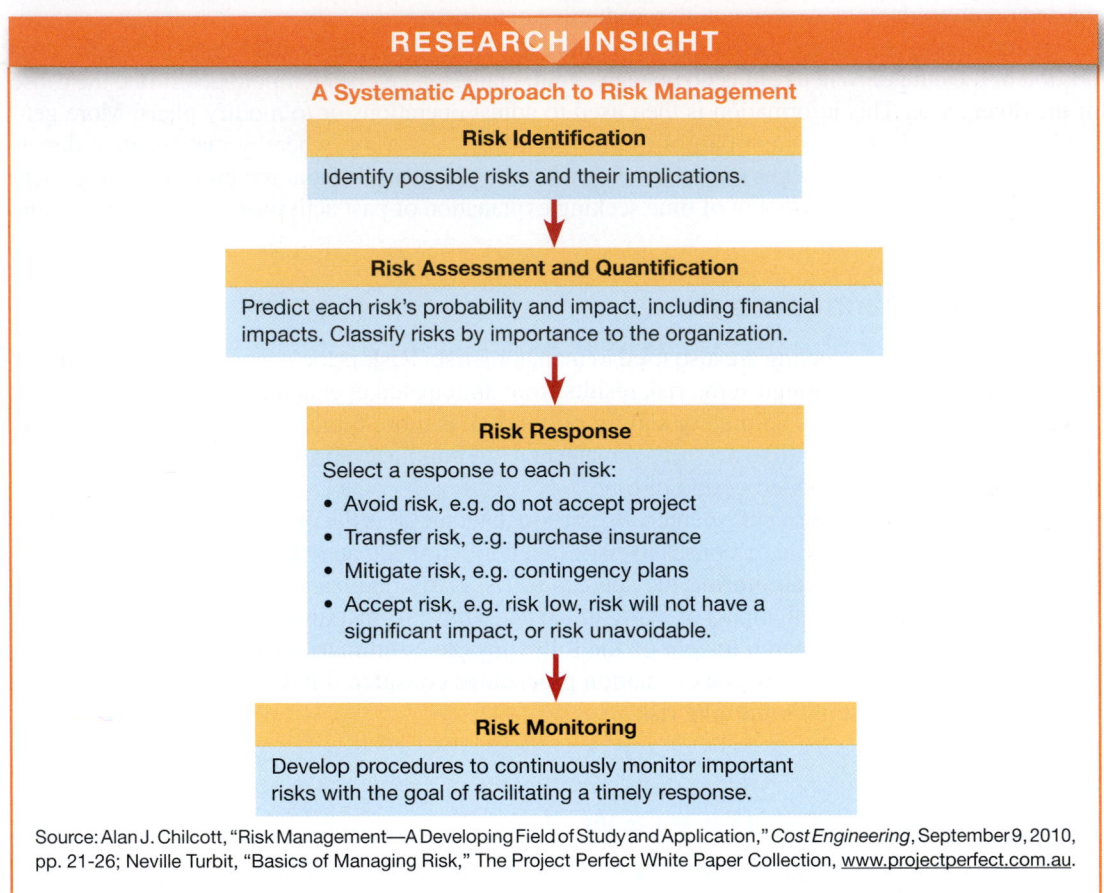

RESEARCH INSIGHT

A Systematic Approach to Risk Management

Risk Identification

Identify possible risks and their implications.

Risk Assessment and Quantification

Predict each risk's probability and impact, including financial impacts. Classify risks by importance to the organization.

Risk Response

Select a response to each risk:
- Avoid risk, e.g. do not accept project
- Transfer risk, e.g. purchase insurance
- Mitigate risk, e.g. contingency plans
- Accept risk, e.g. risk low, risk will not have a significant impact, or risk unavoidable.

Risk Monitoring

Develop procedures to continuously monitor important risks with the goal of facilitating a timely response.

Source: Alan J. Chilcott, "Risk Management—A Developing Field of Study and Application," *Cost Engineering*, September 9, 2010, pp. 21-26; Neville Turbit, "Basics of Managing Risk," The Project Perfect White Paper Collection, www.projectperfect.com.au.

Activity-Based Approach

The **activity-based approach** is a type of output/input method, but it reduces the distortions in the transformation through emphasis on the expected cost of the planned activities that will be consumed for a process, department, service, product, or other budget objective. Overhead costs are budgeted on the basis of the cost objective's anticipated consumption of activities, not based only on some broad-based cost driver such as direct labor hours or machine hours.

The amount of each activity cost driver used by each budget objective (for example, product or service) is determined and multiplied by the cost per unit of the activity cost driver. The result is an estimate of the costs of each product or service based on cost drivers such as assembly-line setup or inspections, as well as the traditional volume-based drivers such as direct labor hours or units of direct materials consumed. Activity-based budgeting predicts costs of budget objectives by adding all costs of the activity cost drivers that each product or service is budgeted to consume. In evaluating the proposed budget, management would focus their attention on identifying the optimal set of activities rather than just the output/input relationships.

Incremental Approach

The **incremental approach** budgets costs for a coming period as a dollar or percentage change from the amount budgeted for (or spent during) some previous period. This approach is often used when the relationships between inputs and outputs are weak or nonexistent. For example, it is difficult to establish a clear relationship between sales volume and advertising expenditures. Consequently, the budgeted amount of advertising for a future period is often based on the budgeted or actual advertising expenditures in a previous period. If budgeted advertising expenditures for 2017 were $200,000, the budgeted expenditures for 2018 would be some increment, say 5 percent, above $200,000. In evaluating the proposed 2018 budget, management would accept the $200,000 base and focus attention on justifying the increment.

The incremental approach is widely used in government and not-for-profit organizations. In seeking a budget appropriation, a manager using the incremental approach need only justify proposed expenditures in excess of the previous budget. The primary advantage of the incremental approach is that it simplifies the budget process by considering only the increments in the various budget items. A major disadvantage is that existing waste and inefficiencies could escalate year after year.

Minimum Level Approach

Using the **minimum level approach**, an organization establishes a base amount for budget items and requires explanation or justification for any budgeted amount above the minimum (base). This base is usually significantly less than the base used in the incremental approach. It likely is the minimum amount necessary to keep a program or organizational unit viable. For example, the corporate director of product development would need some basic amount to avoid canceling ongoing projects. Additional increments might also be included, first to support the current level of product development and second to undertake desirable new projects.

BUSINESS INSIGHT

Budgeting for Uncertainty   As a firm builds its master budget, budgeting for uncertainty is essential. The financial struggles of **Kodak** can be seen as a cautionary tale for mature firms dealing with technological uncertainty. Kodak was decidedly ahead of the digital camera trend, creating its first prototype in the 1970s. Kodak's technology was foiled by its approach to uncertainty. Traditional approaches to long-term strategy and budgeting focus on forecasting trends and committing to the best single strategy. Kodak knew that the future of photography was digital but chose to bet on its core business rather than making risky investments in new products that would undermine its core.

Analysts at **Bain and Company** argue that firms should budget for a "range of futures," by:

1. Deciding what uncertainties could affect the company. (The potential of digital photography is just such an uncertainty.)
2. Develop probable scenarios for the future. Consider the upsides and downsides of each scenario. (Kodak clearly knew that digital photography was a potential scenario.)
3. Match strategic plans to scenarios, balancing investment with flexibility to adjust to various states of the world.
4. Establish signals that trigger adoption of scenarios.

Though Kodak had the technology to adapt to the new market the company was unable, or unwilling, to restructure its business accordingly. If the management team had agreed that they would shift toward digital cameras when digital had 15% market share, it would have been positioned to switch. By preparing for multiple uncertain futures and setting triggers, managers pre-commit to difficult decisions, and are prepared to be flexible.

General Electric's $200 million "multimodal" factory in Pune, India, is an example of this flexible scenario-based approach. Leadership was confident that four different businesses would need capacity in India, but the mix was uncertain. Rather than commit to a mix, GE built flexibility into the factory. The advanced facility they built has 1,500 employees and a 67-acre footprint that is designed to switch between production of jet engines, locomotives, wind turbines, and water treatment equipment depending on future demand. Rather than committing to one business model, GE has prepared for several possible scenarios.

Source: Martin Toner, Nikhil Ojha, Piet de Paepe, and Miguel Simoes de Melo, "A Strategy for Thriving in Uncertainty," *Bain Brief*, Bain & Company, August 12, 2015.

Some organizations, especially units of government, employ a variation of the minimum level approach, identified as zero-based budgeting. Under **zero-based budgeting** every dollar of expenditure must be justified. The essence of zero-based budgeting is breaking an organizational unit's total budget into program packages with related costs. Management then ranks all program packages on the basis of the perceived benefits in relationship to their costs. Program packages are then funded for the budget period using this ranking. High-ranking packages are most likely to be funded and low-ranking packages are least likely to be funded.

Budgeting for objectives is a variation on the minimum level approach that combines elements of activity-based and zero-based budgeting with a need to live within fixed financial constraints. The minimum level approach improves on the incremental approach by questioning the necessity for costs included in the base of the incremental approach, but it is very time consuming. All three approaches are often used within the same organization. A pharmaceutical company might use the output/input or the activity-based approach to budget distribution expenditures, the incremental approach to budget administrative salaries, and the minimum level approach to budget research and development.

MID-CHAPTER REVIEW 2

To illustrate the various approaches to budgeting discussed above, assume that **McNeil**, a division of **Johnson & Johnson**, manufactures two products in institutional quantities, Regular Strength Tylenol and Tylenol Extra Strength. Suppose last period, McNeil produced 18,000 units of Regular and 45,000 units of Extra Strength at a total unit cost of $38 for Regular and $32 for Extra Strength. Also suppose the current period, overall costs are expected to rise about 3.5 percent over the last period. Assume estimated overhead costs of $408,500 for the next period include the cost of assembly-line setups, engineering and maintenance, and inspections. Total estimated assembly hours is 50,000 hours; therefore, the estimated overhead cost per assembly hour is $8.17. Other predicted data for the next period follow:

	Regular	Extra Strength
Direct materials (per unit)	$20.00	$14.50
Direct labor hours of assembly time (per unit)	0.5	0.8
Assembly labor cost (per hour)	$18	$18
Total estimated production (in units)	20,000	50,000
Total setup hours	1,000	1,500
Total engineering and maintenance hours	500	600
Total inspections	650	580
Setup cost (per setup hour)	$25	$25
Engineering and maintenance (per hour)	$35	$35
Inspection cost (per inspection)	$250	$250

REQUIRED

a. Calculate McNeil's budgeted cost per unit to produce Regular and Extra Strength Tylenol during the next period, assuming it uses an output/input approach and budgets overhead cost based only on assembly hours.

b. Repeat *a.*, assuming McNeil uses an activity-based approach and budgets overhead cost based on budgeted activity costs.

c. Repeat *a.*, assuming McNeil uses an incremental approach for budgeting overhead cost.

d. Explain how the minimum level approach differs from the above methods.

The solution to this review problem can be found on page 965.

LO3 Explain the relations among elements of a master budget and develop a basic budget.

3

MASTER BUDGET

The culmination of the budgeting process is the preparation of a **master budget** for the entire organization that considers all interrelationships among organization units. The master budget groups together all budgets and supporting schedules and coordinates all financial and operational activities, placing them into an organization-wide set of budgets for a given time period.

Because it explicitly considers organizational interrelationships, the master budget is more complex than budgets developed for products, services, organization units, or specific processes. The elements of the master budget depend on the nature of the business, its products or services, processes and organization, and management needs.

A major goal of developing a master budget is to ensure the smooth functioning of a business throughout the budget period and the organization's operating cycle. As shown in **Exhibit 21.1**, the operating cycle involves the conversion of cash into other assets, which are intended to produce revenues in excess of their costs. The cycle generally follows a path from cash, to inventories, to receivables (via sales or services), and back to cash. There are, of course, intermediate processes such as the purchase or manufacture of inventories, payments of accounts payable, and the collection of receivables. The master budget is merely a detailed model of the firm's operating cycle that includes all internal processes.

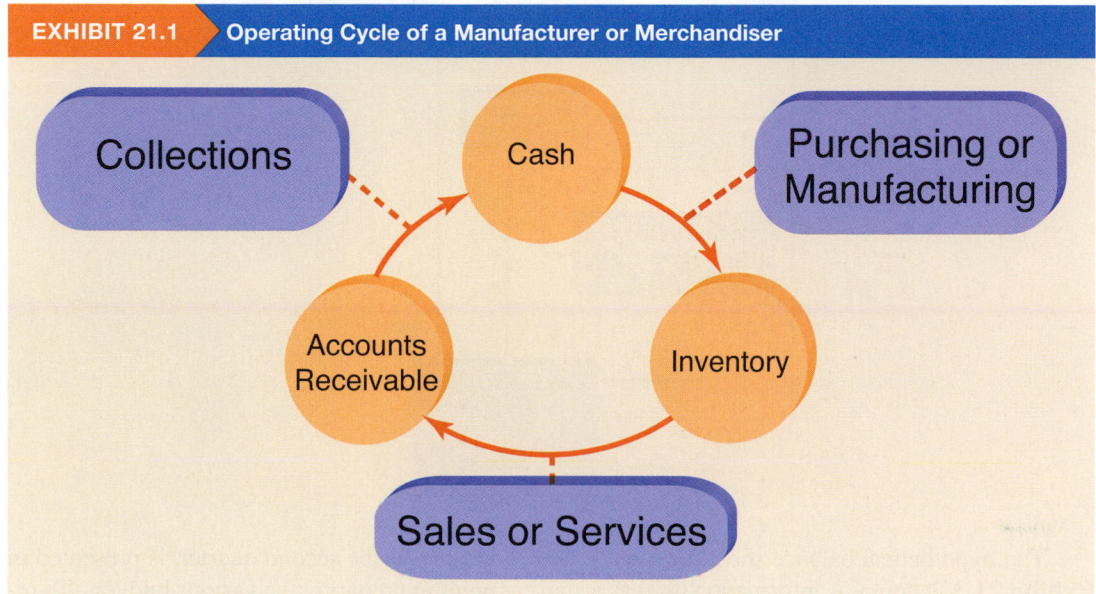

EXHIBIT 21.1 Operating Cycle of a Manufacturer or Merchandiser

Most for-profit organizations begin the budgeting process with the development of the sales budget and conclude with the development of budgeted financial statements. **Exhibit 21.2** depicts the annual budget assembly process in a retail merchandising organization. Most of the budget data flow from sales toward cash and then toward the budgeted financial statements.

To illustrate the procedures involved in budget assembly, a hypothetical monthly budget for the second quarter of 2017 is developed for **REI**, a retail organization specializing in gear and apparel for outdoor and fitness activities. The assembly sequence follows the overview illustrated in **Exhibit 21.2**. Each element of the budget process in **Exhibit 21.2** is illustrated in a separate exhibit. Because of the numerous elements in the budget process illustrated for REI, you will find it useful to refer to **Exhibit 21.2** often.

The activities of a business can be summarized under three broad categories: operating activities, financing activities, and investing activities. To simplify the illustration, assume that REI engaged in no investing activities during the budget period and that the only anticipated financing activity is short-term borrowing. Normal profit-related activities performed in conducting the daily affairs of an organization are called **operating activities**. Assume the operating activities of REI include the following:

1. Purchasing inventory intended for sale.
2. Selling goods or services.
3. Purchasing and using goods and services classified as selling expenses.
4. Purchasing and using goods and services classified as general and administrative expenses.

In addition to preparing the budget for each operating activity, companies prepare a cash budget for cash receipts and disbursements related to their operating activities as well as for financing and investing activities. The importance of cash planning makes this budget a vital part of the total budget process. Management must, for example, be aware in advance of the need to borrow and have some idea when borrowed funds can be repaid.

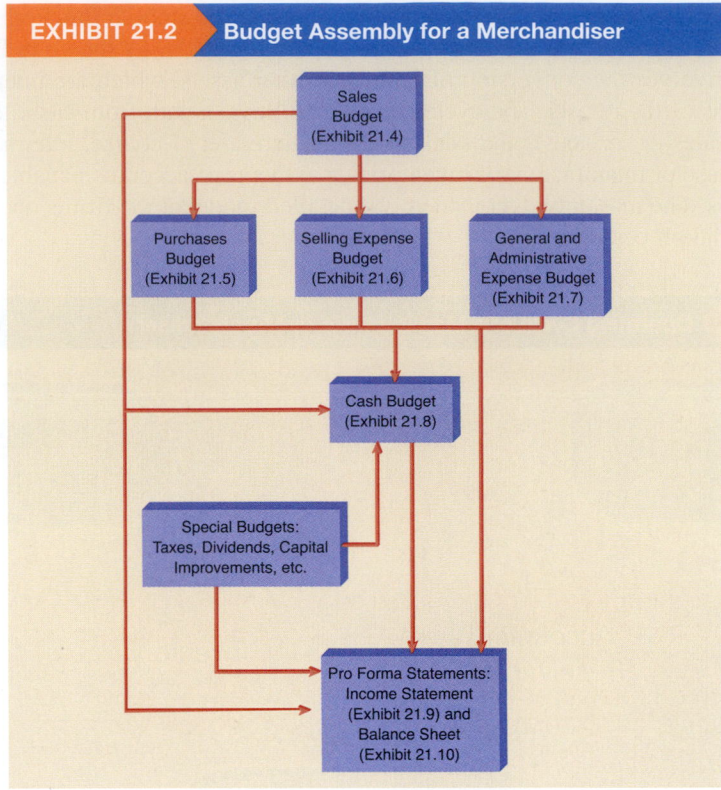

EXHIBIT 21.2 Budget Assembly for a Merchandiser

The hypothetical balance sheet for April 1, 2017, the start of the second quarter, is presented in **Exhibit 21.3**. It contains information used as a starting point in preparing the various budgets. To reduce complexity, we use the output/input approach to budget variable costs and assume that the budgets for other costs were previously developed using the incremental approach. Budgets to be prepared include those for sales, purchases, selling expense, general and administrative expense, and cash.

Beginning of the period balance sheet.

The balance sheet at the beginning of the budgeted period contains information used as a starting point in preparing the various budgets.

EXHIBIT 21.3 Initial Balance Sheet

REI
Balance Sheet
April 1, 2017

Assets			
Current assets			
Cash		$ 15,000	
Accounts receivable, net		59,200	
Merchandise Inventory		157,000	$231,200
Fixed assets			
Buildings and equipment	$460,000		
Less accumulated depreciation	(124,800)	335,200	
Land		60,000	395,200
Total assets			$626,400
Liabilities and Stockholders' Equity			
Current liabilities			
Accounts payable		$ 84,000	
Taxes payable*		35,000	$119,000
Stockholders' equity			
Capital stock		350,000	
Retained earnings		157,400	507,400
Total liabilities and stockholders' equity			$626,400

*Quarterly income taxes are paid within 30 days of the end of each quarter.

Sales Budget

The **sales budget** includes a forecast of sales revenue, and it can also contain a forecast of unit sales and sales collections. Because sales drive almost all other activities in a for-profit organization, developing a sales budget is the starting point in the budgeting process. Managers use the best available information to accurately forecast future market conditions. These forecasts, when considered along with merchandise available, marketing and promotion plans, and expected pricing policies, should lead to the most dependable sales budget. Assume the sales budget of REI is in **Exhibit 21.4**.

EXHIBIT 21.4	Sales Budget					
	REI					
	Sales Budget					
	For the Second Quarter Ending June 30, 2017					
	April	**May**	**June**	**Quarter Total**	**July**	
Sales.	$190,000	$228,000	$250,000	$668,000	$309,000	

Sales budget.

Developing a sales budget is the starting point in the budgeting process.

The information in the sales budget along with predictions of the expected portion of cash sales and the timing of collections from credit sales are used to calculate cash receipts. In the event of a projected cash shortfall, management could consider ways to increase cash sales or to accelerate the collection of receipts from credit sales.

Purchases Budget

The **purchases budget** indicates the merchandise that must be acquired to meet sales needs and ending inventory requirements. It can be referred to as a merchandise budget if it contains only purchases of merchandise for sale. However, for a manufacturer it would include purchase of raw materials. The purchases budget, shown in **Exhibit 21.5**, includes only purchases of merchandise.

EXHIBIT 21.5	Purchases Budget				
	REI				
	Purchases Budget				
	For the Second Quarter Ending June 30, 2017				
	April	**May**	**June**	**Quarter Total**	**July**
Budgeted sales (Exhibit 21.4).	$190,000	$228,000	$250,000	$668,000	$309,000
Current cost of goods sold*.	$114,000	$136,800	$150,000	$400,800	
Desired ending inventory**.	168,400	175,000	192,700	192,700	
Total needs.	282,400	311,800	342,700	593,500	
Less beginning inventory***.	(157,000)	(168,400)	(175,000)	(157,000)	
Purchases.	$125,400	$143,400	$167,700	$436,500	

Purchases budget.

The purchases budget indicates the merchandise that must be acquired to meet sales needs and ending inventory requirements.

*Cost of goods sold is 60 percent of selling price

**Fifty percent of inventory required for next month's budgeted sales plus base inventory of $100,000.
April: ($228,000 May sales × 0.60 cost × 0.50 desired ending inventory) + $100,000
May: ($250,000 June sales × 0.60 cost × 0.50 desired ending inventory) + $100,000
June :($309,000 July sales × 0.60 cost × 0.50 desired ending inventory) + $100,000

***Fifty percent of current month sales × 0.60 cost plus base inventory of $100,000. Note monthly beginning inventory.
Same as previous month's ending inventory.

In reviewing REI's purchases budget, note the following:

- Because REI sells a wide variety of items, the purchases budget is expressed in terms of sales dollars, with the assumed cost of merchandise averaging 60 percent of the selling price. Management also keeps detailed records for budgeting the number of units of items carried. An organization that only sold a small number of items might present the sales budget in units as well as dollars.

- Assume management desires to have 50 percent of the inventory needed to fill the following month's sales in stock at the end of the previous month.

- To provide for a possible delay in the receipt of inventory and to meet variations in customer demand, assume REI maintains an additional base inventory of $100,000.

- The total inventory needs equal current sales plus desired ending inventory, including the base inventory.

- Budgeted purchases are computed as total inventory needs less the beginning inventory.

The information in the purchases budget and the information on expected timing of payments for purchases are used to budget cash disbursements for purchases. In the event of a projected cash shortfall, management can consider ways to delay the purchase of inventory or the payment for inventory purchases.

Selling Expense Budget

The **selling expense budget** presents the expenses the organization plans to incur in connection with sales and distribution. In the selling expense budget, **Exhibit 21.6**, the budgeted variable selling expenses are determined as a percentage of budgeted sales dollars. The budgeted fixed selling expenses are based on amounts obtained from the manager of the sales department. To simplify the presentation of the cash budget, assume REI pays its selling expenses in the month they are incurred.

Selling expense budget.	**EXHIBIT 21.6**	Selling Expense Budget			
	REI				
The selling expense budget presents the expenses the organization plans to incur in connection with sales and distribution.	**Selling Expense Budget**				
	For the Second Quarter Ending June 30, 2017				
		April	**May**	**June**	**Quarter Total**
	Budgeted sales (Exhibit 21.4)...............	$190,000	$228,000	$250,000	$668,000
	Variable selling expenses				
	Setup/Display (1% sales)..................	$ 1,900	$ 2,280	$ 2,500	$ 6,680
	Commissions (2% sales).................	3,800	4,560	5,000	13,360
	Miscellaneous (1% sales).................	1,900	2,280	2,500	6,680
	Total	7,600	9,120	10,000	26,720
	Fixed selling expenses				
	Advertising	2,250	2,250	2,250	6,750
	Office	1,250	1,250	1,250	3,750
	Miscellaneous............................	1,000	1,000	1,000	3,000
	Total	4,500	4,500	4,500	13,500
	Total selling expenses	$ 12,100	$ 13,620	$ 14,500	$ 40,220

General and Administrative Expense Budget

The **general and administrative expense budget** presents the expenses the organization plans to incur in connection with the general administration of the organization. Included are expenses for the accounting department, the computer center, and the president's office, for example. REI's assumed general and administrative expense budget is presented in **Exhibit 21.7**.

The depreciation of $2,000 per month is a noncash item and is not carried forward to the cash budget. No variable general and administrative costs are included because most expenditures categorized as general and administrative are related to top-management operations that do not vary with unit-level cost drivers. To simplify the presentation of the cash budget, assume that general and administrative expenses, except depreciation, are paid in the month they are incurred.

EXHIBIT 21.7	General and Administrative Expense Budget

REI
General and Administrative Expense Budget
For the Second Quarter Ending June 30, 2017

	April	May	June	Quarter Total
General and administrative expenses				
Compensation	$25,000	$25,000	$25,000	$75,000
Insurance	2,000	2,000	2,000	6,000
Depreciation	2,000	2,000	2,000	6,000
Utilities	3,000	3,000	3,000	9,000
Miscellaneous...............................	1,000	1,000	1,000	3,000
Total general and administrative expenses	$33,000	$33,000	$33,000	$99,000

General and administrative expense budget.

The general and administrative expense budget presents the expenses the organization plans to incur in connection with the general administration of the organization.

Cash Budget

The **cash budget** summarizes all cash receipts and disbursements expected to occur during the budget period. Cash is critical to survival. Income is like food and cash is like water. Food is necessary to survive and prosper over time, but you can get along without food for a short period of time. You cannot survive very long without water. Hence, cash budgeting is very important, especially in a small business where cash receipts from sales lag purchases of inventory. As pointed out in the following Business Insight, cash budgets are also critical for managing the impact of changing customer preferences.

BUSINESS INSIGHT

Budgeting within a Consumer Products Giant   Budgeting within a large diversified multinational corporation is challenging when the business spans many markets and countries. **Unilever** operates segments across the globe with product lines from dairy to skin care, so the company must make sure they have the ability to invest in new products in these areas while insulating its performance from exchange rate fluctuations. In the first quarter of 2016, Unilever PCL posted an increase in both volume and price of sales but a 2% decrease in revenue. To limit its exposure to exchange rates, Unilever has adopted strict cost controls and is restructuring its portfolio of brands to keep up with shifting demand.

Unilever's food business has been lagging behind other areas, especially personal care. Originally a Dutch margarine producer, Unilever is considering dropping the butter substitute altogether. Unilever is shifting resources to focus on men's skin and hair care as men are spending more time and money on their appearance and customers are returning to real butter. Rob Candelino, VP of hair care marketing at Unilever, says that "This generation of man—on all aspects of how they are taking care of themselves—is caring much more than previous generations." Therefore, the company is developing new products and has recently acquired the Dollar Shave Club, a low-cost direct provider of shaving supplies for men.

Careful cash budgeting is essential for Unilever in managing the impact of changing customer preferences and global economic fluctuations while still investing in continued growth.

Sources: Saabira Chaudhuri, "Unilever Sales Fall on Currencies, Offsetting Better Volume, Prices," *Wall Street Journal*, April 14, 2016.
Sharon Terlep, "Dollar Shave Club's $1 Billion Deal: A Victory for Simplicity over Technology," *Wall Street Journal*, July 20, 2016.
Elizabeth Holmes, "Young Men Are Obsessed with Their Hair" *Wall Street Journal*, March 1, 2016.
Saabira Chaudhuri, "Will Margarine Become Toast at Unilever?" *Wall Street Journal*, January 19, 2016.

After it makes sales predictions, an organization uses information regarding credit terms, collections policy, and prior collection experience to develop a cash collections budget. Collections on sales normally include receipts from the current period's sales and collections from sales of prior periods. An allowance for bad debts, which reduces each period's collections, is also predicted. Other items often included are cash sales, sales discounts, allowances for volume discounts, and seasonal changes of sales prices and collections. REI's assumed cash budget is in **Exhibit 21.8**. Note the following important points:

Cash budget.

The cash budget summarizes all cash receipts and disbursements expected to occur during the budget period.

EXHIBIT 21.8   Cash Budget

REI
Cash Budget
For the Second Quarter Ending June 30, 2017

	April	May	June	Quarter Total
Budgeted sales (Exhibit 21.4).	$190,000	$228,000	$250,000	$668,000
Cash balance, beginning	$ 15,000	$ 15,770	$ 44,850	$ 15,000
Collections on sales				
Cash sales (50% sales).	95,000	114,000	125,000	
Credit sales				
Current month (25% credit sales)	23,750	28,500	31,250	
Prior month (74% credit sales)	59,200*	70,300	84,360	
Total.	177,950	212,800	240,610	631,360
Cash available for operations.	192,950	228,570	285,460	646,360
Disbursements				
Purchases (Exhibit 21.5)				
Current month (20% purchases).	25,080	28,680	33,540	
Prior month (80% purchases)	84,000**	100,320	114,720	
Total.	109,080	129,000	148,260	386,340
Selling expenses (Exhibit 21.6).	12,100	13,620	14,500	40,220
General & Administrative Expenses				
(Exhibit 21.7, excluding depreciation)	31,000	31,000	31,000	93,000
Taxes (Exhibit 21.3).	35,000			35,000
Total	(187,180)	(173,620)	(193,760)	(554,560)
Excess (deficiency) cash available over disbursements	5,770	54,950	91,700	91,800
Short-term financing***				
New loans.	10,000			10,000
Repayments		(10,000)		(10,000)
Interest	—	(100)	—	(100)
Net cash from financing	10,000	(10,100)	—	(100)
Cash balance, ending.	$ 15,770	$ 44,850	$ 91,700	$ 91,700

*April 1 accounts receivable.

**April 1 accounts payable.

***Loans are obtained in $1,000 increments at the start of the month to maintain a minimum balance of $15,000 at all times. Repayments are made at the end of the month, as soon as adequate cash is available. Assume interest of 12 percent per year (1 percent per month) is paid when the loan is repaid.

- Management estimates that one-half of all sales are for cash and the other half are on the company's credit card. (When sales are on bank credit cards, the collection is immediate, less any bank user fee; however, assume charges using REI's credit card are collected by the company from the customer.) Twenty-five percent of the credit card sales are collected in the month of sale, and 74 percent are collected in the following month. Bad debts are budgeted at 1 percent of credit sales. This resource flow is graphically illustrated as follows:

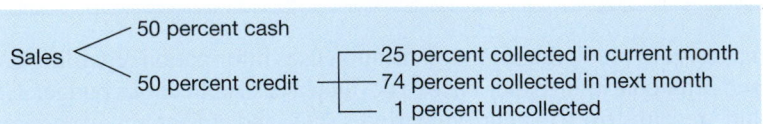

- Assume payments for purchases are made 20 percent in the month purchased and 80 percent in the next month.

- Information on cash expenditures for selling expenses and for general and administrative expenses is based on budgets for these items. The monthly cash expenditures for general and administrative expenses are $31,000 rather than $33,000. The $2,000 difference relates to depreciation, which does not require use of cash.

- Assume REI's income taxes are determined on the basis of predicted taxable income following IRS rules. Estimated tax payments are made during the month following the end of each quarter. Hence, the taxes payable on April 1 are paid during April.

- The cash budget shows cash operating deficiencies and surpluses expected to occur at the end of each month; this is used to plan for borrowing and loan payment.

- Suppose the cash maintenance policy for REI specifies that a minimum balance of $15,000 is to be maintained.

- Assume REI has a line of credit with a bank, with any interest on borrowed funds computed at the simple interest rate of 12.0 percent per year, or 1.0 percent per month. All necessary borrowing is assumed to occur at the start of each month in increments of $1,000. Repayments are assumed to occur at the end of the month. Interest is paid when loans are repaid.

- The cash budget indicates REI needs to borrow $10,000 in April. The $10,000 plus interest is repaid in May.

If REI had any cash disbursements for dividends or capital expenditures they would be included in the cash budget. These items, along with information on income taxes, would be shown in special budgets.

Budgeted Financial Statements

The preparation of the master budget culminates in the preparation of budgeted financial statements. **Budgeted financial statements** are pro forma statements that reflect the "as-if" effects of the budgeted activities on the actual financial position of the organization. That is, the statements reflect the results of operations assuming all budget predictions are correct. Spreadsheets that permit the user to immediately determine the impact of any assumed changes facilitate developing budgeted financial statements. The budgeted income statement can follow the functional format traditionally used for financial accounting or the contribution format introduced in Chapter 15. In either case, the balance sheet amounts reflect the corresponding budgeted entries.

Exhibit 21.9 presents the budgeted income statement for the quarter ending June 30, 2017. If all predictions made in the operating budget are correct, REI will produce a net income of $51,540 for the quarter. Almost every item on the budgeted income statement comes from one of the budget schedules.

EXHIBIT 21.9	Budgeted Income Statement

REI
Budgeted Income Statement
For the Second Quarter Ending June 30, 2017

Sales (Exhibit 21.4)..		$668,000
Cost of goods sold:*		
Beginning inventory (Exhibit 21.3)	$157,000	
Purchases (Exhibit 21.5)...................................	436,500	
Cost of merchandise available.............................	593,500	
Ending inventory (Exhibit 21.5)............................	(192,700)	(400,800)
Gross profit..		267,200
Other expenses:...		
Bad debt (1% of credit sales)**............................	3,340	
Selling (Exhibit 21.6).....................................	40,220	
General and administrative (Exhibit 21.7)...................	99,000	(142,560)
Income from operations......................................		124,640
Interest expense (Exhibit 21.8)...............................		(100)
Net income from operations..................................		124,540
Allowance for income taxes***................................		(73,000)
Net income..		$ 51,540

*Also computed at sales × 0.6
**$668,000 × 0.5 credit sales × 0.01 bad debts
***Provided by accounting

The budgeted balance sheet, presented in **Exhibit 21.10** shows REI's financial position as of June 30, 2017, assuming that all budget predictions are correct. Sources of the budgeted balance sheet data are included as part of the exhibit.

EXHIBIT 21.10	Budgeted Balance Sheet		

REI
Balance Sheet
June 30, 2017

Assets:			
Current assets			
Cash (Exhibit 21.8)		$ 91,700	
Accounts receivable, net*		92,500	
Merchandise inventory (Exhibits 21.5 and 21.9)		192,700	$376,900
Fixed assets			
Buildings and equipment (Exhibit 21.3)	$460,000		
Less accumulated depreciation			
(Exhibit 21.3 plus depreciation Exhibit 21.7).................	(130,800)	329,200	
Land (Exhibit 21.3)		60,000	389,200
Total assets.			$766,100
Liabilities and Stockholders' Equity			
Current liabilities			
Accounts payable**....................................		$134,160	
Taxes payable (Exhibit 21.9)		73,000	$207,160
Stockholders' equity			
Capital stock (Exhibit 21.3)		350,000	
Retained earnings (Exhibit 21.3 plus net income Exhibit 21.9)....		208,940	558,940
Total liabilities and stockholders' equity........................			$766,100

*June credit sales collected in July, $250,000 × 0.50 × 0.74.
**June purchases paid in July, $167,700 × 0.80.

Finalizing the Budget

After studying the REI example, you might conclude that developing the master budget is a mechanical process. That is not the case. Understanding the basics of budget assembly is not the end; it is a tool to assist in efficient and effective budgeting. Before finalizing the budget, the following two questions must be addressed:

- Is the proposed budget feasible?
- Is the proposed budget acceptable?

To be feasible, the organization must be able to actually implement the proposed budget. Without the assumed line of credit, REI's budget is not feasible because the company would run out of cash sometime in April. Knowing this, management can take timely corrective action. Possible actions include obtaining equity financing, issuing long-term debt, reducing the amount of inventory on hand at the end of each quarter, or obtaining a line of credit. Other constraints that would make the budget infeasible include the availability of merchandise and, in the case of a manufacturing organization, production capacity.

Once management determines that the budget is feasible, they still need to determine if it is acceptable. To evaluate acceptability, management might consider various financial ratios, such as return on assets. They might compare the return provided by the proposed budget with past returns, industry averages, or some organizational goal.

MID-CHAPTER REVIEW 3

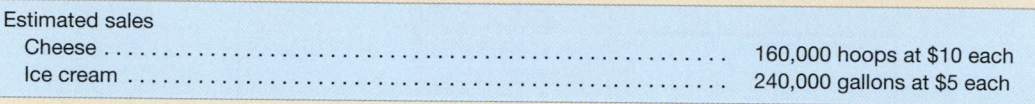

Budget for a Merchandising Organization

Bleu Mont Dairy is a wholesale distributor of artisan cheese and ice cream. Suppose the following information is available for April 2017.

Estimated sales	
Cheese	160,000 hoops at $10 each
Ice cream	240,000 gallons at $5 each

Estimated costs	
Cheese	$8 per hoop
Ice cream	$2 per gallon

Desired inventories	Beginning	Ending
Cheese	10,000	12,000
Ice cream	4,000	5,000

Assumed financial information follows:

- Beginning cash balance is $400,000.
- Purchases of merchandise are paid 60 percent in the current month and 40 percent in the following month. Purchases totaled $1,800,000 in March and are estimated to be $2,000,000 in May.
- Employee wages and salaries are paid for in the current month. Employee expenses for April totaled $156,000.
- Overhead expenses are paid in the next month. The accounts payable amount for these expenses from March is $80,000 and for May will be $90,000. April's overhead expenses total $80,000.
- Sales are on credit and are collected 70 percent in the current period and the remainder in the next period. March's sales were $3,000,000, and May's sales are estimated to be $3,200,000. Bad debts average 1 percent of sales.
- Selling and administrative expenses are paid monthly and total $450,000, including $40,000 of depreciation.
- All unit costs for April are the same as they were in March.

REQUIRED

Prepare the following for April:

a. Sales budget in dollars.
b. Purchases budget.
c. Cash budget.
d. Budgeted income statement.

The solution to this review problem can be found on pages 965–966.

BUDGET DEVELOPMENT IN MANUFACTURING ORGANIZATIONS

LO4 Explain and develop a basic manufacturing cost budget.

4

The importance of inventory in various organizations was introduced in Chapter 17 where **Exhibit 17.1** (page 771) summarized inventory and related expense accounts for service, merchandising, and manufacturing organizations. Recall that service organizations usually have a low percentage of their assets invested in inventory, usually consisting of the supplies needed to facilitate operations. In contrast, merchandising organizations usually have a high percentage of their total assets invested in inventory, with the largest inventory investment in merchandise purchased for resale. The preceding illustration of the development of a master budget was for a merchandising organization. In this section, we will illustrate the the development of a master budget for a manufacturing organization. We will contrast the assembly of a budget for a merchandiser in **Exhibit 21.2** with the assembly of a budget for a manufacturer in **Exhibit 21.11**.

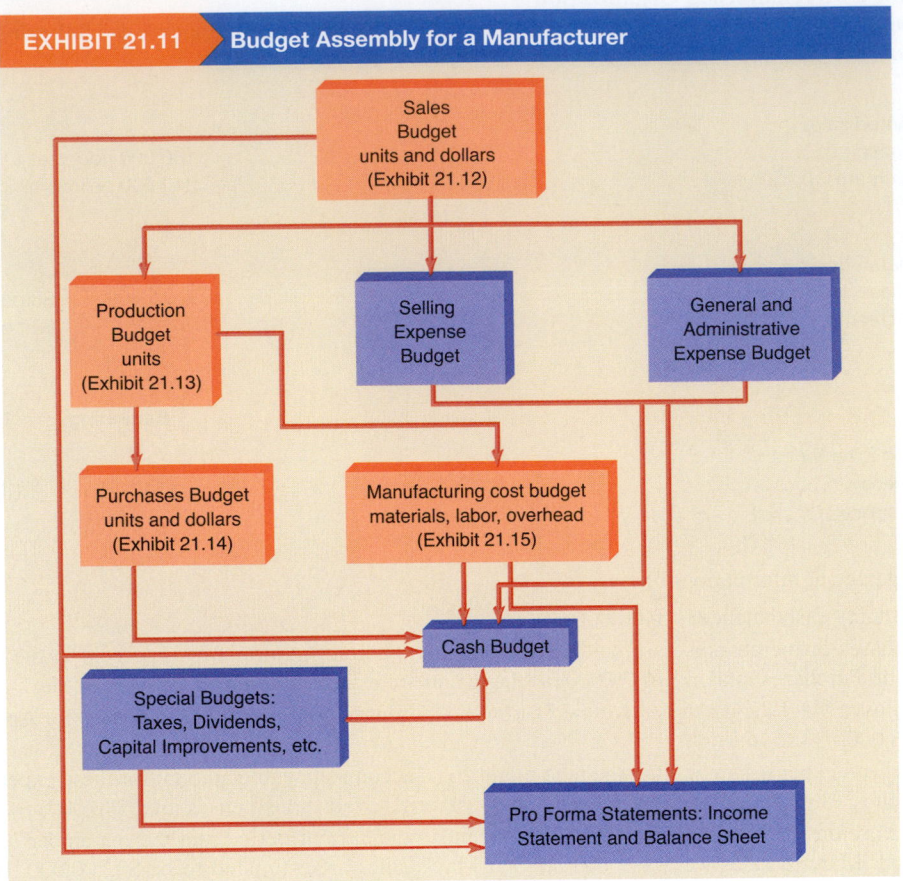

EXHIBIT 21.11   Budget Assembly for a Manufacturer

Production Budget

Because manufacturing organizations convert raw materials into finished goods that are sold to customers, there are additional steps in developing their master budget. The management of a manufacturing organization must determine the production volume required to support sales and finished goods ending inventory requirements (production budget). Then, based on available inventories or raw materials and the raw materials required for production, management develops a purchases budget.

Manufacturing sales budget.

Because unit information is necessary to determine production requirements, the sales budget is expressed in units as well as dollars.

EXHIBIT 21.12   Sales Budget

REI
Sales Budget (Trekpacks)
For the Second Quarter Ending June 30, 2017

	April	May	June	Quarter Total	July
Sales—Units..........................	0	400	500	900	600
Sales—Dollars ($100 each)	0	$40,000	$50,000	$90,000	$60,000

EXHIBIT 21.13	Production Budget			
REI **Production Budget (Trekpacks)** **For the Second Quarter Ending June 30, 2017**				
	April	**May**	**June**	**Quarter Total**
Budgeted Sales	0	400	500	900
Desired ending inventory				
40% following month sales.	160	200	240	240
Total requirements	160	600	740	1,140
Less beginning inventory	0	(160)	(200)	0
Budgeted production	160	440	540	1,140

Manufacturing Cost Budget

In addition to a selling expense budget and a general and administrative expense budget, management needs also to develop a manufacturing cost budget, which is similar in design to a statement of cost of goods manufactured (see **Exhibit 17.6**, page 784) except that it is prepared in advance of production rather than after production. Reflecting these additional steps, the cash budget includes payments for direct labor and manufacturing overhead, based on information in the manufacturing cost budget, and payments for purchases of raw materials based on the purchases budget. Note cash disbursements are for materials purchased rather than materials used in production.

Continuing our REI example, assume that management is considering the option of manufacturing a high-quality backpack, tentatively named the "Trekpack" as an alternative to purchasing a similar item from an outside vendor. Unit variable and monthly fixed cost estimates associated with the manufacture of Trekpacks follow:

Unit costs:		
Direct materials:		
Fabric: 2 square yards at $10 per yard	$20	
Hardware kits (buckles, straps, etc.).	5	$ 25
Direct labor 0.5 hours at $30 per hour		15
Variable overhead, per unit.		8
Total variable costs per unit		$ 48
Fixed costs per month (rent, utilities, supervision).		$6,000

Because management anticipates an average monthly production volume of 500 Trekpacks, the average fixed cost per unit, a predetermined overhead rate, is $12 ($6,000/500).

For budgeting purposes, management uses a standard cost, a budget per unit of product, for valuing inventories and forecasting the cost of goods sold. The standard cost of a Trekpack is $60:

Direct materials	$25
Direct labor.	15
Variable overhead.	8
Fixed overhead.	12
Standard cost.	$60

Management, planning to introduce this new product in May, developed the sales budget shown in **Exhibit 21.12**. In this case, because unit information is necessary to determine production requirements, the sales budget is expressed in units as well as dollars.

Introducing Trekpacks in May requires some April production. To meet the initial sales requirement for the start of each month, management desires end-of-month inventories equal to 40 percent of the following month's budgeted sales. The sales budget and ending inventory plans, along with information on beginning inventories, is used to develop the production budget in **Exhibit 21.13**.

The production budget, along with information on beginning inventories of raw materials and planned ending inventory levels (500 square yards of fabric and 200 kits) is then used to budget the purchases in **Exhibit 21.14** for raw materials in units and dollars. The production budget, along with standard variable and predicted fixed cost information is also used to develop the manufacturing cost budget in **Exhibit 21.15**.

Purchases budget.

The production budget, along with information on beginning inventories of raw materials and planned ending inventory levels is then used to budget the purchases for raw materials in units and dollars.

EXHIBIT 21.14   Purchase Budget

REI
Purchases Budget
For the Second Quarter Ending June 30, 2017

	April	May	June	Quarter Total
Fabric:				
Current needs (2 yards per unit)	320	880	1,080	2,280
Desired ending inventory (500 yards)	500	500	500	500
Total requirements	820	1,380	1,580	2,780
Less beginning inventory	(0)	(500)	(500)	(0)
Fabric purchases in yards.	820	880	1,080	2,780
Assembly kits:				
Current needs (1 per unit)	160	440	540	1,140
Desired ending inventory (200 kits).	200	200	200	200
Total requirements	360	640	740	1,340
Less beginning inventory	(0)	(200)	(200)	(0)
Kit purchases in units	360	440	540	1,340
Purchases (Dollars)				
Fabric at $10 per yard.	$ 8,200	$ 8,800	$10,800	$27,800
Kits at $5 each	1,800	2,200	2,700	6,700
Total purchases in dollars.	$10,000	$11,000	$13,500	$34,500

Manufacturing cost budget.

The production budget, along with standard variable and predicted fixed cost information is also used to develop the manufacturing cost budget.

EXHIBIT 21.15   Manufacturing Cost Budget

REI
Manufacturing Cost Budget
For the Second Quarter Ending June 30, 2017

	April	May	June	Quarter Total
Direct materials				
Fabric used in production (production × 2 yards × $10). . . .	$ 3,200	$ 8,800	$10,800	$22,800
Kits used in production (production × 1 kit × $5)	800	2,200	2,700	5,700
Total	4,000	11,000	13,500	28,500
Direct labor (production × 1/2 hour × $30)	2,400	6,600	8,100	17,100
Manufacturing overhead				
Variable ($8 per unit)	1,280	3,520	4,320	9,120
Fixed	6,000	6,000	6,000	18,000
Total	7,280	9,520	10,320	27,120
Total manufacturing costs	$13,680	$27,120	$31,920	$72,720

Because it does not require the introduction of new concepts, the cash budget and the pro-forma financial statements for REI with the manufacturing of Trekpacks are not presented. Keep in mind that the cash budget will include disbursements for purchases shown in **Exhibit 21.14** and for direct labor, variable overhead, and fixed overhead shown in **Exhibit 21.15**. A pro-forma functional income statement using absorption costing will include the predicted cost of goods sold for Trekpacks at a $60 standard cost per unit. A contribution income statement using variable costing would include the cost of goods sold for Trekpacks at a $48 standard cost per unit with all fixed manufacturing costs expensed in the period incurred. Finally, the pro-forma balance sheet will include standard costs of any June raw materials (500 square yards at $10 per yard and 200 kits at $5 each), work in process (none), and finished goods. Any unpaid liabilities for purchases of raw materials, direct labor, and manufacturing overhead would also be shown under current liabilities. Note that completing the cash budget and the pro-forma statements requires information on the timing of payments for the purchases of raw materials, direct labor, and manufacturing overhead.

MID-CHAPTER REVIEW 4

Budget for a Manufacturer

Assume **DeWalt**, a subsidiary of **Stanley Black and Decker**, manufactures and sells two industrial products in a single plant. Suppose a new manager wants to have quarterly budgets and has prepared the following information for the first quarter of 2017:

Budgeted sales

Drills	60,000 at $100 each
Saws	40,000 at $125 each

Budgeted inventories

	Beginning	Ending
Drills, finished	20,000 units	25,000 units
Saws, finished	8,000 units	10,000 units
Metal, direct materials	32,000 pounds	36,000 pounds
Plastic, direct materials	29,000 pounds	32,000 pounds
Handles, direct materials	6,000 each	7,000 each

Standard variable costs per unit

	Drills		Saws	
Direct materials				
Metal	5 pounds × $8.00	$40.00	4 pounds × $8.00	$32.00
Plastic	3 pounds × $5.00	15.00	3 pounds × $5.00	15.00
Handles	1 handle × $3.00	3.00		
Total		58.00		47.00
Direct labor	2 labor hours × $12.00	24.00	3 labor hours × $16.00	48.00
Variable manufacturing Overhead	2 hours × $1.50	3.00	3 hours × $1.50	4.50
Total		$85.00		$99.50

Assume fixed manufacturing overhead is $214,000 per quarter (including noncash expenditures of $156,000) and is allocated on total units produced. Financial information follows:

- Beginning cash balance is $1,800,000.
- Sales are on credit and are collected 50 percent in the current period and the remainder in the next period. Last quarter's sales were $8,400,000. There are no bad debts.
- Purchases of direct materials and labor costs are paid for in the quarter acquired.
- Manufacturing overhead expenses are paid in the quarter incurred.
- Selling and administrative expenses are all fixed and are paid in the quarter incurred. They are budgeted at $340,000 per quarter, including $90,000 of depreciation.

REQUIRED

For the first quarter of 2017, prepare the following:
a. Sales budget in dollars.
b. Production budget in units.
c. Purchases budget.
d. Manufacturing cost budget.
e. Cash budget.
f. Budgeted contribution income statement. (*Hint:* See Chapter 15.)

The solution to this review problem can be found on pages 967–969.

LO5 Analyze the relationship between budget development and manager behavior.

BUDGET DEVELOPMENT AND MANAGER BEHAVIOR

Organizations are composed of individuals who perform a wide variety of activities in pursuit of the organization's goals. To accomplish these goals, management must recognize the effects that budgeting and performance evaluation methods have on the behavior of the organization's employees.

Employee Participation

Budgeting should be used to promote productive employee behavior directed toward meeting the organization's goals. While no two organizations use exactly the same budgeting procedures, two approaches to employee involvement in budgeting represent possible end points on a continuum. These approaches are sometimes referred to as top-down and bottom-up methods.

With a **top-down** or **imposed budget**, top management identifies the primary goals and objectives for the organization and communicates them to lower management levels. Because relatively few people are involved in top-down budgeting, an imposed budget saves time. It also minimizes the slack that managers at lower organizational levels are sometimes prone to build into their budgets. However, this nonparticipative approach to budgeting can have undesirable motivational consequences. Personnel who do not participate in budget preparation might lack a commitment to achieve their part of the budget.

With a **bottom-up** or **participative budget**, managers at all levels—and in some cases, even nonmanagers—are involved in budget preparation. Budget proposals originate at the lowest level of management possible and are then integrated into the proposals for the next level, and so on, until the proposals reach the top level of management, which completes the budget.

Participation helps ensure that important issues are considered and that employees understand the importance of their roles in meeting the organization's goals. It also provides opportunities for problem solving and fosters employee commitment to agreed-upon goals. Hence, budget predictions are likely to be more accurate, and the people responsible for the budget are more likely to strive to accomplish its objectives. These self-imposed budgets reinforce the concept of participative management and should strengthen the overall budgeting process.

Participative approaches to budgeting have a few disadvantages. Because they require the involvement of many people, the preparation period is longer than that for an imposed budget. Another disadvantage is the tendency of some managers to intentionally understate revenues or overstate expenses to provide **budgetary slack**. A manager might do this to reduce his or her concern regarding unfavorable performance reviews or to make it easier to obtain favorable performance reviews. If a department consistently produces favorable variances (actual results versus budget) with little apparent effort, this might be a symptom of budgetary slack.

YOU MAKE THE CALL

You are the Chief Financial Officer   As the CFO of a relatively new and fast-growing entrepreneurial enterprise, you and the other top managers have previously emphasized technical and marketing innovation and creativity over planning and budgeting. But now with growing competition and the maturing of the company's products, you recognized that a culture of better financial planning must be established if the company is to succeed in the long run. You feel that the financial staff has the best expertise and understanding of the business to prepare effective budgets, but you are concerned about the motivational effects of excluding the lower-level managers from the process and are seeking advice. [Answer, p. 949.]

Budgeting Periods

Although most organizations use a one-year budget period, some organizations budget for shorter or longer periods. In addition to fixed-length budget periods, two other types of budget periods commonly used are life cycle budgeting and continuous budgeting.

When a fixed time period is not particularly relevant to planning, an organization can use **life cycle budgeting**, which involves developing a budget for a project's entire life. An ice cream vendor at the beach might develop a budget for the season. A general contractor might budget costs for the entire (multiple-year) time required to construct a building.

Under **continuous budgeting**, the budget (sometimes called a **rolling budget**) is based on a moving time frame. For example, an organization on a continuous four-quarter budget system adds a quarter to the budget at the end of each quarter of operations, thereby always maintaining a budget for four quarters into the future. Under this system, plans for a full year into the future are always available, whereas under a fixed annual budget, operating plans for a full year ahead are available only at the beginning of the budget year. Because managers are constantly involved in this type of budgeting, the budget process becomes an active and integral part of the management process. Managers are forced to be future oriented throughout the year rather than just once each year.

Forecasts

Budget preparation requires the development of a variety of forecasts. The sales forecast is based on a variety of interrelated factors such as historical trends, product innovation, general economic conditions, industry conditions, and the organization's strategic position for competing on the basis of price, product differentiation, or market niche. Many organizations first determine the industry forecast for a given product or service and then extract from it their sales estimations.

Although the sales forecast is primary to most organizations, there are many other forecasts of varying importance that must be made, including (a) the collection period for sales on account, (b) percent of uncollectable sales on account, (c) cost of materials, supplies, utilities, and so forth, (d) employee turnover, (e) time required to perform activities, (f) interest rates, and (g) development time for new products or services.

BUSINESS INSIGHT

Developing Honesty in Budgeting   Often the budgeting process involves soliciting information from mid-level managers, and honesty in this participative process is essential. Lower-level managers often have much better information about their sphere of the company's operations, but often these managers have financial incentives to misreport.

Experiments by researchers at the University of Indiana and the University of Kentucky suggest that publishing rankings of division performance can eliminate these incentives. When mid-level managers are ranked by their department's contribution to firm performance, their budget reports become quite accurate. This result is independent of the manager's compensation structure. Firms who rely heavily on information from mid-level managers should be careful to construct incentive and recognition structures that encourage honest reporting.

Source: Jason L. Brown, Joseph G. Fisher, Matthew Sooy, and Geoffrey B. Sprinkle, "The Effect of Rankings on Honesty in Budget Reporting", *Accounting, Organizations and Society*, 39, no. 4 (May 2014): 237–46. http://dx.doi.org/10.1016/j.aos.2014.03.001.

Ethics

Because most wrongful activities related to budgeting are unethical, rather than illegal, organizations often have difficulty dealing with them. However, when managers' actions cross the gray area between ethical and fraudulent behavior, organizations are not reluctant to dismiss employees or even pursue legal actions against them.

Although most managers have a natural inclination to be conservative in developing their budgets, at some level the blatant padding or building slack into the budget becomes unethical. In an extreme case, it might even be considered theft if an inordinate level of budgetary slack creates favorable performance variances that lead to significant bonuses or other financial gain for the manager. Another form of falsifying budgets occurs when managers include expense categories in their budgets that are not needed in their operations and subsequently use the funds to pad other budget categories. The deliberate falsification of budgets is unethical behavior and is grounds for dismissal in most organizations.

Ethical issues might also arise in the reporting of performance results, which usually compares actual data with budgeted data. Examples of unethical reporting of actual performance data include misclassification of expenses, overstating revenues or understating expenses, postponing or accelerating the recording of activities at the end of the accounting period, or creating fictitious activities.

Open Book Management

If an organization is to obtain the full benefit of budgeting, support for the budget must be obtained from employees at all levels. Many organizations, especially smaller ones, have used open book management to obtain employee support for the budget. **Open book management** involves sharing financial and related information with employees, teaching employees to understand financial numbers, encouraging employees to use the information in their work, and sharing financial results with employees, perhaps through a bonus program. The following Research Insight examines the success of open book management in small companies.

Properly used, an operating budget is an effective mechanism for motivating employees to higher levels of performance and productivity. Improperly developed and administered, budgets can foster feelings of animosity toward management and the budget process. Behavioral research has generally concluded that when employees participate in the preparation of budgets and believe that the budgets represent fair standards for evaluating their performance, they receive personal satisfaction from accomplishing the goals set in the budgets.

RESEARCH INSIGHT

Open Book Management Opens the Door to Profits   Open book management has its roots at **Springfield Remanufacturing Corp.** (SRC). In the late 1970s, SRC was a subsidiary of **International Harvester** and was losing money. International Harvester sent a new plant manager, Jack Stack, to turn SRC around. Stack made SRC profitable by sharing information and using gamification techniques to improve firm performance. Stack's performance game is based on three principles:

1. Transparency: Make the business's goals and planning transparent, then continually educate employees about the plan.
2. Involvement: Involve employees in both planning and ownership.
3. Measurement: Create a "Critical Number," a measure of performance that the whole organization is invested in working toward.

The key to this approach is that all employees understand how their work fits into the larger success of the organization, and share the proceeds from success. In this context, sharing financial information with employees empowers them to find solutions to problems and inefficiencies throughout the organization.

This approach was so successful that in 1983 Stack and 12 employees bought SRC from International Harvester and have since grown the business to 1,400 employee-owners and 31 businesses, including a corporate training and education practice. The success of these practices extends far beyond SRC. Research by the McGill University Institute for Health and Social Policy finds that firms large and small are able to improve efficiency and profitability by following SRC's model.

Sources: Neil Amato, "Opening the Books, Growing the Business," *The CGMA Magazine*, June 1, 2016.
Jody Heymann, with Magda Berrera, "Profit at the Bottom of the Ladder," *Harvard Business School Press*, 2010.

CHAPTER-END REVIEW

Items 1. though 4. represent manager behaviors related to operational budgeting.
1. Budgetary Slack
2. Participative Budget
3. Open Book Management
4. Life-Cycle Budgeting

REQUIRED
Identify the above term that most appropriately describes the scenarios below:

_____ *a.* The marketing department is asked to provide an estimate as to how much it will spend on print ads during the next fiscal year.

_____ *b.* The marketing department provides a budget amount for print ads for the next fiscal year that includes the expected expenditures plus 10% to account for uncertainty.

_____ *c.* Tristan Renken owns and operates a food truck that sells Mexican food along the beaches in Chicago. Tristan only operates the food truck during the summer and developed a budget to estimate how much he will make during the upcoming summer season.

_____ *d.* Top management hosts semi-annual meetings to discuss the budget and current performance vs. the budget. Management provides employees with tools to help gauge their own performance against the budgeted expectations.

The solution to this review problem can be found on page 970.

GUIDANCE ANSWERS . . . YOU MAKE THE CALL

You are the Chief Financial Officer You seem to be leaning toward using a top-down approach to budgeting. While this method may produce an effective set of benchmarks for planning and evaluation, it does not maximize the benefits of budgeting. A key element in any effective budgeting system is that it must be embraced by the managers whose performance will be evaluated by it. If the budget is imposed from the top down, it is far less likely to be embraced by managers than if they have participated from the beginning of the budget development process. The most effective budgeting systems are those that are strongly embraced by managers at all levels, which is most readily achieved through a participative (bottom-up) approach.

KEY TERMS

activity-based approach, 930
bottom-up budget, 946
budget, 928
budgetary slack, 946
budgeted financial
    statements, 939
cash budget, 937
continuous budgeting, 946
general and administrative
    expense budget, 936

imposed budget, 946
incremental approach, 930
life cycle budgeting, 946
management by exception, 929
master budget, 932
minimum level approach, 931
open book management, 947
operating activities, 933
operating budgets, 928
output/input approach, 929

participative budget, 946
purchases budget, 935
risk, 929
risk management, 929
rolling budget, 946
sales budget, 935
selling expense budget, 936
top-down budget, 946
zero-based budgeting, 931

Assignments with the MBC logo in the margin are available in *BusinessCourse*.
See the Preface of the book for details.

MULTIPLE CHOICE

1. Each of the following is a true statement regarding the budgeting process, except:
   a. The budget is the basis for evaluating performance.
   b. Budgets represent a guide for accomplishing goals and objectives.
   c. The budget is developed by the finance team and its primary purpose is to predict costs.
   d. An organization's budget model can be used to evaluate the financial impact of a risk.

2. Budgeted sales of the East End Burger Joint for the first quarter of the year are as follows:

January	$50,000
February	60,000
March	68,000

   The cost of sales averages 40 percent of sales revenue and management desires ending inventories equal to 25 percent of the following month's sales. Assuming the January 1 inventory is $5,000, the January purchases budget is:
   a. $19,000
   b. $21,000
   c. $31,000
   d. $69,000

3. Syracuse Distribution's sales budget for the first quarter follows:

January	$250,000
February	300,000
March	290,000

All sales are on account (credit) with 50 percent collected in the month of sale, 30 percent collected in the month after sale, and 20 percent collected in the second month after sale. There are no uncollectable accounts. The March cash receipts are:

a. $140,000
b. $235,000
c. $285,000
d. None of the above

4. Refer to question 2 and determine the accounts receivable at the end of March:

a. $147,000
b. $205,000
c. $235,000
d. $285,000

5. Presented is selected second quarter budget data for the Arnold Company

	Sales
April	20,000 units
May	30,000 units
June	36,000 units

Additional information:
- Each unit of finished product requires three pounds of raw materials.
- Arnold maintains ending finished goods inventories equal to 20 percent of the following month's budgeted sales.
- Arnold maintains raw materials inventories equal to 25 percent of the following month's budgeted production.
- April 1 inventories are in line with Arnold's inventory policy.

Arnold's budgeted purchases (in pounds) for April is:

a. 66,000 pounds
b. 72,900 pounds.
c. 89,400 pounds
d. None of the above

6. Presented is additional information for the Arnold Company (refer to question 4):
- Price per pound of raw materials $20
- Direct labor per unit of finished product   0.40 hours at $25 per hour
- Total monthly factory overhead $200,000 + $10 per direct labor hour

Arnold's total manufacturing cost budget for April is:

a. $880,000
b. $1,680,000
c. $1,828,000
d. $1,966,000

QUESTIONS

Q21-1. What are the primary phases in the planning and control cycle?

Q21-2. Does budgeting require formal or informal planning? What are some advantages of this style of management?

Q21-3. Identify the advantages and disadvantages of the incremental approach to budgeting.

Q21-4. Explain the minimum level approach to budgeting.

Q21-5. How does activity-based budgeting predict a cost objective's budget?

Q21-6. Explain the continuous improvement concept of budgeting.

Q21-7. Which budget brings together all other budgets? How is this accomplished?

Q21-8. What budgets are normally used to support the cash budget? What is the net result of cash budget preparations?

Q21-9. Define *budgeted financial statements*.

Q21-10. Identify the two budgets that are part of the master budget of a manufacturing organization but not part of the master budget of a merchandising organization.

Q21-11. Contrast the top-down and bottom-up approaches to budget preparation.

Q21-12. Is budgetary slack a desirable feature? Can it be prevented? Why or why not?

Q21-13. Why are annual budgets not always desirable? What are some alternative budget periods?

Q21-14. Explain how continuous budgeting works.

Q21-15. In addition to the sales forecast, what forecasts are used in budgeting?

Q21-16. Why should motivational considerations be a part of budget planning and utilization? List several ways to motivate employees with budgets.

MINI EXERCISES

M21-17. Output/Input Budget

LO2

Vinyard Clinic has the following resource input information available for a routine physical examination.

- Each exam normally requires 1.25 hours of examining room time, including:
  - ○ 45 minutes of nursing services,
  - ○ 30 minutes of physician services
- Each exam also utilizes one package of examination supplies costing $30 each.
- Including benefits, physicians earn $75/hour and nurses earn $32/hour.
- Variable overhead is budgeted at $35 per examining room hour and fixed overhead is budgeted at $6,000 per month.

REQUIRED

Prepare an output/input budget for October when 500 routine examinations are planned. Discuss some of the likely benefits to Vinyard Clinic of dedicating time to go through the budgeting process.

M21-18. Incremental Budget

LO2

Wood County uses an incremental approach to budgeting. The 2016 cash budget for the Wood County Department of Motor Vehicles is presented as follows:

Supplies	$15,000
Temporary and seasonal wages.	23,000
Wages of full-time employees	185,000
Supervisor salaries.	47,000
Rent	39,000
Insurance	21,000
Utilities	23,000
Miscellaneous.	11,000
Contingencies and equipment	35,000
Total	$399,000

REQUIRED

Prepare an incremental cash budget for 2017, assuming the planned total budget increase is 2.5 percent. Budget details include a budget increment for salaries and wages of 4 percent, no change in rent, and 2 percent increases in the budget for supplies and miscellaneous. Utility companies have received approvals for rate increases amounting to 4 percent and insurance companies have announced an increase in premiums of 6 percent. (*Hint:* The Contingencies and equipment 2017 budget is a plug.)

LO3

M21-19. Purchases Budget in Units and Dollars

Budgeted sales of Wirtz Music Shop for the first six months of 2017 are as follows:

Month	Unit Sales	Month	Unit Sales
January..................	155,000	April	240,000
February..................	185,000	May......................	205,000
March.....................	225,000	June	265,000

Beginning inventory for 2017 is 35,000 units. The budgeted inventory at the end of a month is 40 percent of units to be sold the following month. Purchase price per unit is $5.

REQUIRED

Prepare a purchases budget in units and dollars for each month, January through May.

LO3

M21-20. Cash Budget

Patrick's Retail Company is planning a cash budget for the next three months. Estimated sales revenue is as follows:

Month	Sales Revenue	Month	Sales Revenue
January................	$350,000	March.................	$250,000
February...............	300,000	April	200,000

All sales are on credit; 60 percent is collected during the month of sale, and 40 percent is collected during the next month. Cost of goods sold is 80 percent of sales. Payments for merchandise sold are made in the month following the month of sale. Operating expenses total $52,000 per month and are paid during the month incurred. The cash balance on February 1 is estimated to be $35,000.

REQUIRED

Prepare monthly cash budgets for February, March, and April.

LO4

M21-21. Production and Purchases Budgets in Units

At the end of business on June 30, 2017, the PE Rug Company had 150,000 square yards of rugs and 650,000 pounds of raw materials on hand. Budgeted sales for the third quarter of 2017 are:

Month	Sales
July...	260,000 sq. yards
August	230,000 sq. yards
September	190,000 sq. yards
October	210,000 sq. yards

The PE Rug Company wants to have sufficient square yards of finished product on hand at the end of each month to meet 40 percent of the following month's budgeted sales and sufficient pounds of raw materials to meet 30 percent of the following month's production requirements. Five pounds of raw materials are required to produce one square yard of carpeting.

REQUIRED

Prepare a production budget for the months of July, August, and September and a purchases budget in units for the months of July and August.

LO4

M21-22. Manufacturing Cost Budget

Hubert Products produces a product with the following standard costs:

Unit costs:		
Direct materials:		
Wood: 11 square feet at $25......................................	$275	
Hardware kits (screws, etc).....................................	15	$ 290
Direct labor 0.5 hours at $36 per hour		18
Variable overhead, per unit..		10
Total variable costs per unit		$ 318
Fixed costs per month (rent, utilities, supervision)......................		$75,000

Management plans to produce 9,000 units in April 2017.

REQUIRED

Prepare a manufacturing cost budget for April 2017.

EXERCISES

E21-23. Activity-Based Budget

Highlands Industries has the following budget information available for February:

Units manufactured	30,000
Factory administration	$65,000
Assembly	½ hour per unit × $12
Direct materials	2 pounds per unit × $4
Inspection	$250 per batch of 1,000 units
Manufacturing overhead	$5 per unit
Product development	$20,000
Setup cost	$15 per batch of 1,000 units

REQUIRED

a. Use activity based costing to prepare a manufacturing cost budget for February. Clearly distinguish between unit, batch, and facility-level costs.

b. The operating managers at Highland Industries are concerned that the budgeting process is too time-consuming and diverts attention from their current day-to-day responsibilities. Discuss the reasons that Highland should continue budgeting.

E21-24. Product and Department Budgets Using Activity-Based Approach

The following data are from the general records of the Loading Department of Jonah Freight Company for November.

- Cleaning incoming trucks, 20 minutes.
- Obtaining and reviewing shipping documents for loading truck and instructing loaders, 30 minutes.
- Loading truck, 1 hour and 30 minutes.
- Cleaning shipping dock and storage area after each loading, 10 minutes.
- Employees perform both cleaning and loading tasks and are currently averaging $22 per hour in wages and benefits.
- The supervisor spends 10 percent of her time overseeing the cleaning activities; 60 percent overseeing various loading activities; and the remainder of her time making general plans and managing the department. Her current salary is $5,400 per month.
- Other overhead of the department amounts to $10,800 per month, 20 percent for cleaning and 80 percent for loading.

REQUIRED

Prepare an activities budget for cleaning and loading in the Loading Department for November, assuming 20 working days and the loading of an average of 15 trucks per day.

E21-25. Activity-Based Budgeting

St. Sophia's Hospital is preparing its budget for the coming year. It uses an activity-based approach for all costs except physician care. Its emergency room has three activity areas with cost drivers as follows:

1. *Reception*—paperwork of incoming patients. Cost driver is the number of forms completed.
2. *Treatment*—initial diagnosis and treatment of patients. Cost driver is the number of diagnoses treated.
3. *Cleaning*—general cleaning plus preparing treatment facilities for next patient. Cost driver is the number of people visiting emergency room (patients plus person(s) accompanying them).

Activity Area	Cost Driver Rates	Budgeted Amount of Cost Driver	
		Outpatients	Admitted Patients
Reception	$ 60	8,400 forms	6,500 forms
Treatment	120	8,000 diagnoses	5,400 diagnoses
Cleaning	21	7,400 people	3,400 people

REQUIRED

a. Prepare the total budgeted cost for each activity.

b. How might you adjust the budget approach if you found that outpatients were kept in the emergency room for one hour on average while admitted patients remained for two hours?

c. What advantage does an activity-based approach have over the hospital's former budgeting method of basing the next year's budget on the last year's actual amount plus a percentage increase?

LO3 **E21-26. Sales Budget**

Awesome T-Shirt Shop has very seasonal sales. For 2017, management is trying to decide whether to establish a sales budget based on average sales or on sales estimated by quarter. The unit sales for 2017 are expected to be 8 percent higher than 2016 sales. Unit shirt sales by quarter for 2016 were as follows:

	Children's	Women's	Men's	Total
Winter quarter.	200	200	100	500
Spring quarter	200	250	200	650
Summer quarter	400	300	200	900
Fall quarter	200	250	100	550
Total	1,000	1,000	600	2,600

Children's T-shirts sell for $8 each, women's sell for $12, and men's sell for $13.

REQUIRED

Assuming an 8 percent increase in sales, prepare a sales budget for each quarter of 2017 using the following:

a. Average quarterly sales. (*Hint:* Winter quarter children's shirts are 270 [1,000 × 1.08 ÷ 4].)

b. Actual quarterly sales. (*Hint:* Winter quarter children's shirts are 216 [200 × 1.08].)

c. Suggest advantages of each method.

LO3 **E21-27. Cash Budget & Short-Term Financing**

Presented are partial October, November, and December cash budgets for Holiday Events:

HOLIDAY EVENTS Partial Cash Budgets For the Months of October, November, and December			
	October	November	December	Total
Cash balance, beginning	$23,000	$?	$?	$?
Collections on sales	35,000	40,000	80,000	?
Cash available for operations	?	?	?	?
Disbursements for operations	(50,000)	(60,000)	(40,000)	?
Ending cash before borrowings or replacements	?	?	?	?
Short-term finance:	?	?	?	?
New loans	?	?	?	?
Repayments	?	?	?	?
Interest	?	?	?	?
Cash balance, ending.	$?	$?	$?	$?

Loans are obtained in increments of $1,000 at the start of each month to maintain a minimum end-of-month balance of $12,000. Interest is one percent simple interest (no compounding) per month, payable when the loan is repaid. Repayments are made as soon as possible, subject to the minimum end-of-month balance.

REQUIRED

Complete the short-term financing section of the cash budget.

LO3 **E21-28. Purchases and Cash Budgets**

On July 1, MTC Wholesalers had a cash balance of $175,000 and accounts payable of $99,000. Actual sales for May and June, and budgeted sales for July, August, September, and October are:

Month	Actual Sales	Month	Budgeted Sales
May....................	$150,000	July........................	$ 90,000
June	160,000	August	80,000
		September	100,000
		October	120,000

All sales are on credit with 75 percent collected during the month of sale, 20 percent collected during the next month, and 5 percent collected during the second month following the month of sale. Cost of goods sold averages 70 percent of sales revenue. Ending inventory is one-half of the next month's predicted cost of sales. The other half of the merchandise is acquired during the month of sale. All purchases are paid for in the month after purchase. Operating costs are estimated at $28,000 each month and are paid during the month incurred.

REQUIRED
Prepare purchases and cash budgets for July, August, and September.

E21-29. Cash Receipts

LO3

The sales budget for Andrew Inc. is forecasted as follows:

Month	Sales Revenue
May..	$170,000
June	210,000
July..	230,000
August	170,000

To prepare a cash budget, the company must determine the budgeted cash collections from sales. Historically, the following trend has been established regarding cash collection of sales:

- 50 percent in the month of sale.
- 25 percent in the month following sale.
- 20 percent in the second month following sale.
- 5 percent uncollectible.

The company gives a 2 percent cash discount for payments made by customers during the month of sale. The accounts receivable balance on April 30 is $34,000, of which $10,000 represents uncollected March sales and $24,000 represents uncollected April sales.

REQUIRED
Prepare a schedule of budgeted cash collections from sales for May, June, and July. Include a three-month summary of estimated cash collections.

E21-30. Cash Disbursements

LO3

Timber Company is in the process of preparing its budget for next year. Cost of goods sold has been estimated at 70 percent of sales. Lumber purchases and payments are to be made during the month preceding the month of sale. Wages are estimated at 15 percent of sales and are paid during the month of sale. Other operating costs amounting to 10 percent of sales are to be paid in the month following the month of sale. Additionally, a monthly lease payment of $14,000 is paid for computer services. Sales revenue is forecast as follows:

Month	Sales Revenue
February	$170,000
March	210,000
April	220,000
May..	260,000
June	240,000
July...	280,000

REQUIRED
Prepare a schedule of cash disbursements for April, May, and June.

LO3 **E21-31. Cash Disbursements**

Assume that Ringwood Manufacturing manages its cash flow from its home office. Ringwood controls cash disbursements by category and month. In setting its budget for the next six months, beginning in July, it used the following managerial guidelines:

Category	Guidelines
Purchases............	Pay half in current and half in following month.
Payroll...............	Pay 70 percent in current month and 30 percent in following month.
Loan payments........	Pay total amount due each month.

Predicted activity for selected months follow:

Category	May	June	July	August
Purchases..........................	$ 60,000	$ 74,000	$ 79,000	$ 85,000
Payroll..........................	130,000	140,000	150,000	130,000
Loan payments......................	40,000	40,000	45,000	45,000

REQUIRED

Prepare a schedule showing cash disbursements by account for July and August.

LO3 **E21-32. Budgeted Income Statement**

Quality Wool Company, a merchandising company, is developing its master budget for 2018. The income statement for 2017 is as follows:

QUALITY WOOL COMPANY Income Statement For Year Ending December 31, 2017	
Gross sales......................................	$1,000,000
Less estimated uncollectible accounts	(10,500)
Net sales......................................	989,500
Cost of goods sold...................................	(580,000)
Gross profit......................................	409,500
Operating expenses (including $35,000 depreciation)......................	(250,500)
Net income......................................	$ 159,000

The following are management's goals and forecasts for 2018:

1. Selling prices will increase by 6 percent, and sales volume will increase by 4 percent.
2. The cost of merchandise will increase by 3 percent.
3. All operating expenses are fixed and are paid in the month incurred. Price increases for operating expenses will be 10 percent. The company uses straight-line depreciation.
4. The estimated uncollectibles are 2 percent of budgeted sales.

REQUIRED

Prepare a budgeted functional income statement for 2018.

LO3 **E21-33. Budgeted Income Statement with CVP**

Madison Booksellers is planning a budget for 2018. The estimate of sales revenue is $1,600,000 and of cost of goods sold is 70 percent of sales revenue. Depreciation on the office building and fixtures is budgeted at $60,000. Salaries and wages are budgeted at $100,000. Advertising has been budgeted at $90,000, and utilities should amount to $70,000. Income tax is estimated at 40 percent of operating income.

REQUIRED

a. Prepare a budgeted income statement for 2018.
b. Assuming management desired an after-tax income of $105,000, determine the necessary sales volume.

E21-34. Production and Purchases Budgets

At the beginning of October, Comfy Cushions had 1,600 cushions and 10,500 pounds of raw materials on hand. Budgeted sales for the next three months are:

Month	Sales
October	8,000 cushions
November	10,000 cushions
December	13,000 cushions

Comfy Cushions wants to have sufficient raw materials on hand at the end of each month to meet 25 percent of the following month's production requirements and sufficient cushions on hand at the end of each month to meet 20 percent of the following month's budgeted sales. Five pounds of raw materials, at a standard cost of $0.90 per pound, are required to produce each cushion.

REQUIRED

a. Prepare a production budget for October and November.
b. Prepare a purchases budget in units and dollars for October.

E21-35. Production and Purchases Budgets

Drainage Solutions Culverts produces small culverts for water drainage under two-lane dirt roads. Budgeted unit sales for the next several months are:

Month	Sales
September	2,300
October	1,800
November	1,100
December	800

At the beginning of September, 575 units of finished goods were in inventory. During the final third of the year, as road construction declines, plans are to have an inventory of finished goods equal to 25 percent of the following month's sales. Each unit of finished goods requires 600 pounds of raw materials at a cost of $5 per pound. Management wishes to maintain month-end inventories of raw materials equal to 50 percent of the following month's needs. Five hundred thousand pounds of raw materials were on hand at the start of September.

REQUIRED

a. Prepare a production budget for September, October, and November.
b. Prepare a purchases budget in units and dollars for September and October.

PROBLEMS

P21-36. Cash Budget

Cash budgeting for Nichole Mango, a merchandising firm, is performed on a quarterly basis. The company is planning its cash needs for the third quarter of 2017, and the following information is available to assist in preparing a cash budget. Budgeted income statements for July through October 2017 are as follows:

	July	August	September	October
Sales	$22,000	$28,000	$32,000	$40,000
Cost of goods sold	(11,000)	(15,000)	(17,000)	(21,000)
Gross profit	11,000	13,000	15,000	19,000
Less other expenses				
Selling	3,300	4,000	4,400	5,200
Administrative	3,600	5,000	4,200	4,600
Total	(6,900)	(9,000)	(8,600)	(9,800)
Net income	$ 4,100	$ 4,000	$ 6,400	$ 9,200

Additional information follows:

1. Other expenses, which are paid monthly, include $2,000 of depreciation per month.
2. Sales are 40 percent for cash and 60 percent on credit.
3. Credit sales are collected 25 percent in the month of sale, 65 percent one month after sale, and 10 percent two months after sale. May sales were $16,000, and June sales were $17,000.
4. Merchandise is paid for 50 percent in the month of purchase; the remaining 50 percent is paid in the following month. Accounts payable for merchandise at June 30 totaled $7,000.
5. The company maintains its ending inventory levels at 20 percent of the cost of goods to be sold in the following month. The inventory at June 30 is $2,200.
6. An equipment note of $6,000 per month is being paid through August.
7. The company must maintain a cash balance of at least $6,000 at the end of each month. The cash balance on June 30 is $6,100.
8. The company can borrow from its bank as needed. Borrowings and repayments must be in multiples of $100. All borrowings take place at the beginning of a month, and all repayments are made at the end of a month. When the principal is repaid, interest on the repayment is also paid. The interest rate is 12 percent per year.

REQUIRED

a. Prepare a monthly schedule of budgeted operating cash receipts for July, August, and September.
b. Prepare a monthly purchases budget and a schedule of budgeted cash payments for purchases for July, August, and September.
c. Prepare a monthly cash budget for July, August, and September. Show borrowings from the company's bank and repayments to the bank as needed to maintain the minimum cash balance.

LO3 **P21-37. Cash Budget**

The Williams Supply Company sells for $40 one product that it purchases for $25. Budgeted sales in total dollars for the year are $1,400,000. The sales information needed for preparing the July budget follows:

Month	Sales Revenue
May.	$34,000
June	48,000
July.	56,000
August	64,000

Account balances at July 1 include these:

Cash.	$24,000
Merchandise inventory.	17,500
Accounts receivable (sales).	25,760
Accounts payable (purchases).	16,250

The company pays for one-half of its purchases in the month of purchase and the remainder in the following month. End-of-month inventory must be 50 percent of the budgeted sales in units for the next month. A 2 percent cash discount on sales is allowed if payment is made during the month of sale. Experience indicates that 50 percent of the billings will be collected during the month of sale, 40 percent in the following month, 8 percent in the second following month, and 2 percent will be uncollectible. Total budgeted selling and administrative expenses (excluding bad debts) for the fiscal year are estimated at $210,000, of which one-half is fixed expense (inclusive of a $21,000 annual depreciation charge). Fixed expenses are incurred evenly during the year. The other selling and administrative expenses vary with sales. Expenses are paid during the month incurred.

REQUIRED

a. Prepare a schedule of estimated cash collections for July.
b. Prepare a schedule of estimated July cash payments for purchases.
c. Prepare schedules of July selling and administrative expenses, separately identifying those requiring cash disbursements.
d. Prepare a cash budget in summary form for July.

P21-38. Budgeting Purchases, Revenues, Expenses, and Cash in a Service Organization   **LO3**

Wauconda Medical Center is located in a summer resort community. During the summer months the center operates an outpatient clinic for the treatment of minor injuries and illnesses. The clinic is administered as a separate department within the hospital. It has its own staff and maintains its own financial records. All patients requiring extensive or intensive care are referred to other hospital departments.

An analysis of past operating data for the out-patient clinic reveals the following:

- Staff: Seven full-time employees with total monthly salaries of $56,000. On a monthly basis, one additional staff member is hired for every 500 budgeted patient visits in excess of 3,000, at a cost of $5,000 per month.
- Facilities: Monthly facility costs, including depreciation of $3,000, total $10,000.
- Supplies: The supplies expense averages $12 per patient visit. The center maintains an end-of-month supplies inventory equal to ten percent of the predicted needs of the following month, with a minimum ending inventory of $3,000, which is also the desired inventory at the end of August.
- Additional variable patient costs, such as medications, are charged directly to the patient by the hospital pharmacy.
- Payments: All staff and maintenance expenses are paid in the month the cost is incurrent. Supplies are purchased at cost directly from the hospital with an immediate transfer of cash from the clinic cash account to the hospital cash account.
- Collections: The average bill for services rendered is $80. Of the total bills, 40 percent are paid in cash at the time the service is rendered, 10 percent are never paid, and the remaining 50 percent are covered by insurance. In the past, insurance companies have disallowed 20 percent of the claims filed and paid the balance two months after services are rendered.
- May 30 status: At the end of May, the clinic had $14,000 in cash and supplies costing $4,000.

Budgeted patient visits for next summer are as follows:

Month	Patient visits
June	2,500
July	3,500
August	4,000

REQUIRED

For the Wauconda Outpatient Clinic:

a. Prepare a supplies purchases budget for June, July, and August, with a total column.
b. Prepare a revenue and expense budget for June, July, and August with a total column.
c. Prepare a cash budget for June, July and August with a total column. (*Hint:* See requirement *d.*)
d. Explain why you were unable to develop a feasible cash budget and make any appropriate recommendations for management's consideration.

P21-39. Developing a Master Budget for a Merchandising Organization   **LO3**

Dils Brothers Department Store prepares budgets quarterly. The following information is available for use in planning the second quarter budgets for 2017.

DILS BROTHERS DEPARTMENT STORE
Balance Sheet
March 31, 2017

Assets		Liabilities and Stockholders' Equity	
Cash	$ 4,000	Accounts payable	$31,000
Accounts receivable	31,000	Dividends payable	15,000
Inventory	36,000	Rent payable	3,000
Prepaid insurance	3,000	Stockholders' equity	50,000
Fixtures	25,000		
Total assets	$99,000	Total liabilities and equity	$99,000

Actual and forecasted sales for selected months in 2017 are as follows:

Month	Sales Revenue
January.	$70,000
February	60,000
March	50,000
April	60,000
May.	70,000
June	80,000
July.	100,000
August	90,000

Monthly operating expenses are as follows:

Wages and salaries	$27,000
Depreciation	100
Utilities	1,500
Rent	3,000

Cash dividends of $15,000 are declared during the third month of each quarter and are paid during the first month of the following quarter. Operating expenses, except insurance, rent, and depreciation are paid as incurred. Rent is paid during the following month. The prepaid insurance is for five more months. Cost of goods sold is equal to 50 percent of sales. Ending inventories are sufficient for 120 percent of the next month's cost of sales. Purchases during any given month are paid in full during the following month. All sales are on account, with 50 percent collected during the month of sale, 40 percent during the next month, and 10 percent during the month thereafter. Money can be borrowed and repaid in multiples of $1,000 at an interest rate of 12 percent per year. The company desires a minimum cash balance of $4,000 on the first of each month. At the time the principal is repaid, interest is paid on the portion of principal that is repaid. All borrowing is at the beginning of the month, and all repayment is at the end of the month. Money is never repaid at the end of the month it is borrowed.

REQUIRED

a. Prepare a purchases budget for each month of the second quarter ending June 30, 2017.
b. Prepare a cash receipts schedule for each month of the second quarter ending June 30, 2017. Do not include borrowings.
c. Prepare a cash disbursements schedule for each month of the second quarter ending June 30, 2017. Do not include repayments of borrowings.
d. Prepare a cash budget for each month of the second quarter ending June 30, 2017. Include budgeted borrowings and repayments.
e. Prepare an income statement for each month of the second quarter ending June 30, 2017.
f. Prepare a budgeted balance sheet as of June 30, 2017.

LO4 **P21-40. Developing a Master Budget for a Manufacturing Organization**

Cubs Incorporated manufactures a product with a selling price of $60 per unit. Units and monthly cost data follow:

Variable:	
Selling and administrative.	$ 5 per unit sold
Direct materials.	12 per unit manufactured
Direct labor	12 per unit manufactured
Variable manufacturing overhead	6 per unit manufactured
Fixed:	
Selling and administrative.	$17,000 per month
Manufacturing (including depreciation of $11,000)	34,000 per month

Cubs Inc. pays all bills in the month incurred. All sales are on account with 50 percent collected the month of sale and the balance collected the following month. There are no sales discounts or bad debts.

Cubs Inc. desires to maintain an ending finished goods inventory equal to 20 percent of the following month's sales and a raw materials inventory equal to 10 percent of the following month's production. January 1, 2017, inventories are in line with these policies.

Actual unit sales for December and budgeted unit sales for January, February, and March of 2017 are as follows:

CUBS INCORPORATED Sales Budget For the Months of January, February, and March 2017				
Month	December	January	February	March
Sales—Units..................	11,250	10,000	15,000	13,000
Sales—Dollars	$675,000	$600,000	$900,000	$780,000

Additional information:
- The January 1 beginning cash is projected as $6,000.
- For the purpose of operational budgeting, units in the January 1 inventory of finished goods are valued at variable manufacturing cost.
- Each unit of finished product requires one unit of raw materials.
- Cubs Inc. intends to pay a cash dividend of $12,000 in January

REQUIRED

a. A production budget for January and February.
b. A purchases budget in units for January.
c. A manufacturing cost budget for January.
d. A cash budget for January.
e. A budgeted contribution income statement for January.

P21-41. Risk Management in a Manufacturing Organization LO4

REQUIRED

Continuing problem P21-40, management is concerned that their supplier of raw materials will have a strike. Determine the budget implications if management plans to increase the January-end raw materials inventory to 130 percent of February's production needs. Offer any recommendations you believe appropriate.

P21-42. Developing a Master Budget for a Manufacturing Organization: Challenge Problem LO4

Electric Monkey Computer Accessories assembles a computer networking device from kits of imported components. You have been asked to develop a quarterly and annual operating budget and pro-forma income statements for 2017. You have obtained the following information:

Beginning-of-year balances			
Cash	$50,000.00		
Accounts receivable (previous quarter's sales)..........	$61,200		
Raw materials.....................................	653 kits		
Finished goods....................................	510 units		
Accounts payable..................................	$33,255.00		
Borrowed funds	$20,000.00		
Desired end-of-year inventory balances			
Raw materials.....................................	500 kits		
Finished goods....................................	270 units		
Desired end-of-quarter balances			
Cash	$20,000.00		
Raw materials as a portion of the following quarter's production	0.20		
Finished goods as a portion of the following quarter's sales..................................	0.15		
Manufacturing costs			
Standard cost per unit	Units	Unit price	Total
Raw materials	1 kit	$50.00	$50.00
Direct labor hours at rate	0.8 hour	$25.00	20.00
Variable overhead/labor hour	0.8 hour	$10.00	8.00
Total standard variable cost			$78.00
Fixed cost per quarter			
Cash	$50,000.00		
Depreciation	10,000.00		
Total...	$60,000.00		

Continued

Continued from previous page

Selling and administrative costs				
Variable cost per unit		$6.00		
Fixed costs per quarter				
Cash		$25,000.00		
Depreciation		5,000.00		
Total..		$30,000.00		
Interest rate per quarter		0.04		
Portion of sales collected				
Quarter of sale		0.75		
Subsequent quarter		0.24		
Bad debts.....................................		0.01		
Portion of purchases paid				
Quarter of purchase		0.70		
Subsequent quarter		0.30		
Unit selling price...................................		$150.00		
Sales forecast				
Quarter	First	Second	Third	Fourth
Unit sales	3,400	2,500	3,000	4,100

Additional information

- All cash payments except purchases are made quarterly as incurred.
- All borrowings occur at the start of a quarter.
- All repayments on borrowings occur at the end of a quarter.
- At the time the principal is repaid, interest is paid on the portion of principal that is repaid.
- Borrowings and repayments may be made in any amount.

REQUIRED

a. A sales budget for each quarter and the year. (*Hint:* Use of spreadsheet software strongly recommended for this problem.)

b. A production budget for each quarter and the year.

c. A purchases budget for each quarter and the year.

d. A manufacturing cost budget for each quarter and the year.

e. A selling and administrative expense budget for each quarter and the year.

f. A cash budget for each quarter and the year.

g. A pro-forma contribution income statement for each quarter and the year.

CASES AND PROJECTS

LO5 **C21-43. Behavioral Implications of Budgeting**

Cindy Jones, controller of Systematic Designs, believes that effective budgeting greatly assists in meeting the organization's goals and objectives. She argues that the budget serves as a blueprint for the operating activities during each reporting period, making it an important control device. She believes that sound management evaluations can be based on the comparisons of performance and budgetary schedules and that employees respond more favorably when they participate in the budgetary process. Kevin Dobbs, treasurer of Systematic Designs, agrees that budgeting is essential for overall organization success, but he argues that human resources are too valuable to spend much time planning and preparing the budgetary process. He thinks that the roles people play in budgetary preparation are not important in the final analysis of a budget's effectiveness.

REQUIRED

Contrast the participative versus imposed budgeting concepts and indicate how the ideas of Jones and Dobbs fit the two categories.

LO5 **C21-44. Behavioral Considerations and Budgeting**

Anthony Wagner, the controller in the Division of Transportation for the state, recognizes the importance of the budgetary process for planning, control, and motivation purposes. He believes that a properly implemented participative budgeting process for planning purposes and a management by exception reporting procedure based on that budget will motivate his subordinates to improve productivity within their particular departments. Based on this philosophy, Wagner has implemented the following budget procedures.

- An appropriation target figure is given to each department manager. This amount is the maximum funding that each department can expect to receive in the next fiscal year.
- Department managers develop their individual budgets within the following spending constraints as directed by the controller's staff.
    1. Expenditure requests cannot exceed the appropriation target.
    2. All fixed expenditures should be included in the budget; these should include items such as contracts and salaries at current levels.
    3. All government projects directed by higher authority should be included in the budget in their entirety.
- The controller consolidates the departmental budget requests from the various departments into one budget that is to be submitted for the entire division.
- Upon final budget approval by the legislature, the controller's staff allocates the appropriation to the various departments on instructions from the division manager. However, a specified percentage of each department's appropriation is held back in anticipation of potential budget cuts and special funding needs. The amount and use of this contingency fund are left to the discretion of the division manager.
- Each department is allowed to adjust its budget when necessary to operate within the reduced appropriation level. However, as stated in the original directive, specific projects authorized by higher authority must remain intact.
- The final budget is used as the basis of control for a management by exception form of reporting. Excessive expenditures by account for each department are highlighted on a monthly basis. Department managers are expected to account for all expenditures over budget. Fiscal responsibility is an important factor in the overall performance evaluation of department managers.

Wagner believes that his policy of allowing the department managers to participate in the budget process and then holding them accountable for their performance is essential, especially during these times of limited resources. He also believes that department managers will be positively motivated to increase the efficiency and effectiveness of their departments because they have provided input into the initial budgetary process and are required to justify any unfavorable performances.

REQUIRED
a. Explain the operational and behavioral benefits that generally are attributed to a participative budgeting process.
b. Identify deficiencies in Wagner's participative budgetary policy for planning and performance evaluation purposes. For each deficiency identified, recommend how the deficiency can be corrected.

(CMA Adapted)

C21-45. Budgetary Slack with Ethical Considerations   **LO5**
Karen Bailey was promoted to department manager of a production unit in Parkway Industries three years ago. She enjoys her job except for the evaluation measures that are based on the department's budget. After three years of consistently poor annual evaluations based on a set annual budget, she has decided to improve the evaluation situation. At a recent budget meeting of junior-level managers, the topic of budgetary slack was discussed as a means to maintain some consistency in budgeting matters. As a result of this meeting, Bailey decided to take the following steps in preparing the upcoming year's budget:

1. Use the top quartile for all wage and salary categories.
2. Select the optimistic values for the estimated production ranges for the coming year. These are provided by the marketing department.
3. Use the average of the three months in the current year with poorest production efficiency as benchmarks of success for the coming year.
4. Base equipment charges (primarily depreciation) on replacement values furnished by the purchasing department.
5. Base other fixed costs on current cost plus an inflation rate estimated for the coming year.
6. Use the average of the ten newly hired employees' performance as a basis of labor efficiency for the coming year.

REQUIRED

a. For each item on Bailey's list, explain whether it will create budgetary slack. Use numerical examples as necessary to illustrate.

b. Given the company's use of static budgets as one of the performance evaluation measures of its managers, can the managers justify the use of built-in budgetary slack?

c. What would you recommend as a means for Bailey to improve the budgeting situation in the company? Provide some specific examples of how the budgeting process might be improved.

LO5   C21-46. Budgetary Slack with Ethical Considerations

Norton Company, a manufacturer of infant furniture and carriages, is in the initial stages of preparing the annual budget for next year. Scott Ford recently joined Norton's accounting staff and is interested to learn as much as possible about the company's budgeting process. During a recent lunch with Marge Atkins, sales manager, and Pete Granger, production manager, Ford initiated the following conversation:

Ford: Since I'm new around here and am going to be involved with the preparation of the annual budget, I'd be interested to learn how the two of you estimate sales and production numbers.

Atkins: We start out very methodically by looking at recent history, discussing what we know about current accounts, potential customers, and the general state of consumer spending. Then we add that usual dose of intuition to come up with the best forecast we can.

Granger: I usually take the sales projections as the basis for my projections. Of course, we have to make an estimate of what this year's closing inventories will be, which is sometimes difficult.

Ford: Why does that present a problem? There must have been an estimate of closing inventories in the budget for the current year.

Granger: Those numbers aren't always reliable since Marge makes some adjustments to the sales numbers before passing them on to me.

Ford: What kind of adjustments?

Atkins: Well, we don't want to fall short of the sales projections, so we generally give ourselves a little breathing room by lowering the initial sales projection anywhere from 5 to 10 percent.

Granger: So, you can see why this year's budget is not a very reliable starting point. We always have to adjust the projected production rates as the year progresses; of course, this changes the ending inventory estimates. By the way, we make similar adjustments to expenses by adding at least 10 percent to the estimates; I think everyone around here does the same thing.

REQUIRED

a. Marge Atkins and Pete Granger have described the use of budgetary slack.
    1. Explain why Atkins and Granger behave in this manner, and describe the benefits they expect to realize from the use of budgetary slack.
    2. Explain how the use of budgetary slack can adversely affect Atkins and Granger.

b. As a management accountant, Scott Ford believes that the behavior described by Marge Atkins and Pete Granger could be unethical and that he might have an obligation not to support this behavior. Explain why the use of budgetary slack could be unethical.

(CMA Adapted)

SOLUTIONS TO REVIEW PROBLEMS

Mid-Chapter Review 1

SOLUTION

Operating managers frequently regard budgeting as a time-consuming task that diverts attention from current problems. The development of a budget can be difficult and time-consuming, although it is a necessary process. Organizations that plan will have a focus and their work and tasks will better support the organization's goals and objectives. Without a plan, although managers and employees might be busy, they may not be working on tasks that move their companies forward in a thoughtful way. The plan will allow them to more efficiently focus efforts on tasks that are productive toward the organization's goals. Generally, the budgeting process will: compel planning; promote communication and coordination; provide a guide to action and a basis of evaluation; and act as an aid in risk management.

Mid-Chapter Review 2

SOLUTION

a.   Under the output/input approach, the output of units dictates the expected cost inputs. Here budgeted overhead costs are based on the number of budgeted assembly hours.

	Regular	Extra Strength
Direct materials (20,000 × $20)	$400,000	
(50,000 × $14.50)...................................		$ 725,000
Direct assembly labor (20,000 × 0.5 × $18)	180,000	
(50,000 × 0.8 × $18)		720,000
Overhead (20,000 × 0.5 × $8.17)	81,700	
(50,000 × 0.8 × $8.17).............................		326,800
Total budgeted cost	$661,700	$1,771,800
Unit Cost	$33.085	$35.436

b.   Under the activity-based approach, budgeted overhead costs are based on expected activities to produce the products, not only on assembly hours.

	Regular	Extra Strength
Direct materials (20,000 × $20)	$400,000	
(50,000 × $14.50).....................................		$ 725,000
Direct assembly labor (20,000 × 0.5 × $18)	180,000	
(50,000 × 0.8 × $18)		720,000
Setup (1,000 hours × $25).............................	25,000	
(1,500 hours × $25)		37,500
Engineering and Maintenance (500 hours × $35)	17,500	
(600 hours × $35).....................................		21,000
Inspections (650 inspections × $250)	162,500	
(580 inspections × $250)		145,000
Total budgeted cost	$785,000	$1,648,500
Unit cost...	$39.25	$32.97

c.   Under the incremental approach to budgeting, the cost per unit would be budgeted at last period's cost, plus an increment for expected additional costs in the current period. Based on last period's actual cost of $38 for Regular and $32 for Extra Strength, and using the 3.5 percent overall expected increase in costs, the current period's budgeted cost would be $39.33 for Regular and $33.12 for Extra Strength.

d.   Under the minimum level approach, the company begins with either a zero or very low cost estimate, and then requires all additional costs beyond this minimum to be justified by the production managers. This approach forces managers to evaluate thoroughly all elements of cost each period.

Mid-Chapter Review 3

SOLUTION

a.

BLEU MONT DAIRY Sales Budget For Month of April 2017			
	Units	Price	Sales
Cheese...	160,000	$10	$1,600,000
Ice cream	240,000	5	1,200,000
Total			$2,800,000

b.

BLEU MONT DAIRY Purchases Budget For Month of April 2017			
	Cheese	**Ice Cream**	**Total**
Units			
Sales needs	160,000	240,000	
Desired ending inventory	12,000	5,000	
Total	172,000	245,000	
Less beginning inventory	(10,000)	(4,000)	
Purchases.	162,000	241,000	
Dollars			
Sales needs	$1,280,000	$480,000	
Desired ending inventory	96,000	10,000	
Total	1,376,000	490,000	
Less beginning inventory	(80,000)	(8,000)	
Purchases needed	$1,296,000	$482,000	$1,778,000

c.

BLEU MONT DAIRY Cash Budget For Month of April 2017		
Cash balance, beginning		$ 400,000
Collections on sales		
Current month's sales ($2,800,000 × 0.70)	$1,960,000	
Previous month's sales ($3,000,000 × 0.29).	870,000	2,830,000
Cash available from operations		3,230,000
Less budgeted disbursements		
March purchases ($1,800,000 × 0.40).	720,000	
April purchases ($1,778,000 × 0.60)	1,066,800	
Wages and salaries.	156,000	
Overhead (March).	80,000	
Selling and administrative ($450,000 − $40,000 depreciation)	410,000	(2,432,800)
Cash balance, ending.		$ 797,200

d.

BLEU MONT DAIRY Budgeted Income Statement For Month of April 2017			
Sales (sales budget).			$2,800,000
Allowance for bad debts			(28,000)
Net sales.			2,772,000
Costs of merchandise sold			
Cheese (160,000 × $8).	$1,280,000		
Ice cream (240,000 × $2).	480,000	$1,760,000	
Wages and salaries	156,000		
Overhead	80,000		
Selling and administrative	450,000	686,000	(2,446,000)
Net income.			$ 326,000

Mid-Chapter Review 4

SOLUTION

a.

DEWALT Sales Budget For First Quarter of 2017			
	Units	Price	Sales
Drills	60,000	$100	$ 6,000,000
Saws...	40,000	125	5,000,000
Total			$11,000,000

b.

DEWALT Production Budget For First Quarter of 2017		
	Drills	Saws
Budget sales..	60,000	40,000
Plus desired ending inventory	25,000	10,000
Total inventory requirements	85,000	50,000
Less beginning inventory	(20,000)	(8,000)
Budgeted production	65,000	42,000

c.

DEWALT Purchases Budget For First Quarter of 2017			
	Drills	Saws	Total
Metal purchases			
Production units (production budget).............	65,000	42,000	
Metal (pounds)	× 5	× 4	
Production needs (pounds)...................	325,000	168,000	493,000
Desired ending inventory (pounds)			36,000
Total metal needs (pounds).....................			529,000
Less beginning inventory (pounds)			(32,000)
Purchases needed (pounds).....................			497,000
Cost per pound			× $8
Total metal purchases			$3,976,000
Plastic purchases			
Production units (production budget).............	65,000	42,000	107,000
Plastic (pounds)			× 3
Production needs (pounds).....................			321,000
Desired ending inventory (pounds).............			32,000
Total plastic needs (pounds)..................			353,000
Less beginning inventory (pounds)..............			(29,000)
Purchases needed (pounds).....................			324,000
Cost per pound..............................			× $5
Total plastic purchases............................			$1,620,000

continued

Continued from previous page

DEWALT Purchases Budget For First Quarter of 2017			
	Drills	**Saws**	**Total**
Handle purchases			
Production units (production budget).............	65,000		65,000
Handles......................................			× 1
Production needs			65,000
Desired ending inventory			7,000
Total handle needs			72,000
Less beginning inventory			(6,000)
Purchases needed			66,000
Cost per handle			× $3
Total handle purchases			$198,000
Total purchases			
Metal...........................			$3,976,000
Plastic........................			1,620,000
Handles.......................			198,000
Total purchases			$5,794,000

d.

DEWALT Manufacturing Cost Budget For First Quarter of 2017			
	Drills	**Saws**	**Total**
Direct materials			
Metal			
Production units (production budget)	65,000	42,000	
Metal per unit of product (pounds)	× 5	× 4	
Production needs for metal (pounds)	325,000	168,000	
Unit cost	× $8	× $8	
Cost of metal issued to production	$2,600,000	$1,344,000	$3,944,000
Plastic			
Production units (production budget).............	65,000	42,000	
Plastic (pounds)	× 3	× 3	
Production needs for plastic (pounds)	195,000	126,000	
Unit cost	× $5	× $5	
Cost of plastic issued to production	$ 975,000	$ 630,000	1,605,000
Handles			
Production units (production budget).............	65,000		
Handles....................................	× 1		
Production needs for handles..................	65,000		
Unit cost	× $3		
Cost of handles issued to production	$ 195,000		195,000
Total			5,744,000

continued

DEWALT
Manufacturing Cost Budget
For First Quarter of 2017

	Drills	Saws	Total
Direct labor			
Budgeted production	65,000	42,000	
Direct labor hours per unit	× 2	× 3	
Total direct labor hours.	130,000	126,000	
Labor rate	× $12	× $16	
Labor expenditures	$1,560,000	$2,016,000	3,576,000
Variable manufacturing overhead			
Direct labor hours.	130,000	126,000	
Variable manufacturing overhead rate	× $1.50	× $1.50	
Total variable overhead	$ 195,000	$ 189,000	384,000
Fixed manufacturing overhead.			214,000
Total			$9,918,000

e.

DEWALT
Cash Budget
For First Quarter of 2017

Cash balance, beginning		$ 1,800,000
Collections on sales		
Current quarter's sales ($11,000,000 × 0.50).	$5,500,000	
Previous quarter's sales ($8,400,000 × 0.50).	4,200,000	9,700,000
Cash available from operations		11,500,000
Less budgeted disbursements		
Materials (purchases budget)	5,794,000	
Labor (manufacturing cost budget)	3,576,000	
Manufacturing overhead (manufacturing cost budget)		
([$384,000 + 214,000] − 156,000 noncash).	442,000	
Selling and administrative ($340,000 − $90,000 depreciation)		
	250,000	(10,062,000)
Cash balance, ending.		$ 1,438,000

f.

DEWALT
Contribution Income Statement
For First Quarter of 2017

Sales (sales budget).		$11,000,000
Less variable costs of goods sold		
Drills (60,000 × $85.00)	$5,100,000	
Saws (40,000 × $99.50)	3,980,000	(9,080,000)
Gross profit.		1,920,000
Less fixed costs		
Manufacturing overhead.	214,000	
Selling and administrative expenses	340,000	(554,000)
Net income.		$ 1,366,000

SOLUTION

    2   *a.* The marketing department is asked to provide an estimate as to how much it will spend on print ads during the next fiscal year.

    1   *b.* The marketing department provides a budget amount for print ads for the next fiscal year that includes the expected expenditures plus 10% to account for uncertainty.

    4   *c.* Tristan Renken owns and operates a food truck that sells Mexican food along the beaches in Chicago. Tristan only operates the food truck during the summer and developed a budget to estimate how much he will make during the upcoming summer season.

    3   *d.* Top management hosts semi-annual meetings to discuss the budget and current performance vs. the budget. Management provides employees with tools to help gauge their own performance against the budgeted expectations.

22

Standard Costs and Performance Reports

LEARNING OBJECTIVES

1. Explain responsibility accounting. (p. 974)

2. Differentiate between static and flexible budgets for performance reporting. Prepare a flexible budget. (p. 977)

3. Determine the components of standard cost variance analysis. Formulate and interpret direct materials cost variances. (p. 980)

4. Formulate and interpret direct labor cost variances. (p. 984)

5. Formulate and interpret overhead cost variances. (p. 986)

6. Calculate revenue variances and prepare a performance report for a revenue center. (p. 990)

7. Formulate and interpret fixed overhead cost variances (Appendix 22A). (p. 993)

8. Reconcile budgeted and actual income (Appendix 22B). (p. 995)

SOUTHWEST AIRLINES
www.southwest.com

In the last chapter, we discussed how budgeting was critical to planning within a business. But planning is only half of the story; at the end of the period, the operating results are compared to the budget. By evaluating the differences between the budgeted and the actual results, a manager can identify areas of the business that need attention. We call these differences *budget variances*, and a thorough analysis of these variances aids the manager in controlling the human and physical resources of the business.

To effectively control the business through variance analysis, it is important that the lines of responsibility are clearly defined among the managers. Managers (and the people that evaluate their results) need to understand who is responsible for revenues, costs, profits, capital investments, or some combination of those elements. This assignment of responsibility prevents managers from "passing the buck" when something goes wrong. Consider the case of **Southwest Airlines**, the Dallas, Texas–based airline, which completed a merger with **Air Tran**. When a structural shift such as a merger takes place, the lines of responsibility may be temporarily blurred. This can impede not only variance analysis, but also the integration of the merged entities.

While other airlines have bolstered revenue by charging fees for baggage, additional legroom, Wi-Fi, and changed flights, Southwest's strategy has been to offer passengers inexpensive and flexible flight arrangements with no hidden fees for baggage or other basic services. Inconsistencies between Southwest and Air Tran were prevalent in the merged business. Southwest permits customers to buy early boarding privileges, but Air Tran did not. Bags fly free on Southwest, but not on Air Tran. There is no business class on Southwest, whereas Air Tran passengers frequently received complementary upgrades to business class. The two reservation systems could not easily rebook passengers across the two airlines, and their frequent flier miles were not transferrable between the two airlines.

Even today, the merged airline is likely to encounter differences between expected and actual operating results. Some of the variances may relate to usage or efficiency, whereas others may relate to the dollar amount spent on a resource.

For example, the airline could use more or less fuel than is expected and the price paid per gallon of fuel could differ from expectations. Flight personnel may work more or fewer hours than expected and scheduling issues may result in paying higher- or lower-than-average wages than expected for the number of hours worked. Variance analysis can be extended to issues such as bag handling, overbooking, and number of passenger complaints.

Even though mergers can decrease the level of competition within an industry, customers still have some choice of airlines available to them. Managers prefer timely notification of potential variances so they still have time to "right the ship" before the end of the reporting period. In this chapter, we focus on performance assessment and variance analysis.

Management accounting tools aid in the assessment of the performance of the firm as a whole and all of its various components. Feedback in the form of performance reports is essential if the benefits of budgeting and other types of planning are to be fully realized. To control current operations and to improve future operations, managers must know how actual results compare with the current budget. These performance reports should be prepared in accordance with the concept of **responsibility accounting**, which is the structuring of performance reports addressed to individual (or group) members of an organization to emphasize the factors they control.

This chapter focuses on responsibility accounting and performance assessment. We examine responsibility accounting and identify various types of responsibility centers. We then take a close look at performance assessment for cost centers and conclude by considering performance reports for revenue centers. Responsibility accounting for major business segments is considered in Chapter 23.

Source: Micah Solomon, "Customer Service: What Southwest Knows and You Don't (Hint: Being Nice Isn't Enough)," *Forbes*, September 22, 2013; Alanna Petroff, "Airlines Rake in $27 Billion in Customer Fees," *CNN Money*, September 19, 2013; Scott McCartney, "Airlines Mergers and Aggravations," *Wall Street Journal*, July 18, 2013, pp. D1–D3; Scott McCartney, "Dear Airline, Here's the Problem …," *Wall Street Journal*, April 4, 2013, pp. D1–D4; and Scott McCartney, "Reality Check: Why Airlines Are Shrinking Flight Times," *Wall Street Journal*, June 14, 2012, pp. D1–D2.

CHAPTER ORGANIZATION

Standard Costs and Performance Reports				
Responsibility Accounting	**Performance Reporting for Cost Centers**	**Variance Analysis for Costs**	**Performance Reports for Revenue Centers**	**Additional Topics in Standard Costing (Appendix 22A and 22B)**
• Performance Reporting and Organization Structures • Types of Responsibility Centers • Financial and Nonfinancial Performance Measures	• Development of Flexible Budgets • Flexible Budgets Emphasize Performance • Standard Costs and Performance Reports	• Components of Standard Cost Analysis • Establishing and Using Standards for Direct Materials • Establishing and Using Standards for Direct Labor • Establishing and Using Standards for Variable Overhead • Fixed Overhead Variances	• Inclusion of Controllable Costs • Revenue Centers as Profit Centers	• Establishing and Using Fixed Overhead Variances • Reconciling Budgeted and Actual Income

eLectures
MBC

LO1 Explain responsibility accounting.

1

RESPONSIBILITY ACCOUNTING

Performance reports that include comparisons of actual results with plans or budgets serve as assessment tools and attention-directors to help managers control activities. According to the concept of *management by exception,* the absence of significant differences indicates that activities are proceeding as planned whereas the presence of significant differences indicates a need to either take corrective action or revise plans. These evaluations and actions are made within the framework of an organization's overall mission, goals, and strategies.

Responsibility accounting reports are customized to emphasize the activities of specific organizational units. For example, a performance report addressed to the head of a production department contains manufacturing costs controllable by the department head; it should not contain costs (such as advertising, sales commissions, or the president's salary) that the head of the production department cannot control. Including noncontrollable costs in the report distracts the manager's attention from the controllable costs, thereby diluting a manager's efforts to deal with controllable items.

If too much pressure is placed on managers to meet performance targets, they may take actions that are not in the best interest of the organization. The Business Insight that follows presents a classic example of such actions referred to as channel stuffing. The designers of an organization's responsibility accounting system need to be aware of the potential pressures that such a system can place on managers. The decision-making model of the organization should be such that managers are not influenced to make undesirable decisions just to receive bonuses or promotions.

Performance Reporting and Organization Structures

Before implementing a responsibility accounting system, all areas of authority and responsibility within an organization must be clearly defined. Organization charts and other documents should be examined to determine an organization's authority and responsibility structure. **Organization structure** is the arrangement of lines of authority and responsibility within an organization. These structures vary widely. Some companies have functional-based structures along the lines of marketing, production, research, and so forth; others use products, services, customers, or geography as the basis of organization. When an attempt is made to implement a responsibility accounting system, management could find instances of overlapping duties, authority not commensurate with responsibility, and expenditures for which no one appears responsible. The identification and resolution of these problems can be a major benefit of implementing a responsibility accounting system.

BUSINESS INSIGHT

Meeting Targets by Channel Stuffing   Good business requires good measurement, and GAAP requires measurement too. Financial accountants measure performance and communicate it to capital markets. Management accountants do the same for internal decision-making and stewardship. Bonuses are tied to these numbers, as are stock market performance and promotions. Where there are incentives for performance, there are incentives for unethical practices. Channel stuffing, as *Business Insider*'s Jim Edwards says, is the "oldest—and worst—trick in the book."

Channel stuffing occurs when a company ships more product to retailers than they need, and then books these increased shipments as sales. The immediate effect is that revenue goes up, but this technique almost always backfires. In the following period, the retailers have more than enough inventory, and revenues fall again. At this point the game is up, unless the company turns to more fraudulent methods. Often, firms will take the excess inventory back as sales returns and maintain the overshipping, thus increasing sales but also increasing return expense. This is a red flag for the SEC. **Diageo**, maker of Johnny Walker and Smirnoff, is being investigated by the SEC for just this impropriety. While it remains to be seen what action the SEC will take in this case, as not all channel stuffing amounts to fraud, it is important for firms to monitor this sort of behavior.

Source: "What is channel stuffing and how might it affect your business?" PwC Fraud Academy Blog, May 12, 2016; Jim Edwards, "The SEC wants to know if Diageo used the oldest — and worst — trick in the book to fudge its numbers," *Business Insider*, July 24, 2015.

Although performance reports can be developed for areas of responsibility as narrow as a single worker, the basic responsibility unit in most organizations begins with the department and progresses to division and corporate levels. In manufacturing plants, separate performance reports may be prepared for each production and service department, and then summarized into a performance report for all manufacturing activities. In large universities, reports may be prepared for individual departments such as history, philosophy, and English, and then summarized into a performance report of a college, such as Liberal Arts.

Types of Responsibility Centers

Based on the nature of their responsibility, responsibility centers can be classified as cost centers, revenue centers, profit centers, or investment centers.

Cost Center   A **cost center** manager is only responsible for costs; there is no revenue responsibility. A cost center can be as small as a segment of a department or large enough to include a major aspect of the organization, such as all manufacturing activities. Typical examples of cost centers include the following:

Organization	Cost Center
Manufacturing plant	Tooling department
	Assembly activities
Retail store	Inventory control function
	Maintenance department
Hospital	Radiology
	Emergency room
College	History department
	Registrar's office
City government	Public safety (police and fire)
	Road maintenance

Revenue Center   A **revenue center** manager is responsible for the generation of sales revenues. Even though the basic performance report of a revenue center emphasizes sales, revenue centers are likely to be assigned responsibility for the controllable costs they incur in generating revenues. If revenues and costs are evaluated separately, the center has dual responsibility as a revenue center and as a cost center. If controllable costs are deducted from revenues to obtain some bottom-line contribution, the center is, in fact, being treated more like a profit center than a revenue center.

Profit Center A **profit center** manager is responsible for revenues, costs, and the resulting profits. A profit center could be an entire organization, but it is more frequently a segment of an organization such as a product line, marketing territory, or store. In the context of performance evaluation, the word "profit" does not necessarily refer to the bottom line of an income statement; instead, it likely refers to the profit center's contribution to common corporate costs and profit. Profit is computed as the center's revenues less all costs directly associated with operating the center. Having limited authority regarding the size of total assets, the profit center manager is not held responsible for the relationship between profits and assets. In recent years many hospitals have been treating critical care and clinical service departments as profit centers to encourage physician chiefs to manage their departments as small businesses. The following Research Insight examines some of the issues associated with this movement.

RESEARCH INSIGHT

When Profit Centers Break Down   Profit centers may be a poor fit for health care. In a 2008 article, Dr. David Young contends that there are four central problems with profit-based performance evaluation in hospitals:

1. Departments vary in their profitability for fundamental reasons unrelated to performance. Cardiovascular surgery will be more profitable than pediatrics due to the fundamental structure of health care rather than through performance.
2. Both transfer pricing and use of outside services are complicated, and in some cases impossible. It is impossible for the orthopedic surgery department to use outside radiology in some procedures, as that would require leaving the hospital.
3. The trend in health care is to integrate care across departments. For example, a trend in women's health is to integrate clinical and critical care seamlessly. This makes financially separating clinical and critical care both difficult and possibly counterproductive.
4. A focus on operating profit creates incentives for critical care departments not to treat low-income or uninsured patients.

Dr. Young's arguments are supported by a recent study of hospital profitability, which shows that hospital profitability is strongly determined by the market in which the hospital functions. Factors such as market power and the socioeconomic status of patients are important determinants of profitability and are clearly out of the control of individual departments within the hospital.

Sources: Young, David W. "Profit centers in clinical care departments an idea whose time has gone: a case can be made for converting a hospital's clinical care departments from profit centers into standard expense centers." *Healthcare Financial Management* Mar. 2008: 66+. Academic OneFile. Web. 25 July 2016.
Bai, G., & Anderson, G. F. (2016). A more detailed understanding of factors associated with hospital profitability. *Health Affairs*, 35(5), 889-897. DOI: 10.1377/hlthaff.2015.1193.
Harris Meyer, "Not-for-profits dominate top-10 list of hospitals with biggest surpluses," *Modern Healthcare*, May 2, 2016.

Investment Center An **investment center** manager is responsible for the relationship between its profits and the total assets invested in the center. Investment center managers have a high degree of organization autonomy. In general, the management of an investment center is expected to earn a target profit per dollar invested. Investment center managers are evaluated on the basis of how well they use the total resources entrusted to their care to earn a profit. An investment center is the broadest and most inclusive type of responsibility center. Managers of these centers have more authority and responsibility than other managers and are primarily responsible for planning, organizing, and controlling firm activities. Because of their authority regarding the size of corporate assets, they are held responsible for the relationship between profits and assets. Investment centers are discussed further in Chapter 23.

Financial and Nonfinancial Performance Measures

This chapter's emphasis is on financial performance reports. Dollar-based financial reports have several advantages over other financial measures. Their "bottom line" impact is readily apparent. If actual fixed costs exceed budgeted fixed costs by $10,000, the before-tax income of an organization is $10,000 less than it would be without the extra fixed costs. Additionally, because dollars are additive and applicable to all organizational units, financial measures are easily summarized and reported up the organization chart.

It is important to keep in mind that although financial measures may indicate results are not in accordance with the budget, they do not indicate the root cause of financial deviations. The identification and analysis of the root cause of financial variances requires asking questions and, frequently, the use of nonfinancial data. Managers and employees at lower levels of the organization are often better served by performance reports focusing on data directly related to their job, such as units processed or customers served per hour. Although financial performance is still critical to **Southwest Airline**'s top management and still used to evaluate managers, aircraft and routes, the focus for the evaluation should include customer satisfaction. Other examples of nonfinancial performance measures include: defects per thousand units in a manufacturing plant, average and longest waiting time in a restaurant, nursing staff hours per patient day in a hospital, response time for a fire department, and customer satisfaction at a retail store or bank.

When organizations seek to improve financial performance beyond what is possible with current products, procedures, or services, the initial focus is most often on nonfinancial measures. **Trader Joe's** grocery stores might benchmark the length of their cash-register waiting times against **Whole Foods**.

MID-CHAPTER REVIEW 1

Eli's Cheesecake is a family-owned business based out of Chicago, IL. Eli's operates its corporate office, bakery, retail store, and café from one location on the west side of the city and recently opened a Cheesecake Café at Chicago's O'Hare Airport.

REQUIRED

Peruse Eli's website at http://www.elicheesecake.com to become more familiar with the company. Listed below are likely reporting centers for Eli's. Identify the type of responsibility center that would most likely be assigned to each reporting center: (1) Cost Center; (2) Revenue Center; (3) Profit Center; or (4) Investment Center.

_____ Bakery
_____ Accounting department
_____ Product line—Original Plain Cheesecake
_____ Human resources department
_____ Cheesecake Café at O'Hare Airport

The solution to this review problem can be found on page 1011.

PERFORMANCE REPORTING FOR COST CENTERS

LO2 Differentiate between static and flexible budgets for performance reporting. Prepare a flexible budget.

Financial performance reports for cost centers include a comparison of actual and budgeted (or allowed) costs and identify the difference as a **variance**. *Allowed costs* in performance reports are the flexible budget amounts for the actual level of activity. The variance is favorable if actual costs are less than budgeted (or allowed) costs and unfavorable if actual costs are more than budgeted (or allowed) costs. These comparisons are made in total and individually for each type of controllable cost assigned to the cost center.

Development of Flexible Budgets

A budget that is based on a prediction of sales and production is called a **static budget**. The operating budget explained in Chapter 21 is a static budget. Budgets can also be set for a series of possible production and sales volumes, or budgets can be adjusted to a particular level of production after the fact. These budgets, based on cost-volume relationships, are called **flexible budgets**; they are used to determine what costs should be for a level of activity. For example, if the college cafeteria budgets $15,000 for food during April for 5,000 meals but provides 6,000 meals, the budget needs to be adjusted by the original food budget rate of $3 ($15,000/5,000 meals). If $17,500 was spent on food during the month, the analysis might appear as follows:

Budget Item	Actual	Budget	Difference
Static analysis			
Food.........................	$17,500	5,000 meals × $3 = $15,000	$2,500 over budget
Flexible analysis			
Food.........................	$17,500	6,000 meals × $3 = $18,000	$500 under budget

The cafeteria manager is better evaluated based on what actually happened with the flexible budget than with the static budget, especially if the manager had no control over how many student meals were requested.

For a complete example of a flexible budget, assume that **Tumi**, which produces high-quality bags, luggage, and accessories, produces only one product, a computer bag. Also assume Tumi has only three departments: production, sales, and administration. Focusing on the production department, the flexible budget cost-estimating equations for total monthly production costs of computer bags are based on the production standards for variable and fixed costs. The standards follow:

Variable costs
    Direct materials—2 pounds per bag at $5 per pound, or $10 per bag
    Direct labor—0.25 hour per bag at $24 per hour, or $6 per bag
    Variable overhead—2 pounds of direct material per bag at $4 per pound, or $8 per bag
Fixed costs—$52,000

If management plans to produce 10,000 computer bags in July, the budgeted manufacturing costs are $292,000:

TUMI
Manufacturing Cost Budget
For Month of July

Manufacturing costs	
Variable costs	
Direct materials (10,000 bags × 2 pounds × $5).....................................	$100,000
Direct labor (10,000 bags × 0.25 hours × $24)	60,000
Variable overhead (10,000 bags × 2 pounds × $4)	80,000
Fixed costs..	52,000
Total	$292,000

Flexible Budgets Emphasize Performance

If actual production happened to equal budgeted production, the production department is evaluated by comparing the actual and budgeted costs. If production needs change, perhaps due to an unexpected increase or decrease in sales volume, the production department should attempt to make appropriate changes. When the actual production volume is anything other than the originally budgeted amount, the production department's financial responsibility for costs should be based on the actual level of production.

For the purpose of evaluating the financial performance of cost centers, a flexible budget is tailored, after the fact, to the actual level of activity. A **flexible budget variance** is computed for each cost as the difference between the actual cost and the flexible budget cost. Assume actual production for July totaled 11,000 bags rather than 10,000 bags. Examples of a performance report for July manufacturing costs based on static and flexible budgets are presented in **Exhibit 22.1**. When the production department's financial performance is evaluated using the static budget, the actual cost of producing 11,000 bags is compared to the budgeted cost of producing 10,000 bags. The result is a series of unfavorable static budget variances totaling $20,000.

When the production department's financial performance is evaluated by comparing actual costs with costs allowed in a flexible budget drawn up for the actual production volume, the results are mixed. Direct materials have a $2,000 favorable variance. Direct labor has a $4,000 unfavorable variance. The variable overhead variance is $7,000 favorable. The fixed overhead

EXHIBIT 22.1	Flexible Budgets and Performance Evaluation

TUMI
Production Department Performance Report
For Month of July

	Based on Static Budget			Based on Flexible Budget		
	Actual	**Original Budget**	**Static Budget Variance**	**Actual**	**Flexible Budget***	**Flexible Budget Variance**
Volume	11,000	10,000		11,000	11,000	
Variable costs						
Direct materials.	$108,000	$100,000	$ 8,000 U	$108,000	$110,000	$2,000 F
Direct labor	70,000	60,000	10,000 U	70,000	66,000	4,000 U
Variable overhead	81,000	80,000	1,000 U	81,000	88,000	7,000 F
Fixed costs.	53,000	52,000	1,000 U	53,000	52,000	1,000 U
Totals	$312,000	$292,000	$20,000 U	$312,000	$316,000	$4,000 F

* Flexible budget manufacturing costs: (Actual level × Budgeted per bag cost)
Direct materials (11,000 bags × 2 pounds × $5)
Direct labor (11,000 bags × 0.25 labor hour × $24)
Variable overhead (11,000 bags × 2 pounds × $4)

variance remains $1,000 unfavorable since the static and flexible fixed budgets stay the same. The net flexible budget variance is $4,000 favorable, a substantial change from the static variance of $20,000 unfavorable.

Flexible budget variances provide a much better indicator of performance than static budget variances that do not consider the increased level of production (11,000 bags rather than 10,000 bags). When production exceeds the planned level, the static budget variances are usually unfavorable. Likewise, when actual production is substantially below the planned level of activity, the static variances are usually favorable. While it is important to isolate and determine the cause of any variation between planned and actual production, the financial-based performance report is not the appropriate place to mix volume-created variances with those related to the actual production levels.

Standard Costs and Performance Reports

A **standard cost** indicates what it should cost to provide an activity or produce one batch or unit of product under planned and efficient operating conditions. In a standard costing environment, the flexible budget is based on standard unit costs. Traditionally, standard costs have been developed from an engineering analysis or from an analysis of historical data adjusted for expected changes in the product, production technology, or costs. When standards are developed using historical data, management must be careful to ensure that past inefficiencies are excluded from current standards.

To obtain the full benefit of standard costs, the standards must be based on realistic expectations. Suppose the standard cost for direct labor for **Tumi** is $6.00 per bag, (computed as 0.25 direct labor hours × $24 per hour). Some organizations intentionally set "tight" standards to motivate employees toward higher levels of production. The management of Tumi might set their standards for direct labor at 0.22 hours per bag rather than at the expected 0.25 hours per bag, hoping that employees will strive toward the lower time and, consequently, the lower cost of $5.28 ($24 × 0.22). The use of tight standards often causes planning and behavioral problems. Management expects them to result in unfavorable variances. Accordingly, tight standards should not be used to budget input requirements and cash flows because management expects to incur more labor costs than the standards allow. The use of tight standards can have undesirable behavioral effects if employees find that a second set of standards is used in the "real" budget or if they are constantly subject to unfavorable performance reports. These employees could come to distrust the entire budgeting and performance evaluation system, or they may quit trying to achieve any of the organization's standards.

Tight standards are more likely to occur in an imposed budget than in a participation budget. In a participation budget, the problem may be to avoid overstating the costs required to produce a product. Loose standards may fail to properly motivate employees and can make the company uncompetitive due to costs that are higher than competitors'.

MID-CHAPTER REVIEW 2

Suppose you receive the following performance report from the accounting department for your first month as plant manager for a new company. Your supervisor, the vice president of manufacturing, has concerns that the report does not provide an accurate picture of your performance in the area of cost control.

	Actual	Budgeted	Variance
Units..	10,000	12,000	2,000 U
Costs			
Direct materials	$ 299,000	$ 360,000	$ 61,000 F
Direct labor.............................	345,500	432,000	86,500 F
Variable factory overhead..........	180,000	216,000	36,000 F
Fixed factory overhead	375,000	360,000	15,000 U
Total costs	$1,199,500	$1,368,000	$168,500 F

REQUIRED
Prepare a revised budget that better reflects your performance.

The solution to this review problem can be found on page 1011.

VARIANCE ANALYSIS FOR COSTS
Components of Standard Cost Analysis

LO3 Determine the components of standard cost variance analysis. Formulate and interpret direct materials cost variances.

To use and interpret standard cost variances properly, managers must understand the processes and activities that drive costs. Cost variances are merely signals. They do not explain why costs differ from expectations. Underlying causes of variances must be investigated before final judgment is passed on the effectiveness and efficiency of an operation or activity.

Standard cost variance analysis is a systematic approach to examining flexible budget variances. Actual costs are determined from the organization's financial transactions. Flexible budget costs are determined by multiplying standard quantities allowed for the output times the standard price per unit. For a company using activity-based costing, each manufacturing activity could have its own standard costs that focus on underlying concepts and cost drivers, and companies even develop their own set of variances.

Standard cost variance analysis identifies the general causes of the total flexible budget variance by breaking it into separate price and quantity variances for each production component. Two possible reasons that actual cost could differ from flexible budget cost for a given amount of output produced are (1) a difference between actual and standard prices paid for the production components—the price variance—and (2) a difference between the actual quantity and the standard quantity allowed for the production components—the quantity variance. Variances have different names for different cost categories as follows:

Cost Category	Price Variance Name	Quantity Variance Name
Direct materials	Materials price variance	Materials quantity variance
Direct labor	Labor rate variance	Labor efficiency variance
Variable overhead	Variable overhead spending variance	Variable overhead efficiency variance

Fixed overhead is excluded from the unit standard costs because, within the relevant range of normal activity, it does not vary with the volume of production. To facilitate product costing, however, many organizations develop a standard fixed overhead cost per unit.

In the following sections, we analyze the flexible budget cost variances for materials, labor and variable overhead. Our illustration is based on the following hypothetical July activity and costs of **Tumi**'s production department.

TUMI **Actual Manufacturing Costs** **For Month of July**	
Actual bags completed	11,000
Manufacturing costs	
Unit level costs	
Direct materials (24,000 pounds × $4.50)	$108,000
Direct labor (2,800 hours × $25.00)	70,000
Variable overhead	81,000
Fixed overhead costs	53,000
Total	$312,000

RESEARCH INSIGHT

When Are Variances Evidence of Fraud?   Standard cost variances can help firms hold managers and employees accountable for their work. Dr. Cecily Raiborn and her coauthors argue that variance analysis can also help strengthen internal controls, ultimately detecting fraud early and pointing to areas of the company that are weak. If purchasing managers are receiving kickbacks from suppliers, the behavior may show up in frequent, slightly unfavorable price variances. If employees are stealing materials for resale or personal use, the firm may see unfavorable materials variances.

This sort of data analysis for indicators of fraud is important enough for auditors that the Big Four auditing firms are developing tools to automate this process. **KPMG** recently partnered with **IBM** to use Watson's artificial intelligence engine to comb through financial data for just the sort of behaviors that will show up in the variances discussed here. **EY** (formerly Ernst & Young) has poured $400 million into their own tools for this analysis. Automating the data analysis allows all of the client's transactions to be considered, not just the top-level numbers that come out in variance analysis.

Such tools find patterns that raise suspicion, which can be variances or issues as simple as sales clustered just before the quarter end and expenses clustered just after. These tools do the work of combing through the firm's data for suspicious patterns, but it remains the job of management accountants and auditors to determine whether the patterns are operational or fraudulent.

Sources: Cecily Raiborn, Janet Butler, and Lucian Zelazny, "Standard Costing Variances: Potential Red Flags of Fraud?" *Cost Management*, 2013.
Michael Rapoport, "Auditing firms count on technology for backup," *The Wall Street Journal*, March 7, 2016.

Note that detailed information on actual pounds and an actual rate is not provided for variable overhead. That is because variable overhead represents a pool of related costs driven by a number of factors rather than a single cost with a single driver. Although the basis used in budgeting variable overhead may, and should, have a high correlation with actual variable overhead, it is a surrogate for the multiple cost elements that comprise variable overhead. Issues related to variable overhead are discussed in greater detail later in this chapter.

Establishing and Using Standards for Direct Materials

The two basic elements contained in the standards for direct materials are the *standard price* and the *standard quantity*. Materials standards indicate how much an organization should pay for each input unit of direct materials and the quantity of direct materials it should use to produce one unit of output. The standard price per unit of direct materials should include all reasonable costs necessary to acquire the materials. These costs include the invoice price of materials, less planned discounts plus freight, insurance, special handling, and any other costs related to the acquisition of the materials. The standard quantity represents the number of units of raw materials allowed for the production of one unit of finished product. This amount should include the amount dictated by the physical characteristics of the process and the product, plus a reasonable allowance for normal spoilage, waste, and other inefficiencies. The quantity standard can be determined by engineering analysis, professional judgment, or by averaging the actual amount used for several periods. An average of actual past materials usage may not be a good standard because it could include excessive wastes and inefficiencies in the standard quantity.

Direct Materials Variances   The **materials price variance** is the difference between the actual materials cost and the standard cost of actual materials inputs. The **materials quantity variance** is the difference between the standard cost of actual materials inputs and the flexible budget cost for materials. The direct materials variances for **Tumi** follow.

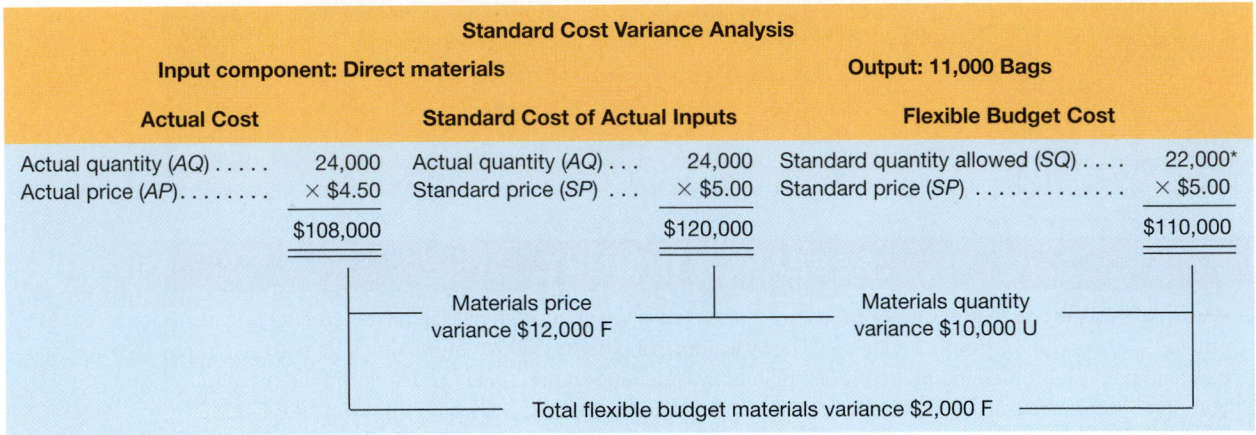

*11,000 bags × 2 pounds per bag

Tumi had a favorable materials price variance of $12,000 because the actual cost of materials used ($108,000) was less than the standard cost of actual materials used ($120,000). The price variance can also be computed using a formula approach as the actual quantity (AQ) used times the difference between the actual price (AP) and the standard price (SP). Tumi paid $0.50 per pound below the standard price for 24,000 pounds for a total savings of $12,000:

$$\text{Materials price variance} = \text{AQ}(\text{AP} - \text{SP})$$

$$= 24{,}000(\$4.50 - \$5.00)$$
$$= 24{,}000 \times \$0.50$$
$$= \$12{,}000 \text{ F}$$

The unfavorable quantity variance of $10,000 occurred because the standard cost of actual materials used, $120,000 (24,000 × $5), was higher than the cost of materials allowed by the flexible budget, $110,000 (22,000 × $5). A total of 22,000 pounds of materials is allowed to produce 11,000 units of finished outputs. This is computed as 11,000 finished bags times 2.0 pounds of direct materials per bag. The materials quantity variance can also be computed using a formula approach as the standard price (SP) per pound times the difference between the number of pounds actually used (AQ) and the number of pounds allowed (SQ):

$$\text{Materials quantity variance} = \text{SP}(\text{AQ} - \text{SQ})$$

$$= \$5(24{,}000 - 22{,}000)$$
$$= \$5 \times 2{,}000$$
$$= \$10{,}000 \text{ U}$$

Interpreting Materials Variances   As highlighted in the following two Business Insights, after computing variances, managers are in a better position to analyze their business' results and to make better and more relevant decisions. A *favorable materials price variance* indicates that the employee responsible for materials purchases paid less per unit than the price allowed by the standards. This could result from receiving discounts for purchasing more than the normal quantities, effective bargaining by the employee, purchasing substandard-quality materials, purchasing from a distress seller, or other factors. Ordinarily, when a favorable price variance is reported, the employee's performance is interpreted as favorable. However, if the favorable price variance results from the purchase of materials of lower than standard quality or from a purchase in more than desirable quantities, the employee's performance would be questionable. All large variances, including favorable variances, should be thoroughly investigated for causes and corrections.

BUSINESS INSIGHT

Variance Analysis Helps Hospitals Understand Impact of Policy   To understand the impact of California's Hospital Fair Pricing Act (CHFPA), Professor Ge Bai of Washington and Lee University applied variance analysis to California hospitals' expense recovery data. Expense recovery is simply the rate at which the hospital is able to recover the costs of serving a patient by collecting from insurers.

The CHFPA stipulates that hospitals can only charge low-income, uninsured patients Medicare rates for services. The act also makes it more difficult to collect payment from these patients. Dr. Bai's study shows that the CHFPA decreases the rate of expense recovery from low-income patients and increases the share of these patients in the health-care system, consistent with the aims of the CHFPA. His study also shows that hospitals appear to be offsetting the cost of treating more low-income patients at lower rates by collecting more aggressively from both public programs and from private insurance companies.

Source: Ge Bai (2016) Applying Variance Analysis to Understand California Hospitals' Expense Recovery Status by Patient Groups. *Accounting Horizons:* June 2016, Vol. 30, No. 2, pp. 211-223.

An *unfavorable materials price variance* means that the purchasing employee paid more per unit for materials than the price allowed by the standards. This could be caused by failure to buy in sufficient quantities to receive normal discounts; purchase of higher-quality materials than called for in the product specifications; failure to place materials orders on a timely basis; failure to bargain for the best available prices; or other factors. An unfavorable variance does not always mean that the employee performed unfavorably. Many noncontrollable factors surround the purchasing function, including unanticipated price increases, the need to increase production to meet unanticipated sales, and supply chain problems such as a work stoppage at a vendor.

BUSINESS INSIGHT

Unfavorable Price Variance? Buy a Farm   Demand for organic ingredients is outpacing supply. Sales of organic food tripled from 2003 to 2013, and supply of some products is not keeping up. Not only are prices rising (unfavorable rate variance) but shortages are also interrupting supply chains for large food companies (unfavorable efficiency variance). In 2015, **Nature's Path Foods Inc.** decided that they had had enough. So they bought a 2,800-acre farm in Montana. Nature's Path had been dealing with supply shortages and unpredictable prices, once even importing ingredients from Sweden on very short notice. The company plans to invest $2 million each year in purchasing and converting farmland.

It turns out that changing a farm from conventional to organic requires a transition period that is tough for farmers. It takes between one and three years to transition a farm. During transition, the farm is using more costly organic practices, but farmers cannot sell their products as organic. **Chipotle Mexican Grill Inc.** and **Pacific Foods of Oregon Inc.** are trying to help farmers switch by offering financing and training. The maker of Garden of Eatin' corn chips, **Hain Celestial Group Inc.** is offering farmers long-term contracts to lock in corn supply and to help offset some of the risks farmers face.

When supply is erratic, companies may find that capital budgeting choices that include purchasing their suppliers make sense.

Source: Ilan Brat, "Hunger for Organic Foods Stretches Supply Chain," *The Wall Street Journal*, April 3, 2015.

A *favorable materials quantity variance* means that the actual quantity of raw materials used was less than the quantity allowed for the units produced. This could result from factors such as less materials waste than allowed by the standards, better than expected machine efficiency, direct materials of higher quality than required by the standards, and more efficient use of direct materials by employees. An *unfavorable materials quantity variance* occurs when the quantity of raw materials used exceeds the quantity allowed for the units produced. This could result from incurring more waste than provided for in the standards, poorly maintained machinery requiring larger amounts of raw materials, raw materials of lower quality than required by the standards, or poorly trained employees who were unable to use the materials at the level of efficiency required by the standards.

MID-CHAPTER REVIEW 3

Suppose the flexible budget performance report for **REI**'s camping chair product for March follows.

	Actual Costs	Flexible Budget Cost	Flexible Budget Variances
Output units	5,000	5,000	
Direct materials	$104,125	$100,000	$ 4,125 U
Direct labor.	82,400	75,000	7,400 U
Variable manufacturing overhead			
Category 1	31,000	30,000	1,000 U
Category 2	18,000	20,000	2,000 F
Fixed manufacturing overhead.	42,000	40,000	2,000 U
Total	$277,525	$265,000	$12,525 U

The standard unit cost for folding chairs follows:

Direct materials (4 pounds × $5.00 per pound).	$20
Direct labor (1.25 hours × $12.00 per hour).	15
Variable overhead, Category 1 (1.25 hours × $4.80).	6
Variable overhead, Category 2 ($4 per finished unit)	4
Total standard variable cost per unit	$45

Actual cost of materials is based on 21,250 pounds of direct materials purchased and used at $4.90 per pound; actual cost of assembly is based on 7,000 labor hours. Variable overhead is applied on labor hours for Category 1 and finished units for Category 2.

REQUIRED
Calculate all standard cost variances for direct materials.

The solution to this review problem can be found on page 1012.

Establishing and Using Standards for Direct Labor

LO4 Formulate and interpret direct labor cost variances.

To evaluate management performance in controlling labor costs, it is necessary to determine the *standard labor rate* for each hour allowed and the *standard time allowed* to produce a unit. Setting labor rate standards can be quite simple or extremely complex. If all employees have the same wage rate, determining the standard cost is relatively easy: Simply adopt the normal wage rate as the standard labor rate. If there are variations in employee wage rates, the standard labor rate should be based on the expected mix of employee wage rates.

The standard labor time per unit can be determined by an engineering approach or an empirical observation approach. When using an engineering approach, industrial engineers ascertain the amount of time required to produce a unit of finished product by applying time and motion methods or other available techniques. Normal operating conditions are assumed in arriving at the labor standard. Therefore, allowances must be made for normal machine downtime, employee personal breaks, and so forth. Under the empirical approach, the average time required to produce a unit under normal operating conditions is used as a basis for the standard.

Direct Labor Variances   Using the general variance model that was used for materials, we can compute the labor rate and efficiency variances. The **labor rate variance** is the difference between the actual cost and the standard cost of actual labor inputs. The **labor efficiency variance** is the difference between the standard cost of actual inputs and the flexible budget cost for labor.

Tumi's labor standards provide for 0.25 hour of labor per bag produced at $24 per hour. During July, 2,800 hours were used at a cost of $25 per hour. Using these data, the labor rate (price) variance and labor efficiency (quantity) variance can be computed as shown in the following illustration.

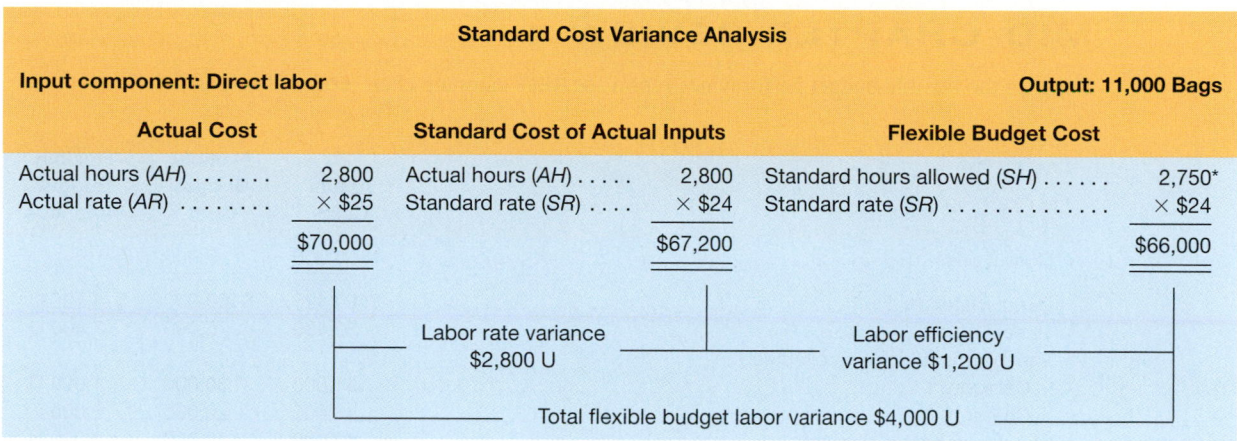

*11,000 bags × 0.25 hours per bag

The labor rate variance can also be computed in formula form as the actual number of hours used times the difference between the actual rate and the standard rate.

$$\textbf{Labor rate variance} = \textbf{AH(AR} - \textbf{SR)}$$

$$= \textbf{2,800(\$25} - \textbf{\$24)}$$
$$= \textbf{2,800} \times \textbf{\$1}$$
$$= \textbf{\$2,800 U}$$

This computation of the labor rate variance shows that the company paid $1 more than the standard rate for each of the 2,800 hours worked.

Since 11,000 units of product were finished during the period and 0.25 hour of labor was allowed for each bag, the total number of standard hours allowed was 2,750 (11,000 bags × 0.25 hours). The labor efficiency variance can also be computed as the standard rate times the difference between the actual labor hours and the standard hours allowed:

$$\textbf{Labor efficiency variance} = \textbf{SR(AH} - \textbf{SH)}$$

$$= \textbf{\$24(2,800} - \textbf{2,750)}$$
$$= \textbf{\$24} \times \textbf{50}$$
$$= \textbf{\$1,200 U}$$

Tumi's labor efficiency variance indicates that the company used 50 more labor hours than allowed. By itself, this inefficiency caused an unfavorable variance of $1,200.

Interpreting Labor Variances   The possible explanations for labor rate variances are rather limited. An *unfavorable labor rate variance* can be caused by the use of higher paid laborers than the standards provided. An increase in wage rates not reflected in the standards can also cause an unfavorable labor rate variance. A *favorable labor rate variance* occurs if lower paid workers were used or if actual wage rates declined.

Unfavorable labor efficiency variances occur when the actual labor hours exceed the number of hours allowed for the actual output. This could be caused by using poorly trained workers or poorly maintained machinery or by the use of low-quality materials. Low employee morale and generally poor working conditions could also adversely affect the efficiency.

Favorable labor efficiency variances occur when the actual labor hours are less than the number of hours allowed for the actual output. This above-normal efficiency can be caused by the company's use of higher-skilled (and higher-paid) workers, better machinery, or higher-quality raw materials than the standards require. High employee morale, improved job satisfaction, or generally improved working conditions could also account for the above-normal efficiency of the workers.

MID-CHAPTER REVIEW 4

Suppose the flexible budget performance report for **REI**'s camping chair product for March follows.

	Actual Costs	Flexible Budget Cost	Flexible Budget Variances
Output units	5,000	5,000	
Direct materials	$104,125	$100,000	$ 4,125 U
Direct labor.	82,400	75,000	7,400 U
Variable manufacturing overhead			
Category 1	31,000	30,000	1,000 U
Category 2	18,000	20,000	2,000 F
Fixed manufacturing overhead.	42,000	40,000	2,000 U
Total	$277,525	$265,000	$12,525 U

The standard unit cost for folding chairs follows:

Direct materials (4 pounds × $5.00 per pound).	$20
Direct labor (1.25 hours × $12.00 per hour).	15
Variable overhead, Category 1 (1.25 hours × $4.80)	6
Variable overhead, Category 2 ($4 per finished unit)	4
Total standard variable cost per unit	$45

Actual cost of materials is based on 21,250 pounds of direct materials purchased and used at $4.90 per pound; actual cost of assembly is based on 7,000 labor hours. Variable overhead is applied on labor hours for Category 1 and finished units for Category 2.

REQUIRED
Calculate all standard cost variances for direct labor.

The solution to this review problem can be found on page 1012.

LO5 Formulate and interpret variable overhead cost variances.

Establishing and Using Standards for Variable Overhead

The traditional unit-level approach to cost estimation, budgeting, and variance analysis separates overhead costs into fixed and variable elements. This separation is necessary because fixed costs are primarily driven by factors related to capacity and variable costs are primarily driven by factors related to volume.

Because it includes many heterogeneous costs, manufacturing overhead poses a unique problem in establishing standards for the standard quantity and the standard price of inputs. Direct materials have a natural physical measure of quantity such as tons, barrels, pounds, and liters. Similarly, labor or assembly is measurable in hours. However, no single quantity measure is common to all overhead items. Overhead is a cost group that can simultaneously include costs measurable in hours, pounds, liters and kilowatts.

The most frequent approach to dealing with the problem of multiple quantity measures in variable manufacturing overhead is to use a single surrogate (or substitute) measure to represent the quantity of all items in a given group. Typical substitute measures include machine hours, units of finished product, direct labor hours, and direct labor dollars. The variable overhead standard is then stated in terms of this surrogate measure.

Variable Overhead Variances   The **variable overhead spending variance** is the difference between the actual variable overhead cost and the standard variable overhead cost for the actual inputs of the surrogate measure. The **variable overhead efficiency variance** is the difference between the standard variable overhead cost for the actual inputs of the surrogate measure and the flexible budget cost allowed for variable overhead based on outputs.

Assume for Tumi, the actual variable overhead in July was $81,000. This represents the actual cost of overhead items such as indirect materials and indirect labor. Pounds of materials is Tumi's surrogate measure for quantity for variable overhead allowed and used. This means that the standard costs allowed for variable overhead varies with the pounds of direct materials allowed. Hence the standard cost of actual inputs is calculated as actual pounds of direct materials (AQ) times the standard variable overhead rate per pound (SR):

$$\textbf{Standard cost of actual inputs} = (\textbf{AQ} \times \textbf{SR})$$
$$= 24{,}000 \times \$4$$
$$= \$96{,}000$$

The flexible budget cost for variable overhead allowed for the actual outputs is based on the 22,000 pounds of direct materials allowed (SQ) for the bags produced during the period (11,000 bags × 2 pounds). The allowed quantities are multiplied by the standard variable overhead rate (SR). The resulting variable overhead flexible budget cost is $88,000:

$$\textbf{Flexible budget cost} = (\textbf{SQ} \times \textbf{SR})$$
$$= 22{,}000 \times \$4$$
$$= \$88{,}000$$

Using these data, the variable overhead spending (price) variance and the variable overhead efficiency (quantity) variance follow.

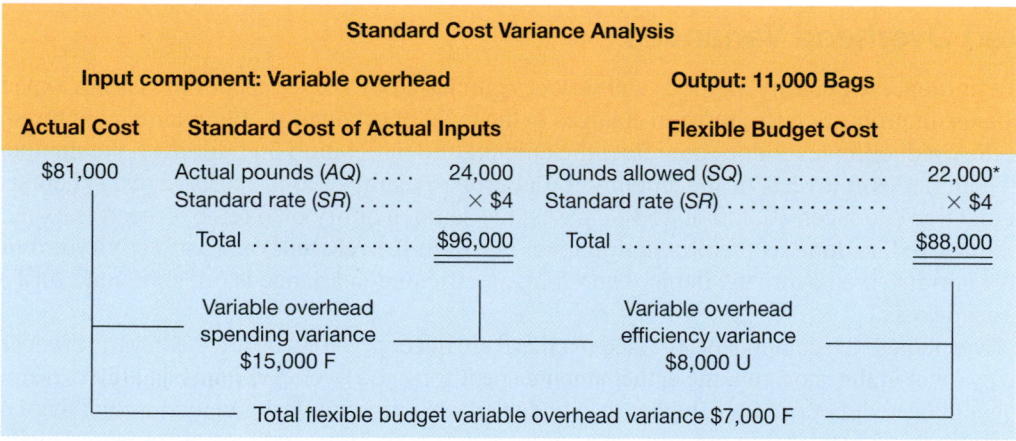

*11,000 bags × 2 lbs.

An alternative to the computation of the variable overhead effectiveness variance follows:

$$\textbf{Variable overhead efficiency variance} = \textbf{SR(AQ} - \textbf{SQ)}$$
$$= \$4(24{,}000 - 22{,}000)$$
$$= \$8{,}000 \textbf{ U}$$

This approach emphasizes that the 2,000 extra pounds used should have increased variable overhead by $8,000 at the standard rate of $4 per pound.

Interpreting Variable Overhead Variances   A *favorable spending variance* encompasses all factors that cause actual expenditures to be less than the amount expected for the actual inputs of the measurement base, including consumption and payment. Conversely, an *unfavorable spending variance* results when the actual expenditures are more than expected for the inputs of the measurement base. This is caused by consuming more overhead items than expected, or by paying more than the expected amount for overhead items consumed, or by both. Thus, the term *spending variance* is used instead of *price variance*.

The key to understanding the variable overhead spending variance is recognizing that the amount of variable overhead cost allowed is determined by the level of the surrogate measurement base used. Any deviation from this spending budget causes a spending variance to occur.

The variable overhead efficiency variance measures the difference between the standard variable overhead cost for the actual quantity of the surrogate measurement base and the standard variable overhead cost for the allowed quantity of the surrogate measurement base. This variance measures the amount of variable overhead that should have been saved (or incurred) because of the efficient (or inefficient) use of the surrogate measurement base. It provides no information about the degree of efficiency in using variable overhead items such as indirect materials and indirect labor. This information is reflected in the spending variance.

YOU MAKE THE CALL

You Are the Vice President of Manufacturing   Your company has had a practice for many years of budgeting variable overhead costs based on direct labor hours. The managerial accountants have argued that if direct labor hours are controlled, variable overhead costs will take care of themselves since direct labor hours drive variable overhead costs. You (and your plant managers) have become very skeptical of this policy because in recent years variable overhead variances have been very erratic—sometimes being large favorable amounts and other times being large unfavorable amounts. You are beginning to plan for the coming budget year. How do you think you should budget variable overhead and evaluate managers who control these costs? [Answer, p. 996]

Fixed Overhead Variances

By definition, the quantity of goods and services purchased by fixed expenditures is not expected to change in proportion to short-run changes in the level of production. For example, in the short run, the production level does not affect the amount of depreciation on buildings, the number of fixed salaried employees, or the amount of real property subject to property taxes. Whether the organization produces 10,000 or 15,000 cases, the same quantity of fixed overhead is expected to be incurred, as long as the production level is within the relevant range of activity provided by the current fixed overhead items. Therefore, an efficiency variance is not computed for fixed overhead costs.

Even though the components of fixed overhead are not expected to be affected by the production activity level in the short run, the actual amount spent for fixed overhead items can differ from the amount budgeted. For example, higher than budgeted supervisors' salaries could be paid, there may be unanticipated increases in property taxes or insurance premiums, and the cost of leased facilities may increase. Fixed overhead costs in excess of the amount budgeted are reflected in the fixed overhead budget variance. The **fixed overhead budget variance** is, simply, the difference between budgeted and actual fixed overhead. Using the assumed fixed costs of **Tumi** as an example:

$$\text{Fixed overhead budget variance} = \text{Actual fixed overhead} - \text{Budgeted fixed overhead}$$
$$= \$53,000 - \$52,000$$
$$= \$1,000 \text{ U}$$

The fixed overhead budget variance is always the same as the total fixed overhead flexible budget variance. Because budgeted fixed overhead is the same for all outputs within the relevant range, the budget variance explains the total flexible budget variance between actual and allowed fixed overhead. Similar to variable overhead, fixed overhead variances can be caused by a combination of price and quantity factors. Fixed overhead variances are examined further in Appendix 22A.

BUSINESS INSIGHT

The Correct Diagnosis Is the Efficient Diagnosis   Misdiagnosis in the medical field is rampant. At its core, misdiagnosis is simply misidentifying a problem—a pathologist doesn't identify cancerous cells that exist, or a doctor may diagnose a patient as having cancer when, in fact, the patient does not. Second opinions of diagnoses raise questions in 25% of cases and prevent procedures that are costly for both the health-care system and the patient. On the other hand, second opinions can also catch missed diagnoses and help patients avoid costly convalescence. But getting a second opinion isn't always easy, especially in rural areas. Currently, lab samples must be physically transported across the country for diagnosis. **GE** is working with the US FDA to introduce a digital diagnosis system that allows samples to move more easily across the country for primary and secondary diagnoses. Getting the diagnosis right will have positive effects on both the patient's quality of life and medical bills and will yield better information for the hospital's budgeting process.

Sources: Laura Landro, "New Ways Doctors Reach Agreement on Patient Diagnoses," *The Wall Street Journal*, June 9, 2015.

MID-CHAPTER REVIEW 5

Suppose the flexible budget performance report for **REI**'s camping chair product for March follows.

	Actual Costs	Flexible Budget Cost	Flexible Budget Variances
Output units	5,000	5,000	
Direct materials	$104,125	$100,000	$ 4,125 U
Direct labor	82,400	75,000	7,400 U
Variable manufacturing overhead			
Category 1	31,000	30,000	1,000 U
Category 2	18,000	20,000	2,000 F
Fixed manufacturing overhead	42,000	40,000	2,000 U
Total	$277,525	$265,000	$12,525 U

The standard unit cost for folding chairs follows:

Direct materials (4 pounds × $5.00 per pound)	$20
Direct labor (1.25 hours × $12.00 per hour)	15
Variable overhead, Category 1 (1.25 hours × $4.80)	6
Variable overhead, Category 2 ($4 per finished unit)	4
Total standard variable cost per unit	$45

Actual cost of materials is based on 21,250 pounds of direct materials purchased and used at $4.90 per pound; actual cost of assembly is based on 7,000 labor hours. Variable overhead is applied on labor hours for Category 1 and finished units for Category 2.

REQUIRED
Calculate all standard cost variances for variable manufacturing overhead.

The solution to this review problem can be found on page 1012.

PERFORMANCE REPORTS FOR REVENUE CENTERS

The financial performance reports for revenue centers include a comparison of actual and budgeted revenues. Controllable costs can be deducted from revenues to obtain some bottom-line contribution margin. If the center is then evaluated on the basis of this contribution, it is being treated as a profit center.

If the organization is to meet its budgeted profit goal for a period, with its budgeted fixed and variable costs, the organization's revenue centers must meet their original revenue budgets. Consequently, the original budget (a static budget) rather than a flexible budget is used to evaluate the financial performance of revenue centers.

Assume that Tumi's July sales budget called for the sale of 10,000 bags at $40.00 each. If Tumi actually sold 11,000 bags at $38.50 each, the total revenue variance is $23,500 favorable:

Actual revenues (11,000 × $38.50)	$423,500
Budgeted revenues (10,000 × $40)	(400,000)
Revenue variance	$ 23,500 F

The **revenue variance** is the difference between the budgeted sales volume at the budgeted selling price and the actual sales volume at the actual selling price. Because Tumi's actual revenues exceeded budgeted revenues, the revenue variance is favorable. It can be presented as follows:

> **Revenue variance = (Actual volume × Actual price) − (Budgeted volume × Budgeted price)**

The separate impact of changing prices and volume on revenue is analyzed with the sales price and sales volume variances. The **sales price variance** is computed as the change in selling price times the actual sales volume:

> **Sales price variance = (Actual selling price − Budgeted selling price) × Actual sales volume**

For Tumi, the sales price variance for July follows:

$$\text{Sales price variance} = (\$38.50 - \$40.00) \times 11{,}000 \text{ bags}$$
$$= \$16{,}500 \text{ U}$$

The **sales volume variance** indicates the impact of the change in sales volume on revenues, assuming there was no change in selling price. The sales volume variance is computed as the difference between the actual and the budgeted sales volumes times the budgeted selling price:

> **Sales volume variance = (Actual sales volume − Budgeted sales volume) × Budgeted selling price**

For Tumi, the sales volume variance for July follows:

$$\text{Sales volume variance} = (11{,}000 \text{ bags} - 10{,}000 \text{ bags}) \times \$40$$
$$= \$40{,}000 \text{ F}$$

The net of the sales price and the sales volume variances is equal to the revenue variance:

Sales price variance	$16,500 U
Sales volume variance	40,000 F
Revenue variance	$23,500 F

Interpretation of these variances is subjective. In this case, we could say that if the increase in sales volume had not been accompanied by a decline in selling price, revenues would have increased $40,000 instead of $23,500. The $1.50 per unit decline in selling price cost the company $16,500 in revenues. Alternatively, we might note that a $1.50 reduction in the unit selling price was more than offset by an increase in sales volume. An economic analysis could explain the relationship as volume being sensitive to price (price elasticity).

In any case, variances are merely signals that actual results are not proceeding according to plan. They help managers identify potential problems and opportunities. An investigation into their cause(s) could even indicate that a manager who received a favorable variance was doing a poor job, whereas a manager who received an unfavorable variance was doing an outstanding job. Consider Tumi's favorable revenue variance. This occurred because actual sales exceeded budgeted sales by 1,000 bags (10 percent), which on the surface indicates good performance. But what if the total market for the company's products exceeded the company's forecast by 15 percent? In this hypothetical case, Tumi's sales volume falls below its expected percentage share of the market; the favorable variance could occur (despite a poor marketing effort) because of strong customer demand that competitors could not fill.

Inclusion of Controllable Costs

Controllable costs should also be considered when evaluating the overall performance of revenue centers. A failure to consider costs could encourage uneconomic selling practices, such as excessive advertising and entertaining, and spending too much time on small accounts. The controllable costs of revenue centers include variable and fixed selling costs. These costs are sometimes further classified into order-getting and order-filling costs. **Order-getting costs** are incurred to obtain customers' orders (for example, advertising, salespersons' salaries and commissions, travel, telephone, and entertainment). **Order-filling costs** are distribution costs incurred to place finished goods in the hands of purchasers (for example, storing, packaging, and transportation).

The performance of a revenue center in controlling costs can be evaluated with the aid of a flexible budget drawn up for the actual level of activity. Assume that Tumi's July budget for the sales department calls for fixed costs of $10,000 and variable costs of $5 per bag sold. If the actual fixed and variable selling expenses for July are $9,500 and $65,000, respectively, the total cost variances assigned to the sales department, detailed in **Exhibit 22.2**, are $9,500 unfavorable. In evaluating the sales department's performance as both a cost center and a revenue center, management should consider these cost variances as well as the revenue variances. Although the revenue variances are based on the original budget, the cost variances are based on the flexible budget.

EXHIBIT 22.2	Sales Department Performance Report for Controllable Costs		

TUMI
Sales Department Performance Report for Controllable Costs
For Month of July

		Based on Flexible Budget	
	Actual	Flexible Budget*	Flexible Budget Variance
Bags....................................	11,000	11,000	
Selling expenses			
Variable.............................	$65,000	$55,000	$10,000 U
Fixed................................	9,500	10,000	500 F
Total	$74,500	$65,000	$ 9,500 U

* Flexible budget formulas:
  Variable selling expenses ($5 per bag)
  Fixed selling expenses($10,000 per month)

Revenue Centers as Profit Centers

Even though we have computed revenue and cost variances for Tumi's sales department, we are still left with an incomplete picture of this revenue center's performance. Is the sales department's performance best represented by the $23,500 favorable revenue variance, by the $9,500 unfavorable cost variance, or by the net favorable variance of $14,000 ($23,500 F − $9,500 U)? Actually, it is inappropriate to attempt to obtain an overall measure of the sales department's performance by combining these separate revenue and selling cost variances. The combination of revenue and cost variances is appropriate only for a profit center; so far, we have left out one important cost that must be assigned to the sales department before it can be treated as a profit center. That cost is the *standard variable cost of goods sold*.

As a profit center, the sales department acquires units from the production department and sells them outside the firm. Its total responsibilities include revenues, the standard variable cost of goods sold, and actual selling expenses. The sales department is assigned the *standard,* rather than the *actual, variable cost of goods sold.* Because the sales department does not control production activities, it should not be assigned actual production costs. Doing so results in passing the production department's variances on to the sales department. Fixed manufacturing costs are not assigned to the sales department because short-run variations in sales volume do not normally affect the total amount of these costs.

To evaluate the sales department as a profit center, the net sales volume variance must be computed. The **net sales volume variance** indicates the impact of a change in sales volume on the contribution margin given the budgeted selling price *and* the standard variable costs. It is computed as the difference between the actual and the budgeted sales volumes times the budgeted unit contribution margin.

Net sales volume variance = (Actual volume − Budgeted volume) × Budgeted contribution margin

Using the $40 budgeted selling price, the standard variable manufacturing costs, and the standard variable selling expenses, the budgeted contribution margin is $11.00:

Sales.		$40.00
Direct materials	$10.00	
Direct labor.	6.00	
Variable manufacturing overhead.	8.00	
Selling.	5.00	(29.00)
Contribution margin		$11.00

The net sales volume variance is computed as follows:

$$\text{Net sales volume variance} = (11{,}000 - 10{,}000) \times \$11.00$$
$$= \$11{,}000 \text{ F}$$

As a profit center, the sales department has responsibility for the sales price variance, the net sales volume variance, and any cost variances associated with its operations. As shown in **Exhibit 22.3**, the sales department variances, as a profit center, net to $15,000 unfavorable:

EXHIBIT 22.3	Sales Department Profit Center Performance Report

TUMI
Sales Department Profit Center Performance Report
For Month of July

Sales price variance.	$16,500 U
Net sales volume variance	11,000 F
Selling expense variance	9,500 U
Sales Department variances, net.	$15,000 U

In an attempt to improve their overall performance, managers often commit themselves to unfavorable variances in some areas, believing that these variances will be more than offset by favorable variances in other areas. When the sales department is evaluated as a revenue center, the favorable sales volume variance more than offsets the price reductions and the higher selling expenses. The more complete evaluation of the sales department as a profit center (with a $15,000 unfavorable variance) gives a very different impression than the evaluation of the sales department as a pure revenue center (with a $23,500 favorable variance) or as a revenue center responsible only for its own direct costs with net favorable variances of $14,000, computed as $23,500 F minus $9,500 U. The performance reports of all the organization's responsibility centers are summarized to reconcile budgeted and actual income in Appendix 22B.

CHAPTER-END REVIEW

Sales Variances Presented is information pertaining to an item sold by Winding Creek General Store:

	Actual	Budget
Unit sales	150	125
Unit selling price.	$26	$25
Unit standard variable costs.	(20)	(20)
Unit contribution margin	$ 6	$ 5
Revenues	$3,900	$3,125
Standard variable costs	(3,000)	(2,500)
Contribution margin at standard costs	$ 900	$ 625

REQUIRED

Compute the revenue, sales price, and the sales volume variances.

The solution to this review problem can be found on page 1013.

APPENDIX 22A: Fixed Overhead Variances

LO7 Formulate and interpret fixed overhead cost variances.

By definition, the quantity of goods and services purchased by fixed expenditures is not expected to change in proportion to short-run changes in the level of production. For example, in the short run, the production level does not affect the amount of depreciation on buildings, the number of fixed salaried employees, or the amount of real property subject to property taxes.

Even though the components of fixed overhead are not expected to be affected by the production activity level in the short run, the actual amount spent for fixed overhead items can differ from the amount budgeted. For example, higher than budgeted supervisors' salaries could be paid, insurance premiums may increase unexpectedly, and price increases could cause the amounts paid for equipment to be higher than expected. Fixed overhead costs in excess of the amount budgeted are reflected in the fixed overhead budget variance. Tumi's fixed overhead budget variance was previously determined as:

$$\text{Fixed overhead budget variance} = \text{Actual fixed overhead} - \text{Budgeted fixed overhead}$$
$$= \$53,000 - \$52,000$$
$$= \$1,000 \text{ U}$$

The fixed overhead budget variance is always the same as the total fixed overhead flexible budget variance. Because budgeted fixed overhead is the same for all outputs within the relevant range, the budget variance explains the total flexible budget variance between actual and allowed fixed overhead.

Recall that predetermined overhead rates are computed by dividing the predicted overhead costs for the period by the predicted activity of the period. The motivation for using a standard fixed overhead rate is the same as the motivation for using a predetermined overhead rate; namely, quicker product costing and assigning identical fixed costs to identical products, regardless of when they are produced during the year.

When a standard fixed overhead rate is used, total fixed overhead costs assigned to production behave as variable costs. As production increases, the total fixed overhead assigned to production increases. Because total budgeted fixed overhead does not vary, differences arise between budgeted and assigned fixed overhead, and managers often inquire about the cause of the differences.

The standard fixed overhead rate is computed as the budgeted fixed costs divided by some budgeted standard level of activity. Assume Tumi applies fixed manufacturing overhead on the basis of machine hours and that 0.40 machine hours are allowed to produce one computer bag. Further assume that the budgeted production is 10,000 computer bag per month, a level that allows 4,000 (10,000 × 0.40) machine hours. The standard fixed overhead rate per machine hour is $13.

$$\text{Standard fixed overhead rate} = \text{Budgeted total fixed overhead} \div \text{Budgeted activity level}$$
$$= \$52,000 \div 4,000 \text{ hours}$$
$$= \$13 \text{ per machine hour}$$

The total fixed overhead assigned to production is computed as the standard rate of $13 multiplied by the standard hours allowed for the units produced. Note that assigned fixed overhead cost equals budgeted fixed overhead only if the allowed activity equals the budgeted activity of 4,000 hours. If less than 4,000 hours are allowed the fixed overhead assigned to production is less than the $52,000 budgeted; if more than 4,000 hours are allowed the fixed overhead assigned to production is more than the amount budgeted.

Even though budgeted fixed overhead is not affected by production below or above 4,000 hours, the fixed overhead assigned to production increases at the rate of $13 per allowed machine hour. The difference between budgeted fixed overhead and fixed overhead assigned to production is called the **fixed overhead volume variance**. This variance is sometimes referred to as the **capacity variance**, a term that emphasizes the maximum output of an operation. The fixed overhead volume variance indicates neither good nor poor performance. Instead, it indicates the difference between the activity allowed for the actual output and the budget level used as the denominator in computing the standard fixed overhead rate.

To explain the difference between actual fixed overhead and fixed overhead assigned to production, two fixed overhead variances are computed: the fixed overhead budget variance and the fixed overhead volume variance. As previously explained, the fixed overhead budget variance represents the difference between actual fixed overhead and budgeted fixed overhead. The fixed overhead budget variance is caused by a combination of price and quantity factors related to the use of fixed overhead goods and services (e.g., depreciation, insurance, supervisors' salaries). The $1,000 unfavorable budget variance for Tumi was caused either by using higher quantities of fixed overhead goods and services, or by paying higher prices than expected for those items, or both.

The fixed overhead volume variance represents the difference between budgeted and assigned fixed overhead and is caused by a difference between the activity level allowed for the actual output and the budgeted activity used in computing the fixed overhead rate. Suppose for Tumi, actual July output of 11,000 bags resulted in 4,400 allowed machine hours and applied fixed overhead of $57,200 (11,000 bags × 0.40 hours × $13). The $5,200 favorable fixed overhead volume variance (budgeted costs of $52,000 minus applied costs of $57,200) indicates that the activity level allowed for the actual output was more than the budgeted activity level. As previously stated, this variance ordinarily cannot be used to control costs. If the budgeted activity is based on production capacity, an unfavorable variance alerts management that facilities are underutilized, and a favorable variance alerts management that facilities are utilized above their expectations. A summary standard cost variance analysis for fixed costs is shown below.

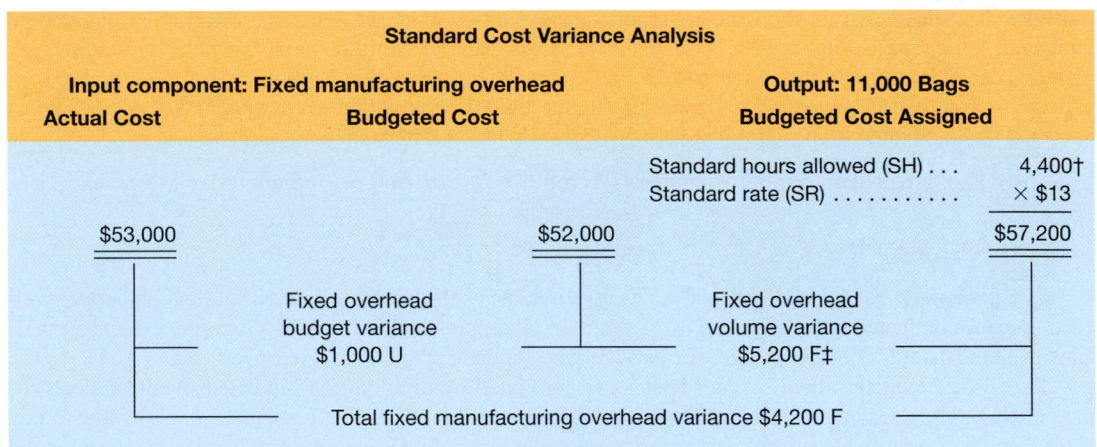

Standard Cost Variance Analysis

Input component: Fixed manufacturing overhead		Output: 11,000 Bags
Actual Cost	**Budgeted Cost**	**Budgeted Cost Assigned**

Standard hours allowed (SH) . . .   4,400†
Standard rate (SR) . . . .   × $13

$53,000 $52,000 $57,200

Fixed overhead budget variance $1,000 U

Fixed overhead volume variance $5,200 F‡

Total fixed manufacturing overhead variance $4,200 F

†11,000 bags × 0.40
‡ Also computed as: (4,400 allowed hours − 4,000 budget hours) × $13 standard rate per hour

APPENDIX 22A REVIEW

Assume that **Marathon Oil** uses a standard cost system for each of its refineries. For the Texas City refinery, the monthly fixed overhead budget is $6,000,000 for a planned output of 2,000,000 barrels. For September, the actual fixed cost was $6,250,000 for 2,100,000 barrels.

REQUIRED
a. Determine the fixed overhead budget variance.
b. If fixed overhead is applied on a per-barrel basis, determine the volume variance.

The solution to this review problem can be found on page 1013.

APPENDIX 22B: Reconciling Budgeted and Actual Income

LO8 Reconcile budgeted and actual income.

Using a contribution format, it is possible to reconcile the difference between budgeted and actual net income for an entire organization. This is done by assigning all costs and revenues to responsibility centers and summarizing the financial performance of each responsibility center. Tumi's budgeted and actual income statements, in a contribution format, for July are presented in **Exhibit 22B.1**.

EXHIBIT 22B.1	Budgeted and Actual Income Statements: Contribution Format

TUMI
Budgeted Income Statement
For Month of July

Sales (10,000 bags × $40).			$400,000
Less variable costs			
Variable cost of goods sold			
Direct materials (10,000 bags × $10)	$100,000		
Direct labor (10,000 bags × $6)	60,000		
Manufacturing overhead (10,000 bags × $8)	80,000	$240,000	
Selling (10,000 bags × $5)		50,000	(290,000)
Contribution margin			110,000
Less fixed costs			
Manufacturing overhead.		52,000	
Selling.		10,000	
Administrative.		4,000	(66,000)
Budgeted net income.			$ 44,000

Actual Income Statement
For the Month of July

Sales (11,000 bags × $38.50)			$423,500
Less variable costs			
Variable cost of goods sold			
Direct materials.	$108,000		
Direct labor.	70,000		
Manufacturing overhead.	81,000	$259,000	
Selling.		65,000	(324,000)
Contribution margin			99,500
Less fixed costs			
Manufacturing overhead.		53,000	
Selling.		9,500	
Administrative.		3,800	(66,300)
Net income.			$ 33,200

We've assumed Tumi contains three responsibility centers: a production department, a sales department, and an administration department. Earlier in the chapter, we discussed both the production and the sales department variances. The sales department's variances in **Exhibit 22.3** net to $15,000 U and the production department's variances in **Exhibit 22.1** net to $4,000 F. Next, we assume that the administration department had a budgeted amount of $4,000 while the actual amount spent was $3,800. Because the administration department is a discretionary cost center, this variance of $200 ($3,800 actual − $4,000 budget) is best identified as being under budget. For consistency in the performance reports, however, it is labeled favorable. By assigning all variances to these three responsibility centers, the reconciliation of budgeted and actual income is as shown in **Exhibit 22B.2**.

EXHIBIT 22B.2	Reconciliation of Budgeted and Actual Income

TUMI
Reconciliation of Budgeted and Actual Income
For Month of July

Budgeted net income.	$44,000
Sales department variances (Exhibit 22.3).	15,000 U
Production department variances (Exhibit 22.1)	4,000 F
Administration department variances ($3,800 actual − $4,000 budgeted)	200 F
Actual net income.	$33,200

APPENDIX 22B REVIEW

Midstate Supply Company has three responsibility centers: sales, production, and administration. The following information pertains to the November activities of Midstate Supply:

Budgeted contribution income.	$18,000
Actual contribution income	27,000
Sales price variance	24,000 F
Sales volume variance	40,000 F
Net sales price variance.	6,000 F
Sales department variable expense variance.	18,000 U
Sales department fixed expense variance	1,500 U
Administration department variances	500 F
Production department variances	2,000 U

REQUIRED
Prepare a reconciliation of budgeted and actual contribution income.

The solution to this review problem can be found on page 1013.

GUIDANCE ANSWERS . . . YOU MAKE THE CALL

You are the Vice President of Manufacturing It appears that direct labor hours may no longer be a reliable basis for budgeting variable overhead in your company. If actual variable overhead costs do not appear to correlate closely with direct labor hours, this could be an indication that the components of variable overhead have changed since direct labor hours was selected as the cost driver. Your cost accountants should consider other unit-level cost drivers for budgeting variable overhead costs. However, an activity-based costing method using multiple overhead cost pools with separate cost drivers might provide a more reliable basis for budgeting and controlling variable overhead costs.

KEY RATIOS

Materials price variance = Actual quantity (Actual price − Standard price)

Materials quantity variance = Standard price (Actual quantity − Standard Quantity)

Labor rate variance = Actual hours (Actual rate − Standard rate)

Labor efficiency variance = Standard rate (Actual hours − Standard hours)

Standard variable overhead cost of actual inputs = (Actual quantity × Standard variable overhead rate)

Flexible variable overhead budget cost = (Standard quantity × Standard variable overhead rate)

Variable overhead efficiency variance = Standard rate (Actual quantity − Standard quantity)

Fixed overhead budget variance = Actual fixed overhead − Budgeted fixed overhead

Revenue variance = (Actual volume × Actual price) − (Budgeted volume × Budgeted price)

Sales price variance = (Actual selling price − Budgeted selling price) × Actual sales volume

Sales volume variance = (Actual sales volume − Budgeted sales volume) × Budgeted selling price

Net sales volume variance = (Actual volume − Budgeted volume) × Budgeted contribution margin

Standard fixed overhead rate = Budgeted total fixed overhead ÷ Budgeted activity level

KEY TERMS

capacity variance, 994

cost center, 975

fixed overhead budget
    variance, 988

fixed overhead volume
    variance, 994

flexible budgets, 977

flexible budget variance, 978

investment center, 976

labor efficiency variance, 985

labor rate (spending)
    variance, 985

materials price variance, 982

materials quantity variance, 982

net sales volume variance, 992

order-filling costs, 991

order-getting costs, 991

organization structure, 974

profit center, 976

responsibility accounting,, 973

revenue center, 975

revenue variance, 990

sales price variance, 990

sales volume variance, 990

standard cost, 979

standard cost variance
    analysis, 980

static budget, 977

variable overhead efficiency
    variance, 987

variable overhead spending
    variance, 987

variance, 977

Assignments with the MBC **logo in the margin are available in** BusinessCourse.
See the Preface of the book for details.

MULTIPLE CHOICE

1. Which of the following statements least describes characteristics of an investment center?
    a. It is responsible for the relationship between its profits and the total assets invested in the center.
    b. It is most frequently a segment of an organization such as a product line, marketing territory, or store.
    c. It is expected to earn a target profit per dollar invested.
    d. It is the broadest and most inclusive type of responsibility center.

2. Presented is an abbreviated performance report for the month of July:

	Actual	Budget	Variance
Units.	5,500	5,000	
Costs:			
Direct materials.	$ 45,500	$ 40,000	$ 5,500 U
Direct labor.	181,500	150,000	31,500 U
Variable factory overhead.	208,000	160,000	48,000 U
Fixed factory overhead.	125,000	120,000	5,000 U
Total costs	$560,000	$470,000	$90,000 U

    The total flexible budget variance is:
    a. $55,000 Unfavorable
    b. $90,000 Unfavorable
    c. $50,000 Favorable
    d. $55,000 Favorable

3. The following additional information is available for the materials costs in question 2:
    * Standard cost per unit produced: 2 liters @ $4.00 per liter
    * Actual use of raw materials 13,000 liters @ $3.50 per liter

    The materials price and materials quantify variances are:
    a. $5,500 F materials price variance and $8,000 U materials quantity variance
    b. $6,500 F materials price variance and $8,000 U materials quantity variance
    c. $6,500 F materials price variance and $12,000 U materials quantity variance
    d. None of the above

4. The following additional information is available for the labor costs in question 2.
   - Standard cost per unit of product 1.5 direct labor hours @ $20 per labor hour
   - Actual use of direct labor is 8,250 hours @ $22 per hour

   The labor rate and the labor efficiency variances are:

   a. $16,500 U labor rate variance and $0 labor efficiency variance
   b. $16,500 F labor rate variance and $0 labor efficiency variance
   c. $16,500 U labor rate variance and $15,000 U labor efficiency variance
   d. None of the above

5. The following additional information is available for the variable overhead costs in question 2:
   - Standard cost per unit of product 2 liters of raw materials @ $16 per liter
   - Actual use of raw materials was 13,000 liters and actual variable overhead was $208,000

   The variable overhead spending and variable overhead efficiency variances are:

   a. $32,000 U spending and $0 efficiency
   b. $32,000 U spending and $16,000 U efficiency
   c. $16,000 U spending and $32,000 U efficiency
   d. $0 spending and $32,000 U efficiency

6. Budgeted June sales of the Tack Shop include 100 western saddles at $650 each. Actual sales were 90 saddles at $725 each. The June sales price and sales volume variances for western saddles are:
   a. $250 F sales price variance and $10 U sales volume variance
   b. $6,750 F sales price variance and $6,500 U sales volume variance
   c. $7,500 F sales price variance and $6,500 U sales volume variance
   d. None of the above

QUESTIONS

Q22-1. What is responsibility accounting? Why should noncontrollable costs be excluded from performance reports prepared in accordance with responsibility accounting?

Q22-2. How can responsibility accounting lead to unethical practices?

Q22-3. Responsibility accounting reports must be expanded to include what nonfinancial areas? Give some examples of nonfinancial measures.

Q22-4. What is a cost center? Give some examples.

Q22-5. How is a cost center different from either an investment or a profit center?

Q22-6. What problems can result from the use of tight standards?

Q22-7. What is a standard cost variance, and what is the objective of variance analysis?

Q22-8. Standard cost variances can usually be broken down into two basic types of variances. Identify and describe these two types of variances.

Q22-9. Identify possible causes for (1) a favorable materials price variance; (2) an unfavorable materials price variance; (3) a favorable materials quantity variance; and (4) an unfavorable materials quantity variance.

Q22-10. How is standard labor time determined? Explain the two ways.

Q22-11. In the standard cost system, what is the appropriate treatment of a change in wage rates (per new labor union contract) that dominate the cost of labor?

Q22-12. Explain the difference between the revenue variance and the sales price variance.

Q22-13. Explain the net sales volume variance and list its components.

Q22-14. Explain the difference between how the *actual costs* and the *standard cost of actual inputs* are computed in variable overhead analysis.

Q22-15. Explain what the net sales volume variance measures.

MINI EXERCISES

M22-16. Flexible Budgets and Performance Evaluation   LO2
Presented is the January performance report for the Production Department of Nowwhat Company.

NOWWHAT COMPANY Production Department Performance Report For Month of January			
	Actual	**Budget**	**Variance**
Volume	40,000	38,000	
Manufacturing costs			
Direct materials.	$160,000	$152,000	$ 8,000 U
Direct labor	295,000	228,000	67,000 U
Variable overhead	162,000	114,000	48,000 U
Fixed overhead	36,000	38,000	2,000 F
Total	$653,000	$532,000	$121,000 U

REQUIRED
a. Evaluate the performance report.
b. Prepare a more appropriate performance report.

M22-17. Materials Variances   LO3
Dark Wind manufactures decorative weather vanes that have a standard materials cost of two
pounds of raw materials at $2.50 per pound. During September 9,500 pounds of raw materials
costing $3.25 per pound were used in making 4,700 weather vanes.

REQUIRED
Determine the materials price and quantity variance.

M22-18. Materials Variances   LO3
Assume that **Pearle Vision** uses standard costs to control the materials in its made-to-order sunglasses. The standards call for 2 ounces of material for each pair of lenses. The standard cost per
ounce of material is $16. During July, the Santa Clara location produced 5,200 pairs of sunglasses
and used 9,700 ounces of materials. The cost of the materials during July was $16.75 per ounce,
and there were no beginning or ending inventories.

Pearle Vision
NYSE :: LUX

REQUIRED
a. Determine the flexible budget materials cost for the completion of the 5,200 pairs of glasses.
b. Determine the actual materials cost incurred for the completion of the 5,200 pairs of glasses
    and compute the total materials variance.
c. How much of the total variance was related to the price paid to purchase the materials?
d. How much of the difference between the answers to requirements (a) and (b) was related to
    the quantity of materials used?

M22-19. Direct Labor Variances   LO4
Assume that **Nortel** manufactures specialty electronic circuitry through a unique photoelectronic
process. One of the primary products, Model ZX40, has a standard labor time of 0.5 hour and
a standard labor rate of $15.00 per hour. During February, the following activities pertaining to
direct labor for ZX40 were recorded:

Nortel
OTCMKTS :: NRTLQ

Direct labor hours used	5,180
Direct labor cost.	$67,000
Units of ZX40 manufactured	9,600

REQUIRED
a. Determine the labor rate variance.
b. Determine the labor efficiency variance.
c. Determine the total flexible budget labor cost variance.

LO4   **M22-20.   Significance of Direct Labor Variances**

The Tomorrow Company's April budget called for labor costs of $184,000. Because the actual labor costs were exactly $184,000, management concluded there were no labor variances.

REQUIRED

Comment on management's conclusion.

LO5   **M22-21.   Variable Overhead Variances**

Sony
NYSE: SNE

Assume that the best cost driver that **Sony** has for variable factory overhead in the assembly department is machine hours. During April, the company budgeted 720,000 machine hours and $6,480,000 for its Texas plant's assembly department. The actual variable overhead incurred was $6,870,000, which was related to 750,000 machine hours.

REQUIRED

a. Determine the variable overhead spending variance.
b. Determine the variable overhead efficiency variance.

LO6   **M22-22.   Sales Variances**

Presented is information pertaining to an item sold by Wheeping Creek General Store:

	Actual	Budget
Unit sales	300	250
Unit selling price.	$52	$50
Unit standard variable costs.	(40)	(40)
Unit contribution margin.	$12	$10
Revenues	$7,800	$6,250
Standard variable costs	(6,000)	(5,000)
Contribution margin at standard costs.	$1,800	$1,250

REQUIRED

Compute the revenue, sales price, and the sales volume variances.

LO7   **M22-23.   Fixed Overhead Variances**

ExxonMobil
NYSE: XOM

Assume that **ExxonMobil** uses a standard cost system for each of its refineries. For the Houston refinery, the monthly fixed overhead budget is $8,000,000 for a planned output of 5,000,000 barrels. For September, the actual fixed cost was $8,750,000 for 5,100,000 barrels.

REQUIRED

a. Determine the fixed overhead budget variance.
b. If fixed overhead is applied on a per-barrel basis, determine the volume variance.

LO8   **M22-24.   Reconciling Budgeted and Actual Income**

Black Supply Company has three responsibility centers: sales, production, and administration. The following information pertains to the November activities of Black Supply:

Budgeted contribution income.	$36,000
Actual contribution income	54,000
Sales price variance.	48,000 F
Sales volume variance	80,000 F
Net sales price variance.	12,000 F
Sales department variable expense variance.	36,000 U
Sales department fixed expense variance	3,000 U
Administration department variances	1,000 F
Production department variances	4,000 U

REQUIRED

Prepare a reconciliation of budgeted and actual contribution income.

EXERCISES

E22-25. Elements of a Flexible Budget

Presented are partial flexible cost budgets for various levels of output.

	Rate per unit		Units	
		2,500	3,750	5,000
Direct materials	a.	$25,000	b.	c.
Direct labor.	d.	e.	7,500	f.
Variable overhead.	$3	g.	h.	i.
Fixed overhead.		j.	k.	l.
Total		m.	n.	$100,000

REQUIRED

Solve for items "a" though "n."

E22-26. Elements of Labor and Variable Overhead Variances

Chelsea Fabricating applies variable overhead to products on the basis of standard direct labor hours. Presented is selected information for last month when 10,000 units were produced.

	Direct labor	Variable overhead
Actual	a.	f.
Standard hours/unit	b.	b.
Actual hours (total)	6,300	6,300
Standard rate/hour	$ 36.00	$ 24.00
Actual rate	$ 37.80	
Flexible budget.	$90,000	$60,000
Labor rate or variable overhead spending variance. .	c.	g.
Efficiency variances	d.	h.
Total flexible budget variance.	e.	$ 3,000 F

REQUIRED

Solve for items "a" through" h."

E22-27. Causes of Standard Cost Variances (Comprehensive)

Following are ten unrelated situations that would ordinarily be expected to affect one or more standard cost variances:

1. A salaried production supervisor is given a raise, but no adjustment is made in the labor cost standards.

2. The materials purchasing manager gets a special reduced price on raw materials by purchasing a train carload. A warehouse had to be rented to accommodate the unusually large amount of raw materials. The rental fee was charged to Rent Expense, a fixed overhead item.

3. An unusually hot August caused the company to use 30,000 kilowatts more electricity than provided for in the variable overhead standards.

4. The local electric utility company raised the charge per kilowatt-hour. No adjustment was made in the variable overhead standards.

5. The plant manager traded in his leased company car for a new one in July, increasing the monthly lease payment by $85.

6. A machine malfunction on the assembly line (caused by using cheap and inferior raw materials) resulted in decreased output by the machine operator and higher than normal machine repair costs. Repairs are treated as variable overhead costs.

7. The production maintenance supervisor decreased routine maintenance checks, resulting in lower maintenance costs and lower machine production output per hour. Maintenance costs are treated as fixed costs.

8. An announcement that vacation benefits had been increased resulted in improved employee morale. Consequently, raw materials pilferage and waste declined, and production efficiency increased.

9. The plant manager reclassified her secretary to administrative assistant and gave him an increase in salary.

10. A union contract agreement calling for an immediate 4 percent increase in production worker wages was signed. No changes were made in the standards.

REQUIRED

For each of these situations, indicate by letter which of the following standard cost variances would be affected. More than one variance will be affected in some cases.

- *a.* Materials price variance.
- *b.* Materials quantity variance.
- *c.* Labor rate variance.
- *d.* Labor efficiency variance.
- *e.* Variable overhead spending variance.
- *f.* Variable overhead efficiency variance.
- *g.* Fixed overhead budget variance.

LO6

Casio Computer
Company, LTD.
PINX:CSIOF

E22-28.   Sales Variances

Assume that **Casio Computer Company, LTD.** sells handheld communication devices for $150 during August as a back-to-school special. The normal selling price is $225. The standard variable cost for each device is $95. Sales for August had been budgeted for 400,000 units nationwide; however, due to the slowdown in the economy, sales were only 375,000.

REQUIRED

Compute the revenue, sales price, sales volume variance, and net sales volume variance.

LO7

E22-29.   Fixed Overhead Variances

Petra Company uses standard costs for cost control and internal reporting. Fixed costs are budgeted at $36,000 per month at a normal operating level of 10,000 units of production output. During October, actual fixed costs were $40,000, and actual production output was 12,000 units.

REQUIRED

- *a.* Determine the fixed overhead budget variance.
- *b.* Assume that the company applied fixed overhead to production on a per-unit basis. Determine the fixed overhead volume variance.
- *c.* Was the fixed overhead budget variance from requirement (a) affected because the company operated above the normal activity level of 10,000 units? Explain.
- *d.* Explain the possible causes for the volume variance computed in requirement (b). How is reporting of the volume variance useful to management?

PROBLEMS

LO2

P22-30.   Multiple Product Performance Report

Case Products manufactures two models of DVD storage cases: regular and deluxe. Presented is standard cost information for each model:

Cost Components	Regular			Deluxe		
Direct materials						
Lumber	2 board feet × $8	=	$16.00	3 board feet × $8	=	$24.00
Assembly kit		=	4.00		=	4.00
Direct labor.	1 hour × $8	=	8.00	1.25 hours × $8	=	10.00
Variable overhead. . . .	1 labor hr. × $4	=	4.00	1.25 labor hrs. × $4	=	5.00
Total			$32.00			$43.00

Budgeted fixed manufacturing overhead is $24,000 per month. During July, the company produced 5,000 regular and 3,000 deluxe storage cases while incurring the following manufacturing costs:

Direct materials	$209,000
Direct labor.	75,000
Variable overhead.	32,000
Fixed overhead.	30,500
Total	$346,500

REQUIRED

Prepare a flexible budget performance report for the July manufacturing activities.

P22-31. **Computation of Variable Cost Variances**

LO3, 4

The following information pertains to the standard costs and actual activity for Repine Company for September:

Standard cost per unit	
Direct materials..............................	4 units of material A × $6.00 per unit
	1 unit of material B × $8.00 per unit
Direct labor.................................	3 hours × $18.00 per hour
Activity for September	
Materials purchased	
Material A	6,750 units × $6.20 per unit
Material B	1,650 units × $8.50 per unit
Materials used	
Material A	6,225 units
Material B	1,508 units
Direct labor used	4,425 hours × $18.80 per hour
Production output............................	1,500 units

There were no beginning direct materials inventories.

REQUIRED

a. Determine the materials price and quantity variances.

b. Determine the labor rate and efficiency variances.

P22-32. **Variance Computations and Explanations**

LO3, 4

Adventure Company manufactures camping tents from a lightweight synthetic fabric. Each tent has a standard materials cost of $42, consisting of 4 yards of fabric at $10.50 per yard. The standards call for 2 hours of assembly at $20 per hour. The following data were recorded for October, the first month of operations:

Fabric purchased	9,000 yards × $10.00 per yard
Fabric used in production of 1,700 tents....................	7,000 yards
Direct labor used	3,600 hours × $21.50 per hour

REQUIRED

a. Compute all standard cost variances for materials and labor.

b. Give one possible reason for each of the preceding variances.

c. Determine the standard variable cost of the 1,700 tents produced, separated into direct materials and labor.

P22-33. **Determining Unit Costs, Variance Analysis, and Interpretation**

LO2, 3, 4, 5

Happy Dog Company, a manufacturer of dog food, produces its product in 1,000-bag batches. The standard cost of each batch consists of 8,000 pounds of direct materials at $0.60 per pound, 48 direct labor hours at $13.25 per hour, and variable overhead cost (based on machine hours) at the rate of $15 per hour with 16 machine hours per batch. The following variable costs were incurred for the last 1,000-bag batch produced:

Direct materials	8,300 pounds costing $4,731 were purchased and used
Direct labor.....................	45 hours costing $675
Variable overhead................	$338
Machine hours used..............	18 hours

REQUIRED

a. Determine the actual and standard variable costs per bag of dog food produced, separated into direct materials, direct labor, and variable overhead.

b. For the last 1,000-bag batch, determine the standard cost variances for direct materials, direct labor, and variable overhead.

c. Explain the possible causes for each of the variances determined in requirement (*b*).

LO3, 4, 5   **P22-34.**   **Computation of Variances and Other Missing Data**

The following data for Bernie Company pertain to the production of 500 units of Product X during December. Selected data items are omitted.

> Direct materials (all materials purchased were used during period)
>   Standard cost per unit: (a) pounds at $3.84 per pound
>   Total actual cost: (b) pounds costing $8,510
>   Standard cost allowed for units produced: $8,640
>   Materials price variance: (c)
>   Materials quantity variance: $216 U
> Direct labor
>   Standard cost: 2 hours at $10.50
>   Actual cost per hour: $10.90
>   Total actual cost: (d)
>   Labor rate variance: (e)
>   Labor efficiency variance: $210 U
> Variable overhead
>   Standard costs: (f) hours at $6.00 per direct labor hour
>   Actual cost: $5,550
>   Variable overhead spending variance: (g)
>   Variable overhead efficiency variance: (h)

REQUIRED

Complete the missing amounts lettered (a) through (h).

LO3, 4, 5   **P22-35.**   **Flexible Budgets and Performance Evaluation**

Kathy Vanderbosch, supervisor of housecleaning for Hotel Valhalla, was surprised by her summary performance report for March given below.

HOTEL VALHALLA
Housekeeping Performance Report
For the Month of March

Actual	Budget	Variance	%Variance
$198,511	$186,400	$12,111 U	6.497% U

Kathy was disappointed. She thought she had done a good job controlling housekeeping labor and towel usage, but her performance report revealed an unfavorable variance of $12,111. She had been hoping for a bonus for her good work, but now expected a series of questions from her manager.

The cost budget for housekeeping is based on standard costs. At the beginning of a month, Kathy receives a report from Hotel Valhalla's Sales Department outlining the planned room activity for the month. Kathy then schedules labor and purchases using this information. The budget for the housekeeping was based on 8,000 room nights. Each room night is budgeted based on the following standards for various materials, labor, and overhead:

Shower supplies.........................	3 bottles @ $0.35 each
Towels*...................................	1 @ $2.25
Laundry	10 lbs. @ $0.35 a lb.
Labor	½ hour @ $14.00 an hour
VOH	$7.00 per labor hour
FOH	$6 a room night (based on 8,000 room nights)

*Replacements for towels evaluated by housekeeping as inappropriate for cleaning and reuse.

With 8,900 room nights sold, actual costs and usage for housekeeping during April were:

> $9,311 for 26,500 bottles of shower supplies.
> $17,502 for 7,900 towels.
> $31,882 for 88,500 lbs. of laundry.
> $60,200 for 4,350 labor hours.
> $30,150 in total VOH.
> $49,466 in FOH.

REQUIRED

a. Develop a complete budget column for the above performance report presented to Kathy. Break it down by expense category. The following format, with additional lines for expense categories, is suggested:

Account	Actual	Budget	Variance
Shower Supplies	$ 9,311	?	?
⋮	⋮	⋮	⋮
Total	$198,511	$186,400	$12,111 U

b. Evaluate the usefulness of the cost center performance report presented to Kathy.
c. Prepare a more logical performance report where standard allowed is based on actual output. Also, split each variance into its price/rate/spending and quantity/efficiency components (except fixed of course). The following format, with additional lines for expense categories, is suggested:

Account	Actual	Flexible Budget	Total Variance	Price/Rate/ Spending Variance	Quantity/ Efficiency Variance
Shower Supplies	$ 9,311	?	?	?	?
⋮	⋮	⋮	⋮		
Total	$198,511	?	?		

d. Explain to Kathy's boss what your report suggests about Kathy's department performance.
e. Identify additional nonfinancial performance measures management might consider when evaluating the performance of the housekeeping department and Kathy as a manager.

P22-36.   Flexible Budget Performance Evaluation with Process Costing   LO3, 4, 5

The Evanston Company produces a single product on a continuous basis. On July 1, 600 units, 75 percent complete as to materials and 50 percent complete as to conversion, were in process. During January, 1,500 units were started and 1,800 units were completed. The July 31 ending work-in-process inventory contained 300 units, 50 percent complete as to materials and 25 percent complete as to conversion.

Evanston uses standard costs for planning and control. The following standard costs are based on a monthly volume of 1,200 equivalent units with fixed budgeted at $9,750 per month.

Direct materials [(2 square meters per unit × $16.00 per meter) × 1,200]	$38,400
Direct labor [(1.5 hours per unit × $40 per hour) × 1,200]	72,000
Variable overhead [(1.5 labor hours per unit × $10.00 per hour) × 1,200]	18,000
Fixed manufacturing overhead...	9,750

Actual July production costs were:

Direct materials	$55,000
Direct labor..	94,360
Manufacturing overhead	29,350

REQUIRED

a. Determine the equivalent units of materials and conversion manufactured during July.
b. Based on the July equivalent units of materials and conversion, prepare a July performance report for the Evanston Company.
c. Explain the treatment of overhead in the July performance report.

LO3, 4, 5   **P22-37.**   **Measuring the Effects of Decisions on Standard Cost Variances (Comprehensive)**

The following five unrelated situations affect one or more standard cost variances for materials, labor (assembly), and overhead:

1. Sally Smith, a production worker, announced her intent to resign to accept another job paying $1.75 more per hour. To keep Sally, the production manager agreed to raise her salary from $7.00 to $9.50 per hour. Sally works an average of 175 regular hours per month.

2. At the beginning of the month, a supplier of a component used in our product notified us that, because of a minor design improvement, the price will be increased by 15 percent above the current standard price of $125 per unit. As a result of the improved design, we expect the number of defective components to decrease by 90 units per month. On average, 1,300 units of the component are purchased each month. Defective units are identified prior to use and are not returnable.

3. In an effort to meet a deadline on a rush order in Department A, the plant manager reassigned several higher-skilled workers from Department B, for a total of 360 labor hours. The average salary of the Department B workers was $3.05 more than the standard $7.25 per hour rate of the Department A workers. Since they were not accustomed to the work, the average Department B worker was able to produce only 36 units per hour instead of the standard 48 units per hour. (Consider only the effect on Department A labor variances.)

4. Robbie Wallace is an inspector who earns a base salary of $900 per month plus a piece rate of 40 cents per bundle inspected. His company accounts for inspection costs as manufacturing overhead. Because of a payroll department error in June, Robbie was paid $500 plus a piece rate of 70 cents per bundle. He received gross wages totaling $1,200.

5. The materials purchasing manager purchased 6,000 units of component K2X from a new source at a price $19 below the standard unit price of $225. These components turned out to be of extremely poor quality with defects occurring at three times the standard rate of 6 percent. The higher rate of defects reduced the output of workers (who earn $11 per hour) from 20 units per hour to 15 units per hour on the units containing the discount components. Each finished unit contains one K2X component. To appease the workers (who were irate at having to work with inferior components), the production manager agreed to pay the workers an additional $0.30 for each of the components (good and bad) in the discount batch. Variable manufacturing overhead is applied at the rate of $3.50 per direct labor hour. The defective units also caused a 20-hour increase in total machine hours. The actual cost of electricity to run the machines is $2.50 per hour.

REQUIRED

For each of the preceding situations, determine which standard cost variance(s) will be affected, and compute the amount of the effect for one month on each variance. Indicate whether the effect is favorable or unfavorable. Assume that the standards are not changed in response to these situations. (Round calculations to two decimal places.)

LO7   **P22-38.**   **Fixed Overhead Budget and Volume Variance**

Four-Leaf Clover Company assigns fixed overhead costs to inventory for external reporting purposes by using a predetermined standard overhead rate based on direct labor hours. The standard rate is based on a normal activity level of 25,000 standard allowed direct labor hours per year. There are five standard allowed hours for each unit of output. Budgeted fixed overhead costs are $360,000 per year. During 2017, the company produced 5,200 units of output, and actual fixed costs were $375,000.

REQUIRED

a. Determine the standard fixed overhead rate used to assign fixed costs to inventory.
b. Determine the amount of fixed overhead assigned to inventory in 2017.
c. Determine the fixed overhead budget variance.

LO8   **P22-39.**   **Profit Center Performance Report**

Bach Tunes is a classical music retailer specializing in the Internet sale of MP3 albums of the works of J. S. Bach. Although prices vary with album popularity and file sizes, the albums sell for an average of $15.75 each and Bach Tunes pays a fixed royalty of $7.25 per MP3 album. With the exception of royalty fees, the operating costs of Bach Tunes are fixed. Presented are budgeted and actual income statements for the month of September.

BACH TUNES
Budgeted and Actual Contribution Statements
For Month of September

	Actual	Budget
Unit sales	6,400	6,200
Unit selling price.	$15.25	$15.75
Sales revenue.	$97,600	$97,650
Cost of goods sold.	(54,650)	(51,000)
Gross profit.	42,950	46,650
Operating costs	(15,000)	(18,000)
Contribution to corporate costs and profits.	$27,950	$28,650

REQUIRED

Compute variances to assist in evaluating the performance of Bach Tunes as a profit center. What was the likely cause of the shortfall in profits?

P22-40.   Profit Center Performance Report

LO2, 3, 4, 5, 6, 7, 8

Falafel Hut operates fast food restaurants in the food courts of shopping malls. It's main product is a serving of falafel that requires ground chick peas (direct material) and food preparation (direct labor). The April budget for Falafel Hut's Parkside restaurant was:

- Sales 30,600 servings at $4.50 each
- Standard food cost of $0.75 per serving (1/3 pound @ $2.25 per pound)
- Standard direct labor of $0.50 per serving (1/30th hour @ $15.00 per hour)
- Fixed occupancy expenses (equip and rent) of $8,000

Actual April performance of the Parkside restaurant was:

- Sales 27,000 servings at $4.80 each
- Food cost of $18,490 for 8,600 pounds
- Direct labor cost of $15,675 for 1,100 hours
- Fixed occupancy expenses of $8,200

In early May, the manager received the following financial performance report:

FALAFEL HUT—PARKSIDE
Performance Report
For the Month of April

	Actual	Budgeted	Variance
Revenues	$129,600	$137,700	$8,100 U
Food Cost.	(18,490)	(22,950)	4,460 F
Labor Cost	(15,675)	(15,300)	375 U
Occupancy	(8,200)	(8,000)	200 U
Profit.	$ 87,235	$ 91,450	$4,215 U

REQUIRED

a. Partition variance into variances for 1) selling price and net sales volume, 2) food variances for price and quantity, and 3) labor variances for rate and efficiency.
b. Using the results of your analysis, prepare an alternative reconciliation of budgeted and actual profit. Be sure to include the occupancy variance.
c. Explain why the total variances for sales, food, and labor in your reconciliation differ from those originally presented to the restaurant manager.

P22-41.   Comprehensive Performance Report

LO2, 3, 4, 5, 6, 7, 8

Instant Computing is a contract manufacturer of laptop computers sold under brand named companies. Presented are Instant's budgeted and actual contribution income statements for October. The company has three responsibility centers: Production, Selling and Distribution, and Administration. Production and Administration are cost centers while Selling and Distribution is a profit center.

INSTANT COMPUTING
Budgeted Contribution Income Statement
For Month of October

Sales (1,800 × $250)			$450,000
Less variable costs			
Variable cost of goods sold			
Direct materials (1,800 × $50)	$90,000		
Direct labor (1,800 × $20)	36,000		
Manufacturing overhead (1,800 × $15)	27,000	$153,000	
Selling and Distribution (1,800 × $60)		108,000	(261,000)
Contribution margin			189,000
Less fixed costs			
Manufacturing overhead		80,000	
Selling and Distribution		60,000	
Administrative		21,000	(161,000)
Net income			$ 28,000

INSTANT COMPUTING
Actual Contribution Income Statement
For Month of October

Sales (2,500 × $275)			$687,500
Less variable costs			
Cost of goods sold			
Direct materials	$125,000		
Direct labor	57,500		
Manufacturing overhead	48,750	$231,250	
Selling and Distribution		188,000	(419,250)
Contribution margin			268,250
Less fixed costs			
Manufacturing overhead		78,000	
Selling and Distribution		75,000	
Administrative		43,000	(196,000)
Net income (loss)			$ 72,250

REQUIRED

a. Prepare a performance report for Production that compares actual and allowed costs.
b. Prepare a performance report for Selling and Distribution that compares actual and allowed costs.
c. Determine the sales price and the net sales volume variances.
d. Prepare a report that summarizes the performance of Selling and Distribution.
e. Determine the amount by which Administration was over or under budget.
f. Prepare a report reconciling budgeted and actual net income. Your report should focus on the performance of each responsibility center.

CASES AND PROJECTS

LO1   C22-42.   Discretionary Cost Center Performance Reports

TruckMax had been extremely profitable, but the company has been hurt in recent years by competition and a failure to introduce new consumer products. In 2014, Tom Lopez became head of Consumer Products Research (CPR) and began a number of product development projects. Under his leadership the group had good ideas that led to the introduction of several promising products. Nevertheless, when 2015 financial results were reviewed, CPR's report revealed large unfavorable variances leading management to criticize Lopez for poor cost control. Management was quite concerned about cost control because profits were low, and the company's cash budget indicated that additional borrowing would be required throughout 2016 to cover out-of-pocket costs. Because of his inability to exert proper cost control, Lopez was relieved of his responsibilities in 2016, and Gabriella Garcia became head of Consumer Products Research. Garcia vowed to improve the performance of CPR and scaled back CPR's development activities to obtain favorable financial performance reports.

By the end of 2017, the company had improved its market position, profitability, and cash position. At this time, the board of directors promoted Garcia to president, congratulating her for the contribution CPR made to the revitalization of the company, as well as her success in improving the financial performance of CPR. Garcia assured the board that the company's financial performance would improve even more in the future as she applied the same cost-reducing measures that had worked so well in CPR to the company as a whole.

REQUIRED

a. For the purpose of evaluating financial performance, what responsibility center classification should be given to the Consumer Products Research Department? What unique problems are associated with evaluating the financial performance of this type of responsibility center?

b. Compare the performances of Lopez and Garcia in the role as head of Consumer Products Research. Did Garcia do a much better job, thereby making her deserving of the promotion? Why or why not?

C22-43.   **Developing Cost Standards for Materials and Labor**   **LO2**

After several years of operating without a formal system of cost control, DeWalt Company, a tools manufacturer, has decided to implement a standard cost system. The system will first be established for the department that makes lug wrenches for automobile mechanics. The standard production batch size is 100 wrenches. The actual materials and labor required for eight randomly selected batches from last year's production are as follows:

Batch	Materials Used (in pounds)	Labor Used (in hours)
1	504.0	10.00
2	508.0	9.00
3	506.0	9.00
4	521.0	5.00
5	516.0	8.00
6	518.0	7.00
7	520.0	6.00
8	515.0	8.00
Average	513.5	7.75

Management has obtained the following recommendations concerning what the materials and labor quantity standards should be:

- The manufacturer of the equipment used in making the wrenches advertises in the toolmakers' trade journal that the machine the company uses can produce 100 wrenches with 500 pounds of direct materials and 5 labor hours. Company engineers believe the standards should be based on these facts.
- The accounting department believes more realistic standards would be 505 pounds and 5 hours.
- The production supervisor believes the standards should be 512 pounds and 7.75 hours.
- The production workers argue for standards of 522 pounds and 8 hours.

REQUIRED

a. State the arguments for and against each of the recommendations, as well as the probable effects of each recommendation on the quantity variance for materials and labor.

b. Which recommendation provides the best combination of cost control and motivation to the production workers? Explain.

C22-44.   **Behavioral Effect of Standard Costs**   **LO1, 2, 3, 4, 5**

Merit Inc. has used a standard cost system for evaluating the performance of its responsibility center managers for three years. Top management believes that standard costing has not produced the cost savings or increases in productivity and profits promised by the accounting department. Large unfavorable variances are consistently reported for most cost categories, and employee morale has fallen since the system was installed. To help pinpoint the problem with the system, top management asked for separate evaluations of the system by the plant manager, the controller, and the human resources director. Their responses are summarized here.

Plant Manager—The standards are unrealistic. They assume an ideal work environment that does not allow materials defects or errors by the workers or machines. Consequently, morale has gone down and productivity has declined. Standards should be based on expected actual prices and recent past averages for efficiency. Thus, if we improve over the past, we receive a favorable variance.

Controller—The goal of accounting reports is to measure performance against an absolute standard and the best approximation of that standard is ideal conditions. Cost standards should be comparable to "par" on a golf course. Just as the game of golf uses a handicap system to allow for differences in individual players' skills and scores, it could be necessary for management to interpret variances based on the circumstances that produced the variances. Accordingly, in one case, a given unfavorable variance could represent poor performance; in another case, it could represent good performance. The managers are just going to have to recognize these subtleties in standard cost systems and depend on upper management to be fair.

Human Resources Director—The key to employee productivity is employee satisfaction and a sense of accomplishment. A set of standards that can never be met denies managers of this vital motivator. The current standards would be appropriate in a laboratory with a controlled environment but not in the factory with its many variables. If we are to recapture our old "team spirit," we must give the managers a goal that they can achieve through hard work.

REQUIRED

Discuss the behavioral issues involved in Merit Inc.'s standard cost dilemma. Evaluate each of the three responses (pros and cons) and recommend a course of action.

LO8 **C22-45.** **Evaluating a Companywide Performance Report**

Mr. Chandler, the production supervisor, bursts into your office, carrying the company's 2017 performance report and thundering, "There is villainy here, sir! And I shall get to the bottom of it. I will not stop searching until I have found the answer! Why is Mr. Richards so down on my department? I thought we did a good job last year. But Richards claims my production people and I cost the company $31,500! I plead with you, sir, explain this performance report to me." Trying to calm Chandler, you take the report from him and ask to be left alone for 15 minutes. The report is as follows:

DICKENS COMPANY, LIMITED
Performance Report
For Year 2017

	Actual	Budget	Variance
Unit sales	7,500	5,000	
Sales	$262,500	$225,000	$37,500 F
Less manufacturing costs			
Direct materials	55,500	47,500	8,000 U
Direct labor	48,000	32,500	15,500 U
Manufacturing overhead	40,000	32,000*	8,000 U
Total	(143,500)	(112,000)	(31,500) U
Gross profit	119,000	113,000	6,000 F
Less selling and administrative expenses			
Selling (all fixed)	57,800	40,000	17,800 U
Administrative (all fixed)	55,000	50,000	5,000 U
Total	(112,800)	(90,000)	(22,800)
Net income	$ 6,200	$ 23,000	$16,800 U
Performance summary			
Budgeted net income			$23,000
Sales department variances			
Sales revenue	$ 37,500 F		
Selling expenses	17,800 U	$19,700 F	
Administration department variances		5,000 U	
Production department variances		31,500 U	16,800 U
Actual net income			$ 6,200

*Includes fixed manufacturing overhead of $22,000.

REQUIRED

a. Evaluate the performance report. Is Mr. Richards correct, or is there "villainy here"?

b. Assume that the Sales Department is a profit center and that the Production and Administration Departments are cost centers. Determine the responsibility of each for cost, revenue, and income variances, and prepare a report reconciling budgeted and actual net income. Your report should focus on the performance of each responsibility center.

SOLUTIONS TO REVIEW PROBLEMS

Mid-Chapter Review 1

SOLUTION

There is some discretion as to how each of the reporting units below would be classified by Eli's. However, likely classifications would be as follows:

Bakery—Cost Center: In this case, the bakery is the "manufacturing facility." Typically, a manufacturing facility is a cost center. The bakery is responsible for producing high-quality products in the most cost-effective way possible.

Accounting—Cost Center

Product line/Original Plain Cheesecake—Profit Center: Typically, a product line is a profit center. The product manager of the Original Plain Cheesecake is likely responsible for the revenues, costs, and resulting profits of his or her product line. A product line is not typically an investment center as many of the production assets are shared with other products; therefore, any decisions regarding the overall bakery assets will be made at a higher level in the organization.

Human resources—Cost Center

Cheesecake Café at O'Hare Airport—Investment Center: The Café at O'Hare will have separate assets such as a display case, cash register, and refrigerators. It will be responsible for attractive displays and customer service. So it is likely that the Café will be evaluated based on its target profit per dollar invested.

Mid-Chapter Review 2

SOLUTION

The performance report prepared by the accounting department was based on a "static" budget. A better basis for evaluating your performance is to compare actual performance with a flexible budget. By dividing the budgeted variable costs amounts by 12,000 units, the budgeted unit variable costs amounts can be determined as follows:

Direct materials cost.	$360,000 ÷ 12,000 units = $30 per unit
Direct labor.	$432,000 ÷ 12,000 units = $36 per unit
Variable factory overhead.	$216,000 ÷ 12,000 units = $18 per unit

Using these budgeted unit values, a flexible budget can be prepared as follows:

	Actual	Flexible Budget	Variance
Units.	10,000	10,000	
Costs			
Direct materials	$ 299,000	$ 300,000	$ 1,000 F
Direct labor.	345,500	360,000	14,500 F
Variable factory overhead.	180,000	180,000	
Fixed factory overhead.	375,000	360,000	15,000 U
Total plant costs.	$1,199,500	$1,200,000	$ 500 F

The plant did not produce the number of units originally budgeted. Therefore, from a cost control standpoint, a flexible budget is a better basis for evaluating performance because it compares the actual cost of producing 10,000 units with a budget also based on 10,000 units. Based on the flexible budget, your performance is still quite good; however, it is much less favorable than it appeared using a static budget.

Mid-Chapter Review 3

SOLUTION

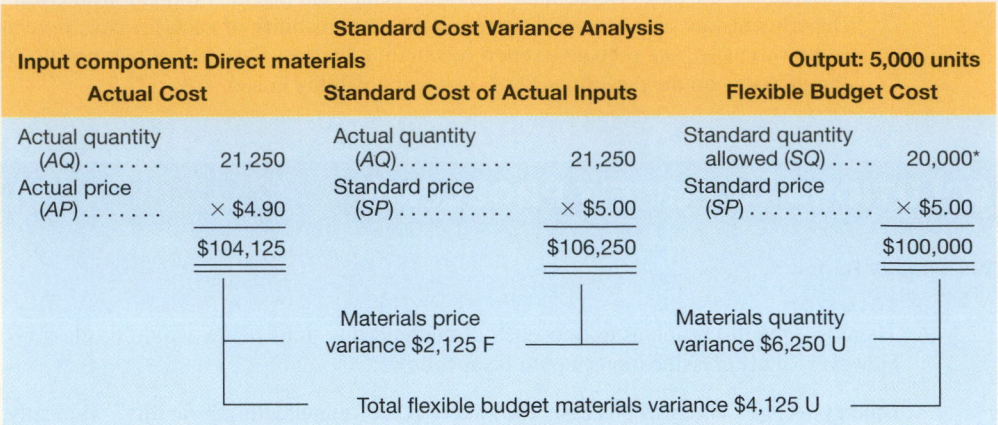

*5,000 units × 4 pounds per unit produced

Mid-Chapter Review 4

SOLUTION

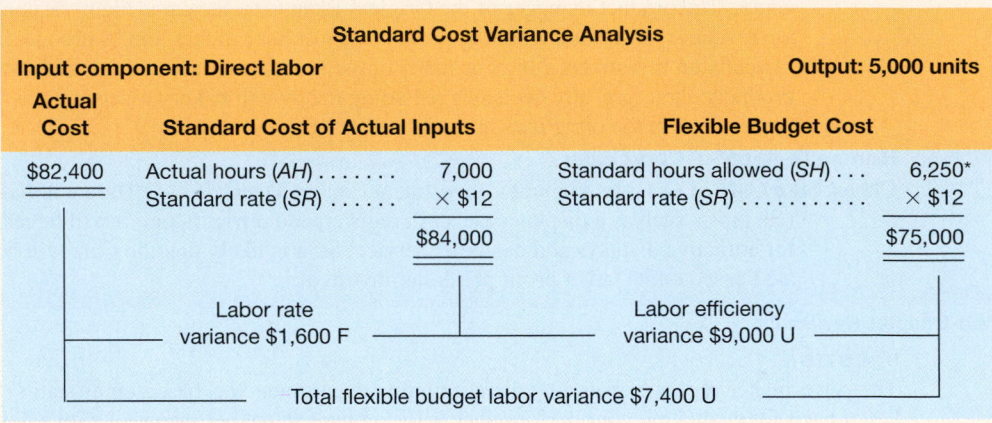

*5,000 units × 1.25 hours per unit

Mid-Chapter Review 5

SOLUTION

Standard Cost Variance Analysis					
Input component: Variable overhead				**Output: 5,000 units**	
Actual Costs		**Standard Cost of Actual Inputs**		**Flexible Budget Cost**	
Category 1 ..	$31,000	Actual labor hours ...	7,000	Standard hours allowed	6,250
Category 2 ..	18,000	Standard rate	× $4.80	Standard rate	× $4.80
Total	$49,000	Driver total	$33,600	Driver total	$30,000
		Finished units	5,000	Finished units	5,000
		Standard rate	× $4.00	Standard rate	× $4.00
		Driver total	$20,000	Driver total	$20,000
		Total	$53,600	Total	$50,000

Variable overhead spending variance $4,600 F

Variable overhead efficiency variance $3,600 U

Total flexible budget variable overhead variance $1,000 F

Chapter-End Review

SOLUTION

Revenue variance	=	(AQ × AP) − (BQ × BP)
	=	(150 × $26) − (125 × $25)
	=	$775 F

Sales price variance	=	(AP − BP) × AQ
	=	($26 − $25) × 150
	=	$150 F

Sales volume variance	=	(AQ − BQ) × BP
	=	(150 − 125) × $25
	=	$625 F

Appendix 22A Review

SOLUTION

a.

Actual fixed overhead cost	$6,250,000
Budgeted fixed overhead cost	(6,000,000)
Fixed overhead budget variance	$ 250,000 U

b.

Fixed overhead rate = $6,000,000/2,000,000 = $3.00/barrel	
Budgeted fixed overhead cost	$6,000,000
Applied fixed overhead (2,100,000 × $3.00 barrels)	(6,300,000)
Volume variance	$ 300,000 F

Appendix 22B Review

SOLUTION

MIDSTATE SUPPLY COMPANY Reconciliation of Budgeted and Actual Contribution Income For the Month of November		
Budgeted income		$18,000
Sales department variances:		
Sales price variance	$24,000 F	
Net sales price variance	6,000 F	
Variable expenses	18,000 U	
Fixed expenses	1,500 U	10,500 F
Administration department variances		500 F
Production department variances		2,000 U
Actual income		$27,000

Note: The important point is to leave out the sales volume variance and to properly consider the impact of favorable and unfavorable variances on income.

23

Segment Reporting, Transfer Pricing, and Balanced Scorecard

LEARNING OBJECTIVES

1. Define a strategic business segment, and prepare and use segment reports. (p. 1016)

2. Explain transfer pricing and assess alternative transfer-pricing methods. (p. 1021)

3. Determine and contrast return on investment and residual income. (p. 1026)

4. Describe the balanced scorecard as a comprehensive performance measurement system. (p. 1034)

VOLKSWAGEN

www.VW.com

On the shores of the Mittelland Canal, in the shadow of Wolfsburg Castle, stands the 73 million square-foot factory of **Volkswagen** (VW). Along with employing 50,000 workers, VW's presence is felt throughout the region from the Volkswagen Arena to the VW-owned Ritz Carlton to Autostadt, VW's sprawling theme park housing the most popular car museum in the world, the ZeitHaus. But VW's products go beyond its flagship brand to include Audi, Porsche, Lamborghini, Bentley, Bugatti, Ducati, SEAT, Skoda, MAN, Scania, and Volkswagen Commercial Vehicles, encompassing a total of 280 different vehicle models. Likewise, VW's reach extends far beyond Germany. VW also has manufacturing or assembly plants in Mexico, Slovakia, China, India, Indonesia, Russia, Brazil, Argentina, Portugal, Spain, Poland, Czech Republic, Bosnia and Herzegovina, South Africa, and the United States.

Given the company's diversity by product line and geographic region, preparing the VW's financial and operating reports by segment assists VW managers in determining where the company should expand or contract its operations. However, the sheer complexity and volume of the company's business make the allocation of common costs across segments a difficult proposition. If managers' performance evaluations are tied to these segmented results, conflicts will undoubtedly arise regarding which allocated costs are within each manager's control.

One of VW's initiatives to manage the business across product and geographic lines is the introduction of modular tool-kit assemblies. This system allows the company to build all of its vehicles using four basic setups: a different tool kit for small, midsize, sports, or large/SUV vehicles. Doing this allows VW to standardize its engineering platforms and reduce inventory costs by using shared components wherever possible. With standardization comes an increase in transfers of components across product line and geographic divisions. However, what is the correct "price" to charge between internal divisions? The "selling" division would like to maximize its divisional performance by charging the highest price possible on the transfer, while the "buying" division would prefer to minimize its costs by paying the lowest price possible to the selling division. And each country in which VW manufactures and assembles its vehicles resides in a different tax jurisdiction such that the choice of a transfer price has real economic consequences for the overall corporate entity.

Another complicating factor in VW's diversity of operations stems from evaluating the performance of the company's divisions. The company will want to compare its return on investment—that is, the income generated for each dollar of investment—across divisions to determine which managers and markets are delivering the best results. But the age of the capital investments, along with financial accounting rules governing depreciation and research and development costs, can distort these performance metrics. In this chapter, we will discuss performance measures that overcome the weaknesses of traditional performance ratios by taking into account leverage, taxation, level of investment, and the cost of accessing financial capital to make those investments. Further, we will examine performance evaluation models that are future oriented and emphasize nonfinancial measures such as innovation and learning, internal processes, and customer satisfaction in addition to financial performance.

Source: Kenneth Rapoza, "Volkswagen Stakes Out Greater Turf in China," *Forbes*, May 14, 2013; Joann Muller, "How Volkswagen Will Rule the World," *Forbes*, April 17, 2013; and Vanessa Fuhrmans and Friedrich Geiger, "A Weaker Outlook in Europe Slams Volkswagen's Stock," *Wall Street Journal*, February 23, 2013, p. B3.

CHAPTER ORGANIZATION

Segment Reporting, Transfer Pricing, and Balanced Scorecard			
Strategic Business Segments and Segment Reporting	**Transfer Pricing**	**Investment Center Evaluation Measures**	**Balanced Scorecard**
• Multilevel Segment Income Statements • Interpreting Segment Reports	• Management Considerations • Determining Transfer Prices	• Return on Investment • Investment Center Income • Investment Center Asset Base • Other Valuation Issues • Residual Income • Economic Value Added	• Balanced Scorecard Framework • Balanced Scorecard and Strategy

Organizations that maintain multiple product lines or that operate in several industries or in multiple markets often adopt a decentralized organization structure in which managers of major business units or strategic segments enjoy a high degree of autonomy. Examples of strategic business segments include the **Porsche division of Volkswagen** and the Asia Pacific Group of **The Coca-Cola Company**. Sometimes companies establish segments within segments such as at Coca-Cola, whose Asia Pacific Group has separate business units for individual countries (Japan, Korea, etc.). In organizations such as Volkswagen and Coca-Cola, upper management typically sets specific performance and profitability objectives for each segment and allows the manager of the segment the decision-making freedom to achieve those objectives.

This chapter explains the ways that an organization evaluates strategic business segments. It also considers transfer pricing and some of the problems that occur when one segment provides goods or services to another segment in the same organization.

STRATEGIC BUSINESS SEGMENTS AND SEGMENT REPORTING

eLectures

MBC

LO1 Define a strategic business segment, and prepare and use segment reports.

1

A **strategic business segment** has its own mission and set of goals. Its mission influences the decisions that top managers make in both short-run and long-run situations. The organization structure dictates to a large extent the type of financial segment reporting and other measures used to evaluate the segment and its managers. In decentralized organizations, for example, the reporting units (typically called *divisions*) normally are quasi-independent companies, often having their own computer system, cost accounting system, and administrative and marketing staffs. With this type structure, top management monitors the segments to ensure that these independent units are functioning for the benefit of the entire organization.

Although segment reports are normally produced to coincide with managerial lines of responsibility, some companies also produce segment reports for smaller slices of the business that do not represent separate responsibility centers. These parts of the business are not significant enough to be identified as "strategic" business units as defined, but management could want information about them on a continuing basis.

For example, **AT&T** has several strategic business units, including wireless, wireline, and advertising solutions. Financial reports are prepared for each of these units. Within the wireline segment, AT&T can also prepare segment reports on a more detailed basis to determine the profitability of its smaller segments, such as phone-only and data service customers. Most public companies are required to provide some segment information in their annual reports.

The point is that segment reporting is not constrained by lines of responsibility. A segment report can be prepared for any part of the business for which management believes more detailed information is useful in managing that portion of the business.

BUSINESS INSIGHT

Strategic Segment Organization   Only three automakers have sold 10 million vehicles in a year. The first two were **General Motors** and **Volkswagen**, and both companies famously struggled after hitting the 10 million mark. **Toyota**'s sales have been above 10 million vehicles for two years running, and the firm has had its struggles. Senior executives at Toyota have expressed concern that this scale of production, sales, and distribution is difficult to manage.

In order to remain nimble and competitive, Toyota has reorganized operations, shifting from a geographic organization to one based on product lines. Toyota President Akio Toyoda has said that as companies reach the 10 million milestone, reorganization is inevitable at all levels. "We can't talk about our future without finding new ways to do our jobs," Toyoda said. Analysts who cover the auto industry feel that this attitude is key to Toyota's ability to adjust more swiftly to challenges such as recalls and natural disasters.

One of the key ways that this new structure can help is by streamlining Toyota's product lines. Previously, Toyota modified the marketing and design of its vehicles to the target geography. The Vitz compact, sold in Japan, has a closely related model, the Yaris, sold only in Europe and the United States, while India has the Etios. What Japanese and American customers recognize as the Prius C is marketed in Europe as the Aqua. This geographical focus served Toyota well as it grew to its current size. Now there are gains to be had by simplifying the product lines, partially due to the size of the company, but also due to the global familiarity with Toyota vehicles. All companies should be prepared to modify internal structures as the firm evolves.

Sources: Naomi Tajitsu, "Toyota Shakes Up Corporate Structure to Focus on Product Lines," *Reuters*, March 2, 2016. Yoko Kubota, "Toyota Plans Organizational Shake-Up," *Wall Street Journal*, February 29, 2016.

Segment reports are income statements for portions or segments of a business. Segment reporting is used primarily for internal purposes, although generally accepted accounting principles also require some disclosure of segment information for public corporations. Even though there are many different types of segment reports, at least three steps are basic to the preparation of all segment reports:

1. Identify the segments.
2. Assign direct costs to segments.
3. Allocate indirect costs to segments.

The format of segment income statements varies depending on the approach adopted by a company for reporting income statements internally. The income statement formats illustrated earlier in this text, including the functional format and the contribution format, can be used for segment reporting. Data availability can, however, dictate the format used. Regardless of the format adopted, it is essential that costs be separable into those directly traceable to the segments and those not directly traceable to segments. See **Exhibit 23.1**, below, for how the three steps above can be incorporated in the development of segment income.

EXHIBIT 23.1

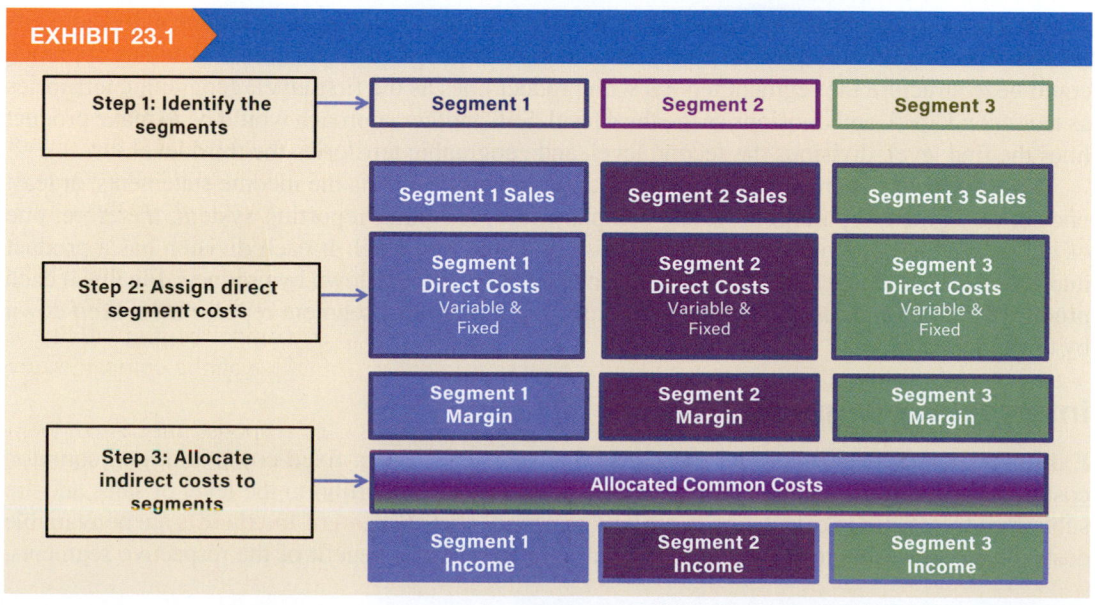

Determining the segment reporting structure is often a more difficult decision than choosing the format for the segment income statements. Companies must decide whether to structure segment reporting along the lines of responsibility reporting, and whether segment reports will be prepared only on one level or on several levels.

For example, assume **Cisco** has two market divisions, three products, and two geographic territories. Suppose Cisco's two divisions include the National Division (serving large national accounts) and the Regional Division (serving smaller regional and local accounts). Further assume Cisco's three main product lines are switching, routing, and wireless. The company is organized into two geographic territories, United States and International. If Cisco were using only a single-level segment reporting approach for all three groupings, one report would show the total company income statement broken down into the two divisions, a second report would show the total company income statement broken down into the three products, and a third report would show the total company income statement broken down into the two geographic territories.

Multilevel Segment Income Statements

If top management of Cisco wants to know how much a particular product is contributing to the income of one of the two divisions or how much income a particular product in one of its two geographic territories contributes, it is necessary to prepare multilevel segment income statements. Since Cisco sells three products and operates through two divisions in two territories, many combinations of divisions, products, and territories could be used in structuring the company's multilevel segment reporting. The goal is not to slice and dice the revenue and cost data in as many ways as possible but to provide useful and meaningful information to management. Therefore, deciding what type of reporting structure is most useful in managing the company is important.

This decision will be constrained to a great extent by data availability and cost. If there were no data constraints, Cisco could look at the company's net income for every possible combination of division, product, and territory. The more data required to support a reporting system, however, the more costly it is to maintain the system, so management must determine the value and the cost of the additional information and make an appropriate cost-benefit judgment.

Panel A of **Exhibit 23.2** illustrates hypothetical multilevel segment reporting for Cisco in which the first level shows the total company income statement segmented into the two market divisions, National Accounts and Regional Accounts. Panel B of **Exhibit 23.2** shows a second-level report for Cisco in which the National Division's segment income statement is broken down into its three product lines, switching, routing, and wireless. Panel C then provides a third-level income statement for the National Division's switching product line sales in each of the company's two geographic territories, the U.S. and International territories. The example in **Exhibit 23.2** shows only part of the segment reports for Cisco. The complete three-level set of segment reports would also break down the Regional Accounts Division into its product lines and all product lines for both divisions into geographic territories.

In the Cisco example in **Exhibit 23.2**, the first reporting level is the company's divisions, its second reporting level is product lines, and the third is geographic territories. Another approach could be to structure the segment reports with product lines as the first level, geographic territories as the second level, and divisions as the third level. Still another approach would be to make product lines the first level, divisions the second level, and geographic territories the third level.

Regardless of how many different ways the company segments the income statements, at least one set of segment reports follows the company's responsibility reporting system; therefore, one of the segment reports has the operating divisions as the first level. If each division has a product manager for each product, the division segment reports are broken down by products. Finally, if each product within each division has a territory manager, the product segment reports are broken down by territories.

Interpreting Segment Reports

Exhibit 23.2 reports costs in four categories: variable costs, direct fixed costs, allocated common costs, and unallocated common costs. Variable costs vary in proportion to the level of sales and are subtracted from sales in calculating contribution margin. **Direct segment fixed costs** are nonvariable costs directly traceable to the segments incurred for the specific benefit of the respective segments.

EXHIBIT 23.2	Multilevel Segment Reports

Panel A: First-Level Segment Report of Cisco—For Divisions (in thousands)

	Segments (Divisions)		
	National Accounts	Regional Accounts	Company Total
Sales.	$100,000	$200,000	$300,000
Less variable costs.	(55,000)	(95,000)	(150,000)
Contribution margin	45,000	105,000	150,000
Less direct fixed costs	(20,000)	(60,000)	(80,000)
Division margin.	25,000	45,000	70,000
Less allocated segment costs	(10,000)	(25,000)	(35,000)
Division income	$ 15,000	$ 20,000	35,000
Less unallocated common costs			(12,000)
Net income			$ 23,000

Panel B: Second-Level Segment Report of the National Division—For Products (in thousands)

	Segments (Products)			National Accounts Total
	Switching	Routing	Wireless	
Sales.	$30,000	$40,000	$30,000	$100,000
Less variable costs.	(15,000)	(19,000)	(21,000)	(55,000)
Contribution margin	15,000	21,000	9,000	45,000
Less direct fixed costs	(9,000)	(4,000)	(2,000)	(15,000)
Product margin.	6,000	17,000	7,000	30,000
Less allocated segment costs	(5,000)	(4,000)	(1,000)	(10,000)
Product income	$ 1,000	$13,000	$ 6,000	20,000
Less unallocated common costs				(5,000)
National Division income				$ 15,000

Panel C: Third-Level Segment Report of the Switching Product Line in the National Division—For Geographic Territories (in thousands)

	Segments (Territories)		Switching Total
	U.S.	International	
Sales.	$20,000	$10,000	$30,000
Less variable costs.	(11,000)	(4,000)	(15,000)
Contribution margin	9,000	6,000	15,000
Less direct fixed costs	(3,000)	(4,000)	(7,000)
Territory margin.	6,000	2,000	8,000
Less allocated segment costs	(2,000)	(3,000)	(5,000)
Territory income	$ 4,000	$(1,000)	3,000
Less unallocated common costs			(2,000)
Switching income.			$ 1,000

Segment margin equals the contribution margin minus the direct segment fixed costs. For Cisco, segment margins are referred to as *division margins, product margins,* and *territory margins.* Segment margins represent the amount that a segment contributes directly to the company's profitability in the short run.

Common segment costs are incurred for the common benefit of all related segments shown on a segment income statement. In some cases, allocating some common costs is reasonable even though they cannot be directly traced to the various segments based on benefits received. For example, if segments share common space, allocating all space-related costs to the segments based on building space occupied could be appropriate. If there is no reasonable basis for allocating common costs, they should not be allocated to the segments. In Panel C of **Exhibit 23.2**, if advertising costs to promote the company's switching products on national television could not be reasonably allocated to the two geographic territories, they would be charged to the switching product line as an unallocated common cost, not to the individual territories.

If some portion of common costs can be reasonably allocated to the segments, those allocated costs are subtracted from the segment margins to determine segment income. Hence, **segment income** represents all revenues of the segment minus all costs directly or indirectly charged to it.

To properly interpret segment income, we should ask whether segment income represents the amount by which net income of the company will change if that segment is discontinued. For example, if Cisco discontinues the wireless product line in the National Division, does this mean that Cisco's net income will decrease by $6 million? Also, does it mean that if the National Division stops selling switching products in the International territory, Cisco's net income will increase by $1 million?

The answer to these questions depends on whether the costs allocated to the segments are avoidable. **Avoidable common costs** are allocated common costs that eventually can be avoided (that is, can be eliminated) if a segment is discontinued. If all allocated common costs are avoidable, the effect of discontinuing the segment on corporate profitability equals the amount of segment income. In most cases, the short-term impact of discontinuing a segment equals the segment margin because allocated costs are capacity costs that cannot be adjusted in the short run. Over time, the company should be able to adjust capacity and eliminate some, or possibly all, of the allocated common costs or find productive uses for that capacity in other segments of the business. The unallocated common costs cannot be changed readily in the short term or the long term without causing major disruptions to the company and its strategy. Therefore, over the long term, the impact of discontinuing a segment should be, approximately, it's segment income.

If Cisco discontinues selling switching products in the International territory (see **Exhibit 23.2**, Panel C) the short-term effect on the company's profits will probably be a $2 million reduction of profits, which equals the International territory's margin. The revenues and costs that make up the International territory margin would all be lost if switching sales were discontinued in the International territory, but the $3 million of common costs allocated to the International territory would continue, at least in the short term. Over the long term, however, after adjusting the capacity for selling this product in the International territory and eliminating the $3 million of allocated common costs, the effect of discontinuing switching products in the International territory on profits should be an increase of about $1 million, which is the amount of the segment loss for switching products in the International territory.

To summarize, generally, segment margin is relevant for measuring the short-term effects of decisions to continue or discontinue a segment; however, segment income is relevant for measuring the long-term effects of decisions to continue or discontinue.

MID-CHAPTER REVIEW 1

Refer to the Cisco example in **Exhibit 23.2**, Panel B. The following additional information is provided for the wireless product line in the National Division:

Sales—U.S. territory.	$12,000
Sales—International territory	18,000
Direct fixed cost—U.S. territory	500
Direct fixed cost—International territory	800
Allocated segment costs—U.S. territory	200
Allocated segment costs—International territory.	600

REQUIRED

a. Prepare a geographic territory segment report of the wireless product line in the National division. Assume variable costs are always the same percent of sales for wireless products.

b. Explain why the total of the Territory Margins for geographic segments of the wireless product line does not equal the product margin of the wireless product segment in Panel B of Exhibit 23.2.

The solution to this review problem can be found on page 1054.

TRANSFER PRICING

LO2 Explain transfer pricing and assess alternative transfer-pricing methods.

To determine whether each division is achieving its organizational objectives, managers must be accountable for the goods and services they acquire, both externally and internally. When goods or services are exchanged internally between segments of a decentralized organization, the way that the transferor and the transferee will report the transfer must be determined, either by negotiations between the two segments or by corporate policy. A **transfer price** is the internal value assigned a product or service that one division provides to another. The transfer price is recognized as revenue by the division providing goods or services and as expense (or cost) by the division receiving them. Transfer-pricing transactions normally occur between profit or investment centers rather than between cost centers of an organization; however, managers often consider cost allocations between cost centers as a type of transfer price. The focus in this chapter is on transfers between responsibility centers that are evaluated based on profits.

Management Considerations

The desire of the selling and buying divisions of the same company to maximize their individual performance measures often creates transfer-pricing conflicts within an organization. Acting as independent units, divisions could take actions that are not in the best interest(s) of the organization as a whole. The three examples that follow illustrate the need for organizations to maintain a *corporate* profit-maximizing viewpoint while attempting to allow *divisional* autonomy and responsibility.

Suppose **Sony Corporation** has five divisions, some of which transfer products and product components to other Sony divisions. Suppose the Monitors and Displays (M&D) Division manufactures two products, Yokia Mount and PVMA. It sells Yokia Mount externally for $50 per unit and transfers PVMA to the Television Division for $60 per unit. The costs associated with the two products follow:

Monitors and Displays Division	Product	
	Yokia Mount	PVMA
Variable costs		
Direct materials.	$15	$14
Direct labor	5	10
Variable manufacturing overhead	5	16
Selling	4	0
Fixed Costs		
Fixed manufacturing overhead	6	15
Total	$35	$55

An external company has just proposed to supply a PVMA substitute product to the Television Division at a price of $52. From the company's viewpoint, this is merely a make or buy decision. The relevant costs are the differential outlay costs of the alternative actions. Assuming that the fixed manufacturing costs of the M&D Division are unavoidable, the relevant costs of this proposal from the company's perspective are as follows:

Buy.		$52
Make		
Direct materials.	$14	
Direct labor.	10	
Variable manufacturing overhead	16	(40)
Difference.		$12

From the corporate viewpoint, the best decision is for the product to be transferred since the relevant cost is $40 rather than to buy it from an external source for $52. The decision for the Television Division management is basically one of cost minimization: Buy from the source that charges the lowest price. If the M&D Division is not willing to transfer PVMA at a price of $52 or less, the Television Division management could go to the external supplier to maximize the division's profits. (Although the Television Division's managers are concerned about the cost of PVMA, they are also concerned about the quality of the goods. If the $52 product does not meet its quality standards, the Television Division could decide to buy from the M&D Division at the higher price. For this discussion, assume that the internal and external products are identical; therefore, acting in its best interest, the Television Division purchases PVMA for $52 from the external source unless the M&D Division can match the price.)

Prior to Television's receipt of the external offer, the M&D Division had been transferring PVMA to the Television Division's for $60. The M&D Division must decide whether to reduce the contribution margin on its transfers of PVMA to the Television Division and, therefore, lower divisional profits or to try to find an alternative use for its resources. Of course, corporate management could intervene and require the internal transfer even though it would hurt M&D Division's profits.

As the second example, assume that the M&D Division has the option to sell an equivalent amount of PVMA externally for $60 per unit if the Television Division discontinues its transfers from the M&D Division. Now the decision for M&D's management is simple: Sell to the buyer willing to pay the most. From the corporate viewpoint, it is best for the M&D Division to sell to the external buyer for $60 and for Television to purchase from the external provider for $52.

To examine a slightly different transfer-pricing conflict, assume that the M&D Division can sell all the Yokia that it can produce (it is operating at capacity). Also assume that there is no external market for PVMA, but there is a one-to-one trade-off between the production of Yokia and PVMA, which use equal amounts of the M&D Division's limited capacity.

The corporation still regards this as a make or buy decision, but the costs of producing PVMA have changed. The cost of PVMA now includes an outlay cost and an opportunity cost. The outlay cost of PVMA is its variable cost of $40 ($14 + $10 + $16), as previously computed. PVMA's opportunity cost is the net benefit foregone if the M&D Division's limited capacity is used to produce PVMA rather than Yokia:

Selling price of Yokia		$50
Outlay costs of Yokia		
Direct materials	$15	
Direct labor	5	
Variable manufacturing overhead	5	
Variable selling	4	(29)
Opportunity cost of making PVMA		$21

Accordingly, the relevant costs in the make or buy decision follow.

Make		
Outlay cost of PVMA	$40	
Opportunity cost of PVMA	21	$61
Buy		$52

From the corporate viewpoint, the Television Division should purchase PVMA from the outside supplier for $52 because in this case it costs $61 to make the product. If there were no outside suppliers, the corporation's relevant cost of manufacturing PVMA would be $61. This is another way of saying that the Television Division should not acquire PVMA internally unless its revenues cover all outlay costs (including the $40 in the M&D Division) and provide a contribution of at least $21 ($61 − $40). From the corporate viewpoint, the relevant costs in make or buy decisions are the external price, the outlay costs to manufacture, and the opportunity cost to manufacture. The opportunity cost is zero if there is excess capacity.

The transfer of goods and services between divisions of a company located in different countries that have unequal tax structures often attracts the attention of the taxing authorities. Companies are sometimes accused of trying to minimize their total tax costs by setting transfer prices that shift profits from the division in the higher-tax-rate country to the division in the lower-tax-rate country. For example, assume that IBM has a division in Denmark that produces software that it sells to its systems division in the U.S. Denmark's corporate tax rate is about 50 percent; whereas, the U.S. rate is about 35 percent. By setting a transfer price at the lowest possible level, the profits of the Danish division will be less, and those of the American division will be higher, resulting in lower overall taxes for the company. The taxing authorities in the high-tax-rate country always insist that the transfer price for goods and services sold to divisions in other countries be at least as high as fair market value of the goods or services transferred out. The following Business Insight discusses a recent attempt by the IRS to collect taxes of more than $521 million from **Guidant Corp.** related to improper transfer prices.

BUSINESS INSIGHT

Transfer Pricing and the IRS   In late 2010, **Boston Scientific Corp.** reported that the IRS had ruled that its **Guidant Corp.** division owed $521.1 million in taxes plus interest as a result of an audit of Guidant's prior year's tax returns. The company indicated that the IRS was "assessing additional taxes related to transfer prices on technology license agreements between some of Guidant's U.S. and foreign businesses."

Boston Scientific asked the U.S. Tax court to throw out the case based on two complaints about the methodology the IRS used. First, Boston Scientific argued that the IRS should have determined the separate taxable income for each Guidant business involved in the complaint. Second, Boston Scientific argued that the IRS failed to make the appropriate adjustments to the transactions in question. In early 2016 the court ruled that the case should go forward.

Sources: "IRS Wins on Question of Aggregation in 'Guidant' Case," *Bloomberg BNA*, March 1, 2016.
"Boston Scientific Owes Half Billion in Taxes, IRS Says; Company to Fight Ruling on Guidant Division," *Boston Globe*, December 22, 2010.

Determining Transfer Prices

As illustrated, the transfer price of goods or services can be subject to much controversy. The most widely used and discussed transfer prices are covered in this section. Although a price must be agreed upon for each item or service transferred between divisions, the selection of the pricing method depends on many factors. The conditions surrounding the transfer determine which of the alternative methods discussed subsequently is selected.

Although no method is likely to be ideal, one must be selected if the profit or investment center concept is used. In considering each method, observe that each transfer results in a revenue entry on the supplier's books and a cost entry on the receiver's books. Transfers can be considered as sales by the supplier and as purchases by the receiver.

Market Price   When there is an existing market with established prices for an intermediate product and the transfer actions of the company will not affect prices, market prices are ideal transfer prices. If divisions are free to buy and sell outside the firm, the use of market prices preserves divisional autonomy and leads divisions to act in a manner that maximizes corporate goal congruence. Unfortunately, not all product transfers have equivalent external markets. Furthermore, the divisions should carefully evaluate whether the market price is competitive or controlled by one or two large companies. When substantial selling expenses are associated with outside sales, many firms specify the transfer price as market price less selling expenses. The internal sale may not require the incurrence of costs to get and fill the order.

To illustrate using the hypothetical Sony example, assume that product Yokia of the M&D Division can be sold competitively at $50 per unit or transferred to a third division, the Medical Equipment Division, for additional processing. Under most situations, the M&D Division will never sell Yokia for less than $50, and the Medical Equipment Division will likewise never pay more than $50 for it. However, if any variable expenses related to marketing and shipping can be eliminated by divisional transfers, these costs are generally subtracted from the competitive market price. In our illustration in which variable selling expenses are $4 for Yokia, the transfer price could be reduced to $46 ($50 − $4). A price between $46 and $50 would probably be better than either extreme price. To the extent that these transfer prices represent a nearly competitive situation, the profitability of each division can then be fairly evaluated.

Variable Costs If excess capacity exists in the supplying division, establishing a transfer price equal to variable costs leads the purchasing division to act in a manner that is optimal from the corporation's viewpoint. The buying division has the corporation's variable cost as its own variable cost as it enters the external market. Unfortunately, establishing the transfer price at variable cost causes the supplying division to report zero profits or a loss equal to any fixed costs. If excess capacity does not exist, establishing a transfer price at variable cost would not lead to optimal action because the supplying division would have to forego external sales that include a markup for fixed costs and profits. If PVMA could be sold externally for $60, the M&D Division would not want to transfer PVMA to the Television Division for a $40 transfer price based on the following variable costs:

Direct materials	$14
Direct labor	10
Variable manufacturing overhead	16
Total variable costs	$40

The M&D Division would much rather sell outside the company for $60, which covers variable costs and provides a profit contribution margin of $20:

Selling price of PVMA	$60
Variable costs	(40)
Contribution margin	$20

Variable Costs Plus Opportunity Costs From the organization's viewpoint, this is the optimal transfer price. Because all relevant costs are included in the transfer price, the purchasing division is led to act in a manner optimal for the overall company, whether or not excess capacity exists.

With excess capacity in the supplying division, the transfer price is the variable cost per unit. Without excess capacity, the transfer price is the sum of the variable and opportunity costs. Following this rule in the previous example, if the M&D Division had excess capacity, the transfer price of PVMA would be set at PVMA's variable costs of $40 per unit. At this transfer price, the Television Division would buy PVMA internally, rather than externally at $52 per unit. If the M&D Division cannot sell PVMA externally but can sell all the Yokia it can produce and is operating at capacity, the transfer price per unit would be set at $61, the sum of PVMA's variable and opportunity costs ($40 + $21). (Refer back two pages.) At this transfer price, the Television Division would buy PVMA externally for $52. In both situations, the management of the Television Division has acted in accordance with the organization's profit-maximizing goal.

There are two problems with this method. First, when the supplying division has excess capacity, establishing the transfer price at variable cost causes the supplying division to report zero profits or a loss equal to any fixed costs. Second, determining opportunity costs when the supplying division produces several products is difficult. If the problems with the previously mentioned transfer-pricing methods are too great, three other methods can be used: absorption cost plus markup, negotiated prices, and dual prices.

Absorption Cost Plus Markup According to absorption costing, all variable and fixed manufacturing costs are product costs. Pricing internal transfers at absorption cost eliminates the supplying division's reported loss on each product that can occur using a variable cost transfer price. Absorption cost plus markup provides the supplying division a contribution toward unallocated costs. In "cost-plus" transfer pricing, "cost" should be defined as standard cost rather than as actual cost. This prevents the supplying division from passing on the cost of inefficient operations to other divisions, and it allows the buying division to know its cost in advance of purchase. Even though cost-plus transfer prices may not maximize company profits, they are widely used. Their popularity stems from several factors, including ease of implementation, justifiability, and perceived fairness. Once everyone agrees on absorption cost plus markup pricing rules, internal disputes are minimized.

Negotiated Prices   *Negotiated transfer prices* are used when the supplying and buying divisions independently agree on a price. As with market-based transfer prices, negotiated transfer prices are believed to preserve divisional autonomy. Negotiated transfer prices can lead to some suboptimal decisions, but this is regarded as a small price to pay for other benefits of decentralization. When they use negotiated transfer prices, some corporations establish arbitration procedures to help settle disputes between divisions. However, the existence of an arbitrator with any real or perceived authority reduces divisional autonomy.

Negotiated prices should have market prices as their ceiling and variable costs as their floor. Although frequently used when an external market for the product or component exists, the most common use of negotiated prices occurs when no identical-product external market exists. Negotiations could start with a floor price plus add-ons such as overhead and profit markups or with a ceiling price less adjustments for selling and administrative expenses and allowances for quantity discounts. When no identical-product external market exists, the market price for a similar completed product can be used, less the estimated cost of completing the product from the transfer stage to the completed stage.

Dual Prices   Dual prices exist when a company allows a difference in the supplier's and receiver's transfer prices for the same product. This method should minimize internal squabbles of division managers and problems of conflicting divisional and corporate goals. The supplier's transfer price normally approximates market price, which allows the selling division to show a "normal" profit on items that it transfers internally. The receiver's price is usually the internal cost of the product or service, calculated as variable cost plus opportunity cost. This ensures that the buying division will make an internal transfer when it is in the best interest of the company to do so.

In most cases, a market-based transfer price achieves the optimal outcome for both the divisions and the company as a whole. As discussed earlier, an exception occurs when a division is operating below full capacity and has no alternative use for its excess capacity. In this case, it is best for the company to have an internal transfer; therefore, to ensure that the receiving division makes an internal transfer, the company must require the internal transfer as long as its price does not exceed the established market rate. The only time an external price is more attractive when excess capacity exists is when the external price is below the variable cost of the providing internal division, and that scenario is highly unlikely.

A potential transfer-pricing problem exists when divisions exchange goods or services for which no established market exists. For example, suppose that a company is operating its information technology (IT) service department as a profit center that transfers services to other profit center departments using a cost-plus transfer price. If the departments using IT services can choose to use those services or to replicate them inside their departments, users might not make a decision that is best for the company. It could be best for the company to have all IT services come from the IT department, but other profit centers could believe that they can provide those services for themselves at lower cost. In this case, the company must decide how important it is to maintain the independence of its profit center. In the interest of maintaining a strong profit center philosophy, top management can decide that it is acceptable to suboptimize by allowing profit centers to provide IT services for themselves.

The ideal transfer-pricing arrangement is seldom the same for both the providing and receiving divisions for every situation. In these cases, what is good for one division is likely not to be good for the other division resulting in no transfer, even though a transfer could achieve corporate goals. These conflicts are sometimes overcome by having a higher-ranking manager impose a transfer price and insist that a transfer be made. Managers in organizations that have a policy of decentralization, however, often regard these orders as undermining their autonomy. Therefore, the imposition of a price could solve the corporate profit optimization problem but create other problems regarding the company's organization strategy. Transfer pricing thus becomes a problem with no ideal solutions.

The previous discussion has focused on the challenges of establishing transfer prices that motivate managers to make decisions that are beneficial to their divisions as well as the overall company. However, research, discussed in the following Research Insight box, concluded that there are often price benefits when dealing with outside vendors, if the company has the option of acquiring the goods or services internally.

MID-CHAPTER REVIEW 2

University Poster Company has a Publication Division that is currently producing and selling 200,000 posters per year but has a capacity of 300,000 posters. The variable costs of each poster are $16, and the annual fixed costs are $1,350,000. The posters sell for $24 on the open market. The company's Retail Division wants to buy 100,000 posters at $13.50 each. The Publication Division manager refuses the order because the price is below variable cost. The Retail Division manager argues that the order should be accepted because it will lower the fixed cost per poster from $6.75 to $4.50.

REQUIRED
a. Should the Retail Division order be accepted? Why or why not?
b. From the viewpoints of the Publication Division and the company, should the order be accepted if the manager of the Retail Division intends to sell each print on the outside market for $44 after incurring additional costs of $10 per print?
c. What action should the company take, assuming it believes in divisional autonomy?

The solution to this review problem can be found on pages 1054–1055.

LO3 Determine and contrast return on investment and residual income.

3

INVESTMENT CENTER EVALUATION MEASURES

Two of the most common measures of investment center performance, return on investment and residual income, are discussed in the following sections. Several supporting components of these measures that help clarify the applications are also presented. (Earlier in the book, we explained the advantages of separating operating and nonoperating items to compute sales, assets, income, and so forth. We can similarly separate operating and nonoperating items for performance measurement. In this case, all measures would be adjusted to yield operating sales, operating assets, operating income, and so forth. Then, the following analysis would apply to those operating metrics and would reflect the operating performance of each center.)

Return on Investment

Return on investment (ROI) is a measure of the earnings per dollar of investment. This assumes that financing decisions are made at the corporate level rather than the division level. Hence, the corporation's investment in the division equals the division's asset base. The return on investment of an investment center is computed by dividing the income of the center by its asset base (usually total assets):

$$\text{ROI} = \frac{\text{Investment center income}}{\text{Investment center asset base}}$$

ROI can be disaggregated into investment turnover times the return-on-sales ratio:

$$\text{ROI} = \text{Investment turnover} \times \text{Return-on-sales}$$

where

$$\text{Investment turnover} = \frac{\text{Sales}}{\text{Investment center asset base}}$$

and

$$\text{Return-on-sales} = \frac{\text{Investment center income}}{\text{Sales}}$$

When investment turnover is multiplied by return-on-sales, the product is the same as investment center income divided by investment center asset base:

$$\text{ROI} = \frac{\text{Sales}}{\text{Investment center base}} \times \frac{\text{Investment center income}}{\text{Sales}} = \frac{\text{Investment center income}}{\text{Investment center asset base}}$$

Once ROI has been computed, it is compared to some previously identified performance criteria. These include the investment center's previous ROI, overall company ROI, the ROI of similar divisions, or the ROI of nonaffiliated companies that operate in similar markets. The breakdown of ROI into investment turnover and return-on-sales is useful in determining the source of variance in overall performance.

To illustrate the computation and use of ROI, suppose the following information is available concerning the 2017 operations of **Procter & Gamble Co. (P&G)** (in thousands):

Division	Asset Base	Sales	Divisional Income
Beauty	$8,000,000	$12,000,000	$1,440,000
Healthcare	4,000,000	8,000,000	960,000
Grooming	7,500,000	5,000,000	1,650,000
Fabric & Homecare	3,800,000	5,700,000	1,026,000

Using this information and the preceding equations, a set of performance measures are shown in **Exhibit 23.3**. To illustrate, the Beauty Division earned a return on its investment base of 18 percent ($1,440,000 ÷ $8,000,000), consisting of an investment turnover of 1.50 ($12,000,000 ÷ $8,000,000) and a return-on-sales of 0.12 ($1,440,000 ÷ $12,000,000). Using such an analysis, the company has three measurement criteria with which to evaluate the performance of the Beauty Division: (1) ROI, (2) investment turnover, and (3) return-on-sales.

EXHIBIT 23.3	Performance Evaluation Data

PROCTER & GAMBLE CO.
Performance Measures
For Year Ending June 30, 2017

	Performance Measures		
	Investment Turnover ×	Return-on-Sales =	ROI
Operating unit			
Beauty	1.50	0.12	0.18
Healthcare	2.00	0.12	0.24
Grooming	0.67	0.33	0.22
Fabric & Homecare	1.50	0.18	0.27
Company performance criteria			
Projected minimums	1.20	0.15	0.18

For 2017, P&G chose to evaluate its divisions based on company ROI and its interrelated components of investment turnover and return-on-sales. Because each division is different in size, the company evaluation standard is not a simple average of the divisions but is based on desired relationships between assets, sales, and income.

Based on ROI, the Fabric & Homecare Division had the best performance, the Healthcare Division excelled in investment turnover, and the Grooming Division had the highest return-on-sales. From **Exhibit 23.3**, the Fabric & Homecare Division had the best year because it was the only division that exceeded each of the company's performance criteria. For 2017, each division equaled or exceeded the minimum ROI established by the company even though the component criteria of ROI were not always achieved.

To properly evaluate each division, the company should study the underlying components of ROI. For the Beauty Division, management would want to know why the minimum investment turnover was exceeded while the return-on-sales minimum was not. The Beauty Division could have incurred unfavorable cost variances by producing inefficiently. As a result of inefficient production, the return-on-sales declined to a point below the minimum desired level. Evaluating a large operating division based on one financial indicator is difficult. Management should select several key indicators of performance when conducting periodic reviews of its operating segments.

A similar analysis of ROI and its components is useful for planning. In developing plans for 2018, management wants to know the possible effect of changes in the major elements of ROI for the Beauty Division. Sensitivity analysis can be used to predict the impact of changes in sales, the investment center asset base, or the investment center income.

Assuming the investment asset base is unchanged, a projected ROI can be determined for the Beauty Division for a sales goal of $16,000,000 and an income goal of $1,600,000:

$$\text{ROI} = \frac{\text{Sales}}{\text{Investment center asset base}} \times \frac{\text{Investment center income}}{\text{Sales}}$$

$$= \frac{\$16,000,000}{\$8,000,000} \times \frac{\$1,600,000}{\$16,000,000}$$

$$= 2.0 \times 0.10$$

$$= 0.20, \text{ or } 20 \text{ percent.}$$

ROI increased from 18 to 20 percent, even though the return-on-sales decreased from 12 to 10 percent. The change in turnover from 1.5 to 2.0 more than offset the reduced return-on-sales.

Sensitivity analysis can involve changing only one factor or a combination of factors in the ROI model. When more than one factor is changed, it is important to analyze exactly how much change is caused by each factor.

RESEARCH INSIGHT

Nonprofit Donations Decrease When Donors Believe Managers Are Overpaid   Over 1.4 million nonprofit organizations across the United States received more than $260 billion in donations during the year 2009. Yet with the weakening economy, contributors to nonprofit organizations are less willing to tolerate inflated salaries of the charity's executives. Specifically, donors decrease their contributions to the organization when the media reports an increase in executive compensation. On average, organizations that draw media coverage over executive compensation increases grow 15 percent less over the two years surrounding the media mention than their peer organizations. However, when this increase is reported on Form 990 for the Internal Revenue Service (IRS), only sophisticated donors reduce their contributions. Small donors may not know where to seek the compensation information out on their own, and larger donors have a greater stake in the stewardship of their donated funds. Among these larger donors, the study reports that contributions decrease by 3 percent for every $100,000 increase in executive compensation.

Source: Steven Balsam and Erica E. Harris, "The Impact of CEO Compensation on Nonprofit Donations," *The Accounting Review* 89, no. 2 (March 2014): 425 -50.

Statistics such as ROI, investment turnover, and return-on-sales mean little by themselves. They take on meaning only when compared with an objective, a trend, another division, a competitor, or an industry average. Many businesses establish minimum ROIs for each of their divisions, expecting them to attain or exceed this minimum return. The salaries, bonuses, and promotions of division managers can be tied directly to their division's ROI. Without other evaluation techniques, managers often strive for ROI maximization, sometimes to the long-run detriment of the entire organization.

Investment Center Income

Despite the relevance and conceptual simplicity of ROI, a division's ROI cannot be determined until management decides how to measure divisional income and investment. Divisional income equals divisional revenues less divisional operating expenses. Determining divisional revenues is usually a relatively easy task since revenues are typically generated and recorded at the division level, but determining total operating expenses for divisions is more complicated. Because many expenses are incurred at the corporate level for the common benefit of the various operating divisions and to support corporate headquarters operations, the cost assignment issues discussed early in this chapter affect investment center income.

Direct division expenses are always included in division operating expenses, but there are conflicting viewpoints about how to deal with common corporate expenses. As stated earlier in this chapter, in corporate annual reports, many companies are required to provide segment revenues and expenses segmented by product lines, geographic territories, customer markets, and so on. Companies also show operating income for their various segments in their annual reports, but they include a category called *corporate* or *unallocated* for company expenses that cannot be reasonably allocated to the various segments. ("Unallocated" typically includes costs for corporate staffs, certain goodwill writeoffs, and nonoperational gains and losses.) For example, the **Ericsson Inc.** 2015 annual report includes the following breakdown of its operating income by segments (stated in millions of Swedish kronas):

Networks	12,943 SEK
Global services.	8,215
Support solutions.	1,504
Modems[1]	7
Unallocated	(864)
Total operating income.	21,805 SEK

[1] Modems was closed during the second half of 2015

For internal segment reporting, some companies do not allocate corporate costs that cannot be associated closely with individual segments. Other companies insist on allocating all common corporate costs to the operating divisions to emphasize that the company does not earn a profit until revenues have covered all costs. Some top managers believe that since only operating divisions produce revenues, they should also bear all costs, including corporate costs. These managers want to ensure that the sum of the division income for the various segments equals the total income for the company.

Division managers do not control corporate costs; therefore, these costs are seldom relevant in evaluating a division manager's performance. To deal with this conflict, some companies allocate some, or possibly all, common corporate costs in reporting segment operating income, but for ROI calculation purposes exclude allocated corporate costs that are not closely associated with the divisions. These companies include in the ROI calculation costs that represent an identifiable benefit to the divisions but not general corporate costs that provide no identifiable benefits to the divisions. In practice, the treatment of corporate costs for division performance evaluation varies widely.

Investment Center Asset Base

Because the primary purpose for computing ROI is to evaluate the effectiveness of a division's operating management in using the assets entrusted to them, most organizations define *investment* as the average total assets of a division during the evaluation period. For most companies, the *investment base* is defined as each division's operating assets. These normally include those assets held for productive use, such as accounts receivable, inventory, and plant and equipment. Nonproductive assets, such as land for a future plant site, are not included in the investment base of a division but in the investment base for the company.

General corporate assets allocated to divisions should not be included in their bases. Although the divisions might need additional administrative facilities if they were truly independent, they have no control over the headquarters' facilities. The joint nature and use of corporate facility-level expenses make any allocation arbitrary.

Other Valuation Issues

Once divisional investment and income have been operationally defined and ROI computations have been made, the significance of the resulting ratios can still be questioned. Return on investment can be overstated in terms of constant dollars because inflation as well as arbitrary inventory and depreciation procedures cause an undervaluation of the inventory and fixed assets included in the investment center asset base. Asset measurement is particularly troublesome if inventories are valued at last-in, first-out (LIFO) cost and fixed assets were acquired many years ago. A division manager could hesitate to replace an old, inefficient asset with a new, efficient one because the replacement could lower income and ROI through an increased investment base and increased depreciation.

To improve the comparability between divisions with old and new assets when computing ROI, some firms value assets at original cost rather than at net book value (cost less accumulated depreciation). This procedure does not reflect inflation, however. An old asset that cost $120,000 ten years ago is still being compared with an asset that costs $200,000 today. A better solution could be to value old assets at their replacement cost, although replacement costs are often difficult to determine.

YOU MAKE THE CALL

You are the Division Vice President Division managers in your company are evaluated primarily based on division return on investment, and you recently received financial reports for your division for the most recent period and discovered that the ROI for your division was 14.5%; whereas, the target ROI for your division set by the CFO and the CEO was 15%. What action can you take to try to avoid missing your performance target for the next period? [Answer, p. 1038]

Residual Income

Residual income is an often-mentioned alternative to ROI for measuring investment center performance. **Residual income** is the excess of investment center income over the minimum rate or dollar of return. The *minimum rate of return* represents the rate that can be earned on alternative investments of similar risks, which is the opportunity cost of the investment. The *minimum dollar return* is computed as a percentage of the investment center's asset base. When residual income is the primary basis of evaluation, the management of each investment center is encouraged to maximize residual income rather than ROI. (We can again measure assets, sales, income, and so forth, as excluding all nonoperating components; similarly, the investment base can be measured as operating assets less operating liabilities).

To illustrate the computation, assume that a company requires a minimum return of 12 percent on each division's investment base. The residual income of a division with an annual net operating income of $2,000,000 and an investment base of $15,000,000 is $200,000 as computed here:

Division income	$2,000,000
Minimum return ($15,000,000 × 0.12)	(1,800,000)
Residual income.	$ 200,000

Economic Value Added

A variation of residual income, referred to as **economic value added** or **EVA**®, is also often used as a basis for evaluating investment center performance. (The term EVA is a registered trademark of the financial consulting firm of Stern Stewart and Company.) EVA is equal to income after taxes less the cost of capital employed. The three significant changes from the residual income computation in applying EVA are the use of an organization's weighted average cost of capital as the minimum return, *net assets* as the evaluation base, and after-tax income. **Weighted average cost of capital** is an average of the after-tax cost of all long-term borrowing and the cost of equity[1]; **net assets** are total assets less current liabilities. Economic value is added only if a division's taxable income exceeds its net cost of investing. (We can again measure assets, sales, income, and so forth, as excluding all nonoperating components; similarly, the net asset base can be measured as operating assets less operating liabilities.)

Using the preceding situation, assume that the company has a cost of capital of 10 percent, $1,800,000 in current liabilities, and a 30 percent tax rate. The economic value-added is $80,000, computed as follows:

Division income after taxes ($2,000,000 × 0.70)	$1,400,000
Cost of capital employed [($15,000,000 − $1,800,000) × 0.10]	(1,320,000)
Economic value added.	$ 80,000

Another differentiating characteristic of the EVA model is that it usually corrects for potential distortions in economic net income caused by generally accepted accounting principles (GAAP). In calculating EVA, the user can abandon any accounting principles that are viewed as distorting the measurement of wealth creation. In practice, EVA consultants have identified up to 150 different adjustments to GAAP income and equity that must be made to restore equity and income to their true economic values. Most companies use no more than about five adjustments (such as the capitalization of research and development cost and the elimination of goodwill write-offs).

Proponents of EVA argue that it is the best measure of managerial performance from the standpoint of maximizing the market value added to a firm through managerial decisions. They maintain that **market value added (MVA)**, which is the increase in market value of the firm for the period, is the definitive measure of wealth creation and that MVA is maximized by maximizing EVA. By maximizing the excess of economic net income over the cost of all outside capital invested in the firm, the firm should maximize its MVA in the long run.

One might ask why we should use EVA to estimate managerial contribution to the maximization of MVA, when we could simply measure how much market value has been added to the firm by considering changes in stock prices. In practice this does not work well because of short-run changes in market prices caused by overall market factors, not just firm-specific factors, and the inability of market prices to reflect divisional wealth creation that is not transparent. Also, many firms are not publicly traded, which makes determining market value changes problematic. Finally, companies want to measure managerial performance over specific segments of a firm, as well as the firm as a whole, but market values for individual segments are seldom available.

EVA provides a good operational metric for assessing managers' performance in terms of maximizing MVA over time. It is a model that can be used to guide managerial action. Companies that use EVA for evaluating performance use it in making a broad range of decisions such as evaluating capital expenditure proposals, adding or dropping a product line, or acquiring another company. Only alternatives that provide economic value are accepted. The following Businesss Insight box discusses how **Whole Foods** uses EVA to guide decisions about store locations.

---

[1] Weighted average cost of capital computations are covered in introductory corporate finance textbooks.

Which Measure Is Best?

Many executives view residual income or EVA as a better measure of managers' performance than ROI. They believe that residual income and EVA encourages managers to make profitable investments that managers might reject if being measured exclusively by ROI.

To illustrate, assume that three divisions of **Monsanto** have an opportunity to make an investment of $100,000 that requires $10,000 of additional current liabilities and that will generate a return of 20 percent. The manager of the Chemical Division is evaluated using ROI, the manager of the Agriculture Division is evaluated using residual income, and the manager of the Nutrition Division is evaluated using economic value added. The current ROI of each division is 24 percent. Each division has a current income of $120,000, a minimum return of 18 percent on invested capital, and a cost of capital of 14 percent. If each division has a current investment base of $500,000, current liabilities of $40,000, and a tax rate of 30 percent, the effect of the proposed investment on each division's performance is as follows:

	Current	+	Proposed	=	Total
Chemical Division					
Investment center income/Asset base	$120,000		$ 20,000		$140,000
	$500,000		$100,000		$600,000
ROI	24%		20%		23.3%
Agriculture Division					
Asset base	$500,000		$100,000		$600,000
Investment center income	$120,000		$ 20,000		$140,000
Minimum return (0.18 × base)	(90,000)		(18,000)		(108,000)
Residual income	$ 30,000		$ 2,000		$ 32,000
Nutrition Division					
Assets	$500,000		$100,000		$600,000
Current liabilities	(40,000)		(10,000)		(50,000)
Evaluation base	$460,000		$ 90,000		$550,000
Investment center income	$120,000		$ 20,000		$140,000
Income taxes (30%)	(36,000)		(6,000)		(42,000)
Income after taxes	84,000		14,000		98,000
Cost of capital (0.14 × base)	(64,400)		(12,600)		(77,000)
Economic value added	$ 19,600		$ 1,400		$ 21,000

The Chemical Division manager will not want to make the new investment because it reduces the current ROI from 24 percent to 23.3 percent. This is true, even though the company's minimum return is only 18 percent. Not wanting to explain a decline in the division's ROI, the manager will probably reject the opportunity even though it could have benefited the company as a whole.

The Agriculture Division manager will probably be happy to accept the new project because it increases residual income by $2,000. Any investment that provides a return more than the required minimum of 18 percent will be acceptable to the Agriculture Division manager. Given a profit maximization goal for the organization, the residual income method is preferred over ROI evaluations because it encourages division managers to accept all projects with returns above the 18 percent cutoff. The same is true for the Nutrition Division manager, although the EVA increase is not as high as that of the residual income because it has a different base.

The primary disadvantage of the residual income and EVA methods as comparative evaluation tools is that they measure performance in absolute dollars rather than percentages. Although they can be used to compare period-to-period results of the same division or with similar-size divisions, they cannot be used effectively to compare the performance of divisions of substantially different sizes. For example, the residual income of a multimillion dollar sales division should be higher than that of a half-million-dollar sales division. Because most performance evaluations and comparisons are made between units or alternative investments of different sizes, ROI continues to be extensively used. The following Business Insight box discusses the changing role of IT as the need for data management and analysis grows.

BUSINESS INSIGHT

Measuring the Value of an IT Project   Historically, a company's IT department has been a support department for the core business. According to research by **The Hackett Group**, the modern IT group has the opportunity to redefine its role as the need for data management and analysis grows. The issue facing leaders of IT departments is that traditional metrics for IT departments focus on minimizing costs. To redefine the role of the IT department, managers need to redefine the way department performance is measured. The Hackett Group recommends the use of key performance indicators (KPIs), developed with input from stakeholders across the organization, that focus on the transformative contribution of the IT department. In the past, IT supported the software and hardware that employees used to do their jobs. Now the IT group can support managers with information they can use to implement their strategic decisions.

Source: "IT Strives to Reinvent Itself Despite Budget Restrictions While Delivering Improved Information and Analytics," *The Hackett Group*, April 1, 2014.

MID-CHAPTER REVIEW 3

KBR Inc., a decentralized engineering and construction organization, has three divisions, Engineering, Construction, and Military. Assume corporate management desires a minimum return of 15 percent on its investments and has a 20 percent tax rate. Suppose the divisions' 2017 results follow (in thousands):

Division	Income	Investment
Engineering.	$30,000	$200,000
Construction.	50,000	250,000
Military	22,000	100,000

The company is planning an expansion project in 2018 that will cost $50,000,000 and return $9,000,000 per year.

REQUIRED
a. Compute the ROI for each division for 2017.
b. Compute the residual income for each division for 2017.
c. Rank the divisions according to their ROI and residual income.
d. Assume that other income and investments will remain unchanged. Determine the effect of the project by itself. What is the effect on ROI and residual income, if the new project is added to each division?

The solution to this review problem can be found on page 1055.

LO4 Describe the balanced scorecard as a comprehensive performance measurement system.

BALANCED SCORECARD

Although financial measures have been emphasized throughout this text, several sections stress that other measures, specifically qualitative measures, are important in evaluating managerial performance. This section examines one popular method of performance evaluation using *both* financial and nonfinancial information.

We might ask: why not use just financial measures? First, no single financial measure captures all performance aspects of an organization. More than one measure must be used. Second, financial measures have reporting time lags that could hinder timely decision making. Third, financial measures might not accurately capture the information needed for current decision making because of the delay that sometimes occurs between making financial investments and receiving their results. For example, building a new nuclear power plant can take several years with the investment in total assets increasing the entire time without generating any revenues.

Balanced Scorecard Framework

Comprehensive performance measurement systems are one suggested solution. The basic premise is to establish a set of diverse key performance indicators to monitor performance. The **balanced scorecard** is a performance measurement system that includes financial and operational measures related to a firm's goals and strategies. The balanced scorecard comprises several categories of measurements, the most common of which include the following:

- Financial
- Customer satisfaction
- Internal processes
- Innovation and learning

A balanced scorecard is usually a set of reports required of all common operating units in an organization. To facilitate the periodic evaluation of performance, a cover sheet (or sheets for a large operation) can be used to summarize the performance of each area using the established criteria for each category.

For example, **Einstein Brothers** might have a balanced scorecard that looks something like the one in **Exhibit 23.4**. This balanced scorecard uses four categories for evaluation and includes financial and nonfinancial information. Each category being monitored has information from the previous period and the standard related to the category. The report should always include the current period, at least one previous period, and some standard. Each store manager should attach documentation and an appropriate explanation as to the change in the measurements during the reporting period.

EXHIBIT 23.4 Balanced Scorecard Illustration			
	Standard	**Prior Period**	**Current Period**
Key financial indicators			
Cash flow	$ 25,000	$ 28,000	$ 21,000
Return on investment (ROI).	0.18	0.22	0.19
Sales.	$4,400,000	$4,494,000	$4,342,000
Key customer indicators			
Average customers per hour	75	80	71
Number of customer complaints per period.	22	21	17
Number of sales returns per period	10	8	5
Key operating indicators			
Bagels sold/produced per day ratio.	0.96	0.93	0.91
Daily units lost (burned, dropped, etc.).	25	32	34
Employee turnover per period	0.10	0.07	0.00
Key growth and innovation indicators			
New products introduced during period.	1	1	0
Products discontinued during period.	1	1	1
Number of sales promotions	3	3	2
Special offers, discounts, etc.	4	5	3

In making assessments with the evaluation categories, it is important to consider both trailing and leading performance measures. *Trailing measures* look backward at historical data while *leading measures* provide some idea of what to expect currently or in the near future. For example, in the financial category, ROI is a trailing indicator while a budget of production units and costs for the next period is a leading indicator. In the customer category, the number of sales invoices per store might tell us whether each store is maintaining its customer base (a trailing indicator) while the number of product complaints per 1000 invoices might be a leading indicator of customer satisfaction, quality control problems, and future sales.

The use of balanced scorecard systems to monitor and assess managerial and organizational performance is increasing worldwide. The following Business Insight discusses some of the complexities involved in the **Department of Education**'s implementation of the College Scorecard.

BUSINESS INSIGHT

Understanding Your Strategy: The First Step to a Balanced Scorecard   Since 2013, the **Department of Education** has been applying a modified version of the balanced scorecard to universities. The College Scorecard was developed to help prospective students evaluate universities before applying. Like all balanced scorecard approaches, the efficacy of the College Scorecard depends on how well what is measured reflects the underlying economics of the business or organization, which is reflected in both the praise and criticism of the College Scorecard. Proponents of the scorecard point to measurement of alumni debt and salaries as powerful reflections of important economic realities that prospective students should consider. Critics of the College Scorecard note that the data in the Scorecard does not allow students to compare themselves by major. A history major considering two schools can only compare average students at the two schools, not history majors at the two schools. Critics also point to the fact that the scorecard only considers full-time students who start and finish at the same school.

With all balanced scorecard approaches to performance evaluation, two essential considerations underpin success. First, the scorecard must be based on a clear understanding of the business activity. Second, the limitations of what can be measured should be carefully considered. Users of the scorecard approach must be careful to craft measurements that accurately reflect the underlying value creation process.

Sources: Peter McPherson and Andrew Kelly, "The College Scorecard Strikes Out," *Wall Street Journal*, March 16, 2015. Jonathan Rothwell, "Understanding the College Scorecard," *Brookings*, September 28, 2015.

A balanced scorecard gives management a perspective of the organization's performance on a recurring set of criteria. Since each reporting unit knows what reports are expected, no one is surprised by changing monthly requests for data. Because the multiple perspectives provide management a broad analysis of the organization's performance, it allows them to determine how and where the goals and objectives are either being achieved or not achieved.

For most management teams, the balanced scorecard highlights trade-offs between measures. For example, a substantial increase in customer satisfaction can result in a short-run decrease in ROI because the extra effort to please customers is expensive, thereby reducing ROI. A balanced scorecard can be filtered down the organization with successively lower-level operating units having their own scorecards that mimic those of the higher-level units. This provides all levels of management an opportunity to evaluate operations from more than just a financial perspective.

RESEARCH INSIGHT

A Picture May Be Worth a Higher Stock Price   In his book *The Winter of Our Discontent*, John Steinbeck wrote, "For the most part people are not curious except about themselves." Psychologists define narcissism as a sense of self-importance, uniqueness, entitlement, self-absorption, arrogance, and vanity. However, some of these same traits are correlated with leadership qualities. In a recent study, researchers investigate the link between CEO narcissism and financial performance, specifically, earnings per share (EPS) and stock price.

They measure CEO narcissism by examining the size and composition of the CEO's photograph in the annual report and components of the CEO's compensation package. They find that narcissistic managers are more likely to take actions that increase sales and production levels, such as extending lenient credit terms, offering sales discounts, and overproducing. There is no evidence that these same managers attempt to manage earnings through accrual-related actions.

Source: Kari Joseph Olsen, Kelsey Kay Dworkis, and S. Mark Young, "CEO Narcissism and Accounting: A Picture of Profits," *Journal of Management Accounting Research* 26, no. 2 (Fall 2014): 243 -67.

As with all management tools and techniques, the use of the balanced scorecard must be incorporated with the other information sources within the organization. Just as the accounting information system cannot stand alone in managing a business, neither can the balanced scorecard. Some areas could need extensive accounting information in great detail to make the best possible decision while other areas need great detail in production or service integration to be at the right place at the right time. By using a multi-faceted approach to managing, the organization should be able to better establish an operating strategy that coincides with its overall goals and objectives.

Balanced Scorecard and Strategy

When a balanced scorecard system is fully utilized to monitor and evaluate an organization's progress, it becomes a system for operationalizing the organization's strategy. Having a goal to maximize shareholder value or generate a certain income does not constitute a strategy. Maximizing shareholder value can be an overarching corporate goal, but it will not likely be realized without a well-developed strategy that identifies and establishes a balanced set of goals on various dimensions of performance.

A balanced scorecard can be the primary vehicle for translating strategy into action and establishing accountability for performance. The balanced scorecard identifies the areas of managerial action that are believed to be the drivers of corporate achievement. If the corporate goal is to increase ROI or residual income, the balanced scorecard should include key performance indicators that drive these measures.

An interesting parallel to the successful management of a company can be drawn by considering the key performance indicators the manager of a professional baseball team uses in setting goals and evaluating progress. The manager of the New York Yankees does not just tell his players and managers at the beginning of the baseball season that the team's goal is to win the World Series or even a certain number of ball games. The win-loss record is only one metric used to set goals and evaluate performance for a baseball team. The manager looks at many different drivers of success related to hitting, pitching, and fielding, including the earned-run averages of the pitchers, the batting and on-base averages of hitters, the number of errors per game by fielders, and the number of bases stolen by base runners. At the end of the season, the manager measures success not just by whether the Yankees won the World Series, but also by the batting average, number of home runs, and number of bases stolen by individual players, and whether or not a team member won a Golden Glove award or the Cy Young award. These are all measures by which to evaluate achievement and strategic accomplishment. By achieving the goals for each of these areas of the game, the win-loss ratio will take care of itself. If the win-loss results are not acceptable, then the manager adjusts his strategic goals with respect to the key performance indicators (or the manager is dismissed).

Like a baseball team, a company can use a balanced scorecard to develop performance metrics for managers from the top of the company to the lowest-level department. The scorecard becomes a vehicle for communicating the factors that are key to the success of managers, factors that upper management will monitor in evaluating the success of lower managers in carrying out the corporate strategy. To make balanced scorecards more user friendly, several companies use performance monitoring **dashboards**, which are computer generated graphics that present scorecard results using graphics, some of which mimic the instrument displays on an automobile dashboard.

The following Business Insight provides an illustration of dashboard graphics.

BUSINESS INSIGHT

Balanced Scorecard Dashboard Balanced scorecard dashboards provide information about an organization in an "at-a-glance" format. Many software companies now provide utilities for generating dashboards from SAP, Excel, QuickBooks, and other databases. The following is an example of a dashboard for Sonatica, a fictional company, designed by Dundas Dashboard for assessment of financial performance. The shaded tabs present financial information graphics for Sales and Support. Additional screens would provide performance data on other scorecard dimensions such as internal processes, customers, and innovation and growth.

continued

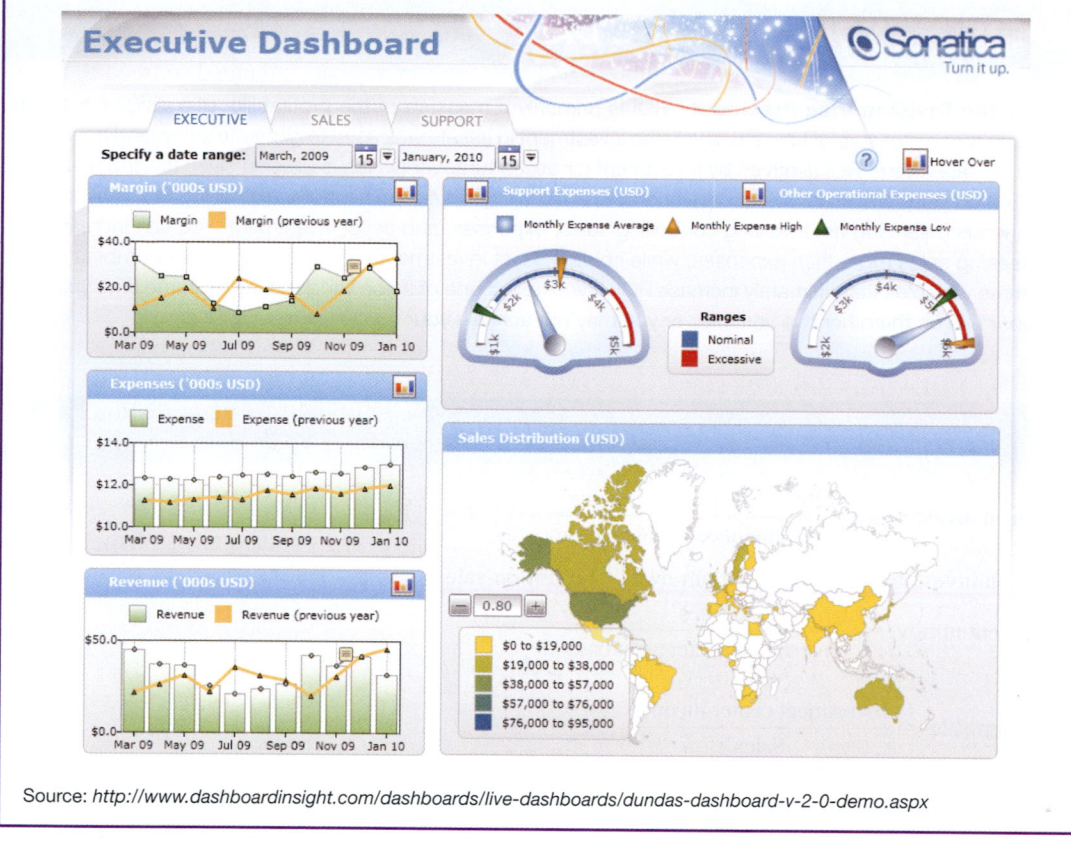

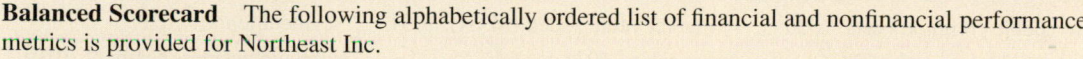

Source: *http://www.dashboardinsight.com/dashboards/live-dashboards/dundas-dashboard-v-2-0-demo.aspx*

CHAPTER-END REVIEW

Balanced Scorecard   The following alphabetically ordered list of financial and nonfinancial performance metrics is provided for Northeast Inc.

Average call wait	New product acceptance rate
Average customer survey rating	New product revenue
Employee turnover ratio	New product ROI
Expense as a % of revenue	Net profit
Expense variance %	Net profit margin
Fulfillment %	Number of complaints
Headcount growth	Number of defects reported
Industry quality rating	Service error rate
Job offer acceptance rate	Time to market on new products
Market share	Unique repeat customer count
New customer count	Year over year revenue growth
New customer sales value	

REQUIRED

a. Assign the above metrics to the four balanced scorecard categories of (1) Financial Success, (2) Customer Satisfaction and Brand Improvement, (3) Business Process Improvement, (4) Learning and Growth of Motivated Workforce.

b. Comment on the use of balanced scorecard versus a single financial measure such as ROI or EVA.

The solution to this review problem can be found on page 1056.

GUIDANCE ANSWERS . . . YOU MAKE THE CALL

You are the Division Vice President   ROI is primarily a measure of the profitability of a division's assets, which is in turn a measure of how effectively the investment in assets was used to generate sales, and how profitable those sales were. ROI is driven by investment (or asset) turnover (which is division sales divided by assets) and return on sales (which is division net income divided division sales). Therefore, increasing ROI is similar to a simultaneous balancing act involving controlling sales, expenses, and asset investment. You can increase ROI by increasing sales more than expenses, while holding asset investment constant, or by other combinations of these three variables that ultimately increase ROI. If you adjust one of these variables, at the same time you must keep your eye on the other two variables or you may not achieve your goal of increasing ROI.

KEY RATIOS

$$\text{Return on investment} = \frac{\text{Investment center income}}{\text{Investment center asset base}}$$

$$\text{Return on investment} = \text{Investment turnover} \times \text{Return-on-sales}$$

$$\text{Investment turnover} = \frac{\text{Sales}}{\text{Investment center asset base}}$$

$$\text{Return-on-sales} = \frac{\text{Investment center income}}{\text{Sales}}$$

$$\text{Return on investment} = \frac{\text{Sales}}{\text{Investment center base}} \times \frac{\text{Investment center income}}{\text{Sales}} = \frac{\text{Investment center income}}{\text{Investment center asset base}}$$

KEY TERMS

avoidable common costs, 1020

balanced scorecard, 1034

common segment costs, 1019

dashboards, 1036

direct segment fixed costs, 1018

economic value added or
    EVA®, 1031

market value added (MVA), 1031

net assets, 1031

residual income, 1030

return on investment (ROI), 1026

segment income, 1020

segment margin, 1019

segment reports, 1017

strategic business segment, 1016

transfer price, 1021

weighted average cost of
    capital, 1031

Assignments with the 🔴 **logo in the margin are available in** BusinessCourse.
See the Preface of the book for details.

MULTIPLE CHOICE

Multiple Choice Answers
1. c   2. d   3. a   4. c   5. a   6. d

1. Northern Communications Inc. has two divisions (Individual and Business) and has the following information available for the current year:

Sales revenue—Individual	$3,000,000
Sales revenue—Business	5,000,000
Variable costs—Individual	1,200,000
Variable costs—Business	2,250,000
Direct fixed costs, Individual	400,000
Direct fixed costs, Business	550,000
Allocated fixed costs—Individual	250,000
Allocated fixed costs—Business	350,000
Unallocated common fixed costs	150,000

Northern Communications Inc.'s Business segment income is
a. $2,400,000
b. $2,200,000
c. $1,850,000
d. $1,765,250

2. Refer to the previous question. The following information is available for the Individual Division, which has two product lines (Land and Mobile):

Sales revenue—Land	$1,200,000
Sales revenue—Mobile	1,800,000
Variable costs—Land	680,000
Variable costs—Mobile	520,000
Direct fixed costs—Land	150,000
Direct fixed costs—Mobile	125,000
Allocated fixed costs—Land	100,000
Allocated fixed costs—Mobile	150,000
Unallocated common fixed costs	125,000

The product margin for Land is
a. $270,000
b. $170,000
c. $520,000
d. $370,000

3. Varcore Inc. is currently acquiring a key component from it's sister company, Farcore Inc. at a transfer price of $10 per unit. Farcore's variable cost of purchasing the unit is $4, and it's fixed cost per unit is $3 per unit. Farcore does not have any excess capacity and can sell all it makes to external customers at $10 per unit. Varcore has been offered a price of $9 per unit for the component from another vendor and is insisting that Farcore reduce its price to $9. Which of the following statements below is false regarding this scenario?
    a. Varcore should not accept the outside offer because the variable cost of purchasing it inside is only $4 per unit.
    b. Varcore should purchase the unit externally because the internal cost of purchasing the unit internally is a variable cost of $4 per unit plus an opportunity cost of $6 per unit, or $10.
    c. The company will be better off if Farcore rejects Varcore's demand and instead sells the units that Varcore would buy to outside customers.
    d. Since Farcore is operating at full capacity and has other external customers ready to purchase additional units, the best transfer price is its regular market price.

4. Shealy's Lawn and Garden Supply Company has recently acquired a lawn sod company that grows turf grasses for lawns. Previously, Shealy's was purchasing sod from other suppliers at 50 cents per square foot. The new sod division, which has substantial excess capacity, is able to produce grass sod at a cost of 35 cents per square foot, including direct materials and direct labor cost of 25 cents, variable overhead of 5 cents, and fixed overhead of 5 cents per square foot. The supply division manager argues that the transfer price should be no more than 35 cents per square foot. What transfer price between the sod and the supply divisions will lead the manger of the supply division to act in a manner that will maximize company profits?
    a. 50 cents
    b. 25 cents
    c. 30 cents
    d. 35 cents

5. SGA Inc., a division of AGS Inc., had sales of $4,000,000, total assets of $2,000,000, and net income of $400,000. Senior management of AGS Inc. has set a target minimum rate of return for SGA Inc. of 18%. Calculate SGA's residual income.
    a. $40,000
    b. $36,000
    c. $72,000
    d. None of the above

6. Which of the following is not one of the four most common categories of measurement presented in a balanced scorecard?
   a. Financial
   b. Internal processes
   c. Innovation and learning
   d. External processes

QUESTIONS

Q23-1. What is the relationship between segment reports and product reports?

Q23-2. What is a reporting objective? How is it determined?

Q23-3. Can a company have more than one type of first-level statement in segment reporting?

Q23-4. Explain the relationships between any two levels of statements in segment reporting.

Q23-5. Distinguish between direct and indirect segment costs.

Q23-6. What types of information are needed before management should decide to drop a segment?

Q23-7. In what types of organizations and for what purpose are transfer prices used?

Q23-8. What problems arise when transfer pricing is used?

Q23-9. When do transfer prices lead to suboptimization? How can suboptimization be minimized? Can it be eliminated? Why or why not?

Q23-10. For what purpose do organizations use return on investment? Why is this measure preferred to net income?

Q23-11. What advantages do residual income and EVA have over ROI for segment evaluations?

Q23-12. Contrast the difference between residual income and EVA.

Q23-13. Explain how a balanced scorecard helps with the evaluation process of internal operations.

Q23-14. How can a balanced scorecard be used as a strategy implementation tool?

MINI EXERCISES

LO1

M23-15. **Multiple Levels of Segment Reporting**

Connect Inc. manufactures four different lines of computer devices: modems, routers, servers, and drives. Each of the product lines is produced in all of the company's three plants: Beckley, Huntington, and Charleston. Marketing efforts of the company are divided into five regions: East, West, South, North, and Central.

REQUIRED

a. Develop a reporting schematic that illustrates how the company might prepare single-level reports segmented on three different bases.

b. Develop a segment reporting schematic that has three different levels. Be sure to identify each segment's level. Briefly explain why you chose the primary-level segment.

LO1

M23-16. **Income Statements Segmented by Territory**

Writing Inc. has two product lines. The September income statements of each product line and the company are as follows:

WRITING INC.
Product Line and Company Income Statements
For Month of September

	Pens	Pencils	Total
Sales.	$45,000	$45,000	$90,000
Less variable expenses	(18,000)	(18,000)	(36,000)
Contribution margin	27,000	27,000	54,000
Less direct fixed expenses.	(13,500)	(10,500)	(24,000)
Product margin.	$13,500	$16,500	30,000
Less common fixed expenses			(9,000)
Net income.			$21,000

Pens and pencils are sold in two territories, Vermont and Washington, as follows:

	Vermont	Washington
Pen sales	$27,000	$18,000
Pencil sales	13,500	31,500
Total sales.	$40,500	$49,500

The common fixed expenses are traceable to each territory as follows:

Vermont fixed expenses.	$3,000
Washington fixed expenses	4,500
Home office administration fixed expenses.	1,500
Total common fixed expenses	$9,000

The direct fixed expenses of pens, $13,500, and of pencils, $10,500, cannot be identified with either territory. The company's accountants were unable to allocate any of the common fixed expenses to the various segments.

REQUIRED

Prepare income statements segmented by territory for September, including a column for the entire firm.

M23-17. **Income Statements Segmented by Products**

Francisco Consulting Firm provides three types of client services in three health-care-related industries. The income statement for July is as follows:

LO1

FRANCISCO CONSULTING FIRM
Income Statement
For Month of July

Sales.		$450,000
Less variable costs.		(325,000)
Contribution margin		125,000
Less fixed expenses		
Service	$35,000	
Selling and administrative.	32,500	(67,500)
Net income.		$ 57,500

The sales, contribution margin ratios, and direct fixed expenses for the three types of services are as follows:

	Hospitals	Physicians	Nursing Care
Sales.	$175,000	$125,000	$150,000
Contribution margin ratio	25%	35%	25%
Direct fixed expenses of services.	$ 10,000	$ 9,000	$ 8,000
Allocated common fixed services expense	$ 500	$ 500	$ 750

REQUIRED

Prepare income statements segmented by client categories. Include a column for the entire firm in the statement.

LO2 **M23-18. Internal or External Acquisitions: No Opportunity Costs**

The Van Division of Travel Vans Corporation has offered to purchase 180,000 wheels from the Wheel Division for $76 per wheel. At a normal volume of 500,000 wheels per year, production costs per wheel for the Wheel Division are as follows:

Direct materials	$26
Direct labor.	20
Variable overhead.	12
Fixed overhead.	30
Total	$88

The Wheel Division has been selling 500,000 wheels per year to outside buyers at $106 each. Capacity is 700,000 wheels per year. The Van Division has been buying wheels from outside suppliers at $100 per wheel.

REQUIRED

a. Should the Wheel Division manager accept the offer? Show computations.

b. From the standpoint of the company, will the internal sale be beneficial?

LO2 **M23-19. Transfer Prices at Full Cost with Excess Capacity: Divisional Viewpoint**

Karakomi Cameras Inc. has a Disposables Division that produces a camera that sells for $13.00 per unit in the open market. The cost of the product is $9.50 (variable manufacturing of $5.00, plus fixed manufacturing of $4.50). Total fixed manufacturing costs are $315,000 at the normal annual production volume of 70,000 units. The Overseas Division has offered to buy 20,000 units at the full cost of $9.50. The Disposables Division has excess capacity, and the 20,000 units can be produced without interfering with the current outside sales of 70,000 units. The total fixed cost of the Disposables Division will not change.

REQUIRED

Explain whether the Disposables Division should accept or reject the offer. Show calculations.

LO2 M23-20. Transfer Pricing with Excess Capacity: Divisional and Corporate Viewpoints

Affordable Art Company has a Print Division that is currently producing 100,000 prints per year but has a capacity of 150,000 prints. The variable costs of each print are $28, and the annual fixed costs are $1,200,000. The prints sell for $40 in the open market. The company's Retail Division wants to buy 50,000 prints at $22 each. The Print Division manager refuses the order because the price is below variable cost. The Retail Division manager argues that the order should be accepted because it will lower the fixed cost per print from $12 to $8.

REQUIRED

a. Should the Retail Division order be accepted? Why or why not?

b. From the viewpoints of the Print Division and the company, should the order be accepted if the manager of the Retail Division intends to sell each print in the outside market for $37 after incurring additional costs of $8 per print?

c. What action should the company take, assuming it believes in divisional autonomy?

LO3 **M23-21. ROI and Residual Income: Impact of a New Investment**

The Stallion Division of Motortown Motors had an operating income of $675,000 and net assets of $2,700,000. Motortown Motors has a target rate of return of 23 percent.

REQUIRED

a. Compute the return on investment.

b. Compute the residual income.

c. The Stallion Division has an opportunity to increase operating income by $100,000 with an $675,000 investment in assets.
  1. Compute the Stallion Division's return on investment if the project is undertaken. (Round your answer to three decimal places.)
  2. Compute the Stallion Division's residual income if the project is undertaken.

M23-22.   ROI: Fill in the Unknowns **LO3**
Provide the missing data in the following situations:

	Eastern Division	Western Division	Southern Division
Sales.	?	$6,000,000	?
Net operating income.	$180,000	$ 360,000	$120,000
Operating assets	?	?	$600,000
Return on investment.	25%	18%	?
Return on sales	0.05	?	0.08
Investment turnover	?	?	2.5

M23-23.   Selection of Balanced Scorecard Items **LO4**
The Worldwide Auditors' Association is a professional association. Its current membership totals 97,600 worldwide. The association operates from a central headquarters in New Zealand but has local membership units throughout the world. The local units hold monthly meetings to discuss recent developments in accounting and to hear professional speakers on topics of interest. The association's journal, *Worldwide Auditor,* is published monthly with feature articles and topical interest areas. The association publishes books and reports and sponsors continuing education courses. A statement of revenues and expenses follows:

WORLDWIDE AUDITORS' ASSOCIATION Statement of Revenues and Expenses For Year Ending November 30, 2017 ($ in thousands)		
Revenues		$55,054
Expenses		
Salaries.	$29,000	
Other personnel costs	6,786	
Occupancy costs	5,650	
Reimbursement to local units.	1,600	
Other membership services	1,000	
Printing and paper	640	
Postage and shipping.	242	
General and administrative.	1,076	(45,994)
Excess of revenues over expenses		$ 9,060

Additional information follows:
- Membership dues are $400 per year, of which $100 is considered to cover a one-year subscription to the association's journal. Other benefits include membership in the association and unit affiliation.
- One-year subscriptions to *Worldwide Auditor* are sold to nonmembers for $160 each. A total of 2,500 of these subscriptions were sold. In addition to subscriptions, the journal generated $400,000 in advertising revenue. The cost per magazine was $40.
- A total of 30,000 technical reports were sold by the Books and Reports Department at an average unit selling price of $90. Average costs per publication were $24.
- The association offers a variety of continuing education courses to both members and nonmembers. During 2017, the one-day course, which cost participants an average of $500 each, was attended by 31,300 people. A total of 1,985 people took two-day courses at a cost of $800 per person.
- General and administrative expenses include all other costs incurred by the corporate staff to operate the association.
- The organization has net capital assets of $90,060,000 and had an actual cost of capital of 9 percent.

REQUIRED

a. Give some examples of key financial performance indicators (no computations needed) that could be part of a balanced scorecard for the IAA.

b. Give some examples of key customer and operating performance indicators (no computations needed) that could be part of a balanced scorecard for IAA.

EXERCISES

LO2 **E23-24.** **Appropriate Transfer Prices: Opportunity Costs**

J. Carter Peanut Butter Company recently acquired a peanut-processing company that has a normal annual capacity of 4,000,000 pounds and that sold 2,800,000 pounds last year at a price of $3.50 per pound. The purpose of the acquisition is to furnish peanuts for the peanut butter plant, which needs 1,600,000 pounds of peanuts per year. It has been purchasing peanuts from suppliers at the market price. Production costs per pound of the peanut-processing company are as follows:

Direct materials	$0.90
Direct labor	0.52
Variable overhead	0.22
Fixed overhead at normal capacity	0.30
Total	$1.94

Management is trying to decide what transfer price to use for sales from the newly acquired Peanut Division to the Peanut Butter Division. The manager of the Peanut Division argues that $3.50, the market price, is appropriate. The manager of the Peanut Butter Division argues that the cost price of $1.94 (or perhaps even less) should be used since fixed overhead costs should be recomputed. Any output of the Peanut Division up to 2,800,000 pounds that is not sold to the Peanut Butter Division could be sold to regular customers at $3.50 per pound.

REQUIRED

a. Compute the annual gross profit for the Peanut Division using a transfer price of $3.50.

b. Compute the annual gross profit for the Peanut Division using a transfer price of $1.94.

c. What transfer price(s) will lead the manager of the Peanut Butter Division to act in a manner that will maximize company profits?

LO2 **E23-25.** **Negotiating a Transfer Price with Excess Capacity**

The Foundry Division of Findlay Pumps Inc. produces metal parts that are sold to the company's Assembly Division and to outside customers. Operating data for the Foundry Division for 2017 are as follows:

	To the Assembly Division	To Outside Customers	Total
Sales			
400,000 parts × $6.00	$2,400,000		
300,000 parts × $6.50		$1,950,000	$4,350,000
Variable expenses at $3.00	(1,200,000)	(900,000)	(2,100,000)
Contribution margin	1,200,000	1,050,000	2,250,000
Fixed expenses*	(700,000)	(525,000)	1,225,000
Net income	$ 500,000	$ 525,000	$1,025,000

*Allocated on the basis of unit sales.

The Assembly Division has just received an offer from an outside supplier to supply parts at $4.50 each. The Foundry Division manager is not willing to meet the $4.50 price. She argues that it costs her $4.75 per part to produce and sell to the Assembly Division, so she would show no profit on the Assembly Division sales. Sales to outside customers are at a maximum, 300,000 parts.

REQUIRED
a. Verify the Foundry Division's $4.75 unit cost figure.
b. Should the Foundry Division meet the outside price of $4.50 for Assembly Division sales? Explain.
c. Could the Foundry Division meet the $4.50 price and still show a net profit for sales to the Assembly Division? Show computations.

E23-26. **Dual Transfer Pricing**

The Athens Company has two divisions, Alpha and Delta. Delta Division produces a product at a variable cost of $7 per unit, and sells 150,000 units to outside customers at $12 per unit and 40,000 units to Alpha Division at variable cost plus 40 percent. Under the dual transfer price system, Alpha Division pays only the variable cost per unit. Delta Division's fixed costs are $275,000 per year. Alpha Division sells its finished product to outside customers at $25 per unit. Alpha has variable costs of $5 per unit, in addition to the costs from Delta Division. Alpha Division's annual fixed costs are $180,000. There are no beginning or ending inventories.

REQUIRED
a. Prepare the income statements for the two divisions and the company as a whole.
b. Why is the income for the company less than the sum of the profit figures shown on the income statements for the two divisions? Explain.

E23-27. **ROI and Residual Income: Basic Computations**

LO3

Watkins Associated Industries is a highly diversified company with three divisions: Trucking, Seafood, and Construction. Assume that the company uses return on investment and residual income as two of the evaluation tools for division managers. The company has a minimum desired rate of return on investment of 15 percent with a 30 percent tax rate. Selected operating data for three divisions of the company follow.

Watkins Associated
Industries

	Trucking Division	Seafood Division	Construction Division
Sales.................	$1,250,000	$800,000	$950,000
Operating assets	650,000	300,000	400,000
Net operating income....	146,250	52,800	79,600

REQUIRED
a. Compute the return on investment for each division. (Round answers to three decimal places.)
b. Compute the residual income for each division.

E23-28. **ROI and Residual Income: Assessing Performance**

LO3

Refer to the computations in the previous exercise E23-27. Assess the performance of the division managers, basing your conclusions on ROI. Assess the performance of the division managers, basing your conclusions on Residual Income. Which manager is doing the best job?

E23-29. **ROI, Residual Income, and EVA with Different Bases**

LO3

Envision Company has a target return on capital of 12 percent. The following financial information is available for October ($ thousands):

	Software Division (Value Base)		Consulting Division (Value Base)		Venture Capital Division (Value Base)	
	Book	Current	Book	Current	Book	Current
Sales...........	$100,000	$100,000	$200,000	$200,000	$800,000	$800,000
Income	12,250	11,700	16,400	20,020	56,730	51,920
Assets..........	70,000	90,000	100,000	110,000	610,000	590,000
Liabilities.......	10,000	10,000	14,000	14,000	40,000	40,000

REQUIRED
a. Compute the return on investment using both book and current values for each division. (Round answers to three decimal places.)
b. Compute the residual income for both book and current values for each division.
c. Compute the economic value added income for both book and current values for each division if the tax rate is 30 percent and the weighted average cost of capital is 10 percent.
d. Does book value or current value provide a better basis for performance evaluation? Which division do you consider the most successful?

LO4

E23-30. **Balanced Scorecard Preparation**

The following information is in addition to that presented in Mini Exercise 23-23 for the World-wide Auditors' Association. For the year ended November 30, 2017, the organization had set a membership goal of 100,000 members with the following anticipated results:

Worldwide Auditors' Association Planned Revenues and Expenses For Year Ending November 30, 2017 ($ in thousands)		
Revenues		$55,859.6
Expenses		
Salaries	27,900.0	
Other personnel costs	6,975.0	
Occupancy costs	3,859.6	
Reimbursement to local units.	1,480.0	
Other membership services	1,050.0	
Printing and paper	525.0	
Postage and shipping.	220.0	
General and administrative.	1,090.0	(43,099.6)
Excess of revenues over expenses		$12,760.0

Additional information follows:
- Membership dues were increased from $360 to $400 at the beginning of the year.
- One-year subscriptions to *Worldwide Auditor* were anticipated to be 2,400 units.
- Advertising revenue was budgeted at $320,000. Each magazine was budgeted at a cost of $36.
- A total of 29,000 technical reports were anticipated at an average price of $80 with average costs of $22.
- The budgeted one-day courses had an anticipated attendance of 33,000 with an average fee of $450. The two-day courses had an anticipated attendance of 3,000 with an average fee of $770 per person.
- The organization began the year with net capital assets of $88,000,000 with a planned cost of capital of 9 percent.

REQUIRED

a. Prepare a balanced scorecard for IAA for November 2017 with calculated key performance indicators presented in two columns for planned performance and actual performance—include key financial, customer, and operating performance indicators.

b. Which of the evaluation areas you selected indicated success and which indicated failure?

c. Give some explanations of the successes and failures.

PROBLEMS

LO1

P23-31. **Multiple Segment Reports**

Worldwide Communications, Incorporated, sells telecommunication products throughout the world in three sales territories: Europe, Asia, and the Americas. For July, all $650,000 of administrative expense is traceable to the territories, except $100,000, which is common to all units and cannot be traced or allocated to the sales territories. The percentage of product line sales made in each of the sales territories and the assignment of traceable fixed expenses follow:

	Sales Territory			
	Europe	**Asia**	**The Americas**	**Total**
Handset sales.	50%	30%	20%	100%
Switchboard sales	40	40	20	100
Automated switches sales	10	30	60	100
Fixed administrative expense.	$200,000	$200,000	$150,000	$ 550,000
Fixed selling expense.	$350,000	$650,000	$650,000	$1,650,000

The manufacturing takes place in one large facility with three distinct manufacturing operations. Selected product-line cost data follow.

	Handset	Switchboard	Automated Switches	Total
Variable costs....................	$ 18	$ 790	$ 1,975	
Depreciation and supervision..........	200,000	200,000	170,000	$ 600,000*
Other mfg. overhead (common)...				150,000
Fixed administrative expense (common).........................				650,000
Fixed selling expense (common).....................................				1,550,000

*Includes common costs of $30,000

The unit sales and selling prices for each product follow.

	Unit Sales	Selling Price
Handset...	10,500	$ 50
Switchboard....................................	2,500	1,500
Automated......................................	2,000	3,200

REQUIRED

a. Prepare an income statement for July segmented by product line. Include a column for the entire firm.

b. Prepare an income statement for July segmented by sales territory. Include a column for the entire firm.

c. Prepare an income statement for July by product line for The Americas sales territory. Include a column for the territory as a whole.

d. Discuss the value of multilevel segment reporting as a managerial tool. Compare and contrast the benefits of the reports generated in parts a, b, and c.

P23-32. Segment Reporting and Analysis   LO1
California Bread Company bakes three products: donuts, bread, and pasteries. It sells them in the cities of San Francisco and San Jose. For March, its first month of operation, the following income statement was prepared:

CALIFORNIA BREAD COMPANY Territory and Company Income Statements For Month of March			
	San Francisco	San Jose	Total
Sales....................................	$4,200	$1,000	$5,200
Cost of goods sold......................	(3,000)	(600)	(3,600)
Gross profit.............................	1,200	400	1,600
Selling and administrative expenses	(800)	(450)	(1,250)
Net income.............................	$ 400	$ (50)	$ 350

Sales and selected variable expense data are as follows:

	Products		
	Donuts	Bread	Pastries
Fixed baking expenses.....................................	$ 400	$ 280	$200
Variable baking expenses as a percentage of sales	50%	50%	60%
Variable selling expenses as a percentage of sales..........	4%	4%	6%
City of San Francisco, sales...........................	$1,700	$1,800	$700
City of San Jose, sales................................	$ 400	$ 300	$300

The fixed selling expenses were $770 for March, of which $320 was a direct expense of the San Francisco market and $450 was a direct expense of the San Jose market. Fixed administrative expenses were $260, which management has decided not to allocate when using the contribution approach.

REQUIRED

a. Prepare a segment income statement showing the territory margin for each sales territory for March. Include a column for the entire firm.

b. Prepare segment income statements showing the product margin for each product. Include a column for the entire firm.

c. If the pastries line is dropped and fixed baking expenses do not change, what is the product margin for donuts and bread?

d. What other type of segmentation might be useful to California Bread. Explain.

LO1 **P23-33.** **Segment Reporting and Analysis**

College Textbook Publishers Inc. has prepared income statements segmented by divisions, but management is still uncertain about actual performance. Financial information for May is given as follows:

	Textbook Division	Professional Division	Company Total
Sales.	$100,000	$205,000	$305,000
Less variable expenses			
Manufacturing.	16,000	102,500	118,500
Selling and administrative.	2,200	12,300	14,500
Total	(18,200)	(114,800)	(133,000)
Contribution margin	81,800	90,200	172,000
Less direct fixed expenses.	(10,000)	(100,000)	(110,000)
Net income.	$ 71,800	$ (9,800)	$ 62,000

Management is concerned about the Professional Division and requests additional analysis. Additional information regarding May operations of the Professional Division is as follows:

	Professional Division		
	Accounting Books Segment	Executive Books Segment	Management Books Segment
Sales.	$70,000	$70,000	$65,000
Variable manufacturing expenses as a percentage of sales.	60%	40%	50%
Other variable expenses as a percentage of sales.	6%	6%	6%
Direct fixed expenses.	$25,000	$36,750	$25,000
Allocated common fixed expenses	$ 2,000	$ 1,000	$ 3,000

The professional accounting books are sold to auditors and controllers. The current information on these markets is as follows:

	Accounting Books Segment		
	Auditors Market	Controllers Market	Total
Sales.	$15,000	$55,000	$70,000
Variable manufacturing expenses as a percentage of sales.	60%	60%	—
Other variable expenses as a percentage of sales.	6%	6%	—
Direct fixed expenses.	$ 7,500	$15,000	$22,500
Allocated common fixed expenses	$ 750	$ 1,000	$ 1,750

REQUIRED

a. Prepare an income statement segmented by product for the Professional Division. Include a column for the division as a whole.

b. Prepare an income statement segmented by market for the Accounting Books Segment of the Professional Division.

c. Evaluate which Accounting Books Segment the Professional Division should keep or discontinue in the short run.

d. What is the correct long-run decision? Explain fully, including any possible risks associated with your recommendation.

P23-34.   Segment Reports and Cost Allocations   LO1

All Things Greek Inc. has three sales divisions. One of the key evaluation inputs for each division manager is the performance of his or her division based on division income. The division statements for August are as follows:

	Alpha	Beta	Gamma	Total
Sales..........................	$200,000	$250,000	$225,000	$675,000
Cost of sales...................	100,000	120,000	115,000	335,000
Division overhead..............	50,000	55,000	55,000	160,000
Division expenses..............	(150,000)	(175,000)	(170,000)	(495,000)
Division contribution...........	50,000	75,000	55,000	180,000
Corporate overhead............	(35,000)	(45,000)	(40,000)	(120,000)
Division income	$ 15,000	$ 30,000	$ 15,000	$ 60,000

The Gamma manager is unhappy that his profitability is the same as that of the Alpha Division and one-half that of the Beta Division when his sales are halfway between these two divisions. The manager knows that his division must carry more product lines because of customer demands, and many of these additional product lines are not very profitable. He has not dropped these marginal product lines because of idle capacity; all of the products cover their own variable costs. After analyzing the product lines with the lowest profit margins, the divisional controller for Gamma provided the following to the manager:

Sales of marginal products.....................................	$45,000	
Cost of sales..	$25,000	
Avoidable fixed costs.......................................	11,000	(36,000)
Product margin...		9,000
Proportion of corporate overhead		(8,000)
Product income		$ 1,000

Although these products were 20 percent of Gamma's total sales, they contributed only about 7 percent of the division's profits. The controller also noted that the corporate overhead allocation was based on a formula of sales and divisional contribution margin.

REQUIRED

a. Prepare a set of segment statements for August assuming that all facts remain the same except that Gamma's weak product lines are dropped and corporate overhead is allocated as follows: Alpha, $40,000; Beta, $47,500; and Gamma, $32,500. Does the Gamma Division appear better after this action? What will be the responses of the other two division managers?

b. Suggest improvements for All Things Greek's reporting process that will better reflect the actual operations of the divisions. Keep in mind the utilization of the reporting process to assist in the evaluation of the managers. What other changes could be made to improve the manager evaluation process?

P23-35.   ROI, Residual Income, and EVA: Impact of a New Investment   LO3

EEG Inc. is a decentralized organization with four autonomous divisions. The divisions are evaluated on the basis of the change in their return on invested assets. Operating results in the Commercial Division for 2017 follow:

EEG INC.—COMMERCIAL DIVISION Income Statement For Year Ending December 31, 2017	
Sales.	$1,562,500
Less variable expenses	(800,000)
Contribution margin	762,500
Less fixed expenses.	(500,000)
Net operating income.	$ 262,500

Operating assets for the Commercial Division currently average $1,500,000. The Commercial Division can add a new product line for an investment of $250,000. Relevant data for the new product line are as follows:

Sales.	$375,000
Variable expenses (% of sales).	0.60
Fixed expenses	$125,000
Increase in current liabilities.	$ 10,000

REQUIRED

a. Determine the effect on ROI of accepting the new product line. (Round calculations to three decimal places.)

b. If a return of 6 percent is the minimum that any division should earn and residual income is used to evaluate managers, would this encourage the division to accept the new product line? Explain and show computations.

c. If EVA is used to evaluate managers, should the new product line be accepted if the weighted average cost of capital is 6 percent and the income tax rate is 30 percent?

LO3 **P23-36.** **Valuing Investment Center Assets**

Six Flags Theme Parks Inc.

NYSE :: SIX

Six Flags Theme Parks Inc. operates theme parks in the United States, Mexico, and Europe. One of its first theme parks, Six Flags over Georgia, was built in the 1960s in Atlanta on a large tract of land that has appreciated enormously over the years. Although most of the rides and other attractions have a fairly short life, some of the major buildings that are still in use on the property have been fully depreciated since they were built. Assume that Six Flags over Georgia operates as an investment center with total assets that have a book value of $100 million and current liabilities of $10 million. Assume also that in 2017, this particular theme park had sales of $120 million and pretax division income of $20 million. The replacement cost of all the assets in this park is estimated to be $160 million. The company has a 35 percent tax rate and a target return of 10% and a cost of capital of 8%.

REQUIRED

a. Calculate the ROI, residual income, and EVA for Six Flags over Georgia using book value as the valuation basis for the investment center asset base.

b. Repeat requirement (a) using replacement cost as the investment center asset value.

c. Which valuation, accounting book value or replacement cost do you think the company uses to evaluate the managers of its various theme parks? Discuss.

LO2, 3 **P23-37.** **Transfer Pricing with and without Capacity Constraints**

Elise Carpets Inc. has just acquired a new backing division that produces a rubber backing, which it sells for $3.30 per square yard. Sales are about 1,200,000 square yards per year. Since the Backing Division has a capacity of 2,000,000 square yards per year, top management is thinking that it might be wise for the company's Tufting Division to start purchasing from the newly acquired Backing Division. The Tufting Division now purchases 600,000 square yards per year from an outside supplier at a price of $3.00 per square yard. The current price is lower than the competitive $3.30 price as a result of the large quantity discounts. The Backing Division's cost per square yard follows.

Direct materials	$1.80
Direct labor.	0.45
Variable overhead.	0.37
Fixed overhead (1,200,000 level)	0.15
Total cost	$2.77

REQUIRED

a. If both divisions are to be treated as investment centers and their performance evaluated by the ROI formula, what transfer price would you recommend? Why?

b. If fixed costs are assumed not to change, determine the effect on corporate profits of making the backing.

c. Based on your transfer price, would you expect the ROI in the Backing Division to increase, decrease, or remain unchanged? Explain.

d. What would be the effect on the ROI of the Tufting Division using your transfer price? Explain.

e. Assume that the Backing Division is now selling 2,000,000 square yards per year to retail outlets. What transfer price would you recommend? What will be the effect on corporate profits?

f. If the Backing Division is at capacity and decides to sell to the Tufting Division for $3.00 per square yard, what will be the effect on the company's profits?

P23-38. **Transfer Pricing and Special Orders**   LO2

Washington State Products has several manufacturing divisions. The Seattle Division produces a component part that is used in the manufacture of electronic equipment. The cost per part for July is as follows:

Variable cost.	$160
Fixed cost (at 2,000 units per month capacity)	120
Total cost per part	$280

Some of Seattle Division's output is sold to outside manufacturers, and some is sold internally to the Redmond Division. The price per part is $400. The Redmond Division's cost and revenue structure follow.

Selling price per unit.		$2,000
Less variable costs per unit		
Cost of parts from the Seattle Division.	$400	
Other variable costs	800	(1,200)
Contribution margin per unit		800
Less fixed costs per unit (at 2,000 units per month)		(200)
Net income per unit		$ 600

The Redmond Division received a one-time order for 10 units. The buyer wants to pay only $970 per unit.

REQUIRED

a. From the perspective of the Redmond Division, should the $970 price be accepted? Explain.

b. If both divisions have excess capacity, would the Redmond Division's action benefit the company as a whole? Explain.

c. If the Redmond Division has excess capacity but the Seattle Division does not and can sell all of its parts to outside manufacturers, what would be the advantage or disadvantage of accepting the ten-unit order at the $970 price to the Redmond Division?

d. To make a decision that is in the best interest of the company, what transfer-pricing information does the Redmond Division need?

P23-39. **Balanced Scorecard**   LO4

The Willowbrook Community Bank recently decided to adopt a balanced scorecard system of performance evaluation. Below is a list of primary performance goals for four major performance categories that have been identified by corporate management and the board of directors.

1. Financial Perspective—Maintain and grow the bank financially
   a. Increase customer deposits
   b. Manage financial risk
   c. Provide profits for the stockholders
2. Customer Perspective—Maintain and grow the customer base
   a. Increase customer satisfaction
   b. Increase number of depositors & customer retention
   c. Increase quality of deposits

3. Internal Perspective—Improve internal processes
   a. Achieve best practices for processing transactions
   b. Improve employee satisfaction
   c. Improve employee promotion opportunities

4. Learning and Innovation—Improve market differentiation
   a. Beat competitors in introducing new products
   b. Become first mover in establishing customer benefit for customers
   c. Become recognized as an innovator in the industry

REQUIRED

a. For each of the 12 goals above suggest at least one measure of performance to measure the achievement of the goal.
b. At what level of the organization should the balanced scorecard be implemented as a means of evaluating performance? Explain.

CASES AND PROJECTS

LO2 **C23-40.**   **Transfer Price Decisions**

IBM Corporation
NYSE :: IBM

The Consulting Division of **IBM Corporation** is often involved in assignments for which IBM computer equipment is sold as part of a systems installation. The Computer Equipment Division is frequently a vendor of the Consulting Division in cases for which the Consulting Division purchases the equipment from the Computer Equipment Division. The Consulting Division does not view itself as a sales arm of the Computer Equipment Division but as a strong competitor to the major consulting firms of information systems. The Consulting Division's goal is to maximize its profit contribution to the company, not necessarily to see how much IBM equipment it can sell. If the Consulting Division is truly an autonomous investment center, it has the freedom to purchase equipment from competing vendors if the consultants believe that a competitor's products serve the needs of a client better than the comparable IBM product in a particular situation.

REQUIRED

a. In this situation, should corporate management be concerned about whether the Consulting Division sells IBM products or those of other computer companies? Should the Consulting Division be required to sell only IBM products?
b. Discuss the transfer-pricing issues that both the Computer Equipment Division manager and the Consulting Division manager should consider. If top management does not have a policy on pricing transfers between these two divisions, what alternative transfer prices should the division managers consider?
c. What is your recommendation regarding how the managers of the Consulting and Computer Equipment Divisions can work together in a way that will benefit each of them individually and the company as a whole?

LO2 **C23-41.**   **Transfer Pricing at Absorption Cost**

The Injection Molding Division of Universal Sign Company produces molded parts that are sold to the Sign Division. This division uses the parts in constructing signs that are sold to various businesses. The Molding Division contains two operations, injection and finishing. The unit variable cost of materials and labor used in the injection operation is $100. The fixed injection overhead is $800,000 per year. Current production (20,000 units) is at full capacity. The variable cost of labor used in the finishing operation is $16 per part. The fixed overhead in this operation is $340,000 per year. The company uses an absorption-cost transfer price. The price data for each operation presented to the Sign Division by the Molding Division follow.

Injection		
Variable cost per unit	$100	
Fixed overhead cost per unit ($800,000 ÷ 20,000 units)	40	$140
Finishing		
Labor cost per unit	16	
Fixed overhead cost per unit ($340,000 ÷ 20,000 units)	17	33
Total cost per unit		$173

An outside company has offered to lease machinery to the Sign Division that would perform the finishing portion of the parts manufacturing for $200,000 per year. With the new machinery, the labor cost per part would remain at $16. If the Molding Division transfers the units for $140, the following analysis can be made:

Current process		
Finishing process costs (20,000 × $33).........................		$660,000
New process		
Machine rental cost per year	$200,000	
Labor cost ($16 × 20,000 units).............................	320,000	(520,000)
Savings..		$140,000

The manager of the Sign Division wants approval to acquire the new machinery.

REQUIRED

a. How would you advise the company concerning the proposed lease?

b. How could the transfer-pricing system be modified or the transfer-pricing problem eliminated?

C23-42.   Transfer Pricing Dispute   **LO2**

MBR Inc. consists of three divisions that were formerly three independent manufacturing companies. Bader Corporation and Roper Company merged in 2016, and the merged corporation acquired Mitchell Company in 2017. The name of the corporation was subsequently changed to MBR Inc., and each company became a separate division retaining the name of its former company.

The three divisions have operated as if they were still independent companies. Each division has its own sales force and production facilities. Each division management is responsible for sales, cost of operations, acquisition and financing of divisional assets, and working capital management. The corporate management of MBR evaluates the performance of the divisions and division management on the basis of return on investment.

Mitchell Division has just been awarded a contract for a product that uses a component manufactured by the Roper Division and also by outside suppliers. Mitchell used a cost figure of $3.80 for the component manufactured by Roper in preparing its bid for the new product. Roper supplied this cost figure in response to Mitchell's request for the average variable cost of the component; it represents the standard variable manufacturing cost and variable selling and distribution expenses.

Roper has an active sales force that is continually soliciting new prospects. Roper's regular selling price for the component Mitchell needs for the new product is $6.50. Sales of this component are expected to increase. The Roper management has indicated, however, that it could supply Mitchell the required quantities of the component at the regular selling price less variable selling and distribution expenses. Mitchell's management has responded by offering to pay standard variable manufacturing cost plus 20 percent.

The two divisions have been unable to agree on a transfer price. Corporate management has never established a transfer-pricing policy because interdivisional transactions have never occurred. As a compromise, the corporate vice president of finance suggested a price equal to the standard full manufacturing cost (i.e., no selling and distribution expenses) plus a 15 percent markup. The two division managers have also rejected this price because each considered it grossly unfair.

The unit cost structure for the Roper component and the three suggested prices follow.

Standard variable manufacturing cost..	$3.20
Standard fixed manufacturing cost	1.20
Variable selling and distribution expenses..................................	0.60
	$5.00
Regular selling price less variable selling and distribution expenses ($6.50 − $0.60).......	$5.90
Standard full manufacturing cost plus 15% ($4.40 × 1.15)........................	$5.06
Variable manufacturing plus 20% ($3.20 × 1.20)................................	$3.84

REQUIRED

a. What should be the attitude of the Roper Division's management toward the three proposed prices?

b. Is the negotiation of a price between the Mitchell and Roper Divisions a satisfactory method of solving the transfer-pricing problem? Explain your answer.

c. Should the corporate management of MBR Inc. become involved in this transfer-price controversy? Explain your answer.

(CMA Adapted)

SOLUTIONS TO REVIEW PROBLEMS

Mid-Chapter Review 1

SOLUTION

a.

	Segments (Territories)		Wireless Total
	U.S.	International	
Sales.	$12,000	$18,000	$30,000
Less variable costs.	(8,400)	(12,600)	(21,000)
Contribution margin	3,600	5,400	9,000
Less direct fixed costs	(500)	(800)	(1,300)
Territory margin.	3,100	4,600	7,700
Less allocated segment costs	(200)	(600)	(800)
Territory income	$ 2,900	$ 4,000	6,900
Less unallocated common costs			(900)
Wireless income.			$ 6,000

b.   The Product Margin for the wireless product line in Panel B was $7,000 and reflected $2,000 of direct fixed costs that were attributable to that product line in the National Division. However, when the wireless product segment income statement is further segmented into geographic segments, only $1,300 of the $2,000 could be directly traced to the two geographic territories. Therefore, $700 of costs that were direct costs at the product segment level became common costs (either allocated or unallocated) at the territory segment level. This reflects the general notion that as segmentation is extended down to lower and lower levels, the total amount of common costs increase and direct costs decrease. Hence, segmentation rarely is extended to more than three levels.

Mid-Chapter Review 2

SOLUTION

a.   No.

	Current Sales	Proposed Sales
Selling price	$ 24.00	$ 13.50
Variable costs.	(16.00)	(16.00)
Unit contribution margin.	$ 8.00	$ (2.50)
Unit sales	× 200,000	× 100,000
Contribution margin	$1,600,000	$(250,000)

Currently, the division is making $250,000 on 100,000 posters ($1,600,000 − $1,350,000 fixed costs); but under the proposal, with a $250,000 negative contribution, it would revert to a break-even situation:

Current contribution margin		$1,600,000
Fixed costs.	$1,350,000	
Loss on special order.	250,000	(1,600,000)
Net income.		$ 0

As a general rule, a project should never be undertaken if the contribution margin is negative.

b.   What the Retail Division does with the posters after receiving them is of no concern to the Production Division. Hence, the Production Division would still object to a transfer price of $13.50. However, for the company, the proposal does have a contribution of $18 per unit ($44 − $16 − $10). Consequently, the order is desirable from the viewpoint of the company.

c. If the company believes in autonomous divisions, it should not require the Production Division to sell, nor should it dictate a higher transfer price. On the other hand, the company may want to create incentives to encourage (but not require) the two division managers to reach some compromise transfer price that would increase the contribution and profits of both divisions.

Mid-Chapter Review 3

SOLUTION

a.
$$\text{Return on investment} = \frac{\text{Investment center income}}{\text{Investment center asset base}}$$

$$\text{Engineering Division} = \$30,000 \div \$200,000$$
$$= 0.15, \text{ or 15 percent}$$

$$\text{Construction Division} = \$50,000 \div \$250,000$$
$$= 0.20, \text{ or 20 percent}$$

$$\text{Military Division} = \$22,000 \div \$100,000$$
$$= 0.22, \text{ or 22 percent}$$

b.
$$\text{Residual income} = \text{Investment center income} - (\text{Investment center asset base} \times \text{Minimum return})$$

$$\text{Engineering Division} = \$30,000 - (0.15 \times \$200,000)$$
$$= \$0.00$$

$$\text{Construction Division} = \$50,000 - (0.15 \times \$250,000)$$
$$= \$12,500$$

$$\text{Military Division} = \$22,000 - (0.15 \times \$100,000)$$
$$= \$7,000$$

c. ROI ranks the Military Division first, the Construction Division second, and the Engineering Division third. Residual income ranks the Construction Division first, the Military Division second, and the Engineering Division third. Because the investments for each division are different, it is somewhat misleading to rank the divisions according to residual income. The Construction Division had the highest residual income, but it also had the largest investment. The Military Division's residual income was 56 percent of the Construction Division's income but only 40 percent of the investment of the Construction Division. This fact, along with the best ROI ranking, probably justifies the Military Division being evaluated as the best division of KBR.

d. Return on investment:

$$\text{Investment} = \$9,000 \div \$50,000$$
$$= 0.18, \text{ or 18 percent}$$

$$\text{Engineering Division} = (\$30,000 + \$9,000) \div (\$200,000 + \$50,000)$$
$$= 0.156, \text{ or 15.6 percent}$$

$$\text{Construction Division} = (\$50,000 + \$9,000) \div (\$250,000 + \$50,000)$$
$$= 0.1967, \text{ or 19.67 percent}$$

$$\text{Military Division} = (\$22,000 + \$9,000) \div (\$100,000 + \$50,000)$$
$$= 0.2067, \text{ or 20.67 percent}$$

ROI will increase for the Engineering Division but decrease for the Construction and Military Divisions, even though the project's ROI of 18 percent exceeds the company's minimum return of 15 percent.

Residual income:

$$\text{Engineering Division} = (\$30,000 + \$9,000) - [0.15 \times (\$200,000 + \$50,000)]$$
$$= \$1,500$$

$$\text{Construction Division} = (\$50,000 + \$9,000) - [0.15 \times (\$250,000 + \$50,000)]$$
$$= \$14,000$$

$$\text{Military Division} = (\$22,000 + \$9,000) - [0.15 \times (\$100,000 + \$50,000)]$$
$$= \$8,500$$

Because the project's ROI exceeds the company's minimum return, the residual income of all divisions will increase.

SOLUTION

a. Financial Success

Expense as a % of revenue

Expense variance %

New product ROI

Net profit

Net profit margin

Year-over-year revenue growth

New product revenue

Customer Satisfaction and Brand Improvement

Number of complaints

Market share

Average customer survey rating

New customer count

New customer sales value

Unique repeat customer count

Business Process Improvement

Average call wait

Service error rate

Fulfillment %

Industry quality rating

New product acceptance rate

Number of defects reported

Time to market on new products

Learning and Growth of Motivated Workforce

Employee turnover ratio

Headcount growth

Job offer acceptance rate

Note that some of the key performance indicators could be included in more than one category. For example New Product ROI is an indicator of the success of introducing new products, but it is also an indicator of financial success.

b. The balanced scorecard has been quite successful in helping companies to better focus managers' attention on the factors that drive ultimate success. If only a general performance metric such as ROI or EVA is used to evaluate performance, managers are left on their own to figure out for themselves the components of managerial performance that drive improvements in the overall indicator. Balanced scorecard provides a framework and structure for carefully thinking about the key performance indicators that drive ultimate success. Once top management has identified the key performance indicators with input from all levels, some or all of the indicators can be used to evaluate managers and employees throughout the organization.

24

Capital Budgeting Decisions

AMAZON
www.amazon.com

Seattle-based **Amazon.com Inc.** started out as an online bookseller in 1995 and quickly expanded its product offerings to DVDs, electronics, jewelry, apparel, and now a full spectrum of consumer goods. Amazon sells more goods online than all other Internet retailers, including **Staples**, **Apple**, **Walmart**, and **Best Buy**. Amazon's meteoric rise was no doubt fueled by well-chosen capital investments, including its website infrastructure that highlighted customer-centric features such as the first shopping carts, one-click buying, email purchase confirmations, and post-shipping follow-ups. Over the years Amazon has kept its prices low by leveraging its purchasing volume, thereby staving off its competition. To maintain its position, Amazon has foregone profits in favor of continual improvement of its business model. In an effort to gain more control over its fulfillment process, Amazon has invested billions of dollars in warehouses and inventory management information systems. As a result, Amazon has been able to offer expedited shipping on its orders since 2005. This program, called Amazon Prime, offers customers two-day shipping for an annual fee of $99.

Amazon could never be accused of complacency. In fact, Amazon Prime is no longer fast enough; some competitors offer same-day delivery in select cities. Increased competition helps explain why Amazon continues to invest in new warehouses. In order to serve a larger segment of the population, the company is building its warehouses closer to urban areas, and this means those investments have become more expensive. Amazon's capital investments don't stop at just warehouses. Software systems that sort items by delivery date and optimize storage space have allowed Amazon to double the number of items it can ship per facility. Amazon is also beginning to open brick-and-mortar bookstore locations, including stores in Oregon, Washington, California, and New York. In 2017, Amazon made its first Prime Air drone delivery; testing its ability to make deliveries using drones.

Amazon's management team needs to tread carefully in evaluating these new investments. Amazon's managers should be asking themselves these questions: How will these investments be financed, and at what cost can we raise the needed funds? What tax deductions or incentives might defray some of the costs of this

investment? How long before the investment has been recouped through increased revenues? Does this estimate consider increases in operating costs? In other words, Amazon needs to determine which capital investments will have a positive effect on operating results.

The company will have to look beyond the cost of the buildings. Inventory storage costs, insurance on both the buildings and the increased volume of goods stored inside of them, and shipping and delivery costs all have increased. At the end of 2016, the company employed over 180,000 full-time U. S. workers and announced plans to add an additional 100,000 employees by the middle of 2018.

While Amazon has a vast customer base and has established itself as one of the most-recognized brands in online retailing, its competitors are not standing on the sidelines. Furthermore, regulatory changes will require that Amazon and other online retailers collect sales tax on sales in several states, including California, Texas, Florida, and New Jersey, further eroding their competitive edge over traditional brick-and-mortar competitors. This chapter will detail important tools that Amazon and managers can use to increase the probability that their capital investments will be sound.

Source: Amazon, "Press Release: Amazon to Create More Than 100,000 New, Full-Time, Full-Benefit Jobs across the U.S. over the Next 18 Months," *Amazon.Com*, January 12, 2017; Jenna Amatulli, "A Brick-And-Mortar Amazon Bookstore Is Coming To NYC," *Huffington Post*, January 10, 2017; Kate Abbey-Lambertz, "Amazon's Flying Warehouse Idea Isn't Even Its Biggest Challenge," *Huffington Post*, December 30, 2016; Peter Cohan, "How You Can Use The Three Big Ideas Behind Amazon's Success," *Forbes*, September 4, 2013; Tim Worstall, "Fascinating Number: Amazon Is Larger Than the Next Dozen Internet Retailers Combined," *Forbes*, September 1, 2013; Danielle Kucera, "Why Amazon Is on a Warehouse Building Spree," *Bloomberg Businessweek*, August 29, 2013; Tom Gara, "Amazon Losing Its Price Edge," *Wall Street Journal*, August 20, 2013, p. B2.

CHAPTER ORGANIZATION

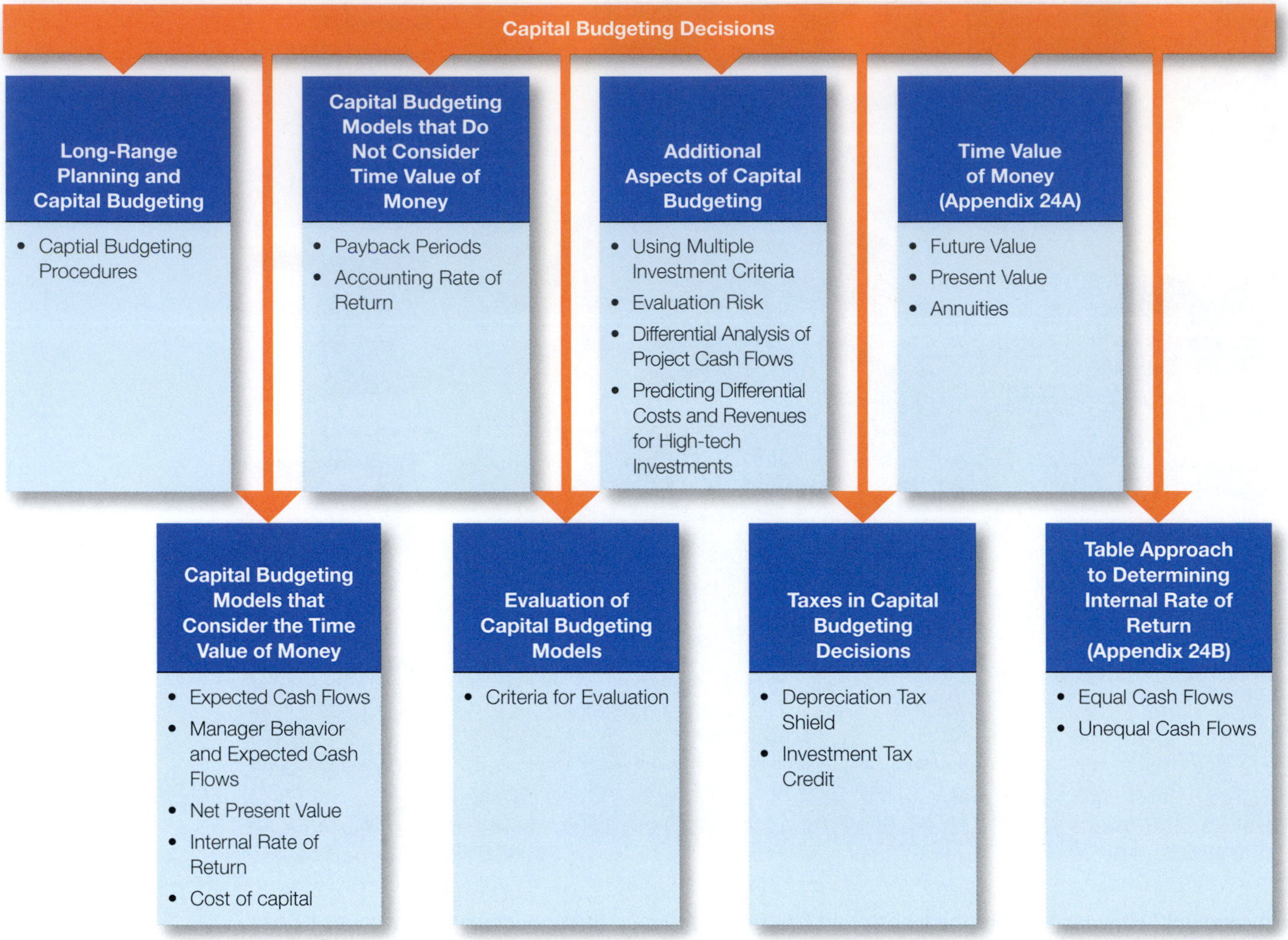

| Capital Budgeting Decisions |

Long-Range Planning and Capital Budgeting

- Capital Budgeting Procedures

Capital Budgeting Models that Do Not Consider Time Value of Money

- Payback Periods
- Accounting Rate of Return

Additional Aspects of Capital Budgeting

- Using Multiple Investment Criteria
- Evaluation Risk
- Differential Analysis of Project Cash Flows
- Predicting Differential Costs and Revenues for High-tech Investments

Time Value of Money (Appendix 24A)

- Future Value
- Present Value
- Annuities

Capital Budgeting Models that Consider the Time Value of Money

- Expected Cash Flows
- Manager Behavior and Expected Cash Flows
- Net Present Value
- Internal Rate of Return
- Cost of capital

Evaluation of Capital Budgeting Models

- Criteria for Evaluation

Taxes in Capital Budgeting Decisions

- Depreciation Tax Shield
- Investment Tax Credit

Table Approach to Determining Internal Rate of Return (Appendix 24B)

- Equal Cash Flows
- Unequal Cash Flows

LO1 Explain the role of capital budgeting in long-range planning.

1

Capital expenditures are investments of financial resources in projects to develop or introduce new products or services, to expand current production or service capacity, or to change current production or service facilities. Capital expenditures are made with the expectation that the new product, process, or service will generate future financial inflows that exceed the initial costs. Capital expenditure decisions affect structural cost drivers. They are made infrequently but once made are difficult to change. They commit the organization to the use of certain facilities and activities to satisfy customer needs. In making large capital expenditure decisions, such as for **Amazon**'s warehouse facilities, management is risking the future existence of the company.

Although capital expenditure decisions are fraught with risk, management accounting provides the concepts and tools needed to organize information and evaluate the alternatives. This systematic organization and analysis is the essence of capital budgeting. This chapter introduces important capital budgeting concepts and models, and it explains the proper use of accounting data in these models.

Capital budgeting is a process that involves identifying potentially desirable projects for capital expenditures, evaluating capital expenditure proposals, and selecting proposals that meet minimum criteria. A number of quantitative models are available to assist managers in evaluating capital expenditure proposals.

The best capital budgeting models are conceptually similar to the short-range planning models used in Chapters 15 and 16. They all emphasize cash flows and focus on future costs (and revenues) that differ among decision alternatives. The major difference is that capital budgeting models involve cash flows over several years, whereas short-range planning models involve cash flows for a year or less. When the cash flows associated with a proposed activity extend over several years, an adjustment is necessary to make the cash flows comparable when they are expected to occur at different points in time.

The *time value of money concept* explains why monies received or paid at different points in time must be adjusted to comparable values. The time value of money is introduced in Appendix 24A at the end of this chapter.

LONG-RANGE PLANNING AND CAPITAL BUDGETING

Most organizations plan not only for operations in the current period but also for the longer term, perhaps 5, 10, or even 20 years in the future. Most planning beyond the next budget year is called *long-range planning*.

Increased uncertainty and business alternatives add to the difficulty of planning as the horizon lengthens. Even though long-range planning is difficult and involves uncertainties, management must make long-range planning and capital expenditure decisions. Capital expenditure decisions will be made. The question is: How will they be made? Will they be made on the basis of the best information available? Will care be taken to ensure that capital expenditure decisions are in line with the organization's long-range goals? Will the potential consequences, both positive and negative, of capital expenditures be considered? Will important alternative uses of the organization's limited financial resources be considered in a systematic manner? Will managers be held accountable for the capital expenditure programs they initiate? The alternative to a systematic approach to capital budgeting is the haphazard expenditure of resources on the basis of a hunch, immediate need, or persuasion—without accountability by the person(s) making the decisions.

The steps of an effective capital budgeting process are outlined in **Exhibit 24.1**. A basic requirement for a systematic approach to capital budgeting is a defined mission, a set of long-range goals, and a business strategy. These elements provide focus and boundaries that reduce the types of capital expenditure decisions management considers. If, for example, **Dunkin' Donuts**'s goal is to become the largest fast-food restaurant chain in North America, its management should not consider a proposal to purchase and operate a bus line.

A well-defined business strategy will likewise guide capital expenditure decisions. If **Cisco Systems** is following a strategy to obtain technological leadership, it might seriously consider a proposal to meet customer needs by investing in innovative production facilities but would not consider a proposal to purchase and refurbish used (but seemingly cost-efficient) equipment. The following Business Insight box identifies companies that focus capital budgeting decisions on the strategic goal of energy efficiency; and therefore, reducing expenses.

BUSINESS INSIGHT

Using the Capital Budget to Save Money   Most capital investments produce positive cash flows by increasing revenues. Energy efficiency reduces key expenses. Companies involved in the CDP investor engagement program, an initiative aimed at helping firms implement sustainability programs, have found that energy efficiency projects generate an internal rate of return of 33% and an average payback of just three years.

Organizations with expenses from owning and operating buildings, like the city of Washington DC, are making energy efficiency a top priority. City managers are partnering with **First Fuel**, maker of an energy auditing software package, to evaluate and manage energy use in the 400 buildings (30 million square feet) that they operate. The District expects to cut their energy bill by 20% based on First Fuel's recommendations.

Energy efficiency is also a priority for companies that operate large data centers. Electricity is the main ongoing expense of a data center. **Google** has successfully piloted the use of the machine learning algorithms to manage energy use. The amount of information involved in solving Google's energy optimization problem is tough for the human mind to comprehend. Their DeepMind-based system will reduce energy use by 15%. This is an impressive move from a company whose energy use rivaled that of the nation of Laos in 2011.

Most capital budget decisions are about deciding to spend money in order to make money. Budgeting for energy efficiency is about spending money to save money.

Sources: Sarah Murray, "It Pays for Companies to Be Part of the Scenery," *Financial Times*, June 1, 2015.
Adam Vaughan, "Google Uses AI to Cut Data Centre Energy Use by 15%," *The Guardian*, July 20, 2016.
Sarah Shemkus "First Fuel Software Aims to Make Energy Efficiency Easier, Quicker," *The Guardian*, April 28, 2014.

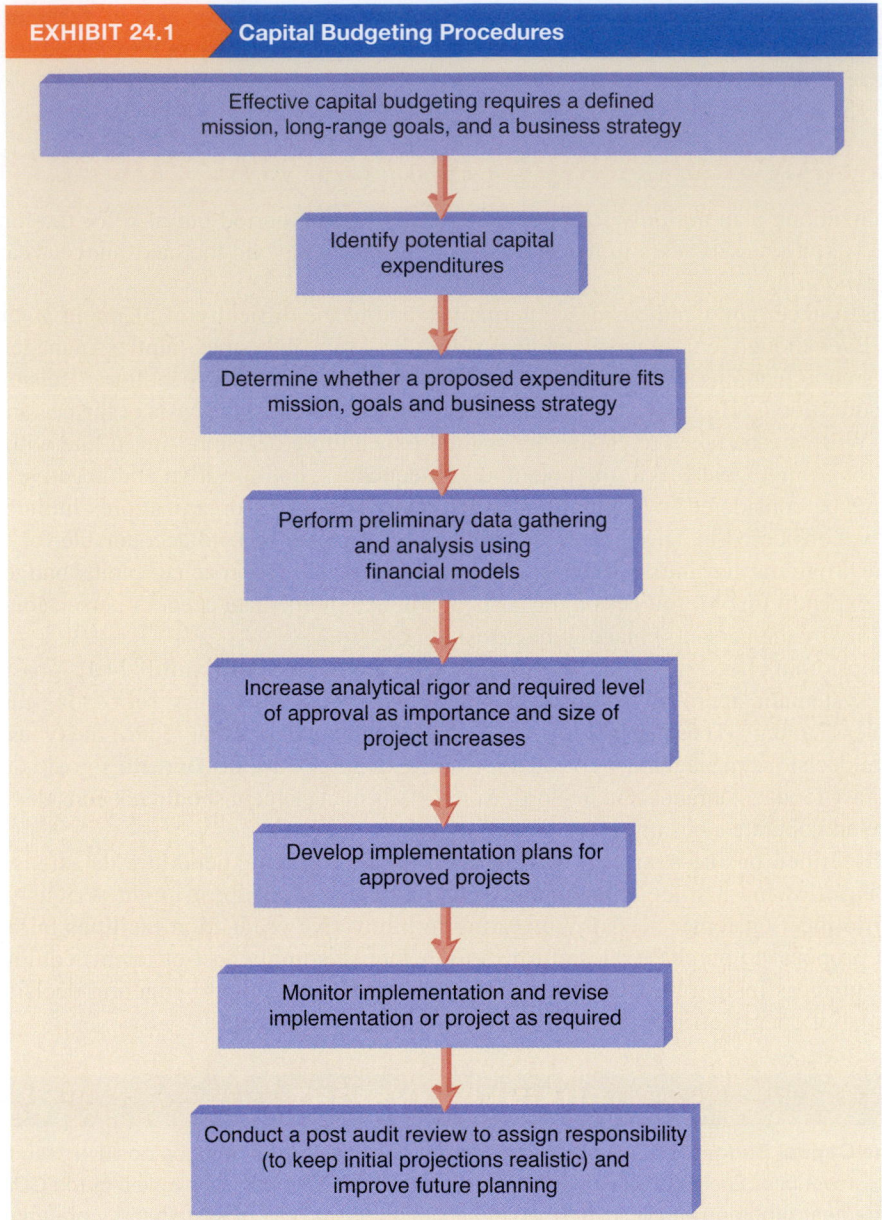

EXHIBIT 24.1   Capital Budgeting Procedures

Effective capital budgeting requires a defined mission, long-range goals, and a business strategy

Identify potential capital expenditures

Determine whether a proposed expenditure fits mission, goals and business strategy

Perform preliminary data gathering and analysis using financial models

Increase analytical rigor and required level of approval as importance and size of project increases

Develop implementation plans for approved projects

Monitor implementation and revise implementation or project as required

Conduct a post audit review to assign responsibility (to keep initial projections realistic) and improve future planning

Management should also develop procedures for the review, evaluation, approval, and post-audit of capital expenditure proposals. In a large organization, a capital budgeting committee that provides guidance to managers in the formulation of capital expenditure proposals is key to these procedures. This committee also reviews, analyzes, and approves or rejects major capital expenditure proposals. Major projects often require the approval of top management and even the board of directors. The capital budgeting committee should include persons knowledgeable in capital budgeting models; financing alternatives and costs; operating procedures; cost estimation and prediction methods; research and development efforts; the organization's goals and basic strategy; and the expectations of the organization's stockholders or owners. A management accountant who is generally expert in data collection, retrieval, and analysis is normally part of the capital budgeting committee.

Not all capital expenditure proposals require committee approval or are subject to formal evaluation. With the approval of top management, the committee might provide guidelines indicating the type and dollar amount of capital expenditures that managers at each level of the organization can make without formal evaluation or committee approval, or both. The guidelines might state that expenditures of less than $20,000 do not require committee approval and that only expenditures of more than $100,000 must be evaluated using capital budgeting models.

Typically, managers at higher levels have greater discretion in making capital expenditures. In a college or university, a department chairperson could have authority to purchase office and instructional equipment with a maximum limit of $10,000 per year. A dean may have authority to renovate offices or classrooms with a maximum limit of $50,000 per year, but the conversion of the power plant from one fuel source to another at a cost of $400,000 could require the formal review of a capital budgeting committee and final approval of the board of trustees.

The post-audit of approved capital expenditure proposals is an important part of a well-formulated approach to capital budgeting. A *post-audit* involves the development of project performance reports comparing planned and actual results. Project performance reports should be provided to the manager who initiated the capital expenditure proposal, the manager assigned responsibility for the project (if a different person), the project manager's supervisor, and the capital budgeting committee. These reports help keep the project on target (especially during the initial investment phase), identify the need to reevaluate the project if the initial analysis was in error or significant environmental changes occur, and improve the quality of investment proposals. When managers know they will be held accountable for the results of projects they initiate, they are likely to put more care into the development of capital expenditure proposals and take a greater interest in approved projects. Problems can occur when decision makers are rewarded for undertaking major projects but are not held responsible for the consequences that occur several years later.

A post-audit review of approved projects also helps the capital budgeting committee do a better job in evaluating new proposals. The committee might learn how to adjust proposals for the biases of individual managers, learn of new factors that should be considered in evaluating proposals, and avoid the routine approval of projects that appear desirable by themselves but are related to larger projects that are not meeting management's expectations. As summarized in the following Business Insight, capital budgeting models play an important role in strategic decision making.

BUSINESS INSIGHT

SodaStream and Pepsi, Partners Not Competitors   **SodaStream**, an Israeli company, has skyrocketed to success in the United States over the last decade. SodaStream makes a countertop soda maker with a dizzying array of flavorings. Distribution deals with **Walmart** and **Bed Bath & Beyond** have made SodaStream a new player in the US soda market even as US soda industry volumes have fallen steadily.

SodaStream's marketing and design focus on reusability and low waste at a time when consumers are becoming increasingly conscious of the waste from cans and bottles of soda. In response to this trend, Pepsi has partnered with SodaStream and Bed Bath & Beyond to make **Pepsi** flavors for SodaStream available in stores. As this partnership evolves, Pepsi's decision makers will depend on net present value analysis as they discuss the decision to continue the partnership or possibly to acquire SodaStream.

Source: Mike Esterl, "PepsiCo Expands Soda Partnership with Home Carbonation Maker SodaStream," *Wall Street Journal*, September 11, 2015.

YOU MAKE THE CALL

You Are the Vice President of Finance   You have recently accepted the position of VP of finance for a rapidly growing biotech company. Last year the company made capital expenditures of $10 million and you anticipate that annual capital expenditures will exceed $30 million in a couple of years. You believe it is time to develop a more formal approach to making capital expenditure decisions. Where do you begin? [Answer p. 1087]

MID-CHAPTER REVIEW 1

Below is a list of terms relevant to capital budgeting decisions.

1. Capital budgeting
2. Capital expenditures
3. Time value of money concept
4. Long range planning
5. Post audit

continued

continued from previous page

REQUIRED

For each of the statements below, select the most relevant term from the above list. Each term above may be used more than once.

_____ *a.* Investment of financial resources with the expectation it will generate future financial inflows that exceed the initial cost.

_____ *b.* Process that involves identifying desirable projects, evaluating proposals, and selecting proposals that meet minimum criteria.

_____ *c.* Involves the development of project performance comparing planned and actual results.

_____ *d.* Concepts and tools that organize information and evaluate alternatives.

_____ *e.* Explains why monies received or paid at different points in time must be adjusted to comparable values.

_____ *f.* Requires an adjustment to make cash flows comparable when they are expected to occur at different points in time.

_____ *g.* Planning beyond the next budget year.

_____ *h.* Helps the capital budgeting committee do a better job in evaluating new proposals.

The solution to this review problem can be found on pages 1101–1102.

LO2 Analyze capital budgeting decisions using models that consider the time value of money, such as net present value and internal rate of return.

CAPITAL BUDGETING MODELS THAT CONSIDER TIME VALUE OF MONEY

The capital budgeting models in this chapter have gained wide acceptance by for-profit and not-for-profit organizations. Our primary focus is on the *net present value* and the *internal rate of return models*, which are superior because they consider the time value of money. Later discussions will consider more traditional capital budgeting models, such as the payback period and the accounting rate of return that, while useful under certain circumstances, do not consider the time value of money. Although we briefly consider the cost of financing capital expenditures, we leave a detailed treatment of this topic, as well as a detailed examination of the sources of funds for financing investments, to books on financial management.

Expected Cash Flows

The focus of capital budgeting models that consider the time value of money is on future cash receipts and future cash disbursements that differ under decision alternatives. It is often convenient to distinguish between the following three phases of a project's cash flows:

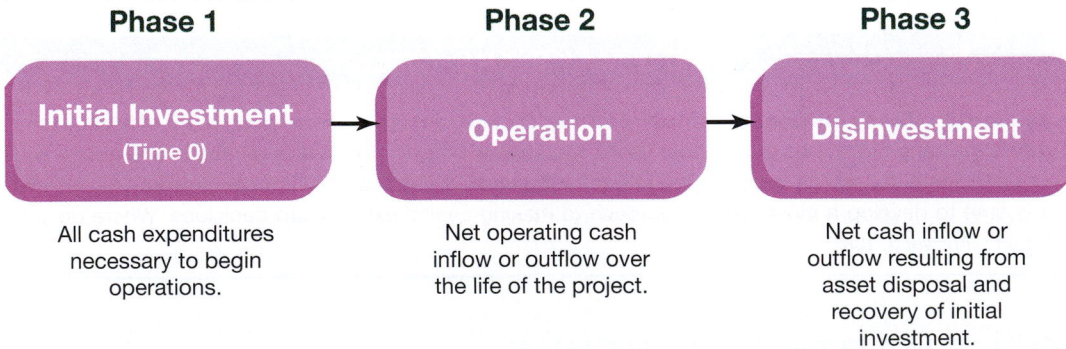

Phase 1	**Phase 2**	**Phase 3**
Initial Investment (Time 0)	**Operation**	**Disinvestment**
All cash expenditures necessary to begin operations.	Net operating cash inflow or outflow over the life of the project.	Net cash inflow or outflow resulting from asset disposal and recovery of initial investment.

All cash expenditures necessary to begin operations are classified as part of the project's *initial investment phase*. Expenditures to acquire property, plant, and equipment are part of the initial investment. Less obvious, but equally important, are expenditures to acquire working capital to purchase inventories and recruit and train employees. Although the initial investment phase often extends over many years, in our examples, we assume that the initial investment takes place at a single point in time.

Cash receipts from sales of goods or services, as well as normal cash expenditures for materials, labor, and other operating expenses, occur during the operation phase. The *operation phase* is typically broken down into one-year periods; for each period, operating cash expenditures are subtracted from operating cash receipts to determine the net operating cash inflow or outflow for the period.

The *disinvestment phase* occurs at the end of the project's life when assets are disposed of for their salvage value and any initial investment of working capital is recovered. Also included are any expenditures to dismantle facilities and dispose of waste. Although this phase might extend over many years, in our examples, we assume disinvestment takes place at a single point in time.

To illustrate the analysis of a project's cash flows, assume the management of Mobile Taqueria is considering a capital expenditure proposal to operate a new shop in a resort community. Each Mobile Taqueria is located in a specially constructed motor vehicle that moves on a regular schedule throughout the community it serves. The predicted cash flows associated with the project, which has an expected life of five years, are presented in **Exhibit 24.2**.

EXHIBIT 24.2	Analysis of a Project's Predicted Cash Flows			
Initial investment (at time 0)				
Vehicle and equipment			$ (90,554)	**Phase 1**
Inventories and other working capital.			(4,000)	
Total investment cash outflow			$ (94,554)	
Operation (per year for 5 years)				
Sales.			$ 175,000	
Cash expenditures				
Food	$47,000			
Labor.	65,000			**Phase 2**
Supplies	9,000			
Fuel and utilities	8,000			
Advertising	4,000			
Miscellaneous	12,000		(145,000)	
Net annual cash inflow			$ 30,000	
Disinvestment (at the end of 5 years)				
Sale of vehicle and equipment			$ 8,000	
Recovery of investment in inventories and other working capital			4,000	**Phase 3**
Total disinvestment cash inflow			$ 12,000	

Manager Behavior and Expected Cash Flows

Accurately predicting the cash flows associated with a capital expenditure proposal is critical to properly evaluating the proposal. Managers might be overly optimistic with their predictions, and they are sometimes tempted to modify predictions to justify capital expenditures. Perhaps they are interested in personal rewards. They might also want to avoid a loss of prestige or employment for themselves or to keep a local facility operating for the benefit of current employees and the local economy. Unfortunately, if a major expenditure does not work out, not only the local plant but also the entire company could be forced out of business. For example, under pressure to increase current sales, automobile leasing companies could be tempted to overstate cash receipts during the disinvestment phase of a lease.

Net Present Value

A project's **net present value**, usually computed as of the time of the initial investment, is the present value of the project's net cash inflows from operations and disinvestment less the amount of the initial investment. Chapter Appendix 24A contains an introduction to the time value of money, including net present value fundamentals. In computing a project's net present value, the cash flows occurring at different points in time are adjusted for the time value of money using a **discount rate** that is the minimum rate of return required for the project to be acceptable. Projects with positive net present values (or values at least equal to zero) are acceptable, and projects with negative net present values are unacceptable. Two methods to compute net present value follow.

Table Approach   Assuming that management uses a 12 percent discount rate, the net present value of the proposed investment in a Mobile Taqueria is shown in **Exhibit 24.3 (a)** to be $20,398. Since the net present value is more than zero, the investment in the Mobile Taqueria is expected to be profitable, even when adjusted for the time value of money.

We can verify the amounts and computations in **Exhibit 24.3**. Start by tracing the cash flows back to **Exhibit 24.2**. Next, determine the 12 percent present value factors by referring to **Exhibit 24A.1** and 24A.2 in Chapter Appendix 24A. The initial investment is assumed to occur at a single point in time (identified as time 0), the start of the project. In net present value computations, all cash flows are restated in terms of their value at time 0. Hence, time 0 cash flows have a present value factor of 1. To simplify computations, all other cash flows are assumed to occur at the end of years 1 through 5, even if they occurred during the year. Although further refinements could be made to adjust for cash flows occuring throughout each year, such adjustments are seldom necessary. Observe that net operating cash inflows are treated as an *annuity*, whereas cash flows for the initial investment and disinvestment are treated as *lump-sum amounts*. If net operating cash flows varied from year to year, we would treat each year's cash flow as a separate amount.

Spreadsheet Approach   functions that compute the present value of a series of cash flows. With this software, simply enter a column or row containing the net cash flows for each period and the appropriate formula. The discount rate of 0.12 is entered as part of the formula. Sample spreadsheet input to determine the net present value of the proposed investment in a Mobile Taqueria is shown on the left in **Exhibit 24.3 (b)**. The spreadsheet output is shown on the right, in **Exhibit 24.3 (b)**.

EXHIBIT 24.3	Net Present Value of a Project's Predicted Cash Flows

(a) Table approach:

	Predicted Cash Inflows (outflows) (A)	Year(s) of Cash Flows (B)	12% Present Value Factor (C)	Present Value of Cash Flows (A) × (C)
Initial investment	$(94,554)	0	1.00000	$ (94,554)
Operation	30,000	1–5	3.60478	108,143
Disinvestment.	12,000	5	0.56743	6,809
Net present value of all cash flows.				$ 20,398

(b) Spreadsheet approach:

Input:

	A	B
1	Year of cash flow	Cash flow
2	1	$30,000
3	2	30,000
4	3	30,000
5	4	30,000
6	5	42,000
7	Present value	=NPV(0.12,B2:B6)
8	Initial investment at time 0	(94,554)
9	Net present value	=B7+B8

Output:

	A	B
1	Year of cash flow	Cash flow
2	1	$ 30,000
3	2	30,000
4	3	30,000
5	4	30,000
6	5	42,000
7	Present value	$114,952.41
8	Initial investment at time 0	(94,554.00)
9	Net present value	$ 20,398.41

Two cautionary notes follow:

1. The spreadsheet formula for the net present value assumes that the first cash flow occurs at time "1," rather than at time "0." Hence, we cannot include the initial investment in the data set analyzed by the spreadsheet formula when computing the net present value. Instead, the initial investment is subtracted from the present value of future cash flows.

2. Arrange the cash flows subsequent to the initial investment from *top* to bottom in a column, or *left* to right in a row.

Internal Rate of Return

The **internal rate of return (IRR)**, often called the **time-adjusted rate of return**, is the discount rate that equates the present value of a project's cash inflows with the present value of the project's cash outflows. Other ways to describe IRR include: (1) The minimum rate that could be paid for the money invested in a project without losing money, and (2) The discount rate that results in a project's net present value equaling zero.

All practical applications of the IRR model use a calculator or spreadsheet. Thus, we illustrate determining an IRR with a spreadsheet. A table approach to determining a project's internal rate of return is illustrated in Appendix 24B of this chapter.

With spreadsheet software, simply enter a column or row containing the net cash flows for each period and the appropriate formula. Spreadsheet input for Mobile Taqueria's investment proposal is shown in **Exhibit 24.4**. The spreadsheet formula for the IRR assumes that the first cash flow occurs at time "0."

The spreadsheet approach requires an initial prediction or guess of the project's internal rate of return. Although the closeness of the prediction to the final solution affects computational speed, for textbook examples almost any number can be used. We use an initial estimate of 0.08 in all illustrations. Because the IRR formula assumes that the first cash flow occurs at time 0, the initial investment is included in the data analyzed by the IRR formula. Again, we must order the cash flows from top to bottom in a column or left to right in a row. As shown on the right column in **Exhibit 24.4**, the spreadsheet software computes the IRR as 20 percent.

Although a project's IRR should be compared to the discount rate established by management, such a discount rate is often unknown. In these situations, computing the IRR still provides insights into a project's profitability.

EXHIBIT 24.4	Spreadsheet Approach to Determining Internal Rate of Return

Input:

	A	B
1	Year of cash flow	Cash flow
2	0	$(94,554)
3	1	30,000
4	2	30,000
5	3	30,000
6	4	30,000
7	5	42,000
8	IRR	=IRR(B2:B7,0.08)*

Output:

	A	B
1	Year of cash flow	Cash flow
2	0	$(94,554)
3	1	30,000
4	2	30,000
5	3	30,000
6	4	30,000
7	5	42,000
8	IRR	0.20

*The formula is "=IRR(Input data range, guess)." The guess, which is any likely rate of return, is used as an initial starting point in determining the solution. We use 0.08 in all illustrations.

The calculated internal rate of return is compared to the discount rate established by management to evaluate investment proposals. If the proposal's IRR is greater than or equal to the discount rate, the project is acceptable; if it is less than the discount rate, the project is unacceptable. Because Mobile Taqueria has a 12 percent discount rate, the project is acceptable using the IRR model.

Although a computer and appropriate software quickly and accurately perform tedious computations, computational ease increases the opportunity for inappropriate use. The ability to plug numbers into a computer or calculator and obtain an output labeled NPV or IRR could mislead the unwary into believing that capital budgeting models are easy to use. This is not true. Training and professional judgment are required to identify relevant costs, to implement procedures to obtain relevant cost information, and to make a good decision once results are available. Capital budgeting models are merely decision aids. Managers, not models, make the decisions. To better illustrate underlying concepts, all subsequent textbook illustrations use a table approach.

Cost of Capital

When discounting models are used to evaluate capital expenditure proposals, management must determine the discount rate (1) used to compute a proposal's net present value or (2) used as the standard for evaluating a proposal's IRR. An organization's cost of capital is often used as this discount rate.

The **cost of capital** is the average cost an organization pays to obtain the resources necessary to make investments. This average rate considers items such as the:

- Effective interest rate on debt (notes or bonds).
- Effective dividend rate on preferred stock.
- Discount rate that equates the present value of all dividends expected on common stock over the life of the organization to the current market value of the organization's common stock.

The cost of capital for a company that has no debt or preferred stock equals the cost of equity capital, computed as follows:

$$\text{Cost of equity capital} = \frac{\text{Current annual dividend per common share}}{\text{Current market price per common share}} + \text{Expected dividend growth rate}$$

Procedures for determining the cost of capital for more complex capital structures are covered in finance books. Investing in a project that has an internal rate of return equal to the cost of capital should not affect the market value of the firm's securities. Investing in a project that has a return higher than the cost of capital should increase the market value of a firm's securities. If, however, a firm invests in a project that has a return less than the cost of capital, the market value of the firm's securities should fall.

The cost of capital is the minimum return acceptable for investment purposes. Any investment proposal not expected to yield this minimum rate should normally be rejected. Because of difficulties encountered in determining the cost of capital, many organizations adopt a discount rate or a target rate of return without complicated mathematical analysis.

MID-CHAPTER REVIEW 2

Consider the following investment proposal:

Initial investment	
Depreciable assets	$27,740
Working capital	3,000
Operations (per year for 4 years)	
Cash receipts	25,000
Cash expenditures	15,000
Disinvestment	
Salvage value of plant and equipment	2,000
Recovery of working capital	3,000

REQUIRED
Determine each of the following:

a. Net present value at a 10 percent discount rate.
b. Internal rate of return. (Refer to Appendix 24B if using the table approach.)

The solution to this review problem can be found on pages 1102–1103.

CAPITAL BUDGETING MODELS THAT DO NOT CONSIDER TIME VALUE

Years ago, capital budgeting models that do not consider the time value of money were more widely used than discounting models. Although most large organizations use net present value or internal rate of return as their primary evaluation tool, they often use nondiscounting models as an initial screening device. Further, as discussed in the following Research Insight, nondiscounting models remain entrenched in small businesses. We consider two nondiscounting models, the *payback period* and the *accounting rate of return*.

LO3 Analyze capital budgeting decisions using methods that do not consider the time value of money, such as payback period and accounting rate of return.

RESEARCH INSIGHT

Size and Education Matter in Capital Budgeting   A survey of small businesses (with an average of 10 employees) by **Danielson and Scott** shows that owners make capital expenditure decisions based on "gut feel" much more often than on other methods predicted by theory. Owners' gut feelings were followed by a payback period, then accounting rate of return—only a few firms reported using discounted cash flows. Danielson and Scott emphasize the following points:

1. Capital investments by small businesses tend not to be discretionary. The firm often either invests or goes out of business.
2. Use of a payback period increases with the formal education of the owner, and owners with advanced degrees are most likely to have a formal business plan and use discounted future cash flows.
3. Accounting rate of return is most common for firms that are planning to expand, or are required to provide financial information to banks.

Graham and Harvey surveyed Fortune 500 CFOs and CFOs of smaller members of the Financial Executives Institute. CFOs generally have advanced degrees in business, and 46% of these firms have sales over $1 billion dollars. In this group most firms use multiple models for budgeting, and their use fits much more with the theory:

1. 76% use internal rate of return.
2. 75% use net present value.
3. More than 50% use a payback period.
4. About 20% use accounting rate of return.

Even in this sample, the smaller firms (sales under $100 million) are less likely to use net present value than larger firms. Follow-up research in Canada and Europe has confirmed that these results generalize beyond the United States and the Fortune 500, with two additional insights. First, there is a long-term trend toward use of discounted cash flows in all firms, and second, the wealth of the firm's home nation also affects the sophistication of modeling.

Sources: Morris Danielson and Johnathan Scott, "The Capital Budgeting Decisions of Small Businesses," *Journal of Applied Finance* (Fall/Winter 2006): 46–56.
John Graham and Campbell Harvey, "The Theory and Practice of Corporate Finance: Evidence from the Field," *Journal of Financial Economics* (May–June 2001): 187–243.
Karim Bennouna, Geoffrey G. Meredith, and Teresa Marchant, "Improved Capital Budgeting Decision Making: Evidence from Canada," *Management Decision* 48, no. 2 (2010): 225–47.
Gyorgy Andor, Sunil K. Mohanty, and Tamas Toth, "Capital Budgeting Practices: A Survey of Central and Eastern European Firms," *Emerging Markets Review* 23 (June 2015): 148–72, http://dx.doi.org/10.1016/j.ememar.2015.04.002.

Payback Period

The **payback period** is the time required to recover the initial investment in a project from operations. The payback decision rule states that acceptable projects must have less than some maximum payback period designated by management. Payback emphasizes management's concern with liquidity and the need to minimize risk through a rapid recovery of the initial investment. It is frequently used for small expenditures having such obvious benefits that the use of more sophisticated capital budgeting models is not required or justified.

When a project is expected to have equal annual operating cash inflows, its payback period is computed as follows:

$$\text{Payback period} = \frac{\text{Initial investment}}{\text{Annual operating cash inflows}}$$

For Mobile Taqueria's investment proposal, outlined in **Exhibit 24.2**, the payback period is 3.15 years:

$$\text{Payback period} = \frac{\$94,554}{\$30,000}$$

$$= 3.15$$

Determining the payback period for a project having unequal cash flows is slightly more complicated. Assume that **Costco Wholesale** is evaluating a capital expenditure proposal that requires an initial investment of $50,000,000 and has the following expected net cash inflows:

Year	Net Cash Inflow
1	$15,000,000
2	25,000,000
3	40,000,000
4	20,000,000
5	10,000,000

To compute the payback period, we must determine the net unrecovered amount at the end of each year. In the year of full recovery, the net cash inflows are assumed to occur evenly and are prorated based on the unrecovered investment at the start of the year. Full recovery of Costco's investment proposal is expected to occur in Year 3:

Year	Net Cash Inflow	Unrecovered Investment
0	$ 0	$50,000,000
1	15,000,000	35,000,000
2	25,000,000	10,000,000
3	40,000,000	0

Therefore, $10,000,000 of $40,000,000 is needed in Year 3 to complete the recovery of the initial investment. This provides a proportion of 0.25 ($10,000,000 ÷ $40,000,000) and a payback period of 2.25 years (2 years plus 0.25 of Year 3). This project is acceptable if management specified a maximum payback period of three years. Because they occur after the payback period, the net cash inflows of Years 4 and 5 are ignored.

Accounting Rate of Return

The **accounting rate of return** is the average annual increase in net income that results from the acceptance of a capital expenditure proposal divided by either the initial investment or the average investment in the project. This method differs from other capital budgeting models in that it focuses on accounting income rather than on cash flow. In most capital budgeting applications, accounting net income is approximated as net cash inflow from operations minus expenses not requiring the use of cash, such as depreciation.

Consider Mobile Taqueria's capital expenditure proposal whose cash flows were outlined in **Exhibit 24.2**. The vehicle and equipment costs are $90,554 and have a disposal value of $8,000 at the end of five years, resulting in an average annual increase in net income of $13,489:

Annual net cash inflow from operations.	$30,000
Less average annual depreciation [($90,554 − $8,000) ÷ 5].	(16,511)
Average annual increase in net income	$13,489

Considering the investment in inventories and other working capital, the initial investment is $94,554 ($90,554 + $4,000), and the *accounting rate of return on initial investment* is 14.27 percent:

$$\text{Accounting rate of return on initial investment} = \frac{\text{Average annual increase in net income}}{\text{Initial investment}} = \frac{\$13,489}{\$94,554} = 0.1427$$

The average investment, computed as the initial investment plus the expected value of any disinvestment, all divided by 2, is $53,277 [($94,554 + $12,000) ÷ 2]. The *accounting rate of return on average investment* is 25.32 percent:

$$\text{Accounting rate of return on average investment} = \frac{\text{Average annual increase in net income}}{\text{Average investment}} = \frac{\$13,489}{\$53,277} = 0.2532$$

When using the accounting rate of return, management specifies either the initial investment or average investment plus some minimum acceptable rate. Management rejects capital expenditure proposals with a lower accounting rate of return but accepts proposals with an accounting rate of return higher than or equal to the minimum.

MID-CHAPTER REVIEW 3

Consider the following investment proposal:

Initial investment	
Depreciable assets	$27,740
Working capital	3,000
Operations (per year for 4 years)	
Cash receipts	25,000
Cash expenditures	15,000
Disinvestment	
Salvage value of plant and equipment	2,000
Recovery of working capital	3,000

REQUIRED

Determine each of the following:

a. Payback period.
b. Accounting rate of return on initial investment and on average investment.

The solution to this review problem can be found on page 1103.

EVALUATION OF CAPITAL BUDGETING MODELS

LO4 Evaluate the strengths and weaknesses of alternative capital budgeting models.

As a single criterion for evaluating capital expenditure proposals, capital budgeting models that consider the time value of money are superior to models that do not consider it. The payback model concerns merely how long it takes to recover the initial investment from a project, yet investments are not made with the objective of merely getting the money back. Indeed, not investing has a payback period of 0. Investments are made to earn a profit. Hence, what happens after the payback period is more important than is the payback period itself. The payback period model, when used as the sole investment criterion, has a fatal flaw in that it fails to consider cash flows after the payback period. Despite this flaw, payback is a rough-and-ready approach to getting a handle on investment proposals. Sometimes a project is so attractive using payback that, when its life is considered, no further analysis is necessary.

For total life evaluations, the accounting rate of return is superior to the payback period because it does consider a capital expenditure proposal's profitability. Using the accounting rate of return, a project that merely returns the initial investment will have an average annual increase in net income of 0 and an accounting rate of return of 0. The problem with the accounting rate of return is that it fails to consider the timing of cash flows. It treats all cash flows within the life of an investment proposal equally despite the fact that cash flows occurring early in a project's life are more valuable than cash flows occurring late in a project's life. Early period cash flows can earn additional profits by being invested elsewhere. Consider the two investment proposals summarized in **Exhibit 24.5**. Both have an accounting rate of return of 5 percent, but Proposal A is superior to Proposal B because most of its cash flows occur in the first two years. Because of the timing of the cash flows when discounted at an annual rate of 10 percent, Proposal A has a net present value of $1,120 while Proposal B has a negative net present value of $(10,928).

EXHIBIT 24.5	Evaluating Capital Budgeting Models with Differences in Cash Flow Timing

Accounting rate of return analysis of Projects A and B

	Project A	Project B
Predicted net cash inflow from operations		
Year 1	$ 50,000	$ 10,000
Year 2	50,000	10,000
Year 3	10,000	50,000
Year 4	10,000	50,000
Total	120,000	120,000
Total depreciation...............................	(100,000)	(100,000)
Total net income.................................	$ 20,000	$ 20,000
Project life.....................................	÷ 4 years	÷ 4 years
Average annual increase in net income............	$ 5,000	$ 5,000
Initial investment	÷ 100,000	÷ 100,000
Accounting rate of return on initial investment ...	0.05	0.05

Net present value analysis of Project A

	Predicted Cash Inflows (outflows)	Year(s) of Cash Flows	10% Present Value Factor	Present Value of Cash Flows
Initial investment	$(100,000)	0	1.00000	$(100,000)
Operation	50,000	1–2	1.73554	86,777
Operation	10,000	3–4	3.16987 − 1.73554	14,343
Net present value of all cash flows				$ 1,120

Net present value analysis of Project B

	Predicted Cash Inflows (outflows)	Year(s) of Cash Flows	10% Present Value Factor	Present Value of Cash Flows
Initial investment	$(100,000)	0	1.00000	$(100,000)
Operation	10,000	1–2	1.73554	17,355
Operation	50,000	3–4	3.16987 − 1.73554	71,717
Net present value of all cash flows				$ (10,928)

The net present value and the internal rate of return models both consider the time value of money and project profitability. They almost always provide the same evaluation of individual projects whose acceptance or rejection will not affect other projects. An exception can occur when periods of net cash outflows are mixed with periods of net cash inflows. Under these circumstances, an investment proposal could have multiple internal rates of return. The net present value and the internal rate of return models, however, have two basic differences that often lead to differences in the evaluation of competing investment proposals:

1. The net present value model gives explicit consideration to investment size. The internal rate of return model does not.

2. The net present value model assumes that all net cash inflows are reinvested at the discount rate; the internal rate of return model assumes that all net cash inflows are reinvested at the project's internal rate of return.

When there is a difference in the size of competing investment proposals and funds not invested in the accepted proposal can only be invested at the cost of capital, the net present value method is superior.

BUSINESS INSIGHT

Patient Capital In the UK, "patient capital" is outpacing traditional venture capital investment. Where venture capital (VC) groups expect returns after a fixed period, usually around 10 years, patient capital is characterized by willingness to wait and see. Of investments in new UK tech firms, 36% came from patient capital investors, while 34% came from traditional VCs. These two sources combined total just shy of $2 billion of funding.

Firms also use the patient capital principle to budget capital for activities such as research and development (R&D). The success of **Corning**'s Gorilla Glass highlights what can go right with patient capital. Corning saw revenue from sales of Gorilla Glass, which was originally developed in the 1960s, go from $0 to $1 billion in 2007 when the glass was selected as the surface of the iPhone.

Because patient capital requires patient investors or owners, less established firms need to be creative to allow time for their investments to make good. Drugmaker **Celator** used a combination of quick returns from improving the delivery of existing leukemia drugs and funding from the **Leukemia and Lymphoma Society** to buy time while their revolutionary treatment for acute myeloid leukemia went through clinical trials. Now that the drug is widely used, investors' patience is being rewarded.

Sources: Muran Ahmed, "Patient Capital Overtakes VC for UK Tech Groups," *Financial Times*, November 1, 2015.
Martin Tillier, "Corning (GLW) and Coherent (COHR): Old Tech Companies Still Worth Investing In," *Nasdaq News*, January 8, 2014.
Brian Gormley, "Venture Investors in Celator Pharma Rewarded for Taking the Long View," *Wall Street Journal*, June 1, 2016.

MID-CHAPTER REVIEW 4

Olive Theory Pizzeria is considering three different unrelated capital investments in 2018. Presented is information pertaining to each investment proposal.

	Proposal A	Proposal B	Proposal C
Initial investment.	$45,000	$45,000	$45,000
Cash flow from operations			
Year 1	40,000	22,500	45,000
Year 2	5,000	22,500	
Year 3	22,500	22,500	
Disinvestment			
Life (years)	3 years	3 years	1 year

REQUIRED
Determine each of the following:

a. Rank these investment proposals using the payback period, the accounting rate of return on initial investment, and the net present value criteria. Assume that the organization's cost of capital is 10 percent. Round all calculations to two decimal places.

b. Explain the difference in rankings. Which investment would you recommend?

The solution to this review problem can be found on page 1104.

ADDITIONAL ASPECTS OF CAPITAL BUDGETING

The capital budgeting models discussed do not make investment decisions. Rather, they help managers separate capital expenditure proposals that meet certain criteria from those that do not. Managers can then focus on those proposals that pass the initial screening.

Using Multiple Investment Criteria

In performing this initial screening, management can use a single capital budgeting model or multiple models, including some we have not discussed. Management might specify that proposals must be in line with the organization's long-range goals and business strategy, have a maximum payback period of three years, have a positive net present value when discounted at 14 percent, and have an initial investment of less than $500,000. The maximum payback period might be intended to reduce risk, the present value criterion might be to ensure an adequate return to investors, and the maximum investment size might reflect the resources available for investment.

Nonquantitative factors such as market position, operational performance improvement, and strategy implementation often play a decisive role in management's final decision to accept or reject a capital expenditure proposal that has passed the initial screening. Also important at this point are top management's attitudes toward risk and financing alternatives, their confidence in the professional judgment of other managers making investment proposals, their beliefs about the future direction of the economy, and their evaluation of alternative investments. In the following sections, we will focus on evaluating risk, differential analysis of project cash flows, predicting differential costs and revenues for high-tech investments, and evaluating mutually exclusive investments.

Evaluating Risk

All capital expenditure proposals involve risk, including risk related to:

- Cost of the initial investment.
- Time required to complete the initial investment and begin operations.
- Whether the new facilities will operate as planned.
- Life of the facilities.
- Customers' demand for the product or service.
- Final selling price.
- Operating costs.
- Disposal values.

Projected cash flows (such as those summarized for the Mobile Taqueria proposal in **Exhibit 24.2**) are based on management's best predictions. Although these predictions are likely to reflect the professional judgment of economists, marketing personnel, engineers, and accountants, they are far from certain.

Many techniques have been developed to assist in the analysis of the risks inherent in capital budgeting. Suggested approaches include the following:

- *To adjust the discount rate for individual projects based on management's perception of the risks associated with a project.* A project perceived as being almost risk free might be evaluated using a discount rate of 12 percent; a project perceived as having moderate risk may be evaluated using a discount rate of 16 percent; and a project perceived as having high risk might be evaluated using a discount rate of 20 percent.

- *To compute several internal rates of return and/or net present values for a project.* For example, a project's net present value might be computed three times: first assuming the most optimistic projections of cash flows; second assuming the most likely projections of cash flows; and third assuming the most pessimistic projections of cash flows. The final decision is then based on management's attitudes toward risk. A project whose most likely outcome is highly profitable would probably be rejected if its pessimistic outcome might lead to bankruptcy.

- *To subject a capital expenditure proposal to sensitivity analysis*, a study of the responsiveness of a model's dependent variable(s) to changes in one or more of its independent variables. Management might want to know, for example, the minimum annual net cash inflows that will provide an internal rate of return of 12 percent with other cost and revenue projections being as expected.

Differential Analysis of Project Cash Flows

All previous examples assume that capital expenditure proposals produce additional net cash inflows, but this is not always the case. Units of government and not-for-profit organizations might provide services that do not produce any cash inflows. For-profit organizations might be required to make capital expenditures to maintain product quality or to bring facilities up to environmental or safety standards. In these situations, it is impossible to compute a project's payback period, accounting rate of return, or internal rate of return. It is possible, however, to compute the present value of all life cycle costs associated with alternative ways of providing the service or meeting the environmental or safety standard. Here, the alternative with the smallest negative net present value is preferred.

Capital expenditure proposals to reduce operating costs by upgrading facilities might not provide any incremental cash inflows. Again, we can use a total cost approach and calculate the present value of the costs associated with each alternative, with the low-cost alternative being preferred. Alternatively, we can perform a differential analysis of cash flows and, treating any reduced operating costs as if they were cash inflows, compute the net present value or the internal rate of return of the cost reduction proposal. Recall from Chapter 16 that a relevant cost analysis focuses on the costs that differ under alternative actions. Once the differential amounts have been determined, they can be adjusted for the time value of money. To illustrate the differential approach, we consider an example introduced in Chapter 16.

Let's again assume Beats produces a variety of electronic components, including 10,000 units per year of a component used in wireless headsets. Further assume the machine currently used in manufacturing the headset components is two years old and has a remaining useful life of four years. It cost $90,000 and has an estimated salvage value of zero dollars at the end of its useful life. Its current book value (original cost less accumulated depreciation) is $60,000, but its current disposal value is only $35,000.

Management is evaluating the desirability of replacing the machine with a new machine. The new machine costs $80,000, has a useful life of four years, and a predicted salvage value of zero dollars at the end of its useful life. Although the new machine has the same productive capacity as the old machine, its predicted operating costs are lower because it requires less electricity. Furthermore, because of a computer control system, the new machine will require less frequent and less expensive inspections and adjustments. Finally, the new machine requires less maintenance.

An analysis of the cash flows associated with this cost reduction proposal, separated into the three phases of the project's life, are presented in **Exhibit 24.6**. Because the proposal does not have a disposal value, this portion of the analysis could have been omitted. (A detailed explanation of the relevant costs included in this analysis is in **Exhibit 16.1** and the accompanying Chapter 16 discussion of relevant costs.) Assuming that Beats has a discount rate of 12 percent, the proposal's net present value (computed in **Exhibit 24.7**) is $2,686, and the proposal is acceptable.

EXHIBIT 24.6	Differential Analysis of Predicted Cash Flows		
		One Year Totals	
	Keep Old Machine (A)	**Replace with New Machine (B)**	**Difference (income effect of replacement) (A) − (B)**
Initial investment			
Cost of new machine		$80,000	$(80,000)
Disposal value of old machine		(35,000)	35,000
Net initial investment			$(45,000)
Annual operating cash savings			
Conversion			
Old machine (10,000 units × $5)	$50,000		
New machine (10,000 units × $4).		$40,000	$10,000
Inspection and adjustment			
Old machine (10 setups × $500 per setup)	5,000		
New machine (5 setups × $300 per setup).		1,500	3,500
Machine maintenance			
Old machine ($200 per month × 12 months).	2,400		
New machine ($200 per year)		200	2,200
Net annual cost savings			$15,700
Disinvestment at end of life			
Old machine	$ 0		
New machine		$ 0	

EXHIBIT 24.7	Differential Analysis of Predicted Cash Flows			
	Predicted Cash Inflows (outflows) (A)	**Year(s) of Cash Flows (B)**	**12% Present Value Factor (C)**	**Present Value of Cash Flows (A) × (C)**
Initial investment.	$(45,000)	0	1.00000	$(45,000)
Operation	15,700	1–4	3.03735	47,686
Disinvestment.	0	4	0.63552	0
Net present value of all cash flows.				$ 2,686

Predicting Differential Costs and Revenues for High-Tech Investments

Care must be taken when evaluating proposals for investments in technological innovations such as flexible manufacturing systems and computer integrated manufacturing. The three types of errors to consider are: (1) investing in unnecessary or overly complex equipment, (2) overestimating cost saving, and (3) underestimating incremental sales.

Investing in Unnecessary or Overly Complex Equipment   A common error is to simply compare the cost associated with the current inefficient way of doing things with the predicted cost of performing the identical operations with more modern equipment. Although capital budgeting models might suggest that such investments are justifiable, the result could be the costly and rapid completion of non-value-added activities. Consider the following examples.

- A company invests in an automated system to speed the movement of work in process between workstations without first evaluating the plant layout. The firm is still unable to compete with other companies having better organized plants that allow lower cycle times, lower work-in-process inventories, and lower manufacturing costs. Management should have evaluated the plant layout before investing in new equipment. They may have found that rearranging the factory floor would have reduced materials movement and eliminated the need for the investment.

- A company invests in an automated warehouse to permit the rapid storage and retrieval of goods while competitors work to eliminate excess inventory. The firm is left with large inventories and a large investment in the automated warehouse while competitors, not having to earn a return on similar investments, are able to charge lower prices. Management should have evaluated the need for current inventory levels and perhaps shifted to a just-in-time approach to inventory management before considering the investment in an automated warehouse.

- A company hires staff to perform quality inspections while competitors implement total quality management and seek to eliminate the need for quality inspections. While defective products or services are now identified before they affect customers, they still exist. Furthermore, the company has higher expenditures than competitors, resulting in a less competitive cost structure. The inspections might not have been needed if management had shifted from inspecting for conformance to an emphasis on "doing it right the first time."

- A company invests in automated welding equipment to more efficiently produce printer casings while competitors simplify the product design and shift from welded to molded plastic casings. Although the cost of producing the welded casings might be lower, the company's cost structure is still not competitive.

All of these examples illustrate the limitations of capital budgeting models and the need for good judgment. *In the final analysis, managers, not models, make decisions.* Management must carefully evaluate the situations and determine whether they have considered the proper alternatives and all important cash flows.

Overestimating Cost Savings   When a number of activities drive manufacturing overhead costs, estimates of overhead cost savings based on a single activity cost driver can significantly overestimate cost savings. Assume, for example, that a company containing both machine-intensive and labor-intensive operations develops a cost-estimating equation for overhead with labor as the only independent variable. Because of this, all overhead costs are associated with labor. The predicted cost savings can be computed as the sum of predicted reductions in labor plus predicted reductions in overhead; the predicted reductions in overhead are computed as the overhead per direct labor dollar or labor hour multiplied by the predicted reduction in direct labor dollars or labor hours. Because a major portion of the overhead is driven by factors other than direct labor, reducing direct labor will not provide the predicted savings. Capital budgeting models might suggest that the investment is acceptable, but the models are based on inaccurate cost data.

Management should beware of overly simplistic computations of cost savings. This is an area in which management needs the assistance of well-trained management accountants and engineers.

Underestimating Incremental Sales or Cost Savings   In evaluating proposals for investments in new equipment, management often assumes that the baseline for comparison is the current sales level, but this might not be the case. If competitors are investing in equipment to better meet customer needs and to reduce costs, a failure to make similar investments might result in uncompetitive prices and declining, rather than steady, sales. Hence, the baseline for sales without the investment is overstated, and the incremental sales of the investment is understated. Not considering the likely decline in sales understates the incremental sales associated with the investment and biases the results against the proposed investment.

Investments in manufacturing technologies, such as flexible manufacturing systems (FMS) and computer integrated manufacturing (CIM), do more than simply allow the efficient production of current products. Such investments also make possible the rapid, low-cost switching to new products. The result is expanded sales opportunities.

Such investments might also produce cost savings further down the value chain, either within or outside the company. Beats' decision to acquire a new machine might have the unanticipated consequence of reducing customer warranty claims or increasing sales because customers are attracted to a higher-quality product.

Unfortunately, because such opportunities are difficult to quantify, they are often ignored in the evaluation of capital expenditure proposals. The solution to this dilemma involves the application of management's professional judgment, a willingness to take risks based on this professional judgment, and recognition that certain investments transcend capital budgeting models in that they involve strategic as well as long-range planning. At this level of planning, qualitative decisions concerning the nature of the organization are at least as important as quantified factors.

MID-CHAPTER REVIEW 5

Hilltop Ski Resort is considering making a capital investment in a new ski lift. Hilltop's finance team assessed the investment using the net present value model and predicts the ski lift will generate a positive net present value cash flow over the life of the asset.

REQUIRED

Identify and discuss additional factors that Hilltop's management should consider after the initial screening of the capital investment in the ski lift, before making a final evaluation of the investment.

The solution to this review problem can be found on page 1104.

LO6 Determine the net present value of investment proposals with consideration of taxes.

TAXES IN CAPITAL BUDGETING DECISIONS

To focus on capital budgeting concepts, we deferred consideration of the impact of taxes. Because income taxes affect cash flows and income, their consideration is important in evaluating investment proposals in for-profit organizations.

The cost of investments in plant and equipment is not deducted from taxable revenues in determining taxable income and income taxes at the time of the initial investment. Instead, the amount of the initial investment is deducted as depreciation over the operating life of an asset. To illustrate the impact of taxes on cash flows, assume:

- Revenues and operating cash receipts are the same each year.
- Depreciation is the only noncash expense of an organization.

Depreciation Tax Shield

Depreciation does not require the use of cash (the funds were spent at the initial investment), but depreciation is said to provide a "tax shield" because it reduces cash payments for income taxes. The **depreciation tax shield** (the reduction in taxes due to the deductibility of depreciation from taxable revenues) is computed as follows:

> **Depreciation tax shield = Depreciation × Tax rate**

The value of the depreciation tax shield is illustrated using Mobile Taqueria's capital expenditure proposal summarized in **Exhibit 24.2**. Mobile Taqueria's annual straight line depreciation of $16,511 is computed as the initial investment of $90,554 minus the predicted disposal value of $8,000, all divided by the predicted five year life $16,511 [($90,554 − $8,000)/5]. With an assumed tax rate of 34 percent, the annual depreciation tax shield is $5,614 ($16,511 depreciation × 0.34 tax rate). The increase in annual cash flows provided by the depreciation tax shield is illustrated in **Exhibit 24.8**. Examine this exhibit, paying particular attention to the lines for depreciation, income taxes, and net annual cash flow.

The U.S. Tax Code contains guidelines concerning the depreciation of various types of assets. (Analysis of these guidelines is beyond the scope of this text.) Tax guidelines allow organizations a choice in tax depreciation procedures between straight-line depreciation and an accelerated depreciation method detailed in the Tax Code. Because of the time value of money, profitable businesses should usually select the tax depreciation procedure that provides the earliest depreciation. To illustrate the effect of accelerated depreciation on taxes and capital budgeting, we use double-declining balance depreciation rather than the accelerated method detailed in the Code. When making capital expenditure decisions, managers should, of course, refer to the most current version of the Tax Code to determine the specific depreciation guidelines in effect at that time.

Exhibits 24.9 and **24.10** illustrate the effect of two alternative depreciation procedures, straight-line and double-declining balance, on the net present value of Mobile Taqueria's proposed investment. The cash flows for this investment were presented in **Exhibit 24.2**, and the effect of taxes on the investment's annual cash flows were examined in **Exhibit 24.8**. Ignoring taxes, the investment was shown (in **Exhibit 24.3**) to have a positive net present value of $20,398 at a discount rate of 12 percent. With taxes, the investment has a positive net present value of $3,866 using straight-line depreciation and $6,082 using double-declining balance depreciation. Although taxes and cash flows are identical over the entire life of the project, the use of double-declining balance depreciation for taxes results in a higher net present value because it results in lower cash expenditures for taxes in the earlier years of an asset's life.

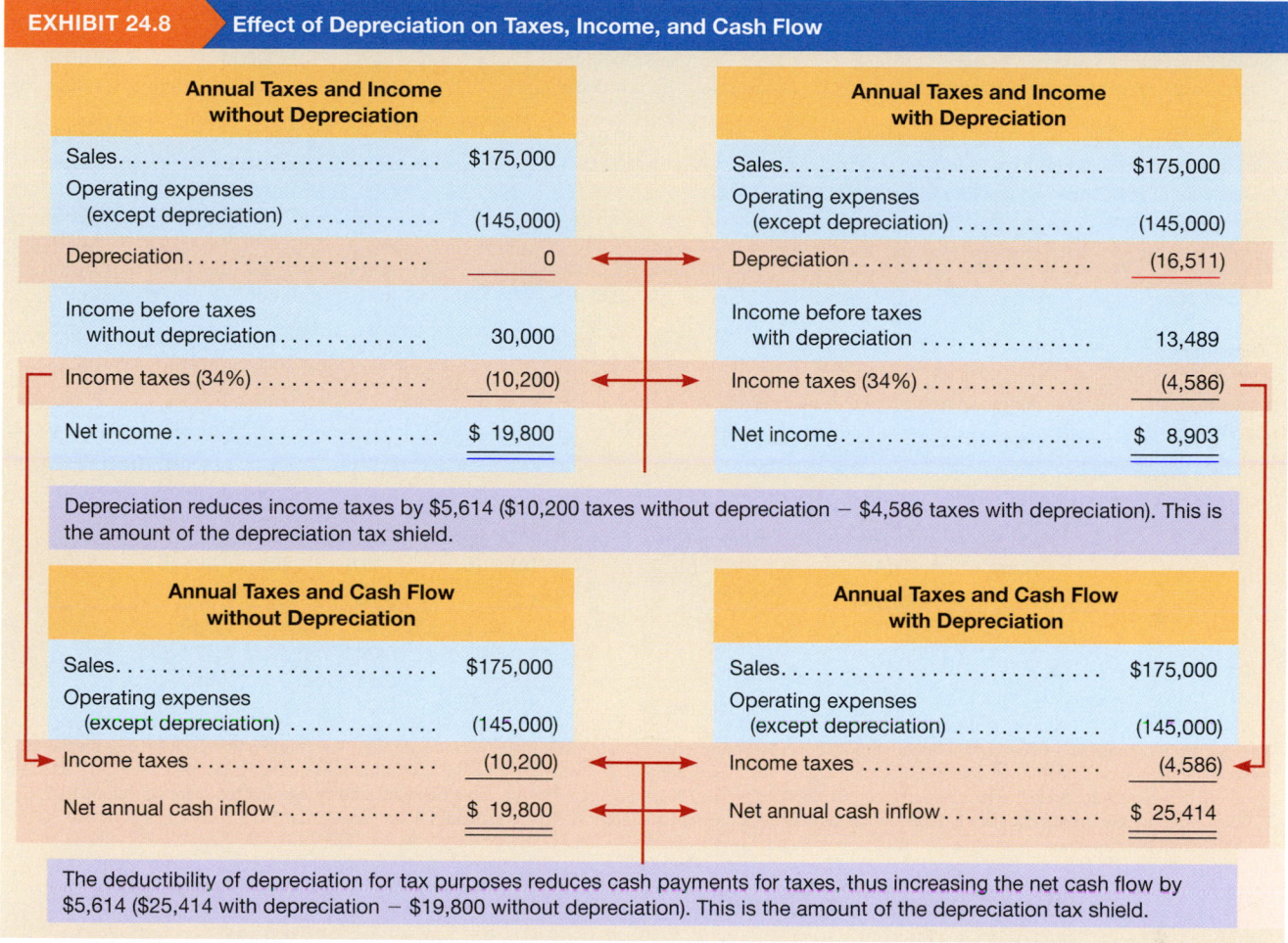

EXHIBIT 24.8   Effect of Depreciation on Taxes, Income, and Cash Flow

Annual Taxes and Income without Depreciation	
Sales........................	$175,000
Operating expenses (except depreciation)	(145,000)
Depreciation......................	0
Income before taxes without depreciation.............	30,000
Income taxes (34%)...............	(10,200)
Net income........................	$ 19,800

Annual Taxes and Income with Depreciation	
Sales........................	$175,000
Operating expenses (except depreciation)	(145,000)
Depreciation......................	(16,511)
Income before taxes with depreciation	13,489
Income taxes (34%)...............	(4,586)
Net income........................	$ 8,903

Depreciation reduces income taxes by $5,614 ($10,200 taxes without depreciation − $4,586 taxes with depreciation). This is the amount of the depreciation tax shield.

Annual Taxes and Cash Flow without Depreciation	
Sales........................	$175,000
Operating expenses (except depreciation)	(145,000)
Income taxes	(10,200)
Net annual cash inflow..............	$ 19,800

Annual Taxes and Cash Flow with Depreciation	
Sales........................	$175,000
Operating expenses (except depreciation)	(145,000)
Income taxes	(4,586)
Net annual cash inflow..............	$ 25,414

The deductibility of depreciation for tax purposes reduces cash payments for taxes, thus increasing the net cash flow by $5,614 ($25,414 with depreciation − $19,800 without depreciation). This is the amount of the depreciation tax shield.

EXHIBIT 24.9   Analysis of Capital Expenditures Including Tax Effects: Straight-Line Depreciation

	Predicted Cash Inflows (outflows) (A)	Year(s) of Cash Flows (B)	12% Present Value Factor (C)	Present Value of Cash Flows (A) × (C)
Initial investment				
Vehicle and equipment............................	$(90,554)	0	1.00000	$ (90,554)
Inventory and other working capital..................	(4,000)	0	1.00000	(4,000)
Operations				
Annual taxable income without depreciation...........	30,000	1–5	3.60478	108,143
Taxes on income ($30,000 × 0.34)..................	(10,200)	1–5	3.60478	(36,769)
Depreciation tax shield*	5,614	1–5	3.60478	20,237
Disinvestment				
Sale of vehicle and equipment......................	8,000	5	0.56743	4,539
Inventory and other working capital..................	4,000	5	0.56743	2,270
Net present value of all cash flows				$ 3,866

*Computation of depreciation tax shield:

Annual straight-line depreciation	$16,511
Tax rate..	× 0.34
Depreciation tax shield............................	$ 5,614

EXHIBIT 24.10	Analysis of Capital Expenditures Including Tax Effects: DDB Depreciation			
	Predicted Cash Inflows (outflows) (A)	Year(s) of Cash Flows (B)	12% Present Value Factor (C)	Present Value of Cash Flows (A) × (C)
Initial investment				
Vehicle and equipment	$(90,554)	0	1.00000	$ (90,554)
Inventory and other working capital	4,000	0	1.00000	(4,000)
Operations				
Annual taxable income without depreciation	30,000	1–5	3.60478	108,143
Taxes on income ($30,000 × 0.34)	(10,200)	1–5	3.60478	(36,769)
Depreciation tax shield*				
Year 1	12,315	1	0.89286	10,996
Year 2	7,389	2	0.79719	5,890
Year 3	4,434	3	0.71178	3,156
Year 4	2,660	4	0.63552	1,690
Year 5	1,270	5	0.56743	721
Disinvestment				
Sale of vehicle and equipment	8,000	5	0.56743	4,539
Inventory and other working capital	4,000	5	0.56743	2,270
Net present value of all cash flows				$ 6,082

*Computation of depreciation tax shield:

Year	Depreciation Base† (A)	Annual Rate (B)	Annual Depreciation (C) = (A) × (B)	Tax Rate (D)	Tax Shield (E) = (C) × (D)
1 . . .	$90,554	2/5	$36,222	0.34	$12,315
2 . . .	54,332	2/5	21,733	0.34	7,389
3 . . .	32,599	2/5	13,040	0.34	4,434
4 . . .	19,559	2/5	7,824	0.34	2,660
5 . . .	11,735	balance	3,735	0.34	1,270

†The depreciation base is reduced by the amount of all previous depreciation. The annual rate is twice the straight-line rate. For simplicity, we depreciated the remaining balance in the fifth year and did not switch to straight-line depreciation when the straight-line amount exceeds the double-declining balance amount. This would happen in the fourth year, when $19,559 ÷ 2 = $9,780. Although the depreciable base excludes the predicted disposal value of $8,000, under double declining balance depreciation, an asset is only depreciated down to its disposal value. Hence, Year 5 depreciation is computed as the $11,735 depreciable base minus the $8,000 disposal value.

Investment Tax Credit

From time to time, for the purpose of stimulating investment and economic growth, the U.S. federal government has implemented an investment tax credit. An **investment tax credit** reduces taxes in the year a new asset is placed in service by some stated percentage of the cost of the asset. In recent years tax credits, such as the credits for purchasing hybrid automobiles, have been used to stimulate investments that reduce the emission of greenhouses gases. Typically, this is done without reducing the depreciation base of the asset for tax purposes. An investment tax credit reduces cash payments for taxes and, hence, is treated as a cash inflow for capital budgeting purposes. This additional cash inflow increases the probability that a new asset will meet a taxpayer's capital expenditure criteria.

CHAPTER-END REVIEW

Assume that Architecture Design is considering a proposal to change the company's manual design system to a computer-aided design system. The new system is expected to save 9,000 design hours per year; an operating cost savings of $45 per hour. The annual cash expenditures of operating the new system are estimated to be $200,000. The new system would require an initial investment of $550,000. The estimated life of this system is 5 years with no salvage value. The tax rate is 35 percent, and Architecture Design uses straight-line depreciation for tax purposes. Architecture Design has a cost of capital of 14 percent.

REQUIRED
a. Compute the annual after-tax cash flows related to the new design system.
b. Assume that management intends to use double declining balance depreciation with a switch to straight-line depreciation (applied to any undepreciated balance) starting in Year 4. Determine the project's net present value.

The solution to this review problem can be found on page 1105.

APPENDIX 24A: Time Value of Money

LO7 Compute basic present value cash flow amounts.

When asked to choose between $500 today or an IOU for $500 to be paid one year later, rational decision makers choose the $500 today. Two reasons for this involve the time *value of money* and the *risk*. A dollar today is worth more than a dollar tomorrow or at some future time. Having a dollar provides flexibility. It can be spent, buried, or invested in a number of projects. If invested in a savings account, it will amount to more than one dollar at some future time because of the effect of interest. The interest paid by a bank (or borrower) for the use of money is analogous to the rent paid for the use of land, buildings, or equipment. Furthermore, we live in an uncertain world, and, for a variety of reasons, the possibility exists that an IOU might not be paid.

Future Value

Future value is the amount that a current sum of money earning a stated rate of interest will accumulate to at the end of a future period. Suppose we deposit $500 in a savings account at a financial institution that pays interest at the rate of 10 percent per year. At the end of the first year, the original deposit of $500 will total $550 ($500 × 1.10). If we leave the $550 for another year, the amount will increase to $605 ($550 × 1.10). It can be stated that $500 today has a future value in one year of $550, or conversely, that $550 one year from today has a present value of $500. Interest of $55 ($605 − $550) was earned in the second year, whereas interest of only $50 was earned in the first year. This happened because interest during the second year was earned on the principal plus interest from the first year ($550). When periodic interest is computed on principal plus prior periods' accumulated interest, the interest is said to be *compounded*. Compound interest is used throughout this text.

To determine future values at the end of one period (usually a year), multiply the beginning amount (present value) by 1 plus the interest rate. When multiple periods are involved, the future value is determined by repeatedly multiplying the beginning amount by 1 plus the interest rate for each period. When $500 is invested for two years at an interest rate of 10 percent per year, its future value is computed as $500 × 1.10 × 1.10. The following equation is used to figure future value:

$$fv = pv(1 + i)^n$$

where:

$$fv = \text{future value amount}$$
$$pv = \text{present value amount}$$
$$i = \text{interest rate per period}$$
$$n = \text{number of periods}$$

For our $500 deposit, the equation becomes:

$$fv \text{ of } \$500 = pv(1 + i)^n$$
$$= \$500(1 + 0.10)^2$$
$$= \$605$$

In a similar manner, once the interest rate and number of periods are known, the future value amount of any present value amount is easily determined.

Present Value

Present value is the current worth of a specified amount of money to be received at some future date at some interest rate. Solving for *pv* in the future value equation, the new present value equation is determined as follows:

$$pv = \frac{fv}{(1 + i)^n}$$

Using this equation, the present value of $8,800 to be received in one year, discounted at 10 percent, is computed as follows:

$$pv \text{ of } \$8,800 = \frac{\$8,800}{(1 + 0.10)^1}$$
$$= \frac{\$8,800}{(1.10)}$$
$$= \$8,000$$

Thus, when the discount rate is 10 percent, the present value of $8,800 to be received in one year is $8,000. The present value equation is often expressed as the future value amount times the present value of $1:

$$pv = fv \times \frac{\$1}{(1+i)^n}$$

Using the equation for the present value of $1, the present value of $8,800 to be received in one year, discounted at 10 percent, is computed as follows:

$$pv \text{ of } \$8,800 = \$8,800 \times \frac{\$1}{(1+0.10)^1}$$

$$= \$8,800 \times 0.90909$$

$$= \$8,000$$

The present value of $8,800 two periods from now is $7,273, computed as [$8,800 ÷ (1.10)²] or [$8,800 × $1 ÷ (1.10)²].

If a calculator or computer with spreadsheet software is not available, present value computations can be done by hand. Tables, such as **Exhibit 24A.1** for the present value of $1 at various interest rates and time periods, can be used to simplify hand computations. Using the factors in **Exhibit 24A.1**, the present value of any future amount can be determined. For example, with an interest rate of 10 percent, the present value of the following future amounts to be received in one period are as follows:

Future Value Amount		Present Value Factor of $1		Present Value
$ 100	×	0.90909	=	$ 90.91
628	×	0.90909	=	570.91
4,285	×	0.90909	=	3,895.45
9,900	×	0.90909	=	8,999.99

To further illustrate the use of **Exhibit 24A.1**, consider the following application. Suppose Beats wants to invest its surplus cash at 12 percent to have $10,000 to pay off a long-term note due at the end of five years. **Exhibit 24A.1** shows that the present value factor of $1, discounted at 12 percent per year for five years, is 0.56743. Multiplying $10,000 by 0.56743, the present value is determined to be $5,674:

$$pv \text{ of } \$10,000 = \$10,000 \times \text{Present value factor for } \$1$$

$$= \$10,000 \times 0.56743$$

$$= \$5,674$$

Therefore, if Beats invests $5,674 today, it will have $10,000 available to pay off its note in five years.

Managers also use present value tables to make investment decisions. Assume that Monroe Company can make an investment that will provide a cash flow of $12,000 at the end of eight years. If the company demands a rate of return of 14 percent per year, what is the most it will be willing to pay for this investment? From **Exhibit 24A.1**, we find that the present value factor for $1, discounted at 14 percent per year for eight years, is 0.35056:

$$pv \text{ of } \$12,000 = \$12,000 \times \text{Present value factor for } \$1$$

$$= \$12,000 \times 0.35056$$

$$= \$4,207$$

If the company demands an annual return of 14 percent, the most it would be willing to invest today is $4,207.

Annuities

Not all investments provide a single sum of money. Many investments provide periodic cash flows called *annuities*. An **annuity** is a series of equal cash flows received or paid over equal intervals of time. Suppose that $100 will be received at the end of each of the next three years. If the discount rate is 10 percent, the present value of this annuity can be determined by summing the present value of each receipt:

Year 1 $100 × $1 ÷ (1 + 0.10)¹ = $ 90.90
Year 2 $100 × $1 ÷ (1 + 0.10)² =   82.65
Year 3 $100 × $1 ÷ (1 + 0.10)³ =   75.13

Total. $248.68

Alternatively, the following equation can be used to compute the present value of an annuity with cash flows at the end of each period:

$$pva = \frac{a}{i} \times \left[1 - \frac{1}{(1+i)^n} \right]$$

where:

pva = present value of an annuity (also called the annuity factor)
i = prevailing rate per period
n = number of periods
a = annuity amount

This equation was used to compute the factors presented in **Exhibit 24A.2** for an annuity amount of $1. The present value of an annuity of $1 per period for three periods discounted at 10 percent per period is as follows:

$$pva\ of\ \$1 = \frac{1}{0.10} \times \left[1 - \frac{1}{(1+0.10)^3} \right]$$

$$= 2.48685$$

Using this factor, the present value of a $100 annuity can be computed as $100 × 2.48685, which yields $248.689. To determine the present value of an annuity of any amount, the annuity factor for $1 can be multiplied by the annuity amount.

To further illustrate the use of **Exhibit 24A.2**, assume that Red Kite Company is considering an investment in a piece of equipment that will produce net cash inflows of $2,000 at the end of each year for five years. If the company's desired rate of return is 12 percent, an investment of $7,210 will provide such a return:

$$pva\ of\ \$2,000 = \$2,000 \times \begin{array}{c}\textbf{Present value for an annuity of \$1}\\\textbf{for five periods discounted at 12\%}\end{array}$$

$$= \$2,000 \times 3.60478$$

$$= \$7,210$$

Here, the $2,000 annuity is multiplied by 3.60478, the factor for an annuity of $1 for five periods found in **Exhibit 24A.2**, discounted at 12 percent per period.

Another use of **Exhibit 24A.2** is to determine the amount that must be received annually to provide a desired rate of return on an investment. Assume that **Corning** invests $33,550 in a piece of machinery and desires a return of the investment plus interest of 8 percent in equal year-end payments for ten years. The minimum amount that must be received each year is determined by solving the equation for the present value of an annuity:

$$pva = a \times (pva\ of\ \$1)$$

$$a = \frac{pva}{pva\ of\ \$1}$$

From **Exhibit 24A.2**, we see that the 8 percent factor for ten periods is 6.71008. Dividing the $33,550 investment by 6.71008, the required annuity is computed to be $5,000:

$$a = \frac{\$33,550}{6.71008}$$

$$= \$5,000$$

Unequal Cash Flows

Many investment situations do not produce equal periodic cash flows. When this occurs, the present value for each cash flow must be determined independently because the annuity table can be used only for equal periodic cash flows. **Exhibit 24A.1** is used to determine the present value of each future amount separately. To illustrate, assume that the **Atlanta Braves** wish to acquire the contract of a popular baseball player who is known to attract large crowds. Management believes this player will return incremental cash flows to the team at the end of each of the next three years in the amounts of $2,500,000, $4,000,000, and $1,500,000. After three years, the player anticipates retiring. If the team's owners require a minimum return of 14 percent on their investment, how much would they be willing to pay for the player's contract?

EXHIBIT 24A.1	Present Value of $1

$$\text{Present value of } \$1 = \frac{1}{(1+i)^n}$$

Discount rate (*i*)

Periods (n)	4%	6%	8%	10%	12%	14%	16%	18%	20%	22%	24%	26%	28%
1	0.96154	0.94340	0.92593	0.90909	0.89286	0.87719	0.86207	0.84746	0.83333	0.81967	0.80645	0.79365	0.78125
2	0.92456	0.89000	0.85734	0.82645	0.79719	0.76947	0.74316	0.71818	0.69444	0.67186	0.65036	0.62988	0.61035
3	0.88900	0.83962	0.79383	0.75131	0.71178	0.67497	0.64066	0.60863	0.57870	0.55071	0.52449	0.49991	0.47684
4	0.85480	0.79209	0.73503	0.68301	0.63552	0.59208	0.55229	0.51579	0.48225	0.45140	0.42297	0.39675	0.37253
5	0.82193	0.74726	0.68058	0.62092	0.56743	0.51937	0.47611	0.43711	0.40188	0.37000	0.34111	0.31488	0.29104
6	0.79031	0.70496	0.63017	0.56447	0.50663	0.45559	0.41044	0.37043	0.33490	0.30328	0.27509	0.24991	0.22737
7	0.75992	0.66506	0.58349	0.51316	0.45235	0.39964	0.35383	0.31393	0.27908	0.24859	0.22184	0.19834	0.17764
8	0.73069	0.62741	0.54027	0.46651	0.40388	0.35056	0.30503	0.26604	0.23257	0.20376	0.17891	0.15741	0.13878
9	0.70259	0.59190	0.50025	0.42410	0.36061	0.30751	0.26295	0.22546	0.19381	0.16702	0.14428	0.12493	0.10842
10	0.67556	0.55839	0.46319	0.38554	0.32197	0.26974	0.22668	0.19106	0.16151	0.13690	0.11635	0.09915	0.08470
11	0.64958	0.52679	0.42888	0.35049	0.28748	0.23662	0.19542	0.16192	0.13459	0.11221	0.09383	0.07869	0.06617
12	0.62460	0.49697	0.39711	0.31863	0.25668	0.20756	0.16846	0.13722	0.11216	0.09198	0.07567	0.06245	0.05170
13	0.60057	0.46884	0.36770	0.28966	0.22917	0.18207	0.14523	0.11629	0.09346	0.07539	0.06103	0.04957	0.04039
14	0.57748	0.44230	0.34046	0.26333	0.20462	0.15971	0.12520	0.09855	0.07789	0.06180	0.04921	0.03934	0.03155
15	0.55526	0.41727	0.31524	0.23939	0.18270	0.14010	0.10793	0.08352	0.06491	0.05065	0.03969	0.03122	0.02465
16	0.53391	0.39365	0.29189	0.21763	0.16312	0.12289	0.09304	0.07078	0.05409	0.04152	0.03201	0.02478	0.01926
17	0.51337	0.37136	0.27027	0.19784	0.14564	0.10780	0.08021	0.05998	0.04507	0.03403	0.02581	0.01967	0.01505
18	0.49363	0.35034	0.25025	0.17986	0.13004	0.09456	0.06914	0.05083	0.03756	0.02789	0.02082	0.01561	0.01175
19	0.47464	0.33051	0.23171	0.16351	0.11611	0.08295	0.05961	0.04308	0.03130	0.02286	0.01679	0.01239	0.00918
20	0.45639	0.31180	0.21455	0.14864	0.10367	0.07276	0.05139	0.03651	0.02608	0.01874	0.01354	0.00983	0.00717

EXHIBIT 24A.2	Present Value of an Annuity of $1

$$\text{Present value of an annuity of } \$1 = \frac{1}{i} \times \left[1 - \frac{1}{(1+i)^n} \right]$$

Ditscount rate (*i*)

Periods (n)	4%	6%	8%	10%	12%	14%	16%	18%	20%	22%	24%	26%	28%
1	0.96154	0.94340	0.92593	0.90909	0.89286	0.87719	0.86207	0.84746	0.83333	0.81967	0.80645	0.79365	0.78125
2	1.88609	1.83339	1.78326	1.73554	1.69005	1.64666	1.60523	1.56564	1.52778	1.49153	1.45682	1.42353	1.39160
3	2.77509	2.67301	2.57710	2.48685	2.40183	2.32163	2.24589	2.17427	2.10648	2.04224	1.98130	1.92344	1.86844
4	3.62990	3.46511	3.31213	3.16987	3.03735	2.91371	2.79818	2.69006	2.58873	2.49364	2.40428	2.32019	2.24097
5	4.45182	4.21236	3.99271	3.79079	3.60478	3.43308	3.27429	3.12717	2.99061	2.86364	2.74538	2.63507	2.53201
6	5.24214	4.91732	4.62288	4.35526	4.11141	3.88867	3.68474	3.49760	3.32551	3.16692	3.02047	2.88498	2.75938
7	6.00205	5.58238	5.20637	4.86842	4.56376	4.28830	4.03857	3.81153	3.60459	3.41551	3.24232	3.08331	2.93702
8	6.73274	6.20979	5.74664	5.33493	4.96764	4.63886	4.34359	4.07757	3.83716	3.61927	3.42122	3.24073	3.07579
9	7.43533	6.80169	6.24689	5.75902	5.32825	4.94637	4.60654	4.30302	4.03097	3.78628	3.56550	3.36566	3.18421
10	8.11090	7.36009	6.71008	6.14457	5.65022	5.21612	4.83323	4.49409	4.19247	3.92318	3.68186	3.46481	3.26892
11	8.76048	7.88687	7.13896	6.49506	5.93770	5.45273	5.02864	4.65601	4.32706	4.03540	3.77569	3.54350	3.33509
12	9.38507	8.38384	7.53608	6.81369	6.19437	5.66029	5.19711	4.79322	4.43922	4.12737	3.85136	3.60595	3.38679
13	9.98565	8.85268	7.90378	7.10336	6.42355	5.84236	5.34233	4.90951	4.53268	4.20277	3.91239	3.65552	3.42718
14	10.56312	9.29498	8.24424	7.36669	6.62817	6.00207	5.46753	5.00806	4.61057	4.26456	3.96160	3.69485	3.45873
15	11.11839	9.71225	8.55948	7.60608	6.81086	6.14217	5.57546	5.09158	4.67547	4.31522	4.00129	3.72607	3.48339
16	11.65230	10.10590	8.85137	7.82371	6.97399	6.26506	5.66850	5.16235	4.72956	4.35673	4.03330	3.75085	3.50265
17	12.16567	10.47726	9.12164	8.02155	7.11963	6.37286	5.74870	5.22233	4.77463	4.39077	4.05911	3.77052	3.51769
18	12.65930	10.82760	9.37189	8.20141	7.24967	6.46742	5.81785	5.27316	4.81219	4.41866	4.07993	3.78613	3.52945
19	13.13394	11.15812	9.60360	8.36492	7.36578	6.55037	5.87746	5.31624	4.84350	4.44152	4.09672	3.79851	3.53863
20	13.59033	11.46992	9.81815	8.51356	7.46944	6.62313	5.92884	5.35275	4.86958	4.46027	4.11026	3.80834	3.54580

To solve this problem, it is necessary to determine the present value of the expected future cash flows. Here we use **Exhibit 24A.1** to find the $1 present value factors at 14 percent for Periods 1, 2, and 3. The cash flows are then multiplied by these factors:

Year		Annual Cash Flow		Present Value of $1 at 14 Percent		Present Value Amount
1		$2,500,000	×	0.87719	=	$2,192,975
2		4,000,000	×	0.76947	=	3,077,880
3		1,500,000	×	0.67497	=	1,012,455
Total						$6,283,310

The total present value of the cash flows for the three years, $6,283,310, represents the maximum amount the team would be willing to pay for the player's contract.

Deferred Returns

Many times, organizations make investments for which they receive no cash until several periods have passed. The present value of an investment discounted at 12 percent per year, which has a $2,000 return only at the end of Years 4, 5, and 6, can be determined as follows:

Year		Amount		Present Value of $1 at 12 Percent		Present Value Amount
1		$ 0	×	0.89286	=	$ 0
2		0	×	0.79719	=	0
3		0	×	0.71178	=	0
4		2,000	×	0.63552	=	1,271
5		2,000	×	0.56743	=	1,135
6		2,000	×	0.50663	=	1,013
Total						$3,419

Computation of the present value of the deferred annuity can also be performed using the annuity tables if the cash flow amounts are equal for each period. The present value of an annuity for six years minus the present value of an annuity for three years yields the present value of an annuity for Years 4 through 6.

Present value of an annuity for 6 years at 12 percent: $2,000 × 4.11141 =	$8,223
Present value of an annuity for 3 years at 12 percent: 2,000 × 2.40183 =	(4,804)
Present value of the deferred annuity.	$3,419

APPENDIX 24A REVIEW

Using the equations and tables in Appendix 24A of this chapter, determine the answers to each of the following independent situations:

a. The future value in two years of $2,000 deposited today in a savings account with interest compounded annually at 6 percent.

b. The present value of $8,000 to be received in four years, discounted at 12 percent.

c. The present value of an annuity of $2,000 per year for five years discounted at 14 percent.

d. An initial investment of $32,010 is to be returned in eight equal annual payments. Determine the amount of each payment if the interest rate is 12 percent.

e. A proposed investment will provide cash flows of $20,000, $8,000, and $6,000 at the end of Years 1, 2, and 3, respectively. Using a discount rate of 20 percent, determine the present value of these cash flows.

f. Find the present value of an investment that will pay $5,000 at the end of Years 10, 11, and 12. Use a discount rate of 14 percent.

The solution to this review problem can be found on page 1106.

APPENDIX 24B: Table Approach to Determining Internal Rate of Return

We consider the use of present value tables to determine the internal rate of return of a series of cash flows with (1) equal net cash flows after the initial investment and (2) unequal net cash flows after the initial investment.

Equal Cash Inflows

An investment proposal's internal rate of return is easily determined when a single investment is followed by a series of equal annual net cash flows. The general relationship between the initial investment and the equal annual cash inflows is expressed as follows:

$$\text{Initial investment} = \text{Present value factor for an annuity of \$1} \times \text{Annual net cash inflow}$$

Solve for the appropriate present value factor as follows:

$$\text{Present value factor for an annuity of \$1} = \frac{\text{Initial investment}}{\text{Annual net cash inflows}}$$

Once the present value factor is calculated, use **Exhibit 24A.2** and go across the row corresponding to the expected life of the project until a table factor equal to or closest to the project's computed present value factor is found. The corresponding percentage for the present value factor is the proposal's internal rate of return. If a table factor does not exactly equal the proposal's present value factor, a more accurate answer can be obtained by interpolation (which is not discussed in this text).

To illustrate, assume that Mobile Taqueria's proposed investment has a zero disinvestment value. Using all information in **Exhibit 24.2** (except that for disinvestment), the proposal's present value factor is 3.15180:

$$\text{Present value factor for an annuity of \$1} = \frac{\text{Initial investment}}{\text{Annual net cash inflows}}$$

$$= \frac{\$94,554}{\$30,000}$$

$$= 3.15180$$

Using **Exhibit 24A.2**, go across the row for five periods; the closest table factor is 3.12717, which corresponds to an internal rate of return of 18 percent.

Unequal Cash Inflows

If periodic cash flows subsequent to the initial investment are unequal, the simple procedure of determining a present value factor and looking up the closest corresponding factor in **Exhibit 24A.2** cannot be used. Instead, a trial-and-error approach must be used to determine the internal rate of return.

The first step is to select a discount rate estimated to be close to the proposal's IRR and to compute the proposal's net present value. If the resulting net present value is zero, the selected discount rate is the actual rate of return. However, it is unlikely that the first rate selected will be the proposal's IRR. If the computation results in a positive net present value, the actual IRR is higher than the initially selected rate. In this case, the next step is to compute the proposal's net present value using a higher rate. If the second computation produces a negative net present value, the actual IRR is less than the selected rate. Therefore, the actual IRR is between the first and the second rates. This trial-and-error approach continues until a discount rate is found that equates the proposal's cash inflows and outflows. For Mobile Taqueria's investment proposal outlined in **Exhibit 24.2**, the details of the trial-and-error approach are presented in **Exhibit 24B.1**.

In **Exhibit 24B.1** the first rate produced a negative net present value, indicating that the proposal's IRR is less than 24 percent. To produce a positive net present value, a smaller rate was selected for the second trial. Since the second rate produced a positive net present value, the proposal's true IRR must be between 16 and 24 percent. The 20 percent rate selected for the third trial produced a net present value of $(13) which is approximately zero, indicating that this is the proposal's IRR.

EXHIBIT 24B.1	Internal Rate of Return with Unequal Cash Flows

First trial with a 24 percent discount rate

	Predicted Cash Inflows (outflows) (A)	Year(s) of Cash Flows (B)	24% Present Value Factor (C)	Present Value of Cash Flows (A) × (C)
Initial investment.	$(94,554)	0	1.00000	$(94,554)
Operation	30,000	1–5	2.74538	82,361
Disinvestment.	12,000	5	0.34111	4,093
Net present value of all cash flows.				$ (8,100)

Second trial with a 16 percent discount rate

	Predicted Cash Inflows (outflows) (A)	Year(s) of Cash Flows (B)	16% Present Value Factor (C)	Present Value of Cash Flows (A) × (C)
Initial investment.	$(94,554)	0	1.00000	$(94,554)
Operation	30,000	1–5	3.27429	98,229
Disinvestment.	12,000	5	0.47611	5,713
Net present value of all cash flows.				$ 9,388

Third trial with a 20 percent discount rate

	Predicted Cash Inflows (outflows) (A)	Year(s) of Cash Flows (B)	20% Present Value Factor (C)	Present Value of Cash Flows (A) × (C)
Initial investment.	$(94,554)	0	1.00000	$(94,554)
Operation	30,000	1–5	2.99061	89,718
Disinvestment.	12,000	5	0.40188	4,823
Net present value of all cash flows.				$ (13)

APPENDIX 24B REVIEW

The internal rate of return is often referred to as the time-adjusted rate of return. It is the discount rate that equates the present value of a project's cash inflows with the present value of the project's cash outflows.

REQUIRED

a. Discuss the process, when using the table approach to determining internal rate of return, when the project involves equal cash flows.

b. Discuss the process, when using the table approach to determining the internal rate of return, when periodic cash flows subsequent to the initial investment are unequal.

The solution to this review problem can be found on page 1106.

GUIDANCE ANSWERS . . . YOU MAKE THE CALL

You are the Vice President of Finance   There is no single correct response to this question. It is useful to start by learning how other companies in similar circumstances handle capital expenditure decisions. This might be done through personal contacts or through professional organizations, such as the Financial Executives Institute. Another starting point might be the formation of a small capital budgeting committee, which could be expanded as necessary once formal procedures were in place. Early tasks of the committee might include developing guidelines for the size of expenditures at various organizational levels subject to committee review and developing guidelines for the criteria used in formal reviews. You would want to ensure that the CEO is in agreement with these proposals. If the company has a board of directors, you would also want some mutual understanding of the board's role in the approval of capital expenditures. Finally, you would want to make clear the importance of a post-audit review.

KEY RATIOS

$$\text{Cost of equity capital} = \frac{\text{Current annual dividend per common share}}{\text{Current market price per common share}} + \text{Expected dividend growth rate}$$

$$\text{Payback period} = \frac{\text{Initial investment}}{\text{Annual operating cash inflows}}$$

$$\text{Accounting rate of return on initial investment} = \frac{\text{Average annual increase in net income}}{\text{Initial investment}}$$

$$\text{Accounting rate of return on average investment} = \frac{\text{Average annual increase in net income}}{\text{Average investment}}$$

Depreciation tax shield = Depreciation × Tax rate

$fv = pv(1 + i)n$

Where: fv = future value amount, pv = present value amount, i = interest rate per period, n = number of periods.

$$pv = \frac{fv}{(1+i)^n}$$

Where: fv = future value amount, pv = present value amount, i = interest rate per period, n = number of periods.

$$pva = \frac{a}{i} \times \left[1 - \frac{1}{(1+i)^n} \right]$$

Where: pva = present value of an annuity, i = prevailing rate per period, n = number of periods, a = annuity amount.

$$\text{Present value factor for an annuity of } \$1 = \frac{\text{Initial investment}}{\text{Annual net cash flows}}$$

KEY TERMS

accounting rate of return 1070	depreciation tax shield 1078	net present value 1065
annuity 1082	discount rate 1065	payback period 1069
capital budgeting 1060	future value 1081	present value 1081
capital expenditures 1060	internal rate of return (IRR) 1067	time-adjusted rate of return 1067
cost of capital 1068	investment tax credit 1080	

Assignments with the MBC logo in the margin are available in **myBusinessCourse**.
See the Preface of the book for details.

MULTIPLE CHOICE

1. Which of the following statements is not a characteristic of an effective capital budgeting process?

    a. Requires an adjustment to make cash flows comparable when they are expected to occur at different points in time.

    b. Develops implementation plans for approved projects.

    c. All projects should be required to go through formal review of a capital budgeting committee.

    d. Conducts a post audit review to assign responsibility and improve future planning.

Use the tables in Exhibits 24A.1 and 24A.2 in Appendix 24A to answer questions 2, 3, and 4.

2. Max is considering an investment proposal that requires an initial investment of $91,100, has predicted cash inflows of $30,000 per year for four years and no salvage value. At a discount rate of 10 percent the projects net present value is:

    a. $4,000
    b. $20,490
    c. $24,490
    d. $95,100

3. The internal rate of return of the investment proposal presented in question 2 is:

    a. 8 percent
    b. 10 percent
    c. 12 percent
    d. Less than 8 percent

4. The Pepper Shop is evaluating a capital expenditure proposal with the following predicted cash flows:

Initial investment.	$(40,000)
Operations, each year for four years	15,000
Salvage.	5,000

    At a discount rate of 12 percent, the project's net present value is:

    a. $2,375
    b. $5,555
    c. $8,735
    d. $20,740

5. The payback period of the investment proposal presented in question 4 is:
    a. 0.37 years
    b. 0.50 years
    c. 2.00 years
    d. 2.67 years

6. The accounting rate of return on the initial investment presented in question 4 is:
    a. 0.125
    b. 0.156
    c. 0.219
    d. 0.375

7. Each of the following statements is true regarding capital budgeting decisions, except:
    a. Capital expenditure proposals involve risk.
    b. A common error is to invest in unnecessary or overly complex equipment.
    c. Capital budgeting models cannot be relied on when a project is projected to have cash flows over a period of time greater than 3 years.
    d. When a number of activities drive manufacturing overhead costs, estimates of overhead cost based on a single activity driver can significantly overestimate cost savings.

8. For a typical $120,000 investment in equipment with a 5-year life and no salvage value, determine the present value of the tax shield using straight-line depreciation. Assume an income tax rate of 35 percent and a discount rate of 16 percent.
    a. $24,000
    b. $8,400
    c. $27,502
    d. $30,511

9. Compute the present value of an investment at 10% per year, which has a 3,000 return only at the end of Years 3, 4 and 5.
    a. $11,372.37
    b. $6,165.72
    c. $16,578.99
    d. $13,066

10. Assume that the Yogurt Shoppe has a proposed investment of $68,500 with a zero disinvestment value. The life of the investment is expected to be 5 years and the annual net cash inflows are expected to be $20,000. Determine the investment proposal's IRR using the tables on page 1084 of Appendix 24A.
   a.   18%
   b.   16%
   c.   14%
   d.   12%

QUESTIONS

Q24-1. What is the relationship between long-range planning and capital budgeting?

Q24-2. What tasks are often assigned to the capital budgeting committee?

Q24-3. What purposes are served by a post-audit of approved capital expenditure proposals?

Q24-4. Into what three phases are a project's cash flows organized?

Q24-5. State three alternative definitions or descriptions of the internal rate of return.

Q24-6. Why is the cost of capital an important concept when discounting models are used for capital budgeting?

Q24-7. What weakness is inherent in the payback period when it is used as the sole investment criterion?

Q24-8. What weakness is inherent in the accounting rate of return when it is used as an investment criterion?

Q24-9. Why are the net present value and the internal rate of return models superior to the payback period and the accounting rate of return models?

Q24-10. State two basic differences between the net present value and the internal rate of return models that often lead to differences in the evaluation of competing investment proposals.

Q24-11. Identify several nonquantitative factors that are apt to play a decisive role in the final selection of projects for capital expenditures.

Q24-12. In what way does depreciation affect the analysis of cash flows for a proposed capital expenditure?

MINI EXERCISES

LO2, 7

M24-13.   Time Value of Money: Basics

Using the equations and tables in Appendix 24A of this chapter, determine the answers to each of the following independent situations:

a. The future value in two years of $3,000 deposited today in a savings account with interest compounded annually at 6 percent.

b. The present value of $12,000 to be received in four years, discounted at 12 percent.

c. The present value of an annuity of $3,000 per year for five years discounted at 14 percent.

d. An initial investment of $48,015 is to be returned in eight equal annual payments. Determine the amount of each payment if the interest rate is 12 percent.

e. A proposed investment will provide cash flows of $30,000, $12,000, and $9,000 at the end of Years 1, 2, and 3, respectively. Using a discount rate of 20 percent, determine the present value of these cash flows.

f. Find the present value of an investment that will pay $7,500 at the end of Years 10, 11, and 12. Use a discount rate of 14 percent.

LO2, 7

M24-14.   Time Value of Money: Basics

Using the equations and tables in Appendix 24A of this chapter, determine the answers to each of the following independent situations:

a. The future value in two years of $7,500 invested today in a certificate of deposit with interest compounded annually at 10 percent.

b. The present value of $9,000 to be received in five years, discounted at 8 percent.

c. The present value of an annuity of $22,500 per year for four years discounted at 12 percent.

d. An initial investment of $44,220 is to be returned in six equal annual payments. Determine the amount of each payment if the interest rate is 16 percent.

e. A proposed investment will provide cash flows of $9,000, $12,000, and $10,000 at the end of Years 1, 2, and 3, respectively. Using a discount rate of 16 percent, determine the present value of these cash flows.

f. Find the present value of an investment that will pay $9,000 at the end of Years 8, 9, and 10. Use a discount rate of 12 percent.

M24-15. **NPV and IRR: Equal Annual Net Cash Inflows**

LO2

Kailey James Company is evaluating a capital expenditure proposal that requires an initial investment of $14,900, has predicted cash inflows of $4,000 per year for 12 years, and has no salvage value.

REQUIRED

a. Using a discount rate of 14 percent, determine the net present value of the investment proposal.

b. Determine the proposal's internal rate of return. (Refer to Appendix 24B if you use the table approach.)

c. What discount rate would produce a net present value of zero?

M24-16. **NPV and IRR: Equal Annual Net Cash Inflows**

LO2

Winter Fun Company is evaluating a capital expenditure proposal that requires an initial investment of $54,768, has predicted cash inflows of $12,000 per year for seven years, and has no salvage value.

REQUIRED

a. Using a discount rate of 14 percent, determine the net present value of the investment proposal.

b. Determine the proposal's internal rate of return. (Refer to Appendix 24B if you use the table approach.)

c. What discount rate would produce a net present value of zero?

M24-17. **Payback Period and Accounting Rate of Return: Equal Annual Operating Cash Flows without Disinvestment**

LO3

Juliana is considering an investment proposal with the following cash flows:

Initial investment—depreciable assets.	$40,000
Net cash inflows from operations (per year for 10 years).	5,000
Disinvestment.	0

REQUIRED

a. Determine the payback period

b. Determine the accounting rate of return on initial investment

c. Determine the accounting rate of return on average investment

M24-18. **Payback Period and Accounting Rate of Return: Equal Annual Operating Cash Flows with Disinvestment**

LO3

Minn is considering an investment proposal with the following cash flows:

Initial investment—depreciable assets.	$90,000
Net cash inflows from operations (per year for 10 years).	15,000
Disinvestment—depreciable assets.	12,000

REQUIRED

a. Determine the payback period

b. Determine the accounting rate of return on initial investment

c. Determine the accounting rate of return on average investment

M24-19. **Payback Period and Accounting Rate of Return: Equal Annual Operating Cash Flows with Disinvestment**

LO3

Roopali is considering an investment proposal with the following cash flows:

Initial investment—depreciable assets.	$45,000
Initial investment—working capital.	5,000
Net cash inflows from operations (per year for 7 years).	10,000
Disinvestment—depreciable assets.	3,000
Disinvestment—working capital.	2,000

REQUIRED

a. Determine the payback period
b. Determine the accounting rate of return on initial investment
c. Determine the accounting rate of return on average investment

EXERCISES

LO2, 8

Goodrich Petroleum
Corporation
OTCQX :: GDPP

E24-20. **NPV and IRR: Unequal Annual Net Cash Inflows**

Assume that **Goodrich Petroleum Corporation** is evaluating a capital expenditure proposal that has the following predicted cash flows:

Initial investment..	$(45,880)
Operation	
Year 1..	15,000
Year 2..	25,000
Year 3..	20,000
Salvage..	0

REQUIRED

a. Using a discount rate of 10 percent, determine the net present value of the investment proposal.
b. Determine the proposal's internal rate of return. (Refer to Appendix 24B if you use the table approach.)

LO2, 8   **E24-21.** **NPV and IRR: Unequal Annual Net Cash Inflows**

Rocky Road Company is evaluating a capital expenditure proposal that has the following predicted cash flows:

Initial investment..	$(90,220)
Operation	
Year 1..	41,275
Year 2..	60,000
Year 3..	20,000
Salvage..	0

REQUIRED

a. Using a discount rate of 14 percent, determine the net present value of the investment proposal.
b. Determine the proposal's internal rate of return. (Refer to Appendix 24B if you use the table approach.)

LO2, 3, 8   **E24-22.** **Payback Period, IRR, and Minimum Cash Flows**

The management of Mohawk Limited is currently evaluating the following investment proposal:

	Time 0	Year 1	Year 2	Year 3	Year 4
Initial investment.............	$150,000	—	—	—	—
Net operating cash inflows.....	—	$50,000	$50,000	$50,000	$50,000

REQUIRED

a. Determine the proposal's payback period.
b. Determine the proposal's internal rate of return. (Refer to Appendix 24B if you use the table approach.)
c. Given the amount of the initial investment, determine the minimum annual net cash inflows required to obtain an internal rate of return of 16 percent. Round the answer to the nearest dollar.

LO2, 3   **E24-23.** **Time-Adjusted Cost-Volume-Profit Analysis**

Honeydukes Treat Shop is considering the desirability of producing a new chocolate candy called Pleasure Bombs. Before purchasing the new equipment required to manufacture Pleasure Bombs, Neville Long, the shop's proprietor performed the following analysis:

Unit selling price.	$2.18
Variable manufacturing and selling costs.	(1.73)
Unit contribution margin.	$0.45
Annual fixed costs	
Depreciation (straight-line for 4 years)	$22,500
Other (all cash)	45,000
Total	$67,500

Annual break-even sales volume = $67,500 ÷ $0.45 = 150,000 units

Because the expected annual sales volume is 160,000 units, Long decided to undertake the production of Pleasure Bombs. This required an immediate investment of $87,000 in equipment that has a life of four years and no salvage value. After four years, the production of Pleasure Bombs will be discontinued.

REQUIRED

a. Evaluate the analysis performed by Long.

b. If Honeydukes Treat Shop has a time value of money of 8 percent, should it make the investment with projected annual sales of 160,000 units?

c. Considering the time value of money, what annual unit sales volume is required to break even?

E24-24. **Time-Adjusted Cost-Volume-Profit Analysis with Income Taxes**   LO6

Assume the same facts as given in Exercise E24-23 for the Honeydukes Treat Shop.

REQUIRED

With a 40 percent tax rate and a 8 percent time value of money, determine the annual unit sales required to break even on a time-adjusted basis. Assume straight-line depreciation is used to determine tax payments.

E24-25. **Payback Period and IRR of a Cost Reduction Proposal—Differential Analysis**   LO2, 3

A light-emitting diode (LED) is a semiconductor diode that emits narrow-spectrum light. Although relatively expensive when compared to incandescent bulbs, they use significantly less energy and last six to ten times longer, with a slow decline in performance rather than an abrupt failure.

Metropolitan City currently has 80,000 incandescent bulbs in traffic lights at approximately 12,000 intersections. It is estimated that replacing all the incandescent bulbs with LED will cost $46.02 million. However, the investment is also estimated to save the City $8.85 million per year in energy costs.

REQUIRED

a. Determine the payback period of converting Metropolitan City traffic lights to LEDs.

b. If the average life of an incandescent streetlight is one year and the average life of an LED street-light is seven years, should the City finance the investment in LED's at an interest rate of five percent per year? Justify your answer.

E24-26. **Payback Period and NPV of a Cost Reduction Proposal—Differential Analysis**   LO2, 3, 5

Hermione decided to purchase a new automobile. Being concerned about environmental issues, she is leaning toward the hybrid rather than the gasoline only model. Nevertheless, as a new business school graduate, she wants to determine if there is an economic justification for purchasing the hybrid, which costs $1,595 more than the regular model. She has determined that city/highway combined gas mileage of the hybrid and regular models are 30 and 24 miles per gallon respectively. Hermione anticipates she will travel an average of 12,000 miles per year for the next several years.

REQUIRED

a. Determine the payback period of the incremental investment if gasoline costs $2.75 per gallon.

b. Assuming that Hermione plans to keep the car about six years and does not believe there will be a trade-in premium associated with the hybrid model, determine the net present value of the incremental investment at six percent time value of money.

c. Determine the cost of gasoline required for a payback period of three years.

d. At $4.60 per gallon, determine the gas mileage required for a payback period of three years.

E24-27.   Payback Period and NPV of Alternative Automobile Purchase

Wendy Li decided to purchase a new Honda Civic. Being concerned about environmental issues she is leaning toward a Honda Civic Hybrid rather than the completely gasoline-powered LX model. Nevertheless, she wants to determine if there is an economic justification for purchasing the Hybrid, which costs $4,950 more than the LX. Based on a mix of city and highway driving she predicts that the average gas mileage of each car is 40 MPG for the Hybrid and 30 MPG for the LX. Wendy also anticipates she will drive an average of 12,000 miles per year and that gasoline will cost an average of $2.75 per gallon over the next four years. She also plans to replace whichever car she purchases at the end of four years when the resale values of the Hybrid and the LX are predicted to be $12,000 and $8,500 respectively.

REQUIRED

a. Determine the payback period of the incremental investment associated with purchasing the Hybrid.
b. Determine the net present value of the incremental investment associated with purchasing the Hybrid at an ten percent time value of money.
c. Determine the cost of gasoline required for a payback period of three years on the incremental investment.
d. Identify other factors Wendy should consider before making her decision.

PROBLEMS

P24-28.   Ranking Investment Proposals: Payback Period, Accounting Rate of Return, and Net Present Value

Presented is information pertaining to the cash flows of three mutually exclusive investment proposals:

	Proposal A	Proposal B	Proposal C
Initial investment.	$60,000	$60,000	$60,000
Cash flow from operations			
Year 1	50,000	30,000	60,000
Year 2	6,000	30,000	
Year 3	29,000	25,000	
Disinvestment.	0	0	0
Life (years)	3 years	3 years	1 year

REQUIRED

a. Rank these investment proposals using the payback period, the accounting rate of return on initial investment, and the net present value criteria. Assume that the organization's cost of capital is 12 percent. Round calculations to four decimal places.
b. Explain the difference in rankings. Which investment would you recommend?

P24-29.   Cost Reduction Proposal: IRR, NPV, and Payback Period

PA Chemical currently discharges liquid waste into Pittsburgh's municipal sewer system. However, the Pittsburgh municipal government has informed PA that a surcharge of $5 per thousand cubic liters will soon be imposed for the discharge of this waste. This has prompted management to evaluate the desirability of treating its own liquid waste.

A proposed system consists of three elements. The first is a retention basin, which would permit unusual discharges to be held and treated before entering the downstream system. The second is a continuous self-cleaning rotary filter required where solids are removed. The third is an automated neutralization process required where materials are added to control the alkalinity-acidity range.

The system is designed to process 600,000 liters a day. However, management anticipates that only about 250,000 liters of liquid waste would be processed in a normal workday. The company operates 300 days per year. The initial investment in the system would be $900,000, and annual operating costs are predicted to be $162,000. The system has a predicted useful life of ten years and a salvage value of $70,000.

REQUIRED
a. Determine the project's net present value at a discount rate of 16 percent.
b. Determine the project's approximate internal rate of return. (Refer to Appendix 24B if you use the table approach.)
c. Determine the project's payback period.

P24-30. **NPV with Income Taxes: Straight-Line versus Accelerated Depreciation**   **LO2, 6**
Carl William, Inc. is a conservatively managed boat company whose motto is, "The old ways are the good ways." Management has always used straight-line depreciation for tax and external reporting purposes. Although they are reluctant to change, they are aware of the impact of taxes on a project's profitability.

REQUIRED
For a typical $180,000 investment in equipment with a five-year life and no salvage value, determine the present value of the advantage resulting from the use of double-declining balance depreciation as opposed to straight-line depreciation. Assume an income tax rate of 35 percent and a discount rate of 16 percent. Also assume that there will be a switch from double-declining balance to straight-line depreciation in the fourth year.

P24-31. **Payback Period and NPV: Taxes and Straight-Line Depreciation**   **LO2, 3, 6**
Assume that **United Technologies Corporation** is evaluating a proposal to change the company's manual design system to a computer-aided design (CAD) system. The proposed system is expected to save 13,500 design hours per year; an operating cost savings of $55 per hour. The annual cash expenditures of operating the CAD system are estimated to be $300,000. The CAD system requires an initial investment of $750,000. The estimated life of this system is five years with no salvage value. The tax rate is 35 percent, and United Technologies uses straight-line depreciation for tax purposes. United Technologies has a cost of capital of 14 percent.

United Technologies
Corporation
NYSE :: UTX

REQUIRED
a. Compute the annual after-tax cash flows related to the CAD project.
b. Compute each of the following for the project:
  1. Payback period.
  2. Net present value.

P24-32. **NPV: Taxes and Accelerated Depreciation**   **LO6**
Assume the same facts as given in P24-31, except that management intends to use double-declining balance depreciation with a switch to straight-line depreciation (applied to any undepreciated balance) starting in Year 4.

REQUIRED
Determine the project's net present value.

P24-33. **NPV Total and Differential Analysis of Replacement Decision**   **LO2**
Fritz Gilgen is evaluating a proposal to purchase a new processor that would cost $180,000 and have a salvage value of $18,000 in five years. Fritz's cost of capital is 14 percent. It would provide annual operating cash savings of $22,500, as follows:

	Old Processor	New Processor
Salaries.	$51,000	$66,000
Supplies	9,000	7,500
Utilities	19,500	9,000
Cleaning and maintenance.	33,000	7,500
Total cash expenditures	$112,500	$90,000

If the new processor is purchased, Fritz will sell the old processor for its current salvage value of $52,500. If the new processor is not purchased, the old processor will be disposed of in five years at a predicted scrap value of $4,500. The old processor's present book value is $75,000. If kept, the old processor will require repairs predicted to cost $60,000 in one year.

REQUIRED
a. Use the total cost approach to evaluate the alternatives of keeping the old processor and purchasing the new processor. Indicate which alternative is preferred.
b. Use the differential cost approach to evaluate the desirability of purchasing the new processor.

LO2   **P24-34.**   **NPV Total and Differential Analysis of Replacement Decision**

Pure White Automatic Laundry must either have a complete overhaul of its current dry-cleaning system or purchase a new one. Its cost of capital is 18 percent. Pure White's accountant has developed the following cost projections:

	Present System	New System
Purchase cost (new)............................	$60,000	$75,000
Remaining book value	22,500	
Overhaul needed	30,000	
Annual cash operating costs	52,500	30,000
Current salvage value...........................	15,000	
Salvage value in 5 years.........................	4,500	16,500

If Pure White keeps the old system, it will have to be overhauled immediately. With the overhaul, the old system will have a useful life of five more years.

REQUIRED

a. Use the total cost approach to evaluate the alternatives of keeping the old system and purchasing the new system. Indicate which alternative is preferred.

b. Use the differential cost approach to evaluate the desirability of purchasing the new system.

LO2, 5   **P24-35.**   **NPV Differential Analysis of Replacement Decision**

The management of Dusseldorf Manufacturing Company is currently evaluating a proposal to purchase a new, innovative drill press as a replacement for a less efficient piece of similar equipment, which would then be sold. The cost of the equipment, including delivery and installation, is $270,000. If the equipment is purchased, Dusseldorf will incur a $7,500 cost in removing the present equipment and revamping service facilities. The present equipment has a book value of $150,000 and a remaining useful life of ten years. Because of new technical improvements that have made the present equipment obsolete, it now has a disposal value of only $60,000. Management has provided the following comparison of manufacturing costs:

	Present Equipment	New Equipment
Annual production (units)	400,000	400,000
Annual costs		
Direct labor (per unit)	$0.113	$0.075
Overhead		
Depreciation (10% of asset's book value)	$15,000	$27,000
Other....................................	$72,000	$30,000

Additional information follows:

- Management believes that if the current equipment is not replaced now, it will have to wait ten years before replacement is justifiable.
- Both pieces of equipment are expected to have a negligible salvage value at the end of ten years.
- Management expects to sell the entire annual production of 400,000 units.
- Dusseldorf's cost of capital is 12 percent.

REQUIRED

Evaluate the desirability of purchasing the new equipment.

CASES AND PROJECTS

LO2, 3, 5   **C24-36.**   **Payback, ARR, and IRR: Evaluating the Sale of Government Assets (Requires**
Morgan Stanley   **Spreadsheet)**
NYSE :: MS   In 2008 the City of Chicago agreed to lease 35,000 parking meters to a **Morgan Stanley**-led partnership for a one-time sum of $1.15 billion. The lease has been criticized as an example of "one-shot" deals arrived at behind closed doors to balance a current budget at the expense of future generations. Some have observed that deals such as this are akin to individuals using their retirement savings to meet current needs, instead of planning for the future. "These deals are rarely done under the light of public scrutiny," says Richard G. Little, director of the Keston Institute for Public

Finance at the University of Southern California. "Often the facts come out long after the deal is done."

Since the lease was signed, helped by parking-fee hikes, the partnership has earned a profit before taxes and depreciation of $0.80 per dollar of revenue. Projected revenues over the 75-year life of the lease are now projected at $11.6 billion.

Defending the city's action, Gene Saffold, Chicago's chief financial officer, stated that "The concession agreement was absolutely the best deal for Chicagoans. ... The net present value of $11.6 billion in revenue over the life of the 75-year agreement is consistent with $1.15 billion.[1]

REQUIRED

Evaluate the 75-year lease and determine if the projected revenues are consistent with the initial investment. To simplify your analysis assume equal revenues and operating costs in all periods, no investment required in working capital, and no salvage value at the end of the lease. Suggested elements of your solution include:

a. Determine the payback period in the absence of taxes.
b. Determine the accounting rate of return on the initial investment in the absence of taxes.
c. Determine the accounting rate of return on the initial investment with a tax rate of 0.34.
d. Determine the internal rate of return in the absence of taxes.
e. Determine the internal rate of return with a tax rate of 0.34.
f. Summary of analysis and conclusions.

C24-37. **Determining Terms of Automobile Leases (Requires Spreadsheet)**   **LO2, 5**

Avant-Garde Motor Company has asked you to develop lease terms for the firm's popular Avant-Garde Challenger, which has an average selling price (new) of $26,000. You know that leasing is attractive because it assists consumers in obtaining new vehicles with a small down payment and "reasonable" monthly payments. Market analysts have told you that to attract the widest number of young professionals, the Challenger must have an initial down payment of no more than $1,000, monthly payments of no more than $470, and lease terms of no more than three years. When the lease expires, Avant-Garde will sell the used Challengers at the automobile's resale market price at that time. It is difficult to predict the future price of the increasingly popular Challenger, but you have obtained the following information on the average resale prices of used Challengers:

Age	Resale Price
1 year	$21,000
2 years	19,500
3 years	17,000
4 years	14,500
5 years	13,500

Avant-Garde's cost of capital is 18 percent per year, or 1.5 percent per month.

REQUIRED

a. With the aid of spreadsheet software, develop a competitive and profitable lease payment program. Assuming a $1,000 down payment, calculate the program's monthly payments for 2, 3, 4 and 5 year leases. Assume the down payment and the first lease payment are made immediately and that all subsequent lease payments are made at the start of the month. [Hint: Most software packages include a function such as the following: PMT (rate,nper,pv,fv,type), where rate = the time value of money; nper = the number of periods; pv = the present value; fv = the future value; and type = 0 (when the payment is at the end of the period) or 1 (when the payment is at the beginning of the period). For monthly payments, rate should be set at the annual rate divided by 12, and npr should be set at the number of months in the lease. Here, fv is the residual value. Consider the residual value as a future value and enter it as a negative number, indicating the lessor has not paid the full cost of the car.]
b. Reevaluate the lease program assuming a down payment of $2,000.
c. Reevaluate the lease program assuming a down payment of $1,000 and a $2,000 increase in residual values.
d. Reevaluate the lease program assuming a down payment of $2,000 and a $2,000 increase in residual values.
e. What is your final recommendation? What risks are associated with your recommendation? Are there any other actions to consider?

---

[1] "Windfall for Investors, A Loss for the Windy City," *Bloomberg Businessweek*, August 29, 2010, pp. 44-45; Ianthe Jeanne Dugan, "Facing Budget Gaps, Cities Sell Parking, Airports, Zoo," *The Wall Street Journal*, August 23, 2010, pp. A1, A12.

LO3, 5 **C24-38.** **Evaluating Data and Using Payback Period for an Investment Proposal**

To determine the desirability of investing in a 21-inch monitor (as opposed to the typical 17-inch monitor that comes with a new personal computer), researchers developed an experiment testing the time required to perform a set of tasks. The tasks included the following:

- Setting up a meeting using electronic mail.
- Reviewing meeting requests.
- Checking an on-line schedule.
- Embedding a video file into a document.
- Searching a customer database to find a specific set of contracts.
- Copying a database into a spreadsheet.
- Modifying a slide presentation.

The researchers assumed this was a typical set of tasks performed by a manager. They determined that there was a 9 percent productivity gain using the 21-inch monitor. One test manager commented that the largest productivity gain came from being able to have multiple applications open at the same time and from being able to view several files at once.

REQUIRED

Accepting the 9 percent productivity gain as accurate, what additional information is needed to determine the payback period of an investment in one 21-inch monitor that is to be used by a manager? Make any necessary assumptions and obtain whatever data you can (perhaps from computer component advertisements) to determine the payback period for the proposed investment.

LO2, 4, 5, 8 **C24-39.** **IRR and NPV with Performance Evaluation Conflict**

Pepperoni Pizza Company owns and operates fast-service pizza parlors throughout North America. The firm operates on a regional basis and provides almost complete autonomy to the manager of each region. Regional managers are responsible for long-range planning, capital expenditures, personnel policies, pricing, and so forth. Each year the performance of regional managers is evaluated by determining the accounting return on fixed assets in their regions; a return of 14 percent is expected. To determine this return, regional net income is divided by the book value of fixed assets at the start of the year. Managers of regions earning a return of more than 16 percent are identified for possible promotion, and managers of regions with a return of less than 12 percent are subject to replacement.

Mr. Light, with a degree in hotel and restaurant management, is the manager of the Northeast region. He is regarded as a "rising star" and will be considered for promotion during the next two years. Light has been with Pepperoni for a total of three years. During that period, the return on fixed assets in his region (the oldest in the firm) has increased dramatically. He is currently considering a proposal to open five new parlors in the Boston area. The total project involves an investment of $650,000 and will double the number of Pepperoni pizzas sold in the Northeast region to a total of 600,000 per year. At an average price of $6 each, total sales revenue will be $3,600,000.

The expenses of operating each of the new parlors include variable costs of $4 per pizza and fixed costs (excluding depreciation) of $80,000 per year. Because each of the new parlors has only a five-year life and no salvage value, yearly straight-line depreciation will be $26,000 [($650,000 ÷ 5 parlors) ÷ 5 years].

REQUIRED

a. Evaluate the desirability of the $650,000 investment in new pizza parlors by computing the internal rate of return and the net present value. Assume a time value of money of 14 percent. (Refer to Appendix 24B if you use the table approach.)

b. If Light is shrewd, will he approve the expansion? Why or why not? (Additional computations are suggested.)

C24-40. **NPV and Project Reevaluation with Taxes, Straight-Line Depreciation**　**LO2, 5, 6**
In 2015, the Bayside Chemical Company prepared the following analysis of an investment proposal for a new manufacturing facility:

	Predicted Cash Inflows (outflows) (A)	Year(s) of Cash Flows (B)	12% Present Value Factor (C)	Present Value of Cash Flows (A) × (C)
Initial investment				
Fixed assets	$(810,000)	0	1.00000	$ (810,000)
Working capital	(100,000)	0	1.00000	(100,000)
Operations				
Annual taxable income				
without depreciation	310,000	1–5	3.60478	1,117,482
Taxes on income ($310,000 × 0.40)	(124,000)	1–5	3.60478	(446,993)
Depreciation tax shield	64,800*	1–5	3.60478	233,590
Disinvestment				
Site restoration	80,000	5	0.56743	(45,394)
Tax shield of restoration ($80,000 × 0.40)	32,000	5	0.56743	18,158
Working capital	100,000	5	0.56743	56,743
Net present value of all cash flows				$　23,586

*Computation of depreciation tax shield:
Annual straight-line depreciation ($810,000 ÷ 5)	$162,000
Tax rate	× 0.40
Depreciation tax shield	$ 64,800

Because the proposal had a positive net present value when discounted at Bayside's cost of capital of 12 percent, the project was approved; all investments were made at the end of 2016. Shortly after production began in January 2017, a government agency notified Bayside of required additional expenditures totaling $200,000 to bring the plant into compliance with new federal emission regulations. Bayside has the option either to comply with the regulations by December 31, 2017, or to sell the entire operation (fixed assets and working capital) for $250,000 on December 31, 2017. The improvements will be depreciated over the remaining four-year life of the plant using straight-line depreciation. The cost of site restoration will not be affected by the improvements. If Bayside elects to sell the plant, any book loss can be treated as an offset against taxable income on other operations. This tax reduction is an additional cash benefit of selling.

REQUIRED
a. Should Bayside sell the plant or comply with the new federal regulations? To simplify calculations, assume that any additional improvements are paid for on December 31, 2017.
b. Would Bayside have accepted the proposal in 2016 if it had been aware of the forthcoming federal regulations?
c. Do you have any suggestions that might increase the project's net present value? (No calculations are required.)

C24-41. **Post-Audit and Reevaluation of Investment Proposal: NPV**　**LO1, 2, 5**
Anthony Company's capital budgeting committee is evaluating a capital expenditure proposal for the production of a high definition television receiver to be sold as an add-on feature for personal computers. The proposal calls for an independent contractor to construct the necessary facilities by December 31, 2017, at a total cost of $250,000. Payment for all construction costs will be made on that date. An additional $50,000 in cash will also be made available on December 31, 2017, for working capital to support sales and production activities.

Management anticipates that the receiver has a limited market life; there is a high probability that by 2024 all new PCs will have built-in high definition receivers. Accordingly, the proposal specifies that production will cease on December 31, 2023. The investment in working capital will be recovered on that date, and the production facilities will be sold for $30,000. Predicted net cash inflows from operations for 2018 through 2023 are as follows:

2018	$100,000
2019	100,000
2020	100,000
2021	40,000
2022	40,000
2023	40,000

Anthony Company has a time value of money of 14 percent. For capital budgeting purposes, all cash flows are assumed to occur at the end of each year.

REQUIRED

a. Evaluate the capital expenditure proposal using the net present value method. Should Anthony accept the proposal?

b. Assume that the capital expenditure proposal is accepted, but construction delays caused by labor problems and difficulties in obtaining the necessary construction permits delay the completion of the project. Payments totaling $200,000 were made to the construction company on December 31, 2017, for that year's construction. However, completion is now scheduled for December 31, 2018, and an additional $100,000 will be required to complete construction. If the project is continued, the additional $100,000 will be paid at the end of 2018, and the plant will begin operations on January 1, 2019.

Because of the cost overruns, the capital budgeting committee requests a reevaluation of the project in early 2018, before agreeing to any additional expenditures. After much effort, the following revised predictions of net operating cash inflows are developed:

2019	$120,000
2020	100,000
2021	40,000
2022	40,000
2023	40,000

The working capital investment and disinvestment and the plant salvage values have not changed, except that the cash for working capital would now be made available on December 31, 2018. Use the net present value method to reevaluate the initial decision to accept the proposal. Given the information currently available about the project, should it have been accepted in 2017? (*Hint:* Determine the net present value as of December 31, 2017, assuming management has not committed Anthony to the proposal.)

c. Given the situation that exists in early 2018, should management continue or cancel the project? Assume that the facilities have a current salvage value of $50,000. (*Hint:* Assume that the decision is being made on January 1, 2018.)

LO1, 2, 5 **C24-42.** **Post-Audit and Reevaluation of Investment Proposal: IRR**

Throughout his four years in college, Ronald King worked at the local Beef Burger Restaurant in College City. Although the working conditions were good and the pay was not bad, Ron believed he could do a much better job of managing the restaurant than the current owner-manager. In particular, Ron believed that the proper use of marketing campaigns and sales incentives, such as selling a second burger for a 25 percent discount, could increase annual sales by 40 percent.

Just before graduation in 2016, Ron inherited $500,000 from his great uncle. He seriously considered buying the restaurant. It seemed like a good idea because he liked the town and its college atmosphere, knew the business, and always wanted to work for himself. He also knew that the current owner wanted to sell the restaurant and retire to Florida. As part of a small business management course, Ron developed the following income statement for the restaurant's 2015 operations:

BEEF BURGER RESTAURANT: COLLEGE CITY Income Statement For Year Ended December 31, 2015		
Sales.		$450,000
Expenses		
Cost of food	$150,000	
Supplies	20,000	
Employee expenses	140,000	
Utilities	28,000	
Property taxes.	20,000	
Insurance	10,000	
Advertising	8,000	
Depreciation	60,000	436,000
Net income.		$ 14,000

Ron believed that the cost of food and supplies were all variable, the employee expenses and utilities were one-half variable and one-half fixed in 2015, and all other expenses were fixed. If Ron purchased the restaurant and followed through on his plans, he believed there would be a 40 percent increase in unit sales volume and all variable costs. Of the fixed costs, only advertising would increase by $12,000. The use of discounts and special promotions would, however, limit the increase in sales revenue to only 30 percent even though sales volume increased 40 percent.

REQUIRED

a. Determine
   1. The current annual net cash inflow.
   2. The predicted annual net cash inflow if Ron executes his plans and his assumptions are correct.
b. Ron believes his plan would produce equal net cash inflows during each of the next 15 years, the period remaining on a long-term lease for the land on which the restaurant is built. At the end of that time, the restaurant would have to be demolished at a predicted net cost of $80,000. Assuming Ron would otherwise invest the money in stock expected to yield 12 percent, determine the maximum amount he should pay for the restaurant.
c. Assume that Ron accepts an offer from the current owner to buy the restaurant for $350,000. Unfortunately, although the expected increase in sales volume does occur, customers make much more extensive use of the promotions than Ron had anticipated. As a result, total sales revenues are 8 percent below projections. Furthermore, to improve employee attitudes, Ron gave a 10 percent raise immediately after purchasing the restaurant. Reevaluate the initial decision using the actual sales revenue and the increase in labor costs, assuming conditions will remain unchanged over the remaining life of the project. Was the investment decision a wise one? (Round calculations to the nearest dollar.)
d. Ron can sell the restaurant to a large franchise operator for $250,000. Alternatively, he believes that additional annual marketing expenditures and changes in promotions costing $20,000 per year could bring the sales revenues up to their original projections, with no other changes in costs. Should Ron sell the restaurant or keep it and make the additional expenditures? (Round calculations to the nearest dollar.) (*Hint:* Ron has just bought the restaurant.)

SOLUTIONS TO REVIEW PROBLEMS

Mid-Chapter Review 1

SOLUTION

a. **Capital expenditures**—Investment of financial resources with the expectation it will generate future financial inflows that exceed the initial cost.
b. **Capital budgeting**—Process that involves identifying desirable projects, evaluating proposals, and selecting proposals that meet minimum criteria.
c. **Post Audit**—Involves the development of project performance comparing planned and actual results.
d. **Capital budgeting**—Concepts and tools that organize information and evaluate alternatives.
e. **Time value of money concept**—Explains why monies received or paid at different points in time must be adjusted to comparable values.

f. **Capital budgeting**—Requires an adjustment to make cash flows comparable when they are expected to occur at different points in time.

g. **Long-Range Planning**—Planning beyond the next budget year.

h. **Post Audit**—Helps the capital budgeting committee do a better job in evaluating new proposals.

Mid-Chapter Review 2

SOLUTION

Basic computations:

Initial investment	
Depreciable assets	$(27,740)
Working capital	(3,000)
Total cash outflow	$(30,740)
Operation	
Cash receipts	$ 25,000
Cash expenditures	(15,000)
Net cash inflow	$ 10,000
Disinvestment	
Sale of depreciable assets	$ 2,000
Recovery of working capital	3,000
Total cash inflow	$ 5,000

a.   Net present value at a 10 percent discount rate:

	Predicted Cash Inflows (outflows) (A)	Year(s) of Cash Flows (B)	10% Present Value Factor (C)	Present Value of Cash Flows (A) × (C)
Initial investment.....................	$(30,740)	0	1.00000	$(30,740)
Operation	10,000	1–4	3.16987	31,699
Disinvestment........................	5,000	4	0.68301	3,415
Net present value of all cash flows.....................................				$ 4,374

b.   Internal rate of return:

Using a spreadsheet, the proposal's internal rate of return is readily determined to be 16 percent:

	A	B
1	Year of cash flow	Cash flow
2	0	$(30,740)
3	1	10,000
4	2	10,000
5	3	10,000
6	4	15,000
7	IRR	0.16

The table approach requires additional analysis. Because the proposal has a positive net present value when discounted at 10 percent, its internal rate of return must be higher than 10 percent. Through a trial-and-error approach, the internal rate of return is determined to be 16 percent.

	Predicted Cash Inflows (outflows) (A)	Year(s) of Cash Flows (B)	16% Present Value Factor (C)	Present Value of Cash Flows (A) × (C)
Initial investment....................	$(30,740)	0	1.00000	$(30,740)
Operation	10,000	1–4	2.79818	27,982
Disinvestment.....................	5,000	4	0.55229	2,761
Net present value of all cash flows......				$ 3

Mid-Chapter Review 3

SOLUTION

Basic computations:

Initial investment		
Depreciable assets...		$27,740
Working capital..		3,000
Total		$30,740
Operation		
Cash receipts..		$25,000
Cash expenditures		(15,000)
Net cash inflow..		$10,000
Disinvestment		
Sale of depreciable assets		$ 2,000
Recovery of working capital..		3,000
Total		$ 5,000

a.   Payback period = $30,740 ÷ $10,000
                = 3.074 years

b.   Accounting rate of return on initial and average investments:

Annual net cash inflow from operations.............................	$10,000
Less average annual depreciation [($27,740 − $2,000) ÷ 4]..............	(6,435)
Average annual increase in net income	$ 3,565

Average investment   = ($30,740 + $5,000) ÷ 2

                            = $17,870

Accounting rate of return on   = $ 3,565
initial investment $30,740

                            = 0.1160, or 11.6%

Accounting rate of return on   = $ 3,565
average investment $17,870

                            = 0.1995, or 19.95%

Mid-Chapter Review 4

SOLUTION

a.

	Proposal A	Proposal B	Proposal C
Payback period:	2 years	2 years	1 year
Accounting rate of return:			
Total increase in income before depreciation . . .	$67,500	$67,500	$45,000
Total depreciation	(45,000)	(45,000)	(45,000)
Total increase in income	$22,500	$22,500	$0
Life in years.	÷ 3	÷ 3	÷ 1
Average annual increase in net income	$7,500	$7,500	$0
Initial investment.	÷45,000	÷45,000	÷45,000
Accounting rate of return	0.1667	0.1667	0.0

Net present value at 12 percent:

Year	Factor	Present Values		
1	0.90909	$36,363.60	$20,454.53	$40,909.05
2	0.82645	4,132.25	18,595.13	
3	0.75131	16,904.48	16,904.48	
Total		57,400.33	55,954.14	40,909.05
Initial investment.		(45,000.00)	(45,000.00)	(45,000.00)
Net present value		$12,400.33	$10,954.14	$ (4,090.95)

Rankings:

Payback	2–3	2–3	1
Accounting rate of return	1–2	1–2	3
Net present value	1	2	3

b. While the accounting rate of return and the net present value criteria consider profitability, payback considers only the time required to recover the investment. Proposal C provides for the shortest payback; hence, it ranks first using the payback criterion even though Proposal C does not provide a profit.

Proposals A and B have identical total cash flows over their lives; hence, they have identical accounting rates of return. However, the timing of their cash flows differs. Because Proposal A has higher early-period cash flows, its net present value is higher than that of Proposal B. Of the three criteria used, only net present value considers both profitability and the timing of cash flows.

Mid-Chapter Review 5

SOLUTION

In making the final decision to accept or reject a capital expenditure proposal that has passed the initial screening, non-quantitative factors should also be considered. Very important at this point are management's attitudes toward risk and financing alternatives, their confidence in the professional judgment of managers making investment proposals, their beliefs about the future direction of the economy, and their evaluation of alternative investments.

Specific to Hilltop's investment decision, their management might consider factors such as:

- Will new models of the ski lift be available in the next few years that will be more efficient and/or safer?
- How is the economy and do they expect to be able to sustain the number of skiers that they have had in recent years?
- How likely is it that they will see a decline in customers?
- Are there any other revenue generating uses for the space, such as snowmobile rentals, that might be a better alternative to skiing?

Chapter-End Review

SOLUTION

a.

Operating cost savings (9,000 hours × $45)	$405,000
Operating costs of CAD/CAM system	(200,000)
Before-tax cash savings.	205,000
Income taxes without tax shield at 35 percent	(71,750)
Depreciation tax shield [($550,000/5 years) × 0.35]	38,500
Relevant annual after-tax cash flows	$171,750

b.

	Predicted Cash Inflows (Outflows) (A)	Year(s) of Cash Flows (B)	12% Present Value Factor (C)	Present Value of Cash Flows (A) × (C)
Initial investment	$(550,000)	0	1.00000	$(550,000)
Operations				
Annual taxable income without depreciation .	205,000	1-5	3.43308	703,781
Taxes on income ($205,000 × 0.35).	(71,750)	1-5	3.43308	(246,323)
Depreciation tax shield*				
Year 1	$77,000	1	0.87719	67,544
Year 2	46,200	2	0.76947	35,550
Year 3	27,720	3	0.67497	18,710
Year 4	20,790	4	0.59208	12,309
Year 5	20,790	5	0.51937	10,798
Net present value of all cash flows.				$ 52,369

*Computation of depreciation tax shield[†]:

Year	Depreciation Base[†] (A)	Annual Rate (B)	Annual Depreciation (C) = (A) × (B)	Tax Rate (D)	Tax Shield (E) = (C) × (D)
1 . . .	$550,000	2/5	$220,000	0.35	$77,000
2 . . .	330,000	2/5	132,000	0.35	46,200
3 . . .	198,000	2/5	79,200	0.35	27,720
4 . . .	118,800	1/2	59,400	0.35	20,790
5 . . .	59,400	balance	59,400	0.35	20,790

[†]The depreciation base is reduced by the amount of any previous depreciation. The annual rate is twice the straight-line rate.

Appendix 24A Review

SOLUTION

a. $fv = pv (1 + r)^n$
    $= \$2,000 (1 + 0.06)^2$
    $= \$2,247.20$

    or
    $\$2,000/0.89000 = \$2,247$

b. $pv = \$8,000 \times 0.63552$
    $= \$5,084$

c. $pva = \$2,000 \times 3.43308$
    $= \$6,866$

d. $a = \$32,010/4.96764$
    $= \$6,444$

e.

Year	Cash Flow		Present Value at 20%		Present Value Amount
1	$20,000	×	0.83333	=	$16,667
2	8,000	×	0.69444	=	5,556
3	6,000	×	0.57870	=	3,472
Total					$25,695

f.

Present value of an annuity for 12 years at 14 percent ($5,000 × 5.66029)	$28,301
Present value of an annuity for 9 years at 14 percent ($5,000 × 4.94637)	(24,732)
Present value of the deferred annuity.	$ 3,569

or
$\$5,000 \times (5.66029 - 4.94637) = \$3,570$

Appendix 24B Review

SOLUTION

a. First solve for the appropriate present value factor using the equation:

    Present value factor for an annuity of $1 = Initial investment/Annual net cash flows

    Next, once the present value factor is calculated, use Exhibit 24A.2 and go across the row corresponding to the expected life of the project until a table factor equal to or closest to the projects computed present value factor is found. The corresponding percentage for the present value factor is the proposals internal rate of return.

b. If periodic cash flows subsequent to the initial investment are unequal, a trial-and-error approach must be used to determine the internal rate of return. The first step is to select a discount rate estimated to be close to the proposal's IRR and to compute the proposal's net present value. If the resulting net present value is zero, the selected discount rate is the actual rate of return. However, it is unlikely that the first rate selected will be the proposal's IRR. If the computation results in a positive net present value, the actual IRR is higher than the initially selected rate. In this case, the next step is to compute the proposal's net present value using a higher rate. If the second computation produces a negative net present value, the actual IRR is less than the selected rate. Therefore, the actual IRR is between the first and the second rates. This trial-and-error approach continues until a discount rate is found that equates the proposal's cash inflows and outflows.

A

Compound Interest and the Time-Value of Money

Suppose you were lucky enough to hold a winning lottery ticket that allowed you to choose when you would receive your prize. Most of us would answer: Now! But let's say this ticket gave you the option of receiving $20,000 now, or $24,000 two years from now. Which would you choose?

Of course, $24,000 is better than $20,000. But the choice is not that simple. If you take the $20,000 today, you can buy a new car, pay next semester's tuition, or invest the money in the stock market. If you wait, you'll receive the larger prize, but you may have to take the bus for the next two years, postpone your college studies, or pass up on a great investment opportunity.

This is the essence of what is called the **time-value of money**. A dollar received today is worth more than a dollar received two years in the future. Having cash in our possession gives us the opportunity to spend or invest that cash today. Cash received in the future cannot be spent or invested today.[1]

The easiest way to illustrate the time-value of money is to assume that we collect the $20,000 cash prize today and invest it in a money-market account that guarantees a 10% return on your investment. In one year, the investment would be worth $22,000—which is the original $20,000 investment plus $2,000 interest ($20,000 × 10%). At the end of two years, the investment would be worth $24,200 [= $22,000 + ($22,000 × 10%) = $22,000 × 1.10].

In the second year, the investment earns a return of $2,200, which is $22,000 × 10%. The interest earned in the second year is greater than the interest earned in year one because the interest earned in the first year earns interest in year two. This interest earned on interest is called **compound interest**. As interest accumulates on an investment, both the original investment and the accumulated interest will earn a return in subsequent periods. Interest calculated on the original investment, but not on interest accrued in prior periods, is called **simple interest**.

This Appendix explains and illustrates the concepts of time-value of money and compound interest. It is divided into three sections. The first two address future value concepts and present value concepts, respectively. In the last section, we illustrate the use of spreadsheet software to compute present and future values.

---

[1] The time value of money is primarily due to lost opportunities. However, the risk associated with some future cash flows will influence our assessment of their time value. That is, there may be some uncertainty associated with a future payment. For instance, in our lottery ticket example, there may be a possibility that the payer could default on the $24,000 payment. Risk is reflected in time value calculations by using higher interest rates for risky cash flows.

FUTURE VALUE CONCEPTS

As illustrated above, $20,000 invested today to earn a return of 10% per year will accumulate interest and be worth $24,200 in two years. The $24,200 is referred to as the *future value* of $20,000 because it represents what $20,000 invested today at 10% would be worth two years in the future. The **future value** of any amount is the amount that an investment is worth at a given future date if invested at a given rate of compound interest.

Assume that we allow our $20,000 investment to continue to earn interest for three years. The interest will continue to compound and the future value will continue to grow. This is illustrated in **Exhibit A.1**.

EXHIBIT A.1	Future Value of $20,000	
Initial investment.		$20,000
Interest earned in year 1 (initial investment × 10%)		2,000
Investment plus accumulated interest (future value) in 1 year.		22,000
Interest earned in year 2 (year 1 amount × 10%)		2,200
Investment plus accumulated interest (future value) in 2 years		24,200
Interest earned in year 3 (year 2 amount × 10%)		2,420
Investment plus accumulated interest (future value) in 3 years		$26,620

As **Exhibit A.1** illustrates, the future value of $20,000 invested for three years at 10% per year is $26,620. This can be calculated as $26,620 = $20,000 × 1.10 × 1.10 × 1.10 = $20,000 × (1.10)^3. Similarly, if the interest rate is 8%, the future value is $25,194 = $20,000 × (1.08)^3. That is, to determine the future value of an amount n periods in the future, we multiply the present value by one plus the interest rate, raised to the nth power:

$$\text{Future Value} = \text{Present Value} \times (1 + \text{interest rate})^n$$

The future value of any amount depends on two factors: time and rate. That is, how many periods (e.g., years or months) into the future do we want to project the future value and what rate of return (or interest rate) do we use? There are two simple methods that we can use to obtain future values. The first method uses tables presented at the end of this Appendix. **Table A.1** presents the future value of a single amount. To use the table, move across the top of the table to choose the appropriate interest rate and then move down the column to choose the number of periods in the future. **Table A.1** shows that future value increases in the number of periods and in the interest rate.

For example, if we move across the top to the 10% column and then down to period 3, **Table A.1** provides a value of 1.33100. This is the future value of $1 in three periods at 10% interest per period and is called the **future value factor**. If we want to calculate the future value of $20,000, we multiply the *future value factor* from **Table A.1** by $20,000:

Initial Amount	×	Future Value Factor	=	Future Value
$20,000	×	1.33100	=	$26,620

The future value can also be calculated using a financial calculator. Financial calculators require four inputs to calculate a fifth value, which is the solution. We illustrate the use of a calculator with the following graphic:

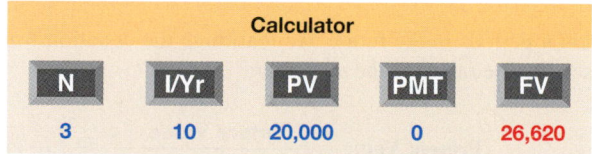

On the financial calculator, N is the number of periods (3), I/Yr is the interest rate per period (10), PV is the current, or present, value ($20,000), PMT refers to a periodic payment (0 in our example) and FV is the future value. Because we are calculating the future value in this illustration, that value is highlighted in red as the solution.[2]

Whether we use the tables at the end of the Appendix or a financial calculator, it is important to recognize that these computations are based on an interest rate *per period*. Most interest rates are stated on an annual, or *per year*, basis. However, for compound interest calculations, a period need not be equal to a year.

---

[2] Actually, most calculators return a solution of −26,620. The calculator interprets the PV as an investment (cash out) and FV as the return (cash in). So, if PV is entered as a positive amount, then FV will come back negative, and vice versa.

Therefore, we must always be careful to adjust our interest rate *per year* to the appropriate interest rate *per period* and use the corresponding number of time periods in our calculations.

To illustrate, assume that our $20,000 investment paid 8% annual interest, *compounded quarterly*. Although the interest rate is quoted as 8% *per year*, the rate is actually 2% every three-month *period* (=8%/4). Hence, in three years, we would have twelve periods. To determine the future value, we would go down the 2% column in **Table A.1** to the 12-period row to get a future value factor of 1.26824.

Initial Amount	×	**Future Value Factor**	=	**Future Value**
$20,000	×	**1.26824**	=	**$25,365**

Alternatively, using the financial calculator:

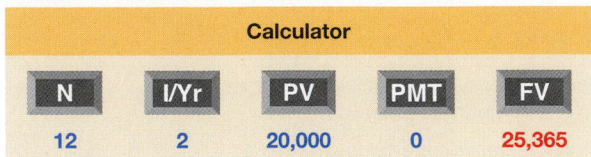

Calculator				
N	**I/Yr**	**PV**	**PMT**	**FV**
12	2	20,000	0	25,365

That is, the future value of $20,000 invested for three years at 8%, compounded quarterly, is $25,365.

PRESENT VALUE CONCEPTS

The concept of *present value* is the inverse of future value. Rather than determining how much an amount today is worth in the future, present value determines how much a future amount is worth today. The **present value** of an amount is the value *today* of a cash flow occurring at a future date given a rate of compound interest. As was the case with future value, present values depend on two factors: time and rate.

Present value is a particularly useful concept because it allows us to compare cash flows occurring at different times in the future. We can do this because we can calculate the value of each cash flow at a common point in time—today. For example, let's say we want to compare two investments. Investment A pays $15,000 in two years. Investment B pays $16,000 in three years. We cannot compare these two investments directly, because the payoffs occur in different amounts at different times in the future.[3] However, we can determine how much each payoff is worth today. If the appropriate interest rate is 8%, the present value of Investment A is $12,860 and the present value of Investment B is $12,701. (We demonstrate how to compute these amounts below.) Hence, Investment A is worth more today than Investment B. By determining the value of each cash payoff at the same point in time (today) we can easily compare the alternatives.

Present Value of a Single Amount

To determine the present value of a single cash payment occurring one period in the future, we simply divide the future cash flow by one plus the interest rate (the interest rate is also called the **discount rate**):[4]

$$\text{Present Value} = \frac{\text{Future Value}}{(1 + \text{discount rate})}$$

If the cash flow occurs *n* periods in the future, we rearrange the equation from the previous page and divide by one plus the discount rate raised to the *n*th power:

$$\text{Present Value} = \frac{\text{Future Value}}{(1 + \text{discount rate})^n}$$

---

[3] The reason that this comparison is difficult is that Investment A pays a return in two years while Investment B doesn't pay a return until year 3. One way to understand this complexity is to ask: What will happen to the cash earned on Investment A during the third year? Or, alternatively, if we invest the return on Investment A for an additional year, how much would we earn after three years? By comparing present values, we are implicitly assuming that any cash payoffs from either investment could be reinvested at the rate of return used to calculate the present value.

[4] The term "discount rate" is often used when referring to present values. This is because when future cash flows are valued using present value calculations, the present value is always less than the future cash amount. Hence, we say that the future value is "discounted" to the present value using the "discount rate."

There are two simple methods for obtaining the present value of a single cash flow occurring at any date in the future. The first method relies on **Table A.2** at the end of this Appendix. We use **Table A.2** in the same way we used **Table A.1** to calculate future values. First, we choose the column representing the appropriate discount rate, and then we move down the column to select the number of periods in the future. The value in the table is the **present value factor**, which decreases in the number of periods and the interest rate. We then multiply the future amount by the *present value factor* to get the present value.

For example, consider Investment A. From **Table A.2**, the present value factor for 8% and two periods is 0.85734. The present value of $15,000 received in two years, discounted at 8% per year is calculated as follows:

Future Amount	×	**Present Value Factor**	=	**Present Value**
$15,000	×	0.85734	=	$12,860

The present value can also be computed using a financial calculator. In this case, N=2; I/Yr = 8; PMT = 0; FV = 15,000 and PV is our answer (highlighted in red).

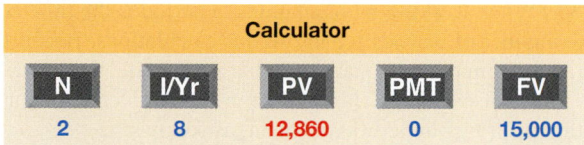

By similar means we can compute the present value of Investment B. The present value factor for 8%, and three periods is 0.79383. The present value of $16,000 received in three years, discounted at 8% per year is:

Future Amount	×	**Present Value Factor**	=	**Present Value**
$16,000	×	0.79383	=	$12,701

Or, using the financial calculator, we get the same answer as follows:

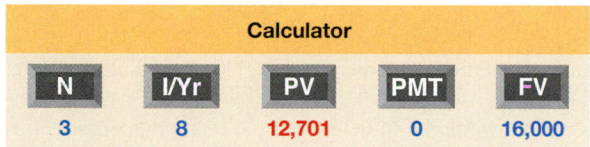

Present Value of an Annuity

Sometimes, we are faced with determining the present value of a series of regular, equal payments, called an **annuity**. For example, let's say we have an investment that pays $7,000 each year for the next three years. We can calculate the present value of each payment and then sum the results to get the present value of the entire annuity. Assume the appropriate discount rate is 6% per year. From **Table A.2**, the present value factors for a 6% discount rate are 0.94340 for one period, 0.89000 for two periods, and 0.83962 for three periods. The calculation of the present value is presented in **Exhibit A.2** (rounded to the nearest whole dollar):

EXHIBIT A.2	Present Value of an Annuity of 3 Payments of $7,000 Discounted at 6%		
Future Payment	×	**Present Value Factor**	=	**Present Value**
1	$7,000	0.94340	6,604
2	7,000	0.89000	6,230
3	7,000	0.83962	5,877
			$18,711

While this method of computing the present value of an annuity is accurate, it can be tedious for annuities with many cash payments. **Table A.3** at the end of this Appendix presents present value factors for annuities of various lengths. This table is used in the same way as **Table A.2**: first we choose the column reflecting our discount rate, and then we choose the row representing the number of payments. From **Table A.3**, the present value factor for an annuity of three payments discounted at 6% is 2.67301. To calculate the present value of an annuity, we multiply the periodic payment by the present value factor:

Payment	×	**Present Value Factor**	=	**Present Value**
$7,000	×	2.67301	=	$18,711

Or alternatively, using a financial calculator, we enter N=3, I/Yr=6, PMT=7,000, FV=0, and the solution is the PV, highlighted in red:

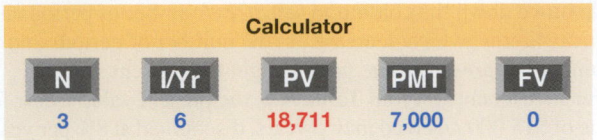

Installment Loans

One useful application of the present value of an annuity is to value an *installment loan*. An **installment loan** is a loan that requires a series of equal payments, or installments, each of which includes interest and some of the original principal. Assume that we take out a bank loan requiring 12 quarterly payments of $2,000 and an annual interest rate of 8%. When working with annuities, a period is the time between payments and the number of payments is the number of periods we use in our calculations. Because the payments are made quarterly, the 8% annual rate is compounded quarterly. That is, the effective interest rate is 2% per quarter. To calculate the loan amount, we use **Table A.3** to get the present value factor for 12 payments discounted at 2%, and then multiply the factor by our $2,000 payment, as follows:

Payment × **Present Value Factor** = **Present Value**
$2,000 × 10.57534 = $21,151

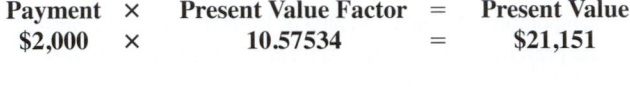

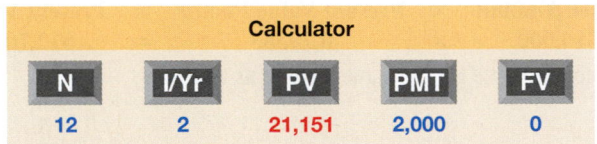

That is, if we agreed to make 12 quarterly payments of $2,000, including an interest charge of 2% per quarter, we could borrow $21,151.

A more common calculation would be to determine the loan payment given the amount borrowed. For example, if we borrow $30,000 and agree to repay the loan in 24 equal monthly payments at a 12% annual interest rate (1% per month), what monthly payment would we need to make to repay the loan plus interest? To compute the payment, we divide the present value (the loan amount) by the present value factor from **Table A.3** (1%, 24 periods) as follows:

Present Value ÷ **Present Value Factor** = **Payment**
$30,000 ÷ 21.24339 = $1,412.20

Using a financial calculator, we can calculate the payment (PMT) directly, given the other inputs:

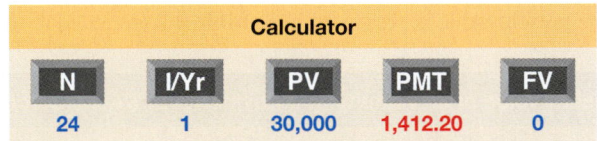

Bond Valuation

From Chapter 9, we know that a typical corporate bond has a face value of $1,000 and pays periodic interest payments every six months based on the stated (or coupon) interest rate. That is, the face value and the stated rate of a bond allow us to lay out the cash flows that will be paid to the bondholder. We also know that bonds are valued using the market interest rate, which may be different from the stated rate.

Bonds represent a combination of an annuity of the periodic interest payments and a single future payment of the face value, or principal payment, sometimes called a **balloon payment**. In order to value a bond, we must calculate the present value of each of these two components. Let's assume that we wish to value a $1,000, 5-year, 7% bond that pays a semi-annual coupon payment. The face value is $1,000 and the semi-annual payment is $35 (= $1,000 × 7%/2). Let's assume a market interest rate (yield) of 8% (which is 4% every six months). The bond is valued as the sum of two parts:

1. Use **Table A.2** to compute the value of the principal (balloon) payment.
2. Use **Table A.3** to compute the value of the annuity of interest (coupon) payments.

This calculation is illustrated in **Exhibit A.3**:

EXHIBIT A.3	Calculating a Bond Value Using Present Value Tables (4%, 10 periods)				
	Cash Flow	×	**Present Value Factor**	=	**Present Value**
Face value: 1 payment of $1,000 at the end of 5 years (**Table A.2**—4%, 10 periods)	$1,000	×	0.67556	=	675.56
Semi-annual coupon payments: 10-payment annuity of $35 every six months (**Table A.3**—4%, 10 periods)	$35	×	8.11090	=	283.88
					$959.44

The bond value can also be calculated using a financial calculator, with the following inputs: N=10; I/Yr=4; PMT=35; FV=1,000. The solution is the PV:

	Calculator			
N	I/Yr	PV	PMT	FV
10	4	959.45	35	1,000

The calculator automatically adds the present value of the annuity (10 payments of $35) to the present value of the single amount ($1,000 principal value) to get the bond value. That is, the market is willing to invest $959.45 in a $1,000, 5-year, 7% bond that pays interest semi-annually, and this amount is what would be received in proceeds from issuing the bond. The difference between $1,000 and $959.45 can be attributed to the difference between the 7% coupon rate of interest and the 8% required by investors.

Calculating Bond Yields

Sometimes we know the future cash payments and the present value of those payments, but not the discount rate used to compute the present value. This would be useful, for example, if we knew the price of a bond but wanted to determine the yield.

   To illustrate the calculation of a bond yield, assume that we have a $1,000, 8-year, 5% bond that is currently priced at 104 (104% of par value or $1,040). The semiannual interest payment is $25 (= $1,000 × 5%/2) and the principal amount of $1,000 is due in 8 years (16 semiannual periods). We input the following values: N=16; PV=1,040; PMT=25; FV=1,000. The solution is returned by pressing the I/Yr button:

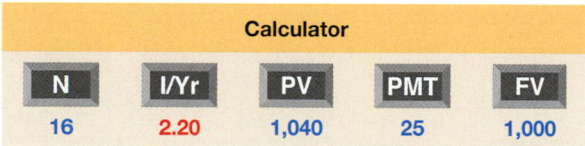

	Calculator			
N	I/Yr	PV	PMT	FV
16	2.20	1,040	25	1,000

In this case, the calculator returns a solution of 2.20%. This is the interest rate *per period* that discounts the future payments on the bond to the present value of $1,040. Because each period is six months, we must double this rate to get the bond yield (or market rate of interest), which is always quoted on an annual basis. Thus, the yield on this bond is 4.4% (= 2.2% × 2).[5]

Future Value of Annuities

On occasion, we may have a future funding target that will be met by making period payments. For instance, we may wish to accumulate a down payment for a residence or accumulate a retirement balance to draw upon in future years. For this analysis, we must examine the future value created by an annuity, i.e., a series of payments.

   Suppose we wish to accumulate a down payment by making quarterly payments into an account that earns 4% per year (1% per quarter). Payments of $2,000 would be made at the beginning of each quarter

---

[5] Technically, in order to obtain the result illustrated here, the amounts for PMT and FV must be entered with the same sign, but the PV amount must be entered with the opposite sign. For example, if we enter PV = −1,040, PMT = 25 and FV = 1,000, we would get the result above.

and would continue for five years. How much would accumulate over the five years? The future value of each payment can be determined using **Table A.1**, but **Table A.4** accumulates the amounts in a convenient format. An annuity of $2,000 per quarter for 20 quarters at 1% per period would produce a future value of:

Payment	×	**Future Value Factor**	=	**Future Value**
$2,000	×	**22.2392**	=	**$44,478.40**

This analysis would also allow for testing the sensitivity of the amount to various factors. For instance, making payments for 6 years, would increase the balance to $54,486.40. Investing in an account that provided 2% interest per quarter would accumulate $49,566.60 after five years.

USING EXCEL TO COMPUTE TIME VALUE

Spreadsheet software, such as Microsoft Excel© is extremely useful for performing a variety of time-value calculations. In this section, we illustrate a few of the features of Excel.

Future Value Calculations

Calculating future value in Excel is straightforward by using the formula for future value or using the function wizard feature. Assume we wish to compute the future value of $12,000 invested today at 6% interest for four years. The formula for this calculation is:

$$=12000*1.06\wedge4$$

Excel returns the value 15149.72. An alternative method of making this calculation is by using the function wizard. The function wizard is accessed by clicking on the *fx* icon in the formula bar at the top of the spreadsheet.

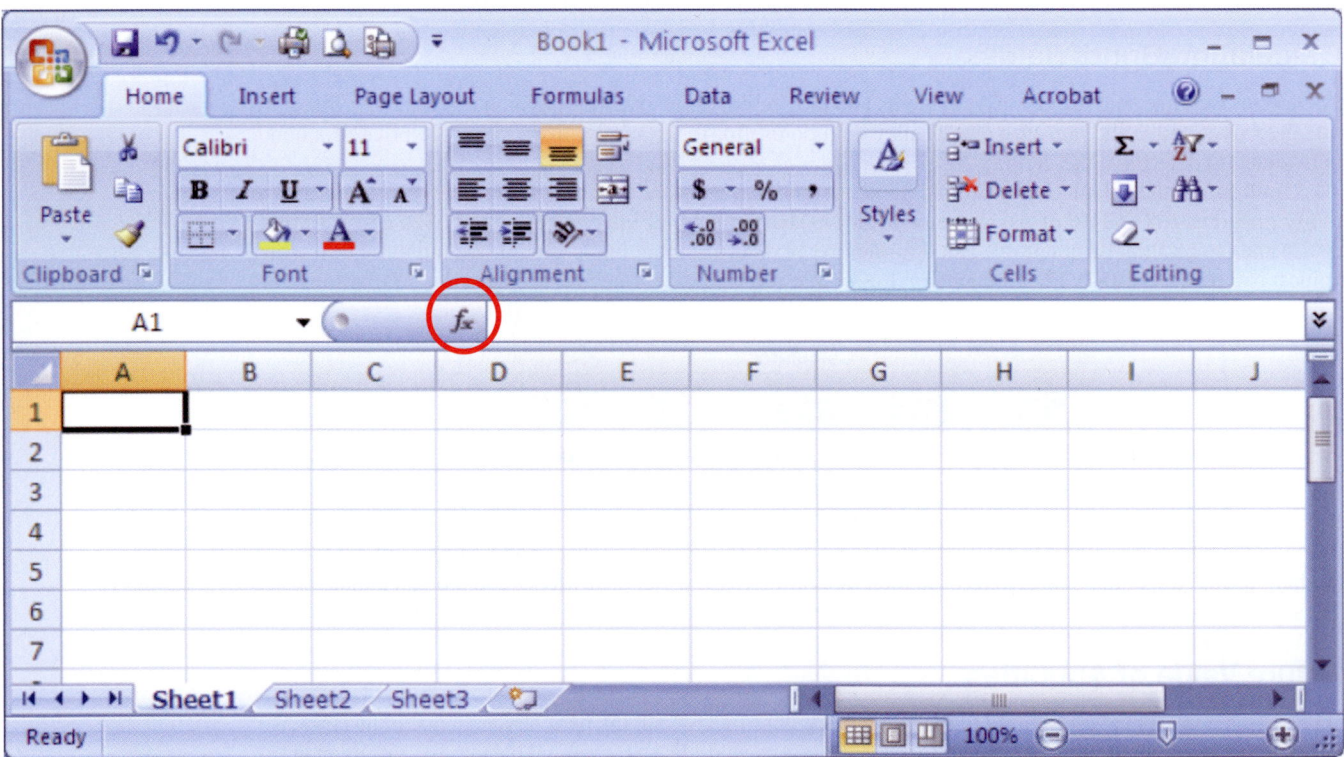

Clicking on the *fx* icon opens a dialog box that offers a variety of built-in functions. The dialog box appears as follows:

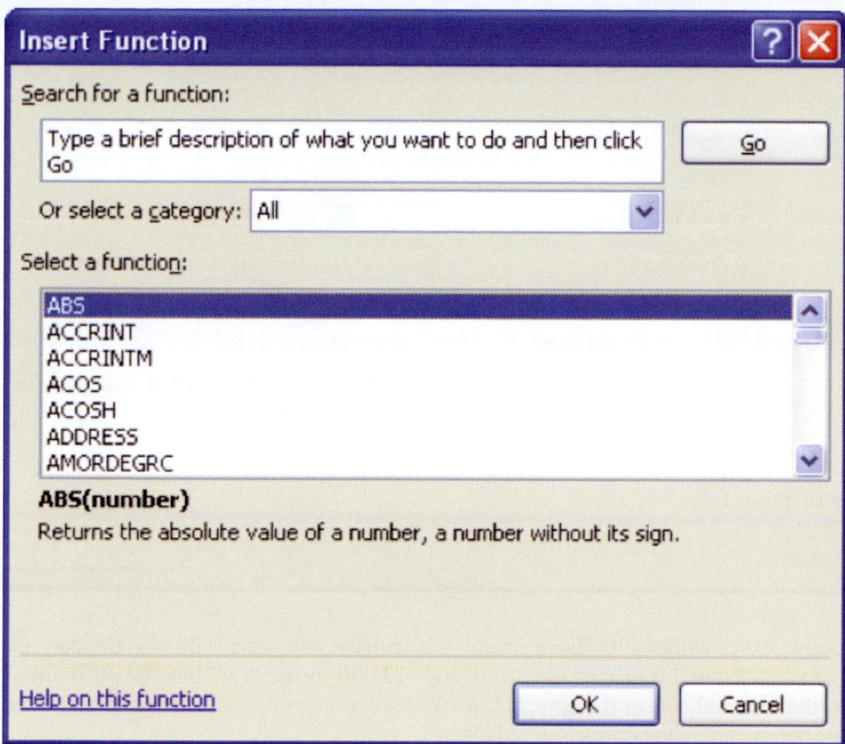

Now, the user can scroll through the long list of built-in Excel functions or customize the search by selecting a category of functions. In the screen shot below, the category of functions described as "Financial" is selected. Scrolling through the list, we select the FV function (for future value).

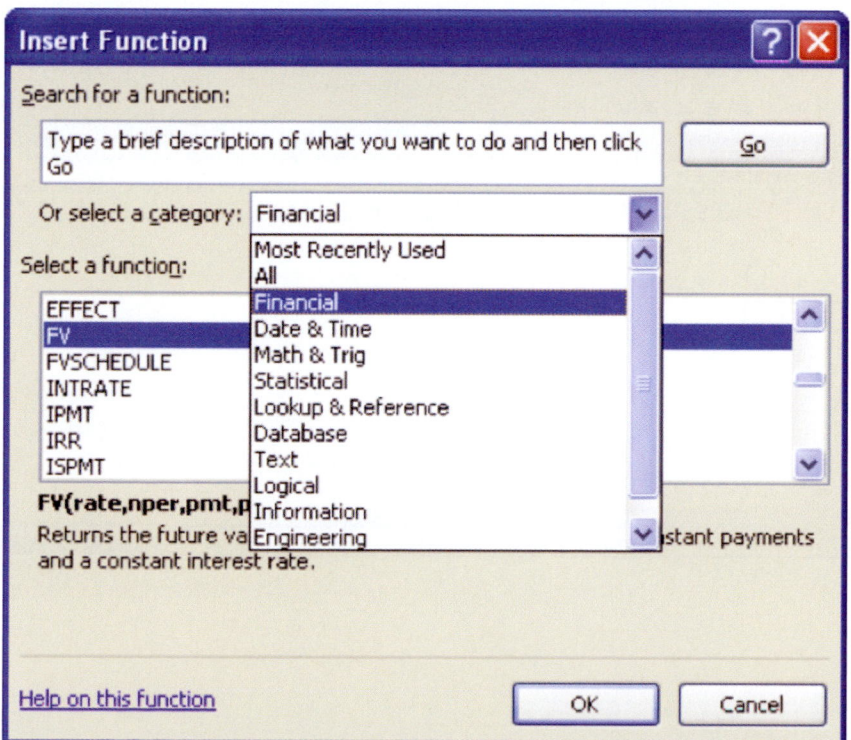

Once the FV function is selected, a new dialog box appears:

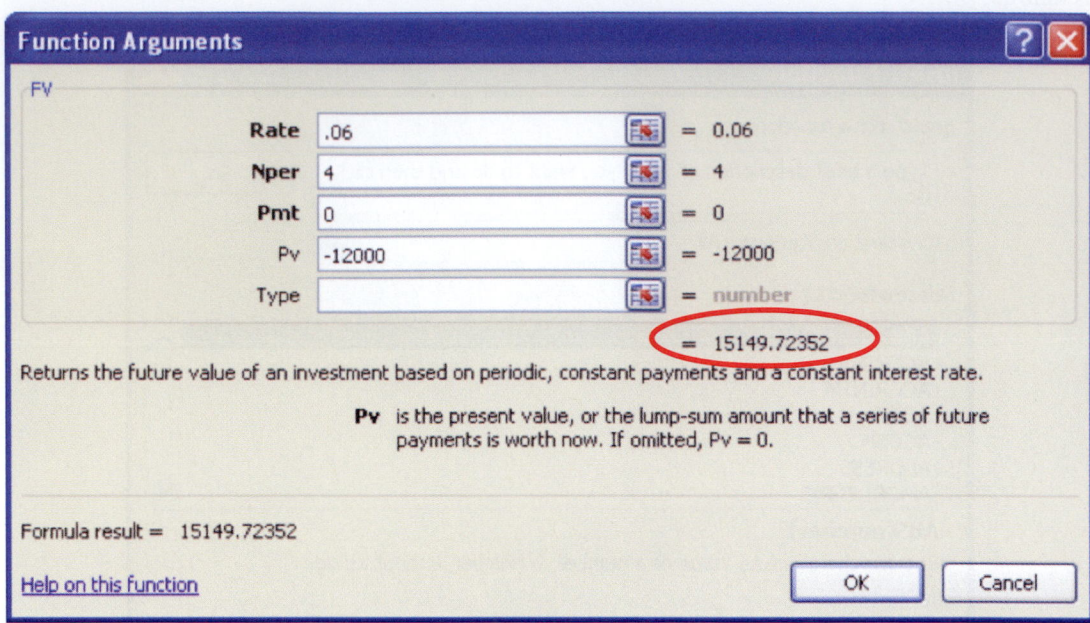

At this point, Excel works a lot like a financial calculator. We enter 0.06 into the box labeled "Rate," 4 in the box labeled "Nper," 0 in the "Pmt" box and -12,000 in the "Pv" box. Excel returns the value of $15,149.72 in the selected cell in the spreadsheet. The solution to the calculation is also presented in the dialog box just below the inputs (circled in red above).

One advantage of Excel, is that it allows the user to enter cell locations as function arguments in the dialog box. This can be useful if we wish to gauge the impact of changing an argument. For instance, we could enter the following in a spreadsheet:

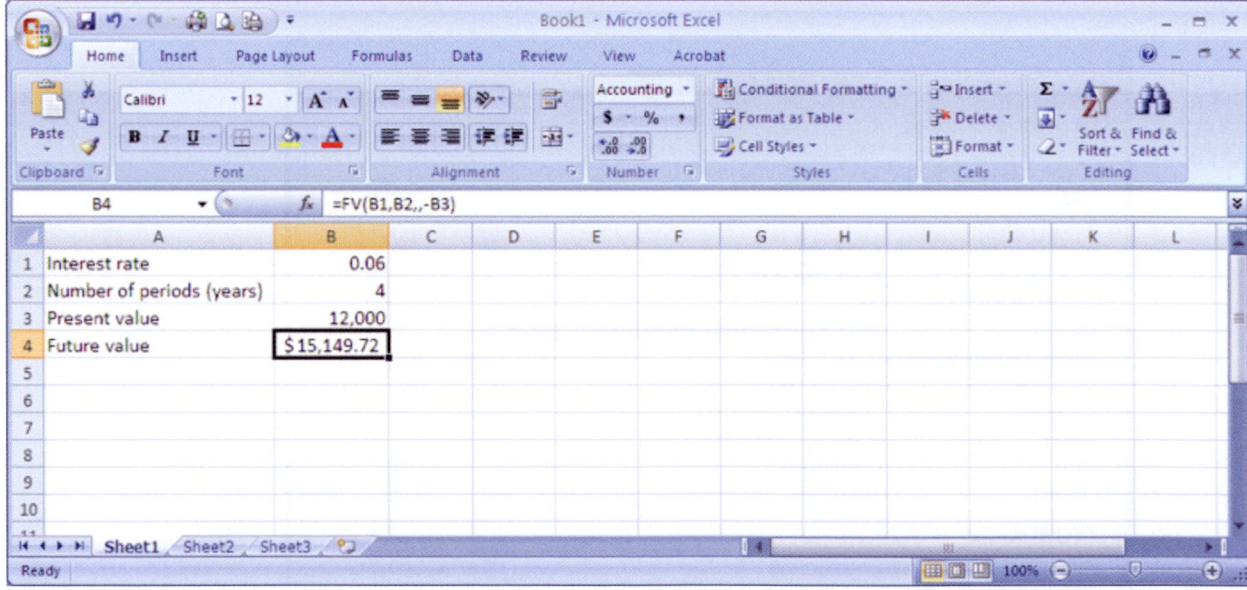

The amount presented as the "Future value" is actually returned by the dialog box below:

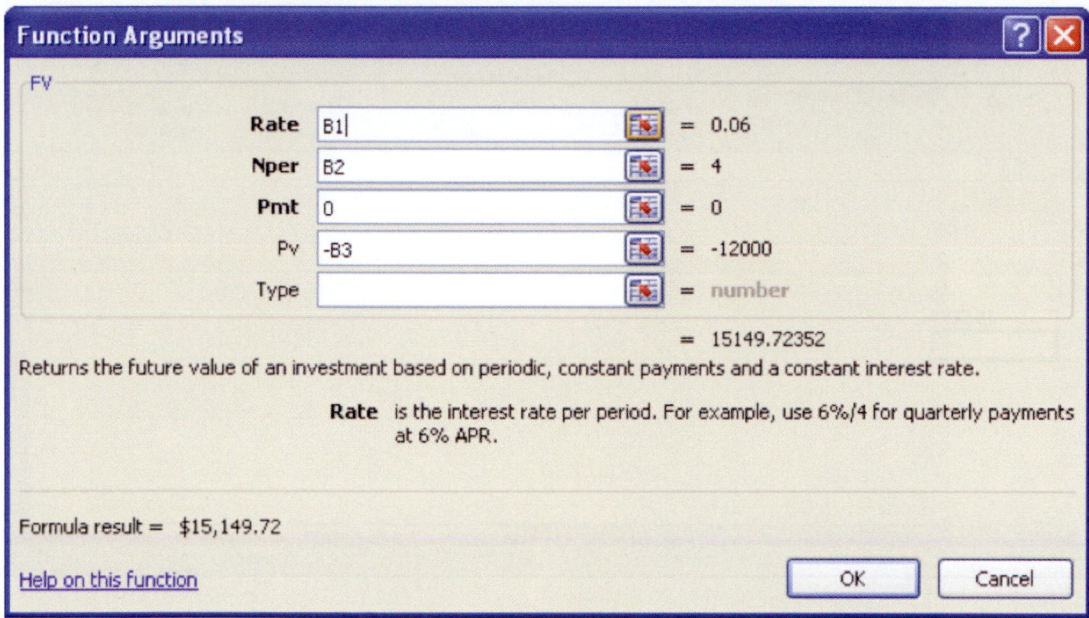

When we enter cell locations (e.g. "B1") in the boxes for function arguments, the function wizard uses the value in that cell as the argument. The benefit of this is that we can now change an argument and recalculate the future value without revisiting the function wizard dialog box. For example, let's say we wish to determine what the future value of our investment would be if we held our investment for five years instead of four years. We simply replace the "4" in cell B2 with a "5" as follows:

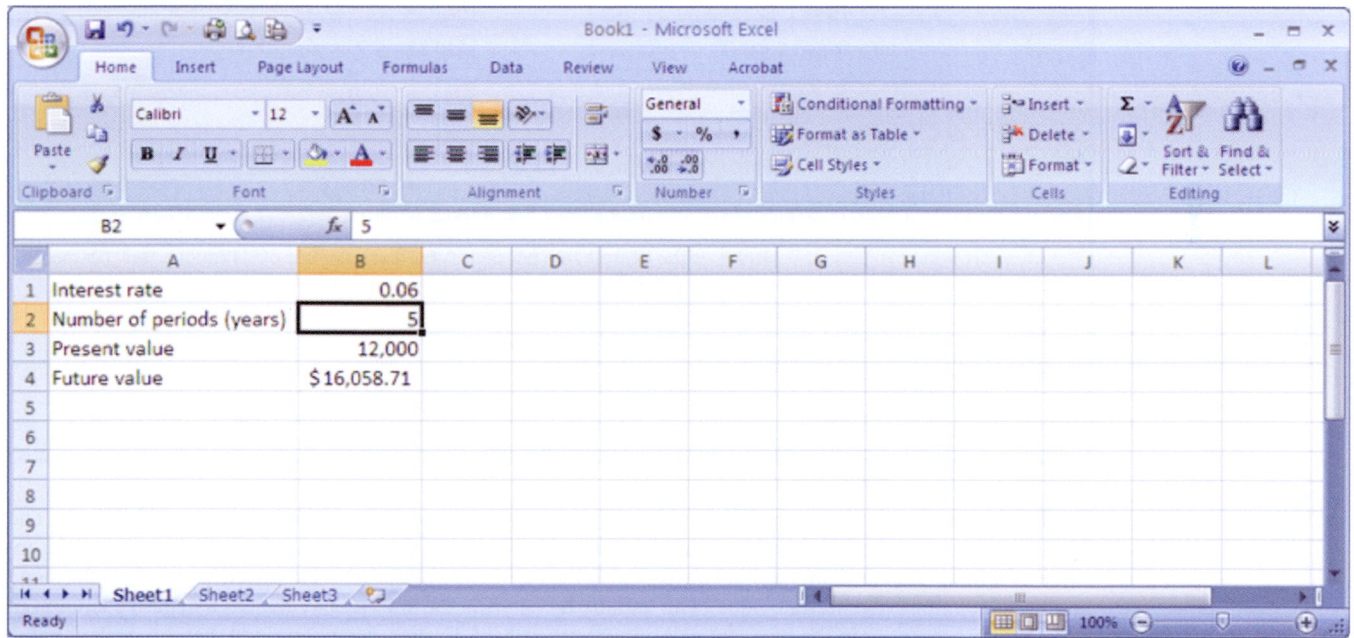

Excel automatically returns the value of $16,058.71 as the future value (cell B4).

Present Value Calculations

Computing present value is as straightforward as future value. The function to use is "PV" for present value. Let's assume we wish to calculate the present value of $15,000 that we expect to receive in two years discounted at 8% per year. Earlier, we determined that the present value is $12,860. To make this calculation using Excel, we enter each of the arguments in the spreadsheet as follows:

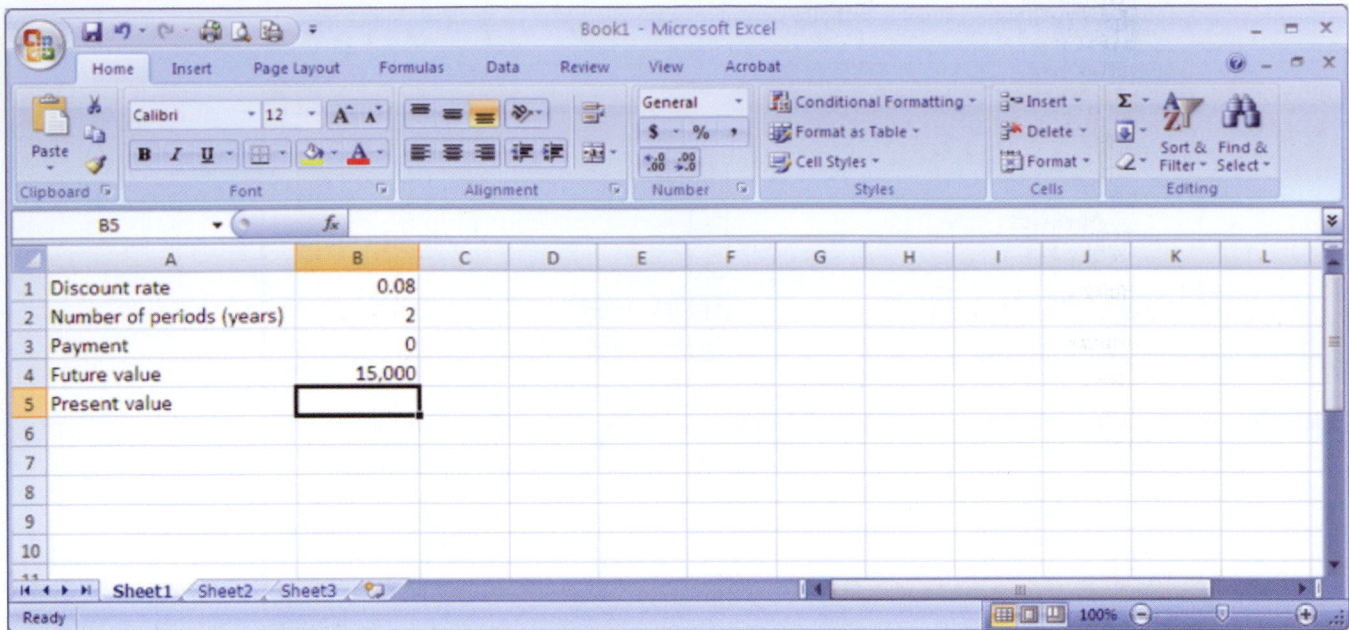

We then use the function wizard to access the "PV" function:

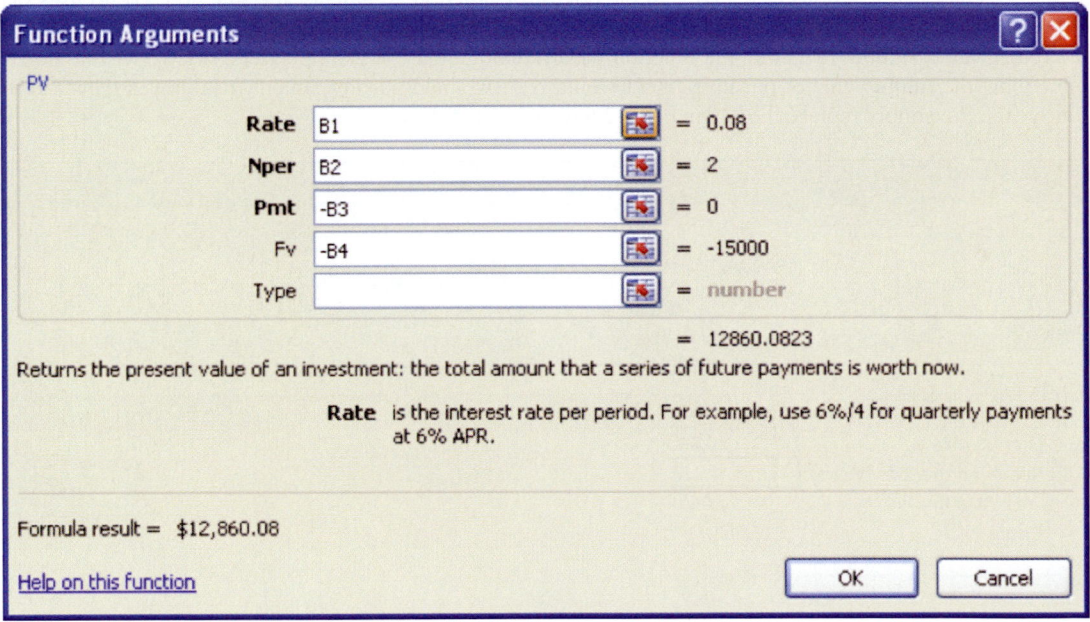

The PV function is similar to the FV function. The amount returned is the present value of $12,860.08. The "Pmt" argument in the PV function is used for annuity payments. In this example, we wanted the present value of a lump-sum amount paid in two years, so the payment was set to 0. However, we can use the same function to compute the present value of an annuity by entering the annuity payment as a negative amount in the "Pmt" argument or in the payment cell of our spreadsheet. Earlier, we determined that the present value of a series of $7,000 payments received annually for three years and discounted at 6% is $18,711. To compute this amount using Excel, we list the payment (Pmt) as 7,000 and the future value (FV) as 0:

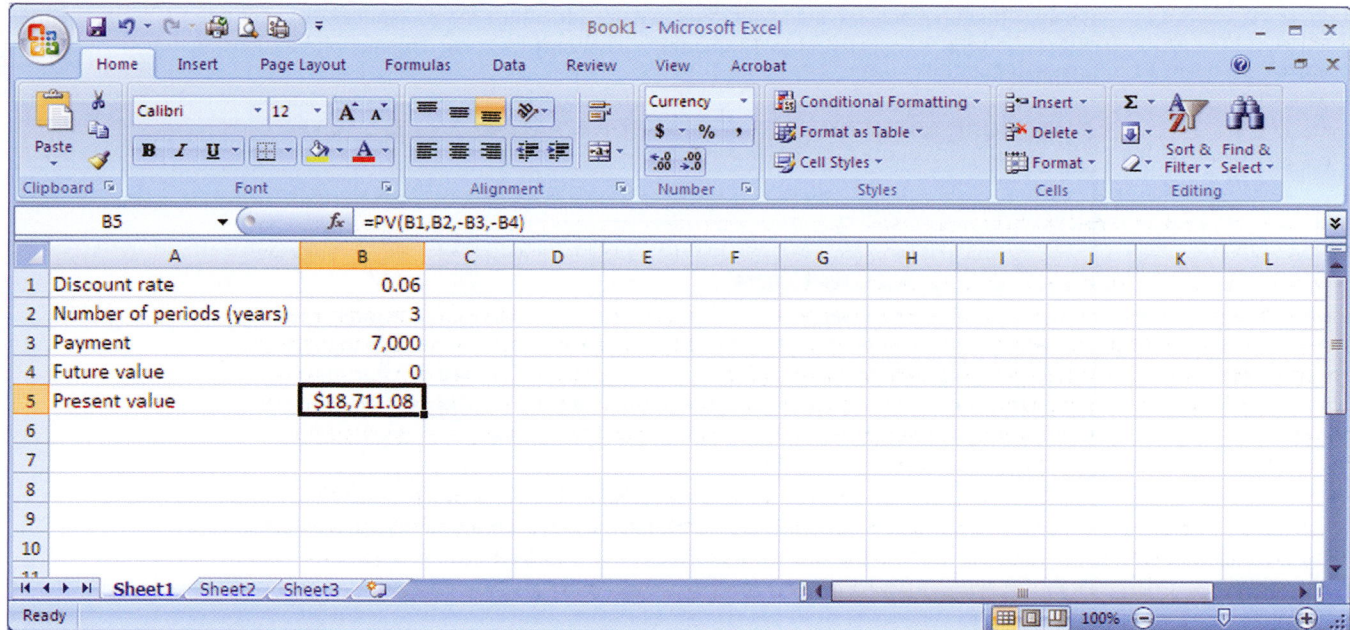

Similarly, our installment loan that requires 12 quarterly payments of $2,000 at 8% interest per year (2% per quarter) would have a present value of $21,150.68, which is computed as follows:

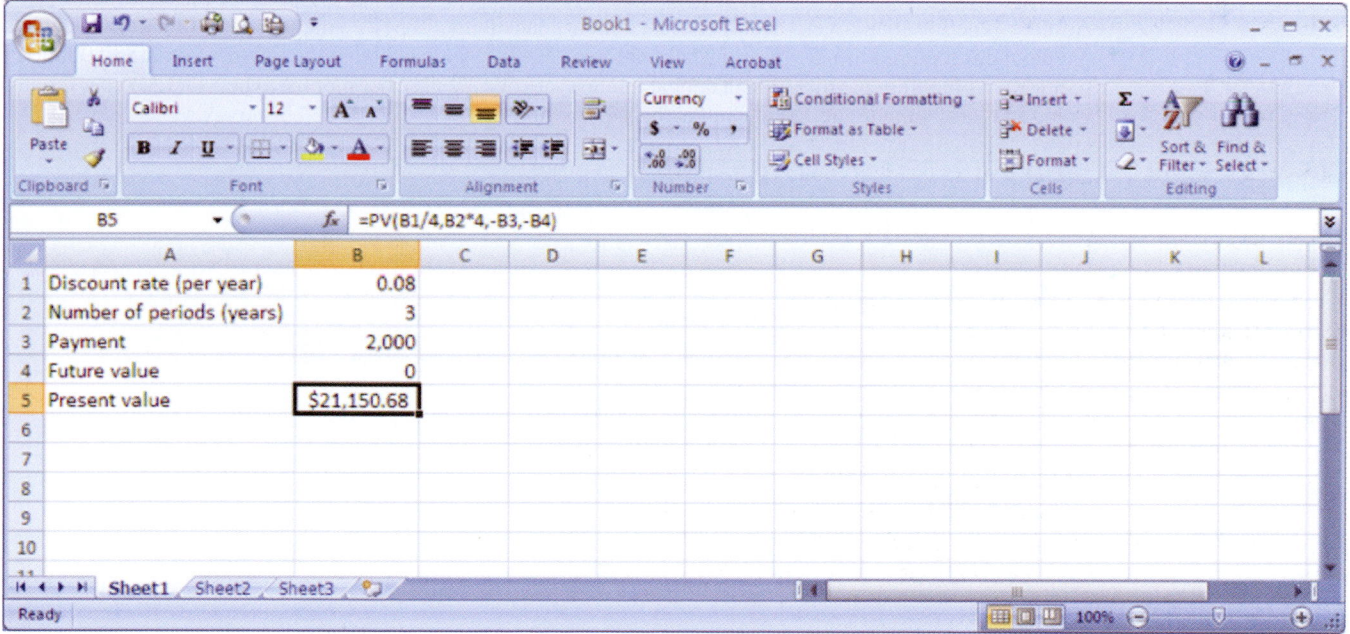

Because the payments are made quarterly, we need to adjust the 8% annual discount rate to 2% per quarter (8%/4) and the 3 year period to 12 quarterly payments (3 × 4). This is done in the function wizard as illustrated below:

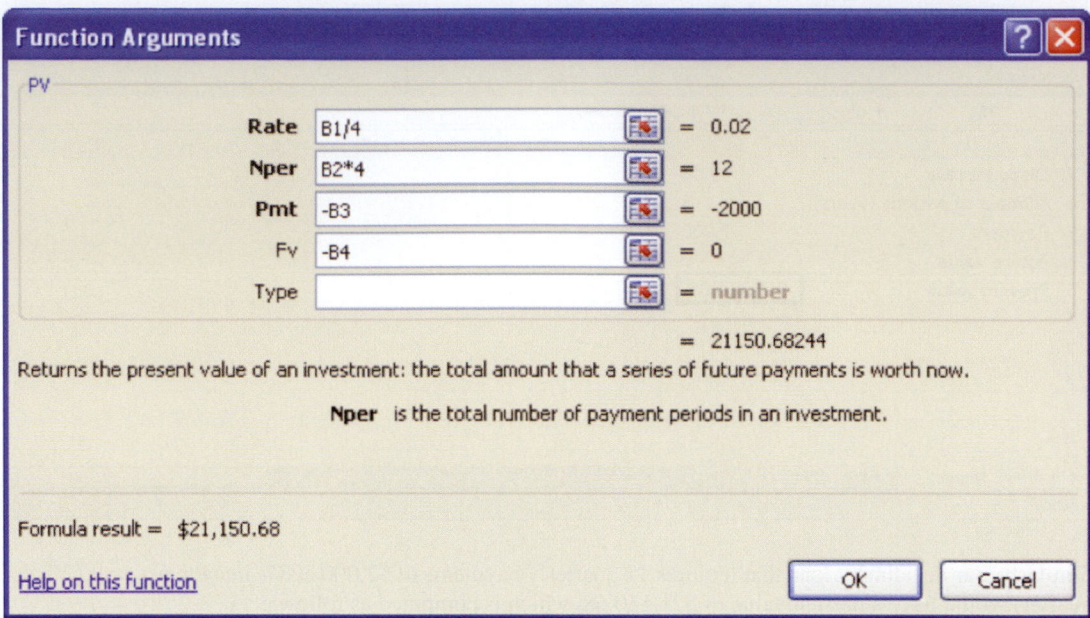

Another function that is very useful for installment loans is the "PMT" function. This function calculates the payment required to pay off an installment loan. Earlier, we calculated the payment on a $30,000 loan requiring 24 monthly payments at an annual interest rate of 12% (1% per month) to be $1,412.20 per month. Using the PMT function in Excel, we get the same result:

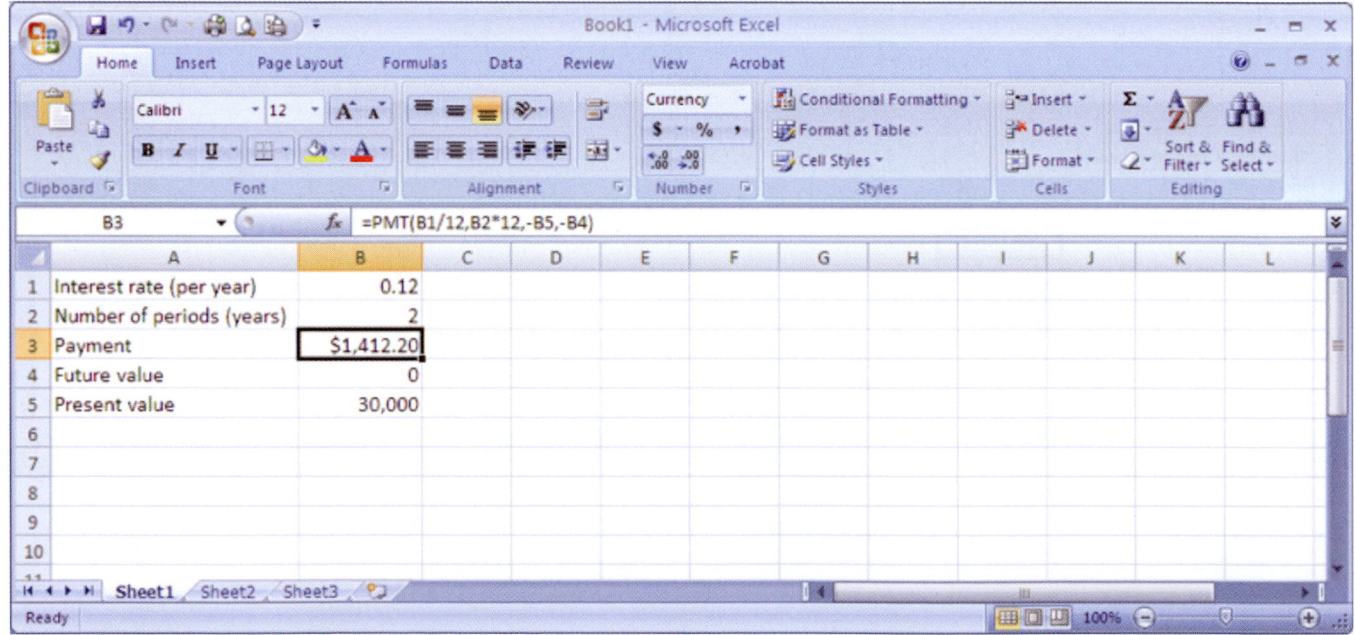

Here we need to divide the annual interest rate by 12 and multiply the number of years by 12 in order to allow for monthly compounding.

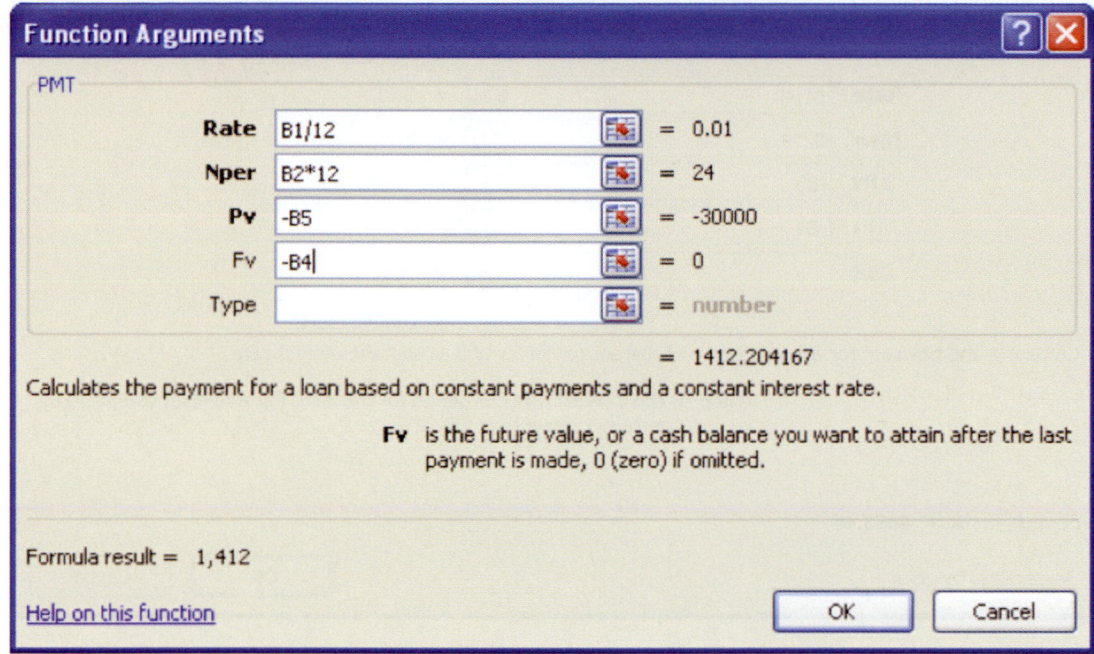

Excel is very useful for setting up loan amortization tables. These tables lay out the loan payments and calculate the interest and principal included in each payment. To illustrate, assume we borrow $5,000 at 4% annual interest, and agree to repay the loan in 8 quarterly payments (four payments per year for two years). The quarterly payment is $653.45 calculated as follows:

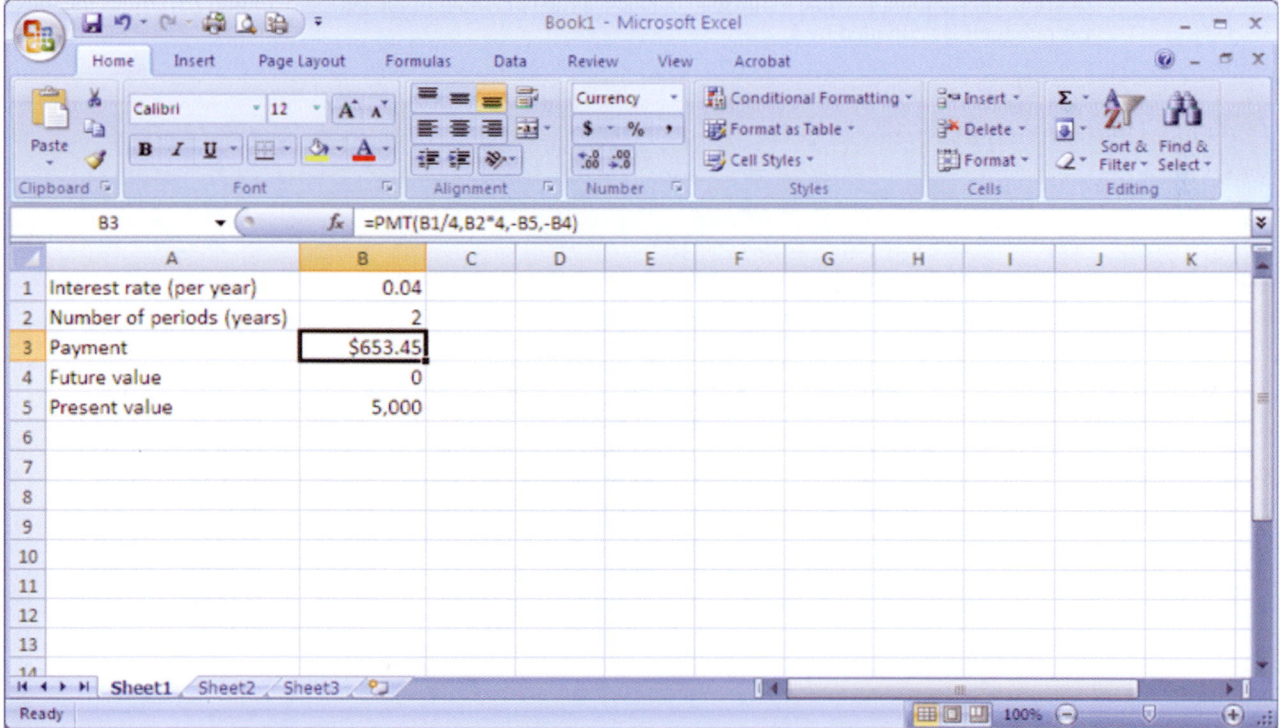

The function box appears as follows:

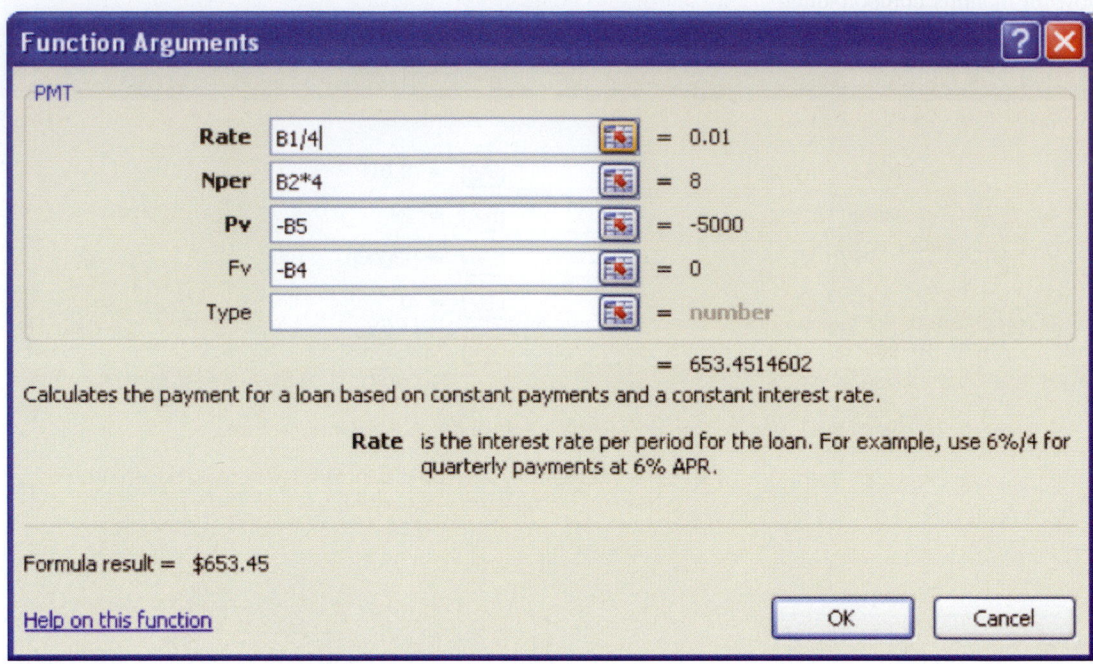

The loan amortization table can be set up on the same worksheet or in a separate sheet linked to the payment calculation. Here we use the same worksheet.

The first column [D] lists the period (1 through 8). In the second column [E], we list the loan balance at the beginning of each period. For the first period, the beginning balance is the loan amount of $5,000. Thereafter, the beginning balance is set equal to the ending balance from the previous period, which is in column [I]. Column [F] lists the quarterly payment of $653.45. In column [G], we compute the interest each quarter. This amount is equal to the loan balance at the beginning of the period (Column [E]) times the interest rate (cell B1) divided by 4.

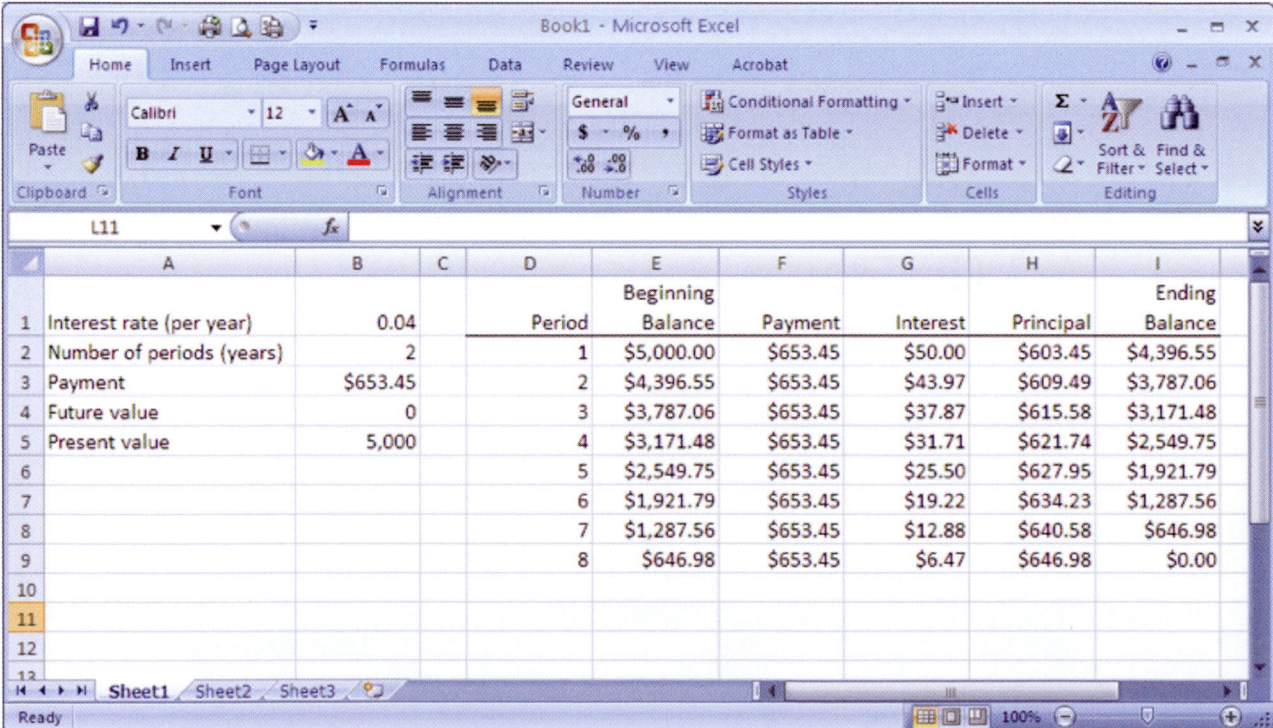

In column [H] we compute the principal component of each payment. This amount is the payment (column [F]) minus the interest (column [G]). Finally, the ending balance (column [I]) is the beginning balance (column [E]) minus the principal (column [H]). Note that the ending balance in period 8 is $0 (the loan has been completely paid off).

Loan amortization tables are especially useful for accountants because the table computes the amounts we enter for each payment. To illustrate, to record the original $5,000 loan, we make the following journal entry:

Cash (+A).	5,000.00	
Loan payable (+L).		5,000.00

Now, each period, we make a loan payment of $653.45 and that payment is part interest expense and part loan principal. To determine the split between interest and principal, we consult the loan amortization table. For instance, in period 1, the payment is split as $50.00 of interest and $603.45 of principal. To record this payment, we would make the following journal entry:

Interest expense (+E, −SE)	50.00	
Loan payable (−L).	603.45	
Cash (−A).		653.45

Finally, Excel allows us to easily compute the present value of a series of irregular cash flows. To do this we use the NPV function. (NPV stands for *Net Present Value*.) To compute NPV we need a series of cash flows at regular time intervals, such as one payment per year. If we skip a period, we must enter a 0 for that period. The cash flows can be a mixture of positive and negative cash flows (for instance receipts and payments). In the following spreadsheet, we present a series of seven cash flows and calculate the present value of these payments discounted at 5% using the NPV function.

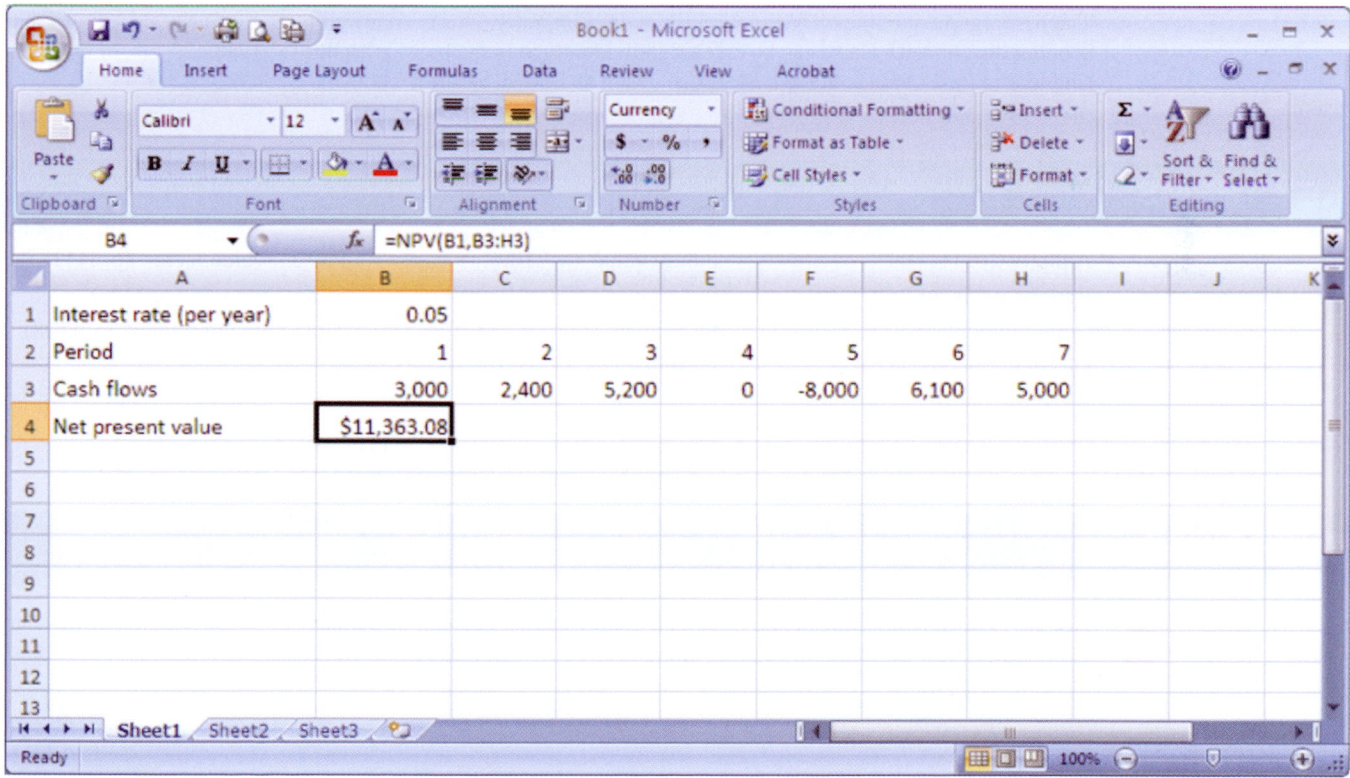

The spreadsheet shows a net present value of $11,363.08. The function wizard dialog box for the NPV function is presented below:

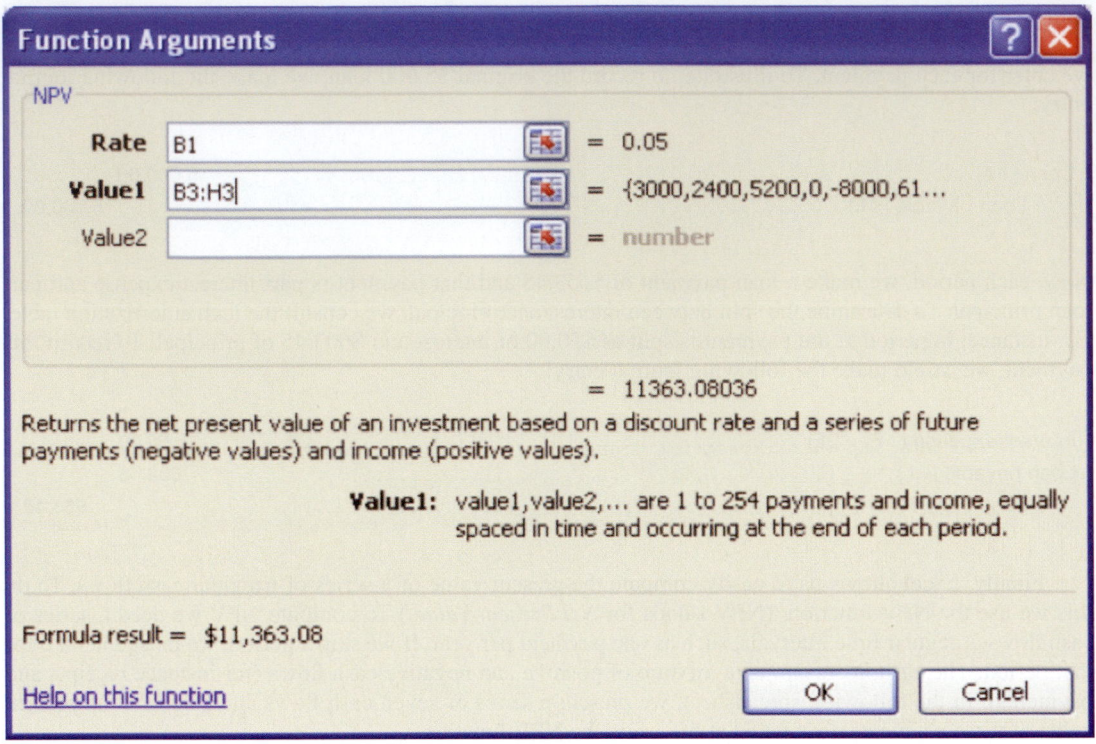

The first argument in the NPV function is the discount rate. This is followed by the series of cash flows that is being discounted. These can be entered individually in in the box for "Value1," "Value2," etc. or by referring to a range of values in the spreadsheet, such as B3:H3, as shown above.

KEY TERMS

Annuity (p. 1111)	Future value (p. 1109)	Present value factor (p. 1111)
Balloon payment (p. 1112)	Future value factor (p. 1109)	Simple interest (p. 1108)
Compound interest (p. 1108)	Installment loan (p. 1112)	Time-value of money (p. 1108)
Discount rate (p. 1110)	Present value (p. 1110)	

Assignments with the logo in the margin are available in BusinessCourse.
See the Preface of the book for details.

EXERCISES

EA-1. Dawn Riley deposited $4,000 in a money market account on January 2, 2016. How much will her savings be worth on January 2, 2022 if the money market account earns a return of

    a. 4%?
    b. 6%?
    c. 8%?

EA-2. Jason Shields invested $7,500 in an account that pays a 12% return. How much will the account be worth in four years if the interest is compounded

    a. annually?
    b. quarterly?
    c. monthly?

EA-3. Leslie Porter is planning a trip to Europe upon graduation in two years. She anticipates that her trip will cost $14,000. She would like to set aside an amount now to save for the trip. How much should she set aside if her savings earns 4% interest compounded quarterly?

EA-4. Matt Wilson has an investment opportunity that promises to pay him $24,000 in four years. He could earn 6% if he invested his money elsewhere. What is the maximum amount that he should be willing to invest in this opportunity?

EA-5. Robert Smith purchased a used car for $14,000. To pay for his purchase, he borrowed $12,500 from a local bank at 12%. The loan requires that Robert repay the loan by making 36 monthly payments. How much will Robert have to pay each month to repay the loan?

EA-6. Refer to Exercise EA-5. How much interest will Robert Smith pay as part of his first monthly payment?

EA-7. Sandy Nguyen just graduated from college and has $40,000 in student loans. The loans bear interest at a rate of 8% and require quarterly payments.

    a. What amount should Sandy pay each quarter if she wishes to pay off her student loans in six years?

    b. Sandy can only afford to pay $1,500 per quarter. How long will it take Sandy to repay these loans?

EA-8. In 2015, Cart Inc. adopted a plan to accumulate funds for environmental remediation beginning July 2, 2020 at an estimated cost of $20 million. Cart plans to make five equal annual payments into a fund earning 6% interest compounded annually. The first deposit is scheduled for July 1, 2015. Determine the amount of the required annual deposit.

EA-9. On May 1, 2015, Ott, Inc. sold merchandise to Fox Inc. Fox signed a noninterest bearing note requiring payment of $60,000 annually for 7 years. The first payment is due May 1, 2016. The prevailing rate for similar notes on that date is 9%. What amount should Ott, Inc. report as revenue in 2015 and 2016?

EA-10. Rex Corporation accepted a $10,000, 5% interest bearing note from Brooks Inc. on December 1, 2015 in exchange for machinery with a list sales price of $9,500. The note is payable on December 1, 2018. If the prevailing interest rate is 8%, what revenues should Rex report in its income statement for the year ended December 31, 2015?

EA-11. Rye Company is considering purchasing a new machine with a useful life of ten years, at which time its salvage value is estimated to be $50,000. Management estimates a net increase in operating cash inflow due to the new machine at $200,000 per year. What is the maximum amount the company should be willing to pay for the machine if the relevant cost of capital associated with this type of investment is 12%?

EA-12. Debra Wilcox won $7 million in the California lottery. She must choose how she wants the prize to be paid to her. First, Debra can elect to receive 26 annual payments, with the first payment due immediately. Second, she can elect to receive a single payment immediately for the entire amount. However, if she elects the single payment option, the winning prize is reduced to one-half the winnings ($3.5 million). Which option should Debra choose if her cost of capital (discount rate) is

    a. 8%?

    b. 4%?

    c. What rate would make Debra indifferent between these two options?

EA-13. Linda Reed, an executive at VIP Inc. has earned a performance bonus. She has the option of accepting $60,000 now or $100,000 5 years from now. What would you advise her to do? Explain and support with calculations.

EA-14. On September 1, 2015, Luft, Inc. deposited $400,000 in a debt retirement fund. The company needs $955,000 cash to settle a maturing debt September 1, 2023. What is the minimal rate of compound interest required to assure the debt will be paid when due?

EA-15. Wolf Inc. establishes a construction fund on July 1, 2015, by making a single deposit of $360,000. At the end of each year, Wolf will deposit an additional $60,000. The fund guarantees a 12% return each year. How much will be in the fund on June 30, 2019?

EA-16. Sylvia Owen, owner of I-Haul Trucking is considering expanding operations from Seattle to the Portland area. Expansion is estimated to cost $10 million including the required new facilities and additional trucks. Owen has elected to finance the expansion by borrowing from her local bank at a yearly interest rate of 10%. She has agreed to repay the loan in twenty equal payments over a 10-year period to begin in six months. (Payments will be made at the end of every half-year period.)

a.   What will Ms. Owen's periodic payments be?
b.   How much of her first payment will be interest expense?
c.   Assume that after five years, Ms. Owen decided to pay off the loan early. How much would she owe at that time?

EA-17.   On November 1, 2015, Ybarra Construction Company issued $200,000 of 5-year bonds that pay interest at an annual rate of 5%. The interest payments are due every six months (that is, the interest is compounded semi-annually). At the end of the five-year period, Ybarra must pay the bond holders a balloon payment of $200,000.

a.   What would the issue price of the bonds be if the prevailing interest rate is (i) 4%? (ii) 6%?
b.   Compute the market price of these bonds on November 1, 2017 assuming that the prevailing market interest rate at that time is 8%.

EA-18.   On August 1, 2015, Paradise Airlines agreed to lease a passenger jet from Boeing Corporation. The 20-year lease requires an annual payment of $450,000. If Paradise were to purchase the jet, it could borrow the necessary funds at a 9% interest rate.

a.   What is the present value of the lease payments if the first payment is due on August 1, 2016?
b.   What is the present value of the lease payments if the first payment is due on August 1, 2015?

EA-19.   Burnham Corporation is comparing two alternatives for leasing a machine.

Alternative A is a lease that requires six annual payments of $8,000 with the first payment due immediately.
Alternative B is a lease that requires two payments of $11,000 and three payments of $9,000 with the first payment due one year from now.

a.   Which alternative should Burnham choose if the relevant discount rate is 5%?
b.   Which alternative should Burnham choose if the relevant interest rate is 7%?

EA-20.   On January 2, 2016, DeSantis Company is comparing two alternatives for leasing a machine.

Alternative A is a lease that requires 24 quarterly payments of $3,000 with the first payment due on March 31, 2016.
Alternative B is a lease that requires five annual payments of $14,300 with the first payment due on December 31, 2016.

Which alternative should DeSantis choose if the appropriate discount rate is 8% compounded quarterly?

EA-21.   Despite his relative youth, Samuel Hunter has started planning for his retirement. At present, he has $2,400 he can invest, and he believes that he will be able to invest that amount each year for the next 39 years—40 contributions in total.

a.   If his investment earns 4% per year for the 40 years, how much will Samuel have accumulated at the end of 40 years?
b.   If Samuel delays investing for 10 years, how will that affect the balance accumulated at the end of 40 years?
c.   If Samuel begins investing now and finds an investment earning 5% per year for 40 years, how much more will he have accumulated than if he earns 4%?

EA-22.   Janice Utley is saving for a real estate investment. If she invests $1,000 now and then at the beginning of each of the next 35 months (36 months in total) at an interest rate of 1% per month, what will be the investment balance at the end of month 36?

TABLE A.1	Future Value of Single Amount											$f = (1 + i)^t$
	Interest Rate											
Period	0.01	0.02	0.03	0.04	0.05	0.06	0.07	0.08	0.09	0.10	0.11	0.12
1	1.01000	1.02000	1.03000	1.04000	1.05000	1.06000	1.07000	1.08000	1.09000	1.10000	1.11000	1.12000
2	1.02010	1.04040	1.06090	1.08160	1.10250	1.12360	1.14490	1.16640	1.18810	1.21000	1.23210	1.25440
3	1.03030	1.06121	1.09273	1.12486	1.15763	1.19102	1.22504	1.25971	1.29503	1.33100	1.36763	1.40493
4	1.04060	1.08243	1.12551	1.16986	1.21551	1.26248	1.31080	1.36049	1.41158	1.46410	1.51807	1.57352
5	1.05101	1.10408	1.15927	1.21665	1.27628	1.33823	1.40255	1.46933	1.53862	1.61051	1.68506	1.76234
6	1.06152	1.12616	1.19405	1.26532	1.34010	1.41852	1.50073	1.58687	1.67710	1.77156	1.87041	1.97382
7	1.07214	1.14869	1.22987	1.31593	1.40710	1.50363	1.60578	1.71382	1.82804	1.94872	2.07616	2.21068
8	1.08286	1.17166	1.26677	1.36857	1.47746	1.59385	1.71819	1.85093	1.99256	2.14359	2.30454	2.47596
9	1.09369	1.19509	1.30477	1.42331	1.55133	1.68948	1.83846	1.99900	2.17189	2.35795	2.55804	2.77308
10	1.10462	1.21899	1.34392	1.48024	1.62889	1.79085	1.96715	2.15892	2.36736	2.59374	2.83942	3.10585
11	1.11567	1.24337	1.38423	1.53945	1.71034	1.89830	2.10485	2.33164	2.58043	2.85312	3.15176	3.47855
12	1.12683	1.26824	1.42576	1.60103	1.79586	2.01220	2.25219	2.51817	2.81266	3.13843	3.49845	3.89598
13	1.13809	1.29361	1.46853	1.66507	1.88565	2.13293	2.40985	2.71962	3.06580	3.45227	3.88328	4.36349
14	1.14947	1.31948	1.51259	1.73168	1.97993	2.26090	2.57853	2.93719	3.34173	3.79750	4.31044	4.88711
15	1.16097	1.34587	1.55797	1.80094	2.07893	2.39656	2.75903	3.17217	3.64248	4.17725	4.78459	5.47357
16	1.17258	1.37279	1.60471	1.87298	2.18287	2.54035	2.95216	3.42594	3.97031	4.59497	5.31089	6.13039
17	1.18430	1.40024	1.65285	1.94790	2.29202	2.69277	3.15882	3.70002	4.32763	5.05447	5.89509	6.86604
18	1.19615	1.42825	1.70243	2.02582	2.40662	2.85434	3.37993	3.99602	4.71712	5.55992	6.54355	7.68997
19	1.20811	1.45681	1.75351	2.10685	2.52695	3.02560	3.61653	4.31570	5.14166	6.11591	7.26334	8.61276
20	1.22019	1.48595	1.80611	2.19112	2.65330	3.20714	3.86968	4.66096	5.60441	6.72750	8.06231	9.64629
21	1.23239	1.51567	1.86029	2.27877	2.78596	3.39956	4.14056	5.03383	6.10881	7.40025	8.94917	10.80385
22	1.24472	1.54598	1.91610	2.36992	2.92526	3.60354	4.43040	5.43654	6.65860	8.14027	9.93357	12.10031
23	1.25716	1.57690	1.97359	2.46472	3.07152	3.81975	4.74053	5.87146	7.25787	8.95430	11.02627	13.55235
24	1.26973	1.60844	2.03279	2.56330	3.22510	4.04893	5.07237	6.34118	7.91108	9.84973	12.23916	15.17863
25	1.28243	1.64061	2.09378	2.66584	3.38635	4.29187	5.42743	6.84848	8.62308	10.83471	13.58546	17.00006
26	1.29526	1.67342	2.15659	2.77247	3.55567	4.54938	5.80735	7.39635	9.39916	11.91818	15.07986	19.04007
27	1.30821	1.70689	2.22129	2.88337	3.73346	4.82235	6.21387	7.98806	10.24508	13.10999	16.73865	21.32488
28	1.32129	1.74102	2.28793	2.99870	3.92013	5.11169	6.64884	8.62711	11.16714	14.42099	18.57990	23.88387
29	1.33450	1.77584	2.35657	3.11865	4.11614	5.41839	7.11426	9.31727	12.17218	15.86309	20.62369	26.74993
30	1.34785	1.81136	2.42726	3.24340	4.32194	5.74349	7.61226	10.06266	13.26768	17.44940	22.89230	29.95992
31	1.36133	1.84759	2.50008	3.37313	4.53804	6.08810	8.14511	10.86767	14.46177	19.19434	25.41045	33.55511
32	1.37494	1.88454	2.57508	3.50806	4.76494	6.45339	8.71527	11.73708	15.76333	21.11378	28.20560	37.58173
33	1.38869	1.92223	2.65234	3.64838	5.00319	6.84059	9.32534	12.67605	17.18203	23.22515	31.30821	42.09153
34	1.40258	1.96068	2.73191	3.79432	5.25335	7.25103	9.97811	13.69013	18.72841	25.54767	34.75212	47.14252
35	1.41660	1.99989	2.81386	3.94609	5.51602	7.68609	10.67658	14.78534	20.41397	28.10244	38.57485	52.79962
36	1.43077	2.03989	2.89828	4.10393	5.79182	8.14725	11.42394	15.96817	22.25123	30.91268	42.81808	59.13557
37	1.44508	2.08069	2.98523	4.26809	6.08141	8.63609	12.22362	17.24563	24.25384	34.00395	47.52807	66.23184
38	1.45953	2.12230	3.07478	4.43881	6.38548	9.15425	13.07927	18.62528	26.43668	37.40434	52.75616	74.17966
39	1.47412	2.16474	3.16703	4.61637	6.70475	9.70351	13.99482	20.11530	28.81598	41.14478	58.55934	83.08122
40	1.48886	2.20804	3.26204	4.80102	7.03999	10.28572	14.97446	21.72452	31.40942	45.25926	65.00087	93.05097

TABLE A.2	Present Value of Single Amount										$p = 1/(1+i)^t$
	Interest Rate										
Period	0.01	0.02	0.03	0.04	0.05	0.06	0.07	0.08	0.09	0.10	0.11	0.12
1	0.99010	0.98039	0.97087	0.96154	0.95238	0.94340	0.93458	0.92593	0.91743	0.90909	0.90090	0.89286
2	0.98030	0.96117	0.94260	0.92456	0.90703	0.89000	0.87344	0.85734	0.84168	0.82645	0.81162	0.79719
3	0.97059	0.94232	0.91514	0.88900	0.86384	0.83962	0.81630	0.79383	0.77218	0.75131	0.73119	0.71178
4	0.96098	0.92385	0.88849	0.85480	0.82270	0.79209	0.76290	0.73503	0.70843	0.68301	0.65873	0.63552
5	0.95147	0.90573	0.86261	0.82193	0.78353	0.74726	0.71299	0.68058	0.64993	0.62092	0.59345	0.56743
6	0.94205	0.88797	0.83748	0.79031	0.74622	0.70496	0.66634	0.63017	0.59627	0.56447	0.53464	0.50663
7	0.93272	0.87056	0.81309	0.75992	0.71068	0.66506	0.62275	0.58349	0.54703	0.51316	0.48166	0.45235
8	0.92348	0.85349	0.78941	0.73069	0.67684	0.62741	0.58201	0.54027	0.50187	0.46651	0.43393	0.40388
9	0.91434	0.83676	0.76642	0.70259	0.64461	0.59190	0.54393	0.50025	0.46043	0.42410	0.39092	0.36061
10	0.90529	0.82035	0.74409	0.67556	0.61391	0.55839	0.50835	0.46319	0.42241	0.38554	0.35218	0.32197
11	0.89632	0.80426	0.72242	0.64958	0.58468	0.52679	0.47509	0.42888	0.38753	0.35049	0.31728	0.28748
12	0.88745	0.78849	0.70138	0.62460	0.55684	0.49697	0.44401	0.39711	0.35553	0.31863	0.28584	0.25668
13	0.87866	0.77303	0.68095	0.60057	0.53032	0.46884	0.41496	0.36770	0.32618	0.28966	0.25751	0.22917
14	0.86996	0.75788	0.66112	0.57748	0.50507	0.44230	0.38782	0.34046	0.29925	0.26333	0.23199	0.20462
15	0.86135	0.74301	0.64186	0.55526	0.48102	0.41727	0.36245	0.31524	0.27454	0.23939	0.20900	0.18270
16	0.85282	0.72845	0.62317	0.53391	0.45811	0.39365	0.33873	0.29189	0.25187	0.21763	0.18829	0.16312
17	0.84438	0.71416	0.60502	0.51337	0.43630	0.37136	0.31657	0.27027	0.23107	0.19784	0.16963	0.14564
18	0.83602	0.70016	0.58739	0.49363	0.41552	0.35034	0.29586	0.25025	0.21199	0.17986	0.15282	0.13004
19	0.82774	0.68643	0.57029	0.47464	0.39573	0.33051	0.27651	0.23171	0.19449	0.16351	0.13768	0.11611
20	0.81954	0.67297	0.55368	0.45639	0.37689	0.31180	0.25842	0.21455	0.17843	0.14864	0.12403	0.10367
21	0.81143	0.65978	0.53755	0.43883	0.35894	0.29416	0.24151	0.19866	0.16370	0.13513	0.11174	0.09256
22	0.80340	0.64684	0.52189	0.42196	0.34185	0.27751	0.22571	0.18394	0.15018	0.12285	0.10067	0.08264
23	0.79544	0.63416	0.50669	0.40573	0.32557	0.26180	0.21095	0.17032	0.13778	0.11168	0.09069	0.07379
24	0.78757	0.62172	0.49193	0.39012	0.31007	0.24698	0.19715	0.15770	0.12640	0.10153	0.08170	0.06588
25	0.77977	0.60953	0.47761	0.37512	0.29530	0.23300	0.18425	0.14602	0.11597	0.09230	0.07361	0.05882
26	0.77205	0.59758	0.46369	0.36069	0.28124	0.21981	0.17220	0.13520	0.10639	0.08391	0.06631	0.05252
27	0.76440	0.58586	0.45019	0.34682	0.26785	0.20737	0.16093	0.12519	0.09761	0.07628	0.05974	0.04689
28	0.75684	0.57437	0.43708	0.33348	0.25509	0.19563	0.15040	0.11591	0.08955	0.06934	0.05382	0.04187
29	0.74934	0.56311	0.42435	0.32065	0.24295	0.18456	0.14056	0.10733	0.08215	0.06304	0.04849	0.03738
30	0.74192	0.55207	0.41199	0.30832	0.23138	0.17411	0.13137	0.09938	0.07537	0.05731	0.04368	0.03338
31	0.73458	0.54125	0.39999	0.29646	0.22036	0.16425	0.12277	0.09202	0.06915	0.05210	0.03935	0.02980
32	0.72730	0.53063	0.38834	0.28506	0.20987	0.15496	0.11474	0.08520	0.06344	0.04736	0.03545	0.02661
33	0.72010	0.52023	0.37703	0.27409	0.19987	0.14619	0.10723	0.07889	0.05820	0.04306	0.03194	0.02376
34	0.71297	0.51003	0.36604	0.26355	0.19035	0.13791	0.10022	0.07305	0.05339	0.03914	0.02878	0.02121
35	0.70591	0.50003	0.35538	0.25342	0.18129	0.13011	0.09366	0.06763	0.04899	0.03558	0.02592	0.01894
36	0.69892	0.49022	0.34503	0.24367	0.17266	0.12274	0.08754	0.06262	0.04494	0.03235	0.02335	0.01691
37	0.69200	0.48061	0.33498	0.23430	0.16444	0.11579	0.08181	0.05799	0.04123	0.02941	0.02104	0.01510
38	0.68515	0.47119	0.32523	0.22529	0.15661	0.10924	0.07646	0.05369	0.03783	0.02673	0.01896	0.01348
39	0.67837	0.46195	0.31575	0.21662	0.14915	0.10306	0.07146	0.04971	0.03470	0.02430	0.01708	0.01204
40	0.67165	0.45289	0.30656	0.20829	0.14205	0.09722	0.06678	0.04603	0.03184	0.02209	0.01538	0.01075

TABLE A.3	Present Value of Ordinary Annuity											$p = \{1 - [1/(1+i)^t]\}/i$
	Interest Rate											
Period	**0.01**	**0.02**	**0.03**	**0.04**	**0.05**	**0.06**	**0.07**	**0.08**	**0.09**	**0.10**	**0.11**	**0.12**
1	0.99010	0.98039	0.97087	0.96154	0.95238	0.94340	0.93458	0.92593	0.91743	0.90909	0.90090	0.89286
2	1.97040	1.94156	1.91347	1.88609	1.85941	1.83339	1.80802	1.78326	1.75911	1.73554	1.71252	1.69005
3	2.94099	2.88388	2.82861	2.77509	2.72325	2.67301	2.62432	2.57710	2.53129	2.48685	2.44371	2.40183
4	3.90197	3.80773	3.71710	3.62990	3.54595	3.46511	3.38721	3.31213	3.23972	3.16987	3.10245	3.03735
5	4.85343	4.71346	4.57971	4.45182	4.32948	4.21236	4.10020	3.99271	3.88965	3.79079	3.69590	3.60478
6	5.79548	5.60143	5.41719	5.24214	5.07569	4.91732	4.76654	4.62288	4.48592	4.35526	4.23054	4.11141
7	6.72819	6.47199	6.23028	6.00205	5.78637	5.58238	5.38929	5.20637	5.03295	4.86842	4.71220	4.56376
8	7.65168	7.32548	7.01969	6.73274	6.46321	6.20979	5.97130	5.74664	5.53482	5.33493	5.14612	4.96764
9	8.56602	8.16224	7.78611	7.43533	7.10782	6.80169	6.51523	6.24689	5.99525	5.75902	5.53705	5.32825
10	9.47130	8.98259	8.53020	8.11090	7.72173	7.36009	7.02358	6.71008	6.41766	6.14457	5.88923	5.65022
11	10.36763	9.78685	9.25262	8.76048	8.30641	7.88687	7.49867	7.13896	6.80519	6.49506	6.20652	5.93770
12	11.25508	10.57534	9.95400	9.38507	8.86325	8.38384	7.94269	7.53608	7.16073	6.81369	6.49236	6.19437
13	12.13374	11.34837	10.63496	9.98565	9.39357	8.85268	8.35765	7.90378	7.48690	7.10336	6.74987	6.42355
14	13.00370	12.10625	11.29607	10.56312	9.89864	9.29498	8.74547	8.24424	7.78615	7.36669	6.98187	6.62817
15	13.86505	12.84926	11.93794	11.11839	10.37966	9.71225	9.10791	8.55948	8.06069	7.60608	7.19087	6.81086
16	14.71787	13.57771	12.56110	11.65230	10.83777	10.10590	9.44665	8.85137	8.31256	7.82371	7.37916	6.97399
17	15.56225	14.29187	13.16612	12.16567	11.27407	10.47726	9.76322	9.12164	8.54363	8.02155	7.54879	7.11963
18	16.39827	14.99203	13.75351	12.65930	11.68959	10.82760	10.05909	9.37189	8.75563	8.20141	7.70162	7.24967
19	17.22601	15.67846	14.32380	13.13394	12.08532	11.15812	10.33560	9.60360	8.95011	8.36492	7.83929	7.36578
20	18.04555	16.35143	14.87747	13.59033	12.46221	11.46992	10.59401	9.81815	9.12855	8.51356	7.96333	7.46944
21	18.85698	17.01121	15.41502	14.02916	12.82115	11.76408	10.83553	10.01680	9.29224	8.64869	8.07507	7.56200
22	19.66038	17.65805	15.93692	14.45112	13.16300	12.04158	11.06124	10.20074	9.44243	8.77154	8.17574	7.64465
23	20.45582	18.29220	16.44361	14.85684	13.48857	12.30338	11.27219	10.37106	9.58021	8.88322	8.26643	7.71843
24	21.24339	18.91393	16.93554	15.24696	13.79864	12.55036	11.46933	10.52876	9.70661	8.98474	8.34814	7.78432
25	22.02316	19.52346	17.41315	15.62208	14.09394	12.78336	11.65358	10.67478	9.82258	9.07704	8.42174	7.84314
26	22.79520	20.12104	17.87684	15.98277	14.37519	13.00317	11.82578	10.80998	9.92897	9.16095	8.48806	7.89566
27	23.55961	20.70690	18.32703	16.32959	14.64303	13.21053	11.98671	10.93516	10.02658	9.23722	8.54780	7.94255
28	24.31644	21.28127	18.76411	16.66306	14.89813	13.40616	12.13711	11.05108	10.11613	9.30657	8.60162	7.98442
29	25.06579	21.84438	19.18845	16.98371	15.14107	13.59072	12.27767	11.15841	10.19828	9.36961	8.65011	8.02181
30	25.80771	22.39646	19.60044	17.29203	15.37245	13.76483	12.40904	11.25778	10.27365	9.42691	8.69379	8.05518
31	26.54229	22.93770	20.00043	17.58849	15.59281	13.92909	12.53181	11.34980	10.34280	9.47901	8.73315	8.08499
32	27.26959	23.46833	20.38877	17.87355	15.80268	14.08404	12.64656	11.43500	10.40624	9.52638	8.76860	8.11159
33	27.98969	23.98856	20.76579	18.14765	16.00255	14.23023	12.75379	11.51389	10.46444	9.56943	8.80054	8.13535
34	28.70267	24.49859	21.13184	18.41120	16.19290	14.36814	12.85401	11.58693	10.51784	9.60857	8.82932	8.15656
35	29.40858	24.99862	21.48722	18.66461	16.37419	14.49825	12.94767	11.65457	10.56682	9.64416	8.85524	8.17550
36	30.10751	25.48884	21.83225	18.90828	16.54685	14.62099	13.03521	11.71719	10.61176	9.67651	8.87859	8.19241
37	30.79951	25.96945	22.16724	19.14258	16.71129	14.73678	13.11702	11.77518	10.65299	9.70592	8.89963	8.20751
38	31.48466	26.44064	22.49246	19.36786	16.86789	14.84602	13.19347	11.82887	10.69082	9.73265	8.91859	8.22099
39	32.16303	26.90259	22.80822	19.58448	17.01704	14.94907	13.26493	11.87858	10.72552	9.75696	8.93567	8.23303
40	32.83469	27.35548	23.11477	19.79277	17.15909	15.04630	13.33171	11.92461	10.75736	9.77905	8.95105	8.24378

TABLE A.4	Future Value of Annuity Paid at Beginning of Period											
	Interest Rate											
Period	**0.01**	**0.02**	**0.03**	**0.04**	**0.05**	**0.06**	**0.07**	**0.08**	**0.09**	**0.10**	**0.11**	**0.12**
1	1.0100	1.0200	1.0300	1.0400	1.0500	1.0600	1.0700	1.0800	1.0900	1.1000	1.1100	1.1200
2	2.0301	2.0604	2.0909	2.1216	2.1525	2.1836	2.2149	2.2464	2.2781	2.3100	2.3421	2.3744
3	3.0604	3.1216	3.1836	3.2465	3.3101	3.3746	3.4399	3.5061	3.5731	3.6410	3.7097	3.7793
4	4.1010	4.2040	4.3091	4.4163	4.5256	4.6371	4.7507	4.8666	4.9847	5.1051	5.2278	5.3528
5	5.1520	5.3081	5.4684	5.6330	5.8019	5.9753	6.1533	6.3359	6.5233	6.7156	6.9129	7.1152
6	6.2135	6.4343	6.6625	6.8983	7.1420	7.3938	7.6540	7.9228	8.2004	8.4872	8.7833	9.0890
7	7.2857	7.5830	7.8923	8.2142	8.5491	8.8975	9.2598	9.6366	10.0285	10.4359	10.8594	11.2997
8	8.3685	8.7546	9.1591	9.5828	10.0266	10.4913	10.9780	11.4876	12.0210	12.5795	13.1640	13.7757
9	9.4622	9.9497	10.4639	11.0061	11.5779	12.1808	12.8164	13.4866	14.1929	14.9374	15.7220	16.5487
10	10.5668	11.1687	11.8078	12.4864	13.2068	13.9716	14.7836	15.6455	16.5603	17.5312	18.5614	19.6546
11	11.6825	12.4121	13.1920	14.0258	14.9171	15.8699	16.8885	17.9771	19.1407	20.3843	21.7132	23.1331
12	12.8093	13.6803	14.6178	15.6268	16.7130	17.8821	19.1406	20.4953	21.9534	23.5227	25.2116	27.0291
13	13.9474	14.9739	16.0863	17.2919	18.5986	20.0151	21.5505	23.2149	25.0192	26.9750	29.0949	31.3926
14	15.0969	16.2934	17.5989	19.0236	20.5786	22.2760	24.1290	26.1521	28.3609	30.7725	33.4054	36.2797
15	16.2579	17.6393	19.1569	20.8245	22.6575	24.6725	26.8881	29.3243	32.0034	34.9497	38.1899	41.7533
16	17.4304	19.0121	20.7616	22.6975	24.8404	27.2129	29.8402	32.7502	35.9737	39.5447	43.5008	47.8837
17	18.6147	20.4123	22.4144	24.6454	27.1324	29.9057	32.9990	36.4502	40.3013	44.5992	49.3959	54.7497
18	19.8109	21.8406	24.1169	26.6712	29.5390	32.7600	36.3790	40.4463	45.0185	50.1591	55.9395	62.4397
19	21.0190	23.2974	25.8704	28.7781	32.0660	35.7856	39.9955	44.7620	50.1601	56.2750	63.2028	71.0524
20	22.2392	24.7833	27.6765	30.9692	34.7193	38.9927	43.8652	49.4229	55.7645	63.0025	71.2651	80.6987
21	23.4716	26.2990	29.5368	33.2480	37.5052	42.3923	48.0057	54.4568	61.8733	70.4027	80.2143	91.5026
22	24.7163	27.8450	31.4529	35.6179	40.4305	45.9958	52.4361	59.8933	68.5319	78.5430	90.1479	103.6029
23	25.9735	29.4219	33.4265	38.0826	43.5020	49.8156	57.1767	65.7648	75.7898	87.4973	101.1742	117.1552
24	27.2432	31.0303	35.4593	40.6459	46.7271	53.8645	62.2490	72.1059	83.7009	97.3471	113.4133	132.3339
25	28.5256	32.6709	37.5530	43.3117	50.1135	58.1564	67.6765	78.9544	92.3240	108.1818	126.9988	149.3339
26	29.8209	34.3443	39.7096	46.0842	53.6691	62.7058	73.4838	86.3508	101.7231	120.0999	142.0786	168.3740
27	31.1291	36.0512	41.9309	48.9676	57.4026	67.5281	79.6977	94.3388	111.9682	133.2099	158.8173	189.6989
28	32.4504	37.7922	44.2189	51.9663	61.3227	72.6398	86.3465	102.9659	123.1354	147.6309	177.3972	213.5828
29	33.7849	39.5681	46.5754	55.0849	65.4388	78.0582	93.4608	112.2832	135.3075	163.4940	198.0209	240.3327
30	35.1327	41.3794	49.0027	58.3283	69.7608	83.8017	101.0730	122.3459	148.5752	180.9434	220.9132	270.2926
31	36.4941	43.2270	51.5028	61.7015	74.2988	89.8898	109.2182	133.2135	163.0370	200.1378	246.3236	303.8477
32	37.8690	45.1116	54.0778	65.2095	79.0638	96.3432	117.9334	144.9506	178.8003	221.2515	274.5292	341.4294
33	39.2577	47.0338	56.7302	68.8579	84.0670	103.1838	127.2588	157.6267	195.9823	244.4767	305.8374	383.5210
34	40.6603	48.9945	59.4621	72.6522	89.3203	110.4348	137.2369	171.3168	214.7108	270.0244	340.5896	430.6635
35	42.0769	50.9944	62.2759	76.5983	94.8363	118.1209	147.9135	186.1021	235.1247	298.1268	379.1644	483.4631
36	43.5076	53.0343	65.1742	80.7022	100.6281	126.2681	159.3374	202.0703	257.3759	329.0395	421.9825	542.5987
37	44.9527	55.1149	68.1594	84.9703	106.7095	134.9042	171.5610	219.3159	281.6298	363.0434	469.5106	608.8305
38	46.4123	57.2372	71.2342	89.4091	113.0950	144.0585	184.6403	237.9412	308.0665	400.4478	522.2667	683.0102
39	47.8864	59.4020	74.4013	94.0255	119.7998	153.7620	198.6351	258.0565	336.8824	441.5926	580.8261	766.0914
40	49.3752	61.6100	77.6633	98.8265	126.8398	164.0477	213.6096	279.7810	368.2919	486.8518	645.8269	859.1424

Glossary

A

absorption costing An approach to product costing that treats both variable and fixed manufacturing costs as product costs.

accelerated cost recovery system (ACRS, MACRS) A system of accelerated depreciation for tax purposes introduced in 1981 (ACRS) and modified starting in 1987 (MACRS); it prescribes depreciation rates by asset classification for assets acquired after 1980

accelerated depreciation (method) Depreciation method in which more depreciation expense is recorded early in an asset's useful life and less in its later life

access control matrix A computerized file that lists the type of access that each computer user is entitled to have to each file and program in the computer system

account An individual record of increases and decreases for an item in the accounting system

accounting The process of identifying, measuring, and communicating financial information to help people make economic decisions

accounting cycle The sequence of activities used to accumulate and report financial statements during a fiscal year

accounting entity An economic unit that has identifiable boundaries and that is the focus for the accumulation and reporting of financial information

accounting equation The basic financial relationship that investing equals financing, commonly expressed as assets = liabilities + equity

accounting period The time period, typically one year (or quarter), to which periodic accounting reports are related

accounting rate of return The average annual increase in net income that results from acceptance of a capital expenditure proposal divided by either the initial investment or the average investment in the project.

accounting system The structured collection of people, policies, procedures, equipment, files, and records that a company uses to collect, record, classify, process, store, report, and interpret financial data

accounts payable Amounts owed to suppliers for goods and services purchased on credit

accounts payable turnover Ratio defined as cost of goods sold divided by average accounts payable

accounts receivable Amounts due to a company from customers arising from the sale of products on credit

accounts receivable aging method A procedure that uses an aging schedule to determine the year-end balance needed in the allowance for uncollectible accounts account

accounts receivable turnover (ART) Annual net sales divided by average accounts receivable (net)

accrual accounting The recognition of revenue when earned and the matching of expenses when incurred

accruals Adjustments that reflect revenues earned but not received or recorded and expenses incurred but not paid or recorded

accrued expense An expense incurred before payment is made, such as wages, utilities, and taxes; recognized with an adjusting entry

accrued income Any revenues or income for an accounting period that have been earned and realized, but are not received or billed

accrued liabilities Obligations for expenses that have been recognized and recorded but not yet paid

accrued revenue The value of services provided that have not as yet been billed or paid for by a client

accumulated depreciation A contra asset reported in the balance sheet; reflects the total depreciation recorded for an asset up to the balance sheet date

accumulated other comprehensive income or loss Accumulated changes in equity that are not reported in the income statement

accumulated postretirement obligation (APBO) A liability for benefits, such as health care benefits, to be paid after an employee retires

acid test ratio More specific than the current ratio as a test of short-term solvency, the acid test ratio (also known as the quick ratio) measures the availability of cash and other current monetary assets that can be quickly generated into cash to pay current liabilities. The general equation for the acid test ratio is: (Cash + Marketable securities + Current receivables)/Current liabilities.

activities list *see* operations list.

activity A unit of work.

activity-based budgeting An approach to budgeting that uses an activity cost hierarchy to budget physical inputs and costs as a function of planned activity. It is mechanically similar to the output/input approach to budgeting where physical inputs and costs are budgeted as a function of planned activity.

activity-based costing (ABC) Used to develop cost information by determining the cost of activities and tracing their costs to cost objectives on the basis of the cost objective's utilization of units of activity.

activity-based management (ABM) The identification and selection of activities to maximize the value of the activities while minimizing their cost from the perspective of the final consumer.

activity cost drivers Specific units of work (activities) performed to serve customer needs that consume costly resources.

activity costing The determination of the cost of specific activities performed to fill customer needs.

activity dictionary A standardized list of processes and related activities.

additional paid-in capital Amounts received from the primary owners of a company in addition to the par or stated value of common stock

adjusted trial balance A listing of all general ledger account balances prepared after adjustments are recorded and posted

adjusting The process of adjusting the historical financial statements prior to the projection of future results; also called recasting and reformulating

adjusting entries Journal entries made at the end of an accounting period to reflect accrual accounting; rarely involve cash; usually affect a balance sheet account (an asset or liability account) and an income statement account (an expense or revenue account)

aging analysis Estimate of expected uncollectible accounts based on the number of days past invoices are outstanding

aging schedule An analysis that shows how long customers' accounts receivable balances have remained unpaid

allowance for uncollectible accounts An estimate of the receivables that a company will be unable to collect; reported as a contra-asset

allowance method An accounting procedure whereby the amount of uncollectible accounts expense is estimated and recorded in the period in which the related credit sales occur

Altman's Z-score A predictor of potential bankruptcy based on multiple ratios

American Institute of Certified Public Accountants (AICPA) Professional organization of CPAs in the United States

amortization The systematic allocation of an account balance to expense; usually refers to the periodic writing off of an intangible asset

annuity A pattern of cash flows in which equal amounts are spaced equally over a number of periods

appraisal costs Quality costs incurred to identify nonconforming products or services before they are delivered to customers.

arm's length Any transaction between two unrelated parties

articles of incorporation A document prepared by persons organizing a corporation in the United States that sets forth the structure and purpose of the corporation and specifics regarding the stock to be issued

articulation The linkage of financial statements within and across accounting periods

assembly efficiency variance The difference between the standard cost of actual assembly inputs and the flexible budget cost for assembly.

assembly rate variance The difference between the actual cost and the standard cost of actual assembly inputs.

asset a resource owned by the company that is expected to provide the company future economic benefits

asset turnover The sales to average assets ratio, which reflects effectiveness in generating sales from assets; also called total asset turnover

asset utilization The efficiency a company has in turning over assets

asset write-downs Restructuring activity where long-term assets or unsalable inventory is reduced in value in the company financial reports; also called write-offs or charge-offs

audit An examination of a company's financial statements by a firm of independent certified public accountants

audited Financial statements that have been reviewed by an independent party (such as an audit firm); financial statements that present fairly and in all material respects the company's financial condition and the results of its operations

audit report A report issued by independent auditors that includes the final version of the financial statements, accompanying notes, and the auditor's opinion on the financial statements

authorized stock The maximum number of shares in a class of stock that a corporation may issue

automatic identification systems (AIS) The use of bar coding of products and production processes that allows inventory and production information to be entered into a computer without writing or keying.

available-for-sale (AFS) securities Investments in securities that management intends to hold for capital gains and dividend revenue

average cash cycle (ACC) The average period of time from when cash is invested in inventories until they are sold; the addition of the average collection period and modified average inventory days outstanding less the modified average payable days outstanding

average collection period (ACP) A measure related to accounts receivable turnover, which is defined as average accounts receivable divided by average daily sales

average cost (AC) Inventory costing method that views cost of goods sold as an average of the cost to purchase all inventories available for sale during a particular period

average inventory days outstanding (AIDO) A companion measure to inventory turnover computed as average inventory divided by average daily cost of goods sold; also called days inventory outstanding

average payable days outstanding A ratio defined as average accounts payable divided by average daily cost of goods sold

B

backflush costing An inventory accounting system used in conjunction with JIT in which costs are assigned initially to cost of goods sold. At the end of the period, costs are backed out of cost of goods sold and assigned to appropriate inventory accounts for any inventories that may exist.

bad debt expense The cost of uncollectible accounts; also called provision for uncollectible accounts

balanced scorecard A performance measurement system that includes financial and operational measures which are related to the organizational goals. The basic premise is to establish a set of indicators that can be used to monitor performance progress and then compare the goals that are established with the results.

balance sheet A financial report based on the accounting equation that lists a company's assets, liabilities, and equity at a certain point in time

balloon payment A lump sum payment due when a bond or other loan matures

bank reconciliation A schedule that accounts for all differences between the ending balance on the bank statement and the ending balance of the general ledger's cash account, as well as determining the reconciled cash balance at the end of the month

basic EPS Earnings per share, defined as net income less dividends on preferred stock divided by weighted average of common shares outstanding for the year

batch level activity An activity performed for each batch of product produced.

bearer One of the terms that may be used to designate the payee on a promissory note; means the note is payable to whoever holds the note

benchmarking A systematic approach to identifying the best practices to help an organization take action to improve performance.

big bath Situation where a company recognizes large write-offs in a period of already depressed income

bill of materials A document that specifies the kinds and quantities of raw materials required to produce one unit of product.

board of directors Governing body of a corporation; elected by the shareholders to represent shareholder interests and oversee management

bond A long-term debt instrument that promises to pay interest periodically and a principal amount at maturity, usually issued by the borrower to a group of lenders; bonds may incorporate a wide variety of provisions relating to security for the debt involved, methods of paying the periodic interest, retirement provisions, and conversion options

book value The dollar amount carried in the accounts of a particular item; the value of an item less its accumulated depreciation; also called net book value or carrying value

book value per share The net book value of a company available to common shareholders, defined as stockholders' equity less preferred stock divided by the number of common shares outstanding

borrows at a discount When the face amount of the note is reduced by a calculated cash discount to determine the cash proceeds

bottom-up budget A budget where managers at all levels—and in some cases even non-managers—become involved in the budget preparation.

break-even point The unit or dollar sales volume where total revenues equal total costs.

budget A formal plan of action expressed in monetary terms.

budget committee A committee responsible for supervising budget preparation. It serves as a review board for evaluating requests for discretionary cost items and new projects.

budget office An organizational unit responsible for the preparation, distribution, and processing of forms used in gathering budget data. It handles most of the work of actually formulating the budget schedules and reports.

budgetary slack Occurs when managers intentionally understate revenues or overstate expenses in order to produce favorable variances for the department.

budgeted financial statements Hypothetical statements that reflect the "as if" effects of the budgeted activities on the actual financial position of the organization. They reflect what the results of operations will be if all the predictions in the budget are correct.

budgeting Projecting the operations of an organization and their financial impact on the future.

bundled sales Two or more products sold together under one lump-sum price

C

calendar year A fiscal year that runs from January 1 to December 31

call provision A company's right to repurchase its own bond

capacity costs Operating expenses related to providing the ability to produce and sell products and provide services to customers; includes costs such as depreciation, rent, utilities, insurance and other related costs; *see* committed fixed costs

capital The assets that provide value to the company

capital budgeting A process that involves the identification of potentially desirable projects for capital expenditures, the subsequent evaluation of capital expenditure proposals, and the selection of proposals that meet certain criteria.

capital expenditures Financial outlays to acquire property, plant, and equipment; sometimes abbreviated as CAPEX

capital lease A lease that transfers to the lessee substantially all of the benefits and risks related to ownership of the property; the lessee records the leased property as an asset and establishes a liability for the lease obligation

capital lease method Method of reporting leases that requires both the lease asset and lease liability to be reported on the balance sheet

capital markets Financing sources that often involve a company's issuance of securities (stocks, bonds, and notes)

capitalization The recording of an asset's cost as an asset on the balance sheet rather than as an expense on the income statement; these costs are transferred to expense as the asset is used up

capitalization of interest A process that adds interest to an asset's initial cost if a period of time is required to prepare the asset for use

capitalized To include a portion of an asset's cost on the balance sheet

capitalized interest Interest incurred during construction that is recorded as a part of the cost of a self-constructed (rather than purchased) asset

cash Currency, bank deposits, certificates of deposit, and other cash equivalents

cash accounting Accounting method where revenues are only recognized when received in cash and expenses are only recognized when paid in cash; sometimes referred to as cash-basis accounting

cash and cash equivalents A balance sheet account that combines cash with certain short-term, highly liquid investments

cash budget Summarizes all cash receipts and disbursements expected to occur during the budget period.

cash (operating) cycle The period of time from when cash is invested in inventories until inventory is sold and receivables are collected

cash discounts A price reduction offered by suppliers to buyers if payment is made within a specified time period; usually established as part of the credit terms and stated as a percentage of the purchase price

cash equivalents Short-term, highly liquid investments that are easily convertible into a known cash amount and are relatively unaffected by interest rate changes

cash flow from operations divided by net income An objective performance measure; the higher this ratio, the higher the quality of income

centralization When top management controls the major functions of an organization (such as manufacturing, sales, accounting, computer operations, marketing, research and development, and management control).

certificate of deposit (CD) An investment security available at financial institutions generally offering a fixed rate of return for a specified period of time

chained target costing Bringing in suppliers as part of the coordination process to attain a competitively priced product that is delivered to the customer in a timely manner.

change in accounting estimate Modification to a previous estimate of an uncertain future event, such as the useful life of a depreciable asset, uncollectible accounts receivable, and warranty expenses; applied currently and prospectively only

change in accounting principle Adoption of a generally accepted accounting principle that differs from one previously used for reporting purposes. Accounting changes require full disclosure in the footnotes of the financial statements describing justification and the effect on cumulative income or loss of the change.

channel stuffing When a company uses its market power over customers or distributors to induce them to purchase more goods than necessary to meet their normal needs

chart of accounts Form that facilitates transaction analysis and the preparation of general ledger entries

check A written order directing a particular bank to pay a specified amount of money to a person named on the check

clean surplus accounting Income that explains successive equity balances

closing procedures Part of the accounting cycle in which the balances of temporary accounts are transferred into permanent accounts

coefficient of determination (R2) A measure of the percent of variation in the dependevt variable that is explained by variations in the independent variable when the least-squares estimation equation is used.

collateral Mortgages on assets a company owns as security for debt financing

collectibility risk The chance that items sold on credit will not be paid in full

commitments A contractual arrangement by which both parties to the contract still have acts to perform

committed fixed costs (capacity costs) Costs required to maintain the current service or production capacity or to fill a previous legal commitment.

common-size comparative financial statement A financial statement in which each item is presented as a percentage of a key figure such as sales or total assets

common cost A cost incurred for the benefit of two or more cost objectives—an indirect cost.

common segment costs Costs related to more than one segment and not directly traceable to a particular segment. These costs are referred to as common costs because they are incurred at one level for the benefit of two or more segments at a lower level.

common size statement A financial statement that has had all its accounts converted into percentages. As such, a common size statement is very useful for detecting items that are out of line, that deviate from some present amount, or that may be indications of other problems.

common stock The basic ownership class of corporate capital stock, carrying the rights to vote, share in earnings, participate in future stock issues, and share in any liquidation proceeds after prior claims have been settled

comparative balance sheet Financial statement that compares the assets, liabilities, and equity of a company over several distinct periods

comparative financial statements A frequently encountered form of horizontal analysis that compares dollar and percentage changes for important items and classification totals

comparative income statement Financial statement that compares the revenues and expenses of a company over several distinct periods

compensating balance A minimum amount that a bank requires a firm to maintain in a bank account as part of a borrowing arrangement

competitor analysis The comparison of a firm's financial measures to similar measures or other firms in the industry or to industry averages

completed contract method Revenue recognition method in which revenue is deferred until the contract is complete

complex capital structure Stockholders' equity that includes dilutive securities outstanding; required to report diluted EPS (earnings per share)

compound interest Interest that accrues on outstanding interest

compound journal entry A journal entry that involves more than two accounts

comprehensive income The total income reported by the company, including net profit and all other changes to stockholders' equity other than those arising from capital (stock) transactions; typical components of other comprehensive income (OCI) are unrealized gains (losses) on available-for-sale securities and derivatives, minimum pension liability adjustment, and foreign currency translation adjustments

computer-aided design (CAD) A method of design that involves the use of computers to design products.

computer-aided manufacturing (CAM) A manufacturing method that involves the use of computers to control the operation of machines.

computer-integrated manufacturing (CIM) The ultimate extension of the CAD, CAM, and FMS concepts to a completely automated and computer-controlled factory where production is self-operating once a product is designed and the decision to produce is made.

conceptual framework Guidelines developed by the FASB to provide a structure for considering future standards, as well as to guide accountants in areas where standards do not currently exist

conservatism An accounting principle stating that judgmental determinations should tend toward understatement rather than overstatement of net assets and income

consignment A type of sale in which a consignor delivers product to a consignee, but retains ownership until the consignee sells the product to the ultimate customer

consistency An accounting principle stating that, unless otherwise disclosed, accounting reports should be prepared on a basis consistent with the preceding period

consolidated financial statements An aggregation (an adding up) of financial statements of the parent company and all its subsidiary companies, less any intercompany activities

contingency A possible future event; significant contingent liabilities must be disclosed in the notes to the financial statements

contingent liability A potential obligation, the eventual occurrence of which usually depends on some future event beyond the control of the firm; contingent liabilities may originate with such events as lawsuits, credit guarantees, and environmental damages

continuous budgeting Budgeting based on a moving time frame that extends over a fixed period. The budget system adds an identical time period to the budget at the end of each period of operations, thereby always maintaining a budget of exactly the same time length.

continuous improvement (Kaizen) budgeting An approach to budgeting that incorporates a targeted improvement (reduction) in costs; management requests that a given process will be improved during the budgeting process. This may be applied to every budget category or to specific areas selected by management. Kaizen budgeting is based upon prior performance and anticipated operating conditions during the upcoming period.

continuous improvement (Kaizen) costing Establishing cost reduction targets for products or services that an organization is currently providing to customers.

continuous improvement An approach to activity-based management where the employees constantly evaluate products, services, and processes, seeking ways to do better.

contra-asset account A means to offset an asset account without directly reducing that account

contra accounts Accounts used to record reductions in or offsets to a related account

contract rate The rate of interest stated on a bond certificate

contributed capital The net funding that a company receives from issuing and reacquiring its equity shares; the difference between what the company receives from issuing shares and the cost it takes to buy them back

contribution income statement An income statement format in which variable costs are subtracted from revenues to figure contribution margin, and fixed costs are then subtracted from contribution margin to calculate net income.

contribution margin ratio The portion of each dollar of sales revenue contributed toward covering fixed costs and earning a profit.

contribution margin The difference between total revenues and total variable costs; this amount goes toward covering fixed costs and providing a profit.

controlling The process of ensuring that results agree with plans.

controlling influence When a company owns a majority of another company's voting stock, such that it has the ability to elect a majority of the board of directors and, as a result, the ability to affect its strategic direction and hiring of executive management

conversion cost The combined costs of direct labor and manufacturing overhead incurred to convert raw materials into finished goods.

conversion feature Contract provision that allows bondholders or preferred shareholders to convert their shares into common stock at a predetermined conversion ratio

convertible bond A bond incorporating the holder's right to convert the bond to capital stock under prescribed terms

convertible securities Debt and equity securities that provide the holder with an option to convert those securities into other securities

cookie jar reserve Accounting method in which income is shifted from the current period to a future period

copyright An exclusive right that protects an owner against the unauthorized reproduction of a specific written work or artwork

core (persistent) components Elements of income that are most likely to persist and are most relevant for projecting future financial performance

core income A company's income from its usual business activities that is expected to continue (persist) into the future

corporation A form of business organization that is a separate legal entity from its owners; characterized by a large number of owners who own shares of equity and who are not involved in managing the day-to-day operations of the company

cost allocation base A measure of volume of activity, such as direct labor hours or machine hours, that determines how much of a cost pool is assigned to each cost objective.

cost behavior How costs respond to changes in an activity cost driver.

cost center A responsibility center whose manager is responsible only for managing costs.

cost driver A factor that causes or influences costs.

cost driver analysis The study of factors that influence costs.

cost estimation The determination of the relationship between activity and cost.

cost flow assumption One of several alternative methods used to account for inventory and cost of goods sold when input prices change

cost method Accounting method in which investment is continually reported at its historical cost, and cash dividends and interest are recognized in current income

cost objective An object to which costs are assigned. Examples include departments, products, and services.

cost of capital The average cost of obtaining the resources necessary to make investments.

cost of goods sold An expense reflecting the cost of merchandise or manufactured products sold to customers

cost of goods sold percentage The ratio of cost of goods sold divided by net sales

cost of production report Used in a process costing system; summarizes unit and cost data for each department or process for each period.

cost pool A collection of related costs, such as departmental manufacturing overhead, that is assigned to one or more cost objectives, such as products.

cost prediction The forecasting of future costs.

cost prediction error The difference between a predicted future cost and the actual amount of the cost when, or if, it is incurred.

cost principle An accounting principle stating that asset measures are based on the prices paid to acquire the assets

cost reduction proposal A proposed action or investment intended to reduce the cost of an activity that the organization is committed to keeping.

cost-volume-profit (CVP) analysis A technique used to examine the relationships among total volume of some independent variable, total costs, total revenues, and profits during a time period (typically a month or a year).

cost-volume-profit graph An illustration of the relationships among activity volume, total revenues, total costs, and profits.

coupon bond A bond with coupons for interest payable to bearer attached to the bond for each interest period; whenever interest is due, the bondholder detaches a coupon and deposits it with his or her bank for collection

coupon (contract or stated) rate The interest rate stated in the bond contract; used to compute interest payments during the bond's life

covenants Contractual requirements that the loan recipient maintain minimum levels of capital to safeguard lenders

credit card fee A fee charged retailers for credit card services provided by financial institutions; the fee is usually stated as a percentage of credit card sales

credit (entry) An entry on the right-hand side of an account; used to record decreases in assets and increases in liabilities and stockholders' equity

credit guarantee A guarantee of another company's debt by cosigning a note payable; a guarantor's contingent liability that is usually disclosed in a balance sheet footnote

credit memo A document prepared by a seller to inform the purchaser that the seller has reduced the amount owed by the purchaser due to a return or an allowance

creditors Those to whom a company owes money; those who provide debt financing

credit period The maximum amount of time, usually stated in days, that the purchaser of merchandise has to pay the seller

credit sales A business transaction between companies where no cash immediately changes hands; also called sales on account

credit terms The prescribed payment period for purchases on credit with discount specified for early payment

cumulative (preferred stock) A feature associated with preferred stock whereby any dividends in arrears must be paid before dividends may be paid on common stock

cumulative effect of a change in principle The cumulative effect on net income to the date of a change in accounting principle

currency translation adjustment The unrecognized gain or loss on assets and liabilities denominated in foreign currencies

current assets The most liquid assets, which can be converted into cash within one year or one operating cycle

current liabilities Obligations such as accounts payable, accrued liabilities, unearned revenues, short-term notes payable, and current maturities of long-term debt that are due within one year

current maturities of long-term debt Long-term borrowings that are scheduled to mature in whole or in part during the upcoming year, including accrued interest

current rate method Method of translating foreign currency transactions under which balance sheet amounts are translated using exchange rates in effect at the period-end consolidation date and income statement amounts using the average exchange rate for the period

current ratio Measure of liquidity defined as current assets divided by current liabilities; a ratio greater than 1.0 implies positive net working capital

customer level activity An activity performed to obtain or maintain each customer.

customer profitability analysis A presentation showing the profits of individual or categories of customers net of the cost of serving and supporting those customers.

customer profitability profile A graphical presentation showing the cumulative profits from the most profitable to the least profitable customer

cycle efficiency The ratio of value-added to nonvalue-added manufacturing activities.

cycle time The total time required to complete a process. It is composed of the times needed for setup, processing, movement, waiting, and inspection.

 D

dashboards Software programs that tabulate and display scorecard results using graphics that mimic the instrument displays on an automobile dashboard

days sales in inventory Inventories divided by average cost of goods sold

days sales in receivables A measure of both solvency and performance, the days receivable outstanding tells how long it takes to convert accounts receivable into cash or how well the firm is managing the credit extended to customers. The general equation for days receivable outstanding is: Ending receivables/Average daily sales.

debenture bond A bond that has no specific property pledged as security for the repayment of funds borrowed

debit (entry) An entry on the left-hand side of an account; used to record increases in assets and decreases in liabilities and stockholders' equity

debt-to-equity (DE) A common measure of financial leverage, defined as total liabilities divided by stockholder's equity

debt-to-equity ratio A measure of long-term solvency, the debt-to-equity ratio indicates the balance between the amounts of capital that creditors and owners provide. The general equation for the debt-to-equity ratio is: Total liabilities/Total stockholders' equity.

decentralization The delegation of decision-making authority to successively lower management levels in an organization. The lower in the organization the authority is delegated, the greater the decentralization.

declining-balance method An accelerated depreciation method that allocates depreciation expense to each year by applying a constant percentage to the declining book value of the asset

default The nonpayment of interest and principal or the failure to adhere to various terms and conditions of an investment

deferral An accounting adjustment in which assets and revenues received in advance of a certain accounting period are allocated as expenses and revenues during that period

deferred income taxes The difference between income tax expense as reported in the income statement and income taxes due to taxing authorities; reported in the balance sheet as either an asset or liability

deferred performance liabilities Obligations that will be satisfied, not by paying cash, but instead, by providing products or services to customers

deferred revenue A liability representing revenues received in advance; also called unearned revenue

deferred revenue *see* unearned revenue

deferred tax asset Situation when tax reporting income is less than financial reporting income; the deferred tax asset expires when the temporary difference reverses

deferred tax liability Taxes to be paid in the future when taxable income is higher than financial reporting income; also called deferred taxes

deferred tax valuation allowance Reduction in a reported deferred tax asset to adjust for the amount that is not likely to be realized

defined benefit plan Pension plan in which the company makes periodic payments to an employee after retirement, generally based on years of service and employee's age

defined contribution plan Pension plan in which a company makes periodic contributions to a current employee's account, which the employee may drawn upon following retirement; many plans require an employee matching contribution

definite life A determinable period of time that an intangible asset, such as a patent or franchise right, exists

degree of operating leverage A measure of operating leverage, often computed as the contribution margin divided by income before taxes.

denominator variance see fixed overhead volume variance.

depletion The process of transferring costs from the resource account into inventory as resources are used up

deposits in transit Deposits not yet recorded by the bank

depreciation The decline in value of equipment and assets due to wear, deterioration, and obsolescence; process of allocating costs of equipment, vehicles, and buildings to the periods benefiting from their use

depreciation accounting The process of allocating the cost of equipment, vehicles, and buildings (not land) to expense over the time period benefiting from their use

depreciation and amortization expenses Write-offs of previously recorded assets added to net income as it is converted to net operating cash flow

depreciation base The capitalized cost of an asset less the estimated residual value

depreciation method Means of calculating the reduction in an asset's value over its useful life

depreciation rate Method of depreciation equal to one divided by the item's useful life

depreciation tax shield The reduction in taxes due to the deductibility of depreciation from taxable revenues.

derivatives Financial instruments that are utilized by companies to reduce various kinds of risk

descriptive model A model that merely specifies the relationships between a series of independent and dependent variables.

design for manufacture Explicitly considering the costs of manufacturing and servicing a product while it is being designed.

detection control An internal control a company adopts to discover problems soon after they arise

differential cost analysis An approach to the analysis of relevant costs that focuses on the costs that differ under alternative actions.

diluted earnings per share (EPS) Earnings per share that includes stock options and convertible securities in the calculations

dilutive securities Securities that can be converted into shares of common stock and would therefore reduce (or dilute) the earnings per share upon conversion

direct association Recognizing a cost directly associated with a specific source of revenue at the same time the related revenue is recognized

direct costing *see* variable costing.

direct department cost A cost directly traceable to a department upon its incurrence.

direct labor Wages earned by production employees for the time they spend working on the conversion of raw materials into finished goods.

direct materials The costs of primary raw materials that are converted into finished goods.

direct method (for cost allocation) A method of allocating service department costs to producing departments based only on the amount of services provided to the producing departments; it does not recognize any interdepartmental services.

direct method (for statement of cash flow) Accounting method that presents net cash flow from operating activities by showing the major categories of operating cash receipts and payments

direct segment fixed costs Costs that would not be incurred if the segment being evaluated were discontinued. They are specifically identifiable with a particular segment.

disclosure The act of providing financial and nonfinancial information to external users

discontinued operations Any separately identifiable component of a company that management abandons, sells or intends to sell

discount Situation where a bond's coupon rate is less than market rate

discount bond A bond that is sold for less than its par (face) value

discount on notes payable A contra account that is subtracted from the Notes Payable amount on the balance sheet; as the life of the note elapses, the discount is reduced and charged to interest expense

discount period The maximum amount of time, usually stated in days, that the purchaser of merchandise has to pay the seller if the purchaser wants to claim the cash discount

discount rate The interest rate used in present value calculations

discounted cash flow (DCF) model The value of a security is equal to the present value of the expected free cash flows to the firm, discounted at the weighted average cost of capital (WACC)

discounting The exchanging of notes receivable for cash at a financial institution at an amount that is less than the face value of the notes

discretionary cost center A cost center that does not have clearly defined relationships between effort and accomplishment.

discretionary fixed costs Costs set at a fixed amount each period at the discretion of management.

dividend discount model The value of a security today is equal to the present value of that security's expected dividends, discounted at the weighted average cost of capital

dividend payout ratio Dividend payments divided by net income

dividend preference The order in which shareholders receive dividends; preferred shareholders take precedence over common shareholders

dividends account A temporary equity account used to accumulate owner dividends from the business

dividend yield Annual dividends per share divided by the market price per share

division margin The amount each division contributes toward covering common corporate expenses and generating corporate profits. It is computed by subtracting all direct fixed expenses identifiable with each division from the contribution margin.

double declining balance (DDB) method An accelerated depreciation method that computes the depreciation rate as twice the straight-line rate times the remaining balance of the asset

double entry accounting system The dual effects where, in order to maintain the equality of the accounting equation, each transaction must affect at least two accounts

 E

earned When referring to revenue, the seller's execution of its duties under the terms of the agreement, with the resultant passing of title to the buyer with no right of return or other contingencies

earned capital The cumulative net income (losses) retained by the company; income not paid to shareholders as dividends

earned income Income in which the seller has executed its duties under the terms of the sales agreement and the title has passed to the buyer

earnings before interest (EBI) Measures the income generated by a firm before taking into account any of its financing costs; computed as Net income + [Interest expense × (1 − Statutory tax rate)]

earnings before interest and taxes (EBIT) Measures the income generated by a firm before interest expense and income taxes

earnings management Discretionary choices management makes that mask the underlying economic performance of a company

earnings per share A measure of performance, earnings per share are disclosed on the income statement. The general equation for basic earnings per share is: Net income less preferred stock dividends/ Weighted average number of common shares outstanding for the period.

earnings quality A measure of earnings in terms of sustainability, the ability for income to persist in future periods

earnings smoothing Earnings management with a goal to provide an earnings stream with less variability

economic consequences Issues resulting from accounting changes

economic profit The number of inventory units sold multiplied by the difference between the sales price and the replacement cost of the inventories (approximated by the cost of the most recently purchased inventories)

economic value added (EVA) Net operating profits after tax less a charge for the use of capital equal to beginning capital utilized in the business multiplied by the weighted average cost of capital

EDGAR Database maintained by the SEC where financial statements are available for download

effective cost The cost to a bond's issuing company for offering the bond, generally as cash interest paid plus the discount or premium incurred

effective interest method A method of amortizing bond premium or discount that results in a constant rate of interest each period and varying amounts of premium or discount amortized each period

effective interest rate The rate determined by dividing the total discount amount by the cash proceeds on a note payable when the borrower borrowed at a discount

effective rate The current rate of interest in the market for a bond or other debt instrument; when issued, a bond is priced to yield the market (effective) rate of interest at the date of issuance

effective tax rate The average tax rate applied to pretax earnings; computed by dividing reported income tax expense by reported pretax earnings

efficient markets hypothesis Capital markets are said to be efficient if at any given time, current equity (stock) prices reflect all relevant information that determines those equity prices

electronic data interchange (EDI) The electronic communication of data between organizations.

employee severance costs Accrued (estimated) costs for termination of employees as part of a restructuring program

employee stock options A form of compensation that grants a select group of employees the right to purchase a fixed number of company shares at a fixed price for a predetermined time period

enterprise resource planning (ERP) Enterprise management information systems that provide organizations an integrated set of operating, financial, and management systems.

equity Capital provided by the company's owners, including stock, retained earnings, and additional paid-in capital; the owners' claim in the company

equity carve outs Corporate divestitures that are generally motivated by the belief that consolidated financial statements obscure the performance of individual business units

equity method Accounting method that reports investment on the balance sheet at an amount equal to the percentage of the investee's equity owned by the investor

equity valuation model A means of defining the value of an equity security in terms of the present value of future forecasted amounts

equivalent completed units The number of completed units that is equal, in terms of production effort, to a given number of partially completed units.

ethics The moral quality, fitness, or propriety of a course of action that can injure or benefit people; also, the values, rules, and justifications that governs one's way of life.

executory contract Situation such as a purchase order where a future sacrifice is probable and the amount of the sacrifice can be reasonably estimated, but the transaction that caused the obligation has not yet occurred

expense Outflow or use of assets, including costs of products and services sold, operating costs, and interest on debt, to generate revenue

expense to sales (ETS) A ratio measuring the percentage of each sales dollar that goes to cover a specific expense item; computed by dividing the expense by sales revenue

expensed Situation when a cost is recorded in the income statement and labeled as an expense

external failure costs Quality costs incurred when nonconforming products or services are delivered to customers.

extraordinary items Material gains or losses that are not related to normal business operations; must be both unusual in nature and infrequent in occurrence

 F

face amount The principal amount of a bond, which is repaid at maturity

facility level activity An activity performed to maintain general manufacturing or marketing capabilities.

factoring Selling an account receivable to another company, typically a finance company or a financial institution, for less than its face value

fair value The value of an asset based on current rates in the general public

fair value option Provides companies with the option of using fair value to measure the value of most financial assets and liabilities

feedback value A characteristic of information that enables users to confirm or correct prior expectations

file A collection of related records.

financial accounting The process of recording, summarizing, and analyzing financial transactions designed primarily for decision makers outside of the company

Financial Accounting Standards Board (FASB) Standard-setting organization which publishes accounting standards governing the preparation of financial reports

financial assets Normally consist of excess resources held for future expansion or unexpected needs; they are usually invested in the form of other companies' stock, corporate or government bonds, and real estate

financial leverage The proportionate use of borrowed funds in the capital structure, computed as net financial obligations (NFO) divided by average equity; financial leverage is considered favorable if the return on assets is higher than the fixed rate on borrowed funds and unfavorable if the fixed rate is greater than the return it generates.

financial reporting The process of preparing financial statements (income statement, balance sheet, and statement of cash flows) for a firm in accordance with generally accepted accounting principles

financial reporting objectives A component of the conceptual framework that specifies that financial statements should provide information (1) useful for investment and credit decisions, (2) helpful in assessing an entity's ability to generate future cash flows, and (3) about an entity's resources, claims to those resources, and the effects of events causing changes in these items

financial statement analysis Identifying and examining relationships between numbers within the financial statements and trends in these relationships from one period to the next

financial statement effects template Form that captures each transaction and its financial statement effects on the balance sheet and income statement

financial statement elements A part of the conceptual framework that identifies the significant components—such as assets, liabilities, stockholders' equity, revenues, and expenses—used to put financial statements together

financing activities Methods companies use to fund investment resources

finished goods Inventory account that records completed manufactured items waiting to be sold

finished goods inventory The dollar amount of inventory that has completed the production process and is awaiting sale to customers

first-in, first-out (FIFO) method One of the prescribed methods of inventory costing; FIFO assumes that the first costs incurred for the purchase or production of inventory are the first costs relieved from inventory when goods are sold

fiscal year The annual (one year) accounting period adopted by a company for its financial activities

five forces of competitive intensity Industry competition, bargaining power of buyers, bargaining power of suppliers, threat of substitution, threat of entry

fixed assets An alternate label for long-term assets; may also be called property, plant, and equipment (PPE)

fixed commitments ratio The ratio of operating cash flow to fixed commitments; computed as operating cash flow divided by fixed commitments

fixed costs Expenses that do not change with changes in sales volume (over a reasonable range)

fixed manufacturing overhead All fixed costs associated with converting raw materials into finished goods.

fixed overhead budget variance The difference between budgeted and actual fixed overhead.

fixed overhead volume variance The difference between total budgeted fixed overhead and total standard fixed overhead assigned to production.

fixed selling and administrative costs All fixed costs other than those directly associated with converting raw materials into finished goods.

flexible budgets Budgets that are drawn up for a series of possible production and sales volumes or adjusted to a particular level of production after the fact. These budgets, based on cost-volume or cost-activity relationships, are used to determine what costs should have been for an attained level of activity.

flexible budget variance Computed for each cost as the difference between the actual cost and the flexible budget cost of producing a given quantity of product or service.

flexible manufacturing systems (FMS) An extension of computer-aided manufacturing techniques through a series of manufacturing operations. These operations include the automatic movement of units between operations and the automatic and rapid setup of machines to produce each product.

for-profit organization An organization that has profit as a primary mission.

forecast The projection of financial results over the forecast horizon and terminal periods

forecast error Differences between amounts reported in the financial statements and amounts forecasted in pro forma financial statements

foreign currency transaction The $US equivalent of an asset or liability denominated in a foreign currency

foreign exchange gain or loss The gain (loss) recognized in the income statement relating to the change in the $US equivalent of an asset or liability denominated in a foreign currency

franchise A contractual agreement that gives a company the right to operate a particular business in an area for a particular period of time

free cash flow The net cash flow from operations less capital expenditures and dividends

full absorption cost *see* absorption costing.

full costing *see* absorption costing.

full costs Include all costs, regardless of their behavior patterns (variable or fixed) or activity level.

full disclosure principle An accounting principle stipulating the disclosure of all facts necessary to make financial statements useful to readers

fully diluted earnings per share *see* diluted earnings per share

functional currency The currency representing the primary currency in which a business unit conducts its operations

functional income statement A type of income statement where costs are classified according to function, rather than behavior. It is typically included in external financial reports.

fundamental analysis Method of using a company's financial information to estimate its value, which is used in buy-sell strategies

funded status The difference between a company's pension plan assets and the projected benefit obligation

future benefits Revenues or some other compensation a company expects to receive in a later period

future value The amount that a specific investment is worth at a future date if invested at a given rate of compound interest

future value factor A value that is multiplied by a current amount to obtain its equivalent value at a future date; the value of $1 invested for a number of periods at a specified interest rate

G

gain on bond retirement Situation where the repurchase price of a bond is less than the net bonds payable

general and administrative expense budget Presents the expenses the organization plans to incur in connection with the general administration of the organization. Included are expenses for such things as the accounting department, the computer center, and the president's office.

general journal A flexible journal that allows any type of business transaction to be included

general ledger A grouping of all of an entity's accounts that are used to prepare the basic financial statements

generally accepted accounting principles (GAAP) An overall set of standards and procedures accountants have developed that apply to the preparation of financial statements

goal A definable, measurable objective.

going concern concept An accounting principle that assumes that, in the absence of evidence to the contrary, a business entity will have an indefinite life

goodwill An intangible asset recorded when a company acquires another company, consisting of the value of a company above and beyond the fair value of its specific assets

gross margin The difference between net sales and cost of goods sold; also called gross profit

gross profit The difference between revenues (at selling prices) and cost of goods sold (at purchasing price or manufacturing cost)

gross profit margin (GPM) (percentage) A measure that reflects the net impact of sales on profitability, defined as gross profit divided by net sales

gross profit on sales The difference between net sales and cost of goods sold; also called gross margin

H

held-to-maturity (HTM) securities Debt securities that management holds on to for their full term

high-low method of cost estimation Utilizes data from two time periods, a representative high activity period and a representative low activity period, to estimate fixed and variable costs.

historical cost The original acquisition cost, less the portion that that has expired or been transferred to the income statement

holding company The parent company of a subsidiary

holding gain The increase in replacement cost since the inventories were acquired, which equals the number of units sold multiplied by the difference between the current replacement cost and the original acquisition cost

horizon period The forecast period for which detailed estimates are made, typically 5–10 years

horizontal analysis An examination of data across two or more consecutive time periods, which assists in analyzing company performance and predicting future performance

I

immediate recognition Costs recognized as expenses in a period when they were incurred, even though they cannot be directly linked to specific revenues

impairment Loss of property, plant, and equipment value determined by comparing the sum of expected future cash flows to the asset's net book value

imposed budget *see* top-down budget.

in-process research and development An intangible asset whose cost must be written off immediately upon purchase

income Also called net income, equals revenue minus expense, and is the increase in net assets (equity) resulting from the company's operations

income smoothing The discretionary management practice of choosing the timing of transactions in order to minimize fluctuations and maintain steady improvements in net income

income statement A financial report on operating activities that lists revenues less expenses over a period of time, yielding a company's net income

incremental budgeting An approach to budgeting where costs for a coming period are budgeted as a dollar or percentage change from the amount budgeted for (or spent during) some previous period.

indefinite lives Situation where an intangible asset's expected useful life extends far enough into the future that it is practically impossible to accurately determine

indirect department cost A cost reassigned, or allocated, to a department from another cost objective.

indirect method Accounting method for preparing the statement of cash flows in which the operating section begins with net income and converts it to cash flows from operations

indirect segment costs *see* common segment costs.

inspection time The amount of time it takes units to be inspected.

installment loan Loan that requires a fixed periodic payment for a fixed duration of time

insufficient write-down Impairment of assets to a larger degree than is recognized

intangible assets Assets such as trademarks and patents that supply the owner rights rather than physical objects

integer programming A variation of linear programming that determines the solution in whole numbers.

intercorporate investments Investments in the securities of other companies

interdepartmental services Services provided by one service department to other service departments.

interest cost Interest accrued on outstanding pension liability, which is added to the liability each year

internal auditing A company function that provides independent appraisals of the company's financial statements, its internal controls, and its operations

internal controls Policies and procedures used to protect assets, ensure reliable accounting, promote efficient operations, and urge adherence to company policies

internal failure costs Quality costs incurred when materials, components, products, or services are identified as defective before delivery to customers.

internal rate of return (IRR) Often called the time-adjusted rate of return, the discount rate that equates the present value of a project's cash inflows with the present value of the project's cash outflows.

International Accounting Standards Board (IASB) The governing body established to develop acceptable accounting standards on a worldwide basis

International Financial Reporting Standards (IFRS) Guidelines developed by the IASB with the intention of unifying all public companies under one global set of reporting standards

inventory Goods purchased or produced for sale to customers

inventory carrying costs Costs of holding inventories, including warehousing, logistics, insurance, financing, and the risk of loss due to theft, damage, or technological or fashion change

inventory quality The rate at which inventory is turned over; the faster the turnover, the higher the quality

inventory shrinkage The cost associated with an inventory shortage; the amount by which the perpetual inventory exceeds the physical inventory

inventory turnover (in dollars) Often regarded as a measure of both solvency and performance, inventory turnover tells how long it takes to convert inventory into current monetary assets and how well the firm is managing investments in inventory. The general equation for inventory turnover is: Cost of goods sold/Average inventory cost.

inventory turnover (in units) The annual demand in units divided by the average inventory in units.

inventory turnover (INVT) Measure of inventory management computed as cost of goods sold divided by average inventory

investing activities Methods companies use to acquire and dispose of assets in the course of production and sales

investing creditors Those who primarily finance investing activities

investment center A responsibility center whose manager is responsible for the relationship between its profits and the total assets invested in the center. In general, the management of an investment center is expected to earn a target profit per dollar invested.

investment returns The increase in pension investments resulting from interest, dividends, and capital gains on the investment portfolio

investment tax credit A reduction in income taxes of a percent of the cost of a new asset in the year the new asset is placed in service.

invoice A document that the seller sends to the purchaser to request payment for items that the seller shipped to the purchaser

invoice price The price that a seller charges the purchaser for merchandise

IOU A slang term for a receivable

irrelevant costs Costs that do not differ among competing decision alternatives.

issued stock Shares of stock that have been sold and issued to stockholders; issued stock may be either outstanding or in the treasury

J

job cost sheet A document used to track the status of and accumulate the costs for a specific job in a job cost system.

job order production The manufacturing of products in single units or in batches of identical units.

job production *see* job order production.

joint costs All materials and conversion costs of joint products incurred prior to the split-off point.

joint products Two or more products simultaneously produced by a single process from a common set of inputs.

journal A tabular record in which business activities are analyzed in terms of debits and credits and recorded in chronological order before they are entered in the general ledger; also called book of original entry

journal entries An accounting entry in a company's financial records that accountants use to represent individual transactions

just-in-time (JIT) inventory management A comprehensive inventory management philosophy that stresses policies, procedures, and attitudes by managers and other workers that result in the efficient production of high-quality goods while maintaining the minimum level of inventories.

just-in-time (JIT) inventory philosophy Receive inventory from suppliers into the production process just at the point it is needed

K

Kaizen costing *see* continuous improvement costing.

kanban system *see* materials pull system.

L

labor efficiency variance The difference between the standard cost of actual labor inputs and the flexible budget cost for labor.

labor rate (spending) variance The difference between the actual cost and the standard cost of actual labor inputs.

land improvements Improvements with limited lives made to land sites, such as paved parking lots and driveways

last-in, first-out (LIFO) method One of the prescribed methods of inventory costing; LIFO assumes that the last costs incurred for the purchase or production of inventory are the first costs relieved form inventory when goods are sold

lean accounting A system of product cost assignment where costs are assigned to value streams of multiple products rather than to individual products

leaning on the trade An increase in accounts payable, which results in an increase in net cash flows from operating activities

lean production A philosophy of inventory production and management that emphasizes increased coordination throughout the value chain, reduced inventory, reduced production times, increased product quality, and increased employee involvement and empowerment

lease A contract between a lessor (owner) and lessee (tenant) for the rental of property

lease asset The value of a leased item

leasehold improvements Expenditures made by a lessee to alter or improve leased property

leasehold The rights transferred from the lessor to the lessee by a lease

lease liability The payments required to lease an item

least-squares regression analysis Uses a mathematical technique to fit a cost estimating equation to the observed data in a manner that minimizes the sum of the vertical squared estimating errors between the estimated and actual costs at each observation.

lessee A party to a lease who wishes to use the asset

lessor The owner of property who transfers the right to use the property to another party by a lease

leveraging The use of borrowed funds in the capital structure of a firm; the expectation is that the funds will earn a return higher than the rate of interest on the borrowed funds

liability A probable future economic sacrifice resulting from a past or current event

licenses *see* operating rights

life-cycle budgeting An approach to budgeting when the entire life of the project represents a more useful planning horizon than an artificial period of one year.

life-cycle costs From the seller's perspective, all costs associated with a product or service ranging from those incurred with initial conception through design, pre-production, production, and after-production support. From the buyer's perspective, all costs associated with a purchased product or service, including initial acquisition costs and subsequent costs of operation, maintenance, repair, and disposal.

LIFO conformity rule IRS requirement to cost inventories using LIFO for tax purposes if they are costed using LIFO for financial reporting purposes

LIFO layer New layer added to inventory at an updated price each time inventory is purchased in companies using LIFO inventory costing; the most recent costs are transferred to cost of goods sold

LIFO liquidation Situation when, in companies using LIFO inventory costing, quantity of inventory sold exceeds that purchased, in which case the costs of older inventory is transferred to cost of good sold

LIFO reserve The difference between the cost of inventories using FIFO and the cost using LIFO

linear algebra method (reciprocal) method A method of allocating service department costs using a series of linear algebraic equations, which are solved simultaneously, to allocate service department costs both interdepartmentally among service departments and to the producing departments.

linear programming An optimizing model used to assist managers in making decisions under constrained conditions when linear relationships exist between all variables.

liquidation preference In the event of a company's failure, preferred shareholders are reimbursed in full before common shareholders are paid

liquidation value per share The amount that would be received by a holder of a share of stock if the corporation liquidated

liquidity The ease of converting noncash assets into cash

list price The suggested price or reference price of merchandise in a catalog or price list

long-term debt Amounts borrowed from creditors that are scheduled to be repaid more than one year into the future

long-term debt-to-equity A common measure of leverage that focuses on long-term financing, defined as long-term debt divided by stockholders' equity

long-term investments Investments that the company does not intend to sell in the near future

long-term liabilities Debt obligations not due to be settled within the normal operating cycle or one year, whichever is longer

long-term operating asset turnover The rate that reflects capital intensity relative to sales, defined as net sales divided by average long-term operating assets

loss on bond retirement Situation if a bond's issuer pays more to retire the bonds than the amount carried on its balance sheet

lower of cost or market (LCM) GAAP requirement to write down the carrying amount of inventories on the balance sheet if the reported cost (using FIFO, for example) exceeds market value (determined by current replacement cost)

lower of cost or market (LCM) Process of reporting inventories at the lower of its cost or its current market value

M

maker Owner of a checking account

managed fixed costs *see* discretionary fixed costs.

management accounting A discipline concerned with financial and related information used by managers and other persons inside specific organizations to make strategic, organizational, and operational decisions.

management by exception An approach to performance assessment whereby management directs attention only to those activities not proceeding according to plan.

management discussion and analysis (MD&A) The section of the 10-K report in which a company provides a detailed discussion of its business activities

managerial accounting The process of recording, summarizing, and analyzing financial transactions designed primarily for decision makers within the company

manufacturers Companies that convert raw materials and components into finished products through the application of skilled labor and machine operations

manufacturing cost budget A budget detailing the direct materials, direct labor, and manufacturing overhead costs that should be incurred by manufacturing operations to produce the number of units called for in the production budget.

manufacturing costs Expenses associated with product production, including materials, labor, and overhead

manufacturing margin The result when direct manufacturing costs (variable costs) are deducted from product sales.

manufacturing organizations Organizations that process raw materials into finished products for sale to others.

manufacturing overhead All manufacturing costs other than direct materials and direct labor.

margin of safety The amount by which actual or planned sales exceed the break-even point.

marginal cost The varying increment in total cost required to produce and sell an additional unit of product.

marginal revenue The varying increment in total revenue derived from the sale of an additional unit.

marginal tax rate The tax rate that applies to the marginal dollar of income; the tax rate generally applied to nonoperating revenues and expenses

mark-to-market Method of valuing assets that results in an adjustment of an asset's carrying amount to its fair value

market method accounting Securities are reported at current market values (marked-to-market) on the statement date

market (yield) rate This is the interest rate that investors expect to earn on the investment in this debt security; this rate is used to price the bond issue

market segment level activity Performed to obtain or maintain operations in a market segment.

market value per share The current price at which shares of stock may be bought or sold

market value The published price (as listed on a stock exchange) multiplied by the number of shares owned

marketable securities Short-term investments that can be quickly sold to raise cash

markup The difference between an item's selling price and the cost incurred to produce it

master budget The grouping together of all budgets and supporting schedules. This budget coordinates all the financial and operational activities and places them into an organization wide set of budgets for a given time period.

matching Recognizing expenses in the same period that the associated revenue is recognized

matching principle An accounting guideline that states that income is determined by relating expenses, to the extent feasible, with revenues that have been recorded

materiality An accounting guideline that states that transactions so insignificant that they would not affect a user's actions or perception of the company may be recorded in the most expedient manner

materials inventory The physical component of inventory; the other components of manufactured inventory are labor costs and overhead costs

materials price variance The difference between the actual materials cost and the standard cost of actual materials inputs.

materials pull system An inventory production flow system in which employees at each station work to replenish the inventory used by employees at subsequent stations. The building of excess inventories is strictly prohibited. When the number of units in inventory reaches a specified limit, work at the station stops until workers at a subsequent station pull a unit from the in-process storage area.

materials push system An inventory production flow system in which employees work to reduce the pile of inventory building up at their work stations. Workers at each station remove materials from an in-process storage area, complete their operation, and place the output in another in-process storage area. Hence, they push the work to the next work station.

materials quantity variance The difference between the standard cost of actual materials inputs and the flexible budget cost for materials.

materials requisition form A document used to record the type and quantity of each raw material issued to the factory.

maturity date The date on which a note or bond matures

measuring unit concept An accounting guideline noting that the accounting unit of measure is the basic unit of money

merchandise inventory A stock of products that a company buys from another company and makes available for sale to its customers

merchandising firm A company that buys finished products, stores the products for varying periods of time, and then resells the products

merchandising organizations Organizations that buy and sell goods without performing manufacturing operations.

method of comparables model Equity valuation or stock values are predicted using price multiples, which are defined as stock price divided by some key financial statement number such as net income, net sales, book value of equity, total assets, or cash flow; companies are then compared with their competitors

minimum level budgeting An approach to budgeting that establishes a base amount for all budget items and requires explanation or justification for any budgeted amount above the minimum (base).

minority interest An ownership in a company that is less than a majority or controlling interest

minority interest The equity claim of a shareholder owning less than a majority or controlling interest in the company

mission The basic purpose toward which an organization's activities are directed.

mixed costs Costs that contain a fixed and a variable cost element.

model A simplified representation of some real-world phenomenon.

modified accelerated cost recovery system (MACRS) *see* accelerated cost recovery system

movement time The time units spend moving between work or inspection stations.

mutually exclusive investments Two or more capital expenditure proposals where the acceptance of one investment automatically causes the rejection of the other(s).

N

natural resources Assets occurring in a natural state, such as timber, petroleum, natural gas, coal, and other mineral deposits

net-of-discount method Inventory capitalized at the net cost, assuming that a cash discount will be taken by the buyer

net asset based valuation model Equity is valued as reported assets less reported liabilities

net assets Assets minus liabilities

net book value (NBV) The cost of the asset less accumulated depreciation; also called carrying value

net financial expense Net operating profit after tax less net income

net financial obligations (NFO) The difference between financial (nonoperating) obligations and financial (nonoperating) assets; positive if obligations exceed assets

net financial rate Net financial expense divided by average net financial obligations

net income The difference between revenues and expenses when revenues exceed expenses

net interest rate (NIR) The average interest rate after taxes on total liabilities; calculated as [Interest expense $\times$ (1 $-$ Statutory tax rate)]/Average total liabilities

net loss The difference between revenues and expenses when expenses exceed revenues

net operating assets (NOA) Current and long-term operating assets less current and long-term operating liabilities

net operating assets turnover (NOAT) A measure of turnover defined as sales divided by average net operating assets

net operating profit after tax (NOPAT) Sales less operating expenses (including taxes)

net operating profit margin (NOPM) The amount of operating profit produced as a percentage of each sales dollar; excludes all nonoperating revenues and expenses; calculated as Net operating profit after tax (NOPAT) divided by Sales revenue

net operating working capital (NOWC) Operating current assets less operating current liabilities

net operating working capital turnover (NOWCT) Management's effectiveness in using operating working capital, defined as net sales divided by average net operating working capital

net present value The present value of a project's net cash inflows from operations and disinvestment less the amount of the initial investment.

net profit margin The income to sales ratio, which reflects the profitability of sales; also called simply profit margin

net realizable value The value of a company's receivables, less an allowance for uncollectible accounts

net sales The total revenue generated by a company through merchandise sales less the revenue given up through sales returns and allowances and sales discounts

net sales volume variance Indicates the impact of a change in sales volume on the contribution margin, given the budgeted selling price and the standard variable costs. It is computed as the difference between the actual and the budgeted sales volumes times the budgeted unit contribution margin.

net working capital The difference between current assets and current liabilities; also called working capital

neutrality A characteristic of information that is free of any bias intended to attain a predetermined result or to induce a particular mode of behavior

no-par stock Stock that does not have a par value

nominal cost Cash interest paid on a debt

nominal rate The rate of interest stated on a bond certificate or other debt instrument

non-operating revenues and expenses Costs related to the company's financing and investing activities, including interest revenue and interest expense

non-value-added activity An activity that does not add value to a product or service from the viewpoint of the customer.

noncash investing and financing activities Significant financial events that do not affect current cash flows, such as issuance of stocks and bonds in exchange for property, plant, and equipment

noncurrent assets Assets not used up or converted to cash in one year; include Long-term financial investments, Property, plant, and equipment (PPE), and Intangible and other assets

noncurrent liabilities Obligations such as long-term debt and other long-term liabilities that are to be paid after one year

nonoperating expenses Expenses that relate to the company's financing activities and include interest income and interest expense, gains and losses on sales of securities, and income or loss on discontinued operations

non pro rata distribution A case where stockholders can accept or reject the distribution of shares

nonrecurring Revenues and expenses that are unlikely to arise in the future and are largely irrelevant to predictions of future performance

NOPAT Net operating profit after tax

normal operating cycle For a particular business, the average period of time between the use of cash in its typical operating activity and the subsequent collection of cash from customers

not-for-profit organization An organization that does not have profit as a primary goal.

not-sufficient-funds check A check from an individual or company that had an insufficient cash balance in the bank when the holder of the check presented it to the bank for payment

notes payable Account assigned to a company's financial borrowings

notes receivable Receivables that are based on a formal written promise to pay a specified amount and a predetermined date

notes to financial statements Footnotes in which companies discuss their accounting policies and estimates used in preparing the statements

O

objective function In linear programming models, the goal to be minimized or maximized.

objectivity principle An accounting principle requiring that, whenever possible, accounting entries are based on objectively determined evidence

off-balance-sheet financing A company's financial obligations that are not reported as liabilities in the balance sheet

on-balance-sheet financing The reporting of financing effects, namely current and noncurrent liabilities, on the balance sheet

operating activities Methods companies use to produce, promote, and sell its products and services

operating asset turnover The ratio obtained by dividing sales by average net operating assets

operating budget Detailed plans to guide operations throughout the budget period.

operating cash flow to capital expenditures ratio A measure that helps assess a firm's ability to replace its property, plant, and equipment, or expand as needed; calculated as operating cash flows from operating activities divided by annual capital expenditures

operating cash flow to current liabilities ratio A measure of the ability to liquidate current liabilities, calculated as net cash flow from operating activities divided by average current liabilities

operating cash flow to liabilities (OCFL) A method to compare operating flows to liabilities, defined as net cash flow from operations divided by total liabilities

operating creditors Those who primarily finance operating activities

operating cycle The time between paying cash for goods or employee services and receiving cash from customers

operating expense The usual and customary costs a company incurs to support its main business activities, including cost of goods sold, selling expenses, depreciation expenses, amortization expenses, and research and development expenses

operating expense margin (OEM) The ratio obtained by dividing any operating expense item or category by sales

operating lease A lease by which the lessor retains the usual risks and rewards of owning the property

operating lease method Method of reporting leases where neither the lease asset nor the lease liability is on the balance sheet

operating leverage A measure of the extent that an organization's costs are fixed.

operating profit margin The ratio obtained by dividing NOPAT by sales

operating rights A contractual agreement similar to franchise rights, but typically granted by government agencies

operational audit An evaluation of activities, systems, and internal controls within a company to determine their efficiency, effectiveness, and economy

operations list A document that specifies the manufacturing operations and related times required to produce one unit or batch of product.

opportunity cost The net cash inflow that could be obtained if the resources committed to one action were used in the most desirable other alternative.

optimal solution In linear programming models, the feasible solution than maximizes or minimizes the value of the objective function, depending on the decision maker's goal.

optimizing model A model that suggests a specific choice between decision alternatives.

options *see* stock options

order-filling costs Costs incurred to place finished goods in the hands of purchasers (for example, storing, packaging, and transportation).

order-getting costs Costs incurred to obtain customers' orders (for example, advertising, salespersons' salaries and commissions, travel, telephone, and entertainment).

order level activity An activity performed for each sales order.

ordinary annuity A series of fixed payments made at the end of each period over a specified time period

organization chart An illustration of the formal relationships existing between the elements of an organization.

organization costs Expenditures incurred in launching a business (usually a corporation), including attorney's fees and various fees paid to the state

organization structure The arrangement of lines of responsibility within the organization.

organizational-based cost systems Used for financial reporting, these systems focus on organizational units such as a company, plant, or department rather than on processes and activities.

organizational cost drivers Choices concerning the organization of activities and the involvement of persons inside and outside the organization in decision making.

organizing The process of making the organization into a well-ordered whole.

other long-term liabilities Various obligations, such as pension liabilities and long-term tax liabilities, that will be satisfied at least one year in the future

other post-employment benefits (OPEB) Benefits, other than pension benefits, such as health care and insurance benefits, provided by a company to retired employees

other postretirement benefits Items such as health care and insurance benefits offered to retired employees

outcomes assessment *see* performance measurement.

outlay costs Costs that require future expenditures of cash or other resources.

output/input budgeting An approach to budgeting where physical inputs and costs are budgeted as a function of planned unit level activities. The budgeted inputs are a function of the planned outputs.

outsourcing The external acquisition of services or components.

outstanding checks Checks not yet recorded by the bank

outstanding stock Shares of stock that are currently owned by stockholders (excludes treasury stock)

overfunded Situation where pension plan assets exceed pension liabilities

owners' equity The interest of owners in the assets of an entity; equal to the difference between the entity's assets and liabilities; also called stockholders' equity

P

packing list A document that lists the items of merchandise contained in a carton and the quantity of each item; the packing list is usually attached to the outside of the carton

paid-in capital The amount of capital contributed to a corporation by various transactions; the primary source of paid-in capital is from the issuance of shares of stock

par (bonds) Face value of the bond

parent company A company owning one or more subsidiary companies

parsimonious method to multiyear forecasting Forecasting multiple years using only sales growth, net operating profit margin (NOPM), and the turnover of net operating assets (NOAT)

participation budget *see* bottom-up budget.

participation feature Contract provision that allows preferred shareholders to share ratably with common shareholders in dividends

partnership A form of business entity characterized by two or more owners who are also usually involved in managing the business

par value Face value of a bond; in stocks, an arbitrary amount set by company organizers at the time of formation

passive influence Indicating lack of control of, or active participation in, the affairs of an investee company.

password A string of characters that a computer user enters into a computer terminal to prove to the computer that the person using the computer is truly the person named in the user identification code

patent An exclusive right to produce a product or use a technology

payback period The time required to recover the initial investment in a project from operations.

payee The person named on a check who will receive compensation

payer The bank that will compensate the recipient of a check

payment approval form A document that authorizes the payment of an invoice

pension plan A plan to pay benefits to employees after they retire from the company; the plan may be a defined contribution plan or a defined benefit plan

percentage-of-completion method Revenue recognition method which recognizes revenue by determining the costs incurred under the contract relative to its total expected costs

percentage of net sales method A procedure that determines the uncollectible accounts expense for the year by multiplying net credit sales by the estimated uncollectible percentage

percentage of sales A means to estimate uncollectible accounts that computes bad debts expense as a percentage of total sales

percent change Financial statement adjustment computed by dollar change (analysis period amount less base period amount) divided by base period amount, with the result multiplied by 100

performance measurement The determination of the extent to which actual outcomes correspond to planned outcomes.

period costs Expired costs not related to manufacturing inventory; they are recognized as expenses when incurred.

periodic interest payment Interest payments made in the form of equal cash flows at periodic intervals

period statement A financial statement accumulating information for a specific period of time; examples are the income statement, the statement of stockholders' equity, and the statement of cash flows

permanent account An account used to prepare the balance sheet; that is, asset, liability, and equity capital (capital stock and retained earnings) accounts; any balance in a permanent account at the end of an accounting period is carried forward to the next period

permanent difference A difference in amount between two financial statements that does not reverse in time

persistent An amount that is expected to be maintained in future periods; see also recurring

physical inventory A year-end procedure that involves counting the quantity of each inventory item, determining the unit cost of each item, multiplying the unit cost times quantity, and summing the costs of all the items to determine the total inventory at cost

physical model A scaled-down version or replica of physical reality.

plan assets The assets of a pension plan that involve investments in stocks and bonds

planning The process of selecting goals and strategies to achieve those goals.

planning activities The process of identifying a company's goals, and the strategies adopted to reach those goals

plant assets Land, buildings, equipment, vehicles, furniture, and fixtures that a firm uses in its operations; sometimes referred to by the acronym PPE

pooling of interests method A method of accounting for business combinations under which the acquired company is recorded on the acquirer's balance sheet at its book value, rather than market value; this method is no longer acceptable under GAAP for acquisitions occurring after 2001

position statement A financial statement, such as the balance sheet, that presents information as of a particular date

post-closing trial balance Accounting balance prepared after closing entries are recorded and posted to verify the equality between debits and credits in the general ledger after the adjusting and closing process

postdated check A check from another person or company with a date that is later than the current date; a postdated check does not become cash until the date of the check

posting The transfer of debit and credit entries from the journal to their related general ledger accounts

practical capacity The maximum possible activity, allowing for normal repairs and maintenance.

predetermined manufacturing overhead rate An overhead rate established at the start of each year by dividing the predicted overhead costs for the year by the predicted volume of activity in the overhead base for the year.

predictive value A characteristic of information referring to its ability to increase the accuracy of a forecast

preemptive right The right of a stockholder to maintain his or her proportionate interest in a corporation by having the right to purchase an appropriate share of any new stock issue

preferred stock Stock that possesses priority over common stock, such as first right to dividends or liquidation payout

premium When a bond's coupon rate is greater than the market rate

premium bond A bond that is sold for more than its par (face) value

prepaid expenses Costs paid in advance for rent, insurance, or other services

present value The amount of money a stock or bond is worth at the current time

present value factor A value that is multiplied by a future amount to obtain its equivalent value at the current date; the value of $1 received in the future discounted for a number of periods at a specified discount rate

present value index The present value of the project's subsequent cash flows divided by the initial investment.

prevention control An internal control companies adopt to deter problems before they arise

prevention costs Quality costs incurred to prevent nonconforming products from being produced or nonconforming services from being performed.

price discrimination Illegally charging different purchasers different prices.

price earnings ratio A measure of performance, price earnings ratio compares the current market price with earnings per share of stock and arrives at a multiple of earnings represented by the selling price. Calculated as: Current market price per common share divided by Earnings per share

price fixing The organized setting of prices by competitors.

process A collection of related activities intended to achieve a common purpose.

process manufacturing A manufacturing environment where production is on a continuous basis.

process map (or process flowchart) A schematic overview of all the activities required to complete a process. Each major activity is represented by a rectangle on the map.

process reengineering The fundamental redesign of a process to serve internal or external customers.

processing time The time spent working on units.

product costs All costs incurred in the manufacturing of products; they are carried in the accounts as an asset (inventory) until the product is sold, at which time they are recognized as an expense (cost of goods sold).

production order A document that contains a job's unique identification number and specifies details for the job such as the quantity to be produced, the total raw materials requirements, the manufacturing operations and other activities to be performed, and perhaps even the time when each manufacturing operation should be performed.

product level activity An activity performed to support the production of each different type of product.

product margin Computed as product sales less direct product costs.

productivity The relationship between outputs and inputs.

profit center A responsibility center whose manager is responsible for revenues, costs, and resulting profits. It may be an entire organization, but it is more frequently a segment of an organization such as a product line, marketing territory, or store.

profit margin (PM) A ratio measuring profit, before interest expense, that is generated from each dollar of sales revenue; calculated as Earnings before interest (EBI) divided by Sales revenue

profit-volume graph Illustrates the relationship between volume and profits; it does not show revenues and costs.

profitability The ability of a company to generate net income

profitability analysis An examination of the relationships between revenues, costs, and profits.

pro forma financial statements Hypothetical statements prepared to reflect specific assumptions about a company and its transactions; often referring to forecasted financial statements

pro forma income GAAP income from continuing operations (excluding discontinued operations and extraordinary items), less transitory items

pro rata distribution Shares distributed to stockholders on a pro rata basis

project-level activity An activity performed to support the completion of each project.

projected benefit obligation (PBO) Pension liabilities that represent future obligations to current and former employees

promissory note A written promise to pay a certain sum of money on demand or at a determinable future time

property, plant, and equipment (PPE) Tangible assets recorded on a balance sheet, including land, factory buildings, warehouses, office buildings, office equipment, and other items used in the operation of a business

provision for income tax Income tax expense

Public Company Accounting Oversight Board (PCAOB) Board established by the Sarbanes-Oxley Act to approve auditing standards and monitor the quality of financial statements and audits

purchase method The prescribed method of accounting for business combinations; under the purchase method, assets and liabilities of the acquired company are recorded at fair value, together with identifiable intangible assets; the balance is ascribed to goodwill

purchase order A document that formally requests a supplier to sell and deliver specific quantities of particular items of merchandise at specified prices

purchase requisition An internal document that requests that the purchasing department order particular items of merchandise

purchases budget Indicates the merchandise or materials that must be acquired to meet current needs and ending inventory requirements.

Q

qualitative characteristics of accounting information The characteristics of accounting information that contribute to decision usefulness; the primary qualities are relevance and reliability

quality circles Groups of employees involved in the production of products who have the authority, within certain parameters, to address and resolve quality problems as they occur, without seeking management approval.

quality Conformance to customer expectations.

quality costs Costs incurred because poor quality of conformance does (or may) exist.

quality of conformance The degree of conformance between a product and its design specifications.

quality of design The degree of conformance between customer expectations for a product or service and the design specifications of the product or service.

quality of earnings The extent to which reported income reflects the underlying economic performance of a company

quantitative model A set of mathematical relationships.

quarterly data Selected quarterly financial information that is reported in annual reports to stockholders

quick ratio (QR) A ratio that reflects a company's ability to meet its current liabilities without liquidating inventories

R

raw materials and supplies Inventory account that records items used in production processes

raw materials inventories The physical ingredients and components that will be converted by machines and/or human labor into a finished product.

realized (or realizable) When referring to revenue, the receipt of an asset or satisfaction of a liability as a result of a transaction or event

realized or realizable income Income in which the company's net assets increase

receivables quality The likelihood of collecting on a receivables account, which a company can change by extending credit terms, taking on longer-paying customers, and increasing the allowance provision

recognition criteria The criteria that must be met before a financial statement element may be recorded in the accounts; essentially, the item must meet the definition of an element and must be measurable

reconciled cash balance A company's cash balance after accounting for deposits in transit and outstanding checks

record A related set of alphabetic and/or numeric data items.

recurring An amount that is expected to be reported again in future periods; *see* also persistent

redeem Company repurchasing their bonds prior to maturity

registered bond A bond for which the issuer (or the trustee) maintains a record of owners and, at the appropriate times, mails out interest payments

relational (cause-and-effect) cost center A cost center that has clearly defined relationships between effort and accomplishment (cause and effect).

relevance The usefulness of information to those who use financial statements in decision making

relevant costs Future costs that differ between competing decision alternatives.

relevant range The range of activity within which a linear cost function is valid.

reliability The ability to objectively determine and accurately measure a value, such as historical cost

remeasurement The computation of gain or loss in the translation of subsidiaries denominated in a foreign currency into $US when the temporal method is used

representational faithfulness A characteristic of accounting information referring to the degree with which it reflects the underlying economic events it purports to measure

residual (or salvage) value The expected realizable value of an asset at the end of its useful life

residual income for investment center Excess of investment center income over the minimum rate of return set by top management. The minimum dollar return is computed as a percentage of the investment center's asset base.

residual net operating income (ROPI) model An equity valuation approach that equates the firm's value to the sum of its net operating assets (NOA) and the present value of its residual operating income (ROPI)

residual operating income Net operating profits after tax (NOPAT) less the product of net operating assets (NOA) at the beginning of the period multiplied by the weighted average cost of capital (WACC)

responsibility accounting The structuring of performance reports addressed to individual (or group) members of an organization in a manner that emphasizes the factors they are able to control. The focus is on specific units within the organization that are responsible for the accomplishment of specific activities or objectives.

restructuring costs Expenses typically associated with activities such as consolidating production facilities, reorganizing sales operations, outsourcing activities, or discontinuing product lines

retailers Companies that buy products from wholesale distributors and sell the products to individual customers, the general public

retained earnings Earned capital, the cumulative net income and loss, of the company (from its inception) that has not been paid to shareholders as dividends

retained earnings reconciliation The reconciliation of retained earnings from the beginning to the end of the year; the change in retained earnings includes, at a minimum, the net income (loss) for the period and dividends paid, if any, but may include other components as well; also called statement of retained earnings

return The amount of money earned on an investment, often expressed as investment income divided by the amount invested; also called yield

return on assets (ROA) A computation of net income divided by average total assets; also called return on invested capital

return on common stockholders' equity A financial ratio computed as net income less preferred stock dividends divided by average common stockholders' equity; sometimes referred to by the acronym ROCE

return on equity (ROE) The ultimate measure of performance from the shareholders' perspective, computed as net income divided by average equity

return on financial leverage (ROFL) A measure of the effect that financial leverage has on Return on equity (ROE); calculated as Return on equity (ROE) minus Return on assets (ROA)

return on investment The ratio obtained by dividing income by average investment; sometimes referred to by the acronym ROI

return on investment for investment center A measure of the earnings per dollar of investment. The return on investment of an investment center is computed by dividing the income of the center by its asset base (usually average total assets). It can also be computed as investment turnover times the return-on-sales ratio.

return on net operating assets (RNOA) A measure of operating returns; calculated as Net operating profit after taxes (NOPAT) divided by Average net operating assets (NOA)

return on sales An overall test of operating efficiency defined as net income divided by net sales revenue; Increase in net assets (assets less liabilities) as a result of business activities

revenue The increase in equity resulting from the sale of goods and services to customers

revenue center A responsibility center whose manager is responsible for the generation of sales revenues.

revenue recognition The timing and amount of revenue reported by a company

revenue recognition criteria Requirements that must be met for income to be recognized on the income statement; according to GAAP, revenue must be realized/realizable and earned

revenue recognition principle An accounting principle requiring that revenue be recognized when earned and realized (or realizable)

revenue variance The difference between the budgeted sales volume at the budgeted selling price and the actual sales volume at the actual selling price.

right of return The allowance for a customer to return a product within a specified period of time

risk-free rate The market rate of interest defined as the yield on U.S. Government borrowings, computed as yield rate less spread

risk The uncertainty of expected return, which is an intrinsic part of each investment

Robinson-Patman Act Prohibits price discrimination when purchasers compete with one another in the sale of their products or services to third parties.

rolling budget *see* continuous budgeting.

S

sale on account A sale of merchandise made on a credit basis

sales budget A forecast of sales revenue for a future period. It may also contain a forecast of sales collections.

sales mix The relative portion of unit or dollar sales derived from each product or service.

sales price variance The impact on revenues of a change in selling price, given the actual sales volume. It is computed as the change in selling price times the actual sales volume.

sales volume variance Indicates the impact on revenues of change in sales volume, assuming there was no change in selling price. It is computed as the difference between the actual and the budgeted sales volumes times the budgeted selling price.

salvage value The expected net recovery when a plant asset is sold or removed from service; also called residual value

Sarbanes-Oxley Act Act passed in 2002 which requires a company's CEO and CFO to personally sign a statement attesting to the accuracy and completeness of financial statements

scatter diagram A graph of past activity and cost data, with individual observations represented by dots.

secured bond A bond that pledges specific property as security for meeting the terms of the bond agreement

Securities and Exchange Commision (SEC) Commision created by the 1934 Securities Act to regulate the issuance and trading of securities

security valuation A determination of the value of equity securities

segment income All revenues of a segment minus all costs directly or indirectly charged to it.

segment margin The amount that a segment contributes toward the common (indirect) costs of the organization and toward profits. It is computed as segment sales less direct segment costs.

segment reports Income statements that show operating results for portions or segments of a business. Segment reporting is used primarily for internal purposes, although generally accepted accounting principles also require disclosure of segment information for some public corporations.

segments Subdivisions of a firm for which supplemental financial information is disclosed

sell-off The outright sale of a business unit

selling expense budget Presents the expenses the organization plans to incur in connection with sales and distribution.

semi-variable costs *see* mixed costs.

sensitivity analysis The process of examining the effect of alternative assumptions on the pro forma statements; helps to identify these effects before a decision is made so that costly mistakes can be avoided

serial bond A bond issue that staggers the bond maturity dates over a series of years

service cost The additional pension benefits earned by employees each year

service cost (pensions) The increase in the pension obligation due to employees working another year for the employer

service costing The process of assigning costs to services performed.

service department A department that provides support services to production and/or other support departments.

service organizations Nonmanufacturing organizations that perform work for others, including banks, hospitals, and real estate agencies.

setup time The time required to prepare equipment to produce a specific product.

shareholders' equity *see* equity

shares authorized The number of shares that a corporation can issue without amending its corporate charter

shares issued The actual number of shares that have been sold to stockholders by a corporation

shares outstanding The number of issued shares less the number of shares repurchased as treasury stock

Sherman Antitrust Act Prohibits price fixing.

short-term interest-bearing debt Short-term bank borrowings and notes expected to mature in whole or in part during the upcoming year

short-term notes payable Short-term debt payable to banks or other creditors

short term borrowings Debt payable to banks or other creditors that is due within one year or within one operating cycle

significant influence The ability of an investor to affect an investee's financing or operating policies

simple capital structure Stockholders' equity with no dilutive securities outstanding

simplex method A mathematical approach to solving linear programming models containing three or more variables.

sinking fund provision A bond feature that requires the borrower to retire a portion of the bonds each year or, in some cases, to make payments each year to a trustee who is responsible for managing the resources needed to retire the bonds at maturity

sole proprietorship A form of business characterized by a single owner who typically manages the daily operations

solvency Refers to the firm's ability to pay its debts as they become due.

solvency analysis A review of a company's ability to meet its financial obligations, which is aided by financial leverage ratios

source document Any written document or computer record evidencing an accounting transaction, such as a bank check or deposit slip, sales invoice, or cash register tape

special purpose entity *see* variable interest entity

spin-off A form of equity carve out in which a company distributes subsidiary shares it owns as dividends to its shareholders, making shareholders owners of the subsidiary

split-off A form of equity carve out in which divestiture is accomplished by the parent company's exchange of stock in the subsidiary in return for shares in the parent owned by its shareholders

split-off point The point in the process where joint products become separately identifiable.

spread The difference between the net financial return (NFR) and the return on net operating activities (RNOA); also called risk premium

standard cost A budget that indicates what it should cost to provide an activity or produce one batch or unit of product under efficient operating conditions.

standard cost variance analysis A system for examining the flexible budget variance, which is the difference between the actual cost and flexible budget cost of producing a given quantity of product or service.

stated value A nominal amount that may be assigned to each share of no-par stock and accounted for much as if it were a par value

statement of cash flows A financial report that identifies net cash flows into and out of a company from operating, investing, and financing activities over a period of time

statement of cost of goods manufactured A report that summarizes the cost of goods completed and transferred into finished goods inventory during the period.

statement of financial position A financial statement showing a firm's assets, liabilities, and stockholders' equity at a specific date; also called a balance sheet

statement of owner's equity A financial statement presenting information on the events causing a change in stockholders' equity during a period; the statement presents the beginning balance, additions to, deductions from, and the ending balance of stockholders' equity for the period

statement of responsibility Form included with each financial statement of a publicly traded company assuring management is responsible for the statements, they have been prepared using GAAP, and they are audited by an outside organization

statement of stockholders' equity A financial statement that reports on changes in key equity accounts over a period of time; also called a statement of equity

static budget A budget based on a prior prediction of expected sales and production.

step costs Costs that are constant within a narrow range of activity but shift to a higher level with an increased range of activity. Total step costs increase in a step-like fashion as activity increases.

step method A method of allocating service department costs that gives partial recognition to interdepartmental services by using a methodology that allocates service department costs sequentially to both the remaining service departments and the producing departments.

stock dividends The payment of dividends in shares of stock

stockholders Owners of a corporation; holders of shares of stock in a corporation

stockholders' equity *see* equity

stock option A stock right giving the holder the right to acquire a share of stock at a preset price within a specified period of time; used to compensate officers and other employees

stock rights A stockholder's option to acquire a specified number of shares of capital stock under prescribed conditions and within a stated period

stock split A distribution (or increase in the number) of shares of common stock accompanied by a proportionate decrease in the par value

stock warrant A certificate that provides the holder with stock rights

storyboard A process map developed by employees who perform the component activities within a process.

straight-line depreciation Determination of annual depreciation expense by dividing the asset's cost by its estimated useful life

strategic business segment A segment that has its own mission and set of goals to be achieved. The mission of the segment influences the decisions that its top managers make in both short-run and long-run situations.

strategic cost management Making decisions concerning specific cost drivers within the context of an organization's business strategy, its internal value chain, and its place in a larger value chain stretching from the development and use of resources to the final consumers.

strategic plan A guideline or framework for making specific medium-range or short-run decisions.

strategic position How an organization wants to place itself in comparison to the competition.

strategic position analysis An organization's basic way of competing to sell products or services.

strategy A course of action that will assist in achieving one or more goals.

structural cost drivers Fundamental choices about the size and scope of operations and technologies employed in delivering products or services to customers. These choices affect the types of activities and the costs of activities performed to satisfy customer needs.

suboptimization When managers or operating units, acting in their own best interests, make decisions that are not in the best interest of the organization as a whole.

subsequent events Events occurring shortly after a fiscal year-end that will be reported as supplemental information to the financial statements of the year just ended

subsidiaries Companies that are owned by the parent company

subsidiary ledger A set of accounts or records that contains detailed information about the items included in the balance of one general ledger account

sum-of-the-years'-digits method An accelerated depreciation method that allocates depreciation expense to each year in a fractional proportion, the denominator of which is the sum of the years' digits in the useful life of the asset and the numerator of which is the remaining useful life of the asset at the beginning of the current depreciation period

summary of significant accounting policies A financial statement disclosure, usually the initial note to the statements, which identifies the major accounting policies and procedures used by the firm

sunk costs Costs resulting from past decisions that cannot be changed.

suppliers Providers of merchandise for resale or materials needed for operating activities

systematic allocation Costs that benefit more than one accounting period and cannot be associated with specific revenues

 T

T-account A graphic representation of an account, shaped like a large T, which uses one side to record increases to the account and the other side to record decreases

tangible assets Assets that have physical substance, such as property, plant, and equipment

target costing Establishes the allowable cost of a product or service by starting with determining what customers are willing to pay for the product or service and then subtracting a desired profit on sales.

temporary account An account used to gather information for an accounting period; at the end of the period, the balance is transferred to a permanent stockholders' equity account; revenue, expense, and dividends accounts are temporary accounts

temporary difference A difference in amount between two financial statements that reverses in time

terminal period The forecast period following the horizon period

term loan A long-term borrowing, evidenced by a note payable, which is contracted with a single lender

theory of constraints Every process has a bottleneck (constraining resource), and production cannot take place faster than it is processed through the bottleneck. The theory's goal is to maximize throughput in a constrained environment.

throughput Sales revenue minus direct materials costs; *see also* theory of constraints.

time-adjusted rate of return *see* internal rate of return.

timeliness A characteristic of information that is received by decision makers before it loses its capacity to influence decisions

times interest earned (TIE) A determination of how much income is available to service debt, defined as earnings before interest and taxes divided by interest expense

times interest earned ratio A measure of long-term solvency and interest-paying ability; measured as income before interest expense and income taxes divided by interest expense

time value of money The recognition that the value of an amount of money depends on when the money is received;

tombstone An announcement of debt offered to the public

top-down budget A budget where top management decides on the primary goals and objectives for the organization and communicates them to lower management levels.

total compensation cost The sum of gross pay, payroll taxes, and fringe benefits paid by the employer

trade credit The financing used to purchase inventories on credit from other companies

trade discount An amount, usually based on quantity of merchandise purchased, that the seller subtracts from the list price of merchandise to determine the invoice price

trademark A registered name, logo, package design, image, jingle, or slogan associated with a product

trade name An exclusive and continuing right to use a certain term or name to identify a brand or family of products

trading on the equity The use of borrowed funds in the capital structure of a firm; the expectation is that the funds will earn a return higher than the rate of interest on the borrowed funds

trading securities Investments in securities that management intends to actively buy and sell for trading profits as market prices fluctuate

transfer price The internal value assigned a product or service that one division provides to another.

transitory components Elements of income that are not recurring; financial projections are improved if these are excluded from them

transitory items Transactions or events that are not likely to recur

translation adjustment The change in the value of the net assets of a subsidiary whose assets and liabilities are denominated in a foreign currency

treasury stock Shares of outstanding stock that have been acquired by the issuing corporation; a contra equity account

trend analysis A type of horizontal analysis in which a base period is chosen and all subsequent period amounts are defined relative to the base

trend percentages A comparison of the same financial item over two or more years, stated as a percentage of a base-year amount

trial balance A list of the account titles in the general ledger, their respective debit or credit balances, and the totals of the debit and credit amounts

U

unadjusted trial balance Account balances before any adjustments are made

uncollectible accounts expense The expense stemming from the inability of a business to collect an amount previously recorded as a receivable; sometimes called bad debts expense; normally classified as a selling or administrative expense

underfunded Situation where pension liabilities exceed pension plan assets

unearned revenue Cash received for products or services to be provided at a later time

unit contribution margin The difference between the unit selling price and the unit variable costs.

unit level activity An activity performed for each unit of product produced or sold.

unit level approach An approach to analyzing cost behavior that assumes changes in costs are best explained by changes in the number of units or sales dollars of products or services provided for customers.

units-of-production method A common depreciation method in which the useful life of the asset is defined in terms of the number of units of service provided by the asset

unrealized holding gain A gain resulting from holding an asset such as inventory as prices are rising

unrecognized prior service cost An accounting adjustment to a pension that represents the portion of the liability earned by employees prior to the plan's inception or a plan amendment

useful life The period of time over which the asset in expected to provide economic benefits to the company

V

value The worth in usefulness or importance of a product or service to the customer.

value-added activity An activity that adds value to a product or service from the viewpoint of the customer.

value chain The set of value-producing activities stretching from basic raw materials to the final consumer.

value chain analysis The study of value-producing activities, stretching from basic raw materials to the final consumer of a product or service.

value stream Consists of the production processes for similar products. Each value stream in a lean company not only has lean processes; it also has a lean accounting system because most costs should be directly traceable to one of the value streams.

variable costs Expenses that change in proportion to changes in sales volume

variable costing An approach to product costing that treats variable manufacturing costs as product costs and fixed manufacturing costs as period costs.

variable cost ratio Variable costs as a portion of sales revenue.

variable interest entity (VIE) Any form of business organization (such as corporation, partnership, trust) that is established by a sponsoring company and provides benefits to that company in the form of asset securitization or project financing; VIEs were formerly known as special purpose entities (SPEs)

variable manufacturing overhead All variable costs, except direct labor and direct materials, associated with converting raw materials into finished goods.

variable overhead effectiveness variance The difference between the standard variable overhead cost for the actual inputs and the flexible budget cost for variable overhead based on outputs.

variable overhead spending variance The difference between the actual variable overhead cost and the standard variable overhead cost for the actual inputs.

variable selling and administrative costs All variable costs other than those directly associated with converting raw materials into finished goods.

variance A comparison of actual and budgeted (or allowed) costs or revenues which are usually identified in financial performance reports.

verifiability A characteristic of accounting information referring to the ability of an independent auditor to reproduce the accounting information by examining the underlying economic events and transactions

vertical analysis A means of overcoming size differences among companies by expressing income statement items as a percentage of net sales and all balance sheet items as a percentage of total assets

vesting period A period of time during which the employee is not allowed to exercise a stock option; also refers to a period after which an employee retains his or her pension benefits even if employment is terminated

virtual integration The use of information technology and partnership concepts to allow two or more entities along a value chain to act as if they were a single economic entity.

voucher Another name for the payment approval form

W

waiting time The time units spend in temporary storage waiting to be processed, moved, or inspected.

warranties Guarantees against product defects for a designated period of time after sale

wasting assets Assets consumed as they are used, including natural resources such as oil reserves, mineral deposits, or timberland; *see* natural resources

weighted average cost of capital (WACC) The discount rate where the weights are the relative percentages of debt and equity in the capital structure and are applied to the expected returns on debt and equity, respectively

weighted average method In process costing, a costing method that spreads the combined beginning inventory cost and current manufacturing costs (for materials, labor, and overhead) over the units completed and those in ending inventory on an average basis.

work-in-process inventories Partially completed goods consisting of raw materials that are in the process of being converted into a finished product.

working capital A measure of solvency, working capital is the difference between current assets and current liabilities and is the net amount of working funds available in the short run. The general equation for working capital is: Current assets minus Current liabilities.

work in process Inventory account that tracks the value of items currently being produced

work in process inventory The cost of inventories that are in the manufacturing process and have not yet reached completion

work ticket A document used to record the time a job spends in a specific manufacturing operation.

Z

z-score The outcome of the Altman Z-score bankruptcy prediction model

zero-based budgeting A variation of the minimum level approach to budgeting where every dollar of expenditure must be justified.

zero coupon bond A bond that offers no periodic interest payments but that is issued at a substantial discount from its face value

Index

Note: Page numbers followed by 'e' denotes exhibit and those followed by 'n' denotes notes.

Note: Page numbers followed by 'e' denotes exhibit and those followed by 'n' denotes notes.

Note: Page numbers followed by 'e' denotes exhibit and those followed by 'n' denotes notes.

Note: Page numbers followed by 'e' denotes exhibit and those followed by 'n' denotes notes.

Note: Page numbers followed by 'e' denotes exhibit and those followed by 'n' denotes notes.

Note: Page numbers followed by 'e' denotes exhibit and those followed by 'n' denotes notes.

Note: Page numbers followed by 'e' denotes exhibit and those followed by 'n' denotes notes.

Note: Page numbers followed by 'e' denotes exhibit and those followed by 'n' denotes notes.

Note: Page numbers followed by 'e' denotes exhibit and those followed by 'n' denotes notes.

Note: Page numbers followed by 'e' denotes exhibit and those followed by 'n' denotes notes.

Note: Page numbers followed by 'e' denotes exhibit and those followed by 'n' denotes notes.

Note: Page numbers followed by 'e' denotes exhibit and those followed by 'n' denotes notes.

Note: Page numbers followed by 'e' denotes exhibit and those followed by 'n' denotes notes.

Note: Page numbers followed by 'e' denotes exhibit and those followed by 'n' denotes notes.

Note: Page numbers followed by 'e' denotes exhibit and those followed by 'n' denotes notes.

Note: Page numbers followed by 'e' denotes exhibit and those followed by 'n' denotes notes.

Note: Page numbers followed by 'e' denotes exhibit and those followed by 'n' denotes notes.

Note: Page numbers followed by 'e' denotes exhibit and those followed by 'n' denotes notes.

Note: Page numbers followed by 'e' denotes exhibit and those followed by 'n' denotes notes.